OXFORD PAPERBACK THESAURUS

Oxford
Paperback
Thesaurus

FOURTH EDITION

Edited by
Maurice Waite

OXFORD
UNIVERSITY PRESS

OXFORD
UNIVERSITY PRESS

Great Clarendon Street, Oxford, OX2 6DP,
United Kingdom

Oxford University Press is a department of the University of Oxford.
It furthers the University's objective of excellence in research, scholarship,
and education by publishing worldwide. Oxford is a registered trade mark of
Oxford University Press in the UK and in certain other countries

First Edition published in 1994
Second Edition published in 2001
Third Edition published in 2006
Fourth Edition published in 2012

5

British Library Cataloguing in Publication Data

Data available

Library of Congress Cataloguing in Publication Data

Data available

ISBN 978-0-19-964095-9

Printed in Great Britain by Clays Ltd, St Ives plc

Contents

Preface

A thesaurus (from the Greek for 'storehouse' or 'treasure') helps you to express yourself more accurately and in more interesting and varied ways. By listing groups of words that have similar meanings to each other, it offers a choice of alternative words (synonyms) that can be used in place of one that you already have in mind. It also shows words that mean the opposite of the word in question (also known as 'antonyms').

The *Oxford Paperback Thesaurus* is an invaluable tool for writing memos and reports at work, essays and dissertations at school or college, letters to friends or potential employers, or in creative writing for a living or for pleasure.

This new edition is based on the latest research from Oxford Dictionaries. We are responsible for the largest language research programme in the world, which constantly monitors language use of all types. Our primary source for new and revised material is the Oxford English Corpus, a dynamic database of more than two billion words which provides a detailed picture of 21st-century English from around the world.

For this edition we have added more than 500 new synonyms. For example, an assignation or meeting can now be a *tweetup*, a bully may be known as an *attack dog*, another way to confine people is to *kettle* them, and those who censor material also *redact* it, while a mistake or error is a *fail*.

In the centre of the book you will find the Wordfinder section. This consists of extensive lists of words in categories such as animals, items of food and drink, parts of the body, plants, computing and Internet terms, and many others. These lists are ideal for helping you solve crosswords and other puzzles or just reminding you of a word that is on the tip of your tongue.

Consulting a book can still be the quickest and most convenient way of finding the word you want, as well as being an enjoyable method of browsing in its own right. But to explore the language further try Oxford Dictionaries Online. This free site is updated regularly and allows you to search our largest dictionary of current English. It also offers information on usage, grammar, and writing, our Word of the Day, a language blog, and more. The subscription-based Oxford Dictionaries Pro features smart-linked, fully searchable dictionaries and thesauruses, audio pronunciations, millions of example sentences, and specialist language reference resources. Find Oxford Dictionaries Online at www.oxforddictionaries.com.

Guide to the thesaurus entry

headword

numbered sense of the headword

air n. **1** *hundreds of birds hovered in the air* **sky**, atmosphere, airspace, ether; literary heavens. **2** *open the windows to get some air into the room* **breeze**, draught, wind; breath/blast of air, gust/puff of wind. **3** *an air of defiance* **expression**, appearance, look, impression, aspect, aura, mien, countenance, manner, bearing, tone. **4** *women putting on airs* **affectations**, pretension, pretentiousness, posing, posturing, airs and graces; Brit. informal side. **5** *a traditional Scottish air* **tune**, melody, song; literary lay.

core synonym—the closest synonym to the headword

example of use, to help distinguish different senses

▸ v. **1** *a chance to air your views* **express**, voice, make public, ventilate, articulate, state, declare, give expression/voice to, have one's say. **2** *the windows were opened to air the room* **ventilate**, freshen, refresh, cool. **3** *the film was aired nationwide* **broadcast**, transmit, screen, show, televise, telecast.

forward slash used to show more than one possibility

part of speech of the headword (*see opposite for abbreviations*)

label indicating the region of the world in which the following synonym is used (*see opposite for abbreviations*)

label indicating the level or style of English in which the following synonyms are used (*see opposite for explanations*)

luxurious adj. **1** *a luxurious hotel* **opulent**, sumptuous, deluxe, grand, palatial, splendid, magnificent, well appointed, extravagant, fancy; Brit. informal plush, posh, classy, ritzy, swanky; Brit. informal swish; N. Amer. informal swank. **2** *a luxurious lifestyle* **self-indulgent**, sensual, pleasure-loving, pleasure-seeking, epicurean, hedonistic, sybaritic, lotus-eating.
– OPPOSITES plain, basic, abstemious.

words meaning the opposite of the headword; most have entries of their own, where a wider choice will be found

night n. night-time; (hours of) darkness, dark.
– OPPOSITES day.
□ **night and day** all the time, around the clock; (morning, noon, and night); (day in, day out), ceaselessly, endlessly, incessantly, unceasingly, interminably, constantly, perpetually, continually, relentlessly; informal 24-7.

brackets to show more than one possibility

phrase for which synonyms are given

brackets around a phrase, to avoid confusion

Most of the synonyms given are part of standard English, but some are used only in certain styles or situations. These are grouped at the end of their sense and have labels in front of them:

informal, e.g. *swig* as a synonym for *drink*: normally used only in speech or informal writing.

formal, e.g. *dwelling* as a synonym for *home*: normally used only in writing such as official documents.

technical, e.g. *neonate* as a synonym for *baby*: normally used only in technical and specialist language. Words used in specific fields are labelled Medicine, Nautical, etc.

literary, e.g. *strand* as a synonym for *beach*: found only or mainly in literature.

dated, e.g. *miffy* as a synonym for *bad-tempered*: no longer used by most, but still sometimes by older people.

historical, e.g. *privateer*, a type of *pirate*: only used today to refer to things that are no longer part of modern life.

humorous, e.g. *libation* as a synonym for *drink*: used with the intention of sounding funny or playful.

archaic, e.g. *meat* as a synonym for any kind of *food*: not used today except for old-fashioned effect.

Synonyms used exclusively or mainly in a particular part of the world are also labelled British, Northern English, Scottish, Irish, North American, Australian, or New Zealand.

Abbreviations used in the thesaurus

Parts of speech		Regional labels	
adj.	adjective	Austral.	Australian
adv.	adverb	Brit.	British
conj.	conjunction	N. Amer.	North American
exclam.	exclamation	N. English	Northern English
n.	noun	NZ	New Zealand
prep.	preposition		
v.	verb		

Aa

aback adv.
□ **take someone aback** surprise, shock, stun, stagger, astound, astonish, startle, take by surprise; dumbfound, nonplus, stop someone in their tracks; shake (up), jolt, throw, unnerve, disconcert, unsettle, bewilder; informal flabbergast, knock sideways, floor; Brit. informal knock for six.

abandon v. **1** *the party abandoned policies which made it unelectable* **renounce**, relinquish, dispense with, disclaim, disown, disavow, discard, wash one's hands of; give up, drop, jettison, do away with, axe; informal ditch, scrap, scrub, junk; formal forswear. **2** *by that stage, she had abandoned painting* **give up**, stop, cease, drop, forgo, desist from, have done with, abstain from, discontinue, break off, refrain from, quit, evacuate. **3** *he abandoned his wife and children* **desert**, leave, leave high and dry, turn one's back on, cast aside, break (up) with; jilt, strand, leave stranded, leave in the lurch, throw over; informal walk out on, run out on, dump, ditch; Brit. informal give someone the push, bin off; literary forsake. **4** *the skipper gave the order to abandon ship* **vacate**, leave, depart from, withdraw from, quit, evacuate. **5** *a vast expanse of territory was abandoned to the invaders* **relinquish**, surrender, give up, cede, yield, leave. **6** *she abandoned herself to the sensuousness of the music* **indulge in**, give way to, give oneself up to, yield to, lose oneself in.
– OPPOSITES keep, retain, continue.
▸ n. *reckless abandon* **uninhibitedness**, recklessness, lack of restraint, lack of inhibition, wildness, impulsiveness, impetuosity, immoderation, wantonness.
– OPPOSITES self-control.

abandoned adj. **1** *an abandoned child* **deserted**, forsaken, cast aside/off; jilted, stranded, rejected; informal dumped, ditched. **2** *an abandoned tin mine* **unused**, disused, neglected, idle; deserted, unoccupied, uninhabited, empty. **3** *a wild, abandoned dance* **uninhibited**, reckless, unrestrained, wild, unbridled, impulsive, impetuous; immoderate, wanton.

abase v. **humble**, humiliate, belittle, demean, lower, degrade, debase, cheapen, discredit, bring low; (**abase oneself**) grovel, kowtow, bow and scrape, toady, fawn; informal crawl, suck up to someone, lick someone's boots.

abasement n. **humiliation**, belittlement, lowering, degradation, debasement.

abashed adj. **embarrassed**, ashamed, shamefaced, remorseful, conscience-stricken, mortified, humiliated, humbled, chagrined, crestfallen, sheepish, red-faced, blushing, discountenanced, with one's tail between one's legs.

abate v. **1** *the storm had abated* **subside**, die down/away/out, lessen, ease (off), let up, decrease, diminish, moderate, decline, fade, dwindle, recede, tail off, peter out, taper off, wane, ebb, weaken, come to an end; old use remit. **2** *nothing abated his crusading zeal* **decrease**, lessen, diminish, reduce, moderate, ease, soothe, dampen, calm, tone down, allay, temper.
– OPPOSITES intensify, increase.

abatement n. **1** *the storm still rages with no sign of abatement* **subsiding**, dying down/away/out, lessening, easing (off), decrease, moderation, decline, ebb. **2** *noise abatement* **decrease**, reduction, lowering.

abattoir n. **slaughterhouse**; Brit. butchery; old use shambles.

abbey n. **monastery**, **convent**, priory, cloister, friary, nunnery; historical charterhouse.

abbreviate v. **shorten**, reduce, cut, contract, condense, compress, abridge, truncate, pare down, prune, shrink, telescope; summarize, abstract, precis, synopsize, digest, edit.
– OPPOSITES lengthen, expand.

abbreviated adj. **shortened**, reduced, cut, condensed, abridged, concise, compact, succinct; summary, thumbnail, synoptic; formal compendious.
– OPPOSITES long.

abbreviation n. **short form**, contraction, acronym, initialism, symbol, diminutive; elision.

abdicate v. **1** *the king abdicated in 1936* **resign**, retire, stand down, step down, bow out, renounce the throne; old use demit. **2** *Ferdinand abdicated the throne* **resign from**, relinquish, renounce, give up, surrender, vacate, cede; Law disclaim; formal abjure. **3** *the state abdicated all responsibility for their welfare* **disown**, reject, renounce, give up, refuse, relinquish, repudiate, abandon, turn one's back on, wash one's hands of; formal abjure; literary forsake.

abdication n. **1** *Edward VIII's abdication* **resignation**, retirement; relinquishment,

a

renunciation, surrender; formal abjuration; old use demission. **2** *an abdication of responsibility* **disowning**, renunciation, rejection, refusal, relinquishment, repudiation, abandonment.

abdomen n. **stomach**, belly, gut, middle, intestines; informal tummy, tum, insides, guts, pot, paunch, maw, breadbasket; Austral. informal bingy; dated corporation.

> **WORD LINKS**
>
> **abdominal, ventral, coeliac** relating to the abdomen
> **laparotomy** a surgical incision of the abdomen
> **peritoneum** a membrane lining the cavity of the abdomen

abdominal adj. **gastric**, intestinal, stomach, stomachic, enteric, duodenal, visceral, coeliac, ventral.

abduct v. **kidnap**, carry off, seize, capture, run away/off with, make off with, spirit away, hold hostage, hold to ransom; informal snatch.

aberrant adj. **deviant**, deviating, divergent, abnormal, atypical, anomalous, irregular, rogue; strange, odd, peculiar, uncommon, freakish; twisted, warped, perverted.
– OPPOSITES normal, typical.

aberration n. *a statistical aberration* **anomaly**, deviation, departure from the norm, divergence, abnormality, irregularity, variation, freak, rarity, oddity, peculiarity, curiosity; mistake.

abet v. **assist**, aid, help, lend a hand, support, back, encourage; cooperate with, collaborate with, work with, collude with, be in collusion with, be hand in glove with, side with; second, endorse, sanction; promote, champion, further, expedite, connive at.
– OPPOSITES hinder.

abeyance n. **suspension**, a state of suspension, a state of uncertainty, remission; (**in abeyance**) pending, suspended, deferred, postponed, put off, put to one side, unresolved, up in the air; informal in cold storage, on ice, on the back burner, hanging fire.

abhor v. **detest**, hate, loathe, despise, execrate, regard with disgust, shrink from, recoil from, shudder at; formal abominate.
– OPPOSITES love, admire.

abhorrence n. **hatred**, loathing, detestation, execration, revulsion, abomination, disgust, repugnance, horror, odium, aversion.

abhorrent adj. **detestable**, hateful, loathsome, despicable, abominable, execrable, repellent, repugnant, repulsive, revolting, disgusting, distasteful, horrible, horrid, horrifying, awful, heinous, reprehensible, obnoxious, odious, nauseating, offensive, contemptible.
– OPPOSITES admirable.

abide v. **1** *he expected everybody to abide by the rules* **comply with**, obey, observe, follow, keep to, hold to, conform to, adhere to, stick to, stand by, act in accordance with, uphold, heed, accept, go along with, acknowledge,

respect, defer to. **2** informal *I can't abide the smell of cigarettes* **tolerate**, bear, stand, put up with, endure, take, countenance; informal stomach; Brit. informal stick; formal brook; old use suffer. **3** *at least one memory will abide* **continue**, remain, survive, last, persist, linger, stay, live on.
– OPPOSITES flout, disobey.

abiding adj. **enduring**, lasting, persisting, long-lasting, lifelong, continuing, remaining, surviving, standing, durable, everlasting, perpetual, eternal, unending, constant, permanent, unchanging, steadfast, immutable.
– OPPOSITES short-lived, ephemeral.

ability n. **1** *the ability to read and write* **capacity**, capability, potential, potentiality, power, faculty, aptness, facility; wherewithal, means. **2** *the president's leadership ability* **talent**, skill, expertise, adeptness, aptitude, skilfulness, savoir faire, prowess, mastery, accomplishment; competence, proficiency; dexterity, adroitness, deftness, cleverness, flair, finesse, gift, knack, genius; qualification, resources; informal know-how.

abject adj. **1** *abject poverty* **wretched**, miserable, hopeless, pathetic, pitiful, pitiable, piteous, sorry, woeful, lamentable, degrading, appalling, atrocious, awful. **2** *an abject sinner* **contemptible**, base, low, vile, worthless, debased, degraded, despicable, ignominious, mean, unworthy, ignoble. **3** *an abject apology* **obsequious**, grovelling, fawning, toadyish, servile, cringing, sycophantic, submissive, craven.

abjure v. formal **renounce**, relinquish, reject, forgo, disavow, abandon, deny, repudiate, give up, wash one's hands of; eschew, abstain from, refrain from; informal kick, pack in; Brit. informal jack in; Law disaffirm; literary forsake; formal forswear, abnegate.

ablaze adj. **1** *several vehicles were ablaze* **on fire**, alight, aflame, in flames, flaming, burning, blazing; literary afire. **2** *every window was ablaze with light* **lit up**, alight, gleaming, glowing, aglow, illuminated, bright, shining, radiant, shimmering, sparkling, flashing, dazzling, luminous, incandescent. **3** *his eyes were ablaze with fury* **passionate**, impassioned, aroused, excited, stimulated, eager, animated, intense, ardent, fervent, frenzied.

able adj. **1** *he will soon be able to resume his duties* **capable of**, competent to, equal to, up to, fit to, prepared to, qualified to; allowed to, free to, in a position to. **2** *an able student* **intelligent**, clever, talented, skilful, skilled, accomplished, gifted; proficient, apt, good, adroit, adept; capable, competent, efficient, effective.
– OPPOSITES incompetent, incapable.

able-bodied adj. **healthy**, fit, in good health, robust, strong, sound, sturdy, vigorous, hardy, hale and hearty, athletic, muscular, strapping, burly, brawny, lusty; in good shape, in trim, in fine fettle, fighting

fit, as fit as a fiddle, as fit as a flea; informal husky; dated stalwart.
– OPPOSITES infirm, frail, disabled.

ablutions plural n. formal **washing**, cleansing, bathing, showering, scrubbing; wash, bath, shower, toilet, soak, dip, douche; rare lavage, lavation.

abnegation n. formal **1** *a serious abnegation of their responsibilities* **renunciation**, rejection, refusal, abandonment, abdication, surrender, relinquishment, repudiation, denial; formal abjuration. **2** *people capable of abnegation and unselfishness* **self-denial**, self-sacrifice, abstinence, temperance, continence, asceticism, abstemiousness, austerity.
– OPPOSITES acceptance, self-indulgence.

abnormal adj. **unusual**, uncommon, atypical, untypical, non-typical, unrepresentative, rare, isolated, irregular, anomalous, deviant, divergent, aberrant, freak, freakish; **strange**, odd, peculiar, curious, bizarre, weird, queer; eccentric, idiosyncratic, quirky; unexpected, unfamiliar, unconventional, surprising, unorthodox, singular, exceptional, extraordinary, out of the ordinary, out of the way; unnatural, perverse, perverted, twisted, warped, unhealthy, distorted; Brit. out of the common; informal funny, freaky, kinky.
– OPPOSITES normal, typical, common.

abnormality n. **1** *babies born with physical or mental abnormalities* **malformation**, deformity, irregularity, flaw, defect. **2** *the abnormality of such behaviour* **unusualness**, atypicality, irregularity, anomalousness, deviation, divergence, aberrance, aberration, freakishness, strangeness, oddness, peculiarity, unexpectedness, singularity.

abode n. formal **home**, house, place of residence, accommodation, seat; quarters, lodgings, rooms; address; informal pad, digs; formal dwelling, dwelling place, residence, habitation.

abolish v. **put an end to**, get rid of, scrap, end, stop, terminate, axe, eradicate, eliminate, exterminate, destroy, annihilate, stamp out, obliterate, wipe out, extinguish, quash, expunge, extirpate; annul, cancel, invalidate, nullify, void, dissolve; rescind, repeal, revoke, overturn; discontinue, remove, excise, drop, jettison; informal do away with, ditch, junk, scrub, dump, chop, give something the chop, knock something on the head; formal abrogate.
– OPPOSITES retain, create.

abolition n. **scrapping**, ending, termination, eradication, elimination, extermination, destruction, annihilation, obliteration, extirpation; annulment, cancellation, invalidation, nullification, dissolution; revocation, repeal, discontinuation, removal; formal abrogation.

abominable adj. **loathsome**, detestable, hateful, odious, obnoxious, despicable, contemptible, damnable, diabolical; disgusting, revolting, repellent, repulsive, offensive, repugnant, abhorrent, reprehensible, atrocious, horrifying, execrable, foul, vile, wretched, base, horrible, awful, dreadful, appalling, nauseating; horrid, nasty, disagreeable, unpleasant, distasteful; informal terrible, shocking, God-awful; Brit. informal beastly; dated cursed, accursed.
– OPPOSITES good, admirable.

abominate v. formal **detest**, loathe, hate, abhor, despise, execrate, shudder at, recoil from, shrink from, be repelled by.
– OPPOSITES like, love.

abomination n. **1** *in both wars, internment was an abomination* **atrocity**, disgrace, horror, obscenity, outrage, evil, crime, monstrosity, anathema, bane. **2** *he had a Calvinist abomination of indulgence* **detestation**, loathing, hatred, aversion, antipathy, revulsion, repugnance, abhorrence, odium, execration, disgust, horror, hostility.
– OPPOSITES liking, love.

aboriginal adj. *the area's aboriginal inhabitants* **indigenous**, native; original, earliest, first; ancient, primitive, primeval, primordial; rare autochthonous.
▶ n. *the social structure of the aboriginals* **native**, aborigine, original inhabitant; rare autochthon, indigene.

abort v. **1** *I decided not to abort the pregnancy* **terminate**, end. **2** *the organism can cause pregnant ewes to abort* **miscarry**, have a miscarriage. **3** *the crew aborted the take-off* **halt**, stop, end, axe, call off, cut short, discontinue, terminate, arrest; informal pull the plug on. **4** *the mission aborted* **come to a halt**, end, terminate, fail, miscarry, go wrong, fall through, collapse, founder, come to grief.

abortion n. **termination**, miscarriage; rare feticide.

abortive adj. **unsuccessful**, failed, vain, thwarted, futile, useless, worthless, ineffective, ineffectual, to no effect, inefficacious, fruitless, unproductive, unavailing, to no avail, sterile, nugatory; old use bootless.
– OPPOSITES successful, fruitful.

abound v. **1** *cafes and bars abound in the narrow streets* **be plentiful**, be abundant, be numerous, proliferate, superabound, be thick on the ground; informal grow on trees, be two/ten a penny. **2** *a stream which abounded with trout and eels* **be full of**, overflow with, teem with, be packed with, be crowded with, be thronged with; be alive with, be crawling with, be overrun by/with, swarm with, bristle with, be infested with, be thick with; informal be lousy with, be stuffed with, be jam-packed with, be chock-a-block with, be chock-full of.

abounding adj. **abundant**, plentiful, superabundant, considerable, copious, ample, lavish, luxuriant, profuse, boundless, prolific, inexhaustible, generous; galore; literary plenteous.
– OPPOSITES meagre, scanty.

a

about prep. **1** *a book about ancient Greece* **regarding**, concerning, with reference to, referring to, with regard to, with respect to, respecting, relating to, on, touching on, dealing with, relevant to, connected with, in connection with, on the subject of, in the matter of, apropos, re. **2** *two hundred people were milling about the room* **around**, round, throughout, over, through.

▸ adv. **1** *there were babies crawling about in the grass* **around**, here and there, to and fro, back and forth, from place to place, hither and thither, in all directions. **2** *I knew he was about somewhere* **near**, nearby, around, hereabouts, not far off/away, close by, in the vicinity, in the neighbourhood. **3** *the explosion caused about £15,000 worth of damage* **approximately**, roughly, around, round about, in the region of, circa, of the order of, something like; or so, or thereabouts, there or thereabouts, more or less, give or take a few, not far off; Brit. getting on for; informal as near as dammit; N. Amer. informal in the ballpark of.
□ **about to** (just) going to, ready to, all set to, preparing to, intending to, soon to; on the point of, on the verge of, on the brink of, within an ace of.

about-turn Brit. n. **1** *he saluted and did an about-turn* **about-face**, volte-face, turnaround, turnabout, U-turn, rowback; informal U-ey, one-eighty. **2** *the government was forced to make an about-turn* **volte-face**, U-turn, reversal, retraction, backtracking, swing, swerve; change of heart, change of mind, sea change.

above prep. **1** *a tiny window above the door* **over**, higher (up) than; on top of, atop, on, upon. **2** *those above the rank of Colonel* **superior to**, senior to, over, higher (up) than; in charge of, commanding. **3** *you must be above suspicion* **beyond**, not liable to, not open to, not vulnerable to, out of reach of; immune to, exempt from. **4** *the Chinese valued pearls above gold* **more than**, over, before, rather than, in preference to, instead of. **5** *an increase above the rate of inflation* **greater than**, more than, higher than, exceeding, in excess of, over, over and above, beyond, surpassing, upwards of.
– OPPOSITES below, under, beneath.

▸ adv. **1** *in the darkness above, something moved* **overhead**, on/at the top, high up, on high, up above, high above one's head, aloft. **2** *the two cases described above* **earlier**, previously, before, formerly.

▸ adj. *the above example* **preceding**, previous, earlier, former, foregoing, prior, above-stated, aforementioned, aforesaid.
□ **above all** most importantly, before everything, beyond everything, first of all, most of all, chiefly, primarily, in the first place, first and foremost, mainly, principally, predominantly, especially, essentially, basically, in essence, at bottom; informal at the end of the day, when all is said and done.

above oneself conceited, proud, arrogant, swollen-headed, self-important, cocky, haughty, disdainful, snobbish, snobby, supercilious; informal stuck-up, high and mighty, snooty, uppity, big-headed, too big for one's boots.

above board adj. *the proceedings were completely above board* **legitimate**, lawful, legal, licit, honest, fair, open, frank, straight, overt, candid, forthright, unconcealed, trustworthy, unequivocal; informal legit, kosher, pukka, by the book, fair and square, square, on the level, on the up and up, upfront.
– OPPOSITES dishonest, shady.

abrade v. **wear away**, wear down, erode, scrape away, corrode, eat away at, gnaw away at.

abrasion n. **1** *he had abrasions to his forehead* **graze**, cut, scrape, scratch, gash, laceration, injury, contusion; sore, ulcer; Medicine trauma. **2** *the metal is resistant to abrasion* **erosion**, wearing away/down, corrosion.

abrasive adj. **1** *abrasive kitchen cleaners* **corrosive**, corroding, erosive; caustic, harsh, coarse, coarse-grained. **2** *her abrasive manner* **caustic**, cutting, biting, acerbic; rough, harsh, hard, tough, sharp, curt, brusque, stern, severe; wounding, nasty, cruel, callous, insensitive, unfeeling, unsympathetic, inconsiderate; N. Amer. acerb.
– OPPOSITES kind, gentle.

abreast adv. **1** *they walked three abreast* **in a row**, side by side, alongside, level, beside each other, shoulder to shoulder. **2** *try to keep abreast of current affairs* **up to date with**, up with, in touch with, informed about, acquainted with, knowledgeable about, conversant with, familiar with, au courant with, au fait with.

abridge v. **shorten**, cut, cut short/down, curtail, truncate, trim, crop, clip, pare down, prune; abbreviate, condense, contract, compress, reduce, decrease, shrink; summarize, sum up, abstract, precis, synopsize, put in a nutshell, edit; rare epitomize.
– OPPOSITES lengthen.

abridged adj. **shortened**, cut, cut down, concise, condensed, abbreviated; summary, outline, thumbnail; bowdlerized, censored, expurgated; informal potted.

abridgement n. **summary**, abstract, synopsis, precis, outline, résumé, sketch, digest.

abroad adv. **1** *he regularly travels abroad* **overseas**, out of the country, to/in foreign parts. **2** *rumours were abroad* **in circulation**, circulating, current, everywhere, in the air; about, around; at large.

abrogate v. formal **repeal**, revoke, rescind, repudiate, overturn, annul, cancel, invalidate, nullify, void, negate, dissolve, countermand, declare null and void, discontinue; reverse, retract, remove, withdraw, abolish, put an end to, do away with, get rid of, end, stop, quash, scrap; Law disaffirm.
– OPPOSITES institute, introduce.

abrogation n. formal **repeal**, revocation, repudiation, overturning, annulment, cancellation, invalidation, nullification, negation, dissolution, discontinuation; reversal, retraction, removal, withdrawal, abolition; Law rescission; formal disaffirmation.

abrupt adj. **1** *an abrupt halt | an abrupt change of subject* **sudden**, unexpected, without warning, unanticipated, unforeseen, precipitate, surprising, startling; quick, swift, rapid, hurried, hasty, immediate, instantaneous. **2** *an abrupt manner* **curt**, brusque, blunt, short, sharp, terse, brisk, crisp, gruff, rude, discourteous, uncivil, snappish, unceremonious, offhand, rough, harsh; bluff, no-nonsense, to the point; informal snappy. **3** *abrupt, epigrammatic paragraphs* **disjointed**, jerky, uneven, disconnected, inelegant. **4** *an abrupt slope* **steep**, sheer, precipitous, bluff, sharp, sudden; perpendicular, vertical, dizzy, vertiginous.
– OPPOSITES gradual, gentle.

abscess n. **ulcer**, ulceration, cyst, boil, blister, sore, pustule, carbuncle, pimple, wen, whitlow, canker; inflammation, infection, eruption.

abscond v. **run away**, escape, bolt, flee, make off, take flight, take off, decamp; make a break for it, take to one's heels, make a quick getaway, beat a hasty retreat, run for it, make a run for it; disappear, vanish, slip away, steal away, sneak away; informal do a moonlight flit, clear out, cut and run, show a clean pair of heels, skedaddle, skip, head for the hills, do a disappearing act, fly the coop, take French leave, scarper, vamoose; Brit. informal do a bunk, do a runner; N. Amer. informal take a powder.

absence n. **1** *his absence from the office* **non-attendance**, non-appearance, absenteeism; **truancy**, playing truant; leave, holiday, vacation, sabbatical. **2** *the absence of any other suitable candidate* **lack**, want, non-existence, unavailability, deficiency, dearth; need.
– OPPOSITES presence.

absent adj. **1** *she was absent from work* **away**, off, out, non-attending, truant; off duty, on holiday, on leave; gone, missing, lacking, unavailable, non-existent; informal AWOL. **2** *an absent look* **distracted**, preoccupied, inattentive, vague, absorbed, abstracted, unheeding, oblivious, distrait, absent-minded, dreamy, far away, in a world of one's own, lost in thought, in a brown study; blank, empty, vacant; informal miles away.
– OPPOSITES present, attentive, alert.
▸ v. *Rose absented herself from the occasion* **stay away**, be absent, withdraw, retire, take one's leave, remove oneself.

absent-minded adj. **forgetful**, distracted, preoccupied, inattentive, vague, scatterbrained, abstracted, unheeding, oblivious, distrait, in a brown study, wool-gathering; lost in thought, pensive, thoughtful, brooding; informal miles away, having a mind/memory like a sieve.

absolute adj. **1** *absolute silence | an absolute disgrace* **complete**, total, utter, out-and-out, outright, entire, perfect, pure, decided; thorough, thoroughgoing, undivided, unqualified, unadulterated, unalloyed, unmodified, unreserved, downright, undiluted, consummate, unmitigated, sheer, arrant, rank, dyed-in-the-wool. **2** *the absolute truth* **definite**, certain, positive, unconditional, categorical, unquestionable, incontrovertible, undoubted, unequivocal, decisive, conclusive, confirmed, infallible. **3** *absolute power* **unlimited**, unrestricted, unrestrained, unbounded, boundless, infinite, ultimate, total, supreme, unconditional. **4** *an absolute monarch* **autocratic**, despotic, dictatorial, tyrannical, tyrannous, authoritarian, arbitrary, autonomous, sovereign, autarchic, anti-democratic, omnipotent. **5** *absolute moral standards* **universal**, fixed, independent, non-relative, non-variable, absolutist.
– OPPOSITES partial, qualified, limited, conditional.

absolutely adv. *you're absolutely right* **completely**, totally, utterly, perfectly, entirely, wholly, fully, quite, thoroughly, unreservedly; definitely, certainly, positively, unconditionally, categorically, unquestionably, undoubtedly, without (a) doubt, without question, surely, unequivocally; exactly, precisely, decisively, conclusively, manifestly, in every way/respect, one hundred per cent, every inch, to the hilt; informal dead.
▸ exclam. informal *'Have I made myself clear?' 'Absolutely!'* **yes**, indeed, of course, definitely, certainly, quite, without (a) doubt, without question, unquestionably; affirmative, by all means.

absolution n. **forgiveness**, pardon, exoneration, remission, dispensation, indulgence, clemency, mercy; discharge, acquittal; freedom, deliverance, release; vindication; informal let-off; formal exculpation; old use shrift.

absolve v. **1** *this fact does not absolve you from responsibility* **exonerate**, discharge, acquit, vindicate; release, relieve, liberate, free, deliver, clear, exempt, let off; formal exculpate. **2** Christianity *I absolve you from your sins* **forgive**, pardon.
– OPPOSITES blame, condemn.

absorb v. **1** *a sponge-like material which absorbs water* **soak up**, suck up, draw up/in, take up/in, blot up, mop up, sop up. **2** *she absorbed the information in silence* **assimilate**, digest, take in. **3** *the company was absorbed into the new concern* **incorporate**, assimilate, integrate, take in, subsume, include, co-opt, swallow up. **4** *these roles absorb most of his time and energy* **use (up)**, consume, take up, occupy. **5** *she was totally absorbed in her book* **engross**, captivate, occupy, preoccupy, engage, rivet, grip, hold, interest, intrigue, immerse, involve, enthral, spellbind, fascinate.

a

absorbent adj. **porous**, spongy, sponge-like, permeable, pervious, absorptive; technical spongiform; rare sorbefacient.

absorbing adj. **fascinating**, interesting, captivating, gripping, engrossing, compelling, compulsive, enthralling, riveting, spellbinding, intriguing, thrilling, exciting; informal unputdownable.
– OPPOSITES boring, uninteresting.

absorption n. **1** *the absorption of water soaking up*, sucking up; technical osmosis. **2** *the company's absorption into a larger concern* **incorporation**, assimilation, integration, inclusion. **3** *her total absorption in the music* **involvement**, immersion, raptness, engrossment, occupation, preoccupation, engagement, captivation, fascination, enthralment.

abstain v. **1** *Benjamin abstained from wine* **refrain**, desist, hold back, forbear; give up, renounce, avoid, shun, eschew, forgo, go without, do without; refuse, decline; informal cut out; formal abjure. **2** *most pregnant women abstain, or drink very little* **be teetotal**, take the pledge; informal be on the wagon. **3** *262 voted against, 38 abstained* **not vote**, decline to vote.

abstemious adj. **self-denying**, temperate, abstinent, moderate, self-disciplined, restrained, self-restrained, sober, austere, ascetic, puritanical, spartan, self-abnegating, hair-shirt.
– OPPOSITES self-indulgent.

abstinence n. **self-denial**, self-restraint; teetotalism, temperance, sobriety, abstemiousness, abstention.

abstract adj. **1** *abstract concepts* **theoretical**, conceptual, notional, intellectual, metaphysical, philosophical, academic; rare ideational. **2** *abstract art* **non-representational**, non-pictorial.
– OPPOSITES actual, concrete.
▸ v. **1** *staff abstract material for an online database* **summarize**, precis, abridge, condense, compress, shorten, cut down, abbreviate, synopsize; rare epitomize. **2** *a scheme to abstract more water from the river* **extract**, pump, draw (off), withdraw, remove, take out/away; separate, isolate.
▸ n. *an abstract of her speech* **summary**, synopsis, precis, résumé, outline, abridgement, digest, summation; N. Amer. wrap-up; old use argument.

abstracted adj. **preoccupied**, distracted, absent-minded, in a world of one's own, with one's head in the clouds, daydreaming, dreamy, inattentive, thoughtful, pensive, lost in thought, deep in thought, immersed in thought, wool-gathering, in a brown study, musing, brooding, absent, distrait; informal miles away.
– OPPOSITES attentive.

abstraction n. **1** *philosophical abstractions* **concept**, idea, notion, thought, theory, hypothesis. **2** *she sensed his momentary abstraction* **preoccupation**, distraction, absent-mindedness, dreaminess, inattentiveness, inattention, wool-gathering; thoughtfulness, pensiveness.

abstruse adj. **obscure**, arcane, esoteric, little known, recherché, rarefied, recondite, difficult, hard, puzzling, perplexing, cryptic, Delphic, complex, complicated, involved, over/above one's head, incomprehensible, unfathomable, impenetrable, mysterious.

absurd adj. **preposterous**, ridiculous, ludicrous, farcical, laughable, risible, idiotic, stupid, foolish, silly, inane, imbecilic, insane, hare-brained; unreasonable, irrational, illogical, nonsensical, pointless, senseless; informal crazy; Brit. informal barmy, daft.
– OPPOSITES reasonable, sensible.

absurdity n. **preposterousness**, ridiculousness, ludicrousness, risibility, idiocy, stupidity, foolishness, folly, silliness, inanity, insanity; unreasonableness, irrationality, illogicality, pointlessness, senselessness; informal craziness.

abundance n. **profusion**, plentifulness, profuseness, copiousness, amplitude, lavishness, host, cornucopia, riot; plenty, quantities, scores, multitude; informal millions, sea, ocean(s), wealth, lot(s), heap(s), mass(es), stack(s), pile(s), load(s), bags, bucketload(s), mountain(s), ton(s), slew, scads, oodles; Brit. informal shedload; N. Amer. informal gobs; formal plenitude.
– OPPOSITES lack, scarcity.

abundant adj. *an abundant supply of food* **plentiful**, copious, ample, profuse, rich, lavish, liberal, generous, bountiful, large, huge, great, bumper, overflowing, prolific, teeming; in plenty, in abundance; informal a gogo, galore; literary plenteous, bounteous.
– OPPOSITES scarce, sparse.
□ **be abundant** abound, be plentiful, be numerous, be in abundance, proliferate, be thick on the ground; informal grow on trees, be two/ten a penny.

abuse v. **1** *the judge abused his power* **misuse**, misapply, misemploy; exploit, take advantage of. **2** *he was accused of abusing children* **mistreat**, maltreat, ill-treat, treat badly; molest, interfere with, indecently assault, sexually abuse, sexually assault; injure, hurt, harm, damage. **3** *the referee was abused by players from both teams* **insult**, be rude to, swear at, curse, call someone names, taunt, shout at, revile, inveigh against, vilify, slander, cast aspersions on; Brit. informal slag off.
▸ n. **1** *the abuse of power* **misuse**, misapplication, misemployment; exploitation. **2** *the abuse of children* **mistreatment**, maltreatment, ill-treatment; molestation, interference, indecent assault, sexual abuse, sexual assault; injury, hurt, harm, damage. **3** *the scheme is open to administrative abuse* **corruption**, injustice, wrongdoing, wrong, misconduct, misdeed(s), offence(s), crime(s), sin(s). **4** *torrents of abuse* **insults**, curses, jibes, expletives, swear words; swearing, cursing, name-calling; invective, vilification, vituperation, slander; Brit. informal verbal(s), industrial language; N. Amer. informal trash talk;

old use contumely.

abusive adj. **insulting**, rude, vulgar, offensive, disparaging, belittling, derogatory, disrespectful, denigratory, uncomplimentary, pejorative, vituperative; defamatory, slanderous, libellous, scurrilous, blasphemous; informal bitchy; old use contumelious.

abut v. **adjoin**, be adjacent to, border, neighbour, join, touch, meet, reach, be contiguous with.

abysmal adj. *some of the teaching was abysmal* **very bad**, dreadful, awful, terrible, appalling, frightful, atrocious, disgraceful, deplorable, shameful, hopeless, lamentable, laughable; informal rotten, crummy, pathetic, pitiful, woeful, useless, lousy, dire, poxy, the pits; Brit. informal chronic, shocking, pants.

abyss n. **chasm**, gorge, ravine, canyon, fissure, rift, crevasse, hole, gulf, pit, cavity, void, bottomless pit.

academic adj. **1** *an academic institution* **educational**, scholastic, instructional, pedagogical. **2** *his academic turn of mind* **scholarly**, studious, literary, well read, intellectual, clever, erudite, learned, educated, cultured, bookish, highbrow, pedantic, donnish, cerebral; informal brainy; dated lettered. **3** *the debate has been largely academic* **theoretical**, conceptual, notional, philosophical, hypothetical, speculative, conjectural, suppositional, putative; impractical, unrealistic, ivory-tower.
▸ n. *a group of Russian academics* **scholar**, lecturer, don, teacher, tutor, professor, fellow, man/woman of letters, thinker, bluestocking; informal egghead, bookworm; formal pedagogue.

> **WORD LINKS**
> **colloquium**, **symposium** an academic conference
> **dissertation** a long essay written for a university degree or diploma
> **mortar board** a hat worn as part of formal academic dress
> **subfusc** formal dress worn for exams
> **viva** an oral exam for an academic qualification

academy n. **college**, school, university, institute, seminary, conservatory, conservatoire.

accede v. formal **1** *he acceded to the government's demands* **agree to**, consent to, assent to, acquiesce in, comply with, go along with, concur with, surrender to, yield to, give in to, give way to, defer to. **2** *Elizabeth I acceded to the throne in 1558* **succeed to**, come to, assume, inherit, take. **3** *Albania acceded to the IMF in 1990* **join**, become a member of, sign up to.

accelerate v. **1** *the car accelerated down the hill* **speed up**, go faster, gain momentum, increase speed, pick up speed, gather speed, put on a spurt. **2** *inflation started to accelerate* **increase**, rise, go up, leap up, surge, escalate, spiral. **3** *the university accelerated the planning process* **hasten**, expedite, precipitate, speed up, quicken,

make faster, step up, advance, further, forward, promote, stimulate, spur on; informal crank up.
– OPPOSITES decelerate, delay.

acceleration n. **1** *the car's acceleration is sensational* **increase in speed**, increasing speed. **2** *the acceleration of the industrial process* **hastening**, precipitation, speeding up, quickening, stepping up, advancement, furtherance, boost, stimulation, spur. **3** *an acceleration in the divorce rate* **increase**, rise, leap, surge, escalation.

accent n. **1** *a Scottish accent* **pronunciation**, intonation, enunciation, articulation, inflection, tone, modulation, cadence, timbre, manner of speaking, delivery; brogue, burr, drawl, twang. **2** *the accent is on the first syllable* **stress**, emphasis, accentuation, force, prominence; beat; technical ictus. **3** *the accent is on comfort* **emphasis**, stress, priority; importance, prominence. **4** *an acute accent* **mark**, diacritic, diacritical mark.
▸ v. *fabrics which accent the background colours in the room* **draw attention to**, point up, underline, underscore, accentuate, highlight, spotlight, foreground, feature, play up, bring to the fore, heighten, stress, emphasize.

accentuate v. **draw attention to**, point up, underline, underscore, accent, highlight, spotlight, foreground, feature, play up, bring to the fore, heighten, stress, emphasize.

accept v. **1** *he accepted a pen as a present* **receive**, take, get, gain, obtain, acquire. **2** *he accepted the job immediately* **take on**, undertake, assume, take responsibility for. **3** *she accepted an invitation to lunch* **say yes to**, reply in the affirmative, agree to. **4** *she was accepted as one of the family* **welcome**, receive, embrace, adopt. **5** *he accepted Ellen's explanation* **believe**, regard as true, give credence to, credit, trust; informal buy, swallow. **6** *we have agreed to accept his decision* **go along with**, agree to, consent to, acquiesce in, concur with, assent to, comply with, abide by, follow, adhere to, act in accordance with, defer to, yield to, surrender to, bow to, give in to, submit to, respect; formal accede to. **7** *she will just have to accept the consequences* **tolerate**, endure, put up with, bear, take, submit to, stomach, swallow; reconcile oneself to, resign oneself to, get used to, adjust to, learn to live with, make the best of; face up to.
– OPPOSITES refuse, reject.

acceptable adj. **1** *an acceptable standard of living* **satisfactory**, adequate, reasonable, quite good, fair, decent, good enough, sufficient, sufficiently good, fine, not bad, all right, average, tolerable, passable, middling, moderate; informal OK, so-so, fair-to-middling. **2** *a most acceptable present* **welcome**, appreciated; pleasing, agreeable, delightful, desirable, satisfying, gratifying, to one's liking. **3** *the risk had seemed acceptable at the time* **bearable**, tolerable, allowable, admissible, sustainable, justifiable, defensible.

acceptance n. **1** *the acceptance of an award* **receipt**, receiving, taking, obtaining. **2** *the acceptance of responsibility* **undertaking**, assumption. **3** *acceptances to an invitation* **yes**, affirmative reply, confirmation. **4** *her acceptance as one of the family* **welcome**, favourable reception, adoption. **5** *his acceptance of Matilda's explanation* **belief**, credence, trust, faith. **6** *their acceptance of the decision* **compliance**, acquiescence, agreement, consent, concurrence, assent, adherence, deference, surrender, submission, respect. **7** *the acceptance of pain* **toleration**, endurance, forbearance.

accepted adj. **recognized**, acknowledged, established, traditional, orthodox; usual, customary, common, normal, general, prevailing, accustomed, familiar, popular, expected, routine, standard, stock; literary wonted.

access n. **1** *the building has a side access* **entrance**, entry, way in, means of entry; approach, means of approach. **2** *they were denied access to the stadium* **admission**, admittance, entry, entrée, ingress, right of entry. **3** *students have access to a photocopier* **(the) use of**, permission to use. **4** *an access of rage* **fit**, attack, outburst, outpouring, eruption, explosion, burst, outbreak, flare-up, blow-up, blaze, paroxysm, bout, rush; outflow, outflowing, welling up.
▸ v. *the program used to access the data* **retrieve**, gain access to, obtain; read.

accessible adj. **1** *the village is only accessible on foot* | *an easily accessible reference tool* **reachable**, attainable, approachable; obtainable, available; informal get-at-able. **2** *his accessible style of writing* **understandable**, comprehensible, easy to understand, intelligible. **3** *Professor Cooper is very accessible* **approachable**, friendly, agreeable, obliging, congenial, affable, cordial, welcoming, easy-going, pleasant.

accession n. **1** *the Queen's accession to the throne* **succession**, assumption, inheritance. **2** *accession to the Treaty of Rome was effected in 1971* **assent**, consent, agreement; acceptance, acquiescence, compliance, concurrence. **3** *recent accessions to the museum* **addition**, acquisition, new item, gift, purchase.

accessorize v. **complement**, enhance, set off, show off; go with, accompany; decorate, adorn, ornament, trim.

accessory n. **1** *camera accessories such as tripods and flashguns* **attachment**, extra, addition, add-on, adjunct, appendage, appurtenance, fitment, supplement. **2** *fashion accessories* **adornment**, embellishment, ornament, ornamentation, decoration; frills, trimmings. **3** *she was charged as an accessory to murder* **accomplice**, partner in crime, associate, collaborator, fellow conspirator; henchman.
▸ adj. *an accessory gearbox* **additional**, extra, supplementary, supplemental, auxiliary, ancillary, secondary, subsidiary, reserve, add-on.

accident n. **1** *an accident at work* **mishap**, misadventure, unfortunate incident, mischance, misfortune, disaster, tragedy, catastrophe, calamity; technical casualty. **2** *an accident on the motorway* **crash**, collision, smash, bump, car crash, road traffic accident, RTA; derailment; N. Amer. **wreck**; informal smash-up, pile-up; Brit. informal prang, shunt. **3** *it is no accident that there is a similarity between them* **chance**, mere chance, coincidence, twist of fate, freak, hazard; fluke, serendipity; fate, fortuity, fortune, providence, happenstance.

accidental adj. **1** *an accidental meeting* **chance**, fortuitous, adventitious, fluky, coincidental, casual, serendipitous, random; unexpected, unforeseen, unanticipated, unlooked-for, unintentional, unintended, inadvertent, unplanned, unpremeditated, unthinking, unwitting. **2** *the location is accidental and contributes nothing to the poem* **incidental**, unimportant, by the way, by the by, supplementary, subsidiary, subordinate, secondary, accessory, peripheral, tangential, extraneous, extrinsic, irrelevant, non-essential, inessential.
– OPPOSITES intentional, deliberate.

accidentally adv. **by accident**, by chance, by a twist of fate, as luck would have it, fortuitously, by a fluke, by happenstance, coincidentally, adventitiously; unexpectedly, unintentionally, inadvertently, unwittingly.

acclaim v. *the booklet has been widely acclaimed by teachers* **praise**, applaud, cheer, commend, approve, welcome, pay tribute to, speak highly of, eulogize, compliment, celebrate, sing the praises of, rave about, heap praise on, wax lyrical about, lionize, exalt, admire, hail, extol, honour, hymn; N. Amer. informal **ballyhoo**; formal laud.
– OPPOSITES criticize.
▸ n. *she has won acclaim for her commitment to democracy* **praise**, applause, cheers, ovation, tribute, accolade, acclamation, salutes, plaudits, bouquets; approval, approbation, admiration, congratulations, commendation, welcome, homage; compliment, a pat on the back.
– OPPOSITES criticism.

acclaimed adj. **celebrated**, admired, highly rated, lionized, honoured, esteemed, exalted, well thought of, well received, acknowledged; eminent, great, renowned, distinguished, prestigious, illustrious, pre-eminent.

acclamation n. **praise**, applause, cheers, ovation, tribute, accolade, acclaim, salutes, plaudits, bouquets; approval, admiration, approbation, congratulations, commendation, homage; compliment, a pat on the back.
– OPPOSITES criticism.

acclimatization n. **adjustment**, adaptation, accommodation, habituation, acculturation, familiarization, inurement; naturalization; N. Amer. acclimation.

acclimatize v. **adjust**, adapt, accustom, accommodate, habituate, acculturate; get used, become inured, reconcile oneself, resign oneself; familiarize oneself; find one's feet, get one's bearings, become seasoned, become naturalized; N. Amer. acclimate.

accolade n. **1** *he received the accolade of knighthood* **honour**, privilege, award, gift, title; prize, laurels, bays, palm. **2** *the hotel won a top accolade from the inspectors* **tribute**, commendation, praise, testimonial, compliment, pat on the back; salutes, plaudits, congratulations, bouquets; informal rave.

accommodate v. **1** *refugees were accommodated in army camps* **lodge**, house, put up, billet, quarter, board, take in, shelter, give someone a roof over their head; harbour. **2** *the cottages accommodate up to six people* **hold**, take, have room for. **3** *our staff will make every effort to accommodate you* **help**, assist, aid, oblige; meet the needs/wants of, cater for, fit in with, satisfy. **4** *she tried to accommodate herself to her new situation* **adjust**, adapt, accustom, habituate, acclimatize, acculturate, get accustomed, get used, come to terms with; N. Amer. acclimate. **5** *the bank would be glad to accommodate you with a loan* **provide**, supply, furnish, grant.

accommodating adj. **obliging**, cooperative, helpful, eager to help, adaptable, amenable, considerate, unselfish, generous, willing, kindly, hospitable, neighbourly, kind, friendly, pleasant, agreeable; Brit. informal decent.

accommodation n. **1** *temporary accommodation* **housing**, lodging(s), living quarters, quarters, rooms; home, billet; shelter, a roof over one's head; informal digs, pad; formal abode, residence, place of residence, dwelling, dwelling place, habitation. **2** *lifeboat accommodation for 1,178 people* **space**, room, seating; places. **3** *an accommodation between the two parties was reached* **arrangement**, understanding, settlement, accord, deal, bargain, compromise. **4** *their accommodation to changing economic circumstances* **adjustment**, adaptation, habituation, acclimatization, acculturation; inurement; N. Amer. acclimation.

accompaniment n. **1** *a musical accompaniment* **backing**, support, background, soundtrack. **2** *the wine makes a superb accompaniment to cheese* **complement**, supplement, addition, adjunct, appendage, companion, accessory.

accompany v. **1** *the driver accompanied her to the door* **go with**, travel with, keep someone company, tag along with, partner, escort, chaperone, attend, show, see, usher, conduct. **2** *the illness is often accompanied by nausea* **occur with**, co-occur with, coexist with, go with, go together with, go hand in hand with, appear with, attend by. **3** *he accompanied the choir on the piano* **back**, play with, play for, support.

accomplice n. **partner in crime**, associate, accessory, confederate, collaborator, fellow conspirator; henchman; informal sidekick.

accomplish v. **fulfil**, achieve, succeed in, realize, attain, manage, bring about/off, carry out/through, execute, effect, perform, do, discharge, complete, finish, consummate, conclude; formal effectuate.

accomplished adj. **skilled**, skilful, expert, masterly, virtuoso, master, consummate, complete, proficient, talented, gifted, adept, adroit, deft, dexterous, able, good, competent, capable, efficient, experienced, seasoned, trained, practised, professional, polished, ready, apt; informal great, mean, nifty, crack, ace, wizard; Brit. informal a dab hand at; N. Amer. informal crackerjack.

accomplishment n. **1** *the reduction of inflation was a remarkable accomplishment* **achievement**, act, deed, exploit, performance, attainment, effort, feat, move, coup. **2** *typing was another of her accomplishments* **talent**, skill, gift, ability, attainment, achievement, forte, knack. **3** *a poet of considerable accomplishment* **expertise**, skill, skilfulness, talent, adeptness, adroitness, deftness, dexterity, ability, prowess, mastery, competence, capability, proficiency, aptitude, artistry, art; informal know-how.

accord v. **1** *the national assembly accorded him more power* **give**, grant, present, award, vouchsafe; confer on, bestow on, vest in, invest with. **2** *his views accorded with mine* **correspond**, agree, tally, match, concur, be consistent, harmonize, be in harmony, be compatible, be in tune, correlate; conform to; informal square.
– OPPOSITES withhold, disagree, differ.
▸ n. **1** *a peace accord* **pact**, treaty, agreement, settlement, deal, entente, concordat, protocol, contract, convention. **2** *the two sides failed to reach accord* **agreement**, consensus, unanimity, harmony, unison, unity; formal concord.
□ **of one's own accord** voluntarily, of one's own free will, of one's own volition, by choice; willingly, freely, readily.
with one accord unanimously, in complete agreement, with one mind, without exception, as one, of one voice, to a man.

accordance n. *a ballot held in accordance with trade union rules* **in agreement with**, in conformity with, in line with, true to, in the spirit of, observing, following, heeding.

according adj. **1** *she had a narrow escape, according to the doctors* **as stated by**, as claimed by, on the authority of, in the opinion of. **2** *cook the rice according to the instructions* **as specified by**, as per, in accordance with, in compliance with, in agreement with. **3** *salary will be fixed according to experience* **in proportion to**, proportional to, commensurate with, in relation to, relative to, in line with, corresponding to.

a

accordingly adv. **1** *they appreciated the danger and acted accordingly* **appropriately**, correspondingly, suitably. **2** *accordingly, he returned home to Yorkshire* **therefore**, for that reason, consequently, so, as a result, as a consequence, in consequence, hence, thus, that being the case, ergo.

accost v. **speak to**, call to, shout to, hail, address; approach, confront, detain, stop; informal buttonhole, collar; Brit. informal nobble.

account n. **1** *his account of the incident* **description**, report, version, story, narration, narrative, statement, explanation, exposition, delineation, portrayal, tale; chronicle, history, record, log, weblog, blog; view, impression. **2** *the firm's quarterly accounts* **financial record**, ledger, balance sheet, financial statement; (**accounts**) books. **3** *I pay the account off in full each month* **bill**, invoice, tally; debt, charges; N. Amer. check; informal tab. **4** *his background is of no account* **importance**, import, significance, consequence, substance, note; formal moment.
▸ v. *her visit could not be accounted a success* **consider**, regard as, reckon, hold to be, think, look on as, view as, see as, judge, adjudge, count, deem, rate.
□ **account for 1** *they must account for the delay* **explain**, answer for, give reasons for, rationalize, justify. **2** *excise duties account for over half the price of Scotch* **constitute**, make up, comprise, form, compose, represent.
on account of because of, owing to, due to, as a consequence of, thanks to, by/in virtue of, in view of.
on no account never, under no circumstances, not for any reason.

accountability n. **responsibility**, liability.

accountable adj. **1** *the government was held accountable for the food shortage* **responsible**, liable, answerable; to blame. **2** *the game's popularity is barely accountable* **explicable**, explainable; understandable, comprehensible.

accoutrements plural n. **equipment**, paraphernalia, stuff, things, apparatus, tackle, kit, implements, material(s), rig, outfit, regalia, appurtenances, impedimenta, odds and ends, bits and pieces, bits and bobs, trappings, accessories.

accredit v. **1** *he was accredited with being one of the world's fastest sprinters* **recognize as**, credit with. **2** *the discovery of distillation is usually accredited to the Arabs* **ascribe**, attribute. **3** *professional bodies accredit these research degrees* **recognize**, authorize, approve, certify, license.

accredited adj. **official**, appointed, recognized, authorized, approved, certified, licensed.

accretion n. **1** *the accretion of sediments* **accumulation**, formation, collecting, cumulation, accrual; growth, increase. **2** *architectural accretions* **addition**, extension, appendage, add-on, supplement.

accrue v. **1** *financial benefits will accrue from restructuring* **result**, arise, follow, ensue; be caused by. **2** *interest is added to the account as it accrues* **accumulate**, collect, build up, mount up, grow, increase.

accumulate v. **gather**, collect, amass, stockpile, pile up, heap up, store (up), hoard, cumulate, lay in/up; increase, multiply, accrue; run up.

accumulation n. **mass**, build-up, pile, heap, stack, collection, stock, store, stockpile, reserve, hoard; amassing, gathering, cumulation, accrual, accretion.

accuracy n. **correctness**, precision, exactness; factuality, literalness, fidelity, faithfulness, truth, truthfulness, veracity, authenticity, realism, verisimilitude.

accurate adj. **1** *accurate information | an accurate representation of the situation* **correct**, precise, exact, right, error-free, perfect; **factual**, fact-based, literal, faithful, true, truthful, true to life, authentic, realistic; informal on the mark, on the nail; Brit. informal spot on, bang on; N. Amer. informal on the money, on the button; formal veracious. **2** *an accurate shot* **well aimed**, on target, unerring, deadly, lethal, sure, true, on the mark.

accursed adj. dated **hateful**, detestable, loathsome, foul, abominable, damnable, odious, obnoxious, despicable, horrible, horrid, ghastly, awful, dreadful, terrible; annoying, irritating, infuriating, exasperating; informal damned, damn, blasted, pesky, pestilential, infernal; Brit. informal beastly.
– OPPOSITES pleasant.

accusation n. **allegation**, charge, claim, assertion, imputation; indictment; arraignment; suit, lawsuit; Law, Brit. plaint; N. Amer. impeachment.

accuse v. **1** *four people were accused of assault* **charge with**, indict for, arraign for; summons, cite, prefer charges against; N. Amer. impeach for. **2** *the companies were accused of causing job losses* **blame for**, lay the blame on, hold responsible for, hold accountable for; condemn for, criticize for, denounce for; lay at the door of; informal point the finger at, stick on, pin on.
– OPPOSITES absolve, exonerate.

accustom v. **adapt**, adjust, acclimatize, habituate, accommodate, acculturate; reconcile oneself, become reconciled, get used to, come to terms with, learn to live with, become inured; N. Amer. acclimate.

accustomed adj. **customary**, usual, normal, habitual, regular, routine, ordinary, typical, traditional, established, common, general; literary wonted.

ace informal n. *a rowing ace* **expert**, master, genius, virtuoso, maestro, adept, past master, doyen, champion, star; informal demon, hotshot, wizard, whizz; Brit. informal dab hand; N. Amer. informal maven, crackerjack.
– OPPOSITES amateur.
▸ adj. *an ace tennis player* **excellent**, first-rate,

first-class, top-tier, marvellous, wonderful, magnificent, outstanding, superlative, formidable, virtuoso, masterly, expert, champion, consummate, skilful, adept; informal great, terrific, tremendous, superb, fantastic, sensational, fabulous, fab, crack, hotshot, A1, mean, demon, awesome, magic, tip-top, top-notch; Brit. informal smashing, brilliant, brill.
– OPPOSITES mediocre.

acerbic adj. **sharp**, sarcastic, sardonic, mordant, trenchant, cutting, razor-edged, biting, stinging, searing, scathing, caustic, astringent, abrasive; N. Amer. acerb; Brit. informal sarky; N. Amer. informal snarky.

ache n. **1** *a stomach ache* **pain**, cramp, twinge, pang; gnawing, stabbing, stinging, smarting; soreness, tenderness, irritation, discomfort. **2** *the ache in her heart* **sorrow**, sadness, misery, grief, anguish, suffering, pain, agony, torture, hurt.
▶ v. **1** *my legs were aching* **hurt**, be sore, be painful, be in pain, throb, pound, twinge; smart, burn, sting; Brit. informal give someone gyp, play up. **2** *her heart ached for poor Philippa* **grieve**, sorrow, be in distress, be miserable, be in anguish, bleed. **3** *Marie ached for his affection* **long**, yearn, hunger, thirst, hanker, pine, itch; crave, desire.

achieve v. **attain**, reach, arrive at; realize, bring off/about, pull off, accomplish, carry out/through, fulfil, execute, perform, engineer, conclude, complete, finish, consummate; earn, win, gain, acquire, obtain, come by, get, secure, clinch, net; informal wrap up, wangle, swing; formal effectuate.

achievement n. **1** *the achievement of a high rate of economic growth* **attainment**, realization, accomplishment, fulfilment, implementation, execution, performance; conclusion, completion, close, consummation. **2** *they felt justifiably proud of their achievement* **accomplishment**, attainment, feat, performance, undertaking, act, action, deed, effort, exploit; work, handiwork.

Achilles' heel n. **weak spot**, weak point, weakness, soft underbelly, shortcoming, failing, imperfection, flaw, defect, chink in one's armour.
– OPPOSITES strength.

aching adj. **1** *his aching back* **painful**, achy, sore, stiff, hurt, tender, uncomfortable; hurting, in pain, throbbing, pounding, smarting, burning, stinging. **2** *her aching heart* **sorrowful**, sad, miserable, grieving, upset, distressed, anguished, grief-stricken, heavy.

acid adj. **1** *a slightly acid flavour* **acidic**, **sour**, tart, bitter, sharp, acrid, pungent, acerbic, vinegary, acetic, acetous. **2** *acid remarks* **acerbic**, sarcastic, sharp, sardonic, scathing, cutting, razor-edged, biting, stinging, caustic, trenchant, mordant, bitter, acrimonious, astringent, harsh, abrasive, wounding, hurtful, unkind, vitriolic,

venomous, waspish, spiteful, malicious; N. Amer. acerb; informal bitchy, catty; Brit. informal sarky; N. Amer. informal snarky.
– OPPOSITES sweet, pleasant.

acknowledge v. **1** *the government acknowledged the need to begin talks* **admit**, accept, grant, allow, concede, confess, own, recognize. **2** *he did not acknowledge Colin, but hurried past* **greet**, salute, address; nod to, wave to, raise one's hat to, say hello to. **3** *Douglas was glad to acknowledge her help* **express gratitude for**, show appreciation for, thank someone for. **4** *few people acknowledged my letters* **answer**, reply to, respond to.
– OPPOSITES reject, deny, ignore.

acknowledged adj. **recognized**, accepted, approved, accredited, confirmed, declared, confessed, avowed.

acknowledgement n. **1** *acknowledgement of the need to take new initiatives* **acceptance**, admission, concession, confession, recognition. **2** *a smile of acknowledgement* **greeting**, welcome, salutation. **3** *she left without a word of acknowledgement* **thanks**, gratitude, appreciation, recognition. **4** *I sent off the form, but there was no acknowledgement* **answer**, reply, response.

acme n. **peak**, pinnacle, zenith, height, high point, crown, crest, summit, top, apex, apogee; climax, culmination.
– OPPOSITES nadir.

acolyte n. **assistant**, helper, attendant, minion, underling, lackey, henchman; follower, disciple, supporter, votary; informal sidekick, groupie, hanger-on.

acquaint v. *he will need to acquaint himself with the regulations* **familiarize**, make familiar, make aware of, inform of, advise of, apprise of, let know, get up to date; brief, prime; informal fill in on, gen up on, clue in on.

acquaintance n. **1** *a business acquaintance* **contact**, associate, colleague. **2** *my acquaintance with George* **association**, relationship, contact. **3** *the pupils had little acquaintance with the language* **familiarity with**, knowledge of, experience of, awareness of, understanding of, comprehension of, grasp of.

acquainted adj. **1** *she was well acquainted with Gothic literature* **familiar**, conversant, at home, up to date, abreast, au fait, au courant, well versed, knowledgeable, well informed; informed, apprised; informal genned-up, clued-in; formal cognizant. **2** *I am not personally acquainted with him* **friendly**, on friendly terms.

acquiesce v. *he acquiesced in the cover-up* **accept**, consent to, agree to, allow, concede, assent to, concur with, give the nod to; comply with, go along with, cooperate with, give in to, bow to, yield to, submit to.

acquiescence n. **consent**, agreement, acceptance, concurrence, assent, leave; compliance, concession, cooperation; submission.

a

acquiescent adj. **compliant**, cooperative, willing, obliging, agreeable, amenable, tractable, persuadable, pliant, unprotesting; submissive, self-effacing, unassertive, yielding, biddable, docile.

acquire v. **obtain**, come by, get, receive, gain, earn, win, come into, be given; buy, purchase, procure, possess oneself of, secure, pick up; informal get one's hands on, get hold of, land, bag, score.
– OPPOSITES lose.

acquirement n. **1** *her many acquirements* **attainment**, achievement, accomplishment, skill, talent. **2** *the acquirement of money* **acquisition**, obtaining, gaining, earning, winning, procurement.

acquisition n. **1** *a new acquisition* **purchase**, gain, accession, addition, investment, possession; informal buy. **2** *the acquisition of funds* **obtaining**, acquirement, gaining, earning, winning, procurement, collection.

acquisitive adj. **greedy**, covetous, avaricious, possessive, grasping, grabbing, predatory, avid, rapacious, mercenary, materialistic; informal money-grubbing.

acquisitiveness n. **greed**, greediness, covetousness, cupidity, possessiveness, avarice, avidity, rapaciousness, rapacity, materialism.

acquit v. **1** *the jury acquitted her* **clear**, exonerate, find innocent, absolve; discharge, release, free, set free; informal let off (the hook); formal exculpate. **2** *the boys acquitted themselves well* **behave**, conduct oneself, perform, act; formal comport oneself.
– OPPOSITES convict.

acquittal n. **clearing**, exoneration; discharge, release, freeing; informal let-off; formal exculpation.
– OPPOSITES conviction.

acrid adj. **pungent**, bitter, sharp, sour, tart, harsh, acid, acidic, vinegary, acetic, acetous, stinging, burning.

acrimonious adj. **bitter**, angry, rancorous, caustic, acerbic, scathing, sarcastic, acid, harsh, sharp, cutting; virulent, spiteful, vicious, vitriolic, hostile, venomous, nasty, bad-tempered, ill-natured, mean, malign, malicious, malignant, waspish; informal bitchy, catty.

acrimony n. **bitterness**, anger, rancour, resentment, ill feeling, ill will, bad blood, animosity, hostility, enmity, antagonism, waspishness, spleen, malice, spitefulness, venom.
– OPPOSITES goodwill.

acrobat n. **tumbler**, gymnast, tightrope walker, wire walker, trapeze artist; rare funambulist.

acrobatics plural n. **1** *staggering feats of acrobatics* **gymnastics**, tumbling; agility; rare funambulism. **2** *the acrobatics required to negotiate an international contract* **mental agility**, skill, quick thinking, alertness, inventiveness.

act v. **1** *the Government must act to remedy the situation* **take action**, take steps, take

measures, move, react. **2** *he was acting on the orders of the party leader* **follow**, act in accordance with, obey, heed, comply with; fulfil, meet, discharge. **3** *an estate agent acting for a prospective buyer* **represent**, act on behalf of; stand in for, fill in for, deputize for, take the place of. **4** *Alison began to act oddly* **behave**, conduct oneself, react; formal comport oneself. **5** *the scents act as a powerful aphrodisiac* **operate**, work, function, serve. **6** *the drug acted directly on the blood vessels* **affect**, have an effect on, work on; have an impact on, impact on, influence. **7** *he acted in a highly successful film* **perform**, play a part, take part, appear; informal tread the boards. **8** *we laughed, but most of us were just acting* **pretend**, play-act, put it on, fake it, feign it, dissemble, dissimulate.
▶ n. **1** *acts of kindness* | *a criminal act* **deed**, action, feat, exploit, move, gesture, performance, undertaking, stunt, operation; achievement, accomplishment. **2** *the act raised the tax on tobacco* **law**, decree, statute, bill, Act of Parliament, enactment, resolution, edict, dictum, ruling, measure; N. Amer. formal ordinance. **3** *the first act of the play* **section**, division, subsection, part, segment. **4** *a music hall act* **performance**, turn, routine, number, sketch, skit. **5** *it was all just an act* **pretence**, show, front, facade, masquerade, charade, posture, pose, affectation, sham, fake; informal a put-on.
□ **act up** informal **1** *all children act up from time to time* **misbehave**, behave badly, get up to mischief; Brit. informal play up. **2** *the engine was acting up* **malfunction**, go wrong, be defective, be faulty; informal be on the blink; Brit. informal play up.

acting n. *the theory and practice of acting* **drama**, the theatre, the stage, the performing arts, thespianism, dramatics, dramaturgy, stagecraft, theatricals; informal treading the boards.
▶ adj. *the bank's acting governor* **temporary**, interim, caretaker, pro tem, provisional, stopgap; deputy, stand-in, fill-in; N. Amer. informal pinch-hitting.
– OPPOSITES permanent.

action n. **1** *there can be no excuse for their actions* **deed**, act, move, undertaking, exploit, manoeuvre, endeavour, effort, exertion; behaviour, conduct, activity. **2** *the need for local community action* **measures**, steps, activity, movement, work, operation. **3** *a man of action* **energy**, vitality, vigour, forcefulness, drive, initiative, spirit, liveliness, vim, pep; activity; informal get-up-and-go. **4** *the action of hormones on the pancreas* **effect**, influence, working; power. **5** *he missed all the action while he was away* **excitement**, activity, happenings, events, incidents; informal goings-on. **6** *twenty-nine men died in the action* **fighting**, hostilities, battle, conflict, combat, warfare; engagement, clash, encounter, skirmish. **7** *a civil action for damages* **lawsuit**, legal action, suit (at law), case, prosecution, litigation, proceedings.

activate v. **operate**, switch on, turn on, start (up), set going, trigger (off), set in motion, actuate, energize; trip.

active adj. **1** *despite her illness she remained active* **energetic**, lively, sprightly, spry, mobile, vigorous, vital, dynamic, sporty; busy, occupied; informal on the go, full of beans. **2** *an active member of the union* **hard-working**, busy, industrious, diligent, tireless, contributing, effective, enterprising, involved, enthusiastic, keen, committed, devoted, zealous. **3** *the watermill was active until 1960* **operative**, working, functioning, functional, operating, operational, in action, in operation; live; informal up and running.
– OPPOSITES listless, passive.

activity n. **1** *there was a lot of activity in the area* **bustle**, hustle and bustle, busyness, action, liveliness, movement, life, stir, flurry; happenings, occurrences, proceedings, events, incidents; informal toing and froing, comings and goings. **2** *a wide range of activities* **pursuit**, occupation, interest, hobby, pastime, recreation, diversion; venture, undertaking, enterprise, project, scheme, business, entertainment; act, action, deed, exploit.

actor, **actress** n. **performer**, player, trouper, thespian; film star, matinee idol, star, starlet; informal ham; Brit. informal luvvie; N. Amer. informal hambone.

> **WORD LINKS**
> **thespian**, **histrionic** relating to actors
> **audition** a try-out to see if an actor is suitable for a role
> **greasepaint** make-up used by actors
> **understudy** an actor who learns another's role in case of an emergency

actual adj. **real**, true, genuine, authentic, verified, attested, confirmed, definite, hard, plain, veritable; existing, existent, manifest, substantial, factual, de facto, bona fide; informal real live.
– OPPOSITES notional.

actuality n. *the journalistic debate about actuality and fiction* **reality**, fact, truth, real life.
□ **in actuality** really, in (actual) fact, in point of fact, actually, as a matter of fact, in reality, in truth, if truth be told, to tell the truth; old use in sooth.

actually adv. *I looked upset but actually I was terribly excited* **really**, in (actual) fact, in point of fact, as a matter of fact, in reality, in actuality, in truth, if truth be told, to tell the truth; old use in sooth.

actuate v. **1** *the sprinkler system was actuated by the fire* **activate**, operate, switch on, turn on, start (up), set going, trigger (off), trip, set in motion, energize. **2** *the defendant was actuated by malice* **motivate**, prompt, stimulate, move, drive, influence, incite, spur on, impel.

acumen n. **astuteness**, shrewdness, acuity, sharpness, sharp-wittedness, cleverness, smartness, brains; judgement, understanding, awareness, sense, common sense, canniness, discernment, wisdom, wit, sagacity, perspicacity, insight, perception, penetration; informal nous, savvy, know-how, horse sense; N. Amer. informal smarts; formal perspicuity.

acute adj. **1** *the acute food shortages* **severe**, critical, drastic, dire, dreadful, terrible, awful, grave, bad, serious, desperate, parlous, dangerous. **2** *acute stomach pains* **sharp**, severe, stabbing, excruciating, agonizing, racking, searing. **3** *his acute mind* **astute**, shrewd, sharp, sharp-witted, razor-sharp, rapier-like, quick, quick-witted, agile, nimble, clever, intelligent, brilliant, smart, canny, discerning, perceptive, perspicacious, penetrating, insightful, incisive, piercing, discriminating, sagacious, wise, judicious; informal on the ball, quick off the mark, quick on the uptake, streetwise, savvy; N. Amer. informal heads-up. **4** *an acute sense of smell* **keen**, sharp, good, penetrating, discerning, sensitive.
– OPPOSITES mild, dull.

acutely adv. **extremely**, exceedingly, very, markedly, severely, intensely, deeply, profoundly, keenly, painfully, desperately, tremendously, enormously, thoroughly, heartily; informal awfully, terribly.
– OPPOSITES slightly.

adage n. **saying**, maxim, axiom, proverb, aphorism, apophthegm, saw, dictum, precept, motto, truism, platitude, cliché, commonplace.

adamant adj. **unshakeable**, immovable, inflexible, unwavering, unswerving, uncompromising, resolute, resolved, determined, firm, steadfast; stubborn, unrelenting, unyielding, unbending, rigid, obdurate, inexorable, intransigent, dead set.

adapt v. **1** *we've adapted the hotels to suit their needs* **modify**, alter, change, adjust, convert, redesign, restyle, refashion, remodel, reshape, revamp, rework, rejig, redo, reconstruct, reorganize; customize, tailor; improve, amend, refine; informal tweak. **2** *he has adapted well to his new home* **adjust**, acclimatize oneself, accommodate oneself, habituate oneself, become habituated, get used, orient oneself, reconcile oneself, come to terms, get one's bearings, find one's feet, acculturate, assimilate, blend in, fit in; N. Amer. acclimate.

adaptable adj. **1** *competent and adaptable staff* **flexible**, versatile, cooperative, accommodating, amenable. **2** *an adaptable piece of furniture* **versatile**, modifiable, convertible, alterable, adjustable, changeable; multi-purpose, all-purpose.

adaptation n. **1** *the adaptation of old buildings* **conversion**, alteration, modification, redesign, remodelling, revamping, reconstruction. **2** *the adaptation of an ethnic community to British society* **adjustment**, acclimatization, accommodation, habituation, acculturation,

a

assimilation, integration; N. Amer. acclimation.

add v. **1** *the front porch was added in 1751* **attach**, build on, join, append, affix, connect, annex; include, incorporate. **2** *they added all the figures up* **total**, count (up), compute, reckon up, tally; Brit. tot up. **3** *the subsidies added up to £1700* **amount to**, come to, run to, make, total, equal, number. **4** *the recent riots add up to a deepening crisis* **amount to**, constitute; signify, signal, mean, indicate, denote, point to, be evidence of, be symptomatic of; informal spell. **5** *her decision just added to his woe* **increase**, magnify, amplify, augment, intensify, heighten, deepen; exacerbate, aggravate, compound, reinforce; add fuel to the fire, fan the flames, rub salt in the wound. **6** *she added that she had every confidence in Laura* **go on to say**, state further, continue, carry on.
− OPPOSITES subtract.
□ **add up** informal *the situation just didn't add up* make sense, stand to reason, hold up, hold water, ring true, be convincing.

addendum n. **appendix**, codicil, postscript, afterword, tailpiece, rider, coda, supplement; adjunct, appendage, addition, add-on, attachment.

addict n. **1** *a heroin addict* **abuser**, user; informal junkie, druggy, -freak, -head, pill popper; N. Amer. informal hophead. **2** *informal skiing addicts* **enthusiast**, fan, lover, devotee, aficionado; informal freak, nut, fiend, fanatic, maniac.

addicted adj. **1** *he was addicted to tranquillizers* **dependent on**; informal hooked on. **2** *she became addicted to the theatre* **devoted to**, obsessed with, fixated on, fanatical about, passionate about, a slave to; informal hooked on, mad on, crazy about.

addiction n. **1** *his heroin addiction* **dependency**, dependence, habit; informal monkey. **2** *a slavish addiction to fashion* **devotion to**, dedication to, obsession with, infatuation with, passion for, love of, mania for, enslavement to.

addictive adj. **habit-forming**; compulsive; Brit. informal moreish.

addition n. **1** *the soil is improved by the addition of compost* **adding**, incorporation, inclusion, introduction. **2** *an addition to the existing regulations* **supplement**, adjunct, addendum, appendage, add-on, extra; rider.
□ **in addition 1** *conditions were harsh and in addition some soldiers fell victim to snipers* **also**, as well, what's more, additionally, furthermore, moreover, into the bargain, to boot. **2** *eight presidential candidates in addition to the General* **besides**, as well as, on top of, plus, over and above.

additional adj. **extra**, added, supplementary, supplemental, further, auxiliary, ancillary; more, other, another, new, fresh.

additionally adv. **also**, in addition, as well, too, besides, on top of (that), moreover, further, furthermore, what's more, over and above that, into the bargain, to boot; old use withal.

additive n. **added ingredient**, addition; preservative, colouring; Brit. informal E-number.

addled adj. **muddled**, confused, muzzy, fuddled, befuddled, dazed, disoriented, disorientated, fuzzy; informal woozy.

address n. **1** *the address on the envelope* **inscription**, superscription; directions. **2** *our officers called at the address* **house**, flat, apartment, home; formal residence, dwelling, dwelling place, habitation, abode, domicile. **3** *his address to the European Parliament* **speech**, lecture, talk, monologue, dissertation, discourse, oration, peroration; sermon, homily, lesson.
▸ v. **1** *I addressed the envelope by hand* **inscribe**, superscribe. **2** *the preacher addressed a crowded congregation* **talk to**, give a talk to, speak to, make a speech to, give a lecture to, lecture, hold forth to; preach to. **3** *the question of how to address one's parents-in-law* **call**, name, designate; speak to, write to; formal denominate. **4** *correspondence should be addressed to the Banking Ombudsman* **direct**, send, communicate, convey, remit. **5** *the minister failed to address the issue of subsidies* **attend to**, apply oneself to, tackle, see to, deal with, confront, get to grips with, get down to, turn one's hand to, take in hand, undertake, concentrate on, focus on, devote oneself to.

adduce v. **cite**, quote, name, mention, instance, point out, refer to; put forward, present, offer, advance, propose, proffer.

adept adj. *an adept negotiator* **expert**, proficient, accomplished, skilful, talented, masterly, consummate, virtuoso; adroit, dexterous, deft, artful; brilliant, splendid, marvellous, formidable, outstanding, first-rate, first-class, excellent, fine; informal great, top-notch, tip-top, A1, ace, mean, hotshot, crack, nifty, deadly; Brit. informal a dab hand at; N. Amer. informal crackerjack.
− OPPOSITES inept.
▸ n. *kung fu adepts* **expert**, past master, master, genius, maestro, doyen; informal wizard, demon, ace, hotshot, whizz; N. Amer. informal maven, crackerjack.
− OPPOSITES amateur.

adequacy n. **1** *the adequacy of the existing services* **satisfactoriness**, acceptability, acceptableness; sufficiency. **2** *he had deep misgivings about his own adequacy* **capability**, competence, ability, aptitude, suitability; effectiveness, fitness; formal efficacy.

adequate adj. **1** *he lacked adequate financial resources* **sufficient**, enough, requisite. **2** *the company provides an adequate service* **acceptable**, passable, reasonable, satisfactory, tolerable, fair, decent, quite good, pretty good, goodish, moderate, unexceptional, unremarkable, undistinguished, ordinary, average, not bad, all right, middling; informal OK, so-so, fair-to-middling, nothing to write home about. **3** *the workstations were small but seemed adequate to the task* **equal to**, up to, capable of, suitable for, able to do, fit for, sufficient for.

adhere v. **1** *a dollop of cream adhered to her nose* **stick (fast)**, cohere, cling, bond, attach; be stuck, be fixed, be glued. **2** *they adhere scrupulously to Judaic law* **abide by**, stick to, hold to, comply with, act in accordance with, conform to, submit to; follow, obey, heed, observe, respect, uphold, fulfil.
– OPPOSITES flout, ignore.

adherent n. **follower**, supporter, upholder, defender, advocate, disciple, votary, devotee, partisan, member, friend, stalwart, sectary; believer, worshipper.
– OPPOSITES opponent.

adhesion n. **1** *the adhesion of the gum strip to the paper fibres* **sticking**, adherence. **2** *the front tyres were struggling for adhesion* **traction**, grip, purchase.

adhesive n. *a spray adhesive* **glue**, fixative, gum, paste, cement; N. Amer. mucilage; N. Amer. informal stickum.
▸ adj. *adhesive mortar* **sticky**, tacky, gluey, gummed; viscous, viscid; technical adherent; informal icky.

adieu n. & exclam. **goodbye**, farewell, until we meet again; informal bye-bye, ta-ta, bye, cheerio, cheers, ciao, so long; informal dated toodle-oo, toodle-pip.

ad infinitum adv. **forever**, for ever and ever, evermore, always, for all time, until the end of time, in perpetuity, until hell freezes over; perpetually, eternally, endlessly, interminably, unceasingly, unendingly; Brit. for evermore; informal until the cows come home, until the twelfth of never, until doomsday, until kingdom come; old use for aye.

adjacent adj. **adjoining**, neighbouring, next-door, abutting, contiguous, proximate; (**adjacent to**) close to, near, next to, by, by the side of, bordering on, beside, alongside, attached to, touching, cheek by jowl with.

adjoin v. **be next to**, be adjacent to, border (on), abut, be contiguous with, communicate with, extend to; join, conjoin, connect with, touch, meet.

adjoining adj. **connecting**, connected, interconnecting, adjacent, neighbouring, bordering, next-door; contiguous, proximate; attached, touching.

adjourn v. **1** *the hearing was adjourned* **suspend**, break off, discontinue, interrupt, prorogue, stay, recess. **2** *sentencing was adjourned until June 9* **postpone**, put off/ back, defer, delay, hold over, shelve. **3** *they adjourned to the sitting room for liqueurs* **withdraw**, retire, retreat, take oneself; formal repair, remove; literary betake oneself.

adjournment n. **suspension**, discontinuation, interruption, postponement, deferment, deferral, stay, prorogation; break, pause, recess.

adjudge v. **judge**, deem, find, pronounce, proclaim, rule, hold, determine; consider, think, rate, reckon, perceive, regard as, view as, see as, believe to be.

adjudicate v. **judge**, try, hear, examine, arbitrate; pronounce on, give a ruling on, pass judgement on, decide, determine, settle, resolve.

adjudication n. **judgement**, decision, pronouncement, ruling, settlement, resolution, arbitration, finding, verdict, sentence; Law determination.

adjudicator n. **judge**, arbitrator, arbiter; referee, umpire, line judge, linesman.

adjunct n. **supplement**, addition, extra, add-on, accessory, accompaniment, complement, appurtenance; attachment, appendage, addendum.

adjust v. **1** *Kate had adjusted to her new life* **adapt**, become accustomed, get used, accommodate, acclimatize, orient oneself, reconcile oneself, habituate oneself, assimilate; come to terms with, blend in with, fit in with, find one's feet in; N. Amer. acclimate. **2** *he adjusted the brakes* **modify**, alter, regulate, tune, fine-tune, calibrate, balance; adapt, rearrange, change, rejig, rework, revamp, remodel, reshape, convert, tailor, improve, enhance, customize; repair, fix, correct, rectify, overhaul, put right; informal tweak.

adjustable adj. **alterable**, adaptable, modifiable, convertible, variable, multiway, versatile.

adjustment n. **1** *a period of adjustment* **adaptation**, accommodation, acclimatization, habituation, acculturation, naturalization, assimilation; N. Amer. acclimation. **2** *the car will run on unleaded petrol with no adjustment* **modification**, alteration, regulation, adaptation, rearrangement, change, reconstruction, customization, refinement; repair, correction, amendment, overhaul, improvement.

ad-lib v. *she ad-libbed half the speech* **improvise**, extemporize, speak impromptu, play it by ear, make it up as one goes along; informal busk it, wing it.
▸ adv. *she spoke ad lib* **impromptu**, extempore, without preparation, without rehearsal, extemporaneously; informal off the cuff, off the top of one's head.
▸ adj. *a live, ad-lib commentary* **impromptu**, extempore, extemporaneous, extemporary, improvised, unprepared, unrehearsed, unscripted; informal off-the-cuff, spur-of-the-moment.

administer v. **1** *the union is administered by a central executive* **manage**, direct, control, operate, regulate, conduct, handle, run, organize, supervise, superintend, oversee, preside over, govern, rule, lead, head, steer; be in control of, be in charge of, be responsible for, be at the helm of, helm; informal head up. **2** *the lifeboat crew administered first aid* **dispense**, issue, give, provide, apply, allot, distribute, hand out, dole out, disburse. **3** *a gym shoe was used to administer punishment* **inflict**, mete out, deal out, deliver.

administration n. **1** *the day-to-day administration of the company* **management**, direction, control, command, charge, conduct, operation, running, leadership, government, governing, superintendence, supervision, regulation, overseeing. **2** *the previous Labour administration* **government**, cabinet, ministry, regime, executive, authority, directorate, council, leadership, management; parliament, congress, senate; rule, term of office, incumbency. **3** *the administration of anti-inflammatory drugs* **provision**, issuing, issuance, application, dispensing, dispensation, distribution, disbursement.

administrative adj. **managerial**, management, directorial, executive, organizational, supervisory, regulatory.

administrator n. **manager**, director, executive, controller, head, chief, leader, governor, superintendent, supervisor; informal boss.

admirable adj. **commendable**, praiseworthy, laudable, estimable, meritorious, creditable, exemplary, honourable, worthy, deserving, respectable, worthwhile, good, sterling, fine, masterly, great.
– OPPOSITES deplorable.

admiration n. **respect**, approval, approbation, appreciation, (high) regard, esteem; commendation, acclaim, applause, praise, compliments, tributes, accolades, plaudits; formal laudation.
– OPPOSITES scorn.

admire v. **1** *I admire your courage* **respect**, approve of, esteem, think highly of, rate highly, hold in high regard, applaud, praise, commend, acclaim. **2** *Simon had admired her for a long time* **adore**, love, worship, dote on, be enamoured of, be infatuated with; be taken with, be attracted to, find attractive; informal carry a torch for, have a thing about.
– OPPOSITES despise.

admirer n. **1** *a great admirer of Henry James* **fan**, devotee, enthusiast, aficionado; supporter, adherent, follower, disciple. **2** *a handsome admirer of hers* **suitor**, wooer, sweetheart, lover, boyfriend, young man; literary swain; dated beau.

admissible adj. **valid**, allowable, allowed, permissible, permitted, acceptable, satisfactory, justifiable, defensible, supportable, well founded, tenable, sound; legitimate, lawful, legal, licit; informal OK, legit, kosher, pukka.

admission n. **1** *membership entitles you to free admission* **admittance**, entry, entrance, right of entry, access, right of access, ingress; entrée. **2** *admission is fifty pence* **entrance fee**, entry charge, ticket. **3** *a written admission of liability* **confession**, acknowledgement, acceptance, concession, disclosure, divulgence.

admit v. **1** *he unlocked the door to admit her* **let in**, allow entry, permit entry, take in, usher in, show in, receive, welcome. **2** *he was admitted as a scholar to Winchester College* **accept**, take on, receive, enrol, enlist, register, sign up. **3** *Paul admitted that he was angry* **confess**, acknowledge, own, concede, grant, accept, allow; reveal, disclose, divulge. **4** *he admitted three offences of reckless driving* **confess (to)**, plead guilty to, own up to, make a clean breast of.
– OPPOSITES exclude, deny.

admittance n. **entry**, right of entry, admission, entrance, access, right of access, ingress; entrée.
– OPPOSITES exclusion.

admonish v. **1** *he was severely admonished by his father* **reprimand**, rebuke, scold, reprove, reproach, upbraid, chastise, chide, berate, criticize, take to task, pull up, read the Riot Act to, haul over the coals; informal tell off, dress down, bawl out, rap over the knuckles, give someone hell; Brit. informal tick off, give someone a rocket, have a go at, carpet, tear someone off a strip; N. Amer. informal chew out; formal castigate; rare reprehend. **2** *she admonished him to drink less* **advise**, recommend, counsel, urge, exhort, bid, enjoin, warn; formal adjure.

admonition n. **1** *a breach of the rules which led to an admonition* **reprimand**, rebuke, reproof, remonstrance, reproach, reproval, stricture, criticism, recrimination, scolding, censure; informal telling-off, dressing-down, talking-to, tongue-lashing, rap over the knuckles, slap on the wrist, flea in one's ear, earful; Brit. informal rocket, rollicking, wigging, ticking-off; formal castigation. **2** *an admonition to proceed carefully* **exhortation**, warning, piece of advice, recommendation, counsel.

adolescence n. **teenage years**, teens, youth; pubescence, puberty.

adolescent n. *an awkward adolescent* **teenager**, youngster, young person, youth, boy, girl; juvenile, minor; informal teen, tweenie, teenybopper.
▶ adj. **1** *an adolescent boy* **teenage**, pubescent, young; juvenile; informal teen. **2** *adolescent silliness* **immature**, childish, juvenile, infantile, puerile, jejune.
– OPPOSITES adult, mature.

adopt v. **1** *they adopted local customs* **embrace**, take on/up, espouse, assume; appropriate, arrogate. **2** *the people adopted him as their patron saint* **choose**, select, pick, vote for, elect, settle on, decide on, opt for; name, nominate, appoint.
– OPPOSITES abandon.

adorable adj. **lovable**, appealing, charming, cute, sweet, enchanting, bewitching, captivating, engaging, endearing, dear, darling, delightful, lovely, beautiful, attractive, gorgeous, winsome, winning, fetching; Scottish & N. English bonny.
– OPPOSITES hateful.

adoration n. **1** *the girl gazed at him with adoration* **love**, devotion, care, fondness; admiration, high regard, awe, idolization, worship, hero-worship, adulation. **2** *our* *day of prayer and adoration* **worship**, glory, glorification, praise, thanksgiving, homage, exaltation, extolment, veneration, reverence; old use magnification.

adore v. **1** *he adored his mother* **love**, be devoted to, dote on, hold dear, cherish, treasure, prize, think the world of; admire, hold in high regard, look up to, idolize, worship; informal put on a pedestal. **2** *the people had come to pray and adore God* **worship**, glorify, praise, revere, reverence, exalt, extol, venerate, pay homage to; formal laud; old use magnify. **3** informal *I adore oysters* **like**, love, be very fond of, be very keen on, be partial to, have a weakness for; delight in, revel in, relish, savour; informal be crazy about, be wild about, have a thing about, be hooked on, go a bundle on; Brit. informal be potty about.
– OPPOSITES hate.

adorn v. **decorate**, embellish, ornament, enhance; beautify, prettify, grace, bedeck, deck (out), dress (up), trim, swathe, wreathe, festoon, garland, array, emblazon; literary bedizen, caparison.

adornment n. **decoration**, embellishment, ornamentation, ornament, enhancement; beautification, prettification; frills, accessories, trimmings, finishing touches.

adrift adj. **1** *their empty boat was spotted adrift* **drifting**, unmoored, unanchored. **2** Brit. informal *the pipe of my breathing apparatus came adrift* **loose**, free; detached, unsecured, unfastened, untied, unknotted, undone. **3** *he was adrift in a strange country* **lost**, off course; disorientated, disoriented, confused, (all) at sea; drifting, rootless, unsettled, directionless, aimless, purposeless, without purpose. **4** Brit. informal *his instincts were not entirely adrift.* See **wrong** (sense 1 of the adjective).

adroit adj. **skilful**, adept, dexterous, deft, nimble, able, capable, skilled, expert, masterly, masterful, master, practised, polished, slick, proficient, accomplished, gifted, talented; quick-witted, quick-thinking, clever, smart, sharp, cunning, wily, resourceful, astute, shrewd, canny; informal nifty, crack, mean, wizard, demon, ace, A1, on the ball, savvy; N. Amer. informal crackerjack.
– OPPOSITES inept, clumsy.

adroitness n. **skill**, skilfulness, prowess, expertise, adeptness, dexterity, deftness, nimbleness, ability, capability, mastery, proficiency, accomplishment, artistry, art, facility, aptitude, flair, finesse, talent; quick-wittedness, cleverness, sharpness, cunning, astuteness, shrewdness, resourcefulness, savoir faire; informal know-how, savvy.

adulation n. **hero-worship**, worship, idolization, adoration, admiration, veneration, awe, devotion, glorification, praise, flattery, blandishments.

adulatory adj. **flattering**, complimentary, highly favourable, enthusiastic, glowing, reverential, rhapsodic, eulogistic, laudatory; fulsome, honeyed.
– OPPOSITES disparaging.

adult adj. **1** *an adult woman* **mature**, grown-up, fully grown, full-grown, fully developed, of age. **2** *an adult movie* **pornographic**, obscene, smutty, dirty, rude, erotic, sexy, suggestive, titillating; informal porn, porno, naughty, blue, X-rated, skin.

adulterate v. **make impure**, degrade, debase, spoil, taint, contaminate; doctor, tamper with, dilute, water down, weaken; bastardize, corrupt; informal cut, spike, dope.
– OPPOSITES purify.

adulterer n. **philanderer**, deceiver, womanizer, ladies' man, Don Juan, Casanova, Lothario; informal cheat, two-timer, love rat; formal fornicator.

adulterous adj. **unfaithful**, faithless, disloyal, untrue, inconstant, false, false-hearted, deceiving, deceitful, treacherous; extramarital; informal cheating, two-timing.
– OPPOSITES faithful.

adultery n. **infidelity**, unfaithfulness, falseness, disloyalty, cuckoldry, extramarital sex; affair, liaison, amour; informal carryings-on, hanky-panky, a bit on the side, playing around; formal fornication.
– OPPOSITES fidelity.

advance v. **1** *the battalion advanced rapidly* **move forward**, proceed, press on, push on, push forward, make progress, make headway, gain ground, approach, come closer, draw nearer, near; old use draw nigh. **2** *the court may advance the date of the hearing* **bring forward**, put forward, move forward. **3** *the move advanced his career* **promote**, further, forward, help, aid, assist, boost, strengthen, improve, benefit, foster. **4** *our technology has advanced in the last few years* **progress**, make progress, make headway, develop, evolve, make strides, move forward (in leaps and bounds), move ahead; improve, thrive, flourish, prosper. **5** *the hypothesis I wish to advance in this article* **put forward**, present, submit, suggest, propose, introduce, offer, adduce, moot. **6** *a relative advanced him some money* **lend**, loan, put up, come up with; Brit. informal sub.
– OPPOSITES retreat, hinder, postpone, retract, borrow.

▶ n. **1** *the advance of the aggressors* **progress**, forward movement; approach. **2** *a significant medical advance* **breakthrough**, development, step forward, step in the right direction, (quantum) leap; find, finding, discovery, invention. **3** *share prices showed significant advances* **increase**, rise, upturn, upsurge, upswing, growth; informal hike. **4** *the writer is going to be given a huge advance* **down payment**, retainer, prepayment, deposit, front money, money up front, proposition. **5** *unwelcome sexual advances* **pass**, proposition.

▶ adj. **1** *an advance party of settlers* **preliminary**, sent (on) ahead, first, exploratory; pilot, test, trial. **2** *advance warning* **early**, prior, beforehand.

□ **in advance** beforehand, before, ahead of time, earlier, previously; in readiness.

a

advanced adj. **1** *advanced manufacturing techniques* **state-of-the-art**, new, modern, up to date, up to the minute, the newest, the latest; progressive, avant-garde, ahead of the times, pioneering, innovatory, sophisticated. **2** *advanced further-education courses* **higher-level**, higher, tertiary.
– OPPOSITES primitive.

advancement n. **1** *the advancement of computer technology* **development**, progress, evolution, growth, improvement, advance, furtherance; headway. **2** *employees must be offered opportunities for advancement* **promotion**, preferment, career development, upgrading, a step up the ladder, progress, improvement, betterment, growth.

advantage n. **1** *the advantages of belonging to a union* **benefit**, value, good point, strong point, asset, plus, bonus, boon, blessing, virtue; attraction, beauty, usefulness, helpfulness, convenience, profit. **2** *they appeared to be gaining the advantage over their opponents* **upper hand**, edge, lead, whip hand, trump card; superiority, dominance, ascendancy, supremacy, power, mastery. **3** *there is no advantage to be gained from delaying the process* **benefit**, profit, gain, good; informal mileage, percentage.
– OPPOSITES disadvantage, drawback, detriment.

advantageous adj. **1** *an advantageous position* **superior**, dominant, powerful; good, fortunate, lucky, favourable. **2** *the arrangement is advantageous to both sides* **beneficial**, of benefit, helpful, of assistance, useful, of use, of value, of service, profitable, fruitful; convenient, expedient, in everyone's interests.
– OPPOSITES disadvantageous, detrimental.

advent n. **arrival**, appearance, emergence, materialization, occurrence, dawn, birth, rise, development; approach, coming.
– OPPOSITES disappearance.

adventitious adj. **1** *he felt that the conversation was not entirely adventitious* **unplanned**, unpremeditated, accidental, chance, fortuitous, serendipitous, coincidental, casual, random. **2** *the adventitious population* **foreign**, alien, non-native.
– OPPOSITES premeditated.

adventure n. **1** *her recent adventures in Italy* **exploit**, escapade, deed, feat, experience; stunt. **2** *they set off in search of adventure* **excitement**, thrill, stimulation; risk, danger, hazard, peril, uncertainty, precariousness.

adventurer n. **daredevil**, hero, heroine; swashbuckler, knight errant.

adventurous adj. **1** *an adventurous traveller* **daring**, daredevil, intrepid, venturesome, bold, fearless, brave, unafraid, unshrinking, dauntless; informal gutsy, spunky. **2** *adventurous activities* **risky**, dangerous, perilous, hazardous, precarious, uncertain; exciting, thrilling.
– OPPOSITES cautious.

adversary n. **opponent**, rival, enemy, antagonist, combatant, challenger, contender, competitor, opposer; opposition, competition; literary foe.
– OPPOSITES ally, supporter.

adverse adj. **1** *adverse weather conditions* **unfavourable**, disadvantageous, inauspicious, unpropitious, unfortunate, unlucky, untimely, untoward. **2** *the drug's adverse side effects* **harmful**, dangerous, injurious, detrimental, hurtful, deleterious. **3** *an adverse response from the public* **hostile**, unfavourable, antagonistic, unfriendly, ill-disposed, negative.
– OPPOSITES favourable, auspicious, beneficial.

adversity n. **misfortune**, ill luck, bad luck, trouble, difficulty, hardship, distress, disaster, suffering, affliction, sorrow, misery, tribulation, woe, pain, trauma; mishap, misadventure, accident, upset, reverse, setback, crisis, catastrophe, tragedy, calamity, trial, cross, burden, blow, vicissitude, issue; hard times, trials and tribulations.

advertise v. **publicize**, make public, make known, announce, broadcast, proclaim, trumpet, call attention to, bill; promote, market, beat/bang the drum for, trail, huckster; informal push, plug, hype, boost; N. Amer. informal ballyhoo, flack.

advertisement n. **notice**, announcement, bulletin; commercial, promotion, blurb, write-up; poster, leaflet, pamphlet, flyer, bill, handbill, handout, circular, brochure, sign, placard; informal ad, push, plug, puff, bumf; Brit. informal advert.

advice n. **guidance**, counselling, counsel, help, direction; information, recommendations, guidelines, suggestions, hints, tips, pointers, ideas, opinions, views.

advisability n. **wisdom**, desirability, preferability, prudence, sense, appropriateness, aptness, fitness, suitability, judiciousness; expediency, advantage, benefit, profit, profitability.

advisable adj. **wise**, desirable, preferable, well, best, sensible, prudent, proper, appropriate, apt, suitable, fitting, judicious, recommended, suggested; expedient, politic, advantageous, beneficial, profitable, in one's (best) interests.

advise v. **1** *her grandmother advised her about marriage* **counsel**, give guidance, guide, offer suggestions, give hints/tips/pointers. **2** *he advised caution* **advocate**, recommend, suggest, urge, encourage, enjoin. **3** *you will be advised of the requirements* **inform**, notify, give notice, apprise, warn, forewarn; acquaint with, make familiar with, make known to, update about; informal fill in on.

adviser n. **counsellor**, mentor, guide, consultant, confidant, confidante; coach, teacher, tutor, guru.

advisory adj. **consultative**, consultatory, advising; recommendatory.
– OPPOSITES executive.

advocacy n. **support**, backing, promotion, championing; recommendation, prescription; N. Amer. boosterism.

advocate n. *an advocate of children's rights* **champion**, upholder, supporter, backer, promoter, proponent, exponent, spokesman, spokeswoman, spokesperson, campaigner, fighter, crusader; propagandist, apostle, apologist; N. Amer. booster.
– OPPOSITES critic.
▸v. *heart specialists advocate a diet low in cholesterol* **recommend**, prescribe, advise, urge; support, back, favour, uphold, subscribe to, champion, speak for, argue for, lobby for, promote.

aegis n. **protection**, backing, support, patronage, sponsorship, charge, care, guidance, guardianship, trusteeship, agency, safeguarding, shelter, umbrella, aid, assistance; auspices.

aeon n. **ages**, an age, an eternity, a long time, a lifetime; years; informal donkey's years; Brit. informal yonks.

aesthetic adj. **artistic**, tasteful, in good taste; graceful, elegant, exquisite, beautiful, attractive, pleasing, lovely.

affability n. **friendliness**, amiability, geniality, congeniality, cordiality, warmth, pleasantness, likeability, good humour, good nature, kindliness, kindness, courtesy, courteousness, civility, approachability, amenability, sociability, gregariousness, neighbourliness.

affable adj. **friendly**, amiable, genial, congenial, cordial, warm, pleasant, nice, likeable, personable, charming, agreeable, sympathetic, good-humoured, good-natured, kindly, kind, courteous, civil, gracious, approachable, accessible, amenable, sociable, outgoing, gregarious, clubbable, neighbourly, welcoming, hospitable, obliging; Scottish couthy.
– OPPOSITES unfriendly.

affair n. **1** *what you do is your affair* **business**, concern, matter, responsibility, province, preserve; problem, worry; Brit. informal lookout. **2** *his financial affairs* **transactions**, concerns, matters, activities, dealings, undertakings, ventures, business. **3** *the board admitted responsibility for the affair* **event**, incident, happening, occurrence, eventuality, episode; case, matter, business. **4** *his affair with Anthea was over* **relationship**, love affair, affaire (de cœur), romance, fling, flirtation, dalliance, liaison, involvement, intrigue, amour; informal hanky-panky; Brit. informal carry-on.

affect[1] v. **1** *this development may have affected the judge's decision* **influence**, have an effect on, act on, work on, have an impact on; change, alter, modify, transform, form, shape, sway, bias. **2** *he was visibly affected by the experience* **move**, touch, make an impression on, hit (hard), tug at someone's heartstrings; **upset**, trouble, distress, disturb, agitate, shake (up). **3** *the disease affected his lungs* **attack**, infect; hit, strike.

affect[2] v. **1** *he deliberately affected a republican stance* **assume**, take on, adopt, embrace, espouse. **2** *Paul affected an air of injured innocence* **pretend**, feign, fake, simulate, make a show of, make a pretence of, sham; informal put on; N. Amer. informal make like.

affectation n. **1** *George had always abhorred affectation* **pretension**, pretentiousness, artificiality, posturing, posing; airs (and graces); informal la-di-da; Brit. informal side. **2** *an affectation of calm* **facade**, front, show, appearance, pretence, simulation, posture, pose.

affected adj. **pretentious**, artificial, contrived, unnatural, stagy, studied, mannered, ostentatious; insincere, unconvincing, feigned, false, fake, sham, simulated; informal la-di-da, phoney, pretend, put on.
– OPPOSITES natural, unpretentious, genuine.

affecting adj. **touching**, moving, emotive, emotional; stirring, soul-stirring, heart-warming; poignant, pathetic, pitiful, piteous, tear-jerking, heart-rending, heartbreaking, disturbing, distressing, upsetting, sad, haunting.

affection n. **fondness**, love, liking, tenderness, warmth, devotion, endearment, care, caring, attachment, friendship; warm feelings.

affectionate adj. **loving**, fond, adoring, devoted, caring, doting, tender, warm, warm-hearted, soft-hearted, friendly; demonstrative, cuddly; informal touchy-feely, lovey-dovey.
– OPPOSITES cold.

affiliate v. **associate with**, unite with, combine with, join (up) with, join forces with, link up with, ally with, align with, federate with, amalgamate with, merge with; attach to, annex to, incorporate into, integrate into.

affiliated adj. **associated**, allied, related, federated, confederated, amalgamated, unified, connected, linked; in league, in partnership.

affiliation n. **association**, connection, alliance, alignment, link, attachment, tie, relationship, fellowship, partnership, coalition, union; amalgamation, incorporation, integration, federation, confederation.

affinity n. **1** *her affinity with animals and birds* **empathy**, rapport, sympathy, accord, harmony, relationship, bond, fellow feeling, like-mindedness, closeness, understanding; liking, fondness; informal chemistry. **2** *the semantic affinity between the two words* **similarity**, resemblance, likeness, kinship, relationship, association, link, analogy, similitude, correspondence.
– OPPOSITES aversion, dislike, dissimilarity.

affirm v. **1** *he affirmed that they would lend military assistance* **declare**, state, assert, proclaim, pronounce, attest, swear, avow, guarantee, pledge, give an undertaking;

formal **aver**; rare **asseverate**. **2** *the referendum affirmed the republic's right to secede* **uphold**, support, confirm, ratify, endorse.
– OPPOSITES deny.

affirmation n. **1** *an affirmation of faith* **declaration**, statement, assertion, proclamation, pronouncement, attestation; oath, avowal, guarantee, pledge; deposition; formal **averment**; rare **asseveration**. **2** *the poem ends with an affirmation of pastoral values* **confirmation**, ratification, endorsement.
– OPPOSITES denial.

affirmative adj. *an affirmative answer* **positive**, assenting, consenting, corroborative, favourable.
– OPPOSITES negative.

▶ n. *she took his grunt as an affirmative* **agreement**, acceptance, assent, acquiescence, concurrence; OK, yes.
– OPPOSITES disagreement.

affix v. **1** *he affixed a stamp to the envelope* **stick**, glue, paste, gum; attach, fasten, fix; clip, tack, pin; tape. **2** formal *affix your signature to the document* **append**, add, attach.
– OPPOSITES detach.

afflict v. **trouble**, burden, distress, cause suffering to, beset, harass, worry, oppress; torment, plague, blight, bedevil, rack, smite, curse; old use **ail**.

affliction n. **1** *a herb reputed to cure a variety of afflictions* **disorder**, disease, malady, complaint, ailment, illness, indisposition, handicap; scourge, plague, trouble. **2** *he bore his affliction with great dignity* **suffering**, distress, pain, trouble, misery, wretchedness, hardship, misfortune, adversity, sorrow, torment, tribulation, woe.

affluence n. **wealth**, prosperity, fortune; riches, money, resources, assets, possessions, property, substance, means.
– OPPOSITES poverty.

affluent adj. **wealthy**, rich, prosperous, well off, moneyed, well-to-do; propertied, substantial, of means, of substance, plutocratic; informal **well heeled**, rolling in it, made of money, filthy rich, stinking rich, loaded, on easy street, worth a packet.
– OPPOSITES poor, impoverished.

afford v. **1** *can you afford a new car?* **pay for**, have the money for; run to, stretch to, manage. **2** *it took more time than he could afford* **spare**, allow (oneself). **3** *the rooftop terrace affords beautiful views* **provide**, supply, furnish, offer, give, make available, yield.

affray n. Law, dated **fight**, brawl, confrontation, clash, skirmish, scuffle, tussle; fracas, altercation, disturbance, breach of the peace; informal **scrap**, dust-up, punch-up, set-to, shindig, free-for-all; Brit. informal, Sport **afters**.

affront n. *an affront to public morality* **insult**, offence, indignity, slight, snub, put-down, provocation, injury; outrage, atrocity, scandal; informal **slap in the face**, kick in the teeth.

▶ v. *she was affronted by his familiarity* **insult**, offend, mortify, provoke, pique, wound, hurt; put out, irk, displease, bother, rankle, vex, gall; outrage, scandalize, disgust; informal **put someone's back up**, needle.

aficionado n. **connoisseur**, expert, authority, specialist, pundit; enthusiast, devotee; informal **buff**, freak, nut, fiend, maniac, fanatic, addict.

aflame adj. **burning**, ablaze, alight, on fire, in flames, blazing; literary **afire**.

afloat adv. & adj. **buoyant**, floating, buoyed up, on/above the surface, (keeping one's head) above water.

afoot adj. & adv. **happening**, going on, around, about, abroad, stirring, circulating, in circulation, at large, in the air/wind; brewing, looming, in the offing, on the horizon.

aforesaid adj. **previously mentioned**, aforementioned, aforenamed; foregoing, preceding, earlier, previous; above.

afraid adj. **1** *they ran away because they were afraid* **frightened**, scared, terrified, fearful, petrified, scared witless, scared to death, terror-stricken, terror-struck, frightened/scared out of one's wits, shaking in one's shoes, shaking like a leaf; intimidated, alarmed, panicky; faint-hearted, cowardly; informal **scared stiff**, in a (blue) funk, in a cold sweat; N. Amer. informal **afeared**; old use **affrighted**. **2** *don't be afraid to ask awkward questions* **reluctant**, hesitant, unwilling, disinclined, loath, slow, chary, shy. **3** *I'm afraid that your daughter is ill* **sorry**, sad, distressed, regretful, apologetic.
– OPPOSITES brave, confident.

afresh adv. **anew**, again, over/once again, once more, another time.

after prep. **1** *he made a speech after the performance* **following**, subsequent to, at the close/end of, in the wake of; formal **posterior to**. **2** *after the way he treated my sister I never want to speak to him again* **because of**, as a result/consequence of, in view of, owing to, on account of. **3** *is he still going to marry her, after all that's happened?* **despite**, in spite of, regardless of, notwithstanding. **4** *the policeman ran after him* **in pursuit of**, in someone's direction, following. **5** *they asked after Dad* **about**, concerning, regarding, with regard/respect/reference to. **6** *I'm after information, and I'm willing to pay for it* **in search of**, in quest/pursuit of, trying to find, looking for. **7** *the village was named after a Roman officer* **in honour of**, as a tribute to. **8** *animal studies after Bandinelli* **in the style of**, in the manner of, in imitation of; similar to, like, characteristic of.
– OPPOSITES before, preceding.

▶ adv. **1** *the week after, we went to Madrid* **later**, afterwards, after this/that, subsequently. **2** *porters were following on after with their bags* **behind**, in the rear, at the back, in someone's wake.
– OPPOSITES previously, before, ahead.

after-effect n. **repercussion**, aftermath, consequence; Medicine sequela.

afterlife n. **life after death**, the next world, the hereafter, the afterworld; immortality.

aftermath n. **repercussions**, after-effects, consequences, effects, results, fruits.

afterwards adv. **later**, later on, subsequently, then, next, after this/that; at a later time/date, in due course.

again adv. **1** *her spirits lifted again* **once more**, another time, afresh, anew. **2** *this can add half as much again to the price* **extra**, in addition, additionally, on top. **3** *again, evidence was not always consistent* **also**, furthermore; moreover, besides.
□ **again and again** repeatedly, over and over (again), time and (time) again, many times, many a time; often, frequently, continually, constantly.

against prep. **1** *a number of delegates were against the motion* **opposed to**, in opposition to, hostile to, averse to, antagonistic towards, inimical to, unsympathetic to, resistant to, at odds with, in disagreement with; informal anti, agin. **2** *he was swimming against the tide* **in opposition to**, counter to, contrary to, in the opposite direction to. **3** *his age is against him* **disadvantageous to**, unfavourable to, damaging to, detrimental to, prejudicial to, deleterious to, harmful to, injurious to, a drawback for. **4** *she leaned against the wall* **touching**, in contact with, up against, on.
− OPPOSITES in favour of, pro.

age n. **1** *people of the same age* **number of years**, length of life; generation, age group. **2** *her hearing had deteriorated with age* **elderliness**, old age, oldness, senescence, seniority, maturity; one's advancing/ declining years; literary eld; old use caducity. **3** *the Elizabethan age* **era**, epoch, period, time. **4** informal *you haven't been in touch with me for ages* **a long time**, days/months/years on end, an eternity; informal ages and ages, donkey's years, a month of Sundays; Brit. informal yonks.
▸ v. *Cabernet Sauvignon ages well | the experience has aged her* **mature**, mellow, ripen; grow/become/make old, (cause to) decline.

aged adj. **elderly**, old, mature, older, senior, ancient, senescent, advanced in years, in one's dotage, long in the tooth, as old as the hills, past one's prime, not as young as one used to be; informal getting on, over the hill, no spring chicken.
− OPPOSITES young.

agency n. **1** *an advertising agency* **business**, organization, company, firm, office, bureau. **2** *the infection is caused by the agency of insects* **action**, activity, means, effect, influence, force, power, vehicle, medium. **3** *regional policy was introduced through the agency of the Board of Trade* **intervention**, intercession, involvement, good offices; auspices, aegis.

agenda n. **list of items**, schedule, programme, timetable, line-up, list, plan.

agent n. **1** *the sale was arranged through an agent* **representative**, emissary, envoy, go-between, proxy, negotiator, broker, spokesperson, spokesman, spokeswoman; informal rep. **2** *a travel agent* **agency**, business, organization, company, firm, bureau. **3** *a CIA agent* **spy**, secret agent, undercover agent, operative, fifth columnist, mole, Mata Hari; N. Amer. informal spook, G-man; old use intelligencer. **4** *the agents of destruction* **performer**, author, executor, perpetrator, producer, instrument, catalyst. **5** *a cleansing agent* **medium**, means, instrument, vehicle.

agglomeration n. **collection**, mass, cluster, lump, clump, pile, heap; accumulation, build-up; miscellany, jumble, hotchpotch, mixed bag.

aggravate v. **1** *the new law could aggravate the situation* **worsen**, make worse, exacerbate, inflame, compound; add fuel to the fire/flames, add insult to injury, rub salt in the wound. **2** informal *you don't have to aggravate people to get what you want* **annoy**, irritate, exasperate, put out, nettle, provoke, antagonize, get on someone's nerves, ruffle (someone's feathers), try someone's patience; Brit. rub up the wrong way; informal peeve, needle, bug, miff, hack off, get someone's goat, get under someone's skin, get up someone's nose; Brit. informal wind up, nark, get at, get across, get on someone's wick; N. Amer. informal tick off.
− OPPOSITES alleviate, improve.

aggravation n. **1** *the recession led to the aggravation of unemployment problems* **worsening**, exacerbation, compounding. **2** informal *no amount of money is worth the aggravation* **nuisance**, annoyance, irritation, hassle, trouble, difficulty, inconvenience, bother; informal aggro.

aggregate n. **1** *the specimen is an aggregate of rock and mineral fragments* **collection**, mass, agglomeration, assemblage; mixture, mix, combination, blend; compound, alloy, amalgam. **2** *he won with an aggregate of 325* **total**, sum total, sum, grand total.
▸ adj. *an aggregate score* **total**, combined, gross, overall, composite.

aggression n. **1** *an act of aggression* **hostility**, aggressiveness, belligerence, bellicosity, force, violence; pugnacity, pugnaciousness, militancy, warmongering. **2** *he played the game with unceasing aggression* **confidence**, self-confidence, boldness, determination, forcefulness, vigour, energy, dynamism, zeal.

aggressive adj. **1** *aggressive and disruptive behaviour* **violent**, confrontational, antagonistic, truculent, pugnacious, macho; quarrelsome, argumentative. **2** *aggressive foreign policy* **warmongering**, warlike, warring, belligerent, bellicose, hawkish, militaristic; offensive, expansionist; informal gung-ho. **3** *an aggressive promotional drive* **assertive**, pushy, forceful, vigorous, energetic, dynamic; bold, audacious; informal in-your-face, feisty.
− OPPOSITES peaceable, peaceful.

a

aggressor n. **attacker**, assaulter, assailant; invader.

aggrieved adj. **1** *the manager looked aggrieved at the suggestion* **resentful**, affronted, indignant, disgruntled, discontented, upset, offended, piqued, riled, nettled, vexed, irked, irritated, annoyed, put out, chagrined; informal peeved, miffed, in a huff; Brit. informal cheesed off; N. Amer. informal sore, steamed. **2** *the aggrieved party* **wronged**, injured, harmed.
– OPPOSITES pleased.

aghast adj. **horrified**, appalled, dismayed, thunderstruck, stunned, shocked, shell-shocked, staggered; informal flabbergasted; Brit. informal gobsmacked.

agile adj. **1** *she was as agile as a monkey* **nimble**, lithe, supple, limber, acrobatic, fleet-footed, light-footed, light on one's feet; informal nippy, twinkle-toed; literary fleet, lightsome. **2** *an agile mind* **alert**, sharp, acute, shrewd, astute, perceptive, quick-witted.
– OPPOSITES clumsy, stiff.

agitate v. **1** *any mention of Clare agitates my grandmother* **upset**, perturb, fluster, ruffle, disconcert, unnerve, disquiet, disturb, worry, distress, unsettle; informal rattle, faze; N. Amer. informal discombobulate. **2** *she agitated for the appointment of more women* **campaign**, strive, battle, fight, struggle, push, press. **3** *agitate the water to disperse the oil* **stir**, whisk, beat.

agitated adj. **upset**, perturbed, flustered, ruffled, disconcerted, unnerved, disquieted, disturbed, anxious, worried, distressed, unsettled; nervous, on edge, tense, keyed up; informal rattled, fazed, in a dither, in a flap, in a state, in a lather, jittery, jumpy, in a tizz/tizzy; Brit. informal having kittens, in a (flat) spin; N. Amer. informal discombobulated.
– OPPOSITES calm, relaxed.

agitation n. **1** *Freddie gritted his teeth in agitation* **anxiety**, perturbation, disquiet, distress, concern, alarm, worry. **2** *an upsurge in nationalist agitation* **campaigning**, striving, battling, fighting, struggling. **3** *the vigorous agitation of the components* **stirring**, whisking, beating.

agitator n. **troublemaker**, rabble-rouser, agent provocateur, demagogue, incendiary; revolutionary, firebrand, rebel, insurgent, subversive; informal stirrer.

agnostic n. **sceptic**, doubter, doubting Thomas; unbeliever, disbeliever, non-believer; rationalist; rare nullifidian.
– OPPOSITES believer, theist.

ago adv. **in the past**, before, earlier, back, since, previously; formal heretofore.

agog adv. **eager**, excited, impatient, keen, anxious, avid, in suspense, on tenterhooks, on the edge of one's seat, on pins and needles, waiting with bated breath.

agonize v. **worry**, fret, fuss, brood, upset oneself, rack one's brains, wrestle with oneself, be worried/anxious, feel uneasy, exercise oneself; informal stew; old use pore on.

agonizing adj. **excruciating**, harrowing, racking, searing, extremely painful, acute, severe, torturous, tormenting, piercing; informal hellish, killing; formal grievous.

agony n. **pain**, hurt, suffering, torture, torment, anguish, affliction, trauma; pangs, throes; rare excruciation.

agrarian adj. **agricultural**, rural, rustic, pastoral, countryside, farming; literary georgic, sylvan, Arcadian, agrestic.

agree v. **1** *I agree with you* **concur**, be of the same mind/opinion, see eye to eye, be in sympathy, be united, be as one man. **2** *they had agreed to a ceasefire* **consent**, assent, acquiesce, accept, approve, say yes, give one's approval, give the nod; formal accede. **3** *the plan and the drawing do not agree with each other* **match (up)**, accord, correspond, conform, coincide, fit, tally, be in harmony/agreement, be consistent/equivalent; informal square. **4** *they agreed on a price* **settle**, decide, arrive at, negotiate, reach an agreement, come to terms, strike a bargain, make a deal, shake hands.
– OPPOSITES differ, contradict, reject.

agreeable adj. **1** *an agreeable atmosphere of rural tranquillity* **pleasant**, pleasing, enjoyable, pleasurable, nice, to one's liking, appealing, charming, delightful. **2** *an agreeable fellow* **likeable**, charming, amiable, affable, pleasant, nice, friendly, good-natured, sociable, genial, congenial. **3** *we should get together for a talk, if you're agreeable* **willing**, amenable, in accord/agreement.
– OPPOSITES unpleasant.

agreement n. **1** *all heads nodded in agreement* **accord**, concurrence, consensus; assent, acceptance, consent, acquiescence, endorsement. **2** *an agreement on military cooperation* **contract**, compact, treaty, covenant, pact, accord, concordat, protocol. **3** *there is some agreement between my view and that of the author* **correspondence**, consistency, compatibility, accord; similarity, resemblance, likeness, similitude.
– OPPOSITES discord.

agricultural adj. **1** *an agricultural labourer* **farm**, farming, agrarian; rural, rustic, pastoral, countryside; literary georgic, sylvan, Arcadian, agrestic. **2** *agricultural land* **farmed**, farm, agrarian, cultivated, tilled.
– OPPOSITES urban.

agriculture n. **farming**, cultivation, husbandry, tillage, agribusiness, agronomy.

> **WORD LINKS**
> **agrarian** relating to agriculture
> **arable** referring to land used for growing crops
> **fallow** referring to land which is not currently planted with crops
> **harvest** the gathering in of crops
> **pasture** land used for grazing cattle or sheep

aground adv. & adj. **grounded**, ashore, beached, stuck, shipwrecked, high and dry, on the rocks, on the ground/bottom.

ahead adv. **1** *he peered ahead, but could see nothing* **forward(s)**, towards the front, frontwards. **2** *he had ridden on ahead* **in front**, at the head, in the lead, at the fore, in the vanguard, in advance. **3** *she was preparing herself for what lay ahead* **in the future**, in time, in time to come, in the fullness of time, at a later date, after this, henceforth, later on, in due course, next. **4** *they are ahead by six points* **leading**, winning, in the lead, (out) in front, first, coming first.
– OPPOSITES behind.
☐ **ahead of 1** *Blanche went ahead of the others* **in front of**, before. **2** *we have a demanding trip ahead of us* **in store for**, waiting for. **3** *two months ahead of schedule* **in advance of**, before, earlier than. **4** *in terms of these amenities, Britain is ahead of other European countries* **more advanced than**, further on than, superior to, surpassing, exceeding, better than.

aid n. **1** *with the aid of his colleagues he prepared a manifesto* **assistance**, support, help, backing, cooperation, succour; a helping hand. **2** *humanitarian aid* **relief**, charity, financial assistance, donations, contributions, subsidies, handouts, subvention; debt remission; historical alms. **3** *a hospital aid* **helper**, assistant, girl/man Friday.
– OPPOSITES hindrance.
▸v. **1** *he provided an army to aid the King of England* **help**, assist, abet, come to someone's aid, give assistance, lend a hand, be of service; avail, succour, sustain. **2** *lavender can aid restful sleep* **facilitate**, promote, encourage, help, further, boost; speed up, hasten, accelerate, expedite.
– OPPOSITES hinder.

aide n. **assistant**, helper, adviser, right-hand man, man/girl Friday, adjutant, deputy, second (in command), lieutenant, wingman; subordinate, junior, underling, acolyte; N. Amer. cohort.

ailing adj. **1** *his ailing mother* **ill**, unwell, sick, sickly, poorly, weak, indisposed, in poor/ bad health, infirm, debilitated, delicate, valetudinarian, below par; Brit. off colour; informal laid up, under the weather. **2** *the country's ailing economy* **failing**, in poor condition, weak, poor, deficient.
– OPPOSITES healthy.

ailment n. **illness**, disease, disorder, affliction, malady, complaint, infirmity; informal bug, virus; Brit. informal lurgy.

aim v. **1** *he aimed the rifle* **point**, direct, train, sight, line up. **2** *she aimed at the target* **take aim**, fix on, zero in on, draw a bead on. **3** *undergraduates aiming for a first degree* **work towards**, intend, destine, direct, try for, strive for, aspire to; formal essay. **4** *this system is aimed at the home entertainment market* **target**, intend, tailor, market, pitch. **5** *we aim to give you the best possible service* **intend**, mean, have in mind/view; plan, resolve, propose, design.

▸n. *our aim is to develop gymnasts to the top level* **objective**, object, goal, end, target, design, desire, desired result, intention, intent, plan, purpose, object of the exercise; ambition, aspiration, wish, dream, hope, raison d'être.

aimless adj. **1** *Flavia set out on an aimless walk* **purposeless**, objectless, goalless, without purpose, without goal. **2** *aimless men standing outside the bars* **unoccupied**, idle, at a loose end; purposeless, undirected.
– OPPOSITES purposeful.

air n. **1** *hundreds of birds hovered in the air* **sky**, atmosphere, airspace, ether; literary heavens. **2** *open the windows to get some air into the room* **breeze**, draught, wind; breath/blast of air, gust/puff of wind. **3** *an air of defiance* **expression**, appearance, look, impression, aspect, aura, mien, countenance, manner, bearing, tone. **4** *women putting on airs* **affectations**, pretension, pretentiousness, posing, posturing, airs and graces; Brit. informal side. **5** *a traditional Scottish air* **tune**, melody, song; literary lay.
▸v. **1** *a chance to air your views* **express**, voice, make public, ventilate, articulate, state, declare, give expression/voice to; have one's say. **2** *the windows were opened to air the room* **ventilate**, freshen, refresh, cool. **3** *the film was aired nationwide* **broadcast**, transmit, screen, show, televise, telecast.

WORD LINKS

aerial relating to the air
aerate, ventilate introduce air into something
aerodynamics the science concerned with the movement of objects through the air
aeronautics the study of travel through the air
alfresco in the open air
rarefied referring to air of lower pressure than usual
vacuum a space from which air has been removed

---

airborne adj. **flying**, in flight, in the air, on the wing.

airily adv. **lightly**, breezily, flippantly, casually, nonchalantly, heedlessly, without consideration.
– OPPOSITES seriously.

airing n. **1** *the airing of different views* **expression**, voicing, venting, ventilation, articulation, stating, declaration, communication. **2** *I hope the BBC gives the play another airing* **broadcast**, transmission, screening, showing, televising, telecast.

airless adj. **stuffy**, close, stifling, suffocating, oppressive; unventilated, badly/poorly ventilated.
– OPPOSITES airy, ventilated.

airport n. **airfield**, airstrip; Brit. aerodrome; N. Amer. airdrome; informal drome.

airtight adj. **1** *an airtight container* **sealed**, hermetically sealed, closed/shut tight. **2** *an airtight alibi* **indisputable**, unquestionable, incontrovertible, undeniable, incontestable, irrefutable, watertight, beyond dispute/ question/doubt.

a

airy adj. **1** *the conservatory is light and airy* **well ventilated**, fresh; spacious, uncluttered; light, bright. **2** *an airy gesture* **nonchalant**, casual, breezy, flippant, insouciant, heedless. **3** *airy clouds* **delicate**, soft, fine, feathery, insubstantial.
– OPPOSITES stuffy.

airy-fairy adj. informal **impractical**, unrealistic, idealistic, fanciful.
– OPPOSITES practical.

aisle n. **passage**, passageway, gangway, walkway.

ajar adj. & adv. **slightly open**, half open, agape.
– OPPOSITES closed, wide open.

akin adj. **similar**, related, close, near, corresponding, comparable, equivalent; connected, alike, analogous.
– OPPOSITES unlike.

alacrity n. **eagerness**, willingness, readiness; enthusiasm, ardour, fervour, keenness; promptness, haste, swiftness, dispatch, speed.

alarm n. **1** *the girl spun round in alarm* **fear**, anxiety, apprehension, trepidation, nervousness, unease, distress, agitation, consternation, disquiet, perturbation, fright, panic. **2** *a smoke alarm* **siren**, warning sound, danger/distress signal; warning device, alarm bell; old use tocsin.
– OPPOSITES calmness, composure.
▸ v. *the news had alarmed her* **frighten**, scare, panic, unnerve, distress, agitate, upset, disconcert, shock, dismay, disturb; informal rattle, spook, scare the living daylights out of; Brit. informal put the wind up.

alarming adj. **frightening**, unnerving, shocking; distressing, upsetting, disconcerting, perturbing, dismaying, disquieting, disturbing; informal scary.
– OPPOSITES reassuring.

alarmist n. **scaremonger**, gloom-monger, doom-monger, doomster, doomsayer, Cassandra.
– OPPOSITES optimist.

alchemy n. **chemistry**; magic, sorcery, witchcraft.

alcohol n. **liquor**, intoxicating liquor, strong/alcoholic drink, drink, spirits; informal booze, hooch, the hard stuff, firewater, rotgut, moonshine, grog, tipple, the demon drink, the bottle; Brit. informal gut-rot; N. Amer. informal juice; technical ethyl alcohol, ethanol.

> **WORD LINKS**
>
> **alcoholism, dipsomania** addiction to alcohol
> **temperance, teetotalism** the practice of never drinking alcohol
> **bibulous** too fond of drinking alcohol
> **crapulent** relating to the drinking of alcohol or to drunkenness
> **cirrhosis** a liver disease that can be caused by alcoholism
> **Dutch courage** confidence gained by drinking alcohol
> **hair of the dog** an alcoholic drink taken to cure a hangover

alcoholic adj. *alcoholic drinks* **intoxicating**, inebriating, containing alcohol; strong, hard, stiff; formal spirituous.
▸ n. *he is an alcoholic* **dipsomaniac**, drunk, drunkard, heavy/hard/serious drinker, problem drinker, alcohol abuser; tippler, sot, inebriate; informal boozer, lush, alky, dipso, soak, tosspot, wino, sponge, barfly; US informal juicehead; Austral./NZ informal hophead; old use toper.

alcove n. **recess**, niche, nook, inglenook, bay.

alert adj. **1** *police have asked neighbours to keep alert* **vigilant**, watchful, attentive, observant, wide awake, circumspect; on the lookout, on one's guard/toes, on the qui vive; informal keeping one's eyes open/peeled. **2** *mentally alert* **quick-witted**, sharp, bright, quick, keen, perceptive, wide awake, on one's toes; informal on the ball, quick on the uptake, all there, with it.
– OPPOSITES inattentive.
▸ n. **1** *a state of alert* **vigilance**, watchfulness, attentiveness, alertness, circumspection. **2** *a flood alert* **warning**, notification, notice; siren, alarm, signal, danger/distress signal.
▸ v. *police were alerted by a phone call* **warn**, notify, apprise, forewarn, put on one's guard; informal tip off, clue in.

alias n. *he is known under several aliases* **assumed name**, false name, pseudonym, sobriquet, incognito; pen/stage name, nom de plume/guerre.
▸ adv. *Cassius Clay, alias Muhammad Ali* **also known as**, aka, also called, otherwise known as.

alibi n. *we've both got a good alibi for last night* **defence**, justification, explanation, reason; informal story, line.

alien adj. **1** *alien cultures* **foreign**, overseas, non-native. **2** *an alien landscape* **unfamiliar**, unknown, strange, peculiar; exotic, foreign. **3** *a vicious role alien to his nature* **incompatible**, opposed, conflicting, contrary, in conflict, at variance; rare oppugnant. **4** *alien beings* **extraterrestrial**, unearthly; Martian.
– OPPOSITES native, familiar, earthly.
▸ n. **1** *an illegal alien* **foreigner**, non-native, immigrant, emigrant, émigré, incomer. **2** *the alien's spaceship crashed* **extraterrestrial**, ET; Martian; informal little green man.

alienate v. **1** *his homosexuality alienated him from his conservative father* **estrange**, divide, distance, put at a distance, isolate, cut off; set against, turn away, drive away, disunite, set at variance/odds, drive a wedge between. **2** Law *they tried to prevent the land from being alienated* **transfer**, pass on, hand over; Law convey, devolve.

alienation v. **1** *a sense of alienation from society* **isolation**, detachment, estrangement, distance, separation, division; cutting off, turning away. **2** Law *most leases contain restrictions against alienation* **transfer**, passing on, handing over; Law conveyance, devolution.

alight[1] v. **1** *he alighted from the train* **get off**, step off, disembark, pile out; detrain, deplane. **2** *a swallow alighted on a branch* **land**, come to rest, settle, perch; old use light.
– OPPOSITES get on, board.

alight[2] adj. **1** *the bales of hay were alight* **burning**, ablaze, aflame, on fire, in flames, blazing; literary afire. **2** *her face was alight with laughter* **lit up**, gleaming, glowing, aglow, ablaze, bright, shining, radiant.

align v. **1** *the desks are aligned in straight rows* **line up**, put in order, put in rows/columns, place, position, situate, set, range. **2** *he aligned himself with the workers* **ally**, affiliate, associate, join, side, unite, combine, join forces, form an alliance, team up, band together, throw in one's lot, make common cause.

alike adj. *all the doors looked alike* **similar**, (much) the same, indistinguishable, identical, uniform, interchangeable, cut from the same cloth, like (two) peas in a pod, (like) Tweedledum and Tweedledee; informal much of a muchness.
– OPPOSITES different.
▸ adv. *great minds think alike* **similarly**, (just) the same, in the same way, identically.

alimony n. **financial support**, maintenance, support; child support.

alive adj. **1** *he was last seen alive on Boxing Day* **living**, live, breathing, animate, sentient; informal alive and kicking; old use quick. **2** *the synagogue has kept the Jewish faith alive* **active**, existing, in existence, existent, functioning, in operation; on the map. **3** *the thrills that kept him really alive* **animated**, lively, full of life, alert, active, energetic, vigorous, spry, sprightly, vital, vivacious, buoyant, exuberant, ebullient, zestful, spirited; informal full of beans, bright-eyed and bushy-tailed, chirpy, chipper, peppy, full of vim and vigour. **4** *teachers need to be alive to their pupils' backgrounds* **alert**, awake, aware, conscious, mindful, heedful, sensitive, familiar; informal wise; formal cognizant. **5** *the place was alive with mice* **teeming**, swarming, overrun, crawling, bristling, infested; crowded, packed; informal lousy.
– OPPOSITES dead, inanimate, inactive, lethargic.

all determiner **1** *all the children went | all creatures need sleep* **each of**, each/every one of, every single one of; every (single), each and every. **2** *the sun shone all week* **the whole of the**, the complete, the entire. **3** *in all honesty | with all speed* **complete**, entire, total, full; greatest (possible), maximum.
– OPPOSITES no, none of.
▸ pron. **1** *all are welcome* **everyone**, everybody, each/every person. **2** *all of the cups were broken* **each one**, the sum, the total, the whole lot. **3** *they took all of it* **everything**, every part, the whole/total amount, the (whole) lot, the entirety.
– OPPOSITES none, nobody, nothing.
▸ adv. *he was dressed all in black* **completely**, fully, entirely, totally, wholly, absolutely, utterly; in every respect, in all respects, without reservation/exception.
– OPPOSITES partly.

allay v. **reduce**, diminish, decrease, lessen, assuage, alleviate, ease, relieve, soothe, soften, calm, take the edge off.
– OPPOSITES increase, intensify.

allegation n. **claim**, assertion, charge, accusation, declaration, statement, contention, argument, affirmation, attestation; formal averment.

allege v. **claim**, assert, charge, accuse, declare, state, contend, argue, affirm, attest, testify, swear; formal aver.

alleged adj. **supposed**, so-called, claimed, professed, purported, ostensible, putative, unproven.

allegedly adv. **reportedly**, supposedly, reputedly, purportedly, ostensibly, apparently, putatively, by all accounts, so the story goes.

allegiance n. **loyalty**, faithfulness, fidelity, obedience, adherence, homage, devotion; historical fealty; formal troth.
– OPPOSITES disloyalty, treachery.

allegorical adj. **symbolic**, metaphorical, figurative, representative, emblematic.

allegory n. **parable**, analogy, metaphor, symbol, emblem.

allergic adj. **1** *she was allergic to nuts* **hypersensitive**, sensitive, sensitized. **2** informal *boys are allergic to washing* **averse**, opposed, hostile, inimical, antagonistic, antipathetic, resistant, (dead) set against.

allergy n. **1** *an allergy to feathers* **hypersensitivity**, sensitivity, allergic reaction. **2** informal *their allergy to free enterprise* **aversion**, antipathy, opposition, hostility, antagonism, dislike, distaste.

alleviate v. **reduce**, ease, relieve, take the edge off, deaden, dull, diminish, lessen, weaken, lighten, attenuate, allay, assuage, palliate, damp, soothe, help, soften, temper.
– OPPOSITES aggravate.

alley n. **passage**, passageway, alleyway, back alley, backstreet, lane, path, pathway, walk, allée.

alliance n. **1** *a defensive alliance* **association**, union, league, confederation, federation, confederacy, coalition, consortium, affiliation, partnership. **2** *an alliance between medicine and morality* **relationship**, affinity, association, connection.

allied adj. **1** *a group of allied nations* **federated**, confederated, associated, in alliance, in league, in partnership; unified, united, amalgamated, integrated. **2** *agricultural and allied industries* **associated**, related, connected, interconnected, linked; similar, like, comparable, equivalent.
– OPPOSITES independent, unrelated.

all-important adj. **vital**, essential, indispensable, crucial, key, vitally important, of the utmost importance; critical, life-and-death, paramount, pre-eminent,

high-priority; urgent, pressing, burning.
– OPPOSITES inessential.

allocate v. allot, assign, distribute, apportion, share out, portion out, deal out, dole out, give out, dish out, parcel out, ration out, divide out/up; informal divvy up.

allocation n. 1 *the efficient allocation of resources* **allotment**, assignment, distribution, apportionment, sharing out, handing out, dealing out, doling out, giving out, dishing out, parcelling out, rationing out, dividing out/up; informal divvying up. 2 *our annual allocation of funds* **allowance**, allotment, quota, share, ration, grant, slice; informal cut; Brit. informal whack.

allot v. allocate, assign, apportion, distribute, issue, grant; earmark for, designate for, set aside for; hand out, deal out, dish out, dole out, give out; informal divvy up.

allotment n. 1 *the allotment of shares by a company* **allocation**, assignment, distribution, apportionment, issuing, sharing out, handing out, dealing out, doling out, giving out, dishing out, parcelling out, rationing out, dividing out/up; informal divvying up. 2 *each member received an allotment of new shares* **quota**, share, ration, grant, allocation, allowance, slice; informal cut; Brit. informal whack.

all out adv. *I'm working all out to finish my novel* **strenuously**, energetically, vigorously, hard, with all one's might (and main), eagerly, enthusiastically, industriously, diligently, assiduously, sedulously, indefatigably, with application/perseverance; informal like mad, like crazy; Brit. informal like billy-o.
– OPPOSITES lackadaisically.
▸ adj. *an all-out attack* **strenuous**, energetic, vigorous, forceful, forcible; spirited, mettlesome, plucky, determined, resolute, aggressive, eager, keen, enthusiastic, zealous, ardent, fervent.
– OPPOSITES half-hearted.

allow v. 1 *the police allowed him to go home* **permit**, let, authorize, give permission/authorization/leave, sanction, grant someone the right, license, enable, entitle; consent, assent, give one's consent/assent/blessing, give the nod, acquiesce, agree, approve; informal give the go-ahead, give the thumbs up, give the OK, give the green light; formal accede. 2 *allow an hour or so for driving* **set aside**, allocate, allot, earmark, designate, assign. 3 *the house was demolished to allow for road widening* **provide**, get ready, cater, take into consideration, take into account, make provision, make preparations, prepare, plan, make plans. 4 *she allowed that all people had their funny little ways* **admit**, acknowledge, recognize, agree, accept, concede, grant.
– OPPOSITES prevent, forbid.

allowable adj. *the maximum allowable number of users* **permissible**, permitted, allowed, admissible, acceptable, legal, lawful, legitimate, licit, authorized,

sanctioned, approved, in order; informal OK, legit.
– OPPOSITES forbidden.

allowance n. 1 *your baggage allowance* **quota**, allocation, allotment, share, ration, grant, limit, portion, slice. 2 *her father gave her an allowance* **payment**, pocket money, sum of money, contribution, grant, subsidy, maintenance, financial support. 3 *a tax allowance* **concession**, reduction, decrease, discount.
▢ **make allowance(s) for 1** *you must make allowances for delays* **take into consideration**, take into account, bear in mind, have regard to, provide for, plan for, make plans for, get ready for, cater for, allow for, make provision for, make preparations for, prepare for. 2 *she made allowances for his faults* **excuse**, make excuses for, forgive, pardon, overlook.

alloy n. **mixture**, mix, amalgam, fusion, meld, blend, compound, combination, composite, union; technical admixture.

all-powerful adj. **omnipotent**, almighty, supreme, pre-eminent; dictatorial, despotic, totalitarian, autocratic, anti-democratic.
– OPPOSITES powerless.

all right adj. 1 *the tea was all right* **satisfactory**, acceptable, adequate, fairly good, passable, reasonable; informal so-so, OK. 2 *are you all right?* **unhurt**, uninjured, unharmed, unscathed, in one piece, safe (and sound); well, fine, alive and well; informal OK. 3 *it's all right for you to go now* **permissible**, permitted, allowed, allowable, admissible, acceptable, legal, lawful, legitimate, licit, authorized, sanctioned, approved, in order; informal OK, legit.
– OPPOSITES unsatisfactory, hurt, forbidden.
▸ adv. 1 *the system works all right* **satisfactorily**, adequately, fairly well, passably, acceptably, reasonably; informal OK. 2 *it's him all right* **definitely**, certainly, unquestionably, undoubtedly, indubitably, undeniably, assuredly, without (a) doubt, beyond the shadow of a doubt; old use in sooth, verily.
▸ exclam. *all right, I'll go* **very well (then)**, right (then), fine, good, yes, agreed, wilco; informal OK, okey-dokey, roger; Brit. informal righto.

allude v. **refer**, touch on, suggest, hint, imply, mention (in passing), make an allusion to; formal advert.

allure n. *the allure of Paris* **attraction**, lure, draw, pull, appeal, allurement, enticement, temptation, charm, seduction, fascination.
▸ v. *will sponsors be allured by such opportunities?* **attract**, lure, entice, tempt, appeal to, captivate, draw, win over, charm, seduce, fascinate, whet the appetite of, make someone's mouth water.
– OPPOSITES repel.

alluring adj. **enticing**, tempting, attractive, appealing, inviting, captivating, fetching, seductive; enchanting, charming, fascinating; informal come-hither.

a

allusion n. **reference**, mention, suggestion, hint, comment, remark.

ally n. *close political allies* **associate**, colleague, friend, confederate, partner, supporter.
– OPPOSITES enemy, opponent.
▶v. **1** *he allied his racing experience with business acumen* **combine**, marry, couple, merge, amalgamate, join, fuse. **2** *the Catholic powers allied with Philip II* **unite**, combine, join (up), join forces, band together, team up, collaborate, side, align oneself, form an alliance, throw in one's lot, make common cause.
– OPPOSITES split.

almanac n. **yearbook**, calendar, register, annual; manual, handbook.

almighty adj. **1** *I swear by almighty God* **all-powerful**, omnipotent, supreme, pre-eminent. **2** *informal an almighty explosion* **very great**, huge, enormous, immense, colossal, massive, prodigious, stupendous, tremendous, monumental, mammoth, vast, gigantic, giant, mighty, Herculean, epic; very loud, deafening, ear-splitting, ear-piercing, booming, thundering, thunderous; informal whopping, thumping, astronomical, mega, monster, humongous, jumbo; Brit. informal whacking, ginormous.
– OPPOSITES powerless, insignificant.

almost adv. **nearly**, (just) about, more or less, practically, virtually, all but, as good as, close to, near, well-nigh, nigh on, not quite, not far from/off, to all intents and purposes; approaching, bordering on, verging on; informal pretty nearly/much/well.

alms plural n. historical **gift(s)**, donation(s), handout(s), offering(s), charity, baksheesh, largesse; rare donative.

aloft adj. & adv. **1** *he hoisted the Cup aloft* **upwards**, up, high, into the air/sky, skyward, heavenward. **2** *the airships stayed aloft for many hours* **in the air**, in the sky, high up, up (above), on high, overhead.
– OPPOSITES down.

alone adj. & adv. **1** *she was alone in the house* **by oneself**, on one's own, all alone, solitary, single, singly, solo, solus; unescorted, partnerless, companionless; Brit. informal on one's tod, on one's lonesome, on one's Jack Jones; Austral./NZ informal on one's Pat Malone. **2** *he managed alone* **unaided**, unassisted, without help/assistance, single-handedly, solo, on one's own. **3** *she felt terribly alone* **lonely**, isolated, solitary, deserted, abandoned, forlorn, friendless. **4** *a house standing alone* **apart**, by itself/oneself, separate, detached, isolated. **5** *you alone can inspire me* **only**, solely, just; and no one else, and nothing else, no one but, nothing but.
– OPPOSITES in company, with help, among others.

along prep. **1** *she walked along the corridor* **down**, from one end of —— to the other. **2** *trees grew along the river bank* **beside**, by the side of, on the edge of, alongside.
□ **along with** together with, accompanying, accompanied by; at the same time as; as well as, in addition to, plus, besides.

aloof adj. **distant**, detached, unfriendly, unsociable, remote, unapproachable, formal, stiff, austere, withdrawn, reserved, unforthcoming, uncommunicative; informal stand-offish.
– OPPOSITES familiar, friendly.

aloud adv. **audibly**, out loud, for all to hear.
– OPPOSITES silently.

alphabet n. **ABC**, letters, writing system, syllabary.

already adv. **1** *Anna had suffered a great deal already* **by this/that time**, by now/then, thus/so far, before now/then, until now/then, up to now/then. **2** *is it 3 o'clock already?* **as early as this/that**, as soon as this/that, so soon.

also adv. **too**, as well, besides, in addition, additionally, furthermore, further, moreover, into the bargain, on top of (that), what's more, to boot, equally; informal and all; old use withal, forbye.

alter v. **1** *Eliot was persuaded to alter the passage* **change**, make changes to, make different, make alterations to, adjust, make adjustments to, adapt, amend, modify, revise, revamp, rework, redo, refine, vary, transform; informal tweak; technical permute. **2** *the state of affairs had altered* **change**, become different, undergo a (sea) change, adjust, adapt, transform, evolve.
– OPPOSITES preserve, stay the same.

alteration n. **change**, adjustment, adaptation, modification, variation, revision, amendment; rearrangement, reordering, restyling, rejigging, reworking, revamping; sea change, transformation; humorous transmogrification.

altercation n. **argument**, quarrel, squabble, fight, shouting match, disagreement, difference of opinion, falling-out, dispute, disputation, wrangle, war of words; informal tiff, run-in, slanging match, spat, scrap; Brit. informal row, barney, ding-dong, bust-up, bit of argy-bargy; Brit. informal, Sport afters; N. Amer. informal rhubarb; old use broil, miff.

alternate v. **1** *rows of trees alternate with dense shrub* **be interspersed**, rotate, follow one another; take turns, take it in turns, work/act in sequence. **2** *we could alternate the groups so that no one felt they had been left out* **give turns to**, take in turn, rotate, take in rotation; swap, exchange, interchange.
▶adj. **1** *she attended on alternate days* **every other**, every second. **2** *place the leeks and noodles in alternate layers* **alternating**, interchanging, following in sequence, sequential. **3** N. Amer. *an alternate plan*. See **alternative** (sense 1 of the adjective).

alternative adj. **1** *an alternative route* **different**, other, another, second, possible, substitute, replacement; standby, emergency, reserve, back-up, auxiliary, fallback; N. Amer. alternate. **2** *an alternative lifestyle* **unorthodox**, unconventional, non-standard,

a

unusual, uncommon, out of the ordinary, radical, revolutionary, nonconformist, avant-garde; informal off the wall, oddball, offbeat, way-out.

▶n. *we have no alternative* **option**, choice, other possibility; substitute, replacement.

alternatively adv. **on the other hand**, as an alternative, or; otherwise, instead, if not, then again; N. Amer. alternately.

although conj. **in spite of the fact that**, despite the fact that, notwithstanding (the fact) that, even though/if, for all that, while, whilst.

altitude n. **height**, elevation, distance above the sea/ground.

altogether adv. **1** *he wasn't altogether happy* **completely**, totally, entirely, absolutely, wholly, fully, thoroughly, utterly, perfectly, one hundred per cent, in all respects. **2** *we have five offices altogether* **in all**, all told, in toto. **3** *altogether it was a great evening* **on the whole**, overall, all in all, all things considered, on balance, on average, for the most part, in the main, in general, generally, by and large.

altruism n. **unselfishness**, selflessness, compassion, kindness, public-spiritedness; charity, benevolence, beneficence, philanthropy, humanitarianism; literary bounty, bounteousness.
– OPPOSITES selfishness.

always adv. **1** *he's always late* **every time**, each time, at all times, all the time, without fail, consistently, invariably, regularly, habitually, unfailingly. **2** *she's always complaining* **continually**, continuously, constantly, forever, perpetually, incessantly, ceaselessly, unceasingly, endlessly, the entire time; informal 24-7. **3** *the place will always be dear to me* **forever**, for always, for good (and all), for evermore, for ever and ever, until the end of time, eternally, for eternity, until hell freezes over; informal for keeps, until the cows come home; old use for aye. **4** *you can always take it back to the shop* **as a last resort**, no matter what, in any event/case, come what may.
– OPPOSITES never, seldom, sometimes.

amalgamate v. **combine**, merge, unite, fuse, blend, meld; join (together), join forces, band (together), link (up), team up, go into partnership; literary commingle.
– OPPOSITES separate.

amalgamation n. **combination**, union, blend, mixture, fusion, coalescence, synthesis, composite, amalgam.

amass v. **gather**, collect, assemble; accumulate, stockpile, store (up), cumulate, accrue, lay in/up, garner; informal stash (away).
– OPPOSITES dissipate.

amateur n. **1** *the crew were all amateurs* **non-professional**, non-specialist, layman, layperson; dilettante. **2** *what a bunch of amateurs* **bungler**, incompetent, bumbler; Brit. informal bodger.
– OPPOSITES professional, expert.

▶adj. **1** *an amateur sportsman* **non-professional**, non-specialist, lay; dilettante. **2** *their amateur efforts* **incompetent**, inept, unskilful, inexpert, amateurish, clumsy, maladroit, bumbling; Brit. informal bodged.

amateurish adj. See **amateur** (sense 2 of the adjective).

amatory adj. **sexual**, erotic, amorous, romantic, sensual, passionate, sexy; informal randy, steamy, naughty.

amaze v. **astonish**, astound, surprise, stun, stagger, nonplus, shock, startle, stupefy, stop someone in their tracks, leave open-mouthed, leave aghast, take someone's breath away, dumbfound; informal bowl over, flabbergast; Brit. informal knock for six; (**amazed**) thunderstruck, at a loss for words, speechless; Brit. informal gobsmacked.

amazement n. **astonishment**, surprise, shock, stupefaction, incredulity, disbelief, speechlessness, awe, wonder, wonderment.

amazing adj. **astonishing**, astounding, surprising, stunning, staggering, shocking, startling, stupefying, breathtaking; awesome, awe-inspiring, sensational, remarkable, spectacular, stupendous, phenomenal, extraordinary, incredible, unbelievable; informal mind-blowing, flabbergasting; literary wondrous.

ambassador n. **1** *the American ambassador* **envoy**, plenipotentiary, emissary, (papal) nuncio, representative, diplomat; old use legate. **2** *a great ambassador for the sport* **campaigner**, representative, promoter, champion, supporter, backer; N. Amer. booster.

> **WORD LINKS**
> **attaché** a person on an ambassador's staff
> **chargé d'affaires** an ambassador's deputy
> **embassy** an ambassador's official home or offices

ambience n. **atmosphere**, air, aura, climate, mood, feel, feeling, vibrations, character, quality, impression, flavour, look, tone; informal vibes.

ambiguity n. **ambivalence**, equivocation; obscurity, vagueness, abstruseness, doubtfulness, uncertainty; formal dubiety.

ambiguous adj. **equivocal**, ambivalent, open to debate/argument, arguable, debatable; obscure, unclear, vague, abstruse, doubtful, dubious, uncertain.
– OPPOSITES clear.

ambit n. **scope**, extent, range, breadth, width, reach, sweep; terms of reference, field of reference, jurisdiction, remit; area, sphere, field, realm, compass.

ambition n. **1** *young people with ambition* **drive**, determination, enterprise, initiative, eagerness, motivation, enthusiasm, zeal, commitment, a sense of purpose; informal get-up-and-go. **2** *her ambition was to become a model* **aspiration**, intention, goal, aim, objective, object, purpose, intent, plan, desire, wish, design, target, dream.

ambitious adj. **1** *an energetic and ambitious politician* **aspiring**, determined, forceful, pushy, enterprising, motivated, driven, enthusiastic, energetic, zealous, committed,

purposeful, power-hungry; informal go-ahead, go-getting. **2** *he was ambitious to make it to the top* **eager**, determined, intent on, enthusiastic, anxious, hungry, impatient, striving. **3** *an ambitious task* **difficult**, exacting, demanding, formidable, challenging, hard, arduous, onerous, tough; old use toilsome.
– OPPOSITES laid-back.

ambivalent adj. **equivocal**, uncertain, unsure, doubtful, indecisive, inconclusive, irresolute, in two minds, undecided, torn, in a dilemma, on the horns of a dilemma, in a quandary, on the fence, hesitating, wavering, vacillating, equivocating, blowing hot and cold; informal iffy.
– OPPOSITES unequivocal, certain.

amble v. **stroll**, saunter, wander, ramble, promenade, walk, go for a walk, take a walk; informal mosey, tootle; Brit. informal pootle, mooch; formal perambulate.

ambush n. *the soldiers were killed in an ambush* **surprise attack**, trap; old use ambuscade.
▶ v. *twenty youths ambushed their patrol car* **attack**, surprise, pounce on, lay a trap for, lie in wait for, waylay; N. Amer. bushwhack; old use ambuscade.

ameliorate v. **improve**, make better, better, make improvements to, enhance, help, benefit, boost, amend; relieve, ease, mitigate; informal tweak, patch up.
– OPPOSITES worsen.

amenable adj. **1** *an amenable child* **compliant**, acquiescent, biddable, manageable, controllable, governable, persuadable, tractable, responsive, pliant, malleable, complaisant, easily handled; rare persuasible. **2** *many cancers are amenable to treatment* **susceptible**, receptive, responsive; old use susceptive.
– OPPOSITES uncooperative.

amend v. **revise**, alter, change, modify, qualify, adapt, adjust; edit, copy-edit, rewrite, redraft, rephrase, reword, rework, revamp.

amends plural n. *I wanted to make amends* **compensation**, recompense, reparation, restitution, redress, atonement, expiation.
□ **make amends** compensate, recompense, indemnify, make it up to; atone for, make up for, make good, expiate.

amenity n. *basic amenities* **facility**, service, convenience, resource, appliance, aid, comfort, benefit, advantage.

amiable adj. **friendly**, affable, amicable, cordial; warm, warm-hearted, good-natured, nice, pleasant, agreeable, likeable, genial, good-humoured, charming, easy to get on with, companionable, sociable, personable; informal chummy; Brit. informal matey; N. Amer. informal regular.
– OPPOSITES unfriendly, disagreeable.

amicable adj. **friendly**, good-natured, cordial, easy, easy-going, neighbourly, harmonious, cooperative, civilized.
– OPPOSITES unfriendly.

amid prep. **1** *the jeep was concealed amid pine trees* **in the middle of**, surrounded by, among, amongst; literary amidst, in the midst of. **2** *the truce collapsed amid fears of a revolt* **at a time of**, in an atmosphere of, against a background of; as a result of.

amiss adj. *an inspection revealed nothing amiss* **wrong**, awry, faulty, out of order, defective, unsatisfactory, incorrect; inappropriate, improper.
– OPPOSITES right, in order.
□ **not come/go amiss** be welcome, be appropriate, be useful.
take something amiss be offended, take offence, be upset.

amity n. **friendship**, friendliness, harmony, harmoniousness, understanding, accord, cooperation, amicableness, goodwill, cordiality, warmth; formal concord.
– OPPOSITES animosity, enmity.

ammunition n. *police seized arms and ammunition* **bullets**, shells, projectiles, missiles, rounds, shot, slugs, cartridges, munitions; informal ammo.

amnesty n. *an amnesty for political prisoners* **pardon**, pardoning, reprieve; release, discharge; informal let-off.
▶ v. *the guerrillas were amnestied* **pardon**, reprieve; release, discharge, liberate, free, spare; informal let off, let off the hook.

amok adv.
□ **run amok** go berserk, get out of control, rampage, riot, run riot, go on the rampage; informal raise hell.

among, amongst prep. **1** *you're among friends* **surrounded by**, in the company of, amid, in the middle of; literary amidst, in the midst of. **2** *a child was among the injured* **included in**, one/some of. **3** *he distributed the proceeds among his creditors* **between**, to each of.

amoral adj. **unprincipled**, without standards/morals/scruples, unethical.
– OPPOSITES principled.

amorous adj. **lustful**, sexual, erotic, amatory, ardent, passionate, impassioned; in love, enamoured, lovesick; informal lovey-dovey, kissy, smoochy, goo-goo, hot; Brit. informal randy; old use sportive.
– OPPOSITES unloving.

amorphous adj. **shapeless**, formless, structureless, indeterminate.
– OPPOSITES shaped, definite.

amount n. **quantity**, number, total, aggregate, sum, quota, group, size, mass, weight, volume, bulk, quantum.
□ **amount to 1** *the bill amounted to £50* **add up to**, come to, run to, be, make, total; Brit. tot up to. **2** *the delays amounted to maladministration* **constitute**, comprise, be tantamount, come down, boil down; signify, signal, mean, indicate, suggest, denote, point to, be evidence, be symptomatic; literary betoken. **3** *her relationships had never amounted to anything significant* **become**, grow/develop into, prove to be, turn out to be.

the full amount the grand total, the total, the aggregate; informal the whole caboodle/shebang, the full nine yards.

ample adj. **1** *there is ample time for discussion* **enough**, sufficient, adequate, plenty of, more than enough, enough and to spare. **2** *an ample supply of wine* **plentiful**, abundant, copious, profuse, rich, lavish, liberal, generous, bountiful, large, huge, great, bumper; informal a gogo, galore; literary plenteous. **3** *his ample tunic* **spacious**, capacious, roomy, sizeable; voluminous, loose-fitting, baggy, sloppy; formal commodious.
– OPPOSITES insufficient, meagre.

amplify v. **1** *many frogs amplify their voices* **make louder**, louden, turn up, magnify, intensify, increase, boost, step up, raise. **2** *these notes amplify our statement* **expand**, enlarge on, elaborate on, add to, supplement, develop, flesh out, add detail to, go into detail about.
– OPPOSITES reduce, quieten.

amplitude n. **magnitude**, size, volume; extent, range, compass; breadth, width.

amputate v. **cut off**, sever, remove (surgically), saw/chop off.

amulet n. **lucky charm**, charm, talisman, fetish, mascot, totem, idol, juju; old use periapt.

amuse v. **1** *her annoyance simply amused him* **entertain**, make laugh, delight, divert, cheer (up), please, charm, tickle; informal tickle pink, crack up; Brit. informal crease up. **2** *he amused himself by writing poetry* **occupy**, engage, busy, employ, distract, absorb, engross, hold someone's attention; interest, entertain, divert.
– OPPOSITES bore.

amusement n. **1** *we looked with amusement at the cartoon* **mirth**, merriment, light-heartedness, hilarity, glee, delight, gaiety, joviality, fun; enjoyment, pleasure, high spirits, cheerfulness. **2** *I read the book for amusement* **entertainment**, pleasure, leisure, relaxation, fun, enjoyment, interest, diversion; informal R & R; N. Amer. informal rec; old use disport. **3** *a wide range of amusements* **activity**, entertainment, diversion; game, sport.

amusing adj. **entertaining**, funny, comical, humorous, light-hearted, jocular, witty, mirthful, hilarious, droll, diverting, chucklesome; informal wacky, side-splitting, rib-tickling.
– OPPOSITES boring, solemn.

anaemic adj. **1** *his anaemic face* **colourless**, bloodless, pale, pallid, wan, ashen, grey, sallow, pasty-faced, whey-faced, peaky, sickly, etiolated. **2** *an anaemic description of her feelings* **feeble**, weak, insipid, wishy-washy, vapid, bland; lame, tame, lacklustre, spiritless, lifeless, ineffective, ineffectual, etiolated; informal pathetic.

anaesthetic n. **narcotic**, painkiller, painkilling drug, pain reliever, sedative, anodyne, analgesic; general, local.

analgesic adj. **painkilling**, pain-relieving, anodyne, narcotic, palliative.

analogous adj. **comparable**, parallel, similar, like, corresponding, related, kindred, equivalent; formal cognate.
– OPPOSITES unrelated.

analogy n. **similarity**, parallel, correspondence, likeness, resemblance, correlation, relation, kinship, equivalence, similitude.
– OPPOSITES dissimilarity.

analyse v. **examine**, inspect, survey, study, scrutinize, look over; investigate, explore, probe, research, go over (with a fine-tooth comb), review, evaluate, break down, dissect, anatomize.

analysis n. **examination**, investigation, inspection, survey, study, scrutiny; exploration, probe, research, review, evaluation, interpretation, anatomization, dissection.

analytical, **analytic** adj. **systematic**, logical, scientific, methodical, (well) organized, ordered, orderly, meticulous, rigorous.
– OPPOSITES unsystematic.

anarchic adj. **lawless**, without law and order, in disorder/turmoil, unruly, chaotic, turbulent.
– OPPOSITES ordered.

anarchist n. **nihilist**, insurgent, agitator, subversive, terrorist, revolutionary, revolutionist, insurrectionist.

anarchy n. **lawlessness**, nihilism, mobocracy, revolution, insurrection, disorder, chaos, tumult, turmoil.
– OPPOSITES government, order.

anathema n. **1** *racial hatred was anathema to her* **abhorrent**, hateful, repugnant, repellent, offensive; **abomination**, outrage, bane, bugbear, bête noire. **2** *the Vatican Council issued an anathema* **curse**, ban, excommunication, proscription, debarment, denunciation.

anatomy n. **1** *a cat's anatomy* **structure**, make-up, composition, constitution, form. **2** *an anatomy of society* **analysis**, examination, inspection, survey, study, investigation, review, evaluation.

ancestor n. **1** *he could trace his ancestors back to King James I* **forebear**, forefather, predecessor, antecedent, progenitor, primogenitor. **2** *the instrument is an ancestor of the lute* **forerunner**, precursor, predecessor.
– OPPOSITES descendant, successor.

ancestral adj. **inherited**, hereditary, familial.

ancestry n. **ancestors**, forebears, forefathers, progenitors, antecedents; family tree, pedigree; lineage, genealogy, roots.

anchor n. **1** *a ship's anchor* **kedge**, killick, bower, grapnel, ground tackle. **2** *the anchor of the new coalition* **mainstay**, cornerstone, linchpin, bulwark, foundation. **3** *a CBS news anchor* **presenter**, announcer, anchorman, anchorwoman, broadcaster.

▶v. **1** *the ship was anchored in the bay* **moor**, berth, be at anchor; old use harbour. **2** *the fish anchors itself to the coral* **secure**, fasten, attach, affix, fix.

anchorage n. **moorings**, moorage, roads, roadstead, harbour.

anchorite n. historical **hermit**, recluse, ascetic; historical stylite; old use eremite.

ancient adj. **1** *ancient civilizations* **early**, prehistoric, primeval, primordial, primitive, of long ago; literary of yore; old use foregone. **2** *an ancient custom* **old**, very old, age-old, archaic, antediluvian, time-worn, time-honoured. **3** *I feel positively ancient* **antiquated**, aged, elderly, decrepit, antediluvian, in one's dotage; old-fashioned, out of date, outmoded, démodé, passé; informal out of the ark; Brit. informal past its/one's sell-by date.

– OPPOSITES recent, contemporary.

> **WORD LINKS**
>
> **archaeology** the study of ancient civilizations by examining excavated objects
> **palaeography** the study of ancient writing systems
> **palaeontology** the study of fossil animals and plants

ancillary adj. **additional**, auxiliary, supporting, helping, extra, supplementary, accessory; Medicine adjuvant; rare adminicular.

and conj. **together with**, along with, with, as well as, in addition to, also, too; besides, furthermore; informal plus.

anecdotal adj. *anecdotal evidence* **unscientific**, unreliable, based on hearsay.

anecdote n. **story**, tale, narrative; urban myth; informal yarn.

anew adv. **again**, afresh, once more/again, over again.

angel n. **1** *God sent an angel* **messenger of God**, divine being, archangel, seraph. **2** *she's an absolute angel* **paragon of virtue**, saint; gem, treasure, darling, dear; informal star; Brit. informal dated brick. **3** informal *a financial angel* **backer**, sponsor, benefactor, promoter, patron.

– OPPOSITES devil.

angelic adj. **1** *angelic beings* **divine**, heavenly, celestial, holy, seraphic; literary empyrean. **2** *Sophie's angelic appearance* **innocent**, pure, virtuous, good, saintly, wholesome.

– OPPOSITES demonic, infernal.

anger n. *his face was livid with anger* **annoyance**, vexation, exasperation, crossness, irritation, irritability, indignation, pique; rage, fury, wrath, outrage, irascibility, ill temper/humour; informal aggravation; literary ire, choler.

– OPPOSITES pleasure, good humour.

▶v. *she was angered by his terse reply* **annoy**, irritate, exasperate, irk, vex, put out; enrage, incense, infuriate, make someone's hackles rise; Brit. rub up the wrong way; informal make someone's blood boil, get someone's back up, make someone see red, get someone's

dander up, rattle someone's cage; aggravate, get someone, rile, hack off; Brit. informal wind up, nark; N. Amer. informal tee off, tick off, burn up, gravel; informal dated give someone the pip.

– OPPOSITES pacify, placate.

angle¹ n. **1** *the wall is sloping at an angle of 33° **gradient**, slant, inclination. **2** *the angle of the roof* **corner**, intersection, point, apex. **3** *consider the problem from a different angle* **perspective**, point of view, viewpoint, standpoint, position, aspect, slant, direction.

▶v. **1** *Anna angled her camera towards the tree* **tilt**, slant, direct, turn. **2** *angle your answer so that it is relevant* **present**, slant, orient, twist, bias.

angle² v. *he was angling for an invitation* **try to get**, seek to obtain, fish for, hope for, be after.

angler n. **fisherman**, rod; old use fisher.

angry adj. **1** *Vivienne got angry* **irate**, annoyed, cross, vexed, irritated, indignant, irked; furious, enraged, infuriated, in a temper, incensed, raging, incandescent, fuming, seething, beside oneself, outraged; informal (hopping) mad, wild, livid, apoplectic, as cross as two sticks, hot under the collar, up in arms, foaming at the mouth, steamed up, in a lather/paddy, fit to be tied; Brit. informal aerated, shirty; N. Amer. informal sore, bent out of shape, teed off, ticked off; Austral./NZ informal ropeable, snaky; literary wrathful; old use wroth. **2** *an angry debate* **heated**, passionate, stormy, 'lively'; bad-tempered, ill-tempered, acrimonious, bitter. **3** *angry sores* **inflamed**, red, swollen, sore, painful.

– OPPOSITES pleased, good-humoured.

□ **get angry** lose one's temper, go berserk, flare up; informal go mad/crazy/wild, go bananas, hit the roof, go through the roof, go up the wall, see red, go off the deep end, fly off the handle, blow one's top, blow a fuse/gasket, lose one's rag, flip (one's lid), have a fit, foam at the mouth, explode, go non-linear, go ballistic; Brit. informal go spare, do one's nut; N. Amer. informal flip one's wig, blow one's lid/stack, have a conniption fit.

angst n. **anxiety**, fear, apprehension, worry, foreboding, trepidation, malaise, disquiet, disquietude, unease, uneasiness.

anguish n. **agony**, pain, torment, torture, suffering, distress, angst, misery, sorrow, grief, heartache, desolation, despair; literary dolour.

– OPPOSITES happiness.

anguished adj. **agonized**, tormented, tortured; grief-stricken, wretched, heartbroken, desolate, devastated; informal cut up; literary dolorous.

angular adj. **1** *an angular shape* **sharp-cornered**, pointed, V-shaped, Y-shaped. **2** *an angular face* **bony**, raw-boned, lean, rangy, spare, thin, gaunt.

– OPPOSITES rounded, curving.

animal n. **1** *endangered animals* **creature**, beast, living thing; (**animals**) wildlife, fauna; N. Amer. informal critter. **2** *the man was an animal* **brute**, beast, monster, devil, demon, fiend; informal swine, bastard, pig.

▸**adj. 1** *animal life* **zoological**, animalistic; rare zoic. **2** *a grunt of animal passion* **carnal**, fleshly, bodily, physical; brutish, unrefined, uncultured, coarse.

WORD LINKS

zoology the study of animals
ethology the study of animal behaviour
invertebrate an animal without a backbone
vertebrate an animal with a backbone
marsupial a mammal whose young are carried and suckled in a pouch
monotreme a mammal which lays eggs
quadruped an animal with four feet
menagerie, **zoo** a collection of wild animals kept for display to the public
vivarium an enclosure for keeping animals in semi-natural conditions
bestiary a medieval book describing different animals

---

animate v. *a sense of excitement animated the whole school* **enliven**, vitalize, breathe (new) life into, energize, invigorate, revive, vivify, liven up; inspire, inspirit, exhilarate, thrill, excite, fire, arouse, rouse; N. Amer. light a fire under; informal buck up, pep up, give someone a buzz.
– OPPOSITES depress.
▸**adj.** *an animate being* **living**, alive, live, breathing; old use quick.
– OPPOSITES inanimate.

animated adj. **lively**, spirited, high-spirited, energetic, full of life, excited, enthusiastic, eager, alive, active, vigorous, vibrant, vital, vivacious, buoyant, exuberant, ebullient, effervescent, bouncy, bubbly, perky; informal bright-eyed and bushy-tailed, full of beans, bright and breezy, chirpy, chipper, peppy.
– OPPOSITES lethargic, lifeless.

animosity n. **antipathy**, hostility, friction, antagonism, enmity, animus, bitterness, rancour, resentment, dislike, ill feeling/will, bad blood, hatred, hate, loathing; malice, spite, spitefulness.
– OPPOSITES goodwill, friendship.

annals plural n. **records**, archives, chronicles, accounts, registers; Law muniments.

annex v. **1** *ten amendments were annexed to the constitution* **add**, append, attach, tack on, tag on. **2** *Charlemagne annexed northern Italy* **take over**, take possession of, appropriate, seize, conquer, occupy.
▸**n.** (also **annexe**) **extension**, addition; wing; N. Amer. ell.

annexation n. **seizure**, occupation, invasion, conquest, takeover, appropriation.

annihilate v. **destroy**, wipe out, obliterate, wipe off the face of the earth; kill, slaughter, exterminate, eliminate, liquidate; informal take out, rub out, snuff out, waste.
– OPPOSITES create.

anniversary n. **jubilee**, commemoration.

annotate v. **comment on**, add notes/footnotes to, gloss, interpret; old use margin.

annotation n. **note**, notation, comment, gloss, footnote; commentary, explanation, interpretation.

announce v. **1** *their financial results were announced* **make public**, make known, report, declare, state, give out, notify, publicize, broadcast, publish, advertise, circulate, proclaim, blazon abroad. **2** *Victor announced the guests* **introduce**, present, name. **3** *strains of music announced her arrival* **signal**, indicate, give notice of, herald, proclaim; literary betoken.

announcement n. **1** *an announcement by the Minister* **statement**, report, declaration, proclamation, pronouncement, rescript; bulletin, communiqué; N. Amer. advisory. **2** *the announcement of the decision* **declaration**, notification, reporting, publishing, broadcasting, proclamation; old use annunciation.

announcer n. **presenter**, anchorman, anchorwoman, anchor; newsreader, newscaster, broadcaster.

annoy v. **irritate**, vex, make angry/cross, anger, exasperate, irk, gall, pique, put out, antagonize, get on someone's nerves, ruffle someone's feathers, make someone's hackles rise, nettle; Brit. rub up the wrong way; informal aggravate, peeve, hassle, miff, rile, needle, get (to), bug, hack off, get up someone's nose, get someone's goat, get someone's back up, give someone the hump, drive mad/crazy, drive round the bend/twist, drive up the wall, get someone's dander up; Brit. informal wind up, nark, get on someone's wick; N. Amer. informal tee off, tick off, burn up, rankle, gravel; informal dated give someone the pip.
– OPPOSITES please, gratify.

annoyance n. **1** *much to his annoyance, Louise didn't even notice* **irritation**, exasperation, vexation, indignation, anger, displeasure, chagrin; informal aggravation. **2** *they found him an annoyance* **nuisance**, pest, bother, irritant, inconvenience, thorn in one's flesh; informal pain (in the neck), bind, bore, hassle; N. Amer. informal nudnik, burr under someone's saddle; Austral./NZ informal nark.

annoyed adj. **irritated**, cross, angry, vexed, exasperated, irked, piqued, displeased, put out, disgruntled, nettled, in a bad mood, in a temper; informal aggravated, peeved, miffed, miffy, riled, hacked off, hot under the collar; Brit. informal not best pleased, narked, shirty; N. Amer. informal teed off, ticked off, sore, bent out of shape; Austral./NZ informal snaky, crook; old use wroth.

annoying adj. **irritating**, infuriating, exasperating, maddening, trying, tiresome, troublesome, bothersome, irksome, vexing, vexatious, galling; informal aggravating, pesky.

annual adj. **yearly**, once-a-year; year-long, twelve-month.

annually adv. **yearly**, once a year, each year, per annum.

annul v. **declare null and void**, nullify, invalidate, void; repeal, reverse, rescind, revoke; Law vacate; formal abrogate; old use recall.
– OPPOSITES restore, enact.

anodyne n. **painkiller**, painkilling drug, pain reliever, analgesic, narcotic.
▸ adj. *the conversation was anodyne* **bland**, inoffensive, innocuous, neutral, unobjectionable.

anoint v. **1** *the head of the infant was anointed* **smear/rub with oil**; old use anele. **2** *he was anointed and crowned* **consecrate**, bless, ordain; formal hallow.

anomalous adj. **abnormal**, atypical, irregular, aberrant, exceptional, freak, freakish, odd, bizarre, peculiar, unusual, out of the ordinary.
– OPPOSITES normal, typical.

anomaly n. **oddity**, peculiarity, abnormality, irregularity, inconsistency, incongruity, aberration, quirk.

anon adv. informal **soon**, shortly, in a little while, presently, before long, by and by; dated directly; literary ere long.

anonymous adj. **1** *an anonymous donor* **unnamed**, of unknown name, nameless, incognito, unidentified, unknown; rare innominate. **2** *an anonymous letter* **unsigned**, unattributed. **3** *an anonymous housing estate* **characterless**, nondescript, impersonal, faceless.
– OPPOSITES known, identified.

another determiner **1** *have another drink* **one more**, a further, an additional; an extra, a spare. **2** *she left him for another man* **a different**, some other, an alternative.
– OPPOSITES the same.

answer n. **1** *her answer was unequivocal* **reply**, response, rejoinder, reaction; retort, riposte; informal comeback. **2** *the answer is 150* **solution**, key. **3** *a new filter is the answer* **solution**, remedy, way out.
– OPPOSITES question.
▸ v. **1** *Steve was about to answer* **reply**, respond, rejoin; retort, riposte. **2** *he has yet to answer the charges* **rebut**, refute, defend oneself against. **3** *a man answering this description* **match**, fit, correspond to, be similar to. **4** *we're trying to answer the needs of our audience* **satisfy**, meet, fulfil, fill, measure up to. **5** *I answer to the Commissioner* **report**, work for/under, be subordinate, be accountable, be answerable, be responsible.
▢ **answer someone back** respond cheekily to, be cheeky to, be impertinent to, talk back to, cheek; N. Amer. informal sass.
answer for 1 *he will answer for his crime* **pay for**, be punished for, suffer for; make amends for, make reparation for, atone for. **2** *the government has a lot to answer for* **be accountable for**, be responsible for, be liable for, take the blame for; informal take the rap for.

answerable adj. **accountable**, responsible, liable; subject.

ant n.

WORD LINKS
formic relating to ants
myrmecology the study of ants

---

antagonism n. **hostility**, friction, enmity, antipathy, animus, opposition, dissension, rivalry; acrimony, bitterness, rancour, resentment, aversion, dislike, ill/bad feeling, ill will; Brit. informal needle.
– OPPOSITES rapport, friendship.

antagonist n. **adversary**, opponent, enemy, rival; (**antagonists**) opposition, competition.
– OPPOSITES ally.

antagonistic adj. **1** *he was antagonistic to the reforms* **hostile**, against, (dead) set against, opposed, inimical, antipathetic, ill-disposed, resistant, in disagreement; informal anti. **2** *an antagonistic group of bystanders* **hostile**, aggressive, belligerent, bellicose, pugnacious; rare oppugnant.
– OPPOSITES pro.

antagonize v. **anger**, annoy, provoke, vex, irritate, alienate; Brit. rub up the wrong way; informal aggravate, rile, needle, rattle someone's cage, get someone's back up, get someone's dander up; Brit. informal nark, get on someone's wick.
– OPPOSITES pacify, placate.

antecedent n. **1** *her antecedents have been traced* **ancestor**, forefather, forebear, progenitor, primogenitor; (**antecedents**) ancestry, family tree, lineage, genealogy, roots. **2** *the guitar's antecedent* **precursor**, forerunner, predecessor.
– OPPOSITES descendant.
▸ adj. *antecedent events* **previous**, earlier, prior, preceding, precursory; formal anterior.
– OPPOSITES subsequent.

antedate v. **precede**, predate, come/go before.

antediluvian adj. **1** *antediluvian animals* **prehistoric**, primeval, primordial, primal, ancient, early. **2** *his antediluvian attitudes* **out of date**, outdated, outmoded, old-fashioned, antiquated, behind the times, passé.

anteroom n. **antechamber**, vestibule, lobby, foyer; Architecture narthex.

anthem n. **hymn**, song, chorale, psalm, paean.

anthology n. **collection**, selection, compendium, treasury, miscellany; old use garland.

anticipate v. **1** *the police did not anticipate trouble* **expect**, foresee, predict, be prepared for, bargain on, reckon on; N. Amer. informal figure on. **2** *Elaine anticipated her meeting with Will* **look forward to**, await, lick one's lips over. **3** *warders can't always anticipate the actions of prisoners* **pre-empt**, forestall, second-guess; informal beat someone to the punch. **4** *her plays anticipated her film work* **foreshadow**, precede, antedate, come/go before.

anticipation n. **1** *my anticipation is that we will see a rise in rates* **expectation**, prediction, forecast. **2** *her eyes sparkled with anticipation* **expectancy**, expectation, excitement, suspense.
▢ **in anticipation of** in the expectation of,

a

in preparation for, ready for.

anticlimax n. **let-down**, disappointment, bathos, comedown, non-event; disillusionment; Brit. damp squib; informal washout.

antics plural n. **capers**, pranks, larks, high jinks, skylarking; Brit. informal monkey tricks.

antidote n. **1** *the antidote to this poison* **antitoxin**, antiserum, antivenin. **2** *laughter is a good antidote to stress* **remedy**, cure, nostrum.

antipathetic adj. **hostile**, against, (dead) set against, opposed, antagonistic, ill-disposed, unsympathetic; informal anti, down on.
– OPPOSITES pro.

antipathy n. **hostility**, antagonism, animosity, aversion, animus, enmity, dislike, distaste, hatred, hate, abhorrence, loathing.
– OPPOSITES liking, affinity.

antiquated adj. **outdated**, out of date, outmoded, outworn, behind the times, old-fashioned, anachronistic, old-fangled, passé, démodé; informal out of the ark, mouldy; N. Amer. informal horse-and-buggy, mossy, clunky.
– OPPOSITES modern, up to date.

antique n. **collector's item**, period piece, antiquity, object of virtu, objet d'art.
▶ adj. **1** *antique furniture* **old**, antiquarian, collectable. **2** *statues of antique gods* **ancient**, of long ago; literary of yore. **3** *antique work practices.* See **antiquated**.
– OPPOSITES modern, state-of-the-art.

antiquity n. **1** *the civilizations of antiquity* **ancient times**, the ancient past, classical times, the distant past. **2** *Islamic antiquities* **antique**, period piece, collector's item. **3** *a church of great antiquity* **age**, oldness, ancientness.

antiseptic adj. **1** *an antiseptic substance* **disinfectant**, germicidal, bactericidal. **2** *antiseptic bandages* **sterile**, aseptic, germ-free, uncontaminated, disinfected. **3** *their antiseptic surroundings* **characterless**, colourless, soulless; clinical, institutional.
– OPPOSITES contaminated.
▶ n. **disinfectant**, germicide, bactericide.

antisocial adj. **1** *antisocial behaviour* **objectionable**, offensive, unacceptable, distasteful, disruptive; sociopathic. **2** *I'm feeling a bit antisocial* **unsociable**, unfriendly, uncommunicative, reclusive, misanthropic.

antithesis n. **(direct) opposite**, converse, reverse, inverse, obverse, the other side of the coin; informal the flip side.

antithetical adj. **(directly) opposed**, contrasting, contrary, contradictory, conflicting, incompatible, irreconcilable, inconsistent, poles apart, at variance/odds; rare oppugnant.
– OPPOSITES identical, like.

anxiety n. **1** *his anxiety grew* **worry**, concern, apprehension, apprehensiveness, uneasiness, unease, fearfulness, fear, disquiet, disquietude, perturbation, agitation, angst, nervousness, nerves, tension, tenseness; informal butterflies (in one's stomach), jitteriness, twitchiness, collywobbles, jim-jams. **2** *an anxiety to please* **eagerness**, keenness, desire.
– OPPOSITES serenity.

anxious adj. **1** *I'm anxious about her* **worried**, concerned, apprehensive, fearful, uneasy, perturbed, troubled, bothered, disturbed, distressed, fretful, agitated, nervous, edgy, unquiet, on edge, tense, overwrought, worked up, keyed up, worried sick, with one's stomach in knots, with one's heart in one's mouth; informal uptight, on tenterhooks, with butterflies in one's stomach, like a cat on a hot tin roof, jittery, jumpy, twitchy, in a stew/twitter, all of a dither/lather, in a tizz/tizzy, het up; Brit. informal strung up, windy, having kittens, in a (flat) spin, like a cat on hot bricks; N. Amer. informal antsy, spooky, squirrelly, in a twit; Austral./NZ informal toey; dated overstrung. **2** *she was anxious for news* **eager**, keen, desirous, impatient.
– OPPOSITES carefree, unconcerned.

anyhow adv. **1** *anyhow, it doesn't really matter* **anyway**, in any case/event, at any rate; however, be that as it may; N. Amer. informal anyways. **2** *her clothes were strewn about anyhow* **haphazardly**, carelessly, heedlessly, negligently, in a muddle; informal all over the place; Brit. informal all over the shop; N. Amer. informal all over the lot.

apace adv. literary **quickly**, fast, swiftly, rapidly, speedily, briskly, without delay, post-haste, expeditiously.
– OPPOSITES slowly.

apart adv. **1** *the villages are two miles apart* **away from each other**. **2** *Isabel stood apart* **to one side**, aside, separately, alone, by oneself/itself. **3** *his parents are living apart* **separately**, independently, on one's own. **4** *the car was blown apart* **to pieces/bits**, up; literary asunder.
□ **apart from** except for, but for, aside from, with the exception of, excepting, excluding, bar, barring, besides, other than; informal outside of; formal save.

apartment n. **1** *a rented apartment* **flat**, penthouse; Austral. home unit; N. Amer. informal crib. **2** *the royal apartments* **suite (of rooms)**, rooms, living quarters, accommodation.

apathetic adj. **uninterested**, indifferent, unconcerned, unmoved, uninvolved, unemotional, emotionless, dispassionate, lukewarm, unmotivated; informal couldn't-care-less; rare Laodicean.

apathy n. **indifference**, lack of interest/enthusiasm, unconcern, uninterestedness, unresponsiveness, impassivity, dispassion, dispassionateness, lethargy, languor, ennui, accidie.
– OPPOSITES enthusiasm, passion.

ape n. **primate**, simian; monkey; technical anthropoid.
▶ v. *he aped Barbara's accent* **imitate**, mimic, copy, do an impression of; informal take off,

send up; old use monkey.

aperture n. **opening**, hole, gap, slit, slot, vent, crevice, chink, crack, interstice; technical orifice, foramen.

apex n. **1** *the apex of a pyramid* **tip**, peak, summit, pinnacle, top, vertex. **2** *the apex of his career* **climax**, culmination, apotheosis; peak, pinnacle, zenith, acme, apogee, high(est) point.
– OPPOSITES bottom, nadir.

aphorism n. **saying**, maxim, axiom, adage, epigram, dictum, gnome, proverb, saw, tag, apophthegm.

aphrodisiac n. **love potion**, philtre.
▶ adj. **erotic**, sexy, sexually arousing.

apiece adv. **each**, respectively, per item; informal a throw.

aplenty adj. **in abundance**, in profusion, galore, in large quantities/numbers, by the dozen; informal a gogo, by the truckload.

aplomb n. **poise**, self-assurance, self-confidence, calmness, composure, collectedness, level-headedness, sangfroid, equilibrium, equanimity; informal unflappability.

apocryphal adj. **fictitious**, made-up, untrue, fabricated, false, spurious; unverified, unauthenticated, unsubstantiated.
– OPPOSITES authentic.

apologetic adj. **regretful**, sorry, contrite, remorseful, penitent, repentant; conscience-stricken, shamefaced, ashamed.
– OPPOSITES unrepentant.

apologia n. **defence**, justification, vindication, explanation; argument, case.

apologist n. **defender**, supporter, upholder, advocate, proponent, exponent, propagandist, champion, campaigner.
– OPPOSITES critic.

apologize v. **say sorry**, express regret, be apologetic, ask forgiveness, ask for pardon, eat humble pie.

apology n. **1** *I owe you an apology* **expression of regret**, one's regrets; Austral./NZ informal beg-pardon; literary amende honorable. **2** informal *an apology for a flat* **travesty**, inadequate/poor example; informal excuse.

apoplectic adj. informal **furious**, enraged, infuriated, incensed, raging; incandescent, fuming, seething; informal (hopping) mad, livid, as cross as two sticks, foaming at the mouth, fit to be tied; literary wrathful.

apostate n. **dissenter**, heretic, defector, turncoat; old use recreant; rare tergiversator.
– OPPOSITES follower.

apostle n. **1** *the twelve apostles* **disciple**, follower. **2** *the apostles of the Slavs* **missionary**, evangelist, proselytizer. **3** *an apostle of capitalism* **advocate**, apologist, proponent, exponent, promoter, supporter, upholder, champion; N. Amer. booster.

apotheosis n. **culmination**, climax, peak, pinnacle, zenith, acme, apogee, high(est) point.
– OPPOSITES nadir.

appal v. **horrify**, shock, dismay, distress, outrage, scandalize; disgust, repel, revolt, sicken, nauseate, offend, make someone's blood run cold.

appalling adj. **1** *an appalling crime* **shocking**, horrific, horrifying, horrible, terrible, awful, dreadful, ghastly, hideous, horrendous, frightful, atrocious, abominable, abhorrent, outrageous, gruesome, grisly, monstrous, heinous, egregious. **2** *your schoolwork is appalling* **dreadful**, awful, terrible, frightful, atrocious, abysmal, disgraceful, deplorable, hopeless, lamentable; informal rotten, crummy, pathetic, pitiful, woeful, useless, lousy, dire; Brit. informal chronic, shocking, pants.

apparatus n. **1** *laboratory apparatus* **equipment**, gear, rig, tackle, gadgetry; appliance, instrument, machine, mechanism, device, contraption. **2** *the apparatus of government* **structure**, system, framework, organization, network.

apparel n. formal **clothes**, clothing, garments, dress, attire, wear, garb; informal gear, togs, duds; Brit. informal clobber, kit; N. Amer. informal threads; old use raiment, habit, habiliments.

apparent adj. **1** *their relief was all too apparent* **evident**, plain, obvious, clear, manifest, visible, discernible, perceptible; unmistakable, crystal clear, palpable, patent, blatant, as plain as a pikestaff, writ large; informal as plain as the nose on one's face, written all over one's face. **2** *his apparent lack of concern* **seeming**, ostensible, outward, superficial; supposed, alleged, professed.
– OPPOSITES unclear.

apparently adv. **seemingly**, evidently, it seems/appears (that), as far as one knows, by all accounts; ostensibly, outwardly, on the face of it, so the story goes, so I'm told, allegedly, reputedly.

apparition n. **1** *a monstrous apparition* **ghost**, phantom, spectre, spirit, wraith; vision, hallucination; informal spook; literary phantasm, revenant, shade, visitant, wight; rare eidolon. **2** *the apparition of a strange man* **appearance**, manifestation, materialization, emergence; visitation.

appeal v. **1** *police are appealing for information* **plead**, ask, call, request, make a plea. **2** *Andrew appealed to me to help them* **implore**, beg, entreat, call on, plead with, exhort, ask, request, petition; formal adjure; literary beseech. **3** *the thought of travelling appealed to me* **attract**, be attractive to, interest, take someone's fancy, fascinate, tempt, entice, allure, lure, draw, whet someone's appetite; informal float someone's boat.
▶ n. **1** *an appeal for help* **plea**, urgent/earnest request, entreaty, cry, call, petition, supplication, cri de cœur; rare obsecration. **2** *the cultural appeal of the island* **attraction**, attractiveness, allure, charm; fascination, magnetism, drawing power, pull. **3** *the court allowed the appeal* **retrial**, re-examination.

appealing adj. **attractive**, engaging, alluring, enchanting, captivating, bewitching, fascinating, tempting, enticing, seductive, irresistible, winning, winsome, charming, desirable; Brit. informal tasty; dated taking.
– OPPOSITES disagreeable, off-putting.

appear v. **1** *a cloud of dust appeared on the horizon* **become visible**, come into view/sight, materialize, pop up. **2** *fundamental differences were beginning to appear* **be revealed**, emerge, surface, manifest itself, become apparent/evident, come to light; arise, crop up. **3** informal *Bill still hadn't appeared* **arrive**, turn up, put in an appearance, come, get here/there; informal show (up), pitch up, fetch up, roll in, blow in, rock up. **4** *they appeared to be completely devoted* **seem**, look, give the impression, come across as, strike someone as. **5** *the paperback edition didn't appear for two years* **become available**, come on the market, go on sale, come out, be published, be produced. **6** *he appeared on Broadway* **perform**, play, act.
– OPPOSITES vanish.

appearance n. **1** *her dishevelled appearance* **look(s)**, air, aspect, mien. **2** *an appearance of respectability* **impression**, air, (outward) show; semblance, facade, veneer, front, pretence. **3** *the sudden appearance of her daughter* **arrival**, advent, coming, emergence, materialization. **4** *the appearance of these symptoms* **occurrence**, manifestation, development.

appease v. **1** *an attempt to appease his critics* **conciliate**, placate, pacify, propitiate, reconcile, win over; informal sweeten. **2** *I'd wasted a lot of money to appease my vanity* **satisfy**, fulfil, gratify, indulge; assuage, relieve, take the edge off.
– OPPOSITES provoke, inflame.

appeasement n. **1** *a policy of appeasement* **conciliation**, placation, pacification, propitiation, reconciliation; peacemaking, peace-mongering. **2** *appeasement for battered consciences* **satisfaction**, fulfilment, gratification, indulgence; assuagement, relief.
– OPPOSITES provocation.

appellation n. formal **name**, title, designation, tag, sobriquet, byname, nickname, cognomen; informal moniker, handle; formal denomination.

append v. **add**, attach, affix, tack on, tag on; formal subjoin.

appendage n. **1** *I am not just an appendage to the family* **addition**, attachment, adjunct, addendum, appurtenance, accessory. **2** *a pair of feathery appendages* **protuberance**, projection; technical process.

appendix n. **supplement**, addendum, postscript, codicil; coda, epilogue, afterword, tailpiece, back matter.

appertain v.
□ **appertain to** pertain to, be pertinent to, apply to, relate to, concern, be concerned with, have to do with, be relevant to, have reference to, have a bearing on, bear on; old use regard.

appetite n. **1** *a walk sharpens the appetite* **hunger**, ravenousness, hungriness; taste, palate; rare edacity. **2** *my appetite for learning* **craving**, longing, yearning, hankering, hunger, thirst, passion; enthusiasm, keenness, eagerness, desire; informal yen; old use appetency.

appetizer n. **starter**, first course, hors d'oeuvre, amuse-gueule, antipasto.

appetizing adj. **1** *an appetizing lunch* **mouth-watering**, inviting, tempting; tasty, delicious, flavoursome, toothsome, delectable; informal scrumptious, scrummy, yummy, moreish. **2** *the least appetizing part of election campaigns* **appealing**, attractive, inviting, alluring.
– OPPOSITES bland, unappealing.

applaud v. **1** *the audience applauded* **clap**, give a standing ovation, put one's hands together; show one's appreciation; informal give someone a big hand. **2** *police have applauded the decision* **praise**, commend, acclaim, salute, welcome, celebrate, express admiration for, express approval of, look on with favour, approve of, sing the praises of, pay tribute to, speak highly of, take one's hat off to, express respect for.
– OPPOSITES boo, criticize.

applause n. **1** *a massive round of applause* **clapping**, handclapping, (standing) ovation; acclamation. **2** *the museum's design won general applause* **praise**, acclaim, acclamation, admiration, commendation, adulation, favour, approbation, approval, respect; compliments, accolades, tributes.

appliance n. **1** *domestic appliances* **device**, machine, instrument, gadget, contraption, apparatus, utensil, implement, tool, mechanism, contrivance, labour-saving device; informal gizmo, mod con. **2** *the appliance of science* **application**, use, exercise, employment, implementation, utilization, practice, applying, discharge, execution, prosecution, enactment; formal praxis.

applicable adj. *the laws applicable to the dispute* **relevant**, appropriate, pertinent, appurtenant, apposite, germane, material, significant, related, connected; fitting, suitable, apt, befitting, to the point, useful, helpful; formal ad rem.
– OPPOSITES inappropriate, irrelevant.

applicant n. **candidate**, interviewee, competitor, contestant, contender, entrant; claimant, suppliant, supplicant, petitioner, postulant; prospective student/employee, job-seeker, job-hunter, auditioner.

application n. **1** *an application for an overdraft* **request**, appeal, petition, entreaty, plea, solicitation, supplication, requisition, suit, approach, claim, demand. **2** *the application of anti-inflation policies* **implementation**, use, exercise, employment, utilization, practice, applying, discharge, execution, prosecution, enactment; formal praxis. **3** *the argument is clearest in its application to the theatre* **relevance**, relevancy, bearing, significance, pertinence, aptness, appositeness, germaneness, importance. **4** *the application of make-up* **putting on**, rubbing in, applying. **5** *an application to relieve muscle pain* **ointment**, lotion, cream, rub, salve, emollient, preparation, liniment, embrocation, balm, unguent, poultice. **6** *the job takes a great deal of application* **diligence**, industriousness, industry, assiduity, commitment, dedication, devotion, conscientiousness, perseverance, persistence, tenacity, doggedness, sedulousness; concentration, attention, attentiveness, steadiness, patience, endurance; effort, hard work, labour, endeavour. **7** *a vector graphics application* **program**, software, routine.

apply v. **1** *300 people applied for the job* **put in an application**, put in, try, bid, appeal, petition, sue, register, audition; request, seek, solicit, claim, ask, try to obtain. **2** *the Act did not apply to Scotland* **be relevant**, have relevance, have a bearing, appertain, pertain, relate, concern, affect, involve, cover, deal with, touch; be pertinent, be appropriate, be significant. **3** *she applied some ointment* **put on**, rub in, work in, spread, smear. **4** *a steady pressure should be applied* **exert**, administer, implement, use, exercise, employ, utilize, bring to bear.
□ **apply oneself** be diligent, be industrious, be assiduous, show commitment, show dedication; work hard, exert oneself, make an effort, try hard, do one's best, give one's all, buckle down, put one's shoulder to the wheel, keep one's nose to the grindstone; strive, endeavour, struggle, labour, toil; pay attention, commit oneself, devote oneself; persevere, persist; informal put one's back in it, knuckle down, get stuck in.

appoint v. **1** *he was appointed chairman* **nominate**, name, designate, install as, commission, engage, co-opt; select, choose, elect, vote in; Military detail. **2** *the arbitrator shall appoint a date for the meeting* **specify**, determine, assign, designate, allot, set, fix, arrange, choose, decide on, establish, settle, ordain, prescribe, decree.
– OPPOSITES reject.

appointed adj. **1** *at the appointed time* **scheduled**, arranged, prearranged, specified, decided, agreed, determined, assigned, designated, allotted, set, fixed, chosen, established, settled, preordained, ordained, prescribed, decreed. **2** *a well appointed room* **furnished**, decorated, outfitted, fitted out, provided, supplied.

appointment n. **1** *a six o'clock appointment* **meeting**, engagement, interview, arrangement, consultation, session; date, rendezvous, assignation, tweetup; commitment, fixture; literary tryst. **2** *the appointment of directors* **nomination**, naming, designation, installation,

commissioning, engagement, co-option; selection, choosing, election, voting in; Military detailing. **3** *he held an appointment at the university* **job**, post, position, situation, employment, place, office; dated station.

apportion v. **share**, divide, allocate, distribute, allot, assign, give out, hand out, mete out, deal out, dish out, dole out; ration, measure out; split; informal divvy up.

apposite adj. **appropriate**, suitable, fitting, apt, befitting; relevant, pertinent, appurtenant, to the point, applicable, germane, material, congruous, felicitous; formal ad rem.
– OPPOSITES inappropriate.

appraisal n. **1** *an objective appraisal of the book* **assessment**, evaluation, estimation, judgement, rating, gauging, sizing up, summing-up, consideration. **2** *a free insurance appraisal* **valuation**, estimate, estimation, quotation, pricing; survey.

appraise v. **1** *they appraised their handiwork* **assess**, evaluate, judge, rate, gauge, review, consider; informal size up. **2** *his goods were appraised at £1,800* **value**, price, estimate, quote; survey.

appreciable adj. **considerable**, substantial, significant, sizeable, goodly, fair, reasonable, marked; perceptible, noticeable, visible; informal tidy.
– OPPOSITES negligible.

appreciate v. **1** *I'd appreciate your advice* **be grateful**, be thankful, be obliged, be indebted, be in your debt, be appreciative. **2** *the college appreciated her greatly* **value**, treasure, admire, respect, hold in high regard, think highly of, think much of. **3** *we appreciate the problems* **recognize**, acknowledge, realize, know, be aware of, be conscious of, be sensitive to, understand, comprehend; informal be wise to. **4** *a home that will appreciate in value* **increase**, gain, grow, rise, go up, escalate, soar, rocket.
– OPPOSITES disparage, depreciate, decrease.

appreciation n. **1** *he showed his appreciation* **gratitude**, thanks, gratefulness, thankfulness, recognition. **2** *her appreciation of literature* **valuing**, treasuring, admiration, respect, regard, esteem, high opinion. **3** *an appreciation of the value of teamwork* **acknowledgement**, recognition, realization, knowledge, awareness, consciousness, understanding, comprehension. **4** *the appreciation of the franc against the pound* **increase**, gain, growth, rise, inflation, escalation. **5** *an appreciation of the professor's work* **review**, critique, criticism, critical analysis, assessment, evaluation, judgement, rating; Brit. informal crit.
– OPPOSITES ingratitude, unawareness, depreciation, decrease.

appreciative adj. **1** *we are appreciative of all your efforts* **grateful**, thankful, obliged, indebted, in someone's debt. **2** *an appreciative audience* **supportive**, encouraging, sympathetic, responsive;

a

enthusiastic, admiring, approving, complimentary.
– OPPOSITES ungrateful, disparaging.

apprehend v. **1** *the thieves were quickly apprehended* **arrest**, catch, capture, seize; take prisoner, take into custody, detain, put in jail, put behind bars, imprison, incarcerate; informal collar, nab, nail, run in, pinch, bust, pick up, pull in, feel someone's collar; Brit. informal nick, do. **2** *they are slow to apprehend danger* **appreciate**, recognize, discern, perceive, make out, take in, realize, grasp, understand, comprehend; informal get the picture; Brit. informal twig, suss (out).

apprehension n. **1** *he was filled with apprehension* **anxiety**, worry, unease, nervousness, nerves, misgivings, disquiet, concern, tension, trepidation, perturbation, consternation, angst, dread, fear, foreboding; informal butterflies, the willies, the heebie-jeebies. **2** *her quick apprehension of their wishes* **appreciation**, recognition, discernment, perception, realization, grasp, understanding, comprehension, awareness. **3** *the apprehension of a perpetrator* **arrest**, capture, seizure; detention, imprisonment, incarceration; informal nabbing, bust.
– OPPOSITES confidence.

apprehensive adj. **anxious**, worried, uneasy, nervous, concerned, agitated, tense, afraid, scared, frightened, fearful; informal on tenterhooks, trepidatious.
– OPPOSITES confident.

apprentice n. **trainee**, learner, probationer, novice, beginner, starter; pupil, student; N. Amer. tenderfoot; informal rookie; N. Amer. informal greenhorn.
– OPPOSITES veteran.

apprenticeship n. **traineeship**, training period, studentship, novitiate; historical indentureship.

apprise v. **inform**, tell, notify, advise, brief, make aware, enlighten, update, keep posted; informal clue in, fill in, put wise, put in the picture.

approach v. **1** *she approached the altar* **move towards**, come/go towards, advance towards, go/come/draw/move nearer, go/come/draw/move closer, near; close in, gain on; reach, arrive at. **2** *the trade deficit is approaching £20 million* **border on**, verge on, approximate, touch, nudge, get on for, near, come near to, come close to. **3** *she approached him about leaving his job* **speak to**, talk to; make advances, make overtures, make a proposal, sound out, proposition. **4** *he approached the problem in the best way* **tackle**, set about, address oneself to, undertake, get down to, launch into, embark on, go about, get to grips with.
– OPPOSITES leave.
▶ n. **1** *the traditional British approach* **method**, procedure, technique, modus operandi, MO, style, way, manner; strategy, tactic, system, means, line of action. **2** *he considered an approach to the High Court* **proposal**, proposition, submission, application, appeal,

plea, request. **3** dated *his approaches were repulsed* **advances**, overtures, suggestions, attentions; suit. **4** *the dog barked at the approach of any intruder* **advance**, coming, nearing; arrival, appearance; advent. **5** *the approach to the castle* **driveway**, drive, access road, road, avenue; way.

approachable adj. **1** *students found the staff approachable* **friendly**, welcoming, pleasant, agreeable, congenial, affable, cordial; obliging, communicative, helpful. **2** *the south landing is approachable by boat* **accessible**, attainable, reachable; informal get-at-able.
– OPPOSITES aloof, inaccessible.

approbation n. **approval**, acceptance, endorsement, appreciation, respect, admiration, commendation, praise, congratulations, acclaim, esteem, applause.
– OPPOSITES criticism.

appropriate adj. *this isn't the appropriate time* **suitable**, proper, fitting, apt, right; relevant, pertinent, apposite; convenient, opportune; seemly, befitting; formal ad rem; old use meet.
– OPPOSITES unsuitable.
▶ v. **1** *the barons appropriated church lands* **seize**, commandeer, expropriate, annex, arrogate, sequestrate, sequester, take over, hijack; steal, take; informal swipe, nab, bag; Brit. informal pinch, half-inch, nick. **2** *his images have been appropriated by advertisers* **plagiarize**, copy; poach, steal, 'borrow'; informal rip off. **3** *we are appropriating funds for these expenses* **allocate**, assign, allot, earmark, set aside, devote, apportion.

approval n. **1** *their proposals went to the ministry for approval* **acceptance**, agreement, consent, assent, permission, leave, the nod; rubber stamp, sanction, endorsement, ratification, authorization, validation; support, backing; informal the go-ahead, the green light, the OK, the thumbs up. **2** *Lily looked at him with approval* **approbation**, appreciation, favour, liking, admiration, regard, esteem, respect, praise. **3** *we will send you the goods on approval* **trial**, sale or return; Brit. informal appro.
– OPPOSITES refusal, dislike.

approve v. **1** *his boss doesn't approve of his lifestyle* **agree with**, hold with, endorse, support, back, uphold, subscribe to, recommend, advocate, be in favour of, favour, think well of, like, appreciate, take kindly to; be pleased with, admire, applaud, praise. **2** *the government approved the proposals* **accept**, agree to, consent to, assent to, give one's blessing to, bless, rubber-stamp, give the nod; ratify, sanction, endorse, authorize, validate, pass; support, back; informal give the go-ahead, give the green light, give the OK, give the thumbs-up.
– OPPOSITES condemn, refuse.

approximate adj. *all measurements are approximate* **estimated**, rough, imprecise, inexact, coarse-grained, indefinite, broad, loose; N. Amer. informal ballpark.
– OPPOSITES precise.

▸v. *this scenario probably approximates to the truth* **be/come close to**, be/come near to, approach, border on, verge on; resemble, be similar to, be not unlike.

approximately adv. **roughly**, about, around, circa, round about, more or less, in the neighbourhood of, in the region of, of the order of, something like, give or take (a few); near to, close to, nearly, almost, approaching; Brit. getting on for; informal pushing; N. Amer. informal in the ballpark of.
– OPPOSITES precisely.

approximation n. **1** *the figure is only an approximation* **estimate**, estimation, guess, rough calculation; informal guesstimate; N. Amer. informal ballpark figure. **2** *an approximation to the truth* **semblance**, resemblance, likeness, similarity, correspondence.

appurtenances plural n. **accessories**, trappings, appendages, accoutrements, equipment, paraphernalia, impedimenta, bits and pieces, things; informal stuff.

a priori adj. *a priori reasoning* **theoretical**, deduced, deductive, inferred, postulated, suppositional; scientific.
▸adv. *the results cannot be predicted a priori* **theoretically**, deductively, scientifically.

apron n. **pinafore**, overall; N. Amer. informal pinny.

apropos prep. *he was asked a question apropos his resignation* **with reference to**, with regard to, with respect to, regarding, concerning, on the subject of, connected with, about, re.
▸adj. *the word 'conglomerate' was decidedly apropos* **appropriate**, pertinent, relevant, apposite, apt, applicable, suitable, germane, material.
– OPPOSITES inappropriate.

apt adj. **1** *a very apt description of how I felt* **suitable**, fitting, appropriate, befitting, relevant, applicable, apposite; Brit. informal spot on. **2** *they are apt to get a mite slipshod* **inclined**, given, likely, liable, disposed, predisposed, prone. **3** *an apt pupil* **clever**, quick, bright, sharp, smart, intelligent, able, gifted, adept, astute.
– OPPOSITES inappropriate, unlikely, slow.

aptitude n. **talent**, gift, flair, bent, skill, knack, facility, ability, capability, potential, capacity, faculty, genius.

aquatic adj. **marine**, water, saltwater, freshwater, seawater, sea, oceanic, river; technical pelagic, thalassic.

aqueduct n. **conduit**, race, channel, watercourse, sluice, sluiceway, spillway; bridge, viaduct.

aquiline adj. **hooked**, curved, bent, angular; beak-like.

arable adj. **farmable**, cultivable, cultivatable; fertile, productive, fecund.

arbiter n. **1** *an arbiter between Moscow and Washington.* See **arbitrator**. **2** *the great arbiter of fashion* **authority**, judge, controller, director; master, expert, pundit.

arbitrary adj. **1** *an arbitrary decision* **capricious**, whimsical, random, chance, unpredictable; casual, wanton, unmotivated, motiveless, unreasoned, unsupported, irrational, illogical, groundless, unjustified. **2** *the arbitrary power of a prince* **autocratic**, dictatorial, autarchic, undemocratic, despotic, tyrannical, authoritarian; absolute, uncontrolled, unlimited, unrestrained.
– OPPOSITES reasoned, democratic.

arbitrate v. **adjudicate**, judge, referee, umpire; mediate, conciliate, intervene, intercede; settle, decide, resolve, pass judgement.

arbitration n. **adjudication**, judgement, arbitrament; mediation, conciliation, intervention, interposition.

arbitrator n. **adjudicator**, arbiter, judge, referee, umpire, linesman, line judge; mediator, conciliator, intervenor, intercessor, go-between.

arbour n. **bower**, alcove, grotto, recess, pergola, gazebo.

arc n. *the arc of a circle* **curve**, arch, crescent, semicircle, half-moon; curvature, convexity.
▸v. *I sent the ball arcing out over the river* **curl**, curve; arch.

arcade n. **1** *a classical arcade* **gallery**, colonnade, cloister, loggia, portico, peristyle, stoa. **2** Brit. *she went to a cafe in the arcade* **shopping centre**, shopping precinct; N. Amer. plaza, mall, shopping mall.

arcane adj. **mysterious**, secret, covert, clandestine; enigmatic, esoteric, obscure, abstruse, recondite, recherché, impenetrable, opaque.

arch¹ n. **1** *a stone arch* **archway**, vault, span, dome. **2** *the arch of his spine* **curve**, bow, bend, arc, curvature, convexity; hunch, crook.
▸v. *she arched her eyebrows* **curve**, arc; raise.

arch² adj. *an arch grin* **mischievous**, teasing, saucy, knowing, playful, roguish, impish, cheeky, tongue-in-cheek.

arch- comb. form *his arch-enemy* **chief**, principal, foremost, leading, main, major, prime, premier, greatest; informal number-one.
– OPPOSITES minor.

archaic adj. **obsolete**, out of date, old-fashioned, outmoded, behind the times, bygone, anachronistic, antiquated, superannuated, antediluvian, olde worlde, old-fangled; ancient, old, extinct, defunct; informal out of the ark; literary of yore.
– OPPOSITES modern.

arched adj. **vaulted**, domed, curved, bowed; literary embowed.

archetypal adj. **quintessential**, classic, most typical, representative, model, exemplary, textbook, copybook; stock, stereotypical, prototypical.
– OPPOSITES atypical.

archetype n. **quintessence**, essence, typification, representative, model, embodiment, prototype, stereotype; original, pattern, standard, paradigm.

architect n. **1** *the architect of Durham Cathedral* **designer**, planner, draughtsman. **2** *the architect of the National Health Service*

originator, author, creator, founder, (founding) father; engineer, inventor, mastermind; literary begetter.

architecture n. **1** *modern architecture* **building design**, building style, planning, building, construction; formal architectonics. **2** *the architecture of a computer system* **structure**, construction, organization, layout, design, build, anatomy, make-up; informal set-up.

archive n. **1** *she delved into the family archives* **records**, annals, chronicles, accounts; papers, documents, files; history; Law muniments. **2** *the National Sound Archive* **record office**, registry, repository, museum, chancery.
▶ v. *the videos are archived for future use* **file**, log, catalogue, document, record, register; store, cache.

arctic adj. **1** *Arctic waters* **polar**, far northern; literary hyperborean; technical boreal. **2** *arctic weather conditions* **freezing**, cold, wintry, frozen, icy, glacial, gelid, sub-zero, polar, Siberian.
– OPPOSITES Antarctic, tropical.
▶ n. **far north**, North Pole, Arctic Circle.
– OPPOSITES Antarctic.

ardent adj. **passionate**, fervent, zealous, wholehearted, vehement, intense, fierce; enthusiastic, keen, eager, avid, committed, dedicated.
– OPPOSITES apathetic.

ardour n. **passion**, fervour, zeal, vehemence, intensity, fire, emotion; enthusiasm, eagerness, gusto, keenness, dedication.

arduous adj. **onerous**, taxing, difficult, hard, heavy, laborious, burdensome, strenuous, vigorous, back-breaking; demanding, tough, challenging, formidable; exhausting, tiring, punishing, gruelling; informal killing; Brit. informal knackering; old use toilsome.
– OPPOSITES easy.

area n. **1** *an inner-city area* **district**, region, zone, sector, quarter; locality, locale, neighbourhood, parish, patch; tract, belt; informal neck of the woods; Brit. informal manor; N. Amer. informal turf, hood. **2** *specific areas of scientific knowledge* **field**, sphere, discipline, realm, domain, sector, province, territory, line. **3** *the dining area* **section**, space; place, room. **4** *the area of a circle* **expanse**, extent, size, scope, compass; dimensions, proportions.

arena n. **1** *an ice-hockey arena* **stadium**, amphitheatre, coliseum; ground, field, ring, rink, pitch, court; N. Amer. bowl, park; historical circus. **2** *the political arena* **scene**, sphere, realm, province, domain, sector, forum, territory, world.

argot n. **jargon**, slang, idiom, cant, parlance, vernacular, patois; dialect, speech, language; informal lingo.

arguable adj. **1** *he had an arguable claim for asylum* **tenable**, defendable, defensible, supportable, sustainable, able to hold water; reasonable, viable, acceptable. **2** *it is arguable whether these routes are worthwhile*

debatable, questionable, open to question, controversial, contentious, doubtful, uncertain, moot.
– OPPOSITES untenable, certain.

arguably adv. **possibly**, conceivably, feasibly, plausibly, probably, maybe, perhaps.

argue v. **1** *they argued that the government was to blame* **contend**, assert, maintain, insist, hold, claim, reason, swear, allege; Law depose; formal aver, represent, opine. **2** *the children are always arguing* **quarrel**, disagree, row, squabble, fall out, bicker, fight, wrangle, dispute, feud, have words, cross swords, lock horns, be at each other's throats; informal argufy, spat; old use altercate. **3** *it is hard to argue the point* **dispute**, debate, discuss, controvert.

argument n. **1** *he had an argument with Tony* **quarrel**, disagreement, squabble, fight, dispute, wrangle, clash, altercation, feud, contretemps, disputation, falling-out; informal tiff, slanging match; Brit. informal row, barney; Brit. informal, Sport afters. **2** *arguments for the existence of God* **reasoning**, justification, explanation, rationalization; case, defence, vindication; evidence, reasons, grounds. **3** old use *the argument of the book* **theme**, topic, subject matter; summary, synopsis, precis, gist, outline.

argumentative adj. **quarrelsome**, disputatious, captious, contrary, cantankerous, contentious; belligerent, bellicose, combative, antagonistic, truculent, pugnacious; rare oppugnant.

arid adj. **1** *an arid landscape* **dry**, dried up, waterless, moistureless, parched, scorched, baked, thirsty, droughty, desert; **barren**, infertile. **2** *this town has an arid, empty feel* **dreary**, dull, drab, dry, sterile, colourless, uninspiring, flat, boring, uninteresting, lifeless.
– OPPOSITES wet, fertile, vibrant.

arise v. **1** *many problems arose* **come to light**, become apparent, appear, emerge, crop up, turn up, surface, spring up; occur; literary befall, come to pass. **2** *injuries arising from defective products* **result**, proceed, follow, ensue, derive, stem, originate; be caused by. **3** formal *the beast arose* **stand up**, rise, get to one's feet, get up.

aristocracy n. **nobility**, peerage, gentry, upper class, ruling class, elite, high society, establishment, haut monde; aristocrats, lords, ladies, peers (of the realm), nobles, noblemen, noblewomen; informal upper crust, top drawer, aristos; Brit. informal nobs, toffs.
– OPPOSITES working class.

aristocrat n. **nobleman**, noblewoman, lord, lady, peer (of the realm), peeress, grandee; informal aristo; Brit. informal toff, nob.
– OPPOSITES commoner.

aristocratic adj. **1** *an aristocratic family* **noble**, titled, upper-class, blue-blooded, high-born, well born, elite; Brit. upmarket; informal upper crust, top drawer; Brit. informal posh; old use gentle. **2** *an aristocratic manner* **refined**, polished, courtly, dignified,

decorous, gracious, fine, gentlemanly, ladylike; haughty, proud.
– OPPOSITES working-class, vulgar.

arm[1] n. **1** *the arm of her jacket* **sleeve**. **2** *an arm of the sea* **inlet**, creek, cove, fjord, bay, voe; estuary, firth, strait(s), sound, channel. **3** *the political arm of the group* **branch**, section, department, division, wing, sector, detachment, offshoot, extension. **4** *the long arm of the law* **reach**, power, authority, influence.

> **WORD LINKS**
> **brachial** relating to an arm

arm[2] v. **1** *he armed himself with a revolver* **equip**, provide, supply, furnish, issue, fit out. **2** *arm yourself against criticism* **prepare**, forearm, make ready, brace, steel, fortify.

armada n. **fleet**, flotilla, squadron; literary navy.

armaments plural n. **arms**, weapons, weaponry, firearms, guns, ordnance, artillery, munitions, materiel.

armistice n. **truce**, ceasefire, peace, suspension of hostilities.

armour n. **protective covering**, armour plate; historical chain mail, coat of mail, panoply.

armoured adj. **armour-plated**, steel-plated, ironclad; bulletproof, bombproof; reinforced, toughened.

armoury n. **arsenal**, arms depot, arms cache, ordnance depot, magazine, ammunition dump.

arms plural n. **1** *the illegal export of arms* **weapons**, weaponry, firearms, guns, ordnance, artillery, armaments, munitions, materiel. **2** *the family arms* **crest**, coat of arms, emblem, heraldic device, insignia, escutcheon, shield.

> **WORD LINKS**
> **heraldic** relating to coats of arms
> **heraldry** the system by which coats of arms are drawn up
> **escutcheon** a shield or emblem bearing a coat of arms
> **dexter** the right-hand side of a coat of arms
> **sinister** the left-hand side of a coat of arms

army n. **1** *the invading army* **armed force**, military force, land force, military, soldiery, infantry, militia; troops, soldiers; old use host. **2** *an army of tourists* **crowd**, swarm, multitude, horde, mob, gang, throng, mass, flock, herd, pack.

> **WORD LINKS**
> **military** relating to soldiers or armed forces
> **vanguard** the leading part of an advancing army
> **rearguard** the soldiers protecting a retreating army

aroma n. **smell**, odour, fragrance, scent, perfume, bouquet, nose; literary redolence.

aromatic adj. **fragrant**, scented, perfumed, fragranced, odoriferous; literary redolent.

around adv. **1** *there were houses scattered around* **on every side**, on all sides, throughout, all over (the place), everywhere; about, here and there. **2** *he turned around* **in the opposite direction**, to face the other way, backwards, to the rear. **3** *there was no one around* **nearby**, near, about, close by, close (at hand), at hand, in the vicinity, at close range.
▶ prep. **1** *the palazzo is built around a courtyard* **on all sides of**, about, encircling, surrounding. **2** *they drove around town* **about**, all over, in/to all parts of. **3** *around three miles* **approximately**, about, round about, circa, roughly, something like, more or less, in the region of, in the neighbourhood of, give or take (a few); nearly, close to, approaching; Brit. getting on for; N. Amer. informal in the ballpark of.

arouse v. **1** *they had aroused his suspicion* **induce**, prompt, trigger, stir up, bring out, kindle, fire, spark off, provoke, engender, cause, foster; literary enkindle. **2** *his ability to arouse the masses* **stir up**, rouse, galvanize, excite, electrify, stimulate, inspire, inspirit, move, fire up, whip up, get going, inflame, agitate, goad, incite. **3** *his touch aroused her* **excite**, stimulate (sexually), titillate; informal turn on, get going, give a thrill to, light someone's fire. **4** *she was aroused from her sleep* **wake (up)**, awaken, bring to/round, rouse; Brit. informal knock up; literary waken.
– OPPOSITES allay, pacify, turn off.

arraign v. **1** *he was arraigned for murder* **indict**, prosecute, put on trial, bring to trial, take to court, lay/file/prefer charges against, summons, cite; accuse of, charge with; N. Amer. impeach; informal do; old use inculpate. **2** *they bitterly arraigned the government* **criticize**, censure, attack, condemn, chastise, lambaste, rebuke, admonish, remonstrate with, take to task, berate, reproach; informal knock, slam, blast, lay into; Brit. informal slate, slag off; formal castigate, excoriate.
– OPPOSITES acquit, praise.

arrange v. **1** *she arranged the flowers* **order**, set out, lay out, array, position, dispose, present, display, exhibit; group, sort, organize, tidy. **2** *they hoped to arrange a meeting* **organize**, fix (up), plan, schedule, pencil in, contrive, settle on, decide, determine, agree. **3** *he arranged the piece for a full orchestra* **adapt**, set, score, orchestrate.

arrangement n. **1** *the arrangement of the furniture* **positioning**, disposition, order, presentation, display; grouping, organization, alignment. **2** *the arrangements for my trip* **preparation**, plan, provision; planning, groundwork. **3** *we had an arrangement* **agreement**, deal, understanding, bargain, settlement, pact, modus vivendi. **4** *an arrangement of Beethoven's symphonies* **adaptation**, orchestration, instrumentation.

arrant adj. *what arrant nonsense!* **utter**, complete, total, absolute, downright, outright, thorough, out-and-out, sheer, pure, unmitigated, unqualified; blatant, flagrant; Brit. informal right.

a

array n. **1** *a huge array of cars* **range**, collection, selection, assortment, diversity, variety; arrangement, assemblage, line-up, formation; display, exhibition, exposition. **2** *she arrived in silken array* **dress**, attire, clothing, garb, garments; finery; formal apparel.

▶ v. **1** *a buffet was arrayed on the table* **arrange**, assemble, group, order, range, place, position, set out, lay out, dispose; display. **2** *he was arrayed in grey flannel* **dress**, attire, clothe, garb, deck (out), outfit, get up, turn out; old use apparel, habit.

arrears plural n. *rent arrears* **debts**, money owing, outstanding payment(s), liabilities, dues.

– OPPOSITES credit.

□ **in arrears** behind, behindhand, late, overdue, in the red, in debt.

arrest v. **1** *police arrested him for murder* **apprehend**, take into custody, take prisoner, detain, put in jail; informal pick up, pull in, pinch, bust, nab, do, collar; Brit. informal nick. **2** *the spread of the disease can be arrested* **stop**, halt, check, block, hinder, restrict, limit, inhibit, impede, curb; prevent, obstruct; literary stay. **3** *she tried to arrest his attention* **attract**, capture, catch, hold, engage; absorb, occupy, engross.

– OPPOSITES release, start.

▶ n. **1** *a warrant for your arrest* **detention**, apprehension, seizure, capture. **2** *a cardiac arrest* **stoppage**, halt, interruption.

arresting adj. *an arresting image* **striking**, eye-catching, conspicuous, engaging, impressive, imposing, spectacular, dramatic, breathtaking, awe-inspiring, dazzling, stunning; remarkable, outstanding, distinctive.

– OPPOSITES inconspicuous.

arrival n. **1** *they awaited Ruth's arrival* **coming**, appearance, entrance, entry, approach. **2** *staff greeted the late arrivals* **comer**, entrant, incomer; visitor, caller, guest. **3** *the arrival of democracy* **emergence**, appearance, advent, coming, dawn, onset, inauguration, origin, birth.

– OPPOSITES departure, end.

arrive v. **1** *more police arrived* **come**, turn up, get here/there, make it, appear, enter, present oneself, come along, materialize; informal show (up), roll in/up, blow in, rock up, show one's face. **2** *we arrived at his house* **reach**, get to, come to, make, make it to, gain, end up at; informal wind up at. **3** *they arrived at an agreement* **reach**, achieve, attain, gain, accomplish; work out, draw up, put together, strike, settle on; informal clinch. **4** *the wedding finally arrived* **happen**, occur, take place, come about; present itself, crop up; literary come to pass. **5** *quadraphony had arrived* **emerge**, appear, surface, dawn, be born, come into being, arise.

– OPPOSITES depart, leave.

arriviste n. **social climber**, status-seeker, would-be, self-seeker; upstart, parvenu(e), vulgarian; informal go-getter; (**arrivistes**) nouveau riche, new money.

arrogant adj. **haughty**, conceited, self-important, egotistic, full of oneself, superior; overbearing, pompous, bumptious, imperious, overweening; proud, immodest; informal high and mighty, too big for one's boots, big-headed; rare hubristic.

– OPPOSITES modest.

arrogate v. **assume**, take, claim, appropriate, seize, expropriate, wrest, usurp, commandeer.

arrow n. **1** *a bow and arrow* **shaft**, bolt, dart; historical quarrel. **2** *the arrow pointed right* **pointer**, indicator, marker, needle.

WORD LINKS

fletcher (in the past) a person who made arrows
flight the tail of an arrow
nock a notch at the end of an arrow
quiver a case for carrying arrows
toxophilite a student or lover of archery

---

arsenal n. **1** *Britain's nuclear arsenal* **weapons**, weaponry, arms, armaments. **2** *mutineers broke into the arsenal* **armoury**, arms depot, arms cache, ordnance depot, magazine, ammunition dump.

arson n. **incendiarism**, pyromania; Brit. fire-raising.

arsonist n. **incendiary**, pyromaniac; Brit. fire-raiser; informal firebug, pyro; N. Amer. informal torch.

art n. **1** *he studied art* **fine art**, artwork, design. **2** *the art of writing* **skill**, craft, technique, knack, facility, ability. **3** *she uses art to achieve her aims* **cunning**, artfulness, slyness, craftiness, guile; deceit, duplicity, artifice, wiles.

artery n. *the main arteries out of town* **main road**, trunk road, high road, highway.

artful adj. **sly**, crafty, cunning, wily, scheming, devious, Machiavellian, sneaky, tricky, conniving, designing, calculating; canny, shrewd; deceitful, duplicitous, disingenuous, underhand; informal foxy, shifty; old use subtle.

– OPPOSITES ingenuous.

article n. **1** *small household articles* **object**, thing, item, artefact, commodity, product. **2** *an article in The Times* **report**, account, story, write-up, feature, item, piece (of writing), column, review, commentary. **3** *the crucial article of the treaty* **clause**, section, subsection, point, item, paragraph, division, subdivision, part, portion.

articulate adj. *an articulate speaker* **eloquent**, fluent, effective, persuasive, lucid, expressive, silver-tongued; intelligible, comprehensible, understandable.

– OPPOSITES unintelligible.

▶ v. *they were unable to articulate their emotions* **express**, voice, vocalize, put in words, communicate, state; air, ventilate, vent, pour out; utter, say, speak, enunciate, pronounce; informal come out with.

articulated adj. **hinged**, jointed, segmented; technical articulate.

artifice n. **trickery**, deceit, deception, duplicity, guile, cunning, artfulness, wiliness, craftiness, slyness, chicanery; fraud, fraudulence.

artificial adj. **1** *artificial flowers* **synthetic**, fake, faux, imitation, mock, ersatz, substitute, replica, reproduction; man-made, manufactured, fabricated; plastic; informal pretend. **2** *an artificial smile* **insincere**, feigned, false, unnatural, contrived, put-on, exaggerated, actorly, forced, laboured, strained, hollow; informal pretend, phoney.
– OPPOSITES natural, genuine.

artillery n. **ordnance**, (big) guns, cannon(s), cannonry.

artisan n. **craftsman**, craftswoman, craftsperson; skilled worker, technician; smith, wright, journeyman; old use artificer.

artist n. **1** *a Belfast mural artist* **painter**, illustrator, draughtsman, designer, creator, originator, producer; old master. **2** *the surgeon is an artist with the knife* **expert**, master, maestro, past master, virtuoso, genius; informal pro, ace; Brit. informal dab hand.
– OPPOSITES novice.

artiste n. **entertainer**, performer, showman, artist; player, musician, singer, dancer, actor, actress; star.

artistic adj. **1** *he's very artistic* **creative**, imaginative, inventive, expressive; sensitive, perceptive, discerning. **2** *artistic dances* **aesthetic**, aesthetically pleasing, beautiful, attractive, fine; decorative, ornamental; tasteful, stylish, elegant, exquisite.
– OPPOSITES unimaginative, inelegant.

artistry n. **creative skill**, creativity, art, skill, talent, genius, brilliance, flair, proficiency, virtuosity, finesse, style; craftsmanship, workmanship.

artless adj. **natural**, ingenuous, naive, simple, innocent, childlike, guileless; candid, open, sincere, unaffected.
– OPPOSITES scheming.

as conj. **1** *she saw him as he disappeared* **while**, just as, even as, just when, at the time that, at the moment that. **2** *we all felt as Frank did* **in the (same) way that**, the (same) way; informal like. **3** *do as you're told* **what**, that which. **4** *they were free, as the case had not been proved* **because**, since, seeing that/ as, in view of the fact that, owing to the fact that; informal on account of; literary for. **5** *try as she did, she couldn't smile* **though**, although, even though, in spite of the fact that, despite the fact that, notwithstanding that, for all that, albeit, however. **6** *relatively short distances, as Paris to Lyons* **such as**, like, for instance, for example, e.g..
▶prep. **1** *he was dressed as a policeman* **like**, in the guise of. **2** *I'm speaking to you as your friend* **in the role of**, being, acting as.
☐ **as for/as to** concerning, with respect to, on the subject of, in the matter of, as regards, with regard to, regarding, with reference to, re, in re, apropos, vis-à-vis.
as yet so far, thus far, yet, still, up till now, up to now.

ascend v. **climb**, go up/upwards, move up/ upwards, rise (up); mount, scale, conquer;

take to the air, take off.
– OPPOSITES descend.

ascendancy n. **dominance**, domination, supremacy, superiority, paramountcy, predominance, primacy, dominion, hegemony, authority, control, command, power, rule, sovereignty, lordship, leadership, influence.
– OPPOSITES subordination.

ascendant adj. **rising (in power)**, on the rise, on the way up, up-and-coming, flourishing, prospering, burgeoning.
– OPPOSITES declining.

ascent n. **1** *the first ascent of the Matterhorn* **climb**, scaling, conquest. **2** *a balloon ascent* **rise**, climb, launch, take-off, lift-off, blast-off. **3** *the ascent grew steeper* **(upward) slope**, incline, rise, upward gradient, inclination, acclivity.
– OPPOSITES descent, drop.

ascertain v. **find out**, discover, get to know, work out, make out, fathom (out), learn, deduce, divine, discern, see, understand, comprehend; establish, determine, verify, confirm; informal figure out; Brit. informal suss (out).

ascetic adj. *an ascetic life* **austere**, self-denying, abstinent, abstemious, self-disciplined, self-abnegating; simple, puritanical, monastic; reclusive, eremitic, hermitic; celibate, chaste.
– OPPOSITES sybaritic.
▶n. *a desert ascetic* **abstainer**, puritan, recluse, hermit, solitary; fakir, Sufi, dervish, sadhu, muni; historical anchorite; old use eremite.
– OPPOSITES sybarite.

ascribe v. **attribute**, assign, put down, accredit, credit, chalk up, impute; blame on, lay at the door of; connect with, associate with.

ash n. **cinders**, ashes, clinker.

ashamed adj. **1** *the poor are made to feel ashamed* **sorry**, shamefaced, abashed, sheepish, guilty, contrite, remorseful, repentant, penitent, regretful, rueful, apologetic; embarrassed, mortified. **2** *he was ashamed to admit it* **reluctant**, loath, unwilling, disinclined, indisposed, afraid.
– OPPOSITES proud, pleased.

ashen adj. **pale**, wan, pasty, grey, colourless, pallid, white, waxen, ghostly, bloodless.

ashore adv. **on to (the) land**, on to the shore; shorewards, landwards; on (dry) land.

aside adv. **1** *they stood aside* **to one side**, to the side, on one side; apart, away, separately. **2** *that aside, he seemed a nice man* **apart**, notwithstanding.
▶n. *'Her parents died,' said Mrs Manton in an aside* **whispered remark**, confidential remark, stage whisper; digression, incidental remark, obiter dictum, deviation.
☐ **aside from** apart from, besides, in addition to, not counting, barring, other than, but (for), excluding, not including, except (for), excepting, leaving out, save (for).

asinine adj. **foolish**, stupid, brainless, mindless, senseless, idiotic, imbecilic, ridiculous, ludicrous, absurd, nonsensical, fatuous, silly, inane, witless, empty-headed; informal half-witted, dumb, moronic; Brit. informal daft; Scottish & N. English informal glaikit.
– OPPOSITES intelligent, sensible.

ask v. **1** *he asked what time we opened* **enquire**, query, want to know; question, interrogate, quiz. **2** *they want to ask a few questions* **put (forward)**, pose, raise, submit. **3** *don't be afraid to ask for advice* **request**, demand; solicit, seek, crave, apply, petition, call, appeal, sue. **4** *let's ask them to dinner* **invite**, bid, summon, have someone over/round.
– OPPOSITES answer.

askance adv. *they look askance at anything foreign* **suspiciously**, sceptically, cynically, mistrustfully, distrustfully, doubtfully, dubiously; disapprovingly, contemptuously, scornfully, disdainfully.
– OPPOSITES approvingly.

askew adj. **crooked**, lopsided, tilted, angled, at an angle, skew, skewed, slanted, aslant, awry, squint, out of true, to/on one side, uneven, off-centre, asymmetrical; informal cockeyed, wonky; Brit. informal skew-whiff.
– OPPOSITES straight.

asleep adj. **1** *she was asleep in bed* **sleeping**, napping, catnapping, dozing, drowsing; informal snoozing, dead to the world; Brit. informal kipping; humorous in the land of Nod; literary slumbering. **2** *my leg's asleep* **numb**, numbed, benumbed, dead, insensible, insensate, unfeeling.
– OPPOSITES awake.

aspect n. **1** *the photos depict every aspect of life* **feature**, facet, side, characteristic, particular, detail; angle, slant. **2** *his face had a sinister aspect* **appearance**, look, air, cast, mien, demeanour, expression; atmosphere, mood, quality, ambience, feeling. **3** *a summer house with a southern aspect* **outlook**, view, exposure; situation, position, location. **4** *the front aspect of the hotel* **face**, elevation, facade, side.

asperity n. **harshness**, sharpness, abrasiveness, severity, acerbity, astringency, tartness, sarcasm.

aspersions plural n. **vilification**, disparagement, denigration, defamation, condemnation, criticism, denunciation, slander, libel, calumny; slurs, smears, insults, slights; informal mud-slinging, bad-mouthing; Brit. informal slagging off; formal castigation.
□ **cast aspersions on** vilify, disparage, denigrate, defame, run down, impugn, belittle, criticize, condemn, decry, denounce, pillory; malign, slander, libel, discredit; informal pull apart, throw mud at, knock, bad-mouth; Brit. informal rubbish, slate, slag off.

asphyxiate v. **suffocate**, choke to death, smother, stifle; throttle, strangle.

aspiration n. **desire**, hope, dream, wish, longing, yearning; aim, ambition, expectation, goal, target.

aspire v. **desire**, hope, dream, long, yearn, set one's heart on, wish, want, be desirous of; aim, seek, pursue, set one's sights on.

aspiring adj. **would-be**, aspirant, hopeful, budding; potential, prospective, future; ambitious, determined, driven; informal wannabe.

ass n. **1** *he rode on an ass* **donkey**, jackass, jenny; Scottish cuddy; Brit. informal moke, neddy. **2** informal *don't be a silly ass* **fool**, idiot, dolt, simpleton, imbecile; informal ninny, nincompoop, dimwit, donkey, chump, halfwit, dum-dum, loon, jackass, cretin, jerk, nerd, fathead, blockhead, numbskull, dunce, dipstick, lamebrain, pea-brain, thickhead, woodenhead, pinhead, airhead, birdbrain; Brit. informal nitwit, twit, clot, plonker, berk, prat, plank, pillock, wally, twerp, charlie, muppet, twonk, herbert; Scottish informal nyaff, balloon, gowk; N. Amer. informal schmuck, bozo, turkey, goofball, putz, wiener, weeny, hoser; Austral./NZ informal drongo, galah; dated tomfool, muttonhead.

assail v. **1** *the army moved in to assail the enemy* **attack**, assault, pounce on, set upon/about, fall on, charge, rush, storm; informal lay into, tear into, pitch into. **2** *she was assailed by doubts* **plague**, torment, rack, beset, dog, trouble, disturb, worry, bedevil, nag, vex. **3** *critics assailed the policy* **criticize**, censure, attack, condemn, pillory, revile; informal knock, slam; Brit. informal slate, slag off; formal castigate.

assailant n. **attacker**, mugger, assaulter.

assassin n. **murderer**, killer, gunman; executioner; informal hitman, hired gun; literary slayer; dated homicide.

assassinate v. **murder**, kill, slaughter; eliminate, execute; N. Amer. terminate; informal hit; literary slay.

assassination n. **murder**, killing, slaughter; homicide; political execution, elimination; N. Amer. termination; informal hit; literary slaying.

assault v. **1** *he assaulted a police officer* **attack**, hit, strike, punch, beat up, thump; pummel, pound, batter; informal clout, wallop, belt, clobber, bop, biff, sock, deck, slug, plug, lay into, do over, rough up; Austral. informal quilt; literary smite. **2** *they left to assault the hill* **attack**, assail, pounce on, set upon, strike, fall on, swoop on, rush, storm, besiege. **3** *he first assaulted then murdered her* **rape**, sexually assault, molest, interfere with.
▸ n. **1** *he was charged with assault* **battery**, violence; sexual assault, rape; Brit. grievous bodily harm, GBH, actual bodily harm, ABH. **2** *an assault on the city* **attack**, strike, onslaught, offensive, charge, push, thrust, invasion, bombardment, sortie, incursion, raid, blitz, campaign.

assay n. *new plate was brought for assay* **evaluation**, assessment, appraisal, analysis, examination, tests, inspection, scrutiny.
▸ v. *gold is assayed to determine its purity* **evaluate**, assess, appraise, analyse, examine, test, inspect, scrutinize, probe.

assemblage n. **collection**, accumulation, conglomeration, gathering, group, grouping, cluster, aggregation, mass, number; assortment, selection, array.

assemble v. **1** *a crowd had assembled* **gather**, collect, get together, congregate, convene, meet, muster, rally; formal foregather. **2** *he assembled the suspects* **bring/call together**, gather, collect, round up, marshal, muster, summon; formal convoke. **3** *how to assemble the kite* **construct**, build, fabricate, manufacture, erect, set up, put/piece together, connect, join.
– OPPOSITES disperse, dismantle.

assembly n. **1** *an assembly of dockers* **gathering**, meeting, congregation, convention, rally, convocation, assemblage, group, body, crowd, throng, company; informal get-together. **2** *the labour needed in car assembly* **construction**, manufacture, building, fabrication, erection.

assent n. *they are likely to give their assent* **agreement**, acceptance, approval, approbation, consent, acquiescence, compliance, concurrence, the nod; sanction, endorsement, confirmation; permission, leave, blessing; informal the go-ahead, the green light, the OK, the thumbs up.
– OPPOSITES dissent, refusal.
▸ v. *he assented to the change* **agree to**, accept, approve, consent to, acquiesce in, concur in, give one's blessing to, give the nod; sanction, endorse, confirm; informal give the go-ahead, give the green light, give the OK, OK, give the thumbs up; formal accede to.
– OPPOSITES refuse.

assert v. **1** *they asserted that all aboard were safe* **declare**, maintain, contend, argue, state, claim, propound, proclaim, announce, pronounce, swear, insist, avow; formal aver, opine; rare asseverate. **2** *we find it difficult to assert our rights* **insist on**, stand up for, uphold, defend, contend, establish, press/push for, stress.
□ **assert oneself** behave/speak confidently, be assertive, put oneself forward, make one's presence felt; informal put one's foot down.

assertion n. **1** *I questioned his assertion* **declaration**, contention, statement, claim, opinion, proclamation, announcement, pronouncement, protestation, avowal; formal averment; rare asseveration. **2** *an assertion of the right to march* **defence**, upholding; insistence on.

assertive adj. **confident**, self-confident, bold, decisive, assured, self-assured, self-possessed; authoritative, strong-willed, forceful, insistent, determined, commanding, pushy; informal feisty; dated pushful.
– OPPOSITES timid.

assess v. **1** *the committee's power is hard to assess* **evaluate**, judge, gauge, rate, estimate, appraise, get the measure of, determine, weigh up, analyse; informal size up. **2** *the damage was assessed at £5 billion* **value**, calculate, work out, determine, fix, cost, price, estimate.

assessment n. **1** *a teacher's assessment of the pupil's abilities* **evaluation**, judgement, rating, estimation, appraisal, analysis, opinion. **2** *some assessments valued the estate at £2 million* **valuation**, calculation, costing, pricing, estimate.

asset n. **1** *he sees his age as an asset* **benefit**, advantage, blessing, good point, strong point, strength, forte, virtue, recommendation, attraction, resource, boon, merit, bonus, plus, pro. **2** *the seizure of all their assets* **property**, resources, estate, holdings, possessions, effects, goods, valuables, belongings, chattels.
– OPPOSITES liability.

assiduous adj. **diligent**, careful, meticulous, thorough, sedulous, attentive, conscientious, punctilious, painstaking, rigorous, particular; persevering.

assign v. **1** *a young doctor was assigned the task* **allocate**, allot, give, set; charge with, entrust with. **2** *she was assigned to a new post* **appoint**, promote, delegate, commission, post, co-opt; select for, choose for, install in; Military detail. **3** *we assign large sums of money to travel budgets* **earmark**, designate, set aside, reserve, appropriate, allot, allocate, apportion. **4** *he assigned the opinion to the Prince* **ascribe**, attribute, put down, accredit, credit, chalk up, impute; pin on, lay at the door of. **5** *he may assign the money to a third party* **transfer**, make over, give, pass, hand over/down, convey, consign; Law attorn, devise.

assignation n. **rendezvous**, date, appointment, meeting, tweetup; literary tryst.

assignment n. **1** *I'm going to finish this assignment tonight* **task**, piece of work, job, duty, chore, mission, errand, undertaking, exercise, business, endeavour, enterprise; project, homework. **2** *the assignment of tasks* **allocation**, allotment, issuance, designation; sharing out, apportionment, distribution, handing out, dispensation. **3** *the assignment of property* **transfer**, making over, giving, handing down, consignment; Law conveyance, devise, attornment.

assimilate v. **1** *the amount of information he can assimilate* **absorb**, take in, acquire, pick up, grasp, comprehend, understand, learn, master; digest, ingest. **2** *many tribes were assimilated by Turkic peoples* **subsume**, incorporate, integrate, absorb, engulf, acculturate; co-opt, adopt, embrace, admit.

assist v. **1** *I spend my time assisting the chef* **help**, aid, abet, lend a (helping) hand to, oblige, accommodate, serve; collaborate with, work with; support, back (up), second; informal pitch in with; Brit. informal muck in with. **2** *the exchange rates assisted the firm's expansion* **facilitate**, aid, ease, expedite, spur, promote, boost, benefit, foster, encourage, stimulate, precipitate, accelerate, advance, further, forward.
– OPPOSITES hinder, impede.

a

assistance n. **help**, aid, support, backing, reinforcement, succour, relief, intervention, cooperation, collaboration; a (helping) hand, a good turn; informal a break, a leg up.
– OPPOSITES hindrance.

assistant n. **1** *a photographer's assistant* **subordinate**, deputy, second (in command), number two, lieutenant, right-hand man/woman, aide, personal assistant, PA, attendant, mate, apprentice, junior, auxiliary; hired hand, hired help, helper, man/girl Friday; informal sidekick, gofer; Brit. informal dogsbody, skivvy. **2** *an assistant in the local shop* **sales assistant**, salesperson, saleswoman/girl, salesman, server, checkout operator; seller, vendor; N. Amer. clerk; informal counter-jumper; dated shop boy/girl.

associate v. **1** *the colours that we associate with fire* **link**, connect, relate, identify, equate, bracket, set side by side. **2** *I was forced to associate with them* **mix**, keep company, mingle, socialize, go around, rub shoulders, fraternize, consort, have dealings; N. Amer. rub elbows; informal hobnob, hang out/around/round, be thick with; Brit. informal hang about. **3** *the firm is associated with a local charity* **affiliate**, align, connect, join, attach, team up, be in league, ally; merge, integrate, confederate.
▸ n. *his business associate* **partner**, colleague, co-worker, workmate, comrade, ally, confederate; connection, contact, acquaintance; collaborator; informal crony; Brit. informal oppo; Austral./NZ informal offsider.

associated adj. **1** *salaries and associated costs* **related**, connected, linked, correlated, similar, corresponding; attendant, accompanying, incidental. **2** *their associated company* **affiliated**, allied, integrated, amalgamated, federated, confederated, syndicated, connected, related.
– OPPOSITES unrelated.

association n. **1** *a trade association* **alliance**, consortium, coalition, union, league, guild, syndicate, federation, confederation, confederacy, conglomerate, cooperative, partnership, affiliation. **2** *the association between man and environment* **relationship**, relation, interrelation, connection, interconnection, link, bond, union, tie, attachment, interdependence, affiliation.

assorted adj. **various**, miscellaneous, mixed, varied, varying, diverse, eclectic, multifarious, sundry; literary divers.

assortment n. **mixture**, variety, array, mixed bag, mix, miscellany, selection, medley, diversity, ragbag, potpourri, salmagundi, farrago, gallimaufry, omnium gatherum.

assuage v. **1** *a pain that could never be assuaged* **relieve**, ease, alleviate, soothe, mitigate, allay, palliate, abate, suppress, subdue, tranquillize; moderate, lessen, diminish, reduce. **2** *her hunger was quickly assuaged* **satisfy**, gratify, appease, fulfil, indulge, relieve, slake, sate, satiate, quench, check.

– OPPOSITES aggravate, intensify.

assume v. **1** *I assumed he wanted me to keep the book* **presume**, suppose, take it (as given), take for granted, take as read, conjecture, surmise, conclude, deduce, infer, reckon, reason, think, fancy, believe, understand, gather; N. Amer. figure; old use ween. **2** *he assumed a Southern accent* **affect**, adopt, impersonate, put on, simulate, feign, fake. **3** *the disease may assume epidemic proportions* **acquire**, take on. **4** *they are to assume more responsibility* **accept**, shoulder, bear, undertake, take on/up, manage, handle, deal with. **5** *he assumed control of their finances* **seize**, take (over), appropriate, commandeer, expropriate, hijack, wrest, usurp.

assumed adj. **false**, fictitious, invented, made-up, fake, bogus, sham, spurious, make-believe, improvised, adopted; informal pretend, phoney; Brit. informal cod.
– OPPOSITES genuine.

assumption n. **1** *an informed assumption* **supposition**, presumption, belief, expectation, conjecture, speculation, surmise, guess, premise, hypothesis; conclusion, deduction, inference, notion, impression. **2** *her assumption of ease* **pretence**, simulation, affectation. **3** *the early assumption of community obligation* **acceptance**, shouldering, tackling, undertaking. **4** *the assumption of power by revolutionaries* **seizure**, arrogation, appropriation, expropriation, commandeering, confiscation, hijacking, wresting.

assurance n. **1** *her calm assurance* **self-confidence**, confidence, self-assurance, self-possession, nerve, poise, aplomb, level-headedness; calmness, composure, sangfroid, equanimity; informal cool, unflappability. **2** *you have my assurance* **word (of honour)**, promise, pledge, vow, avowal, oath, bond, undertaking, guarantee, commitment. **3** *there is no assurance of getting one's money back* **guarantee**, certainty, certitude, surety, confidence, expectation. **4** *life assurance* **insurance**, indemnity, indemnification, protection, security, cover.
– OPPOSITES self-doubt, uncertainty.

assure v. **1** *we must assure him of our loyal support* **reassure**, convince, satisfy, persuade, guarantee, promise, tell; affirm, pledge, swear, vow. **2** *he wants to assure a favourable vote* **ensure**, secure, guarantee, seal, clinch, confirm; informal sew up. **3** *they guarantee to assure your life* **insure**, provide insurance, cover, indemnify.

assured adj. **1** *an assured voice* **confident**, self-confident, self-assured, self-possessed, poised, phlegmatic, level-headed; calm, composed, equanimous, imperturbable, unruffled; informal unflappable, together. **2** *an assured supply of weapons* **guaranteed**, certain, sure, secure, reliable, dependable, sound; infallible, unfailing; informal sure-fire.
– OPPOSITES doubtful, uncertain.

astonish v. **amaze**, astound, stagger, surprise, startle, stun, confound, dumbfound, stupefy, daze, nonplus, take aback, leave open-mouthed, leave aghast; informal flabbergast, bowl over; Brit. informal knock for six.

astonished adj. **amazed**, astounded, staggered, surprised, startled, stunned, thunderstruck, aghast, taken aback, dumbfounded, dumbstruck, stupefied, dazed, nonplussed, awestruck; informal flabbergasted; Brit. informal gobsmacked.

astonishing adj. **amazing**, astounding, staggering, surprising, breathtaking; remarkable, extraordinary, incredible, unbelievable, phenomenal; informal mind-boggling.

astonishment n. **amazement**, surprise, stupefaction, incredulity, disbelief, speechlessness, awe, wonder.

astound v. **amaze**, astonish, stagger, surprise, startle, stun, confound, dumbfound, stupefy, daze, nonplus, take aback, leave open-mouthed, leave aghast; informal flabbergast, bowl over; Brit. informal knock for six.

astounding adj. **amazing**, astonishing, staggering, surprising, breathtaking; remarkable, extraordinary, incredible, unbelievable, phenomenal; informal mind-boggling.

astray adv. **1** *the shots went astray* **off target**, wide of the mark, awry, off course. **2** *the older boys lead him astray* **into wrongdoing**, into sin, into iniquity, away from the straight and narrow.

astringent adj. **1** *the lotion has an astringent effect on pores* **constricting**, constrictive, contracting; styptic. **2** *her astringent words* **severe**, sharp, stern, harsh, acerbic, acidulous, caustic, mordant, trenchant; scathing, cutting, incisive, waspish; N. Amer. acerb.

astrology n. **horoscopy**; horoscopes; rare astromancy.

astronaut n. **spaceman/woman**, cosmonaut, taikonaut, space cadet; N. Amer. informal jock.

astronomical adj. **1** *astronomical alignments* **planetary**, stellar; celestial. **2** informal *the sums he has paid are astronomical* **huge**, enormous, very large, prodigious, monumental, colossal, vast, gigantic, massive; substantial, considerable, sizeable, hefty; inordinate; informal astronomic, whopping, humongous; Brit. informal ginormous.
– OPPOSITES tiny.

astute adj. **shrewd**, sharp, acute, quick, clever, intelligent, bright, smart, canny, intuitive, perceptive, insightful, incisive, sagacious, wise; informal on the ball, quick on the uptake, savvy; Brit. informal suss; N. Amer. informal heads-up; rare argute.
– OPPOSITES stupid.

asunder adv. literary *the fabric of society may be torn asunder* **apart**, up, in two; to pieces,

to shreds.

asylum n. **1** *he appealed for political asylum* **refuge**, sanctuary, shelter, safety, protection, security, immunity; a safe haven. **2** *his father was confined to an asylum* **psychiatric hospital**, mental hospital, mental institution, mental asylum; informal madhouse, loony bin, funny farm; N. Amer. informal bughouse; dated lunatic asylum; old use bedlam.

asymmetrical adj. **lopsided**, unsymmetrical, uneven, unbalanced, crooked, awry, askew, skew, squint, misaligned; disproportionate, unequal, irregular; informal cockeyed; Brit. informal skew-whiff, wonky.

atheism n. **non-belief**, disbelief, unbelief, scepticism, doubt, agnosticism; nihilism.

atheist n. **non-believer**, disbeliever, unbeliever, sceptic, doubter, doubting Thomas, agnostic; nihilist; rare nullifidian.
– OPPOSITES believer.

athlete n. **sportsman**, sportswoman, sportsperson; Olympian; runner; N. Amer. informal jock.

athletic adj. **1** *his athletic physique* **muscular**, muscly, sturdy, strapping, well built, strong, powerful, robust, able-bodied, vigorous, hardy, lusty, hearty, brawny, burly, broad-shouldered, Herculean; **fit**, in good shape, in trim; informal sporty, husky, hunky, beefy; literary thewy, stark. **2** *athletic events* **sporting**, sports; Olympic.
– OPPOSITES puny.

atmosphere n. **1** *the gases present in the atmosphere* **air**, sky, airspace; literary the heavens, the firmament, the blue, the azure, the ether. **2** *the hotel has a relaxed atmosphere* **ambience**, air, mood, feel, feeling, character, tone, tenor, aura, quality, undercurrent, flavour; informal vibe.

> **WORD LINKS**
> **meteorology** the study of the atmosphere
> **barometer** an instrument measuring atmospheric pressure
> **isobar** a line on a map connecting points with the same atmospheric pressure

atom n. **1** *they build tiny circuits atom by atom* **particle**, molecule, bit, piece, fragment, fraction. **2** *there wasn't an atom of truth in the allegations* **grain**, iota, jot, whit, mite, scrap, shred, ounce, scintilla; Irish stim; informal smidgen.

> **WORD LINKS**
> **nucleus** the central core of an atom
> **ion** an atom with a net electric charge
> **anion** an ion with a negative electric charge
> **cation** an ion with a positive electric charge

atone v. **make amends**, make reparation, make up for, compensate, pay, recompense, expiate, make good, offset; do penance.

atrocious adj. **1** *atrocious cruelties* **brutal**, barbaric, barbarous, savage, vicious; wicked, cruel, nasty, heinous, monstrous, vile, inhuman, black-hearted, fiendish, ghastly,

horrible; abominable, outrageous, hateful,
disgusting, despicable, contemptible,
loathsome, odious, abhorrent, sickening,
horrifying, unspeakable, execrable,
egregious. **2** *the weather was atrocious*
appalling, dreadful, terrible, abysmal,
unpleasant, miserable; informal dire, rotten,
lousy, God-awful; Brit. informal shocking,
chronic, pants.
– OPPOSITES admirable, superb.

atrocity n. **1** *press reports detailed a
number of atrocities* **abomination**, cruelty,
enormity, outrage, horror, monstrosity,
obscenity, violation, crime, abuse. **2** *conflict
and atrocity around the globe* **barbarity**,
barbarism, brutality, savagery, inhumanity,
cruelty, wickedness, evil, iniquity, horror.

atrophy v. **1** *muscles atrophy in microgravity*
waste away, become emaciated, wither,
shrivel (up), shrink; decay, decline,
deteriorate, degenerate, weaken. **2** *the
Labour campaign atrophied* **dwindle**,
deteriorate, decline, wane, fade, peter out,
crumble, disintegrate, collapse, slump, go
downhill.
– OPPOSITES strengthen, flourish.
▸n. *muscular atrophy* **wasting**, emaciation,
withering, shrivelling, shrinking; decay,
decline, deterioration, degeneration,
weakening, debilitation, enfeeblement.
– OPPOSITES strengthening.

attach v. **1** *a lead weight is attached to the
cord* **fasten**, fix, affix, join, connect, link,
secure, make fast, tie, bind, chain; stick,
adhere, glue, fuse; append. **2** *he attached
himself to the Liberal Party* **affiliate**,
associate, align, ally, unite, integrate, join;
be in league with, form an alliance with.
3 *they attached importance to research*
ascribe, assign, attribute, accredit, impute.
4 *the medical officer attached to HQ* **assign**,
appoint, allocate, second; Military detail.
– OPPOSITES detach, separate.

attached adj. **1** *I'm not interested in you—I'm
attached* **married**, engaged, spoken for,
involved; informal hitched, spliced, going
steady; dated betrothed; formal wed, wedded;
literary affianced; old use espoused. **2** *she was
very attached to her brother* **fond of**, devoted
to; informal mad about, crazy about.
– OPPOSITES single.

attachment n. **1** *he has a strong attachment
to his mother* **bond**, closeness, devotion,
loyalty; fondness for, love for, affection for,
feeling for; relationship with. **2** *the shower
had a massage attachment* **accessory**, fitting,
fitment, extension, add-on, appendage.
3 *the attachment of safety restraints* **fixing**,
fastening, linking, coupling, connection.
4 *he was on attachment from another
regiment* **assignment**, appointment,
secondment, transfer; Military detail. **5** *his
family's Conservative attachment* **affiliation**,
association, alliance, alignment, connection;
links, ties, sympathies.

attack v. **1** *Chris had been brutally attacked*
assault, assail, set upon, beat up; batter,
pummel, punch; N. Amer. beat up on; informal

do over, work over, rough up; Brit. informal duff
up. **2** *the French had still not attacked* **strike**,
charge, pounce; bombard, shell, blitz, strafe,
fire. **3** *the clergy attacked government policies*
criticize, censure, condemn, pillory, savage,
revile, vilify; informal knock, slam, bash, lay
into; Brit. informal slate, slag off, rubbish; N. Amer.
informal pummel. **4** *they have to attack the
problem soon* **address**, attend to, deal with,
confront, apply oneself to, get to work on,
undertake, embark on; informal get stuck into,
get cracking on, get weaving on. **5** *the virus
attacks the liver* **affect**, have an effect on,
strike; infect, damage, injure.
– OPPOSITES defend, praise, protect.
▸n. **1** *an attack on their home* **assault**,
onslaught, offensive, strike, blitz, raid,
charge, rush, invasion, incursion. **2** *she
wrote a devastating personal attack on him*
criticism, censure, rebuke, admonishment,
reprimand, reproval; condemnation,
denunciation, revilement, vilification;
tirade, diatribe, polemic; informal roasting,
caning; Brit. informal slating, rollicking, blast.
3 *an asthmatic attack* **fit**, seizure, spasm,
convulsion, paroxysm, outburst, bout.
– OPPOSITES defence, commendation.

attacker n. **assailant**, assaulter, aggressor;
mugger, rapist, killer, murderer.

attain v. **achieve**, accomplish, reach, obtain,
gain, procure, secure, get, hook, net, win,
earn, acquire; realize, fulfil; informal clinch,
bag, wrap up.

attainable adj. **achievable**, obtainable,
accessible, within reach, securable,
realizable; practicable, workable, realistic,
reasonable, viable, feasible, possible; informal
doable, get-at-able.

attainment n. **1** *the attainment of common
goals* **achievement**, accomplishment,
realization, fulfilment, completion; formal
effectuation, reification. **2** *educational
attainment* **achievement**, accomplishment,
proficiency, competence; qualification; skill,
aptitude, ability.

attempt v. *I attempted to answer the question*
try, strive, aim, venture, endeavour, seek,
undertake, make an effort; have a go at, try
one's hand at; informal go all out, bend over
backwards, bust a gut, have a crack at, have
a shot at, have a stab at; formal essay; old use
assay.
▸n. *an attempt to put the economy to rights*
effort, endeavour, try, venture, trial; informal
crack, go, shot, stab; formal essay; old use assay.

attend v. **1** *they attended a carol service* **be
present at**, sit in on, take part in; appear
at, present oneself at, turn up at, visit, go
to; informal show up at, show one's face at.
2 *he had not attended to the regulations* **pay
attention**, pay heed, be attentive, listen;
concentrate, take note, bear in mind, take
into consideration, heed, observe, mark.
3 *the wounded were attended to nearby* **care
for**, look after, minister to, see to; tend,
treat, nurse, help, aid, assist, succour; informal
doctor. **4** *he attended to the boy's education*
deal with, see to, manage, organize, sort

out, handle, take forward, take care of, take charge of, take in hand, tackle. **5** *the queen was attended by an usher* **escort**, accompany, chaperone, squire, guide, lead, conduct, usher, shepherd; assist, help, serve, wait on. **6** *her giddiness was attended with a fever* **be accompanied by**, occur with, coexist with, be associated with, connected with, be linked with; be produced by, originate from/ in, stem from, result from, arise from.
– OPPOSITES miss, disregard, ignore, neglect.

attendance n. **1** *you requested the attendance of a doctor* **presence**, appearance; attention. **2** *their gig attendances grew* **audience**, turnout, house, gate; crowd, congregation, gathering; Austral. informal muster.
– OPPOSITES absence.
□ **in attendance** present, here, there, near, nearby, at hand, available; assisting, supervising.

attendant n. **1** *a sleeping car attendant* **steward**, waiter, waitress, garçon, porter, servant; N. Amer. waitperson. **2** *a royal attendant* **escort**, companion, retainer, aide, lady-in-waiting, equerry, chaperone; servant, manservant, valet, gentleman's gentleman, maidservant, maid; N. Amer. houseman; Brit. informal skivvy; Military, dated batman.
▶ adj. *new discoveries and the attendant excitement* **accompanying**, associated, related, connected, concomitant; resultant, resulting, consequent.

attention n. **1** *the issue needs further attention* **consideration**, contemplation, deliberation, thought, study, observation, scrutiny, investigation, action. **2** *he tried to attract the attention of a policeman* **awareness**, notice, observation, heed, regard, scrutiny, surveillance. **3** *adequate medical attention* **care**, treatment, ministration, succour, relief, aid, help, assistance. **4** *he was effusive in his attentions* **overtures**, approaches, suit, wooing, courting; compliments, flattery.

attentive adj. **1** *a bright and attentive scholar* **perceptive**, observant, alert, acute, aware, heedful, vigilant; intent, focused, committed, studious, diligent, conscientious, earnest; informal not missing a trick, on the ball. **2** *the most attentive of husbands* **conscientious**, considerate, thoughtful, kind, caring, solicitous, understanding, sympathetic, obliging, accommodating, gallant, chivalrous; dutiful, responsible.
– OPPOSITES inconsiderate.

attenuated adj. **1** *attenuated fingers* **thin**, slender, narrow, slim, skinny, spindly, bony; literary extenuated; rare attenuate. **2** *his muscle activity was much attenuated* **weakened**, reduced, lessened, decreased, diminished, impaired.
– OPPOSITES plump, broad, strengthened.

attest v. **certify**, corroborate, confirm, verify, substantiate, authenticate, evidence, demonstrate, show, prove; endorse, support, affirm, bear out, give credence to, vouch for; formal evince.

– OPPOSITES disprove.

attic n. **loft**, roof space, cock loft; garret, mansard.

attire n. *Thomas preferred formal attire* **clothing**, clothes, garments, dress, wear, outfits, garb, costume; informal gear, togs, duds, get-up; Brit. informal clobber; N. Amer. informal threads; formal apparel; old use raiment, habiliments.
▶ v. *she was attired in black crêpe* **dress (up)**, clothe, garb, robe, array, costume, swathe, deck (out), turn out, fit out, trick out/up, rig out; informal get up; old use apparel, invest, habit.

attitude n. **1** *you seem ambivalent in your attitude* **view**, viewpoint, outlook, perspective, stance, standpoint, position, inclination, orientation, approach, reaction; opinion, ideas, convictions, feelings, thinking. **2** *an attitude of prayer* **position**, posture, pose, stance.

attorney n. **lawyer**, legal practitioner, legal executive, legal representative, member of the bar, barrister, counsel; Brit. Queen's Counsel, QC; Scottish advocate; N. Amer. counselor(-at-law); informal brief.

attract v. **1** *positive ions are attracted to the negatively charged terminal* **draw**, pull, magnetize. **2** *he was attracted by her smile* **entice**, allure, lure, tempt, charm, win over, woo, engage, enchant, entrance, captivate, beguile, bewitch, seduce; excite, titillate, arouse; informal turn on.
– OPPOSITES repel.

attraction n. **1** *the stars are held together by gravitational attraction* **pull**, draw; magnetism. **2** *she had lost whatever attraction she had ever had* **appeal**, attractiveness, desirability, seductiveness, seduction, allure, animal magnetism; charisma, charm, beauty, good looks; informal come-on. **3** *the fair offers sideshows and other attractions* **entertainment**, activity, diversion, interest.
– OPPOSITES repulsion.

attractive adj. **1** *a more attractive career* **appealing**, inviting, tempting, irresistible; agreeable, pleasing, interesting. **2** *she has no idea how attractive she is* **good-looking**, beautiful, pretty, handsome, lovely, stunning, striking, arresting, gorgeous, prepossessing, fetching, captivating, bewitching, beguiling, engaging, charming, enchanting, appealing, delightful; sexy, seductive, alluring, tantalizing, irresistible, ravishing, desirable; Scottish & N. English bonny; informal fanciable, tasty, hot, easy on the eye, drop-dead gorgeous; Brit. informal fit; N. Amer. informal cute, foxy; Austral./NZ informal spunky; literary beauteous; old use comely, fair.
– OPPOSITES uninviting, ugly.

attribute v. *they attributed their success to him* **ascribe**, assign, accredit, credit, impute; put down, chalk up, hold responsible, pin on; connect with, associate with.
▶ n. **1** *he has all the attributes of a top player* **quality**, characteristic, trait, feature,

a

element, aspect, property, sign, hallmark, mark, distinction. **2** *the hourglass is the attribute of Father Time* **symbol**, mark, sign, hallmark, trademark.

attrition n. **1** *a gradual attrition of the market economy* **wearing down/away**, weakening, debilitation, enfeebling, sapping, attenuation. **2** *the attrition of the edges of the teeth* **abrasion**, friction, erosion, corrosion, grinding, wearing (away); deterioration, damaging; rare detrition.

attune v. **accustom**, adjust, adapt, acclimatize, condition, accommodate, assimilate; N. Amer. acclimate.

atypical adj. **unusual**, untypical, uncommon, unconventional, unorthodox, off-centre, irregular, abnormal, aberrant, deviant, unrepresentative; strange, odd, peculiar, bizarre, weird, queer, freakish; exceptional, singular, rare, out of the way, out of the ordinary, extraordinary; Brit. out of the common; informal funny, freaky.
– OPPOSITES normal.

auburn adj. **reddish-brown**, red-brown, Titian (red), tawny, russet, chestnut, copper, coppery, rufous.

au courant adj. **up to date**, au fait, in touch, familiar, at home, acquainted, conversant; abreast, apprised, in the know, well informed, knowledgeable, well versed, enlightened; informal clued-up, wise to, hip to.

audacious adj. **1** *his audacious exploits* **bold**, daring, fearless, intrepid, brave, courageous, valiant, heroic, plucky; daredevil, devil-may-care, death-or-glory, reckless, madcap; venturesome, mettlesome; informal gutsy, spunky, ballsy; literary temerarious. **2** *an audacious remark* **impudent**, impertinent, insolent, presumptuous, cheeky, irreverent, discourteous, disrespectful, insubordinate, ill-mannered, unmannerly, rude, brazen, shameless, pert, defiant, cocky, bold (as brass); informal brass-necked, fresh, lippy, mouthy, saucy; N. Amer. informal sassy, nervy; old use malapert, contumelious.
– OPPOSITES timid, polite.

audacity n. **1** *a traveller of extraordinary audacity* **boldness**, daring, fearlessness, intrepidity, bravery, courage, heroism, pluck, grit; recklessness; spirit, mettle; informal guts, gutsiness, spunk; Brit. informal bottle; N. Amer. informal moxie. **2** *he had the audacity to contradict me* **impudence**, impertinence, insolence, presumption, cheek, bad manners, effrontery, nerve, gall, defiance, temerity; informal brass (neck), chutzpah; Brit. informal sauce; N. Amer. informal sass.

audible adj. **hearable**, perceptible, discernible, detectable, appreciable; clear, distinct, loud.
– OPPOSITES faint.

audience n. **1** *the audience applauded* **spectators**, **listeners**, viewers, onlookers, concertgoers, theatregoers, patrons; crowd, throng, congregation, turnout; house, gallery, stalls; Brit. informal punters. **2** *the radio station has a teenage audience* **market**,

public, following, fans; listenership, viewership. **3** *an audience with the Pope* **meeting**, consultation, conference, hearing, reception, interview.

audit n. *an audit of the party accounts* **inspection**, examination, scrutiny, probe, investigation, assessment, appraisal, evaluation, review, analysis.
▸ v. *we audited their accounts* **inspect**, examine, survey, go through, scrutinize, check, probe, vet, investigate, enquire into, assess, appraise, evaluate, review, analyse, study.

auditorium n. **theatre**, hall, assembly room; chamber, room.

au fait adj. **familiar**, acquainted, conversant, at home, up to date, au courant, in touch; abreast, apprised, in the know, well informed, knowledgeable, well versed, enlightened; informal clued-up, wise to, hip to.

augment v. **increase**, add to, supplement, top up, build up, enlarge, expand, extend, raise, multiply, swell; magnify, amplify, escalate; improve, boost; informal up, jack up, hike up, bump up.
– OPPOSITES decrease.

augur v. *these successes augur well for the future* **bode**, portend, herald, be a sign, warn, forewarn, foreshadow, be an omen, presage, indicate, signify, signal, promise, threaten, spell, denote; predict, prophesy; literary betoken, foretoken, forebode.

august adj. **distinguished**, respected, eminent, venerable, hallowed, illustrious, prestigious, renowned, celebrated, honoured, acclaimed, esteemed, exalted; great, important, lofty, noble; imposing, impressive, awe-inspiring, stately, grand, dignified.

aura n. **atmosphere**, ambience, air, quality, character, mood, feeling, feel, flavour, tone, tenor; emanation, vibration; informal vibe.

auspices plural n. **patronage**, aegis, umbrella, protection, keeping, care; support, backing, guardianship, trusteeship, guidance, supervision.

auspicious adj. **favourable**, propitious, promising, rosy, good, encouraging; opportune, timely, lucky, fortunate, providential, felicitous, advantageous.

austere adj. **1** *an outwardly austere man* **severe**, stern, strict, harsh, steely, flinty, dour, grim, cold, frosty, unemotional, unfriendly; formal, stiff, reserved, aloof, forbidding; grave, solemn, serious, unsmiling, unsympathetic, unforgiving; hard, unyielding, unbending, inflexible, illiberal; informal hard-boiled. **2** *an austere life* **ascetic**, self-denying, self-disciplined, non-indulgent, frugal, spartan, puritanical, abstemious, abstinent, self-sacrificing, strict, temperate, sober, simple, restrained; celibate, chaste. **3** *the buildings were austere* **plain**, simple, basic, functional, modest, unadorned, unembellished, unfussy, restrained; stark, bleak, bare, clinical, spartan, ascetic; informal no frills.
– OPPOSITES genial, immoderate, ornate.

authentic adj. **1** *an authentic document* **genuine**, real, bona fide, true, veritable, simon-pure; legitimate, lawful, legal, valid; informal the real McCoy, the real thing, pukka, kosher; Austral./NZ informal dinkum. **2** *an authentic depiction of the situation* **reliable**, dependable, trustworthy, authoritative, honest, faithful; accurate, factual, true, truthful; formal veridical, veracious.
– OPPOSITES fake, unreliable.

authenticate v. **1** *the evidence will authenticate his claim* **verify**, validate, prove, substantiate, corroborate, confirm, support, back up, attest to, give credence to. **2** *a mandate authenticated by the popular vote* **validate**, ratify, confirm, seal, sanction, endorse.

authenticity n. **1** *the authenticity of the painting* **genuineness**, bona fides; legitimacy, legality, validity. **2** *the authenticity of this account* **reliability**, dependability, trustworthiness, credibility; accuracy, truth, veracity, fidelity.

author n. **1** *modern Canadian authors* **writer**, wordsmith; novelist, playwright, poet, essayist, biographer; columnist, reporter; informal penman, penwoman, scribe, scribbler. **2** *the author of the peace plan* **originator**, creator, instigator, founder, father, architect, designer, deviser, producer; cause, agent.

> **WORD LINKS**
> **auctorial** relating to an author
> **amanuensis** an author's assistant
> **autograph, holograph** an author's handwritten manuscript
> **juvenilia** works produced by an author when young
> **manuscript** an author's handwritten or typed work, submitted for printing
> **pen name, pseudonym** a false name used by an author

authoritarian adj. *his authoritarian manner* **autocratic**, dictatorial, despotic, tyrannical, draconian, oppressive, repressive, illiberal, undemocratic, anti-democratic; disciplinarian, domineering, overbearing, high-handed, peremptory, imperious, strict, rigid, inflexible; informal bossy.
– OPPOSITES democratic, liberal.
▸ n. *the army is dominated by authoritarians* **autocrat**, despot, dictator, tyrant; disciplinarian, martinet.

authoritative adj. **1** *authoritative information* **reliable**, dependable, trustworthy, sound, authentic, valid, attested, verifiable; accurate. **2** *the authoritative edition* **definitive**, most reliable, best; authorized, accredited, recognized, accepted, approved. **3** *his authoritative manner* **assured**, confident, assertive; commanding, masterful, lordly; domineering, imperious, overbearing, authoritarian; informal bossy.
– OPPOSITES unreliable, timid.

authority n. **1** *a rebellion against those in authority* **power**, jurisdiction, command, control, charge, dominance, rule, sovereignty, supremacy; influence; informal clout. **2** *the authority to arrest drug traffickers* **authorization**, right, power, mandate, prerogative, licence. **3** *the money was spent without parliamentary authority* **authorization**, permission, consent, leave, sanction, licence, dispensation, assent, acquiescence, agreement, approval, endorsement, clearance; informal the go-ahead, the thumbs up, the OK, the green light. **4** *the authorities* **officials**, officialdom; government, administration, establishment; police; informal the powers that be. **5** *a minister may have great authority within his department* **influence**, sway, control, leverage, power, command, weight; reputation, standing, kudos, status, stature, prestige, gravitas, image, esteem; credibility, plausibility, integrity; informal clout, pull. **6** *an authority on the stock market* **expert**, specialist, aficionado, pundit, doyen(ne), guru, sage; informal boffin. **7** *he cites the nuns' testimony as an authority* **source**, reference, citation, quotation, passage. **8** *on good authority* **evidence**, testimony, witness, attestation, word, avowal; Law deposition.

authorization n. **permission**, consent, leave, sanction, licence, dispensation, clearance, the nod; assent, agreement, approval, endorsement; authority, right, power, mandate; informal the go-ahead, the thumbs up, the OK, the green light.
– OPPOSITES refusal.

authorize v. **1** *they authorized further action* **sanction**, permit, allow, approve, consent to, assent to; ratify, endorse, validate; informal give the green light, give the go-ahead, OK, give the thumbs up. **2** *the troops were authorized to fire* **empower**, mandate, commission; entitle.
– OPPOSITES forbid.

authorized adj. **approved**, recognized, sanctioned; accredited, licensed, certified; official, lawful, legal, legitimate.
– OPPOSITES unofficial.

autobiography n. **memoirs**, life story, personal history.

autocracy n. **absolutism**, totalitarianism, dictatorship, despotism, tyranny, monocracy, autarchy.
– OPPOSITES democracy.

autocrat n. **absolute ruler**, dictator, despot, tyrant, monocrat.

autocratic adj. **despotic**, tyrannical, dictatorial, totalitarian, autarchic; undemocratic, anti-democratic, one-party, monocratic; domineering, draconian, overbearing, high-handed, peremptory, imperious; harsh, rigid, inflexible, illiberal, oppressive.

autograph n. *fans wanted his autograph* **signature**; N. Amer. informal John Hancock.
▸ v. *Jack autographed copies of his book* **sign**.

automatic adj. **1** *automatic garage doors* **mechanized**, mechanical, automated, computerized, electronic, robotic;

self-activating. **2** *an automatic reaction* **instinctive**, involuntary, unconscious, reflex, knee-jerk, instinctual, subconscious; spontaneous, impulsive, unthinking, mechanical; informal gut. **3** *he is the automatic choice for the team* **inevitable**, unavoidable, inescapable, unpreventable, mandatory, compulsory; certain, definite, undoubted, assured.
– OPPOSITES manual, deliberate.

autonomous adj. **self-governing**, self-ruling, self-determining, independent, sovereign, free.

autonomy n. **self-government**, self-rule, home rule, self-determination, independence, sovereignty, freedom.

autopsy n. **post-mortem**, PM, necropsy.

auxiliary adj. **1** *an auxiliary power source* **additional**, supplementary, supplemental, extra, reserve, back-up, emergency, fallback, other. **2** *auxiliary nursing staff* **ancillary**, assistant, support.
▸ n. *a nursing auxiliary* **assistant**, helper, ancillary.

avail v. **1** *guests can avail themselves of the facilities* **use**, take advantage of, utilize, employ. **2** *his arguments cannot avail him* **help**, aid, assist, benefit, profit, be of service. □ **to no avail** in vain, without success, unsuccessfully, fruitlessly, for nothing.

available adj. **1** *refreshments will be available* **obtainable**, accessible, to/at hand, at one's disposal, handy, convenient; on sale, procurable; untaken, unengaged, unused; informal up for grabs, on tap, gettable. **2** *I'll see if he's available* **free**, unoccupied; present, in attendance; contactable.
– OPPOSITES busy, engaged.

avalanche n. **1** **snowslide**, icefall; rockslide, landslide, landslip; Brit. snow-slip. **2** *an avalanche of press comment* **barrage**, volley, flood, deluge, torrent, tide, shower, wave.

avant-garde adj. **innovative**, innovatory, original, experimental, left-field, inventive, ahead of the times, new, modern, advanced, forward-looking, state-of-the-art, trendsetting, pioneering, progressive, groundbreaking, trailblazing, revolutionary; unfamiliar, unorthodox, unconventional, off-centre; informal offbeat, way-out.
– OPPOSITES conservative.

avarice n. **greed**, acquisitiveness, cupidity, covetousness, rapacity, materialism, mercenariness, Mammonism; informal money-grubbing.
– OPPOSITES generosity.

avenge v. **requite**, punish, repay, pay back, take revenge for, get even for.

avenue n. **1** *tree-lined avenues* **road**, street, drive, parade, boulevard, broadway, thoroughfare. **2** *possible avenues of research* **line**, path; method, approach.

aver v. formal **declare**, maintain, claim, assert, state, swear, avow, vow; rare asseverate.

average n. *the price is above the national average* **mean**, median, mode; norm, standard, rule, par.

▸ adj. **1** *the average temperature in May* **mean**, median, modal. **2** *a woman of average height* **ordinary**, standard, normal, typical, regular. **3** *a very average director* **mediocre**, second-rate, undistinguished, ordinary, middle-of-the-road, unexceptional, unexciting, unremarkable, unmemorable, indifferent, pedestrian, lacklustre, forgettable, amateurish; informal OK, so-so, fair-to-middling, no great shakes, not up to much; Brit. informal not much cop; N. Amer. informal bush-league; NZ informal half-pie.
– OPPOSITES outstanding, exceptional.
□ **on average** normally, usually, ordinarily, generally, in general, for the most part, as a rule, typically; overall, by and large, on the whole.

averse adj. **opposed**, against, antipathetic, hostile, ill-disposed, resistant; disinclined, reluctant, loath; informal anti.
– OPPOSITES keen.

aversion n. **dislike**, antipathy, distaste, abhorrence, hatred, loathing, detestation, hostility; reluctance, disinclination; old use disrelish.
– OPPOSITES liking.

avert v. **1** *she averted her head* **turn aside**, turn away. **2** *an attempt to avert political chaos* **prevent**, avoid, stave off, ward off, forestall, preclude.

aviator n. dated **pilot**, airman/woman, flyer; dated aeronaut.

avid adj. **keen**, eager, enthusiastic, ardent, passionate, zealous; devoted, dedicated, wholehearted, earnest; Brit. informal as keen as mustard.
– OPPOSITES apathetic.

avoid v. **1** *I avoid situations that stress me* **keep away from**, steer clear of, give a wide berth to, fight shy of. **2** *he is trying to avoid responsibility* **evade**, dodge, sidestep, escape, run away from; informal duck, wriggle out of, get out of, cop out of; Austral./NZ informal duck-shove. **3** *she moved to avoid a blow* **dodge**, duck, get out of the way of. **4** *you've been avoiding me all evening* **shun**, stay away from, evade, keep one's distance, elude, hide from; ignore. **5** *he should avoid drinking alcohol* **refrain from**, abstain from, desist from, eschew.
– OPPOSITES confront, face up to, seek out.

avoidable adj. **preventable**, stoppable, avertable, escapable.
– OPPOSITES inescapable.

avow v. **assert**, declare, state, maintain, swear, vow, insist; rare asseverate; formal aver.

avowed adj. **self-confessed**, self-declared, acknowledged, admitted; open, overt.

await v. **1** *Peter was awaiting news* **wait for**, expect, anticipate. **2** *many dangers await them* **be in store for**, lie ahead of, lie in wait for, be waiting for.

awake v. **1** *she awoke the following morning* **wake (up)**, awaken, stir, come to, come round; literary waken. **2** *the alarm awoke him at 7.30* **wake (up)**, awaken, rouse, arouse; Brit. informal knock up. **3** *they finally awoke to the* *extent of the problem* **realize**, become aware of, become conscious of; informal get wise to.

▸adj. **1** *she was still awake* **wakeful**, sleepless, restless, restive; old use watchful. **2** *too few are awake to the dangers* **aware of**, conscious of, mindful of, alert to; formal cognizant of; old use ware of.

– OPPOSITES asleep, oblivious.

awaken v. **1** *I awakened early | the jolt awakened her.* See **awake** (senses 1 & 2). **2** *he had awakened strong emotions in her* **arouse**, rouse, bring out, engender, evoke, trigger, stir up, stimulate, kindle; revive; literary enkindle.

award v. *the society awarded him a silver medal* **give**, grant, accord, assign; confer on, bestow on, present to, endow with, decorate with.

▸n. **1** *an award for high-quality service* **prize**, trophy, medal, decoration; reward; informal gong. **2** *a libel award* **payment**, settlement, compensation. **3** *the Arts Council gave him an award of £1,500* **grant**, scholarship, endowment; Brit. bursary. **4** *the award of an honorary doctorate* **conferral**, conferment, bestowal, presentation.

aware adj. **1** *she is aware of the dangers* **conscious of**, mindful of, informed about, acquainted with, familiar with, alive to, alert to; informal wise to, in the know about, hip to; formal cognizant of; old use ware of. **2** *we need to be more environmentally aware* **knowledgeable**, enlightened, well informed, au fait; informal clued-up, genned-up, plugged-in; Brit. informal switched-on.

– OPPOSITES ignorant.

awareness n. **consciousness**, recognition, realization; understanding, grasp, appreciation, knowledge, insight, familiarity; formal cognizance.

awash adj. **1** *the road was awash* **flooded**, under water, submerged, submersed. **2** *the city was awash with journalists* **inundated**, flooded, swamped, teeming, overflowing, overrun; informal knee-deep in.

away adv. **1** *she began to walk away* **off**, from here, from there. **2** *stay away from the trouble* **at a distance from**, apart from. **3** *Bernice pushed him away* **aside**, off, to one side. **4** *we'll be away for two weeks* **elsewhere**, abroad; gone, absent; on holiday, on vacation.

awe n. **wonder**, wonderment; admiration, reverence, respect; dread, fear.

awe-inspiring adj. See **awesome**.

awesome adj. **breathtaking**, awe-inspiring, magnificent, amazing, stunning, staggering, imposing, stirring, impressive; formidable, fearsome; informal mind-boggling, mind-blowing; literary wondrous; old use awful.

– OPPOSITES unimpressive.

awestruck adj. **amazed**, wonderstruck, awed, lost for words, open-mouthed; terrified, afraid, fearful.

awful adj. **1** *the place smelled awful* **disgusting**, nasty, terrible, dreadful, ghastly, horrible, vile, foul, revolting, repulsive, repugnant, odious, sickening, nauseating; informal yucky, sick-making, gross, rank; Brit. informal beastly; literary noisome. **2** *an awful book* **dreadful**, terrible, abysmal, frightful, atrocious, appalling, execrable; inadequate, inferior, substandard, lamentable; informal crummy, pathetic, rotten, woeful, lousy, dire, poxy; Brit. informal duff, rubbish, pants. **3** *an awful accident* **serious**, grave, bad, terrible, dreadful. **4** *you look awful—go and lie down* **ill**, unwell, sick, peaky, queasy, nauseous; Brit. off colour, poorly; informal rough, lousy, rotten, terrible, dreadful; Brit. informal grotty, ropy; Scottish informal wabbit, peely-wally; Austral./NZ informal crook; dated queer, seedy. **5** *I felt awful for getting so angry* **remorseful**, guilty, ashamed, contrite, sorry, regretful, repentant, self-reproachful.

– OPPOSITES wonderful.

awfully adv. **1** informal *an awfully nice man* **very**, extremely, really, immensely, exceedingly, thoroughly, dreadfully, exceptionally, remarkably, extraordinarily; N. English right; informal terrifically, terribly, devilishly, seriously, majorly; Brit. informal jolly, ever so, dead, well; N. Amer. informal real, mighty, awful; informal dated frightfully; old use exceeding. **2** informal *thanks awfully* **very much**, a lot; informal a million. **3** *we played awfully* **very badly**, terribly, dreadfully, abysmally, atrociously, appallingly, execrably; informal pitifully, diabolically.

awhile adv. **for a moment**, for a (little) while, for a short time; informal for a bit.

awkward adj. **1** *the box was awkward to carry* **difficult**, tricky; cumbersome, lumbersome, unwieldy; Brit. informal fiddly. **2** *an awkward time* **inconvenient**, inappropriate, inopportune, unseasonable, difficult. **3** *he put her in a very awkward position* **embarrassing**, uncomfortable, unpleasant, delicate, tricky, problematic(al), troublesome, thorny; humiliating, compromising; informal sticky, dicey, hairy; Brit. informal dodgy. **4** *she felt awkward alone with him* **uncomfortable**, uneasy, tense, nervous, edgy, unquiet; self-conscious, embarrassed. **5** *his awkward movements* **clumsy**, ungainly, uncoordinated, graceless, inelegant, gauche, gawky, wooden, stiff; unskilful, maladroit, inept, blundering; informal clodhopping, ham-fisted, ham-handed, cack-handed; Brit. informal all (fingers and) thumbs. **6** Brit. *you're being damned awkward* **unreasonable**, uncooperative, unhelpful, disobliging, difficult, obstructive; contrary, perverse; stubborn, obstinate; Brit. informal bloody-minded, bolshie; N. Amer. informal balky; formal refractory.

– OPPOSITES easy, convenient, at ease, graceful, amenable.

awning n. **canopy**, shade, sunshade, shelter, cover; Brit. blind, sunblind.

awry adj. **1** *something was awry* **amiss**, wrong; informal up. **2** *his wig looked awry* **askew**, crooked, lopsided, tilted, skewed, skew, squint, to one side, off-centre, uneven;

a

informal cockeyed; Brit. informal skew-whiff, wonky.
– OPPOSITES straight.

axe n. **hatchet**, cleaver, tomahawk, adze, poleaxe; Brit. chopper; historical battleaxe.
▶v. **1** *the show was axed* **cancel**, withdraw, drop, scrap, discontinue, terminate, end; informal ditch, dump, pull the plug on. **2** *500 staff were axed* **dismiss**, make redundant, lay off, let go, discharge, get rid of; informal sack, fire, give someone the sack, give someone their marching orders; Brit. informal give someone their cards.

axiom n. **accepted truth**, general truth, dictum, truism; maxim, adage, aphorism, apophthegm, gnome.

axis n. **1** *the earth revolves on its axis* **centre line**, vertical, horizontal. **2** *the Anglo-American axis* **alliance**, coalition, bloc, union, confederation, confederacy, league.

axle n. **shaft**, spindle, rod, arbor, mandrel, pivot.

azure adj. **sky-blue**, bright blue, blue; literary cerulean; rare cyanic.

Bb

babble v. **1** *Betty babbled away* **prattle**, rattle on, gabble, chatter, jabber, twitter, go on, run on, prate, ramble, burble, blather, blether; informal gab, yak, yabber, yatter, yammer, blabber, jaw, gas, shoot one's mouth off; Brit. informal witter, rabbit, chunter, natter, waffle; N. Amer. informal run off at the mouth. **2** *a brook babbled gently* **burble**, murmur, gurgle, purl, tinkle; literary plash.
▶n. *his inarticulate babble* **prattle**, gabble, chatter, jabber, prating, rambling, blather, blether; informal gab, yak, yabbering, yatter; Brit. informal wittering, waffle, natter, chuntering.

babe n. literary See **baby** (noun).

babel n. **clamour**, din, racket, confused noise, tumult, uproar, hubbub; babble, babbling, shouting, yelling, screaming; informal hullabaloo; Brit. informal row.

baby n. *a newborn baby* **infant**, newborn, child, tot, little one, bambino; Scottish & N. English bairn; informal sprog, bundle of joy, tiny; literary babe, babe in arms; technical neonate.
▶adj. *baby carrots* **miniature**, mini, little, small, small-scale, scaled-down, toy, pocket, midget, dwarf, fun-size; Scottish wee; N. Amer. vest-pocket; informal teeny, teeny-weeny, teensy, teensy-weensy, itsy-bitsy, itty-bitty, tiddly, bite-sized; Brit. informal titchy; N. Amer. informal little-bitty.
▶v. *her aunt babied her* **pamper**, mollycoddle, spoil, cosset, coddle, indulge, overindulge, pet, nanny, pander to.

babyish adj. **childish**, immature, infantile, juvenile, puerile, adolescent.
– OPPOSITES mature.

back n. **1** *she's broken her back* **spine**, backbone, spinal column, vertebral column. **2** *the back of the house* **rear**, rear side, other side; Nautical stern. **3** *the back of the queue* **end**, tail end, rear end, tail; N. Amer. tag end. **4** *the back of a postcard* **reverse**, other side, underside; verso; informal flip side.
– OPPOSITES front, head, face.
▶adv. **1** *Michael pushed his chair back* **backwards**, behind one, to one's rear, rearwards; away, off. **2** *a few months back* **ago**, earlier, previously, before, in the past.
– OPPOSITES forward.
▶v. **1** *the record companies backed the scheme with a few hundred pounds* **sponsor**, finance, put up the money for, fund, subsidize, underwrite; informal foot the bill for, pick up the tab for; N. Amer. informal bankroll, stake.

2 *most people backed the idea* **support**, endorse, sanction, approve of, give one's blessing to, smile on, favour, advocate, promote, uphold, champion; vote for, ally oneself with, stand behind, side with, be on the side of, defend, take up the cudgels for; second; informal throw one's weight behind. **3** *he backed the horse at 33–1* **bet on**, gamble on, stake money on. **4** *he backed away* **reverse**, draw back, step back, move backwards, back off, pull back, retreat, withdraw, give ground, backtrack, retrace one's steps.
– OPPOSITES oppose, advance.
▶adj. **1** *the back seats* **rear**, rearmost, hind, hindmost, hinder, posterior. **2** *a back copy* **past**, old, previous, earlier, former, out of date.
– OPPOSITES front, future.
  □ **back down** give in, concede defeat, surrender, yield, submit, climb down, concede, reconsider; backtrack, back-pedal.
back out of renege on, go back on, withdraw from, pull out of, retreat from, fail to honour, abandon, default on, repudiate, back-pedal on.
back something up substantiate, corroborate, confirm, support, bear out, endorse, bolster, reinforce, lend weight to.
back someone up support, stand by, give one's support to, side with, be on someone's side, take someone's side, take someone's part; vouch for.

> **WORD LINKS**
> **dorsal, lumbar** relating to the back
> **supine** lying on one's back

backbiting n. **malicious talk**, spiteful talk, slander, libel, defamation, abuse, character assassination, disparagement, denigration; slurs, aspersions; informal bitching, bitchiness, cattiness, mud-slinging, bad-mouthing; Brit. informal slagging off, rubbishing.

backbone n. **1** *an injured backbone* **spine**, spinal column, vertebral column, vertebrae; back; Anatomy dorsum, rachis. **2** *infantry are the backbone of most armies* **mainstay**, cornerstone, foundation, keystone, buttress, pillar. **3** *he has enough backbone to see us through* **strength of character**, strength of will, firmness of purpose, firmness, resolution, resolve, grit, determination, fortitude, mettle, spirit; informal guts, spunk; Brit. informal bottle.

b

back-breaking adj. **gruelling**, arduous, strenuous, onerous, punishing, crushing, demanding, exacting, taxing, exhausting, draining; informal killing; Brit. informal knackering; old use toilsome.
– OPPOSITES easy.

backchat n. Brit. informal **impudence**, impertinence, cheek, cheekiness, effrontery, insolence, rudeness, rude retorts; answering back, talking back; informal mouth, lip; N. Amer. informal sass, smart mouth, back talk; rare contumely.

backer n. **1** *£3 million was provided by the project's backers* **sponsor**, investor, underwriter, financier, patron, benefactor, benefactress; informal angel. **2** *the backers of the proposition* **supporter**, defender, advocate, promoter, proponent; seconder; N. Amer. booster.

backfire v. *Bernard's plan backfired on him* **rebound**, boomerang, come back; fail, miscarry, go wrong; informal blow up in someone's face; old use redound on.

background n. **1** *a background of palm trees* **backdrop**, backcloth, surrounding(s), setting, scene. **2** *students from many different backgrounds* **social circumstances**, family circumstances; environment, class, culture, tradition; upbringing. **3** *her nursing background* **experience**, record, history, past, training, education, grounding, knowledge. **4** *the political background* **circumstances**, context, conditions, situation, environment, milieu, scene, scenario.
– OPPOSITES foreground.
□ **in the background** *maybe there was a sugar daddy in the background* behind the scenes, out of the public eye, out of the spotlight, out of the limelight, backstage; inconspicuous, unobtrusive, unnoticed.

backhanded adj. **ambiguous**, indirect, oblique, equivocal; double-edged, two-edged; tongue-in-cheek.
– OPPOSITES direct.

backing n. **1** *he has the backing of his colleagues* **support**, help, assistance, aid; approval, endorsement, sanction, blessing. **2** *financial backing* **sponsorship**, funding, patronage; money, investment, funds, finance; grant, contribution, subsidy. **3** *musical backing* **accompaniment**; harmony, obbligato.

backlash n. **adverse reaction**, adverse response, counterblast, comeback; retaliation, reprisal.

backlog n. **accumulation**, logjam, pile-up.

back-pedal v. *the government has back-pedalled on its plans* **change one's mind**, go into reverse, backtrack, back down, climb down, do an about-face, do a U-turn, row back, renege, go back on, back out of, fail to honour, withdraw, take back, default on; Brit. do an about-turn.

backslide v. *many things can cause slimmers to backslide* **relapse**, lapse, regress, retrogress, weaken, lose one's resolve, give in to temptation, go astray, leave the straight and narrow.
– OPPOSITES persevere.

backslider n. **recidivist**, regressor; apostate, fallen angel.

back-up n. **help**, support, assistance, aid; reinforcements, reserves, additional resources.

backward adj. **1** *a backward look* **rearward**, to/towards the rear, to/towards the back, behind one, reverse. **2** *the decision was a backward step* **retrograde**, retrogressive, regressive, for the worse, in the wrong direction, downhill, negative. **3** *an economically backward country* **underdeveloped**, undeveloped; primitive, benighted. **4** *he was not backward in displaying his talents* **hesitant**, reticent, reluctant; shy, diffident, bashful, timid; unwilling, afraid, loath, averse.
– OPPOSITES forward, progressive, advanced, confident.
▸ adv. *the car rolled slowly backward.* See **backwards**.

backwards adv. **1** *Penny glanced backwards* **towards the rear**, rearwards, backward, behind one. **2** *count backwards from twenty to ten* **in reverse**, in reverse order.
– OPPOSITES forwards.

backwash n. **1** *a ship's backwash* **wake**, wash, slipstream, backflow. **2** *the backwash of the Cuban missile crisis* **repercussions**, reverberations, after-effects, aftermath, fallout.

backwoods plural n. **the back of beyond**, the wilds, the hinterlands, a backwater; N. Amer. the backcountry, the backland; informal the middle of nowhere, the sticks; N. Amer. informal the boondocks, the boonies; Austral./NZ informal beyond the black stump.
▸ adj. **provincial**, rural, hillbilly, country, primitive, crude, simple.

bacteria plural n. **microorganisms**, microbes, germs, bacilli, pathogens; informal bugs.

bad adj. **1** *bad workmanship* **substandard**, poor, inferior, second-rate, second-class, unsatisfactory, inadequate, unacceptable, not up to scratch, not up to par, deficient, imperfect, defective, faulty, shoddy, amateurish, careless, negligent, miserable, sorry; incompetent, inept, inexpert, ineffectual; informal crummy, rotten, pathetic, useless, woeful, bum, lousy, ropy, not up to snuff; Brit. informal duff, rubbish, pants. **2** *the alcohol had a really bad effect on me* **harmful**, damaging, detrimental, injurious, hurtful, inimical, destructive, ruinous, negative; unhealthy, unwholesome; formal deleterious. **3** *the bad guys* **wicked**, sinful, immoral, evil, morally wrong, corrupt, base, black-hearted, reprobate, amoral; criminal, villainous, nefarious, iniquitous, dishonest, dishonourable, unscrupulous, unprincipled; informal crooked, bent, dirty; dated dastardly. **4** *you bad girl!* **naughty**, badly behaved, disobedient, wayward, wilful, self-willed, defiant, unruly, insubordinate, undisciplined. **5** *bad news* **unpleasant**,

b

disagreeable, unwelcome; unfortunate, unlucky, unfavourable; terrible, dreadful, awful, grim, distressing. **6** *a bad time to arrive* **inauspicious**, unfavourable, inopportune, unpropitious, unfortunate, disadvantageous, adverse, inappropriate, unsuitable, untoward. **7** *a bad accident* **severe**, serious, grave, critical, acute; formal grievous. **8** *the meat's bad* **rotten**, off, decayed, decomposed, decomposing, putrid, putrefied, mouldy, mouldering; sour, rancid, rank, unfit for human consumption; addled. **9** *if you still feel bad, stay in bed.* See **ill** (sense 1 of the adjective). **10** *a bad knee* **injured**, wounded, diseased, sore; Brit. informal gammy, knackered; Austral./NZ informal crook. **11** *I felt bad about leaving them* **guilty**, conscience-stricken, remorseful, guilt-ridden, ashamed, contrite, sorry, regretful, shamefaced, uncomfortable. **12** *a bad cheque* **invalid**, worthless; counterfeit, fake, false, bogus, fraudulent; informal phoney, dud. **13** *bad language* **offensive**, vulgar, crude, foul, obscene, rude, coarse, smutty, dirty, filthy, indecent, indecorous; blasphemous, profane.
– OPPOSITES good, beneficial, virtuous, well behaved, minor, slight, fresh, unrepentant.

badge n. **1** *a name badge* pin, brooch; N. Amer. button. **2** *a badge of success* **sign**, symbol, indication, signal, mark; hallmark, trademark.

badger v. **pester**, harass, bother, plague, torment, hound, nag, chivvy, harry, keep on at, go on at; informal hassle, bug.

badinage n. **banter**, repartee, witty conversation, raillery, wordplay, cut and thrust; witticisms, bons mots, ripostes, sallies, quips; N. Amer. informal josh.

badly adv. **1** *the job had been very badly done* **poorly**, incompetently, ineptly, inexpertly, inefficiently, imperfectly, deficiently, defectively, unsatisfactorily, inadequately, incorrectly, faultily, shoddily, amateurishly, carelessly, negligently; informal crummily, pitifully, woefully. **2** *try not to think badly of me* **unfavourably**, ill, critically, disapprovingly. **3** *stop behaving badly* **naughtily**, disobediently, wilfully, reprehensibly, mischievously. **4** *he had been badly treated* **cruelly**, wickedly, unkindly, harshly, shamefully; unfairly, unjustly, wrongly, improperly. **5** *it turned out badly* **unsuccessfully**, unfavourably, adversely, unfortunately, unhappily, unluckily. **6** *some of the victims are badly hurt* **severely**, seriously, gravely, acutely, critically; formal grievously. **7** *she badly needs help* **desperately**, sorely, intensely, seriously, very much, greatly, exceedingly.
– OPPOSITES well, slightly.

bad-tempered adj. **irritable**, irascible, tetchy, testy, grumpy, grouchy, crotchety, in a (bad) mood, cantankerous, curmudgeonly, ill-tempered, ill-humoured, peevish, having got out of bed on the wrong side, cross, as cross as two sticks, fractious, pettish, crabby; informal snappish, on a short fuse; Brit. informal

shirty, stroppy, ratty; N. Amer. informal cranky, ornery; Austral./NZ informal snaky; informal dated miffy.
– OPPOSITES good-humoured, affable.

baffle v. **perplex**, puzzle, bewilder, mystify, bemuse, confuse, confound, nonplus; informal flummox, faze, stump, beat, fox, be all Greek to, floor; N. Amer. informal discombobulate, buffalo.
– OPPOSITES enlighten.

baffling adj. **puzzling, bewildering**, perplexing, mystifying, bemusing, confusing, unclear; inexplicable, incomprehensible, impenetrable, cryptic, opaque.
– OPPOSITES clear, comprehensible.

bag n. **1** *I dug around in my bag for my lipstick* **handbag**, shoulder bag, clutch bag, evening bag, pochette; N. Amer. pocketbook, purse; historical reticule, scrip. **2** *she began to unpack her bags* **suitcase**, case, valise, portmanteau, holdall, grip, overnighter; backpack, rucksack, knapsack, haversack, kitbag, duffel bag; satchel; (**bags**) luggage, baggage.
▸v. **1** *locals bagged the most fish* **catch**, land, capture, trap, snare, ensnare; kill, shoot. **2** *he bagged seven medals* **get**, secure, obtain, acquire, pick up; win, achieve, attain; commandeer, grab, appropriate, take; informal get one's hands on, land, net.

baggage n. **luggage**, suitcases, cases, bags.

baggy adj. **loose-fitting**, loose, roomy, generously cut, full, ample, voluminous, billowing; oversized, shapeless, ill-fitting, tent-like, sack-like.
– OPPOSITES tight.

bail n. *he was released on bail* **surety**, security, assurance, indemnity, indemnification; bond, guarantee, pledge; old use gage.
☐ **bail someone/something out** rescue, save, relieve; finance, help (out), assist, aid; informal save someone's bacon/neck/skin.

bait n. **1** *the fish let go of the bait* **lure**, worm, fly, troll, jig, plug. **2** *was she the bait to lure him into a trap?* **enticement**, lure, decoy, snare, trap, siren, carrot, attraction, draw, magnet, incentive, temptation, inducement; informal come-on.
▸v. *he was baited at school* **taunt**, tease, goad, pick on, torment, persecute, plague, harry, harass, hound; informal needle; Brit. informal wind up, nark.

bake v. **1** *bake the fish for 15–20 minutes* **cook**, oven-bake, roast, dry-roast, pot-roast; rare oven. **2** *the earth was baked by the sun* **scorch**, burn, sear, parch, dry (up), desiccate; N. Amer. broil.

balance n. **1** *I tripped and lost my balance* **stability**, equilibrium, steadiness, footing. **2** *political balance in broadcasting* **fairness**, justice, impartiality, egalitarianism, even-handedness; parity, equity, equilibrium, equipoise, evenness, symmetry, correspondence, uniformity, equality, equivalence, comparability. **3** *this stylistic development provides a balance to the rest of the work* **counterbalance**, counterweight,

stabilizer, compensation. **4** *we need to maintain the proper balance of nutrients in the soil* **proportion(s)**, ratio, combination, mix, mixture; interaction, relationship. **5** *the balance of the rent* **remainder**, outstanding amount, rest, residue, difference, remaining part.
– OPPOSITES instability.
▶v. **1** *she balanced the book on her head* **steady**, stabilize, poise, level. **2** *he balanced his radical remarks with more familiar declarations* **counterbalance**, balance out, offset, even out/up, counteract, compensate for, make up for. **3** *she manages to balance work and family life* **combine**, mix, offset, even out/up; juggle. **4** *their income and expenditure do not balance* **correspond**, agree, tally, match up, concur, coincide, be in agreement, be consistent, equate, be equal. **5** *you need to balance cost against benefit* **weigh**, weigh up, compare, evaluate, consider, assess, appraise, judge.
□ **in the balance** uncertain, undetermined, unsettled, unresolved, unsure, pending, in limbo, up in the air, at a turning point, critical, at a critical stage, at a crisis.
on balance overall, all in all, all things considered, taking everything into consideration/account, by and large, on average.

balanced adj. **1** *a balanced view* **fair**, equitable, just, unbiased, unprejudiced, objective, impartial, dispassionate. **2** *a balanced diet* **mixed**, varied; healthy, sensible. **3** *a balanced individual* **level-headed**, well balanced, well adjusted, mature, stable, sensible, practical, realistic, with both feet on the ground, pragmatic, reasonable, rational, sane, even-tempered, commonsensical; informal together.
– OPPOSITES partial, unhealthy, neurotic.

balcony n. **1** *the balcony of the villa* veranda, loggia, terrace, patio. **2** *the applause from the balcony* **gallery**, upper circle; informal the gods.

bald adj. **1** *a bald head* **hairless**, smooth, shaven, depilated; bald-headed. **2** *a bald patch on the front tyre* **bare**, worn, smooth. **3** *a bald statement* **plain**, simple, unadorned, unvarnished, unembellished, undisguised, unveiled, stark, severe, austere, brutal, harsh; blunt, direct, forthright, plain-spoken, straight, straightforward, candid, honest, truthful, realistic, frank, outspoken; informal upfront.
– OPPOSITES hairy, vague.

balderdash n. See **nonsense** (sense 1).

baldness n. **hair loss**, hairlessness; Medicine alopecia.

bale[1] n. *a bale of cotton* **bundle**, truss, bunch, pack, package, parcel.

bale[2] v.
□ **bale out** See **bail**.

baleful adj. **menacing**, threatening, unfriendly, hostile, antagonistic, evil, evil-intentioned, vindictive, malevolent, malicious, malignant, malign, sinister; harmful, injurious, dangerous, noxious, pernicious, deadly, venomous, poisonous; literary malefic, maleficent.
– OPPOSITES benevolent, friendly.

balk v. **1** *I balk at paying that much* **be unwilling to**, draw the line at, jib at, be reluctant to, hesitate over; eschew, resist, scruple to, refuse to, take exception to; draw back from, flinch from, shrink from, recoil from, demur from, not like to, hate to. **2** *they were balked by traffic* **impede**, obstruct, thwart, hinder, prevent, check, stop, curb, halt, bar, block, forestall, frustrate.
– OPPOSITES accept, assist.

ball[1] n. **1** *a ball of dough | a cricket ball* **sphere**, globe, orb, globule, spherule, spheroid, ovoid. **2** *a musket ball* **bullet**, pellet, slug, projectile.

ball[2] n. *a fancy-dress ball* **dance**, dinner dance, masked ball, masquerade; N. Amer. hoedown, prom; informal hop, disco, bop.

ballad n. **song**, folk song, shanty, ditty, canzone; poem, tale, saga.

balloon n. hot-air balloon, barrage balloon; airship, dirigible, Zeppelin; envelope, gasbag; informal blimp.
▶v. **1** *her long skirt ballooned in the wind* **swell (out)**, puff out/up, bulge (out), bag, belly (out), fill (out), billow (out). **2** *the company's debt has ballooned* **increase rapidly**, soar, rocket, shoot up, escalate, mount, surge, spiral; informal go through the roof, skyrocket.

ballot n. **vote**, poll, election, referendum, plebiscite, show of hands.

ballyhoo n. informal **publicity**, advertising, promotion, marketing, propaganda, push, puffery, build-up, boosting; fuss, excitement; informal hype, spiel, hoo-ha, hullabaloo, splash.

balm n. **1** *a skin balm* **ointment**, lotion, cream, salve, liniment, embrocation, rub, gel, emollient, unguent, balsam, moisturizer; dated pomade; technical demulcent, humectant; old use unction. **2** *balm for troubled spirits* **relief**, comfort, ease, succour, consolation, cheer, solace; literary easement.
– OPPOSITES astringent, misery.

balmy adj. **mild**, gentle, temperate, summery, calm, tranquil, clement, fine, pleasant, benign, soothing, soft.
– OPPOSITES harsh, wintry.

bamboozle v. informal See **trick** (verb).

ban v. **1** *smoking was banned* **prohibit**, forbid, veto, proscribe, disallow, outlaw, make illegal, embargo, bar, debar, block, stop, suppress, interdict; Law enjoin, restrain. **2** *Gary was banned from the playground* **exclude**, banish, expel, eject, evict, drive out, force out, oust, remove, get rid of; informal boot out, kick out; Brit. informal turf out.
– OPPOSITES permit, admit.
▶n. **1** *a ban on smoking* **prohibition**, veto, proscription, embargo, bar, suppression, stoppage, interdict, interdiction, moratorium, injunction. **2** *a ban from international football* **exclusion**, banishment, expulsion, ejection, eviction, removal.
– OPPOSITES permission, admission.

b

banal adj. **trite**, hackneyed, clichéd, platitudinous, vapid, commonplace, ordinary, common, stock, conventional, stereotyped, overused, overdone, overworked, stale, worn out, time-worn, tired, threadbare, hoary, hack, unimaginative, unoriginal, uninteresting, dull; informal old hat, corny, played out; N. Amer. informal cornball, dime-store.
– OPPOSITES original.

banality n. **1** *the banality of most sitcoms* **triteness**, vapidity, staleness, unimaginativeness, lack of originality, prosaicness, dullness; informal corniness. **2** *they exchanged banalities* **platitude**, cliché, truism, commonplace, old chestnut, bromide.
– OPPOSITES originality, epigram, witticism.

band¹ n. **1** *a band round her waist* **belt**, sash, girdle, strap, tape, ring, hoop, loop, circlet, circle, cord, tie, string, thong, ribbon, fillet, strip; literary cincture. **2** *the green band round his pullover* **stripe**, strip, streak, line, bar, belt, swathe; technical stria, striation.

band² n. **1** *a band of robbers* **group**, gang, mob, pack, troop, troupe, company, party, crew, body, working party, posse; team, side, line-up; association, society, club, circle, fellowship, partnership, guild, lodge, order, fraternity, confraternity, sodality, brotherhood, sisterhood, sorority, union, alliance, affiliation, institution, league, federation, clique, set, coterie; informal bunch. **2** *the band played on* **(musical) group**, pop group, ensemble, orchestra; informal combo.
▸ v. *local people banded together* **join (up)**, team up, join forces, pool resources, club together, get together; amalgamate, unite, form an alliance, form an association, affiliate, federate.
– OPPOSITES split up.

bandage n. *she had a bandage on her foot* **dressing**, covering, gauze, compress, plaster, tourniquet; trademark Elastoplast, Band-Aid.
▸ v. *she bandaged my knee* **bind**, bind up, dress, cover, wrap, swaddle, strap (up).

bandit n. *they were robbed by bandits* **robber**, thief, raider, mugger; freebooter, outlaw, hijacker, looter, marauder, gangster; dated desperado; literary brigand; historical rustler, highwayman, footpad, reaver; Scottish historical mosstrooper.

bandy¹ adj. *bandy legs* **bowed**, curved, bent; bow-legged, bandy-legged.
– OPPOSITES straight.

bandy² v. **1** *lots of figures were bandied about* **spread (about/around)**, put about, toss about, discuss, rumour, mention, repeat; literary bruit about/abroad. **2** *I'm not going to bandy words with you* **exchange**, swap, trade.

bane n. **scourge**, plague, curse, blight, pest, nuisance, headache, nightmare, trial, hardship, cross to bear, burden, thorn in one's flesh/side, bitter pill, affliction, trouble, misery, woe, tribulation, misfortune; informal pain.

bang n. **1** *the door slammed with a bang* **thud**, thump, bump, crack, crash, smack, boom, clang, clap, knock, tap, clunk, clonk; stamp, stomp, clump, clomp; report, explosion, detonation; informal wham, whump, whomp. **2** *a nasty bang on the head* **blow**, knock, thump, bump, hit, smack, crack; informal bash, whack, thwack.
▸ v. **1** *he banged the table with his fist* **hit**, strike, beat, thump, hammer, knock, rap, pound, thud, punch, bump, smack, crack, slap, slam, welt, cuff, pummel, buffet; informal bash, whack, thwack, clobber, clout, clip, wallop, belt, biff, bop, sock, lam, whomp; Brit. informal slosh; N. Amer. informal boff, bust, slug, whale. **2** *fireworks banged in the air* **go bang**, thud, thump, boom, clap, pound, crack, crash, explode, detonate, burst, blow up.
▸ adv. informal **1** *bang in the middle of town | bang on time* **precisely**, exactly, right, directly, immediately, squarely, dead; promptly, prompt, dead on, on the stroke of ——, on the dot of ——; sharp, on the dot; informal smack, slap, slap bang, plumb; N. Amer. informal on the button, on the nose, smack dab, spang. **2** *bang up to date* **completely**, absolutely, totally, entirely, wholly, fully, thoroughly, in all respects, utterly, perfectly, quite, altogether, one hundred per cent.

bangle n. **bracelet**, wristlet, anklet, armlet.

banish v. **1** *he was banished for his crime* **exile**, expel, deport, eject, expatriate, extradite, repatriate, transport; cast out, oust, evict, throw out, exclude, shut out, ban. **2** *he tried to banish his fear* **dispel**, dismiss, disperse, scatter, dissipate, drive away, chase away, shut out, quell, allay.
– OPPOSITES admit, engender.

banister n. **handrail**, railing, rail; baluster; balustrade.

bank¹ n. **1** *the banks of Lake Michigan* **edge**, side, embankment, levee, border, verge, boundary, margin, rim, fringe; literary marge, bourn, skirt. **2** *a grassy bank* **slope**, rise, incline, gradient, ramp; mound, ridge, hillock, hummock, knoll; bar, reef, shoal, shelf; accumulation, pile, heap, mass, drift. **3** *a bank of switches* **array**, row, line, tier, group, series.
▸ v. **1** *they banked up the earth* **pile (up)**, heap (up), stack (up); accumulate, amass, assemble, put together. **2** *the aircraft banked* **tilt**, lean, tip, slant, incline, angle, slope, list, camber, pitch, dip, cant.

> **WORD LINKS**
> **riparian, riverine** relating to or found on a riverbank

bank² n. **1** *money in the bank* **financial institution**, merchant bank, savings bank, finance company, finance house; Brit. building society; N. Amer. savings and loan (association), thrift. **2** *a blood bank* **store**, reserve, accumulation, stock, stockpile, supply, pool, fund, cache, hoard, deposit; storehouse, reservoir, repository, depository, archive.
▸ v. *I banked the money* **deposit**, pay in.

b

◻ **bank on** rely on, depend on, count on, bargain on, plan on, reckon on, calculate on; anticipate, expect; be confident of, be sure of, pin one's hopes/faith on; N. Amer. informal figure on.

banknote n. **note**; N. Amer. **bill**; US informal **greenback**; US & historical **Treasury note**; (**banknotes**) paper money.

bankrupt adj. **1** *the company was declared bankrupt* **insolvent**, failed, ruined, in debt, owing money, in the red, in arrears; Brit. in administration, in receivership; informal **bust**, belly up, gone to the wall, broke, flat broke; informal dated **smashed**; Brit. informal **skint**, stony broke, in Queer Street; Brit. informal dated in Carey Street. **2** *this government is bankrupt of ideas* **bereft**, devoid, empty, destitute; completely lacking, without, in need of, wanting; informal **minus**, sans.
– OPPOSITES solvent.
▶ v. *the strike nearly bankrupted the union* **ruin**, impoverish, bring someone to their knees, wipe out, break, pauperize; rare **beggar**.

bankruptcy n. *many companies were facing bankruptcy* **insolvency**, liquidation, failure, (financial) ruin; Brit. administration, receivership.
– OPPOSITES solvency.

banner n. **1** *students waved banners* **placard**, sign, poster, notice. **2** *banners fluttered above the troops* **flag**, standard, ensign, colour(s), pennant, banderole, guidon; Brit. pendant; Nautical burgee.

banquet n. **feast**, dinner; informal **spread**, blowout; Brit. informal **nosh-up**, slap-up meal; Brit. informal dated **tuck-in**.
– OPPOSITES snack.

banter n. *a brief exchange of harmless banter* **repartee**, conversation, raillery, wordplay, cut and thrust, badinage; N. Amer. informal **josh**.
▶ v. *sightseers were bantering with the guards* **joke**, jest, quip; informal **josh**, wisecrack.

baptism n. **1** *the baptism ceremony* **christening**, naming; rare **lustration**. **2** *his baptism as a politician* **initiation**, debut, introduction, inauguration, launch, rite of passage.

baptize v. **1** *he was baptized as a baby* **christen**; rare **lustrate**. **2** *they were baptized into the church* **admit**, initiate, enrol, recruit, convert. **3** *he was baptized Enoch* **name**, give the name, call, dub; formal **denominate**.

bar n. **1** *an iron bar* **rod**, pole, stick, batten, shaft, rail, paling, spar, strut, crosspiece, beam. **2** *a bar of chocolate* **block**, slab, cake, tablet, brick, loaf, wedge, ingot. **3** *your drinks are on the bar* **counter**, table, buffet, stand. **4** *she had a drink in a bar* **hostelry**, tavern, inn, taproom; Brit. pub, public house; informal **watering hole**; Brit. informal **local**, boozer; dated **alehouse**; N. Amer. historical **saloon**. **5** *a bar to promotion* **obstacle**, impediment, hindrance, obstruction, block, hurdle, barrier, stumbling block. **6** Brit. *members of the Bar* **barristers**, advocates, counsel. **7** *the bar across the river mouth* **sandbank**, shoal, shallow, reef.

– OPPOSITES aid.
▶ v. **1** *they have barred the door* **bolt**, lock, fasten, secure, block, barricade, obstruct. **2** *I was barred from entering* **prohibit**, debar, preclude, forbid, ban, interdict, inhibit; exclude, keep out; obstruct, hinder, block; Law **enjoin**.
– OPPOSITES open, admit.
▶ prep. *everyone bar me.* See **except** (preposition).

barb n. **1** *the hook has a nasty barb* **spike**, prong, spur, thorn, needle, prickle, spine, quill. **2** *the barbs from his critics* **insult**, sneer, jibe, cutting remark, shaft, slight, brickbat, slur, jeer, taunt; (**barbs**) abuse, disparagement, scoffing, scorn, sarcasm, goading; informal **dig**, put-down.

barbarian n. **savage**, animal, brute, beast; ruffian, thug, lout, vandal, hoodlum, hooligan; informal **roughneck**; Brit. informal **yobbo**, yob, lager lout.
▶ adj. **savage**, uncivilized, barbaric, primitive, heathen, wild, brutish, Neanderthal.
– OPPOSITES civilized.

barbaric adj. **1** *barbaric crimes* **brutal**, barbarous, brutish, bestial, savage, vicious, wicked, cruel, ruthless, merciless, villainous, murderous, heinous, monstrous, vile, inhuman, infernal, dark, fiendish, diabolical. **2** *barbaric cultures* **savage**, barbarian, primitive, heathen, wild, brutish, Neanderthal.
– OPPOSITES civilized.

barbarity n. **1** *the barbarity of slavery* **brutality**, brutalism, cruelty, bestiality, barbarism, barbarousness, savagery, viciousness, wickedness, villainy, baseness, inhumanity. **2** *the barbarities of the last war* **atrocity**, act of brutality, act of savagery, crime, outrage, enormity.
– OPPOSITES benevolence.

barbarous adj. See **barbaric** (sense 1).

barbed adj. **hurtful**, wounding, cutting, stinging, mean, spiteful, nasty, cruel, vicious, unkind, snide, scathing, pointed, bitter, acid, caustic, sharp, vitriolic, venomous, poisonous, hostile, malicious, malevolent, vindictive; informal **bitchy**, catty.
– OPPOSITES kindly.

bard n. literary See **poet**.

bare adj. **1** *he was bare to the waist* **naked**, unclothed, undressed, uncovered, stripped, with nothing on, nude, in the nude, stark naked; informal **without a stitch on**, in one's birthday suit, in the raw, in the altogether, in the buff; Brit. informal **starkers**; Scottish informal in the scud; N. Amer. informal **buck naked**. **2** *a bare room* **empty**, unfurnished, cleared; stark, austere, spartan, unadorned, unembellished, unornamented, plain. **3** *a cupboard bare of food* **empty**, devoid, bereft; without, lacking, wanting, free from. **4** *a bare landscape* **barren**, bleak, exposed, desolate, stark, arid, desert, lunar; treeless, deforested. **5** *the bare facts* **basic**, essential, fundamental, plain, straightforward, simple, pure, stark, bald, cold, hard, brutal, harsh. **6** *a bare minimum*

mere, no more than, simple; slim, slight, slender, paltry, minimum.
– OPPOSITES clothed, furnished, embellished, lush.
▸ v. *he bared his arm* **uncover**, strip, lay bare, undress, unclothe, denude, expose.
– OPPOSITES cover.

barefaced adj. **flagrant**, blatant, glaring, obvious, undisguised, unconcealed, naked; shameless, unabashed, unashamed, impudent, audacious, unblushing, brazen, brass-necked.

barely adv. **hardly**, scarcely, just, only just, narrowly, by the skin of one's teeth, by a hair's breadth; almost not; informal by a whisker.
– OPPOSITES easily.

bargain n. **1** *I'll make a bargain with you* **agreement**, arrangement, understanding, deal; contract, pact, compact; pledge, promise. **2** *this binder is a bargain at £1.98* **(good) value for money**, good buy; informal snip, steal, giveaway.
– OPPOSITES rip-off.
▸ v. *they bargained over the contract* **haggle**, negotiate, discuss terms, hold talks, deal, barter, dicker; formal treat.
□ **bargain for/on** expect, anticipate, be prepared for, allow for, plan for, reckon with, take into account/consideration, contemplate, imagine, envisage, foresee, predict; count on, rely on, depend on, bank on, plan on, reckon on; N. Amer. informal figure on.
into the bargain also, as well, in addition, additionally, besides, on top of (that), over and above that, to boot, for good measure; N. Amer. in the bargain.

barge n. lighter, canal boat; Brit. narrowboat, wherry; N. Amer. scow.
▸ v. *he barged us out of the way* **push**, shove, force, elbow, shoulder, jostle, bulldoze, muscle.
□ **barge in** burst in, break in, butt in, cut in, interrupt, intrude, encroach; gatecrash; informal horn in.

bark[1] n. *the bark of a dog* **woof**, yap, yelp, bay.
▸ v. **1** *the dog barked* **woof**, yap, yelp, bay. **2** *'Okay, outside!' he barked* **shout**, snap, cry, yell, roar, bellow, bawl, thunder; informal holler.
– OPPOSITES whisper.

bark[2] n. *the bark of a tree* **rind**, skin, peel, covering; integument; cork; technical cortex.
▸ v. *he barked his shin* **scrape**, graze, scratch, abrade, scuff, rasp, skin.

> **WORD LINKS**
> **corticate** relating to bark
> **decorticate** remove the bark from

barmy adj. Brit. informal See **mad**.

barn n. **outbuilding**, shed, outhouse, shelter; stable, stall; Brit. byre; old use grange, garner.

baron n. **1** *he was created a baron* **lord**, noble, nobleman, aristocrat, peer. **2** *a press baron* **magnate**, tycoon, mogul, captain of industry, nabob, mandarin.

baroque adj. **1** *the baroque exuberance of his printed silk shirts* **ornate**, fancy, over-elaborate, extravagant, rococo, fussy, busy, ostentatious, showy. **2** *baroque prose* **flowery**, florid, flamboyant, high-flown, high-sounding, magniloquent, grandiloquent, orotund, overblown, convoluted, pleonastic; informal highfalutin, purple; rare fustian.
– OPPOSITES plain.

barrack v. Brit. & Austral./NZ **jeer**, heckle, shout at/down; interrupt, boo, hiss.
– OPPOSITES applaud.

barracks plural n. **garrison**, camp, encampment, depot, billet, quarters, fort, cantonment.

barrage n. **1** *an artillery barrage* **bombardment**, cannonade; gunfire, shelling; salvo, volley, fusillade; historical broadside. **2** *a barrage of criticism* **deluge**, stream, storm, torrent, onslaught, flood, spate, tide, avalanche, hail, blaze; abundance, mass, profusion. **3** *a barrage across the river* **dam**, barrier, weir, dyke, embankment, wall.

barrel n. **cask**, keg, butt, vat, tun, drum, hogshead, kilderkin, pin, pipe; historical firkin.

> **WORD LINKS**
> **cooper** a maker of barrels
> **spigot, spile** a small plug for the vent of a barrel
> **stave** a plank from which barrels are made

barren adj. **1** *barren land* **unproductive**, infertile, unfruitful, sterile, arid, desert, empty, bleak, lifeless. **2** old use *a barren woman* **infertile**, sterile, childless; technical infecund. **3** *a barren exchange of courtesies* **pointless**, futile, worthless, profitless, valueless, unrewarding, purposeless, useless, vain, aimless, hollow, empty.
– OPPOSITES fertile.

barricade n. *a barricade across the street* **barrier**, roadblock, blockade; obstacle, obstruction.
▸ v. *they barricaded the building* **seal (up)**, close up, block off, shut off/up; defend, protect, fortify, occupy.

barrier n. **1** *the barrier across the entrance* **fence**, railing, barricade, hurdle, bar, blockade, roadblock. **2** *a barrier to international trade* **obstacle**, obstruction, hurdle, stumbling block, bar, block, impediment, hindrance, curb.

barring prep. **except for**, with the exception of, excepting, if there is/are no, bar, discounting, short of, apart from, but for, other than, aside from, excluding, omitting, leaving out, save for, saving; informal outside of.

barrister n. **counsel**, Queen's Counsel, QC, lawyer; Scottish advocate; N. Amer. attorney, counselor(-at-law); informal brief; **(barristers)** Brit. the Bar.

barter v. **1** *they bartered grain for salt* **trade**, swap, exchange, sell. **2** *you can barter for souvenirs* **haggle**, bargain, negotiate, discuss terms, deal, dicker; formal treat.
▸ n. *an economy based on barter* **trading**, trade,

b

exchange, business, commerce, buying and selling, dealing.

base[1] n. **1** *the base of the tower* **foundation**, bottom, foot, support, stand, pedestal, plinth. **2** *the system uses existing technology as its base* **basis**, foundation, bedrock, starting point, source, origin, root(s), core, key component, heart, backbone. **3** *the troops returned to their base* **headquarters**, camp, site, station, settlement, post, centre, starting point.
– OPPOSITES top.
▸v. **1** *he based his idea on a movie* **found**, build, construct, form, ground, root; (**be based on**) derive from, spring from, stem from, originate in, have its origin in, issue from. **2** *the company was based in London* **locate**, situate, position, install, station, site, establish, garrison.

base[2] adj. *base motives* **sordid**, ignoble, low, low-minded, mean, immoral, improper, unseemly, unscrupulous, unprincipled, dishonest, dishonourable, shameful, bad, wrong, evil, wicked, iniquitous, sinful.
– OPPOSITES noble.

baseless adj. *baseless accusations* **groundless**, unfounded, ill-founded, without foundation; unsubstantiated, unproven, unsupported, uncorroborated, unconfirmed, unverified, unattested; unjustified, unwarranted; speculative, conjectural; unsound, unreliable, spurious, specious, trumped up, fabricated, untrue.
– OPPOSITES valid.

basement n. **cellar**, vault, crypt, undercroft; Brit. lower ground floor; Scottish dunny.

bash informal v. **1** *she bashed him with her stick* **strike**, hit, beat, thump, slap, smack, clip, bang, knock, batter, pound, pummel; informal wallop, clout, belt, whack, thwack, clobber, bop, biff, sock; old use smite. **2** *they bashed into one another* **crash**, run, bang, smash, slam, cannon, knock, bump; collide with, hit, meet head-on.
▸n. **1** *a bash on the head* **blow**, rap, hit, knock, bang, slap, crack, thump, tap, clip; informal wallop, clout, belt, whack, thwack, bop, biff, sock. **2** *Harry's birthday bash.* See **party** (sense 1 of the noun). **3** Brit. *I'll have a bash at it.* See **attempt**.

bashful adj. **shy**, reserved, diffident, inhibited, retiring, reticent, reluctant, shrinking; hesitant, timid, apprehensive, nervous, wary.
– OPPOSITES bold, confident.

basic adj. **1** *basic human rights* **fundamental**, essential, primary, principal, cardinal, elementary, elemental, quintessential, intrinsic, central, pivotal, critical, key, focal; vital, necessary, indispensable. **2** *basic cooking facilities* **plain**, simple, unsophisticated, straightforward, adequate; unadorned, undecorated, unornamented, without frills; spartan, stark, severe, austere, limited, meagre, rudimentary, patchy, sketchy, minimal; unfussy, homely, homespun; rough (and ready), crude,

makeshift; informal bog-standard.
– OPPOSITES secondary, unimportant, elaborate.

basically adv. **fundamentally**, essentially, in essence; firstly, first of all, first and foremost, primarily; at heart, at bottom, au fond; principally, chiefly, above all, most of all, mostly, mainly, on the whole, by and large, substantially; intrinsically, inherently; informal at the end of the day, when all is said and done.

basics plural n. **fundamentals**, essentials, rudiments, (first) principles, foundations, preliminaries, groundwork; essence, basis, core; informal nitty-gritty, brass tacks, nuts and bolts, ABC.

basin n. **1** *she poured water into the basin* **bowl**, dish, pan. **2** *a basin among low hills* **valley**, hollow, dip, depression.

basis n. **1** *the basis of his method* **foundation**, support, base; reasoning, rationale, defence; reason, grounds, justification, motivation. **2** *the basis of discussion* **starting point**, base, point of departure, beginning, premise, fundamental point/principle, principal constituent, main ingredient, cornerstone, core, heart, thrust, essence, kernel, nub. **3** *on a part-time basis* **footing**, condition, status, position; arrangement, system, method.

bask v. **1** *I basked in the sun* **laze**, lie, lounge, relax, sprawl, loll; sunbathe, sun oneself. **2** *she's basking in all the glory* **revel**, delight, luxuriate, wallow, take pleasure, rejoice, glory, indulge oneself; enjoy, relish, savour, lap up.

basket n. **wickerwork box**, hamper, creel, pannier, punnet, trug.

bass adj. **low**, deep, low-pitched, resonant, sonorous, rumbling, booming, resounding; baritone.
– OPPOSITES high.

bastard n. **1** old use *he had fathered a bastard* **illegitimate child**; dated love child; Brit. dated by-blow; old use natural child/son/daughter. **2** informal *he's a real bastard.* See **scoundrel**.
▸adj. **1** old use *a bastard child* **illegitimate**, born out of wedlock; old use natural. **2** *a bastard Darwinism* **adulterated**, alloyed, impure, inferior; hybrid, mongrel, patchwork.

bastardize v. **adulterate**, corrupt, contaminate, weaken, dilute, taint, pollute, debase, distort.

bastion n. **1** *the town wall and bastions* **projection**, outwork, breastwork, barbican; Architecture bartizan. **2** *a bastion of respectability* **stronghold**, bulwark, defender, support, supporter, guard, protection, protector, defence, prop, mainstay.

batch n. **group**, quantity, lot, bunch, mass, cluster, raft, set, collection, bundle, pack; consignment, shipment.

bath n. **1** *he lay soaking in the bath* **bathtub**, tub, hot tub, whirlpool, sauna, steam bath, Turkish bath; trademark jacuzzi. **2** *she had a quick bath* **wash**, soak, dip; shower.

b

bathe v. **1** *she bathed and dressed* **bath**, wash, soak, shower. **2** *I bathed in the local swimming pool* **swim**, go swimming, take a dip. **3** *they bathed his wounds* **clean**, wash, rinse, wet, soak, immerse. **4** *the room was bathed in light* **suffuse**, permeate, pervade, envelop, flood, cover, wash, fill.
▸ n. *we had a bathe* **swim**, dip, paddle.

bathing costume Brit. n. **swimsuit**, bathing suit; swimming trunks, bikini; swimwear; Brit. swimming costume; informal cossie; Austral./NZ informal bathers.

bathos n. **anticlimax**, let-down, disappointment, disillusionment; absurdity; informal comedown.

baton n. **1** *the conductor's baton* **stick**, rod, staff, wand. **2** *police batons* **truncheon**, club, cudgel, bludgeon, stick, mace, shillelagh; N. Amer. nightstick, blackjack; Brit. informal cosh.

battalion n. **1** *an infantry battalion* regiment, brigade, force, division, squadron, squad, company, section, detachment, contingent, legion, corps, cohort. **2** *a battalion of supporters*. See **crowd** (sense 1 of the noun).

batten n. *a timber batten* **bar**, bolt, rail, shaft; board, strip.
▸ v. *Stephen was battening down the shutters* **fasten**, fix, secure, clamp, lash, make fast, nail, seal.

batter v. **pummel**, pound, hit repeatedly, rain blows on, buffet, belabour, thrash, beat up; informal knock about/around, beat the living daylights out of, lay into, lace into, do over, rough up.

battered adj. **damaged**, shabby, run down, worn out, falling to pieces, falling apart, dilapidated, rickety, ramshackle, crumbling, the worse for wear, on its last legs.

battery n. **1** *a flat battery* **cell**, accumulator. **2** *a gun battery* **emplacement**, artillery unit; cannonry, ordnance. **3** *a battery of equipment* **array**, set, bank, group, row, line, line-up, collection. **4** *a battery of tests* **series**, sequence, range, string, succession. **5** *assault and battery* **violence**, assault, mugging; Brit. grievous bodily harm, GBH, actual bodily harm, ABH.

battle n. **1** *he was killed in the battle* **fight**, armed conflict, clash, struggle, skirmish, engagement, fray, duel; war, campaign, crusade; fighting, warfare, combat, action, hostilities; informal scrap, dogfight, shoot-out. **2** *a legal battle* **conflict**, clash, contest, competition, struggle; disagreement, argument, altercation, dispute, controversy.
▸ v. **1** *conservation groups battled to save the house* **fight**, struggle, strive, work, campaign, lobby; war, feud. **2** *the company was battling lawsuits alleging copyright infringement* **contest**, combat, contend with, resist, withstand, stand up to, confront. **3** *Mark battled his way to the bar* **force**, push, elbow, shoulder, fight; struggle, labour.

battleaxe n. **1** *a severe blow from a battleaxe* **poleaxe**, axe, pike, halberd, tomahawk, war mattock. **2** informal *she's a real battleaxe*.

See **harridan**.

battle cry n. *the battle cry of the feminist movement* **slogan**, motto, watchword, catchphrase; mantra.

battlefield n. **battleground**, field of battle, field of operations, combat zone, theatre (of war), front.

battlement n. **castellation**, crenellation, parapet, rampart, wall.

batty adj. informal See **mad** (sense 1).

bauble n. **trinket**, knick-knack, ornament, frippery, gewgaw, gimcrack, bibelot; N. Amer. kickshaw; N. Amer. informal tchotchke.

baulk v. See **balk**.

bawdy adj. **ribald**, indecent, risqué, racy, rude, spicy, sexy, suggestive, titillating, naughty, improper, indelicate, indecorous, off colour, earthy, broad, locker-room, Rabelaisian; pornographic, obscene, vulgar, crude, coarse, gross, lewd, dirty, filthy, smutty, unseemly, salacious, prurient, lascivious, licentious, near the bone, near the knuckle; informal X-rated, blue, raunchy, nudge-nudge; euphemistic adult.
– OPPOSITES clean, innocent.

bawl v. **1** *'Come on!' he bawled* **shout**, yell, roar, bellow, screech, scream, shriek, howl, whoop, bark, trumpet, thunder; informal yammer, holler. **2** *the children continued to bawl* **cry**, sob, weep, shed tears, wail, whine, howl, squall, ululate; Scottish informal greet.
– OPPOSITES whisper.

bay¹ n. *ships were anchored in the bay* **cove**, inlet, indentation, gulf, bight, basin, fjord, arm; natural harbour, anchorage.

bay² n. *there was a bay let into the wall* **alcove**, recess, niche, nook, opening, hollow, cavity, inglenook; compartment.

bay³ v. *the hounds bayed* **howl**, bark, yelp, yap, cry, bellow, roar. **2** *the crowd bayed for an encore* **clamour**, shout, call, press, yell, scream, shriek, roar; demand, insist on.
□ **at bay** at a distance, away, off, at arm's length.

bayonet n. *a man armed with a bayonet* sword, knife, blade, spear, lance, pike, javelin; literary brand.
▸ v. *stragglers were bayoneted* **stab**, spear, knife, gore, spike, stick, impale, run through, transfix, gash, slash.

bazaar n. **1** *a Turkish bazaar* **market**, market place, souk, mart, exchange. **2** *the church bazaar* **fete**, fair, carnival; fund-raiser, charity event; Brit. jumble sale, bring-and-buy sale, car boot sale; N. Amer. tag sale.

be v. **1** *there was once a king* **exist**, have being, have existence; live, be alive, have life, breathe, draw breath, be extant. **2** *is there a cafe here?* **be present**, be around, be available, be near, be nearby, be at hand. **3** *the trial is tomorrow at half past one* **occur**, happen, take place, come about, arise, crop up, transpire, fall, materialize, ensue; literary come to pass, befall, betide. **4** *the bed is over there* **be situated**, be located, be found, be present, be set, be positioned, be placed, be installed. **5** *it has been like this for hours*

remain, stay, last, continue, survive, endure, persist, prevail; wait, linger, hold on, hang on; formal obtain. **6** *I'm at college* **attend**, go to, be present at, take part in; frequent, haunt, patronize.

beach n. *a sandy beach* **seaside**, seashore, shore, coast, coastline, coastal region, littoral, seaboard, foreshore, water's edge; sands, lido; dated plage; literary strand.

▶ v. **1** *they beached the boat* **land**, ground, strand, run aground, run ashore. **2** *65 dolphins have been beached on Cornish shores this year* **ground**, strand, maroon, wash up/ashore.

beachcomber n. **scavenger**, forager, collector; informal scrounger.

beached adj. **stranded**, grounded, aground, ashore, marooned, high and dry, stuck.

beacon n. **signal**, light, flare, fire, bonfire; lighthouse, light-tower.

bead n. **1** *a string of beads* **ball**, pellet, pill, globule, sphere, spheroid, oval, ovoid, orb, round; (**beads**) necklace, rosary, chaplet. **2** *beads of sweat* **droplet**, drop, blob, dot, dewdrop, teardrop.

beak n. **1** *a bird's beak* **bill**, nib, mandible; Scottish & N. English **neb**. **2** informal *he blew his beak loudly.* See **nose** (sense 1 of the noun).

beaker n. **cup**, tumbler, glass, mug, drinking vessel.

beam n. **1** *an oak beam* **joist**, lintel, rafter, purlin; spar, girder, balk, timber, plank; support, strut; scantling, transom, stringer. **2** *a beam of light coming from the window* **ray**, shaft, stream, streak, pencil, finger; flash, gleam, glow, glimmer, glint, flare. **3** *the beam on her face* **grin**, smile, happy expression.
– OPPOSITES frown.

▶ v. **1** *the signal is beamed out* **broadcast**, transmit, relay, send/put out, disseminate; direct, aim. **2** *the sun beamed down* **shine**, radiate, glare, gleam. **3** *he beamed broadly* **grin**, smile, smirk; informal be all smiles.
– OPPOSITES frown.

□ **off beam** informal mistaken, incorrect, inaccurate, wrong, erroneous, off target, out, on the wrong track, wide of the mark, awry.

bear¹ v. **1** *she was bearing a box of cookies* **carry**, bring, transport, move, convey, take, fetch, deliver; informal tote. **2** *the bag bore my name* **display**, exhibit, be marked with, show, carry, have. **3** *will it bear his weight?* **support**, carry, hold, prop up. **4** *they can't bear the cost alone* **sustain**, carry, support, shoulder, absorb, take on. **5** *she bore no grudge* **harbour**, foster, entertain, cherish, nurse, nurture, brood over. **6** *such a solution does not bear close scrutiny* **withstand**, stand up to, stand, put up with, take, cope with, handle, sustain, accept. **7** *I can't bear having him around* **endure**, tolerate, put up with, stand, abide, submit to, experience, undergo, go through, countenance, brave, weather, stomach, support; Scottish thole; informal hack, swallow; Brit. informal stick, wear, be doing with; formal brook; old use suffer. **8** *she bore*

a son **give birth to**, bring forth, deliver, be delivered of, have, produce, spawn; N. Amer. birth; informal drop; literary beget. **9** *a shrub that bears yellow berries* **produce**, yield, give forth, give, grow, provide, supply. **10** *bear left at the junction* **veer**, curve, swerve, fork, diverge, deviate, turn, bend.

□ **bear oneself** conduct oneself, carry oneself, acquit oneself, act, behave, perform; formal comport oneself.

bear down on advance on, close in on, move in on, converge on.

bear fruit yield results, get results, succeed, meet with success, be successful, be effective, be profitable, work; informal pay off, come off, do the trick, do the business.

bear something in mind take into account, take into consideration, remember, consider, be mindful, mind, mark, heed.

bear on be relevant to, appertain to, pertain to, relate to, have a bearing on, have relevance to, apply to, be pertinent to.

bear something out confirm, corroborate, substantiate, endorse, vindicate, give credence to, support, ratify, warrant, uphold, justify, prove, authenticate, verify.

bear up remain cheerful, grin and bear it; cope, manage, get by, muddle through; informal hack it.

bear with be patient with, show forbearance towards, make allowances for, tolerate, put up with, endure.

bear witness/testimony to testify to, be evidence of, be proof of, attest to, evidence, prove, vouch for; demonstrate, show, establish, indicate, reveal, bespeak.

bear² n.

┌─────────────────────────────┐
│ **WORD LINKS**   │
│ **ursine** relating to bears │
└─────────────────────────────┘

bearable adj. **tolerable**, endurable, supportable, sustainable.

beard n. *a black beard* **facial hair**, whiskers, stubble, five o'clock shadow, bristles; goatee, imperial, Vandyke.

▶ v. *I bearded him when he was on his own* **confront**, face, challenge, brave, come face to face with, meet head on; defy, oppose, stand up against, square up to, dare, throw down the gauntlet to.

bearded adj. **unshaven**, whiskered, whiskery, bewhiskered; stubbly, bristly.
– OPPOSITES clean-shaven.

bearer n. **1** *a lantern-bearer* **carrier**, porter. **2** *the bearer of bad news* **messenger**, agent, bringer, conveyor, carrier, emissary. **3** *the bearer of the documents* **holder**, possessor, owner.

bearing n. **1** *a man of military bearing* **posture**, stance, carriage, gait; Brit. deportment; formal comportment. **2** *a rather regal bearing* **demeanour**, manner, air, aspect, attitude, behaviour, mien, style. **3** *this has no bearing on the matter* **relevance**, pertinence, connection, appositeness, germaneness, importance, significance, application. **4** *a bearing of 015° direction*, orientation, course, trajectory,

b

heading, tack, path, line, run. **5** *he tormented her beyond bearing* **endurance**, tolerance, toleration. **6** *I lost my bearings* **orientation**, sense of direction; whereabouts, location, position.

beast n. **1** *the beasts of the forest* **animal**, creature, brute; N. Amer. informal critter. **2** *he is a cruel beast* **monster**, brute, savage, barbarian, animal, swine, pig, ogre, fiend, sadist, demon, devil.

beastly adj. Brit. informal **1** *politics is a beastly profession* **awful**, horrible, rotten, nasty, foul, objectionable, unpleasant, disagreeable, offensive, vile, hateful, detestable; informal terrible, God-awful. **2** *he was beastly to her* **unkind**, malicious, mean, nasty, unpleasant, unfriendly, spiteful, cruel, vicious, base, foul, malevolent, despicable, contemptible; informal horrid, rotten.
– OPPOSITES pleasant, kind.

beat v. **1** *they were beaten with truncheons* **hit**, strike, batter, thump, bang, hammer, punch, knock, thrash, pound, pummel, slap, rain blows on; assault, attack, abuse; cudgel, club, birch; informal wallop, belt, bash, whack, thwack, clout, clobber, slug, tan, biff, bop, sock, deck, plug, beat the living daylights out of, give someone a good hiding. **2** *the waves beat all along the shore* **break on/ against**, dash against; lash, strike, lap, wash; splash, ripple, roll; literary plash, lave. **3** *the metal is beaten into a die* **hammer**, forge, form, shape, mould, work, stamp, fashion, model. **4** *her heart was still beating* **pulsate**, pulse, palpitate, vibrate, throb; pump, pound, thump, thud, hammer, drum; pitter-patter, go pit-a-pat. **5** *the eagle beat its wings* **flap**, flutter, thresh, thrash, wave, vibrate, oscillate. **6** *beat the cream into the mixture* **whisk**, mix, blend, whip. **7** *she beat a path through the grass* **tread**, tramp, trample, wear, flatten, press down. **8** *the team they need to beat* **defeat**, conquer, win against, get the better of, vanquish, trounce, rout, overpower, overcome, subdue; informal lick, thrash, whip, wipe the floor with, clobber. **9** *he beat the record* **surpass**, exceed, better, improve on, go one better than, eclipse, transcend, top, trump, cap.
▸ n. **1** *the song has a good beat* **rhythm**, pulse, metre, time, measure, cadence; stress, accent. **2** *the beat of hooves* **pounding**, banging, thumping, thudding, booming, hammering, battering, crashing. **3** *the beat of her heart* **pulse**, pulsation, vibration, throb, palpitation, reverberation; pounding, thump, thud, hammering, drumming; pit-a-pat. **4** *a policeman on his beat* **circuit**, round, route, way, path.
▸ adj. informal *phew, I'm beat!* See **exhausted** (sense 1).
▫ **beat it** informal See **run** (sense 2 of the verb).
beat someone/something off repel, fight off, fend off, stave off, repulse, drive away/ back, force back, beat back, push back, put to flight.
beat someone up assault, attack, mug,

thrash; informal knock about/around, do over, work over, rough up, fill in, lay into, lace into, sail into, beat the living daylights out of, let someone have it; Brit. informal duff someone up; N. Amer. informal beat up on.

beatific adj. **1** *a beatific smile* **rapturous**, joyful, ecstatic, seraphic, blissful, serene, happy, beaming. **2** *a beatific vision* **blessed**, exalted, sublime, heavenly, holy, divine, celestial, paradisiacal, glorious.

beatify v. **canonize**, bless, sanctify, hallow, consecrate, make holy.

beatitude n. **blessedness**, benediction, grace; bliss, ecstasy, exaltation, supreme happiness, divine joy/rapture; saintliness, sainthood.

beau n. dated **1** *Sally and her beau* **boyfriend**, sweetheart, lover, darling, partner, significant other, escort, young man, admirer, suitor. **2** *an eighteenth-century beau* **dandy**, fop, man about town; informal dated swell; dated popinjay; old use coxcomb.

beautiful adj. **attractive**, pretty, handsome, good-looking, alluring, prepossessing, lovely, charming, delightful, appealing, engaging, winsome; ravishing, gorgeous, stunning, arresting, glamorous, bewitching, beguiling; graceful, elegant, exquisite, aesthetic, artistic, decorative, magnificent; Scottish & N. English bonny; informal tasty, divine, knockout, drop-dead gorgeous, fanciable; Brit. informal smashing; N. Amer. informal cute, foxy; Austral./NZ informal beaut, spunky; literary beauteous; old use comely, fair.
– OPPOSITES ugly.

beautify v. **adorn**, embellish, enhance, decorate, ornament, garnish, gild, smarten, prettify, enrich, glamorize, spruce up, deck (out), trick out, grace; informal get up, do up, do out, tart up.
– OPPOSITES spoil, uglify.

beauty n. **1** *the great beauty of the scenery | he was struck by her beauty* **attractiveness**, prettiness, good looks, comeliness, allure; loveliness, charm, appeal, heavenliness, winsomeness, grace, elegance, exquisiteness; splendour, magnificence, grandeur, impressiveness, decorativeness; gorgeousness, glamour; Scottish & N. English bonniness; literary beauteousness, pulchritude. **2** *she is a beauty* **beautiful woman**, belle, vision, Venus, goddess, beauty queen, English rose, picture; informal looker, good-looker, lovely, stunner, knockout, bombshell, dish, cracker, peach, eyeful, bit of all right; Brit. informal smasher. **3** *the beauty of this plan* **advantage**, attraction, strength, benefit, boon, blessing, good thing, strong point, virtue, merit, selling point.
– OPPOSITES ugliness, drawback.

> **WORD LINKS**
> **aesthetic** concerned with beauty or the appreciation of beauty

becalmed adj. **motionless**, still, at a standstill, at a halt, unmoving, stuck.

b

because conj. **since**, as, in view of the fact that, owing to the fact that, seeing that/as; informal on account of; literary for.
– OPPOSITES despite.
□ **because of** on account of, as a result of, as a consequence of, owing to, due to; thanks to, by/in virtue of; formal by reason of.

beckon v. 1 *the guard beckoned to Benny* **gesture**, signal, wave, gesticulate, motion. 2 *the countryside beckons you* **entice**, invite, tempt, coax, lure, charm, attract, draw, call.

become v. 1 *she became rich* **grow**, get, turn, come to be, get to be; literary wax. 2 *he became a tyrant* **turn into**, change into, be transformed into, be converted into. 3 *he became Foreign Secretary* **be appointed (as)**, be assigned as, be nominated as, be elected (as), be made. 4 *the dress becomes her* **suit**, flatter, look good on; set off, show to advantage; informal do something for. 5 *it ill becomes him to preach the gospel* **befit**, suit; formal behove.
□ **become of** happen to, be the fate of, be the lot of, overtake; literary befall, betide.

becoming adj. **flattering**, attractive, lovely, pretty, handsome; stylish, elegant, chic, tasteful; old use comely.

bed n. 1 *she got into bed* **couch**, cot, cradle, berth, billet; informal the sack, the hay; Brit. informal one's pit; Scottish informal one's kip. 2 *a flower bed* **patch**, plot, border, strip. 3 *built on a bed of stones* **base**, foundation, support, prop, substructure, substratum. 4 *a river bed* **bottom**, floor, ground.
▶ v. 1 *the tiles are bedded in mortar* **embed**, set, fix, insert, inlay, implant, bury, base, plant, settle. 2 *time to bed out the seedlings* **plant (out)**, transplant.
□ **go to bed** retire, call it a day; go to sleep, take a nap, get some sleep; informal hit the sack, hit the hay, turn in, snatch forty winks, get some shut-eye; Brit. informal get some kip; N. Amer. informal catch some Zs.

bedclothes plural n. **bedding**, sheets and blankets; bedlinen; bedcovers, covers.

bedding n. See **bedclothes**.

bedeck v. **decorate**, adorn, ornament, embellish, furnish, garnish, trim, deck, grace, enrich, dress up, trick out; swathe, wreathe, festoon; informal get up, do out; literary furbelow.

bedevil v. **afflict**, torment, beset, assail, beleaguer, plague, blight, rack, oppress, harry, curse, dog; harass, distress, trouble, worry, torture.

bedlam n. **uproar**, pandemonium, commotion, mayhem, confusion, disorder, chaos, anarchy, lawlessness; furore, upheaval, hubbub, hurly-burly, turmoil, riot, ruckus, rumpus, tumult; informal hullabaloo, ructions, snafu.
– OPPOSITES calm.

bedraggled adj. **dishevelled**, disordered, untidy, unkempt, tousled, disarranged, in a mess; N. Amer. informal mussed.
– OPPOSITES neat, clean, dry.

bedridden adj. **confined to bed**, immobilized; informal laid up, flat on one's back.

bedrock n. *this fact is the bedrock of our authority* **core**, basis, base, foundation, roots, heart, backbone, principle, essence, nitty-gritty; informal nuts and bolts.

bedspread n. **bedcover**, coverlet, quilt, throw-over, blanket; Brit. eiderdown; N. Amer. throw, spread, comforter; dated counterpane.

bee n.

WORD LINKS
apian relating to bees
apiary a place where bees are kept
drone a male bee which does no work but can fertilize a queen
queen a reproductive female bee
worker a neuter bee which performs the basic work of a colony
honeycomb a wax structure made by bees
royal jelly a substance produced by honeybee workers
varroa a serious parasite of the honeybee

beef informal n. 1 *there's plenty of beef on him* **muscle**, brawn, bulk; strength, power. 2 *his beef was about the cost* **complaint**, criticism, objection, cavil, quibble, grievance, grumble, grouse; informal gripe, grouch, moan, whinge.
▶ v. *security was being beefed up* **toughen up**, strengthen, build up, reinforce, consolidate, invigorate, improve.

beefy adj. informal **muscular**, brawny, hefty, burly, hulking, strapping, well built, solid, strong, powerful, heavy, robust, sturdy; informal hunky, husky.
– OPPOSITES puny.

beer n. **ale**, brew; Brit. informal bitter, lager, wallop; Austral./NZ informal sherbet.

WORD LINKS
hop a plant whose dried flowers are used in brewing beer
malt grain used for brewing beer
wort a solution made from soaking malt, used in brewing beer
tankard, stein a large beer mug
widget a device used in some beer cans to give a creamy head

beetle v. informal *he beetled past* **scurry**, scamper, scuttle, bustle, hurry, hasten, rush, dash; informal scoot, zip.

beetling adj. **projecting**, protruding, prominent, overhanging, sticking out, jutting out.

befall v. literary 1 *the same fate befell him* **happen to**, overtake, come upon, be visited on. 2 *tell us what befell* **happen**, occur, take place, come about, transpire, materialize; ensue, follow, result; N. Amer. informal go down; literary come to pass, betide; formal eventuate.

befitting adj. *he couldn't have chosen a more befitting slogan* **appropriate**, apt, fit, suitable, suited, proper, right, in keeping, compatible, consistent; old use meet.

befogged adj. **confused**, muddled, fuddled, befuddled, groggy, dizzy, muzzy; informal

dopey, woozy, not with it.
– OPPOSITES lucid.

before prep. **1** *he dressed up before going out* **prior to**, previous to, earlier than, preparatory to, in preparation for, preliminary to, in anticipation of, in expectation of; in advance of, ahead of, leading up to, on the eve of; rare anterior to. **2** *he appeared before the judge* **in front of**, in the presence of, in the sight of. **3** *death before dishonour* **in preference to**, rather than, sooner than.
– OPPOSITES after.
▶ adv. *she has ridden before* **previously**, before now/then, until now/then, up to now/then; earlier, formerly, hitherto, in the past, in days gone by; formal heretofore.
– OPPOSITES behind.

beforehand adv. **in advance**, in readiness, ahead of time; before, before now/then, earlier (on), previously, already, sooner.
– OPPOSITES afterwards.

befriend v. **make friends with**; look after, help, protect, stand by.

befuddled adj. **confused**, muddled, addled, bewildered, disorientated, all at sea, fazed, perplexed, dazed, dizzy, stupefied, groggy, muzzy, foggy, fuzzy, dopey, woozy; informal mixed up; N. Amer. informal discombobulated.
– OPPOSITES clear.

beg v. **1** *he begged on the streets* **ask for money**, seek charity, seek alms; informal sponge, cadge, scrounge, bum; Brit. informal scab; N. Amer. informal mooch; Austral./NZ informal bludge. **2** *we begged for mercy* **ask for**, request, plead for, appeal for, call for, sue for, solicit, seek, press for. **3** *he begged her not to go* **implore**, entreat, plead with, appeal to, supplicate, pray to, importune; ask, request, call on, petition; literary beseech.

beget v. literary **1** *he begat a son* **father**, sire, have, bring into the world, give life to, bring into being, spawn. **2** *violence begets violence* **cause**, give rise to, lead to, result in, bring about, create, produce, generate, engender, spawn, occasion, bring on, precipitate, prompt, provoke, kindle, trigger, spark off, touch off, stir up, whip up, induce, inspire, promote; literary enkindle.

beggar n. **1** *he never turned any beggar from his kitchen door* **tramp**, beggarman, beggarwoman, vagrant, vagabond, mendicant; N. Amer. hobo; informal scrounger, sponger, cadger, freeloader; Brit. informal dosser; N. Amer. informal bum, moocher, mooch, schnorrer; Austral./NZ informal bagman, bludger; rare clochard. **2** informal *the lucky beggar!* See **person**.
▶ v. *the fare beggared her for a week* **impoverish**, make poor, reduce to penury, bankrupt, make destitute, pauperize, ruin, wipe out, break, cripple; bring someone to their knees.

beggarly adj. **1** *a beggarly sum* **meagre**, paltry, pitiful, miserable, miserly, ungenerous, scant, scanty, skimpy, puny, inadequate, insufficient, insubstantial; informal measly, stingy, pathetic, piddling, piffling, mingy; formal exiguous. **2** *in beggarly circumstances* **wretched**, miserable, sordid, squalid, shabby, mean; poor, poverty-stricken, impoverished, distressed, needy, destitute.
– OPPOSITES considerable, affluent.

beggary n. **poverty**, penury, destitution, ruin, ruination, indigence, impecuniousness, impoverishment, need, privation, pauperism, mendicity, want, hardship, reduced circumstances, straitened circumstances, debt, financial ruin; rare pauperdom.

begin v. **1** *we began work* **start**, commence, set about, go about, embark on, launch into, get down to, take up; initiate, set in motion, institute, inaugurate, get ahead with; informal get cracking on, get going on. **2** *he began by saying hello* **open**, lead off, get under way, get going, get off the ground, start (off), go ahead, commence; informal start the ball rolling, kick off, get the show on the road, fire away, take the plunge. **3** *when did the illness begin?* **appear**, arise, become apparent, make an appearance, spring up, crop up, turn up, come into existence, come into being, originate, start, commence, develop; literary come to pass.
– OPPOSITES finish, end, disappear.

beginner n. **novice**, starter, (raw) recruit, newcomer, tyro, fledgling, neophyte, initiate, fresher, freshman, cub, probationer; postulant, novitiate; N. Amer. tenderfoot; informal rookie, new kid (on the block), newie, newbie; N. Amer. informal greenhorn, probie.
– OPPOSITES expert, veteran.

beginning n. **1** *the beginning of socialism* **dawn**, birth, inception, conception, origination, genesis, emergence, rise, start, commencement, starting point, launch, onset, outset; day one; informal kick-off. **2** *the beginning of the article* **opening**, start, commencement, first part, introduction, preamble, opening statement. **3** *the therapy has its beginnings in China* **origin**, source, roots, starting point, birthplace, fons et origo, cradle, spring, early stages, fountainhead; genesis, creation; literary fount, well spring.
– OPPOSITES end, conclusion.

begrudge v. **1** *she begrudged Brian his affluence* **envy**, grudge; resent, be jealous of, be envious of. **2** *don't begrudge the cost* **resent**, feel aggrieved about, feel bitter about, be annoyed about, be resentful of, grudge, mind, object to, take exception to, regret; give unwillingly, give reluctantly.

beguile v. **1** *she was beguiled by its beauty* **charm**, attract, enchant, entrance, win over, woo, captivate, bewitch, spellbind, dazzle, hypnotize, mesmerize, seduce. **2** *the programme has been beguiling children for years* **entertain**, amuse, delight, please, occupy, absorb, engage, distract, divert, fascinate, enthral, engross.
– OPPOSITES repel, bore.

beguiling adj. **charming**, enchanting, entrancing, charismatic, captivating, bewitching, spellbinding, hypnotizing, mesmerizing, magnetic, alluring, enticing, tempting, inviting, seductive, irresistible; informal come-hither.
– OPPOSITES unappealing.

behalf n.
□ **on behalf of/on someone's behalf**
1 *I am writing on behalf of my client* **for**, in the name of, in place of, on the authority of, at the behest of. **2** *a campaign on behalf of cycling* **in the interests of**, in support of, for, for the benefit of, for the good of, for the sake of.

behave v. **1** *she behaved badly* **conduct oneself**, act, acquit oneself, bear oneself; formal comport oneself; old use deport oneself. **2** *the children behaved themselves* **act correctly**, act properly, conduct oneself well, be well behaved, be good; be polite, mind one's manners, mind one's Ps and Qs.
– OPPOSITES misbehave.

behaviour n. **1** *his behaviour was inexcusable* **conduct**, bearing, etiquette; actions, doings; manners, ways; N. Amer. deportment; formal comportment. **2** *the behaviour of these organisms* **functioning**, action, performance, operation, working, reaction, response.

behead v. **decapitate**, cut someone's head off, guillotine.

behest n. literary **instruction**, requirement, demand, insistence, bidding, request, wish, desire, will; command, order, decree, ruling, directive; informal say-so.

behind prep. **1** *he hid behind a tree* **at the back/rear of**, beyond, on the far/other side of; N. Amer. in back of. **2** *a guard ran behind him* **after**, following, at the back/rear of, hard on the heels of, in the wake of. **3** *he was behind the bombings* **responsible for**, at the bottom of, the cause of, the source of, the organizer of; to blame for, culpable of, guilty of. **4** *they have the nation behind them* **supporting**, backing, for, on the side of, in agreement with; financing; informal rooting for.
– OPPOSITES in front of, ahead of.
▶ adv. **1** *a man followed behind* **after**, afterwards, at the back/end, in the rear. **2** *I looked behind* **over one's shoulder**, to/towards the back, to/towards the rear, backwards. **3** *we're behind, so don't stop* **(running) late**, behind schedule, behindhand, not on time, behind time. **4** *he was behind with his subscription* **in arrears**, overdue; late, unpunctual, behindhand.
– OPPOSITES ahead.
▶ n. informal *he sat on his behind.* See **bottom** (sense 6 of the noun).

behindhand adj. **behind**, behind schedule/time; late, belated, unpunctual, slow.
– OPPOSITES ahead.

behold v. literary **see**, observe, view, look at, watch, survey, gaze at/upon, regard, contemplate, inspect, eye; catch sight of,

glimpse, spot, spy, notice; literary espy, descry.

beholden adj. **indebted**, in someone's debt, obligated, under an obligation; grateful, owing a debt of gratitude.

behove v. formal **1** *it behoves me to go* **be incumbent on**, be obligatory for, be required of, be expected of, be appropriate for. **2** *it ill behoves them to comment* **befit**, become, suit.

beige adj. **fawn**, pale brown, buff, sand, sandy, oatmeal, biscuit, coffee, coffee-coloured, café au lait, camel, ecru.

being n. **1** *she is warmed by his very being* **existence**, living, life, reality, actuality, essential nature, lifeblood, vital force; Philosophy esse. **2** *God is alive in the being of man* **soul**, spirit, nature, essence, inner being, inner self, psyche; heart, bosom, breast; Philosophy quiddity, pneuma. **3** *an enlightened being* **creature**, life form, living entity, living thing, (living) soul, individual, person, human (being).

belabour v. **1** *he belaboured the driver about the head* **beat**, hit, strike, smack, batter, pummel, pound, buffet, rain blows on, thrash; N. Amer. beat up on; informal wallop, whack, clout, clobber, bop, biff, sock, plug; N. Amer. informal whale; old use smite. **2** *he was belaboured in the press* **criticize**, attack, berate, censure, condemn, denounce, denigrate, revile, pillory, flay, lambaste, savage, tear/pull to pieces, run down; informal knock, slam, pan, bash, take apart, crucify, hammer, lay into, roast; Brit. informal slate, rubbish, slag off; N. Amer. informal pummel, cut up; formal castigate, excoriate. **3** *don't belabour the point* **over-elaborate**, labour, dwell on, harp on about, hammer away at; overdo, overplay, overdramatize, make too much of, place too much emphasis on; informal flog to death, drag out, make a big thing of, blow out of all proportion.
– OPPOSITES praise, understate.

belated adj. **late**, overdue, behindhand, behind time, behind schedule, delayed, tardy, unpunctual.
– OPPOSITES early.

belch v. **1** *onions make me belch* **bring up wind**; informal **burp**; Scottish & N. English informal rift. **2** *the furnace belched flames* **emit**, give off, give out, pour out, discharge, disgorge, spew out, spit out, vomit, cough up; literary disembogue.
▶ n. *he gave a loud belch* informal **burp**; Scottish & N. English informal rift; formal eructation.

beleaguered adj. **1** *the beleaguered garrison* **besieged**, under siege, blockaded, surrounded, encircled, hemmed in, under attack. **2** *a beleaguered government* **hard-pressed**, troubled, in difficulties, under pressure, under stress, with one's back to the wall, in a tight corner, in a tight spot; informal up against it; Brit. informal under the cosh.

belie v. **1** *his eyes belied his words* **contradict**, be at odds with, call into question, give the lie to, show/prove to be false, disprove, debunk, discredit, controvert, negative; formal

confute. **2** *his image belies his talent* **conceal**, cover, disguise; misrepresent, falsify, give a false idea/account of.
– OPPOSITES testify to, reveal.

belief n. **1** *it's my belief that age is irrelevant* **opinion**, view, conviction, judgement, thinking, way of thinking, idea, impression, theory, conclusion, notion. **2** *belief in God* **faith**, trust, reliance, confidence, credence. **3** *traditional beliefs* **ideology**, principle, ethic, tenet, canon; doctrine, teaching, dogma, article of faith, creed, credo.
– OPPOSITES disbelief, doubt.

believable adj. **credible**, plausible, tenable, able to hold water, conceivable, likely, probable, possible, feasible, reasonable, having a ring of truth.
– OPPOSITES inconceivable.

believe v. **1** *I don't believe you* **be convinced by**, trust, have confidence in, consider honest, consider truthful. **2** *do you believe his story?* **accept**, be convinced by, give credence to, credit, trust, put confidence in; informal swallow, buy, go for. **3** *I believe he worked for you* **think**, be of the opinion that, have an idea that, imagine, suspect, suppose, assume, presume, take it, conjecture, surmise, conclude, deduce, understand, be given to understand, gather, fancy, guess, dare say; informal reckon, figure; old use ween.
– OPPOSITES doubt.
▫ **believe in** have faith in, pin one's faith on, trust in, have every confidence in, cling to, set (great) store by, value, be convinced by, be persuaded by; subscribe to, approve of; informal swear by, rate.

believer n. **devotee**, adherent, disciple, follower, supporter, upholder, worshipper.
– OPPOSITES infidel, sceptic.

belittle v. **disparage**, denigrate, run down, deprecate, depreciate, downgrade, play down, trivialize, minimize, make light of, treat lightly; informal do down, pooh-pooh; formal derogate; rare misprize.
– OPPOSITES praise, magnify.

bell n.

> **WORD LINKS**
>
> **belfry** the place in a tower in which bells are housed
> **campanile** a bell tower
> **campanology** bell-ringing
> **change** the order in which a peal of bells can be rung

belle n. **beauty**, vision, picture, pin-up, beauty queen, English rose, goddess, Venus; informal looker, good-looker, lovely, stunner, knockout, bombshell, dish, cracker, bobby-dazzler, peach, honey, eyeful, sight for sore eyes, bit of all right; Brit. informal smasher.

bellicose adj. **belligerent**, aggressive, hostile, antagonistic, pugnacious, truculent, confrontational, contentious, militant, combative; informal spoiling for a fight; Brit. informal stroppy, bolshie; N. Amer. informal scrappy; rare oppugnant.
– OPPOSITES peaceable.

belligerent adj. **1** *a belligerent stare* **hostile**, aggressive, threatening, antagonistic, pugnacious, bellicose, truculent, confrontational, contentious, militant, combative; informal spoiling for a fight; Brit. informal stroppy, bolshie; N. Amer. informal scrappy; rare oppugnant. **2** *the belligerent states* **warring**, at war, combatant, fighting, battling.
– OPPOSITES peaceable, neutral.

bellow v. *she bellowed in his ear* **roar**, shout, bawl, thunder, trumpet, boom, bark, yell, shriek, howl, scream; raise one's voice; informal holler.
– OPPOSITES whisper.
▶ n. *a bellow of pain* **roar**, shout, bawl, bark, yell, yelp, shriek, howl, scream; informal holler.
– OPPOSITES whisper.

belly n. *he scratched his belly* **stomach**, abdomen, paunch, middle, midriff, girth; informal tummy, tum, gut, guts, insides, pot, pot belly, beer belly, beer gut, breadbasket; Scottish informal kyte; N. Amer. informal bay window; dated corporation.
▶ v. *her skirt bellied out* **billow (out)**, bulge (out), balloon (out), bag (out), fill (out); distend.
– OPPOSITES sag, flap.

belong v. **1** *the house belongs to his mother* **be owned by**, be the property of, be the possession of, be held by, be in the hands of. **2** *I belong to a trade union* **be a member of**, be in, be affiliated to, be allied to, be associated with, be linked to, be an adherent of. **3** *the garden belongs to the basement flat* **be part of**, be attached to, be an adjunct of, go with. **4** *these creatures belong with bony fish* **be classed**, be classified, be categorized, be included, be located, be situated, be found, lie. **5** *she doesn't belong here* **fit in**, be suited to, have a rightful place, have a home; informal go, click.

belonging n. **affiliation**, acceptance, association, attachment, integration, closeness; rapport, fellow feeling, fellowship.
– OPPOSITES alienation.

belongings plural n. **possessions**, effects, worldly goods, chattels, property; paraphernalia; informal gear, tackle, kit, things, stuff, bits and pieces, bits and bobs; Brit. informal clobber, gubbins.

beloved adj. *her beloved brother* **darling**, dear, dearest, precious, adored, much loved, cherished, treasured, prized, highly regarded, admired, esteemed, worshipped, revered, venerated, idolized.
– OPPOSITES hated.
▶ n. *he watched his beloved* **sweetheart**, love, darling, dearest, lover, girlfriend, boyfriend, young lady, young man, lady friend, man friend; informal steady, baby, angel, honey, pet; literary swain; dated beau; old use paramour, doxy.

below prep. **1** *the water rushed below them* **beneath**, under, underneath, further down than, lower than. **2** *the sum is below average* **less than**, lower than, under, not as much

as, smaller than. **3** *a captain is below a major*
lower than, under, inferior to, subordinate
to, subservient to.
– OPPOSITES above, over.
▸ adv. **1** *I could see what was happening below*
further down, lower down, in a lower
position, underneath, beneath. **2** *the*
statements below **underneath**, following,
further on, at a later point.

belt n. **1** *the belt of her coat* **girdle**, sash,
strap, cummerbund, band; literary cincture;
historical baldric. **2** *farmers in the cotton belt*
region, area, district, zone, sector, territory;
tract, strip, stretch. **3** informal *a belt across the*
face **blow**, punch, smack, crack, slap, bang,
thump, knock, box; informal clout, bash, clip,
biff, whack, thwack, wallop, sock, swipe; Brit.
informal slosh; N. Amer. informal boff, bust, slug,
whale.
▸ v. **1** *she belted the children in* **fasten**, tie,
bind; literary gird. **2** informal *a guy belted him in*
the face **hit**, strike, smack, slap, bang, beat,
punch, thump, welt; informal clout, bash, biff,
whack, thwack, wallop, sock, slog, clobber,
bop, lam, larrup; N. Amer. informal boff, bust,
slug, whale; old use smite. **3** informal *he belted*
down the hill. See **speed** (sense 1 of the
verb).
□ **below the belt** unfair, unjust,
unacceptable, inequitable; unethical,
unprincipled, immoral, unscrupulous,
unsporting, sneaky, dishonourable,
dishonest, underhand; informal low-down,
dirty; Brit. informal out of order, off, a bit thick,
not cricket.
belt up informal be quiet, quieten down, be
silent, fall silent, hush, stop talking, hold
your tongue; informal shut up, shut your face/
mouth/trap, button your lip, pipe down, cut
the cackle, put a sock in it; Brit. informal shut
your gob, wrap up; N. Amer. informal save it,
can it.

bemoan v. **lament**, bewail, mourn, grieve
over, sorrow over, cry over; deplore,
complain about; old use plain over.
– OPPOSITES rejoice at, applaud.

bemused adj. **bewildered**, confused,
puzzled, perplexed, baffled, mystified,
nonplussed, muddled, dumbfounded, at
sea, at a loss, taken aback, disoriented,
disconcerted; informal flummoxed,
bamboozled, clueless, fazed; N. Amer. informal
discombobulated.

bemusement n. **bewilderment**, confusion,
puzzlement, perplexity, bafflement,
befuddlement, stupefaction, mystification,
disorientation; informal bamboozlement;
N. Amer. informal discombobulation.

bench n. **1** *he sat on a bench* **pew**, form, stall,
settle. **2** *a laboratory bench* **workbench**,
work table, worktop, work surface, counter.
3 *the bench heard the evidence* **judges**,
magistrates, judiciary; court.

benchmark n. **standard**, point of reference,
gauge, criterion, specification, canon,
convention, guide, guideline, guiding
principle, norm, touchstone, yardstick,
barometer, indicator, measure, model,

exemplar, pattern.

bend v. **1** *the frames can be bent to fit your*
face **curve**, crook, flex, angle, hook, bow,
arch, buckle, warp, contort, distort, deform.
2 *the highway bent to the left* **turn**, curve,
incline, swing, veer, deviate, diverge, fork,
change course, curl, loop. **3** *he bent down to*
tie his shoe **stoop**, bow, crouch, hunch, lean
down/over. **4** *they want to bend me to their*
will **mould**, shape, manipulate, direct, force,
press, influence, incline, sway. **5** *he bent*
his mind to the question **direct**, turn, train,
steer, set.
– OPPOSITES straighten.
▸ n. *he came to a bend in the road* **curve**, turn,
corner, kink, angle, arc, crescent, twist,
crook, deviation, deflection, loop; dog-leg,
oxbow, zigzag; Brit. hairpin bend, hairpin
turn, hairpin; rare incurvation.
– OPPOSITES straight.
□ **bend over backwards** informal try one's
hardest, do one's best, do one's utmost, do
all one can, give one's all, make every effort;
informal do one's damnedest, go all out, pull
out all the stops, bust a gut, move heaven
and earth.

beneath prep. **1** *we sat beneath the trees*
under, underneath, below, at the foot
of, at the bottom of; lower than. **2** *the*
rank beneath theirs **inferior to**, below,
not so important as, lower in status than,
subordinate to, subservient to. **3** *such an*
attitude was beneath her **unworthy of**,
unbecoming to, degrading to, below.
– OPPOSITES above.

benediction n. **1** *the priest said a*
benediction **blessing**, prayer, invocation;
grace. **2** *filled with heavenly benediction*
blessedness, beatitude, bliss, grace.

benefactor, benefactress n. **patron**,
supporter, backer, sponsor; donor,
contributor, subscriber; informal angel.

beneficent adj. **benevolent**, charitable,
altruistic, humanitarian, neighbourly,
public-spirited, philanthropic; generous,
magnanimous, munificent, unselfish,
unstinting, open-handed, liberal, lavish,
bountiful; literary bounteous.
– OPPOSITES unkind, mean.

beneficial adj. **advantageous**, favourable,
helpful, useful, of use, of benefit, of
assistance, valuable, of value, profitable,
rewarding, gainful.
– OPPOSITES disadvantageous.

beneficiary n. **heir**, heiress, inheritor,
legatee; recipient; Law devisee, cestui que
trust; Scottish Law heritor.

benefit n. **1** *for the benefit of others* **good**,
sake, welfare, well-being, advantage,
comfort, ease, convenience; help, aid,
assistance, service. **2** *the benefits of working*
for a large firm **advantage**, reward, merit,
boon, blessing, virtue; bonus; value; informal
perk; formal perquisite. **3** *state benefit* **social**
security, welfare; charity, donations, gifts,
financial assistance; informal the dole; Scottish
informal the buroo, the broo.

– OPPOSITES detriment, disadvantage.

▶v. **1** *the deal benefited them both* **be advantageous to**, be beneficial to, be of advantage to, be to the advantage of, profit, do good to, be of service to, serve, be useful to, be of use to, be helpful to, be of help to, help, aid, assist, be of assistance to; better, improve, strengthen, boost, advance, further. **2** *they may benefit from drugs* **profit**, gain, reap benefits, reap reward, make money; make the most of, exploit, turn to one's advantage, put to good use, do well out of; informal cash in, make a killing.

– OPPOSITES damage, suffer.

benevolence n. **kindness**, kind-heartedness, big-heartedness, goodness, goodwill, charity, altruism, humanitarianism, compassion, philanthropism; generosity, magnanimity, munificence, unselfishness, open-handedness, beneficence; literary bounty, bounteousness.

– OPPOSITES spite, miserliness.

benevolent adj. **1** *a benevolent patriarch* **kind**, kindly, kind-hearted, big-hearted, good-natured, good, benign, compassionate, caring, altruistic, humanitarian, philanthropic; generous, magnanimous, munificent, unselfish, open-handed, beneficent; literary bounteous. **2** *a benevolent institution* **charitable**, non-profit-making, non-profit, not-for-profit; formal eleemosynary.

– OPPOSITES unkind, tight-fisted.

benighted adj. **ignorant**, unenlightened, uneducated, uninformed, backward, simple; primitive, uncivilized, unsophisticated, philistine, barbarian, barbaric, barbarous; literary nescient; old use rude.

– OPPOSITES enlightened.

benign adj. **1** *a benign grandfatherly role* **kindly**, kind, warm-hearted, good-natured, friendly, warm, affectionate, agreeable, genial, congenial, cordial, approachable, tender-hearted, gentle, sympathetic, compassionate, caring, well disposed, benevolent. **2** *a benign climate* **temperate**, mild, gentle, balmy, soft, pleasant; healthy, wholesome, salubrious. **3** Medicine *a benign tumour* **harmless**, non-malignant, non-cancerous, innocent; Medicine benignant.

– OPPOSITES unfriendly, hostile, unhealthy, unfavourable, malignant.

bent adj. **1** *the bucket had a bent handle* **twisted**, crooked, warped, contorted, deformed, misshapen, out of shape, irregular; bowed, arched, curved, angled, hooked, kinked; N. Amer. informal pretzeled. **2** Brit. informal *a bent policeman.* See **corrupt** (sense 1 of the adjective).

– OPPOSITES straight.

▶n. *an artistic bent* **inclination**, leaning, tendency; talent, gift, flair, aptitude, facility, skill, capability, capacity; predisposition, disposition, instinct, orientation, predilection, proclivity, propensity.

□ **bent on** intent on, determined on, set on, insistent on, resolved on, hell-bent on; committed to, single-minded about, obsessed with, fanatical about, fixated on.

benumbed adj. **numb**, unfeeling, insensible, stupefied, groggy, foggy, fuzzy, muzzy, dazed, dizzy; befuddled, fuddled, disoriented, confused, bewildered, all at sea; informal dopey, woozy, mixed up; N. Amer. informal discombobulated.

– OPPOSITES perceptive.

bequeath v. **leave (in one's will)**, will, make over, pass on, hand on/down, entrust, grant, transfer; donate, give; bestow on, confer on; endow with; Law demise, devise, convey.

bequest n. **legacy**, inheritance, endowment, settlement; estate, heritage; bestowal, bequeathal; Law devise; Law, dated hereditament.

berate v. **scold**, rebuke, reprimand, reproach, reprove, admonish, chide, criticize, upbraid, take to task, pull up, read someone the Riot Act, haul over the coals; informal tell off, give someone a talking-to, give someone a telling-off, give someone a dressing-down, give someone a roasting, rap over the knuckles, send someone away with a flea in their ear, bawl out, come down on, tear into, slap down, blast; Brit. informal tick off, have a go at, carpet, give someone a rocket, give someone a rollicking, tear someone off a strip; Brit. informal dated give someone a wigging; N. Amer. informal chew out, ream out, take to the woodshed; Austral. informal monster; formal castigate; dated call down, rate; rare reprehend, objurgate.

– OPPOSITES praise.

bereaved adj. **orphaned**, widowed; mourning, grieving.

bereavement n. **death in the family**, loss, passing (away), demise; formal decease.

bereft adj. **deprived**, robbed, stripped, devoid, bankrupt; wanting, in need of, lacking, without; informal minus, sans, clean out of.

berserk adj. **mad**, crazy, insane, out of one's mind, hysterical, frenzied, crazed, demented, maniacal, manic, frantic, raving, wild, out of control, amok, on the rampage; informal off one's head, off the deep end, ape, bananas, bonkers, nuts, hyper; Brit. informal spare, crackers, barmy; N. Amer. informal postal.

berth n. **1** *a 4-berth cabin* **bunk**, bed, cot, couch, hammock. **2** *the vessel left its berth* **mooring**, dock.

▶v. **1** *the ship berthed in London Docks* **dock**, moor, land, tie up, make fast. **2** *the boats each berth six* **accommodate**, sleep.

□ **give someone/something a wide berth** avoid, shun, keep away from, stay away from, steer clear of, keep at arm's length, have nothing to do with; dodge, sidestep, circumvent, skirt round.

beseech v. literary **implore**, beg, entreat, plead with, appeal to, call on, supplicate, importune, pray to, ask, request, petition.

beset v. **1** *he is beset by fears* **plague**, bedevil, assail, beleaguer, afflict, torment, rack, oppress, trouble, worry, harass, dog. **2** *they*

b

were beset by enemy forces **surround**, besiege, hem in, shut in, fence in, box in, encircle, ring round.

beside prep. **1** *Kate walked beside him* **alongside**, by/at the side of, next to, parallel to, abreast of, at someone's elbow; adjacent to, next door to, cheek by jowl with; bordering, abutting, neighbouring. **2** *beside Paula, she felt clumsy* **compared with/to**, in comparison with/to, by comparison with, next to, against, contrasted with, in contrast to/with.
□ **beside oneself** distraught, overcome, out of one's mind, frantic, desperate, distracted, at one's wits' end, frenzied, wound up, worked up; hysterical, unhinged, mad, crazed, berserk, demented.
beside the point See **point**[1].

besides prep. *who did you ask besides Mary?* **in addition to**, as well as, over and above, above and beyond, on top of; apart from, other than, aside from, but for, save for, not counting, excluding, not including, except, with the exception of, excepting, leaving aside; N. Amer. informal outside of; old use forbye.
▸ adv. **1** *there's a lot more besides* **in addition**, as well, too, also, into the bargain, on top of that, to boot; old use therewithal. **2** *besides, he's a man* **furthermore**, moreover, further; anyway, anyhow, in any case, be that as it may; informal what's more; N. Amer. informal anyways.

besiege v. **1** *the English army besieged Leith* **lay siege to**, beleaguer, blockade, surround; old use invest. **2** *fans besieged his hotel* **surround**, mob, crowd round, swarm round, throng round, ring round, encircle. **3** *guilt besieged him* **oppress**, torment, torture, rack, plague, afflict, haunt, harrow, beset, beleaguer, trouble, bedevil, prey on. **4** *he was besieged with requests* **overwhelm**, inundate, deluge, flood, swamp, snow under; bombard.

besmirch v. literary **sully**, tarnish, blacken, drag through the mud/mire, stain, taint, smear, disgrace, dishonour, bring discredit to, damage, ruin.
– OPPOSITES honour, enhance.

besotted adj. **infatuated**, smitten, in love, head over heels in love, obsessed; doting on, greatly enamoured of; informal bowled over by, swept off one's feet by, struck on, crazy about, mad about, wild about, gone on, carrying a torch for; Brit. informal potty about.

bespatter v. **splatter**, spatter, splash, speck, fleck, spot; dirty, soil; Scottish & Irish slabber; informal splotch, splodge, splosh.

bespeak v. **1** *a tree-lined road which bespoke money* **indicate**, be evidence of, be a sign of, denote, point to, testify to, evidence, reflect, demonstrate, show, manifest, display, signify; reveal, betray; informal spell; literary betoken. **2** *he had bespoken a room* **order**, reserve, book; informal bag.
– OPPOSITES belie.

best adj. **1** *the best hotel in Paris* **finest**, greatest, top, foremost, leading, pre-

eminent, premier, prime, first, chief, principal, supreme, of the highest quality, superlative, par excellence, unrivalled, second to none, without equal, nonpareil, unsurpassed, peerless, matchless, unparalleled, unbeaten, unbeatable, optimum, optimal, ultimate, incomparable, ideal, perfect; highest, record-breaking; informal star, number-one, a cut above the rest, top-drawer; formal unexampled. **2** *do whatever you think best* **most advantageous**, most useful, most suitable, most fitting, most appropriate; most prudent, most sensible, most advisable.
– OPPOSITES worst.
▸ adv. **1** *the best-dressed man* **to the highest standard**, in the best way. **2** *the food he liked best* **most**, to the highest/greatest degree. **3** *this is best done at home* **most advantageously**, most usefully, most suitably, most fittingly, most appropriately; most sensibly, most prudently, most wisely; better.
– OPPOSITES worst, least.
▸ n. **1** *only the best will do* **finest**, choicest, top, cream, choice, prime, elite, crème de la crème, flower, jewel in the crown, nonpareil; informal tops, pick of the bunch. **2** *she dressed in her best* **best clothes**, finery, Sunday best; informal best bib and tucker, glad rags. **3** *give her my best* **best wishes**, regards, kind/kindest regards, greetings, compliments, felicitations, respects; love.
▸ v. informal *she was not to be bested* **defeat**, beat, get the better of, outdo, outwit, outsmart, worst, be more than a match for, prevail over, vanquish, trounce, triumph over; surpass, outclass, outshine, put someone in the shade, overshadow, eclipse; informal lick, get one over on.
□ **do one's best** do one's utmost, try one's hardest, make every effort, do all one can, give one's all; informal bend over backwards, do one's damnedest, go all out, pull out all the stops, bust a gut, break one's neck, move heaven and earth.

bestial adj. **1** *Stanley's bestial behaviour* **savage**, brutish, brutal, barbarous, barbaric, cruel, vicious, violent, inhuman, subhuman; depraved, degenerate, perverted, immoral, warped. **2** *man's bestial ancestors* **animal**, beast-like, animalistic; rare zoic.
– OPPOSITES civilized, humane.

bestir v.
□ **bestir oneself** exert oneself, make an effort, rouse oneself, get going, get moving, get on with it; informal shake a leg, look lively, get cracking, get weaving, get one's finger out, get off one's backside; Brit. informal dated stir one's stumps.

bestow v. **confer on**, grant, accord, afford, endow someone with, vest in, present, award, give, donate, entrust with, vouchsafe.

bestride v. **1** *the oilfield bestrides the border* **extend across**, lie on both sides of, straddle, span, bridge. **2** *he bestrode his horse* **straddle**, sit/stand astride. **3** *Italy bestrode Europe in opera* **dominate**, tower over/above.

best-seller n. great success, brand leader; informal hit, smash (hit), blockbuster, chart-topper, chartbuster.
– OPPOSITES failure, flop.

best-selling adj. **very successful**, very popular; informal number-one, chart-topping, hit, smash.

bet v. **1** *he bet £10 on the favourite* **wager**, gamble, stake, risk, venture, hazard, chance; put/lay money, speculate; informal punt; Brit. informal have a flutter, chance one's arm. **2** informal *I bet it was your idea* **be certain**, be sure, be convinced, be confident; expect, predict, forecast, guess; Brit. informal put one's shirt on.
▶n. **1** *a £20 bet* **wager**, gamble, stake, ante; Brit. informal flutter, punt. **2** informal *my bet is that they'll lose* **prediction**, forecast, guess; opinion, belief, feeling, view, theory. **3** informal *your best bet is to go early* **option**, choice, alternative, course of action, plan.

bête noire n. **bugbear**, pet hate, bogey; a thorn in one's flesh/side, the bane of one's life; N. Amer. bugaboo.
– OPPOSITES favourite.

betoken v. literary **1** *a small gift betokening regret* **indicate**, be a sign of, be evidence of, evidence, manifest, mean, signify, denote, represent, show, demonstrate, bespeak; informal spell. **2** *the blue sky betokened a day of good weather* **foretell**, signal, give notice of, herald, proclaim, prophesy, foreshadow, presage, be a harbinger of, portend, augur, be an omen of, be a sign of, be a warning of, warn of, bode; literary foretoken, forebode.

betray v. **1** *he betrayed his own brother* **break one's promise to**, be disloyal to, be unfaithful to, break faith with, play someone false; inform on/against, give away, denounce, sell out, stab in the back; informal split on, rat on, peach on, stitch up, do the dirty on, sell down the river, squeal on; Brit. informal grass on, shop, sneak on; N. Amer. informal rat out, drop a/the dime on, finger; Austral./NZ informal dob on, point the bone at. **2** *he betrayed a secret* **reveal**, disclose, divulge, tell, give away, leak; unmask, expose; let slip, let out, let drop, blurt out; informal blab, spill.
– OPPOSITES be loyal to, hide.

betrayal n. **disloyalty**, treachery, bad faith, faithlessness, falseness, Punic faith; duplicity, deception, double-dealing; breach of faith, breach of trust, stab in the back; double-cross, sell-out; literary perfidy.
– OPPOSITES loyalty.

betrayer n. **traitor**, back-stabber, Judas, double-crosser; renegade, quisling, double agent, collaborator, informer, mole, stool pigeon; turncoat, defector; informal snake in the grass, rat, scab; Brit. informal grass, supergrass, nark; N. Amer. informal fink, stoolie.

betrothal n. dated **engagement**, marriage contract; old use espousal.

betrothed adj. dated **engaged (to be married)**, promised/pledged in marriage, attached; informal spoken for; literary affianced; old use plighted, espoused.
– OPPOSITES unattached.

better adj. **1** *better facilities* **superior**, finer, of higher quality; preferable; informal a cut above, streets ahead, head and shoulders above, ahead of the pack/field. **2** *there couldn't be a better time* **more advantageous**, more suitable, more fitting, more appropriate, more useful, more valuable, more desirable. **3** *are you better?* **healthier**, fitter, stronger; well, cured, healed, recovered; recovering, on the road to recovery, making progress, improving, on the mend.
– OPPOSITES worse, inferior.
▶adv. **1** *I played better today* **to a higher standard**, in a superior/finer way. **2** *this may suit you better* **more**, to a greater degree/extent. **3** *the money could be better spent* **more wisely**, more sensibly, more suitably, more fittingly, more advantageously.
▶v. **1** *he bettered the record* **surpass**, improve on, beat, exceed, top, cap, trump, eclipse. **2** *refugees who want to better their lot* **improve**, ameliorate, raise, advance, further, lift, upgrade, enhance.
– OPPOSITES worsen.

betterment n. **improvement**, amelioration, advancement, development, upgrading, enhancement.

between prep. **1** *Philip stood between his parents* **in the middle of**, with one on either side; old use betwixt. **2** *the bond between her and her mother* **connecting**, linking, joining, uniting, allying.

bevel n. **slope**, slant, angle, cant, chamfer.

beverage n. See **drink** (sense 1 of the noun).

bevy n. **group**, crowd, herd, flock, horde, army, galaxy, assemblage, gathering, band, body, pack; knot, cluster; informal bunch, gaggle, posse.

bewail v. **lament**, bemoan, mourn, grieve over, sorrow over, cry over; deplore, complain about; old use plain over.
– OPPOSITES rejoice at, applaud.

beware v. **be on your guard**, watch out, look out, mind out, be alert, be on the lookout, keep your eyes open/peeled, keep an eye out, keep a sharp lookout, be on the qui vive; take care, be careful, be cautious, have a care, watch your step; Brit. school slang dated cave; Golf fore; Hunting ware.

bewilder v. **baffle**, mystify, bemuse, perplex, puzzle, confuse, confound, nonplus; informal flummox, faze, stump, beat, fox, be all Greek to, floor; N. Amer. informal discombobulate, buffalo.
– OPPOSITES enlighten.

bewildered adj. **baffled**, mystified, bemused, perplexed, puzzled, confused, nonplussed, at sea, at a loss, disorientated, taken aback; informal flummoxed, bamboozled; N. Amer. informal discombobulated.

bewitch v. **1** *that evil woman bewitched him* **cast/put a spell on**, enchant; possess, witch, curse; N. Amer. hex, hoodoo; Austral. point the bone at. **2** *she was bewitched by her*

b

surroundings **captivate**, enchant, entrance, enrapture, charm, beguile, delight, fascinate, enthral.
– OPPOSITES repel.

beyond prep. **1** *beyond the trees* **on the far side of**, on the other side of, further away than, behind, past, after. **2** *beyond six o'clock* **later than**, past, after. **3** *inflation beyond 10 per cent* **greater than**, more than, exceeding, in excess of, above, over and above, above and beyond, upwards of. **4** *little beyond food was provided* **apart from**, except, other than, besides; informal outside of; formal save.
▸ adv. *a house with a garden beyond* **further away**, further off.

bias n. **1** *he accused the media of bias* **prejudice**, partiality, partisanship, favouritism, unfairness, one-sidedness; bigotry, intolerance, discrimination, a jaundiced eye; leaning, tendency, inclination, predilection. **2** *a dress cut on the bias* **diagonal**, cross, slant, angle.
– OPPOSITES impartiality.
▸ v. *this may have biased the result* **prejudice**, influence, colour, sway, weight, predispose; distort, skew, slant.

biased adj. **prejudiced**, partial, partisan, one-sided, blinkered; bigoted, intolerant, discriminatory; jaundiced, distorted, warped, twisted, skewed.
– OPPOSITES impartial.

bibliophile n. **book lover**, avid reader; informal bookworm; rare bibliomaniac.

bicker v. **squabble**, argue, quarrel, wrangle, fight, disagree, dispute, spar, have words, be at each other's throats, lock horns; informal scrap, argufy, spat; old use altercate.
– OPPOSITES agree.

bicycle n. **cycle**, two-wheeler, pedal cycle; informal bike, pushbike.

bid¹ v. **1** *United bid £1 million for the striker* **offer**, make an offer of, put in a bid of, put up, tender, proffer, propose. **2** *she is bidding for a place in the England team* **try to obtain**, try to get, make a pitch for, make a bid for.
▸ n. **1** *a bid of £3,000* **offer**, tender, proposal. **2** *a bid to cut crime* **attempt**, effort, endeavour, try; informal crack, go, shot, stab; formal essay.

bid² v. **1** *she bid him farewell* **wish**, utter. **2** literary *I did as he bade me* **order**, command, tell, instruct, direct, enjoin, charge. **3** literary *he bade his companions enter* **invite to**, ask to, request to.

biddable adj. **obedient**, acquiescent, compliant, tractable, amenable, complaisant, cooperative, dutiful, submissive; rare persuasible.
– OPPOSITES disobedient, uncooperative.

bidding n. **command**, order, instruction, decree, injunction, demand, mandate, direction, summons, call; wish, desire; request; literary behest; old use hest.

big adj. **1** *a big building* **large**, sizeable, substantial, great, huge, immense, enormous, extensive, colossal, massive,

mammoth, vast, tremendous, gigantic, giant, monumental, mighty, gargantuan, elephantine, titanic, mountainous, Brobdingnagian; towering, tall, high, lofty; outsize, oversized; goodly; capacious, voluminous, spacious; king-size(d), man-size(d), family-size(d), economy-size(d); informal jumbo, whopping, thumping, bumper, mega, humongous, monster, astronomical, almighty, dirty great, socking great; Brit. informal whacking, ginormous; formal commodious. **2** *a big man* **well built**, sturdy, brawny, burly, broad-shouldered, muscular, muscly, rugged, lusty, Herculean, bulky, hulking, strapping, thickset, stocky, solid, hefty; tall, huge, gigantic; fat, stout, portly, plump, fleshy, paunchy, corpulent, obese; informal hunky, beefy, husky; literary thewy, stark. **3** *my big brother* **grown-up**, adult, mature, grown; elder, older. **4** *a big decision* **important**, significant, major, momentous, weighty, consequential, far-reaching, key, vital, critical, crucial. **5** informal *a big man in the government* **powerful**, important, prominent, influential, high-powered, leading; N. Amer. major-league. **6** informal *he has big plans* **ambitious**, far-reaching, grandiose, on a grand scale. **7** *she's got a big heart* **generous**, kind, kindly, caring, compassionate, loving. **8** informal *African bands are big in Britain* **popular**, successful, in demand, sought-after, all the rage; informal hot, in, cool, trendy, now, hip; Brit. informal dated all the go.
– OPPOSITES small, minor, modest.
□ **too big for one's boots** informal conceited, full of oneself, swollen-headed, cocky, arrogant, cocksure, above oneself, self-important; vain, self-satisfied, pleased with oneself, smug, complacent; informal big-headed; literary vainglorious.

big-headed adj. informal **conceited**, full of oneself, swollen-headed, cocky, arrogant, cocksure, above oneself, self-important; vain, self-satisfied, pleased with oneself, smug, complacent; informal too big for one's boots; literary vainglorious.
– OPPOSITES modest.

big-hearted adj. **generous**, magnanimous, munificent, open-handed, bountiful, unstinting, unselfish, altruistic, charitable, philanthropic, benevolent; kind, kindly, kind-hearted; literary bounteous.
– OPPOSITES mean.

bigot n. **dogmatist**, partisan, sectarian; racist, sexist, chauvinist, jingoist.

bigoted adj. **prejudiced**, biased, partial, one-sided, sectarian, discriminatory; opinionated, dogmatic, intolerant, narrow-minded, blinkered, illiberal; racist, sexist, chauvinistic, jingoistic; jaundiced, warped, twisted, distorted.
– OPPOSITES open-minded.

bigotry n. **prejudice**, bias, partiality, partisanship, sectarianism, discrimination; dogmatism, intolerance, narrow-mindedness; racism, sexism, chauvinism, jingoism.
– OPPOSITES open-mindedness.

bigwig n. informal **VIP**, important person, notable, dignitary, grandee; celebrity; informal somebody, heavyweight, big shot, big noise, big gun, big cheese, big fish; Brit. informal brass hat; N. Amer. informal big wheel.
– OPPOSITES nonentity.

bijou adj. **small**, little, compact, snug, cosy.

bilge n. informal See **nonsense** (sense 1).

bilious adj. **1** *I felt bilious* **nauseous**, sick, queasy, nauseated, green about the gills; N. Amer. informal barfy. **2** *his bilious disposition* **bad-tempered**, irritable, irascible, tetchy, testy, crotchety, ill-tempered, ill-natured, ill-humoured, peevish, fractious, pettish, crabby, waspish, prickly, crusty, shrewish, quick-tempered; N. Amer. informal cranky, ornery. **3** *a bilious green and pink colour scheme* **lurid**, garish, loud, violent; sickly, nauseating.
– OPPOSITES well, good-humoured, muted.

bilk v. informal See **swindle** (verb).

bill¹ n. **1** *a bill for £6* **invoice**, account, statement, list of charges; N. Amer. check; humorous the damage; N. Amer. informal tab; old use reckoning, score. **2** *a parliamentary bill* **draft law**, proposal, measure. **3** *she was top of the bill* **programme (of entertainment)**, line-up; N. Amer. playbill. **4** N. Amer. *a $10 bill* **banknote**, note; US informal greenback; US & historical Treasury note. **5** *he had been posting bills* **poster**, advertisement, public notice, announcement; flyer, leaflet, handbill; Brit. fly-poster; N. Amer. dodger; informal ad; Brit. informal advert.
▶ v. **1** *please bill me for the work* **invoice**, charge, debit. **2** *the concert went ahead as billed* **advertise**, announce; schedule, programme, timetable; N. Amer. slate. **3** *he was billed as the new Sean Connery* **describe**, call, style, label, dub; promote, publicize, talk up; informal hype.

bill² n. *a bird's bill* **beak**; Scottish & N. English neb; technical mandibles.

billet n. *the troops' billets* **quarters**, rooms; accommodation, lodging, housing; barracks, cantonment.
▶ v. *two soldiers were billeted here* **accommodate**, quarter, put up, lodge, house; station, garrison.

billow n. **1** *billows of smoke* **cloud**, mass. **2** old use *the billows that break upon the shore* **wave**, roller, boomer, breaker.
▶ v. **1** *her dress billowed around her* **puff up/out**, balloon (out), swell, fill (out), belly out. **2** *smoke billowed from the chimney* **swirl**, spiral, roll, undulate, eddy; pour, flow.

billowing adj. **rolling**, swirling, undulating, surging, heaving, billowy, swelling, rippling.

bin n. **container**, receptacle, holder; drum, canister, caddy, can, tin.

bind v. **1** *they bound her hands and feet* **tie (up)**, fasten (together), hold together, secure, make fast, attach; rope, strap, lash, truss, tether. **2** *Shelley bound up the wound with a clean dressing* **bandage**, dress, cover, wrap; strap up, tape up. **3** *the experience had bound them together* **unite**, join, bond, knit together, draw together, yoke together. **4** *we have not bound ourselves to join* **commit oneself**, undertake, pledge, vow, promise, swear, give one's word. **5** *the edges are bound in a contrasting colour* **trim**, hem, edge, border, fringe; finish. **6** *they are bound by the agreement* **constrain**, restrict, restrain, trammel, tie hand and foot, straitjacket, tie down, shackle; hamper, hinder, inhibit.
– OPPOSITES untie, separate.
▶ n. informal **1** *starting so early is a bind* **nuisance**, annoyance, inconvenience, bore, bother, source of irritation, irritant, trial; informal pain, pain in the neck/backside, headache, hassle, drag; N. Amer. informal pain in the butt. **2** *he is in a political bind* **predicament**, difficult/awkward situation, quandary, dilemma, plight, cleft stick; informal spot, tight spot, hole.

binding adj. **irrevocable**, unalterable, inescapable, unbreakable, contractual; compulsory, obligatory, mandatory, incumbent.

binge n. informal **drinking bout**, debauch; informal bender, session, booze-up, blind; Scottish informal skite; N. Amer. informal jag, toot; dated souse; literary bacchanal, bacchanalia; old use wassail.

biography n. **life story**, life history, life, memoir; informal bio, biog.

biological adj. **biotic**, biologic, organic, living; botanic, botanical, zoological.
– OPPOSITES inorganic, non-living.

bird n. fowl; chick, fledgling, nestling; **(birds)** avifauna; informal feathered friend, birdie.

> **WORD LINKS**
>
> **avian** relating to birds
> **aviary** a large enclosure for keeping birds
> **aviculture** the breeding of birds
> **ornithology** the study of birds
> **passerine** referring to all birds that have feet adapted for perching
> **twitcher** a birdwatcher devoted to spotting rare birds

birth n. **1** *the birth of a child* **childbirth**, delivery, nativity, birthing; formal parturition; dated confinement; old use accouchement, childbed. **2** *the birth of science* **beginning(s)**, emergence, genesis, dawn, dawning, rise, start. **3** *he is of noble birth* **ancestry**, lineage, blood, descent, parentage, family, extraction, origin, genealogy, heritage, stock, kinship.
– OPPOSITES death, demise, end.
□ **give birth to** have, bear, produce, be delivered of, bring into the world; N. Amer. birth; informal drop; dated mother; old use bring forth.

> **WORD LINKS**
>
> **natal** relating to one's birth
> **antenatal** before childbirth
> **perinatal** close to the time of birth
> **postnatal**, **post-partum** after childbirth
> **midwife** a nurse trained to help women give birth
> **neonate** a baby that has just been born
> **obstetrics** the branch of medicine concerned with childbirth
> **viviparous** giving birth to live young

b

birthmark n. **naevus**, mole, blemish.

birthright n. **patrimony**, inheritance, heritage; right, due, prerogative, privilege; primogeniture.

biscuit n. Brit. **cracker**, wafer; N. Amer. cookie; informal bicky.

bisect v. **cut in half**, halve, divide/cut/split in two, split down the middle; cross, intersect.

bisexual adj. **1** *bisexual crustaceans* **hermaphrodite**, hermaphroditic, intersex; androgynous, epicene; technical monoclinous, gynandrous, gynandromorphic. **2** *a bisexual actor* **ambisexual**; informal AC/DC, bi, swinging both ways, ambidextrous; N. Amer. informal switch-hitting.

bishop n. diocesan, metropolitan, suffragan; formal prelate.

> **WORD LINKS**
>
> **episcopal** relating to a bishop
> **bishopric, diocese, see** the district for which a bishop is responsible
> **episcopate** a bishop's period of office
> **crozier** a bishop's hooked staff
> **mitre** a bishop's headdress
> **encyclical** a letter sent by the Pope to all Roman Catholic bishops

bishopric n. **diocese**, see.

bit n. **1** *a bit of bread* **piece**, portion, segment, section, part; chunk, lump, hunk, slice; fragment, scrap, shred, crumb, grain, speck; spot, drop, pinch, dash, soupçon, modicum; morsel, mouthful, bite, sample; iota, jot, tittle, whit, atom, particle, trace, touch, suggestion, hint, tinge; snippet, snatch; informal smidgen, tad. **2** *wait a bit* **moment**, minute, second, (little) while; informal sec, jiffy; Brit. informal mo, tick.
– OPPOSITES lot.
□ **a bit** rather, fairly, slightly, somewhat, quite, moderately; informal pretty, sort of, kind of.
bit by bit gradually, little by little, in stages, step by step, piecemeal, slowly.
in a bit soon, in a (little) while, in a second, in a minute, in a moment, shortly; informal anon, in a jiffy, in two shakes; Brit. informal in a tick, in two ticks, in a mo; N. Amer. informal in a snap; dated directly; literary ere long.

bitch n. informal **1** *she's such a bitch* **shrew**, vixen, she-devil, hellcat; informal cow, cat; old use grimalkin. **2** *a bitch of a job* **nightmare**; informal bastard, bummer, —— from hell, swine, pig, stinker.
▸ v. **1** *big men bitched about the price of oil* **complain**, whine, grumble, grouse; informal whinge, moan, grouch, gripe. **2** *he's always bitching about colleagues* **criticize**, run down, speak ill of, slander, malign; informal knock, pull to pieces, take apart, bad-mouth, do a hatchet job on; N. Amer. informal trash; Brit. informal slag off.

bitchy adj. informal See **spiteful**.

bite v. **1** *the dog bit his arm* **sink one's teeth into**, chew, munch, crunch, champ, tear at. **2** *the acid bites into the copper* **corrode**, eat into, eat away at, burn (into), etch, dissolve.

3 *my boots failed to bite* **grip**, hold, get a purchase. **4** *the measures begin to bite* **take effect**, have an effect, be effective, work, act, have results. **5** *a hundred or so retailers should bite* **accept**, agree, respond; be lured, be enticed, be tempted; take the bait.
▸ n. **1** *he took a bite at his sandwich* **chew**, munch, nibble, gnaw, nip, snap. **2** *he ate it in two bites* **mouthful**, piece, bit, morsel. **3** *do you fancy a bite?* **snack**, light meal, mouthful, soupçon; refreshments; informal a little something. **4** *the appetizer had a fiery bite* **piquancy**, pungency, spiciness, strong flavour, tang, zest, sharpness, tartness; informal kick, punch, zing.

biting adj. **1** *biting comments* **vicious**, harsh, cruel, savage, cutting, sharp, bitter, scathing, caustic, acid, acrimonious, acerbic, stinging; vitriolic, hostile, spiteful, venomous, mean, nasty; informal bitchy, catty. **2** *the biting wind* **freezing**, icy, arctic, glacial; bitter, piercing, penetrating, raw, wintry.
– OPPOSITES mild.

bitter adj. **1** *bitter coffee* **sharp**, acid, acidic, acrid, tart, sour, biting, unsweetened, vinegary; N. Amer. acerb; technical acerbic. **2** *a bitter woman* **resentful**, embittered, aggrieved, grudge-bearing, begrudging, rancorous, spiteful, jaundiced, ill-disposed, sullen, sour, churlish, morose, petulant, peevish; informal with a chip on one's shoulder. **3** *a bitter blow* **painful**, unpleasant, disagreeable, nasty, cruel, awful, distressing, upsetting, harrowing, heartbreaking, heart-rending, agonizing, traumatic, tragic, chilling; formal grievous. **4** *a bitter wind* **freezing**, icy, arctic, glacial; biting, piercing, penetrating, raw, wintry. **5** *a bitter row* **acrimonious**, virulent, angry, rancorous, spiteful, vicious, vitriolic, savage, ferocious, hate-filled, venomous, poisonous, acrid, nasty, ill-natured.
– OPPOSITES sweet, magnanimous, content, welcome, warm, amicable.

bitterness n. **1** *the bitterness of the medicine* **sharpness**, acidity, acridity, tartness, sourness, harshness; technical acerbity. **2** *his bitterness grew* **resentment**, rancour, indignation, grudge, spite, sullenness, sourness, churlishness, moroseness, petulance, pique, peevishness. **3** *the bitterness of war* **trauma**, pain, agony, grief; unpleasantness, disagreeableness, nastiness; heartache, heartbreak, distress, desolation, despair, tragedy. **4** *there was no bitterness between them* **acrimony**, hostility, antipathy, antagonism, enmity, animus, friction, rancour, vitriol, hatred, loathing, venom, poison, nastiness, ill feeling, ill will, bad blood.
– OPPOSITES sweetness, magnanimity, contentment, warmth, goodwill.

bitty adj. informal **disjointed**, incoherent, fragmented, fragmentary, scrappy, piecemeal; inconsistent, unsystematic, jumbled; uneven, erratic, patchy.
– OPPOSITES coherent.

bizarre adj. **strange**, peculiar, odd, funny, curious, outlandish, outré, eccentric, unconventional, unorthodox, queer, extraordinary; informal weird, wacky, oddball, way out, freaky, off the wall, offbeat; Brit. informal rum; N. Amer. informal wacko.
– OPPOSITES normal.

blab v. informal **1** *she blabbed to the press* **talk**, give the game away; informal let the cat out of the bag, spill the beans; Brit. informal blow the gaff, cough. **2** *I do not blab secrets* **blurt out**, let slip, let out, tell, reveal, betray, disclose, give away, divulge, leak; informal let on, spill.

blabber v. informal See **chat** (verb).

blabbermouth n. informal **talker**, chatterer, prattler; N. Amer. blatherskite; informal chatterbox, windbag, gasbag; Brit. informal natterer.

black adj. **1** *a black horse* **dark**, pitch-black, jet-black, coal-black, inky; Heraldry sable; rare nigrescent. **2** *a black night* **unlit**, dark, starless, moonless; literary tenebrous, Stygian. **3** *the blackest day of the war* **tragic**, disastrous, calamitous, catastrophic, cataclysmic, fateful, wretched, woeful, awful, terrible; formal grievous. **4** *Mary was in a black mood* **miserable**, unhappy, sad, wretched, broken-hearted, heartbroken, grief-stricken, grieving, sorrowful, sorrowing, anguished, desolate, despairing, disconsolate, downcast, dejected, cheerless, melancholy, morose, gloomy, glum, mournful, doleful, funereal, dismal, forlorn, woeful, abject; informal blue; literary dolorous. **5** *black humour* **cynical**, macabre, weird, unhealthy, ghoulish, morbid, perverted, gruesome; informal sick. **6** *a black look*. See **angry** (sense 1).
– OPPOSITES white, clear, bright, joyful.
▶ v. **1** *the steps of the houses were neatly blacked* **blacken**, darken; dirty, make sooty, make smoky, stain, grime, soil. **2** *she blacked his eye* **bruise**, contuse; hit, punch, injure. **3** Brit. dated *trade union members blacked the work* **boycott**, embargo, blacklist, proscribe.
□ **black out** faint, lose consciousness, pass out, swoon; informal flake out, go out.
in the black in credit, in funds, debt-free, solvent, financially sound, creditworthy.
black and white 1 *a black-and-white picture* **monochrome**, greyscale. **2** *I wish to see the proposals in black and white* **in print**, printed, written down, set down, on paper, recorded, on record, documented. **3** *in black-and-white terms* **categorical**, unequivocal, absolute, uncompromising, unconditional, unqualified, unambiguous, clear, clear-cut.

blackball v. **reject**, debar, bar, ban, vote against, blacklist, exclude, shut out.
– OPPOSITES admit.

blacken v. **1** *pollutants blackening the air* **darken**, dirty, stain, soil, make sooty, make smoky, pollute. **2** *the sky blackened* **darken**, dim, grow dim, cloud over. **3** *someone has blackened my name* **sully**, tarnish, besmirch, drag through the mud/mire, stain, taint, smear, disgrace, dishonour, bring discredit to, damage, ruin; slander, defame.

– OPPOSITES whiten, clean, lighten, brighten, clear.

blacklist v. **boycott**, ostracize, avoid, embargo, steer clear of, ignore; refuse to employ; Brit. dated black.

black magic n. **sorcery**, witchcraft, wizardry, necromancy, the black arts, devilry; malediction, voodoo, witching, witchery.

blackmail n. *he was accused of blackmail* **extortion**, demanding money with menaces; informal hush money; formal exaction.
▶ v. **1** *he was blackmailing the murderer* **extort money from**, threaten, hold to ransom; informal demand hush money from. **2** *she blackmailed me to work for her* **coerce**, pressurize, pressure, force; informal lean on, put the screws on, twist someone's arm.

blackout n. **1** *a power blackout* **power cut**, power failure; brown-out. **2** *a news blackout* **suppression**, silence, censorship, reporting restrictions. **3** *he had a blackout* **fainting fit**, faint, loss of consciousness, passing out, swoon, collapse; Medicine syncope.

blame v. **1** *he always blames others* **hold responsible**, hold accountable, condemn, accuse, find/consider guilty, assign fault/liability/guilt to; old use inculpate. **2** *they blame youth crime on unemployment* **ascribe to**, attribute to, impute to, lay at the door of, put down to; informal pin.
– OPPOSITES absolve.
▶ n. *he was cleared of all blame for the accident* **responsibility**, guilt, accountability, liability, culpability, fault.

blameless adj. **innocent**, guiltless, above reproach, irreproachable, unimpeachable, in the clear, exemplary, perfect, virtuous, pure, impeccable; informal squeaky clean.
– OPPOSITES blameworthy.

blameworthy adj. **culpable**, reprehensible, indefensible, inexcusable, guilty, criminal, delinquent, wrong, evil, wicked; to blame, at fault, reproachable, responsible, answerable, erring, errant, in the wrong.
– OPPOSITES blameless.

blanch v. **1** *the cold light blanched her face* **turn pale**, whiten, lighten, bleach, wash out, fade. **2** *his face blanched* **pale**, turn pale, turn white, whiten, lose its colour, lighten, fade, blench. **3** *blanch the spinach leaves* **scald**, boil briefly.
– OPPOSITES colour, darken.

bland adj. **1** *bland food* **tasteless**, flavourless, insipid, weak, watery, spiceless, wishy-washy. **2** *a bland film* **uninteresting**, dull, boring, tedious, monotonous, dry, drab, dreary, wearisome; unexciting, unimaginative, uninspiring, uninspired, lacklustre, vapid, flat, stale, trite, vacuous, wishy-washy. **3** *a bland expression* **unemotional**, emotionless, dispassionate, passionless; unexpressive, cool, impassive; expressionless, blank, wooden, stony, deadpan, hollow, undemonstrative, imperturbable.
– OPPOSITES tangy, interesting, emotional.

blandishments plural n. **flattery**, cajolery, coaxing, wheedling, persuasion, honeyed words, smooth talk, blarney; informal sweet talk, soft soap, buttering up.

blank adj. **1** *a blank sheet of paper* **empty**, unmarked, unused, clear, free, bare, clean, plain. **2** *a blank face* **expressionless**, deadpan, wooden, stony, impassive, unresponsive, poker-faced, vacuous, empty, glazed, fixed, lifeless, inscrutable. **3** *'What?' said Maxim, looking blank* **baffled**, mystified, puzzled, perplexed, stumped, at a loss, stuck, bewildered, nonplussed, bemused, lost, uncomprehending, (all) at sea, confused; informal flummoxed, bamboozled. **4** *a blank refusal* **outright**, absolute, categorical, unqualified, complete, flat, straight, positive, certain, explicit, unequivocal, clear, clear-cut.
– OPPOSITES full, expressive, qualified.
▶ n. **space**, gap, lacuna.

blanket n. *a blanket of cloud* **covering**, layer, coating, carpet, overlay, cloak, mantle, veil, pall, shroud.
▶ adj. *a blanket ban on tobacco advertising* **complete**, total, comprehensive, overall, general, mass, umbrella, inclusive, all-inclusive, all-round, wholesale, outright, across the board, sweeping, indiscriminate, thorough; universal, global, worldwide, international, nationwide, countrywide, coast-to-coast.
– OPPOSITES partial, piecemeal.
▶ v. **1** *snow blanketed the mountains* **cover**, coat, carpet, overlay; cloak, shroud, swathe, envelop; literary mantle. **2** *double glazing blankets the noise a bit* **muffle**, deaden, soften, mute, silence, quieten, smother, dampen.
– OPPOSITES amplify.

blare v. *sirens blared* **blast**, sound loudly, trumpet, clamour, boom, roar, thunder, bellow, resound.
– OPPOSITES murmur.
▶ n. *the blare of the siren* **blast**, trumpeting, clamour, boom, roar, thunder, bellow.
– OPPOSITES murmur.

blarney n. **blandishments**, honeyed words, smooth talk, flattery, cajolery, coaxing, wheedling, persuasion; charm offensive; informal sweet talk, soft soap, smarm, buttering up.

blasé adj. **indifferent**, unconcerned, uncaring, casual, nonchalant, offhand, uninterested, apathetic, unimpressed, unmoved, unresponsive, phlegmatic; informal laid-back.
– OPPOSITES concerned, responsive.

blaspheme v. **swear**, curse, take the Lord's name in vain; informal cuss; old use execrate.

blasphemous adj. **sacrilegious**, profane, irreligious, irreverent, impious, ungodly, godless.
– OPPOSITES reverent.

blasphemy n. **profanity**, sacrilege, irreligion, irreverence, taking the Lord's name in vain, swearing, curse, cursing, impiety, desecration; old use execration.
– OPPOSITES reverence.

blast n. **1** *the blast from the bomb* **shock wave**, pressure wave. **2** *Friday's blast killed two people* **explosion**, detonation, discharge, burst. **3** *a sudden blast of cold air* **gust**, rush, gale, squall, wind, draught, waft, puff, flurry. **4** *the shrill blast of the trumpets* **blare**, wail, roar, screech, shriek, hoot, honk, beep.
▶ v. **1** *bombers were blasting enemy airfields* **blow up**, bomb, blow (to pieces), dynamite, explode; shell, strafe, bombard. **2** *guns were blasting away* **fire**, shoot, blaze, let fly, discharge. **3** *he blasted his horn* **honk**, beep, toot, sound. **4** *radios blasting out pop music* **blare**, boom, roar, thunder, bellow, pump, shriek, screech. **5** *Fowler was blasted with an airgun* **shoot**, gun down, mow down, cut down; informal pot, plug. **6** informal *he blasted the pupils for being late.* See **reprimand** (verb).
◻ **blast off** be launched, take off, lift off, leave the ground, become airborne, take to the air.

blasted adj. informal See **damned** (sense 2).

blast-off n. **launch**, lift-off, take-off, ascent, firing.
– OPPOSITES touchdown.

blatant adj. **flagrant**, glaring, obvious, undisguised, unconcealed, open; shameless, barefaced, unabashed, unashamed, unblushing, brazen, brass-necked.
– OPPOSITES inconspicuous, shamefaced.

blather v. *he just blathered on* **prattle**, babble, chatter, twitter, prate, go on, run on, rattle on, yap, jibber-jabber, maunder, ramble, burble, drivel; informal yak, yatter; Brit. informal witter, rabbit, chunter, waffle.
▶ n. *mindless blather* **prattle**, chatter, twitter, babble, prating, gabble, jabber, rambling; informal yatter, twaddle; Brit. informal wittering, chuntering.

blaze n. **1** *firemen fought the blaze* **fire**, flames, conflagration, inferno, holocaust. **2** *a blaze of light* **glare**, gleam, flash, burst, flare, streak, radiance, brilliance, beam. **3** *a blaze of anger* **outburst**, burst, eruption, flare-up, explosion, outbreak; blast, attack, fit, spasm, paroxysm, access, rush, storm.
▶ v. **1** *the fire blazed merrily* **burn**, be alight, be on fire, be in flames, flame. **2** *headlights blazed* **shine**, flash, flare, glare, gleam, glint, dazzle, glitter, glisten. **3** *soldiers blazed away* **fire**, shoot, blast, let fly.

blazon v. **1** *their name is blazoned across the sails* **display**, exhibit, present, spread, emblazon, plaster. **2** *the newspapers blazoned the news abroad* **publicize**, make known, make public, announce, report, communicate, spread, circulate, give out, publish, broadcast, trumpet, proclaim, promulgate.

bleach v. **1** *the blinds had been bleached by the sun* **turn white**, whiten, turn pale, blanch, lighten, fade, decolour, decolorize, peroxide. **2** *they saw bones bleaching in the sun* **turn white**, whiten, turn pale, pale, blanch, lose its colour, lighten, fade.
– OPPOSITES darken.

bleak adj. **1** *a bleak landscape* **bare**, exposed, desolate, stark, desert, lunar, open, empty, windswept; treeless, without vegetation, denuded. **2** *the future is bleak* **unpromising**, unfavourable, unpropitious, inauspicious; discouraging, disheartening, depressing, dim, gloomy, black, dark, grim, hopeless.
– OPPOSITES lush, promising.

bleary adj. **blurred**, blurry, unfocused; fogged, clouded, dull, misty, watery, rheumy; old use blear.
– OPPOSITES clear.

bleat v. **1** *the sheep were bleating* **baa**; N. Amer. informal blat. **2** *don't bleat to me about fairness* **complain**, grouse, carp, fuss, snivel; Scottish & Irish gurn; informal gripe, beef, whinge, bellyache, moan, go on; N. English informal mither; N. Amer. informal kvetch.

bleed v. **1** *his arm was bleeding* **lose blood**, haemorrhage. **2** *the doctor bled him* **draw blood from**; Medicine exsanguinate; old use phlebotomize. **3** *one colour bled into another* **flow**, run, seep, filter, percolate, leach. **4** *sap was bleeding from the trunk* **flow**, run, ooze, seep, exude, weep. **5** *the country was bled dry by poachers* **drain**, sap, deplete, milk, exhaust. **6** *my heart bleeds for them* **grieve**, ache, sorrow, mourn, lament, feel, suffer; sympathize with, pity.

blemish n. **1** *not a blemish marred her skin* **imperfection**, flaw, defect, fault, deformity, discoloration, disfigurement; bruise, scar, pit, pock, scratch, cut, gash; mark, streak, spot, smear, speck, blotch, smudge, smut; birthmark; Medicine stigma. **2** *government is not without blemish* **defect**, fault, failing, flaw, imperfection, foible, vice; shortcoming, weakness, deficiency, limitation; taint, stain, dishonour, disgrace.
– OPPOSITES virtue.
▶v. **1** *nothing blemished the coast* **mar**, spoil, impair, disfigure, blight, deface, mark, scar; ruin. **2** *his reign has been blemished by controversy* **sully**, tarnish, besmirch, blacken, blot, taint; spoil, mar, ruin, disgrace, damage, undermine, degrade, dishonour; formal vitiate.
– OPPOSITES enhance.

blench v. **flinch**, start, shy (away), recoil, shrink, pull back, cringe, wince, quail, cower.

blend v. **1** *blend the ingredients until smooth* **mix**, mingle, combine, merge, fuse, meld, coalesce, integrate, intermix; stir, whisk, fold in; technical admix; literary commingle. **2** *the new buildings blend with the older ones* **harmonize**, go (well), fit (in), be in tune, be compatible; coordinate, match, complement.
▶n. *a blend of bananas, raisins, and ginger* **mixture**, mix, combination, amalgamation, amalgam, union, marriage, fusion, meld, synthesis; technical admixture.

bless v. **1** *the chaplain blessed the couple* **ask/invoke God's favour for**. **2** *the Cardinal blessed the memorial plaque* **consecrate**, sanctify, dedicate (to God), make holy, make sacred; formal hallow. **3** *bless the name of the Lord* **praise**, worship, glorify, honour,

exalt, pay homage to, venerate, reverence, hallow; old use magnify. **4** *the gods blessed us with magical voices* **endow**, bestow, furnish, accord, give, favour, grace; confer on; literary endue. **5** *I bless the day you came here* **give thanks for**, be grateful for, thank; appreciate. **6** *the government refused to bless the undertaking* **sanction**, consent to, endorse, agree to, approve, back, support; informal give the thumbs up to, give the green light to, OK.
– OPPOSITES curse, trouble, rue, oppose.

blessed adj. **1** *a blessed place* **holy**, sacred, hallowed, consecrated, sanctified; ordained, canonized, beatified. **2** *blessed are the meek* **favoured**, fortunate, lucky, privileged, enviable. **3** *the fresh air made a blessed change* **welcome**, pleasant, agreeable, refreshing, favourable, gratifying, heartening, much needed.
– OPPOSITES cursed, wretched, unwelcome.

blessing n. **1** *may God give us his blessing* **protection**, favour. **2** *a special blessing from the priest* **benediction**, invocation, prayer, intercession; grace. **3** *she gave the plan her blessing* **sanction**, endorsement, approval, approbation, favour, consent, assent, agreement; backing, support; informal the thumbs up. **4** *it was a blessing they didn't have far to go* **boon**, godsend, advantage, benefit, help, bonus, plus; stroke of luck, windfall; literary benison.
– OPPOSITES condemnation, affliction.

blight n. **1** *potato blight* **disease**, canker, infestation, fungus, mildew, mould. **2** *the blight of aircraft noise* **affliction**, scourge, bane, curse, plague, menace, misfortune, woe, trouble, ordeal, trial, nuisance, pest.
– OPPOSITES blessing.
▶v. **1** *a tree blighted by leaf curl* **infect**, mildew; kill, destroy. **2** *scandal blighted the careers of several politicians* **ruin**, wreck, spoil, mar, frustrate, disrupt, undo, end, scotch, destroy, shatter, devastate, demolish; informal mess up, foul up, put paid to, put the kibosh on, stymie; Brit. informal scupper; old use bring to naught.

blind adj. **1** *he has been blind since birth* **sightless**, unsighted, visually impaired, visionless, unseeing; partially sighted, purblind; informal as blind as a bat. **2** *she was ignorant, but not blind* **imperceptive**, unperceptive, insensitive, slow, obtuse, uncomprehending; stupid, unintelligent; informal dense, dim, thick, dumb, dopey; Brit. informal dozy; Scottish & N. English informal glaikit. **3** *you should be blind to failure* **unmindful of**, mindless of, careless of, heedless of, oblivious to, insensible to, unconcerned about, indifferent to. **4** *blind acceptance of conventional opinion* **uncritical**, unreasoned, unthinking, unconsidered, mindless, undiscerning, indiscriminate. **5** *a blind rage* **wild**, uncontrolled, unbridled, uncontrollable, unrestrained, furious, towering. **6** *a blind alley* **without exit**, blocked, closed, barred, impassable; dead-end.

b

– OPPOSITES sighted, perceptive, mindful, discerning.

▸ v. **1** *he was blinded in a car crash* **make blind**, deprive of sight, render sightless; put someone's eyes out. **2** *scaffolding blinded the windows* **obscure**, cover, blot out, mask, shroud, block, eclipse, obstruct. **3** *he was blinded by his faith* **deprive of judgement**, deprive of reason, deprive of sense. **4** *they try to blind you with science* **overawe**, intimidate, daunt, deter, discourage, cow, abash, subdue, dismay; disquiet, discomfit, unsettle, disconcert; confuse, bewilder, confound, perplex, overwhelm; informal faze, psych out.

▸ n. **1** *a window blind* **screen**, shade, sunshade, curtain, awning, canopy; louvre, jalousie, shutter. **2** *some crook had sent the card as a blind* **deception**, camouflage, smokescreen, front, facade, cover, pretext, masquerade, feint; trick, ploy, ruse, machination.

blindly adv. **1** *he stared blindly ahead* **sightlessly**, unseeingly. **2** *he ran blindly upstairs* **impetuously**, impulsively, recklessly, heedlessly, uncontrolledly. **3** *they blindly followed US policy* **uncritically**, unthinkingly, mindlessly, indiscriminately.

blink v. **1** *his eyes did not blink* **flutter**, flicker, wink, bat; technical nictitate, nictate. **2** *several red lights began to blink* **flash**, flicker, wink. **3** *no one even blinks at the 'waitresses' in drag* **be surprised**, look twice; informal boggle.

blinkered adj. **narrow-minded**, inward-looking, parochial, provincial, insular, small-minded, close-minded, short-sighted; hidebound, inflexible, entrenched, prejudiced, bigoted; Brit. parish-pump.
– OPPOSITES broad-minded.

bliss n. **1** *she gave a sigh of bliss* **joy**, happiness, pleasure, delight, ecstasy, elation, rapture, euphoria. **2** *religions promise perfect bliss after death* **blessedness**, benediction, beatitude, glory, heavenly joy, divine happiness; heaven, paradise.
– OPPOSITES misery, hell.

blissful adj. **ecstatic**, euphoric, joyful, elated, rapturous, on cloud nine, in seventh heaven; delighted, thrilled, overjoyed, joyous; informal over the moon, on top of the world; Austral. informal wrapped.

blister n. **1** *a blister on each heel* **bleb**; Medicine bulla, pustule, vesicle, vesication. **2** *check for blisters in the roofing felt* **bubble**, swelling, bulge, protuberance.

blistering adj. **1** *blistering heat* **intense**, extreme, ferocious, fierce; **scorching**, searing, blazing, burning, fiery; informal boiling, baking, roasting, sweltering. **2** *a blistering attack on the government* **savage**, vicious, fierce, bitter, harsh, scathing, devastating, caustic, searing, vitriolic. **3** *a blistering pace* **very fast**, breakneck; informal blinding.
– OPPOSITES mild, leisurely.

blithe adj. **1** *a blithe disregard for the rules* **casual**, indifferent, unconcerned, unworried, untroubled, uncaring, careless, heedless, thoughtless; nonchalant, blasé. **2** literary *his blithe, smiling face* **happy**, cheerful, jolly, merry, joyful, joyous, blissful, ecstatic, euphoric, elated; literary blithesome; dated gay.
– OPPOSITES thoughtful, sad.

blitz n. *the 1940 blitz on London* **bombardment**, bombing, onslaught, barrage; campaign, attack, assault, raid, strike, blitzkrieg.

▸ v. *the town was blitzed in the war* **bombard**, attack, bomb, shell, torpedo, strafe; destroy, devastate, ravage.

blizzard n. **snowstorm**, white-out.

bloated adj. **swollen**, distended, tumefied, bulging, inflated, enlarged, expanded, dilated.

blob n. **1** *a blob of cold gravy* **drop**, droplet, globule, bead, bubble; informal glob. **2** *a blob of ink* **spot**, dab, blotch, blot, dot, smudge; informal splotch, splodge.

▸ v. *masking fluid is blobbed on freely* **daub**, dab, spot, slop.

bloc n. **alliance**, coalition, federation, confederation, league, union, partnership, axis, body, association, group.

block n. **1** *a block of cheese* **chunk**, hunk, lump, wedge, cube, brick, slab, piece; Brit. informal wodge. **2** *an apartment block* **building**, complex, structure, development. **3** *a block of shares* **batch**, group, set, quantity, tranche. **4** *a sketching block* **pad**, notepad, sketch pad, jotter, tablet. **5** *a block to Third World development* **obstacle**, bar, barrier, impediment, hindrance, check, hurdle, stumbling block, handicap, deterrent. **6** *a block in the pipe* **blockage**, obstruction, stoppage, congestion, occlusion, clot.
– OPPOSITES aid.

▸ v. **1** *weeds can block drainage ditches* **clog (up)**, stop up, choke, plug, obstruct, gum up, dam up, bung up, congest, jam, close; Brit. informal gunge up; technical occlude. **2** *picket lines blocked access to the factory* **hinder**, hamper, obstruct, impede, inhibit, restrict, limit; halt, stop, bar, check, prevent. **3** *he blocked a shot on the goal line* **parry**, stop, deflect, fend off, hold off, repel, repulse.
– OPPOSITES facilitate.

▫ **block something off** close up, shut off, seal off, barricade, bar, obstruct.
block something out 1 *trees blocked out the light* **conceal**, keep out, blot out, exclude, obliterate, blank out, stop. **2** *block out an area in charcoal* **rough out**, sketch out, outline, delineate, draft.

blockade n. **1** *a naval blockade of the island* **siege**. **2** *they erected blockades in the streets* **barricade**, barrier, roadblock; obstacle, obstruction.

▸ v. *rebels blockaded the capital* **barricade**, block off, shut off, seal; **besiege**, surround.

blockage n. **obstruction**, stoppage, block, occlusion, congestion.

bloke n. Brit. informal See **fellow** (sense 1).

blonde, blond adj. **fair**, light, yellow, flaxen, tow-coloured, golden, platinum, ash blonde, strawberry blonde; bleached, peroxide.
– OPPOSITES dark.

blood n. **1** *he had lost too much blood* gore, vital fluid; literary lifeblood, ichor. **2** *a woman of noble blood* **ancestry**, lineage, bloodline, descent, parentage, family, birth, extraction, origin, genealogy, heritage, stock, kinship.

> **WORD LINKS**
>
> **corpuscle** a blood cell
> **haemoglobin** the protein in the blood that transports oxygen
> **plasma** the colourless part of the blood
> **anaemia** a shortage of haemoglobin in the blood
> **septicaemia, toxaemia** blood poisoning
> **leukaemia** a blood disease in which increased numbers of white cells are produced
> **haematology** the branch of medicine relating to blood
> **haemophilia** a medical condition in which the blood cannot clot properly
> **haemorrhage** an escape of blood from a ruptured blood vessel
> **styptic** able to stop bleeding

blood-curdling adj. **terrifying**, frightening, spine-chilling, chilling, hair-raising, horrifying, alarming; eerie, sinister, horrible; Scottish eldritch; informal scary.

bloodless adj. **1** *a bloodless revolution* **non-violent**, peaceful, peaceable, pacifist. **2** *his face was bloodless* **anaemic**, pale, wan, pallid, ashen, colourless, chalky, waxen, white, grey, pasty, drained, drawn, deathly. **3** *a bloodless Hollywood mogul* **heartless**, unfeeling, cruel, ruthless, merciless, pitiless, uncharitable; cold, hard, stony-hearted, cold-blooded, callous. **4** *a bloodless chorus* **feeble**, spiritless, lifeless, listless, half-hearted, unenthusiastic, lukewarm.
– OPPOSITES bloody, ruddy, charitable, powerful.

bloodshed n. **slaughter**, massacre, killing, wounding; carnage, butchery, bloodletting, bloodbath; violence, fighting, warfare, battle; literary slaying.

bloodthirsty adj. **murderous**, homicidal, violent, vicious, barbarous, barbaric, savage, brutal, cut-throat; fierce, ferocious, inhuman.

bloody adj. **1** *his bloody nose* **bleeding**. **2** *bloody medical waste* **bloodstained**, blood-soaked, gory; old use sanguinary. **3** *a bloody civil war* **vicious**, ferocious, savage, fierce, brutal, murderous, gory; old use sanguinary. **4** informal *a bloody nuisance!* See **damned**.

bloody-minded adj. Brit. informal **uncooperative**, awkward, disobliging, recalcitrant, unaccommodating, inflexible, uncompromising, contrary, perverse, obstinate, stubborn; difficult; informal pig-headed; Brit. informal bolshie, stroppy.
– OPPOSITES compliant.

bloom n. **1** *orchid blooms* **flower**, blossom, floweret, floret. **2** *a girl in the bloom of youth* **prime**, perfection, acme, peak, height, heyday; salad days. **3** *the bloom of her skin*

radiance, lustre, sheen, glow, freshness; blush, rosiness, pinkness, colour.
▶ v. **1** *the geraniums bloomed* **flower**, blossom, open; mature. **2** *the children bloomed in the Devonshire air* **flourish**, thrive, prosper, progress, burgeon; informal be in the pink.
– OPPOSITES wither, decline.

blossom n. *pink blossoms* **flower**, bloom, floweret, floret.
▶ v. **1** *the snowdrops have blossomed* **bloom**, flower, open, unfold; mature. **2** *the whole region had blossomed* **develop**, grow, mature, progress, evolve; flourish, thrive, prosper, bloom, burgeon.
– OPPOSITES fade, decline.

blot n. **1** *an ink blot* **spot**, dot, mark, blotch, smudge, patch, dab; informal splotch; Brit. informal splodge. **2** *the only blot on a clean campaign* **blemish**, taint, stain, blight, flaw, fault; disgrace, dishonour. **3** *a blot on the landscape* **eyesore**, monstrosity, carbuncle, mess; informal sight.
▶ v. **1** *blot the excess water* **soak up**, absorb, sponge up, mop up; dry up/out; dab, pat. **2** *the writing was messy and blotted* **smudge**, smear, blotch, mark. **3** *he had blotted our name forever* **tarnish**, taint, stain, blacken, sully, mar; dishonour, disgrace, besmirch.
– OPPOSITES honour.
□ **blot something out 1** *Mary blotted out her picture* **erase**, obliterate, delete, efface, rub out, blank out, expunge; cross out, strike out. **2** *clouds were starting to blot out the stars* **conceal**, hide, obscure, exclude, obliterate; shadow, eclipse. **3** *he urged her to blot out the memory* **erase**, efface, eradicate, expunge, wipe out.

blotch n. **1** *pink flowers with dark blotches* **patch**, smudge, dot, spot, blot, dab, daub; informal splotch; Brit. informal splodge. **2** *his face was covered in blotches* **patch**, mark, freckle, birthmark, discoloration, eruption, naevus.
▶ v. *her face was blotched and swollen* **spot**, mark, smudge, streak, blemish.

blotchy adj. **mottled**, dappled, blotched, patchy, spotty, spotted, smudged, marked; informal splotchy; Brit. informal splodgy.

blow¹ v. **1** *the icy wind blew around us* **gust**, puff, flurry, blast, roar, bluster, rush, storm. **2** *his ship was blown on to the rocks* **sweep**, carry, toss, drive, push, force. **3** *leaves blew across the road* **drift**, flutter, waft, float, glide, whirl, move. **4** *he blew a smoke ring* **exhale**, puff; emit, expel, discharge, issue. **5** *Uncle Albert was puffing and blowing* **wheeze**, puff, pant, gasp. **6** *he blew a trumpet* **sound**, blast, toot, pipe, trumpet; play. **7** *a rear tyre had blown* **burst**, explode, blow out, split, rupture, puncture. **8** *the bulb had blown* **fuse**, short-circuit, burn out, break, go. **9** informal *he blew his money on gambling* **squander**, waste, misspend, throw away, fritter away, go through, lose, lavish, dissipate, use up; spend recklessly; informal splurge; Brit. informal dated blue. **10** informal *don't blow this opportunity* **spoil**, ruin, bungle, mess up, fudge; **waste**, lose, squander; informal botch, muff, screw up, foul up; Brit. informal cock up, bodge. **11** *his cover was blown* **expose**, reveal, uncover, disclose, divulge, unveil, betray, leak.

□ **blow out 1** *the matches will not blow out in a strong wind* **be extinguished**, go out, be put out, stop burning. **2** *the windows blew out* **shatter**, rupture, crack, smash, splinter, disintegrate; burst, explode, fly apart; informal bust.

blow something out extinguish, put out, snuff, douse, quench, smother.

blow over abate, subside, drop off, lessen, ease (off), let up, diminish, fade, dwindle, slacken, recede, tail off, peter out, pass, die down, fizzle out.

blow up 1 *a lorryload of shells blew up* **explode**, detonate, go off, ignite, erupt. **2** *he blows up at whoever's in his way* **lose one's temper**, get angry, rant and rave, go berserk, flare up, erupt; informal go mad, go crazy, go wild, go ape, hit the roof, fly off the handle. **3** *a crisis blew up* **break out**, erupt, flare up, boil over; emerge, arise.

blow something up 1 *they blew the plane up* **bomb**, blast, destroy; explode, detonate. **2** *blow up the balloons* **inflate**, pump up, fill up, puff up, swell, expand, aerate. **3** *things get blown up out of all proportion* **exaggerate**, overstate, overstress, overestimate, magnify, amplify; aggrandize, embellish, elaborate. **4** *I blew the picture up on a photocopier* **enlarge**, magnify, expand, increase.

blow² n. **1** *a blow on the head* **knock**, **bang**, hit, punch, thump, smack, crack, rap; informal whack, thwack, bash, clout, sock, wallop. **2** *losing his wife must have been a blow* **shock**, surprise, bombshell, thunderbolt, jolt; calamity, catastrophe, disaster, upset, setback.

blowout n. **1** *the steering is automatic in the event of blowouts* **puncture**, flat tyre, burst tyre; informal flat. **2** *informal this meal is our last real blowout* **feast**, banquet, celebration, party; informal shindig, do, binge; Brit. informal beanfeast, bunfight, nosh-up.

blowsy adj. **untidy**, sloppy, scruffy, messy, dishevelled, unkempt, frowzy, slovenly; coarse; **red-faced**, ruddy, florid, raddled.
– OPPOSITES tidy, respectable.

blowy adj. **windy**, windswept, blustery, gusty, breezy; stormy, squally.
– OPPOSITES still.

blubber¹ n. *whale blubber* **fat**, fatty tissue.

blubber² v. informal *she started to blubber* **cry**, sob, weep, howl, snivel; informal blub, boohoo.

bludgeon n. *hooligans wielding bludgeons* **cudgel**, club, stick, truncheon, baton; N. Amer. nightstick, blackjack; Brit. informal cosh.
▶v. **1** *he was bludgeoned to death* **batter**, cudgel, club, beat, thrash; informal clobber. **2** *I let him bludgeon me into marriage* **coerce**, force, compel, pressurize, pressure, bully, browbeat, hector, dragoon, steamroller; informal strong-arm, railroad.

blue adj. **1** *bright blue eyes* **sky-blue**, azure, cobalt, sapphire, navy, Oxford blue,
Cambridge blue, ultramarine, aquamarine, cyan; literary cerulean. **2** informal *Mum was feeling a bit blue* **depressed**, down, sad, unhappy, melancholy, miserable, gloomy, dejected, downhearted, downcast, despondent, low, glum; informal down in the dumps, down in the mouth, fed up. **3** informal *a blue movie* **pornographic**, racy, risqué, naughty, spicy; indecent, dirty, lewd, smutty, filthy, obscene, sordid; erotic, arousing, sexy, titillating, explicit; informal porn, porno, X-rated, raunchy; euphemistic adult.
– OPPOSITES happy, clean.

blueprint n. **1** *blueprints of the aircraft plan*, design, diagram, drawing, sketch, map, layout, representation. **2** *a blueprint for similar measures in other countries* **model**, plan, template, framework, pattern, example, guide, prototype, pilot.

blues plural n. informal *a fit of blues* **depression**, sadness, unhappiness, melancholy, misery, sorrow, gloom, dejection, despondency, despair; the doldrums.

bluff¹ n. *this offer was denounced as a bluff* **deception**, subterfuge, pretence, sham, fake, deceit, feint, hoax, fraud, charade; trick, ruse, scheme, machination; informal put-on.
▶v. **1** *they are bluffing to hide their guilt* **pretend**, sham, fake, feign, lie, hoax, pose, posture, masquerade, dissemble. **2** *I managed to bluff the board into believing me* **deceive**, delude, mislead, trick, fool, hoodwink, dupe, hoax, beguile, gull; informal con, kid, have on.

bluff² adj. *a bluff man* **plain-spoken**, straightforward, blunt, direct, no-nonsense, frank, open, candid, forthright, unequivocal; hearty, genial, good-natured; informal upfront.

bluff³ n. *an impregnable high bluff* **cliff**, promontory, headland, crag, bank, peak, escarpment, scarp.

blunder n. *he shook his head at his blunder* **mistake**, error, gaffe, slip, oversight, faux pas; informal botch, slip-up, boo-boo, fail; Brit. informal clanger, boob; N. Amer. informal blooper.
▶v. **1** *the government admitted it had blundered* **make a mistake**, err, miscalculate, bungle, trip up, be wrong; informal slip up, screw up, blow it, goof; Brit. informal boob. **2** *she blundered down the steps* **stumble**, lurch, stagger, flounder, struggle, fumble, grope.

blunt adj. **1** *a blunt knife* **unsharpened**, dull, worn, edgeless. **2** *the leaf is broad with a blunt tip* **rounded**, flat, obtuse, stubby. **3** *a blunt message* **straightforward**, frank, plain-spoken, candid, direct, bluff, forthright, unequivocal; brusque, abrupt, curt, terse, bald, brutal, harsh; stark, undisguised, unvarnished; informal upfront.
– OPPOSITES sharp, pointed, subtle.
▶v. **1** *ebony blunts tools very rapidly* **dull**, make less sharp. **2** *age hasn't blunted my passion for life* **dull**, deaden, dampen, numb, weaken, sap, cool, temper, allay, abate; diminish, reduce, decrease, lessen, deplete.
– OPPOSITES sharpen, intensify.

b

blur v. **1** *she felt tears blur her vision* **cloud**, fog, obscure, dim, make hazy, unfocus, soften; literary bedim; old use blear. **2** *films blur the difference between villains and victims* **obscure**, make vague, confuse, muddle, muddy, obfuscate, cloud, weaken. **3** *memories of the picnic had blurred* **become dim**, dull, numb, deaden, mute; lessen, decrease, diminish.
– OPPOSITES sharpen, focus.
▶ n. *a blur on the horizon* **shape**, form, smudge; haze, cloud, mist.

blurred adj. **indistinct**, blurry, fuzzy, hazy, misty, foggy, shadowy, faint; unclear, vague, indefinite, unfocused, obscure, nebulous.

blurt v.
□ **blurt something out** burst out with, exclaim, call out; divulge, disclose, reveal, betray, let slip, give away; informal blab, gush, let on, spill the beans, let the cat out of the bag; dated ejaculate.

blush v. *Joan blushed at the compliment* **redden**, turn/go pink, turn/go red, flush, colour, burn up; feel shy, feel embarrassed.
▶ n. *the darkness hid her fiery blush* **flush**, rosiness, pinkness, bloom, high colour.

bluster v. **1** *he started blustering about the general election* **rant**, thunder, bellow, sound off; be overbearing; informal throw one's weight about/around. **2** *storms bluster in from the sea* **blast**, gust, storm, roar, rush.
▶ n. *his bluster turned to cooperation* **ranting**, thundering, hectoring, bullying; bombast, bumptiousness, braggadocio.

blustery adj. **stormy**, gusty, blowy, windy, squally, wild, tempestuous, turbulent; howling, roaring.
– OPPOSITES calm.

board n. **1** *a wooden board* **plank**, beam, panel, slat, batten, timber, lath. **2** *the board of directors* **committee**, council, panel, directorate, commission, group. **3** *your room and board will be free* **food**, meals, provisions, refreshments, diet, table, bread; keep, maintenance; informal grub, nosh, eats, chow; Brit. informal scoff.
▶ v. **1** *he boarded the aircraft* **get on**, go aboard, enter, mount, ascend; embark, emplane, entrain; catch; informal hop on. **2** *a number of students boarded with them* **lodge**, live, reside, be housed; N. Amer. room; informal put up, have digs. **3** *they run a facility for boarding dogs* **accommodate**, lodge, take in, put up, house; keep, feed, cater for.

boast v. **1** *his mother had been boasting about him* **brag**, crow, swagger, swank, gloat, show off; exaggerate, overstate; informal talk big, lay it on thick; Austral./NZ informal skite. **2** *the hotel boasts a fine restaurant* **possess**, have, own, enjoy, pride oneself/itself on.
▶ n. **1** *I said I would win and it wasn't an idle boast* **brag**, self-praise; claim, exaggeration, overstatement; informal swank; Austral./NZ informal skite; rare fanfaronade. **2** *the hall is the boast of the county* **pride**, joy, wonder, delight, treasure, gem.

boastful adj. **bragging**, swaggering, bumptious, puffed up, full of oneself; cocky, conceited, arrogant, egotistical; informal swanky, big-headed; N. Amer. informal blowhard; literary vainglorious.
– OPPOSITES modest.

boat n. *a rowing boat* **vessel**, craft, watercraft, ship; literary keel, barque.
▶ v. *he insisted on boating into the lake* **sail**, yacht, cruise.

bob v. **1** *their yacht bobbed about* **move up and down**, bounce, toss, skip, dance, jounce; wobble, jiggle, joggle, jolt, jerk. **2** *the bookie's head bobbed* **nod**, incline, dip; wag, waggle. **3** *the maid bobbed and left the room* **curtsy**, bow.
▶ n. **1** *a bob of his head* **nod**, inclination, dip; wag, waggle. **2** *the maid scurried away with a bob* **curtsy**, bow, obeisance.

bode v. **augur**, portend, herald, be a sign of, warn of, foreshadow, be an omen of, presage, indicate, signify, promise, threaten, spell, denote, foretell; prophesy, predict; literary betoken, forebode.

bodily adj. *bodily sensations* **physical**, corporeal, corporal, somatic, fleshly; concrete, real, actual, tangible.
– OPPOSITES spiritual, mental.
▶ adv. *he hauled her bodily from the van* **forcefully**, forcibly, violently; wholly, completely, entirely.

body n. **1** *the human body* **figure**, frame, form, physique, anatomy, skeleton; soma; informal bod. **2** *he was hit by shrapnel in the head and body* **torso**, trunk. **3** *the bodies were put in the fire* **corpse**, carcass, skeleton; remains; informal stiff; Medicine cadaver. **4** *the body of the article* **main part**, central part, core, heart, hub. **5** *the body of the ship* **bodywork**, hull; fuselage. **6** *a body of water* **expanse**, mass, area, stretch, tract, sweep, extent. **7** *a growing body of evidence* **quantity**, amount, volume, collection, mass, corpus. **8** *the representative body of the employers* **association**, organization, group, party, company, society, circle, syndicate, guild, corporation, contingent. **9** *a heavenly body* **object**, entity. **10** *add body to your hair* **fullness**, thickness, substance, bounce, lift, shape.
□ **body and soul** completely, entirely, totally, utterly, fully, thoroughly, wholeheartedly, unconditionally, to the hilt.

> **WORD LINKS**
> **corporal, corporeal, somatic** relating to the body
> **anatomy** the study of the structure of the body
> **biorhythm** a recurring cycle in the functioning of the body
> **palpate** examine a part of the body by touch

bodyguard n. **minder**, guard, protector, guardian, defender; informal heavy.

boffin n. Brit. informal **expert**, specialist, authority, genius, mastermind; **scientist**, technician, inventor; informal egghead, Einstein.

b

bog n. **marsh**, swamp, mire, quagmire, morass, slough, fen, wetland; Brit. carr; Scottish & N. English moss.
□ **bog someone/something down** mire, stick, entangle, ensnare, embroil; hamper, hinder, impede, delay, stall, detain; swamp, overwhelm.

bogey n. **1** *water bogies frighten children from pools* **evil spirit**, bogle, spectre, phantom, hobgoblin, demon; informal spook. **2** *the guild is the bogey of bankers* **bugbear**, pet hate, bane, anathema, abomination, nightmare, horror, dread, curse; N. Amer. bugaboo.

boggle v. informal **1** *this data makes the mind boggle* **marvel**, wonder, be astonished, be overwhelmed, be staggered; gape, goggle; informal gawk. **2** *you never boggle at plain speaking* **demur**, balk; shrink from, shy away from, be shy about; hesitate, waver, falter; informal be cagey about.

boggy adj. **marshy**, swampy, miry, fenny, muddy, waterlogged, wet, soggy, sodden, squelchy; spongy, heavy, sloughy.

bogus adj. **fake**, spurious, false, fraudulent, sham, deceptive; **counterfeit**, forged, feigned; make-believe, dummy, pseudo; informal phoney, pretend.
– OPPOSITES genuine.

bohemian n. *he is an artist and a real bohemian* **nonconformist**, avant-gardist, free spirit, dropout; hippy, beatnik.
– OPPOSITES conservative.
▶ adj. *his family disapproved of his bohemian life* **unconventional**, nonconformist, unorthodox, avant-garde, irregular, alternative; artistic; informal arty-farty, way-out, offbeat.
– OPPOSITES conventional.

boil¹ v. **1** *boil the potatoes* **cook**, simmer; bring to the boil. **2** *the soup is boiling* **simmer**, bubble, stew. **3** *a huge cliff with the sea boiling below* **churn**, seethe, froth, foam; literary roil. **4** *she boiled at his lack of consideration* **fume**, seethe, rage, smoulder, bristle, be angry, be furious; get worked up; informal see red, get steamed up.
▶ n. bring the stock to the boil **boiling point**, 100 degrees centigrade.
□ **boil something down** condense, reduce, concentrate, thicken.
boil down to come down to, amount to, add up to, be in essence.

boil² n. *a boil on her neck* **swelling**, spot, pimple, blister, pustule, eruption, carbuncle, wen, abscess, ulcer; technical furuncle.

boiling adj. **1** *boiling water* **at boiling point**, at 100 degrees centigrade; very hot, piping hot; bubbling. **2** informal *it was a boiling day* **very hot**, scorching, blistering, sweltering, sultry, torrid; informal roasting, baking.
– OPPOSITES freezing.

boisterous adj. **1** *a boisterous game of handball* **lively**, animated, exuberant, spirited; rowdy, unruly, wild, uproarious, unrestrained, undisciplined, uninhibited, uncontrolled, rough, disorderly, riotous;

noisy, loud, clamorous; informal rumbustious, Tiggerish. **2** *a boisterous wind* **blustery**, gusty, windy, stormy, wild, squally, tempestuous; howling, roaring; informal blowy.
– OPPOSITES restrained, calm.

bold adj. **1** *bold adventurers* **daring**, intrepid, brave, courageous, valiant, valorous, fearless, dauntless, audacious, daredevil; adventurous, heroic, plucky, spirited, confident, assured; informal gutsy, spunky, feisty. **2** *a bold pattern* **striking**, vivid, bright, strong, eye-catching, prominent; gaudy, lurid, garish. **3** *departure times are in bold type* **heavy**, thick.
– OPPOSITES timid, pale.

bolshie adj. Brit. informal **uncooperative**, awkward, disobliging, unhelpful, recalcitrant, contrary, perverse, obstinate, stubborn, difficult, unreasonable, exasperating, trying; Brit. informal bloody-minded, stroppy.
– OPPOSITES compliant.

bolster n. *the bed was strewn with bolsters* **pillow**, cushion, pad.
▶ v. *a break would bolster her morale* **strengthen**, reinforce, boost, fortify, renew; support, buoy up, shore up, maintain, aid, help; augment, increase.
– OPPOSITES undermine.

bolt n. **1** *the bolt on the shed door* **bar**, lock, catch, latch, fastener. **2** *nuts and bolts* **rivet**, pin, peg, screw. **3** *a bolt whirred over my head* **arrow**, quarrel, dart, shaft; literary reed. **4** *a bolt of lightning* **flash**, shaft, streak, burst, flare. **5** *Mark made a bolt for the door* **dash**, dart, run, sprint, leap, bound. **6** *a bolt of cloth* **roll**, reel, spool; quantity, amount.
▶ v. **1** *he bolted the door* **lock**, bar, latch, fasten, secure. **2** *the lid was bolted down* **rivet**, pin, peg, screw; fasten, fix. **3** *Anna bolted from the room* **dash**, dart, run, sprint, hurtle, rush, fly, shoot, bound; flee; informal tear, scoot, leg it. **4** *he bolted down his breakfast* **gobble**, gulp, wolf, guzzle, devour; informal demolish, polish off, scoff, shovel down, hoover up, trough; Brit. informal shift, gollop; N. Amer. informal scarf, snarf.
□ **a bolt from/out of the blue** shock, surprise, bombshell, thunderbolt, revelation; informal turn-up for the books.

bomb n. **1** *bombs burst on the runway* **explosive**, incendiary (device). **2** *the fight against the bomb* **nuclear weapons**, nuclear bombs, atom bombs, A-bombs, weapons of mass destruction, WMD. **3** Brit. informal *a new superstore will cost a bomb*. See **fortune** (sense 5).
▶ v. **1** *their headquarters were bombed* **bombard**, blast, shell, blitz, strafe, pound; attack, assault; blow up, destroy, demolish, flatten, devastate. **2** Brit. informal *she bombed across Texas*. See **speed** (sense 1 of the verb). **3** informal *the film bombed at the box office*. See **fail** (sense 1).

bombard v. **1** *gun batteries bombarded the islands* **shell**, pound, blitz, strafe, bomb; assail, attack, assault, batter, blast, pelt. **2** *we were bombarded with information* **inundate**, swamp, flood, deluge, snow under; besiege, overwhelm.

bombast n. **bluster**, pomposity, empty talk, humbug, turgidity, verbosity, verbiage; pretentiousness, ostentation, grandiloquence; informal hot air; rare fustian.

bombastic adj. **pompous**, blustering, turgid, verbose, orotund, high-flown, high-sounding, overwrought, pretentious, ostentatious, grandiloquent; informal highfalutin; rare fustian.

bona fide adj. **authentic**, genuine, real, true, actual; legal, legitimate, lawful, valid, proper; informal legit, pukka, the real McCoy.
– OPPOSITES bogus.

bonanza n. **windfall**, godsend, boon, blessing, bonus, stroke of luck; informal jackpot.

bond n. **1** *the women forged a close bond* **friendship**, relationship, fellowship, partnership, association, affiliation, alliance, attachment. **2** *the prisoner struggled with his bonds* **chains**, fetters, shackles, manacles, irons, restraints. **3** *I've broken my bond* **promise**, pledge, vow, oath, word (of honour), guarantee, assurance; agreement, contract, pact, bargain, deal.
▸ v. *the extensions are bonded to your hair* **join**, fasten, fix, affix, attach, secure, bind, stick, fuse.

bondage n. **slavery**, enslavement, servitude, subjugation, subjection, oppression, domination, exploitation, persecution; historical serfdom, vassalage; old use enthralment.
– OPPOSITES liberty.

bone n.

WORD LINKS
osseous consisting of bone
orthopaedics the branch of medicine concerned with bones
ossify turn into bone or bony tissue
osteopathy treatment involving manipulation of the bones and muscles
osteoporosis a condition in which the bones become brittle
caries the decay of a bone or tooth

bonhomie n. **geniality**, affability, conviviality, cordiality, amiability, sociability, friendliness, warmth, joviality.
– OPPOSITES coldness.

bon mot n. **witticism**, quip, pun, pleasantry, jest, joke; informal wisecrack, one-liner.

bonny adj. Scottish & N. English **beautiful**, attractive, pretty, gorgeous, fetching, prepossessing; lovely, nice, sweet, cute, appealing, endearing, adorable, lovable, charming, winsome; informal divine; Austral./ NZ informal beaut; literary beauteous; old use fair, comely.
– OPPOSITES unattractive.

bonus n. **1** *the extra work's a real bonus* **benefit**, advantage, boon, blessing, godsend, stroke of luck, asset, plus, pro, attraction, extra; informal perk; formal perquisite. **2** *she's on a good salary and she gets a bonus*

gratuity, handout, gift, present, reward, prize; incentive, inducement; informal perk, sweetener; formal perquisite.
– OPPOSITES disadvantage.

bon viveur, **bon vivant** n. **hedonist**, pleasure-seeker, sensualist, sybarite, voluptuary; epicure, gourmet, gastronome.
– OPPOSITES puritan.

bony adj. **gaunt**, angular, skinny, thin, lean, spare, spindly, skin and bone, skeletal, emaciated, underweight; informal like a bag of bones.
– OPPOSITES plump.

booby n. See **idiot**.

book n. **1** *he published his first book in 1610* **volume**, tome, publication, title; novel, storybook, treatise, manual; paperback, hardback, softback. **2** *he scribbled in his book* **notepad**, notebook, pad, memo pad, exercise book; logbook, ledger, journal, diary; Brit. jotter, pocketbook; N. Amer. scratch pad. **3** *the council had to balance its books* **accounts**, records; account book, record book, ledger, balance sheet.
▸ v. **1** *she booked a table at the restaurant* **reserve**, make a reservation for, prearrange, order; informal bag; formal bespeak. **2** *we booked a number of events in the Festival* **arrange**, programme, schedule, timetable, line up, lay on; N. Amer. slate.
□ **by the book** according to the rules, within the law, lawfully, legally, legitimately; honestly, fairly; informal on the level, fair and square.
book in register, check in, enrol.

WORD LINKS
bibliography a list of books
bibliophile a book lover
recto the right-hand page of an open book
verso the left-hand page of an open book
colophon a publisher's emblem or imprint

booking n. **reservation**, prearrangement; appointment, date.

bookish adj. **studious**, scholarly, academic, intellectual, highbrow, erudite, learned, educated, knowledgeable; cerebral, serious, earnest, thoughtful.

booklet n. **pamphlet**, brochure, leaflet, handbill, flyer, tract; N. Amer. folder, mailer.

boom n. **1** *the boom of the waves on the rocks* **reverberation**, resonance, thunder, echoing, crashing, drumming, pounding, roar, rumble. **2** *an unprecedented boom in sales* **upturn**, upsurge, upswing, increase, advance, growth, boost, escalation, improvement.
– OPPOSITES slump.
▸ v. **1** *thunder boomed overhead* **reverberate**, resound, resonate; rumble, thunder, blare; echo; crash, roll, clap, explode, bang. **2** *a voice boomed at her* **bellow**, roar, thunder, shout, bawl; informal holler. **3** *the market continued to boom* **flourish**, burgeon, thrive, prosper, progress, improve, pick up, expand, mushroom, snowball.
– OPPOSITES whisper, slump.

boomerang v. **backfire**, recoil, reverse, rebound, come back, ricochet; be self-defeating; informal blow up in one's face.

booming adj. **1** *a booming voice* **resonant**, sonorous, ringing, resounding, reverberating, carrying, thunderous, strident, stentorian, strong, powerful. **2** *booming business* **flourishing**, burgeoning, thriving, prospering, prosperous, successful, strong, buoyant; profitable, fruitful, lucrative; expanding.

boon[1] n. *their help was such a boon* **blessing**, godsend, bonus, plus, benefit, advantage, help, aid, asset; stroke of luck; informal perk; formal perquisite.
– OPPOSITES curse.

boon[2] adj. *a boon companion* **close**, intimate, bosom, inseparable, faithful; favourite, best.

boor n. **lout**, oaf, ruffian, thug, barbarian, Neanderthal, brute, beast; informal clod, yahoo, roughneck, peasant, pig; Brit. informal yobbo, yob, oik.

boorish adj. **coarse**, uncouth, rude, ill-bred, ill-mannered, uncivilized, unrefined, common, rough, thuggish, loutish; vulgar, unsavoury, gross, brutish, Neanderthal; informal cloddish, plebby; Brit. informal yobbish; Austral. informal ocker.
– OPPOSITES refined.

boost n. **1** *a boost to one's morale* **uplift**, lift, spur, encouragement, help, inspiration, stimulus, fillip. **2** *a boost in sales* **increase**, expansion, upturn, upsurge, upswing, rise, escalation, improvement, advance, growth, boom; informal hike.
– OPPOSITES decrease.
▸ v. **1** *he phones her to boost her morale* **improve**, raise, uplift, increase, enhance, encourage, heighten, help, promote, foster, stimulate, invigorate, revitalize; informal buck up. **2** *they used advertising to boost sales* **increase**, raise, escalate, improve, strengthen, inflate, push up, promote, advance, foster, stimulate; facilitate, help, assist, aid; informal hike, bump up.
– OPPOSITES decrease.

boot[1] n. **1** *muddy boots* **gumboot**, wellington, wader, walking boot, riding boot, moon boot, thigh boot, ankle boot, pixie boot, desert boot; informal welly; trademark Dr Martens; historical top boot. **2** informal *a boot in the stomach* **kick**, blow, knock.
▸ v. **1** *his shot was boomed away by the goalkeeper* **kick**, punt, bunt, tap; propel, drive, knock. **2** *boot up your computer* **start up**, fire up, activate.

boot[2] n.
□ **to boot** as well, also, too, besides, into the bargain, in addition, additionally, on top, what's more, moreover, furthermore.

booth n. **1** *booths for different traders* **stall**, stand, kiosk. **2** *a phone booth* **cubicle**, kiosk, box, enclosure, cabin.

bootleg adj. **illegal**, illicit, unlawful, unauthorized, unlicensed, pirated; contraband, smuggled, black-market.

bootlicker n. informal **sycophant**, toady, fawner, flatterer, creep, crawler, lickspittle, truckler, groveller, kowtower; informal yes-man; old use toad-eater.

booty n. **loot**, plunder, pillage, haul, spoils, stolen goods, ill-gotten gains, pickings; informal swag.

booze informal n. *fill him up with food and booze* **alcohol**, alcoholic drink, (intoxicating) liquor, drink, spirits, intoxicants; informal grog, firewater, rotgut, the hard stuff, the bottle, Dutch courage, hooch, moonshine; Brit. informal bevvies; N. Amer. informal juice, the sauce.
▸ v. *I was boozing with my mates* **drink (alcohol)**, tipple, imbibe, indulge; informal hit the bottle, knock a few back, swill; Brit. informal bevvy; N. Amer. informal bend one's elbow.

boozer n. **1** informal *he's a notorious boozer* **drinker**, drunk, drunkard, alcoholic, dipsomaniac, tippler, imbiber, sot, inebriate; informal lush, alky, dipso, soak, tosspot, wino, sponge, barfly; US informal juicehead; Austral./NZ informal hophead; old use toper. **2** Brit. informal *I'm off down the boozer* **bar**, wine bar, inn, roadhouse; Brit. pub, public house; N. Amer. tavern; informal watering hole; Brit. informal local; dated alehouse; N. Amer. historical saloon; old use hostelry.

bop n. Brit. informal **1** *I fancy a bop* **dance**; informal boogie, jive. **2** *a college bop* **discotheque**; informal disco, hop.
▸ v. informal *they were bopping to disco music* **dance**, jig; informal boogie, jive, groove, disco, rock, stomp, hoof it; N. Amer. informal get down, cut a/the rug.

border n. **1** *the border of a medieval manuscript* **edge**, margin, perimeter, circumference, periphery; rim, fringe, verge; sides. **2** *the Soviet border* **frontier**, boundary, borderline, perimeter; marches, bounds.
▸ v. **1** *the fields were bordered by hedges* **surround**, enclose, encircle, circle, edge, fringe, bound, flank. **2** *the straps are bordered with gold braid* **edge**, fringe, hem, trim, pipe, finish. **3** *the forest bordered on Broadmoor* **adjoin**, abut, be next to, be adjacent to, be contiguous with, touch, join, meet, reach.
□ **border on** verge on, approach, come close to, be comparable to, approximate to, be tantamount to, be similar to, resemble.

borderline n. *the borderline between old and antique* **dividing line**, divide, division, demarcation line, line, cut-off point; threshold, margin, border, boundary.
▸ adj. *borderline cases* **marginal**, uncertain, indefinite, unsettled, undecided, doubtful, indeterminate, unclassifiable, equivocal; questionable, debatable, controversial, contentious, problematic; informal iffy.

bore[1] v. *bore a hole in the ceiling* **drill**, pierce, perforate, puncture, punch, cut; tunnel, burrow, mine, dig, gouge, sink.
▸ n. **1** *a well bore* **borehole**, hole, well, shaft, pit. **2** *the canon has a bore of 890 millimetres* **calibre**, diameter, gauge.

bore² v. *the television news bored Philip* **stultify**, pall on, stupefy, weary, tire, fatigue, send to sleep, leave cold; bore to death, bore to tears; informal turn off.
– OPPOSITES interest.
▶ n. *you can be such a bore* **tedious person/ thing**, tiresome person/thing, bother, nuisance, pest, annoyance, trial, vexation, thorn in one's flesh/side; informal drag, pain (in the neck), headache, hassle; N. Amer. informal nudnik.

boredom n. **weariness**, ennui, apathy, unconcern, accidie; frustration, dissatisfaction, restlessness, restiveness; tedium, dullness, monotony, repetitiveness, flatness, dreariness; informal deadliness.

boring adj. **tedious**, dull, monotonous, repetitive, unrelieved, unvaried, unimaginative, uneventful; characterless, featureless, colourless, lifeless, insipid, uninteresting, unexciting, uninspiring, jejune, flat, bland, dry, stale, tired, banal, lacklustre, stodgy, dreary, humdrum, mundane; mind-numbing, soul-destroying, wearisome, tiring, tiresome, irksome, trying, frustrating; informal deadly, not up to much; Brit. informal samey; N. Amer. informal dullsville.
– OPPOSITES interesting, lively.

borrow v. **1** *we borrowed a lot of money* **loan**, take as a loan; lease, hire; informal cadge, scrounge, bum; Brit. informal scab; N. Amer. informal mooch; Austral./NZ informal bludge. **2** informal *they 'borrowed' all of his tools* **take**, help oneself to, appropriate, commandeer, abscond with, carry off; steal, purloin; informal filch, rob, swipe, nab, rip off, lift, 'liberate', snaffle; Brit. informal nick, pinch, half-inch, whip, knock off; N. Amer. informal heist, glom. **3** *adventurous chefs borrow foreign techniques* **adopt**, take on, acquire, embrace.
– OPPOSITES lend.

bosom n. **1** *the gown was set low over her bosom* **bust**, chest; breasts, mammary glands, mammae; informal boobs, knockers, bubbies; Brit. informal bristols, charlies, baps; N. Amer. informal bazooms; old use embonpoint. **2** literary *the family took Gill into its bosom* **protection**, shelter, safety, refuge; heart, core; literary midst. **3** *love was kindled within his bosom* **heart**, breast, soul, core, spirit.
▶ adj. *bosom friends* **close**, boon, intimate, inseparable, faithful, constant, devoted; good, best, firm, favourite.

boss informal n. *the boss of a large company* **head**, chief, principal, director, president, chief executive, chair, manager(ess); supervisor, foreman, overseer, controller; employer, owner, proprietor, patron; Brit. gangmaster; informal number one, kingpin, top dog, bigwig; Brit. informal gaffer, governor; N. Amer. informal head honcho, padrone, sachem, big kahuna.
▶ v. *you have no right to boss me about* **order about/around**, dictate to, lord it over, bully, push around/about, domineer, dominate, pressurize, browbeat; call the shots, lay down the law; informal bulldoze, walk all over, railroad.

bossy adj. informal **domineering**, pushy, overbearing, imperious, officious, high-handed, authoritarian, dictatorial, controlling; informal high and mighty.
– OPPOSITES submissive.

botch informal v. *examiners botched the marking* **bungle**, mismanage, mishandle, make a mess of; informal mess up, make a hash of, muff, fluff, foul up, screw up; Brit. informal bodge, cock up; N. Amer. informal flub.
▶ n. *I've made a botch of things* **mess**, blunder, failure, wreck, fiasco, debacle; informal hash, foul-up, fail; Brit. informal bodge, cock-up, pig's ear.
– OPPOSITES success.

bother v. **1** *no one bothered her* **disturb**, trouble, inconvenience, pester, badger, harass, molest, plague, nag, hound, harry, annoy, upset, irritate; informal hassle, bug, get up someone's nose, get in someone's hair; N. English informal mither; N. Amer. informal ride. **2** *the incident was too small to bother about* **mind**, care, concern oneself, trouble oneself, worry oneself; informal give a damn, give a hoot. **3** *there was something bothering him* **worry**, trouble, concern, perturb, disturb, disquiet, disconcert, unnerve; fret, upset, distress, agitate, gnaw at, weigh down; informal rattle.
▶ n. **1** *I don't want to put you to any bother* **trouble**, effort, exertion, inconvenience, fuss, pains; informal hassle. **2** *the food was such a bother to cook* **nuisance**, pest, palaver, rigmarole, job, trial, bind, bore, drag, inconvenience, trouble, problem; informal hassle, headache, pain (in the neck). **3** *a spot of bother in the public bar* **disorder**, fighting, trouble, ado, disturbance, agitation, commotion, uproar; NZ bobsy-die; informal hoo-ha, aggro, argy-bargy, kerfuffle.

bothersome adj. **annoying**, irritating, vexatious, maddening, exasperating; tedious, wearisome, tiresome; troublesome, trying, taxing, awkward; informal aggravating, pesky, pestilential.

bottle n. **1** *a bottle of whisky* **carafe**, flask, decanter, pitcher, flagon, carboy, demijohn. **2** Brit. informal *no one had the bottle to stand up to McGregor* **courage**, bravery, valour, nerve, confidence, daring, audacity, pluck, spirit, grit, mettle, spine, backbone; informal guts, spunk, gumption; N. Amer. informal moxie.
□ **bottle something up** suppress, repress, restrain, withhold, hold in, rein in, inhibit, smother, stifle, contain, conceal, hide; informal keep a lid on.

bottleneck n. **traffic jam**, jam, congestion, hold-up, gridlock, tailback; constriction, narrowing, restriction, obstruction, blockage; informal snarl-up.

bottom n. **1** *the bottom of the stairs* **foot**, lowest part, lowest point, base; foundation, substructure, underpinning. **2** *the bottom of the car* **underside**, underneath, undersurface, undercarriage, underbelly. **3** *the bottom of Lake Ontario* **floor**, bed, depths. **4** *the bottom of his garden* **farthest point**, far end, extremity. **5** *the bottom of his*

b

class **lowest level**, lowest position. **6** Brit. *I've got a tattoo on my bottom* **rear (end)**, rump, seat; buttocks, cheeks; Scottish bahookie; informal behind, backside, BTM, sit-upon, derrière; Brit. informal bum, botty, jacksie; N. Amer. informal butt, fanny, tush, tail, buns, booty, heinie, bippy; humorous fundament, posterior, stern; Anatomy nates. **7** *police got to the bottom of the mystery* **origin**, cause, root, source, basis, foundation; heart, kernel; reality, essence.
– OPPOSITES top, surface.
▸ adj. *she sat on the bottom step* **lowest**, last, bottommost; technical basal.
– OPPOSITES top.

bottomless adj. **1** *the bottomless pits of hell* **fathomless**, unfathomable, endless, infinite, immeasurable. **2** *George's appetite was bottomless* **unlimited**, limitless, boundless, infinite, inexhaustible, endless, never-ending, everlasting; vast, huge, enormous.
– OPPOSITES limited.

bough n. **branch**, limb, arm, offshoot.

boulder n. **rock**, stone; Austral./NZ gibber.

boulevard n. **avenue**, street, road, drive, lane, parade, broadway, thoroughfare.

bounce v. **1** *the ball bounced* **rebound**, spring back, ricochet, jounce; N. Amer. carom. **2** *William bounced down the stairs* **bound**, leap, jump, spring, bob, hop, skip, trip, prance.
▸ n. **1** *he reached the door in a single bounce* **bound**, leap, jump, spring, hop, skip. **2** *the pitch's uneven bounce* **springiness**, resilience, elasticity, give. **3** *she had lost her bounce* **vitality**, vigour, energy, vivacity, liveliness, animation, sparkle, verve, spirit, enthusiasm, dynamism; cheerfulness, happiness, buoyancy, optimism; informal get-up-and-go, pep, zing.
□ **bounce back** recover, revive, rally, pick up, be on the mend; perk up, cheer up, brighten up, liven up; informal buck up.

bouncing adj. **vigorous**, thriving, flourishing, blooming; **healthy**, strong, robust, fit, in fine fettle; informal in the pink.

bouncy adj. **1** *a bouncy bridge* **springy**, flexible, resilient, elastic, stretchy, rubbery. **2** *a rather bouncy ride* **bumpy**, jolting, jerky, jarring, rough; informal jumpy. **3** *she was always bouncy* **lively**, energetic, perky, frisky, jaunty, dynamic, vital, vigorous, vibrant, animated, spirited, buoyant, bubbly, sparkling, vivacious; enthusiastic, upbeat; informal peppy, zingy, chirpy.

bound[1] adj. **1** *he raised his bound ankles* **tied**, chained, fettered, shackled, secured. **2** *she seemed bound to win* **certain**, sure, very likely, destined. **3** *you're bound by the Official Secrets Act to keep quiet* **obligated**, obliged, compelled, required, constrained. **4** *religion and morality are bound up with one another* **connected**, linked, tied, united, allied.

bound[2] v. *hares bound in the fields* **leap**, jump, spring, bounce, hop; skip, bob, dance, prance, gambol, gallop.

▸ n. *he crossed the room with a single bound* **leap**, jump, spring, bounce, hop.

bound[3] v. **1** *corporate freedom is bounded by law* **limit**, restrict, confine, circumscribe, demarcate, delimit. **2** *the heath is bounded by a hedge* **enclose**, surround, encircle, circle, border; close in/off, hem in. **3** *the garden was bounded by Mill Lane* **border**, adjoin, abut; be next to, be adjacent to.

boundary n. **1** *the boundary between Israel and Jordan* **border**, frontier, borderline, partition. **2** *the boundary between art and advertising* **dividing line**, divide, division, borderline, cut-off point. **3** *the boundary of his estate* **bounds**, confines, limits, margins, edges, fringes; border, periphery, perimeter. **4** *the boundaries of accepted behaviour* **limits**, parameters, bounds, confines; ambit, compass.

boundless adj. **limitless**, unlimited, unbounded, untold, immeasurable, abundant; inexhaustible, endless, infinite, interminable, unfailing, ceaseless, everlasting.
– OPPOSITES limited.

bounds plural n. **1** *we keep rents within reasonable bounds* **limits**, confines, proportions. **2** *land within the forest bounds* **borders**, boundaries, confines, limits, margins, edges; periphery, perimeter.
□ **out of bounds** off limits, restricted; forbidden, banned, proscribed, illegal, illicit, unlawful, unacceptable, taboo; informal no go.

bountiful adj. **1** *their bountiful patron* **generous**, magnanimous, munificent, open-handed, unselfish, unstinting, lavish; benevolent, beneficent, charitable. **2** *a bountiful supply of fresh food* **abundant**, plentiful, ample, copious, bumper, superabundant, inexhaustible, prolific, profuse; lavish, generous, handsome, rich; informal whopping; literary plenteous.
– OPPOSITES mean, meagre.

bounty n. **1** *a bounty for each man killed* **reward**, prize, award, commission, premium, dividend, bonus, gratuity, tip, donation, handout; incentive, inducement; money; informal perk, sweetener; formal perquisite. **2** literary *I thank the Lord for all his bounty* **generosity**, magnanimity, munificence, largesse, lavishness; benevolence, beneficence, charity, goodwill; blessings, favours.

bouquet n. **1** *her bridal bouquet* **bunch of flowers**, posy, nosegay, tussie-mussie, spray, corsage. **2** *bouquets go to Ann for a well-planned event* **compliment**, commendation, tribute, accolade; praise, congratulations, applause. **3** *the Chardonnay has a fine bouquet* **aroma**, nose, smell, fragrance, perfume, scent, odour.

bourgeois adj. **1** *a bourgeois family* **middle-class**, propertied; **conventional**, conservative, conformist; provincial, suburban, small-town. **2** *bourgeois decadence* **capitalistic**, materialistic, money-oriented, commercial.

– OPPOSITES proletarian, communist.
▶ n. *a proud bourgeois* **member of the middle class**, property owner.

bout n. **1** *a short bout of exercise* **spell**, period, time, stretch, stint, session; burst, flurry, spurt. **2** *a coughing bout* **attack**, fit, spasm, paroxysm, convulsion, eruption, outburst. **3** *he is fighting only his fifth bout* **contest**, match, round, heat, competition, event, meeting, fixture; fight, prizefight; Brit. clash.

bovine adj. **1** *large, bovine eyes* **cow-like**, calf-like, taurine. **2** *an expression of bovine amazement* **stupid**, slow, ignorant, unintelligent, imperceptive, half-baked, vacuous, mindless, witless, doltish; informal dumb, dense, dim, dim-witted, dopey, birdbrained, pea-brained; Brit. informal dozy, daft; Scottish & N. English informal glaikit.
▶ n. **cow**, heifer, bull, bullock, calf, ox; N. Amer. informal boss, bossy; Farming beef.

bow¹ v. **1** *the officers bowed* **incline the body**, incline the head, nod, salaam, curtsy, bob. **2** *the mast quivered and bowed* **bend**, buckle, stoop, curve, flex, deform. **3** *the government bowed to foreign pressure* **yield**, submit, give in, surrender, succumb, capitulate, defer, conform; comply with, accept, heed, observe. **4** *a footman bowed her in* **usher**, conduct, show, lead, guide, direct, steer, shepherd.
▶ n. *a perfunctory bow* **obeisance**, salaam, bob, curtsy, nod; old use reverence.
□ **bow out** withdraw, resign, retire, step down, pull out, back out; give up, quit, leave; informal pack in, chuck (in); Brit. informal jack in.

bow² n. *the bow of the tanker* **prow**, front, stem, nose, head, cutwater; Brit. humorous sharp end.

bow³ n. **1** *she tied a bow in her hair* **loop**, knot; ribbon. **2** *he bent the rod into a bow* **arc**, curve, bend; crescent, half-moon. **3** *an archer's bow* **longbow**, crossbow; Archery recurve.

bowdlerize v. **expurgate**, censor, blue-pencil, cut, edit; sanitize, water down, emasculate.

bowel n. **1** *a disorder of the bowels* **intestine(s)**, small intestine, large intestine, colon; informal guts, insides. **2** *the bowels of the ship* **interior**, inside, core, belly; depths, recesses; informal innards.

bower n. **arbour**, pergola, grotto, alcove, sanctuary.

bowl¹ v. **1** *he bowled a hundred or so balls* **pitch**, throw, propel, hurl, toss, lob, loft, fling, launch, deliver; spin, roll; informal chuck, sling, bung, heave, buzz; dated shy. **2** *the car bowled along the roads* **hurtle**, speed, shoot, sweep, career, hare, fly; informal belt, tear, scoot; Brit. informal bomb; N. Amer. informal clip.
□ **bowl someone over 1** *the explosion bowled us over* **knock down/over**, fell, floor, prostrate. **2** informal *I have been bowled over by your generosity* **overwhelm**, astound, astonish, overawe, dumbfound, stagger, stun, daze, shake, take aback, leave aghast; informal knock sideways, flabbergast, blow away; Brit. informal knock for six.

bowl² n. **1** *she cracked two eggs into a bowl* **dish**, basin, pot, crock, crucible, mortar; container, vessel, receptacle; historical jorum, porringer. **2** *the town lay in a shallow bowl* **valley**, hollow, dip, depression, trough, crater. **3** N. Amer. *the Hollywood Bowl* **stadium**, arena, amphitheatre, coliseum; enclosure, ground; informal park.

box¹ n. **1** *a box of cigars* **carton**, pack, packet; case, crate, chest, coffer, casket; container, receptacle. **2** *a telephone box* **booth**, cubicle, kiosk, cabin, hut; compartment, carrel, alcove, bay, recess.
▶ v. *Muriel boxed up his clothes* **package**, pack, parcel, wrap, bundle, bale, crate.
□ **box something/someone in** hem in, fence in, close in, shut in; trap, confine, kettle, imprison, intern; surround, enclose, encircle.

box² v. **1** *he began boxing professionally* **fight**, prizefight, spar; battle, brawl; informal scrap. **2** *he boxed my ears* **cuff**, smack, strike, hit, thump, slap, swat, punch, jab, wallop; Scottish & N. English skelp; informal belt, bop, biff, sock, clout, clobber, whack, plug, slug; Brit. informal slosh, dot; N. Amer. informal boff, bust.
▶ n. *a box on the ear* **cuff**, hit, thump, slap, smack, swat, punch, jab, hook; Scottish & N. English skelp; informal belt, bop, biff, sock, clout, whack, plug, slug.

boxer n. **fighter**, pugilist, ringster, prizefighter, kick-boxer; informal bruiser, scrapper.

boxing n. **pugilism**, the noble art, fighting, sparring, fisticuffs; kick-boxing, prizefighting; the (prize) ring.

boy n. **lad**, schoolboy, male child, youth, young man, stripling; Scottish & N. English laddie; derogatory brat. See also **child**.

boycott v. *they boycotted the elections* **spurn**, snub, shun, avoid, abstain from, wash one's hands of, turn one's back on, reject, veto.
– OPPOSITES support.
▶ n. *a boycott on the use of tropical timbers* **ban**, veto, embargo, prohibition, sanction, restriction; avoidance, rejection, refusal.

boyfriend n. **lover**, sweetheart, beloved, darling, dearest, young man, man friend, man, escort, suitor; **partner**, significant other; informal fella, flame, fancy man, toy boy, sugar daddy; N. Amer. informal squeeze; literary swain; dated beau; old use paramour.

boyish adj. **youthful**, young, childlike, adolescent, teenage; immature, juvenile, infantile, childish, babyish, puerile.

brace n. **1** *the saw is best used with a brace* **vice**, clamp, press. **2** *power drills run faster than a brace* **drill**, boring tool, rotary tool. **3** *the aquarium is supported by wooden braces* **prop**, beam, joist, batten, rod, post, strut, stay, support, stanchion, bracket. **4** *a brace on his right leg* **support**, caliper. **5** *a brace of partridges* **pair**, couple, duo, twosome; two. **6** Printing *the term within braces* **bracket**, parenthesis.
▶ v. **1** *the plane's wing is braced by a system of rods* **support**, shore up, prop up, hold up,

b

buttress, underpin; strengthen, reinforce. **2** *he braced his hand on the railing* **steady**, secure, stabilize, fix, poise; tense, tighten. **3** *brace yourself for disappointment* **prepare**, get ready, gear up, nerve, steel, galvanize, gird, strengthen, fortify; informal psych oneself up.

bracelet n. **bangle**, band, circlet, armlet, wristlet; manilla, rakhi, kara.

bracing adj. **invigorating**, refreshing, stimulating, energizing, exhilarating, reviving, restorative, rejuvenating, revitalizing, rousing, fortifying, strengthening; **fresh**, brisk, keen.

bracket n. **1** *each speaker is fixed on a separate bracket* **support**, prop, stay, batten, joist; rest, mounting, rack, frame. **2** *put the words in brackets* **parenthesis**; Printing brace. **3** *a higher tax bracket* **group**, category, grade, band, classification, set, division, order.
▶ v. *women were bracketed with minors* **group**, classify, class, categorize, grade, list, sort, place, assign; couple, pair, twin; liken, compare.

brackish adj. **slightly salty**, saline, salt.

brag v. **boast**, crow, swagger, swank, bluster, gloat, show off; blow one's own trumpet, sing one's own praises; informal talk big, lay it on thick; Austral./NZ informal skite.

braggart n. *he was a prodigious braggart and a liar* **boaster**, bragger, swaggerer, poser, poseur, egotist; informal big-head, loudmouth, show-off, swank; N. Amer. informal showboat, blowhard; Austral./NZ informal skite; Brit. informal dated swankpot.

braid n. **1** *straps bordered with gold braid* **cord**, bullion, thread, tape, binding, rickrack, ribbon; cordon, torsade; Military slang scrambled egg. **2** *his hair is in braids* **plait**, pigtail, twist; cornrows, dreadlocks.
▶ v. **1** *she began to braid her hair* **plait**, entwine, intertwine, interweave, weave, twist, twine. **2** *the sleeves are braided in scarlet* **trim**, edge, border, pipe, hem, fringe.

brain n. **1** *the disease attacks certain cells in the brain* **cerebrum**, cerebral matter, encephalon. **2** *success requires brains as well as brawn* **intelligence**, intellect, brainpower, cleverness, wit(s), reasoning, wisdom, acumen, discernment, judgement, understanding, sense; informal nous, grey matter, savvy; N. Amer. informal smarts. **3** informal *Janice is the brains of the family* **clever person**, intellectual, intellect, thinker, mind, scholar; genius, Einstein; informal egghead, bright spark; Brit. informal brainbox, clever clogs; N. Amer. informal brainiac, rocket scientist.

> **WORD LINKS**
>
> **cerebral, encephalic** relating to the brain
> **encephalitis** inflammation of the brain
> **hydrocephalus** fluid in the brain
> **lobotomy** an operation involving cutting into part of the brain

brainless adj. **stupid**, **foolish**, witless, unintelligent, ignorant, idiotic, simple-minded, empty-headed, half-baked; informal dumb, half-witted, brain-dead, moronic, cretinous, thick, dopey, dozy, birdbrained, pea-brained, dippy, wooden-headed; Brit. informal divvy; Scottish & N. English informal glaikit; N. Amer. informal chowderheaded.

brain-teaser n. informal **puzzle**, problem, riddle, conundrum, poser.

brainwash v. **indoctrinate**, condition, re-educate, persuade, influence, programme.

brainy adj. informal **clever**, intelligent, bright, brilliant, gifted; intellectual, erudite, academic, scholarly, studious, bookish; informal smart; Brit. informal swotty.
– OPPOSITES stupid.

brake n. *a brake on research* **curb**, check, restraint, restriction, constraint, control, limitation.
▶ v. *she braked at the traffic lights* **slow (down)**, decelerate, reduce speed.
– OPPOSITES accelerate.

branch n. **1** *the branches of a tree* **bough**, limb, arm, offshoot. **2** *a branch of the river* **tributary**, feeder, side stream. **3** *the judicial branch of government* **division**, subdivision, section, subsection, department, sector, part, side, wing. **4** *the corporation's New York branch* **office**, bureau, agency; subsidiary, offshoot, satellite.
▶ v. **1** *the place where the road branches* **fork**, bifurcate, divide, subdivide, split. **2** *narrow paths branched off the road* **diverge from**, deviate from, split off from; fan out from, radiate from.
□ **branch out** expand, open up, extend; diversify, broaden one's horizons.

brand n. **1** *a new brand of margarine* **make**, line, label, marque; type, kind, sort, variety; trade name, trademark, proprietary name. **2** *her particular brand of humour* **type**, kind, sort, variety, class, category, genre, style, ilk; N. Amer. stripe. **3** *the brand on a sheep* **identification**, marker, earmark. **4** *the brand of dipsomania* **stigma**, shame, disgrace; taint, blot, mark.
▶ v. **1** *the letter M was branded on each animal* **mark**, stamp, burn, sear. **2** *the scene was branded on her brain* **engrave**, stamp, etch, imprint. **3** *the media branded us as communists* **stigmatize**, mark out; denounce, discredit, vilify; label.

brandish v. **wave**, flourish, shake, wield; swing, swish; display, flaunt.

brash adj. **1** *a brash man* **self-assertive**, pushy, cocksure, cocky, self-confident, arrogant, bold, audacious, brazen; forward, impudent, insolent, rude. **2** *brash colours* **garish**, gaudy, loud, flamboyant, showy, tasteless; informal flashy, tacky.
– OPPOSITES meek, muted.

brassy adj. **1** **brazen**, forward, bold, self-assertive, pushy, cocksure, cocky, brash; shameless, immodest; loud, vulgar, showy, ostentatious; informal flashy. **2** *brassy music* **loud**, blaring, noisy, deafening, strident; raucous, harsh, dissonant, discordant, cacophonous; tinny.
– OPPOSITES demure, soft.

brat n. derogatory **rascal**, wretch, imp; minx, chit; informal monster, horror, whippersnapper.

bravado n. **boldness**, swaggering, bluster; machismo; boasting, bragging, bombast, braggadocio; informal showing off.

brave adj. **courageous**, plucky, valiant, valorous, intrepid, heroic, lionhearted, bold, fearless, daring, audacious; unflinching, unshrinking, unafraid, dauntless, doughty, mettlesome, stout-hearted, spirited; informal game, gutsy, spunky.
– OPPOSITES cowardly.
▸ n. dated an Indian brave **warrior**, soldier, fighter.
▸ v. fans braved freezing temperatures to see them play **endure**, put up with, bear, withstand, weather, suffer, go through; face, confront, defy.

bravery n. **courage**, pluck, valour, intrepidity, nerve, daring, fearlessness, audacity, boldness, dauntlessness, stout-heartedness, heroism; backbone, grit, spine, spirit, mettle; informal guts, spunk; Brit. informal bottle; N. Amer. informal moxie.

bravo exclam. **well done**, congratulations; encore.

bravura n. a display of bravura **skill**, brilliance, virtuosity, expertise, artistry, talent, ability, flair.
▸ adj. a bravura performance **virtuoso**, masterly, outstanding, excellent, superb, brilliant, first-class, top-tier; informal mean, ace, A1.

brawl n. a drunken brawl **fight**, skirmish, scuffle, tussle, fray, melee, free-for-all, scrum; fisticuffs; informal scrap, dust-up, set-to; Brit. informal punch-up, ruck; Brit. informal, Football afters; Scottish informal rammy; N. Amer. informal rough house, brannigan; Law, dated affray.
▸ v. he ended up brawling with photographers **fight**, skirmish, scuffle, tussle, exchange blows, grapple, wrestle; informal scrap; N. Amer. informal rough-house.

brawn n. **physical strength**, muscle(s), burliness, huskiness, toughness, power, might; informal beef, beefiness.

brawny adj. **strong**, muscular, muscly, well built, powerful, mighty, Herculean, strapping, burly, sturdy, husky, rugged; bulky, hefty, meaty, solid; informal beefy, hunky, hulking.
– OPPOSITES puny, weak.

bray v. 1 a donkey brayed **neigh**, whinny, hee-haw. 2 Billy brayed with laughter **roar**, bellow, trumpet.

brazen adj. **bold**, **shameless**, unashamed, unabashed, unembarrassed; defiant, impudent, impertinent, cheeky; barefaced, blatant, flagrant; Brit. informal saucy.
– OPPOSITES timid.
□ **brazen it out** put on a bold front, stand one's ground, be defiant, be unrepentant, be unabashed.

breach n. 1 a clear breach of the regulations **contravention**, violation, infringement, infraction, transgression, neglect; Law delict. 2 a breach between government and Church **rift**, schism, division, gulf, chasm; disunion, estrangement, discord, dissension, disagreement; split, break, rupture, scission; Brit. informal bust-up. 3 a breach in the sea wall **break**, rupture, split, crack, fracture; opening, gap, hole, fissure.
▸ v. 1 the river breached its bank **break (through)**, burst, rupture; informal bust. 2 the changes breached union rules **break**, contravene, violate, infringe; defy, disobey, flout, fly in the face of; Law infract.

breadth n. 1 a breadth of 100 metres **width**, broadness, wideness, thickness; span; diameter. 2 the breadth of his knowledge **range**, extent, scope, depth, reach, compass, scale, degree.

break v. 1 the mirror broke **shatter**, smash, crack, snap, fracture, fragment, splinter, fall to bits, fall to pieces; split, burst; informal bust. 2 she had broken her leg **fracture**, crack. 3 the bite had barely broken the skin **pierce**, puncture, penetrate, perforate; cut. 4 the coffee machine has broken **stop working**, break down, give out, go wrong, malfunction, crash; informal go kaput, conk out, be on the blink, give up the ghost; Brit. informal pack up. 5 traders who break the law **contravene**, violate, infringe, breach; defy, flout, disobey, fly in the face of. 6 his concentration was broken **interrupt**, disturb, interfere with. 7 they broke for coffee **stop**, pause, have a rest; N. Amer. recess; informal knock off, take five. 8 a pile of carpets broke his fall **cushion**, soften the impact of, take the edge off. 9 the film broke box-office records **exceed**, surpass, beat, better, cap, top, outdo, outstrip, eclipse; informal leave standing. 10 habits are very difficult to break **give up**, relinquish, drop; informal kick, shake, pack in, quit. 11 the strategies used to break the union **destroy**, crush, quash, defeat, vanquish, overcome, overpower, overwhelm, suppress, cripple; weaken, subdue, cow, undermine. 12 her self-control finally broke **give way**, crack, cave in, yield, go to pieces. 13 four thousand pounds wouldn't break him **bankrupt**, ruin, pauperize. 14 he tried to break the news gently **reveal**, disclose, divulge, impart, tell; announce, release. 15 he broke the encryption code **decipher**, decode, decrypt, unravel, work out; informal figure out. 16 the day broke fair and cloudless **dawn**, begin, start, emerge, appear. 17 a political scandal broke **erupt**, break out. 18 the weather broke **change**, alter, shift. 19 waves broke against the rocks **crash**, dash, beat, pound, lash. 20 her voice broke as she relived the experience **falter**, quaver, quiver, tremble, shake.
– OPPOSITES repair, keep, resume.
▸ n. 1 the magazine has been published without a break since 1950 **interruption**, interval, gap, hiatus; discontinuation, suspension, disruption, cut-off; stop, stoppage, cessation. 2 a break in the weather **change**, alteration, variation. 3 let's have a break **rest**, respite,

b

recess; stop, pause; interval, intermission; informal breather, time out, downtime. **4** *a weekend break* **holiday**; N. Amer. vacation; Brit. informal vac. **5** *a break in diplomatic relations* **rift**, schism, split, break-up, severance, rupture; Brit. informal bust-up. **6** *a break in the wall* **gap**, opening, space, hole, breach, chink, crack, fissure; tear, split. **7** informal *the actress got her first break in 1951* **opportunity**, chance, opening.

□ **break away 1** *she attempted to break away from his grip* **escape**, get away, run away, flee, make off; break free, break loose, get out of someone's clutches; informal leg it, cut and run. **2** *a group broke away from the main party* **leave**, secede from, split off from, separate from, part company with, defect from; form a splinter group.
break down 1 *his van broke down.* See **break** (sense 4 of the verb). **2** *pay negotiations broke down* **fail**, collapse, founder, fall through, disintegrate; informal fizzle out. **3** *Vicky broke down, sobbing loudly* **burst into tears**; lose control, be overcome, go to pieces, crumble, disintegrate; informal crack up, lose it.
break something down 1 *the police broke the door down* **knock down**, kick down, smash in, pull down, tear down, demolish. **2** *break big tasks down into smaller parts* **divide**, separate. **3** *graphs show how the information can be broken down* **analyse**, categorize, classify, sort out, itemize, organize; dissect.
break in 1 *thieves broke in and took her cheque book* **commit burglary**, break and enter; force one's way in, burst in. **2** *'I don't want to interfere,' Mrs Hendry broke in* **interrupt**, butt in, cut in, interject, interpose, intervene, chime in; Brit. informal chip in.
break into 1 *thieves broke into a house in Perth Street* **burgle**, rob; force one's way into, burst into. **2** *Phil broke into the discussion* **interrupt**, butt into, cut in on, intervene in. **3** *he broke into a song* **burst into**, launch into.
break off snap off, come off, become detached, become separated.
break something off 1 *I broke off a branch from the tree* **snap off**, pull off, sever, detach. **2** *they threatened to break off diplomatic relations* **end**, terminate, stop, cease, call a halt to, finish, dissolve; **suspend**, discontinue; informal pull the plug on.
break out 1 *he broke out of the detention centre* **escape from**, abscond from, flee from; get free. **2** *fighting broke out* **flare up**, start suddenly, erupt, burst out.
break up 1 *the meeting broke up* **end**, finish, stop, terminate, adjourn; N. Amer. recess. **2** *the crowd began to break up* **disperse**, scatter, disband, part company. **3** *Danny and I broke up last year* **split up**, separate, part (company); divorce. **4** informal *the whole cast broke up* **burst out laughing**, dissolve into laughter; informal fall about, crack up, crease up; theatrical slang corpse.

break something up 1 *police tried to break up the crowd* **disperse**, scatter, disband. **2** *I'm not going to let you break up my marriage* **wreck**, ruin, destroy.
breakable adj. **fragile**, delicate, flimsy, insubstantial; destructible; formal frangible.
breakaway adj. *a breakaway group* **separatist**, secessionist, schismatic, splinter; rebel, renegade.
breakdown n. **1** *the breakdown of the negotiations* **failure**, collapse, disintegration, foundering. **2** *on the death of her father she suffered a breakdown* **nervous breakdown**; informal crack-up. **3** *the breakdown of the computer system* **malfunction**, failure, crash. **4** *a breakdown of the figures* **analysis**, classification, examination, investigation, dissection.
breaker n. **wave**, roller, comber, white horse; informal boomer; N. Amer. informal kahuna.
break-in n. **burglary**, robbery, theft, raid; informal smash-and-grab.
breakneck adj. *the breakneck pace of change* **extremely fast**, rapid, speedy, high-speed, lightning, whirlwind.
□ **at breakneck speed** dangerously fast, at full tilt, flat out, ventre à terre; informal hell for leather, like the wind, like a bat out of hell, like greased lightning; Brit. informal like the clappers.
breakthrough n. **advance**, development, step forward, success, improvement; discovery, innovation, revolution.
– OPPOSITES setback.
break-up n. **1** *the break-up of negotiations* **end**, dissolution; breakdown, failure, collapse, disintegration. **2** *their break-up was very amicable* **separation**, split, parting, divorce; estrangement, rift; Brit. informal bust-up. **3** *the break-up of the Soviet Union* **division**, partition.
breakwater n. **sea wall**, jetty, mole, groyne, pier.
breast n. **1** *the curve of her breasts* mammary gland, mamma; (**breasts**) **bosom(s)**, bust, chest; informal boobs, knockers, bubbies; Brit. informal bristols, charlies, baps; N. Amer. informal bazooms. **2** *feelings of frustration were rising up in his breast* **heart**, bosom, soul, core.

WORD LINKS

mastectomy the surgical removal of a breast
mammogram a breast X-ray

---

breath n. **1** *I took a deep breath* **inhalation**, inspiration, gulp of air; exhalation, expiration; Medicine respiration. **2** *I had barely enough breath to reply* **wind**; informal puff. **3** *a breath of wind* **puff**, waft, faint breeze. **4** *a breath of scandal* **hint**, suggestion, trace, touch, whisper, suspicion, whiff, undertone.
□ **take someone's breath away** astonish, astound, amaze, stun, startle, stagger, shock, take aback, dumbfound, jolt, shake up; awe, overawe, thrill; informal knock sideways, flabbergast, blow away, bowl over; Brit. informal knock for six.

b

WORD LINKS

respiratory relating to breath
respirator a device enabling someone to breathe artificially
hyperventilation abnormally rapid breathing
apnoea a condition in which a person temporarily stops breathing
halitosis bad breath

breathe v. **1** *she breathed deeply* inhale and exhale, respire, draw breath; puff, pant, blow, gasp, wheeze; Medicine inspire, expire; literary suspire. **2** *at least I'm still breathing* be alive, be living, live. **3** *he would breathe new life into his firm* instil, infuse, inject, impart. **4** *'Together at last,' she breathed* whisper, murmur, purr, sigh, say.

breather n. informal break, rest, respite, breathing space, pause, interval, recess.

breathless adj. **1** *Will arrived flushed and breathless* out of breath, panting, puffing, gasping, wheezing; winded, puffed out, short of breath; informal out of puff. **2** *the crowd were breathless with anticipation* agog, open-mouthed, waiting with bated breath, on the edge of one's seat, on tenterhooks, in suspense; excited, impatient.

breathtaking adj. spectacular, magnificent, wonderful, awe-inspiring, awesome, astounding, astonishing, amazing, stunning, incredible; thrilling, exciting; informal sensational, out of this world; literary wondrous.

breed v. **1** *elephants breed readily in captivity* reproduce, produce offspring, procreate, multiply; mate. **2** *she was born and bred in the village* bring up, rear, raise, nurture. **3** *the political system bred discontent* cause, bring about, give rise to, lead to, produce, generate, foster, result in; stir up; literary beget.
▶ n. **1** *a breed of cow* variety, stock, strain; type, kind, sort. **2** *a new breed of journalist* type, kind, sort, variety, class, genre, generation; N. Amer. stripe.

breeding n. **1** *individual birds pair for breeding* reproduction, procreation; mating. **2** *the breeding of rats* rearing, raising, nurturing. **3** *her aristocratic breeding* upbringing, rearing; parentage, family, pedigree, blood, birth. **4** *people of rank and breeding* (good) manners, gentility, refinement, cultivation, polish, urbanity; informal class.

breeding ground n. *the school is a breeding ground for communists* nursery, cradle, nest, den; hotbed.

breeze n. **1** *a breeze ruffled the leaves* gentle wind, puff of air, gust; Meteorology light air(s); literary zephyr. **2** informal *travelling through London was a breeze* easy task, five-finger exercise, walkover; child's play, nothing; informal doddle, piece of cake, cinch, kids' stuff, cakewalk, walk in the park; N. Amer. informal duck soup, snap; Austral./NZ informal bludge; dated snip.
▶ v. informal *Roger breezed into her office* saunter, stroll, sail, sweep, cruise.

breezy adj. **1** *a bright, breezy day* windy, fresh, brisk, airy; blowy, blustery, gusty. **2** *his breezy manner* jaunty, cheerful, cheery, brisk, carefree, easy, casual, relaxed, informal, light-hearted, lively, buoyant, sunny; informal upbeat, bright-eyed and bushy-tailed; dated gay.

brevity n. **1** *the report is notable for its brevity* conciseness, concision, succinctness, economy of language, pithiness, shortness, incisiveness, compactness. **2** *the brevity of human life* shortness, briefness, transience, ephemerality, impermanence.
– OPPOSITES verbosity.

brew v. **1** *this beer is brewed in Frankfurt* ferment, make. **2** *I'll brew some tea* prepare, infuse, make, stew; Brit. informal mash. **3** *there's trouble brewing* develop, loom, impend, be imminent, be on the horizon, be in the offing, be just around the corner.
▶ n. **1** *home brew* beer, ale. **2** *a hot reviving brew* drink, beverage; tea, coffee. **3** *a dangerous brew of political turmoil and violent conflict* mixture, mix, blend, combination, amalgam.

bribe v. *he used his wealth to bribe officials* buy off, pay off, suborn; informal grease someone's palm, keep someone sweet, fix, square; Brit. informal nobble.
▶ n. *he accepted bribes* inducement, incentive, carrot, douceur; informal backhander, pay-off, kickback, sweetener; Brit. informal bung; N. Amer. informal schmear.

WORD LINKS

venal able to be bribed

bribery n. subornation, corruption; N. Amer. payola; informal palm-greasing, graft, hush money.

bric-a-brac n. ornaments, knick-knacks, trinkets, bibelots, gewgaws, gimcracks; paraphernalia, bits and pieces, bits and bobs, odds and ends, things, stuff; informal junk.

brick n. **1** *bricks and mortar* breeze block, adobe, clinker; header, stretcher, bondstone; Brit. airbrick. **2** *a brick of ice cream* block, cube, bar, cake.

bridal adj. *the bridal party* wedding, nuptial, marriage, matrimonial, marital, conjugal.

bride n. wife, marriage partner; newly-wed.

bridge n. **1** *a bridge over the river* viaduct, flyover, overpass, aqueduct. **2** *a bridge between rival groups* link, connection, bond, tie.
▶ v. **1** *a walkway bridged the motorway* span, cross (over), extend across, traverse, arch over. **2** *an attempt to bridge the gap between cultures* join, link, connect, unite; straddle; overcome, reconcile.

WORD LINKS

pontine relating to bridges
cantilever a type of long beam or girder used in bridge construction
bascule a movable section forming part of a bridge that can be raised to allow ships to pass
pontoon a floating object supporting a temporary bridge

b

> **span** the part of a bridge between its supports
> **truss** a supporting framework for a bridge

bridle n. *a horse's bridle* **harness**, headgear.
▶v. **1** *she bridled at his tone* **bristle**, take offence, take umbrage, be affronted, be offended, get angry. **2** *he bridled his indignation* **curb**, restrain, hold back, control, check, rein in/back; suppress, stifle; informal keep a/the lid on.

brief adj. **1** *a brief account* **concise**, succinct, short, pithy, incisive, abridged, condensed, compressed, abbreviated, compact, thumbnail, potted; formal compendious. **2** *a brief visit* **short**, flying, fleeting, hasty, hurried, quick, cursory, perfunctory; temporary, short-lived, momentary, transient; informal quickie. **3** *a pair of brief shorts* **skimpy**, scanty, short; revealing. **4** *the boss was rather brief with him* **brusque**, abrupt, curt, short, blunt, sharp.
– OPPOSITES lengthy.
▶n. **1** *my brief is to reorganize the project* **instructions**, directions, directive, briefing, remit, mandate; job, task; guidelines, guidance. **2** *a barrister's brief* **case**, summary, argument, contention; dossier, information. **3** Brit. informal *his brief's eloquence saved him.* See **lawyer**.
▶v. *employees were briefed about the decision* **inform**, tell, update, notify, advise, apprise; prepare, prime, instruct; informal fill in, clue in, put in the picture.

briefing n. **1** *a press briefing* **conference**, meeting, interview; N. Amer. backgrounder. **2** *this briefing explains the systems* **information**, rundown, guidance; instructions, directions, guidelines.

briefly adv. **1** *Henry paused briefly* **momentarily**, temporarily, for a moment, fleetingly. **2** *briefly, the plot is as follows* **in short**, in brief, to cut a long story short, in a word, in sum, in a nutshell, in essence.

briefs plural n. **underpants**, pants, knickers, Y-fronts, G-string, thong; N. Amer. shorts, undershorts; informal panties, undies, frillies; Brit. informal kecks, smalls, trolleys.

brigade n. **1** *a brigade of soldiers* **unit**, contingent, battalion, regiment, division, squadron, company, platoon, section, corps, troop. **2** *the volunteer ambulance brigade* **squad**, team, group, band, party, crew, force, outfit.

brigand n. literary See **bandit**.

bright adj. **1** *the bright surface of the metal* **shining**, brilliant, dazzling, beaming, glaring, sparkling, flashing, glittering, scintillating, gleaming, glowing, luminous, radiant; shiny, lustrous, glossy. **2** *a bright morning* **sunny**, sunshiny, cloudless, clear, fair, fine. **3** *bright colours* **vivid**, brilliant, intense, strong, bold, glowing, rich; gaudy, lurid, garish. **4** *bright flowers* **colourful**, brightly-coloured, vivid, vibrant; dated gay. **5** *a bright guitar sound* **clear**, vibrant, ringing, pellucid; high-pitched, sharp. **6** *a bright young graduate* **clever**, intelligent, quick-witted, smart, canny, astute, intuitive,

perceptive; ingenious, resourceful; gifted, brilliant; informal brainy. **7** *he felt remarkably bright* **happy**, cheerful, cheery, jolly, merry, sunny, beaming; lively, exuberant, buoyant, bubbly, bouncy, perky, chirpy; Brit. Tiggerish; dated gay. **8** *a bright future* **promising**, rosy, optimistic, hopeful, favourable, propitious, auspicious, encouraging, good, golden.
– OPPOSITES dull, dark, stupid.

brighten v. **1** *sunshine brightened the room* **illuminate**, light up, lighten, make bright, make brighter, cast/shed light on. **2** *you can brighten up the shadiest of corners* **enhance**, embellish, enrich, dress up, prettify, beautify; informal jazz up. **3** *Sarah brightened up as she thought of Emily's words* **cheer up**, perk up, rally; be enlivened, feel heartened, be uplifted, be encouraged, take heart; informal buck up, pep up.

brilliance n. **1** *a philosopher of great brilliance* **genius**, talent, ability, prowess, skill, expertise, aptitude, flair, finesse, panache; greatness, distinction; intelligence, wisdom, sagacity, intellect. **2** *the brilliance and beauty of Paris* **splendour**, magnificence, grandeur, resplendence. **3** *the brilliance of the sunshine* **brightness**, vividness, intensity, sparkle, glitter, glittering, glow, blaze, beam, luminosity, radiance.

brilliant adj. **1** *a brilliant student* **gifted**, talented, able, adept, skilful; bright, intelligent, clever, smart, astute, intellectual; elite, superior, first-class, first-rate, excellent, top-tier; informal brainy. **2** *his brilliant career* **superb**, glorious, glittering, illustrious, impressive, remarkable, exceptional; informal stellar. **3** Brit. informal *we had a brilliant time* **excellent**, marvellous, superb, very good, first-rate, first-class, wonderful, splendid; informal great, terrific, tremendous, fantastic, sensational, fabulous, fab, ace, cool, awesome, magic, wicked; Brit. informal smashing, brill; Austral./NZ informal bonzer. **4** *a shaft of brilliant light* **bright**, shining, blazing, dazzling, vivid, intense, gleaming, glaring, luminous, radiant; literary irradiant, coruscating. **5** *brilliant green* **vivid**, intense, bright, bold, dazzling.
– OPPOSITES stupid, bad, dark.

brim n. **1** *the brim of his hat* peak, visor, shield, shade. **2** *the cup was filled to its brim* **rim**, lip, brink, edge.
▶v. **1** *the pan was brimming with water* **be full (up)**, be filled to the top; overflow, run over. **2** *her eyes were brimming with tears* **fill**, fill up; overflow.

brimful adj. **full (up)**, brimming, filled/full to the brim, filled to capacity, overfull, running over; informal chock-full.
– OPPOSITES empty.

brindle, brindled adj. **tawny**, brownish, brown; **dappled**, streaked, mottled, speckled, flecked.

bring v. **1** *he brought over a tray* **carry**, fetch, bear, take; convey, transport; move, haul, shift. **2** *Philip brought his bride to his mansion* **escort**, conduct, guide, lead,

usher, show, shepherd. **3** *the wind changed and brought rain* **cause**, produce, create, generate, precipitate, lead to, give rise to, result in; stir up, whip up, promote; literary beget. **4** *the police contemplated bringing charges* **put forward**, prefer, lay, submit, present, initiate, institute. **5** *this job brings him a regular salary* **earn**, make, fetch, bring in, yield, net, gross, return, produce; command, attract.
□ **bring something about 1** *the affair that brought about her death* **cause**, produce, give rise to, result in, lead to, occasion, bring to pass; provoke, generate, engender, precipitate; formal effectuate. **2** *he brought the ship about* **turn (round/around)**, reverse, change the direction of.
bring something back 1 *the smell brought back memories* **remind one of**, put one in mind of, bring/call to mind, conjure up, evoke, summon up; take one back. **2** *bring back capital punishment* **reintroduce**, reinstate, reinstitute, re-establish, revive, resurrect.
bring something down 1 *we will bring down the price* **decrease**, reduce, lower, cut, drop; informal slash. **2** *the unrest brought down the government* **unseat**, overturn, topple, overthrow, depose, oust.
bring something forward propose, suggest, advance, raise, table, present, move, submit, lodge.
bring something in 1 *he brought in a private member's bill* **introduce**, launch, inaugurate, initiate, institute. **2** *the event brings in one million pounds each year.* See **bring** (sense 5).
bring something off achieve, accomplish, attain, bring about, pull off, manage, realize, complete, finish; execute, perform, discharge; formal effectuate.
bring something on See **bring something about** (sense 1).
bring something out 1 *they were bringing out a new magazine* **launch**, establish, begin, start, found, set up, instigate, inaugurate, market; publish, print, issue, produce. **2** *the shawl brings out the colour of your eyes* **accentuate**, highlight, emphasize, accent, set off.
bring someone round 1 *she administered artificial respiration and brought him round* **wake up**, rouse, bring to. **2** *we would have brought him round, given time* **persuade**, convince, talk round, win over, sway, influence.
bring oneself to force oneself to, make oneself, bear to.
bring someone up rear, raise, care for, look after, nurture, provide for.
bring something up mention, allude to, touch on, raise, broach, introduce; voice, air, suggest, propose, submit, put forward, bring forward, table.

brink n. **1** *the brink of the abyss* **edge**, verge, margin, rim, lip; border, boundary, perimeter, periphery, limit(s). **2** *two countries on the brink of war* **verge**,

threshold, point, edge.

brio n. **vigour**, vivacity, gusto, verve, zest, enthusiasm, vitality, dynamism, animation, spirit, energy; informal pep, vim, get-up-and-go.

brisk adj. **1** *a brisk pace* **quick**, rapid, fast, swift, speedy, hurried; energetic, lively, vigorous; informal nippy. **2** *the bar was doing a brisk trade* **busy**, bustling, lively, hectic; good. **3** *his tone became brisk* **no-nonsense**, decisive, businesslike; brusque, abrupt, short, sharp, curt, blunt, terse, gruff; informal snappy. **4** *a brisk breeze* **bracing**, fresh, crisp, invigorating, refreshing, stimulating, energizing; biting, keen, chilly, cold; informal nippy.
− OPPOSITES slow, quiet.

bristle n. **1** *the bristles on his chin* **hair**, whisker; (**bristles**) stubble, five o'clock shadow; Zoology seta. **2** *a hedgehog's bristles* **spine**, prickle, quill, barb.
▸ v. **1** *the hair on the back of his neck bristled* **rise**, stand up, stand on end; literary horripilate. **2** *she bristled at his tone* **bridle**, take offence, take umbrage, be affronted, be offended; get angry, be irritated. **3** *the roof bristled with antennae* **abound**, overflow, be full, be packed, be crowded, be jammed, be covered; informal be thick, be jam-packed, be chock-full.

bristly adj. **1** *bristly little bushes* **prickly**, spiky, thorny, scratchy, brambly. **2** *the bristly skin of his cheek* **stubbly**, hairy, fuzzy, unshaven, whiskered, whiskery; scratchy, rough, coarse, prickly; Zoology hispid.
− OPPOSITES smooth.

brittle adj. **1** *glass is a brittle material* **breakable**, fragile, delicate; splintery; formal frangible. **2** *a brittle laugh* **harsh**, hard, sharp, grating. **3** *a brittle young woman* **edgy**, nervy, anxious, unstable, highly strung, tense, excitable, skittish, neurotic; informal uptight, jumpy.
− OPPOSITES flexible, resilient, soft, relaxed.

broach v. **1** *I broached the matter with my parents* **bring up**, raise, introduce, talk about, mention, touch on, air. **2** *he broached a barrel of beer* **pierce**, puncture, tap; **open**, uncork; informal crack open.

broad adj. **1** *a broad flight of steps* **wide**. **2** *the leaves are two inches broad* **wide**, across, in breadth, in width. **3** *a broad expanse of prairie* **extensive**, vast, immense, great, spacious, expansive, sizeable, sweeping, rolling. **4** *a broad range of opportunities* **comprehensive**, inclusive, extensive, wide, all-embracing, eclectic, unlimited. **5** *this report gives a broad outline* **general**, non-specific, unspecific, rough, approximate, basic; loose, vague. **6** *a broad hint* **obvious**, unsubtle, explicit, direct, plain, clear, straightforward, bald, patent, transparent, undisguised, overt. **7** *his broad humour has been toned down* **indecent**, coarse, indelicate, ribald, risqué, racy, rude, suggestive, naughty, off colour, earthy, smutty, dirty, filthy, vulgar; informal blue, near the knuckle. **8** *a broad Somerset accent* **pronounced**,

b

noticeable, strong, thick. **9** *he was attacked in broad daylight* **full**, complete, total; clear, bright.
– OPPOSITES narrow, limited, detailed, subtle.

broadcast v. **1** *the show will be broadcast worldwide* **transmit**, relay, air, beam, show, televise, telecast, videocast, podcast, screen. **2** *the result was broadcast far and wide* **report**, announce, publicize, proclaim; spread, circulate, air, blazon, trumpet. **3** *don't broadcast too much seed* **scatter**, sow, disperse, sprinkle, spread, distribute.
▶ n. *radio and television broadcasts* **programme**, show, production, transmission, telecast, screening; informal prog.

broaden v. **1** *her smile broadened* **widen**, expand, stretch (out), draw out, spread; deepen. **2** *the government tried to broaden its political base.* **expand**, enlarge, extend, widen, swell; increase, augment, add to, amplify; develop, enrich, improve, build on.

broadly adv. **1** *the pattern is broadly similar for men and women* **in general**, on the whole, as a rule, in the main, mainly, predominantly; loosely, roughly, approximately. **2** *he was smiling broadly now* **widely**, openly.

broad-minded adj. **liberal**, tolerant, open-minded, freethinking, indulgent, progressive, permissive, unshockable; unprejudiced, unbiased, unbigoted.
– OPPOSITES intolerant.

broadside n. **1** historical *the gunners fired broadsides* **salvo**, volley, cannonade, barrage, blast, fusillade. **2** *a broadside against the economic reforms* **criticism**, censure, polemic, diatribe, tirade; attack, onslaught; literary philippic.

brochure n. **booklet**, prospectus, catalogue; pamphlet, leaflet, handbill, handout; N. Amer. folder.

broil v. N. Amer. **grill**, toast, barbecue, bake; cook.

broke adj. informal See **penniless**.

broken adj. **1** *a broken bottle* **smashed**, shattered, fragmented, splintered, crushed, snapped; in bits, in pieces; destroyed, disintegrated; cracked, split; informal in smithereens. **2** *a broken arm* **fractured**, damaged, injured. **3** *his video's broken* **damaged**, faulty, defective, not working, malfunctioning, in disrepair, inoperative, out of order, broken-down, down; informal on the blink, kaput, bust, busted, conked out, acting up, done for; Brit. informal knackered. **4** *broken skin* **cut**, ruptured, punctured, perforated. **5** *a broken marriage* **failed**, ended, unsuccessful. **6** *broken promises* **flouted**, violated, infringed, contravened, disregarded, ignored. **7** *he was left a broken man* **defeated**, beaten, subdued; demoralized, dispirited, discouraged, crushed, humbled; dishonoured, ruined. **8** *a night of broken sleep* **interrupted**, disturbed, fitful, disrupted, discontinuous, intermittent, unsettled, troubled. **9** *he pressed on over the broken ground* **uneven**,

rough, irregular, bumpy; rutted, pitted. **10** *she spoke in broken English* **halting**, hesitating, disjointed, faltering, imperfect.
– OPPOSITES whole, working, uninterrupted, smooth, perfect.

broken-down adj. **1** *a broken-down hotel* **dilapidated**, run down, ramshackle, tumbledown, in disrepair, battered, crumbling, deteriorated, gone to rack and ruin. **2** *a broken-down car* **defective**, broken, faulty; not working, malfunctioning, inoperative, non-functioning; informal kaput, conked out, clapped out, done for; Brit. informal knackered.
– OPPOSITES smart.

broken-hearted adj. **heartbroken**, grief-stricken, desolate, devastated, inconsolable, miserable, depressed, melancholy, wretched, sorrowful, forlorn, heavy-hearted, woeful, doleful, downcast, woebegone, sad, down; informal down in the mouth; literary heartsick.
– OPPOSITES overjoyed.

broker n. *a top City broker* **dealer**, broker-dealer, agent; middleman, intermediary, mediator; factor, liaison; stockbroker.
▶ v. *an agreement brokered by the secretariat* **arrange**, organize, orchestrate, work out, settle, clinch, bring about; negotiate, mediate.

bronze n. *Scotland won the bronze* **bronze medal**, third prize.

bronzed adj. **tanned**, suntanned, tan, bronze, brown, reddish-brown.

brooch n. **breastpin**, pin, clip, badge.

brood n. **1** *the bird flew to feed its brood* **offspring**, young, progeny; family, hatch, clutch; formal progeniture. **2** informal *Gill was the youngest of the brood* **family**; children, offspring, youngsters, progeny; informal kids.
▶ v. **1** *once the eggs are laid the male broods them* **incubate**, hatch. **2** *he slumped in his armchair, brooding* **worry**, fret, agonize, mope, sulk; think, ponder, contemplate, meditate, muse, ruminate.

brook¹ n. *a babbling brook* **stream**, streamlet, rill, brooklet, runnel, runlet, gill; N. English beck; Scottish & N. English burn; S. English bourn; N. Amer. & Austral./NZ creek.

brook² v. formal *we brook no violence* **tolerate**, allow, stand, bear, abide, put up with, endure; accept, permit, countenance; informal stomach, stand for, hack; Brit. informal stick; old use suffer.

brothel n. **whorehouse**; N. Amer. bordello; Brit. informal knocking shop; N. Amer. informal cathouse, creepjoint; euphemistic massage parlour; Law disorderly house; old use bawdy house, house of ill fame, house of ill repute.

brother n. **1** *they were brothers in crime* **colleague**, associate, partner, comrade, fellow, friend; informal pal, chum; Brit. informal mate. **2** *a brother of the Carmelite Order* **monk**, cleric, friar, religious, monastic.

> **WORD LINKS**
>
> **fraternal** relating to a brother
> **fratricide** the killing of one's brother or sister

brotherhood n. **1** *the ideals of justice and brotherhood* **comradeship**, fellowship, brotherliness, fraternalism, kinship; camaraderie, club, lodge, circle. **2** *a Masonic brotherhood* **society**, fraternity, association, alliance, union, league, guild, order, body, community, club, lodge, circle.

brotherly adj. **1** *brotherly rivalry* **fraternal**, sibling. **2** *brotherly love* **friendly**, comradely; affectionate, amicable, kind, devoted, loyal.

brow n. **1** *the doctor wiped his brow* **forehead**, temple; Zoology frons. **2** *heavy black brows* **eyebrow**. **3** *the brow of the hill* **summit**, peak, top, mountaintop, crest, crown, head, pinnacle, apex.

browbeat v. **bully**, hector, intimidate, force, coerce, compel, dragoon, bludgeon, pressure, pressurize, tyrannize, terrorize, menace; harass, harry, hound; informal bulldoze, railroad.

brown adj. **1** *she has brown eyes* **hazel**, chocolate-coloured, coffee-coloured, cocoa-coloured, nut-brown; brunette; sepia, mahogany, umber, burnt sienna; beige, buff, tan, fawn, camel, café au lait, caramel, chestnut. **2** *his skin was brown* **tanned**, suntanned, browned, bronze, bronzed; dark, swarthy, dusky. **3** *brown bread* **wholemeal**; unrefined.
▸ v. *the grill browns food evenly* **grill**, toast, singe, sear, crisp (up); barbecue, bake, cook.

browned off adj. informal **irritated**, annoyed, irked, put out, peeved, disgruntled; disheartened, depressed; informal fed up, hacked off; Brit. informal brassed off, cheesed off, narked.

browse v. **1** *I browsed among the little shops* **look around/round**, window-shop, peruse. **2** *she browsed through the newspaper* **scan**, skim, glance, look, peruse; thumb, leaf, flick; dip into. **3** *three cows were browsing in the meadow* **graze**, feed, crop; ruminate.
▸ n. *this brochure is well worth a browse* **scan**, read, skim, glance, look.

bruise n. *a bruise across her forehead* **contusion**, lesion, mark, injury; swelling, lump, bump, welt; Medicine ecchymosis.
▸ v. **1** *her face was badly bruised* **contuse**, injure, mark, discolour. **2** *every one of the apples is bruised* **mark**, discolour, blemish; damage, spoil. **3** *Eric's ego was bruised* **upset**, offend, insult, affront, hurt, wound, injure, crush.

brunette adj. **brown-haired**, dark, dark-haired.

brunt n. **(full) force**, impact, shock, burden, pressure, weight; effect, repercussions, consequences.

brush¹ n. **1** *a dustpan and brush* **broom**, sweeper, besom, whisk. **2** *he gave the seat a brush with his hand* **clean**, sweep, wipe, dust. **3** *a fox's brush* **tail**. **4** *the brush of his lips against her cheek* **touch**, stroke, skim, graze, nudge, contact; kiss. **5** *a brush with the law* **encounter**, clash, confrontation, conflict, altercation, incident; informal run-in, to-do; Brit. informal spot of bother; Brit. informal,

Football afters.
▸ v. **1** *he spent his day brushing the floors* **sweep**, clean, buff, scrub. **2** *she brushed her hair* **groom**, comb, neaten, tidy, smooth, arrange, fix, do; curry. **3** *she felt his lips brush her cheek* **touch**, stroke, caress, skim, sweep, graze, contact; kiss. **4** *she brushed a wisp of hair away* **push**, move, sweep, clear.
▫ **brush something aside** disregard, ignore, dismiss, shrug off, wave aside; overlook, pay no attention to, take no notice of, neglect, forget about, turn a blind eye to; reject, spurn; laugh off, make light of, trivialize; informal pooh-pooh.

brush someone off rebuff, dismiss, spurn, reject; slight, scorn, disdain; ignore, disregard, snub, cut, turn one's back on, give someone the cold shoulder, freeze out; jilt, cast aside, discard, throw over, drop, leave; informal knock back.

brush up (on) revise, read up, go over, relearn, cram, study; improve, sharpen (up), polish up; hone, refine, perfect; informal bone up; Brit. informal swot up, gen up.

brush² n. *an area covered in dense brush* **undergrowth**, underwood, scrub, brushwood, shrubs, bushes; N. Amer. underbrush, chaparral.

brush-off n. informal **rejection**, refusal, rebuff, repulse; snub, slight, cut; informal knock-back; N. Amer. informal kiss-off.

brusque adj. **curt**, abrupt, blunt, short, sharp, terse, brisk, peremptory, gruff, bluff; offhand, discourteous, impolite, rude; informal snappy.
– OPPOSITES polite.

brutal adj. **1** *a brutal attack* **savage**, cruel, vicious, ferocious, barbaric, barbarous, wicked, murderous, bloodthirsty, cold-blooded, callous, heartless, merciless, sadistic; heinous, monstrous, abominable, atrocious. **2** *brutal honesty* **unsparing**, unstinting, unembellished, unvarnished, bald, naked, stark, blunt, direct, straightforward, frank, outspoken, forthright, plain-spoken; complete, total.
– OPPOSITES gentle.

brutalize v. **1** *the men were brutalized by life in the trenches* **desensitize**, dehumanize, harden, toughen, inure. **2** *they were brutalized by the police* **attack**, assault, beat, batter; abuse.

brute n. **1** *a callous brute* **savage**, beast, monster, animal, barbarian, fiend, ogre; sadist; thug, lout, ruffian; informal swine, pig. **2** *the alsatian was a vicious-looking brute* **animal**, beast, creature; N. Amer. informal critter.
▸ adj. *brute force* **physical**, bodily, crude, violent.

bubble n. *the bubbles in his mineral water* **globule**, bead, blister; air pocket; (**bubbles**) sparkle, fizz, effervescence, froth.
▸ v. **1** *this wine bubbled nicely on the tongue* **sparkle**, fizz, effervesce, foam, froth. **2** *the milk was bubbling above the flame* **boil**, simmer, seethe, gurgle. **3** *she was bubbling over with enthusiasm* **overflow**, brim over,

be filled, gush; burst.

bubbly adj. **1** *a bubbly wine* **sparkling**, bubbling, fizzy, effervescent, gassy, aerated, carbonated; spumante, pétillant, mousseux; frothy, foaming. **2** *she was bubbly and full of life* **vivacious**, animated, ebullient, lively, high-spirited, zestful; sparkling, bouncy, buoyant, carefree; merry, happy, cheerful, perky, sunny, bright; Brit. Tiggerish; informal upbeat, chirpy.
– OPPOSITES still, listless.
▶ n. informal *a bottle of bubbly* **champagne**, sparkling wine; mousseux, spumante, cava; informal champers, fizz.

buccaneer n. old use **pirate**, marauder, raider, freebooter, plunderer, cut-throat, privateer.

buck v. *it takes guts to buck the system* **resist**, oppose, defy, fight, kick against.
□ **buck up** informal cheer up, perk up, take heart, pick up, bounce back.
buck someone up informal cheer up, buoy up, ginger up, perk up, hearten, uplift, encourage, enliven, give someone a lift; informal pep up.

bucket n. **1** *a bucket of cold water* **pail**, scuttle, can, tub. **2** informal *everyone wept buckets* **floods**, gallons, oceans.
▶ v. Brit. informal **1** *it was bucketing down* **rain heavily**, rain cats and dogs, rain hard, pour, pelt, lash, teem; Brit. tip. **2** *the car came bucketing out of a side road.* See **speed** (sense 1 of the verb).

buckle n. *a belt buckle* **clasp**, clip, catch, hasp, fastener.
▶ v. **1** *he buckled the belt round his waist* **fasten**, do up, hook, strap, secure, clasp, clip. **2** *pillars were put in to stop the walls buckling* **bend**, warp, twist, curve, bulge, arc, arch; crumple, collapse, give way.
□ **buckle down** get (down) to work, set to work, get down to business; work hard, apply oneself, make an effort, be industrious, be diligent, focus; informal pull one's finger out; Brit. informal get stuck in.

bucolic adj. **rustic**, rural, pastoral, country, countryside; literary Arcadian, sylvan, georgic.

bud n. *fresh buds* **sprout**, shoot; Botany plumule.
▶ v. *trees began to bud* **sprout**, shoot, germinate, swell; dated vegetate.

budding adj. **promising**, up-and-coming, rising, in the making, aspiring, future, prospective, potential, fledgling, developing; informal would-be, wannabe.

budge v. **1** *the horses wouldn't budge* **move**, shift, stir, go. **2** *I couldn't budge the door* **dislodge**, shift, move; open. **3** *they refuse to budge on the issue* **give way**, give in, yield, change one's mind, acquiesce, compromise, do a U-turn. **4** *our customers won't be budged on price alone* **influence**, sway, convince, persuade, induce, entice, tempt, lure, cajole, bring round.

budget n. **1** *your budget for the week* **financial plan**, forecast; accounts, statement. **2** *the defence budget* **allowance**, allocation, quota; grant, award, funds,

resources, capital.
▶ v. **1** *we have to budget £7,000 for the work* **allocate**, allot, allow, earmark, designate, set aside. **2** *the work was initially budgeted at $100m* **cost**, price; value; estimate, schedule. **3** *you should budget for periods of unemployment* **allow**, plan, be ready/ prepared, make allowances.
▶ adj. *a budget hotel* **cheap**, inexpensive, economy, low-cost, low-price, cut-price, discount, bargain.
– OPPOSITES expensive.

buff[1] adj. *a plain buff envelope* **beige**, yellowish, yellowish-brown, light brown, fawn, sandy, wheaten, biscuit, camel.
▶ v. *he buffed the glass* **polish**, burnish, shine, clean, rub.
□ **in the buff** informal See **naked** (sense 1).

buff[2] n. informal *a film buff* **enthusiast**, fan, devotee, lover, admirer; expert, aficionado, authority, pundit; informal freak, nut, fanatic, addict.

buffer n. *a buffer against market fluctuations* **cushion**, bulwark, shield, barrier, guard, safeguard.
▶ v. *a massage helped to buffer the strain* **cushion**, absorb, soften, lessen, diminish, moderate, allay.
– OPPOSITES intensify.

buffet[1] n. **1** *a sumptuous buffet* **cold table**, self-service meal, smorgasbord. **2** *a station buffet* **cafe**, cafeteria, snack bar, canteen, restaurant. **3** *the plates are kept in the buffet* **sideboard**, cabinet, cupboard.

buffet[2] v. **1** *rough seas buffeted the coast* **batter**, pound, lash, strike, hit. **2** *he has been buffeted by bad publicity* **afflict**, trouble, harm, burden, bother, beset, harass, torment, blight, bedevil.
▶ n. **shock**, upset, setback, crisis, blow; misfortune, trouble, problem, hardship, adversity; affliction, sorrow, tribulation, tragedy, vicissitude.

buffoon n. *he regarded the chaplain as a buffoon* **fool**, idiot, dunce, ignoramus, simpleton, jackass; informal chump, blockhead, nincompoop, numbskull, dope, twit, nitwit, halfwit, clot, birdbrain, twerp.

bug n. **1** *bugs were crawling everywhere* **insect**, mite; informal creepy-crawly, beastie. **2** informal *a stomach bug* **illness**, ailment, disorder, infection, disease, sickness, complaint, upset, condition; bacterium, germ, virus; Brit. informal lurgy. **3** informal *he caught the journalism bug* **obsession**, enthusiasm, craze, fad, mania, passion, fixation. **4** *the bug planted on his phone* **listening device**, hidden microphone, wire, wiretap, tap. **5** *the program developed a bug* **fault**, error, defect, flaw; virus; informal glitch, gremlin.
▶ v. **1** *her conversations were bugged* **record**, eavesdrop on, spy on, overhear; wiretap, tap, monitor. **2** informal *she really bugs me.* See **annoy**.

bugbear n. **pet hate**, bête noire, bogey; bane, irritation, vexation, anathema, thorn in one's flesh/side; nightmare, horror; informal peeve, pain (in the neck), hang-up; N. Amer. bugaboo.

build v. 1 *a supermarket had been built* **construct**, erect, put up, assemble. 2 *they were building a snowman* **make**, construct, form, create, fashion, model, shape. 3 *they are building a business strategy* **establish**, found, set up, institute, inaugurate, initiate.
▸n. *a man of slim build* **physique**, frame, body, figure, form, shape, stature, proportions; informal vital statistics.
□ **build something in/into** incorporate in/into, include in, absorb into, subsume into, assimilate into.
build on expand on, enlarge on, develop, elaborate, flesh out, embellish, amplify; refine, improve, perfect.
build up increase, grow, mount up, intensify, escalate; strengthen.
build something up 1 *he built up a huge business* **establish**, set up, found, institute, start, create; develop, expand, enlarge. 2 *he built up his stamina* **boost**, strengthen, increase, improve, augment, raise, enhance, swell; informal beef up. 3 *I have built up a collection of prints* **accumulate**, amass, collect, gather; stockpile, hoard.

builder n. 1 *a canal builder* **designer**, planner, architect, deviser, creator, maker, constructor. 2 *the builders must finish the job in time* **construction worker**, bricklayer, labourer; Brit. ganger; Brit. dated navvy.

building n. 1 *a brick building* **structure**, construction, erection, pile; property, premises, establishment; formal edifice. 2 *the building of power stations* **construction**, erection, fabrication, assembly.

WORD LINKS
architecture the design and construction of buildings

build-up n. 1 *the build-up of military strength* **increase**, growth, expansion, escalation, development, proliferation. 2 *the build-up of carbon dioxide* **accumulation**, accretion. 3 *the build-up for the World Cup* **publicity**, promotion, advertising, marketing; informal hype, ballyhoo.

built-in adj. 1 *a built-in cupboard* **fitted**, integral, integrated, incorporated. 2 *built-in advantages* **inherent**, intrinsic, inbuilt; essential, implicit, basic, fundamental, deep-rooted.

bulb n. **tuber**, corm, rhizome.

bulbous adj. **bulging**, protuberant, round, fat, rotund; swollen, tumid, distended, bloated.

bulge n. 1 *a bulge in his pocket* **swelling**, bump, lump, protuberance, prominence. 2 informal *a bulge in the population* **surge**, upsurge, rise, increase, escalation.
▸v. *his eyes were bulging* **swell**, stick out, puff out, balloon (out), fill out, belly, distend; project, protrude, stand out.

bulk n. 1 *the sheer bulk of the bags* **size**, volume, dimensions, proportions, mass, scale, magnitude, immensity, vastness. 2 *the bulk of entrants were British* **majority**, generality, main part, major part, lion's share, preponderance; most, almost all.
– OPPOSITES minority.
▸v. *some meals are bulked out with fat* **expand**, pad out, fill out, eke out; augment, increase.
□ **bulk large** be important, loom large, dominate; be significant, be influential, be of consequence, carry weight; count, matter, signify.

bulky adj. 1 *bulky items of refuse* **large**, big, huge, sizeable, substantial, massive; king-size, outsize, oversized, considerable; **cumbersome**, unmanageable, unwieldy, ponderous, heavy, weighty; informal jumbo, whopping, hulking; Brit. informal ginormous. 2 *a bulky man* **heavily built**, stocky, thickset, sturdy, well built, burly, strapping, solid, heavy, hefty, meaty; stout, fat, plump, chubby, portly, rotund, round, chunky; overweight, obese, fleshy, corpulent; informal tubby, pudgy, roly-poly, beefy, porky, blubbery; Brit. informal podgy.
– OPPOSITES small, slight.

bull n.

WORD LINKS
taurine relating to a bull
matador, toreador, torero, picador types of bullfighter
Minotaur a mythological creature that was half-man and half-bull

bulldoze v. 1 *they plan to bulldoze the park* **demolish**, knock down, tear down, pull down, flatten, level, raze, clear. 2 *he bulldozed his way through* **force**, push, shove, barge, elbow, shoulder, jostle; plunge, crash, sweep, bundle. 3 informal *she tends to bulldoze everyone* **bully**, hector, browbeat, intimidate, steamroller, dragoon, bludgeon, domineer, pressurize, tyrannize, strong-arm; informal railroad, lean on, boss.

bullet n. **ball**, shot; informal slug; (**bullets**) lead.

bulletin n. 1 *a news bulletin* **report**, dispatch, story, press release, newscast, flash; statement, announcement, message, communication, communiqué. 2 *the society's monthly bulletin* **newsletter**, news-sheet, proceedings; newspaper, magazine, digest, gazette, review.

bullish adj. **confident**, positive, assertive, self-assertive, assured, self-assured, bold, determined; optimistic, buoyant, sanguine; informal feisty, upbeat.

bully n. *the village bully* **persecutor**, oppressor, tyrant, tormentor, intimidator; tough guy, bully boy, thug, attack dog.
▸v. 1 *the others bully him* **persecute**, oppress, tyrannize, browbeat, intimidate, strong-arm, dominate; informal push around/about. 2 *she was bullied into helping* **coerce**, pressure, pressurize, press, push; force, compel; badger, goad, prod, browbeat, bludgeon, intimidate, dragoon, strong-arm; informal bulldoze, railroad, lean on.

b

b

bulwark n. **1** *ancient bulwarks* **wall**, rampart, fortification, parapet, stockade, palisade, barricade, embankment, earthwork. **2** *a bulwark of liberty* **protector**, defender, protection, guard, defence, supporter, buttress; mainstay, bastion, stronghold.

bum[1] n. Brit. informal See **bottom** (sense 6 of the noun).

bum[2] informal n. **1** N. Amer. *the bums sleeping on the sidewalk*. See **tramp** (sense 1 of the noun). **2** *you lazy bum* **idler**, loafer, good-for-nothing, ne'er-do-well, layabout, lounger, shirker; informal waster, loser, scrounger.
▸ v. **1** *he bummed around Florida* **loaf**, lounge, idle, moon, amble, wander, drift, meander, dawdle; informal mooch; N. Amer. informal lollygag. **2** *they bummed money off him* **beg**, borrow; informal scrounge, cadge, sponge; Brit. informal scab; N. Amer. informal mooch; Austral./NZ informal bludge.
▸ adj. *a bum deal* **bad**, poor, second-rate, third-rate, second-class, unsatisfactory, inadequate, unacceptable; dreadful, awful, terrible, deplorable, lamentable; informal crummy, rotten, pathetic, lousy, pitiful, dire, poxy; Brit. informal duff, rubbish.
– OPPOSITES efficient.

bumble v. **1** *they bumbled around the house* **blunder**, lurch, stumble, stagger, lumber, flounder, totter. **2** *the speakers bumbled* **mutter**, mumble, stumble, babble, burble, drivel, gibber.

bumbling adj. **blundering**, bungling, inept, clumsy, maladroit, awkward, muddled; oafish, clodhopping, lumbering; crude; informal botched, ham-fisted, cack-handed.
– OPPOSITES efficient.

bump n. **1** *I landed with a bump* **jolt**, crash, smash, smack, crack, bang, thud, thump; informal whack, thwack, bash, wallop. **2** *I was woken by a bump* **bang**, crack, boom, clang, knock, thud, thump, clunk, crash, smash; stomp, clump, clomp; informal whump. **3** *a bump in the road* **hump**, lump, ridge, bulge, knob, protuberance. **4** *a bump on his head* **swelling**, lump, bulge, injury, contusion; outgrowth, growth, carbuncle, protuberance; Anatomy bulla.
▸ v. **1** *cars bumped into each other* **hit**, crash, smash, slam, bang, knock, run, plough; ram, collide with, strike; N. Amer. informal impact. **2** *a car bumping along the road* **bounce**, jolt, jerk, rattle, shake.
□ **bump into** informal meet (by chance), encounter, run into/across, come across, chance on, happen on.

bumper adj. **abundant**, rich, bountiful, good, fine; large, big, huge, plentiful, profuse, copious; informal whopping; literary plenteous, bounteous.
– OPPOSITES meagre.

bumpkin n. **yokel**, peasant, provincial, rustic, country cousin, countryman/woman; Irish informal culchie; N. Amer. informal hayseed, hillbilly, hick; Austral. informal bushy.

bumptious adj. **self-important**, conceited, arrogant, self-assertive, pushy, swollen-headed, pompous, overbearing, cocky, swaggering; proud, haughty, overweening, egotistical; informal snooty, uppity.
– OPPOSITES modest.

bumpy adj. **1** *a bumpy road* **uneven**, rough, rutted, pitted, potholed, holey; lumpy, rocky. **2** *a bumpy ride* **bouncy**, rough, uncomfortable, jolting, lurching, jerky, jarring, bone-shaking. **3** *a bumpy start* **inconsistent**, variable, irregular, fluctuating, intermittent, erratic, patchy; rocky, unsettled, unstable, turbulent, chaotic, full of ups and downs.
– OPPOSITES smooth.

bunch n. **1** *a bunch of flowers* **bouquet**, posy, nosegay, tussie-mussie, spray, corsage; wreath, garland. **2** *a bunch of keys* **cluster**, clump, knot; group. **3** informal *a great bunch of people* **group**, set, circle, company, collection, bevy, band; informal gang, crowd, load. **4** N. Amer. informal *a whole bunch of things*. See **lot** (pronoun).
▸ v. **1** *he bunched the reins in his hand* **bundle**, clump, cluster, group, gather; pack. **2** *his trousers bunched around his ankles* **gather**, ruffle, pucker, fold, pleat. **3** *the runners bunched up behind him* **cluster**, huddle, gather, congregate, collect, amass, group, crowd.

bundle n. *a bundle of clothes* **bunch**, roll, clump, wad, parcel, sheaf, bale, bolt; pile, stack, heap, mass; informal load, wodge.
▸ v. **1** *she bundled up her things* **tie**, pack, parcel, wrap, roll, fold, bind, truss, bale. **2** *she was bundled in furs* **wrap**, envelop, clothe, cover, muffle, swathe, swaddle, shroud, drape, enfold. **3** informal *he was bundled into a van* **hustle**, manhandle, frogmarch, hurry, rush; shove, push, thrust.

bung n. **stopper**, plug, cork, spigot, spile, seal; N. Amer. stopple.

bungle v. **mishandle**, mismanage, mess up, spoil, ruin; informal botch, muff, fluff, make a hash of, foul up, screw up; Brit. informal make a pig's ear of, cock up; N. Amer. informal flub, goof up.

bungler n. **blunderer**, incompetent, amateur, bumbler, clown; informal botcher, butterfingers; Brit. informal bodger; N. Amer. informal jackleg.

bungling adj. **incompetent**, blundering, amateurish, inept, unskilful, clumsy, awkward, bumbling; informal ham-fisted, cack-handed.

bunk[1] n. *he slept in a bunk* **berth**, cot, bed.

bunk[2] Brit. informal v. *he bunked off school* **(play) truant from**, skip, avoid, shirk; informal sag off; Brit. informal skive off; N. Amer. informal play hookey from, goof off, cut; Austral./NZ informal wag.
□ **do a bunk** See **abscond**.

bunk[3] n. informal *what bunk you talk!* See **nonsense** (sense 1).

buoy n. *a mooring buoy* **float**, marker, beacon.
▸ v. *the party was buoyed by an election victory*

cheer (up), hearten, rally, invigorate, uplift, lift, encourage, stimulate, inspirit; informal pep up, perk up, buck up.
– OPPOSITES depress.

buoyancy n. **1** *the drum's buoyancy* **ability to float**, lightness, floatability. **2** *her natural buoyancy* **cheerfulness**, happiness, light-heartedness, joy, bounce, sunniness, breeziness, jollity; liveliness, ebullience, high spirits, vivacity, vitality, verve, sparkle, zest; optimism; informal pep. **3** *the buoyancy of the market* **vigour**, strength, resilience, growth, improvement, expansion.

buoyant adj. **1** *a buoyant substance* **able to float**, floating, floatable. **2** *a buoyant mood* **cheerful**, cheery, happy, light-hearted, carefree, bright, merry, joyful, bubbly, bouncy, sunny, jolly; lively, jaunty, high-spirited, perky; optimistic, confident, positive; informal peppy, upbeat. **3** *sales were buoyant* **booming**, strong, vigorous, thriving; improving, expanding, mushrooming, snowballing.

burble v. **1** *the exhaust was burbling* **gurgle**, bubble, murmur, purr, whir, drone, hum, rumble. **2** *he burbled on* **prattle**, blather, blether, babble, gabble, prate, drivel, rattle, ramble, maunder, go on, run on; informal jabber, blabber, yatter, gab; Brit. informal rabbit, witter, waffle, chunter; N. Amer. informal run off at the mouth.

burden n. **1** *they shouldered their burdens* **load**, cargo, weight; pack, bundle. **2** *a financial burden* **responsibility**, onus, charge, duty, obligation, liability; trouble, care, problem, worry, difficulty, strain, encumbrance. **3** *the burden of his message* **gist**, substance, drift, thrust, meaning, significance, essence, import, message.
▶ v. **1** *he was burdened with a heavy pack* **load**, charge, weigh down, encumber, hamper; overload, overburden. **2** *avoid burdening them with guilt* **oppress**, trouble, worry, harass, upset, distress; haunt, afflict, strain; stress, tax, overwhelm.

burdensome adj. **onerous**, oppressive, troublesome, weighty, worrisome, stressful; vexatious, irksome, trying, difficult; arduous, strenuous, hard, laborious, exhausting, tiring, taxing, demanding, punishing, gruelling.

bureau n. **1** *an oak bureau* **desk**, writing table, secretaire, escritoire; Brit. davenport. **2** *a marriage bureau* **agency**, service, office, business, company, firm. **3** *the intelligence bureau* **department**, division, branch, section.

bureaucracy n. **1** *the ranks of the bureaucracy* **civil service**, government, administration; establishment, system, powers that be; ministries, authorities. **2** *unnecessary bureaucracy* **red tape**, rules and regulations, protocol, officialdom, paperwork.

bureaucrat n. **official**, administrator, civil servant, minister, functionary, mandarin; Brit. jack-in-office; derogatory apparatchik.

bureaucratic adj. **1** *bureaucratic structure* **administrative**, official, governmental, ministerial, state, civic. **2** *current practice is far too bureaucratic* **rule-bound**, rigid, inflexible, complicated.

burgeon v. **flourish**, thrive, prosper, improve; expand, escalate, swell, grow, boom, mushroom, snowball, rocket.

burglar n. **housebreaker**, robber, cat burglar, thief, raider, looter, safe-breaker/cracker; intruder; N. Amer. informal yegg; informal dated cracksman.

burglary n. **1** *a sentence for burglary* **housebreaking**, breaking and entering, theft, stealing, robbery, larceny, thievery, looting. **2** *a series of burglaries* **break-in**, theft, robbery, raid; informal smash-and-grab; N. Amer. informal heist.

burgle v. **rob**, loot, steal from, plunder, rifle, pillage; break into; informal do.

burial n. **burying**, interment, committal, inhumation, entombment; funeral, obsequies; formal exequies; old use sepulture.
– OPPOSITES exhumation.

> **WORD LINKS**
> **funerary**, **sepulchral**, **mortuary** relating to burial
> **barrow**, **tumulus** an ancient burial mound
> **shroud**, **winding sheet** a piece of cloth in which a dead body is wrapped for burial.
> See also **funeral**.

burial ground n. **cemetery**, graveyard, churchyard, necropolis, garden of remembrance; Scottish kirkyard; N. Amer. memorial park; informal boneyard; historical potter's field; old use God's acre.

burlesque n. **parody**, caricature, satire, lampoon, skit; informal send-up, take-off, spoof.

burly adj. **strapping**, well built, sturdy, brawny, strong, muscular, muscly, thickset, big, hefty, bulky, stocky, Herculean; informal hunky, beefy, husky, hulking.
– OPPOSITES puny.

burn v. **1** *the coal was burning* **be on fire**, be alight, be ablaze, blaze, go up (in smoke), be in flames, be aflame; smoulder, glow. **2** *he burned the letters* **set fire to**, set on fire, set alight, set light to, light, ignite, touch off; incinerate; informal torch. **3** *I burned my arm* **scorch**, singe, sear, char, blacken, brand; scald; Medicine cauterize. **4** *her face burned* **be hot**, be warm, be feverish, be on fire; blush, redden, go red, flush, colour. **5** *she was burning with curiosity* **be consumed**, be eaten up, be obsessed, be tormented, be beside oneself. **6** *Meredith burned to know the secret* **yearn**, long, ache, desire, want, wish, hanker, crave, hunger, thirst; informal have a yen, yen, itch, be dying. **7** *the energy they burn up* **consume**, use up, expend, get/go through, eat up; dissipate.

burning adj. **1** *burning coals* **blazing**, flaming, fiery, ignited, glowing, red-hot, smouldering; raging, roaring. **2** *burning desert sands* **hot**, red-hot, fiery, blistering,

b

b

scorching, searing, sweltering, torrid; informal baking, boiling (hot), roasting, sizzling. **3** *a burning desire* **intense**, passionate, deep-seated, profound, wholehearted, strong, ardent, fervent, urgent, fierce, eager, frantic, consuming, uncontrollable. **4** *the burning issues of the day* **important**, crucial, significant, vital, essential, pivotal; urgent, pressing, compelling, critical.

burnish v. **polish (up)**, shine, buff (up), rub (up).

burp informal v. **belch**, bring up wind; Scottish & N. English informal **rift**.
▶n. **belch**; wind; Scottish & N. English informal **rift**; formal eructation.

burrow n. *a rabbits' burrow* **warren**, tunnel, hole, dugout; lair, set, den, earth.
▶v. *the mouse burrows a hole* **tunnel**, dig (out), excavate, grub, mine, bore, channel; hollow out, gouge out.

burst v. **1** *one balloon burst* **split (open)**, rupture, break, tear. **2** *a shell burst* **explode**, blow up, detonate, go off. **3** *smoke burst through the hole* **break**, erupt, surge, gush, rush, stream, flow, pour, spill; spout, spurt, jet, spew. **4** *he burst into the room* **plunge**, charge, barge, plough, hurtle, career, rush, dash, tear. **5** *she burst into tears* **break out in**, erupt in, have a fit of.
▶n. **1** *mortar bursts* **explosion**, detonation, blast, eruption, bang. **2** *a burst of gunfire* **volley**, salvo, fusillade, barrage, discharge; hail, rain. **3** *a burst of activity* **outbreak**, eruption, flare-up, blaze, attack, fit, rush, gale, storm, surge, upsurge, spurt; informal splurt.
□ **burst out** *'I don't care!' she burst out* exclaim, blurt, cry, shout, yell; dated ejaculate.

bury v. **1** *the dead were buried* **inter**, lay to rest, entomb; informal plant; literary inhume. **2** *she buried her face in her hands* **hide**, conceal, cover, enfold, engulf, tuck, cup, sink. **3** *the bullet buried itself in the wood* **embed**, sink, implant, submerge; drive into. **4** *he buried himself in his work* **absorb**, engross, immerse, occupy, engage, busy, involve.
– OPPOSITES exhume.

bush n. **1** *a rose bush* **shrub**; (**bushes**) undergrowth, shrubbery. **2** *it's easy to get lost in the bush* **wilds**, wilderness; backwoods, hinterland(s); N. Amer. backcountry; backland(s); Austral./NZ outback, backblocks, booay; N. Amer. informal boondocks, tall timbers; Austral./NZ informal Woop Woop, beyond the black stump.

bushy adj. **thick**, shaggy, fuzzy, bristly, fluffy, woolly; luxuriant; informal jungly.
– OPPOSITES sleek, wispy.

busily adv. **energetically**, vigorously, enthusiastically; industriously, purposefully, diligently.

business n. **1** *she has to smile in her business* **work**, line (of work), occupation, profession, career, employment, job, position; vocation, calling; field, sphere, trade, craft; informal

racket, game; old use employ. **2** *who do you do business with?* **trade**, trading, commerce, dealing, traffic, merchandising; dealings, transactions, negotiations. **3** *her own business* **firm**, company, concern, enterprise, venture, organization, operation, undertaking; office, agency, franchise, practice; informal outfit, set-up. **4** *none of your business* **concern**, affair, responsibility, duty, function, obligation; problem, worry; informal pigeon, bailiwick; Brit. informal lookout. **5** *an odd business* **affair**, matter, thing, case, circumstance, situation, event, incident, happening, occurrence; episode.

WORD LINKS
corporate relating to a business corporation

businesslike adj. **professional**, efficient, slick, competent, methodical, disciplined, systematic, orderly, organized, structured, practical, pragmatic.

businessman, **businesswoman** n. **entrepreneur**, business person, industrialist, manufacturer, tycoon, magnate, employer; dealer, trader, broker, merchant, buyer, seller, marketeer, merchandiser, vendor, tradesman, retailer, supplier; Brit. informal flogger.

bust[1] n. **1** *her large bust* **chest**, bosom; breasts, mammary glands, mammae; informal boobs, knockers, bubbies; Brit. informal bristols, charlies; N. Amer. informal bazooms. **2** *a bust of Caesar* **sculpture**, carving, effigy, statue; head and shoulders.

bust[2] informal v. **1** *the lock has bust* **break**, crack, snap, smash, fracture, shatter, disintegrate; split, burst. **2** *he promised to bust the mafia* **overthrow**, destroy, topple, bring down, ruin, break, overturn, overcome, defeat, get rid of, oust, dislodge. **3** *they were busted for drugs*. See **arrest** (sense 1 of the verb). **4** N. Amer. *my apartment got busted*. See **raid** (sense 3 of the verb).
□ **go bust** fail, collapse, fold, go under, founder; go bankrupt, go into receivership, go into liquidation, be wound up; informal crash, go broke, go to the wall, go belly up, flop, flatline.

bustle v. **1** *people bustled about* **rush**, dash, hurry, scurry, scuttle, scamper, scramble; run, tear, charge; informal scoot, beetle, buzz, zoom. **2** *she bustled us into the kitchen* **hustle**, bundle, sweep, push, whisk.
▶n. *the bustle of the market* **activity**, action, liveliness, hustle and bustle, excitement; tumult, hubbub, whirl; informal toing and froing, comings and goings.

bustling adj. **busy**, crowded, swarming, teeming, thronged; buzzing, hectic, lively.
– OPPOSITES deserted.

busy adj. **1** *they are busy raising money* **occupied (in)**, engaged in, involved in, employed in, working at, hard at work (on); rushed off one's feet, hard-pressed; on the job, absorbed, engrossed, immersed, preoccupied; informal (as) busy as a bee, on the go, hard at it; Brit. informal on the hop. **2** *she is*

busy at the moment **unavailable**, engaged, occupied; working, on duty; informal tied up. **3** *a busy day* **hectic**, active, lively, full, eventful; energetic, tiring. **4** *the town was busy* **crowded**, bustling, hectic, swarming, teeming, full, thronged; informal buzzy. **5** *a busy design* **ornate**, over-elaborate, overblown, overwrought, overdone, fussy, cluttered, overworked.
– OPPOSITES idle, free, quiet.
▶ v. *he busied himself with paperwork* **occupy**, involve, engage, concern, absorb, engross, immerse, preoccupy; distract, divert.

busybody n. **meddler**, interferer, mischief-maker, troublemaker; gossip, scandalmonger; eavesdropper, gawker; informal nosy parker, snoop, snooper, rubberneck; Brit. informal gawper; informal dated Paul Pry.

but conj. **1** *he stumbled but didn't fall* **yet**, nevertheless, nonetheless, even so, however, still, notwithstanding, despite that, in spite of that, for all that, all the same, just the same; though, although. **2** *I am clean but you aren't* **whereas**, conversely, but then, then again, on the other hand, by/in contrast, on the contrary. **3** *one cannot but sympathize* **(do) other than**, (do) otherwise than; except.
▶ prep. *everyone but him* **except (for)**, apart from, other than, besides, aside from, with the exception of, bar, excepting, excluding, leaving out, save (for), saving.
▶ adv. *he is but a shadow of his former self* **only**, just, simply, merely, no more than, nothing but; a mere; N. English nobbut.
□ **but for** except for, if it were not for, were it not for, barring, notwithstanding.

butch adj. informal **masculine**, manly; mannish, manlike, unfeminine, unladylike; informal macho.
– OPPOSITES effeminate.

butcher n. **1** *a butcher's shop* **meat seller**, meat trader; slaughterer; Scottish flesher. **2** *a Nazi butcher* **murderer**, slaughterer, killer, assassin; N. Amer. terminator; literary slayer; dated cut-throat, homicide.
▶ v. **1** *the goat was butchered* **slaughter**, cut up, carve up, joint. **2** *they butchered 150 people* **massacre**, murder, slaughter, kill, destroy, exterminate, assassinate; N. Amer. terminate; informal dispose of; literary slay. **3** *the studio butchered the film* **spoil**, ruin, mutilate, mangle, mess up, wreck; informal make a hash of, screw up.

butchery n. **1** Brit. **abattoir**, slaughterhouse, meat market. **2** *the butchery in the war* **slaughter**, massacre, mass murder; genocide; literary slaying.

butt[1] v. *she butted him* **ram**, headbutt, bunt; bump, buffet, push, shove; N. English tup.
□ **butt in** interrupt, break in, cut in, chime in, interject, intervene, interfere; informal poke one's nose in, put one's oar in; Brit. informal chip in.

butt[2] n. *the butt of a joke* **target**, victim, object, subject; laughing stock.

butt[3] n. **1** *the butt of a gun* **stock**, end, handle, hilt, haft, helve. **2** *a cigarette butt* **stub**, end, tail end, stump, remnant; informal fag end, dog end. **3** N. Amer. informal *sitting on his butt.* See **bottom** (sense 6 of the noun).
▶ v. *the shop butts up against the house* **adjoin**, abut, be next to, be adjacent to, border (on), neighbour, be connected to; join, touch.

butt[4] n. *a brandy butt* **barrel**, cask, keg, vat, tun; tub, bin, drum, canister.

butter v.
□ **butter someone up** informal flatter, court, wheedle, persuade, blarney, coax, get round, prevail on; be obsequious towards, be sycophantic towards, toady to, fawn on, make up to, play up to, ingratiate oneself with, curry favour with; informal suck up to, be all over, keep someone sweet, sweet-talk, soft-soap.

butterfly n.

> **WORD LINKS**
>
> **lepidopterist** a person who collects or studies butterflies
> **caterpillar** the larva of a butterfly
> **chrysalis** the pupa of a butterfly

buttocks plural n. **cheeks**; rear (end), rump, seat; Brit. bottom; Scottish bahookie; informal behind, backside, BTM, sit-upon, derrière; Brit. informal bum, botty, jacksie; N. Amer. informal butt, fanny, tush, tail, buns, booty, heinie, bippy; humorous fundament, posterior, stern; Anatomy nates.

button n. **1** *shirt buttons* **fastener**, stud, toggle; hook, catch, clasp. **2** *press the button* **switch**, knob, control; lever, handle.

buttonhole v. informal See **accost**.

buttress n. **1** *stone buttresses* **prop**, support, abutment, shore, pier, reinforcement, stanchion. **2** *a buttress against social collapse* **safeguard**, defence, protection, guard; support, prop; bulwark.
▶ v. *authority was buttressed by religion* **strengthen**, reinforce, fortify, support, bolster, shore up, underpin, cement, uphold, defend, back up.

buxom adj. **large-breasted**, big-breasted, bosomy, big-bosomed; shapely, ample, plump, rounded, full-figured, voluptuous, curvaceous, Rubenesque; informal busty, chesty, well endowed, curvy.

buy v. **1** *they bought a new house* **purchase**, acquire, obtain, get, pick up, snap up; take, procure, pay for; invest in; informal get hold of, score. **2** *he could not be bought* **bribe**, buy off, suborn, corrupt; informal grease someone's palm, give a backhander to, get at, fix, square; Brit. informal nobble.
– OPPOSITES sell.
▶ n. informal *a good buy* **purchase**, investment, acquisition, gain; deal, bargain.

buyer n. **purchaser**, customer, consumer, shopper, investor; (**buyers**) clientele, patronage, market; Law vendee.

buzz n. **1** *the buzz of the bees* **hum**, humming, buzzing, murmur, drone; Brit. informal zizz. **2** *an insistent buzz from her control panel*

noise, beep, bleep, purr, ring, note, tone, warble, alarm. **3** informal *give me a buzz*. See **call** (sense 3 of the noun). **4** informal *the buzz is that he's gone*. See **rumour**. **5** informal *I get a buzz out of flying* **thrill**, stimulation, glow, tingle; informal kick, hit; N. Amer. informal charge.

▶ v. **1** *bees buzzed* **hum**, drone, bumble, murmur; Brit. informal zizz. **2** *the intercom soon buzzed* **sound**, beep, bleep, purr, warble, ring. **3** informal *he buzzed around* **bustle**, scurry, scuttle, hurry, rush, race, dash, tear, chase; informal scoot, beetle, whizz, zoom, zip. **4** *the club is buzzing with excitement* **hum**, throb, vibrate, pulse, bustle.

by prep. **1** *I broke it by forcing the lid* **through**, as a result of, because of, by dint of, by way of, via, by means of; with the help of, with the aid of, by virtue of. **2** *be there by midday* **no later than**, in good time for, at, before. **3** *a house by the lake* **next to**, beside, alongside, by/at the side of, adjacent to, side by side with; near, close to, neighbouring, adjoining, bordering, overlooking; connected to, contiguous with, attached to. **4** *go by the building* **past**, in front of, beyond. **5** *all right by me* **according to**, with, as far as —— is concerned.

▶ adv. *people hurried by* **past**, on, along.
□ **by and by** eventually, ultimately, finally, in the end, one day, some day, sooner or later, in time, in a while, in the long run, in the fullness of time, in time to come, at length, in the future, in due course.
by oneself alone, on one's own, singly, separately, solitarily, unaccompanied, companionless, unattended, unescorted, solo; unaided, unassisted, without help, by one's own efforts, under one's own steam, independently, single-handed(ly), off one's own bat, on one's own initiative; informal by one's lonesome; Brit. informal on one's tod, on one's Jack Jones.

bygone adj. **past**, former, olden, earlier, previous, one-time, long-ago, of old, ancient, antiquated; departed, dead, extinct, defunct, out of date, outmoded; literary of yore.
– OPPOSITES present, recent.

by-law n. Brit. **local law**, regulation, rule.

bypass n. **ring road**, detour, diversion, alternative route; Brit. relief road.
▶ v. **1** *bypass the farm* **go round**, go past, make a detour round; avoid. **2** *an attempt to bypass the problem* **avoid**, evade, dodge, escape, elude, circumvent, get round, skirt, sidestep, steer clear of; informal duck. **3** *they bypassed the regulations* **ignore**, pass over, omit, neglect; informal short-circuit.

by-product n. **side effect**, consequence, entailment, corollary; ramification, repercussion, spin-off, fallout; fruits; Brit. knock-on effect.

bystander n. **onlooker**, looker-on, passer-by, non-participant, observer, spectator, eyewitness, witness, watcher; informal gawper, rubberneck.

byword n. **1** *the office was a byword for delay* **perfect example**, classic case, model, exemplar, embodiment, incarnation, personification, epitome, typification. **2** *reality was his byword* **slogan**, motto, maxim, mantra, catchword, watchword, formula; middle name.

Cc

cab n. **1** *she hailed a cab* **taxi**, taxi cab;
Brit. minicab, hackney carriage; N. Amer.
hack; historical fiacre. **2** *a truck driver's cab*
(driver's) compartment, cabin.

cabal n. **clique**, faction, coterie, cell, sect,
camarilla; pressure group, ginger group.

cabaret n. **1** *the evening's cabaret*
entertainment, (floor) show, performance.
2 *the cabarets of Montreal* **nightclub**, club,
boîte; N. Amer. cafe; informal nightspot, niterie,
clip joint; N. Amer. informal honky-tonk.

cabin n. **1** *a first-class cabin* **berth**, stateroom,
deckhouse; historical roundhouse. **2** *a cabin by
the lake* **hut**, log cabin, shanty, shack; chalet;
Scottish bothy; N. Amer. cabana; Austral. mia-mia;
old use cot; N. Amer. old use shebang. **3** *the
driver's cabin* **cab**, compartment.

cabinet n. **1** *a walnut cabinet* **cupboard**,
bureau, chest of drawers. **2** *a cabinet
meeting* **senior ministers**, ministry, council,
executive.

cable n. **1** *a thick cable moored the ship*
rope, cord, line, guy; Nautical hawser, stay,
bridle, topping lift; N. Amer. choker. **2** *electric
cables* **wire**, lead, cord; power line; Brit.
flex. **3** historical *he immediately sent a cable*
telegram, telemessage, radiogram; informal
wire; historical cablegram.
▶ v. *the secretariat cabled a reply* **radio**, send,
transmit; informal wire.

cache n. **1** *a cache of arms* **hoard**, store,
stockpile, stock, supply, reserve; arsenal;
informal stash. **2** *a niche used as a cache* **hiding
place**, secret place; informal hidey-hole; informal
dated stash.

cachet n. **prestige**, prestigiousness, status,
standing, kudos, snob value, stature, pre-
eminence, eminence; street credibility.

cackle v. **1** *the geese cackled at him* **squawk**,
cluck. **2** *Noel cackled with glee* **laugh loudly**,
guffaw, crow, chortle, chuckle.

cacophonous adj. **loud**, noisy, ear-
splitting, raucous, discordant, dissonant,
inharmonious, unmelodious, unmusical,
tuneless; old use absonant.
– OPPOSITES harmonious.

cacophony n. **din**, racket, noise, discord,
dissonance, discordance.

cad n. dated See **scoundrel**.

cadaver n. Medicine **corpse**, (dead) body,
remains, carcass; informal stiff; old use corse.

cadaverous adj. **(deathly) pale**, pallid,
ashen, grey, whey-faced, etiolated, corpse-
like; as thin as a rake, bony, skeletal,
emaciated, skin and bone, haggard, gaunt,
drawn, pinched, hollow-cheeked, hollow-
eyed; informal like a bag of bones, anorexic; old
use starveling.
– OPPOSITES rosy, plump.

cadence n. **rhythm**, tempo, metre, beat,
pulse; intonation, modulation, lilt.

cadge v. informal **borrow**; informal scrounge,
bum, touch someone for, sponge; Brit. informal
scab; N. Amer. informal mooch; Austral./NZ informal
bludge.

cadre n. **corps**, body, team, group.

cafe n. **snack bar**, cafeteria, buffet; coffee
bar/shop, tea room/shop; bistro, brasserie;
N. Amer. diner; informal eatery, noshery; Brit.
informal caff.

cafeteria n. **self-service restaurant**,
canteen, cafe, buffet.

cage n. *animals in cages* **enclosure**, pen,
pound; coop, hutch; birdcage, aviary; N. Amer.
corral.
▶ v. *many animals are caged* **confine**, shut in/
up, pen, coop up, immure, impound; N. Amer.
corral.

cagey adj. informal **secretive**, guarded, non-
committal, tight-lipped, reticent, evasive;
informal playing one's cards close to one's
chest.
– OPPOSITES open.

cahoots plural n.
□ **in cahoots** informal in league, colluding, in
collusion, conspiring, collaborating, hand
in glove.

cajole v. **persuade**, wheedle, coax, talk into,
prevail on, blarney; informal sweet-talk, soft-
soap, twist someone's arm; old use blandish.

cajolery n. **persuasion**, wheedling, coaxing,
inveiglement, cajolement; blandishments,
blarney; informal sweet talk, soft soap, arm-
twisting; formal suasion.

cake n. **1** *cream cakes* **bun**, pastry, gateau.
2 *a cake of soap* **bar**, tablet, block, slab, lump.
▶ v. **1** *boots caked with mud* **coat**, encrust,
plaster, cover. **2** *the blood was beginning to
cake* **clot**, congeal, coagulate, solidify, set,
inspissate.

calamitous adj. **disastrous**, catastrophic,
cataclysmic, devastating, dire, tragic; literary
direful.

calamity n. **disaster**, catastrophe, tragedy,
cataclysm, adversity, tribulation, affliction,
misfortune, misadventure.
– OPPOSITES godsend.

C

calculate v. **1** *the interest is calculated on a daily basis* **compute**, work out, reckon, figure; add up/together, count up, tally, total; Brit. tot up. **2** *his words were calculated to wound her* **intend**, mean, design. **3** *we had calculated on a quiet Sunday* **expect**, anticipate, reckon, bargain; N. Amer. informal figure on.

calculated adj. **deliberate**, premeditated, planned, pre-planned, preconceived, intentional, intended; Law, dated prepense.
– OPPOSITES unintentional.

calculating adj. **cunning**, crafty, wily, shrewd, scheming, devious, designing, Machiavellian; informal foxy; old use subtle.
– OPPOSITES ingenuous.

calculation n. **1** *the calculation of the overall cost* **computation**, reckoning, adding up, counting up, working out, figuring; Brit. totting up. **2** *political calculations* **assessment**, judgement; forecast, projection, prediction.

calendar n. **1** **almanac**. **2** *my social calendar* **schedule**, programme, diary.

calibre n. **1** *a man of his calibre* **quality**, merit, distinction, stature, excellence, pre-eminence; ability, expertise, talent, capability, capacity, proficiency. **2** *rugby of this calibre* **standard**, level, quality. **3** *the calibre of a gun* **bore**, diameter, gauge.

call v. **1** *'Wait for me!' she called* **cry (out)**, shout, yell, bellow, roar, bawl, scream, vociferate; informal holler. **2** *Mum called me in the morning* **wake (up)**, awaken, rouse; Brit. informal knock up; literary waken. **3** *I'll call you tomorrow* **phone**, telephone, get someone on the phone, give someone a call; Brit. ring (up), give someone a ring; informal call up, give someone a buzz; Brit. informal give someone a bell/tinkle, get someone on the blower; N. Amer. informal get someone on the horn. **4** *Rose called a taxi* **summon**, send for, order. **5** *he called at Ashgrove Cottage* **pay a (brief) visit to**, visit, pay a call on, call/drop/look in on, drop/stop by, pop into. **6** *the prime minister called a meeting* **convene**, summon, assemble; formal convoke. **7** *they called their daughter Hannah* **name**, christen, baptize; designate, style, term, dub; formal denominate. **8** *I would call him a friend* **describe as**, regard as, look on as, consider to be.
▶ n. **1** *I heard calls from the auditorium* **cry**, shout, yell, roar, scream, exclamation, vociferation; informal holler. **2** *the call of the water rail* **cry**, song, sound. **3** *I'll give you a call tomorrow* **phone call**, telephone call; Brit. ring; informal buzz; Brit. informal bell, tinkle. **4** *he paid a call on Harold* **visit**, social call. **5** *a call for party unity* **appeal**, request, plea, entreaty. **6** *the last call for passengers on flight BA701* **summons**, request. **7** *there's no call for that kind of language* **need**, necessity, reason, justification, excuse. **8** *there's no call for expensive wine here* **demand**, desire, market. **9** *the call of the Cairngorms* **attraction**, appeal, lure, allure, spell, pull, draw.

□ **call for 1** *desperate times call for desperate measures* **require**, need, necessitate; justify, warrant. **2** *I'll call for you around seven* **pick up**, collect, fetch.
call something off cancel, abandon, scrap, drop, axe; informal scrub, nix; N. Amer. informal redline.
call on 1 *I might call on her later* **visit**, pay a call on, go and see, look/drop in on; N. Amer. visit with; informal look up, pop in on. **2** *he called on the government to hold a plebiscite* **appeal to**, ask, request, petition, urge. **3** *we are able to call on qualified staff* **have recourse to**, avail oneself of, draw on, make use of.
call the shots be in charge, be in control, be at the helm/wheel, be in the driving seat, pull the strings; informal run the show, be the boss.
call to mind 1 *this calls to mind Cézanne's works* **evoke**, bring to mind, call up, conjure up. **2** *I cannot call to mind where I have seen you* **remember**, recall, recollect.
call someone up 1 *they called up the reservists* **enlist**, recruit, conscript; US draft. **2** *he was called up for the England team* **select**, pick, choose; Brit. cap.
on call on duty, on standby, available.

call girl n. **prostitute**, whore, sex worker, fille de joie; informal tart, pro, working girl; N. Amer. informal hooker, hustler; euphemistic escort, masseuse; dated woman of the streets; old use strumpet, harlot, trollop.

calling n. **profession**, occupation, vocation, career, work, employment, job, business, trade, craft, line (of work); old use employ.

callous adj. **heartless**, unfeeling, uncaring, cold, cold-hearted, hard, as hard as nails, hard-hearted, stony-hearted, insensitive, lacking compassion, hard-bitten, unsympathetic.
– OPPOSITES kind, compassionate.

callow adj. **immature**, inexperienced, juvenile, adolescent, naive, green, raw, untried, unworldly, unsophisticated; informal wet behind the ears.
– OPPOSITES mature.

calm adj. **1** *she seemed very calm* **serene**, tranquil, relaxed, unruffled, unperturbed, unflustered, untroubled; equable, even-tempered, placid, unexcitable, unemotional, phlegmatic; composed, {cool, calm, and collected}, cool-headed, self-possessed; informal unflappable, unfazed. **2** *the night was calm* **windless**, still, tranquil, quiet. **3** *the calm waters of the lake* **tranquil**, still, smooth, glassy, like a millpond; literary stilly.
– OPPOSITES excited, nervous, stormy.
▶ n. **1** *calm prevailed* **tranquillity**, stillness, calmness, quiet, quietness, quietude, peace, peacefulness. **2** *his usual calm deserted him* **composure**, coolness, calmness, self-possession, sangfroid, serenity, tranquillity, equanimity, equability, placidness, placidity; informal cool, unflappability.
▶ v. **1** *I tried to calm him down* **soothe**, pacify, placate, mollify, appease, conciliate; Brit. quieten (down); Austral. square off; literary

dulcify. **2** *she forced herself to calm down* **compose oneself**, recover/regain one's composure, control oneself, pull oneself together, simmer down, cool down/off, take it easy; Brit. quieten down; informal chill out, get a grip, keep one's shirt on, wind down; N. Amer. informal hang/stay loose, decompress.
– OPPOSITES excite, upset.

calumny n. **slander**, defamation (of character), character assassination, libel; vilification, traducement, obloquy, verbal abuse, revilement, scurrility; informal mud-slinging; formal calumniation; old use contumely.

camaraderie n. **friendship**, comradeship, fellowship, companionship; mutual support, team spirit, esprit de corps.

camouflage n. **1** *pieces of turf served for camouflage* **disguise**, concealment. **2** *her indifference was merely camouflage* **facade**, (false) front, smokescreen, cover-up, mask, blind, screen, masquerade, dissimulation, pretence.
▶ v. *the caravan was camouflaged with branches* **disguise**, hide, conceal, keep hidden, mask, screen, cover (up).

camp¹ n. **1** *an army camp* **bivouac**, encampment; campsite, camping ground. **2** *the liberal and conservative camps* **faction**, wing, group, lobby, caucus, bloc, coterie, sect, cabal.
▶ v. *they camped in a field* **pitch tents**, set up camp, encamp, bivouac.

camp² informal adj. **1** *a highly camp actor* **effeminate**, effete, mincing; informal campy, limp-wristed; Brit. informal poncey. **2** *camp humour* **exaggerated**, theatrical, actorly, affected; informal over the top, OTT, camped up.
– OPPOSITES macho.
◻ **camp it up** posture, behave theatrically/affectedly, overact; informal ham it up.

campaign n. **1** *Napoleon's Russian campaign* **military operation(s)**, manoeuvre(s); crusade, war, battle, offensive, attack. **2** *the campaign to reduce vehicle emissions* **crusade**, drive, push, struggle; operation, strategy, battle plan.
▶ v. **1** *they are campaigning for political reform* **crusade**, fight, battle, push, press, strive, struggle, lobby. **2** *she campaigned as a political outsider* **run/stand for office**, canvass, electioneer; N. Amer. stump.

campaigner n. **crusader**, fighter, activist; champion, advocate, promoter.

can n. **tin**, canister; jerrycan, oilcan.

canal n. **1** *barges chugged up the canal* **inland waterway**, watercourse. **2** *the ear canal* **duct**, tube, passage.

cancel v. **1** *the match was cancelled* **call off**, abandon, scrap, drop, axe; informal scrub, nix; N. Amer. informal redline. **2** *his visa has been cancelled* **annul**, invalidate, nullify, declare null and void, void; revoke, rescind, retract, countermand, withdraw; Law vacate, discharge. **3** *rising unemployment cancelled out earlier economic gains* **neutralize**,

counterbalance, counteract, balance (out), countervail; negate, nullify, wipe out, negative.

cancer n. **1** *most skin cancers are curable* **malignant growth**, cancerous growth, tumour, malignancy; technical carcinoma, sarcoma, melanoma, lymphoma, myeloma. **2** *racism is a cancer* **evil**, blight, scourge, poison, canker, plague; old use pestilence.

> **WORD LINKS**
>
> **carcinogen** a substance that can cause cancer
> **oncology** the branch of medicine dealing with cancer
> **metastasis** the development of secondary tumours elsewhere in the body from the primary cancer site

candid adj. **1** *his responses were remarkably candid* **frank**, outspoken, forthright, blunt, open, honest, truthful, sincere, direct, plain-spoken, bluff; informal upfront, on the level; N. Amer. informal on the up and up; old use round, free-spoken. **2** *candid shots* **unposed**, informal, uncontrived, impromptu, natural.
– OPPOSITES guarded.

candidate n. **1** *candidates should be computer-literate* **(job) applicant**, job-seeker, interviewee; contender, nominee, possible; Brit. informal runner. **2** *A-level candidates* **examinee**, entrant.

candour n. **frankness**, openness, honesty, candidness, truthfulness, sincerity, forthrightness, directness, plain-spokenness, bluffness, bluntness, outspokenness; informal telling it like it is.

cane n. **1** *a silver-topped cane* **(walking) stick**, staff; alpenstock; crook; Austral./NZ waddy. **2** *tie the shoot to a cane* **stick**, stake, upright, pole. **3** *he was beaten with a cane* **stick**, rod, birch; N. Amer. informal paddle; historical ferule.
▶ v. *Matthew was caned for bullying* **beat**, strike, hit, flog, thrash, lash, birch, flagellate; informal give someone a hiding, larrup; N. Amer. informal whale.

canker n. **1** *this plant is susceptible to canker* **fungal disease**, plant rot; blight. **2** *ear cankers* **ulcer**, ulceration, infection, sore, abscess. **3** *racism remains a canker*. See **cancer** (sense 2).

cannabis n. **marijuana**, hashish, bhang, hemp, kif, ganja, sinsemilla, skunkweed; informal hash, dope, grass, skunk, pot, blow, draw, the weed, reefer; Brit. informal wacky baccy; N. Amer. informal locoweed.

cannibal n. **man-eater**, people-eater.

cannon n. **mounted gun**, field gun, piece of artillery; mortar, howitzer; historical carronade, bombard, culverin, falconet, serpentine; Brit. historical pom-pom.
▶ v. *the couple behind cannoned into us* **collide with**, hit, run into, crash into, plough into.

cannonade n. **bombardment**, shelling, gunfire, artillery fire, barrage, pounding.

canny adj. **shrewd**, astute, smart, sharp, sharp-witted, discerning, penetrating, discriminating, perceptive, perspicacious,

wise, sagacious; cunning, crafty, wily; N. Amer. as sharp as a tack; informal savvy; Brit. informal suss, sussed; N. Amer. informal heads-up; dated long-headed; rare argute.
– OPPOSITES foolish.

canoe n. **kayak**, dugout, outrigger, bidarka, pirogue, waka.

canon[1] n. **1** *the canons of fair play and equal opportunity* **principle**, rule, law, tenet, precept; standard, convention, criterion, measure. **2** *a set of ecclesiastical canons* **law**, decree, edict, statute, dictate, decretal. **3** *the Shakespeare canon* **(list of) works**, writings, oeuvre.

canon[2] n. *a canon assists the bishop* **prebendary**, minor canon.

canonical adj. **1** *the canonical method* **recognized**, authoritative, authorized, accepted, sanctioned, approved, established, orthodox. **2** *canonical rites* **according to ecclesiastical law**, official, sanctioned.
– OPPOSITES unorthodox.

canopy n. **awning**, shade, sunshade; baldachin, tester, chuppah, velarium.

cant[1] n. **1** *religious cant* **hypocrisy**, sanctimoniousness, sanctimony, humbug, pietism. **2** *thieves' cant* **slang**, jargon, idiom, argot, patois, speech, terminology, language; informal lingo, -speak, -ese.

cant[2] v. *the deck canted some twenty degrees* **tilt**, lean, slant, slope, incline; tip, list, bank, heel.
▸ n. *the cant of the walls* **slope**, slant, tilt, angle, inclination.

cantankerous adj. **bad-tempered**, irascible, irritable, grumpy, grouchy, crotchety, tetchy, testy, crusty, curmudgeonly, ill-tempered, ill-humoured, peevish, cross, fractious, pettish, crabbed, crabby, prickly, touchy; informal snappish, snappy, chippy; Brit. informal shirty, stroppy, narky, ratty; N. Amer. informal cranky, ornery; Austral./NZ informal snaky; informal dated miffy.
– OPPOSITES affable.

canteen n. **1** *the staff canteen* **restaurant**, cafeteria, refectory, mess hall; Brit. Military NAAFI; N. Amer. lunchroom. **2** *a canteen of water* **container**, flask, bottle.

canvass v. **1** *he's canvassing for the Green Party* **campaign**, electioneer; N. Amer. stump; Brit. informal doorstep. **2** *they promised to canvass all members* **poll**, question, ask, survey, interview. **3** *they're canvassing support* **seek**, try to obtain. **4** *early retirement was canvassed as a solution* **propose**, suggest, discuss, debate, consider.

canyon n. **ravine**, gorge, gully, defile, couloir; chasm, abyss, gulf; N. Amer. gulch, coulee.

cap n. **1** *a white plastic cap* **lid**, top, stopper, cork, bung, stopple; N. Amer. stopple. **2** *cap and gown* **mortar board**, academic cap; Brit. square; dated trencher. **3** *the cap on spending* **(upper) limit**, ceiling; curb, check.
▸ v. **1** *mountains capped with snow* **top**, crown, cover, coat. **2** *his innings capped a great day* **round off**, crown, be a fitting climax to.

3 *they tried to cap each other's stories* **beat**, better, improve on, surpass, outdo, outshine, top, upstage. **4** Brit. *he was capped for England* **choose**, select, pick, give someone the nod. **5** *budgets will be capped* **set a limit on**, limit, restrict; curb, control, peg.

capability n. **ability**, capacity, power, potential; competence, proficiency, accomplishment, adeptness, aptitude, faculty, experience, skill, skilfulness, talent, flair; informal know-how.

capable adj. *a very capable young woman* **competent**, able, efficient, effective, proficient, accomplished, adept, handy, experienced, skilful, skilled, talented, gifted; informal useful.
– OPPOSITES incompetent.
□ **be capable of 1** *I'm quite capable of looking after myself* **have the ability to**, be equal to (the task of), be up to; informal have what it takes to. **2** *the strange events are capable of rational explanation* **be open/ susceptible to**, admit of, allow of.

capacious adj. **roomy**, spacious, ample, big, large, sizeable, generous; formal commodious.
– OPPOSITES cramped, small.

capacity n. **1** *the capacity of the freezer* **volume**, size, magnitude, dimensions, measurements, proportions. **2** *his capacity to inspire trust.* See **capability**. **3** *in his capacity as Commander-in-Chief* **position**, post, job, office; role, function.

cape[1] n. *a woollen cape* **cloak**, mantle, cope, wrap, stole, tippet, poncho; historical pelisse, pelerine, mantlet.

cape[2] n. *the ship rounded the cape* **headland**, promontory, point, head, foreland; horn, hook, bill, ness, mull.

caper v. *children were capering about* **skip**, dance, romp, frisk, gambol, cavort, prance, frolic, leap, hop, jump; rare curvet, rollick.
▸ n. **1** *she did a little caper* **dance**, skip, hop, leap, jump, curvet, gambado. **2** informal *I'm too old for this kind of caper* **escapade**, stunt, prank, trick, mischief, antics, high jinks, skylarking; informal lark, shenanigans.

capital n. **1** *Warsaw is the capital of Poland* **first city**, seat of government, metropolis. **2** *he had enough capital to pull off the deal* **money**, finance(s), funds, the wherewithal, the means, assets, wealth, resources, investment capital; informal dough, bread, loot; Brit. informal dosh, brass, lolly, spondulicks; US informal greenbacks; N. Amer. informal bucks; Austral./NZ informal Oscar. **3** *he wrote the name in capitals* **capital letter**, upper-case letter, block capital; informal cap.
▸ adj. **1** *capital letters* **upper-case**, block. **2** informal dated *he's a really capital fellow.* See **splendid** (sense 2).

capitalism n. **private enterprise**, free enterprise, the free market.
– OPPOSITES communism.

capitalist n. **financier**, investor, industrialist; magnate, tycoon.

capitalize v. *the capacity to capitalize new ventures* **finance**, fund, underwrite, provide capital for, back; N. Amer. informal **bankroll**, stake.

◻ **capitalize on** take advantage of, profit from, make the most of, exploit; informal **cash in on**.

capitulate v. **surrender**, give in, yield, concede defeat, give up the struggle, submit; lay down one's arms, raise/show the white flag, throw in the towel/sponge.
– OPPOSITES resist, hold out.

caprice n. **1** *his wife's caprices* **whim**, whimsy, vagary, fancy, fad, quirk, eccentricity, foible. **2** *the staff tired of his caprice* **fickleness**, changeableness, volatility, capriciousness, unpredictability.

capricious adj. **fickle**, inconstant, changeable, variable, mercurial, volatile, unpredictable, temperamental; whimsical, fanciful, flighty, quirky, faddish.
– OPPOSITES consistent.

capsize v. **overturn**, turn over, turn upside down, upend, flip/tip/keel over, turn turtle; Nautical pitchpole; old use **overset**.
– OPPOSITES right.

capsule n. **1** *he swallowed a capsule* **pill**, tablet, lozenge, pastille, drop; informal **tab**. **2** *the bottle's capsule* **cover**, seal, cap, top. **3** *a space capsule* **module**, craft, probe.

captain n. **1** *the ship's captain* **commander**, master; informal **skipper**. **2** *the team's captain* **leader**, head; informal **boss**, skipper. **3** *a captain of industry* **magnate**, tycoon, industrialist; chief, head, leader, principal; informal **boss**, number one, bigwig, big shot/gun, honcho, top dog; N. Amer. informal **kahuna**, top banana.
▸ v. *a vessel captained by a cut-throat* **command**, run, be in charge of, control, manage, govern; informal **skipper**.

caption n. **title**, heading, wording, head, legend, rubric, slogan.

captious adj. **critical**, fault-finding, quibbling, cavilling; hypercritical, pedantic, hair-splitting; informal **nitpicking, pernickety**.
– OPPOSITES forgiving.

captivate v. **enthral**, charm, enchant, bewitch, fascinate, beguile, entrance, enrapture, delight, attract, allure.
– OPPOSITES repel, bore.

captive n. *release the captives* **prisoner**, convict, detainee, inmate; prisoner of war, POW, internee; informal **jailbird**, con; Brit. informal (old) **lag**; N. Amer. informal **yardbird**.
▸ adj. *captive wild animals* **confined**, caged, incarcerated, locked up; jailed, imprisoned, in prison, interned, detained, in captivity, under lock and key, behind bars.

captivity n. **imprisonment**, confinement, internment, incarceration, detention; old use **duress, durance**.
– OPPOSITES freedom.

captor n. **jailer**, guard, incarcerator, keeper.

capture v. **1** *the spy was captured in Moscow* **catch**, apprehend, seize, arrest; take prisoner/captive, imprison, detain, put/throw in jail, put behind bars, put under lock and key, incarcerate; informal **nab, collar, lift**,

pick up, pull in; Brit. informal **nick**. **2** *guerrillas captured a strategic district* **occupy**, invade, conquer, seize, take (possession of). **3** *the music captured the atmosphere of a summer morning* **express**, reproduce, represent, encapsulate. **4** *the tales of pirates captured the children's imaginations* **engage**, attract, catch, seize, hold.
– OPPOSITES free.
▸ n. *the capture of the gunmen* **arrest**, apprehension, seizure, imprisonment.

car n. **1** *he drove up in his car* **motor (car)**, automobile; informal **wheels**; N. Amer. informal **auto**. **2** *the dining car* **carriage**, coach; Brit. **saloon**.

carafe n. **flask**, jug, pitcher, decanter, flagon.

caravan n. **1** *a fishing holiday in a caravan* **mobile home**, camper, caravanette; N. Amer. **trailer**; Brit. trademark **Dormobile**. **2** *a Gypsy caravan* **wagon**, covered cart. **3** *a refugee caravan* **convoy**, procession, column, train.

carbuncle n. **boil**, sore, abscess, pustule, wen, whitlow; technical **furuncle**.

carcass n. **1** *a lamb carcass* **corpse**, (dead) body, remains; Medicine **cadaver**; informal **stiff**; old use **corse**. **2** *informal shift your carcass* **body**, self; informal **backside**; N. Amer. informal **butt**.

card n. **1** *a piece of stiff card* **cardboard**, pasteboard, board. **2** *I'll send her a card* **greetings card**, postcard. **3** *she produced her card* **identification**, ID, credentials; business card. **4** *she paid with her card* **credit card**, debit card, cash card, swipe card; informal **plastic**.
◻ **on the cards** informal **likely**, possible, probable, expected, in the wind, in the offing.

cardinal adj. **fundamental**, basic, main, chief, primary, prime, principal, paramount, pre-eminent, highest, key, essential.
– OPPOSITES unimportant.

care n. **1** *the care of the child* **safe keeping**, supervision, custody, charge, protection, control, responsibility; guardianship, wardship. **2** *handle with care* **caution**, carefulness, heedfulness, heed, attention, attentiveness. **3** *she chose her words with care* **discretion**, judiciousness, forethought, thought, regard, heed, mindfulness; accuracy, precision. **4** *the cares of the day* **worry**, anxiety, trouble, concern, stress, pressure, strain; sorrow, woe, hardship. **5** *constant care for others* **concern**, consideration, thought, regard, solicitude.
– OPPOSITES neglect, carelessness.
▸ v. *the teachers didn't care about our work* **be concerned**, worry (oneself), trouble/concern oneself, bother, mind, be interested; informal **give a damn/hoot/rap**.
◻ **care for 1** *he cares for his children* **love**, be fond of, be devoted to, treasure, adore, dote on, think the world of, worship, idolize. **2** *would you care for a cup of coffee?* **like**, want, desire, fancy, feel like. **3** *the hospice cares for the terminally ill* **look after**, take care of, tend, attend to, minister to, nurse; be responsible for, keep safe, keep an eye on.

C

career n. **1** *a business career* **profession**, occupation, vocation, calling, employment, line (of work), walk of life, métier. **2** *a chequered career* **existence**, life, course, passage, path.
▶ adj. *a career politician* **professional**, permanent, full-time.
▶ v. *they careered down the hill* **rush**, hurtle, streak, shoot, race, bolt, dash, speed, run, whizz, zoom, flash, blast, charge, hare, fly, pelt, go like the wind; informal belt, scoot, tear, zap, zip, whip, go like a bat out of hell; Brit. informal bomb, bucket; N. Amer. informal hightail, clip.

carefree adj. **unworried**, untroubled, blithe, airy, nonchalant, insouciant, happy-go-lucky, free and easy, easy-going, relaxed; informal laid-back.
– OPPOSITES careworn.

careful adj. **1** *be careful when you go up the stairs* **cautious**, heedful, alert, attentive, watchful, vigilant, wary, on guard, circumspect. **2** *Roland was careful of his reputation* **mindful**, heedful, protective. **3** *careful with money* **prudent**, thrifty, economical, sparing, frugal, scrimping, abstemious; informal stingy. **4** *careful consideration of the facts* **attentive**, conscientious, painstaking, meticulous, diligent, assiduous, sedulous, scrupulous, punctilious, methodical; informal pernickety; old use nice.
– OPPOSITES careless, extravagant.

careless adj. **1** *careless motorists* **inattentive**, incautious, negligent, remiss, heedless, irresponsible, impetuous, reckless. **2** *careless work* **shoddy**, slapdash, slipshod, scrappy, slovenly, sloppy, negligent, lax, slack, disorganized, hasty, hurried; informal slap-happy. **3** *a careless remark* **thoughtless**, insensitive, indiscreet, unguarded, incautious, inadvertent. **4** *she was very careless of investments* **negligent**, heedless, improvident, unconcerned, indifferent, oblivious. **5** *careless masculine grace* **unstudied**, artless, casual, effortless, nonchalant, insouciant, languid.
– OPPOSITES careful, meticulous.

caress v. **stroke**, touch, fondle, brush, skim, nuzzle.

caretaker n. **janitor**, attendant, porter, custodian, concierge; N. Amer. superintendent.
▶ adj. *the caretaker manager* **temporary**, short-term, provisional, substitute, acting, interim, pro tem, stand-in, fill-in, stopgap; N. Amer. informal pinch-hitting.
– OPPOSITES permanent.

careworn adj. **worried**, anxious, harassed, strained, stressed; drained, drawn, gaunt, haggard; informal hassled.
– OPPOSITES carefree.

cargo n. **freight**, load, haul, consignment, delivery, shipment; goods, merchandise; old use lading.

caricature n. *a caricature of the Prime Minister* **cartoon**, parody, satire, lampoon, burlesque; informal send-up, take-off.
▶ v. *she has turned to caricaturing her fellow actors* **parody**, satirize, lampoon, make fun of, burlesque; informal send up, take off.

caring adj. **kind**, kind-hearted, warm-hearted, tender; concerned, attentive, thoughtful, solicitous, considerate; affectionate, loving, doting, fond; sympathetic, understanding, compassionate, feeling.
– OPPOSITES cruel.

carnage n. **slaughter**, massacre, mass murder, butchery, bloodbath, bloodletting; holocaust, pogrom, ethnic cleansing.

carnal adj. **sexual**, sensual, erotic, lustful, lascivious, libidinous, lecherous, licentious; physical, bodily, corporeal, fleshly.
– OPPOSITES spiritual.

carnival n. **1** *the town's carnival* **festival**, fiesta, fete, gala, jamboree, celebration. **2** N. Amer. *he worked at a carnival* **funfair**, circus, fair, amusement show.

carnivorous adj. **meat-eating**, predatory, of prey.
– OPPOSITES herbivorous.

carol n. *children sang carols* **Christmas song**, hymn, canticle.
▶ v. *Boris carolled happily* **sing**, trill, warble, chirp; old use wassail.

carouse v. **drink and make merry**, revel, celebrate, roister; informal booze, go boozing, go on a bender, paint the town red, party, rave, make whoopee, whoop it up; old use wassail.

carp v. **complain**, cavil, grumble, grouse, whine, bleat, nag; informal gripe, grouch, beef, bellyache, moan, bitch, whinge; Brit. informal be on at someone; N. English informal mither; N. Amer. informal kvetch.
– OPPOSITES praise.

carpenter n. **woodworker**, joiner, cabinetmaker; Brit. informal chippy.

carpet n. **1** *a Turkish carpet* **rug**, mat, matting, floor covering. **2** *a carpet of wild flowers* **covering**, blanket, layer, cover, cloak, mantle.
▶ v. **1** *the gravel was carpeted in moss* **cover**, coat, overlay, overspread, blanket. **2** Brit. informal *an officer was carpeted for leaking information.* See **reprimand** (verb).

carriage n. **1** *a railway carriage* **coach**, car; Brit. saloon. **2** *a horse and carriage* **wagon**, hackney, hansom, gig, landau, trap. **3** *the carriage of bikes on trains* **transport**, transportation, conveyance, carrying, movement, shipment. **4** *an erect carriage* **posture**, bearing, stance, gait; attitude, manner, demeanour; Brit. deportment.

carrier n. **bearer**, conveyor, transporter; porter, courier, haulier.

carry v. **1** *she carried the box into the kitchen* **convey**, transfer, move, take, bring, bear, lug, fetch; informal cart, hump. **2** *a coach operator carrying 12 million passengers a year* **transport**, convey, move, handle. **3** *satellites carry the signal over the Atlantic* **transmit**, conduct, relay, communicate, convey, dispatch, beam. **4** *the dinghy can carry the weight of the baggage* **support**, sustain,

stand; prop up, shore up, bolster. **5** *managers carry most responsibility* **undertake**, accept, assume, bear, shoulder, take on (oneself). **6** *she was carrying his baby* **be pregnant with**, bear, expect; technical be gravid with. **7** *she carried herself with assurance* **conduct**, bear, hold; act, behave, acquit; formal comport; old use deport. **8** *a resolution was carried* **approve**, vote for, accept, endorse, ratify; agree to, assent to, rubber-stamp; informal OK, give the thumbs up to. **9** *I carried the whole audience* **win over**, sway, convince, persuade, influence; motivate, stimulate. **10** *today's paper carried an article on housing policy* **publish**, print, communicate, distribute; broadcast, transmit. **11** *we carry a wide range* **sell**, stock, keep (in stock), offer, have (for sale), retail, supply. **12** *most toxins carry warnings* **display**, bear, exhibit, show, be marked with. **13** *it carries a penalty of two years' imprisonment* **entail**, involve, result in, occasion, have as a consequence. **14** *his voice carried across the quay* **be audible**, travel, reach.
▢ **be/get carried away** lose self-control, get overexcited, go too far; informal flip, lose it.

carry something off 1 *she carried off four awards* **win**, secure, gain, achieve, collect; informal land, net, bag, scoop. **2** *he has carried it off* **succeed**, triumph, be victorious, be successful, do well, make good; informal crack it.

carry on 1 *they carried on arguing* **continue**, keep (on), go on; persist in, persevere in; informal stick with/at. **2** informal *the English way of carrying on* **behave**, act, conduct oneself, acquit oneself; formal comport oneself; old use deport oneself. **3** informal *she was carrying on with other men* **have an affair**, commit adultery, have a fling; informal play around, mess about/around; Brit. informal play away; N. Amer. informal fool around. **4** informal *I was always carrying on* **misbehave**, behave badly, get up to mischief, cause trouble, get up to no good, be naughty; clown about/around, fool about/around, mess about/around; informal act up; Brit. informal muck about/around, play up.

carry something on engage in, conduct, undertake, be involved in, carry out, perform.

carry something out 1 *they carried out a caesarean* **conduct**, perform, implement, execute. **2** *I carried out my promise to her* **fulfil**, carry through, honour, redeem, make good; keep, observe, abide by, comply with, adhere to, stick to, keep faith with.

carry-on n. Brit. informal **fuss**, commotion, trouble, bother, excitement, palaver; informal hoo-ha, ballyhoo, song and dance, performance, kerfuffle.

cart n. **1** *a horse-drawn cart* **wagon**, carriage, dray; old use wain. **2** *a man with a cart took their luggage* **handcart**, pushcart, trolley, barrow.
▶v. informal *he had the wreckage carted away* **transport**, convey, haul, move, shift, take; carry, lug, heft; informal hump.

carton n. **box**, package, cardboard box, container, pack, packet.

cartoon n. **1** *a cartoon of the Prime Minister* **caricature**, parody, lampoon, satire; informal take-off, send-up. **2** *he was reading cartoons* **comic strip**, comic, graphic novel. **3** *they watched cartoons on television* **animated film**, animation. **4** *detailed cartoons for a full-size portrait* **sketch**, rough, outline, preliminary drawing, underdrawing, artist's impression; Computing wireframe.

cartridge n. **1** *a toner cartridge* **cassette**, magazine, canister, container. **2** *a rifle cartridge* **bullet**, round, shell, charge, shot.

carve v. **1** *he carved horn handles* **sculpt**, sculpture; cut, hew, whittle; form, shape, fashion. **2** *I carved my initials on the tree* **engrave**, etch, incise, score. **3** *he carved the roast chicken* **slice**, cut up, chop.
▢ **carve something up** divide, partition, apportion, subdivide, split up, break up; share out, dole out; informal divvy up.

carving n. **sculpture**, model, statue, statuette, figure, figurine.

WORD LINKS
glyptic relating to carving
---

cascade n. **waterfall**, cataract, falls, rapids, white water.
▶v. *rain cascaded from the roof* **pour**, gush, surge, spill, stream, flow, issue, spurt, jet.

case¹ n. **1** *a classic case of overreaction* **instance**, occurrence, manifestation, demonstration, exposition, exhibition; example, illustration, specimen, sample, exemplification. **2** *if that is the case I will have to find somebody else* **situation**, position, state of affairs, the lie of the land; circumstances, conditions, facts, how things stand; Brit. state of play; informal score. **3** *the officers on the case* **investigation**, enquiry, examination, exploration, probe, search, inquest. **4** *urgent cases* **patient**, sick person, invalid, sufferer, victim. **5** *he lost his case* **lawsuit**, (legal) action, legal dispute, suit, trial, legal/judicial proceedings, litigation. **6** *a strong case* **argument**, contention, reasoning, logic, defence, justification, vindication, exposition, thesis.

case² n. **1** *a cigarette case* **container**, box, canister, receptacle, holder; dated etui. **2** *a seed case* **casing**, cover, covering, sheath, sheathing, envelope, sleeve, jacket, integument. **3** Brit. *she threw some clothes into a case* **suitcase**, (travelling) bag, valise, portmanteau; (**cases**) luggage, baggage. **4** *a case of wine* **crate**, box, pack. **5** *a glass display case* **cabinet**, cupboard.
▶v. **1** *the rifle is cased in wood* **cover**, surround, encase, sheathe, envelop. **2** informal *a thief casing the joint* **reconnoitre**, inspect, examine, survey, explore; informal recce, check out.

cash n. **1** *a wallet stuffed with cash* **money**, currency, hard cash; (bank) notes, coins, change; N. Amer. bills; informal dough, bread, loot, moolah; Brit. informal dosh, brass, lolly,

readies, spondulicks; US informal **greenbacks**;
N. Amer. informal **bucks**, **dinero**; Austral./NZ informal
Oscar; Brit. dated **l.s.d.** **2** *a lack of cash* **finance**,
money, resources, funds, assets, the means,
the wherewithal.
– OPPOSITES cheque, credit.
▶v. *the bank cashed her cheque* **exchange**,
change, convert into cash/money; honour,
pay, accept; Brit. **encash**.
◻ **cash in on** take advantage of, exploit,
milk; make money from, profit from; informal
make a killing out of.

cashier¹ n. *the cashier took the cheque* **clerk**,
bank clerk, teller, banker, treasurer, bursar,
purser.

cashier² v. Military *he was found guilty and
cashiered* **dismiss**, discharge, expel, throw/
cast out, get rid of; informal **sack**, **fire**, **kick/
boot out**, give someone their marching
orders, give someone the bullet, give
someone the elbow/push.

casing n. **cover**, case, shell, envelope, sheath,
sheathing, sleeve, jacket, housing.

casino n. **gambling house**, gambling club,
gambling den; dated gaming house.

cask n. **barrel**, keg, butt, tun, vat, drum,
hogshead; historical puncheon, firkin.

casket n. **1** *a small casket* **box**, chest, case,
container, receptacle. **2** N. Amer. *the casket
of a dead soldier* **coffin**; informal box; humorous
wooden overcoat.

cast v. **1** *he cast the stone into the stream*
throw, toss, fling, pitch, hurl, lob; informal
chuck, sling, bung; dated shy. **2** *fishermen
cast their nets* **spread**, throw, open out.
3 *she cast a fearful glance over her shoulder*
direct, shoot, throw, send. **4** *each citizen
cast a vote* **register**, record, enter, file, vote.
5 *the fire cast a soft light* **emit**, give off,
send out, radiate. **6** *the figures cast shadows*
form, create, produce; project, throw. **7** *the
stags' antlers are cast each year* **shed**, lose,
discard, slough off. **8** *a figure cast by hand*
mould, fashion, form, shape, model; sculpt,
sculpture, forge. **9** *they were cast as extras*
choose, select, pick, name, nominate.
▶n. **1** *a cast of the writer's hand* **mould**, die,
matrix, shape, casting, model. **2** *a cast of the
dice* **throw**, toss, fling, pitch, hurl, lob; informal
chuck, sling, bung; dated shy. **3** *an enquiring
cast of mind* **type**, sort, kind, character,
variety, class, style, stamp, nature. **4** *a cast in
one eye* **squint**, strabismus. **5** *the cast of 'The
Barber of Seville'* **actors**, performers, players,
company; dramatis personae, characters.
◻ **cast something aside** discard, reject,
throw away/out, get rid of, dispose of,
abandon.
cast someone away shipwreck, wreck;
strand, leave stranded, maroon.
cast down depressed, downcast, unhappy,
sad, miserable, gloomy, down, low; dejected,
dispirited, discouraged, disheartened,
downhearted, demoralized, disconsolate,
crestfallen; informal blue.

caste n. **(social) class**, social order, rank,
level, stratum, echelon, status; dated estate,
station.

castigate v. formal **reprimand**, rebuke,
admonish, chastise, chide, upbraid, reprove,
reproach, scold, berate, take to task,
lambaste, give someone a piece of one's
mind, haul over the coals, censure; informal tell
off, give someone an earful, give someone
a roasting, rap someone on the knuckles,
slap someone's wrist, dress down, bawl out,
give someone hell, pitch into, lay into, blast;
Brit. informal tick off, have a go at, carpet, tear
someone off a strip, give someone what
for, give someone a rocket; N. Amer. informal
chew out, ream out; Austral. informal monster;
dated give someone a rating; rare reprehend,
objurgate.
– OPPOSITES praise, commend.

castle n. **fortress**, fort, stronghold,
fortification, keep, citadel.

castrate v. **neuter**, geld, cut, desex, sterilize,
fix; N. Amer. & Austral. alter; Brit. informal doctor; old
use emasculate.

casual adj. **1** *a casual attitude to life*
indifferent, apathetic, uncaring,
unconcerned; lackadaisical, blasé,
nonchalant, insouciant, offhand, flippant,
easy-going, free and easy, blithe, carefree,
devil-may-care; informal laid-back. **2** *a
casual remark* **offhand**, spontaneous,
unpremeditated, unthinking, unconsidered,
impromptu, throwaway, unguarded; informal
off-the-cuff. **3** *a casual glance* **cursory**,
perfunctory, superficial, passing, fleeting,
hasty, brief, quick. **4** *a casual acquaintance*
slight, superficial. **5** *casual work* **temporary**,
part-time, freelance, impermanent, irregular,
occasional. **6** *casual sex* **promiscuous**,
recreational, extramarital, free. **7** *a casual
meeting changed his life* **chance**, accidental,
unplanned, unintended, unexpected,
unforeseen, unanticipated, fortuitous,
serendipitous, adventitious. **8** *a casual shirt*
informal, comfortable, leisure, sportif,
everyday; informal sporty. **9** *the inn's casual
atmosphere* **relaxed**, friendly, informal,
unceremonious, easy-going, free and easy;
informal laid-back.
– OPPOSITES careful, planned, formal.
▶n. *we employ ten casuals* **temporary worker**,
part-timer, freelance, freelancer; informal
temp.

casualty n. **victim**, fatality, loss, MIA;
(**casualties**) dead and injured, missing (in
action).

casuistry n. **sophistry**, specious reasoning,
speciousness.

cat n. **feline**, tomcat, tom, kitten, mouser;
informal pussycat, pussy, puss, kitty; Brit. informal
moggie, mog; old use grimalkin.

WORD LINKS
feline relating to cats
ailurophobia fear of cats

cataclysm n. **disaster**, catastrophe, calamity,
tragedy, devastation, holocaust, ruin,
ruination, upheaval, convulsion.

cataclysmic adj. **disastrous**, catastrophic, calamitous, tragic, devastating, ruinous, terrible, violent, awful.

catacombs plural n. **underground cemetery**, crypt, vault, tomb, ossuary.

catalogue n. 1 *a library catalogue* **directory**, register, index, list, listing, record, archive, inventory. 2 *a mail-order catalogue* **brochure**, magalogue, mailer; N. Amer. informal wish book.

▶ v. *the collection is fully catalogued* **classify**, categorize, systematize, index, list, archive, make an inventory of, inventory, record, itemize.

catapult n. *a boy fired the catapult* **sling**, slingshot; Austral./NZ shanghai; historical ballista, trebuchet.

▶ v. *Sam was catapulted into the sea* **propel**, launch, hurl, fling, send flying, fire, blast, shoot.

cataract n. **waterfall**, cascade, falls, rapids, white water.

catastrophe n. **disaster**, calamity, cataclysm, holocaust, ruin, ruination, tragedy; adversity, blight, trouble, trial, tribulation.

catastrophic adj. **disastrous**, calamitous, cataclysmic, ruinous, tragic, fatal, dire, awful, terrible, dreadful; literary direful.

catcall n. **whistle**, boo, hiss, jeer, raspberry, hoot, taunt; (**catcalls**) scoffing, abuse, taunting, derision.

catch v. 1 *he caught the ball* **seize**, grab, snatch, seize/grab/take hold of, grasp, grip, clutch, clench; receive, get, intercept. 2 *we've caught the thief* **capture**, seize; apprehend, arrest, take prisoner/captive, take into custody; trap, snare, ensnare; net, hook, land; informal nab, collar, run in, bust; Brit. informal nick. 3 *her heel caught in a hole* **become trapped**, become entangled, snag. 4 *she caught the 7.45 bus* **be in time for**, make, get; board, get on, step aboard. 5 *they were caught siphoning petrol* **discover**, find, come upon/across, stumble on, chance on; surprise, catch red-handed, catch in the act. 6 *it caught his imagination* **engage**, capture, attract, draw, grab, grip, seize; hold, absorb, engross. 7 *she caught a trace of aftershave* **perceive**, notice, observe, discern, detect, note, make out; Brit. informal clock. 8 *I couldn't catch what she was saying* **hear**, perceive, discern, make out; understand, comprehend, grasp, apprehend; informal get, get the drift of, figure out; Brit. informal twig, suss (out). 9 *it caught the flavour of the sixties* **evoke**, conjure up, call to mind, recall, encapsulate, capture. 10 *the blow caught her on the side of her face* **hit**, strike, slap, smack, bang. 11 *he caught malaria* **contract**, get, become infected with, be taken ill with, develop, come down with, be struck down with; Brit. go down with; informal take ill with; N. Amer. informal take sick with. 12 *the kindling wouldn't catch* **ignite**, start burning, catch fire, kindle. 13 *the generator caught immediately* **start (running)**, fire, begin working.

– OPPOSITES drop, release, miss.

▶ n. 1 *he inspected the catch* **haul**, net, bag, yield. 2 informal *Giles is a good catch* **eligible man/woman**, marriage prospect. 3 *he slipped the catch* **latch**, lock, fastener, clasp, hasp. 4 *he is always looking for the catch* **snag**, disadvantage, drawback, stumbling block, hitch, fly in the ointment, pitfall, complication, problem, hiccup, difficulty; trap, trick, snare; informal con. 5 *a catch in her voice* **tremor**, unevenness, shake, quiver, wobble.

□ **catch on 1** *radio soon caught on* **become popular/fashionable**, take off, boom, flourish, thrive. 2 *I caught on fast* **understand**, comprehend, learn, see the light; informal cotton on, latch on, get the picture/message, get wise.

catch (someone) up draw level (with), reach; gain on.

catching adj. informal **infectious**, contagious, communicable, transmittable, transmissible; dated infective.

catchphrase n. **saying**, quotation, quote, slogan, catchword; N. Amer. informal tag line.

catchword n. **motto**, watchword, slogan, byword, catchphrase; informal buzzword.

catchy adj. **memorable**, unforgettable; appealing, popular; singable, melodious, tuneful.

categorical adj. **unqualified**, unconditional, unequivocal, absolute, explicit, unambiguous, definite, direct, downright, outright, emphatic, positive, point-blank, conclusive, without reservations, out-and-out; formal apodictic.

– OPPOSITES qualified, equivocal.

categorize v. **classify**, class, group, grade, rate, designate; order, arrange, sort, rank; file, catalogue, list, index.

category n. **class**, classification, group, grouping, bracket, heading, set; type, sort, kind, variety, species, breed, brand, make, model; grade, order, rank.

cater v.

□ **cater for 1** *we cater for vegetarians* **provide food for**, feed, serve, cook for; dated victual. 2 *a resort catering for older holidaymakers* **serve**, provide for, meet the needs of, accommodate. 3 *he seemed to cater for all tastes* **take into account/consideration**, allow for, consider, bear in mind, make provision for, have regard for.

cater to satisfy, indulge, pander to, gratify, accommodate, minister to, give in to, fulfil.

caterwaul v. **howl**, wail, bawl, cry, yell, scream, screech, yowl, ululate.

catharsis n. **purging**, purgation, purification, cleansing, (emotional) release, relief; Psychoanalysis abreaction.

catholic adj. **diverse**, diversified, wide, broad, broad-based, eclectic, liberal; comprehensive, all-encompassing, all-embracing, all-inclusive.

– OPPOSITES narrow.

cattle plural n. **cows**, bovines, oxen, bulls; stock, livestock.

C

catty adj. informal *a catty remark.* See **spiteful**.

caucus n. **1** in North America & NZ *caucuses will be held in eleven states* **meeting**, assembly, gathering, congress, conference, convention, rally, convocation. **2** in the UK *the right-wing caucus* **faction**, camp, bloc, group, set, band, ring, cabal, coterie, pressure group, ginger group.

cause n. **1** *the cause of the fire* **source**, root, origin, beginning(s), starting point; mainspring, base, basis, foundation, fountainhead; originator, author, creator, producer, agent; formal radix. **2** *there is no cause for alarm* **reason**, grounds, justification, call, need, necessity, occasion, excuse, pretext. **3** *the cause of human rights | a good cause* **principle**, ideal, belief, conviction; object, end, aim, objective, purpose; charity. **4** *he went to plead his cause* **case**, suit, lawsuit, action, dispute.
– OPPOSITES effect, result.
▸ v. *this disease can cause blindness* **bring about**, give rise to, lead to, result in, create, produce, generate, engender, spawn, bring on, precipitate, prompt, provoke, trigger, make happen, induce, inspire, promote, foster; literary beget, enkindle.
– OPPOSITES result from.

caustic adj. **1** *a caustic cleaner* **corrosive**, corroding, mordant, acid. **2** *a caustic comment* **sarcastic**, cutting, biting, mordant, sharp, bitter, scathing, derisive, sardonic, ironic, scornful, trenchant, acerbic, vitriolic, acidulous; Brit. informal sarky; formal mordacious.

cauterize v. Medicine **burn**, sear, singe, scorch; disinfect, sterilize.

caution n. **1** *proceed with caution* **care**, carefulness, heedfulness, heed, attention, attentiveness, alertness, watchfulness, vigilance, circumspection, discretion, prudence. **2** *a first offender may receive a caution* **warning**, admonishment, injunction; reprimand, rebuke, reproof, scolding; informal telling-off, dressing-down, talking-to; Brit. informal ticking-off, carpeting.
▸ v. **1** *advisers cautioned against tax increases* **advise**, warn, counsel, urge. **2** *he was cautioned by the police* **warn**, admonish; reprimand, rebuke, reprove, scold; informal tell off, give someone a dressing-down, give someone a talking-to; Brit. informal give someone a ticking-off, carpet.

cautious adj. **careful**, heedful, attentive, alert, watchful, vigilant, circumspect, prudent.
– OPPOSITES reckless.

cavalcade n. **procession**, parade, motorcade, cortège; Brit. march past.

cavalier n. old use *foot soldiers and cavaliers* **horseman**, equestrian; cavalryman, trooper, knight.
▸ adj. *a cavalier disregard for danger* **offhand**, indifferent, casual, dismissive, insouciant, unconcerned; supercilious, patronizing, condescending, disdainful, scornful, contemptuous; informal couldn't-care-less.

cavalry plural n. historical **mounted troops**, cavalrymen, troopers, horse; historical dragoons, lancers, hussars.

cave n. **cavern**, grotto, pothole, underground chamber.
□ **cave in 1** *the roof caved in* **collapse**, fall in/down, give (way), crumble, subside. **2** *the manager caved in to their demands* **yield**, surrender, capitulate, give in, back down, make concessions, throw in the towel/sponge.

caveat n. **warning**, caution, admonition; proviso, condition, stipulation, provision, clause, rider, qualification.

caveman, cavewoman n. **cave-dweller**, troglodyte, primitive man/woman, prehistoric man/woman.

cavern n. **large cave**, grotto, underground chamber/gallery.

cavernous adj. **vast**, huge, large, immense, spacious, roomy, airy, capacious, voluminous, extensive, deep; hollow, gaping, yawning; formal commodious.
– OPPOSITES small.

cavil v. **complain**, carp, grumble, grouse, whine, bleat, quibble, niggle; informal gripe, grouch, beef, bellyache, moan, bitch, whinge, kick up a fuss; Brit. informal chunter, create; N. English informal mither; N. Amer. informal kvetch.

cavity n. **space**, chamber, hollow, hole, pocket, pouch; orifice, aperture; socket, gap, crater, pit.

cavort v. **skip**, dance, romp, jig, caper, frisk, gambol, prance, frolic, lark; bounce, trip, leap, jump, bound, spring, hop; rare rollick.

cease v. **1** *hostilities had ceased* **come to an end**, come to a halt, end, halt, stop, conclude, terminate, finish, draw to a close, be over. **2** *they ceased all military activity* **bring to an end**, bring to a halt, end, halt, stop, conclude, terminate, finish, wind up, discontinue, suspend, break off; informal leave off.
– OPPOSITES start, continue.

ceaseless adj. **continual**, constant, continuous; incessant, unceasing, unending, endless, never-ending, interminable, non-stop, uninterrupted, unremitting, relentless, unrelenting, unrelieved, sustained, persistent, eternal, perpetual.
– OPPOSITES intermittent.

cede v. **surrender**, concede, relinquish, yield, part with, give up; hand over, deliver up, give over, make over, transfer; abandon, forgo, sacrifice; literary forsake.

ceiling n. **upper limit**, maximum, limitation.

celebrate v. **1** *they were celebrating their wedding anniversary* **commemorate**, observe, mark, keep, honour, remember, memorialize. **2** *let's all celebrate!* **enjoy oneself**, make merry, have fun, have a good time, have a party, revel, roister, carouse; N. Amer. step out; informal party, go out on the town, paint the town red, whoop it up, make whoopee, live it up, have a ball. **3** *the priest celebrated mass* **perform**, observe, officiate at. **4** *he was celebrated for his achievements* **praise**, extol, glorify, eulogize, reverence, honour, pay tribute to; formal laud; old use emblazon.

celebrated adj. **acclaimed**, admired, highly rated, lionized, revered, honoured, esteemed, exalted, vaunted, well thought of; eminent, great, distinguished, prestigious, illustrious, pre-eminent, estimable, notable, of note, of repute; formal lauded.
– OPPOSITES unsung.

celebration n. **1** *the celebration of his 50th birthday* **commemoration**, observance, marking, keeping. **2** *a cause for celebration* **jollification**, merrymaking, enjoying oneself, carousing, revelry, revels, festivities; informal partying. **3** *a birthday celebration* **party**, function, gathering, festivities, festival, fete, carnival, jamboree; informal do, bash, rave; Brit. informal rave-up, knees-up, beanfeast, bunfight, beano. **4** *the celebration of the Eucharist* **observance**, performance, officiation, solemnization.

celebrity n. **1** *his celebrity grew* **fame**, prominence, renown, eminence, pre-eminence, stardom, popularity, distinction, note, notability, prestige, stature, repute, reputation. **2** *a sporting celebrity* **famous person**, VIP, very important person, personality, (big) name, famous/household name, star, superstar; informal celeb, somebody, someone, megastar.
– OPPOSITES obscurity.

celestial adj. **1** *a celestial body* **(in) space**, heavenly, astronomical, extraterrestrial, stellar, planetary. **2** *celestial beings* **heavenly**, holy, saintly, divine, godly, godlike, ethereal, immortal, angelic, seraphic, cherubic.
– OPPOSITES earthly, hellish.

celibate adj. **unmarried**, single, unwed; chaste, virginal, virgin, maidenly, maiden, intact, abstinent, self-denying.

cell n. **1** *a prison cell* **room**, cubicle, chamber; dungeon, oubliette, lock-up. **2** *each cell of the honeycomb* **compartment**, cavity, hole, hollow, section. **3** *terrorist cells* **unit**, faction, arm, section, coterie, group.

cellar n. **basement**, vault, underground room, lower ground floor; crypt, undercroft.
– OPPOSITES attic.

cement n. *polystyrene cement* **adhesive**, glue, fixative, gum, paste; superglue, epoxy resin; N. Amer. mucilage; N. Amer. informal stickum.
▶v. *he cemented the sample to a microscope slide* **stick**, bond; fasten, fix, affix, attach, secure, bind, glue, gum, paste.

cemetery n. **graveyard**, churchyard, burial ground, necropolis; informal boneyard; historical potter's field; old use God's acre.

censor n. *the film censors* **expurgator**, bowdlerizer; examiner, inspector, editor.
▶v. *letters home were censored* **cut**, delete parts of, make cuts in, blue-pencil, redact; edit, expurgate, bowdlerize, sanitize; informal clean up.

censorious adj. **hypercritical**, overcritical, disapproving, condemnatory, denunciatory, deprecatory, disparaging, reproachful, reproving, censuring, captious; formal castigatory.
– OPPOSITES complimentary.

censure v. *he was censured for his conduct.* See **reprimand** (verb).
▶n. *a note of censure* **condemnation**, criticism, attack, abuse; reprimand, rebuke, admonishment, reproof, reproval, upbraiding, disapproval, reproach, reprehension, obloquy; formal excoriation, castigation; rare objurgation.
– OPPOSITES approval.

central adj. **1** *occupying a central position* **middle**, centre, halfway, midway, mid, median, medial, mean; Anatomy mesial. **2** *central London* **inner**, innermost, middle, mid. **3** *their central campaign issue* **main**, chief, principal, primary, leading, foremost, first, most important, predominant, dominant, key, crucial, vital, essential, basic, fundamental, core, prime, premier, paramount, major, overriding; informal number-one.
– OPPOSITES side, outer, subordinate.

centralize v. **concentrate**, consolidate, amalgamate, condense, unify, streamline, focus, rationalize.
– OPPOSITES devolve.

centre n. *the centre of the town* **middle**, nucleus, heart, core, hub; middle point, midpoint, halfway point, mean, median.
– OPPOSITES edge.
▶v. *the story centres on a doctor* **focus**, concentrate, pivot, revolve, be based.

centrepiece n. **highlight**, main feature, high point/spot, best part, climax; focus of attention, focal point, centre of attention/interest, magnet, cynosure.

ceremonial adj. *a ceremonial occasion* **formal**, official, state, public; ritual, ritualistic, prescribed, stately, courtly, solemn.
– OPPOSITES informal.
▶n. *diplomatic ceremonial* **ritual**, ceremony, rite, formality, pomp, protocol; formal praxis.

ceremonious adj. **dignified**, majestic, imposing, impressive, solemn, stately, formal, courtly; regal, imperial, elegant, grand, glorious, splendid, magnificent, resplendent, portentous; informal starchy.

ceremony n. **1** *a wedding ceremony* **rite**, ritual, ceremonial, observance; service, sacrament, liturgy, worship, celebration. **2** *the new Queen was proclaimed with due ceremony* **pomp**, protocol, formalities, niceties, decorum, etiquette, punctilio, politesse.

certain adj. **1** *I'm certain he's guilty* **sure**, confident, positive, convinced, in no doubt, satisfied, assured, persuaded. **2** *it is certain that more changes are in the offing* **unquestionable**, sure, definite, beyond question, not in doubt, indubitable, undeniable, irrefutable, indisputable; obvious, evident, recognized, confirmed, accepted, acknowledged, undisputed, undoubted, unquestioned, as sure as eggs is eggs. **3** *they are certain to win* **sure**, very likely, bound, destined. **4** *certain defeat* **inevitable**, assured, destined, predestined; unavoidable, inescapable, inexorable, ineluctable. **5** *there is no certain cure for this* **reliable**, dependable, trustworthy, foolproof, tried and tested, effective, guaranteed, sure, unfailing, infallible; informal sure-fire; dated sovereign. **6** *a certain sum of money* **determined**, definite, fixed, established, precise. **7** *a certain lady* **particular**, specific, individual, special. **8** *to a certain extent that is true* **moderate**, modest, medium, middling; limited, small.
– OPPOSITES doubtful, possible, unlikely.

certainly adv. **1** *this is certainly a late work* **unquestionably**, surely, assuredly, definitely, beyond/without question, without doubt, indubitably, undeniably, irrefutably, indisputably; obviously, patently, evidently, plainly, clearly, unmistakably, undoubtedly, as sure as eggs is eggs. **2** *our revenues are certainly lower* **admittedly**, without question, definitely, undoubtedly, without a doubt.
– OPPOSITES possibly.
▸ exclam. *'Shall we eat now?' 'Certainly.'* **yes**, definitely, absolutely, sure, by all means, indeed, of course, naturally; affirmative; Brit. dated rather.

certainty n. **1** *she knew with certainty that he was telling the truth* **confidence**, sureness, positiveness, conviction, certitude, assurance. **2** *he accepted defeat as a certainty* **inevitability**, foregone conclusion; informal sure thing; Brit. informal cert, dead cert.
– OPPOSITES doubt, possibility.

certificate n. **guarantee**, certification, document, authorization, authentication, credentials, accreditation, licence, diploma.

certify v. **1** *the aircraft was certified as airworthy* **verify**, guarantee, attest, validate, confirm, substantiate, endorse, vouch for, testify to; provide evidence, give proof, prove, demonstrate. **2** *a certified hospital* **accredit**, recognize, license, authorize, approve, warrant.

certitude n. **certainty**, confidence, sureness, positiveness, conviction, assurance.
– OPPOSITES doubt.

cessation n. **end**, ending, termination, stopping, halting, ceasing, finish, finishing, stoppage, conclusion, winding up, discontinuation, abandonment, suspension, breaking off, cutting short.
– OPPOSITES start, resumption.

cession n. **surrender**, surrendering, ceding, concession, relinquishment, yielding, giving up; handing over, transfer; abandonment, sacrifice; literary forsaking.

chafe v. **1** *the collar chafed his neck* **abrade**, graze, rub against, gall, scrape, scratch; Medicine excoriate. **2** *I chafed her feet* **rub**, warm (up). **3** *material chafed by the rock* **wear away/down**, erode, abrade, scour, scrape away. **4** *the bank chafed at the restrictions* **be angry**, be annoyed, be irritated, fume, be exasperated, be frustrated.

chaff[1] n. **1** *separating the chaff from the grain* **husks**, hulls, pods, shells, bran; N. Amer. shucks. **2** *the proposals were so much chaff* **rubbish**, dross; N. Amer. garbage, trash; Austral./NZ mullock; informal junk.

chaff[2] n. *good-natured chaff* **banter**, repartee, teasing, ragging, joking, jesting, raillery, badinage, wisecracks, witticism(s); informal kidding, ribbing; formal persiflage.
▸ v. *the pleasures of chaffing your mates* **tease**, make fun of, poke fun at, rag; informal take the mickey out of, rib, josh, kid, have on, pull someone's leg; Brit. informal wind up; N. Amer. informal goof on, rag on, razz; Austral./NZ informal poke mullock at, poke borak at; informal dated twit; old use make sport of.

chagrin n. **annoyance**, irritation, vexation, exasperation, displeasure, dissatisfaction, discontent; anger, rage, fury, wrath, indignation, resentment; embarrassment, mortification, humiliation, shame.
– OPPOSITES delight.

chain n. **1** *he was held in chains* **fetters**, shackles, irons, leg irons, manacles, handcuffs; informal cuffs, bracelets; historical bilboes; old use darbies, gyves. **2** *a chain of events* **series**, succession, string, sequence, train, course. **3** *a chain of shops* **group**, multiple shop/store, multiple.
▸ v. *she chained her bicycle to the railings* **secure**, fasten, tie, tether, hitch; restrain, shackle, fetter, manacle, handcuff.

chair n. **1** *he sat down on a chair* **seat**, armchair, stool; Brit. informal pew. **2** *the chair of the committee.* See **chairman**. **3** *a university chair* **professorship**.
▸ v. *she chairs the economic committee* **preside over**, take the chair of; lead, direct, run, manage, control, be in charge of.

chairman, chairwoman n. **chair**, chairperson, president, leader, convener; spokesperson, spokesman, spokeswoman.

chalk v.
  □ **chalk something up 1** *he has chalked up another success* **achieve**, attain, accomplish, gain, earn, win, make, get, obtain, notch up, rack up. **2** *I forgot completely—chalk it up to age* **attribute**, assign, ascribe, put down; blame on, pin on, lay at the door of.

> **WORD LINKS**
> **calcareous** containing chalk

chalky adj. **1** *chalky skin* **pale**, bloodless, pallid, colourless, wan, ashen, white, pasty.

2 *chalky bits at the bottom of the glass* **powdery**, gritty, granular; old use pulverulent.

challenge n. **1** *he accepted the challenge* **dare**, provocation; summons. **2** *a challenge to his leadership* **test**, questioning, dispute, stand, opposition, confrontation. **3** *it was proving quite a challenge* **problem**, difficult task, test, trial.

▶v. **1** *we challenged their statistics* **question**, disagree with, dispute, take issue with, protest against, call into question, object to. **2** *he challenged one of my men to a duel* **dare**, summon, throw down the gauntlet to. **3** *changes that would challenge them* **test**, tax, strain, make demands on; stretch, stimulate, inspire, excite.

challenging adj. **demanding**, testing, taxing, exacting; stretching, exciting, stimulating, inspiring; difficult, tough, hard, formidable, onerous, arduous, strenuous, gruelling; formal exigent.
– OPPOSITES easy, uninspiring.

chamber n. **1** *a debating chamber* **room**, hall, assembly room, auditorium. **2** *the left chamber of the heart* **compartment**, cavity; Anatomy auricle, ventricle.

champagne n. **sparkling wine**; vin mousseux, spumante, Sekt, cava; informal champers, bubbly, fizz.

champion n. **1** *the world champion* **winner**, title-holder, defending champion, gold medallist; prizewinner, victor (ludorum); informal champ, number one. **2** *a champion of change* **advocate**, proponent, promoter, supporter, defender, upholder, backer, exponent; campaigner, lobbyist, crusader, apologist; N. Amer. booster. **3** *historical the king's champion* **knight**, man-at-arms, warrior.

▶v. *championing the rights of tribal peoples* **advocate**, promote, defend, uphold, support, back, stand up for, take someone's part; campaign for, lobby for, fight for, crusade for, stick up for.
– OPPOSITES oppose.

chance n. **1** *there was a chance he might be released* **possibility**, prospect, probability, likelihood, likeliness, expectation, anticipation; risk, threat, danger. **2** *I gave her a chance to answer* **opportunity**, opening, occasion, turn, time, window (of opportunity); N. Amer. & Austral./NZ show; informal shot, look-in. **3** *Nigel took an awful chance* **risk**, gamble, venture, speculation, long shot, leap in the dark. **4** *pure chance* **accident**, coincidence, serendipity, fate, destiny, fortuity, providence, happenstance; good fortune, (good) luck, fluke.

▶adj. *a chance discovery* **accidental**, fortuitous, adventitious, fluky, coincidental, serendipitous; unintentional, unintended, inadvertent, unplanned.
– OPPOSITES intentional.

▶v. **1** *I chanced to meet him* **happen**. **2** informal *she chanced another look* **risk**, hazard, venture, try; formal essay.
◻ **by chance** fortuitously, by accident, accidentally, coincidentally, serendipitously; unintentionally, inadvertently.

chance on come across/upon, run across/into, happen on, light on, stumble on, find by chance, meet (by chance); informal bump into; old use run against.

chancy adj. informal **risky**, unpredictable, uncertain, precarious; unsafe, insecure, tricky, high-risk, hazardous, perilous, parlous; informal dicey, hairy; Brit. informal dodgy.
– OPPOSITES predictable.

change v. **1** *this could change the face of Britain* | *things have changed* **alter**, make/ become different, adjust, adapt, amend, modify, revise, refine; reshape, refashion, redesign, restyle, revamp, rework, remodel, reorganize, reorder; vary, transform, transfigure, transmute, transmogrify, metamorphose; informal tweak. **2** *he's changed his job* **exchange**, substitute, swap, switch, replace, alternate, interchange.
– OPPOSITES preserve, keep.

▶n. **1** *a change of plan* **alteration**, modification, variation, revision, amendment, adjustment, adaptation; remodelling, reshaping, rearrangement, reordering, restyling, reworking; metamorphosis, transformation, evolution, mutation; humorous transmogrification. **2** *a change of government* **exchange**, substitution, swap, switch, replacement, alternation, interchange. **3** *I've no change* **coins**, loose/small change, (hard) cash, silver, coppers, specie.

changeable adj. **1** *the weather will be changeable* | *changeable moods* **variable**, inconstant, varying, changing, fluctuating, irregular; erratic, inconsistent, unstable, unsettled, turbulent, changeful, protean; fickle, capricious, temperamental, volatile, mercurial, unpredictable, blowing hot and cold; informal up and down; literary fluctuant. **2** *the colours are changeable* **alterable**, adjustable, modifiable, variable, mutable, exchangeable, interchangeable, replaceable.
– OPPOSITES constant.

changeless adj. **unchanging**, unvarying, timeless, static, fixed, permanent, constant, unchanged, consistent, uniform, undeviating; stable, steady, unchangeable, unalterable, invariable, immutable.
– OPPOSITES variable.

channel n. **1** *the English Channel* **strait(s)**, sound, narrows, (sea) passage. **2** *the water ran down a channel* **duct**, gutter, conduit, trough, culvert, sluice, spillway, race, drain. **3** *a channel for their extraordinary energy* **use**, medium, vehicle, way of harnessing; release (mechanism), safety valve, vent. **4** *a channel of communication* **means**, medium, instrument, mechanism, agency, vehicle, route, avenue.

▶v. **1** *she channelled out a groove* **hollow out**, gouge (out), cut (out). **2** *many countries channel their aid through charities* **convey**, transmit, conduct, direct, guide, relay, pass on, transfer.

chant n. **1** *the protesters' chants* **shout**, cry, (rallying) call, slogan. **2** *the melodious chant of the monks* **incantation**, intonation, singing, song, recitative.

▸v. **1** *protesters were chanting slogans* **shout**, chorus, repeat. **2** *the choir chanted Psalm 118* **sing**, intone, incant.

chaos n. **disorder**, disarray, disorganization, confusion, mayhem, bedlam, pandemonium, havoc, turmoil, tumult, commotion, disruption, upheaval, uproar; a muddle, a mess, a shambles; anarchy, lawlessness; informal hullabaloo, all hell broken loose.
– OPPOSITES order.

chaotic adj. **disorderly**, disordered, in disorder, in chaos, in disarray, disorganized, topsy-turvy, in pandemonium, in turmoil, in uproar; in a muddle, in a mess, messy, in a shambles; anarchic, lawless; Brit. informal shambolic.

chap[1] v. *my skin chapped in the wind* **become raw**, become sore, become inflamed, chafe, crack.

chap[2] n. Brit. informal *he's a nice chap* **man**, boy, character; informal fellow, guy, geezer; Brit. informal bloke, lad, bod; N. Amer. informal dude, hombre; Brit. informal dated cove.

chaperone n. *Aunt Millie went as chaperone* **companion**, duenna, escort, protectress, protector, minder.
▸v. *she was chaperoned by her mother* **accompany**, escort, attend, watch over, keep an eye on, protect, mind.

chapter n. **1** *the first chapter of the book* **section**, division, part, portion. **2** *a new chapter in our history* **period**, phase, page, stage, epoch, era. **3** N. Amer. *a local chapter of the American Cancer Society* **branch**, division, subdivision, section, department, lodge, wing, arm. **4** *the cathedral chapter* **governing body**, council, assembly, convocation, synod, consistory.

char v. **scorch**, burn, singe, sear, blacken; informal toast.

character n. **1** *a forceful character | the character of a town* **personality**, nature, disposition, temperament, temper, mentality, make-up; features, qualities, properties, traits; spirit, essence, identity, ethos, complexion, tone, feel, feeling. **2** *a woman of character* **integrity**, honour, moral strength/fibre, rectitude, uprightness; fortitude, strength, backbone, resolve, grit, will power; informal guts, gutsiness; Brit. informal bottle. **3** *a stain on his character* **reputation**, (good) name, standing, stature, position, status. **4** informal *a bit of a character* **eccentric**, oddity, madcap, crank, individualist, nonconformist, rare bird; informal oddball; Brit. informal odd bod; informal dated card, caution. **5** *a boorish character* **person**, man, woman, soul, creature, individual, figure, customer; informal cookie; Brit. informal bod, guy; informal dated body, dog. **6** *the characters develop throughout the play* **persona**, role, part; (**characters**) dramatis personae. **7** *thirty characters* **letter**, figure, symbol, sign, mark.

characteristic n. *interesting characteristics* **attribute**, feature, (essential) quality, property, trait, aspect, element, facet;

mannerism, habit, custom, idiosyncrasy, peculiarity, quirk, oddity, foible.
▸adj. *his characteristic eloquence* **typical**, usual, normal, predictable, habitual; distinctive, particular, special, especial, peculiar, idiosyncratic, singular, unique.

characterize v. **1** *the period was characterized by scientific advancement* **distinguish**, make distinctive, mark, typify, set apart. **2** *the women are characterized as prophets of doom* **portray**, depict, present, represent, describe; categorize, class, style, brand.

charade n. **farce**, pantomime, travesty, mockery, parody, act, masquerade.

charge v. **1** *he didn't charge much* **ask (in payment)**, levy, demand, exact; bill, invoice. **2** *the subscription will be charged to your account* **bill**, debit from, take from. **3** *two men were charged with affray* **accuse**, indict, arraign; prosecute, try, put on trial; N. Amer. impeach; old use inculpate. **4** *they charged him with reforming the system* **entrust**, burden, encumber, saddle, tax. **5** *the cavalry charged the tanks* **attack**, storm, assault, assail, fall on, swoop on, descend on; informal lay into, tear into. **6** *we charged into the crowd* **rush**, storm, stampede, push, plough, launch oneself, go headlong; informal steam; N. Amer. informal barrel. **7** *charge your glasses! | the guns were charged* **fill (up)**, top up; load (up), arm, prepare to fire. **8** *his work was charged with energy* **suffuse**, pervade, permeate, saturate, infuse, imbue, fill. **9** *I charge you to stop* **order**, command, direct, instruct, enjoin; formal adjure; literary bid.
▸n. **1** *all customers pay a charge* **fee**, payment, price, tariff, amount, sum, fare, levy. **2** *he pleaded guilty to the charge* **accusation**, allegation, indictment, arraignment; N. Amer. impeachment; old use inculpation. **3** *an infantry charge* **attack**, assault, offensive, onslaught, drive, push, thrust. **4** *the child was in her charge* **care**, protection, safe keeping, control; custody, guardianship, wardship; hands; old use ward. **5** *his charge was to save the business* **duty**, responsibility, task, job, assignment, mission, function; Brit. informal pigeon. **6** *the safety of my charge* **ward**, protégé, dependant. **7** *the judge gave a careful charge to the jury* **instruction**, direction, directive, order, command, dictate, exhortation. **8** N. Amer. informal *I get a real charge out of working hard* **thrill**, tingle, glow; excitement, stimulation, enjoyment, pleasure; informal kick, buzz.
▫ **in charge of** responsible for, in control of, at the helm/wheel of; managing, running, administering, directing, supervising, overseeing, controlling; informal running the show.

charisma n. **charm**, presence, (force of) personality, strength of character; (animal) magnetism, attractiveness, appeal, allure.

charismatic adj. **charming**, fascinating, magnetic, captivating, beguiling, attractive, appealing, alluring.

charitable adj. **1** *charitable activities*
philanthropic, humanitarian, altruistic,
benevolent, public-spirited; non-profit-
making; formal eleemosynary. **2** *charitable
people* **big-hearted**, generous, open-handed,
free-handed, munificent, bountiful,
beneficent; literary bounteous. **3** *he was
charitable in his judgements* **magnanimous**,
generous, liberal, tolerant, easy-going,
broad-minded, considerate, sympathetic,
lenient, indulgent, forgiving.

charity n. **1** *an AIDS charity* **non-profit-
making organization**, voluntary
organization, charitable institution;
fund, trust, foundation. **2** *we don't need
charity* **financial assistance**, aid, welfare,
(financial) relief; handouts, gifts, presents,
largesse; historical alms. **3** *his actions are
motivated by charity* **philanthropy**,
humanitarianism, humanity, altruism,
public-spiritedness, social conscience,
benevolence, beneficence, munificence.
4 *show a bit of charity* **goodwill**, compassion,
consideration, concern, kindness,
kind-heartedness, tender-heartedness,
tenderness, sympathy, indulgence, tolerance,
leniency, caritas; literary bounteousness.

charlatan n. **quack**, mountebank, sham,
fraud, fake, impostor, hoodwinker, hoaxer,
cheat, deceiver, double-dealer, (confidence)
trickster, swindler, fraudster; informal phoney,
shark, con man/artist, flimflammer; Brit.
informal twister; N. Amer. informal bunco artist,
gold brick, chiseller; Austral. informal magsman,
illywhacker; dated confidence man/woman.

charm n. **1** *people were captivated by her
charm* **attractiveness**, beauty, glamour,
loveliness; appeal, allure, desirability,
seductiveness, sexual/animal magnetism,
charisma; informal pulling power. **2** *these
traditions retain a lot of charm* **appeal**,
drawing power, attraction, allure,
fascination. **3** *magical charms* **spell**,
incantation, conjuration, rune, magic
formula/word; N. Amer. mojo, hex. **4** *a lucky
charm* **talisman**, fetish, amulet, mascot,
totem, juju; old use periapt.
▶v. **1** *he charmed them with his singing* **delight**,
please, win (over), attract, captivate, allure,
lure, dazzle, fascinate, enchant, enthral,
enrapture, seduce, spellbind. **2** *he charmed
his mother into agreeing* **coax**, cajole,
wheedle; informal sweet-talk, soft-soap; old use
blandish.

charming adj. **delightful**, pleasing,
pleasant, agreeable, likeable, endearing,
lovely, lovable, adorable, appealing,
attractive, good-looking, prepossessing;
alluring, delectable, ravishing, winning,
winsome, fetching, captivating, enchanting,
entrancing, fascinating, seductive; informal
heavenly, divine, gorgeous, easy on the eye;
Brit. informal smashing; literary beauteous; old use
fair, comely.
– OPPOSITES repulsive.

chart n. **1** *check your ideal weight on the chart*
graph, table, diagram, histogram; bar chart,
pie chart, flow chart; Computing graphic. **2** *the*
pop charts **top twenty**, list, listing; dated hit
parade.
▶v. **1** *the changes were charted accurately*
tabulate, plot, graph, record, register,
represent; make a chart/diagram of. **2** *the
book charted his progress* **follow**, trace,
outline, describe, detail, record, document,
chronicle, log.

charter n. **1** *a Royal charter* **authority**,
authorization, sanction, dispensation,
consent, permission; permit, licence,
warrant, franchise. **2** *the UN Charter*
constitution, code, canon; fundamental
principles, rules, laws. **3** *the charter of a
yacht* **hire**, hiring, lease, leasing, rent, rental,
renting; booking, reservation, reserving.
▶v. *they chartered a bus* **hire**, lease, rent; book,
reserve.

chary adj. **wary**, cautious, circumspect,
heedful, careful, on one's guard; distrustful,
mistrustful, sceptical, suspicious, dubious,
hesitant, reluctant, leery, nervous,
apprehensive, uneasy; informal cagey, iffy.

chase¹ v. **1** *the dogs chased the fox* **pursue**,
run after, give chase to, follow; hunt, track,
trail; informal tail. **2** *chasing young girls* **woo**,
pursue, run after, make advances to, flirt
with, pay court to; informal chat up, come on
to; dated court, romance, set one's cap at,
make love to. **3** *she chased away the donkeys*
drive, send, scare; informal send packing.
4 *she chased away all thoughts of him* **dispel**,
banish, dismiss, drive away, shut out, put out
of one's mind. **5** *photographers chased on to
the runway* **rush**, dash, race, speed, streak,
shoot, charge, scramble, scurry, hurry, fly,
pelt; informal scoot, belt, tear, zip, whip; N. Amer.
informal boogie, hightail, clip; old use hie.
▶n. *they gave up the chase* **pursuit**, hunt, trail.

chase² v. *the figures are chased on the dish*
engrave, etch, carve, inscribe, cut, chisel.

chasm n. **1** *a deep chasm* **gorge**, abyss,
canyon, ravine, gully, gulf, defile, couloir,
crevasse, fissure, crevice; N. Amer. gulch,
coulee. **2** *the chasm between their views*
breach, gulf, rift; difference, separation,
division, dissension, schism, scission.

chassis n. **framework**, frame, structure,
substructure, shell, casing, bodywork, body.

chaste adj. **1** *chaste girlhood* **virginal**,
virgin, intact, maidenly, unmarried, unwed;
celibate, abstinent, self-restrained, self-
denying, continent; innocent, virtuous, pure
(as the driven snow), sinless, undefiled,
unsullied; Christianity immaculate; literary vestal.
2 *a chaste kiss on the cheek* **non-sexual**,
platonic, innocent. **3** *the dark, chaste interior*
plain, simple, bare, unadorned, undecorated,
unornamented, unembellished, functional,
no-frills, austere.
– OPPOSITES promiscuous, passionate.

chasten v. **subdue**, humble, cow, squash,
deflate, flatten, take down a peg or two, put
someone in their place; informal cut down to
size, settle someone's hash.

chastise v. **1** *the staff were chastised
for arriving late* **scold**, upbraid, berate,

c

reprimand, reprove, rebuke, admonish, chide, censure, lambaste, lecture, give someone a piece of one's mind, take to task, haul over the coals; informal tell off, dress down, bawl out, give someone an earful, give someone a roasting, come down on someone like a ton of bricks, have someone's guts for garters, slap someone's wrist, rap over the knuckles, give someone hell; Brit. informal carpet, tick off, have a go at, tear someone off a strip, give someone what for, give someone a rocket; N. Amer. informal chew out, ream out; Austral. informal monster; dated give someone a rating; formal castigate; old use chasten; rare reprehend, objurgate. **2** dated *her mistress chastised her with a whip.* See **beat** (sense 1 of the verb).
– OPPOSITES praise.

chastity n. **celibacy**, chasteness, virginity, abstinence, self-restraint, self-denial, continence; singleness, maidenhood; innocence, purity, virtue, morality; Christianity immaculateness.

chat n. *I popped in for a chat* **talk**, conversation, gossip, chatter, heart-to-heart, tête-à-tête, blather; informal jaw, gas, confab; Brit. informal natter, chinwag, rabbit; N. Amer. informal rap, bull session; formal confabulation, colloquy.
▸v. *they chatted with their guests* **talk**, gossip, chatter, speak, converse, tittle-tattle, prattle, jabber, babble; informal gas, jaw, chew the rag/fat, yap, yak, yabber, yatter, yammer; Brit. informal natter, rabbit, chunter, have a chinwag; N. Amer. informal shoot the breeze/bull, visit; Austral./NZ informal mag; formal confabulate; old use clack.
▫ **chat someone up** informal flirt with, make advances to; informal come on to; dated make love to, set one's cap at, romance.

chatter n. *she tired him with her chatter* **chat**, talk, gossip, chit-chat, patter, jabbering, jabber, prattling, prattle, babbling, babble, tittle-tattle, blathering, blather; informal yabbering, yammering, yattering, yapping; Brit. informal nattering, chuntering, rabbiting on; formal confabulation, colloquy; old use clack.
▸v. *they chattered excitedly.* See **chat** (verb).

chatterbox n. informal **talker**, chatterer, prattler, blabber; N. Amer. blatherskite; informal windbag, gasbag, blabbermouth; Brit. informal natterer.

chatty adj. **1** *he was a chatty person* **talkative**, communicative, expansive, unreserved, gossipy, gossiping, garrulous, loquacious, voluble, verbose; informal mouthy, gabby, gassy; Brit. informal able to talk the hind legs off a donkey. **2** *a chatty letter* **conversational**, gossipy, informal, casual, familiar, friendly; informal newsy.
– OPPOSITES taciturn.

chauvinist adj. *chauvinist sentiments* **jingoistic**, chauvinistic, excessively patriotic, excessively nationalistic, flag-waving, xenophobic, racist, racialist, ethnocentric; sexist, male chauvinist, anti-feminist, misogynist, woman-hating.
▸n. *he's a chauvinist* **sexist**, anti-feminist, misogynist, woman-hater; informal male

chauvinist pig, MCP.

cheap adj. **1** *cheap tickets* **inexpensive**, low-priced, low-cost, economical, competitive, affordable, reasonable, budget, economy, bargain, cut-price, reduced, discounted, discount, rock-bottom, giveaway, bargain-basement; informal dirt cheap. **2** *plain without looking cheap* **poor-quality**, second-rate, third-rate, substandard, low-grade, inferior, vulgar, shoddy, trashy, tawdry, meretricious, cheapjack, gimcrack, Brummagem, pinchbeck; informal rubbishy, cheapo, junky, tacky, kitsch; Brit. informal naff, duff; N. Amer. informal two-bit, dime-store. **3** *the cheap exploitation of suffering* **despicable**, contemptible, immoral, unscrupulous, unprincipled, unsavoury, distasteful, vulgar, ignoble, shameful; old use scurvy. **4** *he made me feel cheap* **ashamed**, humiliated, mortified, debased, degraded. **5** N. Amer. informal *he made the other guests look cheap.* See **mean²** (sense 1).
– OPPOSITES expensive.

cheapen v. **1** *cheapening the cost of exports* **reduce**, lower (in price), cut, mark down, discount; informal slash. **2** *Hetty never cheapened herself* **demean**, debase, degrade, lower, humble, devalue, abase, discredit, disgrace, dishonour, shame, humiliate, mortify, prostitute.

cheat v. **1** *customers were cheated* **swindle**, defraud, deceive, trick, dupe, hoodwink, double-cross, gull; informal diddle, rip off, con, fleece, shaft, sting, bilk, rook, gyp, finagle, flimflam, put one over on, pull a fast one on; N. Amer. informal sucker, gold-brick, stiff; Austral. informal pull a swifty on; formal mulct; cozen; old use chicane. **2** *she cheated Ryan out of his fortune* **deprive of**, deny; informal do out of. **3** *the boy cheated death* **avoid**, escape, evade, elude; foil, frustrate, thwart. **4** *cheating husbands* **commit adultery**, be unfaithful, stray; informal two-time, play about/around; Brit. informal play away.
▸n. **1** *a liar and a cheat* **swindler**, cheater, fraudster, (confidence) trickster, deceiver, hoaxer, hoodwinker, double-dealer, double-crosser, sham, fraud, fake, charlatan, quack, mountebank; informal con man/artist, shark, sharper, phoney, flimflammer; Brit. informal twister; N. Amer. informal grifter, bunco artist, gold brick, chiseller; Austral. informal magsman, illywhacker; dated confidence man. **2** *a sure cheat for generating cash* **swindle**, fraud, deception, deceit, hoax, sham, trick, ruse; informal con.

check v. **1** *troops checked all vehicles | I checked her background* **examine**, inspect, look at/over, scrutinize, survey; study, investigate, research, probe, look into, enquire into; informal check out, give something a/the once-over. **2** *he checked that the gun was cocked* **make sure**, confirm, verify. **3** *two defeats checked their progress* **halt**, stop, arrest, cut short; bar, obstruct, hamper, impede, inhibit, frustrate, foil, thwart, curb, block, stall, hold up, retard, delay, slow down; literary stay. **4** *her tears could* *not be checked* **suppress**, repress, restrain, control, curb, rein in, stifle, hold back, choke back; informal keep a lid on.

▶n. **1** *a check of the records* **examination**, inspection, scrutiny, scrutinization, perusal, study, investigation, probe, analysis; test, trial, monitoring; check-up; informal once-over, look-see. **2** *a check on the abuse of authority* **control**, restraint, constraint, curb, limitation. **3** N. Amer. *the waitress arrived with the check* **bill**, account, invoice, statement; N. Amer. informal tab; old use reckoning.

□ **check in** report (one's arrival), book in, register.

check out leave, vacate, depart; pay the bill, settle up.

check something out informal **1** *the police checked out dozens of leads* **investigate**, look into, enquire into, probe, research, examine, go over; assess, weigh up, analyse, evaluate; follow up; informal give something a/the once-over; N. Amer. informal scope out. **2** *she checked herself out in the mirror* **look at**, survey, regard, inspect, contemplate; informal have a gander/squint at; Brit. informal have a dekko/ butcher's at, clock; N. Amer. informal eyeball.

keep something in check curb, restrain, hold back, keep a tight rein on, rein in/back; control, govern, master, suppress, stifle; informal keep a lid on.

check-up n. **examination**, inspection, evaluation, analysis, survey, probe, test, appraisal; check, health check; informal once-over, going-over.

cheek n. *that's enough of your cheek!* **impudence**, impertinence, insolence, cheekiness, presumption, effrontery, gall, pertness, impoliteness, disrespect, bad manners, overfamiliarity, cockiness; answering back, talking back; informal brass (neck), lip, mouth, chutzpah; Brit. informal sauce, backchat; N. Amer. informal sass, sassiness, nerviness, back talk; old use assumption.

▶v. *they were cheeking the dinner lady* **answer back**, talk back, be cheeky, be impertinent; Brit. informal backchat; N. Amer. informal sass, be sassy.

> **WORD LINKS**
> **buccal, malar** relating to the cheeks

cheeky adj. **impudent**, impertinent, insolent, presumptuous, forward, pert, bold (as brass), brazen, cocky, overfamiliar, discourteous, disrespectful, impolite, bad-mannered; informal brass-necked, lippy, mouthy, fresh, saucy; N. Amer. informal sassy, nervy; old use assumptive.
– OPPOSITES respectful, polite.

cheep v. **chirp**, chirrup, twitter, tweet, peep, chitter, chirr, trill, warble, sing.

cheer n. **1** *the cheers of the crowd* **hurrah**, hurray, whoop, bravo, shout; hosanna, alleluia; (**cheers**) acclaim, acclamation, clamour, applause, ovation. **2** *a time of cheer* **happiness**, joy, joyousness, cheerfulness, cheeriness, gladness, merriment, gaiety, jubilation, jollity, jolliness, high spirits, joviality, jocularity, conviviality, light-

heartedness; merrymaking, pleasure, rejoicing, revelry. **3** *Christmas cheer* **fare**, food, foodstuffs, eatables, provender; drink, beverages; informal eats, nibbles, nosh, grub, chow; Brit. informal scoff; dated victuals; formal comestibles; literary viands.
– OPPOSITES boo, sadness.

▶v. **1** *they cheered their team* **acclaim**, hail, salute, shout for, hurrah, hurray, applaud, clap, put one's hands together for; bring the house down; informal holler for, give someone a big hand; N. Amer. informal ballyhoo. **2** *the bad weather did little to cheer me* **raise someone's spirits**, make happier, brighten, buoy up, enliven, exhilarate, hearten, gladden, uplift, perk up, encourage, inspirit; informal buck up.
– OPPOSITES boo, depress.

□ **cheer someone on** encourage, urge on, spur on, drive on, motivate, inspire, fire (up), inspirit; N. Amer. light a fire under.

cheer up perk up, brighten (up), become more cheerful, liven up, rally, revive, bounce back, take heart; informal buck up.

cheer someone up See **cheer** (sense 2 of the verb).

cheerful adj. **1** *he arrived looking cheerful* **happy**, jolly, merry, bright, glad, sunny, joyful, joyous, light-hearted, in good/high spirits, full of the joys of spring, sparkling, bubbly, exuberant, buoyant, ebullient, cock-a-hoop, elated, gleeful, breezy, cheery, jaunty, animated, radiant, lively, jovial, genial, good-humoured; carefree, unworried, untroubled, without a care in the world; informal upbeat, chipper, chirpy, peppy, bright-eyed and bushy-tailed, full of beans; dated gay; formal jocund; literary gladsome, blithe, blithesome. **2** *a cheerful room* **pleasant**, attractive, agreeable, cheering, bright, sunny, happy, friendly, welcoming.
– OPPOSITES sad.

cheerio exclam. Brit. informal **goodbye**, farewell, adieu, au revoir, ciao, adios, auf Wiedersehen, sayonara; Austral./NZ hooray; informal bye, bye-bye, so long, see you (later), later(s); Brit. informal cheers, ta-ta, ta-ra; informal dated pip pip, toodle-oo.

cheerless adj. **gloomy**, dreary, dull, dismal, bleak, drab, sombre, dark, dim, dingy, funereal; austere, stark, bare, comfortless, unwelcoming, uninviting; miserable, wretched, joyless, depressing, disheartening, dispiriting.

cheers exclam. informal *he raised his glass and said 'Cheers!'* **here's to you**, good health, your health, skol, prosit, salut; informal bottoms up, down the hatch; Brit. informal here's mud in your eye; Brit. informal dated cheerio, chin-chin.

cheery adj. See **cheerful** (sense 1).

chef n. **cook**, cordon bleu cook, food preparer; chef de cuisine, chef de partie; pastry cook, saucier; N. Amer. informal short-order cook.

chef-d'œuvre n. **masterpiece**, masterwork, finest work, magnum opus, pièce de résistance, tour de force.

chequered adj. **1** *a chequered tablecloth* **checked**, multicoloured, many-coloured. **2** *a chequered history* **varied**, mixed, full of ups and downs, vicissitudinous; unstable, irregular, erratic, inconstant; informal up and down.

cherish v. **1** *a woman he could cherish* **adore**, hold dear, love, dote on, be devoted to, revere, esteem, admire; think the world of, set great store by, hold in high esteem; care for, look after, protect, preserve, keep safe. **2** *I cherish her letters* **treasure**, prize, value highly, hold dear. **3** *they cherished dreams of glory* **harbour**, entertain, possess, hold (on to), cling to, foster, nurture.

cherub n. **1** *she was borne up to heaven by cherubs* **angel**, seraph. **2** *a cherub of 18 months* **baby**, infant, toddler; pretty/lovable child, innocent child, little angel; informal (tiny) tot, tiny; literary babe (in arms).

cherubic adj. **angelic**, sweet, cute, adorable, appealing, lovable; innocent, seraphic, saintly.

chest n. **1** *a bullet wound in the chest* **breast**, upper body, torso, trunk, ribcage; technical thorax. **2** *the matron had a large chest* **bust**, bosom; old use embonpoint. **3** *an oak chest* **box**, case, casket, crate, trunk, coffer, strongbox.
□ **get something off one's chest** informal confess, disclose, divulge, reveal, make known, make public, make a clean breast of, bring into the open, get a load off one's mind.

> **WORD LINKS**
> **pectoral, thoracic** relating to the chest

chew v. *Carolyn chewed a mouthful of toast* **masticate**, munch, champ, crunch, nibble, gnaw, eat, consume; formal manduce.
□ **chew something over** meditate on, ruminate on, think about/over/through, mull over, consider, weigh up, ponder on, deliberate on, reflect on, muse on, dwell on, give thought to, turn over in one's mind; brood over, puzzle over, rack one's brains about; N. Amer. think on; informal kick around/about, bat around/about; formal cogitate about; old use pore on.

chic adj. **stylish**, smart, elegant, sophisticated, dressy, dapper, dashing, trim; fashionable, high-fashion, in vogue, up to date, up to the minute, contemporary, à la mode; informal trendy, with it, snazzy, snazzy, natty, swish; N. Amer. informal fly, spiffy, kicky, tony.
– OPPOSITES unfashionable.

chicanery n. **trickery**, deception, deceit, deceitfulness, duplicity, dishonesty, deviousness, unscrupulousness, underhandedness, subterfuge, fraud, fraudulence, sharp practice, skulduggery, swindling, cheating, duping, hoodwinking; informal crookedness, monkey business, hanky-panky, shenanigans; Brit. informal jiggery-pokery; N. Amer. informal monkeyshines; old use management, knavery.

chicken n. **fowl**, hen, cock, chick.

chide v. **scold**, chastise, upbraid, berate, reprimand, reprove, rebuke, admonish, censure, lambaste, lecture, give someone a piece of one's mind, take to task, haul over the coals; informal tell off, dress down, bawl out, give someone an earful, give someone a roasting, come down on someone like a ton of bricks, have someone's guts for garters, slap someone's wrist, rap over the knuckles, give someone hell; Brit. informal carpet, tick off, have a go at, tear someone off a strip, give someone what for, give someone a rocket; N. Amer. informal chew out, ream out; Austral. informal monster; formal castigate; dated give someone a rating; old use chasten; rare reprehend, objurgate.
– OPPOSITES praise.

chief n. **1** *a Highland chief* **leader**, chieftain, head, headman, ruler, overlord, master, commander, seigneur, liege (lord), potentate. **2** *the chief of the central bank* **head**, principal, chief executive, president, chair, chairman, chairwoman, chairperson, governor, director, manager, manageress; employer, proprietor; N. Amer. chief executive officer, CEO; informal skipper, numero uno, (head) honcho, boss; Brit. informal gaffer, guv'nor; N. Amer. informal padrone, sachem.
▶ adj. **1** *the chief rabbi* **head**, leading, principal, premier, highest, foremost, supreme, arch. **2** *their chief aim* **main**, principal, most important, primary, prime, first, cardinal, central, key, crucial, essential, pre-eminent, predominant, paramount, overriding; informal number-one.
– OPPOSITES subordinate, minor.

chiefly adv. **mainly**, in the main, primarily, principally, predominantly, mostly, for the most part; usually, habitually, typically, commonly, generally, on the whole, largely, by and large, as a rule, almost always.

child n. **youngster**, little one, boy, girl; baby, newborn, infant, toddler; schoolboy, schoolgirl, minor, junior; son, daughter, descendant; (children) offspring, progeny; Scottish & N. English bairn, laddie, lassie, lass; informal kid, kiddie, kiddiewink, nipper, tiny, (tiny) tot, shaver, young 'un, lad; Brit. informal sprog; N. Amer. informal rug rat; Austral./NZ informal ankle-biter; derogatory brat, guttersnipe; literary babe (in arms).

> **WORD LINKS**
> **infantile** relating to babies and young children
> **crèche** a place where babies and young children are cared for during the working day
> **nursery** a room for children, or a school for very young children
> **paediatrics** the branch of medicine dealing with children
> **paedophile** a person who is sexually attracted to children
> **infanticide** the killing of a young child

childbirth n. **labour**, delivery, giving birth, birthing; formal parturition; dated confinement; literary travail; old use lying-in, accouchement, childbed.

childhood n. **youth**, early years/life, infancy, babyhood, boyhood, girlhood, pre-teens, prepubescence, minority; the springtime of life, one's salad days; formal nonage, juvenescence.
– OPPOSITES adulthood.

childish adj. **1** *childish behaviour* **immature**, babyish, infantile, juvenile, puerile; silly, inane, jejune, foolish, irresponsible. **2** *a round childish face* **childlike**, youthful, young, young-looking, girlish, boyish.
– OPPOSITES mature, adult.

childlike adj. **1** *grandmother looked almost childlike* **youthful**, young, young-looking, girlish, boyish. **2** *geniuses tend to be rather childlike* **innocent**, artless, guileless, unworldly, unsophisticated, naive, ingenuous, trusting, unsuspicious, unwary, credulous, gullible; unaffected, without airs, uninhibited, natural, spontaneous; informal wet behind the ears.

chill n. **1** *a chill in the air* **coldness**, chilliness, coolness, nip, iciness, rawness, bitterness. **2** *he had a chill* **cold**, dose of flu; old use grippe. **3** *the chill in their relations* **unfriendliness**, lack of warmth, chilliness, coldness, coolness.
– OPPOSITES warmth.
▶ v. **1** *the dessert is best chilled* **make cold**, make colder, cool (down/off); refrigerate, ice. **2** *his quiet tone chilled Ruth* **scare**, frighten, petrify, terrify, alarm; make someone's blood run cold, chill to the bone/marrow, make someone's flesh crawl; informal scare the pants off; Brit. informal put the wind up; old use affright.
– OPPOSITES warm.
▶ adj. *a chill wind* **cold**, chilly, cool, fresh; wintry, frosty, icy, ice-cold, icy-cold, glacial, polar, arctic, raw, bitter, bitterly cold, biting, freezing, frigid, gelid; informal nippy; Brit. informal parky.
□ **chill out** informal See **relax** (sense 1).

chilly adj. **1** *the weather had turned chilly* **cold**, cool, crisp, fresh, wintry, frosty, icy, ice-cold, icy-cold, chill, glacial, polar, arctic, raw, bitter, bitterly cold, freezing, frigid, gelid; informal nippy; Brit. informal parky. **2** *I woke up feeling chilly* **cold**, frozen (stiff), frozen to the core/marrow/bone, freezing (cold), bitterly cold, shivery, chilled. **3** *a chilly reception* **unfriendly**, unwelcoming, cold, cool, frosty, gelid; informal stand-offish, offish.
– OPPOSITES warm.

chime v. **1** *the bells began to chime* **ring**, peal, toll, sound; ding, dong, clang, boom; literary knell. **2** *the clock chimed eight o'clock* **strike**, sound.
▶ n. *the chimes of the bells* **peal**, pealing, ringing, carillon, toll, tolling; ding-dong, clanging, tintinnabulation; literary knell.
□ **chime in 1** *'Yes, you do that,' Doreen chimed in* **interject**, interpose, interrupt, butt in, cut in, join in; Brit. informal chip in. **2** *his remarks chimed in with the ideas of Adam Smith* **accord**, correspond, be consistent, be compatible, agree, be in agreement, fit in, be in tune, be consonant; informal square.

chimera n. **illusion**, fantasy, delusion, dream, fancy.

chimney n. **stack**, smokestack; flue, funnel, vent.

china n. **1** *a china cup* **porcelain**. **2** *a table laid with the best china* **dishes**, plates, cups and saucers, crockery, tableware, dinner service, tea service.

chink[1] n. *a chink in the curtains* **opening**, gap, space, hole, aperture, crack, fissure, crevice, cranny, cleft, split, slit, slot.

chink[2] v. *the glasses chinked* **jingle**, jangle, clink, tinkle.

chip n. **1** *wood chips* **fragment**, sliver, splinter, spell, shaving, paring, flake. **2** *a chip in the glass* **nick**, crack, scratch; flaw, fault. **3** *fish and chips* chipped potatoes, potato chips; Brit. French fried potatoes; N. Amer. French fries. **4** *gambling chips* **counter**, token, jetton; N. Amer. check.
▶ v. **1** *the teacup was chipped* **nick**, crack, scratch; damage. **2** *the plaster had chipped* **break (off)**, crack, crumble. **3** *chip the flint to the required shape* **whittle**, hew, chisel.
□ **chip in 1** *'He's right,' Gloria chipped in* **interrupt**, interject, interpose, cut in, chime in, butt in. **2** *parents and staff chipped in to raise the cash* **contribute**, make a contribution/donation, club together, pay; informal fork out, shell out, cough up; Brit. informal stump up; N. Amer. informal kick in.

chirp v. **tweet**, twitter, chirrup, cheep, peep, chitter, chirr; sing, warble, trill.

chirpy adj. informal See **cheerful** (sense 1).

chit-chat n. informal **small talk**, chat, chatting, chatter, prattle; Brit. informal nattering, chuntering.

chivalrous adj. **1** *his chivalrous treatment of women* **gallant**, gentlemanly, honourable, respectful, considerate; courteous, polite, gracious, well mannered, mannerly; old use gentle. **2** *chivalrous pursuits* **knightly**, noble, chivalric; brave, courageous, bold, valiant, valorous, heroic, daring, intrepid.
– OPPOSITES rude, cowardly.

chivalry n. **1** *acts of chivalry* **gallantry**, gentlemanliness, considerateness; courtesy, courteousness, politeness, graciousness, mannerliness, good manners. **2** *the values of chivalry* **knight errantry**, courtly manners, knightliness, courtliness, nobility; bravery, courage, boldness, valour, heroism, daring, intrepidity.
– OPPOSITES rudeness.

chivvy v. **nag**, badger, hound, harass, harry, pester, keep on at, go on at; informal hassle, bug, breathe down someone's neck; N. Amer. informal ride.

choice n. **1** *their choice of candidate | freedom of choice* **selection**, election, choosing, picking; decision, say, vote. **2** *you have no other choice* **option**, alternative, possible course of action. **3** *an extensive choice of wines* **range**, variety, selection, assortment. **4** *the perfect choice* **appointee**, nominee, candidate, selection.
▶ adj. **1** *choice plums* **superior**, first-class,

C

first-rate, prime, premier, grade A, best, finest, excellent, select, quality, high-quality, top, top-quality, top-tier, high-grade, prize, fine, special; hand-picked, carefully chosen; informal tip-top, A1, top-notch. **2** *a few choice words* **rude**, abusive, insulting, offensive.
– OPPOSITES inferior.

choir n. **singers**, chorus; US chorale.

> **WORD LINKS**
> **choral** relating to a choir
> **chorister** a member of a church choir

choke v. **1** *Christopher started to choke* **gag**, retch, cough, fight for breath. **2** *thick dust choked her* **suffocate**, asphyxiate, smother, stifle. **3** *she had been choked to death* **strangle**, throttle; asphyxiate, suffocate; informal strangulate. **4** *the guttering was choked with leaves* **clog (up)**, bung up, stop up, block, obstruct, plug; technical occlude.
□ **choke something back** suppress, hold back, fight back, bite back, swallow, check, restrain, control, repress, smother, stifle; informal keep a/the lid on.

choleric adj. **bad-tempered**, irascible, irritable, grumpy, grouchy, crotchety, tetchy, testy, crusty, cantankerous, curmudgeonly, ill-tempered, peevish, cross, fractious, crabbed, crabby, waspish, prickly, peppery, touchy, short-tempered; informal snappish, snappy, chippy, short-fused; Brit. informal shirty, stroppy, narky, ratty; N. Amer. informal cranky, ornery, soreheaded; Austral./NZ informal snaky.
– OPPOSITES good-natured, affable.

choose v. **1** *we chose a quiet country hotel* **select**, pick (out), opt for, plump for, settle on, decide on, fix on; appoint, name, nominate, vote for. **2** *I'll stay as long as I choose* **wish**, want, desire, feel/be inclined, please, like, see fit.

choosy adj. informal **fussy**, finicky, fastidious, over-particular, difficult/hard to please, exacting, demanding; informal picky, pernickety; N. Amer. informal persnickety; old use nice.

chop v. **1** *chop the potatoes into pieces* **cut up**, cut into pieces, chop up, cube, dice; N. Amer. hash. **2** *chopping wood* **chop up**, cut up, cut into pieces, hew, split. **3** *four fingers were chopped off* **sever**, cut off, hack off, slice off, lop off, saw off, shear off. **4** *they chopped down large areas of rainforest* **cut down**, fell, hack down. **5** informal *their training courses were chopped* **reduce drastically**, cut; abolish, axe, scrap; informal slash.
□ **the chop** Brit. informal notice; informal the sack, the boot, the elbow, the push, one's marching orders; Brit. informal one's cards.

chopper n. Brit. **axe**, cleaver, hatchet.

choppy adj. **rough**, turbulent, heavy, heaving, stormy, tempestuous, squally.
– OPPOSITES calm.

chore n. **task**, job, duty, errand; (**chores**) (domestic) work.

chortle v. **chuckle**, laugh, giggle, titter, tee-hee, snigger.

chorus n. **1** *the chorus sang powerfully* **choir**, ensemble, choral group, choristers, (group of) singers. **2** *they sang the chorus* **refrain**.
□ **in chorus** in unison, together, simultaneously, as one; in concert, in harmony.

christen v. **1** *she was christened Sara* **baptize**, name, give the name of, call. **2** *a group who were christened 'The Magic Circle'* **call**, name, dub, style, term, designate, label, nickname, give the name of; formal denominate.

chronic adj. **1** *a chronic illness* **persistent**, long-standing, long-term; incurable. **2** *chronic economic problems* **constant**, continuing, ceaseless, unabating, unending, persistent, long-lasting; severe, serious, acute, grave, dire. **3** *a chronic liar* **inveterate**, hardened, dyed-in-the-wool, incorrigible; compulsive; informal pathological. **4** Brit. informal *the film was chronic*. See **substandard**.
– OPPOSITES acute, temporary.

chronicle n. *a chronicle of the region's past* **record**, written account, history, annals, archive(s); log, diary, journal.
▶ v. *the events that followed have been chronicled* **record**, put on record, write down, set down, document, register, report.

chronicler n. **annalist**, historian, archivist, diarist, recorder, reporter.

chronological adj. **sequential**, consecutive, in sequence, in order (of time).

chubby adj. **plump**, tubby, fat, rotund, portly, dumpy, chunky, well upholstered, well covered, well rounded; informal roly-poly, pudgy, blubbery; Brit. informal podgy; N. Amer. informal zaftig, corn-fed; old use pursy.
– OPPOSITES skinny.

chuck v. informal **1** *he chucked the letter onto the table* **throw**, toss, fling, hurl, pitch, cast, lob; informal sling, bung, buzz; Austral. informal hoy; NZ informal bish. **2** *I chucked the rubbish* **throw away/out**, discard, dispose of, get rid of, dump, bin, scrap, jettison; informal ditch, junk; N. Amer. informal trash. **3** *I've chucked my job* **give up**, leave, resign from; informal quit, pack in; Brit. informal jack in. **4** *Mary chucked him for another guy* **leave**, throw over, finish with, break off with, jilt; informal dump, ditch, give someone the elbow; Brit. informal give someone the push, give someone the big E.

chuckle v. **chortle**, giggle, titter, tee-hee, snicker, snigger.

chum n. informal **friend**, companion, intimate; playmate, classmate, schoolmate, workmate; informal pal, spar, crony; Brit. informal mate, oppo, china, mucker; N. Amer. informal buddy, amigo, compadre, homeboy.
– OPPOSITES enemy, stranger.

chummy adj. informal **friendly**, on good terms, close, familiar, intimate; informal thick, matey, pally, buddy-buddy, palsy-walsy.

chunk n. **lump**, hunk, wedge, block, slab, square, nugget, brick, cube, bar, cake; informal wodge; N. Amer. informal gob.

chunky adj. **1** *a chunky young man* **stocky**, sturdy, thickset, heavily built, well built,

burly, bulky, brawny, solid, heavy; Austral./NZ nuggety; Brit. informal fubsy. **2** *a chunky sweater* **thick**, bulky, heavy-knit.
– OPPOSITES slight, light.

church n. **1** *a village church* **place of worship**, house of God; cathedral, minster, abbey, chapel, basilica; Scottish & N. English kirk. **2** *the Methodist Church* **denomination**, sect, creed; faith.

> **WORD LINKS**
>
> **ecclesiastical** relating to the Christian Church
> **liturgy** a set form of public Christian worship
> **synod** an official meeting of ministers etc. of a Christian Church
> **canon law** the laws of the Christian Church
> **consistory** (in the Church of England) a court presided over by a bishop
> **excommunicate** officially bar someone from the sacraments of the Christian Church

churchyard n. **graveyard**, cemetery, necropolis, burial ground, garden of remembrance; Scottish kirkyard; N. Amer. memorial park; old use God's acre.

churlish adj. **rude**, ill-mannered, ill-bred, discourteous, impolite, unmannerly, uncivil, unchivalrous; inconsiderate, uncharitable, surly, sullen; informal ignorant.
– OPPOSITES polite.

churn v. **1** *village girls churned the milk* **stir**, agitate, beat, whip, whisk. **2** *the sea churned* **heave**, boil, swirl, toss, seethe; literary roil. **3** *the propellers churned up the water* **disturb**, stir up, agitate; literary roil.
□ **churn something out** produce, make, turn out; informal crank out, bang out.

chute n. **1** *a refuse chute* **channel**, slide, shaft, funnel, conduit. **2** *water chutes* **(water) slide**, flume.

cigarette n. filter tip, king-size; informal ciggy, cig, smoke, cancer stick, coffin nail; Brit. informal fag, snout, roll-up.

cinch n. informal **1** *it's a cinch* **easy task**, child's play, five-finger exercise, gift, walkover; informal doddle, piece of cake, walk in the park, picnic, breeze, kids' stuff, cakewalk, pushover; Brit. informal doss; N. Amer. informal duck soup, snap; Austral./NZ informal bludge, snack; dated snip. **2** *he was a cinch to take a prize* **certainty**, sure thing; Brit. informal (dead) cert.
– OPPOSITES challenge.

cinders plural n. **ashes**, ash, embers.

cinema n. **1** *the local cinema* multiplex, cinematheque; N. Amer. movie theatre/house; dated picture palace/theatre; historical nickelodeon. **2** *I hardly ever go to the cinema* **the pictures**, the movies; informal the flicks. **3** *British cinema* **films**, movies, pictures, motion pictures.

cipher n. **1** *information in cipher* **code**, secret writing, cryptograph. **2** *working as a cipher* **nobody**, nonentity, unimportant person. **3** dated *a row of ciphers* **zero**, nought, nil, O.

circa prep. **approximately**, (round) about, around, in the region of, roughly, of the order of, or so, or thereabouts, more or less; informal as near as dammit; N. Amer. informal in the ballpark of.
– OPPOSITES exactly.

circle n. **1** *a circle of gold stars* **ring**, band, hoop, circlet; halo, disc; technical annulus. **2** *her circle of friends* **group**, set, company, coterie, clique; crowd, band; informal gang, bunch, crew. **3** *illustrious circles* **sphere**, world, milieu; society.
▶ v. **1** *seagulls circled above* **wheel**, move round, revolve, rotate, whirl, spiral. **2** *satellites circling the earth* **go round**, travel round, circumnavigate; orbit, revolve round. **3** *the abbey was circled by a wall* **surround**, encircle, ring, enclose, encompass; literary gird.

circuit n. **1** *two circuits of the village green* **lap**, turn, round, circle. **2** Brit. *a racing circuit* **track**, racetrack, running track, course. **3** *the judge's circuit* **tour (of duty)**, rounds.

circuitous adj. **1** *a rather circuitous route* **roundabout**, indirect, winding, meandering, serpentine. **2** *a circuitous discussion* **indirect**, oblique, roundabout, circumlocutory, periphrastic.
– OPPOSITES direct.

circular adj. *a circular window* **round**, disc-shaped, ring-shaped, annular.
▶ n. *a free circular* **leaflet**, pamphlet, handbill, flyer; N. Amer. mailer, folder, dodger.

circulate v. **1** *the news was widely circulated* **spread (about/around)**, communicate, disseminate, make known, make public, broadcast, publicize, advertise; distribute, give out, pass around. **2** *fresh air circulates freely* **flow**, course, move round. **3** *they circulated among their guests* **socialize**, mingle.

circumference n. **1** *the circumference of the pit* **perimeter**, border, boundary; edge, rim, verge, margin, fringe; literary marge, bourn. **2** *the circumference of his arm* **girth**, width.

circumlocution n. **periphrasis**, discursiveness, long-windedness, verbosity, verbiage, wordiness, prolixity, redundancy, pleonasm, tautology, repetitiveness, repetitiousness.

circumscribe v. **restrict**, limit, keep within bounds, curb, confine, restrain; regulate, control.

circumspect adj. **cautious**, wary, careful, chary, guarded, on one's guard; watchful, alert, attentive, heedful, vigilant, leery; informal cagey, playing one's cards close to one's chest.
– OPPOSITES unguarded.

circumstances plural n. **1** *favourable economic circumstances* **situation**, conditions, state of affairs, position; (turn of) events, incidents, occurrences, happenings; factors, context, background, environment; informal circs. **2** *Jane explained the circumstances to him* **the facts**, the details, the particulars, how things stand, the lie of the land; Brit. the state of play; N. Amer. the lay of the land; informal what's what, the score. **3** *reduced circumstances* **financial position**, lot, lifestyle; resources, means, finances, income; dated station in life.

c

circumstantial adj. **1** *they have only circumstantial evidence* **indirect**, inferred, deduced, conjectural; inconclusive, unprovable. **2** *the picture was so circumstantial that it began to be convincing* **detailed**, particularized, comprehensive, thorough, exhaustive; explicit, specific.

circumvent v. **avoid**, get round/past, evade, bypass, sidestep, dodge; N. Amer. end-run; informal duck.

cistern n. **tank**, reservoir, container, butt.

citadel n. **fortress**, fort, stronghold, fortification, castle, burg; old use hold.

citation n. **1** *a citation from an eighteenth-century text* **quotation**, quote, extract, excerpt, passage, line; reference, allusion; N. Amer. cite. **2** *a citation for gallantry* **commendation**, (honourable) mention. **3** Law *a traffic citation* **summons**, subpoena, writ, court order.

cite v. **1** *cite the passage in full* **quote**, reproduce. **2** *he cited the case of Leigh v. Gladstone* **refer to**, make reference to, mention, allude to, adduce, instance; specify, name. **3** *he has been cited many times* **commend**, pay tribute to, praise.

citizen n. **1** *a British citizen* **subject**, national, passport holder, native. **2** *the citizens of Edinburgh* **inhabitant**, resident, native, townsman, townswoman; formal denizen; old use burgher; Brit. old use burgess.

city n. **town**, municipality, metropolis, megalopolis; conurbation, urban area, metropolitan area; Scottish burgh; informal big smoke; N. Amer. informal burg.

> WORD LINKS
> civic, metropolitan, urban relating to a city

civic adj. **municipal**, city, town, urban, metropolitan; public, civil, community.

civil adj. **1** *a civil marriage* **secular**, non-religious, lay; formal laic. **2** *civil aviation* **non-military**, civilian. **3** *a civil war* **internal**, domestic, interior, national. **4** *he behaved in a civil manner* **polite**, courteous, well mannered, well bred, gentlemanly, chivalrous, gallant, ladylike; cordial, genial, pleasant, affable.
– OPPOSITES religious, military, international, rude.

civilian n. **non-military person**, non-combatant, ordinary/private citizen; informal civvy.

civility n. **1** *he treated me with civility* **courtesy**, courteousness, politeness, good manners, graciousness, consideration, respect, politesse, comity. **2** *she didn't waste time on civilities* **polite remark**, politeness, courtesy; formality.
– OPPOSITES rudeness.

civilization n. **1** *a higher stage of civilization* **human development**, advancement, progress, enlightenment, culture, refinement, sophistication. **2** *ancient civilizations* **culture**, society, nation, people.

civilize v. **enlighten**, improve, educate, instruct, refine, cultivate, polish, socialize, humanize; informal edify.

civilized adj. **polite**, courteous, well mannered, civil, gentlemanly, ladylike, mannerly; cultured, cultivated, refined, polished, sophisticated; enlightened, educated, advanced, developed.
– OPPOSITES rude, unsophisticated.

civil servant n. **public servant**, government official; bureaucrat, mandarin, official, administrator, functionary.

clad adj. **dressed**, clothed, attired, got up, garbed, rigged out, costumed; wearing, sporting; old use apparelled.

claim v. **1** *Davies claimed that she was lying* **assert**, declare, profess, maintain, state, hold, affirm, avow; argue, contend, allege; formal aver; old use avouch. **2** *no one claimed the items* **lay claim to**, assert ownership of, formally request. **3** *you can claim compensation* **request**, ask for, apply for; demand, exact. **4** *the fire claimed four lives* **take**, cause/result in the loss of.
> n. **1** *her claims that she was raped* **assertion**, declaration, profession, affirmation, avowal, protestation; contention, allegation. **2** *a claim for damages* **request**, application; demand, petition. **3** *we have first claim on their assets* **entitlement to**, title to, right to.

claimant n. **applicant**, candidate, supplicant; petitioner, plaintiff, litigant, appellant.

clairvoyance n. **second sight**, psychic powers, ESP, extrasensory perception, sixth sense; telepathy.

clairvoyant n. **psychic**, fortune teller, crystal-gazer; medium, spiritualist; telepathist, telepath, mind reader.
> adj. *I'm not clairvoyant* **psychic**, having second sight, having a sixth sense; telepathic.

clamber v. **scramble**, climb, scrabble, claw one's way.

clammy adj. **1** *his clammy hands* **moist**, damp, sweaty, sticky; slimy, slippery. **2** *the clammy atmosphere* **damp**, dank, wet; humid, close, muggy, heavy.
– OPPOSITES dry.

clamorous adj. **noisy**, loud, vocal, vociferous, raucous, rowdy; importunate, demanding, insistent, vehement.
– OPPOSITES quiet.

clamour n. **1** *her voice rose above the clamour* **din**, racket, rumpus, loud noise, uproar, tumult, shouting, yelling, screaming, baying, roaring; commotion, brouhaha, hue and cry, hubbub; informal hullabaloo; Brit. informal row. **2** *the clamour for her resignation* **demand(s)**, call(s), urging. **3** *the clamour of protectionists* **protests**, complaints, outcry.
> v. **1** *clamouring crowds* **yell**, shout loudly, bay, scream, roar. **2** *scientists are clamouring for a ban* **demand**, call, press, push, lobby.

clamp n. **1** *a clamp was holding the wood* **brace**, vice, press, clasp; Music capo (tasto); Climbing jumar. **2** *clamps had been fitted to the car* **immobilizer**, wheel clamp; N. Amer. boot.
> v. **1** *the sander is clamped on to the workbench*

fasten, secure, fix, attach; screw, bolt. **2** *a pipe was clamped between his teeth* **clench**, grip, hold, press, clasp. **3** *his car was clamped* **immobilize**, wheel-clamp; N. Amer. boot.
□ **clamp down on** suppress, prevent, stop, put a stop/end to, stamp out; crack down on, limit, restrict, control, keep in check.

clampdown n. informal **suppression**, prevention, stamping out; crackdown, restriction, restraint, curb, check.

clan n. **1** *the Macleod clan* **group of families**, sept; family, house, dynasty, tribe; Anthropology sib, kinship group. **2** *a clan of art collectors* **group**, set, circle, clique, coterie; crowd, band; informal gang, bunch.

clandestine adj. **secret**, covert, furtive, surreptitious, stealthy, cloak-and-dagger, hole-and-corner, closet, backstairs, hugger-mugger; Military black; informal hush-hush.

clang n. *the clang of the church bells* **reverberation**, ringing, ring, ding-dong, bong, peal, chime, toll.
▶ v. *the huge bells clanged* **reverberate**, resound, ring, bong, peal, chime, toll.

clanger n. Brit. informal See **blunder** (noun).

clank n. *the clank of rusty chains* **jangling**, clanging, rattling, clinking, jingling; clang, jangle, rattle, clangour, clink, jingle.
▶ v. *I could hear the chain clanking* **jangle**, rattle, clink, clang, jingle.

clannish adj. **cliquey**, cliquish, insular, exclusive; unfriendly, unwelcoming.

clap v. **1** *the audience clapped* **applaud**, clap one's hands, give someone a round of applause, put one's hands together; informal give someone a (big) hand; N. Amer. informal give it up. **2** *he clapped Owen on the back* **slap**, strike, hit, smack, thump; pat; informal whack, thwack. **3** *the dove clapped its wings* **flap**, beat, flutter.
▶ n. **1** *everybody gave him a clap* **round of applause**, handclap; informal hand. **2** *a clap on the shoulder* **slap**, blow, smack, thump; pat; informal whack, thwack. **3** *a clap of thunder* **crack**, crash, bang, boom; thunderclap.

claptrap n. See **nonsense** (sense 1).

clarify v. **1** *their report clarified the situation* **make clear**, shed/throw light on, elucidate, illuminate; **explain**, explicate, define, spell out, clear up. **2** *clarified butter* **purify**, refine; filter, fine.
– OPPOSITES confuse.

clarity n. **1** *the clarity of his account* **lucidity**, clearness, coherence; formal perspicuity. **2** *the clarity of the image* **sharpness**, clearness, crispness, definition. **3** *the crystal clarity of the water* **limpidity**, limpidness, clearness, transparency, translucence, pellucidity.
– OPPOSITES vagueness, blurriness, opacity.

clash n. **1** *clashes between armed gangs* **confrontation**, skirmish, fight, battle, engagement, encounter, conflict. **2** *an angry clash* **argument**, altercation, confrontation, shouting match; contretemps, quarrel, disagreement, dispute; Brit. slanging match; informal run-in; Brit. informal, Football afters. **3** *a clash of tweeds and a striped shirt* **mismatch**,

discordance, discord, lack of harmony. **4** *a clash of dates* **coincidence**, concurrence; conflict. **5** *the clash of cymbals* **striking**, bang, clang, crash.
▶ v. **1** *protesters clashed with police* **fight**, skirmish, contend, come to blows, come into conflict; do battle. **2** *the prime minister clashed with union leaders* **disagree**, differ, wrangle, dispute, cross swords, lock horns, be at loggerheads. **3** *her red coat clashed with her hair* **be incompatible**, not match, not go, be discordant. **4** *the dates clash* **conflict**, coincide, occur simultaneously. **5** *she clashed the cymbals together* **bang**, strike, clang, crash.

clasp v. **1** *Ruth clasped his hand* **grasp**, grip, clutch, hold tightly; take hold of, seize, grab. **2** *he clasped Joanne in his arms* **embrace**, hug, enfold, fold, envelop; hold, squeeze.
▶ n. **1** *a gold clasp* **fastener**, fastening, catch, clip, pin; buckle, hasp. **2** *his tight clasp* **embrace**, hug, cuddle; grip, grasp.

class n. **1** *a hotel of the first class* **category**, grade, rating, classification, group, grouping. **2** *a new class of heart drug* **kind**, sort, type, variety, genre, brand; species, genus, breed, strain; N. Amer. stripe. **3** *the middle class* **social division**, social stratum, rank, level, echelon, group, grouping; social status; dated estate; old use condition. **4** *there are 30 pupils in the class* **form**, study group, set, stream. **5** *a maths class* **lesson**, period; seminar, tutorial, workshop. **6** informal *a woman of class* **style**, stylishness, elegance, chic, sophistication, taste, refinement, quality, excellence.
▶ v. *the 12-seater is classed as a commercial vehicle* **classify**, categorize, group, grade; order, sort, codify; bracket, designate, label, pigeonhole.
▶ adj. informal *a class player.* See **excellent**.

classic adj. **1** *the classic work on the subject* **definitive**, authoritative; outstanding, first-rate, first-class, best, finest, excellent, superior, masterly. **2** *a classic example of Norman design* **typical**, archetypal, quintessential, vintage; model, representative, perfect, prime, textbook. **3** *a classic style* **simple**, elegant, understated; traditional, timeless, ageless.
– OPPOSITES atypical.
▶ n. *a classic of the genre* **definitive example**, model, epitome, paradigm, exemplar; great work, masterpiece.

classical adj. **1** *classical mythology* **ancient Greek**, Hellenic, Attic; Latin, ancient Roman. **2** *classical music* **traditional**, long-established; serious, highbrow, heavyweight. **3** *a classical style* **simple**, pure, restrained, plain, austere; well proportioned, harmonious, balanced, symmetrical, elegant.
– OPPOSITES modern.

classification n. **1** *the classification of diseases* **categorization**, categorizing, classifying, grouping, grading, ranking, organization, sorting, codification, systematization. **2** *a series of classifications* **category**, class, group, grouping, grade, grading, ranking, bracket.

C

classify v. **categorize**, group, grade, rank, rate, order, organize, range, sort, type, codify, bracket, systematize, systemize; catalogue, list, file, index; old use assort.

classy adj. informal **stylish**, high-class, superior, exclusive, chic, elegant, smart, sophisticated; Brit. upmarket; N. Amer. high-toned; informal posh, ritzy, plush, swanky; Brit. informal swish.

clatter v. **rattle**, clank, clink, clunk, clang.

clause n. **section**, paragraph, article, subsection; stipulation, condition, proviso, rider.

claw n. **1** *a bird's claw* **talon**, nail; technical unguis. **2** *a crab's claw* **pincer**, nipper; technical chela.

▸ v. *her fingers clawed his shoulders* **scratch**, lacerate, tear, rip, scrape, graze, dig into.

clay n. **1** *the soil is mainly clay* **earth**, soil, loam. **2** *potter's clay* argil, china clay, kaolin, adobe, ball clay, pug; fireclay.

clean adj. **1** *keep the wound clean* **washed**, scrubbed, cleansed, cleaned; spotless, unsoiled, unstained, unsullied, unblemished, immaculate, pristine, dirt-free, as clean as a whistle; hygienic, sanitary, disinfected, sterilized, sterile, aseptic, decontaminated; laundered; informal squeaky clean. **2** *a clean sheet of paper* **blank**, empty, clear, plain; unused, new, pristine, fresh, unmarked. **3** *clean air* **pure**, clear, fresh, crisp, refreshing; unpolluted, uncontaminated. **4** *a clean life* **virtuous**, good, upright, upstanding; honourable, respectable, reputable, decent, righteous, moral, exemplary; innocent, pure, chaste; informal squeaky clean. **5** *the firm is clean* **innocent**, guiltless, blameless, guilt-free, crime-free, above suspicion; informal squeaky clean. **6** *a good clean fight* **fair**, honest, sporting, sportsmanlike, honourable, according to the rules; informal on the level. **7** informal *they are trying to stay clean* **sober**, teetotal, dry, non-drinking; **drug-free**, off drugs; informal on the wagon. **8** *a clean cut* **neat**, smooth, crisp, straight, precise. **9** *a clean break* **complete**, thorough, total, absolute, conclusive, decisive, final, irrevocable. **10** *clean lines* **simple**, elegant, graceful, streamlined, smooth.

– OPPOSITES dirty, polluted.

▸ adv. informal *I clean forgot* **completely**, entirely, totally, fully, quite, utterly, absolutely.

▸ v. **1** *Dad cleaned the windows* **wash**, cleanse, wipe, sponge, scrub, mop, rinse, scour, swab, hose down, sluice (down), disinfect; shampoo; literary lave. **2** *I got my clothes cleaned* **launder**, dry-clean. **3** *she cleaned the fish* **gut**, draw, dress; formal eviscerate.

– OPPOSITES dirty.

□ **come clean** informal tell the truth, tell all, make a clean breast of it; confess, own up, admit guilt, admit to one's crimes/sins; informal fess up.

cleanse v. **1** *the wound was cleansed* **clean (up)**, wash, bathe, rinse, disinfect. **2** *cleansing the environment of traces of lead*

rid, clear, free, purify, purge. **3** *only God can cleanse us from sin* **purify**, purge, absolve, free; deliver.

clear adj. **1** *he gave clear instructions* **understandable**, comprehensible, intelligible, plain, uncomplicated, explicit, lucid, coherent, simple, straightforward, unambiguous, clear-cut, crystal clear; formal perspicuous. **2** *a clear case of harassment* **obvious**, evident, plain, crystal clear; sure, definite, unmistakable, manifest, indisputable, patent, incontrovertible, irrefutable, beyond doubt, beyond question; palpable, visible, discernible, conspicuous, overt, blatant, glaring; as plain as a pikestaff, as plain as day; informal as plain as the nose on one's face. **3** *clear water* **transparent**, limpid, pellucid, translucent, crystal clear; unclouded. **4** *a clear blue sky* **bright**, cloudless, unclouded, without a cloud in the sky. **5** *her clear complexion* **unblemished**, spot-free. **6** *Rosa's clear voice* **distinct**, bell-like, as clear as a bell. **7** *the road was clear* | *a clear view* **unobstructed**, unblocked, passable, open; unrestricted, unhindered. **8** *the algae were clear of toxins* **free**, devoid, without, unaffected by; rid, relieved. **9** *a clear conscience* **untroubled**, undisturbed, unperturbed, unconcerned, having no qualms; peaceful, at peace, tranquil, serene, calm, easy. **10** *two clear days' notice* **whole**, full, entire, complete.

– OPPOSITES vague, opaque, cloudy, obstructed.

▸ adv. **1** *stand clear of the doors* **away from**, apart from, at a (safe) distance from, out of contact with. **2** *Tommy's voice came loud and clear* **distinctly**, clearly, as clear as a bell, plainly, audibly. **3** *he has time to get clear away* **completely**, entirely, fully, wholly, totally, utterly; informal clean.

▸ v. **1** *the sky cleared briefly* **brighten (up)**, lighten, clear up, become bright/brighter/lighter, become fine/sunny. **2** *the drizzle had cleared* **disappear**, go away, end; peter out, fade, wear off, decrease, lessen, diminish. **3** *together they cleared the table* **empty**, unload, unburden, strip. **4** *clearing drains* **unblock**, unstop. **5** *staff cleared the building* **evacuate**, empty; leave. **6** *Karen cleared the dirty plates* **remove**, take away, carry away, tidy away/up. **7** *I'm clearing my debts* **pay (off)**, repay, settle, discharge. **8** *I cleared the bar at my first attempt* **go over**, pass over, sail over; jump (over), vault (over), leap (over), hurdle. **9** *he was cleared by an appeal court* **acquit**, declare innocent, find not guilty; absolve, exonerate; informal let off (the hook); formal exculpate. **10** *I was cleared to work on the atomic project* **authorize**, give permission, permit, allow, pass, accept, endorse, license, sanction, give approval/consent to; informal OK, give the OK, give the thumbs up, give the green light, give the go-ahead. **11** *I cleared £50,000 profit* **net**, make/realize a profit of, take home, pocket; gain, earn, make, get, bring in, pull in.

□ **clear off** informal go away, get out, leave; be

off with you, shoo, on your way; informal beat it, push off, shove off, scram, scoot, buzz off, clear out; Brit. informal hop it, sling your hook; Austral./NZ informal rack off; N. Amer. informal bug off, take a hike; literary begone.

clear something out 1 *we cleared out the junk room* **empty (out)**; tidy (up), clear up. **2** *clear out the rubbish* **get rid of**, throw out/away, discard, dispose of, dump, bin, scrap, jettison; informal chuck (out/away), ditch, get shut of; Brit. informal get shot of; N. Amer. informal trash.

clear up See **clear** (sense 1 of the verb).

clear something up 1 *clear up the garden* **tidy (up)**, put in order, straighten up, clean up, spruce up. **2** *we've cleared up the problem* **solve**, resolve, straighten out, find an/the answer to; get to the bottom of, explain; informal crack, figure out, suss out.

clearance n. **1** *slum clearance* **removal**, clearing, demolition. **2** *you must have Home Office clearance* **authorization**, permission, consent, approval, blessing, leave, sanction, licence, dispensation, assent, agreement, endorsement; informal the green light, the go-ahead, the thumbs up, the OK, the say-so. **3** *the clearance of a debt* **repayment**, payment, paying (off), settling, discharge. **4** *there is plenty of clearance* **space**, room (to spare), margin, leeway.

clear-cut adj. **definite**, distinct, clear, well defined, precise, specific, explicit, unambiguous, unequivocal, black and white, cut and dried.
– OPPOSITES vague.

clearing n. **glade**, dell, gap, opening.

clearly adv. **1** *write clearly* **intelligibly**, plainly, distinctly, comprehensibly, with clarity; legibly, audibly; formal perspicuously. **2** *clearly, substantial changes are needed* **obviously**, evidently, patently, unquestionably, undoubtedly, without doubt, indubitably, plainly, undeniably, incontrovertibly, irrefutably, doubtless, it goes without saying, needless to say.

cleave[1] v. **1** *cleaving wood for the fire* **split (open)**, cut (up), hew, hack, chop up; literary sunder; old use rive. **2** *cleaving a path through the traffic* **plough**, drive, bulldoze, carve.

cleave[2] v.
▫ **cleave to** literary **1** *her tongue clove to the roof of her mouth* **stick (fast) to**, adhere to, be attached to. **2** *cleaving too closely to Moscow's line* **adhere to**, hold to, abide by, be loyal/faithful to.

cleaver n. **chopper**, hatchet, axe, knife; butcher's knife, kitchen knife.

cleft n. **1** *a deep cleft in the rocks* **split**, slit, crack, fissure, crevice, rift, break, fracture, rent, breach. **2** *the cleft in his chin* **dimple**.
▸ adj. *a cleft tail* **split**, divided, cloven.

clemency n. **mercy**, mercifulness, leniency, lenience, mildness, indulgence, quarter; compassion, humanity, pity, sympathy.
– OPPOSITES ruthlessness.

clench v. **1** *he stood there clenching his hands* **squeeze together**, clamp together, close/

shut tightly; make into a fist. **2** *he clenched the back of the chair* **grip**, grasp, grab, clutch, clasp, hold tightly, seize, press, squeeze.

clergy n. **clergymen**, clergywomen, churchmen, churchwomen, clerics, priests, ecclesiastics, men/women of God; ministry, priesthood, holy orders, the church, the cloth.
– OPPOSITES laity.

> **WORD LINKS**
> **clerical** relating to the clergy
> **ordain** make someone a priest or minister
> **ordinand** a person preparing for ordination

clergyman, clergywoman n. **priest**, churchman, churchwoman, man/woman of the cloth, man/woman of God; cleric, minister, preacher, chaplain, father, ecclesiastic, bishop, pastor, vicar, rector, parson, curate, deacon, deaconess; Scottish kirkman; N. Amer. dominie; informal reverend, padre, Holy Joe, sky pilot; Austral. informal josser.

clerical adj. **1** *clerical jobs* **office**, desk, back-room; administrative, secretarial; white-collar. **2** *a clerical collar* **ecclesiastical**, church, priestly, religious, spiritual, sacerdotal; holy, divine.
– OPPOSITES secular.

clerk n. **office worker**, clerical worker, administrator; bookkeeper; cashier, teller; informal pen-pusher; historical scrivener.

clever adj. **1** *a clever young woman* **intelligent**, bright, smart, astute, quick-witted, shrewd; talented, gifted, brilliant, capable, able, competent, apt; educated, learned, knowledgeable, wise; informal brainy, savvy. **2** *a clever scheme* **ingenious**, canny, cunning, crafty, artful, slick, neat. **3** *she was clever with her hands* **skilful**, dexterous, adroit, adept, deft, nimble; skilled, talented, gifted. **4** *a clever remark* **witty**, amusing, droll, humorous, funny.
– OPPOSITES stupid.

cliché n. **platitude**, hackneyed phrase, commonplace, banality, truism, stock phrase, trite phrase; informal old chestnut; dated bromide.

click n. **clack**, snick, snap, pop, tick; clink.
▸ v. **1** *cameras clicked* **clack**, snap, snick, tick, pop; clink. **2** informal *that night it clicked* **become clear**, fall into place, come home, make sense, dawn, register, get through, sink in. **3** informal *we just clicked* **take to each other**, get along, be compatible, be like-minded, feel a rapport, be on the same wavelength, see eye to eye; informal hit it off, get on like a house on fire. **4** informal *this issue hasn't clicked with the voters* **go down well**, prove popular, be a hit, succeed.

client n. **customer**, buyer, purchaser, shopper, consumer, user; patient; patron, regular; (**clients**) clientele, patronage, public, market; Brit. informal punter; Law vendee.

clientele n. **clients**. See **client**.

cliff n. **precipice**, rock face, crag, bluff, ridge, escarpment, scar, scarp, overhang.

C

climactic adj. **final**, ending, closing, concluding, ultimate; exciting, thrilling, gripping, riveting, dramatic, hair-raising; crucial, decisive, critical.

climate n. **1** *a mild climate* **weather conditions**, weather; atmospheric conditions. **2** *they come from colder climates* **region**, area, zone, country, place; literary clime. **3** *the political climate* **atmosphere**, mood, feeling, ambience, tenor; tendency, ethos, attitude, milieu; informal vibe(s).

climax n. **1** *the climax of his career* **peak**, pinnacle, height, high(est) point, top; acme, zenith; culmination, crowning point, crown, crest; highlight, high spot, high water mark. **2 orgasm**; ejaculation.
– OPPOSITES nadir.
▸ v. *the event will climax with a concert* **culminate**, peak, reach a pinnacle, come to a crescendo, come to a head.

climb v. **1** *we climbed the hill* **ascend**, mount, scale, scramble up, clamber up, shin up; go up, walk up; conquer, gain. **2** *the plane climbed* **rise**, ascend, go up, gain altitude. **3** *the road climbs steeply* **slope upwards**, rise, go uphill, incline upwards. **4** *the shares climbed to 550 pence* **increase**, rise, go up; shoot up, soar, rocket. **5** *he climbed through the ranks* **advance**, rise, move up, progress, work one's way. **6** *he climbed out of his car* **clamber**, scramble; step.
– OPPOSITES descend, drop, fall.
▸ n. *a steep climb* **ascent**, clamber.
– OPPOSITES descent.
□ **climb down 1** *Sandy climbed down the ladder* **descend**, go/come down, move down, shin down. **2** *the Government had to climb down* **back down**, admit defeat, surrender, capitulate, yield, give in, give way, submit; retreat, backtrack; eat one's words, eat humble pie; do a U-turn, row back; Brit. do an about-turn; N. Amer. informal eat crow.

clinch v. **1** *he clinched the deal* **secure**, settle, conclude, close, pull off, bring off, complete, confirm, seal, finalize; informal sew up, wrap up. **2** *these findings clinched the matter* **settle**, decide, determine; resolve; informal sort out. **3** *they clinched the title* **win**, secure; be victorious, come first, triumph, prevail. **4** *they clinch every nail* **secure**, fasten, fix, pinion. **5** *the boxers clinched* **grapple**, wrestle, struggle, scuffle.
– OPPOSITES lose.
▸ n. *a passionate clinch* **embrace**, hug, cuddle, squeeze, hold, clasp.

cling v. *rice grains tend to cling together* **stick**, adhere, hold, cohere, bond, bind.
□ **cling (on) to 1** *she clung to him* **hold on**, clutch, grip, grasp, clasp, attach oneself to, hang on; embrace, hug. **2** *they clung to their beliefs* **adhere to**, hold to, stick to, stand by, abide by, cherish, remain true to, have faith in; informal swear by, stick with.

clinic n. **medical centre**, health centre, outpatients' department, surgery, doctor's.

clinical adj. **1** *he seemed so clinical* **detached**, impersonal, dispassionate,

objective, uninvolved, distant, remote, aloof, removed, cold, indifferent, neutral, unsympathetic, unfeeling, unemotional. **2** *the room was clinical* **plain**, simple, unadorned, unembellished, stark, austere, spartan, bleak, bare; clean; functional, basic, institutional, impersonal, characterless.
– OPPOSITES emotional, luxurious.

clip¹ n. **1** *a briefcase clip* **fastener**, clasp, hasp, catch, hook, buckle, lock. **2** *a diamanté clip* **brooch**, pin, badge. **3** *his clip was empty* **magazine**, cartridge, cylinder.
▸ v. *he clipped the pages together* **fasten**, attach, fix, join; pin, staple, tack.

clip² v. **1** *I clipped the hedge* **trim**, prune, cut, snip, shorten, crop, shear, pare; lop; neaten, shape. **2** *clip the coupon below* **remove**, cut out, snip out, tear out, detach. **3** *his lorry clipped a van* **hit**, strike, touch, graze, glance off, run into. **4** *Mum clipped his ear* **hit**, cuff, strike, smack, slap, box; informal clout, whack, wallop, clobber, biff, sock.
▸ n. **1** *I gave the dog a clip* **trim**, cut, crop, haircut; shear. **2** *a film clip* **extract**, excerpt, snippet, cutting, fragment; trailer. **3** informal *a clip round the ear* **smack**, cuff, slap, box; informal clout, whack, wallop, biff, sock. **4** informal *the truck went at a good clip* **speed**, rate, pace, velocity; informal lick.

clipping n. **cutting**, snippet, extract, excerpt.

clique n. **coterie**, set, circle, ring, in-crowd, group; club, society, fraternity, sorority; cabal, caucus; informal gang.

cloak n. **1** *the cloak over his shoulders* **cape**, robe, mantle, shawl, pashmina, wrap, stole, tippet; poncho, serape, djellaba; cope. **2** *a cloak of secrecy* **cover**, veil, mantle, shroud, screen, mask, shield, blanket.
▸ v. *a peak cloaked in mist* **conceal**, hide, cover, veil, shroud, mask, obscure, cloud; envelop, swathe, surround.

clobber¹ n. Brit. informal *get your clobber on.* See **clothes**.

clobber² v. informal *I'll clobber him.* See **hit** (sense 1 of the verb).

clock n. **1** *a grandfather clock* **timepiece**, timekeeper, timer; chronometer, chronograph. **2** informal *the car had 50,000 miles on the clock* **milometer**, counter; taximeter.
▸ v. informal **1** *the UK clocked up record exports* **register**, record, log, notch up; achieve, attain, accomplish, make; informal chalk up, bag. **2** Brit. *Liz soon clocked the change.* See **notice** (verb).

clod n. **1** *clods of earth* **lump**, clump, chunk, hunk, wedge. **2** informal *an insensitive clod.* See **idiot**.

clog n. *a wooden clog* sabot.
▸ v. *the pipes were clogged* **block**, obstruct, congest, jam, choke, bung up, plug, stop up, fill up; Brit. informal gunge up.

cloister n. **1** *the convent cloisters* **walkway**, covered walk, arcade, loggia, gallery. **2** *I was educated in the cloister* **abbey**, monastery, friary, convent, priory, nunnery.
▸ v. *they were cloistered at home* **confine**,

isolate, shut away, sequester, seclude, closet.

cloistered adj. **secluded**, sequestered, sheltered, protected, insulated; shut off, isolated, confined; solitary, monastic, reclusive.

close[1] adj. **1** *the town is close to Leeds* **near**, adjacent; in the vicinity of, in the neighbourhood of, within reach of; neighbouring, adjoining, abutting, alongside, on the doorstep, a stone's throw away; nearby, at hand, at close quarters; informal within spitting distance; old use nigh. **2** *flying in close formation* **dense**, compact, tight, close-packed, packed, solid; crowded, cramped, congested. **3** *I was close to tears* **near**, on the verge of, on the brink of, on the point of. **4** *a very close match* **evenly matched**, even, with nothing to choose between them, neck and neck, nip and tuck; informal fifty-fifty, even-steven(s). **5** *close relatives* **immediate**, direct, near. **6** *close friends* **intimate**, dear, bosom; close-knit, inseparable, attached, devoted, faithful; special, good, best, fast, firm; informal (as) thick as thieves. **7** *a close resemblance* **strong**, marked, distinct, pronounced. **8** *a close examination* **careful**, detailed, thorough, minute, searching, painstaking, meticulous, rigorous, scrupulous, conscientious; attentive, focused. **9** *keep a close eye on them* **vigilant**, watchful, keen, alert. **10** *a close translation* **strict**, faithful, exact, precise, literal; word for word, verbatim. **11** *he's close about his deals* **reticent**, secretive, uncommunicative, unforthcoming, tight-lipped, guarded, evasive. **12** *Sylvie was close with money* **mean**, miserly, niggardly, parsimonious, penny-pinching; informal tight-fisted, stingy, tight. **13** *the weather was close* **humid**, muggy, stuffy, airless, heavy, sticky, sultry, oppressive, stifling.
– OPPOSITES far, distant, one-sided, slight, loose, generous, fresh.
▸ n. Brit. *a small close of houses* **cul-de-sac**, street, road; courtyard, quadrangle, enclosure.

close[2] v. **1** *she closed the door* **shut**, pull to, push to, slam; fasten, secure. **2** *close the hole* **block (up/off)**, stop up, plug, seal (up/off), shut up/off, cork, stopper, bung (up); clog (up), choke, obstruct. **3** *the enemy were closing fast* **catch up**, creep up, near, approach, gain ground. **4** *the gap is closing* **narrow**, reduce, shrink, lessen, get smaller, diminish, contract. **5** *his arms closed around her* **meet**, join, connect; form a circle. **6** *he closed the meeting* **end**, conclude, finish, terminate, wind up, break off, halt, discontinue, dissolve; adjourn, suspend. **7** *the factory is to close* **shut down**, close down, cease production, cease trading, be wound up, go out of business, go bankrupt, go into receivership, go into liquidation; informal fold, go to the wall, go bust. **8** *he closed a deal* **clinch**, settle, secure, seal, confirm, establish; transact, pull off, complete, conclude, fix, agree, finalize;

informal **wrap up**.
– OPPOSITES open, widen, begin.
▸ n. *the close of the talks* **end**, finish, conclusion, termination, cessation, completion, resolution; climax, denouement.
– OPPOSITES beginning.

closet n. *a clothes closet* **cupboard**, wardrobe, cabinet, locker.
▸ adj. *a closet gay* **secret**, covert, private; surreptitious, clandestine, underground, furtive.
▸ v. *David was closeted in his den* **shut away**, sequester, seclude, cloister, confine, isolate.

closure n. **closing down**, shutdown, winding up; termination, discontinuation, cessation, finish, conclusion; failure; informal folding.

clot n. **1** *blood clots* **lump**, clump, mass; thrombus, thrombosis, embolus; informal glob; Brit. informal gob. **2** Brit. informal *a clumsy clot.* See **fool** (sense 1 of the noun).
▸ v. *the blood is likely to clot* **coagulate**, set, congeal, curdle, thicken, solidify.

> **WORD LINKS**
>
> **coronary** a blockage of the blood flow to the heart, caused by a clot in an artery
> **embolectomy**, **thrombectomy** the surgical removal of a blood clot

cloth n. **1** *a maker of cloth* **fabric**, material, textile(s). **2** *a cloth to wipe the table* **rag**, wipe, duster, sponge; flannel, towel; Austral. washer; UK trademark J-cloth. **3** *a gentleman of the cloth* **the clergy**, the church, the priesthood, the ministry; clergymen, clerics, priests.

> **WORD LINKS**
>
> **draper**, **mercer** a person who sells cloth

clothe v. **1** *they were clothed in silk* **dress**, attire, robe, garb, array, costume, swathe, deck (out), turn out, fit out, rig (out); informal get up; old use apparel, habit, invest. **2** *a valley clothed in conifers* **cover**, blanket, carpet; envelop, swathe.

clothes plural n. **clothing**, garments, attire, garb, dress, wear, costume; informal gear, togs, duds, get-up, garms; Brit. informal clobber; N. Amer. informal threads; formal apparel; old use raiment, habiliments, vestments.

> **WORD LINKS**
>
> **sartorial** relating to clothes
> **clothier** a maker or seller of clothes
> **couturier** a person who designs and sells fashionable clothes
> **tailor** a person who makes men's clothes for individual customers
> **mannequin** a dummy used to display clothes in a shop window

clothing n. See **clothes**.

cloud n. **1** *dark clouds* **storm cloud**, cloud bank; mackerel sky. **2** *a cloud of exhaust smoke* **mass**, billow; pall, mantle, blanket. **3** *a cloud of rooks* **flock**, swarm, mass, multitude, host, throng, crowd.
▸ v. **1** *the sky clouded* **become overcast**, cloud over, lour, blacken, darken. **2** *the sand is*

churned up, clouding the water **make cloudy**, make murky, dirty, darken, blacken. **3** *anger clouded my judgement* **confuse**, muddle, obscure, fog, muddy, mar.

□ **on cloud nine** ecstatic, rapturous, joyful, elated, blissful, euphoric, in seventh heaven, walking on air, transported, in raptures, delighted, thrilled, overjoyed, very happy; informal over the moon, on top of the world; Austral. informal wrapped.

cloudy adj. **1** *a cloudy sky* **overcast**, clouded; dark, grey, black, leaden, murky; sombre, dismal, heavy, gloomy; sunless, starless; hazy, misty, foggy. **2** *cloudy water* **murky**, muddy, milky, dirty, opaque, turbid. **3** *his eyes grew cloudy* **tearful**, moist, watery; misty, blurred; informal teary, weepy; formal lachrymose. **4** *avoid cloudy phrases* **vague**, imprecise, foggy, hazy, confused, muddled, nebulous, obscure.
– OPPOSITES clear.

clout informal n. **1** *a clout on the ear* **smack**, slap, thump, punch, blow, hit, cuff, box, clip; informal whack, wallop. **2** *his clout in the business world* **influence**, power, weight, sway, leverage, control, say; dominance, authority; informal teeth, muscle.
▶v. *he clouted me* **hit**, strike, punch, smack, slap, cuff, thump, buffet; informal wallop, belt, whack, clobber, sock, bop, biff.

cloven adj. **split**, divided, cleft.

clown n. **1** *a circus clown* **comic entertainer**, comedian; historical jester, fool, zany; old use merry andrew. **2** *the class clown* **joker**, comedian, comic, humorist, wag, wit, prankster, jester, buffoon; informal laugh, kidder, wisecracker; Austral./NZ informal hard case. **3** *bureaucratic clowns* **fool**, idiot, dolt, ass, simpleton, ignoramus; bungler, blunderer; informal moron, jackass, chump, numbskull, nincompoop, halfwit, bonehead, fathead, birdbrain; Brit. informal prat, berk, twit, nitwit, twerp.
▶v. *Harvey clowned around* **fool around/about**, play the fool, play about/around, monkey about/around; joke, jest; informal mess about/around, lark (about/around), horse about/around; Brit. informal muck about/around; dated play the giddy goat.

cloy v. **sicken**, disgust; become sickening, become nauseating, pall; be excessive.

cloying adj. **sickly**, syrupy, saccharine, oversweet; sickening, nauseating; mushy, slushy, sloppy; mawkish, sentimental; Brit. twee; informal over the top, OTT, gooey, cheesy, corny; N. Amer. informal cornball, sappy.

club[1] n. **1** *a canoeing club* **society**, association, organization, institution, group, circle, band, body, ring, crew; alliance, league, union. **2** *the city has great clubs* **nightclub**, disco, discotheque, bar; informal niterie. **3** *the top club in the league* **team**, squad, side, line-up.
□ **club together** pool resources, join forces, team up, band together, get together, pull together, collaborate, ally; informal have a whip-round.

club[2] n. *a wooden club* **cudgel**, truncheon, bludgeon, baton, stick, mace, bat; N. Amer. blackjack, nightstick; Brit. informal cosh.
▶v. *he was clubbed with an iron bar* **cudgel**, bludgeon, bash, beat, hit, strike, batter, belabour; informal clout, clobber; Brit. informal cosh.

clue n. **1** *police are searching for clues* **hint**, indication, sign, signal, pointer, trace, indicator; lead, tip, tip-off; evidence, information. **2** *a crossword clue* **question**, problem, puzzle, riddle, poser, conundrum.
□ **clue someone in/up** informal inform, notify, make aware, prime; keep up to date, keep posted; informal tip off, give the low-down, fill in on, gen up on, put in the picture, put wise, keep up to speed.

not have a clue informal have no idea, be ignorant, not have an inkling; be baffled, be mystified, be at a loss; informal be clueless, not have the faintest.

clump n. **1** *a clump of trees* **cluster**, thicket, group, bunch, assemblage. **2** *a clump of earth* **lump**, clod, mass, gobbet, wad; informal glob; Brit. informal gob.
▶v. **1** *galaxies clump together* **cluster**, group, collect, gather, assemble, congregate, mass. **2** *they were clumping around upstairs* **stamp**, stomp, clomp, tramp, lumber; thump, thud, bang; informal galumph.

clumsy adj. **1** *she was terribly clumsy* **awkward**, uncoordinated, ungainly, graceless, inelegant; inept, maladroit, unskilful, unhandy, accident-prone, like a bull in a china shop, all fingers and thumbs; informal cack-handed, ham-fisted, butterfingered, having two left feet; N. Amer. informal klutzy. **2** *a clumsy contraption* **unwieldy**, cumbersome, bulky, awkward. **3** *a clumsy remark* **gauche**, awkward, graceless; unsubtle, uncouth, boorish, crass; tactless, insensitive, thoughtless, undiplomatic, indelicate, ill-judged.
– OPPOSITES graceful, elegant, tactful.

cluster n. **1** *clusters of berries* **bunch**, clump, mass, knot, group, clutch, bundle, truss. **2** *a cluster of spectators* **crowd**, group, knot, huddle, bunch, throng, flock, pack, band; informal gang, gaggle.
▶v. *they clustered around the television* **congregate**, gather, collect, group, assemble; huddle, crowd, flock.

clutch[1] v. *she clutched his arm* **grip**, grasp, clasp, cling to, hang on to, clench, hold.
□ **clutch at** reach for, snatch at, make a grab for, catch at, claw at.

clutch[2] n. **1** *a clutch of eggs* **group**, batch. **2** *a clutch of awards* **group**, collection; raft, armful; informal load, bunch.

clutches plural n. **power**, control, domination, command, rule, tyranny; hands, hold, grip, grasp, claws, jaws; custody.

clutter n. **1** *a clutter of toys* **mess**, jumble, litter, heap, tangle, muddle, hotchpotch. **2** *a desk full of clutter* **disorder**, chaos, disarray, untidiness, mess, confusion; litter, rubbish.
▶v. *the garden was cluttered with tools* **litter**,

mess up, disarrange; be strewn, be scattered; literary bestrew.

coach[1] n. **1** *a journey by coach* bus, minibus; dated omnibus, charabanc. **2** *a railway coach* carriage, wagon, compartment, van, Pullman; N. Amer. car. **3** *a coach and horses* horse-drawn carriage, trap, hansom (cab), gig.

coach[2] n. *a football coach* instructor, trainer; teacher, tutor, mentor, guru.

▸v. *he coached Richard in maths* instruct, teach, tutor, school, educate; drill, cram; train.

coagulate v. congeal, clot, thicken, gel; solidify, harden, set, dry.

coalesce v. merge, unite, join together, combine, fuse, mingle, blend; amalgamate, consolidate, integrate, homogenize, converge.

coalition n. alliance, union, partnership, bloc, caucus; federation, league, association, confederation, consortium, syndicate, combine; amalgamation, merger.

coarse adj. **1** *coarse blankets* rough, scratchy, prickly, wiry. **2** *his coarse features* large, rough, rough-hewn, heavy; ugly. **3** *a coarse boy* oafish, loutish, boorish, uncouth, rude, impolite, ill-mannered, uncivil; vulgar, common, rough, uncultured, crass. **4** *a coarse innuendo* vulgar, crude, rude, off colour, dirty, filthy, smutty, indelicate, improper, unseemly, crass, tasteless, lewd, prurient; informal blue, farmyard.

– OPPOSITES soft, delicate, refined.

coarsen v. **1** *hands coarsened by work* roughen, toughen, harden. **2** *I had been coarsened by the army* desensitize, dehumanize; dull, deaden.

– OPPOSITES soften, refine.

coast n. *the west coast* seaboard, coastal region, coastline, seashore, shore, foreshore, shoreline, seaside, waterfront, littoral; literary strand.

▸v. *the car coasted down a hill* freewheel, cruise, taxi, drift, glide, sail.

coat n. **1** *a winter coat* overcoat, jacket. **2** *a dog's coat* fur, hair, wool, fleece; hide, pelt, skin. **3** *a coat of paint* layer, covering, coating, skin, film, wash; plating, glaze, varnish, veneer, patina; deposit.

▸v. *the tube was coated with wax* cover, paint, glaze, varnish, wash; surface, veneer, laminate, plate, face; daub, smear, cake, plaster.

coating n. See **coat** (sense 3 of the noun).

coax v. persuade, wheedle, cajole, get round; beguile, seduce, inveigle, manoeuvre; informal sweet-talk, soft-soap, butter up, twist someone's arm.

cobble v.

□ **cobble something together** prepare roughly/hastily, make roughly/hastily, throw together; improvise, contrive, rig (up), whip up; informal rustle up; Brit. informal knock up.

cock n. rooster, cockerel, capon.

▸v. **1** *he cocked his head* tilt, tip, angle, incline, dip. **2** *she cocked her little finger* bend, flex,

crook, curve. **3** *the dog cocked its leg* lift, raise, hold up.

cockeyed adj. informal **1** *that picture is cockeyed* crooked, awry, askew, lopsided, tilted, off-centre, skewed, skew, squint, misaligned; Brit. informal skew-whiff, wonky. **2** *a cockeyed scheme* absurd, preposterous, ridiculous, ludicrous, farcical, laughable, risible, idiotic, stupid, foolish, silly, inane, imbecilic, half-baked, hare-brained; impractical, unfeasible; irrational, illogical, nonsensical; informal crazy; Brit. informal barmy, daft.

cocksure adj. arrogant, conceited, overweening, overconfident, cocky, proud, vain, self-important, swollen-headed, egotistical, presumptuous; smug, patronizing, pompous; informal high and mighty.

– OPPOSITES modest.

cocky adj. arrogant, conceited, overweening, overconfident, cocksure, swollen-headed, self-important, egotistical, presumptuous, boastful, self-assertive; bold, forward, insolent, cheeky.

– OPPOSITES modest.

cocoon v. **1** *he cocooned her in a towel* wrap, swathe, swaddle, muffle, cloak, enfold, envelop, cover, fold. **2** *he was cocooned in the upper classes* protect, shield, shelter, screen, cushion, insulate, isolate, cloister.

coddle v. pamper, cosset, mollycoddle; spoil, indulge, overindulge, pander to; wrap in cotton wool; baby, mother, wait on hand and foot.

– OPPOSITES neglect.

code n. **1** *a secret code* cipher, key; hieroglyphics; cryptogram. **2** *a strict social code* morality, convention, etiquette, protocol. **3** *the penal code* law(s), rules, regulations; constitution, system.

> **WORD LINKS**
>
> **cryptography** the art of writing or solving codes
> **encrypt, encode, encipher** convert something into code
> **decrypt, decipher, crack** make a coded message intelligible

codify v. systematize, systemize, organize, arrange, order, structure; tabulate, catalogue, list, sort, index, classify, categorize, file, log.

coerce v. pressure, pressurize, press, push, constrain; force, compel, oblige, browbeat, bludgeon, bully, threaten, intimidate, dragoon, twist someone's arm; informal railroad, squeeze, lean on.

coercion n. force, compulsion, constraint, duress, oppression, enforcement, harassment, intimidation, threats, arm-twisting, pressure.

coffer n. **1** *every church had a coffer* strongbox, money box, cash box, money chest, treasure chest, safe; casket, box. **2** *the Imperial coffers* fund(s), reserves, resources, money, finances, wealth, cash, capital, purse; treasury, exchequer.

coffin n. sarcophagus; N. Amer. casket; informal box; humorous wooden overcoat.

> **WORD LINKS**
> **bier, catafalque** a platform on which a coffin is placed before burial
> **pall-bearer** a person helping to carry a coffin at a funeral

cogent adj. **convincing**, compelling, strong, forceful, powerful, potent, weighty, effective; valid, sound, plausible, telling; impressive, persuasive, eloquent, credible, influential; conclusive, authoritative; logical, reasoned, rational, reasonable, lucid, coherent, clear.

cogitate v. formal **think (about)**, contemplate, consider, mull over, meditate, muse, ponder, reflect, deliberate, ruminate; dwell on, brood on, chew over, weigh up; informal put on one's thinking cap.

cognate adj. formal **associated**, related, connected, allied, linked; similar, like, alike, akin, kindred, comparable, parallel, corresponding, analogous.

cognition n. **perception**, discernment, apprehension, learning, understanding, comprehension, insight; reasoning, thinking, thought.

cognizance n. formal See **awareness**.

cognizant adj. formal See **aware** (sense 1).

cohabit v. **live together**, live with; informal shack up (with); informal dated live in sin.

cohere v. 1 *the stories cohere into a convincing whole* **stick together**, hold together, be united, bind, fuse. 2 *this view does not cohere with others* **be consistent**, hang together.

coherent adj. **logical**, reasoned, reasonable, rational, sound, cogent, consistent; clear, lucid, articulate; intelligible, comprehensible.
– OPPOSITES muddled.

cohesion n. **unity**, togetherness, solidarity, bond, coherence; connection, linkage.

cohort n. 1 *a Roman army cohort* **unit**, force, corps, division, brigade, battalion, regiment, squadron, company, troop, contingent, legion. 2 *the 1940–4 birth cohort of women* **group**, grouping, category, class, set, division, batch, list; age group, generation.

coil n. *coils of rope* **loop**, twist, turn, curl, convolution; spiral, helix, corkscrew.
▶ v. *he coiled her hair around his finger* **wind**, loop, twist, curl, curve, bend, twine, entwine; spiral, corkscrew.

coin n. 1 *a gold coin* **piece**. 2 *large amounts of coin* **coinage**, coins, specie; (loose) change, small change, silver, copper(s), gold.
▶ v. 1 *guineas were coined* **mint**, stamp, strike, cast, punch, die, mould, forge, make. 2 *he coined the term* **invent**, create, make up, conceive, originate, think up, dream up.

> **WORD LINKS**
> **numismatic** relating to coins
> **numismatics** the collecting of coins

coincide v. 1 *the events coincided* **occur simultaneously**, happen together, be concurrent, concur, coexist. 2 *their interests do not always coincide* **tally**, correspond, agree, accord, concur, match, fit, be consistent, equate, harmonize, be compatible, dovetail, correlate; informal square.
– OPPOSITES differ.

coincidence n. 1 *too close to be mere coincidence* **accident**, chance, serendipity, fortuity, providence, happenstance, fate; a fluke. 2 *the coincidence of inflation and unemployment* **co-occurrence**, coexistence, conjunction, simultaneity, contemporaneity, concomitance. 3 *a coincidence of interests* **correspondence**, agreement, accord, concurrence, consistency, conformity, harmony, compatibility.

coincident adj. 1 *algae blooms coincident with dolphin deaths* **concurrent**, coinciding, simultaneous, contemporaneous, concomitant, coexistent. 2 *their aims are coincident* **in agreement**, in harmony, in accord, consistent, compatible, congruent, in step, in tune; the same.

coincidental adj. 1 *a coincidental resemblance* **accidental**, chance, fluky, random; fortuitous, adventitious, serendipitous; unexpected, unforeseen, unintentional, inadvertent, unplanned. 2 *the coincidental disappearance of the two men* **simultaneous**, concurrent, coincident, contemporaneous, concomitant.

coitus n. technical See **sex** (sense 1).

cold adj. 1 *a cold day* **chilly**, chill, cool, freezing, icy, snowy, wintry, frosty, frigid, gelid; bitter, biting, raw; informal nippy, brass monkeys, arctic; Brit. informal parky. 2 *I'm very cold* **chilly**, chilled, cool, freezing, frozen, shivery, numb, benumbed; hypothermic. 3 *a cold reception* **unfriendly**, inhospitable, unwelcoming, forbidding, cool, frigid, frosty, glacial, lukewarm, indifferent, unfeeling, unemotional, formal, stiff.
– OPPOSITES hot, warm.

> **WORD LINKS**
> **hypothermia** a condition caused by extreme cold

cold-blooded adj. **cruel**, callous, sadistic, inhuman, inhumane, pitiless, merciless, ruthless, unforgiving, unfeeling, uncaring, heartless; savage, brutal, barbaric, barbarous; cold, cold-hearted, unemotional.

cold-hearted adj. **unfeeling**, unloving, uncaring, unsympathetic, unemotional, unfriendly, uncharitable, unkind, insensitive; hard-hearted, stony-hearted, heartless, hard, cold.

collaborate v. 1 *they collaborated on the project* **cooperate**, join forces, team up, band together, work together, participate, combine, ally; pool resources, club together. 2 *they collaborated with the enemy* **fraternize**, conspire, collude, cooperate, consort, sympathize.

collaborator n. **1** *his collaborator on the book* **co-worker**, partner, associate, colleague, confederate; assistant. **2** *a wartime collaborator* **quisling**, fraternizer, collaborationist, colluder, (enemy) sympathizer; traitor, fifth columnist.

collapse v. **1** *the roof collapsed* **cave in**, fall in, subside, fall down, give (way), crumple, sag, slump. **2** *he collapsed last night* **faint**, pass out, black out, lose consciousness, keel over, swoon; informal flake out, conk out. **3** *she collapsed in tears* **break down**, go to pieces, lose control, be overcome, crumble; informal crack up. **4** *peace talks collapsed* **break down**, fail, fall through, fold, founder, miscarry, come to grief, be unsuccessful; end; informal flop, fizzle out, flatline.
▸n. **1** *the collapse of the roof* **cave-in**, subsidence. **2** *her collapse on stage* **fainting fit**, faint, blackout, loss of consciousness, swoon; Medicine syncope. **3** *the collapse of the talks* **breakdown**, failure, disintegration; end. **4** *he suffered a collapse* **(nervous) breakdown**, personal crisis, psychological trauma; informal crack-up.

collar n. **1** *a shirt collar* **neckband**, choker; historical ruff, gorget, bertha. **2** *a collar round the pipe* **ring**, band, collet, sleeve, flange.
▸v. informal **1** *he collared a thief* **apprehend**, arrest, catch, capture, seize; take prisoner, take into custody, detain; informal nab, pinch, bust, pick up, pull in, feel someone's collar; Brit. informal nick. **2** *she collared me in the street* **accost**, waylay, hail, approach, detain, stop, halt, catch, confront, importune; informal buttonhole; Brit. informal nobble.

collate v. **1** *the system is used to collate information* **collect**, gather, accumulate, assemble; combine, aggregate, put together; arrange, organize. **2** *we must collate these two sources* **compare**, contrast, set side by side, juxtapose, weigh against.

collateral n. **security**, surety, guarantee, guaranty, insurance, indemnity, indemnification; backing.

colleague n. **co-worker**, fellow worker, workmate, teammate, associate, partner, collaborator, ally, confederate; Brit. informal oppo.

collect v. **1** *he collected the rubbish* **gather**, accumulate, assemble; amass, stockpile, pile up, heap up, store (up), hoard, save; mass, accrue. **2** *a crowd soon collected* **gather**, assemble, meet, muster, congregate, convene, converge, flock together. **3** *I must collect the children* **fetch**, go/come to get, call for, meet. **4** *they collect money for charity* **raise**, appeal for, ask for, solicit; obtain, acquire, gather. **5** *he paused to collect himself* **recover**, regain one's composure, pull oneself together, steady oneself; informal get a grip (on oneself). **6** *she collected her thoughts* **muster**, summon (up), gather, get together, marshal.
– OPPOSITES disperse, distribute.

collected adj. **calm**, cool, self-possessed, self-controlled, composed, poised; serene, tranquil, relaxed, unruffled, unperturbed, untroubled; placid, quiet, sedate, phlegmatic; informal unfazed, together, laid-back.
– OPPOSITES excited, hysterical.

collection n. **1** *a collection of stolen items* **hoard**, pile, heap, stack, stock, store, stockpile; accumulation, reserve, supply, bank, pool, fund, mine, reservoir. **2** *a collection of shoppers* **group**, crowd, body, assemblage, gathering, throng; knot, cluster; multitude, bevy, party, band, horde, pack, flock, swarm, mob; informal gang, load, gaggle. **3** *a collection of Victorian dolls* **set**, series; array, assortment. **4** *a collection of short stories* **anthology**, selection, compendium, treasury, compilation, miscellany, potpourri. **5** *a collection for the poor* **donations**, contributions, gifts, subscription(s); informal whip-round; historical alms. **6** *a church collection* **offering**, offertory, tithe.

collective adj. **common**, shared, joint, combined, mutual, communal, pooled; united, allied, cooperative, collaborative.
– OPPOSITES individual.

college n. **1** *a college of technology* **school**, academy, university, polytechnic, institute, seminary, conservatoire, conservatory. **2** *the College of Heralds* **association**, society, club, institute, body, fellowship, guild, lodge, order, fraternity, league, union, alliance.

collide v. **1** *the trains collided with each other* **crash**, impact; hit, strike, run into, bump into, meet head-on, cannon into, plough into; N. Amer. informal barrel into. **2** *politics and metaphysics collide* **conflict**, clash; differ, diverge, disagree, be at odds, be incompatible.

collision n. **1** *a collision on the ring road* **crash**, accident, impact, smash, bump, hit; Brit. RTA (road traffic accident); N. Amer. wreck; informal pile-up; Brit. informal prang, shunt. **2** *a collision between two ideas* **conflict**, clash; disagreement, incompatibility, contradiction.

colloquial adj. **informal**, conversational, everyday, non-literary; unofficial, idiomatic, slangy, vernacular, popular, demotic.
– OPPOSITES formal.

collude v. **conspire**, connive, collaborate, plot, scheme; informal be in cahoots.

colonist n. **settler**, colonizer, colonial, pioneer; immigrant, incomer, newcomer; N. Amer. historical homesteader.
– OPPOSITES native.

colonize v. **settle (in)**, people, populate; occupy, take over, seize, capture, subjugate.

colonnade n. **row of columns**; portico, stoa, peristyle.

colony n. **1** *a French colony* **territory**, dependency, protectorate, satellite, settlement, outpost, province. **2** *the British colony in New York* **population**, community. **3** *an artists' colony* **community**, commune; quarter, district, ghetto.

colossal adj. **huge**, massive, enormous, gigantic, very big, giant, mammoth, vast,

C

cosmic, immense, monumental, prodigious, mountainous, titanic, towering, king-size(d); informal monster, whopping, humongous, jumbo; Brit. informal ginormous.
– OPPOSITES tiny.

colour n. **1** *the lights changed colour* **hue**, shade, tint, tone, coloration. **2** *oil colour* **paint**, pigment, colourant, dye, stain, tint, wash. **3** *the colour in her cheeks* **redness**, pinkness, rosiness, ruddiness, blush, flush, bloom. **4** *people of every colour* **skin colouring**, skin tone, colouring; race, ethnic group. **5** *anecdotes add colour to the text* **vividness**, life, liveliness, vitality, excitement, interest, richness, zest, spice, piquancy, impact, force; informal oomph, pizzazz, punch, kick; literary salt. **6** *the colours of the Oxford City club* **strip**, kit, uniform, costume, livery, regalia. **7** *the regimental colours*. See **flag¹** (noun).
▶ v. **1** *the wood was coloured blue* **tint**, dye, stain, paint, pigment, wash. **2** *she coloured up* **blush**, redden, go pink, go red, flush. **3** *the experience coloured her outlook* **influence**, affect, taint, warp, skew, distort, bias, prejudice. **4** *they colour evidence to make a story saleable* **exaggerate**, overstate, embroider, embellish, dramatize, enhance, varnish; falsify, misreport, manipulate.

> **WORD LINKS**
> **chromatic** relating to colour
> **chromogenic** producing colour
> **deuteranopia, protanopia, tritanopia** different forms of colour blindness
> **monochromatism** complete colour blindness
> **spectrum** a band of colours produced by separating light into parts with different wavelengths

colourful adj. **1** *a colourful picture* **brightly coloured**, vivid, vibrant, brilliant, radiant, rich; gaudy, glaring, garish; multicoloured, multicolour, rainbow, varicoloured, harlequin, polychromatic, psychedelic; informal jazzy. **2** *a colourful account* **vivid**, graphic, lively, animated, dramatic, fascinating, interesting, stimulating, scintillating, evocative.

colourless adj. **1** *a colourless liquid* **uncoloured**, white, bleached; literary achromatic. **2** *her colourless face* **pale**, pallid, wan, anaemic, bloodless, ashen, white, waxen, pasty, peaky, sickly, drained, drawn, ghostly, deathly. **3** *a colourless personality* **uninteresting**, dull, boring, tedious, dry, dreary; unexciting, bland, weak, insipid, vapid, vacuous, feeble, wishy-washy, lame, lifeless, spiritless, anaemic, bloodless; nondescript, characterless.
– OPPOSITES colourful, rosy.

column n. **1** *arches supported by massive columns* **pillar**, post, support, upright, baluster, pier, pile, pilaster, stanchion; obelisk, monolith. **2** *a column in the paper* **article**, piece, item, story, report, account, write-up, feature, review, notice, editorial, leader. **3** *we walked in a column* **line**, file, queue, procession, train, cavalcade, convoy;

informal crocodile.

columnist n. **writer**, contributor, journalist, correspondent, newspaperman, newspaperwoman, newsman, newswoman; wordsmith, penman; critic, reviewer, commentator; informal scribbler, pen-pusher, hack(ette), journo.

coma n. **state of unconsciousness**; Medicine persistent vegetative state, PVS.

comatose adj. **1** *he was comatose after the accident* **unconscious**, in a coma, insensible, insensate. **2** informal *she lay comatose in the sun* **inert**, inactive, lethargic, sluggish, torpid, languid; somnolent, sleeping, dormant.

comb v. **1** *she combed her hair* **groom**, brush, untangle, smooth, straighten, neaten, tidy, arrange; curry. **2** *the wool was combed* **separate**, dress, card, tease, hackle, heckle. **3** *police combed the area* **search**, scour, explore, sweep, probe, hunt through, forage through, poke about/around in, go over, go over with a fine-tooth comb; leave no stone unturned.

combat n. *he was killed in combat* **battle**, fighting, action, hostilities, conflict, war, warfare.
▶ v. *they tried to combat the disease* **fight**, battle, tackle, attack, counter, resist, withstand; impede, block, thwart, inhibit; stop, halt, prevent, check, curb.

combatant n. **1** *a combatant in the war* **fighter**, soldier, serviceman/woman, warrior, trooper. **2** *combatants in the computer market* **contender**, adversary, opponent, competitor, challenger, rival.
▶ adj. *combatant armies* **warring**, at war, opposing, belligerent, fighting, battling.

combative adj. **pugnacious**, aggressive, antagonistic, quarrelsome, argumentative, contentious, hostile, truculent, belligerent, bellicose, militant; informal spoiling for a fight.
– OPPOSITES conciliatory.

combination n. **1** *a combination of ancient and modern* **amalgamation**, amalgam, merge, blend, mixture, mix, fusion, marriage, coalition, integration, incorporation, synthesis, composite. **2** *he acted in combination with his brother* **cooperation**, collaboration, association, union, partnership, league.

combine v. **1** *he combines comedy with tragedy* **amalgamate**, integrate, incorporate, merge, mix, fuse, blend; bind, join, marry, unify. **2** *teachers combined to tackle the problem* **cooperate**, collaborate, join forces, get together, club together, unite, team up, throw in one's lot; informal gang up.

combustible adj. **inflammable**, flammable, incendiary, ignitable.

combustion n. **burning**; kindling, ignition.

come v. **1** *come and listen* **move nearer**, move closer, approach, advance, draw close/closer, draw near/nearer; proceed; old use draw nigh. **2** *they came last night* **arrive**, get here/there, make it, appear, come on the scene; approach, enter, turn up, come along, materialize; informal show (up), roll in/up, blow in, show one's face. **3** *they came to a stream* **reach**, arrive at, get to, make it to, make, gain; come across, run across, happen on, chance on, come upon, stumble on; end up at; informal wind up at. **4** *the dress comes to her ankles* **extend**, stretch, reach, come as far as. **5** *she comes from Belgium* **be from**, be a native of, hail from, originate in; live in, reside in. **6** *attacks came without warning* **happen**, occur, take place, come about, transpire, fall, present itself, crop up, materialize, arise, arrive, appear; ensue, follow; literary come to pass, befall. **7** *the car does not come in red* **be available**, be for sale; be made, be produced. **8** informal **climax**, orgasm.

– OPPOSITES go, leave.

□ **come about** happen, occur, take place, transpire, fall; crop up, materialize, arise, appear, surface; ensue, follow; literary come to pass, befall.
come across 1 *they came across his friends* **meet/find by chance**, meet, run into, run across, come upon, chance on, stumble on, happen on; discover, encounter, find, locate; informal bump into. **2** *the emotion comes across* **be communicated**, be perceived, get across, be clear, be understood, register, sink in, strike home. **3** *she came across as cool* **seem**, appear, look, sound; Brit. come over; N. Amer. come off.
come along 1 *the puppies are coming along nicely* **progress**, develop, shape up; come on, turn out; improve, get better, pick up, rally, recover. **2** *Come along!* **hurry (up)**, be quick, get a move on, come on, look lively, speed up, move faster; informal get moving, get cracking, step on it, move it, buck up, shake a leg, make it snappy, get a wiggle on; Brit. informal get your skates on; dated make haste.
come apart break up, fall to bits, fall to pieces, disintegrate, come unstuck, separate, split, tear.
come between alienate, estrange, separate, divide, split up, break up, disunite, set at odds.
come by obtain, acquire, gain, get, find, pick up, procure, secure; buy, purchase; informal get one's hands on, get hold of, bag, score, swing.
come down to amount to, add up to, constitute, boil down to, be equivalent to.
come down with fall ill with, fall sick with, be taken ill with, show symptoms of, become infected with, get, catch, develop, contract, fall victim to; Brit. go down with.
come forward volunteer, offer one's services, make oneself available.
come into inherit, be left, be willed, be bequeathed.
come in for receive, experience, sustain, undergo, go through, encounter, face, be subjected to, bear, suffer.
come off 1 *this soufflé rarely comes off* **succeed**, work, turn out well, work out, go as planned, get results. **2** *she always came off worse* **end up**, finish up.
come on progress, develop, shape up, take

shape, come along, turn out; improve.
come out 1 *it came out that he'd been to Rome* **become known**, become apparent, come to light, emerge, transpire; get out, be discovered, be uncovered, be revealed, leak out, be disclosed. **2** *my book is coming out* **be published**, be issued, be released, be brought out, be printed, go on sale. **3** *the flowers have come out* **bloom**, flower, open. **4** *it will come out all right* **end**, finish, conclude, work out, turn out; informal pan out.
come out with utter, say, let out, blurt out, burst out with.
come round 1 *he has just come round from anaesthetic* **regain consciousness**, come to, come to one's senses, recover, revive, awake, wake up. **2** *I came round to her view* **be converted**, be won over (by), agree (with), change one's mind, be persuaded (by); give way, yield, relent. **3** *Friday the 13th comes round every few months* **occur**, take place, happen, come up, crop up, arise; recur, reoccur, return, reappear. **4** *come round for a drink* **visit**, call (in/round), look in, stop by, drop by/in/round/over, come over; informal pop in/round/over.
come through survive, get through, ride out, weather, live through, pull through; withstand, stand up to, endure, surmount, overcome; informal stick out.
come to 1 *the bill came to £17.50* **amount to**, add up to, run to, total, equal; Brit. tot up to. **2** *I came to in the hospital* **regain consciousness**, come round, come to one's senses, recover, revive, awake, wake up.
come up arise, occur, happen, come about, transpire, emerge, surface, crop up, turn up, pop up.
come up to *he never came up to her expectations* measure up to, match up to, live up to, fulfil, satisfy, meet, equal, compare with; be good enough; informal hold a candle to.
come up with produce, devise, think up; propose, put forward, submit, suggest, recommend, advocate, introduce, moot.
comeback n. **1** *he made a determined comeback* **resurgence**, recovery, return, rally, upturn; Brit. fightback. **2** informal *one of my best comebacks* **retort**, riposte, return, rejoinder; answer, reply, response.
comedian n. **1** *a famous comedian* **comic**, comedienne, funny man/woman, humorist, gagster, stand-up; N. Amer. tummler. **2** *Dad was such a comedian* **joker**, jester, wit, wag, comic, wisecracker, jokester; prankster, clown, fool, buffoon; informal laugh, hoot, case; informal dated card, caution.
comedienne n. See **comedian** (sense 1).
comedown n. informal **1** *a bit of a comedown for a sergeant* **loss of status**, loss of face, humiliation, belittlement, demotion, degradation, disgrace. **2** *it's such a comedown after Christmas* **anticlimax**, let-down, disappointment, disillusionment, deflation, decline.
comedy n. **1** *he excels in comedy* **light entertainment**, comic play, comic film,

C

farce, situation comedy, satire, pantomime, comic opera; burlesque, slapstick; informal sitcom. **2** *the comedy in their work* **humour**, fun, funny side, comical aspect, absurdity, drollness, farce.
– OPPOSITES tragedy, gravity.

comely adj. old use See **attractive** (sense 2).

come-on n. informal **inducement**, incentive, attraction, lure, pull, draw, enticement, bait, carrot, temptation; fascination, charm, appeal, allure.

comeuppance n. informal **just deserts**, just punishment, due, retribution, requital.

comfort n. **1** *travel in comfort* **ease**, relaxation, repose, serenity, tranquillity, contentment, cosiness; luxury, opulence, prosperity; bed of roses. **2** *words of comfort* **consolation**, solace, condolence, sympathy, commiseration; support, reassurance, cheer.
▶ v. *a friend tried to comfort her* **console**, solace, condole with, commiserate with, sympathize with; support, succour, ease, reassure, soothe, calm; cheer, hearten, uplift; informal buck up.
– OPPOSITES distress, depress.

comfortable adj. **1** *a comfortable lifestyle* **pleasant**, free from hardship; affluent, well-to-do, luxurious, opulent. **2** *a comfortable room* **cosy**, snug, warm, pleasant, agreeable; restful, homelike, homely; informal comfy. **3** *comfortable clothes* **loose**, loose-fitting, casual; informal comfy. **4** *a comfortable pace* **leisurely**, unhurried, relaxed, easy, gentle, sedate, undemanding, slow; informal laid-back. **5** *they feel comfortable with each other* **at ease**, relaxed, secure, safe, unworried, contented, happy.
– OPPOSITES hard, spartan, tense.

comforting adj. **consoling**, sympathetic, compassionate, solicitous, tender, warm, caring, loving; supportive, reassuring, soothing, calming; cheering, heartening, encouraging.

comfortless adj. **1** *a comfortless house* **gloomy**, dreary, dismal, bleak, grim, sombre; joyless, cheerless, depressing, disheartening, dispiriting, unwelcoming, uninviting; austere, spartan, institutional. **2** *he left her comfortless* **miserable**, heartbroken, grief-stricken, unhappy, sad, distressed, desolate, devastated, inconsolable, disconsolate, downcast, downhearted, dejected, cheerless, depressed, melancholy, gloomy, glum; informal blue, down in the mouth, down in the dumps.
– OPPOSITES cosy, happy.

comic adj. *a comic play* **humorous**, funny, droll, amusing, hilarious, uproarious; comical, farcical, silly, slapstick, zany; witty, jocular, chucklesome; informal priceless, side-splitting, rib-tickling; informal dated killing.
– OPPOSITES serious.
▶ n. **1** *a music hall comic* **comedian**, comedienne, funny man/woman, comedy actor/actress, humorist, wit; joker, clown; informal kidder, wisecracker. **2** *Tony read his comic* **cartoon paper**, comic paper, comic

book, graphic novel; informal funny.

comical adj. **1** *he could be quite comical* **funny**, comic, humorous, droll, witty, jocular, hilarious, amusing, diverting, entertaining, chucklesome; informal jokey, wacky, waggish, side-splitting, rib-tickling, priceless, a scream, a laugh; informal dated killing, a card, a caution. **2** *they look comical in those suits* **silly**, absurd, ridiculous, laughable, risible, ludicrous, preposterous, foolish; informal wacky, crazy.
– OPPOSITES sensible.

coming adj. *the coming election* **forthcoming**, imminent, impending, approaching; future, expected, anticipated; close, at hand, in store, in the offing, in the pipeline, on the horizon, on the way; informal on the cards.
▶ n. *the coming of spring* **approach**, advance, advent, arrival, appearance, emergence, onset.

command v. **1** *he commanded his men to retreat* **order**, tell, direct, instruct, call on, require; literary bid. **2** *Jones commanded a tank squadron* **be in charge of**, be in command of, be the leader of; head, lead, control, direct, manage, supervise, oversee; informal head up. **3** *they command great respect* **receive**, get, gain, secure.
▶ n. **1** *officers shouted commands* **order**, instruction, directive, direction, commandment, injunction, demand, stipulation, requirement, exhortation, bidding, request. **2** *he had 160 men under his command* **authority**, control, charge, power, direction, dominion, guidance; leadership, rule, government, management, supervision, jurisdiction. **3** *a brilliant command of English* **knowledge**, mastery, grasp, comprehension, understanding.

commandeer v. **seize**, take, requisition, appropriate, expropriate, sequestrate, sequester, confiscate, annex, take over, claim, pre-empt; hijack, arrogate, help oneself to; informal walk off with; Law distrain; Scottish Law poind.

commander n. **leader**, head, chief, overseer, controller; commander-in-chief, commanding officer, CO, officer; informal boss, boss man, skipper, numero uno, number one, top dog, kingpin, head honcho; Brit. informal gaffer, guv'nor.

commanding adj. **1** *a commanding position* **dominant**, dominating, controlling, superior, powerful, prominent, advantageous, favourable. **2** *a commanding voice* **authoritative**, masterful, assertive, firm, emphatic, insistent, imperative; peremptory, imperious, dictatorial; informal bossy.

commemorate v. **celebrate**, pay tribute to, pay homage to, honour, salute, toast; remember, recognize, acknowledge, observe, mark.

commemorative adj. **memorial**, remembrance; celebratory.

commence v. **begin**, start; get the ball rolling, get going, get under way, get off the ground, set about, embark on, launch into, lead off; open, initiate, inaugurate; informal kick off, get the show on the road.
– OPPOSITES conclude.

commencement n. **beginning**, start, opening, outset, onset, launch, initiation, inception, origin; informal kick-off.

commend v. **1** *we should commend him* **praise**, compliment, congratulate, applaud, salute, honour; sing the praises of, pay tribute to, take one's hat off to, pat on the back; formal laud. **2** *I commend her to you without reservation* **recommend**, suggest, propose; endorse, advocate, vouch for, speak for, support, back. **3** formal *I commend them to your care* **entrust**, trust, deliver, commit, hand over, give, turn over, consign, assign.
– OPPOSITES criticize.

commendable adj. **admirable**, praiseworthy, creditable, laudable, estimable, meritorious, exemplary, noteworthy, honourable, respectable, fine, excellent.
– OPPOSITES reprehensible.

commendation n. **1** *letters of commendation* **praise**, congratulation, appreciation; acclaim, credit, recognition, respect, esteem, admiration, homage, tribute. **2** *a commendation for bravery* **award**, accolade, prize, honour, (honourable) mention, citation.

commensurate adj. **1** *they had privileges but commensurate duties* **equivalent**, equal, corresponding, correspondent, comparable, proportionate, proportional. **2** *a salary commensurate with your qualifications* **appropriate to**, in keeping with, in line with, consistent with, corresponding to, according to, relative to; dependent on, based on.

comment n. **1** *their comments on her appearance* **remark**, observation, statement, utterance; pronouncement, judgement, reflection, opinion, view; criticism. **2** *a great deal of comment* **discussion**, debate; interest. **3** *a comment in the margin* **note**, annotation, footnote, gloss, commentary, explanation.
▶ v. **1** *they commented on the food* **remark on**, speak about, talk about, discuss, mention. **2** *'It will soon be night,' he commented* **remark**, observe, reflect, say, state, declare, announce; interpose, interject.

commentary n. **1** *the test match commentary* **narration**, description, account, report, review. **2** *textual commentary* **explanation**, elucidation, interpretation, exegesis, analysis; assessment, appraisal, criticism; notes, comments, blog, vlog.

commentator n. **1** *a television commentator* **narrator**, announcer, presenter, anchor, anchorman, anchorwoman; reporter, journalist, newscaster, sportscaster; informal talking head. **2** *a political commentator* **analyst**, pundit, monitor, observer; writer, speaker.

commerce n. **trade**, trading, buying and selling, business, dealing, traffic; (financial) transactions, dealings.

commercial adj. **1** *a vessel built for commercial purposes* **trade**, trading, business, private enterprise, mercantile, sales. **2** *we turn good ideas into commercial products* **lucrative**, moneymaking, money-spinning, profitable, remunerative, fruitful, gainful; viable, successful. **3** *public opinion was commercial* **profit-orientated**, money-orientated, materialistic, mercenary.
▶ n. *a TV commercial* **advertisement**, promotion, display; informal ad, plug; Brit. informal advert.

commercialized adj. **profit-orientated**, money-orientated, commercial, materialistic, mercenary.

commiserate v. **offer sympathy**, be sympathetic, offer condolences, condole, sympathize, empathize, feel pity, feel sorry; feel for, comfort, console.

commiseration n. **condolence(s)**, sympathy, pity, comfort, solace, consolation; compassion, understanding.

commission n. **1** *the dealer's commission* **percentage**, brokerage, share, portion, dividend, premium, fee, consideration, bonus; informal cut, take, rake-off, slice; Brit. informal whack, divvy. **2** *the commission of building a palace* **task**, employment, job, project, mission, assignment, undertaking; duty, charge, responsibility. **3** *items made under royal commission* **warrant**, licence, sanction, authority. **4** *an independent commission* **committee**, board, council, panel, directorate, delegation. **5** *the commission of an offence* **perpetration**, committing, committal, execution.
▶ v. **1** *he was commissioned to paint a portrait* **engage**, contract, charge, employ, hire, recruit, retain, appoint, enlist, co-opt, book, sign up. **2** *they commissioned a sculpture* **order**; authorize; formal bespeak.
▢ **in commission** in service, in use; working, functional, operative, up and running, in operation, in working order.
out of commission not in service, not in use, unserviceable; not working, inoperative, out of order; down.

commit v. **1** *he committed a murder* **carry out**, do, perpetrate, engage in, enact, execute, effect, accomplish; be responsible for; informal pull off. **2** *she was committed to their care* **entrust**, consign, assign, deliver, give, hand over, relinquish; formal commend. **3** *they committed themselves to the project* **pledge**, devote, apply, give, dedicate. **4** *the judge committed him to prison* **consign**, send, deliver, confine. **5** *her husband had her committed* **hospitalize**, confine, institutionalize, put away; certify; Brit. section.

commitment n. **1** *the pressure of his commitments* **responsibility**, obligation, duty, tie, liability; task; engagement, arrangement. **2** *her commitment to her students* **dedication**, devotion, allegiance,

C

loyalty, faithfulness, fidelity. **3** *he made a commitment* **vow**, promise, pledge, oath; contract, pact, deal; decision, resolution.

committed adj. **devout**, devoted, dedicated, loyal, faithful, staunch, firm, steadfast, unwavering, wholehearted, keen, passionate, ardent, fervent, motivated, driven, sworn, pledged; dutiful, diligent; informal card-carrying, true blue, deep-dyed.
– OPPOSITES apathetic.

commodious adj. formal **roomy**, capacious, spacious, ample, generous, sizeable, large, big, extensive.
– OPPOSITES cramped.

commodity n. **item**, material, product, article, object; import, export.

common adj. **1** *the common folk* **ordinary**, normal, average, unexceptional; simple. **2** *a very common art form* **usual**, ordinary, familiar, regular, frequent, recurrent, everyday; standard, typical, conventional, stock, commonplace, run-of-the-mill. **3** *a common belief* **widespread**, general, universal, popular, mainstream, prevalent, prevailing, rife, established, conventional, traditional, orthodox, accepted. **4** *the common good* **collective**, communal, community, public, popular, general; shared, combined. **5** *they are far too common* **uncouth**, vulgar, coarse, rough, boorish, unladylike, ungentlemanly, ill-bred, uncivilized, unsophisticated, unrefined; lowly, low-born, low-class, inferior, proletarian, plebeian; informal plebby; Brit. informal common as muck.
– OPPOSITES unusual, rare, individual, refined.
▶ n. Brit. informal *use your common!* See **common sense**.

commonly adv. **often**, frequently, regularly, repeatedly, time and (time) again, all the time, routinely, habitually, customarily; N. Amer. oftentimes; informal lots.

commonplace adj. **1** *a commonplace writing style* **ordinary**, run-of-the-mill, unremarkable, unexceptional, average, mediocre, pedestrian, prosaic, lacklustre, dull, bland, uninteresting, mundane, hackneyed, trite, banal, clichéd, predictable, stale, tired, unoriginal; informal (plain) vanilla, bog-standard, a dime a dozen; Brit. informal common or garden; N. Amer. informal bush-league. **2** *a commonplace occurrence* **common**, normal, usual, ordinary, familiar, routine, standard, everyday, daily, regular, frequent, habitual, typical.
– OPPOSITES original, unusual.
▶ n. **1** *early death was a commonplace* **everyday event**, routine. **2** *a great store of commonplaces* **platitude**, cliché, truism, hackneyed phrase, trite phrase, old chestnut, banality; dated bromide.

common sense n. **sensibleness**, (good) sense, (native) wit, judgement, level-headedness, prudence, discernment, canniness, astuteness, shrewdness, wisdom, insight, perception, perspicacity; practicality,

capability, resourcefulness, enterprise; informal horse sense, gumption, nous, savvy; Brit. informal **common**; N. Amer. informal smarts.
– OPPOSITES folly.

commotion n. **disturbance**, uproar, tumult, rumpus, ruckus, brouhaha, furore, hue and cry, fuss, stir, storm; turmoil, disorder, confusion, chaos, mayhem, havoc, pandemonium; unrest, fracas, riot, breach of the peace; Irish, N. Amer., & Austral. donnybrook; informal ruction(s), ballyhoo, kerfuffle, hoo-ha, to-do, hullabaloo; Brit. informal carry-on, row, aggro, argy-bargy; Law, dated affray.

communal adj. **1** *the kitchen was communal* **shared**, joint, common. **2** *they farm on a communal basis* **collective**, cooperative, community, communalist, combined.
– OPPOSITES private, individual.

commune n. *she lives in a commune* **collective**, cooperative, communal settlement, kibbutz.
▶ v. **1** *we pray to commune with God* **communicate**, speak, talk, converse, interface. **2** *she likes to commune with nature* **empathize**, identify, have a rapport, feel at one; relate to, feel close to.

communicable adj. **contagious**, **infectious**, transmittable, transmissible, transferable, spreadable; informal catching; dated infective.

communicate v. **1** *he communicated the news to his boss* **convey**, tell, impart, relay, transmit, pass on, announce, report, recount, relate, present; divulge, disclose, mention; spread, disseminate, promulgate, broadcast. **2** *they communicate daily* **liaise**, be in touch, be in contact, have dealings, interface, commune, meet; talk, speak, converse; informal have a confab, powwow. **3** *learn how to communicate better* **get one's message across**, explain oneself, be understood, get through to someone. **4** *the disease is communicated easily* **transmit**, transfer, spread, carry, pass on. **5** *each bedroom communicates with a bathroom* **connect with**, join up with, open on to, lead into.

communication n. **1** *the communication of news* **transmission**, conveyance, divulgence, divulgation, disclosure; dissemination, promulgation, broadcasting. **2** *there was no communication between them* **contact**, dealings, relations, connection, association, socializing, intercourse; correspondence, dialogue, talk, conversation, discussion; dated commerce. **3** *an official communication* **message**, statement, announcement, report, dispatch, communiqué, letter, bulletin, correspondence. **4** *road and rail communications* **links**, connections; services, routes.

communicative adj. **forthcoming**, expansive, expressive, unreserved, uninhibited, vocal, outgoing, frank, open, candid; talkative, chatty, loquacious; informal gabby.

communion n. **1** *a sense of communion with others* **affinity**, fellowship, kinship, friendship, fellow feeling, togetherness, closeness, harmony, understanding, rapport, connection, communication, empathy, accord, unity. **2** *Christ's presence at Communion* **Eucharist**, Holy Communion, Lord's Supper, Mass.

communiqué n. **official communication**, press release, bulletin, message, missive, dispatch, statement, report, announcement, declaration, proclamation; N. Amer. advisory; informal memo.

communism n. **collectivism**, state ownership, (radical) socialism; Sovietism, Bolshevism, Marxism, Leninism, Trotskyism, Maoism.

communist n. & adj. **collectivist**, leftist, (radical) socialist, anti-capitalist; Soviet, Bolshevik, Bolshevist, Marxist, Leninist, Trotskyist, Trotskyite, Maoist; informal derogatory commie, Bolshie, red, lefty.

community n. **1** *work done for the community* **population**, populace, people, citizenry, (general) public, collective; residents, inhabitants, citizens. **2** *a rural community* **district**, region, zone, area, locality, locale, neighbourhood; informal neck of the woods, turf; Brit. informal manor; N. Amer. informal hood, nabe. **3** *gays are not one homogeneous community* **group**, body, set, circle, clique, faction; informal gang, bunch. **4** *a monastic community* **brotherhood**, sisterhood, fraternity, sorority, sodality, colony, order. **5** *community of interests* **similarity**, likeness, comparability, correspondence, agreement, closeness, affinity. **6** *the community of goods* **joint ownership**, common ownership, shared possession.

commute v. **1** *they commute on a train* **travel to and from work**, travel back and forth. **2** *his sentence was commuted* **reduce**, lessen, lighten, shorten, cut, attenuate, moderate. **3** *knight service was commuted for a payment* **exchange**, change, substitute, swap, trade, switch.
– OPPOSITES increase.

commuter n. **(daily) traveller**, passenger; informal straphanger.

compact[1] adj. **1** *a compact rug* **dense**, close-packed, tightly packed; thick, tight, firm. **2** *a compact camera* **small**, little, petite, miniature, mini, small-scale; Scottish wee; informal teeny, teeny-weeny; Brit. informal dinky; N. Amer. little-bitty. **3** *her tale is compact* **concise**, succinct, condensed, brief, pithy; short and sweet; informal snappy; formal compendious.
– OPPOSITES loose, large, rambling.
▸ v. *the snow has been compacted* **compress**, condense, pack down, press down, tamp (down), flatten.

compact[2] n. *the warring states signed a compact* **treaty**, pact, accord, agreement, contract, bargain, deal, settlement, covenant, concordat; pledge, promise, bond.

companion n. **1** *Harry and his companion* **associate**, partner, escort, compatriot, confederate; friend, intimate, confidant(e),

comrade; informal pal, chum, crony, sidekick; Brit. informal mate, oppo, china, mucker; N. Amer. informal buddy, amigo, compadre; Austral./NZ informal offsider. **2** *a lady's companion* **attendant**, aide, helper, assistant, valet, equerry, lady-in-waiting; chaperone; carer, minder. **3** *the tape is a companion to the book* **complement**, counterpart, twin, match; accompaniment, supplement, addition, adjunct, accessory. **4** *The Gardener's Companion* **handbook**, manual, guide, reference book, ABC, primer, vade mecum; informal bible.

companionable adj. **friendly**, affable, cordial, genial, congenial, amiable, easygoing, good-natured, comradely; sociable, convivial, outgoing, gregarious; informal chummy, pally; Brit. informal matey; N. Amer. informal buddy-buddy, clubby.

companionship n. **friendship**, fellowship, closeness, togetherness, amity, intimacy, rapport, camaraderie, brotherhood, sisterhood; company, society, social contact.

company n. **1** *an oil company* **firm**, business, corporation, establishment, agency, office, bureau, institution, organization, concern, enterprise; conglomerate, consortium, syndicate, multinational; informal outfit. **2** *I enjoy his company* **companionship**, friendship, fellowship, amity, camaraderie; society, association. **3** *I'm expecting company* **guests**, visitors, callers, people; someone. **4** *a company of poets* **group**, crowd, party, band, assembly, cluster, flock, herd, troupe, throng, congregation; informal bunch, gang. **5** *a company of infantry* **unit**, section, detachment, troop, corps, squad, squadron, platoon, battalion, division.

> **WORD LINKS**
> **corporate** relating to a business company

comparable adj. **1** *comparable incomes* **similar**, close, near, approximate, akin, equivalent, commensurate, proportional, proportionate; like, matching. **2** *nobody is comparable with him* **equal to**, as good as, in the same league as, able to hold a candle to, on a par with, on a level with; a match for.

comparative adj. **relative**; in/by comparison.

compare v. **1** *we compared the data sets* **contrast**, juxtapose, collate, differentiate, weigh up. **2** *he was compared to Wagner* **liken**, equate, analogize; class with, bracket with, set side by side with. **3** *the porcelain compares with Dresden's fine china* **be as good as**, be comparable to, bear comparison with, be the equal of, match up to, be on a par with, be in the same league as, come close to, hold a candle to, be not unlike; match, resemble, emulate, rival, approach.
□ **beyond compare** without equal, second to none, in a class of one's own; peerless, matchless, unmatched, incomparable, inimitable, supreme, outstanding, consummate, unique, singular, perfect.

C

comparison n. 1 *a comparison of the results* **juxtaposition**, collation, differentiation. 2 *there's no comparison between them* **resemblance**, likeness, similarity, correspondence, correlation, parallel, parity, comparability.

compartment n. 1 *a secret compartment* **section**, part, bay, recess, chamber, cavity; pocket. 2 *they put science and religion in separate compartments* **domain**, field, sphere, department; category, pigeonhole, bracket, group, set.

compartmentalize v. **categorize**, pigeonhole, bracket, group, classify, characterize, stereotype, label, brand; sort, rank, rate.

compass n. **scope**, range, extent, reach, span, breadth, ambit, limits, parameters, bounds.

compassion n. **pity**, sympathy, empathy, fellow feeling, care, concern, solicitude, sensitivity, warmth, love, tenderness, mercy, leniency, tolerance, kindness, humanity, charity.
– OPPOSITES indifference, cruelty.

compassionate adj. **sympathetic**, empathetic, understanding, caring, solicitous, sensitive, warm, loving; merciful, lenient, tolerant, considerate, kind, humane, charitable, big-hearted.

compatibility n. **like-mindedness**, similarity, affinity, closeness, fellow feeling, harmony, rapport, empathy, sympathy.

compatible adj. 1 *they were never compatible* **(well) suited**, well matched, like-minded, in tune, in harmony; reconcilable. 2 *her bruising is compatible with a fall* **consistent**, congruous, congruent; in keeping.

compatriot n. **fellow countryman/woman**, countryman, countrywoman, fellow citizen.

compel v. 1 *he compelled them to leave their land* **force**, pressurize, pressure, press, push, urge; dragoon, browbeat, bully, intimidate; oblige, require; make; informal lean on, put the screws on. 2 *they can compel compliance* **exact**, extort, demand, insist on, force, necessitate.

compelling adj. 1 *a compelling performance* **enthralling**, captivating, gripping, riveting, spellbinding, mesmerizing, absorbing, irresistible. 2 *a compelling argument* **convincing**, persuasive, cogent, irresistible, powerful, strong, weighty, plausible, credible, sound, valid, telling, conclusive, irrefutable, unanswerable.
– OPPOSITES boring, weak.

compendious adj. formal **succinct**, pithy, short and to the point, concise, compact, condensed, compressed, abridged, summarized, synoptic; informal snappy.
– OPPOSITES expanded.

compendium n. **collection**, compilation, anthology, treasury, digest; summary, synopsis, precis, outline.

compensate v. 1 *you must compensate for what you did* **make amends**, make up, make reparation, recompense, atone, requite, pay; expiate, make good, rectify. 2 *we agreed to compensate him for his loss* **recompense**, repay, pay back, reimburse, remunerate, recoup, requite, indemnify. 3 *his flair compensated for his faults* **balance (out)**, counterbalance, counteract, offset, make up for, cancel out, neutralize, negative.

compensation n. **recompense**, repayment, reimbursement, remuneration, requital, indemnification, indemnity, redress; damages; N. Amer. informal comp.

compère n. **host**, presenter, anchor, anchorman/woman, master of ceremonies, MC, announcer; N. Amer. informal emcee.

compete v. 1 *they competed in a tennis tournament* **take part**, participate, play, be a competitor, be involved; enter, go in for. 2 *they had to compete with other firms* **contend**, vie, battle, wrangle, jockey, go head-to-head; strive against, pit oneself against; challenge, take on. 3 *no one can compete with him* **rival**, challenge, keep up with, keep pace with, compare with, match, be in the same league as, come near to, come close to, touch; informal hold a candle to.

competence n. 1 *my technical competence* **capability**, ability, competency, proficiency, accomplishment, expertise, adeptness, skill, prowess, mastery, talent; informal savvy, know-how. 2 *the competence of the system* **adequacy**, appropriateness, suitability, fitness; effectiveness; formal efficacy. 3 *matters within the competence of the courts* **authority**, power, control, jurisdiction, ambit, scope, remit.

competent adj. 1 *a competent carpenter* **capable**, able, proficient, adept, adroit, accomplished, complete, skilful, skilled, gifted, talented, expert; good, excellent; informal great, mean, wicked, nifty, ace. 2 *she spoke competent French* **adequate**, acceptable, satisfactory, reasonable, fair, decent, not bad, all right, average, tolerable, passable, moderate, middling; informal OK, okay, so-so. 3 *the court was not competent to hear the case* **fit**, suitable, suited, appropriate; qualified, empowered, authorized.
– OPPOSITES inadequate, unfit.

competition n. 1 *Stephanie won the competition* **contest**, tournament, match, game, heat, fixture, event; trials, stakes. 2 *I'm not interested in competition* **rivalry**, competitiveness, vying; conflict, feuding, fighting; informal keeping up with the Joneses. 3 *we must stay ahead of the competition* **opposition**, other side, field; enemy; challengers, opponents, rivals, adversaries; literary foe.

competitive adj. 1 *a competitive player* **ambitious**, driven, zealous, keen, pushy, combative, aggressive; informal go-ahead. 2 *a highly competitive industry* **ruthless**, aggressive, fierce; informal dog-eat-dog, cut-throat. 3 *competitive prices* **reasonable**, moderate, keen; low, inexpensive, cheap, budget, bargain, reduced, discount; rock-

bottom, bargain-basement.
– OPPOSITES apathetic, exorbitant.

competitor n. **1** *the competitors in the race* **contestant**, contender, challenger, participant, entrant; runner, player. **2** *our European competitors* **rival**, challenger, opponent, adversary; competition, opposition.
– OPPOSITES ally.

compilation n. **collection**, selection, anthology, treasury, compendium, album, corpus, collectanea; potpourri.

compile v. **assemble**, put together, make up, collate, compose, organize, arrange; gather, collect.

complacency n. **smugness**, self-satisfaction, self-congratulation, self-regard; gloating, triumph, pride; satisfaction, contentment.

complacent adj. **smug**, self-satisfied, self-congratulatory, self-regarding; gloating, triumphant, proud; pleased, satisfied, content, contented; informal like the cat that got the cream, I'm-all-right-Jack; N. Amer. informal wisenheimer.

complain v. **protest**, grumble, whine, bleat, carp, cavil, grouse, make a fuss; object, speak out, oppose, criticize, find fault; informal whinge, kick up a fuss, bellyache, moan, gripe, beef, bitch, sound off; Brit. informal chunter, create; N. Amer. informal kvetch.

complaint n. **1** *they lodged a complaint* **protest**, objection, grievance, grouse, cavil, quibble, grumble; charge, accusation, criticism; informal beef, gripe, whinge; Law, Brit. plaint. **2** *little cause for complaint* **protestation**, objection, exception, grievance, grumbling; criticism, fault-finding, condemnation, disapproval, dissatisfaction; informal whingeing, grousing, bellyaching, nitpicking. **3** *a kidney complaint* **disorder**, disease, infection, affliction, illness, ailment, sickness; condition, problem, upset, trouble; informal bug, virus.

complaisant adj. **willing**, acquiescent, agreeable, amenable, cooperative, accommodating, obliging; biddable, compliant, docile, obedient.

complement n. **1** *the perfect complement to the food* **accompaniment**, companion, addition, supplement, accessory, trimming. **2** *a full complement of lifeboats* **amount**, total, contingent, capacity, allowance, quota.
▶ v. *this sauce complements the dessert* **accompany**, go with, round off, set off, suit, harmonize with; enhance, complete.

complementary adj. **harmonious**, compatible, corresponding, matching, twin, complemental; supportive, reciprocal, interdependent.
– OPPOSITES incompatible.

complete adj. **1** *the complete interview* **entire**, whole, full, total; uncut, unabridged. **2** *their research was complete* **finished**, ended, concluded, completed, finalized; accomplished, achieved, discharged, settled, done; informal wrapped up, sewn up, polished

off. **3** *a complete fool* **absolute**, out-and-out, utter, total, real, downright, thoroughgoing, veritable, prize, perfect, unqualified, unmitigated, sheer, arrant; N. Amer. informal full-bore; Brit. informal right.
– OPPOSITES partial, unfinished.
▶ v. **1** *he had to complete his training* **finish**, end, conclude, finalize, wind up; informal wrap up, sew up, polish off. **2** *the outfit was completed with a veil* **finish off**, round off, top off, crown, cap, complement. **3** *complete the application form* **fill in/out**, answer.

completely adv. **totally**, entirely, wholly, thoroughly, fully, utterly, absolutely, perfectly, unreservedly, unconditionally, quite, altogether, downright; in every way, in every respect, one hundred per cent, every inch, to the hilt; informal dead, deadly.

completion n. **realization**, accomplishment, achievement, fulfilment, consummation, finalization, resolution; finish, end, conclusion, close, cessation.

complex adj. **1** *a complex situation* **complicated**, involved, intricate, convoluted, elaborate, impenetrable, Gordian; difficult, knotty, tricky, thorny; Brit. informal fiddly. **2** *a complex structure* **compound**, composite, multiplex.
– OPPOSITES simple.
▶ n. **1** *a complex of roads* **network**, system, nexus, web, tissue; combination, aggregation. **2** informal *he had a complex about losing his hair* **obsession**, fixation, preoccupation; neurosis; informal hang-up, thing.

complexion n. **1** *a pale complexion* **skin**, skin colour, skin tone; pigmentation. **2** *this puts an entirely new complexion on things* **perspective**, angle, slant, interpretation; appearance, light, look. **3** *governments of all complexions* **type**, kind, sort; nature, character, stamp, ilk, kidney.

complexity n. **complication**, problem, difficulty; twist, turn, intricacy.

compliance n. **1** *compliance with international law* **obedience to**, observance of, adherence to, conformity to, respect for. **2** *he mistook her silence for compliance* **acquiescence**, agreement, assent, consent, acceptance; complaisance, pliability, docility, meekness, submission.
– OPPOSITES violation, defiance.

compliant adj. **acquiescent**, amenable, biddable, tractable, complaisant, accommodating, cooperative; obedient, docile, malleable, pliable, submissive, tame, yielding, controllable, unresisting, persuadable, persuasible.
– OPPOSITES recalcitrant.

complicate v. **make (more) difficult**, make complicated, mix up, confuse, muddle; informal mess up, screw up, snarl up.
– OPPOSITES simplify.

complicated adj. **complex**, intricate, involved, convoluted, tangled, impenetrable, knotty, tricky, thorny, labyrinthine, tortuous, Gordian; confusing, bewildering, perplexing;

Brit. informal **fiddly**.
– OPPOSITES straightforward.

complication n. **1** *a complication concerning ownership* **difficulty**, problem, issue, obstacle, hurdle, stumbling block; drawback, snag, catch, hitch, fly in the ointment; Brit. spanner in the works; informal hiccup, prob, headache, facer. **2** *the complication of life in our society* **complexity**, complicatedness, intricacy, convolutedness.
– OPPOSITES straightforwardness.

complicity n. **collusion**, involvement, collaboration, connivance; conspiracy.

compliment n. **1** *an unexpected compliment* **flattering remark**, tribute, accolade, commendation, bouquet, pat on the back; (**compliments**) praise, acclaim, admiration, flattery, blandishments, honeyed words. **2** *my compliments on your cooking* **congratulations**, commendations, praise; N. Amer. informal kudos. **3** *Margaret sends her compliments* **greetings**, regards, respects, good wishes, best wishes, salutations, felicitations.
– OPPOSITES insult.
▶v. *they complimented his performance* **praise**, pay tribute to, speak highly/well of, flatter, wax lyrical about, make much of, commend, acclaim, applaud, salute, honour; congratulate, pat on the back.
– OPPOSITES criticize.

complimentary adj. **1** *complimentary remarks* **flattering**, appreciative, congratulatory, admiring, approving, commendatory, favourable, glowing, adulatory; informal rave. **2** *complimentary tickets* **free (of charge)**, gratis, for nothing; courtesy; informal on the house.
– OPPOSITES derogatory.

comply v. *Myra complied with his wishes* **abide by**, observe, obey, adhere to, conform to, follow, respect; agree to, assent to, go along with, yield to, submit to, defer to; satisfy, fulfil.
– OPPOSITES ignore, disobey.

component n. *the components of electronic devices* **part**, piece, bit, element, constituent, ingredient; unit, module, section.
▶adj. *the molecule's component elements* **constituent**, integral; basic, essential.

comport v.
□ **comport oneself** formal behave, conduct oneself, act, acquit oneself; old use deport oneself.

compose v. **1** *a poem composed by Shelley* **write**, formulate, devise, make up, think up, produce, invent, concoct; pen, author, draft; literary rhyme. **2** *compose a still life* **organize**, arrange, set out. **3** *the congress is composed of ten senators* **make up**, constitute, form, comprise.
□ **compose oneself** calm down, control oneself, regain one's composure, pull oneself together, collect oneself, steady oneself, keep one's head; informal get a grip, keep one's cool; N. Amer. informal decompress.

composed adj. **calm**, collected, cool (as a cucumber), self-controlled, self-possessed; serene, tranquil, relaxed, at ease, unruffled, unperturbed, untroubled; equable, even-tempered, imperturbable; informal unflappable, together, laid-back.
– OPPOSITES excited.

composer n. **melodist**, symphonist, songwriter, songster, writer; informal tunesmith, songsmith.

composite adj. *a composite structure* **compound**, complex; combined, blended, mixed.
▶n. *a composite of plastic and metal* **amalgamation**, amalgam, combination, compound, fusion, synthesis, mixture, blend; alloy.

composition n. **1** *the composition of the council* **make-up**, constitution, configuration, structure, formation, form, framework, fabric, anatomy, organization; informal set-up. **2** *a literary composition* **work (of art)**, creation, opus, oeuvre, piece, arrangement. **3** *the composition of a poem* **writing**, creation, formulation, invention, concoction, compilation. **4** *a school composition* **essay**, paper, study, piece of writing; N. Amer. informal theme. **5** *the composition of the painting* **arrangement**, disposition, layout; proportions, balance, symmetry. **6** *an adhesive composition* **mixture**, compound, amalgam, blend, mix.

compost n. **fertilizer**, mulch, manure, bonemeal, fishmeal, guano; humus, peat; plant food, top-dressing.

composure n. **self-control**, self-possession, calm, equanimity, equilibrium, serenity, tranquillity; aplomb, poise, presence of mind, sangfroid; imperturbability, placidness, impassivity; informal cool.

compound n. *a compound of two elements* **amalgam**, amalgamation, combination, composite, blend, mixture, mix, fusion, synthesis; alloy.
▶adj. *a compound substance* **composite**, complex; blended, fused, combined.
– OPPOSITES simple.
▶v. **1** *a smell compounded of dust and mould* **be composed of**, be made up of, be formed from. **2** *soap compounded with disinfectant* **mix**, combine, blend, amalgamate, fuse, synthesize. **3** *his illness compounds their problems* **aggravate**, exacerbate, worsen, add to, augment, intensify, heighten, increase, magnify; complicate.
– OPPOSITES alleviate.

comprehend v. **1** *Katie couldn't comprehend his message* **understand**, grasp, take in, see, apprehend, follow, make sense of, fathom, get to the bottom of; unravel, decipher, interpret; informal work out, figure out, make head or tail of, get one's head around, take on board, get the drift of, catch on to, get; Brit. informal twig, suss (out). **2** formal *a divine order comprehending all men* **comprise**, include, encompass, embrace, involve, contain.
– OPPOSITES exclude.

comprehensible adj. **intelligible**, understandable, accessible; lucid, coherent, clear, plain, explicit, unambiguous, straightforward, fathomable.
– OPPOSITES opaque.

comprehension n. **understanding**, grasp, conception, apprehension, cognition; ken, knowledge, awareness, perception; interpretation.
– OPPOSITES ignorance.

comprehensive adj. **inclusive**, all-inclusive, complete; thorough, full, extensive, all-embracing, exhaustive, detailed, in-depth, encyclopedic, universal, catholic; far-reaching, radical, sweeping, across the board, wholesale; broad, wide-ranging; informal wall-to-wall.
– OPPOSITES limited.

compress v. **1** *the skirt can be compressed into a bag* **squeeze**, press, squash, crush, cram, jam, stuff; tamp, pack, compact; constrict; informal scrunch. **2** *Polly compressed her lips* **purse**, press together, pucker. **3** *the text was compressed* **abridge**, condense, shorten, cut, abbreviate, truncate; summarize, precis.
– OPPOSITES expand.

comprise v. **1** *the country comprises twenty states* **consist of**, be made up of, be composed of, contain, encompass, incorporate; include; formal comprehend. **2** *this breed comprises half the herd* **make up**, constitute, form, compose; account for.

compromise n. **1** *they reached a compromise* **agreement**, understanding, settlement, terms, deal, trade-off, bargain; middle ground, happy medium, balance. **2** *a happy marriage needs compromise* **give and take**, concession, cooperation.
▸ v. **1** *we compromised* **meet each other halfway**, come to an understanding, make a deal, make concessions, find a happy medium, strike a balance; give and take. **2** *his actions could compromise his reputation* **undermine**, weaken, damage, harm; jeopardize, prejudice; discredit, dishonour, shame, embarrass.

compulsion n. **1** *he is under no compulsion to go* **obligation**, constraint, coercion, duress, pressure, intimidation. **2** *a compulsion to tell the truth* **urge**, impulse, need, desire, drive; obsession, fixation, addiction; temptation.

compulsive adj. **1** *a compulsive desire* **irresistible**, uncontrollable, compelling, overwhelming, urgent; obsessive. **2** *compulsive eating* **obsessive**, obsessional, addictive, uncontrollable. **3** *a compulsive liar* **inveterate**, chronic, incorrigible, incurable, hardened, hopeless, persistent; obsessive, addicted, habitual; informal pathological, hooked. **4** *it's compulsive viewing* **fascinating**, compelling, gripping, riveting, engrossing, enthralling, captivating.

compulsory adj. **obligatory**, mandatory, required, requisite, necessary, essential; imperative, unavoidable, enforced, demanded, prescribed.
– OPPOSITES optional.

compunction n. **scruples**, misgivings, qualms, worries, unease, uneasiness, doubts, reluctance, reservations; guilt, regret, contrition, self-reproach.

compute v. **calculate**, work out, reckon, determine, evaluate, quantify; add up, count up, tally, total, totalize; Brit. tot up.

comrade n. **companion**, friend; colleague, associate, partner, co-worker, workmate; informal pal, chum, crony; Brit. informal mate, oppo; N. Amer. informal buddy.

con informal v. & n. See **swindle**.

concatenation n. **series**, sequence, succession, chain.

concave adj. **incurved**, curved inwards, hollow, depressed, sunken; indented, recessed.
– OPPOSITES convex.

conceal v. **1** *clouds concealed the sun* **hide**, screen, cover, obscure, block out, blot out, mask, shroud, secrete. **2** *he concealed his true feelings* **hide**, cover up, disguise, mask, veil; keep secret, keep dark, draw a veil over; suppress, repress, bottle up; informal keep a/ the lid on, keep under one's hat.
– OPPOSITES reveal, confess.

concealed adj. **hidden**, not visible, out of sight, invisible, covered, disguised, camouflaged, obscured; private, secret.

concealment n. **1** *the concealment of his weapon* **hiding**, secretion. **2** *the concealment of the bushes* **cover**, shelter, protection, screen; privacy, seclusion; secrecy. **3** *the deliberate concealment of facts* **suppression**, hiding, cover-up, hushing up; whitewash.

concede v. **1** *I had to concede that I'd overreacted* **admit**, acknowledge, accept, allow, grant, recognize, own, confess; agree. **2** *he conceded the Auvergne to the king* **surrender**, yield, give up, relinquish, cede, hand over.
– OPPOSITES deny, retain.
□ **concede defeat** capitulate, give in, surrender, yield, give up, submit, raise the white flag; back down, climb down, throw in the towel.

conceit n. **1** *his extraordinary conceit* **vanity**, narcissism, conceitedness, egotism, self-admiration, self-regard; pride, arrogance, hubris, self-importance; self-satisfaction, smugness; informal big-headedness; literary vainglory. **2** *the conceits of Shakespeare's verse* **image**, imagery, metaphor, simile, trope. **3** *the conceit of time travel* **idea**, notion, fancy.
– OPPOSITES humility.

conceited adj. **vain**, narcissistic, self-centred, egotistic, egotistical, egocentric; proud, arrogant, boastful, full of oneself, self-important, immodest, swaggering; self-satisfied, smug; supercilious, haughty, snobbish; informal big-headed, too big for one's boots, stuck-up, high and mighty, uppity, snotty; Brit. informal toffee-nosed; N. Amer. informal chesty; literary vainglorious.

conceivable adj. **imaginable**, possible; plausible, tenable, credible, believable, thinkable, feasible; understandable, comprehensible.

conceive v. **1** *she was unable to conceive* **become pregnant**, become impregnated. **2** *the project was conceived in 1977* **think up**, think of, dream up, devise, formulate, design, originate, create, develop; hatch; informal cook up. **3** *I could hardly conceive what it must be like* **imagine**, envisage, visualize, picture, think, envision; grasp, appreciate, apprehend.

concentrate v. **1** *the government concentrated its efforts* **focus**, direct, centre, centralize. **2** *she concentrated on the film* **focus on**, pay attention to, keep one's mind on, devote oneself to; be absorbed in, be engrossed in, be immersed in; informal get stuck into. **3** *troops concentrated on the horizon* **collect**, gather, congregate, converge, mass, cluster, rally. **4** *the liquid is filtered and concentrated* **condense**, boil down, reduce, thicken.
– OPPOSITES disperse, dilute.
▸n. *a fruit concentrate* **extract**, decoction, distillation.

concentrated adj. **1** *a concentrated effort* **strenuous**, concerted, intensive, intense, all-out. **2** *a concentrated solution* **condensed**, reduced, evaporated, thickened; undiluted, strong.
– OPPOSITES half-hearted, diluted.

concentration n. **1** *a task which requires concentration* **close attention**, attentiveness, application, single-mindedness, absorption. **2** *the concentration of effort* **focusing**, centralization. **3** *large concentrations of barnacle geese* **gathering**, cluster, mass, flock, congregation, assemblage.
– OPPOSITES inattention.

concept n. **idea**, notion, conception, abstraction; theory, hypothesis; belief, conviction, opinion; image, impression, picture.

conception n. **1** *bleeding can occur seven to ten days after conception* **fertilization**, impregnation, insemination. **2** *the product's conception* **inception**, genesis, origination, creation, invention; beginning, origin. **3** *his original conception* **plan**, scheme, project, proposal; intention, aim, idea. **4** *my conception of democracy* **idea**, concept, notion, understanding, abstraction; theory, hypothesis; perception, image, impression. **5** *they had no conception of our problems* **understanding**, comprehension, appreciation, grasp, knowledge; idea, inkling; informal clue.

concern v. **1** *the report concerns the war* **be about**, deal with, cover; discuss, go into, examine, study, review, analyse; relate to, pertain to. **2** *that doesn't concern you* **affect**, involve, be relevant to, apply to, have a bearing on, impact on; be important to, interest. **3** *I won't concern myself with your affairs* **involve oneself in**, take an interest in, busy oneself with, devote one's time to, bother oneself with. **4** *one thing still concerns me* **worry**, disturb, trouble, bother, perturb, unsettle, make anxious.
▸n. **1** *a voice full of concern* **anxiety**, worry, disquiet, apprehensiveness, unease, consternation. **2** *his concern for others* **solicitude**, solicitousness, consideration, care, sympathy, regard. **3** *housing is the concern of the council* **responsibility**, business, affair, charge, duty, job; province, preserve; problem, worry; informal pigeon, bag, bailiwick; Brit. informal lookout. **4** *issues that are of concern to women* **interest**, importance, relevance, significance. **5** *Aboriginal concerns* **affair**, issue, matter, question, consideration. **6** *a publishing concern* **company**, business, firm, organization, operation, corporation, establishment, house, office, agency; informal outfit, set-up.
– OPPOSITES indifference.

concerned adj. **1** *her mother looked concerned* **worried**, anxious, upset, perturbed, troubled, distressed, uneasy, apprehensive, agitated. **2** *he is concerned about your welfare* **solicitous**, caring; attentive to, considerate of. **3** *all concerned parties* **interested**, involved, affected; connected, related, implicated.

concerning prep. **about**, regarding, relating to, with reference to, referring to, with regard to, as regards, with respect to, respecting, dealing with, on the subject of, in connection with, re, apropos of.

concert n. **musical performance**, show, production, presentation; recital; informal gig.
□ **in concert** together, jointly, in combination, in collaboration, in cooperation, in league, side by side; in unison.

concerted adj. **1** *make a concerted effort* **strenuous**, vigorous, intensive, intense, concentrated, all-out. **2** *concerted action* **joint**, united, collaborative, collective, combined, cooperative.
– OPPOSITES half-hearted, individual.

concession n. **1** *the government made several concessions* **compromise**, allowance, exception, sop. **2** *a concession of failure* **admission**, acknowledgement, acceptance, recognition, confession. **3** *the concession of territory* **surrender**, relinquishment, sacrifice, handover. **4** *tax concessions* **reduction**, cut, discount, deduction, decrease; rebate; informal break. **5** *a logging concession* **right**, privilege; licence, permit, franchise, warrant, authorization.
– OPPOSITES denial, acquisition.

conciliate v. **1** *he tried to conciliate the peasantry* **appease**, placate, pacify, mollify, assuage, soothe, humour, reconcile, win over, make peace with. **2** *he conciliated in the dispute* **mediate**, act as peacemaker, arbitrate; pour oil on troubled waters.
– OPPOSITES provoke.

conciliator n. **peacemaker**, mediator, go-between, middleman, intermediary, intercessor; dove.
– OPPOSITES troublemaker.

conciliatory adj. **propitiatory**, placatory, appeasing, pacifying, pacific, mollifying, peacemaking.

concise adj. **succinct**, pithy, incisive, brief, short and to the point, short and sweet; abridged, condensed, compressed, abbreviated, compact, potted; informal snappy.
– OPPOSITES lengthy, wordy.

conclave n. **(private) meeting**, gathering, assembly, conference, council, summit; informal parley, powwow, get-together.

conclude v. **1** *the meeting concluded at ten* **finish**, end, draw to a close, be over, stop, cease. **2** *he concluded the press conference* **bring to an end**, close, wind up, terminate, dissolve; round off; informal wrap up. **3** *an attempt to conclude a ceasefire* **negotiate**, broker, agree, settle, clinch, finalize, tie up; bring about, arrange, effect, engineer; informal sew up. **4** *I concluded that he was rather unpleasant* **deduce**, infer, gather, judge, decide, conjecture, surmise; N. Amer. figure; informal reckon.
– OPPOSITES commence.

conclusion n. **1** *the conclusion of his speech* **end**, ending, finish, close, termination, wind-up, cessation; culmination, denouement, coda. **2** *the conclusion of a trade agreement* **negotiation**, brokering, settlement, completion, arrangement, resolution. **3** *his conclusions have been verified* **deduction**, inference, interpretation, reasoning; opinion, judgement, verdict; assumption, presumption, supposition.
– OPPOSITES beginning.
  □ **in conclusion** finally, in closing, to conclude, last but not least; to sum up, in short.

conclusive adj. **1** *conclusive proof* **incontrovertible**, undeniable, indisputable, irrefutable, unquestionable, unassailable, convincing, certain, decisive, definitive, definite, positive, categorical, unequivocal; airtight, watertight. **2** *a conclusive win* **emphatic**, resounding, convincing.
– OPPOSITES unconvincing.

concoct v. **1** *she began to concoct her dinner* **prepare**, make, assemble; informal fix, rustle up; Brit. informal knock up. **2** *this story she has concocted* **make up**, dream up, fabricate, invent, trump up; formulate, hatch, brew; informal cook up.

concoction n. **1** *a concoction containing gin and vodka* **mixture**, brew, preparation, potion. **2** *a strange concoction of styles* **blend**, mixture, mix, combination, hybrid. **3** *her story is an improbable concoction* **fabrication**, invention, falsification; informal fairy story, fairy tale.

concomitant adj. formal **attendant**, accompanying, associated, related, connected; resultant, consequent.
– OPPOSITES unrelated.

concord n. formal **1** *council meetings rarely ended in concord* **agreement**, harmony, accord, consensus, concurrence, unity. **2** *a concord was to be drawn up* **treaty**, agreement, accord, pact, compact, settlement.
– OPPOSITES discord.

concourse n. **1** *the station concourse* **entrance**, foyer, lobby, hall. **2** formal *a vast concourse of onlookers* **crowd**, group, gathering, assembly, body, company, throng, flock, mass.

concrete adj. **1** *concrete objects* **solid**, material, real, physical, tangible, palpable, substantial, visible, existing. **2** *concrete proof* **definite**, firm, positive, conclusive, definitive; real, genuine, bona fide.
– OPPOSITES abstract, imaginary.

concubine n. old use **mistress**, kept woman; lover; informal fancy woman, bit on the side; old use paramour.

concur v. **1** *we concur with this view* **agree**, be in agreement, go along, fall in, be in sympathy; see eye to eye, be of the same mind, be of the same opinion. **2** *the two events concurred* **coincide**, be simultaneous, be concurrent, coexist.
– OPPOSITES disagree.

concurrent adj. **1** *nine concurrent life sentences* **simultaneous**, coincident, contemporaneous, parallel. **2** *concurrent lines* **convergent**, converging, meeting, intersecting.

concussion n. **1** *he suffered concussion* temporary unconsciousness; brain injury. **2** *the concussion of the blast* **force**, impact, shock, jolt.

condemn v. **1** *he condemned the suspended players* **censure**, criticize, denounce, revile, blame, chastise, berate, reprimand, rebuke, reprove, take to task, find fault with; informal slam, blast, lay into; Brit. informal slate, slag off; formal castigate. **2** *he was condemned to death* **sentence**; convict, find guilty. **3** *the house has been condemned* **declare unfit**, declare unsafe. **4** *her mistake had condemned her* **incriminate**, implicate; old use inculpate. **5** *his illness condemned him to a lonely life* **doom**, destine, damn; consign, assign.
– OPPOSITES praise.

condemnation n. **censure**, criticism, strictures, denunciation, vilification; reproof, disapproval; informal flak, a bad press; formal castigation.

condemnatory adj. **censorious**, critical, damning; reproving, reproachful, deprecatory, disapproving, unfavourable; formal castigatory.

condemned adj. **1** *a condemned building* **unsafe**, dangerous, hazardous, perilous, precarious, insecure, treacherous; **dilapidated**, ramshackle, rickety, run down, broken-down, worn out, deteriorating, deteriorated, decrepit, tumbledown, crumbling, in (a state of) disrepair, neglected, in ruins, ruined. **2** *condemned meat* **unhealthy**, unsafe, contaminated, unsound, infected, blighted, unwholesome, septic, rotten, bad. **3** *condemned prisoners* **convicted**, sentenced, censured, doomed,

C

damned, lost.
– OPPOSITES safe, in good repair, wholesome, innocent, reprieved.

condensation n. **1** *windows misty with condensation* **moisture**, water droplets, steam. **2** *the condensation of the vapour* **precipitation**, liquefaction, deliquescence. **3** *a condensation of recent literature* **abridgement**, summary, synopsis, precis, digest. **4** *the condensation of the report* **shortening**, abridgement, abbreviation, summarization.

condense v. **1** *the water vapour condenses* **precipitate**, liquefy, become liquid, deliquesce. **2** *he condensed the play* **abridge**, shorten, cut, abbreviate, compact; summarize, synopsize, precis; truncate, curtail.
– OPPOSITES vaporize, expand.

condensed adj. **1** *a condensed text* **abridged**, shortened, cut, compressed, abbreviated, reduced, truncated, concise; outline, thumbnail; informal potted. **2** *condensed soup* **concentrated**, evaporated, reduced; strong, undiluted.
– OPPOSITES diluted.

condescend v. **1** *don't condescend to your reader* **patronize**, talk down to, look down one's nose at, look down on, put down. **2** *he condescended to see us* **deign**, stoop, descend, lower oneself, demean oneself; vouchsafe, see fit, consent.

condescending adj. **patronizing**, supercilious, superior, snobbish, snobby, disdainful, lofty, haughty; informal snooty, stuck-up; Brit. informal toffee-nosed.

condition n. **1** *check the condition of your wiring* **state**, shape, order; Brit. informal nick. **2** *they lived in appalling conditions* **circumstances**, surroundings, environment, situation, setting, habitat; informal circs, set-up. **3** *she was in tip-top condition* **fitness**, health, form, shape, trim, fettle. **4** *a liver condition* **disorder**, problem, complaint, illness, disease, ailment, sickness, affliction, infection, upset; informal bug, virus; Brit. informal lurgy. **5** *a condition of employment* **stipulation**, constraint, prerequisite, precondition, requirement, rule, term, specification, provision, proviso.
▶ v. **1** *their choices are conditioned by the economy* **constrain**, control, govern, determine, decide; affect, touch, impact on; form, shape, guide, sway, bias. **2** *our minds are conditioned by habit* **train**, teach, educate, guide; accustom, adapt, habituate, mould, inure. **3** *condition the boards with water* **treat**, prepare, prime, temper, process, acclimatize, acclimate, season. **4** *a product to condition your skin* **improve**, nourish, tone (up), moisturize.

conditional adj. **1** *their approval is conditional on success* **subject to**, dependent on, contingent on, based on, determined by, controlled by, tied to. **2** *a conditional offer* **contingent**, dependent, qualified, with reservations, limited, provisional, provisory.

condolences plural n. **sympathy**, commiseration(s), compassion, pity, support, comfort, consolation, understanding.

condom n. **contraceptive**, sheath; N. Amer. prophylactic; Brit. trademark Durex, Femidom; Brit. informal johnny; N. Amer. informal rubber, safe; Brit. informal dated French letter; dated protective.

condone v. **disregard**, accept, allow, let pass, turn a blind eye to, overlook, forget; forgive, pardon, excuse, let go.
– OPPOSITES condemn.

conducive adj. **favourable**, beneficial, advantageous, opportune, propitious, encouraging, promising, convenient, good, helpful, instrumental, productive, useful.
– OPPOSITES unfavourable.

conduct n. **1** *they complained about her conduct* **behaviour**, performance, demeanour; actions, activities, deeds, doings, exploits; habits, manners; formal comportment. **2** *the conduct of the elections* **management**, running, direction, control, supervision, regulation, administration, organization, coordination, orchestration, handling.
▶ v. **1** *the election was conducted lawfully* **manage**, direct, run, administer, organize, coordinate, orchestrate, handle, control, oversee, supervise, regulate, carry out/on. **2** *he was conducted through the corridors* **escort**, guide, lead, usher, show; shepherd, see, bring, take, help. **3** *aluminium conducts heat* **transmit**, convey, carry, transfer, impart, channel, relay; disseminate, diffuse, radiate.
□ **conduct oneself** behave, act, acquit oneself, bear oneself; formal comport oneself; old use deport oneself.

conduit n. **channel**, duct, pipe, tube, gutter, trench, culvert, cut, sluice, spillway, flume, chute.

confectionery n. **sweets**, chocolates, bonbons; N. Amer. candy; informal sweeties; old use sweetmeats.

confederacy n. **federation**, confederation, alliance, league, association, coalition, consortium, syndicate, group, circle; bloc, axis.

confederate adj. *confederate councils* **federal**, confederated, federated, allied, associated, united.
– OPPOSITES split.
▶ n. *he met his confederate in the street* **associate**, partner, accomplice, helper, assistant, ally, collaborator, colleague; Brit. informal oppo; Austral./NZ informal offsider.

confederation n. **alliance**, league, confederacy, federation, association, coalition, consortium, conglomerate, cooperative, syndicate, group, circle; society, union.

confer v. **1** *she conferred a knighthood on him* **bestow**, present to, grant to, award to, decorate with, honour with, give to, endow with, extend to, vouchsafe to. **2** *she went to confer with her colleagues* **consult**, talk, speak, converse, have a chat, have a tête-à-tête, parley; informal have a confab, powwow.

conference n. **1** *an international conference* **congress**, meeting, convention, seminar, colloquium, symposium, forum, summit. **2** *he gathered them for a conference* **discussion**, consultation, debate, talk, conversation, dialogue, chat, tête-à-tête, parley; informal confab; formal confabulation.

confess v. **1** *he confessed that he had done it* **admit**, acknowledge, reveal, disclose, divulge, avow, declare, profess; own up, tell all; informal fess up. **2** *they could not make him confess* **own up**, plead guilty, accept the blame; tell the truth, tell all, make a clean breast of it; informal come clean, spill the beans, let the cat out of the bag, get something off one's chest, let on; Brit. informal cough. **3** *I confess I don't know* **acknowledge**, admit, concede, grant, allow, own, declare, affirm.
– OPPOSITES deny.

confession n. **admission**, acknowledgement, profession; revelation, disclosure, divulgence, avowal; guilty plea.

confidant, **confidante** n. **close friend**, bosom friend, best friend; intimate, familiar; informal chum, pal, crony; Brit. informal mate, oppo, mucker; N. Amer. informal buddy.

confide v. **1** *he confided his fears to his mother* **reveal**, disclose, divulge, lay bare, betray, impart, declare, intimate, uncover, expose, vouchsafe, tell; confess, admit, give away; informal blab, spill. **2** *I need him to confide in* **open one's heart to**, unburden oneself to, confess to, tell all to.

confidence n. **1** *I have little confidence in these figures* **trust**, belief, faith, credence, conviction. **2** *she's brimming with confidence* **self-assurance**, self-confidence, self-possession, assertiveness; poise, aplomb, phlegm; courage, boldness, mettle, nerve. **3** *the girls exchanged confidences* **secret**, confidentiality, intimacy.
– OPPOSITES scepticism, doubt.

confident adj. **1** *we are confident that business will improve* **optimistic**, hopeful, sanguine; sure, certain, positive, convinced, in no doubt, satisfied, assured, persuaded. **2** *a confident girl* **self-assured**, assured, self-confident, positive, assertive, self-possessed, self-reliant, poised; cool-headed, phlegmatic, level-headed, unperturbed, imperturbable, unruffled, at ease; informal together.

confidential adj. **1** *a confidential chat* **private**, personal, intimate, quiet; secret, sensitive, classified, restricted, unofficial, unrevealed, undisclosed, unpublished; informal hush-hush, mum; formal sub rosa; old use privy. **2** *a confidential friend* **trusted**, trustworthy, trusty, faithful, reliable, dependable; close, bosom, intimate.

confidentially adv. **privately**, in private, in confidence, between ourselves/themselves, off the record, quietly, secretly, in secret, behind closed doors; formal sub rosa.

configuration n. **arrangement**, layout, geography, design, organization, order,

grouping, positioning, disposition, alignment; shape, form, appearance, formation, structure, format.

confine v. **1** *they were confined in the house* **enclose**, incarcerate, imprison, intern, impound, hold captive, trap, kettle; shut in/up, keep, lock in/up, coop (up); fence in, hedge in, wall in/up. **2** *he confined his remarks to the weather* **restrict**, limit.

confined adj. **cramped**, constricted, restricted, limited, small, narrow, compact, tight, poky, uncomfortable, inadequate.
– OPPOSITES roomy.

confinement n. **1** *solitary confinement* **imprisonment**, internment, incarceration, custody, captivity, detention, restraint; house arrest. **2** *the confinement of an animal* **caging**, enclosure; quarantine. **3** dated *she went to hospital for her confinement* **labour**, delivery, birthing; birth, childbirth; formal parturition; old use lying-in, childbed.

confines plural n. **limits**, margins, extremities, edges, borders, boundaries, fringes, marches; periphery, perimeter.

confirm v. **1** *records confirm the latest evidence* **corroborate**, verify, prove, validate, authenticate, substantiate, justify, vindicate, support, uphold, back up. **2** *he confirmed that help was on the way* **affirm**, reaffirm, assert, assure someone, repeat; promise, guarantee. **3** *his appointment was confirmed by the President* **ratify**, validate, sanction, endorse, formalize, authorize, warrant, accredit, approve, accept.
– OPPOSITES contradict, deny.

confirmation n. **1** *independent confirmation of the deaths* **corroboration**, verification, proof, testimony, endorsement, authentication, substantiation, evidence. **2** *confirmation of your appointment* **ratification**, approval, authorization, validation, sanction, endorsement, formalization, accreditation, acceptance.

confirmed adj. **established**, long-standing, committed, dyed-in-the-wool, through and through; staunch, loyal, faithful, devoted, dedicated, steadfast; habitual, compulsive, persistent; unapologetic, unashamed, inveterate, chronic, incurable; informal deep-dyed, card-carrying.

confiscate v. **impound**, seize, commandeer, requisition, appropriate, expropriate, sequester, sequestrate, take (away); Law distrain; Scottish Law poind, poinding.
– OPPOSITES return.

confiscation n. **seizure**, requisition, appropriation, expropriation, sequestration; Law distraint, distrainment; Scottish Law poind.

conflagration n. **fire**, blaze, flames, inferno, firestorm.

conflict n. **1** *industrial conflicts* **dispute**, quarrel, squabble, disagreement, dissension, clash; discord, friction, strife, antagonism, hostility, disputation, contention; feud, schism. **2** *the Vietnam conflict* **war**, campaign, battle, fighting, (armed) confrontation, engagement, encounter,

struggle, hostilities; warfare, combat. **3** *a conflict between his business and domestic life* **clash**, incompatibility, incongruity, friction; mismatch, variance, difference, divergence, contradiction, inconsistency.
– OPPOSITES agreement, peace, harmony.
▶v. *their interests sometimes conflict* **clash**, be incompatible, vary, be at odds, be in conflict, differ, diverge, disagree, contrast, collide.

conflicting adj. **contradictory**, incompatible, inconsistent, irreconcilable, incongruous, contrary, opposite, opposing, antithetical, clashing, discordant, divergent; at odds.

confluence n. **convergence**, meeting, junction, conflux, watersmeet.

conform v. **1** *visitors have to conform to our rules* **comply with**, abide by, obey, observe, follow, keep to, stick to, adhere to, uphold, heed, accept, go along with, fall in with, respect, defer to; satisfy, meet, fulfil. **2** *they refuse to conform* **follow convention**, be conventional, fit in, adapt, adjust, follow the crowd; comply, acquiesce, toe the line, follow the rules; submit, yield; informal play it by the book, play by the rules. **3** *goods must conform to their description* **match**, fit, suit, answer, agree with, be like, correspond to, be consistent with, measure up to, tally with, square with.
– OPPOSITES flout, rebel.

conformist n. **conventionalist**, traditionalist, conservative, stickler, formalist, diehard, reactionary; informal stick-in-the-mud, stuffed shirt.
– OPPOSITES eccentric, rebel.

confound v. **1** *the figures confounded analysts* **amaze**, astonish, dumbfound, stagger, surprise, startle, stun, nonplus; throw, shake, discompose, bewilder, baffle, mystify, bemuse, perplex, puzzle, confuse; take aback, shake up, catch off balance; informal flabbergast, blow someone's mind, blow away, flummox, faze, stump, beat, fox; N. Amer. informal discombobulate. **2** *he has always confounded expectations* **contradict**, counter, invalidate, negate, go against, throw a coach and horses through; quash, explode, demolish, shoot down, destroy, disprove; informal shoot full of holes.

confront v. **1** *Jones confronted the burglar* **challenge**, square up to, face (up to), come face to face with, meet, accost, waylay; stand up to, brave, beard, tackle; informal collar; Brit. informal nobble. **2** *the problems that confront us* **trouble**, bother, burden, distress, worry, oppress, annoy, strain, stress, tax, torment, plague, blight, curse; face, beset. **3** *they must confront their problems* **tackle**, address, face, get to grips with, grapple with, take on, attend to, see to, deal with, take care of, handle, manage; informal get stuck into. **4** *she confronted him with the evidence* **present**, face.
– OPPOSITES avoid.

confrontation n. **conflict**, clash, fight, battle, encounter, head-to-head, face-off,

engagement, skirmish; hostilities, fighting; informal set-to, run-in, dust-up, showdown; Brit. informal, Football afters.

confuse v. **1** *don't confuse students with too much detail* **bewilder**, baffle, mystify, bemuse, perplex, puzzle, confound, nonplus; informal flummox, faze, stump, fox; N. Amer. informal discombobulate. **2** *the authors have confused the issue* **complicate**, muddle, jumble, garble, blur, obscure, cloud. **3** *some confuse strokes with heart attacks* **mix up**, muddle up, confound; mistake for.
– OPPOSITES enlighten, simplify.

confused adj. **1** *they are confused about what is going on* **bewildered**, bemused, puzzled, perplexed, baffled, mystified, nonplussed, muddled, dumbfounded, at sea, at a loss, taken aback, disoriented, disconcerted; informal flummoxed, bamboozled, clueless, fazed; N. Amer. informal discombobulated. **2** *her confused elderly mother* **demented**, bewildered, muddled, addled, befuddled, disoriented, disorientated; unbalanced, unhinged; senile. **3** *a confused recollection* **vague**, unclear, indistinct, imprecise, blurred, hazy, woolly, shadowy, dim; imperfect, sketchy. **4** *a confused mass of bones* **disorderly**, disordered, disorganized, disarranged, out of order, untidy, muddled, jumbled, mixed up, chaotic, topsy-turvy; informal higgledy-piggledy; Brit. informal shambolic.
– OPPOSITES lucid, clear, precise, neat.

confusing adj. **bewildering**, baffling, unclear, perplexing, puzzling, mystifying, disconcerting; ambiguous, misleading, inconsistent, contradictory; unaccountable, inexplicable, impenetrable, unfathomable; complex, complicated.

confusion n. **1** *there is confusion about the new system* **uncertainty**, incertitude, unsureness, doubt, ignorance; formal dubiety. **2** *she stared in confusion* **bewilderment**, bafflement, perplexity, puzzlement, mystification, befuddlement; shock, daze, wonder, wonderment, astonishment; informal bamboozlement; N. Amer. informal discombobulation. **3** *her life was in utter confusion* **disorder**, disarray, disorganization, untidiness, chaos, mayhem; turmoil, tumult, disruption, upheaval, uproar, hurly-burly, muddle, mess; informal shambles. **4** *a confusion of boxes* **jumble**, muddle, mess, heap, tangle; informal shambles.
– OPPOSITES certainty, order.

confute v. formal **disprove**, contradict, controvert, refute, deny, rebut, belie, negate, invalidate, explode, discredit, debunk, quash, drive a coach and horses through; informal shoot full of holes; formal gainsay.
– OPPOSITES prove.

congeal v. **coagulate**, clot, thicken, gel, inspissate, cake, set, curdle.

congenial adj. **1** *very congenial people* **like-minded**, compatible, kindred, well suited; companionable, sociable, sympathetic, comradely, convivial, hospitable, genial,

personable, agreeable, friendly, pleasant, likeable, amiable, nice. **2** *a congenial environment* **pleasant**, pleasing, agreeable, enjoyable, pleasurable, nice, appealing, satisfying, gratifying, delightful, relaxing, welcoming, hospitable; suitable, well suited, favourable.
– OPPOSITES unpleasant.

congenital adj. **1** *congenital defects* **inborn**, inherited, hereditary, innate, inbred, constitutional, inbuilt, natural, inherent. **2** *a congenital liar* **inveterate**, compulsive, persistent, chronic, regular, habitual, obsessive, confirmed; incurable, incorrigible, irredeemable, hopeless; unashamed, shameless; informal pathological.
– OPPOSITES acquired.

congested adj. **crowded**, overcrowded, full, overflowing, packed, jammed, thronged, teeming, swarming; obstructed, blocked, clogged, choked; informal snarled up, gridlocked, jam-packed; Brit. informal like Piccadilly Circus.
– OPPOSITES clear.

congestion n. **crowding**, overcrowding; obstruction, blockage; traffic jam, bottleneck; informal snarl-up, gridlock.

conglomerate n. **1** *the conglomerate was broken up* **corporation**, combine, group, consortium, partnership; firm, company, business, multinational. **2** *a conglomerate of disparate peoples* **mixture**, mix, combination, amalgamation, union, marriage, fusion, composite, synthesis; miscellany, hotchpotch.
▸ adj. *a conglomerate mass* **aggregate**, agglomerate, amassed, combined.
▸ v. *the debris conglomerated into planets* **coalesce**, unite, join, combine, merge, fuse, consolidate, amalgamate, integrate, mingle, intermingle.

congratulate v. **1** *she congratulated him on his marriage* **send one's best wishes**, wish someone good luck; drink someone's health, toast. **2** *they are to be congratulated* **praise**, commend, applaud, salute, honour; pay tribute to, regard highly, pat on the back, take one's hat off to.
– OPPOSITES criticize.
▫ **congratulate oneself** take pride, feel proud, flatter oneself, preen oneself, pat oneself on the back; feel satisfaction, take pleasure, glory, bask, delight.

congratulations plural n. **1** *her congratulations on their wedding* **good wishes**, best wishes, compliments, felicitations. **2** *you all deserve congratulations* **praise**, commendation, applause, salutes, honour, acclaim, cheers, bouquets; approval, admiration, compliments, adulation; a pat on the back; N. Amer. informal kudos.

congregate v. **assemble**, gather, collect, come together, convene, rally, rendezvous, muster, meet, cluster, group.
– OPPOSITES disperse.

congregation n. **1** *the chapel congregation* **parishioners**, parish, churchgoers, flock, faithful, followers, believers, fellowship, communicants, laity, brethren; throng, company, assemblage, audience. **2** *congregations of birds* **gathering**, assembly, flock, swarm, bevy, pack, group, body, crowd, mass, multitude, horde, host, mob, throng.

congress n. **1** *an annual congress of mathematicians* **conference**, convention, seminar, colloquium, symposium, forum, meeting, assembly, gathering, rally, summit. **2** *elections for the new Congress* **legislature**, legislative assembly, parliament, convocation, diet, council, senate, chamber, house.

congruence n. **compatibility**, consistency, conformity, match, balance, consonance, congruity; agreement, accord, consensus, harmony, unity; formal concord.
– OPPOSITES conflict.

conical adj. **cone-shaped**, tapered, tapering, pointed, funnel-shaped; informal pointy; Zoology conoid.

conjectural adj. **speculative**, suppositional, suppositious, theoretical, hypothetical, putative, notional; postulated, inferred, presumed, assumed, presupposed, tentative.

conjecture n. *the information is merely conjecture* **speculation**, guesswork, surmise, fancy, presumption, assumption, theory, postulation, supposition; inference, extrapolation; estimate; informal guesstimate, a shot in the dark.
– OPPOSITES fact.
▸ v. *I conjectured that the game was over* **guess**, speculate, surmise, infer, fancy, imagine, believe, think, suspect, presume, assume, hypothesize, suppose.
– OPPOSITES know.

conjugal adj. **marital**, matrimonial, nuptial, marriage, bridal; Law spousal; literary connubial.

conjunction n. **co-occurrence**, concurrence, coincidence, coexistence, simultaneity, contemporaneity, concomitance, synchronicity, synchrony.

conjure v. **1** *he conjured a cigarette out of the air* **produce**, make something appear, materialize, magic, summon. **2** *the picture that his words conjured up* **bring to mind**, call to mind, evoke, summon up, recall, recreate; echo, allude to, suggest, awaken.

conjuring n. **magic**, illusion, sleight of hand, legerdemain; formal prestidigitation.

conjuror n. **magician**, illusionist; formal prestidigitator.

connect v. **1** *electrodes were connected to the device* **attach**, join, fasten, fix, affix, couple, link, secure, hitch; stick, adhere, fuse, pin, screw, bolt, clamp, clip, hook (up); add, append. **2** *customs connected with Easter* **associate**, link, couple; identify, equate, bracket, relate to.

connection n. **1** *the connection between commerce and art* **link**, relationship, relation, interconnection, interdependence,

association; bond, tie, tie-in, correspondence, parallel, analogy. **2** *a poor connection in the plug* **attachment**, joint, fastening, coupling. **3** *he has the right connections* **contact**, friend, acquaintance, ally, colleague, associate; relation, relative, kin.
□ **in connection with** regarding, concerning, with reference to, with regard to, with respect to, respecting, relating to, in relation to, on, connected with, on the subject of, in the matter of, apropos, re, in re.

connivance n. **collusion**, complicity, collaboration, involvement, assistance; tacit consent, conspiracy, intrigue.

connive v. **1** *wardens connived at offences deliberately* **ignore**, overlook, disregard, pass over, take no notice of, make allowances for, turn a blind eye to, wink at, excuse, condone, let go; look the other way. **2** *the government connived with security forces* **conspire**, collude, collaborate, intrigue, be hand in glove, plot, scheme; informal be in cahoots.

conniving adj. **scheming**, cunning, crafty, calculating, devious, wily, sly, tricky, artful, guileful; manipulative, Machiavellian, disingenuous, deceitful, underhand, treacherous; informal foxy.

connoisseur n. **expert**, authority, specialist, pundit, savant; arbiter of taste, aesthete; gourmet, epicure, gastronome; informal buff; N. Amer. informal maven.

connotation n. **overtone**, undertone, undercurrent, implication, hidden meaning, nuance, hint, echo, vibrations, association, intimation, suggestion, suspicion, insinuation.

connote v. **imply**, suggest, indicate, signify, hint at, give the impression of, smack of, be associated with, allude to.

conquer v. **1** *the Franks conquered the Visigoths* **defeat**, beat, vanquish, trounce, triumph over, be victorious over, get the better of, worst; overcome, overwhelm, overpower, overthrow, subdue, subjugate, quell, quash, crush, rout; informal lick, best, hammer, clobber, thrash, paste, demolish, annihilate, wipe the floor with, walk all over, make mincemeat of, massacre, slaughter; Brit. informal stuff; N. Amer. informal cream, shellac, skunk. **2** *Peru was conquered by Spain* **seize**, take (over), appropriate, subjugate, capture, occupy, invade, annex, overrun. **3** *the first men to conquer Mount Everest* **climb**, ascend, mount, scale, top, crest. **4** *the way to conquer fear* **overcome**, get the better of, control, master, get a grip on, deal with, cope with, surmount, rise above, get over; quell, quash, beat, triumph over; informal lick.
– OPPOSITES lose.

conqueror n. **vanquisher**, conquistador; victor, winner, champion, conquering hero.

conquest n. **1** *the conquest of the Aztecs* **defeat**, annihilation, overthrow, subjugation, rout, mastery, crushing; victory over, triumph over. **2** *their conquest of the valley* **seizure**, takeover,

capture, occupation, invasion, acquisition, appropriation, subjugation, subjection. **3** *the conquest of Everest* **ascent**. **4** *she's his latest conquest* **catch**, acquisition, prize, slave; admirer, fan, worshipper; lover, boyfriend, girlfriend; informal fancy man, fancy woman.
– OPPOSITES surrender.

conscience n. **sense of right and wrong**, moral sense, inner voice; morals, standards, values, principles, ethics, beliefs; compunction, scruples, qualms.

conscience-stricken adj. **guilt-ridden**, remorseful, ashamed, shamefaced, apologetic, sorry; chastened, contrite, guilty, regretful, rueful, repentant, penitent, self-reproachful, abashed, sheepish, compunctious.
– OPPOSITES unrepentant.

conscientious adj. **diligent**, industrious, punctilious, painstaking, sedulous, assiduous, dedicated, careful, meticulous, thorough, attentive, hard-working, studious, rigorous, particular; religious, strict.
– OPPOSITES casual.

conscious adj. **1** *the patient was conscious* **aware**, awake, alert, responsive, sentient, compos mentis. **2** *he became conscious of people talking* **aware of**, alert to, mindful of, sensible of; formal cognizant of; old use ware of. **3** *a conscious effort* **deliberate**, intentional, intended, purposeful, purposive, knowing, considered, calculated, wilful, premeditated, planned, volitional; Law, dated prepense.
– OPPOSITES unaware.

conscript v. *they were conscripted into the army* **call up**, enlist, recruit; US draft; historical press, impress.
▸ n. *an army conscript* recruit; US draftee.
– OPPOSITES volunteer.

consecrate v. **sanctify**, bless, make holy, make sacred; dedicate to God, devote, reserve, set apart; anoint, ordain; formal hallow.

consecutive adj. **successive**, succeeding, following, in succession, running, in a row, one after the other, back-to-back, continuous, straight, uninterrupted; informal on the trot.

consensus n. **1** *there was consensus among delegates* **agreement**, harmony, concurrence, accord, unity, unanimity, solidarity; formal concord. **2** *the consensus was that they should act* **general opinion**, majority opinion, common view.
– OPPOSITES disagreement.

consent n. *the consent of all members* **agreement**, assent, acceptance, approval, approbation; permission, authorization, sanction, leave; backing, endorsement, support; informal go-ahead, thumbs up, green light, OK.
– OPPOSITES dissent.
▸ v. *she consented to surgery* **agree**, assent, yield, give in, submit; allow, give permission for, sanction, accept, approve, go along with.
– OPPOSITES forbid.

consequence n. 1 *a consequence of inflation* **result**, upshot, outcome, out-turn, effect, repercussion, ramification, corollary, concomitant, aftermath; fruit(s), product, by-product, end result; informal pay-off; Medicine sequela. 2 *the past is of no consequence* **importance**, import, significance, account, substance, note, mark, prominence, value, concern, interest; formal moment.
– OPPOSITES cause.

consequent adj. **resulting**, resultant, ensuing, consequential; following, subsequent, successive; attendant, accompanying, concomitant; collateral, associated, related.

consequential adj. 1 *a fire and the consequential smoke damage* **resulting**, resultant, ensuing, consequent; following, subsequent; attendant, accompanying, concomitant; collateral, associated, related. 2 *one of his more consequential initiatives* **important**, significant, major, momentous, weighty, material, appreciable, memorable, far-reaching, serious.
– OPPOSITES insignificant.

consequently adv. **as a result**, as a consequence, so, thus, therefore, ergo, accordingly, hence, for this/that reason, because of this/that, on this/that account; inevitably, necessarily.

conservation n. **preservation**, protection, safeguarding, safe keeping; care, guardianship, husbandry, supervision; upkeep, maintenance, repair, restoration; ecology, environmentalism.

conservative adj. 1 *the conservative wing of the party* **right-wing**, reactionary, traditionalist; Brit. Tory, blimpish; US Republican; informal true blue. 2 *the conservative trade-union movement* **traditionalist**, traditional, conventional, orthodox, old-fashioned, dyed-in-the-wool, hidebound, unadventurous, set in one's ways; moderate, middle-of-the-road; informal stick-in-the-mud. 3 *a conservative suit* **conventional**, sober, modest, plain, unobtrusive, restrained, subtle, low-key, demure; informal square, straight. 4 *a conservative estimate* **low**, cautious, understated, moderate, reasonable.
– OPPOSITES socialist, radical, ostentatious.
▶ n. *liberals and conservatives have found common ground* **right-winger**, reactionary, rightist, diehard; Brit. Tory, blimp; US Republican.

conservatory n. 1 *a frost-free conservatory* **summer house**, belvedere; glasshouse, greenhouse, hothouse. 2 *a teaching job at the conservatory* **conservatoire**, music school, drama school.

conserve v. *fossil fuel should be conserved* **preserve**, protect, save, safeguard, keep, look after; sustain, prolong, perpetuate; store, reserve, husband.
– OPPOSITES squander.
▶ n. *cherry conserve* **jam**, preserve, jelly, marmalade, confiture.

consider v. 1 *Isabel considered her choices* **think about**, contemplate, reflect on, examine, review; mull over, ponder, deliberate on, chew over, meditate on, ruminate on; assess, evaluate, weigh up, appraise; informal size up. 2 *I consider him irresponsible* **deem**, think, believe, judge, adjudge, rate, count, find; regard as, hold to be, reckon to be, view as, see as. 3 *he considered the ceiling* **look at**, contemplate, observe, regard, survey, view, scrutinize, scan, examine, inspect; informal check out; N. Amer. informal eyeball. 4 *the inquiry will consider those issues* **take into consideration**, take account of, make allowances for, bear in mind, be mindful of, remember, mind, mark, respect, heed, note, make provision for.
– OPPOSITES ignore.

considerable adj. 1 *a considerable amount of money* **sizeable**, substantial, appreciable, significant; goodly, fair, hefty, handsome, decent, worthwhile; ample, plentiful, abundant, great, large, generous; informal tidy, not to be sneezed at. 2 *a considerable success* **much**, great, a lot of, lots of, a great deal of, plenty of, a fair amount of. 3 *a considerable cricketer* **distinguished**, noteworthy, important, significant, prominent, eminent, influential, illustrious; renowned, celebrated, acclaimed.
– OPPOSITES paltry, minor.

considerably adv. **greatly**, (very) much, a great deal, a lot, lots; significantly, substantially, appreciably, markedly, noticeably; informal plenty, seriously.

considerate adj. **attentive**, thoughtful, solicitous, mindful, heedful; obliging, accommodating, helpful, cooperative, patient; kind, unselfish, compassionate, sympathetic, caring, charitable, altruistic, generous; polite, sensitive, tactful.

consideration n. 1 *your case needs careful consideration* **thought**, deliberation, reflection, contemplation, rumination, meditation; examination, inspection, scrutiny, analysis, discussion; attention, regard; formal cogitation. 2 *his health is the prime consideration* **factor**, issue, matter, concern, detail, aspect, feature. 3 *firms should show more consideration* **attentiveness**, concern, care, thoughtfulness, solicitude; kindness, understanding, respect, sensitivity, tact, discretion; compassion, charity, benevolence. 4 *I might do it, for a consideration* **payment**, fee, premium, remuneration, compensation; commission, percentage, dividend; informal cut, slice, piece of the action; formal emolument.
– OPPOSITES disregard.
□ **take something into consideration** consider, give thought to, take into account, allow for, provide for, plan for, make provision for, accommodate, bargain for, reckon with; foresee, anticipate.

considering prep. *considering his size he was speedy* **bearing in mind**, taking into

consideration, taking into account, keeping in mind, in view of, in the light of.
▸ adv. informal *he'd been lucky, considering* **all things considered**, all in all, on the whole, at the end of the day, when all's said and done.

consign v. **1** *he was consigned to prison* **send**, deliver, hand over, turn over, sentence; confine in, imprison in, incarcerate in, lock up in; informal put away, put behind bars; Brit. informal bang up. **2** *the picture was consigned for sale* **assign**, allocate, place, put, remit, hand down. **3** *the package was consigned by a local company* **send (off)**, dispatch, transmit, convey, post, mail, ship. **4** *I consigned her picture to the bin* **deposit**, commit, banish, relegate.

consignment n. **delivery**, shipment, load, boatload, lorryload, truckload, cargo; batch; goods.

consist v. **1** *the exhibition consists of 180 drawings* **be composed**, be made up, be formed; comprise, contain, include, incorporate. **2** *style consists in the choices that writers make* **be inherent**, lie, reside, be present, be contained; be expressed by.

consistency n. **1** *the trend shows a degree of consistency* **uniformity**, constancy, regularity, evenness, steadiness, stability, equilibrium; dependability, reliability. **2** *cream of pouring consistency* **thickness**, density, viscosity, heaviness, texture; firmness, solidity.

consistent adj. **1** *consistent opinion-poll evidence* **constant**, regular, uniform, steady, stable, even, unchanging, undeviating; dependable, reliable, predictable. **2** *her injuries were consistent with a knife attack* **compatible**, congruous, consonant, in tune, in line, reconcilable; corresponding to, conforming to.
− OPPOSITES irregular, incompatible.

consolation n. **comfort**, solace, sympathy, compassion, pity, commiseration; relief, help, (moral) support, encouragement, reassurance.

console[1] v. *she tried to console him* **comfort**, solace, condole with, sympathize with, commiserate with, show compassion for; help, support, cheer (up), hearten, encourage, reassure, soothe.
− OPPOSITES upset.

console[2] n. *a digital console* **control panel**, instrument panel, dashboard, keyboard, keypad; informal dash.

consolidate v. **1** *we consolidated our position in the market* **strengthen**, secure, stabilize, reinforce, fortify; enhance, improve. **2** *consolidate the results into an action plan* **combine**, unite, merge, integrate, amalgamate, fuse, synthesize, bring together, unify.

consonance n. **agreement**, accord, harmony, unison; compatibility, congruity, congruence; formal concord.

consonant adj.
□ **consonant with** in agreement with,

consistent with, in accordance with, in harmony with, compatible with, congruous with, in tune with.

consort n. *the queen and her consort* **partner**, companion, mate; spouse, husband, wife.
▸ v. *he consorted with other women* **associate**, keep company, mix, go around, spend time, socialize, fraternize, have dealings; informal run around, hang around/round, hang out, be thick; Brit. informal hang about.

conspicuous adj. **easily seen**, clear, visible, noticeable, discernible, perceptible, detectable; obvious, manifest, evident, apparent, marked, pronounced, prominent, patent, crystal clear; striking, eye-catching, overt, blatant, writ large; distinct, recognizable, unmistakable, inescapable; informal as plain as the nose on one's face, standing out like a sore thumb, standing out a mile.

conspiracy n. **1** *a conspiracy to manipulate the race results* **plot**, scheme, plan, machination, ploy, trick, ruse, subterfuge; informal racket. **2** *conspiracy to murder* **plotting**, collusion, intrigue, connivance, machination, collaboration; treason.

conspirator n. **plotter**, schemer, intriguer, colluder, collaborator, conniver, machinator.

conspire v. **1** *they admitted conspiring to steal cars* **plot**, scheme, plan, intrigue, machinate, collude, connive, collaborate, work hand in glove; informal be in cahoots. **2** *circumstances conspired against them* **act together**, work together, combine, unite, join forces; informal gang up.

constancy n. **1** *constancy between lovers* **fidelity**, faithfulness, loyalty, commitment, dedication, devotion; dependability, reliability, trustworthiness. **2** *the constancy of Henry's views* **steadfastness**, resolution, resolve, firmness, fixedness; determination, perseverance, tenacity, doggedness, staunchness, staying power, obstinacy. **3** *a constancy of human motive* **consistency**, permanence, persistence, durability, endurance; uniformity, immutability, regularity, stability, steadiness.

constant adj. **1** *the constant background noise* **continual**, continuous, persistent, sustained, round-the-clock; ceaseless, unceasing, perpetual, incessant, never-ending, eternal, endless, unabating, non-stop, unrelieved; interminable, unremitting, relentless. **2** *a constant speed* **consistent**, regular, steady, uniform, even, invariable, unvarying, unchanging, undeviating. **3** *a constant friend* **faithful**, loyal, devoted, true, fast, firm, unswerving; steadfast, staunch, dependable, trustworthy, trusty, reliable, dedicated, committed. **4** *constant vigilance* **steadfast**, steady, resolute, determined, tenacious, dogged, unwavering, unflagging.
− OPPOSITES fitful, variable, fickle.
▸ n. *dread of cancer has been a constant* **unchanging factor**, given.

constantly adv. **always**, all the time, continually, continuously, persistently;

round-the-clock, night and day, {morning, noon, and night}; endlessly, non-stop, incessantly, unceasingly, perpetually, eternally, forever; interminably, unremittingly, relentlessly; Scottish aye; informal 24-7.
– OPPOSITES occasionally.

consternation n. **dismay**, perturbation, distress, disquiet, discomposure; surprise, amazement, astonishment; alarm, panic, fear, fright, shock.
– OPPOSITES satisfaction.

constituent adj. *constituent parts* **component**, integral; elemental, basic, essential, inherent.
▸ n. **1** *MPs must listen to their constituents* **voter**, elector. **2** *the constituents of tobacco* **component**, ingredient, element; part, piece, bit, unit; section, portion.

constitute v. **1** *farmers constituted 10 per cent of the population* **amount to**, add up to, account for, form, make up, compose, comprise. **2** *this constitutes a breach of copyright* **be equivalent to**, be, embody, be tantamount to, be regarded as. **3** *the courts were constituted in 1875* **inaugurate**, establish, initiate, found, create, set up, start, form, organize, develop; commission, charter, invest, appoint, install, empower.

constitution n. **1** *the constitution guarantees our rights* **charter**, social code, law; bill of rights; rules, regulations, fundamental principles. **2** *the chemical constitution of the dye* **composition**, make-up, structure, construction, arrangement, configuration, formation, anatomy; informal set-up. **3** *she has the constitution of an ox* **health**, physique, physical condition, shape, fettle.

constitutional adj. **1** *constitutional powers* **legal**, lawful, legitimate, authorized, permitted; sanctioned, ratified, warranted, constituted, statutory, chartered, vested, official; by law. **2** *a constitutional weakness* **inherent**, intrinsic, innate, fundamental, essential, organic; congenital, inborn, inbred.
▸ n. dated *she went out for a constitutional.* See **walk** (sense 1 of the noun).

constrain v. **1** *he felt constrained to explain* **compel**, force, drive, impel, oblige, coerce, prevail on, require; press, push, pressure, pressurize. **2** *prices were constrained by state controls* **restrict**, limit, curb, check, restrain, contain, straitjacket, rein in, hold back, keep down.

constrained adj. *his constrained manner* **unnatural**, awkward, self-conscious, forced, stilted, strained; restrained, reserved, reticent, guarded.
– OPPOSITES relaxed.

constraint n. **1** *financial constraints* **restriction**, limitation, curb, check, restraint, control, damper, rein, straitjacket; hindrance, impediment, obstruction, handicap. **2** *they were able to talk without constraint* **inhibition**, uneasiness,

embarrassment; restraint, reticence, guardedness, formality; self-consciousness, awkwardness, stiltedness.

constrict v. **1** *fat constricts the blood vessels* **narrow**, make narrower, tighten, compress, contract, squeeze, strangle, strangulate; old use straiten. **2** *fear of crime constricts many people's lives* **restrict**, impede, limit, inhibit, obstruct, interfere with, hinder, hamper.
– OPPOSITES expand, dilate.

constriction n. **tightness**, pressure, compression, contraction; obstruction, blockage, impediment; Medicine stricture, stenosis.

construct v. **1** *a new motorway was being constructed* **build**, erect, put up, set up, raise, establish, assemble, manufacture, fabricate, create, make. **2** *he constructed a faultless argument* **formulate**, form, put together, create, devise, design, compose, work out; fashion, mould, shape, frame.
– OPPOSITES demolish.

construction n. **1** *the construction of a new airport* **building**, erection, putting up, setting up, establishment; assembly, manufacture, fabrication, creation. **2** *the station was a spectacular construction* **structure**, building, pile; formal edifice. **3** *you could put an honest construction on their conduct* **interpretation**, reading, meaning, explanation, explication, construal; informal take.

constructive adj. **useful**, helpful, productive, positive, encouraging; practical, valuable, profitable, worthwhile.

construe v. **interpret**, understand, read, see, take, take to mean, regard.

consul n. **ambassador**, diplomat, chargé d'affaires, attaché, envoy, emissary, plenipotentiary; old use legate.

consult v. **1** *you need to consult a solicitor* **seek advice from**, ask, take counsel from, call on, speak to, turn to, have recourse to; informal pick someone's brains. **2** *the government must consult with interested parties* **confer**, have discussions, talk things over, exchange views, communicate, parley, deliberate; informal put their heads together. **3** *she consulted her diary* **refer to**, turn to, look at.

consultant n. **1** *an engineering consultant* **adviser**, expert, specialist, authority, pundit. **2** *a consultant at Guy's hospital* **senior doctor**, specialist.

consultation n. **1** *the need for further consultation with industry* **discussion**, dialogue, discourse, debate, negotiation, deliberation. **2** *a 30-minute consultation* **meeting**, talk, discussion, interview, audience, hearing; appointment, session; formal confabulation, colloquy.

consume v. **1** *vast amounts of food and drink were consumed* **eat**, devour, ingest, swallow, gobble up, wolf down, guzzle, feast on, snack on; **drink**, gulp down, imbibe, sup; informal tuck into, put away, polish off, scoff, hoover up, dispose of, pig oneself on, trough, down, neck, sink, swill; Brit. informal gollop, shift; N. Amer. informal scarf (down/up), snarf (down/up). **2** *natural resources are being consumed at an alarming rate* **use (up)**, utilize, expend; deplete, exhaust; waste, squander, drain, dissipate, fritter away. **3** *the fire consumed fifty houses* **destroy**, demolish, lay waste, wipe out, annihilate, devastate, gut, ruin, wreck. **4** *Carolyn was consumed with guilt* **eat up**, devour, obsess, grip, overwhelm; absorb, preoccupy.

consumer n. **purchaser**, buyer, customer, shopper; user, end-user; client; (**the consumer** or **consumers**) the public, the market.

consuming adj. **absorbing**, compelling, compulsive, besetting, obsessive, overwhelming; intense, ardent, strong, powerful, burning, raging, fervid, profound, deep-seated.

consummate v. *the deal was finally consummated* **complete**, conclude, finish, accomplish, achieve; execute, carry out, perform; informal sew up, wrap up; formal effectuate.
▶ adj. *his consummate skill* | *a consummate politician* **supreme**, superb, superlative, superior, accomplished, expert, proficient, skilful, skilled, masterly, master, first-class, talented, gifted, polished, practised, perfect, ultimate; complete, total, utter, absolute, pure.

consumption n. **1** *food unfit for human consumption* **eating**, drinking, ingestion. **2** *the consumption of fossil fuels* **use**, using up, utilization, expending, depletion; waste, squandering, dissipation.

contact n. **1** *a disease transmitted through direct contact with rats* **touch**, touching; proximity, exposure. **2** *foreign diplomats were asked to avoid all contact with him* **communication**, correspondence, touch; association, connection, intercourse, relations, dealings; old use traffic. **3** *he had many contacts in Germany* **connection**, acquaintance, associate, friend.
▶ v. *anyone with information should contact the police* **get in touch with**, communicate with, make contact with, approach, notify; telephone, phone, call, ring up, speak to, talk to, write to; informal get hold of.

contagion n. dated **disease**, infection, illness, plague, blight; informal bug, virus; old use pestilence.

contagious adj. **infectious**, communicable, transmittable, transmissible, spreadable; informal catching; dated infective.

contain v. **1** *the archive contains much unpublished material* **include**, comprise, take in, incorporate, involve, encompass, embrace; consist of, be made up of, be composed of. **2** *the boat contained four people* **hold**, carry, accommodate, seat. **3** *he must contain his anger* **restrain**, curb, rein in, suppress, repress, stifle, subdue, quell, swallow, bottle up, hold in, keep in check; control, master.

container n. **receptacle**, vessel, holder, repository.

contaminate v. **pollute**, adulterate; defile, debase, corrupt, taint, infect, foul, spoil, soil, stain, sully; poison; literary befoul.
– OPPOSITES purify.

contemplate v. **1** *she contemplated her image in the mirror* **look at**, view, regard, examine, inspect, observe, survey, study, scrutinize, scan, stare at, gaze at, eye. **2** *he contemplated his fate* **think about**, ponder, reflect on, consider, mull over, muse on, dwell on, deliberate over, meditate on, ruminate on, chew over, brood on/about, turn over in one's mind; formal cogitate. **3** *he was contemplating action for damages* **consider**, think about, have in mind, intend, plan, propose; envisage, foresee.

contemplation n. **1** *the contemplation of beautiful objects* **viewing**, examination, inspection, observation, survey, study, scrutiny. **2** *the monks sat in quiet contemplation* **thought**, reflection, meditation, consideration, rumination, deliberation, reverie, introspection, brown study; formal cogitation, cerebration.

contemplative adj. **thoughtful**, pensive, reflective, meditative, musing, ruminative, introspective, brooding, deep/lost in thought, in a brown study.

contemporary adj. **1** *contemporary sources of the time*, of the day, contemporaneous, concurrent, coeval, coexisting, coexistent. **2** *contemporary society* **modern**, present-day, present, current, present-time. **3** *a very contemporary design* **modern**, up to date, up to the minute, fashionable; modish, latest, recent; informal trendy, with it.
– OPPOSITES old-fashioned, out of date.
▶ n. *Chaucer's contemporaries* **peer**, fellow; formal compeer.

contempt n. **1** *she regarded him with contempt* **scorn**, disdain, disrespect, scornfulness, contemptuousness, derision; disgust, loathing, hatred, abhorrence; old use despite. **2** *he is guilty of contempt of court* **disrespect**, disregard, slighting.
– OPPOSITES respect.

contemptible adj. **despicable**, detestable, hateful, reprehensible, deplorable, unspeakable, disgraceful, shameful, ignominious, abject, low, mean, cowardly, unworthy, discreditable, petty, worthless, shabby, cheap, beyond contempt, beyond the pale, sordid; old use scurvy.
– OPPOSITES admirable.

contemptuous adj. **scornful**, disdainful, disrespectful, insulting, insolent, derisive, mocking, sneering, scoffing, withering, scathing, snide; condescending, supercilious, proud, haughty, superior, arrogant, dismissive, aloof; informal high and mighty, snotty, sniffy; old use contumelious.
– OPPOSITES respectful.

contend v. **1** *the pilot had to contend with torrential rain* **cope with**, face, grapple with, deal with, take on, pit oneself against.

2 *three main groups were contending for power* **compete**, vie, contest, fight, battle, tussle, go head-to-head; strive, struggle. **3** *he contends that the judge was wrong* **assert**, maintain, hold, claim, argue, insist, state, declare, profess, affirm; allege; formal aver.

content¹ adj. *she seemed content with life* **contented**, satisfied, pleased, gratified, fulfilled, happy, cheerful, glad; unworried, untroubled, at ease, at peace, tranquil, serene.
– OPPOSITES discontented, dissatisfied.
▶v. *her reply seemed to content him* **satisfy**, please; soothe, pacify, placate, appease, mollify.
▶n. *a time of content.* See **contentment**.

content² n. **1** *foods with a high fibre content* **amount**, proportion, quantity. **2** *the contents of a vegetarian sausage* **constituents**, ingredients, components, elements. **3** *the book's list of contents* **chapters**, sections, divisions. **4** *the content of the essay* **subject matter**, subject, theme, argument, thesis, message, thrust, substance, matter, material, text, ideas.

contented adj. *a contented man.* See **content¹** (adjective).

contention n. **1** *a point of contention* **disagreement**, dispute, disputation, argument, discord, conflict, strife, dissension, disharmony. **2** *the Marxist contention that capitalism equals exploitation* **argument**, claim, plea, submission, allegation, assertion, declaration; opinion, stand, position, view, belief, thesis, case.
– OPPOSITES agreement.
□ **in contention** in competition, competing, contesting, contending, vying; striving, struggling.

contentious adj. **1** *a contentious issue* **controversial**, disputable, debatable, disputed, open to debate, moot, vexed. **2** *a contentious debate* **heated**, vehement, fierce, violent, intense, impassioned. **3** *contentious people.* See **quarrelsome**.

contentment n. **contentedness**, content, satisfaction, gratification, fulfilment, happiness, pleasure, cheerfulness; ease, comfort, well-being, peace, equanimity, serenity, tranquillity.

contest n. **1** *a boxing contest* **competition**, match, tournament, game, meet, event, trial, bout, heat, fixture, tie, race. **2** *the contest for the party leadership* **fight**, battle, tussle, struggle, competition, race.
▶v. **1** *he intended to contest the seat* **compete for**, contend for, vie for, fight for, try to win, go for, throw one's hat in the ring. **2** *we contested the decision* **oppose**, object to, challenge, take a stand against, take issue with, question, call into question. **3** *the issues have been hotly contested* **debate**, argue about, dispute, quarrel over.

contestant n. **competitor**, participant, player, contender, candidate, aspirant, entrant; rival, opponent, adversary, antagonist.

context n. **1** *the wider historical context* **circumstances**, conditions, factors, state of affairs, situation, background, scene, setting. **2** *a quote taken out of context* **frame of reference**, contextual relationship; text, subject, theme, topic.

contiguous adj. **adjacent**, neighbouring, adjoining, bordering, next-door; abutting, connecting, touching, in contact, proximate.

continent adj. **self-restrained**, self-disciplined, abstemious, abstinent, self-denying, ascetic; chaste, celibate, monkish, monastic, virginal.

contingency n. **eventuality**, (chance) event, incident, happening, occurrence, juncture, possibility, fortuity, accident, chance, emergency.

contingent adj. **1** *the merger is contingent on government approval* **dependent on**, conditional on, subject to, determined by, hinging on, resting on. **2** *contingent events* **chance**, accidental, fortuitous, possible, unforeseeable, unpredictable, random, haphazard.
▶n. **1** *a contingent of Japanese businessmen* **group**, party, body, band, company, cohort, deputation, delegation; informal bunch, gang. **2** *a contingent of marines* **detachment**, unit, group.

continual adj. **1** *a service disrupted by continual breakdowns* **frequent**, repeated, constant, recurrent, recurring, regular. **2** *she was in continual pain* **constant**, continuous, unending, never-ending, unremitting, unabating, relentless, unrelenting, round-the-clock, unrelieved, chronic, uninterrupted, unbroken.
– OPPOSITES occasional, temporary.

continuance n. See **continuation**.

continuation n. **carrying on**, continuance, extension, prolongation, protraction, perpetuation.
– OPPOSITES end.

continue v. **1** *he was unable to continue with his job* **carry on**, proceed, pursue, go on, keep on, persist, press on, persevere, keep at; informal stick at, soldier on. **2** *discussions continued throughout the year* **go on**, carry on, last, extend, be prolonged, run on, drag on. **3** *we are keen to continue this relationship* **maintain**, keep up, sustain, keep going, keep alive, preserve. **4** *his willingness to continue in office* **remain**, stay, carry on, keep going. **5** *we continued our conversation after supper* **resume**, pick up, take up, carry on with, return to, recommence.
– OPPOSITES stop, break off.

continuing adj. **ongoing**, continuous, sustained, persistent, steady, relentless, uninterrupted, unabating, unremitting, unrelieved, unceasing.
– OPPOSITES sporadic.

continuity n. **continuousness**, uninterruptedness, flow, progression.

continuous adj. **continual**, uninterrupted, unbroken, constant, ceaseless, incessant, steady, sustained, solid, continuing, ongoing,

C

unceasing, without a break, non-stop, round-the-clock, persistent, unremitting, relentless, unrelenting, unabating, unrelieved, without respite, endless, unending, never-ending, perpetual, everlasting, eternal, interminable; consecutive, running; N. Amer. without surcease.
– OPPOSITES intermittent.

contort v. **twist**, bend out of shape, distort, misshape, warp, buckle, deform.

contour n. **outline**, shape, form; lines, curves, figure; silhouette, profile.

contraband n. *contraband was suspected* **smuggling**, illegal traffic, black-marketeering, bootlegging; the black market.
▸ adj. *contraband goods* **smuggled**, black-market, bootleg, under the counter, illegal, illicit, unlawful; prohibited, banned, proscribed, forbidden; informal hot.

contract n. *a legally binding contract* **agreement**, commitment, arrangement, settlement, understanding, compact, covenant, bond; deal, bargain; Law indenture.
▸ v. **1** *the market for such goods began to contract* **shrink**, get smaller, decrease, diminish, reduce, dwindle, decline. **2** *her stomach muscles contracted* **tighten**, tense, flex, constrict, draw in, narrow.
3 *she contracted her brow* **wrinkle**, knit, crease, purse, pucker. **4** *his name was soon contracted to 'Jack'* **shorten**, abbreviate, cut, reduce; elide. **5** *the company contracted to rebuild the stadium* **undertake**, pledge, promise, covenant, commit oneself, engage, agree, enter an agreement, make a deal.
6 *she contracted German measles* **develop**, catch, get, pick up, come down with, be struck down by, be stricken with, succumb to; Brit. go down with. **7** *he contracted a debt of £3,300* **incur**, run up.
– OPPOSITES expand, relax, lengthen.
□ **contract something out** subcontract, outsource, farm out.

contraction n. **1** *the contraction of the industry* **shrinking**, shrinkage, decline, decrease, diminution, dwindling. **2** *the contraction of muscles* **tightening**, tensing, flexing. **3** *my contractions started at midnight* **labour pains**, labour; cramps; literary travail. **4** *'goodbye' is a contraction of 'God be with you'* **abbreviation**, short form, shortened form, elision, diminutive.

contradict v. **1** *he contradicted the government's account of the affair* **deny**, refute, rebut, dispute, challenge, counter, controvert; formal gainsay. **2** *nobody dared to contradict him* **argue against**, go against, challenge, oppose; formal gainsay. **3** *this research contradicts previous computer models* **conflict with**, be at odds with, be at variance with, be inconsistent with, run counter to, disagree with.
– OPPOSITES confirm, agree with.

contradiction n. **1** *the contradiction between his faith and his lifestyle* **conflict**, clash, disagreement, opposition,

inconsistency, mismatch, variance. **2** *a contradiction of his statement* **denial**, refutation, rebuttal, countering, counterstatement.
– OPPOSITES confirmation, agreement.

contradictory adj. **opposed**, in opposition, opposite, antithetical, contrary, contrasting, conflicting, at variance, at odds, opposing, clashing, divergent, discrepant, different; inconsistent, incompatible, irreconcilable.

contraption n. **device**, gadget, apparatus, machine, appliance, mechanism, invention, contrivance; informal gizmo, widget; Brit. informal gubbins; Austral. informal bitzer.

contrary adj. **1** *contrary views* **opposite**, opposing, opposed, contradictory, clashing, conflicting, antithetical, incompatible, irreconcilable. **2** *she was sulky and contrary* **perverse**, awkward, difficult, uncooperative, unhelpful, obstructive, disobliging, recalcitrant, wilful, self-willed, stubborn, obstinate, mulish, pig-headed, intractable; informal cussed; Brit. informal bloody-minded, bolshie, stroppy; N. Amer. informal balky; formal refractory; old use froward.
– OPPOSITES compatible, accommodating.
▸ n. *in fact, the contrary is true* **opposite**, reverse, converse, antithesis.
□ **contrary to** in conflict with, against, at variance with, at odds with, in opposition to, counter to, incompatible with.

contrast n. **1** *the contrast between rural and urban trends* **difference**, dissimilarity, disparity, distinction, contradistinction, divergence, variance, variation, differentiation; contradiction, incongruity, opposition, polarity; formal dissimilitude. **2** *Jane was a complete contrast to Sarah* **opposite**, antithesis; foil, complement.
– OPPOSITES similarity.
▸ v. **1** *a view which contrasts with his earlier opinion* **differ from**, be at variance with, be contrary to, conflict with, go against, be at odds with, be in opposition to, disagree with, clash with. **2** *people contrasted her with her sister* **compare**, set side by side, juxtapose; measure against; distinguish from, differentiate from.
– OPPOSITES resemble, liken.

contravene v. **1** *he contravened the Official Secrets Act* **break**, breach, violate, infringe; defy, disobey, flout. **2** *the prosecution contravened the rights of the individual* **conflict with**, be in conflict with, be at odds with, be at variance with, run counter to.
– OPPOSITES comply with.

contravention n. **breach**, violation, infringement, neglect, dereliction.

contretemps n. **argument**, quarrel, squabble, disagreement, difference of opinion, dispute; informal tiff, set-to, run-in, spat; Brit. informal row, barney; Scottish informal rammy.

contribute v. **1** *the government contributed a million pounds* **give**, donate, put up, subscribe, hand out, grant, bestow, present, provide, supply, furnish; informal chip in, pitch in, fork out, shell out, cough up; Brit. informal stump up; N. Amer. informal kick in, ante up, pony up. **2** *an article contributed by Dr Clouson* **supply**, provide, submit. **3** *numerous factors contribute to job satisfaction* **play a part in**, be instrumental in, be a factor in, have a hand in, be conducive to, make for, lead to, cause; formal conduce to.

contribution n. **1** *voluntary financial contributions* **donation**, gift, offering, present, handout, grant, subsidy, allowance, endowment, subscription; formal benefaction; historical alms. **2** *contributions from local authors* **article**, piece, story, item, chapter, paper, essay.

contributor n. **1** *the magazine's regular contributors* **writer**, columnist, correspondent. **2** *campaign contributors* **donor**, benefactor, subscriber, supporter, backer, subsidizer, patron, sponsor.

contrite adj. **remorseful**, repentant, penitent, regretful, sorry, apologetic, rueful, sheepish, hangdog, ashamed, chastened, shamefaced, conscience-stricken, guilt-ridden, in sackcloth and ashes.

contrition n. **remorse**, repentance, penitence, sorrow, sorrowfulness, regret, ruefulness, pangs of conscience; shame, guilt, compunction; old use rue.

contrivance n. **1** *a mechanical contrivance* **device**, gadget, machine, appliance, contraption, apparatus, mechanism, implement, tool, invention; informal gizmo, widget; Austral. informal bitzer. **2** *her matchmaking contrivances* **scheme**, stratagem, tactic, manoeuvre, move, plan, ploy, gambit, wile, trick, ruse, plot, machination.

contrive v. **bring about**, engineer, manufacture, orchestrate, stage-manage, create, devise, concoct, construct, plan, fabricate, plot, hatch; informal wangle, set up.

contrived adj. **forced**, strained, studied, artificial, affected, put-on, pretended, false, feigned, manufactured, unnatural; laboured, overdone, elaborate.
- OPPOSITES natural.

control n. **1** *China retained control over the region* **jurisdiction**, sway, power, authority, command, dominance, government, mastery, leadership, rule, sovereignty, supremacy, ascendancy; charge, management, direction, supervision, superintendence. **2** *strict import controls* **restraint**, constraint, limitation, restriction, check, curb, brake, rein; regulation. **3** *her control deserted her* **self-control**, self-restraint, self-possession, composure, calmness; informal cool. **4** *easy-to-use controls* **switch**, knob, button, dial, handle, lever. **5** *mission control* **headquarters**, HQ, base, centre of operations, command post.
▶ v. **1** *one family had controlled the company since its formation* **be in charge of**, run, manage, direct, administer, head, preside over, supervise, superintend, steer;

command, rule, govern, lead, dominate, hold sway over, be at the helm; informal head up, be in the driving seat, run the show. **2** *she struggled to control her temper* **restrain**, keep in check, curb, check, contain, hold back, bridle, rein in, suppress, repress, master. **3** *public spending was controlled* **limit**, restrict, curb, cap, constrain; informal put the brakes on.

controversial adj. **contentious**, disputed, at issue, moot, disputable, debatable, arguable, vexed, tendentious.

controversy n. **disagreement**, dispute, argument, debate, dissension, contention, disputation, altercation, wrangle, wrangling, quarrel, quarrelling, war of words, storm; cause célèbre; Brit. informal row.

contusion n. **bruise**, discoloration, black-and-blue mark, injury; Medicine ecchymosis.

conundrum n. **1** *the conundrums facing policy-makers in the 1980s* **problem**, difficult question, vexed question, difficulty, quandary, dilemma; informal poser, facer. **2** *Roderick enjoyed conundrums and crosswords* **riddle**, puzzle, word game; informal brain-teaser.

convalesce v. **recuperate**, get better, recover, get well, get back on one's feet.

convalescence n. **recuperation**, recovery, return to health, rehabilitation, improvement.

convalescent adj. **recuperating**, recovering, getting better, on the road to recovery, improving, on the mend.

convene v. **1** *he convened a secret meeting* **summon**, call, call together, order; formal convoke. **2** *the committee convened for its final session* **assemble**, gather, meet, come together, congregate; formal foregather.

convenience n. **1** *the convenience of the arrangement* **expedience**, advantage, opportuneness, propitiousness, timeliness; suitability, appropriateness. **2** *for convenience, the handset is wall-mounted* **ease of use**, usability, usefulness, utility, serviceability, practicality. **3** *the kitchen has all the modern conveniences* **appliance**, (labour-saving) device, gadget; amenity, facility; informal gizmo, mod con.

convenient adj. **1** *a convenient time* **suitable**, appropriate, fitting, fit, suited, opportune, timely, well timed, favourable, advantageous, seasonable, expedient. **2** *a hotel that's convenient for the beach* **near (to)**, close to, within easy reach of, well situated for, handy for, not far from, just round the corner from; informal a stone's throw from, within spitting distance of.

convent n. **nunnery**, priory, abbey, religious community.

convention n. **1** *social conventions* **custom**, usage, practice, tradition, way, habit, norm; rule, code, canon, punctilio; propriety, etiquette, protocol; formal praxis; (**conventions**) mores. **2** *a convention signed by 74 countries* **agreement**, accord, protocol, compact, pact, treaty, concordat, entente;

C

contract, bargain, deal. **3** *the party's biennial convention* **conference**, meeting, congress, assembly, gathering, summit, convocation, synod, conclave.

conventional adj. **1** *the conventional wisdom of the day* **orthodox**, traditional, established, accepted, received, mainstream, prevailing, prevalent, accustomed, customary. **2** *a conventional railway* **normal**, standard, regular, ordinary, usual, established, typical, common. **3** *a very conventional woman* **conservative**, traditional, traditionalist, conformist, bourgeois, old-fashioned, of the old school, small-town, suburban; informal straight, square, stick-in-the-mud, fuddy-duddy. **4** *a conventional piece of work* **unoriginal**, formulaic, predictable, stock, unadventurous, unremarkable.
– OPPOSITES unorthodox, original.

converge v. **1** *Oxford Circus, a station where three lines converge* **meet**, intersect, cross, connect, link up, coincide, join, unite, merge. **2** *90,000 fans converged on Wembley* **close in on**, bear down on, approach, move towards.
– OPPOSITES diverge, leave.

conversant adj. **familiar**, acquainted, au fait, au courant, at home, well versed, well informed, knowledgeable, informed, abreast, up to date; informal up to speed, clued-up, genned-up; formal cognizant.

conversation n. **discussion**, talk, chat, gossip, tête-à-tête, heart-to-heart, head-to-head, exchange, dialogue; informal confab, jaw, chit-chat; Brit. informal chinwag, natter; N. Amer. informal gabfest, schmooze; Austral./NZ informal yarn; formal confabulation, colloquy.

conversational adj. **1** *conversational English* **informal**, chatty, relaxed, friendly; colloquial, idiomatic. **2** *a conversational man* **talkative**, chatty, communicative, forthcoming, expansive, loquacious, garrulous.

converse[1] v. *they conversed in low voices* **talk**, speak, chat, have a conversation, discourse, communicate; informal chew the fat/rag, jaw; Brit. informal natter; N. Amer. informal visit, shoot the breeze/bull; Austral./NZ informal mag; formal confabulate.

converse[2] n. *the converse is also true* **opposite**, reverse, obverse, contrary, antithesis, other side of the coin; informal flip side.

conversion n. **1** *the conversion of waste into energy* **change**, changing, transformation, metamorphosis, transfiguration, transmutation, sea change; humorous transmogrification. **2** *the conversion of the building* **adaptation**, alteration, modification, reconstruction, rebuilding, redevelopment, redesign, renovation, rehabilitation. **3** *his religious conversion* **rebirth**, regeneration, reformation.

convert v. **1** *plants convert the sun's energy into chemical energy* **change**, turn, transform, metamorphose, transfigure, transmute; humorous transmogrify; technical permute. **2** *the factory was converted into flats* **adapt**, turn, change, alter, modify, rebuild, reconstruct, redevelop, refashion, redesign, restyle, revamp, renovate, rehabilitate; N. Amer. bring up to code; informal do up; N. Amer. informal rehab. **3** *they sought to convert sinners* **proselytize**, evangelize, bring to God, redeem, save, reform, re-educate, cause to see the light.
▸ n. *Christian converts* **proselyte**, neophyte, new believer; Christianity catechumen.

convey v. **1** *taxis conveyed guests to the station* **transport**, carry, bring, take, fetch, bear, move, ferry, shuttle, shift, transfer. **2** *he conveyed the information to me* **communicate**, pass on, make known, impart, relay, transmit, send, hand on, relate, tell, reveal, disclose. **3** *it's impossible to convey how I felt* **express**, communicate, get across/over, put across/over, indicate, say. **4** *he conveys an air of competence* **project**, exude, emit, emanate.

conveyance n. **1** *the conveyance of agricultural produce* **transportation**, transport, carriage, carrying, transfer, movement, delivery; haulage, portage, cartage, shipment, freightage. **2** formal *three-wheeled conveyances* **vehicle**, means/method of transport; car, bus, coach, van, lorry, truck, bicycle, motorbike, motorcycle.

convict v. *he was convicted of indecent assault* **find guilty**, sentence; Brit. informal be done for.
– OPPOSITES acquit.
▸ n. *two escaped convicts* **prisoner**, inmate; trusty; criminal, offender, lawbreaker, felon; informal jailbird, con, (old) lag, crook; N. Amer. informal yardbird.

conviction n. **1** *his conviction for murder* **declaration of guilt**, sentence, judgement. **2** *his political convictions* **belief**, opinion, view, thought, persuasion, idea, position, stance, article of faith. **3** *she spoke with conviction* **certainty**, certitude, assurance, confidence, sureness, no shadow of a doubt.
– OPPOSITES acquittal, uncertainty.

convince v. **1** *he convinced me that I was wrong* **make certain**, persuade, satisfy, prove to; assure, put/set someone's mind at rest. **2** *I convinced her to marry me* **persuade**, induce, prevail on, get, talk into, win over, cajole, inveigle.

convincing adj. **1** *a convincing argument* **cogent**, persuasive, plausible, powerful, potent, strong, forceful, compelling, irresistible, telling, conclusive. **2** *a convincing 5–0 win* **resounding**, emphatic, decisive, conclusive.

convivial adj. **friendly**, genial, affable, amiable, congenial, agreeable, good-humoured, cordial, warm, sociable, outgoing, gregarious, clubbable, companionable, hail-fellow-well-met, cheerful, jolly, jovial, lively; enjoyable, festive; Scottish couthy.

conviviality n. **friendliness**, geniality, affability, amiability, bonhomie, congeniality, cordiality, warmth, good nature, sociability, gregariousness, cheerfulness, good cheer, joviality, jollity, gaiety, liveliness.

convocation n. **assembly**, gathering, meeting, conference, convention, congress, council, symposium, colloquium, conclave, synod.

convoke v. formal **convene**, summon, call together, call.

convoluted adj. **complicated**, complex, involved, elaborate, serpentine, labyrinthine, tortuous, tangled, Byzantine; confused, confusing, bewildering, baffling.
– OPPOSITES straightforward.

convolution n. **1** *crosses adorned with elaborate convolutions* **twist**, turn, coil, spiral, twirl, curl, helix, whorl, loop, curlicue; Architecture volute. **2** *the convolutions of the plot* **complexity**, intricacy, complication, twist, turn, entanglement.

convoy n. *a convoy of vehicles* **group**, fleet, cavalcade, motorcade, cortège, caravan, line, train.
▶ v. *the ship was convoyed by army gunboats* **escort**, accompany, attend, flank; protect, defend, guard.

convulse v. **shake uncontrollably**, fit, go into spasms, thrash about.

convulsion n. **1** *she had convulsions* **fit**, seizure, paroxysm, spasm, attack; throes; Medicine ictus. **2** *the audience collapsed in convulsions* **fits of laughter**, paroxysms of laughter, uncontrollable laughter; informal hysterics. **3** *the political convulsions of the period* **upheaval**, eruption, cataclysm, turmoil, turbulence, tumult, disruption, agitation, disturbance, unrest, disorder.

convulsive adj. **spasmodic**, jerky, paroxysmal, violent, uncontrollable.

cook v. **1** *Iris had cooked dinner* **prepare**, make, put together; informal fix, rustle up; Brit. informal knock up. **2** informal *he'd been cooking the books* **falsify**, alter, doctor, tamper with, interfere with, massage, manipulate; Brit. informal fiddle. **3** informal *what's cooking?* See **happen** (sense 1).
☐ **cook something up** informal concoct, devise, contrive, fabricate, trump up, hatch, plot, plan, invent, make up, think up, dream up.

cooking n. **cuisine**, cookery, baking; food.

> **WORD LINKS**
> **culinary** relating to cooking
> **gastronomy** the practice of cooking and eating good food
> **haute cuisine** high-quality cooking

cool adj. **1** *a cool breeze* **chilly**, chill, cold, bracing, brisk, crisp, fresh, refreshing, invigorating; draughty; informal nippy; Brit. informal parky. **2** *a cool response* **unenthusiastic**, lukewarm, tepid, indifferent, uninterested, apathetic, half-hearted; unfriendly, distant, remote, aloof, cold, chilly, frosty, unwelcoming, unresponsive, offhand, uncommunicative, undemonstrative; informal stand-offish. **3** *his ability to keep cool in a crisis* **calm**, {cool, calm, and collected}, composed, as cool as a cucumber, collected, cool-headed, level-headed, self-possessed, controlled, self-controlled, poised, serene, tranquil, unruffled, unperturbed, unmoved, untroubled, imperturbable, placid, phlegmatic; informal unflappable, together, laid-back. **4** *a cool lack of morality* **bold**, audacious, nerveless; brazen, shameless, unabashed. **5** *she thinks she's so cool* **fashionable**, stylish, chic, up to the minute, sophisticated; informal trendy, funky, with it, hip, big, happening, groovy; N. Amer. informal kicky, tony, fly. **6** informal *a cool song.* See **excellent**.
– OPPOSITES warm, enthusiastic, agitated.
▶ n. **1** *the cool of the evening* **chill**, chilliness, coldness, coolness. **2** *Ken lost his cool* **self-control**, control, composure, self-possession, calmness, equilibrium, calm; aplomb, poise, sangfroid, presence of mind.
– OPPOSITES warmth.
▶ v. **1** *cool the sauce in the fridge* **chill**, refrigerate. **2** *her reluctance did nothing to cool his interest* **lessen**, moderate, diminish, reduce, dampen. **3** *Simpson's ardour had cooled* **subside**, lessen, diminish, decrease, abate, moderate, die down, fade, dwindle, wane. **4** *after a while, she cooled off* **calm down**, recover/regain one's composure, compose oneself, control oneself, pull oneself together, simmer down.
– OPPOSITES heat, inflame, intensify.

coop n. *a hen coop* **pen**, run, cage, hutch, enclosure.
▶ v. *he hates being cooped up at home* **confine**, shut in/up, cage (in), pen up/in, keep, detain, trap, incarcerate, immure.

cooperate v. **1** *police and social services cooperated in the operation* **collaborate**, work together, work side by side, pull together, band together, join forces, team up, unite, combine, pool resources, make common cause, liaise. **2** *he was happy to cooperate* **be of assistance**, assist, help, lend a hand, be of service, do one's bit; informal play ball.

cooperation n. **1** *cooperation between management and workers* **collaboration**, joint action, combined effort, teamwork, partnership, coordination, liaison, association, synergy, give and take, compromise. **2** *thank you for your cooperation* **assistance**, helpfulness, help, helping hand, aid.

cooperative adj. **1** *a cooperative effort* **collaborative**, collective, combined, common, joint, shared, mutual, united, concerted, coordinated. **2** *pleasant and cooperative staff* **helpful**, eager to help, obliging, accommodating, willing, amenable, adaptable.

coordinate v. **1** *exhibitions coordinated by a team of international scholars* **organize**, arrange, order, systematize, harmonize, correlate, synchronize, bring together, fit together, dovetail. **2** *care workers coordinate at a local level* **cooperate**, liaise, collaborate, work together, negotiate, communicate, be in contact. **3** *floral designs coordinate with the decor* **match**, complement, set off; harmonize, blend, fit in, go.

cop informal n. *a traffic cop.* See **police officer**.
▶ v. *he tried to cop out of his responsibilities.* See **avoid** (sense 2).

cope v. **1** *she couldn't cope on her own* **manage**, survive, subsist, look after oneself, fend for oneself, shift for oneself, carry on, get by/through, bear up, hold one's own, keep one's end up, keep one's head above water; informal make it, hack it. **2** *his inability to cope with the situation* **deal with**, handle, manage, address, face (up to), confront, tackle, get to grips with, get through, weather, come to terms with.

copious adj. **abundant**, superabundant, plentiful, ample, profuse, full, extensive, generous, bumper, lavish, fulsome, liberal, overflowing, in abundance, many, numerous; informal a gogo, galore; literary plenteous.
– OPPOSITES sparse.

copse n. **thicket**, grove, wood, coppice, stand, clump, brake; Brit. spinney; N. Amer. & Austral./NZ brush; old use hurst, holt, boscage.

copulate v. See **have sex** at **sex**.

copulation n. See **sex** (sense 1).

copy n. **1** *a copy of the report* **duplicate**, facsimile, photocopy, carbon (copy), mimeograph, mimeo, photostat; transcript; reprint; trademark Xerox. **2** *a copy of a sketch by Leonardo da Vinci* **replica**, reproduction, replication, print, imitation, likeness; counterfeit, forgery, fake; informal knock-off.
▶ v. **1** *each form had to be copied* **duplicate**, photocopy, xerox, photostat, mimeograph, run off, reproduce. **2** *portraits copied from original paintings by Reynolds* **reproduce**, replicate; forge, fake, counterfeit. **3** *their sound was copied by a lot of jazz players* **imitate**, reproduce, emulate, follow, echo, mirror, parrot, mimic, ape; plagiarize, steal; informal rip off.

coquettish adj. **flirtatious**, flirty, provocative, seductive, inviting, kittenish, coy, arch, teasing, playful; informal come-hither, vampish.

cord n. **string**, thread, thong, lace, ribbon, strap, tape, tie, line, rope, cable, wire, ligature; twine, yarn, elastic, braid, braiding.

cordial adj. *a cordial welcome* **friendly**, warm, genial, affable, amiable, pleasant, fond, affectionate, warm-hearted, good-natured, gracious, hospitable, welcoming, hearty.
▶ n. *fruit cordial* **squash**, crush, concentrate.

cordon n. *a cordon of 500 police* **barrier**, line, row, chain, ring, circle; picket line.
▶ v. *troops cordoned off the area* **close off**, shut off, seal off, fence off, separate off, isolate, enclose, surround.

core n. **1** *the earth's core* **centre**, interior, middle, nucleus; recesses, bowels, depths; informal innards; literary midst. **2** *the core of the argument* **heart**, heart of the matter, nucleus, nub, kernel, marrow, meat, essence,

quintessence, crux, gist, pith, substance, basis, fundamentals; informal nitty-gritty, brass tacks, nuts and bolts.
▶ adj. *the core issue* **central**, key, basic, fundamental, principal, primary, main, chief, crucial, vital, essential; informal number-one.
– OPPOSITES peripheral.

cork n. **stopper**, stop, plug, bung, peg, spigot, spile; N. Amer. stopple.

corner n. **1** *the cart lurched round the corner* **bend**, curve, crook, dog-leg; turn, turning, junction, fork, intersection; Brit. hairpin bend. **2** *a charming corner of Italy* **district**, region, area, section, quarter, part; informal neck of the woods. **3** *he found himself in a tight corner* **predicament**, plight, tight spot, mess, muddle, difficulty, problem, dilemma, quandary; informal pickle, jam, stew, fix, hole, hot water, bind.
▶ v. **1** *he was eventually cornered by police dogs* **drive into a corner**, run to earth, bring to bay, cut off, block off, trap, hem in, pen in, surround, enclose; capture, catch. **2** *crime syndicates have cornered the stolen car market* **gain control of**, take over, control, dominate, monopolize; capture; informal sew up.

cornerstone n. **foundation**, basis, keystone, mainspring, mainstay, linchpin, bedrock, base, backbone, key, centrepiece, core, heart, centre, crux.

corny adj. informal **banal**, trite, hackneyed, commonplace, clichéd, predictable, stereotyped, platitudinous, tired, stale, overworked, overused, well worn; mawkish, sentimental, cloying, syrupy, sugary, saccharine; mushy, slushy, sloppy; Brit. twee; informal cheesy, schmaltzy, cutesy, toe-curling; Brit. informal soppy; N. Amer. informal cornball, hokey.

corollary n. **consequence**, (end) result, upshot, effect, repercussion, product, by-product; Brit. knock-on effect.

coronet n. See **crown** (sense 1 of the noun).

corporal adj. **bodily**, fleshly, corporeal, somatic, carnal, physical, material.
– OPPOSITES spiritual.

corporation n. **1** *the chairman of the corporation* **company**, firm, business, concern, operation, house, organization, agency, trust, partnership, conglomerate, group, chain, multinational; informal outfit, set-up. **2** Brit. *the corporation refused two planning applications* **council**, town council, municipal authority.

corporeal adj. **bodily**, fleshly, carnal, corporal, human, mortal, earthly, physical, material, tangible, concrete, real, actual.

corps n. **1** *an army corps* **unit**, division, detachment, section, company, contingent, squad, squadron, regiment, battalion, brigade, platoon. **2** *a corps of trained engineers* **group**, body, band, cohort, party, gang, pack; team, crew.

corpse n. **dead body**, body, carcass, skeleton, remains; informal stiff; Medicine cadaver; old use corse.

WORD LINKS

autopsy, **post-mortem** an examination of a dead body to find out the cause of death

embalm preserve a corpse from decay

mortuary, **morgue** a place where corpses are kept until burial or cremation

winding sheet, **shroud** a length of cloth in which a corpse is wrapped for burial

necrophilia sexual intercourse with corpses

corpulent adj. **fat**, obese, overweight, plump, portly, stout, chubby, paunchy, beer-bellied, heavy, bulky, chunky, well upholstered, well padded, well covered, meaty, fleshy, rotund, broad in the beam; informal tubby, pudgy, beefy, porky, roly-poly, blubbery; Brit. informal podgy, fubsy; N. Amer. informal corn-fed.
– OPPOSITES thin.

correct adj. **1** *the correct answer* **right**, accurate, true, exact, precise, unerring, faithful, strict, faultless, flawless, error-free, perfect, word-perfect; informal on the mark, on the nail; Brit. informal spot on, bang on; N. Amer. informal on the money, on the button. **2** *correct behaviour* **proper**, seemly, decorous, decent, respectable, right, suitable, fit, fitting, befitting, appropriate, apt; approved, accepted, conventional, customary, traditional, orthodox, comme il faut.
– OPPOSITES wrong, improper.
▶ v. **1** *proof-read your work and correct any mistakes* **rectify**, put right, set right, right, amend, emend, remedy, repair. **2** *an attempt to correct the trade imbalance* **counteract**, offset, counterbalance, compensate for, make up for, neutralize. **3** *the brakes need correcting* **adjust**, regulate, fix, set, standardize, normalize, calibrate, fine-tune.

correction n. **rectification**, rectifying, righting, amendment, emendation, repair, remedy; old use reparation.

corrective adj. **remedial**, therapeutic, restorative, curative, reparative, rehabilitative.

correctly adv. **1** *the questions were answered correctly* **accurately**, right, unerringly, precisely, faultlessly, flawlessly, perfectly, without error; dated aright. **2** *she behaved correctly at all times* **properly**, decorously, with decorum, decently, suitably, fittingly, appropriately, well.

correlate v. **1** *socio-economic status often correlates with educational achievement* **correspond**, match, parallel, agree, tally, tie in, be consistent, be compatible, be consonant, coordinate, dovetail, relate, conform; informal square; N. Amer. informal jibe. **2** *consumption of such foods was correlated with a decreased risk for certain cancers* **connect**, establish a connection between, associate, relate.
– OPPOSITES contrast.

correlation n. **connection**, association, link, tie-in, tie-up, relation, relationship, interrelationship, interdependence, interconnection, interaction; parallel, correspondence.

correspond v. **1** *their policies do not correspond with their statements* **correlate**, agree, be in agreement, be consistent, be compatible, be consonant, accord, be in tune, concur, coincide, tally, tie in, dovetail, fit in; match, parallel; informal square; N. Amer. informal jibe. **2** *a rank corresponding to the British rank of sergeant* **be equivalent**, be analogous, be comparable, equate. **3** *Debbie and I corresponded for years* **exchange letters**, write, communicate, keep in touch/contact.

correspondence n. **1** *there is some correspondence between the two variables* **correlation**, agreement, consistency, compatibility, consonance, conformity, similarity, resemblance, parallel, comparability, accord, concurrence, coincidence. **2** *his private correspondence* **letters**, messages, missives, mail, post; communication.

correspondent n. *the paper's foreign correspondent* **reporter**, journalist, columnist, writer, contributor, newspaperman, newspaperwoman, commentator; Brit. pressman; informal stringer, newshound, journo.
▶ adj. *a correspondent improvement in quality* **corresponding**, parallel, matching, equivalent, comparable, similar, analogous, commensurate.

corresponding adj. **commensurate**, parallel, correspondent, matching, correlated, relative, proportional, proportionate, comparable, equivalent, analogous.

corridor n. **passage**, passageway, aisle, gangway, hall, hallway, gallery, arcade.

corroborate v. **confirm**, verify, endorse, ratify, authenticate, validate, certify; support, back up, uphold, bear out, bear witness to, attest to, testify to, vouch for, give credence to, substantiate, sustain.
– OPPOSITES contradict.

corrode v. **1** *the iron had corroded* **rust**, become rusty, tarnish; wear away, disintegrate, crumble, perish, spoil; oxidize. **2** *acid rain corrodes buildings* **wear away**, eat away (at), gnaw away (at), erode, abrade, consume, destroy.

corrosive adj. **caustic**, corroding, erosive, abrasive, burning, stinging; destructive, damaging, harmful, harsh.

corrugated adj. **ridged**, fluted, grooved, furrowed, crinkled, crinkly, puckered, creased, wrinkled, wrinkly, crumpled; technical striate, striated.

corrupt adj. **1** *a corrupt official* | *corrupt practices* **dishonest**, unscrupulous, dishonourable, unprincipled, unethical, amoral, untrustworthy, venal, underhand, double-dealing, fraudulent, bribable, buyable; criminal, illegal, unlawful, nefarious; informal crooked, shady, dirty, mucky, sleazy; Brit. informal bent, dodgy. **2** *the earth was corrupt in God's sight* **immoral**, depraved, degenerate, reprobate, vice-ridden, perverted, debauched, dissolute, dissipated, bad, wicked, evil, base, sinful, ungodly, unholy, irreligious, profane, impious, impure; informal warped. **3** *a corrupt text* **impure**, bastardized, debased, adulterated.

– OPPOSITES honest, ethical, pure.

▸v. **1** *the fear of firms corrupting politicians in the search for contracts* **bribe**, suborn, buy (off), pay off; informal grease someone's palm, give someone a backhander/sweetener, get at, square; Brit. informal nobble. **2** *a book that might corrupt its readers* **deprave**, pervert, debauch, degrade, warp, lead astray, defile, pollute, sully; old use demoralize. **3** *the apostolic writings had been corrupted* **alter**, tamper with, interfere with, bastardize, debase, adulterate.

corruption n. **1** *political corruption* **dishonesty**, unscrupulousness, double-dealing, fraud, fraudulence, misconduct, crime, criminality, wrongdoing; bribery, subornation, venality, extortion, profiteering, jobbery; N. Amer. payola; informal graft, crookedness, sleaze; formal malversation. **2** *his fall into corruption* **immorality**, depravity, vice, degeneracy, perversion, debauchery, dissoluteness, decadence, wickedness, evil, sin, sinfulness, ungodliness; formal turpitude. **3** *these figures have been subject to corruption* **alteration**, bastardization, debasement, adulteration.

– OPPOSITES honesty, morality, purity.

corsair n. old use See **pirate** (sense 1 of the noun).

corset n. **girdle**, panty girdle, foundation (garment), corselette; Brit. roll-on; informal dated waspie; historical stays.

cortège n. **1** *the funeral cortège* **procession**, parade, cavalcade, motorcade, convoy, caravan, train, column, file, line. **2** *the prince's cortège* **entourage**, retinue, train, suite; attendants, companions, followers, retainers.

cosmetic adj. *most of the changes were merely cosmetic* **superficial**, surface, skin-deep, outward, exterior, external.

– OPPOSITES fundamental.

▸n. *a new range of cosmetics* **make-up**, beauty products, maquillage, face paint; informal warpaint, paint, slap.

cosmic adj. **1** *cosmic bodies* **extraterrestrial**, in space, from space. **2** *an epic of cosmic dimensions* **vast**, huge, immense, enormous, massive, colossal, prodigious, immeasurable, incalculable, unfathomable, fathomless, measureless, infinite, limitless, boundless.

cosmonaut n. **astronaut**, spaceman/woman, taikonaut, space traveller, space cadet; N. Amer. informal jock.

cosmopolitan adj. **1** *the student body has a cosmopolitan character* **multicultural**, multiracial, international, worldwide, global. **2** *a cosmopolitan audience* **worldly**, worldly-wise, well travelled, experienced, cultivated, cultured, sophisticated, suave, urbane, glamorous, fashionable; informal jet-setting, cool.

– OPPOSITES provincial.

cosset v. **pamper**, indulge, overindulge, mollycoddle, coddle, baby, pet, mother, nanny, nursemaid, pander to, feather-bed, spoil; wrap in cotton wool, wait on someone hand and foot.

cost n. **1** *the cost of the equipment* **price**, asking price, market price, selling price, fee, tariff, fare, toll, levy, charge, rental; value, valuation, quotation, rate, worth; humorous damage. **2** *the human cost of the conflict* **sacrifice**, loss, expense, penalty, toll, price. **3** *we need to make £10,000 to cover our costs* **expenses**, outgoings, disbursements, overheads, running costs, operating costs, fixed costs; expenditure, spending, outlay.

▸v. **1** *the chair costs £186* **be priced at**, sell for, be valued at, fetch, come to, amount to; informal set someone back, go for; Brit. informal knock someone back. **2** *the proposal has not yet been costed* **put a price on**, price, value, put a value on, put a figure on.

costly adj. **1** *costly machinery* **expensive**, dear, high-cost, highly priced, overpriced; Brit. over the odds; informal steep, pricey. **2** *a costly mistake* **catastrophic**, disastrous, calamitous, ruinous; damaging, harmful, injurious, deleterious, woeful, awful, terrible, dreadful; formal grievous.

– OPPOSITES cheap.

costume n. **1** *Elizabethan costumes* **(set of) clothes**, garments, robes, outfit, ensemble; dress, clothing, attire, garb, uniform, livery; informal get-up, gear, togs; Brit. informal clobber, kit; N. Amer. informal threads; formal apparel; old use habit, habiliments, raiment. **2** Brit. *if you'd like a dip, we can lend you a costume.* See **swimsuit**.

cosy adj. **1** *a cosy country cottage* **snug**, comfortable, warm, homelike, homey, homely, welcoming; safe, sheltered, secure; N. Amer. down-home, homestyle; informal comfy, snug as a bug (in a rug). **2** *a cosy chat* **intimate**, relaxed, informal, friendly.

coterie n. **clique**, set, circle, inner circle, crowd, in-crowd, band, community; informal gang.

cottage n. **small house**, lodge, chalet, cabin; shack, shanty; in Russia dacha; Scottish bothy, but and ben; Austral. informal weekender; literary bower; old use cot.

couch n. *she seated herself on the couch* **settee**, sofa, divan, chaise longue, chesterfield, love seat, settle, ottoman; Brit. put-you-up; N. Amer. daybed, davenport, studio couch.

▸v. *his reply was couched in deferential terms* **express**, phrase, word, frame, put, formulate, style, convey, say, state, utter.

cough v. *he coughed loudly* **hack**, hawk, bark, clear one's throat, hem.

▸n. *a loud cough* **hack**, bark; informal frog in one's throat.

□ **cough something up** pay (up), come up with, hand over, dish out, part with; informal fork out, shell out, lay out; Brit. informal stump up; N. Amer. informal ante up, pony up.

> **WORD LINKS**
> **tussive** relating to coughing
> **expectorant** a medicine used to treat coughs

council n. **1** *the town council* **local authority**, local government, municipal authority, administration, executive, chamber, assembly; Brit. corporation. **2** *the Schools Council* **advisory body**, board, committee, commission, assembly, panel; synod, convocation. **3** *that evening, she held a family council* meeting, gathering, conference, conclave, assembly.

counsel n. **1** *his wise counsel* **advice**, guidance, counselling, direction, information; recommendations, suggestions, guidelines, hints, tips, pointers, warnings. **2** *the counsel for the defence* **barrister**, lawyer; Scottish advocate; N. Amer. attorney, counselor(-at-law); informal brief.
▶ v. *he counselled the team to withdraw from the deal* **advise**, recommend, direct, advocate, encourage, urge, warn, caution; guide, give guidance.

counsellor n. **adviser**, consultant, guide, mentor; expert, specialist.

count v. **1** *she counted the money again* **add up**, add together, reckon up, figure up, total, tally, calculate, compute; Brit. tot up; formal enumerate; dated cast up. **2** *a company with 250 employees, not counting overseas staff* **include**, take into account, take account of, take into consideration, allow for. **3** *I count it a privilege to be asked* **consider**, think, feel, regard, look on as, view as, hold to be, judge, deem, account. **4** *it's your mother's feelings that count* **matter**, be of consequence, be of account, be significant, signify, be important, carry weight; informal cut any ice.
▶ n. **1** *at the last count, the committee had 579 members* **calculation**, computation, reckoning, tally; formal enumeration. **2** *her white blood cell count* **amount**, number, total.
□ **count on 1** *you can count on me* **rely on**, depend on, bank on, trust (in), be sure of, have (every) confidence in, believe in, put one's faith in, take for granted, take as read. **2** *they hadn't counted on Rangers' indomitable spirit* **expect**, reckon on, anticipate, envisage, allow for, be prepared for, bargain for/on; N. Amer. informal figure on.
out for the count informal See **unconscious** (sense 1 of the adjective).

countenance n. *his strikingly handsome countenance* **face**, features, physiognomy, profile; (facial) expression, look, appearance, aspect, mien; informal mug; Brit. informal mush, phizog, phiz, clock, boat race; N. Amer. informal puss; literary visage, lineaments.
▶ v. *he would not countenance the use of force* **tolerate**, permit, allow, agree to, consent to, give one's blessing to, go along with, hold with, put up with, endure, stomach, swallow; Scottish thole; informal stand for; formal brook.

counter[1] n. *a pile of counters* **token**, chip, disc, jetton, plaque; piece, man, marker;

N. Amer. check.

counter[2] v. **1** *workers countered accusations of dishonesty with claims of oppression* **respond to**, parry, hit back at, answer, retort to. **2** *the second argument is more difficult to counter* **oppose**, dispute, argue against/with, contradict, controvert, negate, counteract; challenge, contest; formal gainsay, confute.
– OPPOSITES support.
▶ adj. *a counter bid* **opposing**, opposed, opposite.
□ **counter to** against, in opposition to, contrary to, at variance with, in defiance of, in contravention of, in conflict with, at odds with.

counteract v. **1** *new measures to counteract drug trafficking* **prevent**, thwart, frustrate, foil, impede, curb, hinder, hamper, check, put a stop/end to, defeat. **2** *a drug to counteract the possible effect on her heart* **offset**, counterbalance, balance (out), cancel out, even out, counterpoise, countervail, compensate for, make up for, remedy; neutralize, nullify, negate, invalidate.
– OPPOSITES encourage, exacerbate.

counterbalance v. **compensate for**, make up for, offset, balance (out), even out, counterpoise, counteract, equalize, neutralize; nullify, negate, undo.

counterfeit adj. *counterfeit cassettes* **fake**, faked, bogus, forged, imitation, spurious, substitute, ersatz; informal phoney.
– OPPOSITES genuine.
▶ n. *the notes were counterfeits* **fake**, forgery, copy, reproduction, imitation; fraud, sham; informal phoney, knock-off.
– OPPOSITES original.
▶ v. **1** *his signature was hard to counterfeit* **fake**, forge, copy, reproduce, imitate. **2** *he grew tired of counterfeiting interest* **feign**, simulate, pretend, fake, sham.

countermand v. **revoke**, rescind, reverse, undo, repeal, retract, withdraw, quash, overturn, overrule, cancel, annul, invalidate, nullify, negate; Law disaffirm, discharge, vacate; formal abrogate; old use recall.
– OPPOSITES uphold.

counterpane n. dated See **bedspread**.

counterpart n. **equivalent**, opposite number, peer, equal, coequal, parallel, complement, analogue, match, twin, mate, fellow, brother, sister; formal compeer.

countless adj. **innumerable**, numerous, untold, legion, without number, numberless, unnumbered, limitless, multitudinous, incalculable; informal umpteen, no end of, a slew of, loads of, stacks of, heaps of, masses of, oodles of, zillions of; N. Amer. informal gazillions of; literary myriad.
– OPPOSITES few.

countrified adj. **rural**, rustic, pastoral, bucolic, country; idyllic, unspoilt; literary Arcadian, sylvan, georgic.
– OPPOSITES urban.

country n. **1** *foreign countries* **nation**, (sovereign) state, kingdom, realm, territory, province, principality, palatinate, duchy.

C

C

2 *he risked his life for his country* **homeland**, native land, fatherland, motherland, the land of one's fathers. **3** *the whole country took to the streets* **people**, public, population, populace, citizenry, nation, body politic; electors, voters, taxpayers, grass roots; Brit. informal Joe Public. **4** *thickly forested country* **terrain**, land, territory, parts; landscape, scenery, setting, surroundings, environment. **5** *she hated living in the country* **countryside**, green belt, great outdoors; provinces, rural areas, backwoods, back of beyond, hinterland; Austral./NZ outback, bush, back country, backblocks, booay; informal sticks, middle of nowhere; N. Amer. informal boondocks, boonies, tall timbers; Austral. informal beyond the black stump.
▶ adj. *country pursuits* **rural**, countryside, outdoor, rustic, pastoral, bucolic; literary sylvan, Arcadian, georgic.
– OPPOSITES urban.

countryman, countrywoman n. **1** *the traditions of his countrymen* **compatriot**, fellow citizen. **2** *the countryman takes a great interest in the weather* **country dweller**, country cousin, son/daughter of the soil, farmer; rustic, yokel, bumpkin, peasant, provincial; Irish informal culchie; N. Amer. informal hayseed, hick, hillbilly, rube; Austral. informal bushy; old use swain, hind, kern, carl, cottier.

countryside n. **1** *beautiful unspoilt countryside* **landscape**, scenery, surroundings, setting, environment; country, terrain, land. **2** *I was brought up in the countryside.* See **country** (sense 5 of the noun).

county n. *the northern counties* **shire**, province, territory, administrative unit, region, district, area.
▶ adj. Brit. *a county lady* **upper-class**, aristocratic, landed, landowning; informal upper-crust, top-drawer, {huntin', shootin', and fishin'}, tweedy.

coup n. **1** *a violent military coup* **seizure of power**, coup d'état, putsch, overthrow, takeover, deposition; (palace) revolution, rebellion, revolt, insurrection, mutiny, insurgence, uprising. **2** *a major publishing coup* **success**, triumph, feat, accomplishment, achievement, scoop, master stroke, stroke of genius.

coup de grâce n. **death blow**, finishing blow, kiss of death; informal KO, kayo.

coup d'état n. See **coup** (sense 1).

couple n. **1** *a couple of girls* **pair**, duo, twosome, two, brace, span, yoke; old use twain. **2** *a honeymoon couple* **husband and wife**, twosome, partners, lovers; informal item.
▶ v. **1** *a sense of hope is coupled with a sense of loss* **combine**, accompany, mix, incorporate, link, associate, connect, ally; add to, join to; formal conjoin. **2** *a cable is coupled to one of the wheels* **connect**, attach, join, fasten, fix, link, secure, tie, bind, strap, rope, tether, truss, lash, hitch, yoke, chain, hook (up).
– OPPOSITES detach.

coupon n. **1** *money-off coupons* **voucher**, token, ticket, slip; N. Amer. informal ducat, comp, rain check. **2** *fill in the coupon below* **form**, tear-off slip.

courage n. **bravery**, courageousness, pluck, pluckiness, valour, fearlessness, intrepidity, nerve, daring, audacity, boldness, grit, hardihood, heroism, gallantry; informal guts, spunk; Brit. informal bottle; N. Amer. informal moxie, cojones, sand.
– OPPOSITES cowardice.

courageous adj. **brave**, plucky, fearless, valiant, valorous, intrepid, heroic, lionhearted, bold, daring, daredevil, audacious, undaunted, unflinching, unshrinking, unafraid, dauntless, indomitable, doughty, mettlesome, venturesome, stout-hearted, gallant, death-or-glory; N. Amer. rock-ribbed; informal game, gutsy, spunky, ballsy, have-a-go.
– OPPOSITES cowardly.

courier n. **1** *the documents were sent by courier* **messenger**, dispatch rider, runner. **2** *a courier for a package holiday company* **representative**, (tour) guide; dragoman; N. Amer. tour director; informal rep.

course n. **1** *the island was not far off our course* **route**, way, track, direction, tack, path, line, trail, trajectory, bearing, heading, orbit. **2** *the course of history* **progression**, development, progress, advance, evolution, flow, movement, sequence, order, succession, rise, march, passage, passing. **3** *what is the best course to adopt?* **procedure**, plan (of action), course/line of action, MO, modus operandi, practice, approach, technique, way, means, policy, strategy, programme; formal praxis. **4** *a waterlogged course* **racecourse**, racetrack, track, ground. **5** *a French course* **programme/course of study**, curriculum, syllabus; classes, lectures, studies. **6** *a course of antibiotics* **programme**, series, sequence, system, schedule, regimen.
▶ v. *tears coursed down her cheeks* **flow**, pour, stream, run, rush, gush, cascade, flood, roll.
□ **in due course** at the appropriate time, when the time is ripe, in time, in the fullness of time, in the course of time, at a later date, by and by, sooner or later, in the end, eventually.
of course naturally, as might be expected, as you/one would expect, needless to say, certainly, to be sure, as a matter of course, obviously, it goes without saying; informal natch.

court n. **1** *the court found him guilty* **court of law**, law court, bench, bar, judicature, tribunal, chancery, assizes; Military court martial. **2** *walking in the castle court* **courtyard**, quadrangle, square, close, enclosure, plaza, piazza, cloister; informal quad. **3** *the King's court* **royal household**, retinue, entourage, train, suite, courtiers, attendants. **4** *she made her way to the queen's court* **royal residence**, palace, castle, chateau.
▶ v. **1** *a newspaper editor who was courted by senior politicians* **curry favour with**,

cultivate, try to win over, make up to, ingratiate oneself with; informal suck up to, butter up; N. Amer. informal shine up to; old use blandish. **2** *he was busily courting public attention* **seek**, pursue, go after, strive for, solicit. **3** *he's often courted controversy* **risk**, invite, attract, bring on oneself. **4** dated *he's courting her sister* **woo**, go out with, pursue, run after, chase, pay court to; informal date, see, go steady with; Austral. informal track (square) with; dated set one's cap at, romance, seek the hand of, make love to.

WORD LINKS

judicial, juridical relating to a court of law
defendant a person sued or accused in a court of law
plaintiff a person who brings a case in a court of law
litigate take a dispute or claim to a court of law
summons, subpoena an order instructing someone to attend a court of law
perjury the offence of deliberately lying in a court of law when under oath
sub judice being considered by a court of law and not permitted to be publicly discussed.
See also **law**.

---

courteous adj. **polite**, well mannered, civil, respectful, well behaved, well bred, well spoken, mannerly; gentlemanly, chivalrous, gallant; gracious, obliging, considerate, pleasant, cordial, urbane, polished, refined, courtly, civilized; old use fair-spoken.
– OPPOSITES rude.

courtesan n. old use See **prostitute** (noun).

courtesy n. **politeness**, courteousness, good manners, civility, respect, respectfulness; chivalry, gallantry; graciousness, consideration, thought, thoughtfulness, cordiality, urbanity, courtliness.

courtier n. **attendant**, lord, lady, lady-in-waiting, steward, equerry, page, squire; historical liegeman.

courtly adj. **refined**, polished, suave, cultivated, civilized, elegant, urbane, debonair; polite, civil, courteous, gracious, well mannered, well bred, chivalrous, gallant, gentlemanly, ladylike, aristocratic, dignified, decorous, formal, ceremonious, stately.
– OPPOSITES uncouth.

courtship n. **1** *a whirlwind courtship* **romance**, (love) affair; engagement. **2** *his courtship of Emma* **wooing**, courting, suit, pursuit; old use addresses.

courtyard n. **quadrangle**, cloister, square, plaza, piazza, close, enclosure; informal quad.

cove n. *a small sandy cove* **bay**, inlet, fjord, anchorage; Scottish (sea) loch; Irish lough.

covenant n. *a breach of the covenant* **contract**, agreement, undertaking, commitment, guarantee, warrant, pledge, promise, bond, indenture; pact, deal, settlement, arrangement, understanding.
▶v. *the landlord covenants to repair the property* **undertake**, contract, guarantee, pledge, promise, agree, engage, warrant, commit oneself, bind oneself.

cover v. **1** *she covered her face with a towel* **protect**, shield, shelter; hide, conceal, veil. **2** *his car was covered in mud* **cake**, coat, encrust, plaster, smother, daub, bedaub. **3** *snow covered the fields* **blanket**, overlay, overspread, carpet, coat; literary mantle. **4** *a course covering all aspects of the business* **deal with**, consider, take in, include, involve, comprise, incorporate, embrace. **5** *the trial was covered by a range of newspapers* **report on**, write about, describe, commentate on, publish/broadcast details of. **6** *he turned on the radio to cover their conversation* **mask**, disguise, hide, camouflage, muffle, stifle, smother. **7** *I'm covering for Jill* **stand in for**, fill in for, deputize for, take over from, relieve, take the place of, sit in for, understudy, hold the fort; informal sub for; N. Amer. informal pinch-hit for. **8** *can you make enough to cover your costs?* **pay (for)**, be enough for, fund, finance; pay back, make up for, offset. **9** *your home is covered against damage and loss* **insure**, protect, secure, underwrite, assure, indemnify. **10** *we covered ten miles each day* **travel**, journey, go, do, traverse.
– OPPOSITES expose.
▶n. **1** *a protective cover* **covering**, sleeve, wrapping, wrapper, envelope, sheath, housing, jacket, casing, cowling; awning, canopy, tarpaulin. **2** *a manhole cover* **lid**, top, cap. **3** *a book cover* **binding**, jacket, dust jacket, dust cover, wrapper. **4** *she pulled the covers over her head* **bedclothes**, bedding, sheets, blankets. **5** *a thick cover of snow* **coating**, coat, covering, layer, carpet, blanket, overlay, dusting, film, sheet, veneer, crust, skin, cloak, mantle, veil, pall, shroud. **6** *panicking onlookers ran for cover* **shelter**, protection, refuge, sanctuary, haven, hiding place. **7** *there is considerable game cover around the lake* **undergrowth**, vegetation, greenery, woodland, trees, bushes, brush, scrub, plants; covert, thicket, copse, coppice. **8** *the company was a cover for an international swindle* **front**, facade, smokescreen, screen, blind, camouflage, disguise, mask, cloak. **9** Brit. *your policy provides cover against damage by subsidence* **insurance**, protection, security, assurance, indemnification, indemnity, compensation.
□ **cover something up** conceal, hide, keep secret/dark, hush up, draw a veil over, suppress, sweep under the carpet, gloss over; informal whitewash, keep a/the lid on.

coverage n. **reportage**, reporting, description, treatment, handling, presentation, investigation, commentary; reports, articles, pieces, stories.

covering n. **1** *a canvas covering* **awning**, canopy, tarpaulin, cowling, casing, housing; wrapping, wrapper, cover, envelope, sheath, sleeve, jacket, lid, top, cap. **2** *a covering of snow* **layer**, coating, coat, carpet, blanket, overlay, topping, dusting, film, sheet, veneer, crust, skin, cloak, mantle, veil.
▶adj. *a covering letter* **accompanying**, explanatory, introductory, prefatory.

coverlet n. **bedspread**, bedcover, cover, throw, duvet, quilt; Brit. eiderdown; N. Amer. spread, comforter; dated counterpane.

covert adj. **secret**, furtive, clandestine, surreptitious, stealthy, cloak-and-dagger, hole-and-corner, backstairs, under-the-table, hugger-mugger, concealed, hidden, private, undercover, underground; Military black; informal hush-hush.
– OPPOSITES overt.

cover-up n. **whitewash**, concealment, false front, facade, camouflage, disguise, mask.
– OPPOSITES exposé.

covet v. **desire**, yearn for, crave, have one's heart set on, want, wish for, long for, hanker after/for, hunger after/for, thirst for.

covetous adj. **grasping**, greedy, acquisitive, desirous, possessive, envious, green with envy, green-eyed.

covey n. **group**, gang, troop, troupe, party, company, band, bevy, flock; knot, cluster; informal bunch, gaggle, posse, crew.

cow v. **intimidate**, daunt, browbeat, bully, tyrannize, scare, terrorize, frighten, dishearten, unnerve, subdue; informal psych out, bulldoze.

coward n. **weakling**, milksop, namby-pamby, mouse; informal chicken, scaredy-cat, yellow-belly, sissy, baby; Brit. informal big girl's blouse; N. Amer. informal pantywaist, pussy; Austral./NZ informal dingo, sook; old use poltroon, caitiff.
– OPPOSITES hero.

cowardly adj. **faint-hearted**, lily-livered, spineless, chicken-hearted, craven, timid, timorous, fearful, pusillanimous; informal yellow, chicken, weak-kneed, gutless, yellow-bellied, wimpish, wimpy; Brit. informal wet; old use recreant.
– OPPOSITES brave.

cowboy n. **1** *cowboys on horseback* **cattleman**, cowhand, cowman, cowherd, herder, herdsman, drover, stockman, rancher, gaucho, vaquero; N. Amer. informal cowpuncher, cowpoke, broncobuster; N. Amer. dated buckaroo. **2** informal *the builders were complete cowboys* **rogue**, rascal, scoundrel, cheat, swindler, fraudster, fly-by-night.

cower v. **cringe**, shrink, crouch, recoil, flinch, pull back, draw back, tremble, shake, quake, blench, quail, grovel.

coy adj. **arch**, simpering, coquettish, flirtatious, kittenish, skittish; demure, shy, modest, bashful, reticent, diffident, self-effacing, shrinking, timid.
– OPPOSITES brazen.

crabbed adj. **1** *her crabbed handwriting* **cramped**, ill-formed, bad, illegible, unreadable, indecipherable; shaky, spidery. **2** *a crabbed old man.* See **crabby**.

crabby adj. **irritable**, cantankerous, irascible, bad-tempered, grumpy, grouchy, crotchety, tetchy, testy, crusty, curmudgeonly, ill-tempered, ill-humoured, peevish, cross, fractious, pettish, crabbed, prickly, waspish; informal snappish, snappy, chippy; Brit. informal shirty, stroppy, narky, ratty; N. Amer. informal cranky, ornery; Austral./NZ informal snaky.

– OPPOSITES affable.

crack n. **1** *a crack in the glass* **split**, break, chip, fracture, rupture; crazing. **2** *a crack between two rocks* **space**, gap, crevice, fissure, cleft, breach, rift, cranny, chink, interstice. **3** *the crack of a rifle* **bang**, report, explosion, detonation, pop; clap, crash. **4** *a crack on the head* **blow**, bang, hit, knock, rap, punch, thump, bump, smack, slap; informal bash, whack, thwack, clout, wallop, clip, biff, bop. **5** informal *we'll have a crack at it* **attempt**, try; informal go, shot, stab, whack; formal essay. **6** informal *cheap cracks about her clothes* **joke**, witticism, quip; jibe, barb, taunt, sneer, insult; informal gag, wisecrack, funny, dig.
▸ v. **1** *the glass cracked in the heat* **break**, split, fracture, rupture, snap. **2** *she cracked him across the forehead* **hit**, strike, smack, slap, beat, thump, knock, rap, punch; informal bash, whack, thwack, clobber, clout, clip, wallop, belt, biff, bop, sock; Brit. informal slosh; N. Amer. informal boff, bust, slug. **3** *the witnesses cracked* **break down**, give way, cave in, go to pieces, crumble, lose control, yield, succumb. **4** informal *the naval code proved harder to crack* **decipher**, interpret, decode, break, solve, resolve, work out, find the key to; informal figure out, suss out.
▸ adj. *a crack shot* **expert**, skilled, skilful, formidable, virtuoso, masterly, consummate, excellent, first-rate, first-class, marvellous, wonderful, magnificent, outstanding, superlative; deadly; informal great, superb, fantastic, ace, hotshot, mean, demon; Brit. informal brilliant; N. Amer. informal crackerjack.
– OPPOSITES incompetent.
□ **crack down on** suppress, prevent, stop, put a stop to, put an end to, stamp out, eliminate, eradicate; clamp down on, get tough on, come down hard on, limit, restrain, restrict, check, keep in check, control, keep under control.
crack up informal break down, have a breakdown, lose control, go to pieces, go out of one's mind, go mad; informal lose it, fall/come apart at the seams, go crazy, freak out.

cracked adj. **1** *a cracked cup* **chipped**, broken, crazed, fractured, splintered, split; damaged, defective, flawed, imperfect. **2** informal *you're cracked!* See **mad** (sense 1).

crackle v. **sizzle**, fizz, hiss, crack, snap, sputter, crepitate; technical decrepitate.

cradle n. **1** *the baby's cradle* **crib**, bassinet, Moses basket, cot, carrycot. **2** *the cradle of democracy* **birthplace**, fount, fountainhead, source, spring, fountain, origin, place of origin, seat; literary wellspring.
▸ v. *she cradled his head in her arms* **hold**, support, pillow, cushion, shelter, protect; rest, prop (up).

craft n. **1** *a player with plenty of craft* **skill**, skilfulness, ability, capability, competence, art, talent, flair, artistry, dexterity, craftsmanship, expertise, proficiency, adroitness, adeptness, deftness, virtuosity. **2** *the historian's craft* **activity**, occupation, profession, work, line of work, pursuit. **3** *she used craft and diplomacy* **cunning**,

C

craftiness, guile, wiliness, artfulness, deviousness, slyness, trickery, duplicity, dishonesty, deceit, deceitfulness, deception, intrigue, subterfuge; wiles, ploys, ruses, schemes, stratagems, tricks. **4** *a sailing craft* **vessel**, ship, boat; literary barque.

craftsman, **craftswoman** n. **artisan**, artist, skilled worker; expert, master; old use artificer, mechanic.

craftsmanship n. **workmanship**, artistry, craft, art, handiwork, work; skill, skilfulness, expertise, technique.

crafty adj. **cunning**, wily, guileful, artful, devious, sly, tricky, scheming, calculating, designing, sharp, shrewd, astute, canny; duplicitous, dishonest, deceitful; informal foxy; old use subtle.
– OPPOSITES honest.

crag n. **cliff**, bluff, ridge, precipice, height, peak, tor, escarpment, scarp.

craggy adj. **1** *the craggy cliffs* **steep**, precipitous, sheer, perpendicular; rocky, rugged, ragged. **2** *his craggy face* **rugged**, rough-hewn, strong, manly; weather-beaten, weathered.

cram v. **1** *wardrobes crammed with clothes* **fill**, stuff, pack, jam, fill to overflowing, fill to the brim, overload; crowd, throng, overcrowd. **2** *they all crammed into the car* **crowd**, pack, pile, squash, wedge oneself, force one's way. **3** *he crammed his clothes into a suitcase* **thrust**, push, shove, force, ram, jam, stuff, pack, pile, squash, compress, squeeze, wedge. **4** *most of the students are cramming for exams* **revise**; informal swot, mug up, bone up.

cramp n. *stomach cramps* **muscle spasm**, pain, shooting pain, pang, stitch; Medicine clonus, hyperkinesis.
▶v. *tighter rules will cramp economic growth* **hinder**, impede, inhibit, hamper, constrain, hamstring, interfere with, restrict, limit, shackle; slow down, check, arrest, curb, retard.

cramped adj. **1** *dark, cramped accommodation* **poky**, uncomfortable, confined, restricted, constricted, small, tiny, narrow; crowded, packed, congested; old use strait. **2** *cramped handwriting* **small**, crabbed, illegible, unreadable, indecipherable.
– OPPOSITES spacious.

crane n. **derrick**, winch, hoist, davit, windlass; block and tackle.

cranium n. **skull**, head; N. Amer. informal brainpan.

crank[1] v. *you crank the engine by hand* **start**, turn (over), get going.
□ **crank something up** informal increase, intensify, amplify, heighten, escalate, add to, augment, build up, expand, extend, raise; speed up, accelerate; informal jack up, hike up, step up, bump up, pump up.

crank[2] n. *they're nothing but a bunch of cranks* **eccentric**, oddity, madman/madwoman, lunatic; informal oddball, freak, weirdo, crackpot, loony, nut, nutcase, head case,

maniac; Brit. informal nutter; N. Amer. informal screwball, kook.

cranky adj. **1** informal *a cranky diet* **eccentric**, bizarre, weird, peculiar, odd, strange, unconventional, left-field, unorthodox, outlandish; silly, stupid, mad, crazy, idiotic; informal wacky, crackpot, nutty; Brit. informal daft, potty; N. Amer. informal wacko. **2** N. Amer. informal *the children were tired and cranky*. See **irritable**.

cranny n. **chink**, crack, crevice, slit, split, fissure, rift, cleft, opening, gap, aperture, cavity, hole, hollow, niche, corner, nook, interstice.

crash v. **1** *the car crashed into a tree* **smash into**, collide with, be in collision with, hit, strike, ram, cannon into, plough into, meet head-on, run into; N. Amer. impact. **2** *he crashed his car* **smash**, wreck; Brit. write off; Brit. informal prang; N. Amer. informal total. **3** *waves crashed against the shore* **dash**, batter, pound, lash, slam, be hurled. **4** *thunder crashed overhead* **boom**, crack, roll, clap, explode, bang, blast, blare, resound, reverberate, rumble, thunder, echo. **5** informal *his clothing company crashed* **collapse**, fold, fail, go under, go bankrupt, become insolvent, cease trading, go into receivership, go into liquidation, be wound up; informal go broke, go bust, go to the wall, go belly up, flatline.
▶n. **1** *a crash on the motorway* **accident**, collision, smash, road traffic accident, RTA; derailment; N. Amer. wreck; informal pile-up; Brit. informal prang, shunt. **2** *a loud crash* **bang**, smash, smack, crack, bump, thud, clatter, clunk, clonk, clang; report, detonation, explosion; noise, racket, clangour, din. **3** *the crash of her company* **collapse**, failure, bankruptcy, insolvency, liquidation.
▶adj. *a crash course* **intensive**, concentrated, rapid, short; accelerated-learning, total-immersion.

crass adj. **stupid**, insensitive, mindless, thoughtless, witless, oafish, boorish, asinine, coarse, gross, graceless, tasteless, tactless, clumsy, heavy-handed, blundering; informal ignorant, pig-ignorant.
– OPPOSITES intelligent.

crate n. **case**, packing case, chest, tea chest, box; container, receptacle.

crater n. **hollow**, bowl, basin, hole, cavity, depression; Geology caldera, maar, solfatara.

crave v. **long for**, yearn for, desire, want, wish for, hunger for, thirst for, sigh for, pine for, hanker after, covet, lust after, ache for, set one's heart on, dream of, be bent on; informal have a yen for, itch for, be dying for; old use desiderate.

craven adj. **cowardly**, lily-livered, faint-hearted, chicken-hearted, spineless, timid, timorous, fearful, pusillanimous, weak, feeble; informal yellow, chicken, weak-kneed, gutless, yellow-bellied, wimpish; contemptible, abject, ignominious; Brit. informal wet; old use recreant.
– OPPOSITES brave.

C

craving n. **longing**, yearning, desire, want, wish, hankering, hunger, thirst, appetite, greed, lust, ache, need, urge; informal yen, itch.

crawl v. **1** *they crawled under the table* **creep**, worm one's way, go on all fours, go on hands and knees, wriggle, slither, squirm, scrabble. **2** informal *I'm not going to go crawling to him* **grovel to**, ingratiate oneself with, be obsequious to, kowtow to, pander to, toady to, truckle to, bow and scrape to, dance attendance on, curry favour with, make up to, fawn on/over; informal suck up to, lick someone's boots, butter up. **3** *the place was crawling with soldiers* **be full of**, overflow with, teem with, be packed with, be crowded with, be alive with, be overrun with, swarm with, be bristling with, be infested with, be thick with; informal be lousy with, be stuffed with, be jam-packed with, be chock-a-block with, be chock-full of.

craze n. **fad**, fashion, trend, vogue, enthusiasm, mania, passion, rage, obsession, compulsion, fixation, fetish, fancy, taste, fascination, preoccupation; informal thing.

crazed adj. **mad**, insane, out of one's mind, deranged, demented, certifiable, lunatic, psychopathic; wild, raving, berserk, manic, maniac, frenzied; informal crazy, mental, off one's head, out of one's head, raving mad. See also **crazy** (sense 1).
– OPPOSITES sane.

crazy adj. informal **1** *a crazy old man* **mad**, insane, out of one's mind, deranged, demented, not in one's right mind, crazed, lunatic, non compos mentis, unhinged, mad as a hatter, mad as a March hare; informal mental, off one's head, nutty (as a fruitcake), off one's rocker, not right in the head, round the bend, raving mad, bats, batty, bonkers, cuckoo, loopy, loony, bananas, loco, with a screw loose, touched, gaga, doolally, not all there, away with the fairies; Brit. informal barmy, crackers, barking, potty, round the twist, off one's trolley, not the full shilling; N. Amer. informal nutso, out of one's tree, meshuga, wacko, gonzo; Canadian informal spinny; Austral./NZ informal bushed. **2** *a crazy idea* **stupid**, foolish, idiotic, silly, absurd, ridiculous, ludicrous, preposterous, farcical, laughable, risible, nonsensical, imbecilic, hare-brained, half-baked, impracticable, unworkable, ill-conceived, senseless; informal cockeyed; Brit. informal barmy, daft. **3** *he's crazy about her* **passionate about**, very keen on, enamoured of, infatuated with, smitten with, devoted to; very enthusiastic about, fanatical about; informal wild/mad/nuts about, gone on; Brit. informal potty about.
– OPPOSITES sane, sensible, apathetic.

creak v. **squeak**, grate, rasp; groan, complain.

cream n. **1** *skin creams* **lotion**, ointment, moisturizer, emollient, unguent, cosmetic; salve, rub, embrocation, balm, liniment. **2** *the cream of the world's photographers* **best**, finest, pick, flower, crème de la crème, elite, A-list.
– OPPOSITES dregs.
▸ adj. *a cream dress* **off-white**, whitish, cream-coloured, creamy, ivory, yellowish-white.

creamy adj. **1** *a creamy paste* **smooth**, thick, velvety, whipped; rich, buttery. **2** *creamy flowers* **off-white**, whitish, cream-coloured, cream, ivory, yellowish-white.
– OPPOSITES lumpy.

crease n. **1** *trousers with knife-edge creases* **fold**, line, ridge; pleat, tuck; furrow, groove, corrugation. **2** *the creases at the corners of her eyes* **wrinkle**, line, crinkle, pucker; (**creases**) crow's feet.
▸ v. *her skirt was creased and stained* **crumple**, wrinkle, crinkle, line, scrunch up, rumple, ruck up.

create v. **1** *she has created a work of stunning originality* **produce**, generate, bring into being, make, fabricate, fashion, build, construct; design, devise, originate, frame, develop, shape, form, forge. **2** *regular socializing creates a good team spirit* **bring about**, give rise to, lead to, result in, cause, breed, generate, engender, produce, make for, promote, foster, sow the seeds of, contribute to. **3** *the governments planned to create a free-trade zone* **establish**, found, initiate, institute, constitute, inaugurate, launch, set up, form, organize, develop. **4** *she was created a life peer in 2004* **appoint**, make; invest as, install as.
– OPPOSITES destroy.

creation n. **1** *the creation of a coalition government* **establishment**, formation, foundation, initiation, institution, inauguration, constitution; production, generation, fabrication, fashioning, building, construction, origination, development. **2** *the whole of creation* **the world**, the universe, the cosmos; the living world, the natural world, nature, life, living things. **3** *Dickens's literary creations* **work**, work of art, production, opus, oeuvre; achievement.
– OPPOSITES destruction.

creative adj. **inventive**, imaginative, innovative, innovatory, experimental, original; artistic, expressive, inspired, visionary; enterprising, resourceful; informal blue-sky.

creativity n. **inventiveness**, imagination, imaginativeness, innovation, innovativeness, originality, individuality; artistry, inspiration, vision; enterprise, initiative, resourcefulness.

creator n. **author**, writer, designer, deviser, maker, producer; originator, inventor, architect, mastermind, prime mover; literary begetter.

creature n. **1** *the earth and its creatures* **animal**, beast, brute; living thing, living being; N. Amer. informal critter. **2** *you're such a lazy creature!* **person**, individual, human being, character, soul, wretch, customer; informal devil, beggar, sort, type; Brit. informal bod; old use wight. **3** *she was denounced as a creature of the liberals* **lackey**, minion, hireling, servant, puppet, tool, cat's paw, pawn; informal stooge, yes-man; Brit. informal poodle.

credence n. 1 *the government placed little credence in the scheme* **belief**, faith, trust, confidence, reliance. 2 *later reports lent credence to this view* **credibility**, plausibility; old use credit.

credentials plural n. **documents**, documentation, papers, identity papers, bona fides, ID, ID card, identity card, passport, proof of identity; certificates, diplomas, certification.

credibility n. 1 *the whole tale lacks credibility* **plausibility**, believability, tenability, probability, feasibility, likelihood, credence; authority, cogency; old use credit. 2 *the party lacked moral credibility* **trustworthiness**, reliability, dependability, integrity.

credible adj. **believable**, plausible, tenable, able to hold water, conceivable, likely, probable, possible, feasible, reasonable, with a ring of truth, persuasive.

credit n. 1 *he never got much credit for the show's success* **praise**, commendation, acclaim, acknowledgement, recognition, kudos, glory, esteem, respect, admiration, tributes, bouquets, thanks, gratitude, appreciation; informal brownie points. 2 *the speech did his credit no good in the House of Commons* **reputation**, repute, image, (good) name, character, prestige, standing, status, estimation, credibility.
▶ v. 1 *the wise will seldom credit all they hear* **believe**, accept, give credence to, trust, have faith in; informal buy, swallow, fall for, take something as gospel. 2 *the scheme's success can be credited to the team's frugality* **ascribe**, attribute, assign, accredit, chalk up, put down.
□ **on credit** on hire purchase, on (the) HP, by instalments, on account; informal on tick, on the slate; Brit. informal on the never-never.

creditable adj. **commendable**, praiseworthy, laudable, admirable, honourable, estimable, meritorious, worthy, deserving, respectable.
– OPPOSITES deplorable.

credulous adj. **gullible**, naive, over-trusting, over-trustful, easily taken in, impressionable, unsuspecting, unsuspicious, unwary, unquestioning; innocent, ingenuous, inexperienced, unsophisticated, unworldly, wide-eyed; informal born yesterday, wet behind the ears.
– OPPOSITES suspicious.

creed n. 1 *people of many creeds and cultures* **faith**, religion, religious belief, religious persuasion, Church, denomination, sect. 2 *his political creed* **system of belief**, (set of) beliefs, principles, articles of faith, ideology, credo, doctrine, teaching, dogma, tenets, canons.

creek n. **inlet**, bay, estuary, bight, fjord, sound; Scottish firth, frith; in Orkney & Shetland voe.

creep v. 1 *Tim crept out of the house* **tiptoe**, steal, sneak, slip, slink, sidle, pad, edge, inch; skulk, prowl. 2 informal *they're always creeping to the boss* **grovel to**, ingratiate oneself with, curry favour with, toady to, truckle to, kowtow to, bow and scrape to, pander to, fawn on/over, make up to; informal crawl to, suck up to, lick someone's boots, butter up.

creeper n. **climbing plant**, trailing plant; vine, climber, rambler.

creepy adj. informal **frightening**, eerie, disturbing, sinister, weird, hair-raising, menacing, threatening; Scottish eldritch; informal spooky, scary.

crescent n. **half-moon**, sickle-shape, demilune, lunula, lunette; arc, curve, bow.

crest n. 1 *the bird's crest* **comb**, plume, tuft of feathers. 2 *the crest of the hill* **summit**, peak, top, mountaintop, tip, pinnacle, brow, crown, apex. 3 *the Duke of Wellington's crest* **insignia**, regalia, badge, emblem, heraldic device, coat of arms, arms; Heraldry bearing, charge.

crestfallen adj. **downhearted**, downcast, despondent, disappointed, disconsolate, disheartened, discouraged, dispirited, dejected, depressed, desolate, in the doldrums, sad, glum, gloomy, dismayed, doleful, miserable, unhappy, woebegone, forlorn; informal blue, down in the mouth, down in the dumps.
– OPPOSITES cheerful.

crevasse n. **chasm**, abyss, fissure, cleft, crack, split, breach, rift, hole, cavity.

crevice n. **crack**, fissure, cleft, chink, interstice, cranny, nook, slit, split, rift, fracture, breach; opening, gap, hole.

crew n. 1 *the ship's crew* **sailors**, mariners, hands, ship's company, ship's complement. 2 *a crew of cameramen and sound engineers* **team**, group, company, unit, corps, party, gang. 3 informal *a crew of inebriated locals* **crowd**, group, band, gang, mob, pack, troop, swarm, herd, posse; informal bunch, gaggle.

crib n. 1 *the baby's crib* **cot**, cradle, bassinet, Moses basket, carrycot. 2 *the oxen's cribs* **manger**, stall, feeding trough, fodder rack.
▶ v. informal *she cribbed the plot from a Shakespeare play* **copy**, plagiarize, poach, appropriate, steal, 'borrow'; informal rip off, lift; Brit. informal nick, pinch.

crick v. **strain**, twist, rick, sprain, pull, wrench; injure, hurt, damage.

crime n. 1 *kidnapping is a very serious crime* **offence**, unlawful act, illegal act, felony, misdemeanour, misdeed, wrong; Law tort. 2 *the increase in crime* **lawbreaking**, delinquency, wrongdoing, criminality, misconduct, illegality, villainy; informal crookedness; Law malfeasance. 3 *a crime against humanity* **sin**, evil, immoral act, wrong, atrocity, abomination, disgrace, outrage.

> **WORD LINKS**
>
> **felonious** relating to or involved in crime
> **forensic** relating to the use of scientific methods to investigate crime
> **criminology** the scientific study of crime
> **alibi** evidence that one was elsewhere when a crime took place
> **accessory** a person who helps someone to

C

commit a crime without taking part in it
principal a person directly responsible for a crime
agent provocateur a person employed to tempt
others to commit a crime and so be prosecuted
entrap trick someone into committing a crime
and so be prosecuted

criminal n. *a convicted criminal* **lawbreaker**,
offender, villain, delinquent, felon,
convict, malefactor, wrongdoer, culprit,
miscreant; thief, burglar, robber, armed
robber, gunman, gangster, terrorist; informal
crook, con, jailbird, (old) lag; N. Amer. informal
hood, yardbird; Austral./NZ informal crim; Law
malfeasant.
▸adj. **1** *criminal conduct* **unlawful**, illegal,
against the law, illicit, lawless, felonious,
delinquent, fraudulent, actionable, culpable;
villainous, nefarious, corrupt, wrong, bad,
evil, wicked, iniquitous; informal crooked;
Brit. informal bent; Law malfeasant. **2** informal
a criminal waste of taxpayer's money
deplorable, shameful, reprehensible,
disgraceful, inexcusable, unforgivable,
unpardonable, outrageous, monstrous,
shocking, scandalous, wicked.
– OPPOSITES lawful.

crimp v. **pleat**, flute, corrugate, ruffle,
fold, crease, crinkle, pucker, gather; pinch,
compress, press together, squeeze together.

crimped adj. *crimped blonde hair* **curly**,
wavy, curled, frizzy, ringlety.

cringe v. **1** *she cringed as he bellowed in her
ear* **cower**, shrink, recoil, shy away, flinch,
blench, draw back; shake, tremble, quiver,
quail, quake. **2** *it makes me cringe when
I think of it* **wince**, shudder, squirm, feel
embarrassed/mortified.

crinkle v. **wrinkle**, crease, pucker, furrow,
corrugate, line; rumple, scrunch up, ruck up.

crinkly adj. **wrinkled**, wrinkly, crinkled,
creased, crumpled, rumpled, crimped,
corrugated, fluted, puckered, furrowed;
wavy.

cripple v. **1** *the accident crippled her* **disable**,
paralyse, immobilize, lame, incapacitate,
handicap. **2** *the company had been crippled
by the recession* **devastate**, ruin, destroy,
wipe out; paralyse, hamstring, bring to
a standstill, put out of action, put out of
business, bankrupt, break, bring someone to
their knees.

crippled adj. **disabled**, paralysed,
incapacitated, physically handicapped,
lame, immobilized, bedridden, confined to a
wheelchair; euphemistic physically challenged;
old use halt.

crisis n. **1** *the situation had reached a crisis*
critical point, turning point, crossroads,
climacteric, head, moment of truth, zero
hour, point of no return, Rubicon, doomsday;
informal crunch. **2** *the current economic crisis*
emergency, disaster, catastrophe, calamity;
predicament, plight, mess, trouble, dire
straits, difficulty, extremity.

crisp adj. **1** *crisp bacon* **crunchy**, crispy,
brittle, crumbly, friable, breakable; firm, dry.
2 *a crisp autumn day* **invigorating**, bracing,

brisk, fresh, refreshing, exhilarating, tonic,
energizing; cool, chill, chilly, cold; informal
nippy; Brit. informal parky. **3** *her answer was
crisp* **brisk**, decisive, businesslike, no-
nonsense, incisive, to the point, matter-
of-fact, brusque; terse, succinct, concise,
brief, short, short and sweet, laconic; informal
snappy. **4** *crisp white bedlinen* **smooth**,
uncreased, ironed; starched.
– OPPOSITES soft, sultry, rambling.

criterion n. **standard**, specification,
measure, gauge, test, scale, benchmark,
yardstick, touchstone, barometer; principle,
rule, law, canon.

critic n. **1** *a literary critic* **reviewer**,
commentator, evaluator, analyst, judge,
pundit. **2** *critics of the government*
detractor, attacker, fault-finder.

critical adj. **1** *a highly critical report*
censorious, condemnatory, condemning,
denunciatory, disparaging, disapproving,
scathing, fault-finding, judgemental,
negative, unfavourable; informal nitpicking,
picky. **2** *a critical essay* **evaluative**,
analytical, interpretative, expository,
explanatory. **3** *the situation is critical*
grave, serious, dangerous, risky, perilous,
hazardous, precarious, touch-and-go, in
the balance, uncertain, parlous, desperate,
dire, acute, life-and-death. **4** *the choice
of materials is critical for product safety*
crucial, vital, essential, of the essence, all-
important, paramount, fundamental, key,
pivotal, decisive, deciding, climacteric.
– OPPOSITES complimentary, unimportant.

criticism n. **1** *she was stung by his criticism*
censure, condemnation, denunciation,
disapproval, disparagement, opprobrium,
fault-finding, attack, broadside, brickbats,
stricture, recrimination; informal flak, a bad
press, panning; Brit. informal stick, slating; formal
excoriation. **2** *literary criticism* **evaluation**,
assessment, appraisal, analysis, judgement,
commentary, interpretation, explanation,
explication, elucidation.

criticize v. **find fault with**, censure,
denounce, condemn, attack, lambaste,
pillory, rail against, inveigh against, arraign,
cast aspersions on, pour scorn on, disparage,
denigrate, give a bad press to, run down;
informal knock, pan, slam, hammer, lay into,
pull to pieces, pick holes in; Brit. informal slag
off, slate, rubbish; N. Amer. informal pummel,
trash; Austral./NZ informal bag, monster; formal
excoriate.
– OPPOSITES praise.

critique n. **analysis**, evaluation, assessment,
appraisal, appreciation, criticism, review,
study, commentary, exposition, exegesis.

crock n. **1** *a crock of honey* **pot**, jar; jug,
pitcher, ewer; container, receptacle, vessel.
2 *a pile of dirty crocks.* See **crockery**.
3 informal *he's a bit of an old crock* **invalid**,
valetudinarian; geriatric, dotard; informal
crumbly, wrinkly.

crockery n. **dishes**, crocks, china, tableware;
plates, bowls, cups, saucers.

crony n. informal **friend**, companion, bosom friend, intimate, confidant(e), familiar, associate, comrade; informal pal, chum, sidekick; Brit. informal mate; N. Amer. informal buddy, amigo, compadre; old use compeer.

crook n. **1** informal *a small-time crook* **criminal**, lawbreaker, offender, villain, delinquent, felon, convict, malefactor, culprit, wrongdoer; rogue, scoundrel, cheat, swindler, racketeer, confidence trickster; thief, robber, burglar; informal (old) lag, shark, con man, con, jailbird; N. Amer. informal hood, yardbird; Austral./NZ informal crim; Law malfeasant. **2** *the crook of a tree branch* **bend**, fork, curve, angle.
▶v. *he crooked his finger and called the waiter* **cock**, flex, bend, curve, curl.

crooked adj. **1** *narrow, crooked streets* **winding**, twisting, zigzag, meandering, tortuous, serpentine. **2** *a crooked spine* **bent**, twisted, misshapen, deformed, malformed, contorted, out of shape, wry, warped, bowed, distorted; Scottish thrawn. **3** *the picture over the bed looked crooked* **lopsided**, askew, awry, off-centre, uneven, out of true, out of line, asymmetrical, tilted, at an angle, aslant, slanting, squint; Scottish agley; informal cockeyed; Brit. informal skew-whiff, wonky. **4** informal *a crooked cop | crooked deals* **dishonest**, unscrupulous, unprincipled, untrustworthy, corrupt, corruptible, buyable, venal; criminal, illegal, unlawful, nefarious, fraudulent; Brit. informal bent, dodgy.
– OPPOSITES straight, honest.

croon v. **sing softly**, hum, warble, trill.

crop n. **1** *some farmers lost their entire crop* **harvest**, year's growth, yield; fruits, produce. **2** *a bumper crop of mail* **batch**, lot, assortment, selection, collection, supply, intake. **3** *the bird's crop* **craw**; gullet, throat. **4** *a rider's crop* **whip**, switch, cane, stick.
▶v. **1** *she's had her hair cropped* **cut short**, cut, clip, shear, shave, lop off, chop off, hack off; dock. **2** *a flock of sheep were cropping the turf* **graze on**, browse on, feed on, nibble, eat. **3** *the hay was cropped several times this summer* **harvest**, reap, mow; gather (in), collect, pick, bring home.
□ **crop up** happen, occur, arise, turn up, spring up, pop up, emerge, materialize, surface, appear, come to light, present itself; literary come to pass, befall; old use hap.

> **WORD LINKS**
>
> **agronomy** the science of crop production
> **arable** referring to land used for growing crops
> **monoculture** the cultivation of a single crop in a particular area
> **rotate** grow different crops one after the other on an area of land
> **tilth** the condition of soil prepared for growing crops

cross n. **1** *a bronze cross* **crucifix**, rood. **2** *we all have our crosses to bear* **burden**, trouble, worry, trial, tribulation, affliction, curse, bane, misfortune, adversity, hardship, vicissitude; millstone, albatross, thorn in one's flesh/side; misery, woe, pain, sorrow,

suffering; informal hassle, headache. **3** *a cross between a yak and a cow* **hybrid**, hybridization, cross-breed, half-breed, mongrel; mixture, amalgam, blend, combination.
▶v. **1** *they crossed the hills on foot* **travel across**, traverse, range over; negotiate, navigate, cover. **2** *a lake crossed by a fine stone bridge* **span**, bridge; extend/stretch across, pass over. **3** *the point where the two roads cross* **intersect**, meet, join, connect, criss-cross. **4** *no one dared cross him* **oppose**, resist, defy, obstruct, impede, hinder, hamper; contradict, argue with, quarrel with, stand up to, take a stand against, take issue with; formal gainsay. **5** *the breed was crossed with the similarly coloured Friesian* **hybridize**, cross-breed, interbreed, cross-fertilize, cross-pollinate.
▶adj. *Jane was getting cross* **angry**, annoyed, irate, irritated, in a bad mood, vexed, irked, piqued, out of humour, put out, displeased; irritable, short-tempered, bad-tempered, snappish, crotchety, grouchy, grumpy, fractious, testy, tetchy, crabby; informal mad, hot under the collar, peeved, riled, snappy, on the warpath, up in arms, steamed up, in a paddy; Brit. informal aerated, shirty, stroppy, ratty, not best pleased; N. Amer. informal sore, bent out of shape, teed off, ticked off; Austral./NZ informal ropeable, snaky, crook.
– OPPOSITES pleased.
□ **cross something out** delete, strike out, ink out, score out, edit out, blue-pencil, cancel, obliterate; Printing dele.

cross-examine v. **interrogate**, question, cross-question, quiz, catechize, give someone the third degree; informal grill, pump, put someone in/through the wringer/mangle.

cross-grained adj. **bad-tempered**, cantankerous, irascible, grumpy, grouchy; awkward, perverse, contrary, uncooperative, unhelpful, obstructive, disobliging, recalcitrant, stubborn, obstinate, mulish, pig-headed, intractable; informal cussed; Brit. informal bloody-minded, bolshie, stroppy; N. Amer. informal balky; formal refractory.
– OPPOSITES good-humoured.

crossing n. **1** *a busy road crossing* **junction**, crossroads, intersection, interchange; level crossing. **2** *a short ferry crossing* **journey**, passage, voyage.

crosswise, crossways adv. **diagonally**, obliquely, transversely, aslant, cornerwise, at an angle, on the bias; N. Amer. cater-cornered, kitty-corner.

crotch n. **groin**, crutch; lap.

crotchet n. **whim**, whimsy, fancy, notion, vagary, caprice; foible, quirk, eccentricity; old use megrim.

crotchety adj. **bad-tempered**, irascible, irritable, grumpy, grouchy, cantankerous, short-tempered, tetchy, testy, curmudgeonly, ill-tempered, ill-humoured, peevish, cross, fractious, pettish, waspish, crabbed, crabby, crusty, prickly, touchy; informal snappish, snappy, chippy; Brit. informal shirty, stroppy,

narky, ratty; N. Amer. informal cranky, ornery; Austral./NZ informal snaky.
– OPPOSITES good-humoured.

crouch v. **squat**, bend (down), hunker down, hunch over, stoop, kneel (down); duck, cower; N. Amer. informal scooch.

crow v. **1** *a cock crowed* **cry**, squawk, screech, caw. **2** *try to avoid crowing about your success* **boast**, brag, trumpet, swagger, swank, gloat, show off, preen oneself, sing one's own praises, blow one's own trumpet; informal talk big, lay it on thick; Austral./NZ informal skite.

crowd n. **1** *a crowd of people* **throng**, horde, mass, multitude, host, army, herd, flock, drove, swarm, sea, troupe, pack, press, crush, mob, rabble; collection, company, gathering, assembly, assemblage, congregation; informal gaggle, bunch, gang, posse; old use rout.
2 *she wanted to stand out from the crowd* **majority**, multitude, common people, populace, general public, masses, rank and file; Brit. informal Joe Public. **3** *he's been hanging round with Hurley's crowd* **set**, group, circle, clique, coterie; camp; informal gang, crew, lot. **4** *the final attracted a capacity crowd* **audience**, spectators, listeners, viewers; house, turnout, attendance, gate; congregation; Brit. informal punters.
▸v. **1** *reporters crowded round her* **cluster**, flock, swarm, mill, throng, huddle, gather, assemble, congregate, converge. **2** *the guests all crowded into the dining room* **surge**, push one's way, jostle, elbow one's way; squeeze, pile, cram. **3** *the quayside was crowded with holidaymakers* **throng**, pack, jam, cram, fill. **4** *stop crowding me* **pressurize**, pressure, harass, hound, pester, harry, badger, nag; informal hassle, lean on.

crowded adj. **packed**, full, filled to capacity, full to bursting, congested, overcrowded, overflowing, teeming, swarming, thronged, populous, overpopulated; busy; informal jam-packed, stuffed, chock-a-block, chock-full, bursting at the seams, full to the gunwales, wall-to-wall; Austral./NZ informal chocker.
– OPPOSITES deserted.

crown n. **1** *a jewelled crown* **coronet**, diadem, circlet; literary coronal; historical taj. **2** *the world heavyweight crown* **title**, award, accolade, distinction; trophy, cup, medal, plate, shield, belt, prize; laurels, bays, palm. **3** *his family were loyal servants of the Crown* **monarch**, sovereign, king, queen, emperor, empress; monarchy, royalty; informal royals. **4** *the crown of the hill* **top**, crest, summit, peak, pinnacle, tip, head, brow, apex.
▸v. **1** *David II was crowned in 1331* **enthrone**, install; invest, induct. **2** *a teaching post at Harvard crowned his career* **round off**, cap, be the climax of, be the culmination of, top off, consummate, perfect, complete, put the finishing touch(es) to. **3** *a steeple crowned by a gilded weathercock* **top**, cap, tip, head, surmount. **4** informal *someone crowned him with a poker.* See **hit** (sense 1 of the verb).

crucial adj. **1** *negotiations were at a crucial stage* **pivotal**, critical, key, climacteric, decisive, deciding; life-and-death.

2 *confidentiality is crucial in this case* **all-important**, of the utmost importance, of the essence, critical, pre-eminent, paramount, essential, vital.
– OPPOSITES unimportant.

crude adj. **1** *crude oil* **unrefined**, unpurified, unprocessed, untreated; unmilled, unpolished; coarse, raw, natural. **2** *a crude barricade* **primitive**, simple, basic, homespun, rudimentary, rough, rough and ready, rough-hewn, make-do, makeshift, improvised, unfinished; dated rude. **3** *crude jokes* **vulgar**, rude, naughty, suggestive, bawdy, off colour, indecent, obscene, offensive, lewd, salacious, licentious, ribald, coarse, uncouth, indelicate, tasteless, crass, smutty, dirty, filthy, scatological; informal blue.
– OPPOSITES refined, sophisticated.

cruel adj. **1** *a cruel man* **brutal**, savage, inhuman, barbaric, barbarous, brutish, bloodthirsty, murderous, vicious, sadistic, wicked, evil, fiendish, diabolical, monstrous, abominable; callous, ruthless, merciless, pitiless, remorseless, uncaring, heartless, stony-hearted, hard-hearted, cold-blooded, cold-hearted, unfeeling, unkind, inhumane; dated dastardly; literary fell. **2** *her death was a cruel blow* **harsh**, severe, bitter, harrowing, heartbreaking, heart-rending, painful, agonizing, traumatic; formal grievous.
– OPPOSITES compassionate.

cruelty n. **brutality**, savagery, inhumanity, barbarity, barbarousness, brutishness, bloodthirstiness, viciousness, sadism, wickedness; callousness, ruthlessness.

cruise n. *a cruise down the Nile* **boat trip**, sea trip; voyage, journey.
▸v. **1** *she cruised across the Atlantic* **sail**, voyage, journey. **2** *a taxi cruised past* **drive slowly**, drift; informal mosey, tootle; Brit. informal pootle.

crumb n. **fragment**, bit, morsel, particle, speck, scrap, shred, sliver, atom, grain, trace, tinge, mite, iota, jot, whit, ounce, scintilla, soupçon; informal smidgen, tad.

crumble v. **disintegrate**, fall apart, fall to pieces, fall to bits, break up, collapse, fragment; decay, fall into decay, deteriorate, degenerate, go to rack and ruin, decompose, rot, moulder, perish.

crumbly adj. **brittle**, breakable, friable, powdery, granular; short; crisp, crispy.

crumple v. **1** *she crumpled the note in her fist* **crush**, scrunch up, screw up, squash, squeeze; Brit. scrumple. **2** *his trousers were dirty and crumpled* **crease**, wrinkle, crinkle, rumple, ruck up. **3** *her resistance crumpled* **collapse**, give way, cave in, go to pieces, break down, crumble, be overcome.

crunch v. *she crunched the biscuit with relish* **munch**, chomp, champ, scrunch, bite into.
▸n. informal *when the crunch comes, she'll be forced to choose* **moment of truth**, critical point, crux, crisis, decision time, zero hour, point of no return; showdown.

crusade n. **1** *the medieval crusades* **holy war**; Islam jihad. **2** *a crusade against crime*

campaign, drive, push, movement, effort, struggle; battle, war, offensive.

▸v. *she likes crusading for the cause of the underdog* **campaign**, fight, do battle, battle, take up arms, take up the cudgels, work, strive, struggle, agitate, lobby, champion, promote.

crusader n. **campaigner**, fighter, champion, advocate; reformer.

crush v. **1** *essential oils are released when the herbs are crushed* **squash**, squeeze, press, compress; pulp, mash, macerate, mangle; flatten, trample on, tread on; informal squidge, splat; N. Amer. informal smush. **2** *your dress will get crushed* **crease**, crumple, rumple, wrinkle, crinkle, scrunch up, ruck up; Brit. scrumple up. **3** *crush the biscuits with a rolling pin* **pulverize**, pound, grind, break up, smash, crumble; mill; technical triturate, comminute; old use bray, levigate. **4** *he crushed her in his arms* **hug**, squeeze, hold tight, embrace, enfold. **5** *the new regime crushed all popular uprisings* **suppress**, put down, quell, quash, stamp out, put an end to, overcome, overpower, defeat, triumph over, break, repress, subdue, extinguish. **6** *Alan was crushed by her words* **mortify**, humiliate, abash, chagrin, deflate, demoralize, flatten, squash; devastate, shatter, put someone in their place; informal shoot down in flames, cut down to size, knock the stuffing out of.

▸n. **1** *the crush of people* **crowd**, throng, horde, swarm, sea, mass, pack, press, mob; old use rout. **2** informal *a teenage crush* **infatuation**, obsession, love, passion; informal pash, puppy love, calf love. **3** *lemon crush* **squash**, fruit juice, cordial, drink.

crust n. **1** *a crust of ice* **covering**, layer, coating, cover, coat, sheet, thickness, film, skin, topping; encrustation, scab. **2** informal *I'm just trying to earn an honest crust* **living**, livelihood, income, daily bread, means of subsistence; informal bread and butter.

crusty adj. **1** *crusty French bread* **crisp**, crispy, well baked; crumbly, brittle, friable. **2** *a crusty old man* **irritable**, cantankerous, irascible, bad-tempered, ill-tempered, grumpy, grouchy, crotchety, short-tempered, tetchy, testy, crabby, curmudgeonly, peevish, cross, fractious, pettish, crabbed, prickly, waspish, peppery, cross-grained; informal snappish, snappy, chippy; Brit. informal stroppy, narky, ratty; N. Amer. informal cranky, ornery; Austral./NZ informal snaky.
– OPPOSITES soft, good-natured.

crux n. **nub**, heart, essence, central point, main point, core, centre, nucleus, kernel; informal the bottom line.

cry v. **1** *Mandy started to cry* **weep**, shed tears, sob, wail, cry one's eyes out, bawl, howl, snivel, whimper, squall, mewl, bleat; lament, grieve, mourn, keen; Scottish greet; informal boohoo, blub, blubber, turn on the waterworks; Brit. informal grizzle; literary pule. **2** *'Wait!' he cried* **call**, shout, exclaim, sing out, yell, shriek, scream, screech, bawl, bellow, roar, vociferate, squeal, yelp; informal holler; dated ejaculate.

– OPPOSITES laugh, whisper.

▸n. **1** *Leonora had a good cry* **sob**, weep, crying fit. **2** *a cry of despair* **call**, shout, exclamation, yell, shriek, scream, screech, bawl, bellow, roar, howl, yowl, squeal, yelp, interjection; informal holler; dated ejaculation. **3** *fund-raisers have issued a cry for help* **appeal**, plea, entreaty, cry from the heart, cri de cœur.

□ **cry off** informal back out, pull out, cancel, withdraw, beg off, excuse oneself, change one's mind; informal get cold feet, cop out.

crypt n. **tomb**, vault, mausoleum, burial chamber, sepulchre, catacomb, ossuary, undercroft.

cryptic adj. **enigmatic**, mysterious, confusing, mystifying, perplexing, puzzling, obscure, abstruse, arcane, oracular, Delphic, ambiguous, elliptical, oblique; informal as clear as mud.
– OPPOSITES clear.

cubbyhole n. **small room**, booth, cubicle; den, snug; N. Amer. cubby.

cube n. **1** *a shape that was neither a cube nor a sphere* **hexahedron**, cuboid, parallelepiped. **2** *a cube of soap* **block**, lump, chunk, brick.

cuddle v. **1** *she picked up the baby and cuddled her* **hug**, embrace, clasp, hold tight, hold/fold in one's arms. **2** *the pair were kissing and cuddling* **embrace**, hug, caress, pet, fondle; informal canoodle, smooch; informal dated spoon, bill and coo. **3** *I cuddled up to him* **snuggle**, nestle, curl, nuzzle, burrow against.

cuddly adj. **huggable**, cuddlesome; plump, curvaceous, rounded, buxom, soft, warm; attractive, endearing, lovable; N. Amer. informal zaftig.

cudgel n. *a thick wooden cudgel* **club**, bludgeon, stick, truncheon, baton, blackthorn, shillelagh, mace; N. Amer. blackjack, billy, nightstick; Brit. life preserver; Brit. informal cosh.

▸v. *she was cudgelled to death* **bludgeon**, club, beat, batter, bash; Brit. informal cosh.

cue n. **signal**, sign, indication, prompt, reminder; nod, word, gesture.

cuff v. *Cullam cuffed him on the head* **hit**, strike, slap, smack, thump, beat, punch; informal clout, wallop, belt, whack, thwack, bash, clobber, bop, biff, sock; Brit. informal slosh; N. Amer. informal boff, slug; old use smite.

□ **off the cuff** informal **1** *an off-the-cuff remark* **impromptu**, extempore, ad lib; unrehearsed, unscripted, unprepared, improvised, spontaneous, unplanned. **2** *I spoke off the cuff* **without preparation**, without rehearsal, impromptu, ad lib; informal off the top of one's head.

cuisine n. **cooking**, cookery; haute cuisine, cordon bleu, nouvelle cuisine.

cul-de-sac n. **no through road**, blind alley, dead end.

cull v. **1** *anecdotes culled from Greek history* **select**, choose, pick, take, obtain, glean. **2** *he sees culling deer as a necessity* **slaughter**, kill, destroy.

C

culminate v. *the festival culminated in a dramatic fire-walking ceremony* **come to a climax**, come to a head, peak, climax, reach a pinnacle; build up to, lead up to; end with, finish with, conclude with.

culmination n. **climax**, pinnacle, peak, high point, highest point, height, high water mark, top, summit, crest, zenith, crowning moment, apotheosis, apex, apogee; consummation, completion, finish, conclusion.
– OPPOSITES nadir.

culpable adj. **to blame**, guilty, at fault, in the wrong, answerable, accountable, responsible, blameworthy, censurable.
– OPPOSITES innocent.

culprit n. **guilty party**, offender, wrongdoer, miscreant; criminal, malefactor, lawbreaker, felon, delinquent; informal baddy, crook.

cult n. **1** *a religious cult* **sect**, denomination, group, movement, church, persuasion, body, faction. **2** *the cult of youth in Hollywood* **obsession with**, fixation on, mania for, passion for, idolization of, devotion to, worship of, veneration of.

cultivate v. **1** *the peasants cultivated the land* **till**, plough, dig, hoe, farm, work, fertilize, mulch. **2** *they were encouraged to cultivate basic food crops* **grow**, raise, rear, plant, sow. **3** *Tessa tried to cultivate her* **win someone's friendship**, woo, court, pay court to, keep sweet, curry favour with, ingratiate oneself with; informal get in someone's good books, butter up, suck up to; N. Amer. informal shine up to. **4** *he wants to cultivate his mind* **improve**, better, refine, elevate; educate, train, develop, enrich.

cultivated adj. **cultured**, educated, well read, civilized, enlightened, discerning, discriminating, refined, polished; sophisticated, urbane, cosmopolitan.

cultivation n. See **farming**.

cultural adj. **1** *cultural differences* **ethnic**, racial, folk; societal, lifestyle. **2** *cultural achievements* **aesthetic**, artistic, intellectual; educational, edifying, civilizing.

culture n. **1** *20th century popular culture* **the arts**, the humanities, intellectual achievement; literature, music, painting, philosophy. **2** *a man of culture* **intellectual/artistic awareness**, education, cultivation, enlightenment, discernment, discrimination, good taste, taste, refinement, polish, sophistication. **3** *Afro-Caribbean culture* **civilization**, society, way of life, lifestyle; customs, traditions, heritage, habits, ways, mores, values. **4** *the culture of crops* **cultivation**, farming; agriculture, husbandry, agronomy.

cultured adj. **cultivated**, intellectually/artistically aware, artistic, enlightened, civilized, educated, well educated, well read, well informed, learned, knowledgeable, discerning, discriminating, refined, polished, sophisticated; informal arty.
– OPPOSITES ignorant.

culvert n. **channel**, conduit, watercourse, trough; drain, gutter.

cumbersome adj. **1** *a cumbersome diving suit* **unwieldy**, unmanageable, awkward, clumsy, inconvenient, incommodious; bulky, large, heavy, hefty, weighty, burdensome; informal hulking, clunky. **2** *cumbersome procedures* **complicated**, complex, involved, inefficient, unwieldy, slow.
– OPPOSITES manageable, straightforward.

cumulative adj. **increasing**, accumulative, growing, mounting; collective, aggregate, amassed; Brit. knock-on.

cunning adj. *a cunning scheme* **crafty**, wily, artful, guileful, devious, sly, scheming, designing, calculating, Machiavellian; shrewd, astute, clever, canny; deceitful, deceptive, duplicitous; informal foxy; old use subtle.
– OPPOSITES honest.
▶ n. *his political cunning* **guile**, craftiness, deviousness, slyness, trickery, duplicity; shrewdness, astuteness.

cup n. **1** *a cup and saucer* **teacup**, coffee cup, demitasse; mug, beaker; historical chalice. **2** *the winner was presented with a silver cup* **trophy**, award, prize.

cupboard n. **cabinet**, sideboard, dresser, armoire, credenza, buffet; Brit. chiffonier; informal glory hole.

cupidity n. **greed**, avarice, avariciousness, acquisitiveness, covetousness, rapacity, materialism, mercenariness, Mammonism; informal money-grubbing, an itching palm.
– OPPOSITES generosity.

cur n. **1** *a mangy cur* **mongrel**, tyke; N. Amer. yellow dog; NZ kuri; informal mutt; Austral. informal mong, bitzer. **2** informal *Neil was beginning to feel like a cur.* See **scoundrel**.

curable adj. **remediable**, treatable, medicable, operable.

curative adj. **healing**, therapeutic, medicinal, remedial, corrective, restorative, tonic, health-giving; old use sanative.

curator n. **custodian**, keeper, conservator, guardian, caretaker, steward.

curb n. *a curb on public spending* **restraint**, restriction, check, brake, rein, control, limitation, limit, constraint; informal crackdown; literary trammel.
▶ v. *he tried to curb his temper* **restrain**, hold back/in, keep back, repress, suppress, fight back, bite back, keep in check, check, control, rein in, contain, bridle, subdue; informal keep a/the lid on.

curdle v. **clot**, coagulate, congeal, solidify, thicken; turn, sour, ferment.

cure v. **1** *he was cured of the disease* **heal**, restore to health, make well/better; old use cleanse. **2** *economic equality cannot cure all social ills* **rectify**, remedy, put/set right, right, fix, mend, repair, heal, make better; solve, sort out, be the answer/solution to; eliminate, end, put an end to. **3** *some farmers cured their own bacon* **preserve**, smoke, salt, dry, pickle.
▶ n. **1** *a cure for cancer* **remedy**, medicine,

medication, medicament, antidote, antiserum; treatment, therapy; old use physic. **2** *interest rate cuts are not the cure for the problem* **solution**, answer, antidote, nostrum, panacea, cure-all; informal quick fix, magic bullet.

cure-all n. **panacea**, cure for all ills, sovereign remedy, heal-all, nostrum; informal magic bullet.

curio n. **trinket**, knick-knack, bibelot, ornament, bauble; objet d'art, collector's item, object of virtu, rarity, curiosity; N. Amer. kickshaw.

curiosity n. **1** *his evasiveness roused my curiosity* **interest**, spirit of inquiry, inquisitiveness. **2** *the shop is a treasure trove of curiosities* **oddity**, curio, conversation piece, object of virtu, collector's item.

curious adj. **1** *she was curious to know what had happened* **intrigued**, interested, eager/dying to know, agog; inquisitive. **2** *her curious behaviour* **strange**, odd, peculiar, funny, unusual, bizarre, weird, eccentric, queer, unexpected, unfamiliar, extraordinary, abnormal, out of the ordinary, anomalous, surprising, incongruous, unconventional, unorthodox; informal offbeat; Brit. out of the common; Scottish unco; Brit. informal rum.
– OPPOSITES uninterested, ordinary.

curl v. **1** *smoke curled up from his cigarette* **spiral**, coil, wreathe, twirl, swirl; wind, curve, bend, twist (and turn), loop, meander, snake, corkscrew, zigzag. **2** *Ruth curled her arms around his neck* **wind**, twine, entwine, wrap. **3** *she washed and curled my hair* **crimp**, perm, tong. **4** *they curled up together on the sofa* **nestle**, snuggle, cuddle; N. Amer. snug down.
▸ n. **1** *the tangled curls of her hair* **ringlet**, corkscrew, kink; kiss-curl. **2** *a curl of smoke* **spiral**, coil, twirl, swirl, twist, corkscrew, curlicue, helix.

curly adj. **wavy**, curling, curled, ringlety, crimped, permed, frizzy, kinky, corkscrew.
– OPPOSITES straight.

currency n. **1** *foreign currency* **money**, legal tender, cash, banknotes, notes, coins, coinage, specie; N. Amer. bills. **2** *a term which has gained new currency* **prevalence**, circulation, exposure; acceptance, popularity, traction.

current adj. **1** *current issues and events* **contemporary**, present-day, modern, present, contemporaneous; topical, in the news, live, burning. **2** *the idea is still current* **prevalent**, prevailing, common, accepted, in circulation, circulating, on everyone's lips, popular, widespread. **3** *a current driving licence* **valid**, usable, up to date. **4** *the current prime minister* **incumbent**, present, in office, in power; reigning.
– OPPOSITES past, out of date, former.
▸ n. **1** *a current of air* **flow**, stream, backdraught, slipstream; airstream, thermal, updraught, draught; undercurrent, undertow, tide. **2** *the current of human life*

course, progress, progression, flow, tide, movement. **3** *the current of opinion* **trend**, drift, direction, tendency.

curriculum n. **syllabus**, course/programme of study, subjects, modules.

curse n. **1** *she put a curse on him* **malediction**, the evil eye; N. Amer. hex; Irish cess; informal jinx; formal imprecation; literary anathema. **2** *the curse of racism* **evil**, blight, scourge, plague, cancer, canker, poison. **3** *the curse of unemployment* **affliction**, burden, cross to bear, bane. **4** *muffled curses* **swear word**, expletive, oath, profanity, four-letter word, dirty word, obscenity, blasphemy; informal cuss, cuss word; formal imprecation.
▸ v. **1** *it seemed as if the family had been cursed* **put a curse on**, put the evil eye on, hoodoo, anathematize, damn; N. Amer. hex; informal jinx; old use imprecate. **2** *she was cursed with feelings of inadequacy* **afflict**, trouble, plague, bedevil. **3** *drivers cursed and sounded their horns* **swear**, blaspheme, take the Lord's name in vain; informal cuss, turn the air blue, eff and blind; old use execrate.

cursed adj. **1** *a cursed city* **damned**, doomed, ill-fated, ill-starred; informal jinxed; literary accursed, star-crossed. **2** informal dated *those cursed children*. See **annoying**.

cursory adj. **perfunctory**, desultory, casual, superficial, token; hasty, quick, hurried, rapid, brief, passing, fleeting.
– OPPOSITES thorough.

curt adj. **terse**, brusque, abrupt, clipped, blunt, short, monosyllabic, summary; snappish, sharp, tart; gruff, offhand, unceremonious, ungracious, rude, impolite, discourteous, uncivil; informal snappy.
– OPPOSITES expansive.

curtail v. **1** *economic policies designed to curtail spending* **reduce**, cut, cut down, decrease, lessen, pare down, trim, retrench; restrict, limit, curb, rein in/back; informal slash. **2** *his visit was curtailed* **shorten**, cut short, truncate.
– OPPOSITES increase, lengthen.

curtain n. *he drew the curtains* **window hanging**, screen, blind; N. Amer. drape.
▸ v. *the bed was curtained off from the rest of the room* **conceal**, hide, screen, shield; separate, isolate.

curtsy v. *she curtsied to the king* **bend one's knee**, drop/bob a curtsy, genuflect.
▸ n. *she made a curtsy* **bob**, genuflection, obeisance.

curvaceous adj. **shapely**, voluptuous, sexy, full-figured, buxom, full-bosomed, bosomy, Junoesque; cuddly; informal curvy, well endowed, pneumatic, busty; old use comely.
– OPPOSITES skinny.

curve n. *the serpentine curves of the river* **bend**, turn, loop, curl, twist, hook; arc, arch, bow, half-moon, undulation, curvature.
▸ v. *the road curved back on itself* **bend**, turn, loop, wind, meander, undulate, snake, spiral, twist, coil, curl; arc, arch.

> **WORD LINKS**
> **sinuous** having many curves

C

> **concave** curving inwards
> **convex** curving outwards

curved adj. **bent**, arched, bowed, crescent, curving, wavy, sinuous, serpentine, meandering, undulating, curvilinear, curvy.
– OPPOSITES straight.

cushion n. *a cushion against inflation* **protection**, buffer, shield, defence, bulwark.
▶ v. **1** *she cushioned her head on her arms* **support**, cradle, prop (up), rest. **2** *to cushion the blow, wages and pensions were increased* **soften**, lessen, diminish, decrease, mitigate, temper, allay, alleviate, take the edge off, dull, deaden. **3** *residents are cushioned from the outside world* **protect**, shield, shelter, cocoon.

cushy adj. informal *a cushy job* **easy**, undemanding; comfortable, secure; Brit. informal jammy.
– OPPOSITES difficult.

custodian n. **curator**, keeper, conservator, guardian, overseer, superintendent; caretaker, steward, protector.

custody n. *the parent who has custody of the child* **care**, guardianship, charge, keeping, safe keeping, wardship, responsibility, protection, tutelage; custodianship, trusteeship; old use ward.
◻ **in custody** in prison, in jail, imprisoned, incarcerated, locked up, under lock and key, interned, detained; on remand; informal behind bars, doing time, inside; Brit. informal banged up.

custom n. **1** *his unfamiliarity with the local customs* **tradition**, practice, usage, observance, way, convention, formality, ceremony, ritual; shibboleth, sacred cow, unwritten rule; mores; formal praxis. **2** *it is our custom to visit the Lake District in October* **habit**, practice, routine, way; policy, rule; formal wont. **3** Brit. *if you keep me waiting I will take my custom elsewhere* **business**, patronage, trade.

customarily adv. **usually**, traditionally, normally, as a rule, generally, ordinarily, commonly; habitually, routinely.
– OPPOSITES occasionally.

customary adj. **1** *customary social practices* **usual**, traditional, normal, conventional, familiar, accepted, routine, established, time-honoured, regular, prevailing. **2** *her customary good sense* **usual**, accustomed, habitual; literary wonted.
– OPPOSITES unusual.

customer n. **consumer**, buyer, purchaser, patron, client; shopper; Brit. informal punter.

customs plural n. See **tax** (sense 1 of the noun).

cut v. **1** *the knife slipped and cut his finger* **gash**, slash, lacerate, sever, slit, pierce, penetrate, wound, injure; scratch, graze, nick, snick, incise, score; lance. **2** *cut the meat into small pieces* **chop**, cut up, slice, dice, cube, mince; carve; N. Amer. hash. **3** *cut back the new growth to about half its length* **trim**, snip, clip, crop, barber, shear, shave;

pare; prune, pollard, poll, lop, dock; mow. **4** *I went to cut some flowers* **pick**, pluck, gather; literary cull. **5** *lettering had been cut into the stonework* **carve**, engrave, incise, etch, score; chisel, whittle. **6** *the government cut public expenditure* **reduce**, cut back/down on, decrease, lessen, retrench, trim, slim down; rationalize, downsize, slenderize; mark down, discount, lower; informal slash. **7** *the text has been substantially cut* **shorten**, abridge, condense, abbreviate, truncate; edit; bowdlerize, expurgate. **8** *you need to cut at least ten lines per page* **delete**, remove, take out, excise, blue-pencil. **9** *oil supplies to the area had been cut* **discontinue**, break off, suspend, interrupt; stop, end, put an end to. **10** *the point where the line cuts the vertical axis* **cross**, intersect, bisect; meet, join. **11** dated *the banker's wife cut her at church* **snub**, ignore, shun, give someone the cold shoulder, cold-shoulder, cut dead, look right through, rebuff, turn one's back on; informal freeze out.
▶ n. **1** *a cut on his jaw* **gash**, slash, laceration, incision, wound, injury; scratch, graze, nick, snick. **2** *a cut of beef* **joint**, piece, section. **3** informal *the directors are demanding their cut* **share**, portion, bit, quota, percentage; informal slice of the cake, rake-off, piece of the action; Brit. informal whack. **4** *his hair was in need of a cut* **haircut**, trim, clip, crop. **5** *a smart cut of the whip* **blow**, slash, stroke. **6** *he followed this with the unkindest cut of all* **insult**, slight, affront, slap in the face, jibe, barb, cutting remark; informal put-down, dig. **7** *a cut in interest rates* **reduction**, cutback, decrease, lessening; N. Amer. rollback. **8** *the elegant cut of his jacket* **style**, design; tailoring, lines, fit.
◻ **cut back** *companies cut back on foreign investment* reduce, cut, cut down on, decrease, lessen, retrench, economize on, trim, slim down, scale down; rationalize, downsize, pull/draw in one's horns, tighten one's belt; informal slash.

cut someone/something down 1 *24 hectares of trees were cut down* **fell**, chop down, hack down, saw down, hew. **2** *he was cut down in his prime* **kill**, slaughter, shoot down, mow down, gun down; informal take out, blow away; literary slay.

cut and dried definite, decided, settled, explicit, specific, precise, unambiguous, clear-cut, unequivocal, black and white, hard and fast.

cut in interrupt, butt in, break in, interject, interpose, chime in; Brit. informal chip in.

cut someone/something off 1 *they cut off his finger* **sever**, chop off, hack off; amputate. **2** *oil and gas supplies were cut off* **discontinue**, break off, disconnect, suspend; stop, end, bring to an end. **3** *a community cut off from the mainland by the flood waters* **isolate**, separate, keep apart; seclude, closet, cloister, sequester.

cut out stop working, stop, fail, give out, break down; informal die, give up the ghost, conk out; Brit. informal pack up.

cut someone/something out 1 *cut out all the diseased wood* **remove**, take out, excise, extract; snip out, clip out. **2** *it's best to cut out alcohol altogether* **give up**, refrain from, abstain from, go without; informal quit, leave off, pack in, lay off, knock off. **3** *his mother cut him out of her will* **exclude**, leave out, omit, eliminate.

cut something short break off, shorten, truncate, curtail, terminate, end, stop, abort, bring to an untimely end.

cut someone short interrupt, cut off, butt in on, break in on.

cutback n. **reduction**, cut, decrease; economy, saving; N. Amer. rollback.
– OPPOSITES increase.

cute adj. **endearing**, adorable, lovable, sweet, lovely, appealing, engaging, delightful, dear, darling, winning, winsome, attractive, pretty; informal cutesy, twee; Brit. informal dinky.

cut-price adj. **cheap**, marked down, reduced, on (special) offer, discount; N. Amer. cut-rate.

cut-throat n. dated *a band of robbers and cut-throats* **murderer**, killer, assassin; informal hitman; dated homicide.
▶ adj. *cut-throat competition between rival firms* **ruthless**, merciless, fierce, intense, aggressive, dog-eat-dog.

cutting n. **1** *a newspaper cutting* **clipping**, clip, snippet; article, piece, column, paragraph. **2** *plant cuttings* **scion**, slip; graft. **3** *fabric cuttings* **piece**, bit, fragment; trimming.
▶ adj. **1** *a cutting remark* **hurtful**, wounding, barbed, pointed, scathing, acerbic, mordant, caustic, acid, sarcastic, sardonic, snide, spiteful, malicious, mean, nasty, cruel, unkind; informal bitchy, catty; Brit. informal sarky; N. Amer. informal snarky. **2** *cutting winter winds* **icy**, icy-cold, freezing, arctic, Siberian, glacial, bitter, chilling, chilly, chill; biting, piercing, penetrating, raw, keen, sharp.
– OPPOSITES friendly, warm.

cut up adj. informal *he's pretty cut up about it.* See **upset** (sense 1 of the adjective).

cycle n. **1** *the cycle of birth, death, and rebirth* **round**, rotation; pattern, rhythm. **2** *the painting is one of a cycle of seven* **series**, sequence, succession, run; set. **3** *cycles may be hired from the station.* See **bicycle**.

cyclical adj. **recurrent**, recurring, regular, repeated; periodic, seasonal, circular.

cyclone n. **hurricane**, typhoon, tropical storm, storm, superstorm, tornado, windstorm, whirlwind, tempest; Austral. willy-willy; N. Amer. informal twister.

cynic n. **sceptic**, doubter, doubting Thomas; pessimist, prophet of doom, doomsayer, Cassandra; informal doom (and gloom) merchant.
– OPPOSITES idealist.

cynical adj. **sceptical**, doubtful, distrustful, suspicious, disbelieving; pessimistic, negative, world-weary, disillusioned, disenchanted, jaundiced, sardonic.
– OPPOSITES idealistic.

cynicism n. **scepticism**, doubt, distrust, mistrust, suspicion, disbelief; pessimism, negativity, world-weariness, disenchantment.
– OPPOSITES idealism.

cyst n. **growth**, lump; abscess, wen, boil, carbuncle.

Dd

d

dab v. *she dabbed disinfectant on the cut* **pat**, press, touch, blot, mop, swab; daub, apply, wipe, stroke.
▸ n. **1** *a dab of glue* **drop**, spot, smear, splash, speck, taste, trace, touch, hint, bit; informal smidgen, tad, lick. **2** *apply concealer with light dabs* **pat**, touch, blot, wipe.

dabble v. **1** *they dabbled their feet in rock pools* **splash**, dip, paddle, trail; immerse. **2** *he dabbled in politics* **toy with**, dip into, flirt with, tinker with, trifle with, play with, dally with.

dabbler n. **amateur**, dilettante, layman, layperson; tinkerer, trifler.
– OPPOSITES professional.

daemon n. **numen**, genius (loci), attendant spirit, tutelary spirit.

daft adj. Brit. informal **1** *a daft idea* **absurd**, preposterous, ridiculous, ludicrous, farcical, laughable; idiotic, stupid, foolish, silly, inane, fatuous, hare-brained, half-baked; informal crazy, cockeyed; Brit. informal barmy. **2** *are you daft?* **simple-minded**, stupid, idiotic, slow, witless, feeble-minded, empty-headed, vacuous, vapid; unhinged, insane, mad; informal thick, dim, dopey, dumb, dim-witted, half-witted, birdbrained, pea-brained, slow on the uptake, soft in the head, brain-dead, not all there, touched, crazy, mental, nuts, batty, bonkers; Brit. informal potty, not the full shilling, barmy, crackers; N. Amer. informal chowderheaded. **3** *she's daft about him* **infatuated with**, enamoured of, smitten with, besotted by, very fond of; informal crazy, mad, nuts; Brit. informal potty; informal dated sweet on.
– OPPOSITES sensible.

daily adj. *a daily event* **everyday**, day-to-day, quotidian, diurnal, circadian.
▸ adv. *the museum is open daily* **every day**, once a day, day after day, diurnally.

dainty adj. **1** *a dainty china cup* **delicate**, fine, neat, elegant, exquisite; Brit. informal dinky. **2** *a dainty morsel* **tasty**, delicious, choice, palatable, luscious, mouth-watering, delectable, toothsome; appetizing, inviting, tempting; informal scrumptious, yummy, scrummy, finger-licking, moreish. **3** *a dainty eater* **fastidious**, fussy, finicky, finical, faddish; particular, discriminating; informal choosy, pernickety, picky; Brit. informal faddy.
– OPPOSITES unwieldy, unpalatable, undiscriminating.
▸ n. *home-made dainties* **delicacy**, titbit, fancy, luxury, treat; nibble, savoury, appetizer,

confection, bonbon; informal goody; old use sweetmeat.

dais n. **platform**, stage, podium, rostrum, stand, apron; soapbox, stump.

dale n. **valley**, vale; hollow, basin, gully, gorge, ravine; Brit. dene, combe; N. English clough; Scottish glen, strath; literary dell.

dally v. **1** *don't dally on the way to work* **dawdle**, delay, loiter, linger, waste time; lag, trail, straggle, fall behind; amble, meander, drift; informal dilly-dally; old use tarry. **2** *he likes dallying with film stars* **trifle**, toy, amuse oneself, flirt, play fast and loose, philander, carry on; informal play around.
– OPPOSITES hurry.

dam n. *the dam burst* **barrage**, barrier, wall, embankment, barricade, obstruction.
▸ v. *the river was dammed* **block (up)**, obstruct, bung up, close; technical occlude.

damage n. **1** *did the thieves do any damage?* **harm**, destruction, vandalism; injury, impairment, desecration, vitiation, detriment; ruin, havoc, devastation. **2** humorous *what's the damage?* **cost**, price, expense, charge, total. **3** *she won £4,300 damages* **compensation**, recompense, restitution, redress, reparation(s); indemnification, indemnity; N. Amer. informal comp.
▸ v. *the parcel had been damaged* **harm**, deface, mutilate, mangle, impair, injure, disfigure, vandalize; tamper with, sabotage; ruin, destroy, wreck; N. Amer. informal trash; formal vitiate.
– OPPOSITES repair.

damaging adj. **harmful**, detrimental, injurious, hurtful, inimical, dangerous, destructive, ruinous, deleterious; bad, malign, adverse, undesirable, prejudicial, unfavourable; unhealthy, unwholesome.
– OPPOSITES beneficial.

damn v. **1** *they were all damning him* **curse**, put the evil eye on, hoodoo; anathematize; N. Amer. hex; informal jinx; old use imprecate. **2** *we are not going to damn the new product* **condemn**, censure, criticize, attack, denounce, revile; find fault with, deprecate, disparage; informal slam, lay into, blast; Brit. informal slate, slag off, have a go at.
– OPPOSITES bless, praise.
▸ n. informal *I don't care a damn* **jot**, whit, iota, rap, scrap, bit; informal hoot, two hoots.

damnable adj. **1** *it's a damnable nuisance* **unpleasant**, disagreeable, objectionable, horrible, horrid, awful, nasty, dreadful, terrible; annoying, irritating, maddening, exasperating; hateful, detestable, loathsome, abominable; Brit. informal beastly. **2** *suicide was thought damnable* **sinful**, wicked, evil, iniquitous, heinous, base, execrable.

damnation n. **condemnation to hell**, eternal punishment, perdition, doom, hellfire; curse, anathema; N. Amer. hex; formal imprecation; old use execration.

damned adj. **1** *damned souls* **cursed**, doomed, lost, condemned to hell; anathematized; literary accursed. **2** informal *this damned car won't start* **wretched**; informal blasted, bloody, damn, damnable, flaming, rotten; Brit. informal blessed, flipping, blinking, blooming, bleeding, ruddy; informal dated confounded; dated accursed.

damning adj. **incriminating**, condemnatory, damnatory; damaging, derogatory; conclusive, strong.

damp adj. *her hair was damp* **moist**, moistened, wettish, dampened, dampish; humid, steamy, muggy, clammy, sweaty, sticky, dank, moisture-laden, wet, wetted, rainy, drizzly, showery, misty, foggy, vaporous, dewy.
– OPPOSITES dry.
▸ n. *the damp in the air* **moisture**, dampness, humidity, wetness, wet, water, condensation, steam, vapour; clamminess, dankness; rain, dew, drizzle, precipitation, spray; perspiration, sweat.
– OPPOSITES dryness.
▸ v. **1** *sweat damped his hair*. See **dampen** (sense 1). **2** *nothing damped my enthusiasm*. See **dampen** (sense 2).

dampen v. **1** *the rain dampened her face* **moisten**, damp, wet, dew, water; literary bedew. **2** *nothing could dampen her enthusiasm* **lessen**, decrease, diminish, reduce, moderate, damp, put a damper on, throw cold water on, cool, discourage; suppress, extinguish, quench, stifle, curb, limit, check, restrain, inhibit, deter.
– OPPOSITES dry, heighten.

damper n. **curb**, check, restraint, restriction, limit, limitation, constraint, rein, brake, control, impediment; chill, pall, gloom.

dampness n. See **damp** (noun).

damsel n. literary See **girl** (sense 2).

dance v. **1** *he danced with her* sway, trip, twirl, whirl, pirouette, gyrate; informal bop, disco, shake a leg, hoof it, cut a rug, trip the light fantastic; N. Amer. informal get down. **2** *little girls danced round me* **caper**, cavort, frisk, frolic, skip, prance, gambol, jig; leap, jump, hop, bounce. **3** *flames danced in the fireplace* **flicker**, leap, dart, play, flit, quiver; twinkle, shimmer.
▸ n. *the school dance* **ball**, discotheque; masquerade; N. Amer. prom, hoedown; informal disco, hop, bop.

WORD LINKS

terpsichorean relating to dancing
choreography the sequence of steps in a ballet or other dance

---

dancer n. danseur, danseuse; informal bopper, hoofer.

dandle v. **bounce**, jiggle, dance, rock.

dandy n. *he became something of a dandy* **fop**, man about town, bright young thing, glamour boy, rake; informal sharp dresser, snappy dresser, trendy, dude, pretty boy; informal dated swell, popinjay; dated beau; historical macaroni; old use buck, coxcomb.
▸ adj. N. Amer. informal *our trip was dandy*. See **excellent**.

danger n. **1** *an element of danger* **peril**, hazard, risk, jeopardy; perilousness, riskiness, precariousness, uncertainty, instability, insecurity. **2** *he is a danger to society* **menace**, hazard, threat, risk. **3** *a serious danger of fire* **possibility**, chance, risk, probability, likelihood, fear, prospect.
– OPPOSITES safety.

dangerous adj. **1** *a dangerous animal* **menacing**, threatening, treacherous; savage, wild, vicious, murderous, desperate; rare minacious. **2** *dangerous wiring* **hazardous**, perilous, risky, high-risk, unsafe, unpredictable, precarious, insecure, touch-and-go, chancy, treacherous; informal dicey, hairy; Brit. informal dodgy.
– OPPOSITES harmless, safe.

dangle v. **1** *a chain dangled from his belt* **hang (down)**, droop, swing, sway, wave, trail, stream. **2** *he dangled the keys* **wave**, swing, jiggle, brandish, flourish. **3** *he dangled money in front of the locals* **offer**, hold out; entice someone with, tempt someone with.

dangling adj. **hanging**, drooping, droopy, suspended, pendulous, pendent, trailing, flowing, tumbling.

dank adj. **damp**, musty, chilly, clammy, moist, wet, unaired, humid.
– OPPOSITES dry.

dapper adj. **smart**, spruce, trim, debonair, neat, well dressed, well groomed, well turned out, elegant, chic, dashing; informal snazzy, snappy, natty, sharp; N. Amer. informal spiffy, fly.
– OPPOSITES scruffy.

dapple v. **dot**, spot, fleck, streak, speck, speckle, mottle, marble.

dappled adj. **speckled**, blotched, blotchy, spotted, spotty, dotted, mottled, marbled, flecked, freckled; piebald, pied, brindle, pinto, tabby; patchy, variegated; informal splotchy, splodgy.

dare v. **1** *nobody dared to say a word* **be brave enough**, have the courage; venture, have the nerve, have the temerity, be so bold as, have the audacity; risk, hazard, take the liberty of; N. Amer. take a flyer; informal stick one's neck out, go out on a limb. **2** *she dared him to go* **challenge**, defy, invite, bid, provoke, goad; throw down the gauntlet.
▸ n. *she accepted the dare* **challenge**, provocation, goad; gauntlet, invitation.

daredevil n. *a young daredevil crashed his car* **madcap**, hothead, adventurer, exhibitionist, swashbuckler; stuntman; Brit. tearaway; informal show-off.

d

d

▸ adj. *a daredevil skydiver* **daring**, bold, audacious, intrepid, fearless, madcap, death-or-glory, dauntless; heedless, reckless, rash, impulsive, impetuous, foolhardy, incautious, imprudent; Brit. tearaway, harum-scarum.
– OPPOSITES cowardly, cautious.

daring adj. *a daring attack* **bold**, audacious, intrepid, venturesome, fearless, brave, unafraid, undaunted, dauntless, valiant, valorous, heroic, dashing; madcap, rash, reckless, heedless; informal gutsy, spunky.
▸ n. *his sheer daring* **boldness**, audacity, temerity, fearlessness, intrepidity, bravery, courage, valour, heroism, pluck, spirit, mettle; recklessness, rashness, foolhardiness; informal nerve, guts, spunk, grit; Brit. informal bottle; N. Amer. informal moxie, sand.

dark adj. **1** *a dark night* **black**, pitch-black, jet-black, inky; unlit, unilluminated; starless, moonless; dingy, gloomy, dusky, shadowy, shady; literary Stygian. **2** *a dark secret* **mysterious**, secret, hidden, concealed, veiled, covert, clandestine; enigmatic, arcane, esoteric, obscure, abstruse, impenetrable, incomprehensible, cryptic; Military black. **3** *dark hair* **brunette**, dark brown, chestnut, sable, jet-black, ebony. **4** *dark skin* **swarthy**, dusky, olive, black, ebony; tanned, bronzed. **5** *dark days* **tragic**, disastrous, calamitous, catastrophic, cataclysmic; dire, awful, terrible, dreadful, horrible, horrendous, atrocious, nightmarish, harrowing; wretched, woeful. **6** *dark thoughts* **gloomy**, dismal, pessimistic, negative, downbeat, bleak, grim, fatalistic, black, sombre; despairing, despondent, hopeless, cheerless, melancholy, glum, grave, morose, mournful, doleful. **7** *a dark look* **moody**, brooding, sullen, dour, scowling, glowering, angry, forbidding, threatening, ominous. **8** *dark deeds* **evil**, wicked, sinful, immoral, bad, iniquitous, ungodly, unholy, base; vile, unspeakable, foul, monstrous, shocking, atrocious, abominable, hateful, despicable, odious, horrible, heinous, execrable, diabolical, fiendish, murderous, barbarous, black; sordid, degenerate, depraved; dishonourable, dishonest, unscrupulous; informal low-down, dirty, crooked, shady.
– OPPOSITES bright, blonde, pale, happy, good.
▸ n. **1** *he's afraid of the dark* **darkness**, blackness, gloom, murkiness, shadow, shade; dusk, twilight, gloaming. **2** *she went out after dark* **night**, night-time, darkness; nightfall, evening, twilight, sunset.
– OPPOSITES light, day.
□ **in the dark** informal unaware, ignorant, oblivious, uninformed, unenlightened, unacquainted.

darken v. **1** *the sky darkened* **grow dark**, blacken, dim, cloud over, lour; shade, fog. **2** *his mood darkened* **blacken**, become angry, become annoyed; sadden, become gloomy, become unhappy, become depressed, become dejected, become dispirited, become troubled.

darkness n. **1** *lights shone in the darkness* **dark**, blackness, gloom, dimness, murkiness, shadow, shade; dusk, twilight, gloaming. **2** *darkness fell* **night**, night-time, dark. **3** *the forces of darkness* **evil**, wickedness, sin, iniquity, immorality; devilry, the Devil.

darling n. **1** *good night, darling* **dear**, dearest, love, lover, sweetheart, sweet, beloved; informal honey, angel, pet, sweetie, sugar, babe, baby, poppet, treasure. **2** *the darling of the media* **favourite**, pet, idol, hero, heroine; Brit. informal blue-eyed boy/girl.
▸ adj. **1** *his darling wife* **dear**, dearest, precious, adored, loved, beloved, cherished, treasured, esteemed, worshipped. **2** *a darling little hat* **adorable**, appealing, charming, cute, sweet, enchanting, bewitching, endearing, dear, delightful, lovely, beautiful, attractive, gorgeous, fetching; Scottish & N. English bonny.

darn v. *he was darning his socks* **mend**, repair, reinforce; sew up, stitch, patch.
▸ n. *a sweater with darns in the elbows* **patch**, repair, reinforcement, stitch.

dart n. **1** *a poisoned dart* **small arrow**, flechette, bolt; missile, projectile. **2** *she made a dart for the door* **dash**, rush, run, bolt, break, start, charge, sprint, bound, leap, dive; scurry, scamper, scramble.
▸ v. **1** *Karl darted across the road* **dash**, rush, tear, run, bolt, fly, shoot, charge, race, sprint, bound, leap, dive, gallop, scurry, scamper, scramble; informal scoot. **2** *he darted a glance at her* **direct**, cast, throw, shoot, send, flash.

dash v. **1** *he dashed home* **rush**, race, run, sprint, bolt, dart, gallop, career, charge, shoot, hurtle, hare, fly, speed, zoom, scurry, scuttle, scamper; informal tear, belt, pelt, scoot, zip, whip, hotfoot it, leg it; Brit. informal bomb, go like the clappers; N. Amer. informal barrel. **2** *he dashed the glass to the ground* **hurl**, smash, crash, slam, throw, toss, fling, pitch, cast, project, propel, send; informal chuck, heave, sling, bung; N. Amer. informal peg; dated shy. **3** *rain dashed against the walls* **be hurled**, crash, smash; batter, strike, beat, pound, lash. **4** *her hopes were dashed* **shatter**, destroy, wreck, ruin, crush, devastate, demolish, blight, overturn, scotch, spoil, frustrate, thwart, check; informal banjax, do for, blow a hole in, put paid to; Brit. informal scupper.
– OPPOSITES dawdle, raise.
▸ n. **1** *a dash for the door* **rush**, race, run, sprint, bolt, dart, leap, charge, bound, break; scramble. **2** *a dash of salt* **pinch**, touch, sprinkle, taste, spot, drop, dab, speck, smattering, sprinkling, splash, bit, modicum, little; informal smidgen, tad, lick. **3** *he led off with such dash* **verve**, style, flamboyance, gusto, zest, confidence, self-assurance, elan, flair, vigour, vivacity, sparkle, brio, panache, éclat, vitality, dynamism; informal pizzazz, pep, oomph.

dashing adj. **1** *a dashing pilot* **debonair**, devil-may-care, raffish, sporty, spirited, lively, dazzling, energetic, animated, exuberant, flamboyant, dynamic, bold, intrepid, daring, adventurous, plucky,

swashbuckling; romantic, attractive, gallant.
2 *he looked exceptionally dashing* **stylish**,
smart, elegant, chic, dapper, spruce, trim,
debonair; fashionable, modish, voguish;
informal trendy, with it, hip, sharp, snazzy,
classy, natty, swish; N. Amer. informal fly, spiffy.

dastardly adj. dated **wicked**, evil, heinous,
villainous, diabolical, fiendish, barbarous,
cruel, black, dark, rotten, vile, monstrous,
abominable, despicable, degenerate, sordid;
bad, base, mean, low, dishonourable,
dishonest, unscrupulous, unprincipled;
informal low-down, dirty, shady, rascally,
scoundrelly, crooked; Brit. informal beastly.
– OPPOSITES noble.

data n. **facts**, figures, statistics, details,
particulars, specifics; information,
intelligence, material, input; informal info, gen.

date n. **1** *the only date he has to remember*
day (of the month), occasion, time; year;
anniversary. **2** *a later date is suggested for this*
bridge **age**, time, period, era, epoch, century,
decade, year. **3** *a lunch date* **appointment**,
meeting, engagement, rendezvous,
assignation; commitment. **4** informal *a date for*
tonight **partner**, escort, girlfriend, boyfriend;
informal steady, bird, fella.
▸v. **1** *the sculpture can be dated accurately*
assign a date to, ascertain the date of, put
a date on. **2** *the building dates from the*
16th century **was made in**, was built in,
originates in, comes from, belongs to, goes
back to. **3** *the best films don't date* **become**
old-fashioned, become outmoded, become
dated, show its age. **4** informal *he's dating Jill*
go out with, take out, go around with, be
involved with, see, woo; informal go steady
with; dated court.
□ **to date** so far, thus far, yet, as yet, up to
now, till now, until now, up to the present
(time), hitherto.

dated adj. **old-fashioned**, outdated,
outmoded, passé, behind the times, archaic,
obsolete, antiquated; unfashionable,
unstylish; crusty, olde worlde, prehistoric,
antediluvian; informal old hat, out, out of the
ark.
– OPPOSITES modern.

daub v. *he daubed a rock with paint* **smear**,
bedaub, plaster, splash, spatter, splatter,
cake, cover, smother, coat.
▸n. *daubs of paint* **smear**, smudge, splash, blot,
spot, patch, blotch; informal splodge, splotch.

daunt v. **discourage**, deter, demoralize, put
off, dishearten, dispirit; intimidate, abash,
take aback, throw, cow, overawe, awe,
frighten, scare, unman, dismay, disconcert,
discompose, perturb, unsettle, unnerve;
throw off balance; informal rattle, faze,
shake up.
– OPPOSITES hearten.

daunting adj. **intimidating**, formidable,
disconcerting, unnerving, unsettling,
dismaying; discouraging, disheartening,
dispiriting, demoralizing; forbidding,
ominous, awesome, frightening, fearsome.
– OPPOSITES reassuring, inviting.

dauntless adj. **fearless**, determined,
resolute, indomitable, intrepid, doughty,
plucky, spirited, mettlesome; undaunted,
undismayed, unflinching, unshrinking,
bold, audacious, valiant, brave, courageous,
daring; informal gutsy, spunky, feisty.

dawdle v. **1** *they dawdled over breakfast*
linger, dally, take one's time, be slow, waste
time, idle; delay, procrastinate, stall;
dilly-dally; old use tarry. **2** *Ruth dawdled home*
amble, stroll, trail, walk slowly, move at a
snail's pace; informal mosey, tootle; Brit. informal
pootle, mooch.
– OPPOSITES hurry.

dawn n. **1** *we got up at dawn* **daybreak**,
sunrise, first light, daylight, cockcrow; first
thing in the morning; N. Amer. sunup. **2** *the*
dawn of civilization **beginning**, start, birth,
inception, origination, genesis, emergence,
advent, appearance, arrival, dawning, rise,
origin, onset; unfolding, development,
infancy; informal kick-off.
– OPPOSITES dusk, end.
▸v. **1** *Thursday dawned crisp and sunny* **begin**,
break, arrive, emerge. **2** *a bright new future*
has dawned **begin**, start, commence, be born,
appear, arrive, emerge; arise, rise, break,
unfold, develop. **3** *the reality dawned on*
him **occur to**, come to, strike, hit, enter/
cross someone's mind, register with, suggest
itself.
– OPPOSITES end.

day n. **1** *I stayed for a day* **twenty-four-hour**
period, twenty-four hours. **2** *enjoy the beach*
during the day **daytime**, daylight; waking
hours. **3** *the leading architect of the day*
period, time, age, era, generation. **4** *in his*
day he had great influence **heyday**, prime,
time; peak, height, zenith, ascendancy;
youth, springtime, salad days.
– OPPOSITES night, decline.
□ **day after day** repeatedly, again and
again, over and over (again), time and
(time) again, frequently, often, time after
time; {day in, day out}, night and day, all the
time; persistently, recurrently, constantly,
continuously, continually, relentlessly,
regularly, habitually, unfailingly, always;
N. Amer. oftentimes; informal 24-7; literary oft,
oft-times.
day by day 1 *day by day they were forced to*
retreat **gradually**, slowly, progressively; bit
by bit, inch by inch, little by little, inchmeal.
2 *they follow the news day by day* **daily**, every
day, day after day; diurnally.

WORD LINKS

diurnal of or during the daytime
equinox either of the times of the year when day
　and night are of equal length
solstice the longest or shortest days of the year

---

daybreak n. **dawn**, crack of dawn, sunrise,
first light, first thing in the morning,
cockcrow; daylight; N. Amer. sunup.
– OPPOSITES nightfall.

daydream n. **1** *she was lost in a daydream*
reverie, trance, fantasy, vision, fancy, brown
study; inattentiveness, wool-gathering,

d

preoccupation, absorption, self-absorption, absent-mindedness, abstraction. **2** *a big house was one of her daydreams* **dream**, pipe dream, fantasy, castle in the air, castle in Spain, fond hope; wishful thinking; informal pie in the sky.

▶ v. *stop daydreaming!* **dream**, muse, stare into space; fantasize, be in cloud cuckoo land, build castles in the air, build castles in Spain.

daydreamer n. **dreamer**, fantasist, fantasizer, romantic, wishful thinker, idealist; visionary, theorizer, utopian, Walter Mitty.

daylight n. **1** *do the test in daylight* **natural light**, sunlight. **2** *she only went there in daylight* **daytime**, day; broad daylight. **3** *police moved in at daylight* **dawn**, daybreak, break of day, crack of dawn, sunrise, first light, early morning, cockcrow; N. Amer. sunup.
– OPPOSITES darkness, night-time, nightfall.
□ **see daylight 1** *Sam finally saw daylight* **understand**, comprehend, realize, see the light; informal cotton on, catch on, latch on, get the picture, get the message, get it; Brit. informal twig. **2** *his project never saw daylight* **be completed**, be accomplished, see (the) light of day.

day-to-day adj. **regular**, everyday, daily, routine, habitual, frequent, normal, standard, usual, typical.

daze v. **1** *he was dazed by his fall* **stun**, stupefy; knock unconscious, knock out; informal knock the stuffing out of. **2** *she was dazed by the revelations* **astound**, amaze, astonish, startle, dumbfound, stupefy, overwhelm, stagger, shock, confound, bewilder, take aback, nonplus, shake up; informal flabbergast, knock sideways, bowl over, blow away; Brit. informal knock for six.
▶ n. *she is in a daze* **stupor**, trance, haze; spin, whirl, muddle, jumble.

dazzle v. **1** *she was dazzled by the headlights* **blind temporarily**, deprive of sight. **2** *I was dazzled by the exhibition* **overwhelm**, overcome, impress, move, stir, affect, touch, awe, overawe, leave speechless, take someone's breath away; spellbind, hypnotize; informal bowl over, blow away, knock out.
▶ n. **1** *dazzle can be a problem to sensitive eyes* **glare**, brightness, brilliance, shimmer, radiance, shine. **2** *the dazzle of the limelight* **sparkle**, glitter, brilliance, glory, splendour, magnificence, glamour; attraction, lure, allure, draw, appeal; informal razzle-dazzle, razzmatazz.

dazzling adj. **1** *the sunlight was dazzling* **bright**, blinding, glaring, brilliant. **2** *a dazzling performance* **impressive**, remarkable, extraordinary, outstanding, exceptional; incredible, amazing, astonishing, phenomenal, coruscating, breathtaking, thrilling; excellent, wonderful, magnificent, marvellous, superb, first-rate, superlative, matchless; informal mind-blowing, out of this world, fabulous, fab, super, sensational, ace, A1, cool, awesome; Brit.

informal smashing, brill.

dead adj. **1** *my parents are dead* **passed on/ away**, expired, departed, gone, no more; late, lost, lamented; perished, fallen, slain, slaughtered, killed, murdered; lifeless, extinct; informal (as) dead as a doornail, six feet under, pushing up daisies; formal deceased; euphemistic with God, asleep. **2** *patches of dead ground* **barren**, lifeless, bare, desolate, sterile. **3** *a dead language* **obsolete**, extinct, defunct, disused, abandoned, discarded, superseded, vanished, forgotten; archaic, antiquated, ancient; literary of yore. **4** *the phone was dead* **not working**, out of order, inoperative, inactive, in disrepair, broken, malfunctioning, defective; informal kaput, conked out, on the blink, bust; Brit. informal knackered. **5** *a dead leg* **numb**, numbed, deadened, desensitized, unfeeling; paralysed, crippled, incapacitated, immobilized, frozen. **6** *she has dead eyes* **emotionless**, unemotional, unfeeling, impassive, unresponsive, indifferent, dispassionate, inexpressive, wooden, stony, cold; deadpan, flat; blank, vacant. **7** *his affection for her was dead* **extinguished**, quashed, stifled; finished, over, gone, no more; ancient history. **8** *a dead town* **uneventful**, uninteresting, unexciting, uninspiring, dull, boring, flat, quiet, sleepy, slow, lacklustre, lifeless; informal one-horse, dead-and-alive; N. Amer. informal dullsville. **9** *dead silence* **complete**, absolute, total, utter, out-and-out, thorough, unmitigated. **10** *a dead shot* **unerring**, unfailing, impeccable, sure, true, accurate, precise; deadly, lethal; Brit. informal spot on, bang on.
– OPPOSITES alive, fertile, modern, lively, poor.
▶ adv. **1** *he was dead serious* **completely**, absolutely, totally, utterly, deadly, perfectly, entirely, quite, thoroughly; definitely, certainly, positively, categorically, unquestionably, undoubtedly, surely; one hundred per cent. **2** *flares were seen dead ahead* **directly**, exactly, precisely, immediately, right, straight, due, squarely; informal bang, slap bang. **3** Brit. informal *it's dead easy.* See **very**.

deadbeat n. informal **layabout**, loafer, idler, good-for-nothing; informal waster; Brit. informal skiver; N. Amer. informal bum; literary wastrel.

deaden v. **1** *ether was used to deaden the pain* **numb**, dull, blunt, suppress; alleviate, mitigate, diminish, reduce, lessen, ease, soothe, relieve, assuage. **2** *the wood panelling deadened any noise* **muffle**, mute, smother, stifle, dull, damp (down); silence, quieten, soften; cushion, buffer, absorb. **3** *laughing might deaden us to the moral issue* **desensitize**, numb, anaesthetize; harden (one's heart), toughen.
– OPPOSITES intensify, amplify, sensitize.

deadline n. **time limit**, limit, finishing date, target date, cut-off point.

deadlock n. **1** *the strike reached a deadlock* **stalemate**, impasse, checkmate, stand-off; standstill, halt, (full) stop, dead end.

2 Brit. *the deadlock is opened with a key* **bolt**, lock, latch, catch; Scottish sneck, snib.

deadly adj. **1** *these drugs can be deadly* **fatal**, lethal, mortal, death-dealing, life-threatening; dangerous, injurious, harmful, detrimental, deleterious, unhealthy; noxious, toxic, poisonous; literary deathly. **2** *deadly enemies* **mortal**, irreconcilable, implacable, unappeasable, unforgiving, remorseless, merciless, pitiless; bitter, hostile, antagonistic. **3** *deadly seriousness* **intense**, great, marked, extreme. **4** *he was deadly pale* **deathly**, ghostly, ashen, white, pallid, wan, pale; ghastly. **5** *his aim is deadly* **unerring**, unfailing, impeccable, perfect, flawless, faultless; sure, true, precise, accurate, exact; Brit. informal spot on, bang on. **6** informal *life here can be deadly*. See **boring**.
– OPPOSITES harmless, mild, inaccurate, exciting.
▶ adv. *deadly calm* **completely**, absolutely, totally, utterly, perfectly, entirely, wholly, quite, dead, thoroughly, one hundred per cent.

deadpan adj. **blank**, expressionless, unexpressive, impassive, inscrutable, poker-faced, straight-faced; stony, wooden, vacant, fixed, lifeless.
– OPPOSITES expressive.

deaf adj. **1** *she is deaf and blind* **hard of hearing**; informal deaf as a post. **2** *she was deaf to their pleading* **unmoved by**, untouched by, unaffected by, indifferent to, unresponsive to, unconcerned by; unaware of, oblivious to, impervious to.

deafening adj. **very loud**, very noisy, ear-splitting, ear-shattering, overwhelming, almighty, mighty, tremendous; booming, thunderous, roaring, resounding, resonant, reverberating.
– OPPOSITES quiet.

deal n. *completion of the deal* **agreement**, understanding, pact, bargain, covenant, contract, treaty; arrangement, compromise, settlement; terms; transaction, sale, account; Law indenture.
▶ v. **1** *how to deal with difficult children* **cope with**, handle, manage, treat, take care of, take charge of, take in hand, sort out; tackle, take on; control; act towards, behave towards. **2** *the article deals with advances in chemistry* **concern**, be about, have to do with, discuss, consider, cover, pertain to; tackle, study, explore, investigate, examine, review, analyse. **3** *the company deals in high-tech goods* **trade in**, buy and sell; sell, purvey, supply, stock, market, merchandise; traffic, smuggle; informal push; Brit. informal flog. **4** *the cards were dealt* **distribute**, give out, share out, divide out, hand out, pass out, pass round, dole out, dispense, allocate; informal divvy up. **5** *the court dealt a blow to government reforms* **deliver**, administer, dispense, inflict, give, impose; aim.
□ **a great deal/a good deal** a lot, a large amount, a fair amount, much, plenty; informal lots, loads, heaps, bags, masses, tons; Brit. informal a shedload.

dealer n. **1** *an antique dealer* **trader**, tradesman, tradesperson, merchant, salesman/woman, seller, vendor, purveyor, pedlar, hawker; buyer, merchandiser, distributor, supplier, shopkeeper, retailer, wholesaler; trademark in US e-tailer; Brit. stockist; Brit. informal flogger. **2** *a dealer in a bank* **stockbroker**, broker-dealer, broker, agent.

dealing n. **1** *dishonest dealing* **business methods**, business practices, business, commerce, trading, transactions; behaviour, conduct, actions. **2** *the UK's dealings with China* **relations**, relationship, association, connections, contact, intercourse; negotiations, bargaining, transactions; trade, trading, business, commerce, traffic; informal truck, doings.

dean n. *the dean of the college* **faculty head**, department head, college head, provost, university official; chief, director, principal, president, governor.

dear adj. **1** *a dear friend* **beloved**, loved, adored, cherished, precious; esteemed, respected, worshipped; close, intimate, bosom, boon, best. **2** *her pictures were too dear to part with* **precious**, treasured, valued, prized, cherished, special. **3** *such a dear man* **endearing**, adorable, lovable, appealing, engaging, charming, captivating, winsome, lovely, nice, pleasant, delightful, sweet, darling. **4** *rather dear meals* **expensive**, costly, high-priced, overpriced, exorbitant, extortionate; Brit. over the odds; informal pricey, steep, stiff.
– OPPOSITES hated, disagreeable, cheap.
▶ n. **1** *don't worry, my dear* **darling**, dearest, love, beloved, sweetheart, sweet, precious, treasure; informal sweetie, sugar, honey, baby, pet, sunshine, poppet. **2** *he's such a dear* **lovable person**; darling, sweetheart, pet, angel, gem, treasure; informal star.

dearly adv. **1** *I love my son dearly* **very much**, a great deal, greatly, deeply, profoundly, extremely; fondly, devotedly, tenderly. **2** *our freedom has been bought dearly* **at great cost**, at a high price, with much suffering, with much sacrifice.

dearth n. **lack**, scarcity, shortage, shortfall, want, deficiency, insufficiency, inadequacy, paucity, sparseness, scantiness, rareness; absence.
– OPPOSITES surfeit.

death n. **1** *her father's death* **demise**, dying, end, passing, loss of life; eternal rest, quietus; murder, assassination, execution, slaughter, massacre; informal curtains; formal decease; old use expiry. **2** *the death of their dream* **end**, finish, termination, extinction, extinguishing, collapse, destruction, eradication, obliteration. **3** *Death gestured towards a grave* **the Grim Reaper**, the Dark Angel, the Angel of Death.
– OPPOSITES life, birth.
□ **put someone to death** execute, hang, behead, guillotine, decapitate, electrocute, shoot, gas, crucify, stone; kill, murder, assassinate, eliminate, terminate, exterminate, destroy; informal bump off, polish

d

d

off, do away with, do in, knock off, top, string up, take out, stiff, blow away; N. Amer. informal ice, rub out, waste, whack, smoke; literary slay.

> **WORD LINKS**
>
> **fatal, lethal, mortal** causing death
> **terminal** (of an illness) predicted to lead to death
> **moribund, in extremis** at the point of death
> **necromancy** the prediction of the future by supposedly communicating with the dead
> **obituary** a short biography of someone, published in a newspaper after their death
> **posthumous** happening or awarded after a person's death
> **thanatology** the scientific study of death

deathless adj. **immortal**, undying, imperishable, indestructible; enduring, everlasting, eternal; timeless, ageless.
– OPPOSITES mortal, ephemeral.

deathly adj. **deathlike**, deadly, ghostly, ghastly; ashen, chalky, white, pale, pallid, bloodless, wan, anaemic, pasty.

debacle n. **fiasco**, failure, catastrophe, disaster, mess, ruin; downfall, collapse, defeat; informal foul-up, screw-up, hash, botch, washout, fail; Brit. informal cock-up, pig's ear, bodge; N. Amer. informal snafu.

debar v. **1** *women were debarred from the club* **exclude**, ban, bar, disqualify, declare ineligible, preclude, shut out, lock out, keep out, reject, blackball; N. Amer. disfellowship. **2** *the unions were debarred from striking* **prevent**, prohibit, proscribe, disallow, ban, interdict, block, stop; forbid to; Law enjoin, estop.
– OPPOSITES admit, allow.

debase v. **1** *the moral code has been debased* **degrade**, devalue, demean, cheapen, prostitute, discredit, drag down, tarnish, blacken, blemish; disgrace, dishonour, shame; damage, harm, undermine. **2** *the added copper debases the silver* **reduce in value**, reduce in quality, depreciate; contaminate, adulterate, pollute, taint, sully, corrupt; dilute, alloy.
– OPPOSITES enhance.

debased adj. **1** *their debased amusements* **immoral**, debauched, dissolute, perverted, degenerate, wicked, sinful, vile, base, iniquitous, corrupt; lewd, lascivious, lecherous, prurient, indecent. **2** *the myth lives on in a debased form* **corrupt**, corrupted, bastardized, adulterated, diluted, tainted, sullied.
– OPPOSITES honourable, original.

debatable adj. **arguable**, disputable, questionable, open to question, controversial, contentious; doubtful, dubious, uncertain, unsure, unclear; borderline, inconclusive, moot, unsettled, unresolved, unconfirmed, undetermined, undecided, up in the air; informal iffy.

debate n. *a debate on the reforms* **discussion**, discourse, parley, dialogue; argument, dispute, wrangle, war of words; argumentation, disputation, dissension, disagreement, contention, conflict;

negotiations, talks; informal confab, powwow.
▶ v. **1** *MPs will debate our future* **discuss**, talk over/through, talk about, thrash out, argue, dispute; informal kick around/about, bat around/about. **2** *he debated whether to call her* **consider**, think over/about, chew over, mull over, weigh up, ponder, deliberate, contemplate, muse, meditate; formal cogitate.

debauch v. **corrupt**, debase, deprave, warp, pervert, lead astray, ruin.

debauched adj. **dissolute**, dissipated, degenerate, corrupt, depraved, sinful, unprincipled, immoral; lascivious, lecherous, lewd, lustful, libidinous, licentious, promiscuous, loose, wanton, abandoned; decadent, profligate, intemperate, sybaritic.
– OPPOSITES wholesome.

debauchery n. **dissipation**, degeneracy, corruption, vice, depravity; immodesty, indecency, perversion, iniquity, wickedness, sinfulness, impropriety, immorality; lasciviousness, salaciousness, lechery, lewdness, lust, promiscuity, wantonness, profligacy; decadence, intemperance, sybaritism; formal turpitude.

debilitate v. **weaken**, enfeeble, enervate, devitalize, sap, drain, exhaust, weary, fatigue, prostrate; undermine, impair, indispose, incapacitate, cripple, disable, paralyse, immobilize, lay low; informal knock out, do in.
– OPPOSITES invigorate.

debility n. **frailty**, weakness, enfeeblement, enervation, devitalization, lassitude, exhaustion, weariness, fatigue, prostration; incapacity, indisposition, infirmity, illness, sickness, sickliness; informal weediness; Medicine asthenia.

debonair adj. **suave**, urbane, sophisticated, cultured, self-possessed, self-assured, confident, charming, gracious, courteous, gallant, chivalrous, gentlemanly, refined, polished, well bred, genteel, dignified, courtly; well groomed, elegant, stylish, smart, dashing; informal smooth, swish, sharp, cool.
– OPPOSITES unsophisticated.

debrief v. **question**, quiz, interview, examine, cross-examine, interrogate, probe, sound out; informal grill, pump.

debris n. **detritus**, refuse, rubbish, waste, litter, scrap, dross, chaff, flotsam and jetsam; lumber, rubble, wreckage; remains, scraps, dregs; N. Amer. trash, garbage; Austral./NZ mullock; informal dreck, junk.

debt n. **1** *he couldn't pay his debts* **bill**, account, dues, arrears, charges; financial obligation, outstanding payment, money owing; N. Amer. check; informal tab. **2** *his debt to the author* **indebtedness**, obligation; gratitude, appreciation, thanks.
□ **in debt** owing money, in arrears, overdrawn; insolvent, bankrupt, ruined; Brit. in liquidation; informal in the red, in Queer Street, on the rocks.
in someone's debt indebted to, beholden to, obliged to, duty-bound to, honour-

bound to, obligated to; grateful, thankful, appreciative.

debtor n. **borrower**, mortgagor; bankrupt, insolvent, defaulter.
– OPPOSITES creditor.

debunk v. **explode**, deflate, quash, drive a coach and horses through, discredit, disprove, contradict, controvert, invalidate, negate; challenge, call into question; informal shoot full of holes, blow sky-high; formal confute.
– OPPOSITES confirm.

debut n. **first appearance**, first performance, launch, coming out, entrance, premiere, introduction, inception, inauguration; informal kick-off.

decadence n. **1** *the decadence of modern society* **dissipation**, degeneracy, debauchery, corruption, depravity, vice, sin, moral decay, immorality; immoderateness, intemperance, licentiousness, self-indulgence, hedonism. **2** *the decadence of nations* **decline**, fall, decay, degeneration, deterioration, degradation, retrogression.
– OPPOSITES morality, rise.

decadent adj. **1** *decadent city life* **dissolute**, dissipated, degenerate, corrupt, depraved, sinful, unprincipled, immoral; licentious, abandoned, profligate, intemperate; sybaritic, hedonistic, pleasure-seeking, self-indulgent. **2** *the decadent empire* **declining**, decaying, ebbing, degenerating, deteriorating.

decamp v. **1** *he decamped with the profits* **abscond**, make off, run off/away, flee, bolt, take flight, disappear, vanish, steal away, sneak away, escape, make a run for it, leave, depart; informal split, scram, vamoose, cut and run, do a disappearing act, head for the hills, go AWOL; Brit. informal do a bunk, do a runner, scarper; N. Amer. informal take a powder, go on the lam. **2** old use *the armies decamped* **strike one's tents**, break camp, move on.

decant v. **pour out/off**, draw off, siphon off, drain, tap; transfer.

decapitate v. **behead**, guillotine; old use decollate.

decay v. **1** *the corpses had decayed* **decompose**, rot, putrefy, go bad, go off, spoil, fester, perish, deteriorate; degrade, break down, moulder, mortify, shrivel, wither. **2** *the cities continue to decay* **deteriorate**, degenerate, decline, go downhill, slump, slide, go to rack and ruin, go to seed; disintegrate, fall to pieces, fall into disrepair; fail, collapse; informal go to pot, go to the dogs, go down the toilet; Austral./NZ informal go to the pack.
▸n. **1** *signs of decay* **decomposition**, putrefaction, festering; rot, mould, mildew, fungus. **2** *tooth decay* **rot**, corrosion, decomposition; caries, cavities, holes. **3** *the decay of American values* **deterioration**, degeneration, debasement, degradation, decline, weakening, atrophy; crumbling, disintegration, collapse.

decayed adj. **decomposed**, decomposing, rotten, putrescent, putrid, bad, off, spoiled, perished; mouldy, festering, fetid, rancid, rank; maggoty, wormy, flyblown.

decaying adj. **1** *decaying fish* **decomposing**, decomposed, rotting, rotten, putrescent, putrid, bad, off, perished; mouldy, festering, fetid, rancid, rank; maggoty, wormy, flyblown. **2** *a decaying city* **declining**, degenerating, dying, crumbling; run down, tumbledown, ramshackle, shabby, decrepit, in decline, in ruins, on the way out.

deceased adj. formal **dead**, expired, departed, gone, no more, passed on/away; late, lost, lamented; perished, fallen, slain, slaughtered, killed, murdered; lifeless, extinct; informal (as) dead as a doornail, six feet under, pushing up daisies; euphemistic with God, asleep.

deceit n. **1** *her endless deceit* **deception**, deceitfulness, duplicity, double-dealing, fraud, cheating, trickery, chicanery, deviousness, slyness, wiliness, guile, bluff, lying, pretence, treachery; informal crookedness, monkey business, jiggery-pokery; N. Amer. informal monkeyshines. **2** *their life is a deceit* **sham**, fraud, pretence, hoax, fake, blind, artifice; trick, stratagem, device, ruse, scheme, dodge, machination, deception, subterfuge; cheat, swindle; informal con, set-up, scam, flimflam; N. Amer. informal bunco.
– OPPOSITES honesty.

deceitful adj. **1** *a deceitful woman* **dishonest**, untruthful, mendacious, insincere, false, disingenuous, untrustworthy, unscrupulous, unprincipled, two-faced, duplicitous, double-dealing, underhand, crafty, cunning, sly, scheming, calculating, treacherous, Machiavellian; informal sneaky, tricky, foxy, crooked; Brit. informal bent. **2** *a deceitful allegation* **fraudulent**, counterfeit, fabricated, invented, concocted, made up, trumped up, untrue, false, bogus, fake, spurious, fallacious, deceptive, misleading; euphemistic economical with the truth.

deceive v. **1** *she was deceived by a con man* **swindle**, defraud, cheat, trick, hoodwink, hoax, dupe, take in, mislead, delude, fool, outwit, lead on, inveigle, beguile, double-cross, gull; informal con, bamboozle, do, gyp, diddle, swizzle, rip off, shaft, pull a fast one on, take for a ride, pull the wool over someone's eyes, sell a pup to; N. Amer. informal sucker, snooker, stiff. **2** *he deceived her with another woman* **be unfaithful to**, cheat on, betray, play someone false; informal two-time.

decelerate v. **slow down/up**, ease up, slack up, reduce speed, brake.

decency n. **1** *standards of taste and decency* **propriety**, decorum, good taste, respectability, dignity, correctness, good form, etiquette; morality, virtue, modesty, delicacy. **2** *he didn't have the decency to tell me* **courtesy**, politeness, good manners, civility, respect; consideration, thoughtfulness, tact, diplomacy.

d

d

decent adj. **1** *a decent Christian burial* **proper**, correct, appropriate, apt, fitting, suitable; respectable, dignified, decorous, seemly; nice, tasteful; conventional, accepted, standard, traditional, orthodox; comme il faut; informal pukka. **2** Brit. informal *a very decent chap* **honourable**, honest, trustworthy, dependable; respectable, upright, clean-living, virtuous, good; obliging, helpful, accommodating, unselfish, generous, kind, thoughtful, considerate; neighbourly, hospitable, pleasant, agreeable, amiable. **3** *a job with decent pay* **satisfactory**, reasonable, fair, acceptable, adequate, sufficient, ample; not bad, all right, tolerable, passable, suitable; informal OK, okay, up to snuff.
– OPPOSITES unpleasant, unsatisfactory.

deception n. **1** *they obtained money by deception* **deceit**, deceitfulness, duplicity, double-dealing, fraud, cheating, trickery, chicanery, deviousness, slyness, wiliness, guile, bluff, lying, pretence, treachery; informal crookedness, monkey business, jiggery-pokery; N. Amer. informal monkeyshines. **2** *it was all a deception* **trick**, deceit, sham, fraud, pretence, hoax, fake, blind, artifice, stratagem, device, ruse, scheme, dodge, machination, subterfuge; cheat, swindle; informal con, set-up, scam, flimflam; N. Amer. informal bunco.

deceptive adj. **1** *distances are very deceptive* **misleading**, illusory, illusionary, specious; ambiguous; distorted; literary illusive. **2** *deceptive practices* **deceitful**, duplicitous, fraudulent, counterfeit, underhand, cunning, crafty, sly, guileful, scheming, treacherous, Machiavellian; disingenuous, untrustworthy, unscrupulous, unprincipled, dishonest, insincere, false; informal crooked, sharp, shady, sneaky, tricky, foxy; Brit. informal bent.

decide v. **1** *she decided to become a writer* **resolve**, determine, make up one's mind, make a decision; elect, choose, opt, plan, aim, have the intention, have in mind, set one's sights on. **2** *research to decide a variety of questions* **settle**, resolve, determine, work out, answer; informal sort out, figure out. **3** *the court is to decide the case* **adjudicate**, arbitrate, adjudge, judge; hear, try, examine; sit in judgement on, pronounce on, give a verdict on, rule on.

decided adj. **1** *they have a decided advantage* **distinct**, clear, marked, pronounced, obvious, striking, noticeable, unmistakable, patent, manifest; definite, certain, positive, emphatic, undeniable, indisputable, unquestionable; assured, guaranteed. **2** *he was very decided* **determined**, resolute, firm, strong-minded, strong-willed, emphatic, dead set, unwavering, unyielding, unbending, inflexible, unshakeable, unrelenting, obstinate, stubborn; N. Amer. rock-ribbed. **3** *our future is decided* **settled**, established, resolved, determined, agreed, designated, chosen, ordained, prescribed; set, fixed; informal sewn up, wrapped up.

decidedly adv. **distinctly**, clearly, markedly, obviously, noticeably, unmistakably, patently, manifestly; definitely, certainly, positively, absolutely, downright, undeniably, unquestionably; extremely, exceedingly, exceptionally, particularly, especially, very; N. English right; informal terrifically, devilishly, ultra, mega, majorly; Brit. informal jolly, ever so, dead, well; N. Amer. informal real, mighty, awful; old use exceeding.

deciding adj. **determining**, decisive, conclusive, key, pivotal, crucial, critical, significant, major, chief, principal, prime.

decipher v. **1** *he deciphered the code* **decode**, decrypt, break, work out, solve, interpret, translate; make sense of, get to the bottom of, unravel; informal crack, figure out; Brit. informal twig, suss (out). **2** *the writing was hard to decipher* **make out**, discern, perceive, read, follow, fathom, make sense of, interpret, understand, comprehend, grasp.
– OPPOSITES encode.

decision n. **1** *they came to a decision* **resolution**, conclusion, settlement, commitment, resolve, determination; choice, option, selection. **2** *the judge's decision* **verdict**, finding, ruling, recommendation, judgement, pronouncement, adjudication, arbitrament; order, rule; findings, results; Law determination; N. Amer. resolve. **3** *his order had a ring of decision* **decisiveness**, determination, resolution, resolve, firmness, strong-mindedness, purpose, purposefulness.

decisive adj. **1** *a decisive man* **resolute**, firm, strong-minded, strong-willed, determined; purposeful, forceful, dead set, unwavering, unyielding, unbending, inflexible, unshakeable, obstinate, stubborn; N. Amer. rock-ribbed. **2** *the decisive factor* **deciding**, conclusive, determining; key, pivotal, critical, crucial, significant, influential, major, chief, principal, prime.

deck v. **1** *the street was decked with bunting* **decorate**, bedeck, adorn, ornament, trim, trick out, garnish, cover, hang, festoon, garland, swathe, wreathe; embellish, beautify, prettify, enhance, grace, set off; informal get up, do up, do out, tart up; literary bejewel, bedizen, caparison, furbelow. **2** *Ingrid was decked out in blue* **dress (up)**, clothe, attire, garb, robe, drape, turn out, fit out, rig out, outfit, costume; informal doll up, get up, do up.

declaim v. **1** *a preacher declaiming from the pulpit* **make a speech**, give an address, deliver a sermon; speak, hold forth, orate, preach, lecture, sermonize, moralize; informal sound off, spout, speechify, preachify. **2** *he loved to hear him declaim poetry* **recite**, read aloud, read out loud, read out; deliver; informal spout. **3** *he declaimed against the evils of society* **speak out**, rail, inveigh, fulminate, rage, thunder; rant, expostulate; condemn, criticize, attack, decry, disparage.

declamation n. **speech**, address, lecture, sermon, homily, discourse, oration, recitation, disquisition, monologue.

declaration n. **1** *they issued a declaration* **announcement**, statement, communication, pronouncement, proclamation, communiqué, edict; N. Amer. advisory. **2** *the declaration of war* **proclamation**, notification, announcement, revelation, disclosure, broadcasting. **3** *a declaration of faith* **assertion**, profession, affirmation, acknowledgement, revelation, disclosure, manifestation, confirmation, testimony, validation, certification, attestation; pledge, avowal, vow, oath, protestation.

declare v. **1** *she declared her political principles* **proclaim**, announce, state, reveal, air, voice, articulate, express, vent, set forth, publicize, broadcast; informal come out with, shout from the rooftops. **2** *he declared that they were guilty* **assert**, maintain, state, affirm, contend, argue, insist, hold, profess, claim, avow, swear; formal aver. **3** *his speech declared him a gentleman* **show to be**, reveal as, confirm as, prove to be.

decline v. **1** *she declined all invitations* **turn down**, reject, brush aside, refuse, rebuff, spurn, repulse, dismiss; forgo, deny oneself, pass up; abstain from, say no; informal give the thumbs down to, give something a miss, give someone the brush-off; Brit. informal knock back. **2** *the number of traders has declined* **decrease**, reduce, lessen, diminish, dwindle, contract, shrink, fall off, tail off; drop, fall, go down, slump, plummet; informal nosedive, crash. **3** *standards steadily declined* **deteriorate**, degenerate, decay, crumble, collapse, slump, slip, slide, go downhill, worsen; weaken, wane, ebb; informal go to pot, go to the dogs, go down the toilet; Austral./NZ informal go to the pack.
– OPPOSITES accept, increase, rise.
▶ n. **1** *a decline in profits* **reduction**, decrease, downturn, downswing, devaluation, depreciation, diminution, ebb, drop, slump, plunge; informal nosedive, crash. **2** *forest decline* **deterioration**, degeneration, degradation, shrinkage; death, decay. □ **in decline** declining, decaying, crumbling, collapsing, failing; disappearing, dying, moribund; informal on its last legs, on the way out.

decode v. **decipher**, decrypt, work out, solve, interpret, translate; make sense of, get to the bottom of, unravel, find the key to; informal crack, figure out; Brit. informal twig, suss (out).

decompose v. **1** *the chemical prevents corpses decomposing* **decay**, rot, putrefy, go bad, go off, spoil, fester, perish, deteriorate; degrade, break down, moulder, mortify, shrivel, wither. **2** *some minerals decompose rapidly* **break up**, fragment, disintegrate, crumble, dissolve; break down, decay. **3** *decompose words into simpler elements* **separate**, divide, break down, dissect, resolve, reduce.

decomposition n. **1** *an advanced state of decomposition* **decay**, putrefaction, putrescence, putridity. **2** *the decomposition of granite* **disintegration**, dissolution; breaking down, decay. **3** *the decomposition of*

a sentence **separation**, division, breakdown; dissection, dissolution, resolution, analysis, reduction.

decontaminate v. **sanitize**, sterilize, disinfect, clean, cleanse, purify; fumigate.

decor n. **decoration**, furnishing, ornamentation; colour scheme.

decorate v. **1** *the door was decorated with a wreath* **ornament**, adorn, trim, embellish, garnish, furnish, enhance, grace, prettify; festoon, garland, bedeck. **2** *he started to decorate his home* **paint**, **wallpaper**, paper; refurbish, furbish, renovate, redecorate; informal do up, spruce up, do over, fix up, give something a facelift. **3** *he was decorated for courage* **give a medal to**, honour, cite, reward.

decoration n. **1** *a ceiling with rich decoration* **ornamentation**, adornment, trimming, embellishment, garnishing, gilding; beautification, prettification; enhancements, enrichments, frills, accessories, trimmings, finery, frippery. **2** *internal decoration.* See **decor**. **3** *a Christmas tree decoration* **ornament**, bauble, trinket, knick-knack, spangle; trimming, tinsel. **4** *a decoration won on the battlefield* **medal**, award, star, ribbon; laurel, trophy, prize; Military slang fruit salad; Brit. informal gong.

decorative adj. **ornamental**, embellishing, garnishing; fancy, ornate, attractive, pretty, showy.
– OPPOSITES functional.

decorous adj. **proper**, seemly, decent, becoming, befitting, tasteful; correct, appropriate, suitable, fitting; tactful, polite, well mannered, genteel, respectable; formal, restrained, modest, demure, gentlemanly, ladylike.
– OPPOSITES unseemly.

decorum n. **1** *he had acted with decorum* **propriety**, seemliness, decency, good taste, correctness; politeness, courtesy, good manners; dignity, respectability, modesty, demureness. **2** *a breach of decorum* **etiquette**, protocol, good form, custom, convention; formalities, niceties, punctilios, politeness.
– OPPOSITES impropriety.

decoy n. *a decoy to distract their attention* **lure**, bait, red herring; enticement, inducement, temptation, attraction, carrot; snare, trap.
▶ v. *he was decoyed to the mainland* **lure**, entice, tempt; entrap, snare, trap.

decrease v. **1** *pollution levels decreased* **lessen**, reduce, drop, diminish, decline, dwindle, fall off; die down, abate, subside, tail off, ebb, wane; plummet, plunge. **2** *decrease the amount of fat in your body* **reduce**, lessen, lower, cut, curtail; slim down, tone down, deplete, minimize; informal slash.
– OPPOSITES increase.
▶ n. *a decrease in crime* **reduction**, drop, decline, downturn, cut, cutback, diminution, ebb, wane.
– OPPOSITES increase.

d

decree n. 1 *a presidential decree* **order**, edict, command, commandment, mandate, proclamation, dictum, fiat; law, statute, act; formal ordinance. 2 *a court decree* **judgement**, verdict, adjudication, ruling, resolution, decision.
▶ v. *he decreed that a stadium should be built* **order**, command, rule, dictate, pronounce, proclaim, ordain; direct, decide, determine.

decrepit adj. 1 *a decrepit old man* **feeble**, infirm, weak, weakly, frail; disabled, incapacitated, crippled, doddering, tottering; old, elderly, aged, ancient, senile; informal past it, over the hill, no spring chicken. 2 *a decrepit house* **dilapidated**, rickety, run down, tumbledown, ramshackle, derelict, ruined, in (a state of) disrepair, gone to rack and ruin; battered, decayed, crumbling, deteriorating.
– OPPOSITES strong, sound.

decry v. **denounce**, condemn, criticize, censure, attack, rail against, run down, pillory, lambaste, vilify, revile; disparage, deprecate, cast aspersions on; informal slam, blast, knock; Brit. informal slate.
– OPPOSITES praise.

dedicate v. 1 *she dedicated her life to the sick* **devote**, commit, pledge, give, surrender, sacrifice; set aside, allocate, consign. 2 *a book dedicated to a noblewoman* **inscribe**, address; assign. 3 *the chapel was dedicated to the Virgin Mary* **devote**, assign; bless, consecrate, sanctify; formal hallow.

dedicated adj. 1 *a dedicated socialist* **committed**, devoted, staunch, firm, steadfast, resolute, unwavering, loyal, faithful, true, dyed-in-the-wool; wholehearted, single-minded, enthusiastic, keen, earnest, zealous, driven, ardent, passionate, fervent; informal card-carrying, deep-dyed. 2 *data is accessed by a dedicated machine* **exclusive**, custom built, customized.
– OPPOSITES indifferent.

dedication n. 1 *sport requires dedication* **commitment**, application, diligence, industry, resolve, enthusiasm, zeal, conscientiousness, perseverance, persistence, tenacity, drive, staying power; hard work, effort. 2 *her dedication to the job* **devotion**, commitment, loyalty, adherence, allegiance. 3 *the book has a dedication to his wife* **inscription**, address, message. 4 *the dedication of the church* **blessing**, consecration, sanctification, benediction.
– OPPOSITES apathy.

deduce v. **conclude**, reason, work out, infer; glean, divine, intuit, understand, assume, presume, conjecture, surmise, reckon; informal figure out; Brit. informal suss out.

deduct v. **subtract**, take away, take off, debit, dock, discount; abstract, remove; informal knock off.
– OPPOSITES add.

deduction n. 1 *the deduction of tax* **subtraction**, removal, debit, abstraction. 2 *gross pay, before deductions* **stoppage**,

subtraction. 3 *she was right in her deduction* **conclusion**, inference, supposition, hypothesis, assumption, presumption; suspicion, conviction, belief, reasoning.

deed n. 1 *knightly deeds* **act**, action; feat, exploit, achievement, accomplishment, endeavour, undertaking, enterprise. 2 *unity must be established in deed and word* **fact**, reality, actuality. 3 *mortgage deeds* **legal document**, contract, indenture, instrument.

deem v. **consider**, regard as, judge, adjudge, hold to be, view as, see as, take for, class as, count, find, esteem, suppose, reckon; think, believe, feel.

deep adj. 1 *a deep ravine* **cavernous**, yawning, gaping, huge, extensive; bottomless, fathomless, unfathomable; old use profound. 2 *two inches deep* **in depth**, downwards, inwards, in vertical extent. 3 *deep affection* **intense**, heartfelt, wholehearted, deep-seated, deep-rooted; sincere, genuine, earnest, enthusiastic, great. 4 *a deep sleep* **sound**, heavy, intense. 5 *a deep thinker* **profound**, serious, philosophical, complex, weighty; abstruse, esoteric, recondite, mysterious, obscure; intelligent, intellectual, learned, wise, scholarly; discerning, penetrating, perceptive, insightful. 6 *he was deep in concentration* **rapt**, absorbed, engrossed, preoccupied, immersed, lost, gripped, intent, engaged. 7 *a deep mystery* **obscure**, mysterious, secret, unfathomable, opaque, abstruse, recondite, esoteric, enigmatic, arcane; puzzling, baffling, mystifying, inexplicable. 8 *his deep voice* **low-pitched**, low, bass, rich, powerful, resonant, booming, sonorous. 9 *a deep red* **dark**, intense, rich, strong, bold, warm.
– OPPOSITES shallow, superficial, high, light.
▶ n. literary *creatures of the deep* **the sea**, the ocean; informal the drink; Brit. informal the briny; literary the profound.
▶ adv. 1 *I dug deep* **far down**, way down, to a great depth. 2 *he brought them deep into woodland* **far**, a long way, a great distance.

deepen v. 1 *his love for her had deepened* **grow**, increase, intensify, strengthen, heighten, amplify, augment; informal step up; Brit. informal hot up. 2 *they deepened the hole* **dig out**, dig deeper, excavate.

deeply adv. **profoundly**, greatly, enormously, extremely, very much; strongly, powerfully, intensely, keenly, acutely; thoroughly, completely, entirely; informal well, seriously, majorly.

deep-rooted adj. **deep-seated**, deep, profound, fundamental, basic; established, ingrained, entrenched, unshakeable, inveterate, inbuilt; secure; persistent, abiding, lingering.
– OPPOSITES superficial.

deep-seated adj. See **deep-rooted**.

deer n.

> **WORD LINKS**
> **cervine** relating to deer
> **venison** meat from a deer
> **gralloch** the entrails of a dead deer

deface v. **vandalize**, disfigure, mar, spoil, ruin, sully, damage, blight, impair; N. Amer. informal trash.

de facto adv. *the republic is de facto two states* **in practice**, in effect, in fact, in reality, really, actually.
▸adj. *de facto control* **actual**, real, effective.

defamation n. **libel**, slander, calumny, character assassination, vilification; scandalmongering, malicious gossip, aspersions, muckraking, abuse; disparagement, denigration; smear, slur; informal mud-slinging.

defamatory adj. **libellous**, slanderous, scandalmongering, malicious, vicious, backbiting, muckraking, abusive; disparaging, denigratory, insulting; informal mud-slinging, bitchy, catty; formal calumnious, calumniatory.

defame v. **libel**, slander, malign, cast aspersions on, smear, traduce, give someone a bad name, run down, speak ill of, vilify, besmirch, stigmatize, disparage, denigrate, discredit, decry; informal do a hatchet job on, drag through the mud; N. Amer. slur; informal bad-mouth; Brit. informal slag off; formal calumniate.
– OPPOSITES compliment.

default n. **1** *the incidence of defaults on loans* **non-payment**, failure to pay, non-remittance. **2** *I became a teacher by default* **inaction**, omission, lapse, neglect, negligence, disregard; absence, non-appearance.
▸adj. **normal**, standard, usual, typical, stock, ordinary, customary, habitual, accustomed, everyday, regular, routine; **unvarying**, invariable, unchanging, predictable, obvious; **favourite**, choice, preferred, ideal; **instinctive**, automatic, involuntary, unconscious.
– OPPOSITES atypical, varying, conscious, deliberate.
▸v. **1** *the customer defaulted* **fail to pay**, not pay, renege, back out; go back on one's word; informal welsh, bilk. **2** *the program will default to its own style* **revert**, select automatically.

defaulter n. **1** *a mortgage defaulter* **non-payer**, debt-dodger; tax-dodger; N. Amer. delinquent. **2** Brit. Military *the defaulters' room* **offender**, wrongdoer, felon, delinquent.

defeat v. **1** *the army which defeated the Scots* **beat**, conquer, win against, triumph over, get the better of, vanquish; rout, trounce, overcome, overpower, crush, subdue; informal lick, thrash, whip, wipe the floor with, make mincemeat of, clobber, slaughter, demolish, cane; Brit. informal stuff; N. Amer. informal cream, skunk. **2** *these complex plans defeat their purpose* **thwart**, frustrate, foil, ruin, scotch, debar, snooker, derail; obstruct, impede, hinder, hamper; informal put the kibosh on, put paid to, stymie; Brit. informal scupper, nobble. **3** *the motion was defeated* **reject**, overthrow, throw out, dismiss, outvote, turn down; informal give the thumbs down. **4** *how to make it work defeats me* **baffle**,

perplex, bewilder, mystify, bemuse, confuse, confound, throw; informal beat, flummox, faze, stump, fox.
▸n. **1** *a crippling defeat* **loss**, conquest; rout, trouncing; informal thrashing, hiding, drubbing, licking, pasting, massacre, slaughter. **2** *the defeat of his plans* **failure**, downfall, collapse, ruin; rejection, frustration, abortion, miscarriage; undoing, reverse.
– OPPOSITES victory, success.

defeatist adj. *a defeatist attitude* **pessimistic**, fatalistic, negative, cynical, despondent, despairing, hopeless, bleak, gloomy.
– OPPOSITES optimistic.
▸n. **pessimist**, fatalist, cynic, prophet of doom, doomster; misery, killjoy, worrier; informal quitter, wet blanket.
– OPPOSITES optimist.

defect[1] n. *he spotted a defect in my work* **fault**, flaw, imperfection, deficiency, weakness, weak spot, inadequacy, shortcoming, limitation, failing; kink, deformity, blemish; mistake, error; Computing bug; informal glitch, gremlin.

defect[2] v. *his chief intelligence officer defected* **desert**, change sides, turn traitor, rebel, renege; abscond, quit, escape; break faith; secede from, revolt against; informal rat on; Military go AWOL; literary forsake; rare tergiversate.

defection n. **desertion**, absconding, decamping, flight; apostasy, secession; treason, betrayal, disloyalty; literary perfidy; rare tergiversation.

defective adj. **1** *a defective seat belt* **faulty**, flawed, imperfect, shoddy, inoperative, malfunctioning, out of order, unsound; in disrepair, broken; informal on the blink; Brit. informal knackered, duff. **2** *these methods are defective* **lacking**, wanting, deficient, inadequate, insufficient.
– OPPOSITES perfect.

defector n. **deserter**, turncoat, traitor, renegade, Judas, quisling; informal rat; rare tergiversator.

defence n. **1** *the defence of the fortress* **protection**, guarding, security, fortification; resistance, deterrent. **2** *the enemy's defences* **barricade**, fortification; fortress, keep, rampart, bulwark, bastion. **3** *he spoke in defence of his boss* **vindication**, justification, support, advocacy, endorsement; apology, explanation, exoneration. **4** *more spending on defence* **armaments**, weapons, weaponry, arms; the military, the armed forces. **5** *the prisoner's defence* **vindication**, explanation, mitigation, justification, rationalization, excuse, alibi, reason, plea, pleading; testimony, declaration, case.

defenceless adj. **1** *defenceless animals* **vulnerable**, helpless, powerless, impotent, weak, susceptible. **2** *the country is wholly defenceless* **undefended**, unprotected, unguarded, unshielded, unarmed; vulnerable, assailable, exposed, insecure, pregnable.
– OPPOSITES resilient.

defend v. **1** *a fort built to defend Ireland* **protect**, guard, safeguard, secure, shield; fortify, garrison, barricade; uphold, support, watch over. **2** *he defended his policy* **justify**, vindicate, argue for, support, make a case for, plead for; excuse, explain. **3** *the manager defended his players* **support**, back, stand by, stick up for, stand up for, argue for, champion, endorse; informal throw one's weight behind.
– OPPOSITES attack, criticize.

defendant n. **accused**, prisoner (at the bar); appellant, litigant, respondent; suspect.
– OPPOSITES plaintiff.

defender n. **1** *defenders of the environment* **protector**, guard, guardian, preserver; custodian, watchdog, keeper, overseer, superintendent, caretaker. **2** *a defender of colonialism* **supporter**, upholder, backer, champion, advocate, apologist, proponent, exponent, promoter; adherent, believer. **3** *he passed two defenders and scored* **fullback**, back, sweeper; (**defenders**) back four.

defensible adj. **1** *a defensible attitude* **justifiable**, arguable, tenable, defendable, supportable; plausible, sound, sensible, reasonable, rational, logical; acceptable, valid, legitimate; excusable, pardonable, understandable. **2** *a defensible territory* **secure**, safe, fortified; invulnerable, impregnable, impenetrable, unassailable.
– OPPOSITES untenable, vulnerable.

defensive adj. **1** *troops in defensive positions* **defending**, protective; wary, watchful. **2** *a defensive response* **self-justifying**, oversensitive, prickly, paranoid, neurotic; informal uptight, twitchy.

defer[1] v. *the committee will defer their decision* **postpone**, put off, delay, hold over/ off, put back; shelve, suspend, stay, mothball; N. Amer. put over, table, take a rain check on; informal put on ice, put on the back burner, put in cold storage.

defer[2] v. *they deferred to Joseph's judgement* **yield**, submit, give way, give in, surrender, capitulate, acquiesce; respect, honour.

deference n. **respect**, respectfulness, dutifulness; submissiveness, submission, obedience, surrender, accession, capitulation, acquiescence, complaisance, obeisance.
– OPPOSITES disrespect.

deferential adj. **respectful**, humble, obsequious; dutiful, obedient, submissive, subservient, yielding, acquiescent, complaisant, compliant, tractable, biddable, docile.

deferment n. **postponement**, deferral, suspension, delay, adjournment, interruption, pause; respite, stay, moratorium, reprieve, grace.

defiance n. **resistance**, opposition, non-compliance, disobedience, insubordination, dissent, recalcitrance, subversion, rebellion; contempt, disregard, scorn, insolence, truculence.
– OPPOSITES obedience.

defiant adj. **intransigent**, resistant, obstinate, uncooperative, non-compliant, recalcitrant; obstreperous, truculent, dissenting, disobedient, insubordinate, subversive, rebellious, mutinous; informal feisty; Brit. informal stroppy, bolshie.
– OPPOSITES cooperative.

deficiency n. **1** *a vitamin deficiency* **insufficiency**, lack, shortage, want, dearth, inadequacy, deficit, shortfall; scarcity, paucity, absence, undersupply, deprivation, shortness. **2** *the team's big deficiency* **defect**, fault, flaw, imperfection, weakness, weak point, inadequacy, shortcoming, limitation, failing.
– OPPOSITES surplus, strength.

deficient adj. **1** *a diet deficient in vitamin A* **lacking**, wanting, inadequate, insufficient, limited, poor, scant; short of/on, low on. **2** *deficient leadership* **defective**, faulty, flawed, inadequate, imperfect, shoddy, weak, inferior, unsound, substandard, second-rate, poor; Brit. informal duff.

deficit n. **shortfall**, deficiency, shortage, undersupply; debt, arrears; negative amount, loss.
– OPPOSITES surplus.

defile v. **1** *her capacity for love had been defiled* **spoil**, sully, mar, impair, debase, degrade; poison, taint, tarnish; destroy, ruin. **2** *the sacred bones were defiled* **desecrate**, profane, violate; contaminate, pollute, debase, degrade, dishonour.

definable adj. **determinable**, ascertainable, known, definite, clear-cut, precise, exact, specific.

define v. **1** *the dictionary defines it succinctly* **explain**, expound, interpret, elucidate, describe, clarify; give the meaning of, put into words. **2** *he defined the limits of the middle class* **determine**, establish, fix, specify, designate, decide, stipulate, set out; demarcate, delineate. **3** *the farm buildings defined against the fields* **outline**, delineate, silhouette.

definite adj. **1** *a definite answer* **explicit**, specific, express, precise, exact, clear-cut, direct, plain, outright; fixed, established, confirmed, concrete. **2** *definite evidence* **certain**, sure, positive, conclusive, decisive, firm, concrete, unambiguous, unequivocal, clear, unmistakable, proven; guaranteed, assured, cut and dried. **3** *she had a definite dislike for Robert* **unmistakable**, unequivocal, unambiguous, certain, undisputed, decided, marked, distinct. **4** *a definite geographical area* **fixed**, marked, demarcated, delimited, stipulated, particular.
– OPPOSITES vague, ambiguous, indeterminate.

definitely adv. **certainly**, surely, for sure, unquestionably, without doubt, without question, undoubtedly, indubitably, positively, absolutely; undeniably, unmistakably, plainly, clearly, obviously, patently, palpably, transparently, unequivocally, as sure as eggs is eggs.

definition n. **1** *the definition of 'intelligence'* **meaning**, denotation, sense; interpretation, explanation, elucidation, description, clarification, illustration. **2** *the definition of the picture* **clarity**, visibility, sharpness, crispness, acuteness; resolution, focus, contrast.

definitive adj. **1** *a definitive decision* **conclusive**, final, ultimate; unconditional, unqualified, absolute, categorical, positive, definite. **2** *the definitive guide* **authoritative**, exhaustive, best, finest, consummate; classic, standard, recognized, accepted, official.

deflate v. **1** *he deflated the tyres* **let down**, flatten, void; puncture. **2** *the balloon deflated* **go down**, collapse, shrink, contract. **3** *the news had deflated him* **subdue**, humble, cow, chasten; dispirit, dismay, discourage, dishearten; squash, crush, bring down, take the wind out of someone's sails; informal knock the stuffing out of. **4** *the budget deflated the economy* **reduce**, slow down, diminish; devalue, depreciate, depress.
– OPPOSITES inflate.

deflect v. **1** *she wanted to deflect attention from herself* **turn aside/away**, divert, avert, sidetrack; distract, draw away; block, parry, fend off, stave off. **2** *the ball deflected off the wall* **bounce**, glance, ricochet; diverge, deviate, veer, swerve, slew.

deform v. **disfigure**, bend out of shape, contort, buckle, warp; damage, impair.

deformed adj. **misshapen**, distorted, malformed, contorted, out of shape; twisted, crooked, warped, buckled, gnarled; crippled, humpbacked, hunchbacked, disfigured, grotesque; injured, damaged, mutilated, mangled.

deformity n. **malformation**, misshapenness, distortion, crookedness; imperfection, abnormality, irregularity; disfigurement; defect, flaw, blemish.

defraud v. **swindle**, cheat, rob; deceive, dupe, hoodwink, double-cross, trick; informal con, do, sting, diddle, rip off, shaft, bilk, rook, gyp, fleece, put one over on, sell a pup to; N. Amer. informal sucker, snooker, stiff; Austral. informal pull a swifty on.

defray v. **pay (for)**, cover, meet, square, settle, clear, discharge; foot the bill for; N. Amer. informal pick up the tab for.

deft adj. **skilful**, adept, adroit, dexterous, agile, nimble, handy; able, capable, skilled, proficient, accomplished, expert, polished, slick, professional, masterly; clever, shrewd, astute, canny, sharp; informal nifty, nippy.
– OPPOSITES clumsy.

defunct adj. **disused**, unused, inoperative, non-functioning, unusable, obsolete; no longer existing, discontinued; extinct.
– OPPOSITES working, extant.

defuse v. **1** *he tried to defuse the grenade* **deactivate**, disarm, disable, make safe. **2** *strategies to defuse potentially explosive situations* **ease**, calm, take the heat out of;

settle, resolve; pour oil on troubled waters. **3** *an attempt to defuse the tension* **reduce**, lessen, diminish, lighten, relieve, ease, alleviate, moderate, mitigate.
– OPPOSITES activate, intensify.

defy v. **1** *he defied European law* **disobey**, go against, flout, fly in the face of, disregard, ignore; break, violate, contravene, breach, infringe; informal cock a snook at. **2** *his actions defy belief* **elude**, escape, defeat; frustrate, thwart, baffle. **3** *he glowered, defying her to mock him* **challenge**, dare.
– OPPOSITES obey.

degeneracy n. **corruption**, decadence, moral decay, dissipation, dissolution, profligacy, vice, immorality, sin, sinfulness, ungodliness; debauchery; formal turpitude.

degenerate adj. **1** *a degenerate form of classicism* **debased**, degraded, corrupt, impure; formal vitiated. **2** *her degenerate brother* **corrupt**, decadent, dissolute, dissipated, debauched, reprobate, profligate; sinful, ungodly, immoral, unprincipled, amoral, dishonourable, disreputable, unsavoury, sordid, low, ignoble.
– OPPOSITES pure, moral.
▶ n. *a group of degenerates* **reprobate**, debauchee, profligate, libertine, roué, loose-liver.
▶ v. **1** *their quality of life had degenerated* **deteriorate**, decline, slip, slide, worsen, lapse, slump, go downhill, regress, retrogress; go to rack and ruin; informal go to pot, go to the dogs, hit the skids, go down the toilet. **2** *the muscles started to degenerate* **waste (away)**, atrophy, weaken.
– OPPOSITES improve.

degradation n. **1** *poverty brings with it degradation* **humiliation**, shame, loss of self-respect, abasement, indignity, ignominy. **2** *the degradation of women* **demeaning**, debasement, discrediting. **3** *the degradation of the tissues* **deterioration**, degeneration, atrophy, decay; breakdown.

degrade v. **1** *prisons should not degrade prisoners* **demean**, debase, cheapen, devalue; shame, humiliate, humble, mortify, abase, dishonour; dehumanize, brutalize. **2** *the polymer will not degrade* **break down**, deteriorate, degenerate, decay.
– OPPOSITES dignify.

degraded adj. **1** *I feel so degraded* **humiliated**, demeaned, cheapened, cheap, ashamed. **2** *his degraded sensibilities* **degenerate**, corrupt, depraved, dissolute, dissipated, debauched, immoral, base, sordid.
– OPPOSITES proud, moral.

degrading adj. **humiliating**, demeaning, shameful, mortifying, ignominious, undignified, inglorious, wretched; informal infra dig.

degree n. **level**, standard, grade, mark; amount, extent, measure; magnitude, intensity, strength; proportion, ratio.
□ **by degrees** gradually, little by little, bit by bit, inch by inch, step by step, slowly;

d

piecemeal.

to a degree to some extent, to a certain extent, up to a point.

dehydrate v. **1** *alcohol dehydrates the skin* **dry (out)**, desiccate, dehumidify, effloresce. **2** *frogs can dehydrate quickly* **dry up/out**, lose water.
– OPPOSITES hydrate.

deify v. **1** *she was deified by the early Romans* **worship**, revere, venerate, reverence, hold sacred; immortalize. **2** *he was deified by the press* **idolize**, lionize, hero-worship, extol; idealize, glorify, aggrandize; informal put on a pedestal.
– OPPOSITES demonize.

deign v. **condescend**, stoop, lower oneself, demean oneself, humble oneself; consent, vouchsafe; informal come down from one's high horse.

deity n. **god**, goddess, divine being, supreme being, divinity, immortal; creator, demiurge; godhead.

dejected adj. **downcast**, downhearted, despondent, disconsolate, dispirited, crestfallen, disheartened; depressed, crushed, desolate, heartbroken, in the doldrums, sad, unhappy, doleful, melancholy, miserable, woebegone, forlorn, wretched, glum, gloomy; informal blue, down in the mouth, down in the dumps, fed up; Brit. informal brassed off, cheesed off.
– OPPOSITES cheerful.

delay v. **1** *we were delayed by the traffic* **detain**, hold up, make late, slow up/down, bog down, hinder, hamper, impede, obstruct. **2** *they delayed no longer* **linger**, dally, drag one's feet, be slow, hold back, dawdle, waste time; procrastinate, stall, hang fire, mark time, temporize, hesitate, dither, shilly-shally; informal dilly-dally; old use tarry. **3** *he may delay the cut in interest rates* **postpone**, put off, defer, hold over, shelve, suspend, stay; reschedule; N. Amer. put over, table; informal put on ice, put on the back burner, put in cold storage.
– OPPOSITES hurry, advance.
▶ n. **1** *drivers will face lengthy delays* **hold-up**, wait, detainment; hindrance, impediment, obstruction, setback. **2** *the delay of his trial* **postponement**, deferral, deferment, stay, respite; adjournment. **3** *I set off without delay* **procrastination**, stalling, hesitation, dithering, dallying, dawdling.

delectable adj. **1** *a delectable meal* **delicious**, mouth-watering, appetizing, flavoursome, flavourful, toothsome, palatable; succulent, luscious, tasty; informal scrumptious, delish, scrummy, yummy; Brit. informal moreish; N. Amer. informal finger-licking, nummy. **2** *the delectable Ms Davis* **delightful**, lovely, captivating, charming, enchanting, appealing, beguiling; beautiful, attractive, ravishing, gorgeous, stunning, alluring, sexy, seductive, desirable, luscious; informal divine, heavenly, dreamy; Brit. informal tasty.
– OPPOSITES unpalatable, unattractive.

delectation n. humorous **enjoyment**, gratification, delight, pleasure, satisfaction, relish; entertainment, amusement, titillation.

delegate n. *trade union delegates* **representative**, envoy, emissary, commissioner, agent, deputy, commissary; spokesperson, spokesman/woman; ambassador, plenipotentiary.
▶ v. **1** *she must delegate routine tasks* **assign**, entrust, pass on, hand on/over, turn over, devolve, depute, transfer. **2** *they were delegated to negotiate with the States* **authorize**, commission, depute, appoint, nominate, mandate, empower, charge, choose, designate, elect.

delegation n. **1** *the delegation from South Africa* **deputation**, delegacy, legation, (diplomatic) mission, commission; delegates, representatives, envoys, emissaries, deputies. **2** *the delegation of tasks to others* **assignment**, entrusting, giving, devolution, deputation, transference.

delete v. **remove**, cut out, take out, edit out, expunge, excise, eradicate, cancel; cross out, strike out, blue-pencil, ink out, scratch out, obliterate, white out; rub out, erase, efface, wipe out, blot out; Printing dele.
– OPPOSITES add.

deleterious adj. **harmful**, damaging, detrimental, injurious; bad, adverse, disadvantageous, unfavourable, unfortunate, undesirable.
– OPPOSITES beneficial.

deliberate adj. **1** *a deliberate attempt to provoke him* **intentional**, calculated, conscious, intended, planned, studied, knowing, wilful, wanton, purposeful, purposive, premeditated, pre-planned; voluntary, volitional; Law, dated prepense. **2** *small, deliberate steps* **careful**, cautious; measured, regular, even, steady. **3** *a deliberate worker* **methodical**, systematic, careful, painstaking, meticulous, thorough.
– OPPOSITES accidental, hasty, careless.
▶ v. *she deliberated on his words* **think about/over**, ponder, consider, contemplate, reflect on, muse on, meditate on, ruminate on, mull over, give thought to, weigh up; brood over, dwell on; N. Amer. think on.

deliberately adv. **1** *he deliberately hurt me* **intentionally**, on purpose, purposely, by design, knowingly, wittingly, consciously, purposefully; wilfully, wantonly; Law with malice aforethought. **2** *he walked deliberately down the aisle* **carefully**, cautiously, slowly, steadily, evenly.

deliberation n. **1** *after much deliberation, I accepted* **thought**, consideration, reflection, contemplation, meditation, rumination; formal cogitation. **2** *he replaced the glass with deliberation* **care**, carefulness, caution, steadiness.

delicacy n. **1** *the fabric's delicacy* **fineness**, exquisiteness, delicateness, daintiness; airiness; flimsiness, gauziness, silkiness. **2** *the children's delicacy* **sickliness**, ill

health, frailty, fragility, weakness, debility;
infirmity, valetudinarianism. **3** *the delicacy
of the situation* **difficulty**, trickiness;
sensitivity, ticklishness, awkwardness.
4 *treat this matter with delicacy* **care**,
sensitivity, tact, discretion, diplomacy,
subtlety, sensibility. **5** *an Australian delicacy*
choice food, gourmet food, dainty, treat,
luxury, bonne bouche; speciality.

delicate adj. **1** *delicate embroidery* **fine**,
exquisite, intricate, dainty; flimsy,
gauzy, filmy, floaty, diaphanous, wispy,
insubstantial. **2** *a delicate shade of blue*
subtle, soft, muted; pastel, pale, light.
3 *delicate china cups* **fragile**, breakable, frail;
formal frangible. **4** *his wife is delicate* **sickly**,
unhealthy, frail, feeble, weak, debilitated;
unwell, infirm; formal valetudinarian. **5** *a
delicate issue* **difficult**, tricky, sensitive,
ticklish, awkward, problematical, touchy,
prickly; embarrassing; informal sticky, dicey.
6 *the matter required delicate handling*
careful, sensitive, tactful, diplomatic,
discreet, kid-glove, softly-softly. **7** *his
delicate palate* **discriminating**, discerning;
fastidious, fussy, finicky, dainty; informal
picky, choosy, pernickety. **8** *a delicate
mechanism* **sensitive**, precision, precise.
– OPPOSITES coarse, lurid, strong, robust,
clumsy.

delicious adj. **1** *a delicious meal* **delectable**,
mouth-watering, appetizing, tasty,
flavoursome, flavourful, toothsome,
palatable; succulent, luscious; informal
scrumptious, delish, scrummy, yummy; Brit.
informal moreish; N. Amer. informal finger-licking,
nummy. **2** *a delicious languor stole over her*
delightful, exquisite, lovely, pleasurable,
pleasant; informal heavenly, divine.
– OPPOSITES unpalatable, unpleasant.

delight v. **1** *her manners delighted him*
please greatly, charm, enchant, captivate,
entrance, thrill; gladden, gratify, appeal
to; entertain, amuse, divert; informal send,
tickle pink, bowl over. **2** *Fabia delighted in
his touch* **take pleasure**, revel, luxuriate,
wallow, glory; adore, love, relish, savour, lap
up; informal get a kick out of, get a buzz out
of, get a thrill out of, dig; N. Amer. informal get a
charge out of.
– OPPOSITES dismay, disgust, dislike.
▸ n. *she squealed with delight* **pleasure**,
happiness, joy, glee, gladness; excitement,
amusement; bliss, rapture, elation, euphoria.
– OPPOSITES displeasure.

delighted adj. **pleased**, glad, happy, thrilled,
overjoyed, ecstatic, elated; on cloud nine,
walking on air, in seventh heaven, jumping
for joy; enchanted, charmed; amused,
diverted; gleeful, cock-a-hoop; informal over
the moon, tickled pink, as pleased as Punch,
on top of the world, as happy as Larry,
blissed out; Brit. informal chuffed; N. English informal
made up; Austral. informal wrapped.

delightful adj. **1** *a delightful evening*
pleasant, lovely, pleasurable, enjoyable;
amusing, entertaining, diverting; gratifying,
satisfying; marvellous, wonderful, splendid,

sublime, thrilling; informal great, super,
fabulous, fab, terrific, heavenly, divine,
grand; Brit. informal brilliant, brill, smashing;
N. Amer. informal peachy, ducky; Austral./NZ
informal beaut, bonzer. **2** *the delightful
Sally* **charming**, enchanting, captivating,
bewitching, appealing; sweet, endearing,
cute, lovely, adorable, delectable, delicious,
gorgeous, ravishing, beautiful, pretty;
Scottish & N. English bonny; informal dreamy,
divine.

delimit v. **determine**, establish, set, fix,
demarcate, define, delineate.

delineate v. **1** *the aims of the study as
delineated by the boss* **describe**, set forth/
out, present, outline, depict, represent; map
out, define, specify, identify. **2** *a section
delineated in red marker pen* **outline**, trace,
block in, mark (out/off), delimit.

delinquency n. **1** *teenage delinquency*
crime, wrongdoing, lawbreaking,
lawlessness, misconduct, misbehaviour;
misdemeanours, offences, misdeeds.
2 formal *grave delinquency on the host's
part* **negligence**, dereliction of duty,
irresponsibility.

delinquent adj. **1** *delinquent teenagers*
lawless, lawbreaking, criminal; errant,
badly behaved, troublesome, difficult,
unruly, disobedient, uncontrollable. **2** formal
delinquent parents face tough penalties
negligent, neglectful, remiss, irresponsible,
lax, slack; N. Amer. derelict.
– OPPOSITES dutiful.
▸ n. *teenage delinquents* **offender**, wrongdoer,
malefactor, lawbreaker, culprit, criminal;
hooligan, vandal, ruffian, hoodlum; young
offender; informal tearaway.

delirious adj. **1** *she was delirious but had
lucid intervals* **incoherent**, raving, babbling,
irrational; feverish, frenzied; deranged,
demented, unhinged, mad, insane, out of
one's mind. **2** *the delirious crowd* **ecstatic**,
euphoric, elated, thrilled, overjoyed, beside
oneself, walking on air, on cloud nine, in
seventh heaven, carried away, transported,
rapturous; hysterical, wild, frenzied; informal
blissed out, over the moon, on a high.

delirium n. **1** *she had fits of delirium*
derangement, dementia, madness, insanity;
incoherence, irrationality, hysteria,
feverishness, hallucination. **2** *the delirium
of desire* **ecstasy**, rapture, transports, wild
emotion, passion, wildness, excitement,
frenzy, feverishness, fever; euphoria,
elation.
– OPPOSITES lucidity.

deliver v. **1** *the parcel was delivered to his
house* **bring**, take, convey, carry, transport;
send, dispatch, remit. **2** *the money was
delivered up to the official* **hand over**, turn
over, make over, sign over; surrender, give
up, yield, cede; consign, commit, entrust,
trust. **3** *he was delivered from his enemies*
save, rescue, free, liberate, release, extricate,
emancipate, redeem. **4** *the court delivered
its verdict* **utter**, give, make, read, broadcast;

d

pronounce, announce, declare, proclaim, hand down, return, set forth. **5** *she delivered a blow to his head* **administer**, deal, inflict, give; informal land. **6** *he delivered the first ball* **bowl**, pitch, hurl, throw, cast, lob. **7** *the trip delivered everything she wanted* **provide**, supply, furnish. **8** *we must deliver on our commitments* **fulfil**, live up to, carry out, carry through, make good; informal deliver the goods, come across. **9** *she returned home to deliver her child* **give birth to**, bear, be delivered of, have, bring into the world; N. Amer. birth; informal drop.

deliverance n. **1** *their deliverance from prison* **liberation**, release, delivery, discharge, rescue, emancipation; salvation. **2** *the tone he adopted for such deliverances* **utterance**, statement, announcement, pronouncement, declaration, proclamation; lecture, speech.

delivery n. **1** *the delivery of the goods* **conveyance**, carriage, transportation, transport, distribution; dispatch, remittance; freightage, haulage, shipment. **2** *we get several deliveries a day* **consignment**, load, shipment. **3** *the deliveries take place in hospital* **birth**, childbirth; formal parturition. **4** *her delivery was stilted* **speech**, pronunciation, enunciation, articulation, elocution; utterance, recitation, recital, execution.

delude v. **mislead**, deceive, fool, take in, trick, dupe, hoodwink, gull, lead on; informal con, pull the wool over someone's eyes, lead up the garden path, take for a ride; N. Amer. informal sucker, snooker; Austral. informal pull a swifty on.

deluge n. **1** *homes were swept away by the deluge* **flood**, torrent; Brit. spate. **2** *the deluge turned the pitch into a swamp* **downpour**, torrential rain; thunderstorm, rainstorm, cloudburst. **3** *a deluge of complaints* **barrage**, volley; flood, torrent, avalanche, stream, spate, rush, outpouring.
▶ v. **1** *homes were deluged by the rains* **flood**, inundate, submerge, swamp, drown. **2** *we have been deluged with calls* **inundate**, overwhelm, overrun, flood, swamp, snow under, engulf, bombard.

delusion n. **1** *a common male delusion* **misapprehension**, misconception, misunderstanding, mistake, error, misinterpretation, misconstruction, misbelief; fallacy, illusion, fantasy. **2** *a web of delusion* **deception**, trickery.

deluxe adj. **luxurious**, luxury, sumptuous, palatial, opulent, lavish; grand, high-class, quality, exclusive, choice, fancy; expensive, costly; Brit. upmarket; informal plush, posh, classy, ritzy, swanky, pricey; Brit. informal swish; N. Amer. informal swank.
– OPPOSITES basic, cheap.

delve v. **1** *she delved in her pocket* **rummage**, search, hunt, scrabble about/around, root about/around, ferret, fish about/around in, dig; go through, rifle through; Brit. informal rootle around in. **2** *we must delve deeper*

into the matter **investigate**, enquire, probe, explore, research, look into, go into.

demagogue n. **rabble-rouser**, political agitator, soapbox orator, firebrand; informal tub-thumper.

demand n. **1** *I gave in to her demands* **request**, call, command, order, dictate, ultimatum, stipulation. **2** *the demands of a young family* **requirement**, need, desire, wish, want; claim, imposition. **3** *the big demand for such toys* **market**, call, appetite, desire; run on, rush on.
▶ v. **1** *workers demanded wage increases* **call for**, ask for, request, push for, hold out for; insist on, claim. **2** *Harvey demanded that I tell him the truth* **order**, command, enjoin, urge; literary bid. **3** *'Where is she?' he demanded* **ask**, inquire, question, interrogate; challenge. **4** *an activity demanding detailed knowledge* **require**, need, necessitate, call for, involve, entail. **5** *they demanded complete anonymity* **insist on**, stipulate, make a condition of; expect, look for.
□ **in demand** sought-after, desired, coveted, wanted, requested; marketable, desirable, popular, all the rage, at a premium, like gold dust; informal big, trendy, hot.

demanding adj. **1** *a demanding task* **difficult**, challenging, taxing, exacting, tough, hard, onerous, burdensome, formidable; arduous, uphill, rigorous, gruelling, back-breaking, punishing. **2** *a demanding child* **nagging**, clamorous, importunate, insistent; trying, tiresome, hard to please.
– OPPOSITES easy.

demarcate v. **separate**, divide, mark (out/off), delimit, delineate; bound.

demarcation n. **1** *clear demarcation of function* **separation**, distinction, differentiation, division, delimitation, definition. **2** *territorial demarcations* **boundary**, border, borderline, frontier; dividing line, divide.

demean v. **discredit**, lower, degrade, debase, devalue; cheapen, abase, humble, humiliate, disgrace, dishonour.
– OPPOSITES dignify.

demeaning adj. **degrading**, humiliating, shameful, mortifying, abject, ignominious, undignified, inglorious; informal infra dig.

demeanour n. **manner**, air, attitude, appearance, look, mien; bearing, carriage; behaviour, conduct; formal comportment.

demented adj. **mad**, insane, deranged, out of one's mind, crazed, lunatic, unbalanced, unhinged, disturbed, non compos mentis; informal crazy, mental, off one's head, off one's rocker, nutty, round the bend, raving mad, batty, cuckoo, loopy, loony, bananas, screwy, touched, gaga, not all there, out to lunch; Brit. informal barmy, bonkers, crackers, barking, round the twist, off one's trolley, not the full shilling; N. Amer. informal buggy, nutso, squirrelly, wacko.
– OPPOSITES sane.

dementia n. **mental illness**, madness, insanity, derangement, lunacy; Alzheimer's (disease).

demise n. **1** *her tragic demise* **death**, dying, passing, loss of life, end, quietus; formal decease; old use expiry. **2** *the demise of the Ottoman empire* **end**, break-up, disintegration, fall, downfall, collapse.
– OPPOSITES birth.

demobilize v. **disband**, decommission, discharge; Brit. informal demob.

democracy n. **representative government**, elective government, constitutional government; self-government, autonomy; republic, commonwealth.
– OPPOSITES dictatorship.

democratic adj. **elected**, representative, parliamentary, popular; egalitarian, classless; self-governing, autonomous, republican.

demolish v. **1** *they demolished a block of flats* **knock down**, pull down, tear down, bring down, destroy, flatten, raze (to the ground), level, bulldoze, topple; blow up; dismantle, disassemble. **2** *he demolished her credibility* **destroy**, ruin, wreck; refute, disprove, discredit, overturn, explode, drive a coach and horses through; informal shoot full of holes, do for. **3** *our team were demolished.* See **trounce**. **4** informal *she demolished a sausage roll.* See **devour** (sense 1).
– OPPOSITES construct, strengthen.

demolition n. **1** *the demolition of the building* **destruction**, levelling, bulldozing, clearance; obliteration. **2** *the demolition of his theory* **destruction**, refutation. **3** informal *New Zealand's demolition of England.* See **defeat** (sense 1 of the noun).

demon n. **1** *the demons from hell* **devil**, fiend, evil spirit, cacodemon; incubus, succubus; hellhound. **2** *the man was a demon* **monster**, ogre, fiend, devil, brute, savage, beast, barbarian, animal. **3** *Surrey's fast-bowling demon* **genius**, expert, master, virtuoso, maestro, past master, marvel; star; informal hotshot, whizz, buff, pro, ace. **4** *the demon of creativity.* See **daemon**.
– OPPOSITES angel, saint.

demonic, **demoniac**, **demoniacal** adj. **1** *demonic powers* **devilish**, fiendish, diabolical, satanic, Mephistophelian, hellish, infernal; evil, wicked. **2** *the demonic intensity of his playing* **frenzied**, wild, feverish, frenetic, frantic, furious, manic, like one possessed.

demonstrable adj. **verifiable**, provable, attestable; verified, proven, confirmed; obvious, clear, clear-cut, evident, apparent, manifest, patent, distinct, noticeable; unmistakable, undeniable.

demonstrate v. **1** *his findings demonstrate that boys commit more crimes* **show**, indicate, determine, establish, prove, confirm, verify, corroborate, substantiate. **2** *she was asked to demonstrate quilting* **give a demonstration of**; display, show, illustrate, exemplify. **3** *his work demonstrated an analytical ability*

reveal, bespeak, indicate, signify, signal, denote, show, display, exhibit; bear witness to, testify to; imply, intimate, give away. **4** *they demonstrated against the Government* **protest**, rally, march; stage a sit-in, picket, strike, walk out; mutiny, rebel.

demonstration n. **1** *there is no demonstration of God's existence* **proof**, substantiation, confirmation, affirmation, corroboration, verification, validation; evidence, indication, witness, testament. **2** *a demonstration of woodcarving* **exhibition**, presentation, display, exposition, teach-in; informal demo, expo, taster. **3** *his paintings are a demonstration of his talent* **manifestation**, indication, sign, mark, token, embodiment; expression. **4** *an anti-racism demonstration* **protest**, march, rally, lobby, sit-in; stoppage, strike, walkout, picket (line); informal demo.

demonstrative adj. **1** *a very demonstrative family* **expressive**, open, forthcoming, communicative, unreserved, emotional, effusive, gushing; affectionate, cuddly, loving, warm, friendly, approachable; informal touchy-feely, lovey-dovey. **2** *the successes are demonstrative of their skill* **indicative**, indicatory, suggestive, illustrative. **3** *demonstrative evidence of his theorem* **convincing**, definite, positive, telling, conclusive, certain, decisive; incontrovertible, irrefutable, undeniable, indisputable, unassailable.
– OPPOSITES reserved, inconclusive.

demoralize v. **dishearten**, dispirit, deject, cast down, depress, dismay, daunt, discourage, unman, unnerve, crush, shake, throw, cow, subdue; break someone's spirit; informal knock the stuffing out of, knock sideways; Brit. informal knock for six.
– OPPOSITES hearten.

demoralized adj. **dispirited**, disheartened, downhearted, dejected, downcast, low, depressed, despairing; disconsolate, crestfallen, disappointed, dismayed, daunted, discouraged; crushed, humbled, subdued.

demote v. **downgrade**, relegate, declass, reduce in rank; depose, unseat, displace, oust; Military cashier, disrate.
– OPPOSITES promote.

demotic adj. **popular**, vernacular, colloquial, idiomatic, vulgar, common; informal, everyday, slangy.
– OPPOSITES formal.

demur v. *Steed demurred when the suggestion was made* **object**, take exception, take issue, protest, cavil, dissent; voice reservations, be unwilling, be reluctant, balk, think twice; drag one's heels, refuse; informal boggle, kick up a fuss.
▸ n. *they accepted without demur* **objection**, protest, protestation, complaint, dispute, dissent, opposition, resistance; reservation, hesitation, reluctance, disinclination; doubts, qualms, misgivings, second thoughts; a murmur, a word.

demure adj. **modest**, unassuming, meek, mild, reserved, retiring, quiet, shy, bashful, diffident, reticent, timid, shrinking, coy; decorous, decent, seemly, ladylike, respectable, proper, virtuous, pure, innocent, chaste; sober, sedate, staid, prim, goody-goody, strait-laced; informal butter-wouldn't-melt.
– OPPOSITES brazen.

den n. **1** *the mink left its den* **lair**, sett, earth, drey, burrow, hole, dugout, covert, shelter, hiding place, hideout. **2** *a notorious drinking den* **haunt**, site, hotbed, nest, pit, hole; informal joint, dive. **3** *the poet scribbled in his den* **study**, studio, library; sanctum, retreat, sanctuary, hideaway, snug, cubbyhole; informal hidey-hole.

denial n. **1** *the reports met with a denial* **contradiction**, refutation, rebuttal, repudiation, disclaimer; negation, dissent; Law disaffirmation. **2** *the denial of insurance to certain people* **refusal**, withholding; rejection, rebuff, repulse, veto, turndown; informal knock-back; N. Amer. formal declination. **3** *the denial of worldly values* **renunciation**, eschewal, repudiation, disavowal, rejection, abandonment, surrender, relinquishment.

denigrate v. **disparage**, belittle, deprecate, decry, cast aspersions on, criticize, attack; speak ill of, give someone a bad name, defame, slander, libel; run down, abuse, insult, revile, malign, vilify; N. Amer. slur; informal bad-mouth, pull to pieces; Brit. informal rubbish, slate, slag off; formal calumniate.
– OPPOSITES extol.

denizen n. formal **inhabitant**, resident, townsman/woman, native, local; occupier, occupant, dweller; old use burgher.

denominate v. formal **call**, name, term, designate, style, dub, label, entitle.

denomination n. **1** *a Christian denomination* **religious group**, sect, cult, movement, body, branch, persuasion, order, school; Church. **2** *banknotes in a number of denominations* **value**, unit, size. **3** formal *the invention's denomination still stands today* **name**, title, term, designation, epithet, label, tag; informal handle, moniker; formal appellation.

denote v. **1** *the headdresses denoted warriors* **designate**, indicate, be a mark of, signify, signal, symbolize, represent, mean; typify, characterize, distinguish, mark, identify. **2** *his manner denoted an inner strength* **suggest**, point to, smack of, indicate, show, reveal, intimate, imply, convey, betray, bespeak; informal spell.

denouement n. **1** *the film's denouement* **finale**, final scene, epilogue, coda, end, ending, finish, close; culmination, climax, conclusion, resolution, solution. **2** *the debate had an unexpected denouement* **outcome**, upshot, consequence, result, end; informal pay-off.
– OPPOSITES beginning, origin.

denounce v. **1** *the pope denounced abortion* **condemn**, criticize, attack, censure, decry, revile, vilify, discredit, damn, reject; proscribe; malign, rail against, run down; N. Amer. slur; informal knock, slam, hit out at, lay into; Brit. informal slate, slag off; formal castigate. **2** *he was denounced as a traitor* **expose**, betray, inform on; incriminate, implicate, cite, name, accuse; old use inculpate.
– OPPOSITES praise.

dense adj. **1** *a dense forest* **thick**, close-packed, tightly packed, closely set, crowded, compact, solid, tight; overgrown, jungly, impenetrable, impassable. **2** *dense smoke* **thick**, heavy, opaque, soupy, murky, smoggy; concentrated, condensed. **3** informal *they were dense enough to believe me* **stupid**, unintelligent, ignorant, brainless, mindless, foolish, slow, witless, simple-minded, empty-headed, vacuous, vapid, idiotic, imbecilic; informal thick, dim, moronic, dumb, dopey, dozy, wooden-headed, lamebrained, birdbrained, pea-brained; Brit. informal daft.
– OPPOSITES sparse, thin, clever.

density n. **solidity**, solidness, denseness, thickness, substance, mass; compactness, tightness, hardness.

dent n. **1** *I made a dent in his car* **indentation**, dint, dimple, dip, depression, hollow, crater, pit, trough. **2** *a nasty dent in their finances* **reduction**, depletion, deduction, cut.
– OPPOSITES increase.
▶ v. **1** *Jamie dented his bike* **dint**, indent, mark. **2** *the experience dented her confidence* **diminish**, reduce, lessen, shrink, weaken, erode, undermine, sap, shake, damage, impair.

denude v. **strip**, clear, deprive, bereave, rob; lay bare, uncover, expose; deforest, defoliate; dated divest.
– OPPOSITES cover.

deny v. **1** *the report was denied by witnesses* **contradict**, repudiate, challenge, contest, oppose; disprove, debunk, explode, discredit, refute, rebut, invalidate, negate, nullify, quash; informal shoot full of holes; formal gainsay; Law disaffirm. **2** *he denied the request* **refuse**, turn down, reject, rebuff, repulse, decline, veto, dismiss; informal knock back, give the thumbs down to. **3** *she had to deny her parents* **renounce**, eschew, repudiate, disavow, disown, wash one's hands of, reject, discard, cast aside, abandon, give up; formal forswear; literary forsake.
– OPPOSITES confirm, accept.

deodorant n. *an underarm deodorant* **antiperspirant**, body spray, perfume, scent.

deodorize v. **freshen**, sweeten, purify, disinfect, sanitize, sterilize; fumigate, aerate, air, ventilate.

depart v. **1** *James departed after lunch* **leave**, go (away), withdraw, absent oneself, abstract oneself, quit, exit, decamp, retreat, retire; make off, run off/away; set off/out, get under way, be on one's way; informal make tracks, up sticks, clear off/out, take off, split; Brit. informal sling one's hook. **2** *the budget departed from the norm* **deviate**, diverge, digress, drift, stray, veer; differ, vary;

contrast with.
– OPPOSITES arrive.

departed adj. **dead**, expired, gone, no more, passed on/away; perished, fallen; informal six feet under, pushing up daisies; formal deceased; euphemistic with God, asleep.

department n. **1** *the public health department* **division**, section, sector, unit, branch, arm, wing; office, bureau, agency, ministry. **2** *rural departments* **district**, canton, province, territory, state, county, shire, parish; region, area. **3** *the food is Kay's department* **domain**, territory, province, area, line; responsibility, duty, function, business, affair, charge, task, concern; informal pigeon, baby, bag, bailiwick.

departure n. **1** *he tried to delay her departure* **leaving**, going, leave-taking, withdrawal, exit, egress, retreat. **2** *a departure from normality* **deviation**, divergence, digression, shift; variation, change. **3** *an exciting departure for film-makers* **change**, innovation, novelty, rarity.

depend v. **1** *her career depends on a good reference* **be contingent on**, be conditional on, be dependent on, hinge on, hang on, rest on, rely on; be decided by. **2** *my family depends on me* **rely on**, lean on; count on, bank on, trust (in), have faith in, believe in; pin one's hopes on.

dependable adj. **reliable**, trustworthy, trusty, faithful, loyal, unfailing, sure, steadfast, stable; honourable, sensible, responsible.

dependant n. **child**, minor; ward, charge, protégé; relative; (**dependants**) offspring, progeny.

dependence n. See **dependency** (senses 1–3).

dependency n. **1** *her dependency on her husband* **dependence**, reliance; need for. **2** *the association of retirement with dependency* **helplessness**, dependence, weakness, defencelessness, vulnerability. **3** *drug dependency* **addiction**, dependence, reliance; craving, compulsion, fixation, obsession; abuse. **4** *a British dependency* **colony**, protectorate, province, outpost, satellite state; holding, possession. **5** *a dependency of the firm* **subsidiary**, adjunct, offshoot, auxiliary, attachment, satellite, derivative.
– OPPOSITES independence.

dependent adj. **1** *your placement is dependent on her decision* **conditional**, contingent, based; subject to, determined by, influenced by. **2** *the army is dependent on volunteers* **reliant on**, relying on, counting on; sustained by. **3** *she is dependent on drugs* **addicted to**, reliant on; informal hooked on. **4** *he is ill and dependent* **reliant**, needy; helpless, weak, infirm, invalid, incapable; debilitated, disabled. **5** *a UK dependent territory* **subsidiary**, subject; satellite, ancillary; puppet.

depict v. **1** *the painting depicts the Last Supper* **portray**, represent, picture, illustrate, delineate, reproduce, render; draw, paint. **2** *the process depicted by Darwin's theory* **describe**, detail, relate; present, set forth, set out, outline, delineate; represent, portray, characterize.

depiction n. **1** *a depiction of Aphrodite* **picture**, painting, portrait, drawing, sketch, artist's impression, study, illustration; image, likeness. **2** *the film's depiction of women* **portrayal**, representation, presentation, characterization.

deplete v. **exhaust**, use up, consume, expend, drain, empty, milk; reduce, decrease, diminish; slim down, cut back.
– OPPOSITES augment.

depletion n. **exhaustion**, use, consumption, expenditure; reduction, decrease, diminution; impoverishment.

deplorable adj. **1** *your conduct is deplorable* **disgraceful**, shameful, dishonourable, unworthy, inexcusable, unpardonable, unforgivable; reprehensible, despicable, abominable, contemptible, execrable, heinous, beyond the pale. **2** *the garden is in a deplorable state* **lamentable**, regrettable, unfortunate, wretched, atrocious, appalling, awful, terrible, dreadful, abysmal, diabolical; sorry, poor, inadequate; informal dire, woeful, lousy; formal grievous.
– OPPOSITES admirable.

deplore v. **1** *we deplore violence* **abhor**, find unacceptable, frown on, disapprove of, take a dim view of, take exception to; detest, despise; condemn, denounce. **2** *he deplored their lack of flair* **regret**, lament, mourn, rue, bemoan, bewail, complain about, grieve over, sigh over.
– OPPOSITES applaud.

deploy v. **1** *forces were deployed at strategic points* **position**, station, post, place, install, locate, situate, site, establish; base; distribute, dispose. **2** *she deployed all her skills* **use**, utilize, employ, take advantage of, exploit; bring into service, call on, turn to, resort to.

deport v. **expel**, banish, exile, transport, expatriate, extradite, repatriate; evict, oust, throw out; informal kick out, boot out, send packing; Brit. informal turf out.
– OPPOSITES admit.

deportment n. **1** Brit. *poise is concerned with good deportment* **posture**, carriage, bearing, stance, gait; formal comportment. **2** N. Amer. *unprofessional deportment* **behaviour**, conduct, performance; manners, practices, actions.

depose v. **1** *the president was deposed* **overthrow**, unseat, dethrone, topple, remove, supplant, displace; dismiss, oust, drum out, throw out, expel, eject; informal chuck out, boot out, get rid of, show someone the door; Brit. informal turf out. **2** Law *a witness deposed that he had seen me* **swear**, testify, attest, assert, declare, claim; rare asseverate.

deposit n. **1** *a thick deposit of ash*
accumulation, sediment; layer, covering,
coating, blanket. **2** *a copper deposit* **seam**,
vein, lode, layer, stratum, bed. **3** *they paid a
deposit* **down payment**, advance payment,
prepayment, instalment, retainer, stake.
▸ v. **1** *she deposited her books on the table* **put
(down)**, place, set (down), unload, rest;
drop; informal dump, park, plonk; N. Amer. informal
plunk. **2** *the silt deposited by flood water*
leave (behind), precipitate, dump; wash up,
cast up. **3** *the gold was deposited at the bank*
lodge, bank, house, store, stow, put away;
informal stash, squirrel away.

deposition n. **1** *the King's deposition*
overthrow, downfall, removal,
dethronement, displacement, dismissal,
expulsion, ejection; N. Amer. ouster. **2** Law
depositions from witnesses **statement**,
affidavit, attestation, affirmation,
submission, declaration; testimony,
evidence. **3** *the deposition of calcium*
depositing, accumulation, build-up,
precipitation.

depository n. **repository**, cache, store,
storeroom, storehouse, warehouse; vault,
strongroom, safe, treasury; container,
receptacle; informal lock-up.

depot n. **1** *the bus depot* **terminal**, terminus,
station, garage; headquarters, base. **2** *an
arms depot* **storehouse**, warehouse, store,
repository, depository, cache; arsenal,
magazine, armoury, ammunition dump.

deprave v. **corrupt**, lead astray, warp,
subvert, pervert, debauch, debase, degrade,
defile, sully, pollute.

depraved adj. **corrupt**, perverted, deviant,
degenerate, debased, immoral, unprincipled;
debauched, dissolute, licentious, lecherous,
prurient, indecent, sordid; wicked, sinful,
vile, iniquitous, nefarious; informal warped,
twisted, pervy, sick.

depravity n. **corruption**, vice, perversion,
deviance, degeneracy, immorality,
debauchery, dissipation, profligacy,
licentiousness, lechery, prurience, obscenity,
indecency; wickedness, sin, iniquity; informal
perviness; formal turpitude.

deprecate v. **1** *the school deprecates this
behaviour* **deplore**, abhor, disapprove of,
frown on, take a dim view of, take exception
to, detest, despise; criticize, censure. **2** *he
deprecates the value of television* **belittle**,
disparage, denigrate, run down, discredit,
decry, play down, trivialize, underrate,
undervalue, underestimate, depreciate; scoff
at, sneer at, scorn, disdain; informal pooh-pooh.
– OPPOSITES praise, overrate.

deprecatory adj. **1** *deprecatory remarks*
disapproving, censorious, critical, scathing,
damning, condemnatory, denunciatory,
disparaging, denigratory, derogatory,
negative, unflattering; disdainful, derisive,
snide. **2** *a deprecatory smile* **apologetic**,
rueful, regretful, sorry, remorseful, contrite,
penitent, repentant; shamefaced, sheepish.

depreciate v. **1** *these cars will depreciate*
decrease in value, lose value, fall in price.
2 *the decision to depreciate property* **devalue**,
cheapen, reduce, lower in price, mark down,
cut, discount; informal slash. **3** *they depreciate
the importance of art* **belittle**, disparage,
denigrate, decry, deprecate, underrate,
undervalue, underestimate, diminish,
trivialize; disdain, sneer at, scoff at, scorn;
informal knock, bad-mouth, sell short, pooh-
pooh, do down; Brit. informal rubbish.

depredation n. **plundering**, plunder,
looting, pillaging, robbery; devastation,
destruction, damage, rape; ravages, raids.

depress v. **1** *the news depressed him* **sadden**,
dispirit, cast down, get down, dishearten,
demoralize, crush, shake, desolate, weigh
down, oppress; upset, distress, grieve, haunt,
harrow; informal give someone the blues, make
someone fed up. **2** *new economic policies
depressed sales* **slow down**, reduce, lower,
weaken, impair; limit, check, inhibit, restrict.
3 *imports will depress farm prices* **reduce**,
lower, cut, cheapen, keep down, discount,
deflate, depreciate, devalue, diminish, axe;
informal slash. **4** *depress each key in turn*
press, push, hold down; thumb, tap; operate,
activate.
– OPPOSITES encourage, raise.

depressant n. **sedative**, tranquillizer,
calmative, sleeping pill, soporific, opiate,
hypnotic; informal downer, trank, sleeper,
dope; Medicine neuroleptic.
– OPPOSITES stimulant.

depressed adj. **1** *he felt lonely and depressed*
sad, unhappy, miserable, gloomy, glum,
melancholy, dejected, disconsolate,
downhearted, downcast, down, despondent,
dispirited, low, heavy-hearted, morose,
dismal, desolate; tearful, upset; informal blue,
down in the dumps, down in the mouth, fed
up. **2** *a depressed economy* **weak**, enervated,
devitalized, impaired; inactive, flat, slow,
slack, sluggish, stagnant. **3** *depressed prices*
reduced, low, cut, cheap, marked down,
discounted, discount; informal slashed. **4** *a
depressed town* **poverty-stricken**, poor,
disadvantaged, deprived, needy, distressed;
run down; informal slummy. **5** *a depressed
fracture* **sunken**, hollow, concave, indented,
recessed.
– OPPOSITES cheerful, strong, inflated,
prosperous, raised.

depressing adj. **1** *depressing thoughts*
upsetting, distressing, painful,
heartbreaking; dismal, bleak, black, sombre,
gloomy, grave, unhappy, melancholy, sad;
wretched, doleful; informal morbid, blue.
2 *a depressing room* **gloomy**, bleak, dreary,
grim, drab, sombre, dark, dingy, funereal,
cheerless, joyless, comfortless, uninviting.

depression n. **1** *she ate to ease her depression*
unhappiness, sadness, melancholy,
melancholia, misery, sorrow, woe, gloom,
despondency, low spirits, heavy heart,
despair, desolation, hopelessness; upset,
tearfulness; informal the dumps, the doldrums,
the blues, the black dog, a (blue) funk;

Psychiatry dysthymia. **2** *an economic depression* **recession**, slump, decline, downturn, standstill; stagnation; Economics stagflation. **3** *a depression in the ground* **hollow**, indentation, dent, dint, cavity, concavity, dip, pit, hole, sinkhole, trough, crater; basin, bowl.

deprivation n. **1** *unemployment and deprivation* **poverty**, impoverishment, penury, privation, hardship, destitution; need, want, distress, indigence, beggary, ruin; straitened circumstances; rare pauperdom. **2** *deprivation of political rights* **dispossession**, withholding, withdrawal, removal, divestment, expropriation, seizure, confiscation; denial, forfeiture, loss; absence, lack.
– OPPOSITES wealth.

deprive v. **dispossess**, strip, divest, relieve, bereave, deny, rob; cheat out of; informal do out of.

deprived adj. **disadvantaged**, underprivileged, poverty-stricken, impoverished, poor, destitute, needy, unable to make ends meet; Brit. on the breadline.

depth n. **1** *the depth of the caves* **deepness**, distance downwards, distance inwards; drop, vertical extent; old use profundity. **2** *the depth of his knowledge* **extent**, range, scope, breadth, width; magnitude, scale, degree. **3** *her lack of depth* **profundity**, deepness, wisdom, understanding, intelligence, sagacity, discernment, penetration, insight, astuteness, acumen, shrewdness; formal perspicuity. **4** *a work of great depth* **complexity**, intricacy; profundity, gravity, weight. **5** *depth of colour* **intensity**, richness, deepness, vividness, strength, brilliance. **6** *the depths of the sea* **deepest part**, bottom, floor, bed; abyss.
– OPPOSITES shallowness, triviality, surface.
□ **in depth** thoroughly, extensively, comprehensively, rigorously, exhaustively, completely, fully; meticulously, scrupulously, painstakingly.

deputation n. **delegation**, delegacy, legation, commission, committee, (diplomatic) mission; contingent, group, party.

depute v. **1** *he was deputed to handle negotiations* **appoint**, designate, nominate, assign, commission, charge, choose, select, elect; empower, authorize. **2** *the judge deputed smaller cases to others* **delegate**, transfer, hand over, pass on, consign, assign, entrust, give.

deputize v. **stand in**, sit in, fill in, cover, substitute, replace, take someone's place, understudy, be a locum, relieve, take over; hold the fort, step into the breach; act for, act on behalf of; informal sub.

deputy n. *he handed over to his deputy* **second (in command)**, number two, subordinate, junior, assistant, personal assistant, PA, aide, helper, right-hand man/woman, underling, man/girl Friday; substitute, stand-in, fill-in, relief, understudy, locum tenens; representative, proxy, agent, spokesperson; Scottish depute; informal sidekick, locum, temp.
▶ adj. *her deputy editor* **assistant**, substitute, stand-in, acting, reserve, fill-in, caretaker, temporary, provisional, stopgap, surrogate; pro tempore, ad interim; informal second-string.

deranged adj. **insane**, mad, disturbed, unbalanced, unhinged, unstable, irrational; crazed, demented, berserk, frenzied, lunatic, certifiable; non compos mentis; informal touched, crazy, mental; Brit. informal barmy, barking (mad), round the twist.
– OPPOSITES rational.

derelict adj. **1** *a derelict building* **dilapidated**, ramshackle, run down, tumbledown, in ruins, falling apart; rickety, creaky, deteriorating, crumbling; neglected, untended, gone to rack and ruin. **2** *a derelict airfield* **disused**, abandoned, deserted, discarded, rejected, neglected, untended. **3** N. Amer. *he was derelict in his duty* **negligent**, neglectful, remiss, lax, careless, sloppy, slipshod, slack, irresponsible, delinquent.
▶ n. *the derelicts who survive on the streets* **tramp**, vagrant, vagabond, down-and-out, homeless person, drifter; beggar, mendicant; outcast; informal dosser, bag lady; N. Amer. informal hobo, bum.

dereliction n. **1** *buildings were reclaimed from dereliction* **dilapidation**, disrepair, deterioration, ruin, rack and ruin; abandonment, neglect, disuse. **2** *dereliction of duty* **negligence**, neglect, delinquency, failure; carelessness, laxity, sloppiness, slackness, irresponsibility; oversight, omission.

deride v. **ridicule**, mock, scoff at, jibe at, make fun of, poke fun at, laugh at, pillory; disdain, disparage, denigrate, dismiss, slight; sneer at, scorn, insult; informal knock, pooh-pooh, take the mickey out of.
– OPPOSITES praise.

de rigueur adj. **1** *straight hair was de rigueur* **fashionable**, in fashion, in vogue, modish, up to date, up to the minute, all the rage; informal trendy, with it. **2** *an address is de rigueur for business cards* **customary**, standard, conventional, normal, orthodox, usual, comme il faut; compulsory; informal done.

derision n. **mockery**, ridicule, jeers, sneers, taunts; disdain, disparagement, denigration, disrespect, insults; scorn, contempt; lampooning, satire.

derisive adj. **mocking**, jeering, scoffing, teasing, derisory, snide, sneering; disdainful, scornful, contemptuous, taunting, insulting; scathing, sarcastic; informal snidey; Brit. informal sarky.

derisory adj. **1** *a derisory sum* **inadequate**, insufficient, tiny, small; trifling, paltry, pitiful, miserly, miserable; negligible, token, nominal; ridiculous, laughable, ludicrous, preposterous, insulting; informal measly, stingy, lousy, pathetic, piddling, piffling, mingy, poxy. **2** *derisory calls from the crowd.* See **derisive**.

derivation n. **1** *the derivation of theories from empirical observation* **deriving**, induction, deduction, inference; extraction, eliciting. **2** *the derivation of a word* **origin**, etymology, root, etymon, provenance, source; origination, beginning, foundation, basis, cause; development, evolution.

derivative adj. *her poetry was derivative* **imitative**, unoriginal, uninventive, unimaginative, uninspired; copied, plagiarized, plagiaristic, second-hand; trite, hackneyed, clichéd, stale, stock, banal; informal copycat, cribbed, old hat.
– OPPOSITES original.
▶ n. **1** *a derivative of opium* **by-product**, subsidiary product; spin-off. **2** *a derivative of a verb* **derived word**.

derive v. **1** *he derives consolation from his poetry* **obtain**, get, take, gain, acquire, procure, extract, attain, glean. **2** *'coffee' derives from the Turkish 'kahveh'* **originate in**, stem from, descend from, spring from, be taken from. **3** *his fortune derives from property* **originate in**, be rooted in; stem from, come from, spring from, proceed from, issue from.

derogate v. formal **1** *his contribution was derogated by critics* **disparage**, denigrate, belittle, deprecate, deflate, decry, discredit, cast aspersions on, run down, criticize; defame, vilify, abuse, insult, attack, pour scorn on; informal pull apart, drag through the mud, knock, slam, bash, bad-mouth; Brit. informal rubbish, slate, slag off. **2** *the act would derogate from the king's majesty* **detract from**, devalue, diminish, reduce; lessen, depreciate; demean, cheapen. **3** *rules which derogate from an Act of Parliament* **deviate**, diverge, depart, digress, stray; differ, vary; conflict with, be incompatible with.
– OPPOSITES praise, increase.

derogatory adj. **disparaging**, denigratory, deprecatory, disrespectful, demeaning; critical, pejorative, negative, unfavourable, uncomplimentary, unflattering, insulting; offensive, personal, abusive, rude, nasty, mean, hurtful; defamatory, slanderous, libellous; informal bitchy, catty.
– OPPOSITES complimentary.

descend v. **1** *the plane started descending* **go down**, come down; drop, fall, sink, dive, plummet, plunge, nosedive. **2** *she descended the stairs* **climb down**, go down, come down; shin down. **3** *the road descends to a village* **slope**, dip, slant, go down, fall away. **4** *she saw Leo descend from the bus* **alight**, disembark, get down, get off, dismount. **5** *they would not descend to such mean tricks* **stoop**, lower oneself, demean oneself, debase oneself; resort, be reduced, go as far as. **6** *the army descended into chaos* **degenerate**, deteriorate, decline, sink, slide, fall. **7** *troops descended on the town* **attack**, assail, assault, storm, invade, swoop on, charge. **8** *he is descended from a Flemish family* **be a descendant of**, originate from, issue from, spring from, derive from. **9** *his estates descended to his son* **be handed down**, be passed down; be inherited by.
– OPPOSITES ascend, climb.

descendant n. **successor**, scion; heir; (**descendants**) offspring, progeny, family, lineage; Law issue; old use seed, fruit of one's loins.
– OPPOSITES ancestor.

descent n. **1** *the plane began its descent* **dive**, drop; fall, pitch. **2** *their descent of the mountain* **downward climb**. **3** *a steep descent* **slope**, incline, dip, drop, gradient, declivity, slant; hill. **4** *his descent into alcoholism* **decline**, slide, fall, degeneration, deterioration, regression. **5** *she is of Italian descent* **ancestry**, parentage, ancestors, family, antecedents; extraction, origin, derivation, birth; lineage, line, genealogy, heredity, stock, pedigree, blood, bloodline; roots, origins. **6** *the descent of property* **inheritance**, succession. **7** *the sudden descent of the cavalry* **attack**, assault, raid, onslaught, charge, thrust, push, drive, incursion, foray.

describe v. **1** *he described his experiences* **report**, recount, relate, tell of, set out, chronicle; detail, catalogue, give a rundown of; explain, illustrate, discuss, comment on. **2** *she described him as a pathetic figure* **designate**, pronounce, call, label, style, dub; characterize, class; portray, depict, brand, paint. **3** *the pen described a circle* **delineate**, mark out, outline, trace, draw.

description n. **1** *a description of my travels* **account**, report, rendition, explanation, illustration; chronicle, narration, narrative, story, commentary; portrayal, portrait; details. **2** *the description of coal as 'bottled sunshine'* **designation**, labelling, naming, dubbing, pronouncement; characterization, classification, branding; portrayal, depiction. **3** *vehicles of every description* **sort**, variety, kind, type, category, order, breed, class, designation, specification, genre, genus, brand, make, character, ilk; N. Amer. stripe.

descriptive adj. **illustrative**, expressive, graphic, detailed, lively, vivid, striking; explanatory, elucidatory, explicative.

desecrate v. **violate**, profane, defile, debase, degrade, dishonour; vandalize, damage, destroy, deface.

desert[1] v. **1** *his wife deserted him* **abandon**, leave, turn one's back on; throw over, jilt, break up with; leave high and dry, leave in the lurch, leave behind, strand, maroon; informal walk out on, run out on, drop, dump, ditch; Brit. informal give someone the push; literary forsake. **2** *his allies were deserting the cause* **renounce**, repudiate, relinquish, wash one's hands of, abandon, turn one's back on, betray, disavow; formal abjure; literary forsake. **3** *soldiers deserted in droves* **abscond**, defect, run away, make off, decamp, flee, turn tail, take French leave, depart, quit; Military go AWOL.

desert[2] n. *an African desert* **wasteland**, wastes, wilderness, wilds, barren land; dust bowl.
▸adj. **1** *desert conditions* **arid**, dry, moistureless, parched, scorched, hot; barren, bare, stark, infertile, unfruitful, dehydrated, sterile. **2** *a desert island* **uninhabited**, empty, lonely, desolate, bleak; wild, uncultivated.
– OPPOSITES fertile.

deserted adj. **1** *a deserted wife* **abandoned**, thrown over, jilted, cast aside; neglected, stranded, marooned; forlorn, bereft; informal dumped, ditched, dropped; literary forsaken. **2** *a deserted village* **empty**, uninhabited, unoccupied, unpeopled, abandoned, evacuated, vacant; untenanted, tenantless, neglected; desolate, lonely, godforsaken.
– OPPOSITES populous.

deserter n. **absconder**, runaway, fugitive, truant, escapee; renegade, defector, turncoat, traitor.

desertion n. **1** *his wife's desertion of him* **abandonment**, leaving, jilting. **2** *the desertion of the president's colleagues* **defection**; betrayal, renunciation, repudiation, apostasy; formal abjuration. **3** *soldiers were executed for desertion* **absconding**, running away, going absent without leave; defection, treason; Military going AWOL.

deserve v. **merit**, earn, warrant, rate, justify, be worthy of, be entitled to, have a right to, be qualified for.

deserved adj. **well earned**, merited, warranted, justified, justifiable; rightful, due, right, just, fair, fitting, appropriate, suitable, proper, apt; old use meet.

deserving adj. **1** *the deserving poor* **worthy**, meritorious, commendable, praiseworthy, admirable, estimable, creditable, respectable, decent, honourable, righteous. **2** *a lapse deserving of punishment* **meriting**, warranting, justifying, suitable for, worthy of.

desiccated adj. **dried**, dry, dehydrated, powdered.
– OPPOSITES moist.

desideratum n. **requirement**, prerequisite, need, indispensable thing, sine qua non, essential, requisite, necessary.

design n. **1** *a design for the offices* **plan**, blueprint, drawing, sketch, artist's impression, outline, map, plot, diagram, draft, representation, scheme, model. **2** *tableware with a gold design* **pattern**, motif, device; style, composition, make-up, layout, construction, shape, form. **3** *his design of reaching the top* **intention**, aim, purpose, plan, intent, objective, object, goal, end, target; hope, desire, wish, dream, aspiration, ambition.
▸v. **1** *the church was designed by Hicks* **plan**, outline, map out, draft, draw. **2** *they designed a new engine* **invent**, originate, create, think up, come up with, devise, formulate, conceive; make, produce, develop, fashion; informal dream up. **3** *this paper is designed to provoke discussion* **intend**, aim; devise, contrive, purpose, plan; tailor, fashion, adapt, gear; mean, destine.
□ **by design** deliberately, intentionally, on purpose, purposefully; knowingly, wittingly, consciously, calculatedly.

designate v. **1** *some firms designate a press officer* **appoint**, nominate, depute, delegate; select, choose, pick, elect, name, identify, assign. **2** *the rivers are designated 'Sites of Special Scientific Interest'* **classify**, class, label, tag; name, call, entitle, term, dub; formal denominate.

designation n. **1** *the designation of a leader* **appointment**, nomination, naming, selection, election. **2** *the designation of nature reserves* **classification**, specification, definition, earmarking, pinpointing. **3** *the designation 'Generalissimo'* **title**, name, epithet, tag; nickname, byname, sobriquet; informal moniker, handle; formal denomination, appellation.

designer n. **1** *a designer of farmhouses* **creator**, planner, deviser, inventor, originator; maker; architect, builder. **2** *young designers made the dress* **couturier**, tailor, costumier, dressmaker.

designing adj. **scheming**, calculating, conniving; cunning, crafty, artful, wily, devious, guileful, manipulative; treacherous, sly, underhand, deceitful, double-dealing; informal crooked, foxy.

desirability n. **1** *the desirability of the property* **appeal**, attractiveness, allure; agreeableness, worth, excellence. **2** *the desirability of a different economy* **advisability**, advantage, expedience, benefit, merit, value, profit, profitability. **3** *her obvious desirability* **attractiveness**, sexual attraction, beauty, good looks; charm, seductiveness; informal sexiness.

desirable adj. **1** *a desirable location* **attractive**, sought-after, in demand, popular, desired, covetable, enviable; appealing, agreeable, pleasant; valuable, good, excellent; informal to die for. **2** *it is desirable that they should meet* **advantageous**, advisable, wise, sensible, recommendable; helpful, useful, beneficial, worthwhile, profitable, preferable. **3** *a very desirable woman* **(sexually) attractive**, beautiful, pretty, appealing; seductive, alluring, enchanting, beguiling, captivating, bewitching, irresistible; informal sexy, beddable, hot; Brit. informal fit.
– OPPOSITES unattractive, unwise, ugly.

desire n. **1** *a desire to see the world* **wish**, want, aspiration, fancy, inclination, impulse; yearning, longing, craving, hankering, hunger; eagerness, enthusiasm, determination; informal yen, itch. **2** *his eyes glittered with desire* **lust**, sexual attraction, passion, sensuality, sexuality; lasciviousness, lechery, salaciousness, libidinousness; informal the hots, raunchiness, horniness; Brit. informal randiness.
▸v. **1** *they desired peace* **want**, wish for,

d

long for, yearn for, crave, hanker after, be desperate for, be bent on, covet, aspire to; fancy; informal have a yen for, yen for. **2** *she desired him* **be attracted to**, lust after, burn for, be infatuated by; informal fancy, have the hots for, have a crush on, be mad about.

desired adj. **1** *cut the cloth to the desired length* **required**, necessary, proper, right, correct; appropriate, suitable; preferred, chosen, selected. **2** *the desired results* **wished for**, wanted, coveted; sought-after, longed for, yearned for.

desirous adj. **eager**, desiring, anxious, keen, craving, yearning, longing, hungry; ambitious, aspiring; covetous, envious; informal dying, itching.

desist v. **abstain**, refrain, forbear, hold back, keep; stop, cease, discontinue, suspend, give up, break off, drop, dispense with, eschew; informal lay off, give over, quit, pack in.
– OPPOSITES continue.

desk n. **writing table**, bureau, escritoire, secretaire; Brit. davenport.

desolate adj. **1** *desolate moorlands* **bleak**, stark, bare, dismal, grim; wild, inhospitable; deserted, uninhabited, godforsaken, abandoned, unpeopled, untenanted, empty; unfrequented, unvisited, isolated, remote. **2** *she is desolate* **miserable**, despondent, depressed, disconsolate, devastated, despairing, inconsolable, broken-hearted, grief-stricken, crushed, bereft; sad, unhappy, downcast, down, dejected, forlorn, upset, distressed; informal blue, cut up.
– OPPOSITES populous, joyful.
▸ v. **1** *droughts desolated the plains* **devastate**, ravage, ruin, lay waste to; level, raze, demolish, wipe out, obliterate. **2** *she was desolated by the loss of her husband* **dishearten**, depress, sadden, cast down, make miserable, weigh down, crush, upset, distress; informal shatter.

desolation n. **1** *the desolation of the Gobi desert* **bleakness**, starkness, barrenness, sterility; wildness; isolation, loneliness, remoteness. **2** *a feeling of utter desolation* **misery**, sadness, unhappiness, despondency, sorrow, depression, grief, woe; broken-heartedness, wretchedness, dejection, devastation, despair, anguish, distress.

despair n. **hopelessness**, disheartenment, discouragement, desperation, distress, anguish, unhappiness; despondency, depression, disconsolateness, melancholy, misery, wretchedness; defeatism, pessimism.
– OPPOSITES hope, joy.
▸ v. **lose hope**, abandon hope, give up, lose heart, be discouraged, be despondent, be demoralized, resign oneself; be pessimistic, look on the black side.
◻ **be the despair of** be the bane of, be the scourge of, be a burden on, be a trial to, be a thorn in the flesh/side of.

despairing adj. **hopeless**, in despair, dejected, depressed, despondent, disconsolate, gloomy, miserable, wretched, desolate, inconsolable; disheartened,

discouraged, demoralized, devastated; defeatist, pessimistic.

despatch v. & n. See **dispatch**.

desperado n. dated **bandit**, criminal, outlaw, lawbreaker, villain, renegade; robber, cutthroat, gangster, pirate.

desperate adj. **1** *a desperate look* **despairing**, hopeless; anguished, distressed, wretched, desolate, forlorn, distraught, fraught; out of one's mind, at one's wits' end, beside oneself, at the end of one's tether. **2** *a desperate attempt to escape* **last-ditch**, last-gasp, eleventh-hour, do-or-die, final; frantic, frenzied, wild; futile, hopeless, doomed. **3** *a desperate shortage of teachers* **grave**, serious, critical, acute, risky, precarious; dire, awful, terrible, dreadful; urgent, pressing, crucial, vital, drastic, extreme; informal chronic. **4** *they were desperate for food* **in great need of**, urgently requiring, in want of; eager, longing, yearning, hungry, crying out; informal dying. **5** *a desperate act* **violent**, dangerous, lawless; reckless, rash, hasty, impetuous, foolhardy, incautious, hazardous, risky; death-or-glory, do-or-die.

desperately adv. **1** *he screamed desperately for help* **in desperation**, in despair, despairingly, in anguish, in distress; wretchedly, hopelessly, desolately, forlornly. **2** *they are desperately ill* **seriously**, critically, gravely, severely, acutely, dangerously, perilously; very, extremely, dreadfully; hopelessly, irretrievably; informal terribly. **3** *he desperately wanted to talk* **urgently**, pressingly; intensely, eagerly.

desperation n. **hopelessness**, despair, distress; anguish, agony, torment, misery, wretchedness; disheartenment, discouragement.

despicable adj. **contemptible**, loathsome, hateful, detestable, reprehensible, abhorrent, abominable, awful, heinous; odious, vile, low, mean, abject, shameful, ignominious, shabby, ignoble, disreputable, discreditable, unworthy; informal dirty, rotten, low-down; Brit. informal beastly; old use scurvy.
– OPPOSITES admirable.

despise v. **detest**, hate, loathe, abhor, execrate, deplore, dislike; scorn, disdain, look down on, deride, sneer at, revile; spurn, shun; formal abominate.
– OPPOSITES adore.

despite prep. **in spite of**, notwithstanding, regardless of, in the face of, for all, even with.

despoil v. **1** *a village despoiled by invaders* **plunder**, pillage, rob, ravage, raid, ransack, rape, loot, sack; devastate, lay waste, ruin. **2** *the robbers despoiled him of all he had* **rob**, strip, deprive, dispossess, denude, divest, relieve, clean out.

despondency n. **hopelessness**, despair, disheartenment, discouragement, low spirits, wretchedness; melancholy, gloom, misery, desolation, disappointment, dejection, sadness, unhappiness; informal the blues, heartache.

d

despondent adj. **disheartened**, discouraged, dispirited, downhearted, downcast, crestfallen, down, low, disconsolate, despairing, wretched; melancholy, gloomy, morose, dismal, woebegone, miserable, depressed, dejected, sad; informal blue, down in the mouth, down in the dumps.
– OPPOSITES hopeful, cheerful.

despot n. **tyrant**, oppressor, dictator, absolute ruler, totalitarian, autocrat.

despotic adj. **autocratic**, dictatorial, totalitarian, absolutist, undemocratic, anti-democratic, unaccountable; one-party, autarchic, monocratic; tyrannical, tyrannous, oppressive, repressive, draconian, illiberal.
– OPPOSITES democratic.

despotism n. **tyranny**, dictatorship, totalitarianism, absolute rule, absolutism; oppression, repression; autocracy, monocracy, autarchy.

dessert n. **pudding**, sweet, second course, last course; Brit. informal afters, pud.

destabilize v. **undermine**, weaken, damage, subvert, sabotage, unsettle, upset, disrupt.
– OPPOSITES strengthen.

destination n. **journey's end**, end of the line; terminus, stop, stopping place, port of call; goal, target, end.

destined adj. **1** *he is destined to lead a troubled life* **fated**, ordained, predestined, meant; certain, sure, bound, assured, likely; doomed. **2** *computers destined for Pakistan* **heading**, bound, en route, scheduled; intended, meant, designed, designated, allotted, reserved.

destiny n. **1** *master of his own destiny* **future**, fate, fortune, doom; lot; old use portion. **2** *she was sent by destiny* **fate**, providence; predestination; divine decree, God's will, kismet, the stars; luck, fortune, chance; karma.

destitute adj. **1** *she was left destitute* **penniless**, poor, impoverished, poverty-stricken, impecunious, without a penny to one's name; needy, in straitened circumstances, distressed, badly off; Brit. on the breadline; informal hard up, (flat) broke, strapped (for cash), cash-strapped, without a brass farthing, without two pennies to rub together, without a bean; Brit. informal stony broke, skint; N. Amer. informal stone broke, without a red cent. **2** *we were destitute of clothing* **devoid**, bereft, deprived, in need; lacking, without, deficient in, wanting.
– OPPOSITES rich.

destitution n. **poverty**, impoverishment, penury, pennilessness, privation, pauperism; hardship, need, want, straitened circumstances, dire straits, deprivation, (financial) distress.

destroy v. **1** *their offices were destroyed by bombing* **demolish**, knock down, level, raze (to the ground); fell; wreck, ruin, shatter; blast, blow up, dynamite, explode, bomb. **2** *traffic would destroy the conservation area* **spoil**, ruin, wreck, disfigure, blight, mar,

impair, deface, scar, injure, harm, devastate, damage, wreak havoc on. **3** *illness destroyed his career chances* **wreck**, ruin, spoil, disrupt, undo, upset, put an end to, put a stop to, terminate, frustrate, blight, crush, quash, dash, scotch; devastate, demolish, sabotage; Brit. throw a spanner in the works of; informal mess up, muck up, foul up, put paid to, put the kibosh on, do for, queer, blow a hole in; Brit. informal scupper; old use bring to naught. **4** *the horse had to be destroyed* **kill**, put down, put to sleep, slaughter, terminate, exterminate. **5** *we had to destroy the enemy* **annihilate**, wipe out, obliterate, wipe off the face of the earth, eliminate, eradicate, liquidate, finish off, erase; kill, slaughter, massacre, exterminate; informal take out, rub out, snuff out; N. Amer. informal waste.
– OPPOSITES build, preserve, spare.

destruction n. **1** *the destruction by allied bombers* **demolition**, wrecking, ruination, blasting, bombing; wreckage, ruins. **2** *the destruction of the countryside* **spoliation**, devastation, ruination, blighting, disfigurement, impairment, scarring, harm, desolation. **3** *the destruction of cattle* **slaughter**, killing, putting down, extermination, termination. **4** *the destruction of the enemies' forces* **annihilation**, obliteration, elimination, eradication, liquidation; killing, slaughter, massacre, extermination.

destructive adj. **1** *the most destructive war* **devastating**, ruinous, disastrous, catastrophic, calamitous, cataclysmic; harmful, damaging, detrimental, deleterious, injurious, crippling; violent, savage, fierce, brutal, deadly, lethal. **2** *destructive criticism* **negative**, hostile, vicious, unfriendly; unhelpful, obstructive, discouraging.

desultory adj. **casual**, cursory, superficial, token, perfunctory, half-hearted, lukewarm; random, aimless, erratic, unmethodical, unsystematic, chaotic, inconsistent, irregular, intermittent, sporadic, fitful.
– OPPOSITES keen.

detach v. **1** *he detached the lamp from its bracket* **unfasten**, disconnect, disengage, separate, uncouple, remove, loose, unhitch, unhook, free, disunite; pull off, cut off, break off. **2** *he detached himself from the crowd* **free**, separate, segregate; move away, split off; leave, abandon. **3** *he has detached himself from his family* **dissociate**, divorce, alienate, separate, segregate, isolate, cut off; break away, disaffiliate, defect; leave, quit, withdraw from, break with.
– OPPOSITES attach, join.

detached adj. **1** *a detached collar* **unfastened**, disconnected, separated, separate, loosened; untied, unhitched, undone, unhooked, unbuttoned; free, severed, cut off. **2** *a detached observer* **dispassionate**, disinterested, objective, uninvolved, outside, neutral, unbiased, unprejudiced, impartial, non-partisan; indifferent, aloof, remote, distant,

d

impersonal. **3** *a detached house* **standing alone**, separate.

detachment n. **1** *she looked on everything with detachment* **objectivity**, dispassion, disinterest, open-mindedness, neutrality, impartiality; indifference, aloofness. **2** *a detachment of soldiers* **unit**, detail, squad, troop, contingent, outfit, task force, patrol, crew; platoon, company, corps, regiment, brigade, battalion. **3** *the detachment of the wallpaper* **loosening**, disconnection, disengagement, separation; removal.

detail n. **1** *the picture is correct in every detail* **particular**, respect, feature, characteristic, attribute, specific, aspect, facet, part, unit, component, constituent; fact, piece of information, point, element, circumstance, consideration. **2** *that's just a detail* **unimportant point**, trivial fact, triviality, technicality, nicety, subtlety, trifle, fine point, incidental, inessential, nothing. **3** *records with a considerable degree of detail* **precision**, exactness, accuracy, thoroughness, carefulness, scrupulousness, particularity. **4** *a guard detail* **unit**, detachment, squad, troop, contingent, outfit, task force, patrol. **5** *I got the toilet detail* **duty**, task, job, chore, charge, responsibility, assignment, function, mission, engagement, occupation, undertaking, errand.
▶ v. **1** *the report details our objections* **describe**, explain, expound, relate, catalogue, list, spell out, itemize, particularize, identify, specify; state, declare, present, set out, frame; cite, quote, instance, mention, name. **2** *troops were detailed to prevent the escape* **assign**, allocate, appoint, delegate, commission, charge; send, post; nominate, vote, elect, co-opt.
□ **in detail** thoroughly, in depth, exhaustively, minutely, closely, meticulously, rigorously, scrupulously, painstakingly, carefully; completely, comprehensively, fully, extensively.

detailed adj. **comprehensive**, full, complete, thorough, exhaustive, all-inclusive; elaborate, minute, intricate; explicit, specific, precise, exact, accurate, meticulous, painstaking; itemized, blow-by-blow.
– OPPOSITES general.

detain v. **1** *they were detained for questioning* **hold**, take into custody, take (in), confine, imprison, lock up, put in jail, intern; arrest, apprehend, seize; informal pick up, run in, haul in, nab, collar; Brit. informal nick. **2** *don't let me detain you* **delay**, hold up, make late, keep, slow up/down; hinder, hamper, impede, obstruct.
– OPPOSITES release.

detect v. **1** *no one detected the smell of diesel* **notice**, perceive, discern, be aware of, note, make out, spot, recognize, distinguish, remark, identify, diagnose; catch, sense, see, smell, scent, taste; Brit. informal clock. **2** *they are responsible for detecting fraud* **discover**, uncover, find out, turn up, unearth, dig up, root out, expose, reveal. **3** *help the police to detect crime* **solve**, clear up, get to the

bottom of; informal crack. **4** *the hackers were detected* **catch**, hunt down, track down, find, expose, reveal, unmask, smoke out; apprehend, arrest; informal nail.

detection n. **1** *the detection of methane* **discernment**, perception, awareness, recognition, identification, diagnosis; sensing, sight, smelling, tasting. **2** *the detection of insider dealing* **discovery**, uncovering, unearthing, exposure, revelation. **3** *the detection rate for burglary* **solving**, clear-up. **4** *he managed to escape detection* **capture**, identification, exposure; apprehension, arrest.

detective n. **investigator**, private investigator, private detective, operative; Brit. enquiry agent; informal private eye, PI, sleuth, snoop; N. Amer. informal shamus, gumshoe; informal dated dick.

detention n. **custody**, imprisonment, confinement, incarceration, internment, detainment, captivity; arrest, house arrest; quarantine.

deter v. **1** *the high cost deterred many* **discourage**, dissuade, put off, scare off; dishearten, demoralize, daunt, intimidate. **2** *the presence of a caretaker deters crime* **prevent**, stop, avert, fend off, stave off, ward off, block, halt, check; hinder, impede, hamper, obstruct, foil, forestall, counteract, inhibit, curb.
– OPPOSITES encourage.

detergent n. *washing detergent* **cleaner**, cleanser; washing powder, washing-up liquid; soap.
▶ adj. *detergent action* **cleaning**, cleansing; surface-active.

deteriorate v. **1** *his health deteriorated* **worsen**, decline, degenerate; fail, slump, slip, go downhill, go backwards, wane, ebb; informal go to pot. **2** *these materials deteriorate if stored wrongly* **decay**, degrade, degenerate, break down, decompose, rot, go off, spoil, perish; break up, disintegrate, crumble, fall apart.
– OPPOSITES improve.

deterioration n. **1** *a deterioration in law and order* **decline**, collapse, failure, drop, downturn, slump, slip, retrogression. **2** *deterioration of the roof structure* **decay**, degradation, degeneration, breakdown, decomposition, rot; atrophy, weakening; break-up, disintegration, dilapidation.

determinate adj. **fixed**, settled, specified, established, defined, explicit, known, determined, definitive, conclusive, express, precise, categorical, positive, definite.

determination n. **1** *it took great determination to win* **resolution**, resolve, will power, strength of character, single-mindedness, purposefulness, intentness; staunchness, perseverance, persistence, tenacity, staying power; strong-mindedness, backbone; stubbornness, doggedness, obstinacy; spirit, courage, pluck, grit, stout-heartedness; Brit. Dunkirk spirit; informal guts, spunk; formal pertinacity. **2** *the determination* *of the rent* **setting**, specification, settlement, designation, arrangement, establishment, prescription. **3** *the determination of the speed of light* **calculation**, discovery, ascertainment, establishment, deduction, divination, diagnosis, discernment, verification, confirmation.

determine v. **1** *chromosomes determine the sex of the embryo* **control**, decide, regulate, direct, dictate, govern; affect, influence, mould. **2** *he determined to sell up* **resolve**, decide, make up one's mind, choose, elect, opt; formal purpose. **3** *the rent shall be determined by an accountant* **specify**, set, fix, decide on, settle, assign, designate, arrange, choose, establish, ordain, prescribe, decree. **4** *determine the composition of the fibres* **ascertain**, find out, discover, learn, establish, calculate, work out, make out, deduce, diagnose, discern; check, verify, confirm; informal figure out.

determined adj. **1** *he was determined to have his way* **intent on**, bent on, set on, insistent on, resolved to, firm about, committed to; single-minded about, obsessive about. **2** *a very determined man* **resolute**, purposeful, purposive, adamant, single-minded, unswerving, unwavering, undaunted, intent, insistent; steadfast, staunch, stalwart; persevering, persistent, indefatigable, tenacious; strong-minded, strong-willed, unshakeable, steely, four-square, dedicated, committed; stubborn, dogged, obstinate, inflexible, intransigent, unyielding, immovable; N. Amer. rock-ribbed; formal pertinacious.

determining adj. **deciding**, decisive, conclusive, final, definitive, key, pivotal, crucial, critical, major, chief, prime.

deterrent n. **disincentive**, discouragement, damper, curb, check, restraint; obstacle, hindrance, impediment, obstruction, block, barrier, inhibition.
– OPPOSITES incentive.

detest v. **abhor**, hate, loathe, despise, shrink from, be unable to bear, find intolerable, dislike, disdain, have an aversion to; formal abominate.
– OPPOSITES love.

detestable adj. **abhorrent**, hateful, loathsome, despicable, abominable, execrable, repellent, repugnant, repulsive, revolting, disgusting, distasteful, horrible, horrid, awful; heinous, reprehensible, obnoxious, odious, offensive, contemptible.

dethrone v. **depose**, unseat, uncrown, oust, topple, overthrow, bring down, dislodge, displace, supplant, usurp, eject, drum out.
– OPPOSITES crown.

detonate v. **1** *the charge detonated under the engine* **explode**, go off, blow up, shatter, erupt; ignite; bang, blast, boom. **2** *they detonated the bomb* **set off**, explode, discharge, let off, touch off, trigger; ignite, kindle.

detonation n. **explosion**, discharge, blowing up, ignition; blast, bang, report.

detour n. **diversion**, roundabout route, indirect route, scenic route; bypass, ring road; digression, deviation; Brit. relief road.

detract v. **1** *my reservations should not detract from the book's excellence* **belittle**, take away from, diminish, reduce, lessen, minimize, play down, trivialize, decry, depreciate, devalue, deprecate. **2** *the patterns will detract attention from each other* **divert**, distract, draw away, deflect, avert.

detractor n. **critic**, disparager, denigrator, deprecator, belittler, attacker, fault-finder, backbiter; slanderer, libeller; informal knocker.

detriment n. **harm**, damage, injury, hurt, impairment, loss, disadvantage, disservice, mischief.
– OPPOSITES benefit.

detrimental adj. **harmful**, damaging, injurious, hurtful, inimical, deleterious, destructive, ruinous, disastrous, bad, malign, adverse, undesirable, unfavourable, unfortunate; unhealthy, unwholesome.
– OPPOSITES benign.

detritus n. **debris**, waste, refuse, rubbish, litter, scrap, flotsam and jetsam, lumber, rubble; remains, remnants, fragments, scraps, dregs, leavings, sweepings, dross, scum; N. Amer. trash, garbage; Austral./NZ mullock; informal dreck.

devalue v. **belittle**, depreciate, disparage, denigrate, decry, deprecate, treat lightly, discredit, underrate, undervalue, underestimate, deflate, diminish, trivialize, run down; informal knock, sell short, put down, pooh-pooh, do down, pick holes in; Brit. informal rubbish.

devastate v. **1** *the city was devastated by an earthquake* **destroy**, ruin, wreck, lay waste, ravage, demolish, raze (to the ground), level, flatten. **2** *he was devastated by the news* **shatter**, shock, stun, daze, dumbfound, traumatize, crush, overwhelm, overcome, distress; informal knock sideways; Brit. informal knock for six.

devastating adj. **1** *a devastating cyclone* **destructive**, ruinous, disastrous, catastrophic, calamitous, cataclysmic; harmful, damaging, injurious, detrimental; crippling, violent, savage, fierce, dangerous, fatal, deadly, lethal. **2** *devastating news* **shattering**, shocking, traumatic, overwhelming, crushing, distressing, terrible. **3** informal *he presented devastating arguments* **incisive**, highly effective, penetrating, cutting; withering, blistering, searing, scathing, fierce, savage, stinging, biting, caustic, harsh, unsparing.

devastation n. **1** *the hurricane left a trail of devastation* **destruction**, ruin, desolation, havoc, wreckage; ruins, ravages. **2** *the devastation of Prussia* **destruction**, wrecking, ruination, despoliation; demolition, annihilation. **3** *the devastation you have caused the family* **shock**, trauma, distress, stress, strain, pain, anguish, suffering, upset, agony, misery, heartache.

d

develop v. **1** *the industry developed rapidly* **grow**, expand, spread; advance, progress, evolve, mature; prosper, thrive, flourish, blossom. **2** *a plan was developed* **initiate**, instigate, set in motion; originate, invent, form, establish, generate. **3** *children should develop their talents* **expand**, augment, broaden, supplement, reinforce; enhance, refine, improve, polish, perfect. **4** *a row developed* **start**, begin, emerge, erupt, break out, burst out, arise, break, unfold, happen. **5** *he developed the disease last week* **fall ill with**, be stricken with, succumb to; contract, catch, get, pick up, come down with, become infected with.

development n. **1** *the development of the firm* **evolution**, growth, maturation, expansion, enlargement, spread, progress; success. **2** *the development of an idea* **forming**, establishment, initiation, instigation, origination, invention, generation. **3** *keep abreast of developments* **event**, occurrence, happening, circumstance, incident, situation, issue. **4** *a housing development* **estate**, complex, site.

deviant adj. *deviant behaviour* **aberrant**, abnormal, atypical, anomalous, irregular, non-standard; nonconformist, perverse, uncommon, unusual; freakish, strange, odd, peculiar, bizarre, eccentric, idiosyncratic, unorthodox, exceptional; warped, perverted; informal kinky, quirky.
– OPPOSITES normal.
▶ n. *we were seen as deviants* **nonconformist**, eccentric, maverick, individualist; outsider, misfit; informal oddball, weirdo, freak; N. Amer. informal screwball, kook.

deviate v. **diverge**, digress, drift, stray, slew, veer, swerve; get sidetracked, branch off; differ, vary, run counter to, contrast with.

deviation n. **divergence**, digression, departure; difference, variation, variance; aberration, abnormality, irregularity, anomaly, inconsistency, discrepancy.

device n. **1** *a device for measuring pressure* **implement**, gadget, utensil, tool, appliance, apparatus, instrument, machine, mechanism, contrivance, contraption; informal gizmo, widget. **2** *an ingenious legal device* **ploy**, tactic, move, stratagem, scheme, plot, trick, ruse, manoeuvre, machination, contrivance, expedient, dodge, wile; Brit. informal wheeze. **3** *their shields bear his device* **emblem**, symbol, logo, badge, crest, insignia, coat of arms, escutcheon, seal, mark, design, motif; monogram, hallmark, trademark.

devil n. **1** *God and the Devil* **Satan**, Beelzebub, Lucifer, the Lord of the Flies, the Prince of Darkness; informal Old Nick. **2** *they drove out the devils from their bodies* **evil spirit**, demon, cacodemon, fiend, bogie; informal spook. **3** *look what the cruel devil has done* **brute**, beast, monster, fiend; villain, sadist, barbarian, ogre. **4** *he's a naughty little devil* **rascal**, rogue, imp, fiend, monkey, wretch; informal monster, horror, scamp, tyke; Brit. informal perisher; N. Amer. informal varmint. **5** informal *the poor devils looked ill* **wretch**,

unfortunate, creature, soul, person, fellow; informal thing, beggar.

devilish adj. **1** *a devilish grin* **diabolical**, fiendish, demonic, satanic, demoniac, demoniacal; hellish, infernal. **2** *a devilish torture* **wicked**, evil, iniquitous, vile, foul, abominable, unspeakable, loathsome, monstrous, atrocious, heinous, hideous, odious, horrible, appalling, dreadful, awful, terrible, ghastly, abhorrent, despicable, depraved, dark, black, immoral; vicious, cruel, savage, barbaric. **3** *a devilish job* **difficult**, tricky, ticklish, troublesome, thorny, awkward, problematic.

devil-may-care adj. **reckless**, rash, incautious, heedless, impetuous, impulsive, daredevil, hot-headed, wild, foolhardy, audacious, death-or-glory; nonchalant, casual, breezy, flippant, insouciant, happy-go-lucky, easy-going, unworried, untroubled, unconcerned, harum-scarum; Brit. tearaway.

devilment n. See **devilry** (sense 2).

devilry, deviltry n. **1** *some devilry was afoot* **wickedness**, evil, sin, iniquity, vileness, badness, wrongdoing, dishonesty, unscrupulousness, villainy, delinquency, devilishness, fiendishness; informal crookedness, shadiness. **2** *she had a perverse sense of devilry* **mischief**, mischievousness, naughtiness, badness, perversity, impishness; misbehaviour, troublemaking, misconduct; pranks, tricks, roguery, devilment; informal monkey business, shenanigans. **3** *they dabbled in devilry* **black magic**, sorcery, witchcraft, wizardry, necromancy, enchantment, spell-working, incantation; the supernatural, occultism, the occult, the black arts, divination, voodoo, witchery; N. Amer. mojo, orenda.

devious adj. **1** *the devious ways in which they bent the rules* **underhand**, deceitful, dishonest, dishonourable, unethical, unprincipled, immoral, unscrupulous, fraudulent, dubious, unfair, treacherous, duplicitous; crafty, cunning, calculating, artful, conniving, scheming, sly, wily; sneaky, furtive, secret, clandestine, surreptitious, covert; N. Amer. snide, snidey; informal crooked, shady, dirty, low-down; Brit. informal dodgy. **2** *a devious route around the coast* **circuitous**, roundabout, indirect, meandering, tortuous.

devise v. **conceive**, think up, dream up, work out, formulate, concoct; design, invent, coin, originate; compose, construct, fabricate, create, produce, develop; discover, hit on, hatch, contrive; informal cook up.

devitalize v. **weaken**, enfeeble, debilitate, enervate, sap, drain, tax, exhaust, weary, tire (out), fatigue, wear out, prostrate; indispose, incapacitate, lay low; informal knock out, do in, shatter, whack, bush, frazzle, poop; Brit. informal knacker.
– OPPOSITES strengthen.

devoid adj. **free**, empty, vacant, bereft, denuded, deprived, destitute, bankrupt; (**devoid of**) lacking, without, wanting; informal minus.

devolution n. **decentralization**, delegation; redistribution, transfer; surrender, relinquishment.

devolve v. **delegate**, depute, pass (down/on), hand down/over/on, transfer, transmit, assign, consign, convey, entrust, turn over, give, cede, surrender, relinquish, deliver; bestow, grant.

devote v. **allocate**, assign, allot, commit, give (over), apportion, consign, pledge; dedicate, consecrate; set aside, earmark, reserve, designate.

devoted adj. **loyal**, faithful, true (blue), staunch, steadfast, constant, committed, dedicated, devout; fond, loving, affectionate, caring, admiring.

devotee n. **1** *a devotee of rock music* **enthusiast**, fan, lover, aficionado, admirer; informal buff, freak, nut, fiend, fanatic, addict, maniac. **2** *devotees thronged the temple* **follower**, adherent, supporter, advocate, disciple, votary, member, stalwart, fanatic, zealot; believer, worshipper.

devotion n. **1** *her devotion to her husband* **loyalty**, faithfulness, fidelity, constancy, commitment, adherence, allegiance; dedication; fondness, love, admiration, affection, care. **2** *a life of devotion* **devoutness**, piety, religiousness, spirituality, godliness, holiness, sanctity. **3** *morning devotions* **(religious) worship**, religious observance; prayers, vespers, matins; prayer meeting, church service.

devotional adj. **religious**, sacred, spiritual, divine, church, ecclesiastical.
– OPPOSITES secular.

devour v. **1** *he devoured his meal* **eat hungrily**, eat greedily, gobble (up/down), guzzle, gulp (down), bolt (down), cram down, gorge oneself on, wolf (down), feast on, consume, eat up; informal pack away, demolish, dispose of, make short work of, polish off, scoff, shovel down, stuff oneself with, pig oneself on, put away, get outside of. **2** *flames devoured the house* **consume**, engulf, envelop; destroy, demolish, lay waste, devastate; gut, ravage, ruin, wreck. **3** *he was devoured by remorse* **afflict**, plague, bedevil, trouble, harrow, rack; consume, swallow up, overcome, overwhelm.

devout adj. **1** *a devout Christian* **pious**, religious, devoted, dedicated, reverent, God-fearing; holy, godly, saintly, faithful, dutiful, righteous, churchgoing, orthodox. **2** *a devout soccer fan* **dedicated**, devoted, committed, loyal, faithful, staunch, genuine, firm, steadfast, unwavering, sincere, wholehearted, keen, enthusiastic, zealous, passionate, ardent, fervent, active, sworn, pledged; informal card-carrying, true blue, deep-dyed.

dexterity n. **1** *painting china demanded dexterity* **deftness**, adeptness, adroitness, agility, nimbleness, handiness, ability, talent, skill, proficiency, expertise, experience, efficiency, mastery, delicacy, knack, artistry, finesse. **2** *his political dexterity* shrewdness, astuteness, sharp-wittedness, acumen, acuity, intelligence; ingenuity, inventiveness, cleverness, smartness; canniness, sense, discernment, insight, understanding, penetration, perception, perspicacity, discrimination; cunning, artfulness, craftiness; informal nous, horse sense, savvy.

dexterous adj. **1** *a dexterous flick of the wrist* **deft**, adept, adroit, agile, nimble, neat, handy, able, capable, skilful, skilled, proficient, expert, practised, polished; efficient, effortless, slick, professional, masterly; informal nifty, mean, ace. **2** *his dexterous accounting abilities* **shrewd**, ingenious, inventive, clever, intelligent, brilliant, smart, sharp, acute, astute, canny, intuitive, discerning, perceptive, insightful, incisive, judicious; cunning, artful, crafty, wily; informal on the ball, quick off the mark, quick on the uptake, brainy, savvy; Brit. informal suss.
– OPPOSITES clumsy, stupid.

diabolical, diabolic adj. **1** *his diabolical skill* **devilish**, fiendish, satanic, demonic, demoniacal, hellish, infernal, evil, wicked, ungodly, unholy. **2** informal *a diabolical performance* **very bad**, dreadful, awful, terrible, disgraceful, shameful, lamentable, deplorable, appalling, atrocious, abysmal; inferior, substandard, unsatisfactory, inadequate, second-rate, third-rate, shoddy, inept; informal crummy, dire, dismal, God-awful, rotten, pathetic, pitiful, lousy; Brit. informal duff, rubbish, ropy, pants.

diadem n. **crown**, coronet, tiara, circlet, chaplet; literary coronal; historical taj.

diagnose v. **identify**, determine, distinguish, recognize, detect, pinpoint.

diagnosis n. **1** *the diagnosis of coeliac disease* **identification**, detection, recognition, determination, discovery, pinpointing. **2** *the results confirmed his diagnosis* **opinion**, judgement, verdict, conclusion.

diagonal adj. **crosswise**, crossways, slanting, slanted, aslant, squint, oblique, angled, at an angle, cornerways, cornerwise; N. Amer. cater-cornered, kitty-cornered.

diagram n. **drawing**, line drawing, sketch, artist's impression, representation, draft, illustration, picture, plan, outline, delineation, figure; Computing graphic.

diagrammatic adj. **graphic**, graphical, representational, representative, schematic, simplified.

dial v. **phone**, telephone, call, ring.

dialect n. **regional language**, local language, local speech, vernacular, patois, idiom; regionalisms, localisms; informal lingo.

dialectic n. **discussion**, debate, dialogue, logical argument, reasoning, argumentation, polemics; formal ratiocination.

dialogue n. **1** *a book consisting of a series of dialogues* **conversation**, talk, discussion, interchange, discourse; chat, tête-à-tête; informal confab; formal colloquy, confabulation; old use converse. **2** *they called for a serious*

d

d

political dialogue **discussion**, exchange, debate, exchange of views, talk, head-to-head, consultation, conference, parley; talks, negotiations; informal powwow; N. Amer. informal skull session.

diameter n. **breadth**, width, thickness; calibre, bore, gauge.

diametrical, diametric adj. **direct**, absolute, complete, exact, extreme, polar, antipodal.

diaphanous adj. **sheer**, fine, delicate, light, thin, insubstantial, floaty, flimsy, filmy, silken, chiffony, gossamer, gossamer-thin, gauzy; translucent, transparent, see-through.
– OPPOSITES thick, opaque.

diarrhoea n. loose motions; informal the runs, the trots, gippy tummy, holiday tummy, Delhi belly, Montezuma's revenge; Brit. informal the squits; N. Amer. informal turista; old use the flux.
– OPPOSITES constipation.

diary n. **1** *he put the date in his diary* **appointment book**, engagement book, personal organizer; trademark Filofax. **2** *her World War II diaries* **journal**, memoir, chronicle, log, logbook, history, annal, record; weblog, blog, vlog; N. Amer. daybook.

diatribe n. **tirade**, harangue, onslaught, attack, polemic, denunciation, broadside, fulmination, condemnation, censure, criticism; informal blast; literary philippic.

dicey adj. informal **risky**, uncertain, unpredictable, touch-and-go, precarious, unsafe, dangerous, fraught with danger, hazardous, perilous, high-risk, difficult; informal chancy, hairy, iffy; Brit. informal dodgy; N. Amer. informal gnarly.
– OPPOSITES safe.

dichotomy n. **contrast**, difference, polarity, conflict; gulf, chasm, division, separation, split; rare contrariety.

dicky adj. Brit. informal **weak**, unhealthy, ailing, poorly, sickly, frail; unsound, unreliable, unsteady.
– OPPOSITES robust.

dictate v. **1** *the tsar's attempts to dictate policy* **prescribe**, lay down, impose, set down, order, command, decree, ordain, direct, determine, decide, control, govern. **2** *you are in no position to dictate to me* **give orders to**, order about/around, lord it over; lay down the law; informal boss about/around, push around/about, throw one's weight about/around. **3** *choice is often dictated by availability* **determine**, control, govern, decide, influence, affect.
▸ n. *the dictates of his superior* **order**, command, commandment, decree, edict, ruling, dictum, diktat, directive, direction, instruction, pronouncement, mandate, requirement, stipulation, injunction, demand; formal ordinance; literary behest.

dictator n. **autocrat**, absolute ruler, despot, tyrant, oppressor, autarch.

dictatorial adj. **1** *a dictatorial regime* **autocratic**, undemocratic, totalitarian, authoritarian, autarchic, despotic, tyrannical, tyrannous, absolute, unrestricted, unlimited, unaccountable, arbitrary. **2** *his dictatorial manner* **domineering**, autocratic, authoritarian, oppressive, imperious, officious, overweening, overbearing, peremptory, dogmatic, high and mighty; severe, strict; informal bossy, high-handed.
– OPPOSITES democratic, meek.

dictatorship n. **absolute rule**, undemocratic rule, despotism, tyranny, autocracy, autarchy, authoritarianism, totalitarianism, Fascism; oppression, repression.
– OPPOSITES democracy.

diction n. **1** *his careful diction* **enunciation**, articulation, elocution, locution, pronunciation, speech, intonation, inflection; delivery. **2** *the need for contemporary diction in poetry* **phraseology**, phrasing, turn of phrase, wording, language, usage, vocabulary, terminology, expressions, idioms.

dictionary n. **lexicon**, wordbook, word list, glossary.

> **WORD LINKS**
> **lexicography** the compilation of dictionaries

dictum n. **1** *he received the head's dictum with evident reluctance* **pronouncement**, proclamation, direction, injunction, dictate, command, commandment, order, decree, edict, mandate, diktat. **2** *the old dictum 'might is right'* **saying**, maxim, axiom, proverb, adage, aphorism, saw, precept, epigram, motto, truism, commonplace; expression, phrase, tag.

didactic adj. **instructive**, instructional, educational, educative, informative, informational, edifying, improving, preceptive, pedagogic, moralistic.

die v. **1** *her father died last year* **pass away**, pass on, lose one's life, expire, breathe one's last, meet one's end, meet one's death, lay down one's life, perish, go the way of all flesh, go to one's last resting place, go to meet one's maker, cross the great divide; informal give up the ghost, kick the bucket, croak, flatline, buy it, turn up one's toes, cash in one's chips, shuffle off this mortal coil; Brit. informal snuff it, peg out, pop one's clogs; N. Amer. informal bite the big one, buy the farm; old use decease, depart this life. **2** *the wind had died down* **abate**, subside, drop, lessen, ease (off), let up, moderate, fade, dwindle, peter out, wane, ebb, relent, weaken; melt away, dissolve, vanish, disappear; old use remit. **3** *the engine died* **fail**, cut out, give out, stop, break down, stop working; informal conk out, go kaput, give up the ghost; Brit. informal pack up. **4** informal *she's dying to meet you* **long**, yearn, burn, ache; informal itch.
– OPPOSITES live, intensify.

diehard adj. **hard-line**, reactionary, ultra-conservative, conservative, traditionalist, dyed-in-the-wool, deep-dyed, intransigent, inflexible, uncompromising, rigid, entrenched, set in one's ways; staunch, steadfast; informal blimpish.

diet¹ n. *health problems related to your diet* **selection of food**, food, foodstuffs; informal grub, nosh.

▶ v. *she dieted for most of her life* **be on a diet**, eat sparingly; slim, lose weight, watch one's weight; N. Amer. reduce; informal weight-watch; N. Amer. informal slenderize.

diet² n. *the diet's lower house* **legislative assembly**, legislature, parliament, congress, senate, council, assembly.

differ v. **1** *the second set of data differed from the first* **contrast with**, be different/ dissimilar to, be unlike, vary from, diverge from, deviate from, conflict with, run counter to, be incompatible with, be at odds with, go against, contradict. **2** *the two sides differed over this issue* **disagree**, conflict, be at variance/odds, be in dispute, not see eye to eye.
– OPPOSITES resemble, agree.

difference n. **1** *the difference between the two sets of data* **dissimilarity**, contrast, distinction, differentiation, variance, variation, divergence, disparity, deviation, polarity, gulf, gap, imbalance, contradiction, contradistinction; formal dissimilitude. **2** *we've had our differences in the past* **disagreement**, difference of opinion, dispute, argument, quarrel, wrangle, contretemps, altercation; informal tiff, set-to, run-in, spat; Brit. informal row. **3** *I am willing to pay the difference* **balance**, remainder, rest, remaining amount, residue.
– OPPOSITES similarity.

different adj. **1** *people with different lifestyles* **dissimilar**, unalike, unlike, contrasting, contrastive, divergent, differing, varying, disparate; poles apart, incompatible, mismatched, conflicting, clashing; informal like chalk and cheese. **2** *suddenly everything in her life was* **changed**, altered, transformed, new, unfamiliar, unknown, strange. **3** *two different occasions* **distinct**, separate, individual, discrete, independent. **4** informal *he wanted to try something different* **unusual**, out of the ordinary, unfamiliar, novel, new, fresh, original, unconventional, exotic, uncommon.
– OPPOSITES similar, related, ordinary.

differential adj. **1** *the differential achievements of boys and girls* **different**, dissimilar, contrasting, unalike, divergent, disparate, contrastive. **2** *the differential features between benign and malignant tumours* **distinctive**, distinguishing.
– OPPOSITES similar.

differentiate v. **1** *he was unable to differentiate between fantasy and reality* **distinguish**, discriminate, make/draw a distinction, tell the difference, tell apart. **2** *this differentiates their business from all other booksellers* **make different**, distinguish, set apart, single out, separate, mark off.

differentiation n. **distinction**, distinctness, difference; separation, demarcation, delimitation.

difficult adj. **1** *a very difficult job* **hard**, strenuous, arduous, laborious, tough, onerous, burdensome, demanding, punishing, gruelling, back-breaking, exhausting, tiring, fatiguing, wearisome; informal hellish, killing, no picnic; old use toilsome. **2** *she found maths very difficult* **hard**, complicated, complex, involved, impenetrable, unfathomable, over/ above one's head, beyond one, puzzling, baffling, perplexing, confusing, mystifying; problematic, intricate, knotty, thorny, ticklish. **3** *a difficult child* **troublesome**, tiresome, trying, exasperating, awkward, demanding, perverse, contrary, recalcitrant, unmanageable, obstreperous, uncooperative, unhelpful, uncooperative, disobliging; hard to please, fussy, finicky; formal refractory. **4** *you've come at a difficult time* **inconvenient**, awkward, inopportune, unfavourable, unfortunate, inappropriate, unsuitable, untimely, ill-timed. **5** *the family have been through very difficult times* **bad**, tough, grim, dark, black, hard, adverse, distressing; straitened, hard-pressed.
– OPPOSITES easy, simple, accommodating.

difficulty n. **1** *the difficulty of balancing motherhood with a career* **strain**, trouble, problems, toil, struggle, laboriousness, arduousness; informal hassle, stress. **2** *practical difficulties* **problem**, complication, issue, snag, hitch, pitfall, handicap, impediment, hindrance, obstacle, hurdle, obstruction, barrier, stumbling block, fly in the ointment; Brit. spanner in the works; informal headache, hiccup. **3** *Charles got into difficulties* **trouble**, predicament, plight, hard times, dire straits; quandary, dilemma; informal deep water, a fix, a jam, a spot, a scrape, a stew, a hole, a pickle.
– OPPOSITES ease.

diffidence n. **shyness**, bashfulness, modesty, self-effacement, meekness, unassertiveness, timidity, humility, hesitancy, reticence, insecurity, self-doubt, uncertainty, self-consciousness.

diffident adj. **shy**, bashful, modest, self-effacing, unassuming, meek, unconfident, unassertive, timid, timorous, humble, shrinking, reticent, hesitant, insecure, self-doubting, doubtful, uncertain, unsure, self-conscious; informal mousy.
– OPPOSITES confident.

diffuse v. *such ideas were diffused widely in the 1970s* **spread**, spread around, send out, disseminate, scatter, disperse, distribute, put about, circulate, communicate, purvey, propagate, transmit, broadcast, promulgate.

▶ adj. **1** *a diffuse community centred on the church* **spread out**, scattered. **2** *a diffuse narrative* **verbose**, wordy, prolix, long-winded, long-drawn-out, discursive, rambling, wandering, meandering, maundering, digressive, circuitous,

d

roundabout, circumlocutory, periphrastic; Brit. informal **waffly**.

diffusion n. **spread**, dissemination, scattering, dispersal, distribution, circulation, propagation, transmission, broadcasting, promulgation.

dig v. **1** *she began to dig the heavy clay soil* **turn over**, work, break up; till, harrow, plough. **2** *he took a spade and dug a hole* **excavate**, dig out, quarry, hollow out, scoop out, gouge out; cut, bore, tunnel, burrow, mine. **3** *the bodies were hastily dug up* **exhume**, disinter, unearth. **4** *Winnie dug her elbow into his ribs* **poke**, prod, jab, stab, shove, ram, push, thrust, drive. **5** *he'd been digging into my past* **delve**, probe, search, inquire, look, investigate, research, examine, scrutinize; informal check out. **6** *I dug up some disturbing information* **uncover**, discover, find (out), unearth, dredge up, root out, ferret out, turn up, reveal, bring to light, expose. **7** informal dated *I dig talking with him.* See **enjoy** (sense 1).
▸n. **1** *a dig in the ribs* **poke**, prod, jab, stab, shove, push. **2** informal *they're always making digs at each other* **snide remark**, cutting remark, jibe, jeer, taunt, sneer, insult, barb, insinuation; informal wisecrack, crack, put-down.

digest v. *Liz digested this information* **assimilate**, absorb, take in, understand, comprehend, grasp; consider, think about, reflect on, ponder, contemplate, mull over.
▸n. *a digest of their findings* **summary**, synopsis, abstract, precis, résumé, summation; compilation; N. Amer. informal wrap-up.

digit n. **1** *the door code has ten digits* **numeral**, number, figure, integer. **2** *our frozen digits* **finger**, thumb, toe; extremity.

dignified adj. **stately**, noble, courtly, majestic, distinguished, proud, august, lofty, exalted, regal, lordly, imposing, impressive, grand; solemn, serious, grave, formal, proper, ceremonious, decorous, reserved, composed, sedate.

dignify v. **ennoble**, enhance, distinguish, add distinction to, honour, grace, exalt, magnify, glorify, elevate.

dignitary n. **worthy**, personage, VIP, grandee, notable, notability, pillar of society, luminary, leading light, big name; informal heavyweight, bigwig, top brass, top dog, big gun, big shot, big noise, big cheese, big chief, supremo; N. Amer. informal big wheel, big kahuna, big enchilada, top banana.

dignity n. **1** *the dignity of the Crown* **stateliness**, nobility, majesty, regality, courtliness, augustness, loftiness, lordliness, grandeur; solemnity, gravity, gravitas, formality, decorum, propriety, sedateness. **2** *he had lost his dignity* **self-respect**, pride, self-esteem, self-worth, amour propre. **3** *Cnut promised dignities to the noblemen* **high rank**, high standing, high station, status, elevation, eminence, honour, glory, greatness.

digress v. **deviate**, go off at a tangent, get off the subject, get sidetracked, lose the thread, diverge, turn aside/away, depart, drift, stray, wander.

digression n. **deviation**, detour, diversion, departure, divergence, excursus; aside, incidental remark.

digs plural n. informal **lodgings**, rooms, accommodation, living quarters; flat, house, home; informal pad, place; Brit. informal bedsit; formal abode, dwelling, dwelling place, residence, domicile, habitation.

dilapidated adj. **run down**, tumbledown, ramshackle, broken-down, in disrepair, shabby, battered, rickety, shaky, unsound, crumbling, in ruins, ruined, decayed, decaying, decrepit; neglected, uncared-for, untended, the worse for wear, falling to pieces, falling apart, gone to rack and ruin, gone to seed.

dilate v. **1** *her nostrils dilated* **enlarge**, widen, expand, distend. **2** *Diane dilated on the joys of her married life* **expatiate**, expound, enlarge, elaborate, speak/write at length.
– OPPOSITES contract.

dilatory adj. **1** *he had been dilatory in appointing a solicitor* **slow**, tardy, unhurried, sluggish, sluggardly, snail-like, tortoise-like, lazy. **2** *dilatory procedural tactics* **delaying**, stalling, temporizing, procrastinating, time-wasting, Fabian.
– OPPOSITES fast.

dilemma n. **quandary**, predicament, catch-22, vicious circle, plight, mess, muddle; difficulty, problem, trouble, perplexity, confusion, conflict; informal no-win situation, fix, tight spot/corner; Brit. informal sticky wicket.
□ **on the horns of a dilemma** between the devil and the deep blue sea, between Scylla and Charybdis; informal between a rock and a hard place.

dilettante n. **dabbler**, amateur, non-professional, non-specialist, layman, layperson.
– OPPOSITES professional.

diligence n. **conscientiousness**, assiduousness, assiduity, hard work, application, concentration, effort, care, industriousness, rigour, meticulousness, thoroughness; perseverance, persistence, tenacity, dedication, commitment, tirelessness, indefatigability, doggedness.

diligent adj. **industrious**, hard-working, assiduous, conscientious, particular, punctilious, meticulous, painstaking, rigorous, careful, thorough, sedulous, earnest; persevering, persistent, tenacious, zealous, dedicated, committed, unflagging, untiring, tireless, indefatigable, dogged; old use laborious.
– OPPOSITES lazy.

dilly-dally v. informal **waste time**, dally, dawdle, loiter, linger, take one's time, delay, temporize, stall, procrastinate, pussyfoot around, drag one's feet; dither, hesitate, falter, vacillate, waver; Brit. haver, hum and

haw; informal shilly-shally, let the grass grow under one's feet; old use tarry.
– OPPOSITES hurry.

dilute v. **1** *strong bleach can be diluted with water* **make weaker**, weaken, water down; thin out, thin; doctor, adulterate; informal cut. **2** *the original plans have been diluted* **weaken**, moderate, tone down, water down. ▸adj. *a dilute acid.* See **diluted**.

diluted adj. **weak**, dilute, thin, watered down, watery; adulterated.
– OPPOSITES concentrated.

dim adj. **1** *the dim light* **faint**, weak, feeble, soft, pale, dull, subdued, muted, wishy-washy. **2** *long dim corridors* **dark**, badly lit, ill-lit, dingy, dismal, gloomy, murky; literary tenebrous. **3** *a dim figure* **indistinct**, ill-defined, unclear, vague, shadowy, nebulous, obscured, blurred, blurry, fuzzy. **4** *dim memories* **vague**, imprecise, imperfect, unclear, indistinct, sketchy, hazy, blurred, shadowy. **5** informal *I'm awfully dim.* See **stupid** (sense 1). **6** *their prospects for the future looked dim* **gloomy**, unpromising, unfavourable, discouraging, disheartening, depressing, dispiriting, hopeless.
– OPPOSITES bright, distinct, encouraging.
▸v. **1** *the lights were dimmed* **turn down**, lower, dip, soften, subdue, mute; literary bedim. **2** *my memories have not dimmed with time* **fade**, become vague, dwindle, blur. **3** *the fighting dimmed hopes of peace* **diminish**, reduce, lessen, weaken, undermine.
– OPPOSITES brighten, sharpen, intensify.

dimension n. **1** *the dimensions of the room* **size**, measurements, proportions, extent; length, width, breadth, depth, area, volume, capacity; footage, acreage. **2** *the dimension of the problem* **size**, scale, extent, scope, magnitude; importance, significance. **3** *the cultural dimensions of the problem* **aspect**, feature, element, facet, side.

diminish v. **1** *the pain will gradually diminish* **decrease**, lessen, decline, reduce, subside, die down, abate, dwindle, fade, slacken off, moderate, let up, ebb, wane, recede, die away/out, peter out; old use remit. **2** *new legislation diminished the courts' authority* **reduce**, decrease, lessen, curtail, cut, cut down/back, constrict, restrict, limit, curb, check; weaken, blunt, erode, undermine, sap. **3** *she lost no opportunity to diminish him* **belittle**, disparage, denigrate, defame, deprecate, run down; decry, demean, cheapen, devalue; formal derogate.
– OPPOSITES increase.

diminution n. **reduction**, decrease, lessening, decline, dwindling, moderation, fading, weakening, ebb.

diminutive adj. **tiny**, small, little, petite, elfin, minute, miniature, mini, minuscule, compact, pocket, toy, midget, undersized, short; Scottish wee; informal teeny, weeny, teeny-weeny, teensy-weensy, itty-bitty, itsy-bitsy, tiddly, dinky, baby, pint-sized, knee-high to a grasshopper; Brit. informal titchy; N. Amer. informal little-bitty.
– OPPOSITES enormous.

dimple n. **indentation**, hollow, cleft, dint.

dimwit n. informal See **fool** (sense 1 of the noun).

dim-witted adj. informal See **stupid** (senses 1 & 2).

din n. *he shouted above the din* **noise**, racket, rumpus, cacophony, babel, hubbub, tumult, uproar, commotion, clangour, clatter; shouting, yelling, screaming, caterwauling, clamour, outcry; Scottish & N. English stramash; informal hullabaloo; Brit. informal row.
– OPPOSITES silence.
▸v. **1** *she had had the evils of drink dinned into her* **instil**, inculcate, drive, drum, hammer, drill, ingrain; indoctrinate, brainwash. **2** *the sound dinning in my ears* **blare**, blast, clang, clatter, crash, clamour.

dine v. **1** *we dined at a restaurant* **have dinner**, have supper, eat; dated sup, break bread. **2** *they dined on lobster* **eat**, feed on, feast on, banquet on, partake of; informal tuck into.

dingy adj. **gloomy**, dark, dull, badly/poorly lit, murky, dim, dismal, dreary, drab, sombre, grim, cheerless; dirty, grimy, shabby, faded, worn, dowdy, seedy, run down.
– OPPOSITES bright.

dinky adj. Brit. informal **small**, little, petite, dainty, neat, diminutive, mini, miniature; sweet, cute, dear, adorable; Scottish wee; informal teeny, teeny-weeny, teensy-weensy; N. Amer. informal little-bitty.

dinner n. **evening meal**, supper, main meal; lunch; feast, banquet, dinner party; Brit. tea; informal spread, blowout; Brit. informal nosh-up, slap-up meal; formal repast.

dint n. **dent**, indentation, hollow, depression, dip, dimple, cleft, pit.
□ **by dint of** by means of, by virtue of, on account of, as a result of, as a consequence of, owing to, on the strength of, due to, thanks to, by; formal by reason of.

diocese n. **bishopric**, see.

dip v. **1** *he dipped a rag in the water* **immerse**, submerge, plunge, duck, dunk, lower, sink. **2** *the sun dipped below the horizon* **sink**, set, drop, go/drop down, fall, descend; disappear, vanish. **3** *the president's popularity has dipped* **decrease**, fall, drop, fall off, decline, diminish, dwindle, slump, plummet, plunge; informal hit the floor. **4** *the road dipped* **slope down**, descend, go down; drop away, fall, sink. **5** *he dipped his headlights* **dim**, **lower**, turn down. **6** *you might have to dip into your savings* **draw on**, use, make use of, have recourse to, spend. **7** *an interesting book to dip into* **browse through**, skim through, look through, flick through, glance at, peruse, run one's eye over.
– OPPOSITES rise, increase.
▸n. **1** *a relaxing dip in the pool* **swim**, bathe; paddle. **2** *give the fish a ten-minute dip in a salt bath* **immersion**, plunge, ducking, dunking. **3** *chicken satay with peanut dip* **sauce**, relish, dressing. **4** *the hedge at the*

d

bottom of the dip **slope**, incline, decline, descent; hollow, concavity, depression, basin, indentation. **5** *a dip in sales* **decrease**, fall, drop, downturn, decline, falling-off, slump, reduction, diminution, ebb.

diplomacy n. **1** *diplomacy failed to win them independence* **statesmanship**, statecraft, negotiation(s), discussion(s), talks, dialogue; international relations, foreign affairs. **2** *Jack's quiet diplomacy* **tact**, tactfulness, sensitivity, discretion, subtlety, finesse, soft skills, delicacy, savoir faire, politeness, thoughtfulness, care, judiciousness, prudence.

diplomat n. **ambassador**, attaché, consul, chargé d'affaires, envoy, emissary, plenipotentiary; old use legate.

diplomatic adj. **1** *diplomatic activity* **ambassadorial**, consular, foreign-office. **2** *he tried to be diplomatic* **tactful**, sensitive, subtle, delicate, polite, discreet, thoughtful, careful, judicious, prudent, politic, clever, skilful.
– OPPOSITES tactless.

dire adj. **1** *the dire economic situation* **terrible**, dreadful, appalling, frightful, awful, atrocious, grim, alarming; grave, serious, disastrous, ruinous, hopeless, irretrievable, wretched, desperate, parlous; formal grievous. **2** *he was in dire need of help* **urgent**, desperate, pressing, crying, sore, grave, serious, extreme, acute, drastic. **3** *dire warnings of fuel shortages* **ominous**, gloomy, grim, dismal, unpropitious, inauspicious, unfavourable, pessimistic. **4** informal *the concert was dire.* See **awful** (sense 2).

direct adj. **1** *the most direct route* **straight**, undeviating, unswerving; shortest, quickest. **2** *a direct flight* **non-stop**, unbroken, uninterrupted, through. **3** *he is very direct* **frank**, candid, straightforward, honest, open, blunt, plain-spoken, outspoken, forthright, downright, no-nonsense, matter-of-fact, not afraid to call a spade a spade; informal upfront. **4** *direct contact with the president* **face to face**, personal, head-on, immediate, first-hand, tête-à-tête. **5** *a direct quotation* **verbatim**, word for word, to the letter, faithful, exact, precise, accurate, correct. **6** *the direct opposite* **exact**, absolute, complete, diametrical.
▶ v. **1** *an economic elite directed the nation's affairs* **manage**, govern, run, administer, control, conduct, handle, be in charge/control of, preside over, lead, head, rule, be at the helm of, helm; supervise, superintend, oversee, regulate, orchestrate, coordinate; informal run the show, call the shots/tune, be in the driving seat. **2** *was that remark directed at me?* **aim at**, target at, address to, intend for, mean for, design for. **3** *a man in uniform directed them to the hall* **give directions**, show the way, guide, lead, conduct, accompany, usher, escort. **4** *the judge directed the jury to return a not guilty verdict* **instruct**, tell, command, order, charge, require; literary bid.

direction n. **1** *a northerly direction* **way**, route, course, line, run, bearing, orientation. **2** *the newspaper's political direction* **orientation**, inclination, leaning, tendency, bent, bias, preference; drift, tack, attitude, tone, tenor, mood, current, trend. **3** *his direction of the project* **administration**, management, conduct, handling, running, supervision, superintendence, regulation, orchestration; control, command, rule, leadership, guidance. **4** *explicit directions about nursing care* **instruction**, order, command, prescription, rule, regulation, requirement.

directive n. **instruction**, direction, command, order, charge, injunction, prescription, rule, ruling, regulation, law, dictate, decree, dictum, edict, mandate, fiat; formal ordinance.

directly adv. **1** *they flew directly to New York* **straight**, right, as the crow flies, by a direct route. **2** *I went directly after breakfast* **immediately**, at once, instantly, right away, straight away, post-haste, without delay, without hesitation, forthwith; quickly, speedily, promptly; informal pronto. **3** *the houses directly opposite* **exactly**, right, immediately; diametrically; informal bang. **4** *she spoke simply and directly* **frankly**, candidly, openly, bluntly, forthrightly, without beating around the bush.

director n. **administrator**, manager, chairman, chairwoman, chairperson, chair, head, chief, principal, leader, governor, president; managing director, MD, chief executive, CEO; supervisor, controller, overseer; informal boss, kingpin, top dog, gaffer, head honcho, numero uno; N. Amer. informal Mister Big.

directory n. **index**, list, listing, register, catalogue, record, archive, inventory.

dirge n. **elegy**, lament, threnody, requiem, dead march; Irish keen; Irish & Scottish coronach.

dirt n. **1** *his face was streaked with dirt* **grime**, filth; dust, soot, smut; muck, mud, mire, sludge, slime, ooze, dross; smudges, stains; informal crud, yuck, grunge; Brit. informal grot, gunge. **2** *the packed dirt of the road* **earth**, soil, loam, clay, silt; ground. **3** informal *dog dirt.* See **excrement**. **4** informal *they tried to dig up dirt on the President* **scandal**, gossip, revelations, rumour(s); information.

dirty adj. **1** *a dirty sweatshirt | dirty water* **soiled**, grimy, grubby, filthy, mucky, stained, unwashed, greasy, smeared, smeary, spotted, smudged, cloudy, muddy, dusty, sooty; unclean, sullied, impure, tarnished, polluted, contaminated, defiled, foul, unhygienic, insanitary, unsanitary; informal cruddy, yucky, icky; Brit. informal manky, gungy, grotty; literary befouled, besmirched, begrimed. **2** *a dirty joke* **indecent**, obscene, rude, naughty, vulgar, smutty, coarse, crude, filthy, bawdy, suggestive, ribald, racy, salacious, risqué, offensive, off colour, lewd, pornographic, explicit, X-rated; informal blue; euphemistic adult. **3** *dirty tricks* **dishonest**,

deceitful, unscrupulous, dishonourable,
unsporting, ungentlemanly, below the belt,
unfair, unethical, unprincipled; crooked,
double-dealing, underhand, sly, crafty,
devious, sneaky; Brit. informal out of order, not
cricket. **4** informal *a dirty cheat* **despicable**,
contemptible, hateful, vile, low, mean,
unworthy, worthless, beyond contempt,
sordid; informal rotten; old use scurvy. **5** *a dirty
look* **malevolent**, resentful, hostile, black,
dark; angry, cross, indignant, annoyed,
disapproving; informal peeved. **6** *dirty weather*
unpleasant, nasty, foul, inclement, bad;
rough, stormy, squally, gusty, windy, blowy,
rainy; murky, overcast, louring.
– OPPOSITES clean, innocent, honourable,
pleasant.
▶ **v.** *the dog had dirtied her dress* **soil**, stain,
muddy, blacken, mess up, mark, spatter,
bespatter, smudge, smear, splatter; sully,
pollute, foul, defile; literary befoul, besmirch,
begrime.
– OPPOSITES clean.

disability n. **handicap**, disablement,
incapacity, impairment, infirmity, defect,
abnormality; condition, disorder, affliction.

disable v. **1** *an injury that could disable
somebody for life* **incapacitate**, put out of
action, debilitate; handicap, cripple, lame,
maim, immobilize, paralyse. **2** *the bomb
squad disabled the device* **deactivate**, defuse,
disarm. **3** *he was disabled from holding public
office* **disqualify**, prevent, preclude.

disabled adj. **handicapped**, incapacitated;
debilitated, infirm, out of action; crippled,
lame, paralysed, immobilized, bedridden;
euphemistic physically challenged, differently
abled.
– OPPOSITES able-bodied.

disabuse v. **disillusion**, set straight,
open someone's eyes, correct, enlighten,
disenchant, shatter someone's illusions.

disadvantage n. **drawback**, snag,
downside, stumbling block, fly in the
ointment, catch, hindrance, obstacle,
impediment; flaw, defect, weakness, fault,
handicap, con, trouble, difficulty, problem,
complication, nuisance; Brit. disbenefit,
spanner in the works; informal minus.
– OPPOSITES benefit.

disadvantaged adj. **deprived**,
underprivileged, depressed, in need, needy,
poor, impoverished, indigent, hard up; Brit. on
the breadline.

disadvantageous adj. **unfavourable**,
adverse, unfortunate, unlucky, bad;
detrimental, prejudicial, deleterious,
harmful, damaging, injurious, hurtful;
inconvenient, inopportune, ill-timed,
untimely, inexpedient.

disaffected adj. **dissatisfied**, disgruntled,
discontented, malcontent, frustrated,
alienated; disloyal, rebellious, mutinous,
seditious, dissident, up in arms; hostile,
antagonistic, unfriendly.
– OPPOSITES contented.

disagree v. **1** *no one was willing to disagree
with him* **take issue**, challenge, contradict,
oppose; be at variance/odds, not see eye
to eye, differ, dissent, be in dispute,
debate, argue, quarrel, wrangle, clash, be
at loggerheads, cross swords, lock horns;
formal gainsay. **2** *their accounts disagree on
details* **differ**, be dissimilar, be different,
vary, diverge; contradict each other, conflict,
clash, contrast. **3** *the spicy food disagreed
with her* **make ill**, make unwell, nauseate,
sicken, upset.

disagreeable adj. **1** *a disagreeable smell*
unpleasant, displeasing, nasty, offensive,
off-putting, obnoxious, objectionable,
horrible, horrid, dreadful, frightful,
abominable, odious, repugnant, repulsive,
repellent, revolting, disgusting, foul,
vile, nauseating, sickening, unpalatable.
2 *a disagreeable man* **bad-tempered**, ill-
tempered, curmudgeonly, cross, crabbed,
irritable, grumpy, peevish, sullen, prickly;
unfriendly, unpleasant, nasty, mean, mean-
spirited, rude, surly, discourteous, impolite,
brusque, abrupt, churlish, disobliging.
– OPPOSITES pleasant.

disagreement n. **1** *there was some
disagreement over possible solutions* **dissent**,
dispute, difference of opinion, variance,
controversy, disaccord, discord, contention,
division. **2** *a heated disagreement* **argument**,
debate, quarrel, wrangle, squabble, falling-
out, altercation, dispute, disputation, war
of words, contretemps; informal tiff, set-to,
spat, ding-dong; Brit. informal row, barney;
Scottish informal rammy. **3** *the disagreement
between the results of the two assessments*
difference, dissimilarity, variation,
variance, discrepancy, disparity, divergence,
deviation, nonconformity, incompatibility,
contradiction, conflict, clash, contrast; formal
dissimilitude.

disallow v. **reject**, refuse, dismiss, say no
to; ban, bar, block, debar, forbid, prohibit;
cancel, invalidate, overrule, quash, overturn,
countermand, reverse, throw out, set aside;
informal give the thumbs down to.

disappear v. **1** *by 4 o'clock the mist had
disappeared* **vanish**, pass from sight, be
lost to view/sight, recede from view; fade
(away), melt away, clear, dissolve, disperse,
evaporate, dematerialize; literary evanesce.
2 *this way of life has disappeared* **die out**,
die, cease to exist, come to an end, end, pass
away, pass into oblivion, perish, vanish.
– OPPOSITES materialize.

disappoint v. **1** *I'm sorry to have
disappointed you* **let down**, fail, dissatisfy,
dash someone's hopes; upset, dismay,
sadden, disenchant, disillusion, shatter
someone's illusions, disabuse. **2** *his hopes
were disappointed* **thwart**, frustrate, foil,
dash, put a/the damper on; informal throw cold
water on.
– OPPOSITES fulfil.

disappointed adj. **upset**, saddened,
let down, cast down, disheartened,
downhearted, downcast, depressed,

dispirited, discouraged, despondent, dismayed, crestfallen, distressed, chagrined; disenchanted, disillusioned; displeased, discontented, dissatisfied, frustrated, disgruntled; informal choked, miffed, cut up; Brit. informal gutted, as sick as a parrot.
– OPPOSITES pleased.

disappointing adj. **regrettable**, unfortunate, sorry, discouraging, disheartening, dispiriting, depressing, dismaying, upsetting, saddening; dissatisfactory, unsatisfactory; informal not all it's cracked up to be.

disappointment n. **1** *she tried to hide her disappointment* **sadness**, regret, dismay, sorrow; dispiritedness, despondency, distress, chagrin; disenchantment, disillusionment; displeasure, dissatisfaction, disgruntlement. **2** *the trip was a bit of a disappointment* **let-down**, non-event, anticlimax; Brit. damp squib; informal washout, lead balloon.
– OPPOSITES satisfaction.

disapprobation n. See **disapproval**.

disapproval n. **disapprobation**, objection, dislike; dissatisfaction, disfavour, displeasure, distaste, exception; criticism, censure, condemnation, denunciation, deprecation.

disapprove v. **1** *he disapproved of gamblers* **object to**, have a poor opinion of, look down one's nose at, take exception to, dislike, take a dim view of, look askance at, frown on, be against, not believe in; deplore, criticize, censure, condemn, denounce, decry, deprecate. **2** *the board disapproved the plan* **reject**, veto, refuse, turn down, disallow, throw out, dismiss, rule against; informal give the thumbs down to.

disapproving adj. **reproachful**, reproving, critical, censorious, condemnatory, disparaging, denigratory, deprecatory, unfavourable; dissatisfied, displeased, hostile.

disarm v. **1** *the UN must disarm the country* **demilitarize**, demobilize. **2** *the militia refused to disarm* **lay down one's arms**, demilitarize; literary turn swords into ploughshares. **3** *police disarmed the bomb* **defuse**, disable, deactivate, put out of action, make harmless. **4** *the warmth in his voice disarmed her* **win over**, charm, persuade, thaw; mollify, appease, placate, pacify, conciliate, propitiate.

disarmament n. **demilitarization**, demobilization, decommissioning; arms reduction, arms limitation, arms control; the zero option.

disarming adj. **winning**, charming, irresistible, persuasive, beguiling; conciliatory, mollifying.

disarrange v. **disorder**, throw into disarray/disorder, put out of place, disorganize, disturb, displace; mess up, make untidy, make a mess of, jumble, mix up, muddle, turn upside-down, scatter; dishevel, tousle, rumple; informal turn topsy-turvy, make a shambles of; N. Amer. informal muss up.

disarray n. *the room was in disarray* **disorder**, confusion, chaos, untidiness, disorganization, dishevelment, mess, muddle, clutter, jumble, tangle, hotchpotch, shambles.
– OPPOSITES tidiness.
▸ v. *her clothes were disarrayed.* See **disarrange**.

disassemble v. **dismantle**, take apart, take to pieces, take to bits, deconstruct, break up, strip down.

disaster n. **1** *a railway disaster* **catastrophe**, calamity, cataclysm, tragedy, act of God, holocaust; accident. **2** *a string of personal disasters* **misfortune**, mishap, misadventure, mischance, setback, reversal, stroke of bad luck, blow. **3** informal *the film was a disaster* **failure**, fiasco, catastrophe, debacle; informal flop, dud, washout, dead loss.
– OPPOSITES success.

disastrous adj. **catastrophic**, calamitous, cataclysmic, tragic; devastating, ruinous, harmful, dire, terrible, awful, shocking, appalling, dreadful; black, dark, unfortunate, unlucky, ill-fated, ill-starred, inauspicious; formal grievous.

disavow v. **deny**, disclaim, disown, wash one's hands of, repudiate, reject, renounce.

disavowal n. **denial**, rejection, repudiation, renunciation, disclaimer.

disband v. **break up**, disperse, demobilize, dissolve, scatter, separate, go their separate ways, part company.
– OPPOSITES assemble.

disbelief n. **1** *she stared at him in disbelief* **incredulity**, incredulousness, scepticism, doubt, doubtfulness, dubiousness; cynicism, suspicion, distrust, mistrust; formal dubiety. **2** *I'll burn in hell for disbelief* **atheism**, unbelief, godlessness, irreligion, agnosticism, nihilism.

disbelieve v. **not believe**, give no credence to, discredit, discount, doubt, distrust, mistrust, be incredulous, be unconvinced; reject, repudiate, question, challenge; informal take with a pinch of salt.

disbeliever n. **unbeliever**, non-believer, atheist, irreligionist, nihilist; sceptic, doubter, agnostic, doubting Thomas, cynic; rare nullifidian.

disbelieving adj. **incredulous**, doubtful, dubious, unconvinced; distrustful, mistrustful, suspicious, cynical, sceptical.

disburden v. **relieve**, free, liberate, unburden, disencumber, discharge, excuse, absolve.

disburse v. **pay out**, spend, expend, dole out, dish out, hand out, part with, donate, give; informal fork out, shell out, lay out; Brit. informal stump up; N. Amer. informal ante up, pony up.

disc, disk n. **1** *the sun was a huge scarlet disc* **circle**, round, saucer, discus, ring. **2** *an old T-Rex disc* **record**, gramophone record, album, LP, vinyl.

discard v. **dispose of**, throw away/out, get rid of, toss out, jettison, scrap, dispense with, cast aside/off, throw on the scrapheap; reject, repudiate, abandon, drop, have done with, shed; informal chuck (away/out), dump, ditch, bin, junk, get shut of; Brit. informal get shot of; N. Amer. informal trash.
– OPPOSITES keep.

discern v. **perceive**, make out, pick out, detect, recognize, notice, observe, see, spot; identify, determine, distinguish; literary descry, espy.

discernible adj. **visible**, detectable, noticeable, perceptible, observable, distinguishable, recognizable, identifiable; apparent, evident, distinct, appreciable, clear, obvious, manifest, conspicuous.

discerning adj. **discriminating**, judicious, shrewd, clever, astute, intelligent, sharp, selective, sophisticated, tasteful, sensitive, perceptive, percipient, perspicacious, wise, aware, knowing.

discharge v. **1** *he was discharged from the RAF* **dismiss**, eject, expel, throw out, give someone notice, make redundant; release, let go; Military cashier; informal sack, give someone the sack, fire, boot out, give someone the boot, turf out, give someone their cards, give someone their marching orders, give someone the push. **2** *he was discharged from prison* **release**, free, set free, let go, liberate, let out. **3** *oil is routinely discharged from ships* **send out**, release, eject, let out, pour out, void, give off. **4** *the swelling will burst and discharge pus* **emit**, exude, ooze, leak. **5** *he accidentally discharged a pistol* **fire**, shoot, let off; set off, loose off, trigger, explode, detonate. **6** *the ferry was discharging passengers* **unload**, offload, put off; remove; old use unlade. **7** *they discharged their duties efficiently* **carry out**, perform, execute, conduct, do; fulfil, accomplish, achieve, complete. **8** *the executor must discharge the funeral expenses* **pay**, pay off, settle, clear, honour, meet, liquidate, defray, make good; informal square.
– OPPOSITES recruit, imprison, absorb.
▸ n. **1** *his discharge from the service* **dismissal**, release, removal, ejection, expulsion, congé; Military cashiering; informal the sack, the boot. **2** *her discharge from prison* **release**, liberation. **3** *a discharge of diesel oil into the river* **leak**, leakage, emission, release, flow. **4** *a watery discharge from the eyes* **emission**, secretion, excretion, seepage, suppuration; pus, matter; Medicine exudate. **5** *a single discharge of his gun* **shot**, firing, blast; explosion, detonation. **6** *the discharge of their duties* **carrying out**, performance, performing, execution, conduct; fulfilment, accomplishment, completion. **7** *the discharge of all debts* **payment**, repayment, settlement, clearance, meeting, liquidation, defrayal.

disciple n. **1** *the disciples of Jesus* **apostle**, follower. **2** *a disciple of Rousseau* **follower**, adherent, believer, admirer, devotee, acolyte, votary; pupil, student, learner; upholder, supporter, advocate, proponent,

apologist; epigone.

disciplinarian n. **martinet**, hard taskmaster, authoritarian, stickler for discipline; tyrant, despot; N. Amer. ramrod; informal slave-driver.

discipline n. **1** *a lack of proper parental discipline* **control**, training, teaching, instruction, regulation, direction, order, authority, rule, strictness, a firm hand; routine, regimen, drill, drilling. **2** *he was able to maintain discipline among his men* **good behaviour**, orderliness, control, obedience; self-control, self-discipline, self-government, self-restraint. **3** *sociology is a fairly new discipline* **field (of study)**, branch of knowledge, subject, area; speciality, specialty.
▸ v. **1** *she had disciplined herself to ignore the pain* **train**, drill, teach, school, coach; regiment. **2** *she learned to discipline her emotions* **control**, restrain, regulate, govern, keep in check, check, curb, keep a tight rein on, rein in, bridle, tame, bring into line. **3** *he was disciplined by the management* **punish**, penalize, bring to book; reprimand, rebuke, reprove, chastise, upbraid; informal dress down, give someone a dressing-down, rap over the knuckles, give someone a roasting; Brit. informal carpet; formal castigate.

disclaim v. **1** *the school disclaimed responsibility for his death* **deny**, refuse to accept/acknowledge, reject, wash one's hands of. **2** Law *the earl disclaimed his title* **renounce**, relinquish, resign, give up, abandon.
– OPPOSITES accept.

disclose v. **1** *the information must not be disclosed to anyone* **reveal**, make known, divulge, tell, impart, communicate, pass on, vouchsafe; release, make public, broadcast, publish, report, unveil; leak, betray, let slip, let drop, give away; informal let on, blab, spill the beans, let the cat out of the bag; Brit. informal blow the gaff; old use discover, unbosom. **2** *exploratory surgery disclosed an aneurysm* **uncover**, reveal, show, bring to light.
– OPPOSITES conceal.

disclosure n. **1** *she was embarrassed by this unexpected disclosure* **revelation**, declaration, announcement, news, report; exposé, leak. **2** *the disclosure of official information* **publishing**, broadcasting; revelation, communication, release, uncovering, unveiling, exposure; leakage.

discoloration n. **stain**, mark, patch, soiling, streak, spot, blotch, tarnishing; blemish, flaw, defect, bruise, contusion; birthmark, naevus; liver spot, age spot; informal splodge, splotch; Medicine ecchymosis.

discolour v. **stain**, mark, soil, dirty, streak, smear, spot, tarnish, sully, spoil, mar, blemish; blacken, char; fade, bleach.

discoloured adj. **stained**, marked, spotted, dirty, soiled, tarnished, blackened; bleached, faded, yellowed.

discomfit v. **embarrass**, abash, disconcert, nonplus, discompose, discomfort, take aback, unsettle, unnerve, put someone off their stroke, ruffle, confuse, fluster, agitate, disorientate, upset, disturb, perturb, distress; chagrin, mortify; informal faze, rattle; N. Amer. informal discombobulate.

discomfiture n. **embarrassment**, unease, uneasiness, awkwardness, discomfort, discomposure, abashment, confusion, agitation, nervousness, disorientation, perturbation, distress; chagrin, mortification, shame, humiliation; N. Amer. informal discombobulation.

discomfort n. **1** *abdominal discomfort* **pain**, aches and pains, soreness, tenderness, irritation, stiffness; ache, twinge, pang, throb, cramp; Brit. informal gyp. **2** *the discomforts of life at sea* **inconvenience**, difficulty, bother, nuisance, vexation, drawback, disadvantage, trouble, problem, trial, tribulation, hardship; informal hassle. **3** *Ruth flushed and Thomas noticed her discomfort* **embarrassment**, discomfiture, unease, uneasiness, awkwardness, discomposure, confusion, nervousness, perturbation, distress, anxiety; chagrin, mortification, shame, humiliation.
▶v. *his purpose was to discomfort the Prime Minister.* See **discomfit**.

discomposure n. **agitation**, discomfiture, discomfort, uneasiness, unease, confusion, disorientation, perturbation, distress, nervousness; anxiety, worry, consternation, disquiet, disquietude; embarrassment, abashment, chagrin, loss of face; N. Amer. informal discombobulation.

disconcert v. **unsettle**, nonplus, discomfit, throw/catch off balance, take aback, rattle, unnerve, disorient, perturb, disturb, perplex, confuse, bewilder, baffle, fluster, ruffle, shake, upset, agitate, worry, dismay, discountenance; surprise, take by surprise, startle, put someone off (their stroke/ stride), distract; informal throw, faze; N. Amer. informal discombobulate.

disconcerting adj. **unsettling**, unnerving, discomfiting, disturbing, perturbing, troubling, upsetting, worrying, alarming, distracting, off-putting; confusing, bewildering, perplexing.

disconnect v. **1** *the trucks were disconnected from the train* **detach**, disengage, uncouple, decouple, unhook, unhitch, undo, unfasten, unyoke. **2** *she felt as if she had been disconnected from the real world* **separate**, cut off, divorce, sever, isolate, divide, part, disengage, dissociate, remove. **3** *an engineer disconnected the appliance* **deactivate**, shut off, turn off, switch off, unplug.
– OPPOSITES attach.

disconnected adj. **1** *a world that seemed disconnected from reality* **detached**, separate, separated, divorced, cut off, isolated, dissociated, disengaged; apart. **2** *a disconnected narrative* **disjointed**, incoherent, garbled, mixed up, confused, jumbled, rambling, wandering, disorganized, uncoordinated, ill-thought-out.

disconsolate adj. **sad**, unhappy, doleful, woebegone, dejected, downcast, downhearted, despondent, dispirited, crestfallen, cast down, depressed, down, disappointed, disheartened, discouraged, demoralized, low-spirited, forlorn, in the doldrums, melancholy, miserable, long-faced, glum, gloomy; informal blue, choked, down in the mouth, down in the dumps, fed up; literary dolorous.
– OPPOSITES cheerful.

discontent n. **dissatisfaction**, disaffection, discontentment, discontentedness, disgruntlement, grievances, unhappiness, displeasure, bad feelings, resentment, envy; restlessness, unrest, uneasiness, unease, frustration, irritation, annoyance; informal a chip on one's shoulder.
– OPPOSITES satisfaction.

discontented adj. **dissatisfied**, disgruntled, disaffected, discontent, malcontent, unhappy, aggrieved, displeased, resentful, envious; restless, frustrated, irritated, annoyed; informal fed up, fed up to the (back) teeth, browned off, hacked off; Brit. informal cheesed off, brassed off; N. Amer. informal teed off, ticked off.
– OPPOSITES satisfied.

discontinue v. **stop**, end, terminate, put an end to, put a stop to, wind up, finish, call a halt to, cancel, drop, abandon, dispense with, do away with, get rid of, axe, abolish; suspend, interrupt, break off, withdraw; informal cut, pull the plug on, scrap, knock something on the head.

discontinuity n. **disconnectedness**, disconnection, break, disruption, interruption, disjointedness.

discontinuous adj. **intermittent**, sporadic, broken, fitful, interrupted, on and off, disrupted, erratic, disconnected.

discord n. **1** *stress resulting from family discord* **strife**, conflict, friction, hostility, antagonism, antipathy, enmity, bad feeling, ill feeling, bad blood, argument, quarrelling, squabbling, bickering, wrangling, feuding, contention, disagreement, dissension, dispute, difference of opinion, disunity, division, opposition. **2** *the music faded in discord* **dissonance**, discordance, disharmony, cacophony, jangling.
– OPPOSITES accord, harmony.

discordant adj. **1** *the messages from Washington and London were discordant* **different**, in disagreement, at variance, at odds, divergent, discrepant, contradictory, contrary, in conflict, conflicting, opposite, opposed, opposing, clashing; incompatible, inconsistent, irreconcilable. **2** *discordant sounds* **inharmonious**, tuneless, off-key, dissonant, harsh, jarring, grating, jangling, jangly, strident, shrill, screeching, screechy, cacophonous; sharp, flat.
– OPPOSITES harmonious.

discount n. *students get a 10 per cent discount* **reduction**, deduction, markdown, price cut, cut, concession; rebate.
▶ v. **1** *I'd heard rumours, but discounted them* **disregard**, pay no attention to, take no notice of, take no account of, dismiss, ignore, overlook, disbelieve, reject; informal take with a pinch of salt, pooh-pooh. **2** *the RRP is discounted in many stores* **reduce**, mark down, cut, lower; informal knock down. **3** *top Paris hotels discounted 20 per cent off published room rates* **deduct**, take off, rebate; informal knock off, slash.
– OPPOSITES believe, increase.

discountenance v. **1** *she was not discountenanced by the accusation* **disconcert**, discomfit, unsettle, nonplus, throw/catch off balance, take aback, unnerve, disorient, perturb, disturb, perplex, fluster, ruffle, shake, upset, agitate, worry, dismay, discompose, abash; informal throw, faze, rattle; N. Amer. informal discombobulate. **2** *a family environment in which alcohol consumption is discountenanced* **disapprove of**, frown on, take a dim view of, object to.

discourage v. **1** *we want to discourage children from smoking* **deter**, dissuade, disincline, put off, talk out of; advise against, urge against. **2** *she was discouraged by his hostile tone* **dishearten**, dispirit, demoralize, cast down, depress, disappoint, dash someone's hopes; put off, unnerve, daunt, intimidate, cow, crush. **3** *he sought to discourage further conversation* **prevent**, stop, put a stop to, avert, fend off, stave off, ward off; inhibit, hinder, check, curb, put a damper on, throw cold water on.
– OPPOSITES encourage.

discouraged adj. **disheartened**, dispirited, demoralized, deflated, disappointed, let down, disconsolate, despondent, dejected, cast down, downcast, depressed, crestfallen, dismayed, low-spirited, gloomy, glum, pessimistic, unenthusiastic; put off, daunted, intimidated, cowed, crushed; informal down in the mouth, down in the dumps, fed up, unenthused; old use chap-fallen.

discouraging adj. **depressing**, demoralizing, disheartening, dispiriting, disappointing, gloomy, off-putting, unfavourable, unpromising, inauspicious.
– OPPOSITES encouraging.

discourse n. **1** *they prolonged their discourse outside the door* **discussion**, conversation, talk, dialogue, conference, debate, consultation; parley, powwow, chat; informal confab; formal confabulation, colloquy; old use converse. **2** *a discourse on critical theory* **essay**, treatise, dissertation, paper, study, critique, monograph, disquisition, tract; lecture, address, speech, oration; sermon, homily.
▶ v. **1** *he discoursed at length on his favourite topic* **hold forth**, expatiate, pontificate; talk, give a talk, give a speech, lecture, sermonize; preach; informal spout, sound off; formal perorate. **2** *Edward was discoursing with his friends* **converse**, talk, speak, debate, confer,

consult, parley, chat; formal confabulate.

discourteous adj. **rude**, impolite, ill-mannered, bad-mannered, disrespectful, uncivil, unmannerly, unchivalrous, ungentlemanly, unladylike, ill-bred, churlish, boorish, crass, ungracious, graceless, uncouth; insolent, impudent, cheeky, audacious, presumptuous; curt, brusque, blunt, offhand, unceremonious, short, sharp; informal ignorant; old use malapert.
– OPPOSITES polite.

discourtesy n. **rudeness**, impoliteness, ill manners, bad manners, incivility, disrespect, ungraciousness, churlishness, boorishness, ill breeding, uncouthness, crassness; insolence, impudence, impertinence; curtness, brusqueness, abruptness.

discover v. **1** *firemen discovered a body in the debris* **find**, locate, come across/upon, stumble on, chance on, light on, bring to light, uncover, unearth, turn up; track down, run to earth, run to ground. **2** *eventually, I discovered the truth* **find out**, learn, realize, recognize, see, ascertain, work out, fathom out, dig up/out, ferret out, root out; informal figure out, tumble to; Brit. informal twig, rumble, suss out; N. Amer. informal dope out. **3** *scientists discovered a new way of dating fossil crustaceans* **hit on**, come up with, invent, originate, devise, design, contrive, conceive of; pioneer, develop.

discoverer n. **originator**, inventor, creator, deviser, designer; pioneer.

discovery n. **1** *the discovery of the body* **finding**, location, uncovering, unearthing. **2** *the discovery that she was pregnant* **realization**, recognition; revelation, disclosure. **3** *the discovery of new drugs* **invention**, origination, devising; pioneering. **4** *he failed to take out a patent on his discoveries* **find**, finding; invention, breakthrough, innovation.

discredit v. **1** *an attempt to discredit him and his company* **bring into disrepute**, disgrace, dishonour, damage the reputation of, blacken the name of, put/show in a bad light, reflect badly on, compromise, stigmatize, smear, tarnish, taint; N. Amer. slur. **2** *that theory has been discredited* **disprove**, invalidate, explode, drive a coach and horses through, refute; informal debunk, shoot full of holes, blow sky-high; formal confute.
▶ n. **1** *crimes which brought discredit on the administration* **dishonour**, disrepute, disgrace, shame, humiliation, ignominy, infamy, notoriety; censure, blame, reproach, opprobrium; stigma; dated disesteem. **2** *the ships were a discredit to the country* **disgrace**, source of shame, reproach, blot on the escutcheon.
– OPPOSITES honour, glory.

discreditable adj. **dishonourable**, reprehensible, shameful, deplorable, disgraceful, disreputable, blameworthy, ignoble, shabby, objectionable, regrettable, unacceptable, unworthy.
– OPPOSITES praiseworthy.

d

discreet adj. **1** *discreet enquiries* **careful**, circumspect, cautious, wary, chary, guarded; tactful, diplomatic, prudent, judicious, strategic, politic, delicate, sensitive, kid-glove; informal softly-softly. **2** *discreet lighting* **unobtrusive**, inconspicuous, subtle, low-key, understated, subdued, muted, soft, restrained.

discrepancy n. **difference**, disparity, variance, variation, deviation, divergence, disagreement, inconsistency, dissimilarity, mismatch, discordance, incompatibility, conflict; formal dissimilitude.
– OPPOSITES correspondence.

discrete adj. **separate**, distinct, individual, detached, unattached, disconnected, discontinuous, disjunct, disjoined.
– OPPOSITES connected.

discretion n. **1** *you can rely on his discretion* **circumspection**, carefulness, caution, wariness, chariness, guardedness; **tact**, tactfulness, diplomacy, delicacy, sensitivity, prudence, judiciousness. **2** *honorary fellowships awarded at the discretion of the council* **choice**, option, preference, disposition, volition; pleasure, liking, wish, will, inclination, desire.

discretionary adj. **optional**, voluntary, at one's discretion, elective; Law permissive.
– OPPOSITES compulsory.

discriminate v. **1** *he cannot discriminate between fact and opinion* **differentiate**, distinguish, draw a distinction, tell the difference, tell apart; separate, separate the sheep from the goats, separate the wheat from the chaff. **2** *existing employment policies discriminate against women* **be biased**, be prejudiced; treat differently, treat unfairly, put at a disadvantage, disfavour; victimize.

discriminating adj. **discerning**, perceptive, astute, shrewd, judicious, perspicacious, insightful, keen; selective, fastidious, tasteful, refined, sensitive, cultivated, cultured, artistic, aesthetic.
– OPPOSITES indiscriminate.

discrimination n. **1** *racial discrimination* **prejudice**, bias, bigotry, intolerance, narrow-mindedness, unfairness, inequity, favouritism, one-sidedness, partisanship; sexism, chauvinism, racism, racialism, anti-Semitism, heterosexism, ageism, classism; positive discrimination; in S. Africa, historical apartheid. **2** *a man with no discrimination* **discernment**, judgement, perception, perceptiveness, perspicacity, acumen, astuteness, shrewdness, judiciousness, insight; selectivity, (good) taste, fastidiousness, refinement, sensitivity, cultivation, culture.
– OPPOSITES impartiality.

discriminatory adj. **prejudicial**, biased, prejudiced, preferential, unfair, unjust, invidious, inequitable, weighted, one-sided, partisan; sexist, heterosexist, anti-gay, homophobic, chauvinistic, chauvinist, racist, racialist, anti-Semitic, ageist, classist.
– OPPOSITES impartial.

discursive adj. **1** *dull, discursive prose* **rambling**, digressive, meandering, wandering, maundering, diffuse, long, lengthy, wordy, verbose, long-winded, prolix; circuitous, roundabout, circumlocutory; Brit. informal waffly. **2** *an elegant discursive style* **fluent**, flowing, fluid, eloquent, expansive.
– OPPOSITES concise, terse.

discuss v. **1** *I discussed the matter with my wife* **talk over**, talk about, talk through, converse about, debate, confer about, deliberate about, chew over, consider, weigh up, consider the pros and cons of, thrash out; informal kick around/about, bat around/about. **2** *chapter three discusses this topic in detail* **examine**, explore, study, analyse, go into, deal with, treat, consider, concern itself with, tackle.

discussion n. **1** *a long discussion with her husband* **conversation**, talk, dialogue, discourse, conference, debate, exchange of views, consultation, deliberation; powwow, chat, tête-à-tête, heart-to-heart; negotiations, parley; informal confab, chit-chat, rap; N. Amer. informal skull session, bull session; formal confabulation, colloquy; old use converse. **2** *the book's candid discussion of sexual matters* **examination**, exploration, analysis, study; treatment, consideration.

disdain n. *she looked at him with disdain* **contempt**, scorn, scornfulness, contemptuousness, derision, disrespect; disparagement, condescension, superciliousness, hauteur, haughtiness, arrogance, snobbishness, indifference, dismissiveness; distaste, dislike, disgust; old use despite.
– OPPOSITES respect.
▶ v. **1** *she disdained such vulgar exhibitionism* **scorn**, deride, pour scorn on, regard with contempt, sneer at, sniff at, curl one's lip at, look down one's nose at, look down on; despise; informal turn up one's nose at, pooh-pooh; old use contemn. **2** *she disdained his invitation* **spurn**, reject, refuse, rebuff, disregard, ignore, snub; decline, turn down, brush aside.

disdainful adj. **contemptuous**, scornful, derisive, sneering, withering, slighting, disparaging, disrespectful, condescending, patronizing, supercilious, haughty, superior, arrogant, proud, snobbish, lordly, aloof, indifferent, dismissive; informal high and mighty, hoity-toity, sniffy, snotty; old use contumelious.

disease n. **illness**, sickness, ill health; infection, ailment, malady, disorder, complaint, affliction, condition, indisposition, upset, problem, trouble, infirmity, disability, defect, abnormality; pestilence, plague, cancer, canker, blight; informal bug, virus; Brit. informal lurgy; dated contagion.

WORD LINKS

pathological relating to or caused by disease
morbid relating to or indicating disease
pathology the branch of medicine concerned

with the causes and effects of disease
epidemiology the study of the spread and control of disease
aetiology the cause of a disease
prophylactic intended to prevent disease
quarantine a period of isolation for people or animals that may have a disease.
See also **illness**.

diseased adj. **unhealthy**, ill, sick, unwell, ailing, sickly, unsound; infected, septic, contaminated, blighted, rotten, bad, abnormal.

disembark v. **get off**, step off, leave, alight, pile out; go ashore, debark, detrain; land, arrive; N. Amer. deplane.

disembodied adj. **bodiless**, incorporeal, discarnate, spiritual; intangible, insubstantial, impalpable; ghostly, spectral, phantom, wraithlike.

disembowel v. **gut**, draw, remove the guts from; formal eviscerate.

disenchanted adj. **disillusioned**, disappointed, disabused, let down, dissatisfied, discontented; cynical, soured, jaundiced, sick, out of love, indifferent; informal fed up.

disenchantment n. **disillusionment**, disappointment, dissatisfaction, discontent, discontentedness, rude awakening; cynicism.

disengage v. **1** *I disengaged his hand from mine* **remove**, detach, disentangle, extricate, separate, release, free, loosen, loose, disconnect, unfasten, unclasp, uncouple, undo, unhook, unhitch, untie, unyoke. **2** *American forces disengaged from the country* **withdraw**, leave, pull out of, quit, retreat from.
– OPPOSITES attach, enter.

disentangle v. **1** *Allen was disentangling a coil of rope* **untangle**, unravel, untwist, unwind, undo, untie, straighten out, smooth out; comb, card. **2** *he disentangled his fingers from her hair* **extricate**, extract, free, remove, disengage, untwine, release, loosen, detach, unfasten, unclasp, disconnect.

disfavour n. **disapproval**, disapprobation; dislike, displeasure, distaste, dissatisfaction, low opinion; dated disesteem; old use disrelish.

disfigure v. **mar**, spoil, deface, scar, blemish, uglify; damage, injure, impair, blight, mutilate, deform, maim, ruin; vandalize.
– OPPOSITES adorn.

disfigurement n. **1** *the disfigurement of Victorian buildings* **defacement**, spoiling, scarring, uglification, mutilation, damage, vandalizing, ruin. **2** *a permanent facial disfigurement* **blemish**, flaw, defect, imperfection, discoloration, blotch; scar, pockmark; deformity, malformation, abnormality, injury, wound.

disgorge v. **1** *the combine disgorged a stream of grain* **pour out**, discharge, eject, throw out, emit, expel, spit out, spew out, belch forth, spout; vomit, regurgitate. **2** *they were made to disgorge all the profits* **surrender**, relinquish, hand over, give up, turn over, yield.

disgrace n. **1** *he brought disgrace on the family* **dishonour**, shame, discredit, ignominy, degradation, disrepute, ill-repute, infamy, scandal, stigma, opprobrium, obloquy, condemnation, vilification, contempt, disrespect; humiliation, embarrassment, loss of face; Austral. strife; dated disesteem. **2** *the unemployment figures are a disgrace* **scandal**, outrage; discredit, reproach, affront, insult; stain, blemish, blot, blot on the escutcheon, black mark; informal crime, sin.
– OPPOSITES honour.
▸ v. **1** *you have disgraced the family name* **bring shame on**, shame, dishonour, discredit, bring into disrepute, degrade, debase, defame, stigmatize, taint, sully, tarnish, besmirch, stain, blacken, drag through the mud/mire. **2** *he was publicly disgraced* **discredit**, dishonour, stigmatize; humiliate, cause to lose face, chasten, humble, demean, put someone in their place, take down a peg or two, cut down to size.
– OPPOSITES honour.
□ **in disgrace** out of favour, unpopular, in bad odour, under a cloud, disgraced; informal in someone's bad/black books, in the doghouse; NZ informal in the dogbox.

disgraceful adj. **shameful**, shocking, scandalous, deplorable, despicable, contemptible, beyond contempt, beyond the pale, dishonourable, discreditable, reprehensible, base, mean, low, blameworthy, unworthy, ignoble, shabby, inglorious, outrageous, abominable, atrocious, appalling, dreadful, terrible, disgusting, shameless, vile, odious, monstrous, heinous, iniquitous, unspeakable, loathsome, sordid, nefarious; old use scurvy.
– OPPOSITES admirable.

disgruntled adj. **dissatisfied**, discontented, aggrieved, resentful, displeased, unhappy, disappointed, disaffected; angry, irate, annoyed, cross, exasperated, indignant, vexed, irritated, piqued, irked, put out; informal peeved, miffed, fed up, aggravated, hacked off, browned off, riled, peed off, hot under the collar, in a huff; Brit. informal cheesed off, shirty, narked, not best pleased; N. Amer. informal sore, teed off, ticked off.

disguise v. *his controlled voice disguised his true feelings* **camouflage**, conceal, hide, cover up, dissemble, mask, screen, shroud, veil, cloak; paper over, gloss over, put up a smokescreen.
– OPPOSITES expose.
□ **disguise oneself as** dress up as, pretend to be, pass oneself off as, impersonate, pose as; formal personate.

disguised adj. **in disguise**, camouflaged; incognito, under cover.

disgust n. *a look of disgust* **revulsion**, repugnance, aversion, distaste, nausea, abhorrence, loathing, detestation, odium, horror; contempt, outrage; old use disrelish.
– OPPOSITES delight.
▸ v. **1** *the hospital food disgusted me* **revolt**,

d

repel, repulse, sicken, nauseate, turn someone's stomach, make someone's gorge rise; informal turn off; N. Amer. informal gross out. **2** *Toby's behaviour disgusted her* **outrage**, shock, horrify, appal, scandalize, offend.

disgusting adj. **1** *the food was disgusting* **revolting**, repellent, repulsive, sickening, nauseating, stomach-churning, stomach-turning, off-putting, unpalatable, distasteful, foul, nasty; N. Amer. vomitous; informal yucky, icky, gross, rank, sick-making. **2** *I find racism disgusting* **abhorrent**, loathsome, offensive, appalling, outrageous, objectionable, shocking, horrifying, scandalous, monstrous, unspeakable, shameful, vile, odious, obnoxious, detestable, hateful, sickening, contemptible, despicable, deplorable, abominable, beyond the pale; informal gross, ghastly, sick.
– OPPOSITES delicious, appealing.

dish n. **1** *a china dish* **bowl**, plate, platter, salver, paten; container, receptacle; historical porringer; old use trencher, charger. **2** *vegetarian dishes* **recipe**, meal, course; (**dishes**) food, fare. **3** informal *she's quite a dish.* See **beauty** (sense 2).
□ **dish something out** distribute, dispense, issue, hand out/round, give out, pass out/round; deal out, dole out, share out, allocate, allot, apportion.
dish something up serve (up), spoon out, ladle out, scoop out.

disharmony n. **discord**, friction, strife, conflict, hostility, acrimony, bad blood, bad feeling, enmity, dissension, disagreement, feuding, quarrelling; disunity, division, divisiveness.

dishearten v. **discourage**, dispirit, demoralize, cast down, depress, disappoint, dismay, dash someone's hopes; put off, deter, unnerve, daunt, intimidate, cow, crush.
– OPPOSITES encourage.

disheartened adj. **discouraged**, dispirited, demoralized, deflated, disappointed, let down, disconsolate, despondent, dejected, cast down, downcast, depressed, crestfallen, dismayed, low-spirited, gloomy, glum, pessimistic, unenthusiastic; daunted, intimidated, cowed, crushed; informal down in the mouth, down in the dumps, fed up, unenthused; old use chap-fallen.

dishevelled adj. **untidy**, unkempt, scruffy, messy, in a mess, disordered, disarranged, rumpled, bedraggled; uncombed, tousled, tangled, tangly, knotted, knotty, shaggy, straggly, windswept, wind-blown, wild; slovenly, slatternly, blowsy, frowzy; informal ratty; N. Amer. informal mussed (up); old use draggle-tailed.
– OPPOSITES tidy.

dishonest adj. **fraudulent**, corrupt, swindling, cheating, double-dealing; underhand, crafty, cunning, devious, treacherous, unfair, unjust, dirty, unethical, immoral, dishonourable, untrustworthy, unscrupulous, unprincipled, amoral; criminal, illegal, unlawful; false, untruthful,

deceitful, deceiving, lying, mendacious; informal crooked, shady, tricky, sharp, shifty; Brit. informal bent, dodgy; Austral./NZ informal shonky; literary perfidious.

dishonesty n. **fraud**, fraudulence, sharp practice, corruption, cheating, chicanery, double-dealing, deceit, deception, duplicity, lying, falseness, falsity, falsehood, untruthfulness; craft, cunning, trickery, artifice, underhandedness, subterfuge, skulduggery, treachery, untrustworthiness, unscrupulousness, criminality, misconduct; informal crookedness, dirty tricks, shenanigans; Brit. informal jiggery-pokery; literary perfidy.
– OPPOSITES probity.

dishonour n. *the incident brought dishonour upon the police profession* **disgrace**, shame, discredit, humiliation, degradation, ignominy, scandal, infamy, disrepute, ill repute, loss of face, disfavour, ill favour, debasement, opprobrium, obloquy; stigma; dated disesteem.
▶ v. *his family name has been dishonoured* **disgrace**, shame, discredit, bring into disrepute, humiliate, degrade, debase, lower, cheapen, drag down, drag through the mud, blacken the name of, give a bad name to; sully, stain, taint, besmirch, smear, mar, blot, stigmatize.

dishonourable adj. **disgraceful**, shameful, disreputable, discreditable, degrading, ignominious, ignoble, blameworthy, contemptible, despicable, reprehensible, shabby, shoddy, sordid, sorry, base, low, improper, unseemly, unworthy; unprincipled, unscrupulous, corrupt, untrustworthy, treacherous, traitorous; informal shady, dirty; literary perfidious; old use scurvy.

disillusion v. **disabuse**, enlighten, set straight, open someone's eyes; disenchant, shatter someone's illusions, disappoint, make sadder and wiser.
– OPPOSITES deceive.

disillusioned adj. **disenchanted**, disabused, disappointed, let down, discouraged; cynical, sour, negative, world-weary.

disincentive n. **deterrent**, check, discouragement, damper, brake, curb, restraint, inhibitor; obstacle, impediment, hindrance, obstruction, block, barrier.

disinclination n. **reluctance**, unwillingness, lack of enthusiasm, indisposition, hesitancy; aversion, dislike, distaste; objection, demur, resistance, opposition; old use disrelish.
– OPPOSITES enthusiasm.

disinclined adj. **reluctant**, unwilling, unenthusiastic, unprepared, indisposed, ill-disposed, not in the mood, hesitant; loath, averse, antipathetic, resistant, opposed.
– OPPOSITES willing.

disinfect v. **sterilize**, sanitize, clean, cleanse, purify, decontaminate; fumigate.
– OPPOSITES contaminate.

disinfectant n. **antiseptic**, bactericide, germicide, sterilizer, cleanser, decontaminant; fumigant.

disingenuous adj. **insincere**, dishonest, untruthful, false, deceitful, duplicitous, lying, mendacious; hypocritical; old use hollow-hearted.

disinherit v. **cut someone out of one's will**, cut off, dispossess; disown, repudiate, reject, cast off/aside, wash one's hands of, have nothing more to do with, turn one's back on; informal cut off without a penny.

disintegrate v. **break up**, break apart, fall apart, fall to pieces, fragment, fracture, shatter, splinter; explode, blow up, blow apart, fly apart; crumble, deteriorate, decay, decompose, rot, moulder, perish, dissolve, collapse, go to rack and ruin, degenerate; informal bust, be smashed to smithereens.

disinter v. **exhume**, unearth, dig up, disentomb.

disinterest n. **1** *scholarly disinterest* **impartiality**, neutrality, objectivity, detachment, disinterestedness, lack of bias, lack of prejudice; open-mindedness, fairness, fair-mindedness, equity, balance, even-handedness. **2** *he looked at us with complete disinterest* **indifference**, lack of interest, unconcern, impassivity; boredom, apathy.
– OPPOSITES bias.

disinterested adj. **1** *disinterested advice* **unbiased**, unprejudiced, impartial, neutral, non-partisan, detached, uninvolved, objective, dispassionate, impersonal, clinical; open-minded, fair, just, equitable, balanced, even-handed, with no axe to grind, without fear or favour. **2** *he looked at her with disinterested eyes* **uninterested**, indifferent, incurious, unconcerned, unmoved, unresponsive, impassive, passive, detached, unenthusiastic, lukewarm, bored, apathetic; informal couldn't-care-less.

disjointed adj. **unconnected**, disconnected, disunited, discontinuous, fragmented, disorganized, disordered, muddled, mixed up, jumbled, garbled, incoherent, confused; rambling, wandering.

dislike v. *a man she had always disliked* **find distasteful**, regard with distaste, be averse to, have an aversion to, have no liking/taste for, disapprove of, object to, take exception to; hate, detest, loathe, abhor, despise, be unable to bear/stand, shrink from, shudder at, find repellent; informal be unable to stomach; formal abominate; old use disrelish.
▶ n. *she viewed the other woman with dislike* **distaste**, aversion, disfavour, disapproval, disapprobation, enmity, animosity, hostility, antipathy, antagonism; hate, hatred, detestation, loathing, disgust, repugnance, abhorrence, disdain, contempt; old use disrelish.

dislocate v. **1** *she dislocated her hip* **put out of joint**; informal put out; Medicine luxate. **2** *trade was dislocated by a famine* **disrupt**, disturb, throw into disarray, throw into confusion, play havoc with, interfere with,

disorganize, upset; informal mess up.

dislodge v. **1** *replace any stones you dislodge* **displace**, knock out of place/position, move, shift; knock over, upset. **2** *economic sanctions failed to dislodge the dictator* **remove**, force out, drive out, oust, eject, get rid of, evict, unseat, depose, topple, drum out; informal kick out, boot out; Brit. informal turf out.

disloyal adj. **unfaithful**, faithless, false, false-hearted, untrue, inconstant, untrustworthy, unreliable, undependable, fickle; treacherous, traitorous, subversive, seditious, unpatriotic, two-faced, double-dealing, double-crossing, deceitful; dissident, renegade; adulterous; informal back-stabbing, two-timing; literary perfidious; old use hollow-hearted.

disloyalty n. **unfaithfulness**, infidelity, inconstancy, faithlessness, fickleness, unreliability, untrustworthiness, betrayal, falseness; duplicity, double-dealing, treachery, treason, subversion, sedition, dissidence; adultery; informal back-stabbing, two-timing; literary perfidy, perfidiousness.

dismal adj. **1** *a dismal look* **gloomy**, glum, melancholy, morose, doleful, woebegone, forlorn, dejected, depressed, dispirited, downcast, despondent, disconsolate, miserable, sad, unhappy, sorrowful, desolate, wretched; informal blue, fed up, down in the dumps/mouth; literary dolorous. **2** *a dismal hall* **dingy**, dim, dark, gloomy, dreary, drab, dull, bleak, cheerless, depressing, uninviting, unwelcoming. **3** informal *a dismal performance.* See **poor** (sense 2).
– OPPOSITES cheerful, bright.

dismantle v. **take apart**, take to pieces/bits, pull apart, pull to pieces, disassemble, break up, strip (down); knock down, pull down, demolish.
– OPPOSITES assemble, build.

dismay v. *he was dismayed by the change in his friend* **appal**, horrify, shock, shake (up); disconcert, take aback, alarm, unnerve, unsettle, throw off balance, discompose; disturb, upset, distress; informal rattle, faze, knock sideways; Brit. informal knock for six.
– OPPOSITES encourage, please.
▶ n. *they greeted his decision with dismay* **alarm**, shock, surprise, consternation, distress, concern, perturbation, disquiet, discomposure.
– OPPOSITES pleasure, relief.

dismember v. **disjoint**, joint; pull apart, cut up, chop up, butcher.

dismiss v. **1** *the president dismissed five ministers* **give someone their notice**, get rid of, discharge; lay off, make redundant; informal sack, give someone the sack, fire, boot out, give someone the boot/elbow/push, give someone their marching orders, show someone the door; Brit. informal give someone their cards; Military cashier. **2** *the guards were dismissed* **send away**, let go; disband, dissolve, discharge. **3** *he dismissed all morbid thoughts* **banish**, set aside, disregard, brush

off, shrug off, put out of one's mind; reject, deny, repudiate, spurn.
– OPPOSITES engage.

dismissal n. **1** *the threat of dismissal* **one's notice**, discharge; redundancy, laying off; informal the sack, sacking, firing, the push, the boot, the axe, the elbow, one's marching orders; Brit. informal one's cards, the chop; Military cashiering. **2** *a condescending dismissal* **rejection**, repudiation, repulse, non-acceptance.
– OPPOSITES recruitment.

dismissive adj. **contemptuous**, disdainful, scornful, sneering, snide, disparaging, negative; informal sniffy.
– OPPOSITES admiring.

dismount v. **1** *the cyclist dismounted* **alight**, get off/down. **2** *the horse dismounted the trooper* **unseat**, dislodge, throw, unhorse.

disobedient adj. **insubordinate**, unruly, wayward, badly behaved, naughty, delinquent, disruptive, troublesome, rebellious, defiant, mutinous, recalcitrant, uncooperative, wilful, intractable, obstreperous; Brit. informal bolshie; old use contumacious.

disobey v. **defy**, go against, flout, contravene, infringe, transgress, violate; disregard, ignore, pay no heed to.

disobliging adj. **unhelpful**, uncooperative, unaccommodating, unamenable, unreasonable, awkward, difficult; discourteous, uncivil, unfriendly.
– OPPOSITES helpful.

disorder n. **1** *he hates disorder* **untidiness**, disorderliness, mess, disarray, chaos, confusion; clutter, jumble; a muddle, a shambles. **2** *incidents of public disorder* **unrest**, disturbance, disruption, upheaval, turmoil, mayhem, pandemonium; violence, fighting, rioting, lawlessness, anarchy; breach of the peace, fracas, rumpus, melee; Law, dated affray; informal aggro. **3** *a blood disorder* **disease**, infection, complaint, condition, affliction, malady, sickness, illness, ailment, infirmity, irregularity.
– OPPOSITES tidiness, peace.

disordered adj. **1** *her grey hair was disordered* **untidy**, unkempt, messy, in a mess; disorganized, chaotic, confused, jumbled, muddled; N. Amer. informal mussed (up); Brit. informal shambolic. **2** *a disordered digestive system* **dysfunctional**, disturbed, unsettled, unbalanced, upset, poorly.

disorderly adj. **1** *a disorderly desk* **untidy**, disorganized, messy, cluttered; in disarray, in a mess, in a jumble, in a muddle, at sixes and sevens; informal like a bomb's hit it, higgledy-piggledy; Brit. informal shambolic. **2** *disorderly behaviour* **unruly**, boisterous, rough, rowdy, wild, riotous; disruptive, troublesome, undisciplined, lawless, unmanageable, uncontrollable, out of hand, out of control.
– OPPOSITES tidy, docile.

disorganized adj. **1** *a disorganized tool box* **disorderly**, disordered, unorganized, jumbled, muddled, untidy, messy, chaotic,

topsy-turvy, haphazard; in disorder, in disarray, in a mess, in a muddle, in a shambles; informal higgledy-piggledy; Brit. informal shambolic. **2** *muddled and disorganized* **unmethodical**, unsystematic, undisciplined, badly organized, inefficient; haphazard, careless, sloppy, slapdash; informal hit-or-miss.
– OPPOSITES orderly.

disorientated, **disoriented** adj. **confused**, bewildered, (all) at sea; lost, adrift, off-course, having lost one's bearings; informal not knowing whether one is coming or going; old use mazed.

disown v. **reject**, cast off/aside, abandon, renounce, deny; turn one's back on, wash one's hands of, have nothing more to do with; literary forsake.

disparage v. **belittle**, denigrate, deprecate, play down, trivialize, make light of, undervalue, underrate; ridicule, deride, mock, scorn, scoff at, sneer at; run down, defame, discredit, speak badly of, cast aspersions on, impugn, vilify, traduce, criticize; N. Amer. informal slur; informal do down, pick holes in, knock, slam, pan, bad-mouth, pooh-pooh; Brit. informal rubbish, slate; formal calumniate, derogate.
– OPPOSITES praise, overrate.

disparaging adj. **derogatory**, deprecatory, denigratory, belittling; critical, scathing, negative, unfavourable, uncomplimentary, uncharitable; contemptuous, scornful, snide, disdainful; informal bitchy, catty; old use contumelious.
– OPPOSITES complimentary.

disparate adj. **contrasting**, different, differing, dissimilar, unalike, poles apart; varying, various, diverse, diversified, heterogeneous, distinct, separate, divergent; literary divers.
– OPPOSITES homogen(e)ous.

disparity n. **discrepancy**, inconsistency, imbalance; variance, variation, divergence, gap, gulf; difference, dissimilarity, contrast; formal dissimilitude.
– OPPOSITES similarity.

dispassionate adj. **1** *a calm, dispassionate manner* **unemotional**, emotionless, impassive, cool, calm, {cool, calm, and collected}, unruffled, unperturbed, composed, self-possessed, self-controlled, unexcitable; informal laid-back. **2** *a dispassionate analysis* **objective**, detached, neutral, disinterested, impartial, non-partisan, unbiased, unprejudiced; scientific, analytical.
– OPPOSITES emotional, biased.

dispatch v. **1** *all the messages were dispatched* **send (off)**, post, mail, forward, transmit. **2** *the business was dispatched in the morning* **deal with**, finish, conclude, settle, discharge, perform; expedite, push through; informal make short work of. **3** *the good guy dispatched a host of villains* **kill**, put to death, take/end the life of; slaughter, butcher, massacre, wipe out, exterminate, eliminate;

murder, assassinate, execute; informal bump off, do in, do away with, top, take out, blow away; N. Amer. informal ice, rub out, waste; literary slay.

▶n. **1** *goods ready for dispatch* **sending**, posting, mailing. **2** *efficiency and dispatch* **promptness**, speed, speediness, swiftness, rapidity, briskness, haste, hastiness; literary fleetness, celerity; formal expedition. **3** *the latest dispatch from the front* **communication**, communiqué, bulletin, report, statement, letter, message; news, intelligence; informal memo, info, low-down; literary tidings. **4** *the capture and dispatch of the wolf* **killing**, slaughter, massacre, extermination, elimination; murder, assassination, execution; literary slaying.

dispel v. **banish**, eliminate, drive away/off, get rid of; relieve, allay, ease, quell.

dispensable adj. **expendable**, disposable, replaceable, inessential, non-essential; unnecessary, redundant, superfluous, surplus to requirements.

dispensation n. **1** *the dispensation of supplies* **distribution**, supply, supplying, issue, issuing, handing out, doling out, dishing out, sharing out, dividing out; division, allocation, allotment, apportionment. **2** *the dispensation of justice* **administration**, administering, delivery, discharge, dealing out, meting out. **3** *dispensation from National Insurance contributions* **exemption**, immunity, exception, exoneration, reprieve, remission; informal a let-off. **4** *the new constitutional dispensation* **system**, order, arrangement, organization.

dispense v. **1** *servants dispensed the drinks* **distribute**, pass round, hand out, dole out, dish out, share out; allocate, supply, allot, apportion. **2** *the soldiers dispensed summary justice* **administer**, deliver, issue, discharge, deal out, mete out. **3** *dispensing medicines* **prepare**, make up; supply, provide, sell. **4** *the pope dispensed him from his impediment* **exempt**, excuse, except, release, let off, reprieve, absolve.
□ **dispense with 1** *let's dispense with the formalities* **waive**, omit, drop, leave out, forgo; do away with; informal give something a miss. **2** *he dispensed with his crutches* **get rid of**, throw away/out, dispose of, discard; manage without, cope without; informal ditch, scrap, dump, chuck out/away, get shut of; Brit. informal get shot of.

disperse v. **1** *the crowd began to disperse* | *police dispersed the demonstrators* **break up**, split up, disband, scatter, leave, go their separate ways; drive away/off, chase away. **2** *the fog finally dispersed* **dissipate**, dissolve, melt away, fade away, clear, lift. **3** *seeds dispersed by birds* **scatter**, disseminate, distribute, spread, broadcast.
– OPPOSITES assemble, gather.

dispirited adj. **disheartened**, discouraged, demoralized, downcast, low, low-spirited, dejected, downhearted, depressed, disconsolate; informal fed up; Brit. informal

cheesed off.
– OPPOSITES heartened.

dispiriting adj. **disheartening**, depressing, discouraging, daunting, demoralizing.

displace v. **1** *roof tiles displaced by gales* **dislodge**, dislocate, move, shift, reposition; move out of place, knock out of place/position. **2** *the minister was displaced* **depose**, dislodge, unseat, remove (from office), dismiss, eject, oust, expel, force out, drive out; overthrow, topple, bring down; informal boot out, give someone the boot, show someone the door; Brit. informal turf out; dated out. **3** *English displaced the local language* **replace**, take the place of, supplant, supersede.
– OPPOSITES replace, reinstate.

display n. **1** *a display of dolls and puppets* | *a motorcycle display* **exhibition**, exposition, array, arrangement, presentation, demonstration; spectacle, show, parade, pageant. **2** *they vied to outdo each other in display* **ostentation**, ostentatiousness, showiness, extravagance, flamboyance, lavishness, splendour; informal swank, flashiness, glitziness. **3** *his display of concern* **manifestation**, expression, show.
▶v. **1** *the Crown Jewels are displayed in London* **exhibit**, show, put on show/view; arrange, array, present, lay out, set out. **2** *the play displays his many theatrical talents* **show off**, parade, flaunt, reveal; publicize, make known, call/draw attention to; informal hype. **3** *she displayed a vein of sharp humour* **manifest**, show evidence of, reveal; demonstrate, show; formal evince.
– OPPOSITES conceal.

displease v. **annoy**, irritate, anger, irk, vex, pique, gall, nettle; put out, upset; informal aggravate, peeve, needle, bug, rile, miff, hack off; N. Amer. informal tee off, tick off.

displeasure n. **annoyance**, irritation, crossness, anger, vexation, pique, rancour; dissatisfaction, discontent, discontentedness, disgruntlement, disapproval; informal aggravation.
– OPPOSITES satisfaction.

disposable adj. **1** *disposable plates* **throwaway**, expendable, one-use. **2** *disposable income* **available**, usable, spendable.

disposal n. **1** *rubbish ready for disposal* **throwing away**, discarding, jettisoning, scrapping; informal dumping, ditching, chucking (out/away). **2** *we have twenty copies for disposal* **distribution**, handing out, giving out/away, allotment, allocation. **3** *the disposal of the troops in two lines* **arrangement**, arranging, positioning, placement, lining up, disposition, grouping; Military dressing.
□ **at someone's disposal** for use by, in reserve for, in the hands of, in the possession of.

dispose v. **1** *he disposed his attendants in a circle* **arrange**, place, put, position, array, set up, form; marshal, gather, group;

Military dress. **2** *the experience disposed him to be kind* **incline**, encourage, persuade, predispose, make willing, prompt, lead, motivate; sway, influence.
□ **dispose of 1** *the waste was disposed of* **throw away/out**, get rid of, discard, jettison, scrap; informal dump, ditch, chuck (out/away), get shut of; Brit. informal get shot of; N. Amer. informal trash. **2** *he had disposed of all his assets* **part with**, give away, hand over, deliver up, transfer; sell, auction; informal get shut of; Brit. informal get shot of. **3** informal *she disposed of a fourth cake.* See **consume** (sense 1). **4** informal *he robbed her and then disposed of her.* See **kill** (sense 1 of the verb).

disposed adj. **1** *they are philanthropically disposed* **inclined**, predisposed, minded. **2** *we are not disposed to argue* **willing**, inclined, prepared, ready, minded, in the mood. **3** *he was disposed to be cruel* **liable**, apt, inclined, likely, predisposed, prone, tending; capable of.

disposition n. **1** *a nervous disposition* **temperament**, nature, character, constitution, make-up, mentality. **2** *his disposition to clemency* **inclination**, tendency, proneness, propensity, proclivity. **3** *the disposition of the armed forces* **arrangement**, positioning, placement, configuration; set-up, line-up, layout, array; marshalling, mustering, grouping; Military dressing. **4** Law *the disposition of the company's property* **distribution**, disposal, allocation, transfer; sale, auction.
□ **at someone's disposition** at the disposal of, for use by, in reserve for, in the hands of, in the possession of.

dispossess v. **divest**, strip, rob, cheat out of, deprive; informal do out of; old use reave.

disproportionate adj. **out of proportion to**, not appropriate to, not commensurate with; inordinate, unreasonable, excessive, undue.

disprove v. **refute**, prove false, rebut, falsify, debunk, negate, invalidate, contradict, confound, controvert, negative, discredit; informal shoot full of holes, blow out of the water; formal confute, gainsay.

disputable adj. **debatable**, open to debate/question, arguable, contestable, moot, questionable, doubtful, controvertible; informal iffy.

disputation n. **debate**, discussion, dispute, argument, arguing, altercation, dissension, disagreement, controversy; polemics.

dispute n. **1** *a subject of dispute* **debate**, discussion, disputation, argument, controversy, disagreement, quarrelling, dissension, conflict, friction, strife, discord. **2** *they have settled their dispute* **quarrel**, argument, altercation, squabble, falling-out, disagreement, difference of opinion, clash, wrangle; informal tiff, spat, scrap; Brit. informal row, barney, ding-dong; N. Amer. informal rhubarb; old use broil.
– OPPOSITES agreement.
▸ v. **1** *George disputed with him* **debate**,

discuss, exchange views; quarrel, argue, disagree, clash, fall out, wrangle, bicker, squabble; informal have words; old use altercate. **2** *they disputed his proposals* **challenge**, contest, question, call into question, impugn, quibble over, contradict, controvert, argue about, disagree with, take issue with; formal gainsay.
– OPPOSITES accept.

disqualified adj. **banned**, barred, debarred; ineligible.
– OPPOSITES allowed.

disquiet n. *grave public disquiet* **unease**, uneasiness, worry, anxiety, anxiousness, concern, disquietude; perturbation, consternation, upset, malaise, angst; agitation, restlessness, fretfulness; informal jitteriness.
– OPPOSITES calm.
▸ v. *I was disquieted by the news* **perturb**, agitate, upset, disturb, unnerve, unsettle, discompose, disconcert; make uneasy, worry, make anxious; trouble, concern, make fretful, make restless.

disquisition n. **essay**, dissertation, treatise, paper, tract, article; discussion, lecture, address, presentation, speech, talk.

disregard v. *Annie disregarded the remark* **ignore**, take no notice of, pay no attention/heed to; overlook, turn a blind eye to, turn a deaf ear to, shut one's eyes to, gloss over, brush off/aside, shrug off.
– OPPOSITES heed.
▸ n. *blithe disregard for the rules* **indifference**, non-observance, inattention, heedlessness, neglect.
– OPPOSITES attention.

disrepair n. **dilapidation**, decrepitude, shabbiness, ricketiness, collapse, ruin; abandonment, neglect, disuse.

disreputable adj. **1** *he fell into disreputable company* **of bad reputation**, infamous, notorious, louche; dishonourable, dishonest, untrustworthy, unwholesome, villainous, corrupt, immoral; unsavoury, slippery, seedy, sleazy; informal crooked, shady, shifty; Brit. informal dodgy. **2** *filthy and disreputable* **scruffy**, shabby, down at heel, seedy, untidy, unkempt, dishevelled.
– OPPOSITES respectable, smart.

disrepute n. **disgrace**, shame, dishonour, infamy, notoriety, ignominy, bad reputation; humiliation, discredit, ill repute, low esteem, opprobrium, obloquy.
– OPPOSITES honour.

disrespect n. **1** *disrespect for authority* **contempt**, lack of respect, scorn, disregard, disdain. **2** *he meant no disrespect to anybody* **discourtesy**, rudeness, impoliteness, incivility, ill/bad manners; insolence, impudence, impertinence.
– OPPOSITES esteem.

disrespectful adj. **discourteous**, rude, impolite, uncivil, ill-mannered, bad-mannered; insolent, impudent, impertinent, cheeky, flippant, insubordinate.
– OPPOSITES polite.

disrobe v. **undress**, strip, take off one's clothes, remove one's clothes; Brit. informal peel off.

disrupt v. **1** *the strike disrupted public transport* **throw into confusion/disorder/disarray**, cause confusion/turmoil in, play havoc with; disturb, interfere with, upset, unsettle; obstruct, impede, hold up, delay, interrupt, suspend; Brit. throw a spanner in the works of; N. Amer. throw a monkey wrench in the works of. **2** *the explosion disrupted the walls of the crater* **distort**, damage, buckle, warp; shatter; literary sunder.

disruptive adj. **troublesome**, unruly, badly behaved, rowdy, disorderly, undisciplined, attention-seeking, wild; unmanageable, uncontrollable, uncooperative, out of control/hand, obstreperous, truculent; formal refractory.
– OPPOSITES well behaved.

dissatisfaction n. **discontent**, discontentment, disaffection, disquiet, unhappiness, malaise, disgruntlement, vexation, annoyance, irritation, anger; disapproval, disapprobation, disfavour, displeasure.

dissatisfied adj. **discontented**, malcontent, unsatisfied, disappointed, disaffected, unhappy, displeased; disgruntled, aggrieved, vexed, annoyed, irritated, angry, exasperated; informal cheesed off, fed up; Brit. informal brassed off, not best pleased.
– OPPOSITES contented.

dissect v. **1** *the body was dissected* **anatomize**, cut up/open, dismember; vivisect. **2** *the text of the gospels was dissected* **analyse**, examine, study, scrutinize, pore over, investigate, go over with a fine-tooth comb.

dissection n. **1** *the dissection of corpses* **cutting up/open**, dismemberment; autopsy, post-mortem, necropsy, anatomy, vivisection. **2** *a thorough dissection of their policies* **analysis**, examination, study, scrutiny, scrutinization, investigation; evaluation, assessment.

dissemble v. **dissimulate**, pretend, feign, act, masquerade, sham, fake, bluff, posture, hide one's feelings, put on a false front.

dissembler n. **liar**, dissimulator; humbug, bluffer, fraud, impostor, actor, hoaxer, charlatan.

disseminate v. **spread**, circulate, distribute, disperse, promulgate, propagate, publicize, communicate, pass on, put about, make known.

dissension n. **disagreement**, difference of opinion, dispute, dissent, conflict, friction, strife, discord, antagonism; argument, debate, controversy, disputation, contention.

dissent v. *two members dissented* **differ**, disagree, demur, fail to agree, be at variance/odds, take issue; protest, object, dispute, challenge, quibble.
– OPPOSITES agree, accept.
▸n. *murmurs of dissent* **disagreement**, difference of opinion, argument, dispute; disapproval, objection, protest, opposition,
defiance; conflict, friction, strife.
– OPPOSITES agreement.

dissenter n. **dissident**, dissentient, objector, protester, disputant; rebel, renegade, maverick, independent; apostate, heretic; informal bad boy.

dissentient adj. *dissentient voices* **dissenting**, dissident, disagreeing, differing, discordant, contradicting, contrary, anti-; opposing, objecting, protesting, complaining, rebellious, revolutionary; nonconformist, recusant, unorthodox, heterodox, heretical.
▸n. *a dissentient spoke up*. See **dissenter**.

dissertation n. **essay**, thesis, treatise, paper, study, discourse, disquisition, tract, monograph.

disservice n. **unkindness**, bad/ill turn, disfavour; injury, harm, hurt, damage, wrong, injustice.
– OPPOSITES favour.

dissidence n. **disagreement**, dissent, discord, discontent; opposition, resistance, protest, sedition.

dissident n. *a jailed dissident* **dissenter**, objector, protester; rebel, revolutionary, recusant, subversive, agitator, insurgent, insurrectionist, refusenik.
– OPPOSITES conformist.
▸adj. *dissident intellectuals* **dissenting**, disagreeing, dissentient; opposing, objecting, protesting, rebellious, rebelling, revolutionary, recusant, nonconformist.
– OPPOSITES conforming.

dissimilar adj. **different**, differing, unalike, variant, diverse, divergent, heterogeneous, disparate, unrelated, distinct, contrasting; literary divers.

dissimilarity n. **difference(s)**, variance, diversity, heterogeneity, disparateness, disparity, distinctness, contrast, non-uniformity, divergence; formal dissimilitude.

dissimulate v. **pretend**, deceive, feign, act, dissemble, masquerade, pose, posture, sham, fake, bluff, hide one's feelings, be dishonest, put on a false front, lie.

dissimulation n. **pretence**, dissembling, deceit, dishonesty, duplicity, lying, guile, subterfuge, feigning, shamming, faking, bluff, bluffing, posturing, hypocrisy.

dissipate v. **1** *his anger dissipated* **disappear**, vanish, evaporate, dissolve, melt away, melt into thin air, be dispelled; disperse, scatter; literary evanesce. **2** *he dissipated his fortune* **squander**, fritter (away), misspend, waste, be prodigal with, spend recklessly/freely, spend like water; expend, use up, consume, run through, go through; informal blow, splurge.

dissipated adj. **dissolute**, debauched, decadent, intemperate, profligate, self-indulgent, wild, depraved; licentious, promiscuous; drunken.
– OPPOSITES ascetic.

dissipation n. **1** *drunken dissipation* **debauchery**, decadence, dissoluteness, dissolution, intemperance, excess, profligacy, self-indulgence, wildness; depravity,

d

degeneracy; licentiousness, promiscuity; drunkenness. **2** *the dissipation of our mineral wealth* **squandering**, frittering (away), waste, misspending; expenditure, draining, depletion.
– OPPOSITES asceticism.

dissociate v. *the word 'spiritual' has become dissociated from religion* **separate**, detach, disconnect, sever, cut off, divorce; isolate, alienate.
– OPPOSITES relate.
  □ **dissociate oneself from 1** *he dissociated himself from the Church of England* **break away from**, end relations with, sever connections with; withdraw from, quit, leave, disaffiliate from, resign from, pull out of, drop out of, defect from. **2** *he dissociated himself from the statement* **disown**, reject, disagree with, distance oneself from.

dissociation n. **separation**, disconnection, detachment, severance, divorce, split; segregation, division; literary sundering.
– OPPOSITES union.

dissolute adj. **dissipated**, debauched, decadent, intemperate, profligate, self-indulgent, wild, depraved; licentious, promiscuous; drunken.
– OPPOSITES ascetic.

dissolution n. **1** *the dissolution of parliament* **cessation**, conclusion, end, ending, termination, winding up/down, discontinuation, suspension, disbanding; prorogation, recess. **2** technical *the dissolution of a polymer in a solvent* **dissolving**, liquefaction, melting, deliquescence; breaking up, decomposition, disintegration. **3** *the dissolution of the empire* **disintegration**, breaking up; decay, collapse, demise, extinction. **4** *a life of dissolution.* See **dissipation** (sense 1).

dissolve v. **1** *sugar dissolves in water* **break down**; liquefy, deliquesce, disintegrate. **2** *his hopes dissolved* **disappear**, vanish, melt away, evaporate, disperse, dissipate, disintegrate; dwindle, fade (away), wither; literary evanesce. **3** *the crowd dissolved* **disperse**, disband, break up, scatter, go in different directions. **4** *the assembly was dissolved* **disband**, disestablish, bring to an end, end, terminate, discontinue, close down, wind up/down, suspend; prorogue, adjourn. **5** *their marriage was dissolved* **annul**, nullify, void, invalidate, overturn, revoke.
  □ **dissolve into/in** burst into, break (down) into, be overcome with.

dissonant adj. **1** *dissonant sounds* **inharmonious**, discordant, unmelodious, atonal, off-key, cacophonous. **2** *harmonious and dissonant colours* **incongruous**, anomalous, clashing; disparate, different, dissimilar.
– OPPOSITES harmonious.

dissuade v. **discourage**, deter, prevent, divert, stop; talk out of, persuade against, advise against, argue out of.
– OPPOSITES encourage.

distance n. **1** *they measured the distance* **interval**, space, span, gap, extent; length, width, breadth, depth; range, reach. **2** *our perception of distance* **remoteness**; closeness. **3** *a mix of warmth and distance* **aloofness**, remoteness, detachment, unfriendliness; reserve, reticence, restraint, formality; informal stand-offishness.
  ▸v. *he distanced himself from her* **withdraw**, detach, separate, dissociate, isolate, put at a distance.
  □ **in the distance** far away/off, afar, just in view; on the horizon; old use yonder.

distant adj. **1** *distant parts of the world* **faraway**, far-off, far-flung, remote, out of the way, outlying. **2** *the distant past* **long ago**, bygone, olden; ancient, prehistoric; literary of yore. **3** *half a mile distant* **away**, off, apart. **4** *a distant memory* **vague**, faint, dim, indistinct, unclear, indefinite, sketchy, hazy. **5** *a distant family connection* **remote**, indirect, slight. **6** *father was always distant* **aloof**, reserved, remote, detached, unapproachable; withdrawn, reticent, taciturn, uncommunicative, undemonstrative, unforthcoming, unresponsive, unfriendly; informal stand-offish. **7** *a distant look in his eyes* **distracted**, absent-minded, faraway, detached, distrait, vague.
– OPPOSITES near, close, recent.

distaste n. **dislike**, aversion, disinclination, disapproval, disapprobation, disdain, repugnance, hatred, loathing; old use disrelish.
– OPPOSITES liking.

distasteful adj. **1** *distasteful behaviour* **unpleasant**, disagreeable, displeasing, undesirable; objectionable, offensive, unsavoury, unpalatable, obnoxious; disgusting, repellent, repulsive, revolting, repugnant, abhorrent, loathsome, vile. **2** *their eggs are distasteful to predators* **unpalatable**, unsavoury, unappetizing, inedible, disgusting.
– OPPOSITES agreeable, tasty.

distended adj. **swollen**, bloated, dilated, engorged, enlarged, inflated, expanded, extended, bulging, protuberant.

distil v. **1** *the water was distilled* **purify**, refine, filter, treat, process; evaporate and condense. **2** *oil distilled from marjoram* **extract**, press out, squeeze out, express. **3** *whisky is distilled from barley* **brew**, ferment. **4** *the solvent is distilled to leave the oil* **boil down**, reduce, concentrate, condense; purify, refine.

distinct adj. **1** *two distinct categories* **discrete**, separate, different, unconnected; precise, specific, distinctive, contrasting. **2** *the tail has distinct black tips* **clear**, well defined, unmistakable, easily distinguishable; recognizable, visible, obvious, pronounced, prominent, striking.
– OPPOSITES indefinite.

distinction n. **1** *class distinctions* **difference**, contrast, dissimilarity, variance, variation; division, differentiation,

dividing line, gulf, gap; formal dissimilitude.
2 *a painter of distinction* **importance**,
significance, note, consequence; renown,
fame, celebrity, prominence, eminence,
pre-eminence, repute, reputation; merit,
worth, greatness, excellence, quality. **3** *he
had served with distinction* **honour**, credit,
excellence, merit.
– OPPOSITES similarity, mediocrity.

distinctive adj. **distinguishing**,
characteristic, typical, individual, particular,
peculiar, unique, exclusive, special.
– OPPOSITES common.

distinctly adv. **1** *there's something distinctly
odd about him* **decidedly**, markedly,
definitely; clearly, noticeably, obviously,
plainly, evidently, unmistakably, manifestly,
patently; Brit. informal dead. **2** *Laura spoke
quite distinctly* **clearly**, plainly, intelligibly,
audibly, unambiguously.

distinguish v. **1** *distinguishing reality
from fantasy* **differentiate**, tell apart,
discriminate between, tell the difference
between. **2** *he could distinguish shapes in
the dark* **discern**, see, perceive, make out;
detect, recognize, identify; literary descry,
espy. **3** *this is what distinguishes history from
other disciplines* **separate**, set apart, make
distinctive, make different; single out, mark
off, characterize.

distinguishable adj. **discernible**,
recognizable, identifiable, detectable.

distinguished adj. **eminent**, famous,
renowned, prominent, well known;
esteemed, respected, illustrious, acclaimed,
celebrated, great; notable, important,
influential.
– OPPOSITES unknown, obscure.

distinguishing adj. **distinctive**,
differentiating, characteristic, typical,
peculiar, singular, unique.

distorted adj. **1** *a distorted face* **twisted**,
warped, contorted, buckled, deformed,
malformed, misshapen, disfigured, crooked,
awry, out of shape. **2** *a distorted version*
misrepresented, perverted, twisted,
falsified, misreported, misstated, garbled,
inaccurate; biased, prejudiced, slanted,
coloured, loaded, weighted, altered,
changed.

distract v. **divert**, sidetrack, draw away,
disturb, put off.

distracted adj. **preoccupied**, inattentive,
vague, abstracted, distrait, absent-minded,
faraway, in a world of one's own; bemused,
confused, bewildered; troubled, harassed,
worried; informal miles away, not with it.
– OPPOSITES attentive.

distracting adj. **disturbing**, unsettling,
intrusive, disconcerting, bothersome, off-
putting.

distraction n. **1** *a distraction from the
real issues* **diversion**, interruption,
disturbance, interference, hindrance.
2 *frivolous distractions* **amusement**,
entertainment, diversion, recreation, leisure
pursuit, divertissement. **3** *he was driven*

to distraction **frenzy**, hysteria, mental
distress, madness, mania; agitation,
perturbation.

distraught adj. **worried**, upset, distressed,
fraught; overcome, overwrought, beside
oneself, out of one's mind, desperate,
hysterical, worked up, at one's wits' end;
informal in a state.

distress n. **1** *she concealed her distress*
anguish, suffering, pain, agony, torment,
heartache, heartbreak; misery, wretchedness,
sorrow, grief, woe, sadness, unhappiness,
desolation, despair. **2** *a ship in distress*
danger, peril, difficulty, trouble, jeopardy,
risk. **3** *the poor in distress* **hardship**,
adversity, poverty, deprivation, privation,
destitution, indigence, impoverishment,
penury, need, dire straits.
– OPPOSITES happiness, safety, prosperity.
▶ v. *he was distressed by the trial* **cause
anguish/suffering to**, pain, upset, make
miserable; trouble, worry, bother, perturb,
disturb, disquiet, agitate, harrow, torment;
informal cut up.
– OPPOSITES calm, please.

distressing adj. **upsetting**, worrying,
disturbing, disquieting, painful, traumatic,
agonizing, harrowing; sad, saddening,
heartbreaking, heart-rending.
– OPPOSITES comforting.

distribute v. **1** *the proceeds were distributed
among his creditors* **give out**, deal out, dole
out, dish out, hand out/round; allocate,
allot, apportion, share out, divide out/up,
parcel out. **2** *the newsletter is distributed
free* **circulate**, issue, hand out, deliver.
3 *a hundred and thirty different species are
distributed worldwide* **disperse**, scatter,
spread.
– OPPOSITES collect.

distribution n. **1** *the distribution of charity*
giving out, dealing out, doling out, handing
out/round; issue, issuing, dispensation;
allocation, allotment, apportioning, sharing
out, dividing up/out, parcelling out. **2** *the
geographical distribution of plants* **dispersal**,
dissemination, spread; placement, position,
location, disposition. **3** *centres of food
distribution* **supply**, supplying, delivery,
transport, transportation. **4** *the statistical
distribution of the problem* **frequency**,
prevalence, incidence, commonness.

district n. **neighbourhood**, area, region,
locality, locale, community, quarter, sector,
zone, territory; administrative division,
ward, parish; informal neck of the woods.

distrust n. *the general distrust of authority*
mistrust, suspicion, wariness, chariness,
leeriness, lack of trust, lack of confidence;
scepticism, doubt, doubtfulness, cynicism;
misgivings, qualms, disbelief; formal dubiety.
▶ v. *Louise distrusted him* **mistrust**, be
suspicious of, be wary/chary of, be leery of,
regard with suspicion, suspect; be sceptical
of, have doubts about, doubt, be unsure of/
about, have misgivings about, wonder about,
disbelieve (in).

d

d

disturb v. **1** *somewhere where we won't be disturbed* **interrupt**, intrude on, butt in on, barge in on; distract, disrupt, bother, trouble, pester, harass; informal hassle. **2** *don't disturb his papers* **disarrange**, muddle, rearrange, disorganize, disorder, mix up, interfere with, throw into disorder/confusion, turn upside down. **3** *waters disturbed by winds* **agitate**, churn up, stir up; literary roil. **4** *he wasn't disturbed by the allegations* **perturb**, trouble, concern, worry, upset; agitate, fluster, discomfit, disconcert, dismay, distress, discompose, unsettle, ruffle.

disturbance n. **1** *a disturbance to local residents* **disruption**, distraction, interference; bother, trouble, inconvenience, upset, annoyance, irritation, intrusion, harassment; informal hassle. **2** *disturbances among the peasantry* **riot**, fracas, upheaval, brawl, street fight, melee, free-for-all, ruckus, rumpus; Law, dated affray; informal ruction; Brit. informal, Football afters. **3** *emotional disturbance* **trouble**, perturbation, distress, worry, upset, agitation, discomposure, discomfiture; neurosis, illness, sickness, disorder, complaint.

disturbed adj. **1** *disturbed sleep* **disrupted**, interrupted, fitful, intermittent, broken. **2** *disturbed children* **troubled**, distressed, upset, distraught; unbalanced, unstable, disordered, dysfunctional, maladjusted, neurotic, unhinged; informal screwed up, mixed up.

disturbing adj. **worrying**, perturbing, troubling, upsetting; distressing, discomfiting, disconcerting, disquieting, unsettling, dismaying, alarming, frightening.

disunion n. **breaking up**, separation, dissolution, partition.
– OPPOSITES federation.

disunite v. **break up**, separate, divide, split up, partition, dismantle; literary sunder.
– OPPOSITES unify.

disunity n. **disagreement**, dissent, dissension, argument, arguing, quarrelling, feuding; conflict, strife, friction, discord.

disuse n. **non-use**, non-employment, lack of use; neglect, abandonment, desertion, obsolescence; formal desuetude.

disused adj. **unused**, no longer in use, unemployed, idle; abandoned, deserted, vacated, unoccupied, uninhabited.

ditch n. **trench**, trough, channel, dyke, drain, gutter, gully, watercourse, conduit; Archaeology fosse.
▶ v. **1** informal *more and more companies are ditching their final salary pension schemes* **abandon**, get rid of, dispose of, drop, jettison, throw away/out, shelve; informal dump, junk, scrap, axe. **2** informal *she ditched her husband*. See **throw someone over**.

dither v. **hesitate**, falter, waver, vacillate, change one's mind, be in two minds, be indecisive, be undecided; Brit. haver; informal shilly-shally, dilly-dally.

diurnal adj. **daily**, everyday, quotidian, occurring every/each day.

divan n. **settee**, sofa, couch; sofa bed; Brit. put-you-up; N. Amer. studio couch.

dive v. **1** *they dived into the clear water | the plane was diving towards the ground* **plunge**, nosedive, jump head first, bellyflop; plummet, fall, drop, pitch. **2** *the islanders dive for oysters* **swim under water**; snorkel, scuba dive. **3** *they dived for cover* **leap**, jump, lunge, launch oneself, throw oneself, go headlong, duck.
▶ n. **1** *a dive into the pool* **plunge**, nosedive, jump, bellyflop; plummet, fall, drop, swoop, pitch. **2** *a sideways dive* **lunge**, spring, jump, leap. **3** informal *John got into a fight in some dive* **sleazy bar/nightclub**, seedy bar/ nightclub, drinking den; informal drinking joint.

diverge v. **1** *the two roads diverged* **separate**, part, fork, divide, split, bifurcate, go in different directions. **2** *areas where our views diverge* **differ**, be different, be dissimilar; disagree, be at variance/odds, conflict, clash. **3** *he diverged from his text* **deviate**, digress, depart, veer, stray; stray from the point, get off the subject.
– OPPOSITES converge, agree.

divergence n. **1** *the divergence of the human and ape lineages* **separation**, dividing, parting, forking, bifurcation. **2** *a marked political divergence* **difference**, dissimilarity, variance, disparity; disagreement, incompatibility, mismatch; formal dissimilitude. **3** *divergence from standard behaviour* **deviation**, digression, departure, shift, straying; variation, change, alteration.

divergent adj. **differing**, varying, different, dissimilar, unlike, disparate, contrasting, contrastive; conflicting, incompatible, contradictory, at odds, at variance.
– OPPOSITES similar.

divers adj. literary **several**, many, numerous, multiple, manifold, multifarious, multitudinous, sundry, miscellaneous, assorted, various; literary myriad.

diverse adj. **various**, sundry, manifold, multiple; varied, varying, miscellaneous, assorted, mixed, diversified, divergent, heterogeneous, a mixed bag of; different, differing, distinct, unlike, dissimilar; literary divers, myriad.

diversify v. **1** *farmers looking for ways to diversify* **branch out**, expand, extend operations. **2** *a plan aimed at diversifying the economy* **vary**, bring variety to; modify, alter, change, transform; expand, enlarge.

diversion n. **1** *the diversion of 19 rivers* **re-routing**, redirection, deflection, deviation, divergence. **2** *traffic diversions* **detour**, deviation, alternative route. **3** *the noise created a diversion* **distraction**, disturbance, smokescreen. **4** *a city full of diversions* **entertainment**, amusement, pastime, delight, divertissement; fun, recreation, rest and relaxation, pleasure; informal R & R; dated sport.

diversity n. **variety**, miscellany, assortment, mixture, mix, melange, range,

array, multiplicity; variation, variance, diversification, heterogeneity, difference, contrast; formal dissimilitude.
− OPPOSITES uniformity.

divert v. **1** *a plan to divert Siberia's rivers* **re-route**, redirect, change the course of, deflect, channel. **2** *he diverted her from her studies* **distract**, sidetrack, disturb, draw away, be a distraction, put off. **3** *the story diverted them* **amuse**, entertain, distract, delight, enchant, interest, fascinate, absorb, engross, rivet, grip, hold the attention of.

diverting adj. **entertaining**, amusing, enjoyable, pleasing, agreeable, delightful, appealing; interesting, fascinating, intriguing, absorbing, riveting, compelling; humorous, funny, witty, comical, chucklesome.
− OPPOSITES boring.

divest v. **deprive**, strip, dispossess, rob, cheat/trick out of; old use reave.

divide v. **1** *he divided his kingdom into four* **split (up)**, cut up, carve up; dissect, bisect, halve, quarter; literary sunder. **2** *a curtain divided her cabin from the galley* **separate**, segregate, partition, screen off, section off, split off. **3** *the stairs divide at the mezzanine* **diverge**, separate, part, branch (off), fork, split (in two), bifurcate. **4** *Jack divided up the cash* **share out**, allocate, allot, apportion, portion out, ration out, parcel out, deal out, dole out, dish out, distribute, dispense; informal divvy up. **5** *he aimed to divide his opponents* **disunite**, drive apart, break up, split up, set at variance/odds; separate, isolate, estrange, alienate; literary tear asunder. **6** *living things are divided into three categories* **classify**, sort (out), categorize, order, group, grade, rank.
− OPPOSITES unify, join, converge.
▶n. *the sectarian divide* **breach**, gulf, gap, split; borderline, boundary, dividing line.

dividend n. **1** *an annual dividend* **share**, portion, premium, return, gain, profit; informal cut, rake-off; Brit. informal divvy. **2** *the research will produce dividends in the future* **benefit**, advantage, gain; bonus, extra, plus.

divination n. **fortune telling**, divining, prophecy, prediction, soothsaying, augury; clairvoyance, second sight.

divine[1] adj. **1** *a divine being* **godly**, angelic, seraphic, saintly, beatific; heavenly, celestial, holy. **2** *divine worship* **religious**, holy, sacred, sanctified, consecrated, blessed, devotional. **3** informal *divine food*. See **lovely** (sense 3).
− OPPOSITES mortal.
▶n. dated *puritan divines* **theologian**, clergyman, clergywoman, member of the clergy, churchman, churchwoman, cleric, minister, man/woman of the cloth, preacher, priest; informal reverend.

divine[2] v. **1** *Fergus divined how afraid she was* **guess**, surmise, conjecture, deduce, infer; discern, intuit, perceive, recognize, see, realize, appreciate, understand, grasp, comprehend; informal figure (out), savvy; Brit.

informal twig, suss. **2** *they divined that this was an auspicious day* **foretell**, predict, prophesy, forecast, foresee, prognosticate; rare vaticinate.

diviner n. **fortune teller**, clairvoyant, crystal-gazer, psychic, seer, soothsayer, prognosticator, prophesier, oracle, sibyl; rare vaticinator.

divinity n. **1** *they denied Christ's divinity* **divine nature**, divineness, godliness, deity, godhead, holiness. **2** *the study of divinity* **theology**, religious studies, religion, scripture. **3** *a female divinity* **deity**, god, goddess, divine/supreme being.

division n. **1** *the division of the island | cell division* **dividing (up)**, breaking up, break-up, carving up, splitting, dissection, bisection; partitioning, separation, segregation. **2** *the division of his estates* **sharing out**, dividing up, parcelling out, dishing out, allocation, allotment, apportionment; splitting up, carving up; informal divvying up. **3** *the division between nomadic and urban cultures* **dividing line**, divide, boundary, borderline, border, demarcation line. **4** *each class is divided into nine divisions* **section**, subsection, subdivision, category, class, group, grouping, set, family. **5** *an independent division of the executive* **department**, branch, arm, wing, sector, section, subsection, subdivision, subsidiary. **6** *the causes of social division* **disunity**, disunion, conflict, discord, disagreement, dissension, disaffection, estrangement, alienation, isolation.

divisive adj. **alienating**, estranging, isolating, schismatic.
− OPPOSITES unifying.

divorce n. **1** *she wants a divorce* **dissolution**, annulment, (official/judicial) separation. **2** *a growing divorce between the church and people* **separation**, division, split, disunity, estrangement, alienation; schism, gulf, chasm.
− OPPOSITES marriage, unity.
▶v. **1** *her parents have divorced* **dissolve one's marriage**, end one's marriage. **2** *religion cannot be divorced from morality* **separate**, disconnect, divide, dissociate, detach, isolate, alienate, set apart, cut off.

divulge v. **disclose**, reveal, tell, communicate, pass on, publish, broadcast, proclaim; expose, uncover, make public, give away, let slip; informal spill the beans about, let on about.
− OPPOSITES conceal.

dizzy adj. **1** *she felt dizzy* **giddy**, light-headed, faint, unsteady, shaky, muzzy, wobbly; informal woozy. **2** *dizzy heights* **causing dizziness**, causing giddiness, vertiginous. **3** informal *a dizzy blonde*. See **empty-headed**.

do v. **1** *she does most of the manual work* **carry out**, undertake, discharge, execute, perform, accomplish, achieve; bring about, engineer; informal pull off; formal effectuate. **2** *they can do as they please* **act**, behave, conduct oneself, acquit oneself; formal

d

comport oneself. **3** *regular coffee will do*
suffice, be adequate, be satisfactory, fill/
fit the bill, serve one's purpose, meet one's
needs. **4** *the boys will do the dinner* **prepare**,
make, get ready, see to, arrange, organize,
be responsible for, be in charge of; informal
fix. **5** *the company are doing a new range* |
a portrait I am doing **make**, create, produce,
turn out, design, manufacture; paint, draw,
sketch; informal knock up/off. **6** *each room was*
done in a different colour **decorate**, furnish,
ornament, deck out, trick out; informal do
up. **7** *her maid did her hair* **style**, arrange,
adjust; brush, comb, wash, dry, cut; informal
fix. **8** *I am doing a show to raise money* **put**
on, present, produce; perform in, act in,
take part in, participate in. **9** *you've done me*
a favour **grant**, pay, render, give. **10** *show*
me how to do these equations **work out**,
figure out, calculate; solve, resolve. **11** *she's*
doing archaeology **study**, read, learn, take
a course in. **12** *what does he do?* **have as a**
job, have as a profession, be employed at,
earn a living at. **13** *he is doing well at college*
get on/along, progress, fare, manage, cope;
succeed, prosper. **14** *he was doing 80 mph*
drive at, travel at, move at. **15** *the cyclists*
do 30 miles per day **travel (over)**, journey,
cover, traverse, achieve, notch up, log; informal
chalk up. **16** informal *we're doing Scotland this*
summer **visit**, tour, sightsee in.
▶ **n.** Brit. informal *he invited us to a grand do* **party**,
reception, gathering, celebration, function,
social event/occasion, social, soirée; informal
bash, shindig; Brit. informal knees-up, beanfeast,
bunfight; Austral./NZ informal rage, jollo.
□ **do away with 1** *they want to do away*
with the old customs abolish, get rid of,
discard, remove, eliminate, discontinue,
stop, end, terminate, put an end/stop to,
dispense with, drop, abandon, give up; informal
scrap, ditch, dump. **2** informal *she tried to do*
away with her husband. See **kill** (sense 1 of
the verb).
do someone/something down informal
belittle, disparage, denigrate, run down,
deprecate, cast aspersions on, discredit,
vilify, defame, criticize, malign; N. Amer. slur;
informal have a go at, hit out at, knock, slam,
pan, bad-mouth; Brit. informal rubbish, slag off.
do someone/something in informal **1** *the*
poor devil's been done in. See **kill** (sense 1 of
the verb). **2** *the long walk home did me in*
wear out, tire out, exhaust, fatigue, weary,
overtire, drain; informal shatter, take it out of;
Brit. informal knacker. **3** *I did my back in* **injure**,
hurt, damage.
do something out Brit. informal decorate,
furnish, ornament, deck out, trick out; informal
do up.
do someone out of something informal
swindle out of, cheat out of, trick out of,
deprive of; informal con out of, diddle out of.
do something up 1 *she did her bootlace*
up **fasten**, tie (up), lace, knot; make fast,
secure. **2** informal *he's had his house done*
up **renovate**, refurbish, refit, redecorate,
decorate, revamp, make over, modernize,

improve, spruce up, smarten up; informal give
something a facelift; N. Amer. informal rehab.
do without forgo, dispense with, abstain
from, refrain from, eschew, give up, cut out,
renounce, manage without; formal forswear.

docile adj. **compliant**, obedient, pliant,
dutiful, submissive, deferential, unassertive,
cooperative, amenable, accommodating,
biddable, malleable.
– OPPOSITES disobedient, wilful.

dock[1] n. *his boat was moored at the dock*
harbour, marina, port, anchorage; wharf,
quay, pier, jetty, landing stage.
▶ **v.** *the ship docked* **moor**, berth, put in, tie up,
anchor.

dock[2] v. **1** *they docked the money from his*
salary **deduct**, subtract, remove, debit,
take off/away; informal knock off. **2** *workers*
had their pay docked **reduce**, cut, decrease.
3 *the dog's tail was docked* **cut off**, cut short,
shorten, crop, lop; remove, amputate, detach,
sever, chop off, take off.

docket Brit. n. *a docket for every transaction*
document, chit, coupon, voucher, certificate,
counterfoil, bill, receipt; Brit. informal chitty.
▶ **v.** *neatly docketed bundles* **document**, record,
register; label, tag, tab, mark.

doctor n. **physician**, medical practitioner,
GP, general practitioner, consultant,
clinician; informal doc, medic, medico; Brit.
informal quack.
▶ **v. 1** informal *he doctored their wounds* **treat**,
medicate, cure, heal; tend, attend to,
minister to, care for, nurse. **2** *he doctored*
Stephen's drinks **adulterate**, contaminate,
tamper with, lace; informal spike, dope. **3** *the*
reports have been doctored **falsify**, tamper
with, interfere with, alter, change; forge,
fake; informal cook; Brit. informal fiddle (with).

doctrinaire adj. **dogmatic**, rigid, inflexible,
uncompromising; authoritarian, intolerant,
fanatical, zealous, extreme.

doctrine n. **creed**, credo, dogma, belief,
teaching, ideology; tenet, maxim, canon,
principle, precept.

document n. *their solicitor drew up a*
document **(official/legal) paper**, certificate,
deed, contract, legal agreement; Law
instrument, indenture.
▶ **v.** *many aspects of school life have been*
documented **record**, register, report, log,
chronicle, archive, put on record, write
down; detail, note, describe.

documentary adj. **1** *documentary evidence*
recorded, documented, registered, written,
chronicled, archived, on record/paper, in
writing. **2** *a documentary film* **factual**, non-
fictional.
▶ **n.** *a documentary about rural England*
factual programme/film; programme, film,
broadcast.

dodder v. **totter**, teeter, toddle, hobble,
shuffle, shamble, falter.

doddery adj. **tottering**, tottery, staggering,
shuffling, shambling, faltering, shaky,
unsteady, wobbly; feeble, frail, weak.

dodge v. **1** *she dodged into a telephone booth* **dart**, bolt, dive, lunge, leap, spring. **2** *he could easily dodge the two coppers* **elude**, evade, avoid, escape, run away from, lose, shake (off); informal give someone the slip. **3** *the minister tried to dodge the debate* **avoid**, evade, get out of, back out of, sidestep; N. Amer. end-run; informal duck, wriggle out of; Austral./NZ informal duck-shove.
▶ n. **1** *a dodge to the right* **dart**, bolt, dive, lunge, leap, spring. **2** *a clever dodge* | *a tax dodge* **ruse**, ploy, scheme, tactic, stratagem, subterfuge, trick, hoax, wile, cheat, deception, blind; swindle, fraud; informal scam, con (trick); Brit. informal wheeze; N. Amer. informal bunco, grift; Austral. informal lurk, rort.

dodgy adj. Brit. informal **1** *a dodgy second-hand car salesman.* See **dishonest. 2** *the champagne was dodgy* **second-rate**, third-rate, substandard, low-quality; awful, terrible, dreadful, dire; N. Amer. cheapjack; informal not up to much, woeful; Brit. informal ropy, grotty.

doer n. **1** *the doer of unspeakable deeds* **performer**, perpetrator, executor, agent. **2** *Daniel is a thinker more than a doer* **worker**, organizer, man/woman of action; informal mover and shaker, busy bee.

doff v. dated **take off**, remove, strip off, pull off; raise, lift, tip; dated divest oneself of.
– OPPOSITES don.

dog n. *she went for a walk with her dog* **hound**, canine, mongrel; pup, puppy, whelp; informal doggy, pooch, mutt; Austral. informal bitzer.
▶ v. **1** *they dogged him the length of the country* **pursue**, follow, track, trail, shadow, hound; informal tail. **2** *the scheme was dogged by bad weather* **plague**, beset, bedevil, beleaguer, blight, trouble.

> **WORD LINKS**
> **canine** relating to dogs

dogged adj. **tenacious**, determined, resolute, resolved, purposeful, persistent, persevering, single-minded, tireless; strong-willed, steadfast, staunch; formal pertinacious.
– OPPOSITES half-hearted.

dogma n. **teaching**, belief, tenet, principle, precept, maxim, article of faith, canon; creed, credo, set of beliefs, doctrine, ideology.

dogmatic adj. **opinionated**, peremptory, assertive, insistent, emphatic, adamant, doctrinaire, authoritarian, imperious, dictatorial, uncompromising, unyielding, inflexible, rigid.

dogsbody n. Brit. informal **drudge**, menial (worker), factotum, servant, slave, lackey, minion, man/girl Friday; informal gofer; Brit. informal skivvy; N. Amer. informal peon; old use scullion.

doing n. **1** *the doing of the act constitutes the offence* **performance**, performing, carrying out, execution, implementation, implementing, accomplishment, achievement, realization, completion; formal effectuation. **2** *an account of his doings in Paris* **exploit**, activity, act, action, deed, feat, achievement, accomplishment; informal caper. **3** *that would take some doing* **effort**, exertion, (hard) work, application, labour, toil, struggle. **4** Brit. informal *the drawer where he kept the doings* **thing**, so-and-so; informal whatsit, whatnot, doodah, thingummy, thingamajig, thingamabob, what's-its-name, what-d'you-call-it, oojamaflip, oojah; Brit. informal gubbins; N. Amer. informal doohickey, doojigger, dingus.

doldrums plural n. *winter doldrums* **depression**, melancholy, gloom, gloominess, downheartedness, dejection, despondency, low spirits, despair; inertia, apathy, listlessness; N. Amer. blahs; informal blues.
□ **in the doldrums** inactive, quiet, slow, slack, sluggish, stagnant.

dole n. Brit. informal **unemployment benefit**, social security, welfare.
□ **dole something out** deal out, share out, divide up, allocate, allot, distribute, dispense, hand out, give out, dish out/up; informal divvy up.

doleful adj. **mournful**, woeful, sorrowful, sad, unhappy, depressed, gloomy, morose, melancholy, miserable, forlorn, wretched, woebegone, despondent, dejected, disconsolate, downcast, crestfallen, downhearted; informal blue, down in the mouth/dumps; literary dolorous, heartsick.
– OPPOSITES cheerful.

doll n. **1** *the child was hugging a doll* **figure**, figurine, model; toy, plaything; informal dolly. **2** informal *she was quite a doll.* See **beauty** (sense 2).
□ **doll oneself up** informal dress up; informal get/do oneself up, dress up to the nines, put on one's glad rags; Brit. informal tart oneself up.

dollop n. informal **blob**, gobbet, lump, ball; informal glob; Brit. informal gob, wodge.

dolt n. See **idiot**.

doltish adj. See **stupid** (sense 1).

domain n. **1** *they extended their domain* **realm**, kingdom, empire, dominion, province, territory, land. **2** *the domain of art* **field**, area, sphere, discipline, province, world.

dome n. **cupola**, vault, arched roof.

domestic adj. **1** *domestic commitments* **family**, home, household. **2** *she was not at all domestic* **housewifely**, domesticated, house-proud. **3** *small domestic animals* **domesticated**, tame, pet, household. **4** *the domestic car industry* **national**, state, home, internal. **5** *domestic plants* **native**, indigenous.
▶ n. *they worked as domestics* **servant**, domestic worker/help, home help, maid, housemaid, cleaner, housekeeper; Brit. dated charwoman, charlady, char; Brit. informal daily (help).

domesticated adj. **1** *domesticated animals* **tame**, tamed, pet, domestic, trained. **2** *domesticated crops* **cultivated**, naturalized. **3** *I'm quite domesticated really* **housewifely**, house-proud, home-loving, homely.
– OPPOSITES wild.

d

d

domicile formal n. *changes of domicile* **residence**, home, house, address, residency, lodging, accommodation; informal digs; formal dwelling (place), abode, habitation.
□ **be domiciled** *he is now domiciled in Australia* settled, living, resident; formal dwelling.

dominance n. **supremacy**, superiority, ascendancy, pre-eminence, predominance, domination, dominion, mastery, power, authority, rule, command, control, sway; literary puissance.

dominant adj. **1** *the dominant classes* **presiding**, ruling, governing, controlling, commanding, ascendant, supreme, authoritative. **2** *he has a dominant personality* **assertive**, authoritative, forceful, domineering, commanding, controlling, pushy; dated pushful. **3** *the dominant issues in psychology* **main**, principal, prime, premier, chief, foremost, primary, predominant, paramount, prominent; central, key, crucial, core; informal number-one.
– OPPOSITES subservient.

dominate v. **1** *the Russians dominated Iran in the nineteenth century* **control**, influence, exercise control over, command, be in command of, be in charge of, rule, govern, direct, have ascendancy over, have mastery over; informal head up, be in the driver's seat, be at the helm, rule the roost; Brit. informal wear the trousers; N. Amer. informal have someone in one's hip pocket; literary sway. **2** *the Puritan work ethic still dominates* **predominate**, prevail, reign, be prevalent, be paramount, be pre-eminent. **3** *the village is dominated by the viaduct* **overlook**, command, tower above/over, loom over.

domination n. **rule**, government, sovereignty, control, command, authority, power, dominion, dominance, mastery, supremacy, superiority, ascendancy, sway.

domineer v. **browbeat**, bully, intimidate, push around/about, order about/around, lord it over; dictate to, be overbearing, have under one's thumb, rule with a rod of iron; informal boss about/around, walk all over.

domineering adj. **overbearing**, authoritarian, imperious, high-handed, autocratic; masterful, dictatorial, despotic, oppressive, iron-fisted, strict, harsh; informal bossy.

dominion n. **1** *France had dominion over Laos* **supremacy**, ascendancy, dominance, domination, superiority, predominance, pre-eminence, hegemony, authority, mastery, control, command, power, sway, rule, government, jurisdiction, sovereignty, suzerainty. **2** *a British dominion* **dependency**, colony, protectorate, territory, province, possession; historical tributary.

don[1] n. *an Oxford don* **university teacher**, (university) lecturer, fellow, professor, reader, academic, scholar.

don[2] v. *he donned an overcoat* **put on**, get dressed in, dress (oneself) in, get into, slip into/on.

donate v. **give**, give/make a donation of, contribute, make a contribution of, gift, subscribe, grant, bestow; informal chip in, pitch in; Brit. informal stump up; N. Amer. informal kick in.

donation n. **gift**, contribution, subscription, present, handout, grant, offering; charity; formal benefaction; historical alms.

done adj. **1** *the job is done* **finished**, ended, concluded, complete, completed, accomplished, achieved, fulfilled, discharged, executed; informal wrapped up, sewn up, polished off. **2** *is the meat done?* **cooked (through)**, ready. **3** *those days are done* **over (and done with)**, at an end, finished, ended, concluded, terminated, no more, dead, gone, in the past. **4** informal *that's just not done* **proper**, seemly, decent, respectable, right, correct, in order, fitting, appropriate, acceptable, the done thing.
– OPPOSITES incomplete, underdone, ongoing.
▶ exclam. *Done!* **agreed**, all right, very well; informal you're on, OK, okey-dokey; Brit. informal righto, righty-ho.
□ **be/have done with** be/have finished with, be through with, want no more to do with.
done for informal ruined, finished, destroyed, undone, doomed, lost; informal washed-up.
done in informal See **exhausted** (sense 1).

donkey n. *the cart was drawn by a donkey* **ass**, jackass, jenny; mule, hinny; Brit. informal moke.

donnish adj. **scholarly**, studious, academic, bookish, intellectual, learned, highbrow; informal egghead; dated lettered.

donor n. **giver**, contributor, benefactor, benefactress, subscriber; supporter, backer, patron, sponsor; informal angel.

doom n. **1** *his impending doom* **destruction**, downfall, ruin, ruination; extinction, annihilation, death. **2** old use *the day of doom* **Judgement Day**, the Last Judgement, doomsday, Armageddon.
▶ v. *we were doomed to fail* **destine**, fate, predestine, preordain, foredoom, mean; condemn, sentence.

doomed adj. **ill-fated**, ill-starred, cursed, jinxed, foredoomed, damned; literary star-crossed.

door n. **doorway**, portal, opening, entrance, entry, exit.
□ **out of doors** outside, outdoors, in/into the open air, alfresco.

doorkeeper n. **doorman**, concierge, commissionaire.

dope n. informal **1** *he was caught smuggling dope* **(illegal) drugs**, narcotics; cannabis, heroin. **2** *what a dope!* See **fool** (sense 1 of the noun). **3** *they had plenty of dope on Mr Dixon.* See **intelligence** (sense 2).
▶ v. **1** *the horse was doped* **drug**, administer drugs/narcotics to, tamper with, interfere with; sedate; Brit. informal nobble. **2** *they doped his drink* **add drugs to**, tamper with, adulterate, contaminate, lace; informal spike, doctor.

dopey adj. informal **stupefied**, confused, muddled, befuddled, disorientated, groggy, muzzy; informal woozy, not with it.
– OPPOSITES alert.

dormant adj. **asleep**, sleeping, resting; **inactive**, passive, inert, latent, quiescent.
– OPPOSITES awake, active.

dose n. **measure**, portion, dosage, drench; informal hit.

dossier n. **file**, report, case history; account, notes, information, document(s), documentation, data, evidence.

dot n. *a pattern of tiny dots* **spot**, speck, fleck, speckle; full stop, decimal point.
▸ v. 1 *spots of rain dotted his shirt* **spot**, fleck, mark, stipple, freckle, sprinkle; literary bestrew, besprinkle. 2 *restaurants are dotted around the site* **scatter**, pepper, sprinkle, strew; spread, disperse, distribute.
□ **on the dot** informal precisely, exactly, sharp, prompt, dead on, on the stroke of ——; informal bang on; N. Amer. informal on the button, on the nose.

dotage n. **declining years**; advanced years, old age; literary eld.

dote v.
□ **dote on** adore, love dearly, be devoted to, idolize, treasure, cherish, worship, hold dear; indulge, spoil, pamper.

doting adj. **adoring**, loving, besotted, infatuated; affectionate, fond, devoted, caring.

dotty adj. informal See **mad** (sense 1).

double adj. 1 *a double garage | double yellow lines* **dual**, duplex, twin, binary, duplicate, in pairs, coupled, twofold. 2 *a double helping* **doubled**, twofold. 3 *a double meaning* **ambiguous**, equivocal, dual, two-edged, double-edged, ambivalent, cryptic, enigmatic. 4 *a double life* **deceitful**, double-dealing, two-faced, dual; hypocritical, false, duplicitous, insincere, deceiving, dissembling, dishonest.
– OPPOSITES single, unambiguous.
▸ adv. *we had to pay double* **twice (over)**, twice the amount, doubly.
▸ n. 1 *if it's not her, it's her double* **lookalike**, twin, clone, duplicate, exact likeness, replica, copy, facsimile, doppelgänger; informal spitting image, dead ringer, dead spit. 2 *she used a double for the stunts* **stand-in**, substitute.
▸ v. 1 *they doubled his salary* **multiply by two**, increase twofold. 2 *the bottom sheet had been doubled up* **fold (back/up/down/over/under)**, turn back/up/down/over/under, tuck back/up/down/under. 3 *the kitchen doubles as a dining room* **function**, do, (also) serve.
□ **at/on the double** very quickly, as fast as one's legs can carry one, at a run, at a gallop, fast, swiftly, rapidly, speedily, at (full) speed, at full tilt, as fast as possible; informal double quick, like (greased) lightning, like the wind, like a scalded cat, like a bat out of hell; Brit. informal like the clappers, at a rate of knots; N. Amer. informal lickety-split.

double-cross v. **betray**, cheat, defraud, trick, hoodwink, mislead, deceive, swindle, be disloyal to, be unfaithful to, play false; informal do the dirty on, sell down the river.

double-dealing n. **duplicity**, treachery, betrayal, double-crossing, unfaithfulness, untrustworthiness, infidelity, bad faith, disloyalty, breach of trust, fraud, underhandedness, cheating, dishonesty, deceit, deceitfulness, deception, falseness; informal crookedness.
– OPPOSITES honesty.

double entendre n. **ambiguity**, double meaning, innuendo, play on words.

doubly adv. **twice as**, in double measure, even more, especially, extra.

doubt n. 1 *there was some doubt as to the caller's identity* **uncertainty**, unsureness, indecision, hesitation, dubiousness, suspicion, confusion; queries, questions; formal dubiety. 2 *a weak leader racked by doubt* **indecision**, hesitation, uncertainty, insecurity, unease, uneasiness, apprehension; hesitancy, vacillation, irresolution. 3 *there is doubt about their motives* **scepticism**, distrust, mistrust, doubtfulness, suspicion, cynicism, uneasiness, apprehension, wariness, chariness, leeriness; reservations, misgivings, suspicions; formal dubiety.
– OPPOSITES certainty, conviction.
▸ v. 1 *they doubted my story* **disbelieve**, distrust, mistrust, suspect, have doubts about, be suspicious of, have misgivings about, feel uneasy about, feel apprehensive about, query, question, challenge. 2 *I doubt whether he will come* **think something unlikely**, have (one's) doubts about, question, query, be dubious. 3 *stop doubting and believe!* **be undecided**, have doubts, be irresolute, be ambivalent, be doubtful, be unsure, be uncertain, be in two minds, hesitate, shilly-shally, waver, vacillate.
– OPPOSITES trust.
□ **in doubt** 1 *the issue was in doubt* **doubtful**, uncertain, open to question, unconfirmed, unknown, undecided, unresolved, in the balance, up in the air; informal iffy. 2 *if you are in doubt, ask for advice* **irresolute**, hesitant, vacillating, dithering, wavering, ambivalent; doubtful, unsure, uncertain, in two minds, shilly-shallying, undecided, in a quandary/dilemma; informal sitting on the fence. **no doubt** doubtless, undoubtedly, indubitably, doubtlessly, without (a) doubt; unquestionably, undeniably, incontrovertibly, irrefutably; unequivocally, clearly, plainly, obviously, patently.

doubter n. **sceptic**, doubting Thomas, non-believer, unbeliever, disbeliever, cynic, scoffer, questioner, challenger, dissenter.
– OPPOSITES believer.

doubtful adj. 1 *I was doubtful about going* **irresolute**, hesitant, vacillating, dithering, wavering, in doubt, unsure, uncertain, in two minds, shilly-shallying, undecided, in a quandary/dilemma, blowing hot and cold. 2 *it is doubtful whether he will come* **in doubt**, uncertain, open to question, unsure,

d

unconfirmed, not definite, unknown, undecided, unresolved, debatable, in the balance, up in the air; informal iffy. **3** *the whole trip is looking rather doubtful* **unlikely**, improbable, dubious, impossible. **4** *they are doubtful of the methods used* **distrustful**, mistrustful, suspicious, wary, chary, leery, apprehensive; sceptical, unsure, ambivalent, dubious, cynical. **5** *this decision is of doubtful validity* **questionable**, arguable, debatable, controversial, contentious; informal iffy; Brit. informal dodgy.
– OPPOSITES confident, certain, probable, trusting.

doubtless adv. **undoubtedly**, indubitably, doubtlessly, no doubt; unquestionably, indisputably, undeniably, incontrovertibly, irrefutably; certainly, surely, of course, indeed.

doughty adj. **fearless**, dauntless, determined, resolute, indomitable, intrepid, plucky, spirited, bold, valiant, brave, stout-hearted, courageous; informal gutsy, spunky, feisty.

dour adj. **stern**, unsmiling, unfriendly, severe, forbidding, gruff, surly, grim, sullen, solemn, austere, stony.
– OPPOSITES cheerful, friendly.

douse v. **1** *a mob doused the thieves with petrol* **drench**, soak, saturate, wet, splash, slosh. **2** *a guard doused the flames* **extinguish**, put out, quench, smother, dampen down.

dovetail v. **1** *the ends of the logs were dovetailed* **joint**, join, fit together, splice, mortise, tenon. **2** *this will dovetail well with the division's existing activities* **fit in**, go together, be consistent, match, conform, harmonize, be in tune, correspond; informal square; N. Amer. informal jibe.

dowdy adj. **unfashionable**, frumpy, old-fashioned, inelegant, shabby, scruffy, frowzy; Brit. informal mumsy; Austral./NZ informal daggy.
– OPPOSITES fashionable.

down[1] adj. **1** *I'm feeling a bit down* **depressed**, sad, unhappy, melancholy, miserable, wretched, sorrowful, gloomy, dejected, downhearted, despondent, dispirited, low; informal blue, down in the dumps/mouth, fed up. **2** *the computer is down* **not working**, inoperative, malfunctioning, out of order, broken; not in service, out of action, out of commission; informal conked out, bust, (gone) kaput; N. Amer. informal on the fritz.
▸ v. informal *he downed his beer* **drink (up/down)**, gulp (down), guzzle, quaff, drain, toss off, slug, finish off; informal sink, knock back, put away, hoover up; Brit. informal neck; N. Amer. informal chug, scarf (down/up), snarf (down/up).
▸ n. *the ups and downs of running a business* **setbacks**, upsets, reverses, reversals, mishaps, vicissitudes; informal glitches.
□ **have a down on** informal disapprove of, be against, feel antagonism to, be hostile to,

feel ill will towards; informal have it in for, be down on.

down[2] n. *goose down* **soft feathers**, fine hair; fluff, fuzz, floss, lint.

down and out adj. **destitute**, poverty-stricken, impoverished, penniless, insolvent, impecunious; needy, in straitened circumstances, distressed, badly off; homeless, on the streets, vagrant, sleeping rough; informal hard up, (flat) broke, strapped (for cash), without a brass farthing, without two pennies to rub together; Brit. informal stony broke, skint; N. Amer. informal without a red cent, on skid row.
– OPPOSITES wealthy.
▸ n. (**down-and-out**) **poor person**, pauper, indigent; beggar, homeless person, vagrant, tramp, drifter, derelict, vagabond; N. Amer. hobo; Austral. bagman; informal have-not, bag lady; Brit. informal dosser; N. Amer. informal bum.

down at heel adj. **1** *the resort looks down at heel* **run down**, dilapidated, neglected, uncared-for; seedy, insalubrious, squalid, slummy, wretched; informal scruffy, scuzzy; Brit. informal grotty; N. Amer. informal shacky. **2** *a down-at-heel labourer* **scruffy**, shabby, ragged, tattered, mangy, sorry; unkempt, bedraggled, dishevelled, ungroomed, seedy, untidy, slovenly; informal tatty, scuzzy, grungy; Brit. informal grotty; N. Amer. informal raggedy.
– OPPOSITES smart.

downbeat adj. **1** *the mood is decidedly downbeat* **pessimistic**, gloomy, negative, defeatist, cynical, bleak, fatalistic, dark, black; despairing, despondent, depressed, dejected, demoralized, hopeless, melancholy, glum. **2** *his downbeat joviality* **relaxed**, easy-going, easy, casual, informal, nonchalant, insouciant; low-key, subtle, unostentatious, cool; informal laid-back.

downcast adj. **despondent**, disheartened, discouraged, dispirited, downhearted, crestfallen, down, low, disconsolate, despairing; sad, melancholy, gloomy, glum, morose, doleful, dismal, woebegone, miserable, depressed, dejected; informal blue, down in the mouth, down in the dumps.
– OPPOSITES elated.

downfall n. **undoing**, ruin, ruination; defeat, conquest, deposition, overthrow; nemesis, destruction, annihilation, elimination; end, collapse, fall, crash, failure; debasement, degradation, disgrace; Waterloo.
– OPPOSITES rise.

downgrade v. **1** *plans to downgrade three workers* **demote**, lower, reduce/lower in rank; relegate. **2** *I won't downgrade their achievement* **disparage**, denigrate, detract from, run down, belittle; informal bad-mouth.
– OPPOSITES promote, praise.

downhearted adj. **despondent**, disheartened, discouraged, dispirited, disconsolate, downcast, crestfallen, down, low, wretched; melancholy, gloomy, glum, morose, doleful, dismal, woebegone, miserable, depressed, dejected, sorrowful,

sad; informal blue, down in the mouth, down in the dumps.
– OPPOSITES elated.

downmarket adj. Brit. **cheap**, cheap and nasty, inferior; low-class, lowbrow, unsophisticated, rough, insalubrious; informal tacky, rubbishy, dumbed down.

downpour n. **rainstorm**, cloudburst, deluge; thunderstorm; torrential/pouring rain.

downright adj. 1 *downright lies* **complete**, total, absolute, utter, thorough, out-and-out, outright, sheer, arrant, pure, real, veritable, categorical, unmitigated, unadulterated, unalloyed, unequivocal; Brit. informal proper. 2 *her downright attitude* **frank**, straightforward, direct, blunt, plain-spoken, forthright, uninhibited, unreserved; no-nonsense, matter-of-fact, bluff, undiplomatic; explicit, clear, plain, unequivocal, unambiguous; honest, candid, open, sincere; informal upfront.
▸ adv. *that's downright dangerous* **thoroughly**, utterly, positively, profoundly, really, completely, totally, entirely; unquestionably, undeniably, in every respect, through and through; informal plain.

downside n. **drawback**, disadvantage, snag, stumbling block, catch, pitfall, fly in the ointment; handicap, limitation, trouble, difficulty, problem, complication, nuisance; hindrance; weak spot/point; informal minus, flip side.
– OPPOSITES advantage.

down-to-earth adj. **practical**, sensible, realistic, matter-of-fact, responsible, reasonable, rational, logical, balanced, sober, pragmatic, level-headed, commonsensical, sane.
– OPPOSITES idealistic.

downtrodden adj. **oppressed**, subjugated, persecuted, repressed, tyrannized, crushed, enslaved, exploited, victimized, bullied; disadvantaged, underprivileged, powerless, helpless; abused, maltreated.

downward adj. **descending**, downhill, falling, sinking, dipping; earthbound, earthward.

downy adj. **soft**, velvety, smooth, fleecy, fluffy, fuzzy, feathery, furry, woolly, silky.

dowry n. **marriage settlement**, (marriage) portion; old use dot.

doze v. **catnap**, nap, drowse, sleep lightly, rest; informal snooze, snatch forty winks, get some shut-eye; Brit. informal kip; N. Amer. informal catch some Zs; literary slumber.
▸ n. **catnap**, nap, siesta, light sleep, drowse, rest; informal snooze, forty winks; Brit. informal kip, zizz; literary slumber.
□ **doze off** fall asleep, go to sleep, drop off; informal nod off, drift off; N. Amer. informal sack out, zone out.

dozy adj. **drowsy**, sleepy, half asleep, heavy-eyed, somnolent; lethargic, listless, enervated, inactive, languid, weary, tired, fatigued; N. Amer. logy; informal dopey, yawny.

drab adj. 1 *a drab interior* **colourless**, grey, dull, washed out, muted, lacklustre; dingy, dreary, dismal, cheerless, gloomy, sombre. 2 *a drab existence* **uninteresting**, dull, boring, tedious, monotonous, dry, dreary; unexciting, unimaginative, uninspiring, insipid, lacklustre, flat, stale, wishy-washy, colourless; lame, tired, sterile, anaemic, barren, tame; middle-of-the-road, run-of-the-mill, mediocre, nondescript, characterless, mundane, unremarkable, humdrum.
– OPPOSITES bright, cheerful, interesting.

draconian adj. **harsh**, severe, strict, extreme, drastic, stringent, tough; cruel, oppressive, ruthless, relentless, punitive; authoritarian, despotic, tyrannical, repressive; Brit. swingeing.
– OPPOSITES lenient.

draft n. 1 *the draft of his speech* **preliminary version**, rough outline, plan, skeleton, abstract; main points, bare bones. 2 *a draft of the building* **plan**, blueprint, design, diagram, drawing, sketch, map, layout, representation. 3 *a banker's draft* **cheque**, order, money order, bill of exchange, postal order.

drag v. 1 *she dragged the chair backwards* **haul**, pull, tug, heave, lug, draw; trail, trawl, tow; informal yank. 2 *the day dragged* **become tedious**, pass slowly, creep along, hang heavy, wear on, go on too long, go on and on.
▸ n. 1 *the drag of the air brakes* **pull**, resistance, tug. 2 informal *work can be a drag* **bore**, nuisance, bother, trouble, pest, annoyance, trial, vexation; informal pain (in the neck), bind, headache, hassle.
□ **drag on** persist, continue, go on, carry on, extend, run on, be protracted, endure, prevail.
drag something out prolong, protract, draw out, spin out, string out, extend, lengthen, carry on, keep going, continue.

dragoon n. historical *the dragoons charged* **cavalryman**, mounted soldier; historical knight, chevalier, hussar; old use cavalier.
▸ v. *he dragooned his friends into participating* **coerce**, pressure, pressurize, press, push press-gang; force, compel, impel; hound, harass, nag, harry, badger, goad, pester; browbeat, bludgeon, bully, twist someone's arm, strong-arm; informal railroad.

drain v. 1 *a valve for draining the tank* **empty (out)**, void, clear (out), evacuate, unload. 2 *drain off any surplus liquid* **draw off**, extract, withdraw, remove, siphon off, pour out, pour off; milk, bleed, tap, void, filter, discharge. 3 *the water drained away to the sea* **flow**, pour, trickle, stream, run, rush, gush, flood, surge; leak, ooze, seep, dribble, issue, filter, bleed, leach. 4 *more people would just drain our resources* **use up**, exhaust, deplete, consume, expend, get through, sap, strain, tax; milk, bleed. 5 *he drained his drink* **drink (up/down)**, gulp (down), guzzle, quaff, down, imbibe, sup, swallow, finish off, toss off, slug; informal sink, swig, swill (down), polish off, knock back, put away; Brit. informal neck; N. Amer. informal chug.

d

– OPPOSITES fill.

▶n. **1** *the drain filled with water* **sewer**, channel, conduit, ditch, culvert, duct, pipe, gutter, trough; sluice, spillway, race, flume, chute. **2** *a drain on the battery* **strain**, pressure, burden, load, tax, demand.

dram n. **drink**, nip, tot, sip, drop, finger, splash, little, spot, taste.

drama n. **1** *a television drama* **play**, show, piece, theatrical work, dramatization. **2** *he is studying drama* **acting**, the theatre, the stage, the performing arts, dramatic art, stagecraft. **3** *she liked to create a drama* **incident**, scene, spectacle, crisis; excitement, thrill, sensation; disturbance, row, commotion, turmoil; dramatics, theatrics.

dramatic adj. **1** *dramatic art* **theatrical**, theatric, thespian, stage, dramaturgical; formal histrionic. **2** *a dramatic increase* **considerable**, substantial, sizeable, goodly, fair, marked, noticeable, measurable, perceptible, obvious, appreciable; significant, notable, noteworthy, remarkable, extraordinary, exceptional, phenomenal; informal tidy. **3** *there were dramatic scenes in the city* **exciting**, stirring, action-packed, sensational, spectacular; startling, unexpected, tense, gripping, riveting, fascinating, thrilling, hair-raising; rousing, lively, electrifying, impassioned, moving. **4** *dramatic headlands* **striking**, impressive, imposing, spectacular, breathtaking, dazzling, sensational, awesome, awe-inspiring, remarkable, outstanding, incredible, phenomenal. **5** *a dramatic gesture* **exaggerated**, theatrical, ostentatious, actressy, stagy, showy, melodramatic, overdone, actorly, histrionic, affected, mannered, artificial; informal hammy, ham, campy.

– OPPOSITES insignificant, boring.

dramatist n. **playwright**, writer, scriptwriter, screenwriter, scenarist, dramaturge.

dramatize v. **1** *the novel was dramatized for television* **turn into a play/film**, adapt for the stage/screen. **2** *the tabloids dramatized the event* **exaggerate**, overdo, overstate, hyperbolize, magnify, amplify, inflate; sensationalize, embroider, colour, aggrandize, embellish, elaborate; informal blow up (out of all proportion).

drape v. **1** *she draped a shawl round her* **wrap**, wind, swathe, sling, hang. **2** *the chair was draped with blankets* **cover**, envelop, swathe, shroud, deck, festoon, overlay, cloak, wind, enfold, sheathe. **3** *he draped one leg over the arm of his chair* **dangle**, hang, suspend, droop, drop.

drastic adj. **extreme**, serious, desperate, radical, far-reaching, momentous, substantial; heavy, severe, harsh, rigorous, oppressive, draconian.

– OPPOSITES moderate.

draught n. **1** *the draught made Robyn shiver* **current of air**, rush of air; waft, wind, breeze, gust, puff, blast; informal blow. **2** *a*

deep draught of beer **gulp**, drink, swallow, mouthful, slug; informal swig, swill; N. Amer. informal chug.

draw v. **1** *he drew the house* **sketch**, make a drawing (of), delineate, outline, draft, rough out, illustrate, render, represent, trace; portray, depict. **2** *she drew her chair in to the table* **pull**, haul, drag, tug, heave, lug, trail, tow; informal yank. **3** *the train drew into the station* **move**, go, come, proceed, progress, travel, advance, pass, drive; inch, roll, glide, cruise; forge, sweep; back. **4** *she drew the curtains* **close**, shut, pull to, lower; open, part, pull back, pull open, fling open, raise. **5** *he drew some fluid off the knee joint* **drain**, extract, withdraw, remove, suck, pump, siphon, milk, bleed, tap. **6** *he drew his gun* **pull out**, take out, produce, fish out, extract, withdraw; unsheathe. **7** *I drew £50 out of the bank* **withdraw**, take out. **8** *while I draw breath* **breathe in**, inhale, inspire, respire. **9** *she was drawing huge audiences* **attract**, interest, win, capture, catch, engage, lure, entice; absorb, occupy, rivet, engross, fascinate, mesmerize, spellbind, captivate, enthral, grip. **10** *what conclusion can we draw?* **deduce**, infer, conclude, derive, gather, glean.

▶n. **1** *she won the Christmas draw* **raffle**, lottery, sweepstake, sweep, tombola, ballot; N. Amer. lotto. **2** *the match ended in a draw* **tie**, dead heat, stalemate. **3** *the draw of central London* **attraction**, lure, allure, pull, appeal, glamour, enticement, temptation, charm, seduction, fascination, magnetism.

□ **draw on** call on, have recourse to, avail oneself of, turn to, look to, fall back on, rely on, exploit, use, employ, utilize, bring into play.

draw something out 1 *he drew out a gun.* See **draw** (sense 6 of the verb). **2** *they always drew their parting out* prolong, protract, drag out, spin out, string out, extend, lengthen.

draw someone out encourage to talk, put at ease.

draw up stop, pull up, halt, come to a standstill, brake, park; arrive.

draw something up 1 *we drew up a list* compose, formulate, frame, write down, draft, prepare, think up, devise, work out; create, invent, design. **2** *he drew up his forces in battle array* arrange, marshal, muster, assemble, group, order, range, rank, line up, dispose, position, array.

drawback n. **disadvantage**, snag, downside, stumbling block, catch, hitch, pitfall, fly in the ointment; weak spot/point, weakness, imperfection; handicap, limitation, trouble, difficulty, problem, issue, complication; hindrance, obstacle, impediment, obstruction, inconvenience, discouragement, deterrent; Brit. spanner in the works; informal minus, hiccup.

– OPPOSITES benefit.

drawing n. **sketch**, picture, illustration, representation, portrayal, delineation, depiction, composition, study; diagram, outline, design, plan.

drawl v. **say slowly**, speak slowly; drone.

drawn adj. *she looked pale and drawn* **pinched**, haggard, drained, wan, hollow-cheeked; fatigued, tired, exhausted; tense, stressed, strained, worried, anxious, harassed, fraught; informal hassled.

dread v. *I used to dread going to school* **fear**, be afraid of, worry about, be anxious about, have forebodings about; be terrified by, tremble/shudder at, shrink from, quail from, flinch from; informal get cold feet about.
▶ n. *she was filled with dread* **fear**, apprehension, trepidation, anxiety, worry, concern, foreboding, disquiet, unease, angst; fright, panic, alarm; terror, horror; informal the jitters, the heebie-jeebies.
– OPPOSITES confidence.
▶ adj. *a dread secret* **awful**, frightful, terrible, horrible, dreadful; feared, frightening, alarming, terrifying, dire, dreaded.

dreadful adj. **1** *a dreadful accident* **terrible**, frightful, horrible, grim, awful, dire; horrifying, alarming, shocking, distressing, appalling, harrowing; ghastly, fearful, horrendous; tragic, calamitous; formal grievous. **2** *a dreadful meal* **unpleasant**, disagreeable, nasty; frightful, shocking, awful, abysmal, atrocious, disgraceful, deplorable, very bad, répugnant; poor, inadequate, inferior, unsatisfactory, distasteful; informal pathetic, woeful, crummy, rotten, sorry, third-rate, lousy, ropy, God-awful; Brit. informal duff, chronic, rubbish, pants. **3** *you're a dreadful flirt* **outrageous**, shocking; inordinate, immoderate, unrestrained.
– OPPOSITES pleasant, agreeable.

dreadfully adv. **1** *I'm dreadfully hungry* **extremely**, very, really, exceedingly, tremendously, exceptionally, extraordinarily; decidedly, most, particularly; N. English right; informal terrifically, terribly, desperately, awfully, devilishly, mega, seriously, majorly; Brit. informal jolly, ever so, dead, well; N. Amer. informal real, mighty, awful; informal dated frightfully. **2** *she missed James dreadfully* **very much**, much, lots, a lot, a great deal, intensely, desperately. **3** *the company performed dreadfully* **terribly**, awfully, very badly, atrociously, abysmally, appallingly, abominably, poorly; informal pitifully, diabolically.

dream n. **1** *I awoke from my dreams* REM sleep; nightmare; vision, fantasy, hallucination. **2** *she went around in a dream* **daydream**, reverie, trance, daze, stupor, haze; Scottish dwam. **3** *he realized his childhood dream* **ambition**, aspiration, hope; goal, aim, objective, grail, intention, intent, target; desire, wish, yearning; daydream, fantasy, pipe dream. **4** *he's an absolute dream* **delight**, joy, marvel, wonder, gem, treasure; beauty, vision.
▶ v. **1** *she dreamed of her own funeral* **have a dream**, have a nightmare. **2** *I dreamt of making the Olympic team* **fantasize about**, daydream about; **wish for**, hope for, long for, yearn for, hanker after, set one's heart on; aspire to, aim for, set one's sights on. **3** *she's always dreaming* **daydream**, be in a trance, be lost in thought, be preoccupied, be abstracted, stare into space, be in cloud cuckoo land; muse. **4** *I wouldn't dream of being late* **think**, consider, contemplate, conceive.
▶ adj. *his dream home* **ideal**, perfect, fantasy.
□ **dream something up** think up, invent, concoct, devise, hatch, contrive, create, work out, come up with; informal cook up.

dreamer n. **fantasist**, daydreamer; romantic, sentimentalist, idealist, wishful thinker, Don Quixote; Utopian, visionary.
– OPPOSITES realist.

dreamland n. **1** *I drift off to dreamland* **sleep**; humorous the land of Nod. **2** *they must be living in dreamland* **the land of make-believe**, fairyland, cloud cuckoo land; paradise, Utopia, heaven, Shangri-La.

dreamlike adj. **unreal**, illusory, imaginary, unsubstantial, chimerical, ethereal, phantasmagorical, trance-like; surreal; nightmarish, Kafkaesque; hazy, shadowy, faint, indistinct, unclear; literary illusive.

dreamy adj. **1** *a dreamy expression* **daydreaming**, dreaming; pensive, thoughtful, reflective, meditative, ruminative; lost in thought, preoccupied, distracted, rapt, inattentive, wool-gathering, vague, absorbed, absent-minded, with one's head in the clouds, in a world of one's own; informal miles away. **2** *he was dreamy as a child* **idealistic**, romantic, starry-eyed, impractical, unrealistic, Utopian, quixotic; Brit. informal airy-fairy. **3** *a dreamy recollection* **dreamlike**, vague, dim, hazy, shadowy, faint, indistinct, unclear. **4** informal *the prince was really dreamy* **attractive**, handsome, good-looking; appealing, lovely, delightful; informal heavenly, divine, gorgeous, hot, cute.
– OPPOSITES alert, practical, clear, ugly.

dreary adj. **1** *a dreary day at school* **dull**, drab, uninteresting, flat, tedious, wearisome, boring, unexciting, uninspiring, soul-destroying; humdrum, monotonous, uneventful, unremarkable, featureless. **2** *she thought of dreary things* **sad**, miserable, depressing, gloomy, sombre, grave, mournful, melancholic, joyless, cheerless. **3** *a dreary day* **gloomy**, dismal, dull, dark, dingy, murky, overcast; depressing, sombre.
– OPPOSITES exciting, cheerful, bright.

dregs plural n. **1** *the dregs from a bottle of wine* **sediment**, deposit, residue, accumulation, sludge, lees, grounds, settlings; remains; technical residuum; old use grouts. **2** *the dregs of humanity* **scum**, refuse, riff-raff, outcasts, deadbeats; the underclass, the untouchables, the lowest of the low, the great unwashed, the hoi polloi; informal trash; Brit. informal dossers.

drench v. **soak**, saturate, wet through, permeate, douse, souse; drown, swamp, inundate, flood; steep, bathe.

dress v. **1** *he dressed quickly* **put on clothes**, clothe oneself, get dressed. **2** *she was dressed in a suit* **clothe**, attire, garb, deck out, trick out/up, costume, array, robe; informal get up, doll up; old use apparel. **3** *she enjoyed dressing the tree* **decorate**, trim, deck, adorn, ornament, embellish, beautify, prettify; festoon, garland, garnish. **4** *they dressed his wounds* **bandage**, cover, bind, wrap, swathe. **5** *she had to dress the chickens* **prepare**, get ready; clean. **6** *the field was dressed with manure* **fertilize**, enrich, manure, mulch, compost, top-dress.

▶n. **1** *a long blue dress* **frock**, gown, robe, shift. **2** *full evening dress* **clothes**, clothing, garments, attire; costume, outfit, ensemble, garb, turnout; informal gear, get-up, togs, duds, garms, glad rags; Brit. informal clobber; N. Amer. informal threads; formal apparel; old use raiment.

□ **dress up 1** *Angela loved dressing up* **dress smartly**; informal doll oneself up, put on one's glad rags. **2** *Hugh dressed up as Santa Claus* **disguise oneself**, dress; put on fancy dress, put on a costume.

dress something up present, represent, portray, depict, characterize; embellish, enhance, touch up, embroider.

dressing n. **1** *salad dressing* **sauce**, relish, condiment, dip. **2** *they put fresh dressings on her burns* **bandage**, covering, plaster, gauze, lint, compress. **3** *a soil dressing* **fertilizer**, mulch; manure, compost, dung, bonemeal, fishmeal, guano; top-dressing.

dressmaker n. **tailor**, seamstress, needlewoman; outfitter, costumier, clothier; couturier, designer; dated modiste.

dressy adj. **smart**, formal; elaborate, ornate; stylish, elegant, chic, fashionable; informal snappy, snazzy, natty, trendy.
– OPPOSITES casual.

dribble v. **1** *the baby started to dribble* **drool**, slaver, slobber, salivate, drivel, water at the mouth; Scottish & Irish slabber. **2** *rainwater dribbled down her face* **trickle**, drip, fall, drizzle; ooze, seep.

▶n. **1** *there was dribble on his chin* **saliva**, spittle, spit, slaver, slobber, drool. **2** *a dribble of sweat* **trickle**, drip, driblet, stream, drizzle; drop, splash.

dried adj. **dehydrated**, desiccated, dry, dried up, moistureless.

drift v. **1** *his raft drifted down the river* **be carried**, be borne; float, bob, waft, meander. **2** *the guests drifted away* **wander**, meander, stray, potter, dawdle; Brit. informal mooch. **3** *don't allow your attention to drift* **stray**, digress, deviate, diverge, veer, get sidetracked. **4** *snow drifted over the path* **pile up**, bank up, heap up, accumulate, gather, amass.

▶n. **1** *a drift from the country to urban areas* **movement**, shift, flow, transfer, relocation, gravitation. **2** *the pilot had not noticed any drift* **deviation**, digression. **3** *he caught the drift of her thoughts* **gist**, essence, meaning, sense, substance, significance; thrust, import, tenor; implication, intention; direction, course. **4** *a drift of deep snow* **pile**, heap, bank, mound, mass, accumulation.

drifter n. **wanderer**, traveller, transient, roamer, tramp, vagabond, vagrant; N. Amer. hobo.

drill n. **1** *a hydraulic drill* **drilling tool**, boring tool, auger, (brace and) bit, gimlet, awl, bradawl. **2** *they learned military discipline and drill* **training**, instruction, coaching, teaching; (physical) exercises, workout; informal square-bashing. **3** *Estelle knew the drill* **procedure**, routine, practice, regimen, programme, schedule; method, system.

▶v. **1** *drill the piece of wood* **bore a hole in**, make a hole in; bore, pierce, puncture, perforate. **2** *a sergeant drilling new recruits* **train**, instruct, coach, teach, discipline; exercise, put someone through their paces. **3** *his mother had drilled politeness into him* **instil**, hammer, drive, drum, din, implant, ingrain; teach, indoctrinate, brainwash.

drink v. **1** *she drank her coffee* **swallow**, gulp down, quaff, guzzle, sup; imbibe, sip, consume; drain, toss off, slug; informal swig, down, knock back, put away, sink, swill; Brit. informal neck. **2** *he never drank* **drink alcohol**, tipple, indulge; carouse; informal hit the bottle, booze, knock a few back, have one over the eight, get tanked up, go on a bender; Brit. informal bevvy; N. Amer. informal bend one's elbow. **3** *let's drink to success* **toast**, salute.

▶n. **1** *he took a sip of his drink* **beverage**, liquid refreshment; dram, bracer, nightcap, nip, tot; pint; Brit. informal bevvy; humorous libation; old use potation. **2** *she turned to drink* **alcohol**, (intoxicating) liquor, alcoholic drink; informal booze, hooch, the hard stuff, firewater, rotgut, moonshine, the bottle, the sauce, grog, Dutch courage. **3** *she took a drink of her wine* **swallow**, gulp, sip, draught, slug; informal swig, swill; N. Amer. informal chug. **4** *a drink of orange juice* **glass**, cup, mug. **5** informal *he fell into the drink* **the sea**, the ocean, the water; informal the briny, Davy Jones's locker; literary the deep.

□ **drink something in** absorb, assimilate, digest, ingest, take in; be rapt in, be lost in, be fascinated by, pay close attention to.

drinkable adj. **fit to drink**, palatable; pure, clean, safe, unpolluted, untainted, uncontaminated; formal potable.

drinker n. **drunkard**, drunk, inebriate, imbiber, tippler, sot; alcoholic, dipsomaniac, alcohol-abuser; informal boozer, soak, lush, wino, alky, sponge, barfly; US informal juicehead; Austral./NZ informal hophead; old use toper.
– OPPOSITES teetotaller.

drip v. **1** *there was a tap dripping* **dribble**, drop, leak. **2** *sweat dripped from his chin*

drop, dribble, trickle, drizzle, run, splash, plop; leak, emanate, issue.
▸ n. **1** *a bucket to catch the drips* **drop**, dribble, spot, trickle, splash. **2** *informal that drip who fancies you* **weakling**, ninny, milksop, namby-pamby, crybaby, softie, doormat; informal wimp, weed, sissy; Brit. informal wet, big girl's blouse; N. Amer. informal pantywaist, pussy, wuss.

drive v. **1** *I can't drive a car* **operate**, handle, manage; pilot, steer. **2** *he drove to the police station* **travel by car**, motor. **3** *I'll drive you to the airport* **chauffeur**, run, give someone a lift, take, ferry, transport, convey, carry. **4** *the engine drives the front wheels* **power**, propel, move, push. **5** *he drove a nail into the boot* **hammer**, screw, ram, sink, plunge, thrust, propel, knock. **6** *she drove her cattle to market* **impel**, urge; herd, round-up, shepherd. **7** *a desperate mother driven to crime* **force**, compel, prompt, precipitate; oblige, coerce, pressure, goad, spur, prod. **8** *he drove his staff extremely hard* **work**, push, tax, exert.
▸ n. **1** *an afternoon drive* **excursion**, outing, trip, jaunt, tour; ride, run, journey; informal spin. **2** *the house has a long drive* **driveway**, approach, access road. **3** *sexual drive* **urge**, appetite, desire, need; impulse, instinct. **4** *she lacked the drive to succeed* **motivation**, ambition, single-mindedness, will power, dedication, doggedness, tenacity; enthusiasm, zeal, commitment, aggression, spirit; energy, vigour, verve, vitality, pep; informal get-up-and-go. **5** *an anti-corruption drive* **campaign**, crusade, movement, effort, push, appeal. **6** Brit. *a whist drive* **tournament**, competition, contest, event, match.
□ **drive at** suggest, imply, hint at, allude to, intimate, insinuate, indicate; refer to, mean, intend; informal get at.

drivel n. *he was talking complete drivel* **nonsense**, twaddle, claptrap, balderdash, gibberish, rubbish, mumbo jumbo; N. Amer. garbage; informal rot, poppycock, phooey, piffle, tripe, bosh, bull, hogwash, baloney; Brit. informal cobblers, codswallop, waffle, tosh, double Dutch; N. Amer. informal flapdoodle, bushwa; informal dated tommyrot, bunkum.
▸ v. *you always drivel on* **talk nonsense**, talk rubbish, babble, ramble, gibber, blather, blether, prattle, gabble; Brit. informal waffle, witter.

driver v. **motorist**, chauffeur; pilot, operator.

drizzle n. **1** *they shivered in the drizzle* **fine rain**, light shower, spray; N. English mizzle. **2** *a drizzle of sour cream* **trickle**, dribble, drip, stream, rivulet; sprinkle, sprinkling.
▸ v. **1** *it's beginning to drizzle* **rain lightly**, shower, spot; Brit. informal spit; N. English mizzle; N. Amer. sprinkle. **2** *drizzle the cream over the jelly* **trickle**, drip, dribble, pour, splash, sprinkle.

droll adj. **funny**, humorous, amusing, comic, comical, mirthful, hilarious; clownish, farcical, zany, quirky; jocular, light-hearted, facetious, witty, whimsical, wry, tongue-in-cheek; informal waggish, wacky, side-splitting,
rib-tickling.
– OPPOSITES serious.

drone v. **1** *a plane droned overhead* **hum**, buzz, whir, vibrate, murmur, rumble, purr. **2** *he droned on about right and wrong* **speak boringly**, go on and on, talk at length; intone, pontificate; informal spout, sound off, jaw, spiel, speechify.
▸ n. **1** *the drone of aircraft taking off* **hum**, buzz, whir, vibration, murmur, purr. **2** *drones supported by taxpayers' money* **hanger-on**, parasite, leech, passenger; idler, loafer, layabout, good-for-nothing, do-nothing; informal lazybones, scrounger, sponger, cadger, freeloader, bloodsucker, waster, slacker.

drool v. *his mouth was drooling* **salivate**, dribble, slaver, slobber; Scottish & Irish slabber.
▸ n. *a fine trickle of drool* **saliva**, spit, spittle, dribble, slaver, slobber.

droop v. **1** *the dog's tail is drooping* **hang (down)**, dangle, sag, flop; wilt, sink, slump, drop, drape. **2** *his eyelids were drooping* **close**, shut, fall. **3** *the news made her droop* **be despondent**, lose heart, give up hope, become dispirited, become dejected; flag, languish, wilt.

droopy adj. **hanging (down)**, dangling, falling, dropping, draped; bent, bowed, stooping; sagging, flopping, wilting.

drop v. **1** *Eric dropped the box* **let fall**, let go of, lose one's grip on; release, unhand, relinquish. **2** *water drops from the cave roof* **drip**, fall, dribble, trickle, run, plop, leak. **3** *a plane dropped out of the sky* **fall**, descend, plunge, plummet, dive, nosedive, tumble, pitch. **4** *she dropped to her knees* **fall**, sink, collapse, slump, tumble. **5** informal *I was dropping with exhaustion* **collapse**, faint, pass out, black out, swoon, keel over; informal flake out, conk out. **6** *the track dropped from the ridge* **slope downwards**, slant downwards, descend, go down, fall away, sink, dip. **7** *the exchange rate dropped* **decrease**, lessen, reduce, diminish, depreciate; fall, decline, dwindle, sink, slump, plunge, plummet. **8** *pupils can drop history if they wish* **give up**, finish with, withdraw from; discontinue, end, stop, cease, halt; abandon, forgo, relinquish, dispense with, have done with; informal pack in, quit. **9** *he was dropped from the team* **exclude**, discard, expel, oust, throw out, leave out; dismiss, discharge, let go; informal boot out, kick out, turf out. **10** *he dropped his unsuitable friends* **abandon**, desert, throw over; renounce, disown, turn one's back on, wash one's hands of; reject, give up, cast off; neglect, shun; Brit. informal give someone the push; literary forsake. **11** *he dropped all reference to compensation* **omit**, leave out, eliminate, take out, miss out, delete, cut, erase. **12** *the taxi dropped her off* **deliver**, bring, take, convey, carry, transport; leave, unload. **13** *drop the gun on the ground* **put**, place, deposit, set, lay, leave; informal pop, plonk. **14** *she dropped names* **mention**, refer to, hint at; bring up, raise, broach, introduce; show off. **15** *the team has yet to drop a point*

lose, concede, give away.
– OPPOSITES lift, rise, increase, keep, win.
▸n. 1 *a drop of water* **droplet**, blob, globule, bead, bubble, tear, dot; informal glob. 2 *it needs a drop of oil* **small amount**, little, bit, dash, spot; dribble, driblet, sprinkle, trickle, splash; dab, speck, smattering, sprinkling, modicum; informal smidgen, tad. 3 *an acid drop* **sweet**, lozenge, pastille, bonbon; N. Amer. candy. 4 *a small drop in profits* **decrease**, reduction, decline, fall-off, downturn, slump; cut, cutback, curtailment; depreciation. 5 *I walked to the edge of the drop* **cliff**, abyss, chasm, gorge, gully, precipice; slope, descent, incline. 6 *the hangman measured her for the drop* **hanging**, gibbeting; execution; informal stringing up.
– OPPOSITES increase.
□ **drop back/behind** fall back/behind, get left behind, lag behind; straggle, linger, dawdle, dally, hang back, loiter, bring/take up the rear; informal dilly-dally.
drop off 1 *trade dropped off sharply.* See **drop** (sense 7 of the verb). 2 *she kept dropping off* fall asleep, doze (off), nap, catnap, drowse; informal nod off, drift off, snooze, take forty winks.
drop out of *he dropped out of his studies.* See **drop** (sense 8 of the verb).

dropout n. **nonconformist**, hippy, beatnik, bohemian, free spirit, rebel; idler, layabout, loafer; informal oddball, deadbeat, waster, bad boy.

droppings plural n. **excrement**, excreta, faeces, stools, dung, ordure, manure; informal pooh.

dross n. **rubbish**, junk; debris, chaff, detritus, flotsam and jetsam; N. Amer. garbage, trash; informal dreck.

drought n. **dry spell**, lack of rain, shortage of water.

drove n. 1 *a drove of cattle* **herd**, flock, pack. 2 *they came in droves* **crowd**, swarm, horde, multitude, mob, throng, host, mass, army, herd.

drown v. 1 *the valleys were drowned* **flood**, submerge, immerse, inundate, deluge, swamp, engulf. 2 *his voice was drowned out by the footsteps* **make inaudible**, overpower, overwhelm, override; muffle, deaden, stifle, extinguish.

drowse v. *they like to drowse in the sun* **doze**, nap, catnap, rest; informal snooze, get forty winks, get some shut-eye; Brit. informal kip; N. Amer. informal catch some Zs.
▸n. *she had been woken from her drowse* **doze**, light sleep, nap, catnap, rest; informal snooze, forty winks, shut-eye; Brit. informal kip.

drowsy adj. 1 *the tablet made her drowsy* **sleepy**, dozy, heavy-eyed, groggy, somnolent; tired, weary, fatigued, exhausted, yawning, nodding; lethargic, sluggish, torpid, listless, languid; informal snoozy, dopey, yawny, dead beat, all in, dog-tired; Brit. informal knackered. 2 *a drowsy afternoon* **soporific**, sleep-inducing, sleepy, somniferous; narcotic, sedative, tranquillizing; lulling, soothing.
– OPPOSITES alert, invigorating.

drubbing n. 1 *I gave him a good drubbing* **beating**, thrashing, walloping, thumping, battering, pounding, pummelling, slapping, punching, pelting; informal hammering, licking, clobbering, belting, bashing, pasting, tanning, hiding, kicking. 2 informal *Scotland's 3-0 drubbing by France.* See **defeat** (sense 1 of the noun).

drudge n. **menial worker**, slave, galley slave, lackey, servant, labourer, worker, maid/man of all work; informal gofer, runner; Brit. informal dogsbody, skivvy; Brit. dated charwoman, charlady, char.

drudgery n. **hard work**, menial work, donkey work, toil, labour; chores; informal skivvying; Brit. informal graft; Austral./NZ informal (hard) yakka.

drug n. 1 *drugs prescribed by doctors* **medicine**, medication, medicament; remedy, cure, antidote. 2 *she was under the influence of drugs* **narcotic**, stimulant, hallucinogen; informal dope, gear, downer, upper.
▸v. 1 *he was drugged* **anaesthetize**, narcotize; poison; knock out, stupefy; informal dope. 2 *she drugged his coffee* **add drugs to**, tamper with, adulterate, contaminate, lace, poison; informal dope, spike, doctor.

> **WORD LINKS**
>
> **pharmaceutical** relating to medicinal drugs
> **pharmacology** the branch of science concerned with the uses and effects of drugs
> **pharmacy** (Brit. **chemist**; N. Amer. **drugstore**) a shop selling medicinal drugs
> **codex**, **formulary**, **pharmacopoeia** an official list of medicinal drugs with directions for their use or prescription

drugged adj. **stupefied**, insensible, befuddled; delirious, hallucinating, narcotized; anaesthetized, knocked out; informal stoned, high (as a kite), doped, tripping, spaced out, wasted, wrecked, off one's head.
– OPPOSITES sober.

drum n. 1 *the beat of a drum* **percussion instrument**; bongo, tom-tom, snare drum, kettledrum; historical tambour. 2 *the steady drum of raindrops* **beat**, rhythm, patter, tap, pounding, thump, thud, rattle, pitter-patter, pit-a-pat, rat-a-tat, thrum. 3 *a drum of radioactive waste* **canister**, barrel, cylinder, tank, bin, can; container.
▸v. 1 *she drummed her fingers on the desk* **tap**, beat, rap, thud, thump; tattoo, thrum. 2 *the rules were drummed into us at school* **instil**, drive, din, hammer, drill, drub, implant, ingrain, inculcate.
□ **drum someone out** expel, dismiss, throw out, oust; drive out, get rid of; exclude, banish; informal give someone the boot, boot out, kick out, give someone their marching orders, give someone the push, show someone the door, send packing; Military cashier.
drum something up round up, gather, collect; summon, attract; canvass, solicit, petition.

drunk adj. **intoxicated**, inebriated, drunken, incapable, tipsy, the worse for drink, under the influence; informal tight, merry, in one's cups, three sheets to the wind, pie-eyed, plastered, smashed, wrecked, wasted, sloshed, soused, sozzled, blotto, stewed, pickled, tanked (up), off one's face, out of one's head, ratted; Brit. informal legless, bevvied, paralytic, Brahms and Liszt, half cut, out of it, bladdered, trolleyed, slaughtered, mullered, squiffy, tiddly; N. Amer. informal loaded, trashed, juiced, sauced, out of one's gourd, in the bag, zoned; euphemistic tired and emotional; informal dated lit up.
– OPPOSITES sober.
▶n. **drunkard**, inebriate, drinker, tippler, imbiber, sot; heavy drinker, problem drinker, alcoholic, dipsomaniac; informal boozer, soak, lush, wino, alky, sponge, barfly, tosspot; US informal juicehead; Austral./NZ informal hophead, metho; old use toper.
– OPPOSITES teetotaller.

drunken adj. **1** *a drunken driver.* See **drunk** (adjective). **2** *a drunken all-night party* **debauched**, dissipated, carousing, roistering, intemperate, unrestrained, uninhibited, abandoned; bacchanalian, Bacchic; informal boozy.

drunkenness n. **intoxication**, inebriation, insobriety, tipsiness; intemperance, overindulgence, debauchery; heavy drinking, alcoholism, alcohol abuse, dipsomania.

dry adj. **1** *the dry desert* **arid**, parched, droughty, scorched, baked; waterless, moistureless, rainless; dehydrated, desiccated, thirsty, bone dry. **2** *dry leaves* **parched**, dried, withered, shrivelled, wilted, wizened; crisp, crispy, brittle; dehydrated, desiccated. **3** *the hamburgers were dry* **hard**, stale, old, past its best; off. **4** *a dry well* **waterless**, empty. **5** *I'm really dry* **thirsty**, dehydrated; informal parched, gasping. **6** *it was dry work* **thirsty**, thirst-making; hot; strenuous, arduous. **7** *dry toast* **unbuttered**, butterless, plain. **8** *the dry facts* **bare**, simple, basic, fundamental, stark, bald, hard, straightforward. **9** *a dry debate* **dull**, uninteresting, boring, unexciting, tedious, tiresome, wearisome, dreary, monotonous; unimaginative, sterile, flat, bland, lacklustre, stodgy, prosaic, humdrum, mundane; informal deadly. **10** *a dry sense of humour* **wry**, subtle, laconic, sharp; ironic, sardonic, sarcastic, cynical; satirical, mocking, droll; informal waggish; Brit. informal sarky. **11** *a dry response to his cordial advance* **unemotional**, indifferent, impassive, cool, cold, emotionless; reserved, restrained, impersonal, formal, stiff, wooden. **12** *this is a dry state* **teetotal**, Prohibitionist, alcohol-free, non-drinking, abstinent, sober; informal on the wagon. **13** *dry white wine* **crisp**, sharp, piquant, tart, bitter.
– OPPOSITES wet, moist, fresh, lively, emotional, sweet.
▶v. **1** *the sun dried the ground* **parch**, scorch, bake; dehydrate, desiccate, dehumidify.

2 *dry the leaves completely* **dehydrate**, desiccate; wither, shrivel. **3** *he dried the dishes* **towel**, rub; mop up, blot up, soak up, absorb. **4** *she dried her eyes* **wipe**, rub, dab. **5** *methods of drying meat* **desiccate**, dehydrate; preserve, cure, smoke.
– OPPOSITES moisten.
□ **dry up 1** informal *he dried up and didn't say another thing* **stop speaking**, stop talking, fall silent, shut up; forget one's words. **2** *investment may dry up* **dwindle**, subside, peter out, wane, taper off, ebb, come to a halt/end, run out, give out, disappear, vanish.

dual adj. **double**, twofold, binary; duplicate, twin, matching, paired, coupled.
– OPPOSITES single.

dub v. **1** *he was dubbed 'the world's sexiest man'* **nickname**, call, name, label, christen, term, tag, entitle, style; designate, characterize, nominate; formal denominate. **2** *she dubbed a new knight* **knight**, invest.

dubiety n. formal **doubtfulness**, uncertainty, unsureness, incertitude; ambiguity, ambivalence, confusion; hesitancy, doubt.

dubious adj. **1** *I was rather dubious about the idea* **doubtful**, uncertain, unsure, hesitant; undecided, indefinite, unresolved, up in the air; vacillating, irresolute; sceptical, suspicious; informal iffy. **2** *a dubious businessman* **suspicious**, suspect, untrustworthy, unreliable, questionable; informal shady, fishy; Brit. informal dodgy.
– OPPOSITES certain, trustworthy.

duck[1] n. drake, duckling.

duck[2] v. **1** *he ducked behind the wall* **bob down**, bend (down), stoop (down), crouch (down), squat (down), hunch down, hunker down; cower, cringe. **2** *she was ducked in the river* **dip**, dunk, plunge, immerse, submerge, lower, sink. **3** informal *they cannot duck the issue forever* **shirk**, dodge, evade, avoid, elude, escape, back out of, shun, eschew, sidestep, bypass, circumvent; informal cop out of, get out of, wriggle out of, funk; Austral./NZ informal duck-shove.

duct n. **tube**, channel, canal, vessel; conduit, culvert; pipe, pipeline, outlet, inlet, flue, shaft, vent; Anatomy ductus, ductule.

ductile adj. **1** *ductile metals* **pliable**, pliant, flexible, supple, plastic, tensile; soft, malleable, workable, bendable; informal bendy. **2** *a way to make people ductile* **docile**, obedient, submissive, meek, mild, lamblike; willing, accommodating, amenable, cooperative, compliant, malleable, tractable, biddable, persuadable.
– OPPOSITES brittle, intransigent.

dud informal n. *their new product is a dud* **failure**, flop, let-down, disappointment; Brit. damp squib; informal washout, lemon, no-hoper, non-starter, dead loss, lead balloon, fail; N. Amer. informal clinker.
– OPPOSITES success.
▶adj. **1** *a dud typewriter* **defective**, faulty, unsound, inoperative, broken, malfunctioning; informal bust, busted, kaput,

d

conked out; Brit. informal duff, knackered.
2 *a dud £50 note* **counterfeit**, fraudulent,
forged, fake, faked, false, bogus; invalid,
worthless; informal phoney.
– OPPOSITES sound, genuine.

dudgeon n.
□ **in high dudgeon** indignantly, resentfully,
angrily, furiously; in a temper, in anger, with
displeasure; informal in a huff, in a paddy, as
cross as two sticks, seeing red; Brit. informal dated
in a bate, in a wax.

due adj. **1** *their fees were due* **owing**, owed,
payable; outstanding, overdue, unpaid,
unsettled, undischarged; N. Amer. delinquent.
2 *the chancellor's statement is due today*
expected, anticipated, scheduled for,
awaited; required. **3** *the respect due to
a great artist* **deserved by**, merited by,
warranted by; appropriate to, fit for, fitting
for, right for, proper to. **4** *he drove without
due care* **proper**, correct, rightful, suitable,
appropriate, apt; adequate, sufficient,
enough, satisfactory, requisite.
▶ n. **1** *he attracts more criticism than is his due*
rightful treatment, fair treatment, just
punishment; right, entitlement; just deserts;
informal comeuppance. **2** *members have
paid their dues* **fee**, subscription, charge;
payment, contribution.
▶ adv. *he hiked due north* **directly**, straight,
exactly, precisely, dead.
□ **due to 1** *her death was due to an infection*
attributable to, caused by, ascribed to,
because of, put down to. **2** *the train was
cancelled due to staff shortages* **because of**,
owing to, on account of, as a consequence of,
as a result of, thanks to, in view of; formal by
reason of.

duel n. **1** *he was killed in a duel* **mano-a-
mano**, single combat; fight, confrontation,
head-to-head; informal face-off, shoot-out; old
use rencounter. **2** *a snooker duel* **contest**,
match, game, meet, encounter.
▶ v. *they duelled with swords* **fight a duel**, fight,
battle, combat, contend.

duff adj. Brit. informal See **bad** (sense 1).

duffer n. informal See **dunce**.

dulcet adj. **sweet**, soothing, mellow,
honeyed, mellifluous, euphonious, pleasant,
agreeable; melodious, melodic, lilting,
lyrical, silvery, golden.
– OPPOSITES harsh.

dull adj. **1** *a dull novel* **uninteresting**, boring,
tedious, monotonous, unrelieved, unvaried,
unimaginative, uneventful; characterless,
featureless, colourless, lifeless, insipid,
unexciting, uninspiring, jejune, flat, bland,
dry, stale, tired, banal, lacklustre, stodgy,
dreary, humdrum, mundane; mind-numbing,
soul-destroying, wearisome, tiring, tiresome,
irksome; informal deadly, not up to much;
Brit. informal samey; N. Amer. informal dullsville.
2 *a dull morning* **overcast**, cloudy, gloomy,
dark, dismal, dreary, sombre, grey, murky,
sunless. **3** *dull colours* **drab**, dreary, sombre,
dark, subdued, muted, lacklustre, faded,
washed out, muddy. **4** *a dull sound* **muffled**,

muted, quiet, soft, faint, indistinct; stifled,
suppressed. **5** *the chisel became dull* **blunt**,
unsharpened, edgeless, worn down. **6** *a
rather dull child* **unintelligent**, stupid, slow,
witless, vacuous, empty-headed, brainless,
mindless, foolish, idiotic; informal dense, dim,
moronic, cretinous, half-witted, thick, dumb,
dopey, dozy, bovine, slow on the uptake,
wooden-headed, fat-headed. **7** *her cold made
her feel dull* **sluggish**, lethargic, enervated,
listless, languid, torpid, slow, sleepy, drowsy,
weary, tired, fatigued; apathetic; informal dozy,
dopey, yawny.
– OPPOSITES interesting, bright, loud,
resonant, sharp, clever.
▶ v. **1** *the pain was dulled by drugs* **lessen**,
decrease, diminish, reduce, dampen,
blunt, deaden, allay, ease, soothe, assuage,
alleviate. **2** *sleep dulled her mind* **numb**,
benumb, deaden, desensitize, stupefy,
daze. **3** *the leaves are dulled by mildew*
fade, bleach, decolorize, decolour, etiolate.
4 *rain dulled the sky* **darken**, blacken, dim,
veil, obscure, shadow, fog. **5** *the sombre
atmosphere dulled her spirit* **dampen**, lower,
depress, crush, sap, extinguish, smother,
stifle.
– OPPOSITES intensify, enliven, enhance,
brighten.

dullard n. **idiot**, fool, stupid person,
simpleton, ignoramus, oaf, dunce, dolt;
informal duffer, moron, cretin, imbecile,
nincompoop, dope, chump, nitwit, dimwit,
birdbrain, pea-brain, numbskull, fathead,
dumbo, dum-dum, donkey; Brit. informal wally,
berk, divvy; N. Amer. informal doofus, goof, bozo,
dummy; Austral./NZ informal galah.

duly adv. **1** *the document was duly signed*
properly, correctly, appropriately, suitably,
fittingly. **2** *he duly arrived to collect Alice* **at
the right time**, on time, punctually.

dumb adj. **1** *she stood dumb while he shouted*
mute, speechless, tongue-tied, silent, at a
loss for words; taciturn, uncommunicative,
tight-lipped, close-mouthed; informal mum.
2 *he is not as dumb as you'd think*
stupid, unintelligent, ignorant, dense,
brainless, mindless, foolish, slow, dull,
simple, empty-headed, vacuous, vapid,
idiotic, half-baked, imbecilic, bovine; informal
thick, dim, moronic, cretinous, dopey, dozy,
thickheaded, wooden-headed, fat-headed,
birdbrained, pea-brained; Brit. informal daft.
– OPPOSITES clever.

dumbfound v. **astonish**, astound, amaze,
stagger, surprise, startle, stun, confound,
stupefy, daze, nonplus, take aback, stop
someone in their tracks, strike dumb,
leave open-mouthed, leave aghast; informal
flabbergast, floor, knock sideways, bowl
over; Brit. informal knock for six.

dumbfounded adj. **astonished**, astounded,
amazed, staggered, surprised, startled,
stunned, confounded, nonplussed,
stupefied, dazed, dumbstruck, open-
mouthed, speechless, thunderstruck; taken
aback, disconcerted; informal flabbergasted,
flummoxed; Brit. informal gobsmacked.

dummy n. **1** *a shop-window dummy* **mannequin**, model, figure. **2** *the book is just a dummy* **mock-up**, imitation, likeness, lookalike, representation, substitute, sample; replica, reproduction; counterfeit, sham, fake, forgery; informal dupe. **3** informal *you're a dummy.* See **idiot**.
▸ adj. *a dummy attack on the airfield* **simulated**, feigned, pretended, practice, trial, mock, make-believe; informal pretend, phoney.
– OPPOSITES real.

dump n. **1** *take the rubbish to the dump* **tip**, rubbish dump, rubbish heap, dumping ground; dustheap, slag heap. **2** informal *the house is a dump* **hovel**, shack, slum; mess; informal hole, pigsty.
▸ v. **1** *he dumped his bag on the table* **put down**, set down, deposit, place, shove, unload; drop, throw down; informal stick, park, plonk; Brit. informal bung; N. Amer. informal plunk. **2** *they will dump asbestos at the site* **dispose of**, get rid of, throw away/out, discard, bin, jettison; informal ditch, junk. **3** informal *he dumped her* **abandon**, desert, leave, jilt, break up with, finish with, throw over; informal walk out on, rat on, drop, ditch, chuck, give someone the elbow; Brit. informal give someone the big E.

dumpy adj. **short**, squat, stubby; **plump**, stout, chubby, chunky, portly, fat, bulky; informal tubby, roly-poly, pudgy, porky; Brit. informal podgy.
– OPPOSITES tall, slender.

dun[1] adj. *a dun cow* **greyish-brown**, brownish, mousy, muddy, khaki, umber.

dun[2] v. *you can't dun me for her debts* **importune**, press, plague, pester, nag, harass, hound, badger; informal hassle, bug; N. English informal mither.

dunce n. **fool**, idiot, stupid person, simpleton, ignoramus, dullard; informal dummy, dumbo, clot, thickhead, nitwit, dimwit, halfwit, moron, cretin, imbecile, dope, duffer, booby, chump, numbskull, nincompoop, fathead, airhead, birdbrain, pea-brain, ninny, ass; Brit. informal wally, berk, divvy; N. Amer. informal doofus, goof, schmuck, bozo, lummox, wing nut; Austral./NZ informal galah.
– OPPOSITES genius.

dune n. **bank**, mound, hillock, hummock, knoll, ridge, heap, drift.

dung n. **manure**, muck; excrement, faeces, droppings, ordure, cowpats.

dungeon n. **underground prison**, oubliette; cell, jail, lock-up.

dupe v. *they were duped by a con man* **deceive**, trick, hoodwink, hoax, swindle, defraud, cheat, double-cross; gull, mislead, take in, fool, inveigle; informal con, do, rip off, diddle, shaft, bilk, rook, pull the wool over someone's eyes, pull a fast one on, sell a pup to; N. Amer. informal sucker, snooker; Austral. informal pull a swifty on.
▸ n. *an innocent dupe in her game* **victim**, gull, pawn, puppet, instrument; fool, innocent; informal sucker, stooge, sitting duck, muggins, fall guy; Brit. informal mug; N. Amer. informal pigeon, patsy, sap.

duplicate n. *a duplicate of the invoice* **copy**, carbon copy, photocopy, facsimile, mimeograph, photostat, reprint; replica, reproduction, clone; informal dupe; trademark Xerox.
▸ adj. *duplicate keys* **identical**, matching, twin, corresponding, equivalent.
▸ v. **1** *she will duplicate the newsletter* **copy**, photocopy, photostat, xerox, mimeograph, reproduce, replicate, reprint, run off. **2** *a feat difficult to duplicate* **repeat**, do again, redo, replicate.

duplicity n. **deceitfulness**, deceit, deception, double-dealing, double-handedness, dishonesty, fraud, fraudulence, sharp practice, chicanery, trickery, subterfuge, skulduggery, treachery; informal crookedness, shadiness, dirty tricks, shenanigans, monkey business; literary perfidy.
– OPPOSITES honesty.

durability n. **imperishability**, durableness, longevity; resilience, strength, sturdiness, toughness, robustness.
– OPPOSITES fragility.

durable adj. **1** *durable carpets* **hard-wearing**, long-lasting, heavy-duty, tough, resistant, imperishable, indestructible, strong, sturdy. **2** *a durable peace* **lasting**, long-lasting, long-term, enduring, persistent, abiding, stable, secure, firm, deep-rooted, permanent, undying, everlasting.
– OPPOSITES delicate, short-lived.

duration n. **full length**, time, time span, time scale, period, term, span, fullness, length, extent, continuation.

duress n. **coercion**, compulsion, force, pressure, intimidation, constraint; threats; informal arm-twisting.

during prep. **throughout**, through, in, in the course of, for the time of.

dusk n. **twilight**, nightfall, sunset, sundown, evening, close of day; semi-darkness, gloom, murkiness; literary gloaming, eventide.
– OPPOSITES dawn.

dusky adj. **shadowy**, dark, dim, gloomy, murky, shady; unlit, unilluminated; sunless, moonless.
– OPPOSITES bright.

dust n. **1** *the desk was covered in dust* **dirt**, grime, filth, smut, soot; fine powder. **2** *they fought in the dust* **earth**, soil, dirt; ground.
▸ v. **1** *she dusted her mantelpiece* **wipe**, clean, brush, sweep, mop. **2** *dust the cake with icing sugar* **sprinkle**, scatter, powder, dredge, sift, cover, strew.

dust-up n. informal See **scrap**[2] (noun).

dusty adj. **1** *the floor was dusty* **dirty**, grimy, grubby, unclean, soiled, mucky, sooty; undusted; informal grungy, cruddy; Brit. informal grotty. **2** *dusty sandstone* **powdery**, crumbly, chalky, friable; granular, gritty, sandy. **3** *a dusty pink* **muted**, dull, faded, pale, pastel, subtle; greyish, darkish, dirty. **4** Brit. *a dusty answer* **curt**, abrupt, terse, brusque, blunt, short, sharp, tart, gruff, offhand; informal snippy, snappy.
– OPPOSITES clean, bright.

d

dutiful adj. **conscientious**, responsible, dedicated, devoted, attentive; obedient, compliant, submissive, biddable; deferential, reverent, reverential, respectful, good.
– OPPOSITES remiss.

duty n. **1** *she was free of any duty* **responsibility**, obligation, commitment; allegiance, loyalty, faithfulness, fidelity, homage. **2** *it was his duty to attend the king* **job**, task, assignment, mission, function, charge, place, role, responsibility, obligation; dated office. **3** *the duty was raised on alcohol* **tax**, levy, tariff, excise, toll, fee, payment, rate; dues.
☐ **off duty** not working, at leisure, on holiday, on leave, off (work), free.
on duty working, at work, busy, occupied, engaged; informal on the job, tied up.

dwarf n. **1** **person of restricted growth**, small person, short person; midget, pygmy, manikin, homunculus. **2** *the wizard captured the dwarf* **gnome**, goblin, hobgoblin, troll, imp, elf, brownie, leprechaun.
▶ adj. *dwarf conifers* **miniature**, small, little, tiny, toy, pocket, diminutive, baby, fun-size, pygmy, stunted, undersized, undersize; Scottish wee; informal mini, teeny, teeny-weeny, itsy-bitsy, tiddly, pint-sized; Brit. informal titchy; N. Amer. informal little-bitty.
– OPPOSITES giant.
▶ v. **1** *the buildings dwarf the trees* **dominate**, tower over, loom over, overshadow, overtop. **2** *her progress was dwarfed by her sister's success* **overshadow**, outshine, surpass, exceed, outclass, outstrip, outdo, top, trump, transcend; diminish, minimize.

dwell v. formal *gypsies dwell in these caves* **reside**, live, be settled, be housed, lodge, stay; informal put up; formal abide, be domiciled.
☐ **dwell on** linger over, mull over, muse on, brood about/over, think about; be preoccupied by, be obsessed by, eat one's heart out over; harp on about, discuss at length.

dwelling n. formal **residence**, home, house, accommodation, lodging place; lodgings, quarters, rooms; informal place, pad, digs; formal abode, domicile, habitation.

dwindle v. *the population dwindled* **diminish**, decrease, reduce, lessen, shrink; fall off, tail off, drop, fall, slump, plummet;

disappear, vanish, die out; informal nosedive.
– OPPOSITES increase.

dye n. *a blue dye* **colourant**, colouring, colour, dyestuff, pigment, tint, stain, wash.
▶ v. *the gloves were dyed* **colour**, tint, pigment, stain, wash.

dyed-in-the-wool adj. **inveterate**, confirmed, entrenched, established, long-standing, deep-rooted, diehard; complete, absolute, thorough, thoroughgoing, out-and-out, true blue; firm, unshakeable, staunch, steadfast, committed, devoted, dedicated, loyal, unswerving; N. Amer. full-bore; informal deep-dyed, card-carrying.

dying adj. **1** *his dying aunt* **terminally ill**, at death's door, on one's deathbed, near death, fading fast, expiring, moribund, not long for this world, in extremis; informal on one's last legs, having one foot in the grave. **2** *a dying art form* **declining**, vanishing, fading, ebbing, waning; informal on the way out. **3** *her dying words* **final**, last; deathbed.
– OPPOSITES thriving, first.

dynamic adj. **energetic**, spirited, active, lively, zestful, vital, vigorous, forceful, powerful, positive; high-powered, aggressive, bold, enterprising; magnetic, passionate, fiery, high-octane; informal go-getting, peppy, full of get-up-and-go, full of vim and vigour, gutsy, spunky, feisty, go-ahead.
– OPPOSITES half-hearted.

dynamism n. **energy**, spirit, liveliness, zestfulness, vitality, vigour, forcefulness, power, potency, positivity; aggression, drive, ambition, enterprise; magnetism, passion, fire; informal pep, get-up-and-go, guts, feistiness.

dynasty n. **bloodline**, line, ancestral line, lineage, house, family, ancestry, descent, succession, genealogy, family tree; regime, rule, reign, empire, sovereignty.

dyspeptic adj. **bad-tempered**, short-tempered, irritable, snappish, testy, tetchy, touchy, crabby, crotchety, grouchy, cantankerous, peevish, cross, disagreeable, waspish, prickly; informal snappy, on a short fuse; Brit. informal stroppy, ratty, eggy, like a bear with a sore head; N. Amer. informal cranky, ornery.

Ee

each pron. *there are 5000 books and each must be cleaned* **every one**, each one, each and every one, all, the whole lot.
▸ determiner *he visited each month* **every**, each and every, every single.
▸ adv. *they gave a tenner each* **apiece**, per person, per capita, from each, individually, respectively, severally.

eager adj. **1** *small eager faces* **keen**, enthusiastic, avid, fervent, ardent, motivated, wholehearted, dedicated, committed, earnest; informal mad keen, (as) keen as mustard. **2** *we were eager for news* **anxious**, impatient, longing, yearning, wishing, hoping, hopeful; desirous of, hankering after; on the edge of one's seat, on tenterhooks, on pins and needles; informal itching, gagging, dying.
– OPPOSITES apathetic.

eagerness n. **keenness**, enthusiasm, avidity, fervour, zeal, wholeheartedness, earnestness, commitment, dedication; impatience, desire, longing, yearning, hunger, appetite, ambition; informal yen.

eagle n.

> **WORD LINKS**
> **aquiline** like an eagle
> **eyrie** an eagle's nest

ear n. **1** *he had the ear of the president* **attention**, notice, heed, regard, consideration. **2** *he has an ear for a good song* **appreciation**, discrimination, perception.
□ **play it by ear**. See **play**.

> **WORD LINKS**
> **aural, auricular, otic** relating to the ear or hearing
> **binaural** relating to both ears
> **auditory** relating to hearing
> **audiology** the branch of medicine concerned with hearing
> **otology** the study of the anatomy and diseases of the ear
> **tinnitus** ringing or buzzing in the ears
> **grommet** a tube implanted in the eardrum to drain fluid

early adj. **1** *early copies of the book* **advance**, forward; initial, preliminary, first; pilot, trial. **2** *an early death* **untimely**, premature, unseasonable, before time. **3** *early man* **primitive**, ancient, prehistoric, primeval; literary of yore. **4** *an early official statement* **prompt**, timely, quick, speedy, rapid, fast.
– OPPOSITES late, modern, overdue.

▸ adv. **1** *Rachel has to get up early* **in the early morning**; at dawn, at daybreak, at cockcrow, with the lark. **2** *they hoped to leave school early* **before the usual time**; prematurely, too soon, ahead of time, ahead of schedule.
– OPPOSITES late.

earmark v. *the cash had been earmarked for the firm* **set aside**, keep (back), reserve; designate, assign, mark; allocate, allot, devote, pledge, give over.
▸ n. *he has all the earmarks of a leader* **characteristics**, attribute, feature, hallmark, quality.

earn v. **1** *they earned £20,000* **be paid**, take home, gross; receive, get, make, obtain, collect, bring in; informal pocket, bank, rake in, net, bag. **2** *he has earned their trust* **deserve**, merit, warrant, justify, be worthy of; gain, win, secure, establish, obtain, procure, get, acquire; informal clinch.
– OPPOSITES lose.

earnest[1] adj. **1** *he is dreadfully earnest* **serious**, solemn, grave, sober, humourless, staid, intense; committed, dedicated, keen, diligent, zealous; thoughtful, cerebral, deep, profound. **2** *earnest prayer* **devout**, heartfelt, wholehearted, sincere, impassioned, fervent, ardent, intense, urgent.
– OPPOSITES frivolous, half-hearted.
□ **in earnest 1** *we are in earnest about stopping burglaries* **serious**, sincere, wholehearted, genuine; committed, firm, resolute, determined. **2** *he started writing in earnest* **zealously**, purposefully, determinedly, resolutely; passionately, wholeheartedly.

earnest[2] n. *an earnest of a good harvest* **sign**, token, promise, guarantee, pledge, assurance; security, surety, deposit.

earnestly adv. **seriously**, solemnly, gravely, intently; sincerely, resolutely, firmly, ardently, fervently, eagerly.

earnings plural n. **income**, wages, salary, stipend, pay, payment, fees; revenue, yield, profit, takings, proceeds, dividends, return, remuneration.

earth n. **1** *the moon orbits the earth* **world**, globe, planet. **2** *a trembling of the earth* **land**, ground, terra firma; floor. **3** *he ploughed the earth* **soil**, clay, loam; dirt, sod, turf; ground. **4** *the fox's earth* **den**, lair, sett, burrow, warren, hole; retreat, shelter, hideout, hideaway; informal hidey-hole.

e

earthenware n. **pottery**, crockery,
stoneware; china, porcelain; pots.

earthly adj. **1** *the earthly environment*
terrestrial, telluric. **2** *the promise of*
earthly delights **worldly**, temporal, mortal,
human; material; carnal, fleshly, bodily,
physical, corporeal, sensual. **3** informal *there*
is no earthly explanation for this **feasible**,
possible, likely, conceivable, imaginable.
– OPPOSITES extraterrestrial, heavenly.

earthquake n. **(earth) tremor**, shock,
foreshock, aftershock, convulsion; informal
quake, shake, trembler.

earthy adj. **1** *an earthy smell* **soil-like**,
dirt-like. **2** *the earthy Calvinistic tradition*
down-to-earth, unsophisticated, unrefined,
simple, plain, unpretentious, natural.
3 *Emma's earthy language* **bawdy**, ribald,
off colour, racy, rude, vulgar, lewd, crude,
foul, coarse, uncouth, unseemly, indelicate,
indecent, obscene; informal blue, locker-room,
X-rated; Brit. informal fruity, near the knuckle.

ease n. **1** *he defeated them all with ease*
effortlessness, no trouble, simplicity;
deftness, adroitness, proficiency, mastery.
2 *his ease of manner* **naturalness**,
casualness, informality, amiability, affability;
unconcern, composure, nonchalance,
insouciance. **3** *he couldn't find any ease*
peace, calm, tranquillity, serenity; repose,
restfulness, quiet, security, comfort. **4** *a life*
of ease **affluence**, wealth, prosperity, luxury,
plenty; comfort, contentment, enjoyment,
well-being.
– OPPOSITES difficulty, formality, trouble,
hardship.
▸ v. **1** *the alcohol eased his pain* **relieve**,
alleviate, mitigate, soothe, palliate,
moderate, dull, deaden, numb; reduce,
lighten, diminish. **2** *the rain eased off* **abate**,
subside, die down, let up, slacken off,
diminish, lessen, peter out, relent, come to
an end. **3** *work helped to ease her mind* **calm**,
quieten, pacify, soothe, comfort, console;
hearten, gladden, uplift, encourage. **4** *we*
want to ease their adjustment **facilitate**,
expedite, assist, help, aid, advance, further,

forward, simplify. **5** *he eased out the cork*
guide, manoeuvre, inch, edge; slide, slip,
squeeze.
– OPPOSITES aggravate, worsen, hinder.
□ **at ease/at one's ease** relaxed, calm,
serene, tranquil, unworried, contented,
content, happy; comfortable.

easily adv. **1** *I overcame this problem easily*
effortlessly, comfortably, simply; with
ease, without difficulty, smoothly; skilfully,
deftly, smartly; informal no sweat. **2** *he's easily*
the best **undoubtedly**, without doubt,
without question, indisputably, undeniably,
definitely, certainly, clearly, obviously,
patently; by far, far and away, by a mile.

east adj. **eastern**, easterly, oriental.

easy adj. **1** *the task was very easy*
uncomplicated, undemanding,
unchallenging, effortless, painless, trouble-
free, facile, simple, straightforward,
elementary, plain sailing; informal easy as pie,
a piece of cake, child's play, kids' stuff, a
cinch, no sweat, a doddle, a breeze, a walk
in the park; Brit. informal easy-peasy; N. Amer.
informal duck soup, a snap; dated a snip. **2** *easy*
babies **docile**, manageable, amenable,
tractable, compliant, pliant, acquiescent,
obliging, cooperative, easy-going. **3** *an easy*
target **vulnerable**, susceptible, defenceless;
naive, gullible, trusting. **4** *Vic's easy manner*
natural, casual, informal, unceremonious,
unreserved, uninhibited, unaffected,
easy-going, amiable, affable, genial,
good-humoured; carefree, nonchalant,
unconcerned; informal laid-back. **5** *an easy*
life **calm**, tranquil, serene, quiet, peaceful,
untroubled, contented, relaxed, comfortable,
secure, safe; informal cushy. **6** *an easy*
pace **leisurely**, unhurried, comfortable,
undemanding, easy-going, gentle, sedate,
moderate, steady. **7** informal *people think she's*
easy **promiscuous**, free with one's favours,
unchaste, loose, wanton, abandoned,
licentious, debauched; informal sluttish,
whorish, tarty; N. Amer. informal roundheeled.
– OPPOSITES difficult, demanding, formal,
chaste.

easy-going adj. **relaxed**, even-tempered,
placid, mellow, mild, happy-go-lucky,
carefree, free and easy, nonchalant,
insouciant, imperturbable; amiable,
considerate, undemanding, patient, tolerant,
lenient, broad-minded, understanding;
good-natured, pleasant, agreeable; informal
laid-back, unflappable.
– OPPOSITES intolerant.

eat v. **1** *we ate a hearty breakfast* **consume**,
devour, ingest, partake of; gobble (up/
down), bolt (down), wolf (down); swallow,
chew, munch, chomp; informal guzzle, nosh,
put away, scoff, tuck into, demolish, dispose
of, polish off, hoover up, get stuck into, pig
out on, get outside of, trough; Brit. informal
gollop; N. Amer. informal scarf, snarf. **2** *we ate*
at a local restaurant **have a meal**, consume
food, feed, snack; breakfast, lunch, dine;
feast, banquet; informal graze, nosh. **3** *acidic*
water can eat away at pipes **erode**, corrode,

wear away/down/through, burn through, consume, dissolve, disintegrate, crumble, decay; damage, destroy.

eatable adj. **edible**, palatable, digestible; fit to eat, fit for consumption.

eats plural n. informal **food**, sustenance, nourishment, fare; eatables, snacks, titbits; informal nosh, grub, chow, scoff; Brit. informal tuck; N. Amer. informal chuck.

eavesdrop v. **listen in**, spy; monitor, tap, wiretap, record, overhear; informal snoop, bug.

ebb v. **1** *the tide ebbed* **recede**, go out, retreat, flow back, fall back/away, subside. **2** *his courage began to ebb* **diminish**, dwindle, wane, fade away, peter out, decline, flag, let up, decrease, weaken, disappear.
– OPPOSITES increase.
▸n. **1** *the ebb of the tide* **receding**, retreat, subsiding. **2** *the ebb of the fighting* **abatement**, subsiding, easing, dying down, de-escalation, decrease, decline, diminution.

ebony adj. **black**, jet-black, pitch-black, coal-black, sable, inky, sooty, raven, dark.

ebullience n. **exuberance**, buoyancy, cheerfulness, cheeriness, merriment, jollity, sunniness, jauntiness, light-heartedness, high spirits, elation, euphoria, jubilation; animation, sparkle, vivacity, enthusiasm, perkiness; informal bubbliness, chirpiness, bounciness, pep.

ebullient adj. **exuberant**, buoyant, cheerful, joyful, cheery, merry, jolly, sunny, jaunty, light-hearted, elated; animated, sparkling, vivacious, irrepressible; Brit. Tiggerish; informal bubbly, bouncy, peppy, upbeat, chirpy, smiley, full of beans; dated gay.
– OPPOSITES depressed.

eccentric adj. *eccentric behaviour* **unconventional**, uncommon, abnormal, irregular, aberrant, anomalous, odd, queer, strange, peculiar, weird, bizarre, outlandish, freakish, extraordinary; idiosyncratic, quirky, nonconformist, outré; informal way out, offbeat, freaky, oddball, wacky, cranky; Brit. informal rum; N. Amer. informal kooky, wacko.
– OPPOSITES conventional.
▸n. *he was something of an eccentric* **oddity**, odd fellow, character, individualist, individual, free spirit; misfit; informal oddball, queer fish, weirdo, freak, nut, head case, crank; Brit. informal one-off, odd bod, nutter, mentalist; N. Amer. informal wacko, screwball.

eccentricity n. **unconventionality**, singularity, oddness, strangeness, weirdness, quirkiness, freakishness; peculiarity, foible, idiosyncrasy, caprice, whimsy, quirk; informal nuttiness, screwiness, freakiness; N. Amer. informal kookiness.

ecclesiastical adj. **priestly**, ministerial, clerical, ecclesiastic, canonical, sacerdotal; church, churchly, religious, spiritual, holy, divine; informal churchy.

echelon n. **level**, rank, grade, step, rung, tier, position, order.

echo n. **1** *a faint echo of my shout* **reverberation**, reflection, ringing,

repetition, repeat. **2** *the scene she described was an echo of the photograph* **duplicate**, copy, replica, imitation, mirror image, double, match, parallel; informal lookalike, spitting image, dead ringer. **3** *an echo of their love* **trace**, vestige, remnant, ghost, memory, recollection, remembrance; reminder, sign, mark, token, indication, suggestion, hint; evidence.
▸v. **1** *his laughter echoed round the room* **reverberate**, resonate, resound, reflect, ring, vibrate. **2** *Bill echoed Rex's words* **repeat**, restate, reiterate; copy, imitate, parrot, mimic; reproduce, recite, quote, regurgitate; informal recap.

éclat n. **style**, flamboyance, confidence, elan, dash, flair, vigour, gusto, verve, zest, sparkle, brio, panache, dynamism, spirit; informal pizzazz, pep, oomph.

eclectic adj. **wide-ranging**, broad-based, extensive, comprehensive, encyclopedic; varied, diverse, catholic, all-embracing, multifaceted, multifarious, heterogeneous, miscellaneous, assorted.

eclipse n. **1** *the eclipse of the sun* **blotting out**, blocking, covering, obscuring, concealing, darkening; Astronomy occultation. **2** *the eclipse of the empire* **decline**, fall, failure, decay, deterioration, degeneration, weakening, collapse.
▸v. **1** *the sun was eclipsed by the moon* **blot out**, block, cover, obscure, hide, conceal, obliterate, darken; shade; Astronomy occult. **2** *the system was eclipsed by new methods* **outshine**, overshadow, surpass, exceed, outclass, outstrip, outdo, top, trump, transcend, upstage.

economic adj. **1** *economic reform* **financial**, monetary, budgetary, fiscal; commercial. **2** *the firm cannot remain economic* **profitable**, moneymaking, lucrative, remunerative, fruitful, productive; solvent, viable, cost-effective. **3** *an economic alternative to carpeting* **cheap**, inexpensive, low-cost, budget, economy, economical, cut-price, discount, bargain.
– OPPOSITES unprofitable, expensive.

economical adj. **1** *an economical car* **cheap**, inexpensive, low-cost, budget, economy, economic; cut-price, discount, bargain. **2** *a very economical shopper* **thrifty**, provident, prudent, sensible, frugal, sparing, abstemious; mean, parsimonious, penny-pinching, miserly; N. Amer. forehanded; informal stingy.
– OPPOSITES expensive, spendthrift.

economize v. **save (money)**, cut costs; cut back, make cutbacks, retrench, budget, make economies, be thrifty, be frugal, scrimp, cut corners, tighten one's belt, draw in one's horns, watch the/your pennies.

economy n. **1** *the nation's economy* **wealth**, (financial) resources; financial system, financial management. **2** *one can combine good living with economy* **thrift**, thriftiness, providence, prudence, careful budgeting, economizing, saving, scrimping,

restraint, frugality, abstemiousness; N. Amer.
forehandedness.
– OPPOSITES extravagance.

ecstasy n. **rapture**, bliss, elation, euphoria,
transports, rhapsodies; joy, jubilation,
exultation.
– OPPOSITES misery.

ecstatic adj. **enraptured**, elated, in raptures,
euphoric, rapturous, joyful, overjoyed,
blissful; on cloud nine, in seventh heaven,
beside oneself with joy, jumping for joy,
delighted, thrilled, exultant; informal over the
moon, on top of the world, blissed out.

ecumenical adj. **non-denominational**,
universal, catholic, all-embracing, all-
inclusive.
– OPPOSITES denominational.

eddy n. *small eddies at the river's edge* **swirl**,
whirlpool, vortex, maelstrom.
▶ v. *cold air eddied around her* **swirl**, whirl,
spiral, wind, circulate, twist; flow, ripple,
stream, surge, billow.

edge n. **1** *the edge of the lake* **border**,
boundary, extremity, fringe, margin, side;
lip, rim, brim, brink, verge; perimeter,
circumference, periphery, limits, bounds.
2 *she had an edge in her voice* **sharpness**,
severity, bite, sting, asperity, acerbity,
acidity, trenchancy; sarcasm, acrimony,
malice, spite, venom. **3** *they have an edge
over their rivals* **advantage**, lead, head start,
the whip hand, the upper hand; superiority,
dominance, ascendancy, supremacy, primacy.
– OPPOSITES middle, disadvantage.
▶ v. **1** *poplars edged the orchard* **border**, fringe,
verge, skirt; surround, enclose, encircle,
circle, encompass, bound. **2** *a frock edged
with lace* **trim**, pipe, band, decorate, finish;
border, fringe; bind, hem. **3** *he edged closer
to the fire* **creep**, inch, work one's way, pick
one's way, ease oneself; sidle, steal, slink.
□ **on edge** tense, nervous, edgy, anxious,
apprehensive, uneasy, unsettled; twitchy,
nervy, keyed up, restive, skittish, neurotic,
insecure; informal uptight, jumpy, wired; Brit.
informal strung up.

edgy adj. **tense**, nervous, on edge, anxious,
apprehensive, uneasy, unsettled; twitchy,
nervy, keyed up, restive, skittish, neurotic,
insecure; irritable, touchy, tetchy, testy,
crotchety, prickly; informal uptight, jumpy,
wired, snappy; Brit. informal strung up.
– OPPOSITES calm.

edible adj. **safe to eat**, fit for human
consumption, wholesome, good to eat;
consumable, digestible, palatable; formal
comestible.

edict n. **decree**, order, command,
commandment, mandate, proclamation,
pronouncement, dictate, fiat, promulgation;
law, statute, act, bill, ruling, injunction; formal
ordinance.

edification n. formal **education**, instruction,
tuition, teaching, training, tutelage,
pedagogy, guidance; enlightenment,
cultivation, information; improvement,
development.

edifice n. formal **building**, structure,
construction, erection, pile, complex;
property, development, premises.

edify v. formal **educate**, instruct, teach, school,
tutor, train, guide; enlighten, inform,
cultivate, develop, improve, better.

edit v. **1** *she edited the text* **correct**, check,
copy-edit, improve, emend, polish; modify,
adapt, revise, rewrite, reword, rework,
redraft; shorten, condense, cut, abridge;
informal clean up. **2** *this volume was edited
by a consultant* **select**, choose, assemble,
organize, put together. **3** *he edited The Times*
be the editor of, direct, run, manage, head,
lead, supervise, oversee, preside over; informal
be the boss of.

edition n. **issue**, number, volume,
impression, publication; version, revision.

educate v. **teach**, school, tutor, instruct,
coach, train, drill; guide, inform, enlighten;
inculcate, indoctrinate; formal edify.

educated adj. **informed**, literate, schooled,
tutored, well read, learned, knowledgeable,
enlightened; intellectual, academic, erudite,
scholarly, cultivated, cultured; dated lettered.

education n. **1** *the education of young
children* **teaching**, schooling, tuition,
tutoring, instruction, coaching, training,
tutelage, guidance; indoctrination,
inculcation, enlightenment; formal
edification. **2** *a woman of some education*
learning, knowledge, literacy, scholarship,
enlightenment.

> **WORD LINKS**
> **pedagogy** the profession or theory of teaching

educational adj. **1** *an educational
establishment* **academic**, scholastic, school,
learning, teaching, pedagogic, tuitional,
instructional. **2** *an educational experience*
instructive, instructional, educative,
informative, illuminating, pedagogic,
enlightening, didactic, heuristic; formal
edifying.

educative adj. See **educational** (sense 2).

educator n. **teacher**, tutor, instructor,
schoolteacher, schoolmaster, schoolmistress;
educationalist, educationist; lecturer,
professor; guide, mentor, guru; N. Amer.
informal schoolmarm; Brit. informal beak; formal
pedagogue; old use schoolman.

eerie adj. **uncanny**, sinister, ghostly,
unnatural, unearthly, supernatural, other-
worldly; strange, abnormal, odd, weird,
freakish; frightening, spine-chilling, hair-
raising, blood-curdling, terrifying; informal
creepy, scary, spooky, freaky.

efface v. **1** *the words were effaced by the rain*
erase, eradicate, expunge, blot out, rub out,
wipe out, remove, eliminate; delete, cancel,
obliterate, blank out. **2** *he attempted to efface
himself* **make oneself inconspicuous**, keep
out of sight, keep out of the limelight, lie
low, keep a low profile, withdraw.

effect n. **1** *the effect of these changes*
result, consequence, upshot, outcome,
out-turn, repercussions, ramifications; end

result, conclusion, culmination, corollary, concomitant, aftermath; fruit(s), product, by-product; informal pay-off; Medicine sequela. **2** *the effect of the drug* **impact**, action, effectiveness, influence; power, potency, strength; success; formal efficacy. **3** *with effect from tomorrow* **force**, operation, enforcement, implementation, effectiveness; validity, lawfulness, legality, legitimacy. **4** *some words to that effect* **sense**, meaning, theme, drift, import, intent, intention, tenor, significance, message; gist, essence, spirit. **5** *the dead man's effects* **belongings**, possessions, (worldly) goods, chattels; property, paraphernalia; informal gear, tackle, things, stuff, bits and pieces; Brit. informal clobber.
– OPPOSITES cause.
▸ v. *they effected many changes* **achieve**, accomplish, carry out, realize, manage, bring off, execute, conduct, engineer, perform, do, perpetrate, discharge, complete, consummate; cause, bring about, create, produce, make; provoke, occasion, generate, engender, actuate, initiate; formal effectuate.
□ **in effect** really, in reality, in truth, in (actual) fact, effectively, essentially, in essence, practically, to all intents and purposes, all but, as good as, more or less, almost, nearly, just about, well-nigh, nigh on; informal pretty much.
take effect 1 *these measures will take effect in May* **come into force**, come into operation, begin, become valid, become law, apply, be applied. **2** *the drug started to take effect* **work**, act, be effective, produce results.

effective adj. **1** *an effective treatment* **successful**, effectual, potent, powerful; helpful, beneficial, advantageous, valuable, useful; formal efficacious. **2** *a more effective argument* **convincing**, compelling, strong, forceful, potent, weighty, sound, valid; impressive, persuasive, plausible, credible, authoritative; logical, reasonable, lucid, coherent, cogent, eloquent; formal efficacious. **3** *the new law will be effective next week* **operative**, in force, in effect; valid, official, lawful, legal, binding; Law effectual. **4** *Korea was under effective Japanese control* **virtual**, practical, essential, actual, implicit, tacit.
– OPPOSITES weak, invalid, theoretical.

effectiveness n. **success**, productiveness, potency, power; benefit, advantage, value, virtue, usefulness; formal efficacy.

effectual adj. **1** *effectual political action* **effective**, successful, productive, constructive; worthwhile, helpful, beneficial, advantageous, valuable, useful; formal efficacious. **2** Law *an effectual document* **valid**, authentic, bona fide, genuine, official; lawful, legal, legitimate, (legally) binding, contractual.

effeminate adj. **womanish**, effete, foppish, mincing; informal camp, campy, limp-wristed, queenie.
– OPPOSITES manly.

effervesce v. **1** *heat the mixture until it effervesces* **fizz**, sparkle, bubble; froth, foam. **2** *managers must effervesce with praise* **sparkle**, be vivacious, be animated, be ebullient, be exuberant, be bubbly, be effervescent.

effervescence n. **1** *wines of uniform effervescence* **fizz**, fizziness, sparkle, gassiness, carbonation, aeration, bubbliness. **2** *his cheeky effervescence* **vivacity**, liveliness, animation, high spirits, ebullience, exuberance, buoyancy, sparkle, gaiety, jollity, cheerfulness, perkiness, breeziness, enthusiasm, irrepressibility, vitality, zest, energy, dynamism; informal pep, bounce.

effervescent adj. **1** *an effervescent drink* **fizzy**, sparkling, carbonated, aerated, gassy, bubbly; mousseux, pétillant, spumante. **2** *effervescent young people* **vivacious**, lively, animated, high-spirited, bubbly, ebullient, buoyant, sparkling, scintillating, light-hearted, jaunty, happy, jolly, cheery, cheerful, perky, sunny, enthusiastic, irrepressible, vital, zestful, energetic, dynamic; Brit. Tiggerish; informal bright-eyed and bushy-tailed, peppy, bouncy, upbeat, chirpy, full of beans.
– OPPOSITES still, depressed.

effete adj. **1** *effete trendies* **affected**, pretentious, precious, mannered, over-refined; ineffectual; informal la-di-da, pseud; Brit. informal poncey. **2** *an effete young man* **effeminate**, unmanly, girlish, feminine; soft, timid, cowardly, lily-livered, spineless, pusillanimous; informal sissy, wimpish, wimpy. **3** *the fabric of society is effete* **weak**, enfeebled, enervated, worn out, exhausted, finished, drained, spent, powerless, ineffectual.
– OPPOSITES manly, powerful.

efficacious adj. formal **effective**, effectual, successful, productive, constructive, potent; helpful, beneficial, advantageous, valuable, useful.

efficacy n. formal **effectiveness**, success, productiveness, potency, power; benefit, advantage, value, virtue, usefulness.

efficiency n. **1** *we need reforms to bring efficiency* **organization**, order, orderliness, regulation, coherence; productivity, effectiveness. **2** *I compliment you on your efficiency* **competence**, capability, ability, proficiency, adeptness, expertise, professionalism, skill, effectiveness.

efficient adj. **1** *efficient techniques* **organized**, methodical, systematic, logical, orderly, businesslike, streamlined, productive, effective, cost-effective. **2** *an efficient secretary* **competent**, capable, able, proficient, adept, skilful, skilled, effective, productive, organized, businesslike.
– OPPOSITES disorganized, incompetent.

effigy n. **statue**, statuette, sculpture, model, dummy, figurine; guy; likeness, image; bust.

effluent n. **(liquid) waste**, sewage, effluvium, outflow, discharge, emission.

e

effort n. **1** *they made an effort to work together* **attempt**, try, endeavour; informal crack, shot, stab, bash; formal essay. **2** *his score was a fine effort* **achievement**, accomplishment, attainment, result, feat; undertaking, enterprise, work; triumph, success, coup. **3** *the job requires little effort* **exertion**, energy, work, endeavour, application, labour, power, muscle, toil, strain; informal sweat, elbow grease; Brit. informal graft; Austral./NZ informal (hard) yakka.

effortless adj. **easy**, undemanding, unchallenging, painless, simple, uncomplicated, straightforward, elementary; fluent, natural; informal as easy as pie, child's play, kids' stuff, a cinch, no sweat, a doddle, a breeze, a walk in the park; Brit. informal easy-peasy; N. Amer. informal duck soup, a snap.
– OPPOSITES difficult.

effrontery n. **impudence**, impertinence, cheek, insolence, cockiness, audacity, temerity, presumption, nerve, gall, shamelessness, impoliteness, disrespect, bad manners; informal brass (neck), face, chutzpah; Brit. informal sauce; N. Amer. informal sass.

effusion n. **1** *an effusion of poisonous gas* **outflow**, outpouring, rush, current, flood, deluge, emission, discharge, emanation; spurt, surge, jet, stream, torrent, gush, flow. **2** *reporters' flamboyant effusions* **outburst**, outpouring, gushing; wordiness, verbiage.

effusive adj. **gushing**, gushy, unrestrained, extravagant, fulsome, demonstrative, lavish, enthusiastic, lyrical; expansive, wordy, verbose; informal over the top, OTT.
– OPPOSITES restrained.

egg n. **ovum**; gamete, germ cell; (**eggs**) roe, spawn, seed.
◻ **egg someone on** urge, goad, incite, provoke, push, drive, prod, prompt, induce, impel, spur on; encourage, exhort, motivate, galvanize.

> **WORD LINKS**
> **oval, ovate, ovoid** egg-shaped
> **oviparous** egg-laying
> **oology** the study or collecting of birds' eggs

egghead n. informal **intellectual**, thinker, academic, scholar, sage; bookworm, highbrow; expert, genius, Einstein, mastermind; informal brain, whizz; Brit. informal brainbox, boffin; N. Amer. informal brainiac, rocket scientist.
– OPPOSITES dunce.

ego n. **self-esteem**, self-importance, self-worth, self-respect, self-image, self-confidence.

egocentric adj. **self-centred**, egomaniacal, self-interested, selfish, self-seeking, self-absorbed, self-obsessed; narcissistic, vain, self-important.
– OPPOSITES altruistic.

egotism, egoism n. **self-centredness**, egomania, egocentricity, self-interest, selfishness, self-seeking, self-serving, self-regard, self-obsession; self-love, narcissism, self-admiration, vanity, conceit, self-importance; boastfulness.

egotist, egoist n. **self-seeker**, egocentric, egomaniac, narcissist; boaster, brag, braggart; informal swank, show-off, big-head; N. Amer. informal showboat.

egotistic, egoistic adj. **self-centred**, selfish, egocentric, egomaniacal, self-interested, self-seeking, self-absorbed, self-obsessed; narcissistic, vain, conceited, self-important; boastful.

egregious adj. **shocking**, appalling, terrible, awful, horrendous, frightful, atrocious, abominable, abhorrent, outrageous; monstrous, heinous, dire, unspeakable, shameful, unforgivable, intolerable, dreadful; formal grievous.
– OPPOSITES marvellous.

egress n. **1** *the egress from the gallery was blocked* **exit**, way out, escape route. **2** *a means of egress* **departure**, exit, withdrawal, retreat, exodus; escape; vacation.
– OPPOSITES entrance.

eight cardinal number **octet**, eightsome, octuplets; technical octad.

> **WORD LINKS**
> **octuple** consisting of eight parts or things
> **octennial** lasting for or recurring every eight years
> **octagon** a plane figure with eight sides
> **octahedron** a solid figure with eight faces
> **octad** a group or set of eight

ejaculate v. **1** emit semen, climax, orgasm; informal come. **2** *the sperm is ejaculated* **emit**, eject, discharge, release, expel, disgorge; shoot out, squirt out, spurt out. **3** dated *'What?' he ejaculated* **exclaim**, cry out, call out, yell, blurt out, come out with.

ejaculation n. **1** *the ejaculation of fluid* **emission**, ejection, discharge, release, expulsion. **2** dated *the conversation consisted of ejaculations* **exclamation**, interjection; call, shout, yell.

eject v. **1** *the volcano ejected ash* **emit**, spew out, discharge, give off, send out, belch; vent; expel, release, disgorge, spout, vomit, throw up. **2** *the pilot had time to eject* **bail out**, escape, get out. **3** *they were ejected from the hall* **expel**, throw out, turn out, cast out, remove, oust; evict, banish; informal chuck out, kick out, turf out, boot out; N. Amer. informal give someone the bum's rush. **4** *he was ejected from the job* **dismiss**, remove, discharge, oust, expel, axe, throw out, force out, drive out; informal sack, fire, send packing, boot out, chuck out, kick out, give someone their marching orders, give someone the push, show someone the door; Brit. informal give someone their cards, turf out; Military cashier.
– OPPOSITES admit, appoint.

ejection n. **1** *the ejection of electrons* **emission**, discharge, expulsion, release; elimination. **2** *their ejection from the ground* **expulsion**, removal; eviction, banishment, exile. **3** *his ejection from office* **dismissal**, removal, discharge, expulsion; informal the sack, the boot, the push, the (old) heave-ho, the bullet; Brit. informal the chop.

eke v. *I had to eke out my remaining funds* **husband**, use sparingly, be thrifty with, be frugal with, be sparing with, use economically; informal go easy on.
– OPPOSITES squander.
□ **eke out a living** subsist, survive, get by, scrape by, make ends meet, keep body and soul together, keep the wolf from the door, keep one's head above water.

elaborate adj. **1** *an elaborate plan* **complicated**, complex, intricate, involved; detailed, painstaking, careful; tortuous, convoluted, serpentine, Byzantine. **2** *an elaborate plasterwork ceiling* **ornate**, decorated, embellished, adorned, ornamented, fancy, fussy, busy, ostentatious, extravagant, showy, baroque, rococo, florid, wedding-cake.
– OPPOSITES simple, plain.
▶ v. *both sides refused to elaborate on their reasons* **expand on**, enlarge on, add to, flesh out, put flesh on the bones of, add detail to, expatiate on; develop, fill out, embellish, embroider, enhance, amplify.

elan n. **flair**, style, panache, confidence, dash, éclat; energy, vigour, vitality, liveliness, brio, esprit, animation, vivacity, zest, verve, spirit, pep, sparkle, enthusiasm, gusto, eagerness, feeling, fire; informal pizzazz, zing, zip, vim, oomph.

elapse v. **pass**, go by/past, wear on, slip by/away/past, roll by/past, slide by/past, steal by/past, tick by/past.

elastic adj. **1** *elastic material* **stretchy**, elasticated, stretchable, springy, flexible, pliant, pliable, supple, yielding, plastic, resilient. **2** *an elastic concept of nationality* **adaptable**, flexible, adjustable, accommodating, variable, fluid, versatile.
– OPPOSITES rigid.

elasticity n. **1** *the skin's natural elasticity* **stretchiness**, flexibility, pliancy, suppleness, plasticity, resilience, springiness; informal give. **2** *the elasticity of the term* **adaptability**, flexibility, adjustability, fluidity, versatility.

elated adj. **thrilled**, delighted, overjoyed, ecstatic, euphoric, very happy, joyous, gleeful, jubilant, beside oneself, exultant, rapturous, in raptures, walking on air, on cloud nine, in seventh heaven, jumping for joy, in transports of delight; informal on top of the world, over the moon, on a high, tickled pink; Austral. informal wrapped.
– OPPOSITES miserable.

elation n. **euphoria**, ecstasy, happiness, delight, transports of delight, joy, rapture, joyousness, glee, jubilation, exultation, bliss.

elbow v. **push**, shove, force, shoulder, jostle, barge, muscle, bulldoze.

elbow room n. **room to manoeuvre**, room, space, Lebensraum, breathing space, scope, freedom, play, free rein, licence, latitude, leeway.

elder adj. *his elder brother* **older**, senior, big.
▶ n. *the church elders* **leader**, senior figure,

patriarch, father.

elderly adj. *her elderly mother* **aged**, old, advanced in years, ageing, long in the tooth, past one's prime; grey-haired, grey-bearded, grizzled, hoary; in one's dotage, decrepit, doddering, doddery, senescent; informal getting on, past it, over the hill, no spring chicken.
– OPPOSITES youthful.
▶ n. **old people**, senior citizens, (old-age) pensioners, OAPs, retired people; geriatrics; N. Amer. seniors, retirees, golden agers; informal (golden) oldies, wrinklies; N. Amer. informal oldsters, woopies.

elect v. **1** *a new president was elected* **vote for**, vote in, return; choose, pick, select. **2** *she elected to stay behind* **choose**, decide, opt, vote.
▶ adj. *the president elect* **future**, -to-be, designate, chosen, elected, coming, next, appointed, presumptive.
▶ n. **the chosen**, the elite, the favoured; the crème de la crème, A-list.

election n. **ballot**, vote, popular vote; poll; Brit. by-election; US primary.

> **WORD LINKS**
>
> **psephology** the study of elections and trends in voting
> **hustings** the campaigning taking place before an election
> **canvass** visit someone to ask for their vote in an election
> **scrutineer** a person who ensures that an election is organized correctly
> **franchise, suffrage** the right to vote in political elections.
> See also **vote**.

electioneer v. **campaign**, canvass, go on the hustings, doorstep; Brit. informal go out on the knocker.

elector n. **voter**, member of the electorate, constituent; selector.

electric adj. **1** *an electric kettle* **electric-powered**, electrically operated, mains-operated, battery-operated. **2** *the atmosphere was electric* **exciting**, charged, electrifying, thrilling, heady, dramatic, intoxicating, dynamic, stimulating, galvanizing, rousing, stirring, moving; tense, knife-edge, explosive, volatile.

electricity n. **power**, electric power, energy, current, static; Brit. mains; Canadian hydro; Brit. informal leccy; historical galvanism.

electrify v. **excite**, thrill, stimulate, arouse, rouse, inspire, stir (up), exhilarate, intoxicate, galvanize, move, fire (with enthusiasm), fire someone's imagination, invigorate, animate; startle, jolt, shock; N. Amer. light a fire under; informal give someone a buzz, give someone a kick; N. Amer. informal give someone a charge.

elegance n. **1** *he was attracted by her elegance* **style**, stylishness, grace, gracefulness, taste, tastefulness, sophistication; refinement, dignity, beauty, poise, charm, culture; suaveness, urbanity, panache. **2** *the elegance of the idea* **neatness**, simplicity; ingenuity, cleverness, inventiveness.

elegant adj. **1** *an elegant black outfit* **stylish**, graceful, tasteful, sophisticated, classic, chic, smart, fashionable, modish; refined, dignified, poised, beautiful, lovely, charming, artistic, aesthetic; cultivated, polished, cultured; dashing, debonair, suave, urbane. **2** *an elegant solution* **neat**, simple, effective; ingenious, clever, deft, intelligent, inventive.
– OPPOSITES gauche.

elegiac adj. **mournful**, melancholic, melancholy, plaintive, sorrowful, sad, lamenting, doleful; funereal, dirgelike; nostalgic, valedictory, poignant; literary dolorous.
– OPPOSITES cheerful.

elegy n. **lament**, requiem, funeral poem/ song, threnody, dirge, plaint; Irish keen; Irish & Scottish coronach.

element n. **1** *an essential element of the local community* **component**, constituent, part, section, portion, piece, segment, bit; aspect, factor, feature, facet, ingredient, strand, detail, point; member, unit, module, item. **2** *there is an element of truth in this stereotype* **trace**, touch, hint, smattering, soupçon. **3** *the elements of political science* **basics**, essentials, principles, first principles; foundations, fundamentals, rudiments; informal nuts and bolts, ABC. **4** *I braved the elements* **the weather**, the climate, meteorological conditions, atmospheric conditions; the wind, the rain.

elemental adj. **1** *the elemental principles of accountancy* **basic**, primary, fundamental, essential, root, underlying; rudimentary. **2** *elemental forces* **natural**, atmospheric, meteorological, environmental.

elementary adj. **1** *an elementary astronomy course* **basic**, rudimentary, fundamental; preparatory, introductory, initiatory. **2** *a lot of the work is elementary* **easy**, simple, straightforward, uncomplicated, undemanding, painless, child's play, plain sailing; informal as easy as falling off a log, as easy as pie, as easy as ABC, a piece of cake, no sweat, kids' stuff, a walk in the park; Brit. informal easy-peasy.
– OPPOSITES advanced, difficult.

elephantine adj. **enormous**, huge, gigantic, very big, massive, giant, immense, tremendous, colossal, mammoth, gargantuan, vast, prodigious, monumental, titanic; hulking, bulky, heavy, weighty, ponderous, lumbering; informal jumbo, whopping, humongous, monster; Brit. informal whacking, ginormous.
– OPPOSITES tiny.

elevate v. **1** *we need a breeze to elevate the kite* **raise**, lift (up), raise up/aloft, upraise; hoist, hike up, haul up. **2** *he was elevated to Secretary of State* **promote**, upgrade, advance, move up, raise, prefer; ennoble, exalt, aggrandize; informal kick upstairs, move

up the ladder.
– OPPOSITES lower, demote.

elevated adj. **1** *an elevated motorway* **raised**, upraised, high up, aloft; overhead. **2** *elevated language* **lofty**, grand, exalted, fine, sublime; inflated, pompous, bombastic, orotund. **3** *the gentry's elevated status* **high**, higher, high-ranking, of high standing, lofty, superior, exalted, eminent; grand, noble.
– OPPOSITES lowly.

elevation n. **1** *his elevation to the peerage* **promotion**, upgrading, advancement, advance, preferment, aggrandizement; ennoblement; informal step up the ladder, kick upstairs. **2** *1,500 to 3,000 metres in elevation* **altitude**, height. **3** *elevations in excess of 3,000 metres* **height**, hill, mountain, mount; formal eminence. **4** *elevation of thought* **grandeur**, greatness, nobility, loftiness, majesty, sublimity.

elf n. **pixie**, fairy, sprite, imp, brownie; dwarf, gnome, goblin, hobgoblin; leprechaun, puck, troll.

elfin adj. **elflike**, elfish, elvish, pixie-like; puckish, impish, playful, mischievous; dainty, delicate, small, petite, slight, little, tiny, diminutive.

elicit v. **obtain**, draw out, extract, bring out, evoke, call forth, bring forth, induce, prompt, generate, engender, trigger, provoke; formal educe.

eligible adj. **1** *those people eligible to vote* **entitled**, permitted, allowed, qualified, able. **2** *an eligible bachelor* **desirable**, suitable; available, single, unmarried, unattached, unwed.

eliminate v. **1** *a policy that would eliminate inflation* **remove**, get rid of, put an end to, do away with, end, stop, terminate, eradicate, destroy, annihilate, stamp out, wipe out, extinguish; informal knock something on the head. **2** *he was eliminated from the title race* **knock out**, beat; exclude, rule out, disqualify.

elite n. **best**, pick, cream, crème de la crème, flower, nonpareil, elect, A-list; high society, jet set, beautiful people, beau monde, haut monde; aristocracy, nobility, upper class; N. Amer. four hundred.
– OPPOSITES dregs.

elixir n. **potion**, concoction, brew, philtre, decoction, mixture; medicine, tincture; extract, essence, concentrate, distillate, distillation; literary draught; old use potation.

elliptical adj. **1** *an elliptical shape* **oval**, egg-shaped, elliptic, ovate, ovoid, oviform, ellipsoidal; Botany obovate. **2** *elliptical phraseology* **cryptic**, abstruse, ambiguous, obscure, oblique, Delphic; terse, concise, succinct, compact, economic, laconic, sparing.

elocution n. **pronunciation**, enunciation, articulation, diction, speech, intonation, vocalization, modulation; phrasing, delivery, public speaking.

elongate v. **1** *an exercise that elongates the muscles* **lengthen**, extend, stretch (out).

2 *the high notes were elongated* **prolong**, protract, draw out, sustain.
– OPPOSITES shorten.

eloquence n. **fluency**, articulacy, articulateness, expressiveness, silver tongue, persuasiveness, forcefulness, power, potency, effectiveness; oratory, rhetoric, grandiloquence, magniloquence; informal gift of the gab, way with words, blarney.

eloquent adj. **1** *an eloquent speaker* **fluent**, articulate, expressive, silver-tongued, persuasive, strong, forceful, powerful, potent, well expressed, effective, lucid, vivid, graphic; smooth-tongued, glib. **2** *her glance was more eloquent than words* **expressive**, meaningful, suggestive, revealing, telling, significant, indicative.
– OPPOSITES inarticulate.

elsewhere adv. **somewhere else**, in/at/ to another place, in/at/to a different place, hence; not here, not present, absent, away, abroad, out.
– OPPOSITES here.

elucidate v. **explain**, make clear, illuminate, throw/shed light on, clarify, clear up, sort out, unravel, spell out; interpret, explicate; gloss.
– OPPOSITES confuse.

elucidation n. **explanation**, clarification, illumination; interpretation, explication; gloss.

elude v. **evade**, avoid, get away from, dodge, escape from, run (away) from; lose, shake off, give the slip to, slip away from, throw off the scent; informal slip through someone's fingers, slip through the net; old use bilk.

elusive adj. **1** *her elusive husband* **difficult to find**; evasive, slippery. **2** *an elusive quality* **indefinable**, intangible, impalpable, unanalysable; fugitive; ambiguous.

Elysian adj. **heavenly**, paradisal, paradisiacal, celestial, superlunary, divine; literary empyrean.

emaciated adj. **thin**, skeletal, bony, gaunt, wasted, thin as a rake; scrawny, skinny, scraggy, skin and bone, raw-boned, stick-like; starved, underfed, undernourished, underweight, half-starved; cadaverous, shrivelled, shrunken, withered; informal anorexic, like a bag of bones.
– OPPOSITES fat.

emanate v. **1** *warmth emanated from the fireplace* **issue**, spread, radiate, be sent forth/out. **2** *the proposals emanated from a committee* **originate**, stem, derive, proceed, spring, issue, emerge, flow, come. **3** *he emanated an air of power* **exude**, emit, radiate, give off/out, send out/forth.

emanation n. **1** *an emanation of his tortured personality* **product**, consequence, result, fruit. **2** *radon gas emanation* **discharge**, emission, radiation, effusion, outflow, outpouring, flow, leak; technical efflux.

emancipate v. **free**, liberate, set free, release, deliver, discharge; unchain, unfetter, unshackle, untie, unyoke; historical manumit; rare disenthral.

– OPPOSITES enslave.

emancipated adj. **liberated**, independent, unconstrained, uninhibited; free.

emasculate v. **weaken**, enfeeble, debilitate, erode, undermine, cripple; informal water down.

embalm v. **1** *his body had been embalmed* **preserve**, mummify, lay out. **2** *the poem ought to embalm his memory* **preserve**, conserve, enshrine, immortalize.

embankment n. **bank**, mound, ridge, earthwork, causeway, barrier, levee, dam, dyke.

embargo n. *an embargo on oil sales* **ban**, bar, prohibition, stoppage, interdict, proscription, veto, moratorium; restriction, restraint, block, barrier, impediment, obstruction; boycott.
▸ v. *arms sales were embargoed* **ban**, bar, prohibit, stop, interdict, debar, proscribe, outlaw; restrict, restrain, block, obstruct; boycott.
– OPPOSITES allow.

embark v. **1** *he embarked at Dover* **board ship**, go on board, go aboard, take ship; emplane; informal hop on, jump on; dated ship. **2** *he embarked on a new career* **begin**, start, commence, undertake, set about, take up, turn one's hand to, get down to; enter into, venture into, launch into, plunge into, engage in, settle down to; informal get cracking on, get going on, have a go/crack/shot at.

embarrass v. **mortify**, shame, put someone to shame, humiliate, abash, chagrin, make uncomfortable, make self-conscious; discomfit, disconcert, discompose, upset, discountenance, distress; informal show up.

embarrassed adj. **mortified**, red-faced, blushing, abashed, shamed, ashamed, shamefaced, humiliated, chagrined, awkward, self-conscious, uncomfortable, not knowing where to look, sheepish; discomfited, disconcerted, upset, discomposed, flustered, agitated, discountenanced, distressed; shy, bashful, tongue-tied; informal with egg on one's face, wishing the earth would swallow one up.

embarrassing adj. **humiliating**, shaming, shameful, mortifying, ignominious; awkward, uncomfortable, compromising; disconcerting, discomfiting, upsetting, distressing; informal blush-making, cringeworthy, cringe-making, toe-curling.

embarrassment n. **1** *he was scarlet with embarrassment* **mortification**, humiliation, shame, shamefacedness, chagrin, awkwardness, self-consciousness, sheepishness, discomfort, discomfiture, discomposure, agitation, distress; ignominy; shyness, bashfulness. **2** *his current financial embarrassment* **difficulty**, predicament, plight, problem, mess; informal bind, jam, pickle, fix, scrape. **3** *an embarrassment of riches* **surplus**, excess, overabundance, superabundance, glut, surfeit, superfluity; abundance, profusion, plethora.

embassy n. **consulate**, legation, ministry.

embed, imbed v. **implant**, plant, set, fix, lodge, root, insert, place; sink, drive in, hammer in, ram in.

embellish v. **1** *weapons embellished with precious metal* **decorate**, adorn, ornament; beautify, enhance, grace; trim, garnish, gild; deck, bedeck, festoon, emblazon; literary bejewel, bedizen. **2** *the legend was embellished by an American academic* **elaborate**, embroider, expand on, exaggerate.

embellishment n. **1** *architectural embellishments* **decoration**, ornamentation, adornment; beautification, enhancement, trimming, trim, garnishing, gilding. **2** *we wanted the truth, not romantic embellishments* **elaboration**, addition, exaggeration.

ember n. **glowing coal**, live coal; cinder; (**embers**) ashes, residue.

embezzle v. **misappropriate**, steal, thieve, pilfer, purloin, appropriate, abstract, defraud someone of, siphon off, pocket, help oneself to; put one's hand in the till; informal rob, rip off, skim, line one's pockets; Brit. informal pinch, nick, half-inch; formal peculate.

embezzlement n. **misappropriation**, theft, stealing, robbery, thieving, pilfering, purloining, pilferage, appropriation, swindling; fraud, larceny; formal peculation.

embittered adj. **bitter**, resentful, grudge-bearing, rancorous, jaundiced, aggrieved, sour, frustrated, dissatisfied, alienated, disaffected.

emblazon v. **1** *shirts emblazoned with the company name* **adorn**, decorate, ornament, embellish; inscribe. **2** *a flag with a hammer and sickle emblazoned on it* **display**, depict, show.

emblem n. **symbol**, representation, token, image, figure, mark, sign; crest, badge, device, insignia, stamp, seal, heraldic device, coat of arms, shield; logo, trademark.

emblematic, emblematical adj. **1** *a situation emblematic of the industrialized twentieth century* **symbolic**, representative, demonstrative, suggestive, indicative. **2** *emblematic works of art* **allegorical**, symbolic, metaphorical, parabolic, figurative.

embodiment n. **personification**, incarnation, realization, manifestation, expression, representation, actualization, symbol, symbolization; paradigm, epitome, paragon, soul, model; type, essence, quintessence, exemplification, example, exemplar, ideal; formal reification.

embody v. **1** *Gradgrind embodies the spirit of industrial capitalism* **personify**, realize, manifest, symbolize, represent, express, concretize, incarnate, epitomize, stand for, typify, exemplify; formal reify. **2** *the changes in law embodied in the Children Act* **incorporate**, include, contain, encompass; assimilate, consolidate, integrate, organize, systematize; combine.

embolden v. **fortify**, make brave/braver, encourage, hearten, strengthen, brace, stiffen the resolve of; rouse, stir, stimulate, cheer, rally, fire, animate, inspirit, invigorate; informal buck up.
– OPPOSITES dishearten.

embrace v. **1** *he embraced her warmly* **hug**, take/hold in one's arms, hold, cuddle, clasp to one's bosom, clasp, squeeze, clutch; caress; enfold, enclasp, encircle, envelop, entwine oneself around; informal canoodle, smooch; literary embosom. **2** *most western European countries have embraced the concept* **welcome**, welcome with open arms, accept, take up, take to one's heart, adopt; espouse, support, back, champion. **3** *the faculty embraces a wide range of departments* **include**, take in, comprise, contain, incorporate, encompass, cover, involve, embody, subsume, comprehend.
▸ n. *a fond embrace* **hug**, cuddle, squeeze, clinch, caress; bear hug.

embrocation n. **ointment**, lotion, cream, rub, salve, emollient, liniment, balm, unguent.

embroider v. **1** *a cushion embroidered with a pattern of golden keys* **sew**, stitch; decorate, adorn, ornament, embellish. **2** *she embroidered her stories with colourful detail* **elaborate**, embellish, enlarge on, exaggerate, touch up, dress up, gild, colour; informal jazz up.

embroidery n. **1** *the girls were taught embroidery* **needlework**, needlepoint, needlecraft, sewing, tatting, crewel work, tapestry. **2** *fanciful embroidery of the facts* **elaboration**, embellishment, adornment, ornamentation, colouring, enhancement; exaggeration, overstatement, hyperbole.

embroil v. **involve**, entangle, ensnare, enmesh, catch up, mix up, bog down, mire.

embryo n. **1** *a human embryo* **fetus**, fertilized egg, unborn child/baby. **2** *the embryo of a capitalist economy* **germ**, nucleus, seed; rudimentary version, rudiments, basics, beginning, start.

embryonic adj. **1** *an embryonic chick* **fetal**, unborn, unhatched. **2** *an embryonic pro-democracy movement* **rudimentary**, undeveloped, unformed, immature, incomplete, incipient, inchoate; fledgling, budding, nascent, emerging, developing, early, germinal.
– OPPOSITES mature.

emend v. **correct**, rectify, repair, fix; improve, enhance, polish, refine, amend; edit, redact, rewrite, revise, copy-edit, subedit, redraft, recast, rephrase, reword, rework, alter, change, modify.

emerge v. **1** *a policeman emerged from the alley* **come out**, appear, come into view, become visible, surface, materialize, manifest oneself, issue, come forth. **2** *several unexpected facts emerged* **become known**, become apparent, be revealed, come to light, come out, turn up, transpire, unfold, turn out, prove to be the case.

emergence n. **appearance**, arrival, coming, materialization; advent, inception, dawn, birth, origination, start, development, rise.

emergency n. *a military emergency* **crisis**, urgent situation, extremity, exigency; accident, disaster, catastrophe, calamity; difficulty, plight, predicament, danger; informal panic stations.
▸ adj. **1** *an emergency meeting* **urgent**, crisis; impromptu, extraordinary. **2** *emergency supplies* **reserve**, standby, back-up, fallback, in reserve.

emergent adj. **emerging**, developing, rising, dawning, budding, embryonic, infant, fledgling, nascent, incipient.

emigrate v. **move abroad**, move overseas, leave one's country, migrate; relocate, resettle; defect.
– OPPOSITES immigrate.

emigration n. **moving abroad**, moving overseas, expatriation, migration; exodus, diaspora; relocation, resettling; defection.

eminence n. **1** *his eminence as a scientist* **fame**, celebrity, illustriousness, distinction, renown, pre-eminence, notability, greatness, prestige, importance, reputation, repute, note; prominence, superiority, stature, standing. **2** *various legal eminences* **important person**, dignitary, luminary, worthy, grandee, notable, notability, personage, leading light, VIP; informal somebody, someone, big shot, big noise, big gun, heavyweight. **3** formal *the hotel's eminence above the sea* **elevation**, height, rise.

eminent adj. **1** *an eminent man of letters* **illustrious**, distinguished, renowned, esteemed, pre-eminent, notable, noteworthy, great, prestigious, important, influential, outstanding, noted, of note; famous, celebrated, prominent, well known, lionized, acclaimed, exalted, revered, august, venerable. **2** *the eminent reasonableness of their claims* **obvious**, clear, conspicuous, marked, singular, signal; total, complete, utter, absolute, thorough, perfect, downright, sheer.
– OPPOSITES unknown.

eminently adv. **very**, greatly, highly, exceedingly, extremely, particularly, exceptionally, supremely, uniquely; obviously, clearly, conspicuously, markedly, singularly, signally, outstandingly, strikingly, notably, surpassingly; totally, completely, utterly, absolutely, thoroughly, perfectly, downright.

emissary n. **envoy**, ambassador, delegate, attaché, consul, plenipotentiary; agent, representative, deputy; messenger, courier; nuncio; old use legate.

emission n. **discharge**, release, outpouring, outflow, outrush, leak, excretion, secretion, ejection; emanation, radiation, effusion, ejaculation, disgorgement, issuance.

emit v. **1** *the hydrocarbons emitted from vehicle exhausts* **discharge**, release, give out/off, pour out, send forth, throw out, void, vent, issue; leak, ooze, excrete, disgorge, secrete, eject, ejaculate; spout, belch, spew out; emanate, radiate, exude. **2** *he emitted a*

loud cry **utter**, voice, let out, produce, give vent to, come out with, vocalize.
– OPPOSITES absorb.

emollient adj. **1** *a rich emollient shampoo* **moisturizing**, soothing, softening. **2** *an emollient response* **conciliatory**, conciliating, appeasing, soothing, calming, pacifying, assuaging, placating, mollifying, propitiatory.
▸ n. *she applied an emollient* **moisturizer**, cream, lotion, oil, rub, salve, unguent, balm; technical humectant.

emolument n. formal **salary**, pay, payment, wage(s), earnings, allowance, stipend, honorarium, reward, premium; fee, charge, consideration; income, profit, gain, return.

emotion n. **1** *she was good at hiding her emotions* **feeling**, sentiment; reaction, response. **2** *overcome by emotion, she turned away* **passion**, strength of feeling, warmth of feeling. **3** *responses based purely on emotion* **instinct**, intuition, gut feeling; sentiment, the heart.

emotional adj. **1** *an emotional young man* **passionate**, hot-blooded, ardent, fervent, excitable, temperamental, melodramatic, tempestuous; demonstrative, responsive, tender, loving, feeling, sentimental, sensitive. **2** *he paid an emotional tribute to his wife* **poignant**, moving, touching, affecting, powerful, stirring, emotive, heart-rending, heart-warming, impassioned, dramatic; haunting, pathetic, sentimental; informal tear-jerking.
– OPPOSITES unfeeling.

emotionless adj. **unemotional**, unfeeling, dispassionate, passionless, unexpressive, cool, cold, cold-blooded, impassive, indifferent, detached, remote, aloof; toneless, flat, dead, expressionless, blank, wooden, stony, deadpan, vacant.

emotive adj. **controversial**, contentious, inflammatory; sensitive, delicate, difficult, problematic, touchy, awkward, prickly, ticklish.

empathize v. **identify**, sympathize, be in sympathy, understand, share someone's feelings, be in tune; be on the same wavelength as, talk the same language as; relate to, feel for, have insight into; informal put oneself in someone else's shoes.

emperor n. **ruler**, sovereign, king, monarch, potentate; historical tsar, kaiser, mikado.

> **WORD LINKS**
> **imperial** relating to an emperor or empire

emphasis n. **1** *the curriculum gave more emphasis to reading and writing* **prominence**, importance, significance, value; stress, weight, accent, attention, priority, pre-eminence, urgency, force. **2** *the emphasis is on the word 'little'* **stress**, accent, accentuation, weight, prominence; beat; Prosody ictus.

emphasize v. **stress**, underline, highlight, focus attention on, point up, lay stress on, draw attention to, spotlight, foreground,

e

play up, make a point of; bring to the fore, insist on, belabour; accent, accentuate, underscore; informal press home, rub it in.
– OPPOSITES understate.

emphatic adj. **1** *an emphatic denial* **vehement**, firm, wholehearted, forceful, forcible, energetic, vigorous, direct, assertive, insistent; certain, definite, out-and-out, one hundred per cent; decided, determined, categorical, unqualified, unconditional, unequivocal, unambiguous, absolute, explicit, downright, outright, clear. **2** *an emphatic victory* **conclusive**, decisive, decided, unmistakable; resounding; telling; informal thumping, thundering.
– OPPOSITES hesitant, narrow.

empire n. **1** *the Ottoman Empire* **kingdom**, realm, domain, territory; commonwealth; power, world power, superpower. **2** *a worldwide shipping empire* **organization**, corporation, multinational, conglomerate, consortium, company, business, firm, operation. **3** *his dream of empire* **power**, rule, ascendancy, supremacy, command, control, authority, sway, dominance, domination, dominion.

empirical adj. **experiential**, practical, heuristic, first-hand, hands-on; observed, seen.
– OPPOSITES theoretical.

employ v. **1** *she employed a chauffeur* **hire**, engage, recruit, take on, secure the services of, sign up, sign, enrol, appoint; retain; indenture, apprentice. **2** *Sam was employed in carving a stone figure* **occupy**, engage, involve, keep busy, tie up; absorb, engross, immerse. **3** *the team employed subtle psychological tactics* **use**, utilize, make use of, avail oneself of; apply, exercise, practise, put into practice, exert, bring into play, bring to bear; draw on, resort to, turn to, have recourse to.
– OPPOSITES dismiss.

employed adj. **working**, in work, in employment, holding down a job; earning, waged, breadwinning.

employee n. **worker**, member of staff; blue-collar worker, white-collar worker, workman, labourer, (hired) hand; wage-earner, breadwinner; (**employees**) personnel, staff, workforce; informal liveware.

employer n. **1** *his employer gave him a glowing reference* **manager**, manageress, proprietor, director, head man, head woman; informal boss, boss man, skipper; Brit. informal gaffer, governor, guv'nor; N. Amer. informal padrone, sachem. **2** *the largest private sector employer in Sheffield* **firm**, company, business, organization, manufacturer.

employment n. **1** *she found employment as a clerk* **work**, labour, service; job, post, position, situation, occupation, profession, trade, métier, business, line, line of work, calling, vocation, craft, pursuit; old use employ. **2** *the employment of children* **hiring**, hire, engagement, taking on; apprenticing. **3** *the employment of nuclear weapons* **use**, utilization, application, exercise.

emporium n. **shop**, store, outlet, retail outlet; department store, chain store, supermarket, hypermarket, superstore, megastore; establishment.

empower v. **1** *the act empowered Henry to punish heretics* **authorize**, entitle, permit, allow, license, sanction, warrant, commission, delegate, qualify, enable, equip. **2** *movements to empower the poor* **emancipate**, unshackle, set free, liberate.
– OPPOSITES forbid.

empress n. **ruler**, sovereign, queen, monarch, potentate; historical tsarina.

emptiness n. **void**, vacuum, empty space, vacuity, gap, vacancy, hole.

empty adj. **1** *an empty house* **vacant**, unoccupied, uninhabited, untenanted, bare, desolate, deserted, abandoned; clear, free. **2** *an empty threat* **meaningless**, hollow, idle, vain, futile, worthless, useless, insubstantial, ineffective, ineffectual. **3** *without her my life is empty* **futile**, pointless, purposeless, worthless, meaningless, valueless, of no value, useless, of no use, aimless, senseless, hollow, barren, insignificant, inconsequential, trivial. **4** *his eyes were empty* **blank**, expressionless, vacant, deadpan, wooden, stony, impassive, absent, glazed, fixed, lifeless, emotionless, unresponsive.
– OPPOSITES full, serious, worthwhile.
▸ v. **1** *I emptied the dishwasher* **unload**, unpack, void; clear, evacuate; old use unlade. **2** *he emptied out the contents of the case* **remove**, take out, extract, tip out, pour out.
– OPPOSITES fill.

empty-headed adj. **stupid**, foolish, silly, unintelligent, idiotic, brainless, witless, vacuous, vapid, feather-brained, birdbrained, scatterbrained, scatty, thoughtless; informal half-witted, dumb, dim, airheaded, brain-dead, dippy, dizzy, dopey, dozy, soft in the head, slow on the uptake; Brit. informal daft; N. Amer. informal ditzy.
– OPPOSITES intelligent.

emulate v. **imitate**, copy, mirror, echo, follow, model oneself on, take a leaf out of someone's book; match, equal, parallel, be on a par with, be in the same league as, come close to; compete with, contend with, rival, surpass.

enable v. **allow**, permit, let, give the means to, equip, empower, make able, fit; authorize, entitle, qualify; formal capacitate.
– OPPOSITES prevent.

enact v. **1** *the Bill was enacted in 1963* **pass**, make law, legislate; approve, ratify, sanction, authorize; impose, lay down. **2** *members of the church enacted a nativity play* **act out**, act, perform, appear in, stage, mount, put on, present.
– OPPOSITES repeal.

enactment n. **1** *the enactment of a Bill of Rights* **passing**; ratification, sanction, approval, authorization; imposition. **2** *parliamentary enactments* **act**, law, by-law, ruling, rule, regulation, statute, measure;

N. Amer. formal ordinance; (**enactments**) legislation. **3** *the enactment of the play acting*, performing, performance, staging, presentation.

enamoured adj. **in love**, infatuated, besotted, smitten, captivated, enchanted, fascinated, bewitched, beguiled; keen on, taken with; informal mad about, crazy about, wild about, bowled over by, struck on, sweet on, carrying a torch for; literary ensorcelled by.

encampment n. **camp**, military camp, bivouac, cantonment; campsite, camping ground; tents.

encapsulate v. **1** *their conclusions are encapsulated in one sentence* **summarize**, sum up, give the gist of, put in a nutshell; capture, express. **2** *seeds encapsulated in resin* **enclose**, encase, contain, envelop, enfold, sheath, cocoon, surround.

enchant v. **captivate**, charm, delight, enrapture, entrance, enthral, beguile, bewitch, spellbind, fascinate, hypnotize, mesmerize, rivet, grip, transfix; informal bowl someone over.
– OPPOSITES bore.

enchanter n. **wizard**, witch, sorcerer, warlock, magician, necromancer, magus; witch doctor, medicine man, shaman; old use mage; rare thaumaturge.

enchanting adj. **captivating**, charming, delightful, bewitching, beguiling, adorable, lovely, attractive, appealing, engaging, winning, fetching, winsome, alluring, disarming, irresistible, fascinating; dated taking.

enchantment n. **1** *a race of giants skilled in enchantment* **magic**, witchcraft, sorcery, wizardry, necromancy; charms, spells, incantations; N. Amer. mojo; rare thaumaturgy. **2** *the enchantment of the garden by moonlight* **allure**, delight, charm, beauty, attractiveness, appeal, fascination, irresistibility, magnetism, pull, draw, lure. **3** *being with him was sheer enchantment* **bliss**, ecstasy, heaven, rapture, joy.

enchantress n. **witch**, sorceress, magician, fairy; Circe, siren.

encircle v. **surround**, enclose, circle, girdle, ring, encompass; close in, shut in, fence in, wall in, hem in, confine; literary gird, engirdle.

enclose v. **1** *tall trees enclosed the garden* **surround**, circle, ring, girdle, encompass, encircle; confine, close in, shut in, fence in, wall in, hedge in, hem in; literary gird, engirdle. **2** *please enclose a stamped addressed envelope* **include**, insert, put in; send.

> **WORD LINKS**
> **claustrophobia** extreme fear of enclosed spaces

enclosure n. **paddock**, fold, pen, compound, stockade, ring, yard; sty, coop; N. Amer. corral.

encompass v. **1** *the monument is encompassed by Hunsbury Park* **contain**, have within; surround, enclose, encircle. **2** *debates encompassing a vast range of subjects* **cover**, embrace, include,

incorporate, take in, contain, comprise, involve, deal with; formal comprehend.

encounter v. **1** *I encountered a girl I used to know* **meet**, meet by chance, run into, come across/upon, stumble across/on, chance on, happen on; informal bump into; old use run against, rencounter. **2** *we encountered a slight problem* **experience**, run into, come up against, face, be faced with, confront.
▶ n. **1** *an unexpected encounter* **meeting**, chance meeting; old use rencounter. **2** *a violent encounter between police and demonstrators* **battle**, fight, clash, confrontation, struggle, skirmish, engagement; informal run-in, set-to, dust-up, scrap; Brit. informal, Football afters.

encourage v. **1** *the players were encouraged by the crowd's response* **hearten**, cheer, buoy up, uplift, inspire, motivate, spur on, stir, stir up, fire up, stimulate, invigorate, vitalize, revitalize, embolden, fortify, rally; informal buck up, pep up, give a shot in the arm to. **2** *she had encouraged him to go* **persuade**, coax, urge, press, push, pressure, pressurize, prod, goad, egg on, prompt, influence, sway. **3** *the Government was keen to encourage local businesses* **support**, back, champion, promote, further, foster, nurture, cultivate, strengthen, stimulate; help, assist, aid, boost, fuel.
– OPPOSITES discourage, dissuade, hinder.

encouragement n. **1** *she needed a bit of encouragement* **heartening**, cheering up, inspiration, motivation, stimulation, fortification; morale-boosting; informal a shot in the arm. **2** *they required no encouragement to get back to work* **persuasion**, coaxing, urging, pressure, pressurization, prodding, prompting; spur, goad, inducement, incentive, carrot, bait, motive. **3** *the encouragement of foreign investment* **support**, backing, championship, championing, sponsoring, promotion, furtherance, furthering, fostering, nurture, cultivation; help, assistance; N. Amer. boosterism.

encouraging adj. **1** *an encouraging start* **promising**, hopeful, auspicious, propitious, favourable, bright, rosy; heartening, reassuring, cheering, comforting, welcome, pleasing, gratifying. **2** *my parents were very encouraging* **supportive**, understanding, helpful, positive, responsive, enthusiastic.

encroach v. **intrude**, trespass, impinge, obtrude, impose oneself, invade, infiltrate, interrupt, infringe, violate, interfere with, disturb; tread/step on someone's toes; informal horn in on, muscle in on; old use entrench on.

encroachment n. **intrusion**, trespass, invasion, infiltration, incursion, obtrusion, infringement, impingement.

encumber v. **1** *her movements were encumbered by her heavy skirts* **hamper**, hinder, obstruct, impede, cramp, inhibit, restrict, limit, constrain, restrain, bog down, retard, slow (down); inconvenience, disadvantage, handicap. **2** *they are*

e

encumbered with debt **burden**, load, weigh down, saddle; overwhelm, tax, stress, strain, overload, overburden; Brit. informal lumber.

encumbrance n. **1** *he soon found the old equipment a great encumbrance* **hindrance**, obstruction, obstacle, impediment, constraint, handicap, inconvenience, nuisance, disadvantage, drawback; literary trammel; old use cumber. **2** *she knew she was an encumbrance to him* **burden**, responsibility, obligation, liability, weight, load, stress, strain, pressure, trouble, worry; millstone, albatross, cross to bear.

encyclopedic adj. **comprehensive**, complete, thorough, thoroughgoing, full, exhaustive, in-depth, wide-ranging, all-inclusive, all-embracing, all-encompassing, universal, vast; formal compendious.

end n. **1** *the end of the road* **extremity**, furthermost part, limit; margin, edge, border, boundary, periphery; point, tip, tail end; N. Amer. tag end. **2** *the end of the novel* **conclusion**, termination, ending, finish, close, resolution, climax, finale, culmination, denouement; epilogue, coda, peroration. **3** *a cigarette end* **butt**, stub, stump, remnant; informal fag end, dog end. **4** *wealth is a means and not an end in itself* **aim**, goal, purpose, objective, object, holy grail, target; intention, intent, design, motive; aspiration, wish, desire, ambition. **5** *the commercial end of the business* **aspect**, side, section, area, field, part, share, portion, segment, province. **6** *his end might come at any time* **death**, dying, demise, passing, expiry, quietus; doom, extinction, annihilation, extermination, destruction; downfall, ruin, ruination, Waterloo; informal curtains; formal decease.
– OPPOSITES beginning.
▶v. **1** *the show ended with a wedding scene* **finish**, conclude, terminate, come to an end, draw to a close, close, stop, cease; culminate, climax, come to a head. **2** *she ended their relationship* **break off**, call off, bring to an end, put an end to, stop, finish, terminate, discontinue; dissolve, cancel, annul.
– OPPOSITES begin.

endanger v. **imperil**, jeopardize, risk, put at risk, put in danger; threaten, pose a threat to, be a danger to, be detrimental to, damage, injure, harm; old use peril.

endearing adj. **lovable**, adorable, cute, sweet, dear, delightful, lovely, charming, appealing, attractive, engaging, winning, captivating, enchanting, beguiling, winsome; dated taking.

endearment n. **1** *his murmured endearments* **term of affection**, term of endearment, pet name; **(endearments)** sweet nothings, sweet talk. **2** *he spoke to her without endearment* **affection**, fondness, tenderness, feeling, sentiment, warmth, love, liking, care.

endeavour v. *the company endeavoured to expand its activities* **try**, attempt, seek, undertake, aspire, aim, set out; strive, struggle, labour, toil, work, exert oneself, apply oneself, do one's best, do one's utmost, give one's all, be at pains; informal have a go/ shot/stab, give something one's best shot, do one's damnedest, go all out, bend over backwards; formal essay.
▶n. **1** *an endeavour to build a more buoyant economy* **attempt**, try, bid, effort, venture; informal go, crack, shot, stab, bash; formal essay. **2** *several days of endeavour* **effort**, exertion, striving, struggling, labouring, struggle, labour, hard work, application, industry; pains; informal sweat, {blood, sweat, and tears}, elbow grease; Brit. informal graft; Austral./ NZ informal (hard) yakka; literary travail. **3** *an extremely unwise endeavour* **undertaking**, enterprise, venture, exercise, activity, exploit, deed, act, action, move; scheme, plan, project; informal caper.

ending n. **end**, finish, close, closing, conclusion, resolution, summing-up, denouement, finale; cessation, stopping, termination, discontinuation.
– OPPOSITES beginning.

endless adj. **1** *a woman with endless energy* **unlimited**, limitless, infinite, inexhaustible, boundless, unbounded, untold, immeasurable, measureless, incalculable; abundant, abounding, great; ceaseless, unceasing, unending, without end, everlasting, constant, continuous, continual, interminable, unfading, unfailing, perpetual, eternal, enduring, lasting. **2** *as children we played endless games* **countless**, innumerable, untold, legion, numberless, unnumbered, numerous, very many, manifold, multitudinous, multifarious; a great number of, infinite numbers of, a multitude of; informal umpteen, no end of, loads of, stacks of, heaps of, masses of, oodles of, scads of, zillions of; N. Amer. informal gazillions of; literary myriad, divers.
– OPPOSITES limited, few.

endorse v. **support**, back, agree with, approve (of), favour, subscribe to, recommend, champion, stick up for, uphold, affirm, sanction; informal throw one's weight behind.
– OPPOSITES oppose.

endorsement n. **support**, backing, approval, seal of approval, agreement, recommendation, championship, patronage, affirmation, sanction.

endow v. **1** *Henry II endowed a hospital for poor pilgrims* **finance**, fund, pay for, subsidize, support financially, settle money on; establish, found, set up, institute. **2** *nature endowed the human race with intelligence* **provide**, supply, furnish, equip, invest, favour, bless, grace, gift; give, bestow; literary endue.

endowment n. **1** *the endowment of a Chair of Botany* **funding**, financing, subsidizing; establishment, foundation, institution. **2** *a generous endowment* **bequest**, legacy, inheritance; gift, present, grant, award, donation, contribution, subsidy, settlement; formal benefaction. **3** *his natural endowments* **quality**, characteristic, feature, attribute, facility, faculty, ability, talent, gift, strength, aptitude, capability, capacity.

endurable adj. **bearable**, tolerable, supportable, manageable, sustainable.
– OPPOSITES unbearable.

endurance n. **1** *she pushed him beyond the limit of his endurance* **toleration**, tolerance, sufferance, forbearance, patience, acceptance, resignation, stoicism. **2** *the race is a test of endurance* **stamina**, staying power, fortitude, perseverance, persistence, tenacity, doggedness, grit, indefatigability, resolution, determination; Brit. Dunkirk spirit; informal stickability; formal pertinacity.

endure v. **1** *he endured years of pain* **undergo**, go through, live through, experience, meet, encounter; cope with, deal with, face, suffer, tolerate, put up with, brave, withstand, sustain, weather; Scottish thole. **2** *I cannot endure such behaviour* **tolerate**, bear, put up with, suffer, take; informal hack, stand for, stomach, swallow, abide, hold with; Brit. informal stick, wear, be doing with; formal brook. **3** *God's love will endure for ever* **last**, live, live on, go on, survive, abide, continue, persist, remain, stay.
– OPPOSITES fade.

enduring adj. **lasting**, long-lasting, abiding, durable, continuing, persisting, eternal, perennial, permanent, unending, everlasting; constant, stable, steady, steadfast, fixed, firm, unwavering, unfaltering, unchanging.
– OPPOSITES short-lived.

enemy n. **opponent**, adversary, rival, antagonist, combatant, challenger, competitor, opposer, opposition, competition, other side; literary foe.
– OPPOSITES ally.

energetic adj. **1** *an energetic woman* **active**, lively, dynamic, zestful, spirited, animated, vital, vibrant, bouncy, bubbly, exuberant, perky, frisky, sprightly, tireless, indefatigable, enthusiastic; informal peppy, sparky, feisty, full of beans, full of the joys of spring, bright-eyed and bushy-tailed. **2** *energetic exercises* **vigorous**, strenuous, brisk; hard, arduous, demanding, taxing, tough, rigorous. **3** *an energetic advertising campaign* **forceful**, vigorous, high-powered, all-out, determined, bold, powerful, potent; intensive, hard-hitting, pulling no punches, aggressive, high-octane; informal punchy, in-your-face.
– OPPOSITES lethargic, gentle, half-hearted.

energize v. **1** *people are energized by his ideas* **enliven**, liven up, animate, vitalize, invigorate, perk up, excite, electrify, stimulate, stir up, fire up, rouse, motivate, move, drive, spur on, encourage, galvanize; informal pep up, buck up, give a shot in the arm to. **2** *floor sensors energized by standing passengers* **activate**, trigger, trip, operate, actuate, switch on, turn on, start, start up, power.

energy n. **1** *she has so much energy* **vitality**, vigour, life, liveliness, animation, vivacity, spirit, spiritedness, verve, enthusiasm, zest, vibrancy, spark, sparkle, effervescence, exuberance, buoyancy, sprightliness; strength, stamina, forcefulness, power, dynamism, drive; fire, passion, ardour, zeal; informal zip, zing, pep, pizzazz, punch, bounce, oomph, go, get-up-and-go; N. Amer. informal feistiness. **2** *the increasing use of solar energy* **power**.

enervate v. **exhaust**, tire, fatigue, weary, wear out, devitalize, drain, sap, weaken, enfeeble, debilitate, incapacitate, prostrate; informal knock out, do in, shatter, fag out; Brit. informal knacker.
– OPPOSITES invigorate.

enervation n. **fatigue**, exhaustion, tiredness, weariness, lassitude, weakness, feebleness, debilitation, indisposition, prostration.

enfeeble v. **weaken**, debilitate, incapacitate, indispose, lay low; drain, sap, exhaust, tire, fatigue, devitalize.
– OPPOSITES strengthen.

enfold v. **1** *the summit was enfolded in white cloud* **envelop**, engulf, sheathe, swathe, swaddle, cocoon, shroud, veil, cloak, drape, cover; surround, enclose, encase, encircle; literary enshroud, mantle. **2** *he enfolded her in his arms* **clasp**, hold, fold, wrap, squeeze, clutch, gather; embrace, hug, cuddle; literary embosom.

enforce v. **1** *the sheriff enforced the law* **impose**, apply, administer, implement, bring to bear, discharge, execute, prosecute. **2** *they cannot enforce cooperation between the parties* **force**, compel, coerce, exact, extort; old use constrain.

enforced adj. **compulsory**, obligatory, mandatory, involuntary, forced, imposed, required, requisite, stipulated, prescribed, contractual, binding, necessary, unavoidable, inescapable.
– OPPOSITES voluntary.

enfranchise v. **1** *women over thirty were enfranchised in 1918* **give the vote to**, give/grant suffrage to. **2** historical *he enfranchised his slaves* **emancipate**, liberate, free, set free, release; unchain, unyoke, unfetter, unshackle; historical manumit.

engage v. **1** *tasks which engage children's interest* **capture**, catch, arrest, grab, draw, attract, gain, win, hold, grip, captivate, engross, absorb, occupy. **2** *he engaged a nursemaid* **employ**, hire, recruit, take on, secure the services of, enrol, appoint. **3** *he engaged to pay them £10,000* **contract**, promise, agree, pledge, vow, covenant, commit oneself, bind oneself, undertake, enter into an agreement. **4** *the chance to engage in many social activities* **participate in**, take part in, join in, become involved in, go in for, partake in/of, share in, play a part/role in; have a hand in, be a party to, enter into. **5** *infantry units engaged the enemy* **fight**, do battle with, wage war on/

e

against, attack, take on, set upon, clash with, skirmish with; encounter, meet.
– OPPOSITES lose, dismiss.

engaged adj. **1** *he's otherwise engaged* **busy**, occupied, unavailable; informal tied up. **2** *she's engaged to an American guy* promised/pledged in marriage; attached; informal spoken for; dated betrothed; literary affianced; old use plighted, espoused.
– OPPOSITES free, unattached.

engagement n. **1** *they broke off their engagement* **marriage contract**; dated betrothal; old use espousal. **2** *a business engagement* **appointment**, meeting, arrangement, commitment, tweetup; date, assignation, rendezvous; literary tryst. **3** *Britain's continued engagement in open trading* **participation**, involvement, association. **4** *his engagement as a curate* **employment**, appointment; work, job, post, situation. **5** *the first engagement of the war* **battle**, fight, clash, confrontation, encounter, conflict, skirmish; warfare, action, combat, hostilities; informal dogfight.

engaging adj. **charming**, appealing, attractive, pretty, delightful, lovely, pleasing, pleasant, agreeable, likeable, lovable, sweet, winning, winsome, fetching, captivating, enchanting, bewitching; Scottish & N. English bonny; dated taking; old use comely, fair.
– OPPOSITES unappealing.

engender v. **1** *his works engendered considerable controversy* **cause**, be the cause of, give rise to, bring about, occasion, lead to, result in, produce, create, generate, arouse, rouse, inspire, provoke, kindle, trigger, spark, stir up, whip up, induce, incite, instigate, foment; literary beget, enkindle. **2** old use *he engendered six children* **father**, sire, bring into the world, spawn, breed; literary beget.

engine n. **1** *a car engine* **motor**, machine, mechanism. **2** *the main engine of change* **cause**, agent, instrument, originator, initiator, generator. **3** historical *engines of war* **device**, contraption, apparatus, machine, appliance, mechanism, implement, instrument, tool.

engineer n. **1** *a structural engineer* **designer**, planner, builder. **2** *the ship's engineer* **operator**, driver, controller. **3** *the prime engineer of the approach* **originator**, deviser, designer, architect, inventor, developer, creator; mastermind.
▶ v. *he engineered a takeover deal* **bring about**, arrange, pull off, bring off, contrive, manoeuvre, manipulate, negotiate, organize, orchestrate, choreograph, mount, stage, mastermind, originate, manage, stage-manage, coordinate, control, superintend, direct, conduct; informal wangle.

engrained adj. See **ingrained**.

engrave v. **1** *my name was engraved on the ring* **carve**, inscribe, cut (in), incise, chisel, chase, score, notch, etch, imprint, impress. **2** *the image was engraved in his memory* **fix**, set, imprint, stamp, brand,

impress, embed, etch.

engraving n. **etching**, print, impression, lithograph; plate, dry point, woodcut, linocut.

engross v. **absorb**, engage, rivet, grip, hold, interest, involve, occupy, preoccupy; fascinate, captivate, enthral, intrigue.

engrossed adj. **absorbed**, involved, interested, occupied, preoccupied, immersed, caught up, riveted, gripped, focused, rapt, fascinated, intent, captivated, enthralled, intrigued.

engrossing adj. **absorbing**, interesting, riveting, gripping, captivating, compelling, compulsive, fascinating, intriguing, enthralling; informal unputdownable.

engulf v. **inundate**, flood, deluge, immerse, swamp, swallow up, submerge; bury, envelop, overwhelm.

enhance v. **increase**, add to, intensify, heighten, magnify, amplify, inflate, strengthen, build up, supplement, augment, boost, raise, lift, elevate, exalt; improve, enrich, complement.
– OPPOSITES diminish.

enigma n. **mystery**, puzzle, riddle, conundrum, paradox, problem; a closed book; informal poser.

enigmatic adj. **mysterious**, inscrutable, puzzling, mystifying, baffling, perplexing, impenetrable, unfathomable, sphinx-like, Delphic, oracular; cryptic, elliptical, ambiguous, equivocal, paradoxical, obscure, oblique, secret.

enjoin v. **urge**, encourage, admonish, press, instruct, direct, require, order, command, tell, call on, demand, charge; formal adjure; literary bid.

enjoy v. **1** *he enjoys playing the piano* **like**, love, be fond of, be entertained by, take pleasure in, be keen on, delight in, appreciate, relish, revel in, lap up, savour, luxuriate in, bask in; informal get a kick out of, get a thrill out of, get a buzz out of, go a bundle on. **2** *she had always enjoyed good health* **benefit from**, have the benefit of; be blessed with, be favoured with, be endowed with, be possessed of, possess, own, boast.
– OPPOSITES dislike, lack.
□ **enjoy oneself** have fun, have a good time, have the time of one's life; make merry, celebrate, revel; informal party, have a ball, have a whale of a time, whoop it up, let one's hair down.

enjoyable adj. **entertaining**, amusing, diverting, delightful, to one's liking, pleasant, congenial, convivial, lovely, fine, good, great, agreeable, pleasurable, delicious, delectable, satisfying, gratifying; marvellous, wonderful, magnificent, splendid; informal super, fantastic, fabulous, fab, terrific, grand, magic; Brit. informal brilliant, brill, smashing.

enjoyment n. **pleasure**, fun, entertainment, amusement, diversion, recreation, relaxation; delight, happiness, merriment, joy, gaiety, jollity; satisfaction, gratification, liking, relish, gusto; humorous delectation; dated sport.

enlarge v. **1** *they enlarged the scope of their research* **extend**, expand, grow, add to, amplify, augment, magnify, build up, supplement; widen, broaden, stretch, lengthen; elongate, deepen, thicken. **2** *the lymph glands had enlarged* **swell**, distend, bloat, bulge, dilate, tumefy, blow up, puff up, balloon. **3** *he enlarged on this subject* **elaborate on**, expand on, add to, build on, flesh out, put flesh on the bones of, add detail to, expatiate on; develop, fill out, embellish, embroider.
– OPPOSITES reduce, shrink.

enlargement n. **expansion**, extension, growth, amplification, augmentation, addition, magnification, widening, broadening, lengthening; elongation, deepening, thickening; swelling, distension, dilation, tumefaction.

enlighten v. **inform**, tell, make aware, open someone's eyes, notify, illuminate, apprise, brief, update, bring up to date; disabuse, set straight; informal put in the picture, clue in, fill in, put wise, bring up to speed.

enlightened adj. **informed**, well informed, aware, sophisticated, advanced, developed, liberal, open-minded, broad-minded, educated, knowledgeable, wise; civilized, refined, cultured, cultivated.
– OPPOSITES benighted.

enlightenment n. **insight**, understanding, awareness, wisdom, education, learning, knowledge; illumination, awakening, instruction, teaching; sophistication, advancement, development, open-mindedness, broad-mindedness; culture, refinement, cultivation, civilization.

enlist v. **1** *he enlisted in the Royal Engineers* **join up**, join, enrol in, sign up for, volunteer for; Brit. old use take the King's shilling. **2** *he was enlisted in the army* **recruit**, call up, enrol, sign up, conscript; US draft, induct; old use levy. **3** *he enlisted the help of a friend* **obtain**, engage, secure, win, get, procure.

enliven v. **1** *a meeting enlivened by her wit and vivacity* **liven up**, spice up, add spice to, ginger up, perk up, vitalize, leaven; informal pep up, sex up. **2** *the visit had enlivened my mother* **cheer up**, brighten up, liven up, raise someone's spirits, uplift, gladden, buoy up, animate, vivify, vitalize, invigorate, restore, revive, refresh, stimulate, rouse, boost, exhilarate; N. Amer. light a fire under; informal perk up, buck up, pep up.

en masse adv. **(all) together**, as a group, as one, en bloc, as a whole, in a body, wholesale.

enmesh v. **embroil**, entangle, ensnare, snare, trap, entrap, ensnarl, involve, catch up, mix up, bog down, mire.

enmity n. **hostility**, animosity, antagonism, friction, antipathy, animus, acrimony, bitterness, rancour, resentment, aversion, ill feeling, bad feeling, ill will, bad blood, hatred, hate, loathing, odium; malice, spite, spitefulness, venom, malevolence; Brit. informal needle.
– OPPOSITES friendship.

ennoble v. **dignify**, honour, exalt, elevate, raise, enhance, add dignity to, distinguish; magnify, glorify, aggrandize.
– OPPOSITES demean.

ennui n. **boredom**, tedium, listlessness, lethargy, lassitude, languor, weariness, enervation; malaise, dissatisfaction, melancholy, world-weariness, depression, Weltschmerz.

enormity n. **1** *the enormity of the task* **immensity**, hugeness; size, extent, magnitude, greatness. **2** *the enormity of his crimes* **wickedness**, evil, vileness, baseness, depravity; outrageousness, monstrousness, hideousness, heinousness, horror, atrocity; villainy, cruelty, inhumanity, mercilessness, brutality, savagery, viciousness. **3** *the enormities of the regime* **outrage**, horror, evil, atrocity, barbarity, abomination, monstrosity, obscenity, iniquity; crime, sin, violation, wrong, offence, disgrace, injustice, abuse.

enormous adj. **huge**, vast, immense, gigantic, very big, great, giant, massive, colossal, mammoth, tremendous, mighty, monumental, epic, prodigious, mountainous, king-size(d), titanic, towering, elephantine, gargantuan; informal mega, monster, whopping (great), humongous, jumbo, astronomical; Brit. informal whacking (great), ginormous.
– OPPOSITES tiny.

enormously adv. **1** *an enormously important factor* **very**, extremely, really, exceedingly, exceptionally, tremendously, immensely, hugely; singularly, particularly, eminently; informal terrifically, awfully, terribly, seriously, desperately, ultra, damn, damned; Brit. informal ever so, well, dead, jolly; N. Amer. informal real, mighty, darned; informal dated frightfully. **2** *prices vary enormously* **considerably**, greatly, very much, a great deal, a lot.
– OPPOSITES slightly.

enough determiner *they had enough food* **sufficient**, adequate, ample, the necessary; informal plenty of.
– OPPOSITES insufficient.

▸ pron. *there's enough for everyone* **sufficient**, plenty, a sufficient amount, an adequate amount, as much as necessary; a sufficiency, an ample supply; one's fill.

enquire, **inquire** v. **1** *I enquired about part-time training courses* **ask**, make enquiries, question someone, request information. **2** *the commission is to enquire into alleged illegal payments* **investigate**, conduct an enquiry, probe, look into; research, examine, explore, delve into; informal check out.

enquiring, **inquiring** adj. **inquisitive**, curious, interested, questioning, probing, searching; investigative.

enquiry, **inquiry** n. **1** *telephone enquiries* **question**, query. **2** *an enquiry into alleged security leaks* **investigation**, probe, examination, exploration; inquest, hearing.

enrage v. **anger**, infuriate, incense, madden, inflame; antagonize, provoke, exasperate; informal drive mad/crazy, drive up the wall, make someone see red, make someone's blood boil, make someone's hackles rise, get someone's back up, get someone's dander up; N. Amer. informal burn up.
– OPPOSITES placate.

enraged adj. **furious**, infuriated, very angry, irate, incensed, raging, incandescent, fuming, ranting, raving, seething, beside oneself; informal mad, hopping mad, wild, livid, boiling, apoplectic, hot under the collar, on the warpath, foaming at the mouth, steamed up, in a paddy, fit to be tied; literary wrathful.
– OPPOSITES calm.

enrapture v. **delight**, enchant, captivate, charm, enthral, entrance, bewitch, beguile, transport, thrill, excite, exhilarate, intoxicate, take someone's breath away; informal bowl someone over, blow someone's mind; literary ravish.

enrich v. **enhance**, improve, better, add to, augment; supplement, complement; boost, elevate, raise, lift, refine.
– OPPOSITES spoil.

enrol v. **1** *they both enrolled for the course* **register**, sign on/up, put one's name down, apply, volunteer; matriculate; enter, join. **2** *280 new members were enrolled* **accept**, admit, take on, register, sign on/up, recruit, engage; matriculate; impanel.

en route adv. **on the way**, in transit, during the journey, along/on the road, on the move; coming, going, proceeding, travelling.

ensconce v. **settle**, install, plant, position, seat, sit, sit down; establish; informal park, plonk.

ensemble n. **1** *a Bulgarian folk ensemble* **group**, band; company, troupe, cast, chorus, corps; informal combo. **2** *the buildings present a charming provincial ensemble* **whole**, entity, unit, body, set, combination, composite, package; sum, total, totality, entirety, aggregate. **3** *a pink and black ensemble* **outfit**, costume, suit; separates, coordinates; informal get-up.

enshrine v. **set down**, set out, spell out, express, lay down, set in stone, embody, realize, manifest, incorporate, represent, contain, include, preserve, treasure, immortalize, cherish.

enshroud v. literary **envelop**, veil, shroud, swathe, cloak, cloud, enfold, surround, bury; cover, conceal, obscure, blot out, hide, mask; literary mantle.

ensign n. **flag**, standard, colour(s), banner, pennant, pennon, streamer, banderole.

enslavement n. **slavery**, servitude, bondage, forced labour; exploitation, oppression, bonds, chains, fetters, shackles, yoke; historical thraldom.
– OPPOSITES liberation.

ensnare v. **capture**, catch, trap, entrap, snare, net; entangle, embroil, enmesh.

ensue v. **result**, follow, be consequent on, develop, proceed, succeed, emerge, stem, arise, derive, issue; occur, happen, take place, come next/after, transpire, supervene; formal eventuate; literary come to pass, befall.

ensure v. **1** *ensure that the surface is completely clean* **make sure**, make certain, see to it; check, confirm, establish, verify. **2** *legislation to ensure equal opportunities for all* **secure**, guarantee, assure, certify, set the seal on, clinch.

entail v. **involve**, necessitate, require, need, demand, call for; mean, imply; cause, produce, result in, lead to, give rise to, occasion.

entangle v. **1** *their parachutes became entangled* **twist**, intertwine, entwine, tangle, ravel, snarl, knot, coil, mat. **2** *the fish are easily entangled in fine nets* **catch**, capture, trap, snare, ensnare, entrap, enmesh. **3** *he was entangled in a lawsuit* **involve**, implicate, embroil, mix up, catch up, bog down, mire.

entanglement n. **1** *their entanglement in the war* **involvement**, embroilment. **2** *romantic entanglements* **affair**, relationship, love affair, romance, amour, fling, dalliance, liaison, involvement, intrigue; complication.

entente n. **understanding**, agreement, arrangement, entente cordiale, settlement, deal; alliance, treaty, pact, accord, convention, concordat.

enter v. **1** *police entered the house* **go in/into**, come in/into, get in/into, set foot in, cross the threshold of, gain access to. **2** *a bullet entered his chest* **penetrate**, pierce, puncture, perforate; literary transpierce. **3** *he entered politics in 2001* **get involved in**, join, throw oneself into, engage in, embark on, take up; participate in, take part in, play a part/role in, contribute to. **4** *the planning entered a new phase* **reach**, move into, get to, begin, start, commence. **5** *they entered the Army at eighteen* **join**, become a member of, enrol in/for, enlist in, volunteer for, sign up for; take up. **6** *she entered a cookery competition* **go in for**, put one's name down for, register for, enrol for, sign on/up for; compete in, take part in, participate in. **7** *the cashier entered the details in a ledger* **record**, write, set down, put down, take down, note, jot down; put on record, minute, register, log. **8** *please enter your password* **key (in)**, type (in), tap in. **9** Law *he entered a plea of guilty* **submit**, register, lodge, record, file, put forward, present.
– OPPOSITES leave.

enterprise n. **1** *a joint enterprise* **undertaking**, endeavour, venture, exercise, activity, operation, task, business, proceeding; project, scheme, plan, programme, campaign. **2** *a woman with enterprise* **initiative**, resourcefulness, entrepreneurialism, imagination, ingenuity, inventiveness, originality, creativity; quick-wittedness, native wit, cleverness;

enthusiasm, dynamism, drive, ambition, energy; boldness, daring, courage; informal gumption, get-up-and-go, oomph. **3** *a profit-making enterprise* **business**, company, firm, venture, organization, operation, concern, corporation, establishment, partnership; informal outfit, set-up.

enterprising adj. **resourceful**, entrepreneurial, imaginative, ingenious, inventive, creative; quick-witted, clever, bright, sharp, sharp-witted; enthusiastic, dynamic, ambitious, energetic; bold, daring, courageous, adventurous; informal go-ahead.
– OPPOSITES unimaginative.

entertain v. **1** *he wrote stories to entertain them* **amuse**, divert, delight, please, charm, cheer, interest; engage, occupy, absorb, engross. **2** *he entertains foreign visitors* **receive**, play host/hostess to, invite (round/over), throw a party for; wine and dine, feast, cater for, feed, treat, welcome, fete. **3** *I would never entertain such an idea* **consider**, give consideration to, contemplate, think about, give thought to; countenance, tolerate, support; formal brook.

entertainer n. **performer**, artist, artiste.

entertaining adj. **delightful**, enjoyable, diverting, amusing, pleasing, agreeable, appealing, engaging, interesting, fascinating, absorbing, compelling; humorous, funny, comical, chucklesome; informal fun.

entertainment n. **1** *he read for entertainment* **amusement**, pleasure, leisure, recreation, relaxation, fun, enjoyment, interest, diversion; N. Amer. informal rec. **2** *an entertainment for the emperor* **show**, performance, presentation, production, extravaganza, spectacle.

enthral v. **captivate**, charm, enchant, bewitch, fascinate, beguile, entrance, delight; win, ensnare, absorb, engross, rivet, grip, transfix, hypnotize, mesmerize, spellbind.
– OPPOSITES bore.

enthralling adj. **fascinating**, entrancing, enchanting, bewitching, captivating, charming, beguiling, delightful; absorbing, engrossing, compelling, riveting, gripping, exciting, spellbinding; informal unputdownable.

enthuse v. **1** *I enthused about the idea* **rave**, be enthusiastic, gush, wax lyrical, be effusive, rhapsodize; praise to the skies; informal go wild/mad/crazy; N. Amer. informal ballyhoo. **2** *he enthuses people* **motivate**, inspire, stimulate, encourage, spur (on), galvanize, rouse, excite, stir (up), fire, inspirit.

enthusiasm n. **1** *she worked with enthusiasm* **eagerness**, keenness, ardour, fervour, passion, zeal, zest, gusto, energy, verve, vigour, vehemence, fire, spirit, avidity; wholeheartedness, commitment, willingness, devotion, earnestness; informal get-up-and-go. **2** *they put their enthusiasms to good use* **interest**, passion, obsession, mania; inclination, preference, penchant,

predilection, fancy; pastime, hobby, recreation, pursuit.
– OPPOSITES apathy.

enthusiast n. **fan**, devotee, aficionado, lover, admirer, follower; expert, connoisseur, authority, pundit; informal buff, freak, fanatic, nut, fiend, addict, maniac.

enthusiastic adj. **eager**, keen, avid, ardent, fervent, passionate, zealous, vehement; excited, wholehearted, committed, devoted, fanatical, earnest.

entice v. **tempt**, lure, attract, appeal to; invite, persuade, convince, beguile, coax, woo; seduce, lead on; informal sweet-talk.

enticement n. **lure**, temptation, allure, attraction, appeal, draw, pull, bait; charm, seduction, fascination; informal come-on.

enticing adj. **tempting**, alluring, attractive, appealing, inviting, seductive, beguiling, charming; magnetic, irresistible.

entire adj. **1** *I devoted my entire life to him* **whole**, complete, total, full; undivided. **2** *only one of the gates is entire* **intact**, unbroken, undamaged, unimpaired, unscathed, unspoiled, perfect, in one piece. **3** *they are in entire agreement* **absolute**, total, utter, out-and-out, thorough, wholehearted; unqualified, unreserved, outright.
– OPPOSITES partial, broken.

entirely adv. **1** *that's entirely out of the question* **absolutely**, completely, totally, wholly, utterly, quite; altogether, in every respect, thoroughly, downright, one hundred per cent. **2** *a gift entirely for charitable purposes* **solely**, only, exclusively, purely, merely, just, alone.

entirety n. **whole**, total, aggregate, totality, sum total.
– OPPOSITES part.
□ **in its entirety** completely, entirely, totally, fully, wholly; in every respect, in every way, one hundred per cent, all the way, every inch, to the hilt, to the core.

entitle v. **1** *this pass entitles you to visit the museum* **qualify**, make eligible, authorize, allow, permit; enable, empower. **2** *a chapter entitled 'Comedy and Tragedy'* **title**, name, call, label, designate, dub; formal denominate.

entitlement n. **1** *their entitlement to benefits* **right**, prerogative, claim; permission, dispensation, privilege. **2** *your holiday entitlement* **allowance**, allocation, quota, ration, limit.

entity n. **1** *a single entity* **being**, creature, individual, organism, life form; person; body, object, article, thing. **2** *the distinction between entity and nonentity* **existence**, being; life, living, animation; substance, essence, reality, actuality.

entomb v. **inter**, lay to rest, bury; informal plant; literary inhume, sepulchre.

entourage n. **retinue**, escort, cortège, train, suite; court, staff, bodyguard; attendants, companions, retainers.

e

e

entrails plural n. **intestines**, bowels, guts, viscera, internal organs, vital organs; offal; informal insides, innards.

entrance[1] n. 1 *the main entrance* **entry**, way in, access, ingress, approach; door, portal, gate; opening, mouth; entrance hall, foyer, lobby, porch; N. Amer. entryway. 2 *the entrance of Mrs Knight* **appearance**, arrival, entry, ingress, coming. 3 *he was refused entrance* **admission**, admittance, (right of) entry, access, ingress.
– OPPOSITES exit, departure.

entrance[2] v. 1 *I was entranced by her beauty* **enchant**, bewitch, beguile, captivate, mesmerize, hypnotize, spellbind; enthral, engross, absorb, fascinate; stun, overpower, electrify; charm, delight; informal bowl over, knock out. 2 *Orpheus entranced the wild beasts* **cast a spell on**, bewitch, hex, spellbind, hypnotize, mesmerize.

entrant n. 1 *university entrants* **new member**, new arrival, beginner, newcomer, fresher, freshman, recruit; novice, neophyte; N. Amer. tenderfoot; informal rookie; N. Amer. informal greenhorn. 2 *a prize will be awarded to the best entrant* **competitor**, contestant, contender, participant; candidate, applicant.

entrap v. 1 *fishing lines can entrap wildlife* **trap**, snare, ensnare, entangle, enmesh; catch, capture. 2 *he was entrapped by an undercover policeman* **entice**, lure, inveigle; bait, decoy, trap; lead on, trick, deceive, dupe, hoodwink; informal set up, frame; Brit. informal fit up.

entreat v. **implore**, beg, plead with, pray, ask, request; bid, enjoin, appeal to, call on, petition, solicit; literary beseech.

entreaty n. **plea**, appeal, request, petition; suit, application, claim; solicitation, supplication; prayer.

entrée n. 1 *there are a dozen entrées on the menu* **main course**, main dish. 2 *an excellent entrée into the profession* **(means of) entry**, entrance, ingress; route, path, avenue, way, key, passport.

entrench, **intrench** v. **establish**, settle, lodge, set, root, install, plant, embed, seat; informal dig in.

entrenched, **intrenched** adj. **ingrained**, established, confirmed, fixed, firm, deep-seated, deep-rooted; unshakeable, indelible, ineradicable, inexorable.

entrepreneur n. **businessman/woman**, enterpriser, speculator, tycoon, magnate, mogul; dealer, trader; promoter, impresario; informal wheeler-dealer, whizz-kid, mover and shaker, go-getter, high-flyer.

entrust v. 1 *he was entrusted with the task* **charge**, invest, endow; burden, encumber, saddle. 2 *the powers entrusted to the Home Secretary* **assign**, confer on, bestow on, vest in, consign; delegate, depute, devolve; give, grant, vouchsafe. 3 *she entrusted them to the hospital* **hand over**, give custody of, turn over, commit, consign, deliver; formal commend.

entry n. 1 *my moment of entry* **appearance**, arrival, entrance, ingress, coming. 2 *the entry to the flats* **entrance**, way in, access, ingress, approach; door, portal, gate; entrance hall, foyer, lobby; N. Amer. entryway. 3 *he was refused entry* **admission**, admittance, entrance, access, ingress. 4 *entries in the cash book* **item**, record, note, listing; memo, memorandum; account. 5 *data entry* **recording**, archiving, logging, documentation, capture. 6 *we must pick a winner from the entries* **contestant**, competitor, contender, entrant, participant; candidate, applicant; submission, entry form, application.
– OPPOSITES departure, exit.

entwine v. **wind round**, twist round, coil round; weave, intertwine, interlace, interweave; entangle, tangle; twine, braid, plait, knit.

enumerate v. 1 *he enumerated four objectives* **list**, itemize, set out, give; cite, name, specify, identify, spell out, detail, particularize. 2 formal *they enumerated hospital readmission rates* **calculate**, compute, count, add up, tally, total, number, quantify; reckon, work out; Brit. tot up.

enunciate v. 1 *she enunciated each word slowly* **pronounce**, articulate; say, speak, utter, voice, vocalize, sound, mouth. 2 *a document enunciating the policy* **express**, state, put into words, declare, profess, set forth, assert, affirm; put forward, air, proclaim.

envelop v. **surround**, cover, enfold, engulf, encircle, encompass, cocoon, sheathe, swathe, enclose; cloak, screen, shield, veil, shroud.

envelope n. **wrapper**, wrapping, sleeve, cover, covering, casing.

envenom v. **embitter**, sour, poison, jaundice, taint; antagonize.

enviable adj. **desirable**, desired, favoured, sought-after, admirable, covetable, attractive; fortunate, lucky; informal to die for.

envious adj. **jealous**, covetous, desirous; grudging, begrudging, resentful; bitter, green-eyed.

environment n. 1 *birds from many environments* **habitat**, territory, domain; surroundings, conditions. 2 *the hospital environment* **situation**, setting, milieu, background, backdrop, scene, location; context, framework; sphere, world, realm; ambience, atmosphere. 3 *the impact of pesticides on the environment* **the natural world**, nature, the earth, the ecosystem, the biosphere, Mother Nature; wildlife, flora and fauna, the countryside.

> **WORD LINKS**
>
> **ecology** the study of the relationships of living things to their environment
>
> **conservation**, **environmentalism** the preservation or restoration of the natural environment

environmentalist n. **conservationist**, preservationist, ecologist, nature-lover; informal ecofreak, tree hugger.

environs plural n. **surroundings**, surrounding area, vicinity; locality, neighbourhood, district, region; precincts; N. Amer. vicinage.

envisage v. **1** *it was envisaged that the hospital would open soon* **foresee**, predict, forecast, anticipate, expect, think likely. **2** *I cannot envisage what the future holds* **imagine**, contemplate, visualize, envision, picture; conceive of, think of.

envision v. **visualize**, imagine, envisage, picture; conceive of, think of, see; intend, mean.

envoy n. **ambassador**, emissary, diplomat, consul, attaché, chargé d'affaires, plenipotentiary; nuncio; representative, delegate, proxy, surrogate, liaison, spokesperson; agent, intermediary, mediator; informal go-between; historical legate.

envy n. **1** *a pang of envy* **jealousy**, covetousness; resentment, bitterness, discontent; the green-eyed monster. **2** *the firm is the envy of Europe* **finest**, best, pride, top, cream, pick, jewel, flower, glory, leading light, the crème de la crème.
▶v. **1** *I admired and envied her* **be envious of**, be jealous of; begrudge, be resentful of. **2** *we envied her lifestyle* **covet**, desire, aspire to, wish for, want, long for, yearn for, hanker after, crave.

ephemeral adj. **transitory**, transient, fleeting, passing, short-lived, momentary, brief, short; temporary, impermanent, short-term; fly-by-night.
– OPPOSITES permanent.

epic n. **1** *the epics of Homer* **heroic poem**; story, saga, legend, romance, chronicle, myth, fable, tale. **2** *a big Hollywood epic* long film; informal blockbuster.
▶adj. **1** *a traditional epic poem* **heroic**, long, grand, monumental, Homeric, Miltonian. **2** *their epic journey* **ambitious**, heroic, grand, great, Herculean; very long, monumental.

epicene adj. **1** *a sort of epicene beauty* **sexless**, asexual, neuter; androgynous. **2** *he gave an epicene titter* **effeminate**, unmanly, unmasculine, girlie, girlish; informal camp, campy.
– OPPOSITES macho.

epicure n. **gourmet**, gastronome, gourmand, connoisseur; informal foodie.

epicurean n. **hedonist**, sensualist, pleasure-seeker, sybarite, voluptuary, bon viveur; epicure, gourmet, gastronome, connoisseur, gourmand.
▶adj. **hedonistic**, sensualist, pleasure-seeking, self-indulgent, sybaritic, voluptuary, lotus-eating; decadent, unrestrained, extravagant, intemperate, immoderate; gluttonous, gourmandizing.

epidemic n. **1** *an epidemic of typhoid* **outbreak**, plague, pandemic, epizootic.

2 *a joyriding epidemic* **spate**, rash, wave, eruption, outbreak, craze; flood, torrent; upsurge, upturn, increase, growth, rise.
▶adj. *the craze is now epidemic* **rife**, rampant, widespread, wide-ranging, extensive, pervasive; global, universal, ubiquitous; endemic, pandemic, epizootic.

epigram n. **witticism**, quip, jest, pun, bon mot; saying, maxim, adage, aphorism, apophthegm, epigraph; informal one-liner, wisecrack, (old) chestnut.

epigrammatic adj. **concise**, succinct, pithy, aphoristic; incisive, short and sweet; witty, clever, quick-witted, piquant, sharp; informal snappy.
– OPPOSITES expansive.

epilogue n. **afterword**, postscript, PS, coda, codicil, appendix, tailpiece, supplement, addendum, postlude, rider, back matter; conclusion.
– OPPOSITES prologue.

episode n. **1** *the best episode of his career* **incident**, event, occurrence, happening; occasion, interlude, chapter, experience, adventure, exploit; matter, affair, thing. **2** *the final episode of the series* **instalment**, chapter, passage; part, portion, section, component; programme, show. **3** *an episode of illness* **period**, spell, bout, attack, phase; informal dose.

episodic adj. **1** *episodic wheezing* **intermittent**, sporadic, periodic, fitful, irregular, spasmodic, occasional. **2** *an episodic account of the war* **in episodes**, in instalments, in sections, in parts.
– OPPOSITES continuous.

epistle n. formal **letter**, missive, communication, dispatch, note, line; correspondence, news.

epitaph n. **elegy**, commemoration, obituary; inscription, legend.

epithet n. **sobriquet**, nickname, byname, title, name, label, tag; description, designation; informal moniker, handle; formal appellation, denomination.

epitome n. **1** *he was the epitome of respectability* **personification**, embodiment, incarnation, paragon; essence, quintessence, archetype, paradigm, typification; exemplar, model, soul, example; height. **2** *an epitome of a larger work* **summary**, abstract, synopsis, precis, résumé, outline, digest, summation; abridgement, abbreviation, condensation.

epitomize v. **embody**, encapsulate, typify, exemplify, represent, manifest, symbolize, illustrate, sum up; personify; formal reify.

epoch n. **era**, age, period, time, span, stage; aeon.

equable adj. **1** *an equable man* **even-tempered**, calm, composed, collected, self-possessed, relaxed, easy-going; nonchalant, insouciant, mellow, mild, tranquil, placid, stable, level-headed; imperturbable, unexcitable, untroubled, well balanced; informal unflappable, together, laid-back. **2** *an equable climate* **stable**, constant,

uniform, unvarying, consistent, unchanging, changeless; moderate, temperate.
– OPPOSITES temperamental, extreme.

equal adj. **1** *lines of equal length* **identical**, uniform, alike, like, the same, equivalent; matching, comparable, similar, corresponding. **2** *fares equal to a fortnight's wages* **equivalent**, identical, amounting; proportionate to, commensurate with, on a par with. **3** *equal treatment before the law* **unbiased**, impartial, non-partisan, fair, just, equitable; unprejudiced, non-discriminatory, egalitarian; neutral, objective, disinterested. **4** *an equal contest* **evenly matched**, even, balanced, level; on a par, on an equal footing; informal fifty-fifty, level pegging, neck and neck.
– OPPOSITES different, discriminatory.

▶ n. *they did not treat him as their equal* **equivalent**, peer, fellow, coequal; like; counterpart, match, parallel.

▶ v. **1** *two plus two equals four* **be equal to**, be equivalent to, be the same as; come to, amount to, make, total, add up to. **2** *he equalled the world record* **match**, reach, parallel, be level with, measure up to. **3** *the fable equals that of any other poet* **be as good as**, be a match for, measure up to, equate with; be in the same league as, rival, compete with.

□ **equal to** capable of, fit for, up to, good/strong enough for; suitable for, suited to, appropriate for; informal having what it takes.

equality n. **1** *we promote equality for women* **fairness**, equal rights, equal opportunities, equitability, egalitarianism; impartiality, even-handedness; justice. **2** *equality between supply and demand* **parity**, similarity, comparability, correspondence; likeness, resemblance; uniformity, evenness, balance, equilibrium, consistency, agreement, congruence, symmetry.

equalize v. **1** *attempts to equalize their earnings* **make equal**, make even, even out/up, level, regularize, standardize, balance, square, match; bring into line. **2** *Villa equalized in the second half* **level the score**, draw.

equanimity n. **composure**, calm, level-headedness, self-possession, cool-headedness, presence of mind; serenity, tranquillity, phlegm, imperturbability, equilibrium; poise, assurance, self-confidence, aplomb, sangfroid, nerve; informal cool.
– OPPOSITES anxiety.

equate v. **1** *he equates criticism with treachery* **identify**, compare, bracket, class, associate, connect, link, relate, ally. **2** *the rent equates to £24 per square foot* **correspond**, be equivalent, amount; equal. **3** *moves to equate supply and demand* **equalize**, balance, even out/up, level, square, tally, match; make equal, make even, make equivalent.

equation n. **1** *a quadratic equation* **mathematical problem**, sum, calculation, question. **2** *the equation of success*

with riches **identification**, association, connection, matching; equivalence, correspondence, agreement, comparison. **3** *other factors came into the equation* **situation**, problem, case, question; quandary, predicament.

equatorial adj. **tropical**, hot, humid, sultry.
– OPPOSITES polar.

equilibrium n. **1** *the equilibrium of the economy* **balance**, symmetry, equipoise, parity, equality; stability. **2** *his equilibrium was never shaken* **composure**, calm, equanimity, sangfroid; level-headedness, cool-headedness, imperturbability, poise, presence of mind; self-possession, self-command; impassivity, placidity, tranquillity, serenity; informal cool.
– OPPOSITES imbalance, agitation.

equip v. **1** *the boat was equipped with a flare gun* **provide**, furnish, supply, issue, kit out, stock, provision, arm, endow. **2** *the course will equip them for the workplace* **prepare**, qualify, suit.

equipment n. **apparatus**, paraphernalia, articles, appliances, impedimenta; tools, utensils, implements, instruments, hardware, gadgets, gadgetry; stuff, things; kit, tackle; resources, supplies; trappings, appurtenances, accoutrements; informal gear; Military materiel, baggage.

equipoise n. **1** *an equipoise of power* **equilibrium**, balance, evenness, symmetry, parity, equality, equity; stability. **2** *an equipoise to imbalances in savings* **counterweight**, counterbalance, counterpoise, balance; stabilizer.
– OPPOSITES imbalance.

equitable adj. **fair**, just, impartial, even-handed, unbiased, unprejudiced, egalitarian; disinterested, objective, neutral, non-partisan, open-minded; informal fair and square.
– OPPOSITES unfair.

equity n. **1** *the equity of Finnish society* **fairness**, justness, impartiality, egalitarianism; objectivity, balance, open-mindedness. **2** *he owns 25% of the equity in the property* **value**, worth; ownership, rights, proprietorship.

equivalence n. **equality**, sameness, interchangeability, comparability, correspondence; uniformity, similarity, likeness, nearness.

equivalent adj. *a degree or equivalent qualification* **equal**, identical; similar, parallel, analogous, comparable, corresponding, commensurate; approximate, near.

▶ n. *Denmark's equivalent of the Daily Mirror* **counterpart**, parallel, alternative, match, analogue, twin, opposite number; equal, peer.

equivocal adj. **ambiguous**, indefinite, non-committal, vague, imprecise, inexact, inexplicit, hazy; unclear, cryptic, enigmatic; ambivalent, uncertain, unsure, indecisive.
– OPPOSITES definite.

equivocate v. **prevaricate**, be evasive, be non-committal, be vague, be ambiguous, dodge the issue, beat about the bush, hedge one's bets, pussyfoot around; vacillate, shilly-shally, waver; temporize, hesitate, stall; Brit. hum and haw; informal sit on the fence, duck the issue; rare tergiversate.

era n. **epoch**, age, period, time, span, aeon; generation.

eradicate v. **eliminate**, get rid of, remove, obliterate; exterminate, destroy, annihilate, kill, wipe out; abolish, stamp out, extinguish, quash; erase, efface, excise, expunge.

erase v. **1** *they erased his name from all lists* **delete**, rub out, wipe off, blot out, blank out, cancel; efface, expunge, excise, remove, obliterate, eliminate, censor, redact. **2** *the old differences in style were erased* **destroy**, wipe out, obliterate, eradicate, abolish, stamp out, quash.

erect adj. **1** *she held her body erect* **upright**, straight, vertical, perpendicular; standing. **2** *an erect penis* **engorged**, enlarged, swollen, tumescent; hard, stiff. **3** *the dog's fur was erect* **bristling**, standing on end, upright.
– OPPOSITES bent, flaccid, flat.
▶v. **1** *the bridge was erected in 1973* **build**, construct, put up; assemble, put together, fabricate. **2** *the party that erected the welfare state* **establish**, form, set up, found, institute, initiate, create, organize.
– OPPOSITES demolish, dismantle, lower.

erection n. **1** *the erection of a house* **construction**, building, assembly, fabrication, elevation. **2** *a bleak concrete erection* **building**, structure, construction, pile; formal edifice. **3** *erect penis*, phallus; tumescence, tumidity.

erode v. **wear away/down**, abrade, grind down, crumble; weather; eat away at, dissolve, corrode, rot, decay; undermine, weaken, deteriorate, destroy.

erosion n. **wearing away**, abrasion, attrition; weathering; dissolution, corrosion, decay; deterioration, disintegration, destruction; rare detrition.

erotic adj. **sexually arousing**, sexually stimulating, titillating, suggestive; pornographic, sexually explicit, lewd, smutty, hard-core, soft-core, dirty, racy, risqué, ribald, naughty; sexual, sexy, sensual, amatory; seductive, alluring, tantalizing; informal blue, X-rated, steamy, raunchy; euphemistic adult.

err v. *the judge had erred in ruling that the evidence was inadmissible* **make a mistake**, be wrong, be in error, be mistaken, blunder, be incorrect, miscalculate, get it wrong; informal slip up, screw up, goof, make a boo-boo, bark up the wrong tree, get the wrong end of the stick; Brit. informal boob.

errand n. **task**, job, chore, assignment; collection, delivery; mission, undertaking.

errant adj. **1** *he fined the errant councillors* **offending**, guilty, culpable, misbehaving, delinquent, lawbreaking; troublesome, unruly, disobedient. **2** old use *a knight errant travelling*, wandering, itinerant, roaming, roving, voyaging.
– OPPOSITES innocent.

erratic adj. **unpredictable**, inconsistent, changeable, variable, inconstant, irregular, fitful, unstable, turbulent, unsettled, changing, varying, fluctuating, mutable; unreliable, undependable, volatile, mercurial, capricious, fickle, temperamental, moody.
– OPPOSITES consistent.

erring adj. **offending**, guilty, culpable, misbehaving, errant, delinquent, lawbreaking, aberrant, deviant.

erroneous adj. **wrong**, incorrect, mistaken, in error, inaccurate, untrue, false, fallacious; unsound, specious, faulty, flawed; informal off beam, way out.
– OPPOSITES correct.

error n. **mistake**, inaccuracy, miscalculation, blunder, oversight; fallacy, misconception, delusion; misprint, erratum; informal slip-up, bloomer, boo-boo, fail; Brit. informal boob.
□ **in error** wrongly, by mistake, mistakenly, incorrectly; accidentally, by accident, inadvertently, unintentionally, by chance.

ersatz adj. **artificial**, substitute, imitation, synthetic, fake, false, faux, mock, simulated; pseudo, sham, bogus, spurious, counterfeit; manufactured, man-made; informal phoney.
– OPPOSITES genuine.

erstwhile adj. **former**, old, past, one-time, sometime, as was, ex-, late, then; previous; formal quondam.
– OPPOSITES present.

erudite adj. **learned**, scholarly, educated, knowledgeable, well read, well informed, intellectual; intelligent, clever, academic, literary; bookish, highbrow, cerebral; informal brainy; dated lettered.
– OPPOSITES ignorant.

erupt v. **1** *the volcano erupted* **emit lava**, become active, flare up; explode. **2** *lava was erupted* **emit**, discharge, eject, expel, spew out, pour out, disgorge. **3** *fighting erupted* **break out**, flare up, start suddenly; ensue, arise, happen. **4** *a boil erupted on her temple* **appear**, break out, flare up, come to a head, emerge.

eruption n. **1** *a volcanic eruption* **discharge**, ejection, emission; explosion. **2** *an eruption of violence* **outbreak**, flare-up, upsurge, outburst, breakout, explosion; wave, spate. **3** *a skin eruption* **rash**, outbreak, inflammation.

escalate v. **1** *prices have escalated* **increase rapidly**, soar, rocket, shoot up, mount, spiral, climb, go up; informal go through the roof, skyrocket. **2** *the dispute escalated* **grow**, develop, mushroom, increase, heighten, intensify, accelerate.
– OPPOSITES plunge, shrink.

escalation n. **1** *an escalation in oil prices* **increase**, rise, hike, growth, leap, upsurge, upturn, climb. **2** *an escalation of the conflict*

e

intensification, aggravation, exacerbation, magnification, amplification, augmentation; expansion, build-up; deterioration.

escapade n. **exploit**, stunt, caper, antic(s), spree; adventure, venture, mission; deed, feat, trial, experience; incident, occurrence, event.

escape v. **1** *he escaped from prison* **run away/ off**, get out, break out, break free, make a break for it, bolt, flee, take flight, make off, take off, abscond, take to one's heels, make one's getaway, make a run for it; disappear, vanish, slip away, sneak away; informal cut and run, skedaddle, scarper, vamoose, do a vanishing act, fly the coop, take French leave, leg it; Brit. informal do a bunk, do a runner; N. Amer. informal go on the lam. **2** *he escaped his pursuers* **get away from**, escape from, elude, avoid, dodge, shake off; informal give someone the slip. **3** *they escaped injury* **avoid**, evade, dodge, elude, miss, cheat, sidestep, circumvent, steer clear of; shirk; informal duck. **4** *lethal gas escaped* **leak (out)**, seep (out), discharge, emanate, issue, flow (out), pour (out), gush (out), spurt (out), spew (out).
▸ n. **1** *his escape from prison* **getaway**, breakout, bolt, flight; disappearance, vanishing act; informal flit; informal dated spring. **2** *a narrow escape from death* **avoidance of**, evasion of, circumvention of. **3** *a gas escape* **leak**, leakage, spill, seepage, discharge, emanation, outflow, outpouring; gush, stream, spurt. **4** *an escape from boredom* **distraction**, diversion.

escapee n. **runaway**, escaper, absconder; jailbreaker, fugitive; truant; deserter, defector.

escapism n. **fantasy**, fantasizing, daydreaming, daydreams, reverie; imagination, flight(s) of fancy, pipe dreams, wishful thinking, wool-gathering; informal pie in the sky.
– OPPOSITES realism.

eschew v. **abstain from**, refrain from, give up, forgo, shun, renounce, steer clear of, have nothing to do with, fight shy of; relinquish, reject, disavow, abandon, spurn, wash one's hands of, drop; informal kick, pack in; Brit. informal jack in; formal forswear, abjure.

escort n. **1** *a police escort* **guard**, bodyguard, protector, minder, custodian; attendant, chaperone; entourage, retinue, cortège; protection, defence, convoy. **2** *her escort for the evening* **companion**, partner; informal date. **3** *an agency dealing with escorts* **paid companion**, hostess, geisha; gigolo.
▸ v. **1** *he was escorted home by the police* **conduct**, accompany, guide, usher, shepherd, take. **2** *he escorted her in to dinner* **accompany**, partner, take, bring.

esoteric adj. **abstruse**, obscure, arcane, recherché, rarefied, recondite, abstract; enigmatic, inscrutable, cryptic, Delphic; complex, complicated, incomprehensible, opaque, impenetrable, mysterious.

especial adj. **1** *especial care is required* **particular**, (extra) special, superior, exceptional, extraordinary; unusual, out of the ordinary, uncommon, remarkable, singular. **2** *her especial brand of charm* **distinctive**, individual, special, particular, distinct, peculiar, personal, own, unique, specific.

especially adv. **1** *work poured in, especially from Kent* **mainly**, mostly, chiefly, principally, largely; substantially, particularly, primarily, generally, usually, typically. **2** *a committee especially for the purpose* **expressly**, specially, specifically, exclusively, just, particularly, explicitly. **3** *he is especially talented* **exceptionally**, particularly, specially, very, extremely, singularly, distinctly, unusually, extraordinarily, uncommonly, uniquely, remarkably, outstandingly, really; informal seriously, majorly; Brit. informal jolly, dead, well.

espionage n. **spying**, infiltration; eavesdropping, surveillance, reconnaissance, intelligence.

espousal n. **adoption**, embracing, acceptance; support, championship, encouragement, defence; sponsorship, promotion, endorsement, advocacy, approval.

espouse v. **adopt**, embrace, take up, accept, welcome; support, back, champion, favour, prefer, encourage; promote, endorse, advocate.
– OPPOSITES reject.

espy v. literary **catch sight of**, glimpse, see, spot, spy, notice, observe, discern, pick out, detect; literary behold, descry.

essay n. **1** *he wrote an essay* **article**, composition, study, paper, dissertation, thesis, discourse, treatise, disquisition, monograph; commentary, critique; N. Amer. theme. **2** formal *his first essay in telecommunications* **attempt**, effort, endeavour, try, venture, trial, experiment, undertaking.
▸ v. formal *many essayed to travel that way* **attempt**, try, strive, venture, endeavour, seek, undertake.

essence n. **1** *the very essence of economics* **quintessence**, soul, spirit, nature; core, heart, crux, nucleus, substance; principle, fundamental quality, sum and substance, reality, actuality; informal nitty-gritty. **2** *essence of ginger* **extract**, concentrate, distillate, elixir, decoction, juice, tincture; scent, perfume, oil.
□ **in essence** essentially, basically, fundamentally, primarily, principally, chiefly, predominantly, substantially; above all, first and foremost; effectively, virtually, to all intents and purposes; intrinsically, inherently.
of the essence See **essential** (sense 1 of the adjective).

essential adj. **1** *it is essential to remove the paint* **crucial**, necessary, key, vital, indispensable, important, all-important, of

the essence, critical, imperative, mandatory, compulsory, obligatory; urgent, pressing, paramount, pre-eminent, high-priority. **2** *the essential simplicity of his style* **basic**, inherent, fundamental, quintessential, intrinsic, underlying, characteristic, innate, primary, elementary, elemental, central, pivotal, vital. **3** *the essential English gentleman* **ideal**, absolute, complete, perfect, quintessential.
– OPPOSITES unimportant, optional, secondary.
▶ n. **1** *an essential for broadcasters* **necessity**, prerequisite, requisite, requirement, need; condition, precondition, stipulation; sine qua non; informal must. **2** *the essentials of the job* **fundamentals**, basics, rudiments, first principles, foundations, bedrock; essence, basis, core, kernel, crux, sine qua non; informal nitty-gritty, brass tacks, nuts and bolts.

establish v. **1** *they established an office in Moscow* **set up**, start, initiate, institute, form, found, create, inaugurate; build, construct, install. **2** *evidence to establish his guilt* **prove**, demonstrate, show, indicate, signal, exhibit, manifest, attest to, evidence, determine, confirm, verify, certify, substantiate.

established adj. **1** *established practice* **accepted**, traditional, orthodox, habitual, set, fixed, official; usual, customary, common, normal, general, prevailing, accustomed, familiar, expected, routine, typical, conventional, standard. **2** *an established composer* **well known**, recognized, esteemed, respected, famous, prominent, noted, renowned.

establishment n. **1** *the establishment of a democracy* **foundation**, institution, formation, inception, creation, installation; inauguration, start, initiation. **2** *a dressmaking establishment* **business**, firm, company, concern, enterprise, venture, organization, operation; factory, plant, shop, office, practice; informal outfit, set-up. **3** *educational establishments* **institution**, place, premises, foundation, institute. **4** *they dare to poke fun at the Establishment* **the authorities**, the powers that be, the system, the ruling class; informal Big Brother.

estate n. **1** *the Balmoral estate* **property**, grounds, garden(s), park, parkland, land(s), landholding, manor, territory. **2** *a housing estate* **area**, site, development, complex. **3** *a coffee estate* **plantation**, farm, holding; forest, vineyard; N. Amer. ranch. **4** *he left an estate worth £610,000* **assets**, capital, wealth, riches, holdings, fortune; property, effects, possessions, belongings; Law goods and chattels. **5** dated *the estate of matrimony* **state**, condition, situation, position, circumstance.

estate agent n. **property agent**; Brit. house agent; N. Amer. trademark realtor.

esteem n. *she was held in high esteem* **respect**, admiration, acclaim, approbation, appreciation, favour, recognition, honour, reverence; estimation, regard, opinion.

▶ v. **1** *such ceramics are highly esteemed* **respect**, **admire**, value, regard, acclaim, appreciate, like, prize, treasure, favour, revere. **2** formal *I would esteem it a favour if you could speak to him*. See **deem**.

estimate v. **1** *estimate the cost* **calculate roughly**, approximate, guess; evaluate, judge, gauge, reckon, rate, determine; informal guesstimate. **2** *we estimate it to be worth £50,000* **consider**, believe, reckon, deem, judge, rate, gauge; formal opine.
▶ n. **1** *an estimate of the cost* **rough calculation**, approximation, estimation, rough guess, impression; costing, quotation, valuation, evaluation; informal guesstimate. **2** *his estimate of Paul's integrity* **evaluation**, estimation, judgement, rating, appraisal, opinion, view.

estimation n. **1** *an estimation of economic growth* **estimate**, approximation, rough calculation, rough guess, evaluation; informal guesstimate. **2** *he rated highly in Carl's estimation* **assessment**, evaluation, judgement; esteem, opinion, view.

estrange v. **alienate**, antagonize, turn away, drive away, distance; sever, set at odds with, drive a wedge between.

estrangement n. **alienation**, antagonism, antipathy, disaffection, hostility, unfriendliness; variance, difference; parting, separation, divorce, break-up, split, breach, schism.

estuary n. **(river) mouth**, firth; delta.

et cetera adv. **and so on**, and so forth, and the rest, and/or the like, and suchlike, among others, et al., etc.; informal and what have you, and whatnot.

etch v. **1** *the metal is etched with acid* **corrode**, burn into; mark. **2** *a stone etched with tiny designs* **engrave**, carve, inscribe, incise, chase, score, print, mark.

etching n. **engraving**, print, impression, block, plate; woodcut, linocut.

eternal adj. **1** *eternal happiness* **everlasting**, never-ending, endless, perpetual, undying, immortal, abiding, permanent, enduring, infinite, boundless, timeless. **2** *eternal vigilance* **constant**, continual, continuous, perpetual, persistent, sustained, unremitting, relentless, unrelieved, uninterrupted, unbroken, never-ending, non-stop, round-the-clock, endless, ceaseless.
– OPPOSITES transient, intermittent.

eternally adv. **1** *I shall be eternally grateful* **forever**, permanently, perpetually, (for) evermore, for ever and ever, for eternity, in perpetuity, enduringly; N. Amer. forevermore; informal until doomsday, until the cows come home; old use for aye. **2** *the tenants complain eternally* **constantly**, continually, continuously, always, all the time, persistently, repeatedly, regularly; day and night, non-stop; endlessly, incessantly, perpetually; interminably, relentlessly; informal 24-7.

eternity n. **1** *the memory will remain for eternity* **ever**, all time, perpetuity. **2** Theology *souls destined for eternity* **the afterlife**, everlasting life, life after death, the hereafter, the afterworld, the next world; heaven, paradise, immortality. **3** informal *I waited an eternity for you* **a long time**, an age, ages, a lifetime; hours, years, aeons; forever; informal donkey's years, a month of Sundays; Brit. informal yonks.

ethereal adj. **1** *her ethereal beauty* **delicate**, exquisite, dainty, elegant, graceful; fragile, airy, fine, subtle. **2** *theologians discuss ethereal ideas* **celestial**, heavenly, spiritual, other-worldly, paradisal, Elysian.
– OPPOSITES substantial, earthly.

ethical adj. **1** *an ethical dilemma* **moral**, social, behavioural. **2** *an ethical investment policy* **morally correct**, right-minded, principled, irreproachable; righteous, high-minded, virtuous, good, moral; clean, lawful, just, honourable, reputable, respectable, noble, worthy; praiseworthy, commendable, admirable, laudable; whiter than white, saintly, impeccable; informal squeaky clean.

ethics plural n. **moral code**, morals, morality, values, rights and wrongs, principles, ideals, standards (of behaviour), virtues.

ethnic adj. **racial**, race-related, ethnological; cultural, national, tribal, ancestral, traditional.

ethos n. **spirit**, character, atmosphere, climate, mood, feeling, tenor, essence; disposition, rationale, morality, moral code, principles, standards, ethics.

etiquette n. **protocol**, manners, accepted behaviour, rules of conduct, decorum, good form; courtesy, propriety, formalities, niceties, punctilios; custom, convention; informal the done thing; formal politesse.

etymology n. **derivation**, word history, development, origin, source.

eulogize v. **extol**, acclaim, sing the praises of, praise to the skies, wax lyrical about, rhapsodize about, rave about, enthuse about; N. Amer. informal ballyhoo.
– OPPOSITES criticize.

eulogy n. **accolade**, panegyric, paean, tribute, compliment, commendation; praise, acclaim; plaudits, bouquets; formal encomium.
– OPPOSITES attack.

euphemism n. **polite term**, indirect term, substitute, alternative, understatement, genteelism.

euphemistic adj. **polite**, substitute, mild, understated, neutral, evasive; diplomatic, inoffensive, genteel.

euphonious adj. **pleasant-sounding**, sweet-sounding, mellow, mellifluous, dulcet, sweet, honeyed, lyrical, silvery, golden, lilting, soothing; harmonious, melodious; informal easy on the ear.
– OPPOSITES cacophonous.

euphoria n. **elation**, happiness, joy, delight, glee; excitement, exhilaration, jubilation, exultation; ecstasy, bliss, rapture.
– OPPOSITES misery.

euphoric adj. **elated**, happy, joyful, delighted, gleeful; excited, exhilarated,

jubilant, exultant; ecstatic, blissful, rapturous, transported, on cloud nine, in seventh heaven; informal on top of the world, over the moon, on a high.

euthanasia n. **mercy killing**, assisted suicide.

evacuate v. **1** *local residents were evacuated* **remove**, clear, move out, take away. **2** *they evacuated the bombed town* **leave**, vacate, abandon, desert, move out of, quit, withdraw from, retreat from, decamp from, flee, depart from, escape from. **3** *police evacuated the area* **clear**, empty, depopulate. **4** *patients couldn't evacuate their bowels* **empty (out)**, void, open, move, purge; defecate. **5** *he evacuated the contents of his stomach* **expel**, eject, discharge, excrete, void, empty (out).

evacuation n. **1** *the evacuation of civilians* **removal**, clearance, shifting; eviction, deportation. **2** *the evacuation of military bases* **clearance**, depopulation; abandonment, vacation, desertion. **3** *involuntary evacuation of the bowels* **emptying (out)**, voidance, opening, purging; defecation. **4** *dysenteric evacuations* **bowel movement/motion**, stools, excrement, excreta, faeces, waste.

evade v. **1** *they evaded the guards* **elude**, avoid, dodge, escape (from), steer clear of, keep at arm's length, sidestep; lose, leave behind, shake off; N. Amer. end-run; informal give someone the slip. **2** *he evaded the question* **avoid**, dodge, sidestep, bypass, hedge, fence, skirt round, fudge, be evasive about; informal duck, cop out of.
– OPPOSITES confront.

evaluate v. **assess**, judge, gauge, rate, estimate, appraise, analyse, weigh up, get the measure of; informal size up, check out.

evaluation n. **assessment**, appraisal, judgement, gauging, rating, estimation, consideration, analysis.

evanescent adj. literary **vanishing**, fading, evaporating, melting away, disappearing; ephemeral, fleeting, short-lived, short-term, transitory, transient, fugitive, temporary.
– OPPOSITES permanent.

evangelical adj. **1** *evangelical Christianity* **scriptural**, biblical; orthodox, fundamentalist. **2** *an evangelical preacher* **evangelistic**, evangelizing, missionary, crusading, propagandist, propagandizing, proselytizing.

evangelist n. **preacher**, missionary, gospeller, proselytizer, crusader, propagandist.

evangelistic adj. See **evangelical** (sense 2).

evangelize v. **convert**, proselytize, redeem, save, preach to, recruit.

evaporate v. **1** *the water evaporated* **vaporize**, become vapour, volatilize; dry up. **2** *the rock salt is washed and evaporated* **dry out**, dehydrate, desiccate, dehumidify. **3** *the feeling has evaporated* **end**, pass (away), fizzle out, peter out, wear off, vanish, fade, disappear, melt away.
– OPPOSITES condense, wet, materialize.

evasion n. **1** *the evasion of immigration control* **avoidance**, circumvention, dodging, sidestepping. **2** *she grew tired of all the evasion* **prevarication**, evasiveness, beating about the bush, hedging, pussyfooting, equivocation, vagueness, temporization; Brit. humming and hawing; rare tergiversation.

evasive adj. **equivocal**, prevaricating, elusive, ambiguous, non-committal, vague, inexplicit, unclear; roundabout, indirect; informal cagey.

eve n. **1** *the eve of the election* **day before**, evening before, night before; the run-up to. **2** literary *a winter's eve* **evening**, night; literary eventide.
– OPPOSITES morning.

even adj. **1** *an even surface* **flat**, smooth, uniform, featureless; unbroken, undamaged; level, plane. **2** *an even temperature* **uniform**, constant, steady, stable, consistent, unvarying, unchanging, regular. **3** *they all have an even chance* **equal**, the same, identical, like, alike, similar, comparable, parallel. **4** *the score was even* **level**, drawn, tied, all square, balanced; neck and neck; Brit. level pegging; informal even-steven(s). **5** *an even disposition* **even-tempered**, balanced, stable, equable, placid, calm, composed, poised, cool, relaxed, easy, imperturbable, unexcitable, unruffled, untroubled; informal together, laid-back, unflappable.
– OPPOSITES bumpy, irregular, unequal, moody.
▶ v. **1** *the canal bottom was evened out* **flatten**, level (off/out), smooth (off/out), plane; make uniform, make regular. **2** *the union wants to even up our wages* **equalize**, make equal, level up, balance, square; standardize, regularize.
▶ adv. **1** *it got even colder* **still**, yet, more, all the more. **2** *even the best hitters missed the ball* **surprisingly**, unexpectedly, paradoxically. **3** *she is afraid, even ashamed, to ask for help* **indeed**, you could say, veritably, in truth, actually, or rather, nay. **4** *she couldn't even afford food* **so much as**.
□ **even so** nevertheless, nonetheless, all the same, just the same, anyway, anyhow, still, yet, however, notwithstanding, despite that, in spite of that, for all that, be that as it may, in any event, at any rate.
get even have one's revenge, avenge oneself, take vengeance, even the score, settle the score, hit back, give as good as one gets, pay someone back, repay someone, reciprocate, retaliate, take reprisals, exact retribution; give someone their just deserts; informal get one's own back, give someone a taste of their own medicine, settle someone's hash; literary be revenged.

even-handed adj. **fair**, just, equitable, impartial, unbiased, unprejudiced, non-partisan, non-discriminatory; disinterested, detached, objective, neutral.
– OPPOSITES biased.

evening n. **night**, late afternoon, end of day, close of day; twilight, dusk, nightfall, sunset, sundown; literary eve, eventide.

event n. **1** *an annual event* **occurrence**, happening, proceeding, incident, affair, circumstance, occasion, phenomenon; function, gathering; informal bash, do. **2** *the team lost the event* **competition**, contest, tournament, round, heat, match, fixture; race, game, bout; Brit. clash.

even-tempered adj. **serene**, calm, composed, tranquil, relaxed, easy-going, mellow, unworried, untroubled, unruffled, imperturbable, placid, equable, stable, level-headed; informal unflappable, together, laid-back.
– OPPOSITES excitable.

eventful adj. **busy**, action-packed, full, lively, active, hectic, strenuous; momentous, significant, important, historic, consequential, fateful.
– OPPOSITES dull.

eventual adj. **final**, ultimate, concluding, closing, end; resulting, ensuing, consequent, subsequent.

eventuality n. **event**, incident, occurrence, happening, development, phenomenon, situation, circumstance, case, contingency, chance, likelihood, possibility, probability; outcome, result.

eventually adv. **in the end**, in due course, by and by, in time, after some time, after a bit, finally, at last; ultimately, in the long run, at the end of the day, one day, some day, sometime, sooner or later.

eventuate v. formal **1** *you never know what might eventuate.* See **happen** (sense 1). **2** *the fight eventuated in his death* **result in**, end in, lead to, give rise to, bring about, cause.

ever adv. **1** *the best I've ever done* **at any time**, at any point, on any occasion, under any circumstances, on any account; up till now, until now. **2** *he was ever the optimist* **always**, forever, eternally, until hell freezes over; informal until the twelfth of never, until the cows come home, until doomsday. **3** *an ever increasing rate of crime* **continually**, constantly, always, endlessly, perpetually, incessantly, unremittingly. **4** *will she ever learn?* **at all**, in any way.
□ **ever so** Brit. informal very, extremely, exceedingly, especially, immensely, particularly, really, truly; N. English right; informal awfully, terribly, desperately, mega, ultra; Brit. informal well, dead, jolly; N. Amer. informal real, mighty, awful.

everlasting adj. **1** *everlasting love* **eternal**, endless, never-ending, perpetual, undying, abiding, enduring, infinite, boundless, timeless. **2** *his everlasting complaints* **constant**, continual, continuous, persistent, relentless, unrelieved, uninterrupted, unabating, endless, interminable, never-ending, non-stop, incessant.
– OPPOSITES transient, occasional.

evermore adv. **always**, forever, ever, for always, for all time, until hell freezes over, eternally, in perpetuity; ever after, henceforth; Brit. for evermore, forever more; N. Amer. forevermore; informal until the cows come home, until the twelfth of never.

every determiner **1** *he exercised every day* **each**, each and every, every single. **2** *we make every effort to satisfy our clients* **all possible**, the utmost.

everybody pron. **everyone**, every person, each person, all, one and all, all and sundry, the whole world, the public; informal {every Tom, Dick, and Harry}, every man jack, every mother's son.

everyday adj. **1** *the everyday demands of a baby* **daily**, day-to-day, quotidian. **2** *everyday drugs like aspirin* **commonplace**, ordinary, common, usual, regular, familiar, conventional, run-of-the-mill, standard, stock; household; Brit. common or garden; informal bog-standard.
– OPPOSITES unusual.

everyone pron. **everybody**, every person, each person, all, one and all, all and sundry, the whole world, the public; informal {every Tom, Dick, and Harry}, every man jack, every mother's son.

everything pron. **each item**, each thing, every single thing, the (whole) lot; all; informal the whole caboodle, the whole shebang; N. Amer. informal the whole ball of wax.
– OPPOSITES nothing.

everywhere adv. **all over**, all around, in every nook and cranny, far and wide, near and far, high and low, {here, there, and everywhere}; throughout the land, the world over, worldwide; informal all over the place; Brit. informal all over the shop; N. Amer. informal all over the map.
– OPPOSITES nowhere.

evict v. **expel**, eject, oust, remove, dislodge, turn out, throw out, drive out; dispossess, expropriate; informal chuck out, kick out, boot out, bounce; give someone the (old) heave-ho, throw someone out on their ear; Brit. informal turf out; N. Amer. informal give someone the bum's rush; dated out.

eviction n. **expulsion**, ejection, ousting, removal, dislodgement, displacement, banishment; dispossession, expropriation; Law ouster.

evidence n. **1** *they found evidence of his plotting* **proof**, confirmation, verification, substantiation, corroboration, affirmation, attestation. **2** *the court accepted her evidence* **testimony**, statement, attestation, declaration, avowal, submission, claim, contention, allegation; Law deposition, representation, affidavit. **3** *evidence of a struggle* **signs**, indications, pointers, marks, traces, suggestions, hints; manifestation.
▸ v. *the rise of racism is evidenced here* **indicate**, show, reveal, display, exhibit, manifest; testify to, confirm, prove, substantiate, endorse, bear out; formal evince.
– OPPOSITES disprove.
□ **in evidence** noticeable, conspicuous, obvious, perceptible, visible, on view, plain to see; palpable, tangible, unmistakable, undisguised, prominent, striking, glaring; informal as plain as the nose on your face,

sticking out like a sore thumb, sticking out a mile, staring someone in the face.

evident adj. **obvious**, apparent, noticeable, conspicuous, perceptible, visible, discernible, clear, plain, manifest, patent; palpable, tangible, distinct, pronounced, marked, striking, glaring, blatant; unmistakable, indisputable; informal as plain as the nose on your face, sticking out like a sore thumb, sticking out a mile, as clear as day.

evidently adv. **1** *he was evidently dismayed* **obviously**, clearly, plainly, visibly, manifestly, patently, distinctly, markedly; unmistakably, undeniably, undoubtedly, as sure as eggs is eggs. **2** *evidently, she believed herself superior* **seemingly**, apparently, as far as one can tell, from all appearances, on the face of it; it seems (that), it appears (that).

evil adj. **1** *an evil deed* **wicked**, bad, wrong, immoral, sinful, foul, vile, dishonourable, corrupt, iniquitous, depraved, villainous, nefarious, vicious, malicious; malevolent, sinister, demonic, devilish, diabolical, fiendish, dark; monstrous, shocking, despicable, atrocious, heinous, odious, contemptible, horrible, execrable; informal low-down, dirty. **2** *an evil spirit* **harmful**, hurtful, injurious, detrimental, deleterious, inimical, bad, mischievous, pernicious, malignant, malign, baleful; destructive, ruinous. **3** *evil weather* **unpleasant**, disagreeable, nasty, horrible, foul, filthy, vile, inclement.
– OPPOSITES good, beneficial, pleasant.
▸ n. **1** *the evil in our midst* **wickedness**, bad, badness, wrongdoing, sin, immorality, vice, iniquity, degeneracy, corruption, depravity, villainy, nefariousness, malevolence; formal turpitude. **2** *nothing but evil would ensue* **harm**, pain, misery, sorrow, suffering, trouble, disaster, misfortune, catastrophe, affliction, woe, hardship. **3** *the evils of war* **abomination**, atrocity, obscenity, outrage, enormity, crime, monstrosity, barbarity.

evince v. formal **reveal**, show, make plain, manifest, indicate, display, exhibit, demonstrate, evidence, attest to; convey, communicate, proclaim, bespeak.
– OPPOSITES conceal.

eviscerate v. formal **disembowel**, gut, draw, dress.

evocative adj. **reminiscent**, suggestive, redolent; expressive, vivid, graphic, powerful, haunting, moving, poignant.

evoke v. **bring to mind**, put one in mind of, conjure up, summon (up), invoke, elicit, induce, kindle, stimulate, stir up, awaken, arouse; recall, echo, capture.

evolution n. **1** *the evolution of Bolshevism* **development**, advancement, growth, rise, progress, expansion, evolvement; transformation, adaptation, modification, revision. **2** *his interest in evolution* **Darwinism**, natural selection.

evolve v. **develop**, progress, advance; mature, grow, expand, spread; alter, change, transform, adapt, metamorphose; humorous transmogrify.

exacerbate v. **aggravate**, worsen, inflame, compound; intensify, increase, heighten, magnify, add to, amplify, augment; informal add fuel to the fire/flames.
– OPPOSITES reduce.

exact adj. **1** *an exact description* **precise**, accurate, correct, faithful, close, true; literal, strict, faultless, perfect, impeccable; explicit, detailed, minute, meticulous, thorough; informal on the nail, on the mark; Brit. informal spot on, bang on; N. Amer. informal on the money, on the button. **2** *an exact manager* **careful**, meticulous, painstaking, punctilious, conscientious, scrupulous, exacting; methodical, organized, orderly.
– OPPOSITES inaccurate, careless.
▸ v. **1** *she exacted high standards from them* **demand**, require, insist on, request, impose, expect; extract, compel, force, squeeze. **2** *they exacted a terrible vengeance on him* **inflict**, impose, administer, apply.

exacting adj. **1** *an exacting training routine* **demanding**, stringent, testing, challenging, onerous, arduous, laborious, taxing, gruelling, punishing, hard, tough. **2** *an exacting boss* **strict**, stern, firm, demanding, tough, harsh; inflexible, uncompromising, unyielding, unsparing.
– OPPOSITES easy, easy-going.

exactly adv. **1** *it's exactly as I expected it to be* **precisely**, entirely, absolutely, completely, totally, just, quite, in every way, in every respect, one hundred per cent, every inch, to the hilt; informal to a T; N. Amer. informal on the money. **2** *write the quotation out exactly* **accurately**, precisely, correctly, unerringly, faultlessly, perfectly; verbatim, word for word, letter for letter, to the letter, faithfully.

exaggerate v. **overstate**, overemphasize, overestimate, magnify, amplify, aggrandize, inflate; embellish, embroider, elaborate, overplay, dramatize; hyperbolize, stretch the truth; Brit. overpitch; informal lay it on thick, make a mountain out of a molehill, blow out of all proportion, make a big thing of.
– OPPOSITES understate.

exaggerated adj. **overstated**, inflated, magnified, amplified, aggrandized, excessive; hyperbolic, elaborate, overdone, overplayed, overdramatized, actorly, highly coloured, melodramatic, sensational; informal over the top, OTT.

exaggeration n. **overstatement**, overemphasis, magnification, amplification, aggrandizement; dramatization, elaboration, embellishment, embroidery, hyperbole, overkill, gilding the lily.

exalt v. **1** *they exalted their hero* **extol**, praise, acclaim, esteem; pay homage to, revere, venerate, worship, lionize, idolize, look up to; informal put on a pedestal; formal laud. **2** *this power exalts the peasant* **elevate**, promote, raise, advance, upgrade, ennoble, dignify, aggrandize. **3** *his works exalt the emotions*

uplift, elevate, inspire, excite, stimulate, enliven, exhilarate.
– OPPOSITES disparage, lower, depress.

exaltation n. **1** *a heart full of exaltation* **elation**, joy, rapture, ecstasy, bliss, happiness, delight, gladness. **2** *their exaltation of Shakespeare* **praise**, extolment, acclamation, reverence, veneration, worship, adoration, idolization, lionization; formal laudation. **3** *the exaltation of Jesus to God's right hand* **elevation**, rise, promotion, advancement, ennoblement.

exalted adj. **1** *his exalted office* **high**, high-ranking, elevated, superior, lofty, eminent, prestigious, illustrious, distinguished, esteemed. **2** *his exalted aims* **noble**, lofty, high-minded, elevated; inflated, pretentious. **3** *she felt spiritually exalted* **elated**, exultant, jubilant, joyful, rapturous, ecstatic, blissful, transported, happy, exuberant, exhilarated; informal high.

exam n. **test**, examination, assessment; paper, oral, practical; Brit. viva (voce); N. Amer. quiz.

examination n. **1** *artefacts spread out for examination* **scrutiny**, inspection, perusal, study, investigation, consideration, analysis, appraisal, evaluation. **2** *a medical examination* **inspection**, check-up, assessment, appraisal; probe, test, scan; informal once-over, overhaul. **3** *a school examination* **test**, exam, assessment; paper, oral, practical; Brit. viva (voce); N. Amer. quiz. **4** Law *the examination of witnesses* **interrogation**, questioning, cross-examination, inquisition.

examine v. **1** *they examined the bank records* **inspect**, scrutinize, investigate, look at, study, scan, sift, probe, appraise, analyse, review, survey; informal check out. **2** *students were examined after a year* **test**, quiz, question; assess, appraise. **3** Law *name the witnesses to be examined* **interrogate**, question, quiz, cross-examine; catechize, give the third degree to, probe, sound out; informal grill, pump.

examiner n. **tester**, questioner, interviewer, assessor, appraiser, marker, inspector; auditor, analyst; adjudicator, judge, scrutineer.

example n. **1** *a fine example of Chinese porcelain* **specimen**, sample, exemplar, exemplification, instance, case, illustration. **2** *we must follow their example* **precedent**, lead, model, pattern, exemplar, ideal, standard; role model. **3** *he was hanged as an example to others* **warning**, caution, lesson, deterrent, admonition; moral.
□ **for example** for instance, e.g., by way of illustration, such as, as, like; in particular, namely, viz.

exasperate v. **infuriate**, incense, anger, annoy, irritate, madden, enrage, antagonize, provoke, irk, vex, get on someone's nerves, ruffle someone's feathers; Brit. rub up the wrong way; informal aggravate, rile, bug, needle, hack off, get up someone's nose, get

someone's back up, get someone's goat, give someone the hump; Brit. informal nark, wind up, get on someone's wick; N. Amer. informal tee off, tick off.
– OPPOSITES please.

exasperating adj. **infuriating**, annoying, irritating, maddening, provoking, irksome, vexatious, trying, displeasing; informal aggravating.

exasperation n. **irritation**, annoyance, vexation, anger, fury, rage, ill humour, crossness, tetchiness, testiness; disgruntlement, discontent, displeasure; informal aggravation.

excavate v. **1** *she excavated a narrow tunnel* **dig (out)**, bore, hollow out, scoop out; burrow, tunnel, sink, gouge. **2** *numerous artefacts have been excavated* **unearth**, dig up, uncover, reveal; disinter, exhume.

excavation n. **1** *the excavation of a grave* **unearthing**, digging up; disinterment, exhumation. **2** *the excavation of a moat* **digging**, hollowing out, boring, channelling. **3** *implements found in the excavations* **hole**, pit, trench, trough; archaeological site.

exceed v. **1** *the cost will exceed £400* **be more than**, be greater than, be over, go beyond, overreach, top. **2** *Brazil exceeds America in fertile land* **surpass**, outdo, outstrip, outshine, outclass, transcend, top, beat, better, eclipse, overshadow; informal best, leave standing, be head and shoulders above.

exceedingly adv. **extremely**, exceptionally, especially, tremendously, very, really, truly, most; informal terribly, awfully, seriously, mega, ultra; Brit. informal ever so, well, dead, jolly; N. Amer. informal real, mighty; old use exceeding.

excel v. **1** *he excelled at football* **shine**, be excellent, be outstanding, be skilful, be talented, be pre-eminent, reign supreme; stand out, be the best, be unparalleled, be unequalled, be second to none, be unsurpassed. **2** *she excelled him in her work* **surpass**, outdo, outshine, outclass, outstrip, beat, top, transcend, better, pass, eclipse, overshadow; informal best, be head and shoulders above, be a cut above.

excellence n. **distinction**, quality, superiority, brilliance, greatness, merit, calibre, eminence, pre-eminence, supremacy; skill, talent, virtuosity, accomplishment, mastery.

excellent adj. **very good**, superb, outstanding, exceptional, marvellous, wonderful; pre-eminent, perfect, matchless, peerless, supreme, first-rate, first-class, superlative, top-tier, splendid, fine; informal A1, ace, great, terrific, tremendous, fantastic, fabulous, fab, top-notch, class, awesome, magic, wicked, cool, out of this world; Brit. informal brilliant, brill, smashing; Austral. informal bonzer; informal dated spiffing, capital.
– OPPOSITES inferior.

except prep. *every day except Monday* **excluding**, not including, excepting, omitting, not counting, but, besides, apart from, aside from, barring, bar, other than, saving; with the exception of; informal outside of; formal save.
– OPPOSITES including.
▸ v. *you're all crooks, present company excepted* **exclude**, omit, leave out, count out, disregard.
– OPPOSITES include.

exception n. *this case is an exception* **anomaly**, irregularity, deviation, special case, peculiarity, abnormality, oddity; misfit; informal freak.
□ **take exception** object, take offence, take umbrage, demur, disagree; resent, argue against, protest against, oppose, complain about; informal kick up a fuss, kick up a stink.
with the exception of See **except** (preposition).

exceptionable adj. formal See **objectionable**.

exceptional adj. **1** *the drought was exceptional* **unusual**, uncommon, abnormal, atypical, extraordinary, out of the ordinary, rare, unprecedented, unexpected, surprising; odd, strange, freakish, anomalous, peculiar; Brit. out of the common; informal weird, freaky, something else. **2** *her exceptional ability* **outstanding**, extraordinary, remarkable, special, excellent, phenomenal, prodigious; unequalled, unparalleled, unsurpassed, peerless, matchless, first-rate, first-class; informal A1, top-notch.
– OPPOSITES normal, average.

exceptionally adv. **1** *it was exceptionally cold* **unusually**, uncommonly, abnormally, atypically, extraordinarily, unexpectedly, surprisingly; strangely, oddly; informal weirdly, freakily. **2** *an exceptionally acute mind* **exceedingly**, outstandingly, extraordinarily, remarkably, especially, phenomenally, prodigiously.

excerpt n. **extract**, part, section, piece, portion, snippet, clip, bit; reading, citation, quotation, quote, line, passage; N. Amer. cite.

excess n. **1** *an excess of calcium* **surplus**, surfeit, overabundance, superabundance, glut, superfluity; too much. **2** *the excess is turned into fat* **remainder**, rest, residue; leftovers, remnants; surplus, extra, difference. **3** *a life of excess* **overindulgence**, overconsumption, intemperance, immoderation, profligacy, lavishness, extravagance, decadence, self-indulgence.
– OPPOSITES lack, restraint.
▸ adj. *excess skin oils* **surplus**, superfluous, redundant, unwanted, unneeded, excessive; extra.
□ **in excess of** more than, over, above, upwards of, beyond.

excessive adj. **1** *excessive alcohol consumption* **immoderate**, intemperate, imprudent, overindulgent, unrestrained, uncontrolled, lavish, extravagant; superfluous. **2** *the cost is excessive* **exorbitant**, extortionate, unreasonable, outrageous, undue, uncalled for, extreme, inordinate, unwarranted, disproportionate, too much; informal over the top, OTT.

excessively adv. **inordinately**, unduly, unnecessarily, unreasonably, ridiculously, overly; very, extremely, exceedingly, exceptionally, impossibly; immoderately, intemperately, too much.

exchange n. **1** *the exchange of ideas* **interchange**, trade, trading, swapping, traffic, trafficking; old use truck. **2** *a broker on the exchange* **stock exchange**, money market, bourse. **3** *an acrimonious exchange* **conversation**, dialogue, chat, talk, discussion; debate, argument, altercation; informal confab; Brit. informal row, barney; formal confabulation, colloquy.
▶ v. *we exchanged shirts* **trade**, swap, switch, change, interchange; old use truck.
▫ **exchange blows** fight, brawl, scuffle, tussle, engage in fisticuffs; informal scrap; Brit. informal have a punch-up.
exchange words argue, quarrel, squabble, have an argument/disagreement; informal have a slanging match.

excise[1] n. *the excise on spirits* **duty**, tax, levy, tariff.

excise[2] v. **1** *the tumours were excised* **cut out/off/away**, take out, extract, remove; technical resect. **2** *all unnecessary detail should be excised* **delete**, cross out/through, strike out, score out, cancel, put a line through; erase; Computing, informal kill; Printing dele.

excitable adj. **temperamental**, mercurial, volatile, emotional, sensitive, highly strung, unstable, nervous, tense, edgy, twitchy, uneasy, neurotic; informal uptight, jumpy, wired.
– OPPOSITES placid.

excite v. **1** *the prospect of a holiday excited me* **thrill**, exhilarate, animate, enliven, rouse, stir, stimulate, galvanize, electrify, inspirit; informal buck up, pep up, ginger up, give someone a buzz/kick; N. Amer. informal give someone a charge. **2** *she wore a chiffon nightgown to excite him* **arouse (sexually)**, stimulate, titillate, inflame; informal turn someone on, get someone going, float someone's boat. **3** *his clothes excited envy* **provoke**, stir up, rouse, arouse, kindle, trigger (off), spark off, incite, cause; literary enkindle.
– OPPOSITES bore, depress.

excited adj. **1** *they were excited about the prospect* **thrilled**, exhilarated, animated, enlivened, electrified; enraptured, intoxicated, feverish, enthusiastic; informal high (as a kite), fired up. **2** **(sexually) aroused**, stimulated, titillated, inflamed; informal turned on, hot, horny, sexed up; Brit. informal randy; N. Amer. informal squirrelly.

excitement n. **1** *the excitement of seeing a leopard in the wild* **thrill**, pleasure, delight, joy; informal kick, buzz; N. Amer. informal charge. **2** *excitement in her eyes* **exhilaration**, elation, animation, enthusiasm, eagerness, anticipation, feverishness; informal pep, vim, zing. **3** **(sexual) arousal**, passion, stimulation, titillation.

exciting adj. **1** *an exciting story* **thrilling**, exhilarating, stirring, rousing, stimulating, intoxicating, electrifying, invigorating; gripping, compelling, powerful, dramatic. **2** **(sexually) arousing**, (sexually) stimulating, titillating, erotic, sexual, sexy; informal raunchy, steamy.

exclaim v. **cry (out)**, declare, blurt out; call (out), shout, yell; dated ejaculate.

exclamation n. **cry**, call, shout, yell, interjection; dated ejaculation.

exclude v. **1** *women were excluded from many scientific societies* **keep out**, deny access to, shut out, debar, disbar, bar, ban, prohibit. **2** *the clause excluded any judicial review* **eliminate**, rule out, preclude; formal except. **3** *the price excludes postage* **be exclusive of**, not include. **4** *he excluded his name from the list* **leave out**, omit, miss out.
– OPPOSITES admit, include.

exclusion n. **1** *the exclusion of women from the society* **barring**, keeping out, debarment, debarring, disbarring, banning, prohibition. **2** *the exclusion of other factors* **elimination**, ruling out, precluding. **3** *the exclusion of pupils* **expulsion**, ejection, throwing out; suspension.
– OPPOSITES acceptance, inclusion.

exclusive adj. **1** *an exclusive club* **select**, chic, high-class, elite, fashionable, stylish, elegant, premier, grade A; expensive; Brit. upmarket; N. Amer. high-toned; informal posh, ritzy, classy; Brit. informal swish; N. Amer. informal tony. **2** *a room for your exclusive use* **sole**, unshared, unique, only, individual, personal, private. **3** *prices exclusive of VAT* **not including**, excluding, leaving out, omitting, excepting. **4** *mutually exclusive alternatives* **incompatible**, irreconcilable.
– OPPOSITES inclusive.
▶ n. *a six-page exclusive* **scoop**, exposé, special, coup.

excoriate v. **1** Medicine *the skin had been excoriated* **abrade**, rub away/raw, scrape, scratch, chafe; strip away, skin. **2** formal *he was excoriated in the press*. See **criticize**.

excrement n. **faeces**, excreta, stools, droppings; waste matter, ordure, dung; informal pooh, doings; Brit. informal cack, whoopsies, jobbies; N. Amer. informal poop.

┌─────────────────────────────────┐
WORD LINKS
scatological obsessed with excrement and excretion
coprophagy the eating of excrement
└─────────────────────────────────┘

excrescence n. **1** *an excrescence on his leg* **growth**, lump, swelling, nodule, outgrowth. **2** *the new buildings were an excrescence* **eyesore**, blot on the landscape, monstrosity.

excrete v. **expel**, pass, void, discharge, eject, evacuate; defecate, urinate.
– OPPOSITES ingest.

excruciating adj. **agonizing**, severe, acute, intense, violent, racking, searing, piercing, stabbing, raging; unbearable, unendurable; informal splitting, killing.

excursion n. **trip**, outing, jaunt, expedition, journey, tour; day trip/out, drive, run, ride; informal junket, spin.

excusable adj. **forgivable**, pardonable, defensible, justifiable; venial.
– OPPOSITES unforgivable.

excuse v. **1** *eventually she excused him* **forgive**, pardon, absolve, exonerate, acquit; informal let someone off (the hook); formal exculpate. **2** *such conduct can never be excused* **justify**, defend, condone, vindicate; forgive, overlook, disregard, ignore, tolerate, sanction. **3** *she has been excused from her duties* **let off**, release, relieve, exempt, absolve, free.
– OPPOSITES punish, blame, condemn.
▸n. **1** *that's no excuse for stealing* **justification**, defence, reason, explanation, mitigating circumstances, vindication. **2** *an excuse to get away* **pretext**, ostensible reason, pretence; Brit. get-out; informal story, alibi. **3** informal *that pathetic excuse for a man!* **travesty of**, poor specimen of; informal apology for.

execrable adj. **appalling**, awful, dreadful, terrible, frightful, atrocious, abysmal, lamentable, egregious; disgusting, deplorable, disgraceful, reprehensible, abhorrent, loathsome, odious, hateful, vile; informal diabolical, lousy, God-awful; Brit. informal chronic, shocking, pants.
– OPPOSITES admirable.

execrate v. **revile**, denounce, decry, condemn, vilify; detest, loathe, abhor, despise; formal abominate, excoriate.

execute v. **1** *he was convicted and executed* **put to death**, kill; hang, behead, guillotine, electrocute, shoot; informal string up; N. Amer. send to the (electric) chair; N. Amer. informal fry. **2** *the corporation executed a series of financial deals* **carry out**, accomplish, bring off/about, achieve, complete, engineer; informal pull off; formal effectuate. **3** *a well-executed act* **perform**, present, render; stage.

execution n. **1** *the execution of the plan* **implementation**, carrying out, accomplishment, bringing off/about, engineering, attainment, realization. **2** *the execution of the play* **performance**, presentation, rendition, rendering, staging. **3** *thousands were sentenced to execution* **capital punishment**, the death penalty; the gibbet, the gallows, the noose, the rope, the scaffold, the guillotine, the firing squad; N. Amer. the (electric) chair.

executioner n. **hangman**, official killer; historical headsman.

executive adj. *executive powers* **administrative**, decision-making, managerial; law-making.
▸n. **1** *top-level bank executives* **chief**, head, director, senior official, senior manager, CEO, chief executive officer; informal boss, exec, suit. **2** *the executive has increased in number* **administration**, management, directorate; government, legislative body.

exegesis n. **interpretation**, explanation, exposition, explication.

exemplar n. **epitome**, perfect example, model, paragon, ideal, exemplification, textbook example, embodiment, essence, quintessence.

exemplary adj. **1** *her exemplary behaviour* **perfect**, ideal, model, faultless, flawless, impeccable, irreproachable; excellent, outstanding, admirable, commendable, laudable, above/beyond reproach. **2** *exemplary jail sentences* **serving as a deterrent**, cautionary, warning, admonitory; rare monitory. **3** *her works are exemplary of certain feminist arguments* **typical**, characteristic, representative, illustrative.
– OPPOSITES deplorable.

exemplify v. **1** *this story exemplifies current trends* **typify**, epitomize, be a typical example of, be representative of, symbolize. **2** *he exemplified his point with an anecdote* **illustrate**, give an example of, demonstrate.

exempt adj. *they are exempt from all charges* **free**, not liable/subject, exempted, excepted, excused, absolved.
– OPPOSITES subject to.
▸v. *he had been exempted from military service* **excuse**, free, release, exclude, give/grant immunity, spare, absolve; informal let off (the hook); N. Amer. informal grandfather.

exemption n. **immunity**, exception, dispensation, indemnity, exclusion, freedom, release, relief, absolution; informal let-off.

exercise n. **1** *exercise improves your heart* **physical activity**, a workout, working-out; gymnastics, sports, games, physical education, PE, physical training, PT, aerobics, jogging, running; callisthenics; Brit. informal physical jerks. **2** *translation exercises* **task**, piece of work, problem, assignment; Music étude. **3** *the exercise of professional skill* **use**, utilization, employment; practice, application. **4** *military exercises* **manoeuvres**, operations; war games.
▸v. **1** *she exercised every day* **work out**, do exercises, train; informal pump iron. **2** *he must learn to exercise patience* **use**, employ, make use of, utilize; practise, apply. **3** *the problem continued to exercise him* **worry**, trouble, concern, make anxious, bother, disturb, perturb, distress, preoccupy, prey on someone's mind, make uneasy; informal bug, do someone's head in.

exert v. **1** *he exerted considerable pressure on me* **bring to bear**, apply, exercise, employ, use, utilize, deploy. **2** *he had been exerting himself* **make an/every effort**, try hard, strive, endeavour, do one's best/utmost, give one's all, push oneself, drive oneself, work hard; informal go all out, pull out all the stops, bend over backwards, do one's damnedest, move heaven and earth, work one's socks off; N. Amer. informal do one's darnedest, bust one's chops; Austral. informal go for the doctor.

exertion n. **1** *she was panting with the exertion* **effort**, strain, struggle, toil, endeavour, hard work, labour; Brit. informal

graft; Austral./NZ informal yakka; literary travail.
2 *the exertion of pressure* **use**, application,
exercise, employment, utilization.

exhale v. **1** *she exhaled her cigarette smoke*
breathe out, blow out, puff out. **2** *the jungle
exhaled mists of early morning* **give off**,
emanate, send forth, emit.
– OPPOSITES inhale.

exhaust v. **1** *the effort had exhausted him*
tire (out), wear out, overtire, fatigue, weary,
drain, run someone into the ground; informal
do in, take it out of one, wipe out, knock out,
shatter; Brit. informal knacker; N. Amer. informal
poop, tucker out. **2** *the country has exhausted
its reserves* **use up**, run through, go through,
consume, finish, deplete, spend, empty,
drain; informal blow.
– OPPOSITES invigorate, replenish.

exhausted adj. **1** *I'm exhausted* **tired
out**, worn out, weary, dog-tired, bone-
tired, drained, fatigued,
enervated; informal done in, all in, dead beat,
shattered, bushed, knocked out, wiped
out, bushwhacked; Brit. informal knackered,
whacked (out), jiggered; N. Amer. informal
pooped, tuckered out, fried, whipped;
Austral./NZ informal stonkered. **2** *exhausted
reserves* **used up**, consumed, finished,
spent, depleted; empty, drained.

exhausting adj. **tiring**, wearying, taxing,
fatiguing, wearing, enervating, draining,
arduous, strenuous, onerous, demanding,
gruelling; informal killing, murderous; Brit.
informal knackering.

exhaustion n. **1** *sheer exhaustion forced Paul
to give up* **extreme tiredness**, overtiredness,
fatigue, weariness. **2** *the exhaustion of fuel
reserves* **consumption**, depletion, using up,
expenditure; draining, emptying.

exhaustive adj. **comprehensive**, all-
inclusive, complete, full, encyclopedic,
thorough, in-depth; detailed, meticulous,
painstaking.
– OPPOSITES perfunctory.

exhibit v. **1** *the paintings were exhibited at
Sotheby's* **put on display/show**, display,
show, put on public view, showcase; set out,
lay out, array, arrange. **2** *Luke exhibited signs
of jealousy* **show**, reveal, display, manifest;
express, indicate, demonstrate, present; formal
evince.
▸ n. **1** *an exhibit at the British Museum* **object
on display**, item, piece. **2** N. Amer. *people
flocked to the exhibit.* See **exhibition**
(sense 1).

exhibition n. **1** *an exhibition of French
sculpture* **(public) display**, show, showing,
presentation, demonstration, exposition,
showcase; N. Amer. exhibit. **2** *a convincing
exhibition of concern* **display**, show,
demonstration, manifestation, expression.

exhibitionist n. **posturer**, poser, self-
publicist, attention-seeker; extrovert; informal
show-off; N. Amer. informal showboat.

exhilarate v. **thrill**, excite, intoxicate,
elate, delight, enliven, animate, invigorate,
energize, stimulate; informal give someone

a thrill/buzz; N. Amer. informal give someone a
charge.

exhilaration n. **elation**, euphoria,
exultation, exaltation, joy, happiness,
delight, joyousness, jubilation, rapture,
ecstasy.

exhort v. **urge**, encourage, call on, enjoin,
charge, press; bid, appeal to, entreat,
implore; formal adjure; literary beseech.

exhortation n. **1** *no amount of exhortation
had any effect* **urging**, encouragement,
persuasion, pressure; admonishment,
warning. **2** *the government's exhortations*
entreaty, appeal, call, charge, injunction;
admonition, warning.

exhume v. **disinter**, dig up, disentomb.
– OPPOSITES bury.

exigency n. **1** *the exigencies of the continuing
war* **need**, demand, requirement, necessity.
2 *financial exigency* **urgency**, crisis,
difficulty, pressure.

exiguous adj. formal **meagre**, inadequate,
insufficient, small, scanty, paltry, negligible,
modest, deficient, miserly, niggardly,
beggarly; informal measly, stingy, piddling.
– OPPOSITES ample, generous.

exile n. **1** *his exile from the land of his birth*
banishment, expulsion, expatriation,
deportation. **2** *political exiles* **émigré**,
expatriate; displaced person, DP, refugee,
deportee; informal expat.
▸ v. *he was exiled from his country* **expel**,
banish, expatriate, deport, drive out, throw
out, outlaw.

exist v. **1** *animals existing in the distant past*
live, be alive, be living; be, have being, have
existence. **2** *the liberal climate that existed
during his presidency* **prevail**, occur, be
found, be in existence; be the case. **3** *she had
to exist on a low income* **survive**, subsist, live,
support oneself; manage, make do, get by,
scrape by, make ends meet.

existence n. **1** *the industry's continued
existence* **actuality**, being, existing, reality;
survival, continuation. **2** *her suburban
existence* **way of life/living**, life, lifestyle.
▫ **in existence 1** *there are several million
unidentified species in existence* **alive**,
existing, extant, existent. **2** *the only copy
still in existence* **surviving**, remaining, in
circulation.

existent adj. **in existence**, alive, existing,
living, extant; surviving, remaining.

exit n. **1** *the fire exit* **way out**, door, egress,
escape route; doorway, gate, gateway, portal.
2 *take the second exit* **turning**, turn-off, turn;
N. Amer. turnout. **3** *his sudden exit* **departure**,
leaving, withdrawal, going, decamping,
retreat; flight, exodus, escape.
– OPPOSITES entrance, arrival.
▸ v. *the doctor had just exited* **leave**, go (out),
depart, withdraw, retreat.
– OPPOSITES enter.

exodus n. **mass departure**, withdrawal,
evacuation, leaving; migration, emigration;
flight, escape, fleeing.

exonerate v. **1** *the inquiry exonerated them* **absolve**, clear, acquit, find innocent, discharge; formal exculpate. **2** *the pope exonerated the king from his oath* **release**, discharge, free, liberate; excuse, exempt, except, dispense; informal let off.
– OPPOSITES convict.

exorbitant adj. **extortionate**, excessively high, excessive, prohibitive, outrageous, unreasonable, inflated, unconscionable, huge, enormous; Brit. over the odds; informal steep, stiff, over the top, a rip-off; Brit. informal daylight robbery.
– OPPOSITES reasonable.

exorcize v. **1** *exorcizing a spirit* **drive out**, cast out, expel. **2** *they exorcized the house* **purify**, cleanse, purge; rare lustrate.

exotic adj. **1** *exotic birds* **foreign**, non-native, tropical. **2** *exotic places* **foreign**, faraway, far-off, far-flung, distant. **3** *Linda's exotic appearance* **striking**, colourful, eye-catching; unusual, unconventional, out of the ordinary, foreign-looking, extravagant, outlandish; informal offbeat, off the wall.
– OPPOSITES native, nearby, conventional.

expand v. **1** *metals expand when heated* **increase in size**, become larger, enlarge; swell, dilate, inflate; lengthen, stretch, thicken, fill out; rare intumesce. **2** *the company is expanding* **grow**, become/make larger, become/make bigger, increase in size/scope; extend, augment, broaden, widen, develop, diversify, build up; branch out, spread, proliferate. **3** *the minister expanded on the proposals* **elaborate on**, enlarge on, go into detail about, flesh out, develop, expatiate on. **4** *she expanded and flourished* **relax**, unbend, become relaxed, grow friendlier, loosen up.
– OPPOSITES shrink, contract.

expanse n. **area**, stretch, sweep, tract, swathe, belt, region; sea, carpet, blanket, sheet.

expansion n. **1** *expansion and contraction* **enlargement**, swelling, dilation; lengthening, elongation, stretching, thickening. **2** *the expansion of the company* **growth**, increase in size, enlargement, extension, development; spread, proliferation, multiplication. **3** *an expansion of a lecture given last year* **elaboration**, enlargement, amplification, development.
– OPPOSITES contraction.

expansive adj. **1** *expansive moorland* **extensive**, sweeping, rolling. **2** *expansive coverage* **wide-ranging**, extensive, broad, wide, comprehensive, thorough. **3** *Cara became engagingly expansive* **communicative**, forthcoming, sociable, friendly, outgoing, affable, chatty, talkative, garrulous, loquacious, voluble.

expatiate v. **speak/write at length**, go into detail, expound, dwell, dilate, expand, enlarge, elaborate; formal perorate.

expatriate n. *expatriates working overseas* **emigrant**, non-native, émigré, (economic) migrant; informal expat.
– OPPOSITES national.
▶adj. *expatriate workers* **emigrant**, living abroad, non-native, émigré; informal expat.
– OPPOSITES indigenous.
▶v. **1** *he was not tempted to expatriate himself* **settle abroad**, live abroad. **2** *he was expatriated* **exile**, deport, banish, expel.

expect v. **1** *I expect she'll be late* **suppose**, presume, think, believe, imagine, assume, surmise; informal guess, reckon; N. Amer. informal figure. **2** *a 10 per cent rise was expected* **anticipate**, await, look for, hope for, look forward to; contemplate, bargain for/on, bank on; predict, forecast, envisage, envision. **3** *we expect total loyalty* **require**, ask for, call for, want, insist on, demand.

expectancy n. **1** *feverish expectancy* **anticipation**, expectation, eagerness, excitement. **2** *life expectancy* **likelihood**, probability, outlook, prospect.

expectant adj. **1** *expectant fans* **eager**, excited, agog, waiting with bated breath, hopeful; in suspense, on tenterhooks. **2** *an expectant mother* **pregnant**; informal expecting, in the family way, preggers; Brit. informal up the duff/spout, in the (pudding) club; technical gravid; old use with child, in a delicate/interesting condition.

expectation n. **1** *her expectations were unrealistic* **supposition**, assumption, presumption, conjecture, surmise, calculation, prediction. **2** *tense with expectation* **anticipation**, expectancy, eagerness, excitement, suspense.

expecting adj. informal See **expectant** (sense 2).

expedient adj. *a politically expedient strategy* **convenient**, advantageous, in one's own interests, useful, of use, beneficial, of benefit, helpful; practical, pragmatic, politic, prudent, wise, judicious, sensible.
▶n. *a temporary expedient* **measure**, means, method, stratagem, scheme, plan, move, tactic, manoeuvre, device, contrivance, ploy, machination, dodge; Austral. informal lurk.

expedite v. **speed up**, accelerate, hurry, hasten, step up, quicken, precipitate, dispatch; advance, facilitate, ease, make easier, further, promote, aid, push through, urge on, boost, stimulate, spur on, help along.
– OPPOSITES delay.

expedition n. **1** *an expedition to the South Pole* **journey**, voyage, tour, odyssey; exploration, safari, trek, hike. **2** informal *a shopping expedition* **trip**, excursion, outing, jaunt. **3** *all members of the expedition* **group**, team, party, crew, band, squad. **4** formal *use all expedition possible* **speed**, haste, swiftness, quickness, rapidity, briskness; literary fleetness, celerity.

expeditious adj. **speedy**, swift, quick, rapid, fast, brisk, efficient; prompt, punctual, immediate, instant; literary fleet.
– OPPOSITES slow.

expel v. **1** *she was expelled from her party* **throw out**, bar, ban, debar, drum out, oust,

remove, get rid of, dismiss; Military cashier; informal chuck out, sling out, kick/boot out; Brit. informal turf out, give someone the push; N. Amer. informal give someone the bum's rush; dated out. **2** *he was expelled from the country* **banish**, exile, deport, evict, expatriate, drive out, throw out. **3** *Dolly expelled a hiss* **let out**, discharge, eject, issue, send forth.
– OPPOSITES admit.

expend v. **1** *they had already expended $75,000* **spend**, pay out, disburse, dole out, dish out, get through, waste, fritter (away), dissipate; informal fork out, shell out, lay out, cough up, blow, splurge; Brit. informal splash out, stump up; N. Amer. informal ante up. **2** *children expend a lot of energy* **use (up)**, utilize, consume, eat up, deplete, get through.
– OPPOSITES save, conserve.

expendable adj. **1** *an accountant decided he was expendable* **dispensable**, replaceable, non-essential, inessential, unnecessary, not required, superfluous, disposable. **2** *an expendable satellite launcher* **disposable**, throwaway, one-use, single-use.
– OPPOSITES indispensable.

expenditure n. **1** *the expenditure of funds* **spending**, paying out, outlay, disbursement, doling out, waste, wasting, frittering (away), dissipation. **2** *reducing public expenditure* **outgoings**, costs, payments, expenses, overheads, spending, spend.
– OPPOSITES saving, income.

expense n. **1** *Nigel resented the expense* **cost**, price, charge, outlay, spend, fee, tariff, levy, payment; humorous damage. **2** *regular expenses* **outgoing**, payment, outlay, expenditure, charge, bill, overhead. **3** *pollution controls come at the expense of jobs* **sacrifice**, cost, loss.

expensive adj. **costly**, dear, high-priced, overpriced, exorbitant, extortionate; informal steep, pricey, costing an arm and a leg, costing the earth, costing a bomb.
– OPPOSITES cheap, economical.

experience n. **1** *qualifications and experience* **skill**, (practical) knowledge, understanding; background, record, history; maturity, worldliness, sophistication; informal know-how. **2** *an enjoyable experience* **incident**, occurrence, event, happening, episode; adventure, exploit, escapade. **3** *his first experience of business* **involvement in**, participation in, contact with, acquaintance with, exposure to, observation of, awareness of, insight into.
▶ v. *some policemen experience harassment* **undergo**, encounter, meet, come into contact with, come across, come up against, face, be faced with.

> **WORD LINKS**
> **empirical** based on experience rather than theory or logic

experienced adj. **1** *an experienced pilot* **knowledgeable**, skilful, skilled, expert, accomplished, adept, adroit, master, consummate; proficient, trained, competent, capable, well trained, well versed; seasoned, practised, mature, veteran. **2** *she deluded herself that she was experienced* **worldly (wise)**, sophisticated, suave, urbane, mature, knowing, savvy; informal streetwise; Brit. informal sussed.
– OPPOSITES novice, naive.

experiment n. **1** *carrying out experiments* **test**, investigation, trial, examination, observation; assessment, evaluation, appraisal, analysis, study. **2** *these results have been established by experiment* **research**, experimentation, observation, analysis, testing.
▶ v. *they experimented with new ideas* **conduct experiments**, carry out trials/tests, conduct research; test, trial, try out, assess, appraise, evaluate.

experimental adj. **1** *the experimental stage* **exploratory**, investigational, trial, test, pilot; speculative, conjectural, hypothetical, tentative, preliminary, untested, untried. **2** *experimental music* **innovative**, innovatory, new, original, radical, avant-garde, alternative, unorthodox, unconventional, left-field; informal way-out.

expert n. *he is an expert in kendo* **specialist**, authority, pundit; adept, maestro, virtuoso, (past) master, wizard; connoisseur, aficionado; informal ace, buff, pro, whizz, hotshot; Brit. informal dab hand; N. Amer. informal maven, crackerjack.
▶ adj. *an expert chess player* **skilful**, skilled, adept, accomplished, talented, fine; master, masterly, brilliant, virtuoso, magnificent, outstanding, great, exceptional, excellent, first-class, first-rate, top-tier, superb; proficient, good, able, capable, experienced, practised, knowledgeable; informal wizard, ace, crack, mean.
– OPPOSITES incompetent.

expertise n. **skill**, skilfulness, expertness, prowess, proficiency, competence; knowledge, mastery, ability, aptitude, facility, capability; informal know-how.

expiate v. **atone for**, make amends for, make up for, do penance for, pay for, redress, redeem, offset, make good.

expire v. **1** *my contract has expired* **run out**, become invalid, become void, lapse; **end**, finish, stop, come to an end, terminate. **2** *the spot where he expired* **die**, pass away/on, breathe one's last; informal kick the bucket, bite the dust, croak, buy it; Brit. informal snuff it, peg out, pop one's clogs; old use decease, depart this life. **3** technical *afterwards the breath is expired* **breathe out**, exhale, blow out, expel.

expiry n. **1** *the expiry of the lease* **lapse**, expiration. **2** *the expiry of his term of office* **end**, finish, termination, conclusion. **3** old use *the sad expiry of their friend* **death**, demise, passing (away/on), dying; formal decease.

explain v. **1** *a technician explained the procedure* **describe**, give an explanation of, make clear/intelligible, spell out, put into words; elucidate, expound, explicate,

clarify, throw light on; gloss, interpret.
2 *nothing could explain his new-found wealth* **account for**, give a reason for; justify, give a justification for, give an excuse for, vindicate, legitimize.

explanation n. **1** *an explanation of the ideas contained in the essay* **clarification**, simplification; description, report, statement; elucidation, exposition, expounding, explication; gloss, interpretation, commentary, exegesis.
2 *I owe you an explanation* **account**, reason; justification, excuse, alibi, defence, vindication.

explanatory adj. **explaining**, descriptive, describing, illustrative, illuminative, elucidatory.

expletive n. **swear word**, oath, curse, obscenity, profanity, four-letter word, dirty word; informal cuss word, cuss; formal imprecation; (**expletives**) bad language, foul language, strong language, swearing; Brit. informal industrial language.

explicable adj. **explainable**, understandable, comprehensible, accountable, intelligible, interpretable.

explicate v. **explain**, make explicit, clarify, make plain/clear, spell out; interpret, elucidate, expound, illuminate, throw light on.

explicit adj. **1** *explicit instructions* **clear**, plain, straightforward, crystal clear, easily understandable; precise, exact, specific, unequivocal, unambiguous; detailed, comprehensive, exhaustive. **2** *sexually explicit material* **uncensored**, graphic, candid, full-frontal.
– OPPOSITES vague.

explode v. **1** *a bomb has exploded* **blow up**, detonate, go off, burst (apart), fly apart.
2 *exploding the first atomic device* **detonate**, set off, let off, discharge. **3** *he exploded in anger* **lose one's temper**, blow up, get angry, become enraged; informal fly off the handle, hit the roof, blow one's cool/top, go wild, go bananas, see red, go off the deep end; Brit. informal go spare, go crackers; N. Amer. informal blow one's lid/stack. **4** *the city's exploding population* **increase suddenly/rapidly**, mushroom, snowball, escalate, multiply, burgeon, rocket. **5** *exploding the myths about men* **disprove**, refute, rebut, invalidate, negate, negative, controvert, repudiate, discredit, debunk, belie, give the lie to; informal shoot full of holes, blow out of the water; formal confute.
– OPPOSITES defuse.

exploit v. **1** *we should exploit this new technology* **utilize**, use, make use of, turn/put to good use, make the most of, capitalize on, benefit from; informal cash in on. **2** *exploiting the workers* **take advantage of**, abuse, impose on, treat unfairly, misuse, ill-treat; informal walk (all) over, take for a ride, rip off.
▶ n. *his exploits brought him notoriety* **feat**, deed, act, adventure, stunt, escapade;

achievement, accomplishment, attainment; informal lark, caper.

exploitation n. **1** *the exploitation of mineral resources* **utilization**, use. **2** *the exploitation of the poor* **taking advantage**, abuse, misuse, ill-treatment, unfair treatment, oppression.

exploration n. **1** *the exploration of space* **investigation**, study, survey, research, inspection, examination, scrutiny, observation; consideration, analysis, review. **2** *explorations into the mountains* **expedition**, trip, journey, voyage; old use peregrination; (**explorations**) travels.

exploratory adj. **investigative**, investigational, explorative, probing, fact-finding; experimental, trial, test, preliminary, provisional.

explore v. **1** *they explored all the possibilities* **investigate**, look into, consider; examine, research, survey, scrutinize, study, review, go over with a fine-tooth comb; informal check out. **2** *exploring Iceland's north-west* **travel over**, tour, range over; survey, take a look at, inspect, investigate, reconnoitre; informal recce, give something a/the once-over.

explorer n. **traveller**, discoverer, voyager, adventurer; surveyor, scout, prospector.

explosion n. **1** *Edward heard the explosion* **detonation**, eruption, blowing up; bang, blast, boom. **2** *an explosion of anger* **outburst**, flare-up, outbreak, eruption, storm, rush, surge; fit, paroxysm, attack. **3** *the explosion of human populations* **sudden/rapid increase**, mushrooming, snowballing, escalation, multiplication, burgeoning, rocketing.

explosive adj. **1** *explosive gases* **volatile**, inflammable, flammable, combustible, incendiary. **2** *Marco's explosive temper* **fiery**, stormy, violent, volatile, angry, passionate, tempestuous, turbulent, touchy, irascible, hot-headed, short-tempered.
3 *an explosive situation* **tense**, (highly) charged, overwrought; dangerous, perilous, hazardous, sensitive, delicate, unstable, volatile. **4** *explosive population growth* **sudden**, dramatic, rapid; mushrooming, snowballing, escalating, rocketing, accelerating.
▶ n. **bomb**, incendiary device.

exponent n. **1** *an exponent of free-trade policies* **advocate**, supporter, proponent, upholder, backer, defender, champion; promoter, propagandist, campaigner, fighter, crusader, enthusiast, apologist. **2** *a karate exponent* **practitioner**, performer, player.
– OPPOSITES critic, opponent.

export v. **1** *exporting raw materials* **sell overseas/abroad**, send overseas/abroad, trade internationally. **2** *he is trying to export his ideas to America* **transmit**, spread, disseminate, circulate, communicate, pass on; literary bruit about/abroad.
– OPPOSITES import.

expose v. **1** *at low tide the sands are exposed* **reveal**, uncover, lay bare. **2** *he was exposed to asbestos* **make vulnerable**, subject, lay

open, put at risk, put in jeopardy. **3** *they were exposed to liberal ideas* **introduce to**, bring into contact with, make aware of, familiarize with, acquaint with. **4** *he was exposed as a liar* **uncover**, reveal, unveil, unmask, detect, find out; discover, bring to light, bring into the open, make known; denounce, condemn; informal spill the beans on, blow the whistle on.
– OPPOSITES cover.

exposé n. **revelation**, disclosure, exposure; report, feature, piece, column; informal scoop.
– OPPOSITES cover-up.

exposed adj. **unprotected**, unsheltered, open to the elements/weather; vulnerable, defenceless, undefended, pregnable.
– OPPOSITES sheltered.

exposition n. **1** *a lucid exposition* **explanation**, description, elucidation, explication, interpretation; account, commentary, appraisal, assessment, discussion, exegesis. **2** *the exposition will feature 200 exhibits* **exhibition**, (trade) fair, display, show, presentation, demonstration; N. Amer. exhibit.

expository adj. **explanatory**, descriptive, describing, elucidatory, explicatory, explicative, interpretative, exegetic.

expostulate v. **remonstrate**, disagree, argue, take issue, protest, reason, express disagreement, raise objections.

exposure n. **1** *the exposure of the lizard's vivid blue tongue* **revealing**, revelation, uncovering, baring, laying bare. **2** *exposure to harmful chemicals* **subjection**, vulnerability, laying open. **3** *suffering from exposure* **frostbite**, cold, hypothermia. **4** *exposure to great literature* **introduction to**, experience of, contact with, familiarity with, acquaintance with, awareness of. **5** *the exposure of a banking scandal* **uncovering**, revelation, disclosure, unveiling, unmasking, discovery, detection; denunciation, condemnation. **6** *we're getting a lot of exposure* **publicity**, publicizing, advertising, public interest/attention, media interest/attention; informal hype. **7** *the exposure is perfect* **outlook**, aspect, view; position, setting, location.

expound v. **1** *he expounded his theories* **present**, put forward, set forth, propose, propound; explain, detail, spell out, describe. **2** *a treatise expounding Paul's teachings* **explain**, interpret, explicate, elucidate; comment on, give a commentary on.
□ **expound on** elaborate on, expand on, expatiate on, discuss at length.

express¹ v. **1** *community leaders expressed their anger* **communicate**, convey, indicate, show, demonstrate, reveal, make manifest, put across/over, get across/over; articulate, put into words, utter, voice, give voice to; state, assert, proclaim, profess, air, make public, give vent to; formal evince. **2** *all the juice is expressed* **squeeze out**, press out, extract.
□ **express oneself** communicate one's thoughts/opinions/views, put thoughts into

words, speak one's mind, say what's on one's mind.

express² adj. *an express bus* **rapid**, swift, fast, quick, speedy, high-speed; non-stop, direct.
– OPPOSITES slow.
▶ n. *an overnight express* **express train**, fast train, direct train.

express³ adj. **1** *express reference to confidential matters* **explicit**, clear, direct, obvious, plain, distinct, unambiguous, unequivocal; specific, precise, crystal clear, certain, categorical. **2** *one express purpose* **sole**, specific, particular, exclusive, specified, fixed.
– OPPOSITES implied.

expression n. **1** *the free expression of opposition views* **utterance**, uttering, voicing, pronouncement, declaration, articulation, assertion, setting forth; dissemination, circulation, communication, spreading, promulgation. **2** *an expression of sympathy* **indication**, demonstration, show, exhibition, token; communication, illustration, revelation. **3** *an expression of harassed fatigue* **look**, appearance, air, manner, countenance, mien. **4** *a time-worn expression* **idiom**, phrase, idiomatic expression; proverb, saying, adage, maxim, axiom, aphorism, saw, motto, platitude, cliché. **5** *these pieces are very different in expression* **emotion**, feeling, spirit, passion, intensity; style, intonation, tone. **6** *essential oils obtained by expression* **squeezing**, pressing, extraction, extracting.

expressionless adj. **1** *his face was expressionless* **inscrutable**, deadpan, poker-faced; blank, vacant, emotionless, unemotional, inexpressive; glazed, stony, wooden, impassive. **2** *a flat, expressionless tone* **dull**, dry, toneless, monotonous, boring, tedious, flat, wooden, unmodulated, unvarying, devoid of feeling/emotion.
– OPPOSITES expressive, lively.

expressive adj. **1** *an expressive shrug* **eloquent**, meaningful, demonstrative, suggestive. **2** *an expressive song* **emotional**, full of emotion/feeling, passionate, poignant, moving, stirring, evocative, powerful, emotionally charged. **3** *his diction is very expressive of his Englishness* **indicative**, demonstrative, demonstrating, showing, suggesting.
– OPPOSITES expressionless, unemotional.

expressly adv. **1** *he was expressly forbidden to discuss the matter* **explicitly**, clearly, directly, plainly, distinctly, unambiguously, unequivocally; absolutely; specifically, categorically, pointedly, emphatically. **2** *a machine expressly built for spraying paint* **solely**, specifically, particularly, specially, exclusively, just, only, explicitly.

expropriate v. **seize**, take (away/over), appropriate, take possession of, requisition, commandeer, claim, acquire, sequestrate, confiscate; Law distrain.

expulsion n. **1** *expulsion from the party* **removal**, debarment, dismissal, exclusion,

discharge, ejection, drumming out. **2** *the expulsion of bodily wastes* **discharge**, ejection, excretion, voiding, evacuation, elimination, passing.
– OPPOSITES admission.

expunge v. **erase**, remove, delete, rub out, wipe out, efface; cross out, strike out, blot out, blank out; destroy, obliterate, eradicate, eliminate.

expurgate v. **censor**, bowdlerize, blue-pencil, redact, cut, edit; clean up, sanitize, make acceptable, make palatable, water down.

exquisite adj. **1** *exquisite antique glass* **beautiful**, lovely, elegant, fine; magnificent, superb, excellent, wonderful, well-crafted, well-made, perfect; delicate, fragile, dainty, subtle. **2** *exquisite taste* **discriminating**, discerning, sensitive, selective, fastidious; refined, cultivated, cultured, educated. **3** *exquisite agony* **intense**, acute, keen, piercing, sharp, severe, racking, excruciating, agonizing, harrowing, searing; unbearable, unendurable.

extant adj. **still existing**, in existence, existent, surviving, remaining.

extemporary, **extemporaneous** adj. *an extemporaneous address.* See **extempore**.

extempore adj. *an extempore speech* **impromptu**, spontaneous, unscripted, ad lib, extemporary, extemporaneous; improvised, unrehearsed, unplanned, unprepared, off the top of one's head; informal off-the-cuff; formal ad libitum.
– OPPOSITES rehearsed.
▶ adv. *he was speaking extempore* **spontaneously**, extemporaneously, ad lib, without preparation, without rehearsal, off the top of one's head; informal off the cuff; formal ad libitum.

extemporize v. **improvise**, ad lib, play it by ear, think on one's feet; informal busk it, wing it.

extend v. **1** *he attempted to extend his dominions* **expand**, enlarge, increase, make larger/bigger; lengthen, widen, broaden. **2** *the garden extends down to the road* **continue**, carry on, run on, stretch (out), reach, lead. **3** *we have extended our range of services* **widen**, expand, broaden; augment, supplement, increase, add to, enhance, develop. **4** *extending the life of parliament* **prolong**, lengthen, increase; stretch out, protract, spin out, string out. **5** *extend your arms and legs* **stretch out**, spread out, reach out, straighten out. **6** *he extended a hand in greeting* **hold out**, reach out, hold forth; offer, give, outstretch, proffer. **7** *we wish to extend our thanks to Mr Bayes* **offer**, proffer, give, grant, bestow, accord.
– OPPOSITES reduce, narrow, shorten.
▫ **extend to** include, take in, incorporate, encompass.

extended adj. **prolonged**, protracted, long-lasting, long-drawn-out, spun out, dragged out, strung out, lengthy, long.

extension n. **1** *they are planning a new extension* **addition**, add-on, adjunct, annexe, wing, supplementary building; N. Amer. ell. **2** *an extension of knowledge* **expansion**, increase, enlargement, widening, broadening, deepening; augmentation, enhancement, development, growth, continuation. **3** *an extension of opening hours* **prolongation**, lengthening, increase. **4** *I need an extension of time* **postponement**, deferral, delay, more/extra time.

extensive adj. **1** *a mansion with extensive grounds* **large**, large-scale, sizeable, substantial, considerable, ample, expansive, great, vast. **2** *extensive knowledge* **comprehensive**, thorough, exhaustive; broad, wide, wide-ranging, catholic.

extent n. **1** *two acres in extent* **area**, size, expanse, length; proportions, dimensions. **2** *the full extent of her father's illness* **degree**, scale, level, magnitude, scope; size, breadth, width, reach, range.

extenuate v. **excuse**, mitigate, palliate, make allowances/excuses for, defend, vindicate, justify; diminish, lessen, moderate, qualify, play down.

extenuating adj. **mitigating**, excusing, exonerative, palliating, palliative, justifying, justificatory, vindicating; formal exculpatory.

exterior adj. *the exterior walls* **outer**, outside, outermost, outward, external.
– OPPOSITES interior.
▶ n. *the exterior of the building* **outside**, outer surface, external surface, outward appearance, facade.
– OPPOSITES interior.

exterminate v. **kill**, put to death, take/end the life of, dispatch; slaughter, butcher, massacre, wipe out, eliminate, eradicate, annihilate; murder, assassinate, execute; informal do away with, bump off, do in, top, take out, blow away; N. Amer. informal ice, rub out, waste; literary slay.

extermination n. **killing**, murder, assassination, putting to death, execution, dispatch, slaughter, massacre, liquidation, elimination, eradication, annihilation; literary slaying.

external adj. **1** *an external wall* **outer**, outside, outermost, outward, exterior. **2** *an external examiner* **outside**, independent, non-resident, from elsewhere.
– OPPOSITES internal, in-house.

extinct adj. **1** *an extinct species* **vanished**, lost, died out, no longer existing, no longer extant, wiped out, destroyed, gone. **2** *an extinct volcano* **inactive**.
– OPPOSITES extant, dormant.

extinction n. **dying out**, disappearance, vanishing; extermination, destruction, elimination, eradication, annihilation.

extinguish v. **1** *the fire was extinguished* **douse**, put out, stamp out, smother, beat out, dampen down. **2** *all hope was extinguished* **destroy**, end, finish off, put an end to, bring to an end, terminate, remove, annihilate, wipe out, erase, eliminate, eradicate,

obliterate; informal take out, rub out.
– OPPOSITES light.

extirpate v. **weed out**, destroy, eradicate, stamp out, root out, wipe out, eliminate, suppress, crush, put down, put an end to, get rid of.

extol v. **praise enthusiastically**, go into raptures about/over, wax lyrical about, sing the praises of, praise to the skies, acclaim, eulogize, rhapsodize over, rave about, enthuse about/over; informal go wild about, go on about; N. Amer. informal ballyhoo; formal laud; old use panegyrize.
– OPPOSITES criticize.

extort v. **obtain by force**, obtain by threat(s), blackmail someone for, extract, exact, wring, wrest, screw, squeeze; N. Amer. & Austral. informal put the bite on someone for.

extortion n. **demanding money with menaces**, blackmail, extraction; N. Amer. informal shakedown; formal exaction.

extortionate adj. **1** *extortionate prices* **exorbitant**, excessively high, excessive, outrageous, unreasonable, inordinate, inflated; informal over the top, OTT. **2** *an extortionate clause* **grasping**, bloodsucking, avaricious, greedy; exacting, harsh, severe, oppressive; informal money-grubbing.

extortionist n. **racketeer**, extortioner, extorter, blackmailer; informal bloodsucker.

extra adj. *extra income* **additional**, more, added, supplementary, further, auxiliary, ancillary, subsidiary, secondary.
▸ adv. **1** *working extra hard* **exceptionally**, particularly, specially, especially, very, extremely; unusually, extraordinarily, uncommonly, remarkably, outstandingly, amazingly, incredibly, really; informal seriously, mucho, awfully, terribly; Brit. jolly, dead, well; informal dated frightfully. **2** *postage is charged extra* **in addition**, additionally, as well, also, too, besides, on top (of that); old use withal.
▸ n. **1** *an optional extra* **addition**, adjunct, addendum, add-on. **2** *a film extra* **walk-on**, supernumerary, spear-carrier.

extract v. **1** *he extracted the cassette* **take out**, draw out, pull out, remove, withdraw; free, release, extricate. **2** *extracting money* **wrest**, exact, wring, screw, squeeze, obtain by force, obtain by threat(s), extort, blackmail someone for; N. Amer. & Austral. informal put the bite on someone for. **3** *the roots are crushed to extract the juice* **squeeze out**, express, press out, obtain. **4** *the table is extracted from the report* **excerpt**, select, reproduce, copy, take. **5** *ideas extracted from a variety of theories* **derive**, develop, evolve, deduce, infer, obtain; formal educe.
– OPPOSITES insert.
▸ n. **1** *an extract from his article* **excerpt**, passage, citation, quotation; (**excerpts**) analects. **2** *an extract of the ginseng root* **decoction**, distillation, distillate, abstraction, concentrate, essence, juice.

extraction n. **1** *the extraction of gall bladder stones* **removal**, taking out, drawing out,

pulling out, withdrawal; freeing, release, extrication. **2** *the extraction of grape juice* **squeezing**, expressing, pressing, obtaining. **3** *a man of Irish extraction* **descent**, ancestry, parentage, ancestors, family, antecedents; lineage, line, origin, derivation, birth; genealogy, heredity, stock, pedigree, blood, bloodline; roots, origins.
– OPPOSITES insertion.

extradition n. **deportation**, repatriation, expulsion.

extraneous adj. **1** *extraneous considerations* **irrelevant**, immaterial, beside the point, unrelated, unconnected, inapposite, inapplicable. **2** *extraneous noise* **external**, outside, exterior.

extraordinary adj. **1** *an extraordinary coincidence* **remarkable**, exceptional, amazing, astonishing, astounding, sensational, stunning, incredible, unbelievable, phenomenal; striking, outstanding, momentous, impressive, singular, memorable, unforgettable, unique, noteworthy; out of the ordinary, unusual, uncommon, rare, surprising; informal fantastic, terrific, tremendous, stupendous, awesome; literary wondrous. **2** *extraordinary speed* **very great**, tremendous, enormous, immense, prodigious, stupendous, monumental; informal almighty.

extravagance n. **1** *a fit of extravagance* **profligacy**, unthriftiness, improvidence, wastefulness, prodigality, lavishness. **2** *the costliest brands are an extravagance* **luxury**, indulgence, self-indulgence, treat, extra, non-essential. **3** *the extravagance of the decor* **ornateness**, elaborateness, embellishment, ornamentation; ostentation, over-elaborateness. **4** *the extravagance of his compliments* **excessiveness**, exaggeration, outrageousness, immoderation, excess.

extravagant adj. **1** *an extravagant lifestyle* **spendthrift**, profligate, unthrifty, improvident, wasteful, prodigal, lavish. **2** *extravagant gifts* **expensive**, costly, dear, high-priced, high-cost; valuable, precious; informal pricey, costing the earth, costing a bomb. **3** *extravagant prices* **exorbitant**, extortionate, excessive, high, unreasonable. **4** *extravagant praise* **excessive**, immoderate, exaggerated, gushing, unrestrained, effusive, fulsome. **5** *decorated in an extravagant style* **ornate**, elaborate, decorated, ornamented, fancy; over-elaborate, ostentatious, exaggerated, baroque, rococo; informal flash, flashy.
– OPPOSITES thrifty, cheap, plain.

extravaganza n. **spectacular**, display, spectacle, show, pageant.

extreme adj. **1** *extreme danger* **utmost**, very great, greatest (possible), maximum, maximal, highest, supreme, great, acute, enormous, severe, high, exceptional, extraordinary. **2** *extreme measures* **drastic**, serious, desperate, dire, radical, far-reaching, momentous, consequential; heavy, sharp, severe, austere, harsh, tough,

e

strict, rigorous, oppressive, draconian; Brit. swingeing. **3** *extreme views* **radical**, extremist, immoderate, fanatical, revolutionary, rebel, subversive, militant. **4** *extreme sports* **dangerous**, hazardous, risky, high-risk, adventurous. **5** *the extreme north-west* **furthest**, farthest, furthermost, farthermost, very, utmost; old use outmost.
– OPPOSITES slight, moderate.
▶ n. **1** *the two extremes* **opposite**, antithesis, (opposite) pole, antipode. **2** *this attitude is taken to its extreme in the following quote* **limit**, extremity, highest/greatest degree, maximum, height, top, zenith, peak.

extremely adv. **very**, exceedingly, exceptionally, especially, extraordinarily, in the extreme, tremendously, immensely, vastly, hugely, intensely, acutely, singularly, uncommonly, unusually, decidedly, particularly, supremely, highly, remarkably, really, truly, mightily; informal terrifically, awfully, fearfully, terribly, devilishly, majorly, seriously, mega, ultra, damn, damned; Brit. informal ever so, well, hellish, dead, jolly; N. Amer. informal real, mighty, awful, darned; informal dated devilish, frightfully; old use exceeding.
– OPPOSITES slightly.

extremist n. **fanatic**, radical, zealot, fundamentalist, hardliner, militant, activist; informal ultra.
– OPPOSITES moderate.

extremity n. **1** *the eastern extremity* **limit**, end, edge, side, farthest point, boundary, border, frontier; perimeter, periphery, margin; literary bourn, marge. **2** *she lost feeling in her extremities* **hands and feet**, fingers and toes, limbs. **3** *the extremity of the violence* **intensity**, magnitude, acuteness, ferocity, vehemence, fierceness, violence, severity, seriousness, strength, power, powerfulness, vigour, force, forcefulness. **4** *in extremity he will send for her* **dire straits**, trouble, difficulty, hard times, hardship, adversity, misfortune, distress; crisis, emergency, disaster, catastrophe, calamity; predicament, plight, mess, dilemma; informal fix, pickle, jam, spot.

extricate v. **extract**, free, release, disentangle, get out, remove, withdraw, disengage; informal get oneself off the hook.

extrinsic adj. **external**, extraneous, exterior, outside, outward.
– OPPOSITES intrinsic.

extrovert n. *like most extroverts he was a good dancer* **outgoing person**, sociable person, socializer, life and soul of the party.
– OPPOSITES introvert.
▶ adj. *his extrovert personality* **outgoing**, extroverted, sociable, gregarious, genial, affable, friendly, unreserved.
– OPPOSITES introverted.

extrude v. **force out**, thrust out, express, eject, expel, release, emit.

exuberant adj. **1** *exuberant guests dancing on the terrace* **ebullient**, buoyant, cheerful, jaunty, light-hearted, high-spirited,

exhilarated, excited, elated, exultant, euphoric, joyful, cheery, merry, jubilant, vivacious, enthusiastic, irrepressible, energetic, animated, full of life, lively, vigorous; Brit. Tiggerish; informal bubbly, bouncy, chipper, chirpy, full of beans; literary blithe, blithesome. **2** *an exuberant welcome* **effusive**, extravagant, fulsome, expansive, gushing, gushy, demonstrative.
– OPPOSITES gloomy, restrained.

exude v. **1** *milkweed exudes a milky sap* **give off/out**, discharge, release, emit, issue; ooze, weep, secrete, excrete. **2** *slime exudes from the fungus* **ooze**, seep, issue, escape, discharge, flow, leak. **3** *he exuded self-confidence* **emanate**, radiate, ooze, emit; display, show, exhibit, manifest, transmit.

exult v. **1** *her opponents exulted when she left* **rejoice**, be joyful, be happy, be delighted, be elated, be ecstatic, be overjoyed, be cock-a-hoop, be jubilant, be rapturous, be in raptures, be thrilled, jump for joy, be on cloud nine, be in seventh heaven; celebrate, cheer; informal be over the moon, be on top of the world; Austral. informal be wrapped; literary joy; old use jubilate. **2** *he exulted in his triumph* **rejoice at/in**, take delight in, find/take pleasure in, enjoy, revel in, glory in, delight in, relish, savour; be/feel proud of, congratulate oneself on.

exultant adj. **jubilant**, thrilled, triumphant, delighted, exhilarated, happy, overjoyed, joyous, joyful, gleeful, cock-a-hoop, excited, rejoicing, ecstatic, euphoric, elated, rapturous, in raptures, enraptured, on cloud nine, in seventh heaven; informal over the moon; N. Amer. informal wigged out.

exultation n. **jubilation**, rejoicing, happiness, pleasure, joy, gladness, delight, glee, elation, cheer, euphoria, exhilaration, delirium, ecstasy, rapture, exuberance.

eye n. **1** *he rubbed his eyes* **eyeball**; informal peeper; literary orb. **2** *sharp eyes* **eyesight**, vision, sight, powers of observation, (visual) perception. **3** *an eye for a bargain* **appreciation**, awareness, alertness, perception, consciousness, feeling, instinct, intuition, nose. **4** *his watchful eye* **watch**, observance, gaze, stare, regard; observation, surveillance, vigilance, contemplation, scrutiny. **5** *to desert was despicable in their eyes* **opinion**, (way of) thinking, mind, view, viewpoint, attitude, standpoint, perspective, belief, judgement, assessment, analysis, estimation. **6** *the eye of a needle* **hole**, opening, aperture, eyelet, slit, slot. **7** *the eye of the storm* **centre**, middle, heart, core.
▶ v. **1** *he eyed the stranger suspiciously* **look at**, observe, view, gaze at, stare at, regard, contemplate, survey, scrutinize, peruse, glance at; watch, keep an eye on, keep under observation; informal have/take a gander at, check out, size up; Brit. informal have/take a butcher's at, have/take a dekko at, have/take a shufti at, clock; N. Amer. informal eyeball; literary behold. **2** *eyeing young women in the street* **ogle**, leer at, stare at, make eyes at; informal eye up, give someone the glad eye; Brit. informal

gawp at; Austral./NZ informal perv on.

☐ **see eye to eye** agree, concur, be in agreement, be of the same mind/opinion, be in accord, think as one; be on the same wavelength, get on/along.

WORD LINKS

ocular, **ophthalmic** relating to the eye

ophthalmology the branch of medicine concerned with the eye

optometry the occupation of measuring eyesight and detecting eye disease

optician (N. Amer. **optometrist**) a person qualified to prescribe glasses etc. and to detect eye disease

astigmatism a defect in an eye, preventing proper focusing

glaucoma increased pressure in the eyeball, causing loss of sight

cataract a cloudy area on the lens of an eye, causing blurred vision

nystagmus rapid involuntary movements of the eyes

---

eye-catching adj. **striking**, arresting, conspicuous, dramatic, impressive, spectacular, breathtaking, dazzling, amazing, stunning, sensational, remarkable, distinctive, unusual, out of the ordinary.

eyesore n. **ugly sight**, blot (on the landscape), mess, scar, blight, disfigurement, blemish, monstrosity; informal sight.

eyewitness n. **observer**, onlooker, witness, bystander, spectator, watcher, viewer, passer-by; literary beholder.

e

Ff

fable n. **1** *the fable of the wary fox* **tale**, parable, allegory, apologue. **2** *the fables of ancient Greece* **myth**, legend, saga, epic, folk tale, folk story, fairy tale, mythos, mythus; folklore, mythology. **3** *it's a fable that I have a taste for fancy restaurants* **falsehood**, fib, fabrication, made-up story, invention, fiction, falsification, fairy story/tale, cock and bull story; lie, untruth, half-truth, exaggeration; story, rumour, myth; informal tall story; Brit. informal porky (pie).

fabled adj. **1** *a fabled god-giant of Irish myth* **legendary**, mythical, mythic, mythological, fabulous, folkloric, fairy-tale; fictitious, imaginary, imagined, made up. **2** *the fabled quality of French wine* **celebrated**, renowned, famed, famous, well known, prized, noted, notable, acclaimed, esteemed, prestigious, of repute, of high standing.

fabric n. **1** *the finest silk fabric* **cloth**, material, textile, tissue. **2** *the fabric of the building* **structure**, framework, frame, form, composition, construction, foundations.

> **WORD LINKS**
> **draper, mercer** a person who sells fabrics

fabricate v. **1** *he fabricated research data* **falsify**, fake, counterfeit; invent, make up. **2** *fabricating a pack of lies* **concoct**, make up, dream up, invent, trump up; informal cook up. **3** *you will have to fabricate an exhaust system* **make**, create, manufacture, produce; construct, build, assemble, put together, form, fashion.

fabrication n. **1** *the story was a complete fabrication* **invention**, concoction, (piece of) fiction, falsification, lie, untruth, falsehood, fib, myth, made-up story, fairy story/tale, cock and bull story; white lie, half-truth, exaggeration; informal tall story, whopper; Brit. informal porky (pie). **2** *the lintels are galvanized after fabrication* **manufacture**, creation, production; construction, building, assembly, forming, fashioning.

fabulous adj. **1** *fabulous salaries* **tremendous**, stupendous, prodigious, phenomenal, remarkable, exceptional; astounding, amazing, fantastic, breathtaking, staggering, unthinkable, unimaginable, incredible, unbelievable, unheard of, untold, undreamed of, beyond one's wildest dreams; informal mind-boggling, mind-blowing. **2** informal *we had a fabulous time*. See **excellent**. **3** *a fabulous horse-like beast* **mythical**, legendary, mythic,

mythological, fabled, folkloric, fairy-tale; fictitious, imaginary, imagined, made up.

facade n. **1** *a half-timbered facade* **front**, frontage, face, elevation, exterior, outside. **2** *a facade of bonhomie* **show**, front, appearance, pretence, simulation, affectation, semblance, illusion, act, masquerade, charade, mask, cloak, veil, veneer.

face n. **1** *a beautiful face* **countenance**, physiognomy, features; informal mug; Brit. informal mush, dial, clock, phiz, phizog, boat race; N. Amer. informal puss, pan; literary visage, lineaments. **2** *her face grew sad* **(facial) expression**, look, appearance, air, manner, bearing, countenance, mien. **3** *he made a face at the sourness of the drink* **grimace**, scowl, wry face, wince, frown, glower, pout, moue. **4** *a cube has six faces* **side**, aspect, flank, surface, plane, facet, wall, elevation. **5** *a watch face* **dial**, display. **6** *changing the face of the industry* **(outward) appearance**, aspect, nature, image. **7** *he put on a brave face* **front**, show, display, act, appearance, facade, exterior, mask, masquerade, pretence, pose, veneer. **8** *criticism should never cause the recipient to lose face* **respect**, honour, esteem, regard, admiration, approbation, acclaim, approval, favour, appreciation, popularity, prestige, standing, status, dignity; self-respect, self-esteem.

▸ v. **1** *the hotel faces the sea* **look out on**, front on to, look towards, be facing, look over/across, overlook, give on to, be opposite (to). **2** *you'll just have to face facts* **accept**, become reconciled to, get used to, become accustomed to, adjust to, acclimatize oneself to; learn to live with, cope with, deal with, come to terms with, become resigned to. **3** *he faces a humiliating rejection* **be confronted by**, be faced with, encounter, experience, come into contact with, come up against. **4** *the problems facing our police force* **beset**, worry, distress, trouble, bother, confront; harass, oppress, vex, irritate, exasperate, strain, stress, tax; torment, plague, blight, bedevil, curse; formal discommode. **5** *he faced the challenge boldly* **brave**, face up to, encounter, meet (head-on), confront; oppose, resist, withstand. **6** *a wall faced with flint* **cover**, clad, veneer, overlay, surface, dress, laminate, coat, line.

□ **on the face of it** ostensibly, to all appearances, to all intents and purposes, at first glance, on the surface, superficially;

facelift n. **1** *she's planning to have a facelift* **cosmetic surgery**, plastic surgery. **2** informal *the theatre is reopening after a facelift* **renovation**, redecoration, refurbishment, revamp, makeover, overhaul, modernization, refit, restoration, repair, redevelopment, rebuilding, reconstruction; informal refurb.

facet n. **1** *the many facets of the gem* **surface**, face, side, plane. **2** *other facets of his character* **aspect**, feature, side, dimension, characteristic, detail, point, ingredient, strand; component, constituent, element.

facetious adj. **flippant**, flip, glib, frivolous, tongue-in-cheek, joking, jokey, jocular, playful, sportive, teasing, mischievous; witty, amusing, funny, droll, comic, comical, light-hearted; formal jocose.
– OPPOSITES serious.

facile adj. **1** *a facile explanation* **simplistic**, superficial, oversimplified; shallow, glib, jejune, naive; N. Amer. dime-store. **2** *he achieved a facile victory* **effortless**, easy, undemanding, painless, trouble-free; Brit. informal easy-peasy.

facilitate v. **make easy/easier**, ease, make possible, make smooth/smoother, smooth the way for, enable, assist, help (along), aid, oil the wheels of, expedite, speed up, accelerate, forward, advance, promote, further, encourage.
– OPPOSITES impede.

facility n. **1** *car-parking facilities* **provision**, space, means, potential, equipment. **2** *the camera has a zoom facility* **feature**, option, setting; mode. **3** *a wealth of local facilities* **amenity**, resource, service, advantage, convenience, benefit. **4** *a medical facility* **establishment**, centre, place, station, location, premises, site, post, base; informal joint, outfit, set-up. **5** *his facility for drawing* **aptitude**, talent, gift, flair, bent, skill, knack, genius; ability, proficiency, competence, capability, capacity, faculty; expertness, adeptness, prowess, mastery, artistry. **6** *I was turning out poetry with facility* **ease**, effortlessness, no difficulty, no trouble, facileness; deftness, adroitness, dexterity, proficiency, mastery.

facing n. **1** *green velvet facings* **covering**, trimming, lining, interfacing. **2** *brick facing on a concrete core* **cladding**, veneer, skin, surface, facade, front, coating, covering, dressing, overlay, lamination, plating; N. Amer. siding.

facsimile n. **copy**, reproduction, duplicate, photocopy, mimeograph, photostat, replica, likeness, carbon copy, print, reprint, offprint, autotype; fax, telefax; trademark Xerox.
– OPPOSITES original.

fact n. **1** *it is a fact that the water is polluted* **reality**, actuality, certainty; truth, verity, gospel. **2** *every fact was double-checked* **detail**, piece of information, particular, item, specific, element, point, factor, feature, characteristic, ingredient, circumstance, aspect, facet; (**facts**) information. **3** *an accessory after the fact* **event**, happening, occurrence, incident, act, deed.
– OPPOSITES lie, fiction.
□ **in fact** actually, in actuality, in actual fact, really, in reality, in point of fact, as a matter of fact, in truth, to tell the truth; old use in sooth, verily.

faction n. **1** *a faction of the Liberal Party* **clique**, coterie, caucus, cabal, bloc, camp, group, grouping, sector, section, wing, arm, branch, set; ginger group, pressure group. **2** *the council was split by faction* **infighting**, dissension, dissent, dispute, discord, strife, conflict, friction, argument, disagreement, controversy, quarrelling, wrangling, bickering, squabbling, disharmony, disunity, schism.

factious adj. **divided**, split, schismatic, discordant, conflicting, argumentative, disagreeing, disputatious, quarrelling, quarrelsome, clashing, warring, at loggerheads, at odds, rebellious, mutinous.
– OPPOSITES harmonious.

factitious adj. **bogus**, fake, specious, false, counterfeit, fraudulent, spurious, sham, mock, feigned, affected, pretended, contrived, engineered; informal phoney, pseudo, pretend; Brit. informal cod.
– OPPOSITES genuine.

factor n. **element**, part, component, ingredient, strand, constituent, point, detail, item, feature, facet, aspect, characteristic, consideration, influence, circumstance.

factory n. **works**, plant, yard, mill, industrial unit; workshop, shop; old use manufactory.

factotum n. **odd-job man**, handyman, man/maid of all work, jack of all trades, man/girl Friday; Austral. knockabout; informal (Mr) Fixit.

factual adj. **truthful**, true, accurate, authentic, historical, genuine, fact-based; true-to-life, correct, exact, honest, faithful, literal, verbatim, word for word, unbiased, objective, unvarnished; formal veridical.
– OPPOSITES fictitious.

faculty n. **1** *the faculty of speech* **power**, capability, capacity, facility, wherewithal, means; (**faculties**) senses, wits, reason, intelligence. **2** *an unusual faculty for unearthing contributors* **ability**, proficiency, competence, capability, potential, capacity, facility; aptitude, talent, gift, flair, bent, skill, knack, genius; expertise, expertness, adeptness, adroitness, dexterity, prowess, mastery, artistry. **3** *the arts faculty* **department**, school, division, section. **4** *the vicar introduced certain ornaments without the faculty to do so* **authorization**, authority, power, right, permission, consent, leave, sanction, licence, dispensation, assent, acquiescence, agreement, approval, endorsement, clearance; informal the go-ahead, the thumbs up, the OK, the green light, say-so.

f

fad n. **craze**, vogue, trend, fashion, mode, enthusiasm, passion, obsession, mania, rage, compulsion, fixation, fetish, fancy, whim, fascination; informal thing.

faddy adj. Brit. informal **fussy**, finicky, faddish, over-particular, over-fastidious, dainty; informal picky, pernickety; N. Amer. informal persnickety; old use nice.

fade v. **1** *the paintwork has faded* **become pale**, become bleached, lose colour, discolour; grow dull, grow dim. **2** *sunlight had faded the picture* **bleach**, wash out, blanch, whiten, dim, dull. **3** *remove the flower heads as they fade* **wither**, wilt, droop, shrivel, die. **4** *the afternoon light began to fade* **(grow) dim**, grow faint, fail, dwindle, die away, wane, disappear, vanish, melt away; literary evanesce. **5** *the Communist movement was fading away* **decline**, die out, diminish, deteriorate, decay, crumble, collapse, fail, fall, sink, slump, go downhill; informal go to pot, go to the dogs; old use retrograde.
– OPPOSITES brighten, increase.

fag[1] Brit. informal n. *it's too much of a fag!* **chore**, slog, grind, bother, bore; informal pain, sweat.
– OPPOSITES pleasure.
▸ v. *we fagged away all day* **toil**, slave, slog, labour, grind, work hard; informal work one's socks off; Brit. informal graft; Austral./NZ informal bullock; literary travail.
□ **fag someone out** exhaust, tire (out), wear out, fatigue, overtire, weary; informal do in, wipe out, knock out, shatter; Brit. informal knacker; N. Amer. informal poop, tucker out.

fag[2] n. Brit. informal *he was smoking a fag* **cigarette**, filter tip, king-size; informal ciggy, cig, smoke, cancer stick, coffin nail; Brit. informal snout, roll-up.

fagged adj. informal **exhausted**, tired (out), worn out, fatigued, weary, drained, washed out; informal done in, all in, dead beat, dead on one's feet, shattered, bushed; Brit. informal knackered; N. Amer. informal tuckered, pooped.

fail v. **1** *the enterprise had failed* **be unsuccessful**, not succeed, fall through, fall flat, collapse, founder, backfire, meet with disaster, come to nothing/naught; informal flop, bomb. **2** *he failed his examination* **be unsuccessful in**, not pass; not make the grade; informal flunk. **3** *his friends had failed him* **let down**, disappoint; desert, abandon, betray; be disloyal to; literary forsake. **4** *the crops failed* **not grow**, wither. **5** *the daylight failed* **fade**, dim, die away, wane, disappear, vanish. **6** *the ventilation system failed* **break (down)**, stop working, cut out, crash; malfunction, go wrong; informal conk out, go on the blink; Brit. informal pack up, play up. **7** *Ceri's health was failing* **deteriorate**, degenerate, decline, fade, wane, ebb. **8** *900 businesses are failing a week* **collapse**, crash, go under, go bankrupt, go into receivership, go into liquidation, cease trading, be wound up; informal fold, flop, flatline, go bust, go broke, go to the wall.
– OPPOSITES succeed, pass, thrive, work.
□ **without fail** without exception, unfailingly, regularly, invariably, predictably, conscientiously, religiously, whatever happened, no matter what.

failing n. *Jeanne accepted him despite his failings* **fault**, shortcoming, weakness, imperfection, defect, flaw, frailty, foible, idiosyncrasy, vice.
– OPPOSITES strength.
▸ prep. *failing financial assistance, you will be bankrupt* **in the absence of**, lacking, notwithstanding.

failure n. **1** *the failure of the assassination attempt* **lack of success**, non-fulfilment, defeat, collapse, foundering. **2** *all his schemes had been a failure* **fiasco**, debacle, catastrophe, disaster; informal flop, washout, dead loss, fail; N. Amer. informal snafu, clinker. **3** *she was regarded as a failure* **loser**, underachiever, ne'er-do-well, disappointment; informal no-hoper, dead loss. **4** *a failure in duty* **negligence**, remissness, dereliction; omission, oversight. **5** *a crop failure* **inadequacy**, insufficiency, deficiency. **6** *the failure of the camera* **breaking down**, breakdown, malfunction; crash. **7** *company failures* **collapse**, crash, bankruptcy, insolvency, liquidation, closure.
– OPPOSITES success.

faint adj. **1** *a faint mark* **indistinct**, vague, unclear, indefinite, ill-defined, imperceptible, unobtrusive; pale, light, faded. **2** *a faint cry* **quiet**, muted, muffled, stifled; feeble, weak, whispered, murmured, indistinct; low, soft, gentle. **3** *a faint possibility* **slight**, slender, slim, small, tiny, negligible, remote, vague, unlikely, improbable; informal minuscule. **4** *faint praise* **unenthusiastic**, half-hearted, weak, feeble. **5** *I suddenly felt faint* **dizzy**, giddy, light-headed, unsteady; informal woozy.
– OPPOSITES clear, loud, strong.
▸ v. *she thought he would faint* **pass out**, lose consciousness, black out, keel over, swoon; informal flake out, conk out, zonk out, go out like a light.
▸ n. *a dead faint* **blackout**, fainting fit, loss of consciousness, swoon; Medicine syncope.

faint-hearted adj. **timid**, timorous, nervous, nervy, easily scared, fearful, afraid; cowardly, craven, spineless, pusillanimous, lily-livered; informal chicken, chicken-hearted, yellow, yellow-bellied, gutless, sissy, wimpy, wimpish; old use recreant.
– OPPOSITES brave.

fair[1] adj. **1** *the courts were generally fair* **just**, equitable, honest, upright, honourable, trustworthy; impartial, unbiased, unprejudiced, non-partisan, neutral, even-handed; lawful, legal, legitimate; informal legit, on the level; N. Amer. informal on the up and up. **2** *fair weather* **fine**, dry, bright, clear, sunny, cloudless; warm, balmy, clement, benign, pleasant. **3** *fair winds* **favourable**, advantageous, benign; on one's side, in one's favour. **4** *fair hair* **blond(e)**, yellowish, golden, flaxen, light, light brown, tow-coloured, ash blonde; fair-haired, light-haired, golden-haired. **5** *fair skin* **pale**, light,

light-coloured, white, creamy. **6** old use *the fair maiden's heart*. See **beautiful**. **7** *a fair achievement* **reasonable**, passable, tolerable, satisfactory, acceptable, respectable, decent, all right, good enough, pretty good, not bad, average, middling; informal OK, so-so.
– OPPOSITES inclement, unfavourable, dark.
□ **fair and square** honestly, fairly, without cheating, by the book; lawfully, legally, legitimately; informal on the level; N. Amer. informal on the up and up.

fair² n. **1** *a country fair* **fete**, gala, festival, carnival. **2** *an antiques fair* **market**, bazaar, mart, exchange, sale; old use emporium. **3** *a new art fair* **exhibition**, display, show, presentation, exposition; N. Amer. exhibit.

fairly adv. **1** *all pupils were treated fairly* **justly**, equitably, impartially, without bias, without prejudice, even-handedly; lawfully, legally, legitimately, by the book; equally, the same. **2** *the pipes are in fairly good condition* **reasonably**, passably, tolerably, adequately, moderately, quite, relatively, comparatively; informal pretty, kind of, sort of. **3** *he fairly hauled her along the street* **positively**, really, veritably, simply, actually, absolutely; practically, almost, nearly, all but; informal plain.

fair-minded adj. **fair**, just, even-handed, equitable, impartial, non-partisan, unbiased, unprejudiced; honest, honourable, trustworthy, upright, decent; informal on the level; N. Amer. informal on the up and up.

fairy n. **sprite**, pixie, elf, imp, brownie, puck, leprechaun, pishogue, nixie; literary faerie, fay.

fairy tale, **fairy story** n. **1** *the film was inspired by a fairy tale* **folk tale**, folk story, traditional story, myth, legend, fantasy, fable. **2** informal *she accused him of telling fairy tales* **(white) lie**, fib, half-truth, untruth, falsehood, (tall) story, fabrication, invention, piece of fiction; informal whopper, cock and bull story; Brit. informal porky (pie).

faith n. **1** *he justified his boss's faith in him* **trust**, belief, confidence, conviction; optimism, hopefulness, hope. **2** *she gave her life for her faith* **religion**, church, sect, denomination, (religious) persuasion, (religious) belief, ideology, creed, teaching, doctrine.
– OPPOSITES mistrust.
□ **break faith with** be disloyal to, be unfaithful to, be untrue to, betray, play someone false, break one's promise to, fail, let down; double-cross, deceive, cheat, stab in the back; informal do the dirty on.
keep faith with be loyal to, be faithful to, be true to, stand by, stick by, keep one's promise to.

faithful adj. **1** *his faithful assistant* **loyal**, constant, true, devoted, true-blue, unswerving, staunch, steadfast, dedicated, committed; trusty, trustworthy, dependable, reliable. **2** *a faithful copy* **accurate**, precise, exact, errorless, unerring, faultless, true, close, strict; realistic, authentic; informal on the mark, on the nail; Brit. informal spot on,

bang on; N. Amer. informal on the money.
– OPPOSITES inaccurate.

faithless adj. **1** *her faithless lover* **unfaithful**, disloyal, inconstant, false, untrue, adulterous, traitorous; fickle, flighty, untrustworthy, unreliable, undependable; deceitful, two-faced, double-crossing; informal cheating, two-timing, back-stabbing; literary perfidious. **2** *the natives were faithless* **unbelieving**, non-believing, irreligious, disbelieving, agnostic, atheistic; pagan, heathen; rare nullifidian.

fake n. **1** *the sculpture was a fake* **forgery**, counterfeit, copy, pirate(d) copy, sham, fraud, hoax, imitation, mock-up, dummy, reproduction; informal phoney, rip-off, dupe. **2** *that doctor is a fake* **charlatan**, quack, mountebank, sham, fraud, humbug, impostor, hoaxer, cheat, (confidence) trickster, fraudster; informal phoney, con man, con artist.
▸ adj. **1** *fake banknotes* **counterfeit**, forged, fraudulent, sham, imitation, pirate(d), false, bogus; invalid; informal phoney, dud. **2** *fake diamonds* **imitation**, artificial, synthetic, simulated, reproduction, faux, replica, ersatz, man-made, dummy, false, mock, bogus; informal pretend, phoney, pseudo. **3** *a fake accent* **feigned**, faked, put-on, assumed, invented, affected, pseudo; unconvincing, artificial, mock; informal phoney, pseud; Brit. informal cod.
– OPPOSITES genuine, authentic.
▸ v. **1** *the certificate was faked* **forge**, counterfeit, falsify, mock up, copy, pirate, reproduce, replicate; doctor, alter, tamper with. **2** *he faked a yawn* **feign**, pretend, simulate, put on, make-believe, affect.

fall v. **1** *bombs began to fall* **drop**, descend, come down, go down; plummet, plunge, sink, dive, tumble; cascade. **2** *he tripped and fell* **topple over**, tumble over, keel over, fall down/over, go head over heels, go headlong, collapse, take a spill, pitch forward; trip (over), stumble, slip; informal come a cropper; Brit. informal go for six. **3** *the river began to fall* **subside**, recede, ebb, flow back, fall away, go down, sink. **4** *inflation will fall* **decrease**, decline, diminish, fall off, drop off, lessen, dwindle; plummet, plunge, slump, sink; depreciate, cheapen, devalue; informal go through the floor, nosedive, crash. **5** *those who fell in the war* **die**, perish, lose one's life, be killed, be slain, be lost, meet one's death; informal bite the dust, croak, buy it; Brit. informal snuff it; old use decease. **6** *the town fell to the barbarians* **surrender**, yield, submit, give in, capitulate, succumb; be taken by, be defeated by, be conquered by, be overwhelmed by. **7** *Easter falls on 23rd April* **occur**, take place, happen, come about; arise; literary come to pass. **8** *night fell* **come**, arrive, appear, arise, materialize. **9** *she fell ill* **become**, grow, get, turn. **10** *more tasks may fall to him* **be the responsibility of**, be the duty of, be borne by, be one's job; come someone's way.
– OPPOSITES rise, flood, increase.

▶ n. **1** *an accidental fall* **tumble**, trip, spill, topple, slip; collapse; informal nosedive, header, cropper. **2** *a fall in sales* **decline**, fall-off, drop, decrease, cut, dip, reduction, downswing; plummet, plunge, slump; informal nosedive, crash. **3** *the fall of the Roman Empire* **downfall**, collapse, ruin, ruination; failure, decline, deterioration, degeneration; destruction, overthrow, demise. **4** *the fall of the city* **surrender**, capitulation, yielding, submission; defeat. **5** *a steep fall down to the ocean* **descent**, declivity, slope, slant, incline; N. Amer. downgrade. **6** *the fall of man* **sin**, wrongdoing, transgression, error, offence, lapse, fall from grace. **7** *rafting trips below the falls* **waterfall**, cascade, cataract; rapids, white water.
– OPPOSITES increase, rise, ascent.
▫ **fall apart** fall/come to pieces, fall/come to bits, come apart (at the seams); disintegrate, fragment, break up, break apart, crumble, decay, perish; informal bust.
fall asleep doze off, drop off, go to sleep; informal nod off, go off, drift off, crash (out), flake out, conk out, go out like a light; N. Amer. informal sack out.
fall back retreat, withdraw, back off, draw back, pull back, pull away, move away.
fall back on resort to, turn to, look to, call on, have recourse to; rely on, depend on, lean on.
fall behind 1 *the other walkers fell behind* **lag (behind)**, trail (behind), be left behind, drop back, bring up the rear; straggle, dally, dawdle, hang back. **2** *they fell behind on their payments* **get into debt**, get into arrears, default.
fall for informal **1** *she fell for John* **fall in love with**, become infatuated with, lose one's heart to, take a fancy to, be smitten by, be attracted to; informal fancy, have the hots for. **2** *she won't fall for that trick* **be deceived by**, be duped by, be fooled by, be taken in by, believe, trust, be convinced by; informal go for, buy, swallow (hook, line, and sinker).
fall in 1 *the roof fell in* **collapse**, cave in, crash in, fall down; give way, crumble, disintegrate. **2** *the troops fell in* **get in formation**, get in line, line up, take one's position; Military dress.
fall in with 1 *he fell in with a bad crowd* **get involved with**, take up with, join up with, go around with, string along with, make friends with; informal hang out/about with. **2** *he won't fall in with their demands* **comply with**, go along with, support, cooperate with, obey, yield to, submit to, bow to, defer to, adhere to, conform to; agree to, agree with, accept, concur with.
fall off See **fall** (sense 4 of the verb).
fall on attack, assail, assault, fly at, set about, set upon; pounce on, ambush, surprise, rush, storm, charge; informal jump, lay into, pitch into, beat someone up; Brit. informal have a go at.
fall out 1 *let's not fall out* **quarrel**, argue, row, fight, squabble, bicker, have words, disagree, be at odds, clash, wrangle, cross

swords, lock horns, be at loggerheads, be at each other's throats; informal scrap, argufy, argy-bargy. **2** *the soldiers fell out* **move out of formation**, move out of line; stand at ease.
fall short of fail to meet, fail to reach, fail to live up to; be deficient, be inadequate, be insufficient, be wanting, be lacking, disappoint; informal not come up to scratch.
fall through fail, be unsuccessful, come to nothing, miscarry, abort, go awry, collapse, founder, come to grief; informal fizzle out, flop, fold, come a cropper, go down like a lead balloon.

fallacious adj. **erroneous**, false, untrue, wrong, incorrect, flawed, inaccurate, mistaken, misinformed, misguided; specious, spurious, bogus, fictitious, fabricated, made up; groundless, unfounded, unproven, unsupported, uncorroborated; informal phoney, full of holes, off beam.
– OPPOSITES correct.

fallacy n. **misconception**, misbelief, delusion, mistaken impression, misapprehension, misinterpretation, misconstruction, error, mistake; untruth, inconsistency, myth.

fallen adj. **1** *fallen heroes* **dead**, perished, killed, slain, slaughtered, murdered; lost, late, lamented, departed, gone; formal deceased; rare demised. **2** dated *fallen women* **immoral**, loose, promiscuous, unchaste, sinful, impure, sullied, tainted, dishonoured, ruined.

fallible adj. **prone to error**, liable to err; imperfect, flawed, weak.

fallow adj. **1** *fallow farmland* **uncultivated**, unploughed, untilled, unplanted, unsown; unused, dormant, resting, empty, bare. **2** *a fallow trading period* **inactive**, dormant, quiet, slack, slow, stagnant; barren, unproductive.
– OPPOSITES cultivated, busy.

false adj. **1** *a false report* **incorrect**, untrue, wrong, erroneous, fallacious, flawed, distorted, inaccurate, imprecise; untruthful, fictitious, concocted, fabricated, invented, made up, trumped up, unfounded, spurious; counterfeit, forged, fraudulent. **2** *a false friend* **faithless**, unfaithful, disloyal, untrue, inconstant, treacherous, traitorous, two-faced, double-crossing, deceitful, dishonest, duplicitous, untrustworthy, unreliable; untruthful; informal cheating, two-timing, back-stabbing; literary perfidious. **3** *false pearls* **fake**, artificial, imitation, synthetic, simulated, reproduction, faux, replica, ersatz, man-made, dummy, mock; informal phoney, pretend, pseudo.
– OPPOSITES correct, truthful, faithful, genuine.

falsehood n. **1** *a downright falsehood* **lie**, untruth, fib, falsification, fabrication, invention, fiction, story, cock and bull story, flight of fancy; half truth; informal tall story, tall tale, fairy story, fairy tale, whopper; Brit. informal porky (pie); humorous terminological

inexactitude. **2** *he accused me of falsehood*
lying, mendacity, untruthfulness, fibbing,
fabrication, invention, perjury, telling
stories; deceit, deception, pretence, artifice,
double-crossing, treachery; literary perfidy.
– OPPOSITES truth, honesty.

falsify v. **1** *she falsified the accounts* **forge**,
fake, counterfeit, fabricate; alter, change,
doctor, tamper with, fudge, manipulate,
adulterate, corrupt, misrepresent, misreport,
distort, warp, embellish, embroider. **2** *the
theory is falsified by the evidence* **disprove**,
refute, rebut, deny, debunk, negate,
negative, invalidate, contradict, controvert,
confound, demolish, discredit; informal shoot
full of holes, blow out of the water; formal
confute, gainsay.

falsity n. **untruthfulness**, untruth,
fallaciousness, falseness, falsehood,
fictitiousness, inaccuracy; mendacity,
fabrication, dishonesty, deceit.

falter v. **1** *the government faltered* **hesitate**,
delay, drag one's feet, stall; waver, vacillate,
be indecisive, be irresolute, blow hot and
cold; Brit. haver, hum and haw; informal sit on
the fence, dilly-dally, shilly-shally. **2** *she
faltered over his name* **stumble**, stutter,
stammer; hesitate, flounder.

fame n. **renown**, celebrity, stardom,
popularity, prominence; note, distinction,
esteem, importance, account, consequence,
greatness, eminence, prestige, stature,
repute; notoriety, infamy.
– OPPOSITES obscurity.

famed adj. **famous**, celebrated, well known,
prominent, noted, notable, renowned,
respected, esteemed, acclaimed; notorious,
infamous.
– OPPOSITES unknown.

familiar adj. **1** *a familiar task* **well known**,
recognized, accustomed; common,
commonplace, everyday, day-to-day,
ordinary, habitual, usual, customary, routine,
standard, stock, mundane, run-of-the-mill;
literary wonted. **2** *are you familiar with the
subject?* **acquainted**, conversant, versed,
knowledgeable, well informed; skilled,
proficient, at home with, no stranger to, au
fait with, au courant with; informal well up
on, in the know about, genned up on, clued
up on. **3** *a familiar atmosphere* **informal**,
casual, relaxed, easy, comfortable; friendly,
unceremonious, unreserved, open, natural,
unpretentious. **4** *he is too familiar with
the teachers* **overfamiliar**, presumptuous,
disrespectful, forward, bold, impudent,
impertinent.
– OPPOSITES formal.

familiarity n. **1** *he wants greater familiarity
with politics* **acquaintance with**, awareness
of, experience of, insight into, conversancy
with, conversance with; knowledge of,
understanding of, comprehension of,
grasp of, skill in, proficiency in. **2** *she was
affronted by his familiarity* **overfamiliarity**,
presumption, presumptuousness,
forwardness, boldness, audacity, cheek,

impudence, impertinence, disrespect;
liberties. **3** *our familiarity allows us to tease
each other* **closeness**, intimacy, attachment,
affinity, friendliness, friendship, amity;
informal chumminess, palliness; Brit. informal
mateyness.

familiarize v. **acquaint**, make familiar,
make conversant; accustom, habituate,
instruct, teach, educate, school, prime,
introduce; informal clue up, put in the picture,
give the low-down, fill in.

family n. **1** *I met his family* **relatives**,
relations, (next of) kin, kinsfolk, kindred,
one's (own) flesh and blood, nearest and
dearest, people, connections; extended
family; clan, tribe; informal folks. **2** *he had the
right kind of family* **ancestry**, parentage,
pedigree, genealogy, background, family
tree, descent, lineage, bloodline, blood,
extraction, stock; forebears, forefathers,
antecedents, roots, origins. **3** *she is
married with a family* **children**, little ones,
youngsters; offspring, progeny, descendants,
scions, heirs; brood; Law issue; informal kids,
kiddies, tots. **4** *the weaver bird family*
taxonomic group, order, class, genus,
species; stock, strain, line; Zoology phylum.

family tree n. **ancestry**, genealogy,
descent, lineage, line, bloodline, pedigree,
background, extraction, derivation; family,
dynasty, house; forebears, forefathers,
antecedents, roots, origins.

famine n. **1** *a nation threatened by famine*
scarcity of food, food shortages. **2** *the
cotton famine* **shortage**, scarcity, lack,
dearth, deficiency, insufficiency, shortfall,
scantiness, paucity, poverty, drought.
– OPPOSITES plenty.

famished adj. **ravenous**, hungry, starving,
starved, empty, unfed; informal peckish.
– OPPOSITES full.

famous adj. **well known**, prominent,
famed, popular; renowned, noted, eminent,
distinguished, esteemed, celebrated,
respected; of distinction, of repute;
illustrious, acclaimed, great, legendary,
lionized; notorious, infamous.
– OPPOSITES unknown.

fan[1] n. *a ceiling fan* **air-cooler**, air
conditioner, ventilator, blower, aerator.
▶ v. **1** *she fanned her face* **cool**, aerate,
ventilate; freshen, refresh. **2** *they fanned
public fears* **intensify**, increase, agitate,
inflame, exacerbate; stimulate, stir up, whip
up, fuel, kindle, spark, arouse. **3** *the police
squad fanned out* **spread**, branch; outspread.

fan[2] n. *a basketball fan* **enthusiast**, devotee,
admirer, lover; supporter, follower, disciple,
adherent, zealot; expert, connoisseur,
aficionado; informal buff, fiend, freak, nut,
addict, fanatic, groupie; N. Amer. informal jock.

fanatic n. **1** *a religious fanatic* **zealot**,
extremist, militant, dogmatist, devotee,
adherent, sectarian, bigot, partisan, radical,
diehard, ultra; informal maniac. **2** informal *a
keep-fit fanatic*. See **fan**[2].

f

fanatical adj. **1** *they are fanatical about their faith* **zealous**, extremist, extreme, militant, dogmatic, radical, diehard; intolerant, single-minded, blinkered, inflexible, uncompromising. **2** *he was fanatical about tidiness* **enthusiastic**, eager, keen, fervent, ardent, passionate; obsessive, obsessed, fixated, compulsive; informal wild, gung-ho, nuts, crazy; Brit. informal potty.

fancier n. *a pigeon fancier* **enthusiast**, lover, hobbyist; expert, connoisseur, aficionado; breeder; informal buff.

fanciful adj. **1** *a fanciful story* **fantastic**, far-fetched, unbelievable, extravagant; ridiculous, absurd, preposterous; imaginary, made-up, make-believe, mythical, fabulous; informal tall, hard to swallow. **2** *a fanciful girl* **imaginative**, inventive; whimsical, impractical, dreamy, quixotic; in a world of one's own. **3** *a fanciful building* **ornate**, exotic, fancy, imaginative, extravagant, fantastic; curious, bizarre, eccentric, unusual.
– OPPOSITES literal, practical.

fancy v. **1** Brit. informal *I fancied a change of scene* **wish for**, want, desire; long for, yearn for, crave, thirst for, hanker after, dream of, covet; informal have a yen for; old use be desirous of. **2** Brit. informal *she fancied him* **be attracted to**, find attractive, be infatuated with, be taken with, desire; lust after, burn for; informal have a crush on, have the hots for, be crazy about, have a thing about, have a soft spot for, carry a torch for. **3** *I fancied I could see lights* **think**, imagine, believe, be of the opinion, be under the impression; informal reckon.
▸ adj. *fancy clothes* **elaborate**, ornate, ornamental, decorative, adorned, embellished, intricate; ostentatious, showy, flamboyant; luxurious, lavish, extravagant, expensive; informal flash, flashy, bling, jazzy, ritzy, snazzy, posh, classy; Brit. informal swish.
– OPPOSITES plain.
▸ n. **1** *his fancy to own a farm* **desire**, urge, wish; inclination, whim, impulse, notion, whimsy; yearning, longing, hankering, craving; informal yen, itch. **2** *I've a fancy they want to be alone* **idea**, notion, thought, supposition, opinion, belief, impression, understanding; feeling, suspicion, hunch, inkling.

fanfare n. **1** *a fanfare announced her arrival* **trumpet call**, flourish, fanfaronade; old use trump. **2** *the project was greeted with great fanfare* **fuss**, commotion, show, display, ostentation, flashiness, pageantry, splendour; informal ballyhoo, hype, pizzazz, razzle-dazzle, glitz.

fantasize v. **daydream**, dream, muse, make-believe, pretend, imagine; build castles in the air, build castles in Spain, live in a dream world.

fantastic adj. **1** *a fantastic notion* **fanciful**, extravagant, extraordinary, irrational, wild, absurd, far-fetched, nonsensical, incredible, unbelievable, unthinkable, implausible, improbable, unlikely, doubtful, dubious; strange, peculiar, odd, queer, weird, eccentric, whimsical, capricious; visionary, romantic; informal crazy, cockeyed, off the wall. **2** *his fantastic accuracy* **tremendous**, remarkable, great, terrific, impressive, outstanding, phenomenal. **3** *fantastic shapes* **strange**, weird, bizarre, outlandish, queer, peculiar, grotesque, freakish, surreal, exotic; elaborate, ornate, intricate. **4** informal *a fantastic car* **marvellous**, wonderful, sensational, outstanding, superb, excellent, first-rate, first-class, dazzling, out of this world, breathtaking; informal great, terrific, fabulous, fab, mega, super, ace, magic, cracking, cool, wicked, awesome; Brit. informal brilliant, brill, smashing; Austral./NZ informal bonzer; Brit. informal dated spiffing.
– OPPOSITES rational, ordinary.

fantasy n. **1** *a mix of fantasy and realism* **imagination**, fancy, invention, make-believe; creativity, vision; daydreaming, reverie. **2** *his fantasy about being famous* **dream**, daydream, pipe dream, fanciful notion, wish; fond hope, chimera, delusion, illusion; informal pie in the sky.
– OPPOSITES realism.

far adv. **1** *we are far from the palace* **a long way**, a great distance, a good way; afar. **2** *her charm far outweighs any flaws* **much**, considerably, markedly, immeasurably, greatly, significantly, substantially, appreciably, noticeably; to a great extent, by a long way, by far, by a mile, easily.
– OPPOSITES near.
▸ adj. **1** *far places* **distant**, faraway, far-off, remote, out of the way, far-flung, outlying. **2** *the far side of the campus* **further**, more distant; opposite.
– OPPOSITES near.
▫ **by far** by a great amount, by a good deal, by a long way, by a mile, far and away; undoubtedly, without doubt, without question, positively, absolutely, easily; significantly, substantially, appreciably, much; Brit. by a long chalk.
far and away See **by far**.
far and wide everywhere, {here, there, and everywhere}, all over (the world), throughout the land, worldwide; informal all over the place.
far from *staff were far from happy* not, not at all, nowhere near; the opposite of.
go far be successful, succeed, prosper, flourish, thrive, get on (in the world), make good, set the world on fire; informal make a name for oneself, make one's mark, go places, do all right for oneself, find a place in the sun.
go too far go over the top, go to extremes, go overboard.
so far 1 *nobody has noticed so far* **until now**, up to now, up to this point, as yet, thus far, hitherto, up to the present, to date. **2** *his liberalism only extends so far* **to a certain extent**, up to a point, to a degree, within reason, within limits.

faraway adj. **1** *faraway places* **distant**, far off, far, remote, far-flung, outlying, exotic;

obscure, out of the way, off the beaten track. **2** *a faraway look in her eyes* **dreamy**, daydreaming, abstracted, absent-minded, distracted, preoccupied, vague; lost in thought, somewhere else, not with us, in a world of one's own; informal **miles away**.
– OPPOSITES nearby.

farce n. **1** *the stories approach farce* **slapstick (comedy)**, burlesque, vaudeville, buffoonery. **2** *the trial was a farce* **mockery**, travesty, absurdity, sham, pretence, masquerade, charade, joke, waste of time; informal **shambles**.
– OPPOSITES tragedy.

farcical adj. **1** *the idea is farcical* **ridiculous**, preposterous, ludicrous, absurd, laughable, risible, nonsensical; senseless, pointless, useless; silly, foolish, idiotic, stupid, hare-brained; informal **crazy**; Brit. informal **barmy, daft**. **2** *farcical goings-on* **madcap**, zany, slapstick, comic, comical, clownish, amusing; hilarious, uproarious; informal **wacky**.

fare n. **1** *we paid the fare* **ticket price**; price, cost, charge, fee, toll, tariff. **2** *the taxi picked up a fare* **passenger**, traveller, customer; Brit. informal **punter**. **3** *they eat simple fare* **food**, meals, sustenance, nourishment, nutriment, foodstuffs, provender, eatables, provisions; cooking, cuisine; diet, table; informal **grub, nosh, eats, chow, scoff**; formal **comestibles, victuals**.
▶ v. *how are you faring?* **get on**, get along, cope, manage, do, muddle through/along, survive; informal **make out**.

farewell exclam. *farewell, Patrick!* **goodbye**, so long, adieu; au revoir, ciao; informal **bye, bye-bye, cheerio, see you (later), later(s)**; Brit. informal **ta-ta, cheers**; informal dated **toodle-oo, toodle-pip**.
▶ n. *an emotional farewell* **goodbye**, valediction, adieu; leave-taking, parting, departure; send-off.

far-fetched adj. **improbable**, unlikely, implausible, unconvincing, dubious, doubtful, incredible, unbelievable, unthinkable; contrived, fanciful, unrealistic, ridiculous, absurd, preposterous; informal **hard to swallow, fishy**.
– OPPOSITES likely.

farm n. *a farm of 100 acres* **smallholding**, farmstead, plantation, estate; farmland; Brit. **grange, croft**; Scottish **steading**; N. Amer. **ranch**; Austral./NZ **station**.
▶ v. **1** *he farmed locally* **be a farmer**, cultivate the land, work the land; rear livestock. **2** *they farm the land* **cultivate**, till, work, plough, dig, plant. **3** *the family farms sheep* **breed**, rear, keep, raise, tend.
□ **farm something out** contract out, outsource, subcontract, delegate.

farmer n. **agriculturalist**, agronomist, smallholder, grazier; farmhand; Brit. **crofter**; N. Amer. **rancher**; historical **yeoman**.

farming n. **agriculture**, cultivation, husbandry; agronomy, agribusiness; Brit. **crofting**.

far out adj. informal See **unconventional**.

farrago n. **hotchpotch**, mishmash, ragbag, potpourri, jumble, mess, confusion, melange, gallimaufry, hash, assortment, miscellany, mixture, conglomeration, medley; N. Amer. **hodgepodge**.

far-reaching adj. **extensive**, wide-ranging, comprehensive, widespread, all-embracing, overarching, across the board, sweeping, blanket, wholesale; important, significant, radical, major, consequential.
– OPPOSITES limited.

far-sighted adj. **prescient**, visionary, percipient, shrewd, discerning, judicious, canny, prudent.

farther adv. & adj. See **further**.

farthest adj. See **furthest**.

fascinate v. **interest**, captivate, engross, absorb, enchant, enthral, entrance, transfix, rivet, mesmerize, engage, compel; lure, tempt, entice, draw; charm, attract, intrigue, divert, entertain.
– OPPOSITES bore.

fascinating adj. **interesting**, captivating, engrossing, absorbing, enchanting, enthralling, spellbinding, riveting, engaging, compelling, compulsive, gripping, thrilling; alluring, tempting, irresistible; charming, attractive, intriguing, diverting, entertaining.

fascination n. **interest**, preoccupation, passion, obsession, compulsion; allure, lure, charm, attraction, intrigue, appeal, pull, draw.

fascism n. **authoritarianism**, totalitarianism, dictatorship, despotism, autocracy; Nazism, rightism; nationalism, xenophobia, racism, anti-Semitism, jingoism, isolationism; neo-fascism, neo-Nazism.

fascist n. *he was branded a fascist* **authoritarian**, totalitarian, autocrat, extreme right-winger, rightist; Nazi, blackshirt; nationalist, xenophobe, racist, anti-Semite, jingoist; neo-fascist, neo-Nazi.
– OPPOSITES liberal.
▶ adj. *a fascist regime* **authoritarian**, totalitarian, dictatorial, despotic, autocratic, undemocratic, anti-democratic, illiberal; Nazi, extreme right-wing, rightist, militarist; nationalist(ic), xenophobic, racist, jingoistic.
– OPPOSITES democratic.

fashion n. **1** *the fashion for tight clothes* **vogue**, trend, craze, rage, mania, fad; style, look; tendency, convention, custom, practice; informal **thing**. **2** *the world of fashion* **clothes**, clothing design, couture; informal **the rag trade**. **3** *it needs to be run in a sensible fashion* **manner**, way, method, mode, style; system, approach.
▶ v. *the model was fashioned from lead* **construct**, build, make, manufacture, fabricate, produce; cast, shape, form, mould, sculpt; forge, hew, carve.
□ **after a fashion** to a certain extent, in a way, somehow (or other), in a manner of speaking, in its way.
in fashion fashionable, in vogue, up to date, up to the minute, all the rage, chic, à la

f

mode; informal trendy, with it, cool, in, the in thing, hot, big, hip, happening, now, sharp, groovy; N. Amer. tony, fly; Brit. informal dated all the go.

out of fashion unfashionable, dated, old-fashioned, out of date, outdated, outmoded, behind the times; unstylish, unpopular, passé, démodé; informal old hat, out, square, out of the ark.

fashionable adj. **chic**, stylish, in vogue, voguish, in fashion, popular, (bang) up to date, up to the minute, modern, all the rage, modish, à la mode, trendsetting; informal trendy, classy, with it, cool, funky, in, the in thing, hot, big, hip, happening, now, sharp, groovy, snazzy; N. Amer. informal tony, fly; Brit. informal dated all the go.

fast[1] adj. **1** *a fast pace* **speedy**, quick, swift, rapid; fast-moving, high-speed, turbo, sporty; accelerated, express, blistering, breakneck, pell-mell; hasty, hurried; informal nippy, zippy, scorching, blinding, supersonic; Brit. informal cracking; literary fleet. **2** *he held the door fast* **secure**, fastened, tight, firm, closed, shut, to; immovable, unbudgeable. **3** *a fast colour* **indelible**, lasting, permanent, stable. **4** *fast friends* **loyal**, devoted, faithful, firm, steadfast, staunch, true, boon, bosom, inseparable; constant, enduring, unswerving. **5** *a fast woman* **promiscuous**, licentious, dissolute, debauched, impure, unchaste, wanton, abandoned, of easy virtue; sluttish, whorish; intemperate, immoderate, shameless, sinful, immoral; informal easy, tarty; Brit. informal slaggy; N. Amer. informal roundheeled; dated loose.
– OPPOSITES slow, loose, temporary, chaste.
▸ adv. **1** *she drove fast* **quickly**, rapidly, swiftly, speedily, briskly, at speed, at full tilt; hastily, hurriedly, in a hurry, post-haste, pell-mell; like a shot, like a flash, on the double, at the speed of light; informal double quick, p.d.q. (pretty damn quick), nippily, like (greased) lightning, hell for leather, like mad, like the wind, like a scalded cat, like a bat out of hell; Brit. informal like the clappers, at a rate of knots, like billy-o; N. Amer. informal lickety-split; literary apace. **2** *his wheels were stuck fast* **securely**, firmly, immovably, fixedly. **3** *he's fast asleep* **deeply**, sound, completely. **4** *she lived fast and dangerously* **wildly**, dissolutely, intemperately, immoderately, recklessly, self-indulgently, extravagantly.
– OPPOSITES slowly.

fast[2] v. *we must fast and pray* **eat nothing**, abstain from food, refrain from eating, go without food, go hungry, starve oneself; go on hunger strike.
– OPPOSITES eat.

fasten v. **1** *he fastened the door* **bolt**, lock, secure, make fast, chain, seal. **2** *they fastened splints to his leg* **attach**, fix, affix, clip, pin, tack; stick, bond, join. **3** *he fastened his horse to a tree* **tie (up)**, bind, tether, truss, fetter, lash, hitch, anchor, strap, rope. **4** *the dress fastens at the front* **button (up)**, zip (up), do up, close. **5** *his gaze fastened on me* **focus**, fix, be riveted, concentrate, zero in, zoom in,

direct at. **6** *critics fastened on the end of the report* **single out**, concentrate on, focus on, pick out, fix on, seize on.
– OPPOSITES unlock, remove, open, untie, undo.

fastidious adj. **scrupulous**, punctilious, painstaking, meticulous; perfectionist, fussy, finicky, over-particular; critical, overcritical, hypercritical, hard to please, exacting, demanding; informal pernickety, nitpicking, choosy, picky; N. Amer. informal persnickety.
– OPPOSITES lax.

fat adj. **1** *a fat man* **plump**, stout, overweight, large, chubby, portly, flabby, paunchy, pot-bellied, beer-bellied, meaty, of ample proportions; obese, corpulent, gross, fleshy; informal tubby, roly-poly, beefy, porky, blubbery, chunky; Brit. informal podgy, fubsy; old use pursy. **2** *fat bacon* **fatty**, greasy, oily, oleaginous; formal pinguid. **3** *a fat book* **thick**, big, chunky, substantial; long. **4** informal *a fat salary* **large**, substantial, sizeable, considerable; generous, lucrative.
– OPPOSITES thin, lean, small.
▸ n. **1** *whale fat* **blubber**, fatty tissue, adipose tissue. **2** *he was running to fat* **fatness**, plumpness, stoutness, chubbiness, tubbiness, portliness, podginess, flabbiness; obesity, corpulence; informal flab, blubber. **3** *eggs in sizzling fat* **oil**, grease; lard, suet, butter, margarine.

fatal adj. **1** *a fatal disease* **deadly**, lethal, mortal, death-dealing; terminal, incurable, untreatable, inoperable, malignant; literary deathly. **2** *a fatal mistake* **disastrous**, devastating, ruinous, catastrophic, calamitous, dire; costly; formal grievous.
– OPPOSITES harmless, beneficial.

fatalism n. **passive acceptance**, resignation, stoicism.

fatality n. **death**, casualty, mortality, victim; fatal accident.

fate n. **1** *what has fate in store for me?* **destiny**, providence, the stars, chance, luck, serendipity, fortune, kismet, karma. **2** *my fate was in their hands* **future**, destiny, outcome, end, lot. **3** *a similar fate would befall other killers* **death**, demise, end; retribution, sentence. **4** *the Fates will decide* **the weird sisters, the Parcae, the Moirai**.
▸ v. *his daughter was fated to face the same problem* **be predestined**, be preordained, be destined, be meant, be doomed; be sure, be certain, be bound, be guaranteed.

fateful adj. **1** *that fateful day* **decisive**, critical, crucial, pivotal; momentous, important, key, significant, historic, portentous. **2** *the fateful defeat of 1402* **disastrous**, ruinous, calamitous, devastating, tragic, terrible.
– OPPOSITES unimportant.

father n. **1** *his mother and father* **male parent**, patriarch, paterfamilias; informal dad, daddy, pop, pa, old man; Brit. informal dated pater. **2** literary *the religion of my fathers* **ancestor**, forefather, forebear, predecessor, antecedent, progenitor, primogenitor. **3** *the*

father of democracy **originator**, initiator, founder, inventor, creator, maker, author, architect. **4** *the city fathers* **leader**, elder, patriarch, official. **5** *our heavenly Father* **God**, Lord (God). **6** *pray for me, Father* **priest**, pastor, parson, clergyman, cleric, minister, preacher; informal reverend, padre.
– OPPOSITES child, mother, descendant.
▶v. **1** *he fathered six children* **be the father of**, sire, bring into the world, spawn, breed; literary beget; old use engender. **2** *he fathered a strand of applied economics* **establish**, institute, originate, initiate, invent, found, create.

WORD LINKS
paternal relating to a father
paternity fatherhood
patriarchy a form of social organization in which the father is head of the family
patrilineal based on relationship with the father or male line of descent
patricide the killing of one's father

fatherland n. **native land**, native country, homeland, mother country, motherland, land of one's birth.
fatherly adj. **paternal**, fatherlike; protective, supportive, encouraging, affectionate, caring, sympathetic, indulgent.
fathom v. **1** *Charlie tried to fathom her expression* **understand**, comprehend, work out, make sense of, grasp, divine, puzzle out, get to the bottom of; interpret, decipher, decode; informal make head or tail of, tumble to, crack; Brit. informal twig, suss (out), savvy. **2** *fathoming the ocean* **measure the depth of**, sound, plumb.
fatigue n. **1** *his face was grey with fatigue* **tiredness**, weariness, exhaustion, enervation, prostration. **2** Military *kitchen fatigues* **menial work**, drudgery, chores; informal skivvying.
– OPPOSITES energy.
▶v. *the troops were fatigued* **tire (out)**, exhaust, wear out, drain, weary, wash out, overtire, prostrate, enervate; informal knock out, take it out of, do in, fag out, whack, poop, shatter, bush, wear to a frazzle; Brit. informal knacker.
– OPPOSITES invigorate.
fatness n. **plumpness**, stoutness, heaviness, chubbiness, portliness, rotundity, flabbiness, paunchiness; obesity, corpulence; informal tubbiness, podginess.
– OPPOSITES thinness.
fatten v. **1** *fattening livestock* **make fat/fatter**, feed (up), build up. **2** *we're sending her home to fatten up* **put on weight**, gain weight, get heavier, grow fatter, fill out.
– OPPOSITES slim.
fatty adj. **greasy**, oily, fat, oleaginous.
– OPPOSITES lean.
fatuous adj. **silly**, foolish, stupid, inane, idiotic, vacuous, asinine; pointless, senseless, ridiculous, ludicrous, absurd; informal dumb, gormless; Brit. informal daft.
– OPPOSITES sensible.

fault n. **1** *he has his faults* **defect**, failing, imperfection, flaw, blemish, shortcoming, weakness, frailty, foible, vice. **2** *engineers have located the fault* **defect**, flaw, imperfection, bug; error, mistake, inaccuracy; informal glitch, gremlin. **3** *it was not my fault* **responsibility**, liability, culpability, blameworthiness, guilt. **4** *don't blame one child for another's faults* **misdeed**, wrongdoing, offence, misdemeanour, misconduct, indiscretion, peccadillo, transgression.
– OPPOSITES merit, strength.
▶v. *you couldn't fault any of the players* **find fault with**, criticize, attack, censure, condemn, reproach; complain about, quibble about, moan about; informal knock, slam, gripe about, beef about, pick holes in; Brit. informal slag off, have a go at, slate.
□ **at fault** to blame, blameworthy, culpable; responsible, guilty, in the wrong.
to a fault excessively, unduly, overly, immoderately, needlessly.
fault-finding n. **criticism**, captiousness, cavilling, quibbling; complaining, grumbling, carping, moaning; informal griping, grousing, bellyaching.
– OPPOSITES praise.
faultless adj. **perfect**, flawless, without fault, error-free, impeccable, accurate, precise, exact, correct, exemplary.
– OPPOSITES flawed.
faulty adj. **1** *a faulty electric blanket* **malfunctioning**, broken, damaged, defective, not working, out of order; informal on the blink, acting up, kaput, bust; Brit. informal knackered, playing up, duff; N. Amer. informal on the fritz. **2** *her logic is faulty* **defective**, flawed, unsound, inaccurate, incorrect, erroneous, fallacious, wrong.
– OPPOSITES working, sound.
faux pas n. **gaffe**, blunder, mistake, indiscretion, impropriety, solecism; informal boo-boo; Brit. informal boob; N. Amer. informal blooper.
favour n. **1** *will you do me a favour?* **good turn**, service, good deed, (act of) kindness, courtesy. **2** *she looked on him with favour* **approval**, approbation, goodwill, kindness, benevolence. **3** *they showed favour to one of the players* **favouritism**, bias, partiality, partisanship. **4** *you shall receive the king's favour* **patronage**, backing, support, assistance.
– OPPOSITES disservice, disapproval.
▶v. **1** *the party favours electoral reform* **advocate**, recommend, approve of, be in favour of, support, back, champion; campaign for, stand up for, press for, lobby for, promote; informal plug, push for. **2** *Robyn favours loose clothes* **prefer**, go (in) for, choose, opt for, select, pick, plump for, be partial to, like. **3** *father always favoured George* **show favouritism towards**, have a bias towards, think more highly of. **4** *the conditions favoured the other team* **benefit**, be to the advantage of, help, assist, aid, be of service to, do someone a favour. **5** *he*

favoured Lucy with a smile **oblige**, honour, gratify, humour, indulge. **6** informal *Travis favours our father* **resemble**, look like, be similar to, bear a resemblance to, remind one of, take after; informal be the spitting image of, be a dead ringer for.
– OPPOSITES oppose, dislike, hinder.
▫ **in favour of** on the side of, pro, (all) for, giving support to, approving of, sympathetic to.

favourable adj. **1** *a favourable assessment of his ability* **approving**, commendatory, complimentary, flattering, glowing, enthusiastic; good, pleasing, positive; informal rave. **2** *conditions are favourable* **advantageous**, beneficial, in one's favour, good, right, suitable, fitting, appropriate; propitious, auspicious, promising, encouraging. **3** *a favourable reply* **positive**, affirmative, assenting, agreeing, approving; encouraging, reassuring.
– OPPOSITES critical, disadvantageous, negative.

favourably adv. **positively**, approvingly, sympathetically, enthusiastically, appreciatively.

favoured adj. **preferred**, favourite, recommended, chosen, choice.

favourite adj. *his favourite aunt* **best-loved**, most-liked, favoured, dearest; preferred, chosen, choice.
▸ n. **1** *Brutus was Caesar's favourite* **(first) choice**, pick, preference, pet, darling, the apple of one's eye; informal golden boy/girl; Brit. informal blue-eyed boy/girl; N. Amer. informal fair-haired boy/girl. **2** *the favourite fell at the first fence* **expected winner**, front runner.

favouritism n. **partiality**, partisanship, unfair preference, preferential treatment, favour, prejudice, bias, inequality, unfairness, discrimination.

fawn¹ adj. *a fawn carpet* **beige**, yellowish-brown, pale brown, buff, sand, oatmeal, café au lait, camel, ecru, taupe, stone, mushroom.

fawn² v. *they were fawning over the President* **be obsequious to**, be sycophantic to, curry favour with, pay court to, play up to, crawl to, ingratiate oneself with, dance attendance on; informal suck up to, make up to, be all over, creep, grovel; Austral./NZ informal smoodge to.

fawning adj. **obsequious**, servile, sycophantic, flattering, ingratiating, unctuous, oleaginous, grovelling, crawling; informal bootlicking, smarmy.

fear n. **1** *she felt fear at entering the house* **terror**, fright, fearfulness, horror, alarm, panic, agitation, trepidation, dread, consternation, dismay, distress; anxiety, worry, angst, unease, uneasiness, apprehension, apprehensiveness, nervousness, nerves, perturbation, foreboding; informal the creeps, the willies, the heebie-jeebies, jitteriness, twitchiness, butterflies (in the stomach), (blue) funk. **2** *she overcame her fears* **phobia**, aversion, antipathy, dread, bugbear, bogey, nightmare, horror, terror; anxiety, neurosis; informal hang-

up. **3** old use *the love and fear of God* **awe**, wonder, wonderment; reverence, veneration, respect. **4** *there's no fear of me leaving you alone* **likelihood**, likeliness, prospect, possibility, chance, probability; risk, danger.
▸ v. **1** *she feared her husband* **be afraid of**, be fearful of, be scared of, be apprehensive of, dread, live in fear of, be terrified of; be anxious about, worry about, feel apprehensive about. **2** *he fears heights* **have a phobia about**, have a horror of, take fright at. **3** *he feared to tell them* **be too afraid**, be too scared, hesitate, dare not. **4** *they feared for his health* **worry about**, feel anxious about, feel concerned about, have anxieties about. **5** old use *all who fear the Lord* **stand in awe of**, revere, reverence, venerate, respect. **6** *I fear that you may be right* **suspect**, have a (sneaking) suspicion, be inclined to think, be afraid, have a hunch, think it likely.

fearful adj. **1** *they are fearful of being overheard* **afraid**, frightened, scared (stiff), scared to death, terrified, petrified; alarmed, panicky, nervy, nervous, tense, apprehensive, uneasy, worried (sick), anxious; informal jittery, jumpy; Brit. informal in a (blue) funk; old use afeared, affrighted. **2** *the guards were fearful* **nervous**, trembling, quaking, cowed, daunted; timid, timorous, faint-hearted, nervy; informal jittery, jumpy, twitchy, keyed up, in a cold sweat, trepidatious, a bundle of nerves, like a cat on a hot tin roof; Brit. informal having kittens, like a cat on hot bricks; N. Amer. informal spooky. **3** *a fearful accident* **terrible**, dreadful, awful, appalling, frightful, ghastly, horrific, horrible, horrifying, horrendous, terribly bad, shocking, atrocious, abominable, hideous, monstrous, gruesome. **4** informal *he was in a fearful hurry* **(very) great**, extreme, real, dreadful; informal terrible.

fearfully adv. **1** *she opened the door fearfully* **apprehensively**, uneasily, nervously, timidly, timorously, hesitantly, with one's heart in one's mouth. **2** informal *Stephanie looked fearfully glamorous* **extremely**, exceedingly, exceptionally, remarkably, uncommonly, extraordinarily, tremendously, incredibly, very, really; Scottish unco; informal awfully, terribly, dreadfully; Brit. well, ever so, dead; N. Amer. informal real, mighty, awful; dated frightfully.

fearless adj. **bold**, brave, courageous, intrepid, valiant, valorous, gallant, plucky, lionhearted, heroic, daring, audacious, indomitable, doughty; unafraid, undaunted, unflinching; informal gutsy, spunky, ballsy, feisty.
– OPPOSITES timid, cowardly.

fearsome adj. **frightening**, horrifying, terrifying, menacing, chilling, spine-chilling, hair-raising, alarming, unnerving, daunting, formidable, forbidding, dismaying, disquieting, disturbing; informal scary.

feasible adj. **practicable**, practical, workable, achievable, attainable, realizable, viable, realistic, sensible, reasonable, within reason; suitable, possible, expedient,

constructive; informal doable.
– OPPOSITES impractical.

feast n. **1** *a wedding feast* **banquet**,
celebration meal, lavish dinner; treat,
entertainment; revels, festivities; informal
blowout, spread; Brit. informal nosh-up,
beanfeast, bunfight, beano, slap-up meal.
2 *the feast of St Stephen* **(religious) festival**,
feast day, saint's day, holy day, holiday. **3** *a*
feast for the eyes **treat**, delight, joy, pleasure.
▸ v. **1** *they feasted on lobster* **gorge on**, dine
on, eat one's fill of, overindulge in, binge
on; eat, devour, consume, partake of; informal
stuff one's face with, stuff oneself with,
pig oneself on, pig out on. **2** *they feasted*
the deputation **hold a banquet for**, throw
a feast/party for, wine and dine, entertain
lavishly, regale, treat, fete.

feat n. **achievement**, accomplishment,
attainment, coup, triumph; undertaking,
enterprise, venture, operation, exercise,
endeavour, effort, performance, exploit.

feather n. **plume**, quill, flight feather,
tail feather; Ornithology covert, plumule;
(feathers) plumage, feathering, down.

feature n. **1** *a typical feature of French music*
characteristic, attribute, quality, property,
trait, hallmark, trademark; aspect, facet,
factor, ingredient, component, element,
theme; peculiarity, idiosyncrasy, quirk.
2 *her delicate features* **face**, countenance,
physiognomy; informal mug, kisser; Brit. informal
mush, phiz, phizog; N. Amer. informal puss,
pan; literary visage, lineaments. **3** *she made a*
feature of her garden sculptures **centrepiece**,
(special) attraction, highlight, focal point,
focus (of attention). **4** *a series of short*
features **article**, piece, item, report, story,
column, review, commentary, write-up.
▸ v. **1** *Radio Ulster is featuring a week of live*
concerts **present**, promote, make a feature
of, give prominence to, focus attention on,
spotlight, highlight. **2** *she is to feature in a*
major advertising campaign **star**, appear,
participate, play a part.

febrile adj. **feverish**, hot, burning, flushed,
sweating; rare pyretic.

feckless adj. **good-for-nothing**,
irresponsible, lazy, idle, slothful, indolent,
shiftless; useless, worthless, incompetent,
inept, ne'er-do-well; informal no-good, no-
account.

fecund adj. **fertile**, fruitful, productive, high-
yielding; rich, lush, flourishing, thriving;
formal fructuous.
– OPPOSITES barren.

federal adj. **confederate**, federated,
federative; combined, allied, united,
amalgamated, integrated.

federate v. **confederate**, combine, unite,
unify, merge, amalgamate, integrate, join
(up), band together, team up.

federation n. **confederation**, confederacy,
federacy, league; combination, alliance,
coalition, union, syndicate, guild,
consortium, partnership, cooperative,
association, amalgamation.

fed up adj. **exasperated**, irritated, annoyed,
irked, put out, peeved, piqued, disgruntled;
discontented, discouraged, disheartened,
depressed; bored, weary, tired; informal hacked
off, cheesed off, brassed off, narked; Brit.
informal not best pleased; vulgar slang pissed off.
– OPPOSITES happy.

fee n. **payment**, wage, salary, allowance;
price, cost, charge, tariff, rate, amount, sum,
figure; **(fees)** remuneration, dues, earnings,
pay; formal emolument.

feeble adj. **1** *he was very old and feeble* **weak**,
weakly, weakened, frail, infirm, delicate,
sickly, ailing, unwell, poorly, enfeebled,
enervated, debilitated, incapacitated,
decrepit. **2** *a feeble argument* **ineffective**,
ineffectual, inadequate, unconvincing,
implausible, unsatisfactory, poor, weak,
flimsy. **3** *he's too feeble to stand up to his boss*
cowardly, craven, faint-hearted, spineless,
spiritless, lily-livered; timid, timorous,
fearful, unassertive, weak, ineffectual;
informal wimpy, sissy, sissified, gutless,
chicken; Brit. informal wet. **4** *a feeble light* **faint**,
dim, weak, pale, soft, subdued, muted.
– OPPOSITES strong, brave.

feed v. **1** *a large family to feed* **give food to**,
provide (food) for, cater for, cook for; suckle,
breastfeed, bottle-feed; dated victual. **2** *the*
baby spends all day feeding **eat**, snack; informal
nosh, graze. **3** *too many cows feeding in a*
small area **graze**, browse, crop, pasture. **4** *the*
birds feed on a varied diet **live on/off**, exist
on, subsist on, eat, consume. **5** *feeding one's*
self-esteem **strengthen**, fortify, support,
bolster, reinforce, boost, fuel, encourage.
6 *she fed secrets to the Russians* **supply**,
provide, give, deliver, furnish, issue.
▸ n. **1** *feed for goats and sheep* **fodder**, food,
forage, pasturage, herbage, provender; formal
comestibles. **2** informal *they halted for their*
feed **meal**, lunch, dinner, supper; Brit. tea;
informal nosh, scoff; formal repast.

feel v. **1** *she felt the fabric* **touch**, stroke,
caress, fondle, finger, thumb, handle. **2** *she*
felt a breeze on her back **perceive**, sense,
detect, discern, notice, be aware of, be
conscious of. **3** *the patient does not feel pain*
experience, undergo, go through, bear,
endure, suffer. **4** *he felt his way towards the*
door **grope**, fumble, scrabble, pick. **5** *feel*
the temperature of the water **test**, try (out),
assess, gauge. **6** *he feels that he should go*
to the meeting **believe**, think, consider (it
right), be of the opinion, hold, maintain,
judge; informal reckon, figure. **7** *I feel that he*
is only biding his time **sense**, have a (funny)
feeling, get the impression, have a hunch,
intuit. **8** *the air feels damp* **seem**, appear,
strike one as.
▸ n. **1** *the divers worked by feel* **(sense of)**
touch, tactile sense, feeling (one's way).
2 *the feel of the paper* **texture**, surface,
finish; weight, thickness, consistency,
quality. **3** *the feel of a room* **atmosphere**,
ambience, aura, mood, feeling, air,
impression, character, tenor, spirit, flavour;
informal vibrations, vibes. **4** *a feel for languages*

aptitude, knack, flair, bent, talent, gift, faculty, ability.
□ **feel for** sympathize with, be sorry for, pity, feel pity for, feel sympathy for, feel compassion for, be moved by; commiserate with, condole with.
feel like want, would like, wish for, desire, fancy, feel in need of, long for; informal yen for, be dying for.

feeler n. **1** *the fish has two feelers on its head* **antenna**, tentacle, tactile/sensory organ; Zoology antennule. **2** *the minister put out feelers* **tentative enquiry/proposal**, advance, approach, overture, probe.

feeling n. **1** *a loss of feeling in the hands* **(sense of) touch**, feel, tactile sense. **2** *a feeling of nausea* **sensation**, sense, consciousness. **3** *I had a feeling that I would win* **(sneaking) suspicion**, notion, inkling, hunch, funny feeling, feeling in one's bones, fancy, idea; presentiment, premonition; informal gut feeling. **4** *the strength of her feeling* **love**, affection, fondness, tenderness, warmth, warmness, emotion, sentiment; passion, ardour, desire. **5** *out of touch with public feeling* **sentiment**, emotion; opinion, attitude, belief, ideas, views. **6** *he had hurt her feelings* **sensibilities**, sensitivities, self-esteem, pride. **7** *my feeling is that it is true* **opinion**, belief, view, impression, intuition, instinct, hunch, estimation, guess. **8** *a feeling of peace* **atmosphere**, ambience, aura, air, feel, mood, impression, spirit, quality, flavour; informal vibrations, vibes. **9** *a remarkable feeling for language* **aptitude**, knack, flair, bent, talent, gift, faculty, ability.
▸adj. *she was a feeling child* **sensitive**, warm, warm-hearted, tender, tender-hearted, caring, sympathetic, kind, compassionate, understanding, thoughtful.

feign v. **1** *she lay still and feigned sleep* **simulate**, fake, sham, affect, give the appearance of, make a pretence of. **2** *he's not really ill, he's only feigning* **pretend**, put it on, fake, sham, bluff, masquerade, play-act; informal kid.

feigned adj. **pretended**, simulated, affected, artificial, insincere, put-on, fake, false, sham; informal pretend, phoney.
– OPPOSITES sincere.

feint n. **bluff**, blind, ruse, deception, subterfuge, hoax, trick, ploy, device, dodge, sham, pretence, cover, smokescreen, distraction, contrivance; informal red herring.

felicitations plural n. **congratulations**, good/best wishes, (kind) regards, blessings, compliments, respects.

felicitous adj. **1** *his nickname was particularly felicitous* **apt**, well chosen, fitting, suitable, appropriate, apposite, pertinent, germane, relevant. **2** *the room's only felicitous feature* **favourable**, advantageous, good, pleasing.
– OPPOSITES inappropriate, unfortunate.

felicity n. **1** *domestic felicity* **happiness**, joy, joyfulness, joyousness, bliss, delight, cheerfulness; contentedness, satisfaction,

pleasure. **2** *David expressed his feelings with his customary felicity* **eloquence**, aptness, appropriateness, suitability, suitableness, applicability, fitness, relevance, pertinence.
– OPPOSITES unhappiness, inappropriateness.

feline adj. *she moved with feline grace* **catlike**, graceful, sleek, sinuous.
▸n. *her pet feline* **cat**, kitten; informal puss, pussy (cat); Brit. informal moggie, mog; old use grimalkin.

fell[1] v. **1** *all the dead sycamores had to be felled* **cut down**, chop down, hack down, saw down, clear. **2** *she felled him with one punch* **knock down/over**, knock to the ground, strike down, bring down, rugby-tackle, floor, prostrate; knock out, knock unconscious; informal deck, flatten, down, lay out, KO; Brit. informal knock for six.

fell[2] adj.
□ **at/in one fell swoop** all at once, together, at the same time, in one go.

fellow n. **1** informal *he's a decent sort of fellow* **man**, boy; person, individual, soul; informal guy, geezer, lad, fella, character, customer, devil, bastard; Brit. informal chap, bloke; N. Amer. informal dude, hombre; Austral./NZ informal digger; informal dated body, dog, cove. **2** informal *she longed to have a fellow* **boyfriend**, lover. **3** *he exchanged glances with his fellows* **companion**, friend, comrade, partner, associate, co-worker, colleague; informal chum, pal, buddy; Brit. informal mate. **4** *some peasants were wealthier than their fellows* **peer**, equal, contemporary, confrère; old use compeer.
□ **fellow feeling** sympathy, empathy, feeling, compassion, care, concern, solicitude, solicitousness, warmth, tenderness, (brotherly) love; pity, sorrow, commiseration.

fellowship n. **1** *a community bound together in fellowship* **companionship**, companionability, sociability, comradeship, camaraderie, friendship, mutual support; togetherness, solidarity; informal chumminess, palliness; Brit. informal mateyness. **2** *the church fellowship* **association**, society, club, league, union, guild, affiliation, alliance, fraternity, brotherhood, sorority, sodality.

female adj. *typical female attributes* **feminine**, womanly, ladylike; old use feminal.
– OPPOSITES male.
▸n. *the victim was an elderly female.* See **woman** (sense 1).

feminine adj. **1** *a very feminine young woman* **womanly**, girlish, girlie; old use feminal. **2** *he enjoyed feminine company* **female**.
– OPPOSITES masculine, manly.

femininity n. **womanliness**, feminineness, womanly/feminine qualities.

feminism n. **the women's movement**, the feminist movement, women's liberation, female emancipation, women's rights; informal women's lib.

femme fatale n. **seductress**, temptress, siren; informal vamp.

fen n. **marsh**, marshland, salt marsh, fenland, wetland, (peat) bog, swamp, swampland; N. Amer. moor.

fence n. **1** *a gap in the fence* **barrier**, paling, railing, enclosure, barricade, stockade, palisade. **2** *informal a fence dealing mainly in jewellery* **receiver (of stolen goods)**, dealer.
▶v. **1** *they fenced off many acres* **enclose**, surround, circumscribe, encircle, circle, encompass; isolate; literary engirdle; old use compass. **2** *he fenced in his chickens* **confine**, pen in, coop up, shut in/up, separate off; enclose, surround; N. Amer. corral. **3** *the man fenced but Jim persisted* **be evasive**, be vague, be non-committal, equivocate, prevaricate, stall, vacillate, hedge, pussyfoot around, sidestep the issue; informal duck the question/issue.
◻ **(sitting) on the fence** informal undecided, uncommitted, uncertain, unsure, vacillating, wavering, dithering, hesitant, doubtful, ambivalent, in two minds, in a quandary; neutral, impartial, non-partisan, open-minded; Brit. humming and hawing.

fend v. **1** *they were unable to fend off the invasion* **ward off**, head off, stave off, hold off, repel, repulse, resist, fight off, defend oneself against, prevent, stop, block, intercept, hold back.
◻ **fend for oneself** take care of oneself, look after oneself, provide for oneself, shift for oneself, manage by oneself, cope alone, stand on one's own two feet.

feral adj. **1** *feral dogs* **wild**, untamed, undomesticated, untrained. **2** *a feral snarl* **fierce**, ferocious, vicious, savage, predatory, menacing, bloodthirsty.
– OPPOSITES tame, pet.

ferment v. **1** *the beer continues to ferment* **brew**; effervesce, fizz, foam, froth. **2** *an environment that ferments disorder* **cause**, bring about, give rise to, generate, engender, spawn, instigate, provoke, incite, excite, stir up, whip up, foment; literary beget, enkindle.
▶n. *a ferment of revolutionary upheaval* **fever**, furore, frenzy, tumult, storm, rumpus; turmoil, upheaval, unrest, disquiet, uproar, agitation, turbulence, disruption, confusion, disorder, chaos, mayhem; informal kerfuffle, hoo-ha, to-do; Brit. informal aggro.

ferocious adj. **1** *ferocious animals* **fierce**, savage, wild, predatory, aggressive, dangerous. **2** *a ferocious attack* **brutal**, vicious, violent, bloody, barbaric, savage, sadistic, ruthless, cruel, merciless, heartless, bloodthirsty, murderous; literary fell; old use sanguinary. **3** *informal a ferocious headache* **intense**, strong, powerful, fierce, severe, extreme, acute, unbearable; informal hellish.
– OPPOSITES gentle, mild.

ferocity n. **savagery**, brutality, barbarity, fierceness, violence, bloodthirstiness, murderousness; ruthlessness, cruelty, pitilessness, mercilessness, heartlessness.

ferret v. **1** *she ferreted in her handbag* **rummage**, feel, grope, forage, fish, poke about/around; search through, hunt through,

rifle through; Austral./NZ informal fossick through. **2** *ferreting out misdemeanours* **unearth**, uncover, discover, detect, search out, bring to light, track down, dig up, root out, nose out; informal get wise to; Brit. informal rumble.

ferry n. *the ferry from Dover to Calais* **passenger boat/ship**, ferry boat, car ferry; ship, boat, vessel; dated packet (boat).
▶v. **1** *ferrying passengers to and from the Continent* **transport**, convey, carry, ship, run, take, bring, shuttle. **2** *the boat ferried hourly across the river* **go back and forth**, shuttle, run.

fertile adj. **1** *the soil is fertile* **fecund**, fruitful, productive, high-yielding, rich, lush; formal fructuous. **2** *fertile couples* **able to conceive**, able to have children; technical fecund. **3** *a fertile brain* **imaginative**, inventive, innovative, creative, visionary, original, ingenious; productive, prolific.
– OPPOSITES barren.

fertilization n. **conception**, impregnation, insemination; pollination, propagation.

fertilize v. **1** *the field was fertilized* **feed**, mulch, compost, manure, dress, top-dress. **2** *these orchids are fertilized by insects* **pollinate**, cross-pollinate, cross-fertilize.

fertilizer n. **manure**, plant food, compost, dressing, top dressing, dung.

fervent adj. **impassioned**, passionate, intense, vehement, ardent, sincere, fervid, heartfelt; enthusiastic, zealous, fanatical, wholehearted, avid, eager, keen, committed, dedicated, devout; informal mad keen; literary perfervid.
– OPPOSITES apathetic.

fervid adj. **fervent**, ardent, passionate, impassioned, intense, vehement, wholehearted, heartfelt, sincere, earnest; literary perfervid.

fervour n. **passion**, ardour, intensity, zeal, vehemence, emotion, warmth, earnestness, avidity, eagerness, keenness, enthusiasm, excitement, animation, vigour, energy, fire, spirit, zest, fervency, ardency.
– OPPOSITES apathy.

fester v. **1** *his deep wound festered* **suppurate**, become septic, form pus, weep; Medicine maturate, be purulent; old use rankle. **2** *rubbish festered* **rot**, moulder, decay, decompose, putrefy, go bad/off, spoil, deteriorate. **3** *their resentment festered* **rankle**, eat/gnaw away at one's mind, brew, smoulder.

festival n. **1** *the town's autumn festival* **fete**, fair, gala (day), carnival, fiesta, jamboree, celebrations, festivities, eisteddfod. **2** *fasting precedes the festival* **holy day**, feast day, saint's day, commemoration, day of observance.

festive adj. **jolly**, merry, joyous, joyful, happy, jovial, light-hearted, cheerful, jubilant, convivial, high-spirited, mirthful, uproarious; celebratory, holiday, carnival; Christmassy; old use festal.

f

festivity n. **1** *food plays an important part in the festivities* **celebration**, festival, entertainment, party, jamboree; merrymaking, feasting, revelry, jollification; revels, fun and games; informal bash, shindig, shindy; Brit. informal rave-up, knees-up, beanfeast, bunfight, beano. **2** *the festivity of the Last Night of the Proms* **jollity**, merriment, gaiety, cheerfulness, cheer, joyfulness, jubilance, conviviality, high spirits, revelry.

festoon n. *festoons of paper flowers* **garland**, chain, lei, swathe, swag, loop.
▸ v. *the room was festooned with streamers* **decorate**, adorn, ornament, trim, deck (out), hang, loop, drape, swathe, garland, wreathe, bedeck; informal do up/out, get up, trick out; literary bedizen, furbelow.

fetch v. **1** *he went to fetch a doctor* **(go and) get**, go for, call for, summon, pick up, collect, bring, carry, convey, transport. **2** *the land could fetch a million pounds* **sell for**, bring in, raise, realize, yield, make, command, cost, be priced at; informal go for, pull in.
□ **fetch up** informal end up, finish up, turn up, appear, materialize, find itself; informal wind up, show up.

fetching adj. **attractive**, appealing, sweet, pretty, lovely, delightful, charming, prepossessing, captivating, enchanting, irresistible; Scottish & N. English **bonny**; informal divine, heavenly; Brit. informal fit, smashing; old use comely, fair.

fete n. Brit. **gala (day)**, bazaar, fair, festival, fiesta, jubilee, carnival; fund-raiser, charity event.

fetid adj. **stinking**, smelly, foul-smelling, malodorous, reeking, pungent, acrid, high, rank, foul, noxious; Brit. informal niffy, pongy, whiffy, humming; N. Amer. informal funky; literary noisome, miasmic, miasmal.
− OPPOSITES fragrant.

fetish n. **1** *he developed a rubber fetish* **fixation**, obsession, compulsion, mania; weakness, fancy, fascination, fad; informal thing, hang-up. **2** *a voodoo fetish* **juju**, talisman, charm, amulet; totem, idol, image, effigy; old use periapt.

fetter v. **1** *the captive was fettered* **shackle**, manacle, handcuff, clap in irons, put in chains, chain (up); literary enfetter. **2** *these obligations fetter the company's powers* **restrict**, restrain, constrain, limit, hinder, hamper, impede, obstruct, hamstring, inhibit, check, curb, trammel.

fetters plural n. **shackles**, manacles, handcuffs, leg irons, chains, restraints; informal cuffs, bracelets; historical bilboes.

fettle n. **shape**, trim, (physical) fitness, (state of) health; condition, form, (state of) repair, (working) order; Brit. informal nick.

fetus n. **embryo**, fertilized egg, unborn baby/child.

feud n. *tribal feuds* **vendetta**, conflict; rivalry, hostility, enmity, strife, discord; quarrel, argument, falling-out.
▸ v. *he feuded with his teammates* **quarrel**, fight, argue, bicker, squabble, fall out, dispute, clash, differ, be at odds; informal scrap.

fever n. **1** *he developed fever* **feverishness**, high temperature, febrility; Medicine pyrexia; informal temperature. **2** *a fever of excitement* **ferment**, frenzy, furore; ecstasy, rapture. **3** *World Cup fever* **excitement**, frenzy, agitation, passion.

WORD LINKS
febrile having a fever
febrifuge a medicine used to reduce fever

fevered adj. **1** *her fevered brow* **feverish**, febrile, hot, burning; rare pyretic. **2** *a fevered imagination* **excited**, agitated, frenzied, overwrought, fervid.

feverish adj. **1** *she's really feverish* **febrile**, fevered, hot, burning; rare pyretic. **2** *feverish excitement* **frenzied**, frenetic, hectic, agitated, excited, restless, nervous, worked up, overwrought, frantic, furious, hysterical, wild, uncontrolled, unrestrained.

few determiner *police are revealing few details* **not many**, hardly any, scarcely any; a small number of, a small amount of, one or two, a handful of; little.
− OPPOSITES many.
▸ adj. *comforts here are few* **scarce**, scant, meagre, insufficient, in short supply; thin on the ground, few and far between, infrequent, uncommon, rare.
− OPPOSITES plentiful.
□ **a few** a small number, a handful, one or two, a couple, two or three; not many, hardly any.

fiancée, fiancé n. **betrothed**, wife-to-be, husband-to-be, bride-to-be, future wife/husband, prospective spouse; informal intended.

fiasco n. **failure**, disaster, catastrophe, debacle, shambles, farce, mess, wreck; informal flop, washout, fail; Brit. informal cock-up; N. Amer. informal snafu; Austral./NZ informal fizzer.
− OPPOSITES success.

fiat n. **decree**, edict, order, command, commandment, injunction, proclamation, mandate, dictum, diktat.

fib n. *you're telling a fib* **lie**, untruth, falsehood, made-up story, invention, fabrication, deception, (piece of) fiction; (little) white lie, half-truth; informal tall story/tale, whopper; Brit. informal porky (pie).
− OPPOSITES truth.
▸ v. *she had bunked off school, fibbing about a sore throat* **lie**, tell a fib, tell a lie, invent a story, make up a story; informal kid.

fibre n. **1** *fibres from the murderer's jumper* **thread**, strand, filament; technical fibril. **2** *natural fibres* **material**, cloth, fabric. **3** *a man with no fibre.* See **moral fibre**. **4** *you need more fibre in your diet* **roughage**, bulk.

fickle adj. **capricious**, changeable, variable, volatile, mercurial; inconstant, undependable, unsteady, unfaithful, faithless, flighty, giddy, skittish; technical labile; literary mutable.
− OPPOSITES constant.

fiction n. **1** *the traditions of British fiction* **novels**, stories, creative writing, literature. **2** *the president dismissed the allegation as absolute fiction* **fabrication**, invention, lies, fibs, untruth, falsehood, fantasy, nonsense.
– OPPOSITES fact.

fictional adj. **fictitious**, invented, imaginary, made up, make-believe, unreal, fabricated, mythical.
– OPPOSITES real.

fictitious adj. **1** *a fictitious name* **false**, fake, fabricated, sham; bogus, spurious, assumed, affected, adopted, feigned, invented, made up; informal pretend, phoney. **2** *a fictitious character.* See **fictional**.
– OPPOSITES genuine.

fiddle informal n. **1** *she played the fiddle* **violin**, viola. **2** *a VAT fiddle* **fraud**, swindle, confidence trick; informal racket, con trick, flimflam.
▸v. **1** *he fiddled with a beer mat* **fidget**, play, toy, twiddle, fuss, fool about/around; finger, thumb, handle; informal mess about/around; Brit. informal muck about/around. **2** *he fiddled with the dials* **adjust**, tinker, play about/around, meddle, interfere. **3** *fiddling the figures* **falsify**, manipulate, massage, rig, distort, misrepresent, doctor, alter, tamper with, interfere with; informal fix, flimflam, cook (the books).

fiddling adj. informal **trivial**, petty, trifling, insignificant, unimportant, inconsequential, negligible, paltry, footling, minor, small, incidental, of little/no account; informal piddling, piffling.
– OPPOSITES important.

fidelity n. **1** *fidelity to her husband* **faithfulness**, loyalty, constancy; true-heartedness, trustworthiness, dependability, reliability; formal troth. **2** *fidelity to your king* **loyalty**, allegiance, obedience, constancy, homage; historical fealty. **3** *the fidelity of the reproduction* **accuracy**, exactness, precision, preciseness, correctness; strictness, closeness, faithfulness, authenticity.
– OPPOSITES disloyalty.

fidget v. **1** *the audience began to fidget* **wriggle**, squirm, twitch, jiggle, shuffle, be agitated; informal be jittery. **2** *she fidgeted with her scarf* **play**, fuss, toy, twiddle, fool about/around; informal fiddle, mess about/around. **3** *she seemed to fidget him* **make uneasy**, worry, agitate, bother, upset, ruffle.
▸n. **1** *his convulsive fidgets* **twitch**, wriggle, squirm, jiggle, shuffle, tic, spasm. **2** *what a fidget you are!* **restless person**, bundle of nerves. **3** *that woman gives me the fidgets* **restlessness**, nervousness, fidgetiness; informal the jitters, twitchiness.

fidgety adj. **restless**, restive, on edge, uneasy, nervous, nervy, keyed up, anxious, agitated; informal jittery, twitchy.

field n. **1** *a large ploughed field* **meadow**, pasture, paddock, grassland, pastureland, sward; literary lea, mead; old use glebe. **2** *a football field* **pitch**, ground, sports field, playing field, recreation ground. **3** *the field*

of biotechnology **area**, sphere, discipline, province, department, domain, sector, branch, subject; informal bailiwick. **4** *your field of vision* **scope**, range, sweep, reach, extent. **5** *she is well ahead of the field* **competitors**, entrants, competition; applicants, candidates, possibles.
▸v. **1** *she fielded the ball* **catch**, stop, retrieve; return, throw back. **2** *they had fielded an ineligible player* **put in**, send out, play, put up. **3** *they can field an army of about one million* **deploy**, position, range, dispose. **4** *he fielded some awkward questions* **deal with**, handle, cope with, answer, reply to, respond to.
▸adj. **1** *field experience* **practical**, hands-on, applied, experiential, empirical. **2** *field artillery* **mobile**, portable, transportable, movable, manoeuvrable, light.

fiend n. **1** *a fiend had taken possession of him* **demon**, devil, evil spirit, bogie, cacodemon; informal spook. **2** *a fiend bent on global evil-doing* **brute**, beast, villain, barbarian, monster, ogre, sadist, evildoer; informal swine. **3** informal *a drug fiend* **addict**, abuser, user; informal junkie, ——head/freak. **4** informal *I'm a fiend for Mexican food* **enthusiast**, maniac; devotee, fan, lover; informal fanatic, addict, buff, freak, nut.

fiendish adj. **1** *a fiendish torturer* **wicked**, cruel, vicious, evil, malevolent, villainous; brutal, savage, barbaric, barbarous, inhuman, murderous, ruthless, merciless; dated dastardly. **2** *a fiendish plot* **cunning**, clever, ingenious, crafty, canny, wily, devious, shrewd; informal foxy, sneaky. **3** *a fiendish puzzle* **difficult**, complex, challenging, complicated, intricate, involved, knotty, thorny.

fierce adj. **1** *a fierce black mastiff* **ferocious**, savage, vicious, aggressive. **2** *fierce competition* **aggressive**, cut-throat, competitive; keen, intense, strong, relentless. **3** *fierce, murderous jealousy* **intense**, powerful, vehement, passionate, impassioned, fervent, fervid, ardent. **4** *a fierce wind* **powerful**, strong, violent, forceful; stormy, blustery, gusty, tempestuous. **5** *a fierce pain* **severe**, extreme, intense, acute, awful, dreadful; excruciating, agonizing, piercing.
– OPPOSITES gentle, mild.

fiery adj. **1** *fiery breath* **burning**, blazing, flaming; on fire, ablaze; literary afire. **2** *a fiery red* **bright**, brilliant, vivid, intense, deep, rich. **3** *her fiery spirit* **passionate**, impassioned, ardent, fervent, fervid, spirited; quick-tempered, volatile, explosive, aggressive, determined, resolute.

fiesta n. **festival**, carnival, holiday, celebration, party.

fight v. **1** *two men were fighting* **brawl**, exchange blows, attack/assault each other, hit/punch each other; struggle, grapple, wrestle; informal scrap, have a dust-up, have a set-to; Brit. informal have a punch-up; N. Amer. informal rough-house; Austral./NZ informal stoush, go the knuckle. **2** *he fought in the First World*

War **(do) battle**, go to war, take up arms, be a soldier; engage, meet, clash, skirmish. **3** *a war fought for freedom* **engage in**, wage, conduct, prosecute, undertake. **4** *they are always fighting* **quarrel**, argue, row, bicker, squabble, fall out, have a row/fight, wrangle, be at odds, disagree, differ, have words, bandy words, be at each other's throats, be at loggerheads; informal scrap; old use altercate. **5** *fighting against wage reductions* **campaign**, strive, battle, struggle, contend, crusade, agitate, lobby, push, press. **6** *they will fight the decision* **oppose**, contest, contend with, confront, challenge, combat, dispute, quarrel with, argue against/with, strive against, struggle against. **7** *Donaldson fought the urge to put his tongue out* **repress**, restrain, suppress, stifle, smother, hold back, fight back, keep in check, curb, control, rein in, choke back; informal keep the lid on, cork up.

▸n. **1** *a fight outside a club* **brawl**, fracas, melee, rumpus, skirmish, sparring match, struggle, scuffle, altercation, scrum, clash, disturbance; fisticuffs; informal scrap, dust-up, set-to, shindy, shindig; Brit. informal punch-up, bust-up, ruck; Brit. informal, Football afters; N. Amer. informal rough house, brannigan; Austral./NZ informal stoush; Law, dated affray; rare broil. **2** *a heavyweight fight* **boxing match**, bout, match. **3** *Britain's fight against Germany* **battle**, engagement, clash, conflict, struggle; war, campaign, crusade, action, hostilities. **4** *a fight with my girlfriend* **argument**, quarrel, squabble, row, wrangle, disagreement, falling-out, contretemps, altercation, dispute; informal tiff, spat, scrap, slanging match; Brit. informal barney, ding-dong, bust-up. **5** *their fight for control of the company* **struggle**, battle, campaign, push, effort. **6** *she had no fight left in her* **will to resist**, resistance, spirit, courage, pluck, pluckiness, grit, strength, backbone, determination, resolution, resolve, resoluteness, aggression, aggressiveness; informal guts, spunk; Brit. informal bottle; N. Amer. informal sand, moxie.

□ **fight back 1** *use your pent-up anger to fight back* **retaliate**, counter-attack, strike back, hit back, respond, reciprocate, return fire, give tit for tat; formal requite something. **2** *she fought back tears*. See **fight** (sense 7 of the verb).

fight someone/something off repel, repulse, beat off/back, ward off, fend off, keep/hold at bay, drive away/back, force back.

fight shy of flinch from, demur from, recoil from; have scruples about, have misgivings about, have qualms about, be averse to, be chary of, be loath to, be reluctant to, be disinclined to, be afraid to, hesitate to, balk at; informal boggle at; old use disrelish.

fightback n. Brit. **counter-attack**, counteroffensive; rally, recovery; informal comeback.

fighter n. **1** *a guerrilla fighter* **soldier**, fighting man/woman, warrior, combatant, serviceman, servicewoman, trooper; Brit. informal squaddie; old use man-at-arms. **2** *the fighter was knocked to the ground* **boxer**, pugilist, prizefighter; wrestler; informal scrapper, pug.

fighting adj. *a fighting man* **violent**, combative, aggressive, pugnacious, truculent, belligerent, bellicose.
– OPPOSITES peaceful.
▸n. *200 were injured in the fighting* **violence**, hostilities, conflict, action, combat; warfare, war, battles, skirmishing, rioting; Law, dated affray.
– OPPOSITES peace.

figment n. **invention**, creation, fabrication; hallucination, illusion, delusion, fancy, vision.

figurative adj. **metaphorical**, non-literal, symbolic, allegorical, representative, emblematic.
– OPPOSITES literal.

figure n. **1** *the production figure* **statistic**, number, quantity, amount, level, total, sum; (**figures**) data, information. **2** *the second figure was 9* **digit**, numeral, numerical symbol. **3** *he can't put a figure on it* **price**, cost, amount, value, valuation. **4** *I'm good at figures* **arithmetic**, mathematics, sums, calculations, computation, numbers; Brit. informal maths; N. Amer. informal math. **5** *her petite figure* **physique**, build, frame, body, proportions, shape, form. **6** *a dark figure emerged* **silhouette**, outline, shape, form. **7** *a figure of authority* **person**, personage, individual, man, woman, character, personality; representative, embodiment, personification, epitome. **8** *life-size figures* **human representation**, effigy. **9** *geometrical figures* **shape**, pattern, design, motif. **10** *see figure 4* **diagram**, illustration, drawing, picture, plate.
▸v. **1** *a beast figuring in Egyptian legend* **feature**, appear, be featured, be mentioned, be referred to, have prominence. **2** *a way to figure the values* **calculate**, work out, total, reckon, compute, determine, assess, put a figure on; Brit. tot up. **3** informal *I figured that I didn't have a chance* **suppose**, think, believe, consider, expect, take it, suspect, sense; assume, dare say, conclude, take it as read, presume, deduce, infer, gather; N. Amer. guess. **4** informal *'Rosemary's away.' 'That figures.'* **make sense**, seem reasonable, stand to reason, be to be expected, be logical, follow, ring true.

□ **figure on** N. Amer. informal *they figured on paying about $100* **plan on**, count on, rely on, bank on, bargain on, depend on, pin one's hopes on; anticipate, expect to.

figure something out informal *he tried to figure out how to switch on the lamp* **work out**, fathom, puzzle out, decipher, ascertain, make sense of, think through, get to the bottom of; understand, comprehend, see, grasp, get the hang of, get the drift of; informal twig, crack; Brit. informal suss out.

filament n. **fibre**, thread, strand; technical fibril.

file[1] n. **1** *he opened the file* **folder**, portfolio, binder, document case. **2** *we have files on all the major companies* **dossier**, document, record, report; data, information, documentation, annals, archives. **3** *the computer file was searched* **document**, text; databank, database.
▸v. **1** *file the documents correctly* **categorize**, classify, organize, put in place/order, order, arrange, catalogue, record, store, archive. **2** *Debbie has filed for divorce* **apply**, register, ask. **3** *two women have filed a civil suit against him* **bring**, press, lodge, place; formal prefer.

file[2] n. *a file of boys* **line**, column, row, string, chain, procession; Brit. informal crocodile.
▸v. *we filed out into the car park* **walk**, march, parade, troop.

file[3] v. *she filed her nails* **smooth**, buff, rub (down), polish, shape; scrape, abrade, rasp, sandpaper.

filial adj. **dutiful**, devoted, compliant, respectful, affectionate, loving.

filibuster n. *many hours in committee are characterized by filibuster* **delaying tactics**, stonewalling, procrastination, obstruction, temporizing.
▸v. *the opposition are filibustering* **waste time**, stall, play for time, stonewall, procrastinate, buy time, employ delaying tactics.

filigree n. **tracery**, fretwork, latticework, scrollwork, lacework.

fill v. **1** *he filled a bowl with cereal* **make/become full**, fill up, fill to the brim, top up, charge. **2** *guests filled the parlour* **crowd into**, throng, pack (into), occupy, squeeze into, cram (into); overcrowd, overfill. **3** *he began filling his shelves* **stock**, pack, load, supply, replenish, restock, refill. **4** *fill all the holes with a wood-repair compound* **block up**, stop (up), plug, seal, caulk. **5** *the perfume filled the room* **pervade**, permeate, suffuse, be diffused through, penetrate, infuse, perfuse. **6** *he was going to fill a government post* **occupy**, hold, take up; informal hold down. **7** *we had just filled a big order* **carry out**, complete, fulfil, execute, discharge; formal effectuate.
– OPPOSITES empty.
□ **fill in** substitute, deputize, stand in, cover, take over, act as stand-in, take the place of; informal sub, step into someone's shoes/boots; N. Amer. informal pinch-hit.

fill someone in inform of, advise of, tell about, acquaint with, apprise of, brief on, update with; informal put in the picture about, bring up to speed on.

fill something in Brit. complete, answer, fill up; N. Amer. fill out.

fill out grow fatter, become plumper, flesh out, put on weight, get heavier.

fill something out 1 *this account needs to be filled out* expand, enlarge, add to, elaborate on, flesh out; supplement, extend, develop, amplify. **2** N. Amer. *he filled out the forms.* See **fill something in**.

filling n. *filling for cushions* **stuffing**, padding, wadding, filler.
▸adj. *a filling meal* **substantial**, hearty, ample, satisfying, square; heavy, stodgy.

fillip n. **stimulus**, stimulation, boost, incentive, impetus; tonic, spur, push, aid, help; informal shot in the arm.

film n. **1** *a film of sweat* **layer**, coat, coating, covering, cover, sheet, patina, overlay. **2** *Emma was watching a film* **movie**, picture, feature (film), motion picture; informal flick, pic, talkie; dated moving picture. **3** *she would like to work in film* **cinema**, movies, the pictures, the silver screen, celluloid.
▸v. **1** *he immediately filmed the next scene* **record**, shoot, capture, video. **2** *his eyes had filmed over* **cloud**, mist, haze; become blurred, blur; old use blear.

> **WORD LINKS**
> **cinematic** relating to films and the cinema
> **cinematography** the art of camerawork in film-making
> **cineaste, cinephile** a film expert or enthusiast

film star n. **(film) actor/actress**, movie star, leading man/woman, leading lady, lead; celebrity, star, starlet, superstar; informal celeb; dated matinee idol.

filmy adj. **diaphanous**, transparent, see-through, translucent, sheer, gossamer; delicate, fine, light, thin, silky.
– OPPOSITES thick, opaque.

filter n. *a carbon filter* **strainer**, sifter; sieve, riddle; gauze, netting.
▸v. **1** *the farmers filter the water* **sieve**, strain, sift, filtrate, riddle; clarify, purify, refine, treat. **2** *the rain had filtered through her jacket* **seep**, percolate, leak, trickle, ooze.

filth n. **1** *stagnant pools of filth* **dirt**, muck, grime, mud, mire, sludge, slime, ooze; excrement, excreta, dung, manure, ordure, sewage; rubbish, refuse, dross; pollution, contamination, filthiness, uncleanness, foulness, nastiness; N. Amer. garbage; informal crud, grunge; Brit. informal grot, gunge; N. Amer. informal trash. **2** *I felt sick after reading that filth* **pornography**, pornographic literature/films, dirty books, smut, obscenity, indecency; informal porn, porno.

filthy adj. **1** *the room was filthy* **dirty**, mucky, grimy, muddy, slimy, unclean; foul, squalid, sordid, nasty, soiled, sullied; polluted, contaminated, unhygienic, unsanitary; informal cruddy, grungy; Brit. informal grotty; literary besmirched. **2** *his face was filthy* **unwashed**, unclean, dirty, grimy, smeared, grubby, muddy, mucky, black, blackened, stained; literary begrimed. **3** *filthy jokes* **obscene**, indecent, dirty, smutty, rude, improper, coarse, bawdy, vulgar, lewd, racy, off colour, earthy, ribald, risqué, 'adult', pornographic, explicit; informal blue, porn, porno, X-rated; N. Amer. informal raw. **4** *you filthy brute!* **despicable**, contemptible, nasty, low, base, mean, vile, obnoxious; informal dirty (rotten), low-down, no-good. **5** *he was in a filthy mood* **bad**, foul, bad-tempered,

final | fine

ill-tempered, irritable, grumpy, grouchy, cross, fractious, peevish; informal snappish, snappy; Brit. informal shirty, stroppy, narky, ratty; N. Amer. informal cranky, ornery.
– OPPOSITES clean.
▶ adv. *filthy rich* **very**, extremely, tremendously, immensely, remarkably, excessively, exceedingly; informal stinking, awfully, terribly, seriously, mega, ultra, damn.

final adj. **1** *the final year of study* **last**, closing, concluding, finishing, end, terminating, ultimate, eventual. **2** *their decisions are final* **irrevocable**, unalterable, absolute, conclusive, irrefutable, incontrovertible, indisputable, unchallengeable, binding.
– OPPOSITES first, provisional.
▶ n. *the FA Cup final* **decider**, final game/match.
– OPPOSITES qualifier.

finale n. **climax**, culmination; end, ending, finish, close, conclusion, termination; denouement, last act, final scene.
– OPPOSITES beginning.

finality n. **conclusiveness**, decisiveness, decision, definiteness, definitiveness, certainty, certitude; irrevocability, irrefutability, incontrovertibility.

finalize v. **conclude**, complete, clinch, settle, work out, secure, wrap up, wind up, put the finishing touches to; reach an agreement on, agree on, come to terms on; informal sew up.

finally adv. **1** *she finally got her man to the altar* **eventually**, ultimately, in the end, after a long time, at (long) last; in the long run, in the fullness of time. **2** *finally, wrap the ribbon round the edge* **lastly**, last, in conclusion, to conclude, to end. **3** *this should finally dispel that common misconception* **conclusively**, irrevocably, decisively, definitively, for ever, for good, once and for all.

finance n. **1** *he knows about finance* **financial affairs**, money matters, fiscal matters, economics, money management, commerce, business, investment. **2** *short-term finance* **funds**, assets, money, capital, resources, cash, reserves, revenue, income; funding, backing, sponsorship.
▶ v. *the project was financed by grants* **fund**, pay for, back, capitalize, endow, subsidize, invest in; underwrite, guarantee, sponsor, support; N. Amer. informal bankroll.

financial adj. **monetary**, money, economic, pecuniary, fiscal, banking, commercial, business, investment.

financier n. **investor**, speculator, banker, capitalist, industrialist, businessman, businesswoman, stockbroker; informal money man.

find v. **1** *I found the book I wanted* **locate**, spot, pinpoint, unearth, obtain; search out, nose out, track down, root out; come across/upon, run across/into, chance on, light on, happen on, stumble on, encounter; informal bump into; literary espy, descry. **2** *they have found a cure for rabies* **discover**, invent,

come up with, hit on. **3** *the police found her purse* **retrieve**, recover, get back, regain, repossess. **4** *I hope you find peace* **obtain**, acquire, get, procure, come by, secure, gain, earn, achieve, attain. **5** *I found the courage to speak* **summon (up)**, gather, muster (up), screw up, call up. **6** *caffeine is found in coffee and tea* **be (present)**, occur, exist, be existent, appear. **7** *you'll find that it's a lively area* **discover**, become aware, realize, observe, notice, note, perceive, learn. **8** *I find their decision strange* **consider**, think, believe to be, feel to be, look on as, view as, see as, judge, deem, regard as. **9** *he was found guilty* **judge**, adjudge, adjudicate, deem, rule, declare, pronounce. **10** *her barb found its mark* **arrive at**, reach, attain, achieve; hit, strike.
– OPPOSITES lose.
▶ n. **1** *an archaeological find* **discovery**, acquisition, asset. **2** *this table is a real find* **good buy**, bargain; boon.
□ **find out** discover, become aware, learn, detect, discern, perceive, observe, notice, note, get/come to know, realize; bring to light, reveal, expose, unearth, disclose; informal figure out, cotton on, catch on, tumble, get wise, savvy; Brit. informal twig, rumble, suss.

finding n. **1** *the finding of the leak* **discovery**, location, locating, detection, detecting, uncovering. **2** *the tribunal's findings* **conclusion**, decision, verdict, pronouncement, judgement, ruling, rule, decree, order, recommendation; Law determination; N. Amer. resolve.

fine[1] adj. **1** *a fine collection of Regency furniture | fine wines* **excellent**, first-class, first-rate, great, exceptional, outstanding, quality, superior, splendid, magnificent, exquisite, choice, select, premium, prime, supreme, superb, wonderful, superlative, of high quality, second to none; informal A1, top-notch, splendiferous. **2** *a fine lady* **worthy**, admirable, praiseworthy, laudable, estimable, upright, upstanding, respectable. **3** *the initiative is fine, but it's not enough on its own* **all right**, acceptable, suitable, good (enough), passable, satisfactory, adequate, reasonable, tolerable; informal OK. **4** *I feel fine* **in good health**, well, healthy, all right, (fighting) fit, as fit as a fiddle/flea, blooming, thriving, in good shape/condition, in fine fettle; informal OK, in the pink. **5** *a fine day* **fair**, dry, bright, clear, sunny, without a cloud in the sky, warm, balmy, summery. **6** *a fine old house* **impressive**, imposing, striking, splendid, grand, majestic, magnificent, stately. **7** *fine clothes* **elegant**, stylish, expensive, smart, chic, fashionable; fancy, sumptuous, lavish, opulent; informal flashy, swanky, ritzy, plush. **8** *a fine mind* **keen**, quick, alert, sharp, bright, brilliant, astute, clever, intelligent, perspicacious. **9** *fine china* **delicate**, fragile, dainty. **10** *fine hair* **thin**, light, delicate, wispy, flyaway. **11** *a fine point* **sharp**, keen, acute, sharpened, razor-sharp. **12** *fine material* **sheer**, light,

lightweight, thin, flimsy; diaphanous, filmy, gossamer, silky, transparent, translucent, see-through. **13** *a fine gold chain* **pure**, sterling, solid, unmixed, unblended, one hundred per cent. **14** *fine sand* **fine-grained**, powdery, powdered, dusty, ground, crushed; technical comminuted; old use pulverulent. **15** *fine detailed work* **intricate**, delicate, detailed, elaborate, dainty, meticulous. **16** *a fine distinction* **subtle**, ultra-fine, nice, hair-splitting. **17** *people's finer feelings* **elevated**, lofty, exalted; refined, sensitive, cultivated, cultured, civilized, sophisticated. **18** *fine taste* **discerning**, discriminating, refined, cultivated, cultured, critical.
– OPPOSITES poor, unsatisfactory, ill, inclement, thick, coarse.
▶ adv. informal *you're doing fine* **well**, all right, not badly, satisfactorily, adequately, nicely, tolerably; informal OK, good.
– OPPOSITES badly.
▶ v. **1** *it can be fined right down to the required shape* **thin**, make/become thin, narrow, taper, attenuate. **2** *additives for fining wine* **clarify**, clear, purify, refine, filter.

fine² n. *heavy fines* **(financial) penalty**, sanction, fee, charge; formal mulct; Brit. historical amercement.
▶ v. *they were fined for breaking environmental laws* **penalize**, impose a fine on, charge; formal mulct; Brit. historical amerce.

finery n. **regalia**, best clothes, (Sunday) best; informal glad rags, best bib and tucker.

finesse n. **1** *masterly finesse* **skill**, skilfulness, expertise, subtlety, flair, panache, elan, polish, artistry, virtuosity, mastery. **2** *a modicum of finesse* **tact**, tactfulness, discretion, diplomacy, delicacy, sensitivity, perceptiveness, savoir faire. **3** *a clever finesse* **winning move**, trick, stratagem, ruse, manoeuvre, artifice, machination.

finger n. *he wagged his finger at her* **digit**, thumb, index finger, forefinger; informal pinkie.
▶ v. **1** *she fingered her brooch uneasily* **touch**, feel, handle, stroke, rub, caress, fondle, toy with, play (about/around) with, fiddle with. **2** N. Amer. informal *no one fingered the culprit* **identify**, recognize, pick out, spot; inform on, point the finger at; informal rat on, squeal on, tell on, blow the whistle on, snitch on, peach on; Brit. informal grass on.

finicky adj. **fussy**, fastidious, punctilious, over-particular, difficult, exacting, demanding; informal picky, choosy, pernickety; N. Amer. informal persnickety; old use nice.

finish v. **1** *Mrs Porter had just finished the task* **complete**, end, conclude, stop, cease, terminate, bring to a conclusion/end/close, wind up; crown, cap, round off, put the finishing touches to; accomplish, discharge, carry out, do, get done, fulfil; informal wrap up, sew up, polish off. **2** *Sarah has finished school* **leave**, give up, drop; stop, discontinue, have done with, complete; informal pack in, quit. **3** *Hitch finished his dinner* **consume**, eat, devour, drink, finish off, polish off, gulp (down); use (up), exhaust, empty, drain, get

through, run through; informal down. **4** *the programme has finished* **end**, come to an end, stop, conclude, come to a conclusion/end/close, cease. **5** *some items were finished in a black lacquer* **varnish**, lacquer, veneer, coat, stain, wax, shellac, enamel, glaze.
– OPPOSITES start, begin, continue.
▶ n. **1** *the finish of filming* **end**, ending, completion, conclusion, close, closing, cessation, termination; final part/stage, finale, denouement; informal sewing up, polishing off. **2** *a gallop to the finish* **finishing line/post**, tape. **3** *an antiquated paint finish* **veneer**, lacquer, lamination, glaze, coating, covering; surface, texture.
– OPPOSITES start, beginning.
▫ **finish someone/something off 1** *the executioners finished them off* **kill**, take/end the life of, execute, terminate, exterminate, liquidate; informal wipe out, do in, bump off, take out, dispose of, do away with; N. Amer. informal ice, rub out, waste. **2** *financial difficulties finished off the business* **overwhelm**, overcome, defeat, get the better of, worst, bring down; informal drive to the wall, best.

finished adj. **1** *the finished job* **completed**, concluded, terminated, over (and done with), at an end; accomplished, executed, discharged, fulfilled, done; informal wrapped up, sewn up, polished off; formal effectuated. **2** *a finished performance* **accomplished**, polished, flawless, faultless, perfect; expert, proficient, masterly, impeccable, virtuoso, skilful, skilled, professional. **3** *he was finished* **ruined**, defeated, beaten, wrecked, doomed, bankrupt, broken; informal washed up, through.
– OPPOSITES incomplete.

finite adj. **limited**, restricted, fixed, determinate.

fire n. **1** *a fire broke out* **blaze**, conflagration, inferno; flames, burning, combustion. **2** *an electric fire* **heater**, radiator, convector. **3** *he lacked fire* **dynamism**, energy, vigour, animation, vitality, vibrancy, exuberance, zest, elan; passion, ardour, zeal, spirit, verve, vivacity, vivaciousness; enthusiasm, eagerness, gusto, fervour, fervency; informal pep, vim, go, get-up-and-go, oomph. **4** *rapid machine-gun fire* **gunfire**, firing, flak, bombardment. **5** *they directed their fire at the prime minister* **criticism**, censure, condemnation, denunciation, opprobrium, admonishments, brickbats; hostility, antagonism, animosity; informal flak.
▶ v. **1** *howitzers firing shells* **launch**, shoot, discharge, let fly with. **2** *someone fired a gun* **shoot**, discharge, let off, set off. **3** informal *he was fired* **dismiss**, discharge, give someone their notice, lay off, let go, get rid of, axe, cashier; informal sack, give someone the sack, boot out, give someone the boot/bullet, give someone the elbow/push, give someone their marching orders; Brit. informal give someone their cards. **4** *the engine fired* **start**, get started, get going. **5** *the stories fired my imagination* **stimulate**, stir up, excite,

awaken, arouse, rouse, inflame, animate, inspire, motivate.
□ **catch fire** ignite, catch light, burst into flames, go up in flames.
on fire 1 *the restaurant was on fire* **burning**, alight, ablaze, blazing, aflame, in flames; literary afire. **2** *she was on fire with passion* **ardent**, passionate, fervent, excited, eager, enthusiastic.

> **WORD LINKS**
>
> **arson** the criminal act of deliberately setting fire to property
> **pyromania** an obsessive desire to set fire to things
> **incendiary** a bomb designed to cause fires
> **kindling**, **tinder** material used to light a fire
> **Prometheus** (in Greek mythology) a demigod who stole fire from the gods and gave it to humans
> **salamander** a mythical creature said to live in fire

firearm n. **gun**, weapon; informal **shooter**; N. Amer. informal piece, rod, shooting iron.
firebrand n. **radical**, revolutionary, agitator, rabble-rouser, incendiary, subversive, troublemaker.
fireproof adj. **non-flammable**, incombustible, fire resistant, flame resistant, flame retardant, heatproof.
– OPPOSITES inflammable.
firm¹ adj. **1** *the ground is fairly firm* **hard**, solid, unyielding, resistant; solidified, hardened, compacted, compressed, dense, stiff, rigid, frozen, set. **2** *firm foundations* **secure**, secured, stable, steady, strong, fixed, fast, set, taut, tight; immovable, irremovable, stationary, motionless. **3** *a firm handshake* **strong**, vigorous, sturdy, forceful. **4** *I was very firm about what I wanted* **resolute**, determined, decided, resolved, steadfast; adamant, emphatic, insistent, single-minded; sure, certain, definite. **5** *a firm Labour supporter* **wholehearted**, unfaltering, unwavering, unflinching, unswerving, unbending; hard-line, committed, dyed-in-the-wool. **6** *firm friends* **close**, good, boon, intimate, inseparable, dear, special, fast; constant, devoted, loving, faithful, long-standing, steady, steadfast. **7** *firm plans* **definite**, fixed, settled, decided, established, confirmed, agreed; unalterable, unchangeable, irreversible.
– OPPOSITES soft, unstable, limp, indefinite.
firm² n. *an accountancy firm* **company**, business, concern, enterprise, organization, corporation, conglomerate, office, bureau, agency, consortium; informal outfit, set-up.
firmament n. literary **the sky**, heaven; the skies; literary the heavens, the empyrean, the welkin.
first adj. **1** *the first chapter* **earliest**, initial, opening, introductory. **2** *first principles* **fundamental**, basic, rudimentary, primary; key, cardinal, central, chief, vital, essential. **3** *our first priority* **foremost**, principal, highest, greatest, paramount, top, uppermost, prime, chief, leading, main, major; overriding, predominant, prevailing,

central, core, dominant; informal number-one. **4** *first prize* **top**, best, prime, premier, winner's, winning.
– OPPOSITES last, closing.
▸ adv. **1** *the room they had first entered* **at first**, to begin with, first of all, at the outset, initially. **2** *she would eat first* **before anything else**, first and foremost, now. **3** *she wouldn't go—she'd die first!* **in preference**, sooner, rather, more willingly.
▸ n. **1** *from the first, surrealism was theatrical* **the (very) beginning**, the start, the outset, the commencement; informal the word go, the off. **2** informal *it was a first for both of us* **novelty**, new/first experience.
first-class adj. **superior**, first-rate, high-quality, top-quality, top-tier, high-grade, five-star; prime, premier, premium, grade A, best, finest, select, exclusive, excellent, superb; informal tip-top, A1, top-notch.
– OPPOSITES poor.
first-hand adj. **direct**, immediate, personal, hands-on, experiential, empirical.
– OPPOSITES vicarious, indirect.
first name n. **forename**, Christian name, given name.
– OPPOSITES surname.
first-rate adj. **top-quality**, high-quality, top-grade, top-tier, first-class, second to none, fine; superlative, excellent, superb, outstanding, exceptional, exemplary, marvellous, magnificent, splendid; informal tip-top, top-notch, ace, A1, super, great, terrific, tremendous, fantastic; Brit. informal top-hole, smashing; informal dated capital.
fiscal adj. **tax**, budgetary; financial, economic, monetary, money.
fish v. **1** *some people were fishing in the lake* **go fishing**, angle, trawl. **2** *she fished for her purse* **search**, delve, look, hunt; grope, fumble, ferret (about/around), root about/around, rummage (about/around/round). **3** *I'm not fishing for compliments* **angle for**, look for, seek, hope for, solicit, cast about/around/round, be after.
□ **fish something out** pull out, haul out, remove, extricate, extract, retrieve.

> **WORD LINKS**
>
> **piscine** relating to fish
> **piscatorial** relating to fishing
> **ichthyology** the study of fish
> **mariculture**, **pisciculture** the controlled breeding and rearing of fish
> **piscivorous** fish-eating
> **roe**, **spawn** fish eggs
> **milt** the semen of a male fish
> **fry** young fish

fisherman n. **angler**, rod; old use fisher.
fishy adj. **1** *a fishy smell* **fishlike**, piscine. **2** *round fishy eyes* **expressionless**, inexpressive, vacant, lacklustre, glassy. **3** informal *there was something fishy going on* **suspicious**, questionable, dubious, doubtful, suspect; odd, queer, peculiar, strange; informal funny, shady, crooked, bent; Brit. informal dodgy; Austral./NZ informal shonky.

fission n. **splitting**, division, dividing, rupture, breaking, severance.
– OPPOSITES fusion.

fissure n. **opening**, crevice, crack, cleft, breach, crevasse, chasm; break, fracture, fault, rift, rupture, split.

fist n. **clenched hand**; informal duke, meat hook; Brit. informal bunch of fives.

fit¹ adj. **1** *fit for human habitation | he is a fit subject for such a book* **suitable**, good enough; relevant, pertinent, apt, appropriate, suited, apposite, fitting; old use meet. **2** *is he fit to look after a child?* **competent**, able, capable; ready, prepared, qualified, trained, equipped. **3** informal *you look fit to commit murder!* **ready**, prepared, all set, in a fit state, likely, about; informal psyched up. **4** *he looked tanned and fit* **healthy**, well, in good health, in (good) shape, in (good) trim, in good condition, fighting fit, as fit as a fiddle/flea; athletic, muscular, strong, robust, hale and hearty.
– OPPOSITES unsuitable, incapable, unwell.
▸ v. **1** *my overcoat should fit you* **be the right/correct size (for)**, be big/small enough (for), fit like a glove. **2** *have your carpets fitted professionally* **lay**, put in place/position, position, place, fix. **3** *cameras fitted with a backlight button* **equip**, provide, supply, fit out, furnish. **4** *concrete slabs were fitted together* **join**, connect, put together, piece together, attach, unite, link. **5** *a sentence that fits his crimes* **be appropriate to**, suit, match, correspond to, tally with, go with, accord with, correlate to, be congruous with, be congruent with, be consonant with. **6** *an MSc fits you for a professional career* **qualify**, prepare, make ready, train, groom.
▸ n. *the degree of fit between a school's philosophy and practice* **correlation**, correspondence, agreement, consistency, equivalence, match, similarity, compatibility, concurrence.
◻ **fit in** conform, be in harmony, blend in, be in line, be assimilated into.
fit someone/something out/up equip, provide, supply, furnish, kit out, rig out.
fit someone up Brit. informal falsely incriminate; informal frame, set up.

fit² n. **1** *an epileptic fit* **convulsion**, spasm, paroxysm, seizure, attack; Medicine ictus. **2** *a fit of the giggles* **outburst**, outburst, attack, bout, spell. **3** *my mother would have a fit if she knew* **tantrum**, fit of temper, outburst of anger/rage, frenzy; informal paddy, stress; N. Amer. informal blowout; formal boutade.
◻ **in/by fits and starts** spasmodically, intermittently, sporadically, erratically, irregularly, fitfully, haphazardly.

fitful adj. **intermittent**, sporadic, spasmodic, broken, disturbed, disrupted, patchy, irregular, uneven, unsettled.

fitness n. **1** *polo requires tremendous fitness* **good health**, strength, robustness, vigour, athleticism, toughness, physical fitness, muscularity; good condition, good shape, well-being. **2** *his fitness for active service* **suitability**, capability, competence, ability,

aptitude; readiness, preparedness, eligibility.

fitted adj. **1** *a fitted sheet* **shaped**, contoured, fitting tightly/well. **2** *a fitted wardrobe* **built-in**, integral, integrated, fixed. **3** *he wasn't fitted for the job* **(well) suited**, right, suitable; equipped, fit; informal cut out.

fitting n. **1** *a light fitting* **attachment**, connection, part, piece, component, accessory. **2** *bathroom fittings* **furnishings**, furniture, fixtures, fitments, equipment, appointments, appurtenances. **3** *the fitting of catalytic converters* **installation**, installing, putting in, fixing.
▸ adj. *a fitting conclusion* **apt**, appropriate, suitable, apposite; fit, proper, right, seemly, correct; old use meet.
– OPPOSITES unsuitable.

five cardinal number **quintet**, fivesome; quintuplets.

WORD LINKS

quintuple consisting of five parts or things
quinquennial lasting for or recurring every five years
pentad a group or set of five
pentagon a five-sided figure
pentagram, pentangle a five-pointed star
pentameter a line of verse consisting of five metrical feet
pentathlon an athletic event consisting of five different activities

---

fix v. **1** *signs were fixed to lamp posts* **fasten**, attach, affix, secure; join, connect, couple, link; install, implant, embed; stick, glue, pin, nail, screw, bolt, clamp, clip. **2** *his words are fixed in my memory* **stick**, lodge, embed. **3** *his eyes were fixed on the ground* **focus**, direct, level, point, train. **4** *techniques of fixing audience's attention* **attract**, draw; hold, grip, engage, captivate, rivet. **5** *he fixed my washing machine* **repair**, mend, put right, put to rights, get working, restore (to working order); overhaul, service, renovate, recondition. **6** *James fixed it for his parents to watch the show from the wings* **arrange**, organize, contrive, manage, engineer; informal swing, wangle. **7** informal *Laura was fixing her hair* **arrange**, put in order, adjust; style, groom, comb, brush; informal do. **8** informal *Chris will fix supper* **prepare**, cook, make, get; informal rustle up; Brit. informal knock up. **9** *let's fix a date for the meeting* **decide on**, select, choose, resolve on; determine, settle, set, arrange, establish, allot; designate, name, appoint, specify. **10** *chemicals are used to fix the dye* **make permanent**, make fast, set. **11** informal *the fight was fixed* **rig**, arrange fraudulently; tamper with, influence; informal fiddle.
▸ n. informal **1** *they are in a bit of a fix* **predicament**, plight, difficulty, awkward situation, corner, tight spot; mess, mare's nest, dire straits; informal pickle, jam, hole, scrape, bind, sticky situation. **2** *he needed his fix* **dose**; informal hit. **3** *a quick fix for the coal industry* **solution**, answer, resolution, way out, remedy, cure; informal magic bullet. **4** *the result was a complete fix* **fraud**, swindle,

trick, charade, sham; informal set-up, fiddle.
□ **fix something up** organize, arrange, make arrangements for, fix, sort out.

fixated adj. **obsessed**, preoccupied, obsessive; focused, keen, gripped, engrossed, immersed, wrapped up, enthusiastic, fanatical; informal hooked, wild, nuts, crazy; Brit. informal potty.

fixation n. **obsession**, preoccupation, mania, addiction, compulsion; informal thing, bug, craze, fad.

fixed adj. **1** *there are fixed ropes on the rock face* **fastened**, secure, fast, firm; riveted, moored, anchored. **2** *a fixed period of time* **predetermined**, set, established, arranged, specified, decided, agreed, determined, confirmed, prescribed, definite, defined, explicit, precise.

fixture n. **1** *fixtures and fittings* **fixed appliance**, installation, unit. **2** Brit. *their first fixture of the season* **match**, race, game, competition, contest, sporting event; Brit. clash.

fizz v. **1** *the mixture fizzed like mad* **effervesce**, sparkle, bubble, froth; literary spume. **2** *all the screens were fizzing* **crackle**, buzz, hiss, fizzle, crepitate.
▶ n. **1** *the fizz in champagne* **effervescence**, sparkle, fizziness, bubbles, bubbliness, gassiness, carbonation, froth. **2** informal *they all had another glass of fizz* **sparkling wine**, champagne; informal bubbly, champers, sparkler. **3** informal *their set is a little lacking in fizz* **ebullience**, exuberance, liveliness, life, vivacity, animation, vigour, energy, verve, dash, spirit, sparkle, zest; informal pizzazz, pep, zip, oomph. **4** *the fizz of the static* **crackle**, crackling, buzz, buzzing, hiss, hissing, white noise; literary susurration.

fizzle v. *the loudspeaker fizzled* **crackle**, buzz, hiss, fizz, crepitate.
▶ n. **1** *electric fizzle.* See **fizz** (sense 4 of the noun). **2** *the whole thing turned out to be a fizzle* **failure**, fiasco, debacle, disaster; Brit. damp squib; informal flop, washout, let-down, dead loss; N. Amer. informal snafu.
□ **fizzle out** peter out, die off, ease off, cool off; tail off, wither away; informal flatline.

fizzy adj. **effervescent**, sparkling, carbonated, gassy, bubbly, frothy; mousseux, pétillant, spumante, frizzante.
– OPPOSITES still, flat.

flab n. informal **fat**, excessive weight, fatness, plumpness; paunch, pot belly, beer gut.

flabbergast v. informal See **astonish**.

flabbiness n. **fat**, fatness, fleshiness, plumpness, chubbiness, portliness, obesity, corpulence; softness, looseness, flaccidity, droopiness, sag; informal flab, tubbiness.

flabby adj. **1** *his flabby stomach* **soft**, loose, flaccid, slack, untoned, drooping, sagging. **2** *a flabby woman* **fat**, fleshy, overweight, plump, chubby, portly, rotund, broad in the beam, of ample proportions, obese, corpulent; informal tubby, roly-poly, well covered, well upholstered.
– OPPOSITES firm, thin.

flaccid adj. **1** *your muscles are sagging, they're flaccid* **soft**, loose, flabby, slack, lax; drooping, sagging. **2** *his play seemed flaccid* **lacklustre**, lifeless, listless, uninspiring, unanimated, tame.
– OPPOSITES firm, spirited.

flag[1] n. *the Irish flag* **banner**, standard, ensign, pennant, banderole, streamer, jack, gonfalon; colours; Brit. pendant.
▶ v. *flag the misspelt words* **indicate**, identify, point out, mark, label, tag, highlight.
□ **flag someone/something down** hail, wave down, signal to stop, stop, halt.

> **WORD LINKS**
> **vexillology** the study of flags

flag[2] n. *stone flags.* See **flagstone**.

flag[3] v. **1** *they were flagging towards the finish* **tire**, grow tired/weary, weaken, grow weak, wilt, droop. **2** *my energy flags in the afternoon* **fade**, decline, wane, ebb, diminish, decrease, lessen, dwindle; wither, melt away, peter out, die away/down.
– OPPOSITES revive.

flagon n. **jug**, vessel, bottle, carafe, flask, decanter, tankard, ewer, pitcher.

flagrant adj. **blatant**, glaring, obvious, overt, conspicuous, barefaced, shameless, brazen, undisguised, unconcealed; outrageous, scandalous, shocking, disgraceful, dreadful, terrible, gross.

flagstone n. **paving slab**, paving stone, slab, flag, sett.

flail v. **1** *he fell headlong, his arms flailing* **wave**, swing, thrash about, flap about. **2** *I was flailing about in the water* **flounder**, struggle, thrash, writhe, splash. **3** *he flailed their shoulders with his cane* **thrash**, beat, strike, flog, whip, lash, scourge, cane; informal wallop, whack.

flair n. **1** *a flair for publicity* **aptitude**, talent, gift, instinct, (natural) ability, facility, skill, bent, feel. **2** *she dressed with flair* **style**, stylishness, panache, dash, elan, poise, elegance; (good) taste, discernment, discrimination; informal class.

flak n. **1** *my aircraft had been damaged by flak* **anti-aircraft fire**, shelling, gunfire; bombardment, barrage, salvo, volley. **2** informal *he has come in for a lot of flak* **criticism**, censure, disapproval, disapprobation, hostility, complaints; opprobrium, obloquy, calumny, vilification, abuse, brickbats; Brit. informal stick, verbal; formal castigation, excoriation, calumniation.

flake[1] n. *flakes of pastry* **sliver**, wafer, shaving, paring; chip, scale, spillikin; fragment, scrap, shred; technical lamina.
▶ v. *the paint was flaking* **peel (off)**, chip, blister, come off (in layers).

flake[2] v.
□ **flake out** informal *she flaked out in her chair* fall asleep, go to sleep, drop off; collapse, faint, pass out, lose consciousness, black out, swoon; informal conk out, nod off; N. Amer. informal sack out, zone out.

flaky adj. **flaking**, peeling, scaly, blistering, scabrous.

flamboyant adj. **1** *her flamboyant personality* **ostentatious**, exuberant, confident, lively, animated, vibrant, vivacious. **2** *flamboyant jewellery* **colourful**, brightly coloured, bright, vibrant, vivid; dazzling, eye-catching, bold; showy, gaudy, garish, lurid, loud; informal jazzy, flashy, bling; dated gay. **3** *a flamboyant architectural style* **elaborate**, ornate, fancy; baroque, rococo.
– OPPOSITES restrained.

flame n. **1** *a sheet of flames* **fire**, blaze, conflagration, inferno. **2** *the flames of her anger* **passion**, warmth, ardour, fervour, fervency, fire, intensity. **3** informal *an old flame* **sweetheart**, boyfriend, girlfriend, lover, partner; informal steady; dated beau.
▶ v. **1** *logs crackled and flamed* **burn**, blaze, be ablaze, be alight, be on fire, be in flames, be aflame, flare. **2** *Erica's cheeks flamed* **become red**, go red, blush, flush, redden, grow pink/crimson/scarlet, colour, glow.
▢ **in flames** on fire, burning, alight, flaming, blazing, ignited; literary afire.

flameproof adj. **non-flammable**, non-inflammable, flame-resistant, fire-resistant, flame-retardant, uninflammable.
– OPPOSITES flammable.

flaming adj. **1** *a flaming bonfire* **blazing**, ablaze, burning, on fire, in flames, aflame; literary afire. **2** *flaming hair* **bright**, brilliant, vivid; red, reddish-orange, ginger. **3** *a flaming row* **furious**, violent, vehement, frenzied, angry, passionate. **4** *in a flaming temper* **furious**, enraged, fuming, seething, incensed, infuriated, angry, raging; informal livid; literary wrathful. **5** informal *where's that flaming ambulance?* **wretched**; informal damned, damnable, blasted, blessed, confounded; Brit. informal flipping, blinking, blooming, bleeding, effing; Brit. informal dated bally, ruddy; dated cursed, accursed.

flammable adj. **inflammable**, burnable, combustible.

flank n. **1** *the horse's flanks* **side**, haunch, quarter, thigh. **2** *the southern flank of the Eighth Army* **side**, wing; face, aspect.
▶ v. *the garden is flanked by two rivers* **edge**, bound, line, border, fringe.

flannel n. **1** Brit. *she dabbed her face with a flannel* **facecloth**, cloth; N. Amer. washcloth, washrag; Austral. washer. **2** Brit. informal *don't accept any flannel from salespeople* **smooth talk**, flattery, blarney, blandishments, honeyed words; prevarication, equivocation, evasion, doublespeak; informal spiel, soft soap, sweet talk, baloney, hot air; Brit. informal waffle; Austral./NZ informal guyver.
▶ v. Brit. informal *she can tell if you're flannelling* **use flattery**, talk blarney; prevaricate, equivocate, be evasive, blather, stall; Brit. hum and haw; informal soft-soap, sweet-talk; Brit. informal waffle; N. Amer. informal fast-talk; rare tergiversate.

flap v. **1** *the mallards flapped their wings* **beat**, flutter, agitate, wave, wag, swing. **2** *the flag flapped in the breeze* **flutter**, fly, blow, swing, sway, ripple, stir. **3** informal *a deliberate ploy to make us flap* **panic**, go into a panic, become flustered, be agitated, fuss; informal be in a state, be in a tizzy.
▶ n. **1** *pockets with buttoned flaps* **fold**, overlap, covering; lappet. **2** *a few flaps of the wing* **flutter**, fluttering, beat, beating, waving. **3** informal *I'm in a frightful flap* **panic**, fluster; informal state, dither, twitter, blue funk, stew, tizzy; N. Amer. informal twit. **4** informal *she created a flap with her controversial statement* **fuss**, commotion, stir, hubbub, storm, uproar; controversy, brouhaha, furore; informal to-do, ballyhoo, hoo-ha, kerfuffle.

flare n. **1** *the flare of the match* **blaze**, flash, dazzle, burst, flicker. **2** *a flare set off by the crew* **distress signal**, rocket, Very light, beacon, light, signal. **3** *a flare of anger* **burst**, rush, eruption, explosion, spasm, access.
▶ v. **1** *the match flared* **blaze**, flash, flare up, flame, burn; glow, flicker. **2** *her nostrils flared* **spread**, broaden, widen; dilate.
▢ **flare up 1** *the wooden houses flared up like matchsticks* **burn**, blaze, go up in flames. **2** *there are numerous disputes, any one of which might flare up into a major conflict* **erupt**, explode, blow up, break out, escalate. **3** *I flared up at him* **lose one's temper**, become enraged, fly into a temper, go berserk; informal blow one's top, fly off the handle, go mad, go bananas, hit the roof, go up the wall, go off the deep end, lose one's rag, flip (one's lid), explode, have a fit; Brit. informal go spare, go crackers, do one's nut; N. Amer. informal flip one's wig, blow one's lid/stack, have a conniption fit.

flash v. **1** *a torch flashed* **light up**, shine, flare, blaze, gleam, glint, sparkle, burn; blink, wink, flicker, shimmer, twinkle, glimmer, glisten, scintillate; literary glister, coruscate. **2** informal *he was flashing his money about* **show off**, flaunt, flourish, display, parade. **3** *racing cars flashed past* **zoom**, streak, tear, shoot, dash, dart, fly, whistle, hurtle, rush, bolt, race, speed, career, whizz, whoosh, buzz; informal belt, zap; Brit. informal bomb, bucket; N. Amer. informal barrel.
▶ n. **1** *a flash of light* **flare**, blaze, burst; gleam, glint, sparkle, flicker, shimmer, twinkle, glimmer. **2** *a basic uniform with no flashes* **emblem**, insignia, badge; stripe, bar, chevron. **3** *a sudden flash of inspiration* **burst**, outburst, wave, rush, surge, flush.
▶ adj. informal *a flash sports car.* See **flashy**.
▢ **in/like a flash** instantly, suddenly, abruptly, immediately, all of a sudden; quickly, rapidly, swiftly, speedily; in an instant/moment, in a (split) second, in a trice, in the blink of an eye; informal in a jiffy, before you can say Jack Robinson.

flashy adj. informal **ostentatious**, flamboyant, showy, conspicuous, extravagant, expensive; vulgar, tasteless, brash, lurid, garish, loud, gaudy; informal snazzy, fancy, swanky, flash, jazzy, glitzy, bling.
– OPPOSITES understated.

flask n. **bottle**, container; hip flask, vacuum flask; trademark Thermos.

flat¹ adj. **1** *a flat surface* **level**, horizontal; smooth, even, uniform, regular, plane. **2** *the sea was flat* **calm**, still, pacific, glassy, undisturbed, without waves, like a millpond. **3** *a flat wooden box* **shallow**, low-sided. **4** *a pair of flat sandals* **low**, low-heeled, without heels. **5** *his voice was flat* **monotonous**, toneless, droning, boring, dull, tedious, uninteresting, unexciting, soporific; bland, dreary, colourless, featureless, emotionless, expressionless, lifeless, spiritless, lacklustre. **6** *he felt flat and weary* **depressed**, dejected, dispirited, despondent, downhearted, disheartened, low, low-spirited, down, unhappy, blue; without energy, enervated, sapped, weary, tired out, worn out, exhausted, drained; informal down in the mouth/dumps. **7** *the market was flat* **slow**, inactive, sluggish, slack, quiet, depressed. **8** Brit. *a flat battery* **expired**, dead, finished, used up, run out. **9** *a flat tyre* **deflated**, punctured, burst. **10** *a flat fee* **fixed**, set, regular, unchanging, unvarying, invariable. **11** *a flat denial* **outright**, direct, absolute, definite, positive, straight, plain, explicit; firm, resolute, adamant, assertive, emphatic, categorical, unconditional, unqualified, unequivocal.
– OPPOSITES vertical, uneven.
▸ adv. **1** *she lay down flat on the floor* **stretched out**, outstretched, spreadeagled, sprawling, prone, supine, prostrate, recumbent. **2** informal *she turned me down flat* **outright**, absolutely, firmly, resolutely, adamantly, emphatically, insistently, categorically, unconditionally, unequivocally.
▫ **flat out** hard, as hard as possible, for all one's worth, to the full/limit, all out; at full speed, as fast as possible, at full tilt; informal like crazy, like mad, like the wind, like a bomb; Brit. informal like billy-o, like the clappers.

flat² n. *a two-bedroom flat* **apartment**, set of rooms, penthouse; rooms; Austral. home unit; N. Amer. informal crib.

flatten v. **1** *Tom flattened the crumpled paper* **smooth out**, even (out), level (out/off). **2** *the cows flattened the grass* **compress**, press down, crush, squash, compact, trample. **3** *tornadoes can flatten buildings in seconds* **demolish**, raze (to the ground), tear down, knock down, destroy, wreck, devastate, obliterate; N. Amer. informal total. **4** informal *Flynn flattened him with a single punch* **knock down/over**, knock to the ground, fell, floor, prostrate, rugby-tackle; informal deck; Brit. informal knock for six. **5** *I flattened a drunken heckler* **humiliate**, crush, quash, squash, take down a peg or two, put someone in their place; informal put down, cut down to size.

flatter v. **1** *it amused him to flatter her* **compliment**, praise, express admiration for, say nice things about, pay court to, fawn on; cajole, humour, flannel, blarney; informal sweet-talk, soft-soap, butter up, play up to; formal laud. **2** *I was flattered to be asked*

honour, gratify, please, delight; informal tickle pink. **3** *a hairstyle that flattered her* **suit**, become, look good on, go well with; informal do something for.
– OPPOSITES insult, offend.

flatterer n. **sycophant**, groveller, fawner, lackey; informal crawler, toady, bootlicker, yes man, lickspittle; formal encomiast.

flattering adj. **1** *flattering remarks* **complimentary**, praising, favourable, commending, admiring, applauding, appreciative, good; honeyed, sugary, cajoling, flannelling, silver-tongued, honey-tongued; fawning, oily, obsequious, ingratiating, servile, sycophantic; informal sweet-talking, soft-soaping, crawling, bootlicking; formal encomiastic. **2** *it was very flattering to be nominated* **pleasing**, gratifying, honouring, gladdening. **3** *her most flattering dress* **becoming**, enhancing.

flattery n. **praise**, adulation, compliments, blandishments, honeyed words; fawning, blarney, cajolery; informal sweet talk, soft soap, buttering up, toadying; Brit. informal flannel; formal laudation.

flatulence n. **1** *medications that help with flatulence* **(intestinal) gas**, wind; informal farting; formal flatus. **2** *the flatulence of his latest recordings* **pomposity**, pompousness, pretension, pretentiousness, grandiloquence, bombast, turgidity.

flaunt v. **show off**, display ostentatiously, make a (great) show of, put on show/display, parade; brag about, crow about, vaunt; informal flash.

flavour n. **1** *the flavour of prosciutto* **taste**, savour, tang. **2** *salami can give extra flavour* **flavouring**, seasoning, tastiness, tang, relish, bite, piquancy, pungency, spice, spiciness, zest; informal zing, zip. **3** *a strong international flavour* **character**, quality, feel, feeling, ambience, atmosphere, aura, air, mood, tone; spirit, essence, nature; informal vibe. **4** *this excerpt will give a flavour of the report* **impression**, suggestion, hint, taste.
▸ v. *spices for flavouring food* **add flavour to**, add flavouring to, season, spice (up), add piquancy to, ginger up, enrich; informal pep up.

flavouring n. **1** *this cheese is often combined with other flavourings* **seasoning**, spice, herb, additive; condiment, dressing. **2** *vanilla flavouring* **essence**, extract, concentrate, distillate.

flaw n. **defect**, blemish, fault, imperfection, deficiency, weakness, weak spot/point, inadequacy, shortcoming, limitation, failing, foible; Computing bug; informal glitch.
– OPPOSITES strength.

flawed adj. **1** *a flawed mirror* **faulty**, defective, unsound, imperfect; broken, cracked, torn, scratched, deformed, distorted, warped, buckled; Brit. informal duff. **2** *the findings were flawed* **unsound**, defective, faulty, distorted, inaccurate, incorrect, erroneous, imprecise, fallacious, misleading.
– OPPOSITES flawless, sound.

flawless adj. **perfect**, unblemished, unmarked, unimpaired; whole, intact, sound, unbroken, undamaged, mint, pristine; impeccable, immaculate, consummate, accurate, correct, faultless, error-free, unerring; exemplary, model, ideal, copybook.
– OPPOSITES flawed.

flay v. **1** *the saint was flayed alive* **skin**, strip the skin off; Medicine excoriate. **2** *he flayed his critics.* See **criticize**.

fleck n. *flecks of pale blue* **spot**, mark, dot, speck, speckle, freckle, patch, smudge, streak, blotch, dab; informal splosh, splodge; rare macula.
▸ v. *the deer's flanks were flecked with white* **spot**, mark, dot, speckle, bespeckle, freckle, stipple, stud, bestud, blotch, mottle, streak, splash, spatter, bespatter, scatter, sprinkle; Scottish & Irish slabber; informal splosh, splodge.

fledgling n. *a woodpecker fledgling* **chick**, baby bird, nestling.
▸ adj. *fledgling industries* **emerging**, emergent, sunrise, dawning, embryonic, infant, nascent; developing, in the making, budding, up-and-coming, rising.
– OPPOSITES declining, mature.

flee v. **1** *she fled to her room* **run (away/off)**, run for it, make a run for it, take flight, be gone, make off, take off, take to one's heels, make a break for it, bolt, beat a (hasty) retreat, make a quick exit, make one's getaway, escape; informal beat it, clear off/out, vamoose, skedaddle, split, leg it, turn tail, scram; Brit. informal scarper; N. Amer. informal light out, bug out, cut out, peel out; Austral. informal shoot through; old use fly. **2** *they fled the country* **run away from**, leave, escape from; informal skip, quit; old use fly.

fleece n. *a sheep's fleece* **wool**, coat.
▸ v. informal *we were fleeced by a ticket tout.* See **swindle** (verb).

fleecy adj. **fluffy**, woolly, downy, soft, fuzzy, furry, velvety, shaggy; technical floccose, pilose.
– OPPOSITES coarse.

fleet[1] n. *the fleet set sail* **navy**, naval force, (naval) task force, armada, flotilla, squadron, convoy.

fleet[2] adj. literary *as fleet as a greyhound* **nimble**, agile, lithe, lissom, acrobatic, supple, light-footed, light on one's feet, spry, sprightly; quick, fast, swift, rapid, speedy, brisk, smart; informal nippy, zippy, twinkle-toed.

fleeting adj. **brief**, short, short-lived, quick, momentary, cursory, transient, ephemeral, fugitive, passing, transitory; literary evanescent.
– OPPOSITES lasting.

flesh n. **1** *you need more flesh on your bones* **muscle**, meat, tissue, brawn; informal beef. **2** *she carries too much flesh* **fat**, weight; Anatomy adipose tissue; informal blubber, flab. **3** *a fruit with juicy flesh* **pulp**, soft part, marrow, meat. **4** *the pleasures of the flesh* **the body**, human nature, physicality, carnality, animality; sensuality, sexuality.

▫ **one's (own) flesh and blood** family, relative(s), relation(s), blood relation(s), kin, kinsfolk, kinsman, kinsmen, kinswoman, kinswomen, kindred, nearest and dearest, people; informal folks.

flesh out put on weight, gain weight, get heavier, grow fat/fatter, fatten up, get fat, fill out.

flesh something out expand (on), elaborate on, add to, build on, add flesh to, put flesh on (the bones of), add detail to, expatiate on, supplement, reinforce, augment, fill out, enlarge on.

in the flesh in person, before one's (very) eyes, in front of one; in real life, live; physically, bodily, in bodily/human form, incarnate.

fleshly adj. **carnal**, physical, animal, bestial; sexual, sensual, erotic, lustful.
– OPPOSITES spiritual, noble.

fleshy adj. **plump**, chubby, portly, fat, obese, overweight, stout, corpulent, paunchy, well padded, well covered, well upholstered, rotund; informal tubby, pudgy, beefy, porky, roly-poly, blubbery; Brit. informal podgy, fubsy; N. Amer. informal corn-fed; Austral./NZ nuggety.
– OPPOSITES thin.

flex[1] v. **1** *you must flex your elbow* **bend**, crook, hook, cock, angle, double up. **2** *Rachel flexed her cramped muscles* **tighten**, tauten, tense (up), tension, contract.
– OPPOSITES straighten, relax.

flex[2] n. Brit. *an electric flex* **cable**, wire, lead; N. Amer. cord.

flexibility n. **1** *the flexibility of wood* **pliability**, suppleness, pliancy, plasticity; elasticity, stretchiness, springiness, spring, resilience, bounce; informal give. **2** *the flexibility of an endowment loan* **adaptability**, adjustability, variability, versatility, open-endedness, freedom, latitude. **3** *the flexibility shown by the local authority* **willingness to compromise**, accommodation, amenability, cooperation, tolerance.
– OPPOSITES rigidity, inflexibility, intransigence.

flexible adj. **1** *flexible tubing* **pliable**, supple, bendable, pliant, plastic; elastic, stretchy, whippy, springy, resilient, bouncy; informal bendy; old use flexile. **2** *a flexible arrangement* **adaptable**, adjustable, variable, versatile, open-ended, open, free. **3** *the need to be flexible towards tenants* **accommodating**, amenable, willing to compromise, cooperative, tolerant, easy-going.
– OPPOSITES rigid, inflexible, intransigent.

flick n. *a flick of the wrist* **jerk**, snap, flip, whisk.
▸ v. **1** *he flicked the switch* **click**, snap, flip, jerk. **2** *the horse flicked its tail* **swish**, twitch, wave, wag, waggle, shake.
▫ **flick through** thumb (through), leaf through, flip through, skim through, scan, look through, browse through, dip into, glance at/through, peruse, run one's eye over.

flicker v. **1** *the lights flickered* **glimmer**, glint, flare, dance, gutter; twinkle, sparkle, blink, wink, flash, scintillate; literary glister, coruscate. **2** *his eyelids flickered* **flutter**, quiver, tremble, shiver, shudder, spasm, jerk, twitch.

flight n. **1** *the history of flight* **aviation**, flying, air transport, aerial navigation, aeronautics. **2** *a flight to Rome* **plane trip/ journey**, trip/journey by air. **3** *the flight of a cricket ball* **trajectory**, path through the air, track, orbit. **4** *a flight of birds* **flock**, skein, covey, swarm, cloud. **5** *his headlong flight from home* **escape**, getaway, hasty departure, exit, exodus, decamping, breakout, bolt, disappearance; Brit. informal flit.
□ **take flight** flee, run (away/off), run for it, make a run for it, be gone, make off, take off, take to one's heels, make a break for it, bolt, beat a (hasty) retreat, make a quick exit, make one's getaway, escape; informal beat it, clear off/out, vamoose, skedaddle, split, leg it, turn tail, scram; Brit. informal scarper; N. Amer. informal light out, bug out, cut out, peel out; Austral. informal shoot through; old use fly.

flighty adj. **fickle**, inconstant, mercurial, whimsical, capricious, skittish, volatile, impulsive; irresponsible, giddy, reckless, wild, careless, thoughtless.
– OPPOSITES steady, responsible.

flimsy adj. **1** *a flimsy building* **insubstantial**, fragile, breakable, frail, shaky, unstable, wobbly, tottery, rickety, ramshackle, makeshift; jerry-built, badly built, shoddy, gimcrack. **2** *a flimsy garment* **thin**, light, fine, filmy, floaty, diaphanous, sheer, delicate, insubstantial, wispy, gossamer, gauzy. **3** *flimsy evidence* **weak**, feeble, poor, inadequate, insufficient, thin, unsubstantial, unconvincing, implausible, unsatisfactory.
– OPPOSITES sturdy, thick, sound.

flinch v. **1** *he flinched at the noise* **wince**, start, shudder, quiver, jerk, shy. **2** *he never flinched from his duty* **shrink from**, recoil from, shy away from, swerve from, demur from; dodge, evade, avoid, duck, balk at, jib at, quail at, fight shy of.

fling v. *he flung the axe into the river* **throw**, toss, sling, hurl, cast, pitch, lob; informal chuck, heave, bung, buzz; dated shy.
▸ n. *she had a brief fling with him* **affair**, love affair, relationship, romance, affaire (de cœur), amour, flirtation, dalliance, liaison, entanglement, involvement, attachment.

flip v. **1** *the wave flipped the dinghy over | the plane flipped on to its back* **overturn**, turn over, tip over, roll (over), upturn, capsize; upend, invert, knock over; keel over, topple over, turn turtle; old use overset. **2** *he flipped the key through the air* **throw**, flick, toss, fling, sling, pitch, cast, spin, lob; informal chuck, bung; dated shy. **3** *I flipped the transmitter switch* **flick**, click, snap.
□ **flip through** thumb (through), leaf through, flick through, skim through, scan, look through, browse through, dip into, glance at/through, peruse, run one's eye over.

flippancy n. **frivolity**, levity, facetiousness; disrespect, irreverence, impudence, cheek, impertinence; Brit. informal sauce; N. Amer. informal sassiness; dated waggery.
– OPPOSITES seriousness, respect.

flippant adj. **frivolous**, facetious, tongue-in-cheek; disrespectful, irreverent, impudent, cheeky, impertinent; informal flip, saucy, waggish; N. Amer. informal sassy.
– OPPOSITES serious, respectful.

flirt v. **1** *it amused him to flirt with her* **trifle with**, toy with, tease, lead on. **2** *those conservatives who flirted with fascism* **dabble in**, toy with, trifle with, amuse oneself with, play with, tinker with, dip into, scratch the surface of. **3** *he is flirting with danger* **dice with**, court, risk, not fear.
▸ n. *Anna was quite a flirt* **tease**, trifler, philanderer, coquette, heartbreaker; old use fizgig.

flirtation n. **coquetry**, teasing, trifling.

flirtatious adj. **coquettish**, flirty, kittenish, teasing.

flit v. **dart**, dance, skip, play, dash, trip, flutter, bob, bounce.

float v. **1** *oil floats on water* **stay afloat**, stay on the surface, be buoyant, be buoyed up. **2** *the balloon floated in the air* **hover**, levitate, be suspended, hang, defy gravity. **3** *a cloud floated across the moon* **drift**, glide, sail, slip, slide, waft. **4** *they have just floated that idea* **suggest**, put forward, come up with, submit, moot, propose, advance; informal run something up the flagpole. **5** *the company was floated on the Stock Exchange* **launch**, get going, get off the ground, offer, sell, introduce.
– OPPOSITES sink, rush, withdraw.

floating adj. **1** *floating seaweed* **afloat**, buoyant. **2** *floating gas balloons* **hovering**, levitating, suspended, hanging, defying gravity. **3** *floating voters* **uncommitted**, undecided, in two minds, torn, split, uncertain, unsure, wavering, vacillating, indecisive, blowing hot and cold, undeclared; informal sitting on the fence. **4** *a floating population* **unsettled**, transient, temporary, variable, fluctuating, migrant, wandering, nomadic, on the move, migratory, travelling, drifting, roving, roaming, itinerant, vagabond. **5** *a floating exchange rate* **variable**, changeable, changing, fluid, fluctuating.
– OPPOSITES sunken, grounded, committed, settled, fixed.

flock n. **1** *a flock of sheep* **herd**, drove. **2** *a flock of birds* **flight**, congregation, covey, clutch. **3** *flocks of people* **crowd**, throng, horde, mob, rabble, mass, multitude, host, army, pack, swarm, sea; informal gaggle.
▸ v. **1** *people flocked around Jesus* **gather**, collect, congregate, assemble, converge, mass, crowd, throng, cluster, swarm; formal foregather. **2** *tourists flock to the place* **stream**, go in large numbers, swarm, crowd, troop.

flog v. **1** *the thief was flogged* **whip**, scourge, flagellate, lash, birch, switch, cane, thrash, beat, tan/whip someone's hide. **2** Brit. informal *he is flogging his old car* **sell**, put up for sale, offer for sale, trade in, peddle; informal push.

flood n. **1** **inundation**, deluge; torrent, overflow, flash flood, freshet; Brit. spate. **2** *a flood of tears* **outpouring**, torrent, rush, stream, gush, surge, cascade. **3** *a flood of complaints* **succession**, series, string, chain; barrage, volley, battery; avalanche, torrent, stream, tide, spate, storm, shower, cascade.
– OPPOSITES trickle.
▶v. **1** *the whole town was flooded* **inundate**, swamp, deluge, immerse, submerge, drown, engulf. **2** *the river could flood* **overflow**, burst its banks, brim over, run over. **3** *imports are flooding the domestic market* **glut**, swamp, saturate, oversupply. **4** *refugees flooded in* **pour**, stream, flow, surge, swarm, pile, crowd.
– OPPOSITES trickle.

floor n. **1** *he sat on the floor* **ground**, flooring. **2** *the second floor* **storey**, level, deck, tier.
▶v. **1** *he floored his attacker* **knock down**, knock over, bring down, fell, prostrate, rugby-tackle; informal lay out. **2** informal *the question floored him* **baffle**, defeat, confound, perplex, puzzle, nonplus, mystify; informal beat, flummox, stump, fox, make someone scratch their head; N. Amer. informal buffalo; old use pose.

flop v. **1** *he flopped into a chair* **collapse**, slump, crumple, subside, sink, drop. **2** *his hair flopped over his eyes* **hang (down)**, dangle, droop, sag, loll. **3** informal *the play flopped* **be unsuccessful**, fail, not work, fall flat, founder, misfire, backfire, be a disappointment, do badly, lose money, be a disaster; informal bomb, go to the wall, come a cropper, bite the dust, fold, flatline, blow up in someone's face; N. Amer. informal tank.
– OPPOSITES succeed.
▶n. informal *the play was a flop* **failure**, disaster, debacle, catastrophe, loser; Brit. informal damp squib; informal flopperoo, washout, also-ran, dog, lemon, non-starter; N. Amer. informal clinker.
– OPPOSITES success.

floppy adj. **limp**, flaccid, slack, flabby, relaxed; drooping, droopy; loose, flowing.
– OPPOSITES erect, stiff.

florid adj. **1** *a florid complexion* **ruddy**, red, red-faced, rosy, rosy-cheeked, pink; flushed, blushing, high-coloured; old use sanguine. **2** *florid plasterwork* **ornate**, fancy, elaborate, embellished, curlicued, extravagant, flamboyant, baroque, rococo, fussy, busy. **3** *florid English* **flowery**, flamboyant, high-flown, high-sounding, grandiloquent, ornate, fancy, bombastic, elaborate, turgid, pleonastic; informal highfalutin; rare fustian.
– OPPOSITES pale, plain.

flotsam n. **wreckage**, lost cargo, floating remains; rubbish, debris, detritus, waste, dross, refuse, scrap; N. Amer. trash, garbage; informal dreck, junk; Brit. informal grot.

flounce[1] v. *she flounced off to her room* **storm**, stride, sweep, stomp, stamp, march, strut, stalk.

flounce[2] n. *a lace flounce* **frill**, ruffle, ruff, peplum, jabot, furbelow, ruche.

flounder v. **1** *people were floundering in the water* **struggle**, thrash, flail, twist and turn, splash, stagger, stumble, reel, lurch, blunder, squirm, writhe. **2** *she floundered, not knowing quite what to say* **struggle mentally**, be out of one's depth, have difficulty, be confounded, be confused; informal scratch one's head, be flummoxed, be clueless, be foxed, be fazed, be floored, be beaten.

flourish v. **1** *ferns flourish in the shade* **grow**, thrive, prosper, do well, burgeon, increase, multiply, proliferate; spring up, shoot up, bloom, blossom, bear fruit, burst forth, run riot. **2** *the arts flourished* **thrive**, prosper, bloom, be in good health, be vigorous, be in its heyday; progress, make progress, advance, make headway, develop, improve; evolve, make strides, move forward (in leaps and bounds), expand; informal be in the pink, go places, go great guns, get somewhere. **3** *he flourished the sword at them* **brandish**, wave, shake, wield; swing, twirl, swish; display, exhibit, flaunt, show off.
– OPPOSITES die, wither, decline.

flout v. **defy**, refuse to obey, disobey, break, violate, fail to comply with, fail to observe, contravene, infringe, breach, transgress against; ignore, disregard; informal cock a snook at.
– OPPOSITES observe.

flow v. **1** *the water flowed down the channel* **run**, course, glide, drift, circulate; trickle, seep, ooze, dribble, drip, drizzle, spill; stream, swirl, surge, sweep, gush, cascade, pour, roll, rush. **2** *many questions flow from today's announcement* **result**, proceed, arise, follow, ensue, derive, stem, accrue; originate, emanate, spring, emerge; be caused by, be brought about by, be produced by, be consequent on.
▶n. *a good flow of water* **movement**, motion, current, flux, circulation; trickle, ooze, percolation, drip; stream, swirl, surge, gush, rush, spate, tide.

flower n. **1** *blue flowers* **bloom**, blossom, floweret, floret. **2** *the flower of the nation's youth* **best**, finest, pick, choice, cream, the crème de la crème, elite.

> **WORD LINKS**
> **floral** relating to flowers
> **florist** a person who sells flowers
> **floriculture** the cultivation of flowers

flowery adj. **1** *flowery fabrics* **floral**, flower-patterned. **2** *flowery language* **florid**, flamboyant, ornate, fancy, convoluted; high-flown, high-sounding, magniloquent, grandiloquent, baroque, orotund, overblown, pleonastic; informal highfalutin, purple; rare fustian.
– OPPOSITES plain.

f

flowing adj. **1** *long flowing hair* **loose**, free, unconfined, draping. **2** *the new model will have soft, flowing lines* **sleek**, streamlined, aerodynamic, smooth, clean; elegant, graceful; technical faired. **3** *he writes in an easy, flowing style* **fluent**, fluid, free-flowing, effortless, easy, natural, smooth.
– OPPOSITES stiff, curly, jagged, halting.

fluctuate v. **vary**, change, differ, shift, alter, waver, swing, oscillate, alternate, rise and fall, go up and down, see-saw, yo-yo, be unstable.

fluctuation n. **variation**, change, shift, alteration, swing, movement, oscillation, alternation, rise and fall, see-sawing, yo-yoing, instability, unsteadiness.
– OPPOSITES stability.

flue n. **duct**, tube, shaft, vent, pipe, passage, channel, conduit; funnel, chimney, smokestack.

fluent adj. **1** *a fluent speech* **articulate**, eloquent, expressive, communicative, coherent, cogent, illuminating, vivid. **2** *fluent in French* **articulate**; (**be fluent in**) have a (good) command of. **3** *a very fluent running style* **free-flowing**, smooth, effortless, easy, natural, fluid; graceful, elegant; regular, rhythmic.
– OPPOSITES inarticulate, jerky.

fluff n. **1** *fluff on her sleeve* **fuzz**, lint, dust; N. Amer. dustballs, dust bunnies. **2** informal *he only made a few fluffs* **mistake**, error, slip, slip of the tongue; wrong note; informal slip-up; formal lapsus linguae.
▶ v. informal *Penney fluffed the shot | he fluffed his only line* **bungle**, make a mess of, fumble, miss, deliver badly, muddle up, forget; informal mess up, make a hash of, make a botch of, foul up, bitch up, screw up; Brit. informal make a muck of, make a pig's ear of, cock up, make a Horlicks of; N. Amer. informal flub, goof up.
– OPPOSITES succeed in.

fluffy adj. **fleecy**, woolly, fuzzy, hairy, feathery, downy, furry; soft.
– OPPOSITES rough.

fluid n. *the fluid seeps up the tube* **liquid**, watery substance, solution; **gas**, gaseous substance, vapour.
– OPPOSITES solid.
▶ adj. **1** *a fluid substance* **free-flowing**; liquid, liquefied, melted, molten, runny, running; gaseous, gassy. **2** *his plans were still fluid* **adaptable**, flexible, adjustable, open-ended, open, open to change, changeable, variable. **3** *the fluid state of affairs* **fluctuating**, changeable, subject/likely to change, (ever-)shifting, inconstant; unstable, unsettled, turbulent, volatile, mercurial, protean. **4** *he stood up in one fluid movement* **smooth**, fluent, flowing, effortless, easy, continuous; graceful, elegant.
– OPPOSITES solid, firm, static, jerky.

fluke n. **chance**, coincidence, accident, twist of fate; piece of luck, stroke of good luck/fortune.

fluky adj. **lucky**, fortunate, providential, timely, opportune, serendipitous, expedient, heaven-sent, auspicious, propitious; felicitous; chance, fortuitous, accidental, unintended; Brit. informal jammy.
– OPPOSITES planned.

flummox v. informal **baffle**, perplex, puzzle, bewilder, mystify, bemuse, confuse, confound, nonplus; informal faze, stump, beat, fox, make someone scratch their head, be all Greek to, floor; N. Amer. informal discombobulate, buffalo.

flunkey n. **1** *a flunkey brought us drinks* **liveried servant**, lackey, steward, butler, footman, valet, attendant, page. **2** *government flunkeys searched his offices* **minion**, lackey, hireling, subordinate, underling, servant; creature, instrument, cat's paw; informal stooge, gofer; Brit. informal poodle, dogsbody, skivvy.

flurry n. **1** *a flurry of snow* **swirl**, whirl, eddy, billow, shower, gust. **2** *a flurry of activity* **burst**, outbreak, spurt, fit, spell, bout, rash, eruption; fuss, stir, bustle, hubbub, commotion, disturbance, furore; informal to-do, flap. **3** *a flurry of imports* **spate**, wave, flood, deluge, torrent, stream, tide, avalanche; series, succession, string, outbreak, rash, explosion, run, rush.
– OPPOSITES dearth, trickle.
▶ v. *snow flurried through the door* **swirl**, whirl, eddy, billow, gust, blast, blow, rush.

flush[1] v. **1** *she flushed in embarrassment* **blush**, redden, go pink, go red, go crimson, go scarlet, colour (up); old use mantle. **2** *fruit helps to flush toxins from the body* **rinse**, wash, sluice, swill, cleanse, clean; Brit. informal sloosh. **3** *they flushed out the snipers* **drive**, chase, force, dislodge, expel, frighten, scare.
– OPPOSITES pale.
▶ n. **1** *a flush crept over her face* **blush**, reddening, high colour, colour, rosiness, pinkness, ruddiness, bloom. **2** *the first flush of manhood* **bloom**, glow, freshness, radiance, vigour, rush.
– OPPOSITES paleness.

flush[2] adj. informal **1** *the company was flush with cash* **well supplied**, well provided, well stocked, replete, overflowing, bursting, brimful, brimming, loaded, overloaded, teeming, stuffed, swarming, thick, solid; full of, abounding in, rich in, abundant in; informal awash, jam-packed, chock-full of; Austral./NZ informal chocker. **2** *the years when cash was flush* **plentiful**, abundant, in abundance, copious, ample, profuse, superabundant; informal a gogo, galore; literary plenteous, bounteous.
– OPPOSITES lacking, low (on).

flushed adj. **1** *flushed faces* **red**, pink, ruddy, glowing, reddish, pinkish, rosy, florid, high-coloured, healthy-looking, aglow, burning, feverish; blushing, red-faced, embarrassed, shamefaced. **2** *flushed with success* **elated**, excited, thrilled, exhilarated, happy, delighted, overjoyed, joyous, gleeful, jubilant, exultant, ecstatic, euphoric, rapturous; informal blissed out, over the moon, high, on a high; N. Amer. informal wigged out.
– OPPOSITES pale, dismayed.

fluster v. *she was flustered by his presence* **unsettle**, make nervous, unnerve, agitate, ruffle, upset, bother, put on edge, disquiet, disturb, worry, perturb, disconcert, confuse, throw off balance, confound, nonplus; informal rattle, faze; Brit. informal send into a spin; N. Amer. informal discombobulate.
– OPPOSITES calm.
▶ n. *I was in a terrible fluster* **panic**, state of anxiety, nervous state, frenzy, fret; informal dither, flap, tizz, tizzy, twitter, state, sweat; N. Amer. informal twit.
– OPPOSITES state of calm.

fluted adj. **grooved**, channelled, furrowed, ribbed, corrugated, ridged.
– OPPOSITES smooth, plain.

flutter v. **1** *butterflies fluttered around* **flit**, hover, flitter, dance. **2** *a tern was fluttering its wings* **flap**, move up and down, beat, quiver, agitate, vibrate. **3** *she fluttered her eyelashes* **flicker**, bat. **4** *flags fluttered* **flap**, wave, ripple, undulate, quiver; fly. **5** *her heart fluttered* **beat weakly**, beat irregularly, palpitate, miss/skip a beat, quiver, go pit-a-pat; Medicine exhibit arrhythmia.
▶ n. **1** *the flutter of wings* **beating**, flapping, quivering, agitation, vibrating. **2** *a flutter of dark eyelashes* **flicker**, bat. **3** *the flutter of the flags* **flapping**, waving, rippling. **4** *a flutter of nervousness* **tremor**, wave, rush, surge, flash, stab, flush, tremble, quiver, shiver, frisson, chill, thrill, tingle, shudder, ripple, flicker. **5** Brit. informal *he enjoys a flutter on the horses* **bet**, wager, gamble; Brit. informal punt.

flux n. **change**, changeability, variability, inconstancy, fluidity, instability, variation, unsteadiness, fluctuation, shift, movement, oscillation, alternation, rise and fall, see-sawing, yo-yoing.
– OPPOSITES stability.

fly[1] v. **1** *a bird flew overhead* **wing its way**, pass, wing, glide, soar, wheel; hover, hang; take wing, take to the air, mount. **2** *they flew to Paris* **travel**, jet. **3** *military planes flew in food supplies* **airlift**, lift, jet, drop, transport. **4** *he could fly a plane* **pilot**, operate, control, manoeuvre, steer. **5** *the ship was flying a quarantine flag* **display**, show, exhibit; have hoisted. **6** *flags flew in the town* **flutter**, flap, wave. **7** *doesn't time fly?* **go quickly**, fly by/past, pass swiftly, slip past, rush past. **8** *the runners flew by.* See **speed** (sense 1 of the verb). **9** dated *they had to fly the country.* See **flee** (sense 2).
□ **fly at** attack, assault, pounce on, set upon, set about, weigh into, let fly at, turn on, round on, lash out at, hit out at, belabour, fall on; informal lay into, tear into, lace into, sail into, pitch into, wade into, let someone have it, jump; Brit. informal have a go at; N. Amer. informal light into.
let fly See **let**.

fly[2] adj. Brit. informal *she's fly enough not to get conned* **shrewd**, sharp, astute, acute, canny, worldly-wise, knowing, clever; informal streetwise, not born yesterday, smart, no fool, nobody's fool; Brit. informal suss, knowing how many beans make five; Scottish & N. English informal pawky.
– OPPOSITES naive.

fly-by-night adj. **unreliable**, undependable, untrustworthy, disreputable; **dishonest**, deceitful, dubious, unscrupulous; informal iffy, shady, shifty, slippery, crooked; Brit. informal dodgy, bent; Austral./NZ informal shonky.
– OPPOSITES reliable, honest.

flyer, flier n. **1** *frequent flyers* **air traveller**, air passenger, airline customer. **2** *flyers killed in the war* **pilot**, airman, airwoman; N. Amer. informal jock; dated aviator, aeronaut. **3** *flyers promoting a new sandwich bar* **handbill**, bill, handout, leaflet, circular, advertisement; N. Amer. dodger.

flying adj. **1** *a flying beetle* **winged**; airborne, in the air, in flight. **2** *a flying visit* **brief**, short, lightning, fleeting, hasty, rushed, hurried, quick, whistle-stop, cursory, perfunctory; informal quickie.
– OPPOSITES long.

foam n. *the foam on the waves* **froth**, spume, surf; fizz, effervescence, bubbles, head; lather, suds.
▶ v. *the water foamed* **froth**, spume; fizz, effervesce, bubble; lather, ferment, rise; boil, seethe, simmer.

foamy adj. **frothy**, foaming, spumy, bubbly, aerated, bubbling; sudsy; whipped, whisked.

fob v.
□ **fob someone off** *I wasn't going to be fobbed off with excuses* put off, stall, give someone the runaround, deceive; placate, appease.
fob something off on *he fobbed off the chairmanship on Clifford* impose, palm off, unload, dump, get rid of, foist, offload; saddle someone with something, land someone with something, lumber someone with something.

focus n. **1** *schools are a focus of community life* **centre**, focal point, central point, centre of attention, hub, pivot, nucleus, heart, cornerstone, linchpin, cynosure. **2** *the focus is on helping people* **emphasis**, accent, priority, attention, concentration. **3** *the main focus of this chapter* **subject**, theme, concern, subject matter, topic, issue, thesis, point, thread; substance, essence, gist, matter. **4** *the resulting light beams are brought to a focus at the eyepiece* **focal point**, point of convergence.
▶ v. **1** *he focused his binoculars on the tower* **direct**; aim, point, turn, train. **2** *the investigation will focus on areas of social need* **concentrate**, centre, zero in, zoom in; address itself to, pay attention to, pinpoint, revolve around.
□ **in focus** sharp, crisp, distinct, clear, well defined, well focused.
out of focus blurred, unfocused, indistinct, blurry, fuzzy, hazy, misty, cloudy, lacking definition, nebulous.

focused adj. **concentrated**, concentrating, attentive, absorbed, engrossed, rapt, earnest, intense, studious, fixed, steady, steadfast, occupied, preoccupied, wrapped up, alert,

watchful, observant; determined, resolved, firm, committed, single-minded; inflexible, obsessive, obsessed, fanatical, fixated.
– OPPOSITES distracted.

foe n. literary **enemy**, adversary, opponent, rival, antagonist, combatant, challenger, competitor, opposer, opposition, competition, other side.
– OPPOSITES friend.

fog n. **mist**, smog, murk, haze, haar; N. English (sea) fret; informal pea-souper; literary brume, fume.
▸v. **1** *the windscreen fogged up | his breath fogged the glass* **steam up**, mist over, cloud over, film over, make/become misty. **2** *his brain was fogged with sleep* **muddle**, daze, stupefy, fuddle, befuddle, bewilder, confuse, befog; literary bedim, becloud.
– OPPOSITES demist, clear.

foggy adj. **1** *the weather was foggy* **misty**, smoggy, hazy, murky. **2** *she was foggy with sleep | a foggy memory* **muddled**, fuddled, befuddled, confused, at sea, bewildered, dazed, stupefied, numb, groggy, fuzzy, bleary; dark, dim, hazy, shadowy, cloudy, blurred, obscure, vague, indistinct, unclear; informal dopey, woolly, woozy, out of it.
– OPPOSITES clear.

foible n. **weakness**, failing, shortcoming, flaw, imperfection, blemish, fault, defect, limitation; quirk, kink, idiosyncrasy, eccentricity, peculiarity.
– OPPOSITES strength.

foil[1] v. *their escape attempt was foiled* **thwart**, frustrate, counter, balk, impede, obstruct, hamper, hinder, snooker, cripple, scotch, derail, smash; stop, block, prevent, defeat; informal do for, put paid to, stymie, cook someone's goose; Brit. informal scupper, nobble, queer, put the mockers on.
– OPPOSITES assist.

foil[2] n. *the wine was a perfect foil to pasta* **contrast**, complement, antithesis, relief.

foist v. **impose**, force, thrust, offload, unload, dump, palm off, fob off; pass off, get rid of; saddle someone with, land someone with, lumber someone with.

fold[1] v. **1** *I folded the cloth* **double (over/up)**, crease, turn under/up/over, bend; tuck, gather, pleat. **2** *fold the cream into the chocolate mixture* **mix**, blend, stir gently. **3** *he folded her in his arms* **enfold**, wrap, envelop; take, gather, clasp, squeeze, clutch; embrace, hug, cuddle, cradle. **4** *the firm folded last year* **fail**, collapse, founder; go bankrupt, become insolvent, cease trading, go into receivership, go into liquidation, be wound up, be closed (down), be shut (down); informal crash, go bust, go broke, go under, go to the wall, go belly up, flatline.
▸n. *there was a fold in the paper* **crease**, knife-edge; wrinkle, crinkle, pucker, furrow; pleat, gather.

fold[2] n. **1** *the sheep were in their fold* **enclosure**, pen, paddock, pound, compound, ring; N. Amer. corral. **2** *Lloyd George returned to the Liberal fold* **community**, group, body,

company, mass, throng, flock, congregation, assembly.

folder n. **file**, binder, ring binder, portfolio, document case, envelope, sleeve, wallet.

foliage n. **leaves**, leafage; greenery, vegetation, verdure.

folk n. informal **1** *the local folk* **people**, individuals, {men, women, and children}, (living) souls, mortals; citizenry, inhabitants, residents, populace, population; informal peeps; formal denizens. **2** *my folks came from the north* **relatives**, relations, blood relations, family, nearest and dearest, people, kinsfolk, kinsmen, kinswomen, kin, kith and kin, kindred, flesh and blood.

folklore n. **mythology**, lore, oral history, tradition, folk tradition; legends, fables, myths, folk tales, folk stories, old wives' tales; mythos.

follow v. **1** *we'll let the others follow* **come behind**, come after, go behind, go after, walk behind. **2** *he was expected to follow his father in the business* **take the place of**, replace, succeed, take over from; informal step into someone's shoes, fill someone's shoes/boots. **3** *people used to follow the band around* **accompany**, go along with, go around with, travel with, escort, attend, trail around with, string along with; informal tag along with. **4** *the KGB man followed her everywhere* **shadow**, trail, stalk, track, dog, hound; informal tail. **5** *do follow the instructions* **obey**, comply with, conform to, adhere to, stick to, keep to, act in accordance with, abide by, observe, heed, pay attention to. **6** *penalties may follow from such behaviour* **result**, arise, be a consequence of, be caused by, be brought about by, be a result of, come after, develop, ensue, emanate, issue, proceed, spring, flow, originate, stem. **7** *I couldn't follow what he said* **understand**, comprehend, apprehend, take in, grasp, fathom, appreciate, see; informal make head or tail of, get, figure out, savvy, get one's head around, get one's mind around, get the drift of; Brit. informal suss out. **8** *he followed his master in his poetic style* **imitate**, copy, mimic, ape, reproduce, mirror, echo; emulate, take as an example, take as a model, adopt the style of, model oneself on, take a leaf out of someone's book. **9** *he follows Manchester United* **be a fan of**, be a supporter of, support, be a follower of, be an admirer of, be a devotee of, be devoted to.
– OPPOSITES lead, flout, misunderstand.
▫ **follow something through** complete, bring to completion, see something through; continue with, carry on with, keep on with, keep going with, stay with; informal stick something out.

follow something up investigate, research, look into, dig into, delve into, make enquiries into, enquire about, ask questions about, pursue, chase up; informal check out; N. Amer. informal scope out.

follower n. **1** *the president's closest followers* **acolyte**, assistant, attendant, companion, henchman, minion, lackey, servant; informal

hanger-on, sidekick; old use liegeman. **2** *a follower of Caravaggio* **imitator**, emulator, copier, mimic; pupil, disciple; informal copycat. **3** *a follower of Christ* **disciple**, apostle, supporter, defender, champion; believer, worshipper. **4** *followers of Scottish football* **fan**, enthusiast, admirer, devotee, lover, supporter, adherent; N. Amer. informal rooter.
– OPPOSITES leader, opponent.

following n. *his devoted following* **admirers**, supporters, backers, fans, adherents, devotees, advocates, patrons, public, audience, circle, retinue, train.
– OPPOSITES opposition.
▸ adj. **1** *the following day* **next**, ensuing, succeeding, subsequent. **2** *the following questions* **below**, further on, underneath; these; formal hereunder, hereinafter.
– OPPOSITES preceding, aforementioned.

folly n. **foolishness**, foolhardiness, stupidity, idiocy, lunacy, madness, rashness, recklessness, imprudence, injudiciousness, irresponsibility, thoughtlessness, indiscretion; informal craziness; Brit. informal daftness.
– OPPOSITES wisdom.

foment v. **instigate**, incite, provoke, agitate, excite, stir up, whip up, encourage, urge, fan the flames of.

fond adj. **1** *she was fond of dancing* **keen on**, partial to, addicted to, enthusiastic about, passionate about; attached to, attracted to, enamoured of, in love with, having a soft spot for; informal into, hooked on, gone on, sweet on, struck on. **2** *his fond father* **adoring**, devoted, doting, loving, caring, affectionate, warm, tender, kind, attentive. **3** *a fond hope* **unrealistic**, naive, foolish, over-optimistic, deluded, delusory, absurd, vain, Panglossian.
– OPPOSITES indifferent, unfeeling, realistic.

fondle v. **caress**, stroke, pat, pet, finger, tickle, play with; maul, molest; informal paw, grope, feel up, touch up, cop a feel of.

fondness n. **1** *they look at each other with such fondness* **affection**, love, liking, warmth, tenderness, kindness, devotion, endearment, attachment, friendliness. **2** *a fondness for spicy food* **liking**, love, taste, partiality, keenness, inclination, penchant, predilection, relish, passion, appetite; weakness, soft spot; informal thing, yen.
– OPPOSITES hatred.

food n. **1** *French food* **nourishment**, sustenance, nutriment, fare, bread, daily bread; cooking, cuisine; foodstuffs, edibles, provender, refreshments, meals, provisions, rations, solids; informal eats, eatables, nosh, grub, chow, scoff, nibbles; Brit. informal tuck; N. Amer. informal chuck; formal comestibles; literary viands; dated victuals; old use commons, meat, aliment. **2** *food for the cattle* **fodder**, feed, provender, forage.

> **WORD LINKS**
> **alimentary** relating to food or nutrition
> **gourmet, gastronome, gourmand** a connoisseur of good food

foodie n. informal **gourmet**, epicure, gastronome, gourmand.

fool n. **1** *you've acted like a complete fool* **idiot**, ass, halfwit, blockhead, dunce, dolt, dullard, simpleton, clod; informal dope, ninny, nincompoop, chump, dimwit, coot, goon, dumbo, dummy, dum-dum, fathead, numbskull, dunderhead, pudding-head, thickhead, airhead, lamebrain, cretin, moron, nerd, imbecile, pea-brain, birdbrain, jerk, dipstick, donkey, noodle; Brit. informal nit, nitwit, twit, clot, goat, plonker, berk, prat, plank, pillock, wally, git, dork, twerp, charlie, muppet, twonk, mug, herbert; Scottish informal nyaff, balloon, sumph, gowk; N. Amer. informal schmuck, bozo, boob, turkey, schlepper, chowderhead, dumbhead, wing nut, goofball, goof, goofus, galoot, lummox, klutz, putz, hoser, schlemiel, sap, meatball; Austral./NZ informal drongo, dill, alec, galah, boofhead. **2** *she made a fool of me* **laughing stock**, dupe, butt, gull; informal stooge, sucker, mug, fall guy; N. Amer. informal sap. **3** *historical the fool in King James's court* **jester**, court jester, clown, buffoon, joker, zany, merry andrew.
▸ v. **1** *he'd been fooled by a schoolboy* **deceive**, trick, hoax, dupe, take in, mislead, delude, hoodwink, bluff, gull; swindle, defraud, cheat, double-cross; informal con, bamboozle, pull a fast one on, take for a ride, pull the wool over someone's eyes, put one over on, have on, diddle, fiddle, rip off, do, sting, shaft; Brit. informal sell a pup to; N. Amer. informal sucker, snooker, stiff, euchre, hornswoggle; Austral. informal pull a swifty on; literary cozen. **2** *I'm not fooling, I promise* **pretend**, make believe, feign, put on an act, act, sham, fake; joke, jest; informal kid; Brit. informal have someone on.
□ **fool around 1** *someone's been fooling around with the controls* **fiddle**, play (about/around), toy, trifle, meddle, tamper, interfere, monkey about/around; informal mess about/around; Brit. informal muck about/around. **2** N. Amer. informal *my husband's been fooling around* **philander**, womanize, flirt, have an affair, commit adultery; informal play around, mess about/around, carry on, play the field, sleep around; Brit. informal play away.

foolery n. **clowning**, fooling, tomfoolery, buffoonery, silliness, foolishness, stupidity, idiocy; antics, capers; informal larking around, larks, shenanigans; Brit. informal monkey tricks; N. Amer. informal didoes; old use harlequinade.

foolhardy adj. **reckless**, rash, irresponsible, impulsive, hot-headed, impetuous, daredevil, devil-may-care, death-or-glory, madcap, hare-brained, precipitate, hasty, overhasty; literary temerarious.
– OPPOSITES prudent.

foolish adj. **stupid**, silly, idiotic, witless, brainless, mindless, unintelligent, thoughtless, half-baked, imprudent, incautious, injudicious, unwise; ill-advised, ill-considered, impolitic, rash, reckless, foolhardy; informal dumb, dim, dim-witted, half-witted, thick, gormless, hare-brained, crackbrained, pea-brained, wooden-headed;

f

Brit. informal **barmy**, **daft**; Scottish & N. English informal **glaikit**; N. Amer. informal **chowderheaded**.
– OPPOSITES sensible, wise.

foolishness n. **folly**, stupidity, idiocy, imbecility, silliness, inanity, lack of sense, thoughtlessness, imprudence, injudiciousness, irresponsibility, indiscretion, foolhardiness, rashness, recklessness; Brit. informal **daftness**.
– OPPOSITES sense, wisdom.

foolproof adj. **infallible**, dependable, reliable, trustworthy, certain, sure, guaranteed, safe, sound, tried and tested; watertight, airtight, flawless, perfect; informal **sure-fire**; formal **efficacious**.
– OPPOSITES flawed.

foot n. **1** *my feet hurt* informal **tootsies**, **trotters**, **plates of meat**; N. Amer. informal **dogs**. **2** *the animal's foot* **paw**, hoof, trotter, pad. **3** *the foot of the hill* **bottom**, base, lowest part; end; foundation.
□ **foot the bill** informal **pay**, settle up; informal **pick up the tab**, cough up, fork out, shell out, come across; N. Amer. informal **pick up the check**.

> **WORD LINKS**
> **chiropody, podiatry** medical treatment of the feet
> **pedicure** a cosmetic treatment of the feet and toenails
> **pedometer** an instrument for estimating the distance travelled on foot

footing n. **1** *Jenny lost her footing* **foothold**, toehold, grip, purchase. **2** *a solid financial footing* **basis**, base, foundation. **3** *on an equal footing* **standing**, status, position; condition, arrangement, basis; relationship, terms.

footling adj. **trivial**, trifling, petty, insignificant, inconsequential, unimportant, minor, small, time-wasting; informal **piddling**, piffling, fiddling.
– OPPOSITES important, large.

footnote n. **note**, marginal note, annotation, comment, gloss; aside, incidental remark, digression.

footprint n. **footmark**, footstep, mark, impression; pug, slot; (**footprints**) track(s), spoor.

footstep n. **1** *he heard a footstep* **footfall**, step, tread, stomp, stamp. **2** *footsteps in the sand* **footprint**, footmark, mark, impression; (**footsteps**) track(s), spoor.

fop n. **dandy**, poseur, man about town; informal **snappy dresser**, natty dresser, trendy; informal dated **swell**; dated **beau**, **popinjay**; old use **coxcomb**.

foppish adj. **dandyish**, dandified, dapper, dressy; affected, preening, vain; effeminate, girlie, niminy-piminy, mincing; informal **natty**, sissy, camp, campy; Brit. informal **poncey**.

forage v. **hunt**, search, look, rummage (about/around/round), ferret (about/around), root about/around, scratch about/around, nose around/about/round, scavenge; Brit. informal **rootle around**.
▸n. **1** *forage for the horses* **fodder**, feed, food, provender. **2** *a nightly forage for food* **hunt**,

search, look, quest, rummage, scavenge.

foray n. **1** *his first foray into documentary film-making* **venture**; experience of, encounter with. **2** *the garrison made a foray against Richard's camp* **raid**, attack, assault, incursion, swoop, strike, onslaught, sortie, sally, push, thrust. **3** *a brief foray into town* **expedition**, trip, visit, outing.

forbear v. **refrain**, abstain, desist, keep, restrain oneself, stop oneself, hold back, withhold; resist the temptation to; eschew, avoid, decline to.
– OPPOSITES persist.

forbearance n. **tolerance**, patience, resignation, endurance, fortitude, stoicism; leniency, clemency, indulgence; restraint, self-restraint, self-control.

forbearing adj. **patient**, tolerant, easy-going, lenient, clement, forgiving, understanding, accommodating, indulgent; long-suffering, resigned, stoic; restrained, self-controlled.
– OPPOSITES impatient, intolerant.

forbid v. **prohibit**, ban, outlaw, make illegal, veto, proscribe, disallow, embargo, bar, debar, interdict; Law **enjoin**, restrain.
– OPPOSITES permit.

forbidden adj. **prohibited**, verboten, taboo; illegal, illicit, against the law; Islam **haram**; informal **not on**, out, no go; formal **non licet**. See also **forbid**.
– OPPOSITES permitted.

forbidding adj. **1** *a forbidding manner* **hostile**, unwelcoming, unfriendly, off-putting, unsympathetic, unapproachable, grim, stern, hard, tough, frosty. **2** *the dark castle looked forbidding* **threatening**, ominous, menacing, sinister, brooding, daunting, fearsome, frightening, chilling, disturbing, disquieting.
– OPPOSITES friendly, inviting.

force n. **1** *he pushed with all his force* **strength**, power, energy, might, effort, exertion; impact, pressure, weight, impetus. **2** *they used force to achieve their aims* **coercion**, compulsion, constraint, duress, oppression, harassment, intimidation, threats; informal **arm-twisting**. **3** *the force of the argument* **cogency**, weight, effectiveness, soundness, validity, strength, power, significance, influence, authority; informal **punch**; formal **efficacy**. **4** *a force for good* **agency**, power, influence, instrument, vehicle, means. **5** *a peace-keeping force* **body**, body of people, group, outfit, party, team; detachment, unit, squad; informal **bunch**.
– OPPOSITES weakness.

▸v. **1** *he was forced to pay* **compel**, coerce, make, constrain, oblige, impel, drive, pressurize, pressure, press, push, press-gang, bully, dragoon, bludgeon; informal **put the screws on**, lean on, twist someone's arm. **2** *the door had to be forced* **break open**, burst open, knock down, smash down, kick in. **3** *water was forced through a hole* **propel**, push, thrust, shove, drive, press, pump. **4** *they forced a confession out of the kids*

extract, elicit, exact, extort, wrest, wring, drag, screw, squeeze.
□ **in force 1** *the law is now in force* **effective**, in operation, operative, operational, in action, valid. **2** *her fans were out in force* **in great numbers**, in hordes, in full strength.

forced adj. **1** *forced entry* **violent**, forcible. **2** *forced repatriation* **enforced**, compulsory, obligatory, mandatory, involuntary, imposed, required, stipulated, dictated, ordained, prescribed. **3** *a forced smile* **strained**, unnatural, artificial, false, feigned, simulated, contrived, laboured, stilted, studied, mannered, affected, unconvincing, insincere, hollow; informal phoney, pretend, put on.
– OPPOSITES voluntary, natural.

forceful adj. **1** *a forceful personality* **dynamic**, energetic, assertive, authoritative, vigorous, powerful, strong, pushy, driving, determined, insistent, commanding, dominant, domineering; informal bossy, in-your-face, go-ahead, feisty. **2** *a forceful argument* **cogent**, convincing, compelling, strong, powerful, potent, weighty, effective, well founded, telling, persuasive, irresistible, eloquent, coherent.
– OPPOSITES weak, submissive, unconvincing.

forcible adj. **1** *forcible entry* **forced**, violent. **2** *forcible repatriation.* See **forced** (sense 2). **3** *a forcible argument.* See **forceful** (sense 2).

forebear n. **ancestor**, forefather, antecedent, progenitor, primogenitor.
– OPPOSITES descendant.

forebode v. literary **presage**, augur, portend, herald, warn of, forewarn of, foreshadow, be an omen of, indicate, signify, signal, promise, threaten, spell, denote; literary betoken, foretoken.

foreboding n. **1** *a feeling of foreboding* **apprehension**, anxiety, trepidation, disquiet, unease, uneasiness, misgiving, suspicion, worry, fear, fearfulness, dread, alarm; informal the willies, the heebie-jeebies, the jitters. **2** *their forebodings proved justified* **premonition**, presentiment, bad feeling, sneaking suspicion, funny feeling, intuition; old use presage.
– OPPOSITES calm.

forecast v. *they forecast record profits* **predict**, prophesy, prognosticate, foretell, foresee, forewarn of.
▸ n. *a gloomy forecast* **prediction**, prophecy, forewarning, prognostication, augury, divination, prognosis.

forefather n. **forebear**, ancestor, antecedent, progenitor, primogenitor.
– OPPOSITES descendant.

forefront n. **vanguard**, van, spearhead, head, lead, front, fore, front line, cutting edge.
– OPPOSITES rear, background.

forego v. See **forgo**.

foregoing adj. **preceding**, aforesaid, aforementioned, previously mentioned, earlier, above; previous, prior, antecedent.
– OPPOSITES following.

foreground n. **1** *the foreground of the picture* **front**, fore. **2** *in the foreground of the political drama* **forefront**, vanguard, van, spearhead, head, lead, front, fore, front line, cutting edge.

forehead n. **brow**, temple.

foreign adj. **1** *foreign branches of UK banks* **overseas**, exotic, distant, external, alien, non-native. **2** *the concept is very foreign to us* **unfamiliar**, unknown, unheard of, strange, alien; novel, new.
– OPPOSITES domestic, native, familiar.

foreigner n. **alien**, non-native, stranger, outsider; immigrant, settler, newcomer, incomer.
– OPPOSITES native.

> **WORD LINKS**
>
> **xenophobia** an irrational fear or dislike of foreigners
> **deport** expel a foreigner from a country
> **naturalize** admit a foreigner to the citizenship of a particular country

foreman, forewoman n. **supervisor**, overseer, superintendent, team leader; foreperson; Brit. chargehand, captain, ganger, gangmaster; Scottish grieve; N. Amer. informal ramrod, straw boss; Austral. informal pannikin boss; Mining overman.

foremost adj. **leading**, principal, premier, prime, top, top-level, greatest, best, supreme, pre-eminent, outstanding, most important, most prominent, most influential, most illustrious, most notable; N. Amer. ranking; informal number-one.
– OPPOSITES minor.

foreordained adj. **predetermined**, preordained, ordained, predestined, destined, fated.

forerunner n. **1** *archosaurs were the forerunners of dinosaurs* **predecessor**, precursor, antecedent, ancestor, forebear; prototype. **2** *a headache may be the forerunner of other complaints* **prelude**, herald, harbinger, precursor, sign, signal, indication, warning.
– OPPOSITES descendant.

foresee v. **anticipate**, predict, forecast, expect, envisage, envision, see; foretell, prophesy, prognosticate; Scottish spae; literary foreknow.

foreshadow v. **signal**, indicate, signify, mean, be a sign of, suggest, herald, be a harbinger of, warn of, portend, prefigure, presage, promise, point to, anticipate; informal spell; literary forebode, foretoken, betoken; old use foreshow.

foresight n. **forethought**, planning, far-sightedness, vision, anticipation, prudence, care, caution, precaution, readiness, preparedness; N. Amer. forehandedness.
– OPPOSITES hindsight.

forest n. **wood(s)**, woodland, trees, plantation; jungle, rainforest; old use greenwood.

forestall v. **pre-empt**, get in before, steal a march on; anticipate, second-guess; nip in the bud, thwart, frustrate, foil, stave off, ward off, fend off, avert, preclude, obviate, prevent; informal beat someone to it.

forestry n. **forest management**, tree growing, agroforestry; technical arboriculture, silviculture.

foretaste n. **sample**, taster, taste, preview, specimen, example; indication, suggestion, hint, whiff; warning, forewarning, omen; informal try-out.

foretell v. **1** *the locals can foretell a storm* **predict**, forecast, prophesy, prognosticate; foresee, anticipate, envisage, envision, see; Scottish spae. **2** *dreams can foretell the future* **indicate**, foreshadow, prefigure, anticipate, warn of, point to, signal, portend, augur, presage, be an omen of; literary forebode, foretoken, betoken; old use foreshow.

forethought n. **anticipation**, planning, forward planning, provision, precaution, prudence, care, caution; foresight, far-sightedness, vision.
– OPPOSITES impulse, recklessness.

forever adv. **1** *their love would last forever* **for always**, evermore, for ever and ever, for good, for all time, until the end of time, until hell freezes over, eternally; Brit. for evermore; N. Amer. forevermore; informal until the cows come home, until doomsday, until kingdom come; old use for aye. **2** *he was forever banging into things* **always**, continually, constantly, perpetually, incessantly, endlessly, persistently, repeatedly, regularly; non-stop, day and night, {morning, noon, and night}; all the time, the entire time; Scottish aye; informal 24-7.
– OPPOSITES never, occasionally.

forewarn v. **warn**, warn in advance, give advance warning, give fair warning, give notice, apprise, inform; alert, caution, put someone on their guard; informal tip off; Brit. informal tip someone the wink.

forewarning n. **omen**, sign, indication, portent, presage, warning, harbinger, foreshadowing, augury, signal, promise, threat, straw in the wind, writing on the wall, hint; literary foretoken.

foreword n. **preface**, introduction, prologue, preamble; informal intro; formal exordium, prolegomenon, proem.
– OPPOSITES conclusion.

forfeit v. *latecomers will forfeit their places* **lose**, be deprived of, surrender, relinquish, sacrifice, give up, yield, renounce, forgo; informal pass up, lose out on.
– OPPOSITES retain.
▸ n. *they are liable to a forfeit* **penalty**, sanction, punishment, penance; fine; confiscation, loss, relinquishment, forfeiture, surrender; Law sequestration.

forfeiture n. **confiscation**, loss; relinquishment, giving up, surrender, sacrifice; Law sequestration; historical attainder.

forge[1] v. **1** *a smith forged swords* **hammer out**, beat into shape, fashion. **2** *they forged a partnership* **build**, construct, form, create, establish, set up. **3** *he forged her signature* **fake**, falsify, counterfeit, copy, imitate, reproduce, replicate, simulate; informal pirate.

forge[2] v. *they forged through swamps* **advance**, press on, push on, soldier on, march on, push forward, make progress, make headway.
◻ **forge ahead** advance rapidly, progress quickly, make rapid progress, increase speed, put a spurt on, accelerate.

forged adj. **fake**, faked, false, counterfeit, imitation, copied, pirate(d); sham, bogus; informal phoney, dud.
– OPPOSITES genuine.

forger n. **counterfeiter**, faker, copyist, imitator, pirate.

forgery n. **1** *guilty of forgery* **counterfeiting**, falsification, faking, copying, pirating. **2** *the painting was a forgery* **fake**, counterfeit, fraud, sham, imitation, replica, copy, pirate copy; informal phoney.

forget v. **1** *he forgot her address* **fail to remember**, fail to recall, fail to think of. **2** *I forgot to close the door* **neglect**, fail, omit. **3** *you can forget that idea* **stop thinking about**, put out of one's mind, shut out, blank out, pay no heed to, not worry about, ignore, overlook, take no notice of.
– OPPOSITES remember.

forgetful adj. **1** *I'm so forgetful these days* **absent-minded**, amnesic, amnesiac, vague, disorganized, dreamy, abstracted, scatterbrained, with a mind/memory like a sieve; informal scatty. **2** *forgetful of the time* **heedless**, careless, unmindful; inattentive to, negligent about, oblivious to, unconcerned about, indifferent to, not bothered about.
– OPPOSITES reliable, heedful.

forgetfulness n. **absent-mindedness**, amnesia, poor memory, a lapse of memory, vagueness, abstraction; informal scattiness.

forgivable adj. **pardonable**, excusable, condonable, understandable, tolerable, permissible, allowable, justifiable.

forgive v. **1** *she would not forgive him* **pardon**, excuse, exonerate, absolve; make allowances for, harbour no grudge against, bury the hatchet with; let bygones be bygones; informal let off (the hook); formal exculpate. **2** *you must forgive his rude conduct* **excuse**, overlook, disregard, ignore, pass over, make allowances for, allow; turn a blind eye to, turn a deaf ear to, wink at, blink at, indulge, tolerate.
– OPPOSITES blame, punish.

forgiveness n. **pardon**, absolution, exoneration, remission, dispensation, indulgence, clemency, mercy; reprieve, amnesty; informal let-off; old use shrift.
– OPPOSITES mercilessness, punishment.

forgiving adj. **merciful**, lenient, compassionate, magnanimous, humane,

soft-hearted, forbearing, tolerant, indulgent, understanding.
– OPPOSITES merciless, vindictive.

forgo, forego v. **do without**, go without, give up, waive, renounce, surrender, relinquish, part with, drop, sacrifice, abstain from, refrain from, eschew, cut out; informal swear off; formal forswear, abjure.
– OPPOSITES keep.

fork v. **split**, branch (off), divide, subdivide, separate, part, diverge, go in different directions, bifurcate; technical furcate, divaricate, ramify.

forked adj. **split**, branching, branched, bifurcate(d), Y-shaped, V-shaped, pronged, divided; technical divaricate.
– OPPOSITES straight.

forlorn adj. **1** *he sounded forlorn* **unhappy**, sad, miserable, sorrowful, dejected, despondent, disconsolate, wretched, abject, down, downcast, dispirited, downhearted, crestfallen, depressed, melancholy, gloomy, glum, mournful, despairing, doleful, woebegone; informal blue, down in the mouth, down in the dumps, fed up; formal lachrymose. **2** *a forlorn garden* **desolate**, deserted, abandoned, forsaken, forgotten, neglected. **3** *a forlorn attempt* **hopeless**, with no chance of success; useless, futile, pointless, purposeless, vain, unavailing, nugatory; old use bootless.
– OPPOSITES happy, busy, cared for, hopeful, sure-fire.

form n. **1** *the general form of the landscape* | *form is less important than content* **shape**, configuration, formation, structure, construction, arrangement, appearance, exterior, outline, format, layout, design. **2** *the human form* **body**, shape, figure, stature, build, frame, physique, anatomy; informal vital statistics. **3** *the infection takes different forms* **manifestation**, appearance, embodiment, incarnation, semblance, shape, guise. **4** *sponsorship is a form of advertising* **kind**, sort, type, class, classification, category, variety, genre, brand, style; species, genus, family. **5** *put the mixture into a form* **mould**, cast, shape, matrix, die. **6** *what is the form here?* **etiquette**, social practice, custom, usage, use, modus operandi, habit, protocol, procedure, rules, convention, tradition, fashion, style; formal praxis, wont. **7** *you have to fill in a form* **questionnaire**, document, coupon, tear-off slip, paper. **8** *what form is your daughter in?* **class**, year; N. Amer. grade. **9** *in top form* **fitness**, condition, fettle, shape, trim, health; Brit. informal nick. **10** Brit. *a wooden form* **bench**, pew, stall.
– OPPOSITES content.
▶v. **1** *the pads are formed from mild steel* **make**, construct, build, manufacture, fabricate, assemble, put together; create, produce, concoct, devise, contrive, frame, fashion, shape. **2** *he formed a plan* **formulate**, devise, conceive, work out, think up, lay, draw up, put together, produce, fashion, concoct, forge, hatch, develop; informal dream up. **3** *they plan to form a company* **set up**,

establish, found, launch, float, create, bring into being, institute, start, get going, initiate, bring about, inaugurate. **4** *a mist was forming* **materialize**, come into being/ existence, crystallize, emerge, spring up, develop; take shape, appear, loom, show up, become visible. **5** *the horse may form bad habits* **acquire**, develop, get, pick up, contract, slip into, get into. **6** *his men formed themselves into an arrowhead* **arrange**, draw up, line up, assemble, organize, sort, order, range, array, dispose, marshal, deploy. **7** *the parts of society form an integrated whole* **comprise**, make, make up, constitute, compose, add up to. **8** *the city formed a natural meeting point* **constitute**, serve as, act as, function as, perform the function of, do duty for, make. **9** *natural objects are most important in forming the mind of the child* **develop**, mould, shape, train, teach, instruct, educate, school, drill, discipline, prime, prepare, guide, direct, inform, enlighten, inculcate, indoctrinate; formal edify.
▫ **good form** good manners, manners, polite behaviour, correct behaviour, convention, etiquette, protocol; informal the done thing.

formal adj. **1** *a formal dinner* **ceremonial**, ceremonious, ritualistic, ritual, conventional, traditional, stately, courtly, solemn, dignified; elaborate, ornate, dressy. **2** *a very formal manner* **aloof**, reserved, remote, detached, unapproachable; stiff, prim, stuffy, staid, ceremonious, correct, proper, decorous, conventional, precise, exact, punctilious, unbending, inflexible, strait-laced; informal stand-offish. **3** *a formal garden* **symmetrical**, regular, orderly, arranged, methodical, systematic. **4** *formal permission* **official**, legal, authorized, approved, validated, certified, endorsed, documented, sanctioned, licensed, recognized, authoritative. **5** *formal education* **conventional**, mainstream; school, institutional.
– OPPOSITES informal, casual, colloquial, unofficial.

formality n. **1** *the formality of the occasion* **ceremony**, ceremoniousness, ritual, conventionality, red tape, protocol, decorum; stateliness, courtliness, solemnity. **2** *his formality was off-putting* **aloofness**, reserve, remoteness, detachment, unapproachability; stiffness, primness, stuffiness, staidness, correctness, decorum, punctiliousness, inflexibility; informal stand-offishness. **3** *we keep the formalities to a minimum* **official procedure**, bureaucracy, red tape, paperwork. **4** *the medical examination is just a formality* **routine**, routine practice, normal procedure. **5** *promotion looks a formality* **matter of course**, foregone conclusion, inevitability, certainty; informal sure thing.
– OPPOSITES informality.

format n. **design**, style, presentation, appearance, look; form, shape, size; arrangement, plan, structure, scheme, composition, configuration.

formation n. **1** *the formation of the island's sand ridges* **emergence**, genesis, development, evolution, shaping, origination. **2** *the formation of a new government* **establishment**, setting up, start, initiation, institution, foundation, inception, creation, inauguration, launch, flotation. **3** *the aircraft were flying in tight formation* **configuration**, arrangement, pattern, array, alignment, positioning, disposition, order.

formative adj. **1** *at a formative stage* **developmental**, developing, growing, malleable, impressionable, susceptible. **2** *a formative influence* **determining**, controlling, influential, guiding, decisive, forming, shaping, determinative.

former adj. **1** *the former bishop* **one-time**, erstwhile, sometime, ex-, late, as was; **previous**, foregoing, preceding, earlier, prior, past, last. **2** *in former times* **earlier**, old, past, bygone, olden, long-ago, gone by, long past, of old; literary of yore. **3** *the former view* **first-mentioned**, first.
– OPPOSITES future, next, latter.

formerly adv. **previously**, earlier, before, until now/then, hitherto, née, once, as was, once upon a time, at one time, in the past; formal heretofore.

formidable adj. **1** *a formidable curved dagger* **intimidating**, forbidding, daunting, disturbing, alarming, frightening, disquieting, brooding, awesome, fearsome, ominous, foreboding, sinister, menacing, threatening, dangerous. **2** *a formidable task* **onerous**, arduous, taxing, difficult, hard, heavy, laborious, burdensome, strenuous, back-breaking, uphill, Herculean, monumental, colossal; demanding, tough, challenging, exacting; formal exigent; old use toilsome. **3** *a formidable pianist* **capable**, able, proficient, adept, adroit, accomplished, seasoned, skilful, skilled, gifted, talented, masterly, virtuoso, expert, knowledgeable, qualified; impressive, powerful, mighty, terrific, tremendous, great, complete, redoubtable; informal mean, wicked, deadly, nifty, crack, ace, wizard, magic; N. Amer. informal crackerjack.
– OPPOSITES pleasant-looking, comforting, easy, poor, weak.

formless adj. **shapeless**, amorphous, unshaped, indeterminate; structureless, unstructured.
– OPPOSITES shaped, definite.

formula n. **1** *a legal formula* **form of words**, set expression, phrase, saying, aphorism. **2** *a peace formula* **recipe**, prescription, blueprint, plan, method, procedure, technique, system. **3** *a formula for removing grease* **preparation**, concoction, mixture, compound, creation, substance.

formulate v. **1** *the miners formulated a plan* **devise**, conceive, work out, think up, lay, draw up, put together, form, produce, fashion, concoct, contrive, forge, hatch, prepare, develop; informal dream up. **2** *this is how Marx formulated his question* **express**,

phrase, word, put into words, frame, couch, put, articulate, convey, say, state, utter.

fornication n. formal **extramarital sex**, extramarital relations, adultery, infidelity, unfaithfulness, cuckoldry; informal hanky-panky, a bit on the side.

forsake v. literary **1** *he forsook his wife* **abandon**, desert, leave, leave high and dry, turn one's back on, cast aside, break (up) with; jilt, strand, leave stranded, leave in the lurch, throw over; informal walk out on, run out on, dump, ditch, give someone the push. **2** *I won't forsake my vegetarian principles* **renounce**, abandon, relinquish, dispense with, disclaim, disown, disavow, discard, wash one's hands of; give up, drop, jettison, do away with, axe; informal ditch, scrap, scrub, junk; formal forswear.
– OPPOSITES keep to, adopt.

forswear v. formal **renounce**, relinquish, reject, forgo, disavow, abandon, deny, repudiate, give up, wash one's hands of; eschew, abstain from, refrain from; informal kick, pack in, quit, swear off; Law disaffirm; literary forsake; formal abjure, abnegate.
– OPPOSITES adhere to, persist with, take up.

fort n. **fortress**, castle, citadel, blockhouse, burg; stronghold, redoubt, fortification, bastion; fastness.

forte n. **strength**, strong point, speciality, strong suit, talent, special ability, skill, bent, gift, métier; informal thing.
– OPPOSITES weakness.

forth adv. **1** *smoke billowed forth* **out**, outside, away, off, ahead, forward, into view; into existence. **2** *from that day forth* **onwards**, onward, on, forward; for ever, into eternity; until now.

forthcoming adj. **1** *forthcoming events* **imminent**, impending, coming, upcoming, approaching, future; close, (close) at hand, in store, in the wind, in the air, in the offing, in the pipeline, on the horizon, on the way, on us, about to happen. **2** *no reply was forthcoming* **available**, ready, at hand, accessible, obtainable, at someone's disposal, on offer; informal up for grabs, on tap. **3** *he was not very forthcoming about himself* **communicative**, talkative, chatty, loquacious, vocal; expansive, expressive, unreserved, uninhibited, outgoing, frank, open, candid; informal gabby.
– OPPOSITES past, current, uncommunicative.

forthright adj. **frank**, direct, straightforward, honest, candid, open, sincere, outspoken, straight, blunt, plain-spoken, no-nonsense, bluff, matter-of-fact, to the point; informal upfront.
– OPPOSITES secretive, evasive.

forthwith adv. **immediately**, at once, instantly, directly, right away, straight away, post-haste, without delay, without hesitation; quickly, speedily, promptly; informal pronto.
– OPPOSITES sometime.

fortification n. **rampart**, wall, defence, bulwark, palisade, stockade, redoubt, earthwork, bastion, parapet, barricade.

fortify v. **1** *he rode in haste to fortify his castles* **secure**, protect, defend, strengthen. **2** *the wall had been fortified* **strengthen**, reinforce, toughen, consolidate, bolster, shore up, brace, buttress. **3** *I'll have a drink to fortify me* **invigorate**, strengthen, energize, enliven, liven up, animate, vitalize, rejuvenate, restore, revive, refresh; informal pep up, buck up, give a shot in the arm to.
– OPPOSITES weaken, sedate, subdue.

fortitude n. **courage**, bravery, endurance, resilience, mettle, moral fibre, strength of mind, strength of character, strong-mindedness, backbone, spirit, grit, doughtiness, steadfastness; Brit. Dunkirk spirit; informal guts; Brit. informal bottle.
– OPPOSITES faint-heartedness.

fortress n. **fort**, castle, citadel, blockhouse, burg; stronghold, redoubt, fortification, bastion; fastness; bunker.

fortuitous adj. **1** *a fortuitous resemblance* **chance**, adventitious, unexpected, unanticipated, unpredictable, unforeseen, unlooked-for, serendipitous, casual, incidental, coincidental, random, accidental, inadvertent, unintentional, unintended, unplanned, unpremeditated. **2** *United were saved by a fortuitous penalty* **lucky**, fluky, fortunate, providential, advantageous, timely, opportune, serendipitous, heaven-sent; Brit. informal jammy.
– OPPOSITES predictable, unlucky.

fortunate adj. **1** *he was fortunate that the punishment was so slight* **lucky**, favoured, blessed, in luck, having a charmed life, charmed; informal sitting pretty; Brit. informal jammy. **2** *in a fortunate position* **favourable**, advantageous, providential, auspicious, welcome, heaven-sent, beneficial, propitious, fortuitous, opportune, happy, felicitous. **3** *the society gives generously to less fortunate people* **wealthy**, rich, affluent, prosperous, well off, moneyed, well-to-do, well heeled, opulent, comfortable; favoured, privileged.
– OPPOSITES unfortunate, unfavourable, underprivileged.

fortunately adv. **luckily**, by good luck, by good fortune, as luck would have it, propitiously; mercifully, thankfully; thank goodness, thank God, thank heavens.

fortune n. **1** *fortune favoured him* **chance**, accident, coincidence, serendipity, destiny, fortuity, providence; N. Amer. happenstance. **2** *a change of fortune* **luck**, fate, destiny, predestination, the stars, serendipity, karma, kismet, lot. **3** *an upswing in Sheffield's fortunes* **circumstances**, state of affairs, condition, position, situation; plight, predicament. **4** *he made his fortune in steel* **wealth**, riches, substance, property, assets, resources, means, possessions, treasure, estate. **5** informal *this dress cost a fortune* **huge amount**, vast sum, king's ransom, millions, billions; informal small fortune, packet, mint, bundle, pile, wad, arm and a leg, pretty penny, tidy sum, killing, big money; Brit.

informal bomb, loadsamoney, shedloads; N. Amer. informal big bucks, gazillions.
– OPPOSITES pittance.

fortune teller n. **clairvoyant**, crystal-gazer, psychic, prophet, seer, oracle, soothsayer, augur, diviner, sibyl; palmist, palm-reader; Scottish spaewife.

forum n. **1** *forums were held for staff to air grievances* **meeting**, assembly, gathering, rally, conference, seminar, convention, symposium, colloquium; N. Amer. caucus; informal get-together; formal colloquy. **2** *a forum for discussion* **setting**, place, scene, context, stage, framework, backdrop; medium, means, apparatus, auspices. **3** *the Roman forum* **public meeting place**, marketplace, agora.

forward adv. **1** *the traffic moved forward* **ahead**, forwards, onwards, onward, on, further. **2** *the winner stepped forward* **towards the front**, out, forth, into view. **3** *from that day forward* **onward**, onwards, on, forth; for ever, into eternity; until now.
– OPPOSITES backwards.
▸ adj. **1** *in a forward direction* **moving forwards**, moving ahead, onward, advancing, progressing, progressive. **2** *the fortress served as the Austrian army's forward base against the Russians* **front**, advance, foremost, head, leading, frontal. **3** *forward planning* **future**, forward-looking, for the future, prospective. **4** *the girls seemed very forward* **bold**, brazen, brazen-faced, barefaced, brash, shameless, immodest, audacious, daring, presumptuous, familiar, overfamiliar, pert; informal brass-necked, fresh.
– OPPOSITES backward, rear, shy, late.
▸ v. **1** *my mother forwarded me your letter* **send on**, post on, redirect, readdress, pass on. **2** *the goods were forwarded by sea* **send**, dispatch, transmit, carry, convey, deliver, ship. **3** *Sir William forwarded his plan* **advance**, further, promote, assist, carry forward, hasten, hurry along, expedite, accelerate, speed up.

forward-looking adj. **progressive**, enlightened, dynamic, pushing, bold, enterprising, ambitious, pioneering, innovative, modern, avant-garde, positive, reforming, radical; informal go-ahead, go-getting.
– OPPOSITES backward-looking.

forwards adv. See **forward** (adverb).

fossil n. **petrified remains**, petrified impression, remnant, relic; Geology reliquiae.

fossilized adj. **1** *fossilized remains* petrified, ossified. **2** *a fossilized idea* **archaic**, antiquated, antediluvian, old-fashioned, quaint, outdated, outmoded, behind the times, anachronistic; informal prehistoric.

foster v. **1** *he fostered the arts* **encourage**, promote, further, stimulate, advance, forward, cultivate, nurture, strengthen, enrich; help, aid, abet, assist, contribute to, support, back. **2** *they started fostering children* **bring up**, rear, raise, care for, take

care of, look after, nurture, provide for; mother, parent.
– OPPOSITES neglect, suppress.

foul adj. **1** *a foul stench* **disgusting**, revolting, repulsive, repugnant, abhorrent, loathsome, offensive, sickening, nauseating, nauseous, stomach-churning, stomach-turning, distasteful, obnoxious, objectionable, odious, noxious; N. Amer. vomitous; informal ghastly, gruesome, gross, rank, putrid, yucky, skanky, sick-making; Brit. informal beastly; Austral. informal on the nose; literary miasmic, noisome, mephitic. **2** *a foul mess* **dirty**, filthy, mucky, grimy, grubby, muddy, muddied, unclean, unwashed; squalid, sordid, soiled, sullied, scummy; rotten, defiled, decaying, putrid, putrefied, smelly, fetid; informal cruddy, yucky, icky; Brit. informal manky, gungy, grotty; rare feculent. **3** *he had been foul to her* **unkind**, malicious, mean, nasty, unpleasant, unfriendly, horrible, spiteful, cruel, vicious, base, malevolent, despicable, contemptible; informal horrid, rotten; Brit. informal beastly. **4** *foul weather* **inclement**, unpleasant, disagreeable, bad; rough, stormy, squally, gusty, windy, blustery, wild, blowy, rainy, wet; Brit. informal filthy. **5** *foul drinking water* **contaminated**, polluted, infected, tainted, impure, filthy, dirty, unclean; rare feculent. **6** *a foul deed* **evil**, wicked, bad, wrong, immoral, sinful, vile, dishonourable, corrupt, iniquitous, depraved, villainous, nefarious, vicious, malicious; malevolent, sinister, demonic, devilish, diabolical, fiendish, dark; monstrous, shocking, despicable, atrocious, heinous, odious, contemptible, horrible, execrable; informal low-down, dirty. **7** *foul language* **vulgar**, crude, coarse, filthy, dirty, obscene, indecent, indelicate, naughty, lewd, suggestive, smutty, ribald, salacious, scatological, offensive, abusive; informal blue. **8** *a foul tackle* **unfair**, illegal, unsporting, unsportsmanlike, below the belt, dirty.
– OPPOSITES pleasant, kind, fair, clean, righteous, mild, fair.
▶ v. **1** *the river had been fouled with waste* **dirty**, infect, pollute, contaminate, poison, taint, sully, soil, stain, blacken, muddy, splash, spatter, smear, blight, defile, make filthy. **2** *the vessel had fouled her nets* **tangle up**, entangle, snarl, catch, entwine, enmesh, twist.
– OPPOSITES clean up, disentangle.

foul-mouthed adj. **vulgar**, crude, coarse; obscene, rude, smutty, dirty, filthy, indecent, indelicate, offensive, lewd, X-rated, scatological, foul, abusive; informal blue.

found v. **1** *he founded his company in 1989* **establish**, set up, start, begin, get going, institute, inaugurate, launch, float, form, create, bring into being, originate, develop. **2** *they founded a new city* **build**, construct, erect, put up; plan, lay plans for. **3** *their relationship was founded on trust* **base**, build, construct; ground in, root in; rest, hinge, depend.
– OPPOSITES dissolve, liquidate, abandon, demolish.

foundation n. **1** *the foundations of a wall* **footing**, foot, base, substructure, underpinning; bottom, bedrock, substratum. **2** *the report has a scientific foundation* **basis**, starting point, base, point of departure, beginning, premise; principles, fundamentals, rudiments; cornerstone, core, heart, thrust, essence, kernel. **3** *there was no foundation for the claim* **justification**, grounds, defence, reason, rationale, cause, basis, motive, excuse, call, pretext, provocation. **4** *an educational foundation* **institution**, charity, agency.

founder[1] n. *the founder of modern physics* **originator**, creator, (founding) father, prime mover, architect, engineer, designer, developer, pioneer, author, planner, inventor, mastermind; informal godfather; literary begetter.

founder[2] v. **1** *the ship foundered* **sink**, go to the bottom, go down, be lost at sea; informal go to Davy Jones's locker. **2** *the scheme foundered* **fail**, be unsuccessful, not succeed, fall flat, fall through, collapse, backfire, meet with disaster, come to nothing/naught; informal flop, bomb, flatline. **3** *their horses foundered in the river bed* **stumble**, trip, trip up, lose one's balance, lose/miss one's footing, slip, stagger, lurch, totter, fall, tumble, topple, sprawl, collapse.
– OPPOSITES succeed.

foundling n. **abandoned infant**, waif, stray, orphan, outcast; old use wastrel.

fountain n. **1** *a fountain of water* **jet**, spray, spout, spurt, well, fount, cascade. **2** *a fountain of knowledge* **source**, fount, well; reservoir, fund, mass, mine.

four cardinal number **quartet**, foursome, quadruplets.

WORD LINKS

quadruple consisting of four parts or things
quadrennial lasting for or recurring every four years
quadrilateral a plane figure with four sides
quadruped a four-legged animal
quatrain a verse of four lines
tetrahedron a solid with four triangular faces
tetralogy a group of four related books, plays, etc.
tetrad a group or set of four

---

fox n.

WORD LINKS

vulpine relating to foxes
vixen a female fox
brush a fox's tail
mask a fox's head as a hunting trophy

---

foxy adj. informal **crafty**, wily, artful, guileful, devious, sly, scheming, designing, calculating, Machiavellian; shrewd, astute, clever, canny; deceitful, deceptive, duplicitous; old use subtle.

foyer n. **entrance hall**, hall, hallway, entrance, entry, porch, reception area, atrium, concourse, lobby; N. Amer. entryway.

fracas n. **disturbance**, brawl, melee, rumpus, skirmish, struggle, scuffle, scrum, clash, fisticuffs, altercation; informal scrap, dust-up, set-to, shindy, shindig; Brit. informal punch-up, bust-up, ruck; Brit. informal, Football afters; N. Amer. informal rough house, brannigan; Austral./NZ informal stoush; Law, dated affray.

fraction n. **1** *a fraction of the population* **part**, subdivision, division, portion, segment, slice, section, sector; proportion, percentage, ratio, measure. **2** *only a fraction of the collection* **fragment**, snippet, snatch, smattering, selection. **3** *he moved a fraction closer* **little**, bit, touch, soupçon, trifle, mite, shade, jot; informal smidgen, smidge, tad.
– OPPOSITES whole.

fractious adj. **1** *fractious children* **grumpy**, bad-tempered, irascible, irritable, crotchety, grouchy, cantankerous, short-tempered, tetchy, testy, curmudgeonly, ill-tempered, ill-humoured, peevish, cross, pettish, waspish, crabbed, crabby, crusty, prickly, touchy; informal snappish, snappy, chippy; Brit. informal shirty, stroppy, narky, ratty; N. Amer. informal cranky, ornery; Austral./NZ informal snaky. **2** *the fractious parliamentary party* **wayward**, unruly, uncontrollable, unmanageable, out of hand, obstreperous, difficult, headstrong, recalcitrant, intractable; disobedient, insubordinate, disruptive, disorderly, undisciplined; contrary, wilful; formal refractory; old use contumacious.
– OPPOSITES contented, affable, dutiful.

fracture n. **1** *the risk of vertebral fracture* **breaking**, breakage, cracking, fragmentation, splintering, rupture. **2** *tiny fractures in the rock* **crack**, split, fissure, crevice, break, rupture, breach, rift, cleft, chink, interstice; crazing.
▸ v. *the glass fractured* **break**, crack, shatter, splinter, split, rupture; informal bust.

fragile adj. **1** *fragile porcelain* **breakable**, easily broken; delicate, dainty, fine, flimsy; eggshell; formal frangible. **2** *the fragile ceasefire* **tenuous**, shaky, insecure, unreliable, vulnerable, flimsy. **3** *she is still very fragile* **weak**, delicate, frail, debilitated; ill, unwell, ailing, poorly, sickly, infirm, enfeebled.
– OPPOSITES strong, durable, robust.

fragment n. **1** *meteorite fragments* **piece**, bit, particle, speck; chip, shard, sliver, splinter; shaving, paring, snippet, scrap, offcut, flake, shred, wisp, morsel; Scottish skelf. **2** *a fragment of conversation* **snatch**, snippet, scrap, bit.
▸ v. *explosions caused the chalk to fragment* **break up**, break, break into pieces, crack open/apart, shatter, splinter, fracture; disintegrate, fall to pieces, fall apart.

fragmentary adj. **incomplete**, fragmented, disconnected, disjointed, broken, discontinuous, piecemeal, scrappy, bitty, sketchy, uneven, patchy.

fragrance n. **1** *the fragrance of spring flowers* **sweet smell**, scent, perfume, bouquet; aroma, redolence, nose. **2** *a bottle of fragrance* **perfume**, scent, eau de toilette, toilet water; eau de cologne, cologne; aftershave.

fragrant adj. **sweet-scented**, sweet-smelling, scented, perfumed, aromatic, perfumy; literary redolent.
– OPPOSITES smelly.

frail adj. **1** *a frail old lady* **weak**, delicate, feeble, enfeebled, debilitated; infirm, ill, ailing, unwell, sickly, poorly, in poor health. **2** *a frail structure* **fragile**, breakable, easily damaged, delicate, flimsy, insubstantial, unsteady, unstable, rickety; formal frangible.
– OPPOSITES strong, robust.

frailty n. **1** *the frailty of old age* **infirmity**, weakness, enfeeblement, debility; fragility, delicacy; ill health, sickliness. **2** *his many frailties* **weakness**, fallibility; weak point, flaw, imperfection, defect, failing, fault, shortcoming, deficiency, inadequacy, limitation.
– OPPOSITES strength.

frame n. **1** *a tubular metal frame* **framework**, structure, substructure, skeleton, chassis, shell, casing, body, bodywork; support, scaffolding, foundation. **2** *his tall, slender frame* **body**, figure, form, shape, physique, build, size, proportions. **3** *a photograph frame* **setting**, mount, mounting.
▸ v. **1** *he had the picture framed* **mount**, set in a frame. **2** *the legislators who frame the regulations* **formulate**, draw up, draft, plan, shape, compose, put together, form, devise, create, establish, conceive, think up, originate; informal dream up.
□ **frame of mind** mood, state of mind, humour, temper, disposition.

frame-up n. informal **conspiracy**, plot; trick, trap, entrapment; informal put-up job, fit-up, set-up.

framework n. **1** *a metal framework* **frame**, substructure, structure, skeleton, chassis, shell, body, bodywork; support, scaffolding, foundation. **2** *the framework of society* **structure**, shape, fabric, order, scheme, system, organization, construction, configuration, composition; informal make-up.

franchise n. **1** *the extension of the franchise to women* **suffrage**, the vote, the right to vote, voting rights, enfranchisement. **2** *the company lost its TV franchise* **warrant**, charter, licence, permit, authorization, permission, sanction.

frank[1] adj. **1** *he was quite frank with me* **candid**, direct, forthright, plain, plain-spoken, straight, straightforward, straight from the shoulder, explicit, to the point, matter-of-fact; open, honest, truthful, sincere; outspoken, bluff, blunt, unsparing, not afraid to call a spade a spade; informal upfront. **2** *she looked at Sam with frank admiration* **open**, undisguised, unconcealed, naked, unmistakable, clear, obvious, transparent, patent, manifest, evident, perceptible, palpable; blatant, barefaced, flagrant.
– OPPOSITES evasive.

f

frank² v. *the envelope had not been franked* **stamp**, postmark; imprint, print, mark.

frankly adv. **1** *frankly, I'm not very interested* **to be frank**, to be honest, to tell you the truth, to be truthful, in all honesty, as it happens. **2** *he stated the case quite frankly* **candidly**, directly, plainly, straightforwardly, straight from the shoulder, forthrightly, openly, honestly, without beating about the bush, without mincing one's words, without prevarication, point-blank; bluntly, outspokenly, with no holds barred.

frantic adj. **panic-stricken**, panic-struck, panicky, beside oneself, at one's wits' end, distraught, overwrought, worked up, agitated, distressed; frenzied, wild, frenetic, fraught, feverish, hysterical, desperate; informal in a state, in a tizzy/tizz, wound up, het up, in a flap, tearing one's hair out; Brit. informal having kittens, in a flat spin.
– OPPOSITES calm.

fraternity n. **1** *a spirit of fraternity* **brotherhood**, fellowship, kinship, friendship, (mutual) support, solidarity, community, union, togetherness; sisterhood. **2** *the teaching fraternity* **profession**, body of workers; band, group, set, circle. **3** N. Amer. *a college fraternity* **society**, club, association; group, set.

fraternize v. **associate**, mix, consort, socialize, keep company, rub shoulders; N. Amer. rub elbows; informal hang around/round, hang out, run around, knock about/around, hobnob, be thick with.

fraud n. **1** *he was arrested for fraud* **fraudulence**, sharp practice, cheating, swindling, embezzlement, deceit, deception, double-dealing, chicanery. **2** *social security frauds* **swindle**, racket, deception, trick, cheat, hoax; informal scam, con, con trick, rip-off, sting, gyp, diddle, fiddle; N. Amer. informal bunco, hustle, grift. **3** *they exposed him as a fraud* **impostor**, fake, sham, charlatan, quack, mountebank; swindler, fraudster, racketeer, cheat, confidence trickster, liar; informal phoney, con man, con artist.

fraudulent adj. **dishonest**, cheating, swindling, corrupt, criminal, illegal, unlawful, illicit, against the law; deceitful, double-dealing, duplicitous, dishonourable, unscrupulous, unprincipled; informal crooked, shady, dirty; Brit. informal bent, dodgy; Austral./NZ informal shonky.
– OPPOSITES honest.

fraught adj. **1** *their world is fraught with danger* **full of**, filled with, rife with; attended by, accompanied by. **2** *she sounded a bit fraught* **anxious**, worried, stressed, upset, distraught, overwrought, worked up, agitated, distracted, desperate; frantic, panic-stricken, panic-struck, panicky; beside oneself, at one's wits' end, at the end of one's tether; informal wound up, in a state, in a flap, in a cold sweat, tearing one's hair out; Brit. informal having kittens, in a flat spin.

fray¹ v. **1** *cheap fabric soon frays* **unravel**, wear, wear thin, wear out/through, become worn. **2** *her nerves were frayed* **strain**, tax, overtax, put on edge.

fray² n. *two men started the fray* **battle**, fight, engagement, conflict, clash, skirmish, altercation, tussle, struggle, scuffle, melee, brawl; informal scrap, dust-up, set-to; Brit. informal punch-up, bust-up; Brit. informal, Football afters; Scottish informal rammy; Law, dated affray.

frayed adj. **1** *a frayed shirt collar* **worn**, well worn, threadbare, tattered, ragged, holey, moth-eaten, in holes, the worse for wear; informal tatty; N. Amer. informal raggedy. **2** *his frayed nerves* **strained**, fraught, tense, edgy, stressed.

freak n. **1** *a genetically engineered freak* **aberration**, abnormality, irregularity, oddity; monster, monstrosity, mutant; freak of nature. **2** *the accident was a complete freak* **anomaly**, aberration, rarity, oddity, unusual occurrence; fluke, twist of fate. **3** informal *they were dismissed as a bunch of freaks* **oddity**, eccentric, misfit; crank, lunatic; informal oddball, weirdo, nutcase, nut; Brit. informal nutter; N. Amer. informal wacko, kook. **4** informal *a fitness freak* **enthusiast**, fan, devotee, lover, aficionado; informal fiend, nut, fanatic, addict, maniac, buff.
▶ adj. *a freak storm* | *a freak result* **unusual**, anomalous, aberrant, atypical, unrepresentative, irregular, fluky, exceptional, unaccountable, bizarre, queer, peculiar, odd, freakish; unpredictable, unforeseeable, unexpected, unanticipated, surprising; rare, singular, isolated.
– OPPOSITES normal.
▶ v. informal *he freaked out* **go crazy**, go mad, go to pieces, crack, snap, lose control; panic, become hysterical; informal lose it, lose one's cool, crack up; N. Amer. informal go ape, go postal.

freakish adj. *freakish weather*. See **freak** (adjective).

freaky adj. informal See **odd** (senses 1 & 2).

free adj. **1** *admission is free* **without charge**, free of charge, for nothing; complimentary, gratis; informal for free, on the house. **2** *she was free of any pressures* **unencumbered by**, unaffected by, clear of, without, rid of; exempt from, not liable to, safe from, immune to, excused of; informal sans, minus. **3** *I'm free this afternoon* **unoccupied**, not busy, available, between appointments; off duty, off work, off, on holiday, on leave; at leisure, with time on one's hands, with time to spare. **4** *the bathroom's free now* **vacant**, empty, available, unoccupied, not taken, not in use. **5** *a citizen of a proud free nation* **independent**, self-governing, self-governed, self-ruling, self-determining, non-aligned, sovereign, autonomous; democratic. **6** *the killer is still free* **on the loose**, at liberty, at large; loose, unconfined, unbound, untied, unchained, untethered, unshackled, unfettered, unrestrained. **7** *you are free to leave* **able to**, in a position to, capable of; **allowed**, permitted. **8** *the free flow of water* **unimpeded**, unobstructed, unrestricted,

unhampered, clear, open, unblocked. **9** *she was free with her money* **generous**, liberal, open-handed, unstinting, bountiful; lavish, extravagant, prodigal. **10** *his free and hearty manner* **frank**, open, candid, direct, plain-spoken; unrestrained, unconstrained, free and easy, uninhibited.
– OPPOSITES busy, occupied, captive, mean.
▶ v. **1** *three of the hostages were freed* **release**, set free, let go, liberate, discharge, deliver; set loose, let loose, turn loose, untie, unchain, unfetter, unshackle, unleash; literary disenthral; historical manumit. **2** *the victims were freed by firefighters* **extricate**, release, get out, pull out, pull free; rescue, set free. **3** *they wish to be freed from all legal ties* **exempt**, except, excuse, relieve, unburden, disburden.
– OPPOSITES confine, trap.
□ **free and easy** easy-going, relaxed, casual, informal, unceremonious, unforced, natural, open, spontaneous, uninhibited, friendly; tolerant, liberal; informal laid-back.
a free hand free rein, carte blanche, freedom, liberty, licence, latitude, leeway.

freebooter n. **pirate**, marauder, raider; bandit, robber; adventurer, swashbuckler; historical privateer; old use buccaneer, corsair.

freedom n. **1** *a desperate bid for freedom* **liberty**, liberation, release, deliverance, delivery, discharge; literary disenthralment; historical manumission. **2** *national revolution was the only path to freedom* **independence**, self-government, self-determination, self rule, home rule, sovereignty, non-alignment, autonomy; democracy. **3** *freedom from local political accountability* **exemption**, immunity, dispensation; impunity. **4** *patients have more freedom to choose who treats them* **right**, entitlement, privilege, prerogative; scope, latitude, leeway, flexibility, space, breathing space, room, elbow room; licence, leave, free rein, a free hand, carte blanche; informal wiggle room.
– OPPOSITES captivity, subjection, liability.

free-for-all n. **brawl**, fight, scuffle, tussle, struggle, confrontation, clash, altercation, fray, fracas, melee, rumpus, disturbance; breach of the peace; informal dust-up, scrap, set-to, shindy; Brit. informal punch-up, bust-up, barney; Scottish informal rammy; Law, dated affray.

freely adv. **1** *may I speak freely?* **openly**, candidly, frankly, directly, without constraint, without inhibition; truthfully, honestly, without beating about the bush, without mincing one's words, without prevarication. **2** *they gave their time and labour freely* **voluntarily**, willingly, readily; of one's own volition, of one's own accord, of one's own free will, without compulsion.

freethinker n. **nonconformist**, individualist, independent, maverick; agnostic, atheist, non-believer, unbeliever.
– OPPOSITES conformist.

free will n. **self-determination**, freedom of choice, autonomy, liberty, independence.
□ **of one's own free will** voluntarily, willingly, readily, freely, without reluctance,

without compulsion, of one's own accord, of one's own volition, of one's own choosing.

freeze v. **1** *the stream had frozen* **ice over**, ice up, solidify. **2** *the campers stifled in summer and froze in winter* **be very cold**, be numb with cold, turn blue with cold, shiver, be chilled to the bone/marrow. **3** *she froze in horror* **stop dead**, stop in one's tracks, stop, stand (stock) still, go rigid, become motionless, become paralysed. **4** *the prices of basic foodstuffs were frozen* **fix**, hold, peg, set; limit, restrict, cap, confine, regulate; hold/keep down.
– OPPOSITES thaw.
□ **freeze someone out** informal exclude, leave out, shut out, cut out, ignore, ostracize, spurn, snub, shun, cut, cut dead, turn one's back on, cold-shoulder, give someone the cold shoulder, leave out in the cold; Brit. send to Coventry; Brit. informal blank.

> **WORD LINKS**
> **cryonics**, **cryogenics** the practice or technique of deep-freezing the bodies of people who have died of an incurable disease, in the hope of a future cure
> **cryosurgery** surgery using instruments that freeze and destroy unwanted tissue

freezing adj. **1** *a freezing wind* **bitter**, bitterly cold, icy, chill, frosty, glacial, wintry, sub-zero; raw, biting, piercing, penetrating, cutting, numbing; arctic, polar, Siberian. **2** *you must be freezing* **frozen**, extremely cold, numb with cold, chilled to the bone/marrow, frozen stiff, shivery, shivering; informal frozen to death.
– OPPOSITES balmy, hot.

freight n. **1** *freight carried by rail* **goods**, cargo, freightage; load, consignment, delivery, shipment; merchandise. **2** *the importance of air freight* **transportation**, transport, conveyance, freightage, carriage, portage, haulage.

frenetic adj. **frantic**, wild, frenzied, hectic, fraught, feverish, fevered, mad, manic, hyperactive, energetic, intense, fast and furious, turbulent, tumultuous.
– OPPOSITES calm.

frenzied adj. **frantic**, wild, frenetic, hectic, fraught, feverish, fevered, mad, crazed, manic, intense, furious, uncontrolled, out of control.
– OPPOSITES calm.

frenzy n. **1** *the crowd worked themselves into a state of frenzy* **hysteria**, madness, mania, dementedness, delirium, feverishness, fever, wildness, agitation, turmoil, tumult; wild excitement, euphoria, elation, ecstasy. **2** *a frenzy of anger* **fit**, paroxysm, spasm, bout.

frequency n. **rate of occurrence**, incidence, amount, commonness, prevalence; Statistics distribution.

frequent adj. **1** *frequent bouts of chest infection* **recurrent**, recurring, repeated, periodic, continual, one after another, successive; many, numerous, lots of, several. **2** *a frequent business traveller* **habitual**, regular.

f

f

– OPPOSITES occasional.
▶ v. *he frequented chic supper clubs* **visit**, patronize, spend time in, visit regularly, be a regular visitor to, haunt; informal hang out at.

frequenter n. **habitué**, patron, regular, regular visitor, regular customer, regular client, familiar face.

frequently adv. **regularly**, often, very often, all the time, habitually, customarily, routinely; many times, many a time, lots of times, again and again, time and again, over and over again, repeatedly, recurrently, continually; N. Amer. oftentimes; literary oft, oft-times.

fresh adj. **1** *fresh fruit* **newly picked**, garden-fresh, crisp, unwilted; raw, natural, unprocessed. **2** *a fresh sheet of paper* **clean**, blank, empty, clear, white; unused, new, pristine, unmarked, untouched. **3** *a fresh approach* **new**, recent, latest, up to date, modern, modernistic, ultra-modern, newfangled; original, novel, different, innovative, unusual, unconventional, unorthodox; radical, revolutionary; informal offbeat. **4** *fresh recruits* **young**, youthful; new, inexperienced, naive, untrained, unqualified, untried, raw; informal wet behind the ears. **5** *he felt fresh and happy to be alive* **refreshed**, rested, restored, revived; (as) fresh as a daisy, energetic, vigorous, invigorated, full of vim and vigour, lively, vibrant, spry, sprightly, bright, alert, perky; informal full of beans, raring to go, bright-eyed and bushy-tailed, chirpy, chipper. **6** *her fresh complexion* **healthy**, healthy-looking, clear, bright, youthful, blooming, glowing, unblemished; fair, rosy, rosy-cheeked, pink, ruddy. **7** *the night air was fresh* **cool**, crisp, refreshing, invigorating, tonic; pure, clean, clear, uncontaminated, untainted. **8** *a fresh wind* **chilly**, chill, cool, cold, brisk, bracing, invigorating; strong; informal nippy; Brit. informal parky. **9** informal *that young man has been getting a little too fresh* **impudent**, impertinent, insolent, presumptuous, forward, cheeky, disrespectful, rude, brazen, shameless, pert, bold, (as) bold as brass; informal brass-necked, lippy, mouthy, saucy; N. Amer. informal sassy.
– OPPOSITES stale, old, tired, warm.

freshen v. **1** *the cold water freshened him* **refresh**, revitalize, restore, revive, wake up, rouse, enliven, liven up, energize, brace, invigorate; informal buck up, pep up. **2** *he opened a window to freshen the room* **ventilate**, air, aerate, oxygenate; deodorize, purify, cleanse; refresh, cool. **3** *she went to freshen up before dinner* **have a wash**, wash oneself, bathe, shower; tidy oneself (up), spruce oneself up, smarten oneself up, groom oneself, primp oneself; N. Amer. wash up; informal titivate oneself, do oneself up, doll oneself up; Brit. informal tart oneself up; formal or humorous perform one's ablutions. **4** N. Amer. *the waitress freshened their coffee* **refill**, top up, fill up, replenish.

freshman, **freshwoman** n. **first-year student**, undergraduate; newcomer, new

recruit, starter, probationer; beginner, learner, novice; N. Amer. tenderfoot; informal undergrad, rookie; Brit. informal fresher; N. Amer. greenhorn.

fret v. **1** *she was fretting about Jonathan* **worry**, be anxious, feel uneasy, be distressed, be upset, upset oneself, concern oneself; agonize, sigh, pine, brood, eat one's heart out. **2** *his absence began to fret her* **trouble**, bother, concern, perturb, disturb, disquiet, disconcert, distress, upset, alarm, panic, agitate; informal eat away at.

fretful adj. **distressed**, upset, miserable, unsettled, uneasy, ill at ease, uncomfortable, edgy, agitated, worked up, tense, stressed, restive, fidgety; querulous, irritable, cross, fractious, peevish, petulant, out of sorts, bad-tempered, irascible, grumpy, crotchety, captious, testy, tetchy; N. Amer. informal cranky; informal het up, uptight, twitchy, crabby.

friable adj. **crumbly**, easily crumbled, powdery, dusty, chalky, soft; dry, crisp, brittle.

friar n. **monk**, brother, religious, coenobite, contemplative; prior, abbot.

friction n. **1** *a lubrication system which reduces friction* **abrasion**, rubbing, chafing, grating, rasping, scraping; resistance, drag. **2** *there was considerable friction between father and son* **discord**, strife, conflict, disagreement, dissension, dissent, opposition, contention, dispute, disputation, arguing, argument, quarrelling, bickering, squabbling, wrangling, fighting, feuding, rivalry; hostility, animosity, antipathy, enmity, antagonism, resentment, acrimony, bitterness, bad feeling, ill feeling, ill will, bad blood.
– OPPOSITES harmony.

friend n. **1** *a close friend* **companion**, boon companion, bosom friend, best friend, intimate, confidante, confidant, familiar, soul mate, alter ego, second self, playmate, playfellow, classmate, schoolmate, workmate; ally, associate; sister, brother; informal pal, chum, sidekick, crony, main man; Brit. informal mate, china, mucker; N. English informal marrow, marrer; N. Amer. informal buddy, amigo, compadre, homeboy; old use compeer. **2** *the friends of the Royal Botanic Garden* **patron**, backer, supporter, benefactor, benefactress, sponsor; well-wisher, defender, champion; informal angel.
– OPPOSITES enemy.

friendless adj. **alone**, all alone, by oneself, solitary, lonely, with no one to turn to, lone, without friends, companionless, unbefriended, unpopular, unwanted, unloved, abandoned, rejected, forsaken, shunned, spurned, forlorn; N. Amer. lonesome.
– OPPOSITES popular.

friendliness n. **affability**, amiability, geniality, congeniality, bonhomie, cordiality, good nature, good humour, warmth, affection, demonstrativeness, conviviality, joviality, companionability, sociability, gregariousness, camaraderie, neighbourliness, approachability, accessibility, openness, kindness, kindliness, sympathy, amenability, benevolence.

friendly adj. **1** *a friendly woman* **affable**, amiable, genial, congenial, cordial, warm, affectionate, demonstrative, convivial, companionable, sociable, gregarious, outgoing, clubbable, comradely, neighbourly, hospitable, approachable, easy to get on with, accessible, communicative, open, unreserved, easy-going, good-natured, kindly, benign, amenable, agreeable, obliging, sympathetic, well disposed, benevolent; Scottish couthy; informal chummy, pally, clubby; Brit. informal matey; N. Amer. informal buddy-buddy. **2** *friendly conversation* **amicable**, congenial, cordial, pleasant, easy, relaxed, casual, informal, unceremonious; close, intimate, familiar. **3** *a friendly wind swept the boat to the shore* **favourable**, advantageous, helpful; lucky, providential.
– OPPOSITES hostile.

friendship n. **1** *lasting friendships* **relationship**, close relationship, attachment, mutual attachment, association, bond, tie, link, union. **2** *old ties of love and friendship* **amity**, camaraderie, friendliness, comradeship, companionship, fellowship, fellow feeling, closeness, affinity, rapport, understanding, harmony, unity; intimacy, mutual affection.
– OPPOSITES enmity.

fright n. **1** *she was paralysed with fright* **fear**, fearfulness, terror, horror, alarm, panic, dread, trepidation, dismay, nervousness, apprehension, apprehensiveness, perturbation, disquiet; informal jitteriness, twitchiness. **2** *the experience gave everyone a fright* **scare**, shock, surprise, turn, jolt, start; the shivers, the shakes; informal the jitters, the heebie-jeebies, the willies, the creeps, the collywobbles, a cold sweat; Brit. informal the (screaming) abdabs, butterflies (in one's stomach). **3** informal *she looked an absolute fright* **ugly sight**, eyesore, monstrosity; informal mess, sight, state, blot on the landscape.

frighten v. **scare**, startle, alarm, terrify, petrify, shock, chill, panic, shake, disturb, dismay, unnerve, unman, intimidate, terrorize, cow, daunt; strike terror into, put the fear of God into, chill someone to the bone/marrow, make someone's blood run cold; informal scare the living daylights out of, scare stiff, scare someone out of their wits, scare witless, scare to death, scare the pants off, spook, make someone's hair stand on end, make someone jump out of their skin; Brit. informal put the wind up, give someone the heebie-jeebies, make someone's hair curl; Irish informal scare the bejesus out of; old use affright.

frightening adj. **terrifying**, horrifying, alarming, startling, chilling, spine-chilling, hair-raising, blood-curdling, disturbing, unnerving, intimidating, daunting, dismaying, upsetting, harrowing, traumatic; eerie, sinister, fearsome, nightmarish,

macabre, menacing; Scottish eldritch; informal scary, spooky, creepy, hairy.

frightful adj. **1** *a frightful accident* **horrible**, horrific, ghastly, horrendous, serious, awful, dreadful, terrible, nasty, grim, dire, unspeakable; alarming, shocking, terrifying, harrowing, appalling, fearful; hideous, gruesome, grisly; informal horrid; formal grievous. **2** informal *a frightful racket* **awful**, terrible, dreadful, appalling, ghastly, abominable; unpleasant, disagreeable, lamentable, deplorable, insufferable, unbearable; informal God-awful; Brit. informal beastly.

frigid adj. **1** *a frigid January night* **very cold**, bitterly cold, bitter, freezing, frozen, frosty, icy, gelid, chilly, chill, wintry, bleak, sub-zero, arctic, Siberian, polar, glacial; informal nippy; Brit. informal parky. **2** *frigid politeness* **stiff**, formal, stony, wooden, unemotional, passionless, unfeeling, indifferent, unresponsive, unenthusiastic, austere, distant, aloof, remote, reserved, unapproachable; frosty, cold, icy, cool, unsmiling, forbidding, unfriendly, unwelcoming, hostile; informal offish, stand-offish.
– OPPOSITES hot, friendly.

frill n. **1** *a full skirt with a wide frill* **ruffle**, flounce, ruff, furbelow, jabot, peplum, ruche, ruching, fringe; old use purfle. **2** *a comfortable flat with no frills* **ostentation**, ornamentation, decoration, embellishment, fanciness, fuss, chichi, gilding, excess; trimmings, extras, additions, non-essentials, luxuries, extravagances, superfluities.

frilly adj. **ruffled**, flounced, frilled, crimped, ruched, trimmed, lacy, frothy; fancy, ornate.

fringe n. **1** *the city's northern fringe* **perimeter**, periphery, border, borderline, margin, rim, outer edge, edge, extremity, limit; outer limits, limits, borders, bounds, outskirts, marches; literary marge, bourn. **2** *blue curtains with a yellow fringe* **edging**, edge, border, trimming, frill, flounce, ruffle; tassels; old use purfle.
– OPPOSITES middle.
▶ adj. *fringe theatre* **unconventional**, unorthodox, alternative, avant-garde, experimental, innovative, left-field, innovatory, radical, extreme; peripheral; off Broadway; informal offbeat, way out.
– OPPOSITES mainstream.
▶ v. **1** *a robe of gold, fringed with black velvet* **trim**, edge, hem, border, bind, braid; decorate, adorn, ornament, embellish, finish; old use purfle. **2** *the lake is fringed by a belt of trees* **border**, edge, bound, skirt, line, surround, enclose, encircle, circle, girdle, encompass, ring; literary gird.

fringe benefit n. **extra**, added extra, additional benefit, privilege; informal perk; formal perquisite.

frippery n. **1** *a functional building with not a hint of frippery* **ostentation**, showiness, embellishment, adornment, ornamentation, ornament, decoration, trimming, gilding,

f

prettification, gingerbread; finery; informal bells and whistles. **2** *stalls full of fripperies* **trinket**, bauble, knick-knack, gewgaw, gimcrack, bibelot, ornament, novelty, trifle; N. Amer. kickshaw; old use gaud.

frisk v. **1** *the spaniels frisked around my ankles* **frolic**, gambol, cavort, caper, cut capers, scamper, skip, dance, romp, trip, prance, leap, spring, hop, jump, bounce. **2** *the officer frisked him* **search**, body-search, check.

frisky adj. **lively**, bouncy, bubbly, perky, active, energetic, animated, zestful, full of vim and vigour; playful, coltish, skittish, spirited, high-spirited, in high spirits, exuberant; Brit. Tiggerish; informal full of beans, sparky, zippy, peppy, bright-eyed and bushy-tailed; literary frolicsome.

fritter v. **squander**, waste, misuse, misspend, dissipate; overspend, spend like water, be prodigal with, run through, get through; informal blow, splurge, pour/chuck something down the drain; Brit. informal dated blue.
– OPPOSITES save.

frivolity n. **light-heartedness**, levity, joking, jocularity, gaiety, fun, frivolousness, silliness, foolishness, flightiness, skittishness; superficiality, shallowness, vacuity, empty-headedness.

frivolous adj. **1** *a frivolous girl* **skittish**, flighty, giddy, silly, foolish, superficial, shallow, light-minded, irresponsible, thoughtless, feather-brained, empty-headed, pea-brained, birdbrained, vacuous, vapid; informal dizzy, dippy; N. Amer. informal ditzy. **2** *frivolous remarks* **flippant**, glib, facetious, joking, jokey, light-hearted; fatuous, inane, senseless, thoughtless; informal flip. **3** *new rules to stop frivolous lawsuits* **time-wasting**, pointless, trivial, trifling, minor, petty, insignificant, unimportant.
– OPPOSITES sensible, serious.

frizzle[1] v. *a hamburger frizzled in the pan* **sizzle**, crackle, fizz, hiss, spit, sputter, crack, snap; fry, cook.

frizzle[2] v. *their hair was powdered and frizzled* **curl**, coil, crimp, crinkle, kink, wave, frizz.
– OPPOSITES straighten.

frizzy adj. **curly**, curled, corkscrew, ringlety, crimped, crinkly, kinky, frizzed; permed; N. Amer. informal nappy.
– OPPOSITES straight.

frock n. **dress**, gown, robe, shift; garment, costume.

frog n.

> **WORD LINKS**
> **batrachian, anuran** relating to frogs
> **tadpole** the larva of a frog

frolic v. *children frolicked on the sand* **play**, amuse oneself, romp, disport oneself, frisk, gambol, cavort, caper, cut capers, scamper, skip, dance, prance, leap about, jump about; dated sport.
▸ n. *the youngsters enjoyed their frolic* **antic**, caper, game, romp, escapade; (**frolics**) fun (and games), high jinks, merrymaking,

amusement, skylarking.

frolicsome adj. literary **playful**, frisky, fun-loving, jolly, merry, gleeful, light-hearted, exuberant, high-spirited, spirited, lively, perky, skittish, coltish, kittenish; mischievous, impish, roguish; informal peppy, zippy, full of beans.

front n. **1** *the front of the boat* **fore**, foremost part, forepart, anterior, forefront, nose, head; bow, prow; foreground. **2** *a shop front* **frontage**, face, facing, facade; window. **3** *the battlefield surgeons who work at the front* **front line**, firing line, vanguard, van; trenches. **4** *the front of the queue* **head**, beginning, start, top, lead. **5** *she kept up a brave front* **appearance**, air, face, manner, demeanour, bearing, pose, exterior, veneer; (outward) show, act, pretence, affectation. **6** *the shop was a front for his real business* **cover**, cover-up, false front, blind, disguise, facade, mask, cloak, screen, smokescreen, camouflage. **7** informal *he's got a lot of front* **self-confidence**, boldness, forwardness, pushiness, audacity, temerity, presumption, presumptuousness, cockiness, daring; informal nerve, face, neck, brass neck.
– OPPOSITES rear, back.
▸ adj. *the front runners* **leading**, lead, first, foremost; in first place.
– OPPOSITES last.
▸ v. *the houses fronted on a reservoir* **overlook**, look out on/over, face (towards), lie opposite (to); have a view of, command a view of.
◻ **in front** ahead, to/at the fore, at the head, up ahead, at twelve o'clock, in the vanguard, in the van, in the lead, leading, coming first; at the head of the queue; informal up front.

frontier n. **border**, boundary, borderline, dividing line, demarcation line; perimeter, limit, edge, rim; marches, bounds.

frost n. **1** *hedges covered with frost* **ice crystals**, ice, rime, verglas; hoar frost, ground frost, black frost; informal Jack Frost; old use hoar. **2** *there was frost in his tone* **coldness**, coolness, frostiness, ice, iciness, frigidity; hostility, unfriendliness, stiffness; informal stand-offishness.

frosty adj. **1** *a frosty morning* **freezing**, cold, icy-cold, bitter, bitterly cold, chill, wintry, frigid, glacial, arctic; frozen, icy, gelid; informal nippy; Brit. informal parky; literary frore, rimy. **2** *her frosty gaze* **cold**, frigid, icy, glacial, unfriendly, inhospitable, unwelcoming, forbidding, hostile, stony, stern, hard.

froth n. *the froth on top of the beer* **foam**, head; bubbles, frothiness, fizz, effervescence; lather, suds; scum; literary spume.
▸ v. *the liquid frothed up* **bubble**, fizz, effervesce, foam, lather; churn, seethe; literary spume.

frothy adj. **1** *a frothy liquid* **foaming**, foamy, bubbling, bubbly, fizzy, sparkling, effervescent, gassy, carbonated; sudsy; literary spumy, spumous. **2** *a frothy pink evening dress* **frilly**, flouncy, lacy. **3** *a frothy woman's magazine* **lightweight**, light, superficial, shallow, slight, insubstantial; trivial, trifling, frivolous.

frown v. **1** *she frowned at him* **scowl**, glower, glare, lour, make a face, look daggers, give someone a black look; knit/furrow one's brows; informal give someone a dirty look. **2** *public displays of affection were frowned on* **disapprove of**, view with disfavour, dislike, look askance at, not take kindly to, take a dim view of, take exception to, object to, have a low opinion of.
– OPPOSITES smile.

frowsty adj. Brit. **stuffy**, airless, unventilated, fusty, close, muggy, stifling; stale, musty, smelly; N. Amer. funky.
– OPPOSITES airy.

frowzy adj. **1** *a frowzy old biddy* **scruffy**, unkempt, untidy, dishevelled, messy, slovenly, slatternly, bedraggled, down at heel, badly dressed, dowdy; N. Amer. informal raggedy. **2** *a frowzy room* **dingy**, gloomy, dull, drab, dark, dim; stuffy, close, musty, stale, stifling; shabby, seedy, run down; Brit. frowsty, fuggy.

frozen adj. **1** *the frozen ground* **icy**, ice-covered, ice-bound, frosty, frosted, gelid; frozen solid, hard, (as) hard as iron; literary rimy. **2** *his hands were frozen* **freezing**, icy, very cold, chilled to the bone/marrow, numb, numbed, frozen stiff.
– OPPOSITES boiling.

frugal adj. **1** *a hard-working, frugal man* **thrifty**, economical, careful, cautious, prudent, provident, unwasteful, sparing, scrimping; abstemious, abstinent, austere, self-denying, ascetic, monkish, spartan; parsimonious, miserly, niggardly, cheese-paring, penny-pinching, close-fisted; N. Amer. forehanded; informal tight-fisted, tight, stingy. **2** *their frugal breakfast* **meagre**, scanty, scant, paltry, skimpy; plain, simple, spartan, inexpensive, cheap, economical.
– OPPOSITES extravagant, lavish.

fruit n. *the fruits of their labours* **reward**, benefit, profit, product, return, yield, legacy, issue; result, outcome, upshot, consequence, effect.

> **WORD LINKS**
> **carpology** the study of fruits and seeds
> **costermonger** a person selling fruit and vegetables in the street
> **pomiculture** fruit-growing
> **pomology** the science of fruit-growing
> **frugivorous** fruit-eating
> **fruitarian** a person who eats only fruit

fruitful adj. **1** *a fruitful tree* **fertile**, fecund, prolific, high-yielding; fruit-bearing, fruiting. **2** *fruitful discussions* **productive**, constructive, useful, of use, worthwhile, helpful, beneficial, valuable, rewarding, profitable, advantageous, gainful, successful, effective, effectual, well spent.
– OPPOSITES barren, futile.

fruition n. **fulfilment**, realization, actualization, materialization, achievement, attainment, accomplishment, resolution;

success, completion, consummation, conclusion, close, finish, perfection, maturity, maturation, ripening, ripeness; implementation, execution, performance.

fruitless adj. **futile**, vain, in vain, to no avail, to no effect, idle; pointless, useless, worthless, wasted, hollow; ineffectual, ineffective, inefficacious; unproductive, unrewarding, profitless, unsuccessful, unavailing, barren, for naught; abortive; old use bootless.
– OPPOSITES productive.

fruity adj. **1** *his fruity voice* **deep**, rich, resonant, full, mellow, clear, strong, vibrant. **2** Brit. informal *a fruity story* **bawdy**, racy, risqué, naughty, spicy, earthy, ribald, suggestive, titillating; rude, indelicate, vulgar, indecent, improper, dirty, smutty, coarse, off colour; N. Amer. gamy; euphemistic adult; informal blue, near the knuckle, nudge-nudge, raunchy; Brit. informal saucy.

frumpy adj. **dowdy**, frumpish, unfashionable, old-fashioned; drab, dull, shabby, scruffy; Brit. informal mumsy.
– OPPOSITES fashionable.

frustrate v. **1** *his plans were frustrated* **thwart**, defeat, foil, block, stop, put a stop to, counter, spoil, check, balk, disappoint, forestall, dash, scotch, quash, crush, derail, snooker; obstruct, impede, hamper, hinder, hamstring, stand in the way of, spike someone's guns; informal stymie, foul up, screw up, put the kibosh on, banjax, do for; Brit. informal scupper. **2** *the delays frustrated him* **exasperate**, infuriate, annoy, anger, vex, irritate, irk, try someone's patience; disappoint, discontent, dissatisfy, discourage, dishearten, dispirit; informal aggravate, bug, miff, hack off.
– OPPOSITES help, facilitate.

frustration n. **1** *he clenched his fists in frustration* **exasperation**, annoyance, anger, vexation, irritation; disappointment, dissatisfaction, discontentment, discontent; informal aggravation. **2** *the frustration of his attempts to introduce changes* **thwarting**, defeat, prevention, foiling, blocking, spoiling, circumvention, forestalling, disappointment, derailment; obstruction, hampering, hindering; failure, collapse.

fuddled adj. **stupefied**, addled, befuddled, confused, muddled, bewildered, dazed, stunned, muzzy, groggy, foggy, fuzzy, vague, disorientated, disoriented, all at sea; informal dopey, woozy, woolly-minded, fazed, not with it; N. Amer. informal discombobulated.

fuddy-duddy n. informal **(old) fogey**, conservative, traditionalist, conformist; fossil, dinosaur, troglodyte; Brit. museum piece; informal stick-in-the-mud, square, stuffed shirt, dodo.

fudge v. **1** *the minister tried to fudge the issue* **evade**, avoid, dodge, skirt, duck, gloss over; hedge, prevaricate, vacillate, be non-committal, stall, beat about the bush, equivocate; Brit. hum and haw; informal cop out, sit on the fence; rare tergiversate. **2** *the* *government has been fudging figures* **adjust**, manipulate, massage, put a spin on, juggle, misrepresent, misreport, bend; tamper with, tinker with, interfere with, doctor, falsify, distort; informal cook, fiddle with.

▸n. *the latest proposals are a fudge* **compromise**, cover-up; informal cop-out.

fuel n. **1** *the car ran out of fuel* **petrol**, diesel; power source; N. Amer. gasoline, gas. **2** *she added more fuel to the fire* **firewood**, wood, kindling, logs; coal, coke, anthracite; oil, paraffin, kerosene; heat source. **3** *we all need fuel to keep our bodies going* **nourishment**, food, sustenance, nutriment, nutrition. **4** *his antics added fuel to the Republican cause* **encouragement**, ammunition, stimulus, incentive; provocation, goading.

▸v. **1** *power stations fuelled by low-grade coal* **power**, fire, run. **2** *the rumours fuelled anxiety among opposition backbenchers* **fan**, feed, stoke up, inflame, intensify, stimulate, encourage, provoke, incite, whip up; sustain, keep alive.

fug n. Brit. informal **stuffiness**, fustiness, frowstiness, staleness, stuffy atmosphere.

fuggy adj. Brit. informal **stuffy**, smoky, close, muggy, stale, fusty, unventilated, airless, stifling, heavy.
– OPPOSITES airy.

fugitive n. *a hunted fugitive* **escapee**, runaway, deserter, absconder; refugee.

▸adj. **1** *a fugitive criminal* **escaped**, runaway, on the run, on the loose, at large; wanted; informal AWOL; N. Amer. informal on the lam. **2** *the fugitive nature of life* **fleeting**, transient, transitory, ephemeral, fading, momentary, short-lived, short, brief, passing, impermanent, here today and gone tomorrow; literary evanescent.

fulfil v. **1** *he fulfilled a lifelong ambition to visit Israel* **achieve**, attain, realize, actualize, make happen, succeed in, bring to completion, bring to fruition, satisfy. **2** *she failed to fulfil her duties* **carry out**, perform, accomplish, execute, do, discharge, conduct; complete, finish, conclude, perfect. **3** *they fulfilled the criteria* **meet**, satisfy, comply with, conform to, fill, answer.

fulfilled adj. **satisfied**, content, contented, happy, pleased; serene, placid, untroubled, at ease, at peace.
– OPPOSITES discontented.

full adj. **1** *her glass was full* **filled**, filled up, filled to capacity, filled to the brim, brimming, brimful. **2** *streets full of people* **crowded**, packed, crammed, congested; teeming, swarming, thick, thronged, overcrowded, overrun; abounding, bursting, overflowing; informal jam-packed, wall-to-wall, stuffed, chock-a-block, chock-full, bursting at the seams, packed to the gunwales, awash. **3** *all the seats were full* **occupied**, taken, in use, unavailable. **4** *I'm full* **replete**, full up, satisfied, well fed, sated, satiated, surfeited; gorged, glutted; informal stuffed. **5** *she'd had a full life* **eventful**, interesting, exciting, lively, action-packed, busy, energetic,

active. **6** *a full list of available facilities* **comprehensive**, thorough, exhaustive, all-inclusive, all-encompassing, all-embracing, in depth; complete, entire, whole, unabridged, uncut. **7** *a fire engine driven at full speed* **maximum**, top, greatest, highest. **8** *she had a full figure* **plump**, well rounded, rounded, buxom, shapely, ample, curvaceous, voluptuous, womanly, Junoesque; informal busty, curvy, well upholstered, well endowed; N. Amer. informal zaftig. **9** *a full skirt* **loose-fitting**, loose, baggy, voluminous, roomy, capacious, billowing. **10** *his full baritone voice* **resonant**, rich, sonorous, deep, vibrant, full-bodied, strong, fruity, clear. **11** *the full flavour of a Bordeaux* **rich**, intense, full-bodied, strong, deep.
– OPPOSITES empty, hungry, selective, thin.

▸adv. **1** *she looked full into his face* **directly**, right, straight, squarely, square, dead, point-blank; informal bang, slap (bang), plumb. **2** *you knew full well I was leaving* **very**, perfectly, quite; informal darn, damn, damned; Brit. informal jolly, bloody; N. Amer. informal darned.
▢ **in full** in its entirety, in toto, in total, unabridged, uncut.
to the full fully, thoroughly, completely, to the utmost, to the limit, to the maximum, for all one's worth.

full-blooded adj. *a full-blooded price war* **uncompromising**, all-out, out-and-out, no-holds-barred, committed, vigorous, strenuous, intense; unrestrained, uncontrolled, unbridled, hard-hitting, pulling no punches; informal full-on.
– OPPOSITES half-hearted.

full-blown adj. **fully developed**, full-scale, full-blooded, fully fledged, complete, total, thorough, entire; advanced.

full-bodied adj. **full-flavoured**, flavourful, flavoursome, full of flavour, rich, mellow, fruity, robust, strong, well-matured.
– OPPOSITES tasteless.

full-grown adj. **adult**, mature, grown-up, of age; fully grown, fully developed, fully fledged, in one's prime, in full bloom, ripe.
– OPPOSITES infant.

fullness n. **1** *the fullness of the information they provide* **comprehensiveness**, completeness, thoroughness, exhaustiveness, all-inclusiveness. **2** *the fullness of her body* **plumpness**, roundness, roundedness, shapeliness, curvaceousness, voluptuousness, womanliness; informal curviness. **3** *the recording has a fullness and warmth* **resonance**, richness, intensity, depth, vibrancy, strength, clarity.
▢ **in the fullness of time** in due course, when the time is ripe, eventually, in time, in time to come, one day, some day, sooner or later; ultimately, finally, in the end.

full-scale adj. **1** *a full-scale model* **full-size**, life-size. **2** *a full-scale public inquiry* **thorough**, comprehensive, extensive, exhaustive, complete, all-out, all-encompassing, all-inclusive, all-embracing, thoroughgoing, wide-ranging, sweeping, in-depth, far-reaching.

– OPPOSITES small-scale.

fully adv. **1** *I fully agree with him* **completely**, entirely, wholly, totally, quite, utterly, perfectly, altogether, thoroughly, in all respects, in every respect, without reservation, without exception, to the hilt. **2** *fully two minutes must have passed* **at least**, no less than, no fewer than, easily, without exaggeration.
– OPPOSITES partly, nearly.

fully fledged adj. **trained**, qualified, proficient, experienced; mature, fully developed, full grown; Brit. time-served.
– OPPOSITES novice.

fulminate v. **protest**, rail, rage, rant, thunder, storm, vociferate, declaim, inveigh, speak out; denounce, decry, condemn, criticize, censure, disparage, attack, execrate, arraign; informal mouth off about, kick up a stink about; formal excoriate.

fulmination n. **protest**, objection, complaint, rant, tirade, diatribe, harangue, invective, railing, obloquy; denunciation, condemnation, criticism, censure, attack, broadside, brickbats; formal excoriation; literary philippic.

fulsome adj. **excessive**, extravagant, overdone, immoderate, inordinate, over-appreciative, flattering, adulatory, fawning, unctuous, ingratiating, cloying, saccharine; enthusiastic, effusive, rapturous, glowing, gushing, profuse, generous, lavish; informal over the top, OTT, smarmy.

fumble v. **1** *he fumbled for his keys* **grope**, fish, search, feel, scrabble around. **2** *he fumbled about in the dark* **stumble**, blunder, flounder, lumber, stagger, totter, lurch; feel one's way, grope one's way. **3** *the keeper fumbled the ball* **miss**, drop, mishandle; misfield. **4** *he fumbled his lines* **mess up**, make a mess of, bungle, mismanage, mishandle, spoil; informal make a hash of, fluff, botch, muff; Brit. informal cock up; N. Amer. informal flub.
▶ n. *a fumble from the goalkeeper* **slip**, mistake, error, gaffe; informal slip-up, boo-boo; Brit. informal cock-up, boob.

fume n. **1** *a fire giving off toxic fumes* **smoke**, vapour, gas, effluvium; exhaust; pollution. **2** *stale wine fumes* **smell**, odour, stink, reek, stench; Brit. informal pong, niff; Scottish informal guff; N. Amer. informal funk; literary miasma.
▶ v. **1** *fragments of lava were fuming and sizzling* **emit smoke**, emit gas, smoke; old use reek. **2** *Ella was still fuming at his arrogance* **be furious**, be enraged, be very angry, seethe, be livid, be incensed, boil, be beside oneself, spit; rage, rant and rave; informal be hot under the collar, foam at the mouth, see red.

fumigate v. **disinfect**, purify, sterilize, sanitize, decontaminate, cleanse, clean out.
– OPPOSITES soil.

fun n. **1** *I joined in with the fun* **enjoyment**, entertainment, amusement, pleasure; jollification, merrymaking; recreation, diversion, leisure, relaxation; good time, great time; informal R & R (rest and recreation), living it up, a ball, beer and skittles. **2** *she's full of fun* **merriment**, cheerfulness, cheeriness, jollity, joviality, jocularity, high spirits, gaiety, mirth, laughter, hilarity, glee, gladness, light-heartedness, levity. **3** *he became a figure of fun* **ridicule**, derision, mockery, laughter, scorn, contempt, jeering, sneering, jibing, teasing, taunting.
– OPPOSITES boredom, misery.
▶ adj. informal *a fun evening* **enjoyable**, entertaining, amusing, diverting, pleasurable, pleasing, agreeable, interesting.
□ **make fun of** tease, poke fun at, chaff, rag; ridicule, mock, laugh at, taunt, jeer at, scoff at, deride; parody, lampoon, caricature, satirize; informal take the mickey out of, rib, kid, have on, pull someone's leg, send up; Brit. informal wind up; N. Amer. informal goof on, razz.

function n. **1** *the main function of the machine* **purpose**, task, use, role. **2** *my function was to select and train the recruits* **responsibility**, duty, role, concern, province, activity, assignment, obligation, charge; task, job, mission, undertaking, commission; capacity, post, situation, office, occupation, employment, business. **3** *a function attended by local dignitaries* **social event**, party, social occasion, affair, gathering, reception, soirée, jamboree, gala; N. Amer. levee; informal do, bash, shindig; Brit. informal jolly, beanfeast.
▶ v. **1** *the electrical system had ceased to function* **work**, go, run, be in working/running order, operate, be operative. **2** *the museum functions as an educational and study centre* **act**, serve, operate; perform, work, play the role of, do duty as.

functional adj. **1** *a small functional kitchen* **practical**, useful, utilitarian, utility, workaday, serviceable; minimalist, plain, simple, basic, modest, unadorned, unostentatious, no-frills, without frills; impersonal, characterless, soulless, institutional, clinical. **2** *the machine is now fully functional* **working**, in working order, functioning, in service, in use; going, running, operative, operating, in operation, in commission, in action; informal up and running.

functionary n. **official**, office-holder, public servant, civil servant, bureaucrat, administrator, apparatchik; Brit. jack-in-office.

fund n. **1** *an emergency fund for refugees* **collection**, kitty, reserve, pool, purse; endowment, foundation, trust, grant, investment; savings, nest egg; informal stash. **2** *I was very short of funds* **money**, cash, ready money; wealth, means, assets, resources, savings, capital, reserves, the wherewithal; informal dough, bread, loot, dosh; Brit. informal lolly, spondulicks, the readies. **3** *his fund of stories* **stock**, store, supply, accumulation, collection, bank, pool; mine, reservoir, storehouse, treasury, treasure house, hoard, repository.
▶ v. *the agency was funded by the Treasury* **finance**, pay for, back, capitalize, sponsor,

put up the money for, subsidize, underwrite, endow, support, maintain; informal foot the bill for, pick up the tab for; N. Amer. informal bankroll, stake.

fundamental adj. **basic**, underlying, core, foundational, rudimentary, elemental, elementary, basal, root; primary, prime, cardinal, first, principal, chief, key, central, vital, essential, important, indispensable, necessary, crucial, pivotal, critical; structural, organic, constitutional, inherent, intrinsic.
– OPPOSITES secondary, unimportant.

fundamentally adv. *Barbara was, fundamentally, a good person* **essentially**, in essence, basically, at heart, at bottom, deep down, au fond; primarily, above all, first and foremost, first of all; informal at the end of the day, when all is said and done, when you get right down to it.

fundamentals plural n. **basics**, essentials, rudiments, foundations, basic principles, first principles, preliminaries; crux, crux of the matter, heart of the matter, essence, core, heart, base, bedrock; informal nuts and bolts, nitty-gritty, brass tacks, ABC.

funeral n. **burial**, interment, entombment, committal, inhumation, laying to rest; cremation; obsequies, last offices; formal exequies; old use sepulture.

> **WORD LINKS**
> **cortège** a funeral procession
> **dirge** a lament for the dead
> **knell** a bell rung to mark a funeral or death
> **hearse** a vehicle carrying the coffin
> **pall-bearer** a person carrying the coffin
> **wake** a party held after a funeral
> **undertaker** (US **mortician**) a person who makes arrangements for funerals.
> See also **burial**.

funereal adj. **1** *the funereal atmosphere* **sombre**, gloomy, mournful, melancholy, lugubrious, sepulchral, miserable, doleful, woeful, sad, sorrowful, cheerless, joyless, bleak, dismal, depressing, dreary; grave, solemn, serious; literary dolorous. **2** *funereal colours* **dark**, black, drab.
– OPPOSITES cheerful.

fungus n. **mushroom**, toadstool; mould, mildew, rust; Biology saprophyte.

> **WORD LINKS**
> **mycology** the scientific study of fungi

funk informal n. *he put us all into a funk* **panic**, state of fear, fluster; informal cold sweat, state, stew, flap, tizzy, tizz; Brit. informal blue funk, heebie-jeebies; N. Amer. informal twit.
▶ v. *I'm certain he funked it* **avoid**, evade, dodge, run away from, balk at, flinch from; informal chicken out of, duck out of, wriggle out of, cop out of, get out of.

funnel n. **1** *fluid was poured through the funnel* **tube**, pipe, channel, conduit. **2** *smoke poured from the ship's funnels* **chimney**, flue, vent.
▶ v. *the money was funnelled back into Europe*

channel, feed, direct, convey, move, pass; pour, filter.

funny adj. **1** *a very funny film* **amusing**, humorous, witty, comic, comical, droll, chucklesome, facetious, jocular, jokey; hilarious, hysterical, riotous, uproarious; entertaining, diverting, sparkling, scintillating; silly, farcical, slapstick; informal side-splitting, rib-tickling, laugh-a-minute, wacky, zany, waggish, off the wall, a scream, rich, priceless; informal dated killing. **2** *a funny coincidence* **strange**, peculiar, odd, queer, weird, bizarre, curious, freakish, freak, quirky; mysterious, mystifying, puzzling, perplexing; unusual, uncommon, anomalous, irregular, abnormal, exceptional, singular, out of the ordinary, extraordinary; Brit. informal dated rum. **3** *there's something funny about him* **suspicious**, suspect, dubious, untrustworthy, questionable; informal shady, fishy; Brit. informal dodgy.
– OPPOSITES serious, unsurprising, trustworthy.

fur n. **hair**, wool; coat, fleece, pelt; Zoology pelage.

furious adj. **1** *he was furious when he learned about it* **enraged**, infuriated, very angry, irate, incensed, raging, incandescent, fuming, ranting, raving, seething, beside oneself, outraged; informal mad, hopping mad, wild, livid, boiling, apoplectic, hot under the collar, on the warpath, foaming at the mouth, steamed up, in a paddy, fit to be tied; literary wrathful. **2** *a furious debate* **heated**, hot, passionate, fiery, 'lively'; fierce, vehement, violent, wild, unrestrained, tumultuous, turbulent, tempestuous, stormy.
– OPPOSITES calm.

furnish v. **1** *the bedrooms are elegantly furnished* **fit out**, provide with furniture, appoint, outfit; Brit. informal do out. **2** *grooms furnished us with horses for our journey* **supply**, provide, equip, provision, issue, kit out, present, give, offer, afford, purvey, bestow; informal fix up.

furniture n. **furnishings**, fittings, fitments, movables, appointments, effects; Law chattels; informal stuff, things.

furore n. **commotion**, uproar, outcry, fuss, upset, brouhaha, palaver, pother, tempest, agitation, pandemonium, disturbance, hubbub, rumpus, tumult, turmoil; stir, excitement; informal song and dance, to-do, hoo-ha, hullabaloo, ballyhoo, kerfuffle, flap, stink; Brit. informal carry-on.

furrow n. **1** *furrows in a ploughed field* **groove**, trench, rut, trough, channel, hollow. **2** *the furrows on either side of her mouth* **wrinkle**, line, crease, crinkle, crow's foot, corrugation.
▶ v. *his brow furrowed* **wrinkle**, crease, line, crinkle, pucker, screw up, scrunch up, corrugate.

furry adj. **covered with fur**, hairy, downy, fleecy, soft, fluffy, fuzzy, woolly.

further adv. *further, it gave him an excellent excuse not to attend* **furthermore**, moreover, what's more, also, additionally, in addition, besides, as well, too, to boot, on top of that, over and above that, into the bargain, by the same token; old use withal.
▸adj. **1** *the further side of the field* **more distant**, more remote, remoter, further away/off, farther (away/off); far, other, opposite. **2** *further information* **additional**, more, extra, supplementary, supplemental, other; new, fresh.
▸v. *an attempt to further his career* **promote**, advance, forward, develop, facilitate, aid, assist, help, help along, lend a hand to, abet; expedite, hasten, speed up, accelerate, step up, spur on, oil the wheels of, boost, encourage, cultivate, nurture, foster.
– OPPOSITES impede.

furtherance n. **promotion**, furthering, advancement, forwarding, development, facilitation, aiding, assisting, helping, abetting; hastening, acceleration, boosting, encouragement, cultivation, nurturing, fostering.
– OPPOSITES hindrance.

furthermore adv. **moreover**, further, what's more, also, additionally, in addition, besides, as well, too, to boot, on top of that, over and above that, into the bargain, by the same token; old use withal.

furthest adj. **most distant**, most remote, remotest, furthest/farthest away, farthest, furthermost, farthermost; outlying, outer, outermost, extreme, uttermost, ultimate; old use outmost.
– OPPOSITES nearest.

furtive adj. **secretive**, secret, surreptitious, clandestine, hidden, covert, conspiratorial, cloak-and-dagger, hole-and-corner, backstairs, hugger-mugger; sly, sneaky, under-the-table; sidelong, sideways, oblique, indirect; Military black; informal hush-hush, shifty.
– OPPOSITES open.

fury n. **1** *she exploded with fury* **rage**, anger, wrath, outrage, spleen, temper; crossness, indignation, umbrage, annoyance, exasperation; literary ire, choler. **2** *the fury of the storm* **fierceness**, ferocity, violence, turbulence, tempestuousness, savagery; severity, intensity, vehemence, force, forcefulness, power, strength. **3** *she turned on Mother like a fury* **virago**, hellcat, termagant, spitfire, vixen, shrew, harridan, dragon, gorgon; (**Furies**) Greek Mythology Eumenides.
– OPPOSITES good humour, mildness.

fuse v. **1** *a band which fuses rap with rock* **combine**, amalgamate, put together, join, unite, marry, blend, merge, meld, mingle, integrate, intermix, intermingle, synthesize; coalesce, compound, alloy; technical admix; literary commingle. **2** *metal fused to a base of coloured glass* **bond**, stick, bind, weld, solder; melt, smelt. **3** Brit. *a light had fused* **short-circuit**, stop working, trip; informal go, blow.
– OPPOSITES separate.

fusillade n. **salvo**, volley, barrage, bombardment, cannonade, battery, burst, blast, hail, shower, rain, stream; historical broadside.

fusion n. **blend**, blending, combination, amalgamation, joining, union, marrying, bonding, merging, melding, mingling, integration, intermixture, intermingling, synthesis; coalescence.

fuss n. **1** *what's all the fuss about?* **commotion**, excitement, agitation, stir, confusion, disturbance, brouhaha, uproar, furore, palaver, storm in a teacup, much ado about nothing, pother; bother, fluster, flurry, bustle; informal hoo-ha, to-do, ballyhoo, song and dance, performance, pantomime, kerfuffle; Brit. informal carry-on; N. Amer. informal fuss and feathers. **2** *they settled in with very little fuss* **bother**, trouble, inconvenience, effort, exertion, labour; informal hassle. **3** *he didn't put up a fuss* **protest**, complaint, objection, grumble, grouse; informal gripe.
▸v. *he was still fussing about his clothes* **worry**, fret, be anxious, be agitated, make a big thing out of; make a mountain out of a molehill; informal flap, be in a tizzy, be in a stew, make a meal of.

fussy adj. **1** *he's very fussy about what he eats* **finicky**, particular, over-particular, fastidious, discriminating, selective, dainty; hard to please, difficult, exacting, demanding; faddish; informal pernickety, choosy, picky, old womanish; Brit. informal faddy; N. Amer. informal persnickety. **2** *a fussy, frilly bridal gown* **over-elaborate**, over-decorated, ornate, fancy, overdone; busy, cluttered.

fusty adj. **1** *the room smelt fusty* **stale**, musty, dusty; stuffy, airless, unventilated; damp, mildewed, mildewy; Brit. frowsty. **2** *technical tomes written by fusty academics* **old-fashioned**, out of date, outdated, behind the times, antediluvian, backward-looking; fogeyish; informal square, out of the ark.
– OPPOSITES fresh.

futile adj. **fruitless**, vain, pointless, useless, ineffectual, ineffective, of no use, inefficacious, to no effect, in vain, to no avail, unavailing; unsuccessful, failed, thwarted; unproductive, barren, unprofitable, abortive; impotent, hollow, empty, forlorn, idle, hopeless; old use bootless.
– OPPOSITES useful.

futility n. **fruitlessness**, pointlessness, uselessness, vanity, ineffectiveness, inefficacy; failure, barrenness, unprofitability; impotence, hollowness, emptiness, forlornness, hopelessness; old use bootlessness.

future n. **1** *his plans for the future* **time to come**, time ahead; what lies ahead, coming times. **2** *she knew her future lay in acting* **destiny**, fate, fortune; prospects, expectations, chances.
– OPPOSITES past.
▸adj. **1** *a future date* **later**, to come, following, ensuing, succeeding, subsequent, coming.

2 *his future wife* **to be**, destined; intended, planned, prospective.
□ **in future** from now on, after this, in the future, from this day forward, hence, henceforward, subsequently, in time to come; formal hereafter.

fuzz[1] n. *the soft fuzz on his cheeks* **hair**, down; fur, fluff, fleeciness.

fuzz[2] n. informal *we'd better call the fuzz.* See **police** (noun).

fuzzy adj. **1** *her fuzzy hair* **frizzy**, fluffy, woolly; downy, soft; N. Amer. informal **nappy**. **2** *a fuzzy picture* **blurry**, blurred, indistinct, unclear, bleary, misty, distorted, out of focus, unfocused, lacking definition, nebulous; ill-defined, indefinite, vague, hazy, imprecise, inexact, loose, woolly. **3** *my mind was fuzzy* **confused**, muddled, addled, fuddled, befuddled, groggy, disoriented, disorientated, mixed up, fazed, foggy, dizzy, stupefied, benumbed.

Gg

gab informal v. *they were all gabbing away like crazy* **chatter**, chitter-chatter, chat, talk, gossip, gabble, babble, prattle, jabber, blather, blab; informal yak, yackety-yak, yabber, yatter, yammer, blabber, blah-blah, jaw, gas, shoot one's mouth off; Brit. informal witter, rabbit, chunter, natter; N. Amer. informal run off at the mouth.
□ **the gift of the gab** eloquence, fluency, expressiveness, a silver tongue; persuasiveness; informal a way with words, blarney.

gabble v. *he gabbled on in a panicky way* **jabber**, babble, prattle, rattle, blabber, gibber, blab, drivel, twitter, splutter; Brit. informal waffle, chunter, witter.
▸ n. *the boozy gabble of the crowd* **jabbering**, babbling, chattering, gibbering, babble, chatter, rambling; Brit. informal waffle, waffling, chuntering, wittering.

gabby adj. informal See **talkative**.

gad v. informal **gallivant**, flit, travel, roam; Brit. informal swan.

gadabout n. informal **pleasure-seeker**; traveller, globetrotter, wanderer, drifter, bird of passage; informal gallivanter.

gadget n. **appliance**, apparatus, instrument, implement, tool, utensil, contrivance, contraption, machine, mechanism, device, labour-saving device, convenience, invention; informal gizmo, gimmick, widget, mod con.

gaffe n. **blunder**, mistake, error, slip, faux pas, indiscretion, impropriety, miscalculation, gaucherie, solecism; informal slip-up, howler, boo-boo, boner, fluff; Brit. informal boob, bloomer, clanger; N. Amer. informal blooper, goof.

gaffer n. **1** Brit. informal *being the gaffer's gone to her head* **manager**, manageress, foreman, forewoman, overseer, supervisor, superintendent; informal boss, boss man, head honcho, numero uno, number one, kingpin, top dog, big chief, skipper; Brit. informal governor, guv'nor; N. Amer. informal padrone, sachem, big kahuna. **2** informal *an old gaffer* **old man**, elderly man, senior citizen, pensioner, OAP; informal old boy, old codger, old-timer, greybeard, grandad, wrinkly; Brit. informal buffer.

gag¹ v. **1** *a dirty rag was used to gag her mouth* **stop up**, block, plug, stifle, smother, muffle. **2** *the government tried to gag its critics* **silence**, muzzle, mute, muffle, suppress, stifle; censor, curb, check, restrain, fetter, shackle, restrict. **3** *the stench made her gag* **retch**, heave, dry-heave; informal keck.
▸ n. *his scream was muffled by the gag* **muzzle**, tie, restraint.

gag² n. informal *he told a few gags* **joke**, jest, witticism, quip, pun, play on words, double entendre; informal crack, wisecrack, one-liner, funny.

gaiety n. **1** *I was struck by her gaiety* **cheerfulness**, light-heartedness, happiness, merriment, glee, gladness, joy, joie de vivre, joyfulness, joyousness, delight, high spirits, good spirits, good humour, cheeriness, jollity, mirth, joviality, exuberance, elation, liveliness, vivacity, animation, effervescence, sprightliness, zest, zestfulness; informal chirpiness, bounce, pep; literary blitheness. **2** *the hotel restaurant was a scene of gaiety* **merrymaking**, festivity, fun, fun and games, frolics, revelry, jollification, celebration, pleasure; informal partying.
− OPPOSITES misery.

gaily adv. **1** *she skipped gaily along the path* **merrily**, cheerfully, cheerily, happily, joyfully, joyously, light-heartedly, blithely, jauntily, gleefully. **2** *gaily painted boats* **brightly**, colourfully, brilliantly. **3** *she plunged gaily into speculation on the stock market* **heedlessly**, unthinkingly, thoughtlessly, without thinking, carelessly; casually, nonchalantly, airily, breezily, lightly.

gain v. **1** *he gained a scholarship to the college* **obtain**, get, secure, acquire, come by, procure, attain, achieve, earn, win, capture, clinch, pick up, carry off, reap; informal land, net, bag, scoop, wangle, swing, walk away/off with. **2** *they stood to gain from the deal* **profit**, make money, reap benefits, benefit, do well out of; informal make a killing, milk. **3** *she had gained weight* **put on**, increase in. **4** *the others were gaining on us* **catch up with/on**, catch someone up, catch, close in on, near. **5** *we gained the ridge* **reach**, arrive at, get to, come to, make, attain, set foot on; informal hit.
− OPPOSITES lose.
▸ n. **1** *his gain from the deal* **profit**, advantage, benefit, reward; percentage, takings, yield, return, winnings, receipts, proceeds, dividend, interest. **2** *a price gain of 7.5 per cent* **increase**, rise, increment, augmentation, addition.
− OPPOSITES loss, decrease.

g

□ **gain time** play for time, stall, procrastinate, delay, temporize, hold back, hang back, hang fire, dally, drag one's feet.

gainful adj. **profitable**, paid, well paid, remunerative, lucrative, moneymaking; rewarding, fruitful, worthwhile, useful, productive, constructive, beneficial, advantageous, valuable.

gainsay v. formal **deny**, dispute, disagree with, argue with, dissent from, contradict, repudiate, challenge, oppose, contest, counter, controvert, refute, rebut; formal confute.
– OPPOSITES confirm.

gait n. **walk**, step, stride, pace, tread, way of walking; bearing, carriage; Brit. deportment; formal comportment.

gala n. *the annual summer gala* **fete**, fair, festival, carnival, pageant, jubilee, jamboree, party, garden party, celebration; festivities.
▸adj. *a gala occasion* **festive**, celebratory, merry, joyous, joyful; diverting, entertaining, enjoyable, spectacular.

galaxy n. **1** *a distant galaxy* **star system**, solar system, constellation; stars. **2** *a galaxy of the rock world's biggest stars* **host**, multitude, array, gathering, assemblage, assembly, throng, crowd, company, flock, group.

gale n. **1** *a howling gale* **strong wind**, high wind, hurricane, tornado, cyclone, whirlwind; storm, squall, tempest, typhoon, superstorm; N. Amer. windstorm; informal burster, buster. **2** *gales of laughter* **peal**, howl, hoot, shriek, scream, roar; outburst, burst, fit, paroxysm, explosion.

gall[1] n. **1** *she had the gall to ask for money* **effrontery**, impudence, impertinence, cheek, cheekiness, insolence, audacity, temerity, presumption, cockiness, nerve, shamelessness, disrespect, bad manners; informal brass neck, face, chutzpah; Brit. informal sauce; N. Amer. informal sass. **2** *scholarly gall was poured on this work* **bitterness**, resentment, rancour, bile, spleen, malice, spite, spitefulness, malignity, venom, vitriol, poison.

gall[2] v. **1** *it galled him to have to sit in silence* **irritate**, annoy, vex, anger, infuriate, exasperate, irk, pique, nettle, put out, displease, antagonize, get on someone's nerves, make someone's hackles rise; Brit. rub up the wrong way; informal aggravate, peeve, miff, rile, needle, get (to), bug, hack off, get up someone's nose, get someone's goat, get/put someone's back up, get someone's dander up, drive mad/crazy, drive round the bend/twist, drive up the wall; Brit. informal wind up, nark, get on someone's wick, give someone the hump; N. Amer. informal tee off, tick off, rankle; informal dated give someone the pip. **2** *the straps galled their shoulders* **chafe**, abrade, rub (against), rub raw, scrape, graze, skin, scratch, rasp, bark.
▸n. **1** *this was a gall that she frequently had to endure* **irritation**, irritant, annoyance, vexation, nuisance, provocation, bother,

torment, plague, thorn in one's side/flesh; informal aggravation, pain, pain in the neck, bore, headache, hassle; N. Amer. informal pain in the butt. **2** *a bay horse with a gall on its side* **sore**, ulcer, ulceration; abrasion, scrape, scratch, graze, chafe.

gallant adj. **1** *his gallant countrymen* **brave**, courageous, valiant, valorous, bold, plucky, daring, fearless, intrepid, heroic, lionhearted, stout-hearted, doughty, mettlesome, death-or-glory, dauntless, undaunted, unflinching, unafraid; informal gutsy, spunky. **2** *her gallant companion* **chivalrous**, gentlemanly, honourable, courteous, polite, mannerly, attentive, respectful, gracious, considerate, thoughtful.
– OPPOSITES cowardly, discourteous.

gallantry n. **1** *he received medals for gallantry* **bravery**, courage, courageousness, valour, pluck, pluckiness, nerve, daring, boldness, fearlessness, dauntlessness, intrepidity, heroism, stout-heartedness, mettle, grit; informal guts, spunk; Brit. informal bottle; N. Amer. informal moxie. **2** *she acknowledged his selfless gallantry* **chivalry**, chivalrousness, gentlemanliness, courtesy, courteousness, politeness, good manners, attentiveness, graciousness, respectfulness, respect, considerateness.

gallery n. **1** *the National Gallery* **art gallery**, museum. **2** *they sat up in the gallery* **balcony**, circle, upper circle; informal gods. **3** *a long gallery with doors along each side* **passage**, passageway, corridor, walkway, arcade.

galling adj. **annoying**, irritating, vexing, vexatious, infuriating, maddening, irksome, provoking, exasperating, trying, tiresome, troublesome, bothersome, displeasing, disagreeable; informal aggravating.

gallivant v. informal **flit**, jaunt, run; roam, wander, travel, rove; informal gad.

gallop v. *Paul galloped across the clearing* **rush**, race, run, sprint, bolt, dart, dash, career, charge, shoot, hurtle, hare, fly, speed, zoom, streak; informal tear, belt, pelt, scoot, zip, whip, hotfoot it, leg it; Brit. informal bomb, go like the clappers; N. Amer. informal barrel.
– OPPOSITES amble.

gallows plural n. **1** *the wooden gallows* **gibbet**, scaffold, gallows tree, Tyburn tree. **2** *they were condemned to the gallows* **hanging**, being hanged, the noose, the rope, the gibbet, the scaffold, execution; informal the drop.

galore adj. **aplenty**, in abundance, in profusion, in great quantities, in large numbers, by the dozen; to spare; everywhere, all over (the place); informal a gogo, by the truckload; Brit. informal by the shedload.

galvanize v. **jolt**, shock, startle, impel, stir, spur, prod, urge, motivate, stimulate, electrify, excite, rouse, arouse, awaken; invigorate, fire, animate, vitalize, energize, exhilarate, thrill, dynamize, inspire; N. Amer. light a fire under; informal give someone a shot in the arm.

gambit n. **stratagem**, scheme, plan, tactic, manoeuvre, move, course/line of action, device; machination, ruse, trick, ploy; Brit. informal wheeze, wangle.

gamble v. **1** *he started to gamble more often* **bet**, place/lay a bet on something, stake money on something, back the horses, game; informal play the ponies; Brit. informal punt, have a flutter. **2** *investors are gambling that the pound will fall* **take a chance**, take a risk; N. Amer. take a flyer; informal stick one's neck out, go out on a limb; Brit. informal chance one's arm.
▸ n. **1** *his grandfather enjoyed a gamble* **bet**, wager, speculation; game of chance; Brit. informal flutter, punt. **2** *I took a gamble and it paid off* **risk**, chance, hazard, leap in the dark; pig in a poke, pot luck.

gambol v. **frolic**, frisk, cavort, caper, skip, dance, romp, prance, leap, hop, jump, spring, bound, bounce; play; dated sport.

game n. **1** *the children invented a new game* **pastime**, diversion, entertainment, amusement, distraction, divertissement, recreation, sport, activity. **2** *the club haven't lost a game all season* **match**, contest, fixture, tie, tournament; cup tie, final, Cup Final, play-off; Brit. clash. **3** *we were only playing a game on him* **practical joke**, prank, jest, trick, hoax; informal lark. **4** *he's in the banking game* **business**, profession, occupation, trade, industry, line, line of work/business; informal racket. **5** *I spoiled his little game* **scheme**, plot, ploy, stratagem, strategy, gambit, cunning plan, tactics; trick, device, manoeuvre, wile, dodge, ruse, machination, contrivance, subterfuge; informal scam; Brit. informal wheeze; old use shift. **6** *he hunted game in Africa* **wild animals**, wild fowl, big game.
▸ adj. **1** *they weren't game enough to join in* **brave**, courageous, plucky, bold, daring, intrepid, valiant, stout-hearted, mettlesome; fearless, dauntless, undaunted, unflinching; informal gutsy, spunky. **2** *I need a bit of help—are you game?* **willing**, prepared, ready, disposed; eager, keen, enthusiastic.

gamut n. **range**, spectrum, span, scope, sweep, compass, area, breadth, reach, extent, catalogue, scale; variety.

gang n. **1** *a gang of teenagers* **band**, group, crowd, pack, horde, throng, mob, herd, swarm, troop, cluster; company, gathering; informal posse, bunch, gaggle, load. **2** informal *John was one of our gang* **circle**, social circle, social set, group, clique, in-crowd, coterie, lot, ring; informal crew. **3** *a gang of workmen* **crew**, team, group, squad, shift, detachment, unit.
▸ v. *they all ganged up to put me down* **conspire**, cooperate, work together, act together, combine, join forces, team up, get together, unite, ally.

gangling, gangly adj. **lanky**, rangy, tall, thin, skinny, spindly, stringy, bony, angular, scrawny, spare; awkward, uncoordinated, ungainly, gawky, inelegant, graceless, ungraceful; dated spindle-shanked.
– OPPOSITES squat.

gangster n. **hoodlum**, gang member, racketeer, robber, ruffian, thug, villain, lawbreaker, criminal; gunman, terrorist; Mafioso; informal mobster, tough, crook, hitman; US informal wise guy; N. Amer. informal hood; dated desperado.

gaol n. Brit. dated See **jail**.

gaoler n. Brit. dated See **jailer**.

gap n. **1** *a gap in the shutters* **opening**, aperture, space, breach, chink, slit, slot, vent, crack, crevice, cranny, cavity, hole, orifice, interstice, perforation, break, fracture, rift, rent, fissure, cleft, divide. **2** *a gap between meetings* **pause**, intermission, interval, interlude, break, breathing space, breather, respite, hiatus; N. Amer. recess. **3** *a gap in our records* **omission**, blank, lacuna, void, vacuity. **4** *the gap between rich and poor* **chasm**, gulf, rift, split, separation, breach; contrast, difference, disparity, divergence, imbalance.

gape v. **1** *she gaped at him in astonishment* **stare**, stare open-mouthed, stare in wonder, goggle, gaze, ogle; informal rubberneck; Brit. informal gawk, gawp. **2** *a leather jerkin which gaped at every seam* **open wide**, open up, yawn; part, split.

gaping adj. *a gaping hole* **cavernous**, yawning, wide, broad; vast, huge, enormous, immense, extensive.

garb n. *men and women in riding garb* **clothes**, clothing, garments, attire, dress, costume, outfit, wear, uniform, livery, regalia; informal gear, get-up, togs, rig-out, duds; Brit. informal clobber; formal apparel; old use raiment, habiliment, vestments.
▸ v. *both men were garbed in black* **dress**, clothe, attire, fit out, turn out, deck (out), kit out, costume, robe; informal get up; old use apparel.

garbage N. Amer. n. **1** *the garbage is taken to landfill sites* **rubbish**, refuse, waste, detritus, litter, junk, scrap; scraps, scourings, leftovers, remains, slops; N. Amer. trash; Austral./NZ mullock. **2** *most of what he says is garbage* **rubbish**, nonsense, balderdash, claptrap, twaddle, blather; dross; informal hogwash, baloney, tripe, bilge, bull, bunk, poppycock, rot, bosh, piffle, dreck; Brit. informal tosh, codswallop, cobblers, stuff and nonsense; informal dated tommyrot, bunkum.

garble v. **mix up**, muddle, jumble, confuse, obscure, distort; misstate, misquote, misreport, misrepresent, mistranslate, misinterpret, misconstrue, twist.

garden n. cottage garden, flower garden, rock garden, walled garden, knot garden, parterre; vegetable garden, kitchen garden, potager; (**gardens**) park, estate, grounds.
□ **lead someone up the garden path** informal deceive, mislead, delude, hoodwink, dupe, trick, entrap, beguile, take in, fool, pull the wool over someone's eyes, gull; informal con, pull a fast one on, string along, take for a ride, put one over on.

┌─────────────────────────────────────┐
WORD LINKS

horticultural relating to gardens and gardening
arbour, bower a shady or sheltered place in a garden
└─────────────────────────────────────┘

g

summer house a small garden building used for relaxing in fine weather

gazebo, belvedere a summer house with a good view

trellis, pergola a framework for climbing plants in a garden

topiary the art of clipping garden bushes into decorative shapes

gargantuan adj. **huge**, enormous, vast, gigantic, very big, giant, massive, colossal, mammoth, immense, mighty, monumental, mountainous, titanic, towering, tremendous, elephantine, king-size(d), prodigious; informal mega, monster, whopping, humongous, jumbo; Brit. informal whacking, ginormous.
– OPPOSITES tiny.

garish adj. **gaudy**, lurid, loud, over-bright, harsh, glaring, violent, showy, glittering, brassy, brash; tasteless, in bad taste, vulgar, unattractive, bilious; informal flash, flashy, tacky.
– OPPOSITES drab.

garland n. *a garland of flowers* **festoon**, lei, wreath, ring, circle, swag; coronet, crown, coronal, chaplet, fillet.
▶ v. *gardens garlanded with coloured lights* **festoon**, wreathe, swathe, hang; adorn, ornament, embellish, decorate, deck, trim, dress, bedeck, array; literary bedizen, caparison.

garment n. **item of clothing**, article of clothing; (**garments**) clothes, clothing, dress, garb, outfit, costume, attire; informal get-up, rig-out, gear, togs, duds, garms; N. Amer. informal threads; formal apparel.

garner v. **gather**, collect, accumulate, amass, get together, assemble.

garnish v. *garnish the dish with chopped parsley* **decorate**, adorn, ornament, trim, dress, embellish; enhance, grace, beautify, prettify, add the finishing touch to.
▶ n. *keep a few sprigs for a garnish* **decoration**, adornment, trim, trimming, ornament, ornamentation, embellishment, enhancement, finishing touch; Cookery chiffonade.

garret n. **attic**, loft, roof space, cock loft, mansard.

garrison n. **1** *the English garrison had been burned alive* **troops**, militia, soldiers, forces; armed force, military detachment, unit, platoon, brigade, squadron, battalion, corps. **2** *forces from three garrisons* **fortress**, fort, fortification, stronghold, citadel, camp, encampment, cantonment, command post, base, station; barracks.
▶ v. **1** *French infantry garrisoned the town* **defend**, guard, protect, barricade, shield, secure; man, occupy. **2** *troops were garrisoned in various regions* **station**, post, put on duty, deploy, assign, install; base, site, place, position; billet.

garrulity n. **talkativeness**, garrulousness, loquacity, loquaciousness, volubility, verbosity, verboseness, long-windedness, wordiness, chattiness, effusiveness; informal the gift of the gab; Brit. informal wittering; rare logorrhoea.

garrulous adj. **1** *a garrulous old man* **talkative**, loquacious, voluble, verbose, chatty, chattering, gossipy; effusive, expansive, forthcoming, conversational, communicative; informal mouthy, gabby, gassy, windy, having the gift of the gab, having kissed the Blarney Stone; Brit. informal able to talk the hind legs off a donkey, gobby. **2** *his garrulous reminiscences* **long-winded**, wordy, verbose, prolix, long, lengthy, rambling, wandering, maundering, meandering, digressive, diffuse, discursive; gossipy, chatty; informal windy, gassy.
– OPPOSITES taciturn, concise.

gash n. *a gash on his forehead* **laceration**, cut, wound, injury, slash, tear, incision; slit, split, rip, rent; scratch, scrape, graze, abrasion; Medicine lesion.
▶ v. *he gashed his hand on some broken glass* **lacerate**, cut (open), wound, injure, hurt, slash, tear, gouge, puncture, slit, split, rend; scratch, scrape, graze, abrade.

gasp v. **1** *I gasped in surprise* **catch one's breath**, draw in one's breath, gulp; exclaim, cry (out). **2** *he collapsed on the ground, gasping* **pant**, puff, puff and pant, puff and blow, wheeze, breathe hard, choke, fight for breath.
▶ n. *a gasp of dismay* **drawing-in of breath**, gulp; exclamation, cry; dated ejaculation.

gastric adj. *gastric pain* **stomach**, intestinal, enteric, duodenal, coeliac, abdominal, ventral.

gate n. **1** *heavy wooden gates* **barrier**, wicket gate, lychgate, five-barred gate, turnstile; Brit. kissing gate. **2** *she went through the gate* **gateway**, doorway, entrance, exit, egress, opening; door, portal; N. Amer. entryway.

gather v. **1** *we gathered in the hotel lobby* **congregate**, assemble, meet, collect, come/get together, convene, muster, rally, converge; cluster together, crowd, mass, flock together; formal foregather. **2** *he gathered his family together* **summon**, call together, bring together, assemble, convene, rally, round up, muster, marshal. **3** *knick-knacks she had gathered over the years* **collect**, accumulate, amass, garner, accrue; store, stockpile, hoard, put by/away, lay by/in; informal stash away, squirrel away. **4** *they gathered corn from the fields* **harvest**, reap, crop; pick, pluck; collect. **5** *the show soon gathered a fanatical following* **attract**, draw, pull, pull in, collect, pick up. **6** *I gather he's a keen footballer* **understand**, be given to understand, believe, be led to believe, think, conclude, deduce, infer, assume, take it, surmise, fancy; hear, hear tell, learn, discover. **7** *he gathered her to his chest* **clasp**, clutch, pull, embrace, enfold, hold, hug, cuddle, squeeze; literary embosom; old use strain. **8** *his tunic was gathered at the waist* **pleat**, shirr, pucker, tuck, fold, ruffle.
– OPPOSITES disperse.

gathering n. **1** *she rose to address the gathering* **assembly**, meeting, convention, rally, turnout, congress, convocation, conclave, council, synod, forum; congregation, audience, crowd, group, throng, mass, multitude; informal get-together; formal concourse. **2** *the gathering of data for a future book* **collecting**, collection, garnering, amassing, accumulation, accrual, cumulation, building up.

gauche adj. **awkward**, gawky, inelegant, graceless, ungraceful, ungainly, maladroit, inept; lacking in social grace(s), unsophisticated, uncultured, uncultivated, unrefined, raw, inexperienced, unworldly.
– OPPOSITES elegant, sophisticated.

gaudy adj. **garish**, lurid, loud, over-bright, glaring, harsh, violent, showy, glittering, brassy, ostentatious; tasteless, in bad taste, vulgar, unattractive, bilious; informal flash, flashy, tacky.
– OPPOSITES drab, tasteful.

gauge n. **1** *the temperature gauge* **measuring device**, measuring instrument, meter, measure; indicator, dial, scale, display. **2** *exports are an important gauge of economic activity* **measure**, indicator, barometer, point of reference, guide, guideline, touchstone, yardstick, benchmark, criterion, test, litmus test. **3** *guitar strings of a different gauge* **size**, diameter, thickness, width, breadth; measure, capacity, magnitude; bore, calibre.
▶ v. **1** *astronomers can gauge the star's intrinsic brightness* **measure**, calculate, compute, work out, determine, ascertain; count, weigh, quantify, put a figure on. **2** *it is difficult to gauge how effective the ban was* **assess**, evaluate, determine, estimate, form an opinion of, appraise, weigh up, get the measure of, judge, guess; informal guesstimate, size up.

gaunt adj. **1** *a gaunt, greying man* **haggard**, drawn, thin, lean, skinny, spindly, spare, bony, angular, raw-boned, pinched, hollow-cheeked, scrawny, scraggy, as thin as a rake, cadaverous, skeletal, emaciated, skin and bone; wasted, withered; informal like a bag of bones; old use spindle-shanked, starveling. **2** *the gaunt ruin of Pendragon Castle* **bleak**, stark, desolate, bare, gloomy, dismal, sombre, grim, stern, harsh, forbidding, uninviting, cheerless.
– OPPOSITES plump.

gauzy adj. **translucent**, transparent, sheer, see-through, fine, delicate, flimsy, filmy, gossamer-like, diaphanous, chiffony, wispy, floaty, thin, light, insubstantial.
– OPPOSITES opaque, thick.

gawk v. informal **gape**, goggle, gaze, ogle, stare, stare open-mouthed; informal rubberneck; Brit. informal gawp.

gawky adj. **awkward**, ungainly, gangling, gauche, maladroit, clumsy, inelegant, uncoordinated, graceless, ungraceful; unsophisticated, unconfident.
– OPPOSITES graceful.

gay adj. **1** *gay men and women* **homosexual**, lesbian. **2** dated *her children all looked*

chubby and gay **cheerful**, cheery, merry, jolly, light-hearted, carefree, jovial, glad, happy, in good/high spirits, joyful, elated, exuberant, animated, lively, sprightly, vivacious, buoyant, bouncy, bubbly, perky, effervescent, playful; informal chirpy. **3** dated *they were having a gay old time* **jolly**, merry, hilarious, amusing, uproarious, rollicking, entertaining, enjoyable, convivial; festive. **4** dated *gay checked curtains* **bright**, brightly coloured, vivid, brilliant, vibrant; richly coloured, many-coloured, multicoloured; flamboyant, showy, gaudy.
– OPPOSITES heterosexual, gloomy.

gaze v. *he gazed at her* **stare**, look fixedly, gape, goggle, eye, look, study, scrutinize, take a good look; ogle, leer; informal gawk, rubberneck; Brit. informal gawp; N. Amer. informal eyeball.
▶ n. *his piercing gaze* **stare**, fixed look, gape; regard, inspection, scrutiny.

gazebo n. **summer house**, pavilion, belvedere; arbour, bower.

gazette n. **newspaper**, paper, journal, periodical, organ, news-sheet, newsletter, bulletin; informal rag.

gear n. informal **1** *his fishing gear* **equipment**, apparatus, paraphernalia, articles, appliances, impedimenta; tools, utensils, implements, instruments, gadgets; stuff, things; kit, rig, tackle, odds and ends, bits and pieces, bits and bobs; trappings, appurtenances, accoutrements, regalia; Brit. informal clobber, gubbins, odds and sods; old use equipage. **2** *I'll go back to my hotel and pick up my gear* **belongings**, possessions, effects, personal effects, property, paraphernalia, odds and ends, bits and pieces, bits and bobs, bags, baggage; Law chattels; informal things, stuff, kit; Brit. informal clobber. **3** *the best designer gear* **clothes**, clothing, garments, outfits, attire, garb; dress, wear; informal togs, duds, get-up, garms; Brit. informal clobber, kit; N. Amer. informal threads; formal apparel.

gel, **jell** v. **1** *leave the mixture to gel* **set**, stiffen, solidify, thicken, harden; cake, congeal, coagulate, clot. **2** *things started to gel very quickly* **take shape**, fall into place, come together, take form, work out; crystallize.

gelatinous adj. **jelly-like**, glutinous, viscous, viscid, mucilaginous, ropy, sticky, gluey, gummy, slimy; informal gooey.

geld v. **castrate**, neuter, desex, fix; N. Amer. & Austral. alter; Brit. informal doctor.

gelid adj. **frozen**, freezing, icy, glacial, frosty, wintry, snowy; arctic, polar, Siberian.

gem n. **1** *rubies and other gems* **jewel**, precious stone, semi-precious stone, stone; solitaire, brilliant, cabochon; old use bijou. **2** *the gem of the collection* **best**, finest, pride, prize, treasure, flower, pearl, the jewel in the crown; pick, choice, cream, the crème de la crème, elite, acme; informal one in a million, the bee's knees.

g

genealogy n. **lineage**, line (of descent), family tree, bloodline; pedigree, ancestry, extraction, heritage, parentage, birth, family, dynasty, house, stock, blood, roots.

general adj. **1** *this is suitable for general use* **widespread**, common, extensive, universal, wide, popular, public, mainstream; established, conventional, traditional, orthodox, accepted. **2** *a general pay increase* **comprehensive**, overall, across the board, blanket, umbrella, mass, wholesale, sweeping, broad-ranging, inclusive, company-wide; universal, global, worldwide, nationwide. **3** *general knowledge* **miscellaneous**, mixed, assorted, diversified, composite, heterogeneous. **4** *the general practice* **usual**, customary, habitual, traditional, normal, conventional, typical, standard, regular; familiar, accepted, prevailing, routine, run-of-the-mill, established, everyday, ordinary, common. **5** *a general description* **broad**, imprecise, inexact, rough, loose, approximate, unspecific, vague, woolly, indefinite; N. Amer. informal **ballpark**.
– OPPOSITES restricted, localized, specialist, detailed.

generality n. **1** *the debate has moved on from generalities* **generalization**, general statement, general principle, sweeping statement; abstraction, extrapolation. **2** *the generality of this principle* **universality**, comprehensiveness, all-inclusiveness, broadness. **3** *the generality of people are kind* **majority**, greater part/number, best/better part; bulk, mass, preponderance, predominance; most.

generally adv. **1** *summers were generally hot* **normally**, in general, as a rule, by and large, more often than not, almost always, mainly, mostly, for the most part, predominantly, on the whole; usually, habitually, customarily, typically, ordinarily, commonly. **2** *France was moving generally to the left* **overall**, in general terms, generally speaking, all in all, broadly, on average, basically, effectively. **3** *the method was generally accepted* **widely**, commonly, extensively, universally, popularly.

generate v. **1** *moves to generate extra business* **cause**, give rise to, lead to, result in, bring about, create, make, produce, engender, spawn, precipitate, prompt, provoke, trigger, spark off, stir up, induce, promote, foster. **2** *the male most likely to generate offspring* **procreate**, breed, father, sire, spawn, create, produce, have; literary **beget**; old use engender.

generation n. **1** *people of the same generation* **age**, age group, peer group. **2** *generations ago* **ages**, years, aeons, a long time, an eternity; informal donkey's years; Brit. informal **yonks**. **3** *the next generation of computers* **crop**, batch, wave, range.

4 *the generation of novel ideas* **creation**, production, initiation, origination, inception, inspiration. **5** *human generation* **procreation**, reproduction, breeding; creation.

generic adj. **1** *a generic term for two separate offences* **general**, common, collective, non-specific, inclusive, all-encompassing, comprehensive, broad, blanket, umbrella. **2** *generic drugs are cheaper than branded ones* **unbranded**, non-proprietary.
– OPPOSITES specific.

generosity n. **1** *the generosity of our host* **liberality**, lavishness, magnanimity, munificence, open-handedness, free-handedness, unselfishness; kindness, benevolence, altruism, charity, big-heartedness, goodness; literary bounteousness. **2** *the generosity of the food portions* **abundance**, plentifulness, copiousness, lavishness, liberality, largeness.

generous adj. **1** *she is generous with money* **liberal**, lavish, magnanimous, munificent, giving, open-handed, free-handed, bountiful, unselfish, ungrudging, free, indulgent, prodigal; literary bounteous. **2** *it was generous of them to offer* **magnanimous**, kind, benevolent, altruistic, charitable, noble, big-hearted, honourable, good; unselfish, self-sacrificing. **3** *a generous amount of fabric* **lavish**, plentiful, copious, ample, liberal, large, great, abundant, profuse, bumper, opulent, prolific; informal a gogo, galore.
– OPPOSITES mean, selfish, meagre.

genesis n. **1** *the hatred had its genesis in something dark* **origin**, source, root, beginning, start. **2** *the genesis of neurosis* **formation**, development, evolution, emergence, inception, origination, creation, formulation, propagation.

genial adj. **friendly**, affable, cordial, amiable, warm, easy-going, approachable, sympathetic; good-natured, good-humoured, cheerful; neighbourly, hospitable, companionable, comradely, sociable, convivial, outgoing, gregarious; informal chummy, pally; Brit. informal matey.
– OPPOSITES unfriendly.

genitals plural n. **private parts**, genitalia, sexual organs, reproductive organs, pudenda; crotch, groin; informal naughty bits, privates; euphemistic nether regions.

genius n. **1** *the world knew of his genius* **brilliance**, intelligence, intellect, ability, cleverness, brains, erudition, wisdom, fine mind; artistry, flair. **2** *he has a genius for organization* **talent**, gift, flair, aptitude, facility, knack, bent, ability, expertise, capacity, faculty; strength, forte, brilliance, skill, artistry. **3** *he is a genius* **brilliant person**, gifted person, mastermind, Einstein, intellectual, great intellect, brain, prodigy; informal egghead, bright spark; Brit. informal brainbox, clever clogs; N. Amer. informal brainiac, rocket scientist.
– OPPOSITES stupidity, dunce.

genocide n. **mass murder**, mass homicide, massacre; annihilation, extermination, elimination, liquidation, eradication, decimation, butchery, bloodletting; pogrom, ethnic cleansing, holocaust.

genre n. **category**, class, classification, group, set, list; type, sort, kind, variety, style, model, school, stamp, cast, ilk.

genteel adj. **refined**, respectable, decorous, mannerly, well mannered, courteous, polite, proper, correct, seemly; well bred, cultured, sophisticated, ladylike, gentlemanly, dignified, gracious; affected; Brit. informal posh.
– OPPOSITES uncouth.

gentility n. **social superiority**, respectability, punctiliousness, decorum, good manners, politeness, civility, courtesy, correctness; refinement, distinction, breeding, sophistication; graciousness, affectation, ostentation.

gentle adj. **1** *his manner was gentle* **kind**, tender, sympathetic, considerate, understanding, compassionate, benevolent, good-natured; humane, lenient, merciful, clement; mild, placid, serene, sweet-tempered. **2** *a gentle breeze* **light**, soft. **3** *a gentle slope* **gradual**, slight, easy. **4** old use *a woman of gentle birth*. See **noble** (sense 1 of the adjective).
– OPPOSITES brutal, strong, steep, low.

gentleman n. **man**; nobleman, honnête homme; informal gent; old use cavalier.

gentlemanly adj. **chivalrous**, gallant, honourable, noble, courteous, civil, mannerly, polite, gracious, considerate, thoughtful; well bred, cultivated, cultured, refined, suave, urbane.
– OPPOSITES rude.

gentry n. **upper classes**, privileged classes, elite, high society, haut monde, smart set; establishment; informal upper crust, top drawer; Brit. informal nobs, toffs.

genuine adj. **1** *a genuine Picasso* **authentic**, real, actual, original, bona fide, true, veritable; attested, undisputed; informal pukka, the real McCoy, the real thing, kosher; Austral./NZ informal dinkum. **2** *a very genuine person* **sincere**, honest, truthful, straightforward, direct, frank, candid, open; artless, natural, unaffected; informal straight, upfront, on the level; N. Amer. informal on the up and up.
– OPPOSITES bogus, insincere.

genus n. **1** Biology *a large genus of plants* **subdivision**, division, group, subfamily. **2** *a new genus of music* **type**, sort, kind, genre, style, variety, category, class; breed, brand, family, stamp, cast, ilk.

germ n. **1** *this detergent kills germs* **microbe**, microorganism, bacillus, bacterium, virus; informal bug. **2** *a fertilized germ* **embryo**, bud; seed, spore, ovule; egg, ovum. **3** *the germ of an idea* **start**, beginning(s), seed, embryo, bud, root, rudiment; origin, source, potential; core, nucleus, kernel, essence.

germane adj. **relevant**, pertinent, applicable, apposite, material; apropos, to the point, appropriate, apt, fitting, suitable; connected, related, akin; formal ad rem.
– OPPOSITES irrelevant.

germinate v. **1** *the grain is allowed to germinate* **sprout**, shoot (up), bud; develop, grow, spring up; dated vegetate. **2** *the idea began to germinate* **develop**, take root, grow, emerge, evolve, mature, expand, advance, progress.

gestation n. **1** *a gestation of thirty days* **pregnancy**, incubation; development, maturation. **2** *the law underwent a period of gestation* **development**, evolution, formation, emergence, origination.

gesticulate v. **gesture**, signal, motion, wave, sign.

gesticulation n. **gesturing**, gesture, hand movement, signals, signs; wave, indication; body language.

gesture n. **1** *a gesture of surrender* **signal**, sign, motion, indication, gesticulation. **2** *a symbolic gesture* **action**, act, deed, move.
▶ v. *he gestured to her* **signal**, motion, gesticulate, wave, indicate, give a sign.

get v. **1** *where did you get that hat?* **acquire**, obtain, come by, receive, gain, earn, win, come into, take possession of, be given; buy, purchase, procure, secure; gather, collect, pick up, hook, net, land; achieve, attain; informal get one's hands on, get one's mitts on, get hold of, grab, bag, score. **2** *I got your letter* **receive**, be sent, be in receipt of, be given. **3** *your tea's getting cold* **become**, grow, turn, go. **4** *get the children from school* **fetch**, collect, go for, call for, pick up, bring, deliver, convey, ferry, transport. **5** *the chairman gets £650,000 a year* **earn**, be paid, take home, bring in, make, receive, collect, gross; informal pocket, bank, rake in, net, bag. **6** *have the police got their man?* **apprehend**, catch, arrest, capture, seize; take prisoner, take into custody, detain, put in jail, put behind bars, imprison, incarcerate; informal collar, grab, nab, nail, run in, pinch, bust, pick up, pull in, do, feel someone's collar; Brit. informal nick. **7** *I got a taxi* **travel by/on/in**; take, catch, use. **8** *she got flu* **succumb to**, develop, go/come down with, sicken for, fall victim to, be struck down with, be afflicted by/with; become infected with, catch, contract, fall ill with, be taken ill with; Brit. go down with; informal take ill with; N. Amer. informal take sick with. **9** *I got a pain in my arm* **experience**, suffer, be afflicted with, sustain, feel, have. **10** *I didn't get what he said* **hear**, discern, distinguish, make out, perceive, follow, take in. **11** *I don't get the joke* **understand**, comprehend, grasp, see, fathom, follow, perceive, apprehend, unravel, decipher; informal get the drift of, catch on to, latch on to, figure out; Brit. informal twig, suss. **12** *we got there early* **arrive**, reach, come, make it, turn up, appear, come on the scene, approach, enter, present oneself, come along, materialize, show one's face; informal show (up), roll in/up, blow in. **13** *we got her to go* **persuade**, induce, prevail on, influence; wheedle into, talk into, cajole into. **14** *I'll get*

g

supper **prepare**, get ready, cook, make, assemble, muster, concoct; informal fix, rustle up; Brit. informal knock up. **15** informal *I'll get him for that* **take revenge on**, get one's revenge on, get even with, pay back, get back at, give someone their just deserts; Brit. informal get one's own back on. **16** *He scratched his head. 'You've got me there.'* **baffle**, nonplus, perplex, puzzle, bewilder, mystify, bemuse, confuse, confound; informal flummox, faze, stump, beat, fox; N. Amer. informal discombobulate. **17** *what gets me is how neurotic she is* **annoy**, irritate, exasperate, anger, irk, vex, provoke, incense, infuriate, madden, try someone's patience; informal aggravate, peeve, miff, rile, get to, needle, hack off, get someone's back up, get on someone's nerves, get up someone's nose, get someone's goat, drive mad; Brit. informal wind up, nark, get someone's wick; N. Amer. informal tee off, tick off.

□ **get something across** communicate, get over, impart, convey, transmit, make clear, express.

get ahead prosper, flourish, thrive, do well; succeed, make it, advance, get on in the world, go up in the world, make good, become rich; informal go places, get somewhere, make the big time.

get along 1 *does he get along with his family?* **be friendly**, be compatible, get on; agree, see eye to eye, concur, be in accord, be on the same wavelength; informal hit it off. **2** *he was getting along well at school* **fare**, manage, progress, advance, get on, get by, do, cope; succeed.

get at 1 *it's difficult to get at the pipes* **access**, get to, reach, touch. **2** *he had been got at by enemy agents* **corrupt**, suborn, influence, bribe, buy off, pay off; informal fix, square; Brit. informal nobble. **3** informal *what are you getting at?* **imply**, suggest, intimate, insinuate, hint, mean, drive at, allude to. **4** Brit. informal *I don't like being got at* **criticize**, pick on, find fault with, nag; **bully**, victimize, persecute, discriminate against.

get away escape, run away/off, break out, break free, break loose, bolt, flee, take flight, make off, take off, decamp, abscond, make a run for it; slip away, sneak away; informal cut and run, skedaddle, do a disappearing act, scarper, leg it; Brit. informal do a bunk, do a runner.

get away with escape blame for, escape punishment for.

get something back retrieve, regain, win back, recover, recoup, reclaim, repossess, recapture, redeem; find (again), trace.

get by manage, cope, survive, exist, subsist, muddle through/along, scrape by, make ends meet, make do, keep the wolf from the door; informal make out.

get someone down depress, sadden, make unhappy, make gloomy, dispirit, dishearten, demoralize, discourage, crush, weigh down, oppress; upset, distress; informal give someone the blues, make someone fed up.

get off 1 *Sally got off the bus* **alight (from)**, step off, dismount (from), descend (from),

disembark (from), leave, exit. **2** informal *he was arrested but got off* **escape punishment**, be acquitted, be absolved, be cleared, be exonerated.

get on 1 *we got on the train* **board**, enter, step aboard, climb on, mount, ascend, catch; informal hop on, jump on. **2** *how are you getting on?* **fare**, manage, progress, get along, do, cope, get by, survive, muddle through/along; succeed, prosper; informal make out. **3** *he got on with his job* **continue**, proceed, go ahead, carry on, go on, press on, persist, persevere; keep at; informal stick with/at. **4** *we don't get on.* See **get along** (sense 1).

get out of evade, avoid, shirk, avoid, escape, sidestep; informal duck (out of), wriggle out of, cop out of; Austral./NZ informal duck-shove.

get over 1 *I have just got over flu* **recover from**, recuperate from, get better after, shrug off, survive. **2** *we tried to get over this problem* **overcome**, surmount, get the better of, master, get round, find an/the answer to, get a grip on, deal with, cope with, sort out, take care of, crack, rise above; informal lick.

get something over See **get something across**.

get round someone cajole, persuade, wheedle, coax, prevail on, win over, bring round, sway, beguile, charm, inveigle, influence, woo; informal sweet-talk, soft-soap, butter up, twist someone's arm.

get together 1 *get together the best writers* **collect**, gather, assemble, bring together, rally, muster, marshal, congregate, convene, amass; formal convoke. **2** *we must get together soon* **meet (up)**, rendezvous, see each other, socialize.

get up get out of bed, rise, stir, rouse oneself; informal surface; formal arise.

get someone up informal dress, clothe, attire, garb, fit out, turn out, deck (out), trick out/up, costume, array, robe; informal doll up; old use apparel.

getaway n. **escape**, breakout, bolt for freedom, flight; disappearance, vanishing act; Brit. informal flit.

get-together n. **party**, meeting, gathering, social event, tweetup; informal do, bash; Brit. informal rave-up, knees-up, jolly, bunfight, beano.

get-up n. informal **outfit**, clothes, costume, ensemble, suit, clothing, dress, attire, garments, garb; informal gear, togs, duds, garms; Brit. informal clobber, rig-out; N. Amer. informal threads; formal apparel.

get-up-and-go n. informal **drive**, initiative, enterprise, enthusiasm, eagerness, ambition, motivation, dynamism, energy, gusto, vigour, vitality, verve, fire, fervour, zeal, commitment, spirit; informal gumption, oomph, vim, pep.
– OPPOSITES apathy.

ghastly adj. **1** *a ghastly stabbing* **terrible**, frightful, horrible, grim, awful, dire; frightening, terrifying, horrifying, alarming; distressing, shocking, appalling, harrowing; dreadful, horrendous, monstrous,

gruesome, grisly. **2** *informal a ghastly building* **unpleasant**, objectionable, disagreeable, distasteful, horrible, awful, terrible, dreadful, frightful, detestable, insufferable, vile; *informal* horrid. **3** *the patient feels ghastly* **ill**, unwell, peaky, poorly; sick, queasy, nauseous; Brit. off colour; *informal* rough, lousy, rotten, terrible, awful, dreadful; Brit. *informal* grotty, ropy; *Scottish informal* peely-wally; Austral./NZ *informal* crook. **4** *a ghastly pallor* **pale**, white, pallid, pasty, wan, bloodless, peaky, ashen, grey, waxy, blanched, drained, pinched, green, sickly; *informal* like death warmed up.
– OPPOSITES pleasant, charming, fine, healthy.

ghost n. **1** *his ghost haunts the crypt* **spectre**, phantom, wraith, spirit, presence; apparition; *informal* spook. **2** *the ghost of a smile* **trace**, hint, suggestion, impression, suspicion, tinge; glimmer, semblance, shadow, whisper.

ghostly adj. **spectral**, ghostlike, phantom, wraithlike; unearthly, unnatural, supernatural; insubstantial, shadowy; eerie, weird, uncanny; frightening, spine-chilling, hair-raising, blood-curdling, terrifying, chilling, sinister; *informal* creepy, scary, spooky; *literary* phantasmal, phantasmic.

ghoulish adj. **macabre**, grisly, gruesome, grotesque, ghastly; unhealthy, horrible, unwholesome.

giant n. *the forest giant had died* **colossus**, man mountain, behemoth, Brobdingnagian, mammoth, monster; *informal* jumbo.
– OPPOSITES dwarf.
▶adj. *a giant marble statue* **huge**, colossal, massive, enormous, gigantic, very big, mammoth, vast, immense, monumental, mountainous, titanic, towering, elephantine, king-size(d), gargantuan, Brobdingnagian; substantial, hefty; *informal* mega, monster, whopping, humongous, jumbo, hulking, bumper; Brit. *informal* ginormous.
– OPPOSITES miniature.

gibber v. **prattle**, babble, ramble, drivel, jabber, gabble, burble, twitter, flannel, mutter, mumble; *informal* yammer, blabber, jibber-jabber, blather, blether; Brit. *informal* witter, chunter.

gibberish n. **nonsense**, rubbish, balderdash, blather, blether; *informal* drivel, gobbledegook, mumbo jumbo, tripe, hogwash, baloney, bilge, bosh, bull, bunk, guff, eyewash, piffle, twaddle, poppycock; Brit. *informal* cobblers, codswallop, double Dutch, tosh, cack; N. Amer. *informal* garbage, blathers, applesauce.

gibe n. & v. See **jibe**.

giddiness n. **dizziness**, light-headedness; faintness, unsteadiness, shakiness, wobbliness; *informal* wooziness.

giddy adj. **1** *she felt giddy* **dizzy**, light-headed, faint, weak, vertiginous; unsteady, shaky, wobbly, reeling; *informal* woozy. **2** *she was young and giddy* **flighty**, silly, frivolous, skittish, irresponsible, flippant, whimsical, capricious; feather-brained, scatty, thoughtless, heedless, carefree; *informal* dippy;

N. Amer. *informal* ditzy.
– OPPOSITES steady, sensible.

gift n. **1** *he gave the staff a gift* **present**, handout, donation, offering, bestowal, bonus, award, endowment; tip, gratuity, baksheesh; largesse; *informal* prezzie, freebie, perk; *formal* benefaction. **2** *a gift for melody* **talent**, flair, aptitude, facility, knack, bent, ability, expertise, capacity, capability, faculty; endowment, strength, genius, brilliance, skill, artistry.
▶v. *he gifted a composition to the orchestra* **present**, give, bestow, confer, donate, endow, award, accord, grant; hand over, make over.

gifted adj. **talented**, skilful, skilled, accomplished, expert, consummate, masterly, master, first-rate, able, apt, adept, proficient; intelligent, clever, bright, brilliant; precocious; *informal* crack, top-notch, ace.
– OPPOSITES inept.

gigantic adj. **huge**, enormous, vast, extensive, very big, very large, giant, massive, colossal, mammoth, immense, monumental, mountainous, titanic, towering, elephantine, king-size(d), gargantuan; *informal* mega, monster, whopping, humongous, jumbo, hulking, bumper; Brit. *informal* ginormous.
– OPPOSITES tiny.

giggle v. *he giggled at the picture* **titter**, snigger, snicker, tee-hee, chuckle, chortle, laugh.
▶n. *she suppressed a giggle* **titter**, snigger, snicker, tee-hee, chuckle, chortle, laugh.

gigolo n. **playboy**, (male) escort; admirer, lover; *informal* fancy man; Brit. *informal* toy boy.

gild v. **1** *a gilded weathercock* **cover with gold**, paint gold. **2** *he tends to gild the truth* **elaborate**, embellish, embroider, camouflage, disguise, dress up, colour, exaggerate, expand on; *informal* jazz up.

gimcrack adj. **shoddy**, jerry-built, flimsy, insubstantial, thrown together, makeshift; inferior, poor-quality, second-rate, cheap, cheapjack, tawdry, kitschy, trashy; *informal* tacky, junky, rubbishy.

gimmick n. **publicity device**, stunt, contrivance, scheme, stratagem, ploy; *informal* shtick.

gingerly adv. **cautiously**, carefully, with care, warily, charily, circumspectly, delicately; heedfully, watchfully, vigilantly, attentively; hesitantly, timidly.
– OPPOSITES recklessly.

gird v. *literary* **1** *Sir Hector girded on his sword* **fasten**, belt, bind, tie. **2** *the island was girded by rocks* **surround**, enclose, encircle, circle, encompass, border, bound, edge, skirt, fringe; close in, confine. **3** *they girded themselves for war* **prepare**, get ready, gear up; nerve, steel, galvanize, brace, fortify; *informal* psych oneself up.

girdle n. **1** *a diamond-studded girdle* **belt**, sash, cummerbund, waistband, strap, band, girth, cord. **2** *her stockings were held up*

g

g

by her girdle **corset**, corselet, foundation garment, panty girdle; truss.

▸ v. *a garden girdled the house* **surround**, enclose, encircle, circle, encompass, circumscribe, border, bound, skirt, edge; literary gird.

girl n. **1** *a five-year-old girl* **female child**, daughter; schoolgirl; Scottish & N. English lass, lassie; derogatory chit. See also **child. 2** *a tall dark girl* **young woman**, young lady, miss, mademoiselle; Scottish lass, lassie; Irish colleen; informal chick, girlie, filly; Brit. informal bird, bint; N. Amer. informal gal, broad, dame, jane, babe; Austral./NZ informal sheila; literary maid, damsel; old use wench. **3** *his girl left him.* See **girlfriend**.

girlfriend n. **sweetheart**, lover, partner, significant other, girl, woman; fiancée; informal steady; Brit. informal bird; N. Amer. informal squeeze; dated lady (friend), lady-love, betrothed; old use leman.

girlish adj. **girlie**, youthful, childlike, childish, immature; feminine.

girth n. **1** *a tree ten feet in girth* **circumference**, perimeter; width, breadth. **2** *he tied the towel around his girth* **stomach**, midriff, middle, abdomen, belly, gut; informal tummy, tum. **3** *a horse's girth* N. Amer. cinch.

gist n. **essence**, substance, central theme, heart of the matter, nub, kernel, marrow, meat, burden, crux; thrust, drift, sense, meaning, significance, import; informal nitty-gritty.

give v. **1** *he gave them £2000* **present with**, provide with, supply with, furnish with, let someone have; hand (over), offer, proffer; award, grant, bestow, accord, confer, make over; donate, contribute, put up. **2** *can I give him a message?* **convey**, pass on, impart, communicate, transmit; send, deliver, relay; tell. **3** *a baby given into their care* **entrust**, commit, consign, assign; formal commend. **4** *he gave his life for them* **sacrifice**, give up, relinquish; devote, dedicate. **5** *he gave her time to think* **allow**, permit, grant, accord; offer. **6** *this leaflet gives our opening times* **show**, display, set out, indicate, detail, list. **7** *they gave no further trouble* **cause**, make, create, occasion. **8** *garlic gives flavour* **produce**, yield, afford, impart, lend. **9** *he gave a drinks party* **organize**, arrange, lay on, throw, host, hold, have, provide. **10** *Dominic gave a bow* **perform**, execute, make, do. **11** *she gave a shout* **utter**, let out, emit, produce, make. **12** *he gave Harry a beating* **administer**, deliver, deal, inflict, impose. **13** *the door gave* **give way**, cave in, collapse, break, fall apart; bend, buckle.
– OPPOSITES receive, take.

▸ n. informal *there isn't enough give in the jacket* **elasticity**, flexibility, stretch, stretchiness; slack, play.

◻ **give someone away** betray, inform on; informal split on, rat on, peach on, do the dirty on, blow the whistle on, sell down the river; Brit. informal grass on, shop; N. Amer. informal rat out, finger; Austral./NZ informal dob on; English Law turn Queen's/King's evidence.

give something away reveal, disclose, divulge, let slip, leak, let out.

give in capitulate, concede defeat, admit defeat, give up, surrender, yield, submit, back down, give way, defer, relent, throw in the towel/sponge.

give something off/out emit, produce, send out, throw out; discharge, release, exude, vent.

give out run out, be used up, be consumed, be exhausted, be depleted; fail, flag; dry up.

give something out distribute, issue, hand out, pass round, dispense; dole out, dish out, mete out; allocate, allot, share out.

give up See **give in.**

give something up stop, cease, discontinue, desist from, abstain from, cut out, renounce, forgo; resign from, stand down from; informal quit, kick, swear off, leave off, pack in, lay off; Brit. informal jack in.

give and take n. **compromise**, concession; cooperation, reciprocity, teamwork, interplay.

given adj. **1** *a given number of years* **specified**, stated, designated, set, particular, specific; prescribed, agreed, appointed, prearranged, predetermined. **2** *she was given to fits of temper* **prone**, liable, inclined, disposed, predisposed, apt, likely.
– OPPOSITES unspecified.

▸ prep. *given the issue's complexity, a summary is difficult* **considering**, in view of, bearing in mind, in the light of; assuming.

▸ n. *his aggression is taken as a given* **established fact**, reality, certainty.

giver n. **donor**, contributor, donator, benefactor, benefactress, provider; supporter, backer, patron, sponsor, subscriber.

glacial adj. **1** *glacial conditions* **freezing**, cold, icy, ice-cold, sub-zero, frozen, gelid, wintry; arctic, polar, Siberian; bitter, biting, raw, chill. **2** *Polly's tone was glacial* **unfriendly**, hostile, unwelcoming; frosty, icy, cold, chilly.
– OPPOSITES tropical, hot, friendly.

glad adj. **1** *I'm really glad you're coming* **pleased**, happy, delighted, thrilled, overjoyed, cock-a-hoop, elated, gleeful; gratified, grateful, thankful; informal tickled pink, over the moon; Brit. informal chuffed; N. English informal made up; Austral. informal wrapped. **2** *I'd be glad to help* **willing**, eager, happy, pleased, delighted; ready, prepared. **3** *glad tidings* **pleasing**, welcome, happy, joyful, cheering, heartening, gratifying; literary gladsome.
– OPPOSITES dismayed, reluctant, distressing.

gladden v. **delight**, please, make happy, elate; cheer (up), hearten, buoy up, give someone a lift, uplift; gratify; informal give someone a kick, tickle someone pink, buck up.
– OPPOSITES sadden.

gladly adv. **with pleasure**, happily, cheerfully; willingly, readily, eagerly, freely, ungrudgingly; old use fain, lief.

glamorous adj. **1** *a glamorous woman* **beautiful**, attractive, lovely, bewitching, enchanting, beguiling; elegant, chic, stylish, fashionable; charming, charismatic, appealing, alluring, seductive; informal classy, glam. **2** *a glamorous lifestyle* **exciting**, thrilling, stimulating; dazzling, glittering, glossy, colourful, exotic; informal ritzy, glitzy, jet-setting.
– OPPOSITES dowdy, dull.

glamour n. **1** *she had undeniable glamour* **beauty**, allure, attractiveness; elegance, chic, style; charisma, charm, magnetism, desirability. **2** *the glamour of show business* **allure**, attraction, fascination, charm, magic, romance, mystique, exoticism, spell; excitement, thrill; glitter, the bright lights; informal glitz, glam.

glance v. **1** *Rachel glanced at him* **look briefly**, look quickly, peek, peep; glimpse; Scottish keek; informal have a gander; Brit. informal take a dekko, have a shufti, have a butcher's; Austral./NZ informal squiz. **2** *I glanced through the report* **read quickly**, scan, skim, leaf, flick, flip, thumb, browse; dip into. **3** *a bullet glanced off the ice* **ricochet**, rebound, be deflected, bounce; graze, clip. **4** *sunlight glanced off her hair* **reflect**, flash, gleam, glint, glitter, glisten, glimmer, shimmer.
▶ n. *a glance at his watch* **peek**, peep, brief look, quick look, glimpse; Scottish keek; informal gander; Brit. informal dekko, shufti, butcher's; Austral./NZ informal squiz, geek.
□ **at first glance** on the face of it, on the surface, at first sight, to the casual eye, to all appearances; apparently, seemingly, outwardly, superficially, it would seem, it appears, as far as one can see/tell, by all accounts.

glare v. **1** *she glared at him* **scowl**, glower, stare angrily, look daggers, frown, lour, give someone a black look, look threateningly; informal give someone a dirty look. **2** *the sun glared out of the sky* **blaze**, beam, shine brightly, be dazzling, be blinding.
▶ n. **1** *a cold glare* **scowl**, glower, angry stare, frown, black look, threatening look; informal dirty look. **2** *the harsh glare of the lights* **blaze**, dazzle, shine, beam; radiance, brilliance, luminescence.

glaring adj. **1** *glaring lights* **dazzling**, blinding, blazing, strong, bright, harsh. **2** *a glaring omission* **obvious**, conspicuous, unmistakable, inescapable, unmissable, striking; flagrant, blatant, outrageous, gross; overt, patent, transparent, manifest; informal standing/sticking out like a sore thumb.
– OPPOSITES soft, minor.

glass n. **tumbler**, drinking vessel; flute, schooner, balloon, goblet, chalice.

> **WORD LINKS**
> **vitreous** relating to glass
> **vitriform** like glass
> **glazier** a glass-fitter

glasses plural n. **spectacles**, eyewear; N. Amer. eyeglasses; informal specs.

glasshouse n. **greenhouse**, hothouse, conservatory.

glassy adj. **1** *the glassy surface of the lake* **smooth**, mirror-like, gleaming, shiny, glossy, polished, vitreous; slippery, icy; clear, transparent, translucent; calm, still, flat. **2** *a glassy stare* **expressionless**, glazed, blank, vacant, fixed, motionless; emotionless, impassive, lifeless, wooden, vacuous.
– OPPOSITES rough, expressive.

glaze v. **1** *the pots are glazed when dry* **varnish**, enamel, lacquer, japan, shellac, paint; gloss. **2** *pastry glazed with caramel* **cover**, coat; ice, frost. **3** *his eyes glazed over* **become glassy**, go blank; mist over, film over.
▶ n. **1** *pottery with a blue glaze* **varnish**, enamel, lacquer, finish, coating; lustre, shine, gloss. **2** *a cake with an apricot glaze* **coating**, topping; icing, frosting.

gleam v. **shine**, glimmer, glint, glitter, shimmer, sparkle, twinkle, flicker, wink, glisten, flash; literary glister.
▶ n. **1** *a gleam of light* **glimmer**, glint, shimmer, twinkle, sparkle, flicker, flash; beam, ray, shaft. **2** *the gleam of brass* **shine**, lustre, gloss, sheen; glint, glitter, glimmer, sparkle; brilliance, radiance, glow; literary glister. **3** *a gleam of hope* **glimmer**, flicker, ray, spark, trace, suggestion, hint, sign.

glean v. **obtain**, get, take, draw, derive, extract, cull, garner, gather; learn, find out.

glee n. **delight**, pleasure, happiness, joy, gladness, elation, euphoria; amusement, mirth, merriment; excitement, gaiety, exuberance; triumph, jubilation, relish, satisfaction, gratification.
– OPPOSITES disappointment.

gleeful adj. **delighted**, pleased, joyful, happy, glad, overjoyed, elated, euphoric; amused, mirthful, merry, exuberant; cock-a-hoop, jubilant; informal over the moon.

glib adj. **slick**, pat, plausible; smooth-talking, fast-talking, silver-tongued, smooth, urbane, having kissed the Blarney Stone; disingenuous, insincere, facile, shallow, superficial, flippant; informal flip, sweet-talking.
– OPPOSITES sincere.

glide v. **1** *a gondola glided past* **slide**, slip, sail, float, drift, flow; coast, freewheel, roll; skim, skate. **2** *seagulls gliding over the waves* **soar**, wheel, plane; fly. **3** *he glided out of the door* **slip**, steal, slink.

glimmer v. *moonlight glimmered on the lawn* **gleam**, shine, glint, flicker, shimmer, glisten, glow, twinkle, sparkle, glitter, wink, flash; literary glister.
▶ n. **1** *a glimmer of light* **gleam**, glint, flicker, shimmer, glow, twinkle, sparkle, flash, ray. **2** *a glimmer of hope* **gleam**, flicker, ray, trace, sign, suggestion, hint.

glimpse n. *a glimpse of her face* **brief look**, quick look; glance, peek, peep; sight, sighting.
▶ v. *he glimpsed a figure* **catch sight of**, notice, discern, spot, spy, sight, pick out, make out; Brit. informal clock; literary espy, descry.

g

glint v. *the diamond glinted* **shine**, gleam, catch the light, glitter, sparkle, twinkle, wink, glimmer, shimmer, glisten, flash; literary glister.
▸ n. *the glint of the silver* **glitter**, gleam, sparkle, twinkle, glimmer, flash.

glisten v. **shine**, sparkle, twinkle, glint, glitter, glimmer, shimmer, wink, flash; literary glister.

glitter v. *crystal glittered in the candlelight* **shine**, sparkle, twinkle, glint, gleam, shimmer, glimmer, wink, flash, catch the light; literary glister.
▸ n. **1** *the glitter of light on the water* **sparkle**, twinkle, glint, gleam, shimmer, glimmer, flicker, flash; brilliance, luminescence. **2** *the glitter of show business* **glamour**, excitement, thrills, attraction, appeal; dazzle; informal razzle-dazzle, razzmatazz, glitz, ritziness.

gloat v. **delight**, relish, take great pleasure, revel, rejoice, glory, exult, triumph, crow; boast, brag, be smug, congratulate oneself, preen oneself, pat oneself on the back; rub one's hands together; informal rub it in.

global adj. **1** *the global economy* **worldwide**, international, world, intercontinental. **2** *a global view of the problem* **comprehensive**, overall, general, all-inclusive, all-encompassing, encyclopedic, universal, blanket; broad, far-reaching, extensive, sweeping.

globe n. **1** *every corner of the globe* **world**, earth, planet. **2** *the sun is a globe* **sphere**, orb, ball, spheroid, round.

globular adj. **spherical**, spheric, spheroidal, round, globe-shaped, ball-shaped, orb-shaped, rounded, bulbous.

globule n. **droplet**, drop, bead, tear, ball, bubble, pearl; informal blob, glob.

gloom n. **1** *she peered into the gloom* **darkness**, dark, dimness, blackness, murkiness, shadows, shade; dusk, twilight, gloaming. **2** *his gloom deepened* **despondency**, depression, dejection, downheartedness, melancholy, melancholia, unhappiness, sadness, glumness, gloominess, misery, sorrow, woe, wretchedness; despair, pessimism, hopelessness; informal the blues, the dumps.
– OPPOSITES light, happiness.

gloomy adj. **1** *a gloomy room* **dark**, shadowy, sunless, dim, sombre, dingy, dismal, dreary, murky, unwelcoming, cheerless, comfortless, funereal; literary Stygian. **2** *Joanna looked gloomy* **despondent**, downcast, downhearted, dejected, dispirited, disheartened, discouraged, demoralized, crestfallen; depressed, desolate, low, sad, unhappy, glum, melancholy, miserable, fed up, woebegone, mournful, forlorn, morose; Brit. Eeyorish; informal blue, down in the mouth, down in the dumps. **3** *gloomy forecasts about the economy* **pessimistic**, depressing, downbeat, disheartening, disappointing; unfavourable, bleak, bad, black, sombre, grim, cheerless, hopeless.
– OPPOSITES bright, cheerful, optimistic.

glorify v. **1** *they gather to glorify God* **praise**, extol, exalt, worship, revere, reverence, venerate, pay homage to, honour, adore, thank, give thanks to; formal laud; old use magnify. **2** *a poem to glorify the memory of the dead* **ennoble**, exalt, elevate, dignify, enhance, augment, promote; praise, celebrate, honour, extol, lionize, acclaim, applaud, hail; glamorize, idealize, romanticize, enshrine, immortalize; formal laud.
– OPPOSITES dishonour.

glorious adj. **1** *a glorious victory* **illustrious**, celebrated, famous, acclaimed, distinguished, honoured; outstanding, great, magnificent, noble, triumphant. **2** *glorious views* **wonderful**, marvellous, magnificent, superb, sublime, spectacular, lovely, fine, delightful; informal super, great, stunning, fantastic, terrific, tremendous, sensational, heavenly, divine, gorgeous, fabulous, fab, awesome, ace; informal dated capital, spiffing; Brit. informal smashing; literary wondrous, beauteous.
– OPPOSITES undistinguished, horrid.

glory n. **1** *a sport that won him glory* **renown**, fame, prestige, honour, distinction, kudos, eminence, acclaim, praise, bouquets; celebrity, recognition, reputation. **2** *glory be to God* **praise**, worship, adoration, veneration, honour, reverence, exaltation, extolment, homage, thanksgiving, thanks. **3** *a house restored to its former glory* **magnificence**, splendour, resplendence, grandeur, majesty, greatness, nobility; opulence, beauty, elegance. **4** *the glories of Vermont* **wonder**, beauty, delight, marvel, phenomenon; sight, spectacle.
– OPPOSITES shame, obscurity, modesty.
▸ v. *we gloried in our independence* **take pleasure in**, revel in, rejoice in, delight in; relish, savour; congratulate oneself on, be proud of; boast about; informal get a kick out of, get a thrill out of.

gloss[1] n. **1** *the gloss of her hair* **shine**, sheen, lustre, gleam, patina, brilliance, shimmer. **2** *beneath the gloss of success* **facade**, veneer, surface, show, camouflage, disguise, mask, smokescreen; window dressing.
▸ v. **1** *she glossed her lips* **make glossy**, shine, glaze, polish, burnish. **2** *he tried to gloss over his problems* **conceal**, cover up, hide, disguise, mask, veil; shrug off, brush aside, play down, minimize, understate, make light of; informal brush under the carpet.

gloss[2] n. *glosses in the margin* **explanation**, interpretation, exegesis, explication, elucidation; annotation, note, footnote, commentary, comment; translation; historical scholium.
▸ v. *difficult words are glossed in a footnote* **explain**, interpret, explicate, elucidate; annotate; translate, paraphrase.

glossy adj. **1** *a glossy wooden floor* **shiny**, gleaming, lustrous, brilliant, shimmering, glistening, satiny, sheeny, smooth, glassy; polished, lacquered, glazed. **2** *a glossy magazine* **expensive**, high-quality; stylish,

fashionable, glamorous; attractive, artistic; Brit. upmarket, coffee-table; informal classy, ritzy, glitzy.
– OPPOSITES dull, cheap.

glove n. **mitten**, mitt, gauntlet.

glow v. **1** *lights glowed from the windows* **shine**, radiate, gleam, glimmer, flicker, flare; luminesce. **2** *a fire glowed in the hearth* **radiate heat**, smoulder, burn. **3** *she glowed with embarrassment* **flush**, blush, redden, colour (up), go pink, go scarlet; burn. **4** *she glowed with pleasure* **tingle**, thrill; beam.
▶ n. **1** *the glow of the fire* **radiance**, light, shine, gleam, glimmer, incandescence, luminescence; warmth, heat. **2** *a glow spread over her face* **flush**, blush, rosiness, pinkness, redness, high colour; bloom, radiance. **3** *a warm glow deep inside her* **happiness**, contentment, pleasure, satisfaction.

glower v. *she glowered at him* **scowl**, glare, look daggers, frown, lour, give someone a black look; informal give someone a dirty look.
▶ n. *the glower on his face* **scowl**, glare, frown, black look; informal dirty look.

glowing adj. **1** *glowing coals* **bright**, shining, radiant, glimmering, flickering, twinkling, incandescent, luminous, luminescent; lit (up), lighted, illuminated, ablaze; aglow, smouldering. **2** *his glowing cheeks* **rosy**, pink, red, flushed, blushing; radiant, blooming, ruddy, florid; hot, burning. **3** *glowing colours* **vivid**, vibrant, bright, brilliant, rich, intense, strong, radiant, warm. **4** *a glowing report* **complimentary**, favourable, enthusiastic, commendatory, admiring, lionizing, rapturous, rhapsodic, adulatory; fulsome; informal rave.

glue n. *a tube of glue* **adhesive**, fixative, gum, paste, cement; epoxy (resin), size; N. Amer. mucilage; N. Amer. informal stickum.
▶ v. **1** *the planks were glued together* **stick**, gum, paste; affix, fix, cement. **2** *informal she was glued to the television* **be riveted to**, be gripped by, be hypnotized by, be mesmerized by.

glum adj. **gloomy**, downcast, downhearted, dejected, despondent, crestfallen, disheartened; depressed, desolate, unhappy, doleful, melancholy, miserable, woebegone, mournful, forlorn, in the doldrums, morose; informal blue, down in the mouth, down in the dumps, fed up.
– OPPOSITES cheerful.

glut n. *a glut of cars* **surplus**, excess, surfeit, superfluity, overabundance, superabundance, oversupply, plethora.
– OPPOSITES dearth.
▶ v. *the factories are glutted* **cram full**, overfill, overload, oversupply, saturate, flood, inundate, deluge, swamp; informal stuff.

glutinous adj. **sticky**, viscous, viscid, tacky, gluey, gummy, treacly; adhesive; informal gooey, gloopy, cloggy; N. Amer. informal gloppy.

glutton n. **gourmand**, overeater, big eater, gorger, gobbler; informal (greedy) pig, gannet, greedy guts, gutbucket, guzzler.

gluttonous adj. **greedy**, gourmandizing, voracious, insatiable, wolfish; informal piggish, piggy.

gluttony n. **greed**, greediness, overeating, overconsumption, gourmandism, gourmandizing, voracity, insatiability; informal piggishness.

gnarled adj. **1** *a gnarled tree trunk* **knobbly**, knotty, knotted, gnarly, lumpy, bumpy, nodular; twisted, bent, crooked, distorted, contorted. **2** *gnarled hands* **twisted**, bent, misshapen; arthritic; rough, wrinkled, wizened.

gnash v. **grind**, grate, rasp, grit.

gnaw v. **1** *the dog gnawed at a bone* **chew**, champ, chomp, bite, munch, crunch; nibble, worry. **2** *the pressures are gnawing away their independence* **erode**, wear away, wear down, eat away (at); consume, devour. **3** *the doubts gnawed at her* **nag**, plague, torment, torture, trouble, distress, worry, haunt, oppress, burden, hang over, bother, fret; niggle.

go v. **1** *he's gone into town* **move**, proceed, make one's way, advance, progress, pass; walk, travel, journey; literary betake oneself. **2** *the road goes to London* **extend**, stretch, reach; lead. **3** *the money will go to charity* **be given**, be donated, be granted, be presented, be awarded; be devoted; be handed (over). **4** *it's time to go* **leave**, depart, take oneself off, go away, withdraw, absent oneself, make an exit, exit; set off, start out, get under way, be on one's way; decamp, retreat, retire, make off, clear out, run off/away, flee; Brit. make a move; informal make tracks, push off, beat it, take off, skedaddle, scram, split, scoot; Brit. informal sling one's hook. **5** *three years went past* **pass**, elapse, slip by/past, roll by/past, tick away; fly by/past. **6** *a golden age that has gone for good* **disappear**, vanish, be no more, be over, run its course, fade away; finish, end, cease. **7** *all our money had gone* **be used up**, be spent, be exhausted, be consumed, be drained, be depleted. **8** *I'd like to see my grandchildren before I go* **die**, pass away, pass on, lose one's life, expire, breathe one's last, perish, go to meet one's maker; informal give up the ghost, kick the bucket, croak, buy it, turn up one's toes; Brit. informal snuff it, pop one's clogs; N. Amer. informal bite the big one, buy the farm; old use decease, depart this life. **9** *the bridge went suddenly* **collapse**, give way, fall down, cave in, crumble, disintegrate. **10** *his hair had gone grey* **become**, get, turn, grow. **11** *he heard the bell go* **make a sound**, sound, reverberate, resound; ring, chime, peal, toll, clang. **12** *everything went well* **turn out**, work out, develop, come out; result, end (up); informal pan out. **13** *those colours don't go* **match**, be harmonious, harmonize, blend, be suited, be complementary, coordinate, be compatible. **14** *my car won't go* **function**, work, run, operate. **15** *where does the cutlery go?* **belong**, be kept, be found, be located, be situated. **16** *this all goes to prove my point* **contribute**, help, serve; incline, tend.

– OPPOSITES arrive, come, return, clash.

▶ n. informal **1** *his second go* **attempt**, try, effort, bid, endeavour; informal shot, stab, crack, bash, whirl, whack; formal essay. **2** *he has plenty of go in him* **energy**, vigour, vitality, life, liveliness, spirit, verve, enthusiasm, zest, vibrancy, sparkle; stamina, dynamism, drive, push, determination; informal pep, punch, oomph, get-up-and-go.

▫ **go about** set about, begin, embark on, start, commence, address oneself to, get down to, get to work on, get going on, undertake; approach, tackle, attack; informal get cracking on/with.

go along with agree to/with, fall in with, comply with, cooperate with, acquiesce in, assent to, follow; submit to, yield to, defer to.

go away See go (sense 4 of the verb).

go back on renege on, break, fail to honour, default on, repudiate, retract; do an about-face; informal cop out (of), rat on.

go by *we have to go by his decision* obey, abide by, comply with, keep to, conform to, follow, heed, defer to, respect.

go down 1 *the ship went down* **sink**, founder, go under. **2** *interest rates are going down* **decrease**, get lower, fall, drop, decline; plummet, plunge, slump. **3** informal *they went down in the first leg* **lose**, be beaten, be defeated, come to grief. **4** *his name will go down in history* **be remembered**, be recorded, be commemorated, be immortalized.

go down with Brit. fall ill with, get, develop, contract, pick up, succumb to, fall victim to, be struck down with, become infected with.

go far be successful, succeed, be a success, do well, get on, get somewhere, get ahead, make good; informal make a name for oneself, make one's mark.

go for 1 *I went for the tuna* **choose**, pick, opt for, select, plump for, decide on. **2** *the man went for her* **attack**, assault, hit, strike, beat up, assail, set upon, rush at, lash out at; informal lay into, rough up; Brit. informal have a go at, duff up; N. Amer. informal beat up on. **3** *he goes for older women* **be attracted to**, like, fancy; prefer, favour, choose; informal have a thing about.

go in for take part in, participate in, engage in, get involved in, join in, enter into, undertake; practise, pursue; espouse, adopt, embrace.

go into investigate, examine, enquire into, look into, research, probe, explore, delve into; consider, review, analyse.

go off 1 *the bomb went off* **explode**, detonate, blow up. **2** Brit. *the milk's gone off* **go bad**, go stale, go sour, turn, spoil, go rancid; decompose, go mouldy.

go on 1 *the lecture went on for hours* **last**, continue, carry on, run on, proceed; endure, persist; take. **2** *she went on about the sea* **talk at length**, ramble, rattle on, chatter, prattle, gabble, blether, blather, twitter; informal gab, yak, yabber, yatter; Brit. informal witter, rabbit, natter, waffle, chunter; N. Amer. informal run off

at the mouth. **3** *I'm not sure what went on* **happen**, take place, occur, transpire; N. Amer. informal go down; literary come to pass, betide; old use hap.

go out 1 *the lights went out* **be turned off**, be extinguished; stop burning. **2** *he's going out with Kate* **see**, take out, be someone's boyfriend/girlfriend, be involved with; informal date, go steady with, go with; N. Amer. informal dated step out with; dated court, woo.

go over 1 *go over the figures* **examine**, study, scrutinize, inspect, look at/over, scan, check; analyse, appraise, review. **2** *we are going over our lines* **rehearse**, practise, read through, run through.

go round 1 *the wheels were going round* **spin**, revolve, turn, rotate, whirl. **2** *a nasty rumour going round* **be spread**, be circulated, be put about, circulate, pass round, be broadcast.

go through 1 *the terrible things she has gone through* **undergo**, experience, face, suffer, be subjected to, live through, endure, brave, bear, tolerate, withstand, put up with, cope with, weather. **2** *he went through hundreds of pounds* **spend**, use up, run through, get through, expend, deplete; waste, squander, fritter away. **3** *he went through Susie's bag* **search**, look, hunt, rummage, rifle; informal frisk. **4** *I have to go through the report* **examine**, study, scrutinize, inspect, look over, scan, check; analyse, appraise, review. **5** *the deal has gone through* **be completed**, be concluded, be brought off; be approved, be signed, be rubber-stamped.

go under go bankrupt, cease trading, go into receivership, go into liquidation, become insolvent, be liquidated, be wound up, be shut (down); fail; informal go broke, go to the wall, go belly up, fold, flatline.

go without 1 *I went without breakfast* **abstain from**, refrain from, forgo, do without, deny oneself. **2** *the children did not go without* **be deprived**, be in want, go short, go hungry, be in need.

goad n. **1** *he applied his goad to the cows* **prod**, spike, staff, crook, rod. **2** *a goad to political change* **stimulus**, incentive, encouragement, inducement, fillip, spur, prod, prompt; motive, motivation.

▶ v. *we were goaded into action* **provoke**, spur, prod, egg on, hound, badger, incite, rouse, stir, move, stimulate, motivate, prompt; induce, encourage, urge, inspire, impel, pressure, pressurize, dragoon.

go-ahead informal n. *they gave the go-ahead for the scheme* **permission**, consent, leave, licence, dispensation, warrant, clearance; authorization, assent, agreement, approval, endorsement, sanction, blessing, the nod; informal the thumbs up, the OK, the green light.

▶ adj. *go-ahead companies* **enterprising**, resourceful, innovative, disruptive, ingenious, original, creative; progressive, pioneering, modern, forward-looking, enlightened; enthusiastic, ambitious, entrepreneurial, high-powered; bold, daring, audacious, adventurous, dynamic, driven; informal go-getting.

goal n. **objective**, aim, end, target, design, intention, intent, plan, purpose; (holy) grail; ambition, aspiration, wish, dream, desire, hope.

goat n. **1** *a herd of goats* billy (goat), nanny (goat), kid. **2** *be careful of that old goat* **lecher**, libertine, womanizer, seducer, Don Juan, Casanova, Lothario, Romeo; pervert, debauchee, rake; informal lech, ladykiller.

> **WORD LINKS**
> **caprine** relating to goats

gobble v. **guzzle**, bolt, gulp, devour, wolf, cram, gorge (oneself) on; informal tuck into, put away, demolish, polish off, scoff, shovel down, stuff one's face (with), pig oneself (on); Brit. informal gollop, shift; N. Amer. informal scarf (down/up).

gobbledegook n. informal **gibberish**, claptrap, nonsense, rubbish, balderdash, mumbo jumbo, blather, blether; N. Amer. garbage; informal drivel, tripe, hogwash, baloney, bilge, bosh, bull, bunk, guff, eyewash, piffle, twaddle, poppycock, phooey, hooey; Brit. informal cobblers, codswallop, double Dutch, tosh; N. Amer. informal bushwa, applesauce.

go-between n. **intermediary**, middleman, agent, broker, liaison, linkman, contact; negotiator, interceder, intercessor, mediator.

goblet n. **wine glass**, chalice; glass, beaker, tumbler, cup.

goblin n. **hobgoblin**, gnome, dwarf, troll, imp, elf, brownie, fairy, pixie, leprechaun.

god n. **1** *a gift from God* **the Lord**, the Almighty, the Creator, the Maker, the Godhead; Allah, Jehovah, Yahweh; (God) the Father, (God) the Son, the Holy Ghost/Spirit, the Holy Trinity. **2** *sacrifices to appease the gods* **deity**, goddess, divine being, celestial being, divinity, immortal, avatar. **3** *wooden gods* **idol**, graven image, icon, totem, talisman, fetish, juju.

> **WORD LINKS**
> **divine** relating to God or a god
> **theology** the study of God and religious belief
> **deify** worship or treat as a god
> **deism** belief in an all-powerful creator who does not intervene in the universe
> **theism** belief in a god or gods, especially as a creator who intervenes in the universe
> **theocracy** a system of government in which priests rule in the name of God or a god
> **pantheon** all the gods of a people or religion
> **oblation** an offering made to a god
> **libation** a drink poured out as an offering to a god

godforsaken adj. **wretched**, miserable, dreary, dismal, depressing, grim, cheerless, bleak, desolate, gloomy; deserted, neglected, isolated, remote, backward; Brit. informal grotty.
– OPPOSITES charming.

godless adj. **1** *a godless society* **atheistic**, unbelieving, agnostic, sceptical, heretical, faithless, irreligious, ungodly, unholy, impious, profane; infidel, heathen, idolatrous, pagan; satanic, devilish. **2** *godless pleasures* **immoral**, wicked, sinful, wrong, evil, bad, iniquitous, corrupt; irreligious, sacrilegious, profane, blasphemous, impious; depraved, degenerate, debauched, perverted, decadent; impure.
– OPPOSITES religious, virtuous.

godlike adj. **divine**, godly, superhuman; angelic, seraphic; spiritual, heavenly, celestial; sacred, holy, saintly.

godly adj. **religious**, devout, pious, reverent, believing, God-fearing, saintly, holy, prayerful, churchgoing.
– OPPOSITES irreligious.

godsend n. **boon**, blessing, bonus, plus, benefit, advantage, help, aid, asset; stroke of luck; informal perk; formal perquisite.
– OPPOSITES curse.

goggle v. **stare**, gape, gaze, ogle; informal gawk, rubberneck; Brit. informal gawp.

going-over n. informal **1** *his work was subjected to a going-over* **examination**, inspection, investigation, probe, check-up; assessment, review, analysis, appraisal, critique; informal once-over. **2** *the flat needs a going-over* **clean**, dust, mop, scrub; informal vacuum, once-over. **3** *the thugs gave him a going-over* **beating**, thrashing, thumping, pummelling, battering, pelting; assault, attack; informal doing-over, belting, bashing, pasting, walloping, clobbering, hiding.

goings-on plural n. **events**, happenings, affairs, business; mischief, misbehaviour, misconduct, funny business; informal monkey business, hanky-panky, shenanigans; Brit. informal jiggery-pokery, carry-on; N. Amer. informal monkeyshines.

gold n. *she won the gold* **gold medal**, first prize.

> **WORD LINKS**
> **aureate** made of gold, or gold-coloured
> **bullion** gold in bulk or solid bars
> **carat** a measure of the purity of gold
> **alchemy** a medieval form of chemistry, concerned with trying to turn other metals into gold

golden adj. **1** *her golden hair* **blond(e)**, yellow, fair, flaxen, tow-coloured. **2** *a golden time* **successful**, prosperous, flourishing, thriving; favourable, providential, lucky, fortunate; happy, joyful, glorious. **3** *a golden opportunity* **excellent**, fine, superb, splendid; special, unique; favourable, opportune, promising, bright, full of promise; advantageous, profitable, valuable, providential. **4** *the golden girl of tennis* **favourite**, favoured, popular, admired, beloved, pet; acclaimed, applauded, praised; brilliant, consummate, gifted; Brit. informal blue-eyed; formal lauded.
– OPPOSITES dark, unhappy.

gone adj. **1** *I wasn't gone long* **away**, absent, off, out; missing, unavailable. **2** *those days are gone* **past**, over (and done with), no

g

more, done, finished, ended; forgotten, dead and buried. **3** *the milk's all gone* **used up**, consumed, finished, spent, depleted; at an end. **4** *an aunt of mine, long since gone* **dead**, expired, departed, no more, passed on/away; late, lost, lamented; perished, fallen; defunct, extinct; informal six feet under, pushing up daisies; formal deceased; euphemistic with God, asleep, at peace.
– OPPOSITES present, here, alive.

goo n. informal **sticky substance**, ooze, sludge, muck; informal gunk, crud, gloop; Brit. informal gunge; N. Amer. informal glop.

good adj. **1** *a good product* **fine**, superior, quality; excellent, superb, outstanding, magnificent, exceptional, marvellous, wonderful, first-rate, first-class, sterling; satisfactory, acceptable, up to scratch, up to standard, not bad, all right; informal great, OK, A1, ace, terrific, fantastic, fabulous, fab, top-notch, class, awesome, wicked; informal dated capital; Brit. informal smashing, brilliant, brill; Austral. informal beaut, bonzer; Brit. informal dated spiffing, top hole. **2** *a good person* **virtuous**, righteous, upright, upstanding, moral, ethical, high-minded, principled, anti-corruption; exemplary, law-abiding, irreproachable, blameless, guiltless, unimpeachable, honourable, scrupulous, reputable, decent, respectable, noble, trustworthy; meritorious, praiseworthy, admirable; whiter than white, saintly, saintlike, angelic; informal squeaky clean. **3** *the children are good at school* **well behaved**, obedient, dutiful, polite, courteous, respectful, deferential, compliant. **4** *a good thing to do* **right**, correct, proper, decorous, seemly; appropriate, fitting, apt, suitable; convenient, expedient, favourable, opportune, felicitous, timely. **5** *a good driver* **capable**, able, proficient, adept, adroit, accomplished, skilful, skilled, talented, masterly, expert; informal great, mean, wicked, nifty, ace; N. Amer. informal crackerjack. **6** *a good friend* **close**, intimate, dear, bosom, special, best, firm, valued, treasured; loving, devoted, loyal, faithful, constant, reliable, dependable, trustworthy, trusty, true, unfailing, staunch. **7** *the dogs are in good condition* **healthy**, fine, sound, tip-top, hale and hearty, fit, robust, sturdy, strong, vigorous. **8** *a good time was had by all* **enjoyable**, pleasant, agreeable, pleasurable, delightful, great, nice, lovely; amusing, diverting, jolly, merry, lively; informal super, fantastic, fabulous, fab, terrific, grand; Brit. informal brilliant, brill, smashing; N. Amer. informal peachy, ducky; Austral./NZ informal beaut, bonzer. **9** *it was good of you to come* **kind**, kind-hearted, good-hearted, generous, charitable, magnanimous, gracious; altruistic, unselfish, selfless. **10** *a good time to call* **convenient**, suitable, appropriate, fitting, fit; opportune, timely, favourable, advantageous, expedient, felicitous, happy, providential. **11** *milk is good for you* **wholesome**, healthy, healthful, nourishing, nutritious, nutritional, beneficial,

salubrious. **12** *are these eggs good?* **edible**, safe to eat, fit for human consumption; fresh, wholesome, consumable; formal comestible. **13** *good food* **delicious**, tasty, mouth-watering, appetizing, flavoursome, flavourful, delectable, toothsome, palatable, succulent, luscious; informal scrumptious, delish, scrummy, yummy; Brit. informal moreish; N. Amer. informal finger-licking, nummy. **14** *a good reason* **valid**, genuine, authentic, legitimate, sound, bona fide; convincing, persuasive, telling, potent, cogent, compelling. **15** *we waited a good hour* **whole**, full, entire, complete, solid. **16** *a good number of them* **considerable**, sizeable, substantial, appreciable, significant; goodly, fair, reasonable; plentiful, abundant, great, large, generous; informal tidy. **17** *wear your good clothes* **best**, smart, smartest, finest, nicest; special, party, Sunday, formal, dressy. **18** *good weather* **fine**, fair, dry; bright, clear, sunny, cloudless; calm, windless; warm, mild, balmy, clement, pleasant, nice.
– OPPOSITES bad, wicked, naughty, poor, terrible, inconvenient, small, scruffy.

▸ n. **1** *issues of good and evil* **virtue**, righteousness, goodness, morality, integrity, rectitude; honesty, truth, honour, probity; propriety, worthiness, merit; blamelessness, purity. **2** *it's all for your good* **benefit**, advantage, profit, gain, interest, welfare, well-being; enjoyment, comfort, ease, convenience; help, aid, assistance, service; behalf.
– OPPOSITES wickedness, disadvantage.

▸ exclam. *good, that's settled* **fine**, very well, all right, right, right then, yes, agreed; informal okay, OK, okey-dokey, roger; Brit. informal righto, righty-ho.

□ **for good** *those days are gone for good* forever, permanently, for always, (for) evermore, for ever and ever, for eternity, until hell freezes over, never to return; N. Amer. forevermore; informal for keeps, until doomsday, until the cows come home; old use for aye.

in good part *she took the joke in good part* good-naturedly, good-humouredly, without offence, amicably, favourably, tolerantly, indulgently, cheerfully, well.

make good succeed, be successful, be a success, do well, get ahead; prosper, flourish, thrive; informal make it, make the grade, make a name for oneself, make one's mark, get somewhere, arrive.

make something good 1 *he promised to make good any damage* **repair**, mend, fix, put right, see to; restore, remedy, rectify. **2** *they made good their escape* **effect**, conduct, perform, implement, execute, carry out; achieve, accomplish, succeed in, realize, attain, engineer, bring about, bring off. **3** *he will make good his promise* **fulfil**, carry out, implement, discharge, honour, redeem; keep, observe, abide by, comply with, stick to, heed, follow, be bound by, live up to, stand by, adhere to.

goodbye exclam. **farewell**, adieu, au revoir, ciao, auf Wiedersehen, adios; Austral./NZ hooray; informal bye, bye-bye, so long, see you (later), later(s); Brit. informal cheers, cheerio, ta-ta; N. English informal ta-ra; informal dated toodle-oo, toodle-pip.

good-for-nothing adj. *a good-for-nothing layabout* **useless**, worthless, incompetent, inefficient, inept, ne'er-do-well; lazy, idle, slothful, indolent, shiftless; informal no-good, lousy.
– OPPOSITES worthy.
▶ n. *lazy good-for-nothings* **ne'er-do-well**, layabout, do-nothing, idler, loafer, lounger, sluggard, shirker; informal waster, slacker, lazybones, couch potato; Brit. informal skiver.

good-humoured adj. **genial**, affable, cordial, friendly, amiable, easy-going, approachable, good-natured, cheerful, cheery; companionable, comradely, sociable, convivial; informal chummy, pally; Brit. informal matey; N. Amer. informal clubby.
– OPPOSITES grumpy.

good-looking adj. **attractive**, beautiful, pretty, handsome, lovely, stunning, striking, arresting, gorgeous, prepossessing, fetching, captivating, bewitching, beguiling, engaging, charming, enchanting, appealing, delightful; sexy, seductive, alluring, tantalizing, irresistible, ravishing, desirable; Scottish & N. English bonny; informal fanciable, tasty, hot, easy on the eye, drop-dead gorgeous; Brit. informal fit; N. Amer. informal cute, foxy; Austral./NZ informal spunky; literary beauteous; old use comely, fair.
– OPPOSITES ugly.

goodly adj. **large**, largish, sizeable, substantial, considerable, respectable, significant, decent, generous, handsome; informal tidy, serious.
– OPPOSITES paltry.

good-natured adj. **warm-hearted**, friendly, amiable; neighbourly, benevolent, kind, kind-hearted, generous, unselfish, considerate, thoughtful, obliging, helpful, supportive, charitable; understanding, sympathetic, easy-going, accommodating; Brit. informal decent.
– OPPOSITES malicious.

goodness n. **1** *he had some goodness in him* **virtue**, good, righteousness, morality, integrity, rectitude; honesty, truth, truthfulness, honour, probity; propriety, decency, respectability, nobility, worthiness, worth, merit, trustworthiness; blamelessness, purity. **2** *God's goodness towards us* **kindness**, kindliness, tender-heartedness, humanity, mildness, benevolence, graciousness; tenderness, warmth, affection, love, goodwill; sympathy, compassion, care, concern, understanding, tolerance, generosity, charity, leniency, clemency, magnanimity. **3** *slow cooking retains the food's goodness* **nutritional value**, nutrients, wholesomeness, nourishment.

goods plural n. **1** *he dispatched the goods* **merchandise**, wares, stock, commodities, produce, products, articles; imports, exports. **2** *the dead man's goods* **property**, possessions, effects, chattels, valuables; informal things, stuff, junk, gear, kit, bits and pieces; Brit. informal clobber. **3** Brit. *most goods went by train* **freight**, cargo; load, consignment, delivery, shipment.

good-tempered adj. **equable**, even-tempered, imperturbable; unruffled, unflustered, untroubled, well balanced; easy-going, mellow, mild, calm, relaxed, cool, at ease; placid, stable, level-headed; cheerful, upbeat; informal unflappable, laid-back.
– OPPOSITES moody.

goodwill n. **benevolence**, compassion, goodness, kindness, consideration, charity; cooperation, collaboration; friendliness, amity, thoughtfulness, decency, sympathy, understanding, neighbourliness.
– OPPOSITES hostility.

goody-goody adj. informal **self-righteous**, sanctimonious, pious; prim and proper, strait-laced, prudish, priggish, puritanical, moralistic; informal starchy, square.

gooey adj. informal **1** *a gooey mess* **sticky**, viscous, viscid; gluey, tacky, gummy, treacly, syrupy; Brit. claggy; informal gloopy, gungy, icky; N. Amer. informal gloppy. **2** *a gooey film* **sentimental**, mawkish, cloying, sickly, saccharine, sugary, syrupy; slushy, sloppy, mushy, romantic; Brit. twee; informal schmaltzy, lovey-dovey, cheesy, corny, sick-making; Brit. informal soppy; N. Amer. informal cornball, sappy.

goose n.

> **WORD LINKS**
> **anserine** relating to geese
> **gander** a male goose
> **gosling** a young goose

gore[1] n. *the film's gratuitous gore* **blood**, bloodiness; bloodshed, slaughter, carnage, butchery.

gore[2] v. *he was gored by a bull* **pierce**, stab, stick, impale, spear, horn.

gorge n. *the river runs through a gorge* **ravine**, canyon, gully, defile, couloir; chasm, gulf; N. English clough, gill; N. Amer. gulch, coulee.
▶ v. **1** *they gorged themselves on cakes* **stuff**, cram, fill; glut, satiate, overindulge, overfill; informal pig. **2** *vultures gorged on the flesh* **devour**, guzzle, gobble, gulp (down), wolf; informal tuck into, demolish, polish off, scoff (down), down, stuff one's face (with); Brit. informal gollop; N. Amer. informal scarf (down/up).

gorgeous adj. **1** *a gorgeous girl* **good-looking**, attractive, beautiful, pretty, handsome, lovely, stunning, striking, arresting, prepossessing, fetching, captivating, bewitching, charming, enchanting, appealing, delightful; sexy, seductive, alluring, tantalizing, irresistible, ravishing, desirable; Scottish & N. English bonny; informal fanciable, tasty, hot, easy on the eye, drop-dead gorgeous; Brit. informal fit; N. Amer. informal cute, foxy; Austral./NZ informal spunky; literary beauteous; old use comely, fair.

g

g

2 *a gorgeous view* **spectacular**, splendid, superb, wonderful, grand, impressive, awe-inspiring, awesome, amazing, stunning, breathtaking, incredible; informal sensational, fabulous, fantastic. **3** *gorgeous uniforms* **resplendent**, magnificent, sumptuous, luxurious, elegant, opulent; dazzling, brilliant. **4** *informal gorgeous weather* **excellent**, marvellous, superb, very good, first-rate, first-class, wonderful, magnificent, splendid; informal great, glorious, terrific, fantastic, fabulous, fab, ace; Brit. informal smashing, brilliant, brill; Austral./NZ informal bonzer.
– OPPOSITES ugly, drab, terrible.

gory adj. **1** *a gory ritual slaughter* **grisly**, gruesome, violent, bloody, brutal, savage; ghastly, frightful, horrid, fearful, hideous, macabre, horrible, horrific; shocking, appalling, monstrous, unspeakable; informal blood-and-guts, sick-making. **2** *gory pieces of flesh* **bloody**, bloodstained, bloodsoaked.

gospel n. **1** *the Gospel was spread by missionaries* **Christian teaching**, Christian doctrine, Christ's teaching; the word of God, the New Testament. **2** *don't treat this as gospel* **the truth**; fact, actual fact, reality, actuality, factuality, the case, a certainty. **3** *his gospel of non-violence* **doctrine**, dogma, teaching, principle, ethic, creed, credo, ideology, ideal; belief, tenet, canon.

gossamer n. *her dress swirled like gossamer* **cobwebs**; silk, gauze, chiffon.
▸ adj. *a gossamer veil* **gauzy**, gossamery, fine, diaphanous, delicate, filmy, floaty, chiffony, cobwebby, wispy, thin, light, insubstantial, flimsy; translucent, transparent, see-through, sheer.

gossip n. **1** *tell me all the gossip* **tittle-tattle**, tattle, rumour(s), whispers, canards, titbits; scandal, hearsay; informal dirt, buzz; Brit. informal goss; N. Amer. informal scuttlebutt. **2** *they went for a gossip* **chat**, talk, conversation, chatter, heart-to-heart, tête-à-tête, blether, blather; discussion, dialogue; informal chit-chat, jaw, gas, confab, goss; Brit. informal natter, chinwag; N. Amer. informal gabfest; Austral./NZ informal yarn; formal confabulation. **3** *she's such a gossip* **scandalmonger**, gossipmonger, tattler, busybody, muckraker.
▸ v. **1** *she gossiped about his wife* **spread rumours**, spread gossip, tittle-tattle, tattle, talk, whisper, tell tales; informal dish the dirt. **2** *people sat around gossiping* **chat**, talk, converse; informal gas, chew the fat, chew the rag, jaw, yak, yap; Brit. informal natter, chinwag; N. Amer. informal shoot the breeze, shoot the bull; formal confabulate.

gouge v. **scoop out**, hollow out, excavate; cut (out), dig (out), scrape (out), scratch (out).

gourmand n. **glutton**, overeater, big eater, gobbler, gorger; informal (greedy) pig, gannet, greedy guts, gutbucket, guzzler.

gourmet n. **gastronome**, epicure, epicurean; connoisseur; informal foodie.

govern v. **1** *he governs the province* **rule**, preside over, reign over, control, be in charge of, command, lead, dominate; run, head, administer, manage, regulate, oversee, supervise; informal be in the driving seat. **2** *the rules governing social behaviour* **determine**, decide, control, regulate, direct, rule, dictate, shape; affect, influence, sway, act on, mould, modify, impact on.

governess n. **tutor**, instructress, duenna; teacher.

government n. **1** *the government announced cuts* **administration**, executive, regime, authority, powers that be, directorate, council, leadership; cabinet, ministry; informal top brass. **2** *they help him in the government of the country* **rule**, running, leadership, control, administration, regulation, management, supervision.

governor n. **leader**, ruler, chief, head; premier, president, viceroy, chancellor; administrator, principal, director, chairman/woman, chair, superintendent, commissioner, controller; informal boss.

gown n. **dress**, frock, shift, robe.

grab v. **1** *Dot grabbed his arm* **seize**, grasp, snatch, take hold of, grip, clasp, clutch; take. **2** *informal I'll grab another drink* **obtain**, acquire, get; buy, purchase, procure, secure, snap up; gather, collect; achieve, attain; informal get one's hands on, get one's mitts on, get hold of, bag, score, nab.
▸ n. *she made a grab for his gun* **lunge**, snatch.
□ **up for grabs** informal available, obtainable, to be had, for the taking; for sale, on the market; informal for the asking, on tap, gettable.

grace n. **1** *the grace of a ballerina* **elegance**, poise, gracefulness, finesse; suppleness, agility, nimbleness, light-footedness. **2** *he had the grace to look sheepish* **courtesy**, decency, (good) manners, politeness, decorum, respect, tact. **3** *he fell from grace* **favour**, approval, approbation, acceptance, esteem, regard, respect; goodwill. **4** *he lived there by grace of the king* **favour**, goodwill, generosity, kindness, indulgence; formal benefaction. **5** *they have five days' grace to decide* **deferment**, deferral, postponement, suspension, adjournment, delay, pause; respite, stay, moratorium, reprieve. **6** *say grace* **prayer of thanks**, thanksgiving, blessing, benediction.
– OPPOSITES inelegance, effrontery, disfavour.
▸ v. **1** *the occasion was graced by the prince* **dignify**, distinguish, honour, favour; enhance, ennoble, glorify, elevate, aggrandize, upgrade. **2** *a mosaic graced the floor* **adorn**, embellish, decorate, ornament, enhance; beautify, prettify, enrich, bedeck.

graceful adj. **elegant**, fluid, fluent, natural, neat; agile, supple, nimble, light-footed.

graceless adj. **gauche**, maladroit, inept, awkward, unsure, unpolished, unsophisticated, uncultured, unrefined; clumsy, ungainly, ungraceful, inelegant, uncoordinated, gawky, gangling, bumbling; tactless, thoughtless, inconsiderate; informal cack-handed, ham-handed, ham-fisted.

gracious adj. **1** *a gracious hostess* **courteous**, polite, civil, chivalrous, well mannered, mannerly, decorous; tactful, diplomatic; kind, benevolent, considerate, thoughtful, obliging, accommodating, indulgent, magnanimous; friendly, amiable, cordial, hospitable. **2** *gracious colonial buildings* **elegant**, stylish, tasteful, graceful; comfortable, luxurious, sumptuous, opulent, grand, high-class; informal swanky, plush. **3** *God's gracious intervention* **merciful**, compassionate, kind; forgiving, lenient, clement, forbearing, humane, tender-hearted, sympathetic; indulgent, generous, magnanimous, benign, benevolent.
– OPPOSITES rude, crude, cruel.

gradation n. **1** *a gradation of ability* **range**, scale, spectrum, compass, span; progression, hierarchy, ladder, pecking order. **2** *each pay band has a number of gradations* **level**, grade, rank, position, status, stage, standard, echelon, rung, step, notch; class, stratum, group, grouping, set.

grade n. **1** *hotels within the same grade* **category**, set, class, classification, grouping, group, bracket. **2** *his job is of the lowest grade* **rank**, level, echelon, standing, position, class, status, order; step, rung, stratum, tier. **3** N. Amer. *the best grades in the school* **mark**, score; assessment, evaluation, appraisal. **4** N. Amer. *the fifth grade* **year**, form, class.
▶ v. **1** *eggs are graded by size* **classify**, class, categorize, bracket, sort, group, arrange, pigeonhole; rank, evaluate, rate, value. **2** N. Amer. *the essays have been graded* **assess**, mark, score, judge, evaluate, appraise. **3** *the colours grade into one another* **pass**, shade, merge, blend.
□ **make the grade** informal come up to standard, come up to scratch, qualify, pass, pass muster, measure up; succeed, win through; informal be up to snuff, cut it, cut the mustard.

gradient n. **1** *a steep gradient* **slope**, incline, hill, rise, ramp, bank; acclivity, declivity; N. Amer. grade. **2** *the gradient of the line* **steepness**, angle, slant, slope, inclination.

gradual adj. **1** *a gradual transition* **slow**, measured, unhurried, cautious; piecemeal, step-by-step, little-by-little, bit-by-bit; progressive, continuous, systematic, steady. **2** *a gradual slope* **gentle**, moderate, slight, easy.
– OPPOSITES abrupt, steep.

gradually adv. **slowly**, slowly but surely, cautiously, gently, gingerly; piecemeal, little by little, bit by bit, inch by inch, by degrees; progressively, systematically; regularly, steadily.

graduate v. **1** *he wants to teach when he graduates* **qualify**, pass one's exams, get one's degree. **2** *she wants to graduate to serious drama* **progress**, advance, move up. **3** *a proposal to graduate income tax* **rank**, grade, order, group, classify, categorize. **4** *a thermometer graduated in Fahrenheit* **calibrate**, mark off, measure out, grade.

graft[1] n. **1** *grafts may die from lack of water* **scion**, cutting, shoot, offshoot, bud, sprout, sprig. **2** *a skin graft* **transplant**, implant.
▶ v. **1** *graft a bud onto the stem* **affix**, join, insert, splice. **2** *tissue is grafted on to the cornea* **transplant**, implant. **3** *a mansion grafted on to a farmhouse* **attach**, add, join.

graft[2] Brit. informal n. *hard graft*. See **work** (sense 1 of the noun).
▶ v. *they often graft for each other*. See **work** (sense 1 of the verb).

graft[3] n. informal *sweeping measures to curb official graft* **corruption**, bribery, subornation, dishonesty, deceit, fraud, unlawful practices, illegal means; N. Amer. payola; informal palm-greasing, hush money, kickbacks, crookedness, sharp practices.
– OPPOSITES honesty.

grain n. **1** *the local farmers grow grain* **cereal**, cereal crops. **2** *a grain of corn* **kernel**, seed, grist. **3** *grains of sand* **granule**, particle, speck, mote, mite; bit, piece; scrap, crumb, fragment, morsel. **4** *a grain of truth* **trace**, hint, tinge, suggestion, shadow; bit, soupçon; scintilla, ounce, iota, jot, whit, scrap, shred; informal smidgen, smidge, tad. **5** *the grain of the timber* **texture**, surface, finish; weave, pattern.

grammar n. **syntax**, rules of language, morphology; linguistics.

grammatical adj. **1** *the grammatical structure of a sentence* **syntactic**, morphological; linguistic. **2** *a grammatical sentence* **well formed**, idiomatic, correct, proper, acceptable, allowable.

grand adj. **1** *a grand hotel* **magnificent**, imposing, impressive, awe-inspiring, splendid, resplendent, majestic, monumental; palatial, stately, large; luxurious, sumptuous, lavish, opulent; Brit. upmarket; N. Amer. upscale; informal fancy, posh, plush, classy, swanky; Brit. informal swish. **2** *a grand scheme* **ambitious**, bold, epic, big, extravagant. **3** *a grand old lady* **august**, distinguished, illustrious, eminent, esteemed, honoured, venerable, dignified, respectable; pre-eminent, prominent, notable, renowned, celebrated, famous; aristocratic, noble, regal, blue-blooded, high-born, patrician; informal upper-crust; Brit. informal posh, upmarket. **4** *a grand total of £2,000* **complete**, comprehensive, all-inclusive, inclusive; final. **5** *the grand staircase* **main**, principal, central, prime; biggest, largest. **6** informal *you're doing a grand job* **excellent**, very good, marvellous, splendid, first-class, first-rate, wonderful, outstanding, sterling, fine; informal superb, terrific, great, super, ace; Brit. informal smashing, brilliant, brill.
– OPPOSITES inferior, humble, minor, poor.
▶ n. informal *a cheque for ten grand* **thousand pounds/dollars**; informal thou, K; N. Amer. informal G, gee.

grandeur n. **splendour**, magnificence, impressiveness, glory, resplendence, majesty, greatness; stateliness, pomp, ceremony.

g

g

grandfather n. **1** *his grandfather lives here* informal grandad, grandpa, gramps, gramp, grandaddy. **2** *the grandfather of modern liberalism* **founder**, inventor, originator, creator, initiator; father, founding father, pioneer. **3** *our Victorian grandfathers* **forefather**, forebear, ancestor, progenitor, antecedent.

▶ v. N. Amer. informal *some smokers have been grandfathered* **exempt**, excuse, free, exclude, grant immunity, spare, absolve; informal let off (the hook).

grandiloquent adj. **pompous**, bombastic, magniloquent, pretentious, ostentatious, high-flown, orotund, florid, flowery; overwrought, overblown, overdone; informal highfalutin, purple.
– OPPOSITES understated.

grandiose adj. **1** *the court's grandiose facade* **magnificent**, impressive, grand, imposing, awe-inspiring, splendid, resplendent, majestic, glorious, elaborate; palatial, stately, luxurious, opulent; informal plush, swanky, flash. **2** *a grandiose plan* **ambitious**, bold, overambitious, extravagant, high-flown, flamboyant; informal over the top, OTT.
– OPPOSITES humble, modest.

grandmother n. informal grandma, granny, gran, nan, nana.

grant v. **1** *he granted them leave of absence* **allow**, accord, permit, afford, vouchsafe. **2** *he granted them £20,000* **give**, award, bestow on, confer on, present with, provide with, endow with, supply with. **3** *I grant that the difference is not absolute* **admit**, accept, concede, yield, allow, appreciate, recognize, acknowledge, confess; agree.
– OPPOSITES refuse, deny.

▶ n. *a grant from the council* **endowment**, subvention, award, donation, bursary, allowance, subsidy, contribution, handout, allocation, gift; scholarship.

granular adj. **powder**, powdered, powdery, grainy, granulated, gritty.

granulated adj. **powdered**, crushed, crumbed, ground, minced, grated, pulverized.

granule n. **grain**, particle, fragment, bit, crumb, morsel, mote, speck.

graph n. *use graphs to analyse your data* **chart**, diagram; histogram, bar chart, pie chart, scatter diagram.

▶ v. *we graphed the new prices* **plot**, trace, draw up, delineate.

graphic adj. **1** *a graphic representation of language* **visual**, symbolic, pictorial, illustrative, diagrammatic; drawn, written. **2** *a graphic account* **vivid**, explicit, expressive, detailed; uninhibited, powerful, colourful, rich, lurid, shocking; realistic, descriptive, illustrative; telling, effective.
– OPPOSITES vague.

▶ n. Computing *this printer's good enough for graphics* **picture**, illustration, image; diagram, graph, chart.

grapple v. **1** *the policemen grappled with him* **wrestle**, struggle, tussle; brawl, fight, scuffle, battle. **2** *he grappled his prey* **seize**, grab, catch (hold of), take hold of, grasp. **3** *she is grappling with the problems of exile* **tackle**, confront, face, deal with, cope with, get to grips with; apply oneself to, devote oneself to.

grasp v. **1** *she grasped his hands* **grip**, clutch, clasp, hold, clench; catch, seize, grab, snatch, latch on to. **2** *everybody grasped the important points* **understand**, comprehend, follow, take in, perceive, see, apprehend, assimilate, absorb; informal get, catch on to, figure out, get one's head around, take on board; Brit. informal twig, suss (out). **3** *he grasped the opportunity* **take advantage of**, act on; seize, leap at, snatch, jump at, pounce on.
– OPPOSITES release, overlook.

▶ n. **1** *his grasp on her hand* **grip**, hold; clutch, clasp, clench. **2** *his domineering mother's grasp* **control**, power, clutches, command, domination, rule, tyranny. **3** *a prize lay within their grasp* **reach**, scope, power, limits, range; sights. **4** *your grasp of history* **understanding**, comprehension, perception, apprehension, awareness, grip, knowledge; mastery, command.

grasping adj. **avaricious**, acquisitive, greedy, rapacious, mercenary, materialistic; mean, miserly, parsimonious, niggardly, hoarding, selfish, possessive, close; informal tight-fisted, tight, stingy, money-grubbing; N. Amer. informal cheap, grabby.

grass n. **1** *he sat down on the grass* **turf**, sod; lawn, green; literary sward. **2** informal *they smoked grass*. See **cannabis**. **3** Brit. informal *few clubs were without a grass* **informer**, mole, stool pigeon; informal snitch, snout, whistle-blower, rat; Brit. informal supergrass, nark; N. Amer. informal fink, stoolie.

▶ v. Brit. informal *he grassed on the robbers* **inform**, tell; give away, betray, sell out; informal split, blow the whistle, rat, peach, squeal, do the dirty, stitch up, sell down the river; Brit. informal shop; N. Amer. informal finger; Austral./NZ informal dob, pimp.

> **WORD LINKS**
>
> **graminivorous** relating to animals that feed on grass
> **prairie, pampas, steppe, savannah, veld** a large area of grassland without trees (in various parts of the world)

grate v. **1** *she grated the cheese* **shred**, pulverize, mince, grind, granulate, crush, crumble. **2** *her bones grated together* **grind**, rub, rasp, scrape, jar, grit, creak. **3** *the tune grates slightly* **irritate**, set someone's teeth on edge, jar; annoy, nettle, chafe, fret; informal aggravate, get on someone's nerves, get under someone's skin, get someone's goat.

grateful adj. **thankful**, appreciative; indebted, obliged, obligated, in your debt, beholden.

gratification n. **satisfaction**, fulfilment, indulgence, relief, appeasement; pleasure, enjoyment, relish.

gratify v. **1** *it gratified him to be seen with her* **please**, gladden, make happy, delight, make someone feel good, satisfy; informal tickle pink, give someone a kick, buck up. **2** *he gratified his desires* **satisfy**, fulfil, indulge, comply with, pander to, cater to, give in to, satiate, feed, accommodate.
– OPPOSITES displease, frustrate.

grating[1] adj. **1** *the chair made a grating noise* **scraping**, scratching, grinding, rasping, jarring. **2** *a grating voice* **harsh**, raucous, strident, piercing, shrill, screechy; discordant, cacophonous; hoarse, rough, gravelly. **3** *it's written in grating language* **irritating**, annoying, infuriating, irksome, maddening, displeasing, tiresome; jarring, discordant, inharmonious, unsuitable, inappropriate; informal aggravating.
– OPPOSITES harmonious, pleasing, appropriate.

grating[2] n. *a strong iron grating* **grid**, grate, grille, lattice, trellis, mesh.

gratis adv. **free (of charge)**, without charge, for nothing, at no cost, gratuitously; informal on the house, for free.

gratitude n. **gratefulness**, thankfulness, thanks, appreciation, indebtedness; recognition, acknowledgement, credit.

gratuitous adj. **1** *gratuitous violence* **unjustified**, uncalled for, unwarranted, unprovoked, undue; indefensible, unjustifiable; needless, unnecessary, inessential, unmerited, groundless, senseless, wanton, indiscriminate; excessive, immoderate, inordinate, inappropriate. **2** *they offer gratuitous advice* **free**, gratis, complimentary, voluntary, unpaid; free of charge, for nothing; Law pro bono (publico); informal for free, on the house; Brit. informal buckshee.
– OPPOSITES necessary, paid.

gratuity n. formal **tip**, pourboire, baksheesh, gift, present, donation, reward, handout; bonus, extra; informal perk; formal perquisite.

grave[1] n. *she left flowers at his grave* **burying place**, tomb, sepulchre, vault, burial chamber, mausoleum, crypt; last resting place.

grave[2] adj. **1** *a grave matter* **serious**, important, weighty, profound, significant, momentous; critical, acute, urgent, pressing; dire, terrible, awful, dreadful; formal exigent. **2** *Jackie looked grave* **solemn**, serious, sober, unsmiling, grim, sombre; severe, stern, dour.
– OPPOSITES trivial, cheerful.

gravel n. **shingle**, grit, pebbles, stones.

gravelly adj. **1** *a gravelly beach* **shingly**, pebbly, stony, gritty. **2** *his gravelly voice* **husky**, gruff, throaty, deep, croaky, rasping, grating, harsh, rough.

gravestone n. **headstone**, tombstone, stone, monument, memorial.

graveyard n. **cemetery**, churchyard, burial ground, necropolis; informal boneyard; historical potter's field; old use God's acre.

gravitas n. **dignity**, seriousness, solemnity, gravity, sobriety.
– OPPOSITES frivolity.

gravitate v. **move**, head, drift, be drawn, be attracted; tend, lean, incline.

gravity n. **1** *the gravity of the situation* **seriousness**, importance, significance, weight, consequence, magnitude; acuteness, urgency, exigence; awfulness, dreadfulness; formal moment. **2** *the gravity of his demeanour* **solemnity**, seriousness, sombreness, sobriety, severity, grimness, humourlessness; dourness; gloominess.

graze[1] v. *the deer grazed* **feed**, eat, crop, nibble, browse.

graze[2] v. **1** *he grazed his knuckles on the box* **scrape**, abrade, skin, scratch, chafe, bark, scuff, rasp; cut, nick. **2** *his shot grazed the far post* **touch**, brush, shave, skim, kiss, scrape, clip, glance off.
▶ n. *grazes on the skin* **scratch**, scrape, abrasion, cut; Medicine trauma.

grease n. **1** *axle grease* **lubricant**, lubrication, unguent; informal lube. **2** *the kitchen was filmed with grease* **fat**, oil, cooking oil, animal fat; lard, suet.

greasy adj. **1** *a greasy supper* **fatty**, oily, buttery, oleaginous; formal pinguid. **2** *greasy hair* **oily**. **3** *the pitch was very greasy* **slippery**, slick, slimy, slithery, oily; informal slippy, skiddy. **4** *a greasy little man* **ingratiating**, obsequious, sycophantic, fawning, toadying, grovelling; effusive, gushing, gushy; unctuous, oily; informal smarmy, slimy, bootlicking, sucky.
– OPPOSITES lean, dry.

great adj. **1** *they showed great interest* **considerable**, substantial, significant, appreciable, special, serious; exceptional, extraordinary. **2** *a great expanse of water* **large**, big, extensive, expansive, broad, wide, sizeable, ample; vast, immense, huge, enormous, massive; informal humongous, whopping; Brit. informal ginormous. **3** *a great big house* **very**, extremely, exceedingly, exceptionally, especially, really; informal dirty. **4** *you great fool!* **absolute**, total, utter, out-and-out, downright, thoroughgoing, complete; perfect, positive, prize, sheer, arrant, unqualified, consummate, veritable; informal thundering; Brit. informal right, proper. **5** *great writers* **prominent**, eminent, important, distinguished, illustrious, celebrated, honoured, acclaimed, admired, esteemed, revered, renowned, notable, famous, famed, well known; leading, top, major, principal, first-rate, matchless, peerless, star. **6** *the country is now a great power* **powerful**, dominant, influential, strong, potent, formidable, redoubtable; leading, important, foremost, major, chief, principal. **7** *a great castle* **magnificent**, imposing, impressive, awe-inspiring, grand, splendid, majestic, sumptuous, resplendent. **8** *a great sportsman* **expert**, skilful, skilled, adept, accomplished, talented, fine, masterly, master, brilliant, virtuoso, marvellous, outstanding, first class, superb; informal crack, ace, A1, class. **9** *a great fan of rugby* **enthusiastic**, eager, keen, zealous, devoted, ardent, fanatical, passionate,

g

dedicated, committed. **10** *we had a great time* **enjoyable**, delightful, lovely, pleasant, congenial; exciting, thrilling; excellent, marvellous, wonderful, fine, splendid, very good; informal terrific, fantastic, fabulous, fab, super, grand, cool; Brit. informal smashing, brilliant, brill; Austral./NZ informal bonzer, beaut; Brit. informal dated spiffing; N. Amer. informal dated swell.
– OPPOSITES little, small, minor, modest, poor, unenthusiastic, bad.

greatly adv. **very much**, considerably, substantially, appreciably, significantly, markedly, sizeably, seriously, materially, profoundly; enormously, vastly, immensely, tremendously, mightily, abundantly, extremely, exceedingly; informal plenty, majorly.
– OPPOSITES slightly.

greatness n. **1** *a woman destined for greatness* **eminence**, distinction, illustriousness, repute, high standing; importance, significance; celebrity, fame, prominence, renown. **2** *his greatness as a writer* **brilliance**, genius, prowess, talent, expertise, mastery, artistry, virtuosity, skill, proficiency; flair, finesse; calibre, distinction.

greed, **greediness** n. **1** *human greed* **avarice**, cupidity, acquisitiveness, covetousness, rapacity; materialism, mercenariness, Mammonism; informal money-grubbing, money-grabbing. **2** *her mouth salivated with greed* **gluttony**, hunger, voracity, insatiability; gourmandism, intemperance, overeating, overconsumption, self-indulgence; informal piggishness. **3** *their greed for power* **desire**, appetite, hunger, thirst, craving, longing, yearning, hankering; avidity, eagerness; informal yen, itch.
– OPPOSITES generosity, temperance, indifference.

greedy adj. **1** *a greedy eater* **gluttonous**, ravenous, voracious, intemperate, self-indulgent, wolfish; informal piggish, piggy. **2** *a greedy millionaire* **avaricious**, acquisitive, covetous, grasping, materialistic, mercenary, possessive; informal money-grubbing, money-grabbing; N. Amer. informal grabby. **3** *she is greedy for a title* **eager**, avid, hungry, craving, longing, yearning, hankering; impatient, anxious; informal dying, itching, gagging.

green adj. **1** *a green scarf* **viridescent**; olive green, pea green, emerald green, lime green, bottle green, Lincoln green, sea green, eau de Nil; literary virescent, glaucous. **2** *a green island* **verdant**, grassy, leafy, verdurous. **3** *he promotes Green issues* **environmental**, ecological, conservation, eco-. **4** *a green alternative to diesel* **environmentally friendly**, non-polluting; ozone-friendly. **5** *green bananas* **unripe**, immature. **6** *green timber* **unseasoned**, not aged, unfinished; pliable, supple. **7** *green bacon* **raw**, fresh, unsmoked, uncured. **8** *the new lieutenant was very green* **inexperienced**, unversed, callow, immature; new, raw, unseasoned, untried; inexpert, untrained, unqualified,

ignorant; simple, unsophisticated, unpolished; naive, innocent, ingenuous, credulous, gullible, unworldly; informal wet behind the ears, born yesterday. **9** *he went green* **pale**, wan, pallid, ashen, ashen-faced, pasty, pasty-faced, grey, whitish, washed out, whey-faced, waxen, waxy, blanched, drained, pinched, sallow; sickly, nauseous, ill, sick, unhealthy.
– OPPOSITES barren, dry, cured, experienced, ruddy.
▸ n. **1** *a canopy of green over the road* **foliage**, greenery, plants, leaves, leafage, vegetation. **2** *a village green* **lawn**, common, grassy area, sward. **3** *they had roast beef and greens* **vegetables**, leaf vegetables; informal veg, veggies. **4** *Greens are against multinationals* **environmentalist**, conservationist, preservationist, nature-lover, eco-activist.

greenery n. **foliage**, vegetation, plants, green, leaves, leafage, undergrowth, plant life, flora, herbage, verdure.

greenhouse n. **hothouse**, glasshouse, conservatory.

greet v. **1** *she greeted Hank cheerily* **say hello to**, address, salute, hail, halloo; welcome, meet, receive. **2** *the decision was greeted with outrage* **receive**, acknowledge, respond to, react to, take.

greeting n. **1** *he shouted a greeting* **hello**, salute, salutation, address; welcome; acknowledgement. **2** *birthday greetings* **best wishes**, good wishes, congratulations, felicitations; compliments, regards, respects.
– OPPOSITES farewell.

gregarious adj. *he was fun-loving and gregarious* **sociable**, companionable, outgoing, friendly, affable, amiable, genial, convivial, warm, comradely, clubbable; Scottish couthy; informal chummy, pally; Brit. informal matey.
– OPPOSITES unsociable.

grey adj. **1** *a grey suit* **charcoal**, silvery, silver-grey, gunmetal, slate, smoky. **2** *his grey hair* **white**, silver, hoary. **3** *a grey day* **cloudy**, overcast, dull, sunless, gloomy, dreary, dismal, sombre, bleak, murky. **4** *her face looked grey* **ashen**, wan, pale, pasty, pallid, colourless, bloodless, white, waxen; sickly, peaky, drained, drawn, deathly. **5** *the grey daily routine* **characterless**, colourless, nondescript, unremarkable, insipid, jejune, flat, bland, dry, stale; dull, uninteresting, boring, tedious, monotonous. **6** *a grey area* **ambiguous**, doubtful, unclear, uncertain, indefinite, open to question, debatable. **7** *the grey economy* **unofficial**, informal, irregular, back-door.
– OPPOSITES sunny, ruddy, lively, certain.
▸ v. *the population greyed* **age**, grow old, mature.

grid n. **1** *a metal grid* **grating**, mesh, grille, gauze, lattice. **2** *the grid of streets* **network**, matrix, reticulation.

grief n. **1** *he was overcome with grief* **sorrow**, misery, sadness, anguish, pain, distress, heartache, heartbreak, agony, torment,

affliction, suffering, woe, desolation, dejection, despair; mourning, mournfulness, bereavement, lamentation; literary dolour, dole. **2** informal *the police gave me loads of grief* **trouble**, annoyance, bother, irritation, vexation, harassment; informal aggravation, aggro, hassle.
– OPPOSITES joy.
□ **come to grief** fail, meet with disaster, miscarry, go wrong, go awry, fall through, fall flat, founder, come to nothing, come to naught; informal come unstuck, come a cropper, flop, go phut; Brit. informal go pear-shaped.

grief-stricken adj. **sorrowful**, sorrowing, miserable, sad, heartbroken, broken-hearted, anguished, pained, distressed, tormented, suffering, woeful, doleful, desolate, despairing, devastated, upset, inconsolable, wretched; mourning, grieving, mournful, bereaved, lamenting; literary dolorous, heartsick.
– OPPOSITES joyful.

grievance n. **1** *social and economic grievances* **injustice**, wrong, injury, ill, unfairness; affront, insult, indignity. **2** *students voiced their grievances* **complaint**, criticism, objection, grumble, grouse; ill feeling, bad feeling, resentment, bitterness, pique; informal gripe, whinge, moan, grouch, niggle, beef, bone to pick.

grieve v. **1** *she grieved for her father* **mourn**, lament, sorrow, be sorrowful; cry, sob, weep, shed tears, keen, weep and wail, beat one's breast. **2** *it grieved me to leave her* **sadden**, upset, distress, pain, hurt, wound, break someone's heart, make someone's heart bleed.
– OPPOSITES rejoice, please.

grievous adj. formal *his death was a grievous blow* **serious**, severe, grave, bad, critical, dreadful, terrible, awful, crushing, calamitous; painful, agonizing, traumatic, wounding, damaging, injurious; sharp, acute.
– OPPOSITES slight.

grim adj. **1** *his grim expression* **stern**, forbidding, uninviting, unsmiling, dour, formidable, harsh, steely, flinty, stony; cross, churlish, crabbed, surly, sour, ill-tempered; fierce, ferocious, threatening, menacing, implacable, ruthless, merciless; Brit. informal boot-faced. **2** *grim humour* **black**, dark, mirthless, bleak, cynical. **3** *the asylum holds some grim secrets* **dreadful**, dire, ghastly, horrible, horrendous, horrid, terrible, awful, appalling, frightful, shocking, unspeakable, grisly, gruesome, hideous, macabre; depressing, distressing, upsetting, worrying, unpleasant. **4** *a grim little hovel* **bleak**, dreary, dismal, dingy, wretched, miserable, depressing, cheerless, comfortless, joyless, gloomy, uninviting; informal God-awful. **5** *grim determination* **resolute**, determined, firm, decided, steadfast, dead set; obstinate, stubborn, obdurate, unyielding, intractable, uncompromising, unshakeable, unrelenting, relentless, dogged, tenacious.
– OPPOSITES amiable, pleasant.

grimace n. *his mouth twisted into a grimace* **scowl**, frown, sneer; face.
▶v. *Nina grimaced at Joe* **scowl**, frown, sneer, glower, lour; make a face, make faces, pull a face; Brit. gurn.
– OPPOSITES smile.

grime n. *her skirt was smeared with grime* **dirt**, smut, soot, dust, mud, filth, mire; informal muck, yuck, crud; Brit. informal grot, gunge.
▶v. *concrete grimed by diesel exhaust* **blacken**, dirty, stain, soil; literary begrime, besmirch.

grimy adj. **dirty**, grubby, mucky, soiled, stained, smeared, filthy, smutty, sooty, dusty, muddy; informal yucky, cruddy; Brit. informal manky, grotty, gungy; Austral./NZ scungy; literary besmirched, begrimed.
– OPPOSITES clean.

grin v. *he grinned at her* **smile**, smile broadly, beam, smile from ear to ear, grin like a Cheshire cat; smirk; informal be all smiles.
▶n. *a silly grin* **smile**, broad smile; smirk.
– OPPOSITES frown, scowl.

grind v. **1** *the sandstone is ground into powder* **crush**, pound, pulverize, mill, granulate, crumble, smash, press; technical triturate, comminute; old use levigate, bray. **2** *a knife being ground on a wheel* **sharpen**, whet, hone, file, strop; smooth, polish, sand, sandpaper. **3** *one tectonic plate grinds against another* **rub**, grate, scrape, rasp.
▶n. *the daily grind* **drudgery**, toil, hard work, labour, donkey work, exertion, chores, slog; informal fag, sweat; literary travail.
□ **grind away** labour, toil, work hard, slave (away), work one's fingers to the bone, work like a Trojan, work like a dog; informal slog, plug away, beaver away, work one's socks off; Brit. informal graft; literary travail; old use drudge.
grind someone down oppress, crush, persecute, tyrannize, ill-treat, maltreat.

grip v. **1** *she gripped the edge of the table* **grasp**, clutch, hold, clasp, take hold of, clench, grab, seize, cling to; squeeze, press. **2** *Harry was gripped by a sneezing fit* **afflict**, affect, take over, beset, rack, convulse. **3** *we were gripped by the drama* **engross**, enthral, absorb, rivet, spellbind, hold spellbound, bewitch, fascinate, hold, mesmerize, enrapture; interest.
– OPPOSITES release.
▶n. **1** *a tight grip* **grasp**, hold. **2** *the wheels lost their grip on the road* **traction**, purchase, friction, adhesion, resistance. **3** *he was in the grip of an obsession* **control**, power, hold, stranglehold, clutches, command, mastery, influence. **4** *I had a pretty good grip on the situation* **understanding**, comprehension, grasp, perception, awareness, apprehension, conception; formal cognizance. **5** *a leather grip* **travelling bag**, bag, holdall, overnight bag, flight bag, kitbag, Gladstone bag.
□ **come/get to grips with** deal with, cope with, handle, grasp, grasp the nettle of, tackle, undertake, take on, grapple with, face, face up to, confront.

gripe informal v. *he's always griping about something* **complain**, grumble, grouse, protest, whine, bleat; informal moan, bellyache,

beef, bitch, whinge; Brit. informal chunter;
N. Amer. informal kvetch.

▶n. *employees' gripes* **complaint**, grumble,
grouse, grievance, objection; cavil, quibble,
niggle; informal moan, beef, whinge; N. Amer.
informal kvetch.

gripping adj. **engrossing**, enthralling,
absorbing, riveting, captivating,
spellbinding, bewitching, fascinating,
compulsive, compelling, mesmerizing;
thrilling, exciting, action-packed, dramatic,
stimulating; informal unputdownable, page-
turning.
− OPPOSITES boring.

grisly adj. **gruesome**, ghastly, frightful,
horrid, horrifying, fearful, hideous, macabre,
spine-chilling, horrible, horrendous, grim,
awful, dire, dreadful, terrible, horrific,
shocking, appalling, abominable, loathsome,
abhorrent, odious, monstrous, unspeakable,
disgusting, repulsive, repugnant, revolting,
repellent, sickening; informal sick-making,
gross; old use disgustful.

gristly adj. **stringy**, sinewy, fibrous; tough,
leathery, chewy.

grit n. **1** *the grit from the paths* **gravel**,
pebbles, stones, shingle, sand; dust, dirt.
2 *the true grit of a seasoned campaigner*
courage, bravery, pluck, mettle, backbone,
spirit, strength of character, strength of
will, moral fibre, steel, nerve, fortitude,
toughness, hardiness, resolve, resolution,
determination, tenacity, perseverance,
endurance; informal guts, spunk; Brit. informal
bottle.

▶v. *Gina gritted her teeth* **clench**, clamp
together, shut tightly; grind, gnash.

gritty adj. **1** *a gritty floor* **sandy**, gravelly,
pebbly, stony; powdery, dusty. **2** *a gritty
performance* **courageous**, brave, plucky,
mettlesome, stout-hearted, valiant, bold,
spirited, intrepid, tough, determined,
resolute, purposeful, dogged, tenacious;
informal gutsy, spunky.

grizzle v. Brit. informal **cry**, whimper, mewl,
snivel, sob, wail; Scottish greet.

grizzled adj. **grey**, greying, silver, silvery,
snowy, white, salt-and-pepper; grey-haired,
hoary.

groan v. **1** *she groaned and rubbed her
stomach* **moan**, whimper, cry, call out.
2 *they were groaning about the management*
complain, grumble, grouse; informal moan,
niggle, beef, bellyache, bitch, whinge, gripe.
3 *the old wooden door groaned* **creak**, squeak;
grate, rasp.

▶n. **1** *a groan of anguish* **moan**, cry, whimper.
2 *their moans and groans* **complaint**,
grumble, grouse, objection, protest,
grievance; informal grouch, moan, beef,
whinge; informal gripe. **3** *the groan of the
elevator* **creaking**, creak, squeak, grating,
grinding.

groggy adj. **dazed**, muzzy, stupefied, in a
stupor, befuddled, fuddled, disoriented,
disorientated, dizzy, punch-drunk, shaky,
unsteady, wobbly, weak, faint; informal dopey,

woozy, not with it.

groin n. **crotch**, crutch, genitals.

WORD LINKS
inguinal relating to the groin

groom v. **1** *she groomed her pony* **curry**,
brush, comb, clean, rub down. **2** *his dark hair
was carefully groomed* **brush**, comb, arrange,
do; tidy, spruce up, smarten up, preen, primp;
informal fix. **3** *they were groomed for stardom*
prepare, prime, ready, condition, tailor;
coach, train, instruct, drill, teach, school.

▶n. **1** *a groom took his horse* **stable hand**,
stableman, stable lad, stable boy, stable
girl; historical equerry. **2** *the bride and groom*
bridegroom; newly-married man, newly-
wed.

groove n. **furrow**, channel, trench, trough,
canal, gouge, hollow, indentation, rut,
gutter, cutting, cut, fissure; Carpentry rebate.

grooved adj. **furrowed**, fluted, corrugated,
ribbed, ridged.

grope v. **1** *she groped for her glasses* **fumble**,
scrabble, fish, ferret, rummage, feel, search,
hunt; Brit. informal rootle. **2** informal *one of the
men started groping her* **fondle**, touch; informal
paw, maul, feel up, touch up.

gross adj. **1** *the man was pale and gross* **obese**,
corpulent, overweight, fat, big, large, fleshy,
flabby, portly, bloated; informal porky, pudgy,
tubby, blubbery, roly-poly; Brit. informal podgy,
fubsy. **2** *men of gross natures* **boorish**,
coarse, vulgar, loutish, oafish, thuggish,
brutish, philistine, uncouth, crass, common,
unrefined, unsophisticated, uncultured,
uncultivated; informal cloddish; Brit. informal
yobbish. **3** informal *the place smelled gross*
disgusting, repellent, repulsive, abhorrent,
loathsome, foul, nasty, obnoxious,
unpalatable, sickening, nauseating, stomach-
churning; N. Amer. vomitous; informal yucky,
rank, icky, sick-making, gut-churning;
old use disgustful. **4** *a gross distortion of the
truth* **flagrant**, blatant, glaring, obvious,
overt, naked, barefaced, shameless, brazen,
audacious, brass-necked, undisguised,
unconcealed, patent, transparent, manifest,
palpable; out-and-out, utter, complete.
5 *their gross income* **total**, whole, entire,
complete, full, overall, combined, aggregate;
before deductions, before tax.
− OPPOSITES slender, refined, pleasant, net.

▶v. *he grosses over a million dollars a month*
earn, make, bring in, take, get, receive,
collect; informal rake in.

grotesque adj. **1** *a grotesque creature*
malformed, deformed, misshapen,
misproportioned, distorted, twisted,
gnarled, mangled, mutilated; ugly, unsightly,
monstrous, hideous, freakish, unnatural,
abnormal, strange, odd, peculiar; informal
weird, freaky. **2** *grotesque mismanagement
of funds* **outrageous**, monstrous, shocking,
appalling, preposterous; ridiculous,
ludicrous, farcical, unbelievable, incredible.
− OPPOSITES normal.

g

grotto n. **cave**, cavern, hollow; pothole, underground chamber.

grouch informal *an. an ill-mannered grouch* **grumbler**, complainer, moaner; informal grump, sourpuss, crosspatch, whinger; Brit. informal misery, bear with a sore head; N. Amer. informal sorehead, kvetch.

▸ v. *there's not a lot to grouch about* **grumble**, complain, grouse, whine, bleat, carp, cavil; informal moan, whinge, gripe, beef, bellyache, bitch, sound off; Brit. informal chunter; N. Amer. informal kvetch.

grouchy adj. **grumpy**, cross, irritable, bad-tempered, crotchety, crabby, crabbed, cantankerous, curmudgeonly, testy, tetchy, huffy, snappish, waspish, prickly; informal snappy; Brit. informal narky, ratty, like a bear with a sore head, whingy; N. Amer. informal cranky, soreheaded; informal dated miffy.

ground n. **1** *she collapsed on the ground* **floor**, earth, terra firma; flooring; informal deck. **2** *the soggy ground* **earth**, soil, dirt, clay, loam, turf, clod, sod; land, terrain. **3** *the team's home ground* **stadium**, pitch, field, arena, track; N. Amer. bowl; Brit. informal park. **4** *the mansion's grounds* **estate**, gardens, lawns, park, parkland, land, acres, property, surroundings, holding, territory; old use demesne. **5** *grounds for dismissal* **reason**, cause, basis, base, foundation, justification, rationale, argument, premise, occasion, excuse, pretext, motive, motivation. **6** *coffee grounds* **sediment**, precipitate, settlings, dregs, lees, deposit, residue; old use grouts.

▸ v. **1** *the boat grounded on a mud bank* **run aground**, run ashore, beach, land. **2** *an assertion grounded on results of several studies* **base**, found, establish, root, build, construct, form. **3** *they were grounded in classics and history* **instruct**, coach, teach, tutor, educate, school, train, drill, prime, prepare; familiarize with, acquaint with.

groundless adj. **baseless**, without basis, without foundation, ill-founded, unfounded, unsupported, uncorroborated, unproven, empty, idle, unsubstantiated, unwarranted, unjustified, unjustifiable, without cause, without reason, without justification, unreasonable, irrational, illogical, misguided.

groundwork n. **preliminary work**, preliminaries, preparations, spadework, legwork, donkey work; planning, arrangements, organization, homework; basics, essentials, fundamentals, underpinning, foundation.

group n. **1** *the exhibits were divided into three distinct groups* **category**, class, classification, grouping, set, lot, batch, bracket, type, sort, kind, variety, family, species, genus, breed; grade, grading, rank, status. **2** *a group of tourists* **crowd**, party, body, band, company, gathering, congregation, assembly, collection, cluster, flock, pack, troop, gang; informal bunch. **3** *a coup attempt by a group within the parliament* **faction**, division, section, clique, coterie, circle, set, ring,

camp, bloc, caucus, cabal, fringe movement, splinter group. **4** *the women's group* **association**, club, society, league, guild, circle, union. **5** *a small group of trees* **cluster**, knot, collection, mass, clump. **6** *a local folk group* **band**, ensemble, act; informal line-up, combo, outfit.

▸ v. **1** *patients were grouped according to their symptoms* **categorize**, classify, class, catalogue, sort, bracket, pigeonhole, grade, rate, rank. **2** *wooden chairs were grouped round the table* **place**, arrange, assemble, organize, range, line up, dispose. **3** *the two parties grouped together* **unite**, join together/up, team up, join forces, get together, ally, form an alliance, affiliate, combine; collaborate, work together, pull together, cooperate.

grouse v. *she groused about the food* **grumble**, complain, protest, whine, bleat, carp, cavil, make a fuss; informal moan, bellyache, gripe, beef, bitch, grouch, whinge, sound off; Brit. informal chunter, create; N. Amer. informal kvetch.

▸ n. *our biggest grouse was about the noise* **grumble**, complaint, grievance, objection, cavil, quibble; informal moan, beef, gripe, grouch.

grove n. **copse**, wood, thicket, coppice; orchard, plantation; Brit. spinney; old use hurst, holt.

grovel v. **1** *George grovelled at his feet* **prostrate oneself**, lie, kneel, cringe. **2** *she was not going to grovel to him* **be obsequious**, fawn on, kowtow, bow and scrape, toady, truckle, abase oneself, humble oneself; curry favour with, flatter, dance attendance on, make up to, play up to, ingratiate oneself with; informal crawl, creep, suck up to, lick someone's boots.

grow v. **1** *the boys had grown* **get bigger**, get taller, get larger, increase in size. **2** *sales and profits continue to grow* **increase**, swell, multiply, snowball, mushroom, balloon, build up, mount up, pile up; informal skyrocket. **3** *flowers grew among the rocks* **sprout**, germinate, shoot up, spring up, develop, bud, burst forth, bloom, flourish, thrive, run riot. **4** *he grew vegetables* **cultivate**, produce, propagate, raise, rear, nurture, tend; farm. **5** *the family business grew* **expand**, extend, develop, progress, make progress; flourish, thrive, burgeon, prosper, succeed, boom. **6** *the fable grew from an ancient Indian source* **originate**, stem, spring, arise, emerge, issue; develop, evolve. **7** *Leonora grew bored* **become**, get, turn, begin to feel.
– OPPOSITES shrink, decline.

growl v. **snarl**, bark, yap, bay.

grown-up n. *she wanted to be treated like a grown-up* **adult**, (grown) woman, (grown) man, mature woman, mature man.
– OPPOSITES child.

▸ adj. *she has two grown-up daughters* **adult**, mature, of age; fully grown, full-grown, fully developed.

growth n. **1** *population growth* **increase**, expansion, augmentation, proliferation, multiplication, enlargement, mushrooming, snowballing, rise, escalation, build-up. **2** *the growth of plants* **development**, maturation, growing, germination, sprouting; blooming. **3** *the marked growth of local enterprises* **expansion**, extension, development, progress, advance, advancement, headway, spread; rise, success, boom, upturn, upswing. **4** *a growth on his jaw* **tumour**, malignancy, cancer; lump, excrescence, outgrowth, swelling, nodule; cyst, polyp.
– OPPOSITES decrease, decline.

grub n. **1** *a small black grub* **larva**; maggot; caterpillar. **2** informal *pub grub*. See **food** (sense 1).
▶v. **1** *kids grubbing around in the dirt* **dig**, poke, scratch. **2** *they grubbed up the old trees* **dig up**, unearth, uproot, root up/out, pull up/out, tear out. **3** *he began grubbing about in the bin* **rummage**, search, hunt, delve, dig, scrabble, ferret, root, rifle, fish, poke; Brit. informal rootle; Austral./NZ informal fossick through.

grubby adj. **dirty**, grimy, filthy, mucky, unwashed, stained, soiled, smeared, spotted, muddy, dusty, sooty; unhygienic, insanitary; informal cruddy, yucky; Brit. informal manky, grotty, gungy; literary befouled, begrimed.
– OPPOSITES clean.

grudge n. *a former employee with a grudge* **grievance**, resentment, bitterness, rancour, pique, umbrage, dissatisfaction, disgruntlement, bad feelings, hard feelings, ill feelings, ill will, animosity, antipathy, antagonism, enmity, animus; informal a chip on one's shoulder.
▶v. **1** *he grudged the time that the meetings involved* **begrudge**, resent, feel aggrieved about, be resentful of, mind, object to, take exception to. **2** *I don't grudge you your success* **envy**, begrudge, resent, be jealous of, be envious of, be resentful of.

grudging adj. **reluctant**, unwilling, forced, half-hearted, unenthusiastic, hesitant; begrudging, resentful.
– OPPOSITES eager.

gruelling adj. **exhausting**, tiring, fatiguing, wearying, taxing, draining, debilitating; demanding, exacting, difficult, hard, arduous, strenuous, laborious, back-breaking, harsh, severe, stiff, punishing, crippling; informal killing, murderous, hellish; Brit. informal knackering.

gruesome adj. **grisly**, ghastly, frightful, horrid, horrifying, hideous, horrible, horrendous, grim, awful, dire, dreadful, terrible, horrific, shocking, appalling, disgusting, repulsive, repugnant, revolting, repellent, sickening; loathsome, abhorrent, odious, monstrous, unspeakable; informal sick, sick-making, gross; old use disgustful.
– OPPOSITES pleasant.

gruff adj. **1** *a gruff reply | his gruff exterior* **abrupt**, brusque, curt, short, blunt, bluff, no-nonsense; laconic, taciturn; surly, churlish, grumpy, crotchety, crabby, crabbed, cross, bad-tempered, short-tempered, ill-natured, crusty, tetchy, bearish, ungracious, unceremonious; informal grouchy. **2** *a gruff voice* **rough**, guttural, throaty, gravelly, husky, croaking, rasping, raspy, growly, hoarse, harsh; low, thick.
– OPPOSITES friendly, soft.

grumble v. *they grumbled about the disruption* **complain**, grouse, whine, mutter, bleat, carp, cavil, protest, make a fuss; informal moan, bellyache, beef, gripe, bitch, grouch, whinge, sound off; Brit. informal chunter, create; N. English informal mither; N. Amer. informal kvetch.
▶n. *his customers' grumbles* **complaint**, grouse, grievance, protest, cavil, quibble, criticism; informal grouch, moan, whinge, beef, bitch, gripe.

grumpy adj. **bad-tempered**, crabby, ill-tempered, short-tempered, crotchety, tetchy, testy, crabbed, waspish, prickly, touchy, irritable, irascible, crusty, cantankerous, curmudgeonly, bearish, surly, ill-natured, churlish, ill-humoured, peevish, cross, fractious, disagreeable, pettish; informal grouchy, snappy, snappish; Brit. informal shirty, stroppy, narky, ratty, eggy, like a bear with a sore head; N. Amer. informal cranky, ornery, soreheaded; informal dated miffy.
– OPPOSITES good-humoured.

guarantee n. **1** *all repairs have a one-year guarantee* **warranty**, warrant. **2** *a guarantee that the hospital will stay open* **promise**, assurance, word (of honour), pledge, vow, oath, bond, commitment, covenant. **3** *banks usually demand a personal guarantee for loans* **collateral**, security, surety, guaranty, earnest.
▶v. **1** *he agreed to guarantee the loan* **underwrite**, put up collateral for. **2** *can you guarantee he wasn't involved?* **promise**, swear, swear to the fact, pledge, vow, undertake, give one's word, give an assurance, give an undertaking, take an oath, cross one's heart (and hope to die); old use plight.

guard v. **1** *infantry guarded the barricaded bridge* **protect**, stand guard over, watch over, keep an eye on; cover, patrol, police, defend, shield, safeguard, keep safe, secure. **2** *the prisoners were guarded by armed men* **keep under surveillance**, keep under guard, keep watch over, mind. **3** *forest wardens must guard against poachers* **beware of**, keep watch for, be alert to, keep an eye out for, be on the alert/lookout for.
▶n. **1** *border guards* **sentry**, sentinel, security guard, nightwatchman; protector, defender, guardian; lookout, watch; garrison; old use watchman. **2** *her prison guard* **warder**, warden, keeper; jailer; informal screw; old use turnkey. **3** *he let his guard slip and they escaped* **vigilance**, vigil, watch, surveillance, watchfulness, caution, heed, attention, care, wariness. **4** *a metal guard* **safety guard**, safety device, protective device, shield, screen, fender; bumper, buffer.
□ **off (one's) guard** unprepared, unready, inattentive, unwary, with one's defences

down, cold, unsuspecting; informal napping, asleep at the wheel, on the hop.
on one's guard vigilant, alert, on the alert, wary, watchful, cautious, careful, heedful, chary, circumspect, on the lookout, on the qui vive, on one's toes, prepared, ready, wide awake, attentive, observant, keeping one's eyes peeled; informal keeping a weather eye out.

guarded adj. **cautious**, careful, circumspect, wary, chary, on one's guard, reluctant, non-committal, reticent, restrained, reserved; informal cagey.

guardian n. **protector**, defender, preserver, custodian, warden, guard, keeper; conservator, curator, caretaker, steward, trustee.

> **WORD LINKS**
> **tutelary** relating to a guardian

guerrilla n. **freedom fighter**, irregular, member of the resistance, partisan; rebel, radical, revolutionary, revolutionist; terrorist.

guess v. **1** *he guessed she was about 40* **estimate**, hazard a guess, reckon, gauge, judge, calculate; hypothesize, postulate, predict, speculate, conjecture, surmise; informal guesstimate. **2** informal *I guess I owe you an apology* **suppose**, think, imagine, expect, suspect, dare say; informal reckon, figure.
▸ n. *my guess was right* **hypothesis**, theory, prediction, postulation, conjecture, surmise, estimate, belief, opinion, reckoning, judgement, supposition, speculation, suspicion, impression, feeling; informal guesstimate.

guesswork n. **guessing**, conjecture, surmise, supposition, assumptions, presumptions, speculation, hypothesizing, theorizing, prediction; approximations, rough calculations; hunches; informal guesstimates.

guest n. **1** *I have two guests coming to dinner* **visitor**, caller; company; old use visitant. **2** *hotel guests* **resident**, boarder, lodger, paying guest, PG; patron, client; N. Amer. roomer.
– OPPOSITES host.

guest house n. **boarding house**, bed and breakfast, B&B, hotel; pension, pensione.

guff n. informal See **nonsense** (sense 1).

guffaw v. **roar with laughter**, laugh heartily/loudly, roar, bellow, cackle; informal laugh like a drain.

guidance n. **1** *she looked to her father for guidance* **advice**, counsel, direction, instruction, enlightenment, information; recommendations, suggestions, tips, hints, pointers, guidelines. **2** *work continued under the guidance of a project supervisor* **direction**, control, leadership, management, supervision, superintendence, charge; handling, conduct, running, overseeing.

guide n. **1** *our guide took us back to the hotel* **escort**, attendant, courier, cicerone, dragoman; usher; chaperone. **2** *he is my*

inspiration and my guide **adviser**, mentor, counsellor; guru. **3** *the light acted as a guide for shipping* **pointer**, marker, indicator, signpost, mark, landmark; guiding light, sign, signal, beacon. **4** *the techniques outlined are meant as a guide* **model**, pattern, blueprint, template, example, exemplar; standard, touchstone, measure, benchmark, yardstick, gauge. **5** *a pocket guide of Paris* **guidebook**, travelogue, vade mecum; companion, handbook, directory, A to Z; informal bible.
▸ v. **1** *he guided her to her seat* **lead**, lead the way, conduct, show, show someone the way, usher, shepherd, direct, steer, pilot, escort, accompany, attend; see, take, help, assist. **2** *the chairman must guide the meeting* **direct**, steer, control, manage, command, lead, conduct, run, be in charge of, have control of, govern, preside over, superintend, supervise, oversee; handle, regulate. **3** *he was always there to guide me* **advise**, counsel, give advice to, direct, give direction to.

guidebook n. **guide**, travel guide, travelogue, vade mecum; companion, handbook, directory, A to Z; informal bible.

guideline n. **recommendation**, instruction, direction, suggestion, advice; regulation, rule, principle, guiding principle; standard, criterion, measure, gauge, yardstick, benchmark, touchstone; procedure, parameter.

guild n. **association**, society, union, league, organization, company, cooperative, fellowship, club, order, lodge, brotherhood, fraternity, sisterhood, sorority.

guile n. **cunning**, craftiness, craft, artfulness, art, artifice, wiliness, slyness, deviousness; wiles, ploys, schemes, stratagems, manoeuvres, subterfuges, tricks, ruses; deception, deceit, duplicity, underhandedness, double-dealing, trickery.
– OPPOSITES honesty.

guileless adj. **artless**, ingenuous, naive, open, genuine, natural, simple, childlike, innocent, unsophisticated, unworldly, unsuspicious, trustful, trusting; honest, truthful, sincere, straightforward.
– OPPOSITES scheming.

guilt n. **1** *the proof of his guilt* **culpability**, guiltiness, blameworthiness; wrongdoing, wrong, criminality, misconduct, sin. **2** *a terrible feeling of guilt* **self-reproach**, self-condemnation, shame, a guilty conscience, pangs of conscience; remorse, regret, contrition, contriteness, compunction.
– OPPOSITES innocence.

guiltless adj. **innocent**, blameless, not to blame, without fault, above reproach, above suspicion, in the clear, unimpeachable, irreproachable, faultless, sinless, spotless, immaculate, unsullied, uncorrupted, undefiled, untainted, unblemished, untarnished, impeccable; informal squeaky clean, whiter than white, as pure as the driven snow.
– OPPOSITES guilty.

g

guilty adj. **1** *the guilty party* **culpable**, to blame, at fault, in the wrong, blameworthy, responsible; erring, errant, delinquent, offending, sinful, criminal; old use peccant. **2** *I still feel guilty about it* **ashamed**, guilt-ridden, conscience-stricken, remorseful, sorry, contrite, repentant, penitent, regretful, rueful, abashed, shamefaced, sheepish, hangdog; in sackcloth and ashes.
– OPPOSITES innocent, unrepentant.

guise n. **1** *the god appeared in the guise of a swan* **likeness**, outward appearance, appearance, semblance, form, shape, image; disguise. **2** *additional sums paid under the guise of consultancy fees* **pretence**, disguise, front, facade, cover, blind, screen, smokescreen.

gulf n. **1** *our ship sailed into the gulf* **inlet**, bay, creek, bight, cove, fjord, estuary, sound, arm of the sea; Scottish firth, frith. **2** *the ice gave way and a gulf widened slowly* **hole**, crevasse, fissure, cleft, split, rift, pit, cavity, chasm, abyss, void; ravine, gorge, canyon, gully. **3** *a growing gulf between rich and poor* **divide**, division, separation, gap, breach, rift, split, chasm, abyss; difference, contrast, polarity.

gull v. **hoodwink**, fool, dupe, deceive, delude, hoax, trick, mislead, lead on, take in, swindle, cheat, double-cross; informal pull the wool over someone's eyes, pull a fast one on, put one over on, sell a pup to, bamboozle, con, do; N. Amer. informal sucker, snooker; Austral. informal pull a swifty on; literary cozen.

gullet n. **oesophagus**, throat, maw, pharynx; crop, craw; old use throttle, gorge.

gullible adj. **credulous**, naive, over-trusting, over-trustful, easily deceived, easily taken in, exploitable, dupable, impressionable, unsuspecting, unsuspicious, unwary, ingenuous, innocent, inexperienced, unworldly, green; informal wet behind the ears, born yesterday.
– OPPOSITES suspicious.

gully n. **1** *a steep icy gully* **ravine**, canyon, gorge, pass, defile, couloir; S. English chine; N. English clough, gill; N. Amer. gulch, coulee. **2** *water runs from the drainpipe into a gully* **channel**, conduit, trench, ditch, drain, culvert, cut, gutter.

gulp v. **1** *she gulped her juice* **swallow**, quaff, swill down, down; informal swig, knock back; Brit. informal neck; N. Amer. informal chug. **2** *he gulped down the rest of his meal* **gobble**, guzzle, devour, bolt, wolf, cram, stuff; informal put away, demolish, polish off, shovel down, scoff. **3** *Jenny gulped back her tears* **choke back**, fight back, hold back/in, suppress, stifle, smother.
– OPPOSITES sip.
▸ n. *a gulp of cold beer* **mouthful**, swallow, draught; informal swig; N. Amer. informal chug.

gum¹ n. *photographs stuck down with gum* **glue**, adhesive, fixative, paste, epoxy resin; N. Amer. mucilage.
▸ v. *the receipts were gummed into a book* **stick**, glue, paste; fix, affix, attach, fasten.

gum² n.

WORD LINKS
gingival relating to the gums
gingivitis inflammation of the gums

gummy adj. **sticky**, tacky, gluey, adhesive, resinous, viscous, viscid, glutinous, mucilaginous; informal gooey.

gumption n. informal **initiative**, resourcefulness, enterprise, ingenuity, imagination; astuteness, shrewdness, acumen, sense, common sense, wit, mother wit, native wit, practicality; spirit, backbone, pluck, mettle, nerve, courage; informal get-up-and-go, spunk, oomph, nous, savvy, horse sense; N. Amer. informal smarts.

gun n. **firearm**, pistol, revolver, rifle, shotgun, automatic, handgun, machine gun; weapon; informal shooter; N. Amer. informal piece, shooting iron.

gunfire n. **gunshots**, shots, shooting, firing, sniping; artillery fire, strafing, shelling; cannonade, barrage, bombardment, salvo, volley, fusillade.

gunman n. **armed robber**, gangster, terrorist; sniper, gunfighter; assassin, murderer, killer; informal hitman, hired gun, gunslinger, mobster; N. Amer. informal shootist, hood.

gurgle v. *the water swirled and gurgled* **babble**, burble, tinkle, bubble, ripple, murmur, purl, splash; literary plash.
▸ n. *the gurgle of a small brook* **babbling**, tinkling, bubbling, rippling, trickling, murmur, murmuring, purling, splashing; literary plashing.

guru n. **1** *a Hindu guru and mystic* **spiritual teacher**, teacher, tutor, sage, mentor, spiritual leader, leader, master; Hinduism swami, Maharishi. **2** *a management guru* **expert**, authority, pundit, leading light, master, specialist; informal whizz.
– OPPOSITES disciple.

gush v. **1** *water gushed through the weir* **surge**, burst, spout, spurt, jet, stream, rush, pour, spill, well out, cascade, flood; flow, run, issue; Brit. informal sloosh. **2** *everyone gushed about the script* **enthuse**, rave, be enthusiastic, be effusive, rhapsodize, go into raptures, wax lyrical, praise to the skies; informal go mad/wild/crazy, go over the top; N. Amer. informal ballyhoo.
▸ n. *a gush of water* **surge**, stream, spurt, jet, spout, outpouring, outflow, burst, rush, cascade, flood, torrent; technical efflux.

gushing, gushy adj. **effusive**, enthusiastic, overenthusiastic, unrestrained, extravagant, fulsome, lavish, rhapsodic, lyrical; informal over the top, OTT, laid on with a trowel.
– OPPOSITES restrained.

gust n. **1** *a sudden gust of wind* **flurry**, blast, puff, blow, rush; squall. **2** *gusts of laughter* **outburst**, burst, eruption, fit, paroxysm; gale, peal, howl, hoot, shriek, roar.
▸ v. *wind gusted around the chimneys* **blow**, bluster, flurry, roar.

gusto n. **enthusiasm**, relish, appetite, enjoyment, delight, glee, pleasure, satisfaction, appreciation, liking; zest, zeal, fervour, verve, keenness, avidity.
– OPPOSITES apathy, distaste.

gusty adj. **blustery**, windy, breezy; squally, stormy, tempestuous, wild, turbulent; informal blowy.
– OPPOSITES calm.

gut n. **1** *he had an ache in his gut* **stomach**, belly, abdomen, solar plexus; intestines, bowels; informal tummy, tum, insides, innards. **2** *fish heads and guts* **entrails**; intestines, viscera; offal; informal insides, innards; Brit. old use numbles. **3** informal *Nicola had the guts to say what she felt* **courage**, bravery, backbone, nerve, pluck, spirit, boldness, audacity, daring, grit, fearlessness, toughness, determination; informal spunk; Brit. informal bottle; N. Amer. informal moxie.
▸ adj. informal *a gut feeling* **instinctive**, instinctual, intuitive, deep-seated; knee-jerk, automatic, involuntary, spontaneous, unthinking.
▸ v. **1** *clean, scale, and gut the sardines* **remove the guts from**, disembowel, draw; formal eviscerate. **2** *the church was gutted by fire* **devastate**, destroy, demolish, wipe out, lay waste, ravage, consume, ruin, wreck.

gutless adj. informal See **cowardly**.

gutsy adj. informal **brave**, courageous, plucky, bold, daring, fearless, adventurous, audacious, valiant, intrepid, heroic, lionhearted, undaunted, unflinching, unshrinking, unafraid, dauntless, indomitable, doughty, stout-hearted; spirited, determined, resolute, death-or-glory; informal spunky, ballsy, have-a-go.

gutter n. **drain**, sluice, sluiceway, culvert, spillway, sewer; channel, conduit, pipe; trough, trench, ditch, furrow, cut.

guttersnipe n. derogatory **urchin**, ragamuffin, waif, stray; dated gamin; old use mudlark, street Arab.

guttural adj. **throaty**, husky, gruff, gravelly, growly, growling, croaky, croaking, harsh, rough, rasping, raspy; deep, low, thick.

guy informal n. *he's a handsome guy* **man**, fellow, gentleman; youth, boy; informal lad, fella, geezer, gent; Brit. informal chap, bloke; N. Amer. informal dude, hombre; Brit. informal dated cove.
▸ v. *she guyed him about his weight* **make fun of**, poke fun at, laugh at, mock, ridicule, jeer at, scoff at; satirize, lampoon; informal send up, take the mickey out of; N. Amer. informal goof on.

guzzle v. **1** *he guzzled his burger* **gobble**, bolt, wolf, devour; informal tuck into, put away, pack away, scoff, demolish, polish off, hoover up, stuff one's face with, pig oneself on, shovel down, trough; Brit. informal shift; N. Amer. informal snarf down/up, scarf down/up. **2** *she guzzled down the orange juice* **gulp down**, swallow, quaff, down, swill; informal knock back, swig, slug down.

Gypsy, **Gipsy** n. **Romany**, Rom, chal, gitano, gitana, tzigane; traveller, nomad, rover, roamer, wanderer; dialect didicoi; Brit. derogatory tinker.

gyrate v. **rotate**, revolve, wheel, turn round, whirl, circle, pirouette, twirl, swirl, spin, swivel.

g

Hh

habit n. **1** *it was his habit to go for a run every morning* **custom**, practice, routine, pattern, convention, way, norm, tradition, matter of course, rule, usage; formal wont. **2** *her many irritating habits* **mannerism**, way, quirk, foible, trick, trait, idiosyncrasy, peculiarity, singularity, oddity, eccentricity, feature; tendency, propensity, inclination, bent, proclivity, disposition, predisposition. **3** *a scientific habit of mind* **disposition**, temperament, character, nature, make-up, constitution, frame of mind, bent. **4** informal *his cocaine habit* **addiction**, dependence, dependency, craving, fixation, compulsion, obsession, weakness; informal monkey on one's back; N. Amer. informal jones. **5** *a monk's habit* **garments**, dress, garb, clothes, clothing, attire, outfit, costume; informal gear; formal apparel.
□ **in the habit of** accustomed to, used to, given to, inclined to; literary wont to.

habitable adj. **fit to live in**, inhabitable, in good repair, liveable-in; formal tenantable.

habitat n. **natural environment**, natural surroundings, home, domain, haunt; formal habitation.

habitation n. **1** *a house fit for human habitation* **occupancy**, occupation, residence, residency, living in, tenancy; old use inhabitancy. **2** formal *his main habitation* **residence**, place of residence, house, home, seat, lodging place, billet, quarters, living quarters, rooms, accommodation; informal pad, digs; formal dwelling, dwelling place, abode, domicile.

habitual adj. **1** *her father's habitual complaints* **constant**, persistent, continual, continuous, perpetual, non-stop, recurrent, repeated, frequent; interminable, incessant, ceaseless, endless, never-ending; informal eternal. **2** *habitual drinkers* **inveterate**, confirmed, compulsive, obsessive, incorrigible, hardened, ingrained, dyed-in-the-wool, chronic, regular; addicted; informal pathological. **3** *his habitual secretiveness* **customary**, accustomed, regular, usual, normal, set, fixed, established, routine, common, ordinary, familiar, traditional, typical, general, characteristic, standard, time-honoured; literary wonted.
– OPPOSITES occasional, unaccustomed.

habituate v. **accustom**, make used, familiarize, adapt, adjust, attune, acclimatize, acculturate, condition; inure, harden; N. Amer. acclimate.

habitué n. **regular, frequent visitor**, familiar face, patron, frequenter, haunter.

hack¹ v. *I hacked the padlock off* **cut**, chop, hew, lop, saw; slash.
□ **hack it** informal cope, manage, get on/by, carry on, come through, muddle along/through; stand it, tolerate it, bear it, endure it, put up with it; informal handle it, abide it, stick it; Brit. informal be doing with it.
hack someone off informal See **annoy**.

hack² n. **1** *a tabloid hack* **journalist**, reporter, newspaperman, newspaperwoman, writer, Grub Street writer; informal journo, scribbler, hackette; old use penny-a-liner. **2** *office hacks* **drudge**, menial, menial worker, factotum, galley slave; informal gofer; Brit. informal dogsbody, skivvy. **3** *a riding-school hack* **horse**, pony; informal nag; N. Amer. informal plug; Austral./NZ informal moke.

hackle n.
□ **make someone's hackles rise** annoy, irritate, exasperate, anger, incense, infuriate, irk, nettle, vex, put out, provoke, gall, antagonize, get on someone's nerves, ruffle someone's feathers, rankle with; Brit. rub up the wrong way; informal aggravate, peeve, needle, rile, make someone see red, make someone's blood boil, hack off, get someone's back up, get someone's goat, get up someone's nose, get someone's dander up, bug, miff; Brit. informal wind up, nark, get on someone's wick; N. Amer. informal tee off, tick off, burn up; informal dated give someone the pip.

hackneyed adj. **overused**, overdone, overworked, worn out, time-worn, platitudinous, vapid, stale, tired, threadbare; trite, banal, hack, clichéd, hoary, commonplace, common, ordinary, stock, conventional, stereotyped, predictable; unimaginative, unoriginal, uninspired, prosaic, dull, boring, pedestrian, run-of-the-mill, routine; informal old hat, corny, played out.
– OPPOSITES original.

Hades n. See **hell** (sense 1).

haft n. **handle**, shaft, hilt, butt, stock, grip, handgrip, helve, shank.

hag n. **crone**, old woman, gorgon; informal witch, crow, cow, old bag, old boot; old use beldam.

haggard adj. **drawn**, tired, exhausted, drained, careworn, unwell, unhealthy, spent, washed out, rundown; gaunt, pinched,

peaked, peaky, hollow-cheeked, hollow-eyed, thin, emaciated, wasted, cadaverous; pale, wan, grey, ashen.
– OPPOSITES healthy.

haggle v. **barter**, bargain, negotiate, dicker, quibble, wrangle; beat someone down, drive a hard bargain; old use chaffer.

hail[1] v. **1** *a friend hailed him from the upper deck* **call out to**, shout to, halloo, address; greet, say hello to, salute. **2** *he hailed a cab* **flag down**, wave down, signal to. **3** *critics hailed the film as a masterpiece* **acclaim**, praise, applaud, rave about, extol, eulogize, hymn, lionize, sing the praises of, make much of, glorify, cheer, salute, toast; informal big up; N. Amer. informal ballyhoo; formal laud. **4** *Rick hails from Australia* **come from**, be from, be a native of, have one's roots in.

hail[2] n. *a hail of bullets* **barrage**, volley, shower, rain, torrent, burst, stream, storm, avalanche, onslaught; bombardment, cannonade, battery, blast, salvo; historical broadside.
▸ v. *tons of dust hailed down on us* **beat**, shower, rain, fall, pour; pelt, pepper, batter, bombard, assail.

hail-fellow-well-met adj. **convivial**, sociable, outgoing, gregarious, companionable, friendly, genial, affable, amiable, congenial, agreeable, good-humoured; extrovert, uninhibited; Scottish couthy; informal backslapping, chummy, pally, clubbable, clubby, buddy-buddy; Brit. informal matey.
– OPPOSITES unsociable.

hair n. **1** *her thick black hair* **head of hair**, shock of hair, mane, mop; locks, tresses, curls, ringlets. **2** *I like your hair* **hairstyle**, haircut, cut, coiffure; informal hairdo, do, coif. **3** *a dog with short, blue-grey hair* **fur**, wool; coat, fleece, pelt; mane.
□ **a hair's breadth** the narrowest of margins, a narrow margin, the skin of one's teeth, a split second, a nose; informal a whisker. **let one's hair down** informal enjoy oneself, have a good time, have fun, make merry, let oneself go; informal have a ball, whoop it up, paint the town red, live it up, have a whale of a time, let it all hang out.
make someone's hair stand on end horrify, shock, appal, scandalize, stun; make someone's blood run cold; informal make someone's hair curl.
split hairs quibble, cavil, carp, niggle, chop logic; informal nitpick; old use pettifog.

WORD LINKS

trichology the branch of medicine concerned with the hair and scalp
alopecia abnormal hair loss
hirsute having a great deal of hair
depilatory used to remove unwanted hair

---

hairdo n. informal See **hairstyle**.

hairdresser n. **hairstylist**, stylist, coiffeur, coiffeuse; barber; informal crimper.

hairless adj. **bald**, bald-headed; shaven, shaved, shorn, clean-shaven, beardless, smooth, smooth-faced, depilated; tonsured; informal baldy; technical glabrous; old use bald-pated.
– OPPOSITES hairy.

hairpiece n. **wig**, toupee, periwig; merkin; informal rug.

hair-raising adj. **terrifying**, frightening, petrifying, alarming, chilling, horrifying, shocking, spine-chilling, blood-curdling, fearsome, nightmarish; eerie, sinister, weird, ghostly, unearthly; Scottish eldritch; informal hairy, spooky, scary, creepy.

hair-splitting adj. **pedantic**, pettifogging, quibbling, niggling, cavilling, carping, critical, overcritical, hypercritical; informal nitpicking, pernickety, picky; N. Amer. informal persnickety.

hairstyle n. **haircut**, cut, style, hair, coiffure; informal hairdo, do, coif.

hairy adj. **1** *animals with hairy coats* **shaggy**, bushy, long-haired; woolly, furry, fleecy, fuzzy; Botany & Zoology pilose. **2** *his hairy face* **bearded**, bewhiskered, mustachioed; unshaven, stubbly, bristly; formal hirsute. **3** informal *a hairy situation* **risky**, dangerous, perilous, hazardous, touch-and-go; tricky, ticklish, difficult, awkward; informal dicey, sticky; Brit. informal dodgy.

halcyon adj. **happy**, golden, idyllic, palmy, carefree, blissful, joyful, joyous, contented; flourishing, thriving, prosperous, successful; serene, calm, tranquil, peaceful.

hale adj. **healthy**, fit, fighting fit, well, in good health, in fine fettle, as fit as a fiddle/flea; strong, robust, vigorous, hardy, sturdy, hearty, lusty, able-bodied; informal in the pink, as right as rain.

half adj. *a half grapefruit* **halved**, divided in two.
– OPPOSITES whole.
▸ adv. **1** *half-cooked chicken* **partially**, partly, incompletely, inadequately, insufficiently; in part, part, slightly. **2** *I'm half inclined to believe you* **to a certain extent/degree**, to some extent/degree, (up) to a point, in part, partly, in some measure.
– OPPOSITES fully.

half-baked adj. **1** *half-baked theories* **ill-conceived**, hare-brained, ill-judged, impractical, unrealistic, unworkable, ridiculous, absurd; informal crazy, crackpot, cockeyed. **2** *her half-baked young nephew* **foolish**, stupid, silly, idiotic, simple-minded, feeble-minded, empty-headed, feather-brained, feather-headed, brainless, witless, unintelligent, ignorant; informal dim, dopey, dumb, gormless, thick, half-witted, dim-witted, birdbrained; Brit. informal daft, divvy, dozy.
– OPPOSITES sensible.

half-hearted adj. **unenthusiastic**, cool, lukewarm, tepid, apathetic, indifferent, uninterested, unconcerned, languid, listless; perfunctory, cursory, superficial, desultory, feeble, lacklustre.
– OPPOSITES enthusiastic.

h

halfway adj. *the halfway point* **midway**, middle, mid, central, centre, intermediate; Anatomy medial, mesial.
▶adv. **1** *he stopped halfway down the passage* **midway**, in the middle, in the centre; part of the way, part-way. **2** *he seemed halfway friendly* **to some extent/degree**, in some measure, relatively, comparatively, moderately, somewhat, (up) to a point; just about, almost, nearly.
□ **meet someone halfway** compromise, come to terms, reach an agreement, make a deal, make concessions, find the middle ground, strike a balance; give and take.

halfwit n. informal See **fool** (sense 1 of the noun).

half-witted adj. informal See **stupid** (senses 1 & 2).

hall n. **1** *hang your coat in the hall* **entrance hall**, hallway, entry, entrance, lobby, foyer, vestibule; atrium, concourse; passageway, passage, corridor; N. Amer. entryway. **2** *the village hall* **assembly room**, meeting room, chamber; auditorium, concert hall, theatre.

hallmark n. **1** *the hallmark on silver* **assay mark**, official mark, stamp of authenticity. **2** *the tiny bubbles are the hallmark of fine champagnes* **mark**, distinctive feature, characteristic, sign, sure sign, telltale sign, badge, stamp, trademark, indication, indicator.

halloo v. **call out**, shout, cry out, yell, bawl, bellow, roar, whoop; hail, greet; informal holler, yoo-hoo, cooee.

hallowed adj. **holy**, sacred, blessed, consecrated, sanctified; revered, venerated, honoured, sacrosanct, worshipped, divine, inviolable.

hallucinate v. **have hallucinations**, see things, be delirious, fantasize; informal trip, see pink elephants.

hallucination n. **delusion**, illusion, figment of the imagination, vision, apparition, mirage, chimera, fantasy; (**hallucinations**) delirium, phantasmagoria; informal trip, pink elephants.

halo n. **ring of light**, nimbus, aureole, glory, crown of light, corona; technical halation; rare gloriole.

halt v. **1** *Len halted and turned round* **stop**, come to a halt, come to a stop, come to a standstill; pull up, draw up. **2** *a further strike has halted production* **stop**, bring to a stop, put a stop to, bring to an end, put an end to, terminate, end, wind up; suspend, break off, arrest; impede, check, curb, stem, staunch, block, stall, hold back; informal pull the plug on, put the kibosh on.
– OPPOSITES start, continue.
▶n. **1** *the car drew to a halt* **stop**, standstill. **2** *a halt in production* **stoppage**, stopping, discontinuation, break, suspension, pause, interval, interruption, hiatus; cessation, termination, close, end.

halter n. **harness**, head collar, bridle; N. Amer. headstall.

halting adj. **1** *a halting conversation* | *halting English* **hesitant**, faltering, hesitating, stumbling, stammering, stuttering; broken, imperfect. **2** *his halting gait* **unsteady**, awkward, faltering, stumbling, limping, hobbling.
– OPPOSITES fluent.

ham-fisted adj. **clumsy**, bungling, incompetent, amateurish, inept, unskilful, inexpert, maladroit, gauche, awkward, inefficient, bumbling, useless; informal cack-handed, ham-handed; Brit. informal all fingers and thumbs.
– OPPOSITES expert.

hammer n. *a hammer and chisel* **mallet**, beetle, gavel, sledgehammer.
▶v. **1** *the alloy is hammered into a circular shape* **beat**, forge, shape, form, mould, fashion, make. **2** *Sally hammered at the door* **batter**, pummel, beat, bang, pound; strike, hit, knock on, thump on; cudgel, bludgeon, club; informal bash, wallop, clobber, whack, thwack. **3** *they hammered away at their non-smoking campaign* **work hard**, labour, slog away, plod away, grind away, slave away, work like a Trojan, work like a dog, keep one's nose to the grindstone; persist with, persevere with, press on with; informal stick at, peg away, beaver away, plug away, work one's socks off, soldier on; Brit. informal graft away. **4** *anti-racism had been hammered into her* **drum**, instil, inculcate, knock, drive, din; drive home to, impress on; ingrain.
□ **hammer something out** thrash out, work out, agree on, sort out, decide on, bring about, effect, produce, broker, negotiate, reach an agreement on.

hamper[1] n. *a picnic hamper* **basket**, pannier, wickerwork basket; box, container, holder.

hamper[2] v. *the search was hampered by fog* **hinder**, obstruct, impede, inhibit, retard, balk, thwart, foil, curb, delay, set back, slow down, hold up, interfere with; restrict, constrain, trammel, block, check, curtail, frustrate, cramp, bridle, handicap, cripple, hamstring, shackle, fetter; N. Amer. bork; informal stymie.
– OPPOSITES help.

hamstring v. **1** *cattle were killed or hamstrung* **cripple**, lame, disable, incapacitate. **2** *manufacturing companies were hamstrung by the economic chaos* **handicap**, constrain, restrict, cripple, shackle, fetter, encumber, block, frustrate; hamper, hinder, obstruct, impede, trammel, straitjacket, inhibit, balk, thwart, foil; informal stymie; N. Amer. informal bork.
– OPPOSITES help.

hand n. **1** *big, strong hands* **palm**, fist; informal paw, mitt, duke, hook, meat hook; Zoology manus. **2** *the clock's second hand* **pointer**, indicator, needle, arrow, marker. **3** *the frontier posts remained in government hands* **control**, power, charge, authority; command, responsibility, guardianship, management, care, supervision, jurisdiction; possession, keeping, custody; clutches, grasp, thrall; disposal; informal say-so. **4** *let me give you* *a hand* **help**, a helping hand, assistance, aid, support, succour, relief; a good turn, a favour. **5** informal *his fans gave him a big hand* **round of applause**, clap, handclap, ovation, standing ovation; applause, handclapping. **6** *a document written in his own hand* **handwriting**, writing, script, calligraphy. **7** *a factory hand* **worker**, factory worker, manual worker, unskilled worker, blue-collar worker, workman, labourer, operative, hired hand, roustabout; N. Amer. peon; Austral./NZ rouseabout.

▸ **v. 1** *he handed each man a glass* **pass**, give, reach, let someone have, throw, toss; present to; informal chuck, bung. **2** *he handed him into a carriage* **assist**, help, give someone a hand; guide.

▫ **at hand 1** *keep the manual close at hand* **readily available**, available, handy, to hand, within reach, accessible, close (by), near, nearby, at the ready, at one's fingertips, at one's disposal, convenient; informal get-at-able. **2** *the time for starting the campaign is at hand* **imminent**, approaching, coming, about to happen, on the horizon, impending.
hand something down pass on, pass down; bequeath, will, leave, make over, give, gift, transfer; Law demise, devise.
hand in glove in close collaboration, in close association, in close cooperation, very closely, in partnership, in league, in collusion; informal in cahoots.
hand something on give, pass, hand, transfer, grant, cede, surrender, relinquish, yield; part with, let go of; bequeath, will, leave.
hand something out distribute, hand round, give out/round, pass out/round, share out, dole out, dish out, deal out, mete out, issue, dispense; allocate, allot, apportion, disburse; circulate, disseminate.
hand something over yield, give, give up, pass, grant, entrust, surrender, relinquish, cede, turn over, deliver up, forfeit, sacrifice.
to hand readily available, available, handy, at hand, within reach, accessible, ready, close (by), near, nearby, at the ready, at one's fingertips, at one's disposal, convenient; informal get-at-able.
try one's hand have a go, make an attempt; attempt, try, try out, give something a try; informal have a stab, have a shot, have a bash, give something a whirl; formal essay.

WORD LINKS

manual relating to the hands
ambidextrous able to use either hand equally well
dexterity skill in using the hands
artisan a skilled worker who makes things by hand
palmate shaped like an open hand
palmistry the prediction of a person's future by examining their hand

---

handbag n. **bag**, shoulder bag, clutch bag, evening bag, pochette; N. Amer. purse, pocketbook; historical reticule.

handbill n. **notice**, advertisement, flyer, leaflet, circular, handout, pamphlet, brochure; N. Amer. dodger; informal ad; Brit. informal advert.

handbook n. **manual**, instructions, instruction manual, ABC, A to Z; almanac, companion, directory, compendium; guide, guidebook, vade mecum.

handcuff v. **manacle**, shackle, fetter; restrain, clap/put someone in irons; informal cuff.

handcuffs plural n. **manacles**, shackles, irons, fetters, bonds, restraints; informal cuffs, bracelets; old use darbies, gyves.

handful n. **1** *a handful of British firms* **a few**, a small number, a small amount, a small quantity, one or two, some, not many, a scattering, a trickle. **2** informal *the child is a real handful* **nuisance**, problem, bother, irritant, thorn in someone's flesh/side; informal pest, headache, pain, pain in the neck/backside; Scottish informal nyaff, skelf; N. Amer. informal pain in the butt.

handgun n. **pistol**, revolver, gun, side arm, six-shooter, thirty-eight, derringer; N. Amer. informal piece, shooting iron, Saturday night special, rod; trademark Colt.

handicap n. **1** *a visual handicap* **disability**, physical/mental abnormality, defect, impairment, affliction, deficiency. **2** *a handicap to the competitiveness of the industry* **impediment**, hindrance, obstacle, barrier, bar, obstruction, encumbrance, constraint, restriction, check, block, curb; disadvantage, drawback, stumbling block, difficulty, shortcoming, limitation; ball and chain, albatross, millstone round someone's neck; literary trammel.
– OPPOSITES benefit, advantage.
▸ **v.** *lack of funding handicapped the research* **hamper**, impede, hinder, impair, hamstring; restrict, check, obstruct, block, curb, bridle, hold back, constrain, trammel, limit, encumber; informal stymie; N. Amer. informal bork.
– OPPOSITES help.

handicapped adj. **disabled**, incapacitated, disadvantaged; infirm, invalid; euphemistic physically challenged, differently abled.

handicraft n. **craft**, handiwork, craftwork; craftsmanship, workmanship, artisanship, art, skill.

handiwork n. *jewellery which is the handiwork of Chinese smiths* **creation**, product, work, achievement; handicraft, craft, craftwork.

handkerchief n. pocket handkerchief, tissue, paper handkerchief; trademark Kleenex; informal hanky, nose rag, snot rag; literary kerchief.

handle v. **1** *the equipment must be handled with care* **hold**, pick up, grasp, grip, lift; feel, touch, finger; informal paw. **2** *a car which is easy to handle* **control**, drive, steer, operate, manoeuvre, manipulate. **3** *she handled the job formidably* **deal with**, manage, tackle, take care of, take forward, take charge of, attend to, see to, sort out, apply oneself to,

h

h

take in hand. **4** *the advertising company that is handling the account* **administer**, manage, control, conduct, direct, guide, supervise, oversee, be in charge of, take care of, look after. **5** *the traders handled goods manufactured in the Rhineland* **trade in**, deal in, buy, sell, supply, peddle, traffic in, purvey, hawk; tout, market.
▸n. *the knife's handle* **haft**, shank, stock, shaft, grip, handgrip, hilt, helve, butt; knob.

hand-me-down adj. **second-hand**, used, nearly new, handed-down, passed-on, cast-off, worn, old, pre-owned; Brit. informal reach-me-down.
– OPPOSITES new.

handout n. **1** *she existed on handouts* **charity**, aid, benefit, financial support, donations, subsidies; historical alms. **2** *a xeroxed handout* **leaflet**, pamphlet, brochure; handbill, flyer, notice, circular, mailshot.

hand-picked adj. **specially chosen**, selected, invited; select, elite; choice.

handsome adj. **1** *a handsome man* **good-looking**, attractive, personable, striking; informal hunky, dishy, tasty, fanciable; Brit. informal fit; N. Amer. informal cute; Austral./NZ informal spunky. **2** *a handsome woman of 30* **striking**, imposing, prepossessing, elegant, stately, dignified, statuesque, good-looking, attractive, personable. **3** *a handsome profit* **substantial**, considerable, sizeable, princely, large, big, ample, bumper; informal tidy, whopping, not to be sneezed at; Brit. informal whacking, ginormous.
– OPPOSITES ugly, meagre.

handwriting n. **writing**, script, hand, pen; penmanship, calligraphy, chirography; informal scrawl, scribble.

> **WORD LINKS**
> **holograph, autograph** a manuscript handwritten by its author
> **graphology** the study of handwriting

handy adj. **1** *a handy reference tool* **useful**, convenient, practical, easy-to-use, well-designed, user-friendly, user-oriented, helpful, functional, serviceable. **2** *keep your credit card handy* **readily available**, available, at hand, to hand, near at hand, within reach, accessible, ready, close (by), near, nearby, at the ready, at one's fingertips; informal get-at-able. **3** *he's handy with a needle* **skilful**, skilled, dexterous, deft, nimble-fingered, adroit, able, adept, proficient, capable; good with one's hands; informal nifty.
– OPPOSITES inconvenient, inept.

handyman n. **odd-job man**, odd-jobber, factotum, jack of all trades, man of all work; DIY'er; informal Mr Fixit.

hang v. **1** *lights hung from the trees* **be suspended**, hang down, be pendent, dangle, swing, sway; old use depend. **2** *hang your pictures at eye level* **put up**, fix, attach, affix, fasten, post, display, suspend, pin up, nail up. **3** *the room was hung with streamers* **decorate**, adorn, drape, festoon, deck out, trick out, bedeck, array, garland, swathe,

cover, ornament; literary bedizen. **4** *he was hanged for murder* **send to the gallows**, execute; informal string up. **5** *a pall of smoke hung over the city* **hover**, float, drift, be suspended. **6** *the threat of budget cuts is hanging over us* **be imminent**, threaten, be close, be impending, impend, loom, be on the horizon.
□ **hang about** Brit. informal See **hang around**.
hang around informal **1** *they spent their time hanging around in bars* **loiter**, linger, wait around, waste time, kill time, mark time, while away the time, kick/cool one's heels, twiddle one's thumbs; frequent, haunt; informal hang out in. **2** *she's hanging around with a bunch of hippies* **associate**, mix, keep company, socialize, fraternize, consort, rub shoulders; N. Amer. rub elbows; informal hang out, run around, knock about/around, be thick, hobnob.
hang fire delay, hang back, hold back, hold on, stall, pause; procrastinate, vacillate, adopt Fabian tactics; informal hang about/around, sit tight, hold one's horses.
hang on 1 *he hung on to her coat* **hold on**, hold fast, grip, clutch, grasp, hold tightly, cling. **2** *her future hung on his decision* **depend on**, be dependent on, turn on, hinge on, rest on, be contingent on, be determined by, be decided by. **3** *I'll hang on as long as I can* **persevere**, hold out, hold on, go on, carry on, keep on, keep going, keep at it, continue, persist, stay with it, struggle on, plod on, plough on; informal soldier on, stick at it, stick it out, hang in there. **4** informal *hang on, let me think* **wait**, wait a minute, hold on, stop; hold the line; informal hold your horses, sit tight; Brit. informal hang about.

hangdog adj. **shamefaced**, sheepish, abashed, ashamed, guilty-looking, abject, cowed, dejected, downcast, crestfallen, woebegone, disconsolate.
– OPPOSITES unabashed.

hanger-on n. **follower**, flunkey, toady, camp follower, sycophant, parasite, leech; henchman, minion, lackey, vassal, dependant, retainer; acolyte; N. Amer. cohort; informal groupie, sponger, freeloader, passenger, sidekick.

hanging n. *silk wall hangings* **drape**, curtain; drapery.
▸adj. *hanging fronds of honeysuckle* **pendent**, dangling, trailing, tumbling; suspended.

hang-out n. **haunt**, stamping ground, favourite spot, meeting place, territory; den, refuge, retreat; N. Amer. stomping ground.

hang-up n. **neurosis**, phobia, preoccupation, fixation, obsession, idée fixe; inhibition, mental block, psychological block, block, difficulty; informal complex, thing, bee in one's bonnet.

hank n. **coil**, skein, length, roll, loop, twist, piece; lock, ringlet, curl.

hanker v. **yearn**, long, crave, desire, wish, want, hunger, thirst, lust, ache, pant, be eager, be desperate, be eating one's heart out; fancy, pine for, have one's heart set on;

informal **be dying**, **have a yen**, **itch**.

hankering n. **longing**, yearning, craving, desire, wish, hunger, thirst, urge, ache, lust, appetite, fancy; informal yen, itch; old use appetency.
– OPPOSITES aversion.

hanky-panky n. informal **goings-on**, funny business, mischief, misbehaviour, misconduct, chicanery, dishonesty, deception, deceit, trickery, intrigue, skulduggery, subterfuge, machinations; infidelity, unfaithfulness, adultery; informal monkey business, shenanigans, carryings-on; Brit. informal jiggery-pokery.

haphazard adj. **random**, unplanned, unsystematic, unmethodical, disorganized, disorderly, irregular, indiscriminate, chaotic, hit-and-miss, arbitrary, aimless, careless, casual, slapdash, slipshod; chance, accidental; informal higgledy-piggledy.
– OPPOSITES methodical.

hapless adj. **unfortunate**, unlucky, luckless, out of luck, ill-starred, ill-fated, jinxed, cursed, doomed; unhappy, forlorn, wretched, miserable, woebegone; informal down on one's luck; literary star-crossed.
– OPPOSITES lucky.

happen v. **1** *remember what happened last time he was here* **occur**, take place, come about; ensue, result, transpire, materialize, arise, crop up, come up, present itself, supervene; N. Amer. informal go down; formal eventuate; literary come to pass, betide; old use hap. **2** *I wonder what happened to Susie?* **become of**; literary befall, betide. **3** *they happened to be in London* **chance**, have the good/bad luck. **4** *he happened on a linnet's nest* **discover**, find, find by chance, come across, chance on, stumble on, hit on.

happening n. *bizarre happenings* **occurrence**, event, incident, proceeding, affair, circumstance, phenomenon, episode, experience, occasion, development, eventuality.
▸ adj. informal *a happening nightspot* **fashionable**, modern, popular, new, latest, up to date, up to the minute, in fashion, in vogue, le dernier cri; informal trendy, funky, hot, cool, with it, hip, in, big, now, groovy; N. Amer. informal kicky, tony.
– OPPOSITES old-fashioned.

happily adv. **1** *he smiled happily* **contentedly**, cheerfully, cheerily, merrily, delightedly, joyfully, joyously, gaily, gleefully. **2** *I will happily do as you ask* **gladly**, willingly, readily, freely, cheerfully, ungrudgingly, with pleasure; old use fain. **3** *happily, we are living in enlightened times* **fortunately**, luckily, thankfully, mercifully, by good luck, by good fortune, as luck would have it; thank goodness, thank God, thank heavens.

happiness n. **pleasure**, contentment, satisfaction, cheerfulness, merriment, gaiety, joy, joyfulness, joviality, jollity, glee, delight, good spirits, light-heartedness, well-being, enjoyment; exuberance, exhilaration, elation, ecstasy, jubilation, rapture, bliss, blissfulness, euphoria, transports of delight.

happy adj. **1** *Melissa looked happy and excited* **cheerful**, cheery, merry, joyful, jovial, jolly, jocular, gleeful, carefree, untroubled, delighted, smiling, beaming, grinning, in good spirits, in a good mood, light-hearted, pleased, contented, content, satisfied, gratified, buoyant, radiant, sunny, joyous, beatific; thrilled, elated, exhilarated, ecstatic, blissful, euphoric, overjoyed, exultant, rapturous, in seventh heaven, on cloud nine, walking on air, jumping for joy, cock-a-hoop, jubilant; informal chirpy, over the moon, on top of the world, as happy as a sandboy, tickled pink, like a dog with two tails, as pleased as Punch, on a high; Brit. informal chuffed, as happy as Larry; N. English informal made up; N. Amer. informal as happy as a clam; Austral. informal wrapped; literary blithe; formal jocund; dated gay. **2** *we will be happy to advise you* **glad**, pleased, delighted; willing, ready, disposed. **3** *a happy coincidence* **fortunate**, lucky, favourable, advantageous, opportune, timely, well-timed, convenient.
– OPPOSITES sad, unwilling, unfortunate.

happy-go-lucky adj. **easy-going**, carefree, casual, free and easy, devil-may-care, blithe, nonchalant, insouciant, blasé, unconcerned, untroubled, unworried, light-hearted; informal laid-back.
– OPPOSITES anxious.

harangue n. *a ten-minute harangue* **tirade**, diatribe, lecture, polemic, rant, fulmination, broadside, attack, onslaught; criticism, condemnation, censure, admonition; declamation, speech; informal blast; literary philippic.
▸ v. *he harangued his erstwhile colleagues* **rant at**, hold forth to, lecture, shout at; berate, criticize, attack; informal earbash, sound off at, mouth off at.

harass v. **1** *council tenants who harass their neighbours* **persecute**, intimidate, hound, harry, plague, torment, bedevil, pressurize; pester, bother, worry, disturb, trouble, provoke, stress; informal hassle, bug, give someone a hard time; N. English informal mither; N. Amer. informal devil, ride. **2** *they were sent to harass the enemy flanks* **harry**, attack, beleaguer, set upon, assail.

harassed adj. **stressed**, strained, worn out, hard-pressed, careworn, worried, troubled, beleaguered, under pressure, at the end of one's tether; N. Amer. at the end of one's rope; informal hassled; Brit. informal under the cosh.
– OPPOSITES carefree.

harassment n. **persecution**, intimidation, pressure, pressurization, force, coercion; informal hassle.

harbinger n. **herald**, sign, indication, signal, portent, omen, augury, forewarning, presage; forerunner, precursor, messenger; literary foretoken.

harbour n. **1** *a picturesque harbour* **port**, dock, haven, marina; mooring, moorage, anchorage, harbourage; waterfront. **2** *a safe harbour for me* **refuge**, haven, safe haven,

h

shelter, sanctuary, retreat, place of safety, port in a storm.

▸v. **1** *he is harbouring a dangerous criminal* **shelter**, conceal, hide, shield, protect, give sanctuary to; take in, put up, accommodate, house. **2** *Rose had harboured a grudge against him* **bear**, nurse, nurture, cherish, entertain, foster, hold on to, cling to.

hard adj. **1** *hard ground* **firm**, solid, rigid, stiff, resistant, unbreakable, inflexible, impenetrable, unyielding, solidified, hardened, compact, compacted, dense, close-packed, compressed; steely, tough, strong, stony, rock-like, flinty, as hard as iron, as hard as stone; frozen; literary adamantine. **2** *hard physical work* **arduous**, strenuous, tiring, fatiguing, exhausting, wearying, back-breaking, gruelling, heavy, laborious; difficult, taxing, exacting, testing, challenging, demanding, punishing, tough, formidable, onerous, rigorous, uphill, Herculean; informal murderous, killing, hellish; Brit. informal knackering; formal exigent; old use toilsome. **3** *hard workers* **diligent**, hard-working, industrious, sedulous, assiduous, conscientious, energetic, keen, enthusiastic, zealous, earnest, persevering, persistent, unflagging, untiring, indefatigable; studious. **4** *a hard problem* **difficult**, puzzling, perplexing, baffling, bewildering, mystifying, knotty, thorny, problematic, complicated, complex, intricate, involved; insoluble, unfathomable, impenetrable, incomprehensible, unanswerable. **5** *times are hard* **harsh**, grim, difficult, bad, bleak, dire, tough, austere, unpleasant, uncomfortable, straitened, spartan; dark, distressing, painful, awful. **6** *a hard taskmaster* **strict**, harsh, firm, severe, stern, tough, rigorous, demanding, exacting; callous, unkind, unsympathetic, cold, heartless, hard-hearted, unfeeling; intransigent, unbending, uncompromising, inflexible, implacable, stubborn, obdurate, unyielding, unrelenting, unsparing, grim, ruthless, merciless, pitiless, cruel. **7** *a hard winter* **bitterly cold**, cold, bitter, harsh, severe, bleak, freezing, icy, icy-cold, arctic. **8** *a hard blow* **forceful**, heavy, strong, sharp, smart, violent, powerful, vigorous, mighty, hefty, tremendous. **9** *hard facts* **reliable**, definite, true, confirmed, substantiated, undeniable, indisputable, unquestionable, verifiable. **10** *hard liquor* **alcoholic**, strong, intoxicating, potent; formal spirituous. **11** *hard drugs* **addictive**, habit-forming; strong, harmful.
– OPPOSITES soft, easy, lazy, gentle.

▸adv. **1** *George pushed her hard* **forcefully**, forcibly, roughly, powerfully, strongly, heavily, sharply, vigorously, energetically, with all one's might, with might and main. **2** *they worked hard* **diligently**, industriously, assiduously, conscientiously, sedulously, busily, enthusiastically, energetically, doggedly, steadily; informal like mad, like crazy; Brit. informal like billy-o. **3** *this prosperity has been hard won* **with difficulty**, with effort, after a struggle, painfully, laboriously. **4** *her death hit him hard* **severely**, badly, acutely, deeply, keenly, seriously, profoundly, gravely; formal grievously. **5** *it was raining hard* **heavily**, strongly, in torrents, cats and dogs; steadily. **6** *my mother looked hard at me* **closely**, attentively, intently, critically, carefully, keenly, searchingly, earnestly, sharply.
□ **hard and fast** definite, fixed, set, strict, rigid, binding, clear-cut, cast-iron; inflexible, immutable, unchangeable, incontestable.
hard feelings resentment, animosity, ill feeling, ill will, bitterness, bad blood, resentfulness, rancour, malice, acrimony, antagonism, antipathy, animus, friction, anger, hostility, hate, hatred.
hard up informal poor, short of money, badly off, impoverished, impecunious, in reduced circumstances, unable to make ends meet; penniless, destitute, poverty-stricken; informal broke, strapped (for cash); Brit. informal skint.

hard-bitten adj. **hardened**, tough, cynical, unsentimental, hard-headed, case-hardened, as hard as nails; informal hard-nosed, hard-boiled.
– OPPOSITES sentimental.

hard-boiled adj. informal *a hard-boiled undercover agent*. See **hard-bitten**.

hard-core adj. **diehard**, staunch, dedicated, committed, steadfast, dyed-in-the-wool, long-standing; hard-line, extreme, entrenched, radical, intransigent, uncompromising, rigid; informal deep-dyed.

harden v. **1** *this glue will harden in four hours* **solidify**, set, congeal, clot, coagulate, stiffen, thicken, cake, inspissate; freeze, crystallize; ossify, petrify. **2** *their suffering had hardened them* **toughen**, desensitize, inure, case-harden, harden someone's heart; deaden, numb, benumb, anaesthetize; brutalize.
– OPPOSITES liquefy, soften.

hardened adj. **1** *he was hardened to the violence he had seen* **inured**, desensitized, deadened; accustomed, habituated, acclimatized, used. **2** *a hardened criminal* **inveterate**, seasoned, habitual, chronic, compulsive, confirmed, dyed-in-the-wool; incorrigible, incurable, irredeemable, unregenerate. **3** *the silos are hardened against air attack* **strengthened**, fortified, reinforced, toughened.

hard-headed adj. **unsentimental**, practical, pragmatic, businesslike, realistic, sensible, rational, clear-thinking, cool-headed, down-to-earth, matter-of-fact, no-nonsense, with one's/both feet on the ground; tough, hard-bitten; shrewd, astute, sharp, sharp-witted; informal hard-nosed, hard-boiled.

hard-hearted adj. **unfeeling**, heartless, cold, hard, callous, unsympathetic, uncaring, unloving, unconcerned, indifferent, unmoved, unkind, uncharitable, unemotional, cold-hearted, cold-blooded, mean-spirited, stony-hearted, having a heart of stone, as hard as nails, cruel.
– OPPOSITES compassionate.

hard-hitting adj. **uncompromising**, blunt, forthright, frank, honest, direct, tough; critical, unsparing, strongly worded, straight-talking, pulling no punches, not mincing one's words, not beating about the bush.

hardihood n. **bravery**, courage, pluck, valour, intrepidity, nerve, daring, fearlessness, audacity, boldness, dauntlessness, stout-heartedness, heroism; backbone, grit, spine, spirit, mettle; informal guts, spunk; Brit. informal bottle; N. Amer. informal moxie.
– OPPOSITES timidity.

hardiness n. **robustness**, strength, toughness, ruggedness, sturdiness, resilience, stamina, vigour; healthiness, good health.
– OPPOSITES frailty.

hard-line adj. **uncompromising**, strict, extreme, tough, diehard, inflexible, intransigent, intractable, unyielding, single-minded, not giving an inch.
– OPPOSITES moderate.

hardly adv. *we hardly know each other* **scarcely**, barely, only just, slightly.

hard-nosed adj. informal **tough-minded**, unsentimental, no-nonsense, hard-headed, hard-bitten, pragmatic, realistic, down-to-earth, practical, rational, shrewd, astute, businesslike; informal hard-boiled.
– OPPOSITES sentimental.

hard-pressed adj. **1** *the hard-pressed infantry* **under attack**, hotly pursued, harried. **2** *the hard-pressed construction industry* **in difficulties**, under pressure, troubled, beleaguered, harassed, with one's back to/against the wall, in a tight corner, in a tight spot, between a rock and a hard place; overburdened, overworked, overloaded, rushed off one's feet; informal pushed, up against it; Brit. informal under the cosh.

hardship n. **privation**, deprivation, destitution, poverty, austerity, penury, want, need, neediness, impecuniousness; misfortune, distress, suffering, affliction, trouble, pain, misery, wretchedness, tribulation, adversity, trials, trials and tribulations, dire straits; literary travails.
– OPPOSITES prosperity, ease.

hardware n. **equipment**, apparatus, gear, paraphernalia, tackle, kit, machinery; tools, articles, implements, instruments, appliances.

hard-wearing adj. **durable**, strong, tough, resilient, lasting, long-lasting, made to last, stout, well made, rugged, heavy-duty.
– OPPOSITES flimsy.

hard-working adj. **diligent**, industrious, conscientious, assiduous, sedulous, painstaking, persevering, unflagging, untiring, tireless, indefatigable, studious; keen, enthusiastic, zealous, driven.
– OPPOSITES lazy.

hardy adj. **robust**, healthy, fit, strong, sturdy, tough, rugged, hearty, lusty, vigorous, hale and hearty, fit as a fiddle, fighting fit, in fine

fettle, in good health, in good condition; Brit. in rude health; dated stalwart.
– OPPOSITES delicate.

hare-brained adj. **1** *a hare-brained scheme* **ill-judged**, rash, foolish, foolhardy, reckless, madcap, wild, silly, stupid, ridiculous, absurd, idiotic, asinine, imprudent, impracticable, unworkable, unrealistic, unconsidered, half-baked, ill-thought-out, ill-advised, ill-conceived; informal crackpot, crackbrained, cockeyed, crazy; Brit. informal daft, barmy. **2** *a hare-brained young girl* **foolish**, silly, idiotic, unintelligent, empty-headed, scatterbrained, feather-brained, birdbrained, pea-brained, brainless, giddy; informal dippy, dizzy, dopey, dotty, airheaded.
– OPPOSITES sensible, intelligent.

harem n. **seraglio**, zenana; historical gynaeceum.

hark v. literary *hark, I hear a warning note* **listen**, lend an ear, pay attention, attend, mark; old use hearken, give ear.
□ **hark back to** recall, call/bring to mind, evoke, put one in mind of.

harlequin n. **jester**, joker, merry andrew.
▶ adj. *a harlequin pattern* **multicoloured**, many-coloured, colourful, particoloured, varicoloured, many-hued, rainbow, variegated, jazzy, kaleidoscopic, psychedelic, polychromatic, chequered; old use motley.

harm n. **1** *the voltage is not sufficient to cause harm* **injury**, hurt, pain, trauma; damage, impairment, mischief. **2** *I can't see any harm in it* **wrong**, ill, wickedness, evil, iniquity, sin.
– OPPOSITES benefit.
▶ v. **1** *he's never harmed anybody in his life* **injure**, hurt, wound, lay a finger on, maltreat, mistreat, misuse, ill-treat, ill-use, abuse, molest. **2** *this could harm his World Cup prospects* **damage**, spoil, mar, do mischief to, impair.

harmful adj. **damaging**, injurious, detrimental, dangerous, deleterious, unfavourable, negative, disadvantageous, unhealthy, unwholesome, hurtful, baleful, destructive; noxious, hazardous, poisonous, toxic, deadly, lethal; bad, evil, malign, malignant, malevolent, corrupting, subversive, pernicious.
– OPPOSITES beneficial.

harmless adj. **1** *a harmless substance* **safe**, innocuous, benign, gentle, mild, wholesome, non-toxic, non-poisonous, non-irritant; non-addictive. **2** *he seems harmless enough* **inoffensive**, innocuous, unobjectionable, unexceptionable.
– OPPOSITES dangerous.

harmonious adj. **1** *harmonious music* **tuneful**, melodious, melodic, sweet-sounding, mellifluous, dulcet, lyrical; euphonious, euphonic, harmonic, polyphonic; informal easy on the ear. **2** *their harmonious relationship* **friendly**, amicable, cordial, amiable, congenial, easy, peaceful, peaceable, cooperative, compatible, sympathetic, united, attuned, in harmony,

h

h

in rapport, in tune, in accord, of one mind, seeing eye to eye. **3** *a harmonious blend of traditional and modern* **congruous**, coordinated, balanced, in proportion, compatible, well matched, well balanced.
– OPPOSITES discordant, hostile, incongruous.

harmonize v. **1** *colours which harmonize in a pleasing way* **coordinate**, go together, match, blend, mix, balance, tone in; be compatible, be harmonious, suit each other, set each other off. **2** *the need to harmonize tax laws across Europe* **coordinate**, bring in line, systematize, correlate, integrate, synchronize, make consistent, bring in tune.
– OPPOSITES clash.

harmony n. **1** *musical harmony* **euphony**, polyphony; tunefulness, melodiousness, mellifluousness. **2** *the harmony of the whole structure* **balance**, symmetry, congruity, consonance, coordination, compatibility. **3** *the villagers live together in harmony* **accord**, agreement, peace, peacefulness, amity, amicability, friendship, fellowship, cooperation, understanding, consensus, unity, sympathy, rapport, like-mindedness; unison, union, concert, oneness, synthesis; formal concord.
– OPPOSITES dissonance, disagreement.

harness n. *a horse's harness* **tack**, tackle, equipment; trappings; yoke; old use equipage.
▶v. **1** *he harnessed his horse* **hitch up**, put in harness, yoke, couple. **2** *attempts to harness solar energy* **control**, exploit, utilize, use, employ, make use of, put to use; channel, mobilize, apply, capitalize on.

harp v.
□ **harp on about** keep on about, go on about, keep talking about, dwell on, make an issue of; labour the point.

harpoon n. **spear**, trident, dart, barb, gaff, leister.

harridan n. **shrew**, termagant, virago, harpy, vixen, nag, hag, crone, dragon, ogress; fishwife, hellcat, she-devil, gorgon; martinet, tartar; informal old bag, old bat, old cow, bitch, battleaxe, witch; old use scold.

harried adj. **harassed**, beleaguered, flustered, agitated, bothered, vexed, beset, plagued; informal hassled, up against it; Brit. informal under the cosh.

harrow v. **distress**, trouble, bother, afflict, grieve, torment, pain, hurt, mortify.
– OPPOSITES comfort.

harrowing adj. **distressing**, distressful, traumatic, upsetting; shocking, disturbing, painful, haunting, appalling, horrifying.

harry v. **1** *they harried the retreating enemy* **attack**, assail, assault; charge, rush, strike, set upon; bombard, shell, strafe. **2** *the government was harried by a new lobby* **harass**, hound, pressurize, bedevil, torment, pester, bother, worry, badger, nag, plague; informal hassle, bug, lean on, give someone a hard time, get on someone's back.

harsh adj. **1** *a harsh voice* **grating**, jarring, rasping, strident, raucous, brassy, discordant, unharmonious, unmelodious; screeching,

shrill; rough, coarse, hoarse, gruff, croaky. **2** *harsh colours* **glaring**, bright, dazzling; loud, garish, gaudy, lurid, bold. **3** *his harsh rule over them* **cruel**, savage, barbarous, despotic, dictatorial, tyrannical, tyrannous; ruthless, merciless, pitiless, relentless, unmerciful; severe, strict, intolerant, illiberal; hard-hearted, heartless, unkind, inhuman, inhumane. **4** *they took harsh measures to end the crisis* **severe**, stringent, firm, stiff, hard, stern, rigorous, grim, uncompromising; punitive, cruel, brutal. **5** *harsh words* **rude**, discourteous, uncivil, impolite; unfriendly, sharp, bitter, abusive, unkind, disparaging; abrupt, brusque, curt, gruff, short, surly, offhand. **6** *harsh conditions* **austere**, grim, spartan, hard, comfortless, inhospitable, stark, bleak, desolate. **7** *a harsh winter* **hard**, severe, cold, bitter, bleak, freezing, icy; arctic, polar, Siberian. **8** *harsh cream cleaners* **abrasive**, strong, caustic; coarse, rough.
– OPPOSITES soft, subdued, kind, friendly, comfortable, balmy, mild.

harum-scarum adj. **reckless**, impetuous, impulsive, imprudent, rash, wild; daredevil, madcap, hot-headed, hare-brained, foolhardy, incautious, careless, heedless; informal devil-may-care; literary temerarious.
– OPPOSITES cautious.

harvest n. **1** *we all helped with the harvest* **harvesting**, reaping, picking, collecting; formal ingathering. **2** *a poor harvest* **yield**, crop, vintage; fruits, produce. **3** *the experiment yielded a meagre harvest* **return**, result, fruits; product, output, effect; consequence.
▶v. **1** *he harvested the wheat* **gather (in)**, bring in, reap, pick, collect; formal ingather. **2** *he harvested many honours* **acquire**, obtain, gain, get, earn; accumulate, amass, gather, collect; informal land, net, bag, scoop.

hash[1] n. *a whole hash of excuses* **mixture**, assortment, variety, array, mix, miscellany, selection, medley, mishmash, hotchpotch, ragbag, gallimaufry, potpourri; N. Amer. hodgepodge.
□ **make a hash of** informal bungle, fluff, mess up, make a mess of; mismanage, mishandle, ruin, wreck; informal botch, muff, muck up, foul up, screw up, blow; Brit. informal make a pig's ear of, cock up; N. Amer. informal flub.

hash[2] n. informal *she smokes a lot of hash.* See **cannabis**.

hassle informal n. **1** *parking is such a hassle* **inconvenience**, bother, nuisance, problem, trouble, struggle, difficulty, annoyance, irritation, thorn in one's flesh/side, fuss; informal aggravation, aggro, stress, headache, pain (in the neck). **2** N. Amer. *she got into a hassle with that guy.* See **quarrel** (noun).
▶v. *they were hassling him to pay up* **harass**, pester, nag, keep on at, badger, hound, harry, chivvy, bother, torment, plague; informal bug, give someone a hard time, get on someone's back, breathe down someone's neck; N. English informal mither.

hassled adj. informal **harassed**, agitated, stressed (out), harried, frayed, flustered; beleaguered, hounded, plagued, bothered, beset, tormented; under pressure, hot and bothered; informal up against it; Brit. informal under the cosh.
– OPPOSITES calm.

haste n. *working with feverish haste* **speed**, hastiness, hurriedness, swiftness, rapidity, quickness, briskness; formal expedition.
– OPPOSITES delay.
□ **in haste** quickly, rapidly, fast, speedily, with urgency, in a rush, in a hurry.

hasten v. **1** *we hastened back home* **hurry**, rush, dash, race, fly, shoot; scurry, scramble, dart, bolt, sprint, run, gallop; go fast, go quickly, go like lightning, go hell for leather; informal tear, hare, pelt, scoot, zip, zoom, belt, hotfoot it, leg it; Brit. informal bomb, bucket; N. Amer. informal hightail, barrel; dated make haste. **2** *chemicals can hasten ageing* **speed up**, accelerate, quicken, precipitate, advance, hurry on, step up, spur on; facilitate, aid, assist, boost.
– OPPOSITES dawdle, delay.

hastily adv. **1** *Meg retreated hastily* **quickly**, hurriedly, fast, swiftly, rapidly, speedily, briskly, without delay, post-haste; with all speed, as fast as possible, at a run, hotfoot, on the double; informal double quick, p.d.q. (pretty damn quick), nippily, like (greased) lightning, like the wind, like a scalded cat, like a bat out of hell; Brit. informal at a rate of knots, like the clappers; N. Amer. informal lickety-split. **2** *an agreement was hastily drawn up* **hurriedly**, speedily, quickly; on the spur of the moment, prematurely.

hasty adj. **1** *hasty steps* **quick**, hurried, fast, swift, rapid, speedy, brisk; literary fleet. **2** *hasty decisions* **rash**, impetuous, impulsive, reckless, precipitate, spur-of-the-moment, premature, unconsidered, unthinking; literary temerarious.
– OPPOSITES slow, considered.

hat n. **cap**, beret, bonnet; Brit. informal titfer.

> **WORD LINKS**
> **hatter** a person who makes and sells hats
> **milliner** a person who sells women's hats

hatch v. **1** *the duck hatched her eggs* **incubate**, brood, sit on. **2** *the plot that you hatched up last night* **devise**, conceive, concoct, brew, invent, plan, design, formulate; think up, dream up; informal cook up.

hatchet n. **axe**, cleaver, mattock, tomahawk; Brit. chopper.

hate v. **1** *they hate each other* **loathe**, detest, despise, dislike, abhor, execrate; be repelled by, be unable to bear/stand, find intolerable, recoil from, shrink from; formal abominate; old use disrelish. **2** *I hate to bother you* **be sorry**, be reluctant, be loath, be unwilling, be disinclined; regret, dislike.
– OPPOSITES love.
▸n. **1** *feelings of hate* **hatred**, loathing, detestation, dislike, distaste, abhorrence, abomination, execration, aversion; hostility,

enmity, animosity, antipathy, revulsion, disgust, contempt, odium; old use disrelish. **2** *his pet hate is filling in forms* **bugbear**, bane, bête noire, bogey, aversion, thorn in one's flesh/side; N. Amer. bugaboo.
– OPPOSITES love.

hateful adj. **detestable**, horrible, horrid, unpleasant, awful, nasty, disagreeable, despicable, objectionable, insufferable, revolting, loathsome, abhorrent, abominable, execrable, odious, disgusting, distasteful, obnoxious, offensive, vile, heinous; informal ghastly; Brit. informal beastly, God-awful.
– OPPOSITES delightful.

hatred n. **loathing**, hate, detestation, dislike, distaste, abhorrence, abomination, execration; aversion, hostility, ill will, ill feeling, enmity, animosity, antipathy; revulsion, disgust, contempt, odium; old use disrelish.

haughtiness n. **arrogance**, conceit, pride, hubris, hauteur, vanity, self-importance, pomposity, condescension, disdain, contempt; snobbishness, snobbery, superciliousness; informal snootiness.
– OPPOSITES modesty.

haughty adj. **proud**, arrogant, vain, conceited, snobbish, superior, self-important, pompous, supercilious, condescending, patronizing; scornful, contemptuous, disdainful; full of oneself, above oneself; informal stuck-up, snooty, hoity-toity, uppity, uppish, big-headed, high and mighty, la-di-da; Brit. informal toffee-nosed; N. Amer. informal chesty.
– OPPOSITES humble.

haul v. **1** *she hauled the basket along* **drag**, pull, tug, heave, lug, hump, draw, tow; informal yank. **2** *a contract to haul coal* **transport**, convey, carry, ship, ferry, move, shift.
▸n. *the thieves abandoned their haul* **booty**, loot, plunder; spoils, stolen goods, ill-gotten gains; informal swag, boodle.

haunches plural n. **rump**, hindquarters, rear (end), seat; buttocks, thighs, derrière; Brit. bottom; Scottish bahookie; Anatomy nates; informal behind, backside; Brit. informal bum, botty; N. Amer. informal butt, fanny, tush, heinie, bippy; humorous fundament, posterior.

haunt v. **1** *a ghost haunts this house* **appear in**, materialize in; visit. **2** *he haunts street markets* **frequent**, patronize, visit regularly; loiter in, linger in; informal hang out in. **3** *the sight haunted me for years* **torment**, disturb, trouble, worry, plague, burden, beset, beleaguer; prey on, weigh on, gnaw at, nag at, weigh heavily on, obsess; informal bug.
▸n. *a favourite haunt of artists* **hang-out**, stamping ground, meeting place; territory, domain, resort, retreat, spot; N. Amer. stomping ground; Brit. informal patch.

haunted adj. **1** *a haunted house* **possessed**, cursed; ghostly, eerie; informal spooky, scary. **2** *his haunted eyes* **tormented**, anguished, troubled, tortured, worried, disturbed.

haunting adj. **evocative**, emotive, affecting, moving, touching, stirring, powerful; poignant, nostalgic, wistful; memorable, unforgettable, indelible.

hauteur n. **haughtiness**, superciliousness, arrogance, pride, conceit, snobbery, snobbishness, superiority, self-importance; disdain, condescension; airs and graces; informal snootiness, uppishness; Brit. informal side.

have v. **1** *he had a new car* **possess**, own, be in possession of, be the owner of; be blessed with, boast, enjoy; keep, retain, hold, occupy. **2** *the flat has five rooms* **comprise**, consist of, contain, include, incorporate, be composed of, be made up of; encompass; formal comprehend. **3** *they had tea together* **eat**, consume, devour, partake of; drink, imbibe, quaff; informal demolish, dispose of, put away, get outside of, scoff (down); sink, knock back; N. Amer. informal scarf (down/up). **4** *she had a letter from Mark* **receive**, get, be given, be sent, obtain, acquire, come by, take receipt of. **5** *we've decided to have a party* **organize**, arrange, hold, give, host, throw, put on, lay on, set up, fix up. **6** *she's going to have a baby* **give birth to**, bear, be delivered of, bring into the world; informal drop; old use be brought to bed of, beget. **7** *we are having guests for dinner* **entertain**, be host to, cater for, receive; invite round/over, ask round/over, wine and dine; accommodate, put up. **8** *he had trouble finding the restaurant* **experience**, encounter, face, meet, find, run into, go through, undergo. **9** *I have a headache* **be suffering from**, be afflicted by, be affected by, be troubled with; informal be a martyr to. **10** *I had a good time* **experience**; enjoy. **11** *many of them have doubts* **harbour**, entertain, feel, nurse, nurture, sustain, maintain. **12** *he had little patience* **manifest**, show, display, exhibit, demonstrate. **13** *he had them throw Chris out* **make**, ask to, request to, get to, tell to, require to, induce to, prevail on someone to; order to, command to, direct to, force to. **14** *I can't have you insulting me* **tolerate**, endure, bear, stomach, support, accept, put up with, go along with, take, countenance; permit to, allow to; informal stand, abide; Brit. informal stick, be doing with; formal brook. **15** *I have to get up at six* **must**, be obliged to, be required to, be compelled to, be forced to, be bound to. **16** informal *I'd been had* **trick**, fool, deceive, cheat, dupe, take in, hoodwink, swindle; informal do, con, diddle, rip off, shaft; N. Amer. informal sucker, snooker.
– OPPOSITES send, give, visit.
□ **have someone on** Brit. informal play a trick on, play a joke on, joke with, trick, tease, rag, make a monkey (out) of, pull someone's leg; informal kid, rib, take for a ride, lead up the garden path; Brit. informal wind up; N. Amer. informal put on.

haven n. **1** *they stopped in a small haven* **anchorage**, harbour, harbourage, port, moorage, mooring; road, roadstead; cove, inlet, bay. **2** *a safe haven* **refuge**, retreat, shelter, sanctuary, asylum; port in a storm, oasis, sanctum.

haversack n. **knapsack**, rucksack, backpack, pack.

havoc n. **1** *the hurricane caused havoc* **devastation**, destruction, damage, desolation, ruination, ruin; disaster, catastrophe. **2** *hyperactive children create havoc* **disorder**, chaos, disruption, mayhem, bedlam, pandemonium, turmoil, tumult, uproar; commotion, furore; N. Amer. a three-ring circus; informal hullabaloo.

hawk v. **peddle**, sell, tout, vend, trade in, traffic in, push; Brit. informal flog.

hawker n. **pedlar**, trader, seller, dealer, purveyor, vendor, huckster, travelling salesman; Brit. barrow boy, tout; informal pusher; Brit. informal flogger.

hawk-eyed adj. **vigilant**, observant, alert, sharp-eyed, keen-eyed, eagle-eyed; on the alert, on the lookout, with one's eyes skinned/peeled; informal beady-eyed, not missing a trick, on the ball.
– OPPOSITES inattentive.

hay n. **forage**, dried grass, herbage, silage, fodder, straw.
□ **make hay while the sun shines** make the most of an opportunity, take advantage of something, strike while the iron is hot, seize the day, carpe diem.

haywire adj. informal **out of control**, erratic, faulty, malfunctioning, out of order; chaotic, confused, disorganized, disordered, topsy-turvy; informal on the blink; Brit. informal up the spout, shambolic.

hazard n. **1** *the hazards of radiation* **danger**, risk, peril, threat, menace; problem, pitfall. **2** literary *the laws of hazard* **chance**, probability, fortuity, luck, fate, destiny, fortune, providence.
▶ v. **1** *he hazarded a guess* **venture**, advance, put forward, volunteer; conjecture, speculate, surmise; formal opine. **2** *it's too risky to hazard money on* **risk**, jeopardize, gamble, stake, bet, chance; endanger, imperil.

hazardous adj. **risky**, dangerous, unsafe, perilous, precarious, fraught with danger; unpredictable, uncertain, chancy, high-risk, insecure, touch-and-go; informal dicey, hairy; Brit. informal dodgy.
– OPPOSITES safe, certain.

haze n. **1** *a thick haze on the sea* **mist**, fog, cloud; smoke, vapour, steam. **2** *a haze of euphoria* **blur**, daze, confusion, muddle, befuddlement.

hazy adj. **1** *a hazy day* **misty**, foggy, cloudy, overcast; smoggy, murky. **2** *hazy memories* **vague**, indistinct, unclear, faint, dim, nebulous, shadowy, blurred, fuzzy, confused.

head n. **1** *her head hit the wall* **skull**, cranium, crown; informal nut, noodle, noggin, dome; Brit. informal bonce; informal dated conk, noddle. **2** *he had to use his head* **brain(s)**, brainpower, intellect, intelligence; wit(s), wisdom, mind, sense, reasoning, common sense; informal nous, savvy, grey matter; Brit. informal

loaf; N. Amer. informal smarts. **3** *she had a good head for business* **aptitude**, faculty, talent, gift, capacity, ability; mind, brain. **4** *the head of the church* **leader**, chief, controller, governor, superintendent, headman; commander, captain; director, manager; principal, president, premier; informal boss, boss man, kingpin, top dog, Mr Big, skipper, numero uno, head honcho; Brit. informal gaffer, guv'nor; N. Amer. informal sachem, big kahuna. **5** *the head of the queue* **front**, beginning, start, fore, forefront; top. **6** *the head of the river* **source**, origin, well head, headspring, headwater; literary wellspring. **7** *beer with a head* **froth**, foam, bubbles, spume, fizz, effervescence; suds.
– OPPOSITES back, mouth.
▸ adj. *the head waiter* **chief**, principal, leading, main, first, prime, premier, top, highest, supreme, top-ranking; N. Amer. ranking; informal top-notch.
– OPPOSITES subordinate.
▸ v. **1** *the procession was headed by the mayor* **lead**, be at the front of; be first, lead the way. **2** *a team headed by a line manager* **command**, control, lead, run, manage, direct, supervise, superintend, oversee, preside over, rule, govern, captain, helm; informal be the boss of. **3** *he was heading for the exit* **move towards**, make for, aim for, go in the direction of, be bound for, make a beeline for; set out for, start out for.
□ **at the head of** in charge of, controlling, commanding, leading, managing, running, directing, supervising, overseeing; at the wheel of, at the helm of.
come to a head reach a crisis, come to a climax, reach a critical point, reach a crossroads; informal come to the crunch.
go to someone's head 1 *the wine has gone to my head* **intoxicate**, befuddle, make drunk; informal make woozy; formal inebriate. **2** *her victory went to her head* **make conceited**, turn someone's head, puff someone up.
head someone/something off 1 *he went to head off the cars* **intercept**, divert, deflect, redirect, re-route, draw away, turn away. **2** *they headed off a row* **forestall**, avert, ward off, fend off, stave off, hold off, nip in the bud, keep at bay; prevent, avoid, stop.
keep one's head keep/stay calm, keep one's self-control, maintain one's composure; informal keep one's cool, keep one's shirt on.
lose one's head lose control, lose one's composure, lose one's equilibrium, go to pieces; panic, get flustered, get confused, get hysterical; informal lose one's cool, freak out, crack up; Brit. informal go into a (flat) spin, throw a wobbly.

> **WORD LINKS**
> **cephalic** relating to the head
> **concussion** temporary unconsciousness caused by a blow on the head
> **decapitate, behead** cut off a person's head

headache n. **1** *I've got a headache* **pain in the head**, sore head, migraine; neuralgia;

informal head. **2** informal *their behaviour was a headache for Mr Jones* **nuisance**, trouble, problem, issue, bother, bugbear, pest, worry, inconvenience, vexation, irritant, thorn in one's flesh; informal aggravation, hassle, pain (in the neck), bind.
head case n. informal **maniac**, lunatic, madman, madwoman; informal loony, nut, nutcase, fruitcake, crank, crackpot; Brit. informal nutter; N. Amer. informal screwball, crazy, kook, wacko, wing nut; N. Amer. & Austral./NZ informal dingbat.
head first adv. **1** *she dived head first into the water* **headlong**, on one's head. **2** *don't plunge head first into a relationship* **without thinking**, without forethought, precipitously, impetuously, rashly, recklessly, heedlessly, hastily, headlong.
– OPPOSITES cautiously.
heading n. **1** *chapter headings* **title**, caption, legend, subtitle, subheading, rubric, headline. **2** *this topic falls under four main headings* **category**, division, classification, class, section, group, grouping, subject, topic.
headland n. **cape**, promontory, point, head, foreland, peninsula, ness, bluff; Scottish mull.
headlong adv. **1** *he fell headlong into the tent* **head first**, on one's head. **2** *she rushed headlong to join the craze* **without thinking**, without forethought, precipitously, impetuously, rashly, recklessly, carelessly, heedlessly, hastily.
– OPPOSITES cautiously.
▸ adj. *a headlong dash* **breakneck**, whirlwind; reckless, precipitate, precipitous, hasty, careless, heedless.
– OPPOSITES cautious.
headman n. **chief**, chieftain, leader, head, ruler, overlord, master, commander; lord, potentate; N. Amer. sachem.
– OPPOSITES underling.
head-on adj. **1** *a head-on collision* **direct**, front-to-front. **2** *a head-on confrontation* **direct**, face to face, eyeball to eyeball, personal.
headquarters plural n. **head office**, main office, HQ, base, nerve centre, mission control, command post.
headstone n. **gravestone**, tombstone, stone, monument, memorial.
headstrong adj. **wilful**, strong-willed, stubborn, obstinate, unyielding, obdurate; contrary, perverse, wayward, unruly; formal refractory.
– OPPOSITES tractable.
head teacher n. **head**, headmaster, headmistress, principal, director, president, governor; Brit. master.
headway n.
□ **make headway** make progress, progress, make strides, gain ground, advance, proceed, move, get ahead, come along, take shape.
heady adj. **1** *heady wine* **potent**, intoxicating, strong, powerful; alcoholic, vinous; formal spirituous. **2** *the heady days of my youth* **exhilarating**, exciting, thrilling, stimulating, invigorating, electrifying, rousing; informal

h

mind-blowing.
– OPPOSITES boring.

heal v. **1** *he heals sick people* **make better**, make well, cure, treat, restore to health. **2** *his knee had healed* **get better**, get well, be cured, recover, mend, improve. **3** *time will heal the pain of grief* **alleviate**, ease, assuage, palliate, relieve, help, lessen, mitigate, attenuate, allay. **4** *we tried to heal the rift* **put right**, set right, repair, remedy, resolve, correct, settle; conciliate, reconcile, harmonize; informal patch up.
– OPPOSITES aggravate, worsen.

healing adj. **curative**, therapeutic, medicinal, remedial, corrective, reparative; restorative, tonic, health-giving, healthful, beneficial.
– OPPOSITES harmful.

health n. **1** *he was restored to health* **well-being**, healthiness, fitness, good condition, good shape, fine fettle; strength, vigour. **2** *bad health forced him to retire* **physical state**, physical shape, condition, constitution.
– OPPOSITES illness.

healthful adj. **healthy**, health-giving, beneficial, good for one, salubrious; wholesome, nourishing, nutritious.
– OPPOSITES unhealthy.

healthy adj. **1** *a healthy baby* **well**, in good health, fine, fit, in good trim, in good shape, in fine fettle, in tip-top condition; blooming, thriving, hardy, robust, strong, vigorous, fighting fit, fit as a fiddle, the picture of health; Brit. in rude health; informal OK, in the pink, right as rain. **2** *a healthy diet* **health-giving**, healthful, good for one; wholesome, nutritious, nourishing; beneficial, salubrious.
– OPPOSITES ill, unwholesome.

heap n. **1** *a heap of boxes* **pile**, stack, mound, mountain, mass, quantity, load, lot, jumble; collection, accumulation, assemblage, store, hoard. **2** informal *we have heaps of room* **a lot**, a fair amount, much, plenty, a good deal, a great deal, an abundance, a wealth, a profusion; (a great) many, a large number, numerous, scores; informal hundreds, thousands, millions, a load, loads, loadsa, a pile, piles, oodles, stacks, lots, masses, scads, reams, wads, pots, oceans, miles, tons, zillions; Brit. informal a shedload, lashings.
▶ v. *she heaped logs on the fire* **pile (up)**, stack (up), make a mound of; assemble, collect.
□ **heap something on** *they heaped praise on her* shower on, lavish on, load on; bestow on, confer on, give, grant, vouchsafe, favour with.

hear v. **1** *she can't hear* **perceive sound**; have hearing. **2** *she could hear men's voices* **perceive**, make out, discern, catch, get, apprehend; overhear. **3** *they heard that I had moved* **be informed**, be told, find out, discover, learn, gather, glean, ascertain, get word, get wind. **4** *a jury heard the case* **try**, judge; adjudicate (on), adjudge, pass judgement on.

hearing n. **1** *acute hearing* **ability to hear**, auditory perception, sense of hearing, aural faculty. **2** *she moved out of hearing* **earshot**, hearing distance, hearing range, auditory range. **3** *I had a fair hearing* **chance to speak**, opportunity to be heard; interview, audience. **4** *he gave evidence at the hearing* **trial**, court case, inquiry, inquest, tribunal; investigation, inquisition.

> **WORD LINKS**
>
> **auditory**, **aural**, **acoustic** relating to hearing
> **audiology** the branch of medicine concerned with hearing
> **audiometry** the measurement of hearing

hearsay n. **rumour**, gossip, tittle-tattle, tattle, idle talk; stories, tales, on dit; informal the grapevine; Brit. informal goss; N. Amer. informal scuttlebutt.

heart n. **1** *his heart stopped beating* informal ticker. **2** *he poured out his heart* **emotions**, feelings, sentiments; soul, mind, bosom, breast; love, affection, passion. **3** *he has no heart* **compassion**, sympathy, humanity, feeling(s), fellow feeling, brotherly love, tenderness, empathy, understanding; kindness, goodwill. **4** *they may lose heart* **enthusiasm**, keenness, eagerness, spirit, determination, resolve, purpose, courage, nerve, will power, fortitude; informal guts, spunk; Brit. informal bottle. **5** *the heart of the city* **centre**, middle, hub, core, nucleus, eye, bosom. **6** *the heart of the matter* **essence**, crux, core, nub, root, gist, meat, marrow, pith, substance, kernel; informal nitty-gritty.
– OPPOSITES edge.
□ **after one's own heart** like-minded, of the same mind, kindred, compatible, congenial, sharing one's tastes, on the same wavelength.
at heart deep down, basically, fundamentally, essentially, in essence, intrinsically; really, actually, truly, in fact; informal when you get right down to it.
(off) by heart from memory, off pat, by rote, word for word, verbatim, parrot-fashion, word-perfect.
eat one's heart out pine, long, ache, brood, mope, fret, sigh, sorrow, yearn, agonize; grieve, mourn, lament.
have a change of heart change one's mind, change one's tune, have second thoughts, have a rethink, think again, think twice; informal get cold feet.
have a heart be compassionate, be kind, be merciful, be lenient, be sympathetic, be considerate, have mercy.
heart and soul wholeheartedly, enthusiastically, eagerly, zealously; absolutely, completely, entirely, fully, utterly, to the hilt, one hundred per cent.
take heart be encouraged, be heartened, be comforted; cheer up, brighten up, perk up, liven up, revive; informal buck up.
with one's heart in one's mouth in alarm, in fear, fearfully, apprehensively, on edge, with trepidation, in suspense, in a cold sweat, with bated breath, on tenterhooks;

informal **with butterflies in one's stomach**, in a state, in a stew, in a sweat; Brit. informal having kittens; N. Amer. informal in a twit.

> **WORD LINKS**
>
> **cardiac** relating to the heart
> **coronary** relating to the heart's arteries
> **cardiology** the branch of medicine concerned with the heart
> **diastole** the phase of the heartbeat when the muscle relaxes
> **systole** the phase of the heartbeat when the muscle contracts
> **fibrillation** quivering movements of the heart muscle
> **pacemaker** a device for regulating the heart muscle

heartache n. **anguish**, grief, suffering, distress, unhappiness, misery, sorrow, sadness, heartbreak, pain, hurt, agony, angst, despondency, despair, woe, desolation.
– OPPOSITES happiness.

heartbreak n. See **heartache**.

heartbreaking adj. **tragic**, heart-rending, distressing, upsetting, disturbing, sad, painful, traumatic, agonizing, harrowing; pitiful, poignant, plaintive, moving, tear-jerking.
– OPPOSITES comforting.

heartbroken adj. **anguished**, devastated, broken-hearted, heavy-hearted, grieving, grief-stricken, inconsolable, crushed, shattered, desolate, despairing; upset, distressed, miserable, sorrowful, sad, downcast, disconsolate, crestfallen, despondent; informal choked, down in the mouth, down in the dumps, cut up.

heartburn n. **indigestion**, dyspepsia, pyrosis.

hearten v. **cheer (up)**, encourage, raise someone's spirits, boost, buoy up, perk up, ginger up, inspirit, uplift, elate; comfort, reassure; informal buck up, pep up.

heartfelt adj. **sincere**, genuine, from the heart; earnest, profound, deep, wholehearted, ardent, fervent, passionate, enthusiastic, eager; honest, bona fide.
– OPPOSITES insincere.

heartily adv. **1** we heartily welcome the changes **wholeheartedly**, sincerely, genuinely, warmly, profoundly, with all one's heart; eagerly, enthusiastically, earnestly, ardently. **2** they were heartily sick of her **very**, extremely, thoroughly, completely, absolutely, really, exceedingly, immensely, most, downright; N. Amer. quite; informal right, seriously; Brit. informal jolly, dead, well; N. Amer. informal real, mighty.

heartless adj. **unfeeling**, unsympathetic, unkind, uncaring, unconcerned, insensitive, inconsiderate, hard-hearted, stony-hearted, cold-hearted, mean-spirited; cold, callous, cruel, merciless, pitiless, inhuman.
– OPPOSITES compassionate.

heart-rending adj. **distressing**, upsetting, disturbing, heartbreaking, sad, tragic, painful, traumatic, harrowing; pitiful, poignant, plaintive, moving, tear-jerking.

heart-throb n. informal **idol**, pin-up, star, superstar, hero; informal dreamboat.

heart-to-heart adj. a heart-to-heart chat **intimate**, personal, man-to-man, woman-to-woman; candid, honest, truthful, sincere.
▶ n. they had a long heart-to-heart **conversation**, tête-à-tête, one-to-one, head-to-head; chat, talk, word; informal confab; Brit. informal natter, chinwag.

heart-warming adj. **touching**, moving, heartening, stirring, uplifting, pleasing, cheering, gladdening, encouraging, gratifying.
– OPPOSITES distressing.

hearty adj. **1** a hearty character **exuberant**, jovial, ebullient, cheerful, uninhibited, effusive, lively, loud, animated, vivacious, energetic, spirited, dynamic, enthusiastic, eager; warm, cordial, friendly, affable, amiable, good-natured. **2** hearty congratulations **wholehearted**, heartfelt, sincere, genuine, real, true; earnest, fervent, ardent, enthusiastic. **3** a hearty woman of sixty-five **robust**, healthy, hardy, fit, flourishing, blooming, fighting fit, fit as a fiddle; vigorous, sturdy, strong; Brit. in rude health; informal full of vim and vigour. **4** a hearty meal **substantial**, large, ample, sizeable, filling, generous, square, solid; healthy.
– OPPOSITES introverted, half-hearted, frail, light.

heat n. **1** a plant sensitive to heat **warmth**, hotness, warmness, high temperature; hot weather, warm weather, sultriness, mugginess, humidity; heatwave, hot spell. **2** he took the heat out of the dispute **passion**, intensity, vehemence, warmth, fervour, fervency, ardency; enthusiasm, excitement, agitation; anger, fury.
– OPPOSITES cold, apathy.
▶ v. **1** the food was heated **warm (up)**, heat up, make hot, make warm; reheat, cook; Brit. informal hot up. **2** the pipes expand as they heat up **become hot**, become warm, get hotter, get warmer, increase in temperature; Brit. informal hot up. **3** he calmed down as quickly as he had heated up **become impassioned**, become excited, become animated; get angry, become enraged.
– OPPOSITES cool.

> **WORD LINKS**
> **thermal, caloric** relating to heat

heated adj. **1** a heated swimming pool **made warm**, made hot, warmed up; reheated; hot, piping hot. **2** a heated argument **vehement**, passionate, impassioned, animated, spirited, 'lively', intense, fiery; angry, bitter, furious, fierce, stormy, tempestuous. **3** Robert grew heated as he spoke of the risks **excited**, animated, inflamed, worked up, wound up, keyed up; informal het up, in a state.

heater n. **radiator**, convector, fire, brazier, warmer.

h

heath n. **moor**, heathland, moorland, scrub; common land.

heathen n. **1** *bringing Christianity to the heathens* **pagan**, infidel, idolater, idolatress; unbeliever, non-believer, disbeliever, atheist, agnostic, sceptic, heretic; old use paynim. **2** *heathens who spoil good whisky with ice* **philistine**, boor, oaf, ignoramus, lout, vulgarian, plebeian; informal pleb, peasant, yahoo, oik.
– OPPOSITES believer.
▶adj. *a heathen practice* **pagan**, infidel, idolatrous, heathenish; unbelieving, non-believing, atheistic, agnostic, heretical, faithless, godless, irreligious, ungodly, unholy; barbarian, barbarous, uncivilized, uncultured, primitive, ignorant, philistine.

heave v. **1** *she heaved the sofa backwards* **haul**, pull, lug, drag, draw, tug, heft; informal hump, yank. **2** informal *she heaved a brick at him* **throw**, fling, cast, toss, hurl, lob, pitch; informal chuck, sling; Brit. informal bung; N. English & Austral. informal hoy; NZ informal bish. **3** *he heaved a sigh of relief* **let out**, breathe, give, sigh; emit, utter. **4** *the sea heaved* **rise and fall**, roll, swell, surge, churn, seethe, swirl. **5** *she went to the sink and heaved* **retch**, gag; vomit; Brit. be sick; N. Amer. get sick; informal throw up, puke, chunder, chuck up, hurl, spew; Scottish informal boke; N. Amer. informal barf, upchuck.

heaven n. **1** *the good will have a place in heaven* **paradise**, nirvana, Zion; the hereafter, the next world, the next life, the afterworld; Elysium, the Elysian Fields, Valhalla; literary the empyrean. **2** *a good book is my idea of heaven* **bliss**, ecstasy, rapture, contentment, happiness, delight, joy, seventh heaven; paradise, Utopia, nirvana. **3** literary *he observed the heavens* **the sky**, the skies, the upper atmosphere, the stratosphere; literary the firmament, the blue, the (wide) blue yonder, the welkin, the empyrean, the azure, the upper regions, the sphere.
– OPPOSITES hell, misery.
□ **in seventh heaven** ecstatic, euphoric, thrilled, elated, delighted, overjoyed, on cloud nine, walking on air, jubilant, rapturous, jumping for joy, transported, delirious, blissful; informal over the moon, on top of the world, on a high, tickled pink, as pleased as Punch, cock-a-hoop, as happy as a sandboy; Brit. informal as happy as Larry; N. Amer. informal as happy as a clam; Austral. informal wrapped.
□ **move heaven and earth** try one's hardest, do one's best, do one's utmost, do all one can, give one's all, spare no effort, put oneself out; strive, exert oneself, work hard; informal bend over backwards, do one's damnedest, go all out, bust a gut.

> **WORD LINKS**
> **celestial** belonging or relating to heaven

heavenly adj. **1** *heavenly choirs* **divine**, holy, celestial; angelic, seraphic, cherubic; literary empyrean. **2** *heavenly constellations* **celestial**, cosmic, stellar; planetary; extraterrestrial, superterrestrial. **3** informal *a heavenly morning* **delightful**, wonderful, glorious, perfect, excellent, sublime, idyllic, first-class, first-rate; blissful, pleasurable, enjoyable; exquisite, beautiful, lovely, gorgeous, enchanting; informal divine, super, great, fantastic, fabulous, terrific.
– OPPOSITES mortal, infernal, terrestrial, dreadful.

heaven-sent adj. **auspicious**, providential, propitious, felicitous, opportune, golden, favourable, advantageous, serendipitous, lucky, happy, good, fortunate.
– OPPOSITES inopportune.

heavily adv. **1** *Dad walked heavily* **laboriously**, slowly, ponderously, woodenly, stiffly; with difficulty, painfully, awkwardly, clumsily. **2** *we were heavily defeated* **decisively**, conclusively, roundly, soundly; utterly, completely, thoroughly. **3** *he drank heavily* **excessively**, to excess, immoderately, copiously, inordinately, intemperately, a great deal, too much, overmuch. **4** *the area is heavily planted with trees* **densely**, closely, thickly. **5** *I became heavily involved* **deeply**, very, extremely, greatly, exceedingly, tremendously, profoundly; informal terribly, seriously; Brit. informal jolly, ever so.
– OPPOSITES easily, narrowly, moderately.

heavy adj. **1** *a heavy box* **weighty**, hefty, substantial, ponderous; solid, dense, leaden; burdensome; informal hulking, weighing a ton. **2** *a heavy man* **overweight**, fat, obese, corpulent, large, bulky, stout, stocky, portly, plump, paunchy, fleshy; informal hulking, tubby, beefy, porky; Brit. informal podgy. **3** *a heavy blow to the head* **forceful**, hard, strong, violent, powerful, vigorous, mighty, hefty, sharp, smart, severe. **4** *a gardener did the heavy work for me* **arduous**, hard, physical, laborious, difficult, strenuous, demanding, tough, onerous, back-breaking, gruelling; old use toilsome. **5** *a heavy burden of responsibility* **onerous**, burdensome, demanding, challenging, difficult, formidable, weighty; worrisome, stressful, trying, crushing, oppressive. **6** *heavy fog* **dense**, thick, soupy, murky, impenetrable. **7** *a heavy sky* **overcast**, cloudy, clouded, grey, dull, gloomy, murky, dark, black, stormy, leaden, louring. **8** *heavy rain* **torrential**, relentless, copious, teeming, severe. **9** *heavy soil* **clay**, clayey, muddy, sticky, wet; Brit. claggy; informal cloggy. **10** *a heavy fine* **sizeable**, hefty, substantial, colossal, big, considerable; stiff; informal tidy, whopping, steep, astronomical. **11** *heavy seas* **tempestuous**, turbulent, rough, wild, stormy, choppy, squally. **12** *heavy fighting* **intense**, fierce, vigorous, relentless, all-out, severe, serious. **13** *a heavy drinker* **immoderate**, excessive, intemperate, overindulgent, unrestrained, uncontrolled. **14** *a heavy meal* **substantial**, filling, hearty, large, big, ample, sizeable, generous, square, solid. **15** *their diet is heavy on vegetables* **abounding in**, abundant in,

lavish with, profuse with, unstinting with, using a lot of. **16** *he felt heavy and very tired* **lethargic**, listless, sluggish, torpid, languid, apathetic. **17** *a heavy heart* **sad**, sorrowful, melancholy, gloomy, downcast, downhearted, heartbroken, dejected, disconsolate, demoralized, despondent, depressed, crestfallen, desolate, down; informal blue; literary dolorous. **18** *these poems are rather heavy* **tedious**, difficult, dull, dry, serious, heavy going, dreary, boring, turgid, uninteresting; informal deadly. **19** *branches heavy with blossoms* **laden**, loaded, covered, filled, groaning, bursting, teeming, abounding. **20** *a heavy crop* **bountiful**, plentiful, abundant, large, bumper, rich, copious, considerable, sizeable, profuse; informal whopping; literary plenteous. **21** *he has heavy features* **coarse**, rough, rough-hewn, unrefined; rugged, craggy.
– OPPOSITES light, thin, gentle, easy, bright, friable, small, calm, moderate, energetic, cheerful, meagre, delicate.

heavy-handed adj. **1** *they are heavy-handed with the equipment* **clumsy**, awkward, maladroit, unhandy, inept, unskilful; informal ham-handed, ham-fisted, cack-handed; Brit. informal all (fingers and) thumbs. **2** *heavy-handed policing* **insensitive**, oppressive, overbearing, high-handed, harsh, stern, severe, tyrannical, despotic, ruthless, merciless; tactless, undiplomatic, inept.
– OPPOSITES dexterous, sensitive.

heavy-hearted adj. **melancholy**, sad, sorrowful, mournful, gloomy, depressed, desolate, despondent, dejected, downhearted, downcast, crestfallen, disconsolate, glum, miserable, wretched, dismal, morose, woeful, woebegone, doleful, unhappy; informal down in the dumps, down in the mouth, blue; literary dolorous.
– OPPOSITES cheerful.

heckle v. **jeer**, taunt, jibe at, shout down, boo, hiss, harass; Brit. & Austral./NZ barrack; informal give someone a hard time.
– OPPOSITES cheer.

hectic adj. **frantic**, frenetic, frenzied, feverish, manic, busy, active, fast and furious; lively, brisk, bustling, buzzing.
– OPPOSITES leisurely.

hector v. **bully**, intimidate, browbeat, harass, torment, plague; coerce, pressurize, strong-arm; threaten, menace; informal bulldoze; N. Amer. informal bullyrag.

hedge n. **1** *high hedges* **hedgerow**, bushes, fence; windbreak; Brit. quickset. **2** *an excellent hedge against a fall in sterling* **safeguard**, protection, shield, screen, guard, buffer, cushion; insurance, security. **3** *his analysis is full of hedges* **equivocation**, evasion, fudge, quibble, qualification; temporizing, uncertainty, prevarication, vagueness.
▸ v. **1** *fields hedged with hawthorn* **surround**, enclose, encircle, ring, border, edge, bound. **2** *she was hedged in by her education* **confine**, restrict, limit, hinder, obstruct, impede, constrain, trap; hem in. **3** *he hedged at every new question* **prevaricate**, equivocate,

vacillate, quibble, hesitate, stall, dodge the issue, be non-committal, be evasive, be vague, beat about the bush, pussyfoot around, mince one's words; Brit. hum and haw; informal sit on the fence, duck the question. **4** *the company hedged its position on the market* **safeguard**, protect, shield, guard, cushion; cover, insure.

hedonism n. **self-indulgence**, pleasure-seeking, self-gratification, lotus-eating, sybaritism; intemperance, overconsumption, immoderation, extravagance, luxury, high living.
– OPPOSITES self-restraint.

hedonist n. **sybarite**, sensualist, voluptuary, pleasure-seeker, bon viveur, bon vivant; epicure, gastronome.
– OPPOSITES ascetic.

hedonistic adj. **self-indulgent**, pleasure-seeking, sybaritic, lotus-eating, epicurean; unrestrained, intemperate, immoderate, extravagant, decadent.

heed v. *heed the warnings* **pay attention to**, take notice of, take note of, pay heed to, attend to, listen to; bear in mind, be mindful of, mind, mark, consider, take into account, follow, obey, adhere to, abide by, observe, take to heart, be alert to.
– OPPOSITES disregard.
▸ n. *he paid no heed* **attention**, notice, note, regard; consideration, thought, care.

heedful adj. **attentive**, careful, mindful, cautious, prudent, circumspect; alert, aware, wary, chary, watchful, vigilant, on guard, on the alert.

heedless adj. **unmindful**, taking no notice, paying no heed, unheeding, disregardful, neglectful, oblivious, inattentive, blind, deaf; incautious, imprudent, rash, reckless, foolhardy, improvident, unwary.

heel[1] n. **1** *shoes with low heels* **heel piece**; wedge, stiletto. **2** *the heel of a loaf* **tail end**, end, crust, remnant, remainder, remains.
□ **take to one's heels** run away, run off, make a run for it, take flight, take off, make a break for it, flee, make one's getaway, escape; informal beat it, clear off, vamoose, skedaddle, split, cut and run, leg it, hotfoot it, show a clean pair of heels, scram; Brit. informal do a runner, scarper, do a bunk; N. Amer. informal light out, bug out; Austral. informal shoot through.

heel[2] v. *the ship heeled to starboard* **lean over**, list, careen, tilt, tip, incline, keel over.

heft v. **lift (up)**, raise (up), heave, hoist, haul; carry, lug; informal cart, hump, tote.

hefty adj. **1** *a hefty young man* **burly**, heavy, sturdy, strapping, bulky, brawny, husky, strong, muscular, large, big, solid, well built; portly, stout; informal hulking, hunky, beefy. **2** *a hefty kick* **powerful**, violent, hard, forceful, heavy, mighty. **3** *hefty loads of timber* **heavy**, weighty, bulky, big, large, substantial, massive, ponderous; unwieldy, cumbersome, burdensome; informal hulking. **4** *a hefty fine* **substantial**, sizeable, considerable, stiff, extortionate,

h

large, excessive; informal steep, astronomical, whopping.
– OPPOSITES slight, feeble, light, small.

hegemony n. **leadership**, dominance, dominion, supremacy, authority, mastery, control, power, sway, rule, sovereignty.

height n. **1** *the height of the wall* **highness**, tallness, extent upwards, vertical measurement, elevation, stature, altitude. **2** *the mountain heights* **summit**, top, peak, crest, crown, tip, cap, pinnacle, apex, brow, ridge. **3** *the height of their fame* **highest point**, crowning moment, peak, acme, zenith, apogee, pinnacle, climax, high water mark. **4** *the height of bad manners* **epitome**, acme, zenith, quintessence, very limit; ultimate, utmost. **5** *he is terrified of heights* **high places**, high ground; precipices, cliffs.
– OPPOSITES width, nadir.

> **WORD LINKS**
> **altimetry** the measurement of height
> **acrophobia** an extreme fear of heights
> **vertigo** dizziness caused by looking down from a great height

heighten v. **1** *the roof had to be heightened* **make higher**, raise, lift (up), elevate. **2** *her pleasure was heightened by guilt* **intensify**, increase, enhance, add to, augment, boost, strengthen, deepen, magnify, amplify, reinforce.
– OPPOSITES lower, reduce.

heinous adj. **odious**, wicked, evil, atrocious, monstrous, abominable, detestable, contemptible, reprehensible, despicable, egregious, horrific, terrible, awful, abhorrent, loathsome, hideous, unspeakable, execrable; iniquitous, villainous, beyond the pale.
– OPPOSITES admirable.

heir, **heiress** n. **successor**, next in line, inheritor, beneficiary, legatee; descendant, scion; Law devisee; English Law coparcener; Scottish Law heritor.

helix n. **spiral**, coil, corkscrew, curl, twist, gyre, whorl, convolution.

hell n. **1** *they feared hell* **the netherworld**, the Inferno, the infernal regions, the abyss; eternal damnation, perdition; hellfire, fire and brimstone; Hades, Acheron, Gehenna, Tophet, Sheol; literary the pit. **2** *he made her life hell* **a misery**, torture, agony, a torment, a nightmare, an ordeal; anguish, wretchedness, woe.
– OPPOSITES heaven, paradise.
□ **give someone hell** informal **1** *when I found out I gave him hell* **reprimand severely**, rebuke, admonish, chastise, chide, upbraid, reprove, scold, berate, remonstrate with, reprehend, take to task, lambaste; read someone the Riot Act, give someone a piece of one's mind, haul over the coals; informal tell off, dress down, give someone an earful, give someone a roasting, rap over the knuckles, let someone have it, bawl out, come down hard on, lay into, blast; Brit. informal tick off, have a go at, carpet, give someone a rollicking, give someone a mouthful, tear

someone off a strip, give someone what for; N. Amer. informal chew out; formal castigate. **2** *she gave me hell when I was her junior* **harass**, hound, plague, harry, bother, trouble, bully, intimidate, pick on, victimize, terrorize; informal hassle, give someone a hard time.

hell for leather very fast, very quickly, rapidly, speedily, swiftly, hurriedly, at full tilt, at full pelt, headlong, hotfoot, post-haste, helter-skelter, at the speed of light, at breakneck speed; informal like a bat out of hell, like the wind, like greased lightning, like a bomb; Brit. informal like the clappers, at a rate of knots; N. Amer. informal lickety-split.

> **WORD LINKS**
> **infernal** relating to hell

hell-bent adj. **intent**, bent, determined, (dead) set, insistent, fixed, resolved; single-minded, fixated.
– OPPOSITES half-hearted.

hellish adj. **1** *the hellish face of Death* **infernal**, Hadean, diabolical, fiendish, satanic, demonic; evil, wicked. **2** informal *a hellish week* **horrible**, rotten, awful, terrible, dreadful, ghastly, horrid, vile, foul, appalling, atrocious, horrendous, frightful; difficult, unpleasant, nasty, disagreeable; stressful, taxing, tough, hard, frustrating, fraught, traumatic, gruelling; informal murderous, lousy; Brit. informal beastly; N. Amer. informal hellacious.
– OPPOSITES angelic, wonderful.
▸ adv. Brit. informal *it's hellish hard work* **extremely**, very, exceedingly, exceptionally, tremendously, immensely, intensely, unusually, decidedly, particularly, really, truly, mightily; most, so; N. English right; informal terrifically, awfully, fearfully, terribly, devilishly, majorly, seriously, ultra, oh-so, damn, damned; Brit. informal ever so, well, bloody, dead; N. Amer. informal real, mighty, awful; informal dated devilish; old use exceeding.
– OPPOSITES moderately.

helm n. *he took the helm* **tiller**, wheel; steering gear, rudder.
□ **at the helm** in charge, in command, in control, responsible, in authority, at the wheel, in the driving seat, in the saddle; informal holding the reins, running the show, calling the shots.

help v. *can you help me please?* **assist**, aid, lend a (helping) hand to, give assistance to, come to the aid of; be of service to, be of use to; do someone a favour, do someone a service, do someone a good turn, bail someone out, come to the rescue, give someone a leg up; rally round, pitch in; informal get someone out of a tight spot, save someone's bacon, save someone's skin. **2** *this credit card helps cancer research* **support**, contribute to, give money to, donate to; promote, boost, back; further the interests of; N. Amer. informal bankroll. **3** *sore throats are helped by lozenges* **relieve**, soothe, ease, alleviate, make better, improve, assuage, lessen; remedy, cure, heal.
– OPPOSITES hinder, impede, worsen.

▸n. **1** *this could be of help to you* **assistance**, aid, a helping hand, support, succour, advice, guidance, solution; benefit, use, advantage, service, comfort; informal a shot in the arm. **2** *he sought help for his eczema* **relief**, alleviation, improvement, assuagement, healing; a remedy, a cure, a restorative. **3** *they treated the help badly* **domestic worker**, domestic servant, cleaner, cleaning lady, home help, maid, housemaid, hired help, helper; Brit. informal daily (woman), skivvy, Mrs Mop; Brit. dated charwoman, charlady, char.
□ **cannot help** *he could not help laughing* be unable to stop, be unable to refrain from, be unable to keep from.
help oneself to steal, take, appropriate, 'borrow', 'liberate', pocket, purloin, commandeer; informal swipe, nab, filch, snaffle, walk off with, run off with; Brit. informal nick, pinch, whip, knock off.

helper n. **assistant**, aide, helpmate, helpmeet, deputy, auxiliary, second, right-hand man/woman, wingman, attendant, acolyte; co-worker, workmate, teammate, associate, colleague, partner; informal sidekick.

helpful adj. **1** *the staff are extremely helpful* **obliging**, eager to please, kind, accommodating, supportive, cooperative; sympathetic, neighbourly, charitable. **2** *we found your comments helpful* **useful**, of use, beneficial, valuable, profitable, fruitful, advantageous, worthwhile, constructive; informative, instructive. **3** *a helpful new tool* **handy**, useful, convenient, practical, easy-to-use, functional, serviceable; informal neat, nifty.
– OPPOSITES unsympathetic, useless, inconvenient.

helping n. **portion**, serving, piece, slice, share, ration, allocation; informal dollop.

helpless adj. **dependent**, incapable, powerless, impotent, weak; defenceless, vulnerable, exposed, unprotected, open to attack; paralysed, disabled.
– OPPOSITES independent.

helpmate, helpmeet n. **helper**, assistant, attendant; supporter, friend, companion; spouse, partner, mate, husband, wife.

helter-skelter adv. *they ran helter-skelter down the hill* **headlong**, pell-mell, hotfoot, post-haste, hastily, hurriedly, at full pelt, at full tilt, hell for leather; recklessly, precipitately, heedlessly, wildly; informal like a bat out of hell, like the wind, like greased lightning, like a bomb; Brit. informal like the clappers, at a rate of knots; N. Amer. informal lickety-split.
▸adj. *a helter-skelter collection of houses* **disordered**, disorderly, chaotic, muddled, jumbled, untidy, haphazard, disorganized, topsy-turvy; informal higgledy-piggledy; Brit. informal shambolic.
– OPPOSITES orderly.

hem n. *the hem of her dress* **edge**, edging, border, trim, trimming.
▸v. *Nan taught me to hem skirts* **edge**, trim.

□ **hem someone/something in** surround, border, edge, encircle, circle, ring, enclose, skirt, fringe, encompass; restrict, confine, trap, kettle, hedge in, fence in; constrain, restrain, limit, curb, check.

he-man n. informal **muscleman**, strongman, macho man, iron man; Hercules, Samson, Tarzan; informal hunk, tough guy, beefcake, bruiser.
– OPPOSITES wimp.

hence adv. **consequently**, as a consequence, for this reason, therefore, ergo, thus, so, accordingly, as a result, because of that, that being so.

henceforth, henceforward adv. **from now on**, as of now, in (the) future, hence, subsequently, from this day on, from this day forth; formal hereafter.

henchman n. **right-hand man**, assistant, aide, helper; underling, minion, man Friday, lackey, flunkey, stooge; bodyguard, minder; informal sidekick, crony, heavy.

henpecked adj. **browbeaten**, downtrodden, bullied, dominated, subjugated, oppressed, intimidated; meek, timid, cringing; informal under someone's thumb, led by the nose.
– OPPOSITES domineering.

herald n. **1** historical *a herald announced the armistice* **messenger**, courier; proclaimer, announcer, crier. **2** *the first herald of spring* **harbinger**, sign, indicator, indication, signal, prelude, portent, omen; forerunner, precursor; literary foretoken.
▸v. **1** *shouts heralded their approach* **proclaim**, announce, broadcast, publicize, declare, trumpet, blazon, advertise. **2** *the speech heralded a policy change* **signal**, indicate, announce, spell, presage, augur, portend, promise, foretell; usher in, pave the way for, be a harbinger of; literary foretoken, betoken.

Herculean adj. **1** *a Herculean task* **arduous**, gruelling, laborious, back-breaking, onerous, strenuous, difficult, formidable, hard, tough, huge, massive, uphill; demanding, exhausting, taxing; old use toilsome. **2** *his Herculean build* **strong**, muscular, muscly, powerful, robust, solid, strapping, brawny, burly; informal hunky, beefy, hulking.
– OPPOSITES easy, puny.

herd n. **1** *a herd of cows* **drove**, flock, pack, fold; group, collection. **2** *a herd of actors* **crowd**, group, bunch, horde, mob, host, pack, multitude, throng, swarm, company. **3** *they consider themselves above the herd* **the common people**, the masses, the rank and file, the crowd, the commonality, the commonalty, the plebeians; the hoi polloi, the mob, the proletariat, the rabble, the riff-raff, the great unwashed; informal the proles, the plebs.
▸v. **1** *we herded the sheep into the pen* **drive**, shepherd, guide; round up, gather, collect, kettle. **2** *we all herded into the room* **crowd**, pack, flock; cluster, huddle. **3** *they herd reindeer* **tend**, look after, keep, watch (over), mind, guard.

herdsman, herdswoman n. **stockman**, herder, drover, cattleman, cowherd, cowhand, cowman, cowboy, rancher, shepherd; N. Amer. ranchero; N. Amer. informal cowpuncher, cowpoke; old use herd.

here adv. **1** *they lived here* **at/in this place**, at/in this spot, at/in this location. **2** *I am here now* **present**, in attendance, attending, at hand; available. **3** *come here tomorrow* **to this place**, to this spot, to this location, over here, nearer, closer; literary hither. **4** *here is your opportunity* **now**, at this moment, at this point (in time), at this juncture, at this stage.
– OPPOSITES absent.
□ **here and there 1** *clumps of heather here and there* **in various places**, in different places; at random. **2** *they darted here and there* **hither and thither**, around, about, to and fro, back and forth, in all directions.

hereafter adv. formal *nothing I say hereafter is intended to offend* **from now on**, after this, as of now, from this moment forth, from this day forth, from this day forward, subsequently, in (the) future, hence, henceforth, henceforward; formal hereinafter.
▸ n. *our preparation for the hereafter* **life after death**, the afterlife, the afterworld, the next world; eternity, heaven, paradise.

hereditary adj. **1** *a hereditary right* **inherited**; bequeathed, willed, handed-down, passed-down, passed-on, transferred; ancestral, family, familial. **2** *a hereditary disease* **genetic**, genetical, congenital, inborn, inherited, inbred, innate; in the family, in the blood, in the genes.

heredity n. **genetic make-up**, genes, congenital traits; ancestry, descent, extraction, parentage.

heresy n. **dissension**, dissent, nonconformity, heterodoxy, unorthodoxy, apostasy, blasphemy, freethinking; agnosticism, atheism, non-belief; idolatry, paganism; iconoclasm.

heretic n. **dissenter**, nonconformist, apostate, freethinker, iconoclast; agnostic, atheist, non-believer, unbeliever, idolater, idolatress, pagan, heathen; old use paynim.
– OPPOSITES conformist, believer.

heritage n. **1** *they stole his heritage* **inheritance**, birthright, patrimony; legacy, bequest; Law, dated hereditament. **2** *Europe's cultural heritage* **tradition**, history, past, background; culture, customs. **3** *his Greek heritage* **ancestry**, lineage, descent, extraction, parentage, roots, background, heredity.

hermaphrodite n. **androgyne**, intersex, epicene; Biology bisexual, gynandromorph.
▸ adj. *hermaphrodite creatures* **androgynous**, intersex, hermaphroditic, hermaphroditical, epicene; Biology bisexual, gynandrous, gynandromorphic.

hermetic adj. **airtight**, tight, sealed; watertight, waterproof.

hermit n. **recluse**, solitary, loner, ascetic; historical anchorite, anchoress; old use eremite.

hermitage n. **retreat**, refuge, hideaway, hideout, shelter; informal hidey-hole.

hero n. **1** *a war hero* **brave man**, man of courage, man of the hour, lionheart, warrior; champion, victor, conqueror. **2** *a football hero* **star**, superstar, megastar, idol, celebrity, luminary; ideal, paragon, shining example; favourite, darling; informal celeb. **3** *the hero of the film* **male protagonist**, principal male character/role, starring role, star part; male lead, lead (actor), leading man.
– OPPOSITES coward, loser, villain.

heroic adj. **1** *heroic rescuers* **brave**, courageous, valiant, valorous, lionhearted, intrepid, bold, fearless, daring, audacious; unafraid, undaunted, dauntless, doughty, plucky, stout-hearted, mettlesome; gallant, chivalrous, noble; informal gutsy, spunky. **2** *obelisks on a heroic scale* **prodigious**, grand, enormous, huge, massive, titanic, colossal, monumental; epic; informal mega.

heroine n. **1** *she's a heroine—she saved my baby* **brave woman**, hero, woman of courage, woman of the hour; victor, winner, conqueror. **2** *the literary heroine of Moscow* **star**, superstar, megastar, idol, celebrity, luminary; ideal, paragon, shining example; favourite, darling; informal celeb. **3** *the film's heroine* **female protagonist**, principal female character/role; female lead, lead (actress), leading lady; prima donna, diva.

heroism n. **bravery**, courage, valour, intrepidity, boldness, daring, audacity, fearlessness, dauntlessness, pluck, stout-heartedness; backbone, spine, grit, spirit, mettle; gallantry, chivalry; informal guts, spunk; Brit. informal bottle; N. Amer. informal moxie.

hero-worship n. **idolization**, adulation, admiration, lionization, idealization, worship, adoration, veneration.

hesitancy n. See **hesitation**.

hesitant adj. **1** *she is hesitant about buying* **uncertain**, undecided, unsure, doubtful, dubious, sceptical; tentative, nervous, reluctant; indecisive, irresolute, hesitating, dithering, vacillating, blowing hot and cold; ambivalent, in two minds; Brit. havering, humming and hawing; informal iffy. **2** *a hesitant child* **lacking confidence**, diffident, timid, shy, bashful, insecure.
– OPPOSITES certain, decisive, confident.

hesitate v. **1** *she hesitated, unsure of what to say* **pause**, delay, wait, shilly-shally, dither, stall, temporize; be in two minds, be uncertain, be unsure, be doubtful, be indecisive, equivocate, vacillate, waver, blow hot and cold, have second thoughts; Brit. haver, hum and haw; informal dilly-dally. **2** *don't hesitate to contact me* **be reluctant**, be unwilling, be disinclined, scruple; have misgivings about, have qualms about, shrink from, demur from, think twice about, balk at.

hesitation n. **hesitancy**, hesitance, uncertainty, unsureness, doubt, doubtfulness, dubiousness; irresolution, irresoluteness, indecision, indecisiveness;

h

equivocation, vacillation, second thoughts; dithering, stalling, temporization, delay; reluctance, disinclination, unease, ambivalence; formal dubiety.

heterodox adj. **unorthodox**, nonconformist, dissenting, dissident, rebellious, renegade; heretical, blasphemous, apostate, sceptical.
– OPPOSITES orthodox.

heterogeneous adj. **diverse**, varied, varying, miscellaneous, assorted, mixed, sundry, disparate, different, differing, unrelated; motley; literary divers.
– OPPOSITES homogeneous.

heterosexual adj. *a heterosexual man* informal **straight**, hetero, het.
– OPPOSITES homosexual, gay.

hew v. **chop**, hack, cut, lop, axe, cleave; fell; carve, shape, fashion, sculpt, model.

heyday n. **prime**, peak, height, pinnacle, acme, zenith; day, time, bloom; prime of life, salad days.

hiatus n. **pause**, break, gap, lacuna, interval, intermission, interlude, interruption, suspension, lull, respite, time out; N. Amer. recess; informal breather, let-up.

hibernate v. **lie dormant**, lie torpid, sleep; overwinter.

hidden adj. **1** *a hidden camera* **concealed**, secret, invisible, unseen, out of sight; camouflaged, disguised, masked. **2** *a hidden meaning* **obscure**, unclear, concealed, indistinct, indefinite, vague, unfathomable, inexplicable; cryptic, mysterious, secret, covert, abstruse, arcane; ulterior, deep, subliminal, coded; Military black.
– OPPOSITES visible, obvious.

hide[1] v. **1** *he hid the money* **conceal**, secrete, put out of sight; camouflage; lock up, stow away, cache; informal stash. **2** *they hid in an air vent* **conceal oneself**, secrete oneself, hide out, take cover, keep out of sight; lie low, go to ground, go to earth; informal hole up; Brit. informal dated lie doggo. **3** *clouds hid the moon* **obscure**, block out, blot out, obstruct, cloud, shroud, veil, blanket, envelop, eclipse. **4** *he could not hide his dislike* **conceal**, keep secret, cover up, keep dark, keep quiet about, hush up, bottle up, suppress; disguise, mask, camouflage; informal keep under one's hat, keep a/the lid on.
– OPPOSITES flaunt, reveal.

hide[2] n. *the hide should be tanned quickly* **skin**, pelt, coat; leather.

hideaway n. **retreat**, refuge, hiding place, hideout, den, bolt-hole, shelter, sanctuary, sanctum; hermitage; informal hidey-hole.

hidebound adj. **conservative**, reactionary, conventional, orthodox; fundamentalist, diehard, hard-line, dyed-in-the-wool, set in one's ways; narrow-minded, small-minded, intolerant, uncompromising, rigid; prejudiced, bigoted; Brit. blimpish.
– OPPOSITES liberal.

hideous adj. **1** *a hideous smile* **ugly**, repulsive, repellent, unsightly, revolting, gruesome, grotesque, monstrous, ghastly, reptilian; informal as ugly as sin. **2** *hideous*

cases of torture **horrific**, terrible, appalling, awful, dreadful, frightful, horrible, horrendous, horrifying, shocking, sickening, gruesome, ghastly, unspeakable, abhorrent, monstrous, heinous, abominable, foul, vile, odious, execrable.
– OPPOSITES beautiful, pleasant.

hideout n. **hiding place**, hideaway, retreat, refuge, shelter, bolt-hole, safe house, sanctuary, sanctum; informal hidey-hole.

hiding[1] n. informal *they gave him a hiding* **beating**, battering, thrashing, thumping, drubbing, pelting; flogging, whipping, caning, birching; informal licking, belting, bashing, pasting, walloping, clobbering, tanning.

hiding[2] n.
□ **in hiding** *the fugitive is in hiding* **hidden**, concealed, lying low, gone to ground, gone to earth, in a safe house; Brit. informal dated lying doggo.

hiding place n. **hideaway**, hideout, retreat, refuge, shelter, sanctuary, sanctum, bolt-hole, safe house; informal hidey-hole.

hie v. old use See **hurry** (sense 1 of the verb).

hierarchy n. **pecking order**, ranking, grading, ladder, scale.

hieroglyphic n. **1** *hieroglyphics on a stone monument* **symbols**, signs, ciphers, code; cryptograms. **2** *notebooks filled with hieroglyphics* **scribble**, scrawl, illegible writing; shorthand.
▸ adj. **1** *hieroglyphic brass ornamentation* **symbolic**, stylized, emblematic. **2** *hieroglyphic handwriting* **illegible**, indecipherable, unreadable, scribbled, scrawled.

higgledy-piggledy informal adj. *a higgledy-piggledy pile of papers* **disordered**, disorderly, disorganized, untidy, messy, chaotic, jumbled, muddled, confused, unsystematic, irregular; out of order, in disarray, in a mess, in a muddle, haphazard; informal all over the place; Brit. informal shambolic.
– OPPOSITES tidy.
▸ adv. *the cars were parked higgledy-piggledy* **in disorder**, in a muddle, in a jumble, in disarray, untidily, haphazardly, anyhow; informal all over the place, topsy-turvy, every which way, any old how; Brit. informal all over the shop; N. Amer. informal all over the map, all over the lot.

high adj. **1** *a high building* **tall**, lofty, towering, elevated, giant, big; multistorey, high-rise. **2** *a high position in the government* **high-ranking**, high-level, leading, top, top-level, prominent, pre-eminent, foremost, senior; influential, powerful, important, elevated, prime, premier, exalted; N. Amer. ranking; informal top-notch. **3** *high principles* **high-minded**, noble, lofty, moral, ethical, honourable, admirable, upright, honest, virtuous, righteous. **4** *high prices* **inflated**, excessive, unreasonable, expensive, dear, costly, exorbitant, extortionate, prohibitive; Brit. over the odds; informal steep,

stiff, pricey. **5** *high standards* **excellent**, outstanding, exemplary, exceptional, admirable, fine, good, first-class, first-rate, superior, superlative, superb; impeccable, irreproachable, unimpeachable, perfect, flawless; informal A1, top-notch. **6** *high winds* **strong**, powerful, violent, intense, extreme, forceful, stiff; blustery, gusty, squally, tempestuous, turbulent. **7** *the high life* **luxurious**, lavish, extravagant, grand, opulent; sybaritic, hedonistic; Brit. upmarket; N. Amer. upscale; informal fancy, classy, swanky. **8** *I have a high opinion of you* **favourable**, good, positive, approving, admiring, complimentary, commendatory, flattering, glowing, adulatory, rapturous. **9** *a very high note* **high-pitched**, high-frequency; soprano, treble, falsetto, shrill, sharp, piercing, penetrating. **10** informal *they are high on drugs* **intoxicated**, inebriated, drugged, stupefied, befuddled, delirious, hallucinating; informal high as a kite, stoned, tripping, hyped up, spaced out, wasted, wrecked, off one's head. **11** *the partridges were high* **gamy**, smelly, strong-smelling; stinking, reeking, rank, malodorous, bad, off, rotting; Brit. informal pongy, niffy, whiffy; N. Amer. informal funky.
– OPPOSITES short, lowly, amoral, cheap, low, light, abstemious, unfavourable, deep, sober, fresh.
▶ n. *prices were at a rare high* **high level**, high point, peak, high water mark; pinnacle, zenith, acme, height.
– OPPOSITES low.
▶ adv. *a jet flew high overhead* **at great height**, high up, far up, way up, at altitude; in the air, in the sky, on high, aloft, overhead.
– OPPOSITES low.
□ **high and dry** destitute, bereft, helpless, in the lurch, in difficulties; abandoned, stranded, marooned.
high and low everywhere, all over, all around, far and wide, {here, there, and everywhere}, extensively, thoroughly, widely, in every nook and cranny; informal all over the place; Brit. informal all over the shop; N. Amer. informal all over the map.
high and mighty informal self-important, condescending, patronizing, disdainful, supercilious, superior, snobbish, snobby, haughty, conceited, above oneself; informal stuck-up, snooty, hoity-toity, la-di-da, uppity; Brit. informal toffee-nosed.
on a high informal ecstatic, euphoric, delirious, elated, thrilled, overjoyed, beside oneself, walking on air, on cloud nine, in seventh heaven, jumping for joy, in raptures, exultant, jubilant; excited, overexcited; informal blissed out, over the moon, on top of the world; Austral./NZ informal wrapped.
high-born adj. **noble**, aristocratic, well born, titled, patrician, blue-blooded, upper-class; informal upper-crust, top-drawer; Brit. informal posh; old use gentle.
– OPPOSITES lowly.
highbrow adj. *his work has a highbrow following* **intellectual**, scholarly, bookish, academic, educated, donnish, bluestocking;

sophisticated, erudite, learned; informal brainy, egghead.
– OPPOSITES lowbrow.
▶ n. *highbrows who hate pop music* **intellectual**, scholar, academic, bookish person, bluestocking, thinker; informal egghead, brain, bookworm; Brit. informal brainbox, boffin; N. Amer. informal brainiac.
high-class adj. **superior**, upper-class, first-rate; excellent, select, elite, choice, premier, top, top-flight; luxurious, deluxe, high-quality, top-quality, top-tier; Brit. upmarket; informal top-notch, top-drawer, A1, classy, posh.
highfalutin adj. informal See **pretentious**.
high-flown adj. **grand**, extravagant, elaborate, flowery, ornate, overblown, overdone, overwrought, grandiloquent, magniloquent, grandiose, inflated, affected, pretentious, turgid; informal windy, purple, highfalutin, la-di-da.
– OPPOSITES plain.
high-handed adj. **imperious**, arbitrary, peremptory, arrogant, haughty, domineering, pushy, overbearing, heavy-handed, lordly; inflexible, rigid; autocratic, authoritarian, undemocratic, anti-democratic, dictatorial, tyrannical; informal bossy, high and mighty.
high jinks plural n. **antics**, pranks, larks, escapades, stunts, practical jokes, tricks; fun (and games), skylarking, mischief, horseplay, tomfoolery, clowning; informal shenanigans, capers, monkey business; Brit. informal monkey tricks.
highland n. **uplands**, highlands, mountains, hills, heights, moors; upland, tableland, plateau; Brit. wolds.
highlight n. *the highlight of his long career* **high point**, high spot, best part, climax, peak, pinnacle, height, acme, zenith, summit, crowning moment, high water mark.
– OPPOSITES nadir.
▶ v. *he has highlighted shortcomings in the plan* **spotlight**, call attention to, focus on, underline, feature, play up, show up, bring out, accentuate, accent, give prominence to, zero in on, stress, emphasize.
highly adv. **1** *a highly dangerous substance* **very**, extremely, exceedingly, particularly, most, really, thoroughly, decidedly, distinctly, exceptionally, immensely, inordinately, singularly, extraordinarily; N. English right; informal terrifically, awfully, terribly, majorly, seriously, desperately, mega, ultra, oh-so, damn, damned; Brit. informal ever so, well, dead, jolly; N. Amer. informal real, mighty, awful; dated frightfully. **2** *he was highly regarded* **favourably**, well, appreciatively, admiringly, approvingly, positively, glowingly, enthusiastically.
– OPPOSITES slightly, unfavourably.
highly strung adj. **nervous**, nervy, excitable, temperamental, sensitive, unstable; brittle, on edge, edgy, restless, anxious, tense, stressed, overwrought, neurotic; informal uptight, jumpy, twitchy, wired, wound up, het up.
– OPPOSITES easy-going.

high-minded adj. **high-principled**, principled, honourable, moral, upright, upstanding, right-minded, noble, good, honest, decent, ethical, righteous, virtuous, worthy, idealistic.
– OPPOSITES unprincipled.

high-pitched adj. **high**, high-frequency, shrill, sharp, piping, piercing; soprano, treble, falsetto.
– OPPOSITES deep.

high-powered adj. **dynamic**, ambitious, driven, energetic, assertive, enterprising, vigorous; forceful, aggressive, pushy, high-octane; informal go-ahead, go-getting; N. Amer. informal go-go.

high-pressure adj. **forceful**, insistent, persistent, pushy; intensive, high-powered, aggressive, coercive, compelling, thrusting, not taking no for an answer.

high-priced adj. **expensive**, costly, dear; overpriced, exorbitant, extortionate; Brit. over the odds; informal pricey, steep, stiff.

high-sounding adj. **grand**, high-flown, extravagant, elaborate, flowery, ornate, overblown, overdone, overwrought, grandiloquent, magniloquent, grandiose, inflated, affected, pretentious, turgid; informal windy, purple, highfalutin, la-di-da.
– OPPOSITES plain.

high-speed adj. **fast**, quick, rapid, speedy, swift, breakneck, lightning, brisk; express, non-stop, whistle-stop; informal nippy, zippy, supersonic; literary fleet.
– OPPOSITES slow.

high-spirited adj. **lively**, spirited, full of fun, fun-loving, animated, zestful, bouncy, bubbly, sparkling, vivacious, buoyant, cheerful, joyful, exuberant, ebullient, jaunty, irrepressible; Brit. Tiggerish; informal chirpy, peppy, sparky, bright and breezy, full of beans; literary frolicsome.

high spirits plural n. **liveliness**, vitality, spirit, zest, energy, bounce, sparkle, vivacity, buoyancy, cheerfulness, good humour, joy, joyfulness, exuberance, ebullience, joie de vivre; informal pep, zing.

highwayman n. historical **bandit**, robber, outlaw, ruffian, marauder, raider; historical footpad; literary brigand.

hijack v. **commandeer**, seize, take over; skyjack; appropriate, expropriate, confiscate; informal snatch.

hike n. *a five-mile hike* **walk**, trek, tramp, trudge, slog, footslog, march; ramble; Brit. informal yomp.
▶v. *they hiked across the moors* **walk**, trek, tramp, trudge, slog, footslog, march; ramble; informal hoof it, leg it; Brit. informal yomp.
□ **hike something up 1** *Roy hiked up his trousers* **hitch up**, pull up, hoist, lift, raise; informal yank up. **2** *they hiked up the price* **increase**, raise, up, put up, mark up, push up, inflate; informal jack up, bump up.

hilarious adj. **1** *a hilarious story* **very funny**, hysterically funny, hysterical, uproarious, riotous, farcical, rib-tickling; humorous, comic, amusing, entertaining; informal side-splitting, priceless, a scream, a hoot. **2** *a hilarious evening* **amusing**, entertaining, animated, high-spirited, lively, funny, merry, jolly, mirthful, cheerful, uproarious, boisterous; informal wacky.
– OPPOSITES sad, serious.

hilarity n. **amusement**, mirth, laughter, merriment, light-heartedness, levity, fun, humour, jocularity, jollity, gaiety, delight, glee, exuberance, high spirits; comedy.

hill n. **high ground**, prominence, hillock, foothill, hillside, rise, mound, mount, mountain, knoll, hummock, tor, tump, fell, pike, mesa; bank, ridge, slope, incline, gradient; (**hills**) heights, downs; Scottish & Irish drum; Scottish brae; Geology drumlin; formal eminence.

hillock n. **mound**, small hill, prominence, elevation, rise, knoll, hummock, hump, tump, dune; bank, ridge; N. English howe; N. Amer. knob; formal eminence.

hilt n. **handle**, haft, handgrip, grip, shaft, shank, stock, helve.
□ **to the hilt** completely, fully, wholly, totally, entirely, utterly, unreservedly, unconditionally, in every respect, in all respects, one hundred per cent, every inch, to the full, to the maximum extent, all the way, body and soul, heart and soul.

hind adj. **back**, rear, hinder, hindmost, posterior.
– OPPOSITES fore, front.

hinder v. **hamper**, obstruct, impede, inhibit, retard, balk, thwart, foil, curb, delay, arrest, interfere with, set back, slow down, hold back, hold up, stop, halt; restrict, restrain, constrain, block, check, curtail, frustrate, cramp, handicap, cripple, hamstring; Brit. throw a spanner in the works; informal stymie.
– OPPOSITES facilitate.

hindmost adj. **furthest back**, last, rear, rearmost, end, endmost, final, tail.
– OPPOSITES leading.

hindrance n. **impediment**, obstacle, barrier, bar, obstruction, handicap, block, hurdle, restraint, restriction, limitation, encumbrance; complication, delay, drawback, setback, difficulty, inconvenience, snag, catch, hitch, fly in the ointment, stumbling block; Brit. spanner in the works; informal hiccup, facer.
– OPPOSITES help.

hinge v. *our future hinges on the election* **depend**, hang, rest, turn, centre, be contingent, be dependent, be conditional; be determined by, be decided by, revolve around.

hint n. **1** *a hint that he would leave* **clue**, inkling, suggestion, indication, indicator, sign, signal, pointer, intimation, insinuation, innuendo, mention, whisper. **2** *handy hints about painting* **tip**, suggestion, pointer, clue, guideline, recommendation; advice, help; informal how-to, wrinkle. **3** *a hint of mint* **trace**, touch, suspicion, suggestion, dash, soupçon, tinge, modicum, whiff, taste, undertone; informal smidgen, tad.

▸ v. *what are you hinting at?* **imply**, insinuate, intimate, suggest, indicate, signal; allude to, refer to, drive at, mean; informal get at.

hinterland n. **the backwoods**, a backwater, the wilds, the bush, the back of beyond; Austral./NZ the outback, the backblocks, the booay; informal the sticks, the middle of nowhere; N. Amer. informal the boondocks, the tall timbers.

hip adj. informal See **fashionable**.

hippy n. **flower child**, bohemian, dropout, free spirit, nonconformist.

hips plural n. **pelvis**, hindquarters, haunches, thighs.

> **WORD LINKS**
> **sciatic** relating to the hips

hire v. **1** *we hired a car* **rent**, lease, charter. **2** *they hire labour in line with demand* **employ**, engage, recruit, appoint, take on, sign up, enrol, commission, enlist.
– OPPOSITES dismiss.
▸ n. *the hire of the machine* **rental**, rent, hiring, lease, leasing, charter.

hire purchase n. **instalment plan**, deferred payment, HP, credit, finance, easy terms; Brit. informal the never-never.

hirsute adj. formal **hairy**, shaggy, bushy, hair-covered; woolly, furry, fleecy, fuzzy; bearded, unshaven, bristly.

hiss v. **1** *the escaping gas hissed* **fizz**, fizzle, whistle, wheeze; rare sibilate. **2** *the audience hissed* **jeer**, catcall, whistle, hoot; scoff, jibe.
▸ n. **1** *the hiss of the steam* **fizz**, fizzing, whistle, hissing, sibilance, wheeze; rare sibilation. **2** *the speaker received hisses* **jeer**, catcall, whistle; abuse, scoffing, taunting, derision.

historian n. **chronicler**, annalist, archivist, recorder; historiographer, antiquarian, chronologist.

historic adj. **significant**, notable, important, momentous, consequential, memorable, unforgettable, remarkable; famous, famed, celebrated, renowned; landmark, groundbreaking, epoch-making, red-letter; informal earth-shattering.
– OPPOSITES insignificant.

historical adj. **1** *historical evidence* **documented**, recorded, chronicled, archival; authentic, factual, actual, true. **2** *historical figures* **past**, bygone, ancient, old, former; literary of yore.
– OPPOSITES contemporary.

history n. **1** *my interest in history* **the past**, former times, historical events, the olden days, the old days, bygone days, yesterday, antiquity; literary days of yore, yesteryear. **2** *a history of the Civil War* **chronicle**, archive, record, report, narrative, account, study, tale; memoir. **3** *she gave details of her history* **background**, past, life story, experiences; antecedents.

histrionic adj. **melodramatic**, theatrical, dramatic, exaggerated, actorly, actressy, stagy, showy, affected, artificial, overacted, overdone; informal hammy, ham, camp.

histrionics plural n. **dramatics**, theatrics, tantrums, overreaction, melodrama; affectation, staginess, artificiality.

hit v. **1** *she hit her child* **strike**, slap, smack, cuff, punch, thump, swat; beat, thrash, batter, belabour, pound, welt, pummel, box someone's ears; whip, flog, cane; informal whack, wallop, bash, biff, bop, lam, clout, clip, clobber, sock, swipe, crown, beat the living daylights out of, give someone a (good) hiding, belt, tan, lay into, let someone have it, deck; Brit. informal stick one on, dot, slosh; N. Amer. informal slug, boff; Austral./NZ informal dong; literary smite. **2** *a car hit the barrier* **crash into**, run into, smash into, smack into, knock into, bump into, cannon into, plough into, collide with, meet head-on; N. Amer. impact. **3** *the tragedy hit her hard* **devastate**, affect badly, hurt, harm, leave its mark on; upset, shatter, crush, shock, overwhelm, traumatize; informal knock sideways, knock the stuffing out of; Brit. informal knock for six. **4** informal *spending will hit £1,800 million* **reach**, touch, arrive at, rise to, climb to. **5** *it hit me that I had forgotten* **occur to**, strike, dawn on, come to; enter one's head, cross one's mind, come to mind, spring to mind.
▸ n. **1** *he received a hit from behind* **blow**, thump, punch, knock, bang, box, cuff, slap, smack, tap, crack, stroke, welt; impact, collision, bump, crash; informal whack, thwack, wallop, bash, belt, biff, clout, sock, swipe, clip; Brit. informal slosh; N. Amer. informal boff, slug; Austral./NZ dong. **2** *a hit at his friend's religion* **jibe**, taunt, jeer, sneer, barb; informal dig, crack, wisecrack, put-down. **3** *he directed many big hits* **success**, box-office success, sell-out, winner, triumph, sensation; best-seller; informal smash (hit), knockout, crowd-puller, wow, biggie; Brit. informal smasher.
– OPPOSITES compliment, failure.
□ **hit back** retaliate, respond, reply, react, counter, defend oneself.
hit home have the intended effect, strike home, hit the mark, register, be understood, get through, sink in.
hit it off informal get on (well), get along, be friends, be friendly, be compatible, feel a rapport, see eye to eye, be on the same wavelength, take to each other, warm to each other; informal click, get on like a house on fire.
hit on discover, come up with, think of, conceive of, dream up, work out, invent, create, devise, design, pioneer; uncover, stumble on, chance on, light on, come upon.
hit out at criticize, attack, censure, denounce, condemn, lambaste, pillory, rail against, inveigh against, arraign, cast aspersions on, pour scorn on, disparage, denigrate; informal knock, pan, slam, hammer, lay into, pull to pieces, pick holes in; Brit. informal slag off, slate, rubbish; N. Amer. informal pummel, trash; formal excoriate.

hitch v. **1** *she hitched the blanket around her* **pull**, jerk, hike, lift, raise; informal yank. **2** *Tom hitched the pony to his cart* **harness**,

yoke, couple, fasten, connect, attach, tether.
3 informal *they hitched to college* **hitch-hike**;
informal thumb a lift, hitch a lift.
▶ n. *it went without a hitch* **problem**, difficulty,
issue, snag, setback, hindrance, obstacle,
obstruction, complication, impediment,
stumbling block, barrier; hold-up,
interruption, delay; informal headache, glitch,
hiccup.

hitherto adv. **previously**, formerly, earlier,
before, beforehand; so far, thus far, to date,
as yet, until now, until then, till now, till
then, up to now, up to then; formal heretofore.

hit-or-miss, **hit-and-miss** adj. **erratic**,
haphazard, disorganized, undisciplined,
unmethodical, uneven; careless, slapdash,
sloppy, slipshod, casual, cursory, lackadaisical,
perfunctory, random, aimless, undirected,
indiscriminate; informal slap-happy.
– OPPOSITES meticulous.

hoard n. *a secret hoard of gold* **cache**,
stockpile, stock, store, collection, supply,
reserve, reservoir, fund, accumulation;
treasure house, treasure trove; informal stash.
▶ v. *they hoarded rations* **stockpile**, store (up),
stock up on, put aside, put by, lay by, lay up,
set aside, stow away, buy up; cache, amass,
collect, save, gather, garner, accumulate,
squirrel away, put aside for a rainy day;
informal stash away, salt away.
– OPPOSITES squander.

hoarse adj. **rough**, harsh, croaky, throaty,
gruff, husky, guttural, growly, gravelly,
grating, rasping.
– OPPOSITES mellow, clear.

hoary adj. **1** *hoary cobwebs* **greyish-white**,
grey, white, silver, silvery; frosty; literary
rimy. **2** *a hoary ancient* **grey-haired**, white-
haired, silver-haired, grizzled; elderly,
aged, old, long in the tooth; informal getting
on, over the hill. **3** *a hoary old adage* **trite**,
hackneyed, clichéd, banal, commonplace,
predictable, overused, stale, time-worn,
tired, unimaginative, unoriginal, uninspired;
informal old hat, corny; N. Amer. informal cornball.
– OPPOSITES young, original.

hoax n. *the call was a hoax* **practical joke**,
joke, jest, prank, trick; ruse, deception,
fraud, bluff, humbug, confidence trick;
informal con, spoof, scam.
▶ v. *the DJ hoaxed his listeners* **play a
(practical) joke on**, play a prank on, trick,
fool; deceive, hoodwink, delude, dupe, take
in, lead on, bluff, gull, humbug; informal con,
kid, have on, pull a fast one on, put one over
on, take for a ride, lead up the garden path;
N. Amer. informal sucker, snooker.

hoaxer n. **(practical) joker**, prankster,
trickster; fraudster, hoodwinker, swindler;
informal spoofer, con man.

hobble v. **limp**, walk with difficulty, move
unsteadily, walk haltingly; shamble, totter,
dodder, stagger, stumble; Scottish hirple.

hobby n. **pastime**, leisure activity, leisure
pursuit; sideline, diversion, avocation;
recreation, entertainment, amusement,
enthusiasm.

hobgoblin n. **goblin**, imp, sprite, elf,
brownie, pixie, leprechaun, gnome; Scottish
kelpie.

hobnob v. informal **associate**, mix, fraternize,
socialize, keep company, spend time, go
around, mingle, consort, rub shoulders;
N. Amer. rub elbows; informal hang around/
round/out, knock about/around, be thick
with.

hocus-pocus n. **jargon**, mumbo jumbo,
argle-bargle, gibberish, balderdash, claptrap,
nonsense, rubbish, twaddle, garbage; informal
gobbledegook, double Dutch, hokum; N. Amer.
informal flapdoodle; informal dated bunkum.

hog n. **pig**, sow, swine, porker, piglet, boar;
informal piggy.
▶ v. informal *he hogged the limelight* **monopolize**,
dominate, take over, corner, control.
– OPPOSITES share.

hogwash n. informal See **nonsense** (sense 1).

hoi polloi n. **the masses**, the common
people, the populace, the public, the
multitude, the rank and file, the lower
orders, the commonality, the commonalty,
the third estate, the plebeians, the
proletariat; the mob, the herd, the rabble,
the riff-raff, the great unwashed; informal the
plebs, the proles.

hoist v. *we hoisted the mainsail* **raise**, lift
(up), haul up, heave up, jack up, hike up,
winch up, pull up, upraise, uplift, elevate,
erect.
– OPPOSITES lower.
▶ n. *a mechanical hoist* **lifting gear**, crane,
winch, block and tackle, pulley, windlass,
derrick.

hoity-toity adj. informal **snobbish**, snobby,
haughty, disdainful, conceited, proud,
arrogant, supercilious, superior, imperious,
above oneself, self-important; informal high
and mighty, snooty, uppity, uppish, la-di-da;
Brit. informal toffee-nosed.

hold v. **1** *she held a suitcase* **clasp**, clutch,
grasp, grip, clench, cling to, hold on to;
carry, bear. **2** *I wanted to hold her* **embrace**,
hug, clasp, cradle, enfold, squeeze, fold in
one's arms. **3** *do you hold a driving licence?*
possess, have, own, bear, carry, have to
one's name. **4** *the branch held my weight*
support, bear, carry, take, keep up, sustain,
prop up, shore up. **5** *the police were holding
him* **detain**, hold in custody, imprison,
lock up, put behind bars, put in prison, put
in jail, incarcerate, keep under lock and
key, confine, intern; informal put away, put
inside. **6** *try to hold the audience's attention*
maintain, keep, occupy, engross, absorb,
interest, captivate, fascinate, enthral, rivet;
engage, catch, capture, arrest. **7** *he held a
senior post* **occupy**, have, fill; informal hold
down. **8** *the tank held 250 gallons* **take**,
contain, accommodate, fit; have a capacity
of, have room for. **9** *the court held that there
was no evidence* **maintain**, consider, take
the view, believe, think, feel, deem, be of the
opinion; judge, rule, decide; informal reckon;
formal opine. **10** *let's hope the weather holds*

persist, continue, carry on, go on, hold out, keep up, last, endure, stay, remain. **11** *the offer still holds* **be available**, be valid, hold good, stand, apply, remain, exist, be the case, be in force, be in effect. **12** *they held a meeting* **convene**, call, summon; conduct, have, organize, run; *formal* convoke.
– OPPOSITES release, lose, end.
▶ n. **1** *she kept a hold on my hand* **grip**, grasp, clasp, clutch. **2** *Tom had a hold over his father* **influence**, power, control, dominance, authority, leverage, sway, mastery. **3** *the military tightened their hold on the capital* **control**, grip, power, stranglehold, dominion, authority.
□ **get hold of** *informal* **1** *I just can't get hold of saffron* **obtain**, acquire, get, find, come by, pick up, procure; buy, purchase; *informal* get one's hands on. **2** *I'll try to get hold of Mark* **contact**, get in touch with, communicate with, make contact with, reach, notify; phone, call, speak to, talk to; *Brit.* ring (up), get on to.
hold back hesitate, pause, stop oneself, desist, forbear.
hold someone back hinder, hamper, impede, obstruct, check, curb, block, thwart, balk, hamstring, restrain, frustrate, stand in someone's way.
hold something back 1 *Jane held back the tears* **suppress**, fight back, choke back, stifle, smother, subdue, rein in, repress, curb, control, keep a tight rein on; *informal* keep a/the lid on. **2** *don't hold anything back from me* **withhold**, hide, conceal, keep secret, keep hidden, keep quiet about, hush up; *informal* sit on, keep under one's hat.
hold someone/something dear cherish, treasure, prize, appreciate, value highly, care for/about, set great store by; *informal* put on a pedestal.
hold something down 1 *they will hold down inflation* **keep down**, keep low, freeze, fix. **2** *informal she held down two jobs* **occupy**, hold, have, do, fill.
hold forth speak at length, talk at length, go on, sound off; declaim, spout, pontificate, orate, preach, sermonize; *informal* speechify, preachify, drone on.
hold off *the rain held off* stay away, keep off, not come.
hold something off resist, repel, repulse, rebuff, parry, deflect, fend off, stave off, ward off, keep at bay.
hold on 1 *hold on a minute* **wait (a minute)**, just a moment, just a second; stay here, stay put; hold the line; *informal* hang on, sit tight, hold your horses; *Brit. informal* hang about. **2** *if only they could hold on a while* **keep going**, persevere, survive, last, continue, struggle on, carry on, go on, hold out, see it through, stay the course; *informal* soldier on, stick at it, hang in there.
hold on to 1 *he held on to the chair* **clutch**, hold, hang on to, clasp, grasp, grip, cling to. **2** *they can't hold on to their staff* **retain**, keep, hang on to.
hold one's own See **own**.

hold out 1 *we held out against the attacks* **resist**, withstand, hold off, fight off, fend off, keep off, keep at bay, stand up to, stand firm against. **2** *our supplies will hold out* **last**, remain, be extant, continue.
hold something out extend, proffer, offer, present; outstretch, reach out, stretch out, put out.
hold something over postpone, put off, put back, delay, defer, suspend, shelve, hold in abeyance; *N. Amer.* put over, table, take a rain check on; *informal* put on ice, put on the back burner, put in cold storage, mothball.
hold up *the argument doesn't hold up* be convincing, be logical, hold water, bear examination, be sound.
hold something up 1 *they held up the trophy* **display**, hold aloft, exhibit, show (off), flourish, brandish; *informal* flash. **2** *concrete pillars hold up the bridge* **support**, hold, bear, carry, take, keep up, prop up, shore up, buttress. **3** *our flight was held up for hours* **delay**, detain, make late, set back, keep back, retard, slow up. **4** *a lack of cash has held up progress* **obstruct**, impede, hinder, hamper, inhibit, balk, thwart, curb, hamstring, frustrate, foil, interfere with, stop; *informal* stymie. **5** *a raider held up the bank* **rob**; *informal* stick up, mug.
hold water See **water**.
hold with approve of, agree with, be in favour of, endorse, accept, countenance, support, subscribe to, take kindly to; *informal* stand for; *Brit. informal* be doing with.

holder n. **1** *a knife holder* **container**, receptacle, case, casing, cover, covering, housing, sheath; stand, rest, rack. **2** *a British passport holder* **bearer**, owner, possessor, keeper; custodian.

holdings plural n. **assets**, funds, capital, resources, savings, investments, securities, equities, bonds, stocks and shares, reserves; property, possessions.

hold-up n. **1** *I ran into a series of hold-ups* **delay**, setback, hitch, snag, difficulty, problem, issue, trouble; traffic jam, tailback, gridlock; *informal* snarl-up, glitch, hiccup. **2** *a bank hold-up* **(armed) robbery**, (armed) raid; theft, burglary, mugging; *informal* stick-up; *N. Amer. informal* heist.

hole n. **1** *a hole in the roof* **opening**, aperture, gap, space, orifice, vent, chink, breach; crack, leak, rift, rupture; puncture, perforation, cut, split, gash, slit, crevice, fissure. **2** *a hole in the ground* **pit**, ditch, trench, cavity, crater, depression, hollow; well, borehole, excavation, dugout; cave, cavern, pothole. **3** *the badger's hole* **burrow**, lair, den, earth, sett; retreat, shelter. **4** *there are holes in their argument* **flaw**, fault, defect, weakness, shortcoming, inconsistency, discrepancy, loophole; error, mistake. **5** *informal I was living in a real hole* **hovel**, slum, shack, mess; *informal* dump, dive, pigsty, tip. **6** *informal they steal when they are in a hole* **predicament**, difficult situation, awkward situation, (tight) corner, quandary, dilemma; crisis, emergency, difficulty, trouble, plight, dire straits; informal fix, jam, bind, (tight) spot, pickle, sticky situation, hot water; Brit. informal spot of bother.

▶v. *a fuel tank was holed by the attack* **puncture**, perforate, pierce, penetrate, rupture, split, rent, lacerate, gash.

▫ **hole up 1** *the bears hole up in winter* **hibernate**, lie dormant. **2** informal *the snipers holed up in a farmhouse* **hide (out)**, conceal oneself, secrete oneself, shelter, take cover, lie low, go to ground, go to earth; Brit. informal dated lie doggo.

pick holes in informal See **criticize**.

hole-and-corner adj. **secret**, secretive, clandestine, covert, furtive, surreptitious; underhand, devious, stealthy, sneaky, backstairs, hugger-mugger, cloak-and-dagger, under-the-counter; Military black; informal hush-hush.

holiday n. **1** *a ten-day holiday* **vacation**, break, rest, recess; time off, time out, leave, furlough, sabbatical; trip, tour, journey, voyage; informal hols, vac, staycation; formal sojourn. **2** *the twenty-fourth of May is a holiday* **public holiday**, bank holiday, festival, feast day, fiesta, celebration, anniversary, jubilee; saint's day, holy day.

holier-than-thou adj. **sanctimonious**, self-righteous, smug, self-satisfied; priggish, pious, pietistic, Pharisaic; informal goody-goody, preachy.
– OPPOSITES humble.

holler informal v. *he hollers when he wants feeding* **shout**, yell, cry (out), vociferate, call (out), roar, bellow, bawl, bark, howl; boom, thunder.
– OPPOSITES whisper.

▶n. *a euphoric holler* **shout**, cry, yell, roar, bellow, bawl, howl; whoop.
– OPPOSITES whisper.

hollow adj. **1** *each fibre has a hollow core* **empty**, void, unfilled, vacant. **2** *hollow cheeks* **sunken**, deep-set, concave, depressed, indented. **3** *a hollow voice* **dull**, low, flat, toneless, expressionless; muffled, muted. **4** *a hollow victory* **meaningless**, empty, valueless, worthless, useless, pyrrhic, futile, fruitless, profitless, pointless. **5** *a hollow promise* **insincere**, hypocritical, feigned, false, sham, deceitful, cynical, spurious, untrue, two-faced; informal phoney, pretend.
– OPPOSITES solid, worthwhile, sincere.

▶n. **1** *a hollow under the tree* **hole**, pit, cavity, crater, trough, cave, cavern; depression, indentation, dip; niche, nook, cranny, recess. **2** *the village lay in a hollow* **valley**, vale, dale; Brit. dene, combe; N. English clough; Scottish glen, strath; literary dell.

▶v. *a tunnel hollowed out of a mountain* **gouge**, scoop, dig, cut; excavate, channel.

▫ **beat someone hollow** trounce, defeat utterly, crush, rout, overwhelm, outclass; informal hammer, clobber, thrash, drub, lick, paste, crucify, slaughter, massacre, flatten, demolish, destroy, annihilate, walk over, wipe the floor with, make mincemeat of; Brit. informal stuff; N. Amer. informal shellac, cream, skunk.

holocaust n. **cataclysm**, disaster, catastrophe; destruction, devastation, annihilation; massacre, slaughter, mass murder, carnage, butchery; genocide, ethnic cleansing.

holy adj. **1** *holy men* **saintly**, godly, saintlike, pious, pietistic, religious, devout, God-fearing, spiritual; righteous, good, virtuous, sinless, pure; canonized, beatified, ordained. **2** *a Jewish holy place* **sacred**, consecrated, hallowed, sanctified, venerated, revered, divine, religious, blessed, dedicated.
– OPPOSITES sinful, irreligious, cursed.

homage n. **respect**, honour, reverence, worship, admiration, esteem, adulation, acclaim; tribute, acknowledgement, recognition; accolade, panegyric, paean, salute.

▫ **pay homage to** honour, acclaim, applaud, salute, praise, commend, pay tribute to, take one's hat off to; formal laud.

home n. **1** *they fled their homes* **residence**, place of residence, house, flat, apartment, bungalow, cottage; accommodation, property, quarters, lodgings, rooms; a roof over one's head; address, place; informal pad, digs, semi; formal domicile, abode, dwelling (place), habitation. **2** *I am far from my home* **homeland**, native land, home town, birthplace, roots, fatherland, motherland, mother country, country of origin, the old country. **3** *a home for the elderly* **institution**, nursing home, retirement home, rest home, children's home; hospice, shelter, refuge, retreat, asylum, hostel. **4** *the home of fine wines* **domain**, realm, origin, source, cradle, fount, fountainhead.

▶adj. **1** *the UK home market* **domestic**, internal, local, national, interior. **2** *home produce* **home-made**, home-grown, local, family.
– OPPOSITES foreign, international.

▫ **at home 1** *she felt very much at home* **at ease**, comfortable, relaxed, content; in one's element. **2** *he is at home with mathematics* **confident with**, conversant with, proficient in; used to, familiar with, au fait with, au courant with, skilled in, experienced in, well versed in; informal well up on. **3** *she was not at home to friends* **entertaining**, receiving; playing host to.

bring something home to someone make someone realize, make someone understand, make someone aware, make something clear to someone; drive home, press home, impress on someone, draw attention to, focus attention on, underline, highlight, spotlight, emphasize, stress.

home in on focus on, concentrate on, zero in on, centre on, fix on; highlight, spotlight, underline, pinpoint; informal zoom in on.

nothing to write home about informal unexceptional, mediocre, ordinary, commonplace, indifferent, average, middle-of-the-road, run-of-the-mill; tolerable, passable, adequate, fair; informal OK, so-so, bog-standard, (plain) vanilla, no great shakes, not so hot, not up to much; Brit. informal common or garden.

h

h

homeland n. **native land**, country of origin, home, fatherland, motherland, mother country, land of one's fathers, the old country.

homeless adj. *homeless people* **of no fixed abode**, without a roof over one's head, on the streets, vagrant, sleeping rough; destitute, down and out.
▶ n. *charities for the homeless* **people of no fixed abode**, vagrants, down-and-outs, tramps, vagabonds, itinerants, transients, migrants, derelicts, drifters; N. Amer. hoboes; Austral. bagmen; informal bag ladies; Brit. informal dossers; N. Amer. informal bums.

homely adj. **1** *a homely atmosphere* **cosy**, homelike, homey, comfortable, snug, welcoming, friendly, congenial, intimate, warm, hospitable, informal, relaxed, pleasant, cheerful; informal comfy. **2** *homely pursuits* **unsophisticated**, everyday, ordinary, domestic, simple, modest, unpretentious, unassuming; homespun, folksy. **3** N. Amer. *she's rather homely* **unattractive**, plain, unprepossessing, unlovely, ill-favoured, ugly; informal not much to look at; Brit. informal no oil painting.
– OPPOSITES uncomfortable, formal, sophisticated, attractive.

homespun adj. **unsophisticated**, plain, simple, unpolished, unrefined, rustic, folksy; coarse, rough, crude, rudimentary.
– OPPOSITES sophisticated.

homey adj. **1** *the house is homey yet elegant* **cosy**, homelike, homely, comfortable, snug, welcoming, informal, relaxed, intimate, warm, pleasant, cheerful; informal comfy.
2 *peasant life was simple and homey* **unsophisticated**, homely, unrefined, unpretentious, plain, simple, modest.
– OPPOSITES uncomfortable, formal, sophisticated.

homicidal adj. **murderous**, violent, brutal, savage, ferocious, vicious, bloody, bloodthirsty, barbarous, barbaric; deadly, lethal, mortal, death-dealing; literary fell; old use sanguinary.

homicide n. **1** *he was charged with homicide* **murder**, killing, slaughter, butchery, massacre; assassination, execution, extermination; patricide, matricide, infanticide; literary slaying. **2** dated *a convicted homicide* **killer**, assassin, serial killer, butcher, slaughterer; patricide, matricide, infanticide; informal hitman, hired gun; dated cut-throat; literary slayer.

homily n. **sermon**, lecture, discourse, address, lesson, talk, speech, oration.

homogeneous adj. **1** *a homogeneous group* **uniform**, identical, unvaried, consistent, undistinguishable; alike, similar, (much) the same, all of a piece; informal much of a muchness. **2** *we have to compete with homogeneous products* **similar**, comparable, equivalent, like, analogous, corresponding, parallel, matching, related; formal cognate.
– OPPOSITES different.

homogenize v. **make uniform**, make similar, standardize, unite, integrate, fuse, merge, blend, meld, coalesce, amalgamate, combine.
– OPPOSITES diversify.

homologous adj. **similar**, comparable, equivalent, like, analogous, corresponding, correspondent, parallel, matching, related, congruent; formal cognate.
– OPPOSITES different.

hone v. **1** *he was carefully honing the long blade* **sharpen**, whet, strop, grind, file. **2** *a great opportunity to hone my skills as a singer* **improve**, develop, enhance, sharpen; upgrade.
– OPPOSITES blunt.

honest adj. **1** *an honest man* **upright**, honourable, moral, ethical, principled, righteous, right-minded, respectable; virtuous, good, decent, law-abiding, high-minded, upstanding, incorruptible, anti-corruption, truthful, trustworthy, trusty, reliable, conscientious, scrupulous, reputable; informal on the level. **2** *I haven't been honest with you* **truthful**, sincere, candid, frank, open, forthright, straight; straightforward, plain-speaking, matter-of-fact; informal upfront. **3** *an honest mistake* **genuine**, real, authentic, actual, true, bona fide, legitimate, fair and square; informal legit, kosher, on the level, honest-to-goodness.
– OPPOSITES unscrupulous, insincere.

honestly adv. **1** *he earned the money honestly* **fairly**, lawfully, legally, legitimately, honourably, decently, ethically, in good faith, by the book; informal on the level. **2** *we honestly believe this is for the best* **sincerely**, genuinely, truthfully, truly, wholeheartedly; really, actually, to be honest, to tell you the truth, to be frank, in all honesty, in all sincerity; informal Scout's honour.

honesty n. **1** *I can attest to his honesty* **integrity**, uprightness, honourableness, honour, morality, morals, ethics, (high) principles, righteousness, right-mindedness; virtue, goodness, probity, high-mindedness, fairness, incorruptibility, truthfulness, trustworthiness, reliability, dependability. **2** *they spoke with honesty about their fears* **sincerity**, candour, frankness, directness, truthfulness, truth, openness, straightforwardness.

honeyed adj. **sweet**, sugary, saccharine, pleasant, flattering, adulatory, unctuous; dulcet, soothing, soft, mellow, mellifluous.
– OPPOSITES harsh.

honorarium n. **fee**, payment, consideration, allowance; remuneration, pay, expenses, compensation, recompense, reward; formal emolument.

honorary adj. **1** *an honorary doctorate* **titular**, nominal, in name only, unofficial, token. **2** Brit. *an honorary treasurer* **unpaid**, unsalaried, voluntary, volunteer; N. Amer. pro bono (publico).

honour n. **1** *a man of honour* **integrity**, honesty, uprightness, ethics, morals,

morality, (high) principles, righteousness, high-mindedness; virtue, goodness, decency, probity, scrupulousness, worth, fairness, justness, trustworthiness, reliability, dependability. **2** *a mark of honour* **distinction**, privilege, glory, kudos, cachet, prestige, merit, credit; importance, illustriousness, notability; respect, esteem, approbation. **3** *our honour is at stake* **reputation**, (good) name, character, repute, image, kudos, standing, stature, status. **4** *he was welcomed with honour* **acclaim**, acclamation, applause, accolades, tributes, compliments, salutes, bouquets; homage, praise, glory, reverence, adulation, exaltation. **5** *she had the honour of meeting the Queen* **privilege**, pleasure, pride, joy; compliment, favour. **6** *military honours* **accolade**, award, reward, prize, decoration, distinction, medal, ribbon, star, laurel; Military, informal fruit salad; Brit. informal gong.
– OPPOSITES unscrupulousness, shame.
▸v. **1** *we should honour our parents* **esteem**, respect, admire, defer to, look up to; appreciate, value, cherish; reverence, revere, venerate, worship; informal put on a pedestal. **2** *they were honoured at a special ceremony* **applaud**, acclaim, praise, salute, recognize, celebrate, commemorate, commend, hail, lionize, exalt, eulogize, pay homage to, pay tribute to, sing the praises of; formal laud. **3** *he honoured the contract* **fulfil**, observe, keep, obey, heed, follow, carry out, discharge, implement, execute, effect; keep to, abide by, adhere to, comply with, conform to, be true to, live up to. **4** *the cheque was not honoured* **accept**, take, clear, pass, cash; Brit. encash.
– OPPOSITES disgrace, criticize, disobey.

honourable adj. **1** *an honourable man* **honest**, moral, ethical, principled, righteous, right-minded; decent, respectable, virtuous, good, upstanding, upright, worthy, noble, fair, just, truthful, trustworthy, trusty, law-abiding, reliable, reputable, dependable. **2** *an honourable career* **illustrious**, distinguished, eminent, great, glorious, prestigious, noble, creditable.
– OPPOSITES crooked, deplorable.

hoodlum n. **hooligan**, thug, lout, delinquent, tearaway, vandal, ruffian; gangster, mobster, criminal, Mafioso; Austral. larrikin; informal tough, bruiser, roughneck, heavy, hitman; Brit. informal yob, yobbo, bovver boy, lager lout; N. Amer. informal hood.

hoodoo n. **witchcraft**, magic, black magic, sorcery, wizardry, devilry, voodoo, necromancy; N. Amer. mojo.

hoodwink v. **deceive**, trick, dupe, outwit, fool, delude, cheat, take in, hoax, mislead, lead on, defraud, double-cross, swindle, gull; informal con, bamboozle, do, have, sting, gyp, diddle, shaft, rip off, lead up the garden path, pull a fast one on, put one over on, take for a ride, pull the wool over someone's eyes; N. Amer. informal sucker, snooker; Austral. informal pull a swifty on; literary cozen.

hoof n. trotter, foot; Zoology ungula.

hook n. **1** *she hung her jacket on the hook* **peg**. **2** *the dress has six hooks* **fastener**, fastening, catch, clasp, hasp, clip, pin. **3** *I had a fish on the end of my hook* **fish hook**, barb, snare. **4** *a right hook to the chin* **punch**, blow, hit, cuff, thump, smack; Scottish & N. English skelp; informal belt, bop, biff, sock, clout, whack, wallop, slug; N. Amer. informal boff.
▸v. **1** *they hooked baskets onto the ladder* **attach**, hitch, fasten, fix, secure, clasp. **2** *he hooked his thumbs in his belt* **curl**, bend, crook, loop, curve. **3** *he hooked a 24 lb pike* **catch**, land, net, take, bag, snare, trap.
◻ **by hook or by crook** by any means, somehow (or other), no matter how, in one way or another, by fair means or foul.
hook, line, and sinker completely, totally, utterly, entirely, wholly, absolutely, through and through, one hundred per cent, {lock, stock, and barrel}.
off the hook informal out of trouble, in the clear, free; acquitted, cleared, reprieved, exonerated, absolved; informal let off.

hooked adj. **1** *a hooked nose* **curved**, hook-shaped, hook-like, aquiline, angular, bent; Biology falcate, falciform, uncinate. **2** informal *they are hooked on cocaine* **addicted to**, dependent on; informal using; N. Amer. informal have a jones for. **3** informal *he is hooked on crosswords* **keen on**, enthusiastic about, addicted to, obsessed with, fixated on, fanatical about; informal mad about, crazy about, wild about, nuts about; Brit. informal potty about.
– OPPOSITES straight.

hooligan n. **hoodlum**, thug, lout, delinquent, tearaway, vandal, ruffian, troublemaker; Austral. larrikin; informal tough, rough, bruiser, roughneck; Brit. informal yob, yobbo, bovver boy, lager lout; Scottish informal ned.

hoop n. **ring**, band, circle, circlet, loop; technical annulus.

hoot n. **1** *the hoot of an owl* **screech**, shriek, call, cry; tu-whit tu-whoo. **2** *the hoot of a horn* **beep**, honk, toot, blast, blare. **3** *hoots of derision* **shout**, yell, cry, howl, shriek, whoop, whistle; boo, hiss, jeer, catcall. **4** informal *your mum's a real hoot* **amusing person**, character, clown; informal scream, laugh, card, case, one, riot, giggle, barrel of laughs; informal dated caution.
▸v. **1** *an owl hooted* **screech**, shriek, cry, call; tu-whit tu-whoo. **2** *a car horn hooted* **beep**, honk, toot, blare, blast, sound. **3** *they hooted in disgust* **shout**, yell, cry, howl, shriek, whistle; boo, hiss, jeer, catcall.
◻ **give a hoot** informal care, be concerned, mind, be interested, be bothered, get worked up; informal give a damn, give a rap, give a monkey's.

hop v. **1** *he hopped along the road* **jump**, bound, spring, bounce, skip, jig, leap; prance, dance, frolic, gambol. **2** informal *she hopped over the Atlantic* **go**, dash; travel; informal pop, whip; Brit. informal nip.
▸n. **1** *the rabbit had a hop around* **jump**, bound, bounce, prance, leap, spring,

gambol. **2** informal *a short hop by taxi* **journey**, distance, ride, drive, run, trip; flight. **3** informal *come to the hop on Saturday* **dance**, social, party, disco; informal bash, bop, shindig, do; Brit. informal rave-up, knees-up.

◻ **on the hop** Brit. informal **1** *he was caught on the hop* **unprepared**, unready, off guard, unawares, by surprise, with one's defences down; informal napping; Brit. informal with one's trousers down. **2** *we were always kept on the hop* **busy**, occupied, employed, working, at work, on the job; rushed off one's feet; informal on the go.

hope n. **1** *I had high hopes* **aspiration**, desire, wish, expectation, ambition, aim, plan; dream, daydream, pipe dream. **2** *a life filled with hope* **hopefulness**, optimism, expectation, expectancy; confidence, faith, trust, belief, conviction, assurance; promise.
– OPPOSITES pessimism.
▶v. **1** *he's hoping for a medal* **expect**, anticipate, look for, be hopeful of, pin one's hopes on, want; wish for, dream of. **2** *we're hoping to address the issue* **aim**, intend, be looking, have the intention, have in mind, plan, aspire.

hopeful adj. **1** *he remained hopeful* **optimistic**, full of hope, confident, positive, buoyant, sanguine, bullish, cheerful; informal upbeat. **2** *hopeful signs* **promising**, encouraging, heartening, reassuring, auspicious, favourable, optimistic, propitious, bright, rosy.

hopefully adv. **1** *he rode on hopefully* **optimistically**, full of hope, confidently, buoyantly, sanguinely; expectantly. **2** *hopefully it should finish soon* **all being well**, if all goes well, God willing, with luck; most likely, probably; conceivably, feasibly; informal touch wood, fingers crossed.

hopeless adj. **1** *her hopeless appeal* **despairing**, desperate, wretched, forlorn, pessimistic, defeatist, resigned; dejected, downhearted, despondent, demoralized. **2** *a hopeless case* **irremediable**, beyond hope, lost, beyond repair, irreparable, irreversible; past cure, incurable; impossible, no-win, futile, forlorn, unworkable, impracticable; old use bootless. **3** *Joseph was hopeless at maths* **bad**, poor, awful, terrible, dreadful, appalling, atrocious; inferior, incompetent, unskilled; informal pathetic, useless, lousy, rotten; Brit. informal duff, rubbish, pants.

hopelessly adv. **1** *she began to cry hopelessly* **despairingly**, in despair, in distress, desperately; dejectedly, downheartedly, despondently, wretchedly, miserably, forlornly. **2** *she was hopelessly lost* **utterly**, completely, irretrievably, impossibly; extremely, very, desperately, totally, dreadfully; informal terribly.

horde n. **crowd**, mob, pack, gang, troop, army, swarm, mass; throng, multitude, host, band, flock; informal crew, tribe, load.

horizon n. **1** *the sun rose above the horizon* **skyline**. **2** *she wanted to broaden her horizons* **outlook**, perspective, perception;

range of experience, scope, ambit, orbit.
◻ **on the horizon** imminent, impending, close, near, approaching, coming, forthcoming, in prospect, at hand, on the way, about to happen, upon us, in the offing, in the pipeline, in the air, just around the corner; brewing, looming, threatening, menacing; informal on the cards.

horizontal adj. **1** *a horizontal surface* level, flat, plane, smooth, even; straight, parallel. **2** *she was stretched horizontal on a sunbed* **flat**, supine, prone, prostrate.
– OPPOSITES vertical.

horny adj. informal **(sexually) aroused**, excited, stimulated, titillated, inflamed; informal turned on, hot, sexed up; Brit. informal randy.

horrendous adj. See **horrible**.

horrible adj. **1** *a horrible murder* **dreadful**, awful, terrible, shocking, appalling, horrifying, horrific, horrendous, grisly, ghastly, gruesome, harrowing, heinous, vile, unspeakable; nightmarish, macabre, spine-chilling; loathsome, monstrous, abhorrent, hateful, execrable, abominable, atrocious, sickening. **2** *a horrible little man* **nasty**, horrid, disagreeable, unpleasant, awful, dreadful, terrible, appalling, foul, repulsive, repellent, ghastly; obnoxious, hateful, odious, objectionable, insufferable, vile, loathsome, abhorrent; informal frightful, God-awful; Brit. informal beastly.
– OPPOSITES pleasant, agreeable.

horrid adj. **1** *horrid apparitions*. See **horrible** (sense 1). **2** informal *the teachers were horrid*. See **horrible** (sense 2).

horrific adj. **dreadful**, horrendous, horrible, frightful, awful, terrible, atrocious; horrifying, shocking, appalling, harrowing, gruesome; hideous, grisly, ghastly, unspeakable, monstrous, nightmarish, sickening.

horrify v. **1** *she horrified us with ghastly tales* **frighten**, scare, terrify, petrify, alarm, panic, terrorize, fill with fear, scare someone out of their wits, frighten the living daylights out of, make someone's hair stand on end, make someone's blood run cold; informal scare the pants off; Brit. informal put the wind up; N. Amer. informal spook; old use affright. **2** *he was horrified by her remarks* **shock**, appal, outrage, scandalize, offend; disgust, revolt, nauseate, sicken.

horror n. **1** *children screamed in horror* **terror**, fear, fright, alarm, panic; dread, trepidation. **2** *to her horror she found herself alone* **dismay**, consternation, perturbation, alarm, distress; disgust, outrage, shock. **3** *the horror of the tragedy* **awfulness**, frightfulness, savagery, barbarity, hideousness; atrocity, outrage. **4** informal *he's a little horror* **rascal**, devil, imp, monkey; informal terror, scamp, scallywag, tyke; Brit. informal perisher; N. Amer. informal varmint.
– OPPOSITES delight, satisfaction.
◻ **have a horror of** hate, detest, loathe, abhor; formal abominate.

horror-struck, **horror-stricken** adj. **horrified**, terrified, petrified, frightened, afraid, fearful, scared, panic-stricken, scared/frightened to death, scared witless; informal scared stiff.

horse n. **mount**, charger, cob, nag, hack; pony, foal, yearling, colt, stallion, gelding, mare, filly; N. Amer. bronco; Austral./NZ moke, yarraman; informal gee-gee; old use steed.
□ **horse around/about** informal fool around/about, play the fool, act the clown, clown about/around, monkey about/around; informal mess about/around, lark about/around; Brit. informal muck about/around; dated play the giddy goat.

> **WORD LINKS**
> **equine** relating to horses
> **equestrian** relating to horse riding
> **equitation** horse riding
> **gymkhana** a horse-riding competition
> **dressage** controlled movements performed by a horse at the rider's command
> **showjumping** the sport of riding horses over obstacles in an arena
> **stable** a place where horses are kept or trained
> **manège** a riding school
> **stud** a place where horses are kept for breeding
> **farrier**, **blacksmith** a person who shoes horses

horseman, **horsewoman** n. **rider**, equestrian, jockey; cavalryman, trooper; historical hussar, dragoon; old use cavalier.

horseplay n. **tomfoolery**, fooling around, foolish behaviour, clowning, buffoonery; pranks, antics, high jinks; informal shenanigans, monkey business; Brit. informal monkey tricks.

horse sense n. informal See **common sense**.

horticulture n. **gardening**, floriculture, arboriculture, agriculture, cultivation.

hose n. **1** *a garden hose* **pipe**, piping, tube, tubing, duct, outlet, pipeline, siphon. **2** *her hose had laddered.* See **hosiery**.

hosiery n. **stockings**, tights, stay-ups, nylons, hose; socks; N. Amer. pantyhose.

hospitable adj. **welcoming**, friendly, congenial, genial, sociable, convivial, cordial; gracious, well disposed, amenable, helpful, obliging, accommodating, neighbourly, warm, kind, generous, bountiful.

hospital n. **infirmary**, sanatorium, hospice, medical centre, health centre, clinic; Brit. cottage hospital; Military field hospital.

hospitality n. **1** *he is renowned for his hospitality* **friendliness**, warm reception, helpfulness, neighbourliness, warmth, kindness, congeniality, geniality, cordiality, amenability, generosity. **2** *corporate hospitality* entertainment; catering, food.

host[1] n. **1** *the host greeted the guests* **party-giver**, hostess, entertainer. **2** *the host of a TV series* **presenter**, compère, anchor, anchorman, anchorwoman, announcer.
– OPPOSITES guest.
▶v. **1** *the Queen hosted a dinner* **give**, have, hold, throw, put on, provide, arrange, organize. **2** *the show is hosted by Angus*

present, introduce, compère, front, anchor.

host[2] n. **1** *a host of memories* **multitude**, lot, abundance, wealth, profusion; informal load, heap, mass, pile, ton; Brit. informal shedload; literary myriad. **2** *a host of film stars* **crowd**, throng, flock, herd, swarm, horde, mob, army, legion; assemblage, gathering.

hostage n. **captive**, prisoner, detainee, internee.

hostel n. **cheap hotel**, YMCA, YWCA, bed and breakfast, B&B, boarding house, guest house, pension.

hostile adj. **1** *a hostile attack* **unfriendly**, unkind, bitter, unsympathetic, malicious, vicious, rancorous, venomous; antagonistic, aggressive, confrontational, belligerent, truculent. **2** *hostile climatic conditions* **unfavourable**, adverse, bad, harsh, grim, hard, tough, inhospitable, forbidding. **3** *they are hostile to the idea* **opposed**, averse, antagonistic, ill-disposed, unsympathetic, antipathetic; opposing, against; informal anti, down on.
– OPPOSITES friendly, favourable.

hostility n. **1** *he glared at her with hostility* **antagonism**, unfriendliness, malevolence, malice, unkindness, rancour, venom, hatred; aggression, belligerence. **2** *their hostility to the present regime* **opposition**, antagonism, animosity, antipathy, ill will, ill feeling, resentment, aversion, enmity. **3** *a cessation of hostilities* **fighting**, (armed) conflict, combat, warfare, war, bloodshed, violence.

hot adj. **1** *hot food* **heated**, piping (hot), sizzling, steaming, roasting, boiling (hot), searing, scorching, scalding, red-hot. **2** *a hot day* **very warm**, balmy, summery, tropical, scorching, searing, blistering; sweltering, torrid, sultry, humid, muggy, close; informal boiling, baking, roasting. **3** *she felt very hot* **feverish**, fevered, febrile; burning, flushed. **4** *a hot chilli* **spicy**, spiced, highly seasoned, peppery, fiery, strong; piquant, pungent, aromatic. **5** *the competition was too hot* **fierce**, intense, keen, competitive, cut-throat, dog-eat-dog, ruthless, aggressive, strong. **6** informal *the hottest story in Fleet Street* **new**, fresh, recent, late, up to date, up to the minute; just out, hot off the press, breaking. **7** informal *this band is hot* **popular**, in demand, sought-after, in favour; fashionable, in vogue, all the rage; informal big, in, now, hip, trendy, cool. **8** informal *she is hot on local history* **knowledgeable about**, well informed about, au fait with, up on, well versed in, au courant with; informal clued-up, genned-up. **9** informal *hot goods* **stolen**, illegally obtained, illegal, illicit, unlawful; smuggled, bootleg, contraband; Brit. informal dodgy.
– OPPOSITES cold, chilly, mild, dispassionate, weak, old, lawful.
□ **blow hot and cold** vacillate, dither, shilly-shally, waver, be indecisive, change one's mind, be undecided, be uncertain, be unsure; Brit. haver, hum and haw; Scottish swither.
hot on the heels of close behind, directly

h

after, right after, straight after, hard on the heels of, following closely.
hot under the collar informal See **angry** (sense 1).

hot air n. informal **nonsense**, rubbish, garbage, empty talk, wind, blather, claptrap, drivel, balderdash, gibberish; pomposity, bombast; informal guff, bosh, hogwash, poppycock, bilge, twaddle; Brit. informal cobblers, codswallop, tosh; N. Amer. informal flapdoodle.

hotbed n. *a hotbed of crime* **breeding ground**, den, cradle, nest.

hot-blooded adj. **passionate**, amorous, amatory, ardent, lustful, libidinous, lecherous, sexy; informal horny, randy.
– OPPOSITES cold.

hotchpotch n. **mixture**, mix, mixed bag, assortment, random collection, jumble, ragbag, miscellany, medley, potpourri; melange, mishmash, confusion, farrago, gallimaufry; N. Amer. hodgepodge.

hotel n. **inn**, motel, boarding house, guest house, bed and breakfast, B&B, hostel; pension, auberge.

hotfoot adv. **hastily**, hurriedly, speedily, quickly, fast, rapidly, swiftly, without delay; at top speed, at full tilt, headlong, post-haste, pell-mell, helter-skelter; informal like the wind, like greased lightning, like blazes; Brit. informal like the clappers, like billy-o; N. Amer. informal lickety-split.
– OPPOSITES slowly.
□ **hotfoot it** informal hurry, dash, run, race, sprint, bolt, dart, career, charge, shoot, hurtle, hare, fly, speed, zoom, streak; informal tear, belt, pelt, scoot, clip, leg it, go like a bat out of hell; Brit. informal bomb; N. Amer. informal hightail it.

hot-headed adj. **impetuous**, impulsive, headstrong, reckless, rash, irresponsible, foolhardy, madcap; excitable, volatile, fiery, hot-tempered, quick-tempered, unruly, harum-scarum.

hothouse n. **greenhouse**, glasshouse, conservatory, orangery, vinery, winter garden.
▶adj. *the school has a hothouse atmosphere* **intense**, oppressive, stifling; overprotected, pampered, shielded.

hotly adv. **1** *the rumours were hotly denied* **vehemently**, vigorously, strenuously, fiercely, passionately, heatedly; angrily, indignantly. **2** *he was hotly pursued by Boris* **closely**, swiftly, quickly, hotfoot; eagerly, enthusiastically.
– OPPOSITES calmly.

hot-tempered adj. **irascible**, quick-tempered, short-tempered, irritable, fiery, bad-tempered; touchy, volatile, testy, tetchy, fractious, prickly, peppery; informal snappish, snappy, chippy, on a short fuse; Brit. informal narky, ratty, like a bear with a sore head; N. Amer. informal soreheaded.
– OPPOSITES easy-going.

hound n. **(hunting) dog**, canine, mongrel, cur; informal doggy, pooch, mutt; Austral./NZ informal mong, bitzer.

▶v. **1** *she was hounded by the press* **pursue**, chase, follow, shadow, be hot on someone's heels, hunt (down), stalk, track, trail; harass, persecute, harry, pester, bother, badger, torment, bedevil; informal hassle, bug, give someone a hard time; N. Amer. informal devil. **2** *they hounded him out of office* **force**, drive, pressure, pressurize, push, urge, coerce, impel, dragoon, strong-arm; nag, bully, browbeat, chivvy; informal bulldoze, railroad; Brit. informal bounce; N. Amer. informal hustle.

house n. **1** *an estate of 200 houses* **residence**, home, place of residence; homestead; a roof over one's head; formal habitation, dwelling (place), abode, domicile. **2** *you'll wake the whole house!* **household**, family, clan, tribe; informal brood. **3** *the house of Stewart* **family**, clan, tribe; dynasty, line, bloodline, lineage, ancestry, family tree. **4** *a printing house* **firm**, business, company, corporation, enterprise, establishment, institution, concern, organization, operation; informal outfit, set-up. **5** *the country's upper house* **legislative assembly**, legislative body, chamber, council, parliament, congress, senate, diet. **6** *the house applauded* **audience**, crowd, spectators, viewers; congregation; gallery, stalls; Brit. informal punters.
▶v. **1** *they can house twelve employees* **accommodate**, provide accommodation for, give someone a roof over their head, lodge, quarter, board, billet, take in, sleep, put up; harbour, shelter. **2** *this panel houses the main switch* **contain**, hold, store; cover, protect, enclose.
□ **on the house** informal free (of charge), without charge, at no cost, for nothing, gratis; courtesy, complimentary; informal for free; N. Amer. informal comp.

household n. *the household was asleep* **family**, house, occupants; clan, tribe; informal brood.
▶adj. *household goods* **domestic**, family; everyday, workaday.

householder n. **homeowner**, owner, occupant, resident; tenant, leaseholder; proprietor, landlady, landlord, freeholder; Brit. occupier, owner-occupier.

housekeeping n. **household management**, domestic work, homemaking, housewifery; home economics; Brit. housecraft.

house-trained Brit. adj. **domesticated**, trained; N. Amer. housebroken.

housing n. **1** *they invested in housing* **houses**, homes, residences, buildings; accommodation, living quarters; formal dwellings, dwelling places, habitations. **2** *the housing for the antennae* **casing**, covering, case, cover, holder, sheath, jacket, shell, capsule.

hovel n. **shack**, slum, shanty, hut; informal dump, hole.

hover v. **1** *helicopters hovered overhead* **be suspended**, be poised, hang, levitate; fly. **2** *she hovered anxiously nearby* **linger**, loiter, wait about; informal hang around, stick around; Brit. informal hang about.

however adv. **1** *however, gaining weight is not inevitable* **nevertheless**, nonetheless, but, still, yet, though, although, even so, for all that, despite that, in spite of that; anyway, anyhow, be that as it may, having said that, notwithstanding; informal still and all. **2** *however you look at it* **in whatever way**, regardless of how, no matter how.

howl n. **1** *the howl of a wolf* **baying**, howling, bay, cry, yowl, bark, yelp. **2** *a howl of anguish* **wail**, cry, yell, yelp, yowl; bellow, roar, shout, shriek, scream, screech.
▸ v. **1** *dogs howled in the distance* **bay**, cry, yowl, bark, yelp. **2** *a baby started to howl* **wail**, cry, yell, yowl, bawl, bellow, shriek, scream, screech, caterwaul; informal holler. **3** *we howled with laughter* **laugh**, guffaw, roar; be creased up, be doubled up, split one's sides; informal fall about, crack up, be in stitches, be rolling in the aisles.

howler n. informal **mistake**, error, blunder, fault, gaffe, slip; informal slip-up, boo-boo, botch, clanger, fail; Brit. informal boob; N. Amer. informal blooper.

hub n. **1** *the hub of the wheel* **pivot**, axis, fulcrum, centre, middle. **2** *the hub of family life* **centre**, core, heart, focus, focal point, nucleus, kernel, nerve centre.
– OPPOSITES periphery.

hubbub n. **1** *her voice was lost in the hubbub* **noise**, din, racket, commotion, clamour, cacophony, babel, rumpus; Brit. informal row. **2** *she fought through the hubbub* **confusion**, chaos, pandemonium, bedlam, mayhem, disorder, turmoil, tumult, fracas, hurly-burly.

hubris n. **arrogance**, conceit, haughtiness, hauteur, pride, self-importance, pomposity, superciliousness, superiority; informal big-headedness.
– OPPOSITES humility.

huckster n. **trader**, dealer, seller, purveyor, vendor, salesman, pedlar, hawker; informal pusher; Brit. informal flogger.

huddle v. **1** *they huddled together* **crowd**, cluster, gather, bunch, throng, flock, herd, collect, group, congregate; press, pack, squeeze. **2** *he huddled beneath the sheets* **curl up**, snuggle, nestle, hunch up.
– OPPOSITES disperse.
▸ n. **1** *a huddle of passengers* **crowd**, cluster, bunch, knot, group, throng, flock, press, pack; collection, assemblage; informal gaggle. **2** *the team went into a huddle* **consultation**, discussion, debate, talk, parley, meeting, conference; informal confab, powwow.

hue n. **1** *paints in a variety of hues* **colour**, shade, tone, tint. **2** *men of all political hues* **complexion**, type, kind, sort, cast, stamp, character, nature.

hue and cry n. **commotion**, outcry, uproar, fuss, clamour, storm, stir, furore, ruckus, brouhaha, palaver, rumpus; informal hoo-ha, hullabaloo, ballyhoo, kerfuffle, to-do, song and dance; Brit. informal row, stink.

huff n. **bad mood**, sulk, fit of pique, pet; temper, tantrum, rage; informal grump; Brit.

informal strop, paddy; N. Amer. informal snit; Brit. informal dated bate, wax.

huffy adj. **irritable**, irritated, annoyed, cross, grumpy, bad-tempered, crotchety, crabby, cantankerous, moody, petulant, sullen, surly; touchy, testy, tetchy, snappish; informal snappy, cranky; Brit. informal narky, miffed, ratty, eggy, shirty, like a bear with a sore head; N. Amer. informal soreheaded.

hug v. **1** *they hugged each other* **embrace**, cuddle, squeeze, clasp, clutch, cling to, hold close, hold tight, take someone in one's arms, clasp someone to one's bosom; literary embosom. **2** *our route hugged the coastline* **follow closely**, keep close to, stay near to, follow the course of. **3** *we hugged the comforting thought* **cling to**, hold on to, cherish, harbour, nurse, foster, retain, keep in mind.
▸ n. *there were hugs as we left* **embrace**, cuddle, squeeze, bear hug, clinch.

huge adj. **enormous**, vast, immense, large, big, great, massive, colossal, prodigious, gigantic, gargantuan, mammoth, monumental; giant, towering, elephantine, mountainous, titanic; epic, Herculean, Brobdingnagian; informal jumbo, mega, monster, whopping, humongous, hulking, bumper, astronomical; Brit. informal ginormous.
– OPPOSITES tiny.

hugely adv. **very**, extremely, exceedingly, most, really, particularly, tremendously, greatly, decidedly, exceptionally, immensely, inordinately, extraordinarily, vastly; very much, to a great extent; N. English right; informal terrifically, awfully, terribly, majorly, seriously, mega, ultra, oh-so, damn, damned; Brit. informal ever so, well, dead, jolly; N. Amer. informal real, mighty, awful; informal dated devilish, frightfully; old use exceeding.

hulk n. **1** *the rusting hulks of ships* **wreck**, shipwreck, ruin, derelict; shell, skeleton, hull. **2** *a great hulk of a man* **giant**, lump; oaf; informal clodhopper, ape, gorilla; N. Amer. informal lummox.

hulking adj. informal **large**, big, heavy, sturdy, burly, brawny, hefty, strapping; bulky, weighty, massive, ponderous; clumsy, awkward, ungainly, lumbering, lumpish, oafish; informal hunky, beefy, clodhopping.
– OPPOSITES small.

hull[1] n. *the ship's hull* **framework**, body, shell, frame, skeleton, structure.

hull[2] n. *seed hulls* **shell**, husk, pod, case, covering, integument, shuck; Botany pericarp, legume.
▸ v. *the bird uses its beak to hull seeds* **shell**, husk, peel, pare, skin, shuck; technical decorticate.

hullabaloo n. informal **fuss**, commotion, hue and cry, uproar, outcry, clamour, storm, furore, hubbub, ruckus, brouhaha; pandemonium, mayhem, tumult, turmoil, hurly-burly; informal hoo-ha, to-do, kerfuffle, song and dance; Brit. informal carry-on, row, stink.

h

h

hum v. **1** *the engine was humming* **purr**, drone, murmur, buzz, thrum, whir, throb, vibrate; literary bombinate. **2** *she hummed a tune* sing, croon, murmur, drone. **3** *the workshops are humming* **be busy**, be active, be lively, buzz, bustle, be a hive of activity, throb. **4** Brit. informal *this stuff really hums.* See **reek** (verb).
▸ n. *a low hum of conversation* **murmur**, drone, purr, buzz; literary bombination.
□ **hum and haw** Brit. hesitate, dither, vacillate, be indecisive, equivocate, prevaricate, waver, blow hot and cold; Brit. haver; Scottish swither; informal shilly-shally.

human adj. **1** *the human race* anthropoid. **2** *they're only human* **mortal**, flesh and blood; fallible, weak, frail, imperfect, vulnerable, susceptible, erring, error-prone; physical, bodily, fleshly. **3** *the human side of politics* **compassionate**, humane, kind, considerate, understanding, sympathetic, tolerant; approachable, accessible.
– OPPOSITES infallible.
▸ n. *the link between humans and animals* **person**, human being, personage, mortal, member of the human race; man, woman; individual, (living) soul, being; Homo sapiens; earthling.

> **WORD LINKS**
> **anthropology** the study of humankind

humane adj. **compassionate**, kind, considerate, understanding, sympathetic, tolerant; lenient, forbearing, forgiving, merciful, mild, tender, clement, benign, humanitarian, benevolent, charitable.
– OPPOSITES cruel.

humanitarian adj. **1** *a humanitarian act* **compassionate**, humane; unselfish, altruistic, generous, magnanimous, benevolent, merciful, kind, sympathetic. **2** *a humanitarian organization* **charitable**, philanthropic, public-spirited, socially concerned, welfare.
– OPPOSITES selfish.
▸ n. **philanthropist**, altruist, benefactor, social reformer, good Samaritan; do-gooder; old use philanthrope.

humanities plural n. **(liberal) arts**, literature; classics, classical studies, classical literature.

humanity n. **1** *humanity evolved from the apes* **humankind**, mankind, man, people, the human race; Homo sapiens. **2** *the humanity of Christ* **human nature**, humanness, mortality. **3** *he praised them for their humanity* **compassion**, brotherly love, fellow feeling, humaneness, kindness, consideration, understanding, sympathy, tolerance; leniency, mercy, mercifulness, pity, tenderness; benevolence, charity.

humanize v. **civilize**, improve, better; educate, enlighten, instruct; sophisticate, socialize, refine, polish; formal edify.

humankind n. **the human race**, the human species, humanity, human beings, mankind, man, people, mortals; Homo sapiens.

humble adj. **1** *her bearing was humble* **meek**, deferential, respectful, submissive, self-effacing, unassertive; unpresuming, modest, unassuming, self-deprecating; Scottish mim. **2** *a humble background* **lowly**, working-class, lower-class, poor, undistinguished, mean, ignoble, low-born; common, ordinary, simple, inferior, unremarkable, insignificant, inconsequential; informal plebby. **3** *my humble abode* **modest**, plain, simple, ordinary, unostentatious, unpretentious.
– OPPOSITES proud, noble, grand.
▸ v. **1** *he humbled himself to ask for help* **humiliate**, abase, demean, lower, degrade, debase; mortify, shame, eat humble pie; take someone down a peg or two; informal cut down to size, settle someone's hash; N. Amer. informal make someone eat crow. **2** *Wales were humbled by Romania* **defeat**, beat, trounce, rout, overwhelm, get the better of, bring to one's knees; informal lick, clobber, slaughter, massacre, crucify, walk all over; N. Amer. informal shellac, cream.

humbug n. **1** *that is sheer humbug* **hypocrisy**, hypocritical talk, sanctimoniousness, posturing, cant, empty talk; insincerity, dishonesty, falseness, deceit, deception, fraud. **2** *you see what a humbug I am?* **hypocrite**, fraud, fake, plaster saint; charlatan, cheat, deceiver, dissembler; informal phoney; literary whited sepulchre.
▸ v. *Dave is easily humbugged* **deceive**, trick, delude, mislead, fool, hoodwink, dupe, take in, beguile, bamboozle, gull; informal con, kid, have on, put one over on someone.

humdrum adj. **mundane**, dull, dreary, boring, tedious, monotonous, prosaic; unexciting, uninteresting, uneventful, unvaried, unremarkable; routine, ordinary, everyday, day-to-day, quotidian, run-of-the-mill, commonplace, workaday, pedestrian; informal (plain) vanilla.
– OPPOSITES remarkable, exciting.

humid adj. **muggy**, close, sultry, sticky, steamy, oppressive, airless, stifling, suffocating, stuffy, clammy, heavy.
– OPPOSITES fresh.

humiliate v. **embarrass**, mortify, humble, shame, put to shame, disgrace; discomfit, chasten, abash, deflate, crush, squash; debase, demean, degrade; cause to feel small, cause to lose face, take down a peg or two; informal show up, put down, cut down to size, settle someone's hash; N. Amer. informal make someone eat crow.

humiliating adj. **embarrassing**, mortifying, humbling, ignominious, inglorious, shameful; discreditable, undignified, chastening, demeaning, degrading, deflating.

humiliation n. **embarrassment**, mortification, shame, indignity, ignominy, disgrace, dishonour, degradation, discredit, obloquy, opprobrium; loss of pride, loss of face; blow to one's pride, slap in the face, kick in the teeth.
– OPPOSITES honour.

humility n. **modesty**, humbleness, meekness, diffidence, unassertiveness; lack of pride, lack of vanity.
– OPPOSITES pride.

hummock n. **hillock**, hump, mound, knoll, tump, prominence, elevation, rise, dune; N. Amer. knob; formal eminence.

humorist n. **comic writer**, wit, wag; comic, funny man/woman, comedian, comedienne, joker, jokester; clown.

humorous adj. **amusing**, funny, comic, comical, entertaining, diverting, witty, jocular, light-hearted, tongue-in-cheek, chucklesome, wry; hilarious, uproarious, riotous, zany, farcical, droll; informal priceless, side-splitting, rib-tickling, a scream, a hoot, a barrel of laughs, waggish; informal dated killing.
– OPPOSITES serious.

humour n. **1** *the humour of the situation* **comedy**, comical aspect, funny side, funniness, hilarity; absurdity, ludicrousness, drollness; satire, irony. **2** *the stories are spiced up with humour* **jokes**, jests, jesting, quips, witticisms, funny remarks, puns; wit, wittiness, comedy, drollery; informal gags, wisecracks, cracks, waggishness, one-liners. **3** *his good humour was infectious* **mood**, temper, disposition, temperament, state of mind; spirits.
▸ v. *she was always humouring him* **indulge**, accommodate, pander to, cater to, yield to, give way to, give in to, go along with; pamper, spoil, overindulge, mollify, placate, gratify, satisfy.

humourless adj. **serious**, solemn, sober, sombre, grave, grim, dour, unsmiling, stony-faced; gloomy, glum, sad, melancholy, dismal, joyless, cheerless, lugubrious; boring, tedious, dull, dry.
– OPPOSITES jovial.

hump n. *a hump at the base of the spine* **protuberance**, prominence, lump, bump, knob, protrusion, projection, bulge, swelling, hunch; growth, outgrowth.
▸ v. **1** *he humped his body to avoid a blow* **arch**, hunch, bend, bow, curve. **2** informal *he humped boxes up the stairs* **heave**, carry, lug, lift, hoist, heft; informal schlep, tote.
– OPPOSITES straighten.
□ **give someone the hump** informal See **annoy**.

hunch v. **1** *he hunched his shoulders* **arch**, curve, hump, bow. **2** *I hunched up as small as I could* **crouch**, huddle, curl; hunker down, bend, stoop, squat.
– OPPOSITES straighten.
▸ n. **1** *the hunch on his back* **protuberance**, hump, lump, bump, knob, protrusion, prominence, bulge, swelling; growth, outgrowth. **2** *my hunch is that he'll be back* **feeling**, feeling in one's bones, guess, suspicion, impression, inkling, idea, notion, fancy, intuition; informal gut feeling.

hundred cardinal number century; informal ton.

WORD LINKS

centenary, **centennial** the hundredth anniversary of an event

centesimal relating to division into hundredths
centenarian a person who is a hundred or more years old
centurion the commander of a hundred men in the ancient Roman army

---

hunger n. **1** *she was faint with hunger* **lack of food**, hungriness, ravenousness, emptiness; starvation, malnutrition, malnourishment, undernourishment. **2** *a hunger for news* **desire**, craving, longing, yearning, hankering, appetite, thirst; want, need; informal itch, yen.
□ **hunger after/for** desire, crave; long for, yearn for, pine for, ache for, hanker after, thirst for, lust for; want, need; informal have a yen for, itch for, be dying for, be gagging for.

hungry adj. **1** *I was really hungry* **ravenous**, empty, in need of food, hollow, faint from hunger; starving, starved, famished; malnourished, undernourished, underfed; informal peckish; old use esurient. **2** *they are hungry for success* **eager**, keen, avid, longing, yearning, aching, greedy; craving, desirous of, hankering after; informal itching, dying, gagging, hot.
– OPPOSITES full.

hunk n. **1** *a hunk of bread* **chunk**, wedge, block, slab, lump, square, gobbet; Brit. informal wodge. **2** informal *he's such a hunk* **muscleman**, strongman, macho man, iron man, Hercules; informal tough guy, he-man, beefcake, stud; N. Amer. informal studmuffin.
– OPPOSITES wimp.

hunt v. **1** *they hunted deer* **chase**, stalk, pursue, course, run down; track, trail, follow, shadow; informal tail. **2** *police are hunting for her* **search**, look (high and low), scour the area; seek, try to find; cast about/around/round, rummage (about/around/round), root about/around, fish about/around.
▸ n. **1** *the thrill of the hunt* **chase**, pursuit. **2** *police have stepped up their hunt* **search**, look, quest.

hunted adj. **harassed**, persecuted, harried, hounded, beleaguered, troubled, stressed, tormented; careworn, haggard; distraught, desperate; informal hassled.
– OPPOSITES carefree.

hunter n. **huntsman**, huntswoman, trapper, stalker, woodsman; nimrod; predator.

hunting n. **blood sports**, field sports, coursing, fox-hunting; trapping; the chase; old use venery.

hurdle n. **1** *his leg hit a hurdle* **fence**, jump, barrier, barricade, bar, railing, rail. **2** *the final hurdle to overcome* **obstacle**, difficulty, problem, barrier, bar, snag, fly in the ointment, stumbling block, impediment, obstruction, complication, hindrance; Brit. spanner in the works; informal headache.

hurl v. **throw**, toss, fling, pitch, cast, lob, bowl, launch, catapult; project, propel, let fly; informal chuck, heave, sling, buzz, bung; N. Amer. informal peg; Austral. & N. English informal hoy; NZ informal bish; dated shy.

hurly-burly n. **bustle**, hustle and bustle, hubbub, confusion, disorder, uproar, tumult,

pandemonium, mayhem, rumpus; informal hoo-ha, hullabaloo, ballyhoo, kerfuffle.
– OPPOSITES calm, order.

hurricane n. **cyclone**, typhoon, tornado, storm, superstorm, tempest, windstorm, whirlwind, gale; Austral. willy-willy; N. Amer. informal twister.

hurried adj. **1** *hurried glances* **quick**, fast, swift, rapid, speedy, brisk, hasty; cursory, perfunctory, brief, short, fleeting, passing, superficial. **2** *a hurried decision* **hasty**, rushed, speedy, quick; impetuous, impulsive, precipitate, precipitous, rash, incautious, imprudent, spur-of-the-moment.
– OPPOSITES slow, considered.

hurriedly adv. **hastily**, speedily, quickly, fast, rapidly, swiftly, briskly; without delay, at top speed, at full tilt, at the double; headlong, hotfoot, post-haste; informal like the wind, like greased lightning, in double quick time; Brit. informal like the clappers, at a rate of knots, like billy-o; N. Amer. informal lickety-split.

hurry v. **1** *hurry or you'll be late* **be quick**, hurry up, hasten, speed up, press on, push on; run, dash, rush, race, fly; scurry, scramble, scuttle, sprint; informal get a move on, step on it, get cracking, get moving, shake a leg, get a wiggle on, tear, hare, zip, zoom, hotfoot it, leg it; Brit. informal shift, get one's skates on, stir one's stumps; N. Amer. informal get the lead out; dated make haste; old use hie. **2** *she hurried him out* **hustle**, hasten, push, urge, drive, spur, goad, prod; informal gee up.
– OPPOSITES dawdle, delay.
▶ n. *in all the hurry, we forgot* **rush**, haste, flurry, hustle and bustle, confusion, commotion, hubbub, turmoil; race, scramble, scurry.

hurt v. **1** *my back hurts* **be painful**, be sore, be tender, cause pain, cause discomfort; ache, smart, sting, burn, throb; informal be killing; Brit. informal be playing up. **2** *Dad hurt his leg* **injure**, wound, damage, disable, incapacitate, maim, mutilate; bruise, cut, gash, graze, scrape, scratch, lacerate. **3** *his words hurt her* **distress**, pain, wound, sting, upset, sadden, devastate, grieve, mortify; cut to the quick. **4** *high interest rates are hurting the economy* **harm**, damage, be detrimental to, weaken, blight, impede, jeopardize, undermine, ruin, wreck, sabotage, cripple.
– OPPOSITES heal, comfort, benefit.
▶ n. **1** *falling properly minimizes hurt* **harm**, injury, wounding, pain, suffering, discomfort, soreness; aching, smarting, stinging, throbbing. **2** *all the hurt he had caused* **distress**, pain, suffering, grief, misery, anguish, trauma, woe, upset, sadness, sorrow; harm, damage, trouble.
– OPPOSITES joy.
▶ adj. **1** *my hurt hand* **injured**, wounded, bruised, grazed, cut, gashed, sore, painful, aching, smarting, throbbing. **2** *Anne's hurt expression* **pained**, distressed, anguished, upset, sad, mortified, offended; informal miffed, peeved, sore.
– OPPOSITES pleased.

hurtful adj. **1** *hurtful words* **upsetting**, distressing, wounding, painful; unkind, cruel, nasty, mean, malicious, spiteful; cutting, barbed; informal catty, bitchy. **2** *this is hurtful to the interests of women* **detrimental**, harmful, damaging, injurious, disadvantageous, unfavourable, prejudicial, deleterious, ruinous.

hurtle v. **speed**, rush, run, race, bolt, dash, career, whizz, zoom, charge, shoot, streak, gallop, hare, fly, scurry, go like the wind; informal belt, pelt, tear, scoot, go like a bat out of hell; Brit. informal bomb, bucket, go like the clappers; N. Amer. informal hightail, barrel.

husband n. **spouse**, partner, mate, consort, man, helpmate, helpmeet; groom, bridegroom; informal hubby, old man, one's better half; Brit. informal other half.
▶ v. *oil reserves should be husbanded* **conserve**, preserve, save, safeguard, put aside, put by, lay in, reserve, stockpile, hoard; use economically, use sparingly, be frugal with.
– OPPOSITES squander.

husbandry n. **1** *farmers have new methods of husbandry* **farm management**, land management, farming, agriculture, agronomy; cultivation; animal husbandry. **2** *the careful husbandry of their resources* **conservation**, management; economy, thrift, thriftiness, frugality.

hush v. **1** *he tried to hush her* **silence**, quieten (down), shush; gag, muzzle; informal shut up. **2** *the crowd hushed* **fall silent**, stop talking, quieten down; informal pipe down, shut up. **3** *they hushed up the dangers* **keep secret**, conceal, hide, suppress, cover up, keep dark, keep quiet about; obscure, veil, sweep under the carpet; informal sit on, keep under one's hat.
– OPPOSITES disclose.
▶ exclam. *Hush! Someone will hear you* **be quiet**, keep quiet, quieten down, be silent, stop talking, hold your tongue; informal shut up, shut your mouth, shut your face, shut your trap, button your lip, pipe down, put a sock in it, give it a rest, save it, not another word; Brit. informal shut your gob; N. Amer. informal save it, can it.
▶ n. *a hush descended* **silence**, quiet, quietness, stillness, peace, peacefulness, calm, tranquillity.
– OPPOSITES noise.

hush-hush adj. informal See **secret** (sense 1 of the adjective).

husk n. **shell**, hull, pod, case, covering, integument, shuck; Botany pericarp, legume.

husky adj. **1** *a husky voice* **throaty**, gruff, gravelly, hoarse, croaky, rough, guttural, harsh, rasping, raspy. **2** *Paddy was a husky guy* **strong**, muscular, muscly, muscle-bound, brawny, hefty, burly, hulking, chunky, strapping, thickset, solid, powerful, heavy, robust, sturdy, Herculean, well built; informal beefy, hunky.
– OPPOSITES shrill, soft, puny.

hussy n. dated **minx**, coquette, tease, seductress, Lolita, Jezebel; slut, loose woman; informal floozie, tart, vamp; Brit. informal scrubber, slapper, slag; N. Amer. informal tramp; dated trollop; old use jade, strumpet.

hustle v. **1** *they were hustled as they went* **jostle**, shove, push, bump, knock, nudge, elbow, shoulder. **2** *I was hustled away* **manhandle**, push, shove, thrust, frogmarch; rush, hurry, whisk; informal bundle. **3** informal *don't be hustled into anything* **coerce**, force, pressure, pressurize, badger, pester, hound, nag, goad, prod; browbeat, bulldoze, steamroller, dragoon; informal railroad, fast-talk.
□ **hustle and bustle** hurly-burly, bustle, tumult, hubbub, activity, action, liveliness, animation, excitement, agitation, flurry, whirl; informal toing and froing, comings and goings, ballyhoo, hoo-ha, hullabaloo.

hut n. **shack**, shanty, (log) cabin, shelter, shed, lean-to; hovel; Scottish bothy, shieling; N. Amer. cabana.

hybrid n. *a hybrid between a brown and albino mouse* **cross**, cross-breed, mixed-breed, half-breed, half blood; mixture, blend, amalgamation, combination, composite, fusion.
▸ adj. *hybrid roses* **composite**, cross-bred, interbred, mongrel; mixed, blended, compound.

hybridize v. **cross-breed**, cross, interbreed, cross-fertilize, cross-pollinate; mix, blend, combine, amalgamate.

hygiene n. **cleanliness**, sanitation, sterility, purity, disinfection; public health, environmental health.

hygienic adj. **sanitary**, clean, germ-free, disinfected, sterilized, sterile, antiseptic, aseptic, unpolluted, uncontaminated, salubrious, healthy, wholesome; informal squeaky clean.
– OPPOSITES insanitary.

hymn n. **religious song**, song of praise, anthem, canticle, chorale, psalm, carol; spiritual.

hype informal n. *her work relies on hype and headlines* **publicity**, advertising, promotion, marketing, propaganda, exposure; informal plugging, ballyhoo; Brit. informal puff.
▸ v. *a stunt to hype a new product* **publicize**, advertise, promote, push, puff, boost, merchandise, build up, bang the drum for; informal plug.

hyperbole n. **exaggeration**, overstatement, magnification, embroidery, embellishment, excess, overkill; informal purple prose, puffery.
– OPPOSITES understatement.

hypercritical adj. **overcritical**, fault-finding, hair-splitting, carping, cavilling, captious, niggling, quibbling, pedantic, pettifogging, fussy, finicky; informal picky, nitpicking, pernickety; N. Amer. informal persnickety; old use nice.

hypnosis n. **mesmerism**, hypnotism, hypnotic suggestion, auto-suggestion.

hypnotic adj. **mesmerizing**, mesmeric, spellbinding, entrancing, bewitching, irresistible, compelling; soporific, sedative,

numbing; Medicine stupefacient.

hypnotism n. **mesmerism**, hypnosis, hypnotic suggestion, auto-suggestion.

hypnotize v. **1** *he had been hypnotized* **mesmerize**, put into a trance. **2** *they were hypnotized by the dancers* **entrance**, spellbind, enthral, transfix, captivate, bewitch, enrapture, grip, rivet, absorb, magnetize.

hypochondriac n. *a hypochondriac who depends on her pills* **valetudinarian**, valetudinary; neurotic.
▸ adj. *her hypochondriac husband* **valetudinarian**, valetudinary, hypochondriacal, malingering, health-obsessed, neurotic.

hypocrisy n. **sanctimoniousness**, sanctimony, pietism, piousness, false virtue, cant, posturing, speciousness, empty talk; insincerity, falseness, deceit, dishonesty, dissimulation, duplicity.
– OPPOSITES sincerity.

hypocrite n. **sanctimonious person**, pietist, plaster saint, humbug, pretender, deceiver, dissembler; informal phoney; literary whited sepulchre.

hypocritical adj. **sanctimonious**, pietistic, pious, self-righteous, holier-than-thou, superior; insincere, specious, false; deceitful, dishonest, dissembling, two-faced; informal phoney.

hypodermic n. **needle**, syringe; informal hype, spike.

hypothesis n. **theory**, theorem, thesis, conjecture, supposition, postulation, postulate, proposition, premise, assumption; notion, concept, idea.

hypothetical adj. **theoretical**, speculative, conjectured, notional, suppositional, supposed, assumed; academic.
– OPPOSITES actual.

hysteria n. **frenzy**, feverishness, hysterics, fit of madness, derangement, mania; panic, alarm, distress; Brit. informal the screaming abdabs.
– OPPOSITES calm.

hysterical adj. **1** *Janet became hysterical* **overwrought**, overemotional, out of control, frenzied, frantic, wild, feverish; beside oneself, driven to distraction, agitated, berserk, manic, delirious, unhinged, deranged, out of one's mind, raving; informal in a state. **2** informal *her attempts to dance were hysterical* **hilarious**, uproarious, very funny, very amusing, comical, farcical; informal hysterically funny, side-splitting, rib-tickling, a scream, a hoot, a barrel of laughs; dated killing.

hysterics plural n. informal **1** *a fit of hysterics* **hysteria**, wildness, feverishness, irrationality, frenzy, loss of control, delirium, derangement, mania; Brit. informal the screaming abdabs. **2** *the girls collapsed in hysterics* **fits of laughter**, gales of laughter, uncontrollable laughter, convulsions, fits; informal stitches.

h

Ii

ice n. **1** *a lake covered with ice* **frozen water**, icicles; black ice, verglas, frost, rime; N. Amer. glaze. **2** *assorted ices* **ice cream**, water ice, sorbet; N. Amer. sherbet. **3** *the ice in her voice* **coldness**, coolness, frostiness, iciness; hostility, unfriendliness.
▸ v. **1** *the lake has iced over* **freeze (over)**, turn into ice, harden, solidify. **2** *I'll ice the drinks* **cool**, chill, refrigerate. **3** *she had iced the cake* **cover with icing**, glaze; N. Amer. frost.
– OPPOSITES thaw, heat.
□ **on ice** informal See **pending** (sense 1 of the adjective).

> **WORD LINKS**
> **glacial** relating to ice
> **glacier** a slowly moving mass of ice
> **floe** a sheet of floating ice
> **iceberg** a large mass of floating ice

ice-cold adj. **icy**, freezing, glacial, gelid, sub-zero, frozen, wintry; arctic, polar, Siberian; bitter, biting, raw, chilly; literary frore, rimy.
– OPPOSITES hot.

icing n. **glaze**, sugar paste; N. Amer. frosting.

icon n. **image**, idol, portrait, representation, symbol; figure, statue.

iconoclast n. **critic**, sceptic; heretic, unbeliever, dissident, dissenter; rebel, renegade, mutineer.

icy adj. **1** *icy roads* **frosty**, frozen (over), iced over, ice-bound, ice-covered, iced up; slippery; literary rimy. **2** *an icy wind* **freezing**, chill, chilly, biting, bitter, raw, arctic, glacial, Siberian, polar, gelid. **3** *an icy voice* **unfriendly**, hostile, forbidding; cold, cool, chilly, frigid, frosty, glacial, gelid; haughty, stern, hard.

idea n. **1** *the idea of death scares her* **concept**, notion, conception, thought; image, visualization; hypothesis, postulation. **2** *our idea is to open a new shop* **plan**, scheme, design, proposal, proposition, suggestion; aim, intention, objective, object, goal, target. **3** *Liz had other ideas on the subject* **thought**, theory, view, opinion, feeling, belief, conclusion. **4** *I had an idea that it might happen* **sense**, feeling, suspicion, fancy, inkling, hunch, theory, notion, impression. **5** *an idea of the cost* **estimate**, estimation, approximation, guess, conjecture, rough calculation; informal guesstimate.

ideal adj. **1** *ideal flying weather* **perfect**, best possible, consummate, supreme, flawless, faultless, exemplary, classic, model, ultimate, quintessential. **2** *an ideal concept* **abstract**, theoretical, conceptual, notional; hypothetical, speculative, conjectural, suppositional. **3** *an ideal world* **unattainable**, unachievable, impracticable; unreal, fictitious, hypothetical, theoretical, ivory-towered, imaginary, idealized, Utopian, fairy-tale.
– OPPOSITES bad, concrete, real.
▸ n. **1** *she tried to be his ideal* **perfection**, paragon, epitome, ne plus ultra, nonpareil, dream; informal one in a million, the tops, the bee's knees. **2** *an ideal to aim at* **model**, pattern, exemplar, example, paradigm, archetype; yardstick. **3** *liberal ideals* **principle**, standard, value, belief, conviction, persuasion; (**ideals**) morals, morality, ethics, ideology, creed.

idealist n. **Utopian**, visionary, fantasist, romantic, dreamer, daydreamer; Walter Mitty, Don Quixote; N. Amer. fantast.
– OPPOSITES realist.

idealistic adj. **Utopian**, visionary, romantic, quixotic, dreamy, unrealistic, impractical.

idealize v. **romanticize**, be unrealistic about, look at something through rose-tinted spectacles, paint a rosy picture of, glamorize.

ideally adv. **in a perfect world**; preferably, if possible, for preference, by choice, as a matter of choice, (much) rather; all things being equal, theoretically, hypothetically, in theory, in principle, on paper.

idée fixe n. **obsession**, fixation, (consuming) passion, mania, compulsion, preoccupation, infatuation, addiction, fetish; phobia, complex, neurosis; informal bee in one's bonnet, hang-up, thing.

identical adj. **1** *the girls were wearing identical tops* **similar**, (exactly) the same, indistinguishable, uniform, twin, interchangeable, undifferentiated, homogeneous, of a piece, cut from the same cloth; alike, like, matching, like (two) peas in a pod; informal much of a muchness. **2** *I used the identical technique* **the (very) same**, the selfsame, the very, one and the same; aforementioned, aforesaid, aforenamed, above, above-stated; foregoing, preceding.
– OPPOSITES different.

identifiable adj. **distinguishable**, recognizable, known; noticeable, perceptible, discernible, appreciable, detectable, observable, perceivable, visible; distinct, marked, conspicuous, unmistakable, clear.
– OPPOSITES unrecognizable.

identification n. **1** *the identification of the suspect* **recognition**, singling out, pinpointing, naming; discerning, distinguishing; informal fingering. **2** *early identification of problems* **determination**, establishment, ascertainment, discovery, diagnosis, divination; verification, confirmation. **3** *may I see your identification?* **ID**, (identity/identification) papers, bona fides, documents, credentials; ID card, identity card, pass, badge, warrant, licence, permit, passport. **4** *the identification of the party with high taxes* **association**, link, linkage, connection, bracketing. **5** *his identification with the music* **empathy**, rapport, unity, togetherness, bond, sympathy, understanding.

identify v. **1** *Gail identified her attacker* **recognize**, single out, pick out, spot, point out, pinpoint, put one's finger on, put a name to, name, know; discern, distinguish; remember, recall, recollect; informal finger. **2** *I identified four problem areas* **determine**, establish, ascertain, make out, diagnose, discern, distinguish; verify, confirm; informal figure out, get a fix on. **3** *we identify sport with glamour* **associate**, link, connect, relate, bracket, couple. **4** *Peter identifies with the hero* **empathize**, be in tune, have a rapport, feel at one, sympathize; be on the same wavelength as, speak the same language as; understand, relate to, feel for. **5** *they identify him with this painter of the same name* **equate with**, identify as, consider to be, regard as being the same as.

identity n. **1** *the identity of the owner* **name**; specification. **2** *she was afraid of losing her identity* **individuality**, self, selfhood; personality, character, originality, distinctiveness, singularity, uniqueness. **3** *a case of mistaken identity* **identification**, recognition, naming, singling out. **4** *we share an identity of interests* **congruity**, congruence, sameness, oneness, interchangeability; likeness, uniformity, similarity, closeness, accordance, alignment.

ideology n. **beliefs**, ideas, ideals, principles, ethics, morals; doctrine, creed, credo, teaching, theory; tenets, canon(s); conviction(s), persuasion.

idiocy n. **stupidity**, folly, foolishness, foolhardiness, madness, insanity, lunacy; silliness, brainlessness, thoughtlessness, senselessness, irresponsibility, imprudence, ineptitude, inanity, absurdity, ludicrousness, fatuousness; informal craziness; Brit. informal daftness.
– OPPOSITES sense.

idiom n. **1** *a rather dated idiom* **expression**, phrase, turn of phrase, locution. **2** *the poet's idiom is terse* **language**, mode of expression, style, speech, locution, usage, phraseology, phrasing, vocabulary, parlance, jargon, patter; informal lingo.

idiomatic adj. **vernacular**, colloquial, everyday, conversational; natural, grammatical, correct.

idiosyncrasy n. **peculiarity**, oddity, eccentricity, mannerism, quirk, whim, vagary, caprice, kink; fetish, foible, crotchet, habit, characteristic; individuality; unconventionality, unorthodoxy; old use megrim, freak.

idiosyncratic adj. **distinctive**, individual, individualistic, characteristic, peculiar, typical, special, specific, unique, personal; eccentric, unconventional, irregular, anomalous, odd, off-centre, quirky, queer, strange, weird, bizarre, freakish; informal freaky.

idiot n. **fool**, ass, halfwit, blockhead, dunce, dolt, ignoramus, simpleton; informal dope, ninny, nincompoop, chump, dimwit, dumbo, dummy, loon, dork, jackass, bonehead, fathead, numbskull, dunderhead, thickhead, woodenhead, airhead, pinhead, lamebrain, cretin, moron, imbecile, pea-brain, birdbrain, jerk, nerd, donkey; Brit. informal nit, nitwit, twit, clot, plonker, plank, berk, prat, pillock, wally, divvy, twerp, charlie, muppet, twonk, herbert; Scottish informal nyaff, balloon; N. Amer. informal schmuck, bozo, turkey, chowderhead, dingbat, wing nut, hoser; Austral./NZ informal drongo, dill, alec, galah.
– OPPOSITES genius.

idiotic adj. **stupid**, silly, foolish, witless, brainless, mindless, thoughtless, unintelligent; imprudent, unwise, ill-advised, ill-considered, half-baked, foolhardy; absurd, senseless, pointless, nonsensical, inane, fatuous, ridiculous; informal dumb, dim, dim-witted, half-witted, dopey, gormless, hare-brained, pea-brained, wooden-headed, thickheaded; Brit. informal barmy, daft; Scottish & N. English informal glaikit.

idle adj. **1** *an idle fellow* **lazy**, indolent, slothful, work-shy, shiftless, inactive, sluggish, lethargic, listless; slack, lax, lackadaisical, good-for-nothing; informal bone idle. **2** *I was bored with being idle* **unemployed**, jobless, out of work, redundant, between jobs, workless, unwaged, unoccupied; Brit. informal on the dole, 'resting'. **3** *they left the machine idle* **inactive**, unused, unoccupied, unemployed, disused; out of action, inoperative, out of service. **4** *their idle hours* **unoccupied**, spare, empty, vacant, unfilled, available. **5** *idle remarks* **frivolous**, trivial, trifling, minor, petty, lightweight, shallow, superficial, insignificant, unimportant, worthless, paltry, niggling, peripheral, inane, fatuous; unnecessary, time-wasting. **6** *idle threats* **empty**, meaningless, pointless, worthless, vain, insubstantial, futile, ineffective, ineffectual; groundless, baseless.
– OPPOSITES industrious, employed, working, busy, serious.
▸ v. **1** *Lily idled on the window seat* **do nothing**, be inactive, vegetate, take it easy, mark time, kick one's heels, twiddle one's thumbs, kill time, languish, laze, lounge, loll, loaf, slouch; informal hang around, veg out; Brit. informal hang about; N. Amer. informal bum around, lollygag. **2** *Rob idled along the pavement* **saunter**,

stroll, dawdle, drift, potter, amble, maunder, wander, straggle; informal mosey, tootle; Brit. informal pootle, mooch. **3** *he let the engine idle* **tick over**.

idler n. **loafer**, layabout, good-for-nothing, ne'er-do-well, lounger, shirker, sluggard, slug; informal skiver, waster, slacker, slowcoach, slob, lazybones; N. Amer. informal slowpoke; literary wastrel.
– OPPOSITES workaholic.

idol n. **1** *an idol in a shrine* **icon**, effigy, statue, figure, figurine, fetish, totem; graven image, false god, golden calf. **2** *the pop world's latest idol* **hero**, heroine, star, superstar, icon, celebrity; favourite, darling; informal pin-up, heart throb, golden boy/girl; Brit. informal blue-eyed boy/girl.

idolatry n. **1** *he preached against idolatry* **idol worship**, fetishism, iconolatry; paganism, heathenism. **2** *our idolatry of art* **idolization**, fetishization, worship, adulation, adoration, reverence, glorification, lionization, hero-worshipping.

idolize v. **hero-worship**, worship, revere, venerate, deify, lionize; stand in awe of, reverence, look up to, admire, exalt; informal put on a pedestal.

idyll n. **1** *an idyll unspoilt by machines* **perfect time**, ideal time; paradise, heaven (on earth), Shangri-La, Utopia; literary Arcadia. **2** *the poem began as a two-part idyll* **pastoral**, eclogue, georgic, rural poem.

idyllic adj. **perfect**, wonderful, blissful, halcyon, happy; ideal, idealized; heavenly, paradisal, Utopian, Elysian; peaceful, picturesque; literary Arcadian.

if conj. **1** *if the weather is fine, we can walk* **on condition that**, provided (that), providing (that), presuming (that), supposing (that), assuming (that), as long as, given that, in the event that. **2** *if I go out she gets nasty* **whenever**, every time. **3** *I wonder if he noticed* **whether**, whether or not. **4** *a useful, if unintended innovation* **although**, albeit, but, yet, whilst; even though, despite being.
▸ n. *there is one if in all this* **uncertainty**, doubt; condition, stipulation, provision, proviso, constraint, precondition, requirement, specification, restriction.

iffy adj. informal **1** *the windscreen's a bit iffy, but it's a good car* **substandard**, second-rate, low-grade, low-quality; doubtful, dubious, questionable; informal not up to much; Brit. informal dodgy, ropy. **2** *that date is a bit iffy* **tentative**, undecided, unsettled, unsure, unresolved, in doubt; informal up in the air.

ignite v. **1** *he got to safety moments before the petrol ignited* **catch fire**, burst into flames; be set off, explode. **2** *a cigarette ignited the fumes* **light**, set fire to, set on fire, set alight, kindle, touch off; informal set/put a match to. **3** *the campaign failed to ignite voter interest* **arouse**, kindle, trigger, spark, instigate, excite, provoke, stimulate, stir up, whip up, incite, fuel.
– OPPOSITES go out, extinguish.

ignoble adj. **dishonourable**, unworthy, base, shameful, contemptible, despicable, shabby, sordid; improper, unprincipled, discreditable.

ignominious adj. **humiliating**, undignified, embarrassing, ignoble, inglorious.
– OPPOSITES glorious.

ignominy n. **shame**, humiliation, embarrassment; disgrace, dishonour, discredit, degradation, scandal, infamy, indignity, ignobility, loss of face.

ignoramus n. **fool**, ass, halfwit, blockhead, dunce, simpleton; informal dope, ninny, nincompoop, chump, dimwit, imbecile, moron, dumbo, dummy, fathead, numbskull, thickhead, woodenhead, airhead, birdbrain; Brit. informal nit, nitwit, twit, clot, plonker, plank, berk, divvy; Scottish informal balloon; N. Amer. informal schmuck, bozo, turkey; Austral./NZ informal drongo.

ignorance n. **1** *his ignorance of economics* **incomprehension**, unawareness, unconsciousness, unfamiliarity, inexperience, innocence, lack of knowledge; informal cluelessness; literary nescience. **2** *their attitudes are based on ignorance* **lack of knowledge**, lack of education; unenlightenment, benightedness; lack of intelligence, stupidity, foolishness, idiocy.
– OPPOSITES knowledge, education.

ignorant adj. **1** *an ignorant country girl* **uneducated**, untaught, unschooled, untutored, untrained, illiterate, unlettered, unlearned, unread, uninformed, unenlightened, benighted; inexperienced, unworldly, unsophisticated; informal pig-ignorant, thick. **2** *they were ignorant of working-class life* **without knowledge**, unaware, unconscious, unfamiliar, unacquainted, uninformed, unenlightened, inexperienced, naive, innocent, green; informal in the dark, clueless; literary nescient.
– OPPOSITES educated, knowledgeable.

ignore v. **1** *he ignored the customers* **disregard**, take no notice of, pay no attention to, pay no heed to; turn a blind eye to, turn a deaf ear to. **2** *he was ignored by the countess* **snub**, slight, spurn, shun, look right through, cold-shoulder, freeze out; Brit. send to Coventry; informal give someone the brush-off, cut (dead); Brit. informal blank. **3** *doctors ignored her husband's instructions* **set aside**, pay no attention to, take no account of; break, contravene, fail to comply with, fail to observe, disregard, disobey, breach, defy, flout.
– OPPOSITES acknowledge, obey.

ilk n. **type**, sort, class, category, group, set, bracket, genre, kidney, vintage, make, model, brand, stamp, variety.

ill adj. **1** *she was feeling rather ill* **unwell**, sick, not (very) well, ailing, poorly, sickly, peaky, indisposed, infirm; out of sorts, not oneself, under/below par, bad, in a bad way; bedridden, invalided, on the sick list, valetudinarian; queasy, nauseous, nauseated; Brit. off colour; informal under the weather,

laid up, lousy, rough; Brit. informal ropy, grotty; Austral./NZ informal crook; Brit. informal dated queer. **2** *the ill effects of smoking* **harmful**, damaging, detrimental, deleterious, adverse, injurious, hurtful, destructive, pernicious, dangerous; unhealthy, unwholesome, poisonous, noxious; literary malefic, maleficent, nocuous; old use baneful. **3** *ill feeling* **hostile**, antagonistic, acrimonious, inimical, antipathetic; unfriendly, unsympathetic; resentful, spiteful, malicious, vindictive, malevolent, bitter. **4** *an ill omen* **unlucky**, adverse, unfavourable, unfortunate, unpropitious, inauspicious, unpromising, infelicitous, ominous, sinister; literary direful. **5** *ill manners* **rude**, discourteous, impolite; impertinent, insolent, impudent, uncivil, disrespectful; informal ignorant. **6** *ill management* **bad**, poor, unsatisfactory, incompetent, deficient, defective, inexpert.
– OPPOSITES well, healthy, beneficial, auspicious, polite.
▶ n. **1** *the ills of society* **problems**, troubles, difficulties, misfortunes, trials, tribulations; worries, anxieties, concerns; informal headaches, hassles. **2** *he wished them no ill* **harm**, hurt, injury, damage, pain, trouble, misfortune, suffering, distress. **3** *the body's ills* **illnesses**, ailments, disorders, complaints, afflictions, sicknesses, diseases, maladies, infirmities.
▶ adv. **1** *such behaviour ill became the king* **poorly**, badly, imperfectly. **2** *the look on her face boded ill* **unfavourably**, adversely, badly, inauspiciously. **3** *he can ill afford the loss of income* **barely**, scarcely, hardly, only just, just possibly. **4** *things are going ill* **badly**, adversely, unsuccessfully, unfavourably; unfortunately, unluckily, inauspiciously. **5** *we are ill prepared* **inadequately**, unsatisfactorily, insufficiently, imperfectly, poorly, badly.
– OPPOSITES well, auspiciously, satisfactorily.
□ **ill at ease** awkward, uneasy, self-conscious, uncomfortable, embarrassed, out of place, inhibited, gauche; restless, restive, fidgety, discomfited, worried, anxious, on edge, edgy, nervous, tense; informal twitchy, jittery; N. Amer. informal discombobulated, antsy.
speak ill of denigrate, disparage, criticize, be critical of, speak badly of, be malicious about, blacken the name of, run down, insult, abuse, attack, revile, malign, vilify; N. Amer. slur; informal bad-mouth, bitch about; Brit. informal rubbish, slate, slag off; formal derogate; rare asperse.

ill-advised adj. **unwise**, injudicious, misguided, imprudent, ill-considered, ill-judged; foolhardy, hare-brained, rash, reckless; informal crazy, crackpot.
– OPPOSITES judicious.

ill-assorted adj. **mismatched**, incongruous, ill-matched, incompatible; dissimilar, unalike, varied, disparate.

ill-bred adj. **ill-mannered**, bad-mannered, rude, impolite, discourteous, uncivil; boorish, churlish, loutish, vulgar, coarse, crass, uncouth, uncivilized, ungentlemanly, indecorous, unseemly; informal ignorant; Brit. informal yobbish.

ill-considered adj. **rash**, ill-advised, ill-judged, injudicious, imprudent, unwise, hasty; misjudged, ill-conceived, badly thought out, hare-brained; literary temerarious.
– OPPOSITES judicious.

ill-defined adj. **vague**, indistinct, unclear, imprecise; blurred, fuzzy, hazy, woolly.

ill-disposed adj. **hostile**, antagonistic, unfriendly, unsympathetic, antipathetic, inimical, unfavourable, averse, at odds; informal anti.
– OPPOSITES friendly.

illegal adj. **unlawful**, illicit, illegitimate, against the law, criminal, felonious; unlicensed, unauthorized, unsanctioned; outlawed, banned, forbidden, prohibited, proscribed; contraband, black-market, bootleg; Law malfeasant; informal crooked, shady; Brit. informal bent, dodgy.
– OPPOSITES lawful, legitimate.

illegible adj. **unreadable**, indecipherable, unintelligible; scrawled, scribbled, crabbed.

illegitimate adj. **1** *illegitimate share trading* **illegal**, unlawful, illicit, against the law, criminal, felonious; unlicensed, unauthorized, unsanctioned; prohibited, outlawed, banned, forbidden, proscribed; fraudulent, corrupt, dishonest; Law malfeasant; informal crooked, shady; Brit. informal bent, dodgy. **2** *an illegitimate child* **born out of wedlock**; dated born on the wrong side of the blanket, unfathered; old use bastard, natural, misbegotten, baseborn, nameless, spurious.
– OPPOSITES legal, lawful.

ill-fated adj. **doomed**, blighted, damned, cursed, ill-starred, jinxed; literary star-crossed.

ill-favoured adj. **unattractive**, plain, ugly; N. Amer. homely; informal not much to look at; Austral./NZ informal drack.
– OPPOSITES attractive.

ill-founded adj. **baseless**, groundless, without foundation, unjustified; questionable, misinformed, misguided.

ill humour n. **bad mood**, bad temper, irritability, irascibility, cantankerousness, petulance, peevishness, pettishness, pique, crabbiness, testiness, tetchiness, fractiousness, snappishness, waspishness, touchiness, moodiness, sullenness, sulkiness, surliness, annoyance, anger, crossness.

ill-humoured adj. **bad-tempered**, ill-tempered, short-tempered, in a (bad) mood, cross; irritable, irascible, tetchy, testy, crotchety, touchy, cantankerous, curmudgeonly, peevish, fractious, waspish, prickly, pettish; grumpy, grouchy, crabbed, crabby, disagreeable, splenetic, dyspeptic, choleric; informal snappish, snappy, chippy, on a short fuse; Brit. informal shirty, stroppy, ratty, like a bear with a sore head; N. Amer. informal cranky, ornery; Austral./NZ informal snaky; informal dated waxy, miffy.
– OPPOSITES amiable.

i

illiberal adj. **intolerant**, conservative, unenlightened, reactionary, undemocratic, authoritarian, anti-democratic, repressive, totalitarian, despotic, tyrannical, oppressive.

illicit adj. **1** *illicit drugs* **illegal**, unlawful, illegitimate, against the law, criminal, felonious; outlawed, banned, forbidden, prohibited, proscribed; unlicensed, unauthorized, unsanctioned; contraband, black-market, bootleg; Law malfeasant. **2** *an illicit love affair* **taboo**, forbidden, impermissible, unacceptable; secret, clandestine.
– OPPOSITES lawful, legal.

illimitable adj. **limitless**, unlimited, unbounded; endless, unending, never-ending, infinite, immeasurable.

illiteracy n. **1** *illiteracy was widespread* **illiterateness**, inability to read or write. **2** *economic illiteracy* **ignorance**, unawareness, inexperience, unenlightenment, lack of knowledge/ education; literary nescience.

illiterate adj. **1** *an illiterate peasant* **unable to read or write**, unlettered. **2** *politically illiterate* **ignorant**, uneducated, unschooled, untutored, untrained, uninstructed, uninformed; literary nescient.

ill-judged adj. **ill-considered**, unwise, ill-thought-out; imprudent, incautious, injudicious, misguided, ill-advised, impolitic, inexpedient; rash, hasty, thoughtless, careless, reckless.
– OPPOSITES judicious.

ill-mannered adj. **bad-mannered**, discourteous, rude, impolite, uncivil, abusive; insolent, impertinent, impudent, cheeky, presumptuous, disrespectful; badly behaved, ill-behaved, loutish, oafish, uncouth, uncivilized, ill-bred; informal ignorant.
– OPPOSITES polite.

ill-natured adj. **mean**, nasty, spiteful, malicious, disagreeable; ill-tempered, bad-tempered, moody, irritable, irascible, surly, sullen, peevish, petulant, fractious, crabbed, crabby, tetchy, testy, grouchy.

illness n. **sickness**, disease, ailment, complaint, malady, affliction, infection, indisposition; ill health, poor health, infirmity; informal bug, virus; Brit. informal lurgy; dated contagion.

> **WORD LINKS**
> **convalesce**, **recuperate** recover one's health after an illness
> **remission** a temporary period in which a serious illness becomes less severe
> **psychosomatic** relating to physical illness caused or made worse by a mental factor
> **iatrogenic** relating to illness which is caused by medical treatment
> See also **disease**.

illogical adj. **irrational**, unreasonable, unsound, unreasoned, unjustifiable; incorrect, erroneous, invalid, spurious, faulty, flawed, fallacious, unscientific;

specious, sophistic, casuistic; absurd, preposterous, untenable; informal off beam, way out.

ill-starred adj. **ill-fated**, doomed, ill-omened, blighted, damned, cursed, jinxed; unlucky, luckless, unfortunate, hapless; literary star-crossed.
– OPPOSITES blessed.

ill temper n. **bad mood**, irritation, vexation, exasperation, indignation, huff, moodiness, pet, pique; anger, crossness, bad temper; irritability, irascibility, peevishness, tetchiness, testiness; informal grump; Brit. informal paddy, strop; N. Amer. informal blowout, hissy fit; Brit. informal dated bate, wax.

ill-tempered adj. **bad-tempered**, short-tempered, ill-humoured, moody; in a (bad) mood, cross, irritable, irascible, tetchy, testy, crotchety, touchy, cantankerous, curmudgeonly, peevish, fractious, waspish, prickly, pettish; grumpy, grouchy, crabbed, crabby, disagreeable, splenetic, dyspeptic, choleric; informal snappish, snappy, chippy, on a short fuse; Brit. informal shirty, stroppy, ratty; N. Amer. informal cranky, ornery; Austral./NZ informal snaky; informal dated waxy, miffy.

ill-timed adj. **untimely**, mistimed, badly timed; premature, early, hasty, inopportune.
– OPPOSITES timely.

ill-treat v. **abuse**, mistreat, maltreat, ill-use, misuse; manhandle, handle roughly, molest; harm, injure, damage; informal knock about/ around.

ill-treatment n. **abuse**, mistreatment, maltreatment, ill use, ill usage, misuse; manhandling, rough treatment.

illuminate v. **1** *the bundle was illuminated by the torch* **light (up)**, throw light on, brighten, shine on; literary illumine. **2** *the manuscripts were illuminated* **decorate**, illustrate, embellish, adorn, ornament. **3** *documents often illuminate people's thought processes* **clarify**, elucidate, explain, reveal, shed light on, give insight into.
– OPPOSITES darken, conceal.

illuminating adj. **informative**, enlightening, revealing, explanatory, instructive, helpful, educational.

illumination n. **1** *a floodlamp provided illumination* **light**, lighting, radiance, gleam, glow, glare; shining, gleaming, glowing; literary illumining, irradiance, lucency, lambency, effulgence, refulgence. **2** *the illumination of a manuscript* **decoration**, illustration, embellishment, adornment, ornamentation. **3** *these books give illumination on the subject* **clarification**, elucidation, explanation, revelation, explication. **4** *moments of real illumination* **enlightenment**, insight, understanding, awareness; learning, education; formal edification.

illusion n. **1** *he had destroyed her illusions* **delusion**, misapprehension, misconception, false impression; fantasy, fancy, dream, chimera. **2** *the lighting increases the illusion of depth* **appearance**, impression, semblance. **3** *it's just an illusion* **mirage**, hallucination, apparition, figment of the imagination, trick of the light. **4** *magical illusions* **(magic) trick**, conjuring trick; (**illusions**) magic, conjuring, sleight of hand, legerdemain.

illusory adj. **delusory**, delusive; illusionary, imagined, imaginary, fanciful, fancied, unreal; sham, false, fallacious, fake, bogus, mistaken, erroneous, misguided, untrue.
– OPPOSITES genuine.

illustrate v. **1** *the photographs that illustrate the book* **decorate**, adorn, ornament, accompany; add pictures/drawings to, provide artwork for. **2** *this can be illustrated through a brief example* **explain**, elucidate, clarify, make plain, demonstrate, show, emphasize; informal get across/over. **3** *his wit was illustrated by his remark to Lucy* **exemplify**, show, demonstrate, display, represent.

illustrated adj. **with illustrations**, with pictures, with drawings, pictorial.

illustration n. **1** *the illustrations in children's books* **picture**, drawing, sketch, figure, plate, print. **2** *by way of illustration* **exemplification**, demonstration, showing; example, typical case, case in point, analogy. **3** *a career in illustration* **artwork**, (graphic) design; ornamentation, decoration, embellishment.

illustrative adj. **exemplifying**, explanatory, elucidatory, elucidative, explicative, expository, illuminative, exegetic.

illustrious adj. **eminent**, distinguished, acclaimed, notable, noteworthy, prominent, pre-eminent, foremost, leading, important, influential; renowned, famous, famed, well known, celebrated; esteemed, honoured, respected, venerable, august, highly regarded, well thought of, of distinction.
– OPPOSITES unknown.

ill will n. **animosity**, hostility, enmity, acrimony, animus, hatred, hate, loathing, antipathy; ill feeling, bad blood, antagonism, unfriendliness, dislike; spite, spitefulness, resentment, hard feelings, bitterness; old use disrelish.
– OPPOSITES goodwill.

image n. **1** *an image of the Madonna* **likeness**, resemblance; depiction, portrayal, representation; statue, statuette, sculpture, bust, effigy; painting, picture, portrait, drawing, sketch, artist's impression. **2** *images of the planet Neptune* **picture**, photograph, snapshot, photo. **3** *he contemplated his image in the mirror* **reflection**, mirror image, likeness. **4** *the image of this country as democratic* **conception**, impression, idea, perception, notion; mental picture, vision. **5** *biblical images* **simile**, metaphor, metonymy; figure of speech, trope, turn of phrase. **6** *his heart-throb image* **public perception**, persona, profile, face, front, facade, mask, guise. **7** *I'm the image of my grandfather* **double**, living image, lookalike, clone, copy, twin, duplicate, exact likeness, mirror image; informal spitting image, dead ringer; old use similitude. **8** *a graven image* **idol**, icon, fetish, totem.

WORD LINKS
iconography, **iconology** the use or study of images

imaginable adj. **thinkable**, conceivable, supposable, believable, credible, creditable; possible, plausible, feasible; rare cogitable.

imaginary adj. **unreal**, non-existent, fictional, fictitious, pretend, make-believe, mythical, fabulous, fanciful, illusory; made-up, dreamed-up, invented, fancied; old use visionary.
– OPPOSITES real.

imagination n. **1** *a vivid imagination* **creative power**, fancy; informal mind's eye. **2** *you need imagination in dealing with these problems* **creativity**, imaginativeness, creativeness; vision, inspiration, inventiveness, invention, resourcefulness, ingenuity; originality, innovation, innovativeness. **3** *the album captured the public's imagination* **interest**, fascination, attention, passion, curiosity.

imaginative adj. **creative**, visionary, inspired, inventive, resourceful, ingenious; original, innovative, innovatory, unorthodox, unconventional, off-centre; fanciful, whimsical; informal blue-sky.

imagine v. **1** *one can imagine the cloud-capped castle* **visualize**, envisage, envision, picture, see in the mind's eye; dream up, think up/of, conceive. **2** *I imagine he was at home* **assume**, presume, expect, take it (as read), presuppose; suppose, think (it likely), dare say, surmise, believe, be of the view; N. Amer. figure; informal guess, reckon; formal opine.

imbalance n. **disparity**, variance, variation, polarity, contrast, lack of harmony; gulf, breach, gap.

imbed v. See **embed**.

imbibe v. formal **1** *they'd imbibed too much whisky* **drink**, consume, quaff, guzzle, gulp (down); informal knock back, down, sink; Brit. informal neck; N. Amer. informal chug. **2** *he had imbibed liberally* **drink (alcohol)**, tipple; informal booze, knock a few back; N. Amer. informal bend one's elbow, chug; old use tope. **3** *imbibing local history* **assimilate**, absorb, soak up, take in, drink in, learn, acquire, grasp, pick up, familiarize oneself with.

imbroglio n. **complicated situation**, complication, problem, difficulty, predicament, trouble, confusion, entanglement, muddle, mess; informal bind, jam, pickle, fix, corner, hole.

imbue v. **permeate**, saturate, diffuse, suffuse, pervade; impregnate, inject, inculcate, ingrain, inspire; fill.

imitate v. **1** *other artists have imitated his style* **emulate**, copy, model oneself on, follow, echo, parrot; informal rip off. **2** *he imitated Winston Churchill* **mimic**, do an impression of, impersonate, ape; parody, caricature, burlesque, travesty; informal take off, send up; N. Amer. informal make like; formal personate; old use monkey. **3** *the tombs* *imitated houses* **resemble**, look like, be like; echo, mirror; bring to mind, remind one of.

imitation n. **1** *an imitation of a sailor's hat* **copy**, simulation, reproduction, replica. **2** *learning by imitation* **emulation**, copying, echoing, parroting. **3** *a perfect imitation of Francis* **impersonation**, impression, parody, mockery, caricature, burlesque, travesty, lampoon, pastiche; mimicry, mimicking, imitating, aping; informal send-up, take-off, spoof.
▸ adj. *imitation ivory* **artificial**, synthetic, simulated, man-made, manufactured, ersatz, substitute, faux; mock, false, sham, fake, bogus; informal pseudo, phoney.
– OPPOSITES real, genuine.

imitative adj. **1** *imitative crime* **similar**, like, mimicking; informal copycat. **2** *I found the film empty and imitative* **derivative**, unoriginal, unimaginative, uninspired, plagiarized, plagiaristic; clichéd, hackneyed, stale, trite, banal; informal cribbed, old hat. **3** *imitative words* **onomatopoeic**, echoic.

imitator n. **1** *the show's success has sparked off many imitators* **copier**, copyist, emulator, follower, mimic, plagiarist, ape, parrot; informal copycat. **2** *an Elvis imitator* **impersonator**, impressionist, mimicker; parodist, caricaturist, lampooner.

immaculate adj. **1** *an immaculate white shirt* **clean**, spotless, pristine, unsoiled, unstained, unsullied; shining, shiny, gleaming; neat, tidy, spick and span; informal squeaky clean. **2** *immaculate condition* **perfect**, pristine, mint; flawless, faultless, unblemished, unspoiled, undamaged; excellent, impeccable; informal tip-top, A1. **3** *his immaculate record* **unblemished**, spotless, impeccable, unsullied, undefiled, untarnished, stainless; informal squeaky clean.
– OPPOSITES dirty, damaged.

immanent adj. **1** *the protection of liberties immanent in the constitution* **inherent**, intrinsic, innate, latent, essential, fundamental, basic. **2** *God is immanent in His creation* **pervasive**, pervading, permeating; omnipresent.

immaterial adj. **1** *the difference in our ages was immaterial* **irrelevant**, unimportant, inconsequential, insignificant, of no matter/moment, of little account, beside the point, neither here nor there. **2** *the immaterial soul* **intangible**, incorporeal, bodiless, disembodied, impalpable, ethereal, insubstantial; spiritual, unearthly, supernatural.
– OPPOSITES significant, physical.

immature adj. **1** *an immature Stilton* **unripe**, not mature, unmellowed; undeveloped, unformed, unfinished. **2** *an extremely immature girl* **childish**, babyish, infantile, juvenile, puerile, jejune, callow, green, inexperienced, unsophisticated, unworldly, naive; informal wet behind the ears.
– OPPOSITES ripe.

immeasurable adj. **incalculable**, inestimable, innumerable, untold; limitless, boundless, unbounded, unlimited, illimitable, infinite, cosmic, never-ending, interminable, endless, inexhaustible; vast, immense, great, abundant; informal no end of; literary myriad.

immediate adj. **1** *the UN called for immediate action* **instant**, instantaneous, prompt, swift, speedy, rapid, quick, expeditious; sudden, hurried, hasty, precipitate; informal snappy; literary rathe. **2** *their immediate concerns* **current**, present, existing, actual; urgent, pressing. **3** *the immediate past* **recent**, just gone. **4** *our immediate neighbours* **nearest**, near, close, closest, next-door; adjacent, adjoining. **5** *the immediate cause of death* **direct**, primary.
– OPPOSITES delayed, distant.

immediately adv. **1** *it was necessary to make a decision immediately* **straight away**, at once, right away, instantly, now, directly, promptly, forthwith, this/that (very) minute, this/that instant, there and then, here and now, without delay, without further ado, post-haste; quickly, as fast as possible, speedily, as soon as possible, ASAP; informal pronto, in double-quick time, pretty damn quick, p.d.q., toot sweet; old use instanter, forthright. **2** *I sat immediately behind him* **directly**, right, exactly, precisely, squarely, just, dead; informal slap bang; N. Amer. informal smack dab.

immemorial adj. **ancient**, (very) old, age-old, antediluvian, timeless, archaic, long-standing, time-worn, time-honoured; traditional; literary of yore.

immense adj. **huge**, vast, massive, enormous, gigantic, colossal, cosmic, great, very large/big, monumental, towering, tremendous; giant, elephantine, monstrous, mammoth, titanic, king-sized; informal mega, monster, whopping (great), thumping (great), humongous, jumbo; Brit. informal whacking (great), ginormous.
– OPPOSITES tiny.

immensely adv. **extremely**, very, exceedingly, exceptionally, extraordinarily, tremendously, hugely, singularly, distinctly, outstandingly, uncommonly, unusually, decidedly, particularly, eminently, supremely, highly, remarkably, really, truly, mightily, thoroughly, in the extreme; informal terrifically, awfully, fearfully, terribly, devilishly, seriously, mega, damn, damned; Brit. informal ever so, well, bloody, hellish, dead, jolly; N. Amer. informal real, mighty, powerful, awful, darned; informal dated devilish, frightfully; old use exceeding.
– OPPOSITES slightly.

immerse v. **1** *litmus paper turns red on being immersed in acid* **submerge**, dip, dunk, duck, sink; soak, drench, saturate, wet. **2** *new Christians were immersed in the river* **baptize**, christen; informal dated dip; rare lustrate. **3** *Elliot was immersed in his work* **absorb**, engross, occupy, engage, involve, bury; busy, employ, preoccupy; informal lose oneself in.

immigrant n. **newcomer**, settler, incomer, migrant, emigrant; non-native, foreigner, alien.
– OPPOSITES native.

imminent adj. **impending**, close (at hand), near, (fast) approaching, coming, forthcoming, on the way, in the offing, in the pipeline, on the horizon, in the air/wind, expected, anticipated, brewing, looming; informal on the cards.

immobile adj. **1** *she sat immobile for a long time* **motionless**, without moving, still, stock-still, static, stationary; rooted to the spot, rigid, frozen, transfixed, like a statue, not moving a muscle. **2** *she dreaded being immobile* **unable to move**, immobilized; paralysed, crippled.
– OPPOSITES moving.

immobilize v. **put out of action**, disable, make inoperative, inactivate, deactivate, paralyse, cripple; bring to a standstill, halt, stop; clamp, wheel-clamp.

immoderate adj. **excessive**, heavy, intemperate, unrestrained, unrestricted, uncontrolled, unlimited, unbridled, uncurbed, overindulgent, imprudent, reckless; undue, inordinate, unreasonable, unjustified, unwarranted, uncalled for, outrageous; extravagant, lavish, prodigal, profligate.

immodest adj. **indecorous**, improper, indecent, indelicate, immoral; forward, bold, brazen, impudent, shameless, loose, wanton; informal fresh, cheeky, saucy.

immolate v. **sacrifice**, offer up; kill, slaughter, burn.

immoral adj. **unethical**, bad, morally wrong, wrongful, wicked, evil, unprincipled, unscrupulous, dishonourable, dishonest, unconscionable, iniquitous, disreputable, corrupt, depraved, vile, villainous, nefarious, base, miscreant; sinful, impure, unchaste, unvirtuous, shameless, degenerate, debauched, dissolute, reprobate, lewd, licentious, wanton, promiscuous; informal shady, low-down; Brit. informal dodgy, crooked.
– OPPOSITES ethical, chaste.

immorality n. **wickedness**, immoral behaviour, badness, evil, vileness, corruption, dishonesty, dishonourableness; sinfulness, unchastity, sin, depravity, vice, degeneracy, debauchery, dissolution, perversion, lewdness, wantonness, promiscuity; informal shadiness; Brit. informal crookedness; formal turpitude.

immortal adj. **1** *our souls are immortal* **undying**, deathless, eternal, everlasting, never-ending, endless, lasting, enduring; imperishable, indestructible, inextinguishable, immutable. **2** *an immortal children's classic* **timeless**, perennial, classic, time-honoured, enduring; famous, famed, renowned, great, eminent, outstanding, acclaimed, celebrated.
▸n. **1** *Greek temples of the immortals* **god**, goddess, deity, divine being, supreme being, divinity. **2** *one of the immortals of soccer*

great, hero, Olympian.

immortality n. **1** *the immortality of the gods* **eternal life**, everlasting life, deathlessness; indestructibility, imperishability. **2** *the book has achieved immortality* **timelessness**, legendary status, lasting fame/renown.

immortalize v. **commemorate**, memorialize, eternalize; celebrate, eulogize, pay tribute to, honour, salute, exalt, glorify; literary eternize.

immovable adj. **1** *lock your bike to something immovable* **fixed**, secure, stable, moored, anchored, braced, set firm, set fast; stuck, jammed, stiff, unbudgeable. **2** *he sat immovable* **motionless**, unmoving, stationary, still, stock-still, not moving a muscle, rooted to the spot; transfixed, paralysed, frozen. **3** *she was immovable in her loyalties* **steadfast**, unwavering, unswerving, resolute, determined, firm, unshakeable, unfailing, dogged, tenacious, inflexible, unyielding, unbending, uncompromising, iron-willed; N. Amer. rock-ribbed.
– OPPOSITES mobile, moving.

immune adj. **resistant**, not subject, not liable, unsusceptible, not vulnerable; protected from, safe from, secure against, not in danger of.
– OPPOSITES susceptible.

immunity n. **1** *an immunity to malaria* **resistance**, non-susceptibility; ability to fight off, protection against, defences against; immunization against, inoculation against. **2** *immunity from prosecution* **exemption**, exception, freedom, release, dispensation; informal a let-off. **3** *diplomatic immunity* **indemnity**, privilege, prerogative, right, liberty, licence; legal exemption, impunity, protection.

immunize v. **vaccinate**, inoculate, inject; protect from, safeguard against; informal give someone a jab/shot.

immure v. **confine**, intern, shut up, lock up, incarcerate, imprison, jail, put behind bars, put under lock and key, hold captive, hold prisoner; detain, hold.

immutable adj. **fixed**, set, rigid, inflexible, permanent, established; unchanging, unchanged, unvarying, unvaried, static, constant, lasting, enduring.
– OPPOSITES variable.

imp n. **1** *imps are thought to sprout from Satan* **demon**, devil, fiend; hobgoblin, goblin, elf, sprite, puck, cacodemon; old use bugbear. **2** *a cheeky young imp* **rascal**, monkey, devil, troublemaker, wretch, urchin, tearaway; informal scamp, brat, monster, horror, tyke, whippersnapper; Brit. informal perisher; N. Amer. informal hellion, varmint; old use scapegrace, rapscallion.

impact n. **1** *the force of the impact* **collision**, crash, smash, bump, bang, knock. **2** *the job losses will have a major impact* **effect**, influence; consequences, repercussions, ramifications, reverberations.
▸v. **1** N. Amer. *a comet impacted the earth sixty*

million years ago **crash into**, smash into, collide with, hit, strike, smack into, bang into. **2** *high interest rates have impacted on retail spending* **affect**, influence, have an effect, make an impression; hit, touch, change, alter, modify, transform, shape.

impair v. **have a negative effect on**, damage, harm, diminish, reduce, weaken, lessen, decrease, impede, hinder; undermine, compromise; formal vitiate.
– OPPOSITES improve, enhance.

impaired adj. **disabled**, handicapped, incapacitated; euphemistic challenged, differently abled.

impairment n. **disability**, handicap, abnormality, defect, dysfunction.

impale v. **stick**, skewer, spear, spike, transfix; pierce, stab, run through; literary transpierce.

impalpable adj. **intangible**, insubstantial, incorporeal; indefinable, elusive, indescribable.

impart v. **1** *she had news to impart* **communicate**, pass on, convey, transmit, relay, relate, recount, tell, make known, make public, report, announce, proclaim, spread, disseminate, circulate, promulgate, broadcast; disclose, reveal, divulge; informal let on about, blab; old use discover, unbosom. **2** *the brush imparts a good sheen* **give**, bestow, confer, grant, lend, afford, provide, supply.

impartial adj. **unbiased**, unprejudiced, neutral, non-partisan, disinterested, detached, dispassionate, objective, open-minded, equitable, even-handed, fair, just.
– OPPOSITES biased, partisan.

impassable adj. **unpassable**, unnavigable; closed, blocked.

impasse n. **deadlock**, dead end, stalemate, checkmate, stand-off; standstill, halt, (full) stop.

impassioned adj. **emotional**, heartfelt, wholehearted, earnest, sincere, fervent, ardent, passionate, fervid; literary perfervid; rare passional.

impassive adj. **expressionless**, inexpressive, inscrutable, blank, deadpan, poker-faced, straight-faced; stony, wooden, unresponsive.
– OPPOSITES expressive.

impatience n. **1** *he was shifting in his seat with impatience* **restlessness**, restiveness, agitation, nervousness; eagerness, keenness; informal jitteriness. **2** *a burst of impatience* **irritability**, testiness, tetchiness, irascibility, querulousness, peevishness, frustration, exasperation, annoyance, pique.

impatient adj. **1** *Melissa grew impatient* **restless**, restive, agitated, nervous, anxious, ill at ease, edgy, keyed up, nervy; informal twitchy, jumpy, jittery, uptight. **2** *they are impatient to get back home* **anxious**, eager, keen, yearning, longing, aching; informal itching, dying. **3** *an impatient gesture* **irritated**, annoyed, angry, testy, tetchy, snappy, cross, querulous, peevish, piqued; short-tempered; abrupt, curt, brusque, terse, short; informal peeved.
– OPPOSITES calm, reluctant.

impeach v. **1** N. Amer. *moves to impeach the president* **indict**, charge, accuse, lay charges against, arraign, take to court, put on trial, prosecute. **2** *the headlines impeached their clean image* **challenge**, question, call into question, raise doubts about.

impeccable adj. **flawless**, faultless, unblemished, spotless, stainless, perfect, exemplary; sinless, irreproachable, blameless, guiltless; informal squeaky clean.
– OPPOSITES imperfect, sinful.

impecunious adj. **penniless**, poor, impoverished, indigent, insolvent, hard up, poverty-stricken, needy, destitute; in straitened circumstances, unable to make ends meet; Brit. on the breadline; informal (flat) broke, strapped (for cash), cash-strapped, on one's uppers; Brit. informal skint, stony broke, in Queer Street; N. Amer. informal stone broke; formal penurious.
– OPPOSITES wealthy.

impede v. **hinder**, obstruct, hamper, hold back/up, delay, interfere with, disrupt, retard, slow (down); block, check, stop, thwart, frustrate, balk, foil, derail; Brit. throw a spanner in the works; N. Amer. throw a monkey wrench in the works; informal stymie; Brit. informal scupper; N. Amer. informal bork; dated cumber.
– OPPOSITES facilitate.

impediment n. **1** *an impediment to economic improvement* **hindrance**, obstruction, obstacle, barrier, bar, block, check, curb, restriction, limitation; setback, difficulty, problem, issue, snag, hitch, fly in the ointment, stumbling block; Brit. spanner in the works; N. Amer. monkey wrench in the works; informal hiccup; old use cumber. **2** *a speech impediment* **defect**; stammer, stutter, lisp.

impedimenta plural n. **paraphernalia**, trappings, equipment, accoutrements, appurtenances, accessories, bits and pieces, tackle; informal stuff, gear; Brit. informal clobber, gubbins; old use equipage.

impel v. **1** *financial difficulties impelled her to seek work* **force**, compel, constrain, oblige, require, make, urge, press, pressurize, drive, push, spur, prod, goad, incite, prompt, persuade. **2** *vital energies impel him in unforeseen directions* **propel**, drive, move, get going, get moving.

impending adj. **imminent**, close (at hand), near, nearing, approaching, coming, forthcoming, upcoming, to come, on the way, about to happen, in store, in the offing, on the horizon, in the air/wind, brewing, looming, threatening, menacing.

impenetrable adj. **1** *impenetrable armoured plating* **unbreakable**, indestructible, solid, thick, unyielding; impregnable, inviolable, unassailable, unpierceable. **2** *a dark, impenetrable forest* **impassable**, unpassable, inaccessible, unnavigable; dense, thick, overgrown. **3** *an impenetrable clique* **exclusive**, closed, secretive, secret, private; restrictive, restricted, limited.

4 *impenetrable statistics* **incomprehensible**, unfathomable, inexplicable, unintelligible, unclear, baffling, bewildering, puzzling, perplexing, confusing, abstruse, opaque; complex, complicated, difficult; old use wildering.

impenitent adj. **unrepentant**, unrepenting, uncontrite, remorseless, unashamed, unapologetic, unabashed.

imperative adj. **1** *it is imperative that you find him* **vitally important**, of vital importance, all-important, vital, crucial, critical, essential, necessary, indispensable, urgent. **2** *the imperative note in her voice* **peremptory**, commanding, imperious, authoritative, masterful, dictatorial, assertive, firm, insistent.
– OPPOSITES unimportant, submissive.

imperceptible adj. **unnoticeable**, undetectable, indistinguishable, indiscernible, invisible, inaudible, impalpable, unobtrusive; slight, small, subtle, faint, fine, negligible; indistinct, unclear, obscure, vague, indefinite, hard to make out.
– OPPOSITES noticeable.

imperfect adj. **1** *the goods were found to be imperfect* **faulty**, flawed, defective, shoddy, unsound, inferior, unsellable, second-rate, below standard, substandard; damaged, blemished, torn, broken, cracked, scratched; informal not up to scratch, tenth-rate, crummy; Brit. informal duff. **2** *an imperfect form of the manuscript* **incomplete**, unfinished, half-done; unpolished, unrefined, rough. **3** *she spoke imperfect Arabic* **broken**, faltering, halting, hesitant, rudimentary, limited.
– OPPOSITES flawless.

imperfection n. **1** *the glass is free from imperfections* **defect**, fault, flaw, deformity, discoloration, disfigurement; crack, scratch, chip, dent, blemish, stain, spot, mark. **2** *he was aware of his imperfections* **flaw**, fault, failing, deficiency, weakness, weak point, shortcoming, foible, inadequacy, limitation. **3** *the imperfection of the fossil record* **incompleteness**, patchiness, deficiency; roughness, crudeness.
– OPPOSITES strength.

imperial adj. **1** *imperial banners* **royal**, regal, monarchal, monarchial, monarchical, sovereign, kingly, queenly, princely. **2** *her imperial bearing* **majestic**, grand, dignified, proud, stately, noble, aristocratic, regal; magnificent, imposing, impressive. **3** *our customers thought we were imperial* **imperious**, high-handed, peremptory, dictatorial, domineering, bossy, arrogant, overweening, overbearing.

imperil v. **endanger**, jeopardize, risk, put in danger, put in jeopardy, expose to danger; threaten, pose a threat to; old use peril.

imperious adj. **peremptory**, high-handed, commanding, imperial, overbearing, overweening, domineering, authoritarian, dictatorial, authoritative, lordly, assertive, bossy, arrogant; informal pushy, high and mighty.

imperishable adj. **enduring**, everlasting, undying, immortal, perennial, long-lasting; indestructible, inextinguishable, ineradicable, unfading, permanent, never-ending, never dying; literary sempiternal, perdurable.

impermanent adj. **temporary**, transient, transitory, passing, fleeting, momentary, ephemeral, fugitive; short-lived, brief, here today and gone tomorrow; literary evanescent.

impermeable adj. **watertight**, waterproof, damp-proof, airtight, (hermetically) sealed.

impersonal adj. **1** *the hand of fate is impersonal* **neutral**, unbiased, non-partisan, unprejudiced, objective, detached, disinterested, dispassionate, without favouritism. **2** *he remained strangely impersonal* **aloof**, distant, remote, reserved, withdrawn, unemotional, unsentimental, dispassionate, cold, cool, indifferent, unconcerned; formal, stiff, businesslike; informal starchy, stand-offish.
– OPPOSITES biased, warm.

impersonate v. **imitate**, mimic, do an impression of, ape; parody, caricature, burlesque, travesty, satirize, lampoon; masquerade as, pose as, pass oneself off as; informal take off, send up; N. Amer. informal make like; formal personate; old use monkey.

impersonation n. **impression**, imitation, parody, caricature, burlesque, travesty, lampoon, pastiche; informal take-off, send-up; formal personation.

impertinence n. **rudeness**, insolence, impoliteness, bad manners, discourtesy, discourteousness, disrespect, incivility; impudence, cheek, cheekiness, audacity, temerity, effrontery, nerve, gall, boldness, cockiness, brazenness; informal brass (neck); Brit. informal sauce; N. Amer. informal sass, sassiness, chutzpah; old use assumption.

impertinent adj. **1** *she asked a lot of impertinent questions* **rude**, insolent, impolite, ill-mannered, bad-mannered, uncivil, discourteous, disrespectful; impudent, cheeky, audacious, bold, brazen, brash, presumptuous, forward; tactless, undiplomatic; informal brass-necked, saucy; N. Amer. informal sassy; old use contumelious. **2** formal *talk of 'rhetoric' is impertinent to this process* **irrelevant**, inapplicable, inapposite, inappropriate, immaterial, unrelated, unconnected, not germane; beside the point, out of place.
– OPPOSITES polite, relevant.

imperturbable adj. **self-possessed**, composed, {cool, calm, and collected}, cool-headed, self-controlled, serene, relaxed, unexcitable, even-tempered, placid, phlegmatic; unperturbed, unflustered, unruffled; informal unflappable, unfazed, laid-back.
– OPPOSITES excitable.

impervious adj. **1** *he seemed impervious to the chill wind* **unaffected**, untouched, immune, invulnerable, insusceptible, resistant, indifferent, heedless, oblivious;

proof against. **2** *an impervious damp-proof course* **impermeable**, impenetrable, impregnable, waterproof, watertight; (hermetically) sealed.
– OPPOSITES susceptible, permeable.

impetuous adj. **1** *an impetuous decision* **impulsive**, rash, hasty, overhasty, reckless, heedless, foolhardy, incautious, imprudent, injudicious, ill-considered, unthought-out; spontaneous, impromptu, spur-of-the-moment, precipitate, precipitous, hurried, rushed. **2** *an impetuous flow of water* **torrential**, powerful, forceful, vigorous, violent, raging, relentless, uncontrolled; rapid, fast, fast-flowing.
– OPPOSITES considered, sluggish.

impetus n. **1** *the flywheel lost all its impetus* **momentum**, propulsion, impulsion, motive force, driving force, drive, thrust; energy, force, power, push, strength. **2** *the sales force were given fresh impetus* **motivation**, stimulus, incitement, incentive, inducement, inspiration, encouragement, boost; informal a shot in the arm.

impiety n. **1** *a world of impiety and immorality* **godlessness**, ungodliness, unholiness, irreligion, sinfulness, sin, vice, immorality, unrighteousness; apostasy, atheism, agnosticism, paganism, heathenism, non-belief, unbelief. **2** *one impiety will cost me my eternity in paradise* **sin**, transgression, wrongdoing, evildoing, wrong, misdeed, misdemeanour.
– OPPOSITES faith.

impinge v. **1** *these issues impinge on all of us* **affect**, have an effect, touch, influence, make an impact, leave a mark. **2** *the proposed fencing would impinge on a public bridleway* **encroach**, intrude, infringe, invade, trespass, obtrude, cut through, interfere with; violate; old use entrench on. **3** Physics *electrically charged particles impinge on the lunar surface* **strike**, hit, collide with.

impious adj. **godless**, ungodly, unholy, irreligious, sinful, immoral, unrighteous, sacrilegious, profane, blasphemous, irreverent; apostate, atheistic, agnostic, pagan, heathen, faithless, non-believing, unbelieving; rare nullifidian.

impish adj. **1** *he takes an impish delight in shocking the press* **mischievous**, naughty, wicked, rascally, roguish, playful, sportive; mischief-making, full of mischief. **2** *an impish grin* **elfin**, elflike, pixie-like, puckish; mischievous, roguish.

implacable adj. **unappeasable**, unforgiving; intransigent, inflexible, unyielding, unbending, uncompromising, unrelenting, ruthless, remorseless, merciless, heartless, pitiless, cruel, hard, harsh, stern, tough.

implant v. **1** *the collagen is implanted under the skin* **insert**, embed, bury, lodge, place; graft. **2** *he implanted the idea in my mind* **instil**, inculcate, insinuate, introduce, inject, plant, sow, root, lodge.
▸n. *a silicone implant* **transplant**, graft, implantation, insert.

implausible adj. **unlikely**, improbable, questionable, doubtful, debatable; unrealistic, unconvincing, far-fetched, incredible, unbelievable, unimaginable, inconceivable, fantastic, fanciful, ridiculous, absurd, preposterous; informal cock and bull.
– OPPOSITES convincing.

implement n. *garden implements* **tool**, utensil, instrument, device, apparatus, gadget, contraption, appliance, machine, contrivance; informal gizmo.
▸v. *the cost of implementing the new law* **execute**, apply, put into effect/action, put into practice, carry out/through, perform, enact; fulfil, discharge, accomplish, bring about, achieve, realize; formal effectuate.

implicate v. **1** *he had been implicated in a financial scandal* **incriminate**, compromise; involve, connect, embroil, enmesh; old use inculpate. **2** *viruses are implicated in the development of cancer* **involve in**, concern with, associate with, connect with. **3** *when one asks a question one implicates that one desires an answer.* See **imply** (sense 1).

implication n. **1** *he was smarting at their implication* **suggestion**, inference, insinuation, innuendo, hint, intimation, imputation. **2** *important political implications* **consequence**, result, ramification, repercussion, reverberation, effect. **3** *his implication in the murder case* **incrimination**, involvement, connection, entanglement, association; old use inculpation.

implicit adj. **1** *implicit assumptions* **implied**, inferred, understood, hinted at, suggested, deducible; unspoken, unexpressed, undeclared, unstated, tacit, unacknowledged, taken for granted. **2** *assumptions implicit in the way questions are asked* **inherent**, latent, underlying, inbuilt, incorporated. **3** *an implicit trust in human nature* **absolute**, complete, total, wholehearted, perfect, utter; unqualified, unconditional; unshakeable, unquestioning, firm, steadfast.
– OPPOSITES explicit.

implicitly adv. **completely**, absolutely, totally, wholeheartedly, utterly, unconditionally, unreservedly, without reservation.

implied adj. **implicit**, hinted at, suggested, insinuated, inferred, understood, deducible; unspoken, unexpressed, undeclared, unstated, tacit, unacknowledged, taken for granted.
– OPPOSITES explicit.

implore v. **plead with**, beg, entreat, appeal to, ask, request, call on; exhort, urge, enjoin, press, push, petition, bid; literary beseech.

imply v. **1** *are you implying he is mad?* **insinuate**, suggest, hint, intimate, say indirectly, indicate, give someone to understand, make out. **2** *the forecasted traffic increase implies more roads* **involve**, entail; mean, point to, signify, indicate, signal; necessitate, require.

impolite adj. **rude**, bad-mannered, ill-mannered, discourteous, uncivil, disrespectful, inconsiderate, boorish, churlish, ill-bred, ungentlemanly, unladylike, ungracious; insolent, impudent, impertinent, cheeky; loutish, rough, crude, indelicate, indecorous; informal ignorant, lippy; old use malapert, contumelious.

impolitic adj. **imprudent**, unwise, injudicious, incautious, irresponsible; ill-judged, ill-advised, misguided, rash, reckless, foolhardy, foolish, short-sighted; undiplomatic, tactless.
– OPPOSITES prudent.

import v. *the UK imports iron ore* **buy from abroad**, bring in, buy in, ship in.
– OPPOSITES export.
▸n. **1** *a tax on imports* **imported commodity**, foreign commodity. **2** *the import of foreign books* **importation**, importing, bringing in, shipping in. **3** *a matter of great import* **importance**, significance, consequence, momentousness, magnitude, substance, weight, note, gravity, seriousness; formal moment. **4** *the full import of her words* **meaning**, sense, essence, gist, drift, purport, message, thrust, substance, implication.
– OPPOSITES export, insignificance.

importance n. **1** *an event of immense importance* **significance**, momentousness, import, consequence, note, noteworthiness, substance; seriousness, gravity, weightiness, urgency. **2** *she had a fine sense of her own importance* **power**, influence, authority, sway, weight, dominance; prominence, eminence, pre-eminence, notability, worth.
– OPPOSITES insignificance.

important adj. **1** *an important meeting* **significant**, consequential, momentous, of great import, major; critical, crucial, vital, pivotal, decisive, urgent, historic; serious, grave, weighty, material; formal of great moment. **2** *the important thing is that you do well in your exams* **main**, chief, principal, key, major, salient, prime, foremost, paramount, overriding, crucial, vital, critical, essential, significant; central, fundamental; informal number-one. **3** *the school was important to the community* **of value**, valuable, beneficial, necessary, essential, indispensable, vital; of concern, of interest, relevant, pertinent. **4** *he was an important man* **powerful**, influential, of influence, well-connected, high-ranking; prominent, eminent, pre-eminent, notable, noteworthy, of note; distinguished, esteemed, respected, prestigious, celebrated, famous, great; informal major league.
– OPPOSITES trivial, insignificant.

importunate adj. **persistent**, insistent, tenacious, persevering, dogged, unrelenting, tireless, indefatigable; aggressive, high-pressure; informal pushy; formal exigent, pertinacious.

importune v. **1** *he importuned her for some spare change* **beg**, entreat, implore, plead with, appeal to, call on; harass, pester, press, badger, bother, nag, harry; informal hassle; literary beseech. **2** *they arrested me for importuning* **solicit**; informal proposition; N. Amer. informal hustle.

impose v. **1** *he imposed his ideas on the art director* **foist**, force, inflict, press, urge; informal saddle someone with, land someone with. **2** *new taxes will be imposed* **levy**, charge, apply, enforce; set, establish, institute, introduce, bring into effect. **3** *how dare you impose on me like this!* **take advantage of**, exploit, take liberties with, treat unfairly; bother, trouble, disturb, inconvenience, put out, put to trouble.
□ **impose oneself** force oneself, foist oneself; control, take charge of; informal call the shots/tune, be in the driving seat, be in the saddle, run the show.

imposing adj. **impressive**, striking, arresting, eye-catching, dramatic, stunning, spectacular, awesome, formidable, splendid, grand, majestic.
– OPPOSITES modest.

imposition n. **1** *the imposition of an alien culture* **imposing**, foisting, forcing, inflicting. **2** *the imposition of VAT* **levying**, charging, application, applying, enforcement, enforcing; setting, establishment, introduction, institution. **3** *it would be no imposition* **burden**, encumbrance, strain, bother, worry; informal hassle. **4** *the levying of special impositions* **tax**, levy, duty, charge, tariff, toll, impost; formal mulct, exaction.

impossible adj. **1** *gale force winds made fishing impossible* **not possible**, out of the question, unfeasible, impractical, impracticable, non-viable, unworkable; informal undoable, like herding cats. **2** *an impossible dream* **unattainable**, unachievable, unobtainable, hopeless, impractical, implausible, far-fetched, impracticable, unworkable. **3** *food shortages made life impossible* **unbearable**, intolerable, unendurable. **4** informal *an impossible woman* **unreasonable**, objectionable, difficult, awkward; intolerable, unbearable, unendurable; exasperating, maddening, infuriating.
– OPPOSITES attainable, bearable.

impostor n. **impersonator**, masquerader, pretender, deceiver, hoaxer, trickster, fraudster; fake, fraud, sham; informal phoney.

imposture n. **misrepresentation**, pretence, deceit, deception, trickery, artifice, subterfuge; hoax, trick, ruse, dodge; informal con (trick), scam, flimflam; Brit. informal wheeze.

impotent adj. **1** *the legal sanctions are impotent* **powerless**, ineffective, ineffectual, inadequate, weak, useless, worthless, futile; literary impuissant. **2** *forces which man is impotent to control* **unable**, incapable, powerless. **3** *an impotent opposition party* **weak**, powerless, ineffective, feeble.
– OPPOSITES powerful, effective.

impound v. **1** *officials began impounding documents* **confiscate**, appropriate, take possession of, seize, commandeer, expropriate, requisition, sequester, sequestrate; Law distrain. **2** *the cattle were impounded* **pen in**, shut up/in, fence in, enclose, confine, kettle; N. Amer. corral. **3** *unfortunates impounded in prison* **lock up**, incarcerate, imprison, confine, intern, immure, hold captive, hold prisoner.

impoverish v. **1** *the widow had been impoverished* **make poor**, make penniless, reduce to penury, bankrupt, ruin, make insolvent, pauperize. **2** *the trees were impoverishing the soil* **weaken**, sap, exhaust, deplete.

impoverished adj. **1** *an impoverished peasant farmer* **poor**, poverty-stricken, penniless, destitute, indigent, impecunious, needy, pauperized, down and out, on the breadline; bankrupt, ruined, insolvent; informal (flat) broke, stony broke, on one's uppers, hard up, without a bean, on skid row; Brit. informal skint; N. Amer. informal stone broke; formal penurious. **2** *the soil is impoverished* **weakened**, exhausted, drained, sapped, depleted, spent; barren, unproductive, unfertile.
– OPPOSITES rich.

impracticable adj. **unworkable**, unfeasible, non-viable, unachievable, unattainable, unrealizable; impractical.
– OPPOSITES workable, feasible.

impractical adj. **1** *an impractical suggestion* **unrealistic**, unworkable, unfeasible, non-viable, impracticable; ill-thought-out, impossible, absurd, wild; informal cockeyed, crackpot, crazy. **2** *impractical white ankle boots* **unsuitable**, not sensible, inappropriate, unserviceable. **3** *an impractical scholar* **idealistic**, unrealistic, romantic, dreamy, fanciful, quixotic; informal airy-fairy.
– OPPOSITES practical, sensible.

imprecation n. formal **1** *the most dreadful imprecations* **curse**, malediction; N. Amer. hex; literary anathema; old use execration. **2** *a stream of imprecations* **swear word**, curse, expletive, oath, profanity, four-letter word, obscenity; (**imprecations**) swearing, cursing, foul language, strong language; N. Amer. informal cuss word; old use execration.
– OPPOSITES blessing.

imprecise adj. **1** *a rather imprecise definition* **vague**, loose, indefinite, inexplicit, indistinct, non-specific, unspecific, coarse-grained, sweeping, broad, general; hazy, fuzzy, woolly, nebulous, ambiguous, equivocal, uncertain. **2** *an imprecise estimate* **inexact**, approximate, estimated, rough; N. Amer. informal ballpark.
– OPPOSITES exact.

impregnable adj. **1** *an impregnable castle* **invulnerable**, impenetrable, unassailable, inviolable, secure, strong, well fortified, well defended; invincible, unconquerable, unbeatable, indestructible. **2** *an impregnable parliamentary majority* **unassailable**, unbeatable, undefeatable, unshakeable,

invincible, unconquerable, invulnerable.
– OPPOSITES vulnerable.

impregnate v. **1** *a pad impregnated with natural oils* **infuse**, soak, steep, saturate, drench. **2** *make pregnant*, get pregnant, inseminate, fertilize; N. Amer. informal knock up; archaic get with child.

impresario n. **organizer**, (stage) manager, producer; promoter, publicist, showman; director, conductor, maestro.

impress v. **1** *Hazel had impressed him mightily* **make an impression on**, have an impact on, influence, affect, move, stir, rouse, excite, inspire; dazzle, awe, overawe, take someone's breath away, amaze, astonish; informal grab, stick in someone's mind. **2** *goldsmiths impressed his likeness on medallions* **imprint**, print, stamp, mark, emboss, punch. **3** *you must impress upon her the need to save* **emphasize to**, stress to, bring home to, instil in, inculcate into, drum into, knock into, din into.
– OPPOSITES disappoint.

impression n. **1** *he got the impression that she was hiding something* **feeling**, feeling in one's bones, sense, fancy, (sneaking) suspicion, inkling, intuition, hunch; notion, idea, funny feeling; informal gut feeling. **2** *a favourable impression* **opinion**, view, image, picture, perception, judgement, verdict, estimation. **3** *school made a profound impression on me* **impact**, effect, influence. **4** *the cap had left a circular impression* **indentation**, dent, mark, outline, imprint. **5** *he did a good impression of their teacher* **impersonation**, imitation; parody, caricature, burlesque, travesty, lampoon; informal take-off, send-up, spoof; formal personation. **6** *an artist's impression of the gardens* **representation**, portrayal, depiction, rendition, interpretation, picture, drawing. **7** *a revised impression of the 1981 edition* **print run**, imprint, reprint, issue, edition.

impressionable adj. **easily influenced**, suggestible, susceptible, persuadable, pliable, malleable, pliant, ingenuous, trusting, naive, gullible.

impressive adj. **1** *an impressive building* **magnificent**, majestic, imposing, splendid, spectacular, grand, awe-inspiring, stunning, breathtaking; stately, palatial. **2** *they played some impressive football* **admirable**, masterly, accomplished, expert, skilled, skilful, consummate; excellent, outstanding, first-class, first-rate, fine; informal great, mean, nifty, cracking, ace, wizard.
– OPPOSITES ordinary, mediocre.

imprint v. **1** *patterns can be imprinted in the clay* **stamp**, print, impress, mark, emboss. **2** *the image was imprinted on his mind* **fix**, establish, stick, lodge, implant, embed.
▶ n. **1** *her feet left imprints on the floor* **impression**, print, mark, indentation. **2** *colonialism has left its imprint* **impact**, lasting effect, influence, impression.

imprison v. **incarcerate**, send to prison, jail, lock up, put away, intern, detain, hold

prisoner, hold captive; informal send down, put behind bars, put inside; Brit. informal bang up.
– OPPOSITES free, release.

imprisoned adj. **incarcerated**, in prison, in jail, jailed, locked up, interned, detained, held prisoner, held captive; informal sent down, behind bars, doing time, inside; Brit. informal doing porridge, doing bird, banged up.

imprisonment n. **incarceration**, internment, confinement, detention, captivity; informal time; Brit. informal porridge, bird; old use durance.

improbability n. **unlikelihood**, implausibility; doubtfulness, uncertainty, dubiousness.

improbable adj. **1** *it seemed improbable that the hot weather should continue* **unlikely**, doubtful, dubious, debatable, questionable, uncertain; unthinkable, inconceivable, unimaginable, unimagined, incredible. **2** *an improbable exaggeration* **unconvincing**, unbelievable, incredible, ridiculous, absurd, preposterous.
– OPPOSITES certain, believable.

impromptu adj. *an impromptu lecture* **unrehearsed**, unprepared, unscripted, extempore, extemporized, extemporaneous, improvised, spontaneous, unplanned; informal off-the-cuff.
– OPPOSITES prepared, rehearsed.
▸ adv. *they played the song impromptu* **extempore**, spontaneously, extemporaneously, without preparation, without rehearsal; informal off the cuff, off the top of one's head.

improper adj. **1** *it is improper for policemen to accept gifts* **inappropriate**, unacceptable, unsuitable, unprofessional, irregular; unethical, corrupt, immoral, dishonest, dishonourable; informal not cricket. **2** *it was improper for young ladies to drive a young man home* **unseemly**, indecorous, unfitting, unladylike, ungentlemanly, indelicate, impolite; indecent, immodest, immoral. **3** *an extremely improper poem* **indecent**, risqué, off colour, suggestive, naughty, ribald, earthy, smutty, dirty, filthy, vulgar, crude, rude, obscene, lewd; informal blue, raunchy, steamy; Brit. informal fruity, saucy.
– OPPOSITES acceptable, decent.

impropriety n. **1** *a suggestion of impropriety* **wrongdoing**, misconduct, dishonesty, corruption, unscrupulousness, unprofessionalism, irregularity; unseemliness, indecorousness, indelicacy, indecency, immorality. **2** *fiscal improprieties* **transgression**, misdemeanour, offence, misdeed, crime; indiscretion, mistake, peccadillo; old use trespass.

improve v. **1** *ways to improve the service* **make better**, ameliorate, upgrade, refine, enhance, boost, build on, raise; informal tweak; formal meliorate. **2** *communications improved during the 18th century* **get better**, advance, progress, develop; make headway, make progress, pick up, look up. **3** *the dose is not repeated if the patient improves* **recover**,

get better, recuperate, gain strength, rally, revive, get back on one's feet, get over something; be on the road to recovery, be on the mend, turn the corner, take a turn for the better. **4** *resources are needed to improve the offer* **increase**, make larger, raise, augment, supplement, top up; informal up, hike up, bump up.
– OPPOSITES worsen, deteriorate.
□ **improve on** surpass, better, do better than, outdo, exceed, beat, top, cap.

improvement n. **advance**, development, upgrade, refinement, enhancement, advancement, upgrading, amelioration; boost, augmentation, raising; rally, recovery, upswing.

improvident adj. **spendthrift**, thriftless, wasteful, prodigal, profligate, extravagant, free-spending, lavish, immoderate, excessive; imprudent, irresponsible, careless, reckless.
– OPPOSITES thrifty.

improvise v. **1** *she was improvising in front of the cameras* **extemporize**, ad-lib, speak impromptu; informal speak off the cuff, busk it, wing it. **2** *she improvised a sandpit* **contrive**, devise, throw together, cobble together, rig up; Brit. informal knock up; informal whip up, rustle up.

improvised adj. **1** *an improvised speech* **impromptu**, unrehearsed, unprepared, unscripted, extempore, extemporized, spontaneous, unplanned; informal off-the-cuff. **2** *an improvised shelter* **makeshift**, thrown together, cobbled together, rough and ready, make-do.
– OPPOSITES prepared, rehearsed.

imprudent adj. **unwise**, injudicious, incautious, misguided, ill-advised; thoughtless, unthinking, improvident, irresponsible, short-sighted, foolish.
– OPPOSITES sensible.

impudence n. **impertinence**, insolence, effrontery, cheek, cockiness, brazenness; presumption, presumptuousness, disrespect, flippancy, bumptiousness, brashness; rudeness, impoliteness, ill manners, discourteousness, gall; informal brass neck, chutzpah, nerve; Brit. informal sauce; N. Amer. informal sassiness.

impudent adj. **impertinent**, insolent, cheeky, cocky, brazen; presumptuous, forward, disrespectful, insubordinate, flippant, bumptious, brash; rude, impolite, ill-mannered, discourteous, ill-bred; informal brass-necked, saucy, lippy; N. Amer. informal sassy; old use malapert, contumelious.
– OPPOSITES polite.

impugn v. **call into question**, challenge, question, dispute, query, take issue with.

impulse n. **1** *she had an impulse to run and hide* **urge**, instinct, drive, compulsion, itch; whim, desire, fancy, notion. **2** *a man of impulse* **spontaneity**, impetuosity, recklessness, rashness. **3** *passions provide the main impulse of poetry* **inspiration**, stimulation, stimulus, incitement,

motivation, encouragement, spur, catalyst. **4** *impulses from the spinal cord to the muscles* **pulse**, current, wave, signal.
▫ **on (an) impulse** impulsively, spontaneously, on the spur of the moment, without forethought, without premeditation.

impulsive adj. **1** *he had an impulsive nature* **impetuous**, spontaneous, hasty, passionate, emotional, uninhibited; rash, reckless, foolhardy, unwise, madcap, devil-may-care, daredevil. **2** *an impulsive decision* **impromptu**, snap, spontaneous, unpremeditated, spur-of-the-moment, extemporaneous; impetuous, precipitate, hasty, rash; sudden, ill-considered, ill-thought-out.
– OPPOSITES cautious, premeditated.

impunity n. *the impunity enjoyed by military officers* **immunity**, indemnity, exemption (from punishment), non-liability, licence; privilege, special treatment.
– OPPOSITES liability.
▫ **with impunity** without punishment, scot-free, unpunished.

impure adj. **1** *impure gold* **adulterated**, mixed, combined, blended, alloyed; technical admixed. **2** *the water was impure* **contaminated**, polluted, tainted, unwholesome, poisoned; dirty, filthy, foul; unhygienic, unsanitary, insanitary; literary befouled. **3** *impure thoughts* **immoral**, sinful, wrongful, wicked; unchaste, lustful, lecherous, lewd, lascivious, prurient, obscene, indecent, ribald, risqué, improper, crude, coarse; formal concupiscent.
– OPPOSITES clean, chaste.

impurity n. **1** *the impurity of the cast iron* **adulteration**, debasement, degradation. **2** *the impurity of the air* **contamination**, pollution; dirtiness, filthiness, uncleanliness, foulness, unwholesomeness. **3** *the impurities in beer* **contaminant**, pollutant, foreign body; dross, dirt, filth. **4** *sin and impurity* **immorality**, sin, sinfulness, wickedness; unchastity, lustfulness, lechery, lecherousness, lewdness, lasciviousness, prurience, obscenity, dirtiness, crudeness, indecency, ribaldry, impropriety, vulgarity, coarseness; formal concupiscence.

impute v. **attribute**, ascribe, assign, credit; connect with, associate with.

in prep. **1** *she was hiding in a wardrobe* **inside**, within, in the middle of; surrounded by, enclosed by. **2** *he was covered in mud* **with**, by. **3** *he put a fruit gum in his mouth* **into**, inside. **4** *they met in 1921* **during**, in the course of, over. **5** *I'll see you in half an hour* **after**, at the end of, following; within, in less than, in under. **6** *a tax of ten pence in the pound* **to**, per, every, each.
– OPPOSITES outside.
▸ adj. **1** *there was no one in* **present**, (at) home; inside, indoors, in the house/room. **2** informal *beards are in* **fashionable**, in fashion, in vogue, popular, (bang) up to date, modern, modish, chic, à la mode, de rigueur; informal trendy, all the rage, with it, cool, the in

thing, hip. **3** informal *I was in with all the right people* **in favour**, popular, friendly, friends; liked, admired, accepted; informal in someone's good books.
– OPPOSITES out, unfashionable, unpopular.
▫ **in for** due for, in line for; expecting, about to receive.
in on privy to, aware of, acquainted with, informed about/of, apprised of; informal wise to, in the know about, hip to; old use ware of.
ins and outs informal details, particulars, facts, features, characteristics, nuts and bolts; informal nitty gritty.

inability n. **lack of ability**, incapability, incapacity, powerlessness, impotence, helplessness; incompetence, ineptitude, unfitness.

inaccessible adj. **1** *an inaccessible woodland site* **unreachable**, out of reach; cut-off, isolated, remote, in the back of beyond, out of the way, lonely, godforsaken. **2** *the book was elitist and inaccessible* **esoteric**, obscure, abstruse, recondite, arcane; elitist, exclusive, pretentious.

inaccuracy n. **1** *the inaccuracy of recent opinion polls* **incorrectness**, inexactness, imprecision, erroneousness, mistakenness, fallaciousness, faultiness. **2** *the article contained a number of inaccuracies* **error**, mistake, fallacy, slip, oversight, fault, blunder, gaffe; erratum; Brit. literal; informal howler, boo-boo, fail, typo; Brit. informal boob; N. Amer. informal blooper, goof.
– OPPOSITES correctness.

inaccurate adj. **inexact**, imprecise, incorrect, wrong, erroneous, faulty, imperfect, flawed, defective, unsound, unreliable; fallacious, false, mistaken, untrue; informal off beam; Brit. informal adrift.

inaction n. **inactivity**, non-intervention; neglect, negligence, apathy, inertia, indolence.

inactivate v. **disable**, deactivate, make inoperative, immobilize.

inactive adj. **1** *over the next few days I was horribly inactive* **idle**, indolent, lazy, lifeless, slothful, lethargic, inert, sluggish, listless, torpid. **2** *the device remains inactive while the computer is started up* **inoperative**, non-functioning, idle; not working, out of service, unused, not in use.

inactivity n. **1** *years of inactivity* **idleness**, indolence, laziness, lifelessness, slothfulness, lethargy, inertia, sluggishness, listlessness. **2** *government inactivity* **inaction**, non-intervention; neglect, negligence, apathy.
– OPPOSITES action.

inadequacy n. **1** *the inadequacy of available resources* **insufficiency**, deficiency, scarcity, scarceness, sparseness, dearth, paucity, shortage, want, lack, undersupply; paltriness, meagreness; formal exiguity. **2** *her feelings of personal inadequacy* **incompetence**, incapability, unfitness, ineffectiveness, inefficiency, inefficacy, inexpertness, ineptness, uselessness, impotence,

powerlessness. **3** *the inadequacies of the present system* **shortcoming**, defect, fault, failing, weakness, weak point, limitation, flaw, imperfection.
– OPPOSITES abundance, competence.

inadequate adj. **1** *inadequate water supplies* **insufficient**, deficient, poor, scant, scanty, scarce, sparse, in short supply; paltry, meagre, niggardly, limited; informal measly, pathetic; formal exiguous. **2** *inadequate staff* **incapable**, unsatisfactory, not up to scratch, unfit, ineffective, ineffectual, inefficient, unskilful, inexpert, inept, amateurish, substandard, poor, useless, inferior; informal not up to snuff; Brit. informal duff, not much cop, no great shakes.
– OPPOSITES sufficient, competent.

inadmissible adj. **unallowable**, invalid, unacceptable, impermissible, disallowed, forbidden, prohibited, precluded.

inadvertent adj. **unintentional**, unintended, accidental, unpremeditated, unplanned, innocent, uncalculated, unconscious, unthinking, unwitting, involuntary.
– OPPOSITES deliberate.

inadvertently adv. **accidentally**, by accident, unintentionally, unwittingly.

inadvisable adj. **unwise**, ill-advised, imprudent, ill-judged, ill-considered, injudicious, impolitic, foolish, misguided.
– OPPOSITES shrewd.

inalienable adj. **inviolable**, absolute, sacrosanct; untransferable, non-transferable, non-negotiable; Law indefeasible.

inane adj. **silly**, foolish, stupid, fatuous, idiotic, ridiculous, ludicrous, asinine, frivolous, vapid; childish, puerile; informal dumb, gormless, moronic; Brit. informal daft.
– OPPOSITES sensible.

inanimate adj. **lifeless**, insentient, without life; dead, defunct.
– OPPOSITES living.

inapplicable adj. **irrelevant**, immaterial, not germane, not pertinent, unrelated, unconnected, extraneous, beside the point; formal impertinent.
– OPPOSITES relevant.

inapposite adj. **inappropriate**, unsuitable, inapt, out of place, infelicitous, misplaced, ill-judged, ill-advised.
– OPPOSITES appropriate.

inappreciable adj. **imperceptible**, minute, tiny, slight, small; insignificant, inconsequential, unimportant, negligible, trivial, minor; informal piddling, piffling; formal exiguous.
– OPPOSITES considerable.

inappropriate adj. **unsuitable**, unfitting, unseemly, unbecoming, unbefitting, improper; incongruous, out of place/keeping, inapposite, inapt; informal out of order; formal malapropos.
– OPPOSITES suitable.

inapt adj. See **inappropriate**.

inarticulate adj. **1** *an inarticulate young man* **tongue-tied**, lost for words, unable

to express oneself; old use mumchance. **2** *an inarticulate reply* **unintelligible**, incomprehensible, incoherent, unclear, indistinct, mumbled, muffled. **3** *inarticulate rage* **unspoken**, silent, unexpressed, wordless, unvoiced.
– OPPOSITES silver-tongued, fluent.

inattention n. **1** *a moment of inattention* **distraction**, inattentiveness, preoccupation, absent-mindedness, daydreaming, abstraction. **2** *his inattention to duty* **negligence**, neglect, disregard; forgetfulness, carelessness, thoughtlessness, heedlessness.
– OPPOSITES concentration.

inattentive adj. **1** *an inattentive pupil* **distracted**, lacking concentration, preoccupied, absent-minded, daydreaming, dreamy, abstracted, distrait; informal miles away. **2** *inattentive service* **negligent**, neglectful, remiss, slack, sloppy, slapdash, lax; forgetful, careless, thoughtless, heedless.
– OPPOSITES alert.

inaudible adj. **unheard**, out of earshot; indistinct, faint, muted, soft, low, muffled, whispered, muttered, murmured, mumbled.

inaugural adj. **first**, opening, initial, introductory, initiatory.
– OPPOSITES final.

inaugurate v. **1** *he inaugurated a new policy* **initiate**, begin, start, institute, launch, start off, get going, get under way, establish, lay the foundations of; bring in, usher in; informal kick off. **2** *the new President will be inaugurated* **admit to office**, install, instate, swear in; invest, ordain, crown. **3** *the museum was inaugurated in September* **open**, declare open, unveil; dedicate, consecrate; N. Amer. hansel.

inauspicious adj. **unpromising**, unpropitious, unfavourable, unfortunate, infelicitous, ominous; discouraging, disheartening, bleak.
– OPPOSITES promising.

inborn adj. **innate**, congenital, connate, connatural; inherent, natural, inbred, inherited, hereditary, in one's genes.

inbred adj. See **inborn**.

inbuilt adj. **1** *an inbuilt CD-ROM drive* **built-in**, integral, incorporated. **2** *our inbuilt survival instinct* **inherent**, intrinsic, innate, congenital, natural, connatural, connate.

incalculable adj. **inestimable**, indeterminable, untold, immeasurable, incomputable; infinite, endless, limitless, boundless, measureless, cosmic; enormous, immense, huge, vast, innumerable.

incandescent adj. **1** *incandescent fragments of lava* **white-hot**, red-hot, burning, fiery, blazing, ablaze, aflame; glowing, aglow, radiant, bright, brilliant, luminous; literary fervid, rutilant, lucent. **2** *the minister was incandescent* **furious**, enraged, raging, very angry, incensed, seething, infuriated, fuming, irate, in a temper, beside oneself; informal livid, foaming at the mouth, (hopping) mad, wild, apoplectic, steamed up, in a lather, in a paddy; literary wrathful; old use wroth.

incantation n. 1 *he muttered some weird incantations* **chant**, invocation, conjuration, magic spell/formula, rune; N. Amer. hex, mojo; NZ makutu. 2 *ritual incantation* **chanting**, intonation, recitation.

incapable adj. 1 *an incapable government* **incompetent**, inept, inadequate, not good enough, leaving much to be desired, inexpert, unskilful, ineffective, ineffectual, inefficacious, feeble, unfit, unqualified, unequal to the task; informal out of one's depth, not up to it, not up to snuff, useless, hopeless, pathetic, a dead loss. 2 *he was mentally incapable* **incapacitated**, helpless, powerless, impotent.
– OPPOSITES competent.

incapacitated adj. **disabled**, debilitated, indisposed, unfit; immobilized, out of action, out of commission, hors de combat; informal laid up.
– OPPOSITES fit.

incapacity n. 1 *mental incapacity* **disability**, incapability, inability, debility, impairment, indisposition; impotence, powerlessness, helplessness; incompetence, inadequacy, ineffectiveness. 2 *legal incapacity* **disqualification**, lack of entitlement.
– OPPOSITES capability.

incarcerate v. **imprison**, put in prison, send to prison, jail, lock up, put under lock and key, put away, intern, confine, detain, hold, immure, put in chains, clap in irons, hold prisoner, hold captive; Brit. detain at Her Majesty's pleasure; informal send down, put behind bars, put inside; Brit. informal bang someone up.
– OPPOSITES release.

incarceration n. **imprisonment**, internment, confinement, detention, custody, captivity, restraint; informal time; Brit. informal porridge; old use durance, duress.

incarnate adj. **in human form**, in the flesh, in physical form, in bodily form, made flesh; corporeal, physical, fleshly, embodied.

incarnation n. 1 *the incarnation of artistic genius* **embodiment**, personification, exemplification, type, epitome; manifestation, bodily form, avatar. 2 *a previous incarnation* **lifetime**, life, existence.

incautious adj. **rash**, unwise, careless, heedless, thoughtless, reckless, unthinking, imprudent, misguided, ill-advised, ill-judged, injudicious, impolitic, unguarded, foolhardy, foolish; unwary, off-guard, inattentive; informal asleep on the job.
– OPPOSITES circumspect.

incendiary adj. 1 *an incendiary bomb* **combustible**, flammable, inflammable. 2 *an incendiary speech* **inflammatory**, rabble-rousing, provocative, seditious, subversive; contentious, controversial.
▸ n. 1 *an aircraft loaded with incendiaries* **explosive**, bomb, incendiary device.

2 *incendiaries set the village on fire* **arsonist**, fire-bomber, fire-setter; pyromaniac; Brit. fire-raiser; informal firebug, pyro; N. Amer. informal torch. 3 *a political incendiary* **agitator**, demagogue, rabble-rouser, firebrand, troublemaker, agent provocateur, revolutionary, insurgent, subversive.

incense¹ v. *his taunts used to incense me* **enrage**, infuriate, anger, madden, outrage, inflame, exasperate, antagonize, provoke; informal make someone see red, make someone's blood boil, make someone's hackles rise, drive mad/crazy; N. Amer. informal burn up.
– OPPOSITES placate, please.

incense² n. *a whiff of incense* **perfume**, fragrance, scent.

incensed adj. **enraged**, very angry, furious, infuriated, irate, in a temper, raging, incandescent, fuming, seething, beside oneself, outraged; informal mad, hopping mad, wild, livid, apoplectic, hot under the collar, foaming at the mouth, steamed up, in a paddy, fit to be tied; literary wrathful; old use wroth.

incentive n. **inducement**, motivation, motive, reason, stimulus, stimulant, spur, impetus, encouragement, impulse; incitement, goad, provocation; attraction, lure, carrot, bait; informal sweetener, come-on.
– OPPOSITES deterrent.

inception n. **establishment**, institution, foundation, founding, formation, initiation, setting up, origination, constitution, inauguration, opening, day one; beginning, commencement, start, birth, dawn, genesis, origin; informal kick-off.
– OPPOSITES end.

incessant adj. **ceaseless**, unceasing, constant, continual, unabating, interminable, endless, unending, never-ending, everlasting, eternal, perpetual, continuous, non-stop, uninterrupted, unbroken, unremitting, persistent, relentless, unrelenting, unrelieved, sustained.
– OPPOSITES intermittent.

incessantly adv. **constantly**, continually, all the time, non-stop, without stopping, without a break, round the clock, {morning, noon, and night}, interminably, unremittingly, ceaselessly, endlessly; informal 24-7.
– OPPOSITES occasionally.

incidence n. **occurrence**, prevalence; rate, frequency; amount, degree, extent.

incident n. 1 *incidents in his youth* **event**, occurrence, episode, experience, happening, occasion, proceeding, eventuality, affair, business; adventure, exploit, escapade; matter, circumstance, fact, development. 2 *police are investigating the incident* **disturbance**, fracas, melee, commotion, rumpus, scene; fight, skirmish, clash, brawl, free-for-all, encounter, conflict, ruckus, confrontation, altercation, contretemps; informal ruction; Brit. informal, Football afters; Law, dated affray. **3** *the journey was not without incident* **excitement**, adventure, drama; danger, peril.

incidental adj. **1** *incidental details* **less important**, secondary, subsidiary; minor, peripheral, background, by-the-way, by-the-by, non-essential, inessential, unimportant, insignificant, inconsequential, tangential, extrinsic, extraneous. **2** *an incidental discovery* **chance**, accidental, random; fluky, fortuitous, serendipitous, adventitious, coincidental, unlooked-for. **3** *the risks incidental to the job* **connected with**, related to, associated with, accompanying, attending, attendant on, concomitant with.
– OPPOSITES essential, deliberate.

incidentally adv. **1** *incidentally, I haven't had a reply yet* **by the way**, by the by(e), in passing, en passant, speaking of which; parenthetically; informal btw, as it happens. **2** *the infection was discovered incidentally* **by chance**, by accident, accidentally, fortuitously, by a fluke, by happenstance; coincidentally, by coincidence.

incinerate v. **burn**, reduce to ashes, consume by fire, carbonize; cremate.

incipient adj. **developing**, growing, emerging, emergent, dawning, just beginning, inceptive, initial; nascent, embryonic, fledgling, in its infancy, germinal.
– OPPOSITES full-blown.

incise v. **1** *the wound was incised* **cut (open)**, make an incision in, slit (open), lance. **2** *an inscription incised in Roman letters* **engrave**, etch, carve, cut, chisel, inscribe, score, chase.

incision n. **1** *a surgical incision* **cut**, opening, slit. **2** *incisions on the marble* **notch**, nick, snick, scratch, scarification.

incisive adj. **penetrating**, acute, sharp, sharp-witted, razor-sharp, keen, astute, trenchant, shrewd, piercing, perceptive, insightful, percipient, perspicacious, discerning, analytical, clever, smart, quick; concise, succinct, pithy, to the point, crisp, clear; informal punchy.
– OPPOSITES rambling, vague.

incite v. **1** *he was arrested for inciting racial hatred* **stir up**, whip up, encourage, fan the flames of, stoke up, fuel, kindle, ignite, inflame, stimulate, instigate, provoke, excite, arouse, awaken, inspire, trigger, spark off, ferment, foment; literary enkindle, waken. **2** *she incited him to commit murder* **egg on**, encourage, urge, goad, provoke, spur on, drive, stimulate, push, prod, prompt, induce, impel; arouse, rouse, excite, inflame, sting, prick; informal put up to.
– OPPOSITES discourage, deter.

incivility n. **rudeness**, discourtesy, discourteousness, impoliteness, bad manners, disrespect, boorishness, ungraciousness; insolence, impertinence, impudence.
– OPPOSITES politeness.

inclement adj. **cold**, chilly, bleak, wintry, freezing, snowy, icy; wet, rainy, drizzly, damp; stormy, blustery, wild, rough, squally,

windy; unpleasant, bad, foul, nasty, filthy, severe, extreme, harsh.
– OPPOSITES fine.

inclination n. **1** *his political inclinations* **tendency**, propensity, proclivity, leaning, predisposition, disposition, predilection, desire, wish, impulse, bent; liking, penchant, partiality, preference, appetite, fancy, interest, affinity; stomach, taste; informal yen; formal velleity; old use list, humour. **2** *an inclination of his head* **bowing**, bow, bending, nod, nodding, lowering. **3** *an inclination of ninety degrees.* See **incline** (noun).
– OPPOSITES aversion.

incline v. **1** *his prejudice inclines him to overlook obvious facts* **predispose**, lead, make, make of a mind to, dispose, prejudice; prompt, induce, influence, sway; persuade, convince. **2** *I incline to the opposite view* **prefer**, favour, go for; tend, lean, swing, veer, gravitate, be drawn. **3** *he inclined his head* **bend**, bow, nod, bob, lower, dip. **4** *the columns incline away from the vertical* **lean**, tilt, angle, tip, slope, slant, bend, curve, bank, cant, bevel; list, heel.

▶ n. *a steep incline* **slope**, gradient, pitch, ramp, bank, ascent, rise, acclivity, upslope, dip, descent, declivity, downslope; hill; N. Amer. grade, downgrade, upgrade.

inclined adj. **1** *I'm inclined to believe her* **disposed**, minded, of a mind, willing, ready, prepared; predisposed. **2** *she's inclined to gossip* **prone**, given, in the habit of, liable, likely, apt; literary wont.

include v. **1** *activities include sports, drama, music, and chess* **incorporate**, comprise, encompass, cover, embrace, involve, take in, number, contain; consist of, be made up of, be composed of; formal comprehend. **2** *don't forget to include the cost of repairs* **allow for**, count, take into account, take into consideration.
– OPPOSITES exclude.

including prep. **inclusive of**, counting; as well as, plus, together with.

inclusive adj. **1** *an inclusive price* | *an inclusive definition* **all-in**, all-inclusive, comprehensive, in toto, overall, full, all-round, umbrella, catch-all, all-encompassing. **2** *prices are inclusive of VAT* **including**, incorporating, taking in, counting; comprising, covering.

incognito adv. & adj. **under an assumed name**, under a false name, in disguise, disguised, under cover, in plain clothes, camouflaged; secretly, anonymously.

incoherent adj. **1** *a long, incoherent speech* **unclear**, confused, muddled, unintelligible, incomprehensible, hard to follow, disjointed, disconnected, disordered, mixed up, garbled, jumbled, scrambled; rambling, wandering, discursive, disorganized, illogical; inarticulate, mumbling, slurred. **2** *she was incoherent and shivering violently* **delirious**, raving, babbling, hysterical, irrational.
– OPPOSITES lucid.

i

incombustible adj. **non-flammable**, non-combustible; fireproof, flameproof, fire/flame resistant, fire/flame retardant; heatproof, ovenproof.
– OPPOSITES flammable, inflammable.

income n. **earnings**, salary, pay, remuneration, wages, stipend; revenue, receipts, takings, profits, gains, proceeds, turnover, yield, dividend, incomings; means; N. Amer. take; formal emolument.
– OPPOSITES expenditure, outgoings.

incoming adj. **1** *the incoming train* **arriving**, entering; approaching, coming (in). **2** *the incoming president* **newly elected**, newly appointed, succeeding, new, next, future; elect, to-be, designate.
– OPPOSITES outgoing.

incommensurate adj. **out of proportion**, not in proportion, disproportionate, inappropriate, out of keeping; insufficient, inadequate; excessive, inordinate, unreasonable, uncalled for, undue, unfair.
– OPPOSITES proportional.

incommunicable adj. **indescribable**, inexpressible, unutterable, unspeakable, undefinable, ineffable, beyond words, beyond description; overwhelming, intense, profound.

incomparable adj. **without equal**, beyond compare, unparalleled, matchless, peerless, unmatched, without parallel, beyond comparison, second to none, in a class of its own, unequalled, unrivalled, inimitable, nonpareil, par excellence; transcendent, superlative, surpassing, unsurpassed, unsurpassable, supreme, top, outstanding, consummate, singular, unique, rare, perfect; informal one-in-a-million; formal unexampled.

incomparably adv. **far and away**, by far, infinitely, immeasurably, easily; inimitably, supremely, superlatively, uniquely, transcendently.

incompatible adj. **1** *she and McBride are totally incompatible* **unsuited**, mismatched, ill-matched, poles apart, worlds apart, like day and night; Brit. like chalk and cheese. **2** *incompatible economic objectives* **irreconcilable**, conflicting, opposed, opposite, contradictory, antagonistic, antipathetic; clashing, inharmonious, discordant; mutually exclusive. **3** *a theory incompatible with that of his predecessor* **inconsistent with**, at odds with, out of keeping with, at variance with, inconsonant with, different to, divergent from, contrary to, in conflict with, in opposition to, (diametrically) opposed to, counter to, irreconcilable with.
– OPPOSITES well matched, harmonious, consistent.

incompetent adj. **inept**, unskilful, unskilled, inexpert, amateurish, unprofessional, bungling, blundering, clumsy, inadequate, substandard, inferior, ineffective, deficient, inefficient, ineffectual, wanting, lacking, leaving much to be desired; incapable, unfit, unqualified; informal useless,

pathetic, cack-handed, ham-fisted, not up to it, not up to scratch; Brit. informal not much cop.

incomplete adj. **1** *the project is still incomplete* **unfinished**, uncompleted, partial, half-finished, half-done, half-completed. **2** *inaccurate or incomplete information* **deficient**, insufficient, imperfect, defective, partial, patchy, sketchy, fragmentary, fragmented, scrappy, bitty; abridged, shortened; expurgated, bowdlerized.

incomprehensible adj. **unintelligible**, impossible to understand, impenetrable, unclear, indecipherable, beyond one's comprehension, beyond one, beyond one's grasp, complicated, complex, involved, baffling, bewildering, mystifying, puzzling, confusing, perplexing; abstruse, esoteric, recondite, arcane, mysterious, Delphic; informal over one's head, all Greek to someone; Brit. informal double Dutch.
– OPPOSITES intelligible, clear.

inconceivable adj. **unbelievable**, beyond belief, incredible, unthinkable, unimaginable, unimagined, extremely unlikely; impossible, beyond the bounds of possibility, out of the question, preposterous, ridiculous, ludicrous, absurd, incomprehensible; informal hard to swallow.
– OPPOSITES likely.

inconclusive adj. **indecisive**, proving nothing; indefinite, indeterminate, unresolved, unproven, unsettled, still open to question/doubt, debatable, unconfirmed; moot; vague, ambiguous; informal up in the air, left hanging.

incongruous adj. **1** *the women looked incongruous in their smart hats and fur coats* **out of place**, out of keeping, inappropriate, unsuitable, unsuited; wrong, strange, odd, absurd, bizarre, off-key, extraneous. **2** *an incongruous collection of objects* **ill-matched**, ill-assorted, mismatched, unharmonious, discordant, dissonant, conflicting, clashing, jarring, incompatible, different, dissimilar, contrasting, disparate.
– OPPOSITES appropriate, harmonious.

inconsequential adj. **insignificant**, unimportant, of little no/consequence, neither here nor there, incidental, inessential, non-essential, immaterial, irrelevant; negligible, inappreciable, inconsiderable, slight, minor, trivial, trifling, petty; informal piddling, piffling.
– OPPOSITES important.

inconsiderable adj. **insignificant**, negligible, trifling, small, tiny, little, minuscule, nominal, token, petty, slight, minor, inappreciable, insubstantial, inconsequential; informal piffling; formal exiguous.

inconsiderate adj. **thoughtless**, unthinking, insensitive, selfish, self-centred, unsympathetic, uncaring, heedless, unmindful, unkind, uncharitable, ungracious, impolite, discourteous, rude, disrespectful; tactless, undiplomatic,

indiscreet, indelicate; informal ignorant.
– OPPOSITES thoughtful.

inconsistent adj. **1** *his inconsistent behaviour* **erratic**, changeable, unpredictable, variable, varying, changing, changeful, inconstant, unstable, irregular, fluctuating, unsteady, unsettled, uneven; self-contradictory, contradictory, paradoxical; capricious, fickle, flighty, whimsical, unreliable, mercurial, volatile, blowing hot and cold, ever-changing, chameleon-like; informal up and down; technical labile. **2** *he had done nothing inconsistent with his morality* **incompatible with**, conflicting with, in conflict with, at odds with, at variance with, differing from, contrary to, in opposition to, (diametrically) opposed to, irreconcilable with, out of keeping with, out of step with; antithetical to.

inconsolable adj. **heartbroken**, brokenhearted, grief-stricken, beside oneself with grief, devastated, wretched, sick at heart, desolate, despairing, distraught, comfortless; miserable, unhappy, sad; literary heartsick.

inconspicuous adj. **unobtrusive**, unnoticeable, unremarkable, unspectacular, unostentatious, undistinguished, modest, unexceptional, unassuming, discreet, hidden, concealed; unseen, in the background, low-profile.
– OPPOSITES noticeable.

inconstant adj. **fickle**, faithless, unfaithful, false, false-hearted; wayward, unreliable, untrustworthy, capricious, volatile, flighty, unpredictable, erratic, blowing hot and cold; informal cheating, two-timing.
– OPPOSITES faithful.

incontestable adj. **incontrovertible**, indisputable, undeniable, irrefutable, unassailable, beyond dispute, unquestionable, beyond question, indubitable, beyond doubt; airtight, watertight, unarguable, undebatable, emphatic, categorical, certain, definite, definitive, proven, demonstrable, decisive, conclusive.
– OPPOSITES questionable.

incontinent adj. **unrestrained**, uncontrolled, lacking self-restraint, unbridled, unchecked; uncontrollable, ungovernable.

incontrovertible adj. **indisputable**, incontestable, undeniable, irrefutable, unassailable, beyond dispute, unquestionable, beyond question, indubitable, beyond doubt, unarguable, undebatable; certain, sure, definite, definitive, proven, decisive, conclusive, demonstrable, emphatic, categorical, airtight, watertight.
– OPPOSITES questionable.

inconvenience n. **1** *we apologize for any inconvenience caused* **trouble**, bother, problems, disruption, difficulty, disturbance; vexation, irritation, annoyance; informal aggravation, hassle. **2** *his early arrival was clearly an inconvenience* **nuisance**, trouble,

bother, problem, vexation, worry, trial, bind, bore, irritant, thorn in someone's flesh; informal headache, pain, pain in the neck, pain in the backside, drag, aggravation, hassle; N. Amer. informal pain in the butt.
▸ v. *I don't want to inconvenience you* **trouble**, bother, put out, put to any trouble, disturb, impose on, burden; vex, annoy, irritate; informal hassle; formal discommode.

inconvenient adj. **awkward**, difficult, inopportune, untimely, ill-timed, unsuitable, inappropriate, unfortunate; tiresome, irritating, annoying, vexing, bothersome; informal aggravating.

incorporate v. **1** *the region was incorporated into Moldavian territory* **absorb**, include, subsume, assimilate, integrate, take in, swallow up. **2** *the model incorporates some advanced features* **include**, contain, comprise, embody, embrace, build in, encompass. **3** *a small amount of salt is incorporated with the butter* **blend**, mix, mingle, meld, combine; fold in, stir in.

incorporeal adj. **intangible**, impalpable, non-physical; bodiless, disembodied, discarnate; spiritual, ethereal, unsubstantial, insubstantial, transcendental; ghostly, spectral, supernatural.
– OPPOSITES tangible.

incorrect adj. **1** *an incorrect answer* **wrong**, erroneous, in error, mistaken, inaccurate, wide of the mark, off target; untrue, false, fallacious; informal off beam, out, way out, full of holes. **2** *incorrect behaviour* **inappropriate**, wrong, unsuitable, inapt, inapposite; ill-advised, ill-considered, illjudged, injudicious, unacceptable, unfitting, out of keeping, improper, unseemly, unbecoming, indecorous; informal out of order.

incorrigible adj. **inveterate**, habitual, confirmed, hardened, incurable, irredeemable, hopeless, beyond hope, beyond redemption; impenitent, uncontrite, unrepentant, unapologetic, unashamed.

incorruptible adj. **1** *an incorruptible man* **honest**, honourable, trustworthy, principled, high-principled, anti-corruption, unbribable, moral, ethical, good, virtuous. **2** *an incorruptible substance* **imperishable**, indestructible, indissoluble, enduring, everlasting.
– OPPOSITES venal.

increase v. **1** *demand is likely to increase* **grow**, get bigger, get larger, enlarge, expand, swell; rise, climb, escalate, soar, surge, rocket, shoot up, spiral; intensify, strengthen, extend, heighten, stretch, spread, widen; multiply, snowball, mushroom, proliferate, balloon, build up, mount up, pile up, accrue, accumulate; literary wax. **2** *higher expectations will increase user demand* **add to**, make larger, make bigger, augment, supplement, top up, build up, extend, raise, swell, inflate; magnify, intensify, strengthen, heighten, amplify; informal up, jack up, hike up, bump up, crank up.
– OPPOSITES decrease, reduce.

i

▶ n. *the increase in size* | *an increase in demand* **growth**, rise, enlargement, expansion, extension, multiplication, elevation, inflation; increment, addition, augmentation; magnification, intensification, amplification, step up, climb, escalation, surge, upsurge, upswing, spiral, spurt; informal hike.

increasingly adv. **more and more**, progressively, to an increasing extent, ever more.

incredible adj. **1** *I find his story incredible* **unbelievable**, beyond belief, hard to believe, unconvincing, far-fetched, implausible, improbable, highly unlikely, dubious, doubtful; inconceivable, unthinkable, unimaginable, impossible; feeble, weak, thin, lame; informal hard to swallow/take, cock-and-bull. **2** *an incredible feat of engineering* **magnificent**, wonderful, marvellous, spectacular, remarkable, phenomenal, prodigious, breathtaking, extraordinary, unbelievable, amazing, stunning, astounding, astonishing, awe-inspiring, staggering, formidable, impressive, supreme, great, awesome, superhuman; informal fantastic, terrific, tremendous, stupendous, mind-boggling, mind-blowing, out of this world; literary wondrous.

incredulity n. **disbelief**, incredulousness, scepticism, distrust, mistrust, suspicion, doubt, doubtfulness, dubiousness, lack of conviction; cynicism.

incredulous adj. **disbelieving**, unbelieving, sceptical, distrustful, mistrustful, suspicious, doubtful, dubious, unconvinced; cynical.

increment n. **increase**, addition, supplement, gain, augmentation, boost; informal hike.
– OPPOSITES reduction.

incriminate v. **implicate**, involve, enmesh; blame, accuse, denounce, inform against, point the finger at; entrap; informal frame, set up, stick/pin the blame on, rat on; Brit. informal fit up, grass on; old use inculpate.

inculcate v. **1** *the beliefs inculcated in him by his father* **instil**, implant, fix, impress, imprint; hammer into, drum into, drive into, drill into, din into. **2** *they will try to inculcate you with a respect for culture* **imbue**, infuse, inspire, teach.

incumbent adj. **1** *it is incumbent on the government to give a clear lead* **necessary**, essential, required, imperative; compulsory, binding, obligatory, mandatory. **2** *the incumbent president* **current**, present, in office, in power; reigning.
▶ n. *the first incumbent of the post* **holder**, bearer, occupant.

incur v. **bring on oneself**, expose oneself to, lay oneself open to; run up; attract, invite, earn, arouse, cause, give rise to, be liable/subject to, meet with, sustain, experience.

incurable adj. **1** *an incurable illness* **untreatable**, inoperable, irremediable; terminal, fatal, mortal; chronic. **2** *an incurable romantic* **inveterate**, dyed-in-the-wool, confirmed, established, long-established, long-standing, absolute, complete, utter, thorough, thoroughgoing, out-and-out, through and through; unashamed, unapologetic, unrepentant, incorrigible, hopeless.

incursion n. **attack**, assault, raid, invasion, storming, foray, blitz, sortie, sally, advance, push, thrust.
– OPPOSITES retreat.

indebted adj. **beholden**, under an obligation, obliged, obligated, grateful, thankful, in someone's debt, owing a debt of gratitude.

indecent adj. **1** *indecent photographs* **obscene**, dirty, filthy, rude, coarse, naughty, vulgar, gross, crude, lewd, salacious, improper, smutty, off colour; pornographic, offensive, prurient, sordid, scatological; ribald, risqué, racy; informal blue, nudge-nudge, porn, porno, X-rated, raunchy, skin; Brit. informal saucy; euphemistic adult. **2** *indecent clothes* **revealing**, short, brief, skimpy, scanty, low-cut, flimsy, thin, see-through; erotic, arousing, sexy, suggestive, titillating. **3** *indecent haste* **unseemly**, improper, indecorous, unceremonious, indelicate, unbecoming, ungentlemanly, unladylike, unfitting, unbefitting; untoward, unsuitable, inappropriate; in bad taste, tasteless, unacceptable, offensive, crass.

indecipherable adj. **illegible**, unreadable, hard to read, unintelligible, unclear; scribbled, scrawled, hieroglyphic, squiggly, cramped, crabbed.

indecision n. **indecisiveness**, irresolution, hesitancy, hesitation, tentativeness; ambivalence, doubt, doubtfulness, uncertainty, incertitude; vacillation, equivocation, second thoughts; shilly-shallying, dithering, temporizing; Brit. humming and hawing; Scottish swithering; informal dilly-dallying, sitting on the fence; formal dubiety.

indecisive adj. **1** *an indecisive result* **inconclusive**, proving nothing, settling nothing, open, indeterminate, undecided, unsettled, borderline, indefinite, unclear, ambiguous; informal up in the air. **2** *an indecisive leader* **irresolute**, hesitant, tentative, weak; vacillating, equivocating, dithering, wavering, faltering, shilly-shallying; ambivalent, divided, blowing hot and cold, in two minds, in a dilemma, in a quandary, torn; doubtful, unsure, uncertain, undecided, uncommitted; informal iffy, sitting on the fence.

indecorous adj. **improper**, unseemly, unbecoming, undignified, immodest, indelicate, indecent, unladylike, ungentlemanly; inappropriate, incorrect, unsuitable, undesirable, unfitting, in bad taste, ill-bred.

indecorum n. **impropriety**, unseemliness, immodesty, indecency, indelicacy; inappropriateness, unsuitability, undesirability, unacceptability, bad taste.

indeed adv. **1** *there was, indeed, quite a furore as expected*, to be sure; in fact, in point of fact, as a matter of fact, in truth, actually, as it happens/happened, if truth be told; old use in sooth. **2** *'May I join you?' 'Indeed you may.'* yes, certainly, assuredly, of course, naturally, without (a) doubt, without question, by all means; informal you bet, I'll say. **3** *Ian's future with us looked rosy indeed* very, extremely, exceedingly, tremendously, immensely, singularly, decidedly, particularly, remarkably, really.

indefatigable adj. tireless, untiring, unwearied, unwearying, unflagging; determined, tenacious, dogged, single-minded, assiduous, industrious, unswerving, unfaltering, unshakeable, indomitable; persistent, relentless, unremitting.

indefensible adj. **1** *indefensible cruelty* inexcusable, unjustifiable, unjustified, unpardonable, unforgivable; uncalled for, unprovoked, gratuitous, unreasonable, unnecessary. **2** *an indefensible system of dual justice* untenable, unsustainable, insupportable, unwarranted, unwarrantable, unjustifiable, unjustified, flawed, unacceptable. **3** *an indefensible island* defenceless, vulnerable, exposed, open to attack, pregnable, undefended, unfortified, unguarded, unprotected, unarmed.

indefinable adj. hard to define, hard to describe, indescribable, inexpressible, nameless; vague, obscure, impalpable, elusive.

indefinite adj. **1** *an indefinite period* indeterminate, unspecified, unlimited, unrestricted, undecided, undetermined, undefined, unfixed, unsettled, unknown, uncertain; limitless, infinite, endless, immeasurable. **2** *an indefinite meaning* vague, ill-defined, unclear, loose, general, imprecise, inexact, nebulous, blurred, fuzzy, hazy, obscure, ambiguous, equivocal.
– OPPOSITES fixed, clear.

indefinitely adv. for an unspecified period, for an unlimited period, without limit, sine die.

indelible adj. ineradicable, permanent, lasting, persisting, enduring, unfading, unforgettable, haunting, never to be forgotten.

indelicate adj. **1** *an indelicate question* insensitive, tactless, undiplomatic, impolitic, indiscreet. **2** *an indelicate sense of humour* vulgar, rude, crude, bawdy, racy, risqué, ribald, earthy, indecent, improper, naughty, indecorous, off colour, dirty, smutty, salacious; informal blue, nudge-nudge, raunchy; Brit. informal saucy.

indemnify v. **1** *he should be indemnified for his losses* reimburse, compensate, recompense, repay, pay back, remunerate, recoup. **2** *they are indemnified against breach of contract* insure, guarantee, protect, secure, underwrite.

indemnity n. **1** *no indemnity will be given for loss of cash* insurance, assurance, protection, security, indemnification, surety, guarantee, warranty, safeguard. **2** *indemnity from prosecution* immunity, exemption, dispensation, freedom; special treatment, privilege. **3** *the company was paid $100,000 in indemnity* compensation, reimbursement, recompense, repayment, restitution, payment, redress, reparation(s), damages.

indent v. **1** *a coastline indented by many fjords* notch, make an indentation in, scallop, groove, furrow. **2** *you'll have to indent for a new uniform* order, put in an order for, requisition, apply for, put in for, request, ask for, claim, put in a request/claim for, call for.
▶n. Brit. *an indent for silk scarves* order, requisition, purchase order, request, call, application; claim.

indentation n. hollow, depression, dip, dent, dint, cavity, concavity, pit, trough; dimple, cleft; snick, nick, notch; recess, bay, inlet, cove.

indenture n. contract, agreement, compact, covenant, bond, warrant; certificate, deed, document, instrument.

independence n. **1** *the struggle for American independence* self-government, self-rule, home rule, self-determination, sovereignty, autonomy, non-alignment, freedom, liberty. **2** *he valued his independence* self-sufficiency, self-reliance. **3** *the adviser's independence* impartiality, neutrality, disinterest, disinterestedness, detachment, objectivity. **4** *independence of spirit* freedom, individualism, unconventionality, unorthodoxy.

independent adj. **1** *an independent country* self-governing, self-ruling, self-determining, sovereign, autonomous, autarchic, free, non-aligned. **2** *two independent groups of biologists verified the results* separate, different, unconnected, unrelated, dissociated, discrete. **3** *an independent school* private, non-state-run, private-sector, fee-paying; privatized, denationalized. **4** *her grown-up, independent children* self-sufficient, self-supporting, self-reliant, standing on one's own two feet. **5** *independent advice* impartial, unbiased, unprejudiced, neutral, disinterested, uninvolved, uncommitted, detached, dispassionate, objective, non-partisan, non-discriminatory, with no axe to grind, without fear or favour. **6** *an independent spirit* freethinking, free, individualistic, unconventional, maverick, bold, unconstrained, unfettered, untrammelled.
– OPPOSITES subservient, related, public, biased.

independently adv. alone, on one's own, separately, unaccompanied, solo; unaided, unassisted, without help, by one's own efforts, under one's own steam, single-handed(ly), off one's own bat, on one's own initiative.

indescribable adj. **inexpressible,** indefinable, beyond words/description, incommunicable, ineffable; unutterable, unspeakable; intense, extreme, acute, strong, powerful, profound; incredible, extraordinary, remarkable, prodigious.

indestructible adj. **unbreakable,** shatterproof, durable; lasting, enduring, everlasting, perennial, deathless, undying, immortal, inextinguishable, imperishable; literary adamantine.
− OPPOSITES fragile.

indeterminate adj. **1** *an indeterminate period of time* **undetermined,** uncertain, unknown, unspecified, indefinite, unfixed. **2** *some indeterminate background noise* **vague,** indefinite, unspecific, unclear, nebulous, indistinct; amorphous, shapeless, formless; hazy, faint, shadowy, dim.

index n. **1** *the library's subject index* **list,** listing, inventory, catalogue, register, directory. **2** *literature is an index to the condition of civilization* **guide,** sign, indication, indicator, measure, signal, mark, evidence, symptom, token; clue, hint. **3** *the index jumped up the dial* **pointer,** indicator, needle, hand, finger, marker.

indicate v. **1** *sales indicate a growing market for such art* **point to,** be a sign of, be evidence of, evidence, demonstrate, show, testify to, bespeak, be a symptom of, be symptomatic of, denote, connote, mark, signal, signify, suggest, imply; manifest, reveal, betray, display, reflect, represent; formal evince; literary betoken. **2** *the president indicated his willingness to use force* **state,** declare, make known, communicate, announce, mention, reveal, divulge, disclose. **3** *please indicate your choice of prize on the form* **specify,** designate, stipulate; show. **4** *he indicated the room with a sweep of his arm* **point out,** gesture towards.

indicated adj. *in such cases surgery is indicated* **advisable,** recommended, suggested, desirable, preferable, best, sensible, wise, commonsensical, prudent, in someone's (best) interests; necessary, needed, required, called for.

indication n. **sign,** signal, indicator, symptom, mark, manifestation, demonstration, show, evidence; pointer, guide, hint, clue, intimation, omen, augury, portent, warning, forewarning.

indicative adj. **symptomatic,** expressive, suggestive, representative, emblematic, symbolic; typical, characteristic; rare indicatory.

indicator n. **1** *these tests are a reliable indicator of performance* **measure,** gauge, barometer, guide, index, mark, sign, signal; standard, touchstone, yardstick, benchmark, criterion, point of reference, guideline, test, litmus test. **2** *the depth indicator* **meter,** measuring device, measure, gauge, dial. **3** *a position indicator* **pointer,** needle, hand, arrow, marker.

indict v. **charge,** accuse, arraign, take to court, put on trial, prosecute; summons, cite, prefer charges against; N. Amer. impeach.
− OPPOSITES acquit.

indictment n. **charge,** accusation, arraignment; citation, summons; Brit. plaint; N. Amer. impeachment.

indifference n. **1** *his apparent indifference infuriated her* **lack of concern,** unconcern, disinterest, lack of interest, lack of enthusiasm, apathy, nonchalance; boredom, unresponsiveness, impassivity, dispassion, detachment, coolness. **2** *the indifference of the midfield players* **mediocrity,** lack of distinction, amateurism, amateurishness, lack of inspiration.

indifferent adj. **1** *an indifferent shrug* **unconcerned,** uninterested, uncaring, casual, nonchalant, offhand, uninvolved, unenthusiastic, apathetic, lukewarm, phlegmatic; unimpressed, bored, unmoved, unresponsive, impassive, dispassionate, detached, cool. **2** *an indifferent performance* **mediocre,** ordinary, average, middling, middle-of-the-road, uninspired, undistinguished, unexceptional, unexciting, unremarkable, run-of-the-mill, pedestrian, prosaic, lacklustre, forgettable, amateur, amateurish; informal OK, so-so, fair-to-middling, no great shakes, not up to much; Brit. informal not much cop; N. Amer. informal bush-league; NZ informal half-pie.
− OPPOSITES enthusiastic, brilliant.

indigenous adj. **native,** original, aboriginal, autochthonous; earliest, first.

indigent adj. **poor,** impecunious, destitute, penniless, impoverished, insolvent, poverty-stricken; needy, in need, hard up, on the breadline, deprived, disadvantaged, badly off, on one's beam-ends; informal on one's uppers, broke, flat broke, strapped (for cash), without a brass farthing, without a bean/sou, as poor as a church mouse; Brit. informal stony broke, skint, boracic; N. Amer. informal on skid row; formal penurious.
− OPPOSITES rich.

indigestion n. **dyspepsia,** heartburn, pyrosis, acidity, stomach ache; (an) upset stomach, (a) stomach upset; informal bellyache, tummy ache, collywobbles.

indignant adj. **aggrieved,** resentful, affronted, disgruntled, displeased, cross, angry, annoyed, offended, exasperated, irritated, piqued, nettled, in high dudgeon, chagrined; informal peeved, vexed, irked, put out, miffed, aggravated, riled, in a huff; Brit. informal narked, not best pleased; N. Amer. informal sore.

indignation n. **resentment,** umbrage, affront, disgruntlement, displeasure, anger, annoyance, irritation, exasperation, vexation, offence, pique; informal aggravation; literary ire.

indignity n. **shame,** humiliation, loss of self-respect, loss of pride, loss of face, embarrassment, mortification; disgrace, dishonour, stigma, discredit; affront, insult, abuse, mistreatment, injury, offence, injustice, slight, snub, discourtesy, disrespect; informal slap in the face, kick in the teeth.

indirect adj. **1** *an indirect effect* **incidental**, accidental, unintended, secondary, subordinate, ancillary, collateral, concomitant, contingent. **2** *the indirect route* **roundabout**, circuitous, wandering, meandering, serpentine, winding, tortuous, zigzag. **3** *an indirect attack* **oblique**, inexplicit, implicit, implied, allusive.

indirectly adv. **1** *I heard of the damage indirectly* **second-hand**, at second hand, from others; informal on the grapevine, on the bush/jungle telegraph. **2** *he referred to the subject indirectly* **obliquely**, by implication, allusively.

indiscernible adj. **1** *an almost indiscernible change* **unnoticeable**, imperceptible, invisible, hidden, undetectable, indistinguishable, inappreciable; tiny, minute, minuscule, microscopic, nanoscopic, infinitesimal, negligible, inconsequential. **2** *an indiscernible shape* **indistinct**, nebulous, unclear, fuzzy, obscure, vague, indefinite, amorphous, shadowy, dim, hard to make out.
– OPPOSITES distinct.

indiscreet adj. **1** *an indiscreet remark* **imprudent**, unwise, impolitic, injudicious, incautious, irresponsible, ill-judged, ill-advised, misguided, ill-considered, careless, rash, unwary, hasty, reckless, precipitate, impulsive, foolhardy, foolish, short-sighted; undiplomatic, indelicate, tactless, insensitive; inexpedient, untimely, infelicitous. **2** *her indiscreet behaviour* **immodest**, indecorous, unseemly, improper, indecent, indelicate.

indiscretion n. **1** *he was prone to indiscretion* **imprudence**, injudiciousness, incaution, irresponsibility; carelessness, rashness, recklessness, precipitateness, impulsiveness, foolhardiness, foolishness, folly; tactlessness, insensitivity. **2** *his past indiscretions* **blunder**, lapse, gaffe, mistake, faux pas, error, slip, miscalculation, impropriety; misdemeanour, transgression, peccadillo, misdeed; informal slip-up.

indiscriminate adj. **non-selective**, unselective, undiscriminating, uncritical, aimless, hit-or-miss, haphazard, random, arbitrary, unsystematic, undirected; wholesale, general, sweeping, blanket; thoughtless, unthinking, unconsidered, casual, careless.
– OPPOSITES selective.

indispensable adj. **essential**, necessary, all-important, of the utmost importance, of the essence, vital, crucial, key, needed, required, requisite; invaluable.
– OPPOSITES superfluous.

indisposed adj. **1** *my wife is indisposed* **ill**, unwell, sick, on the sick list, poorly, ailing, not (very) well, out of sorts, under/below par; out of action, hors de combat; Brit. off

colour; informal under the weather. **2** *she was indisposed to help him* **reluctant**, unwilling, disinclined, loath, unprepared, not disposed, not minded, averse.
– OPPOSITES well, willing.

indisposition n. **1** *a mild indisposition* **illness**, malady, ailment, disorder, sickness, disease, infection; condition, complaint, problem; informal bug, virus; Brit. informal lurgy. **2** *his indisposition to leave the house* **reluctance**, unwillingness, disinclination, aversion.

indisputable adj. **incontrovertible**, incontestable, undeniable, irrefutable, beyond dispute, unassailable, unquestionable, beyond question, indubitable, not in doubt, beyond doubt, beyond a shadow of a doubt, unarguable, undebatable, airtight, watertight; unequivocal, unmistakable, certain, sure, definite, definitive, proven, decisive, conclusive, demonstrable, self-evident, clear, clear-cut, plain, obvious, manifest, patent, palpable.
– OPPOSITES questionable.

indistinct adj. **1** *the distant shoreline was indistinct* **blurred**, out of focus, fuzzy, hazy, misty, foggy, cloudy, shadowy, dim, nebulous; unclear, obscure, vague, faint, indistinguishable, barely perceptible, hard to see, hard to make out. **2** *the last two digits are indistinct* **indecipherable**, illegible, unreadable, hard to read. **3** *indistinct sounds* **muffled**, muted, low, quiet, soft, faint, inaudible, hard to hear; muttered, mumbled.
– OPPOSITES clear.

indistinguishable adj. **1** *the two girls were indistinguishable* **identical**, difficult to tell apart, like (two) peas in a pod, like Tweedledum and Tweedledee, very similar, two of a kind. **2** *his words were indistinguishable* **unintelligible**, incomprehensible, hard to make out, indistinct, unclear; inaudible.
– OPPOSITES unalike, clear.

individual adj. **1** *exhibitions devoted to individual artists* **single**, separate, discrete, independent; sole, lone, solitary, isolated. **2** *he had his own individual style of music* **characteristic**, distinctive, distinct, typical, particular, peculiar, personal, personalized, special. **3** *a chic and highly individual apartment* **original**, unique, exclusive, singular, idiosyncratic, different, unusual, off-centre, novel, unorthodox, atypical, out of the ordinary.
▸ n. **1** *Peter was a rather stuffy individual* **person**, human being, mortal, soul, creature; man, boy, woman, girl; character, personage; informal type, sort, beggar, cookie, customer, guy, geezer, devil, bastard; Brit. informal bod, gent, punter; informal dated body, cove; old use wight. **2** *she was a real individual* **individualist**, free spirit, nonconformist, original, eccentric, character, maverick, rare bird; Brit. informal one-off.

individualism n. **independence**, freethinking, freedom of thought, originality; unconventionality, eccentricity.

individualist n. **free spirit**, individual, nonconformist, original, eccentric, maverick, rare bird; Brit. informal one-off.
– OPPOSITES conformist.

individualistic adj. **unconventional**, unorthodox, atypical, singular, unique, original, off-centre, nonconformist, independent, freethinking; eccentric, maverick, strange, odd, peculiar, idiosyncratic.

individuality n. **distinctiveness**, distinction, uniqueness, originality, singularity, particularity, peculiarity, differentness, separateness; personality, character, identity, self.

individually adv. **one at a time**, one by one, singly, separately, severally, independently, apart.
– OPPOSITES together.

indoctrinate v. **brainwash**, propagandize, proselytize, inculcate, re-educate, persuade, convince, condition, mould, discipline; instruct, teach, school, drill.

indolence n. **laziness**, idleness, slothfulness, sloth, shiftlessness, inactivity, inaction, inertia, sluggishness, lethargy, languor, languidness, torpor; literary hebetude.

indolent adj. **lazy**, idle, slothful, loafing, work-shy, do-nothing, sluggardly, shiftless, lackadaisical, languid, inactive, inert, sluggish, lethargic, torpid; slack, lax, remiss, negligent, good-for-nothing, feckless; informal bone idle.
– OPPOSITES industrious, energetic.

indomitable adj. **invincible**, unconquerable, unbeatable, unassailable, invulnerable, unshakeable; indefatigable, unyielding, unbending, stalwart, stout-hearted, lionhearted, strong-willed, strong-minded, steadfast, staunch, resolute, firm, determined, intransigent, inflexible, adamant; unflinching, courageous, brave, valiant, heroic, intrepid, fearless, plucky, mettlesome, gritty, steely.
– OPPOSITES submissive.

indubitable adj. **unquestionable**, undoubtable, indisputable, unarguable, undebatable, incontestable, undeniable, irrefutable, incontrovertible, unmistakable, unequivocal, certain, sure, positive, definite, absolute, conclusive, watertight; beyond doubt, beyond the shadow of a doubt, beyond dispute, beyond question, not in question, not in doubt.
– OPPOSITES doubtful.

induce v. **1** *the pickets induced many workers to stay away* **persuade**, convince, prevail on, get, make, prompt, move, inspire, influence, encourage, motivate; coax into, wheedle into, cajole into, talk into, prod into; informal twist someone's arm. **2** *these activities induce a feeling of togetherness* **bring about**, cause, produce, effect, create, give rise to, generate, instigate, engender, occasion, set in motion, lead to, result in, trigger off, spark off, whip up, stir up, kindle, arouse, rouse, foster, promote, encourage; literary beget, enkindle.
– OPPOSITES dissuade, prevent.

inducement n. **incentive**, encouragement, attraction, temptation, stimulus, bait, carrot, lure, pull, draw, spur, goad, impetus, motive, motivation, provocation; bribe, reward; informal come-on, sweetener.
– OPPOSITES deterrent.

induct v. **1** *the new ministers were inducted into the government* **admit to**, allow into, introduce to, initiate into, install in, instate in, swear into; appoint to. **2** *he inducted me into the skills of magic* **introduce to**, acquaint with, familiarize with, make conversant with; ground in, instruct in, teach in, educate in, school in.

indulge v. **1** *Sally indulged her passion for long walks* **satisfy**, gratify, fulfil, feed, accommodate; yield to, give in to, give way to. **2** *she indulged in a fit of sulks* **wallow in**, give oneself up to, give way to, yield to, abandon oneself to, give free rein to; luxuriate in, revel in, lose oneself in. **3** *she did not like her children to be indulged* **pamper**, spoil, overindulge, coddle, mollycoddle, cosset, baby, pet, spoon-feed, feather-bed, wrap in cotton wool; pander to, wait on hand and foot, cater to someone's every whim, kill with kindness; old use cocker.
– OPPOSITES frustrate.
□ **indulge oneself** treat oneself, give oneself a treat; have a spree, splash out; informal go to town, splurge.

indulgence n. **1** *the indulgence of all his desires* **satisfaction**, gratification, fulfilment. **2** *excess indulgence contributed to his ill-health* **self-gratification**, self-indulgence, overindulgence, overconsumption, intemperance, immoderation, excess, excessiveness, lack of restraint, extravagance, decadence, pleasure-seeking, sybaritism. **3** *they viewed holidays as an indulgence* **extravagance**, luxury, treat, non-essential, extra, frill. **4** *her indulgence left him spoilt* **pampering**, coddling, mollycoddling, cosseting, babying. **5** *his parents view his lapses with indulgence* **tolerance**, forbearance, understanding, kindness, compassion, sympathy, forgiveness, leniency.

indulgent adj. **generous**, permissive, easy-going, liberal, tolerant, forgiving, forbearing, lenient, kind, kindly, soft-hearted, compassionate, understanding, sympathetic; fond, doting, soft; compliant, obliging, accommodating.
– OPPOSITES strict.

industrial adj. **1** *industrial areas of the city* **manufacturing**, factory; commercial, business, trade. **2** Brit. *industrial action* **strike**, protest.

industrialist n. **manufacturer**, producer, factory owner; captain of industry, big businessman, magnate, tycoon, capitalist, financier; informal derogatory fat cat.

industrious adj. **hard-working**, diligent,
assiduous, conscientious, steady,
painstaking, sedulous, persevering,
unflagging, untiring, tireless, indefatigable,
studious; busy, as busy as a bee, active,
bustling, energetic, on the go, vigorous,
determined, dynamic, driven, zealous,
productive; with one's shoulder to the
wheel, with one's nose to the grindstone.
– OPPOSITES indolent.

industry n. **1** *British industry
manufacturing*, production; construction.
2 *the publishing industry* **business**, trade,
field, line (of business); informal racket. **3** *the
kitchen was a hive of industry* **activity**,
busyness, energy, vigour, productiveness;
hard work, industriousness, diligence,
application, dedication.

inebriated adj. **drunk**, intoxicated, drunken,
incapable, tipsy, the worse for drink, under
the influence; informal tight, merry, in one's
cups, three sheets to the wind, pie-eyed,
plastered, smashed, wrecked, wasted,
sloshed, soused, sozzled, blotto, stewed,
pickled, tanked (up), off one's face, out
of one's head, ratted; Brit. informal legless,
bevvied, paralytic, Brahms and Liszt, half
cut, out of it, lashed, bladdered, trolleyed,
slaughtered, mullered, squiffy, tiddly; N. Amer.
informal loaded, trashed, juiced, sauced, out
of one's gourd, in the bag, zoned, blitzed,
jacked; euphemistic tired and emotional; informal
dated lit up.
– OPPOSITES sober.

inedible adj. **uneatable**, indigestible,
unsavoury, unpalatable, unwholesome; stale,
rotten, off, bad.

ineffable adj. **1** *the ineffable beauty of the
Everglades* **indescribable**, inexpressible,
beyond words; undefinable, unutterable,
untold, unimaginable; overwhelming,
breathtaking, awesome, staggering, amazing.
2 *the ineffable name of God* **unutterable**,
unmentionable; taboo, forbidden, off limits;
informal no go.

ineffective adj. **1** *an ineffective scheme*
unsuccessful, unproductive, fruitless,
unprofitable, abortive, futile, purposeless,
useless, worthless, ineffectual, inefficient,
inefficacious, inadequate; feeble, inept,
lame; old use bootless. **2** *an ineffective
president* **ineffectual**, inefficient,
inefficacious, unsuccessful, powerless,
impotent, inadequate, incompetent,
incapable, unfit, inept, weak, poor; informal
useless, hopeless.

ineffectual adj. See **ineffective**
(senses 1 & 2).

inefficacious adj. See **ineffective** (sense 1).

inefficient adj. **1** *an inefficient worker*
ineffective, ineffectual, incompetent,
inept, incapable, unfit, unskilful, inexpert,
amateurish; disorganized, unprepared;
negligent, lax, sloppy, slack, careless;
informal lousy, useless. **2** *inefficient processes*
uneconomical, wasteful, unproductive,

time-wasting, slow; deficient, disorganized,
unsystematic.

inelegant adj. **1** *an inelegant bellow
of laughter* **unrefined**, uncouth,
unsophisticated, unpolished, uncultivated;
ill-bred, coarse, vulgar, rude, impolite,
unmannerly. **2** *inelegant dancing* **graceless**,
ungraceful, ungainly, uncoordinated,
awkward, clumsy, lumbering; inept,
unskilful, inexpert; informal having two left
feet.
– OPPOSITES refined, graceful.

ineligible adj. **1** *we are ineligible for a
grant* **unqualified**, ruled out, disqualified,
disentitled; Law incompetent. **2** dated
she was in love with someone ineligible
unmarriageable, unavailable; unsuitable,
unacceptable, undesirable, inappropriate,
unworthy.
– OPPOSITES suitable.

inept adj. **incompetent**, unskilful, unskilled,
inexpert, amateurish; clumsy, awkward,
maladroit, unhandy, bungling, blundering;
unproductive, unsuccessful, ineffectual,
not up to scratch; informal cack-handed, ham-
fisted, butterfingered, klutzy; Brit. informal all
(fingers and) thumbs.
– OPPOSITES competent.

inequality n. **imbalance**, inequity,
inconsistency, variation, variability;
divergence, polarity, disparity, discrepancy,
dissimilarity, difference; bias, prejudice,
discrimination, unfairness.

inequitable adj. **unfair**, unjust,
unequal, uneven, unbalanced, one-sided,
discriminatory, preferential, biased,
partisan, partial, prejudiced.
– OPPOSITES fair.

inequity n. **unfairness**, injustice,
unjustness, discrimination, partisanship,
partiality, favouritism, bias, prejudice.

inert adj. **unmoving**, motionless, immobile,
inanimate, still, stationary, static; dormant,
sleeping; unconscious, comatose, lifeless,
insensible, insensate, insentient; idle,
inactive, sluggish, lethargic, stagnant,
listless, torpid.
– OPPOSITES active.

inertia n. **inactivity**, inaction, inertness;
apathy, accidie, malaise, stagnation,
enervation, lethargy, listlessness, torpor,
idleness, sloth; motionlessness, immobility,
lifelessness; formal stasis.

inescapable adj. **unavoidable**, inevitable,
ineluctable, ineliminable, inexorable,
unpreventable; assured, sure, certain;
necessary, required, compulsory, mandatory;
rare ineludible.
– OPPOSITES avoidable.

inessential adj. **unnecessary**, non-
essential, unwanted, uncalled-for, needless,
redundant, superfluous, excessive, surplus,
dispensable, expendable; unimportant,
peripheral, minor, secondary.

inestimable adj. **immeasurable**,
incalculable, innumerable, unfathomable,
indeterminable, measureless, untold;

limitless, boundless, unlimited, infinite, endless, inexhaustible; informal no end of; literary myriad.
– OPPOSITES few.

inevitable adj. **unavoidable**, unpreventable, inescapable, inexorable, ineluctable; assured, certain, sure; fated, predestined, predetermined; rare ineludible.
– OPPOSITES uncertain.

inevitably adv. **naturally**, necessarily, automatically, as a matter of course, of necessity, inescapably, unavoidably, certainly, surely, definitely, undoubtedly; informal like it or not; formal perforce.

inexact adj. **imprecise**, inaccurate, approximate, rough, crude, coarse-grained, general, vague; incorrect, erroneous, wrong, false; off, out; N. Amer. informal ballpark.

inexcusable adj. **indefensible**, unjustifiable, unwarranted, unpardonable, unforgivable; blameworthy, censurable, reprehensible, deplorable, unconscionable, unacceptable, unreasonable; uncalled-for, unprovoked, gratuitous.

inexhaustible adj. **1** *her patience is inexhaustible* **unlimited**, limitless, illimitable, infinite, boundless, endless, never-ending, unfailing, everlasting, immeasurable, incalculable, inestimable, untold; copious, abundant. **2** *the dancers were inexhaustible* **tireless**, indefatigable, untiring, unfaltering, unflagging, unremitting, persevering, persistent, dogged.
– OPPOSITES limited, weary.

inexorable adj. **1** *the inexorable advance of science* **relentless**, unstoppable, inescapable, inevitable, unavoidable, irrevocable; persistent, continuous, non-stop, steady, interminable, incessant, unceasing, unremitting, unrelenting. **2** *inexorable creditors* **intransigent**, unbending, unyielding, inflexible, adamant, obdurate, immovable, unshakeable; implacable, unappeasable, unforgiving, unsparing, uncompromising, ruthless, relentless, pitiless, merciless.

inexpedient adj. **unadvisable**, injudicious, unwise, impolitic, imprudent, incautious; irresponsible, foolhardy, foolish, ill-advised, ill-considered, inappropriate; disadvantageous, prejudicial.
– OPPOSITES wise.

inexpensive adj. **cheap**, low-priced, low-cost, economical, competitive, affordable, reasonable, budget, economy, bargain, cut-price, reduced, discounted, discount, rock-bottom, giveaway, bargain-basement; informal dirt cheap.

inexperience n. **ignorance**, unworldliness, naivety, naiveness, innocence, greenness, immaturity; literary nescience.

inexperienced adj. **inexpert**, unpractised, untrained, unschooled, unqualified, unskilled, amateur; ignorant, unversed, unseasoned; naive, unsophisticated, callow, immature, green; informal wet behind the ears, wide-eyed.

inexpert adj. **unskilled**, unskilful, amateur, amateurish, unprofessional, inexperienced; inept, incompetent, maladroit, clumsy, bungling, blundering, unhandy; informal cack-handed, ham-fisted, butterfingered.

inexplicable adj. **unaccountable**, unexplainable, incomprehensible, unfathomable, impenetrable, insoluble; baffling, puzzling, perplexing, mystifying, bewildering; mysterious, strange.
– OPPOSITES understandable.

inexpressible adj. **indescribable**, undefinable, unutterable, unspeakable, ineffable, beyond words; unimaginable, inconceivable, unthinkable, untold.

inexpressive adj. **expressionless**, impassive, emotionless; inscrutable, unreadable, blank, vacant, glazed, lifeless, deadpan, wooden, stony; poker-faced, straight-faced.

inextinguishable adj. **irrepressible**, unquenchable, indestructible, undying, unfailing, unceasing, ceaseless, enduring, everlasting, eternal, persistent.

inextricable adj. **1** *our lives are inextricable* **inseparable**, indivisible, entangled, tangled, mixed up. **2** *an inextricable situation* **inescapable**, unavoidable, ineluctable, unpreventable.

infallible adj. **1** *an infallible sense of timing* **unerring**, unfailing, faultless, flawless, impeccable, perfect, precise, accurate, meticulous, scrupulous; Brit. informal spot on. **2** *infallible cures* **unfailing**, guaranteed, dependable, trustworthy, reliable, sure, certain, safe, foolproof, effective; informal sure-fire; formal efficacious.

infamous adj. **1** *an infamous mass murderer* **notorious**, disreputable; legendary, fabled. **2** *infamous misconduct* **abominable**, outrageous, shocking, shameful, disgraceful, dishonourable, discreditable, unworthy; monstrous, atrocious, appalling, dreadful, terrible, heinous, egregious, detestable, loathsome, hateful, vile, unspeakable, unforgivable, iniquitous, scandalous; informal dirty, filthy, low-down; Brit. informal beastly.
– OPPOSITES reputable, honourable.

infamy n. **1** *these acts brought him infamy* **notoriety**, disrepute, ill fame, disgrace, discredit, shame, dishonour, ignominy, scandal, censure, blame, disapprobation, condemnation. **2** *she was punished for her infamy* **wickedness**, evil, vileness, iniquity, depravity, degeneracy, immorality; sin, wrongdoing, offence, abuse; formal turpitude.

infancy n. **1** *she died in infancy* **babyhood**, early childhood. **2** *the infancy of broadcasting* **beginnings**, early days, early stages; seeds, roots; start, commencement, launch, debut, rise, emergence, dawn, birth, inception.
– OPPOSITES end.

infant n. *a fretful infant* **baby**, newborn, young child, (tiny) tot, little one; Medicine neonate; Scottish & N. English bairn, wean; informal tiny, sprog; literary babe.

▸adj. *infant industries* **developing**, emergent, emerging, embryonic, nascent, new, fledgling, budding, up-and-coming.

infantile adj. **childish**, babyish, immature, puerile, juvenile, adolescent; silly, inane, fatuous.

infantry n. **infantrymen**, foot soldiers, foot guards; the ranks; cannon fodder; US GIs; Brit. informal Tommies; Military slang infanteers, grunts; US informal dated dogfaces; historical footmen.

infatuated adj. **besotted**, in love, head over heels, obsessed, taken; enamoured of, attracted to, devoted to, captivated by, enchanted by, bewitched by, under the spell of; informal smitten with, sweet on, keen on, gone on, mad about, crazy about, stuck on, bowled over by, carrying a torch for.

infatuation n. **passion**, love, adoration, desire, feeling, devotion; obsession, fixation, fancy; informal crush, thing, hang-up, pash.

infect v. **1** *the ill can infect their partners* **pass infection to**, spread disease to, contaminate. **2** *nitrates were infecting rivers* **contaminate**, pollute, taint, foul, dirty, blight, damage, ruin; poison. **3** *his high spirits infected everyone* **affect**, influence, impact on, touch; excite, inspire, stimulate, animate.

infection n. **1** *a kidney infection* **disease**, virus; disorder, condition, affliction, complaint, illness, ailment, sickness, infirmity; informal bug; Brit. informal lurgy; dated contagion. **2** *the infection in his wounds* **contamination**, poison; septicity, septicaemia, suppuration, inflammation; germs, bacteria; Medicine sepsis.

infectious adj. **1** *infectious disease* **contagious**, communicable, transmittable, transmissible, transferable, spreadable; epidemic; informal catching; dated infective. **2** *infectious fluids* **contaminating**, germ-laden, polluting; poisonous, toxic, noxious. **3** *her laughter is infectious* **irresistible**, compelling, contagious, catching.

infelicitous adj. **unfortunate**, unsuitable, inappropriate, inapposite, inapt; untimely, inopportune; injudicious, imprudent, indiscreet, indelicate.
– OPPOSITES appropriate.

infelicity n. **mistake**, error, blunder, slip, lapse, solecism.

infer v. **deduce**, conclude, conjecture, surmise, reason; gather, understand, presume, assume, take it; read between the lines; N. Amer. figure; Brit. informal suss (out).

inference n. **deduction**, conclusion, reasoning, conjecture, speculation, presumption, assumption, supposition, reckoning, extrapolation; guesswork.

inferior adj. **1** *she regards him as inferior* **second-class**, lower-ranking, subordinate, junior, minor, second-fiddle, lowly, humble, menial, beneath one. **2** *inferior accommodation* **second-rate**, substandard, low-quality, low-grade, unsatisfactory, shoddy, deficient; poor, bad, awful, dreadful, wretched; Brit. downmarket; informal crummy,

dire, rotten, lousy, third-rate; Brit. informal duff, rubbish, ropy, dodgy.
– OPPOSITES superior, luxury.
▸n. *how dare she treat him as an inferior?* **subordinate**, junior, underling, minion; informal bitch.

infernal adj. **1** *the infernal regions* **hellish**, lower, nether, subterranean, underworld, chthonic; Hadean, Tartarean. **2** informal *an infernal nuisance* **damnable**, wretched; annoying, irritating, infuriating, exasperating; informal damned, damn, flaming, blasted, blessed, pesky, aggravating; Brit. informal blinking, blooming, flipping; Brit. informal dated bally, ruddy.

infertile adj. **1** *infertile soil* **barren**, unfruitful, unproductive, uncultivable; sterile, impoverished, arid. **2** *she was infertile* **sterile**, barren; childless; technical infecund.

infest v. **overrun**, spread through, invade, infiltrate, pervade, permeate, inundate, overwhelm; beset, plague.

infested adj. **overrun**, swarming, teeming, crawling, alive, ridden; plagued, beset.

infidel n. **unbeliever**, disbeliever, non-believer, agnostic, atheist; heathen, pagan, idolater, idolatress, heretic, freethinker, dissenter, nonconformist; old use paynim; rare nullifidian.

infidelity n. **unfaithfulness**, adultery, unchastity; faithlessness, disloyalty, treachery, double-dealing, duplicity, deceit; affair; informal playing around, fooling around, cheating, two-timing; formal fornication; dated cuckoldry.

infiltrate v. **1** *he infiltrated the smuggling operation* **insinuate oneself into**, worm one's way into, sneak into, invade, intrude on, butt into; informal gatecrash, muscle in on. **2** *mineral solutions infiltrate the rocks* **permeate**, penetrate, pervade, seep into/through, soak into, get into, enter.

infiltrator n. **spy**, (secret) agent, plant, intruder, interloper, subversive, informant, informer, mole, entrist, entryist; N. Amer. informal spook.

infinite adj. **1** *the universe is infinite* **boundless**, unbounded, unlimited, limitless, never-ending, interminable, cosmic; immeasurable, fathomless; extensive, vast. **2** *an infinite number of birds* **countless**, uncountable, inestimable, innumerable, numberless, immeasurable, incalculable, untold; great, huge, enormous. **3** *she bathed him with infinite care* **great**, immense, supreme, absolute, real; informal no end of.
– OPPOSITES limited, small.

infinitesimal adj. **minute**, tiny, minuscule, very small; microscopic, nanoscopic, imperceptible, indiscernible; Scottish wee; informal teeny, teeny-weeny, itsy-bitsy, tiddly; Brit. informal titchy; N. Amer. informal little-bitty.
– OPPOSITES huge.

infinity n. **1** *the infinity of space* **endlessness**, infinitude, infiniteness, boundlessness, limitlessness; vastness, immensity. **2** *an* *infinity of different molecules* **infinite number**; abundance, profusion, host, multitude, mass, wealth; informal heap, stack.

infirm adj. **frail**, weak, feeble, debilitated, decrepit, disabled; ill, unwell, sick, sickly, poorly, indisposed, ailing.
– OPPOSITES healthy.

infirmity n. **1** *they were excused due to infirmity* **frailty**, weakness, feebleness, delicacy, debility, decrepitude; disability, impairment; illness, sickness, indisposition, poor health. **2** *the infirmities of old age* **ailment**, malady, illness, disease, disorder, sickness, affliction, complaint, indisposition.

inflame v. **1** *the play inflames anti-Semitism* **incite**, arouse, rouse, provoke, stir up, whip up, kindle, ignite, touch off, foment, inspire, stimulate, agitate. **2** *he inflamed a sensitive situation* **aggravate**, exacerbate, intensify, worsen, compound. **3** *his opinions inflamed his rival* **enrage**, incense, anger, madden, infuriate, exasperate, provoke, antagonize, rile; informal make someone see red, make someone's blood boil.
– OPPOSITES calm, soothe, placate.

inflamed adj. **swollen**, puffed up; red, hot, burning, itchy; raw, sore, painful, tender; infected, septic.

inflammable adj. **flammable**, combustible, incendiary, ignitable; volatile, unstable.
– OPPOSITES fireproof.

inflammation n. **swelling**, puffiness, redness, heat, burning; rawness, soreness, tenderness; infection, festering, septicity.

inflammatory adj. **1** *an inflammatory lung condition* causing inflammation; Medicine erythrogenic. **2** *inflammatory language* **provocative**, incendiary, stirring, rousing, rabble-rousing, seditious, mutinous; like a red rag to a bull; fiery, passionate; controversial, contentious.

inflate v. **1** *the mattress inflated* **blow up**, fill up, fill with air, aerate, puff up/out, pump up; dilate, distend, swell. **2** *the demand inflated prices* **increase**, raise, boost, escalate, put up; informal hike up, jack up, bump up. **3** *the figures were inflated by the press* **exaggerate**, magnify, overplay, overstate, enhance, embellish, touch up; increase, amplify, augment.
– OPPOSITES decrease, understate.

inflated adj. **1** *an inflated balloon* **blown up**, aerated, filled, puffed up/out, pumped up; distended, expanded, engorged, swollen. **2** *inflated prices* **high**, sky-high, excessive, unreasonable, prohibitive, outrageous, exorbitant, extortionate; Brit. over the odds; informal steep. **3** *an inflated opinion of himself* **exaggerated**, magnified, aggrandized, immoderate, overblown, overstated. **4** *inflated language* **high-flown**, extravagant, exaggerated, elaborate, flowery, ornate, overblown, overwrought, grandiloquent, magniloquent, lofty, grandiose; affected, pretentious; informal windy, highfalutin.

inflection n. **1** Grammar *verbal inflections* **conjugation**, declension; form, ending, case.

2 *his voice was without inflection* **stress**, cadence, rhythm, accentuation, intonation, emphasis, modulation, lilt.

inflexible adj. **1** *his inflexible attitude* **stubborn**, obstinate, obdurate, intractable, intransigent, unbending, immovable, unaccommodating; hidebound, single-minded, pig-headed, mulish, uncompromising, adamant, firm, resolute, diehard, dyed-in-the-wool; formal refractory. **2** *inflexible rules* **unalterable**, unchangeable, immutable, unvarying; firm, fixed, set, established, entrenched, hard and fast; stringent, strict. **3** *an inflexible structure* **rigid**, stiff, unyielding, unbending, unbendable; hard, firm, inelastic.
– OPPOSITES accommodating, pliable.

inflict v. **1** *he inflicted an injury on Frank* **impose**, exact, wreak; administer to, deal out to, mete out to, cause to, give to. **2** *I won't inflict my pain on my children* **impose**, force, thrust, foist; saddle someone with, burden someone with.

infliction n. **administration**, delivery, application; imposition, perpetration; formal exaction.

influence n. **1** *the influence of parents on their children* **effect**, impact; control, sway, hold, power, authority, mastery, domination, supremacy; guidance, direction; pressure. **2** *a bad influence on young girls* **example to**, (role) model for, guide for, inspiration to. **3** *political influence* **power**, authority, sway, leverage, weight, pull, standing, prestige, stature, rank; informal clout, muscle, teeth; N. Amer. informal drag.
▶ v. **1** *bosses can influence our careers* **affect**, have an impact on, determine, guide, control, shape, govern, decide; change, alter, transform. **2** *an attempt to influence the jury* **sway**, bias, prejudice, suborn; pressurize, coerce; dragoon, intimidate, browbeat, brainwash; informal twist someone's arm, lean on; Brit. informal nobble.

influential adj. **1** *an influential leader* **powerful**, dominant, controlling, strong, authoritative; important, prominent, distinguished. **2** *he was influential in shaping her career* **instrumental**, significant, important, crucial, pivotal.

influx n. **1** *an influx of tourists* **inundation**, rush, stream, flood, incursion; invasion, intrusion. **2** *influxes of river water* **inflow**, inrush, flood, inundation.

inform v. **1** *she informed him that she was ill* **tell**, notify, apprise, advise, impart to, communicate to, let someone know; brief, prime, enlighten, send word to; informal fill in, clue in/up. **2** *he informed on two villains* **denounce**, give away, betray, incriminate, inculpate, report; sell out, stab in the back; informal rat, squeal, split, tell, blow the whistle, sell down the river, snitch, peach, stitch up; Brit. informal grass, shop, sneak; Scottish informal clype; N. Amer. informal rat out, finger; Austral./NZ informal dob. **3** *the articles were informed by feminism* **suffuse**, pervade, permeate, infuse, imbue; characterize, typify.

informal adj. **1** *an informal discussion* **unofficial**, casual, relaxed, easy-going, unceremonious; open, friendly, intimate; simple, unpretentious, easy, homely, cosy; informal unstuffy, laid-back, chummy, pally, matey. **2** *an informal speech style* **colloquial**, vernacular, idiomatic, demotic, popular; familiar, everyday, unofficial; simple, natural, unpretentious; informal slangy, chatty, folksy. **3** *informal clothes* **casual**, relaxed, comfortable, everyday, sloppy, leisure; informal comfy.
– OPPOSITES formal, official, literary, smart.

informality n. **lack of ceremony**, casualness, unceremoniousness, unpretentiousness; homeliness, cosiness; ease, naturalness, approachability.

information n. **details**, particulars, facts, figures, statistics, data; knowledge, intelligence; instruction, advice, guidance, direction, counsel, enlightenment; news; informal info, gen, the low-down, the dope, the inside story.

informative adj. **instructive**, instructional, illuminating, enlightening, revealing, explanatory; factual, educational, educative, edifying, didactic; informal newsy.

informed adj. **knowledgeable**, enlightened, literate, educated; sophisticated, cultured; briefed, up to date, up to speed, in the picture, in the know, au courant, au fait; informal clued-up, genned-up, plugged-in; Brit. informal switched-on, sussed.
– OPPOSITES ignorant.

informer n. **informant**, betrayer, traitor, Judas, collaborator, stool pigeon, fifth columnist, spy, double agent, infiltrator, plant; telltale, tale teller; N. Amer. tattletale; informal rat, squealer, whistle-blower, snake in the grass, snitch; Brit. informal grass, supergrass, nark, snout; Scottish informal clype; N. Amer. informal fink, stoolie.

infraction n. **infringement**, contravention, breach, violation, transgression; neglect, dereliction, non-compliance; Law delict, contumacy.

infrequent adj. **rare**, uncommon, unusual, exceptional, few (and far between), like gold dust, as scarce as hens' teeth; unaccustomed, unwonted; isolated, scarce, scattered; sporadic, irregular, intermittent; informal once in a blue moon; dated seldom.
– OPPOSITES common.

infringe v. **1** *the bid infringed EU rules* **contravene**, violate, transgress, break, breach; disobey, defy, flout, fly in the face of; disregard, ignore, neglect; go beyond, overstep, exceed; Law infract. **2** *surveillance could infringe personal liberties* **undermine**, erode, diminish, weaken, impair, damage, compromise; limit, curb, check, encroach on.
– OPPOSITES obey, preserve.

infuriate v. **enrage**, incense, anger, madden, inflame; exasperate, antagonize, provoke, rile, annoy, irritate, nettle, gall,

irk, vex, pique, get on someone's nerves, try someone's patience; N. Amer. rankle; informal aggravate, make someone see red, get someone's back up, make someone's blood boil, get up someone's nose, needle, hack off, brown off; Brit. informal wind up, get to, nark, cheese off; N. Amer. informal bug, tick off.
– OPPOSITES please.

infuriating adj. **exasperating**, maddening, annoying, irritating, irksome, vexatious, trying, tiresome; informal aggravating, pesky.

infuse v. **1** *she was infused with a sense of hope* **fill**, suffuse, imbue, inspire, charge, pervade, permeate. **2** *he infused new life into the group* **instil**, breathe, inject, impart, inculcate, introduce, add. **3** *infuse the dried leaves* **steep**, brew, stew, soak, immerse, souse; Brit. informal mash.

ingenious adj. **inventive**, creative, imaginative, original, innovative, pioneering, resourceful, enterprising, inspired; clever, intelligent, smart, brilliant, masterly, talented, gifted, skilful; astute, sharp-witted, quick-witted, shrewd; elaborate, sophisticated.

ingenuous adj. **naive**, innocent, simple, childlike, trusting, trustful, over-trusting, unwary; unsuspicious, unworldly, wide-eyed, inexperienced, green; open, sincere, honest, frank, candid, forthright, artless, guileless, genuine.
– OPPOSITES artful.

inglorious adj. **shameful**, dishonourable, ignominious, discreditable, disgraceful, scandalous; humiliating, mortifying, demeaning, ignoble, undignified, wretched.

ingrained, engrained adj. **1** *ingrained attitudes* **entrenched**, established, deep-rooted, deep-seated, fixed, firm, unshakeable, ineradicable; inveterate, dyed-in-the-wool, abiding, enduring, stubborn. **2** *ingrained dirt* **ground-in**, fixed, implanted, embedded; permanent, indelible, ineradicable, inexpungible.
– OPPOSITES transient, superficial.

ingratiate v.
□ **ingratiate oneself** curry favour with, cultivate, win over, get in someone's good books; toady to, crawl to, grovel to, fawn over, kowtow to, play up to, pander to, flatter, court; informal suck up to, lick someone's boots.

ingratiating adj. **sycophantic**, toadying, fawning, unctuous, obsequious; flattering, insincere; smooth-tongued, silver-tongued, slick; greasy, oily, saccharine; informal smarmy, slimy, creepy, sucky.

ingratitude n. **ungratefulness**, unthankfulness, non-recognition.

ingredient n. **constituent**, component, element; part, piece, bit, strand, portion, unit, feature, aspect, attribute; (**ingredients**) contents, makings.

ingress n. **1** *the doors gave ingress to the station* **entry**, entrance, access, admittance, admission; way in, approach. **2** *the ingress of water* **seepage**, leakage, inundation, inrush,

intrusion, incursion, entry, entrance.
– OPPOSITES exit.

inhabit v. **live in**, occupy; settle (in), people, populate, colonize; dwell in, reside in, tenant, lodge in, have one's home in; formal be domiciled in, abide in.

inhabitable adj. **habitable**, fit to live in, usable; informal liveable-in; formal tenantable.

inhabitant n. **resident**, occupant, occupier, dweller, settler; local, native; (**inhabitants**) population, populace, people, public, community, citizenry, townsfolk, townspeople; formal denizen; old use burgher, habitant.

inhale v. **breathe in**, inspire, draw in, suck in, sniff in, drink in; literary inbreathe.

inharmonious adj. **1** *inharmonious sounds* **unmelodious**, unharmonious, unmusical, tuneless, discordant, dissonant, off-key; harsh, grating, jarring, cacophonous; old use absonant. **2** *an inharmonious modern building* **out of place**, unsuitable, inappropriate, clashing, conflicting, incompatible, mismatched; jarring, discordant. **3** *his relationships are inharmonious* **antagonistic**, quarrelsome, argumentative, disputatious, cantankerous, confrontational, belligerent.
– OPPOSITES musical, fitting, congenial.

inherent adj. **intrinsic**, innate, connate, connatural, immanent, built-in, inborn, ingrained, deep-rooted; essential, fundamental, basic, structural, organic; natural, instinctive, instinctual, congenital, native.
– OPPOSITES acquired.

inherit v. **1** *she inherited his farm* **become heir to**, come into/by, be bequeathed, be left, be willed; Law be devised. **2** *Richard inherited the title* **succeed to**, assume, take over, come into; formal accede to.

inheritance n. **1** *a comfortable inheritance* **legacy**, bequest, endowment, bestowal, bequeathal, provision; birthright, heritage, patrimony; Law devise. **2** *his inheritance of the title* **succession to**, accession to, assumption of, elevation to.

> **WORD LINKS**
> **hereditary** passed on by or relating to inheritance
> **primogeniture** a system by which an eldest son inherits all his parents' property
> **entail** limit the inheritance of a property so that ownership remains within a family

inheritor n. **heir**, heiress, legatee; successor, next in line; Law devisee, grantee, cestui que trust; Scottish Law heritor.

inhibit v. **1** *the obstacles which inhibit change* **impede**, hinder, hamper, hold back, discourage, interfere with, obstruct, slow down, retard; curb, check, suppress, restrict, fetter, cramp, frustrate, stifle, prevent, block, thwart, foil, stop, halt. **2** *she feels inhibited from taking part* **prevent**, disallow, exclude, forbid, prohibit, preclude, ban, bar, interdict.
– OPPOSITES assist, encourage, allow.

inhibited adj. **shy**, reticent, reserved, self-conscious, diffident, bashful, coy; wary, reluctant, hesitant, insecure, unconfident, unassertive, timid; withdrawn, repressed, undemonstrative; informal uptight.

inhibition n. **1** *they overcame their inhibitions* **shyness**, reticence, self-consciousness, reserve, diffidence; wariness, hesitance, hesitancy, insecurity; unassertiveness, timidity; repression, reservation; psychological block; informal hang-up. **2** *the inhibition of publishing* **hindrance**, hampering, discouragement, obstruction, impediment, retardation; suppression, repression, restriction, restraint, constraint, cramping, stifling, prevention; curb, check, bar, barrier.

inhospitable adj. **1** *the inhospitable landscape* **uninviting**, unwelcoming, bleak, forbidding, cheerless, hostile, harsh, inimical; uninhabitable, barren, bare, desolate, stark. **2** *forgive me if I seem inhospitable* **unwelcoming**, unfriendly, unsociable, unsocial, antisocial, unneighbourly, uncongenial; cool, cold, frosty, distant, remote, aloof, indifferent, offhand; uncivil, discourteous, ungracious; ungenerous, unkind, unsympathetic; informal stand-offish.
– OPPOSITES welcoming.

inhuman adj. **1** *inhuman treatment* **cruel**, harsh, inhumane, brutal, callous, sadistic, severe, savage, vicious, barbaric; monstrous, heinous, egregious; merciless, ruthless, pitiless, remorseless, cold-blooded, heartless, hard-hearted; unkind, inconsiderate, unfeeling, uncaring; Brit. informal beastly; dated dastardly. **2** *hellish and inhuman shapes* **non-human**, non-mortal, monstrous, devilish, ghostly; subhuman, animal; strange, odd, unearthly.
– OPPOSITES humane.

inhumane adj. See **inhuman** (sense 1).

inimical adj. **1** *this is inimical to genuine democracy* **harmful**, injurious, detrimental, deleterious, prejudicial, damaging, hurtful, destructive, ruinous; antagonistic, contrary, antipathetic, unfavourable, adverse, opposed, hostile; literary malefic. **2** *he fixed her with an inimical gaze* **hostile**, unfriendly, antagonistic, unkind, unsympathetic, malevolent; unwelcoming, cold, frosty.
– OPPOSITES advantageous, friendly.

inimitable adj. **unique**, exclusive, distinctive, individual, special, idiosyncratic; incomparable, unparalleled, unrivalled, peerless, matchless, unequalled, unsurpassable, superlative, supreme, beyond compare, second to none, in a class of one's own; formal unexampled.

iniquity n. **1** *the iniquity of his conduct* **wickedness**, sinfulness, immorality, impropriety; vice, evil, sin; villainy, criminality; odiousness, atrocity, egregiousness; outrage, monstrosity, obscenity, reprehensibility. **2** *I will forgive their iniquity* **sin**, crime, transgression,

wrongdoing, wrong, violation, offence, vice; atrocity, outrage.
– OPPOSITES goodness, virtue.

initial adj. *the initial stages* **beginning**, opening, commencing, starting, inceptive, embryonic, fledgling; first, early, primary, preliminary, elementary, foundational, preparatory; introductory, inaugural.
– OPPOSITES final.
▶ n. *what do the initials stand for?* **initial letter**; (**initials**) acronym, abbreviation, initialism.
▶ v. **1** *he initialled the warrant* **put one's initials on**, sign, countersign, autograph, endorse, inscribe, witness. **2** *they initialled a new agreement* **ratify**, accept, approve, authorize, validate, recognize.

initially adv. **at first**, at the start, at the outset, in/at the beginning, to begin with, to start with, originally.

initiate v. **1** *the government initiated the scheme* **begin**, start (off), commence; institute, inaugurate, launch, instigate, establish, set up, sow the seeds of, start the ball rolling; originate, pioneer; informal kick off. **2** *he was initiated into a cult* **introduce**, admit, induct, install, incorporate, enlist, enrol, recruit, sign up, swear in; ordain, invest. **3** *they were initiated into the world of maths* **teach about**, instruct in, tutor in, school in, prime in, ground in; familiarize with, acquaint with; indoctrinate, inculcate; informal show someone the ropes.
– OPPOSITES finish, expel.
▶ n. *an initiate on the team* **novice**, starter, beginner, newcomer; learner, student, pupil, trainee, apprentice; new boy, new girl, recruit, tyro, neophyte; postulant, novitiate; informal rookie, new kid (on the block), newie, newbie, greenhorn.

initiative n. **1** *employers are looking for initiative* **enterprise**, resourcefulness, inventiveness, imagination, ingenuity, originality, creativity; drive, dynamism, ambition, motivation, spirit, energy, vision; informal get-up-and-go, pep, punch. **2** *he has lost the initiative* **advantage**, upper hand, edge, lead, whip hand, trump card. **3** *a recent initiative on recycling* **plan**, scheme, strategy, stratagem, measure, proposal, step, action, approach.

inject v. **1** *he injected a dose of codeine* **administer**, introduce; inoculate, vaccinate; informal shoot (up), mainline, fix (up). **2** *a pump injects air into the valve* **insert**, introduce, feed, push, force, shoot. **3** *he injected new life into the team* **introduce**, instil, infuse, imbue, breathe.

injection n. **inoculation**, vaccination, vaccine, immunization, booster; dose; informal jab, shot, hype.

injudicious adj. **imprudent**, unwise, inadvisable, ill-advised, misguided; ill-considered, ill-judged, incautious, hasty, rash, foolish, foolhardy, hare-brained; inappropriate, impolitic, inexpedient; informal dumb.

– OPPOSITES prudent.

injunction n. **order**, ruling, direction, directive, command, instruction; decree, edict, dictum, dictate, fiat, mandate.

injure v. **1** *he injured his foot* **hurt**, wound, damage, harm; cripple, lame, disable; maim, mutilate, deform, mangle, break; Brit. informal knacker; old use scathe. **2** *a libel injured her reputation* **damage**, mar, spoil, ruin, blight, blemish, tarnish, blacken.

injured adj. **1** *his injured arm* **hurt**, wounded, damaged, sore, bruised; crippled, lame, game, disabled; maimed, mutilated, deformed, mangled, broken, fractured; Brit. informal gammy. **2** *the injured party* **wronged**, offended, maltreated, mistreated, ill-used, harmed; defamed, maligned, insulted, dishonoured. **3** *an injured tone* **upset**, hurt, wounded, offended, reproachful, pained, aggrieved, unhappy, put out; Brit. informal not best pleased.
– OPPOSITES healthy, offending.

injurious adj. **harmful**, damaging, deleterious, detrimental, hurtful; disadvantageous, unfavourable, undesirable, adverse, inimical, unhealthy, pernicious; literary malefic.

injury n. **1** *minor injuries* **wound**, bruise, cut, gash, scratch, graze, abrasion, contusion, lesion; Medicine trauma. **2** *they escaped without injury* **harm**, hurt, damage, pain, suffering, impairment, affliction, incapacity. **3** *the injury to her feelings* **offence**, abuse; affront, insult, slight, snub; wrong, wrongdoing, injustice.

injustice n. **1** *the injustice of the world* **unfairness**, unjustness, inequity; cruelty, tyranny, repression, exploitation, corruption; bias, prejudice, discrimination, intolerance. **2** *his sacking was an injustice* **wrong**, offence, crime, sin, misdeed, outrage, atrocity, scandal, disgrace, affront.

inkling n. **idea**, notion, sense, impression, suggestion, indication, whisper, glimmer, (sneaking) suspicion, fancy, hunch; hint, clue, intimation, sign; informal the foggiest (idea), the faintest (idea).

inky adj. **1** *the inky darkness* **black**, jet-black, pitch-black; sable, ebony, dark; literary Stygian. **2** *inky fingers* **ink-stained**, stained, blotchy.

inlaid adj. **inset**, set, studded, lined, panelled; ornamented, decorated; mosaic, intarsia, marquetry.

inland adj. **1** *inland areas* **interior**, inshore, central, internal, upcountry. **2** *inland trade* **domestic**, internal, home, local.
– OPPOSITES coastal, international.
▶ adv. *the goods were carried inland* **upcountry**, inshore, to the interior.

inlet n. **1** **cove**, bay, bight, creek, estuary, fjord, sound; Scottish firth. **2** *a fresh air inlet* **vent**, flue, shaft, duct, channel, pipe, pipeline.

inmate n. **1** *the inmates of the hospital* **patient**, inpatient; convalescent; resident, inhabitant, occupant. **2** *the prison's inmates* **prisoner**, convict, captive, detainee, internee; informal jailbird, con; Brit. informal lag; N. Amer. informal yardbird.

inmost adj. See **innermost**.

inn n. **tavern**, bar, hostelry, taproom; hotel, guest house; Brit. pub, public house; Canadian beer parlour; informal watering hole; dated alehouse.

innards plural n. informal **entrails**, internal organs, viscera, intestines, bowels, guts; informal insides.

innate adj. **inborn**, inbred, congenital, inherent, natural, intrinsic, instinctive, intuitive, unlearned; hereditary, inherited, in the blood, in the family; inbuilt, deep-rooted, deep-seated, connate, connatural.
– OPPOSITES acquired.

inner adj. **1** *inner London* **central**, innermost, mid, middle. **2** *the inner gates* **internal**, interior, inside, inmost, innermost, intramural. **3** *the Queen's inner circle* **privileged**, restricted, exclusive, private, confidential, intimate. **4** *the inner meaning* **hidden**, secret, deep, underlying, unapparent; veiled, esoteric, unrevealed. **5** *one's inner life* **mental**, intellectual, psychological, spiritual, emotional.
– OPPOSITES external, apparent.

innermost adj. **1** *the innermost shrine* **central**, middle, internal, interior. **2** *her innermost feelings* **deepest**, deep-seated, inward, underlying, intimate, private, personal, secret, hidden, concealed, unexpressed, unrevealed, unapparent; true, real, honest.

innkeeper n. **landlord**, landlady, hotelier, hotel owner, proprietor, manager, manageress; licensee, barman, barmaid; Brit. publican.

innocence n. **1** *he protested his innocence* **guiltlessness**, blamelessness, irreproachability. **2** *the innocence of his bride* **virginity**, chastity, chasteness, purity; integrity, morality, decency; dated honour; old use virtue. **3** *she took advantage of his innocence* **naivety**, ingenuousness, credulity, inexperience, gullibility, simplicity, unworldliness, guilelessness, greenness.

innocent adj. **1** *he was entirely innocent* **guiltless**, blameless, in the clear, unimpeachable, irreproachable, above suspicion, faultless; honourable, honest, upright, law-abiding; informal squeaky clean. **2** *innocent fun* **harmless**, innocuous, safe, inoffensive. **3** *nice innocent girls* **virtuous**, pure, moral, decent, righteous, upright, wholesome; demure, modest, chaste, virginal; impeccable, spotless, sinless, unsullied, incorrupt, undefiled; informal squeaky clean, whiter than white. **4** *she is innocent of guile* **free from**, without, lacking (in), clear of, ignorant of, unaware of, untouched by; literary nescient of. **5** *innocent foreigners* **naive**, ingenuous, trusting, credulous, unsuspicious, unwary, unguarded; impressionable, gullible, easily led; inexperienced, unworldly, unsophisticated, green; simple, artless, guileless; informal wet

behind the ears, born yesterday.
– OPPOSITES guilty, sinful, worldly.
▸ n. *an innocent in a strange land* **ingénue**, unworldly person; child; novice; N. Amer. informal greenhorn; literary babe in arms.

innocuous adj. **1** *an innocuous fungus* **harmless**, safe, non-toxic, innocent; edible, eatable. **2** *an innocuous comment* **inoffensive**, unobjectionable, unexceptionable, harmless, mild, tame; anodyne, unremarkable, commonplace, run-of-the-mill.
– OPPOSITES harmful, offensive.

innovation n. **change**, alteration, revolution, upheaval, transformation, metamorphosis; reorganization, restructuring, rearrangement, remodelling; new measures, new methods, modernization, modernism; novelty, newness; informal a shake up, a shakedown.

innovative adj. **original**, innovatory, innovational, new, novel, fresh, unusual, unprecedented, avant-garde, experimental, inventive, ingenious; advanced, modern, state-of-the-art, pioneering, groundbreaking, revolutionary, radical, newfangled.

innovator n. **pioneer**, trailblazer, pathfinder, groundbreaker; developer, modernizer, reformer, reformist, progressive; experimenter, inventor, creator; formal neoteric.

innuendo n. **insinuation**, suggestion, intimation, implication, hint, overtone, undertone, allusion, reference; aspersion, slur.

innumerable adj. **countless**, numerous, untold, legion, without number, numberless, unnumbered, multitudinous, incalculable, limitless; informal umpteen, a slew of, no end of, loads of, stacks of, heaps of, masses of, oodles of, zillions of; N. Amer. informal gazillions of; literary myriad.
– OPPOSITES few.

inoculate v. **immunize**, vaccinate, inject; protect from, safeguard against; informal give someone a jab/shot.

inoculation n. **immunization**, vaccination, vaccine; injection, booster; informal jab, shot.

inoffensive adj. **harmless**, innocuous, unobjectionable, unexceptionable; non-violent, non-aggressive, mild, peaceful, peaceable, gentle; tame, innocent.

inoperable adj. **1** *an inoperable tumour* **untreatable**, incurable, irremediable; malignant; terminal, fatal, deadly, lethal; old use immedicable. **2** *the airfield was left inoperable* **unusable**, out of action, out of service, non-active. **3** *the agreement is now inoperable* **impractical**, unworkable, unfeasible, unrealistic, non-viable, impracticable, unsuitable.
– OPPOSITES curable, workable.

inoperative adj. **1** *the fan is inoperative* **out of order**, out of service, broken, out of commission, unserviceable, faulty, defective; down; informal bust, kaput, on the blink, acting up, shot; Brit. informal knackered. **2** *the*

contract is inoperative **void**, null and void, invalid, ineffective, non-viable; cancelled, revoked, terminated; worthless, valueless, unproductive, abortive.
– OPPOSITES working, valid.

inopportune adj. **inconvenient**, unsuitable, inappropriate, unfavourable, unfortunate, infelicitous, inexpedient; untimely, ill-timed, unseasonable; awkward, difficult.
– OPPOSITES convenient.

inordinate adj. **excessive**, undue, unreasonable, unjustifiable, unwarrantable, disproportionate, unwarranted, unnecessary, needless, uncalled for, exorbitant, extreme; immoderate, extravagant; informal over the top, OTT.
– OPPOSITES moderate.

inorganic adj. **inanimate**, inert; lifeless, dead, defunct, extinct; mineral.

input n. *an error resulted from invalid input data*, details, information, material; facts, figures, statistics, particulars, specifics; informal info.
▸v. *she input data into the file* **feed in**, put in, load, upload, insert; key in, type in; code, store.

inquest n. **inquiry**, investigation, inquisition, probe, examination, review, analysis; hearing.

inquire v. See **enquire**.

inquiring adj. See **enquiring**.

inquiry n. See **enquiry**.

inquisition n. **interrogation**, questioning, quizzing, cross-examination; investigation, inquiry, inquest; informal grilling; Law examination.

inquisitive adj. **curious**, interested, intrigued, agog; prying, spying, eavesdropping, intrusive, busybody, meddlesome; inquiring, questioning, probing; informal nosy, nosy-parker, snoopy.
– OPPOSITES uninterested.

insalubrious adj. **seedy**, unsavoury, sordid, seamy, sleazy, unpleasant, dismal, wretched; slummy, squalid, shabby, ramshackle, tumbledown, dilapidated, neglected, crumbling, decaying; informal scruffy, scuzzy, crummy; Brit. informal grotty; N. Amer. informal shacky.
– OPPOSITES smart.

insane adj. **1** *she was declared insane* **mentally ill**, mentally disordered, of unsound mind, certifiable; psychotic, schizophrenic; mad, deranged, demented, out of one's mind, non compos mentis, sick in the head, unhinged, unbalanced, unstable, disturbed, crazed; informal crazy, (stark) raving mad, not all there, bonkers, cracked, batty, cuckoo, loony, loopy, nuts, screwy, bananas, wacko, off one's rocker, off one's head, round the bend; Brit. informal crackers, barmy, barking (mad), off one's trolley, round the twist, not the full shilling; N. Amer. informal buggy, nutso, out of one's tree; Austral./NZ informal bushed. **2** *an insane suggestion* **foolish**, idiotic, stupid, silly, senseless, nonsensical, absurd, ridiculous, ludicrous, preposterous, fatuous, inane, asinine, hare-brained, half-

baked; impracticable, implausible, irrational, illogical; informal crazy, mad, cockeyed; Brit. informal daft, barmy.
– OPPOSITES sane, sensible.

insanitary adj. **unhygienic**, unsanitary, unhealthy, insalubrious, dirty, filthy, unclean, impure, contaminated, polluted, foul; infected, infested, germ-ridden; informal germy.
– OPPOSITES hygienic.

insanity n. **1** *insanity runs in her family* **mental illness**, madness, dementia; lunacy, instability; mania, psychosis; informal craziness. **2** *it would be insanity to take this loan* **folly**, foolishness, madness, idiocy, stupidity, lunacy, silliness; informal craziness.

insatiable adj. **unquenchable**, unappeasable, uncontrollable; voracious, gluttonous, greedy, hungry, ravenous, wolfish; avid, eager, keen; informal piggy; literary insatiate.

inscribe v. **1** *his name was inscribed above the door* **carve**, write, engrave, etch, cut; imprint, stamp, impress, mark. **2** *a book inscribed to him by the author* **dedicate**, address, name, sign.

inscription n. **1** *the inscription on the sarcophagus* **engraving**, etching; wording, writing, lettering, legend, epitaph, epigraph. **2** *the book had an inscription* **dedication**, message; signature, autograph.

inscrutable adj. **1** *her inscrutable face* **enigmatic**, unreadable, mysterious; unexpressive, inexpressive, emotionless, unemotional, expressionless, impassive, blank, vacant, deadpan, poker-faced, dispassionate. **2** *God's ways are inscrutable* **mysterious**, inexplicable, unexplainable, incomprehensible, impenetrable, unfathomable, opaque, abstruse, arcane, obscure, cryptic.
– OPPOSITES expressive, transparent.

insect n. bug; informal creepy-crawly, beastie; S. African informal gogga.

> **WORD LINKS**
> **entomology** the study of insects

insecure adj. **1** *an insecure young man* **unconfident**, uncertain, unsure, doubtful, hesitant, self-conscious, unassertive, diffident, unforthcoming, shy, timid, retiring, timorous, inhibited, introverted; anxious, fearful, worried; informal mousy. **2** *insecure windows* **unguarded**, unprotected, vulnerable, defenceless, unshielded, exposed, assailable, pregnable; unlocked, unsecured. **3** *an insecure footbridge* **unstable**, rickety, rocky, wobbly, shaky, unsteady, precarious; weak, flimsy, unsound, unsafe; informal jerry-built; Brit. informal dicky, dodgy.
– OPPOSITES confident, stable, insecure.

insecurity n. **1** *he hid his insecurity* **lack of confidence**, self-doubt, diffidence, unassertiveness, timidity, uncertainty, nervousness, inhibition; anxiety, worry, unease. **2** *the insecurity of our situation*

vulnerability, defencelessness, peril, danger; instability, fragility, frailty, shakiness, unreliability.

insensate adj. See **insensible** (sense 1).

insensible adj. **1** *she was insensible on the floor* **unconscious**, insensate, senseless, insentient, inert, comatose, knocked out, passed out, blacked out; stunned, numb, numbed; informal out (cold), out for the count, out of it, zonked (out), dead to the world; Brit. informal spark out. **2** *he was insensible to the risks* **unaware of**, ignorant of, unconscious of, unmindful of, oblivious to; indifferent to, impervious to, deaf to, blind to; unaffected by; informal in the dark about. **3** *he scared even the most insensible person* **insensitive**, dispassionate, cool, emotionless, unfeeling, unconcerned, detached, indifferent, hardened, tough; informal hard-boiled.
– OPPOSITES conscious, aware, sensitive.

insensitive adj. **1** *an insensitive bully* **heartless**, unfeeling, inconsiderate, thoughtless, thick-skinned; hard-hearted, cold-blooded, uncaring, unconcerned, unsympathetic, unkind, callous, cruel, merciless, pitiless. **2** *he was insensitive to her feelings* **impervious to**, oblivious to, unaware of, unresponsive to, indifferent to, unaffected by, unmoved by, untouched by; informal in the dark about.
– OPPOSITES compassionate.

insentient adj. **inanimate**, lifeless, inorganic, inert; insensate, unconscious, comatose, anaesthetized, desensitized, numb; informal dead to the world, out (cold).

inseparable adj. **1** *inseparable friends* **devoted**, bosom, close, fast, firm, good, best, intimate, boon, faithful; informal as thick as thieves. **2** *the laws are inseparable* **indivisible**, indissoluble, inextricable, entangled; (one and) the same.

insert v. **1** *he inserted a tape in the machine* **put**, place, push, thrust, slide, slip, load, fit, slot, lodge, install; informal pop, stick, bung. **2** *she inserted a clause* **enter**, introduce, incorporate, interpolate, interpose, interject.
– OPPOSITES extract, remove.
▸ n. *the newspaper carried an insert* **enclosure**, insertion, inlay, supplement; circular, advertisement, pamphlet, leaflet; informal ad.

inside n. **1** *the inside of a volcano* **interior**, inner part; centre, core, middle, heart. **2** informal *my insides are out of order* **stomach**, gut, bowels, intestines; informal belly, tummy, guts.
– OPPOSITES exterior.
▸ adj. **1** *his inside pocket* **inner**, interior, internal, innermost. **2** *inside information* **confidential**, classified, restricted, privileged, private, secret, exclusive; informal hush-hush.
– OPPOSITES outer, public.
▸ adv. **1** *she ushered me inside* **indoors**, within, in. **2** *how do you feel inside?* **inwardly**, within, secretly, privately, deep down, at heart, emotionally, intuitively, instinctively. **3** informal *if I burgle again I'll be back inside*

in prison, in jail, in custody; locked up, imprisoned, incarcerated; informal behind bars, doing time; Brit. informal banged up.
– OPPOSITES outside.

insider n. **member**, worker, employee, representative; person in the know.

insidious adj. **stealthy**, subtle, surreptitious, cunning, crafty, artful, sly, wily, underhand, backhanded, indirect; informal sneaky.

insight n. **1** *your insight has been invaluable* **intuition**, discernment, perception, awareness, understanding, comprehension, apprehension, appreciation, penetration, acumen, perspicacity, judgement, acuity; vision, prescience, imagination; informal nous, savvy. **2** *an insight into the government* **understanding of**, appreciation of, revelation about; introduction to; informal eye-opener.

insignia n. **badge**, crest, emblem, symbol, sign, device, mark, seal, colours.

insignificant adj. **unimportant**, trivial, trifling, negligible, inconsequential, of no account, inconsiderable; nugatory, paltry, petty, insubstantial, frivolous, pointless, worthless, irrelevant, immaterial, peripheral; informal piddling.

insincere adj. **false**, fake, hollow, artificial, feigned, pretended, put-on; disingenuous, hypocritical, cynical, deceitful, deceptive, duplicitous, double-dealing, two-faced, Janus-faced, lying, untruthful, mendacious; informal phoney, pretend, pseud.

insinuate v. **1** *he insinuated that she lied* **imply**, suggest, hint, intimate, indicate, let it be known, give someone to understand; informal make out, tip someone the wink. **2** *he insinuated his hand under hers* **slide**, slip, manoeuvre, insert, edge.
□ **insinuate oneself into** worm one's way into, ingratiate oneself with, curry favour with; foist oneself on, introduce oneself into; infiltrate, invade, sneak into, intrude on, impinge on; informal muscle in on.

insinuation n. **implication**, inference, suggestion, hint, intimation, innuendo, reference, allusion, indication, undertone, overtone; aspersion, slur, allegation.

insipid adj. **1** *insipid coffee* **tasteless**, flavourless, savourless, bland, weak, wishy-washy; unappetizing, unpalatable. **2** *insipid pictures* **unimaginative**, uninspired, uninspiring, characterless, flat, uninteresting, lacklustre, dull, boring, dry (as dust), jejune, humdrum, run-of-the-mill, commonplace, pedestrian, trite, tired, hackneyed, stale, lame, tame, poor, inadequate, sterile, anaemic.
– OPPOSITES tasty, interesting.

insist v. **1** *be prepared to insist* **stand firm**, stand one's ground, be resolute, be determined, hold out, be emphatic, not take no for an answer; persevere, persist; informal stick to one's guns. **2** *she insisted that they pay up* **demand**, command, require, dictate; urge, exhort. **3** *he insisted that he knew nothing* **maintain**, assert, hold, contend, argue, protest, claim, vow, swear, declare, stress, repeat, reiterate; formal aver.

insistence n. **1** *she sat down at Anne's insistence* **demand**, bidding, command, dictate, instruction, requirement, request, entreaty, exhortation; informal say-so; literary behest. **2** *his insistence that he loved her* **assertion**, declaration, contention, claim, pronouncement, assurance, affirmation, avowal, profession.

insistent adj. **1** *Tony's insistent questioning* **persistent**, determined, adamant, importunate, tenacious, unyielding, dogged, unrelenting, inexorable; demanding, pushy, urgent; emphatic, firm, assertive. **2** *an insistent buzzing* **incessant**, constant, unremitting, repetitive; obtrusive, intrusive.

insobriety n. **drunkenness**, intoxication, inebriation, tipsiness; informal tightness; literary crapulence.

insolent adj. **impertinent**, impudent, cheeky, ill-mannered, bad mannered, unmannerly, rude, impolite, uncivil, discourteous, disrespectful, insubordinate, contemptuous; audacious, bold, cocky, brazen; insulting, abusive; informal fresh, flip, lippy, saucy; N. Amer. informal sassy; old use contumelious, malapert.
– OPPOSITES polite.

insoluble adj. **1** *some problems are insoluble* **unsolvable**, unanswerable, unresolvable; unfathomable, impenetrable, unexplainable, inscrutable, inexplicable. **2** *these minerals are insoluble* **indissoluble**.

insolvency n. **bankruptcy**, liquidation, failure, collapse, (financial) ruin; pennilessness, penury; Brit. receivership.

insolvent adj. **bankrupt**, ruined, liquidated, wiped out; penniless, impoverished, impecunious; Brit. in receivership, without a penny (to one's name); informal bust, (flat) broke, belly-up, gone to the wall, on the rocks, in the red, hard up, strapped for cash; Brit. informal skint, in Queer Street, stony broke, cleaned out; formal penurious.

insomnia n. **sleeplessness**, wakefulness, restlessness; old use watchfulness.

insouciance n. **nonchalance**, unconcern, indifference, heedlessness, calm, equanimity, composure, ease, airiness; informal cool.
– OPPOSITES anxiety.

insouciant adj. **nonchalant**, untroubled, unworried, unruffled, unconcerned, indifferent, blasé, heedless; relaxed, calm, equable, equanimous, serene, composed, easy, carefree, free and easy, happy-go-lucky, light-hearted; informal cool, laid-back.

inspect v. **examine**, check, scrutinize, investigate, vet, test, monitor, survey, study, look over, scan, explore, probe; assess, appraise, review; informal check out, give something a/the once-over.

inspection n. **examination**, check-up, survey, scrutiny, probe, exploration, observation, investigation; assessment, appraisal, review, evaluation; informal once-over, going-over, look-see, overhaul.

inspector n. **examiner**, checker, scrutinizer, scrutineer, investigator, surveyor, assessor, appraiser, reviewer, analyst; observer, overseer, supervisor, monitor, watchdog, ombudsman; auditor.

inspiration n. **1** *she's a real inspiration to others* **stimulus**, stimulation, motivation, fillip, encouragement, influence, muse, spur, lift, boost, incentive, impulse, catalyst; example, model. **2** *his work lacks inspiration* **creativity**, inventiveness, innovation, ingenuity, imagination, originality; artistry, insight, vision; finesse, flair. **3** *she had a sudden inspiration* **bright idea**, revelation; informal brainwave; N. Amer. informal brainstorm. **4** *inspiration pains her* **inhalation**, breathing in; respiration.

inspire v. **1** *the landscape inspired him to write* **stimulate**, motivate, encourage, influence, rouse, move, stir, energize, galvanize, incite; animate, fire, inspirit, incentivize. **2** *the film inspired a musical* **give rise to**, lead to, bring about, cause, prompt, spawn, engender; literary beget. **3** *Charles inspired awe in her* **arouse**, awaken, prompt, induce, ignite, trigger, kindle, produce, bring out; literary enkindle.

inspired adj. **outstanding**, wonderful, marvellous, excellent, magnificent, fine, exceptional, first-class, first-rate, virtuoso, supreme, superlative; innovative, innovatory, innovational, ingenious, original; informal tremendous, superb, super, ace, wicked, awesome, out of this world; Brit. informal brilliant, brill.
– OPPOSITES poor.

inspiring adj. **inspirational**, encouraging, heartening, uplifting, life-affirming, stirring, rousing, stimulating, electrifying; moving, affecting, influential.

instability n. **1** *the instability of political life* **unreliability**, uncertainty, unpredictability, insecurity, perilousness, riskiness; impermanence, inconstancy, changeability, variability, fluctuation, mutability. **2** *emotional instability* **volatility**, unpredictability, variability, capriciousness, vacillation; frailty, infirmity, weakness, irregularity. **3** *the instability of the foundations* **unsteadiness**, unsoundness, shakiness, frailty, fragility.
– OPPOSITES steadiness.

install v. **1** *a photocopier was installed in the office* **put**, position, place, locate, situate, station, site, lodge; insert. **2** *they installed a new president* **swear in**, induct, instate, inaugurate, invest; appoint, take on; ordain, consecrate, anoint; enthrone, crown. **3** *she installed herself behind the table* **ensconce**, establish, position, settle, seat, lodge, plant; sit (down); informal plonk, park; Brit. informal take a pew.
– OPPOSITES remove.

installation n. **1** *the installation of radiators* **installing**, fitting, putting in; insertion. **2** *the installation of the chancellor* **swearing**

in, induction, instatement, inauguration, investiture; ordination, consecration; enthronement, coronation. **3** *a new computer installation* **unit**, appliance, fixture; equipment, machinery. **4** *an army installation* **base**, camp, post, depot, centre, facility; premises.

instalment n. **1** *I pay by monthly instalments* **part payment**; deferred payment; Brit. hire purchase, HP; Brit. informal the never-never. **2** *a story published in instalments* **part**, portion, section, segment, bit; chapter, episode, volume, issue.

instance n. **1** *an instance of racism* **example**, exemplar, occasion, occurrence, case; illustration. **2** formal *proceedings began at the instance of the director* **instigation**, prompting, suggestion; request, entreaty, demand, insistence; wish, desire.
▶ v. *as an example I would instance Jones's work* **cite**, quote, refer to, mention, allude to, give; specify, name, identify, draw attention to, put forward, offer, advance.
□ **in the first instance** initially, at first, at the start, at the outset, in/at the beginning, to begin with, to start with, originally.

instant adj. **1** *instant access to your money* **immediate**, instantaneous, on-the-spot, prompt, swift, speedy, rapid, quick, express, lightning; sudden, precipitate, abrupt; informal snappy, p.d.q. (pretty damn quick). **2** *instant meals* **pre-prepared**, pre-cooked, ready mixed, fast; microwaveable, convenience, TV.
– OPPOSITES delayed.
▶ n. **1** *come here this instant!* **moment**, time, minute, second; juncture, point. **2** *it all happened in an instant* **trice**, moment, minute, (split) second, the twinkling of an eye, flash, no time (at all); informal sec, nanosecond, jiffy, the blink of an eye; Brit. informal mo; N. Amer. informal snap.

instantaneous adj. **immediate**, instant, on-the-spot, prompt, swift, speedy, rapid, quick, express, lightning; sudden, hurried, precipitate; informal snappy, p.d.q. (pretty damn quick).
– OPPOSITES delayed.

instantly adv. **immediately**, at once, straight away, right away, instantaneously; suddenly, abruptly, all of a sudden; forthwith, there and then, here and now, this/that minute, this/that instant; quickly, rapidly, speedily, promptly; in an instant, in a moment, in a (split) second, in a trice, in/like a flash, like a shot, in the twinkling of an eye, in no time (at all), before you know it; informal in a jiffy, pronto, before you can say Jack Robinson, double quick, like (greased) lightning; old use instanter.

instead adv. *travel by train instead* **as an alternative**, in lieu, alternatively; rather, by contrast, for preference, by/from choice; on second thoughts, all things being equal, ideally; N. Amer. alternately.
□ **instead of** as an alternative to, as a substitute for, as a replacement for, in place of, in lieu of, in preference to; rather than,

as opposed to, as against, as contrasted with, before.

instigate v. **1** *they instigated formal proceedings* **set in motion**, get under way, get off the ground, start, commence, begin, initiate, launch, institute, set up, inaugurate, establish, organize; actuate, generate, bring about; start the ball rolling; informal kick off. **2** *he instigated men to refuse allegiance* **incite**, encourage, urge, goad, provoke, spur on, push, press, prompt, induce, prevail on, motivate, influence, persuade, sway; informal put up to.
– OPPOSITES halt, dissuade.

instigation n. **1** *they became involved at his instigation* **prompting**, suggestion; request, entreaty, demand, insistence; wish, desire, persuasion; formal instance. **2** *foreign instigation of the disorder* **initiation**, incitement, provocation, fomentation, encouragement, inducement, inception.

instigator n. **initiator**, prime mover, motivator, architect, designer, planner, inventor, mastermind, originator, author, creator, agent; founder, pioneer, founding father; agitator, fomenter, troublemaker, ringleader.

instil v. **1** *we instil vigilance in our children* **inculcate**, implant, ingrain, impress, imprint, introduce; engender, produce, generate, induce, inspire, promote, foster; drum into. **2** *he instilled Monet with a love of nature* **imbue**, inspire, infuse, inculcate; indoctrinate; teach. **3** *she instilled the eye drops* **administer**, introduce, infuse, inject.

instinct n. **1** *some instinct told me to be careful* **natural tendency**, inherent tendency, inclination, urge, drive, compulsion, need; intuition, feeling, sixth sense, insight; nose. **2** *a good instinct for acting* **talent**, gift, ability, aptitude, skill, flair, feel, genius, knack, bent.

instinctive adj. **intuitive**, natural, instinctual, innate, inborn, inherent; unconscious, subconscious, intuitional; automatic, reflex, knee-jerk, mechanical, spontaneous, involuntary, impulsive; informal gut.
– OPPOSITES learned, voluntary.

institute n. *a research institute* **organization**, establishment, institution, foundation, centre; academy, school, college, university; society, association, federation, body, guild.
▶ v. **1** *we instituted a search* **initiate**, set in motion, get under way, get off the ground, start, commence, begin, launch; set up, inaugurate, found, establish, organize, generate, bring about; start the ball rolling; informal kick off. **2** *he will be instituted as vicar* **install**, instate, induct, invest, inaugurate, swear in, initiate; ordain, consecrate, anoint; appoint, create.
– OPPOSITES end, dismiss.

institution n. **1** *an academic institution* **establishment**, organization, institute, foundation, centre; academy, school, college, university; society, association, body, guild, consortium. **2** *they spent their lives in institutions* **(residential) home**, hospital, asylum. **3** *the institution of the rector* **installation**, instatement, induction, investiture, inauguration; ordination, consecration, anointing, appointment, creation. **4** *the institution of adoption* **practice**, custom, convention, tradition; phenomenon, fact; procedure, usage, method, system, policy; idea, notion, concept. **5** *the institution of legal proceedings* **initiation**, instigation, launch, start, commencement, beginning, inauguration, generation, origination.

institutional adj. **1** *an institutional framework for discussions* **organized**, established, bureaucratic, conventional, procedural, prescribed, set, routine, formal, systematic, systematized, methodical, businesslike, orderly, coherent, structured, regulated. **2** *the rooms are rather institutional* **impersonal**, formal, regimented, uniform, unvaried, monotonous; insipid, bland, uninteresting, dull; unappealing, uninviting, unattractive, unwelcoming, dreary, drab, colourless; stark, spartan, bare, clinical, sterile.

instruct v. **1** *the union instructed them to strike* **order**, direct, command, tell, enjoin, require, call on, mandate, charge; literary bid. **2** *nobody instructed him in how to operate it* **teach**, school, coach, train, enlighten, inform, educate, tutor, guide, prepare, prime. **3** *she instructed a solicitor of her own choice* **employ**, authorize, brief. **4** *the bank was instructed that money would be withdrawn* **inform**, tell, notify, apprise, advise, brief, prime; informal put in the picture, fill in.

instruction n. **1** *do not disobey my instructions* **order**, command, directive, direction, decree, edict, injunction, mandate, dictate, commandment, bidding; requirement, stipulation; informal say-so; literary behest. **2** *read the instructions* **directions**, key, specification; handbook, manual, guide. **3** *he gave instruction in demolition work* **tuition**, teaching, coaching, schooling, tutelage, pedagogy; lessons, classes, lectures; training, drill, preparation, grounding, guidance.

instructive adj. **informative**, instructional, informational, illuminating, enlightening, explanatory, educational, educative, edifying, didactic, pedagogic, heuristic; improving, moralistic, homiletic; useful, helpful.

instructor n. **trainer**, coach, teacher, tutor; adviser, counsellor, guide; educator; formal pedagogue.

instrument n. **1** *a wound made with a sharp instrument* **implement**, tool, utensil; device, apparatus, contrivance, gadget. **2** *check all the cockpit instruments* **measuring device**, gauge, meter; indicator, dial, display. **3** *an instrument of learning* **agent**, agency, cause, channel, medium, means, mechanism,

vehicle, organ. **4** *a mere instrument acting under coercion* **pawn**, puppet, creature, dupe, cog; tool, cat's paw; informal stooge.

instrumental adj. **involved**, active, influential, contributory; helpful, useful, of service; significant, important; **(be instrumental in)** play a part in, contribute to, be a factor in, have a hand in; add to, help, promote, advance, further; be conducive to, make for, lead to, cause.

insubordinate adj. **disobedient**, unruly, wayward, errant, badly behaved, disorderly, undisciplined, delinquent, troublesome, rebellious, defiant, recalcitrant, uncooperative, wilful, intractable, unmanageable, uncontrollable; awkward, difficult, perverse, contrary; Brit. informal bolshie.
– OPPOSITES obedient.

insubordination n. **disobedience**, unruliness, indiscipline, bad behaviour, misbehaviour, misconduct, delinquency; rebellion, defiance, mutiny, revolt; recalcitrance, wilfulness, awkwardness, perversity; informal acting-up; Law contumacy.

insubstantial adj. **1** *an insubstantial structure* **flimsy**, slight, fragile, breakable, weak, frail, unstable, shaky, wobbly, rickety, ramshackle, jerry-built. **2** *insubstantial evidence* **weak**, flimsy, feeble, poor, inadequate, insufficient, tenuous, insignificant, inconsequential, unsubstantial, unconvincing, implausible, unsatisfactory, paltry. **3** *the light made her seem insubstantial* **intangible**, impalpable, untouchable, discarnate, unsubstantial, incorporeal; imaginary, unreal, illusory, spectral, ghostlike, vaporous; Philosophy immaterial.
– OPPOSITES sturdy, sound, tangible.

insufferable adj. **1** *the heat was insufferable* **intolerable**, unbearable, unendurable, insupportable, unacceptable, oppressive, overwhelming, overpowering; more than flesh and blood can stand; informal too much. **2** *his win made him insufferable* **conceited**, arrogant, boastful, cocky, cocksure, full of oneself, self-important, swollen-headed, swaggering; vain, self-satisfied, self-congratulatory, smug; informal big-headed, too big for one's boots; literary vainglorious.
– OPPOSITES bearable, modest.

insufficient adj. **inadequate**, deficient, poor, scant, scanty; not enough, too little, too few, too small; scarce, sparse, in short supply, lacking, wanting; paltry, meagre, niggardly; incomplete, restricted, limited; informal measly, pathetic, piddling.

insular adj. **1** *insular people* **narrow-minded**, small-minded, blinkered, inward-looking, parochial, provincial, small-town, short-sighted, hidebound, set in one's ways, inflexible, rigid, entrenched; illiberal, intolerant, prejudiced, bigoted, biased, partisan, xenophobic; Brit. blimpish. **2** *an insular existence* **isolated**, inaccessible, cut off, segregated, detached, solitary, lonely.

– OPPOSITES broad-minded, cosmopolitan.

insulate v. **1** *pipes must be insulated* **wrap**, sheathe, cover, encase, enclose, envelop; lag, heatproof, soundproof; pad, cushion. **2** *they were insulated from the impact of the war* **protect**, save, shield, shelter, screen, cushion, cocoon; isolate, segregate, sequester, detach, cut off.

insulation n. **1** *a layer of insulation* **lagging**; blanket, jacket, wrap. **2** *insulation from the rigours of city life* **protection**, defence, shelter, screen, shield; isolation, segregation, separation, sequestration, detachment.

insult v. *he insulted my wife* **abuse**, be rude to, call someone names, slight, disparage, discredit, libel, slander, malign, defame, denigrate, cast aspersions on; offend, affront, hurt, humiliate, wound; informal badmouth; Brit. informal slag off; formal derogate, calumniate; rare asperse.
– OPPOSITES compliment.
▶ n. *he hurled insults at us* **abusive remark**, jibe, affront, slight, barb, slur, indignity; injury, libel, slander, defamation; abuse, disparagement, aspersions; informal dig, putdown, slap in the face, kick in the teeth.

insulting adj. **abusive**, rude, offensive, disparaging, belittling, derogatory, deprecatory, disrespectful, denigratory, uncomplimentary, pejorative; disdainful, derisive, scornful, contemptuous; defamatory, slanderous, libellous, scurrilous, blasphemous; informal bitchy, catty.

insuperable adj. **insurmountable**, invincible, unassailable; overwhelming, hopeless, impossible.

insupportable adj. **1** *this view is insupportable* **unjustifiable**, indefensible, inexcusable, unwarrantable, unreasonable; baseless, groundless, unfounded, unsupported, unsubstantiated, unconfirmed, uncorroborated, invalid, untenable, implausible, weak, flawed, specious, defective. **2** *the heat was insupportable* **intolerable**, insufferable, unbearable, unendurable; oppressive, overwhelming, overpowering, more than flesh and blood can stand; informal too much.
– OPPOSITES justified, bearable.

insurance n. **1** *insurance for his new car* **indemnity**, indemnification, assurance, (financial) protection, security, cover. **2** *insurance against a third World War* **protection**, defence, safeguard, security, precaution, provision; immunity; guarantee, warranty; informal backstop.

insure v. **provide insurance for**, indemnify, cover, assure, protect, underwrite; guarantee, warrant.

insurgent adj. *insurgent forces* **rebellious**, rebel, revolutionary, mutinous, insurrectionist; renegade, seditious, subversive.
– OPPOSITES loyal.
▶ n. *the troops are fighting insurgents* **rebel**, revolutionary, revolutionist, mutineer, insurrectionist, agitator, subversive,

renegade; guerrilla, freedom fighter, anarchist, terrorist.
– OPPOSITES loyalist.

insurmountable adj. **insuperable**, unconquerable, invincible, unassailable; overwhelming, hopeless, impossible.

insurrection n. **rebellion**, revolt, uprising, mutiny, revolution, insurgence, riot, sedition; civil disorder, unrest, anarchy; coup (d'état).

intact adj. **whole**, entire, complete, unbroken, undamaged, unimpaired, faultless, flawless, unscathed, untouched, unspoiled, unblemished, unmarked, perfect, pristine, inviolate, undefiled, unsullied, in one piece; sound, solid.
– OPPOSITES damaged.

intangible adj. **1** *the moonlight made things seem intangible* **impalpable**, untouchable, incorporeal, discarnate, abstract; ethereal, insubstantial, airy; ghostly, spectral, unearthly, supernatural; Philosophy immaterial. **2** *an intangible atmosphere* **indefinable**, indescribable, inexpressible, nameless; vague, obscure, unclear, indefinite, subtle, elusive, fugitive.

integral adj. **1** *an integral part of human behaviour* **essential**, fundamental, basic, intrinsic, inherent, constitutive, innate, structural; vital, necessary, requisite. **2** *the dryer has integral cord storage* **built-in**, inbuilt, integrated, incorporated, fitted. **3** *an integral approach to learning* **unified**, integrated, comprehensive, composite, combined, aggregate; complete, whole.
– OPPOSITES peripheral, fragmented.

integrate v. **combine**, amalgamate, merge, unite, fuse, blend, mingle, coalesce, consolidate, meld, intermingle, mix; incorporate, unify, assimilate, homogenize; desegregate.
– OPPOSITES separate.

integrated adj. **1** *an integrated package of services* **unified**, united, consolidated, amalgamated, combined, merged, fused, homogeneous, assimilated, cohesive. **2** *an integrated school* **desegregated**, non-segregated, unsegregated, mixed.

integrity n. **1** *I never doubted his integrity* **honesty**, probity, rectitude, honour, good character, principle(s), ethics, morals, righteousness, morality, virtue, decency, fairness, scrupulousness, sincerity, truthfulness, trustworthiness. **2** *the integrity of the federation* **unity**, unification, coherence, cohesion, togetherness, solidarity. **3** *the structural integrity of the aircraft* **soundness**, strength, sturdiness, solidity, durability, stability, stoutness, toughness.
– OPPOSITES dishonesty, division, fragility.

intellect n. **1** *a film that appeals to the intellect* **mind**, brain(s), intelligence, reason, understanding, thought, brainpower, sense, judgement, wisdom, wits; informal nous, grey matter, brain cells, upper storey; Brit. informal loaf; N. Amer. informal smarts. **2** *one of the finest* *intellects* **thinker**, intellectual, sage; mind, brain.

intellectual adj. **1** *his intellectual capacity* **mental**, cerebral, cognitive, psychological; rational, abstract, conceptual, theoretical, analytical, logical; academic. **2** *an intellectual man* **intelligent**, clever, academic, educated, well read, erudite, cerebral, learned, knowledgeable, literary, bookish, donnish, highbrow, scholarly, studious, enlightened, sophisticated; informal brainy.
– OPPOSITES physical, stupid.
▶ n. *intellectuals are appalled by television* **highbrow**, intelligent person, learned person, academic, bookworm, man/woman of letters, bluestocking; thinker, brain, scholar, sage; genius, Einstein, polymath, mastermind; informal egghead, brains; Brit. informal brainbox, clever clogs, boffin; N. Amer. informal brainiac, rocket scientist.
– OPPOSITES dunce.

intelligence n. **1** *a man of great intelligence* **intellectual capacity**, mental capacity, intellect, mind, brain(s), brainpower, judgement, reasoning, understanding, comprehension; acumen, wit, sense, insight, perception, penetration, discernment, quick-wittedness, smartness, canniness, astuteness, intuition, acuity, cleverness, brilliance, ability, talent; informal braininess. **2** *intelligence from our agents* **information**, facts, details, particulars, data, knowledge, reports; informal low, gen, dope. **3** *military intelligence* **information gathering**, surveillance, observation, reconnaissance, spying, espionage, infiltration, ELINT, Humint; informal recon.

intelligent adj. **1** *an intelligent writer* **clever**, bright, brilliant, quick-witted, quick on the uptake, smart, canny, astute, intuitive, insightful, perceptive, perspicacious, discerning; knowledgeable; able, gifted, talented; informal brainy. **2** *an intelligent being* **rational**, higher-order, capable of thought. **3** *intelligent machines* **self-regulating**, capable of learning, smart.

intelligentsia plural n. **intellectuals**, intelligent people, academics, scholars, literati, culturati, cognoscenti, illuminati, highbrows, thinkers, brains; the intelligent; informal eggheads; Brit. informal boffins.

intelligible adj. **comprehensible**, understandable, accessible, digestible, user-friendly, penetrable, fathomable; lucid, clear, coherent, plain, explicit, precise, unambiguous, self-explanatory.

intemperance n. **1** *they were criticized for intemperance* **overindulgence**, overconsumption, immoderation, excess, extravagance, prodigality, profligacy, lavishness; self-indulgence, self-gratification; debauchery, decadence, dissipation, dissolution. **2** *he said intemperance was a disease* **drinking**, alcoholism, alcohol abuse, dipsomania; drunkenness, intoxication, inebriation, insobriety, tipsiness; formal inebriety; literary crapulence.

intemperate adj. **immoderate**, excessive, undue, inordinate, extreme, unrestrained, uncontrolled; self-indulgent, overindulgent, extravagant, lavish, prodigal, profligate; imprudent, reckless, wild; dissolute, debauched, wanton, dissipated.
– OPPOSITES moderate.

intend v. **plan**, mean, have in mind, have the intention, aim, propose; aspire, hope, expect, be resolved, be determined; want, wish; contemplate, think of, envisage; design, earmark, set aside; formal purpose.

intended adj. *the foul was not intended* **deliberate**, intentional, calculated, conscious, planned, studied, knowing, wilful, wanton, purposeful, done on purpose, premeditated, pre-planned, preconceived; Law aforethought; Law, dated prepense.
– OPPOSITES accidental.
▶ n. informal *do you share everything with your intended?* **fiancé(e)**, betrothed, bride-to-be, wife-to-be, husband-to-be, future wife, future husband, prospective spouse.

intense adj. **1** *intense heat* **extreme**, great, acute, fierce, severe, high; exceptional, extraordinary; harsh, strong, powerful, potent, vigorous; informal serious. **2** *a very intense young man* **passionate**, impassioned, ardent, fervent, zealous, vehement, fiery, emotional; earnest, eager, animated, spirited, vigorous, energetic, fanatical, committed.
– OPPOSITES mild, apathetic.

intensify v. **escalate**, increase, step up, boost, raise, strengthen, augment, reinforce; pick up, build up, heighten, deepen, extend, expand, amplify, magnify; aggravate, exacerbate, worsen, inflame, compound.
– OPPOSITES abate.

intensity n. **1** *the intensity of the sun* **strength**, power, potency, force; severity, ferocity, vehemence, fierceness, harshness; magnitude, greatness, acuteness, extremity. **2** *his eyes had a glowing intensity* **passion**, ardour, fervour, zeal, vehemence, fire, heat, emotion; eagerness, animation, spirit, vigour, strength, energy; fanaticism.

intensive adj. **thorough**, thoroughgoing, in-depth, rigorous, exhaustive, all-out; all-embracing, all-inclusive, comprehensive, complete, full; vigorous, strenuous, detailed, minute, close, meticulous, scrupulous, painstaking, methodical, careful; extensive, widespread, sweeping; determined, resolute, persistent.
– OPPOSITES cursory.

intent n. *he tried to divine his father's intent* **aim**, intention, purpose, objective, object, goal, target; design, plan, scheme; wish, desire, ambition, idea, aspiration.
▶ adj. **1** *he was intent on proving his point* **bent**, set, determined, insistent, resolved, hell-bent, keen; committed to, obsessive about, fanatical about; determined to, anxious to, impatient to. **2** *an intent expression* **attentive**, absorbed, engrossed, fascinated, enthralled, rapt; focused,

earnest, concentrating, intense, studious, preoccupied; alert, watchful.

◻ **to all intents and purposes** in effect, effectively, in essence, essentially, virtually, practically; more or less, just about, all but, as good as, in all but name, as near as dammit; almost, nearly, nigh on; informal pretty much, pretty well.

intention n. **1** *it is his intention to be leader* **aim**, purpose, intent, objective, object, goal, target; design, plan, scheme; resolve, resolution, determination; wish, desire, ambition, idea, dream, aspiration. **2** *he managed, without intention, to upset me* **intent**, intentionality, deliberateness, design, calculation; premeditation, forethought, pre-planning; Law malice aforethought.

intentional adj. **deliberate**, calculated, conscious, intended, planned, meant, studied, knowing, wilful, wanton, purposeful, purposive, done on purpose, premeditated, pre-planned, preconceived; Law aforethought; Law, dated prepense.

intently adv. **attentively**, closely, keenly, earnestly, hard, carefully, fixedly, steadily.

inter v. **bury**, lay to rest, entomb, inurn; informal put six feet under, plant; literary sepulchre, inhume.
– OPPOSITES exhume.

intercede v. **mediate**, intermediate, arbitrate, conciliate, negotiate, moderate; intervene, interpose, step in, act; plead, petition.

intercept v. **stop**, head off, cut off; catch, seize, grab, snatch; obstruct, impede, interrupt, block, check, detain; ambush, challenge, waylay.

intercession n. **mediation**, intermediation, arbitration, conciliation, negotiation; intervention, involvement; pleading, petition, entreaty, agency; diplomacy.

interchange v. **1** *they interchange ideas* **exchange**, trade, swap, barter, bandy, reciprocate; old use truck. **2** *the terms are often interchanged* **substitute**, transpose, exchange, switch, swap (round), change (round), reverse, invert, replace.
▸ n. **1** *the interchange of ideas* **exchange**, trade, swap, barter, give and take, traffic, reciprocation, reciprocity; old use truck. **2** *a motorway interchange* **junction**, intersection, crossing; N. Amer. cloverleaf.

interchangeable adj. **1** *the gun has interchangeable barrels* **exchangeable**, transposable, replaceable. **2** *two more or less interchangeable roads* **similar**, identical, indistinguishable, alike, the same, uniform, twin, undifferentiated; corresponding, commensurate, equivalent, comparable, equal; informal much of a muchness.

intercourse n. **1** *social intercourse* **dealings**, relations, relationships, association, connections, contact; interchange, communication, communion, correspondence; negotiations, bargaining, transactions; trade, traffic; informal truck, doings. **2** *she did not consent to intercourse* **sexual intercourse**, sex, lovemaking, sexual relations, intimacy, coupling, mating, copulation; informal nooky; Brit. informal bonking, rumpy pumpy, how's your father; technical coitus, coition; formal fornication; dated carnal knowledge.

interdict n. *they breached an interdict* **prohibition**, ban, bar, veto, proscription, interdiction, embargo, moratorium, injunction.
– OPPOSITES permission.
▸ v. **1** *they interdicted foreign commerce* **prohibit**, forbid, ban, bar, veto, proscribe, embargo, disallow, debar, outlaw; stop, suppress; Law enjoin, estop. **2** *efforts to interdict asylum seekers* **intercept**, stop, head off, cut off; obstruct, impede, block; detain.
– OPPOSITES permit.

interest n. **1** *we listened with interest* **attentiveness**, attention, absorption; heed, regard, notice; curiosity, inquisitiveness; enjoyment, delight. **2** *places of interest* **attraction**, appeal, fascination, charm, beauty, allure. **3** *this will be of interest to those involved* **concern**, consequence, importance, import, significance, note, relevance, value, weight; formal moment. **4** *her interests include reading* **hobby**, pastime, leisure pursuit, recreation, diversion, amusement, relaxation; passion, enthusiasm; informal thing, bag, cup of tea. **5** *a financial interest in the firm* **stake**, share, claim, investment, stock, equity; involvement, concern. **6** *what is your interest in the case?* **involvement**, partiality, partisanship, preference, loyalty; bias, prejudice. **7** *his attorney guarded his interests* **concern**, business, affair. **8** *her savings earned interest* **dividends**, profits, returns; a percentage.
– OPPOSITES boredom.
▸ v. **1** *a topic that interests you* **appeal to**, be of interest to, attract, intrigue, fascinate; absorb, engross, rivet, grip, captivate; amuse, divert, entertain; arouse one's curiosity, whet one's appetite; informal float someone's boat, tickle someone's fancy. **2** *can I interest you in a drink?* **persuade to have**; sell.
– OPPOSITES bore.
◻ **in someone's interests** of benefit to, to the advantage of; for the sake of, for the benefit of.

interested adj. **1** *an interested crowd* **attentive**, intent, focused, absorbed, engrossed, fascinated, riveted, gripped, captivated, rapt, agog; intrigued, inquisitive, curious; keen, eager; informal all ears, nosy, snoopy. **2** *the government consulted with interested bodies* **concerned**, involved, affected, connected, related. **3** *no interested party can judge the contest* **partisan**, partial, biased, prejudiced, one-sided, preferential.

interesting adj. **absorbing**, engrossing, fascinating, riveting, gripping, compelling, compulsive, captivating, engaging, enthralling; appealing, attractive; amusing, entertaining, stimulating, thought-provoking, diverting, intriguing; informal unputdownable.

interfere v. **1** *don't let emotion interfere with duty* **impede**, obstruct, stand in the way of, hinder, inhibit, restrict, constrain, hamper, handicap, cramp, check, block; disturb, disrupt, influence, affect, confuse. **2** *she tried not to interfere in his life* **butt into**, barge into, pry into, nose into, intrude into, intervene in, get involved in, encroach on, impinge on; meddle in, tamper with; informal poke one's nose into, horn in on, muscle in on, stick one's oar in. **3** Brit. euphemistic *he interfered with local children* **(sexually) abuse**, sexually assault, indecently assault, molest, grope; informal feel up, touch up.

interference n. **1** *they resent state interference* **intrusion**, intervention, intercession, involvement, trespass, obtrusion; meddling, prying. **2** *radio interference* **disruption**, disturbance, static.

interfering adj. **meddlesome**, meddling, intrusive, prying, inquisitive, overcurious, busybody; informal nosy, nosy-parker, snoopy.

interim n. *in the interim they did more research* **meantime**, meanwhile, intervening time.
▸adj. *an interim advisory body* **provisional**, temporary, pro tem, stopgap, short-term, fill-in, caretaker, acting, intervening, transitional, makeshift, improvised, impromptu.
– OPPOSITES permanent.

interior adj. **1** *the house has interior panelling* **inside**, inner, internal, intramural. **2** *the interior deserts of the US* **inland**, inshore, upcountry, inner, innermost, central. **3** *the country's interior affairs* **internal**, home, domestic, national, state, civil, local. **4** *an interior monologue* **inner**, mental, spiritual, psychological; private, personal, intimate, secret.
– OPPOSITES exterior, outer, foreign.
▸n. **1** *the interior of the yacht* **inside**, inner part, depths, recesses, bowels, belly; centre, core, heart. **2** *the country's interior* **centre**, heartland, hinterland.
– OPPOSITES exterior, outside.

interject v. **1** *she interjected a comment* **interpose**, introduce, throw in, interpolate, add. **2** *he interjected before there was a fight* **interrupt**, intervene, cut in, break in, butt in, chime in; put one's oar in; Brit. informal chip in; N. Amer. informal put in one's two cents.

interjection n. **1** *an astonished interjection* **exclamation**; cry, shout, vociferation, utterance; dated ejaculation. **2** *the interjection of a question* **interposition**, interpolation, insertion, addition, introduction.

interlock v. **interconnect**, interlink, engage, mesh, intermesh, join, unite, connect, couple.

interloper n. **intruder**, encroacher, trespasser, invader, infiltrator; uninvited guest; outsider, stranger, alien; informal gatecrasher.

interlude n. **interval**, intermission, break, recess, pause, respite, rest, breathing space, halt, gap, stop, stoppage, hiatus, lull; informal breather, let-up, time out, downtime.

intermediary n. **mediator**, go-between, negotiator, intervenor, interceder, intercessor, arbitrator, arbiter, conciliator, peacemaker; middleman, broker, linkman.

intermediate adj. **halfway**, in-between, middle, mid, midway, median, medial, intermediary, intervening, transitional.

interment n. **burial**, burying, committal, entombment, inhumation; funeral; old use sepulture.

interminable adj. **endless**, never-ending, unending, non-stop, everlasting, ceaseless, unceasing, incessant, constant, continual, uninterrupted, sustained; monotonous, long-winded, overlong, rambling.

intermingle v. **mix**, intermix, mingle, blend, fuse, merge, combine, amalgamate; unite, affiliate, associate, fraternize; literary commingle.

intermission n. **interval**, interlude, entr'acte, break, recess, pause, rest, respite, breathing space, lull, gap, stop, stoppage, halt; cessation, suspension; informal let-up, breather, time out, downtime.

intermittent adj. **sporadic**, irregular, fitful, spasmodic, broken, fragmentary, discontinuous, isolated, random, patchy, scattered; occasional, periodic.
– OPPOSITES continuous.

intern v. *they were interned without trial* **imprison**, incarcerate, impound, jail, put behind bars, detain, hold (captive), lock up, confine; informal put away, put inside, send down; Brit. informal bang up.
▸n. *an intern at a local firm* **trainee**, apprentice, probationer, student, novice, beginner.

internal adj. **1** *an internal courtyard* **inner**, interior, inside, intramural; central. **2** *the state's internal affairs* **domestic**, home, interior, civil, local; national, state. **3** *an internal battle with herself* **mental**, psychological, emotional; personal, private, secret, hidden.
– OPPOSITES external, foreign.

international adj. **global**, worldwide, intercontinental, universal; cosmopolitan, multiracial, multinational.
– OPPOSITES national, local.

interplay n. **interaction**, interchange; teamwork, cooperation, reciprocation, reciprocity, give and take.

interpolate v. **insert**, interpose, enter, add, incorporate, inset, put, introduce.

interpose v. **1** *he interposed himself between the girls* **insinuate**, place, put. **2** *I must interpose a note of caution* **introduce**, insert, interject, add. **3** *they interposed to suppress the custom* **intervene**, intercede, step in, involve oneself; interfere, intrude, butt in, cut in; informal barge in, horn in, muscle in.

i

interpret v. **1** *the rabbis interpreted the Jewish laws* **explain**, elucidate, expound, explicate, clarify, illuminate, shed light on. **2** *the remark was interpreted as an invitation* **understand**, construe, take (to mean), see, regard. **3** *the symbols are difficult to interpret* **decipher**, decode, make intelligible; understand, comprehend, make sense of; informal crack.

interpretation n. **1** *the interpretation of the Bible's teachings* **explanation**, elucidation, expounding, exposition, explication, exegesis, clarification. **2** *she did not care what interpretation he put on her haste* **meaning**, understanding, construal, connotation, explanation, inference. **3** *the interpretation of experimental findings* **analysis**, evaluation, review, study, examination. **4** *his interpretation of the sonata* **rendition**, rendering, execution, presentation, performance, reading, playing, singing.

interpreter n. **1** *a Japanese interpreter* **translator**, dragoman. **2** *a vocal interpreter of his music* **performer**, presenter, exponent; singer, player. **3** *interpreters of Soviet history* **analyst**, evaluator, reviewer, commentator.

interrogate v. **question**, cross-question, cross-examine; quiz; interview, examine, debrief, give someone the third degree; informal pump, grill.

interrogative adj. **questioning**, inquiring, inquisitive, probing, searching, quizzing, quizzical, curious.

interrupt v. **1** *she opened her mouth to interrupt* **cut in (on)**, break in (on), barge in (on), intervene (in), put one's oar in; Brit. put one's pennyworth in; N. Amer. put one's two cents in; informal butt in (on), chime in (on); Brit. informal chip in (on). **2** *the band had to interrupt their tour* **suspend**, adjourn, discontinue, break off; stop, halt, cease, end, bring to an end/close; informal put on ice, put on a back burner. **3** *the coastal plain is interrupted by large lagoons* **break (up)**, punctuate; pepper, strew, dot, scatter. **4** *their view was interrupted by houses* **obstruct**, impede, block, restrict.

interruption n. **1** *he was not pleased at her interruption* **cutting in**, barging in, intervention, intrusion; informal butting in. **2** *an interruption of the power supply* **discontinuation**, breaking off, suspension, stopping, halting, cessation. **3** *an interruption in her career* **interval**, interlude, break, pause, gap.

intersect v. **1** *the lines intersect at right angles* **cross**, criss-cross; technical decussate. **2** *the cornfield is intersected by a track* **bisect**, divide, cut in two/half, cut across/through; cross, traverse.

intersection n. **1** *the intersection of the two curves* **crossing**, criss-crossing. **2** *the driver stopped at an intersection* **(road) junction**, T-junction, interchange, crossroads; Brit. roundabout.

intersperse v. **1** *giant lobelia were interspersed among the rocks* **scatter**, disperse, spread, strew, dot, sprinkle, pepper; literary bestrew. **2** *the beech trees are interspersed with conifers* **intermix**, mix, mingle, punctuate.

interstice n. **space**, gap, aperture, opening, hole, crevice, chink, slit, slot, crack.

intertwine v. **entwine**, interweave, interlace, interwind, twist, coil.

interval n. **1** *a 15-minute interval* **intermission**, interlude, entr'acte, break, recess; half-time. **2** *Baldwin made two speeches in the interval* **interim**, interlude, intervening time/period, meantime, meanwhile. **3** *short intervals of still water* **stretch**, distance, span, area.

intervene v. **1** *had the war not intervened, they might have married* **occur**, happen, take place, arise, crop up, come about; result, ensue, follow; literary come to pass, befall, betide. **2** *she intervened in the row* **intercede**, involve oneself, get involved, interpose oneself, step in; interfere, intrude.

intervention n. **involvement**, intercession, interceding, interposing; interference, intrusion.

interview n. *all applicants will be called for an interview* **meeting**, discussion, conference, examination, interrogation; audience, talk, dialogue, exchange; talks.
▸ v. *we interviewed seventy subjects for the survey* **talk to**, have a discussion/dialogue with; question, interrogate, cross-examine; poll, canvass, survey, sound out; informal grill, pump; Law examine.

interviewer n. **questioner**, interrogator, examiner, assessor, appraiser; journalist, reporter.

interweave v. **1** *the threads are interwoven* **intertwine**, entwine, interlace, splice, braid, plait; twist together, weave together, wind together; Nautical marry. **2** *their fates were interwoven* **interlink**, link, connect; intermix, mix, merge, blend, interlock, knit/bind together.

intestinal adj. **enteric**, gastro-enteric, duodenal, coeliac, gastric, ventral, stomach, abdominal.

intestines plural n. **gut**, guts, entrails, viscera; small intestine, large intestine, bowel; informal insides, innards.

> **WORD LINKS**
> **enteric, visceral** relating to the intestines
> **enteritis** inflammation of the intestine
> **peristalsis** the contraction and relaxation of the muscles of the intestines

intimacy n. **1** *the sisters re-established their old intimacy* **closeness**, togetherness, affinity, rapport, attachment, familiarity, friendliness, amity, affection, warmth; informal chumminess, palliness; Brit. informal mateyness. **2** *the memory of their intimacy* **sexual relations**, (sexual) intercourse, sex, lovemaking, copulation; technical coitus.

intimate¹ adj. **1** *an intimate friend* **close**, bosom, boon, dear, cherished, faithful, fast, firm; informal chummy, pally. **2** *an intimate atmosphere* **friendly**, warm, welcoming, hospitable, relaxed, informal; cosy, comfortable, snug; informal comfy. **3** *intimate thoughts* **personal**, private, confidential, secret; innermost, inner, inward, unspoken, undisclosed. **4** *an intimate knowledge of the industry* **detailed**, thorough, exhaustive, deep, in-depth, profound. **5** *intimate relations* **sexual**, carnal, amorous, amatory.
– OPPOSITES distant, formal.
▸ n. *his circle of intimates* **close friend**, best friend, bosom friend, confidant, confidante; informal chum, pal, crony; Brit. informal mate; N. Amer. informal buddy.

intimate² v. **1** *he intimated his decision* **announce**, state, proclaim, make known, make public, disclose, reveal, divulge. **2** *her feelings were subtly intimated* **imply**, suggest, hint at, insinuate, indicate, signal, allude to, refer to, convey.

intimation n. **1** *the early intimation of session dates* **announcement**, statement, communication, notification, notice, reporting, publishing; disclosure, revelation, divulging. **2** *the first intimation of discord* **suggestion**, hint, indication, sign, signal, inkling, suspicion, impression; clue to, undertone of, whisper of.

intimidate v. **frighten**, menace, terrify, scare, terrorize, cow, subdue; threaten, browbeat, bully, pressure, pressurize, harass, harry, hound; informal lean on, bulldoze, steamroller, railroad, use strong-arm tactics on; Brit. informal put the frighteners on.

intolerable adj. **unbearable**, insufferable, unsupportable, insupportable, unendurable, beyond endurance, more than flesh and blood can stand, too much to bear.
– OPPOSITES bearable.

intolerant adj. **1** *intolerant in religious matters* **bigoted**, narrow-minded, small-minded, parochial, provincial, illiberal, uncompromising; prejudiced, biased, partial, partisan, discriminatory. **2** *foods to which you are intolerant* **allergic**, sensitive, hypersensitive.

intonation n. **1** *she read the sentence with the wrong intonation* **inflection**, pitch, tone, timbre, cadence, cadency, lilt, modulation, speech pattern. **2** *the intonation of hymns* **chanting**, incantation, recitation, singing.

intone v. **chant**, sing, recite; rare cantillate.

intoxicate v. **1** *one glass of wine intoxicated him* **inebriate**, make drunk, make intoxicated, befuddle, go to someone's head; informal make legless, make woozy. **2** *he was intoxicated by cinema* **exhilarate**, thrill, elate, delight, captivate, enthral, entrance, enrapture, excite, stir, rouse, inspire, fire with enthusiasm; informal give someone a buzz, give someone a kick; N. Amer. informal give someone a charge.

intoxicated adj. **drunk**, inebriated, inebriate, drunken, tipsy, under the influence; informal tight, merry, the worse for wear, pie-eyed, in one's cups, three sheets to the wind, plastered, smashed, sloshed, sozzled, well oiled, wrecked, blotto, stewed, pickled, tanked up, soaked, off one's face, out of one's head/skull; Brit. informal paralytic, legless, Brahms and Liszt, half cut, bladdered, trolleyed, slaughtered, lashed, mullered, tiddly; N. Amer. informal loaded, trashed, out of one's gourd, blitzed, jacked; euphemistic tired and emotional; formal bibulous; literary crapulent.
– OPPOSITES sober.

intoxicating adj. **1** *intoxicating drink* **alcoholic**, strong, hard, potent, stiff, intoxicant; formal spirituous. **2** *an intoxicating sense of freedom* **heady**, exhilarating, thrilling, exciting, rousing, stirring, stimulating, invigorating, electrifying; strong, powerful, potent; informal mind-blowing.
– OPPOSITES non-alcoholic.

intoxication n. **drunkenness**, inebriation, insobriety, tipsiness; informal tightness; literary crapulence.

intractable adj. **1** *intractable problems* **unmanageable**, uncontrollable, difficult, awkward, troublesome, demanding, burdensome. **2** *an intractable man* **stubborn**, obstinate, obdurate, inflexible, unadaptable, unbending, unyielding, uncompromising, unaccommodating, uncooperative, difficult, awkward, perverse, contrary, pig-headed; N. Amer. rock-ribbed; informal stiff-necked.
– OPPOSITES manageable, compliant.

intransigent adj. **uncompromising**, inflexible, unbending, unyielding, unshakeable, unwavering, resolute, rigid, unaccommodating, uncooperative, stubborn, obstinate, obdurate, pig-headed, single-minded, iron-willed; informal stiff-necked.
– OPPOSITES compliant.

intrench v. See **entrench**.

intrenched adj. See **entrenched**.

intrepid adj. **fearless**, unafraid, undaunted, unflinching, unshrinking, bold, daring, audacious, adventurous, heroic, dynamic, spirited, indomitable; brave, courageous, valiant, valorous, stout-hearted, stalwart, plucky, doughty; informal gutsy, spunky.
– OPPOSITES fearful.

intricate adj. **complex**, complicated, convoluted, tangled, entangled, twisted; elaborate, ornate, detailed, involuted; Brit. informal fiddly.

intrigue v. **1** *her answer intrigued him* **interest**, be of interest to, fascinate, arouse someone's curiosity, attract. **2** *the ministers were intriguing* **plot**, conspire, make secret plans, scheme, manoeuvre, connive, collude, machinate.
▸ n. **1** *the intrigue that accompanied the selection of a new leader* **plotting**, conspiracy, collusion, conniving, scheming, machination, trickery, sharp practice, double-dealing, underhandedness, subterfuge; informal dirty

tricks. **2** *the king's intrigues with his nobles' wives* **(love) affair**, affair of the heart, liaison, amour, fling, flirtation, dalliance; adultery, infidelity, unfaithfulness; informal fooling around, playing around, hanky-panky; Brit. informal carryings-on.

intriguer n. **conspirator**, co-conspirator, plotter, schemer, colluder, conniver, machinator, Machiavelli.

intriguing adj. **interesting**, fascinating, absorbing, compelling, gripping, riveting, captivating, engaging, enthralling.

intrinsic adj. **inherent**, innate, inborn, inbred, congenital, connate, connatural, natural; deep-rooted, indelible, ineradicable; integral, basic, fundamental, essential.

introduce v. **1** *he has introduced a new system* **institute**, initiate, launch, inaugurate, establish, found; bring in, set in motion, start, begin, commence, get going, get under way, originate, pioneer; informal kick off. **2** *you can introduce new ideas* **propose**, put forward, suggest, table; raise, broach, bring up, mention, air, float. **3** *she introduced Lindsey to the young man* **present (formally)**, make known, acquaint with. **4** *introducing nitrogen into canned beer* **insert**, inject, put, force, shoot, feed. **5** *she introduced a note of severity into her voice* **instil**, infuse, inject, add. **6** *the same presenter introduces the programme each week* **announce**, present, give an introduction to; start off, begin, open.

introduction n. **1** *the introduction of democratic reforms* **institution**, establishment, initiation, launch, inauguration, foundation; start, commencement, inception, origination, pioneering. **2** *an introduction to the king* **(formal) presentation**; meeting, audience. **3** *an introduction to the catalogue* **foreword**, preface, preamble, prologue, prelude; opening (statement), beginning; informal intro; formal proem, prolegomenon. **4** *an introduction to the history of the period* **basic explanation/account of**; the basics, the rudiments, the fundamentals. **5** *a gentle introduction to the life of the school* **initiation**, induction, inauguration.
– OPPOSITES afterword.

introductory adj. **1** *the introductory chapter* **opening**, initial, starting, initiatory, first; prefatory, preliminary. **2** *an introductory course* **elementary**, basic, rudimentary; initiatory, preparatory.
– OPPOSITES final, advanced.

introspection n. **self-analysis**, soul-searching, introversion; contemplation, meditation, thoughtfulness, pensiveness, reflection; informal navel-gazing; formal cogitation.

introspective adj. **inward-looking**, self-analysing, introverted, introvert; contemplative, thoughtful, pensive, meditative, reflective; informal navel-gazing.

introverted adj. **shy**, reserved, withdrawn, reticent, diffident, retiring, quiet;

introspective, introvert, inward-looking, indrawn, self-absorbed; contemplative, thoughtful, pensive, meditative, reflective.
– OPPOSITES extroverted.

intrude v. **1** *intruding on people's privacy* **encroach**, impinge, trespass, infringe, obtrude, invade, violate, disturb, disrupt; informal horn in, muscle in. **2** *he intruded his own personality into his work* **force**, push, obtrude, impose, thrust.

intruder n. **trespasser**, interloper, invader, infiltrator; burglar, housebreaker, thief.

intrusion n. **encroachment**, obtrusion; invasion, incursion, intervention, disturbance, disruption, infringement, impingement.

intrusive adj. **1** *an intrusive journalist* **intruding**, invasive, obtrusive, unwelcome; inquisitive, prying; informal nosy. **2** *opinion polls play an intrusive role in elections* **invasive**, high-profile, prominent; informal in one's face. **3** *intrusive questions* **personal**, prying, forward, impertinent; informal nosy.

intuition n. **1** *he works according to intuition* **instinct**, intuitiveness; sixth sense, clairvoyance, second sight. **2** *this confirms an intuition I had* **hunch**, feeling (in one's bones), inkling, (sneaking) suspicion; premonition, presentiment; informal gut feeling.

intuitive adj. **instinctive**, intuitional, instinctual; innate, inborn, inherent, natural, congenital; unconscious, subconscious, involuntary; informal gut.

inundate v. **1** *many buildings were inundated* **flood**, deluge, overrun, swamp, submerge, engulf. **2** *we have been inundated by complaints* **overwhelm**, overrun, overload, bog down, swamp, besiege, snow under.

inundation n. **flood**, deluge, torrent, flash flood, freshet; Brit. spate.

inure v. **harden**, toughen, season, temper, condition; accustom, habituate, familiarize, acclimatize, adjust, adapt.
– OPPOSITES sensitize.

invade v. **1** *the island was invaded* **occupy**, conquer, capture, seize, take (over), annex, win, gain, secure; march into, overrun, overwhelm, storm. **2** *someone had invaded our privacy* **intrude on**, violate, encroach on, infringe on, trespass on, obtrude on, disturb, disrupt; informal horn in on, muscle in on. **3** *the feeling of betrayal invaded my being* **permeate**, pervade, spread through/over, diffuse through, imbue.
– OPPOSITES withdraw.

invader n. **attacker**, raider, marauder; occupier, conqueror; intruder.

invalid¹ n. *my mother is an invalid* **ill person**, sick person, valetudinarian; patient, convalescent.
▸ adj. *her invalid husband* **ill**, sick, ailing, unwell, infirm, valetudinarian, in poor health; incapacitated, bedridden, frail, feeble, weak, debilitated, sickly, poorly.
– OPPOSITES healthy.
▸ v. *an officer invalided by a chest wound*

disable, incapacitate, indispose, hospitalize, put out of action, lay up; injure, wound, hurt.

invalid² adj. **1** *the law was invalid* (**legally**) **void**, null and void, unenforceable, not binding, illegitimate, inapplicable. **2** *the whole theory is invalid* **false**, untrue, inaccurate, faulty, fallacious, spurious, unconvincing, unsound, weak, wrong, wide of the mark, off target; untenable, baseless, ill-founded, groundless; informal off beam, full of holes.
– OPPOSITES binding, true.

invalidate v. **1** *a low turnout invalidated the ballot* **render invalid**, void, nullify, annul, negate, cancel, overturn, overrule. **2** *this case invalidates the general argument* **disprove**, refute, explode, contradict, rebut, negate, belie, discredit, debunk; weaken, undermine, compromise; informal shoot full of holes; formal confute.

invaluable adj. **indispensable**, crucial, critical, key, vital, irreplaceable, all-important.
– OPPOSITES dispensable.

invariable adj. **unvarying**, unchanging, unvaried; constant, stable, set, steady, predictable, regular, consistent; unchangeable, unalterable, immutable, fixed.
– OPPOSITES varied.

invariably adv. **always**, on every occasion, at all times, without fail, without exception; everywhere, in all places, in all cases/instances; regularly, consistently, repeatedly, habitually, unfailingly.
– OPPOSITES sometimes, never.

invasion n. **1** *the invasion of the islands* **occupation**, conquering, capture, seizure, annexation, annexing, takeover; overrunning, overwhelming, storming. **2** *an invasion of cars* **influx**, inundation, inrush, flood, torrent, deluge, avalanche. **3** *an invasion of my privacy* **violation**, infringement, interruption, intrusion, encroachment, obtrusion, disturbance, disruption, breach.
– OPPOSITES withdrawal.

invective n. **abuse**, insults, vituperation, expletives, swear words, swearing, curses, bad/foul language, obloquy; Brit. informal industrial language; old use contumely.
– OPPOSITES praise.

inveigh v. **fulminate**, declaim, protest, rail, rage, remonstrate; denounce, censure, condemn, decry, criticize; disparage, denigrate, run down, abuse, vilify, impugn; informal kick up a fuss/stink about, bellyache about, sound off about.
– OPPOSITES support.

inveigle v. **cajole**, wheedle, coax, persuade, talk; tempt, lure, entice, seduce, beguile; informal sweet-talk, soft-soap, con; N. Amer. informal sucker; old use blandish.

invent v. **1** *Louis Braille invented an alphabet to help blind people* **originate**, create, innovate, design, devise, contrive, develop; conceive, think up, dream up, come up with, pioneer. **2** *they invented the story for a laugh*

make up, fabricate, concoct, hatch, dream up; informal cook up.

invention n. **1** *the invention of the telescope* **origination**, creation, innovation, devising, contriving, development, design. **2** *medieval inventions* **innovation**, creation, design, contraption, contrivance, construction, device, gadget; informal brainchild. **3** *his invention was flagging* **inventiveness**, originality, creativity, creativeness, imagination, imaginativeness, inspiration. **4** *a journalistic invention* **fabrication**, concoction, (piece of) fiction, story, tale; lie, untruth, falsehood, fib; myth, fantasy; informal tall story, cock and bull story.

inventive adj. **1** *the most inventive composer of his time* **creative**, original, innovational, innovative, imaginative, ingenious, resourceful. **2** *a fresh, inventive comedy* **original**, innovative, unusual, fresh, novel, new; experimental, avant-garde, groundbreaking, unorthodox, unconventional.
– OPPOSITES unimaginative, hackneyed.

inventor n. **originator**, creator, innovator; designer, deviser, developer, maker, producer; author, architect; pioneer, mastermind, father; formal neoteric.

inventory n. *a complete inventory of all their belongings* **list**, listing, catalogue, record, register, checklist, log, archive.
▶ v. *I inventoried his collection* **list**, catalogue, record, register, log.

inverse adj. *inverse snobbery* **reverse**, reversed, inverted, opposite, converse, contrary, counter, antithetical.
▶ n. *alkalinity is the inverse of acidity* **opposite**, converse, obverse, antithesis; informal flip side.

inversion n. **reversal**, transposition; reverse, contrary, antithesis, converse.

invert v. **turn upside down**, upturn, upend, turn around/about, turn inside out, turn back to front, reverse, flip (over).

invest v. **1** *he invested in a cotton mill* **put/plough money into**, provide capital for, fund, back, finance, underwrite; buy into, buy shares in. **2** *they invested £18 million* **spend**, expend, put in, plough in; venture, speculate, risk; informal lay out. **3** *their words were invested with sarcasm* **imbue**, infuse, charge, steep, suffuse, pervade, endow. **4** *the powers invested in the bishop* **vest in**, confer on, bestow on, grant to, entrust to, put in someone's hands. **5** *bishops whom the king had invested* **admit to office**, instate, install, induct, swear in; ordain, crown. **6** old use *invested in the full canonicals of his calling* **clothe**, attire, dress, garb, robe, deck out, accoutre; old use apparel. **7** old use *he invested the fort of Arcot* **besiege**, lay siege to, beleaguer, surround.

investigate v. **enquire into**, look into, go into, probe, explore, scrutinize, conduct an investigation into, make inquiries about; inspect, analyse, study, examine, consider, research; informal check out, suss out; N. Amer. informal scope out.

investigation n. **examination**, inquiry, study, inspection, exploration, consideration, analysis, appraisal; research, scrutiny, scrutinization, perusal; probe, review, survey.

investigator n. **inspector**, examiner, inquirer, explorer, analyser; researcher, factfinder, scrutineer, scrutinizer, prober, searcher; detective.

investiture n. **inauguration**, appointment, installation, instatement, initiation, swearing in; ordination, consecration, crowning, enthronement.

investment n. **1** *you can lose money by bad investment* **investing**, speculation; funding, backing, financing, underwriting; buying shares. **2** *it's a good investment* **venture**, speculation, risk, gamble; asset, acquisition, holding, possession. **3** *an investment of £305,000* **stake**, share, money/capital invested. **4** *a substantial investment of time* **sacrifice**, surrender, loss, forfeiture.

inveterate adj. **1** *an inveterate gambler* **confirmed**, hardened, incorrigible, addicted, compulsive, obsessive; informal pathological. **2** *an inveterate Democrat* **staunch**, steadfast, committed, devoted, dedicated, dyed-in-the-wool, out-and-out, diehard. **3** *mankind's inveterate stupidity* **ingrained**, deep-seated, deep-rooted, entrenched, ineradicable, incurable.

invidious adj. **1** *that put her in an invidious position* **unpleasant**, awkward, difficult; undesirable, unenviable. **2** *an invidious comparison* **unfair**, unjust, iniquitous, unwarranted; deleterious, detrimental.
– OPPOSITES pleasant, fair.

invigorate v. **revitalize**, energize, refresh, revive, vivify, brace, rejuvenate, enliven, liven up, perk up, wake up, animate, galvanize, fortify, stimulate, rouse, exhilarate; informal buck up, pep up.
– OPPOSITES tire.

invincible adj. **invulnerable**, indestructible, unconquerable, unbeatable, indomitable, unassailable; impregnable, inviolable.
– OPPOSITES vulnerable.

inviolable adj. **inalienable**, absolute, unalterable, unchallengeable; sacrosanct, holy, sacred.

inviolate adj. **untouched**, undamaged, unhurt, unharmed, unscathed; unspoiled, unsullied, unstained, undefiled, unprofaned, perfect, pristine, pure; intact, unbroken, whole, entire, complete.

invisible adj. **unable to be seen**, not visible; undetectable, indiscernible, inconspicuous, imperceptible; unseen, unnoticed, unobserved, hidden, obscured, out of sight.

invitation n. **1** *an invitation to dinner* request to attend, call, summons; informal invite. **2** *an open door is an invitation to a thief* **encouragement**, provocation, temptation, lure, magnet, bait, enticement, attraction, allure; informal come-on.

invite v. **1** *they invited us to Sunday lunch* **ask**, summon, have someone over/round, request (the pleasure of) someone's company at. **2** *applications are invited for the posts* **ask for**, request, call for, appeal for, solicit, seek, summon. **3** *airing such views invites trouble* **cause**, induce, provoke, create, generate, engender, foster, encourage, lead to; incite, elicit, bring on oneself, arouse.
▶ n. informal *an invite to a party.* See **invitation** (sense 1).

inviting adj. **tempting**, enticing, alluring, beguiling; attractive, appealing, pleasant, agreeable, delightful; appetizing, mouth-watering; fascinating, enchanting, entrancing, captivating, intriguing, irresistible, seductive.
– OPPOSITES repellent.

invocation n. **1** *her invocation of new methodologies* **citation**, mention, acknowledgement, reference to, allusion to. **2** *the invocation of rain by tribal people* **summoning**, calling up, conjuring up. **3** *an invocation to the Holy Ghost* **prayer**, intercession, supplication, entreaty, petition, appeal; old use orison.

invoice n. *an invoice for the goods* **bill**, account, statement (of charges); N. Amer. check; informal tab; old use reckoning.
▶ v. *we'll invoice you for the damage* **bill**, charge, send an invoice/bill to.

invoke v. **1** *he invoked his statutory rights* **cite**, refer to, adduce, instance; resort to, have recourse to, turn to. **2** *I invoked the Madonna* **pray to**, call on, appeal to, supplicate, entreat, solicit, beg, implore; literary beseech. **3** *invoking the spirits* **summon**, call (up), conjure (up). **4** *middle-class moralities invoke peculiar anxieties* **bring forth**, bring out, elicit, induce, cause, kindle.

involuntary adj. **1** *an involuntary shudder* **reflex**, automatic; spontaneous, instinctive, unconscious, unintentional, uncontrollable. **2** *involuntary repatriation* **compulsory**, obligatory, mandatory, forced, coerced, compelled, imposed, required, prescribed; unwilling, unconsenting, against one's will.
– OPPOSITES deliberate, optional.

involve v. **1** *the inspection involved a lot of work* **require**, necessitate, demand, call for; entail, mean, imply, presuppose. **2** *I try to involve everyone in key decisions* **include**, count in, bring in, take into account, take note of; cover, incorporate, encompass, touch on, embrace, comprehend. **3** *many drug addicts involve themselves in crime* **implicate**, incriminate, inculpate; associate, connect, concern; embroil, entangle, enmesh; informal mix up.
– OPPOSITES preclude, exclude.

involved adj. **1** *social workers involved in the case* **associated**, connected, concerned. **2** *he had been involved in burglaries* **implicated**, incriminated, inculpated, embroiled, entangled, caught up, mixed up. **3** *a long and involved story* **complicated**, intricate, complex, elaborate; convoluted,

impenetrable, unfathomable. **4** *they were totally involved in their work* **engrossed**, absorbed, immersed, caught up, preoccupied, busy, engaged, intent, focused.
– OPPOSITES unconnected, straightforward.

involvement n. **1** *his involvement in a plot to overthrow the government* **participation**, action, hand; collaboration, collusion, complicity, implication, incrimination, inculpation; association, connection, attachment, entanglement. **2** *emotional involvement* **attachment**, friendship, intimacy; relationship, relations, bond.

invulnerable adj. **impervious**, insusceptible, immune; indestructible, impenetrable, impregnable, unassailable, inviolable, invincible, secure; proof against.

inward adj. **1** *a small inward indentation towards the inside*, going in, ingoing; concave. **2** *an inward smile* **internal**, inner, interior, innermost; private, personal, hidden, secret, veiled, masked, concealed, unexpressed; old use privy.
– OPPOSITES outward.
▶ adv. *the door opened inward.* See **inwards**.

inwardly adv. **inside**, internally, within, deep down (inside), in one's heart (of hearts); privately, secretly, confidentially.

inwards adv. **inside**, into the interior, inward, within.

iota n. **(little) bit**, mite, speck, scrap, shred, ounce, scintilla, atom, jot (or tittle); informal smidgen; old use scruple.

irascible adj. **irritable**, quick-tempered, short-tempered, snappish, tetchy, testy, touchy, edgy, crabby, waspish, dyspeptic; crusty, grouchy, cantankerous, curmudgeonly, ill-natured, peevish, querulous, fractious; informal prickly, ratty, snappy.

irate adj. **angry**, furious, infuriated, incensed, enraged, incandescent, fuming, seething, cross, mad; raging, ranting, raving, in a frenzy, beside oneself, outraged, up in arms; indignant, annoyed, irritated, irked, piqued; informal foaming at the mouth, hot under the collar; literary wrathful; old use wroth.

iridescent adj. **shimmering**, glittering, sparkling, dazzling, shining, gleaming, glowing, lustrous, scintillating, opalescent; literary glistering, coruscating, effulgent.

irk v. **irritate**, annoy, gall, pique, nettle, exasperate, try someone's patience; anger, infuriate, madden, incense, get on someone's nerves; antagonize, provoke, ruffle someone's feathers, make someone's hackles rise; Brit. rub up the wrong way; informal get someone's goat, get/put someone's back up, make someone's blood boil, peeve, miff, rile, aggravate, needle, get (to), bug, hack off, brown off, get up someone's nose, give someone the hump, drive mad/crazy, drive up the wall, make someone see red; Brit. informal wind up, cheese off, nark, get on someone's wick; N. Amer. informal tee off, tick off, rankle, ride, gravel.
– OPPOSITES please.

irksome adj. **irritating**, annoying, vexing, vexatious, galling, exasperating, disagreeable; tiresome, wearisome, tedious, trying, troublesome, bothersome, awkward, difficult, boring, uninteresting; infuriating, maddening; informal infernal.

iron n. **1** *a ship built of iron* metal, pig iron, cast iron, wrought iron. **2** *she needed some iron in her soul* **strength**, toughness, resilience, firmness, robustness, steel, grit; informal guts, spunk. **3** *a soldering iron* **tool**, implement, utensil, device. **4** *a hot iron* **flat iron**, electric iron, steam iron, smoothing iron. **5** *they were clapped in irons* **manacles**, shackles, fetters, chains, handcuffs; informal cuffs, bracelets.
▶ adj. **1** *an iron law of politics* **inflexible**, unbreakable, absolute, unconditional, categorical, incontrovertible, infallible. **2** *an iron will* **uncompromising**, unrelenting, unyielding, unbending, resolute, resolved, determined, firm, unwavering, rigid, steadfast.
– OPPOSITES flexible.
▶ v. *she irons his shirts* **press**.
☐ **iron something out 1** *John had ironed out all the minor snags* **resolve**, straighten out, sort out, clear up, settle, put right, solve, remedy, rectify; informal fix, mend. **2** *ironing out differences in national systems* **eliminate**, eradicate, erase, get rid of; harmonize, reconcile.

WORD LINKS

ferric, ferrous relating to or containing iron

---

ironic adj. **1** *Edward's tone was ironic* **sarcastic**, sardonic, dry, caustic, sharp, stinging, scathing, acerbic, acid, bitter, trenchant, mordant, cynical; mocking, satirical, scoffing, derisory, derisive, scornful; Brit. informal sarky. **2** *it's ironic that I've ended up writing* **paradoxical**, incongruous, odd, strange, peculiar, unexpected.
– OPPOSITES sincere.

irony n. **1** *that note of irony in her voice* **sarcasm**, sardonicism, dryness, causticity, sharpness, acerbity, bitterness, trenchancy, mordancy, cynicism; mockery, satire, ridicule, derision, scorn; Brit. informal sarkiness. **2** *the irony of the situation* **paradox**, incongruity, incongruousness, peculiarity.
– OPPOSITES sincerity.

irradiate v. **illuminate**, light (up), cast light on, brighten, shine on; literary illumine.

irrational adj. **unreasonable**, illogical, groundless, baseless, unfounded, unjustifiable; absurd, ridiculous, ludicrous, silly, foolish, senseless.
– OPPOSITES logical.

irreconcilable adj. **1** *irreconcilable views* **incompatible**, at odds, at variance, conflicting, clashing, antagonistic, mutually exclusive, diametrically opposed; disparate, variant, dissimilar, poles apart; rare oppugnant. **2** *irreconcilable enemies* **implacable**, unappeasable, uncompromising,

inflexible; mortal, bitter, deadly, sworn, out-and-out.
– OPPOSITES compatible.

irrecoverable adj. **unrecoverable**, unreclaimable, irretrievable, irredeemable, unsalvageable, gone for ever; written off.

irrefutable adj. **indisputable**, undeniable, unquestionable, beyond question, beyond doubt, incontrovertible, incontestable; conclusive, definite, definitive, decisive, certain, positive.

irregular adj. **1** *irregular features | an irregular coastline* **asymmetrical**, non-uniform, uneven, crooked, misshapen, lopsided, twisted; jagged, ragged, serrated, indented. **2** *irregular surfaces* **rough**, bumpy, uneven, pitted, rutted; lumpy, knobbly, gnarled. **3** *an irregular heartbeat* **inconsistent**, unsteady, uneven, fitful, patchy, variable, varying, changeable, changing, inconstant, erratic, unstable, unsettled, spasmodic, intermittent, fluctuating. **4** *irregular financial dealings* **against the rules**, out of order, improper, illegitimate, unscrupulous, unethical, unprofessional, unacceptable, beyond the pale; informal shady; Brit. informal not cricket; Austral./NZ informal over the fence. **5** *an irregular army* **guerrilla**, underground; paramilitary; partisan, mercenary.
– OPPOSITES straight, smooth.
▸ n. *gun-toting irregulars* **guerrilla**, underground fighter; paramilitary; resistance fighter, partisan, mercenary.

irregularity n. **1** *the irregularity of the coastline* **asymmetry**, non-uniformity, unevenness, crookedness, lopsidedness; jaggedness, raggedness, indentation. **2** *the irregularity of the surface* **roughness**, bumpiness, unevenness; lumpiness, knobbliness. **3** *irregularities in the concrete* **bump**, lump, bulge, hump, protuberance, kink; hole, hollow, pit, crater, depression, dip, indentation, dent; crack, chink, fissure, cranny. **4** *the irregularity of the bus service* **inconsistency**, unsteadiness, unevenness, fitfulness, patchiness, inconstancy, instability, variability, changeableness, fluctuation, unpredictability, unreliability. **5** *financial irregularities* **impropriety**, wrongdoing, misconduct, dishonesty, corruption, immorality; informal shadiness, crookedness. **6** *staff noted any irregularity in operation* **abnormality**, unusualness, strangeness, oddness, singularity, atypicality, anomaly, deviation, aberration, peculiarity, idiosyncrasy.

irregularly adv. **1** *irregularly hexagonal* **asymmetrically**, unevenly. **2** *his heart was beating irregularly* **erratically**, intermittently, in/by fits and starts, fitfully, patchily, haphazardly, unsystematically, unmethodically, inconsistently, unsteadily, unevenly, variably, spasmodically, discontinuously, inconstantly.

irrelevance n. **inapplicability**, unrelatedness, inappropriateness, inappositeness; unimportance, inconsequentiality, insignificance; formal impertinence.

irrelevant adj. **beside the point**, immaterial, not pertinent, not germane, off the subject, unconnected, unrelated, peripheral, extraneous, inapposite; unimportant, inconsequential, insignificant, trivial; formal impertinent.

irreligious adj. **atheistic**, unbelieving, non-believing, agnostic, heretical, faithless, godless, ungodly, impious, profane, infidel, barbarian, heathen, pagan; rare nullifidian.
– OPPOSITES pious.

irreparable adj. **irreversible**, unrectifiable, irrevocable, unrestorable, irrecoverable, unrepairable, beyond repair.
– OPPOSITES repairable.

irreplaceable adj. **unique**, unrepeatable, incomparable, unparalleled; treasured, prized, cherished.

irrepressible adj. **1** *the desire for freedom is irrepressible* **inextinguishable**, unquenchable, uncontainable, uncontrollable, indestructible, undying, everlasting. **2** *his irrepressible personality* **ebullient**, exuberant, buoyant, sunny, breezy, jaunty, light-hearted, high-spirited, vivacious, animated, full of life, lively; Brit. Tiggerish; informal bubbly, bouncy, peppy, chipper, chirpy, full of beans.

irreproachable adj. **impeccable**, exemplary, model, immaculate, outstanding, exceptional, admirable, perfect; above/beyond reproach, blameless, faultless, flawless, unblemished, untarnished, spotless; informal squeaky clean, whiter than white.
– OPPOSITES reprehensible.

irresistible adj. **1** *her irresistible smile* **tempting**, enticing, alluring, inviting, seductive; attractive, desirable, fetching, appealing, captivating, beguiling, enchanting. **2** *an irresistible impulse* **uncontrollable**, overwhelming, overpowering, compelling, compulsive, irrepressible, ungovernable, driving, forceful.

irresolute adj. **indecisive**, hesitant, vacillating, equivocating, dithering, wavering, shilly-shallying; ambivalent, blowing hot and cold, in two minds, in a dilemma, in a quandary, torn; doubtful, in doubt, unsure, uncertain, undecided; informal sitting on the fence.
– OPPOSITES decisive.

irresolution n. **indecisiveness**, indecision, irresoluteness, hesitancy, hesitation; doubt, doubtfulness, unsureness, uncertainty; vacillation, equivocation, wavering, shilly-shallying, blowing hot and cold, dithering, temporizing, temporization; Brit. havering, humming and hawing; informal dilly-dallying, sitting on the fence.

irrespective adj. **regardless of**, without regard to/for, notwithstanding, whatever, no matter what, without consideration of; informal irregardless of.

irresponsible adj. **1** *irresponsible behaviour* **reckless**, rash, careless, thoughtless, incautious, unwise, imprudent, ill-advised, injudicious, misguided, unheeding, hasty, overhasty, precipitate, precipitous, foolhardy, impetuous, impulsive, devil-may-care, hot-headed, delinquent; N. Amer. derelict. **2** *an irresponsible teenager* **immature**, naive, foolish, hare-brained; unreliable, undependable, untrustworthy, flighty, giddy, scatterbrained, harum-scarum.
– OPPOSITES sensible.

irretrievable adj. **irreversible**, unrectifiable, irremediable, irrecoverable, irreparable, unrepairable, beyond repair.
– OPPOSITES reversible.

irreverent adj. **disrespectful**, disdainful, scornful, contemptuous, derisive, disparaging; impertinent, cheeky, flippant, rude, discourteous.
– OPPOSITES respectful.

irreversible adj. **irreparable**, unrepairable, beyond repair, unrectifiable, irremediable, irrevocable, permanent; unalterable, unchangeable, immutable; Law peremptory.

irrevocable adj. **irreversible**, unalterable, unchangeable, immutable, final, binding, permanent; Law peremptory.

irrigate v. **water**, bring water to, soak, flood, inundate.

irritability n. **irascibility**, tetchiness, testiness, touchiness, grumpiness, moodiness, grouchiness, a (bad) mood, cantankerousness, curmudgeonliness, bad temper, short temper, ill humour, peevishness, crossness, fractiousness, pettishness, crabbiness, waspishness, prickliness; Brit. informal shirtiness, stroppiness, rattiness; N. Amer. informal crankiness, orneriness; Austral./NZ informal snakiness; literary choler.

irritable adj. **bad-tempered**, short-tempered, irascible, tetchy, testy, touchy, grumpy, grouchy, moody, crotchety, in a (bad) mood, cantankerous, curmudgeonly, ill-tempered, ill-humoured, peevish, cross, fractious, pettish, crabby, waspish, prickly, splenetic, dyspeptic, choleric; informal snappish, snappy, on a short fuse; Brit. informal shirty, stroppy, ratty; N. Amer. informal cranky, ornery; Austral./NZ informal snaky.
– OPPOSITES good-humoured.

irritant n. **annoyance**, (source of) irritation, thorn in someone's side/flesh, pest, bother, trial, torment, plague, inconvenience, nuisance; informal aggravation, peeve, pain (in the neck), headache; N. Amer. informal nudnik, burr under someone's saddle; Austral./NZ informal nark.

irritate v. **1** *the smallest things may irritate you* **annoy**, vex, make angry, make cross, anger, exasperate, irk, gall, pique, nettle, put out, antagonize, get on someone's nerves, try someone's patience, ruffle someone's feathers, make someone's hackles rise; infuriate, madden, provoke; Brit. rub up the wrong way; informal aggravate, miff, rile,

needle, get to, bug, hack off, get under someone's skin, get/put someone's back up, get up someone's nose, give someone the hump, drive mad/crazy, drive round the bend/twist, drive up the wall; Brit. informal wind up, get on someone's wick; N. Amer. informal tee off, tick off, rankle, ride, gravel. **2** *some sand irritated my eyes* **inflame**, aggravate, hurt, chafe, abrade, scratch, scrape, graze.
– OPPOSITES pacify, soothe.

irritated adj. **annoyed**, cross, angry, vexed, exasperated, irked, piqued, nettled, put out, disgruntled, in a bad mood, in a temper, testy, huffy, in a huff, aggrieved; irate, infuriated, incensed; informal aggravated, peeved, miffed, mad, riled, hacked off, browned off, fed up, hot under the collar; Brit. informal cheesed off, brassed off, not best pleased, ratty, shirty; N. Amer. informal teed off, ticked off, sore; Austral./NZ informal snaky, crook; old use snuffy, wroth.
– OPPOSITES good-humoured.

irritating adj. **annoying**, infuriating, exasperating, maddening, trying, tiresome, vexing, vexatious, irksome, galling; informal aggravating.

irritation n. **1** *she tried not to show her irritation* **annoyance**, exasperation, vexation, indignation, impatience, crossness, displeasure, chagrin, pique; anger, rage, fury, wrath; informal aggravation; literary ire. **2** *I realize my presence is an irritation for you* **irritant**, annoyance, thorn in someone's side/flesh, bother, trial, torment, plague, inconvenience, nuisance; informal aggravation, pain (in the neck), headache; N. Amer. informal nudnik, burr under someone's saddle; Austral./NZ informal nark.
– OPPOSITES delight.

island n. **isle**, islet; atoll; Brit. holm; **(islands)** archipelago.

> **WORD LINKS**
> **insular** relating to an island

isolate v. **1** *she isolated herself from her family* | *the contaminated area was isolated* **separate**, set/keep apart, segregate, detach, cut off, shut away, divorce, alienate, distance; cloister, seclude; cordon off, seal off, close off, fence off. **2** *the laser beam can isolate the offending vehicles* **identify**, single out, pick out, point out, spot, recognize, distinguish, pinpoint, locate.
– OPPOSITES integrate.

isolated adj. **1** *isolated communities* **remote**, out of the way, outlying, off the beaten track, secluded, lonely, in the back of beyond, godforsaken, inaccessible, cut-off; N. Amer. in the backwoods, lonesome; Austral./NZ in the backblocks, in the booay; informal in the middle of nowhere, in the sticks; N. Amer. informal jerkwater, in the tall timbers; Austral./NZ informal Barcoo, beyond the black stump; old use unapproachable. **2** *he lived a very isolated existence* **solitary**, lonely, companionless, friendless; secluded, cloistered, segregated, unsociable, reclusive, hermitic; N. Amer. lonesome. **3** *an isolated incident* **unique**,

lone, solitary; unusual, uncommon, exceptional, anomalous, abnormal, untypical, freak; informal one-off.
– OPPOSITES accessible, sociable, common.

isolation n. **1** *patients who need isolation* **separation**, segregation, seclusion, keeping apart. **2** *their feeling of isolation* **solitariness**, loneliness, friendlessness. **3** *the isolation of some mental hospitals* **remoteness**, seclusion, inaccessibility.
– OPPOSITES contact.

issue n. **1** *the committee discussed the issue* **matter (in question)**, question, point (at issue), affair, case, subject, topic; problem, bone of contention. **2** *the issue of a special stamp* **issuing**, publication, publishing; circulation, distribution, supplying; appearance. **3** *the latest issue of our magazine* **edition**, number, instalment, copy. **4** Law *she died without issue* **offspring**, descendants, heirs, successors, children, progeny, family; informal kids; old use seed, fruit (of one's loins). **5** *an issue of blood* **discharge**, emission, release, outflow, outflowing, outflux; secretion, emanation, exudation, effluence; technical efflux. **6** dated *a favourable issue* **(end) result**, outcome, consequence, upshot, conclusion, end.
▸ v. **1** *the minister issued a statement* **send out**, put out, release, deliver, publish, announce, broadcast, communicate, circulate, distribute, disseminate. **2** *the captain issued the crew with guns* **supply**, provide, furnish, arm, equip, fit out, rig out, kit out; informal fix up. **3** *savoury smells issued from the kitchen* **emanate**, emerge, exude, flow (out/forth), pour (out/forth); be emitted. **4** *large profits might issue from the deal* **result**, follow, ensue, stem, spring, arise, proceed; be the result of, be produced by.
– OPPOSITES withdraw.
▫ **at issue** in question, in dispute, under discussion, under consideration, for debate.
take issue disagree, be in dispute, be in

contention, be at variance, be at odds, argue, quarrel; challenge, dispute, (call into) question; old use disaccord.

itch n. **1** *I have an itch on my back* irritation, itchiness, tingling. **2** informal *the itch to travel* **longing**, yearning, craving, ache, hunger, thirst, urge, hankering; wish, fancy, desire; informal yen.
▸ v. **1** *my chilblains really itch* be itchy, tingle. **2** informal *he itched to do something to help* **long**, yearn, ache, burn, crave, hanker for/after, hunger, thirst, be eager, be desperate; want, wish, desire, fancy, set one's sights on; informal have a yen, be dying, be gagging.

item n. **1** *an item of farm equipment | the main item in a badger's diet* **thing**, article, object, artefact, piece, product; element, constituent, component, ingredient. **2** *the meeting discussed the item* **issue**, matter, affair, case, situation, subject, topic, question, point. **3** *a news item* **report**, story, account, article, piece, write-up, bulletin, feature. **4** *items in the profit and loss account* **entry**, record, statement, listing.

itemize v. **1** *Steinburg itemized thirty-two design faults* **list**, catalogue, inventory, record, document, register, detail, specify, identify; enumerate, number. **2** *an itemized bill* **analyse**, break down, split up.

iterate v. **repeat**, recapitulate, go over/ through again; say again, restate, reiterate; informal recap; old use ingeminate.

itinerant adj. *itinerant traders* **travelling**, peripatetic, wandering, roving, roaming, touring, nomadic, Gypsy, migrant, vagrant, vagabond, of no fixed address/abode.
▸ n. *an itinerants' lodging house* **traveller**, wanderer, roamer, rover, nomad, Gypsy, migrant, transient, drifter, vagabond, vagrant, tramp; dated bird of passage.

itinerary n. **(planned) route**, journey, way, road; travel plan, schedule, timetable, programme, tour.

Wordfinder

Index

Wordfinder

Wordfinder

Animals

Amphibians

axolotl	fire salamander	horned toad	newt	tree frog
bullfrog	flying frog	marsh frog	salamander	
cane toad	frog	natterjack toad	toad	

Birds

adjutant bird	dipper	hen harrier	noddy	seagull
albatross	diver	heron	nuthatch	secretary bird
antbird	dodo	herring gull	ortolan	shag
Arctic tern	dotterel	hobby	osprey	shearwater
auk	dove	honeyguide	ostrich	shelduck
avocet	duck	hooded crow	ouzel	shoebill
bald eagle	dunlin	hoopoe	owl	shoveler
barnacle goose	dunnock	hornbill	oystercatcher	shrike
barn owl	eagle	horned owl	parakeet	siskin
bateleur eagle	eagle owl	house martin	parrot	skua
Bewick's swan	egret	house sparrow	partridge	skylark
bird of paradise	eider duck	hummingbird	peacock	snipe
bittern	emperor	ibis	peafowl	snow bunting
blackbird	penguin	jackdaw	peewit	snow goose
blackcap	emu	jay	pelican	snowy owl
black swan	falcon	kestrel	penguin	song thrush
bluebird	fantail	kingfisher	peregrine falcon	sparrow
blue tit	fieldfare	king penguin	petrel	sparrowhawk
booby	finch	kite	phalarope	spoonbill
bowerbird	flamingo	kittiwake	pheasant	starling
brambling	flycatcher	kiwi	pigeon	stonechat
broadbill	frigate bird	kookaburra	pilot bird	stone curlew
brown owl	fulmar	lammergeier	pintail	stork
budgerigar	gannet	lapwing	pipit	storm petrel
bullfinch	godwit	lark	plover	sunbird
bunting	goldcrest	laughing jackass	ptarmigan	swallow
bustard	golden eagle	linnet	puffin	swan
butcher-bird	goldfinch	little grebe	quail	swift
buzzard	goose	little owl	rail	tawny owl
Canada goose	goshawk	long-tailed tit	raven	teal
canary	great auk	lorikeet	razorbill	tern
capercaillie	great crested	lovebird	red kite	thrush
caracara	grebe	lyrebird	redpoll	tit
cassowary	great tit	macaw	redshank	titmouse
chaffinch	grebe	magpie	redstart	toucan
chicken	green	mallard	redwing	treecreeper
chiffchaff	woodpecker	mandarin duck	reed bunting	turkey
chough	greenfinch	marabou stork	reed warbler	turkey vulture
coal tit	greenshank	marsh harrier	rhea	turtle dove
cockatiel	greylag goose	martin	rhinoceros bird	vulture
cockatoo	griffon vulture	meadowlark	ringdove	wagtail
condor	grouse	merlin	ring ouzel	wallcreeper
coot	guillemot	mistle thrush	roadrunner	warbler
cormorant	guineafowl	moa	robin	waxbill
corncrake	gull	mockingbird	rook	waxwing
crane	gyrfalcon	moorhen	ruddy duck	weaver bird
crossbill	harrier	mute swan	ruff	wheatear
crow	hawfinch	mynah bird	sand martin	whinchat
cuckoo	hawk	nighthawk	sandpiper	whippoorwill
curlew	hawk owl	nightingale	scops owl	whitethroat
dabchick	hedge sparrow	nightjar	screech owl	whooping crane
darter	hen		sea eagle	whydah

Wordfinder

wigeon
willow warbler

woodchat
woodcock

woodlark
woodpecker

wood pigeon
wren

wryneck
yellowhammer

Butterflies and Moths

Adonis blue
argus
atlas moth
birdwing
blue
brimstone
brown
buff-tip
burnet
cabbage moth
cabbage white
Camberwell
  beauty
chalkhill blue
cinnabar
clearwing
clouded yellow

codlin/codling
  moth
comma
common heath
copper
dagger
death's head
  hawkmoth
drinker
eggar
emerald
emperor
ermine
fritillary
gatekeeper
goat moth
grayling
gypsy moth

hairstreak
hawkmoth
heath
io moth
lackey
lappet
leopard moth
lobster moth
luna moth
magpie moth
marbled white
meadow brown
merveille du jour
milkweed
monarch
morpho
Mother Shipton
mourning cloak

noctuid
nymphalid
oak eggar
old lady
painted lady
papilionid
peacock
  butterfly
peppered moth
plume moth
pug
purple emperor
puss moth
pyralid
red admiral
ringlet
satyrid
silk moth

silver Y
skipper
speckled wood
sulphur
swallowtail
swift
tiger moth
tortoiseshell
tortrix
tussock moth
underwing
vapourer
wall brown
wax moth
white admiral
white spot
yellow-tail

Crustaceans

acorn barnacle
barnacle
crab
crawfish
crayfish
crevette
fairy shrimp

fiddler crab
fish louse
freshwater
  crayfish
ghost crab
goose barnacle
hermit crab

horseshoe crab
king crab
king prawn
krill
land crab
langouste
langoustine

lobster
mitten crab
Norway lobster
prawn
sandhopper
shrimp
spider crab

spiny lobster
tiger prawn
woodlouse

Dinosaurs

allosaurus
ankylosaur
apatosaurus
brachiosaurus
brontosaurus
carnosaur

coelurosaur
deinonychus
diplodocus
dromaeosaur
duck-billed
  dinosaur

hadrosaur
iguanodon
megalosaurus
pliosaur
protoceratops
pteranodon

pterodactyl
raptor
saurischian
sauropod
seismosaurus
stegosaur

theropod
triceratops
tyrannosaurus
velociraptor

Fish

albacore
alewife
amberjack
anchovy
anemone fish
angelfish
angel shark
anglerfish
archerfish
balloonfish
bandfish
barbel
barracouta
barracuda
barramundi
basking shark
bass
beluga
bitterling

blackfish
bleak
blenny
blowfish
bluefin
bluefish
blue shark
boarfish
bonefish
bonito
bonnethead
bowfin
boxfish
bream
brill
brisling
brown trout
bullhead
burbot

butterfly fish
butterfly ray
carp
carpet shark
catfish
charr
chimera
chub
climbing perch
clingfish
clownfish
coalfish
cod
coelacanth
coley
conger eel
crappie
dab
dace

damselfish
darter
devil ray
dogfish
dorado
dory
Dover sole
dragonfish
eagle ray
eel
eelpout
electric eel
electric ray
fighting fish
filefish
flatfish
flathead
flounder
fluke

flying fish
flying gurnard
frogfish
garfish
garpike
goatfish
goby
goldfish
goosefish
gourami
grayling
great white
  shark
grenadier
grey mullet
grouper
grunion
gudgeon
guitarfish

gulper eel
gunnel
guppy
gurnard
haddock
hake
halfbeak
halibut
hammerhead
herring
hoki
humpback
  salmon
huss
icefish
John Dory
kingfish
koi carp
labyrinth fish
lamprey
lanternfish
leatherjacket
lemon sole
ling
loach
lumpsucker
lungfish
mackerel
mako
manta

marlin
megamouth
minnow
molly
monkfish
moonfish
moray eel
mudfish
mudminnow
mudskipper
mullet
needlefish
nurse hound
nurse shark
oarfish
orfe
parrotfish
perch
pickerel
pike
pikeperch
pilchard
pilotfish
pipefish
piranha
plaice
pollack
pomfret
porbeagle
porcupine fish

porgy
puffer fish
rabbitfish
rainbow trout
ray
redfish
red mullet
red snapper
ribbonfish
roach
rock bass
rockling
rudd
ruffe
sailfish
salmon
salmon trout
sand eel
sandfish
sand shark
sardine
sawfish
scad
scorpionfish
sea bass
sea bream
sea horse
sea perch
sea robin
sea trout

shad
shark
shark-sucker
sheepshead
shovelhead
silverside
skate
skipjack tuna
skipper
smelt
smooth hound
snake mackerel
snapper
snipefish
sockeye salmon
sole
sparling
spearfish
sprat
stargazer
stickleback
stingray
stonefish
sturgeon
sucker
sunfish
surgeonfish
swordfish
swordtail
tench

tetra
thornback
threadfin
thresher
tiger shark
tilapia
toadfish
tope
triggerfish
trout
tuna
tunny
turbot
walleye
weakfish
weever
whaler
whale shark
whitebait
whitefish
whiting
witch
wobbegong
wolf fish
wrasse
yellowfin
yellowtail
zander

Insects

alderfly
amazon ant
ant
ant lion
aphid
army ant
army worm
assassin bug
bark beetle
bedbug
bee
beetle
black ant
blackfly
blister beetle
blowfly
bluebottle
body louse
boll weevil
bombardier
  beetle
booklouse
borer
botfly
bulldog ant
bumblebee
bush cricket
butterfly
caddis fly
carpenter ant

carpenter bee
carpet beetle
carrion beetle
chafer
chigger
cicada
click beetle
cluster fly
cockchafer
cockroach
Colorado beetle
crab louse
crane fly
cricket
cuckoo bee
cuckoo wasp
daddy-long-legs
damselfly
darter
death-watch
  beetle
devil's coach-
  horse
dragonfly
driver ant
drone fly
dung beetle
dung fly
earwig
filaria

fire ant
firefly
flea
fluke
fly
froghopper
fruit fly
furniture beetle
gadfly
gall wasp
glow-worm
gnat
goliath beetle
grasshopper
greenbottle
greenfly
groundhopper
head louse
Hercules beetle
honey ant
honeybee
hornet
horsefly
housefly
hoverfly
jewel beetle
lacewing
ladybird
lantern fly
leafcutter ant

leafcutter bee
leafhopper
leaf miner
leatherjacket
leech
locust
longhorn beetle
louse
mantis
mason bee
May bug
mayfly
meal beetle
mealy bug
midge
mining bee
mosquito
moth
oil beetle
pharaoh ant
phylloxera
pond skater
praying mantis
rhinoceros
  beetle
robber fly
sandfly
sawfly
scale insect
scarab

scorpion fly
sexton beetle
silverfish
springtail
stag beetle
stick insect
stink bug
stonefly
termite
thrips
thunderbug
thunderfly
toxocara
treehopper
tsetse fly
velvet ant
warble fly
wasp
water beetle
water boatman
water scorpion
weevil
whirligig
white ant
whitefly
witchetty grub
woodwasp

Wordfinder

Wordfinder

Mammals

aardvark
alpaca
angora
anteater
antelope
ape
armadillo
ass
aurochs
baboon
badger
baleen whale
Barbary ape
bat
beaked whale
bear
beaver
beluga
bison
black bear
blue whale
boar
bobcat
bottlenose
 dolphin
bottlenose
 whale
bowhead whale
brown bear
buffalo
bushbaby
camel
capuchin
 monkey
capybara
caracal
caribou
cat
chamois
cheetah
chimpanzee
chinchilla
chipmunk
civet
coati
colobus
colugo

cougar
cow
coyote
coypu
deer
dingo
dog
dolphin
donkey
dormouse
dromedary
duck-billed
 platypus
dugong
duiker
echidna
eland
elephant
elephant seal
elk
ermine
fallow deer
fennec
ferret
fin whale
flying fox
fox
fur seal
galago
gaur
gayal
gazelle
gemsbok
gerbil
gibbon
giraffe
gnu
goat
gopher
gorilla
grampus
grey seal
grizzly bear
guinea pig
hamadryas
hamster
hanuman langur

hare
harp seal
hartebeest
hedgehog
hippo
hog
honey bear
hooded seal
horse
howler monkey
humpback
 whale
hyena
hyrax
ibex
impala
jackal
jaguar
jaguarundi
killer whale
kinkajou
Kodiak bear
kudu
langur
laughing hyena
lemming
lemur
leopard
leopard seal
lion
llama
loris
lynx
macaque
manatee
mandrill
margay
marmoset
marsupial
marten
meerkat
mink
minke whale
mole
mongoose
monkey
monk seal

moose
mountain goat
mountain lion
mouse
mule
muntjac
musk deer
musk ox
narwhal
ocelot
okapi
onager
opossum
orang-utan
orca
oryx
otter
ox
panda
pangolin
panther
peccary
pig
pika
pilot whale
pine marten
pipistrelle
platypus
polar bear
polecat
porcupine
porpoise
possum
potto
proboscis
 monkey
puma
rabbit
raccoon
rat
red deer
red panda
reindeer
rhesus monkey
rhinoceros
right whale
roe deer

rorqual
sable
sea cow
sea elephant
seal
sea lion
sei whale
serval
sheep
shrew
skunk
sloth
sloth bear
snow leopard
spectacled bear
sperm whale
spider monkey
spiny anteater
springbok
squirrel
squirrel monkey
stoat
sun bear
tamarin
tapir
tarsier
tiger
toothed whale
vampire bat
vervet monkey
vole
walrus
wapiti
warthog
waterbuck
water buffalo
weasel
whale
white whale
wild boar
wildcat
wildebeest
wisent
wolverine
yak
zebra
zebu

Marsupials

antechinus
bandicoot
bettong
bilby
brushtail
brushtail possum
cuscus

dasyure
dibbler
dunnart
flying phalanger
glider
kangaroo
koala

mulgara
numbat
opossum
pademelon
phalanger
planigale
possum

potoroo
quokka
quoll
rat kangaroo
ringtail
Tasmanian devil
Tasmanian tiger

thylacine
wallaby
wallaroo
wombat
yapok

Reptiles

adder
alligator

anaconda
asp

axolotl
basilisk

bearded dragon
black mamba

blind snake
blindworm

boa constrictor
boomslang
bull snake
bushmaster
caiman
chameleon
coachwhip
cobra
colubrid
constrictor
copperhead
coral snake
corn snake
crocodile
death adder

diamondback
  terrapin
Egyptian cobra
fer de lance
flying lizard
frilled lizard
Gaboon viper
galliwasp
garter snake
gecko
gharial
giant tortoise
Gila monster
glass lizard
grass snake

green snake
green turtle
hamadryad
hawksbill
hognose snake
horned toad
iguana
indigo snake
king cobra
Komodo dragon
leatherback
lizard
loggerhead
  turtle
mamba

moloch
monitor lizard
pit viper
puff adder
python
rat snake
rattlesnake
reticulated
  python
rinkhals
sea snake
sidewinder
skink
slider
slow-worm

smooth snake
snake
taipan
terrapin
tokay
tortoise
tuatara
turtle
viper
water moccasin
water snake
whip snake

Shellfish and other Molluscs

abalone
angel wings
argonaut
auger shell
cephalopod
chiton
clam
cockle
conch
cone shell
cowrie
cuttlefish
dog whelk

dove shell
duck mussel
edible snail
gaper
gastropod
geoduck
giant clam
harp shell
helmet
jewel box
lamp shell
limpet
mitre

murex
mussel
nautilus
nerite
nudibranch
octopus
ormer
oyster
paper nautilus
paua
pearl oyster
periwinkle
piddock

pteropod
quahog
ramshorn snail
razor shell
scallop
sea butterfly
sea hare
sea slug
shipworm
slug
snail
softshell clam
squid

teredo
tooth shell
triton
turret shell
tusk shell
wedge shell
wentletrap
whelk
winkle

Spiders and other Arachnids

bird-eating
  spider
black widow
camel spider
chigger
crab spider

false scorpion
funnel-web
  spider
harvestman
harvest mite
itch mite

jigger
mite
money spider
raft spider
redback
red spider mite

scorpion
spider mite
sun spider
tarantula
tick
trapdoor spider

whip scorpion
wolf spider

Male and Female Animals

antelope: *buck,*
  doe
badger: *boar,*
  sow
bear: *boar, sow*
bird: *cock, hen*
buffalo: *bull,*
  cow
cat: *tom, queen*
cattle: *bull, cow*
chicken: *cock,*
  hen

deer: *stag, doe*
dog: *dog, bitch*
donkey: *jackass,*
  jenny
duck: *drake,*
  duck
elephant: *bull,*
  cow
ferret: *jack, gill*
fish: *cock, hen*
fox: *dog, vixen*

goat: *billy goat,*
  nanny
goose: *gander,*
  goose
hare: *buck, doe*
horse: *stallion,*
  mare
kangaroo: *buck,*
  doe
leopard:
  leopard,
  leopardess

lion: *lion, lioness*
lobster: *cock,*
  hen
otter: *dog, bitch*
peafowl:
  peacock,
  peahen
pheasant: *cock,*
  hen
pig: *boar, sow*
rabbit: *buck,*
  doe

seal: *bull, cow*
sheep: *ram, ewe*
swan: *cob, pen*
tiger: *tiger,*
  tigress
weasel: *boar,*
  cow
whale: *bull, cow*
wolf: *dog, bitch*
zebra: *stallion,*
  mare

Young Animals

calf (*antelope,*
  buffalo, camel,
  cattle, elephant,
  elk, giraffe,
  rhinoceros,
  seal, whale)

chick (*chicken,*
  hawk,
  pheasant)
colt (*male horse*)

cub (*badger,*
  bear, fox,
  leopard, lion,
  tiger, walrus,
  wolf)

cygnet (*swan*)
duckling (*duck*)
eaglet (*eagle*)
elver (*eel*)
eyas (*hawk*)

fawn (*caribou,*
  deer)
filly (*female*
  horse)
foal (*horse,*
  zebra)

Wordfinder

fry (*fish*)
gosling (*goose*)
joey (*kangaroo, wallaby, possum*)
kid (*goat, roe deer*)

kit (*beaver, ferret, fox, mink, weasel*)
kitten (*cat, cougar, rabbit, skunk*)

lamb (*sheep*)
leveret (*hare*)
owlet (*owl*)
parr (*salmon*)
peachick (*peafowl*)

pickerel (*pike*)
piglet (*pig*)
pup (*dog, rat, seal, wolf*)
puppy (*coyote, dog*)

smolt (*salmon*)
squab (*pigeon*)
tadpole (*frog, toad*)
whelp (*dog, wolf*)

Collective Names for Animals

band (*gorillas*)
bask (*crocodiles*)
bellowing (*bullfinches*)
bevy (*roe deer, quails, larks, pheasants*)
bloat (*hippopotami*)
brood (*chickens*)
bury (*rabbits*)
busyness (*ferrets*)
charm (*finches*)
cloud (*gnats*)
covey (*partridges*)
crash (*rhinoceros*)

cry (*hounds*)
descent (*woodpeckers*)
down (*hares*)
drove (*bullocks*)
exaltation (*larks*)
flight (*birds*)
flock (*sheep*)
gaggle (*geese on land*)
herd (*cattle, elephants*)
hive (*bees*)
hover (*trout*)
kennel (*dogs*)
kindle (*kittens*)
knot (*toads*)
labour (*moles*)
leap (*leopards*)

litter (*kittens, pigs*)
mob (*kangaroos*)
murder (*crows*)
murmuration (*starlings*)
muster (*peacocks, penguins*)
obstinacy (*buffalo*)
pack (*hounds, grouse*)
pandemonium (*parrots*)
parade (*elephants*)
parliament (*owls*)

pod (*seals*)
pride (*lions*)
rookery (*rooks*)
safe (*ducks*)
school (*whales, dolphins, porpoises*)
shoal (*fish*)
shrewdness (*apes*)
siege (*herons*)
skein (*geese in flight*)
skulk (*foxes*)
sloth (*bears*)
span (*mules*)
stare (*owls*)
string (*horses*)
stud (*mares*)

swarm (*bees, flies*)
tiding (*magpies*)
trip (*goats*)
troop (*baboons*)
turmoil (*porpoises*)
turn (*turtles*)
unkindness (*ravens*)
watch (*nightingales*)
yoke (*oxen*)
zeal (*zebras*)

Art

Art Schools, Styles, and Movements

abstract expressionism
Aesthetic Movement
Art Deco
art nouveau
Arts and Crafts
avant-garde
baroque
Beaux Arts
Blaue Reiter
Bloomsbury Group
classicism

conceptual art
constructivism
cubism
Dada
De Stijl
expressionism
fauvism
Florentine school
futurism
Grand Manner
Group of Seven
Impressionism
Jugendstil
magic realism

Mannerism
metaphysical painting
minimalism
modernism
naive art
naturalism
Nazarenes
neoclassicism
neo-Impressionism
neoplasticism
neo-realism

Neue Sachlichkeit
op art
performance art
photorealism
plein-air painting
pop art
post-Impressionism
postmodernism
Pre-Raphaelitism
primitive art
Purism
realism

Renaissance art
rococo
romanticism
socialist realism
social realism
Sturm und Drang
suprematism
surrealism
symbolism
tenebrism
ukiyo-e

Art Techniques and Media

acrylic
action painting
airbrushing
aquarelle
aquatint
batik
ceramics
cityscape
cloisonné
collage

colour wash
Conté
distemper
divisionism
drawing
emulsion
enamel
encaustic
engraving
etching

finger-painting
fresco
frottage
gesso
glaze
gouache
grisaille
impasto
intaglio
kakemono

lino cut
lithography
marbling
marquetry
metalwork
mezzotint
miniature
montage
mosaic
mural

oil painting
painting
pastel
photography
photogravure
photomontage
pointillism
polychromy
screen printing
sculpture

scumbling　　　　sketching　　　　tapestry　　　　wood carving
secco　　　　　　stained glass　　tempera　　　　woodcut
silk-screen　　　sumi-e　　　　　wall painting　　wood engraving
　printing　　　　tachism　　　　watercolour

Body

Human Bones

ankle bone	femur	kneecap	pisiform bone	stapes
anvil	fibula	lacrimal	pubis	sternum
backbone	floating rib	lunate bone	rachis	stirrup
breastbone	frontal bone	malleus	radius	talus
calcaneus	hamate	mandible	rib	tarsal
capitate	hammer	maxilla	ribcage	tarsus
carpal	heel bone	metacarpal	sacrum	temporal bone
carpus	humerus	metatarsal	scaphoid	thigh bone
cheekbone	hyoid	navicular bone	scapula	tibia
clavicle	ilium	occipital bone	shin bone	triquetral
collarbone	incus	palatine bone	shoulder blade	ulna
cranium	innominate	parietal bone	skull	vertebra
cuboid	bone	patella	sphenoid	vertebral column
cuneiform bone	ischium	pelvis	spinal column	zygomatic bone
ethmoid	jawbone	phalanx	spine	

Organs of the Body

anus	ear	kidney	ovary	testicle
appendix	eye	larynx	pancreas	tongue
bladder	gall bladder	liver	rectum	tonsil
brain	genitals	lung	skin	trachea
breast	heart	mouth	spinal cord	uterus
colon	ileum	nose	spleen	vagina
duodenum	intestine	oesophagus	stomach	

Human Teeth

bicuspid	eye tooth	molar	premolar	wisdom tooth
canine	incisor	permanent	primary tooth	
cuspid	milk tooth	tooth	tricuspid	

Parts of the Ear

anvil	cochlea	hammer	organ of Corti	stirrup
auditory canal	eardrum	incus	outer ear	tympanic
auditory nerve	Eustachian tube	inner ear	pinna	membrane
auricle	hair cell	middle ear	stapes	vestibule

Parts of the Eye

aqueous	conjunctiva	eyelid	limbus	rod
humour	cornea	fovea	optic nerve	sclera
blind spot	dilator muscle	iris	orbit	socket
choroid	eyeball	lacrimal glands	pupil	tear glands
cone	eyelash	lens	retina	vitreous humour

Parts of the Heart

aortic valve	mitral valve	pulmonary	semilunar valve	vena cava
atrium	myocardium	artery	tricuspid valve	ventricle
epicardium	pericardium	pulmonary vein	upper chamber	

Clothing

Clothes

aloha shirt
anorak
apron
ascot
baggies
ballgown
bandanna
bandeau
Barbour
  (trademark)
basque
bathing costume
bedjacket
bell-bottoms
belt
Bermuda shorts
bib
biker jacket
bikini
blazer
bloomers
blouse
blouson
boa
board shorts
bodice
body
body stocking
bodysuit
body warmer
bolero
bolo tie
bomber jacket
boot
bootlace tie
bow tie
bra
braces
breeches
breeks
bumsters
Burberry
  (trademark)
burka/burkha/
  burqa
burnous
bustier
cagoule
cape
capri pants
cardigan
cargo pants
carpenter
  trousers
catsuit
chador
chaparajos
chaps

chemise
cheongsam
chinos
churidars
clamdiggers
coat
coat dress
coatee
combat trousers
cords
corduroys
cravat
crew neck
crinoline
crop top
culottes
cummerbund
cut-offs
cutaway
Daisy Dukes
dashiki
denim jacket
denims
dhoti
dinner jacket
dirndl
divided skirt
djellaba
djibba
dolman
domino
donkey jacket
doublet
dress
dressing gown
dress shirt
ducks
duffel coat
dungarees
fichu
flak jacket
flannels
flares
fleece
flying jacket
foulard
frock coat
fustanella
gabardine/
  gabardine
ghaghra
gilet
glove
gown
grandad shirt
grass skirt
greatcoat
guernsey

gymslip
hacking jacket
haik
hair shirt
halter neck
harem pants
hat
henley
hip-huggers
hipsters
hoody/hoodie
hose
hot pants
housecoat
hula skirt
hunting jacket
jacket
jeans
jeggings
jellaba
jerkin
jersey
jibba
jilbab
jodhpurs
joggers
jogging pants
jumper
jumpsuit
kaftan
kagoul
kameez
kebaya
kecks
kilt
kimono
knickers
leather jacket
leathers
lederhosen
leggings
leg warmers
leotard
loden
loincloth
loons
lumberjacket
lumberjack shirt
lungi
mac
macfarlane
mackintosh/
  macintosh
maillot
mandarin jacket
mankini
mantilla
mantle

mantlet
Mao jacket
mask
maternity dress
matinee coat
maxi
maxidress
mess jacket
middy blouse
midi
mini
minidress
miniskirt
mitt
mitten
morning coat
muff
muffler
neckerchief
Nehru jacket
nightdress
nightshirt
nor'wester
Norfolk jacket
obi
oilskins
overalls
overcoat
overtrousers
Oxford bags
palazzo pants
pantaloons
panties
pants
pantyhose
parka
pedal pushers
peignoir
pelisse
pencil skirt
peplum
pinafore
pinafore dress
pinny
plastron
plus fours
polo neck
polo shirt
poncho
puffball skirt
pullover
pyjamas
racerback
raglan
rah-rah skirt
raincoat
redingote
reefer jacket

robe
roll-neck
ruff
rugby shirt
sack dress
safari jacket
sailor suit
salopettes
salwar
Sam Browne
sandal
sari
sarong
sash
scarf
serape/sarape
shalwar
shawl
sheath dress
sheepskin
shell suit
shift dress
shirt dress
shirtwaister
shooting coat
shooting jacket
shorts
shrug
skinnies
skinny-rib
ski pants
skirt
skivvy
skort
slacks
slip
slipover
sloppy joe
smock
smoking jacket
sock
sports jacket
stirrup pants
stock
stocking
stole
string tie
suit
sundress
surcoat
surtout
sweater
sweatpants
sweatshirt
swimming
  costume
swimming
  trunks

swimsuit
swing coat
T-shirt
tabard
tailcoat
tank top
tee
tent dress
tie
tights

tippet
toga
top
topcoat
toreador pants
tracksuit
treggings
trench coat
trews
trousers

trouser suit
trunks
tube dress
tunic
turtleneck
tutu
tux/tuxedo
tweeds
twinset
ulster

underpants
underskirt
veil
vest
V-neck
waistcoat
waterproof
waxed jacket
wedding dress
windbreaker

windcheater
Wonderbra
(trademark)
woollens
woolly
wrap
yashmak
yukata

Footwear

ballet shoe
balmoral
boot
bootee
bovver boot
brogan
brogue
brothel creeper
buskin
carpet slipper
chappal
Chelsea boot
clog
court shoe
cowboy boot
Cuban heel

dap
deck shoe
Derby
desert boot
Dr Martens
(trademark)
elevator shoe
espadrille
flip-flop
galosh
ghillie/gillie
gladiator sandal
gumboot
half-boot
Hessian boot
high heels

high-low
high-top
hobnail boot
jackboot
jelly shoe
kitten heel
lace-up
loafer
moccasin
moon boot
mukluk
mule
napoleon
overboot
overshoe
Oxford

patten
peep-toe
penny loafer
platform
plimsoll
pump
sabot
sandal
shoe
slingback
slip-on
slipper
sneaker
snow boot
snowshoe
step-in

stiletto
tap shoe
tennis shoe
thong
top boot
track shoe
trainer
Turkish slipper
wader
walking boot
wedge
wellington boot
winkle-picker
zori

Headgear

Alice band
balaclava
balmoral
bandeau
baseball cap
beanie
bearskin
beaver hat
beret
biretta
boater
bobble hat
bonnet
bowler
busby
calash
cap
chaplet
circlet
cloche
cloth cap

cocked hat
coif
coolie hat
coronet
cowl
crash helmet
crown
deerstalker
derby
diadem
Dolly Varden
dunce's cap
Dutch cap
earmuffs
fedora
fez
flat cap
garland
glengarry
hairband
hard hat

headband
headscarf
headtie
helmet
high hat
hijab
homburg
hood
jester's cap
jockey cap
Juliet cap
keffiyeh
kepi
khimar
mantilla
mitre
mob cap
mortar board
nightcap
opera hat
panama

patka
peaked cap
picture hat
pillbox hat
pixie hat
poke bonnet
pork-pie hat
sailor hat
skullcap
slouch hat
snap-brim hat
snood
sola topi
sombrero
sou'wester
Stetson (trademark)
stocking cap
stovepipe hat
sun bonnet
sun hat
sun helmet

tam-o'-shanter
tarboosh
ten-gallon hat
tiara
top hat
topi
topper
toque
tricorne
trilby
triple crown
turban
veil
wideawake
wimple
wreath
zucchetto

Fabrics and Fibres

acetate
acrylic
Aertex (trademark)
alpaca
angora
asbestos
astrakhan
bafta

baize
barathea
barkcloth
batiste
Bedford cord
blanketing
bobbinet
bobbin lace

bombazine
Botany wool
bouclé
broadcloth
brocade
buckram
burlap
butter muslin

calico
cambric
camel hair
candlewick
canvas
cashmere
cavalry twill
challis

chambray
Chantilly lace
cheesecloth
chenille
cheviot
chiffon
chinchilla
chino

chintz
ciré
cloqué
coconut matting
coir
cord
corduroy
cotton
crêpe
crêpe de Chine
crépon
cretonne
crewel
Crimplene
  (trademark)
crinoline
crushed velvet
cupro
Dacron (trademark)
damask
denim
devoré
dimity
doeskin
Donegal tweed
drab
Dralon (trademark)
drill
duchesse lace
duchesse satin
duffel
dungaree
dupion
elastane
faille
felt
fishnet
flannel
flannelette
flax
fleece
flock
foulard
frieze

fustian
gaberdine/
  gabardine
gauze
georgette
gimp
gingham
Gore-tex
  (trademark)
gossamer
grasscloth
grenadine
grogram
grosgrain
gros point
guipure
haircloth
Harris tweed
  (trademark)
hemp
herringbone
hessian
holland
Honiton lace
hopsack
horsehair
huckaback
ikat
jaconet
jacquard
jean
jersey
jute
kapok
kemp
Kendal Green
kersey
kerseymere
khadi
khaki
kikoi
lace
lambswool
lamé

lawn
leathercloth
leatherette
leno
Lincoln green
linen
linsey-woolsey
lint
lisle
loden
lurex (trademark)
Lycra (trademark)
lyocell (trademark)
madras
marocain
marquisette
matting
melton
merino
microfibre
micromesh
mohair
moiré
moleskin
moquette
moreen
mousseline
mungo
muslin
nainsook
nankeen
needlecord
net
Nottingham lace
nylon
oakum
oilcloth
oilskin
organdie
organza
organzine
Orlon (trademark)
ottoman
paisley

panne velvet
pashmina
peau-de-soie
percale
petersham
pillow lace
pilot cloth
piqué
plaid
plush
plush velvet
point lace
polycotton
polyester
pongee
poplin
raffia
ramie
rayon
rep
ripstop
sackcloth
sacking
sailcloth
sarsenet
sateen
satin
satinette
saxony
sea-island cotton
seersucker
serge
shahtoosh
sharkskin
sheer
Shetland wool
shoddy
silk
sisal
slub
spandex
spun silk
stockinet
suede

surah
swansdown
tabaret
taffeta
tapestry
tarlatan
tarpaulin
tattersall
tatting
terry
Terylene
  (trademark)
ticking
tiffany
toile
toile de Jouy
torchon
towelling
tricot
tulle
tussore
tweed
twill
Valenciennes
Velcro (trademark)
velour
velvet
velveteen
vicuña
viscose
Viyella (trademark)
voile
waxcloth
webbing
whipcord
wild silk
wincey
winceyette
wool
worsted

Religious Clothing

alb
amice
biretta
cassock
chasuble
clerical collar

cope
cotta
cowl
dalmatic
dog collar
frock

Geneva bands
habit
hood
mitre
pallium
rochet

scapular
shovel hat
skullcap
soutane
stole
surplice

tallith
tippet
tunicle
wimple
yarmulke
zucchetto

Drinks

Alcoholic Drinks

absinthe
advocaat
aguardiente

alcopop
ale
amaretto

amontillado
amoroso
anisette

applejack
aquavit
arak

Armagnac
arrack
Asti

Auslese
Bandol
Bardolino
barley wine
Barolo
Barsac
Beaujolais
Beaune
beer
Beerenauslese
bitter
Blanc de blancs
bock
bourbon
brandy
brown ale
Bull's Blood
burgundy
Côtes du Rhône
Cabernet Franc
Cabernet
   Sauvignon
cachaca
Calvados
canary wine
cask beer
cassis
catawba
cava
Chablis
champagne
Chardonnay
chartreuse
Chenin Blanc
cherry brandy
Chianti
cider

claret
cocktail
cognac
cream sherry
crème de cacao
crème de
   menthe
curaçao
draught beer
Eiswein
Entre-Deux-Mers
fine champagne
fino
fraise
framboise
Frascati
Gamay
genever
Gewürztraminer
gin
ginger wine
grain whisky
grappa
Graves
Grenache
gueuze
hock
ice beer
Irish whiskey
Kabinett
keg beer
kirsch
kümmel
kvass
lager
Lambic
Lambrusco

Liebfraumilch
light ale
limoncello
liqueur
Madeira
Malbec
malmsey
malt
malt whisky
Malvasia
manzanilla
maraschino
Margaux
Marsala
mead
Médoc
Merlot
mescal
Meursault
mild
milk stout
Minervois
Monbazillac
Montepulciano
Montrachet
moscato
Moselle
Müller-Thurgau
Muscadet
muscat
muscatel
Niersteiner
noyau
Nuits St George
oloroso
Orvieto
ouzo

pale ale
palm wine
pastis
perry
Piesporter
Pils
Pilsner/Pilsener
Pinot Blanc
Pinot Grigio
Pinot Noir
port
porter
poteen
Pouilly-Fuissé
Pouilly-Fumé
Prosecco
raki
ratafia
real ale
retsina
Riesling
Rioja
Rosé d'Anjou
rum
rye
sack
Saint Émilion
sake
sambuca
Sancerre
Sangiovese
Saumur
Sauternes
Sauvignon
schnapps
Scotch whisky
scrumpy

Sekt
Sémillon
shandy
sherry
Shiraz
single malt
slivovitz
sloe gin
Soave
sour mash
Spätlese
spruce beer
Spumante
stout
Sylvaner
Syrah
Tavel
tequila
Tia Maria
Tokay
Traminer
Trebbiano
Trocken-
   beerenauslese
triple sec
Valpolicella
Verdelho
Verdicchio
vermouth
vinho verde
Viognier
vodka
Vouvray
whiskey
whisky
wine
Zinfandel

Non-alcoholic Drinks

Americano
arabica
Assam
babycino
barley water
bitter lemon
black tea
bohea
buttermilk
cafe au lait
cafe noir
caffè latte
caffè macchiato
camomile tea
cappuccino
carbonated
   water
Ceylon tea
cherryade
China tea
citron pressé

club soda
   (trademark)
cocoa
coffee
cola
cordial
cream soda
crush
dandelion and
   burdock
Darjeeling
decaf
decaffeinated
   coffee
drinking
   chocolate
Earl Grey
energy drink
espresso
filter coffee
fruit juice

fruit tea
ginger ale
ginger beer
Greek coffee
green tea
gunpowder tea
herbal tea
horchata
hot chocolate
iced tea
Indian tea
infusion
instant coffee
isotonic drink
jasmine tea
Keemun
Lapsang
   Souchong
lassi
latte
lemon tea

lemonade
limeade
malted milk
maté
milkshake
mineral water
mint tea
mocha
mochaccino
mocktail
oolong
orangeade
orange pekoe
orgeat
pekoe
peppermint tea
pouchong
prairie oyster
pressé
redbush
ristretto

robusta
root beer
rosehip tea
Russian tea
sarsaparilla
seltzer
sherbet
smoothie
soda water
soya milk
sports drink
spring water
squash
St Clements
tea
tisane
tonic water
Turkish coffee
yerba maté

Wordfinder

Cocktails and Mixed Drinks

Bellini
B52
Black Russian
black velvet
Bloody Mary
blue lagoon
brandy
 Alexander
Bronx
Buck's Fizz
caipirinha
champagne
 cocktail
cobbler

cosmopolitan
Cuba libre
daiquiri
egg flip
eggnog
G and T
gimlet
gin sling
grog
Harvey
 Wallbanger
highball
Irish coffee
John Collins

Kir
Kir royal
Long Island iced
 tea
mai tai
manhattan
margarita
Martini (trademark)
mint julep
mojito
negroni
nog
old-fashioned
pina colada

pink gin
pink lady
planter's punch
prairie oyster
punch
rattlesnake
rum and black
sangria
screwdriver
sea breeze
sex on the beach
sidecar
Singapore sling
slammer

snakebite
snowball
sour
spritzer
tequila slammer
tequila sunrise
toddy
Tom Collins
whisky mac
whisky sour
White Lady
White Russian
zombie

Food

Bread and Bread Rolls

bagel
baguette
bannock
bap
bara brith
barmbrack
barm cake
bloomer
bridge roll
brioche
bun

challah
chapatti
ciabatta
cob
cornbread
cottage loaf
crumpet
damper
farl
farmhouse loaf
flatbread

focaccia
French stick
fruit loaf
granary bread
 (trademark)
hoagie
kaiser
malt loaf
matzo
milk loaf
muffin

nan/naan
panettone
panino
paratha
petit pain
pikelet
pitta
pone
poppadom
pumpernickel
puri

quartern loaf
roti
rye
soda bread
sourdough
split tin
stollen

Cakes, Biscuits, and Desserts

affogato
angel cake
angel food cake
apfelstrudel
apple charlotte
apple pie
baba
baked Alaska
Bakewell tart
baklava
banana split
Banbury cake
banoffi/banoffee
 pie
Bath bun
Bath Oliver
Battenberg
beignet
Berliner
biscotti
Black Forest
 gateau
blancmange
bombe
bourbon
brack

brandy snap
bread pudding
bread-and-
 butter pudding
Brown Betty
brownie
bun
butterfly cake
cabinet pudding
cassata
charlotte
charlotte russe
cheesecake
chocolate chip
clafoutis
cobbler
compote
cookie
cracknel
cream cracker
cream puff
crème brûlée
crème caramel
crêpe
crêpe Suzette
crispbread

croquembouche
crumble
crumpet
cupcake
custard cream
custard pie
custard tart
Danish pastry
death by
 chocolate
devil's food cake
digestive
doughnut
drop scone
dumpling
Dundee cake
Eccles cake
eclair
egg custard
Eskimo pie
 (trademark)
Eve's pudding
fairy cake
fancy
flapjack
floating island

Florentine
flummery
fool
fortune cookie
frangipane
fruit cocktail
fruit salad
funnel cake
garibaldi
gateau
gelato
Genoa cake
gingerbread
ginger nut
ginger snap
granita
halwa
hasty pudding
hokey-pokey
hot cross bun
ice cream
Jaffa cake
jelly
junket
Knickerbocker
 Glory

kulfi
lady's finger
langue de chat
lardy cake
layer cake
lebkuchen
Lincoln biscuit
macaroon
Madeira cake
madeleine
maid of honour
marble cake
marie biscuit
marquise
matzo
meringue
milk pudding
millefeuille
mince pie
Mississippi mud
 pie
mousse
mousseline
muffin
Nice biscuit
oatcake

pancake
panettone
panforte
panna cotta
parfait
parkin
pashka
pavlova
peach Melba
petit beurre
petit four
plum duff
plum pudding
popover
pound cake
pretzel

profiterole
queen cake
queen of
  puddings
ratafia
red velvet cake
rice pudding
rock cake
roly-poly
rusk
Sachertorte
sago pudding
Sally Lunn
saltine
sandwich
savarin

scone
seed cake
semifreddo
semolina
ship's biscuit
shoo-fly pie
shortbread
shortcake
simnel cake
singing hinny
sorbet
soufflé
sponge
sponge pudding
spotted dick
steamed pudding

stollen
streusel
strudel
suet pudding
summer pudding
sundae
sweetmeal
  biscuit
Swiss roll
syllabub
tart
tarte Tatin
tartlet
tartufo
tipsy cake
tiramisu

torte
treacle tart
trifle
turnover
tutti-frutti
upside-down
  cake
Victoria sponge
waffle
water biscuit
water ice
whip
whoopie pie
yogurt
yule log
zabaglione

Cheeses

asiago
Bel Paese
  (trademark)
blue vinny
Boursin (trademark)
Brie
Caerphilly
Camembert
cantal
Chaumes
Cheddar
Cheshire
chèvre
cottage cheese

cream cheese
crowdie/crowdy
curd cheese
Danish blue
Derby
Dolcelatte
  (trademark)
Double
  Gloucester
Dunlop
Edam
Emmental
feta/fetta
fontina

fromage blanc
fromage frais
Gloucester
Gorgonzola
Gouda
Gruyère
halloumi
havarti
Jarlsberg
  (trademark)
Lancashire
Leicester
Limburger
Manchego

mascarpone
Monterey Jack
mozzarella
Neufchâtel
paneer/panir
Parmesan
Parmigiano
  Reggiano
pecorino
Pont l'Évêque
Port Salut
provolone
quark
Red Leicester

ricotta
Romano
Roquefort
  (trademark)
sage Derby
scamorza
Stilton
taleggio
Tilsit
Wensleydale

Fruit and Nuts

almond
apple
apricot
avocado
banana
betel nut
bilberry
blackberry
blackcurrant
blood orange
blueberry
boysenberry
Brazil nut
breadfruit
butternut
cantaloupe
Cape gooseberry
carambola
cashew
cashew apple
chayote
checkerberry
cherimoya
cherry
cherry plum
chestnut
chincapin

Chinese
  gooseberry
citron
clementine
cloudberry
cob
cobnut
coconut
cola nut
cowberry
crab apple
cranberry
currant
custard apple
damson
date
dewberry
durian
earthnut
elderberry
feijoa
fig
filbert
galia melon
goji berry
gooseberry
gourd

granadilla
grape
grapefruit
greengage
groundnut
guava
hazelnut
hognut
honeydew
  melon
huckleberry
jackfruit
jujube
kiwi fruit
kumquat
lemon
lime
loganberry
longan
loquat
lychee
macadamia
mammee
mandarin
mango
mangosteen
medlar

melon
minneola
monkey nut
mulberry
musk melon
naseberry
navel orange
nectarine
olive
orange
ortanique
papaya
passion fruit
pawpaw
peach
peanut
pear
pecan
persimmon
pineapple
pine nut
piñon
pistachio
plantain
plum
pomegranate
pomelo

prickly pear
pumpkin
quince
rambutan
raspberry
redcurrant
salmonberry
sapodilla
satsuma
serviceberry
sharon fruit
sloesorb
soursop
star anise
star apple
starfruit
strawberry
sugar apple
sweet chestnut
sweetsop
tamarillo
tamarind
tangelo
tangerine
tayberry
thimbleberry
tiger nut

Wordfinder

tomato	Victoria plum	watermelon	wineberry	
Ugli fruit	walnut	white currant	youngberry	
(trademark)	water chestnut	whortleberry		

Herbs and Spices

ajowan	cayenne pepper	fennel	lemon balm	rue
allspice	chervil	fenugreek	lemon grass	saffron
angelica	chicory	feverfew	lemon mint	sage
anise	chilli	five-spice	lovage	savory
aniseed	chives	powder	mace	sorrel
asafoetida	cilantro	galangal	marjoram	spearmint
balsam	cinnamon	garam masala	milk thistle	St John's wort
basil	clary	garlic	mint	star anise
bay leaf	clove	ginger	mustard	sumac
bergamot	coriander	ginseng	nutmeg	sweet balm
black pepper	cumin	grains of	oregano	sweet cicely
borage	curry powder	Paradise	paprika	tarragon
camomile	damiana	green pepper	parsley	thyme
caper	dill	hyssop	pepper	turmeric
caraway	dittany	jalapeño	peppermint	vanilla
cardamom	dong quai	juniper berry	pimento	white pepper
cassia	echinacea	lavender	rosemary	

Meals

afternoon tea	clambake	elevenses	luncheon	supper
banquet	continental	evening meal	meze	takeaway
barbecue	breakfast	feast	midday meal	tapas
barbie	cookout	finger buffet	packed lunch	tea
breakfast	cream tea	harvest supper	picnic	TV dinner
brunch	dinner	high tea	safari supper	wedding
buffet	dinner party	lunch	smorgasbord	breakfast

Pasta

agnolotti	farfalle	macaroni	radiatori	tagliolini
angel hair	farfalline	maltagliati	ravioli	tortelli
bucatini	fedelini	manicotti	rigatoni	tortellini
cannelloni	fettuccine	noodles	rotelle	tortelloni
capelli	fusilli	orecchiette	rotini	tortiglioni
capellini	gramigna	orzo	spaghetti	trenette
cappelletti	lasagne	pappardelle	spaghettini	vermicelli
conchiglie	linguine	penne	strozzapreti	ziti
ditalini	lumache	pipe	tagliatelle	

Sauces

apple sauce	carbonara sauce	hollandaise	pepper sauce	sweet-and-sour
Amatriciana	chasseur sauce	horseradish	pesto	sauce
arrabbiata	chaud-froid	sauce	pizzaiola sauce	Tabasco
Béarnaise sauce	cheese sauce	jus	ponzu	(trademark)
béchamel sauce	chilli sauce	ketchup	puttanesca	tartare sauce
baba ganoush	chimichurri	mint sauce	sauce	teriyaki sauce
barbecue sauce	cranberry sauce	mornay sauce	ragù	tomato ketchup
black bean sauce	curry sauce	mousseline sauce	salsa	tomato sauce
Bolognese sauce	demi-glace	nam pla	salsa verde	velouté
bordelaise sauce	fish sauce	onion sauce	satay sauce	vinaigrette
bread sauce	gravy	oyster sauce	soubise	white sauce
brown sauce	hoisin sauce	parsley sauce	soy sauce	Worcester sauce

Sweets and Confectionery

acid drop	barley sugar	bonbon	bullseye	candy
aniseed ball	boiled sweet	brittle	butterscotch	candyfloss

caramel
chew
chewing gum
chocolate
chocolate drop
coconut ice
comfit
cracknel
crystallized fruit
dolly mixtures
dragée

Easter egg
fondant
fruit drop
fruit gum
fruit pastille
fudge
gobstopper
gulab jamun
gumdrop
halva
humbug

jalebi
jelly
jelly baby
jelly bean
jujube
Kendal mint cake
laddu
liquorice
liquorice allsort
lollipop
lolly

marshmallow
marzipan
mint
nougat
pastille
pear drop
peppermint
peppermint
cream
Pontefract cake
praline

rock
sherbet
sherbet dip
sherbet lemon
sugared almond
toffee
toffee apple
truffle
Turkish delight
walnut whip
wine gum

Vegetables

ackee
acorn squash
aduki/adzuki
bean
alfalfa
artichoke
asparagus
aubergine
bamboo shoots
bean
beet
beetroot
black bean
black-eyed bean
borlotti bean
breadfruit
broad bean
broccoli
Brussels sprout
butter bean
butterhead
lettuce
butternut squash
cabbage
cabbage lettuce
calabrese
cannellini bean
capsicum

cardoon
carrot
cassava
cauliflower
cavolo nero
celeriac
celery
chard
chayote
chervil
chickpea
chicory
Chinese cabbage
Chinese leaves
choi sum
corn on the cob
cos lettuce
courgette
cress
cucumber
curly kale
cush-cush
custard marrow
eggplant
endive
escarole
fava bean
fennel

flageolet
French bean
garbanzo
garden pea
garlic
gherkin
globe artichoke
gourd
greens
haricot bean
Jerusalem
artichoke
kale
kidney bean
kohlrabi
leek
lentil
lettuce
lima bean
lollo rosso
mangetout
manioc
marrow
marrowfat pea
mooli
mung bean
mushroom
mustard

oak leaf lettuce
okra
onion
oyster plant
pak choi
parsnip
pea
pepper
petits pois
pimiento
pinto bean
plantain
potato
pumpkin
puy lentil
radicchio
radish
red cabbage
rocket
romaine
runner bean
rutabaga
salsify
samphire
savoy cabbage
scallion
scarlet runner
scorzonera

sea kale
shallot
snow pea
soybean
spinach
spinach beet
spring greens
spring onion
squash
string bean
sugar pea
sugar snap pea
swede
sweetcorn
sweet pepper
sweet potato
taro
tiger nut
tomato
turnip
vegetable
spaghetti
wasabi
water chestnut
watercress
waxpod
yam
zucchini

Wordfinder

Language and Literature

Literary Schools, Movements, and Groups

Acmeism
Aesthetic
Movement
Angry Young
Men
Augustans
beat generation
Bloomsbury
Group

Cavalier poets
classicism
Dadaism
expressionism
futurism
Georgian poets
Harlem
Renaissance
imagism

Lake Poets
Liverpool poets
magic realism
magical realism
metaphysical
poets
minimalism
modernism
naturalism

neo-realism
neoclassicism
Parnassians
post-
structuralism
postmodernism
primitivism
realism
romanticism

social realism
socialist realism
structuralism
Sturm und
Drang
surrealism
symbolism
Vorticism

Poetry Terms

alcaics
alcaic verse

alexandrine
alexandrine verse

anapaest
aubade

ballad
ballade

blank verse
bucolic

choriambus
clerihew
couplet
dactyl
dactylics
dactylic verse
decasyllabic
dimeter
distich
disyllable
dithyramb
doggerel
eclogue
elegiac couplet
elegy
epic

epigram
epithalamium
epode
epyllion
free verse
georgic
haiku
heptameter
heroic couplet
heroic verse
hexameter
Horatian ode
iamb
iambic
  pentameter
iambics

iambic verse
iambus
idyll
lay
Leonines
limerick
lyric
macaronics
macaronic verse
monody
nursery rhyme
ode
ottava rima
paeon
palinode
pastoral

pentameter
Petrarchan
  sonnet
poem
prothalamium
pyrrhic
rondeau
roundel
saga
sapphics
satire
sestina
sonnet
Spenserian
  stanza
spondee

terza rima
tetrameter
tribrach
trimeter
triolet
triplet
trisyllable
trochaics
trochaic verse
trochee
verse
villanelle
virelay

Types of Drama

burlesque
closet drama
closet play
comedy
comedy of
  manners
commedia
  dell'arte

docudrama
dumbshow
duologue
farce
Grand Guignol
Greek drama
improvisation
kabuki

kitchen-sink
  drama
masque
melodrama
mime
miracle play
monodrama
morality play

mummers' play
mystery play
nativity play
Noh
pantomime
passion play
play
romcom

soap opera
teleplay
tragedy
tragicomedy
two-hander

Types of Fiction

adventure story
Aga saga
allegory
antinovel
bedtime story
Bildungsroman
black comedy
blockbuster
bodice-ripper
bonkbuster
chick lit
cliffhanger
comedy

conte
crime story
detective story
dime novel
epic
epistolary novel
fable
fairy story
fairy tale
fanfic
fan fiction
fantasy
folk story

folk tale
ghost story
gothic novel
graphic novel
historical novel
horror story
legend
mystery
myth
noir
nouveau roman
novel
novelette

novella
parable
picaresque novel
police
  procedural
policier
roman-à-clef
romance
roman-fleuve
romantic novel
saga
science fiction
sci-fi

short story
spine-chiller
stream of
  consciousness
sword and
  sorcery
tear-jerker
thriller
urban myth
western
whodunnit

Phonetic Alphabet

Alpha
Bravo
Charlie
Delta
Echo
Foxtrot

Golf
Hotel
India
Juliet
Kilo
Lima

Mike
November
Oscar
Papa
Quebec
Romeo

Sierra
Tango
Uniform
Victor
Whisky
X-ray

Yankee
Zulu

Punctuation Marks

accent
apostrophe
asterisk
asterism
backslash
brace
bracket

caret
colon
comma
dagger
dash
diacritical mark
ellipsis

em dash
en dash
exclamation
  mark
full stop
hyphen
inverted comma

obelus
parenthesis
period
point
question mark
quotation mark
rule

semicolon
solidus
square bracket
stop
stroke
swung dash
virgule

Medicine

Branches of Medicine

allopathy
andrology
audiology
bariatrics
cardiology
chiropody
community
  medicine
dermatology

embryology
endocrinology
epidemiology
geriatrics
gynaecology
haematology
immunology
laryngology
nephrology

neurology
neurosurgery
nuclear medicine
obstetrics
oncology
ophthalmology
orthopaedics
orthotics
osteopathy

paediatrics
parasitology
pathology
pharmacology
physiotherapy
plastic surgery
proctology
prosthetics
psychiatry

psychosurgery
radiology
surgery
therapeutics
therapy
urology
venereology
veterinary
  medicine

Therapies

acupressure
acupuncture
Alexander
  technique
aromatherapy
art therapy
autogenic
  training
aversion therapy
Ayurveda
Bates method
behaviour
  therapy
behavioural
  therapy
bioenergetics

biofeedback
biotherapy
brachytherapy
bush medicine
chemotherapy
chiropractic
cognitive
  therapy
colour therapy
combination
  therapy
craniosacral
  therapy
crystal healing
cupping
drama therapy

ear candling
eurhythmics
faith healing
family therapy
gene therapy
gestalt therapy
group therapy
heat treatment
herbalism
homeopathy
hormone
  replacement
  therapy
hydropathy
hydrotherapy
hypnotherapy

immunotherapy
McTimoney
  chiropractic
mesotherapy
moxibustion
music therapy
naturopathy
neurolinguistic
  programming
occupational
  therapy
osteopathy
physiotherapy
psychotherapy
radiation
  therapy

radionics
radiotherapy
rebirthing
recreational
  therapy
reflexology
reiki
Rolfing
sex therapy
shiatsu
shock therapy
shock treatment
speech therapy
spiritual healing
zone therapy

Physical Illnesses

acne
ague
Aids
alopecia
altitude sickness
Alzheimer's
  disease
anaemia
angina
ankylosing
  spondylitis
ankylosis
anthrax
appendicitis
arthritis
asbestosis
asthma
ataxia
athlete's foot
avian flu
Bell's palsy
bends
beriberi
bilharzia
bird flu
blackwater fever
botulism

bronchitis
bubonic plague
bursitis
cachexia
cancer
carpal tunnel
  syndrome
cataract
cerebral palsy
chickenpox
cholera
chorea
chronic fatigue
  syndrome
cirrhosis
coeliac disease
cold
colic
colitis
common cold
consumption
coronary heart
  disease
cough
cowpox

Creutzfeldt-
  Jakob disease
  (CJD)
Crohn's disease
croup
cyanosis
cystic fibrosis
cystitis
decompression
  sickness
deep-vein
  thrombosis
  (DVT)
deficiency
  disease
dengue
dermatitis
dermatosis
diabetes
diabetes
  insipidus
diabetes mellitus
diarrhoea
diphtheria
diverticular
  disease

Down's
  syndrome
dysentery
Ebola
eclampsia
eczema
elephantiasis
emphysema
encephalitis
endocarditis
endometriosis
endometritis
enteritis
epilepsy
ergotism
erysipelas
fetal alcohol
  syndrome
fever
fibrositis
filariasis
flu
frozen shoulder
gangrene
gastric flu
gastritis
gastro-enteritis

German measles
gigantism
gingivitis
glandular fever
glaucoma
glue ear
glycaemia
goitre
gonorrhoea
gout
Gulf War
  syndrome
haemophilia
Hansen's disease
hay fever
heat stroke
hepatitis
hepatoma
hernia
herpes
herpes simplex
hives
Hodgkin's
  disease
hookworm
Huntington's
  disease

hydrocephalus
hydrophobia
hypertension
hypoglycaemia
hypothermia
hypoxia
impetigo
infantile
  paralysis
influenza
irritable bowel
  syndrome
ischaemia
jaundice
Kaposi's sarcoma
ketosis
kwashiorkor
laryngitis
Lassa fever
legionella
legionnaires'
  disease
leishmaniasis
leprosy
leptospirosis
leukaemia
listeria
listeriosis
lupus
lupus vulgaris
Lyme disease
lymphoma
malaria
mastitis
measles
meningitis
molluscum
  contagiosum

morning
  sickness
motor neuron
  disease
mountain
  sickness
multiple sclerosis
  (MS)
mumps
muscular
  dystrophy
myalgic
  encephalo-
  myelitis (ME)
narcolepsy
necrotizing
  fasciitis
nephritis
new variant
  Creutzfeldt-
  Jakob disease
  (nvCJD)
non-Hodgkin's
  lymphoma
oedema
ophthalmia
osteomyelitis
osteoporosis
pancreatitis
paratyphoid
Parkinson's
  disease
pellagra
pelvic
  inflammatory
  disease
pericarditis
peritonitis

pernicious
  anaemia
pertussis
phlebitis
pleurisy
pneumonia
poliomyelitis
porphyria
prickly heat
pruritus
psittacosis
psoriasis
puerperal fever
pulmonary
  emphysema
pyaemia
pyrexia
quinsy
rabies
radiation
  sickness
rash
repetitive strain
  injury (RSI)
retinitis
retinopathy
rheumatic fever
rheumatism
rheumatoid
  arthritis
rhinitis
rickets
ringworm
rubella
St Vitus's dance
salmonella
sarcoma
scabies

scarlet fever
schizophrenia
sciatica
scleritis
scleroderma
sclerosis
scrofula
scurvy
seasonal
  affective
  disorder (SAD)
sepsis
septicaemia
severe acute
  respiratory syn-
  drome (SARS)
sexually
  transmitted
  disease (STD)
shingles
sick building
  syndrome
sickle-cell
  anaemia
silicosis
sinusitis
sleeping sickness
smallpox
Spanish flu
spina bifida
spondylosis
strabismus
sunburn
sunstroke
swine flu
Sydenham's
  chorea
syndrome

syphilis
tendinitis
tenosynovitis
tetanus
thrombosis
thrush
tonsillitis
Tourette's
  syndrome
toxaemia
toxic shock
  syndrome
toxocariasis
toxoplasmosis
trench foot
trichinosis
tuberculosis (TB)
typhoid
typhus
undulant fever
urethritis
urticaria
vaginismus
venereal disease
  (VD)
viraemia
virus
vitiligo
Weil's disease
whooping
  cough
yaws
yellow fever

Psychological Illnesses and Conditions

anorexia nervosa
Asperger's
  syndrome
attention deficit
  hyperactivity
  disorder
  (ADHD)
autism
body
  dysmorphic
  disorder
bulimia nervosa
catatonia

clinical
  depression
combat fatigue
de Clerambault's
  syndrome
dementia
dysphoria
dysthymia
eating disorder
erotomania
false memory
  syndrome
gender
  dysphoria

hebephrenia
hyperactivity
hyperkinesis
hypomania
Korsakoff's
  syndrome
manic
  depression
megalomania
multiple-
  personality
  disorder
Munchausen's
  syndrome

Munchausen's
  syndrome by
  proxy
obsessive–
  compulsive
  disorder
panic disorder
paramnesia
paranoia
paraphilia
pica
post-natal
  depression

post-traumatic
  stress disorder
psychosis
schizo-affective
  disorder
schizophrenia
seasonal
  affective
  disorder (SAD)
shell shock

Phobias

air travel: *aerophobia*
American people and things:
  Americophobia
animals: *zoophobia*
beards: *pogonophobia*

beating: *mastigophobia*
bed: *clinophobia*
bees: *apiphobia*
birds: *ornithophobia*
blood: *haemophobia*

blushing: *erythrophobia*
bridges: *gephyrophobia*
burial alive: *taphephobia*
cancer: *carcinophobia*
cats: *ailurophobia*

childbirth: *tocophobia*
children: *paedophobia*
Chinese people and things: *Sinophobia*
clouds: *nephophobia*
coitus: *coitophobia*
cold: *cheimaphobia*
colour: *chromophobia*
comets: *cometophobia*
computers: *cyberphobia*
corpses: *necrophobia*
crowds: *demophobia*
dampness: *hygrophobia*
darkness: *scotophobia*
dawn: *eosophobia*
death: *thanatophobia*
depth: *bathophobia*
dirt: *mysophobia*
disease: *pathophobia*
dogs: *cynophobia*
dreams: *oneirophobia*
drink: *potophobia*
dust: *koniophobia*
electricity: *electrophobia*
English people and things: *Anglophobia*
everything: *panophobia, pantophobia*
eyes: *ommetaphobia*
faeces: *coprophobia*
fatigue: *kopophobia*
fear: *phobophobia*
feathers: *pteronophobia*
fever: *febriphobia*
fire: *pyrophobia*
fish: *ichthyophobia*
flesh: *selaphobia*
floods: *antlophobia*
flowers: *anthophobia*
food: *cibophobia, sitophobia*
foreigners: *xenophobia*
French people and things: *Francophobia, Gallophobia*
fur: *doraphobia*
German people and things: *Germanophobia, Teutophobia*
germs: *spermophobia*
ghosts: *phasmophobia*
giving birth to monsters: *teratophobia*
glass: *nelophobia*
God: *theophobia*
gold: *aurophobia, chrysophobia*
hair: *trichophobia*
heart disease: *cardiophobia*
heat: *thermophobia*
heaven: *uranophobia*
hell: *hadephobia, stygiophobia*

heredity: *patroiophobia*
high buildings: *batophobia*
high places: *hypsophobia*
home: *oikophobia*
homosexuals: *homophobia*
horses: *hippophobia*
ice: *cryophobia*
ideas: *ideophobia*
idleness: *thassophobia*
illness: *nosophobia*
imperfection: *atelophobia*
infinity: *apeirophobia*
inoculation: *trypanophobia, vaccinophobia*
insanity: *lyssophobia, maniphobia*
insects: *entomophobia*
insect stings: *cnidophobia*
Italian people and things: *Italophobia*
justice: *dikephobia*
lakes: *limnophobia*
leprosy: *leprophobia*
light: *photophobia*
lightning: *astrapophobia*
lists: *pinaciphobia*
loneliness: *autophobia, ermitophobia*
machinery: *mechanophobia*
magic: *rhabdophobia*
marriage: *gametophobia*
men: *androphobia*
metal: *metallophobia*
mice: *musophobia*
microbes: *bacillophobia*
mites: *acarophobia*
mobs: *ochlophobia*
motion: *kinetophobia*
music: *musicophobia*
names: *onomatophobia*
narrowness: *anginophobia*
needles: *belonephobia*
new things: *neophobia*
night: *nyctophobia*
nudity: *gymnophobia*
open places: *agoraphobia*
pain: *algophobia*
philosophy: *philosophobia*
pins: *enetophobia*
places: *topophobia*
pleasure: *hedonophobia*
poison: *toxiphobia*
Pope: *papaphobia*
poverty: *peniaphobia*
precipices: *cremnophobia*
priests: *hierophobia*
punishment: *poinephobia*
religious works of art: *iconophobia*
responsibility: *hypegiaphobia*
rivers: *potamophobia*

robbers: *harpaxophobia*
ruin: *atephobia*
Russian people and things: *Russophobia*
saints: *hagiophobia*
Satan: *Satanophobia*
scabies: *scabiophobia*
Scottish people and things: *Scotophobia*
sex: *erotophobia*
shadows: *sciophobia*
sharpness: *acrophobia*
shock: *hormephobia*
sin: *hamartophobia*
sleep: *hypnophobia*
slime: *blennophobia*
small things: *microphobia*
smell: *olfactophobia, osmophobia*
smothering: *pnigerophobia*
snakes: *ophidiophobia*
snow: *chionophobia*
solitude: *eremophobia*
sourness: *acerophobia*
speech: *glossophobia, phonophobia*
speed: *tachophobia*
spiders: *arachnophobia*
standing: *stasophobia*
stars: *siderophobia*
stealing: *kleptophobia*
string: *linonophobia*
stuttering: *laliophobia, lalophobia*
sun: *heliophobia*
swallowing: *phagophobia*
taste: *geumatophobia*
technology: *technophobia*
teeth: *odontophobia*
thunder: *brontophobia, keraunophobia, tonitrophobia*
time: *chronophobia*
touch: *haptophobia*
travel: *hodophobia*
tyrants: *tyrannophobia*
vehicles: *ochophobia*
venereal disease: *syphilophobia*
voids: *kenophobia*
vomiting: *emetophobia*
water: *hydrophobia*
waves: *cymophobia*
weakness: *asthenophobia*
wind: *anemophobia*
women: *gynophobia*
words: *logophobia*
work: *ergophobia*
writing: *graphophobia*

Wordfinder

Types and Forms of Medication

abortifacient
alpha blocker
anaesthetic
analeptic
analgesic
anaphrodisiac
anodyne
anovulant
antacid
anthelmintic
antibacterial
antibiotic
anticoagulant
antidote
anti-emetic
antihistamine
anti-infective
anti-inflammatory
antipruritic
antipsychotic
antipyretic

antiscorbutic
antiseptic
antispasmodic
antitussive
antiviral
anxiolytic
aperient
aphrodisiac
balsam
beta blocker
booster
cachet
calmative
caplet
capsule
carminative
contraceptive
convulsant
cream
curative
cure-all
decongestant

depressant
diaphoretic
digestive
dilator
diuretic
draught
drip
drops
ear drops
emetic
enema
euphoriant
evacuant
expectorant
eye drops
febrifuge
fungicide
gargle
germicide
hypodermic
inhalant
injectable

laxative
linctus
lotion
lozenge
mercurial
muscle relaxant
narcotic
nasal spray
nebulizer
nervine
neuroleptic
nootropic
ointment
painkiller
palliative
pastille
pessary
pill
placebo
poultice
powder
preventive

prophylactic
psychotropic
relaxant
restorative
rub
salve
sedative
sleeping pill
soporific
spray
steroid
stimulant
stupefacient
sudorific
suppository
suppressant
tablet
tonic
tranquillizer
vasodilator
vermifuge

Music and Dance

Musical Genres and Forms

acid house
acid jazz
acid rock
Afrobeat
air
alt.country
ambient
anthem
AOR
aria
aubade
bagatelle
ballad
ballet
barbershop
barcarole
baroque
barrelhouse
bebop
berceuse
bhangra
bluegrass
blues
boogie-woogie
bop
breakbeat
Britpop
cabaletta
calypso
canon
canticle
Cantopop

canzone
canzonetta
capriccio
carol
catch
cavatina
chaconne
chamber music
chanson
chant
chorale
choral music
chorus
classical music
comic opera
concertino
concerto
concerto grosso
cool jazz
coronach
country
country and
    western
country rock
courante
crossover
crunk
cumbia
dadrock
dancehall
dead march
death metal

descant
dirge
disco
ditty
Dixieland
doo-wop
drinking song
drum and bass
dub
dubstep
duet
duo
easy listening
electro
electronica
electropop
emo
entr'acte
étude
Europop
fado
fanfare
fantasia
fantasy
finale
flamenco
flourish
folk
folktronica
free jazz
fugato
fugue

funk
fusion
garage
glam rock
glee
go-go
gospel
Goth
gradual
grand opera
grime
grunge
gumbo
heavy metal
heavy rock
hip hop
honky-tonk
house
humoresque
hymn
impromptu
indie
interlude
intermezzo
introit
jazz
jazz funk
jingle
jit
jive
juju
jungle

klezmer
Krautrock
kwaito
kwela
lament
Lied
light opera
lovers' rock
lullaby
madrigal
march
mariachi
mass
medley
mento
merengue
modern jazz
monody
MOR
motet
moto perpetuo
Motown
movement
musette
musique
    concrète
New Age
New Romantic
new wave
nocturne
nonet
octet

opera
opera buffa
opera seria
operetta
oratorio
overture
parang
part-song
partita
passacaglia
passion
pastoral
pibroch
plainsong
pop
popular music
postlude
power pop
prelude
progressive rock
psalm

psychedelic
punk
qawwali
quartet
quintet
rag
raga
ragga
ragtime
rai
rap
rave
recitative
refrain
reggae
reggaeton
requiem
reverie
rhapsody
rhythm and
 blues

ricercar
ritornello
rock
rockabilly
rock and roll
rocksteady
romance
rondo
round
roundelay
salsa
scena
scherzo
septet
serenade
serenata
setting
sextet
shanty
signature tune
sinfonia

sinfonia
 concertante
sinfonietta
Singspiel
ska
skiffle
soca
soft rock
solo
sonata
sonatina
song
song cycle
soukous
soul
spiritual
Sprechgesang
study
suite
swing
symphonic poem

symphony
talking blues
techno
Tejano
terzetto
Tex-Mex
thrash
threnody
toccata
tone poem
trad jazz
trance
trio
trip hop
two-step
UK garage
variation
voluntary
world music
zouk
zydeco

Musical Instruments

accordion
acoustic guitar
aeolian harp
alpenhorn
althorn
American organ
autoharp
bagpipes
balalaika
banjo
barrel organ
bass clarinet
bass drum
basset horn
bass guitar
bassoon
bass tuba
bass viol
bell
bombarde
bombardon
bongos
bouzouki
bugle
carillon
castanet
celesta
cello
Celtic harp
chamber organ
chitarrone
cimbalom
cinema organ
cithara
citole
cittern
clarinet

clarion
clarsach
claves
clavichord
clavier
conga drum
contrabass
contrabassoon
cor anglais
cornet
cornetto
cymbal
didgeridoo
double bass
drum
dulcimer
electric guitar
electric organ
electronic organ
euphonium
fiddle
fife
fipple flute
flageolet
flugelhorn
flute
fortepiano
French horn
gamba
glockenspiel
gong
grand piano
guitar
Hammond
 organ (trademark)
handbell
harmonica

harmonium
harp
harpsichord
Hawaiian guitar
heckelphone
helicon
hi-hat
horn
hurdy-gurdy
Jew's harp
kazoo
kettledrum
kick drum
krummhorn
lute
lyre
mandola
mandolin
maraca
melodeon
melodica
mouth organ
oboe
oboe d'amore
ocarina
ondes martenot
organ
oud
pedal steel
 guitar
piano
piano accordion
pianoforte
pianola
piano organ
piccolo
pipe

pipe organ
player-piano
portative organ
post horn
psaltery
rattle
rebec
recorder
reed organ
reed pipe
sackbut
samisen
santoor
sarod
sarrusophone
saxhorn
saxophone
serpent
shawm
side drum
sitar
sleigh bell
slide guitar
slide trombone
snare drum
sousaphone
Spanish guitar
spinet
steel drum
string bass
synthesizer
tabla
tabor
tambour
tamboura
tambourine
tamburitza

tam-tam
temple block
tenor drum
tenor horn
theorbo
thumb piano
timpani
tin whistle
tom-tom
triangle
triple harp
trombone
trumpet
tuba
tubular bell
ukulele/ukelele
upright piano
vibraphone
vihuela
viol
viola
viola da gamba
viola d'amore
violin
violoncello
violone
virginals
Wagner tuba
washboard
Welsh harp
whistle
wobbleboard
wood block
Wurlitzer
 (trademark)
xylophone
zither

Wordfinder

Types of Singer

alto	choirgirl	falsetto	mezzo-soprano	soprano
balladeer	chorister	folk singer	minstrel	spinto
baritone	coloratura	gleeman	opera singer	tenor
bass	contralto	Heldentenor	pop singer	treble
basso profundo	countertenor	jongleur	pop star	troubadour
castrato	crooner	Meistersinger	prima donna	
choirboy	diva	mezzo	soloist	

Dances and Types of Dancing

ballet	clog dance	Highland fling	moonwalk	salsa
ballroom	conga	hoedown	morris dance	samba
barn dance	Cossack dance	hokey-cokey	mosh	shake
beguine	cotillion	hornpipe	old-time	shimmy
belly dance	country dance	hula-hula	one-step	shuffle
body popping	cumbia	Irish jig	pas de deux	skank
bolero	disco	Irish reel	paso doble	slam dance
boogaloo	do-si-do	jazz dance	pas seul	snake dance
boogie	ecossaise	jig	Paul Jones	square dance
bop	eightsome reel	jitterbug	pole dancing	stomp
bossa nova	fan dance	jive	polka	strut
Boston	fandango	jota	polonaise	sun dance
break-dancing	farruca	lambada	quadrille	sword dance
butoh	flamenco	Lambeth Walk	quickstep	tango
cakewalk	fling	lap dancing	rain dance	tap dance
cancan	folk dance	limbo	reel	turkey trot
carioca	formation	line dancing	robotic dancing	twist
ceroc	dancing	mambo	rock and roll	twosome reel
cha-cha	foxtrot	maypole dance	ronde	two-step
cha-cha-cha	galop	mazurka	round dance	vogueing
charleston	gavotte	minuet	roundelay	waltz
circle dance	Gay Gordons	moonstomp	rumba	war dance

Plants

Flowering Plants and Shrubs

Aaron's rod	arum lily	bindweed	bulrush	ceanothus
abelia	asphodel	bird of paradise	burdock	celandine
acacia	aspidistra	flower	burnet	centaury
acanthus	aster	bird's-foot trefoil	busy Lizzie	chaffweed
aconite	astilbe	black-eyed	buttercup	chervil
African daisy	astrantia	Susan	butterfly bush	chickweed
African violet	aubretia	blackthorn	butterwort	chicory
agapanthus	avens	bleeding heart	cabbage rose	chinaberry
agave	azalea	bluebell	cactus	Chinese lantern
agrimony	balsam	bog asphodel	calceolaria	chives
aloe	baneberry	bog rosemary	calendula	choisya
alstroemeria	banksia	boneset	camellia	chokeberry
alyssum	barberry	borage	camomile	Christmas cactus
amaranth	barrenwort	bougainvillea	campanula	Christmas rose
amaryllis	bearberry	bramble	campion	chrysanthemum
anemone	bedstraw	broom	candytuft	cicely
angelica	begonia	bryony	canna lily	cinchona
angel's trumpet	belladonna	buckeye	Canterbury bell	cinquefoil
aquilegia	bellflower	buddleia	Cape primrose	clarkia
arabis	bergamot	bugbane	carnation	clematis
arnica	betony	bugle	catmint	cloudberry
arrowgrass	bilberry	bugloss	cattleya	clove pink

clover
cockscomb
coltsfoot
columbine
comfrey
coneflower
convolvulus
coreopsis
cornflower
corydalis
cotoneaster
cottonweed
cow parsley
cowslip
cranesbill
creeping Jenny
crocus
crowfoot
crown imperial
crown of thorns
cuckoo pint
cuckooflower
cyclamen
daffodil
dahlia
daisy
damask rose
dandelion
daphne
deadly
  nightshade
delphinium
dianthus
dill
dittany
dock
dogbane
dog rose
dog violet
dropwort
duckweed
echinacea
edelweiss
eglantine
elder
evening
  primrose
eyebright
feverfew
figwort
firethorn
flax
fleabane
forget-me-not
forsythia
foxglove
frangipani
fraxinella
freesia
fritillary
fuchsia
furze
gaillardia

gardenia
gazania
gentian
geranium
gerbera
gillyflower
gladiolus
globeflower
glory-of-the-
  snow
gloxinia
goat's beard
golden rod
goldilocks
gorse
grape hyacinth
grass of
  Parnassus
groundsel
guelder rose
gypsophila
harebell
hawkbit
hawksbeard
hawkweed
hawthorn
heartsease
heather
hebe
helianthemum
helianthus
heliotrope
hellebore
helleborine
hemlock
herb Christopher
herb Paris
herb Robert
heuchera
hibiscus
hogweed
holly
hollyhock
honesty
honeysuckle
hop
hosta
hyacinth
hydrangea
ice plant
iris
jacaranda
Jack-by-the-
  hedge
Jacob's ladder
japonica
jasmine
jonquil
juneberry
kalanchoe
kalmia
kerria
kingcup

knapweed
knotgrass
laburnum
lady's mantle
lady's slipper
lady's smock
lady's tresses
larkspur
lavatera
lavender
lemon balm
leopard lily
lilac
lily
lily of the valley
lobelia
London pride
loosestrife
lords and ladies
lotus
lovage
love-in-a-mist
love-lies-
  bleeding
lungwort
lupin
madonna lily
magnolia
mahonia
mallow
mandrake
marguerite
marigold
marsh marigold
marshwort
may
mayflower
mayweed
meadow rue
meadow saffron
meadowsweet
Michaelmas
  daisy
mignonette
milfoil
milkwort
mimosa
mint
mistletoe
mock orange
monkey flower
monkshood
montbretia
moonflower
morning glory
motherwort
musk rose
myrtle
narcissus
nasturtium
nemesia
nettle
nicotiana

nigella
night-scented
  stock
nightshade
old man's beard
oleander
orchid
ox-eye daisy
oxlip
oyster plant
pansy
Parma violet
parsley
pasque flower
passion flower
pelargonium
pennyroyal
penstemon
peony
peppermint
periwinkle
petunia
pheasant's eye
phlox
pimpernel
pink
pitcher plant
plantain
plumbago
poinsettia
polyanthus
poppy
potentilla
prickly pear
prickly poppy
primrose
primula
privet
pulsatilla
pyracantha
pyrethrum
ragweed
ragwort
rampion
ramsons
rape
red-hot poker
rhododendron
rock rose
rose
rosebay
  willowherb
rose of Sharon
safflower
St John's wort
salpiglossis
salvia
samphire
sandwort
saxifrage
scabious
scarlet
  pimpernel

scilla
sedum
shamrock
sheep's-bit
shrimp plant
skullcap
snapdragon
snow-in-summer
snowdrop
snowflake
soapwort
Solomon's seal
sorrel
sowthistle
speedwell
spider flower
spider plant
spiderwort
spikenard
spiraea
spurge
spurrey
squill
star of
  Bethlehem
starwort
stitchwort
stock
stonecrop
storksbill
strawflower
streptocarpus
sunflower
sweetbriar
sweet cicely
sweet pea
sweet rocket
sweet william
tansy
tea rose
teasel
thistle
thorn apple
thrift
tiger lily
toadflax
tormentil
tradescantia
traveller's joy
trefoil
tuberose
tulip
turnsole
valerian
Venus flytrap
verbena
veronica
vervain
vetch
viburnum
violet
viper's bugloss
wallflower

water lily
water violet
willowherb
winter jasmine

wintergreen
wintersweet
wisteria
witch hazel

wolfsbane
wood anemone
wood avens
woodruff

wood sorrel
woody
  nightshade
wormwood

yarrow
yerba buena
yucca
zinnia

Trees and Shrubs

acacia
acer
ackee
alder
allspice
almond
angelica
anise
annatto
apple
apricot
araucaria
ash
aspen
avocado
azalea
balsa
balsam fir
bamboo
banksia
banyan
baobab
basswood
bay tree
beech
beefwood
bergamot
birch
blackthorn
bluegum
bodh tree
bog oak
bottlebrush
bottle tree
bo tree
box
box elder
breadfruit
bristlecone pine
broom
buckeye
buckthorn
bullace
bur oak
butternut
cacao
calabash
camellia
camphor tree
candelabra tree
candleberry
candlenut
carambola
carob
cashew

cassava
cassia
casuarina
cedar
cherimoya
cherry
cherry laurel
cherry plum
chestnut
chinaberry
cinnamon
citron
clove
coco de mer
coconut palm
coffee
cola
coolibah
copper beech
coral tree
cork oak
coromandel
cottonwood
crab apple
cryptomeria
curry leaf
custard apple
cypress
damson
dawn redwood
dogwood
Douglas fir
dragon tree
ebony
elder
elm
eucalyptus
euonymus
false acacia
fever tree
ficus
fig
filbert
fir
firethorn
flame tree
frangipani
fuchsia
gean
genipapo
ginkgo
gorse
grapefruit
greengage
guaiacum

guava
gum tree
handkerchief
  tree
hawthorn
hazel
hemlock fir
hickory
holly
holly oak
holm oak
honey locust
honeysuckle
hornbeam
horse chestnut
hydrangea
ilex
iroko
ironbark
ironwood
jacaranda
jackfruit
jack pine
japonica
jasmine
jojoba
jujube
juniper
kalmia
kapok
kermes oak
kola
kumquat
laburnum
lacquer tree
larch
laurel
lemon
Leyland cypress
leylandii
lilac
lime
linden
liquidambar
live oak
locust
lodgepole pine
logwood
Lombardy poplar
London plane
loquat
lychee
macadamia
macrocarpa
madroño

magnolia
mahogany
maidenhair tree
mandarin
mango
mangosteen
mangrove
maple
mastic
maté
may
mimosa
mirabelle
monkey puzzle
mountain ash
mulberry
myrtle
nectarine
Norway spruce
nutmeg
nux vomica
oak
oleaster
olive
osier
pagoda tree
palm
palmyra
papaya
paper mulberry
paperbark
pawpaw
pear
pedunculate oak
persimmon
pine
piñon
pistachio
pitch pine
plane
plum
pomegranate
pomelo
poplar
privet
pussy willow
quassia
quince
rain tree
rambutan
redbud
red cedar
redwood
rhododendron
robinia

roseapple
rosewood
rowan
royal palm
rubber plant
rubber tree
sallow
sandalwood
sapele
sapodilla
sassafras
satinwood
schefflera
Scots pine
senna
sequoia
service tree
silver birch
Sitka
slippery elm
smoke tree
soapberry
spindle
spruce
star anise
stinkwood
stone pine
storax
sugar maple
sumac
sycamore
tallow tree
tamarind
tamarisk
tangerine
tea
teak
tea tree
thuja
tree of heaven
trembling poplar
tulip tree
tulipwood
umbrella tree
viburnum
walnut
wattle
weeping willow
wellingtonia
whitebeam
willow
witch hazel
wych elm
yew
ylang-ylang

Mushrooms, Toadstools, and Other Fungi

agaric
amethyst
  deceiver
armillaria
beefsteak
  fungus
bird's-nest
black bulgar
blewit
blusher
boletus

bracket fungus
button
  mushroom
cep
champignon
chanterelle
dead man's
  fingers
death cap
destroying angel
earthstar

ergot
fairies' bonnets
field mushroom
fly agaric
girolle
grisette
honey fungus
horn of plenty
horse mushroom
ink cap
Jew's ear

liberty cap
morel
mousseron
oyster
  mushroom
parasol
penny bun
polypore
porcini
portobello

puffball
reishi
russula
shiitake
sickener
stinkhorn
straw mushroom
tartufo
truffle

Science

Branches of Science

acoustics
aerodynamics
agriscience
anatomy
anthropology
astronomy
astrophysics
bacteriology
behavioural
  science
biochemistry
biology
botany
chemistry
climatology
computer
  science
cosmology
cryogenics
cybernetics
cytology
dendrology
dynamics

earth science
ecology
economics
electrical
  engineering
electronics
endocrinology
engineering
entomology
epidemiology
ethnology
ethology
exobiology
fluid mechanics
forensics
genetic
  engineering
genetics
geochemistry
geography
geology
geomorphology
geophysics

glaciology
haematology
herpetology
histology
holography
hydrodynamics
hydrology
hydrostatics
ichthyology
immunology
linguistics
marine biology
mathematics
mechanics
medicine
metallurgy
meteorology
microbiology
mineralogy
molecular
  biology
mycology
natural history

neurology
neuroscience
nuclear
  chemistry
nuclear physics
oceanography
oncology
ophthalmology
optics
ornithology
palaeobotany
palaeontology
parasitology
particle physics
pathology
petrology
pharmacology
physics
physiography
physiology
phytology
psychiatry
psychology

quantum
  mechanics
radiology
robotics
seismology
sociobiology
sociology
soil science
spectroscopy
statistics
stratigraphy
taxonomy
tectonics
toxicology
veterinary
  medicine
virology
volcanology/
  vulcanology
zoogeography
zoology
zymurgy

Chemical Elements *Metals

*actinium (Ac)
*aluminium (Al)
*americium (Am)
*antimony (Sb)
argon (Ar)
arsenic (As)
astatine (At)
*barium (Ba)
*berkelium (Bk)
*beryllium (Be)
*bismuth (Bi)
bohrium (Bh)
boron (B)
bromine (Br)
*cadmium (Cd)
*caesium (Cs)
*calcium (Ca)

*californium (Cf)
carbon (C)
*cerium (Ce)
chlorine (Cl)
*chromium (Cr)
*cobalt (Co)
*copper (Cu)
*curium (Cm)
darmstadtium
  (Ds)
dubnium (Db)
*dysprosium
  (Dy)
einsteinium (Es)
*erbium (Er)
*europium (Eu)
*fermium (Fm)

fluorine (F)
*francium (Fr)
*gadolinium
  (Gd)
*gallium (Ga)
germanium (Ge)
*gold (Au)
*hafnium (Hf)
hassium (Hs)
helium (He)
*holmium (Ho)
hydrogen (H)
*indium (In)
iodine (I)
*iridium (Ir)
*iron (Fe)
krypton (Kr)

*lanthanum (La)
*lawrencium (Lr)
*lead (Pb)
*lithium (Li)
*lutetium (Lu)
*magnesium
  (Mg)
*manganese
  (Mn)
*meitnerium
  (Mt)
*mendelevium
  (Md)
*mercury (Hg)
*molybdenum
  (Mo)

*neodymium
  (Nd)
neon (Ne)
*neptunium (Np)
*nickel (Ni)
*niobium (Nb)
nitrogen (N)
*nobelium (No)
*osmium (Os)
oxygen (O)
*palladium (Pd)
phosphorus (P)
*platinum (Pt)
*plutonium (Pu)
*polonium (Po)
*potassium (K)

Wordfinder

*praseodymium (Pr)
*promethium (Pm)
*protactinium (Pa)
*radium (Ra)
radon (Rn)
*rhenium (Re)

*rhodium (Rh)
roentgenium (Rg)
*rubidium (Rb)
*ruthenium (Ru)
rutherfordium (Rf)
*samarium (Sm)
*scandium (Sc)

seaborgium (Sg)
selenium (Se)
silicon (Si)
*silver (Ag)
*sodium (Na)
*strontium (Sr)
sulphur (S)
*tantalum (Ta)
*technetium (Tc)

tellurium (Te)
*terbium (Tb)
*thallium (Tl)
*thorium (Th)
*thulium (Tm)
tin (Sn)
*titanium (Ti)
*tungsten (W)
*uranium (U)

*vanadium (V)
xenon (Xe)
*ytterbium (Yb)
*yttrium (Y)
*zinc (Zn)
*zirconium (Zr)

Chemicals

acetic acid
acetone
acetylene
alcohol
alum
alumina
baking soda
baryta
bicarbonate of soda
boracic acid
borax
calomel

carbolic acid
carbon tetrachloride
carborundum
caustic potash
caustic soda
chloroform
chrome yellow
cinnabar
common salt
corundum
cream of tartar
cyanide

dry ice
Epsom salts
ether
ethyl alcohol
firedamp
folic acid
formaldehyde
formic acid
glycerine
gypsum
hydrochloric acid
jeweller's rouge
laughing gas

lithia
magnesia
marsh gas
nitric oxide
peroxide
plaster of Paris
potash
prussic acid
quicklime
red lead
salt
saltpetre
silica

slaked lime
soda
strontia
sugar
verdigris
vitriol
washing soda
white arsenic
xylene
zirconia

Rocks and Minerals

agate
alabaster
alexandrite
almandine
amber
amethyst
aquamarine
asbestos
balas ruby
baryte
basalt
beryl
bloodstone
Blue John
borax
breccia
cairngorm
calcite
carbuncle
carnelian
cat's-eye
chalcedony
chalk
chert
chromite

chrysolite
chrysoprase
cinnabar
cipolin
citrine
coal
conglomerate
cornelian
corundum
cryolite
diamond
diorite
dolerite
dolomite
emerald
emery
feldspar
fire opal
flint
fluorite
fluorspar
fool's gold
gabbro
galena
garnet

girasol
gneiss
granite
graphite
greenstone
gypsum
haematite
hornblende
hornfels
ironstone
jacinth
jade
jadeite
jasper
lapis lazuli
lava
limestone
magnetite
malachite
manganite
marble
marcasite
marl
mica
mica schist

moonstone
moss agate
mudstone
muscovite
natron
nephrite
obsidian
oil shale
olivine
onyx
oolite
opal
orpiment
pegmatite
peridot
peridotite
phosphorite
pitchblende
porphyry
pumice
pyrites
pyrope
quartz
quartzite
rag

rhyolite
rock salt
ruby
sandstone
sapphire
sardonyx
schist
serpentine
shale
slate
smoky quartz
spinel
steatite
sunstone
talc
topaz
tourmaline
tuff
turquoise
vermiculite
zeolite
zircon

Subatomic Particles

antiparticle
antiproton
antiquark
axion
baryon
boson

electron
fermion
gluon
hadron
Higgs boson
Higgs particle

hyperon
kaon
lambda particle
lepton
meson
muon

neutrino
neutron
nucleon
photon
pion
positron

proton
quark
tau particle
WIMP

Sports and Games

Sports

aerobatics
aerobics
American football
angling
aquaplaning
archery
Association Football
athletics
Australian Rules football
badminton
ballooning
bandy
base-jumping
baseball
basketball
beach volleyball
beagling
billiards
BMX
bobsleighing
boule/boules
bowling
bowls
boxing
bullfighting
bungee jumping
caber tossing
Canadian football
canoeing
canyoning
caving
clay-pigeon shooting
climbing
clock golf
coarse fishing

coursing
cricket
croquet
cross-country running
crown-green bowls
curling
cycle racing
cycling
cyclo-cross
darts
dinghy racing
diving
downhill skiing
Eton fives
falconry
fencing
field hockey
figure-skating
fishing
five-a-side football
fives
flat-green bowls
flat racing
fly-fishing
football
fowling
free skating
freestyling
French cricket
futsal
Gaelic football
game fishing
gliding
goalball
golf
greyhound racing

gymkhana
gymnastics
handball
hang-gliding
harness racing
heli-skiing
hiking
hockey
horse racing
hunting
hurling
hydrospeed
ice dancing
ice hockey
ice skating
jai alai
jet-skiing
jogging
kabaddi
kayaking
keirin
kiteboarding
kitesurfing
korfball
lacrosse
langlauf
lawn tennis
luge
match fishing
mountain biking
mountaineering
netball
ninepins
Nordic walking
orienteering
parachuting
paragliding
parapenting
parasailing
parascending

parkour
pelota
pétanque
pigeon racing
pistol shooting
point-to-point
polo
pool
potholing
powerboat racing
quoits
rackets
racquetball
rafting
real tennis
rock climbing
roller skating
rollerblading
rounders
rowing
Rugby fives
rugby league
rugby union
sailing
scuba-diving
sculling
sea fishing
shinty
shooting
showjumping
skateboarding
skating
skeet
skiing
skijoring
ski jumping
skin-diving
skittles
skydiving

slalom
snooker
snorkelling
snowboarding
soccer
softball
speed skating
spelunking
sprinting
squash
surfing
swimming
synchronized swimming
table tennis
tennis
tenpin bowling
three-day eventing
tobogganing
trap shooting
trotting
volleyball
wakeboarding
walking
water polo
waterskiing
weightlifting
white-water rafting
wild-water racing
wildfowling
wild swimming
windsurfing
wrestling
yachting
Zumba (trademark)

Athletics Events

biathlon
cross-country running
decathlon
discus
duathlon
field event

half-marathon
hammer
heptathlon
high jump
hurdles
javelin
long jump

long-distance race
marathon
middle-distance race
mile
pentathlon

pole vault
race
relay race
shot-put
sprint
steeplechase
tetrathlon

track event
triathlon
triple jump
tug of war
walking

Gymnastics Events

artistic gymnastics
asymmetric bars

beam
floor exercises
high bar

parallel bars
pommel horse

rhythmic gymnastics
rings

sports aerobics
uneven bars
vault

Wordfinder

Martial Arts and Combat Sports

aikido	hapkido	karate	Shotokan	Thai boxing
ba gua	jeet kune do	kendo	Silat	ultimate fighting
boxing	jousting	kick-boxing	sumo wrestling	wing chun
budo	ju-jitsu	Krav Maga	tae kwon do	wrestling
capoeira	judo	kung fu	t'ai chi chu'an	wushu
fencing	kalaripayattu	pa kua	tang soo do	

Motor Sports

autocross	enduro	hill-climbing	motorcycle	scrambling
cross-country	F1	Indy	racing	sidecar racing
demolition derby	Formula One	Indycar	off-roading	speedway
dirt-track racing	go-karting	karting	rallycross	stock-car racing
drag racing	Grand Prix	motocross	rallying	trials

Games

Aunt Sally	cops and	housey-housey	Pac-Man	shovelboard
backgammon	robbers	hunt the thimble	(trademark)	Simon Says
bagatelle	craps	I spy	paintball	snakes and
battleships	darts	jacks	pass the parcel	ladders
billiards	deck quoits	jackstraws	pat-a-cake	snooker
bingo	dice	kabaddi	peekaboo	solitaire
blind man's buff	dominoes	King of the	piggy in the	spillikins
cards	draughts	Castle	middle	spin the bottle
catch	ducks and	kriegspiel	pinball	Subbuteo
cat's cradle	drakes	leapfrog	pitch-and-toss	(trademark)
charades	dungeons and	lotto	poker dice	table football
checkers	dragons	ludo	Poohsticks	tag
chess	fantasy football	mah-jong	pool	team game
chicken	fivestones	marbles	postman's knock	thimblerig
Chinese	follow-my-leader	Monopoly	prisoner's base	tic-tac-toe
chequers	forfeits	(trademark)	quoits	tiddlywinks
Chinese	frisbee (trademark)	murder in the	ring-a-ring o'	tig
whispers	go	dark	roses	treasure hunt
Cluedo (trademark)	halma	musical bumps	roulette	Trivial Pursuit
computer game	hangman	musical chairs	sardines	(trademark)
conkers	hide-and-seek	nim	Scrabble	tug of war
consequences	hoopla	noughts and	(trademark)	word game
	hopscotch	crosses	shove-halfpenny	

Ball Games

American	boule/boules	football	netball	shinty
football	bowling	French cricket	ninepins	skittles
Association	bowls	futsal	pétanque	snooker
Football	cricket	Gaelic football	polo	soccer
Australian Rules	croquet	golf	pool	softball
football	crown-green	handball	rackets	squash
bandy	bowls	hockey	real tennis	table tennis
baseball	Eton fives	hurling	rounders	tennis
basketball	five-a-side	lacrosse	rugby	tenpin bowling
beach volleyball	football	lawn tennis	rugby league	volleyball
billiards	fives	mini rugby	rugby union	water polo

Card Games

baccarat	Black Maria	cheat	euchre	loo
beggar-my-	Boston	chemin de fer	fan-tan	monte
neighbour	brag	cribbage	faro	nap
bezique	bridge	duplicate bridge	gin rummy	Newmarket
blackjack	canasta	écarté	happy families	old maid

ombre	piquet	rummy	solitaire	twenty-one
patience	poker	skat	solo whist	vingt-et-un
pinochle	pontoon	snap	stud poker	whist

Technology

Computing and Internet Terms

access provider	control unit	filter	mailer	read-only
acoustic coupler	coprocessor	firewall	malware	memory
adware	CPU	firmware	manager	register
agent	crash	flash drive	megabyte	rollerball
alias	crawler	flash memory	megapixel	ROM
applet	crimeware	floppy disk	memory	routine
application	cyberattack	format	memory stick	RSS
assembler	cyberbullying	freeware	menu	scanner
autocomplete	cybersecurity	FTP	message board	screen saver
autofill	cursor	games console	microchip	script
backup	daemon	gateway	microcomputer	search engine
bar-code reader	darknet	GIF	minicomputer	search engine
BASIC	data	gigabit	moblog	optimization
baud	data centre	gigapixel	modem	sequencer
BIOS	debugger	graphics card	monitor	serial port
bit	desktop	groupware	motherboard	server
bitmap	dialler	hacker	mouse	servlet
BitTorrent	dialog box	hard disk	mouse mat	shareware
(trademark)	digital	hard drive	navigator	shell program
blog	digitizer	hardware	Net	silicon chip
blogger	disk	home page	network	sniffer
blogroll	disk drive	host	newsgroup	software
board	diskette	HTML	notebook	sound card
bookmark	display	HTTP	offline	spam
boot	domain	hyperlink	online	spellchecker
bot	domain name	hypertext	optical disk	spider
botnet	DOS	icon	output	spreadsheet
browser	dot-matrix	in-box	palmtop	spyware
buffer	printer	information	parser	surf
bug	dot-org	technology	paywall	talkboard
bulletin board	download	inkjet printer	PC	telnet
bus	drive	input	PDA	terminal
byte	DVD	interactive	PDF	text editor
cache	DVD-R	interface	phishing	toggle
cache memory	DVD-ROM	Internet service	plug-in	tool
card	DVD-RW	provider	podcast	toolbar
CD-R	e-banking	intranet	pop-up	tooltip
CD-ROM	e-reader	ISP	port	touch pad
CD-RW	e-tailer	Javascript	portal	touch screen
central	editor	(trademark)	PowerPoint	trackball
processing	email	joystick	(trademark)	transistor
unit	emoticon	JPEG	printed circuit	Trojan Horse
chat room	Ethernet	keyboard	printed circuit	Unicode
chip	exabyte	keypad	board	upload
click	expansion card	kilobyte	printer	URL
click-through	expert system	laptop	printout	user interface
client	FAQ	laser printer	processor	utility
cloud computing	favicon	light pen	program	vaccine
code	fax modem	log in	RAM	VDU
compact disc	file	log out	random-access	video card
computer	filename	loop	memory	viewscreen
console	file-sharing	macro		virtual reality

Wordfinder

virus	wallpaper	web page	World Wide	zip file
visual display	Web	website	Web	
unit	webcam	wiki	worm	
vlog	web hosting	word processor	XML	
vodcast	weblog	workstation	zip	

Energy and Fuels

acetylene	coal	fusion energy	light	renewable
anthracite	coal gas	gas	lignite	energy
atomic power	coke	gasoline	methane	solar energy
bio-diesel	derv	geothermal	natural gas	steam power
biofuel	diesel	energy	nuclear power	tidal power
biogas	electricity	heat	oil	turf
briquette	electromagnetic	hydroelectric	paraffin	unleaded petrol
butane	energy	power	peat	water power
Calor gas	firewood	hydrogen	petrol	wave power
(trademark)	fossil fuel	kerosene	petroleum	wind power
chemical energy	fuel oil	leaded petrol	propane	wood

Engines

aero engine	four-stroke	linear motor	rocket engine	turbo diesel
beam engine	gas turbine	magneto	rotary engine	turbofan
diesel engine	generator	oil engine	scramjet	turbojet
donkey engine	heat engine	outboard	steam engine	turboprop
dynamo	inboard	petrol engine	steam turbine	turboshaft
electric motor	inline engine	piston engine	straight-eight	twin-cam engine
external-	internal-	prop jet	transverse	two-stroke
combustion	combustion	pulse jet	engine	V6
engine	engine	radial engine	thruster	V8
flat-four engine	jet engine	ramjet	turbine	V12

Tools

adze	clamp	glass cutter	needle	sander
air gun	claw hammer	graver	nippers	sandpaper
Allen key	cleaver	grinder	padsaw	saw
(trademark)	compass saw	grouter	paint gun	sawbench
auger	coping saw	hack	panel saw	scarifier
awl	cramp	hacksaw	peen/pein	scraper
axe	cross peen/pein	hammer	hammer	screwdriver
bandsaw	crowbar	hammer drill	perforator	screw tap
beetle	cultivator	hatchet	pestle	scribe
bevel	cutter	hedge clipper	pick	scroll saw
billhook	dibber	hoe	pickaxe	scythe
blowlamp	dibble	hole saw	pincers	secateurs
blowtorch	diestock	jack	pitchfork	shears
bodkin	dovetailer	jackhammer	plane	shovel
borer	drill	jemmy	pliers	sickle
bowsaw	edge tool	jigsaw	priest	slasher
brace	edging shears	jointer	pruning hook	sledgehammer
bradawl	edging tool	keyhole saw	punch	socket spanner
burin	file	knife	rake	soldering iron
burnisher	flail	lathe	ram	spade
burr	float	lawnmower	rasp	spanner
capstan lathe	fork	loppers	reamer	spokeshave
centre bit	former	mallet	riddle	square
centre punch	frame saw	marlinspike	ripsaw	staple gun
chainsaw	fretsaw	mattock	roller	steam hammer
chisel	froe	mortar board	roulette	strickle
chopper	fuller	nail punch	router	swage
circular saw	gimlet	nailer	rule	swingle

tenon saw	trimmer	vice	wire cutter
tilt hammer	trip hammer	wedge	wire stripper
tinsnips	trowel	wheel brace	woodcarver
torque wrench	tweezers	whipsaw	wrench

Units

acre	cycle	hectare	metre	pound
age	day	henry	metric ton	quantum bit
air mile	decade	hertz	microgram	quart
ampere	decalitre	hogshead	microlitre	quarter
angstrom	decametre	horsepower	micrometre	quintal
astronomical	decibel	hour	micron	rad
unit	decilitre	hundredweight	microsecond	radian
atmosphere	decimetre	inch	mile	rem
atomic mass unit	degree	joule	millennium	rod
bale	denier	kelvin	millibar	roentgen
bar	dessertspoon	kilobyte	milligram	rood
barrel	dioptre	kilocalorie	millilitre	scruple
baud	drachm	kilogram	millimetre	second
becquerel	dyne	kilohertz	millisecond	siemens
bel	electronvolt	kilojoule	minim	sievert
bit	ell	kilolitre	minute	span
brake	epoch	kilometre	mole	square
horsepower	erg	kiloton	month	steradian
British thermal	farad	kilovolt	nanometre	stone
unit	fathom	kilowatt	nanosecond	tablespoon
bushel	firkin	kilowatt-hour	nautical mile	teaspoon
byte	fluid drachm	knot	newton	terabyte
cable	fluid ounce	league	noggin	teraflop
calorie	foot	light year	ohm	tesla
candela	furlong	line	ounce	therm
carat	gallon	link	parsec	tog
centigram	gauss	litre	pascal	ton
centilitre	gigabit	lumen	peck	tonne
centimetre	gigabyte	lux	pennyweight	troy ounce
century	gigaflop	Mach number	perch	volt
chain	gigahertz	maxwell	period	watt
cord	gigawatt	megabyte	pica	weber
coulomb	gill	megaflop	pint	week
cubit	grain	megahertz	pipe	yard
cup	gram	megaton	point	year
cupful	gray	megavolt	poise	
curie	hand	megawatt	pole	

Transport

Motor Vehicles

all-terrain vehicle	bus	coupé	fire engine	hardtop
ambulance	cab	dirt bike	flatbed	hatchback
armoured car	cabriolet	double-decker	float	hearse
articulated lorry	Cadillac	bus	forklift truck	heavy goods
automobile	(trademark)	dragster	four-by-four	vehicle (HGV)
autorickshaw	camper	DUKW	four-wheel drive	horsebox
battlebus	car	dumper truck	(4WD)	hot rod
beach buggy	car transporter	dune buggy	go-kart	jeep (trademark)
Black Maria	charabanc	dustcart	golf cart	juggernaut
bowser (trademark)	coach	earth mover	gritter	kart
buggy	concept car	estate	hackney cab	kit car
bulldozer	convertible	fastback	half-track	limousine

lorry
low-loader
microcar
milk float
minelayer
minicab
moped
motorbike
motor caravan
motorcycle
multi-purpose
    vehicle (MPV)
notchback
off-road vehicle
off-roader
omnibus

pantechnicon
passenger-
    carrying
    vehicle
people carrier
personnel carrier
pickup
public service
    vehicle (PSV)
quad bike
racing car
ragtop
rally car
recreational
    vehicle (RV)
refrigerated van

removal van
roadroller
roadster
rover
runabout
saloon
scooter
scrambler
sedan
shooting brake
snowcat
snowmobile
snowplough
soft top
sports car
sportster

sport utility
    vehicle (SUV)
station wagon
stock car
stretch limo
superbike
supercar
supermini
tank
tanker
taxi
taxicab
tourer
touring car
tow truck
tracklayer

tractor
trail bike
trailer
tram
transporter
trolleybus
troop carrier
truck
utility
van
wagon/waggon
wrecker

Carriages and Carts

barouche
brake
breaking cart
brougham
buggy
cab
cabriolet
caravan

carriole
chaise
chariot
clarence
coach
coach-and-four
coupé
covered wagon

curricle
dog cart
dray
droshky
fiacre
fly
gig
hackney

handcart
hansom
landau
ox cart
phaeton
postchaise
rickshaw
stagecoach

tilbury
trailer
trap
trishaw
tumbril
Victoria
wagon/waggon
wagonette

Trains and Rolling Stock

armoured train
bogie
boxcar
brake van
buffet car
bullet train
cable car
caboose
car
carriage
coach
couchette
diesel-electric

diesel
    locomotive
diesel multiple
    unit
dining car
double-header
electric train
engine
express
flatcar
freight train
goods train
goods wagon

guard's van
handcar
high-speed train
hopper
hospital train
locomotive
maglev
mail coach
mail train
metro
milk train
monorail
motor coach

observation car
pannier tank
passenger train
Pullman
railcar
restaurant car
saddle tank
shunter
sleeper
sleeping car
smokebox
smoker

steam
    locomotive
steam train
stopping train
subway train
tank engine
tender
TGV
underground
    train
wagon-lit

Ships and Boats

airboat
aircraft carrier
amphibious
    assault ship
amphibious
    landing craft
auxiliary
barge
barque
barquentine
bateau mouche
bathyscaphe
bathysphere
battlecruiser
battleship
bireme
boatel

brig
brigantine
bulk carrier
bumboat
cabin cruiser
cable ship
caique
canal boat
canoe
capital ship
car ferry
caravel
cargo ship
carrack
catamaran
catboat
clipper

coal ship
coaler
coaster
cockleshell
collier
container ship
coracle
corvette
cruiser
cruise ship
cutter
destroyer
dhow
dinghy
diving bell
dory
dragon boat

dreadnought
dredger
drifter
dugout
E-boat
East Indiaman
factory ship
felucca
ferry
flag boat
flagship
flatboat
freighter
frigate
full-rigger
galleon
galley

galliot
gig
gondola
gulet
gunboat
helicopter carrier
hermaphrodite
    brig
hospital ship
houseboat
hovercraft
hydrofoil
hydroplane
iceboat
ice-breaker
inboard
Indiaman

inflatable dinghy
ironclad
jetboat
jetfoil
jet ski (trademark)
jolly
junk
kayak
keelboat
ketch
landing craft
launch
liberty boat
lifeboat
life raft
lighter
lightship
liner
longboat
longship
lugger
mailboat
man-of-war
merchantman
merchant ship

minehunter
minelayer
minesweeper
monitor
monohull
motor boat
motor torpedo
  boat
motor yacht
multihull
narrowboat
oiler
oil tanker
outboard
outrigger
paddle boat
paddle steamer
pedal boat
pedalo
pilot boat
pink
pinnace
pirogue
pocket
  battleship

pontoon
powerboat
pram
privateer
proa
punt
Q-ship
quinquereme
raft
RIB
rigger
riverboat
roll-on roll-off
rowing boat
rubber dinghy
safety boat
sailing boat
sailing ship
sampan
schooner
scow
scull
sealer
shallop
shell

ship of the line
showboat
side-wheeler
single-hander
skiff
skipjack
slaver
sloop
sloop of war
smack
speedboat
square-rigger
stake boat
steamboat
steamer
steamship
sternwheeler
submarine
submersible
supertanker
supply ship
tall ship
tanker
tender
torpedo boat

trader
training ship
tramp steamer
trawler
trimaran
trireme
troop carrier
troopship
tub
tugboat
U-boat
vaporetto
warship
water bus
water taxi
weekender
whaleboat
whaler
wherry
windjammer
workboat
xebec
yacht
yawl

Aircraft

airliner
airship
autogiro
balloon
biplane
blimp
bomber
chopper
delta-wing
dirigible
dive bomber
drone

fighter
fighter-bomber
floatplane
flying boat
freighter
glider
gunship
gyrocopter
gyroplane
hang-glider
helicopter
hot-air balloon

hydroplane
interceptor
jet
jet plane
jetliner
jumbo jet
jump jet
microlight
minelayer
monoplane
night fighter
paraglider

sailplane
seaplane
ski-plane
spaceplane
spotter
stealth bomber
stealth fighter
swept-wing
tanker
towplane
triplane
troop carrier

tug
turbofan
turbojet
turboprop
warplane
water bomber
whirlybird
widebody
Zeppelin

War

Weapons

A-bomb
air gun
anti-aircraft gun
arquebus
Armalite
  (trademark)
artillery
assault rifle
atom/atomic
  bomb
automatic
axe
ballistic missile
baton
baton round
battleaxe

bayonet
bazooka
blackjack
bludgeon
blunderbuss
Bofors gun
bomb
bowie knife
brass knuckles
breech-loader
Bren gun
broadsword
Browning
buckshot
cannon
cannonball

car bomb
carbine
case knife
catapult
claymore
club
cluster bomb
Colt (trademark)
cordite
cosh
cruise missile
cudgel
cutlass
dagger
daisy-cutter
depth charge

derringer
dirk
dirty bomb
doodlebug
duelling pistol
dumdum bullet
dynamite
épée
Exocet
express rifle
firebomb
flick knife
flintlock
flying bomb
forty-five

fragmentation
  bomb/grenade
fusil
fusion bomb
Gatling gun
gelignite
grapeshot
grenade
guided missile
gun
guncotton
gunpowder
H-bomb
halberd
hand grenade
handgun

harpoon
harpoon gun
harquebus
hatchet
high explosive
horse pistol
howitzer
hydrogen bomb
improvised
  explosive
  device (IED)
intercontinental
  ballistic missile
  (ICBM)
incendiary bomb
incendiary
  device
jackknife
javelin
Kalashnikov
knife
knobkerrie
knuckleduster
kris
kukri

lance
landmine
lathi
Lee-Enfield
letter bomb
Lewis gun
life preserver
limpet mine
Luger (trademark)
mace
machete
machine gun
magnetic mine
mail bomb
matchlock
Mauser (trademark)
Maxim gun
Mills bomb
missile
Molotov cocktail
mortar
musket
neutron bomb
nuclear bomb
nulla-nulla

panga
parang
parcel bomb
pellet
petard
petrol bomb
pike
pistol
plastic bullet
plastic explosive
Polaris
poleaxe
pom-pom
poniard
pump-action
  shotgun
quarterstaff
rapier
revolver
rifle
rocket
rocket-propelled
  grenade (RPG)
rubber bullet
sabre

sawn-off
  shotgun
scimitar
Scud
semi-automatic
Semtex
sheath knife
shell
shillelagh
shotgun
sidearm
siege gun
six-shooter
sjambok
skean
skean-dhu
slug
small arms
small sword
Smith and
  Wesson
  (trademark)
smooth-bore
spear
staff

stave
Sten gun
stick
stiletto
sub-machine
  gun
switchblade
sword
swordstick
thirty-eight
time bomb
tomahawk
tommy gun
torpedo
tracer
trench mortar
Trident
truncheon
Uzi
warhead
Winchester
  (trademark)
yataghan
zip gun

Parts of a Suit of Armour

basinet
beaver
bracer
brassard
breastplate
brigandine
burgonet
camail
casque

chain mail
chausses
coif
corselet
coutere
cuirass
cuisse
gauntlet
gorget

greave
habergeon
hauberk
helmet
jambeau
lance rest
mail
morion
nasal

neck guard
nosepiece
pectoral
plastron
poleyn
pouldron
rerebrace
sabaton
sallet

solleret
tasses
vambrace
ventail
visor

Types of Soldier

archer
artilleryman
beefeater
blue helmet
bowman
cadet
cannoneer
carabineer
cavalier
cavalryman
centurion
commando
conscript
cuirassier
dragoon

drum major
enlisted man
ensign
evzone
foot soldier
freelance
fusilier
grenadier
guardsman
guerrilla
gunner
halberdier
havildar
hoplite
hussar

infantryman
irregular
janissary
klepht
knight
lancer
legionary
legionnaire
marine
mercenary
military
  policeman
militiaman
musketeer

non-
  commissioned
  officer (NCO)
officer
orderly
paratrooper
partisan
pistoleer
point man
ranger
ranker
recruit
redcap
redcoat
regular

reservist
rifleman
sabreur
samurai
sapper
scout
SEAL
sentinel
sentry
sepoy
spearman
swordsman
Territorial
trooper
yeoman

Jj

jab v. *he jabbed the Englishman with his finger* **poke**, prod, dig, nudge, butt, ram; thrust, stab, push.
▶ n. *a jab in the ribs* **poke**, prod, dig, nudge, butt; thrust, stab, push.

jabber v. *they jabbered away non-stop* **prattle**, babble, chatter, twitter, prate, gabble, rattle on/away, blather; informal yak, yap, yabber, yatter, blab, blabber; Brit. informal witter, rabbit, natter; old use twaddle, clack.
▶ n. *stop your jabber!* **prattle**, babble, chatter, chattering, twitter, twittering, gabble, blather; informal yabbering, yatter, blabber; Brit. informal wittering, rabbiting, nattering; old use clack.

jack v.
□ **jack something up 1** *they jacked up the car* **raise**, hoist, lift (up), winch up, lever up, hitch up, elevate. **2** informal *he may need to jack up interest rates* **increase**, raise, put up, up, mark up; informal hike (up), bump up.

jacket n. *a jacket for your hot-water tank will save about £15 a year* **wrapping**, wrapper, wrap, sleeve, sheath, sheathing, cover, covering.

jackpot n. *this week's lottery jackpot* **top prize**, first prize; pool, bonanza.
□ **hit the jackpot** informal win a lot of money, strike it lucky/rich; informal clean up, hit the big time.

jaded adj. **1** *a jaded palate* **satiated**, sated, surfeited, glutted; dulled, blunted, deadened. **2** *she felt really jaded* **tired (out)**, weary, wearied, worn out, exhausted, fatigued, overtired, sapped, drained; informal all in, done (in), dead (beat), dead on one's feet, bushed; Brit. informal knackered, whacked; N. Amer. informal tuckered out.
– OPPOSITES fresh.

jag n. **sharp projection**, point, barb, thorn.

jagged adj. **spiky**, barbed, ragged, rough, uneven, irregular, broken; serrated, sawtooth, indented.
– OPPOSITES smooth.

jail n. *he was thrown into jail* **prison**, penal institution, lock-up, detention centre; N. Amer. penitentiary, jailhouse, stockade, correctional facility; informal clink, slammer, inside, jug, brig, cooler; Brit. informal nick; N. Amer. informal can, pen, slam, pokey; Brit. historical approved school, borstal, bridewell; N. Amer. historical reformatory.
▶ v. *she was jailed for killing her husband* **imprison**, put in prison, send to prison, incarcerate, lock up, put away, intern, detain, hold (prisoner/captive); informal send down, put behind bars, put inside; Brit. informal bang up.
– OPPOSITES acquit, release.

jailer n. **prison officer**, warder, wardress, warden, guard, captor; informal screw; old use turnkey.

jam¹ v. **1** *he jammed a finger in each ear* **stuff**, shove, force, ram, thrust, press, push, stick, squeeze, cram. **2** *hundreds of people jammed into the hall* **crowd**, pack, pile, press, squeeze, cram; throng, mob, occupy, fill, overcrowd, obstruct, block, clog, congest. **3** *the rudder had jammed* **stick**, become stuck, catch, seize (up), become trapped. **4** *dust can jam the mechanism* **immobilize**, paralyse, disable, cripple, put out of action, bring to a standstill.
▶ n. **1** *a traffic jam* **tailback**, hold-up, congestion, bottleneck; N. Amer. gridlock; informal snarl-up. **2** informal *we are in a real jam* **predicament**, plight, tricky situation, difficulty, problem, quandary, dilemma, muddle, mess, imbroglio, mare's nest, dire straits; informal pickle, stew, fix, hole, scrape, bind, (tight) spot, (tight) corner, hot/deep water; Brit. informal spot of bother.

jam² n. *raspberry jam* **preserve**, conserve, jelly, marmalade.

jamb n. **post**, doorpost, upright, frame.

jamboree n. **rally**, gathering, convention, conference; festival, fete, fiesta, gala, carnival, celebration; informal bash, shindig, shindy, junket.

jammy adj. Brit. informal See **lucky** (sense 1).

jangle v. **1** *keys jangled at his waist* **clank**, clink, jingle, tinkle. **2** *the noise jangled her nerves* **grate on**, jar on, irritate, disturb, fray, put/set on edge; informal get on.
▶ n. *the jangle of his chains* **clank**, clanking, clink, clinking, jangling, jingle, jingling, tintinnabulation.

janitor n. **caretaker**, custodian, porter, concierge, doorkeeper, doorman, warden; cleaner, maintenance man; N. Amer. superintendent.

jar¹ n. *a jar of honey* **(glass) container**, pot, crock, receptacle.

jar² v. **1** *each step jarred my whole body* **jolt**, jerk, shake, vibrate. **2** *her shrill voice jarred on him* **grate**, set someone's teeth on edge, irritate, annoy, irk, exasperate, nettle, disturb, discompose; informal rile, aggravate, get on someone's nerves. **3** *the play's symbolism jarred with the realism of its setting* **clash**, conflict, contrast, be incompatible, be at variance, be at odds, be inconsistent, be discordant; informal scream at.

jargon n. **specialized language**, slang, cant, idiom, argot, patter, gobbledegook; informal lingo, -speak, -ese, mumbo jumbo, geekspeak.

jarring adj. **clashing**, conflicting, contrasting, incompatible, incongruous; discordant, dissonant, inharmonious, harsh, grating, strident, shrill, cacophonous.
– OPPOSITES harmonious.

jaundiced adj. **bitter**, resentful, cynical, soured, disenchanted, disillusioned, disappointed, pessimistic, sceptical, distrustful, suspicious, misanthropic.

jaunt n. **(pleasure) trip**, outing, excursion, day trip, day out, mini holiday, short break; tour, drive, ride, run; informal spin, tootle.

jaunty adj. **cheerful**, cheery, happy, merry, jolly, joyful; lively, perky, bright, buoyant, bubbly, bouncy, breezy, full of the joys of spring, in good spirits, exuberant, ebullient; carefree, airy, light-hearted, nonchalant, insouciant, happy-go-lucky; informal bright-eyed and bushy-tailed, full of beans, chirpy; literary blithe, blithesome.
– OPPOSITES depressed, serious.

javelin n. **spear**, harpoon, dart, gig, shaft, assegai.

jaw n. **1** *a broken jaw* **jawbone**, lower/upper jaw; Anatomy mandible, maxilla. **2** *the whale seized a seal pup in its jaws* **mouth**, maw, muzzle; informal chops. **3** informal *we ought to have a jaw*. See **chat** (noun).

WORD LINKS

mandibular, maxillary relating to the jaw
prognathous having a projecting lower jaw
lockjaw, trismus spasm of the jaw muscles, causing the mouth to remain tightly closed

---

jazz v.
□ **jazz something up** informal enliven, liven up, brighten up, add (some) colour to, ginger up, perk up, spice up; informal pep up, sex up.

jazzy adj. **bright**, colourful, brightly coloured, striking, eye-catching, vivid, lively, vibrant, bold, flamboyant, showy, gaudy; informal flashy.
– OPPOSITES dull.

jealous adj. **1** *he was jealous of his brother's popularity* **envious**, covetous, desirous; resentful, grudging, begrudging, green (with envy). **2** *a jealous lover* **suspicious**, distrustful, mistrustful, doubting, insecure, anxious; possessive, proprietorial, overprotective. **3** *they are very jealous of their rights* **protective**, vigilant, watchful, heedful, mindful, careful, solicitous.
– OPPOSITES proud, trusting.

jealousy n. **1** *he was consumed with jealousy* **envy**, covetousness; resentment, resentfulness, bitterness, spite; informal the green-eyed monster. **2** *the jealousy of his long-suffering wife* **suspicion**,

suspiciousness, distrust, mistrust, insecurity, anxiety; possessiveness, overprotectiveness. **3** *an intense jealousy of status* **protectiveness**, vigilance, watchfulness, heedfulness, mindfulness, care, solicitousness.

jeer v. *the demonstrators jeered the police* **taunt**, mock, scoff at, ridicule, sneer at, deride, insult, abuse, jibe (at), scorn, shout disapproval (at); heckle, catcall (at), boo (at), hoot at, whistle at, hiss (at); old use flout at.
– OPPOSITES cheer.
▸ n. *the jeers of the crowd* **taunt**, sneer, insult, shout, jibe, boo, hiss, catcall; derision, teasing, scoffing, abuse, scorn, heckling, catcalling; Brit. & Austral./NZ barracking.
– OPPOSITES applause.

jejune adj. **1** *their jejune opinions* **naive**, innocent, artless, guileless, unworldly, childlike, ingenuous, unsophisticated; credulous, gullible; childish, immature, juvenile, puerile, infantile. **2** *the following poem is rather jejune* **boring**, dull, tedious, dreary; uninteresting, unexciting, uninspiring, unimaginative; humdrum, run-of-the-mill, mundane, commonplace; lacklustre, dry, sterile, lifeless, vapid, flat, bland, banal, trite, prosaic; Brit. informal samey.
– OPPOSITES sophisticated, fascinating.

jell v. See **gel**.

jeopardize v. **threaten**, endanger, imperil, risk, put at risk, put in danger/jeopardy, drive a nail into the coffin of; leave vulnerable; compromise, prejudice, be prejudicial to; be a danger to, pose a threat to; old use peril.
– OPPOSITES safeguard.

jeopardy n. **danger**, peril; at risk.

jerk n. **1** *she gave the reins a jerk* **yank**, tug, pull, wrench, tweak, twitch. **2** *he let the clutch in with a jerk* **jolt**, lurch, bump, start, jar, jog, bang, bounce, shake, shock. **3** informal *I felt a complete jerk*. See **fool** (sense 1 of the noun).
▸ v. **1** *she jerked her arm free* **yank**, tug, pull, wrench, wrest, drag, pluck, snatch, seize, rip, tear. **2** *the car jerked along* **jolt**, lurch, bump, rattle, bounce, shake, jounce.

jerky adj. **1** *jerky movements* **convulsive**, spasmodic, fitful, twitchy, shaky. **2** *the coach drew to a jerky halt* **jolting**, lurching, bumpy, bouncy, jarring.
– OPPOSITES smooth.

jerry-built adj. **shoddy**, badly built, gimcrack, flimsy, insubstantial, rickety, ramshackle, crude, makeshift; inferior, poor-quality, second-rate, third-rate, low-grade.
– OPPOSITES sturdy.

jersey n. **pullover**, sweater; Brit. jumper; informal woolly.

jest n. *jests were bandied about freely* **joke**, witticism, funny remark, gag, quip, sally, pun; informal crack, wisecrack, one-liner.
▸ v. **1** *surely you are jesting* **joke**, quip, gag, pun; tell jokes, crack jokes; informal wisecrack. **2** *she feared that they had not been jesting* **fool (about/around)**, play a practical joke, tease;

informal kid, have someone on, pull someone's leg; N. Amer. informal pull someone's chain, fun; Brit. informal wind someone up.

□ **in jest** in fun, as a joke, tongue in cheek, playfully, jokingly, light-heartedly, facetiously, flippantly, frivolously, for a laugh.

jester n. **1** historical *a court jester* **(court) fool**, court jester, clown; old use merry andrew. **2** *the class jester* **joker**, comedian, comic, humorist, wag, wit, prankster, jokester, clown, buffoon; informal card, case, caution, hoot, scream, laugh, wisecracker, barrel of laughs; Austral./NZ informal hard case.

jet[1] n. **1** *a jet of water* **stream**, spurt, squirt, spray, spout; gush, rush, surge, burst. **2** *carburettor jets* **nozzle**, head, spout. **3** *an executive jet* **jet plane**, jetliner, aircraft, plane; Brit. aeroplane.

▸ v. **1** *they jetted out of Heathrow* **fly**. **2** *puffs of gas jetted out* **squirt**, spurt, shoot, spray; gush, pour, stream, rush, pump, surge, spew, burst.

jet[2] adj. *her glossy jet hair* **black**, jet-black, pitch-black, ink-black, ebony, raven, sable, sooty.

jettison v. **1** *six aircraft jettisoned their loads* **dump**, drop, ditch, discharge, throw out, tip out, unload, throw overboard. **2** *he jettisoned his unwanted papers | the scheme was jettisoned* **discard**, dispose of, throw away/out, get rid of; reject, scrap, axe, abandon, drop; informal chuck (away/out), dump, ditch, bin, junk, get shut of; Brit. informal get shot of; N. Amer. informal trash.
– OPPOSITES retain.

jetty n. **pier**, landing (stage), quay, wharf, dock; breakwater, mole, groyne, dyke; N. Amer. dockominium, levee.

jewel n. **1** *priceless jewels* **gem**, gemstone, (precious) stone, brilliant; baguette; informal sparkler, rock; old use bijou. **2** *the jewel of his collection* **finest example/specimen**, showpiece, pride (and joy), cream, crème de la crème, jewel in the crown, nonpareil, glory, prize, boast, pick, ne plus ultra. **3** *the girl is a jewel* **treasure**, angel, paragon, marvel, find, godsend; informal one in a million, a star, the tops; old use nonsuch.

jewellery n. **jewels**, gems, gemstones, precious stones, bijouterie, costume jewellery, diamanté; old use bijoux.

jib v. **1** *the horse jibbed at the final fence* **stop (short) at**, balk at, shy at; refuse. **2** *some farmers jib at paying large veterinary bills* **balk at**, fight shy of, recoil from, shrink from; be unwilling, be reluctant, be loath, demur at; informal boggle at.
– OPPOSITES clear.

jibe n. *cruel jibes* **snide remark**, cutting remark, taunt, sneer, jeer, insult, barb; informal dig, put-down.

▸ v. *Simon jibed in a sarcastic way* **jeer**, taunt, mock, scoff, sneer.

jiffy n.
□ **in a jiffy** informal (very) soon, in a second, in a minute, in a moment, in a trice, in a

flash, shortly, any second, any minute (now), in no time (at all); N. Amer. momentarily; informal in a sec, in a nanosecond, in a jiff, in two shakes (of a lamb's tail), before you can say Jack Robinson; Brit. informal in a tick, in two ticks, in a mo; N. Amer. informal in a snap, in jig time; dated directly.

jig v. **bob**, jump, spring, skip, hop, prance, bounce, jounce.

jiggle v. **1** *Barrett jiggled his foot* **shake**, joggle, waggle, wiggle. **2** *Thomas jiggled excitedly* **fidget**, wriggle, squirm.

jilt v. **leave**, walk out on, throw over, finish with, break up with; informal chuck, ditch, dump, drop, run out on; Brit. informal give someone the elbow, give someone the big E, give someone the push, bin off; literary forsake.

jingle n. **1** *the jingle of money in the till* **clink**, chink, tinkle, jangle. **2** *the jingle of the bell* **tinkle**, ring, ding, ping, ting-a-ling, chime, tintinnabulation. **3** *advertising jingles* **slogan**, catchphrase; ditty, song, rhyme, tune; N. Amer. informal tag line.

▸ v. **1** *her bracelets jingled noisily* **clink**, chink, tinkle, jangle. **2** *the bell jingled* **tinkle**, ring, ding, ping, chime.

jingoism n. **extreme patriotism**, chauvinism, extreme nationalism, xenophobia; hawkishness, militarism, belligerence, bellicosity.

jinx n. *the jinx struck six days later* **curse**, spell, hoodoo, malediction; the evil eye, black magic, voodoo, bad luck; N. Amer. hex; old use malison.

▸ v. *the family is jinxed* **curse**, cast a spell on, put the evil eye on, hoodoo; Austral. point the bone at; N. Amer. hex; Austral. informal mozz, put the mozz on.

jitters plural n. informal **nervousness**, nerves, edginess, uneasiness, anxiety, anxiousness, tension, agitation, restlessness; stage fright; informal butterflies (in one's stomach), the willies, collywobbles, the heebie-jeebies, jitteriness, the jim-jams.

jittery adj. informal **nervous**, on edge, edgy, tense, anxious, nervy, ill at ease, uneasy, keyed up, overwrought, on tenterhooks, worried, apprehensive; informal with butterflies in one's stomach, like a cat on a hot tin roof, twitchy, jumpy, uptight, het up, in a tizz/tizzy; Brit. informal strung up, like a cat on hot bricks; N. Amer. informal spooky, squirrelly, antsy; Austral./NZ informal toey; dated overstrung.
– OPPOSITES calm.

job n. **1** *my job involves a lot of travelling* **position**, post, situation, appointment; occupation, profession, employment, trade, career, (line of) work, métier, craft; vocation, calling; vacancy, opening; Austral. informal grip; old use employ. **2** *this job will take three months* **task**, piece of work, assignment, project; chore, errand; undertaking, venture, operation, enterprise, business. **3** *it's your job to protect her* **responsibility**, duty, charge, task; role, function, mission; informal

j

department, pigeon. **4** informal *it was a job to get here on time* **difficult task**, problem, trouble, struggle, strain, trial, bother; informal headache, hassle, pain. **5** informal *a bank job* **crime**, felony; raid, robbery, hold-up, burglary, break-in; informal stick-up; N. Amer. informal heist.

> **WORD LINKS**
> **vocational** relating to a job or employment
> **nepotism** the practice of giving jobs to relatives or friends
> **moonlight** do a second job without declaring it for tax purposes
> **sinecure** a paid job involving little or no work
> **tenure** the right to stay permanently in a job

jobless adj. **unemployed**, out of work, out of a job, unwaged, between jobs, redundant, laid off; Brit. informal signing on, on the dole, 'resting'; Austral./NZ informal on the wallaby track.
– OPPOSITES employed.

jockey n. **rider**, horseman, horsewoman, equestrian; Austral. informal hoop.
▸ v. *ministers began jockeying for position* **compete**, contend, vie; struggle, fight, scramble, jostle.

jocular adj. **humorous**, funny, witty, comic, comical, amusing, chucklesome, droll, jokey, hilarious, facetious, tongue-in-cheek, teasing, playful; light-hearted, jovial, cheerful, cheery, merry; formal jocose, ludic.
– OPPOSITES solemn.

jocund adj. formal See **cheerful** (sense 1).

jog v. **1** *he jogged along the road* **run slowly**, jogtrot, dogtrot, trot, lope. **2** *things are jogging along quite nicely* **continue**, proceed, go on, carry on. **3** *a hand jogged his elbow* **nudge**, prod, poke, push, bump, jar. **4** *something jogged her memory* **stimulate**, prompt, stir, activate, refresh. **5** *she jogged her foot up and down* **joggle**, jiggle, bob, bounce, jolt, jerk.
▸ n. *he set off along at a jog* **run**, jogtrot, dogtrot, trot, lope.

joie de vivre n. **gaiety**, cheerfulness, cheeriness, light-heartedness, happiness, joy, joyfulness, high spirits, jollity, joviality, exuberance, ebullience, liveliness, vivacity, verve, effervescence, buoyancy, zest, zestfulness; informal pep, zing; literary blitheness.
– OPPOSITES sobriety.

join v. **1** *the two parts of the mould are joined with clay* **connect**, unite, couple, fix, affix, attach, fasten, stick, glue, fuse, weld, amalgamate, bond, append, link, merge, secure, make fast, tie, bind, chain; formal conjoin. **2** *here the path joins a major road* **meet**, touch, reach, extend to, abut, adjoin, border (on). **3** *I'm off to join the search party* **become a member of**, help in, participate in, join in, get involved in, contribute to, have a hand in; enlist, join up, sign up, affiliate to; play a part, band together, get together, ally, team up, join forces.
– OPPOSITES separate, leave.
▸ n. See **joint**.

joint n. **1** *a leaky joint in the guttering* **join**, junction, juncture, intersection, link, linkage, connection; weld, seam; Anatomy commissure. **2** *the hip joint* **articulation**. **3** *a classy joint* **establishment**, restaurant, bar, club, nightclub. **4** informal *he rolled a joint* **cannabis cigarette**, marijuana cigarette; informal spliff, reefer, bomb, bomber, stick; Brit. informal bifter.
▸ adj. *matters of joint interest | a joint effort* **common**, shared, communal, collective; mutual, cooperative, collaborative, concerted, combined, united.
– OPPOSITES separate.
▸ v. *she jointed the carcass* **cut up**, chop up, butcher, carve.

> **WORD LINKS**
> **arthritis, rheumatism** painful inflammation and stiffness of the joints
> **gout** a disease that causes the joints to swell
> **dislocate** displace a bone from its proper position in a joint
> **sprain** wrench the ligaments of a joint, causing pain and swelling
> **chiropractic** a system of complementary medicine based on manipulation of the joints

jointly adv. **together**, in partnership, in cooperation, cooperatively, in conjunction, in combination, mutually.

joke n. **1** *they were telling jokes* **funny story**, jest, witticism, quip; pun, play on words; informal gag, wisecrack, crack, funny, one-liner, killer, rib-tickler, knee-slapper, thigh-slapper; N. Amer. informal boffola; rare blague. **2** *playing stupid jokes* **trick**, practical joke, prank, stunt, hoax, jape; informal leg-pull, spoof. **3** informal *he soon became a joke to us* **laughing stock**, figure of fun, object of ridicule, Aunt Sally. **4** informal *the present system is a joke* **farce**, travesty, waste of time; N. Amer. informal shuck.
▸ v. **1** *she joked with the guests* **tell jokes**, jest, banter, quip; informal wisecrack, josh. **2** *I'm only joking* **fool (about/around)**, play a trick, play a (practical) joke, tease, hoax, pull someone's leg, mess about/around; informal kid; Brit. informal have someone on, wind someone up; N. Amer. informal fun, shuck, pull someone's chain.

joker n. **humorist**, comedian, comedienne, comic, wit, jester; prankster, practical joker, hoaxer, trickster, clown; informal card, wisecracker, wag.

jolly adj. **cheerful**, happy, cheery, good-humoured, jovial, merry, sunny, joyful, joyous, light-hearted, in high spirits, bubbly, exuberant, ebullient, cock-a-hoop, gleeful, mirthful, genial, fun-loving; informal chipper, chirpy, perky, bright-eyed and bushy-tailed; formal jocund, jocose; dated gay; literary gladsome, blithe, blithesome.
– OPPOSITES miserable.
▸ v. informal *he tried to jolly her along* **encourage**, urge, coax, cajole, persuade.
▸ adv. Brit. informal *a jolly good idea*. See **very** (adverb).

jolt v. **1** *the train jolted the passengers to one side* **push**, thrust, jar, bump, knock, bang; shake, joggle, jog. **2** *the car jolted along* **bump**, bounce, jerk, rattle, lurch, shudder, judder, jounce. **3** *she was jolted out of her reverie* **startle**, surprise, shock, stun, shake, take aback; astonish, astound, amaze, stagger, stop someone in their tracks; informal rock, floor, knock sideways; Brit. informal knock for six.
▸ n. **1** *a series of sickening jolts* **bump**, bounce, shake, jerk, lurch. **2** *he woke up with a jolt* **start**, jerk, jump. **3** *the sight of the dagger gave him a jolt* **fright**, the fright of one's life, shock, scare, surprise; informal turn.

jostle v. **1** *she was jostled by noisy students* **bump into/against**, knock into/against, bang into, cannon into, plough into, jolt; push, shove, elbow; mob. **2** *I jostled my way to the exit* **push**, thrust, barge, shove, force, elbow, shoulder, bulldoze. **3** *people jostled for the best position* **struggle**, vie, jockey, scramble.

jot v. *I've jotted down a few details* **write**, note, make a note of, take down, put on paper; scribble, scrawl.
▸ n. *not a jot of evidence* **iota**, scrap, shred, whit, grain, crumb, ounce, (little) bit, jot or tittle, speck, atom, particle, scintilla, trace, hint; informal smidgen, tad; Austral./NZ informal skerrick; old use scruple.

journal n. **1** *a medical journal* **periodical**, magazine, gazette, digest, review, newsletter, news-sheet, bulletin; newspaper, paper; daily, weekly, monthly, quarterly. **2** *he keeps a journal* **diary**, daily record, log, logbook, chronicle; weblog, blog, vlog; N. Amer. daybook.

journalism n. **1** *a career in journalism* **the newspaper business**, the press, the fourth estate; Brit. Fleet Street. **2** *his incisive style of journalism* **reporting**, writing, reportage, feature writing, news coverage; articles, reports, features, pieces, stories.

journalist n. **reporter**, correspondent, newspaperman, newspaperwoman, newsman, newswoman, columnist, writer, commentator, reviewer; investigative journalist; Brit. pressman; N. Amer. legman, wireman; Austral. roundsman; informal newshound, hack, hackette, stringer, journo; N. Amer. informal newsy.

journey n. *his journey round the world* **trip**, expedition, tour, trek, voyage, cruise, ride, drive, transfer; crossing, passage, flight; travels, wandering, globetrotting; odyssey, pilgrimage; old use peregrination.
▸ v. *they journeyed south* **travel**, go, voyage, sail, cruise, fly, hike, trek, ride, drive, make one's way; tour; old use peregrinate.

joust historical v. *knights jousted with lances* **tourney**; fight, spar, clash; historical tilt.
▸ n. *a medieval joust* **tournament**, tourney; combat, contest, fight; historical tilt.

jovial adj. **cheerful**, jolly, happy, cheery, good-humoured, convivial, genial, good-natured, friendly, amiable, affable, sociable, outgoing; smiling, merry, sunny, joyful, joyous, high-spirited, exuberant; informal chipper, chirpy, perky, bright-eyed and bushy-tailed; formal jocund, jocose; dated gay; literary gladsome, blithe, blithesome.
– OPPOSITES miserable.

joy n. **1** *whoops of joy* **delight**, great pleasure, joyfulness, jubilation, triumph, exultation, rejoicing, happiness, gladness, glee, exhilaration, exuberance, elation, euphoria, bliss, ecstasy, rapture; enjoyment, felicity, joie de vivre; formal jocundity, jouissance. **2** *it was a joy to be with her* **(source of) pleasure**, delight, treat, thrill; informal buzz, kick. **3** Brit. informal *we still had no joy* **success**, satisfaction, luck, successful result.
– OPPOSITES misery, trial.

joyful adj. **1** *his joyful mood* **cheerful**, happy, jolly, merry, sunny, joyous, light-hearted, in good spirits, bubbly, exuberant, ebullient, cock-a-hoop, cheery, smiling, mirthful, radiant; jubilant, overjoyed, thrilled, ecstatic, euphoric, blissful, on cloud nine, elated, delighted, gleeful; jovial, genial, good-humoured, full of the joys of spring; informal chipper, chirpy, peppy, over the moon, on top of the world; Austral./NZ informal wrapped; dated gay; formal jocund; literary gladsome, blithe, blithesome. **2** *joyful news* **pleasing**, happy, good, cheering, gladdening, welcome, heart-warming; literary gladsome. **3** *a joyful occasion* **happy**, cheerful, merry, jolly, festive, joyous.
– OPPOSITES sad, distressing.

joyless adj. **1** *a joyless man* **gloomy**, melancholy, morose, lugubrious, glum, sombre, saturnine, sullen, dour, humourless. **2** *a joyless room* **depressing**, cheerless, gloomy, dreary, bleak, dispiriting, drab, dismal, desolate, austere, sombre; unwelcoming, uninviting, inhospitable; literary drear.
– OPPOSITES cheerful, welcoming.

joyous adj. See **joyful** (senses 1 & 3).

jubilant adj. **overjoyed**, exultant, triumphant, joyful, rejoicing, cock-a-hoop, exuberant, elated, thrilled, gleeful, euphoric, ecstatic, enraptured, in raptures, walking on air, in seventh heaven, on cloud nine; informal over the moon, on top of the world, on a high; N. Amer. informal wigged out; Austral. informal wrapped.
– OPPOSITES despondent.

jubilation n. **exultation**, joy, joyousness, elation, euphoria, ecstasy, rapture, glee, gleefulness, exuberance.

jubilee n. **anniversary**, commemoration; celebration, festival, jamboree; festivities, revelry.

judge n. **1** *the judge sentenced him to five years* **justice**, magistrate, recorder, sheriff; N. Amer. jurist; Brit. informal beak. **2** *a panel of judges will select the winner* **adjudicator**, arbiter, assessor, evaluator, appraiser, examiner, moderator, mediator; umpire, referee, linesman, line judge.

j

j

▶ v. **1** *I judged that she was simply exhausted* **form the opinion**, conclude, decide; consider, believe, think, deem, view; deduce, gather, infer, gauge, estimate, guess, surmise, conjecture; regard as, look on as, take to be, rate as, class as; informal reckon, figure. **2** *the case was judged by a tribunal* **try**, hear; adjudicate, decide, give a ruling/ verdict on. **3** *she was judged innocent of murder* **adjudge**, pronounce, decree, rule, find. **4** *the competition will be judged by Alan Amey* **adjudicate**, arbitrate, mediate, moderate. **5** *entries were judged by a panel of experts* **assess**, appraise, evaluate; examine, review.

> **WORD LINKS**
> **judicial** relating to a judge
> **the judicature, the judiciary** judges as a group

judgement n. **1** *his temper could affect his judgement* **discernment**, acumen, shrewdness, astuteness, (common) sense, perception, perspicacity, percipience, acuity, discrimination, wisdom, wit, judiciousness, prudence, canniness, sharpness, sharp-wittedness, powers of reasoning, reason, logic; informal nous, savvy, horse sense, gumption; Brit. informal common; N. Amer. informal smarts. **2** *a court judgement* **verdict**, decision, adjudication, ruling, pronouncement, decree, finding; sentence. **3** *critical judgement* **assessment**, evaluation, appraisal; review, analysis, criticism, critique. **4** *a judgement on them for their wickedness* **punishment**, retribution, penalty.
  □ **against one's better judgement** reluctantly, unwillingly, grudgingly.
  in my judgement in my opinion, to my mind, to my way of thinking, I believe, I think, as I see it, in my estimation.

judgemental adj. **critical**, censorious, condemnatory, disapproving, disparaging, deprecating, negative, overcritical, hypercritical.

judicial adj. **legal**, juridical, judicatory; official.

judicious adj. **wise**, sensible, prudent, politic, shrewd, astute, canny, sagacious, commonsensical, sound, well advised, well judged, discerning, percipient, intelligent, smart; N. Amer. informal heads-up.
– OPPOSITES ill-advised.

jug n. **pitcher**, ewer, crock, jar, urn; carafe, flask, flagon, decanter; N. Amer. creamer; historical amphora, jorum.

juggle v. **misrepresent**, tamper with, falsify, distort, alter, manipulate, rig, massage, fudge; informal fix, doctor; Brit. informal fiddle.

juice n. **1** *the juice from two lemons* **liquid**, fluid, sap; extract. **2** *cooking juices* **liquid**, liquor. **3** informal *he ran out of juice.* See **petrol**.

juicy adj. **1** *a juicy peach* **succulent**, tender, moist; ripe; old use mellow. **2** informal *juicy gossip* **very interesting**, fascinating, sensational, lurid; scandalous, racy, risqué,

spicy; informal hot. **3** informal *juicy profits* **large**, substantial, sizeable, generous; lucrative, profitable; informal fat, tidy.
– OPPOSITES dry, dull.

jumble n. **1** *the books were in a jumble* **untidy heap**, clutter, muddle, mess, confusion, disarray, disarrangement, tangle; hotchpotch, mishmash, miscellany, motley collection, mixed bag, medley, farrago; N. Amer. hodgepodge. **2** Brit. *bags of jumble* **junk**, bric-a-brac; Brit. lumber.
▶ v. *the photographs are all jumbled up* **mix up**, muddle up, disarrange, disorganize, disorder.

jumbo adj. informal See **huge**.

jump v. **1** *the cat jumped off his lap | Flora began to jump about* **leap**, spring, bound, hop; skip, caper, dance, prance, frolic, cavort. **2** *he jumped the fence* **vault (over)**, leap over, clear, sail over, hop over, hurdle. **3** *pre-tax profits jumped* **rise**, go up, shoot up, soar, surge, climb, increase; informal skyrocket. **4** *the noise made her jump* **start**, jerk, jolt, flinch, recoil; informal jump out of one's skin. **5** *Polly jumped at the chance* **accept eagerly**, leap at, welcome with open arms, seize on, snap up, grab, pounce on. **6** informal *he jumped the red light* **ignore**, disregard, drive through, overshoot; informal run.
▶ n. **1** *the short jump across the gully* **leap**, spring, vault, bound, hop. **2** *the horse cleared the last jump* **obstacle**, barrier; fence, hurdle. **3** *a jump in profits* **rise**, leap, increase, upsurge, upswing; informal hike. **4** *I woke up with a jump* **start**, jerk, involuntary movement, spasm.
  □ **jump the gun** informal act prematurely, act too soon, be overhasty, be precipitate; informal be ahead of oneself.
  jump to it informal hurry up, get a move on, be quick; informal get cracking, shake a leg, look lively, look sharp, pull one's finger out, get a wiggle on; Brit. informal get one's skates on, stir one's stumps; dated make haste.

jumper Brit. n. **sweater**, pullover, jersey; informal woolly.

jumpy adj. informal **1** *he was tired and jumpy* **nervous**, on edge, edgy, tense, nervy, anxious, ill at ease, uneasy, restless, fidgety, keyed up, overwrought, on tenterhooks; informal a bundle of nerves, jittery, like a cat on a hot tin roof, uptight, het up, in a tizz/tizzy; Brit. informal strung up, like a cat on hot bricks; N. Amer. informal spooky, squirrelly, antsy; Austral./NZ informal toey. **2** *jumpy black-and-white footage* **jerky**, jolting, lurching, bumpy, jarring; fitful, convulsive.

junction n. **1** *the junction between the roof and the wall* **join**, joint, intersection, bond, seam, connection, juncture; Anatomy commissure. **2** *the junction of the two rivers* **confluence**, convergence, meeting point, conflux, juncture. **3** *turn right at the next junction* **crossroads**, intersection, interchange, T-junction; turn, turn-off, exit; Brit. roundabout; N. Amer. turnout, cloverleaf.

juncture n. **1** *at this juncture, I am unable to tell you* **point (in time)**, time, moment (in time); period, phase. **2** *the juncture of the pipes.* See **junction** (sense 1). **3** *the juncture of the rivers.* See **junction** (sense 2).

jungle n. **1** *the Amazon jungle* **tropical forest**, (tropical) rainforest. **2** *a jungle of bureaucracy* **complexity**, confusion, complication, chaos; labyrinth, maze, tangle, web.

junior adj. **1** *the junior members of the family* **younger**, youngest. **2** *a junior minister* **low-ranking**, lower-ranking, subordinate, lesser, lower, minor, secondary. **3** *John White Junior* **the Younger**; Brit. minor; N. Amer. II, the Second.
– OPPOSITES senior, older.

junk informal n. *an attic full of junk* **rubbish**, clutter, odds and ends, bits and pieces, bric-a-brac; refuse, litter, scrap, waste, debris, detritus, dross; Brit. lumber; N. Amer. garbage, trash; Austral./NZ mullock; Brit. informal odds and sods.
▶ v. *junk all the rubbish* **throw away/out**, discard, get rid of, dispose of, scrap, toss out, jettison; informal chuck (away/out), dump, ditch, bin, get shut of; Brit. informal get shot of.

junket n. informal **celebration**, party, jamboree, feast, festivity; spree, excursion, outing, trip, jaunt; informal bash, shindy, shindig; Brit. informal beanfeast, jolly, bunfight, beano; Austral. informal jollo.

junta n. **faction**, cabal, clique, party, set, ring, gang, league, confederacy; historical junto.

jurisdiction n. **1** *an area under French jurisdiction* **authority**, control, power, dominion, rule, administration, command, sway, leadership, sovereignty, hegemony. **2** *foreign jurisdictions* **territory**, region, province, district, area, domain, realm.

just adj. **1** *a just and democratic society* **fair**, fair-minded, equitable, even-handed, impartial, unbiased, objective, neutral, disinterested, unprejudiced, open-minded, non-partisan; honourable, upright, decent, honest, righteous, moral, virtuous, principled. **2** *a just reward* **(well) deserved**, (well) earned, merited; rightful, due, fitting, appropriate, suitable; formal condign; old use meet. **3** *just criticism* **valid**, sound, well founded, justified, justifiable, warranted, legitimate.
– OPPOSITES unfair, undeserved.
▶ adv. **1** *I just saw him* **a moment/second ago**, a short time ago, very recently, not long ago. **2** *she's just right for him* **exactly**, precisely, absolutely, completely, totally, entirely, perfectly, utterly, wholly, thoroughly, in all respects; informal down to the ground, to a T,

dead. **3** *we just made it* **narrowly**, only just, by a hair's breadth, by the skin of one's teeth; barely, scarcely, hardly; informal by a whisker. **4** *she's just a child* **only**, merely, simply, (nothing) but, no more than. **5** *the colour's just fantastic* **really**, absolutely, completely, entirely, totally, quite; indeed, truly.
◻ **just about** informal **nearly**, almost, practically, all but, well-nigh, nigh on, virtually, as good as, more or less, to all intents and purposes; informal pretty much.

justice n. **1** *I appealed to his sense of justice* **fairness**, justness, fair play, fair-mindedness, equity, equitableness, even-handedness, impartiality, objectivity, neutrality, disinterestedness, honesty, righteousness, morals, morality. **2** *the justice of his case* **validity**, justification, soundness, well-foundedness, legitimacy. **3** *an order made by the justices* **judge**, magistrate, recorder, sheriff; N. Amer. jurist; Brit. informal beak.

justifiable adj. **valid**, legitimate, warranted, well founded, justified, just, reasonable; defensible, tenable, supportable, acceptable.
– OPPOSITES indefensible.

justification n. **grounds**, reason, basis, rationale, premise, rationalization, vindication, explanation; defence, argument, apologia, apology, case.

justify v. **1** *directors must justify the expenditure* **give grounds for**, give reasons for, give a justification for, explain, give an explanation for, account for; defend, answer for, vindicate. **2** *the situation justified further investigation* **warrant**, be good reason for, be a justification for.

justly adv. **1** *he is justly proud of his achievement* **justifiably**, with (good) reason, legitimately, rightly, rightfully, deservedly. **2** *they were treated justly* **fairly**, with fairness, equitably, even-handedly, impartially, without bias, objectively, without prejudice; informal fairly and squarely.
– OPPOSITES unjustifiably.

jut v. **stick out**, project, protrude, bulge out, overhang, obtrude; old use be imminent.

juvenile adj. **1** *juvenile offenders* **young**, teenage, adolescent, junior, pubescent, prepubescent. **2** *juvenile behaviour* **childish**, immature, puerile, infantile, babyish; jejune, inexperienced, callow, green, unsophisticated, naive, foolish, silly.
– OPPOSITES adult, mature.
▶ n. *many victims are juveniles* **young person**, youngster, child, teenager, adolescent, minor, junior; informal kid.
– OPPOSITES adult.

juxtapose v. **place side by side**, set side by side, mix; compare, contrast.

j

Kk

kaleidoscopic adj. **1** *kaleidoscopic shapes* **multicoloured**, many-coloured, multicolour, many-hued, variegated, particoloured, varicoloured, psychedelic, rainbow, polychromatic. **2** *the kaleidoscopic political landscape* **ever-changing**, changeable, shifting, fluid, protean, variable, inconstant, fluctuating, unpredictable, impermanent. **3** *the kaleidoscopic world we are living in* **multifaceted**, varied; complex, intricate, complicated.
– OPPOSITES monochrome, constant.

kaput informal adj. *the TV's kaput* **broken**, malfunctioning, broken-down, inoperative; informal conked out.
▫ **go kaput** break down, go wrong, stop working; informal conk out.

keel n. *the upturned keel of the boat* **base**, bottom (side), underside.
▫ **keel over 1** *the boat keeled over* **capsize**, turn turtle, turn upside down, founder; overturn, turn over, tip over. **2** *the slightest activity made him keel over* **collapse**, faint, pass out, black out, lose consciousness, swoon.

keen adj. **1** *his publishers were keen to capitalize on his success* **eager**, anxious, intent, impatient, determined, ambitious; informal raring, itching, dying. **2** *a keen birdwatcher* **enthusiastic**, avid, eager, ardent, passionate, fervent, fervid, impassioned; conscientious, committed, dedicated, zealous, driven. **3** *they are keen on horses | a girl he was keen on* **enthusiastic**, interested, passionate; attracted to, fond of, taken with, smitten with, enamoured of, infatuated with; informal struck on, gone on, mad about, crazy about, nuts about. **4** *a keen cutting edge* **sharp**, sharpened, honed, razor-sharp. **5** *keen eyesight* **acute**, sharp, discerning, sensitive, perceptive, clear. **6** *a keen mind* **acute**, penetrating, astute, incisive, sharp, perceptive, piercing, razor-sharp, perspicacious, shrewd, discerning, clever, intelligent, brilliant, bright, smart, wise, canny, percipient, insightful. **7** *a keen wind* **cold**, icy, freezing, harsh, raw, bitter; penetrating, piercing, biting. **8** *a keen sense of duty* **intense**, acute, fierce, passionate, burning, fervent, ardent, strong, powerful.
– OPPOSITES reluctant, unenthusiastic.

keenness n. **1** *the company's keenness to sign a deal* **eagerness**, willingness, readiness, impatience; enthusiasm, fervour, wholeheartedness, zest, zeal, ardour, passion, avidity. **2** *the keenness of the blade* **sharpness**, razor-sharpness. **3** *keenness of hearing* **acuteness**, sharpness, sensitivity, perceptiveness, clarity. **4** *the keenness of his mind* **acuity**, sharpness, incisiveness, astuteness, perspicacity, perceptiveness, shrewdness, insight, cleverness, discernment, intelligence, brightness, brilliance, canniness. **5** *the keenness of his sense of loss* **intensity**, acuteness, strength, power, ferocity.

keep[1] v. **1** *you should keep all the old forms* **retain**, hold on to, keep hold of, not part with; save, store, put by/aside, set aside; N. Amer. set by; informal hang on to, stash away. **2** *I tried to keep calm* **remain**, continue to be, stay, carry on being, persist in being. **3** *he keeps going on about the murder* **persist in**, keep on, carry on, continue. **4** *I shan't keep you long* **detain**, keep waiting, delay, hold up, retard, slow down. **5** *most people kept the rules | he had to keep his promise* **comply with**, obey, observe, conform to, abide by, adhere to, stick to, heed, follow; fulfil, carry out, act on, make good, honour, keep to, stand by. **6** *keeping the old traditions* **preserve**, keep alive/up, keep going, carry on, perpetuate, maintain, uphold, sustain. **7** *the stand where her umbrella was kept* **store**, house, stow, put (away), place, deposit. **8** *the shop keeps a good stock of parchment* **(have in) stock**, carry, have (for sale), hold. **9** *he stole to keep his family* **provide for**, support, feed, keep alive, maintain, sustain; take care of, look after. **10** *she keeps rabbits* **breed**, rear, raise, farm. **11** *his parents kept a shop* **manage**, run, own, be the proprietor of. **12** *God keep you* **look after**, care for, take care of, mind, watch over; protect, keep safe, preserve, defend, guard. **13** *today people do not keep the Sabbath* **observe**, respect, honour, hold sacred; celebrate, mark, commemorate.
– OPPOSITES throw away, break, abandon.
▸ n. *money to pay for his keep* **maintenance**, upkeep, sustenance, board (and lodging), food, livelihood.
▫ **for keeps** informal forever, for ever and ever, for evermore, for always, for good (and all), permanently, in perpetuity; informal until kingdom come, until doomsday; old use for aye.
keep at persevere with, persist with, keep going with, carry on with, press on with, work away at, continue with; informal stick at, peg away at, plug away at, hammer away at.

keep something back 1 *she kept back some of the money* **(keep in) reserve**, put by/aside, set aside; retain, hold back, keep, hold on to, not part with; N. Amer. set by; informal stash away. **2** *she kept back the details* **conceal**, keep secret, keep hidden, withhold, suppress, keep quiet about. **3** *she could hardly keep back her tears* **suppress**, stifle, choke back, fight back, hold back/in, repress, keep in check, contain, smother, swallow, bite back.

keep from refrain from, stop oneself, restrain oneself from, prevent oneself from, forbear from, avoid.

keep someone from something 1 *he could hardly keep himself from laughing* **prevent**, stop, restrain, hold back. **2** *keep them from harm* **preserve**, protect, keep safe, guard, shield, shelter, safeguard, defend.

keep something from someone keep secret, keep hidden, hide, conceal, withhold, suppress, censor, redact; informal keep dark.

keep off 1 *keep off private land* **stay off**, not enter, keep/stay away from. **2** *Maud tried to keep off political subjects* **avoid**, steer clear of, stay away from, evade, sidestep; informal duck. **3** *you should keep off alcohol* **abstain from**, do without, refrain from, give up, forgo, not touch; informal swear off; formal forswear. **4** *I hope the rain keeps off* **stay away**, hold off, not start, not begin.

keep on 1 *they kept on working* **continue**, go on, carry on, persist in, persevere in; soldier on, struggle on, keep going. **2** *the commander kept on about vigilance* **talk constantly**, talk endlessly, keep talking, go on (and on), rant on; informal harp on, witter on, rabbit on.

keep on at nag, go on at, harp on at, badger, chivvy, harass, hound, pester; informal hassle.

keep to 1 *I've got to keep to the rules* **obey**, abide by, observe, follow, comply with, adhere to, respect, keep, stick to, be bound by. **2** *keep to the path* **follow**, stick to, stay on. **3** *please keep to the point* **stick to**, restrict oneself to, confine oneself to.

keep something up continue (with), keep on with, keep going, carry on with, persist with, persevere with.

keep up with 1 *she walked fast to keep up with him* **keep pace with**, keep abreast of; match, equal. **2** *he kept up with events at home* **keep informed about**, keep up to date with, keep abreast of; informal keep tabs on.

keep² n. *the enemy stormed the keep* **fortress**, fort, stronghold, tower, donjon, castle, citadel, bastion.

keeper n. **1** *keeper of the archives* **curator**, custodian, guardian, administrator, overseer, steward, caretaker. **2** *the keeper of an inn* **proprietor**, owner, master/ mistress, landlord/landlady. **3** *you're not her keeper* **guardian**, protector, guard, minder, chaperon/chaperone; carer, nursemaid, nurse.

keeping n. *the document is in the keeping of the county archivist* **safe keeping**, care, custody, charge, possession, trust, protection.
▫ **in keeping with** consistent with, in harmony with, in accord with, in agreement with, in line with, in character with, compatible with; appropriate to, befitting, suitable for.

keepsake n. **memento**, souvenir, reminder, remembrance, token.

keg n. **barrel**, cask, vat, butt, tun, hogshead; historical firkin.

ken n. **knowledge**, awareness, perception, understanding, grasp, comprehension, realization, appreciation, consciousness.

kernel n. **1** *the kernel of a nut* **seed**, grain, core; nut. **2** *the kernel of the argument* **essence**, core, heart, essentials, quintessence, fundamentals, basics, nub, gist, substance; informal nitty-gritty. **3** *a kernel of truth* **nucleus**, germ, grain, nugget.

key n. **1** *the key to the mystery* **answer**, clue, solution, explanation. **2** *the key to success* **route**, basis, foundation, requisite, precondition, means, way, path, passport, secret, formula, recipe. **3** Music *a minor key* **tone**, pitch, timbre, tone colour. **4** *an austerely intellectual key* **style**, character, mood, vein, spirit, feel, feeling, flavour, quality, atmosphere.
▸ adj. *a key figure* **crucial**, central, essential, indispensable, pivotal, critical, dominant, vital, principal, prime, chief, major, leading, main, important, significant.
– OPPOSITES peripheral.

keynote n. **theme**, salient point, gist, substance, burden, tenor, pith, marrow, essence, heart, core, basis, essential feature/ element.

keystone n. **1** *the keystone of the door* **cornerstone**, central stone, quoin. **2** *the keystone of the government's policy* **foundation**, basis, linchpin, cornerstone, base, (guiding) principle, core, heart, centre, crux, fundament.

kick v. **1** *her attacker kicked her* **boot**; Sport punt; Brit. informal put the boot into, welly. **2** informal *he was struggling to kick his drug habit* **give up**, break, abandon, end, stop, cease, desist from, renounce; informal shake, pack in, leave off, quit. **3** *the gun kicked hard* **recoil**, spring back, jump.
▸ n. **1** *a kick on the knee* **blow**; Soccer punt; informal boot. **2** informal *I get a kick out of driving a racing car* **thrill**, excitement, stimulation, tingle; fun, enjoyment, amusement, pleasure, gratification; informal buzz, high; N. Amer. informal charge. **3** informal *a drink with a powerful kick* **effect**, power, potency, strength; tang, zest, bite, piquancy, edge, pungency; informal punch. **4** informal *a health kick* **craze**, enthusiasm, obsession, mania, passion; fashion, vogue, trend; informal fad.
▫ **kick against** resist, rebel against, oppose, struggle/fight against; defy, disobey, reject, spurn.

kick someone/something around informal **1** *we are undervalued and get kicked around* **abuse**, mistreat, maltreat, push

k

around/about, trample on; informal boss about/ around, walk all over. **2** *they began to kick ideas around* **discuss**, talk over, debate, thrash out, consider, toy with, play with.

kick back N. Amer. informal relax, unwind, take it easy, rest, slow down, let up, ease up/off, sit back; informal chill out, cool out; N. Amer. informal hang loose.

kick off informal start, commence, begin, get going, get off the ground, get under way; open, start off, set in motion, launch, initiate, introduce, inaugurate, usher in.

kick someone out informal expel, eject, throw out, oust, evict, get rid of, axe; dismiss, discharge; informal chuck out, send packing, boot out, give someone their marching orders, sack, fire; Brit. informal turf out; N. Amer. informal give someone the bum's rush.

kickback n. **1** *the kickback from the gun* **recoil**, kick, rebound. **2** informal *they paid kickbacks to politicians* **bribe**, payment, inducement; N. Amer. payola; informal pay-off, sweetener, backhander.

kick-off n. informal **beginning**, start, commencement, outset, opening.

kid[1] n. informal *she has three kids* **child**, youngster, little one, baby, toddler, tot, infant, boy/girl, young person, minor, juvenile, adolescent, teenager, youth, stripling; offspring, son/daughter; Scottish bairn; informal kiddie, nipper, kiddiewink, shaver, young 'un, tiny; Brit. informal sprog; N. Amer. informal rug rat; Austral./NZ ankle-biter; derogatory brat; literary babe.

kid[2] v. informal **1** *I'm not kidding* **joke**, tease, jest, chaff, be facetious, fool about/around; informal pull someone's leg, have on, rib; Brit. informal wind up; N. Amer. informal pull someone's chain, fun, shuck. **2** *why did I kid myself that I'd succeed?* **delude**, deceive, fool, trick, hoodwink, hoax, beguile, dupe, gull; informal con, pull the wool over someone's eyes; literary cozen.

kidnap v. **abduct**, carry off, capture, seize, snatch, take as hostage; Brit. informal nobble.

kidney n.

WORD LINKS

renal relating to the kidneys

nephrology the branch of medicine concerning the kidneys

nephritis inflammation of the kidneys

dialysis a method of purifying the blood, as a substitute for the normal function of the kidneys

---

kill v. **1** *gangs killed twenty-seven people* **murder**, take the life of, make away with, assassinate, eliminate, terminate, dispatch, finish off, put to death, execute; slaughter, butcher, massacre, wipe out, annihilate, exterminate, liquidate, mow down, shoot down, cut down, cut to pieces; informal bump off, polish off, do away with, do in, knock off, top, take out, croak, stiff, blow away, dispose of; N. Amer. informal ice, rub out, waste, whack, scrag, smoke; literary slay. **2** *100,000 seals will be killed over the coming days* **destroy**, put down, put to sleep; cull. **3** *this would*

kill all hopes of progress **destroy**, put an end to, end, extinguish, dash, quash, ruin, wreck, shatter, smash, crush, scotch, thwart; informal put paid to, put the kibosh on, stymie; Brit. informal scupper. **4** *we had to kill several hours at the airport* **while away**, fill (up), occupy, beguile, pass, spend, waste. **5** informal *you must rest or you'll kill yourself* **exhaust**, wear out, tire out, overtax, overtire, fatigue, weary, sap, drain, enervate, prostrate; informal knacker. **6** informal *my feet were killing me* **hurt**, torture, torment, cause discomfort to; be painful, be sore, be uncomfortable. **7** *the engines were at a low rev to kill the noise* **muffle**, deaden, stifle, dampen, damp down, smother, reduce, diminish, decrease, suppress, tone down, moderate. **8** *a shot of morphine to kill the pain* **alleviate**, assuage, soothe, allay, dull, blunt, deaden, stifle, suppress, subdue.
▸ n. **1** *the hunter's kill* **prey**, quarry, victim, bag. **2** *the wolf was moving in for the kill* **death blow**, killing, dispatch, finish, end, coup de grâce.

killer n. *police are searching for the killer* **murderer**, assassin, slaughterer, butcher, serial killer, gunman; exterminator, terminator, executioner; informal hitman; literary slayer; dated homicide.

killing n. *a brutal killing* **murder**, assassination, homicide, manslaughter, elimination, putting/doing to death, execution; slaughter, massacre, butchery, carnage, bloodshed, extermination, annihilation; literary slaying.
▸ adj. **1** *a killing blow* **deadly**, lethal, fatal, mortal, death-dealing; murderous, homicidal; literary deathly. **2** informal *a killing schedule* **exhausting**, gruelling, punishing, taxing, draining, wearing, prostrating, crushing, tiring, fatiguing, debilitating, enervating, arduous, tough, demanding, onerous, strenuous, rigorous; informal murderous; Brit. informal knackering.
□ **make a killing** informal make a large profit, make a/one's fortune, make money; informal clean up, make a packet, make a pretty penny; Brit. informal make a bomb; N. Amer. informal make big bucks.

killjoy n. **spoilsport**, prophet of doom; informal wet blanket, party pooper, misery; Austral./NZ informal wowser.

kilter n.
□ **out of kilter** awry, off balance, unbalanced, out of order, disordered, confused, muddled, out of tune, out of step.

kin n. *their own kin* **relatives**, relations, family (members); kindred, kith and kin; kinsfolk, kinsmen, kinswomen, people; informal folks.
▸ adj. *my uncle was kin to the brothers* **related**, akin, allied, connected with, consanguineous; formal cognate.

kind[1] n. **1** *all kinds of gifts | the kinds of bird that could be seen* **sort**, type, variety, style, form, class, category, genre, ilk; genus, species, family, breed, strain. **2** *they were*

different in kind **character**, nature, essence, quality, disposition, make-up; stamp, manner, description, mould, cast, temperament; N. Amer. stripe.
□ **kind of** informal rather, quite, fairly, somewhat, a little, slightly, a shade; informal sort of, a bit, kinda, pretty, a touch, a tad.

kind² adj. *she is such a kind and caring person* **kindly**, good-natured, kind-hearted, warm-hearted, caring, affectionate, loving, warm; considerate, helpful, thoughtful, obliging, unselfish, selfless, altruistic, good, attentive; compassionate, sympathetic, understanding, big-hearted, benevolent, benign, friendly, neighbourly, hospitable, well meaning, public-spirited; generous, liberal, open-handed, bountiful, beneficent, munificent, benignant; Brit. informal decent.
– OPPOSITES inconsiderate, mean.

kind-hearted adj. **kind**, caring, warm-hearted, kindly, benevolent, good-natured, tender, warm, compassionate, sympathetic, understanding; indulgent, altruistic, benign, beneficent, benignant.

kindle v. **1** *he kindled a fire* **light**, ignite, set alight, set light to, set fire to, put a match to. **2** *Elvis kindled my interest in music* **rouse**, arouse, wake, awaken; stimulate, inspire, stir (up), excite, evoke, provoke, fire, inflame, trigger, activate, engender, spark off; literary waken, enkindle.
– OPPOSITES extinguish.

kindliness n. **kindness**, benevolence, warmth, gentleness, tenderness, care, humanity, sympathy, compassion, understanding; generosity, charity, kind-heartedness, warm-heartedness, thoughtfulness, solicitousness.

kindly adj. *a kindly old lady* **kind**, benevolent, kind-hearted, warm-hearted, generous, good-natured; gentle, warm, compassionate, caring, loving, benign, well meaning; helpful, thoughtful, considerate, good-hearted, nice, friendly, neighbourly; Brit. informal decent.
– OPPOSITES unkind, cruel.
▸ adv. **1** *she spoke kindly* **benevolently**, good-naturedly, warmly, affectionately, tenderly, lovingly, compassionately; considerately, thoughtfully, helpfully, obligingly, generously, selflessly, unselfishly, sympathetically. **2** *kindly explain what you mean* **please**, if you please, if you wouldn't mind, have the goodness to; old use prithee, pray.
– OPPOSITES unkindly, harshly.
□ **not take kindly to** resent, object to, take umbrage at, take exception to, take offence at, be annoyed by, be irritated by, be upset by.

kindness n. **1** *he thanked her for her kindness* **kindliness**, kind-heartedness, warm-heartedness, affection, warmth, gentleness, concern, care; consideration, considerateness, helpfulness, thoughtfulness, unselfishness, selflessness, altruism, compassion, sympathy, understanding, big-heartedness,

benevolence, benignity, friendliness, neighbourliness, hospitality, public-spiritedness; generosity, magnanimity, charitableness; Brit. informal decency. **2** *she has done us many a kindness* **kind act**, good deed, good turn, favour, service.

kindred n. **1** *his mother's kindred* **family**, relatives, relations, kin, kith and kin, one's own flesh and blood; kinsfolk, kinsmen, kinswomen, people; informal folks. **2** *ties of kindred* **kinship**, family ties, being related, (blood) relationship, consanguinity, common ancestry.
▸ adj. **1** *industrial relations and kindred subjects* **related**, allied, connected, comparable, similar, like, parallel, associated, analogous; formal cognate. **2** *a kindred spirit* **like-minded**, in sympathy, in harmony, in tune, of one mind, on the same wavelength, akin, similar, like, compatible.
– OPPOSITES unrelated, alien.

king n. **1** *the king of France* **ruler**, sovereign, monarch, crowned head, Crown, emperor, prince, potentate, lord. **2** informal *the king of world football* **star**, leading light, luminary, superstar, giant, master; informal supremo, megastar.
□ **a king's ransom** a huge amount, a vast sum; informal a (small) fortune, a mint, a packet, a pretty penny, big money; Brit. informal a bomb; N. Amer. informal big bucks; Austral. informal big bickies.

> **WORD LINKS**
>
> **regal, royal** relating to a king
> **regicide** the killing of a king, or a person who kills a king

kingdom n. **1** *his kingdom stretched to the sea* **realm**, domain, dominion, country, empire, land, nation, (sovereign) state, province, territory. **2** *Henry's little kingdom* **domain**, province, realm, sphere, dominion, territory, arena, zone. **3** *the plant kingdom* **division**, category, classification, grouping, group.

kingly adj. **1** *kingly power* **royal**, regal, monarchical, sovereign, imperial, princely. **2** *kingly robes* **regal**, majestic, stately, noble, lordly, dignified, distinguished, courtly; splendid, magnificent, grand, glorious, rich, gorgeous, resplendent, princely, superb, sumptuous; informal splendiferous.

kink n. **1** *your fishing line should have no kinks in it* **curl**, twist, twirl, loop, crinkle; knot, tangle, entanglement. **2** *a kink in the road* **bend**, corner, dog-leg, twist, turn, curve; Brit. hairpin bend. **3** *there are still some kinks to iron out* **flaw**, defect, imperfection, problem, complication, hitch, snag, shortcoming, weakness; informal hiccup, glitch. **4** *their sartorial kinks* **peculiarity**, quirk, idiosyncrasy, eccentricity, oddity, foible, whim, caprice.

kinky adj. **1** informal *a kinky relationship* **perverted**, abnormal, deviant, unnatural, depraved, degenerate, perverse; odd, bizarre, weird; informal pervy. **2** informal *kinky underwear* **provocative**, sexy, sexually arousing, erotic, titillating, naughty,

k

indecent, immodest; Brit. informal saucy.
3 *Catriona's long kinky hair* **curly**, crimped, curled, curling, frizzy, frizzed, wavy.

kinsfolk n. **relatives**, relations, kin, kindred, family, kith and kin, kinsmen, kinswomen, people; informal folks.

kinship n. **1** *ties of kinship* **relationship**, being related, family ties, blood ties, common ancestry, kindred, consanguinity. **2** *she felt kinship with the others* **affinity**, sympathy, rapport, harmony, understanding, empathy, closeness, fellow feeling, bond, compatibility; similarity, likeness, correspondence, concordance.

kinsman, **kinswoman** n. **relative**, relation, family member; cousin, uncle, nephew, aunt, niece.

kiosk n. **booth**, stand, stall, counter, news-stand.

kismet n. **fate**, destiny, fortune, providence, God's will, one's lot (in life), karma, predestination, preordination, predetermination; luck, chance; literary one's dole.

kiss v. **1** *he kissed her on the lips* give a kiss to, brush one's lips against, blow a kiss to, air-kiss; informal peck, smooch, canoodle, neck, pet; Brit. informal snog; N. Amer. informal buss; informal dated spoon; formal osculate. **2** *allow your foot just to kiss the floor* **brush (against)**, caress, touch (gently), stroke, skim over.
▸ n. **1** *a kiss on the cheek* air kiss, French kiss; X; informal peck, smack, smacker, smooch; Brit. informal snog; N. Amer. informal buss; formal osculation. **2** *the kiss of the flowers against her cheeks* **gentle touch**, caress, brush, stroke.

kit n. **1** *his toolkit* **equipment**, tools, implements, instruments, gadgets, utensils, appliances, tools of the trade, gear, tackle, hardware, paraphernalia; informal things, stuff, the necessary; Military accoutrements. **2** Brit. informal *their football kit* **clothes**, clothing, rig, outfit, dress, costume, garments, attire, garb, gear, get-up, rig-out; formal apparel. **3** *a model aircraft kit* **set (of parts)**, DIY kit, do-it-yourself kit, self-assembly set, flat-pack. **4** informal *we packed up all our kit* **belongings**, luggage, baggage, paraphernalia, effects, impedimenta; informal things, stuff, gear; Brit. informal clobber.
  □ **kit someone/something out** equip, fit (out/up), furnish, supply, provide, issue; dress, clothe, array, attire, rig out, deck out; informal fix up.

kitchen n. kitchenette, kitchen-diner, cooking area, galley, cookhouse; N. Amer. cookery.

kittenish adj. **playful**, light-hearted, skittish, lively; coquettish, flirtatious, frivolous, flippant, superficial, trivial, shallow, silly; informal flirty, dizzy; literary frolicsome.
– OPPOSITES serious.

knack n. **1** *a knack for making money | it takes practice to acquire the knack* **gift**, talent, flair, genius, instinct, faculty, ability, capability, capacity, aptitude, aptness, bent, forte, facility; **technique**, method, trick, skill, art, expertise; informal the hang of something. **2** *he has a knack of getting injured at the wrong time* **tendency**, propensity, habit, proneness, liability, predisposition.

knackered adj. Brit. informal **1** *you look absolutely knackered.* See **exhausted** (sense 1). **2** *the computer was knackered.* See **broken** (sense 3).

knapsack n. **rucksack**, backpack, haversack, pack, kitbag.

knead v. **1** *kneading the dough* **pummel**, work, pound, squeeze, shape, mould. **2** *she kneaded the base of his neck* **massage**, press, manipulate, rub.

kneel v. **fall to one's knees**, get down on one's knees, genuflect; historical kowtow.

knell n. literary **1** *the knell of the ship's bell* **toll**, tolling, dong, resounding, reverberation; death knell; old use tocsin. **2** *this sounded the knell for the project* **(beginning of the) end**, death knell, death warrant.

knickers Brit. plural n. **underpants**, briefs, French knickers, camiknickers; underwear, lingerie, underclothes, undergarments; Brit. pants; informal panties, undies; Brit. informal knicks, smalls; dated drawers; historical bloomers, pantalettes.

knick-knack n. **ornament**, novelty, gewgaw, bibelot, trinket, trifle, bauble, gimcrack, curio; memento, souvenir; N. Amer. kickshaw; N. Amer. informal tchotchke; old use gaud, whim-wham, bijou.

knife n. *a sharp knife* **cutting tool**, blade, cutter, carver.
▸ v. *the victims had been knifed* **stab**, hack, gash, run through, slash, lacerate, cut, pierce, spike, impale, transfix, bayonet, spear.

knight n. *knights in armour* **cavalier**, cavalryman, horseman; lord, noble, nobleman; historical chevalier, paladin, banneret.
  □ **knight in shining armour** knight on a white charger, rescuer, saviour, champion, hero, defender, protector, guardian (angel).

> **WORD LINKS**
>
> **joust**, **tilt** a medieval contest in which knights on horseback fought with lances
> **tournament**, **tourney** a medieval jousting event
> **chivalry** the code of behaviour that a medieval knight was expected to follow
> **charger**, **destrier** a horse ridden by a medieval knight
> **Round Table** the table at which King Arthur and his knights sat so that no one should have precedence

knightly adj. **1** *tales of knightly deeds* **gallant**, noble, valiant, heroic, courageous, brave, bold, valorous; chivalrous, courteous, honourable. **2** *the knightly classes* **upper-class**, well born, noble, aristocratic; old use gentle.
– OPPOSITES ignoble, low-born.

k

knit v. **1** *disparate regions began to knit together* **unite**, unify, come together, draw together, become closer, bond, fuse, coalesce, merge, meld, blend. **2** *we expect broken bones to knit* **heal**, mend, join, fuse. **3** *Marcus knitted his brows* **furrow**, tighten, contract, gather, wrinkle.
▸n. *silky knits in pretty shades* **knitted garment**, woollen; sweater, pullover, jersey, cardigan; Brit. jumper; informal woolly; Brit. informal cardy.

knob n. **1** *a black bill with a knob at the base* **lump**, bump, protuberance, protrusion, bulge, swelling, knot, node, nodule, ball, boss. **2** *the knobs on the radio* **dial**, button, control, switch. **3** *she turned the knob on the door* **doorknob**, (door) handle. **4** *a few knobs of butter* **nugget**, lump, pat, ball, dollop, piece; N. Amer. informal gob.

knock v. **1** *he knocked on the door* **bang**, tap, rap, thump, pound, hammer; strike, hit, beat. **2** *she knocked her knee on the table* **bump**, bang, hit, strike, crack; injure, hurt, bruise; informal bash, thwack. **3** *he knocked into an elderly man* **collide with**, bump into, bang into, be in collision with, run into, crash into, smash into, plough into; N. Amer. impact; informal bash into. **4** informal *I'm not knocking the company.* See **criticize**.
▸n. **1** *a sharp knock at the door* **tap**, rap, rat-tat, knocking, bang, banging, pounding, hammering, drumming, thump, thud. **2** *the casing is tough enough to withstand knocks* **bump**, blow, bang, jolt, jar, shock; collision, crash, smash, impact. **3** *a knock on the ear* **blow**, bang, hit, slap, smack, crack, punch, cuff, thump, box; informal clip, clout, wallop, thwack, belt, bash. **4** *life's hard knocks* **setback**, reversal, defeat, failure, difficulty, misfortune, bad luck, mishap, (body) blow, disaster, calamity, disappointment, sorrow, trouble, hardship; informal kick in the teeth.
□ **knock about/around** informal **1** *knocking around the Mediterranean* **wander around**, roam around, rove around, range over, travel around, journey around, voyage around, drift around, potter around; informal gad about, gallivant around. **2** *she knocks around with artists* **associate**, consort, keep company, go around, mix, socialize, be friends, be friendly; informal hobnob, hang out, run around, pal around.
knock someone/something about/around beat (up), batter, hit, punch, thump, thrash, slap; maltreat, mistreat, abuse, ill-treat, assault, attack; N. Amer. beat up on; informal rough up, do over, give someone a hiding, clobber, clout, bash, belt, whack, wallop.
knock something back informal swallow, gulp down, drink up, quaff, guzzle, slug; informal down, swig, swill (down), toss off; N. Amer. informal scarf (down/up), snarf (down/up), chug.
knock someone down fell, floor, flatten, bring down, rugby-tackle; knock over, run over/down.
knock something down 1 *the building was knocked down* **demolish**, pull down, tear down, destroy; raze (to the ground), level, flatten, bulldoze. **2** informal *the firm has knocked down its prices* **reduce**, lower, cut, decrease, drop, put down, mark down; informal slash.
knock off informal stop work, finish (working), clock off, leave work.
knock someone out 1 *I hit him and knocked him out* **knock unconscious**, knock senseless; floor, prostrate; informal lay out, put out cold, KO, kayo. **2** *England was knocked out* **eliminate**, beat, defeat, vanquish, overwhelm, trounce. **3** informal *walking that far knocked her out* **exhaust**, wear out, tire (out), overtire, fatigue, weary, drain; informal do in, take it out of, fag out; Brit. informal knacker; N. Amer. informal poop. **4** informal *the view knocked me out* **overwhelm**, stun, stupefy, amaze, astound, astonish, stagger, take someone's breath away; impress, dazzle, enchant, entrance; informal bowl over, flabbergast, knock sideways, blow away; Brit. informal knock for six.
knock something up Brit. informal make, prepare, build, whip up, rig up, throw together, cobble together, improvise, contrive; informal rustle up.

knockout n. **1** *the match was won by a knockout* **stunning blow**, finishing blow, coup de grâce; informal KO, kayo. **2** informal *she's a knockout!* **beauty**, vision, picture, sensation, dream; informal stunner, dish, looker, good-looker, peach, cracker; Brit. informal smasher. **3** informal *a technical knockout* **masterpiece**, sensation, marvel, wonder, triumph, success, feat, coup, master stroke, tour de force.

knoll n. **1** *she walked up the grassy knoll* **hillock**, mound, rise, hummock, hill, hump, tor, bank, ridge, elevation; Scottish brae; formal eminence.

knot n. **1** *tie a small knot* **tie**, twist, loop, join, fastening, bond; tangle, entanglement. **2** *a knot in the wood* **nodule**, gnarl, node; lump, knob, swelling, gall, protuberance, bump; old use knar. **3** *a small knot of people* **cluster**, group, band, huddle, bunch, circle, ring, gathering, company, crowd, throng.
▸v. *their scarves were knotted round their throats* **tie (up)**, fasten, secure, bind, do up.

knotted adj. **tangled**, tangly, knotty, entangled, matted, snarled, unkempt, uncombed, tousled; informal mussed up.

knotty adj. **1** *a knotty legal problem* **complex**, complicated, involved, intricate, convoluted, involuted; difficult, hard, thorny, taxing, awkward, tricky, problematic, troublesome. **2** *knotty roots* **gnarled**, knotted, knurled, nodular, knobbly, lumpy, bumpy. **3** *a knotty piece of thread* **knotted**, tangled, tangly, twisted, entangled, snarled, matted.
– OPPOSITES straightforward.

know v. **1** *she doesn't know I'm here* **be aware**, realize, be conscious, be informed; notice, perceive, see, sense, recognize; informal savvy, latch on. **2** *I don't know his address* **have knowledge of**, be informed of, be apprised of; formal be cognizant of.

k

3 *do you know the rules* **be familiar with**, be conversant with, be acquainted with, have knowledge of, be versed in, have mastered, have learned, have memorized; informal clued-up. **4** *I don't know many people here* **be acquainted with**, have met, be familiar with; be friends with, be friendly with, be on good terms with, be close to, be intimate with; Scottish ken; informal be thick with. **5** *he had known better times* **experience**, go through, live through, undergo, taste. **6** *my brothers don't know a saucepan from a frying pan* **distinguish**, tell (apart), differentiate, discriminate; recognize, pick out, identify.

know-all n. informal **wiseacre**; informal smart alec, wise guy, smarty, smarty-pants; Brit. informal clever clogs, clever Dick; N. Amer. informal know-it-all.

know-how n. informal **knowledge**, expertise, skill, skilfulness, expertness, proficiency, understanding, mastery, technique; ability, capability, competence, capacity, adeptness, dexterity, deftness, aptitude, adroitness, ingenuity, faculty; informal savvy.

knowing adj. **1** *a knowing smile* **significant**, meaningful, eloquent, expressive, suggestive; **arch**, sly, mischievous, impish, teasing, playful. **2** *she's a very knowing child* **sophisticated**, worldly, worldly-wise, urbane, experienced; knowledgeable, well informed, enlightened; shrewd, astute, canny, sharp, wily, perceptive. **3** *a knowing infringement of the rules* **deliberate**, intentional, conscious, calculated, wilful, done on purpose, premeditated, preconceived, planned.

knowingly adv. **deliberately**, intentionally, consciously, wittingly, on purpose, by design, premeditatedly, wilfully.

knowledge n. **1** *his knowledge of history | technical knowledge* **understanding**, comprehension, grasp, command, mastery; expertise, skill, proficiency, expertness, accomplishment, adeptness, capacity, capability; informal know-how. **2** *people anxious to display their knowledge* **learning**, erudition, education, scholarship, schooling, wisdom. **3** *he slipped away without my knowledge* **awareness**, consciousness, realization, cognition, apprehension, perception, appreciation; formal cognizance.

4 *an intimate knowledge of the countryside* **familiarity**, acquaintance, conversance, intimacy. **5** *inform the police of your knowledge* **information**, facts, intelligence, news, reports; informal info, gen.
– OPPOSITES ignorance.

> **WORD LINKS**
>
> **gnostic, epistemic** relating to knowledge
> **epistemology** the branch of philosophy that deals with knowledge
> **omniscience** knowledge of everything
> **polymath** a person with a wide knowledge of many subjects

knowledgeable adj. **1** *a knowledgeable old man* **well informed**, learned, well read, (well) educated, erudite, scholarly, cultured, cultivated, enlightened. **2** *he is knowledgeable about modern art* **acquainted**, familiar, conversant, au courant, au fait; having a knowledge of, up on, up to date with, abreast of; informal clued-up, genned-up; Brit. informal switched-on.
– OPPOSITES ill-informed.

known adj. **1** *a known criminal* **recognized**, well known, widely known, noted, celebrated, notable, notorious; acknowledged, self-confessed, declared, overt. **2** *the known world* **familiar**, known about, well known; studied, investigated.

knuckle v.
□ **knuckle under** surrender, submit, capitulate, give in/up, yield, give way, succumb, climb down, back down, admit defeat, lay down one's arms, throw in the towel/sponge; informal quit, raise the white flag.

kowtow v. **1** *they kowtowed to the Emperor* **prostrate oneself**, bow (down before), genuflect, do/make obeisance, fall on one's knees before, kneel before. **2** *she didn't have to kowtow to a boss* **grovel**, be obsequious, be servile, be sycophantic, fawn on, bow and scrape, toady, truckle, abase oneself, humble oneself; curry favour with, dance attendance on, make up to, ingratiate oneself with; informal crawl, creep, suck up, lick someone's boots; Austral./NZ informal smoodge to.

kudos n. **prestige**, cachet, glory, honour, status, standing, distinction, prestigiousness, fame, celebrity; admiration, respect, esteem, acclaim, praise, credit.

LI

label n. **1** *the price is clearly stated on the label* **tag**, ticket, tab, sticker, marker, docket, chit, chitty. **2** *a designer label* **brand (name)**, trade name, trademark, make, logo. **3** *the label the media came up with for me* **designation**, description, tag; name, epithet, nickname, title, sobriquet, pet name, cognomen; formal denomination, appellation.
▶ v. **1** *label each jar with the date* **tag**, ticket, mark, docket. **2** *tests labelled him an underachiever* **categorize**, classify, class, describe, designate, identify; mark, stamp, brand, condemn, pigeonhole, stereotype, typecast; call, name, term, dub, nickname.

laborious adj. **1** *a laborious job* **arduous**, hard, heavy, difficult, strenuous, gruelling, punishing, exacting, tough, onerous, burdensome, back-breaking, trying, challenging; tiring, fatiguing, exhausting, wearying, wearing, taxing, demanding, wearisome; tedious, boring; old use toilsome. **2** *Doug's laborious style* **laboured**, strained, forced, contrived, affected, stiff, stilted, unnatural, artificial, overwrought, heavy, ponderous, convoluted.
– OPPOSITES easy, effortless.

labour n. **1** *manual labour* **(hard) work**, toil, exertion, industry, drudgery, effort, donkey work, menial work; informal slog, grind, sweat, elbow grease; Brit. informal graft; literary travail, moil. **2** *the conflict between capital and labour* **workers**, employees, workmen, workforce, staff, working people, blue-collar workers, labourers, labour force, proletariat. **3** *the labours of Hercules* **task**, job, chore, mission, assignment. **4** *a difficult labour* **childbirth**, birth, delivery, nativity; contractions, labour pains; formal parturition; literary travail; dated confinement; old use lying-in, accouchement, childbed.
– OPPOSITES rest, management.
▶ v. **1** *a project on which he had laboured for many years* **work (hard)**, toil, slave (away), grind away, struggle, strive, exert oneself, work one's fingers to the bone, work like a Trojan/slave; informal slog away, plug away, peg away; Brit. informal graft; literary travail; old use moil. **2** *Newcastle laboured to break down their defence* **strive**, struggle, endeavour, work, try hard, make every effort, do one's best, do one's utmost, do all one can, give one's all, go all out, fight, put oneself out, apply oneself, exert oneself; informal bend over backwards, pull out all the stops. **3** *there is no need to labour the point* **overemphasize**, belabour, overstress, overdo, strain, overplay, make too much of, exaggerate, dwell on, harp on (about). **4** *Rex was labouring under a misapprehension* **suffer from**, be a victim of, be deceived by, be misled by.

laboured adj. **1** *laboured breathing* **strained**, difficult, forced, laborious. **2** *a rather laboured joke* **contrived**, strained, stilted, forced, unnatural, artificial, overdone, ponderous, over-elaborate, laborious, unconvincing, overwrought.

labourer n. **workman**, worker, working man, labouring man, manual worker, unskilled worker, blue-collar worker, (hired) hand, roustabout, drudge, menial, coolie; Austral./NZ rouseabout; Brit. dated navvy.

labyrinth n. **1** *a labyrinth of little streets* **maze**, warren, network, complex, web, entanglement. **2** *the labyrinth of conflicting regulations* **tangle**, web, morass, jungle, confusion, entanglement, convolution; jumble, mishmash; old use perplexity.

labyrinthine adj. **1** *labyrinthine corridors* **maze-like**, winding, twisting, serpentine, meandering, wandering, rambling. **2** *a labyrinthine system* **complicated**, intricate, complex, involved, tortuous, convoluted, involuted, tangled, elaborate, Byzantine; confusing, puzzling, mystifying, bewildering, baffling.

lace n. **1** *a dress trimmed with white lace* openwork, lacework, tatting; passementerie, bobbinet, needlepoint (lace), filet, bobbin lace, pillow lace, duchesse lace, guipure, rosaline. **2** *brown shoes with laces* **shoelace**, bootlace, shoestring, lacing, thong, tie; old use latchet.
▶ v. **1** *he laced up his running shoes* **fasten**, do up, tie up, secure, knot. **2** *he laced his fingers into mine* **entwine**, intertwine, twine, entangle, interweave, link; braid, plait. **3** *tea laced with rum* **flavour**, mix (in), blend, fortify, strengthen, stiffen, season, spice (up), enrich, liven up; doctor, adulterate; informal spike. **4** *her brown hair was laced with grey* **streak**, stripe, striate, line.
– OPPOSITES untie.

lacerate v. **cut (open)**, gash, slash, tear, rip, rend, shred, score, scratch, scrape, graze; wound, injure, hurt.

laceration n. **1** *the laceration of her hand* **cutting (open)**, gashing, slashing, tearing, ripping, scratching, scraping, grazing, wounding, injury. **2** *a bleeding laceration* **gash**, cut, wound, injury, tear, slash, scratch, scrape, abrasion, graze.

lachrymose adj. formal **1** *she gets quite lachrymose at the mention of his name* **tearful**, weeping, crying, with tears in one's eyes, close to tears, on the verge of tears, sobbing, snivelling, whimpering; emotional, sad, doleful, maudlin, miserable, forlorn; informal weepy; literary dolorous. **2** *a lachrymose novel* **tragic**, sad, poignant, moving, heart-rending, tear-jerking; mawkish, sentimental; Brit. informal soppy.
– OPPOSITES cheerful, comic.

lack n. *a lack of cash* **absence**, want, need, deficiency, dearth, insufficiency, shortage, shortfall, scarcity, paucity, unavailability, scarceness, deficit; formal exiguity.
– OPPOSITES abundance.
▸ v. *she's immature and lacks judgement* **be without**, be in need of, need, be lacking, require, want, be short of, be deficient in, be bereft of, be low on, be pressed for, have insufficient; informal be strapped for.
– OPPOSITES have, possess.

lackadaisical adj. **careless**, lazy, lax, unenthusiastic, half-hearted, lukewarm, indifferent, unconcerned, casual, offhand, blasé, insouciant, relaxed; apathetic, lethargic, listless, sluggish, spiritless, passionless; informal laid-back, couldn't-care-less, easy going.
– OPPOSITES enthusiastic.

lackey n. **1** *lackeys helped them from their carriage* **servant**, flunkey, footman, manservant, valet, steward, butler, equerry, retainer, attendant, houseboy, domestic; Brit. informal skivvy; old use scullion. **2** *a rich man's lackey* **toady**, flunkey, sycophant, flatterer, minion, doormat, stooge, hanger-on, lickspittle; tool, puppet, instrument, pawn, subordinate, underling; informal yes-man, bootlicker.

lacking adj. **1** *proof was lacking* **absent**, missing, non-existent, unavailable. **2** *the advocate general found the government lacking* **deficient**, inadequate, wanting, flawed, faulty, insufficient, unacceptable, imperfect, inferior. **3** *the game was lacking in atmosphere* **without**, devoid of, bereft of; deficient in, low on, short on, in need of.
– OPPOSITES present, plentiful.

lacklustre adj. **uninspired**, uninspiring, unimaginative, dull, humdrum, colourless, characterless, bland, insipid, vapid, flat, dry, lifeless, tame, prosaic, spiritless, lustreless; boring, monotonous, dreary, tedious.
– OPPOSITES inspired.

laconic adj. **1** *his laconic comment* **brief**, concise, terse, succinct, short, pithy; epigrammatic, aphoristic, gnomic. **2** *their laconic press officer* **taciturn**, uncommunicative, reticent, quiet, reserved, silent, unforthcoming, brusque.
– OPPOSITES verbose, loquacious.

lad n. informal **1** *a young lad of eight* **boy**, schoolboy, youth, youngster, juvenile, stripling; informal kid, nipper, whippersnapper;

Scottish informal laddie; derogatory brat. **2** *a hard-working lad* **(young) man**; informal guy, fellow, geezer; Brit. informal chap, bloke; N. Amer. informal dude, hombre; Austral./NZ informal digger.

ladder n. **1** *she climbed down the ladder* steps, stepladder. **2** *the academic ladder* **hierarchy**, scale, grading, ranking, pecking order.

laden adj. **loaded**, burdened, weighed down, overloaded, piled high, fully charged; full, filled, packed, stuffed, crammed; informal chock-full, chock-a-block.

la-di-da adj. informal **snobbish**, pretentious, affected, mannered, pompous, conceited, haughty; informal snooty, stuck-up, high and mighty, hoity-toity, uppity, snotty; Brit. informal posh, toffee-nosed.
– OPPOSITES common.

ladle v. *he was ladling out the contents of the pot* **spoon out**, scoop out, dish up/out, serve.
▸ n. *a soup ladle* **spoon**, scoop, dipper, bailer.

lady n. **1** *several ladies were present* **woman**, female; Scottish & N. English lass, lassie; Brit. informal bird, bint; N. Amer. informal dame, broad, jane; Austral./NZ informal sheila; literary maid, damsel; old use wench. **2** *lords and ladies* **noblewoman**, duchess, countess, peeress, viscountess, baroness; old use gentlewoman.

ladylike adj. **genteel**, polite, refined, well bred, cultivated, polished, decorous, proper, respectable, seemly, well mannered, cultured, sophisticated, elegant; Brit. informal posh.
– OPPOSITES coarse.

lag v. **fall behind**, straggle, fall back, trail (behind), hang back, not keep pace, bring up the rear.
– OPPOSITES keep up.

laggard n. **straggler**, loiterer, lingerer, dawdler, sluggard, slug, snail, idler, loafer; informal lazybones, slacker, slowcoach; N. Amer. informal slowpoke.

lagoon n. inland sea, bay, lake, bight, pool; Scottish loch; Anglo-Irish lough; N. Amer. bayou.

laid-back adj. informal **relaxed**, easy-going, equable, free and easy, casual, nonchalant, insouciant, unexcitable, imperturbable, unruffled, blasé, cool, calm, {cool, calm, and collected}, unperturbed, unflustered, unworried, unconcerned; leisurely, unhurried; stoical, phlegmatic, tolerant; informal unflappable.
– OPPOSITES uptight.

laid up adj. informal **bedridden**, confined to bed, on the sick list, housebound, incapacitated, injured, disabled; ill, sick, unwell, poorly, ailing, indisposed.
– OPPOSITES healthy, active.

lair n. **1** *the lair of a large python* **den**, burrow, hole, tunnel, cave. **2** *a villain's lair* **hideaway**, hiding place, hideout, refuge, sanctuary, haven, shelter, retreat; informal hidey-hole.

laissez-faire n. *laissez-faire is based on self-interest* **free enterprise**, free trade, non-intervention, free-market capitalism, market forces.

lake n. **pond**, pool, tarn, reservoir, lagoon, waterhole, inland sea; Scottish loch, lochan; Anglo-Irish lough; N. Amer. bayou, pothole (lake); literary mere.

> **WORD LINKS**
> **lacustrine** relating to lakes
> **limnology** the scientific study of lakes

lam v. informal See **hit** (sense 1 of the verb).

lambaste v. **criticize**, chastise, censure, take to task, harangue, rail at, rant at, fulminate against, haul over the coals; upbraid, scold, reprimand, rebuke, chide, reprove, admonish, berate; informal lay into, pitch into, tear into, give someone a dressing-down, carpet, tell off, bawl out; Brit. informal tick off, have a go at; N. Amer. informal chew out; formal castigate, excoriate.

lame adj. **1** *the mare was lame* **limping**, hobbling; crippled, disabled, incapacitated; informal gammy; dated game; old use halt. **2** *a lame excuse* **feeble**, weak, thin, flimsy, poor; unconvincing, implausible, unlikely.
– OPPOSITES convincing.

lament n. **1** *the widow's laments* **wail**, wailing, lamentation, moan, moaning, weeping, crying, sob, sobbing, keening. **2** *a lament for the dead* **dirge**, requiem, elegy, threnody, monody; Irish keen; Scottish & Irish coronach; formal epicedium.
▶ v. **1** *the mourners lamented* **mourn**, grieve, sorrow, wail, weep, cry, sob, keen, beat one's breast; old use plain. **2** *he lamented the modernization of the buildings* **bemoan**, bewail, complain about, deplore; protest against, object to, oppose, fulminate against, inveigh against, denounce.
– OPPOSITES celebrate.

lamentable adj. **deplorable**, regrettable, terrible, awful, wretched, woeful, dire, disastrous, desperate, grave, appalling, dreadful, egregious; intolerable, pitiful, shameful, sorrowful, unfortunate.
– OPPOSITES wonderful.

lamentation n. **weeping**, wailing, crying, sobbing, moaning, lament, keening, grieving, mourning.

lamp n. **light**, lantern, torch, flashlight, beacon.

lampoon v. *he was mercilessly lampooned* **satirize**, mock, ridicule, make fun of, caricature, burlesque, parody, spoof, take off, guy, rag, tease; informal send up.
▶ n. *a lampoon of student life* **satire**, burlesque, parody, skit, caricature, impersonation, travesty, mockery, squib, pasquinade; informal send-up, take-off, spoof.

lance n. *a knight with a lance* **spear**, pike, javelin; harpoon.
▶ v. *the boil was lanced* **cut (open)**, slit, incise, puncture, prick, pierce.

land n. **1** *Lyme Park has 1323 acres of land | publicly owned land* **grounds**, fields, open space; property, acres, acreage, estate, lands, real estate; countryside, rural area, green belt; historical demesne. **2** *fertile land* **soil**, earth, loam, topsoil, humus. **3** *many people are leaving the land* **the countryside**, the country, rural areas. **4** *Tunisia is a land of variety* **country**, nation, (nation) state, realm, kingdom, province; region, area, domain. **5** *the lookout sighted land to the east* **terra firma**, dry land; coast, coastline, shore.
▶ v. **1** *Allied troops landed in France* **disembark**, go ashore, debark, alight, get off. **2** *the ship landed at Le Havre* **berth**, dock, moor, (drop) anchor, tie up, put in. **3** *their plane landed at Chicago* **touch down**, come in to land, come down. **4** *a bird landed on the branch* **perch**, settle, come to rest, alight. **5** informal *Nick landed the job of editor* **obtain**, get, acquire, secure, be appointed to, gain, net, win, achieve, attain, bag, carry off; informal swing; Brit. informal blag. **6** informal *they landed her with the bill* **burden**, saddle, encumber; informal dump something on someone; Brit. informal lumber. **7** informal *John landed a punch on Brian's chin* **inflict**, deal, deliver, administer, mete out; informal fetch.
– OPPOSITES sail, take off.
□ **land up** finish up, find oneself, end up; informal wind up, fetch up, show up, roll up, blow in.

> **WORD LINKS**
> **terrestrial** relating to land
> **territorial** relating to the ownership of land

landing n. **1** *a forced landing* **touchdown**; informal greaser. **2** *the ferry landing* **harbour**, berth, dock, jetty, landing stage, pier, quay, wharf, slipway.
– OPPOSITES take-off.

landlady, **landlord** n. **1** *the landlord of the pub* **publican**, licensee, innkeeper, pub-owner, barkeeper; hotel-keeper, hotelier, restaurateur; manager, manageress. **2** *the landlady had objected to the noise* **property owner**, proprietor, proprietress, lessor, householder, landowner.
– OPPOSITES tenant.

landmark n. **1** *the spire is a landmark for ships* **marker**, mark, indicator, beacon. **2** *one of London's most famous landmarks* **monument**, distinctive feature, prominent feature. **3** *the ruling was hailed as a landmark* **turning point**, milestone, watershed, critical point.

landscape n. **scenery**, countryside, topography, country, terrain; outlook, view, prospect, aspect, vista, panorama, perspective, sweep.

landslide n. **1** *floods and landslides* **landslip**, mudslide; avalanche. **2** *the Labour landslide* **decisive victory**, overwhelming majority, triumph, {game, set, and match}.

lane n. **1** *country lanes* **byroad**, byway, track, road, street; alley, alleyway. **2** *cycle lanes | a three-lane highway* **track**, way, course, path.

language n. **1** *the structure of language* **speech**, writing, communication, conversation, speaking, talking, talk, discourse; words, vocabulary. **2** *the English language* **tongue**, mother tongue, native tongue; informal lingo. **3** *the booklet is written* *in simple, everyday language* **wording**, phrasing, phraseology, style, vocabulary, terminology, expressions, turns of phrase, parlance, form/mode of expression, usages, locutions, idiolect, choice of words; speech, dialect, patois, slang, idioms, jargon, argot, cant; informal lingo, geekspeak.

> **WORD LINKS**
>
> **linguistic** relating to language
> **linguistics** the study of language
> **philology** the study of the structure and historical development of languages
> **grammar** the whole structure and rules of a language
> **bilingual** able to speak two languages
> **monolingual, monoglot** speaking only one language
> **polyglot** able to speak several languages

languid adj. **1** *a languid wave of the hand* **relaxed**, unhurried, languorous, slow; listless, lethargic, sluggish, lazy, idle, indolent, apathetic; informal laid-back; old use otiose. **2** *languid days in the sun* **leisurely**, languorous, relaxed, restful, lazy. **3** *she was pale and languid* **sickly**, weak, faint, feeble, frail, delicate; tired, weary, fatigued.
– OPPOSITES energetic.

languish v. **1** *the plants languished and died* **weaken**, deteriorate, decline, go downhill; wither, droop, wilt, fade, waste away. **2** *the general is now languishing in prison* **waste away**, rot, be abandoned, be neglected, be forgotten, suffer, experience hardship.
– OPPOSITES thrive.

languor n. **1** *the sultry languor that was stealing over her* **lassitude**, lethargy, listlessness, torpor, fatigue, weariness, sleepiness, drowsiness; laziness, idleness, indolence, inertia, sluggishness, apathy. **2** *the languor of a hot day* **stillness**, tranquillity, calm, calmness; oppressiveness, heaviness.
– OPPOSITES vigour.

lank adj. **1** *lank, greasy hair* **limp**, lifeless, lustreless, dull; straggling, straight, long. **2** *his lank figure.* See **lanky**.

lanky adj. **tall, thin**, slender, slim, lean, lank, skinny, spindly, spare, gangling, gangly, gawky, rangy.
– OPPOSITES stocky.

lap[1] n. *Henry sat on his gran's lap* **knee**, knees, thighs.
□ **in the lap of the gods** out of one's hands, beyond one's control, in the hands of fate.
live in the lap of luxury be very rich, want for nothing; informal live the life of Riley; N. Amer. informal live high on the hog.

lap[2] n. *a race of eight laps* **circuit**, leg, circle, revolution, round.
▶ v. *she lapped the other runners* **overtake**, outstrip, leave behind, pass, go past; catch up with.

lap[3] v. **1** *waves lapped against the sea wall* **splash**, wash, swish, slosh, break, beat, strike, dash, roll; literary plash. **2** *the dog lapped water out of a puddle* **drink**, lick up, sup, swallow, slurp, gulp.

□ **lap something up** relish, revel in, savour, delight in, wallow in, glory in, enjoy.

lapse n. **1** *a lapse of concentration* **failure**, failing, slip, error, mistake, blunder, fault, omission; informal slip-up, fail. **2** *his lapse into petty crime* **decline**, fall, falling, slipping, drop, deterioration, degeneration, backsliding, regression, retrogression, descent, sinking, slide. **3** *a lapse of time* **interval**, gap, pause, interlude, lull, hiatus, break; passage, course, passing.
▶ v. **1** *the planning permission has lapsed* **expire**, become void, become invalid, run out. **2** *do not let friendships lapse* **(come to an) end**, cease, stop, terminate, pass, fade, wither, die. **3** *morality has lapsed* **deteriorate**, decline, fall (off), drop, worsen, degenerate, go downhill, backslide, regress, retrogress, get worse, sink, wane, slump; informal go to pot, go to the dogs. **4** *she lapsed into silence* **revert**, relapse; drift, slide, slip, sink.

lapsed adj. **1** *a lapsed Catholic* **non-practising**, backsliding, apostate; formal quondam. **2** *a lapsed season ticket* **expired**, void, invalid, out of date.
– OPPOSITES practising, valid.

larceny n. **theft**, stealing, robbery, pilfering, thieving; burglary, housebreaking, breaking and entering; informal filching, swiping; Brit. informal nicking, pinching; formal peculation.

larder n. **pantry**, (food) store, (food) cupboard; cooler, scullery; Brit. buttery; old use spence.

large adj. **1** *a large house | large numbers of people* **big**, great, huge, sizeable, substantial, immense, enormous, colossal, massive, mammoth, vast, cosmic, prodigious, tremendous, gigantic, giant, monumental, stupendous, gargantuan, elephantine, titanic, mountainous, monstrous; towering, tall, high; mighty, voluminous, king-size, giant-size; informal jumbo, whopping (great), thumping (great), mega, humongous, monster, astronomical; Brit. informal whacking (great), ginormous. **2** *a large red-faced man* **big**, burly, heavy, tall, bulky, thickset, chunky, strapping, hulking, hefty, muscular, brawny, solid, powerful, sturdy, strong, rugged; fat, plump, overweight, chubby, stout, meaty, fleshy, portly, rotund, flabby, paunchy, obese, corpulent; informal hunky, beefy, tubby, pudgy; Brit. informal podgy, fubsy; N. Amer. informal zaftig, corn-fed. **3** *a large supply of wool* **abundant**, copious, plentiful, ample, liberal, generous, lavish, bountiful, bumper, boundless, good, considerable, superabundant; literary plenteous. **4** *the measure has large economic implications* **wide-reaching**, far-reaching, wide, sweeping, large-scale, broad, extensive, comprehensive, exhaustive.
– OPPOSITES small, meagre.

□ **at large 1** *fourteen criminals are still at large* **at liberty**, free, (on the) loose, on the run, fugitive; N. Amer. informal on the lam. **2** *society at large* **as a whole**, generally, in general. **3** dated *he spoke at large* **in detail**,

exhaustively, at length, extensively.
by and large on the whole, generally, in general, all things considered, all in all, for the most part, in the main, as a rule, overall, almost always, mainly, mostly; on average, on balance.

largely adv. **mostly**, mainly, to a large/great extent, chiefly, predominantly, primarily, principally, for the most part, in the main; usually, typically, commonly.

large-scale adj. **1** *a large-scale programme* **extensive**, wide-ranging, far-reaching, comprehensive, exhaustive; mass, nationwide, global. **2** *a large-scale map* **enlarged**, blown-up, magnified.

largesse n. **1** *Tupper took advantage of his friend's largesse* **generosity**, liberality, munificence, bounty, beneficence, altruism, charity, open-handedness, philanthropy, magnanimity, benevolence, charitableness, kindness, big-heartedness; formal benefaction. **2** *distributing largesse to the locals* **gifts**, presents, handouts, grants, aid; patronage, sponsorship, backing, help; historical alms.
– OPPOSITES meanness.

lark informal n. **1** *we were just having a bit of a lark* **fun**, amusement, laugh, giggle, joke; escapade, prank, trick, jape, practical joke; informal leg-pull; (**larks**) antics, high jinks, horseplay, mischief, tomfoolery; informal shenanigans, monkey business; Brit. informal monkey tricks; dated sport. **2** *I've got this snowboarding lark sussed* **activity**, affair, matter; nonsense; informal business, caper, malarkey.
▶ v. *he's always larking about* **fool about/around**, play tricks, make mischief, monkey about/around, clown about/around, have fun, skylark; informal mess about/around; Brit. informal muck about/around.

lascivious adj. **lecherous**, lewd, lustful, licentious, libidinous, salacious, lubricious, prurient, dirty, smutty, naughty, suggestive, indecent, ribald; informal horny; Brit. informal randy; formal concupiscent.

lash v. **1** *he lashed her repeatedly* **whip**, flog, beat, thrash, horsewhip, scourge, birch, switch, belt, strap, cane; strike, hit; informal wallop, whack, lam, larrup, give someone a (good) hiding; N. Amer. informal whale. **2** *rain lashed the window panes* **beat against**, dash against, pound, batter, strike, hit, knock. **3** *the tiger began to lash his tail* **swish**, flick, twitch, whip. **4** *fear lashed them into a frenzy* **provoke**, incite, arouse, excite, agitate, stir up, whip up, work up. **5** *two boats were lashed together* **fasten**, bind, tie (up), tether, hitch, knot, rope, make fast.
▶ n. **1** *he brought the lash down upon the prisoner's back* **whip**, horsewhip, switch, scourge, thong, flail, strap, birch, cane; historical knout, cat-o'-nine-tails, cat. **2** *twenty lashes* **stroke**, blow, hit, strike, welt, thwack, thump; informal wallop, whack; old use stripe.
□ **lash out 1** *the president lashed out at the opposition* **criticize**, chastise, censure, attack, condemn, denounce, lambaste,

harangue, pillory; berate, upbraid, rebuke, reproach; informal lay into; formal castigate. **2** *Norman lashed out at Terry with a knife* **hit out**, strike, let fly, take a swing; set upon/about, turn on, round on, attack; informal lay into, tear into, pitch into. **3** informal *they lashed out on a taxi* **spend lavishly**, be extravagant; informal splash out, splurge, shell out, squander money, waste money, fritter money away.

lass n. Scottish & N. English **girl**, young woman, young lady; Scottish lassie; Irish colleen; informal chick, girlie; Brit. informal bird, bint; N. Amer. informal dame, babe, doll, gal, broad; Austral./NZ informal sheila; literary maid, maiden, damsel; old use wench.

lassitude n. **lethargy**, listlessness, weariness, languor, sluggishness, tiredness, fatigue, torpor, lifelessness, apathy.
– OPPOSITES vigour.

last¹ adj. **1** *the last woman in the queue* **rearmost**, hindmost, endmost, at the end, at the back, furthest (back), final, ultimate. **2** *Rembrandt spent his last years in Amsterdam* **closing**, concluding, final, ending, end, terminal; later, latter. **3** *I'd be the last person to say anything against him* **least likely**, most unlikely, most improbable; least suitable, most unsuitable, most inappropriate, least appropriate. **4** *we met last year* **previous**, preceding; prior, former. **5** *this was his last chance* **final**, only remaining.
– OPPOSITES first, early, next.
▶ adv. *the candidate coming last is eliminated* **at the end**, at/in the rear.
▶ n. *the most important business was left to the last* **end**, ending, finish, close, conclusion, finale, termination.
– OPPOSITES beginning.
□ **at last** finally, in the end, eventually, ultimately, at long last, in (the fullness of) time.
the last word *the last word in luxury and efficiency* the best, the peak, the acme, the epitome, the latest; the pinnacle, the apex, the apogee, the ultimate, the height, the zenith, the nonpareil, the crème de la crème; old use the nonsuch.

last² v. **1** *the hearing lasted for six days* **continue**, go on, carry on, keep on/going, proceed, take; stay, remain, persist. **2** *how long will he last as manager?* **survive**, endure, hold on/out, keep going, persevere; informal stick it out, hang on, hack it. **3** *the car is built to last* **endure**, wear well, stand up, bear up; informal go the distance.

last-ditch adj. **last-minute**, last-chance, eleventh-hour, last-resort, desperate, final; informal last-gasp.

lasting adj. **enduring**, long-lasting, long-lived, abiding, continuing, long-term, surviving, persisting, permanent; durable, constant, stable, established, secure, long-standing; unchanging, irreversible, immutable, eternal, undying, everlasting, unending, never-ending, unfading,

changeless, indestructible, unceasing, unwavering, unfaltering.
– OPPOSITES ephemeral.

lastly adv. **finally**, in conclusion, to conclude, to sum up, to end, last, ultimately.
– OPPOSITES firstly.

latch n. *he lifted the latch* **fastening**, catch, fastener, clasp.
▸ v. *Jess latched the back door* **fasten**, secure, make fast.

late adj. **1** *the train was late* **behind time**, behind schedule, behindhand; tardy, running late, overdue, delayed. **2** *her late husband* **dead**, departed, lamented, passed on/away; formal deceased. **3** *the late government* **previous**, preceding, former, past, prior, earlier, as was, sometime, one-time, ex-, erstwhile; formal quondam.
– OPPOSITES punctual, early.
▸ adv. **1** *she had arrived late* **behind schedule**, behind time, behindhand, belatedly, tardily, at the last minute. **2** *I was working late* **after (office) hours**, overtime. **3** *I won't have you staying out late* **late at night**; informal till all hours.
▢ **of late** recently, lately, latterly.

lately adv. **recently**, of late, latterly, in recent times.

lateness n. **unpunctuality**, tardiness, delay.

latent adj. **dormant**, untapped, unused, undiscovered, hidden, concealed, invisible, unseen, undeveloped, unrealized, unfulfilled, potential.

later adj. *a later chapter* **subsequent**, following, succeeding, future, upcoming, to come, ensuing, next; formal posterior; old use after.
– OPPOSITES earlier.
▸ adv. **1** *later, the film rights were sold* **subsequently**, eventually, then, next, later on, after this/that, afterwards, at a later date, in the future, in due course, by and by, in a while, in time. **2** *two days later a letter arrived* **afterwards**, later on, after (that), subsequently, following; formal thereafter.

lateral adj. **1** *lateral movements* **sideways**, sidewise, sideward, edgewise, edgeways, oblique. **2** *lateral thinking* **unorthodox**, inventive, creative, original, imaginative, innovative.

latest adj. **most recent**, newest, just out, just released, fresh, (bang) up to date, up to the minute, state-of-the-art, current, modern, contemporary, fashionable, in fashion, in vogue; informal in, with it, trendy, hip, hot, happening, cool.
– OPPOSITES old.

lather n. **1** *a rich, soapy lather* **foam**, froth, suds, soapsuds, bubbles; literary spume. **2** *the mare was covered with lather* **sweat**, perspiration. **3** informal *Dad was in a right lather* **panic**, fluster, fret, fuss, fever; informal flap, sweat, tizzy, dither, twitter, state, stew; N. Amer. informal twit; literary pother.

latitude n. **1** *Toronto shares the same latitude as Nice* **parallel**. **2** *he gave them a lot of latitude* **freedom**, scope, leeway, (breathing) space, flexibility, liberty, independence, free rein, licence, room to manoeuvre, freedom of action; informal wiggle room.
– OPPOSITES longitude, restriction.

latter adj. **1** *the latter half of the season* **later**, closing, end, concluding, final; latest, most recent. **2** *Russia chose the latter option* **last-mentioned**, second, last, later.
– OPPOSITES former.

latter-day adj. **modern**, present-day, current, contemporary.

latterly adv. **1** *latterly, she had been in more pain* **recently**, lately, of late. **2** *latterly he worked as a political editor* **ultimately**, finally, towards the end.

lattice n. **grid**, latticework, fretwork, open framework, openwork, trellis, trelliswork, network, mesh.

laud v. formal **praise**, extol, hail, applaud, acclaim, commend, sing the praises of, speak highly of, lionize, eulogize, rhapsodize over/about; informal rave about; old use magnify, panegyrize.
– OPPOSITES criticize.

laudable adj. **praiseworthy**, commendable, admirable, meritorious, worthy, deserving, creditable, estimable, exemplary.
– OPPOSITES shameful.

laudation n. formal **praise**, honour, applause, acclaim, acclamation, commendation, admiration, homage, distinction, approval, credit, kudos, glory, esteem, approbation, tribute, congratulations, plaudits; formal encomium.

laudatory adj. **complimentary**, congratulatory, praising, extolling, adulatory, commendatory, approbatory, flattering, celebratory, eulogizing, panegyrical; informal glowing; formal encomiastic.
– OPPOSITES disparaging.

laugh v. **1** *he started to laugh excitedly* **chuckle**, chortle, guffaw, giggle, titter, snigger, snicker, tee-hee, burst out laughing, roar/hoot with laughter, split one's sides, be doubled up; informal be in stitches, be rolling in the aisles, crease up, fall about, crack up. **2** *people laughed at his theories* **ridicule**, mock, deride, scoff at, jeer at, sneer at, jibe at, make fun of, poke fun at, scorn; lampoon, satirize, parody; informal send up, take the mickey out of, pooh-pooh; Austral./NZ informal poke mullock at.
▸ n. **1** *he gave a short laugh* **chuckle**, chortle, guffaw, giggle, titter, tee-hee, snigger, snicker, roar/hoot of laughter, shriek of laughter, belly laugh. **2** informal *he was a right laugh* **joker**, wag, wit, clown, jester, prankster, character; informal card, case, caution, hoot, scream, riot, barrel of laughs; Austral./NZ informal hard case. **3** informal *I entered the contest for a laugh* **joke**, prank, jest, escapade, caper, practical joke; informal lark.
▢ **laugh something off** dismiss, make a joke of, make light of, shrug off, brush aside, scoff at; informal pooh-pooh.

laughable adj. **1** *the idea that nuclear power is safe is laughable* **ridiculous**, ludicrous, absurd, risible, preposterous; foolish, silly, idiotic, stupid, nonsensical, crazy, insane, outrageous; informal cockeyed; Brit. informal daft. **2** *if it wasn't so tragic, it'd be laughable* **funny**, amusing, humorous, hilarious, uproarious, comical, comic, farcical.

laughing stock n. **figure of fun**, dupe, butt, stooge, Aunt Sally; informal fall guy.

laughter n. **1** *the sound of laughter* **laughing**, chuckling, chortling, guffawing, giggling, tittering, sniggering; informal hysterics. **2** *a source of laughter* **amusement**, entertainment, humour, mirth, merriment, gaiety, hilarity, jollity, jocularity, fun.

launch v. **1** *he launched the boat* **set afloat**, put to sea. **2** *they've launched the shuttle* **send into orbit**, blast off, take off, lift off. **3** *a chair was launched at him* **throw**, hurl, fling, pitch, lob, let fly; fire, shoot; informal chuck, heave, sling. **4** *the government launched a new campaign* **set in motion**, get going, get under way, start, commence, begin, embark on, initiate, inaugurate, set up, organize, introduce, bring into being, roll out; informal kick off. **5** *he launched into a tirade* **start**, commence, burst into.

launder v. **wash**, clean; dry-clean.

laundry n. **1** *a big pile of laundry* **(dirty) washing**, dirty clothes. **2** *the facilities include a laundry* **washroom**, laundry room, launderette; N. Amer. trademark laundromat.

laurels plural n. **honours**, tributes, praise, plaudits, accolades, kudos, acclaim, acclamation, credit, glory, honour, distinction, fame, renown, prestige, recognition; informal brownie points; formal laudation.

lavatory n. **toilet**, WC, water closet, (public) convenience, cloakroom, powder room, urinal, privy, latrine, jakes; N. Amer. washroom, bathroom, rest room, men's/ladies' room, commode, comfort station; Nautical head; informal little girls'/boys' room, smallest room; Brit. informal loo, bog, the Ladies, the Gents, khazi, lav; N. Amer. informal can, john; Austral./NZ informal dunny; old use closet, garderobe.

lavish adj. **1** *lavish parties* **sumptuous**, luxurious, gorgeous, costly, expensive, opulent, grand, splendid, rich, fancy; informal posh, bling. **2** *he was lavish with his hospitality* **generous**, liberal, bountiful, open-handed, unstinting, unsparing, free, munificent, extravagant, prodigal. **3** *lavish amounts of champagne* **abundant**, copious, plentiful, liberal, prolific, generous; literary plenteous.
– OPPOSITES meagre, frugal.
▶ v. *she lavished money on her children* **give freely**, spend generously, heap, shower.

law n. **1** *the law of the land* **rules and regulations**, constitution, legislation, legal code. **2** *a new law was passed* **regulation**, statute, enactment, act, bill, decree, edict, rule, ruling, resolution, dictum, command, order, directive, pronouncement, proclamation, dictate, diktat, fiat, by-law; N. Amer. formal ordinance. **3** *a career in the law* **the legal profession**, the bar. **4** *I'll take you to law!* **litigation**, legal action, lawsuit, justice. **5** informal *on the run from the law.* See **police** (noun). **6** *the laws of the game* **rule**, regulation, principle, convention, instruction, guideline. **7** *a moral law* **principle**, rule, precept, directive, injunction, commandment, belief, creed, credo, maxim, tenet, doctrine, canon.

> **WORD LINKS**
>
> **legal** relating to the law or permitted by law
> **judicial, juridical** relating to a court of law
> **litigious** tending to take legal action to settle disputes
> **sue, prosecute** start legal proceedings against someone
> **jurisprudence** the theory or philosophy of law
> **jurist** an expert in law
> See also **court**.

law-abiding adj. **honest**, lawful, righteous, honourable, upright, upstanding, good, decent, virtuous, moral, dutiful, obedient, compliant, disciplined.
– OPPOSITES criminal.

lawbreaker n. **criminal**, felon, wrongdoer, malefactor, evildoer, offender, transgressor, miscreant; villain, rogue, ruffian; Law malfeasant, infractor; informal crook, con, jailbird.

lawful adj. **1** *a verdict of lawful killing* **legitimate**, legal, licit, just, permissible, permitted, allowable, allowed, rightful, sanctioned, authorized, warranted, within the law; informal legit. **2** *a lawful political organization* **law-abiding**, righteous, good, decent, virtuous, moral, orderly, well behaved, peaceful, dutiful, obedient, compliant, disciplined.
– OPPOSITES illegal, criminal.

lawless adj. **1** *a lawless rabble* **anarchic**, disorderly, ungovernable, unruly, disruptive, rebellious, insubordinate, riotous, mutinous. **2** *lawless activities* **illegal**, unlawful, lawbreaking, illicit, illegitimate, criminal, felonious, villainous, miscreant; informal crooked, shady, bent.
– OPPOSITES orderly, legal.

lawlessness n. **anarchy**, disorder, chaos, unruliness, criminality, crime.

lawsuit n. **(legal) action**, suit (at law), case, (legal/judicial) proceedings, litigation, trial.

lawyer n. **solicitor**, legal practitioner, legal adviser, member of the bar, barrister, advocate, counsel, Queen's Counsel, QC; N. Amer. attorney, counselor(-at-law); informal brief.

lax adj. **slack**, slipshod, negligent, remiss, careless, heedless, unmindful, sloppy, slapdash, offhand, casual; easy-going, lenient, permissive, liberal, indulgent, overindulgent.
– OPPOSITES strict.

laxative n. **purgative**, evacuant; Medicine aperient, cathartic.

lay[1] v. **1** *Curtis laid the newspaper on the table* **put (down)**, place, set (down), deposit, rest, situate, locate, position, stow, shove; informal stick, dump, park, plonk; Brit. informal bung. **2** *the act laid the foundation for the new system* **set in place**, set out/up, establish. **3** *I'll lay money that Michelle will be there* **bet**, wager, gamble, stake, risk, venture; give odds, speculate; informal punt. **4** *they are going to lay charges* **bring (forward)**, press, prefer, lodge, register, place, file. **5** *he laid the blame at the Prime Minister's door* **assign**, attribute, ascribe, allot, attach; hold someone responsible/accountable, find guilty, pin the blame on. **6** *we laid plans for the next voyage* **devise**, arrange, make (ready), prepare, work out, hatch, design, plan, scheme, plot, conceive, put together, draw up, produce, develop, formulate; informal cook up. **7** *this will lay a new responsibility on the court* **impose**, apply, entrust, vest, place, put; inflict, encumber, saddle, charge, burden. **8** *the eagles laid two eggs* **produce**; Zoology oviposit.
▫ **lay something aside 1** *farmers laying aside areas for conservation* **put aside**, put to one side, keep, save. **2** *producers must lay aside their conservatism* **abandon**, cast aside, reject, renounce, repudiate, disregard, forget, discard; literary forsake. **3** *protesters led the government to lay the plans aside* **defer**, shelve, suspend, put on ice, mothball, set aside, put off/aside; informal put on the back burner.
lay something bare reveal, disclose, divulge, show, expose, exhibit, uncover, unveil, unmask, make a clean breast of, make known, make public.
lay something down 1 *he laid down his glass* **put down**, set down, place down, deposit, rest; informal dump, plonk down; Brit. informal bung down. **2** *they were forced to lay down their weapons* **relinquish**, surrender, give up, yield, cede; disarm, give in, submit, capitulate. **3** *the ground rules have been laid down* **formulate**, stipulate, set down, draw up, frame; prescribe, ordain, dictate, decree; enact, pass, decide, determine, impose, codify.
lay down the law order someone about/around, ride roughshod over someone; informal boss someone about/around, throw one's weight about/around, push someone about/around.
lay eyes on informal see, spot, observe, regard, view, catch sight of; informal clap/set eyes on; literary behold, espy, descry.
lay hands on 1 *wait till I lay my hands on you!* **catch**, lay/get hold of, get one's hands on, seize, grab, grasp, capture. **2** *it's not easy to lay your hands on decent champagne* **obtain**, acquire, get, come by, find, locate, discover, unearth, uncover, pick up, procure, get one's hands on, get possession of, buy, purchase. **3** *the pastor laid hands on the children* **bless**, consecrate; confirm; ordain.
lay something in stock up with/on, stockpile, store (up), amass, hoard, stow

(away), put aside/away/by, garner, collect, squirrel away; informal salt away, stash (away).
lay into informal **1** *a policeman laying into a protestor*. See **assault** (sense 1 of the verb). **2** *he laid into her with a string of insults*. See **criticize**.
lay it on thick informal exaggerate, overdo it, embellish the truth; flatter, praise; informal pile it on, sweet-talk, soft-soap.
lay off informal give up, stop, refrain from, abstain from, desist from, cut out; informal pack in, leave off, quit.
lay someone off make redundant, dismiss, let go, discharge, give notice to; informal sack, fire, give someone their cards, give someone their marching orders, give someone the boot/push, give someone the (old) heave-ho.
lay something on provide, supply, furnish, line up, organize, prepare, produce, make available; informal fix up.
lay someone out informal knock out/down, knock unconscious, fell, floor, flatten; informal KO, kayo; Brit. informal knock for six.
lay something out 1 *Robyn laid the plans out on the desk* **spread out**, set out, display, exhibit. **2** *a paper laying out our priorities* **outline**, sketch out, rough out, detail, draw up, formulate, work out, frame, draft.
lay waste devastate, wipe out, destroy, demolish, annihilate, raze, ruin, wreck, level, flatten, ravage, pillage, sack, despoil.

lay[2] adj. **1** *a lay preacher* **non-clerical**, non-ordained, secular, temporal; formal laic. **2** *a lay audience* **non-professional**, amateur, non-specialist, non-technical, untrained, unqualified.

layabout n. **idler**, good-for-nothing, loafer, lounger, shirker, sluggard, slug, laggard, slugabed, malingerer; informal skiver, waster, slacker, lazybones; Austral./NZ informal bludger; literary wastrel.

layer n. **coating**, sheet, coat, film, covering, blanket, skin, thickness.

layman n. See **layperson** (senses 1 & 2).

lay-off n. **redundancy**, dismissal, discharge; informal sacking, firing, the sack, the boot, the axe, the elbow.
– OPPOSITES recruitment.

layout n. **1** *the layout of the house* **arrangement**, geography, design, organization; plan, map. **2** *the magazine's layout* **design**, arrangement, presentation, style, format; structure, organization, composition, configuration.

layperson n. **1** *a prayer book for laypeople* **unordained person**, member of the congregation, layman, laywoman. **2** *engineering sounds highly specialized to the layperson* **non-expert**, layman, non-professional, amateur, non-specialist.

laze v. **relax**, unwind, idle, do nothing, loaf (around/about), lounge (around/about), loll (around/about), lie (around/about), take it easy; informal hang around/round, veg (out); N. Amer. informal bum (around).

lazy adj. **(bone) idle**, indolent, slothful, work-shy, shiftless, inactive, sluggish, lethargic;

remiss, negligent, slack, lax, lackadaisical; old use otiose.
– OPPOSITES industrious.

lazybones n. informal **idler**, loafer, layabout, lounger, good-for-nothing, do-nothing, shirker, sluggard, slug, laggard, slugabed; informal skiver, waster, slacker; Austral./NZ informal bludger; literary wastrel.

leach v. **drain**, filter, percolate, filtrate, strain.

lead[1] v. **1** *Michelle led them into the house* **guide**, conduct, show (the way), lead the way, usher, escort, steer, pilot, shepherd; accompany, see, take. **2** *he led us to believe they were lying* **cause**, induce, prompt, move, persuade, influence, drive, condition, make; incline, dispose, predispose. **3** *this might lead to job losses* **result in**, cause, bring on/about, give rise to, be the cause of, make happen, create, produce, occasion, effect, generate, contribute to, promote; provoke, stir up, spark off, arouse, foment, instigate; involve, necessitate, entail; formal effectuate. **4** *he led a march to the city centre* **be at the head/front of**, head, spearhead. **5** *she led a coalition of radicals* **be the leader of**, be the head of, preside over, head, command, govern, rule, be in charge of, be in command of, be in control of, run, control, be at the helm of, helm; administer, organize, manage; reign over; informal head up. **6** *Rangers were leading at half-time* **be ahead**, be winning, be (out) in front, be in the lead, be first. **7** *the champion was leading the field* **be at the front of**, be first in, be ahead of, head; outrun, outstrip, outpace, leave behind, draw away from; outdo, outclass, beat; informal leave standing. **8** *I just want to lead a normal life* **experience**, have, live, spend.
– OPPOSITES follow.

▸n. **1** *I was in the lead early on* **leading position**, first place, van, vanguard; ahead, in front, winning. **2** *they took the lead in the personal computer market* **first position**, forefront, primacy, dominance, superiority, ascendancy; pre-eminence, supremacy, advantage, upper hand, whip hand. **3** *sixth-formers should give a lead to younger pupils* **example**, (role) model, exemplar, paradigm. **4** *playing the lead* **leading role**, star/starring role, title role, principal part; principal character, male lead, female lead, leading man, leading lady. **5** *a labrador on a lead* **leash**, tether, cord, rope, chain. **6** *detectives were following up a new lead* **clue**, pointer, hint, tip, tip-off, suggestion, indication, sign; (**leads**) evidence, information.

▸adj. *the lead position* **leading**, first, top, foremost, front, head; chief, principal, premier.

□ **lead something off** begin, start (off), commence, open; informal kick off.
lead someone on deceive, mislead, delude, hoodwink, dupe, trick, fool, pull the wool over someone's eyes; tease, flirt with; informal string along, lead up the garden path, take for a ride.
lead the way 1 *he led the way to the kitchen*

guide, conduct, show the way. **2** *Britain is leading the way in aerospace technology* **take the initiative**, break (new) ground, blaze a trail.
lead up to precede, happen before; prepare the way for, pave the way for, lay the groundwork for, set the scene for, work round/up to.

lead[2] n. *a lead-lined box.*

┌─────────────────────────────┐
│ **WORD LINKS**   │
│ plumbic, plumbous relating to lead │
└─────────────────────────────┘

leaden adj. **1** *his eyes were leaden with sleep* **dull**, heavy, weighty; listless, lifeless. **2** *he moved on leaden feet* **sluggish**, heavy, lumbering, slow. **3** *leaden prose* **boring**, dull, unimaginative, uninspired, monotonous, heavy, laboured, wooden. **4** *a leaden sky* **grey**, greyish, black, dark; cloudy, gloomy, overcast, dull, murky, sunless, louring, oppressive, threatening; literary tenebrous.

leader n. **1** *the leader of the Democratic Party* **chief**, head, principal; commander, captain; controller, superior, headman; chairman, chairwoman, chairperson, chair; (managing) director, MD, manager, chief executive officer, CEO, superintendent, supervisor, overseer, administrator, employer, master, mistress; ruler, president, premier, governor; monarch, sovereign, king, queen, emperor; informal boss, skipper, gaffer, guv'nor, number one, numero uno, honcho; N. Amer. informal sachem, padrone. **2** *a world leader in the use of video conferencing* **pioneer**, front runner, innovator, trailblazer, groundbreaker, trendsetter, torch-bearer; originator, initiator, founder, architect; formal neoteric.
– OPPOSITES follower, supporter.

leadership n. **1** *the leadership of the Conservative Party* **headship**, directorship, premiership, governorship, governance, administration, captaincy, control, ascendancy, rule, command, power, dominion. **2** *firm leadership* **guidance**, direction, control, management, superintendence, supervision; organization, government.

leading adj. **1** *he played the leading role in his team's victory* **main**, chief, major, prime, most significant, principal, foremost, key, central, focal, paramount, dominant, essential. **2** *the leading industrialized countries* **most powerful**, most important, greatest, chief, pre-eminent, principal, dominant. **3** *last season's leading scorer* **top**, highest, best, first; front, lead; unparalleled, matchless, star.
– OPPOSITES subordinate, minor.

leaf n. **1** *sycamore leaves* **frond**, leaflet, flag; Botany cotyledon, blade, bract. **2** *a sheaf of loose leaves* **page**, sheet, folio.
▸v. *he leafed through the documents* **flick**, flip, thumb, skim, browse, glance, riffle; scan, run one's eye over, peruse.
□ **turn over a new leaf** reform, improve, mend one's ways, make a fresh start, change for the better; informal go straight.

WORD LINKS

foliar, foliaceous relating to leaves
deciduous referring to a tree that sheds its leaves each year
evergreen referring to a tree that retains its leaves throughout the year
defoliant a chemical used to remove leaves from trees and plants

leaflet n. **pamphlet**, booklet, brochure, handbill, circular, flyer, handout, bulletin; N. Amer. folder, dodger.

league n. **1** *a league of nations* **alliance**, confederation, confederacy, federation, union, association, coalition, consortium, affiliation, guild, cooperative, partnership, fellowship, syndicate, consociation. **2** *we won the league last year* **championship**, competition, contest. **3** *the store is not in the same league* **class**, group, category, level.
▸ v. *they leagued together with other companies* **ally**, join forces, join together, unite, band together, affiliate, combine, amalgamate, confederate, team up, join up.
□ **in league with** collaborating with, cooperating with, in alliance with, allied with, conspiring with, hand in glove with; informal in cahoots with.

leak v. **1** *oil leaking from the tanker* **seep (out)**, escape, ooze (out), emanate, issue, drip, dribble, drain, bleed. **2** *the tanks are leaking gasoline* **discharge**, exude, emit, release, drip, dribble, ooze, secrete. **3** *civil servants leaking information* **disclose**, divulge, reveal, make public, tell, impart, pass on, relate, communicate, expose, broadcast, publish, release, let slip, bring into the open; informal blab, let the cat out of the bag, spill the beans, blow the gaff.
▸ n. **1** *check that there are no leaks in the bag* **hole**, opening, puncture, perforation, gash, slit, nick, rent, break, crack, fissure, rupture. **2** *a gas leak* **discharge**, leakage, leaking, oozing, seeping, seepage, drip, escape. **3** *leaks to the media* **disclosure**, revelation, exposé.

leaky adj. **leaking**, dripping; cracked, split, punctured, perforated.
– OPPOSITES watertight.

lean[1] v. **1** *Polly leaned against the door* **rest**, recline, be supported. **2** *trees leaning in the wind* **slant**, incline, bend, tilt, be at an angle, slope, tip, list. **3** *he leans towards existentialist philosophy* **tend**, incline, gravitate; have a preference for, have a penchant for, be partial to, have a liking for, have an affinity with. **4** *a strong shoulder to lean on* **depend**, be dependent, rely, count, bank, have faith in, trust. **5** informal *I got leaned on by villains* **intimidate**, coerce, browbeat, bully, pressurize, threaten, put pressure on; informal twist someone's arm, put the frighteners on, put the screws on.

lean[2] adj. **1** *a tall, lean man* **slim**, thin, slender, spare, wiry, lanky. **2** *a lean harvest* **meagre**, sparse, poor, mean, inadequate, insufficient, paltry, deficient, insubstantial. **3** *lean times* **unproductive**, unfruitful, arid, barren; hard, bad, difficult, tough, impoverished, poverty-stricken.
– OPPOSITES fat, abundant, prosperous.

leaning n. **inclination**, tendency, bent, proclivity, propensity, penchant, predisposition, predilection, partiality, preference, bias, attraction, liking, fondness, taste.

leap v. **1** *he leapt over the gate* **jump (over)**, vault (over), spring over, bound over, hop (over), hurdle, clear. **2** *Claudia leapt to her feet* **spring**, jump (up), bound, dart. **3** *we leapt to the rescue* **rush**, hurry, hasten. **4** *she leapt at the chance* **accept eagerly**, grasp (with both hands), grab, take advantage of, seize (on), jump at. **5** *don't leap to conclusions* **form hastily**, reach hurriedly; hurry, hasten, jump, rush. **6** *profits leapt by 55%* **increase rapidly**, soar, rocket, skyrocket, shoot up, escalate.
▸ n. **1** *an easy leap* **jump**, vault, spring, bound, hop, skip. **2** *a leap of 33%* **rise**, surge, upsurge, upswing, upturn.
□ **in/by leaps and bounds** rapidly, swiftly, quickly, speedily, dramatically.

learn v. **1** *it's good for kids to learn the piano* **master**, become competent in, become proficient in, grasp, take in, absorb, assimilate, digest, familiarize oneself with; study, read up on, be taught, have lessons in; informal get the hang of. **2** *she learnt the poem by heart* **memorize**, learn by heart, commit to memory, learn parrot-fashion, get off/down pat; old use con. **3** *he learned that the school would shortly be closing* **discover**, find out, become aware, be informed, hear (tell); gather, understand, ascertain, establish; informal get wind of the fact; Brit. informal suss out.

learned adj. **scholarly**, erudite, well educated, knowledgeable, widely read, well informed, lettered, cultured, intellectual, academic, literary, bookish, highbrow, studious; informal brainy; formal sapient.
– OPPOSITES ignorant.

learner n. **beginner**, trainee, apprentice, pupil, student, novice, newcomer, starter, probationer, tyro, fledgling, neophyte; N. Amer. tenderfoot; N. Amer. informal greenhorn.
– OPPOSITES veteran.

learning n. **1** *a centre of learning* **study**, studying, education, schooling, tuition, teaching, academic work; research, investigation. **2** *the astonishing range of his learning* **scholarship**, knowledge, education, erudition, intellect, enlightenment, illumination, book learning, information, understanding, wisdom; formal edification.
– OPPOSITES ignorance.

lease n. *a 15-year lease* **leasehold**, rental/hire agreement, charter; rental, tenancy, tenure, period of occupancy.
– OPPOSITES freehold.
▸ v. **1** *the film crew leased a large hangar* **rent**, hire, charter. **2** *they leased the mill to a reputable family* **rent (out)**, let (out), hire (out), sublet, sublease.

leash n. **1** *keep your dog on a leash* **lead**, tether, rope, chain, strap, restraint. **2** *he found himself off the parental leash* **control**, restraint, check, curb, rein, discipline.

least determiner *I have not the least idea what this means* **slightest**, smallest, minutest, tiniest, littlest.
□ **at least** at the minimum, no/not less than, more than.

leather n. *a leather jacket* **skin**, hide.

leathery adj. **1** *leathery skin* **rough**, rugged, wrinkled, wrinkly, furrowed, lined, wizened, weather-beaten, callous, gnarled. **2** *leathery sides of beef* **tough**, hard, gristly, chewy, stringy.

leave¹ v. **1** *I left the hotel* **depart from**, go (away) from, withdraw from, retire from, take oneself off from, exit from, take one's leave of, pull out of, quit, be gone from, decamp from, disappear from, vacate, absent oneself from; say one's farewells/goodbyes, make oneself scarce; informal push off, shove off, clear out/off, cut and run, split, vamoose, scoot, make tracks, up sticks; Brit. informal sling one's hook. **2** *the next morning we left for Leicester* **set off**, head, make; set sail. **3** *he's left his wife* **abandon**, desert, cast aside/off, jilt, leave in the lurch, leave high and dry, throw over; informal dump, ditch, chuck, drop, walk/run out on; Brit. informal give someone the push, give someone the elbow, bin off; literary forsake. **4** *he left his job in November* **resign from**, retire from, step down from, withdraw from, pull out of, give up; informal quit. **5** *she left her handbag on a bus* **leave behind**, forget, lose, mislay. **6** *I thought I'd leave it to the experts* **entrust**, hand over, pass on, refer; delegate. **7** *he left her £100,000* **bequeath**, will, endow, hand down, make over; Law demise, devise. **8** *the speech left some feelings of disappointment* **cause**, produce, generate, give rise to.
– OPPOSITES arrive.
□ **leave someone in the lurch** leave in trouble, let down, leave stranded, leave high and dry, abandon, desert.
leave off informal stop, cease, finish, desist from, keep from, break off, lay off, give up, discontinue, refrain from, eschew; informal quit, knock off, jack in, swear off; formal forswear.
leave someone/something out 1 *Adam left out the address* **miss out**, omit, overlook, forget; skip, miss, jump. **2** *he was left out of the England squad* **exclude**, omit, drop, pass over.

leave² n. **1** *the judge granted leave to appeal* **permission**, consent, authorization, sanction, warrant, dispensation, approval, clearance, blessing, agreement, backing, assent, acceptance, licence, acquiescence; informal the go-ahead, the green light, the OK, the rubber stamp. **2** *he was on leave* **holiday**, vacation, break, time off, furlough, sabbatical, leave of absence; informal hols, vac. **3** *I will now take my leave of you* **departure**, leaving, leave-taking, parting, withdrawal, exit, farewell, goodbye.

leaven n. *leaven is added to the dough* **leavening**, fermentation agent, raising agent.
▸v. **1** *yeast leavens the bread* **raise**, make rise, puff up, expand. **2** *formal proceedings leavened by humour* **permeate**, infuse, pervade, imbue, suffuse; enliven, liven up, invigorate, energize, electrify, ginger up, perk up, brighten up, season, spice; informal buck up, pep up.

leavings plural n. **residue**, remainder, remains, remnants, leftovers, scrapings, scraps, oddments, odds and ends, rejects, dregs, refuse, rubbish.

lecher n. **lecherous man**, libertine, womanizer, debauchee, rake, roué, profligate, wanton, loose-liver, Don Juan, Casanova, Lothario, Romeo; informal lech, dirty old man, goat, wolf; formal fornicator.

lecherous adj. **lustful**, licentious, lascivious, libidinous, prurient, lewd, salacious, lubricious, debauched, dissolute, wanton, dissipated, degenerate, depraved, dirty, filthy; informal randy, horny, goatish; formal concupiscent.
– OPPOSITES chaste.

lecture n. **1** *a lecture on children's literature* **speech**, talk, address, discourse, disquisition, presentation, oration, lesson. **2** *Dave got a severe lecture* **scolding**, chiding, reprimand, rebuke, reproof, reproach, upbraiding, berating, admonishment; informal dressing-down, telling-off, talking-to, tongue-lashing; formal castigation.
▸v. **1** *lecturing on the dangers of drugs* **give a lecture/talk**, talk, make a speech, speak, give an address, discourse, hold forth, declaim, expatiate; informal spout, sound off. **2** *she lectures at Dublin University* **teach**, tutor, give instruction, give lessons. **3** *he was lectured by the headmaster* **scold**, chide, reprimand, rebuke, reprove, reproach, upbraid, berate, chastise, admonish, lambaste, haul over the coals, take to task; informal give someone a dressing-down, give someone a talking-to, tell off, bawl out; Brit. informal tick off, carpet; formal castigate.

lecturer n. **1** *the lecturer is a journalist* **speaker**, speech-maker, orator. **2** *a lecturer in economics* **university/college teacher**, tutor, reader, scholar, don, professor, fellow; academic, academician, preceptor; formal pedagogue.

ledge n. **shelf**, sill, mantel, mantelpiece, shelving; projection, protrusion, overhang, ridge, prominence.

ledger n. **(account) book**, record book, register, log; records, books; balance sheet, financial statement.

lee n. **shelter**, protection, cover, refuge, safety, security.

leech n. **parasite**, bloodsucker, passenger; informal scrounger, sponger, freeloader, junketeer.

leer v. *Henry leered at her* **ogle**, look lasciviously, look suggestively, eye; informal

give someone a/the once-over, lech after/over; Austral./NZ informal perv on.
▶ n. *a sly leer* **lecherous look**, lascivious look, ogle; informal the once-over.

leery adj. **wary**, cautious, careful, guarded, chary, suspicious, distrustful; worried, anxious, apprehensive.

lees plural n. **sediment**, dregs, deposit, grounds, residue, remains, silt, sludge; technical residuum; literary draff; old use grouts.

leeway n. **freedom**, scope, latitude, space, room, liberty, flexibility, licence, free hand, free rein; informal wiggle room.

left adj. **left-hand**, sinistral, at nine o'clock; Heraldry sinister.
– OPPOSITES right.

> **WORD LINKS**
> **port** (old use **larboard**) the left-hand side of a ship
> **verso** the left-hand page in a book

left-handed adj. **1** *a left-handed golfer* **sinistral**; informal southpaw. **2** *a left-handed compliment* **backhanded**, ambiguous, equivocal, double-edged; dubious, indirect, cryptic, ironic, sardonic, insincere, hypocritical.
– OPPOSITES right-handed.

leftover n. **1** *a leftover from the 60s* **residue**, survivor, vestige, legacy. **2** *put the leftovers in the fridge* **leavings**, uneaten food, remainder, scraps, remnants, remains; excess, surplus.
▶ adj. *leftover food* **remaining**, left, uneaten, unconsumed; excess, surplus, superfluous, unused, unwanted, spare.

left-wing adj. **socialist**, communist, leftist, anti-capitalist, Labour, Marxist–Leninist, Bolshevik, Trotskyite, Maoist; informal commie, lefty, red, pink.
– OPPOSITES right-wing, conservative.

leg n. **1** *Lee broke his leg* **(lower) limb**, shank; informal peg, pin; old use member. **2** *a table leg* **upright**, support, prop. **3** *the first leg of a European tour* **part**, stage, portion, segment, section, phase, stretch, lap.
☐ **leg it** informal **1** *if the dog starts growling, leg it!* **run (away)**, flee, make off, make a break for it, escape, hurry; informal hightail it, hotfoot it, make a run for it, cut and run, skedaddle, vamoose, show a clean pair of heels, split, scoot, scram; Brit. informal scarper. **2** *legging it around London* **walk**, march, tramp, trek, trudge, plod, wander, go on foot, go on Shanks's pony; N. Amer. informal schlep.
pull someone's leg tease, rag, make fun of, chaff, jest, joke, play a (practical) joke on, play a trick on, make a monkey out of; hoax, fool, deceive, lead on, hoodwink, dupe, beguile, gull; informal kid, have on, rib, take for a ride, take the mickey out of; Brit. informal wind up; N. Amer. informal put on.

> **WORD LINKS**
> **crural** relating to the legs
> **bandy-legged, bow-legged** having legs that curve outwards
> **knock-kneed** having legs that curve inwards

> **caliper** a metal support for a person's leg
> **crutch** an implement used as a support by a person who is lame

legacy n. **1** *a legacy from a great aunt* **bequest**, inheritance, heritage, bequeathal, bestowal, endowment, gift, patrimony, settlement, birthright; Law, dated hereditament; formal benefaction. **2** *the rancorous legacy of the war* **consequence**, effect, upshot, spin-off, repercussion, aftermath, by-product, result.

legal adj. **1** *all their actions were legal* **lawful**, legitimate, licit, within the law, legalized, valid; permissible, permitted, allowable, allowed, above board, admissible, acceptable; authorized, sanctioned, licensed, constitutional; informal legit. **2** *the legal profession* **judicial**, juridical, judicatory.
– OPPOSITES criminal.

legality n. **lawfulness**, legitimacy, validity, admissibility, permissibility, constitutionality; justice.

legalize v. **make legal**, decriminalize, legitimize, legitimatize, legitimate, permit, allow, authorize, sanction, license; regularize, normalize; informal OK, give the go-ahead to, give the thumbs up to, give the green light to.
– OPPOSITES prohibit.

legate n. **envoy**, emissary, agent, ambassador, representative, nuncio, commissioner, delegate, proxy, deputy, plenipotentiary, messenger.

legatee n. **beneficiary**, inheritor, heir, heiress, recipient; Law devisee; Scottish Law heritor.

legation n. **1** *the British legation* **(diplomatic) mission**, delegation, deputation, contingent; envoys, delegates, diplomats, aides. **2** *the legations were besieged* **embassy**, consulate.

legend n. **1** *the Arthurian legends* **myth**, saga, epic, (folk) tale, (folk) story, fairy tale, fable, mythos, mythus; folklore, lore, mythology, fantasy, oral history, folk tradition. **2** *pop legends* **celebrity**, star, superstar, icon, phenomenon, luminary, giant; informal celeb, megastar. **3** *the wording of the legend* **caption**, inscription, dedication, slogan, heading, title, subtitle, subheading, rubric. **4** *the legend to Figure 5* **explanation**, key, guide.

legendary adj. **1** *legendary kings* **fabled**, heroic, traditional, fairy-tale, storybook, mythical, mythological. **2** *a legendary figure in the trade-union movement* **famous**, celebrated, famed, renowned, acclaimed, illustrious, esteemed, honoured, exalted, venerable, well known, popular, prominent, distinguished, great, eminent, pre-eminent; formal lauded.
– OPPOSITES historical.

legerdemain n. **1** *stage magicians practising legerdemain* **sleight of hand**, conjuring, magic, wizardry; formal prestidigitation; rare thaumaturgy. **2** *a piece of management legerdemain* **trickery**, cunning, artfulness, craftiness, chicanery, skulduggery, deceit, deception, artifice; Brit. informal jiggery-pokery.

legibility n. **readability**, clarity, clearness, neatness.

legible adj. **readable**, easy to read, easily deciphered, clear, plain, neat, intelligible.

legion n. 1 *a Roman legion* **brigade**, regiment, battalion, company, troop, division, squadron, squad, platoon, unit. 2 *the legions of TV cameras* **horde**, throng, multitude, crowd, mass, mob, gang, swarm, flock, herd, score, army.
▸ adj. *her fans are legion* **numerous**, countless, innumerable, incalculable, many, abundant, plentiful; literary myriad.

legislate v. **make laws**, pass laws, enact laws, formulate laws.

legislation n. **law**, body of laws, rules, rulings, regulations, acts, bills, statutes, enactments; N. Amer. formal ordinances.

legislative adj. **law-making**, judicial, juridical, parliamentary, governmental, policy-making.

legislator n. **lawmaker**, lawgiver, parliamentarian, Member of Parliament, MP, congressman, congresswoman, assemblyman, assemblywoman, senator.

legitimate adj. 1 *the only form of legitimate gambling* **legal**, lawful, licit, legalized, authorized, permitted, permissible, allowable, allowed, admissible, sanctioned, approved, licensed, statutory, constitutional; informal legit. 2 *the legitimate heir* **rightful**, lawful, genuine, authentic, real, true, proper, authorized, sanctioned, acknowledged, recognized. 3 *legitimate grounds for unease* **valid**, sound, admissible, acceptable, well founded, justifiable, reasonable, sensible, just, fair, bona fide.
– OPPOSITES illegal, invalid.

legitimize v. **validate**, legitimate, permit, authorize, sanction, license, condone, justify, endorse, support; legalize.
– OPPOSITES outlaw.

leisure n. *the balance between leisure and work* **free time**, spare time, time off; recreation, relaxation, inactivity, pleasure; informal R & R.
– OPPOSITES work.
□ **at your leisure** at your convenience, when it suits you, in your own (good) time, without haste, unhurriedly.

leisurely adj. **unhurried**, relaxed, easy, gentle, sedate, comfortable, restful, undemanding, slow, lazy.
– OPPOSITES hurried.

lend v. 1 *I'll lend you my towel* **loan**, let someone use; advance; Brit. informal sub. 2 *these examples lend weight to his assertions* **add**, impart, give, bestow, confer, provide, supply, furnish, contribute.
– OPPOSITES borrow.
□ **lend an ear** listen, pay attention, take notice, be attentive, concentrate, (pay) heed; informal be all ears; old use hearken.
lend a hand help (out), give a helping hand, assist, make a contribution, do one's bit;

informal pitch in, muck in, get stuck in.
lend itself to be suitable for, be suited to, be appropriate for, be applicable for.

length n. 1 *a length of three or four metres | the whole length of the valley* **extent**, distance, linear measure, span, reach; area, expanse, stretch, range, scope. 2 *a considerable length of time* **period**, duration, stretch, span. 3 *a length of blue silk* **piece**, swatch, measure. 4 *MPs criticized the length of the speech* **protractedness**, lengthiness, extent, extensiveness; prolixity, wordiness, verbosity, verboseness, long-windedness.
□ **at length** 1 *he spoke at length* **for a long time**, for ages, for hours, interminably, endlessly, ceaselessly, unendingly. 2 *he was questioned at length* **thoroughly**, fully, in detail, in depth, comprehensively, exhaustively, extensively. 3 *his search led him, at length, to Seattle* **eventually**, in time, finally, at (long) last, in the end, ultimately.

lengthen v. 1 *he lengthened his stride* **elongate**, make longer, extend; expand, widen, broaden, enlarge. 2 *the days are lengthening* **grow/get longer**, draw out. 3 *you'll need to lengthen the cooking time* **prolong**, make longer, increase, extend, expand, protract, stretch out.
– OPPOSITES shorten.

lengthy adj. 1 *a lengthy civil war* **(very) long**, long-lasting, prolonged, extended. 2 *lengthy discussions* **protracted**, overlong, long-drawn-out; verbose, wordy, prolix, long-winded; tedious, boring, interminable.
– OPPOSITES short.

leniency n. **mercifulness**, mercy, clemency, forgiveness; tolerance, forbearance, humanity, charity, indulgence, mildness; pity, sympathy, compassion, understanding.

lenient adj. **merciful**, clement, forgiving, forbearing, tolerant, charitable, humane, indulgent, easy-going, magnanimous, sympathetic, compassionate.
– OPPOSITES severe.

leper n. **(social) outcast**, pariah, undesirable, persona non grata.

leprechaun n. **pixie**, goblin, elf, sprite, fairy, gnome, imp, brownie.

lesion n. **wound**, injury, bruise, abrasion, contusion; ulcer, ulceration, (running) sore, abscess; Medicine trauma.

less pron. *the fare is less than £1* **a smaller amount**, not so/as much as, under, below.
– OPPOSITES more.
▸ determiner *there was less noise now* **not so much**, smaller, slighter, shorter, reduced; fewer.
▸ adv. *we must use the car less* **to a lesser degree**, to a smaller extent, not so/as much.
▸ prep. *list price less 10 per cent* **minus**, subtracting, excepting, without.
– OPPOSITES plus.

lessen v. 1 *exercise lessens the risk of heart disease* **reduce**, make less/smaller, minimize, decrease; allay, assuage, alleviate, attenuate, palliate, ease, dull, deaden, blunt, moderate, mitigate, dampen, soften, tone down, dilute,

weaken. **2** *the pain began to lessen* **grow less**, grow smaller, decrease, diminish, decline, subside, abate; fade, die down/off, let up, ease off, tail off, drop (off/away), fall, dwindle, ebb, wane, recede. **3** *his behaviour lessened him in their eyes* **diminish**, degrade, discredit, devalue, belittle.
– OPPOSITES increase.

lesser adj. **1** *a lesser offence* **less important**, minor, secondary, subsidiary, marginal, ancillary, auxiliary, supplementary, peripheral; inferior, insignificant, unimportant, petty. **2** *you look down at us lesser mortals* **subordinate**, minor, inferior, second-class, subservient, lowly, humble.
– OPPOSITES greater, superior.

lesson n. **1** *a maths lesson* **class**, session, seminar, tutorial, lecture, period. **2** *they should be industrious at their lessons* **exercises**, assignments, schoolwork, homework. **3** *reading the lesson in assembly* **Bible reading**, scripture, text, reading. **4** *Stuart's accident should be a lesson to all parents* **warning**, deterrent, caution; example, exemplar, message, moral.

lest conj. **(just) in case**, for fear that, in order to avoid.

let v. **1** *let him sleep for now* **allow**, permit, give permission to, give leave to, authorize, sanction, grant the right to, license, empower, enable, entitle; assent to, consent to, agree to, acquiesce in, tolerate, countenance, give one's blessing to, give assent to, give someone/something the nod; informal give the green light to, give the go-ahead to, give the thumbs up to, OK; formal accede to; old use suffer. **2** *they've let their flat* **rent (out)**, let out, lease, hire (out), sublet, sublease.
– OPPOSITES prevent, prohibit.
▫ **let someone down** fail, disappoint, disillusion; abandon, desert, leave stranded, leave in the lurch.
let fly 1 *he let fly with a brick* **hurl**, fling, throw, propel, pitch, lob, toss, launch; shoot, fire, blast; informal chuck, sling, heave. **2** *she let fly at Geoffrey* **lose one's temper with**, lash out at, scold, chastise, chide, rant at, inveigh against, rail against; explode, burst out, let someone have it; informal carpet, give someone a rocket, tear someone off a strip; formal excoriate.
let go of release, loosen one's hold on, relinquish; old use unhand.
let someone go make redundant, dismiss, discharge, lay off, give notice to, axe; informal sack, fire, give someone their cards, give someone their marching orders, send packing, give someone the boot/push, give someone the (old) heave-ho.
let someone in allow to enter, allow in, admit, open the door to; receive, welcome, greet.
let something off detonate, discharge, explode, set off, fire off.
let someone off 1 informal *I'll let you off this time* **pardon**, forgive, grant an amnesty to; be merciful to, have mercy on; acquit,

absolve, exonerate, clear, vindicate; informal let someone off the hook; formal exculpate. **2** *he let me off work* **excuse from**, exempt from, spare from.
let on informal **1** *I never let on that I felt anxious* **reveal**, make known, tell, disclose, mention, divulge, let slip, give away, make public; blab; informal let the cat out of the bag, give the game away. **2** *they all let on they didn't hear me* **pretend**, feign, affect, make out, make believe, simulate.
let something out 1 *I let out a cry of triumph* **utter**, emit, give (vent to), produce, issue, express, voice, release. **2** *she let out that he'd given her a lift home* **reveal**, make known, tell, disclose, mention, divulge, let slip, give away, let it be known, blurt out.
let someone out release, liberate, (set) free, let go, discharge; set/turn loose, allow to leave.
let up informal **1** *the rain has let up* **abate**, lessen, decrease, diminish, subside, relent, slacken, die down/off, ease (off), tail off; ebb, wane, dwindle, fade; stop, cease, finish. **2** *you never let up, do you?* **relax**, ease up/off, slow down; pause, break (off), take a break, rest, stop; informal take a breather.

let-down n. **disappointment**, anticlimax, comedown, non-event, fiasco, setback, blow; informal washout, damp squib.

lethal adj. **fatal**, deadly, mortal, death-dealing, life-threatening, murderous, killing; poisonous, toxic, noxious, venomous; dangerous, destructive, harmful, pernicious; literary deathly, nocuous; old use baneful.
– OPPOSITES harmless, safe.

lethargic adj. **sluggish**, inert, inactive, slow, torpid, lifeless; languid, listless, lazy, idle, indolent, shiftless, slothful, apathetic, weary, tired, fatigued.

lethargy n. **sluggishness**, inertia, inactivity, inaction, slowness, torpor, torpidity, lifelessness, listlessness, languor, languidness, laziness, idleness, indolence, shiftlessness, sloth, apathy, passivity, weariness, tiredness, lassitude, fatigue; literary hebetude.
– OPPOSITES vigour, energy.

letter n. **1** *capital letters* **(alphabetical) character**, sign, symbol, mark, figure, rune; Linguistics grapheme. **2** *she's received a letter from him* **message**, (written) communication, note, line, missive, dispatch; correspondence, news, information, intelligence, word; post, mail; formal epistle. **3** *a man of letters* **(book) learning**, scholarship, erudition, education, knowledge; intellect, intelligence, enlightenment, wisdom, sagacity, culture.
▫ **to the letter** strictly, precisely, exactly, accurately, closely, faithfully, religiously, punctiliously, literally, verbatim, in every detail.

WORD LINKS

epistolary relating to the writing of letters
poste restante a post office department keeping letters until they are collected

postscript a remark added at the end of a letter, following the signature

lettered adj. **learned**, erudite, academic, (well) educated, well read, widely read, knowledgeable, intellectual, well schooled, enlightened, cultured, cultivated, scholarly, bookish, highbrow, studious.
– OPPOSITES ill-educated.

let-up n. informal **abatement**, lessening, decrease, diminishing, diminution, decline, relenting, remission, slackening, weakening, relaxation, dying down, easing off, tailing off, dropping away/off; respite, break, interval, hiatus, suspension, cessation, stop, pause.

level adj. **1** *a smooth and level surface* **flat**, smooth, even, uniform, plane, flush, plumb. **2** *he kept his voice level* **unchanging**, steady, unvarying, even, uniform, regular, constant, invariable, unaltering; calm, unemotional, composed, equable, unruffled, serene, tranquil. **3** *the scores were level* **equal**, even, drawn, tied, all square, neck and neck, level pegging, on a par, evenly matched; informal even-steven(s). **4** *his eyes were level with hers* **aligned**, on the same level as, on a level, at the same height as, in line.
– OPPOSITES uneven, unsteady, unequal.
▸n. **1** *the post is at research-officer level* **rank**, standing, status, position; echelon, degree, grade, gradation, stage, standard, rung; class, stratum, group, grouping, set, classification. **2** *a high level of employment* **quantity**, amount, extent, measure, degree, volume, size, magnitude, intensity, proportion. **3** *the level of water is rising* **height**, highness, altitude, elevation. **4** *the sixth level* **floor**, storey, deck.
▸v. **1** *tilt the tin to level the mixture* **make level**, level out/off, make even, even off/out, make flat, flatten, smooth (out), make uniform. **2** *bulldozers levelled the building* **raze (to the ground)**, demolish, flatten, topple, destroy; tear down, knock down, pull down, bulldoze. **3** *he levelled his opponent with a single blow* **knock down/out**, knock to the ground, lay out, prostrate, flatten, floor, fell; informal KO, kayo. **4** *Carl levelled the score* **equalize**, make equal, equal, even (up), make level. **5** *he levelled his pistol at me* **aim**, point, direct, train, focus, turn. **6** informal *I knew you'd level with me* **be frank**, be open, be honest, be above board, tell the truth, tell all, hide nothing, be straightforward; informal be upfront.
◻ **on the level** informal **genuine**, straight, honest, above board, fair, true, sincere, straightforward; informal upfront; N. Amer. informal on the up and up.

level-headed adj. **sensible**, practical, realistic, prudent, pragmatic, wise, reasonable, rational, mature, judicious, sound, sober, businesslike, no-nonsense, composed, calm, {cool, calm, and collected}, confident, well balanced, equable, cool-headed, self-possessed, having one's feet on the ground; informal unflappable, together.
– OPPOSITES excitable.

lever n. **1** *you can insert a lever and prise the rail off* **crowbar**, bar, jemmy. **2** *he pulled the lever* **handle**, grip, pull, switch.
▸v. *he levered the door open* **prise**, force, wrench, pull, wrest, heave; N. Amer. pry; informal jemmy.

leverage n. **1** *the long handles provide increased leverage* **grip**, purchase, hold; support, anchorage, force, strength. **2** *they have significant leverage in negotiations* **influence**, power, authority, weight, sway, pull, control, say, dominance, advantage, pressure; informal clout, muscle, teeth.

levitate v. **float**, rise (into the air), hover, be suspended, glide, hang, fly, soar up.

levity n. **light-heartedness**, high spirits, vivacity, liveliness, cheerfulness, cheeriness, humour, gaiety, fun, jocularity, hilarity, frivolity, frivolousness, amusement, mirth, laughter, merriment, glee, comedy, wit, wittiness, jollity, joviality.
– OPPOSITES seriousness.

levy v. **1** *a proposal to levy VAT on fuel* **impose**, charge, exact, raise, collect; tax. **2** old use *levying troops* **conscript**, call up, enlist, mobilize, rally, muster, marshal, recruit, raise; US draft.
▸n. **1** *the levy of taxation* **imposition**, raising, collection; formal exaction. **2** *the levy on spirits* **tax**, tariff, toll, excise, duty, imposition, impost; formal mulct.

lewd adj. **1** *a lewd old man* **lecherous**, lustful, licentious, lascivious, dirty, prurient, salacious, lubricious, libidinous, lickerish; debauched, depraved, degenerate, decadent, dissipated, dissolute, perverted; informal horny; Brit. informal randy; formal concupiscent. **2** *a lewd song* **vulgar**, crude, smutty, dirty, filthy, obscene, pornographic, coarse, off colour, unseemly, indecent, salacious; rude, racy, risqué, naughty, earthy, spicy, bawdy, ribald; informal blue, raunchy, X-rated, nudge-nudge, porno; N. Amer. informal raw; euphemistic adult.
– OPPOSITES chaste, clean.

lexicon n. **dictionary**, wordbook, vocabulary list, glossary, word-finder, thesaurus.

liability n. **1** *journalists' liability for defamation* **accountability**, (legal) responsibility; blame, blameworthiness, culpability, guilt, fault. **2** *they have big liabilities* **financial obligations**, debts, arrears, dues. **3** *an electoral liability* **hindrance**, encumbrance, burden, handicap, nuisance, inconvenience, embarrassment; obstacle, impediment, disadvantage, weakness, shortcoming; millstone round one's neck, albatross, Achilles heel; old use cumber. **4** *their liability to the disease* **susceptibility**, vulnerability, proneness, tendency, predisposition, propensity.
– OPPOSITES immunity, asset.

liable adj. **1** *they are liable for negligence* **(legally) responsible**, accountable, answerable, chargeable, blameworthy, at fault, culpable, guilty. **2** *my income is liable to fluctuate wildly* **likely**, inclined, tending,

l

disposed, apt, predisposed, prone, given.
3 *areas liable to flooding* **exposed**, prone,
subject, susceptible, vulnerable, in danger
of, at risk of.

liaise v. **cooperate**, work together,
collaborate; communicate, network,
interface, link up.

liaison n. **1** *the branches work in close
liaison* **cooperation**, contact, association,
connection, collaboration, communication,
alliance, partnership. **2** *Dave was my White
House liaison* **intermediary**, mediator,
middleman, contact, link, linkman,
linkwoman, linkperson, go-between,
representative, agent. **3** *a secret liaison
(love)* **affair**, relationship, romance,
attachment, fling, amour, affair of the heart,
(romantic) entanglement; informal hanky-
panky.

liar n. **fibber**, deceiver, perjurer, false witness,
fabricator; romancer, fabulist; informal
storyteller.

libation n. **1** *they pour libations into
the holy well* **(liquid) offering**, tribute,
oblation. **2** humorous *would you like a small
libation?* **(alcoholic) drink**, beverage, liquid
refreshment; dram, draught, nip, tot; informal
tipple; old use potation.

libel n. *she sued two newspapers for libel*
defamation (of character), character
assassination, calumny, misrepresentation,
scandalmongering; aspersions, denigration,
vilification, disparagement, derogation,
insult, slander, malicious gossip,
traducement; lie, slur, smear, untruth, false
report; informal mud-slinging, bad-mouthing.
▶ v. *she alleged the magazine had libelled her*
defame, malign, slander, blacken someone's
name, sully someone's reputation, speak ill/
evil of, traduce, smear, cast aspersions on,
drag someone's name through the mud/
mire, besmirch, tarnish, taint, tell lies about,
stain, vilify, denigrate, disparage, run down,
stigmatize, discredit; N. Amer. slur; formal
derogate, calumniate.

libellous adj. **defamatory**, denigratory,
vilifying, disparaging, derogatory,
slanderous, false, untrue, traducing,
maligning, insulting, scurrilous; formal
calumnious.

liberal adj. **1** *the values of a liberal society*
tolerant, unprejudiced, unbigoted,
broad-minded, open-minded, enlightened;
permissive, free (and easy), easy-going,
libertarian, indulgent, lenient. **2** *a liberal
social agenda* **progressive**, advanced,
modern, forward-looking, forward-thinking,
progressivist, enlightened, reformist,
radical; informal go-ahead. **3** *a liberal
education* **wide-ranging**, broad-based,
general. **4** *a liberal interpretation of divorce
laws* **flexible**, broad, loose, rough, free,
general, non-literal, non-specific, imprecise,
vague, indefinite. **5** *liberal coatings of
paint* **abundant**, copious, ample, plentiful,
generous, lavish, luxuriant, profuse,
considerable, prolific, rich; literary plenteous.

6 *they were liberal with their cash* **generous**,
open-handed, unsparing, unstinting,
ungrudging, lavish, free, munificent,
bountiful, beneficent, benevolent, big-
hearted, philanthropic, charitable, altruistic,
unselfish; literary bounteous.
– OPPOSITES reactionary, strict, miserly.

liberate v. **(set) free**, release, let out/go,
set/let loose, save, rescue; emancipate,
enfranchise; historical manumit.
– OPPOSITES imprison, enslave.

liberation n. **1** *the liberation of prisoners*
freeing, release, rescue, setting free;
freedom, liberty; emancipation; historical
manumission. **2** *women's liberation*
freedom, equality, equal rights,
emancipation, enfranchisement.
– OPPOSITES confinement, oppression.

liberator n. **rescuer**, saviour, deliverer,
emancipator; historical manumitter.

libertine n. *an unrepentant libertine*
philanderer, playboy, rake, roué, Don Juan,
Lothario, Casanova, Romeo; lecher, seducer,
womanizer, adulterer, debauchee, profligate,
wanton; informal skirt-chaser, ladykiller, lech,
wolf; formal fornicator.
▶ adj. *libertine sexual intercourse* **licentious**,
lustful, libidinous, lecherous, lascivious,
lubricious, dissolute, dissipated, debauched,
wanton, degenerate, depraved, promiscuous,
lewd, prurient, salacious, intemperate,
lickerish; informal loose, fast, goatish; formal
concupiscent.

liberty n. **1** *personal liberty* **freedom**,
independence, free rein, licence, self-
determination, free will, latitude. **2** *the
essence of British liberty* **independence**,
freedom, autonomy, sovereignty, self
government, self rule, self determination;
civil liberties, human rights. **3** *the liberty
to go where one pleases* **right**, birthright,
prerogative, entitlement, privilege,
permission, sanction, authorization,
authority, licence.
– OPPOSITES constraint, slavery.
□ **at liberty 1** *he was at liberty for three
months* **free**, (on the) loose, at large,
unconfined; escaped, out. **2** *your great aunt
was at liberty to divide her estate how she
chose* **free**, permitted, allowed, authorized,
able, entitled, eligible.

libidinous adj. **lustful**, lecherous, lascivious,
lewd, carnal, salacious, prurient, licentious,
libertine, lubricious, dissolute, debauched,
depraved, degenerate, decadent, dissipated,
wanton, promiscuous, lickerish; informal
horny, goatish, wolfish; Brit. informal randy;
formal concupiscent.

libido n. **sex drive**, sexual appetite; (sexual)
desire, passion, sexiness, sensuality,
sexuality, lust, lustfulness; informal horniness;
Brit. informal randiness; formal concupiscence.

licence n. **1** *a driving licence* **permit**,
certificate, document, documentation,
authorization, warrant; certification,
credentials; pass, papers. **2** *teachers had
licence to administer beatings* **permission**,

authority, right, a free hand, leave, authorization, entitlement, privilege, prerogative; liberty, freedom, power. **3** *they manufacture footwear under licence* **franchise**, permission, consent, sanction, warrant, warranty, charter. **4** *the army have too much licence* **freedom**, liberty, free rein, latitude, independence, scope, impunity, carte blanche. **5** *poetic licence* **disregard for the facts**, inventiveness, invention, creativity, imagination, fancy, freedom, looseness. **6** *the licence of the age* **licentiousness**, dissoluteness, dissipation, debauchery, immorality, impropriety, decadence, intemperateness, excess, excessiveness, lack of restraint.

license v. **permit**, allow, authorize, grant/ give authority to, grant/give permission to; certify, empower, entitle, enable, give approval to, let, qualify, sanction.
– OPPOSITES ban.

licentious adj. **dissolute**, dissipated, debauched, degenerate, immoral, naughty, wanton, decadent, depraved, sinful, corrupt; lustful, lecherous, lascivious, libidinous, prurient, lubricious, lewd, promiscuous, lickerish; formal concupiscent.
– OPPOSITES moral.

licit adj. **legitimate**, permissible, admissible, allowable; permitted, allowed, sanctioned, authorized, warranted; lawful, legal, statutory, legalized, licensed; informal legit.
– OPPOSITES forbidden.

lick v. **1** *the spaniel licked his face* **tongue**; lap, slurp. **2** *flames licking round the coal* **flicker**, play, flit, dance. **3** informal *they licked the home side 3-0.* See **defeat** (sense 1 of the verb). **4** informal *the government have inflation licked* **overcome**, get the better of, find an answer/ solution to, conquer, beat, control, master, curb, check.
▸ n. informal **1** *a lick of paint* **dab**, bit, drop, dash, spot, touch, splash; informal smidgen. **2** *they ran up at a fair lick* **speed**, rate, pace, tempo; informal clip.

licking n. informal **1** *Arsenal took a licking* **defeat**, beating, trouncing, thrashing; informal hiding, pasting, hammering, drubbing; N. Amer. informal shellacking. **2** *Ray got the worst licking of his life* **thrashing**, beating, flogging, whipping; informal walloping, hiding, pasting, lathering; N. Amer. informal whaling.

lid n. *the lid of a saucepan* **cover**, top, cap, covering.
□ **put a/the lid on** informal stop, control, end, put an end/stop to, put paid to.
lift the lid off/on informal expose, reveal, make known, make public, bring into the open, disclose, divulge; informal spill the beans, blow the gaff, blab.

lie¹ n. *loyalty to his friends had made him tell lies* **untruth**, falsehood, fib, fabrication, deception, invention, (piece of) fiction, falsification; (little) white lie, half-truth, exaggeration; informal tall story, whopper; Brit. informal porky (pie).
– OPPOSITES truth.

▸ v. *he had lied to the police* **tell a lie**, fib, dissemble, dissimulate, tell a white lie, perjure oneself, commit perjury; informal lie through one's teeth; formal forswear oneself.
□ **give the lie to** disprove, contradict, negate, deny, refute, rebut, controvert, belie, invalidate, discredit, debunk; challenge, call into question; informal shoot full of holes, shoot down (in flames); formal confute, gainsay.

> **WORD LINKS**
> **mendacious** telling lies
> **slander** the crime of making a false and damaging statement about someone
> **libel** the crime of publishing a false and damaging statement about someone
> **perjury** deliberately lying in a court of law after having sworn to tell the truth
> **polygraph** a machine used as a lie detector

lie² v. **1** *he was lying on a bed* **recline**, lie down/back, be recumbent, be prostrate, be supine, be prone, be stretched out, sprawl, rest, repose, lounge, loll. **2** *her handbag lay on a chair* **be placed**, be situated, be positioned, rest. **3** *lying on the border of Switzerland and Austria* **be situated**, be located, be placed, be found, be sited. **4** *his body lies in a crypt* **be buried**, be interred, be laid to rest, rest, be entombed. **5** *the difficulty lies in building real quality into the products* **consist**, be inherent, be present, be contained, exist, reside.
– OPPOSITES stand.
□ **lie heavy on** trouble, worry, bother, torment, oppress, nag, prey on one's mind, plague, niggle at, gnaw at, haunt; informal bug.
lie low hide (out), go into hiding, conceal oneself, keep out of sight, go to earth/ ground; informal hole up; Brit. informal dated lie doggo.

liege n. **(liege) lord**, feudal lord, overlord, master, chief, superior, baron, monarch, sovereign; historical suzerain, seigneur.

lieutenant n. **deputy**, second in command, right-hand man/woman, number two, assistant, aide, wingman; informal sidekick.

life n. **1** *the joy of giving life to a child* **existence**, being, living, animation; sentience, creation, viability. **2** *threats to life on the planet* **living beings/creatures**, the living; fauna, flora, ecosystems, biodiversity; human beings, humanity, humankind, mankind, man. **3** *an easy life* **way of life/ living**, lifestyle, situation, fate, lot. **4** *the last nine months of his life* **lifetime**, life span, days, time on earth, existence. **5** *the life of a Parliament* **duration**, lifetime, existence. **6** *he is full of life* **vivacity**, animation, liveliness, vitality, verve, high spirits, exuberance, zest, buoyancy, enthusiasm, energy, vigour, dynamism, elan, gusto, brio, bounce, spirit, fire; (hustle and) bustle, movement; informal oomph, pizzazz, pep, zing, zip, vim. **7** *the life of the party* **moving spirit**, (vital) spirit, life force, lifeblood, heart, soul. **8** *more than 1,500 lives were lost in the accident* **person**, human being, individual, soul. **9** *a life of Chopin* **biography**, autobiography, life story/history, profile, chronicle, account, portrait; informal biog, bio, biopic. **10** *I'll miss you, but that's life* **the way of the world**, the human condition; fate, destiny, providence, kismet, karma, fortune, luck, chance; informal the way the cookie crumbles.

– OPPOSITES death.

□ **come to life 1** *the sounds of a barracks coming to life* **become active**, come alive, wake up, awaken, arouse, rouse, stir; literary waken. **2** *the carved angel suddenly came to life* **become animate**, come alive. **for dear life** desperately, with all one's might, with might and main, for all one is worth, as fast/hard as possible, like the devil. **give one's life 1** *he would give his life for her* **die**, lay down one's life, sacrifice oneself. **2** *he gave his life to the company* **dedicate oneself**, devote oneself, give oneself, surrender oneself.

WORD LINKS

animate having life
biology the scientific study of living organisms
biosphere the parts of the earth which are inhabited by living things
longevity long life
resurrect restore a dead person to life

---

life-and-death adj. **vital**, of vital importance, crucial, critical, urgent, pivotal, momentous, important, key, serious, grave, significant; informal earth-shattering; formal of great moment.

– OPPOSITES trivial.

lifeblood n. **life (force)**, essential constituent, driving force, vital spark, inspiration, stimulus, essence, crux, heart, soul, core.

life-giving adj. **vitalizing**, animating, energizing, invigorating, stimulating; life-preserving, life-sustaining.

lifeless adj. **1** *a lifeless body* **dead**, departed, perished, gone, no more, passed on/away, stiff, cold, (as) dead as a doornail; formal deceased. **2** *a lifeless rag doll* **inanimate**, without life, inert, insentient. **3** *a lifeless landscape* **barren**, sterile, bare, desolate, stark, arid, infertile, uncultivated, uninhabited; bleak, colourless, characterless, soulless. **4** *a lifeless performance* **lacklustre**, spiritless, apathetic, torpid, lethargic; dull, monotonous, boring, tedious, dreary, unexciting, expressionless, emotionless, colourless, characterless. **5** *lifeless hair* **lank**, lustreless.

– OPPOSITES alive, animate, lively.

lifelike adj. **realistic**, true to life, representational, faithful, exact, precise, detailed, vivid, graphic, natural, naturalistic.

– OPPOSITES unrealistic.

lifelong adj. **lasting**, long-lasting, long-term, constant, stable, established, steady, enduring, permanent.

– OPPOSITES ephemeral.

lifestyle n. **way of life/living**, life, situation, fate, lot; conduct, behaviour, customs, habits, ways, mores.

lifetime n. **1** *he made an exceptional contribution during his lifetime* **lifespan**, life, days, one's time (on earth), existence, one's career; literary one's threescore years and ten. **2** *the lifetime of the present Parliament* **duration**. **3** *it would take a lifetime* **all one's life**, a very long time, an eternity, years (on end), aeons; informal ages (and ages), an age.

lift v. **1** *lift the pack on to your back* **raise**, hoist, heave, haul up, uplift, heft, raise up/aloft, upraise, elevate, hold high; pick up, grab, take up, scoop up, snatch up; winch up, jack up, lever up; informal hump; literary upheave. **2** *the news lifted his spirits* **boost**, raise, buoy up, elevate, cheer up, perk up, uplift, brighten up, ginger up, gladden, encourage, stimulate, revive; informal buck up. **3** *they lift their game on big occasions* **improve**, boost, enhance, revitalize, upgrade, ameliorate. **4** *the fog had lifted* **clear**, rise, disperse, dissipate, disappear, vanish, dissolve. **5** *the ban has been lifted* **cancel**, remove, withdraw, revoke, rescind, annul, void, discontinue, end, stop, terminate. **6** *lifting carrots* **dig up**, pick, pull up, root out, unearth. **7** *the RAF lifted them to safety* **airlift**, fly, helicopter. **8** *he lifted his voice* **amplify**, raise, make louder, increase. **9** informal *he lifted sections from a 1986 article* **plagiarize**, pirate, copy, reproduce, poach; informal crib, rip off. **10** informal *she lifted a wallet*. See **steal** (sense 1 of the verb).

– OPPOSITES drop, put down.

▶ n. **1** *Alice went up in the lift* **elevator**, paternoster (lift); dumb waiter. **2** *give me a lift up* **push**, hoist, heave, thrust, shove. **3** *he gave me a lift to the airport* **(car) ride**, run, drive. **4** *that goal will give his confidence a real lift* **boost**, fillip, stimulus, impetus, encouragement, spur, push; improvement, enhancement; informal shot in the arm.

□ **lift off** take off, become airborne, take to the air, take wing; be launched, blast off.

light[1] n. **1** *the light of candles* **illumination**, brightness, luminescence, luminosity, shining, gleaming, gleam, brilliance, radiance, lustre, glowing, glow, blaze, glare, dazzle; sunlight, moonlight, starlight, lamplight, firelight; ray of light, beam of light; literary effulgence, refulgence, lambency. **2** *put the lights on* **lamp**; headlight, headlamp, sidelight; floodlight; lantern; torch, flashlight. **3** *have you got a light?* **match**, lighter. **4** *we'll be driving in the light* **daylight (hours)**, daytime, day; natural light, sunlight. **5** *he saw the problem in a different light* **aspect**, angle, slant, approach, interpretation, viewpoint, standpoint, context, hue, complexion. **6** *light dawned on Loretta* **understanding**, enlightenment, illumination, comprehension, insight, awareness, knowledge. **7** *an eminent legal light* **expert**, authority, master, leader, guru, leading light, luminary. **8** *he served his party loyally according to his lights* **talent**, skill, ability; intelligence, intellect, knowledge, understanding.

– OPPOSITES darkness.

▶ v. *Alan lit a fire* **set alight**, set light to, set on fire, set fire to, put/set a match to, ignite, kindle, spark (off); old use enkindle.

– OPPOSITES extinguish.

▶ adj. **1** *a light breakfast room* **bright**, full of light, well lit, well illuminated, sunny. **2** *light pastel shades* **light-coloured**, light-toned, pale, pale-coloured, pastel. **3** *light hair* **fair**, light-coloured, blond(e), golden, flaxen.

– OPPOSITES dark, gloomy.

□ **bring something to light** reveal, disclose, expose, uncover, show up, unearth, dig up/out, bring to notice, identify, hunt out, nose out.

come to light be discovered, be uncovered, be unearthed, come out, become known, become apparent, appear, materialize, emerge.

in the light of taking into consideration/account, considering, bearing in mind, taking note of, in view of.

light up *the dashboard lit up* become bright, brighten, lighten, shine, gleam, flare, blaze, glint, sparkle, shimmer, glisten, scintillate.

light something up 1 *a flare lit up the night sky* **make bright**, brighten, illuminate, lighten, throw/cast light on, shine on, irradiate; literary illumine. **2** *her enthusiasm lit up her face* **animate**, irradiate, brighten, cheer up, enliven.

throw/cast/shed light on explain, elucidate, clarify, clear up, interpret.

WORD LINKS

chiaroscuro the treatment of light and shade in art
optics the study of light
photometry the measurement of light
photophobia fear of light
photosynthesis the process by which plants use sunlight to form nutrients
phototropism the turning of a plant towards or away from light

---

light² adj. **1** *it's light and portable* **easy to lift**, not heavy, lightweight; easy to carry, portable. **2** *a light cotton robe* **flimsy**, lightweight, summer-weight, insubstantial, thin; delicate, floaty, gauzy, gossamer, diaphanous. **3** *she is light on her feet* **nimble**, agile, lithe, limber, lissom, graceful; light-footed, fleet-footed, quick, quick-moving, spry, sprightly; informal twinkle-toed; literary fleet, lightsome. **4** *a light soil* **friable**, sandy, easily dug, workable, crumbly, loose. **5** *a light dinner* **small**, modest, simple, easily digested. **6** *light duties* **easy**, simple, undemanding, untaxing; informal cushy. **7** *his eyes gleamed with light mockery* **gentle**, mild, moderate, slight; playful, light-hearted. **8** *light reading* **entertaining**, lightweight, diverting, undemanding, middle-of-the-road; frivolous, superficial, trivial. **9** *a light heart* **carefree**, light-hearted, cheerful, cheery, happy, merry, jolly, blithe, bright, sunny; buoyant, bubbly, jaunty, bouncy, breezy, optimistic, positive, upbeat, ebullient; dated gay. **10** *this is no light matter*

unimportant, insignificant, trivial, trifling, petty, inconsequential, superficial. **11** *light footsteps* **gentle**, delicate, soft, dainty; faint, indistinct. **12** *her head felt light* **dizzy**, giddy, light-headed, faint, vertiginous; informal woozy.

– OPPOSITES heavy.

light³ v.
□ **light on** come across, chance on, hit on, happen on, stumble on/across, blunder on, find, discover, uncover, come up with.

lighten¹ v. **1** *the sky was beginning to lighten* **become/grow lighter**, brighten. **2** *the first touch of dawn lightened the sky* **light up**, brighten, make brighter, illuminate, throw/cast light on, shine on, irradiate; literary illumine. **3** *he used lemon juice to lighten his hair* **whiten**, make whiter, bleach, blanch, make paler; fade, wash out, decolorize.

– OPPOSITES darken.

lighten² v. **1** *lightening the burden of taxation* **make lighter**, lessen, reduce, decrease, diminish, ease; alleviate, mitigate, allay, relieve, palliate, assuage. **2** *an attempt to lighten her spirits* **raise**, lift; cheer (up), brighten, gladden, hearten, perk up, ginger up, enliven, boost, buoy (up), uplift, revive, restore, revitalize.

– OPPOSITES increase, depress.

light-fingered adj. **thieving**, stealing, pilfering, shoplifting, dishonest; informal sticky-fingered, crooked.

– OPPOSITES honest.

light-footed adj. **nimble**, light on one's feet, agile, graceful, lithe, spry, sprightly, limber, lissom; swift, fast, quick, quick-moving, fleet-footed; informal twinkle-toed; literary fleet.

– OPPOSITES clumsy.

light-headed adj. **dizzy**, giddy, faint, muzzy, vertiginous; informal woozy.

light-hearted adj. **carefree**, cheerful, cheery, happy, merry, glad, playful, jolly, jovial, joyful, gleeful, ebullient, high-spirited, lively, blithe, bright, sunny, buoyant, vivacious, bubbly, jaunty, bouncy, breezy; entertaining, amusing, diverting; informal chirpy, upbeat; dated gay.

– OPPOSITES miserable.

lightly adv. **1** *Maisie kissed him lightly on the cheek* **softly**, gently, faintly, delicately. **2** *season very lightly* **sparingly**, slightly, sparsely, moderately, delicately. **3** *her views are not to be dismissed lightly* **carelessly**, airily, heedlessly, without consideration, uncaringly, indifferently, unthinkingly, thoughtlessly, flippantly, breezily, frivolously.

– OPPOSITES hard, heavily.

lightweight adj. **1** *a lightweight jacket* **thin**, light, flimsy, insubstantial; summery. **2** *lightweight entertainment* **trivial**, insubstantial, superficial, shallow, unintellectual, undemanding, frivolous; of little merit/value.

– OPPOSITES heavy.

like[1] v. **1** *I rather like Colonel Maitland* **be fond of**, be attached to, have a soft spot for, have a liking for, have regard for, think well of, admire, respect, esteem; be attracted to, fancy, find attractive, be keen on, be taken with; informal take a shine to, rate. **2** *Maisie likes veal | she likes gardening* **enjoy**, have a taste for, have a preference for, have a liking for, be partial to, find/take pleasure in, be keen on, find agreeable, have a penchant/passion for, find enjoyable; appreciate, love, adore, relish; informal have a thing about, be into, be mad about/for, be hooked on, go a bundle on. **3** *feel free to say what you like* **choose**, please, wish, want, see/think fit, care to, will. **4** *how would she like it if someone did that to her?* **feel about**, regard, think about, consider.
– OPPOSITES hate.

like[2] prep. **1** *you're just like a teacher* **similar to**, the same as, identical to. **2** *the figure landed like a cat* **in the same way as**, in the manner of, in a similar way to. **3** *cities like Birmingham* **such as**, for example, for instance; in particular, namely, viz. **4** *Richard sounded mean, which isn't like him* **characteristic of**, typical of, in character with.
▸ n. *we shan't see his like again* **equal**, match, equivalent, counterpart, twin, parallel; formal compeer.
▸ adj. *a like situation* **similar**, much the same, comparable, corresponding, resembling, alike, analogous, parallel, equivalent, cognate, related, kindred; identical, same, matching.
– OPPOSITES dissimilar.

likeable adj. **pleasant**, nice, friendly, agreeable, affable, amiable, genial, personable, charming, popular, good-natured, engaging, appealing, endearing, convivial, congenial, winning, delightful, enchanting, lovable, adorable, sweet; informal darling, lovely.
– OPPOSITES unpleasant.

likelihood n. **probability**, chance, prospect, possibility, likeliness, odds, feasibility; risk, threat, danger; hope, promise.

likely adj. **1** *it seemed likely that a scandal would break* **probable**, (distinctly) possible, to be expected, odds-on, plausible, imaginable; expected, anticipated, predictable, predicted, foreseeable; informal on the cards. **2** *a likely explanation* **plausible**, reasonable, feasible, acceptable, believable, credible, tenable, conceivable. **3** *a likely story!* **unlikely**, implausible, unbelievable, incredible, untenable, unacceptable, inconceivable. **4** *a likely-looking place* **suitable**, appropriate, apposite, fit, fitting, acceptable, right; promising, hopeful. **5** *a likely lad* **promising**, talented, gifted; informal up-and-coming.
– OPPOSITES improbable, unbelievable.
▸ adv. *he was most likely dead* **probably**, in all probability, presumably, no doubt, doubtlessly; informal (as) like as not.

liken v. **compare**, equate, draw an analogy between, draw a parallel between; link, associate, bracket together.
– OPPOSITES contrast.

likeness n. **1** *her likeness to Anne is quite uncanny* **resemblance**, similarity, correspondence, analogy, uniformity, conformity. **2** *the likeness of a naked woman* **semblance**, guise, appearance, (outward) form, shape, image. **3** *a likeness of the last president* **representation**, image, depiction, portrayal; picture, drawing, sketch, artist's impression, painting, portrait, photograph, study; statue, sculpture.
– OPPOSITES dissimilarity.

likewise adv. **1** *an ambush was out of the question, likewise poison* **also**, in addition, too, as well, to boot; besides, moreover, furthermore. **2** *encourage your family and friends to do likewise* **the same**, similarly, correspondingly, in the same way, in similar fashion.

liking n. **fondness**, love, affection, penchant, attachment; enjoyment, appreciation, taste; passion; preference, partiality, predilection; desire, fancy, inclination.

lilt n. **cadence**, rise and fall, inflection, intonation, rhythm, swing, beat, pulse, tempo.

limb n. **1** *his sore limbs* **arm**, leg, appendage; old use member. **2** *the limbs of the tree* **branch**, bough. **3** *local job centres act as limbs of the Ministry* **section**, branch, offshoot, arm, wing, subdivision, department, division.
□ **out on a limb 1** *the portrayal of Scotland as being out on a limb* **isolated**, segregated, set apart, separate, cut off, solitary. **2** *the government is out on a limb* **in a precarious position**, vulnerable; informal sticking one's neck out.

limber adj. *I have to practise to keep myself limber* **lithe**, supple, nimble, lissom, flexible, fit, agile, acrobatic, loose-jointed, loose-limbed.
– OPPOSITES stiff.
□ **limber up warm up**, loosen up, get into condition, get into shape, practise, train, stretch.

limbo n. *unbaptized infants are thought to live in limbo* **non-existence**, void, oblivion.
□ **in limbo** in abeyance, unattended to, unfinished; suspended, deferred, postponed, put off, pending, on ice, in cold storage; unresolved, undetermined, up in the air; informal on the back burner, on hold.

limelight n. **the focus of attention**, public attention/interest, media attention, the public eye, the glare of publicity, prominence, the spotlight.
– OPPOSITES obscurity.

limit n. **1** *the city limits* **boundary (line)**, border, bound, partition line, frontier, edge, demarcation line; perimeter, outside, outline, confine, periphery, margin, rim. **2** *a limit of 4,500 supporters* **maximum**, ceiling, limitation, upper limit; restriction, check, control, restraint. **3** *resources are stretched to the limit* **utmost**, breaking point, greatest extent. **4** informal *that really is the limit!* **the last straw**, (more than) enough; informal the end, it.

▶ v. *the pressure to limit costs* **restrict**, curb, cap, (hold in) check, restrain, put a brake on, freeze, peg; regulate, control, govern, delimit.

limitation n. **1** *a limitation on the number of newcomers* **restriction**, curb, restraint, control, check; impediment, obstacle, obstruction, bar, barrier, ceiling, block, deterrent. **2** *he is aware of his own limitations* **imperfection**, flaw, defect, failing, shortcoming, weak point, deficiency, failure, frailty, weakness, foible.
– OPPOSITES increase, strength.

limited adj. **1** *limited resources* **restricted**, finite, little, tight, slight, in short supply, short; meagre, scanty, sparse, insubstantial, deficient, inadequate, insufficient, paltry, poor, minimal. **2** *the limited powers of the council* **restricted**, curbed, checked, controlled, restrained, delimited, qualified.
– OPPOSITES ample, boundless.

limitless adj. **boundless**, unbounded, unlimited, illimitable; infinite, endless, never-ending, unending, everlasting, cosmic, untold, immeasurable, bottomless, fathomless; unceasing, interminable, inexhaustible, constant, perpetual.

limp[1] v. *she limped out of the house* **hobble**, walk haltingly, falter.
▶ n. *his limp was very pronounced* **lameness**, hobble, uneven gait; Medicine claudication.

limp[2] adj. **1** *a limp handshake* **soft**, flaccid, loose, slack, lax; floppy, drooping, droopy, sagging. **2** *we were all limp with exhaustion* **tired**, fatigued, weary, exhausted, worn out; weak, lethargic, listless, spiritless. **3** *a limp and lacklustre speech* **uninspired**, uninspiring, insipid, flat, lifeless, vapid.
– OPPOSITES firm, energetic.

limpid adj. **1** *a limpid pool* **clear**, transparent, glassy, crystal clear, crystalline, translucent, pellucid, unclouded. **2** *his limpid writing* **lucid**, clear, plain, understandable, intelligible, comprehensible, coherent, explicit, unambiguous, simple, vivid, sharp, crystal clear; formal perspicuous.
– OPPOSITES opaque.

line[1] n. **1** *he drew a line through the name* dash, rule, bar, score; underline, underscore, stroke, slash, solidus; stripe, strip, band, belt; crosshatching, hachures; technical stria, striation; Brit. oblique. **2** *there were lines round her eyes* **wrinkle**, furrow, crease, crinkle, crow's foot. **3** *the classic lines of the exterior* **contour**, outline, configuration, shape, figure, delineation, profile, silhouette. **4** *he headed the ball over the line* | *the county line* **boundary (line)**, limit, border, borderline, bounding line, frontier, demarcation line, dividing line, edge, margin, perimeter. **5** *behind enemy lines* **position**, formation, front (line);

trenches. **6** *he put the washing on the line* **cord**, rope, string, cable, wire, thread, twine, strand. **7** *a line of soldiers* **file**, rank, column, string, train, procession; row, queue; Brit. informal crocodile. **8** *a line of figures* **column**, row. **9** *a long line of crass decisions* **series**, sequence, succession, chain, string, set, cycle. **10** *the line of flight of some bees* **course**, route, track, path, trajectory, way, run. **11** *they took a very tough line with the industry* | *the party line* **course (of action)**, procedure, technique, tactic, tack; policy, practice, approach, plan, programme, position, stance, philosophy. **12** *her own line of thought* **course**, direction, drift, tack, tendency, trend. **13** *he couldn't remember his lines* **words**, part, script, speech. **14** *their line of work* **(line of) business**, (line of) work, field, trade, occupation, employment, profession, job, career, walk of life; specialty, forte, province, department, sphere, area (of expertise). **15** *a new line of cologne* **brand**, kind, sort, type, variety, make. **16** *a noble line* **ancestry**, family, parentage, birth, descent, lineage, extraction, genealogy, roots, origin, background; stock, bloodline, pedigree. **17** *the opening line of the poem* **sentence**, phrase, clause, utterance; passage, extract, quotation, quote, citation. **18** *I should drop Ralph a line* **note**, letter, card, postcard, message, communication, missive, memorandum; correspondence, word; informal memo; formal epistle.

▶ v. **1** *her face was lined with age* **furrow**, wrinkle, crease. **2** *the driveway was lined by poplars* **border**, edge, fringe, bound, rim.
□ **draw the line at** stop short of, refuse to accept, balk at; object to, take issue with, take exception to.
in line 1 *the poor stood in line for food* **in a queue**, in a row. **2** *the adverts are in line with the editorial style* **in agreement**, in accord, in accordance, in harmony, in step, in compliance. **3** *in line with the bullseye* **in alignment**, aligned, level; abreast, side by side. **4** *the referee kept him in line* **under control**, in order, in check.
in line for a candidate for, in the running for, on the shortlist for, being considered for.
lay it on the line speak frankly/honestly, pull no punches, be blunt, not mince one's words, call a spade a spade; informal give it to someone straight.
line up form a queue/line, queue up, fall in; Military dress; Brit. informal form a crocodile.
line someone/something up 1 *they lined them up and shot them* **arrange in lines**, put in rows, arrange in columns, align, range; Military dress. **2** *we've lined up an all-star cast* **assemble**, get together, organize, prepare, arrange, prearrange, fix up, lay on; book, schedule, timetable.
on the line at risk, in danger, endangered, imperilled.
toe the line conform, obey/observe the rules, comply with the rules, abide by the rules.

line[2] v. *a cardboard box lined with a blanket* **cover**, interline, face, back, pad.
□ **line one's pockets** informal make money, accept bribes, embezzle money; informal feather one's nest, graft, be on the make.

lineage n. **ancestry**, family, parentage, birth, descent, line, extraction, derivation, genealogy, roots, origin, background; stock, bloodline, breeding, pedigree.

lined[1] adj. **1** *lined paper* **ruled**, feint, striped, banded. **2** *his lined face* **wrinkled**, wrinkly, furrowed, wizened.
– OPPOSITES plain, smooth.

lined[2] adj. *lined curtains* **covered**, backed, interlined; faced, padded.

liner n. **1** *a luxury liner* **ship**, ocean liner, passenger vessel, boat. **2** *her eyes were ringed with liner* **eyeliner**, eye pencil, kohl (pencil); lipliner.

line-up n. **1** *a star-studded line-up* **list of performers**, cast, bill, programme. **2** *United's line-up* **list of players**, team, squad, side. **3** *a long line-up of customers* **queue**, line, row, column.

linger v. **1** *the crowd lingered for a long time* **wait (around)**, stay (put), remain; loiter, dawdle, dally, take one's time; informal stick around, hang around/round, hang on; old use tarry. **2** *the infection can linger for many years* **persist**, continue, remain, stay, endure, carry on, last, keep on/up.
– OPPOSITES vanish.

lingerie n. **women's underwear**, underclothes, underclothing, undergarments; nightwear, nightclothes; informal undies, frillies, underthings, unmentionables; Brit. informal smalls.

lingering adj. **1** *lingering doubts* **remaining**, surviving, persisting, abiding, nagging, niggling. **2** *a slow, lingering death* **protracted**, prolonged, long-drawn-out, long-lasting.

lingo n. informal **1** *I can't speak the lingo* **language**, tongue, dialect. **2** *computer lingo* **jargon**, terminology, slang, argot, cant, patter, mumbo jumbo; informal -ese, -speak, gobbledegook.

linguistic adj. **semantic**, lingual, rhetorical, verbal.

lining n. **backing**, interlining, facing, padding, liner.

link n. **1** *a chain of steel links* **loop**, ring, connection, connector, coupling, joint. **2** *the links between transport and the environment* **connection**, relationship, association, linkage, tie-up. **3** *their links with the labour movement* **bond**, tie, attachment, connection, relationship, association, affiliation. **4** *one of the links in*

the organization **component**, constituent, element, part, piece.
▸ v. **1** *four boxes were linked together* **join**, connect, fasten, attach, bind, unite, combine, amalgamate; clamp, secure, fix, tie, couple, yoke. **2** *the evidence linking him with the body* **associate**, connect, relate, join, bracket.

lion n. **1** *a lion ready to attack* **big cat**, king of the beasts; lioness. **2** *a lion amongst men* **hero**, lionheart; conqueror, champion, conquering hero. **3** *the lions of the symphony hall* **celebrity**, dignitary, VIP, luminary, star, superstar, big name, leading light; informal big shot/noise, celeb, megastar.
□ **the lion's share** most, the majority, the larger part/number, the greater part/number, more than half, the bulk.

lionhearted adj. **brave**, courageous, valiant, gallant, intrepid, valorous, fearless, bold, daring; stout-hearted, stalwart, heroic, doughty, plucky; informal gutsy, spunky.
– OPPOSITES cowardly.

lionize v. **celebrate**, fete, glorify, honour, exalt, acclaim, admire, praise, extol, applaud, hail, venerate, eulogize; formal laud; old use panegyrize.

lip n. **1** *the lip of the crater* **edge**, rim, brim, border, verge, brink. **2** informal *I'll have no more of your lip!* **insolence**, impertinence, impudence, cheek, rudeness, audacity, effrontery, disrespect, presumptuousness; informal mouth; Brit. informal sauce, backchat.

liquefy v. **make/become liquid**, condense, liquidize, melt; deliquesce.

liquid adj. **1** *liquid fuels* **fluid**, liquefied; melted, molten, thawed, dissolved; Chemistry hydrous. **2** *her liquid eyes* **clear**, limpid, crystal clear, crystalline, pellucid, unclouded. **3** *a liquid voice* **pure**, clear, mellifluous, dulcet, mellow, sweet, sweet-sounding, soft, melodious, harmonious; rare mellifluent. **4** *liquid assets* **convertible**, disposable, usable, spendable.
– OPPOSITES solid.
▸ n. *a vat of liquid* **fluid**, moisture, wet, wetness; liquor, solution, juice.

liquidate v. **1** *the company was liquidated* **close down**, wind up, put into liquidation, dissolve, disband. **2** *he liquidated his share portfolio* **convert (to cash)**, cash in, sell off/up. **3** *liquidating the public debt* **pay (off)**, pay in full, settle, clear, discharge, square, honour. **4** informal *they were liquidated in bloody purges.* See **kill** (sense 1 of the verb).

liquidize v. **purée**, cream, liquefy, blend.

liquor n. **1** *alcoholic liquor* **alcohol**, spirits, (alcoholic) drink, intoxicating liquor, intoxicant; informal booze, hard stuff, grog, hooch. **2** *strain the liquor into the sauce* **stock**, broth, bouillon, juice, liquid.

lissom adj. **supple**, lithe, limber, graceful, flexible, loose-limbed, agile, nimble; slim, slender, thin, willowy, sleek, trim.

list[1] n. *a list of the world's wealthiest people* **catalogue**, inventory, record, register, roll, file, index, directory, listing, checklist, enumeration.
▶ v. *the accounts are listed alphabetically* **record**, register, make a list of, enter; itemize, enumerate, catalogue, file, log, minute, categorize, inventory; classify, group, sort, rank, alphabetize, index.

list[2] v. *the boat listed to one side* **lean (over)**, tilt, tip, heel (over), careen, cant, pitch, incline, slant, slope, bank.

listen v. **1** *are you listening carefully?* **hear**, pay attention, be attentive, attend, concentrate; keep one's ears open, prick up one's ears; informal be all ears, pin back one's ears; literary hark; old use hearken. **2** *policy-makers should listen to popular opinion* **pay attention**, take heed, heed, take notice, take note, mind, mark, bear in mind, take into consideration/account.
☐ **listen in** eavesdrop, spy, overhear, tap, wiretap, bug, monitor.

listless adj. **lethargic**, enervated, spiritless, lifeless; languid, languorous, inactive, inert, sluggish, torpid.
– OPPOSITES energetic.

litany n. **1** *repeating the litany* **prayer**, invocation, supplication, devotion; old use orison. **2** *a litany of complaints* **recital**, recitation, repetition, enumeration; list, listing, catalogue, inventory.

literacy n. **ability to read and write**, reading/writing skills; (book) learning, education, scholarship, schooling.

literal adj. **1** *the literal sense of the word 'dreadful'* **strict**, factual, plain, simple, exact, straightforward; unembellished, undistorted; objective, correct, true, truthful, accurate, genuine, authentic. **2** *a literal translation* **word-for-word**, verbatim, letter-for-letter; exact, precise, faithful, close, strict, accurate; formal literatim. **3** *his literal, unrhetorical manner* **literal-minded**, down-to-earth, matter-of-fact, no-nonsense, unsentimental; prosaic, unimaginative, pedestrian, uninspired, uninspiring.
– OPPOSITES figurative, loose.
▶ n. Brit. *William corrected two literals* **misprint**, error, mistake, (slip) of the pen, typographical/typing error/mistake, corrigendum, erratum; informal typo, howler.

literally adv. **verbatim**, word for word, letter for letter; exactly, precisely, faithfully, closely, strictly, accurately; formal literatim.

literary adj. **1** *literary works* **written**, poetic, artistic, dramatic. **2** *her literary friends* **scholarly**, learned, intellectual, cultured, erudite, bookish, highbrow, lettered, academic, cultivated; well read, widely read, (well) educated. **3** *literary language* **formal**, written, poetic, dramatic; elaborate, ornate, flowery.

literate adj. **(well) educated**, well read, widely read, scholarly, learned, knowledgeable, lettered, cultured, cultivated, sophisticated, well informed.
– OPPOSITES ignorant.

literature n. **1** *English literature* **written works**, writings, (creative) writing, literary texts, compositions. **2** *the literature on prototype theory* **publications**, published writings, texts, reports, studies. **3** *election literature* **printed matter**, brochures, leaflets, pamphlets, circulars, flyers, handouts, handbills, mailshots, bulletins, documentation, publicity, blurb, notices; informal bumf.

lithe adj. **agile**, graceful, supple, limber, lithesome, loose-limbed, nimble, deft, flexible, lissom.
– OPPOSITES clumsy.

litigant n. **claimant**, litigator, opponent (in law), contender, disputant, plaintiff, complainant, petitioner, appellant, respondent.

litigation n. **(legal/judicial) proceedings**, (legal) action, lawsuit, legal dispute, (legal) case, suit (at law), prosecution, indictment.

litter n. **1** *never drop litter* **rubbish**, refuse, junk, waste, debris, scraps, leavings, fragments, detritus; N. Amer. trash, garbage. **2** *the litter of glasses around her* **clutter**, jumble, muddle, mess, heap, disorder, untidiness, confusion, disarray; informal shambles. **3** *a litter of kittens* **brood**, family; young, offspring, progeny; Law issue. **4** *straw for use as litter* **(animal) bedding**, straw. **5** *a horse-drawn litter* **sedan chair**, palanquin; stretcher.
▶ v. *clothes littered the floor* **make untidy**, mess up, make a mess of, clutter up, be strewn about, be scattered about, cover; informal make a shambles of; literary bestrew.

little adj. **1** *a little writing desk* **small**, small-scale, compact; mini, miniature, tiny, minute, minuscule; toy, baby, pocket, undersized, dwarf, midget, fun-size; Scottish wee; informal teeny-weeny, teensy-weensy, itsy-bitsy, tiddly, half-pint; Brit. informal titchy, dinky; N. Amer. informal vest-pocket. **2** *a little man* **short**, small, slight, petite, diminutive, tiny; elfin, dwarfish, midget, pygmy, Lilliputian; Scottish wee; informal teeny-weeny, pint-sized. **3** *my little sister* **young**, younger, junior, small, baby, infant. **4** *I was a bodyguard for a little while* **brief**, short, short-lived; fleeting, momentary, transitory, transient; fast, quick, hasty, cursory. **5** *a few little problems* **minor**, unimportant, insignificant, trivial, trifling, petty, paltry, inconsequential, nugatory.
– OPPOSITES big, large, elder, important.
▶ determiner *they have little political influence* **hardly any**, not much, slight, scant, limited, restricted, modest, little or no, minimal, negligible.
– OPPOSITES considerable.
▶ adv. **1** *he is little known as a teacher* **hardly**, barely, scarcely, not much, (only) slightly. **2** *this disease is little seen nowadays* **rarely**, seldom, infrequently, hardly (ever), scarcely

I

(ever), not much.
– OPPOSITES well, often.
   □ **a little 1** *add a little water* **some**, a small amount of, a bit of, a touch of, a soupçon of, a dash of, a taste of, a spot of; a shade of, a suggestion of, a trace of, a hint of, a suspicion of; a dribble of, a splash of, a pinch of, a sprinkling of, a speck of; informal a smidgen of, a tad of. **2** *after a little, Oliver came in* **a short time**, a little while, a bit, an interval, a short period; a minute, a moment, a second, an instant; informal a sec, a mo, a jiffy. **3** *this reminds me a little of the Adriatic* **slightly**, faintly, remotely, vaguely; somewhat, a little bit, quite, to some degree, to some extent.
   little by little gradually, slowly, by degrees, by stages, step by step, bit by bit, progressively; subtly, imperceptibly.

liturgical adj. **ceremonial**, ritual, solemn; church.

liturgy n. **ritual**, worship, service, ceremony, rite, observance, celebration, sacrament; tradition, custom, practice, rubric; formal ordinance.

live¹ v. **1** *the greatest mathematician who ever lived* **exist**, be alive, be, have life; breathe, draw breath, walk the earth. **2** *I live in Leeds* **reside**, have one's home, be settled; be housed, lodge; inhabit, occupy, populate; Scottish stay; formal dwell, be domiciled. **3** *they lived quietly* **pass/spend one's life**; behave, conduct oneself; formal comport oneself. **4** *she had lived a difficult life* **experience**, spend, pass, lead, have, go through, undergo. **5** *Freddy lived by his wits* **survive**, make a living, earn one's living, eke out a living; subsist, support oneself, sustain oneself, make ends meet, keep body and soul together. **6** *you should live a little* **enjoy oneself**, enjoy life, have fun, live life to the full.
– OPPOSITES die, be dead.
   □ **live it up** informal live extravagantly, live in the lap of luxury, live in clover; carouse, revel, enjoy oneself, have a good time, roister; informal party, push the boat out, paint the town red, have a ball, make whoopee; N. Amer. informal live high on/off the hog; old use wassail.
   live off/on subsist on, feed on/off, eat, consume.

live² adj. **1** *live bait* **living**, alive, having life, breathing, animate, sentient. **2** *a live performance* **in the flesh**, personal, in person, not recorded. **3** *a live rail* **electrified**, charged, powered, active; informal hot. **4** *live coals* **(red) hot**, glowing, aglow; burning, alight, flaming, aflame, blazing, ignited, on fire; literary afire. **5** *a live grenade* **unexploded**, explosive, active; unstable, volatile. **6** *live issue* **topical**, current, of current interest, controversial; burning, pressing, important.
– OPPOSITES dead, inanimate, recorded.
   □ **live wire** informal energetic person; informal fireball, human dynamo, powerhouse, life and soul of the party.

livelihood n. **(source of) income**, means of support, living, subsistence, keep, maintenance, sustenance, nourishment, daily bread, bread and butter; job, work, employment, occupation.

livelong adj. literary **entire**, whole, total, complete, full, continuous.

lively adj. **1** *a lively young woman* **energetic**, active, animated, dynamic, full of life, outgoing, spirited, high-spirited, vivacious, enthusiastic, vibrant, buoyant, exuberant, effervescent, cheerful; bouncy, bubbly, perky, sparkling, zestful; Brit. Tiggerish; informal full of beans, chirpy, chipper, peppy. **2** *a lively bar* **busy**, crowded, bustling, buzzing; vibrant, boisterous, jolly, festive; informal hopping, buzzy. **3** *a lively debate* **heated**, vigorous, animated, spirited, enthusiastic, forceful; exciting, interesting, memorable. **4** *a lively portrait of the local community* **vivid**, colourful, striking, graphic, bold, strong. **5** *he bowled at a lively pace* **brisk**, quick, fast, rapid, swift, speedy, smart; informal nippy, snappy. **6** *the press is making things lively for the Government* **awkward**, tricky, difficult, challenging, eventful, exciting, busy; informal hairy.
– OPPOSITES quiet, dull.

liven v.
   □ **liven up** brighten up, cheer up, perk up, revive, rally, pick up, bounce back; informal buck up.
   liven someone/something up brighten up, cheer up, enliven, animate, raise someone's spirits, perk up, spice up, ginger up, make lively, wake up, invigorate, revive, refresh, vivify, galvanize, stimulate, stir up, get going; informal buck up, pep up.

liver n.

> **WORD LINKS**
> **hepatic** relating to the liver
> **hepatitis** inflammation of the liver
> **cirrhosis** liver disease caused by alcoholism or hepatitis

livery n. **1** *servants in blue and gold livery* **uniform**, regalia, costume, dress, attire, garb, clothes, clothing, outfit, suit, garments, ensemble; informal get-up, gear, kit; formal apparel; old use raiment, vestments. **2** *the locomotive has reverted to its original two-tone green livery* **colours**, colouring; paintwork, design, format, specification, look; informal spec, paint job.

livid adj. **1** informal *Mum was absolutely livid*. See **furious** (sense 1). **2** *a livid bruise* **purplish**, bluish, dark, discoloured, purple, greyish-blue; bruised; angry.

living n. **1** *she cleaned floors for a living* **livelihood**, (source of) income, means of support, subsistence, keep, maintenance, sustenance, nourishment, daily bread, bread and butter; job, work, employment, occupation. **2** *healthy living* **way of life**, lifestyle, way of living, life; conduct, behaviour, activities, habits.
▸adj. **1** *living organisms* **alive**, live, having life, animate, sentient; breathing, existing, existent; informal alive and kicking. **2** *a living language* **current**, contemporary, present;

in use, active, surviving, extant, persisting, remaining, existing, in existence. **3** *a living image of the man* **exact**, faithful, true to life, authentic.
– OPPOSITES dead, extinct.

living room n. **sitting room**, lounge, front room, reception room, family room.

lizard n.

> **WORD LINKS**
> **saurian** relating to lizards

load n. **1** *MacDowell's got a load to deliver* **cargo**, freight, consignment, delivery, shipment, goods, merchandise; pack, bundle, parcel; lorryload, truckload, shipload, boatload, vanload; old use lading. **2** informal *I bought a load of clothes* **a lot**, a great deal, a large amount/quantity, an abundance, a wealth, a mountain; many, plenty; informal a heap, a mass, a pile, a stack, a ton, lots, heaps, masses, piles, stacks, tons, bucketloads. **3** *a heavy teaching load* **commitment**, responsibility, duty, obligation, charge, burden; trouble, worry, strain, pressure.
▶ v. **1** *we quickly loaded the van* **fill (up)**, pack, lade, charge, stock, stack. **2** *Larry loaded boxes into the jeep* **pack**, stow, store, stack, bundle, cram, stuff; place, deposit, put away. **3** *loading the committee with responsibilities* **burden**, weigh down, saddle, charge; overburden, overwhelm, encumber, tax, strain, trouble, worry. **4** *Richard loaded Marshal with honours* **reward**, ply, regale, shower. **5** *he loaded a gun* **prime**, charge, prepare to fire/use. **6** *load the cassette into the camcorder* **insert**, put, place, slot, slide, slip. **7** *the dice are loaded against him* **bias**, rig, fix; weight.

loaded adj. **1** *a loaded freight train* **full**, filled, laden, packed, stuffed, crammed, brimming, stacked; informal chock-full, chock-a-block. **2** *a loaded gun* **primed**, charged, ready to fire. **3** informal *they are all loaded*. See **rich** (sense 1). **4** *loaded dice* **biased**, rigged, fixed; weighted. **5** *a politically loaded word* **charged**, emotive, sensitive, delicate.

loaf v. *he was just loafing around* **laze**, loll, idle, waste time; informal hang around/round; Brit. informal hang about, mooch about/around; N. Amer. informal bum around.

loafer n. **idler**, layabout, good-for-nothing, lounger, shirker, sluggard, slug, laggard, slugabed; informal skiver, slacker, slob, lazybones.

loan n. *a loan of £7,000* **credit**, advance; mortgage, overdraft; lending, moneylending; Brit. informal sub.
▶ v. *he loaned me his flat* **lend**, advance, give credit; give on loan, lease, charter, hire; Brit. informal sub.
– OPPOSITES borrow.

> **WORD LINKS**
> **collateral** something promised to someone if one is unable to repay a loan
> **default** failure to repay a loan
> **principal** a sum of money lent, on which interest is paid

> **pawnbroker** a person licensed to lend money in exchange for articles left with them
> **usury** the practice of lending money at unreasonably high rates of interest

loath adj. **reluctant**, unwilling, disinclined, ill-disposed; against, averse, opposed, resistant.
– OPPOSITES willing.

loathe v. **hate**, detest, despise, abhor, execrate, have a strong aversion to, not be able to bear/stand, be repelled by; formal abominate.
– OPPOSITES love.

loathing n. **hatred**, hate, detestation, abhorrence, abomination, execration, odium; antipathy, dislike, hostility, animosity, ill feeling, bad feeling, malice, animus, enmity, aversion; repugnance; informal yuck factor.

loathsome adj. **hateful**, detestable, abhorrent, repulsive, odious, repugnant, repellent, disgusting, revolting, sickening, abominable, despicable, contemptible, reprehensible, execrable, damnable; vile, horrible, nasty, obnoxious, gross, foul; informal horrid, yucky; literary noisome.

lob v. **throw**, toss, fling, pitch, hurl, pelt, sling, launch, propel; informal chuck, bung, heave.

lobby n. **1** *the hotel lobby* **entrance (hall)**, hallway, hall, vestibule, foyer, reception area. **2** *the anti-hunt lobby* **pressure group**, interest group, ginger group, movement, campaign, crusade, lobbyists, supporters; faction, camp.
▶ v. **1** *readers are urged to lobby their MPs* **try to influence**, try to persuade, bring pressure to bear on; petition, appeal to, pressurize, importune. **2** *a group lobbying for better rail services* **campaign**, crusade, press, push, ask, call, demand; promote, advocate, champion.

local adj. **1** *the local council* **community**, district, neighbourhood, regional, city, town, municipal, provincial, village, parish. **2** *a local restaurant* **neighbourhood**, nearby, near, at hand, close by; accessible, handy, convenient. **3** *a local infection* **confined**, restricted, contained, localized.
– OPPOSITES national.
▶ n. **1** *complaints from the locals* **local person**, native, inhabitant, resident, parishioner. **2** Brit. informal *a pint in the local*. See **pub**.
– OPPOSITES outsider.

locale n. **place**, site, spot, area; position, location, setting, scene, venue, background, backdrop, environment; neighbourhood, district, region, locality.

locality n. **1** *the locality of the property* **position**, location, whereabouts, place, situation, spot, point, site, scene, setting. **2** *other schools in the locality* **vicinity**, neighbourhood, area, district, region; informal neck of the woods.

localize v. **limit**, restrict, confine, contain, circumscribe, concentrate, delimit.
– OPPOSITES generalize, globalize.

locate v. **1** *spotter planes locate the shoals* **find**, discover, pinpoint, detect, track down, run to earth, unearth, sniff out, smoke out, search out, ferret out, uncover. **2** *a company located near Pittsburgh* **situate**, site, position, place, base; put, build, establish, found, station, install, settle.

location n. **position**, place, situation, site, locality, locale, spot, whereabouts, point; scene, setting, area, environment; bearings, orientation; venue, address; technical locus.

lock[1] n. *the lock on the door* **bolt**, catch, fastener, clasp, bar, hasp, latch.
▸ v. **1** *he locked the door* **bolt**, fasten, bar, secure, seal; padlock, latch, chain. **2** *she locked her wrists together* **join**, interlock, link, mesh, engage, unite, connect, yoke, mate; couple. **3** *the wheels locked* **jam**, stick, seize up, become stuck, become/make immovable, become/make rigid. **4** *he locked her in an embrace* **clasp**, clench, grasp, embrace, hug, squeeze.
– OPPOSITES unlock, open, separate, divide.
□ **lock someone out** keep out, shut out, refuse entrance to, deny admittance to; exclude, bar, debar, ban.
lock someone up imprison, jail, incarcerate, intern, send to prison, put behind bars, put under lock and key, put in chains, clap in irons, cage, pen, coop up; informal send down, put away, put inside.

lock[2] n. *a lock of hair* **tress**, tuft, curl, ringlet, hank, strand, wisp, snippet.

locker n. **cupboard**, cabinet, chest, safe, box, case, coffer; compartment, storeroom.

lock-up n. **1** *drunks were put in the lock-up overnight* **jail**, prison, cell, detention centre; N. Amer. jailhouse; informal slammer, jug, stir, clink; Brit. informal nick; N. Amer. informal cooler, can; Brit. informal dated quod, chokey. **2** *they stored spare furniture in a lock-up* **storeroom**, store, warehouse, depository; garage.

locomotion n. **movement**, motion, moving; travel, travelling; mobility, motility; walking, ambulation, running; progress, progression, passage; formal perambulation.

lodge n. **1** *the porter's lodge* **gatehouse**, cottage. **2** *a hunting lodge* **house**, cottage, cabin, chalet; Brit. shooting box. **3** *a beaver's lodge* **den**, lair, hole, sett; retreat, haunt, shelter. **4** *a Masonic lodge* **section**, branch, wing; hall, clubhouse, meeting room; N. Amer. chapter.
▸ v. **1** *William lodged at our house* **reside**, board, stay, live, have lodgings, have rooms, put up, be quartered, stop; N. Amer. room; informal have digs; formal dwell, be domiciled, sojourn; old use abide. **2** *they were lodged at an inn* **accommodate**, put up, take in, house, board, billet, quarter, shelter. **3** *the government lodged a protest* **submit**, register, enter, put forward, advance, lay, present, tender, proffer, put on record, record, table, file. **4** *the money was lodged in a bank* **deposit**, put, bank; stash, store, stow, put away, squirrel away. **5** *the bullet lodged in his back* **become fixed**, embed itself, become embedded, become implanted, get/become stuck, stick, catch, become caught, wedge.

lodger n. **boarder**, paying guest, PG, tenant; N. Amer. roomer.

lodging n. **accommodation**, rooms, chambers, living quarters, place to stay, a roof over one's head, housing, shelter; informal digs, pad; formal abode, residence, dwelling, dwelling place, habitation.

lofty adj. **1** *a lofty tower* **tall**, high, giant, towering, soaring, sky-scraping. **2** *lofty ideals* **noble**, exalted, high, high-minded, worthy, grand, fine, elevated. **3** *a lofty post in the department* **eminent**, prominent, leading, distinguished, illustrious, celebrated, elevated, esteemed, respected. **4** *lofty disdain* **haughty**, arrogant, disdainful, supercilious, condescending, patronizing, scornful, contemptuous, self-important, conceited, snobbish; informal stuck-up, snooty, snotty; Brit. informal toffee-nosed.
– OPPOSITES low, short, base, lowly, modest.

log n. **1** *a fallen log* **branch**, trunk; piece of wood; (**logs**) timber, firewood. **2** *a log of phone calls* **record**, register, logbook, journal, diary, minutes, chronicle, daybook, record book, ledger, account, tally.
▸ v. **1** *all complaints are logged* **register**, record, make a note of, note down, write down, jot down, put in writing, enter, file, minute. **2** *the pilot had logged 95 hours* **attain**, achieve, chalk up, make, do, go, cover.

loggerheads plural n.
□ **at loggerheads** in disagreement, at odds, at variance, wrangling, quarrelling, locking horns, at daggers drawn, in conflict, fighting, at war; informal at each other's throats.

logic n. **1** *this case appears to defy all logic* **reason**, judgement, logical thought, rationality, wisdom, sense, good sense, common sense, sanity; informal horse sense. **2** *the logic of their argument* **reasoning**, line of reasoning, rationale, argument, argumentation. **3** *the study of logic* **science of reasoning**, dialectics, argumentation; formal ratiocination.

logical adj. **1** *information displayed in a logical fashion* **reasoned**, well reasoned, rational, sound, cogent, well thought out, valid; coherent, clear, well organized, systematic, orderly, methodical, analytical, consistent, objective; informal joined-up. **2** *the logical outcome* **natural**, reasonable, sensible, understandable; predictable, unsurprising, only to be expected, most likely, likeliest, obvious.
– OPPOSITES illogical, irrational, unlikely, surprising.

logistics plural n. **organization**, planning, plans, management, arrangement, administration, orchestration, coordination, execution, handling, running.

logo n. **emblem**, trademark, device, symbol, design, sign, mark; insignia, crest, seal, coat of arms, shield, badge, motif, monogram, colophon.

loiter v. **1** *he loitered at bus stops* **stand about/around**, wait, skulk; loaf, lounge, idle, laze, waste time, linger; informal hang around/round; Brit. informal hang about, mooch about/around; old use tarry. **2** *they loitered along the river bank* **dawdle**, dally, stroll, amble, saunter, meander, drift, potter, take one's time; informal dilly-dally, mosey, tootle; Brit. informal mooch.

loll v. **1** *he lolled in an armchair* **lounge**, sprawl, drape oneself, stretch oneself; slouch, slump; laze, luxuriate, put one's feet up, lean back, recline, relax, take it easy. **2** *her head lolled to one side* **hang (loosely)**, droop, dangle, sag, drop, flop.

lone adj. **1** *a lone police officer* **solitary**, single, solo, unaccompanied, unescorted, alone, by oneself/itself, sole, companionless; detached, isolated, unique; lonely. **2** *a lone parent* **single**, unmarried, unattached, partnerless, husbandless, wifeless; separated, divorced, widowed.

loneliness n. **1** *his loneliness was unbearable* **isolation**, friendlessness, abandonment, rejection, unpopularity; N. Amer. lonesomeness. **2** *the enforced loneliness of a prison cell* **solitariness**, solitude, lack of company, aloneness, separation. **3** *the loneliness of the village* **isolation**, remoteness, seclusion.

lonely adj. **1** *I felt very lonely* **isolated**, alone, friendless, with no one to turn to, forsaken, abandoned, rejected, unloved, unwanted; N. Amer. lonesome. **2** *the lonely life of a writer* **solitary**, unaccompanied, lone, by oneself/itself, companionless. **3** *a lonely road* **deserted**, uninhabited, unfrequented, unpopulated, desolate, isolated, remote, out of the way, secluded, off the beaten track, in the back of beyond, godforsaken; informal in the middle of nowhere.
– OPPOSITES popular, sociable, crowded.

loner n. **recluse**, introvert, lone wolf, hermit, solitary, misanthrope, outsider; historical anchorite.

long[1] adj. *a long silence* **lengthy**, extended, prolonged, extensive, protracted, long-lasting, long-drawn(-out), spun out, dragged out, seemingly endless, lingering, interminable.
– OPPOSITES short, brief.
□ **before long** soon, shortly, presently, in the near future, in a little while, by and by, in a minute, in a moment, in a second; informal anon, in a jiffy; Brit. informal in a tick, in two ticks, in a mo; dated directly; literary ere long.

long[2] v. *I longed for the holidays* **yearn**, pine, ache, hanker for/after, hunger, thirst, itch, be eager, be desperate; crave, dream of, set one's heart on; informal have a yen, be dying.

longing n. *a longing for the countryside* **yearning**, pining, craving, ache, burning, hunger, thirst, hankering; informal yen, itch.
▶ adj. *a longing look* **yearning**, pining, craving, hungry, thirsty, hankering, wistful, covetous.

long-lasting adj. **enduring**, lasting, abiding, long-lived, long-running, long-established, long-standing, lifelong, deep-rooted, time-honoured, traditional, permanent.
– OPPOSITES short-lived, ephemeral.

long-lived adj. See **long-lasting**.

long-standing adj. **well established**, long-established; time-honoured, traditional, age-old; abiding, enduring, long-lived, surviving, persistent, prevailing, perennial, deep-rooted, long-term, confirmed.
– OPPOSITES new, recent.

long-suffering adj. **patient**, stoical, forbearing, tolerant, uncomplaining, resigned; easy-going, indulgent, charitable, accommodating, forgiving.
– OPPOSITES impatient, complaining.

long-winded adj. **verbose**, wordy, lengthy, long, overlong, prolix, prolonged, protracted, long-drawn-out, interminable; discursive, diffuse, rambling, tortuous, meandering, repetitious; informal windy; Brit. informal waffly.
– OPPOSITES concise, succinct, laconic.

look v. **1** *Mrs Wright looked at him* **glance**, gaze, stare, gape, peer; peep, peek, take a look; watch, observe, view, regard, examine, inspect, check out, eye, scan, scrutinize, survey, study, contemplate, consider, take in, ogle; informal take a gander, rubberneck, give someone/something a/the once-over, get a load of; Brit. informal take a dekko, take a butcher's, take a shufti, clock, gawp; N. Amer. informal eyeball; literary behold. **2** *her room looked out on Broadway* **command a view of**, face, overlook, front. **3** *they looked shocked* **seem (to be)**, appear (to be), have the appearance/air of being, give the impression of being, strike someone as being.
– OPPOSITES ignore.
▶ n. **1** *have a look at this report* **glance**, view, examination, study, inspection, observation, scan, survey, peep, peek, glimpse, gaze, stare; informal eyeful, gander, look-see, once-over, squint, recce; Brit. informal shufti, dekko, gawp, butcher's. **2** *the look on her face* **expression**, mien. **3** *that rustic look* **appearance**, air, aspect, bearing, cast, manner, mien, demeanour, facade, impression, effect, feel; informal vibe. **4** *this season's look* **fashion**, style, vogue, mode.
□ **look after** take care of, care for, attend to, minister to, tend, mind, keep an eye on, keep safe, be responsible for, protect; nurse, babysit, childmind.
look back on reflect on, think back to, remember, recall, reminisce about.
look down on disdain, scorn, regard with contempt, look down one's nose at, sneer at, despise.
look for search for, hunt for, try to find, seek, cast about/round for, try to track down, forage for, scout out, quest for/after.
look forward to await with pleasure, eagerly anticipate, lick one's lips over, be unable to wait for, count the days until.
look into investigate, enquire into, ask questions about, go into, probe, explore, follow up, research, study, examine; informal check out, give something a/the once-over;

N. Amer. informal scope out.

look like resemble, bear a resemblance to, look similar to, take after, have the look of, have the appearance of, remind one of, make one think of; informal be the spitting image of, be a dead ringer for.

look on regard, consider, think of, deem, judge, see, view, count, reckon.

look out beware, watch out, mind out, be on (one's) guard, be alert, be wary, be vigilant, be careful, take care, be cautious, pay attention, take heed, keep one's eyes open/peeled, keep an eye out; watch your step.

look something over inspect, examine, scan, cast an eye over, take stock of, vet, view, look through, peruse, run through, read through; informal give something a/the once-over; N. Amer. check out; N. Amer. informal eyeball.

look to 1 *we must look to the future* **consider**, think about, turn one's thoughts to, focus on, take heed of, pay attention to, attend to, address, mind, heed. **2** *they look to the government for help* **turn to**, resort to, have recourse to, fall back on, rely on.

look up improve, get better, pick up, come along/on, progress, make progress, make headway, perk up, rally, take a turn for the better.

look someone up informal visit, pay a visit to, call on, go to see, look in on; N. Amer. visit with, go see; informal drop in on.

look up to admire, have a high opinion of, think highly of, hold in high regard, regard highly, rate highly, respect, esteem, value.

lookalike n. **double**, twin, clone, duplicate, exact likeness, replica, copy, facsimile, Doppelgänger; informal spitting image, dead ringer, dead spit.

lookout n. **1** *he saw the smoke from the lookout* **observation post**, lookout point, lookout station, lookout tower, watchtower. **2** *the lookout sighted sails* **watchman**, watch, guard, sentry, sentinel, picket; historical vedette. **3** informal *it would be a poor lookout for her* **outlook**, prospect, chance of success, future. **4** Brit. informal *that's your lookout* **problem**, concern, business, affair, responsibility, worry; informal pigeon.
□ **be on the lookout/keep a lookout** keep watch, keep an eye out, keep one's eyes peeled, keep a vigil, be alert, be on the qui vive.

loom v. **1** *ghostly shapes loomed out of the fog* **emerge**, appear, come into view, take shape, materialize, reveal itself. **2** *the church loomed above him* **soar**, tower, rise, rear up; overhang, overshadow, dominate. **3** *without reforms, disaster looms* **be imminent**, be on the horizon, impend, threaten, brew, be just around the corner.

loop n. *a loop of rope* **coil**, hoop, ring, circle, noose, oval, spiral, curl, bend, curve, arc, twirl, whorl, twist, hook, zigzag, helix, convolution, incurvation.
▶v. **1** *Dave looped rope around their hands* **coil**, wind, twist, snake, wreathe, spiral, curve, bend, turn. **2** *he looped the cables together*

fasten, tie, join, connect, knot, bind.

loophole n. **let-out**, ambiguity, omission, flaw, inconsistency, discrepancy.

loose adj. **1** *a loose floorboard* **not fixed in place**, not secure, unsecured, unattached; detached, unfastened; wobbly, unsteady, movable. **2** *she wore her hair loose* **untied**, unpinned, unbound, hanging free, down, flowing. **3** *there's a wolf loose* **free**, at large, at liberty, on the loose, escaped; unconfined, untied, unchained, untethered. **4** *a loose interpretation* **vague**, indefinite, inexact, imprecise, approximate; broad, general, rough; liberal. **5** *a loose jacket* **baggy**, generously cut, slack, roomy, boyfriend; oversized, shapeless, bagging, sagging, sloppy. **6** dated *a loose woman* **promiscuous**, of easy virtue, fast, wanton, unchaste, immoral; licentious, dissolute; N. Amer. informal roundheeled; dated fallen; derogatory whorish, sluttish.
– OPPOSITES secure, literal, narrow, tight, chaste.
▶v. **1** *the hounds have been loosed* **free**, set free, unloose, turn loose, set loose, let loose, let go, release; untie, unchain, unfasten, unleash. **2** *the fingers loosed their hold* **relax**, slacken, loosen; weaken, lessen, reduce, diminish, moderate. **3** *Brian loosed off a shot* **fire**, discharge, shoot, let go, let fly with.
– OPPOSITES confine, tighten.
□ **at a loose end** with nothing to do, unoccupied, unemployed, at leisure, idle, adrift, with time to kill; bored, twiddling one's thumbs, kicking one's heels.
break loose escape, make one's escape, get away, get free, break free, free oneself.
let loose See **loose** (sense 1 of the verb).
on the loose free, at liberty, at large, escaped; on the run, fugitive; N. Amer. informal on the lam.

loose-limbed adj. **supple**, limber, lithe, lissom, willowy; agile, nimble.

loosen v. **1** *you simply loosen two screws* **slacken**, unfasten, detach, release, disconnect, undo, unclasp, unlatch, unbolt. **2** *her fingers loosened* slackened, become loose, let go, ease; work loose, work free. **3** *Philip loosened his grip* **weaken**, relax, slacken, loose, lessen, reduce, moderate, diminish. **4** *you need to loosen up* **relax**, unwind, ease up/off; informal let up, hang loose, lighten up, go easy.
– OPPOSITES tighten.

loot n. *a bag full of loot* **booty**, spoils, plunder, stolen goods, contraband, pillage; informal swag, hot goods, ill-gotten gains, boodle.
▶v. *troops looted the cathedral* **plunder**, pillage, despoil, ransack, sack, raid, rifle, rob, burgle; strip, clear out.

lop v. **cut**, chop, hack, saw, hew, slash, axe; prune, sever, clip, trim, snip, dock, crop.

lope v. **stride**, run, bound; lollop.

lopsided adj. **crooked**, askew, awry, off-centre, uneven, out of true, out of line, asymmetrical, tilted, at an angle, aslant, slanting, squint; Scottish agley; informal

cockeyed; Brit. informal skew-whiff, wonky.
– OPPOSITES even, level, balanced.

loquacious adj. **talkative**, voluble, communicative, expansive, garrulous, unreserved, chatty, gossipy, gossiping; informal having the gift of the gab, gabby, gassy; Brit. informal able to talk the hind legs off a donkey.
– OPPOSITES reticent, taciturn.

loquacity n. **talkativeness**, volubility, expansiveness, garrulousness, garrulity, chattiness; informal the gift of the gab.
– OPPOSITES reticence, taciturnity.

lord n. **1** *lords and ladies* **noble**, nobleman, peer, aristocrat, patrician, grandee, seigneur. **2** *it is my duty to obey my lord's wishes* **master**, ruler, leader, chief, superior, monarch, sovereign, king, emperor, prince, governor, commander, suzerain, liege, liege lord. **3** *let us pray to our Lord* **God**, the Father, the Almighty, Jehovah, the Creator; **Jesus Christ**, the Messiah, the Saviour, the Son of God, the Redeemer, the Lamb of God, the Prince of Peace, the King of Kings. **4** *a press lord* **magnate**, tycoon, mogul, captain, baron, king; industrialist, proprietor; informal big shot, honcho; derogatory fat cat.
– OPPOSITES commoner, servant, inferior.
▫ **lord it over someone** order about/around, dictate to, ride roughshod over, pull rank on, tyrannize, have under one's thumb; be overbearing, put on airs, swagger; informal boss about/around, walk all over, push around, throw one's weight about/around.

lordly adj. **1** *lordly titles* **noble**, aristocratic, princely, kingly, regal, royal, imperial, courtly, stately; magnificent, majestic, grand, august. **2** *in lordly tones* **imperious**, arrogant, haughty, self-important, swaggering; supercilious, disdainful, scornful, contemptuous, condescending, patronizing, superior; dictatorial, authoritarian, peremptory, autocratic; informal bossy, high and mighty, snooty, uppity, hoity-toity; Brit. informal toffee-nosed.
– OPPOSITES lowly, humble.

lore n. **1** *Arthurian legend and lore* **mythology**, myths, legends, stories, traditions, folklore, oral tradition, mythos, mythus. **2** *cricket lore* **knowledge**, learning, wisdom; informal know-how, how-tos.

lorry n. **truck**, wagon, van, juggernaut, trailer; articulated lorry, heavy-goods vehicle, HGV; dated pantechnicon.

lose v. **1** *I've lost my watch* **mislay**, misplace, be unable to find, lose track of, leave (behind). **2** *he's lost a lot of blood* **be deprived of**, suffer the loss of. **3** *he lost his pursuers* **escape from**, evade, elude, dodge, avoid, give someone the slip, shake off, throw off, throw off the scent; leave behind, outdistance, outstrip, outrun. **4** *they lost their way* **stray from**, wander from, depart from; go astray. **5** *you've lost your opportunity* **neglect**, waste, squander, fail to grasp, fail to take advantage of, let pass, miss, forfeit; informal pass up, lose out on. **6** *they always lose at football* **be defeated**,

be beaten, be the loser, be conquered, be vanquished, be trounced, be worsted; informal come a cropper, go down, be bested.
– OPPOSITES find, regain, seize, win.

loser n. **1** *the loser still gets the silver medal* **defeated person**, also-ran, runner-up. **2** informal *he's a complete loser* **failure**, non-achiever, underachiever, ne'er-do-well, dead loss; write-off, has-been; informal flop, non-starter, no-hoper, washout, lemon.
– OPPOSITES winner, success.

loss n. **1** *the loss of the documents* **mislaying**, misplacement, forgetting. **2** *loss of earnings* **deprivation**, disappearance, privation, forfeiture, diminution, erosion, reduction, depletion. **3** *the loss of her husband* **death**, dying, demise, passing (away/on), end, quietus; bereavement; formal decease; old use expiry. **4** *British losses in the war* **casualty**, fatality, victim; dead; missing; death toll, number killed/dead/wounded. **5** *a loss of £15,000* **deficit**, debit, debt, indebtedness, deficiency.
– OPPOSITES recovery, profit.
▫ **at a loss** baffled, nonplussed, mystified, puzzled, perplexed, bewildered, bemused, at sixes and sevens, confused, dumbfounded, stumped, stuck, blank; informal clueless, flummoxed, bamboozled, fazed, floored, beaten; N. Amer. informal discombobulated.

lost adj. **1** *her lost keys* **missing**, mislaid, misplaced, vanished, disappeared, gone missing/astray, forgotten, nowhere to be found; absent, not present, strayed. **2** *I think we're lost* **off course**, off track, disorientated, having lost one's bearings, going round in circles, adrift, at sea, stray, astray. **3** *a lost opportunity* **missed**, forfeited, neglected, wasted, squandered, gone by the board; informal down the drain. **4** *lost traditional values* **bygone**, past, former, one-time, previous, old, olden, departed, vanished, forgotten, consigned to oblivion, extinct, dead, gone. **5** *lost species and habitats* **extinct**, died out, defunct, vanished, gone; **destroyed**, wiped out, ruined, wrecked, exterminated, eradicated. **6** *a lost cause* **hopeless**, beyond hope, futile, forlorn, failed, beyond remedy, beyond recovery. **7** *lost souls* **damned**, fallen, irredeemable, irreclaimable, irretrievable, past hope, past praying for, condemned, cursed, doomed, excommunicated; literary accursed. **8** *lost in thought* **engrossed**, absorbed, rapt, immersed, deep, intent, engaged, wrapped up.
– OPPOSITES current, saved.

lot pron. *a lot of money | lots of friends* **a large amount**, a fair amount, a good/great deal, a great quantity, quantities, an abundance, a wealth, a profusion, plenty; many, a great many, a large number, a considerable number, numerous, scores; informal hundreds, thousands, millions, billions, loads, bucketloads, masses, heaps, a pile, piles, oodles, stacks, scads, reams, wads, pots, oceans, a mountain, mountains, miles, tons, zillions, more —— than one can shake

a stick at; Brit. informal a shedload, lashings; N. Amer. informal gobs, a bunch, gazillions.
– OPPOSITES a little, not much, a few, not many.
▶ adv. *I work in pastels a lot* **a great deal**, a good deal, to a great extent; much; often, frequently, regularly.
– OPPOSITES a little, not much.
▶ n. **1** informal *what do your lot think?* **group**, set, crowd, circle, band, crew; informal bunch, gang, mob; Brit. informal shower. **2** *the books were auctioned as a number of lots* **item**, article; batch, set, collection, group, bundle, quantity, assortment, parcel. **3** *his lot in life* **fate**, destiny, fortune, doom; situation, circumstances, state, condition, position, plight, predicament. **4** N. Amer. *some youngsters playing ball in a vacant lot* **patch of ground**, piece of ground, plot, area, tract, parcel; N. Amer. plat.
□ **draw/cast lots** decide randomly, spin/toss a coin, throw dice, draw straws.
throw in one's lot with join forces with, join up with, form an alliance with, ally with, align oneself with, link up with, make common cause with.

lotion n. **ointment**, cream, salve, balm, rub, emollient, moisturizer, lubricant, unguent, liniment, embrocation.

lottery n. **1** *a national lottery* **raffle**, (prize) draw, sweepstake, sweep, tombola, pools; N. Amer. lotto. **2** *the procedure is something of a lottery* **gamble**, pot luck, lucky dip.

loud adj. **1** *loud music* **noisy**, blaring, booming, deafening, roaring, thunderous, thundering, ear-splitting, ear-piercing, piercing; carrying, clearly audible; lusty, powerful, forceful, stentorian; Music forte, fortissimo. **2** *loud complaints* **vociferous**, clamorous, insistent, vehement, emphatic, urgent. **3** *a loud T-shirt* **garish**, gaudy, flamboyant, lurid, glaring, showy, ostentatious; vulgar, tasteless; informal flash, flashy, naff, kitsch, tacky.
– OPPOSITES quiet, soft, gentle, sober, tasteful.

loudly adv. **at high volume**, at the top of one's voice; noisily, deafeningly, thunderously, piercingly; stridently, lustily, powerfully, forcefully; Music forte, fortissimo; informal as if to wake the dead.
– OPPOSITES quietly, softly.

loudmouth n. informal **braggart**, boaster, blusterer, swaggerer; informal blabbermouth, big mouth, motormouth; N. Amer. informal blowhard.

loudspeaker n. **speaker**, monitor, woofer, tweeter; loudhailer, megaphone; public address system, PA (system); informal squawk box.

lounge v. *he just lounges in his room* **laze**, lie, loll, lie back, lean back, recline, stretch oneself, drape oneself, relax, rest, repose, take it easy, put one's feet up, unwind, luxuriate; sprawl, slump, slouch, flop, loaf, idle, do nothing.
▶ n. *she sat in the lounge* **living room**, sitting room, front room, drawing room, morning room, reception room, salon, family room; dated parlour.

lour, lower v. **scowl**, frown, look sullen, glower, glare, give someone black looks, look daggers, look angry; informal give someone dirty looks.
– OPPOSITES smile.

louring, lowering adj. **overcast**, dark, leaden, grey, cloudy, clouded, gloomy, threatening, menacing, promising rain.
– OPPOSITES sunny, bright.

lousy informal adj. **1** *a lousy film.* See **awful** (sense 2). **2** *the lousy, double-crossing snake!* See **despicable**. **3** *I felt lousy.* See **ill** (sense 1 of the adjective).
□ **be lousy with** See **crawl** (sense 3).

lout n. **ruffian**, hooligan, thug, boor, oaf, hoodlum, rowdy; informal tough, roughneck, bruiser, yahoo, lug; Brit. informal yob, yobbo, chav.
– OPPOSITES smoothie, gentleman.

loutish adj. **uncouth**, rude, impolite, unmannerly, ill-mannered, ill-bred, coarse; thuggish, boorish, oafish, uncivilized, wild, rough; informal slobbish; Brit. informal yobbish.
– OPPOSITES polite, well behaved.

lovable adj. **adorable**, dear, sweet, cute, charming, darling, lovely, likeable, delightful, captivating, enchanting, engaging, bewitching, pleasing, appealing, winsome, winning, fetching, endearing.
– OPPOSITES hateful, loathsome.

love n. **1** *his friendship with Helen grew into love* **deep affection**, fondness, tenderness, warmth, intimacy, attachment, endearment; devotion, adoration, doting, idolization, worship; passion, ardour, desire, lust, yearning, infatuation, besottedness. **2** *her love of fashion* **liking**, enjoyment, appreciation, taste, delight, relish, passion, zeal, appetite, zest, enthusiasm, keenness, fondness, soft spot, weakness, bent, leaning, proclivity, inclination, disposition, partiality, predilection, penchant. **3** *their love for their fellow human beings* **compassion**, care, caring, regard, solicitude, concern, friendliness, friendship, kindness, charity, goodwill, sympathy, kindliness, altruism, unselfishness, philanthropy, benevolence, fellow feeling, humanity. **4** *he was her one true love* **beloved**, loved one, love of one's life, dear, dearest, dear one, darling, sweetheart, sweet, angel, honey; lover, inamorato, inamorata, amour; old use paramour. **5** *their love will survive* **relationship**, love affair, romance, liaison, affair of the heart, amour. **6** *my mother sends her love* **best wishes**, regards, good wishes, greetings, kind/kindest regards.
– OPPOSITES hatred.
▶ v. **1** *she loves him dearly* **adore**, be devoted to, hold very dear, think the world of, dote on, idolize, worship; be in love with, be infatuated with, be smitten with, be besotted with; informal be mad/crazy/nuts/wild/potty about, have a pash on, carry a torch for. **2** *Laura loved painting* **like very**

much, delight in, enjoy greatly, have a passion for, take great pleasure in, relish, savour; have a weakness for, be partial to, have a soft spot for, have a taste for, be taken with; informal get a kick out of, have a thing about, be mad/crazy/nuts/wild/potty about, be hooked on, go a bundle on, get off on, get a buzz out of.
– OPPOSITES hate.
□ **fall in love with** become infatuated with, lose one's heart to; informal fall for, be bowled over by, be swept off one's feet by, develop a crush on.
in love with infatuated with, besotted with, enamoured of, smitten with; captivated by, bewitched by, enthralled by, entranced by; devoted to, doting on; informal mad/crazy/nuts/wild/potty about.

> **WORD LINKS**
> **amatory** relating to sexual love
> **assignation, tryst** a lovers' meeting
> **billet-doux** a love letter
> **philtre** a love potion
> **platonic** describing intimate but non-sexual love
> **Cupid, Venus** the Roman god and goddess of love
> **Aphrodite** the Greek name for Venus

love affair n. **1** *he had a love affair with a teacher* **relationship**, affair, romance, liaison, affair of the heart, affaire de cœur, intrigue, fling, amour, involvement, romantic entanglement; flirtation, dalliance; Brit. informal carry-on. **2** *a love affair with the motor car* **enthusiasm**, mania, devotion, passion.

loveless adj. **passionless**, unloving, unfeeling, heartless, cold, icy, frigid.
– OPPOSITES loving, passionate.

lovelorn adj. **lovesick**, unrequited in love, crossed in love; spurned, jilted, rejected; pining, moping.

lovely adj. **1** *a lovely young woman* **beautiful**, pretty, attractive, good-looking, appealing, handsome, adorable, exquisite, sweet, personable, charming; enchanting, engaging, winsome, seductive, gorgeous, alluring, ravishing, glamorous; Scottish & N. English bonny; informal tasty, knockout, stunning, drop-dead gorgeous; Brit. informal smashing, fit; N. Amer. informal cute, foxy; literary beauteous; old use comely, fair. **2** *a lovely view* **scenic**, picturesque, pleasing, easy on the eye; magnificent, stunning, splendid. **3** informal *we had a lovely day* **delightful**, very pleasant, very nice, very agreeable, marvellous, wonderful, sublime, superb, fine, magical; informal terrific, fabulous, heavenly, divine, amazing, glorious.
– OPPOSITES ugly, horrible.

lover n. **1** *she had a secret lover* **boyfriend**, girlfriend, lady-love, beloved, love, darling, sweetheart, inamorata, inamorato; mistress; partner, significant other; informal bit on the side, bit of fluff, toy boy, fancy man, fancy woman; dated beau; old use swain, concubine, paramour. **2** *a dog lover* **devotee**, admirer, fan, enthusiast, aficionado; informal

buff, freak, nut.

lovesick adj. **lovelorn**, pining, languishing, longing, yearning, infatuated; frustrated.

loving adj. **affectionate**, fond, devoted, adoring, doting, solicitous, demonstrative; caring, tender, warm, warm-hearted, close; amorous, ardent, passionate, amatory.
– OPPOSITES cold, cruel.

low¹ adj. **1** *a low fence* **short**, small, little; squat, stubby, stunted, dwarf; shallow. **2** *she was wearing a low dress* **low-cut**, skimpy, revealing, plunging. **3** *low prices* **cheap**, economical, moderate, reasonable, modest, bargain, bargain-basement, rock-bottom. **4** *supplies were low* **scarce**, scanty, scant, skimpy, meagre, sparse, few, little, paltry; reduced, depleted, diminished. **5** *low quality* **inferior**, substandard, poor, bad, low-grade, below par, second-rate, unsatisfactory, deficient, defective. **6** *of low birth* **humble**, lowly, low-ranking, plebeian, proletarian, peasant, poor; common, ordinary. **7** *low expectations* **unambitious**, unaspiring, modest. **8** *a low opinion* **unfavourable**, poor, bad, adverse, negative. **9** *a rather low thing to have done* **despicable**, contemptible, reprehensible, lamentable, disgusting, shameful, mean, abject, unworthy, shabby, uncharitable, base, dishonourable, unprincipled, ignoble, sordid; nasty, cruel, foul, bad; informal rotten, low-down; Brit. informal beastly; dated dastardly; old use scurvy. **10** *low comedy* **uncouth**, uncultured, unsophisticated, rough, rough-hewn, unrefined, tasteless, crass, common, vulgar, coarse, crude. **11** *a low voice* **quiet**, soft, faint, gentle, muted, subdued, muffled, hushed, quietened, whispered, stifled, murmured. **12** *a low note* **bass**, low-pitched, deep, rumbling, booming, sonorous. **13** *she was feeling low* **depressed**, dejected, despondent, downhearted, downcast, low-spirited, down, morose, miserable, dismal, heavy-hearted, mournful, forlorn, woebegone, crestfallen, dispirited; without energy, enervated, flat, sapped, weary; informal down in the mouth, down in the dumps, fed up, blue.
– OPPOSITES high, expensive, plentiful, superior, noble, favourable, admirable, decent, exalted, loud, cheerful, lively.
▸ n. *the dollar fell to an all-time low* **nadir**, low point, lowest point, lowest level, depth, rock bottom.
– OPPOSITES high.

low² v. *cattle were lowing* **moo**, bellow.

lowbrow adj. **mass-market**, tabloid, popular, intellectually undemanding, lightweight, accessible, unpretentious; uncultured, unsophisticated, trashy, philistine, simplistic; Brit. downmarket; informal dumbed-down, rubbishy.
– OPPOSITES highbrow, intellectual.

low-down informal adj. *a low-down trick* **unfair**, mean, despicable, reprehensible, contemptible, lamentable, disgusting, shameful, low, unworthy, shabby, base, dishonourable, unprincipled, sordid,

underhand; informal rotten, dirty; Brit. informal
beastly; dated dastardly; old use scurvy.
– OPPOSITES kind, honourable.
▶ n. *he gave us the low-down* **facts**, information,
story, data, facts and figures, intelligence,
news; informal info, rundown, the score, the
gen, the latest, the word, the dope.

lower[1] adj. **1** *the lower house of parliament*
subordinate, inferior, lesser, junior,
minor, secondary, lower-level, subsidiary,
subservient. **2** *her lower lip* **bottom**,
bottommost, nether, under; underneath,
further down, beneath. **3** *a lower price*
cheaper, reduced, cut, slashed.
– OPPOSITES upper, higher, increased.

lower[2] v. **1** *she lowered the mask* **move down**,
let down, take down, haul down, drop, let
fall. **2** *lower your voice* **soften**, modulate,
quieten, hush, tone down, muffle, turn
down, mute. **3** *they are lowering their prices*
reduce, decrease, lessen, bring down, mark
down, cut, slash, axe, diminish, curtail,
prune, pare (down). **4** *the water level lowered*
subside, fall (off), recede, ebb, wane;
abate, die down, let up, moderate, diminish,
lessen. **5** *don't lower yourself to their level*
degrade, debase, demean, abase, humiliate,
downgrade, discredit, shame, dishonour,
disgrace; belittle, cheapen, devalue; (**lower
oneself**) stoop, sink, descend.
– OPPOSITES raise, increase.

lower[3] v. *he lowered at her.* See **lour**.

low-grade adj. **poor-quality**, inferior,
substandard, second-rate; shoddy, cheap,
reject, trashy, gimcrack; Brit. informal duff, ropy,
twopenny-halfpenny, rubbishy; N. Amer. informal
two-bit, bum, cheapjack.
– OPPOSITES top-quality, first-class.

low-key adj. **restrained**, modest,
understated, muted, subtle, quiet, low-
profile, inconspicuous, unostentatious,
unobtrusive, discreet, toned-down.
– OPPOSITES ostentatious, obtrusive.

lowly adj. **humble**, low, low-born, low-bred,
low-ranking, plebeian, proletarian; common,
ordinary, plain, average, modest, simple;
inferior, ignoble, subordinate, obscure.
– OPPOSITES aristocratic, exalted.

loyal adj. **faithful**, true, devoted; constant,
steadfast, staunch, dependable, reliable,
trusted, trustworthy, trusty, dutiful,
dedicated, unchanging, unwavering,
unswerving; patriotic.
– OPPOSITES treacherous.

loyalty n. **allegiance**, faithfulness,
obedience, adherence, homage, devotion;
steadfastness, staunchness, true-
heartedness, dependability, reliability,
trustiness, trustworthiness, duty, dedication,
commitment; patriotism; historical fealty.
– OPPOSITES treachery.

lozenge n. **1** *the pattern consists of
overlapping lozenges* **diamond**, rhombus.
2 *a throat lozenge* **pastille**, drop; cough
sweet, jujube; dated cachou.

lubricant n. **grease**, oil, lubrication,
lubricator, emollient, lotion, unguent;

informal lube.

lubricate v. **1** *lubricate the washer with
silicone grease* **oil**, **grease**, wax, polish. **2** *oil
money lubricates an elaborate system of
patronage* **facilitate**, ease, smooth the way
for, oil the wheels of.
– OPPOSITES impede.

lucid adj. **1** *a lucid description* **intelligible**,
comprehensible, understandable, cogent,
coherent, articulate; clear, transparent;
plain, simple, vivid, sharp, straightforward,
unambiguous, graphic; formal perspicuous.
2 *he was not lucid enough to explain* **rational**,
sane, in one's right mind, in possession
of one's faculties, compos mentis, able to
think clearly, balanced, clear-headed, sober,
sensible; informal all there.
– OPPOSITES confusing, confused.

luck n. **1** *with luck you'll make it* **good
fortune**, good luck; fluke, stroke of luck;
informal lucky break. **2** *I wish you luck* **success**,
prosperity, good fortune, good luck. **3** *it
is a matter of luck whether it hits or misses*
fortune, fate, destiny, lot, stars, karma,
kismet; fortuity, serendipity; chance,
accident, a twist of fate; Austral./NZ informal
mozzle.
– OPPOSITES misfortune.
□ **in luck** fortunate, lucky, born under a
lucky star; successful, having a charmed life;
Brit. informal jammy.
out of luck unfortunate, unlucky, luckless,
hapless, unsuccessful, cursed, jinxed,
ill-fated; informal down on one's luck; literary
star-crossed.

> **WORD LINKS**
>
> **mascot**, **talisman** a person or thing believed to
> bring good luck
> **jinx** a person or thing believed to bring bad luck

luckily adv. **fortunately**, happily,
providentially, opportunely, by good
fortune, as luck would have it, propitiously;
mercifully, thankfully.
– OPPOSITES unfortunately.

luckless adj. **unlucky**, unfortunate,
unsuccessful, hapless, out of luck, cursed,
jinxed, doomed, ill-fated; informal down on
one's luck; literary star-crossed.
– OPPOSITES lucky.

lucky adj. **1** *the lucky winner* **fortunate**, in
luck, blessed, favoured, born under a lucky
star, charmed; successful, prosperous; born
with a silver spoon in one's mouth; Brit.
informal jammy. **2** *a lucky escape* **providential**,
fortunate, advantageous, timely, opportune,
serendipitous, expedient, heaven-sent,
auspicious; chance, fortuitous, fluky,
accidental.
– OPPOSITES unfortunate.

lucrative adj. **profitable**, profit-making,
gainful, remunerative, moneymaking,
paying, high-income, well paid, bankable;
rewarding, worthwhile; thriving,
flourishing, successful, booming.
– OPPOSITES unprofitable.

lucre n. **money**, cash, funds, capital, finances, riches, wealth, spoils, ill-gotten gains, Mammon; informal dough, bread, loot, moolah; Brit. informal dosh, brass, lolly, spondulicks, wonga, ackers, the ready, readies; old use pelf.

ludicrous adj. **absurd**, ridiculous, farcical, laughable, risible, preposterous, foolish, mad, insane, idiotic, stupid, inane, silly, asinine, nonsensical; informal crazy; rare derisible.
– OPPOSITES sensible.

lug v. **carry**, lift, bear, heave, hoist, shoulder, manhandle; haul, drag, tug, tow, transport, move, convey, shift; informal hump, tote, schlep; Scottish informal humph.

luggage n. **baggage**; bags, suitcases, cases, trunks. See also **bag** (sense 2 of the noun).

lugubrious adj. **mournful**, gloomy, sad, unhappy, doleful, glum, melancholy, woeful, miserable, woebegone, forlorn, long-faced, Eeyorish, sombre, solemn, serious, sorrowful, morose, dour, cheerless, joyless, dismal; funereal, sepulchral; informal down in the mouth; literary dolorous.
– OPPOSITES cheerful.

lukewarm adj. **1** *lukewarm coffee* **tepid**, slightly warm, warmish; at room temperature, chambré. **2** *a lukewarm response* **indifferent**, cool, half-hearted, apathetic, unenthusiastic, tepid, offhand, lackadaisical, perfunctory, non-committal; informal laid-back, unenthused, couldn't-care-less; rare Laodicean.
– OPPOSITES hot, cold, enthusiastic.

lull v. **1** *the sound of the bells lulled us to sleep* **soothe**, calm, hush; rock to sleep. **2** *his suspicions were soon lulled* **assuage**, allay, ease, alleviate, soothe, quiet, quieten; reduce, diminish; quell, banish, dispel. **3** *the noise had lulled* **abate**, die down, subside, let up, moderate, slacken, lessen, dwindle, decrease, diminish.
– OPPOSITES waken, agitate, arouse, intensify.
▸ n. **1** *a lull in the fighting* **pause**, respite, interval, break, hiatus, suspension, interlude, intermission, breathing space; informal let-up, breather. **2** *the lull before the storm* **calm**, stillness, quiet, tranquillity, peace, silence, hush.
– OPPOSITES agitation, activity.

lullaby n. **cradle song**, berceuse.

lumber¹ v. *elephants lumbered past* **lurch**, stumble, trundle, shamble, shuffle, waddle, trudge, clump, stump, plod, tramp; informal galumph.

lumber² n. **1** *a spare room packed with lumber* **jumble**, clutter, odds and ends, bits and pieces, flotsam and jetsam, cast-offs; refuse, rubbish, litter; N. Amer. trash; informal junk, odds and sods, gubbins, clobber. **2** *the lumber trade* **timber**, wood.
▸ v. Brit. informal *she was lumbered with a husband and child* **burden**, saddle, encumber, hamper; load, oppress, trouble, tax; informal land, dump something on someone.
– OPPOSITES free.

lumbering adj. **clumsy**, awkward, heavy-footed, slow, blundering, bumbling, inept, maladroit, uncoordinated, ungainly, ungraceful, gauche, lumpish, hulking, ponderous; informal clodhopping.
– OPPOSITES nimble, agile.

luminary n. **leading light**, guiding light, inspiration, role model, hero, heroine, leader, expert, master, panjandrum; lion, legend, great, giant.
– OPPOSITES nobody.

luminous adj. **shining**, bright, brilliant, radiant, dazzling, glowing, gleaming, scintillating, lustrous; luminescent, phosphorescent, fluorescent, incandescent.
– OPPOSITES dark.

lump¹ n. **1** *a lump of coal* **chunk**, hunk, piece, mass, block, wedge, slab, cake, nugget, ball, brick, cube, pat, knob, clod, gobbet, dollop, wad; informal glob; N. Amer. informal gob. **2** *a lump on his head* **swelling**, bump, bulge, protuberance, protrusion, growth, outgrowth, nodule, hump.
▸ v. *it is convenient to lump them together* **combine**, put, group, bunch, aggregate, unite, pool, merge, collect, throw, consider together.

lump² v. informal *I'm afraid you'll have to lump it* **put up with**, bear, endure, take, tolerate, accept; Scottish thole it.

lumpish adj. **1** *lumpish furniture* **cumbersome**, unwieldy, heavy, hulking, chunky, bulky, ponderous. **2** *a lumpish young girl* **stupid**, obtuse, dense, dim-witted, dull-witted, slow-witted, slow; lethargic, bovine, sluggish, listless; informal thick, dumb, dopey, slow on the uptake, moronic; Brit. informal dozy.
– OPPOSITES elegant, quick-witted, sharp.

lumpy adj. **1** *a lumpy mattress* **bumpy**, knobbly, bulging, uneven, rough, gnarled. **2** *lumpy custard* **clotted**, curdled, congealed, coagulated.

lunacy n. **1** *originality demands a degree of lunacy* **insanity**, madness, mental illness, dementia, mania, psychosis; informal craziness. **2** *the lunacy of gambling* **folly**, foolishness, foolhardiness, stupidity, silliness, idiocy, madness, rashness, recklessness, imprudence, irresponsibility, injudiciousness; informal craziness; Brit. informal daftness.
– OPPOSITES sanity, sense, prudence.

lunatic n. *he drives like a lunatic* **maniac**, madman, madwoman, imbecile, psychopath, psychotic; fool, idiot; eccentric; informal loony, nut, nutcase, head case, psycho, moron; Brit. informal nutter, mentalist; N. Amer. informal screwball, wing nut.
▸ adj. **1** *a lunatic prisoner*. See **mad** (sense 1). **2** *a lunatic idea*. See **mad** (sense 3).

lunch n. **midday meal**, luncheon; Brit. dinner.

lung n.

> **WORD LINKS**
>
> **pulmonary** relating to the lungs
> **pleurisy** inflammation of the membranes around the lungs
> **pneumonia** an infection causing inflammation of the lungs

lunge n. *Darren made a lunge at his attacker* **thrust**, dive, rush, charge, grab.
▸ v. *he lunged at Finn with a knife* **thrust**, dive, spring, launch oneself, rush, make a grab.

lurch v. **1** *he lurched into the kitchen* **stagger**, stumble, wobble, sway, reel, roll, weave, pitch, totter, blunder. **2** *the ship lurched* **sway**, reel, list, heel, rock, roll, pitch, toss, jerk, shake, judder, flounder, swerve.

lure v. *consumers are frequently lured into debt* **tempt**, entice, attract, induce, coax, persuade, inveigle, allure, seduce, win over, cajole, beguile, bewitch, ensnare.
– OPPOSITES deter, put off.
▸ n. *the lure of the stage* **temptation**, enticement, attraction, pull, draw, appeal; inducement, allurement, fascination, interest, magnet; informal come-on.

lurid adj. **1** *lurid food colourings* **bright**, brilliant, vivid, glaring, shocking, fluorescent, flaming, dazzling, intense, gaudy, loud. **2** *the lurid details* **sensational**, sensationalist, exaggerated, overdramatized, extravagant, colourful; salacious, graphic, explicit, unrestrained, prurient, shocking; gruesome, gory, grisly; informal tacky, shock-horror, juicy, full-frontal, full-on.
– OPPOSITES muted, restrained.

lurk v. **skulk**, loiter, lie in wait, lie low, hide, conceal oneself, take cover, keep out of sight.

luscious adj. **1** *luscious fruit* **delicious**, succulent, lush, juicy, mouth-watering, sweet, tasty, appetizing; informal scrumptious, moreish, scrummy, yummy; N. Amer. informal nummy; literary ambrosial. **2** *a luscious Swedish beauty* **sexy**, sexually attractive, nubile, ravishing, gorgeous, seductive, alluring, sultry, beautiful, stunning; informal fanciable, tasty, drop-dead gorgeous, curvy; Brit. informal fit; N. Amer. informal foxy, cute; Austral./NZ informal spunky.
– OPPOSITES unappetizing, plain, scrawny.

lush adj. **1** *lush vegetation* **luxuriant**, rich, abundant, profuse, exuberant, riotous, prolific, vigorous; dense, thick, rank, rampant; informal jungly. **2** *a lush, ripe peach* **succulent**, luscious, juicy, soft, tender, ripe. **3** *a lush apartment* **luxurious**, deluxe, sumptuous, palatial, opulent, lavish, elaborate, extravagant, fancy; informal plush, ritzy, posh, swanky; Brit. informal swish; N. Amer. informal swank.
– OPPOSITES barren, sparse, austere.

lust n. **1** *his lust for her* **sexual desire**, ardour, desire, passion; libido, sex drive, sexuality, biological urge; lechery, lecherousness, lasciviousness; informal horniness, the hots; Brit. informal randiness. **2** *a lust for power* **greed**, desire, craving, covetousness, eagerness, avidity, cupidity, longing, yearning, hunger, thirst, appetite, hankering.
– OPPOSITES dread, aversion.
▸ v. **1** *he lusted after his employer's wife* **desire**, be consumed with desire for, ache for, burn for, pant for; informal have the hots for, lech after/over, fancy, have a thing about/for, drool over, have the horn for. **2** *she lusted*

after adventure **crave**, desire, covet, want, wish for, long for, yearn for, dream of, hanker for, hanker after, hunger for, thirst for, ache for.
– OPPOSITES dread, avoid.

lustful adj. **lecherous**, lascivious, libidinous, licentious, salacious, goatish; wanton, unchaste, impure, naughty, immodest, indecent, dirty, prurient; passionate, sensual, sexy, erotic; informal horny, randy, raunchy; formal concupiscent.
– OPPOSITES chaste, pure.

lustily adv. **heartily**, vigorously, loudly, at the top of one's voice, powerfully, forcefully, strongly; informal like mad, like crazy.
– OPPOSITES feebly, quietly.

lustre n. **1** *her hair lost its lustre* **sheen**, gloss, shine, glow, gleam, shimmer, burnish, polish, patina. **2** *the lustre of the Milky Way* **brilliance**, brightness, radiance, sparkle, dazzle, flash, glitter, glint, gleam, luminosity, luminescence.
– OPPOSITES dullness, dark.

lustreless adj. **dull**, lacklustre, matt, unpolished, tarnished, dingy, dim, dark.
– OPPOSITES lustrous, bright.

lustrous adj. **shiny**, shining, satiny, glossy, gleaming, shimmering, burnished, polished; radiant, bright, brilliant, luminous; dazzling, sparkling, glistening, twinkling.
– OPPOSITES dull, dark.

lusty adj. **1** *lusty young men* **healthy**, strong, fit, vigorous, robust, hale and hearty, energetic; rugged, sturdy, muscular, muscly, strapping, hefty, husky, burly, powerful; informal beefy; dated stalwart. **2** *lusty singing* **loud**, vigorous, hearty, strong, powerful, forceful.
– OPPOSITES feeble, quiet.

luxuriant adj. **lush**, rich, abundant, profuse, exuberant, riotous, prolific, vigorous; dense, thick, rank, rampant; informal jungly.
– OPPOSITES barren, sparse.

luxuriate v. **revel**, bask, delight, take pleasure, wallow; (**luxuriate in**) enjoy, relish, savour, appreciate; informal get a kick out of, get a thrill out of.
– OPPOSITES dislike.

luxurious adj. **1** *a luxurious hotel* **opulent**, sumptuous, deluxe, grand, palatial, splendid, magnificent, well appointed, extravagant, fancy; Brit. upmarket; informal plush, posh, classy, ritzy, swanky; Brit. informal swish; N. Amer. informal swank. **2** *a luxurious lifestyle* **self-indulgent**, sensual, pleasure-loving, pleasure-seeking, epicurean, hedonistic, sybaritic, lotus-eating.
– OPPOSITES plain, basic, abstemious.

luxury n. **1** *we'll live in luxury* **opulence**, luxuriousness, sumptuousness, grandeur, magnificence, splendour, lavishness, the lap of luxury, a bed of roses, milk and honey; informal the life of Riley. **2** *a TV is his only luxury* **indulgence**, extravagance, self-indulgence, treat, extra, non-essential, frill.
– OPPOSITES simplicity, necessity.

lying n. *she was no good at lying* **untruthfulness**, fabrication, fibbing, perjury, white lies; falseness, falsity, dishonesty, mendacity, telling stories, invention, misrepresentation, deceit, duplicity; literary perfidy.
– OPPOSITES honesty.
▸ adj. *he was a lying womanizer* **untruthful**, false, dishonest, mendacious, deceitful, deceiving, duplicitous, double-dealing, two-faced, Janus-faced; literary perfidious.
– OPPOSITES truthful.

lynch v. **execute illegally**, hang; informal string up.

lyric adj. **1** *a lyric poem* **expressive**, emotional, deeply felt, personal, subjective, passionate. **2** *a lyric soprano* **light**, silvery, clear, sweet.
– OPPOSITES harsh.

lyrical adj. **1** *lyrical love poetry* **expressive**, emotional, deeply felt, personal, subjective, passionate. **2** *she was lyrical about her success* **enthusiastic**, rhapsodic, effusive, rapturous, ecstatic, euphoric, carried away.
– OPPOSITES unenthusiastic.

lyrics plural n. **words**, libretto, book, text, lines.

l

Mm

macabre adj. **1** *a macabre ritual* **gruesome**, grisly, grim, gory, morbid, ghastly, unearthly, grotesque, hideous, horrific, shocking, dreadful, loathsome, repugnant, repulsive, sickening. **2** *a macabre joke* **black**, weird, unhealthy; informal sick.

mace n. **club**, cudgel, stick, staff, shillelagh, bludgeon, truncheon; Brit. life preserver; N. Amer. nightstick, billy, billy club, blackjack; Brit. informal cosh.

macerate v. **pulp**, mash, squash, soften, liquefy, soak.

Machiavellian adj. **devious**, crafty, cunning, artful, wily, sly, scheming, treacherous, two-faced, Janus-faced, tricky, double-dealing, unscrupulous, deceitful, dishonest; literary perfidious; informal foxy.
– OPPOSITES straightforward, ingenuous.

machinations plural n. **scheming**, plotting, intrigues, conspiracies, ruses, tricks, wiles, stratagems, tactics, manoeuvring.

machine n. **1** *it is quicker done by machine* **apparatus**, appliance, device, contraption, contrivance, mechanism, engine, gadget, tool. **2** *an efficient publicity machine* **organization**, system, structure, arrangement, machinery; informal set-up.

> **WORD LINKS**
>
> **mechanical** relating to machines
> **engineer** a person who designs and builds machines
> **hardware** machines and other physical components of an electronic system

machinery n. **1** *road-making machinery* **equipment**, apparatus, plant, hardware, gear, tackle; mechanism; instruments, tools; gadgetry, technology. **2** *the machinery of local government* **workings**, organization, system, structure, administration, institution; informal set-up.

machinist n. **operator**, operative, machine-minder.

machismo n. **(aggressive) masculinity**, toughness, male chauvinism, sexism; virility, manliness; informal laddishness.

macho adj. *a macho, non-caring image* **(aggressively) male**, (unpleasantly) masculine; manly, virile, red-blooded; informal butch, laddish.
– OPPOSITES wimpish.
▶ n. **1** *he was a macho at heart* **red-blooded male**, macho man, muscleman; informal he-man, tough guy. **2** *macho is out.* See

machismo.
– OPPOSITES wimp.

mackintosh n. **raincoat**, gaberdine, trench coat, waterproof; Brit. pakamac; N. Amer. slicker; Brit. informal mac; trademark Burberry, Drizabone.

macrocosm n. **1** *the law of the macrocosm* **universe**, cosmos, creation, outer space. **2** *the individual is a microcosm of the social macrocosm* **system**, structure, totality, entirety, complex.
– OPPOSITES microcosm.

mad adj. **1** *he was killed by his mad brother* **insane**, mentally ill, certifiable, deranged, demented, of unsound mind, out of one's mind, not in one's right mind, sick in the head, crazy, crazed, lunatic, non compos mentis, unhinged, disturbed, raving, psychotic, psychopathic, mad as a hatter, mad as a March hare, away with the fairies; informal mental, off one's head, off one's nut, nuts, nutty, off one's rocker, not right in the head, round the bend, stark staring/raving mad, bats, batty, bonkers, dotty, cuckoo, cracked, loopy, loony, doolally, bananas, loco, dippy, screwy, schizoid, touched, gaga, up the pole, not all there, not right upstairs; Brit. informal barmy, crackers, barking, barking mad, round the twist, off one's trolley, not the full shilling; N. Amer. informal nutso, out of one's tree, meshuga, wacko, gonzo; Canadian informal spinny; Austral./NZ informal bushed; NZ informal porangi; **(be mad)** informal have a screw loose, have bats in the/one's belfry; Austral. informal have kangaroos in the/one's top paddock; **(go mad)** lose one's reason, lose one's mind, take leave of one's senses; informal lose one's marbles, crack up. **2** informal *I'm still mad at him* **angry**, furious, infuriated, irate, raging, enraged, fuming, incensed, seeing red, beside oneself; informal livid, spare; informal dated in a wax; Brit. informal aerated; N. Amer. informal sore; literary wrathful; **(go mad)** lose one's temper, rant and rave; informal explode, go off the deep end, go ape, flip, flip one's lid; Brit. informal do one's nut; N. Amer. informal flip one's wig. **3** *some mad scheme* **foolish**, insane, stupid, lunatic, foolhardy, idiotic, senseless, absurd, impractical, silly, inane, asinine, wild, unwise, imprudent; informal crazy, crackpot, crackbrained; Brit. informal daft. **4** informal *he's mad about jazz* **enthusiastic**, passionate; ardent, fervent, avid, fanatical; devoted to, infatuated with, in love with, hot for; informal crazy, dotty, nuts, wild, hooked on, gone on; Brit. informal potty; N. Amer.

m

informal **nutso. 5** *it was a mad dash to get ready* **frenzied**, frantic, frenetic, feverish, hysterical, wild, hectic, manic.
– OPPOSITES sane, pleased, sensible, indifferent, calm.
□ **like mad** informal **1** *I ran like mad* **fast**, quickly, rapidly, speedily, hastily, hurriedly. **2** *he had to fight like mad* **energetically**, enthusiastically, madly, furiously, with a will, for all one is worth, passionately, intensely, ardently, fervently; informal like crazy, hammer and tongs; Brit. informal like billy-o.

madcap adj. **1** *a madcap scheme* **reckless**, rash, foolhardy, foolish, hare-brained, wild, hasty, imprudent, ill-advised; informal crazy, crackpot, crackbrained. **2** *a madcap comedy* **zany**, eccentric, unconventional.

madden v. **1** *what maddens people most is his vagueness* **infuriate**, exasperate, irritate; incense, anger, enrage, provoke, upset, agitate, vex, irk, make someone's hackles rise, make someone see red; informal aggravate, make someone's blood boil, make livid, get up someone's nose, get someone's goat, get someone's back up; Brit. informal nark; N. Amer. informal tee off, tick off. **2** *they were maddened with pain* **drive mad**, drive insane, derange, unhinge, unbalance; informal drive round the bend.

made-up adj. **invented**, fabricated, trumped up, concocted, fictitious, fictional, false, untrue, specious, spurious, bogus, apocryphal, imaginary, mythical.

madhouse n. informal **1** *his father is shut up in a madhouse* **mental hospital**, mental institution, psychiatric hospital, asylum; informal nuthouse, funny farm, loony bin; dated lunatic asylum. **2** *the place was a total madhouse* **bedlam**, mayhem, chaos, pandemonium, uproar, turmoil, disorder, madness, all hell broken loose; N. Amer. three-ring circus.

madly adv. **1** *she was smiling madly* **insanely**, deliriously, wildly, like a lunatic; informal crazily, barmily. **2** *it was fun, hurtling madly downhill fast*, furiously, hurriedly, quickly, speedily, hastily, energetically; informal like mad, like crazy. **3** informal *he loved her madly* **intensely**, fervently, wildly, unrestrainedly, to distraction. **4** informal *his job isn't madly glamorous* **very**, extremely, really, exceedingly, exceptionally, remarkably, extraordinarily, immensely, tremendously, wildly, all that, hugely; informal awfully, terribly, terrifically, fantastically.
– OPPOSITES sanely, slowly, slightly.

madman, madwoman n. **lunatic**, maniac, psychotic, psychopath; informal loony, nut, nutcase, head case, psycho; Brit. informal nutter, mentalist; N. Amer. informal screwball.

madness n. **1** *today madness is called mental illness* **insanity**, mental illness, dementia, derangement; lunacy, instability; mania, psychosis; informal craziness. **2** *it would be madness to do otherwise* **folly**, foolishness, idiocy, stupidity, insanity, lunacy,

silliness; informal craziness. **3** *it's absolute madness in here* **bedlam**, mayhem, chaos, pandemonium, uproar, turmoil, disorder, all hell broken loose; N. Amer. three-ring circus.
– OPPOSITES sanity, common sense, good sense, calm.

maelstrom n. **1** *a maelstrom in the sea* **whirlpool**, vortex, eddy, swirl; literary Charybdis. **2** *the maelstrom of war* **turbulence**, tumult, turmoil, disorder, disarray, chaos, confusion, upheaval, pandemonium, bedlam, whirlwind.

maestro n. **virtuoso**, master, expert, genius, wizard, prodigy; informal ace, whizz, pro, hotshot.
– OPPOSITES tyro, beginner.

magazine n. **journal**, periodical, supplement, fanzine; informal glossy, mag, zine.

magenta adj. **reddish-purple**, purplish-red, crimson, plum, carmine red, fuchsia.

maggot n. **grub**, larva.

magic n. **1** *do you believe in magic?* **sorcery**, witchcraft, wizardry, necromancy, enchantment, the supernatural, occultism, the occult, black magic, the black arts, voodoo, shamanism; charm, hex, spell, jinx; N. Amer. mojo. **2** *he does magic at children's parties* **conjuring tricks**, sleight of hand, legerdemain, illusion, prestidigitation. **3** *the magic of the stage* **allure**, attraction, excitement, fascination, charm, glamour. **4** *a taste of soccer magic* **skill**, brilliance, ability, accomplishment, adeptness, adroitness, deftness, dexterity, aptitude, expertise, art, finesse, talent.
▸adj. **1** *a magic spell* **supernatural**, enchanted, occult. **2** *a magic place* **fascinating**, captivating, charming, glamorous, magical, enchanting, entrancing, spellbinding, magnetic, irresistible, hypnotic. **3** informal *we had a magic time* **marvellous**, wonderful, excellent, admirable; informal terrific, fabulous, fab, brilliant, brill.

> **WORD LINKS**
> **amulet, fetish, juju, talisman** an object thought to have magical powers
> **elixir** a magical potion
> **hex, incantation** a magic spell
> **pentagram, pentangle** a five-pointed star used as a magical symbol

magical adj. **1** *magical incantations* **supernatural**, magic, occult, shamanistic, mystical, paranormal, preternatural, other-worldly. **2** *the news had a magical effect* **extraordinary**, remarkable, exceptional, outstanding, incredible, phenomenal, unbelievable, amazing, astonishing, astounding, stunning, staggering, marvellous, magnificent, wonderful, sensational, breathtaking, miraculous; informal fantastic, fabulous, stupendous, out of this world, terrific, tremendous, brilliant, mind-boggling, mind-blowing, awesome; literary wondrous. **3** *this magical small land* **enchanting**, entrancing, spellbinding, bewitching, beguiling, fascinating, captivating, alluring, enthralling, charming,

m

attractive, lovely, delightful, beautiful; informal dreamy, heavenly, divine, gorgeous.
– OPPOSITES predictable, boring.

magician n. **1 sorcerer**, sorceress, witch, wizard, warlock, enchanter, enchantress, necromancer, shaman. **2 conjuror**, illusionist, prestidigitator.

magisterial adj. **1** *a magisterial pronouncement* **authoritative**, masterful, assured, lordly, commanding, assertive. **2** *his magisterial style of questioning* **domineering**, dictatorial, autocratic, imperious, overbearing, peremptory, high-handed, arrogant, supercilious, patronizing; informal bossy.
– OPPOSITES untrustworthy, humble, hesitant, tentative.

magnanimity n. **generosity**, charity, benevolence, beneficence, big-heartedness, altruism, philanthropy, humanity, chivalry, nobility; clemency, mercy, leniency, forgiveness, indulgence.
– OPPOSITES meanness, selfishness.

magnanimous adj. **generous**, charitable, benevolent, beneficent, big-hearted, handsome, princely, altruistic, philanthropic, chivalrous, noble; forgiving, merciful, lenient, indulgent, clement.
– OPPOSITES mean-spirited, selfish.

magnate n. **tycoon**, mogul, captain of industry, baron, lord, king; industrialist, proprietor; informal big shot, honcho; derogatory fat cat.

magnet n. **1** *you can tell steel by using a magnet* **lodestone**; electromagnet, solenoid. **2** *a magnet for tourists* **attraction**, focus, draw, lure.

magnetic adj. *a magnetic personality* **alluring**, attractive, fascinating, captivating, enchanting, enthralling, appealing, charming, prepossessing, engaging, entrancing, seductive, inviting, irresistible, charismatic.

magnetism n. *his sheer magnetism* **allure**, attraction, fascination, appeal, draw, drawing power, pull, charm, enchantment, seductiveness, magic, spell, charisma.

magnification n. **1** *optical magnification* **enlargement**, enhancement, increase, augmentation, extension, expansion, amplification, intensification. **2** *the magnification of marginal details* **exaggeration**, overstatement, overemphasis, overplaying, dramatization, colouring, embroidery, embellishment, inflation, hyperbole, aggrandizement; informal blowing up (out of all proportion).
– OPPOSITES reduction, understatement.

magnificence n. **splendour**, resplendence, grandeur, impressiveness, glory, majesty, nobility, pomp, stateliness, elegance, sumptuousness, opulence, luxury, lavishness, richness, brilliance, dazzle, skill, virtuosity.
– OPPOSITES modesty, tawdriness, weakness.

magnificent adj. **1** *a magnificent view of the mountains* **splendid**, spectacular, impressive, striking, glorious, superb, majestic, awesome, awe-inspiring, breathtaking. **2** *a magnificent apartment overlooking the lake* **sumptuous**, resplendent, grand, impressive, imposing, monumental, palatial, stately, opulent, luxurious, lavish, rich, dazzling, beautiful, elegant; informal splendiferous, ritzy, posh. **3** *a magnificent performance* **masterly**, skilful, virtuoso, brilliant, coruscating.
– OPPOSITES uninspiring, modest, tawdry, poor, weak.

magnify v. **1** *the lens magnifies the image* **enlarge**, boost, enhance, maximize, increase, augment, extend, expand, amplify, intensify; informal blow up. **2** *the problem gets magnified* **exaggerate**, overstate, overemphasize, overplay, dramatize, colour, embroider, embellish, inflate, make a mountain out of (a molehill); informal blow up (out of all proportion), make a big thing out of.
– OPPOSITES reduce, minimize, understate.

magnitude n. **1** *the magnitude of the task* **immensity**, vastness, hugeness, enormity; size, extent, expanse, greatness, largeness, bigness. **2** *events of tragic magnitude* **importance**, import, significance, weight, consequence, mark, notability, note; formal moment. **3** *a change in magnitude on the Richter scale* **value**, figure, number, measure, order, quantity, vector, index, indicator. **4** *a star of magnitude 4.2* **brightness**, brilliance, radiance, luminosity.
– OPPOSITES smallness, triviality.
□ **of the first magnitude** of the utmost importance, of the greatest significance, very important, of great consequence; formal of great moment.

maid n. **1** *the maid cleared the table* **female servant**, maidservant, housemaid, parlourmaid, lady's maid, chambermaid, maid-of-all-work, domestic; help, cleaner, cleaning woman/lady; Brit. informal daily, skivvy, Mrs Mop; Brit. dated charwoman, charlady, char, tweeny. **2** literary *a village maid and her swain* **girl**, young woman, young lady, lass, miss; Scottish (wee) lassie; literary maiden, damsel, nymph; old use wench.

maiden n. literary See **maid** (sense 2).
▸ adj. **1** *a maiden aunt* **unmarried**, spinster, unwed, unwedded, single, husbandless, celibate. **2** *a maiden voyage* **first**, initial, inaugural, introductory, initiatory.

maidenly adj. **virginal**, immaculate, intact, chaste, pure, virtuous; demure, reserved, retiring, decorous, seemly.
– OPPOSITES fast, slatternly.

mail n. *the mail arrived* **post**, letters, correspondence; postal system, postal service, post office; delivery, collection; email; informal snail mail; N. Amer. the mails.
▸ v. *we mailed the parcels* **send**, post, dispatch, direct, forward, redirect, ship; email.

maim v. **injure**, wound, cripple, disable, incapacitate, impair, mar, mutilate, lacerate, disfigure, deform, mangle.

main adj. *the main item* **principal**, chief, head, leading, foremost, most important, major, ruling, dominant, central, focal, key, prime, master, premier, primary, first, fundamental, supreme, predominant, (most) prominent, pre-eminent, paramount, overriding, cardinal, crucial, critical, pivotal, salient, elemental, essential, staple.
– OPPOSITES subsidiary, minor.
▶ n. literary *the Spanish Main* **sea**, ocean, deep; informal dated the drink; Brit. informal dated the briny.
□ **in the main** See **mainly**.

mainly adv. **mostly**, for the most part, in the main, on the whole, largely, by and large, to a large extent, predominantly, chiefly, principally, primarily; generally, usually, typically, commonly, on average, as a rule, almost always.

mainspring n. **motive**, motivation, impetus, driving force, incentive, impulse, prime mover, reason, fountain, fount, root, generator.

mainstay n. **central component**, central figure, centrepiece, prop, linchpin, cornerstone, pillar, bulwark, buttress, chief support, backbone, anchor, foundation, base, staple.

mainstream adj. **normal**, conventional, ordinary, orthodox, conformist, accepted, established, recognized, common, usual, prevailing, popular.
– OPPOSITES fringe.

maintain v. **1** *they wanted to maintain peace* **preserve**, conserve, keep, retain, keep going, keep alive, keep up, prolong, perpetuate, sustain, carry on, continue. **2** *the council maintains the roads* **keep in good condition**, keep in (good) repair, keep up, service, care for, take good care of, look after. **3** *the costs of maintaining a family* **support**, provide for, keep, sustain; nurture, feed, nourish. **4** *he always maintained his innocence | he maintains that he is innocent* **insist (on)**, declare, assert, protest, affirm, avow, profess, claim, allege, contend, argue, swear (to), hold to; formal aver; rare asseverate.
– OPPOSITES break, discontinue, neglect, deny.

maintenance n. **1** *the maintenance of peace* **preservation**, conservation, keeping, prolongation, perpetuation, carrying on, continuation, continuance. **2** *car maintenance* **upkeep**, service, servicing, repair(s), care, aftercare. **3** *the maintenance of his children* **support**, keeping, upkeep, sustenance; nurture, feeding, nourishment. **4** *absent fathers are forced to pay maintenance* **financial support**, child support, alimony, provision; keep, subsistence, living expenses.
– OPPOSITES breakdown, discontinuation, neglect.

majestic adj. **stately**, dignified, distinguished, solemn, magnificent, grand, splendid, resplendent, glorious, sumptuous, impressive, august, noble, awe-inspiring, monumental, palatial; statuesque, Olympian, imposing, marvellous, sonorous, resounding, heroic.
– OPPOSITES modest, wretched.

majesty n. **1** *the majesty of the procession* **stateliness**, dignity, distinction, solemnity, magnificence, pomp, grandeur, grandness, splendour, resplendence, glory, impressiveness, augustness, nobility. **2** *the majesty invested in the monarch* **sovereignty**, authority, power, dominion, supremacy.
– OPPOSITES modesty, wretchedness.

major adj. **1** *the major English poets* **greatest**, best, finest, most important, chief, main, prime, principal, capital, cardinal, leading, star, foremost, outstanding, first-rate, pre-eminent, arch-. **2** *an issue of major importance* **crucial**, vital, great, considerable, paramount, utmost, prime. **3** *a major factor* **important**, big, significant, weighty, crucial, key, sweeping, substantial. **4** *major surgery* **serious**, complicated, difficult.
– OPPOSITES minor, little, trivial.

majority n. **1** *the majority of cases* **larger part/number**, greater part/number, best/better part, most, more than half; bulk, mass, weight, (main) body, preponderance, predominance, generality, lion's share. **2** *a majority in the election* **(winning) margin**; landslide. **3** *my son has reached his majority* **coming of age**, legal age, adulthood, manhood/womanhood, maturity; age of consent.
– OPPOSITES minority.

make v. **1** *he makes models* **construct**, build, assemble, put together, manufacture, produce, fabricate, create, form, fashion, model. **2** *she made me drink it* **force**, compel, coerce, press, drive, pressure, pressurize, oblige, require; prevail on, dragoon, bludgeon, strong-arm, impel, constrain; informal railroad. **3** *don't make such a noise* **cause**, create, give rise to, produce, bring about, generate, engender, occasion, effect, set up, establish, institute, found, develop, originate; literary beget. **4** *she made a low bow* **perform**, execute, give, do, accomplish, achieve, bring off, carry out, effect. **5** *they made him chairman* **appoint**, designate, name, nominate, select, elect, vote in, install; induct, institute, invest, ordain. **6** *he had made a will* **formulate**, frame, draw up, devise, make out, prepare, compile, compose, put together; draft, write, pen. **7** *I've made a mistake* **perpetrate**, commit, be responsible for, be guilty of, be to blame for. **8** *he's made a lot of money* **acquire**, obtain, gain, get, realize, secure, win, earn; gross, net, clear; bring in, take (in). **9** *he made tea* **prepare**, get ready, put together, concoct, cook, dish up, throw together, whip up, brew; informal fix; Brit. informal mash. **10** *we've got to make a decision* **reach**, come to, settle on, determine on, conclude. **11** *she made a short announcement* **utter**, give, deliver, give voice to, enunciate, recite, pronounce. **12** *the sofa makes a good bed* **be**, act as, serve as, function as, constitute, do duty for. **13** *he just made his train* **catch**, get, arrive/be in time for, arrive at, reach; get to.

– OPPOSITES destroy, lose, miss.

▸ **n. 1** *what is the car?* **brand**, marque, label. **2** *a man of a different make from his brother* **character**, nature, temperament, temper, disposition, kidney, mould, stamp.

□ **make as if/though** feign, pretend, make a show/pretence of, affect, feint, make out; informal put it on.

make away with 1 *she decided to make away with him* **kill**, murder, dispatch, eliminate; informal bump off, do away with, do in, do for, knock off, top, croak, stiff, blow away; N. Amer. informal ice, rub out, smoke, waste; literary slay. **2** *they made away with the evidence* **dispose of**, get rid of, destroy, throw away, jettison, ditch, dump; informal do away with.

make believe pretend, fantasize, daydream, build castles in the air, build castles in Spain, dream, imagine, play-act, play.

make do scrape by, scrape along, get by/along, manage, cope, survive, muddle along/through, improvise, make ends meet, keep the wolf from the door, keep one's head above water; informal make out; (**make do with**) make the best of, get by on, put up with.

make for 1 *she made for the door* **go for/towards**, head for/towards, aim for, make one's way towards, move towards, steer a course towards, be bound for, make a beeline for. **2** *constant arguing doesn't make for a happy marriage* **contribute to**, be conducive to, produce, promote, facilitate, foster; formal conduce to.

make it 1 *he never made it as a singer* **succeed**, be a success, distinguish oneself, get ahead, make good; informal make the grade, arrive, crack it. **2** *she's very ill—is she going to make it?* **survive**, come through, pull through, get better, recover.

make love See **have sex** at **sex**.

make off run away/off, take to one's heels, beat a hasty retreat, flee, make one's getaway, make a quick exit, run for it, make a run for it, take off, take flight, bolt, make oneself scarce, decamp, do a disappearing act; informal clear off/out, beat it, leg it, cut and run, skedaddle, vamoose, hightail it, hotfoot it, show a clean pair of heels, fly the coop, split, scoot, scram; Brit. informal scarper, do a runner; N. Amer. informal take a powder.

make off with take, steal, purloin, pilfer, abscond with, run away/off with, carry off, snatch; kidnap, abduct; informal walk away/off with, swipe, filch, snaffle, nab, lift, 'liberate', 'borrow', snitch; Brit. informal pinch, half-inch, nick, whip, knock off; N. Amer. informal heist, glom.

make out informal *how did you make out?* get on/along, fare, do, proceed, go, progress, manage, survive, cope, get by.

make something out 1 *I could just make out a figure in the distance* **see**, discern, distinguish, perceive, pick out, detect, observe, recognize; literary descry, espy. **2** *he couldn't make out what she was saying* **understand**, comprehend, follow, grasp, fathom, work out, make sense of, interpret, decipher, make head or tail of, get, get the drift of, catch. **3** *she made out that he was violent* **allege**, claim, assert, declare, maintain, affirm, suggest, imply, hint, insinuate, indicate, intimate, impute; formal aver. **4** *he made out a receipt for $20* **write out**, fill out, fill in, complete, draw up.

make something over to someone transfer, sign over, turn over, hand over/on/down, give, leave, bequeath, bestow, pass on, assign, consign, entrust; Law devolve, convey.

make up *let's kiss and make up* be friends again, bury the hatchet, declare a truce, make peace, forgive and forget, shake hands, become reconciled, settle one's differences, mend fences, call it quits.

make something up 1 *exports make up 42% of earnings* **comprise**, form, compose, constitute, account for. **2** *Gina brought a friend to make up a foursome* **complete**, round off, finish. **3** *the pharmacist made up the prescription* **prepare**, mix, concoct, put together. **4** *he made up an excuse* **invent**, fabricate, concoct, dream up, think up, hatch, trump up; devise, manufacture, formulate, coin; informal cook up. **5** *she made up her face* **apply make-up/cosmetics to**, powder, rouge; (**make oneself up**) informal put on one's face, do/paint one's face, apply one's warpaint, doll oneself up.

make up for 1 *she tried to make up for what she'd said* **atone for**, make amends for, compensate for, make recompense for, make reparation for, make redress for, make restitution for, expiate. **2** *job satisfaction can make up for low pay* **offset**, counterbalance, counteract, compensate for; balance, neutralize, cancel out, even up, redeem.

make up one's mind decide, come to a decision, make/reach a decision; come to a conclusion, reach a conclusion; determine, resolve.

make up to informal curry favour with, cultivate, try to win over, court, ingratiate oneself with; informal suck up to, butter up; N. Amer. informal shine up to; old use blandish.

make way move aside, clear the way, make a space, make room, stand back.

make-believe n. *that was sheer make-believe* **fantasy**, pretence, daydreaming, imagination, invention, fancy, dream, fabrication, play-acting, charade, masquerade.

– OPPOSITES reality.

▸ adj. *make-believe adventures* **imaginary**, imagined, made-up, fantasy, dreamed-up, fanciful, fictitious, fictive, feigned, fake, mock, sham, simulated; informal pretend, phoney.

– OPPOSITES real, actual.

maker n. **creator**, manufacturer, constructor, builder, producer, fabricator.

makeshift adj. **temporary**, provisional, stopgap, standby, rough and ready,

improvised, ad hoc, extempore, thrown together, cobbled together.
- OPPOSITES permanent.

make-up n. **1** *she used excessive make-up* **cosmetics**, maquillage; greasepaint, face paint; informal warpaint, slap. **2** *the cellular make-up of plants* **composition**, constitution, structure, configuration, arrangement, organization, formation. **3** *jealousy isn't part of his make-up* **character**, nature, temperament, personality, disposition, mentality, persona, psyche; informal what makes someone tick.

making n. **1** *the making of cars* **manufacture**, mass-production, building, construction, assembly, production, creation, putting together, fabrication, forming, moulding, forging. **2** *she has the makings of a champion* **qualities**, characteristics, ingredients; potential, promise, capacity, capability; essentials, essence, beginnings, rudiments, basics, stuff.
- OPPOSITES destruction.
  □ **in the making** *a hero in the making* budding, up and coming, emergent, developing, nascent, potential, promising, incipient.

maladjusted adj. **disturbed**, unstable, neurotic, unbalanced, unhinged, dysfunctional; informal mixed up, screwed up, hung up, messed up.
- OPPOSITES normal, stable.

maladministration n. formal **mismanagement**, mishandling, misgovernment, misrule, incompetence, inefficiency, bungling; malpractice, misconduct; Law malfeasance; formal malversation.
- OPPOSITES probity, efficiency.

maladroit adj. **bungling**, awkward, inept, clumsy, bumbling, incompetent, unskilful, heavy-handed, gauche, tactless, inconsiderate, undiplomatic, impolitic; informal ham-fisted, cack-handed.
- OPPOSITES adroit, skilful.

malady n. **illness**, sickness, disease, infection, ailment, disorder, complaint, indisposition, affliction, infirmity; informal bug, virus; Brit. informal lurgy; Austral. informal wog.

malaise n. **unhappiness**, uneasiness, unease, discomfort, melancholy, depression, despondency, dejection, angst, Weltschmerz, ennui; lassitude, listlessness, languor, weariness; indisposition, ailment, infirmity, illness, sickness, disease.
- OPPOSITES comfort, well-being.

malapropism n. **wrong word**, solecism, misuse, misapplication, infelicity, slip of the tongue.

malapropos adj. formal **inappropriate**, unsuitable, inapposite, infelicitous, inapt, unseemly, inopportune, ill-timed, untimely.

malcontent n. *a group of malcontents* **troublemaker**, mischief-maker, agitator, dissident, rebel; discontent, complainer, grumbler, moaner; informal stirrer, whinger,

grouch, bellyacher; N. Amer. informal kvetch.
▸ adj. *a malcontent employee* **disaffected**, discontented, dissatisfied, disgruntled, unhappy, annoyed, irritated, displeased, resentful; rebellious, dissentient, troublemaking, grumbling, complaining; informal browned off, hacked off, fed up, peeved, bellyaching; Brit. informal cheesed off, brassed off, not best pleased; N. Amer. informal teed off, ticked off.
- OPPOSITES happy.

male adj. *male sexual jealousy* **masculine**, virile, manly, macho, red-blooded.
- OPPOSITES female.
▸ n. *two males walked past*. See **man** (sense 1 of the noun).

malediction n. **curse**, damnation, oath; spell; N. Amer. hex; formal imprecation; literary anathema; old use execration.
- OPPOSITES blessing.

malefactor n. **wrongdoer**, miscreant, offender, criminal, culprit, villain, lawbreaker, felon, evildoer, delinquent, sinner, transgressor; informal crook, baddy; Austral. informal crim; Law malfeasant; old use trespasser.

malevolence n. **malice**, hostility, hate, hatred, ill will, enmity, ill feeling, balefulness, venom, rancour, malignity, vindictiveness, viciousness, vengefulness; literary maleficence.
- OPPOSITES benevolence.

malevolent adj. **malicious**, hostile, evil-minded, baleful, evil-intentioned, venomous, evil, malign, malignant, rancorous, vicious, vindictive, vengeful; literary malefic, maleficent.
- OPPOSITES benevolent.

malformation n. **deformity**, distortion, crookedness, misshapenness, disfigurement, abnormality, warp.

malformed adj. **deformed**, misshapen, misproportioned, ill-proportioned, disfigured, distorted, crooked, contorted, twisted, wry, warped; abnormal, grotesque, monstrous; Scottish thrawn.
- OPPOSITES perfect, normal, healthy.

malfunction v. *the computer has malfunctioned* **crash**, go wrong, break down, fail, stop working; informal conk out, go kaput, fall over, act up; Brit. informal play up, pack up.
▸ n. *a computer malfunction* **crash**, breakdown, fault, failure, bug; informal glitch.

malice n. **spite**, malevolence, ill will, vindictiveness, vengefulness, revenge, malignity, evil intentions, animus, enmity, rancour; informal bitchiness, cattiness; literary maleficence.
- OPPOSITES benevolence.

malicious adj. **spiteful**, malevolent, evil-intentioned, vindictive, vengeful, malign, mean, nasty, hurtful, mischievous, wounding, cruel, unkind; informal bitchy, catty; literary malefic, maleficent.
- OPPOSITES benevolent.

malign adj. *a malign influence* **harmful**, evil, bad, baleful, hostile, inimical, destructive,

m

malignant, injurious; literary malefic, maleficent.
– OPPOSITES beneficial.
▶ v. *he maligned an innocent man* **defame**, slander, libel, blacken someone's name/character, smear, vilify, speak ill of, cast aspersions on, run down, traduce, denigrate, disparage, slur, abuse, revile; informal bad-mouth, knock; Brit. informal rubbish, slag off; formal derogate, calumniate; rare asperse.
– OPPOSITES praise.

malignant adj. **1** *a malignant disease* **virulent**, very infectious, invasive, uncontrollable, dangerous, deadly, fatal, life-threatening. **2** *a malignant growth* **cancerous**; technical metastatic. **3** *a malignant thought* **spiteful**, malicious, malevolent, evil-intentioned, vindictive, vengeful, malign, mean, nasty, hurtful, mischievous, wounding, cruel, unkind; informal bitchy, catty; literary malefic, maleficent.
– OPPOSITES benign, benevolent.

malinger v. **pretend to be ill**, feign/fake illness, sham; shirk; informal put it on; Brit. informal skive, swing the lead; N. Amer. informal gold-brick.

malingerer n. **shirker**, idler, layabout; informal slacker; Brit. informal skiver, lead-swinger; N. Amer. informal gold brick.

mall n. **shopping precinct**, shopping centre, shopping complex, arcade, galleria; N. Amer. plaza.

malleable adj. **1** *a malleable substance* **pliable**, ductile, plastic, pliant, soft, workable. **2** *a malleable young woman* **easily influenced**, suggestible, susceptible, impressionable, pliable, amenable, compliant, tractable; biddable, complaisant, manipulable, persuadable, like putty in someone's hands.
– OPPOSITES hard, intractable.

malnutrition n. **undernourishment**, malnourishment, poor diet, inadequate diet, unhealthy diet, lack of food.

malodorous adj. **foul-smelling**, evil-smelling, fetid, smelly, stinking (to high heaven), reeking, rank, high, putrid, noxious; informal stinky; Brit. informal niffy, pongy, whiffy, humming; N. Amer. informal funky; literary noisome, mephitic.
– OPPOSITES fragrant.

malpractice n. **wrongdoing**, professional misconduct, breach of ethics, unprofessionalism, unethical behaviour; negligence, carelessness, incompetence.

maltreat v. **ill-treat**, mistreat, abuse, ill-use, misuse, mishandle; knock about/around, hit, beat, strike, manhandle, harm, hurt, persecute, molest; informal beat up, rough up, do over.

maltreatment n. **ill-treatment**, mistreatment, abuse, ill usage, ill usage, misuse, mishandling; violence, harm, persecution, molestation.

mammoth adj. **huge**, enormous, gigantic, giant, colossal, massive, vast, immense, mighty, stupendous, monumental,

Herculean, epic, prodigious, mountainous, monstrous, titanic, towering, elephantine, king-size(d), gargantuan, Brobdingnagian; informal mega, monster, whopping, humongous, bumper, jumbo, astronomical; Brit. informal whacking, whacking great, ginormous.
– OPPOSITES tiny.

man n. **1** *a handsome man* **male**, adult male, gentleman; youth; informal guy, fellow, geezer, gent; Brit. informal bloke, chap, lad, cove; Scottish & Irish informal bodach; N. Amer. informal dude, hombre; Austral./NZ informal digger. **2** *all men are mortal* **human being**, human, person, mortal, individual, personage, soul. **3** *the evolution of man* **the human race**, the human species, Homo sapiens, humankind, humanity, human beings, humans, people, mankind. **4** *the men voted to go on strike* **worker**, workman, labourer, hand, blue-collar worker. See also **staff** (sense 1 of the noun). **5** *have you met her new man?* **boyfriend**, partner, husband, spouse, lover, admirer, fiancé; common-law husband, live-in lover, significant other, cohabitee; informal fancy man, toy boy, sugar daddy, intended; N. Amer. informal squeeze; dated beau, steady, young man; old use leman. **6** *his man brought him a cocktail* **manservant**, valet, gentleman's gentleman, Jeeves, attendant, retainer; page, footman, flunkey; Military, dated batman; N. Amer. houseman.
▶ v. **1** *the office is manned from 9 a.m. to 5 p.m.* **staff**, crew, occupy, people. **2** *firemen manned the pumps* **operate**, work, use, utilize.
□ **man to man** frankly, openly, honestly, directly, candidly, plainly, forthrightly, without beating about the bush; woman to woman.
to a man without exception, with no exceptions, bar none, one and all, everyone, each and every one, unanimously, as one.

> **WORD LINKS**
>
> **male, masculine, virile** relating to men
> **machismo** strong or aggressive male pride
> **emasculate** deprive a man of his male role or identity
> **patriarchy** a system in which men hold the power
> **patrilineal** based on relationship with the father or male line of descent
> **spear side** the male side of a family
> **misandry** hatred of men
> **androcentric** focused or centred on men
> **yang** (in Chinese philosophy) the active male principle of the universe

manacle v. **shackle**, fetter, chain, put/clap in irons, handcuff, restrain; secure; informal cuff.

manacles plural n. **handcuffs**, shackles, chains, irons, fetters, restraints, bonds; informal cuffs, bracelets; Brit. old use darbies.

manage v. **1** *she manages a staff of 80 people* **be in charge of**, run, be head of, head, direct, control, preside over, lead, govern, rule, command, superintend, supervise, oversee, administer, organize, conduct, handle, guide, be at the helm of, helm; informal head up. **2** *how much work can you manage this week?* **accomplish**, achieve, do, carry out, perform, undertake, bring about/off, effect, finish; succeed in, contrive, engineer. **3** *will you be able to manage without him?* **cope**, get along/on, make do, be/fare/do all right, carry on, survive, get by, muddle through/along, fend for oneself, shift for oneself, make ends meet, weather the storm; informal make out, hack it. **4** *she can't manage that horse* **control**, handle, master; cope with, deal with.

manageable adj. **1** *a manageable amount of work* **achievable**, doable, practicable, possible, feasible, reasonable, attainable, viable. **2** *a manageable child* **compliant**, tractable, pliant, pliable, malleable, biddable, docile, amenable, governable, controllable, accommodating, acquiescent, complaisant, yielding. **3** *a manageable tool* **user-friendly**, easy to use, handy.
– OPPOSITES difficult, impossible.

management n. **1** *he's responsible for the management of the firm* **administration**, running, managing, organization; charge, care, direction, leadership, control, governing, governance, ruling, command, superintendence, supervision, overseeing, conduct, handling, guidance, operation. **2** *workers are in dispute with the management* **managers**, employers, directors, board of directors, board, directorate, executives, administrators, administration; owners, proprietors; informal bosses, top brass.

manager n. **1** *the works manager* **executive**, head of department, line manager, supervisor, principal, administrator, head, director, managing director, employer, superintendent, foreman, forewoman, overseer; proprietor; informal boss, chief, head honcho, governor; Brit. informal gaffer, guv'nor. **2** *the band's manager* **organizer**, controller, comptroller; impresario.

mandate n. **1** *he called an election to seek a mandate for his policies* **authority**, approval, acceptance, ratification, endorsement, sanction, authorization. **2** *a mandate from the UN* **instruction**, directive, decree, command, order, injunction, edict, charge, commission, bidding, ruling, fiat; formal ordinance.

mandatory adj. **obligatory**, compulsory, binding, required, requisite, necessary, essential, imperative.
– OPPOSITES optional.

manful adj. **brave**, courageous, bold, plucky, gallant, manly, heroic, intrepid, fearless, stout-hearted, valiant, valorous, dauntless, doughty; resolute, with gritted teeth, determined; informal gutsy, spunky.
– OPPOSITES cowardly.

manfully adv. **bravely**, courageously, boldly, gallantly, pluckily, heroically, intrepidly, fearlessly, valiantly, dauntlessly; resolutely, determinedly, hard, strongly, vigorously,

with might and main, like a Trojan; with all one's strength, to the best of one's abilities, as best one can, desperately.

mange n. **scabies**, scab, rash, eruption, skin infection.

manger n. **trough**, feeding trough, fodder rack, feeder, crib.

mangle v. **1** *the bodies were mangled beyond recognition* **mutilate**, maim, disfigure, damage, injure, crush; hack, cut up, lacerate, tear apart, butcher, maul. **2** *he's mangling the English language* **spoil**, ruin, mar, mutilate, make a mess of, wreck; informal murder, make a hash of, butcher.

mangy adj. **1** *a mangy cat* **scabby**, scaly, scabious, diseased. **2** *a mangy old armchair* **scruffy**, moth-eaten, shabby, worn; dirty, squalid, sleazy, seedy; informal tatty, the worse for wear, scuzzy; Brit. informal grotty.

manhandle v. **1** *he was manhandled by a gang of youths* **push**, shove, jostle, hustle; maltreat, ill-treat, mistreat, maul, molest; informal paw, rough up; N. Amer. informal roust. **2** *we manhandled the piano down the stairs* **heave**, haul, push, shove; pull, tug, drag, lug, carry, lift, manoeuvre; informal hump.

manhood n. **1** *the transition from boyhood to manhood* **maturity**, sexual maturity, adulthood. **2** *an insult to his manhood* **virility**, manliness, machismo, masculinity, maleness; mettle, spirit, strength, fortitude, determination, bravery, courage, intrepidity, valour, heroism, boldness.

mania n. **1** *fits of mania* **madness**, derangement, dementia, insanity, lunacy, psychosis, mental illness; delirium, frenzy, hysteria, raving, wildness. **2** *his mania for gadgets* **obsession**, compulsion, fixation, fetish, fascination, preoccupation, passion, enthusiasm, desire, urge, craving; craze, fad, rage; informal thing, yen.

maniac n. **1** *a homicidal maniac* **lunatic**, madman, madwoman, psychopath; informal loony, fruitcake, nutcase, nut, psycho, head case, headbanger, sicko; Brit. informal nutter, mentalist; N. Amer. informal screwball, crazy, meshuggener, wing nut. **2** informal *a football maniac* **enthusiast**, fan, devotee, aficionado; informal freak, fiend, fanatic, nut, buff, addict.

manic adj. **1** *a manic grin* **mad**, insane, deranged, demented, maniacal, lunatic, wild, crazed, demonic, hysterical, raving, unhinged, unbalanced; informal crazy. **2** *manic activity* **frenzied**, feverish, frenetic, hectic, intense; informal hyper, mad.
– OPPOSITES sane, calm.

manifest v. **1** *she manifested signs of depression* **display**, show, exhibit, demonstrate, betray, present, reveal; formal evince. **2** *strikes manifest bad industrial relations* **be evidence of**, be a sign of, indicate, show, attest, reflect, bespeak, prove, establish, evidence, substantiate, corroborate, confirm; literary betoken.
– OPPOSITES hide, mask.
▶adj. *his manifest lack of interest* **obvious**, clear, plain, apparent, evident, patent,

m

palpable, distinct, definite, blatant, overt, glaring, barefaced, explicit, transparent, conspicuous, undisguised, unmistakable, noticeable, perceptible, visible, recognizable.
– OPPOSITES secret.

manifestation n. 1 *the manifestation of anxiety* **display**, demonstration, show, exhibition, presentation. 2 *manifestations of global warming* **sign**, indication, evidence, token, symptom, testimony, proof, substantiation, mark, reflection, example, instance. 3 *a supernatural manifestation* **apparition**, appearance, materialization, visitation.

manifesto n. **policy statement**, mission statement, platform, programme, declaration, proclamation, pronouncement, announcement.

manifold adj. **many**, numerous, multiple, multifarious, legion, diverse, various, several, varied, different, miscellaneous, assorted, sundry; literary myriad, divers.

manikin n. **midget**, dwarf, homunculus, pygmy, Tom Thumb.

manipulate v. 1 *he manipulated some knobs and levers* **operate**, work; turn, pull. 2 *she manipulated the muscles of his back* **massage**, rub, knead, feel, palpate. 3 *the government tried to manipulate the situation* **control**, influence, use/turn to one's advantage, exploit, manoeuvre, engineer, steer, direct; twist someone round one's little finger. 4 *they accused him of manipulating the data* **falsify**, rig, distort, alter, change, doctor, massage, juggle, tamper with, tinker with, interfere with, misrepresent; informal cook, fiddle.

manipulative adj. **scheming**, calculating, cunning, crafty, wily, shrewd, devious, designing, conniving, Machiavellian, artful, guileful, slippery, slick, sly, unscrupulous, disingenuous; informal foxy.

manipulator n. **exploiter**, user, manoeuvrer, conniver, puppet master, wheeler-dealer; informal operator, thimblerigger.

mankind n. **the human race**, man, humanity, human beings, humans, Homo sapiens, humankind, people, men and women.

manly adj. 1 *his manly physique* **virile**, masculine, strong, all-male, muscular, muscly, strapping, well built, sturdy, robust, rugged, tough, powerful, brawny, red-blooded, vigorous; informal hunky. 2 *their manly deeds* **brave**, courageous, bold, valiant, valorous, fearless, plucky, macho, manful, intrepid, daring, heroic, lionhearted, gallant, chivalrous, swashbuckling, adventurous, stout-hearted, dauntless, doughty, resolute, determined, stalwart; informal gutsy, spunky.
– OPPOSITES effeminate, cowardly.

man-made adj. **artificial**, synthetic, manufactured; imitation, ersatz, simulated, mock, fake, false, faux, plastic.
– OPPOSITES natural, real.

mannequin n. 1 *mannequins in a shop window* **dummy**, model, figure. 2 *mannequins on the catwalk* **model**, fashion model, supermodel; informal clothes horse.

manner n. 1 *it was dealt with in a very efficient manner* **way**, fashion, mode, means, method, system, style, approach, technique, procedure, process, methodology, modus operandi, form. 2 old use *what manner of person is he?* **kind**, sort, type, variety, nature, breed, brand, stamp, class, category, genre, order. 3 *her rather unfriendly manner* **demeanour**, air, aspect, attitude, bearing, cast, behaviour, conduct; mien; formal comportment. 4 *the life and manners of Victorian society* **customs**, habits, ways, practices, conventions, usages. 5 *it's bad manners to stare* **behaviour**, conduct, way of behaving; form. 6 *you ought to teach him some manners* **correct behaviour**, etiquette, social graces, good form, protocol, politeness, decorum, propriety, gentility, civility, Ps and Qs, breeding; informal the done thing; old use convenances.

mannered adj. **affected**, pretentious, unnatural, artificial, contrived, stilted, stiff, forced, put-on, theatrical, actorly, precious, stagy, camp; informal pseudo.
– OPPOSITES natural.

mannerism n. **idiosyncrasy**, quirk, oddity, foible, trait, peculiarity, habit, characteristic.

mannerly adj. See **polite** (sense 1).

mannish adj. **unfeminine**, unwomanly, masculine, unladylike, Amazonian; informal butch.
– OPPOSITES feminine, girlish.

manoeuvre v. 1 *I manoeuvred the car into the space* **steer**, guide, drive, negotiate, navigate, pilot, direct, manipulate, move, work, jockey. 2 *he manoeuvred things to suit himself* **manipulate**, contrive, manage, engineer, devise, plan, fix, organize, arrange, set up, orchestrate, choreograph, stage-manage; informal wangle. 3 *he began manoeuvring for the party leadership* **intrigue**, plot, scheme, plan, lay plans, conspire, pull strings.
▶ n. 1 *a rather tricky parking manoeuvre* **operation**, exercise, activity, move, movement, action. 2 *diplomatic manoeuvres* **stratagem**, tactic, gambit, ploy, trick, dodge, ruse, plan, scheme, operation, device, plot, machination, artifice, subterfuge, intrigue. 3 *military manoeuvres* **training exercises**, exercises, war games, operations.

manse n. **minister's house**, vicarage, parsonage, rectory, deanery.

manservant n. **valet**, attendant, retainer, equerry, gentleman's gentleman, man, Jeeves; steward, butler, footman, flunkey, page, houseboy, lackey; N. Amer. houseman; Military, dated batman.

mansion n. **stately home**, hall, seat, manor, manor house, country house; informal palace, pile; formal residence.
– OPPOSITES hovel.

mantle n. **1** *a dark green velvet mantle* **cloak**, cape, shawl, wrap, stole; historical pelisse. **2** *a thick mantle of snow* **covering**, layer, blanket, sheet, veil, curtain, canopy, cover, cloak, pall, shroud. **3** *the mantle of leadership* **role**, burden, onus, duty, responsibility.
▸v. *heavy mists mantled the forest* **cover**, envelop, veil, cloak, curtain, shroud, swathe, wrap, blanket, conceal, hide, disguise, mask, obscure, surround, clothe; literary enshroud.

manual adj. **1** *manual work* **done with one's hands**, labouring, physical, blue-collar. **2** *a manual typewriter* **hand-operated**, hand, non-automatic.
▸n. *a training manual* **handbook**, instruction book, instructions, guide, companion, ABC, guidebook; informal bible.

manufacture v. **1** *the company manufactures laser printers* **make**, produce, mass-produce, build, construct, assemble, put together, create, fabricate, prefabricate, turn out, process, engineer. **2** *a story manufactured by the press* **make up**, invent, fabricate, concoct, hatch, dream up, think up, trump up, devise, formulate, frame, contrive; informal cook up.
▸n. *the manufacture of aircraft engines* **production**, making, manufacturing, mass-production, construction, building, assembly, creation, fabrication, prefabrication, processing.

manufacturer n. **maker**, producer, builder, constructor, creator; factory owner, industrialist, captain/baron of industry.

manure n. **dung**, muck, excrement, droppings, ordure, guano, cowpats; fertilizer; N. Amer. informal cow chips, horse apples.

manuscript n. **document**, text, script, paper, typescript; codex, palimpsest, scroll; autograph, holograph.

many determiner & adj. **1** *many animals were killed* **numerous**, a great/good deal of, a lot of, plenty of, countless, innumerable, scores of, crowds of, droves of, an army of, a horde of, a multitude of, a multiplicity of, multitudinous, multiple, untold; several, various, sundry, diverse, assorted, multifarious; copious, abundant, profuse, an abundance of, a profusion of; frequent; informal lots of, umpteen, loads of, masses of, stacks of, scads of, heaps of, piles of, bags of, tons of, oodles of, dozens of, hundreds of, thousands of, millions of, billions of, zillions of, a slew of, more —— than one can shake a stick at; Brit. informal a shedload of; N. Amer. informal gazillions of; Austral./NZ informal a swag of; literary myriad, divers. **2** *sacrificing the individual for the sake of the many* **the people**, the common people, the masses, the multitude, the populace, the public, the rank and file; derogatory the hoi polloi, the common herd, the mob, the proletariat, the riff-raff, the great unwashed, the proles.
– OPPOSITES few.

map n. **plan**, chart, cartogram; road map, A to Z, street plan, guide; atlas, globe; sketch map, relief map, contour map; Mercator projection, Peters projection; N. Amer. plat, plot.
▸v. *the region was mapped from the air* **chart**, plot, delineate, draw, depict, portray.
□ **map something out** outline, set out, lay out, sketch out, trace out, rough out, block out, delineate, detail, draw up, formulate, work out, frame, draft, plan, plot out, arrange, design, programme.

> **WORD LINKS**
>
> **cartography** the science of drawing maps
> **contour line** a line on a map joining points of equal height
> **isobar** a line on a map connecting points with the same atmospheric pressure
> **isotherm** a line on a map connecting points with the same temperature
> **orienteering** the sport of finding one's way across country using a map and compass

mar v. **1** *an ugly scar marred his features* **spoil**, impair, disfigure, detract from, blemish, scar; mutilate, deface, deform. **2** *the celebrations were marred by violence* **spoil**, ruin, impair, damage, wreck; harm, hurt, blight, taint, tarnish, sully, stain, pollute; informal foul up; formal vitiate.
– OPPOSITES enhance.

marauder n. **raider**, plunderer, pillager, looter, robber, pirate, freebooter, bandit, highwayman, rustler; literary brigand; old use buccaneer, corsair, reaver, cateran, mosstrooper.

marauding adj. **predatory**, rapacious, thieving, plundering, pillaging, looting, freebooting, piratical.

march v. **1** *the men marched past* **stride**, walk, troop, step, pace, tread; footslog, slog, tramp, hike, trudge; parade, file, process; Brit. informal yomp. **2** *she marched in without even knocking* **stalk**, stride, strut, flounce, storm, stomp, sweep. **3** *time marches on* **advance**, progress, move on, roll on.
▸n. **1** *a 20-mile march* **hike**, trek, tramp, slog, footslog, walk; route march, forced march; Brit. informal yomp. **2** *police sought to ban the march* **parade**, procession, march past, cortège; demonstration; informal demo. **3** *the march of technology* **progress**, advance, progression, development, evolution; passage.

marches plural n. *the Welsh marches* **borders**, boundaries, borderlands, frontiers; historical marcher lands.

margin n. **1** *the margin of the lake* **edge**, side, verge, border, perimeter, brink, brim, rim, fringe, boundary, limits, periphery, bound, extremity; literary marge, bourn, skirt. **2** *there's no margin for error* **leeway**, latitude, scope, room, room for manoeuvre, space, allowance, extra, surplus. **3** *they won by a narrow margin* **gap**, majority, amount, difference.

marginal adj. **1** *the difference is marginal* **slight**, small, tiny, minute, insignificant, minimal, negligible. **2** *a very marginal case* **borderline**, disputable, questionable, doubtful.

m

marijuana n. cannabis, hashish, bhang, hemp, kif, ganja, sinsemilla, skunkweed; informal dope, hash, grass, pot, blow, draw, the weed, skunk; Brit. informal wacky baccy; N. Amer. informal locoweed.

marinate v. souse, soak, steep, immerse, marinade.

marine adj. **1** *marine plants* seawater, sea, saltwater, oceanic; aquatic; technical pelagic, thalassic. **2** *a marine insurance company* maritime, nautical, naval; seafaring, seagoing, ocean-going.

mariner n. sailor, seaman, seafarer; informal Jack tar, tar, sea dog, salt, bluejacket, matelot; N. Amer. informal shellback.

marital adj. matrimonial, married, wedded, conjugal, nuptial, marriage, wedding; Law spousal; literary connubial, epithalamic.

maritime adj. **1** *maritime law* naval, marine, nautical; seafaring, seagoing, sea, ocean-going. **2** *maritime regions* coastal, seaside, littoral.

mark n. **1** *a dirty mark* blemish, streak, spot, fleck, dot, blot, stain, smear, speck, speckle, blotch, smudge, smut, fingermark, fingerprint; bruise, discoloration; birthmark; informal splotch, splodge; technical stigma; literary smirch. **2** *a punctuation mark* symbol, sign, character; diacritic. **3** *books bearing the mark of a well-known bookseller* logo, seal, stamp, imprint, symbol, emblem, device, insignia, badge, brand, trademark, monogram, hallmark, logotype, watermark. **4** *unemployment passed the three million mark* point, level, stage, degree. **5** *a mark of respect* sign, token, symbol, indication, badge, emblem; symptom, evidence, proof. **6** *the war left its mark on him* impression, imprint, traces; effect, impact, influence. **7** *the mark of a civilized society* characteristic, feature, trait, attribute, quality, hallmark, badge, stamp, property, indicator. **8** *he got good marks for maths* grade, grading, rating, score, percentage. **9** *the bullet missed its mark* target, goal, aim, bullseye; objective, object, end.
▶v. **1** *be careful not to mark the paintwork* discolour, stain, smear, smudge, streak, blotch, blemish; dirty, pockmark, bruise; informal splotch, splodge; literary smirch. **2** *her possessions were clearly marked* put one's name on, name, initial, label; hallmark, watermark, brand. **3** *I've marked the relevant passages* indicate, label, flag, tick; show, identify, designate, delineate, denote. **4** *a festival to mark the town's 200th anniversary* celebrate, observe, recognize, acknowledge, keep, honour, solemnize, pay tribute to, salute, commemorate, remember, memorialize. **5** *the incidents marked a new phase in their campaign* represent, signify, be a sign of, indicate, herald. **6** *his style is marked by simplicity and concision* characterize, distinguish, identify, typify, brand, signalize, stamp. **7** *I have a pile of essays to mark* assess, evaluate, appraise, correct; N. Amer. grade. **8** *it'll cause trouble, you mark my words!* take heed of, pay heed to, heed, listen to, take note of, pay attention to, attend to, note, mind, bear in mind, take into consideration.
□ **make one's mark** be successful, distinguish oneself, succeed, be a success, prosper, get ahead/on, make good; informal make it, make the grade, find a place in the sun.

mark something down reduce, decrease, lower, cut, put down, discount; informal slash.

mark someone out 1 *his honesty marked him out from the rest* set apart, separate, single out, differentiate, distinguish. **2** *she is marked out for fame* destine, ordain, predestine, preordain.

mark something up increase, raise, up, put up, hike (up), escalate; informal jack up.

quick off the mark alert, quick, quick-witted, bright, clever, perceptive, sharp, sharp-witted, observant, wide awake, on one's toes; informal on the ball, quick on the uptake.

wide of the mark inaccurate, incorrect, wrong, erroneous, off target, off beam, out, mistaken, misguided, misinformed.

marked adj. noticeable, pronounced, decided, distinct, striking, clear, glaring, blatant, unmistakable, obvious, plain, manifest, patent, palpable, prominent, signal, significant, conspicuous, notable, recognizable, identifiable, distinguishable, discernible, apparent, evident; written all over one.
– OPPOSITES imperceptible.

market n. **1** shopping centre, marketplace, mart, flea market, bazaar, souk, fair; old use emporium. **2** *there's no market for such goods* demand, call, want, desire, need, requirement. **3** *the market is sluggish* trade, trading, business, commerce, buying and selling, dealing.
▶v. *the product was marketed worldwide* sell, retail, vend, merchandise, trade, peddle, hawk; advertise, promote.
□ **on the market** on sale, (up) for sale, on offer, available, obtainable; N. Amer. on the block.

marksman, **markswoman** n. sniper, sharpshooter, good shot; informal crack shot; N. Amer. informal deadeye, shootist.

maroon v. strand, cast away, cast ashore; abandon, leave behind, leave, leave in the lurch, desert; informal leave high and dry.

marriage n. **1** *a proposal of marriage* (holy) matrimony, wedlock. **2** *the marriage took place at St Margaret's* wedding, nuptials, union; old use espousal. **3** *a marriage of jazz, pop, and gospel* union, alliance, fusion, mixture, mix, blend, amalgamation, combination, merger.
– OPPOSITES divorce, separation.

WORD LINKS

conjugal, connubial, marital, matrimonial, nuptial relating to marriage

monogamy the practice of having only one husband or wife at a time

bigamy the crime of marrying someone while

already married to another person
polygamy the practice of having more than one husband or wife at a time
dowry property or money brought by a bride to her marriage
trousseau the clothes and other belongings collected by a bride for her marriage
elope run away secretly to get married
spouse a husband or wife
bachelor a man who has never been married
spinster a woman who has never been married

married adj. **1** *a married couple* **wedded**, wed; informal spliced, hitched. **2** *married bliss* **marital**, matrimonial, conjugal, nuptial; Law spousal; literary connubial.
– OPPOSITES single.

marrow n. *the marrow of his statement* **essence**, core, nucleus, pith, kernel, heart, quintessence, gist, substance, sum and substance, meat, nub; informal nitty-gritty.

marry v. **1** *the couple married last year* **get/be married**, wed, be wed, become man and wife, plight/pledge one's troth; informal tie the knot, walk down the aisle, take the plunge, get spliced, get hitched, say 'I do'. **2** *John wanted to marry her* **wed**; informal make an honest woman of; old use espouse. **3** *the show marries poetry with art* **join**, unite, combine, fuse, mix, blend, merge, amalgamate, link, connect, couple, knit, yoke.
– OPPOSITES divorce, separate.

marsh n. **swamp**, marshland, bog, peat bog, swampland, morass, mire, quagmire, slough, fen, fenland, wetland; N. Amer. bayou; Scottish & N. English moss; old use quag.

> **WORD LINKS**
> **paludal** relating to marshes
> **will-o'-the-wisp, ignis fatuus** a flickering light seen at night over marshes

marshal v. **1** *the king marshalled an army* **assemble**, gather together, collect, muster, call together, draw up, line up, align, array, organize, group, arrange, deploy, position, order, dispose; mobilize, rally, round up. **2** *guests were marshalled to their seats* **usher**, guide, escort, conduct, lead, shepherd, steer, take.

marshy adj. **boggy**, swampy, muddy, squelchy, soggy, waterlogged, miry, fenny; Scottish & N. English mossy; Ecology paludal.
– OPPOSITES dry, firm.

martial adj. **military**, soldierly, soldier-like, army, naval; warlike, fighting, combative, militaristic; informal gung-ho.

martinet n. **disciplinarian**, slave-driver, stickler for discipline, (hard) taskmaster, authoritarian, tyrant.

martyr v. **put to death**, kill, martyrize; burn, burn at the stake, immolate, stone to death, throw to the lions, crucify.

martyrdom n. **death**, suffering, torture, torment, agony, ordeal; killing, sacrifice, crucifixion, immolation, burning, auto-da-fé; Christianity Passion.

marvel v. *she marvelled at their courage* **be amazed**, be astonished, be surprised, be awed, stand in awe, wonder; stare, gape, goggle, not believe one's eyes/ears, be dumbfounded; informal be flabbergasted.
▸ n. *the marvels of technology* **wonder**, miracle, sensation, spectacle, phenomenon; informal something else, something to shout about, eye-opener.

marvellous adj. **1** *his solo climb was marvellous* **amazing**, astounding, astonishing, awesome, breathtaking, sensational, remarkable, spectacular, stupendous, staggering, stunning; phenomenal, prodigious, miraculous, extraordinary, incredible, unbelievable; literary wondrous. **2** *marvellous weather* **excellent**, splendid, wonderful, magnificent, superb, glorious, sublime, lovely, delightful, too good to be true; informal super, great, amazing, fantastic, terrific, tremendous, sensational, heavenly, divine, gorgeous, grand, fabulous, fab, awesome, to die for, magic, ace, wicked, mind-blowing, far out, out of this world; Brit. informal smashing, brilliant, brill; N. Amer. informal boss; Austral./NZ informal beaut, bonzer; Brit. informal dated champion, wizard, corking, ripping, spiffing, top-hole; N. Amer. informal dated swell.
– OPPOSITES commonplace, awful.

masculine adj. **1** *a masculine trait* **male**, man's, men's. **2** *a powerfully masculine man* **virile**, macho, manly, all-male, muscular, muscly, strong, strapping, well built, rugged, robust, brawny, powerful, red-blooded, vigorous; informal hunky. **3** *a rather masculine woman* **mannish**, unfeminine, unwomanly, unladylike, Amazonian; informal butch.
– OPPOSITES feminine, effeminate.

masculinity n. **virility**, manliness, maleness, machismo, vigour, strength, muscularity, ruggedness, robustness.

mash v. *mash the potatoes* **pulp**, crush, purée, cream, smash, squash, pound, beat.
▸ n. *first pound the garlic to a mash* **pulp**, purée, mush, paste.

mask n. **1** *she wore a mask to conceal her face* **disguise**, false face; historical domino, visor; old use vizard. **2** *he dropped his mask of good humour* **pretence**, semblance, veil, screen, front, false front, facade, veneer, blind, false colours, disguise, guise, concealment, cover, cover-up, cloak, camouflage.
▸ v. *poplar trees masked the factory* **hide**, conceal, disguise, cover up, obscure, screen, cloak, camouflage, veil.

masquerade n. **1** *a grand masquerade* **masked ball**, masque, fancy-dress party. **2** *he couldn't keep up the masquerade much longer* **pretence**, deception, pose, act, front, facade, disguise, dissimulation, cover-up, bluff, play-acting, make-believe; informal put-on.
▸ v. *a woman masquerading as a man* **pretend to be**, pose as, pass oneself off as, impersonate, disguise oneself as; formal personate.

Mass n. **Eucharist**, Holy Communion, Communion, the Lord's Supper.

mass n. **1** *a soggy mass of fallen leaves* **pile**, heap; accumulation, aggregation, accretion, concretion, build-up. **2** *a mass of cyclists* **crowd**, horde, large group, throng, host, troop, army, herd, flock, drove, swarm, mob, pack, press, crush, flood, multitude. **3** *the mass of the population* **majority**, greater part/number, best/better part, major part, most, bulk, main body, lion's share. **4** **the common people**, the populace, the public, the people, the rank and file, the crowd, the third estate; derogatory the hoi polloi, the mob, the proletariat, the common herd, the great unwashed. **5** informal *masses of food.* See **lot** (pronoun).
▸ adj. *mass hysteria* **widespread**, general, wholesale, universal, large-scale, extensive, pandemic.
▸ v. *they began massing troops in the region* **assemble**, marshal, gather together, muster, round up, mobilize, rally.

massacre n. **1** *a cold-blooded massacre of innocent civilians* **slaughter**, wholesale/mass slaughter, indiscriminate killing, mass murder, mass execution, annihilation, liquidation, decimation, extermination; carnage, butchery, bloodbath, bloodletting, pogrom, genocide, ethnic cleansing, holocaust, Shoah, night of the long knives; literary slaying. **2** informal *the match was an 8–0 massacre.* See **rout** (sense 2 of the noun).
▸ v. **1** *thousands were brutally massacred* **slaughter**, butcher, murder, kill, annihilate, exterminate, execute, liquidate, eliminate, decimate, wipe out, mow down, cut down, put to the sword, put to death; literary slay. **2** informal *they were massacred in the final.* See **trounce**.

massage n. **rub**, rub-down, rubbing, kneading, palpation, manipulation, pummelling; shiatsu, reflexology, acupressure, hydromassage, Swedish massage, osteopathy; effleurage, Rolfing, tapotement.
▸ v. **1** *he massaged her tired muscles* **rub**, knead, palpate, manipulate, pummel, work. **2** *the statistics have been massaged* **alter**, tamper with, manipulate, doctor, falsify, juggle, fiddle with, tinker with, distort, change, rig, interfere with, misrepresent; informal fix, cook, fiddle.

massive adj. **huge**, enormous, vast, immense, large, big, mighty, great, colossal, tremendous, prodigious, gigantic, gargantuan, mammoth, monstrous, monumental, giant, towering, elephantine, mountainous, titanic; epic, Herculean, Brobdingnagian; informal monster, jumbo, mega, whopping, humongous, hulking, bumper, astronomical; Brit. informal whacking, ginormous.
– OPPOSITES tiny.

mast n. **1** *a ship's mast* **spar**, boom, yard, gaff, foremast, mainmast, topmast, mizzenmast, mizzen, royal mast. **2** *the mast on top of the building* **flagpole**, flagstaff, pole, post, rod, upright; aerial, transmitter, pylon.

master n. **1** historical *he acceded to his master's wishes* **lord**, overlord, lord and master, ruler, sovereign, monarch, liege (lord), suzerain. **2** *the dog's master* **owner**, keeper. **3** *a chess master* **expert**, adept, genius, past master, maestro, virtuoso, professional, doyen, authority; informal ace, pro, wizard, whizz, hotshot; Brit. informal dab hand; N. Amer. informal maven, crackerjack. **4** *the master of the ship* **captain**, commander; informal skipper. **5** *the geography master* **teacher**, schoolteacher, schoolmaster, tutor, instructor, preceptor; formal pedagogue. **6** *their spiritual master* **guru**, teacher, leader, guide, mentor; swami, Maharishi; Roshi.
– OPPOSITES servant, amateur, pupil.
▸ v. **1** *I managed to master my fears* **overcome**, conquer, beat, quell, quash, suppress, control, overpower, triumph over, subdue, vanquish, subjugate, prevail over, govern, curb, check, bridle, tame, defeat, get the better of, get a grip on, get over; informal lick. **2** *it took ages to master the technique* **learn**, become proficient in, know inside out, know backwards; pick up, grasp, understand; informal get the hang of.
▸ adj. **1** *a master craftsman* **expert**, adept, proficient, skilled, skilful, deft, dexterous, adroit, practised, experienced, masterly, accomplished, complete, demon, brilliant; informal crack, ace, mean, wizard; N. Amer. informal crackerjack. **2** *the master bedroom* **principal**, main, chief; biggest.

masterful adj. **1** *a masterful man* **commanding**, powerful, imposing, magisterial, lordly, authoritative; dominating, domineering, overbearing, overweening, imperious. **2** *their masterful handling of the situation* **expert**, adept, clever, masterly, skilful, skilled, adroit, proficient, deft, dexterous, accomplished, polished, consummate; informal crack, ace.
– OPPOSITES weak, inept.

masterly adj. See **masterful** (sense 2).

mastermind v. *he masterminded the whole campaign* **plan**, control, direct, be in charge of, run, conduct, organize, arrange, preside over, orchestrate, stage-manage, engineer, manage, coordinate; conceive, devise, originate, initiate, think up, frame, hatch, come up with; informal be the brains behind.
▸ n. *the mastermind behind the project* **genius**, mind, intellect, author, architect, organizer, originator, prime mover, initiator, inventor; informal brain, brains, bright spark.

masterpiece n. **chef-d'œuvre**, pièce de résistance, masterwork, magnum opus, finest/best work, tour de force.

master stroke n. **stroke of genius**, coup, triumph, coup de maître, tour de force.

mastery n. **1** *her mastery of the language* **proficiency**, ability, capability; knowledge, understanding, comprehension, familiarity, command, grasp, grip. **2** *they played with tactical mastery* **skill**, skilfulness, expertise, dexterity, finesse, adroitness, virtuosity, prowess, deftness, proficiency; informal know-how. **3** *man's mastery over nature*

m

control, domination, command, ascendancy, supremacy, pre-eminence, superiority; triumph, victory, the upper hand, the whip hand, rule, government, power, sway, authority, jurisdiction, dominion, sovereignty.

masticate v. **chew**, munch, champ, chomp, crunch, eat; ruminate, chew the cud; formal manducate.

mat n. **1** *the hall mat* **rug**, runner, carpet, drugget; doormat, hearthrug; dhurrie, numdah; kilim, flokati; N. Amer. floorcloth. **2** *he placed his glass on the mat* **coaster**, doily; Brit. drip mat. **3** *a thick mat of hair* **mass**, tangle, knot, mop, thatch, shock, mane.
▸ v. *his hair was matted with blood* **tangle**, entangle, knot, ravel, snarl up.

match n. **1** *a football match* | *a boxing match* **contest**, competition, game, tournament, tie, cup tie, event, fixture, trial, test, meet, bout, fight; friendly, (local) derby; play-off, replay, rematch; Brit. clash; old use tourney. **2** *he was no match for the champion* **equal**, rival, equivalent, peer, counterpart; formal compeer. **3** *the vase was an exact match of the one she already owned* **lookalike**, double, twin, duplicate, mate, fellow, companion, counterpart, pair; replica, copy; informal spitting image, spit and image, dead spit, dead ringer. **4** *a love match* **marriage**, betrothal, relationship, partnership, union.
▸ v. **1** *the curtains matched the duvet cover* **go with**, coordinate with, complement, suit; be the same as, be similar to. **2** *did their statements match?* **correspond**, be in agreement, tally, agree, match up, coincide, accord, conform, square. **3** *no one can match him at chess* **equal**, be a match for, measure up to, compare with, parallel, be in the same league as, be on a par with, touch, keep pace with, keep up with, emulate, rival, vie with, compete with, contend with; informal hold a candle to.
□ **match up to** measure up to, come up to, meet with, be equal to, be as good as, satisfy, fulfil, answer to.

matching adj. **corresponding**, equivalent, parallel, analogous; coordinating, complementary, toning; paired, twin, identical, like, like (two) peas in a pod, alike.
– OPPOSITES different, clashing.

matchless adj. **incomparable**, unrivalled, inimitable, beyond compare/comparison, unparalleled, unequalled, without equal, peerless, second to none, unsurpassed, unsurpassable, nonpareil, unique, consummate, perfect, rare, transcendent, surpassing; formal unexampled.

matchmaker n. **marriage broker**, shadchan; marriage bureau, dating agency; go-between.

mate n. **1** Brit. informal *he's gone out with his mates* **friend**, companion, boon companion, intimate, familiar, confidant; playmate, playfellow, schoolmate, classmate, workmate; informal pal, chum; Brit. informal china, mucker; N. English informal marrer; N. Amer. informal buddy, amigo, compadre, homeboy; old use compeer. **2** *she's finally found her ideal mate* **partner**, husband, wife, spouse, lover, live-in lover, significant other, companion, helpmate, helpmeet, consort; informal better half, hubby, missus, missis; Brit. informal other half, dutch, trouble and strife. **3** *I can't find the mate to this sock* **match**, fellow, twin, companion, pair, other half, equivalent. **4** *a plumber's mate* **assistant**, helper, apprentice.
▸ v. *pandas rarely mate in captivity* **breed**, couple, copulate.

material n. **1** *the decomposition of organic material* **matter**, substance, stuff, medium. **2** *the materials for a new building* **constituent**, raw material, element, component. **3** *cleaning materials* **things**, items, articles, stuff, necessaries; Brit. informal gubbins. **4** *curtain material* **fabric**, cloth, textiles. **5** *material for a magazine article* **information**, data, facts, facts and figures, statistics, evidence, details, particulars, background, notes; informal info, gen, dope, low-down.
▸ adj. **1** *the material world* **physical**, corporeal, tangible, non-spiritual, mundane, worldly, earthly, secular, temporal, concrete, real, solid, substantial. **2** *she was too fond of material pleasures* **sensual**, physical, carnal, corporal, fleshly, bodily. **3** *information that could be material to the inquiry* **relevant**, pertinent, applicable, germane; apropos, to the point; vital, essential, key. **4** *the storms caused material damage* **significant**, major, important.
– OPPOSITES spiritual, aesthetic, irrelevant.

materialistic adj. **consumerist**, acquisitive, money-oriented, greedy; worldly, capitalistic, bourgeois.

materialize v. **1** *the forecast investment boom did not materialize* **happen**, occur, come about, take place, come into being, transpire; informal come off; formal eventuate; literary come to pass. **2** *Harry materialized at the door* **appear**, turn up, arrive, make/put in an appearance, present oneself/itself, emerge, surface, reveal oneself/itself, show one's face, pop up; informal show up, fetch up, pitch up.

materially adv. **significantly**, greatly, much, very much, to a great extent, considerably, substantially, a great deal, appreciably, markedly, fundamentally, seriously, gravely.

maternal adj. **1** *her maternal instincts* **motherly**, protective, caring, nurturing, loving, devoted, affectionate, fond, warm, tender, gentle, kind, kindly, comforting. **2** *his maternal grandparents* **on one's mother's side**, on the distaff side.

mathematical adj. **1** *mathematical symbols* **arithmetical**, numerical; statistical, algebraic, geometric, trigonometric. **2** *mathematical precision* **rigorous**, meticulous, scrupulous, punctilious, scientific, strict, precise, exact, accurate, pinpoint, correct, careful, unerring.

m

matrimonial adj. **marital**, conjugal, married, wedded; nuptial; Law spousal; literary connubial.

matrimony n. **marriage**, wedlock, union; nuptials.
– OPPOSITES divorce.

matted adj. **tangled**, tangly, knotted, knotty, tousled, dishevelled, uncombed, unkempt, ratty; black English natty.

matter n. **1** *decaying vegetable matter* **material**, substance, stuff. **2** *the heart of the matter* **affair**, business, proceeding, situation, circumstance, event, happening, occurrence, incident, episode, experience; subject, topic, issue, question, point, point at issue, case, concern. **3** *it is of little matter now* **importance**, consequence, significance, note, import, weight; formal moment. **4** *what's the matter?* **problem**, trouble, difficulty, complication; upset, worry. **5** *the matter of the sermon* **content**, subject matter, text, argument, substance. **6** *an infected wound full of matter* **pus**, suppuration, purulence, discharge.
▶ v. *it doesn't matter what you wear* **be important**, make any/a difference, be of importance, be of consequence, signify, be relevant, count; informal cut any ice.
□ **as a matter of fact** actually, in (actual) fact, in point of fact, as it happens, really, believe it or not, in reality, in truth, to tell the truth.

matter-of-fact adj. **unemotional**, practical, down-to-earth, sensible, realistic, rational, sober, unsentimental, pragmatic, businesslike, commonsensical, level-headed, hard-headed, no-nonsense, factual, literal, straightforward, plain, unembellished, unvarnished, unadorned.

mature adj. **1** *a mature woman* **adult**, grown-up, grown, fully grown, full-grown, of age, fully developed, in one's prime. **2** *he's very mature for his age* **sensible**, responsible, adult, level-headed, reliable, dependable; wise, discriminating, shrewd, sophisticated. **3** *mature cheese* **ripe**, ripened, mellow; ready to eat/drink. **4** *on mature reflection, he decided not to go* **careful**, thorough, deep, considered.
– OPPOSITES adolescent, childish.
▶ v. **1** *kittens mature when they are about a year old* **be fully grown**, be full-grown; grow up, come of age, reach adulthood, reach maturity. **2** *leave the cheese to mature* **ripen**, mellow; age. **3** *their friendship didn't have time to mature* **develop**, grow, evolve, bloom, blossom, flourish, thrive.

maturity n. **1** *her progress from childhood to maturity* **adulthood**, majority, coming of age, manhood/womanhood. **2** *he displayed a maturity beyond his years* **responsibility**, sense, level-headedness; wisdom, discrimination, shrewdness, sophistication.

maudlin adj. **1** *maudlin self-pity* **sentimental**, over-sentimental, emotional, overemotional, tearful; informal weepy; formal lachrymose. **2** *a maudlin ballad* **mawkish**, sentimental, over-sentimental, mushy, slushy, sloppy; Brit. twee; informal schmaltzy, cheesy, corny, toe-curling; Brit. informal soppy; N. Amer. informal cornball, three-hankie.

maul v. **1** *he had been mauled by a lion* **savage**, attack, tear to pieces, lacerate, claw, scratch. **2** *she hated being mauled by men* **molest**, feel, fondle, manhandle; informal grope, paw, touch up. **3** *his book was mauled by the critics.* See **criticize**.

maunder v. **1** *he maundered on about his problems* **ramble**, prattle, blather, blether, rattle, chatter, jabber, babble; informal yak, yatter; Brit. informal rabbit, witter, waffle, natter, chunter. **2** *she maundered across the road* **wander**, drift, meander, amble, potter; Brit. informal mooch.

mausoleum n. **tomb**, sepulchre, crypt, vault, charnel house, burial chamber, catacomb, undercroft.

maverick n. **individualist**, free spirit, nonconformist, unorthodox person, original, eccentric; rebel, dissenter, dissident; informal bad boy.
– OPPOSITES conformist.

maw n. **mouth**, jaws, muzzle; throat, gullet; informal trap, chops, kisser; Brit. informal gob.

mawkish adj. **sentimental**, maudlin, mushy, slushy, sloppy, cloying, sickly, saccharine, sugary, syrupy, nauseating; Brit. twee; informal schmaltzy, weepy, cutesy, lovey-dovey, cheesy, corny, sick-making, toe-curling; Brit. informal soppy; N. Amer. informal cornball, hokey, three-hankie.

maxim n. **saying**, adage, aphorism, proverb, motto, saw, axiom, apophthegm, dictum, precept, epigram; truism, cliché.

maximum adj. *the maximum amount* **greatest**, highest, biggest, largest, top, topmost, most, utmost, maximal.
▶ n. *production levels are near their maximum* **upper limit**, limit, utmost, uttermost, greatest, most, extremity, peak, height, ceiling, top.
– OPPOSITES minimum.

maybe adv. **perhaps**, possibly, conceivably, it could be, it is possible, for all one knows; N. English happen; literary peradventure, perchance.

mayhem n. **chaos**, disorder, havoc, bedlam, pandemonium, tumult, uproar, turmoil, commotion, all hell broken loose, maelstrom, trouble, disturbance, confusion, riot, anarchy, violence; informal madhouse.

maze n. **labyrinth**, complex network, warren; web, tangle, jungle, snarl.

meadow n. **field**, paddock; pasture, pastureland; literary lea, mead.

meagre adj. **1** *their meagre earnings* **inadequate**, scanty, scant, paltry, limited, restricted, modest, insufficient, sparse, deficient, negligible, skimpy, slender, poor, miserable, pitiful, puny, miserly, niggardly, beggarly; informal measly, stingy, pathetic, piddling; formal exiguous. **2** *a tall, meagre man* **thin**, lean, skinny, spare, scrawny, scraggy, gangling, gangly, spindly, stringy, bony,

raw-boned, gaunt, underweight, underfed, undernourished, emaciated, skeletal, cadaverous.
– OPPOSITES abundant, fat.

meal n. snack; feast, banquet; informal bite (to eat), spread, blowout, feed; Brit. informal nosh-up; formal repast, collation; literary refection.

> **WORD LINKS**
>
> **prandial** relating to meals
> **appetizer, hors d'oeuvre** a small dish of food eaten before a meal to stimulate the appetite
> **entrée** the main course of a meal
> **dessert** (Brit. **pudding**) the sweet course at the end of a meal

mean[1] v. **1** *flashing lights mean the road is blocked* **signify**, convey, denote, designate, indicate, connote, show, express, spell out; stand for, represent, symbolize; imply, suggest, intimate, hint at, insinuate, drive at, refer to, allude to; literary betoken. **2** *she didn't mean to break it* **intend**, aim, plan, design, have in mind, contemplate, purpose, propose, set out, aspire, desire, want, wish, expect. **3** *he was hit by a bullet meant for a soldier* **intend**, design; destine, predestine. **4** *the closures will mean a rise in unemployment* **entail**, involve, necessitate, lead to, result in, give rise to, bring about, cause, engender, produce. **5** *this means a lot to me* **matter**, be important, be significant. **6** *a red sky in the morning usually means rain* **presage**, portend, foretell, augur, promise, foreshadow, herald, signal, bode; literary betoken, foretoken.

mean[2] adj. **1** *he's too mean to leave a tip* **miserly**, niggardly, close-fisted, parsimonious, penny-pinching, cheese-paring, Scrooge-like; informal tight-fisted, stingy, tight, mingy, money-grubbing; N. Amer. informal cheap; formal penurious; old use near, niggard. **2** *a mean trick* **unkind**, nasty, unpleasant, spiteful, malicious, unfair, cruel, shabby, foul, despicable, contemptible, horrible, obnoxious, vile, odious, loathsome, base, low; informal horrid, hateful, rotten, low-down; Brit. informal beastly. **3** *the truth was obvious to even the meanest intelligence* **inferior**, poor, limited, restricted. **4** *her flat was mean and cold* **squalid**, shabby, dilapidated, sordid, seedy, slummy, sleazy, insalubrious, wretched, dismal, dingy, miserable, run down, down at heel; informal scruffy, scuzzy, crummy, grungy; Brit. informal grotty. **5** *a man of mean birth* **lowly**, humble, ordinary, low, low-born, modest, common, base, proletarian, plebeian, obscure, undistinguished, ignoble; old use baseborn. **6** informal *he's a mean cook.* See **excellent**.
– OPPOSITES generous, kind, luxurious, noble.

mean[3] n. *a mean between saving and splashing out* **middle course**, middle way, midpoint, happy medium, golden mean, compromise, balance; median, norm, average.
▶ adj. *the mean temperature* **average**, median, middle, medial, medium, normal, standard.

meander v. **1** *the river meandered gently* **zigzag**, wind, twist, turn, curve, curl, bend, snake. **2** *we meandered along the path* **stroll**, saunter, amble, wander, ramble, drift, maunder; Scottish stravaig; informal mosey, tootle.

meandering adj. **1** *a meandering stream* **winding**, windy, zigzag, twisting, turning, curving, serpentine, sinuous, twisty. **2** *meandering reminiscences* **rambling**, maundering, circuitous, roundabout, digressive, discursive, indirect, tortuous, convoluted.
– OPPOSITES straight, succinct.

meaning n. **1** *the meaning of his remark* **significance**, sense, signification, import, gist, thrust, drift, implication, tenor, message, essence, substance, purport, intention. **2** *the word has several different meanings* **definition**, sense, explanation, denotation, connotation, interpretation. **3** *my life has no meaning* **value**, validity, worth, consequence, account, use, usefulness, significance, point. **4** *his smile was full of meaning* **expressiveness**, significance, eloquence, implications, insinuations.

> **WORD LINKS**
>
> **semantic** relating to meaning
> **synonym** a word having the same meaning as another
> **antonym** a word having the opposite meaning to another

meaningful adj. **1** *a meaningful remark* **significant**, relevant, important, consequential, telling, material, valid, worthwhile. **2** *a meaningful relationship* **sincere**, deep, serious, in earnest, significant, important. **3** *a meaningful glance* **expressive**, eloquent, pointed, significant, meaning; pregnant, speaking, telltale, revealing, suggestive.
– OPPOSITES inconsequential.

meaningless adj. **1** *a jumble of meaningless words* **unintelligible**, incomprehensible, incoherent. **2** *she felt her life was meaningless* **futile**, pointless, aimless, empty, hollow, vain, purposeless, valueless, useless, of no use, worthless, senseless, trivial, trifling, unimportant, insignificant, inconsequential.
– OPPOSITES worthwhile.

means plural n. **1** *the best means to achieve your goal* **method**, way, manner, mode, measure, technique, expedient, agency, medium, instrument, channel, vehicle, avenue, course, process, procedure. **2** *she doesn't have the means to support herself* **money**, resources, capital, income, finance, funds, cash, the wherewithal, assets; informal dough, bread; Brit. informal dosh, brass, lolly, spondulicks, ackers. **3** *a man of means* **wealth**, riches, affluence, substance, fortune, property, money, capital.
□ **by all means** of course, certainly, definitely, surely, absolutely, with pleasure; N. Amer. informal sure thing.

m

by means of using, utilizing, employing, through, with the help of; as a result of, by dint of, by way of, by virtue of.

by no means not at all, in no way, not in the least, not in the slightest, not the least bit, not by a long shot, certainly not, absolutely not, definitely not, on no account, under no circumstances; Brit. not by a long chalk; informal no way.

meantime adv. See **meanwhile**.

meanwhile adv. **1** *meanwhile, I'll stay here* **for now**, for the moment, for the present, for the time being, meantime, in the meantime, in the interim, in the interval. **2** *cook for a further half hour; meanwhile, make the stuffing* **at the same time**, simultaneously, concurrently, the while.

measurable adj. **1** *a measurable amount* **quantifiable**, assessable, gaugeable, computable. **2** *a measurable improvement* **appreciable**, noticeable, significant, visible, perceptible, definite, obvious.

measure v. **1** *they measured the length of the room* **calculate**, compute, count, meter, quantify, weigh, size, evaluate, assess, gauge, plumb, determine. **2** *I had better measure my words* **choose carefully**, consider, plan. **3** *she did not need to measure herself against some ideal* **compare with**, pit against, set against, test against, judge by.

▶n. **1** *cost-cutting measures* **action**, act, course (of action), deed, proceeding, procedure, step, means, expedient; manoeuvre, initiative, programme, operation. **2** *the Senate passed the measure* **statute**, act, bill, law, legislation. **3** *the original dimensions were in imperial measure* **system**, standard, units, scale. **4** *use a measure to check the size* **ruler**, tape measure, rule, gauge, meter, scale, level, yardstick. **5** *a measure of egg white* **quantity**, amount, portion. **6** *the states retain a measure of independence* **certain amount**, degree; some. **7** *sales are the measure of the company's success* **yardstick**, test, standard, barometer, touchstone, litmus test, criterion, benchmark. **8** *poetic measure* **metre**, cadence, rhythm; foot.
□ **beyond measure** immensely, extremely, vastly, greatly, excessively, immeasurably, incalculably, infinitely.
for good measure as a bonus, as an extra, into the bargain, to boot, in addition, besides, as well.
get/have the measure of evaluate, assess, gauge, judge, weigh up; understand, fathom, read, be wise to, see through; informal have someone's number.
measure something off mark off, measure out, demarcate, delimit, delineate, outline, describe, define, stake out.
measure up pass muster, match up, come up to standard, fit/fill the bill, be acceptable; informal come up to scratch, make the grade, cut the mustard, be up to snuff.
measure someone up evaluate, rate, assess, appraise, judge, weigh up; informal size up.
measure up to meet, come up to, equal,

match, bear comparison with, be on a level with; achieve, satisfy, fulfil.

measured adj. **1** *his measured tread* **regular**, steady, even, rhythmic, rhythmical, unfaltering; slow, dignified, stately, sedate, leisurely, unhurried. **2** *his measured tones* **thoughtful**, careful, carefully chosen, studied, calculated, planned, considered, deliberate, restrained.

measureless adj. **boundless**, limitless, unlimited, unbounded, untold, immense, vast, endless, cosmic, inexhaustible, infinite, illimitable, immeasurable, incalculable.
– OPPOSITES limited.

measurement n. **1** *measurement of the effect is difficult* **quantification**, computation, calculation, mensuration; evaluation, assessment, gauging. **2** *all measurements are given in metric form* **size**, dimension, proportions, magnitude, amplitude; mass, bulk, volume, capacity, extent; value, amount, quantity, area, length, height, depth, weight, width, range.

meat n. **1** *flesh*, animal flesh. **2** *old use meat and drink* **food**, nourishment, sustenance, provisions, rations, fare, foodstuff(s), provender, daily bread; informal grub, eats, chow, nosh, scoff; formal comestibles; dated victuals; literary viands; old use commons. **3** *the meat of the matter* **substance**, pith, marrow, heart, kernel, core, nucleus, nub, essence, essentials, gist, fundamentals, basics; informal nitty-gritty.

> **WORD LINKS**
>
> **carnivore** an animal that feeds on meat
> **carnivorous** feeding on meat
> **butcher** a person whose trade is cutting up and selling meat

meaty adj. **1** *a tall, meaty young man* **beefy**, brawny, burly, muscular, muscly, powerful, sturdy, strapping, well built, solidly built, thickset; fleshy, stout. **2** *a good, meaty story* **interesting**, thought-provoking, three-dimensional, stimulating; substantial, satisfying, meaningful, deep, profound.

mechanical adj. **1** *a mechanical device* **mechanized**, machine-driven, automated, automatic, power-driven, robotic. **2** *a mechanical response* **automatic**, unthinking, robotic, involuntary, reflex, knee-jerk, habitual, routine, unemotional, unfeeling, lifeless; perfunctory, cursory, careless, casual.
– OPPOSITES manual, conscious.

mechanism n. **1** *an electrical mechanism* **machine**, piece of machinery, appliance, apparatus, device, instrument, contraption, gadget; informal gizmo. **2** *the train's safety mechanism* **machinery**, workings, works, movement, action, gears, components. **3** *a formal mechanism for citizens to lodge complaints* **procedure**, process, system, operation, method, technique, means, medium, agency, channel.

mechanize v. **automate**, industrialize, motorize, computerize.

medal n. **decoration**, ribbon, star, badge, laurel, palm, award; honour; Military slang fruit salad; Brit. informal gong.

meddle v. **1** *don't meddle in my affairs* **interfere**, butt in, intrude, intervene, pry; informal poke one's nose in, horn in on, muscle in on, snoop, put/stick one's oar in; N. Amer. informal kibitz. **2** *someone had been meddling with her things* **fiddle**, interfere, tamper, tinker, finger; Brit. informal muck about/around.

meddlesome adj. **interfering**, meddling, intrusive, prying, busybody; informal nosy, nosy-parker.

mediate v. **1** *Austria tried to mediate between the belligerents* **arbitrate**, conciliate, moderate, act as peacemaker, make peace; intervene, step in, intercede, act as an intermediary, liaise. **2** *a tribunal was set up to mediate disputes* **resolve**, settle, arbitrate in, umpire, reconcile, referee; mend, clear up; informal patch up. **3** *he attempted to mediate a solution to the conflict* **negotiate**, bring about, effect; formal effectuate.

mediation n. **arbitration**, conciliation, reconciliation, intervention, intercession, good offices; negotiation, shuttle diplomacy.

mediator n. **arbitrator**, arbiter, negotiator, conciliator, peacemaker, go-between, middleman, intermediary, moderator, intervenor, intercessor, broker, honest broker, liaison officer; umpire, referee, adjudicator, judge.

medicinal adj. **curative**, healing, remedial, therapeutic, restorative, corrective, health-giving; medical; old use sanative.

medicine n. **medication**, medicament, drug, prescription, dose, treatment, remedy, cure; nostrum, panacea, cure-all; old use physic.

WORD LINKS

pharmaceutical relating to medicine
dispensary a room where medicines are prepared
pharmacy (Brit. **chemist**; N. Amer. **drugstore**) a shop selling medicines
codex, formulary, pharmacopoeia an official list of medicinal drugs with directions for their use or prescription

---

medieval adj. **1** *medieval times* **of the Middle Ages**, of the Dark Ages, Dark-Age; Gothic. **2** informal *the plumbing's a bit medieval* **primitive**, antiquated, archaic, antique, antediluvian, old-fashioned, out of date, outdated, outmoded, anachronistic, passé, obsolete; informal out of the ark; N. Amer. informal horse-and-buggy, clunky.
– OPPOSITES modern.

mediocre adj. **ordinary**, average, middling, middle-of-the-road, uninspired, undistinguished, indifferent, unexceptional, unexciting, unremarkable, run-of-the-mill, pedestrian, prosaic, lacklustre, forgettable, amateur, amateurish; informal OK, so-so, (plain) vanilla, fair-to-middling, no great shakes, not up to much; Brit. informal not much cop; N. Amer. informal bush-league; NZ informal half-pie.
– OPPOSITES excellent.

meditate v. **contemplate**, think, consider, ponder, muse, reflect, deliberate, ruminate, chew the cud, brood, mull over; be in a brown study, be deep/lost in thought, debate with oneself; pray; informal put on one's thinking cap; formal cogitate.

meditation n. **contemplation**, thought, thinking, musing, pondering, consideration, reflection, deliberation, rumination, brooding, reverie, brown study, concentration; prayer; formal cogitation.

meditative adj. **pensive**, thoughtful, contemplative, reflective, musing, ruminative, introspective, brooding, deep/lost in thought, in a brown study; prayerful; formal cogitative.

medium n. **1** *using technology as a medium for job creation* **means**, method, way, form, agency, avenue, channel, vehicle, organ, instrument, mechanism. **2** *organisms growing in their natural medium* **habitat**, element, environment, surroundings, milieu, setting, conditions. **3** *she consulted a medium* **spiritualist**, spiritist, necromancer. **4** *a happy medium* **middle way**, middle course, middle ground, middle, mean, median, midpoint; compromise, golden mean.
▶ adj. *medium height* **average**, middling, medium-sized, middle-sized, moderate, normal, standard.

medley n. **assortment**, miscellany, mixture, melange, variety, mixed bag, mix, collection, selection, potpourri, patchwork; motley collection, ragbag, gallimaufry, mishmash, hotchpotch, jumble; N. Amer. hodgepodge.

meek adj. **submissive**, yielding, obedient, compliant, tame, biddable, tractable, acquiescent, deferential, timid, unprotesting, unresisting, like a lamb to the slaughter; quiet, mild, gentle, docile, lamblike, shy, diffident, unassuming, self-effacing.
– OPPOSITES assertive.

meet v. **1** *I met an old friend on the train* **encounter**, meet up with, come face to face with, run into, run across, come across/upon, chance on, happen on, light on, stumble across/on; informal bump into, hook up with. **2** *she first met Paul at a party* **get to know**, be introduced to, make the acquaintance of. **3** *the committee met on Saturday* **assemble**, gather, come together, get together, congregate, convene; formal foregather. **4** *the place where three roads meet* **converge**, connect, touch, link up, intersect, cross, join. **5** *he met death bravely* **face**, encounter, undergo, experience, go through, suffer, endure, bear; cope with, handle. **6** *the announcement was met with widespread hostility* **greet**, receive, answer, treat. **7** *he does not meet the job's requirements* **fulfil**, satisfy, fill, measure up to, match (up to), conform to, come up to, comply with, answer. **8** *shipowners would meet the cost of oil spills* **pay**, settle, clear, honour, discharge, pay off, square.
▶ n. *an athletics meet*. See **meeting** (sense 5).
□ **meet someone halfway** See **halfway**.

m

meeting n. **1** *he stood up to address the meeting* **gathering**, assembly, conference, congregation, convention, summit, forum, convocation, conclave, council of war, rally; N. Amer. caucus; informal get-together. **2** *she demanded a meeting with the minister* **consultation**, audience, interview. **3** *he intrigued her on their first meeting* **encounter**, contact; appointment, assignation, rendezvous, tweetup; literary tryst. **4** *the meeting of land and sea* **convergence**, coming together, confluence, conjunction, union, junction, abutment; intersection, T-junction, crossing. **5** *an athletics meeting* **event**, tournament, meet, rally, competition, match, game, contest.

megalomania n. **delusions of grandeur**, folie de grandeur, thirst for power; self-importance, egotism, conceit, conceitedness.

melancholy adj. *a melancholy expression* **sad**, sorrowful, unhappy, desolate, mournful, lugubrious, gloomy, despondent, dejected, depressed, downhearted, downcast, disconsolate, glum, miserable, wretched, dismal, morose, woeful, woebegone, doleful, joyless, heavy-hearted; informal down in the dumps, down in the mouth, blue.
– OPPOSITES cheerful.
▶ n. *a feeling of melancholy* **sadness**, sorrow, unhappiness, woe, desolation, melancholia, dejection, depression, despondency, gloom, gloominess, misery; informal the dumps, the blues.

melange n. **mixture**, medley, assortment, blend, variety, mixed bag, mix, miscellany, selection, potpourri, patchwork; motley collection, ragbag, gallimaufry, mishmash, hotchpotch, jumble; N. Amer. hodgepodge.

melee, mêlée n. **fracas**, disturbance, rumpus, tumult, commotion, disorder, fray; brawl, fight, scuffle, struggle, skirmish, free-for-all, tussle; informal scrap, set-to, ruction; N. Amer. informal rough house.

mellifluous adj. **sweet-sounding**, dulcet, honeyed, mellow, soft, liquid, silvery, soothing, rich, smooth, euphonious, harmonious, tuneful, musical.
– OPPOSITES cacophonous.

mellow adj. **1** *the mellow tone of his voice* **dulcet**, sweet-sounding, tuneful, melodious, mellifluous; soft, smooth, warm, full, rich. **2** *a mellow wine* **full-bodied**, mature, well matured, full-flavoured, rich, smooth. **3** *a mellow mood* **genial**, affable, amiable, good-humoured, good-natured, amicable, pleasant, relaxed, easy-going; jovial, jolly, cheerful, happy, merry.

melodious adj. **tuneful**, melodic, musical, mellifluous, dulcet, sweet-sounding, silvery, silvery-toned, harmonious, euphonious, lyrical; informal easy on the ear.
– OPPOSITES discordant.

melodramatic adj. **exaggerated**, histrionic, extravagant, overdramatic, overdone, over-sensational, sensationalized, overemotional, sentimental; theatrical, stagy, actressy, actorly; informal hammy.

melody n. **1** *familiar melodies* **tune**, air, strain, theme, song, refrain, piece of music. **2** *his unique gift for melody* **melodiousness**, tunefulness, lyricism, musicality, euphony.

melt v. **1** *the snow was beginning to melt* **liquefy**, thaw, defrost, soften, dissolve, deliquesce. **2** *his smile melted her heart* **soften**, disarm, touch, affect, move. **3** *his anger melted away* **vanish**, disappear, fade away, dissolve, evaporate; literary evanesce.

member n. **1** *a member of the club* **subscriber**, associate, fellow, life member, founder member, card-carrying member. **2** *a member of a mathematical set* **constituent**, element, component, part, portion, piece, unit. **3** old use *many victims had injured members* **limb**, organ; arm, leg, appendage.

membrane n. **layer**, sheet, skin, film, tissue, integument, overlay; technical pellicle.

memento n. **souvenir**, keepsake, reminder, remembrance, token, memorial; trophy, relic.

memoir n. **1** *a touching memoir of her childhood* **account**, history, record, chronicle, narrative, story, portrayal, depiction, sketch, portrait, profile, biography, monograph. **2** *he published his memoirs in 1955* **autobiography**, life story, life, memories, recollections, reminiscences; journal, diary, log, blog, vlog.

memorable adj. **unforgettable**, indelible, catchy, haunting; momentous, significant, historic, notable, noteworthy, important, consequential, remarkable, special, signal, outstanding, extraordinary, striking, vivid, arresting, impressive, distinctive, distinguished, famous, celebrated, renowned, illustrious, glorious.

memorandum n. **1** *a memorandum from the managing director* **message**, communication, note, email, letter, missive; informal memo. **2** *hasty memoranda and jottings-down* **record**, minute, note, aide-memoire, reminder.

memorial n. **1** *the war memorial* **monument**, cenotaph, mausoleum; statue, plaque, cairn; shrine; tombstone, gravestone, headstone. **2** *the Festschrift is a memorial to his life's work* **tribute**, testimonial; remembrance, memento.
▶ adj. *a memorial service* **commemorative**, remembrance, commemorating; monumental.

memorize v. **commit to memory**, remember, learn by heart, get off by heart, learn, learn by rote, become word-perfect in, get off pat; old use con.

memory n. **1** *she is losing her memory* **ability to remember**, powers of recall. **2** *happy memories of her young days* **recollection**, remembrance, reminiscence; impression. **3** *the town built a statue in memory of him* **commemoration**, remembrance; honour, tribute, recognition, respect. **4** *a computer's memory* **memory bank**, store, cache, disk, RAM, ROM.

menace n. **1** *an atmosphere full of menace* **threat**, ominousness, intimidation, warning, ill omen. **2** *a menace to British society* **danger**, peril, risk, hazard, threat; jeopardy. **3** *that child is a menace* **nuisance**, pest, annoyance, plague, torment, troublemaker, mischief-maker, thorn in someone's side/ flesh.
▶v. **1** *the elephants are still menaced by poaching* **threaten**, be a danger to, put at risk, jeopardize, imperil. **2** *a gang of skinheads menaced local residents* **intimidate**, threaten, terrorize, frighten, scare, terrify.

menacing adj. **threatening**, ominous, intimidating, frightening, terrifying, alarming, forbidding, black, thunderous, glowering, unfriendly, hostile, sinister, baleful, warning; formal minatory.
– OPPOSITES friendly.

mend v. **1** *workmen were mending faulty cabling* **repair**, fix, piece together, restore; sew (up), stitch, darn, patch, cobble; rehabilitate, renew, renovate; informal patch up. **2** *'How's Walter?' 'He'll mend.'* **get better**, get well, recover, recuperate, improve; be well, be cured, heal. **3** *quarrels could be mended by talking* **put/set right**, set straight, straighten out, sort out, rectify, remedy, cure, right, resolve, square, settle, put to rights, correct, retrieve, improve, make better. **4** *he mended the fire* **stoke (up)**, make up, add fuel to.
– OPPOSITES break, worsen.

mendacious adj. **lying**, untruthful, dishonest, deceitful, false, dissembling, insincere, disingenuous, hypocritical, fraudulent, double-dealing, two-faced, Janus-faced, two-timing, duplicitous, perjured; untrue, fictitious, falsified, fabricated, fallacious, invented, made up; euphemistic economical with the truth; literary perfidious.
– OPPOSITES truthful.

mendicant n. **beggar**, tramp, vagrant, vagabond; N. Amer. hobo; informal scrounger, sponger; N. Amer. informal bum, mooch, moocher, schnorrer.

menial adj. *a menial job* **unskilled**, lowly, humble, low-grade, low-status, inferior, degrading; routine, humdrum, boring, dull.
▶n. *they were treated like menials* **servant**, drudge, minion, factotum, lackey, galley slave; informal wage slave, gofer; Brit. informal dogsbody, skivvy; N. Amer. informal peon; old use scullion.

menstruation n. **periods**, menses, menorrhoea, menstrual cycle; menarche; informal the curse, monthlies, time of the month.

mensuration n. **measurement**, measuring, calculation, computation, quantification.

mental adj. **1** *mental faculties* **intellectual**, cerebral, brain, rational, cognitive. **2** *a mental disorder* **psychiatric**, psychological, psychogenic. **3** informal *he's completely mental.* See **mad** (sense 1).
– OPPOSITES physical.

mentality n. **1** *I can't understand the mentality of these people* **way of thinking**, mind set, cast of mind, frame of mind, turn of mind, mind, psychology, mental attitude, outlook, disposition, make-up. **2** *a person of limited mentality* **intellect**, intellectual capabilities, intelligence, IQ, (powers of) reasoning, rationality.

mentally adv. **in one's mind**, in one's head, inwardly, intellectually, cognitively.

mention v. **1** *don't mention the war* **allude to**, refer to, touch on; bring up, raise, broach, introduce, moot. **2** *Jim mentioned that he'd met them before* **state**, say, indicate, let someone know, disclose, divulge, reveal. **3** *I'll gladly mention your work to my friends* **recommend**, commend, put in a good word for, speak well of.
▶n. **1** *he made no mention of your request* **reference**, allusion, remark, statement, announcement, indication. **2** *a mention in dispatches* **tribute**, citation, acknowledgement, recognition. **3** *my book got a mention on the show* **recommendation**, commendation, a good word.
□ **not to mention** in addition to, as well as; not counting, not including, to say nothing of, aside from, besides.

mentor n. **1** *his political mentors* **adviser**, guide, guru, counsellor, consultant; confidant(e). **2** *regular meetings between mentor and trainee* **trainer**, teacher, tutor, instructor.

menu n. **bill of fare**, carte du jour, set menu, table d'hôte; list.

mercantile adj. **commercial**, trade, trading, business, merchant, sales.

mercenary adj. **1** *mercenary self-interest* **money-oriented**, grasping, greedy, acquisitive, avaricious, covetous, bribable, venal, materialistic; informal money-grubbing. **2** *mercenary soldiers* **hired**, paid, bought, professional.
▶n. *a group of mercenaries* **soldier of fortune**, professional soldier, hired soldier; informal hired gun; historical freelance, condottiere.

merchandise n. *a wide range of merchandise* **goods**, wares, stock, commodities, lines, produce, products, solutions.
▶v. *a new product that can be easily merchandised* **promote**, market, sell, retail; advertise, publicize, push; informal hype (up), plug.

merchant n. **trader**, dealer, wholesaler, broker, agent, seller, buyer, buyer and seller, vendor, distributor; trademark in US e-tailer; Brit. informal flogger.

merciful adj. **1** *God is merciful* **forgiving**, compassionate, clement, pitying, forbearing,

m

lenient, humane, mild, kind, soft-hearted, tender-hearted, gracious, sympathetic, humanitarian, liberal, tolerant, indulgent, generous, magnanimous, benign, benevolent. **2** *a merciful silence fell* **welcome**, blessed.
– OPPOSITES cruel.
□ **be merciful to** have mercy on, have pity on, show mercy to, spare, pardon, forgive, be lenient on/to; informal go/be easy on, let off.

mercifully adv. **luckily**, fortunately, happily, thank goodness/God/heavens.

merciless adj. **ruthless**, remorseless, pitiless, unforgiving, unsparing, implacable, inexorable, relentless, inflexible, inhumane, inhuman, unsympathetic, unfeeling, intolerant, rigid, severe, cold-blooded, hard-hearted, stony-hearted, heartless, harsh, callous, cruel, brutal, barbarous, cut-throat.
– OPPOSITES compassionate.

mercurial adj. **volatile**, capricious, temperamental, excitable, fickle, changeable, unpredictable, variable, protean, mutable, erratic, quicksilver, inconstant, inconsistent, unstable, unsteady, fluctuating, ever-changing, moody, flighty, wayward, whimsical, impulsive; technical labile.
– OPPOSITES stable.

mercy n. **1** *he showed no mercy to the others* **leniency**, clemency, compassion, grace, pity, charity, forgiveness, forbearance, quarter, humanity; soft-heartedness, tender-heartedness, kindness, sympathy, liberality, indulgence, tolerance, generosity, magnanimity, beneficence. **2** *we must be thankful for small mercies* **blessing**, godsend, boon, favour, piece/stroke of luck.
– OPPOSITES ruthlessness, cruelty.
□ **at the mercy of 1** *they found themselves at the mercy of the tyrant* **in the power of**, under/in the control of, in the clutches of, under the heel of, subject to. **2** *he was at the mercy of the elements* **defenceless against**, vulnerable to, exposed to, susceptible to, prey to, (wide) open to.

mere adj. **no more than**, just, only, merely; no better than.

merely adv. **only**, purely, solely, simply, just, but.

meretricious adj. **worthless**, valueless, cheap, tawdry, trashy, Brummagem, tasteless, kitsch; false, artificial, fake, imitation; informal tacky.

merge v. **1** *the company merged with a European firm* **join (together)**, join forces, amalgamate, unite, affiliate, team up, link (up). **2** *the two organizations were merged* **amalgamate**, bring together, join, consolidate, conflate, unite, unify, combine, incorporate, integrate, link (up), knit, yoke. **3** *the two colours merged* **mingle**, blend, fuse, mix, intermix, intermingle, coalesce; literary commingle.
– OPPOSITES separate.

merger n. **amalgamation**, combination, union, fusion, coalition, affiliation, unification, incorporation, consolidation,

link-up, alliance.
– OPPOSITES split.

merit n. **1** *composers of outstanding merit* **excellence**, quality, calibre, worth, worthiness, credit, value, distinction, eminence. **2** *the merits of the scheme* **good point**, strong point, advantage, benefit, value, asset, plus.
– OPPOSITES inferiority, fault, disadvantage.
▸ v. *the accusation did not merit a response* **deserve**, earn, be deserving of, warrant, rate, justify, be worthy of, be worth, be entitled to, have a right to, have a claim to/on.

meritorious adj. **praiseworthy**, laudable, commendable, admirable, estimable, creditable, worthy, deserving, excellent, exemplary, good.
– OPPOSITES discreditable.

merriment n. **high spirits**, high-spiritedness, exuberance, cheerfulness, gaiety, fun, effervescence, verve, buoyancy, levity, zest, liveliness, cheer, joy, joyfulness, joyousness, jolliness, jollity, happiness, gladness, jocularity, conviviality, festivity, merrymaking, revelry, mirth, glee, gleefulness, laughter, hilarity, light-heartedness, amusement, pleasure.
– OPPOSITES misery.

merry adj. **1** *merry throngs of students* **cheerful**, cheery, in high spirits, high-spirited, bright, sunny, smiling, light-hearted, buoyant, lively, carefree, without a care in the world, joyful, joyous, jolly, convivial, festive, mirthful, gleeful, happy, glad, laughing; informal chirpy; formal jocund; dated gay; literary blithe, blithesome. **2** Brit. informal *after three beers he began to feel quite merry* **tipsy**, mellow, slightly drunk; Brit. informal tiddly, squiffy.
– OPPOSITES miserable.
□ **make merry** have fun, enjoy oneself, celebrate, carouse, feast, {eat, drink, and be merry}, revel, roister; informal party, have a ball.

merry-go-round n. **carousel**; Brit. roundabout.

mesh n. **1** *wire mesh* **netting**, net, network; web, webbing, lattice, latticework. **2** *a mesh of political intrigue* **entanglement**, net, tangle, web.
▸ v. **1** *one gear meshes with the input gear* **engage**, connect, lock, interlock. **2** *our ideas just do not mesh* **harmonize**, fit together, match, dovetail.

mesmerize v. **enthral**, spellbind, entrance, dazzle, bewitch, charm, captivate, enchant, fascinate, transfix, grip, hypnotize.

mess n. **1** *please clear up the mess* **untidiness**, disorder, disarray, clutter, shambles, jumble, muddle, chaos; Brit. informal tip. **2** *cat mess* **excrement**, muck, faeces, excreta. **3** *I've got to get out of this mess* **plight**, predicament, tight spot/corner, difficulty, trouble, quandary, dilemma, problem, muddle, mix-up, imbroglio; informal jam, fix, pickle, stew, hole, scrape. **4** *he made a mess of the project* **muddle**, bungle; informal botch, hash, foul-up;

Brit. informal cock-up; N. Amer. informal snafu.

□ **make a mess of** mismanage, mishandle, bungle, fluff, spoil, ruin, wreck; informal mess up, botch, make a hash of, muck up, foul up; Brit. informal make a pig's ear of, make a Horlicks of, cock up.

mess about/around potter about, pass the time, fiddle about/around, footle about/ around, play about/around, fool about/ around; fidget, toy, trifle, tamper, tinker, interfere, meddle, monkey (about/around); informal piddle about/around; Brit. informal muck about/around, lark (about/around).

mess something up 1 *he messed up my kitchen* dirty; clutter up, disarrange, jumble, dishevel, rumple; N. Amer. informal muss up; literary befoul. **2** informal *Eddie messed things up.* See **make a mess of**.

message n. **1** *are there any messages for me?* **communication**, piece of information, news, note, memorandum, memo, email, posting, tweet, letter, missive, report, bulletin, communiqué, dispatch. **2** *the message of his teaching* **meaning**, sense, import, idea; point, thrust, gist, essence, content, subject (matter), substance, implication, drift, lesson.

□ **get the message** informal understand, get the point, comprehend; informal catch on, latch on, get the picture.

messenger n. **message-bearer**, postman, courier, runner, dispatch rider, envoy, emissary, agent, go-between; historical herald; old use legate.

messy adj. **1** *messy oil spills | messy hair* **dirty**, filthy, grubby, soiled, grimy; mucky, muddy, slimy, sticky, sullied, spotted, stained, smeared, smudged; dishevelled, scruffy, unkempt, rumpled, matted, tousled, bedraggled, tangled; informal yucky; Brit. informal gungy. **2** *a messy kitchen* **disorderly**, disordered, in a muddle, chaotic, confused, disorganized, in disarray, disarranged; untidy, cluttered, in a jumble; informal like a bomb's hit it; Brit. informal shambolic. **3** *a messy legal battle* **complex**, intricate, tangled, confused, convoluted; unpleasant, nasty, bitter, acrimonious.

– OPPOSITES clean, tidy.

metallic adj. **1** *a metallic sound* **tinny**, jangling, jingling, grating, harsh, jarring, dissonant. **2** *metallic paint* **metallized**, burnished; shiny, glossy, lustrous.

metamorphose v. **transform**, change, mutate, transmute, transfigure, convert, alter, modify, remodel, recast, reconstruct; humorous transmogrify; formal transubstantiate.

metamorphosis n. **transformation**, mutation, transmutation, change, alteration, conversion, modification, remodelling, reconstruction; humorous transmogrification; formal transubstantiation.

metaphor n. **figure of speech**, image, trope, analogy, comparison, symbol, word painting/ picture.

metaphorical adj. **figurative**, allegorical, symbolic; imaginative, extended.

– OPPOSITES literal.

metaphysical adj. **1** *metaphysical questions* **abstract**, theoretical, conceptual, notional, philosophical, speculative, intellectual, academic. **2** *Good and Evil are inextricably linked in a metaphysical battle* **transcendental**, spiritual, supernatural, paranormal.

mete v.
□ **mete something out** dispense, hand out, allocate, allot, apportion, issue, deal out, dole out, dish out, assign, administer.

meteor n. **falling star**, shooting star, meteorite, meteoroid, bolide.

meteoric adj. **rapid**, lightning, swift, fast, quick, speedy, accelerated, instant, sudden, spectacular.

– OPPOSITES gradual.

meteorologist n. **weather forecaster**, met officer, weatherman, weatherwoman.

method n. **1** *they use very old-fashioned methods* **procedure**, technique, system, practice, routine, modus operandi, process; strategy, tactic, plan. **2** *there's method in his madness* **order**, orderliness, organization, structure, form, system, logic, planning, design.

– OPPOSITES disorder.

methodical adj. **orderly**, well ordered, well organized, (well) planned, efficient, businesslike, systematic, structured, logical, analytic, disciplined; meticulous, punctilious.

meticulous adj. **careful**, conscientious, diligent, scrupulous, punctilious, painstaking, accurate; thorough, studious, rigorous, detailed, perfectionist, fastidious, methodical, particular.

– OPPOSITES careless.

métier n. **1** *he had another métier besides the priesthood* **occupation**, job, work, profession, business, employment, career, vocation, trade, craft, line (of work); N. Amer. specialty. **2** *television is more my métier* **forte**, strong point, strength, speciality, talent, bent; informal thing, cup of tea.

metropolis n. **capital (city)**, chief town, county town; big city, conurbation, megalopolis; informal big smoke; old use wen.

mettle n. **1** *a man of mettle* **spirit**, fortitude, strength of character, moral fibre, steel, determination, resolve, resolution, backbone, grit, courage, courageousness, bravery, valour, fearlessness, daring; informal guts, spunk; Brit. Dunkirk spirit; Brit. informal bottle. **2** *Frazer was of a very different mettle* **calibre**, character, disposition, nature, temperament, personality, make-up, stamp.

mettlesome adj. **spirited**, game, gritty, intrepid, fearless, courageous, brave, plucky, daring; tenacious, determined, resolved, resolute, indomitable.

mew v. **1** *the cat mewed plaintively* **miaow**, mewl, cry. **2** *above them, seagulls mewed* **cry**, screech.

mewl v. **whimper**, cry, whine; informal grizzle; literary pule.

m

microbe n. **microorganism**, bacillus, bacterium, virus, germ; informal bug.

microscopic adj. **tiny**, very small, minute, infinitesimal, minuscule, nanoscopic; little, micro, diminutive; Scottish wee; informal teeny, weeny, teeny-weeny, teensy-weensy, itsy-bitsy; Brit. informal titchy, tiddly.
– OPPOSITES huge.

midday n. **noon**, twelve noon, high noon, noontide, noonday.
– OPPOSITES midnight.

middle n. **1** *a shallow dish with a spike in the middle* **centre**, midpoint, halfway point, dead centre, focus, hub; eye, heart, core, kernel. **2** *he had a towel round his middle* **midriff**, waist, belly, stomach, abdomen; informal tummy, tum.
– OPPOSITES outside.
▸adj. **1** *the middle point* **central**, mid, mean, medium, medial, median, midway, halfway. **2** *the middle level* **intermediate**, intermediary.

middleman n. **intermediary**, go-between; dealer, broker, agent, factor, wholesaler, distributor.

middling adj. **average**, standard, normal, middle-of-the-road; moderate, ordinary, commonplace, everyday, workaday, tolerable, passable; run-of-the-mill, fair, mediocre, undistinguished, unexceptional, unremarkable; informal OK, so-so, bog-standard, fair-to-middling, (plain) vanilla; NZ informal half-pie.

midget n. *the inhabitants must have been midgets* **small person**, dwarf, homunculus, Lilliputian, manikin, gnome, pygmy; informal shrimp.
▸adj. **1** *a story about midget matadors* **diminutive**, dwarfish, petite, very small, pygmy; informal pint-sized; N. Amer. informal sawn-off. **2** *a midget camera* **miniature**, pocket, dwarf, baby, fun-size.
– OPPOSITES giant.

midnight n. **the middle of the night**, twenty-four hundred hours, the witching hour.
– OPPOSITES midday.

midst literary n. **middle**, centre, heart, core, midpoint, kernel, nub; depth(s); thick; **(in the midst of)** in the course of, halfway through, at the heart/core of.

midway adv. **halfway**, in the middle, at the midpoint, in the centre; part-way.

mien n. **appearance**, look, expression, countenance, aura, demeanour, attitude, air, manner, bearing; formal comportment.

miffed adj. informal See annoyed.

might n. **strength**, force, power, vigour, energy, brawn, powerfulness, forcefulness. □ **with might and main** with all one's strength, as hard as one can, as hard as possible, (with) full force, forcefully, powerfully, strongly, vigorously.

mightily adv. **1** *he is mightily impressive* **extremely**, exceedingly, enormously, immensely, tremendously, hugely, dreadfully, very (much); informal awfully, majorly, mega; N. Amer. informal mighty, plumb; informal dated devilish. **2** *Ann and I laboured mightily* **strenuously**, energetically, powerfully, hard, with all one's might, with might and main, all out, heartily, vigorously, diligently, assiduously, persistently, indefatigably; informal like mad, like crazy; Brit. informal like billy-o.

mighty adj. **1** *a mighty blow* **powerful**, forceful, violent, vigorous, hefty, thunderous. **2** *a mighty warrior* **fearsome**, ferocious; big, tough, robust, muscular, strapping. **3** *mighty industrial countries* **dominant**, influential, strong, powerful, important, predominant. **4** *mighty oak trees* **huge**, enormous, massive, gigantic, big, large, giant, colossal, mammoth, immense; informal monster, whopping (great), thumping (great), humongous, jumbo(-sized); Brit. informal whacking (great), ginormous.
– OPPOSITES feeble, puny, tiny.
▸adv. N. Amer. informal *I'm mighty pleased to see you* **extremely**, exceedingly, enormously, immensely, tremendously, hugely, mightily, very (much); informal awfully, dreadfully, majorly, mega; Brit. informal well, jolly; N. Amer. informal plumb; informal dated devilish, frightfully.

migrant n. *economic migrants* **immigrant**, emigrant; nomad, itinerant, traveller, vagrant, transient, rover, wanderer, drifter.
▸adj. *migrant workers* **travelling**, wandering, drifting, nomadic, roving, roaming, itinerant, vagrant, transient.

migrate v. **1** *rural populations migrated to urban areas* **relocate**, resettle, move (house); emigrate, go abroad, go overseas; N. Amer. pull up stakes; Brit. informal up sticks; dated remove. **2** *wildebeest migrate across the Serengeti* **roam**, wander, drift, rove, travel (around).

migratory adj. **migrant**, migrating, moving, travelling.

mild adj. **1** *a mild tone of voice* **gentle**, tender, soft-hearted, tender-hearted, sensitive, sympathetic, warm, placid, calm, tranquil, serene, peaceable, good-natured, amiable, affable, genial, easy-going. **2** *a mild punishment* **lenient**, light; compassionate, merciful, humane. **3** *he was eyeing her with mild interest* **slight**, faint, vague, minimal, nominal, token, feeble. **4** *mild weather* **warm**, balmy, temperate, clement. **5** *a mild curry* **bland**, insipid.
– OPPOSITES harsh, strong, severe.

mildewy adj. **mouldy**, mildewed, rotten, decaying.

milieu n. **environment**, sphere, background, backdrop, setting, context, atmosphere; location, conditions, surroundings, environs.

militant adj. *militant supporters* **aggressive**, violent, belligerent, bellicose, vigorous, forceful, active, fierce, combative, pugnacious; radical, extremist, extreme, zealous, fanatical.
▸n. *the demands of the militants* **activist**, extremist, radical, Young Turk, zealot.

militaristic adj. **warmongering**, warlike, martial, hawkish, pugnacious, combative, aggressive, belligerent, bellicose; informal gung-ho.
– OPPOSITES peaceable.

military adj. *military activity* **fighting**, service, army, armed, defence, martial.
– OPPOSITES civilian.
▸ n. *the military took power* (**armed**) **forces**, services, militia; army, navy, air force, marines.

> **WORD LINKS**
>
> **enlist** enrol for military service
> **recruit** a newly enlisted person
> **conscript** call up for compulsory military service
> **cashier** dismiss from military service for serious wrongdoing
> **court martial** a court trying members of the armed forces accused of breaking military law
> **munitions, armament, materiel** (US **ordnance**) military weapons, equipment, etc.
> **tattoo** a military display of music, marching, etc.

militate v. *tend to prevent*, work against, hinder, discourage, prejudice, be detrimental to.

milk v. **1** *Pam was milking the cows* draw milk from, express milk from. **2** *a fraudster who milked £3000 from the rich and famous* **draw off**, siphon (off), tap, drain, extract. **3** *he milked his rich clients* **exploit**, take advantage of, cash in on, suck dry; informal bleed, squeeze, fleece.

> **WORD LINKS**
>
> **dairy, lactic** relating to milk
> **lactate** (of a female animal) produce milk
> **casein** the main protein in milk
> **lactose** a compound sugar found in milk
> **pasteurize** make milk safe to eat by heating it
> **curds** a soft substance formed when milk coagulates
> **whey** the watery part of milk remaining after curds have formed

milksop n. **namby-pamby**, coward, weakling; informal drip, mummy's boy, sissy, jellyfish, wimp; Brit. informal wet, big girl's blouse; N. Amer. informal pantywaist, pussy; old use poltroon.

milky adj. **pale**, white, milk-white, whitish, off-white, cream, creamy, chalky, pearly, nacreous, ivory, alabaster.
– OPPOSITES swarthy.

mill n. **1** *a steel mill* **factory**, (processing) plant, works, workshop, shop, foundry, industrial unit. **2** *a pepper mill* **grinder**, quern, crusher.
▸ v. *the wheat is milled into flour* **grind**, pulverize, powder, granulate, pound, crush, press; technical comminute, triturate; old use bray, levigate.
□ **mill around/about** throng, swarm, seethe, crowd.

millstone n. **burden**, encumbrance, dead weight, cross to bear, albatross; duty, obligation, liability, misfortune; old use cumber.

mime n. *a mime of someone fencing* **dumb show**, pantomime.
▸ v. *she mimed picking up a phone* **act out**, pantomime, gesture, simulate, represent.

mimic v. **1** *she mimicked his accent* **imitate**, copy, impersonate, do an impression of, ape, caricature, parody, lampoon, burlesque; informal send up, take off, spoof; old use monkey. **2** *most hoverflies mimic wasps* **resemble**, look like, have the appearance of, simulate; N. Amer. informal make like.
▸ n. *he was a superb mimic* **impersonator**, impressionist, imitator, mimicker; parodist, caricaturist, lampooner, lampoonist; informal copycat; historical zany; old use ape.
▸ adj. *they were waging mimic war* **simulated**, mock, imitation, make-believe, sham; informal pretend, copycat.

mimicry n. **imitation**, imitating, impersonation, copying, aping; old use apery.

minatory adj. formal **menacing**, threatening, baleful, intimidating, admonitory, warning, cautionary; rare minacious, comminatory.

mince v. **1** *mince the meat and onions* **grind**, chop up, cut up, dice; N. Amer. hash. **2** *she minced out of the room* **walk affectedly**; N. Amer. informal sashay.
□ **not mince (one's) words** talk straight, not beat about the bush, call a spade a spade, speak straight from the shoulder, pull no punches; informal tell it like it is; N. Amer. informal talk turkey.

mincing adj. **affected**, dainty, effeminate, niminy-piminy; pretentious; informal camp, sissy; Brit. informal poncey.

mind n. **1** *a good teacher must stretch pupils' minds* **brain**, intelligence, intellect, intellectual capabilities, brains, brainpower, wits, understanding, reasoning, judgement, sense, head; informal grey matter, brainbox, brain cells; Brit. informal loaf; N. Amer. informal smarts. **2** *he kept his mind on the job* **attention**, thoughts, concentration, attentiveness. **3** *the tragedy affected her mind* **sanity**, mental faculties, senses, wits, reason, reasoning, judgement; informal marbles. **4** *his words stuck in her mind* **memory**, recollection. **5** *a great mind* **intellect**, thinker, brain, scholar, academic. **6** *I've a mind to complain* **inclination**, desire, wish, urge, notion, fancy, intention, will. **7** *of the same mind* **opinion**, way of thinking, outlook, attitude, view, viewpoint, point of view.
▸ v. **1** *do you mind if I smoke?* **care**, object, be bothered, be annoyed, be upset, take offence, disapprove, dislike it, look askance; informal give/care a damn, give/care a toss, give/care a hoot, give/care a rap. **2** *mind the step!* **be careful of**, watch out for, look out for, beware of, be on one's guard for, be wary of. **3** *mind you wipe your feet* **be/make sure (that)**, see (that); remember to, don't forget to. **4** *her husband was minding the baby* **look after**, take care of, keep an eye on, attend to, care for, tend. **5** *mind what your mother says* **pay attention to**, heed, pay heed to, attend to, take note/notice of, note, mark, listen to,

m

be mindful of; obey, follow, comply with; old use regard.

□ **be in two minds** be undecided, be uncertain, be unsure, hesitate, waver, vacillate, dither; Brit. haver, hum and haw; informal dilly-dally, shilly-shally.

bear/keep something in mind remember, note, be mindful of, take note of; formal take cognizance of.

cross one's mind occur to one, enter one's mind/head, strike one, hit one, dawn on one.

mind out take care, be careful, watch out, look out, beware, be on one's guard, be wary.

never mind 1 *never mind the cost* **don't bother about**, don't worry about, disregard, forget. **2** *never mind, it's all right now* **don't apologize**, forget it, don't worry about it, it doesn't matter.

out of one's mind 1 *you must be out of your mind!* See **mad** (sense 1). **2** *I've been out of my mind with worry* frantic, beside oneself, distraught, in a frenzy.

to my mind in my opinion, in my view, as I see it, personally, in my estimation, in my book, if you ask me.

WORD LINKS

cognitive, **mental**, **psychological** relating to the mind
psychology the study of the mind
psychiatry the branch of medicine dealing with the mind
ego the part of the mind responsible for a person's sense of identity
id the part of the unconscious mind consisting of inherited instincts and feelings
superego the part of the mind acting as a conscience, reflecting learned social standards

---

mindful adj. aware, conscious, sensible, alive, alert, acquainted, heedful, wary, chary; informal wise, hip; formal cognizant, regardful.
– OPPOSITES heedless.

mindless adj. **1** *a mindless idiot* **stupid**, idiotic, brainless, imbecilic, imbecile, asinine, witless, foolish, empty-headed, slow-witted, obtuse, feather-brained, doltish; informal dumb, pig-ignorant, brain-dead, cretinous, moronic, thick, birdbrained, pea-brained, dopey, dim, half-witted, dippy, fat-headed, boneheaded; N. Amer. informal chowderheaded. **2** *mindless acts of vandalism* **unthinking**, thoughtless, senseless, gratuitous, wanton, indiscriminate, unreasoning. **3** *a mindless task* **mechanical**, automatic, routine; tedious, boring, monotonous, brainless, mind-numbing.
□ **mindless of** indifferent to, heedless of, unaware of, unmindful of, careless of, blind to.

mine n. **1** *a coal mine* **pit**, excavation, quarry, workings, diggings; strip mine; Brit. opencast mine; N. Amer. open-pit mine. **2** *a mine of information* **rich source**, repository, store, storehouse, reservoir, gold mine, treasure house, treasury, reserve, fund, wealth, stock. **3** *he was killed by a mine* **explosive**, landmine.
▸ v. **1** *the iron ore was mined from shallow pits*

quarry, excavate, dig (up), extract, remove; strip-mine. **2** *medical data was mined for relevant statistics* **search**, delve into, scour, scan, read through, survey.

miner n. **pitman**, digger, collier, faceworker, haulier; tinner; dated hewer.

mingle v. **1** *fact and fiction are skilfully mingled in his novels* **mix**, blend, intermingle, intermix, interweave, interlace, combine, merge, fuse, unite, join, amalgamate, meld, mesh; literary commingle; old use commix. **2** *wedding guests mingled in the marquee* **socialize**, circulate, fraternize, get together, associate with others; informal hobnob.
– OPPOSITES separate.

miniature adj. *a miniature railway* **small-scale**, mini; tiny, little, small, minute, baby, toy, pocket, fun-size, dwarf, pygmy, minuscule, diminutive; Scottish wee; N. Amer. vest-pocket; informal teeny, teeny-weeny, teensy, teensy-weensy, itsy-bitsy, eensy, eensy-weensy; Brit. informal titchy, tiddly.
– OPPOSITES giant.

minimal adj. **very little**, minimum, the least (possible); nominal, token, negligible.
– OPPOSITES maximum.

minimize v. **1** *the aim is to minimize costs* **keep down**, keep at/to a minimum, reduce, decrease, cut down, lessen, curtail, diminish, prune; informal slash. **2** *we should not minimize his contribution* **belittle**, make light of, play down, underestimate, underrate, downplay, undervalue, understate; informal pooh-pooh; old use hold cheap; rare misprize.
– OPPOSITES maximize, exaggerate.

minimum n. *costs will be kept to the minimum* **lowest level**, lower limit, bottom level, rock bottom; least, lowest, slightest.
– OPPOSITES maximum.
▸ adj. *the minimum amount of effort* **minimal**, least, smallest, least possible, slightest, lowest, minutest.

minion n. **underling**, henchman, flunkey, lackey, hanger-on, follower, servant, hireling, vassal, stooge; informal yes-man, bootlicker; Brit. informal poodle; N. Amer. informal suck-up.

minister n. **1** *a government minister* **member of the government**, cabinet minister, Secretary of State, undersecretary. **2** *a minister of religion* **clergyman**, clergywoman, cleric, ecclesiastic, pastor, vicar, rector, priest, parson, father, man/woman of the cloth, man/woman of God, churchman, churchwoman; curate, chaplain; informal reverend, padre, Holy Joe, sky pilot; Austral. informal josser. **3** *the British minister in Egypt* **ambassador**, chargé d'affaires, plenipotentiary, envoy, emissary, diplomat, consul, representative; old use legate.
▸ v. *doctors were ministering to the injured* **tend**, care for, take care of, look after, nurse, treat, attend to, see to, administer to, help, assist.

ministrations plural n. **attention**, treatment, help, assistance, aid, care, services.

ministry n. **1** *the ministry for foreign affairs* **(government) department**, bureau, agency, office. **2** *he's training for the ministry* **holy orders**, the priesthood, the cloth, the church. **3** *the ministry of Jesus* **teaching**, preaching, evangelism. **4** *Gladstone's first ministry* **period of office**, term (of office), administration.

minor adj. **1** *a minor problem* **slight**, small; unimportant, insignificant, inconsequential, inconsiderable, subsidiary, negligible, trivial, trifling, paltry, petty; N. Amer. nickel-and-dime; informal piffling, piddling. **2** *a minor poet* **little known**, unknown, lesser, unimportant, insignificant, obscure; N. Amer. minor-league; informal small-time; N. Amer. informal two-bit. **3** Brit. *Smith minor* **junior**, younger.
– OPPOSITES major, important.
▶ n. *the heir to the throne was a minor* **child**, infant, youth, adolescent, teenager, boy, girl; informal kid, kiddie.
– OPPOSITES adult.

minstrel n. historical **musician**, singer, balladeer; historical troubadour, jongleur; literary bard.

mint n. **1** **coinage factory**, money factory. **2** informal *the bank made a mint out of the deal* **a vast sum of money**, a king's ransom, millions, billions; informal a (small) fortune, a tidy sum, a bundle, a packet, a pile; Brit. informal a bomb, big money; N. Amer. informal big bucks; Austral. informal big bickies, motser.
▶ adj. *in mint condition* **brand new**, pristine, perfect, immaculate, unblemished, undamaged, unmarked, unused, first-class, excellent.
▶ v. **1** *the shilling was minted in 1742* **coin**, stamp, strike, cast, forge, manufacture. **2** *the slogan had been freshly minted* **create**, invent, make up, think up, dream up.

minuscule adj. **tiny**, minute, microscopic, nanoscopic, very small, little, micro, diminutive, miniature, baby, dwarf; Scottish wee; informal teeny, teeny-weeny, teensy, teensy-weensy, itsy-bitsy, eensy, eensy-weensy, tiddly; Brit. informal titchy.
– OPPOSITES huge.

minute¹ n. **1** *it'll only take a minute* **moment**, short time, little while, second, bit, instant; informal sec, nanosecond, jiffy; Brit. informal tick, mo, two ticks. **2** *at that minute, Tony walked in* **point (in time)**, moment, instant, juncture. **3** *their objection was noted in the minutes* **record(s)**, proceedings, log, notes; transcript, summary, résumé.
□ **at the minute** Brit. informal **at present**, at the moment, now, currently.
in a minute very soon, in a moment/second/ instant, in a trice, shortly, any minute (now), in a short time, in (less than) no time, before long; N. Amer. momentarily; informal anon, in a jiffy, in a nanosecond, in two shakes, before you can say Jack Robinson; Brit. informal in a tick, in a mo, in two ticks; N. Amer. informal in a snap; literary ere long.
this minute at once, immediately, directly, this second, instantly, straight away, right away/now, forthwith; informal pronto, straight

off, right off, toot sweet; old use straight.
up to the minute latest, newest, up to date, modern, fashionable, smart, chic, stylish, all the rage, in vogue; informal trendy, with it, in.
wait a minute be patient, hold on; informal hang on, hold your horses; Brit. informal hang about.

minute² adj. **1** *minute particles* **tiny**, minuscule, microscopic, nanoscopic, very small, little, micro, diminutive, miniature, baby, toy, dwarf, pygmy, Lilliputian; Scottish wee; informal teeny, teeny-weeny, teensy, teensy-weensy, itsy-bitsy, eensy, eensy-weensy; Brit. informal titchy, tiddly. **2** *a minute chance of success* **negligible**, slight, infinitesimal, minimal, insignificant, inappreciable. **3** *minute detail* **exhaustive**, painstaking, meticulous, rigorous, scrupulous, punctilious, detailed.
– OPPOSITES huge.

minutely adv. **exhaustively**, painstakingly, meticulously, rigorously, scrupulously, punctiliously, in detail.

minutiae plural n. **details**, niceties, finer points, particulars, trivia, trivialities.

minx n. **tease**, seductress, coquette, slut, Lolita; informal floozie, tart, vamp; Brit. informal scrubber, slapper; N. Amer. informal tramp; dated hussy; old use strumpet, trollop.

miracle n. **1** *Christ's first miracle* **supernatural phenomenon**, mystery, prodigy. **2** *Germany's economic miracle* **wonder**, marvel, sensation, phenomenon.

miraculous adj. **1** *the miraculous help of St Blaise* **supernatural**, preternatural, inexplicable, unaccountable, magical. **2** *a miraculous escape* **amazing**, astounding, remarkable, extraordinary, incredible, unbelievable, sensational; informal mind-boggling, mind-blowing.

mirage n. **optical illusion**, hallucination, phantasmagoria, apparition, fantasy, chimera, vision, figment of the imagination; literary phantasm.

mire n. **1** *it's a mire out there* **swamp**, bog, morass, quagmire, slough; swampland, wetland, marshland. **2** *her horse was spattered with mire* **mud**, slime, dirt, filth, muck. **3** *struggling to pull Russia out of the mire* **mess**, difficulty, plight, predicament, tight spot, trouble, quandary, muddle; informal jam, fix, pickle, hot water.
▶ v. **1** *Frank's horse got mired in a bog* **bog down**, sink (down). **2** *the children were mired* **dirty**, soil, muddy; literary begrime. **3** *he has become mired in lawsuits* **entangle**, tangle up, embroil, catch up, mix up, involve.

mirror n. **1** *a quick look in the mirror* **looking glass**, cheval glass; Brit. glass. **2** *the Frenchman's life was a mirror of his own* **reflection**, twin, replica, copy, match, parallel.
▶ v. *pop music mirrored the mood of desperation* **reflect**, match, reproduce, imitate, simulate, copy, mimic, echo, parallel, correspond to.

m

WORD LINKS
catoptric, **specular** relating to mirrors

mirth n. **merriment**, high spirits, mirthfulness, cheerfulness, cheeriness, hilarity, glee, laughter, gaiety, buoyancy, blitheness, euphoria, exhilaration, light-heartedness, joviality, joy, joyfulness, joyousness.
– OPPOSITES misery.

mirthful adj. **merry**, high-spirited, gleeful, cheerful, cheery, jocular, buoyant, euphoric, exhilarated, elated, light-hearted, jovial, joyous, jolly, festive.

mirthless adj. **humourless**, unamused, grim, sour, surly, dour, sullen, sulky, gloomy, mournful, melancholy, doleful, miserable, grumpy.
– OPPOSITES cheerful.

miry adj. **muddy**, slushy, slimy, swampy, marshy, boggy, squelchy, waterlogged.

misadventure n. **accident**, problem, difficulty, misfortune, mishap, setback, reversal (of fortune), stroke of bad luck, blow; failure, disaster, tragedy, calamity, woe, trial, tribulation, catastrophe.

misanthropic adj. **antisocial**, unsociable, unfriendly, reclusive, uncongenial, cynical, jaundiced.

misapply v. **misuse**, mishandle, misemploy, abuse; distort, garble, warp, misinterpret, misconstrue, misrepresent.

misapprehend v. **misunderstand**, misinterpret, misconstrue, misconceive, mistake, misread, get the wrong idea about, take something the wrong way.

misapprehension n. **misunderstanding**, misinterpretation, misreading, misjudgement, misconception, misbelief, the wrong idea, false impression, delusion.

misappropriate v. **embezzle**, expropriate, steal, thieve, pilfer, pocket, help oneself to, make off with; informal swipe, filch, rip off, snitch; Brit. informal pinch, nick, whip, knock off; formal peculate.

misappropriation n. **embezzlement**, expropriation, stealing, theft, thieving, pilfering; formal peculation.

misbegotten adj. **1** *a misbegotten scheme* **ill-conceived**, ill-advised, badly planned, badly thought-out, hare-brained. **2** *you misbegotten hound!* **contemptible**, despicable, wretched, miserable, confounded; informal infernal, damned, flaming; dated cursed, accursed.

misbehave v. **behave badly**, be misbehaved, be naughty, be disobedient, get up to mischief, get up to no good; be bad-mannered, be rude; informal carry on, act up.

misbehaviour n. **bad behaviour**, misconduct, naughtiness, disobedience, mischief, mischievousness; bad/poor manners, rudeness; informal acting-up.

misbelief n. **false belief**, delusion, illusion, fallacy, error, mistake, misconception, misapprehension.

miscalculate v. **misjudge**, make a mistake (about), calculate wrongly, estimate wrongly, overestimate, underestimate, overvalue, undervalue; go wrong, err, be wide of the mark.

miscalculation n. **error of judgement**, misjudgement, mistake, overestimate, underestimate.

miscarriage n. **1** *she's had a miscarriage* **(spontaneous) abortion**, stillbirth. **2** *the miscarriage of the project* **failure**, foundering, ruin, ruination, collapse, breakdown, thwarting, frustration, undoing, non-fulfilment, mismanagement.

miscarry v. **1** *the shock caused her to miscarry* **lose one's baby**, have a miscarriage, abort, have a (spontaneous) abortion. **2** *our plan miscarried* **go wrong**, go awry, go amiss, be ruined, fail, misfire, abort, founder, come to nothing, fall through, fall flat; informal flop, go up in smoke.
– OPPOSITES succeed.

miscellaneous adj. **various**, varied, different, assorted, mixed, sundry, diverse, disparate; diversified, motley, multifarious, heterogeneous; literary divers.

miscellany n. **assortment**, mixture, melange, blend, variety, mixed bag, mix, medley, diversity, collection, selection, assemblage, potpourri, mishmash, hotchpotch, ragbag, salmagundi, gallimaufry, omnium gatherum; N. Amer. hodgepodge.

mischance n. **accident**, misfortune, mishap, misadventure, setback, disaster, tragedy, calamity, catastrophe, reversal, upset, blow; bad luck, ill fortune.

mischief n. **1** *the boys are always getting up to mischief* **naughtiness**, bad behaviour, misbehaviour, mischievousness, misconduct, disobedience; pranks, tricks, larks, capers, nonsense, devilry, funny business; informal monkey business, shenanigans, hanky-panky; Brit. informal monkey tricks, carryings-on, jiggery-pokery. **2** *the mischief in her eyes* **impishness**, roguishness, devilment. **3** informal *you'll do yourself a mischief* **harm**, hurt, injury, damage.

mischievous adj. **1** *a mischievous child* **naughty**, badly behaved, misbehaving, disobedient, troublesome, full of mischief; rascally, roguish. **2** *a mischievous smile* **playful**, teasing, wicked, impish, roguish, arch. **3** *a mischievous allegation* **malicious**, malevolent, spiteful, venomous, poisonous, evil-intentioned, evil, baleful, vindictive, vengeful, vitriolic, rancorous, malign, malignant, pernicious, mean, nasty, harmful, hurtful, cruel, unkind; informal bitchy, catty; literary malefic, maleficent.
– OPPOSITES well behaved.

misconceive v. **misunderstand**, misinterpret, misconstrue, misapprehend, mistake, misread; miscalculate, err, be mistaken, get the wrong idea.

misconception n. **misapprehension**, misunderstanding, mistake, error, misinterpretation, misconstruction, misreading, misjudgement, misbelief, miscalculation, false impression, illusion, fallacy, delusion.

m

misconduct n. **1** *allegations of misconduct* **wrongdoing**, unlawfulness, lawlessness, crime, felony, criminality, sin, sinfulness; unprofessionalism, unethical behaviour, malpractice, negligence, impropriety; formal maladministration, malversation. **2** *misconduct in the classroom* **misbehaviour**, bad behaviour, misdeeds, misdemeanours, disorderly conduct, mischief, naughtiness, rudeness.

misconstruction n. **misunderstanding**, misinterpretation, misapprehension, misconception, misreading, misjudgement, misbelief, miscalculation, false impression.

misconstrue v. **misunderstand**, misinterpret, misconceive, misapprehend, mistake, misread; be mistaken about, get the wrong idea about, get it/someone wrong.

miscreant n. **criminal**, culprit, wrongdoer, malefactor, offender, villain, lawbreaker, evildoer, delinquent, reprobate; Law malfeasant.

misdeed n. **wrongdoing**, wrong, evil deed, crime, felony, misdemeanour, misconduct, offence, error, transgression, sin; old use trespass.

misdemeanour n. **wrongdoing**, evil deed, crime, felony, misdeed, misconduct, offence, error, peccadillo, transgression, sin; old use trespass.

miser n. **penny-pincher**, pinchpenny, niggard, cheese-parer, Scrooge; informal skinflint, meanie, money-grubber, cheapskate; N. Amer. informal tightwad.
– OPPOSITES spendthrift.

miserable adj. **1** *I'm too miserable to eat* **unhappy**, sad, sorrowful, dejected, depressed, downcast, downhearted, down, despondent, disconsolate, wretched, glum, gloomy, dismal, melancholy, woebegone, doleful, forlorn, heartbroken; informal blue, down in the mouth/dumps. **2** *their miserable surroundings* **dreary**, dismal, gloomy, drab, wretched, depressing, grim, cheerless, bleak, desolate; poor, shabby, squalid, seedy, dilapidated. **3** *miserable weather* **unpleasant**, disagreeable, depressing; wet, rainy, stormy; informal rotten. **4** *a miserable old grouch* **grumpy**, sullen, gloomy, bad-tempered, ill-tempered, dour, surly, sour, glum, moody, unsociable, saturnine, lugubrious, irritable, churlish, cantankerous, crotchety, cross, crabby, grouchy, testy, peevish, crusty, waspish. **5** *miserable wages* **inadequate**, meagre, scanty, paltry, small, poor, pitiful, niggardly; informal measly, stingy, pathetic; formal exiguous. **6** *all that fuss about a few miserable pounds* **wretched**, confounded; informal blithering, flaming, blessed, damned, blasted; dated accursed.
– OPPOSITES cheerful, lovely.

miserliness n. **meanness**, niggardliness, close-fistedness, closeness, parsimony, parsimoniousness; informal stinginess, tight-fistedness; N. Amer. cheapness; old use nearness.

miserly adj. **1** *his miserly great-uncle* **mean**, niggardly, parsimonious, close, close-fisted, penny-pinching, cheese-paring, grasping, Scrooge-like; informal stingy, tight, tight-fisted; N. Amer. informal cheap; old use near. **2** *the prize is a miserly £300* **meagre**, inadequate, paltry, negligible, miserable, pitiful, niggardly, beggarly; informal measly, stingy, pathetic; formal exiguous.
– OPPOSITES generous.

misery n. **1** *periods of intense misery* **unhappiness**, distress, wretchedness, suffering, anguish, anxiety, angst, torment, pain, grief, heartache, heartbreak, despair, despondency, dejection, depression, desolation, gloom, melancholy, melancholia, woe, sadness, sorrow; informal the dumps, the blues; literary dolour. **2** *the miseries of war* **affliction**, misfortune, difficulty, problem, ordeal, trouble, hardship, deprivation; pain, sorrow, trial, tribulation, woe. **3** Brit. informal *he's a real old misery* **killjoy**, dog in the manger, spoilsport; informal sourpuss, grouch, grump, party pooper.
– OPPOSITES contentment, pleasure.

misfire v. **go wrong**, go awry, be unsuccessful, fail, founder, fall through/flat; backfire; informal flop, go up in smoke.

misfit n. **nonconformist**, eccentric, maverick, individualist, square peg in a round hole; informal oddball, weirdo, freak, bad boy; N. Amer. informal screwball.

misfortune n. **problem**, difficulty, issue, setback, trouble, adversity, stroke of bad luck, reversal (of fortune), misadventure, mishap, blow, failure, accident, disaster; sorrow, misery, woe, trial, tribulation.

> **WORD LINKS**
>
> **schadenfreude** pleasure gained from another person's misfortune

misgiving n. **qualm**, doubt, reservation; suspicion, distrust, mistrust, lack of confidence, second thoughts; trepidation, scepticism, unease, uneasiness, anxiety, apprehension, disquiet.

misguided adj. **1** *the policy is misguided* **erroneous**, fallacious, unsound, misplaced, misconceived, ill-advised, ill-considered, ill-judged, inappropriate, unwise, injudicious, imprudent. **2** *you are quite misguided* **misinformed**, misled, labouring under a misapprehension, wrong, mistaken, deluded.

mishandle v. **1** *the officer mishandled the situation* **bungle**, fluff, make a mess of, mismanage, spoil, ruin, wreck; informal botch, make a hash of, mess up, muck up; Brit. informal make a pig's ear of, make a Horlicks of. **2** *he mishandled his wife* **bully**, persecute, ill-treat, mistreat, maltreat, abuse, knock about/around, hit, beat; informal beat up. **3** *the equipment could be dangerous if mishandled* **misuse**, abuse, handle/treat roughly.

mishap n. **accident**, trouble, problem, difficulty, issue, setback, adversity, reversal (of fortune), misfortune, blow; failure, disaster, tragedy, catastrophe, calamity.

mishmash n. **jumble**, confusion, hotchpotch, ragbag, patchwork, farrago, assortment, medley, miscellany, mixture, melange, blend, mix, potpourri, conglomeration, gallimaufry, omnium gatherum, salmagundi; N. Amer. hodgepodge.

misinform v. **mislead**, misguide, delude, take in, deceive, lie to, hoodwink; informal lead up the garden path, take for a ride; N. Amer. informal give someone a bum steer.

misinformation n. **disinformation**, false/misleading information; lie, fib; N. Amer. informal bum steer.

misinterpret v. **misunderstand**, misconceive, misconstrue, misapprehend, mistake, misread; confuse, take amiss, be mistaken, get the wrong idea.

misjudge v. **get the wrong idea about**, get wrong, judge incorrectly, estimate wrongly, be wrong about, miscalculate, misread; overestimate, underestimate, overvalue, undervalue, underrate.

mislay v. **lose**, misplace.
– OPPOSITES find.

mislead v. **deceive**, delude, take in, lie to, fool, hoodwink, throw off the scent, pull the wool over someone's eyes, misguide, misinform, give wrong information to; informal lead up the garden path, take for a ride; N. Amer. informal give someone a bum steer.

misleading adj. **deceptive**, confusing, deceiving, equivocal, ambiguous, fallacious, specious, spurious, false.

mismanage v. **bungle**, fluff, make a mess of, mishandle, misconduct, spoil, ruin, wreck; informal botch, make a hash of, mess up, muck up; Brit. informal make a pig's ear of, make a Horlicks of.

mismatch n. **discrepancy**, inconsistency, contradiction, incongruity, incongruousness, conflict, discord, irreconcilability.

mismatched adj. **ill-assorted**, ill-matched, incongruous, unsuited, incompatible, inconsistent, at odds; out of keeping, clashing, dissimilar, unlike, different, at variance, disparate, unrelated, divergent, contrasting.
– OPPOSITES matching.

misogynist n. **woman-hater**, anti-feminist, (male) chauvinist, sexist; informal male chauvinist pig, MCP.

misplace v. **lose**, mislay, put in the wrong place, be unable to find, forget the whereabouts of.
– OPPOSITES find.

misplaced adj. **1** *his comments were misplaced* **misguided**, unwise, ill-advised, ill-considered, ill-judged, inappropriate. **2** *misplaced keys* **lost**, mislaid, missing.

misprint n. **mistake**, error, typographical mistake/error, typing mistake/error, corrigendum, erratum; Brit. literal; informal typo.

misquote v. **misreport**, misrepresent, misstate, take/quote out of context, distort, twist, slant, bias, put a spin on, falsify.

misrepresent v. **give a false account/idea of**, misstate, misreport, misquote, quote/take out of context, misinterpret, put a spin on, falsify, distort.

misrule n. **1** *the misrule of Edward IV* **bad government**, misgovernment, mismanagement, malpractice, incompetence; formal maladministration. **2** *the misrule at football games* **lawlessness**, anarchy, disorder, chaos, mayhem.
– OPPOSITES order.

miss[1] v. **1** *the shot missed her by inches* **fail to hit**, be/go wide of, fall short of. **2** *Mandy missed the catch* **fail to catch**, drop, fumble, fluff, mishandle, misfield, mishit. **3** *I've missed my bus* **be too late for**, fail to catch/get. **4** *I missed what you said* **fail to hear**, mishear. **5** *you can't miss the station* **fail to see/notice**, overlook. **6** *she never missed a meeting* **fail to attend**, be absent from, play truant from, cut, skip; Brit. informal skive off. **7** *don't miss this exciting opportunity!* **let slip**, fail to take advantage of, let go/pass, pass up. **8** *I left early to miss the rush-hour traffic* **avoid**, beat, evade, escape, dodge, sidestep, elude, circumvent, steer clear of, find a way round, bypass. **9** *she missed him when he was away* **pine for**, yearn for, ache for, long for, long to see.
– OPPOSITES hit, catch.
▫ **miss someone/something out** leave out, exclude, miss (off), fail to mention, pass over, skip; Brit. informal give something a miss.

miss[2] n. *a headstrong young miss* **young woman**, young lady, girl, schoolgirl, missy; Scottish lass, lassie; Irish colleen; informal girlie, chick, bit, doll; Brit. informal bird, bint; N. Amer. informal broad, dame; Austral./NZ informal sheila; literary maiden, maid, damsel; old use wench.

misshapen adj. **deformed**, malformed, distorted, crooked, twisted, warped, out of shape, bent, asymmetrical, irregular, misproportioned, ill-proportioned, disfigured, grotesque.

missile n. **projectile**, shell, rocket, weapon, brickbat.

> **WORD LINKS**
>
> **ballistics** the science of missiles and firearms
> **payload, warhead** the explosive head of a missile
> **silo** an underground chamber for guided missiles

missing adj. **1** *his wallet is missing* **lost**, mislaid, misplaced, absent, gone (astray), unaccounted for. **2** *passion was missing from her life* **absent**, not present, lacking, wanting.
– OPPOSITES present.

mission n. **1** *a mercy mission to Romania* **assignment**, commission, expedition, journey, trip, undertaking, operation; task, job, labour, work, duty, charge, trust. **2** *her mission in life* **vocation**, calling, goal, aim, quest, purpose, function. **3** *a trade mission* **delegation**, deputation, commission, legation, delegacy. **4** *a teacher in a mission* **missionary post**, missionary station. **5** *a bombing mission* **sortie**, operation, raid.

missionary n. **evangelist**, apostle, proselytizer, preacher, minister, priest.

missive n. **message**, communication, letter, word, note, memorandum, line, communiqué, dispatch, news; informal memo; formal epistle; literary tidings.

misspent adj. **wasted**, dissipated, squandered, thrown away, frittered away, misused, misapplied.

misstate v. **misreport**, misrepresent, take/quote out of context, distort, twist, put a spin on, falsify.

mist n. *the mist was clearing* **haze**, fog, smog, murk, cloud, Scotch mist; literary brume, fume.
□ **mist over/up** steam up, become misty, fog over/up, film over, cloud over.

mistake n. **1** *I assumed it had been a mistake* **error**, fault, inaccuracy, omission, slip, blunder, miscalculation, misunderstanding, oversight, misinterpretation, gaffe, faux pas, solecism; informal slip-up, boo-boo, howler, boner, fail; Brit. informal boob, clanger, bloomer; N. Amer. informal goof. **2** *spelling mistakes* **misprint**, typographical error/mistake, typing error/mistake, corrigendum, erratum; Brit. literal; informal typo.
▶ v. **1** *men are apt to mistake their own feelings* **misunderstand**, misinterpret, get wrong, misconstrue, misread. **2** *children often mistake vitamin pills for sweets* **confuse with**, mix up with, take for, misinterpret as.
□ **be mistaken** be wrong, be in error, be under a misapprehension, be misinformed, be misguided; informal be barking up the wrong tree, get the wrong end of the stick.
make a mistake go wrong, err, make an error, blunder, miscalculate; informal slip up, make a boo-boo, make a howler; Brit. informal boob; N. Amer. informal drop the ball, goof (up).

mistaken adj. **wrong**, erroneous, inaccurate, incorrect, off beam, false, fallacious, unfounded, misguided, misinformed.
– OPPOSITES correct.

mistakenly adv. **1** *we often mistakenly imagine that when a problem is diagnosed it is solved* **wrongly**, in error, erroneously, incorrectly, falsely, fallaciously, inaccurately. **2** *Matt mistakenly opened the letter* **by accident**, accidentally, inadvertently, unintentionally, unwittingly, unconsciously, by mistake.
– OPPOSITES correctly, intentionally.

mistimed adj. **ill-timed**, badly timed, inopportune, inappropriate, untimely, unseasonable.
– OPPOSITES opportune.

mistreat v. **ill-treat**, maltreat, abuse, knock about/around, hit, beat, strike, molest, injure, harm, hurt; misuse, mishandle; informal beat up, rough up.

mistreatment n. **ill-treatment**, maltreatment, abuse, beating, molestation, injury, harm; mishandling, manhandling.

mistress n. **lover**, girlfriend, kept woman; courtesan, concubine; informal fancy woman, bit on the side; old use paramour.

mistrust v. **1** *I mistrust his motives* **be suspicious of**, be mistrustful of, be distrustful of, be sceptical of, be wary of, be chary of, distrust, have doubts about, have misgivings about, have reservations about, suspect. **2** *don't mistrust your impulses* **question**, challenge, doubt, have no confidence/faith in.
▶ n. **1** *mistrust of Russia was widespread* **suspicion**, distrust, doubt, misgivings, wariness. **2** *their mistrust of David's competence* **questioning**, lack of confidence/faith in, doubt about.

mistrustful adj. **suspicious**, chary, wary, distrustful, doubtful, dubious, uneasy, sceptical, leery.

misty adj. **1** *misty weather* **hazy**, foggy, cloudy; smoggy. **2** *a misty figure* **blurry**, fuzzy, blurred, dim, indistinct, unclear, vague. **3** *misty memories* **vague**, unclear, indefinite, hazy, nebulous.
– OPPOSITES clear.

misunderstand v. **misapprehend**, misinterpret, misconstrue, misconceive, mistake, misread; be mistaken, get the wrong idea; informal be barking up the wrong tree, get (hold of) the wrong end of the stick.

misunderstanding n. **1** *a fundamental misunderstanding of juvenile crime* **misinterpretation**, misconstruction, misreading, misapprehension, misconception, the wrong idea, false impression. **2** *we have had some misunderstandings* **disagreement**, difference (of opinion), dispute, falling-out, quarrel, argument, altercation, squabble, wrangle, row, clash; informal spat, scrap, tiff.

misuse v. **1** *misusing public funds* **put to wrong use**, misemploy, embezzle, use fraudulently; abuse, squander, waste. **2** *she had been misused by her husband* **ill-treat**, maltreat, mistreat, abuse, knock about/around, hit, beat, strike, molest, injure, harm, hurt; mishandle, manhandle; informal beat up, rough up.
▶ n. **1** *a misuse of company assets* **wrong use**, embezzlement, fraud; squandering, waste. **2** *the misuse of drugs* **illegal use**, abuse.

mitigate v. **alleviate**, reduce, diminish, lessen, weaken, lighten, attenuate, take the edge off, allay, ease, assuage, palliate, relieve, tone down.
– OPPOSITES aggravate.

mitigating adj. **extenuating**, exonerative, justificatory, justifying, vindicatory, vindicating, qualifying; formal exculpatory.

mitigation n. **1** *the mitigation of the problems* **alleviation**, reduction, diminution, lessening, easing, weakening, assuagement, palliation, relief. **2** *what did she say in mitigation?* **extenuation**, explanation, excuse.

mix v. **1** *mix all the ingredients together* **blend**, mix up, mingle, combine, put together, jumble; fuse, unite, unify, join, amalgamate, incorporate, meld, marry, coalesce,

m

homogenize, intermingle, intermix; technical admix; literary commingle; old use commix.
2 *she mixes with all sorts* **associate**, socialize, fraternize, keep company, consort; mingle, circulate; N. Amer. **rub elbows**; informal hang out/around, knock about/around, hobnob; Brit. informal hang about. **3** *we just don't mix* **be compatible**, get along/on, be on the same wavelength, be in harmony, see eye to eye, agree; informal hit it off, click.
– OPPOSITES separate.
▶ n. *a mix of ancient and modern* **mixture**, blend, mingling, combination, compound, fusion, alloy, union, amalgamation; medley, melange, collection, selection, assortment, variety, mixed bag, miscellany, potpourri, jumble, hotchpotch, ragbag, patchwork, farrago, gallimaufry, omnium gatherum, salmagundi; N. Amer. hodgepodge.
□ **mix something up 1** *mix up the rusk with milk*. See **mix** (sense 1 of the verb). **2** *I mixed up the dates* confuse, get confused, muddle (up), get muddled up, mistake.
mixed up in involved in, embroiled in, caught up in.

mixed adj. **1** *a mixed collection* **assorted**, varied, variegated, miscellaneous, disparate, diverse, diversified, motley, sundry, jumbled, heterogeneous. **2** *chickens of mixed breeds* **hybrid**, half-caste, cross-bred, interbred. **3** *mixed reactions* **ambivalent**, equivocal, contradictory, conflicting, confused, muddled.
– OPPOSITES homogeneous.

mixed up adj. informal **confused**, (all) at sea, befuddled, bemused, bewildered, muddled; maladjusted, disturbed, neurotic, unbalanced; informal hung up, messed up.

mixer n. **1** *a kitchen mixer* **blender**, food processor, liquidizer, beater, churn. **2** *she was never really a mixer* **sociable person**, socializer, extrovert, socialite.

mixture n. **1** *the pudding mixture* **blend**, mix, brew, combination, concoction; composition, compound, alloy, amalgam. **2** *a strange mixture of people* **assortment**, miscellany, medley, melange, blend, variety, mixed bag, mix, diversity, collection, selection, potpourri, mishmash, hotchpotch, ragbag, patchwork, farrago, gallimaufry, omnium gatherum, salmagundi; N. Amer. hodgepodge. **3** *the animals were a mixture of genetic strands* **cross**, cross-breed, mongrel, hybrid, half-breed, half-caste.

mix-up n. **confusion**, muddle, misunderstanding, mistake, error.

moan n. **1** *moans of pain* **groan**, wail, whimper, sob, cry. **2** *the moan of the wind* **sough**, sigh, murmur. **3** informal *there were moans about the delay* **complaint**, complaining, grouse, grousing, grumble, grumbling, whine, whining, carping; informal gripe, griping, grouch, grouching, bitch, whinge, whingeing, beef, beefing.
▶ v. **1** *he moaned in agony* **groan**, wail, whimper, sob, cry. **2** *the wind moaned in the trees* **sough**, sigh, murmur. **3** informal *you're always moaning about the weather*

complain, grouse, grumble, whine, carp; informal gripe, grouch, bellyache, bitch, beef, whinge; N. English informal mither.

mob n. **1** *troops dispersed the mob* **crowd**, horde, multitude, rabble, mass, throng, group, gang, gathering, assemblage; old use rout. **2** *the mob were excluded from political life* **the common people**, the masses, the rank and file, the commonality, the commonalty, the third estate, the plebeians, the proletariat; the hoi polloi, the lower classes, the rabble, the riff-raff, the great unwashed; informal the proles, the plebs. **3** Brit. informal *he stood out from the rest of the mob* **group**, set, crowd, lot, circle, coterie, clan, faction, pack, band, ring; informal gang, bunch.
▶ v. **1** *he was mobbed by the crowds* **surround**, swarm around, besiege, jostle; harass, set upon, fall on, worry. **2** *reporters mobbed her hotel* **crowd (into)**, fill, pack, throng, press into, squeeze into.

mobile adj. **1** *both patients are mobile* **able to move (around)**, moving, walking; Zoology motile; Medicine ambulant. **2** *her mobile face* **expressive**, eloquent, revealing, animated. **3** *a mobile library* **travelling**, transportable, portable, movable; itinerant, peripatetic. **4** *highly mobile young people* **adaptable**, flexible, versatile, adjustable.
– OPPOSITES motionless, static.

mobility n. **1** *restricted mobility* **ability to move**, movability. **2** *the mobility of Billy's face* **expressiveness**, eloquence, animation. **3** *mobility in the workforce* **adaptability**, flexibility, versatility, adjustability.

mobilize v. **1** *the government mobilized the troops* **marshal**, deploy, muster, rally, call up, assemble, mass, organize, prepare. **2** *mobilizing support for the party* **generate**, arouse, awaken, excite, incite, provoke, foment, prompt, stimulate, stir up, galvanize, encourage, inspire, whip up; literary waken.

mock v. **1** *the local children mocked the old people* **ridicule**, jeer at, sneer at, deride, scorn, make fun of, laugh at, scoff at, tease, taunt; informal take the mickey out of, josh; N. Amer. informal goof on, rag on, pull someone's chain; Austral./NZ informal poke mullock at, sling off at. **2** *they mocked the way he speaks* **parody**, ape, take off, satirize, lampoon, imitate, mimic; informal send up.
▶ adj. *mock leather* **imitation**, artificial, man-made, simulated, synthetic, ersatz, fake, faux, reproduction, dummy, sham, false, spurious, bogus, counterfeit, pseudo; informal pretend, phoney.
– OPPOSITES genuine.

mockery n. **1** *the mockery in his voice* **ridicule**, derision, jeering, sneering, contempt, scorn, scoffing, teasing, taunting, sarcasm. **2** *the trial was a mockery* **travesty**, charade, farce, parody.

mocking adj. **sneering**, derisive, contemptuous, scornful, sardonic, ironic, sarcastic.

mode n. **1** *an informal mode of policing* **manner**, way, fashion, means, method, system, style, approach, technique, procedure, process, practice. **2** *the camera is in manual mode* **function**, position, operation. **3** *the mode for active wear* **fashion**, vogue, style, look, trend; craze, rage, fad.

model n. **1** *a working model* **replica**, copy, representation, mock-up, dummy, imitation, duplicate, reproduction, facsimile. **2** *the American model of airline deregulation* **prototype**, stereotype, archetype, type, version; mould, template, framework, pattern, design, blueprint. **3** *she was a model as a teacher* **ideal**, paragon, perfect example/specimen; perfection, acme, epitome, nonpareil, crème de la crème. **4** *a top model* **fashion model**, supermodel, mannequin; informal clothes horse. **5** *an artist's model* **sitter**, poser, subject. **6** *the latest model of car* **version**, type, design, variety, kind, sort. **7** *this dress is a model* **original (design)**, exclusive; informal one-off.

▸adj. **1** *model trains* **replica**, **toy**, miniature, dummy, imitation, duplicate, reproduction, facsimile. **2** *model farms* **prototypical**, prototypal, archetypal. **3** *a model teacher* **ideal**, perfect, exemplary, classic, flawless, faultless.

moderate adj. **1** *moderate success* **average**, modest, medium, middling, ordinary, common, commonplace, everyday, workaday; tolerable, passable, adequate, fair; mediocre, indifferent, unexceptional, unremarkable, run-of-the-mill; informal OK, so-so, bog-standard, fair-to-middling, (plain) vanilla, no great shakes, not up to much; NZ informal half-pie. **2** *moderate prices* **reasonable**, acceptable; inexpensive, low, fair, modest. **3** *moderate views* **middle-of-the-road**, non-extreme, non-radical. **4** *moderate behaviour* **restrained**, controlled, sober; tolerant, lenient.
– OPPOSITES great, unreasonable, extreme.

▸v. **1** *the wind has moderated* **die down**, abate, let up, calm down, lessen, decrease, diminish; recede, weaken, subside. **2** *you can help to moderate her anger* **curb**, control, check, temper, restrain, subdue; repress, tame, lessen, decrease, lower, reduce, diminish, alleviate, allay, appease, assuage, ease, soothe, calm, tone down; old use remit. **3** *the Speaker moderates the assembly* **chair**, take the chair of, preside over.
– OPPOSITES increase.

moderately adv. **somewhat**, quite, rather, fairly, reasonably, comparatively, relatively, to some extent; tolerably, passably, adequately; informal pretty.

moderation n. **1** *he urged them to show moderation* **self-restraint**, restraint, self-control, self-discipline; temperance, leniency, fairness. **2** *a moderation of their confrontational style* **relaxation**, easing (off), reduction, abatement, weakening, slackening, tempering, softening, diminution, diminishing, lessening; decline, modulation, modification, mitigation, allaying; informal let-up.

modern adj. **1** *modern times* **present-day**, contemporary, present, current, twenty-first-century, latter-day, recent. **2** *her clothes are very modern* **fashionable**, in fashion, in style, in vogue, up to date, all the rage, trendsetting, stylish, voguish, modish, chic, à la mode; the latest, new, newest, newfangled, modernistic, advanced; informal trendy, cool, in, with it, now, hip, happening; N. Amer. informal tony.
– OPPOSITES past, old-fashioned.

modernity n. **contemporaneity**, contemporaneousness, modernness, modernism; fashionableness, vogue; informal trendiness.

modernize v. **1** *they are modernizing their manufacturing facilities* **update**, bring up to date, streamline, rationalize, overhaul; renovate, remodel, refashion, revamp. **2** *we must modernize to survive* **get up to date**, move with the times, innovate; informal get in the swim, get with it.

modest adj. **1** *she was modest about her poetry* **self-effacing**, self-deprecating, humble, unpretentious, unassuming, unostentatious; shy, bashful, self-conscious, diffident, reserved, reticent, coy. **2** *modest success* **moderate**, fair, limited, tolerable, passable, adequate, satisfactory, acceptable, unexceptional. **3** *a modest house* **small**, ordinary, simple, plain, humble, inexpensive, unostentatious, unpretentious. **4** *her modest dress* **decorous**, decent, seemly, demure, proper.
– OPPOSITES conceited, great, grand.

modesty n. **1** *Hannah's modesty cloaks many talents* **self-effacement**, humility, unpretentiousness; shyness, bashfulness, self-consciousness, reserve, reticence, timidity. **2** *the modesty of his aspirations* **limited scope**, moderation. **3** *the modesty of his home* **unpretentiousness**, simplicity, plainness. **4** *her maidenly modesty* **decorum**, decorousness, decency, seemliness, demureness.

modicum n. **small amount**, particle, speck, fragment, scrap, crumb, grain, morsel, shred, dash, drop, pinch, jot, iota, whit, atom, smattering, scintilla, hint, suggestion; informal smidgen, tad; old use scantling.

modification n. **1** *the design is undergoing modification* **alteration**, adjustment, change, adaptation, refinement, revision. **2** *some minor modifications were made* **revision**, refinement, improvement, amendment, adaptation, adjustment, change, alteration. **3** *the modification of his views* **softening**, moderation, tempering, qualification.

modify v. **1** *their economic policy has been modified* **alter**, change, adjust, adapt, amend, revise, reshape, refashion, restyle, revamp, rework, remodel, refine; informal tweak. **2** *he modified his more extreme views* **moderate**, revise, temper, soften, tone down, qualify.

modish adj. **fashionable**, stylish, chic, modern, contemporary, all the rage, in vogue, voguish, up to the minute, à la mode;

m

informal **trendy**, cool, with it, in, now, hip, happening; N. Amer. informal **kicky**, tony.

modulate v. **regulate**, adjust, set, modify, moderate.

modus operandi n. **method (of working)**, way, MO, manner, technique, style, procedure, approach, methodology, strategy, plan, formula; formal **praxis**.

mogul n. **magnate**, tycoon, VIP, notable, personage, baron, captain, king, lord, grandee, nabob; informal **bigwig**, big shot, big noise, top dog; N. Amer. informal **top banana**, big enchilada.

moist adj. **1** *the air was moist* **damp**, dampish, steamy, humid, muggy, clammy, dank, wet, wettish, soggy, sweaty, sticky. **2** *a moist fruitcake* **succulent**, juicy, soft. **3** *her eyes grew moist* **tearful**, watery, misty.
– OPPOSITES dry.

moisten v. **dampen**, wet, damp, water, humidify; literary **bedew**.

moisture n. **wetness**, wet, water, liquid, condensation, steam, vapour, dampness, damp, humidity, clamminess, mugginess, dankness, wateriness.

> **WORD LINKS**
> **desiccated** having had the moisture removed
> **humectant** preserving moisture
> **hygroscopic** tending to absorb moisture from the air
> **saturated** full of moisture

moisturizer n. **lotion**, cream, balm, emollient, salve, unguent, lubricant; technical **humectant**.

mole[1] n. *the mole on his left cheek* **mark**, freckle, blotch, spot, blemish.

mole[2] n. *a well-placed mole* **spy**, (secret) agent, undercover agent, operative, plant, infiltrator; N. Amer. informal **spook**; old use **intelligencer**.

mole[3] n. *the mole protecting the harbour* **breakwater**, groyne, dyke, pier, sea wall, causeway.

molest v. **(sexually) abuse**, (sexually) assault, interfere with, rape, violate; informal **grope**, paw; literary **ravish**.

mollify v. **1** *they mollified the protesters* **appease**, placate, pacify, conciliate, soothe, calm (down). **2** *mollifying the fears of the public* **allay**, assuage, alleviate, mitigate, ease, reduce, moderate, temper, tone down.
– OPPOSITES enrage.

mollycoddle v. *his parents mollycoddle him* **pamper**, cosset, coddle, spoil, indulge, overindulge, pet, baby, nanny, nursemaid, wait on hand and foot, wrap in cotton wool.
▸ n. informal *the boy's a mollycoddle!* See **drip** (sense 2 of the noun).

molten adj. **liquefied**, liquid, fluid, melted, flowing.

moment n. **1** *he thought for a moment* **little while**, short time, bit, minute, instant, (split) second; informal **sec**, nanosecond, jiffy; Brit. informal **tick**, mo, two ticks. **2** *the moment they met* **point (in time)**, time, hour. **3** formal

issues of little moment **importance**, import, significance, consequence, note, weight, concern, interest.

□ **in a moment** very soon, in a minute, in a second, in a trice, shortly, any minute (now), in the twinkling of an eye, in (less than) no time, in no time at all; N. Amer. **momentarily**; informal **in a jiffy**, in a nanosecond, in two shakes (of a lamb's tail), before you can say Jack Robinson, in the blink of an eye; Brit. informal **in a tick**, in two ticks, in a mo; N. Amer. informal **in a snap**; literary **ere long**.

momentarily adv. **1** *he paused momentarily* **briefly**, fleetingly, for a moment, for a second, for an instant. **2** N. Amer. *my husband will be here momentarily*. See **in a moment**.

momentary adj. **brief**, short, short-lived, fleeting, passing, transient, ephemeral; literary **evanescent**.
– OPPOSITES lengthy.

momentous adj. **important**, significant, historic, portentous, critical, crucial, life-and-death, decisive, pivotal, consequential, of consequence, far-reaching; informal **earth-shattering**; formal **of moment**.
– OPPOSITES insignificant.

momentum n. **impetus**, energy, force, power, strength, thrust, speed, velocity.

monarch n. **sovereign**, ruler, Crown, crowned head, potentate; king, queen, emperor, empress, prince, princess.

monarchy n. **1** *a constitutional monarchy* **kingdom**, sovereign state, principality, empire. **2** *hereditary monarchy* **kingship**, sovereignty, autocracy, monocracy, absolutism.

monastery n. **religious community**; friary, abbey, priory, cloister.

monastic adj. **1** *a monastic community* **cloistered**, cloistral, claustral. **2** *a monastic existence* **austere**, ascetic, simple, solitary, monkish, celibate, quiet, cloistered, sequestered, secluded, reclusive, hermit-like, hermitic.

monetary adj. **financial**, fiscal, pecuniary, money, cash, economic, budgetary.

money n. **1** *I haven't got enough money* **(hard) cash**, ready money; the means, the wherewithal, funds, capital, finances, (filthy) lucre; banknotes, notes, coins, change, specie, silver, copper, currency; Brit. **sterling**; N. Amer. bills; N. Amer. & Austral. **roll**; informal **dough**, bread, loot, readies, shekels, moolah, the necessary; Brit. informal **dosh**, brass, lolly, spondulicks; N. Amer. informal **dinero**, bucks, mazuma; US informal **greenbacks**, simoleons, jack, rocks; Austral./NZ informal **Oscar**; Brit. dated **l.s.d.**; old use **pelf**. **2** *she married him for his money* **wealth**, riches, fortune, affluence, (liquid) assets, resources, means. **3** *the money here is better* **pay**, salary, wages, remuneration; formal **emolument**.

□ **for my money** in my opinion, to my mind, in my view, as I see it, personally, in my estimation, in my judgement, if you ask me.

in the money informal rich, wealthy, affluent, well-to-do, well off, prosperous, moneyed, in clover, opulent; informal rolling in it, loaded, stinking rich, well heeled, made of money.

> **WORD LINKS**
>
> **monetary, pecuniary** relating to money
> **numismatics** the study or collection of coins and banknotes
> **avarice, cupidity** greed for money
> **mercenary** interested only in money
> **miser** a person who hoards money and spends as little as possible
> **embezzlement, defalcation, peculation** the stealing of money entrusted to one's care
> **Mammon** money seen as an evil influence or object of worship

moneyed adj. **rich**, wealthy, affluent, well-to-do, well off, prosperous, in clover, opulent, of means, of substance; informal in the money, rolling in it, loaded, stinking/filthy rich, well heeled, made of money.
– OPPOSITES poor.

money-grubbing adj. informal **acquisitive**, avaricious, grasping, money-grubbing, rapacious, mercenary, materialistic; N. Amer. informal grabby.

moneymaking adj. **profitable**, profit-making, remunerative, lucrative, successful, financially rewarding.
– OPPOSITES loss-making.

mongrel n. *a rough-haired mongrel* **cross-breed**, cross, mixed breed, half-breed; tyke, cur, mutt; NZ kuri; Austral. informal mong, bitzer.
▶ adj. *a mongrel bitch* **cross-bred**, of mixed breed, half-breed.
– OPPOSITES pedigree.

monitor n. **1** *monitors covered all entrances* **detector**, scanner, recorder; security camera, CCTV. **2** *UN monitors* **observer**, watchdog, overseer, supervisor. **3** *a computer monitor* **screen**, visual display unit, VDU. **4** Brit. *a school monitor* **prefect**, praepostor; senior boy/girl, senior pupil.
▶ v. *his movements were closely monitored* **observe**, watch, track, keep an eye on, keep under observation, keep watch on, keep under surveillance, record, note, oversee; informal keep tabs on, keep a beady eye on.

monk n. brother, religious, coenobite, contemplative, mendicant; friar; abbot, prior; novice, oblate, postulant; Benedictine, Black Monk, Cluniac, Carthusian, Cistercian, Trappist, White Monk.

> **WORD LINKS**
>
> **monastic** relating to monks
> **monastery** a community of monks
> **cloister** a covered passage round a courtyard in a monastery
> **cowl** a large hood forming part of a monk's habit
> **scapular** a monk's short cloak
> **tonsure** the shaven part of a monk's head

monkey n. **1 primate**, ape. **2** *you little monkey!* See **rascal**.
□ **monkey about/around** fool about/around, play about/around, clown about/around, footle about/around; informal mess about/around, horse about/around, lark (about/around); Brit. informal muck about/around.

monkey with tamper with, fiddle with, interfere with, meddle with, tinker with, play with; informal mess with; Brit. informal muck about/around with.

> **WORD LINKS**
>
> **simian** relating to or resembling monkeys
> **primatology** the study of monkeys
> **troop** a group of monkeys

monkey business n. informal **mischief**, misbehaviour, mischievousness, devilry, devilment, tomfoolery; dishonesty, trickery, chicanery, skulduggery; informal shenanigans, funny business, hanky-panky; Brit. informal monkey tricks, jiggery-pokery; N. Amer. informal monkeyshines.

monocle n. **eyeglass**, glass.

monolith n. **standing stone**, menhir, sarsen (stone), megalith.

monolithic adj. **1** *a monolithic building* **massive**, huge, vast, colossal, gigantic, immense, giant, enormous; featureless, characterless. **2** *the old monolithic Communist party* **inflexible**, rigid, unbending, unchanging, fossilized.

monologue n. **soliloquy**, speech, address, lecture, sermon; formal oration.

monomania n. **obsession**, fixation, consuming passion, mania, compulsion.

monopolize v. **1** *the company has monopolized the market* **corner**, control, take over, gain control/dominance over; old use engross. **2** *he monopolized the conversation* **dominate**, take over, keep to oneself; informal hog.

monotonous adj. **1** *a monotonous job* **tedious**, boring, dull, uninteresting, unexciting, wearisome, tiresome, repetitive, repetitious, unvarying, unchanging, unvaried, humdrum, routine, mechanical, mind-numbing, soul-destroying; colourless, featureless, dreary; informal deadly; Brit. informal samey; N. Amer. informal dullsville. **2** *a monotonous voice* **toneless**, flat, uninflected, soporific.
– OPPOSITES interesting.

monotony n. **1** *the monotony of everyday life* **tedium**, tediousness, lack of variety, dullness, boredom, repetitiveness, repetitiousness, uniformity, wearisomeness, tiresomeness; lack of excitement, uneventfulness, dreariness, colourlessness, featurelessness; informal deadliness. **2** *the monotony of her voice* **tonelessness**, flatness.

monster n. **1** *her husband is a monster* **brute**, fiend, beast, devil, demon, barbarian, savage, animal; informal swine, pig. **2** *the boy's a little monster* **rascal**, imp, monkey, wretch, devil; informal horror, scamp, scallywag, tyke; Brit. informal perisher, pickle; N. Amer. informal varmint, hellion; old use scapegrace, rapscallion. **3** *he's a monster of a man* **giant**, mammoth, colossus, leviathan, titan; informal jumbo.
▶ adj. informal *a monster carp*. See **huge**.

monstrosity n. **1** *a concrete monstrosity* **eyesore**, blot on the landscape, carbuncle, excrescence. **2** *a biological monstrosity* **mutant**, mutation, freak (of nature), monster, abortion.

monstrous adj. **1** *a monstrous creature* **grotesque**, hideous, ugly, ghastly, gruesome, horrible, horrific, horrifying, grisly, disgusting, repulsive, repellent, dreadful, frightening, terrifying, malformed, misshapen. **2** *a monstrous tidal wave.* See **huge**. **3** *monstrous acts of violence* **appalling**, heinous, egregious, evil, wicked, abominable, terrible, horrible, dreadful, vile, outrageous, shocking, disgraceful; unspeakable, despicable, vicious, savage, barbaric, barbarous, inhuman; Brit. informal beastly.
– OPPOSITES lovely, small.

monument n. **1** *a stone monument* **memorial**, statue, pillar, column, obelisk, cross; cenotaph, tomb, mausoleum, shrine. **2** *a monument was placed over the grave* **gravestone**, headstone, tombstone. **3** *a monument to a past era of aviation* **testament**, record, reminder, remembrance, memorial, commemoration.

monumental adj. **1** *a monumental task* **huge**, great, enormous, gigantic, massive, colossal, mammoth, immense, tremendous, mighty, stupendous. **2** *a monumental error of judgement* **terrible**, dreadful, awful, colossal, staggering, huge, enormous, unforgivable, egregious. **3** *Beethoven's monumental works* **impressive**, striking, outstanding, remarkable, magnificent, majestic, stupendous, ambitious, large-scale, grand, awe-inspiring, important, significant, distinguished, memorable, immortal. **4** *a monumental inscription* **commemorative**, memorial, celebratory, commemorating.

mood n. **1** *she's in a good mood* **frame/state of mind**, humour, temper; disposition, spirit, tenor. **2** *he's obviously in a mood* **bad mood**, (bad) temper, sulk, pet, fit of pique; low spirits, the doldrums, the blues; informal the dumps, grump; Brit. informal paddy. **3** *the mood of the film* **atmosphere**, feeling, spirit, ambience, aura, character, tenor, flavour, feel, tone.
□ **in the mood** in the right frame of mind, feeling like, wanting to, inclined to, disposed to, minded to, eager to, willing to.

moody adj. **temperamental**, emotional, volatile, capricious, changeable, mercurial; sullen, sulky, morose, glum, depressed, dejected, despondent, doleful, dour, sour, saturnine; informal blue, down in the dumps/mouth.
– OPPOSITES cheerful.

moon n. **1** satellite.
▸v. **1** *stop mooning about* **waste time**, loaf, idle, mope; Brit. informal mooch; N. Amer. informal lollygag. **2** *he's mooning over her photograph* **mope**, pine, brood, daydream, fantasize, be in a reverie.
□ **once in a blue moon** informal hardly ever, scarcely ever, rarely, very seldom.

over the moon informal See **ecstatic**.

WORD LINKS

lunar relating to the moon
gibbous referring to the moon when it is more than half but less than fully illuminated
harvest moon a full moon in autumn
waning referring to the moon when it is apparently decreasing in size
waxing referring to the moon when it is apparently increasing in size
mare a large plain of volcanic rock on the moon
selenology the scientific study of the moon

---

moonshine n. See **rubbish** (sense 2 of the noun).

moor[1] v. *a boat was moored to the quay* **tie up**, secure, make fast, fix firmly, anchor, berth, dock.

moor[2] n. *a walk on the moor* **upland**, moorland, heath; grouse moor; Brit. fell, wold.

moot adj. *a moot point* **debatable**, open to discussion/question, arguable, questionable, at issue, open to doubt, disputable, controversial, contentious, disputed, unresolved, unsettled, up in the air.
▸v. *the idea was first mooted in the 1930s* **raise**, bring up, broach, mention, put forward, introduce, advance, propose, suggest.

mop n. *her tousled mop of hair* **shock**, mane, tangle, mass.
▸v. *a man was mopping the floor* **wash**, clean, wipe.
□ **mop something up 1** *I mopped up the spilt coffee* **wipe up**, clean up, sponge up. **2** *troops mopped up the last pockets of resistance* **finish off**, deal with, dispose of, take care of, clear up, eliminate.

mope v. **1** *it's no use moping* **brood**, sulk, be miserable, be despondent, pine, eat one's heart out, fret, grieve; informal be down in the dumps/mouth; literary repine. **2** *she was moping about the house* **languish**, moon, idle, loaf; Brit. informal mooch; N. Amer. informal lollygag.
▸n. *she's regarded as a mope* **melancholic**, depressive, pessimist, killjoy; informal sourpuss, party pooper, spoilsport, grouch, grump; Brit. informal misery.

moral adj. **1** *moral issues* **ethical**. **2** *a very moral man* **virtuous**, good, righteous, upright, upstanding, high-minded, principled, honourable, honest, just, noble, incorruptible, scrupulous, respectable, decent, clean-living, law-abiding. **3** *moral support* **psychological**, emotional, mental.
– OPPOSITES dishonourable.
▸n. **1** *the moral of the story* **lesson**, message, meaning, significance, signification, import, point, teaching. **2** *he has no morals* **moral code**, code of ethics, moral standards/values, principles, standards, (sense of) morality, scruples.

morale n. **confidence**, self-confidence, self-esteem, spirit(s), team spirit.

moral fibre n. **strength of character**, fibre, fortitude, resolve, backbone, spine, mettle, firmness of purpose; Brit. Dunkirk spirit.

morality n. **1** *the morality of nuclear weapons* **ethics**, rights and wrongs, ethicality. **2** *a sharp decline in morality* **virtue**, goodness, good behaviour, righteousness, rectitude, uprightness; morals, principles, honesty, integrity, propriety, honour, justice, decency. **3** *orthodox Christian morality* **moral standards**, morals, ethics, standards/ principles of behaviour, mores, standards.

moralize v. **pontificate**, sermonize, lecture, preach; informal preachify.

morass n. **1** *the muddy morass* **quagmire**, swamp, bog, marsh, mire, marshland, slough; N. Amer. moor. **2** *a morass of paperwork* **confusion**, chaos, muddle, tangle, entanglement, imbroglio, jumble, clutter.

moratorium n. **embargo**, ban, prohibition, suspension, postponement, stay, stoppage, halt, freeze, standstill, respite.

morbid adj. *a morbid fascination with contemporary warfare* **ghoulish**, macabre, unhealthy, gruesome, unwholesome; informal sick.
– OPPOSITES wholesome.

mordant adj. **caustic**, trenchant, biting, cutting, acerbic, sardonic, sarcastic, scathing, acid, sharp, keen; critical, bitter, virulent, vitriolic; formal mordacious.

more determiner *I could do with some more clothes* **additional**, further, added, extra, increased, new, other, supplementary.
– OPPOSITES less, fewer.
▸ adv. **1** *he was able to concentrate more on his writing* **to a greater extent**, further, some more, better. **2** *he was rich, and more, he was handsome* **moreover**, furthermore, besides, what's more, in addition, also, as well, too, to boot, on top of that, into the bargain; old use withal, forbye.
▸ pron. *we're going to need more* **extra**, an additional amount/number, an addition, an increase.
– OPPOSITES less, fewer.
▫ **more or less** approximately, roughly, nearly, almost, close to, about, of the order of, in the region of.

moreover adv. **besides**, furthermore, what's more, in addition, also, as well, too, to boot, additionally, on top of that, into the bargain, more; old use withal, forbye.

mores plural n. **customs**, conventions, ways, way of life, traditions, practices, habits; formal praxis.

morgue n. **mortuary**, funeral parlour; Brit. chapel of rest.

moribund adj. **1** *the patient was moribund* **dying**, expiring, on one's deathbed, near death, at death's door, not long for this world. **2** *the moribund shipbuilding industry* **declining**, in decline, waning, dying, stagnating, stagnant, crumbling, on its last legs.
– OPPOSITES thriving.

morning n. **1** *I've got a meeting this morning* **before noon**, before lunch(time), a.m.; literary morn; Nautical & N. Amer. forenoon. **2** *morning is on its way* **dawn**, daybreak, sunrise,

first light, cockcrow; N. Amer. sunup; literary dayspring, dawning, aurora.
▫ **morning, noon, and night** all the time, without a break, constantly, continually, incessantly, ceaselessly, perpetually, unceasingly; informal 24-7.

WORD LINKS
antemeridian, matutinal relating to the morning

moron n. informal See **fool** (sense 1 of the noun).

moronic adj. informal See **stupid** (sense 1).

morose adj. **sullen**, sulky, gloomy, bad-tempered, ill-tempered, dour, surly, sour, glum, moody, ill-humoured, melancholy, melancholic, doleful, Eeyorish, miserable, depressed, dejected, despondent, downcast, unhappy, in low spirits, low, down, grumpy, irritable, churlish, cantankerous, crotchety, cross, crabby, grouchy, testy, snappish, peevish, crusty; informal blue, down in the dumps/mouth, fed up.
– OPPOSITES cheerful.

morsel n. **mouthful**, bite, nibble, bit, soupçon, taste, spoonful, forkful, sliver, drop, dollop, spot, gobbet; titbit, bonne bouche; informal smidgen.

mortal adj. **1** *mortal remains | all men are mortal* **perishable**, physical, bodily, corporeal, fleshly, earthly; human, impermanent, transient, ephemeral. **2** *a mortal blow* **deadly**, fatal, lethal, death-dealing, murderous, terminal. **3** *mortal enemies* **irreconcilable**, deadly, sworn, bitter, out-and-out, implacable. **4** *a mortal sin* **unpardonable**, unforgivable. **5** *living in mortal fear* **extreme**, (very) great, terrible, awful, dreadful, intense, severe, grave, dire, unbearable. **6** *the punishment is out of all mortal proportion* **conceivable**, imaginable, perceivable, possible, earthly.
– OPPOSITES venial.
▸ n. *we are mere mortals* **human (being)**, person, man/woman; earthling.

mortality n. **1** *a sense of his own mortality* **impermanence**, transience, ephemerality, perishability; humanity; corporeality. **2** *the causes of mortality* **death**, loss of life, dying.

mortification n. **1** *scarlet with mortification* **embarrassment**, humiliation, chagrin, discomfiture, discomposure, shame. **2** *the mortification of the flesh* **subduing**, suppression, subjugation, control, controlling; disciplining, chastening, punishment.

mortify v. **1** *I'd be mortified if my friends found out* **embarrass**, humiliate, chagrin, discomfit, shame, abash, horrify, appal. **2** *he was mortified at being excluded* **hurt**, wound, affront, offend, put out, pique, irk, annoy, vex; informal rile. **3** *mortifying the flesh* **subdue**, suppress, subjugate, control; discipline, chasten, punish. **4** *the cut had mortified* **become gangrenous**, fester, putrefy, gangrene, rot, decay, decompose.

m

mortuary n. **morgue**, funeral parlour; Brit. chapel of rest.

most pron. *most of the guests brought flowers* **nearly all**, almost all, the greatest part/number, the majority, the bulk, the preponderance.
– OPPOSITES little, few.
  □ **for the most part** mostly, mainly, in the main, on the whole, largely, by and large, to a large extent, predominantly, chiefly, principally, basically, generally, usually, typically, commonly, as a rule, on balance, on average.

mostly adv. **1** *the other passengers were mostly businessmen* **mainly**, for the most part, on the whole, in the main, largely, chiefly, predominantly, principally, primarily. **2** *I mostly wear jeans* **usually**, generally, in general, as a rule, ordinarily, normally, customarily, typically, most of the time, almost always.

mote n. **speck**, particle, grain, spot, fleck, atom, scintilla.

moth-eaten adj. **threadbare**, worn (out), well worn, old, shabby, scruffy, tattered, ragged; informal tatty, the worse for wear; N. Amer. informal raggedy.

mother n. **1** *I will ask my mother* **female parent**, materfamilias, matriarch; informal ma, mam, mammy, old lady, old woman; Brit. informal mum, mummy; N. Amer. informal mom, mommy; Brit. informal dated mater; dated mama. **2** *the foal's mother* **dam**. **3** *the wish was mother of the deed* **source**, origin, genesis, fountainhead, inspiration, stimulus; literary wellspring.
– OPPOSITES child, father.
▶ v. **1** *she mothered her husband* **look after**, care for, take care of, nurse, protect, tend, raise, rear; pamper, coddle, cosset, fuss over. **2** *she mothered an illegitimate daughter* **give birth to**, have, bear, produce; N. Amer. birth; old use be brought to bed of.
– OPPOSITES neglect.

motherly adj. **maternal**, maternalistic, protective, caring, loving, devoted, affectionate, fond, warm, tender, gentle, kind, kindly, understanding, compassionate.

motif n. **1** *a colourful tulip motif* **design**, pattern, decoration, figure, shape, device, emblem, ornament. **2** *a recurring motif in Pinter's work* **theme**, idea, concept, subject, topic, leitmotif, element, trope.

motion n. **1** *the rocking motion of the boat* | *a planet's motion around the sun* **movement**, moving, locomotion, rise and fall, shifting; progress, passage, passing, transit, course, travel, travelling; technical kinesis. **2** *a motion of the hand* **gesture**, movement, signal, sign, indication; wave, nod, gesticulation. **3** *the motion failed to obtain a majority* **proposal**, proposition, recommendation, suggestion.
▶ v. *he motioned her to sit down* **gesture**, signal, direct, indicate; wave, beckon, nod, gesticulate.
  □ **in motion** moving, on the move, going, travelling, running, functioning, operational.
  set in motion start, commence, begin, activate, initiate, launch, get under way, get going, get off the ground; trigger off, set off, spark off, generate, cause.

motionless adj. **unmoving**, still, stationary, stock-still, immobile, static, not moving a muscle, rooted to the spot, transfixed, paralysed, frozen.
– OPPOSITES moving.

motivate v. **1** *she was primarily motivated by the desire for profit* **prompt**, drive, move, inspire, stimulate, influence, activate, impel, push, propel, spur (on). **2** *it's the teacher's job to motivate the child* **inspire**, stimulate, encourage, spur (on), excite, inspirit, incentivize, fire with enthusiasm.

motivation n. **1** *his motivation was financial* **motive**, motivating force, incentive, stimulus, stimulation, inspiration, inducement, incitement, spur, reason. **2** *staff motivation* **enthusiasm**, drive, ambition, initiative, determination, enterprise; informal get-up-and-go.

motive n. **1** *the motive for the attack* **reason**, motivation, motivating force, rationale, grounds, cause, basis, object, purpose, intention; incentive, inducement, incitement, lure, inspiration, stimulus, stimulation, spur. **2** *religious motives in art* **motif**, theme, idea, concept, subject, topic, leitmotif, trope.
▶ adj. *motive power* **kinetic**, driving, impelling, propelling, propulsive, motor.

motley adj. **miscellaneous**, disparate, diverse, assorted, varied, diversified, heterogeneous.
– OPPOSITES homogeneous.

mottled adj. **blotchy**, blotched, spotted, spotty, speckled, streaked, streaky, marbled, flecked, freckled, dappled, stippled, piebald, skewbald, brindled, brindle; N. Amer. pinto; informal splotchy.

motto n. **maxim**, saying, proverb, aphorism, adage, saw, axiom, apophthegm, formula, expression, phrase, dictum, precept; slogan, catchphrase; truism, cliché, platitude.

mould¹ n. **1** *the molten metal is poured into a mould* **cast**, die, form, matrix, shape, template, pattern, frame. **2** *an actress in the traditional Hollywood mould* **pattern**, form, shape, format, model, kind, type, style; archetype, prototype. **3** *he is a figure of heroic mould* **character**, nature, temperament, disposition; calibre, kind, sort, variety, stamp, type.

▶ v. **1** *a figure moulded from clay* **shape**, form, fashion, model, work, construct, make, create, manufacture, sculpt, sculpture; forge, cast. **2** *moulding US policy* **determine**, direct, control, guide, lead, influence, shape, form, fashion, make.

mould² n. *walls stained with mould* **mildew**, fungus, must, mouldiness, mustiness.

mould³ n. *leaf mould* **earth**, soil, dirt, loam, humus.

moulder v. **decay**, decompose, rot (away), go mouldy, go off, go bad, spoil, putrefy.

mouldy adj. **mildewed**, mildewy, musty, mouldering, fusty; decaying, decayed, rotting, rotten, bad, spoiled, spoilt, decomposing.

mound n. **1** *a mound of leaves* **heap**, pile, stack, mountain; mass, accumulation, assemblage. **2** *high on the mound* **hillock**, hill, knoll, rise, hummock, hump, embankment, bank, ridge, elevation, acclivity; Scottish brae; Geology drumlin. **3** *a burial mound* **barrow**, tumulus; motte.
▶ v. *mound up the rice on a serving plate* **pile (up)**, heap (up).

mount v. **1** *he mounted the stairs* **go up**, ascend, climb (up), scale. **2** *the committee mounted the platform* **climb on to**, jump on to, clamber on to, get on to. **3** *they mounted their horses* **get astride**, bestride, get on to, hop on to. **4** *the museum is mounting an exhibition* **(put on)** display, exhibit, present, install; organize, put on, stage. **5** *the company mounted a takeover bid* **organize**, stage, prepare, arrange, set up; launch, set in motion, initiate. **6** *their losses mounted rapidly* **increase**, grow, rise, escalate, soar, spiral, shoot up, rocket, climb, accumulate, build up, multiply. **7** *cameras were mounted above the door* **install**, place, fix, set, put up, put in position.
– OPPOSITES descend.
▶ n. **1** *he hung on to his mount's bridle* **horse**; old use steed. **2** *a decorated photograph mount* **setting**, backing, support, mounting, frame, stand.

mountain n. **1** *a range of mountains* **peak**, height, mount, prominence, summit, pinnacle, mountaintop, alp; **(mountains)** range, massif, sierra; Scottish ben, Munro. **2** *a mountain of work* **a great deal**, a lot; profusion, abundance, quantity, backlog; informal heap, pile, stack, slew, lots, loads, heaps, piles, tons, masses; N. Amer. informal gobs. **3** *a butter mountain* **surplus**, surfeit, glut, oversupply.

> **WORD LINKS**
> **montane, orographic** relating to mountains or mountainous country
> **avalanche** a mass of snow and ice falling rapidly down a mountainside
> **glacier** a slowly moving mass of ice on a mountain
> **tarn** a small mountain lake

mountainous adj. **1** *a mountainous region* **hilly**, craggy, rocky, alpine; upland, highland.

2 *mountainous waves* **huge**, enormous, gigantic, massive, giant, colossal, immense, tremendous, mighty; informal whopping, thumping, humongous; Brit. informal whacking, ginormous.
– OPPOSITES flat, tiny.

mountebank n. **swindler**, charlatan, confidence trickster, fraud, fraudster, impostor, trickster, hoaxer, quack; informal con man, flimflammer, sharp; N. Amer. informal grifter, bunco artist; Austral. informal magsman, illywhacker.

mourn v. **1** *Isobel mourned her husband* **grieve for**, sorrow over, lament for, weep for, wail/keen over; old use plain for. **2** *he mourned the loss of the beautiful buildings* **deplore**, bewail, bemoan, rue, regret.

mournful adj. **sad**, sorrowful, doleful, melancholy, melancholic, woeful, grief-stricken, miserable, unhappy, heartbroken, broken-hearted, gloomy, dismal, desolate, dejected, despondent, depressed, downcast, disconsolate, woebegone, forlorn, rueful, lugubrious, joyless, cheerless; literary dolorous.
– OPPOSITES cheerful.

mourning n. **1** *a period of mourning* **grief**, grieving, sorrowing, lamentation, lament, keening, wailing, weeping; literary dole. **2** *she was dressed in mourning* **black (clothes)**, (widow's) weeds; old use sables.

mouse n.

> **WORD LINKS**
> **murine** relating to mice
> **musophobia** fear of mice

moustache n. **whiskers**, mustachios, handlebar moustache, walrus moustache, burnsides; informal tash; N. Amer. informal stash.

mousy adj. **1** *mousy hair* **lightish brown**, brownish, brownish-grey, dun-coloured; dull, lacklustre. **2** *a small, mousy woman* **timid**, quiet, fearful, timorous, shy, self-effacing, diffident, unassertive, unforthcoming, withdrawn, introverted, introvert.

mouth n. **1** *open your mouth* **lips**, jaws; maw, muzzle; informal trap, chops, kisser; Brit. informal gob, cakehole; N. Amer. informal puss, bazoo. **2** *the mouth of the cave* **entrance**, opening, entry, way in, access, ingress. **3** *the mouth of the bottle* **opening**, rim, lip. **4** *the mouth of the river* **outfall**, outlet, debouchment; estuary, firth. **5** informal *he's all mouth* **boasting**, bragging, idle talk, bombast, braggadocio; informal hot air. **6** informal *you've got a lot of mouth* **impudence**, cheek, cheekiness, insolence, impertinence, effrontery, presumption, presumptuousness, rudeness, disrespect; informal lip, (brass) neck; Brit. informal sauce, backchat; N. Amer. informal sass, sassiness, back talk.
▶ v. *he mouthed platitudes* **utter**, speak, say; pronounce, enunciate, articulate, voice, express; say insincerely, say for form's sake.
□ **mouth off** informal rant, spout, declaim, sound off.

m

mouthful n. **1** *a mouthful of pizza* **bite**, nibble, taste, bit, piece; spoonful, forkful. **2** *a mouthful of beer* **draught**, sip, swallow, drop, gulp, slug; informal swig. **3** *'sesquipedalian' is a bit of a mouthful* **tongue-twister**, long word, difficult word.

mouthpiece n. **1** *the flute's mouthpiece* **embouchure**. **2** *a mouthpiece for the government* **spokesperson**, spokesman, spokeswoman, agent, representative, propagandist, voice.

movable adj. **1** *movable objects* **portable**, transportable, transferable; mobile. **2** *movable feasts* **variable**, changeable, alterable.
– OPPOSITES fixed.

movables plural n. **possessions**, belongings, effects, property, goods, chattels, paraphernalia, impedimenta; informal gear.
– OPPOSITES fixtures, fittings.

move v. **1** *she moved to the door | don't move!* **go**, walk, proceed, progress, advance; budge, stir, shift, change position. **2** *he moved the chair closer to the fire* **carry**, transport, transfer, shift. **3** *things were moving too fast* **(make) progress**, make headway, advance, develop. **4** *he urged the council to move quickly* **take action**, act, take steps, do something, take measures; informal get moving. **5** *she's moved to Cambridge* **relocate**, move house, move away/out, change address/house, leave, go away, decamp; Brit. informal up sticks; N. Amer. informal pull up stakes. **6** *I was deeply moved by the story* **affect**, touch, impress, shake, upset, disturb, make an impression on. **7** *she was moved to find out more about it* **inspire**, prompt, stimulate, motivate, provoke, influence, rouse, induce, incite. **8** *they are not prepared to move on this issue* **change**, budge, shift one's ground, change one's tune, change one's mind, have second thoughts; do a U-turn, do an about-face; Brit. do an about-turn. **9** *she moves in the pop and art worlds* **circulate**, mix, socialize, keep company, associate; informal hang out/around; Brit. informal hang about. **10** *I move that we adjourn* **propose**, submit, suggest, advocate, recommend, urge.
▸ n. **1** *his eyes followed her every move* **movement**, motion, action; gesture, gesticulation. **2** *his recent move to London* **relocation**, change of house/address, transfer, posting. **3** *the latest move in the war against drugs* **initiative**, step, action, act, measure, manoeuvre, tactic, stratagem. **4** *it's your move* **turn**, go; opportunity, chance.
□ **get a move on** informal hurry up, speed up, move faster; informal get cracking, get moving, step on it, shake a leg, get a wiggle on; Brit. informal get one's skates on, stir one's stumps; dated make haste.
make a move 1 *waiting for the other side to make a move* **do something**, take action, act, take the initiative; informal get moving. **2** Brit. *I'd better be making a move* **leave**, take one's leave, be on one's way, get going, depart, be off; informal push off, shove off, split.
on the move 1 *she's always on the move* **travelling**, in transit, moving, journeying, on the road; informal on the go. **2** *the economy is on the move* **progressing**, making progress, advancing, developing.

movement n. **1** *Rachel made a sudden movement | there was almost no movement* **motion**, move; gesture, gesticulation, sign, signal; action, activity. **2** *the movement of supplies* **transportation**, shift, shifting, conveyance, moving, transfer. **3** *the labour movement* **political group**, party, faction, wing, lobby, camp. **4** *a movement to declare war on poverty* **campaign**, crusade, drive, push. **5** *there have been movements in the financial markets* **development**, change, fluctuation, variation. **6** *the movement towards equality* **trend**, tendency, drift, swing. **7** *some movement will be made by the end of the month* **progress**, progression, advance. **8** *a symphony in three movements* **part**, section, division. **9** *the clock's movement* **mechanism**, machinery, works, workings; informal innards, guts.

movie n. **1** *a horror movie* **film**, (motion) picture, feature (film); informal flick; dated moving picture. **2** *let's go to the movies* **the cinema**, the pictures, the silver screen; informal the flicks, the big screen.

moving adj. **1** *moving parts | a moving train* **in motion**, operating, operational, working, going, on the move, active; movable, mobile. **2** *a moving book* **affecting**, touching, poignant, heart-warming, heart-rending, emotional, disturbing; inspiring, inspirational, stimulating, stirring. **3** *the party's moving force* **driving**, motivating, dynamic, stimulating, inspirational.
– OPPOSITES fixed, stationary.

mow v. *she had mown the grass* **cut (down)**, trim; crop, clip.
□ **mow someone/something down** kill, gun down, shoot down, cut down, cut to pieces, butcher, slaughter, massacre, annihilate, wipe out; informal blow away.

much determiner *did you get much help?* **a lot of**, a great/good deal of, a great/large amount of, plenty of, ample, copious, abundant, plentiful, considerable; informal lots of, loads of, heaps of, masses of, tons of.
– OPPOSITES little.
▸ adv. **1** *it didn't hurt much* **greatly**, to a great extent/degree, a great deal, a lot, considerably, appreciably. **2** *does he come here much?* **often**, frequently, many times, repeatedly, regularly, habitually, routinely, usually, normally, commonly; informal a lot.
▸ pron. *he did so much for our team* **a lot**, a great/good deal, plenty; informal lots, loads, heaps, masses.
□ **much of a muchness** informal very similar, much the same, very alike, practically identical.

muck n. **1** *I'll just clean off the muck* **dirt**, grime, filth, mud, slime, mess; informal crud, gunk, grunge, gloop; Brit. informal gunge, grot; N. Amer. informal guck, glop. **2** *spreading muck on the fields* **dung**, manure, ordure, excrement, excreta, droppings, faeces, sewage; N. Amer. informal cow chips, horse apples.
□ **muck something up** informal make a mess of, mess up, bungle, spoil, ruin, wreck; informal botch, make a hash of, muff, fluff, foul up, louse up; Brit. informal make a pig's ear of, make a Horlicks of; N. Amer. informal goof up.
muck about/around Brit. informal **1** *he was mucking about with his mates* **fool about/around**, play about/around, clown about/around, footle about/around; informal mess about/around, horse about/around, lark (about/around). **2** *someone's been mucking about with the video* **interfere**, fiddle (about/around), play about/around, tamper, meddle, tinker; informal mess (about/around).

mucky adj. **dirty**, filthy, grimy, muddy, grubby, messy, soiled, stained, smeared, slimy, sticky, bespattered; informal cruddy, grungy, gloopy; Brit. informal gungy, grotty; Austral./NZ informal scungy; literary besmirched, begrimed, befouled.
– OPPOSITES clean.

mud n. **mire**, sludge, ooze, silt, clay, dirt, soil.

muddle v. **1** *the papers have got muddled up* **confuse**, mix up, jumble (up), disarrange, disorganize, disorder, disturb, mess up. **2** *it would only muddle you* **bewilder**, confuse, bemuse, perplex, puzzle, baffle, nonplus, mystify.
▸ n. **1** *the files are in a muddle* **mess**, confusion, jumble, tangle, hotchpotch, mishmash, chaos, disorder, disarray, disorganization; N. Amer. hodgepodge. **2** *a bureaucratic muddle* **bungle**, mix-up, misunderstanding; informal foul-up; N. Amer. informal snafu.
□ **muddle along/through** cope, manage, get by/along, scrape by/along, make do.

muddled adj. **1** *a muddled pile of photographs* **jumbled**, in a jumble, in a muddle, in a mess, chaotic, in disorder, in disarray, topsy-turvy, disorganized, disordered, disorderly, mixed up, at sixes and sevens; informal higgledy-piggledy. **2** *she felt muddled* **confused**, bewildered, bemused, perplexed, disorientated, disoriented, in a muddle, befuddled; N. Amer. informal discombobulated. **3** *muddled thinking* **incoherent**, confused, muddle-headed, woolly.
– OPPOSITES orderly, clear.

muddy adj. **1** *muddy ground* **waterlogged**, boggy, marshy, swampy, squelchy, squishy, mucky, slimy, spongy, wet, soft, heavy; old use quaggy. **2** *muddy boots* **mud-caked**, muddied, dirty, filthy, mucky, grimy, soiled; literary begrimed. **3** *muddy water* **murky**, cloudy, muddied, turbid; N. Amer. riled, roily. **4** *a muddy pink* **dingy**, dirty, drab, dull, sludgy.
– OPPOSITES clean, clear.
▸ v. **1** *don't muddy your boots* **make muddy**, dirty, soil, spatter, bespatter; literary besmirch, begrime. **2** *these results muddy the situation*

make unclear, obscure, confuse, obfuscate, blur, cloud, befog.
– OPPOSITES clarify.

muff v. informal **mishandle**, mismanage, mess up, make a mess of, bungle; informal botch, make a hash of, fluff, foul up, louse up; Brit. informal make a pig's ear of, make a Horlicks of; N. Amer. informal goof up.

muffle v. **1** *everyone was muffled up in coats* **wrap (up)**, swathe, enfold, envelop, cloak. **2** *the sound of their footsteps was muffled* **deaden**, dull, dampen, damp down, mute, soften, quieten, tone down, mask, stifle, smother.

muffled adj. **indistinct**, faint, muted, dull, soft, stifled, smothered.
– OPPOSITES loud.

mug[1] n. **1** *a china mug* **beaker**, cup; tankard, glass, stein, flagon; dated seidel; old use stoup. **2** informal *her ugly mug*. See **face** (sense 1 of the noun). **3** Brit. informal *he's no mug*. See **fool** (sense 1 of the noun).
▸ v. informal *he was mugged by three youths* **assault**, attack, set upon, beat up, rob; informal jump, rough up, lay into; Brit. informal duff up, do over.

mug[2] v.
□ **mug something up** informal *she's mugging up the Highway Code* **study**, read up, cram; informal bone up (on); Brit. informal swot; old use con.

muggy adj. **humid**, close, sultry, sticky, oppressive, airless, stifling, suffocating, stuffy, clammy, damp, heavy, fuggy.
– OPPOSITES fresh.

mulish adj. **obstinate**, stubborn, pig-headed, recalcitrant, intransigent, unyielding, inflexible, bullheaded, stiff-necked; Brit. informal bloody-minded, bolshie.

mull v.
□ **mull something over** ponder, consider, think over/about, reflect on, contemplate, turn over in one's mind, chew over, cogitate on, give some thought to; old use pore on.

multicoloured adj. **kaleidoscopic**, psychedelic, colourful, multicolour, many-coloured, many-hued, rainbow, jazzy, varicoloured, variegated, harlequin, polychromatic.
– OPPOSITES monochrome.

multifarious adj. **diverse**, many, numerous, various, varied, diversified, multiple, multitudinous, multiplex, manifold, multifaceted, different, heterogeneous, miscellaneous, assorted; literary myriad, divers.
– OPPOSITES homogeneous.

multiple adj. **numerous**, many, various, different, diverse, several, manifold, multifarious, multitudinous; literary myriad, divers.
– OPPOSITES single.

multiplicity n. **abundance**, scores, mass, host, array, variety; range, diversity, heterogeneity, plurality, profusion; informal loads, stacks, heaps, masses, tons; literary myriad.

m

multiply v. **1** *their difficulties seem to be multiplying* **increase**, grow, accumulate, proliferate, mount up, mushroom, snowball. **2** *the rabbits have multiplied* **breed**, reproduce, procreate.
– OPPOSITES decrease.

multitude n. **1** *a multitude of birds* **a lot**, a great/large number, a great/large quantity, host, horde, mass, swarm, abundance, profusion; scores, quantities, droves; informal slew, lots, loads, masses, stacks, heaps, tons, dozens, hundreds, thousands, millions; N. Amer. informal gazillions. **2** *Father Peter addressed the multitude* **crowd**, gathering, assembly, congregation, flock, throng, horde, mob; formal concourse. **3** *political power in the hands of the multitude* **the (common) people**, the populace, the masses, the rank and file, the commonality, the commonalty, the plebeians; the hoi polloi, the mob, the proletariat, the common herd, the rabble, the proles, the plebs.

multitudinous adj. **numerous**, many, abundant, profuse, prolific, copious, multifarious, innumerable, countless, numberless, infinite; literary divers, myriad.

mum[1] n. Brit. informal *my mum looks after me.* See **mother** (sense 1 of the noun).

mum[2] informal adj. *he was keeping mum* **silent**, quiet, mute, dumb, tight-lipped, unforthcoming, reticent; old use mumchance. □ **mum's the word** say nothing, keep quiet, don't breathe a word, don't tell a soul, keep it secret, keep it to yourself, keep it under your hat; informal don't let on, keep shtum, don't let the cat out of the bag.

mumble v. **mutter**, murmur, speak indistinctly, talk under one's breath.

mumbo jumbo n. **nonsense**, gibberish, claptrap, rubbish, balderdash, blather, hocus-pocus; informal gobbledegook, double Dutch, argle-bargle.

munch v. **chew**, champ, chomp, masticate, crunch, eat; formal manducate.

mundane adj. **1** *her mundane life* **humdrum**, dull, boring, tedious, monotonous, tiresome, wearisome, unexciting, uninteresting, uneventful, unvarying, unremarkable, repetitive, repetitious, routine, ordinary, everyday, day-to-day, run-of-the-mill, commonplace, workaday; informal (plain) vanilla. **2** *the mundane world* **earthly**, worldly, terrestrial, material, temporal, secular; literary sublunary.
– OPPOSITES extraordinary, spiritual.

municipal adj. **civic**, civil, metropolitan, urban, city, town, borough.
– OPPOSITES rural.

municipality n. **borough**, town, city, district; N. Amer. precinct, township; Scottish burgh.

munificence n. **generosity**, open-handedness, magnanimity, lavishness, liberality, philanthropy, charitableness, largesse, big-heartedness, beneficence; literary bounty, bounteousness.

munificent adj. **generous**, bountiful, open-handed, magnanimous, philanthropic, princely, handsome, lavish, liberal, charitable, big-hearted, beneficent; literary bounteous.
– OPPOSITES mean.

murder n. **1** *a brutal murder* **killing**, homicide, assassination, liquidation, extermination, execution, slaughter, butchery, massacre; manslaughter; literary slaying. **2** informal *driving there was murder* **hell (on earth)**, a nightmare, an ordeal, a trial, misery, torture, agony.
▸ v. **1** *someone tried to murder him* **kill**, put/do to death, assassinate, execute, liquidate, eliminate, dispatch, butcher, slaughter, massacre, wipe out; informal bump off, do in, do away with, knock off, blow away, someone's brains out, take out, dispose of; N. Amer. informal ice, rub out, smoke, waste; literary slay. **2** informal *Anna was murdering a Mozart sonata.* See **mangle** (sense 2). **3** informal *he murdered his opponent.* See **trounce**.

murderer, murderess n. **killer**, assassin, serial killer, butcher, slaughterer; informal hitman, hired gun; dated homicide; literary slayer.

murderous adj. **1** *a murderous attack* **homicidal**, brutal, violent, savage, ferocious, fierce, vicious, bloodthirsty, barbarous, barbaric; fatal, lethal, deadly, mortal, death-dealing; old use sanguinary. **2** informal *a murderous schedule* **arduous**, gruelling, strenuous, punishing, onerous, exhausting, taxing, difficult, rigorous; informal killing, hellish.

murky adj. **1** *a murky winter afternoon* **dark**, gloomy, grey, leaden, dull, dim, overcast, cloudy, clouded, sunless, dismal, dreary, bleak; literary tenebrous. **2** *murky water* **dirty**, muddy, cloudy, turbid; N. Amer. riled, roily. **3** *her murky past* **questionable**, suspicious, suspect, dubious, dark, mysterious, secret; informal shady.
– OPPOSITES bright, clear.

murmur n. **1** *his voice was a murmur* **whisper**, undertone, mutter, mumble. **2** *there were murmurs in Tory ranks* **complaint**, grumble, grouse; informal gripe, moan. **3** *the murmur of bees* **hum**, humming, buzz, buzzing, thrum, thrumming, drone; sigh, rustle; literary susurration, murmuration.
▸ v. **1** *he heard them murmuring in the hall* **mutter**, mumble, whisper, talk under one's breath, speak softly. **2** *no one murmured at the delay* **complain**, mutter, grumble, grouse; informal gripe, moan. **3** *the wind was murmuring through the trees* **rustle**, sigh; burble, purl; literary whisper.

muscle n. **1** *he had muscle but no brains* **strength**, power, muscularity, brawn, burliness; informal beef, beefiness; literary thew. **2** *financial muscle* **influence**, power, strength, might, force, forcefulness, weight; informal clout. □ **muscle in** informal interfere with, force one's way into, impose oneself on, encroach on; informal horn in on.

WORD LINKS
isometrics a system of physical exercise in which muscles act against each other
myalgia pain in a muscle
myology the scientific study of muscles

muscular adj. **1** *muscular tissue* **fibrous**, sinewy. **2** *he's very muscular* **strong**, brawny, muscly, sinewy, powerfully built, well muscled, burly, strapping, sturdy, powerful, athletic; Physiology mesomorphic; informal hunky, beefy; literary thewy. **3** *a muscular economy* **vigorous**, robust, strong, powerful, dynamic, potent, active.

muse[1] n. *the poet's muse* **inspiration**, creative influence, stimulus; formal afflatus.

muse[2] v. *I mused on Toby's story* **ponder**, consider, think over/about, mull over, reflect on, contemplate, turn over in one's mind, chew over, give some thought to, cogitate on; think, be lost in contemplation/thought, daydream; old use pore on.

mush n. **1** *some sort of greyish mush* **pap**, pulp, slop, paste, purée, mash; informal gloop, goo, gook; N. Amer. informal glop. **2** *romantic mush* **sentimentality**, mawkishness; informal schmaltz, corn, slush; N. Amer. informal slop.

mushroom n. **fungus**.
▸v. *ecotourism mushroomed in the 1980s* **proliferate**, grow/develop rapidly, burgeon, spread, increase, expand, boom, explode, snowball, rocket, skyrocket; thrive, flourish, prosper.
– OPPOSITES contract.

mushy adj. **1** *cook until the fruit is mushy* **soft**, semi-liquid, pulpy, pappy, sloppy, spongy, squashy, squelchy, squishy; informal gooey, gloopy; Brit. informal squidgy. **2** *a mushy film* **sentimental**, mawkish, emotional, saccharine; informal slushy, schmaltzy, weepy, corny; Brit. informal soppy; N. Amer. informal cornball, sappy, hokey, three-hankie.
– OPPOSITES firm.

musical adj. **tuneful**, melodic, melodious, harmonious, sweet-sounding, sweet, mellifluous, euphonious, euphonic; rare mellifluent.
– OPPOSITES discordant.

musician n. **player**, performer, instrumentalist, accompanist, soloist, virtuoso, maestro; historical minstrel.

musing n. **meditation**, thinking, contemplation, deliberation, pondering, reflection, rumination, introspection, daydreaming, reverie, dreaming, preoccupation, brooding; formal cogitation.

must[1] v. *I must go* **ought to**, should, have (got) to, need to, be obliged to, be required to, be compelled to.
▸n. informal *this video is a must* **not to be missed**, very good; necessity, essential, requirement, requisite.

must[2] n. *a smell of must* **mould**, mustiness, mouldiness, mildew, fustiness.

muster v. **1** *they mustered 50,000 troops* **assemble**, mobilize, rally, raise, summon, gather (together), mass, collect, convene, call up, call to arms, recruit, conscript; US draft; old use levy. **2** *reporters mustered outside her house* **congregate**, assemble, gather together, come together, collect together, convene, mass, rally; formal foregather. **3** *she mustered her courage* **summon (up)**, screw up, call up, rally.
▸n. *the colonel called a muster* **roll call**, assembly, rally, meeting, gathering, assemblage, congregation, convention; parade, review.
□ **pass muster** be good enough, come up to standard, come up to scratch, measure up, be acceptable/adequate, fill/fit the bill; informal make the grade, come/be up to snuff.

musty adj. **1** *the room smelled musty* **mouldy**, stale, fusty, damp, dank, mildewy, smelly, stuffy, airless, unventilated; N. Amer. informal funky. **2** *the play seemed musty* **unoriginal**, uninspired, unimaginative, hackneyed, stale, flat, tired, banal, trite, clichéd, old-fashioned, outdated; informal old hat.
– OPPOSITES fresh.

mutable adj. *the mutable nature of fashion* **changeable**, variable, varying, fluctuating, shifting, inconsistent, unpredictable, inconstant, uneven, unstable, protean; literary fluctuant.
– OPPOSITES invariable.

mutant n. **freak (of nature)**, deviant, monstrosity, monster, mutation.

mutate v. **change**, metamorphose, evolve; transmute, transform, convert; humorous transmogrify.

mutation n. **1** **alteration**, change, variation, modification, transformation, metamorphosis, transmutation; humorous transmogrification. **2** *a genetic mutation* **mutant**, freak (of nature), deviant, monstrosity, monster.

mute adj. **1** *Yasmin remained mute* **silent**, speechless, dumb, unable to speak, unspeaking, tight-lipped, taciturn; informal mum; old use mumchance. **2** *a mute appeal* **wordless**, silent, dumb, unspoken, unvoiced, unexpressed. **3** *the church was mute* **quiet**, silent, hushed.
– OPPOSITES voluble, spoken.
▸v. **1** *the noise was muted by the heavy curtains* **deaden**, muffle, dampen, soften, quieten; stifle, smother, suppress. **2** *Bruce muted his criticisms* **restrain**, soften, tone down, moderate, temper.
– OPPOSITES intensify.

muted adj. **1** *the muted hum of traffic* **muffled**, faint, indistinct, quiet, soft, low. **2** *muted tones* **subdued**, pastel, delicate, subtle, understated, restrained.

mutilate v. **1** *the bodies had been mutilated* **mangle**, maim, disfigure, butcher, dismember; cripple. **2** *the carved screen had been mutilated* **vandalize**, damage, deface, ruin, destroy, wreck, violate, desecrate; N. Amer. informal trash.

mutinous adj. **rebellious**, insubordinate, subversive, seditious, insurgent, insurrectionary, rebel, riotous.

mutiny n. *a mutiny over pay arrears*
insurrection, rebellion, revolt, riot,
uprising, insurgence, insubordination.
▸v. *thousands of soldiers mutinied* **rise up**,
rebel, revolt, riot, disobey/defy authority, be
insubordinate.

mutt n. informal **1** *a long-haired mutt* **mongrel**,
hound, dog, cur; Austral. informal mong, bitzer.
2 *he pitied the poor mutt.* See **fool** (sense 1
of the noun).

mutter v. **1** *a group of men stood muttering*
talk under one's breath, murmur, mumble,
whisper, speak in an undertone. **2** *backbenchers muttered about the reshuffle*
grumble, complain, grouse, carp, whine;
informal moan, gripe, beef, whinge; Brit. informal
chunter; N. Amer. informal kvetch.

mutual adj. **reciprocal**, reciprocated,
requited, returned; common, joint, shared.

muzzle n. *the dog's velvety muzzle* **snout**,
nose, mouth, maw.
▸v. *attempts to muzzle the media* **gag**, silence,
censor, stifle, restrain, check, curb, fetter.

muzzy adj. **1** *she felt muzzy* **groggy**, light-
headed, faint, dizzy, befuddled, befogged;
informal dopey, woozy. **2** *a slightly muzzy
picture* **blurred**, blurry, fuzzy, unfocused,
unclear, ill-defined, foggy, hazy.
– OPPOSITES clear.

myopic adj. **1** *a myopic patient* **short-
sighted**, nearsighted. **2** *the government's
myopic attitude* **unimaginative**, uncreative,
unadventurous, narrow-minded, small-
minded, short-term.
– OPPOSITES long-sighted, far-sighted.

myriad literary n. *myriads of insects* **multitude**,
a large/great number, a large/great quantity,
scores, quantities, mass, host, droves, horde;
informal lots, loads, masses, stacks, tons,
hundreds, thousands, millions; N. Amer. informal
gazillions.
▸adj. *the myriad lights of the city*
innumerable, countless, infinite,
numberless, untold, unnumbered,
immeasurable, multitudinous, numerous;
literary divers.

mysterious adj. **1** *he vanished in mysterious
circumstances* **puzzling**, strange,
peculiar, curious, funny, queer, odd,
weird, bizarre, mystifying, inexplicable,
baffling, perplexing, incomprehensible,
unexplainable, unfathomable. **2** *he was being
very mysterious* **enigmatic**, inscrutable,
secretive, reticent, evasive, furtive,
surreptitious.
– OPPOSITES straightforward.

mystery n. **1** *his death remains a mystery*
puzzle, enigma, conundrum, riddle, secret,
(unsolved) problem. **2** *her past is shrouded
in mystery* **secrecy**, obscurity, uncertainty,
mystique. **3** *a murder mystery* **thriller**,
detective story/novel, murder story; informal
whodunnit.

mystic, mystical adj. **1** *a mystic experience*
spiritual, religious, transcendental,
paranormal, other-worldly, supernatural,
occult, metaphysical. **2** *mystic rites*
symbolic, symbolical, allegorical,
representational, metaphorical. **3** *a figure
of mystical significance* **cryptic**, concealed,
hidden, abstruse, arcane, esoteric,
inscrutable, inexplicable, unfathomable,
mysterious, secret, enigmatic.

mystify v. **bewilder**, puzzle, perplex, baffle,
confuse, confound, bemuse, nonplus, throw;
informal flummox, stump, bamboozle, faze, fox.

mystique n. **charisma**, glamour, romance,
mystery, magic, charm, appeal, allure.

myth n. **1** *ancient Greek myths* **(folk) tale**,
(folk) story, legend, fable, saga, mythos,
mythus; lore, folklore. **2** *the myths
surrounding childbirth* **misconception**,
fallacy, false notion, old wives' tale, fairy
story/tale, fiction; informal (tall) story, cock
and bull story.

mythical adj. **1** *mythical beasts* **legendary**,
mythological, fabled, fabulous, folkloric,
fairy-tale, storybook; fantastical, imaginary,
imagined, fictitious. **2** *her mythical child*
imaginary, fictitious, make-believe, fantasy,
invented, made-up, non-existent; informal
pretend.

mythological adj. **fabled**, fabulous,
folkloric, fairy-tale, legendary, mythical,
mythic, traditional; fictitious, imaginary.

mythology n. **myth(s)**, legend(s), folklore,
folk tales/stories, lore, tradition.

Nn

nab v. informal **catch**, capture, apprehend, arrest, seize; informal nail, cop, pull in, pick up; Brit. informal nick.

nabob n. **very rich person**, tycoon, magnate, millionaire, billionaire, multimillionaire; informal fat cat.

nadir n. **the lowest point/level**, the all-time low, the bottom, rock bottom; informal the pits.
– OPPOSITES zenith.

nag[1] v. **1** *she's constantly nagging me* **harass**, keep on at, go on at, badger, give someone a hard time, chivvy, hound, harry, criticize, find fault with, moan at, grumble at; henpeck; informal hassle; N. Amer. informal ride; Austral. informal heavy. **2** *this has been nagging me for weeks* **trouble**, worry, bother, plague, torment, niggle, prey on one's mind; annoy, irritate; informal bug, aggravate.
▶ n. *she's such a nag* **shrew**, nagger, harpy, termagant, harridan; old use scold.

nag[2] n. *she rode the old nag* **worn-out horse**, old horse, hack; N. Amer. informal plug, crowbait; Austral./NZ informal moke; old use jade.

nagging adj. **1** *his nagging wife* **shrewish**, complaining, grumbling, fault-finding, scolding, carping, criticizing. **2** *a nagging pain* **persistent**, continuous, niggling, unrelenting, unremitting, unabating.

nail n. **1** *fastened with nails* **tack**, spike, pin, rivet; hobnail. **2** *biting her nails* **fingernail**, thumbnail, toenail.
▶ v. **1** *a board was nailed to the wall* **fasten**, attach, fix, affix, secure, tack, hammer, pin. **2** informal *nailing suspects* **catch**, capture, apprehend, arrest, seize; informal nab, cop, pull in, pick up; Brit. informal nick. **3** *the pictures had nailed the lie* **expose**, reveal, uncover, unmask, bring to light, detect, identify.
□ **hard as nails** callous, hard-hearted, heartless, unfeeling, unsympathetic, uncaring, insensitive, unsentimental, hard-bitten, tough, lacking compassion.
on the nail immediately, at once, without delay, straight away, right away, promptly, directly, now, this minute; N. Amer. on the barrelhead.

> **WORD LINKS**
>
> **ungual** relating to fingernails and toenails
> **cuticle** the dead skin at the base of a fingernail or toenail
> **manicure** a cosmetic treatment of the hands and fingernails
> **pedicure** a cosmetic treatment of the feet and toenails

naive adj. **innocent**, unsophisticated, artless, ingenuous, inexperienced, guileless, unworldly, trusting; gullible, credulous, immature, callow, raw, green; informal wet behind the ears.
– OPPOSITES worldly.

naivety n. **innocence**, ingenuousness, guilelessness, unworldliness, trustfulness; gullibility, credulousness, credulity, immaturity, callowness.

naked adj. **1** *a naked woman* **nude**, bare, in the nude, stark naked, having nothing on, stripped, unclothed, undressed, in a state of nature; informal without a stitch on, in one's birthday suit, in the raw/buff, in the altogether, in the nuddy, mother naked; Brit. informal starkers; N. Amer. informal buck naked. **2** *a naked flame* **unprotected**, uncovered, exposed, unguarded. **3** *the naked branches of the trees* **bare**, barren, denuded, stripped, uncovered. **4** *I felt naked and exposed* **vulnerable**, helpless, weak, powerless, defenceless, exposed, open to attack. **5** *the naked truth* | *naked hostility* **undisguised**, plain, unadorned, unvarnished, unqualified, stark, bald; overt, obvious, open, patent, evident, apparent, manifest, unmistakable, blatant.
– OPPOSITES clothed, covered.

nakedness n. **1** *she covered her nakedness* **nudity**, state of undress, bareness. **2** *the nakedness of the landscape* **bareness**, barrenness, starkness.

namby-pamby adj. **weak**, feeble, spineless, effeminate, effete, limp-wristed, ineffectual; informal wet, weedy, wimpy, sissy.

name n. **1** *her name's Gemma* **designation**, honorific, title, tag, epithet, label; informal moniker, handle; formal denomination, appellation. **2** *the top names in the fashion industry* **celebrity**, star, superstar, VIP, leading light, big name, luminary; expert, authority; informal celeb, somebody, megastar, big noise, big shot, bigwig, big gun. **3** *the good name of the firm* **reputation**, character, repute, standing, stature, esteem, prestige, cachet, kudos; renown, popularity, notability, distinction.
▶ v. **1** *they named the child Phoebe* **call**, dub; label, style, term, title, entitle; baptize, christen; formal denominate. **2** *the driver was named as Jason Penter* **identify**, specify. **3** *he has named his successor* **choose**, select, pick, decide on, nominate, designate.

n

WORD LINKS
nominal, onomastic relating to names
anonymous having no name
eponymous referring to a person after whom
something is named
nomenclature a system of names used in a
certain subject
onomastics the study of personal names
toponymy the study of place names

named adj. **1** *a girl named Anne* **called**, by
the name of, baptized, christened, known as;
dubbed, entitled, styled, termed, labelled.
2 *named individuals* **specified**, designated,
identified, cited, mentioned, singled out.

nameless adj. **1** *a nameless photographer*
unnamed, unidentified, anonymous,
incognito, unspecified, unacknowledged,
uncredited; unknown, unsung, uncelebrated.
2 *nameless fears* **unspeakable**, unutterable,
inexpressible, indescribable; indefinable,
vague, unspecified, unspecifiable.

namely adv. **that is (to say)**, to be specific,
specifically, viz, to wit.

nanny n. *the children's nanny* **nursemaid**,
au pair, childminder, childcarer; governess;
dated nurse.
▶v. *stop nannying me* **mollycoddle**, cosset,
coddle, wrap in cotton wool, baby, feather-
bed; spoil, pamper, indulge, overindulge.

nap[1] n. *she's having a nap* **sleep**, catnap, siesta,
doze, lie-down, rest; informal snooze, forty
winks; Brit. informal kip, zizz.
▶v. *they were napping on the sofa* **doze**, sleep,
take a nap, catnap, rest; informal snooze, get
some shut-eye; N. Amer. informal catch some Zs.
□ **catch someone napping** catch off guard,
catch unawares, (take by) surprise, catch
out, find unprepared; informal catch someone
with their trousers/pants down; Brit. informal
catch on the hop.

nap[2] n. *the nap of the velvet* **pile**, fibres,
threads, weave, surface, grain.

narcissism n. **vanity**, self-love, self-
admiration, self-absorption, self-obsession,
conceit, self-centredness, self-regard,
egotism, egoism.
– OPPOSITES modesty.

narcissistic adj. **vain**, self-loving, self-
admiring, self-absorbed, self-obsessed,
conceited, self-centred, self-regarding,
egotistic, egotistical, egoistic.

narcotic n. **soporific (drug)**, opiate,
sleeping pill; painkiller, pain reliever,
analgesic, anodyne, palliative, anaesthetic;
tranquillizer, sedative; informal downer;
Medicine stupefacient.
▶adj. **soporific**, sleep-inducing, opiate;
painkilling, pain-relieving, analgesic,
anodyne, anaesthetic, tranquillizing,
sedative; Medicine stupefacient.

narked adj. Brit. informal See **annoyed**.

narrate v. **tell**, relate, recount, describe,
chronicle, give a report of, report; voice-over.

narration n. **1** *a narration of past events*
account, narrative, chronicle, description,
report, relation, chronicling. **2** *his narration*

of the story **voice-over**, commentary.

narrative n. **account**, chronicle, history,
description, record, report.

narrator n. **1** *the narrator of 'the Arabian
Nights'* **storyteller**, chronicler, romancer;
raconteur, anecdotalist; Austral. informal
magsman. **2** *the film's narrator* **voice-over**,
commentator.
– OPPOSITES listener, audience.

narrow adj. **1** *the path became narrower*
small, tapered, tapering, narrowing; old use
strait. **2** *her narrow waist* **slender**, slim,
slight, spare, attenuated, thin. **3** *a narrow
space* **confined**, cramped, tight, restricted,
limited, constricted. **4** *a narrow range of
products* **limited**, restricted, circumscribed,
small, inadequate, insufficient, deficient.
5 *a narrow view of the world.* See **narrow-
minded**. **6** *nationalism in the narrowest
sense of the word* **strict**, literal, exact, precise.
7 *a narrow escape* **by a very small margin**,
close, near, by a hair's breadth; informal by a
whisker.
– OPPOSITES wide, broad.
▶v. *the path narrowed* | *narrowing the gap
between rich and poor* **get/become/make
narrower**, get/become/make smaller, taper,
diminish, decrease, reduce, contract, shrink,
constrict; old use straiten.

narrowly adv. **1** *one bullet narrowly missed
him* **(only) just**, barely, scarcely, hardly, by
a hair's breadth; informal by a whisker. **2** *she
looked at me narrowly* **closely**, carefully,
searchingly, attentively.

narrow-minded adj. **intolerant**, illiberal,
reactionary, conservative, parochial,
provincial, insular, small-minded, petty,
blinkered, inward-looking, narrow,
hidebound, prejudiced, bigoted; Brit. parish-
pump, blimpish; N. Amer. informal jerkwater.
– OPPOSITES tolerant.

narrows plural n. **strait(s)**, sound, channel,
waterway, (sea) passage.

nascent adj. **just beginning**, budding,
developing, growing, embryonic, incipient,
young, fledgling, evolving, emergent,
dawning, burgeoning.

nastiness n. **1** *my mother tried to shut
herself off from nastiness* **unpleasantness**,
disagreeableness, offensiveness,
vileness, foulness. **2** *her uncharacteristic
nastiness* **unkindness**, unpleasantness,
unfriendliness, disagreeableness, rudeness,
churlishness, spitefulness, maliciousness,
meanness, ill temper, ill nature, viciousness,
malevolence; informal bitchiness, cattiness.
3 *I abhor such nastiness* **obscenity**,
indecency, offensiveness, crudity, vulgarity,
pornography, smuttiness, lewdness,
licentiousness.

nasty adj. **1** *a nasty smell* **unpleasant**,
disagreeable, disgusting, distasteful, awful,
dreadful, horrible, terrible, vile, foul,
abominable, frightful, loathsome, revolting,
repulsive, odious, sickening, nauseating,
repellent, repugnant, horrendous, appalling,
atrocious, offensive, objectionable,

obnoxious, unsavoury, unappetizing, off-putting; noxious, foul-smelling, smelly, stinking, rank, fetid, malodorous, mephitic; informal ghastly, horrid, gruesome, diabolical, yucky, skanky, God-awful, gross; Brit. informal beastly, grotty, whiffy, pongy, niffy; N. Amer. informal lousy, funky; Austral. informal on the nose; literary miasmal, noisome. **2** *the weather turned nasty* **unpleasant**, disagreeable, foul, filthy, inclement; wet, stormy, cold, blustery. **3** *she can be really nasty* **unkind**, unpleasant, unfriendly, disagreeable, rude, churlish, spiteful, malicious, mean, ill-tempered, ill-natured, vicious, malevolent, obnoxious, hateful, hurtful; informal bitchy, catty. **4** *a nasty accident | a nasty cut* **serious**, dangerous, bad, awful, dreadful, terrible, severe; painful, ugly. **5** *she had the nasty habit of appearing unannounced* **annoying**, irritating, infuriating, disagreeable, unpleasant, maddening, exasperating. **6** *they wrote nasty things on the wall* **obscene**, indecent, offensive, crude, rude, dirty, filthy, vulgar, foul, gross, disgusting, pornographic, smutty, lewd; informal sick.
– OPPOSITES nice.

nation n. **country**, (sovereign/nation) state, land, realm, kingdom, republic; fatherland, motherland; people, race.

national adj. **1** *national politics* **state**, public, federal, governmental; civic, civil, domestic, internal. **2** *a national strike* **nationwide**, countrywide, state, general, widespread.
– OPPOSITES local, international.
▸ n. *a French national* **citizen**, subject, native; voter.

nationalism n. **patriotism**, patriotic sentiment, xenophobia, chauvinism, jingoism.

nationalistic adj. **patriotic**, nationalist, xenophobic, chauvinistic, jingoistic.

nationality n. **1** *British nationality* **citizenship**. **2** *all the main nationalities of Ethiopia* **ethnic group**, ethnic minority, tribe, clan, race, nation.

nationwide adj. **national**, countrywide, state, general, widespread, extensive.
– OPPOSITES local.

native n. *a native of Sweden* **inhabitant**, resident, local; citizen, national; aborigine, autochthon; formal dweller.
– OPPOSITES foreigner.
▸ adj. **1** *the native population* **indigenous**, original, first, earliest, aboriginal, autochthonous. **2** *native produce | native plants* **domestic**, home-grown, home-made, local; indigenous. **3** *a native instinct for politics* **innate**, inherent, inborn, instinctive, intuitive, natural; hereditary, inherited, congenital, inbred, connate, connatural. **4** *her native tongue* **mother**, vernacular.
– OPPOSITES immigrant.

nativity n. **birth**, childbirth, delivery; formal parturition.

natter Brit. informal v. *they nattered away.* See **chat** (verb).
▸ n. *she rang up for a natter.* See **chat** (noun).

natty adj. informal **smart**, stylish, fashionable, dapper, debonair, dashing, spruce, well dressed, chic, elegant, trim; N. Amer. trig; informal snazzy, trendy, snappy, nifty; N. Amer. informal sassy, spiffy, fly, kicky.
– OPPOSITES scruffy.

natural adj. **1** *a natural occurrence* **normal**, ordinary, everyday, usual, regular, common, commonplace, typical, routine, standard, established, customary, accustomed, habitual. **2** *natural produce* **unprocessed**, organic, pure, wholesome, unrefined, pesticide-free, additive-free. **3** *Alex is a natural leader* **born**, naturally gifted, untaught. **4** *his natural instincts* **innate**, inborn, inherent, native, instinctive, intuitive; hereditary, inherited, inbred, congenital, connate, connatural. **5** *she seemed very natural* **unaffected**, spontaneous, uninhibited, relaxed, unselfconscious, genuine, open, artless, guileless, ingenuous, unpretentious, without airs. **6** *it was quite natural to think she admired him* **reasonable**, logical, understandable, (only) to be expected, predictable. **7** old use *his natural son* **illegitimate**, born out of wedlock; dated born on the wrong side of the blanket; old use bastard, misbegotten, baseborn.
– OPPOSITES abnormal, artificial, affected.

naturalist n. **natural historian**, life scientist, wildlife expert; biologist, botanist, zoologist, ornithologist, entomologist, ecologist, conservationist, environmentalist.

naturalistic adj. **realistic**, real-life, true-to-life, lifelike, graphic, representational, photographic.
– OPPOSITES abstract.

naturalize v. **1** *he was naturalized in 1950* **grant citizenship to**, give a passport to; enfranchise. **2** *coriander has now been naturalized in southern Britain* **establish**, introduce, acclimatize, domesticate; N. Amer. acclimate.

naturally adv. **1** *he's naturally shy* **by nature**, by character, inherently, innately, congenitally. **2** *try to act naturally* **normally**, in a natural way, unaffectedly, spontaneously, genuinely, unpretentiously; informal natural. **3** *naturally, they wanted everything kept quiet* **of course**, as might be expected, needless to say; obviously, clearly, it goes without saying.
– OPPOSITES self-consciously.

naturalness n. **unselfconsciousness**, spontaneity, spontaneousness, straightforwardness, genuineness, openness, ingenuousness, lack of sophistication, unpretentiousness.

nature n. **1** *the beauty of nature* **the natural world**, Mother Nature, Mother Earth, the environment; the universe, the cosmos; wildlife, flora and fauna, the countryside. **2** *such crimes are, by their very nature, difficult to hide* **essence**, inherent/basic/essential qualities, inherent/basic/essential features, character, complexion. **3** *it was*

n

not in Daisy's nature to be bitchy **character**, personality, disposition, temperament, make-up, psyche, constitution. **4** *experiments of a similar nature* **kind**, sort, type, variety, category, ilk, class, species, genre, style, cast, order, kidney, mould, stamp; N. Amer. stripe.

naturist n. **nudist**.
– OPPOSITES textile.

naughty adj. **1** *a naughty boy* **badly behaved**, disobedient, bad, misbehaved, misbehaving, wayward, defiant, unruly, insubordinate, wilful, delinquent, undisciplined, uncontrollable, ungovernable, unbiddable, disorderly, disruptive, fractious, recalcitrant, wild, wicked, obstreperous, difficult, troublesome, awkward, contrary, perverse, attention-seeking, incorrigible; mischievous, playful, impish, roguish, rascally; informal brattish; formal refractory. **2** *naughty jokes* **indecent**, risqué, rude, racy, ribald, bawdy, suggestive, improper, indelicate, indecorous; vulgar, dirty, filthy, smutty, crude, coarse, obscene, lewd, pornographic; informal raunchy; Brit. informal fruity, saucy; N. Amer. informal gamy; euphemistic adult.
– OPPOSITES well behaved, decent.

nausea n. **1** *symptoms include nausea and a headache* **sickness**, biliousness, queasiness; vomiting, retching, gagging; travel-sickness, seasickness, carsickness, airsickness. **2** *it induces a feeling of nausea* **disgust**, revulsion, repugnance, repulsion, distaste, aversion, loathing, abhorrence; informal yuck factor.

nauseate v. **sicken**, make sick, turn someone's stomach, make someone's gorge rise; N. Amer. informal gross out.

nauseating adj. **sickening**, stomach-churning, nauseous, emetic, sickly; disgusting, revolting, offensive, loathsome, obnoxious, foul; N. Amer. vomitous; informal sick-making, gross, rank, gut-churning.

nauseous adj. **1** *the food made her feel nauseous* **sick**, nauseated, queasy, bilious, green about/at the gills, ill, unwell; seasick, carsick, airsick, travel-sick; N. Amer. informal barfy. **2** *a nauseous stench*. See **nauseating**.

nautical adj. **maritime**, marine, naval, seafaring; boating, sailing.

navigable adj. **passable**, negotiable, traversable; clear, open, unobstructed, unblocked.

navigate v. **1** *he navigated the yacht across the Atlantic* **steer**, pilot, guide, direct, helm, captain; Nautical con; informal skipper. **2** *the upper reaches are dangerous to navigate* **sail (across/over)**, cross, traverse, negotiate. **3** *I'll drive—you can navigate* **map-read**, give directions.

navigation n. **1** *the navigation of the ship* **steering**, piloting, sailing, guiding, directing, guidance. **2** *the skills of navigation* **helmsmanship**, steersmanship, seamanship, map-reading, chart-reading.

navigator n. **helmsman**, steersman, pilot, guide; N. Amer. wheelman.

navvy n. **labourer**, manual worker, workman, worker, hand, coolie, roustabout; Austral./NZ rouseabout; old use mechanic.

navy n. **1** *a 600-ship navy* **fleet**, flotilla, armada. **2** *a navy suit* **navy blue**, dark blue, indigo.

nay adv. **or rather**, (and) indeed, and even, in fact, actually, in truth.

near adv. **1** *her children all live near* **close (by)**, nearby, close/near at hand, in the neighbourhood, in the vicinity, at hand, within reach, on the doorstep, a stone's throw away; informal within spitting distance; old use nigh. **2** *near perfect conditions* **almost**, just about, nearly, well-nigh, practically, virtually.
▸ prep. *a hotel near the seafront* **close to**, close by, a short distance from, in the vicinity of, in the neighbourhood of, within reach of, a stone's throw away from; informal within spitting distance of.
▸ adj. **1** *the nearest house* **close**, nearby, close/near at hand, at hand, a stone's throw away, within reach, accessible, handy, convenient; informal within spitting distance. **2** *the final judgement is near* **imminent**, in the offing, close/near at hand, at hand, (just) round the corner, impending, looming. **3** *a near relation* **closely related**, close, related. **4** *a near escape* **narrow**, close, by a hair's breadth; informal by a whisker.
– OPPOSITES far, distant.
▸ v. **1** *by dawn we were nearing Moscow* **approach**, draw near/nearer to, get close/closer to, advance towards, close in on. **2** *the death toll is nearing 3,000* **verge on**, border on, approach.

nearby adj. *one of the nearby villages* **not far away/off**, close/near at hand, close (by), near, within reach, at hand, neighbouring; accessible, handy, convenient.
– OPPOSITES faraway.
▸ adv. *her mother lives nearby* **close (by)**, close/near at hand, near, a short distance away, in the neighbourhood, in the vicinity, at hand, within reach, on the doorstep, (just) round the corner.

nearly adv. **almost**, (just) about, more or less, practically, virtually, all but, as good as, not far off, well-nigh, to all intents and purposes; not quite; informal pretty much, pretty well.

near miss n. **close thing**, near thing, narrow escape; informal close shave.

nearness n. **1** *the town's nearness to Rome* **closeness**, proximity, propinquity; accessibility, handiness; old use vicinity. **2** *the nearness of death* **imminence**, closeness, immediacy.

nearsighted adj. **short-sighted**, myopic.

neat adj. **1** *the bedroom was neat and clean* **tidy**, orderly, well ordered, in (good) order, shipshape (and Bristol fashion), in apple-pie order, spick and span, uncluttered, straight, trim. **2** *he's very neat* **smart**, spruce, dapper, trim, well groomed, well turned out; N. Amer. trig; informal natty. **3** *her neat script* **well formed**, regular, precise,

elegant, well proportioned. **4** *this neat little gadget* **compact**, well designed, handy; Brit. informal dinky. **5** *his neat footwork* **skilful**, deft, dexterous, adroit, adept, expert; informal nifty. **6** *a neat solution* **clever**, ingenious, inventive. **7** *neat gin* **undiluted**, straight, unmixed; N. Amer. informal straight up.
− OPPOSITES untidy.

neaten v. **tidy (up)**, make neat/neater, straighten (up), smarten (up), spruce up, put in order; N. Amer. informal fix up.

neatly adv. **1** *neatly arranged papers* **tidily**, methodically, systematically; smartly, sprucely. **2** *the point was neatly put* **cleverly**, aptly, elegantly. **3** *a neatly executed header* **skilfully**, deftly, adroitly, adeptly, expertly.

neatness n. **1** *the neatness of the cottage* **tidiness**, orderliness, trimness, spruceness; smartness. **2** *the neatness of her movements* **grace**, gracefulness, nimbleness, deftness, dexterity, adroitness, agility.

nebulous adj. **1** *the figure was nebulous* **indistinct**, indefinite, unclear, vague, hazy, cloudy, fuzzy, misty, blurred, blurry, foggy; faint, shadowy, obscure, formless, amorphous. **2** *nebulous ideas* **vague**, ill-defined, unclear, hazy, uncertain, indefinite, indeterminate, imprecise, unformed, muddled, confused, ambiguous.
− OPPOSITES clear.

necessarily adv. **as a consequence**, as a result, automatically, as a matter of course, certainly, surely, definitely, incontrovertibly, undoubtedly, inevitably, unavoidably, inescapably, ineluctably, of necessity; formal perforce.

necessary adj. **1** *planning permission is necessary* **obligatory**, requisite, required, compulsory, mandatory, imperative, needed, de rigueur; essential, indispensable, vital. **2** *a necessary consequence* **inevitable**, unavoidable, inescapable, inexorable, ineluctable; predetermined, preordained.
▸ n. informal *could you lend me the necessary?* See **money** (sense 1).

necessitate v. **make necessary**, entail, involve, mean, require, demand, call for, be grounds for, warrant, constrain, force.

necessitous adj. **needy**, poor, short of money, disadvantaged, underprivileged, in straitened circumstances, impoverished, poverty-stricken, penniless, impecunious, destitute, pauperized, indigent; Brit. on the breadline, without a penny to one's name; informal on one's uppers, hard up, without two pennies to rub together; Brit. informal in Queer Street; formal penurious.
− OPPOSITES wealthy.

necessity n. **1** *the TV is now regarded as a necessity* **essential**, indispensable item, requisite, prerequisite, necessary, basic, sine qua non, desideratum. **2** *political necessity forced him to resign* **force of circumstance**, obligation, need, call, exigency; force majeure. **3** *the necessity of growing old* **inevitability**, certainty, inescapability, inexorability, ineluctability. **4** *necessity made*

them steal **poverty**, need, neediness, want, deprivation, privation, penury, destitution, indigence.
□ **of necessity** necessarily, inevitably, unavoidably, inescapably, ineluctably; as a matter of course, naturally, automatically, certainly, surely, definitely, incontrovertibly, undoubtedly; formal perforce.

neck n. technical cervix; old use scrag.
▸ v. informal **kiss**, caress, pet; informal smooch, canoodle; Brit. informal snog; N. Amer. informal make out; informal dated spoon.
□ **neck and neck** level, equal, tied, side by side, nip and tuck; Brit. level pegging; informal even-steven(s).

> **WORD LINKS**
>
> **cervical, jugular** relating to the neck
> **Adam's apple** the lump of cartilage at the front of the neck
> **goitre** a swelling of the neck caused by an enlarged thyroid gland
> **scruff** the back of the neck

necklace n. **chain**, choker, necklet; beads, pearls; pendant, locket; historical torc.

necromancer n. **sorcerer**, sorceress, (black) magician, wizard, warlock, witch, enchantress, occultist, diviner; spiritualist, medium.

necromancy n. **sorcery**, (black) magic, witchcraft, witchery, wizardry, the occult, occultism, voodoo, hoodoo; divination; spiritualism.

necropolis n. **cemetery**, graveyard, churchyard, burial ground; informal boneyard; historical potter's field; old use God's acre.

née adj. *Jill Wyatt, née Peters* **born**, formerly, previously; formal heretofore.

need v. **1** *do you need money?* **require**, be in need of, have need of, want; be crying out for, be desperate for; demand, call for, necessitate, entail, involve; lack, be without, be short of. **2** *you needn't come* **have to**, be obliged to, be compelled to. **3** *she needed him so much* **yearn for**, pine for, long for, desire, miss.
▸ n. **1** *there's no need to apologize* **necessity**, obligation, requirement, call, demand. **2** *basic human needs* **requirement**, essential, necessity, want, requisite, prerequisite, demand, desideratum. **3** *their need was particularly pressing* **neediness**, want, poverty, deprivation, privation, hardship, destitution, indigence. **4** *my hour of need* **difficulty**, trouble, distress; crisis, emergency, urgency, extremity.
□ **in need** needy, necessitous, deprived, disadvantaged, underprivileged, poor, impoverished, poverty-stricken, destitute, impecunious, indigent; Brit. on the breadline; formal penurious.

needed adj. **necessary**, required, wanted, desired, lacking; essential, requisite, compulsory, obligatory, mandatory.
− OPPOSITES optional.

needful adj. formal **necessary**, needed, required, requisite; essential, imperative, vital, indispensable.

needle n. **1** *a needle and thread* darner, bodkin. **2** *the virus is transmitted via needles* hypodermic needle, syringe; informal hype, spike. **3** *the needle on the meter* indicator, pointer, marker, arrow, hand. **4** *put the needle on the record* stylus.
▸ v. informal *he needled her too much.* See **annoy**.

needless adj. **unnecessary**, inessential, non-essential, unneeded, undesired, unwanted, uncalled for; gratuitous, pointless; dispensable, expendable, superfluous, redundant, excessive, supererogatory.
– OPPOSITES necessary.
□ **needless to say** of course, as one would expect, not unexpectedly, it goes without saying, obviously, naturally; informal natch.

needlework n. **sewing**, stitching, embroidery, needlepoint, needlecraft, tapestry, crewel work.

needy adj. **poor**, deprived, disadvantaged, underprivileged, necessitous, in need, needful, hard up, in straitened circumstances, poverty-stricken, indigent, impoverished, pauperized, destitute, impecunious, penniless, moneyless; Brit. on the breadline; informal on one's uppers, broke, strapped (for cash), cash-strapped, without two pennies to rub together; Brit. informal skint, stony broke, in Queer Street; N. Amer. informal stone broke; formal penurious.
– OPPOSITES wealthy.

ne'er-do-well n. **good-for-nothing**, layabout, loafer, idler, shirker, sluggard, slugabed, drone; informal waster, lazybones; Brit. informal skiver; N. Amer. informal bum, gold brick; old use wastrel.

nefarious adj. **wicked**, evil, sinful, iniquitous, egregious, heinous, atrocious, vile, foul, abominable, odious, depraved, monstrous, fiendish, diabolical, unspeakable, despicable; villainous, criminal, corrupt, illegal, unlawful; dated dastardly.
– OPPOSITES good.

negate v. **1** *they negated the court's ruling* **invalidate**, nullify, neutralize, cancel; undo, reverse, annul, void, revoke, rescind, repeal, retract, countermand, overrule, overturn; Law avoid; formal abrogate. **2** *he negates the political nature of education* **deny**, dispute, contradict, controvert, refute, rebut, reject, repudiate; formal gainsay.
– OPPOSITES validate, confirm.

negation n. **1** *negation of the findings* **denial**, contradiction, repudiation, refutation, rebuttal; nullification, cancellation, revocation, repeal, retraction; Law disaffirmation; formal abrogation. **2** *evil is not just the negation of goodness* **opposite**, reverse, antithesis, contrary, inverse, converse; absence, want.

negative adj. **1** *a negative reply* **opposing**, opposed, contrary, anti-, dissenting, dissentient. **2** *stop being so negative* **pessimistic**, defeatist, gloomy, cynical, fatalistic, dismissive, antipathetic; unenthusiastic, uninterested, unresponsive.

3 *a negative effect on the economy* **harmful**, bad, adverse, damaging, detrimental, unfavourable, disadvantageous.
– OPPOSITES positive, optimistic, favourable.
▸ n. *he murmured a negative 'no'*, refusal, rejection, veto; dissension, contradiction; denial.
▸ v. **1** *the bill was negatived by the house* **reject**, turn down, refuse, veto, squash; informal give the thumbs down to. **2** *his arguments were negatived* **disprove**, belie, invalidate, refute, rebut, discredit; contradict, deny, negate; formal gainsay. **3** *they tried to negative the effect of the tax* **neutralize**, cancel out, counteract, nullify, negate; offset, balance, counterbalance.
– OPPOSITES ratify, prove.

negativity n. **pessimism**, defeatism, gloom, cynicism, hopelessness, despair, despondency; apathy, indifference.

neglect v. **1** *she neglected the children* **fail to look after**, leave alone, abandon; literary forsake. **2** *he's neglecting his work* **pay no attention to**, let slide, not attend to, be remiss about, be lax about, leave undone, shirk. **3** *don't neglect our advice* **disregard**, ignore, pay no attention to, take no notice of, pay no heed to, overlook; disdain, scorn, spurn. **4** *I neglected to inform her* **fail**, omit, forget.
– OPPOSITES cherish, heed, remember.
▸ n. **1** *the place had an air of neglect* **disrepair**, dilapidation, deterioration, shabbiness, disuse, abandonment. **2** *her doctor was guilty of neglect* **negligence**, dereliction of duty, remissness, carelessness, heedlessness, unconcern, laxity, slackness, irresponsibility; formal delinquency. **3** *the relative neglect of women* **disregard**, ignoring, overlooking, inattention to, indifference to, heedlessness to.
– OPPOSITES care, attention.

neglected adj. **1** *neglected animals* **uncared for**, abandoned; mistreated, maltreated; literary forsaken. **2** *a neglected cottage* **derelict**, dilapidated, tumbledown, ramshackle, untended. **3** *a neglected masterpiece of prose* **disregarded**, forgotten, overlooked, ignored, unrecognized, unnoticed, unsung, underestimated, undervalued, unappreciated.

neglectful adj. See **negligent**.

negligent adj. **neglectful**, remiss, careless, lax, irresponsible, inattentive, heedless, thoughtless, unmindful, forgetful; slack, sloppy; N. Amer. derelict; formal delinquent.
– OPPOSITES dutiful.

negligible adj. **trivial**, trifling, insignificant, unimportant, minor, inconsequential; minimal, small, slight, inappreciable, infinitesimal, nugatory, petty; paltry, inadequate, insufficient, meagre, pitiful; informal minuscule, piddling, measly, poxy; formal exiguous.
– OPPOSITES significant.

negotiable adj. **1** *the salary will be negotiable* **open to discussion**, discussable, flexible, open to modification; unsettled, undecided. **2** *the path was negotiable* **passable**, navigable, crossable, traversable; clear, unblocked, unobstructed. **3** *negotiable cheques* transferable; valid.

negotiate v. **1** *she refused to negotiate* **discuss terms**, talk, consult, parley, confer, debate; compromise; mediate, intercede, arbitrate, moderate, conciliate; bargain, haggle. **2** *he negotiated a new contract* **arrange**, broker, work out, thrash out, agree on; settle, clinch, conclude, pull off, bring off, transact; informal sort out, swing. **3** *I negotiated the obstacles* **get round**, get past, get over, clear, cross; surmount, overcome, deal with, cope with.

negotiation n. **1** *the negotiations resume next week* **discussion(s)**, talks, deliberations; conference, debate, dialogue, consultation; mediation, arbitration, conciliation. **2** *the negotiation of the deal* **arrangement**, brokering; settlement, conclusion, completion, transaction.

negotiator n. **mediator**, arbitrator, arbiter, moderator, go-between, middleman, intermediary, intercessor, intervener, conciliator; representative, spokesperson, broker, bargainer.

neigh v. **whinny**, bray, nicker, snicker, whicker.

neighbourhood n. **1** *a quiet neighbourhood district*, area, locality, locale, quarter, community; part, region, zone; informal neck of the woods; Brit. informal manor; N. Amer. informal hood, nabe. **2** *in the neighbourhood of Canterbury* **vicinity**, environs, purlieus, precincts, vicinage.
□ **in the neighbourhood of** approximately, about, around, roughly, in the region of, of the order of, nearly, almost, close to, just about, practically, there or thereabouts, circa; Brit. getting on for.

neighbouring adj. **adjacent**, adjoining, bordering, connecting, abutting; proximate, near, close (at hand), next-door, nearby, in the vicinity, vicinal.
– OPPOSITES remote.

neighbourly adj. **obliging**, helpful, friendly, kind, amiable, amicable, affable, genial, agreeable, hospitable, companionable, well disposed, civil, cordial, good-natured, nice, pleasant, generous; considerate, thoughtful, unselfish; Brit. informal decent.
– OPPOSITES unfriendly.

nemesis n. **1** *this could be the bank's nemesis* **downfall**, undoing, ruin, ruination, destruction, Waterloo. **2** *the nemesis that his crime deserved* **retribution**, vengeance, punishment, just deserts; fate, destiny.

neologism n. **new word**, new expression, new term, new phrase, coinage; made-up word, nonce-word.

neophyte n. **1** *a neophyte of the monastery* **novice**, novitiate; postulant, catechumen. **2** *cooking classes are offered to neophytes* **beginner**, learner, novice, newcomer; initiate, tyro, fledgling; trainee, apprentice,

probationer; N. Amer. tenderfoot; informal rookie, newbie, newie; N. Amer. informal greenhorn.

ne plus ultra n. **the last word**, the ultimate, the perfect example, the height, the acme, the zenith, the epitome, the quintessence; old use the nonsuch.

nepotism n. **favouritism**, preferential treatment, the old boy network, looking after one's own, bias, partiality, partisanship; Brit. jobs for the boys, the old school tie.
– OPPOSITES impartiality.

nerd n. informal **bore**; informal dork, dweeb, geek; Brit. informal anorak, spod; N. Amer. informal Poindexter.

nerve n. **1** *the nerves that transmit pain* **nerve fibre**, neuron, axon; Physiology dendrite. **2** *the match will be a test of nerve* **confidence**, assurance, cool-headedness, self-possession; courage, bravery, pluck, boldness, intrepidity, fearlessness, daring; determination, will power, spirit, backbone, fortitude, mettle, grit, stout-heartedness; informal guts, spunk; Brit. informal bottle; N. Amer. informal moxie. **3** *he had the nerve to chat her up* **audacity**, cheek, effrontery, gall, temerity, presumption, boldness, brazenness, impudence, impertinence, arrogance, cockiness; informal face, front, brass neck, chutzpah; Brit. informal sauce. **4** *pre-wedding nerves* **anxiety**, tension, nervousness, stress, worry, cold feet, apprehension; informal butterflies (in one's stomach), collywobbles, the jitters, the shakes; Brit. informal the (screaming) abdabs.
□ **get on someone's nerves** irritate, annoy, irk, anger, bother, vex, provoke, displease, exasperate, infuriate, gall, pique, needle, ruffle someone's feathers, try someone's patience; jar on, grate on, rankle; Brit. rub up the wrong way; informal aggravate, get to, bug, miff, peeve, rile, nettle, get up someone's nose, hack off, get someone's goat; Brit. informal nark, get on someone's wick, wind up.

nerve oneself brace oneself, steel oneself, summon one's courage, gear oneself up, prepare oneself; fortify oneself; informal psych oneself up; literary gird one's loins.

> **WORD LINKS**
> **neural** relating to the nerves in the body
> **neuralgia** intense pain along a nerve
> **neuritis** inflammation of a nerve
> **neurology, neuropathology, neurosurgery** branches of medicine concerned with the nerves and the nervous system
> **neuron, neurone** a nerve cell
> **ganglion** a mass of nerve cells
> **synapse** a connection between two nerve cells

nerveless adj. **1** *her nerveless fingers* **inert**, lifeless; weak, powerless, feeble. **2** *a nerveless lack of restraint* **confident**, self-confident, self-assured, self-possessed, cool, calm, {cool, calm, and collected}, composed, relaxed.
– OPPOSITES nervous.

nerve-racking adj. **stressful**, anxious, worrying, fraught, nail-biting, tense,

nervous adj. **1** *a nervous woman* **highly strung**, anxious, edgy, tense, nervy, excitable, skittish, brittle, neurotic; timid, mousy, shy, fearful; informal jumpy. **2** *he was so nervous he couldn't eat* **anxious**, worried, apprehensive, on edge, edgy, tense, stressed, agitated, uneasy, restless, worked up, keyed up, overwrought; fearful, frightened, scared, shaky, in a cold sweat; informal with butterflies in one's stomach, jittery, twitchy, jumpy, in a state, uptight, wired, in a flap, het up; Brit. informal strung up, having kittens; N. Amer. informal spooky, squirrelly. **3** *a nervous disorder* **neurological**, neural.
– OPPOSITES relaxed, calm.

nervous breakdown n. **mental collapse**, breakdown, collapse, crisis, trauma; nervous exhaustion, mental illness; informal crack-up.

nervousness n. **anxiety**, edginess, tension, agitation, stress, worry, apprehension, uneasiness, disquiet, fear, trepidation, perturbation, alarm; Brit. nerviness; informal butterflies (in one's stomach), collywobbles, the jitters, the willies, the heebie-jeebies, the shakes; Brit. informal the (screaming) abdabs.

nervy adj. See **nervous** (sense 1).

nest n. **1** *the birds built a nest* **roost**, eyrie. **2** *the animals disperse rapidly from the nest* **lair**, den, burrow, set. **3** *a cosy love nest* **hideaway**, hideout, retreat, shelter, refuge, snuggery, den; informal hidey-hole. **4** *a nest of intrigue* **hotbed**, den, breeding ground, cradle.

nest egg n. **(life) savings**, cache, funds, reserve.

nestle v. **snuggle**, cuddle, huddle, nuzzle, settle, burrow, snug down.

nestling n. **chick**, fledgling, baby bird.

net¹ n. **1** *fishermen mending their nets* **fishing net**, dragnet, drift net, trawl net, landing net, gill net, cast net. **2** *a dress of green net* **netting**, meshwork, webbing, tulle, fishnet, openwork, lace, latticework. **3** *he managed to escape the net* **trap**, snare.
▶ v. *they netted big criminals* **catch**, capture, trap, entrap, snare, ensnare, bag, hook, land; informal nab, collar.

net² adj. **1** *net earnings* **after tax**, after deductions, take-home, final; informal bottom line. **2** *the net result* **final**, end, ultimate, closing; overall, actual, effective.
– OPPOSITES gross.
▶ v. *she netted £50,000* **earn**, make, get, gain, obtain, acquire, accumulate, take home, bring in, pocket, realize, be paid; informal rake in.

nether adj. **lower**, low, bottom, bottommost, under, basal; underground.
– OPPOSITES upper.

netherworld n. **hell**, the underworld, the infernal regions, the abyss; eternal damnation, perdition; Hades, Acheron, Gehenna, Tophet, Sheol; literary the pit.
– OPPOSITES heaven.

nettle v. **irritate**, annoy, irk, gall, vex, anger, exasperate, infuriate, provoke; upset, displease, offend, affront, pique, get on someone's nerves, try someone's patience, ruffle someone's feathers; Brit. rub up the wrong way; N. Amer. rankle; informal peeve, aggravate, miff, rile, needle, get to, bug, get up someone's nose, hack off, get someone's goat; Brit. informal nark, get on someone's wick, wind up; N. Amer. informal tick off.

network n. **1** *a network of arteries* **web**, lattice, net, matrix, mesh, criss-cross, grid, reticulum, reticulation; Anatomy plexus. **2** *a network of lanes* **maze**, labyrinth, warren, tangle. **3** *a network of friends* **system**, complex, nexus, web.

neurosis n. **mental illness**, mental disorder, psychological disorder; psychoneurosis, psychopathy; obsession, phobia, fixation; Medicine neuroticism.

neurotic adj. **1** Medicine *neurotic patients* **mentally ill**, mentally disturbed, unstable, unbalanced, maladjusted; psychopathic, phobic, obsessive–compulsive. **2** *a neurotic, self-obsessed woman* **overanxious**, oversensitive, nervous, tense, nervy, highly strung, paranoid; obsessive, fixated, hysterical, overwrought, irrational; informal twitchy.
– OPPOSITES stable, calm.

neuter adj. **asexual**, sexless, unsexed; androgynous, epicene.
▶ v. *have your pets neutered* **sterilize**, castrate, spay, geld, cut, fix, desex; N. Amer. & Austral. alter; Brit. informal doctor; old use emasculate.

neutral adj. **1** *she's neutral on this issue* **impartial**, unbiased, unprejudiced, objective, open-minded, non-partisan, disinterested, dispassionate, detached, impersonal, unemotional, indifferent, uncommitted. **2** *Switzerland remained neutral* **unaligned**, non-aligned, unaffiliated, unallied, uninvolved; non-combatant, anti-war. **3** *a neutral topic of conversation* **inoffensive**, bland, unobjectionable, unexceptionable, anodyne, unremarkable, ordinary, commonplace; safe, harmless, innocuous. **4** *a neutral background* **pale**, light; beige, cream, taupe, oatmeal, ecru, buff, fawn, grey; colourless, uncoloured, achromatic; indeterminate, insipid, nondescript, dull, drab.
– OPPOSITES biased, partisan, provocative, colourful.

neutralize v. **counteract**, offset, counterbalance, balance, counterpoise, countervail, compensate for, make up for; cancel out, nullify, negate, negative; equalize.

never adv. **1** *his room is never tidy* **not ever**, at no time, not at any time, not once; literary ne'er. **2** *she will never agree to it* **not at all**, certainly not, not for a moment, under no circumstances, on no account; informal no way, not on your life, not in a million years; Brit. informal not on your nelly.
– OPPOSITES always, definitely.

never-ending adj. **1** *never-ending noise* **incessant**, continuous, unceasing, ceaseless, constant, continual, perpetual, uninterrupted, unbroken, steady, unremitting, relentless, persistent, interminable, non-stop, endless, unending, everlasting, eternal. **2** *never-ending tasks* **endless**, countless, innumerable, untold, unlimited, limitless, boundless; literary myriad.

nevertheless adv. **nonetheless**, even so, however, but, still, yet, though; in spite of that, despite that, be that as it may, for all that, that said, just the same, all the same; notwithstanding, regardless, anyway, anyhow; informal still and all.

new adj. **1** *new technology* **recently developed**, up to date, latest, current, state-of-the-art, contemporary, advanced, recent, modern. **2** *new ideas* **novel**, original, fresh, imaginative, innovative, creative, experimental, contemporary, modernist, up to date; newfangled, ultra-modern, avant-garde, futuristic; informal way out, far out. **3** *is your boat new?* **unused**, brand new, pristine, fresh, in mint condition. **4** *new neighbours moved in* **different**, another, alternative; unfamiliar, unknown, strange; unaccustomed, untried. **5** *they had a new classroom built* **additional**, extra, supplementary, further, another, fresh. **6** *I came back a new woman* **reinvigorated**, restored, revived, improved, refreshed, regenerated, reborn.
– OPPOSITES old, hackneyed, second-hand, present.

> **WORD LINKS**
> **novice, neophyte** a person who is new to something
> **neophobia** fear of new things

newborn adj. *newborn babies* **just born**, recently born.
▸ n. *the bacteria are fatal to newborns* **young baby**, tiny baby, infant; Medicine neonate.

newcomer n. **1** *a newcomer to the village* **(new) arrival**, immigrant, incomer, settler; stranger, outsider, foreigner, alien; N. English offcomer; informal johnny-come-lately, new kid on the block; Austral. informal blow-in. **2** *photography tips for the newcomer* **beginner**, novice, learner; trainee, apprentice, probationer, tyro, initiate, neophyte; N. Amer. tenderfoot; informal rookie, newbie; N. Amer. informal greenhorn.

newfangled adj. **new**, the latest, modern, ultra-modern, up to the minute, state-of-the-art, advanced, contemporary; new-fashioned; informal trendy, flash.
– OPPOSITES dated.

newly adv. **recently**, (only) just, lately, freshly; not long ago, a short time ago, only now, of late; new-.

news n. **report**, announcement, story, account; article, news flash, newscast, headlines, press release, communication, communiqué, bulletin; message, dispatch, statement, intelligence; disclosure, revelation, word, talk, gossip; informal scoop; literary tidings.

newspaper n. **paper**, journal, gazette, news-sheet; tabloid, broadsheet, quality (paper), national (paper), local (paper), daily (paper), weekly (paper); free sheet, scandal sheet; informal rag; N. Amer. informal tab.

newsworthy adj. **interesting**, topical, notable, noteworthy, important, significant, momentous, historic, remarkable, sensational.
– OPPOSITES unremarkable.

next adj. **1** *the next chapter* **following**, succeeding, upcoming, to come. **2** *the next house in the street* **neighbouring**, adjacent, adjoining, next-door, bordering, connected, attached; closest, nearest.
– OPPOSITES previous.
▸ adv. *where shall we go next?* **then**, after, afterwards, after this/that, following that/this, later, subsequently; formal thereafter, thereupon.
– OPPOSITES before.
□ **next to** beside, by, alongside, by the side of, next door to, adjacent to, side by side with; close to, near, neighbouring, adjoining.

nibble v. **1** *he nibbled at a biscuit* **bite**, pick, gnaw, chew, peck, snack on; toy with; taste, sample; informal graze (on); dialect chumble. **2** *the mouse nibbled his finger* **peck**, nip, bite.
▸ n. *nuts and nibbles* **morsel**, mouthful, bite; snack, titbit, canapé, hors d'oeuvre, bonne bouche.

nice adj. **1** *have a nice time* **enjoyable**, pleasant, agreeable, good, satisfying, gratifying, delightful, marvellous; entertaining, amusing, diverting; informal lovely, great; N. Amer. informal neat. **2** *nice people* **pleasant**, likeable, agreeable, personable, congenial, amiable, affable, genial, friendly, charming, delightful, engaging; sympathetic, compassionate, good. **3** *nice manners* **polite**, courteous, civil, refined, polished, genteel, elegant. **4** *that's a rather nice distinction* **subtle**, fine, delicate, minute, precise, strict, close; careful, meticulous, scrupulous. **5** *it's a nice day* **fine**, pleasant, agreeable; dry, sunny, warm, mild.
– OPPOSITES unpleasant, nasty, rough.

nicety n. **1** *legal niceties* **subtlety**, fine point, nuance, refinement, detail. **2** *great nicety of control* **precision**, accuracy, exactness, meticulousness.

niche n. **1** *a niche in the wall* **recess**, alcove, nook, cranny, hollow, bay, cavity, cubbyhole, pigeonhole. **2** *he found his niche in life* **ideal position**, place, function, vocation, calling, métier, job.

nick n. **1** *a slight nick in the blade* **cut**, scratch, incision, snick, notch, chip, gouge, gash; dent, indentation. **2** Brit. informal *she's in the nick.* See **prison**. **3** Brit. informal *he's under arrest at the nick* **police station**, station; N. Amer. precinct, station house; informal cop shop. **4** Brit. informal *the car's in good nick* **condition**, repair, shape, state, order, form, fettle, trim.

n

▸ **v. 1** *I nicked my toe* **cut**, scratch, incise, snick, gouge, gash, score. **2** Brit. informal *she nicked his wallet*. See **steal** (sense 1 of the verb). **3** Brit. informal *Steve's been nicked.* See **arrest** (sense 1 of the verb).
□ **in the nick of time** just in time, not a moment too soon, at the critical moment; N. Amer. informal under the wire.

nickname n. **sobriquet**, byname, tag, label, epithet, cognomen; pet name, diminutive, endearment; informal moniker; formal appellation.

nifty adj. informal **1** *nifty camerawork* **skilful**, deft, agile, capable. **2** *a nifty little gadget* **useful**, handy, practical. **3** *a nifty suit* **fashionable**, stylish, smart.
– OPPOSITES clumsy.

niggardly adj. **1** *a niggardly person* **mean**, miserly, parsimonious, close-fisted, penny-pinching, cheese-paring, grasping, ungenerous, illiberal; informal stingy, tight, tight-fisted; N. Amer. informal cheap. **2** *niggardly rations* **meagre**, inadequate, scanty, scant, skimpy, paltry, sparse, insufficient, deficient, short, lean, small, slender, poor, miserable, pitiful, puny; informal measly, stingy, pathetic, piddling.
– OPPOSITES generous.

niggle v. **1** *his behaviour does niggle me* **irritate**, annoy, bother, provoke, exasperate, upset, gall, irk, rankle with; informal rile, get to, bug. **2** *he niggles on about taxes* **complain**, fuss, carp, cavil, grumble, grouse; informal moan, nitpick.
▸ **n.** *niggles about the lack of equipment* **quibble**, trivial complaint, criticism, grumble, grouse, cavil; informal gripe, moan, beef, grouch.

night n. night-time; (hours of) darkness, dark.
– OPPOSITES day.
□ **night and day** all the time, around the clock, {morning, noon, and night}, {day in, day out}, ceaselessly, endlessly, incessantly, unceasingly, interminably, constantly, perpetually, continually, relentlessly; informal 24-7.

> **WORD LINKS**
> **nocturnal** relating to night
> **nyctophobia** fear of the night

nightclub n. **disco**, discotheque, night spot, club, bar; N. Amer. cafe; informal niterie.

nightfall n. **sunset**, sundown, dusk, twilight, evening, close of day, dark; literary eventide.
– OPPOSITES dawn.

nightly adj. **1** *nightly raids* **every night**, each night, night after night. **2** *his nightly wanderings* **nocturnal**, night-time.
▸ **adv.** *a band plays there nightly* **every night**, each night, night after night.

nightmare n. **1** *she woke from a nightmare* **bad dream**, night terrors; old use incubus. **2** *the journey was a nightmare* **ordeal**, trial, torment, horror, hell, misery, agony, torture, murder; curse, bane.

nightmarish adj. **unearthly**, spine-chilling, hair-raising, horrific, macabre, hideous, unspeakable, gruesome, grisly, ghastly, harrowing, disturbing; informal scary, creepy.

nihilism n. **scepticism**, disbelief, unbelief, agnosticism, atheism; negativity, cynicism, pessimism; rejection, denial.

nihilist n. **sceptic**, disbeliever, unbeliever, agnostic, atheist; negativist, cynic, pessimist.

nil n. **nothing**, none; nought, zero, o; Tennis love; Cricket a duck; N. English nowt; informal zilch, nix, not a dicky bird; Brit. informal sweet Fanny Adams, sweet FA, not a sausage; N. Amer. informal zip, nada, a goose egg; dated cipher; old use naught.

nimble adj. **1** *he was nimble on his feet* **agile**, sprightly, light, spry, lively, quick, graceful, lithe, limber; skilful, deft, dexterous, adroit; informal nippy, twinkle-toed; literary lightsome. **2** *a nimble mind* **quick-witted**, quick, alert, lively, wide awake, observant, astute, perceptive, penetrating, discerning, shrewd, sharp; intelligent, bright, smart, clever, brilliant; informal brainy, quick on the uptake.
– OPPOSITES clumsy, dull.

nincompoop n. informal See **idiot**.

nine cardinal number

> **WORD LINKS**
> **nonagon** a nine-sided figure
> **nonet** a group of nine people or things

nip v. **1** *the child nipped her* **bite**, nibble, peck; pinch, tweak, squeeze, grip. **2** Brit. informal *I'm just nipping out* **rush**, dash, dart, hurry, scurry, scamper; go; informal pop, whip.
▸ **n.** *penguins can give a serious nip* **bite**, peck, nibble; pinch, tweak.
□ **nip something in the bud** cut short, curtail, check, curb, thwart, frustrate, stop, halt, arrest, stifle, obstruct, block, squash, quash, subdue, crack down on, stamp out; informal put the kibosh on.
nip something off cut, snip, trim, clip, prune, lop, dock, crop; remove, take off.

nipple n. **teat**, dug; Anatomy mamilla.

nippy adj. informal **1** *he's too big to be nippy* **agile**, light-footed, nimble, light on one's feet, spry, supple, limber; informal twinkle-toed; literary lightsome. **2** *a nippy hatchback* **fast**, quick, lively; informal zippy. **3** *it's a bit nippy in here* **cold**, chilly, icy, bitter, raw.
– OPPOSITES lumbering, slow, warm.

nirvana n. **paradise**, heaven; bliss, ecstasy, joy, peace, serenity, tranquillity; enlightenment.
– OPPOSITES hell.

nitpicking adj. informal See **pedantic**.

nitty-gritty n. informal **basics**, essentials, fundamentals, substance, essence, quintessence, heart of the matter; nub, crux, gist, meat, kernel, marrow; informal brass tacks, nuts and bolts.

nitwit n. informal See **idiot**.

no adv. absolutely not, under no circumstances, by no means, not at all, negative, never, not really; informal nope, nah,

not on your life, no way; Brit. informal no fear, not on your nelly; old use nay.
– OPPOSITES yes.

nobble v. Brit. informal **1** *he nobbled the jury* **bribe**, suborn, buy, pay off, corrupt, get at; influence, persuade, win over, sway, control, manipulate; informal grease someone's palm, oil someone's palm. **2** *a stable lad nobbled the horse* **drug**, dope; tamper with, interfere with; disable, incapacitate. **3** *I stopped him nobbling her money* **steal**, thieve, embezzle; informal rob. **4** *people tried to nobble her at parties* **accost**, waylay, detain, catch, confront, importune; informal buttonhole.

nobility n. **1** *a member of the nobility* **aristocracy**, aristocrats, peerage, peers (of the realm), lords, nobles, noblemen, noblewomen, patricians; informal aristos; Brit. informal nobs. **2** *the nobility of his deed* **virtue**, goodness, honour, decency, integrity; magnanimity, generosity, selflessness.

noble adj. **1** *a noble family* **aristocratic**, patrician, blue-blooded, high-born, titled; old use gentle. **2** *a noble cause* **righteous**, virtuous, good, honourable, upright, decent, worthy, moral, ethical, reputable, anti-corruption; magnanimous, unselfish, generous. **3** *a noble pine forest* **magnificent**, splendid, grand, stately, imposing, dignified, proud, striking, impressive, majestic, glorious, awesome, monumental, statuesque, regal, imperial.
– OPPOSITES humble, dishonourable, base.
▶ n. *Scottish nobles* **aristocrat**, nobleman, noblewoman, lord, lady, peer (of the realm), peeress, patrician; informal aristo; Brit. informal nob.

nod v. **1** *she nodded her head* **incline**, bob, bow, dip, wag. **2** *he nodded to me to start* **signal**, gesture, gesticulate, motion, sign, indicate.
▶ n. **1** *she gave a nod to the manager* **signal**, indication, sign, cue; gesture. **2** *a quick nod of his head* **inclination**, bob, bow, dip.
□ **give someone the nod 1** *the winger was given the nod* **select**, choose, pick, go for; Brit. cap. **2** *the Lords will give the treaty the nod* **approve**, agree to, sanction, ratify, endorse, rubber-stamp; informal OK, give something the green light, give something the thumbs up.
nod off fall asleep, go to sleep, doze off, drop off; informal drift off, flake out, go out like a light; N. Amer. informal sack out.

node n. **junction**, intersection, interchange, fork, confluence, convergence, crossing.

noise n. **sound**, din, hubbub, clamour, racket, uproar, tumult, commotion, pandemonium, babel; informal hullabaloo; Brit. informal row.
– OPPOSITES silence.

noisy adj. **1** *a noisy crowd* **rowdy**, clamorous, boisterous, turbulent, rackety; chattering, talkative, vociferous, shouting, screaming. **2** *noisy music* **loud**, fortissimo, blaring, booming, deafening, thunderous, tumultuous, clamorous, ear-splitting, piercing, strident, cacophonous, raucous.
– OPPOSITES quiet, soft.

nomad n. **itinerant**, traveller, migrant, wanderer, roamer, rover; Gypsy, Bedouin; transient, drifter, vagabond, vagrant, tramp; dated bird of passage.

nominal adj. **1** *the nominal head of the campaign* **in name only**, titular, formal, official; theoretical, supposed, ostensible, so-called. **2** *a nominal rent* **token**, symbolic; tiny, minute, minimal, small, insignificant, trifling; Brit. peppercorn; informal minuscule, piddling, piffling; N. Amer. informal nickel-and-dime.
– OPPOSITES real, considerable.

nominate v. **1** *you may nominate a candidate* **propose**, recommend, suggest, name, put forward, present, submit. **2** *he nominated his assistant* **appoint**, select, choose, elect, commission, designate, name, delegate.

non-believer n. **unbeliever**, disbeliever, sceptic, doubter, doubting Thomas, cynic, nihilist; atheist, agnostic, freethinker; infidel, pagan, heathen.

nonchalant adj. **calm**, composed, unconcerned, cool, {cool, calm, and collected}, cool as a cucumber; indifferent, blasé, dispassionate, apathetic, casual, insouciant; informal laid-back.
– OPPOSITES anxious.

non-combatant adj. **non-fighting**, non-participating, civilian; pacifist, neutral, non-aligned.

non-committal adj. **evasive**, equivocal, guarded, circumspect, reserved; discreet, uncommunicative, tactful, diplomatic, vague; informal cagey.
□ **be non-committal** prevaricate, give nothing away, dodge the issue, sidestep the issue, hedge, fence, pussyfoot around, beat about the bush, equivocate, temporize, shilly-shally, vacillate, waver; Brit. hum and haw; informal sit on the fence.

non compos mentis adj. See **insane** (sense 1).

nonconformist n. **dissenter**, dissentient, protester, rebel, renegade, schismatic; freethinker, apostate, heretic; individualist, free spirit, maverick, eccentric, original, deviant, misfit, dropout, outsider; informal freak, oddball, odd fish, weirdo, bad boy; N. Amer. informal screwball, kook.

nondescript adj. **undistinguished**, unremarkable, unexceptional, featureless, characterless, unmemorable; ordinary, commonplace, average, run-of-the-mill, mundane; uninteresting, uninspiring, colourless, bland; informal bog-standard; Brit. informal common or garden.
– OPPOSITES distinctive.

none pron. **1** *none of the fish are unusual* **not one**, not a one. **2** *none of this concerns me* **no part**, not a bit, not any. **3** *none can know better than you* **not one**, no one, nobody, not a soul, not a single person, no man.
– OPPOSITES all.
□ **none the —** *we were left none the wiser* not at all, not a bit, not the slightest bit, in no way, by no means any.

n

nonentity n. **nobody**, unimportant person, cipher, non-person, nothing, small fry, lightweight, mediocrity; informal no-hoper, non-starter.
– OPPOSITES celebrity.

non-essential adj. **unnecessary**, inessential, unessential, needless, unneeded, superfluous, uncalled for, redundant, dispensable, expendable, unimportant, extraneous.

nonetheless adv. **nevertheless**, even so, however, but, still, yet, though; in spite of that, despite that, be that as it may, for all that, that said, just the same, all the same; notwithstanding, regardless, anyway, anyhow; informal still and all.

non-existent adj. **imaginary**, imagined, unreal, fictional, fictitious, made up, invented, fanciful; fantastic, mythical; illusory, hallucinatory, chimerical, notional, shadowy, insubstantial; missing, absent; literary illusive.
– OPPOSITES real.

non-intervention n. **laissez-faire**, non-participation, non-interference, inaction, passivity, neutrality; live and let live.

non-observance n. **infringement**, breach, violation, contravention, transgression, non-compliance, infraction; dereliction, neglect.

nonpareil adj. *a nonpareil storyteller* **incomparable**, matchless, unrivalled, unparalleled, unequalled, peerless, beyond compare, second to none, unsurpassed, unbeatable, inimitable; unique, consummate, superlative, supreme; formal unexampled.
– OPPOSITES mediocre.
▸ n. *Britain's nonpareil of the 1980s* **best**, finest, crème de la crème, peak of perfection, elite, jewel in the crown, ne plus ultra, paragon; old use nonsuch.

nonplus v. **surprise**, stun, dumbfound, confound, take aback, disconcert, throw (off balance); puzzle, perplex, baffle, bemuse, bewilder; informal faze, flummox, stump, bamboozle, fox; N. Amer. informal discombobulate.

nonsense n. **1** *he was talking nonsense* **rubbish**, balderdash, gibberish, claptrap, blarney, blather, garbage; informal hogwash, rot, guff, baloney, tripe, drivel, gobbledegook, bilge, bosh, bunk, hot air, piffle, poppycock, phooey, twaddle; Brit. informal cobblers, codswallop, tosh, double Dutch; Scottish & N. English informal havers; N. Amer. informal flapdoodle, bushwa, applesauce; informal dated bunkum, tommyrot. **2** *she stands no nonsense* **mischief**, naughtiness, bad behaviour, misbehaviour, misconduct, misdemeanour; pranks, tricks, clowning, buffoonery, funny business; informal tomfoolery, monkey business, shenanigans, hanky-panky; Brit. informal monkey tricks, jiggery-pokery. **3** *they dismissed the concept as a nonsense* **absurdity**, folly, stupidity, ludicrousness, inanity, foolishness, idiocy, insanity, madness.
– OPPOSITES sense, wisdom.

nonsensical adj. *a nonsensical generalization* **foolish**, insane, stupid, idiotic, illogical, irrational, senseless, absurd, silly, inane, hare-brained, ridiculous, ludicrous, preposterous; informal crazy, crackpot, nutty; Brit. informal daft.
– OPPOSITES logical, sensible.

non-stop adj. *non-stop entertainment* **continuous**, constant, continual, perpetual, incessant, unceasing, ceaseless, uninterrupted, round-the-clock; unremitting, relentless, persistent.
– OPPOSITES occasional.
▸ adv. *we worked non-stop* **continuously**, continually, incessantly, unceasingly, ceaselessly, all the time, constantly, perpetually, round the clock, steadily, relentlessly, persistently; informal 24-7.
– OPPOSITES occasionally.

non-toxic adj. **non-poisonous**, innocuous, harmless, benign, safe, non-irritating, hypoallergenic.
– OPPOSITES toxic.

nook n. **recess**, corner, alcove, niche, bay, inglenook, cavity, cubbyhole, pigeonhole; opening, gap, aperture; hideaway, hiding place, hideout, shelter; informal hidey-hole.

noon n. **midday**, twelve o'clock, twelve hundred hours, high noon, noonday; literary noontime, noontide.

> **WORD LINKS**
> **meridian** relating to noon
> **solstice** each of two times in the year when the sun reaches its highest or lowest point in the sky at noon

no one pron. **nobody**, not a soul, not anyone, not a single person, never a one, none.

norm n. **1** *norms of diplomatic behaviour* **convention**, standard; criterion, yardstick, benchmark, touchstone, rule, formula, pattern, guide, guideline, model, exemplar. **2** *such teams are now the norm* **standard**, usual, the rule; normal, typical, average, unexceptional, par for the course, expected.

normal adj. **1** *they issue books in the normal way* **usual**, standard, ordinary, customary, conventional, habitual, accustomed, expected; typical, stock, common, everyday, regular, routine, established, set, fixed, traditional; literary wonted. **2** *a normal couple* **ordinary**, average, typical, run-of-the-mill, middle-of-the-road, common, conventional, mainstream, unremarkable, unexceptional; N. Amer. garden-variety; informal bog-standard, a dime a dozen; Brit. informal common or garden. **3** *the man was not normal* **sane**, in one's right mind, right in the head, of sound mind, compos mentis, lucid, rational, coherent; informal all there.
– OPPOSITES unusual, abnormal, insane.

normality n. **normalcy**, business as usual, the daily round; routine, order, regularity.

normally adv. **1** *she wanted to walk normally* **naturally**, conventionally, ordinarily; as usual, as normal. **2** *normally we'd keep quiet about this* **usually**, ordinarily, as a

n

rule, generally, in general, mostly, for the most part, by and large, mainly, most of the time, on the whole; typically, customarily, traditionally.

north adj. **northern**, northerly, boreal.

nose n. **1** *a punch on the nose* snout, muzzle, proboscis, trunk; informal beak, conk, snoot, schnozzle, hooter, sniffer; N. Amer. informal schnozz. **2** *he has a good nose* **sense of smell**. **3** *a nose for scandal* **instinct**, feeling, sixth sense, intuition, insight, perception. **4** *wine with a fruity nose* **smell**, bouquet, aroma, fragrance, perfume, scent, odour. **5** *the plane's nose dipped* nose cone, bow, prow, front end; informal droop-snoot.

▸v. **1** *the dog nosed the ball* **nuzzle**, nudge, push. **2** *she's nosing into my business* **pry**, inquire, poke about/around, interfere (in), meddle (in); be a busybody, stick/poke one's nose in; informal be nosy (about), snoop, Austral./NZ informal stickybeak. **3** *he nosed the car into the traffic* **ease**, inch, edge, move, manoeuvre, steer, guide.

□ **by a nose** (only) just, barely, narrowly, by a hair's breadth, by the skin of one's teeth; informal by a whisker.

nose around/about/round investigate, explore, ferret (about/around), rummage, search; delve into, peer into; prowl around; informal snoop about/around/round.

nose something out detect, find, discover, bring to light, track down, dig up, ferret out, root out, uncover, unearth, sniff out.

WORD LINKS

nasal, **rhinal** relating to the nose
aquiline referring to a nose curved like an eagle's beak
retroussé referring to a nose turned up at the tip
Roman referring to a nose with a high bridge
snub referring to a short, turned-up nose
rhinoplasty plastic surgery performed on the nose
rhinitis inflammation of the nose
epistaxis bleeding from the nose

---

nosedive n. **1** *the plane went into a nosedive* **dive**, descent, drop, plunge, plummet, fall. **2** informal *sterling took a nosedive* **fall**, drop, plunge, plummet, tumble, decline, slump; informal crash.
– OPPOSITES climb, rise.
▸v. **1** *the device nosedived to earth* **dive**, plunge, pitch, drop, plummet. **2** informal *costs have nosedived* **fall**, drop, sink, plunge, plummet, tumble, slump, go down, decline; informal crash.
– OPPOSITES soar, rise.

nosegay n. **posy**, bouquet, bunch, spray, sprig, buttonhole, corsage, boutonnière, tussie-mussie.

nosh informal n. *all kinds of nosh.* See **food** (sense 1).
▸v. *they nosh smoked salmon.* See **eat** (sense 1).

nostalgia n. **reminiscence**, remembrance, recollection; wistfulness, regret, sentimentality.

nostalgic adj. **wistful**, evocative, romantic, sentimental; regretful, dewy-eyed, maudlin.

nostrum n. **1** *they have to prove their nostrums work* **medicine**, quack remedy, potion, elixir, panacea, cure-all, wonder drug; informal magic bullet. **2** *right-wing nostrums* **magic formula**, recipe for success, remedy, cure, prescription, answer.

nosy adj. informal **prying**, inquisitive, curious, busybody, spying, eavesdropping, intrusive; informal snooping, snoopy.

notability n. **1** *the village has always enjoyed notability* **noteworthiness**, prominence, importance, significance, eminence; fame, renown, notoriety. **2** *the patronage of notabilities.* See **notable** (noun).

notable adj. **1** *notable examples of workmanship* **noteworthy**, remarkable, outstanding, important, significant, momentous, memorable; marked, striking, impressive; uncommon, unusual, special, exceptional, signal. **2** *a notable author* **prominent**, important, well known, famous, famed, noted, distinguished, great, eminent, illustrious, respected, esteemed, renowned, celebrated, acclaimed, influential, prestigious, of note.
– OPPOSITES unremarkable, unknown.
▸n. *movie stars and other notables* **celebrity**, public figure, VIP, personage, notability, dignitary, worthy, luminary; star, superstar, (big) name; informal celeb, somebody, bigwig, big shot, big cheese, big fish, megastar; Brit. informal nob; N. Amer. informal kahuna, high muckamuck.
– OPPOSITES nonentity.

notably adv. **1** *other countries, notably the USA* **in particular**, particularly, especially, specially; primarily, principally. **2** *these are notably short-lived birds* **remarkably**, especially, specially, very, extremely, exceptionally, singularly, particularly, peculiarly, distinctly, significantly, unusually, extraordinarily, uncommonly, incredibly, really, decidedly, surprisingly, conspicuously; informal seriously; Brit. informal jolly, dead.

notation n. **1** *algebraic notation* **symbols**, alphabet, syllabary, script; code, cipher, hieroglyphics. **2** *notations in the margin* **annotation**, jotting, comment, footnote, entry, memo, gloss, explanation; historical scholium.

notch n. **1** *a notch in the end of the arrow* **nick**, cut, incision, score, scratch, slit, snick, slot, groove, cleft, indentation. **2** *her opinion of Nick dropped a notch* **degree**, level, rung, point, mark, measure, grade.
▸v. *notch the plank* **nick**, cut, score, incise, carve, scratch, slit, snick, gouge, groove, furrow.
□ **notch something up** score, achieve, attain, gain, earn, make; rack up, chalk up; register, record.

note n. **1** *a note in her diary* **record**, entry, item, notation, jotting, memorandum, reminder, aide-memoire; informal memo. **2** *he will take notes of the meeting* **minutes**, records, details; report, account, commentary, transcript, proceedings, transactions; synopsis, summary, outline. **3** *notes in the margins* **annotation**, footnote, commentary, comment; marginalia, exegesis; historical scholium. **4** *he dropped me a note* **message**, communication, letter, line; formal epistle, missive. **5** Brit. *a £20 note* **banknote**; N. Amer. bill; US informal greenback; (**notes**) paper money. **6** *this is worthy of note* **attention**, consideration, notice, heed, observation, regard. **7** *a composer of note* **distinction**, importance, eminence, prestige, fame, celebrity, acclaim, renown, repute, stature, standing, consequence, account. **8** *a note of hopelessness in her voice* **tone**, intonation, inflection, sound; hint, indication, sign, element, suggestion.

▶ v. **1** *we will note your suggestion* **bear in mind**, be mindful of, consider, observe, heed, take notice of, pay attention to, take in. **2** *the letter noted the ministers' concern* **mention**, refer to, touch on, indicate, point out, make known, state. **3** *note the date in your diary* **write down**, put down, jot down, take down, inscribe, enter, mark, record, register, pencil.

notebook n. **notepad**, exercise book; register, logbook, log, diary, daybook, journal, record; Brit. jotter, pocketbook; N. Amer. scratch pad; informal memo pad.

noted adj. **renowned**, well known, famous, famed, prominent, celebrated; notable, of note, important, eminent, distinguished, illustrious, acclaimed, esteemed; of distinction, of repute.
– OPPOSITES unknown.

noteworthy adj. **notable**, interesting, significant, important; remarkable, impressive, striking, outstanding, memorable, unique, special; unusual, extraordinary, singular, rare.
– OPPOSITES unexceptional.

nothing pron. **1** *there's nothing I can do* **not a thing**, not anything, nil, zero; N. English nowt; informal zilch, sweet Fanny Adams, sweet FA, nix, not a dicky bird; Brit. informal damn all, not a sausage; N. Amer. informal zip, nada; old use naught. **2** *forget it—it's nothing* **a trifling matter**, a trifle; neither here nor there; informal no big deal. **3** *he treats her as nothing* **a nobody**, an unimportant person, a nonentity, a cipher, a non-person; Brit. small beer. **4** *the share value fell to nothing* **zero**, nought, 0; Tennis love; Cricket a duck.
– OPPOSITES something.
□ **be/have nothing to do with 1** *it has nothing to do with you* **be unconnected with**, be unrelated to; be irrelevant to, be inapplicable to, be inapposite to. **2** *I'll have nothing to do with him* **avoid**, have no truck with, steer clear of, give a wide berth to.
for nothing 1 *she hosted the show for nothing* **free (of charge)**, gratis, without charge, at no cost; informal for free, on the house. **2** *all this trouble for nothing* **in vain**, to no avail, to no purpose, with no result, needlessly, pointlessly.
nothing but *he's nothing but a nuisance*

merely, only, just, solely, simply, purely, no more than.

nothingness n. **1** *the nothingness of death* **oblivion**, nullity, blankness; void, vacuum; rare nihility. **2** *the nothingness of it all overwhelmed him* **unimportance**, insignificance, triviality, pointlessness, uselessness, worthlessness.

notice n. **1** *nothing escaped his notice* **attention**, observation, awareness, consciousness, perception; regard, consideration, scrutiny; watchfulness, vigilance, attentiveness. **2** *a notice on the wall* **poster**, bill, handbill, advertisement, announcement, bulletin; flyer, leaflet, pamphlet; sign, card; informal ad; Brit. informal advert. **3** *times may change without notice* **notification**, (advance) warning, announcement; information, news, communication, word. **4** *I handed in my notice* **resignation**. **5** *the film got bad notices* **review**, write-up, critique, criticism; Brit. informal crit.

▶ v. *I noticed that the door was open* **observe**, perceive, note, see, discern, detect, spot, distinguish, mark, remark; Brit. informal clock; literary behold.
– OPPOSITES overlook.
□ **take no notice (of)** **ignore**, pay no attention (to), disregard, pay no heed (to), take no account (of), brush aside, shrug off, turn a blind eye (to), pass over, let go, overlook, look the other way.

noticeable adj. **distinct**, evident, obvious, apparent, manifest, patent, plain, clear, marked, conspicuous, unmistakable, undeniable, pronounced, prominent, striking, arresting; perceptible, discernible, detectable, observable, visible, appreciable.

noticeboard n. **pinboard**, cork board, bulletin board; hoarding.

notification n. **1** *the notification of the victim's wife* **informing**, telling, alerting. **2** *she received notification that he was on the way* **information**, word, advice, news, intelligence; communication, message; literary tidings.

notify v. **1** *we will notify you as soon as possible* **inform**, tell, advise, apprise, let someone know, put in the picture; alert, warn. **2** *births should be notified to the registrar* **report**, make known, announce, declare, communicate, disclose.

notion n. **1** *he had a notion that something was wrong* **idea**, belief, conviction, opinion, view, thought, impression, perception; hypothesis, theory; (funny) feeling, (sneaking) suspicion, hunch. **2** *Claire had no notion of what he meant* **understanding**, idea, awareness, knowledge, clue, inkling. **3** *he got a notion to return* **impulse**, inclination, whim, desire, wish, fancy.

notional adj. **hypothetical**, theoretical, speculative, conjectural, suppositional, putative, conceptual; imaginary, fanciful, unreal, illusory.
– OPPOSITES actual.

notoriety n. **infamy**, disrepute, ill repute, bad name, dishonour, discredit; dated ill fame.

notorious adj. **infamous**, scandalous; well known, famous, famed, legendary.

notwithstanding prep. *notwithstanding his workload, he is a dedicated father* **despite**, in spite of, regardless of, for all.
▸ adv. *she is bright—notwithstanding, she is now jobless* **nevertheless**, nonetheless, even so, all the same, in spite of this, despite this, however, still, yet, that said, just the same, anyway, in any event, at any rate.
▸ conj. *notwithstanding that there was no space, they played on* **although**, even though, though, in spite of the fact that, despite the fact that.

nought n. **nil**, zero, o; Tennis love; Cricket a duck.

nourish v. **1** *patients must be well nourished* **feed**, provide for, sustain, maintain. **2** *we nourish the talents of children* **encourage**, promote, foster, nurture, cultivate, stimulate, boost, advance, assist, help, aid, strengthen, enrich. **3** *the hopes Ursula nourished* **cherish**, nurture, foster, harbour, nurse, entertain, maintain, hold, have.

nourishing adj. **nutritious**, nutritive, wholesome, good for one, healthy, health-giving, healthful, beneficial, sustaining.
– OPPOSITES unhealthy.

nourishment n. **food**, sustenance, nutriment, nutrition, subsistence, provisions, provender, fare; informal grub, nosh, chow, eats, scoff; N. Amer. informal chuck; formal comestibles; dated victuals.

nouveau riche plural n. the new rich, parvenus, arrivistes, upstarts, social climbers, vulgarians.

novel[1] n. *curl up with a good novel* **book**, paperback, hardback; **story**, tale, narrative, romance; best-seller; informal blockbuster.

novel[2] adj. *a novel way of making money* **new**, original, unusual, unfamiliar, unconventional, unorthodox; different, fresh, imaginative, innovative, innovatory, innovational, inventive, modern, neoteric, avant-garde, pioneering, groundbreaking, revolutionary; rare, unique, singular, unprecedented; experimental, untested, untried; strange, exotic, newfangled.
– OPPOSITES traditional.

novelist n. **writer**, author, fictionist, man/woman of letters; informal penman, scribbler.

novelty n. **1** *the novelty of our approach* **originality**, newness, freshness, unconventionality, unfamiliarity; difference, imaginativeness, creativity, innovation, modernity. **2** *we sell seasonal novelties* **knick-knack**, trinket, bauble, toy, trifle, gewgaw, gimcrack, ornament; N. Amer. kickshaw.

novice n. **1** *a five-day course for novices* **beginner**, learner, neophyte, newcomer, initiate, tyro, fledgling; apprentice, trainee, probationer, student, pupil; N. Amer. tenderfoot; informal rookie, newie, newbie; N. Amer. informal greenhorn. **2** *a novice who was never ordained* **neophyte**, novitiate;

postulant, proselyte, catechumen.
– OPPOSITES expert, veteran.

novitiate n. **1** *a three-year novitiate* **probationary period**, probation, trial period, test period, apprenticeship, training period, traineeship, training, initiation. **2** *two young novitiates* **novice**, neophyte; postulant, proselyte, catechumen.

now adv. **1** *I'm extremely busy now* **at the moment**, at present, at the present (time/moment), at this moment in time, currently; N. Amer. presently; Brit. informal at the minute. **2** *television is now the main source of news* **nowadays**, today, these days, in this day and age; in the present climate. **3** *you must leave now* **at once**, straight away, right away, right now, this minute, this instant, immediately, instantly, directly, without further ado, promptly, without delay, as soon as possible; informal pronto, straight off, ASAP.
▢ **as of now** from this time on, from now on, henceforth, henceforward, from this day forward, in future; formal hereafter.
for now for the time being, for the moment, for the present, for the meantime; old use for the nonce.
now and again occasionally, now and then, from time to time, sometimes, every so often, (every) now and again, at times, on occasion(s), (every) once in a while, periodically, once in a blue moon.

nowadays adv. **these days**, today, at the present time, in these times, in this day and age, now, currently, at the moment, at present, at this moment in time; in the present climate; N. Amer. presently.

noxious adj. **poisonous**, toxic, deadly, harmful, dangerous, pernicious, damaging, destructive; unpleasant, nasty, disgusting, awful, dreadful, horrible, terrible; vile, revolting, foul, nauseating, appalling, offensive; malodorous, fetid, putrid; informal ghastly, horrid; literary noisome; old use disgustful.
– OPPOSITES innocuous.

nuance n. **fine distinction**, subtle difference; shade, shading, gradation, variation, degree; subtlety, nicety, overtone.

nub n. **crux**, central point, main point, core, heart (of the matter), nucleus, essence, quintessence, kernel, marrow, meat, pith; gist, substance; informal nitty-gritty.

nubile adj. **sexually mature**, marriageable, sexually attractive, desirable, sexy, luscious; informal beddable.

nucleus n. **1** *the nucleus of the banking world* **core**, centre, central part, heart, nub, hub, middle, eye, focus, focal point, pivot, crux. **2** *a nucleus of union men supported him* **small group**, caucus, cell, coterie, clique, faction.

nude adj. **(stark) naked**, bare, unclothed, undressed, disrobed, stripped, unclad, in a state of nature, au naturel; informal without a stitch on, in one's birthday suit, in the raw, in the altogether, in the buff, in the nuddy; Brit. informal starkers; Scottish informal in the scud;

n

N. Amer. informal **buck naked.**
– OPPOSITES clothed.

nudge v. **1** *he nudged Ben* **poke**, elbow, dig, prod, jog, jab. **2** *the canoe nudged a bank* **touch**, bump (against), push (against), run into. **3** *we nudged them into action* **prompt**, encourage, stimulate, prod, galvanize. **4** *unemployment was nudging 3,000,000* **approach**, near, come close to, be verging on, border on.
▸ n. **1** *Maggie gave him a nudge* **poke**, dig (in the ribs), prod, jog, jab, push. **2** *after a nudge, she remembered Lilian* **reminder**, prompt, prompting, prod, encouragement.

nugatory adj. **1** *a nugatory observation* **worthless**, unimportant, inconsequential, valueless, trifling, trivial, insignificant, meaningless. **2** *the shortages will render nugatory our hopes* **futile**, useless, vain, unavailing, null, invalid.

nugget n. **lump**, nub, chunk, piece, hunk, wad, gobbet; N. Amer. informal **gob.**

nuisance n. **annoyance**, inconvenience, bore, bother, irritation, problem, trouble, trial, burden; pest, plague, thorn in one's side/flesh; informal pain (in the neck), hassle, bind, drag, aggravation, headache; Scottish informal **nyaff**, **skelf**; N. Amer. informal **nudnik**; Austral./NZ informal **nark.**
– OPPOSITES blessing.

null adj. **1** *their marriage was declared null* **invalid**, null and void, void; annulled, nullified, cancelled, revoked. **2** *his null life* **characterless**, colourless, empty, insipid, vapid, dull, boring.
– OPPOSITES valid, interesting.

nullify v. **1** *they nullified the legislation* **annul**, render null and void, void, invalidate; repeal, reverse, rescind, revoke, cancel, abolish; countermand, do away with, terminate, quash; Law **vacate**; formal **abrogate.** **2** *the costs would nullify any tax relief* **cancel out**, neutralize, negate, negative.
– OPPOSITES ratify.

numb adj. *his fingers were numb* **without sensation**, without feeling, numbed, benumbed, desensitized, insensible, senseless, unfeeling; anaesthetized; dazed, stunned, stupefied, paralysed, immobilized, frozen.
– OPPOSITES sensitive.
▸ v. *the cold numbed her senses* **deaden**, benumb, desensitize, dull; anaesthetize; daze, stupefy, paralyse, immobilize, freeze.
– OPPOSITES sensitize.

number n. **1** *a whole number* **numeral**, integer, figure, digit; character, symbol; decimal, unit; cardinal number, ordinal number. **2** *a large number of complaints* **amount**, quantity; total, aggregate, tally; quota. **3** *the wedding of one of their number* **group**, company, crowd, circle, party, band, crew, set; informal **gang**. **4** *the band performed another number* **song**, piece (of music), tune, track; routine, sketch, dance, act.
▸ v. **1** *visitors numbered more than two million* **add up to**, amount to, total, come

to. **2** *he numbers the fleet at a thousand* **calculate**, count, total, compute, reckon, tally; assess; Brit. **tot up**; formal **enumerate. 3** *each paragraph is numbered* **assign a number to**, itemize, enumerate. **4** *he numbers her among his friends* **include**, count, reckon, deem. **5** *his days are numbered* **limit**, restrict, fix.
□ **a number of** several, various, quite a few, sundry.

without number countless, innumerable, unlimited, endless, limitless, untold; numberless, uncountable, uncounted; numerous, many, multiple, manifold, legion.

WORD LINKS

numerical relating to numbers
numerology the study of the supposed magical power of numbers
sudoku, kakuro types of number puzzle

---

numberless adj. **innumerable**, countless, unlimited, endless, limitless, untold, uncountable, uncounted; numerous, many, multiple, manifold, legion; informal **more — than one can shake a stick at**; literary **myriad.**

numbing adj. **1** *menthol has a numbing action* **desensitizing**, deadening, benumbing, anaesthetic, anaesthetizing; paralysing. **2** *numbing cold* **freezing**, raw, bitter, biting, arctic. **3** *numbing boredom* **stupefying**, mind-numbing, stultifying; soporific.

numbskull n. informal See **idiot.**

numeral n. **number**, integer, figure, digit; character, symbol, unit.

numerous adj. **(very) many**, a lot of, scores of, countless, numberless, innumerable; several, quite a few, various; plenty of, copious, a quantity of, an abundance of, a profusion of, a multitude of; frequent; informal **umpteen**, lots of, loads of, masses of, stacks of, heaps of, bags of, tons of, oodles of, hundreds of, thousands of, millions of, **more — than one can shake a stick at**; Brit. informal **a shedload of**; N. Amer. informal **gazillions of**; Austral./NZ informal **a swag of**; literary **myriad.**
– OPPOSITES few.

numinous adj. **spiritual**, religious, divine, holy, sacred; mysterious, other-worldly, unearthly, transcendent.

nun n. **sister**, abbess, prioress, Mother Superior, Reverend Mother; novice; bride of Christ, religious, conventual, contemplative, canoness; literary **vestal**; historical **anchoress.**

nuncio n. **(papal) ambassador**, legate, envoy, messenger.

nunnery n. **convent**, priory, abbey, cloister, religious community.

nuptial adj. **matrimonial**, marital, marriage, wedding, conjugal, bridal; married, wedded; Law **spousal**; literary **connubial.**

nuptials plural n. **wedding (ceremony)**, marriage, union; old use **espousal.**

nurse n. **1** *skilled nurses* **carer**, caregiver; informal **Florence Nightingale**, nursey; N. Amer. informal **candy-striper**. **2** *she had been his nurse in childhood* **nanny**, nursemaid, nursery

nurse, childminder, governess, au pair, childcarer, babysitter, ayah.
▶ v. **1** *they nursed smallpox patients* **care for**, take care of, look after, tend, minister to. **2** *I nursed my sore finger* **treat**, medicate, tend; dress, bandage, soothe; informal doctor. **3** *Rosa was nursing her baby* **breastfeed**, suckle, feed. **4** *they nursed old grievances* **harbour**, foster, entertain, bear, have, hold (on to), cherish, cling to, retain. **5** *our unity needs to be nursed* **nurture**, encourage, promote, boost, assist, help, cultivate; protect, safeguard.

nursemaid n. See **nurse** (sense 2 of the noun).

nurture v. **1** *she nurtured her children into adulthood* **bring up**, care for, take care of, look after, tend, rear, raise, support, foster; parent, mother. **2** *we nurtured these plants* **cultivate**, grow, keep, tend. **3** *he nurtured my love of art* **encourage**, promote, stimulate, develop, foster, cultivate, boost, contribute to, assist, help, abet, strengthen, fuel.
– OPPOSITES neglect, hinder.
▶ n. **1** *we are what nature and nurture have made us* **upbringing**, rearing, raising, childcare; training, education. **2** *the nurture of ideas* **encouragement**, promotion, fostering, development, cultivation.
– OPPOSITES nature.

nut n. **1** *nuts in their shells* **kernel**. **2** informal *he smacked her on the nut* **head**, skull, cranium, crown; informal noodle, noggin, dome; Brit. informal bonce; informal dated conk, noddle. **3** informal *some nut arrived at the office* **maniac**, lunatic, madman, madwoman; eccentric; informal loony, nutcase, fruitcake, head case, crank, crackpot, weirdo; Brit. informal nutter, mentalist; N. Amer. informal screwball, crazy; N. Amer. & Austral./NZ informal dingbat. **4** informal *a movie nut* **enthusiast**, fan, devotee, aficionado; informal freak, fiend, fanatic, addict, buff; N. Amer. informal jock.
◻ **do one's nut** informal be very angry, be furious, lose one's temper; informal go mad, go crazy, go wild, go bananas, have a fit, blow one's top, hit the roof, go off the deep end, go ape, flip, lose one's rag; Brit. informal go spare.

off one's nut informal See **mad** (sense 1).

nutriment n. **nourishment**, nutrients, sustenance, goodness, nutrition, food.

nutrition n. **nourishment**, nutriment, nutrients, sustenance, food; informal grub, chow, nosh, scoff; literary viands; dated victuals; old use aliment.

<hr>
WORD LINKS
alimentary relating to food and nutrition
dietitian an expert on diet and nutrition
<hr>

nutritious adj. **nourishing**, good for one, nutritive, nutrimental; wholesome, healthy, healthful, beneficial, sustaining.

nuts adj. informal **1** *they thought we were nuts.* See **mad** (sense 1). **2** *he's nuts about her* **infatuated with**, keen on, devoted to, in love with, smitten with, enamoured of, hot for; informal mad, crazy, nutty, wild, hooked on, gone on; Brit. informal potty.

nuts and bolts plural n. **practical details**, fundamentals, basics, practicalities, essentials, mechanics; informal nitty-gritty, ins and outs, brass tacks.

nutty adj. informal **1** *they're all nutty.* See **mad** (sense 1). **2** *she's nutty about Elvis.* See **nuts** (sense 2).

nuzzle v. **1** *the horse nuzzled at her pocket* **nudge**, nose, prod, push. **2** *she nuzzled up to her boyfriend* **snuggle**, cuddle, nestle, burrow, embrace, hug.

n

Oo

oaf n. **lout**, boor, barbarian, Neanderthal, churl, bumpkin, yokel; fool, idiot, imbecile; informal cretin, ass, goon, oik, yahoo, ape, lump, clod, meathead, bonehead, lamebrain; Brit. informal clot, plonker, berk, pillock, yob, yobbo; Scottish informal nyaff, gowk; N. Amer. informal bozo, dumbhead, lummox, klutz, goofus, clunk, turkey; Austral. informal hoon, dingbat, galah, drongo; old use lubber.

oafish adj. **stupid**, foolish, idiotic; loutish, awkward, gawkish, clumsy, lumbering, ape-like, cloddish, Neanderthal, uncouth, uncultured, boorish, rough, coarse, brutish, ill-mannered, unrefined; informal clodhopping, blockheaded, boneheaded, thickheaded; Brit. informal yobbish; old use lubberly.

oasis n. **1** an oasis near Cairo **watering hole**, watering place, water hole, spring. **2** a cool oasis in a hot summer **refuge**, haven, retreat, sanctuary, sanctum, harbour, asylum.

oath n. **1** an oath of allegiance **vow**, pledge, promise, avowal, affirmation, word (of honour), bond, guarantee; formal troth. **2** he uttered a stream of oaths **swear word**, profanity, expletive, four-letter word, dirty word, obscenity, vulgarity, curse, malediction; informal cuss (word); formal imprecation.

obdurate adj. **stubborn**, obstinate, intransigent, inflexible, unyielding, unbending, pig-headed, mulish, stiff-necked, headstrong, unshakeable, intractable, unpersuadable, immovable, inexorable, uncompromising, iron-willed, adamant, firm, determined; Brit. informal bloody-minded.
– OPPOSITES malleable.

obedient adj. **compliant**, biddable, acquiescent, tractable, amenable, malleable, pliable, pliant; dutiful, good, law-abiding, deferential, respectful, duteous, well trained, well disciplined, manageable, governable, docile, tame, meek, passive, submissive, unresisting, yielding.
– OPPOSITES disobedient, rebellious.

obeisance n. **1** a gesture of obeisance **respect**, homage, worship, adoration, reverence, veneration, honour, submission, deference. **2** she made a deep obeisance **bow**, curtsy, bob, genuflection, salaam; historical kowtow.

obelisk n. **column**, pillar, needle, shaft, monolith, monument.

obese adj. **fat**, overweight, corpulent, gross, stout, fleshy, heavy, portly, paunchy, pot-bellied, beer-bellied, well upholstered, well padded, broad in the beam, bulky, bloated, flabby; informal porky, roly-poly, blubbery; Brit. informal podgy; old use pursy.
– OPPOSITES thin.

obey v. **1** I obeyed him without question **do what someone says**, carry out someone's orders; submit to, defer to, bow to, yield to. **2** he refused to obey the order **carry out**, perform, act on, execute, discharge, implement, fulfil. **3** health and safety regulations have to be obeyed **comply with**, adhere to, observe, abide by, act in accordance with, conform to, respect, follow, keep to, stick to; play it by the book, toe the line.
– OPPOSITES defy, ignore.

obfuscate v. **obscure**, confuse, blur, muddle, complicate, muddy, cloud, befog; muddy the waters.
– OPPOSITES clarify.

obituary n. **death notice**; informal obit; formal necrology.

object n. **1** wooden objects **thing**, article, item, device, gadget; informal doodah, thingamajig, thingamabob, thingummy, whatsit, whatchamacallit, thingy; Brit. informal gubbins; N. Amer. informal doodad, dingus. **2** he became the object of criticism **target**, butt, focus, recipient, victim. **3** his object was to resolve the crisis **objective**, aim, goal, target, purpose, end (in view), plan, object of the exercise, point; ambition, design, intent, intention, idea.
▸ v. teachers objected to the scheme **protest about**, oppose, raise objections to, express disapproval of, take exception to, take issue with, take a stand against, argue against, quarrel with, condemn, draw the line at, demur at, mind, complain about, cavil at, quibble about; beg to differ; informal kick up a fuss/stink about.
– OPPOSITES approve, accept.

objection n. **protest**, protestation, demur, demurral, complaint, expostulation, grievance, cavil, quibble; opposition, argument, counter-argument, disagreement, disapproval, dissent; informal niggle.

objectionable adj. **unpleasant**, disagreeable, distasteful, displeasing, off-putting, undesirable, obnoxious, offensive, nasty, horrible, horrid, disgusting, awful, terrible, dreadful, frightful, appalling, insufferable, odious, vile, foul, unsavoury, repulsive, repellent, repugnant, revolting,

abhorrent, loathsome, hateful, detestable, reprehensible, deplorable; informal ghastly; Brit. informal beastly; formal exceptionable, rebarbative.
– OPPOSITES pleasant.

objective adj. **1** *an interviewer must try to be objective* **impartial**, unbiased, unprejudiced, non-partisan, disinterested, neutral, uninvolved, even-handed, equitable, fair, fair-minded, just, open-minded, dispassionate, detached. **2** *the world of objective knowledge* **factual**, actual, real, empirical, verifiable.
– OPPOSITES biased, subjective.
▶ n. *our objective is to build a profitable business* **aim**, intention, purpose, target, goal, intent, object, object of the exercise, point, end (in view); idea, design, plan, ambition, aspiration, desire, hope.

objectively adv. **impartially**, without bias, without prejudice, even-handedly, dispassionately, detachedly, equitably, fairly, justly, with an open mind, without fear or favour.

objectivity n. **impartiality**, lack of bias/prejudice, fairness, fair-mindedness, neutrality, even-handedness, justice, open-mindedness, disinterest, detachment, dispassion, dispassionateness.

oblation n. **religious offering**, offering, sacrifice, peace offering, burnt offering, first fruits, libation.

obligate v. **oblige**, compel, commit, bind, require, constrain, force, impel, make.

obligation n. **1** *his professional obligations* **duty**, commitment, responsibility; function, task, job, assignment, commission, burden, charge, onus, liability, accountability, requirement, debt; old use devoir. **2** *a sense of obligation* **duty**, compulsion, indebtedness; duress, necessity, pressure, constraint.
□ **under an obligation** beholden, obliged, in someone's debt, indebted, obligated, duty-bound, honour-bound.

obligatory adj. **compulsory**, mandatory, prescribed, required, demanded, statutory, enforced, binding, incumbent; requisite, necessary, imperative, unavoidable, inescapable, essential.
– OPPOSITES optional.

oblige v. **1** *both parties are obliged to accept the decision* **require**, compel, bind, constrain, obligate, leave someone no option, force. **2** *I'll be happy to oblige you* **do someone a favour**, accommodate, help, assist, serve; gratify someone's wishes, indulge, humour.

obliged adj. **thankful**, grateful, appreciative, much obliged; beholden, indebted, in someone's debt.

obliging adj. **helpful**, accommodating, willing, cooperative, considerate, complaisant, agreeable, amenable, generous, kind, neighbourly, hospitable, pleasant, good-natured, amiable, gracious, unselfish, civil, courteous, polite; Brit. informal decent.
– OPPOSITES unhelpful.

oblique adj. **1** *an oblique line* **slanting**, slanted, sloping, at an angle, angled, diagonal, aslant, slant, slantwise, skew, on the skew, askew, squint; N. Amer. cater-cornered. **2** *an oblique reference* **indirect**, inexplicit, roundabout, circuitous, circumlocutory, implicit, implied, elliptical, evasive, backhanded. **3** *an oblique glance* **sidelong**, sideways, furtive, covert, sly, surreptitious.
– OPPOSITES straight, direct.
▶ n. **slash**, forward slash, solidus, backslash, diagonal, virgule.

obliquely adv. **1** *the sun shone obliquely across the tower* **diagonally**, at an angle, slantwise, sideways, sidelong, aslant. **2** *he referred obliquely to the war* **indirectly**, in a roundabout way, not in so many words, circuitously, evasively.

obliterate v. **1** *he tried to obliterate the memory* **erase**, eradicate, expunge, efface, wipe out, blot out, rub out, remove all traces of. **2** *a nuclear explosion that would obliterate a city* **destroy**, wipe out, annihilate, demolish, liquidate, wipe off the face of the earth, wipe off the map; informal zap. **3** *clouds were darkening, obliterating the sun* **hide**, obscure, blot out, block, cover, screen.

oblivion n. **1** *they drank themselves into oblivion* **unconsciousness**, insensibility, stupor, stupefaction; coma, blackout; literary the waters of Lethe. **2** *they rescued him from artistic oblivion* **obscurity**, limbo, anonymity, neglect, disregard.
– OPPOSITES consciousness, fame.

oblivious adj. **unaware**, unconscious, heedless, unmindful, insensible, unheeding, ignorant, blind, deaf, unsuspecting, unobservant; unconcerned, impervious, unaffected.
– OPPOSITES conscious.

obloquy n. **1** *he endured years of contempt and obloquy* **vilification**, opprobrium, vituperation, condemnation, denunciation, abuse, criticism, censure, defamation, denigration, revilement, calumny, insults; informal flak; formal castigation, excoriation; old use contumely. **2** *conduct to which no moral obloquy could reasonably attach* **disgrace**, dishonour, shame, discredit, stigma, humiliation, loss of face, ignominy, odium, opprobrium, disfavour, disrepute, ill repute, infamy, stain, notoriety, scandal.
– OPPOSITES praise, honour.

obnoxious adj. **unpleasant**, disagreeable, nasty, distasteful, offensive, objectionable, unsavoury, unpalatable, awful, terrible, dreadful, frightful, horrible, revolting, repulsive, repellent, repugnant, disgusting, odious, vile, foul, abhorrent, loathsome, nauseating, sickening, hateful, insufferable, intolerable; informal horrid, ghastly, gross, putrid, sick-making, yucky, God-awful; Brit. informal beastly; old use disgustful, loathly.
– OPPOSITES delightful.

obscene adj. **1** *obscene literature* **pornographic**, indecent, smutty, dirty, filthy, X-rated, 'adult', explicit, lewd, rude,

O

vulgar, coarse, crude, immoral, improper, off colour; scatological, profane; informal blue, porn, porno, skin. **2** *an obscene crime* **shocking**, scandalous, vile, foul, atrocious, outrageous, heinous, odious, abhorrent, abominable, disgusting, hideous, repugnant, repulsive, revolting, repellent, loathsome, nauseating, sickening, awful, dreadful, terrible, frightful.

obscenity n. **1** *the book was banned on the grounds of obscenity* **indecency**, immorality, impropriety, smuttiness, smut, lewdness, rudeness, vulgarity, dirt, filth, coarseness, crudity; profanity, profaneness. **2** *the men scowled and muttered obscenities* **expletive**, swear word, oath, profanity, curse, four-letter word, dirty word, blasphemy; informal cuss, cuss word; formal imprecation.

obscure adj. **1** *his origins and parentage remain obscure* **unclear**, uncertain, unknown, in doubt, doubtful, dubious, mysterious, hazy, vague, indeterminate, concealed, hidden. **2** *obscure references to Proust* **mystifying**, puzzling, perplexing, baffling, ambiguous, cryptic, enigmatic, Delphic, oracular, oblique, opaque, elliptical, unintelligible, incomprehensible, impenetrable, unfathomable; abstruse, recondite, arcane, esoteric; informal as clear as mud. **3** *an obscure Peruvian painter* **little known**, unknown, unheard of, undistinguished, unimportant, nameless, minor; unsung, unrecognized, forgotten. **4** *an obscure shape* **indistinct**, faint, vague, nebulous, ill-defined, unclear, blurred, blurry, misty, hazy.
– OPPOSITES clear, plain, famous, distinct.
▶ v. **1** *grey clouds obscured the sun* **hide**, conceal, cover, veil, shroud, screen, mask, cloak, cast a shadow over, shadow, block, obliterate, eclipse, darken. **2** *recent events have obscured the issue* **confuse**, complicate, obfuscate, cloud, blur, muddy; muddy the waters; literary befog.
– OPPOSITES reveal, clarify.

obscurity n. **1** *the discovery rescued him from relative obscurity* **insignificance**, inconspicuousness, unimportance, anonymity; limbo, twilight, oblivion. **2** *poems of impenetrable obscurity* **incomprehensibility**, impenetrability, unintelligibility, opacity. **3** *the obscurities in his poems and plays* **enigma**, puzzle, mystery, difficulty, problem.
– OPPOSITES fame, clarity.

obsequies plural n. **funeral rites**, funeral service, funeral, burial, interment, entombment, inhumation, last offices; formal exequies; old use sepulture.

obsequious adj. **servile**, ingratiating, sycophantic, fawning, unctuous, oily, oleaginous, grovelling, cringing, subservient, submissive, slavish; informal slimy, bootlicking, smarmy.

observable adj. **noticeable**, visible, perceptible, perceivable, detectable, distinguishable, discernible, recognizable,

evident, apparent, manifest, obvious, patent, clear, distinct, plain, unmistakable; old use sensible.

observance n. **1** *strict observance of the rules* **compliance**, adherence, accordance, respect, observation, fulfilment, obedience; keeping, obeying. **2** *religious observances* **rite**, ritual, ceremony, ceremonial, celebration, practice, service, office, festival, tradition, custom, usage, formality, form.

observant adj. **alert**, sharp-eyed, sharp, eagle-eyed, hawk-eyed, having eyes like a hawk, keen-eyed, watchful, heedful, aware; on the lookout, on the qui vive, on guard, attentive, vigilant, having one's eyes open/peeled; informal beady-eyed, not missing a trick, on the ball, focused.
– OPPOSITES inattentive.

observation n. **1** *detailed observation of the animal's behaviour* **monitoring**, watching, scrutiny, examination, inspection, survey, surveillance, attention, consideration, study. **2** *his observations were concise and to the point* **remark**, comment, statement, utterance, pronouncement, declaration; opinion, impression, thought, reflection. **3** *the observation of the law* **observance**, compliance, adherence, respect, obedience; keeping, obeying.

observe v. **1** *she observed that all the chairs were occupied* **notice**, see, note, perceive, discern, spot; literary espy, descry. **2** *she was alarmed to discover he had been observing her* **watch**, look at, eye, contemplate, view, survey, regard, keep an eye on, scrutinize, keep under observation, keep watch on, keep under surveillance, monitor, keep a weather eye on; informal keep tabs on, keep a beady eye on; literary behold. **3** *'You look tired,' she observed* **remark**, comment, say, mention, declare, announce, state, pronounce; formal opine. **4** *both countries agreed to observe the ceasefire* **comply with**, abide by, keep, obey, adhere to, heed, honour, fulfil, respect, follow, consent to, acquiesce in, accept. **5** *townspeople observed the first anniversary of the flood* **commemorate**, mark, keep, memorialize, remember, celebrate.

observer n. **1** *a casual observer might not have noticed* **spectator**, onlooker, watcher, looker-on, fly on the wall, viewer, witness; informal rubberneck; literary beholder. **2** *industry observers expect the deal to be finalized today* **commentator**, reporter; monitor.

obsess v. **preoccupy**, be uppermost in someone's mind, prey on someone's mind, prey on, possess, haunt, consume, plague, torment, hound, bedevil, beset, take control of, take over, have a hold on, eat up, grip.

obsessed adj. **fixated**, possessed, consumed, infatuated, besotted; informal smitten, hung up; N. Amer. informal hipped.

obsession n. **fixation**, ruling/consuming passion, passion, mania, idée fixe, compulsion, preoccupation, infatuation, addiction, fetish, craze; hobby horse; phobia, complex, neurosis; informal bee in one's bonnet, hang-up, thing.

obsessive adj. **all-consuming**, consuming, compulsive, controlling, obsessional, fanatical, neurotic, excessive, besetting, tormenting, inescapable; informal pathological.

obsolescent adj. **dying out**, on the decline, declining, waning, on the wane, disappearing, past its prime, ageing, moribund, on its last legs, out of date, outdated, old-fashioned, outmoded; informal on the way out, past it.

obsolete adj. **out of date**, outdated, outmoded, old-fashioned, démodé, passé; no longer in use, disused, fallen into disuse, superannuated, outworn, antiquated, antediluvian, anachronistic, discontinued, old, dated, archaic, ancient, fossilized, extinct, defunct, dead, bygone; informal out of the ark, prehistoric; Brit. informal past its sell-by date.
– OPPOSITES current, modern.

obstacle n. **barrier**, hurdle, stumbling block, obstruction, bar, block, impediment, hindrance, snag, catch, drawback, hitch, handicap, deterrent, complication, difficulty, problem, fly in the ointment, disadvantage, curb, check; Brit. spanner in the works; literary trammel.
– OPPOSITES advantage, aid.

obstinacy n. **stubbornness**, inflexibility, intransigence, intractability, obduracy, mulishness, pig-headedness, wilfulness, contrariness, perversity, recalcitrance, implacability; persistence, tenacity, tenaciousness, doggedness, single-mindedness, determination; Brit. informal bloody-mindedness, bolshiness; formal pertinacity, refractoriness.

obstinate adj. **stubborn**, unyielding, inflexible, unbending, intransigent, intractable, obdurate, mulish, stubborn as a mule, pig-headed, self-willed, strong-willed, headstrong, wilful, contrary, perverse, recalcitrant, uncooperative, unmanageable, stiff-necked, uncompromising, implacable, unrelenting, immovable, unshakeable; persistent, tenacious, dogged, single-minded, adamant, determined; Brit. informal bloody-minded, bolshie; N. Amer. informal balky; formal refractory, pertinacious.
– OPPOSITES compliant.

obstreperous adj. **unruly**, unmanageable, disorderly, undisciplined, uncontrollable, rowdy, disruptive, truculent, difficult, rebellious, mutinous, riotous, out of control, wild, turbulent, uproarious, boisterous; noisy, loud, clamorous, raucous, vociferous; informal rumbustious; Brit. informal stroppy, bolshie; N. Amer. informal rambunctious; formal refractory.
– OPPOSITES quiet, restrained.

obstruct v. **1** *ensure that air bricks and vents are not obstructed* **block (up)**, clog (up), get in the way of, occlude, cut off, shut off, bung up, choke, dam up; barricade, bar;

Brit. informal gunge up. **2** *he was charged with obstructing the traffic* **hold up**, bring to a standstill, stop, halt, block. **3** *fears that the regime would obstruct the distribution of food* **impede**, hinder, interfere with, hamper, block, interrupt, hold up, stand in the way of, frustrate, thwart, balk, inhibit, hamstring, sabotage; slow down, retard, delay, stonewall, stop, halt, restrict, limit, curb, put a brake on, bridle; N. Amer. informal bork.
– OPPOSITES clear, facilitate.

obstruction n. **obstacle**, barrier, stumbling block, hurdle, bar, block, impediment, hindrance, snag, fly in the ointment, difficulty, catch, drawback, hitch, handicap, deterrent, curb, check, restriction; blockage, stoppage, congestion, bottleneck, hold-up; Brit. spanner in the works; Medicine occlusion.

obstructive adj. **unhelpful**, uncooperative, awkward, difficult, unaccommodating, disobliging, perverse, contrary; Brit. informal bloody-minded, bolshie; N. Amer. informal balky.
– OPPOSITES helpful.

obtain v. **1** *the newspaper obtained a copy of the letter* **get**, acquire, come by, secure, procure, come into the possession of, pick up, be given; gain, earn, achieve, attain; informal get hold of, get/lay one's hands on, get one's mitts on, land. **2** *rules obtaining in other jurisdictions* **prevail**, be in force, apply, exist, be in use, be in effect, stand, hold, be the case.
– OPPOSITES lose.

obtainable adj. **available**, to be had, in circulation, on the market, on offer, in season, at one's disposal, at hand, attainable, procurable, accessible; informal up for grabs, on tap, get-at-able.

obtrusive adj. **conspicuous**, prominent, noticeable, obvious, unmistakable, intrusive, out of place; informal sticking out a mile, sticking out like a sore thumb.
– OPPOSITES unobtrusive, inconspicuous.

obtuse adj. **stupid**, foolish, slow-witted, slow, dull-witted, unintelligent, ignorant, simple-minded; insensitive, imperceptive, uncomprehending; informal dim, dim-witted, dense, dumb, slow on the uptake, half-witted, brain-dead, moronic, cretinous, thick, dopey, dozy, wooden-headed, boneheaded; Brit. informal divvy; Scottish & N. English informal glaikit; N. Amer. informal chowderheaded.
– OPPOSITES clever.

obviate v. **preclude**, prevent, remove, get rid of, do away with, get round, rule out, eliminate, make unnecessary.

obvious adj. **clear**, crystal clear, plain, evident, apparent, manifest, patent, conspicuous, pronounced, transparent, palpable, prominent, marked, decided, distinct, noticeable, perceptible, visible, discernible; unmistakable, indisputable, self-evident, incontrovertible, incontestable, undeniable, as plain as a pikestaff, as clear as day, staring someone in the face; overt, open, undisguised, unconcealed, frank, glaring, blatant, written all over someone; informal as

plain as the nose on your face, sticking out like a sore thumb, sticking out a mile.
– OPPOSITES imperceptible.

obviously adv. **clearly**, evidently, plainly, patently, visibly, discernibly, manifestly, noticeably; unmistakably, undeniably, incontrovertibly, demonstrably, unquestionably, undoubtedly, without doubt, doubtless; of course, naturally, needless to say, it goes without saying.
– OPPOSITES perhaps.

occasion n. **1** *a previous occasion* **time**, instance, juncture, point; event, occurrence, affair, incident, episode, experience; situation, case, circumstance. **2** *a family occasion* **social event**, event, affair, function, celebration, party, get-together, gathering; informal do, bash. **3** *I doubt if the occasion will arise* **opportunity**, right moment, chance, opening, window. **4** *it's the first time I've had occasion to complain* **reason**, cause, call, grounds, justification, need, motive.
▶v. *her situation occasioned a good deal of sympathy* **cause**, give rise to, bring about, result in, lead to, prompt, elicit, call forth, produce, create, arouse, generate, engender, precipitate, provoke, stir up, inspire, spark off, trigger; literary beget.
□ **on occasion** See **occasionally**.

occasional adj. **infrequent**, intermittent, irregular, periodic, sporadic, odd, random, uncommon, few and far between, isolated, rare; N. Amer. sometime.
– OPPOSITES regular, frequent.

occasionally adv. **sometimes**, from time to time, (every) now and then, (every) now and again, at times, every so often, (every) once in a while, on occasion, periodically, at intervals, irregularly, sporadically, infrequently, intermittently, on and off, off and on.
– OPPOSITES often.

occlude v. **block (up)**, stop (up), obstruct, clog (up), close, shut, bung up, choke.

occult n. *his interest in the occult* **the supernatural**, supernaturalism, magic, black magic, witchcraft, sorcery, necromancy, wizardry, the black arts, occultism, diabolism, devil worship, devilry, voodoo, hoodoo, white magic, mysticism; NZ makutu.
▶adj. **1** *occult powers* **supernatural**, magic, magical, mystical, mystic, psychic, preternatural, transcendental; cabbalistic, hermetic. **2** *the typically occult language of the time* **esoteric**, arcane, recondite, abstruse, secret; obscure, incomprehensible, impenetrable, puzzling, perplexing, mystifying, mysterious, enigmatic.

occupancy n. **occupation**, tenancy, tenure, residence, residency, inhabitation, habitation, living, lease, holding, owner-occupancy; formal dwelling.

occupant n. **1** *the occupants of the houses* **resident**, inhabitant, owner, householder, tenant, renter, leaseholder, lessee; addressee; Brit. occupier, owner-occupier; formal dweller. **2** *the first occupant of the post*

incumbent, holder.

occupation n. **1** *his father's occupation* **job**, profession, (line of) work, trade, employment, position, post, situation, business, career, métier, vocation, calling, craft; Austral. informal grip; old use employ. **2** *her leisure occupations* **pastime**, activity, hobby, pursuit, interest, entertainment, recreation, amusement, divertissement. **3** *a property suitable for occupation by older people* **residence**, residency, habitation, inhabitation, occupancy, tenancy, tenure, lease, living in; formal dwelling. **4** *the Roman occupation of Britain* **conquest**, capture, invasion, seizure, takeover, annexation, overrunning, subjugation, subjection, appropriation; colonization, rule, control, suzerainty.

occupational adj. **job-related**, work, professional, vocational, employment, business, career.

occupied adj. **1** *tasks which kept her occupied all day* **busy**, engaged, working, at work, active; informal tied up, hard at it, on the go. **2** *all the tables were occupied* **in use**, full, engaged, taken. **3** *only two of the flats are occupied* **inhabited**, lived-in, tenanted, settled.
– OPPOSITES free, vacant.

occupy v. **1** *Carol occupied the basement flat* **live in**, inhabit, be the tenant of, lodge in; move into, take up residence in; people, populate, settle; Scottish stay in; formal reside in, dwell in. **2** *two windows occupied almost the whole of the end wall* **take up**, fill, fill up, cover, use up. **3** *he occupies a senior post at the Treasury* **hold**, fill, have; informal hold down. **4** *I need something to occupy my mind* **engage**, busy, employ, distract, absorb, engross, preoccupy, hold, interest, involve, entertain, amuse, divert. **5** *the region was occupied by French troops* **capture**, seize, take possession of, conquer, invade, overrun, take over, colonize, garrison, annex, subjugate.

occur v. **1** *the accident occurred at about 3.30* **happen**, take place, come about, transpire, materialize, arise, crop up; N. Amer. informal go down; literary come to pass, befall, betide; old use hap; formal eventuate. **2** *the disease occurs chiefly in tropical climates* **be found**, be present, exist, appear, prevail, present itself, manifest itself, turn up. **3** *an idea occurred to her* **enter one's head/mind**, cross one's mind, come to mind, spring to mind, strike one, hit one, dawn on one, suggest itself.

occurrence n. **1** *vandalism used to be a rare occurrence* **event**, incident, happening, phenomenon, affair, matter, circumstance. **2** *the occurrence of cancer increases with age* **existence**, instance, appearance, manifestation, materialization, development; frequency, incidence, rate, prevalence; Statistics distribution.

ocean n. *the ocean was calm* **the sea**; informal the drink; Brit. informal the briny; literary the deep, the waves, the main.

odd adj. **1** *an odd man* **strange**, peculiar, weird, queer, funny, bizarre, eccentric, unusual, unconventional, outlandish, quirky, zany; informal wacky, kooky, screwy, oddball, offbeat, off the wall. **2** *quite a few odd things had happened* **strange**, unusual, peculiar, funny, curious, bizarre, weird, uncanny, queer, outré, unexpected, unfamiliar, abnormal, atypical, anomalous, different, out of the ordinary, out of the way, exceptional, rare, extraordinary, remarkable, puzzling, mystifying, mysterious, perplexing, baffling, unaccountable, uncommon, irregular, singular, deviant, aberrant, freak, freakish. **3** *we have the odd drink together | he does odd jobs for friends* **occasional**, casual, irregular, isolated, random, sporadic, periodic; miscellaneous, various, varied, sundry. **4** *odd shoes* **mismatched**, unmatched, unpaired; single, lone, solitary, extra, surplus, leftover, remaining.
– OPPOSITES normal, ordinary, regular.
□ **odd man out** outsider, exception, oddity, nonconformist, maverick, individualist, misfit, fish out of water, square peg in a round hole.

oddity n. **1** *she was regarded as a bit of an oddity* **eccentric**, crank, misfit, maverick, nonconformist, rare bird; informal character, oddball, weirdo, crackpot, nut, freak; Brit. informal nutter; N. Amer. informal screwball, kook; informal dated case. **2** *his work remains an oddity in some respects* **anomaly**, aberration, curiosity, rarity. **3** *the oddities of human nature* **peculiarity**, idiosyncrasy, eccentricity, quirk, irregularity, twist.

oddment plural n. **scrap**, remnant, bit, piece, leftover, fragment, snippet, offcut, end, shred, tail end; Brit. informal fag end; (**oddments**) odds and ends, bits and pieces, bits and bobs.

odds plural n. **1** *the odds are that he is no longer alive* **likelihood**, probability, chances, chance, balance. **2** *the odds are in our favour* **advantage**, edge; superiority, supremacy, ascendancy.
□ **at odds 1** *he was at odds with his colleagues* **in conflict**, in disagreement, on bad terms, at cross purposes, at loggerheads, quarrelling, arguing, at daggers drawn, at each other's throats; N. Amer. on the outs. **2** *behaviour at odds with the interests of the company* **at variance**, out of keeping, out of line, in opposition, conflicting, contrary, incompatible, inconsistent, irreconcilable.
odds and ends bits and pieces, bits and bobs, bits, pieces, stuff, paraphernalia, things, sundries, miscellanea, bric-a-brac, knick-knacks, oddments; informal junk; Brit. informal odds and sods, clobber, gubbins.

odious adj. **revolting**, repulsive, repellent, repugnant, disgusting, offensive, objectionable, vile, foul, abhorrent, loathsome, horrible, nauseating, sickening, hateful, detestable, execrable, abominable, monstrous, appalling, reprehensible, deplorable, insufferable, intolerable, despicable, contemptible, unspeakable, atrocious, awful, terrible, dreadful, frightful, obnoxious, unsavoury, unpalatable, unpleasant, disagreeable, nasty, distasteful; informal ghastly, horrid, gross, God-awful; Brit. informal beastly; old use disgustful, loathly.
– OPPOSITES delightful.

odium n. **disgust**, abhorrence, repugnance, revulsion, loathing, detestation, hatred, hate, obloquy, dislike, distaste, disfavour, antipathy, animosity, animus, enmity, hostility, contempt; disgrace, shame, opprobrium, discredit, dishonour.

odorous adj. **smelly**, malodorous, pungent, acrid, foul-smelling, evil-smelling, stinking, reeking, fetid, rank; informal stinky; Brit. informal pongy, niffy; literary miasmic, noisome, mephitic.

odour n. **1** *an odour of sweat* **smell**, stench, stink, reek; Brit. informal pong, whiff, niff, hum; N. Amer. informal funk; literary miasma. **2** *an odour of suspicion* **atmosphere**, air, aura, quality, flavour, savour, hint, suggestion, impression, whiff.

odyssey n. **journey**, voyage, trek, travels, quest, crusade, pilgrimage, wandering, journeying; old use peregrination.

off adj. **1** *Kate's off today* **away**, absent, unavailable, off duty, on holiday, on leave; free, at leisure; N. Amer. on vacation. **2** *the game's off* **cancelled**, postponed, called off. **3** *strawberries are off* **unavailable**, finished, sold out. **4** *the fish was a bit off* **rotten**, bad, stale, mouldy, high, sour, rancid, turned, spoiled, putrid, putrescent. **5** Brit. informal *I felt decidedly off.* See **off colour** (sense 1). **6** Brit. informal *that remark was a bit off* **unfair**, unjust, uncalled for, below the belt, unjustified, unjustifiable, unreasonable, unwarranted, unnecessary; informal a bit much; Brit. informal out of order. **7** Brit. informal *he was really off with me* **unfriendly**, aloof, cool, cold, distant, frosty; informal stand-offish.
□ **off and on** periodically, at intervals, on and off, (every) once in a while, every so often, (every) now and then/again, from time to time, occasionally, sometimes, intermittently, irregularly.

offbeat adj. informal **unconventional**, unorthodox, unusual, off-centre, eccentric, strange, idiosyncratic, outré, bizarre, weird, peculiar, odd, freakish, outlandish, out of the ordinary, Bohemian, alternative, left-field, zany, quirky; informal wacky, freaky, way-out, off the wall, kooky, oddball.
– OPPOSITES conventional.

off colour adj. **1** Brit. *I'm feeling a bit off colour* **unwell**, ill, poorly, out of sorts, indisposed, not oneself, sick, queasy, nauseous, peaky, liverish, green about the gills, run down, washed out, below par; informal under the weather, rough; Brit. informal ropy, off; Scottish informal wabbit, peely-wally;

Austral./NZ informal crook. **2** *off-colour jokes* **smutty**, dirty, rude, crude, suggestive, indecent, indelicate, risqué, racy, bawdy, naughty, blue, vulgar, ribald, broad, salacious, coarse; informal raunchy; Brit. informal fruity, saucy; euphemistic adult.
– OPPOSITES well.

offence n. **1** *he denied having committed any offence* **crime**, illegal/unlawful act, misdemeanour, breach of the law, felony, wrongdoing, wrong, misdeed, peccadillo, sin, transgression, infringement; Law malfeasance; old use trespass. **2** *an offence to basic justice* **affront**, slap in the face, insult, outrage, violation. **3** *I do not want to cause offence* **annoyance**, anger, resentment, indignation, irritation, exasperation, wrath, displeasure, hard/bad/ill feelings, disgruntlement, pique, vexation, animosity.
□ **take offence** be offended, take exception, take something personally, feel affronted, feel resentful, take something amiss, take umbrage, get upset, get annoyed, get angry, get into a huff; Brit. informal get the hump.

offend v. **1** *I'm sorry if I offended him* **hurt someone's feelings**, give offence to, affront, displease, upset, distress, hurt, wound; annoy, anger, exasperate, irritate, vex, pique, gall, irk, nettle, tread on someone's toes; Brit. rub up the wrong way; informal rile, rattle, peeve, needle, put someone's nose out of joint, put someone's back up. **2** *the smell of cigarette smoke offended him* **displease**, be distasteful to, be disagreeable to, be offensive to, disgust, repel, revolt, sicken, nauseate; informal turn off; N. Amer. informal gross out. **3** *criminals who offend again and again* **break the law**, commit a crime, do wrong, sin, transgress; old use trespass.

offended adj. **affronted**, insulted, aggrieved, displeased, upset, hurt, wounded, disgruntled, put out, annoyed, angry, cross, exasperated, indignant, irritated, piqued, vexed, irked, stung, galled, nettled, resentful, in a huff, huffy, in high dudgeon; informal riled, miffed, peeved, aggravated; Brit. informal narked; N. Amer. informal sore.
– OPPOSITES pleased.

offender n. **wrongdoer**, criminal, lawbreaker, miscreant, malefactor, felon, delinquent, culprit, guilty party, sinner, transgressor; Law malfeasant.

offensive adj. **1** *offensive remarks* **insulting**, rude, impertinent, insolent, derogatory, disrespectful, personal, hurtful, wounding, abusive; annoying, exasperating, irritating, galling, provocative, outrageous; discourteous, uncivil, impolite; formal exceptionable. **2** *an offensive smell* **unpleasant**, disagreeable, nasty, distasteful, displeasing, objectionable, off-putting, awful, terrible, dreadful, frightful, obnoxious, horrible, abominable, disgusting, repulsive, repellent, repugnant, revolting, abhorrent, loathsome, odious, vile, foul, sickening, nauseating; informal ghastly, horrid, gross, God-awful, rank; Brit. informal beastly; old use disgustful. **3** *an offensive air action*

hostile, attacking, aggressive, invading, combative, belligerent, on the attack.
– OPPOSITES complimentary, pleasant, defensive.
▸n. *a military offensive* **attack**, assault, onslaught, drive, invasion, push, thrust, charge, sortie, sally, foray, raid, incursion, blitz, campaign.

offer v. **1** *Frank offered another suggestion* **put forward**, proffer, give, present, come up with, suggest, recommend, propose, advance, submit, tender, render. **2** *she offered to help* **volunteer**, volunteer one's services, be at someone's disposal, be at someone's service, step/come forward, show willing. **3** *the product is offered at a competitive price* **put up for sale**, put on the market, sell, market, put under the hammer; Law vend. **4** *he offered $200* **bid**, tender, put in a bid of, put in an offer of. **5** *a job offering good career prospects* **provide**, afford, supply, give, furnish, present, hold out. **6** *she offered no resistance* **attempt**, try, give, show, express; formal essay. **7** *birds were offered to the gods* **sacrifice**, offer up, immolate.
– OPPOSITES withdraw, refuse.
▸n. **1** *offers of help* **proposal**, proposition, suggestion, submission, approach, overture. **2** *the highest offer* **bid**, tender, bidding price.
□ **on offer** on sale, up for sale, on the market; available, obtainable, to be had; N. Amer. on the block.

offering n. **1** *you may place offerings in the charity box* **contribution**, donation, gift, present, handout, widow's mite, charity; formal benefaction; historical alms. **2** *many offerings were made to the goddess* **sacrifice**, oblation, burnt offering, immolation, libation, first fruits.

offhand adj. *an offhand manner* **casual**, careless, uninterested, unconcerned, indifferent, cool, nonchalant, blasé, insouciant, cavalier, glib, perfunctory, cursory, unceremonious, ungracious, dismissive, discourteous, uncivil, impolite, terse, abrupt, curt; informal off, couldn't-care-less, take-it-or-leave-it.
▸adv. *I can't think of a better answer offhand* **on the spur of the moment**, without consideration, extempore, impromptu, ad lib; extemporaneously, spontaneously; informal off the cuff, off the top of one's head.

office n. **1** *her office in Aldersgate Street* **place of work**, place of business, workplace, workroom. **2** *the newspaper's Paris office* **branch**, division, section, bureau, department; agency. **3** *he assumed the office of President* **post**, position, appointment, job, occupation, role, situation, function, capacity. **4** *he was saved by the good offices of his uncle* **assistance**, help, aid, services, intervention, intercession, mediation, agency. **5** dated *the offices of a nurse* **duty**, job, task, chore, obligation, assignment, responsibility, charge, commission.

officer n. **1** *an officer in the army* military officer, commissioned officer, non-commissioned officer, NCO, commanding officer, CO. **2** *all officers carry warrant cards.* See **police officer**. **3** *the officers of the society* **official**, office-holder, committee member, board member; public servant, administrator, executive, functionary, bureaucrat; derogatory apparatchik.

official adj. **1** *an official inquiry* **authorized**, approved, validated, authenticated, certified, accredited, endorsed, sanctioned, licensed, recognized, accepted, legitimate, legal, lawful, valid, bona fide, proper, ex cathedra; informal kosher. **2** *an official function* **ceremonial**, formal, solemn, ceremonious; bureaucratic; informal stuffed-shirt.
– OPPOSITES unauthorized, informal.
▶ n. *a union official* **officer**, office-holder, administrator, executive, appointee, functionary; bureaucrat, mandarin; representative, agent; Brit. jack-in-office; derogatory apparatchik.

officiate v. **1** *he officiated in the first two matches* **be in charge of**, take charge of, preside over; oversee, superintend, supervise, conduct, run. **2** *Father Buckley officiated at the wedding service* **conduct**, perform, celebrate, solemnize.

officious adj. **self-important**, bumptious, self-assertive, pushy, overbearing, overzealous, domineering, opinionated, interfering, intrusive, meddlesome, meddling; informal bossy.
– OPPOSITES self-effacing.

offing n.
□ **in the offing** on the way, coming, (close) at hand, near, imminent, in prospect, on the horizon, in the wings, just around the corner, in the air, in the wind, brewing, upcoming, forthcoming; informal on the cards.

off-key adj. **1** *an off-key rendition of 'Amazing Grace'* **out of tune**, flat, tuneless, discordant, unharmonious. **2** *the cinematic effects are distractingly off-key* **incongruous**, inappropriate, unsuitable, out of place, out of keeping, jarring, dissonant, inharmonious.
– OPPOSITES harmonious.

offload v. **1** *the cargo was being offloaded* **unload**, remove, empty (out), tip (out); old use unlade. **2** *he offloaded 5,000 of the shares* **dispose of**, dump, jettison, get rid of, transfer, shift; palm off, foist, fob off.

off-putting adj. **1** *an off-putting aroma* **unpleasant**, unappealing, uninviting, unattractive, disagreeable, offensive, distasteful, unsavoury, unpalatable, unappetizing, objectionable, nasty, horrible, disgusting, repellent; informal horrid. **2** *her manner was off-putting* **discouraging**, disheartening, demoralizing, dispiriting, daunting, disconcerting, unnerving, unsettling; formal rebarbative.

offset v. **counterbalance**, balance (out), cancel (out), even out/up, counteract, countervail, neutralize, compensate for, make up for, make good, redeem.

offshoot n. **1** *the plant's offshoots* **side shoot**, shoot, sucker, tendril, runner, scion, slip, offset, stolon; twig, branch, bough, limb.

2 *an offshoot of Cromwell's line* **descendant**, scion. **3** *an offshoot of the growth of interest in heritage* **outcome**, result, effect, consequence, upshot, product, by-product, spin-off, development, ramification.

offspring n. **children**, sons and daughters, progeny, family, youngsters, babies, infants, brood; descendants, heirs, successors; Law issue; informal kids; Brit. informal sprogs, brats; derogatory spawn; old use fruit of one's loins.

often adv. **frequently**, many times, many a time, on many/numerous occasions, a lot, as often as not, repeatedly, again and again; regularly, routinely, usually, habitually, commonly, generally, in many cases/ instances, ordinarily; N. Amer. oftentimes; literary oft.
– OPPOSITES seldom.

ogle v. **leer at**, stare at, eye, make eyes at; informal eye up, give someone the glad eye, lech after, undress with one's eyes, give someone the come-on; Austral./NZ informal perv on.

ogre n. **1** *an ogre with two heads* **monster**, giant, troll. **2** *he is not the ogre he sometimes seems to be* **brute**, fiend, monster, beast, barbarian, savage, animal, tyrant; informal bastard, swine, pig.

ogress n. **1** *a one-eyed ogress* **monster**, giantess. **2** *the French teacher was a real ogress* **harridan**, tartar, termagant, gorgon, virago; informal battleaxe.

oily adj. **1** *oily substances* **greasy**, oleaginous; technical sebaceous; formal pinguid. **2** *oily food* **greasy**, fatty, buttery. **3** *an oily man* **unctuous**, ingratiating, smooth-talking, fulsome, flattering; obsequious, sycophantic, oleaginous; informal smarmy, slimy.

ointment n. **lotion**, cream, salve, liniment, embrocation, rub, gel, balm, emollient, unguent; technical humectant.

OK, okay informal exclam. *OK, I'll go with him* **all right**, right, right then, right you are, very well, very good, fine; informal okey-doke(y); Brit. informal righto, righty-ho.
▶ adj. **1** *the film was OK* **satisfactory**, all right, acceptable, competent; adequate, tolerable, passable, reasonable, fair, decent, not bad, average, middling, moderate, unremarkable, unexceptional; informal so-so, fair-to-middling. **2** *Jo's feeling OK now* **fine**, all right, well, in good shape, in good health, fit, healthy, as fit as a fiddle/flea. **3** *it is OK for me to come?* **permissible**, allowable, acceptable, all right, in order, permitted, fitting, suitable, appropriate.
– OPPOSITES unsatisfactory, ill.
▶ n. *he's just given me the OK* **authorization**, approval, seal of approval, agreement, consent, assent, permission, endorsement, ratification, sanction, approbation, confirmation, blessing, leave; informal the go-ahead, the green light, the thumbs up, say-so.
– OPPOSITES refusal.
▶ v. *the move must be okayed by the president* **authorize**, approve, agree to, consent to,

sanction, pass, ratify, endorse, allow, give something the nod, rubber-stamp; informal give the go-ahead, give the green light, give the thumbs up; formal accede to.
– OPPOSITES refuse, veto.

old adj. **1** *old people* **elderly**, aged, older, senior, advanced in years, venerable; in one's dotage, long in the tooth, grey-haired, grizzled, hoary, past one's prime, not as young as one was, ancient, decrepit, doddering, doddery, not long for this world, senescent, senile, superannuated; informal getting on, past it, over the hill, no spring chicken. **2** *old farm buildings* **dilapidated**, broken-down, run down, tumbledown, ramshackle, decaying, crumbling, disintegrating. **3** *old clothes* **worn**, worn out, shabby, threadbare, holey, torn, frayed, patched, tattered, moth-eaten, ragged; old-fashioned, out of date, outmoded; cast-off, hand-me-down; informal tatty. **4** *old cars* **antique**, veteran, vintage. **5** *she's old for her years* **mature**, wise, sensible, experienced, worldly-wise, knowledgeable. **6** *in the old days* **bygone**, past, former, olden, of old, previous, early, earlier, earliest; medieval, ancient, classical, primeval, primordial, prehistoric. **7** *the same old phrases* **hackneyed**, hack, banal, trite, overused, overworked, tired, worn out, stale, clichéd, platitudinous, unimaginative, stock, conventional; out of date, outdated, old-fashioned, outmoded, hoary; informal old hat, corny, played out. **8** *an old girlfriend* **former**, previous, ex-, one-time, sometime, erstwhile; formal quondam.
– OPPOSITES young, new, modern.
  □ **old age** declining years, advanced years, age, oldness, winter/autumn of one's life, senescence, senility, dotage.

old man 1 senior citizen, pensioner, OAP, elder, grandfather; patriarch; informal greybeard, codger; Brit. informal buffer; old use grandsire, ancient. **2** informal *her old man was away.* See **husband** (noun).

old person senior citizen, senior, (old-age) pensioner, OAP, elder, geriatric, dotard, Methuselah; N. Amer. golden ager; informal old stager, old-timer, oldie, wrinkly, crock, crumbly; N. Amer. informal oldster, woopie.

old woman 1 senior citizen, pensioner, OAP, crone; informal old dear; old use beldam, grandam. **2** informal *his old woman threw him out.* See **wife**.

> **WORD LINKS**
> **geriatric** relating to old people or old age
> **geriatrics** the branch of medicine concerning old people
> **gerontology** the scientific study of old age
> **gerontocracy** government by old people
> **senesce** deteriorate with old age
> **Alzheimer's disease** a disorder affecting older people, causing progressive mental deterioration

old-fashioned adj. **out of date**, outdated, dated, out of fashion, outmoded, unfashionable, passé, démodé, frumpy;

outworn, old, old-time, behind the times, archaic, obsolescent, obsolete, ancient, antiquated, superannuated, defunct; medieval, prehistoric, antediluvian, old-fogeyish, conservative, backward-looking, quaint, anachronistic, fusty, moth-eaten, olde worlde; informal old hat, square, not with it, out of the ark; N. Amer. informal horse-and-buggy, clunky, rinky-dink.
– OPPOSITES modern.

old-time adj. **former**, past, bygone, old-fashioned; traditional, folk, old-world, quaint.
– OPPOSITES modern.

Olympian adj. **aloof**, distant, remote, unfriendly, uncommunicative, unforthcoming, cool; informal stand-offish.
– OPPOSITES friendly.

omen n. **portent**, sign, signal, token, forewarning, warning, foreshadowing, prediction, forecast, prophecy, harbinger, augury, auspice, presage; writing on the wall, indication, hint; literary foretoken.

ominous adj. **threatening**, menacing, baleful, forbidding, sinister, inauspicious, unpropitious, portentous, unfavourable, unpromising; black, dark, gloomy; formal minatory; literary direful.
– OPPOSITES promising.

omission n. **1** *the omission of recent publications from his biography* **exclusion**, leaving out; deletion, cut, excision, elimination. **2** *the damage was not caused by any omission on behalf of the carrier* **negligence**, neglect, neglectfulness, dereliction, forgetfulness, oversight, default, lapse, failure.

omit v. **1** *they omitted his name from the list* **leave out**, exclude, leave off, take out, miss out, miss, drop, cut; delete, eliminate, rub out, cross out, strike out. **2** *I omitted to mention our guest lecturer* **forget**, neglect, fail; leave undone, overlook, skip.
– OPPOSITES add, include, remember.

omnipotence n. **all-powerfulness**, supremacy, pre-eminence, supreme power, unlimited power; invincibility.

omnipotent adj. **all-powerful**, almighty, supreme, pre-eminent; invincible, unconquerable.

omnipresent adj. **ubiquitous**, all-pervasive, everywhere; rife, pervasive, prevalent.

omniscient adj. **all-knowing**, all-wise, all-seeing.

omnivorous adj. **1** *most duck species are omnivorous* **able to eat anything**. **2** *an omnivorous reader* **undiscriminating**, indiscriminate, unselective.

on adj. *the computer's on* **functioning**, in operation, working, in use, operating.
– OPPOSITES off.
  ▶ adv. *she droned on* **interminably**, at length, for a long time, continuously, endlessly, ceaselessly, without a pause/break.
  □ **on and off** See **off and on** at **off**.
  on and on for a long time, for ages, for hours, at (great) length, incessantly,

ceaselessly, constantly, continuously, continually, endlessly, unendingly, eternally, forever, interminably, unremittingly, relentlessly, indefatigably, without let-up, without a pause/break, without cease.

once adv. **1** *I only met him once* **on one occasion**, one time, one single time. **2** *he did not once help* **ever**, at any time, on any occasion, at all. **3** *they were friends once* **formerly**, previously, in the past, at one time, at one point, once upon a time, in days/times gone by, in times past, in the (good) old days, long ago; old use sometime, erstwhile, whilom; literary in days/times of yore.
– OPPOSITES often, now.
▸ conj. *he'll be all right once she's gone* **as soon as**, when, after.
□ **at once 1** *you must leave at once* **immediately**, right away, right now, this moment/instant/second/minute, now, straight away, instantly, directly, forthwith, promptly, without delay/hesitation, without further ado; quickly, as fast as possible, as soon as possible, ASAP, speedily; informal like a shot, in/like a flash, before you can say Jack Robinson. **2** *all the guests arrived at once* **at the same time**, at one and the same time, (all) together, simultaneously; as a group, in unison, in concert, in chorus.
once and for all conclusively, decisively, finally, positively, definitely, definitively, irrevocably; for good, for always, forever, permanently.
once in a while occasionally, from time to time, (every) now and then/again, every so often, on occasion, at times, sometimes, off and on, at intervals, periodically, sporadically, intermittently.

oncoming adj. **approaching**, advancing, nearing, forthcoming, on the way, imminent, impending, looming, gathering, (close) at hand, about to happen, to come.

one cardinal number **1** **unit**, item; technical monad. **2** *only one person came* **a single**, a solitary, a sole, a lone. **3** *her one concern was her daughter* **only**, single, solitary, sole. **4** *they have now become one* **united**, a unit, unitary, amalgamated, consolidated, integrated, combined, incorporated, allied, affiliated, linked, joined, unified, in league, in partnership; wedded, married.

onerous adj. **burdensome**, arduous, strenuous, difficult, hard, severe, heavy, back-breaking, oppressive, weighty, uphill, effortful, formidable, laborious, Herculean, exhausting, tiring, taxing, demanding, punishing, gruelling, exacting, wearing, wearisome, fatiguing; old use toilsome.
– OPPOSITES easy.

oneself n.
□ **by oneself** See **by**.

one-sided adj. **1** *a one-sided account* **biased**, prejudiced, partisan, partial, preferential, discriminatory, slanted, inequitable, unfair, unjust. **2** *a one-sided game* **unequal**, uneven, unbalanced.
– OPPOSITES impartial.

one-time adj. **former**, ex-, old, previous, sometime, erstwhile, as was; lapsed; formal quondam.

ongoing adj. **1** *negotiations are ongoing* **in progress**, under way, going on, continuing, taking place, proceeding, progressing, advancing; unfinished. **2** *an ongoing struggle* **continuous**, continuing, uninterrupted, unbroken, non-stop, constant, ceaseless, unceasing, unending, endless, never-ending, unremitting, relentless, unfaltering.

onlooker n. **eyewitness**, witness, observer, looker-on, fly on the wall, spectator, watcher, viewer, bystander; sightseer; informal rubberneck; literary beholder.

only adv. **1** *there was only enough for two* **at most**, at best, (only) just, no/not more than; barely, scarcely, hardly. **2** *he only works on one picture at a time* **exclusively**, solely. **3** *you're only saying that* **merely**, simply, just.
▸ adj. *their only son* **sole**, single, one (and only), solitary, lone, unique; exclusive.

onomatopoeic adj. **imitative**, echoic.

onset n. **start**, beginning, commencement, arrival, (first) appearance, inception, day one; outbreak.
– OPPOSITES end.

onslaught n. **assault**, attack, offensive, advance, charge, onrush, rush, storming, sortie, sally, raid, descent, incursion, invasion, foray, push, thrust, drive, blitz, bombardment, barrage, salvo; historical broadside.

onus n. **burden**, responsibility, liability, obligation, duty, weight, load, charge, encumbrance; cross to bear, millstone round one's neck, albatross.

ooze v. **1** *blood oozed from the wound* **seep**, discharge, flow, exude, trickle, drip, dribble, issue, filter, percolate, escape, leak, drain, empty, bleed, sweat, well; Medicine extravasate. **2** *she was positively oozing charm* **exude**, gush, drip, pour forth, emanate, radiate.
▸ n. **1** *the ooze of blood* **seepage**, seeping, discharge, flow, exudation, trickle, drip, dribble, percolation, escape, leak, leakage, drainage; secretion; Medicine extravasation. **2** *the ooze on the ocean floor* **mud**, slime, alluvium, silt, mire, sludge, muck, dirt, deposit.

opalescent adj. **iridescent**, prismatic, rainbow-like, kaleidoscopic, multicoloured, many-hued, lustrous, shimmering, glittering, sparkling, variegated, shot, moire, opaline, milky, pearly, nacreous.

opaque adj. **1** *opaque glass* **non-transparent**, cloudy, filmy, blurred, smeared, smeary, misty, dirty, muddy, muddied, grimy. **2** *the technical jargon was opaque to her* **obscure**, unclear, mysterious, puzzling, perplexing, baffling, mystifying, confusing, unfathomable, incomprehensible, unintelligible, impenetrable, hazy, foggy; informal as clear as mud.
– OPPOSITES transparent, clear.

O

open adj. **1** *the door's open* **not shut**, not closed, unlocked, unbolted, unlatched, off the latch, unfastened, unsecured; ajar, gaping, yawning. **2** *a blue silk shirt, open at the neck* **unfastened**, not done up, undone, unbuttoned, unzipped, loose. **3** *the main roads are open* **clear**, passable, navigable, unblocked, unobstructed. **4** *open countryside | open spaces* **unenclosed**, rolling, sweeping, extensive, wide (open), unfenced, exposed, unsheltered; spacious, airy, uncrowded, uncluttered; undeveloped, unbuilt-up. **5** *a map was open beside him* **spread out**, unfolded, unfurled, unrolled, extended, stretched out. **6** *the bank wasn't open* **open for business**, open to the public, trading. **7** *the position is still open* **available**, vacant, free, unfilled; informal up for grabs. **8** *the system is open to abuse* **vulnerable**, subject, susceptible, liable, exposed, an easy target for, at risk of. **9** *she was open about her feelings* **frank**, candid, honest, forthcoming, communicative, forthright, direct, unreserved, plain-spoken, outspoken, free-spoken, not afraid to call a spade a spade; informal upfront. **10** *open hostility* **overt**, obvious, patent, manifest, palpable, conspicuous, plain, undisguised, unconcealed, clear, apparent, evident; blatant, flagrant, barefaced, brazen. **11** *the case is still open* **unresolved**, undecided, unsettled, up in the air; open to debate, open for discussion, arguable, debatable, moot. **12** *an open mind* **impartial**, unbiased, unprejudiced, objective, disinterested, non-partisan, non-discriminatory, neutral, dispassionate, detached. **13** *I'm open to suggestions* **receptive**, amenable, willing/ready to listen, responsive. **14** *what other options are open to us?* **available**, accessible, on hand, obtainable, on offer. **15** *an open meeting* **public**, general, unrestricted, non-exclusive, non-restrictive.
– OPPOSITES shut.

▶ v. **1** *she opened the front door* **unfasten**, unlatch, unlock, unbolt, unbar; throw wide. **2** *Katherine opened the parcel* **unwrap**, undo, untie, unseal. **3** *shall I open another bottle?* **uncork**, broach, crack (open). **4** *Adam opened the map* **spread out**, unfold, unfurl, unroll, straighten out. **5** *he opened his heart to her* **reveal**, uncover, expose, lay bare, bare, pour out, disclose, divulge. **6** *we're hoping to open next month* **start trading**, open for business, set up shop, put up one's plate; N. Amer. informal hang out one's shingle. **7** *Sir Bryan opened the meeting* **begin**, start, commence, initiate, set in motion, launch, get going, get under way, set the ball rolling, get off the ground; inaugurate; informal kick off, get the show on the road. **8** *the lounge opens on to a terrace* **give access**, lead, be connected, communicate with.
– OPPOSITES close, shut, end.

> **WORD LINKS**
> **agoraphobia** fear of open spaces

open-air adj. **outdoor**, out-of-doors, outside, alfresco.
– OPPOSITES indoor.

open-handed adj. **generous**, magnanimous, charitable, benevolent, beneficent, munificent, bountiful, altruistic, philanthropic; literary bounteous.
– OPPOSITES tight-fisted.

opening n. **1** *an opening in the centre of the roof* **hole**, gap, aperture, orifice, vent, crack, slit, chink; spyhole, peephole; Anatomy foramen. **2** *the opening in the wall* **doorway**, gateway, entrance, (means of) entry, way in/out, exit. **3** *United created openings but were unable to score* **opportunity**, chance, window (of opportunity), possibility. **4** *an opening with a stockbroker* **vacancy**, position, job. **5** *the opening of the session* **beginning**, start, commencement, outset; introduction, prefatory remarks, opening statement; informal kick-off; formal proem. **6** *a gallery opening* **opening ceremony**, official opening, launch, inauguration; opening/first night, premiere.

openly adv. **1** *drugs were openly on sale* **publicly**, blatantly, flagrantly, overtly. **2** *he spoke openly of his problems* **frankly**, candidly, explicitly, honestly, sincerely, forthrightly, bluntly, without constraint, without holding back, straight from the shoulder.
– OPPOSITES secretly.

open-minded adj. **1** *open-minded attitudes* **unbiased**, unprejudiced, neutral, non-judgemental, non-discriminatory, objective, disinterested; tolerant, liberal, permissive, broad-minded. **2** *musicians need to be open-minded* **receptive**, open (to suggestions), amenable, flexible.
– OPPOSITES prejudiced, narrow-minded.

open-mouthed adj. **astounded**, amazed, in amazement, surprised, stunned, bowled over, staggered, thunderstruck, aghast, stupefied, taken aback, shocked, shell-shocked, speechless, dumbfounded, dumbstruck; informal flabbergasted; Brit. informal gobsmacked.

operate v. **1** *he can operate the machine* **work**, make go, run, use, utilize, handle, control, manage; drive, steer, manoeuvre. **2** *the machine ceased to operate* **function**, work, go, run, be in working/running order, be operative. **3** *the way the law operates in practice* **take effect**, act, apply, be applied, function. **4** *Hechstetter operated the mines until 1634* **direct**, control, manage, run, govern, administer, superintend, head (up), supervise, oversee, be in control/charge of.

operation n. **1** *the slide bars ensure smooth operation* **functioning**, working, running, performance, action. **2** *the operation of the factory* **management**, running, governing, administration, supervision. **3** *a heart bypass operation* **surgery**, surgical procedure. **4** *a military operation* **action**, activity, exercise, undertaking, enterprise, manoeuvre, campaign. **5** *their mining operations*

business, enterprise, company, firm; informal outfit.

□ **in operation** See **operational**.

operational adj. (up and) running, working, functioning, operative, in operation, in use, in action; in working order, workable, serviceable, functional, usable.

operative adj. 1 *the act is not operative at the moment* **in force**, in operation, in effect, valid. 2 *the steam railway is operative.* See **operational**. 3 *the operative word* **key**, significant, relevant, applicable, pertinent, apposite, germane, crucial, critical, pivotal.
– OPPOSITES invalid.

▸n. 1 *the operatives clean the machines* **machinist**, (machine) operator, mechanic, engineer, worker, workman, (factory) hand, blue-collar worker. 2 *an operative of the CIA* (secret) agent, undercover agent, spy, mole, plant, double agent; N. Amer. informal spook; old use intelligencer. 3 *a private operative* (private) detective, (private) investigator, sleuth; informal private eye; N. Amer. informal gumshoe.

operator n. 1 *a machine operator* **machinist**, mechanic, operative, engineer, worker. 2 *a tour operator* **contractor**, entrepreneur, promoter, arranger, fixer. 3 *a ruthless operator* **manipulator**, manoeuvrer, string-puller, mover and shaker, wheeler-dealer; N. Amer. informal wirepuller.

opiate n. drug, narcotic, sedative, tranquillizer, depressant, soporific, anaesthetic, painkiller, analgesic, anodyne; morphine, opium; informal dope; Medicine stupefacient.

opine v. formal suggest, say, declare, observe, comment, remark; think, believe, consider, maintain, imagine, reckon, guess, assume, presume, take it, suppose; N. Amer. informal allow.

opinion n. *she did not share her husband's opinion* **belief**, judgement, thought(s), (way of) thinking, mind, (point of) view, viewpoint, attitude, stance, position, standpoint.
□ **a matter of opinion** open to question, debatable, open to debate, a moot point.
be of the opinion believe, think, consider, maintain, reckon, estimate, feel, be convinced; N. Amer. informal allow; formal opine.
in my opinion as I see it, to my mind, (according) to my way of thinking, personally, in my estimation, if you ask me.

opinionated adj. dogmatic, of fixed views; inflexible, uncompromising, prejudiced, bigoted.

opponent n. 1 *his Republican opponent* **rival**, adversary, opposer, the opposition, fellow contestant, (fellow) competitor, enemy, antagonist, combatant, contender, challenger; literary foe. 2 *an opponent of the reforms* **opposer**, objector, dissenter.
– OPPOSITES ally, supporter.

opportune adj. auspicious, propitious, favourable, advantageous, golden, felicitous; timely, convenient, suitable, appropriate, apt, fitting.
– OPPOSITES disadvantageous.

opportunism n. expediency, pragmatism, Machiavellianism; striking while the iron is hot, making hay while the sun shines.

opportunity n. (lucky) chance, golden opportunity, favourable time/occasion/moment; time, occasion, moment, opening, option, window (of opportunity), possibility, scope, freedom; informal shot, break, look-in.

oppose v. be against, object to, be hostile to, be in opposition to, disagree with, dislike, disapprove of; resist, take a stand against, put up a fight against, stand up to, fight, challenge; take issue with, dispute, argue with/against, quarrel with; informal be anti; formal gainsay.
– OPPOSITES support.

opposed adj. 1 *the population is opposed to the nuclear power plants* **against**, (dead) set against; in opposition, averse, hostile, antagonistic, antipathetic, resistant; informal anti. 2 *their interests were opposed* **conflicting**, contrasting, incompatible, irreconcilable, antithetical, contradictory, clashing, at variance, at odds, divergent, poles apart.
– OPPOSITES in favour of.
□ **as opposed to** in contrast with, as against, as contrasted with, rather than, instead of.

opposing adj. 1 *the two opposing points of view* **conflicting**, contrasting, opposite, incompatible, irreconcilable, contradictory, antithetical, clashing, at variance, at odds, divergent, opposed, poles apart. 2 *opposing sides in the war* **rival**, opposite, enemy. 3 *the opposing page* **opposite**, facing.

opposite adj. 1 *they sat opposite each other* **facing**, face to face with, across from; informal eyeball to eyeball with. 2 *the opposite page* **facing**, opposing. 3 *opposite views* **conflicting**, contrasting, incompatible, irreconcilable, antithetical, contradictory, clashing, at variance, at odds, different, differing, divergent, dissimilar, unalike, disagreeing, opposed, opposing, poles apart. 4 *opposite sides in a war* **rival**, opposing, enemy.
– OPPOSITES same.

▸n. *in fact the opposite was true* **reverse**, converse, antithesis, contrary, inverse, obverse, antipode; the other side of the coin; informal flip side.

opposition n. 1 *the proposal met with opposition* **resistance**, hostility, antagonism, antipathy, objection, dissent, disapproval; defiance, non-compliance, obstruction. 2 *they beat the opposition* **opponents**, opposing side, other side/team, competition, opposers, rivals, adversaries. 3 *the opposition between the public and the private domains* **conflict**, clash, disparity, antithesis, polarity.

oppress v. 1 *the invaders oppressed the people* **persecute**, abuse, maltreat, ill-treat, tyrannize, crush, repress, suppress, subjugate, subdue, keep down, grind down,

O

rule with a rod of iron, ride roughshod over.
2 *the gloom oppressed her* **depress**, make
gloomy/despondent, weigh down, weigh
heavily on, cast down, dampen someone's
spirits, dispirit, dishearten, discourage,
sadden, get down; old use deject.

oppressed adj. **persecuted**, downtrodden,
abused, maltreated, ill-treated, subjugated,
tyrannized, repressed, subdued, crushed;
disadvantaged, underprivileged.

oppression n. **persecution**, abuse,
maltreatment, ill-treatment, tyranny,
repression, suppression, subjection,
subjugation; cruelty, brutality, injustice,
hardship, suffering, misery.

oppressive adj. **1** *an oppressive dictatorship*
harsh, cruel, brutal, repressive, tyrannical,
autocratic, dictatorial, undemocratic, anti-
democratic, despotic; ruthless, merciless,
pitiless. **2** *an oppressive sense of despair*
overwhelming, overpowering, unbearable,
unendurable, intolerable. **3** *it was grey and
oppressive* **muggy**, close, heavy, hot, humid,
sticky, steamy, airless, stuffy, stifling, sultry.
– OPPOSITES lenient.

oppressor n. **persecutor**, tyrant, despot,
autocrat, dictator, subjugator, tormentor.

opprobrious adj. **abusive**, vituperative,
derogatory, disparaging, denigratory,
pejorative, deprecatory, insulting, offensive;
scornful, contemptuous, derisive; informal
bitchy; old use contumelious.

opprobrium n. **1** *the government endured
months of opprobrium* **vilification**, abuse,
vituperation, condemnation, criticism,
censure, denunciation, defamation,
denigration, disparagement, obloquy,
derogation, slander, revilement, calumny,
execration, bad press, invective; informal
flak, mud-slinging, bad-mouthing; Brit.
informal stick; formal castigation, excoriation,
calumniation; old use contumely. **2** *the
opprobrium of being associated with thugs*
disgrace, shame, dishonour, stigma,
humiliation, loss of face, ignominy,
disrepute, infamy, notoriety, scandal.
– OPPOSITES praise, honour.

opt v. **choose**, select, pick (out), decide on, go
for, settle on, plump for.

optimism n. **hopefulness**, hope, confidence,
buoyancy, sanguineness, positiveness,
positive attitude.

optimistic adj. **1** *she felt optimistic about
the future* **positive**, confident, hopeful,
sanguine, bullish, buoyant; informal upbeat.
2 *the forecast is optimistic* **encouraging**,
promising, hopeful, reassuring, favourable,
auspicious, propitious.
– OPPOSITES pessimistic.

optimum adj. **best**, most favourable, most
advantageous, ideal, perfect, prime, optimal.

option n. **choice**, alternative, possibility,
course of action.

optional adj. **voluntary**, discretionary, non-
compulsory, non-mandatory; Law permissive.
– OPPOSITES compulsory.

opulence n. **1** *the opulence of the room*
luxuriousness, sumptuousness, lavishness,
richness, luxury, luxuriance, splendour,
magnificence, grandeur, splendidness; informal
plushness. **2** *a display of opulence* **wealth**,
affluence, richness, riches, prosperity,
prosperousness, money.
– OPPOSITES poverty.

opulent adj. **1** *his opulent home* **luxurious**,
sumptuous, palatial, lavishly appointed, rich,
splendid, magnificent, grand, grandiose,
fancy; informal plush, swanky; Brit. informal swish;
N. Amer. informal swank. **2** *an opulent family*
wealthy, rich, affluent, well off, well-to-
do, moneyed, prosperous, of substance;
informal well heeled, rolling in money, loaded,
stinking/filthy rich, made of money. **3** *her
opulent red hair* **copious**, abundant, profuse,
prolific, plentiful, luxuriant.
– OPPOSITES spartan, poor.

opus n. **composition**, work (of art), oeuvre.

oracle n. **1** *the oracle of Apollo* **prophet**,
prophetess, sibyl, seer, augur,
prognosticator, diviner, soothsayer, fortune
teller. **2** *our oracle on Africa* **authority**,
expert, specialist, pundit, mentor, adviser.

oracular adj. **1** *his every utterance was given
oracular significance* **prophetic**, prophetical,
sibylline, predictive, prescient, prognostic,
divinatory, augural. **2** *oracular responses*
enigmatic, cryptic, abstruse, unclear,
obscure, confusing, mystifying, puzzling,
mysterious, arcane; ambiguous, equivocal.

oral adj. *an oral agreement* **spoken**, verbal,
unwritten, vocal, uttered, said.
– OPPOSITES written.
▸ n. *a French oral* **oral examination**; Brit. viva
(voce).

orate v. **declaim**, make a speech, hold
forth, speak, discourse, pontificate, preach,
sermonize, sound off, spout off; informal spiel;
formal perorate.

oration n. **speech**, address, lecture, talk,
homily, sermon, discourse, declamation;
informal spiel.

orator n. **(public) speaker**, speech-maker,
lecturer, declaimer, rhetorician, rhetor;
informal spieler.

oratorical adj. **rhetorical**, grandiloquent,
magniloquent, high-flown, orotund,
bombastic, grandiose, pompous, pretentious,
overblown, turgid, flowery, florid.

oratory n. **rhetoric**, eloquence,
grandiloquence, magniloquence, public
speaking, speech-making, declamation.

orb n. **sphere**, globe, ball, circle.

orbit n. **1** *the earth's orbit around the sun*
course, path, circuit, track, trajectory,
rotation, revolution, circle. **2** *the problem
comes outside our orbit* **sphere (of
influence)**, area of activity, range, scope,
ambit, compass, jurisdiction, authority,
remit, domain, realm, province, territory;
informal bailiwick.
▸ v. *Mercury orbits the sun* **revolve round**,
circle round, go round, travel round.

orchestrate v. 1 *the piece was orchestrated by Mozart* **arrange**, adapt, score. 2 *orchestrating a campaign of civil disobedience* **organize**, arrange, plan, set up, bring about, mobilize, mount, stage, stage-manage, mastermind, coordinate, direct, engineer.

ordain v. 1 *the Church of England voted to ordain women* **confer holy orders on**, appoint, anoint, consecrate. 2 *the path ordained by God* **predetermine**, predestine, preordain, determine, prescribe, designate. 3 *he ordained that anyone hunting in the forest was to pay a fine* **decree**, rule, order, command, lay down, legislate, prescribe, pronounce.

ordeal n. **unpleasant experience**, painful experience, trial, tribulation, nightmare, trauma, hell (on earth), trouble, difficulty, torture, torment, agony.

order n. 1 *alphabetical order* **sequence**, arrangement, organization, disposition, system, series, succession; grouping, classification, categorization, codification, systematization. 2 *some semblance of order* **tidiness**, neatness, orderliness, trimness. 3 *the police were needed to keep order* **peace**, control, law (and order), lawfulness, discipline, calm, (peace and) quiet, peacefulness, peaceableness. 4 *his sense of order* **orderliness**, organization, method, system; symmetry, uniformity, regularity; routine. 5 *the equipment was in good order* **condition**, state, repair, shape. 6 *I had to obey his orders* **command**, instruction, directive, direction, decree, edict, injunction, mandate, dictate, commandment, rescript; law, rule, regulation, diktat; demand, bidding, requirement, stipulation; informal say-so; formal ordinance; literary behest. 7 *the company has won the order* **commission**, purchase order, request, requisition; booking, reservation. 8 *the lower orders of society* **class**, level, rank, grade, degree, position, category; dated station. 9 *the established social order* **(class) system**, hierarchy, pecking order, grading, ranking, scale. 10 *the higher orders of insects* **taxonomic group**, class, family, species, breed; taxon. 11 *a religious order* **community**, brotherhood, sisterhood. 12 *the Orange Order* **organization**, association, society, fellowship, fraternity, confraternity, sodality, lodge, guild, league, union, club; sect. 13 *skills of a very high order* **type**, kind, sort, nature, variety; quality, calibre, standard.
– OPPOSITES chaos.
▸ v. 1 *he ordered me to return* **instruct**, command, direct, enjoin, tell, require, charge; formal adjure; literary bid. 2 *he ordered that their assets be confiscated* **decree**,

ordain, rule, legislate, dictate, prescribe. 3 *you can order your tickets by phone* **request**, apply for, place an order for; book, reserve; formal bespeak. 4 *the messages are ordered chronologically* **organize**, put in order, arrange, sort out, marshal, dispose, lay out; group, classify, categorize, catalogue, codify, systematize, systemize.
□ **in order 1** *list the dates in order* **in sequence**, in alphabetical order, in numerical order, in order of priority. 2 *he found everything in order* **tidy**, neat, orderly, straight, trim, shipshape (and Bristol fashion), in apple-pie order; in position, in place. 3 *I think it's in order for me to take the credit* **appropriate**, fitting, suitable, acceptable, (all) right, permissible, permitted, allowable; informal okay.
order someone about/around give orders to, dictate to; lay down the law; informal boss about/around, push about/around.
out of order 1 *the lift's out of order* **not working**, not in working order, not functioning, broken, broken-down, out of service, out of commission, faulty, defective, inoperative; down; informal conked out, bust, (gone) kaput; N. Amer. informal on the fritz, out of whack. 2 Brit. informal *that's really out of order* **unacceptable**, unfair, unjust, unjustified, uncalled for, below the belt, unreasonable, unwarranted, beyond the pale; informal not on, a bit much; Brit. informal a bit thick, off, not cricket; Austral./NZ informal over the fence.

orderly adj. 1 *an orderly room* **neat**, tidy, well ordered, in order, trim, in apple-pie order, spick and span; Brit. informal dated shipshape (and Bristol fashion). 2 *the orderly presentation of information* **(well) organized**, efficient, methodical, systematic, meticulous, punctilious; coherent, structured, logical, well planned, well regulated, systematized. 3 *the crowd was orderly* **well behaved**, law-abiding, disciplined, peaceful, peaceable, non-violent.
– OPPOSITES untidy, disorganized.

ordinance n. formal 1 *the president issued an ordinance* **edict**, decree, law, injunction, fiat, command, order, rule, ruling, dictum, dictate, directive, mandate. 2 *religious ordinances* **rite**, ritual, ceremony, sacrament, observance, service.

ordinarily adv. **usually**, normally, as a (general) rule, generally, in general, for the most part, mainly, mostly, most of the time, typically, habitually, commonly, routinely.

ordinary adj. 1 *the ordinary course of events* **usual**, normal, standard, typical, common, customary, habitual, everyday, regular, routine, day-to-day. 2 *my life seemed very ordinary* **average**, normal, run-of-the-mill, standard, typical, middle-of-the-road, conventional, unremarkable, unexceptional, workaday, undistinguished, nondescript, colourless, commonplace, humdrum, mundane, unmemorable, pedestrian, prosaic, quotidian, uninteresting, uneventful, dull, boring, bland, suburban, hackneyed; N. Amer.

O

garden-variety; informal bog-standard, (plain) vanilla, nothing to write home about, no great shakes; Brit. informal common or garden.
– OPPOSITES unusual.
□ **out of the ordinary** unusual, exceptional, remarkable, extraordinary, unexpected, surprising, unaccustomed, unfamiliar, abnormal, atypical, different, special, exciting, memorable, noteworthy, unique, singular, outstanding; unconventional, unorthodox, strange, peculiar, odd, queer, curious, bizarre, outlandish; informal offbeat.

ordnance n. guns, cannon, artillery, weapons, arms; munitions.

ordure n. excrement, excreta, dung, manure, muck, droppings, faeces, stools, night soil, sewage; informal pooh; Brit. informal cack, big jobs; N. Amer. informal poop.

organ n. **1** the internal organs **body part**, biological structure. **2** the official organ of the Communist Party **newspaper**, paper, journal, periodical, magazine, newsletter, gazette, publication, mouthpiece; informal rag.

organic adj. **1** organic matter **living**, live, animate, biological, biotic. **2** organic vegetables **pesticide-free**, additive-free, natural. **3** the love scenes were an organic part of the drama **essential**, fundamental, integral, intrinsic, vital, indispensable, inherent. **4** a society is an organic whole **structured**, organized, coherent, integrated, coordinated, harmonious.

organism n. **1** fish and other organisms **living thing**, being, creature, animal, plant, life form. **2** a complex political organism **structure**, system, organization, entity.

organization n. **1** the organization of conferences **planning**, arrangement, coordination, administration, organizing, running, management. **2** the overall organization of the book **structure**, arrangement, plan, pattern, order, form, format, framework, composition, constitution. **3** his lack of organization **efficiency**, order, orderliness, planning. **4** a large international organization **company**, firm, corporation, institution, group, consortium, conglomerate, agency, association, society; informal outfit.

organize v. **1** organizing and disseminating information **(put in) order**, arrange, sort (out), assemble, marshal, put straight, group, classify, collocate, categorize, catalogue, codify, systematize, systemize; rare methodize. **2** they organized a search party **make arrangements for**, arrange, coordinate, sort out, put together, fix up, set up, orchestrate, take care of, see to/about, deal with, manage, conduct, administrate, mobilize; schedule, timetable, programme; formal concert.

organized adj. **(well) ordered**, well run, well regulated, structured; orderly, efficient, neat, tidy, methodical; informal together.
– OPPOSITES inefficient.

orgiastic adj. **debauched**, wild, riotous, wanton, dissolute, depraved.

orgy n. **1** a drunken orgy **wild party**, debauch, carousal, carouse, revel, revelry; informal binge, booze-up, bender, love-in; Brit. informal rave-up; N. Amer. informal toot; literary bacchanal; old use wassail. **2** an orgy of violence **bout**, excess, spree, surfeit; informal binge.

orient, orientate v. **1** there were no street names to enable her to orient herself **get/find one's bearings**, establish one's location. **2** you need to orientate yourself to your new way of life **adapt**, adjust, familiarize, acclimatize, accustom, attune; N. Amer. acclimate. **3** magazines oriented to the business community **aim**, direct, pitch, design, intend. **4** the fires are oriented in line with the sunset **align**, place, position, dispose.

oriental adj. **eastern**, Far Eastern, Asian; literary orient.

orientation n. **1** the orientation of the radar station **positioning**, location, position, situation, placement, alignment. **2** his orientation to his new way of life **adaptation**, adjustment, acclimatization. **3** broadly Marxist in orientation **attitude**, inclination. **4** orientation courses **induction**, training, initiation, briefing.

orifice n. **opening**, hole, aperture, slot, slit, cleft.

origin n. **1** the origins of life **beginning**, start, commencement, origination, genesis, birth, dawning, dawn, emergence, creation, birthplace, cradle; source, basis, cause, root(s); formal radix. **2** the Latin origin of the word **source**, derivation, root(s), provenance, etymology; N. Amer. provenience. **3** his Scottish origins **descent**, ancestry, parentage, pedigree, lineage, line (of descent), heritage, birth, extraction, family, stock, blood, bloodline.

original adj. **1** the original inhabitants **indigenous**, native, aboriginal, autochthonous; first, earliest, early. **2** original Rembrandts **authentic**, genuine, actual, true, bona fide; informal pukka, kosher. **3** the film is highly original **innovative**, creative, imaginative, innovatory, inventive; new, novel, fresh, refreshing; unusual, unconventional, unorthodox, groundbreaking, disruptive, pioneering, avant-garde, unique, distinctive.
▸ n. **1** a copy of the original **archetype**, prototype, source, master. **2** he really is an original **individualist**, individual, eccentric, nonconformist, free spirit, maverick; informal character, oddball; Brit. informal one-off, odd bod; N. Amer. informal screwball, kook.

originality n. **inventiveness**, ingenuity, creativeness, creativity, innovation, novelty, freshness, imagination, imaginativeness, individuality, unconventionality, uniqueness, distinctiveness.

originally adv. **(at) first**, in/at the beginning, to begin with, initially, in the first place, at the outset.

originate v. **1** *the disease originates from Africa* **arise**, have its origin, begin, start, stem, spring, emerge, emanate. **2** *Bill Levy originated the idea* **invent**, create, initiate, devise, think up, dream up, conceive, formulate, form, develop, generate, engender, produce, mastermind, pioneer; literary beget.

originator n. **inventor**, creator, architect, author, father, mother, initiator, innovator, founder, pioneer, mastermind; formal neoteric; literary begetter.

ornament n. **1** *small tables covered with ornaments* **knick-knack**, trinket, bauble, bibelot, gewgaw, gimcrack, furbelow; informal whatnot, doodah; N. Amer. informal tchotchke; old use whim-wham, kickshaw, bijou. **2** *the dress had no ornament at all* **decoration**, adornment, embellishment, ornamentation, trimming, accessories.
▸ v. *the room was highly ornamented* **decorate**, adorn, embellish, trim, bedeck, deck (out), festoon; literary bedizen, furbelow.

ornamental adj. **decorative**, fancy, ornate, ornamented.

ornamentation n. **decoration**, adornment, embellishment, ornament, trimming, accessories.

ornate adj. **1** *an ornate mirror* **elaborate**, decorated, embellished, adorned, ornamented, fancy, fussy, ostentatious, showy; informal flash, flashy. **2** *ornate language* **elaborate**, flowery, florid, grandiose, pompous, pretentious, high-flown, orotund, magniloquent, grandiloquent, rhetorical, oratorical, bombastic, overwrought, overblown; informal highfalutin, purple.
– OPPOSITES plain.

orotund adj. **1** *Halliwell's orotund voice* **deep**, sonorous, strong, powerful, full, rich, resonant, loud, booming. **2** *the orotund rhetoric of his prose* **pompous**, pretentious, affected, fulsome, grandiose, ornate, overblown, flowery, florid, high-flown, magniloquent, grandiloquent, rhetorical, oratorical; informal highfalutin, purple.

orthodox adj. **1** *orthodox views* **conventional**, mainstream, conformist, (well) established, traditional, traditionalist, prevalent, popular, conservative, unoriginal. **2** *an orthodox Hindu* **conservative**, traditional, observant, devout, strict.
– OPPOSITES unconventional, unorthodox.

orthodoxy n. **1** *a pillar of orthodoxy* **conventionality**, conventionalism, conformism, conservatism, traditionalism, conformity. **2** *Christian orthodoxies* **doctrine**, belief, conviction, creed, dogma, credo, theory, tenet, teaching.

oscillate v. **1** *the pendulum started to oscillate* **swing (to and fro)**, swing back and forth, sway; N. Amer. informal wigwag. **2** *oscillating between fear and bravery* **waver**, swing, fluctuate, alternate, see-saw, yo-yo, sway, vacillate, hover; informal wobble.

oscillation n. **1** *the oscillation of the pendulum* **swinging (to and fro)**, swing, swaying. **2** *his oscillation between commerce and art* **wavering**, swinging, fluctuation, see-sawing, yo-yoing, vacillation.

ossify v. **1** *these cartilages may ossify* **turn into bone**, harden, solidify, rigidify, petrify. **2** *ossified political institutions* **become inflexible**, become rigid, fossilize, rigidify, stagnate.

ostensible adj. **apparent**, outward, superficial, professed, supposed, alleged, purported.
– OPPOSITES genuine.

ostensibly adv. **apparently**, seemingly, on the face of it, to all intents and purposes, outwardly, superficially, allegedly, supposedly, purportedly.

ostentation n. **showiness**, show, ostentatiousness, pretentiousness, vulgarity, conspicuousness, display, flamboyance, gaudiness, brashness, extravagance, ornateness, exhibitionism; informal flashiness, glitz, glitziness, ritziness.

ostentatious adj. **showy**, pretentious, conspicuous, flamboyant, gaudy, brash, vulgar, loud, extravagant, fancy, ornate, over-elaborate; informal flash, flashy, bling, over the top, OTT, glitzy, ritzy; N. Amer. informal superfly.
– OPPOSITES restrained.

ostracism n. **exclusion**, rejection, shunning, spurning, the cold shoulder, snubbing, avoidance; blackballing, blacklisting.

ostracize v. **exclude**, shun, spurn, cold-shoulder, reject, shut out, avoid, ignore, snub, cut dead, keep at arm's length, leave out in the cold; blackball, blacklist; Brit. send to Coventry; informal freeze out; Brit. informal blank.
– OPPOSITES welcome.

other adj. **1** *these homes use other fuels* **alternative**, different, dissimilar, disparate, distinct, separate, contrasting. **2** *are there any other questions?* **more**, further, additional, extra, added, supplementary.

otherwise adv. **1** *hurry up, otherwise we'll be late* **or (else)**, if not. **2** *she's exhausted, but otherwise she's fine* **in other respects**, apart from that. **3** *he could not have acted otherwise* **in any other way**, differently.

other-worldly adj. **ethereal**, dreamy, spiritual, mystic, mystical; unearthly, unworldly, supernatural.
– OPPOSITES realistic.

ounce n. **particle**, scrap, bit, speck, iota, whit, jot, trace, atom, shred, crumb, fragment, grain, drop, spot; informal smidgen.

oust v. **drive out**, expel, force out, throw out, remove (from office/power), eject, get rid of, depose, topple, unseat, overthrow, bring down, overturn, dismiss, dislodge, displace; informal boot out, kick out; Brit. informal turf out; dated out.

out adj. & adv. **1** *she's out at the moment* **not here**, not at home, not in, (gone) away, elsewhere, absent. **2** *the secret was out* **revealed**, (out) in the open, common/public knowledge, known, disclosed, divulged. **3** *the roses are out* **in flower**, flowering,

in (full) bloom, blooming, in blossom, blossoming, open. **4** *the book should be out soon* **available**, obtainable, in the shops, published, in print. **5** *the fire was nearly out* **extinguished**. **6** informal *grunge is out* **unfashionable**, out of fashion, dated, outdated, passé; informal old hat, not with it, not in. **7** *smoking is out* **forbidden**, not permitted, not allowed, proscribed, unacceptable; informal not on. **8** *he was slightly out in his calculations* **mistaken**, inaccurate, incorrect, wrong, in error.
– OPPOSITES in.
▸ v. informal *it was not our intention to out him* **expose**, unmask.
□ **out cold** unconscious, knocked out, out for the count; informal KO'd, kayoed.

out-and-out adj. **utter**, downright, thoroughgoing, absolute, complete, thorough, total, unmitigated, outright, real, perfect, consummate; N. Amer. full-bore; informal deep-dyed; Brit. informal right; Austral./NZ informal fair.
– OPPOSITES partial.

outbreak n. **1** *a fresh outbreak of killings* **eruption**, flare-up, upsurge, outburst, rash, wave, spate, flood, explosion, burst, flurry; formal boutade. **2** *on the outbreak of war* **start**, beginning, commencement, onset, outset.

outburst n. **eruption**, explosion, burst, outbreak, flare-up, access, rush, flood, storm, outpouring, surge, upsurge, outflowing; formal boutade.

outcast n. **pariah**, persona non grata, reject, outsider.

outclass v. **surpass**, be superior to, be better than, outshine, overshadow, eclipse, outdo, outplay, outmanoeuvre, outstrip, get the better of, upstage; top, cap, beat, defeat, exceed; informal be a cut above, be head and shoulders above, run rings round; old use outrival.

outcome n. **(end) result**, consequence, net result, upshot, after-effect, aftermath, conclusion, issue, end (product).

outcry n. **1** *an outcry of passion* **shout**, exclamation, cry, yell, howl, roar, scream; informal holler. **2** *public outcry* **protest(s)**, protestation(s), complaints, objections, furore, fuss, commotion, uproar, outbursts, opposition, dissent; informal hullabaloo, ballyhoo, ructions, stink.

outdated adj. **old-fashioned**, out of date, outmoded, out of fashion, unfashionable, dated, passé, old, behind the times, behindhand, obsolete, antiquated; informal out, old hat, square, not with it, out of the ark; N. Amer. informal horse-and-buggy, clunky.
– OPPOSITES modern.

outdistance v. **1** *the colt outdistanced the train* **outrun**, outstrip, outpace, leave behind, get (further) ahead of; overtake, pass. **2** *the mill outdistanced all its rivals* **surpass**, outshine, outclass, outdo, exceed, transcend, top, cap, beat, better, leave behind; informal leave standing; old use outrival.

outdo v. **surpass**, outshine, overshadow, eclipse, outclass, outmanoeuvre, get the better of, put in the shade, upstage; exceed, transcend, top, cap, beat, better, leave behind, get ahead of; informal be a cut above, be head and shoulders above, run rings round; old use outrival.

outdoor adj. **open-air**, out-of-doors, outside, alfresco, not under cover.
– OPPOSITES indoor.

outer adj. **1** *the outer layer* **outside**, outermost, outward, exterior, external, surface. **2** *outer areas of the city* **outlying**, distant, remote, faraway, furthest, peripheral; suburban.
– OPPOSITES inner.

outface v. **stand up to**, face down, cow, overawe, intimidate.

outfit n. **1** *a new outfit* **costume**, suit, uniform, ensemble, attire, clothes, clothing, dress, garb; informal get-up, gear, togs; Brit. informal kit, rig-out; formal apparel; old use habit, raiment. **2** *a studio lighting outfit* **kit**, equipment, tools, implements, tackle, apparatus, paraphernalia, things, stuff. **3** informal *a local manufacturing outfit* **organization**, enterprise, company, firm, business; group, band, body, team; informal set-up.
▸ v. *enough swords to outfit an army* **equip**, kit out, fit out/up, rig out, supply, arm; dress, attire, clothe, deck out; old use apparel, invest, habit.

outfitter n. **clothier**, tailor, couturier, costumier, dressmaker, seamstress; dated modiste.

outflow n. **discharge**, outflowing, outpouring, outrush, rush, flood, deluge, issue, spurt, jet, cascade, stream, torrent, gush, outburst; flow, flux; technical efflux.

outgoing adj. **1** *outgoing children* **extrovert**, uninhibited, unreserved, demonstrative, affectionate, warm, friendly, genial, cordial, affable, easy-going, sociable, convivial, lively, gregarious, attention-seeking; communicative, responsive, open, forthcoming, frank. **2** *the outgoing president* **departing**, retiring, leaving.
– OPPOSITES introverted, incoming.

outgoings plural n. **expenses**, expenditure, spending, outlay, payments, costs, overheads.

outgrowth n. **protuberance**, swelling, excrescence, growth, lump, bump, bulge; tumour, cancer, boil, carbuncle, pustule.

outing n. **1** *family outings* **(pleasure) trip**, excursion, jaunt, expedition, day out, (mystery) tour, drive, ride, run; informal junket, spin. **2** informal *the outing of public figures* **exposure**, unmasking, revelation.

outlandish adj. **weird**, queer, far out, quirky, zany, eccentric, idiosyncratic, unconventional, unorthodox, funny, bizarre, unusual, singular, extraordinary, strange, unfamiliar, peculiar, odd, curious; informal offbeat, off the wall, way-out, wacky, freaky, kooky, kinky, oddball; N. Amer. informal in left field.
– OPPOSITES ordinary.

o

outlast v. **outlive**, survive, live/last longer than; ride out, weather, withstand.

outlaw n. *bands of outlaws* **fugitive**, (wanted) criminal, outcast, exile, pariah; bandit, robber; dated desperado.

▸ v. **1** *they voted to outlaw fox-hunting* **ban**, bar, prohibit, forbid, veto, make illegal, proscribe, interdict. **2** *she feared she would be outlawed* **banish**, exile, expel.
– OPPOSITES permit.

outlay n. **expenditure**, expenses, spending, outgoings, spend, cost, price, payment, disbursement, investment.

outlet n. **1** *a central-heating outlet* **vent (hole)**, way out, egress, outfall, opening, channel, conduit, duct. **2** *an outlet for farm produce* **market**, retail outlet, marketplace, shop, store. **3** *an outlet for their energies* **means of expression**, (means of) release, vent, avenue, channel.

outline n. **1** *the outline of the building* **silhouette**, profile, shape, contours, form, line, delineation; diagram, sketch, artist's impression; literary lineaments. **2** *an outline of expenditure for each department* **rough idea**, thumbnail sketch, (quick) rundown, summary, synopsis, résumé, precis; essence, main points, gist, (bare) bones, draft, sketch.

▸ v. **1** *the plane was outlined against the sky* **silhouette**, define, demarcate; sketch, delineate, trace. **2** *she outlined the plan briefly* **rough out**, sketch out, draft, give a rough idea of, summarize, precis.

outlive v. **live on after**, live longer than, outlast, survive.

outlook n. **1** *the two men were wholly different in outlook* **point of view**, viewpoint, views, opinion, (way of) thinking, perspective, attitude, standpoint, stance, frame of mind. **2** *a lovely open outlook* **view**, vista, prospect, panorama, scene, aspect. **3** *the outlook for the economy* **prospects**, expectations, hopes, future, lookout.

outlying adj. **distant**, remote, outer, out of the way, faraway, far-flung, inaccessible, off the beaten track.

outmanoeuvre v. **1** *the English army were outmanoeuvred* **outflank**, circumvent, bypass. **2** *he outmanoeuvred his critics* **outwit**, outsmart, out-think, outplay, steal a march on, trick, get the better of; informal outfox, put one over on.

outmoded adj. **out of date**, old-fashioned, out of fashion, outdated, dated, behind the times, antiquated, obsolete, passé; informal old hat, out of the ark.

out of date adj. **1** *this design is out of date* **old-fashioned**, outmoded, out of fashion, unfashionable, frumpish, frumpy, outdated, dated, old, passé, behind the times, behindhand, obsolete, antiquated; informal out, old hat, square, not with it, out of the ark; N. Amer. informal horse-and-buggy, clunky. **2** *many of the facts are out of date* **superseded**, obsolete, expired, lapsed, invalid, (null and) void.
– OPPOSITES fashionable, current.

out of the way adj. **1** *out-of-the-way places* **outlying**, distant, remote, faraway, far-flung, isolated, lonely, godforsaken, inaccessible, off the beaten track. **2** *I find his methods out of the way* **strange**, unusual, peculiar, odd, funny, curious, bizarre, off-centre, weird, queer, unfamiliar, out of the ordinary, extraordinary, remarkable, singular.
– OPPOSITES accessible.

out of work adj. **unemployed**, jobless, out of a job; redundant, laid off; Brit. informal on the dole; Austral. informal on the wallaby track.

outpouring n. *a massive outpouring of high-energy gamma rays* **outflow**, outflowing, outrush, rush, flood, deluge, discharge, issue, spurt, jet, cascade, stream, torrent, gush, flow, flux; technical efflux. **2** *outpourings of nationalist discontent* **outburst**, eruption, explosion, effusion, welling up, surge, upsurge.

output n. **production**, amount/quantity produced, yield, gross domestic product, out-turn; works, writings.

outrage n. **1** *widespread public outrage* **indignation**, fury, anger, rage, disapproval, wrath, resentment. **2** *it is an outrage* **scandal**, offence, insult, injustice, disgrace. **3** *the bomb outrage* **atrocity**, act of violence/wickedness, crime, wrong, barbarism, inhumane act.

▸ v. *his remarks outraged his parishioners* **enrage**, infuriate, incense, anger, scandalize, offend, give offence to, affront, shock, horrify, disgust, appal.

outrageous adj. **1** *outrageous acts of cruelty* **shocking**, disgraceful, scandalous, atrocious, appalling, monstrous, heinous; evil, wicked, abominable, terrible, horrendous, dreadful, foul, nauseating, sickening, vile, nasty, odious, loathsome, unspeakable; Brit. informal beastly. **2** *the politician's outrageous promises* **far-fetched**, (highly) unlikely, doubtful, dubious, questionable, implausible, unconvincing, unbelievable, incredible, preposterous, extravagant, excessive. **3** *outrageous clothes* **eye-catching**, flamboyant, showy, gaudy, ostentatious; shameless, brazen, shocking; informal saucy, flashy.

outré adj. **weird**, queer, outlandish, far out, freakish, quirky, zany, eccentric, off-centre, unconventional, unorthodox, funny, bizarre, fantastic, unusual, singular, extraordinary, strange, unfamiliar, peculiar, odd, out of the way; informal way-out, wacky, freaky, kooky, oddball, off the wall; N. Amer. informal offbeat, in left field.

outright adv. **1** *he rejected the proposal outright* **completely**, entirely, wholly, fully, totally, categorically, absolutely, utterly, flatly, unreservedly. **2** *I told her outright* **explicitly**, directly, forthrightly, openly, frankly, candidly, honestly, sincerely, bluntly, plainly, in plain language, truthfully, to someone's face, straight from the shoulder; Brit. informal straight up. **3** *they were killed outright* **instantly**, instantaneously,

O

immediately, at once, straight away, then and there, on the spot. **4** *paintings have to be bought outright* **all at once**, in one go.

▸adj. **1** *an outright lie* **out-and-out**, absolute, complete, downright, utter, sheer, categorical, unqualified, unconditional. **2** *the outright winner* **definite**, unequivocal, clear, unqualified, incontestable, unmistakable.

outrun v. **run faster than**, outstrip, outdistance, outpace, leave behind, lose; informal leave standing.

outset n. **start**, starting point, beginning, commencement, dawn, birth, origin, inception, opening, launch, inauguration; informal the word go.
– OPPOSITES end.

outshine v. **surpass**, overshadow, eclipse, outclass, put in the shade, upstage, exceed, transcend, top, cap, beat, better; informal be a cut above, be head and shoulders above, run rings round; old use outrival.

outside n. *the outside of the building* **outer/ external surface**, exterior, outer side/layer, case, skin, shell, covering, facade.
▸adj. **1** *outside lights* **exterior**, external, outer, outdoor, out-of-doors. **2** *outside contractors* **independent**, hired, temporary, freelance, casual, external, extramural. **3** *an outside chance* **slight**, slender, slim, small, tiny, faint, negligible, remote, vague.
▸adv. *they went outside | shall we eat outside?* **outdoors**, out of doors.
– OPPOSITES inside.

outsider n. **stranger**, visitor, non-member; foreigner, alien, immigrant, emigrant, émigré; incomer, newcomer, parvenu.

outsize adj. **1** *her outsize handbag* **huge**, oversized, enormous, gigantic, very big/ large, great, giant, colossal, massive, mammoth, vast, immense, tremendous, monumental, prodigious, mountainous, king-sized; informal mega, monster, whopping (great), thumping (great), humongous, jumbo, bumper; Brit. informal whacking (great), ginormous. **2** *an outsize actor* **very large**, big, massive, fat, corpulent, stout, heavy, plump, portly, ample, bulky; informal pudgy, tubby; Brit. informal podgy; old use pursy.

outskirts plural n. **outlying districts**, edges, fringes, suburbs, suburbia; purlieus, borders, environs.

outsmart v. **outwit**, outmanoeuvre, outplay, steal a march on, trick, get the better of; informal outfox, pull a fast one on, put one over on.

outspoken adj. **forthright**, direct, candid, frank, straightforward, honest, open, straight from the shoulder, plain-spoken; blunt, abrupt, bluff, brusque; old use free-spoken.

outspread adj. **fully extended**, outstretched, spread out, fanned out, unfolded, unfurled, (wide) open, opened out.

outstanding adj. **1** *an outstanding painter* **excellent**, marvellous, magnificent, superb, fine, wonderful, superlative, exceptional, first-class, first-rate, top-tier; informal great, terrific, tremendous, super, amazing, fantastic, sensational, fabulous, ace, crack, A1, mean, awesome, out of this world; Brit. informal smashing, brilliant; N. Amer. informal neat; Austral. informal bonzer. **2** *an outstanding decorative element* **remarkable**, extraordinary, exceptional, striking, eye-catching, arresting, impressive, distinctive, unforgettable, memorable, special, momentous, significant, notable, noteworthy; informal out of this world. **3** *how much work is still outstanding?* **to be done**, undone, unattended to, unfinished, incomplete, remaining, pending, ongoing. **4** *outstanding debts* **unpaid**, unsettled, owing, owed, to be paid, payable, due, overdue, undischarged; N. Amer. delinquent.
– OPPOSITES unexceptional.

outstrip v. **1** *he outstripped the police cars* **go faster than**, outrun, outdistance, outpace, leave behind, get (further) ahead of, lose; informal leave standing. **2** *demand far outstrips supply* **surpass**, exceed, be more than, top, eclipse.

outward adj. **external**, outer, outside, exterior; surface, superficial, seeming, apparent, ostensible.
– OPPOSITES inward.

outwardly adv. **externally**, on the surface, superficially, on the face of it, to all intents and purposes, apparently, ostensibly, seemingly.

outweigh v. **be greater than**, exceed, be superior to, prevail over, have the edge on/ over, override, supersede, offset, cancel out, (more than) make up for, outbalance, compensate for.

outwit v. **outsmart**, outmanoeuvre, outplay, steal a march on, trick, gull, get the better of; informal outfox, pull a fast one on, put one over on.

outworn adj. **out of date**, outdated, old-fashioned, out of fashion, outmoded, dated, behind the times, antiquated, obsolete, defunct, passé; informal old hat, out of the ark.
– OPPOSITES up to date.

oval adj. **egg-shaped**, ovoid, ovate, oviform, elliptical; Botany obovate.

ovation n. **(round of) applause**, handclapping, clapping, cheering, cheers, bravos, acclaim, acclamation, tribute, standing ovation; informal (big) hand.

oven n. **(kitchen) stove**, microwave (oven), (kitchen) range; roaster.

over prep. **1** *there will be cloud over most of the country* **above**, on top of, higher than, atop, covering. **2** *he walked over the grass* **across**, around, throughout. **3** *he has three people over him* **superior to**, above, higher up than, in charge of, responsible for. **4** *over 200,000 people live in the area* **more than**, above, in excess of, upwards of. **5** *a discussion over unemployment* **on the subject of**, about, concerning, apropos of, with reference to, regarding, relating to, in connection with.
– OPPOSITES under.

▸ adv. **1** *a flock of geese flew over* **overhead**, on high, above, past, by. **2** *the relationship is over* **at an end**, finished, concluded, terminated, ended, no more, a thing of the past. **3** *he had some money over* **left (over)**, remaining, unused, surplus, in excess, in addition.
 ▫ **over and above** in addition to, on top of, plus, as well as, besides, along with.
 over and over repeatedly, again and again, over and over again, time and (time) again, many times over, frequently, constantly, continually, persistently, ad nauseam.

overact v. **exaggerate**, overdo it, overplay it; informal ham it up, camp it up.

overall adj. *the overall cost* **all-inclusive**, general, comprehensive, universal, all-embracing, gross, net, final, inclusive; wholesale, complete, across the board, global, worldwide.
▸ adv. *overall, things have improved* **generally (speaking)**, in general, altogether, all in all, on balance, on average, for the most part, in the main, on the whole, by and large, to a large extent.

overawe v. **intimidate**, daunt, cow, disconcert, unnerve, subdue, dismay, frighten, alarm, scare, terrify; informal psych out; N. Amer. informal buffalo.

overbalance v. **fall over**, topple over, lose one's balance, tip over, keel over; push over, upend, upset.

overbearing adj. **domineering**, dominating, autocratic, tyrannical, despotic, oppressive, high-handed, bullying; informal bossy.

overblown adj. **overwritten**, florid, grandiose, pompous, over-elaborate, flowery, overwrought, pretentious, high-flown, turgid, grandiloquent, magniloquent, orotund; informal highfalutin.

overcast adj. **cloudy**, clouded (over), sunless, darkened, dark, grey, black, leaden, heavy, dull, murky, dismal, dreary.
– OPPOSITES bright.

overcharge v. **1** *clients are being overcharged* **swindle**, cheat, defraud, fleece, short-change; informal rip off, sting, screw, rob, diddle, do, rook; N. Amer. informal gouge. **2** *the decoration is overcharged* **overstate**, overdo, exaggerate, over-embroider, over-embellish, overwrite, overdraw.

overcome v. **1** *we overcame the home team* **defeat**, beat, conquer, trounce, thrash, rout, vanquish, overwhelm, overpower, get the better of, triumph over, prevail over, win over/against, outdo, outclass, worst, crush; informal drub, slaughter, clobber, hammer, lick, best, crucify, demolish, wipe the floor with, make mincemeat of, blow out of the water, take to the cleaners; Brit. informal stuff; N. Amer. informal shellac, skunk. **2** *they overcame their fear of flying* **get the better of**, prevail over, control, get/bring under control, master, conquer, defeat, beat; get over, get a grip on, curb, subdue; informal lick, best.
▸ adj. *I was overcome* **overwhelmed**, emotional, moved, affected, speechless.

overconfident adj. **cocksure**, cocky, smug, conceited, self-assured, brash, blustering, overbearing, presumptuous, heading for a fall, riding for a fall; informal too big for one's boots.

overcritical adj. **fault-finding**, hypercritical, captious, carping, cavilling, quibbling, hair-splitting, over-particular; fussy, finicky, fastidious, pedantic, overscrupulous, punctilious; informal nitpicking, pernickety; old use overnice.

overcrowded adj. **overfull**, overflowing, full to overflowing/bursting, crammed full, congested, overpopulated, overpeopled, crowded, swarming, teeming; informal bursting/bulging at the seams, full to the gunwales, jam-packed.
– OPPOSITES empty.

overdo v. **1** *she overdoes the cockney scenes* **exaggerate**, overstate, overemphasize, overplay, go overboard with, overdramatize; informal ham up, camp up. **2** *don't overdo the drink* **eat/drink too much of**, overindulge in, eat/drink to excess. **3** *they overdid the beef* **overcook**, burn.
– OPPOSITES understate.
 ▫ **overdo it** work too hard, overwork, burn the candle at both ends, overtax oneself, drive/push oneself too hard, work/run oneself into the ground, wear oneself to a shadow, wear oneself out, bite off more than one can chew, strain oneself; informal kill oneself, knock oneself out.

overdone adj. **1** *the flattery was overdone* **excessive**, too much, undue, immoderate, inordinate, disproportionate, inflated, overstated, overworked, exaggerated, overemphasized, overenthusiastic, over-effusive; theatrical, actorly; informal a bit much, over the top, OTT. **2** *overdone food* **overcooked**, dried out, burnt.
– OPPOSITES understated, underdone.

overdue adj. **1** *the ship is overdue* **late**, behind schedule, behind time, delayed, unpunctual. **2** *overdue payments* **unpaid**, unsettled, owing, owed, payable, due, outstanding, undischarged; N. Amer. delinquent.
– OPPOSITES early, punctual.

overeat v. **gorge (oneself)**, overindulge (oneself), feast, gourmandize, gluttonize; informal binge, make a pig of oneself, pig out, have eyes bigger than one's stomach; N. Amer. informal scarf out.
– OPPOSITES starve.

overemphasize v. **place/lay too much emphasis on**, overstress, place/lay too much stress on, exaggerate, make too much of, overplay, overdo, overdramatize; informal make a big thing about/of, blow up out of all proportion.
– OPPOSITES understate, play down.

overflow v. *a lot of cream had overflowed the edges of the shallow dish* **spill over**, flow over, brim over, well over, pour forth, stream forth, flood.
▸ n. **1** *an overflow from the tank* **overspill**,

spill, spillage, flood. **2** *to accommodate the overflow, five more offices were built* **surplus**, excess, additional people/things, extra people/things, remainder, overabundance, overspill.

overflowing adj. **overfull**, full to overflowing/bursting, spilling over, running over, crammed full, overcrowded, overloaded; informal bursting/bulging at the seams, jam-packed.
– OPPOSITES empty.

overhang v. **stick out (over)**, stand out (over), extend (over), project (over), protrude (over), jut out (over), bulge out (over), hang over.

overhaul v. **1** *I've been overhauling the gearbox* **service**, maintain, repair, mend, fix up, rebuild, renovate, recondition, refit, refurbish; informal do up, patch up. **2** *Kenyon overhauled him in the race* **overtake**, pass, go past/by, go faster than, get/pull ahead of, outstrip.

overhead adv. *a burst of thunder erupted overhead* **(up) above**, high up, in the sky, on high.
– OPPOSITES below.
▸ adj. *overhead lines* **aerial**, elevated, raised, suspended.
– OPPOSITES underground.

overheads plural n. **running costs**, operating costs, fixed costs, budget items, costs, expenses; Brit. oncosts.

overindulge v. **1** *we all overindulge at Christmas* **drink/eat too much**, overeat, overdrink, be greedy, be intemperate, overindulge oneself, overdo it, drink/eat to excess, gorge (oneself), feast, gourmandize, gluttonize; informal binge, stuff oneself, go overboard, make a pig of oneself, pig oneself; N. Amer. informal scarf out. **2** *his mother had overindulged him* **spoil**, give in to, indulge, humour, pander to, pamper, mollycoddle, baby.
– OPPOSITES abstain.

overindulgence n. **intemperance**, immoderation, excess, overeating, overdrinking, overconsumption, gorging; informal binge.
– OPPOSITES abstinence.

overjoyed adj. **ecstatic**, euphoric, thrilled, elated, delighted, on cloud nine, in seventh heaven, jubilant, rapturous, jumping for joy, delirious, blissful, in raptures, as pleased as Punch, cock-a-hoop, as happy as a sandboy, as happy as Larry; informal over the moon, on top of the world, tickled pink; N. Amer. informal as happy as a clam; Austral. informal wrapped.
– OPPOSITES unhappy.

overlay v. *the area was overlaid with marble* **cover**, face, surface, veneer, inlay, laminate, plaster; coat, varnish, glaze.
▸ n. *an overlay of glass-fibre insulation* **covering**, cover, layer, face, surface, veneer, lamination; coat, varnish, glaze, wash.

overload v. **1** *avoid overloading the ship* **overburden**, overcharge, weigh down. **2** *don't overload the wiring* **strain**, overtax,

overwork, overuse, swamp, oversupply, overwhelm.
▸ n. *there was an overload of demands* **excess**, overabundance, superabundance, profusion, glut, surfeit, surplus, superfluity; avalanche, deluge, flood.

overlook v. **1** *he overlooked the mistake* **fail to notice**, fail to spot, miss. **2** *his work has been overlooked* **disregard**, neglect, ignore, pay no attention/heed to, pass over, forget. **3** *she was willing to overlook his faults* **deliberately ignore**, not take into consideration, disregard, take no notice of, make allowances for, turn a blind eye to, excuse, pardon, forgive. **4** *the breakfast room overlooks the garden* **have a view of**, look over/across, look on to, look out on/over, give on to, command a view of.

overly adv. **unduly**, excessively, inordinately, too; wildly, absurdly, ridiculously, outrageously, unreasonably, exorbitantly, impossibly.

overpower v. **1** *the prisoners might overpower the crew* **gain control over**, overwhelm, prevail over, get the better of, gain mastery over, overthrow, overturn, subdue, suppress, subjugate, repress, bring someone to their knees, conquer, defeat, triumph over, worst, trounce; informal thrash, lick, best, clobber, wipe the floor with. **2** *he was overpowered by grief* **overcome**, overwhelm, move, stir, affect, touch, stun, shake, devastate, take aback, leave speechless; informal bowl over, knock sideways; Brit. informal knock/hit for six.

overpowering adj. **1** *overpowering grief* **overwhelming**, oppressive, unbearable, unendurable, intolerable, shattering. **2** *an overpowering smell* **stifling**, suffocating, strong, pungent, powerful; nauseating, offensive, acrid, fetid, mephitic. **3** *overpowering evidence* **irrefutable**, undeniable, indisputable, incontestable, incontrovertible, compelling, conclusive.

overrate v. **overestimate**, overvalue, think too much of, attach too much importance to, praise too highly.
– OPPOSITES underestimate.

overreact v. **react disproportionately**, act irrationally, lose one's sense of proportion, blow something up out of all proportion; Brit. informal go over the top.

override v. **1** *the court could not override her decision* **disallow**, overrule, countermand, veto, quash, overturn, overthrow; cancel, reverse, rescind, revoke, repeal, annul, nullify, invalidate, negate, void; Law vacate; formal abrogate; old use recall. **2** *the government can override all opposition* **disregard**, pay no heed to, take no account of, turn a deaf ear to, ignore, ride roughshod over. **3** *a positive attitude will override any negative thoughts* **outweigh**, supersede, take precedence over, take priority over, offset, cancel out, (more than) make up for, outbalance, compensate for.

overriding adj. **most important**, of greatest importance, of greatest significance, uppermost, top, first (and foremost), highest, pre-eminent, predominant, principal, primary, paramount, chief, main, major, foremost, central, key, focal, pivotal; informal number-one.

overrule v. **countermand**, cancel, reverse, rescind, repeal, revoke, retract, disallow, override, veto, quash, overturn, overthrow, annul, nullify, invalidate, negate, void; Law vacate; formal abrogate; old use recall.

overrun v. **1** *guerrillas overran the barracks* **invade**, storm, occupy, swarm into, surge into, inundate, overwhelm. **2** *the talks overran the deadline* **exceed**, go beyond/over, run over.

oversee v. **supervise**, superintend, be in charge/control of, be responsible for, look after, keep an eye on, inspect, administer, organize, manage, direct, preside over.

overseer n. **supervisor**, foreman, forewoman, team leader, controller, (line) manager, manageress, head (of department), superintendent, captain; Brit. gangmaster; informal boss, chief, governor; Brit. informal gaffer, guv'nor; N. Amer. informal straw boss; Austral. informal pannikin boss; Mining overman.

overshadow v. **1** *a massive hill overshadows the town* **cast a shadow over**, shade, darken, conceal, obscure, screen; dominate, overlook. **2** *this feeling of tragedy overshadowed his story* **cast a pall over**, blight, take the edge off, mar, spoil, ruin. **3** *he was overshadowed by his brilliant elder brother* **outshine**, eclipse, surpass, exceed, be superior to, outclass, outstrip, outdo, upstage; informal be head and shoulders above.

oversight n. **1** *a stupid oversight* **mistake**, error, omission, lapse, slip, blunder; informal slip-up, boo-boo, fail; Brit. informal boob; N. Amer. informal goof. **2** *the omission was due to oversight* **carelessness**, inattention, negligence, forgetfulness, laxity. **3** *school governors have oversight of the curriculum* **supervision**, surveillance, superintendence, charge, care, administration, management.

overstate v. **exaggerate**, overdo, overemphasize, overplay, dramatize, catastrophize, embroider, embellish; informal blow up out of all proportion.
– OPPOSITES understate.

overstatement n. **exaggeration**, overemphasis, dramatization, embroidery, embellishment, enhancement, hyperbole.

overt adj. **undisguised**, unconcealed, plain (to see), clear, apparent, conspicuous, obvious, noticeable, manifest, patent, open, blatant.
– OPPOSITES covert.

overtake v. **1** *a green car overtook the taxi* **pass**, go past/by, get/pull ahead of, leave behind, outdistance, outstrip. **2** *tourism overtook coffee as the main earner of foreign currency* **outstrip**, surpass, overshadow, eclipse, outshine, outclass; dwarf, put in the shade, exceed, top, cap; old use outrival. **3** *the calamity which overtook us* **befall**, happen

to, come upon, hit, strike, overwhelm, overcome, be visited on; literary betide.

overthrow v. **1** *the President was overthrown* **remove (from office/power)**, bring down, topple, depose, oust, displace, unseat. **2** *an attempt to overthrow the established order* **put an end to**, defeat, conquer.
▸ n. **1** *the overthrow of the Shah* **removal (from office/power)**, downfall, fall, toppling, deposition, ousting, displacement, supplanting, unseating. **2** *the overthrow of capitalism* **ending**, defeat, displacement, fall, collapse, downfall, demise.

overtone n. **connotation**, hidden meaning, implication, association, undercurrent, undertone, echo, vibrations, hint, suggestion, insinuation, intimation, suspicion, feeling, nuance.

overture n. **1** *the overture to Don Giovanni* **prelude**, introduction, opening, introductory movement. **2** *the overture to a long debate* **preliminary**, prelude, introduction, lead-in, precursor, start, beginning. **3** *peace overtures* **(opening) move**, approach, advances, feeler, signal, proposal, proposition.

overturn v. **1** *the boat overturned* **capsize**, turn turtle, keel over, tip over, topple over, turn over; Nautical pitchpole; old use overset. **2** *I overturned the stool* **upset**, tip over, topple over, turn over, knock over, upend. **3** *the Senate may overturn this ruling* **cancel**, reverse, rescind, repeal, revoke, retract, countermand, disallow, override, overrule, veto, quash, overthrow, annul, nullify, invalidate, negate, void; Law vacate; formal abrogate; old use recall.

overused adj. **hackneyed**, overworked, worn out, time-worn, tired, played out, clichéd, stale, trite, banal, stock, unoriginal.

overweening adj. **overconfident**, conceited, cocksure, cocky, smug, haughty, supercilious, lofty, patronizing, arrogant, proud, vain, self-important, imperious, overbearing; informal high and mighty, uppish.
– OPPOSITES unassuming.

overweight adj. **fat**, obese, stout, corpulent, gross, fleshy, plump, portly, chubby, rotund, paunchy, pot-bellied, flabby, well upholstered, well padded, broad in the beam; informal porky, tubby, blubbery; Brit. informal podgy, fubsy; old use pursy.
– OPPOSITES skinny.

overwhelm v. **1** *advancing sand dunes could overwhelm the village* **swamp**, submerge, engulf, bury, deluge, flood, inundate. **2** *Spain overwhelmed Russia in the hockey* **defeat (utterly/heavily)**, trounce, rout, beat (hollow), conquer, vanquish, be victorious over, triumph over, worst, overcome, overthrow, crush; informal thrash, lick, best, clobber, wipe the floor with. **3** *she was overwhelmed by a sense of tragedy* **overcome**, move, stir, affect, touch, strike, dumbfound, shake, devastate, leave speechless; informal bowl over, floor, knock sideways; Brit. informal

o

knock/hit for six.

overwhelming adj. **1** *an overwhelming number of players were unavailable* **very large**, enormous, immense, inordinate, massive, huge. **2** *overwhelming desire to laugh* **very strong**, forceful, uncontrollable, irrepressible, irresistible, overpowering, compelling.

overwork v. **1** *we should not overwork* **work too hard**, work/run oneself into the ground, wear oneself to a shadow, work one's fingers to the bone, burn the candle at both ends, overtax oneself, burn oneself out, overdo it, strain oneself, overload oneself, drive/push oneself too hard; informal kill oneself, knock oneself out. **2** *my colleagues did not overwork me* **drive (too hard)**, exploit, drive into the ground, tax, overtax, overburden, put upon, impose on.

overworked adj. **1** *overworked staff* **stressed (out)**, stress-ridden, overtaxed, overburdened, overloaded, exhausted, worn out. **2** *an overworked phrase* **hackneyed**, overused, worn out, tired, played out, clichéd, threadbare, stale, trite, banal, stock, unoriginal.
– OPPOSITES relaxed, original.

overwrought adj. **1** *she was too overwrought to listen* **tense**, agitated, nervous, on edge, edgy, keyed up, worked up, highly strung, neurotic, overexcited, beside oneself, distracted, distraught, frantic, hysterical; informal in a state, in a tizzy, uptight, wound up, het up; Brit. informal strung up. **2** *the painting is overwrought* **over-elaborate**, over-ornate, overblown, overdone, contrived, overworked, strained.
– OPPOSITES calm, understated.

owe v. **be in debt (to)**, be indebted (to), be in arrears (to), be under an obligation (to).

owing adj. *the rent was owing* **unpaid**, to be paid, payable, due, overdue, undischarged, owed, outstanding, in arrears; N. Amer. delinquent.
– OPPOSITES paid.

□ **owing to** because of, as a result of, on account of, due to, as a consequence of, thanks to, in view of; formal by reason of.

own adj. *he has his own reasons* **personal**, individual, particular, private, personalized, unique.
▸v. **1** *I own this house* **be the owner of**, possess, have in one's possession, have (to one's name). **2** *she had to own that she agreed* **admit**, concede, grant, accept, acknowledge, agree, confess.
□ **get one's own back** informal have/get/take one's revenge (on), be revenged (on), hit back, get (back at), get even (with), settle accounts (with), repay, pay someone back, give someone their just deserts, retaliate (against/on), take reprisals (against), exact retribution (on), give someone a taste of their own medicine.
hold one's own stand firm, stand one's ground, keep one's end up, keep one's head above water, compete, survive, cope, get on/along.
on one's own 1 *I am all on my own* **(all) alone**, (all) by oneself, solitary, unaccompanied, companionless; informal by one's lonesome; Brit. informal on one's tod, on one's Jack Jones. **2** *she works well on her own* **unaided**, unassisted, without help, without assistance, (all) by oneself, independently.
own up confess (to), admit to, admit guilt, plead guilty, accept blame/responsibility, tell the truth (about), make a clean breast of it, tell all; informal come clean (about).

owner n. **possessor**, holder, proprietor/proprietress, homeowner, freeholder, landlord, landlady.

> **WORD LINKS**
> **proprietary** relating to an owner or ownership
> **conveyancing** the legal process of transferring property from one owner to another

ownership n. **(right of) possession**, freehold, proprietorship, proprietary rights, title.

ox n. bull, bullock, steer; Farming beef.

Pp

pace n. **1** *he stepped back a pace* **step**, stride. **2** *a slow, steady pace* **gait**, stride, walk, march. **3** *he drove home at a furious pace* **speed**, rate, velocity; informal clip, lick.
▸ v. *she paced up and down* **walk**, stride, tread, march, pound, patrol.

pacific adj. **1** *a pacific community* **peace-loving**, peaceable, pacifist, anti-war, non-violent, non-aggressive, non-belligerent. **2** *their pacific intentions* **conciliatory**, peacemaking, placatory, propitiatory, appeasing, mollifying, mediatory, dovish; formal irenic. **3** *pacific waters* **calm**, still, smooth, tranquil, placid, waveless, unruffled, like a millpond.
– OPPOSITES aggressive, stormy.

pacifism n. **peacemaking**, conscientious objection(s), passive resistance, peace-mongering, non-violence.

pacifist n. **peace-lover**, conscientious objector, passive resister, peacemaker, peace-monger, dove; Brit. informal conchie.
– OPPOSITES warmonger.

pacify v. **placate**, appease, calm (down), conciliate, propitiate, assuage, mollify, soothe.
– OPPOSITES enrage.

pack n. **1** *a pack of cigarettes* **packet**, container, package, box, carton, parcel. **2** *a 45lb pack* **backpack**, rucksack, knapsack, kitbag, bag, load. **3** *a pack of wolves* **group**, herd, troop. **4** *a pack of youngsters* **crowd**, mob, group, band, troupe, party, set, clique, gang, rabble, horde, throng, huddle, mass, assembly, gathering, host; informal crew, bunch.
▸ v. **1** *she helped pack the hamper* **fill (up)**, put things in, load. **2** *they packed their belongings* **stow**, put away, store, box up. **3** *the glasses were packed in straw* **wrap (up)**, package, parcel, swathe, swaddle, encase, enfold, envelop, bundle. **4** *Christmas shoppers packed the store* **throng**, crowd (into), fill (to overflowing), cram, jam, squash into, squeeze into. **5** *pack the cloth against the wall* **compress**, press, squash, squeeze, jam, tamp.
□ **pack something in** informal **1** *she has packed in her job* **resign from**, leave, give up; informal quit, chuck; Brit. informal jack in. **2** *he should pack in smoking* **give up**, abstain from, drop, desist from, refrain from, discontinue; informal quit, leave off; formal forswear.
pack someone off informal send off, dispatch,

bundle off.
pack up 1 Brit. informal *something is bound to pack up over Christmas* **break (down)**, stop working, fail, malfunction, go wrong; informal act up, conk out, go kaput. **2** informal *it's time to pack up* **stop**, call it a day, finish, cease; informal knock off, quit, pack/jack it in.

package n. **1** *the delivery of a package* **parcel**, packet, container, box. **2** *a complete package of services* **collection**, bundle, combination.
▸ v. *goods packaged in recyclable materials* **wrap (up)**, gift-wrap; pack (up), parcel (up), box, encase.

packaging n. **wrapping**, wrappers, packing, covering.

packed adj. **crowded**, full, filled (to capacity), crammed, jammed, solid, overcrowded, overfull, teeming, seething, swarming; informal jam-packed, chock-full, chock-a-block, full to the gunwales, bursting/bulging at the seams.

packet n. **1** *a packet of cigarettes* **pack**, carton, (cardboard) box, container, case, package. **2** informal *that must have cost a packet* **a large sum of money**, a king's ransom, millions, billions; informal a (small) fortune, pots/heaps of money, a mint, a bundle, a pile, a tidy sum, a pretty penny, big money; Brit. informal a bomb, loadsamoney; N. Amer. informal big bucks, gazillions; Austral. informal big bickies, motser.

pact n. **agreement**, treaty, entente, protocol, deal, settlement, concordat; armistice, truce; formal concord.

pad¹ n. **1** *a pad over the eye* **dressing**, pack, padding, wadding, wad. **2** *a seat pad* **cushion**, squab. **3** *making notes on a pad* **notebook**, notepad, writing pad, memo pad, jotter, block, sketch pad, sketchbook; N. Amer. scratch pad.
▸ v. *a quilted jacket padded with duck feathers* **stuff**, fill, pack, wad.
□ **pad something out** expand unnecessarily, fill out, amplify, increase, flesh out, lengthen, spin out, overdo, elaborate.

pad² v. *he padded along towards the bedroom* **walk quietly**, tread warily, creep, tiptoe, steal, pussyfoot.

padding n. **1** *padding around the ankle* **wadding**, cushioning, stuffing, packing, filling, lining. **2** *a concise style with no padding* **verbiage**, verbosity, wordiness, prolixity; Brit. informal waffle.

p

paddle[1] n. *use the paddles to row ashore* **oar**, scull, blade.
▸ v. *we paddled around the bay* **row gently**, pull, scull.

paddle[2] v. *children were paddling in the water* **splash about**, wade; dabble.

paddock n. **field**, meadow, pasture; pen, pound; N. Amer. corral.

paddy n. Brit. informal **rage**, (bad) temper, (bad) mood, pet, fit of pique, tantrum; informal grump, stress; Brit. informal strop; N. Amer. informal blowout, hissy fit.

padlock v. **lock (up)**, fasten, secure.

padre n. **priest**, chaplain, minister (of religion), pastor, father, parson, clergyman, cleric, ecclesiastic, man of the cloth, churchman, vicar, rector, curate, preacher; informal reverend, Holy Joe, sky pilot; Austral. informal josser.

paean n. **song of praise**, hymn, alleluia; plaudit, glorification, eulogy, tribute, panegyric, accolade, acclamation; formal encomium.

pagan n. *pagans worshipped the sun* **heathen**, infidel, idolater, idolatress; old use paynim.
▸ adj. *the pagan festival* **heathen**, ungodly, irreligious, infidel, idolatrous; rare nullifidian.

page[1] n. **1** *a book of 672 pages* **folio**, sheet, side, leaf. **2** *a glorious page in his life* **period**, time, stage, phase, epoch, era, chapter.

page[2] n. **1** *a page in a hotel* **errand boy**, messenger boy; N. Amer. bellboy, bellhop. **2** *a page at a wedding* **attendant**, pageboy, train-bearer.
▸ v. *could you please page Mr Johnson?* **call (for)**, summon, send for.

pageant n. **parade**, procession, cavalcade, tableau (vivant); spectacle, extravaganza, show.

pageantry n. **spectacle**, display, ceremony, magnificence, pomp, splendour, show; informal razzle-dazzle, razzmatazz.

pain n. **1** *she endured great pain* **suffering**, agony, torture, torment, discomfort. **2** *a pain in the stomach* **ache**, aching, soreness, throb, throbbing, sting, stinging, twinge, shooting pain, stab, pang; discomfort, irritation, tenderness. **3** *the pain of losing a loved one* **sorrow**, grief, heartache, heartbreak, sadness, unhappiness, distress, desolation, misery, wretchedness, despair; agony, torment, torture. **4** informal *that child is a pain.* See **nuisance**. **5** *he took great pains to hide his feelings* **care**, effort, bother, trouble.
▸ v. **1** *her foot is still paining her* **hurt**, cause pain, be painful, be sore, be tender, ache, throb, sting, twinge, cause discomfort; informal kill. **2** *the memory pains her* **sadden**, grieve, distress, trouble, perturb, oppress, cause anguish to.
□ **be at pains** try hard, make a great effort, take (great) pains, put oneself out; strive, endeavour, try, do one's best, do one's utmost, go all out; informal bend over backwards.

pained adj. **upset**, hurt, wounded, injured, insulted, offended, aggrieved, displeased, disgruntled, annoyed, angered, angry, cross, indignant, irritated, resentful; informal riled, miffed, aggravated, peeved, hacked off, browned off; Brit. informal narked, cheesed off, not best pleased; N. Amer. informal teed off, ticked off, sore.

painful adj. **1** *a painful arm* **sore**, hurting, tender, aching, throbbing. **2** *a painful experience* **disagreeable**, unpleasant, nasty, bitter, distressing, upsetting, traumatic, miserable, sad, heartbreaking, agonizing, harrowing.

painfully adv. **distressingly**, disturbingly, unendurably, unbearably, uncomfortably, unpleasantly; dreadfully; informal terribly, awfully; informal dated frightfully.

painkiller n. **analgesic**, pain reliever, anodyne, anaesthetic, narcotic; palliative.

painless adj. **1** *any killing of animals should be painless* **without pain**, pain-free. **2** *getting rid of him proved painless* **easy**, trouble-free, effortless, simple, plain sailing; informal as easy as pie, a piece of cake, child's play, a cinch, a walk in the park.
– OPPOSITES painful, difficult.

painstaking adj. **careful**, meticulous, thorough, assiduous, sedulous, attentive, diligent, industrious, conscientious, punctilious, scrupulous, rigorous, particular; pedantic, fussy.
– OPPOSITES slapdash.

paint n. **colouring**, colourant, tint, dye, stain, pigment, colour.
▸ v. **1** *paint the ceiling* **colour**, apply paint to, decorate, whitewash, emulsion, gloss, spray-paint, airbrush. **2** *painting slogans on a wall* **daub**, smear, spray-paint, airbrush. **3** *Rembrandt painted his mother* **portray**, picture, paint a picture of, depict, represent. **4** *you paint a very stark picture of the suffering* **tell**, recount, outline, sketch, describe, depict, evoke, conjure up.
□ **paint the town red** informal **celebrate**, carouse, enjoy oneself, have a good time, have a party; informal go out on the town, whoop it up, make whoopee, live it up, party, have a ball, push the boat out.

painting n. **picture**, illustration, portrayal, depiction, representation, image, artwork, oil, fresco, mural, watercolour, canvas.

p

chiaroscuro the treatment of light and shade in painting and drawing
vernissage a private view of paintings before public exhibition

pair n. **1** *a pair of gloves* **set (of two)**, matching set, two of a kind. **2** *the pair were arrested* **two**, couple, duo, brace, twosome, duplet; twins; old use twain. **3** *a pair of lines* **couplet**; Prosody distich. **4** *the happy pair* **couple**, man/husband and wife.
▶v. *a cardigan paired with a matching skirt* **match**, put together, couple, twin.

pal informal n. *my best pal.* See **friend** (sense 1).
□ **pal up** become friendly, make friends, form a friendship; N. Amer. informal buddy up.

palace n. **royal/official residence**, castle, château, schloss, mansion, stately home.

palatable adj. **1** *palatable meals* **tasty**, appetizing, flavourful, flavoursome, delicious, mouth-watering, toothsome, succulent; informal scrumptious, yummy, scrummy, moreish; formal comestible. **2** *the truth is not always palatable* **pleasant**, acceptable, pleasing, agreeable, to one's liking.
– OPPOSITES disagreeable, unpalatable.

palate n. **1** *the tea burned her palate* **roof of the mouth**, hard/soft palate. **2** *menus to suit the tourist palate* **(sense of) taste**, appetite, stomach. **3** *wine with a peachy palate* **flavour**, savour, taste.

palatial adj. **luxurious**, deluxe, magnificent, sumptuous, splendid, grand, opulent, lavish, stately, regal; fancy; Brit. upmarket; informal plush, swanky, posh, ritzy, swish.
– OPPOSITES modest.

palaver informal n. **fuss (and bother)**, bother, commotion, trouble, rigmarole, folderol; informal song and dance, performance, to-do, carry-on, carrying-on, kerfuffle, hoo-ha, hullabaloo, ballyhoo.

pale[1] n. **1** *the pales of a fence* **stake**, post, pole, picket, upright. **2** *outside the pale of decency* **boundary**, confines, bounds, limits.
□ **beyond the pale** unacceptable, unseemly, improper, unsuitable, unreasonable, intolerable, disgraceful, deplorable, outrageous, scandalous, shocking; informal not on, not the done thing, out of order, out of line; Austral./NZ informal over the fence; formal exceptionable.

pale[2] adj. **1** *she looked pale and drawn* **white**, pallid, pasty, wan, colourless, anaemic, bloodless, washed out, peaky, ashen, grey, whitish, whey-faced, drained, sickly, sallow, as white as a sheet, deathly pale; milky, creamy, cream, ivory, milk-white, alabaster; informal like death warmed up. **2** *pale colours* **light**, light-coloured, pastel, muted, subtle, soft; faded, bleached, washed out. **3** *the pale light of morning* **dim**, faint, weak, feeble. **4** *a pale imitation* **feeble**, weak, insipid, bland, poor, inadequate; uninspired, unimaginative, lacklustre, spiritless, lifeless; informal pathetic.
– OPPOSITES dark.
▶v. **1** *his face paled* **turn white**, turn pale,

blanch, lose colour. **2** *everything else pales by comparison* **pale into insignificance**, become unimportant.

palisade n. **fence**, paling, barricade, stockade.

pall[1] n. **1** *a rich velvet pall* **funeral cloth**, coffin covering. **2** *a pall of black smoke* **cloud**, covering, cloak, veil, shroud, layer, blanket.
□ **cast a pall over** spoil, cast a shadow over, overshadow, cloud, put a damper on.

pall[2] v. *the high life was beginning to pall* **grow tedious**, grow boring, lose its interest, lose its attraction, wear off; weary, sicken, nauseate; irritate, irk.

palliate v. **1** *the treatment works by palliating symptoms* **alleviate**, ease, relieve, soothe, take the edge off, assuage, moderate, temper, diminish, decrease, blunt, deaden. **2** *there is no way to palliate his dirty deed* **disguise**, hide, gloss over, conceal, cover (up), camouflage, mask; excuse, justify, extenuate, mitigate.

palliative adj. *palliative medicine* **soothing**, alleviating, sedative, calmative.
▶n. *antibiotics and palliatives* **painkiller**, analgesic, pain reliever, sedative, tranquillizer, anodyne, calmative, opiate, bromide.

pallid adj. **1** *a pallid child* **pale**, white, pasty, wan, colourless, anaemic, washed out, peaky, whey-faced, ashen, grey, whitish, drained, sickly, sallow; informal like death warmed up. **2** *pallid watercolours* **insipid**, uninspired, colourless, uninteresting, unexciting, unimaginative, lifeless, spiritless, sterile, bland.

pallor n. **paleness**, pallidness, lack of colour, wanness, ashen hue, pastiness, peakiness, greyness, sickliness, sallowness.

pally adj. informal **friendly**, on good terms, close, intimate; informal matey, buddy-buddy.

palm[1] n.
□ **grease someone's palm** informal bribe, buy (off), corrupt, suborn, give an inducement to; informal give a backhander to, give a sweetener to.
have someone in the palm of one's hand have control over, have influence over, have someone eating out of one's hand, have someone on a string; N. Amer. have someone in one's hip pocket.

palm[2] n. *the palm of victory* **prize**, trophy, award, crown, laurel wreath, laurels, bays.

palmistry n. **fortune telling**, palm-reading, clairvoyancy, chiromancy.

palmy adj. **happy**, fortunate, glorious, prosperous, halcyon, golden, rosy.

palpable adj. **1** *a palpable bump* **tangible**, touchable, noticeable, detectable. **2** *his reluctance was palpable* **perceptible**, perceivable, visible, noticeable, discernible, detectable, observable, tangible, unmistakable, transparent, self-evident; obvious, clear, plain (to see), evident, apparent, manifest, staring one in the face, written all over someone.
– OPPOSITES imperceptible.

p

palpitate v. **1** *her heart began to palpitate* **beat rapidly**, pound, throb, pulsate, pulse, thud, thump, hammer, race. **2** *palpitating with terror* **tremble**, quiver, quake, shake (like a leaf).

paltry adj. **1** *a paltry sum of money* **small**, meagre, trifling, insignificant, negligible, inadequate, insufficient, derisory, pitiful, pathetic, miserable, niggardly, beggarly; informal measly, piddling, poxy; formal exiguous. **2** *naval glory struck him as paltry* **worthless**, petty, trivial, unimportant, insignificant, inconsequential, of little account.
− OPPOSITES considerable.

pamper v. **spoil**, indulge, overindulge, cosset, mollycoddle, coddle, baby, wait on someone hand and foot.

pamphlet n. **brochure**, leaflet, booklet, circular, flyer, handbill; N. Amer. mailer, folder, dodger.

pan[1] n. **1** *a heavy pan* **saucepan**, frying pan, wok, skillet. **2** *salt pans* **hollow**, pit, depression, dip, crater, concavity.
▸ v. **1** informal *the movie was panned by the critics.* See **criticize**. **2** *prospectors panned for gold* **sift for**, search for, look for.
− OPPOSITES praise.
□ **pan out 1** *Harold's idea hadn't panned out* **succeed**, be successful, work (out), turn out well. **2** *the deal panned out badly* **turn out**, work out, end (up), come out, fall out, evolve; formal eventuate.

pan[2] v. *the camera panned to the building* **swing (round)**, sweep, move, turn, circle.

panacea n. **universal cure**, cure-all, cure for all ills, universal remedy, elixir, wonder drug; informal magic bullet.

panache n. **flamboyance**, confidence, self-assurance, style, flair, elan, dash, verve, zest, spirit, brio, éclat, vivacity, gusto, liveliness, vitality, energy; informal pizzazz, oomph, zip, zing.

pancake n. **crêpe**, galette; blin, tortilla, tostada, chapatti, dosa, latke, blintze; N. Amer. flapjack, slapjack.

pandemic adj. **widespread**, prevalent, pervasive, rife, rampant.

pandemonium n. **bedlam**, chaos, mayhem, uproar, turmoil, tumult, commotion, confusion, anarchy, furore, hubbub, rumpus; informal hullabaloo.
− OPPOSITES peace.

pander v.
□ **pander to** indulge, gratify, satisfy, cater to, give in to, accommodate, comply with.

pane n. **sheet of glass**, windowpane.

panegyric n. **eulogy**, paean, accolade, tribute; formal encomium.

panel n. **1** *a control panel* **console**, instrument panel, dashboard; instruments, controls, dials. **2** *a panel of judges* **group**, team, body, committee, board.

pang n. **1** *hunger pangs* **(sharp) pain**, shooting pain, twinge, stab, spasm. **2** *a pang of remorse* **qualm**, twinge, prick.

panic n. *a wave of panic* **alarm**, anxiety, nervousness, fear, fright, trepidation, dread, terror, agitation, hysteria, consternation, perturbation, dismay, apprehension; informal flap, fluster, cold sweat, funk, tizzy; N. Amer. informal swivet.
− OPPOSITES calm.
▸ v. **1** *there's no need to panic* **be alarmed**, be scared, be nervous, be afraid, take fright, be agitated, be hysterical, lose one's nerve, get overwrought, get worked up; informal flap, get in a flap, lose one's cool, get into a tizzy, run around like a headless chicken, freak out, get in a stew; Brit. informal get the wind up, go into a (flat) spin, have kittens. **2** *talk of love panicked her* **frighten**, alarm, scare, unnerve; informal freak out; Brit. informal put the wind up.

panic-stricken adj. **alarmed**, frightened, scared (stiff), terrified, terror-stricken, petrified, horrified, horror-stricken, fearful, afraid, panicky, frantic, in a frenzy, nervous, agitated, hysterical, beside oneself, worked up, overwrought; informal in a cold sweat, in a (blue) funk, in a flap, in a fluster, in a tizzy; Brit. informal in a flat spin.

panoply n. **1** *the full panoply of America's military might* **array**, range, collection. **2** *all the panoply of religious liturgy* **trappings**, regalia; splendour, spectacle, ceremony, ritual.

panorama n. **1** *he surveyed the panorama* **(scenic) view**, vista, prospect, scene, scenery, landscape, seascape. **2** *a panorama of the art scene* **overview**, survey, review, presentation, appraisal.

panoramic adj. **1** *a panoramic view* **sweeping**, wide, extensive, scenic, commanding. **2** *a panoramic look at the 20th century* **wide-ranging**, extensive, broad, far-reaching, comprehensive, all-embracing.

pant v. **1** *he was panting as they reached the top* **breathe heavily**, breathe hard, puff (and blow), huff and puff, gasp, wheeze. **2** *it makes you pant for more* **yearn for**, long for, crave, hanker after/for, ache for, hunger for, thirst for, be hungry for, be thirsty for, wish for, desire, want; informal itch for, be dying for; old use be athirst for.
▸ n. *breathing in shallow pants* **gasp**, puff, wheeze, breath.

panting adj. **out of breath**, breathless, short of breath, puffed out, puffing (and blowing), huffing and puffing, gasping (for breath), wheezing, wheezy.

pantry n. **larder**, store, storeroom; Brit. historical still room; old use spence.

pants plural n. **1** Brit. **underpants**, briefs, Y-fronts, boxer shorts, boxers, long johns, (French) knickers, bikini briefs; Brit. camiknickers; N. Amer. shorts, undershorts; informal panties; Brit. informal kecks, knicks, smalls, trolleys; dated drawers, bloomers, unmentionables; N. Amer. dated step-ins. **2** N. Amer. See **trousers**.

pap n. **1** *tasteless pap* **soft food**, mush, slop, pulp, purée, mash; informal goo, gloop, gook; N. Amer. informal glop. **2** *commercial pap* **trivia**, pulp (fiction), rubbish, nonsense, froth; Brit. candyfloss; informal dreck, drivel, trash, twaddle.

paper n. **1** *a sheet of paper* **writing paper**, notepaper; parchment, vellum. **2** *the local paper* **newspaper**, journal, gazette, periodical; tabloid, broadsheet, quality paper, daily, weekly, evening paper, Sunday paper; informal rag; N. Amer. informal tab. **3** *the paper was peeling off the walls* **wallpaper**, wallcovering; Brit. woodchip; trademark Anaglypta. **4** *toffee papers* **wrapper**, wrapping. **5** *a three-hour paper* **exam**, examination, test. **6** *he has just published a paper* **essay**, article, monograph, thesis, work, dissertation, treatise, study, report, analysis, tract, critique, exegesis, review; N. Amer. theme. **7** *personal papers* **documents**, certificates, letters, files, deeds, records, archives, paperwork, documentation; Law muniments. **8** *they asked us for our papers* **identification papers/documents**, identity card, ID, credentials.
▸ v. *we papered the walls* **wallpaper**, hang wallpaper on.
□ **paper over something** cover up, hide, conceal, disguise, camouflage, gloss over. **on paper 1** *he put his thoughts down on paper* **in writing**, in black and white, in print. **2** *the combatants were evenly matched on paper* **in theory**, theoretically, supposedly.

> **WORD LINKS**
> **ream** 500 sheets of paper
> **quire** 25 sheets of paper
> **esparto** a type of grass used to make paper
> **foolscap** a size of paper, about 330 x 200 (or 400) mm
> **watermark** a faint design made in some paper to identify the maker
> **foxed** referring to paper in old books that is discoloured with brown spots
> **origami** the Japanese art of folding paper into decorative shapes

papery adj. **thin**, paper-thin, flimsy, delicate, insubstantial, light, lightweight.

par n.
□ **below par 1** *their performances have been below par* **substandard**, inferior, not up to scratch, under par, below average, second-rate, mediocre, poor, undistinguished; informal not up to snuff; N. Amer. informal bush-league. **2** *I'm feeling below par* **slightly unwell**, not (very) well, not oneself, out of sorts; ill, unwell, poorly, washed out, run down, peaky; Brit. off (colour); informal under the weather, not up to snuff, lousy, rough; Brit. informal ropy, grotty; Austral./NZ informal crook; dated queer.
on a par with as good as, comparable with, in the same class/league as, equivalent to, equal to, on a level with, of the same standard as.
par for the course normal, typical, standard, usual, what one would expect.
up to par good enough, up to the mark, satisfactory, acceptable, adequate, up to

scratch; informal up to snuff.

parable n. **allegory**, moral story/tale, fable, exemplum, apologue.

parade n. **1** *a St George's Day parade* **procession**, march, cavalcade, motorcade, spectacle, display, pageant; review, dress parade, tattoo; Brit. march past. **2** *she made a great parade of doing the housework* **exhibition**, show, display, performance, spectacle, fuss; informal hoo-ha, to-do. **3** *she walked along the parade* **promenade**, walkway, esplanade, mall; N. Amer. boardwalk; Brit. informal prom.
▸ v. **1** *the teams paraded through the city* **march**, process, file, troop. **2** *she paraded up and down* **strut**, swagger, stride. **3** *he was keen to parade his knowledge* **display**, exhibit, make a show of, flaunt, show (off), demonstrate.

paradigm n. **model**, pattern, example, exemplar, standard, prototype, archetype.

paradisal adj. **heavenly**, idyllic, blissful, divine, sublime, perfect.

paradise n. **1** *the souls in paradise* **(the kingdom of) heaven**, the heavenly kingdom, Elysium, the Elysian Fields, Valhalla, Avalon. **2** *Adam and Eve's expulsion from Paradise* **the Garden of Eden**, Eden. **3** *a tropical paradise* **Utopia**, Shangri-La, heaven, idyll, nirvana. **4** *this is sheer paradise!* **bliss**, heaven, ecstasy, delight, joy, happiness, nirvana, heaven on earth.
– OPPOSITES hell.

paradox n. **contradiction (in terms)**, self-contradiction, inconsistency, incongruity, conflict, anomaly; enigma, puzzle, mystery, conundrum.

paradoxical adj. **contradictory**, self-contradictory, inconsistent, incongruous, anomalous; illogical, puzzling, baffling, incomprehensible, inexplicable.

paragon n. **perfect example**, shining example, model, epitome, archetype, ideal, exemplar, nonpareil, embodiment, personification, quintessence, apotheosis, acme; jewel, gem, angel, treasure; informal one in a million, the tops; old use a nonsuch.

paragraph n. **1** *the concluding paragraph* **section**, subdivision, part, subsection, division, portion, segment, passage. **2** *a paragraph in the newspaper* **report**, article, item, piece, write-up, mention.

parallel adj. **1** *parallel lines* **side by side**, aligned, collateral, equidistant. **2** *parallel careers* **similar**, analogous, comparable, corresponding, like, of a kind, akin, related, equivalent, matching. **3** *a parallel universe* **coexisting**, coexistent, concurrent; contemporaneous, simultaneous, synchronous.
– OPPOSITES divergent.
▸ n. **1** *an exact parallel* **counterpart**, analogue, equivalent, likeness, match, twin, duplicate, mirror. **2** *there is an interesting parallel between these figures* **similarity**, likeness, resemblance, analogy, correspondence,

p

equivalence, correlation, relation, symmetry, parity.

▶v. **1** *his experiences parallel mine* **resemble**, be similar to, be like, bear a resemblance to; correspond to, be analogous to, be comparable/equivalent to, equate with/to, correlate with, imitate, echo, remind one of, duplicate, mirror, follow, match. **2** *her performance has never been paralleled* **equal**, match, rival, emulate.

paralyse v. **1** *both of his legs were paralysed* **disable**, cripple, immobilize, incapacitate, debilitate; formal torpefy. **2** *Maisie was paralysed by the sight of him* **immobilize**, transfix, freeze, stun, render motionless. **3** *the capital was paralysed by a general strike* **bring to a standstill**, immobilize, bring to a (grinding) halt, freeze, cripple, disable.

paralysed adj. **disabled**, crippled, handicapped, incapacitated, paralytic, powerless, immobilized, useless; Medicine paraplegic, quadriplegic, tetraplegic, monoplegic, hemiplegic, paretic, paraparetic.

paralysis n. **1** *the disease can cause paralysis* **immobility**, powerlessness, incapacity, debilitation; Medicine paraplegia, quadriplegia, tetraplegia, monoplegia, hemiplegia, diplegia, paresis, paraparesis. **2** *complete paralysis of the ports* **shutdown**, immobilization, stoppage.

paralytic adj. **1** *her hands became paralytic* **paralysed**, crippled, disabled, incapacitated, powerless, immobilized, useless. **2** Brit. informal *everyone was paralytic.* See **drunk** (adjective).

parameter n. **framework**, variable, limit, boundary, limitation, restriction, criterion, guideline.

paramount adj. **most important**, of greatest/prime importance; uppermost, supreme, chief, overriding, predominant, foremost, prime, primary, principal, highest, main, key, central, leading, major, top; informal number-one.

paranoia n. **persecution complex**, delusions, obsession, psychosis.

paranoid adj. **over-suspicious**, paranoiac, suspicious, mistrustful, fearful, insecure; Brit. informal para.

parapet n. **1** *Marian leaned over the parapet* **balustrade**, barrier, wall. **2** *the sandbags making up the parapet* **barricade**, rampart, bulwark, bank, embankment, fortification, defence, earthwork, bastion.

paraphernalia plural n. **equipment**, stuff, things, apparatus, kit, implements, tools, utensils, material(s), appliances, accoutrements, appurtenances, odds and ends, bits and pieces; informal gear; Brit. informal clobber; old use equipage.

paraphrase v. *paraphrasing literary texts* **reword**, rephrase, put/express in other words, rewrite, gloss.

▶n. *this paraphrase of St Paul's words* **rewording**, rephrasing, rewriting, rewrite, rendition, rendering, gloss.

parasite n. **hanger-on**, cadger, leech, passenger; informal bloodsucker, sponger, scrounger, freeloader; N. Amer. informal mooch; Austral./NZ informal bludger.

parcel n. **1** *a parcel of clothes* **package**, packet; pack, bundle, box, case, bale. **2** *a parcel of land* **plot**, piece, patch, tract; Brit. allotment; N. Amer. lot, plat.

▶v. **1** *she parcelled up the papers* **pack (up)**, package, wrap (up), gift-wrap, tie up, bundle up. **2** *parcelling out commercial farmland* **divide up**, portion out, distribute, share out, allocate, allot, apportion, hand out, dole out, dish out; informal divvy up.

parched adj. **1** *the parched earth* **(bone) dry**, dried up/out, arid, desiccated, dehydrated, baked, burned, scorched; withered, shrivelled. **2** informal *I'm parched.* See **thirsty** (sense 1).
– OPPOSITES soaking.

pardon n. **1** *pardon for your sins* **forgiveness**, absolution, clemency, mercy, lenience, leniency. **2** *he offered them a full pardon* **reprieve**, free pardon, amnesty, exoneration, release, acquittal, discharge; formal exculpation.

▶v. **1** *I know she will pardon me* **forgive**, absolve, have mercy on; excuse, condone, overlook. **2** *they were subsequently pardoned* **exonerate**, acquit, amnesty; reprieve, release, free; informal let off; formal exculpate.
– OPPOSITES blame, punish.

▶exclam. *Pardon?* **what (did you say)**, eh, pardon me, I beg your pardon, sorry, excuse me; informal come again.

pardonable adj. **excusable**, forgivable, condonable, understandable, minor, venial, slight.
– OPPOSITES inexcusable.

pare v. **1** *pare the peel from the lemon* **cut (off)**, trim (off), peel (off), strip (off), skin; technical decorticate. **2** *domestic operations have been pared down* **reduce**, diminish, decrease, cut (back/down), trim, slim down, prune, curtail.

parent n. **1** *her parents have divorced* **mother, father**, birth/biological parent, progenitor; adoptive parent, foster-parent, step-parent, guardian; literary begetter. **2** *the parent of rock and roll* **source**, origin, genesis, root, author, architect; precursor, forerunner, predecessor, antecedent; formal radix.

▶v. *those who parent young children* **bring up**, look after, take care of, rear, raise.

> **WORD LINKS**
> **parricide** the killing of a parent

parentage n. **origins**, extraction, birth, family, ancestry, lineage, heritage, pedigree, descent, blood, stock, roots.

parenthetical adj. **incidental**, supplementary, in brackets, in parentheses, parenthetic; explanatory, qualifying.

parenthetically adv. **incidentally**, by the way, by the by(e), in passing, in parenthesis.

parenthood n. **childcare**, child-rearing, motherhood, fatherhood, parenting.

pariah n. **outcast**, persona non grata, leper, undesirable, unperson.

parings plural n. **peelings**, clippings, peel, rind, cuttings, trimmings, shavings.

parish n. **1** *the parish of Poplar* **district**, community. **2** *the vicar scandalized the parish* **parishioners**, churchgoers, congregation, fold, flock, community.

> WORD LINKS
> **parochial** relating to a parish
> **beat the bounds** (in the past) mark parish boundaries by walking round them and striking certain points

parity n. **equality**, equivalence, uniformity, consistency, correspondence, congruity, levelness, unity, coequality.

park n. **1** *we were playing in the park* **public garden**, recreation ground, playground, play area. **2** *fifty acres of park* **parkland**, grassland, woodland, garden(s), lawns, grounds, estate. **3** *the liveliest player on the park* **(playing) field**, football field, pitch.

▸ v. **1** *he parked his car* **leave**, position; stop, pull up. **2** informal *park your bag by the door* **put (down)**, place, deposit, leave, stick, shove, dump; informal plonk; Brit. informal bung.

□ **park oneself** informal sit down, seat oneself, settle (oneself), install oneself; informal plonk oneself.

parlance n. **jargon**, language, phraseology, talk, speech, argot, patois, cant; informal lingo, -ese, -speak.

parley n. *a peace parley* **negotiation**, talk(s), conference, summit, discussion, powwow; informal confab; formal colloquy, confabulation; dated palaver.

▸ v. *the two parties were willing to parley* **discuss terms**, talk, hold talks, negotiate, deliberate; informal powwow.

parliament n. **1** *the Queen's speech to Parliament* **the Houses of Parliament**, Westminster, the (House of) Commons, the (House of) Lords. **2** *the Russian parliament* **legislature**, legislative assembly, congress, senate, (upper/lower) house, (upper/lower) chamber, diet, assembly.

> WORD LINKS
> **Hansard** the official word-for-word record of debates in Parliament
> **statute** a written law passed by a parliament
> **filibuster** prolonged speaking which obstructs progress in a parliament
> **recess** a break between sessions of a parliament
> **prorogue** discontinue a session of a parliament
> **bicameral** referring to a parliament with two chambers
> **Woolsack** (in the UK) the Lord Chancellor's wool-stuffed seat in the House of Lords
> **Black Rod** (in the UK) the chief usher of the House of Lords

parliamentary adj. **legislative**, law-making, governmental, congressional, senatorial, democratic, elected, representative.

parlour n. **1** dated *tea in the parlour* **sitting room**, living room, lounge, front room, drawing room; Brit. reception room. **2** *a beauty parlour* **salon**, shop, establishment, store.

parlous adj. **bad**, dire, dreadful, awful, terrible, grave, serious, desperate, precarious; sorry, poor, lamentable, hopeless; unsafe, perilous, dangerous, risky; informal dicey, hairy, chronic, woeful.

parochial adj. **narrow-minded**, small-minded, provincial, narrow, small-town, conservative, illiberal, intolerant; Brit. parish-pump; N. Amer. informal jerkwater.
– OPPOSITES broad-minded.

parochialism n. **narrow-mindedness**, provincialism, small-mindedness.

parody n. **1** *a parody of the gothic novel* **satire**, burlesque, lampoon, pastiche, pasquinade, caricature, imitation, mockery; informal spoof, take-off, send-up. **2** *a parody of the truth* **distortion**, travesty, caricature, misrepresentation, perversion, corruption, debasement.

▸ v. *parodying schoolgirl fiction* **satirize**, burlesque, lampoon, caricature, mimic, imitate, ape, copy, make fun of, travesty, take off; informal send up.

paroxysm n. **spasm**, attack, fit, burst, bout, convulsion, seizure, outburst, eruption, explosion, access; formal boutade.

parrot v. *they parroted slogans without appreciating their significance* **repeat (mindlessly)**, repeat mechanically, echo.

> WORD LINKS
> **psittacine** relating to parrots
> **psittacosis** a contagious disease which can be passed from parrots to humans as a form of pneumonia

parrot-fashion adv. **mechanically**, by rote, mindlessly, automatically.

parry v. **1** *Sharpe parried the blow* **ward off**, fend off; deflect, hold off, block, counter, repel, repulse. **2** *I parried her constant questions* **evade**, sidestep, avoid, dodge, answer evasively, field, fend off.

parsimonious adj. **mean**, miserly, niggardly, close-fisted, close, penny-pinching, ungenerous, Scrooge-like; informal tight-fisted, tight, stingy, mingy; N. Amer. informal cheap; formal penurious; old use near.
– OPPOSITES generous.

parsimony n. **meanness**, miserliness, parsimoniousness, niggardliness, close-fistedness, closeness, penny-pinching; informal stinginess, minginess, tightness, tight-fistedness; N. Amer. cheapness; formal penuriousness; old use nearness.

parson n. **vicar**, rector, clergyman, cleric, chaplain, pastor, curate, man of the cloth, ecclesiastic, minister, priest, preacher; informal reverend, padre; Austral. informal josser.

part n. **1** *the last part of the cake* | *a large part of their life* **bit**, slice, chunk, lump, hunk, wedge, fragment, scrap, piece;

p

portion, proportion, percentage, fraction.
2 *car parts* **component**, bit, constituent,
element, module. **3** *body parts* **part of the
body**, organ, limb, member. **4** *the third
part of the book* **section**, division, volume,
chapter, act, scene, instalment. **5** *another
part of the country* **district**, neighbourhood,
quarter, section, area, region. **6** *the part of
Juliet* **(theatrical) role**, character, persona.
7 *he's learning his part* **lines**, words, script,
speech; libretto, lyrics, score. **8** *he was
jailed for his part in the affair* **involvement**,
role, function, hand, work, responsibility,
capacity, position, participation,
contribution; informal bit.
– OPPOSITES whole.
▶ v. **1** *the curtains parted* **separate**, divide
(in two), split (in two), move apart. **2** *we
parted on bad terms* **leave**, take one's leave,
say goodbye/farewell, say one's goodbyes/
farewells, go one's (separate) ways, go away,
depart.
– OPPOSITES join, meet.
▶ adj. *a part payment* **incomplete**, partial,
half, semi-, limited, inadequate, insufficient,
unfinished.
– OPPOSITES complete.
▶ adv. *it is part finished* **to a certain
extent/degree**, to some extent/degree,
partly, partially, in part, half, relatively,
comparatively, (up) to a point, somewhat,
not totally, not entirely, (very) nearly,
almost, just about, all but.
– OPPOSITES completely.
  □ **for the most part** See **most**.
  in good part See **good**.
  in part to a certain extent/degree, to some
  extent/degree, partly, partially, slightly, in
  some measure, (up) to a point.
  on the part of (made/done) by, carried out
  by, caused by, from.
  part with give up/away, relinquish, forgo,
  surrender, hand over, deliver up, dispose of.
  take part participate, join in, get involved,
  enter, play a part/role, be a participant,
  contribute, have a hand, help, assist, lend a
  hand; informal get in on the act.
  take part in participate in, engage in, join
  in, get involved in, share in, play a part/
  role in, be a participant in, contribute to, be
  associated with, have a hand in.
  take someone's part support, give one's
  support to, take the side of, side with, stand
  by, stick up for, be supportive of, back (up),
  give one's backing to, be loyal to, defend,
  come to the defence of, champion.
partake v. **1** formal *visitors can partake in
golf* **participate in**, take part in, engage in,
join in, get involved in. **2** *she had partaken
of lunch* **consume**, have, eat, drink, devour,
wolf down; informal polish off. **3** *Bohemia
partakes of both East and West* **have the
qualities/attributes of**, suggest, evoke, be
characterized by.
partial adj. **1** *a partial recovery* **incomplete**,
limited, qualified, imperfect, fragmentary,
unfinished. **2** *a very partial view of the
situation* **biased**, prejudiced, partisan,

one-sided, slanted, skewed, coloured,
unbalanced.
– OPPOSITES complete, unbiased.
  □ **be partial to** like, love, enjoy, have a
  liking for, be fond of, be keen on, have a soft
  spot for, have a taste for, have a penchant
  for; informal adore, be mad about/on, have a
  thing about, be crazy about, be nutty about;
  Brit. informal be potty about; N. Amer. informal
  cotton to; Austral./NZ informal be shook on.
partiality n. **1** *his partiality towards their
cause* **bias**, prejudice, favouritism, favour,
partisanship. **2** *her partiality for brandy*
liking, love, fondness, taste, soft spot,
predilection, penchant, passion.
partially adv. **to a limited extent/degree**, to
a certain extent/degree, partly, in part, not
totally, not entirely, relatively, moderately,
(up) to a point, somewhat, comparatively,
slightly.
participant n. **participator**, contributor,
party, member; entrant, competitor, player,
contestant, candidate.
participate v. **take part**, engage, join,
get involved, share, play a part/role, be a
participant, partake, have a hand in, be
associated with; cooperate, help, assist, lend
a hand.
participation n. **involvement**, part,
contribution, association.
particle n. **1** *minute particles of rock* **(tiny)
bit**, (tiny) piece, speck, spot, fleck; fragment,
sliver, splinter. **2** *he never showed a particle
of sympathy* **iota**, jot, whit, bit, scrap, shred,
crumb, drop, hint, touch, trace, suggestion,
whisper, suspicion, scintilla; informal smidgen.
particular adj. **1** *a particular group of
companies* **specific**, certain, distinct,
separate, discrete, definite, precise;
single, individual. **2** *an issue of particular
importance* **(extra) special**, especial,
exceptional, unusual, singular, uncommon,
notable, noteworthy, remarkable, unique;
formal peculiar. **3** *he was particular about
what he ate* **fussy**, fastidious, finicky,
meticulous, punctilious, discriminating,
selective, painstaking, exacting, demanding;
informal pernickety, choosy, picky; Brit. informal
faddy.
– OPPOSITES general, careless.
▶ n. *the same in every particular* **detail**, item,
point, specific, element, aspect, respect,
regard, particularity, fact, feature.
  □ **in particular 1** *nothing in particular*
  specific, special. **2** *the poor, in particular,
  were hit by rising prices* **particularly**,
  specifically, especially, specially.
particularity n. **1** *the particularity of each
human being* **individuality**, distinctiveness,
uniqueness, singularity, originality. **2** *a great
degree of particularity* **detail**, precision,
accuracy, thoroughness, scrupulousness,
meticulousness.
particularize v. **specify**, detail, itemize,
list, enumerate, spell out, cite, stipulate,
instance.

particularly adv. **1** *the acoustics are particularly good* **especially**, specially, very, extremely, exceptionally, singularly, peculiarly, unusually, extraordinarily, remarkably, outstandingly, amazingly, incredibly, really; informal seriously, majorly, awfully, terribly; Brit. informal jolly, dead, well; informal dated devilish, frightfully. **2** *he particularly asked that I should help you* **specifically**, explicitly, expressly, in particular, especially, specially.

parting n. **1** *an emotional parting* **farewell**, leave-taking, goodbye, adieu, departure; valediction. **2** *they kept their parting quiet* **separation**, break-up, split, divorce, rift, estrangement; Brit. informal bust-up. **3** *the parting of the Red Sea* **division**, dividing, separation, separating, splitting, breaking up/apart, partition, partitioning.
▶ adj. *a parting kiss* **farewell**, goodbye, last, final, valedictory.

partisan n. **1** *Conservative partisans* **supporter**, follower, adherent, devotee, champion; fanatic, fan, enthusiast, stalwart, zealot; N. Amer. booster. **2** *the partisans opened fire from the woods* **guerrilla**, freedom fighter, resistance fighter, underground fighter, irregular (soldier).
▶ adj. *partisan attitudes* **biased**, prejudiced, one-sided, discriminatory, coloured, partial, interested, sectarian, factional.
– OPPOSITES unbiased.

partisanship n. **bias**, prejudice, one-sidedness, discrimination, favour, favouritism, partiality, sectarianism, factionalism.

partition n. **1** *the partition of Palestine* **dividing up**, partitioning, separation, division, dividing, subdivision, splitting (up), breaking up, break-up. **2** *room partitions* **screen**, (room) divider, (dividing) wall, barrier, panel, separator.
▶ v. **1** *the resolution partitioned Poland* **divide (up)**, subdivide, separate, split (up), break up; share (out), parcel out. **2** *the huge hall was partitioned* **subdivide**, divide (up); separate (off), section off, screen off.

partly adv. **to a certain extent/degree**, to some extent/degree, in part, partially, a little, somewhat, not totally, not entirely, relatively, moderately, (up) to a point, in some measure, slightly.
– OPPOSITES completely.

partner n. **1** *business partners* **colleague**, associate, co-worker, fellow worker, collaborator, comrade, teammate; Brit. informal oppo; Austral./NZ informal offsider; old use compeer. **2** *his partner in crime* **accomplice**, confederate, accessory, collaborator, fellow conspirator, helper; informal sidekick. **3** *your relationship with your partner* **spouse**, husband, wife, consort; lover, girlfriend, boyfriend, fiancé, fiancée, significant other, live-in lover, common-law husband/wife, man, woman, mate; informal hubby, missus, old man, old lady/woman, better half, intended, POSSLQ; Brit. informal other half.

partnership n. **1** *close partnership* **cooperation**, association, collaboration, coalition, alliance, union, affiliation, relationship, connection. **2** *thriving partnerships* **company**, firm, business, corporation, organization, association, consortium, syndicate.

party n. **1** *150 people attended the party* **(social) gathering**, (social) function, get-together, celebration, reunion, festivity, jamboree, reception, at-home, soirée, social; dance, ball, ceilidh, frolic, carousal, carouse; N. Amer. fete, hoedown, shower, bake, cookout, levee; Austral. corroboree; informal bash, shindig, rave, disco, do, shebang, bop, hop; Brit. informal rave-up, knees-up, beanfeast, beano, bunfight; N. Amer. informal blast, wingding, kegger; Austral./NZ informal shivoo, rage, ding, jollo, rort. **2** *a party of British tourists* **group**, company, body, gang, band, crowd, pack, contingent; informal bunch, crew, load. **3** *the left-wing parties* **faction**, political party, group, grouping, cabal, junta, bloc, camp, caucus. **4** *don't mention a certain party* **person**, individual, somebody, someone.
▶ v. informal *let's party!* **celebrate**, have fun, enjoy oneself, have a party, have a good time, rave it up, carouse, make merry; informal go out on the town, paint the town red, whoop it up, let one's hair down, make whoopee, live it up, have a ball.
□ **be a party to** get involved in/with, be associated with, be a participant in.

parvenu n. **upstart**, social climber, arriviste.

pass[1] v. **1** *the traffic passing through the village* **go**, proceed, move, progress, make one's way, travel. **2** *a car passed him* **overtake**, go past/by, pull ahead of, overhaul, leave behind. **3** *time passed* **elapse**, go by/past, advance, wear on, roll by, tick by. **4** *he passed the time writing letters* **occupy**, spend, fill, use (up), employ, while away. **5** *pass me the salt* **hand (over)**, let someone have, give, reach. **6** *he passed the ball back* **kick**, hit, throw, lob. **7** *her estate passed to her grandson* **be transferred**, go, be left, be bequeathed, be handed down/on, be passed on; Law devolve. **8** *his death passed almost unnoticed* **happen**, occur, take place, come about, transpire; literary befall. **9** *the storm passed* **come to an end**, fade (away), blow over, run its course, die out, finish, end, cease. **10** *God's peace passes all human understanding* **surpass**, exceed, transcend. **11** *he passed the exam* **be successful in**, succeed in, gain a pass in, get through; informal sail through, scrape through. **12** *the Senate passed the bill* **approve**, vote for, accept, ratify, adopt, agree to, authorize, endorse, legalize, enact; informal OK. **13** *she could not let that comment pass* **go (unnoticed)**, stand, go unremarked, go undisputed. **14** *we should not pass judgement* **declare**, pronounce, utter, express, deliver, issue. **15** *passing urine* **discharge**, excrete, evacuate, expel, emit, release.
– OPPOSITES stop, fail, reject.
▶ n. **1** *you must show your pass* **permit**,

warrant, authorization, licence. **2** *a cross-field pass* **kick**, hit, throw, shot.

▫ **come to pass** literary happen, come about, occur, transpire, arise; literary befall.

make a pass at make (sexual) advances to, proposition; informal come on to, make a play for; N. Amer. informal hit on, make time with, put the make on.

pass away/on See **die** (sense 1).

pass as/for be mistaken for, be taken for, be accepted as.

pass off 1 *the rally passed off peacefully* **take place**, go off, happen, occur, be completed, turn out. **2** *when the dizziness passed off he sat up* **wear off**, fade (away), pass, die down.

pass someone off misrepresent, falsely represent; disguise.

pass out faint, lose consciousness, black out.

pass something over disregard, overlook, ignore, pay no attention to, let pass, gloss over, take no notice of, pay no heed to, turn a blind eye to.

pass something up turn down, reject, refuse, decline, give up, forgo, let pass, miss (out on); informal give something a miss.

pass² n. *a pass through the mountains* **route**, way, road, passage, cut, gap; N. Amer. notch.

passable adj. **1** *the beer was passable* **adequate**, all right, fairly good, acceptable, satisfactory, moderately good, not (too) bad, average, tolerable, fair; mediocre, middling, ordinary, indifferent, unremarkable, unexceptional; informal OK, so-so, nothing to write home about, no great shakes, not up to much; NZ informal half-pie. **2** *the road is still passable* **navigable**, traversable, negotiable, unblocked, unobstructed, open, clear.

passably adv. **quite**, rather, somewhat, fairly, reasonably, moderately, comparatively, relatively, tolerably; informal pretty.

passage n. **1** *their passage through the country* **transit**, progress, passing, movement, motion, travelling. **2** *the passage of time* **passing**, advance, course, march. **3** *a passage from the embassy* **safe conduct**, warrant, visa; admission, access. **4** *the overnight passage* **voyage**, crossing, trip, journey. **5** *clearing a passage to the front door* **way (through)**, route, path. **6** *a passage to the kitchen*. See **passageway** (sense 1). **7** *a passage between the buildings*. **passageway** (sense 2). **8** *the nasal passages* **duct**, orifice, opening, channel; inlet, outlet. **9** *the passage to democracy* **transition**, development, progress, move, change, shift. **10** *the passage of the bill* **enactment**, passing, ratification, approval, adoption, authorization, legalization. **11** *a passage from 'Macbeth'* **extract**, excerpt, quotation, quote, citation, reading, piece, selection.

passageway n. **1** *secret passageways* **corridor**, hall, passage, hallway, walkway, aisle. **2** *a narrow passageway off the main street* **alley**, alleyway, passage, lane, path, pathway, footpath, track, thoroughfare; N. Amer. areaway.

passé adj. See **old-fashioned**.

passenger n. **1** *rail passengers* **traveller**, commuter, fare payer. **2** *we can't afford passengers* **hanger-on**, idler, parasite; informal freeloader.

passing adj. **1** *of passing interest* **fleeting**, transient, transitory, ephemeral, brief, short-lived, temporary, momentary; literary evanescent. **2** *a passing glance* **hasty**, rapid, hurried, brief, quick; cursory, superficial, casual, perfunctory.

▸ n. **1** *the passing of time* **passage**, course, progress, advance. **2** *Jack's passing* **death**, demise, passing away/on, end, loss, quietus; formal decease. **3** *the passing of the new bill* **enactment**, ratification, approval, adoption, authorization, legalization, endorsement.

▫ **in passing** incidentally, by the by/way, en passant.

passion n. **1** *the passion of activists* **fervour**, ardour, enthusiasm, eagerness, zeal, zealousness, vigour, fire, fieriness, energy, fervency, animation, spirit, spiritedness, fanaticism. **2** *he worked himself up into a passion* **(blind) rage**, fit of anger/temper, temper, towering rage, tantrum, fury, frenzy; Brit. informal paddy. **3** *hot with passion* **love**, (sexual) desire, lust, ardour, infatuation, lasciviousness, lustfulness. **4** *his passion for football* **enthusiasm**, love, mania, fascination, obsession, fanaticism, fixation, compulsion, appetite, addiction; informal thing. **5** *English literature is a passion with me* **obsession**, preoccupation, craze, mania, hobby horse. **6** *the Passion of Christ* **crucifixion**, suffering, agony, martyrdom.

– OPPOSITES apathy.

passionate adj. **1** *a passionate entreaty* **intense**, impassioned, ardent, fervent, vehement, fiery, heated, emotional, heartfelt, eager, excited, animated, spirited, energetic, fervid, frenzied, wild, consuming, violent; literary perfervid. **2** *McGregor is passionate about sport* **very keen**, very enthusiastic, addicted; informal mad, crazy, hooked, nuts; N. Amer. informal nutso; Austral./NZ informal shook. **3** *a passionate kiss* **amorous**, ardent, hot-blooded, aroused, loving, sexy, sensual, erotic, lustful; informal steamy, hot, turned on. **4** *a passionate woman* **excitable**, emotional, fiery, volatile, mercurial, quick-tempered, highly strung, impulsive, temperamental.

– OPPOSITES apathetic.

passionless adj. **unemotional**, cold, cold-blooded, emotionless, frigid, cool, unfeeling, unloving, unresponsive, undemonstrative, impassive.

passive adj. **1** *a passive role* **inactive**, non-active, non-participative, uninvolved. **2** *passive victims* **submissive**, acquiescent, unresisting, unassertive, compliant, pliant, obedient, docile, tractable, malleable, pliable. **3** *the woman's face was passive* **emotionless**, impassive, unemotional, unmoved, dispassionate, passionless, detached, unresponsive, undemonstrative,

apathetic, phlegmatic.
– OPPOSITES active.

passport n. **1 travel permit**, (travel) papers, visa, laissez-passer. **2** *qualifications are the passport to success* **key**, path, way, route, avenue, door, doorway.

past adj. **1** *memories of times past* **gone (by)**, over (and done with), no more, done, bygone, former, (of) old, olden, long-ago; literary of yore. **2** *the past few months* **last**, recent, preceding. **3** *a past chairman* **previous**, former, foregoing, erstwhile, as was, one-time, sometime, ex-; formal quondam.
– OPPOSITES present, future.
▶ n. *details about her past* **history**, background, life (story).
▶ prep. **1** *she walked past the cafe* **in front of**, by. **2** *he's past retirement age* **beyond**, in excess of.
▶ adv. *they hurried past* **along**, by, on.
  ◻ **in the past** formerly, previously, in days/years/times gone by, in former times, in the (good) old days, in days of old, in olden times, once (upon a time); literary in days of yore, in yesteryear.

paste n. **1** *blend the ingredients to a paste* **purée**, pulp, mush, blend. **2** *wallpaper paste* **adhesive**, glue, gum, fixative; N. Amer. mucilage. **3** *fish paste* **spread**, pâté.
▶ v. *a notice was pasted on the door* **glue**, stick, gum, fix, affix.

pastel adj. **pale**, soft, light, light-coloured, muted, subtle, subdued, soft-hued.
– OPPOSITES dark, bright.

pastiche n. **1** *a pastiche of literary models* **mixture**, blend, medley, melange, miscellany, mixed bag, potpourri, mix, compound, composite, collection, assortment, conglomeration, hotchpotch, jumble, ragbag; N. Amer. hodgepodge. **2** *a pastiche of 18th-century style* **imitation**, parody; informal take-off.

pastille n. **lozenge**, sweet, drop; tablet, pill.

pastime n. **hobby**, leisure activity/pursuit, sport, game, recreation, amusement, diversion, entertainment, interest, sideline.

past master n. **expert**, master, wizard, genius, old hand, veteran, maestro, connoisseur, authority, grandmaster; informal ace, pro, star, hotshot; Brit. informal dab hand; N. Amer. informal maven, crackerjack.

pastor n. **priest**, minister (of religion), parson, clergyman, cleric, chaplain, padre, ecclesiastic, man of the cloth, churchman, vicar, rector, curate, preacher; informal reverend; Austral. informal josser.

pastoral adj. **1** *a pastoral scene* **rural**, country, countryside, rustic, agricultural, bucolic; literary sylvan, Arcadian. **2** *his pastoral duties* **priestly**, clerical, ecclesiastical, ministerial.
– OPPOSITES urban.

pastry n. **1** *pastries for tea* **tart**, tartlet, pie, pasty, patty. **2** *two layers of pastry* **crust**, piecrust, croute.

pasture n. **grazing (land)**, grassland, grass, pastureland, pasturage, ley; meadow, field; Austral./NZ run; literary lea, mead, greensward.

pasty adj. **pale**, pallid, wan, colourless, anaemic, ashen, white, grey, pasty-faced, washed out, sallow.

pat[1] v. *Brian patted her on the shoulder* **tap**, slap lightly, clap, touch.
▶ n. **1** *a pat on the cheek* **tap**, light blow, clap, touch. **2** *a pat of butter* **piece**, dab, lump, portion, knob, mass, gobbet, ball, curl.
  ◻ **pat someone on the back** congratulate, praise, take one's hat off to; commend, compliment, applaud, acclaim.

pat[2] adj. *pat answers* **glib**, simplistic, facile, unconvincing.
▶ adv. *his reply came rather pat* **opportunely**, conveniently, at just/exactly the right moment, expediently, favourably, appropriately, fittingly, auspiciously, providentially, felicitously, propitiously.
  ◻ **off pat** word-perfect, by heart, by rote, by memory, parrot-fashion.
get something off pat memorize, commit to memory, remember, learn by heart, learn (by rote).

patch n. **1** *a patch over one eye* **cover**, eyepatch, covering, pad. **2** *a reddish patch on her wrist* **blotch**, mark, pop, spot, smudge, speckle, smear, stain, streak, blemish; informal splodge, splotch. **3** *a patch of ground* **plot**, area, piece, strip, tract, parcel; bed; Brit. allotment; N. Amer. lot. **4** Brit. informal *they are going through a difficult patch* **period**, time, spell, phase, stretch; Brit. informal spot.
▶ v. *her jeans were neatly patched* **mend**, repair, sew (up), stitch (up).
  ◻ **patch something up** informal **1** *the houses were being patched up* **repair**, mend, fix hastily. **2** *he's trying to patch things up with his wife* **reconcile**, make up, settle, remedy, put to rights, rectify, clear up, set right, make good, resolve, square.

patchwork n. **assortment**, miscellany, mixture, melange, medley, blend, mixed bag, mix, collection, selection, assemblage, combination, potpourri, jumble, mishmash, ragbag, hotchpotch; N. Amer. hodgepodge.

patchy adj. **1** *their teaching has been patchy* **uneven**, bitty, varying, variable, intermittent, fitful, sporadic, erratic, irregular. **2** *patchy evidence* **fragmentary**, inadequate, insufficient, rudimentary, limited, sketchy.
– OPPOSITES uniform, comprehensive.

patent n. *there is a patent on the chemical* **copyright**, licence, legal protection, registered trademark.
▶ adj. **1** *patent nonsense* **obvious**, clear, plain, evident, manifest, self-evident, transparent, overt, conspicuous, blatant, downright, barefaced, flagrant, undisguised, unconcealed, unmistakable. **2** *patent medicines* **proprietary**, patented, licensed, branded.

paternal adj. **1** *his face showed paternal concern* **fatherly**, fatherlike, patriarchal;

p

protective, solicitous, compassionate, sympathetic. **2** *his paternal grandfather* **on one's father's side**, patrilineal.
– OPPOSITES maternal.

paternity n. **fatherhood**; rare fathership.

path n. **1** *a path down to the beach* **footpath**, pathway, footway, pavement, track, trail, trackway, bridleway, bridle path, lane, alley, alleyway, passage, passageway; cycle path/track; N. Amer. sidewalk, bikeway. **2** *journalists blocked his path* **route**, way, course; direction, bearing, line; orbit, trajectory. **3** *the best path towards a settlement* **course of action**, route, road, avenue, line, approach, tack, strategy, tactic.

pathetic adj. **1** *a pathetic groan* **pitiful**, pitiable, piteous, moving, touching, poignant, plaintive, distressing, upsetting, heartbreaking, heart-rending, harrowing, wretched, forlorn. **2** informal *a pathetic excuse* **feeble**, woeful, sorry, poor, pitiful, lamentable, deplorable, contemptible, inadequate, paltry, insufficient, insubstantial, unsatisfactory.

pathfinder n. **pioneer**, groundbreaker, trailblazer, trendsetter, leader, torch-bearer, pacemaker; formal neoteric.

pathological adj. **1** *a pathological condition* **morbid**, diseased. **2** informal *a pathological liar* **compulsive**, obsessive, inveterate, habitual, persistent, chronic, hardened, confirmed.

pathos n. **poignancy**, tragedy, sadness, pitifulness, piteousness, pitiableness.

patience n. **1** *she tried everyone's patience* **forbearance**, tolerance, restraint, self-restraint, stoicism; calmness, composure, equanimity, serenity, tranquillity, imperturbability, understanding, indulgence. **2** *a task requiring patience* **perseverance**, persistence, endurance, tenacity, assiduity, application, staying power, doggedness, determination, resolve, resolution, resoluteness; formal pertinacity.

patient adj. **1** *I must ask you to be patient* **forbearing**, uncomplaining, tolerant, resigned, stoical; calm, composed, even-tempered, imperturbable, unexcitable, accommodating, understanding, indulgent; informal unflappable, cool. **2** *a good deal of patient work* **persevering**, persistent, tenacious, indefatigable, dogged, determined, resolved, resolute, single-minded; formal pertinacious.
▸ n. *a doctor's patient* **sick person**, case; invalid, convalescent, outpatient, inpatient.

patio n. **terrace**; courtyard, quadrangle, quad; N. Amer. sun deck.

patois n. **vernacular**, (local) dialect, regional language; jargon, argot, cant; informal (local) lingo.

patriarch n. **senior figure**, father, paterfamilias, leader, elder.

patrician n. *the great patricians* **aristocrat**, grandee, noble, nobleman, noblewoman, lord, lady, peer, peeress.
▸ adj. *patrician families* **aristocratic**, noble,

titled, blue-blooded, high-born, upper-class, landowning; informal upper-crust; old use gentle.

patrimony n. **heritage**, inheritance, birthright; legacy, bequest, endowment, bequeathal; Law, dated hereditament.

patriot n. **nationalist**, loyalist; chauvinist, jingoist, flag-waver.

patriotic adj. **nationalist**, nationalistic, loyalist, loyal; chauvinistic, jingoistic, flag-waving.
– OPPOSITES traitorous.

patriotism n. **nationalism**, patriotic sentiment, allegiance/loyalty to one's country; chauvinism, jingoism, flag-waving.

patrol n. **1** *anti-poaching patrols* **vigil**, guard, watch, monitoring, policing, beat-pounding, patrolling; reconnoitre, surveillance; informal recce. **2** *the patrol stopped a suspect* **patrolman, patrolwoman**, sentinel, sentry; scout, scouting party, task force.
▸ v. *a security guard was patrolling a housing estate* **keep guard (on)**, guard, keep watch (on); police, pound the beat (of), make the rounds (of); stand guard (over), keep a vigil (on), defend, safeguard.

patron n. **1** *a patron of the arts* **sponsor**, backer, financier, benefactor, benefactress, contributor, subscriber, donor; philanthropist, promoter, friend, supporter; informal angel. **2** *club patrons* **customer**, client, frequenter, consumer, user, visitor, guest; informal regular.

patronage n. **1** *art patronage* **sponsorship**, backing, funding, financing, promotion, assistance, support. **2** *political patronage* **power of appointment**, favouritism, nepotism, preferential treatment. **3** *a slight note of patronage* **condescension**, patronizing, patronization, disdain, disrespect, scorn, contempt. **4** *thank you for your patronage* **custom**, trade, business.

patronize v. **1** *don't patronize me!* **treat condescendingly**, condescend to, look down on, talk down to, put down, treat like a child, treat with disdain. **2** *they patronized local tradesmen* **do business with**, buy from, shop at, be a customer of, be a client of, deal with, trade with, frequent, support. **3** *he patronized a national museum* **sponsor**, back, fund, finance, be a patron of, support, champion.

patronizing adj. **condescending**, disdainful, supercilious, superior, imperious, scornful, contemptuous; informal uppity, high and mighty.

patter[1] v. **1** *raindrops pattered against the window* **go pitter-patter**, tap, drum, beat, pound, rat-a-tat, go pit-a-pat, thrum. **2** *she pattered across the floor* **scurry**, scuttle, skip, trip.
▸ n. *the patter of rain* **pitter-patter**, tapping, pattering, drumming, beat, beating, pounding, rat-a-tat, pit-a-pat, clack, thrum, thrumming.

patter[2] n. **1** *this witty patter* **prattle**, prating, blather, blither, drivel, chatter, jabber, babble; informal yabbering, yatter; old use

twaddle. **2** *the salesmen's patter* (**sales**)
pitch, sales talk; informal line. **3** *the local
patter* **speech**, language, parlance, dialect;
informal lingo.
▸ v. *she pattered on incessantly* **prattle**, prate,
blather, blither, drivel, chatter, jabber,
babble; informal yabber, yatter; Brit. informal
rabbit, witter.

pattern n. **1** *the pattern on the wallpaper*
design, decoration, motif, marking,
ornament, ornamentation. **2** *a change
in working patterns* **system**, order,
arrangement, form, method, structure,
scheme, plan, format, framework. **3** *this
would set the pattern for a generation*
model, example, criterion, standard,
basis, point of reference, gauge, norm,
yardstick, touchstone, benchmark; blueprint,
archetype, prototype. **4** *textile patterns*
sample, specimen, swatch.
▸ v. *someone else is patterning my life* **shape**,
influence, model, fashion, mould, style,
determine, control.

patterned adj. **decorated**, ornamented,
fancy, adorned, embellished.
– OPPOSITES plain.

paucity n. **scarcity**, sparseness, sparsity,
dearth, shortage, poverty, insufficiency,
deficiency, lack, want; formal exiguity.
– OPPOSITES abundance.

paunch n. **pot belly**, beer belly; informal beer
gut, pot; dated corporation.

pauper n. **poor person**, indigent, down-and-
out; informal have-not.

pause n. *a pause in the conversation* **stop**,
cessation, break, halt, interruption,
check, lull, respite, breathing space,
discontinuation, hiatus, gap, interlude;
adjournment, suspension, rest, wait,
hesitation; informal let-up, breather.
▸ v. *Hannah paused for a moment* **stop**, cease,
halt, discontinue, break off, take a break;
adjourn, rest, wait, hesitate, falter, waver;
informal take a breather.

pave v. *the yard was paved* **tile**, surface, flag.
□ **pave the way for** prepare (the way) for,
make preparations for, get ready for, lay the
foundations for, herald, precede.

pavement n. **footpath**, walkway, footway;
N. Amer. sidewalk.

paw n. **foot**, forepaw, hind paw.
▸ v. **1** *their offspring were pawing each
other* **handle roughly**, pull, grab, maul,
manhandle. **2** *some Casanova tried to paw
her* **fondle**, feel, maul, molest; informal grope,
feel up, touch up, goose.

pawn[1] v. *he pawned his watch* **pledge**, give as
security; informal hock, put in hock.

pawn[2] n. *a pawn in the battle for the throne*
puppet, dupe, hostage, tool, cat's paw,
instrument.

pay v. **1** *I must pay him for his work* **reward**,
reimburse, recompense, give payment to,
remunerate. **2** *you must pay a few pounds
more* **spend**, expend, pay out, dish out,
disburse; informal lay out, shell out, fork out,

cough up; N. Amer. informal ante up, pony up.
3 *he paid his debts* **discharge**, settle, pay
off, clear, liquidate. **4** *hard work will pay
dividends* **yield**, return, produce. **5** *he made
the buses pay* **be profitable**, make money,
make a profit. **6** *it may pay you to be early* **be
advantageous to**, benefit, be of advantage
to, be beneficial to. **7** *paying compliments*
bestow, grant, give, offer. **8** *he will pay for
his mistakes* **suffer (the consequences)**, be
punished, atone, pay the penalty/price.
▸ n. *equal pay for women* **salary**, wages,
payment; earnings, remuneration,
reimbursement, income, revenue; formal
emolument(s).
□ **pay someone back/out** get one's revenge
on, be revenged on, avenge oneself on, get
back at, get even with, settle accounts with,
pay someone out, exact retribution on.
pay something back repay, pay off, give
back, return, reimburse, refund.
pay for defray the cost of, settle up for,
finance, fund; treat someone to; informal foot
the bill for, shell out for, fork out for, cough
up for; N. Amer. informal ante up for, pony up for.
pay something off pay (in full), settle,
discharge, clear, liquidate.
pay off informal meet with success, be
successful, be effective, get results.
pay something out spend, expend, pay,
dish out, put up, part with, hand over; informal
shell out, fork out/up, lay out, cough up.
pay up make payment, settle up, pay (in
full); informal cough up.

payable adj. **due**, owed, owing, outstanding,
unpaid, overdue, in arrears; N. Amer.
delinquent.

payment n. **1** *discounts for early payment*
remittance, settlement, discharge,
clearance, liquidation. **2** *monthly payments*
instalment, premium. **3** *extra payment
for good performance* **salary**, wages,
pay, earnings, fee(s), remuneration,
reimbursement, income; honorarium; formal
emolument(s).

pay-off n. informal **1** *the lure of enormous
pay-offs* **payment**, payout, reward; bribe,
inducement, 'incentive'; N. Amer. payola;
informal kickback, sweetener, backhander;
Austral. informal sling. **2** *a pay-off of £160,000*
return (on investment), yield, payback,
profit, gain, dividend. **3** *a dramatic pay-off*
outcome, denouement, culmination,
conclusion, development, result.

peace n. **1** *can't a man get any peace around
here?* **tranquillity**, calm, restfulness, peace
and quiet, peacefulness, quiet, quietness;
privacy, solitude. **2** *peace of mind* **serenity**,
peacefulness, tranquillity, equanimity, calm,
calmness, composure, ease, contentment,
contentedness. **3** *we pray for peace* **law
and order**, lawfulness, order, peacefulness,
peaceableness, harmony, non-violence; formal
concord. **4** *a lasting peace* **treaty**, truce,
ceasefire, armistice, cessation/suspension of
hostilities.
– OPPOSITES noise, war.

p

peaceable adj. **1** *a peaceable man* **peace-loving**, non-violent, non-aggressive, easy-going, placid, gentle, inoffensive, good-natured, even-tempered, amiable, amicable, friendly, affable, genial, pacific, dovelike, dovish, anti-war; formal irenic. **2** *a peaceable society* **peaceful**, strife-free, harmonious; law-abiding, disciplined, orderly, civilized.
– OPPOSITES aggressive.

peaceful adj. **1** *everything was quiet and peaceful* **tranquil**, calm, restful, quiet, still, relaxing, soothing, undisturbed, untroubled, private, secluded. **2** *his peaceful mood* **serene**, calm, tranquil, composed, placid, at ease, untroubled, unworried, content. **3** *peaceful relations* **harmonious**, at peace, peaceable, on good terms, amicable, friendly, cordial, non-violent.
– OPPOSITES noisy, agitated, hostile.

peacemaker n. **arbitrator**, arbiter, mediator, negotiator, conciliator, go-between, intermediary, pacifier, appeaser, peace-monger, pacifist, peace-lover, dove; informal peacenik.

peak n. **1** *the peaks of the mountains* **summit**, top, crest, pinnacle, apex, crown, cap. **2** *the highest peak* **mountain**, hill, height, mount, alp; Scottish ben, Munro. **3** *the peak of a cap* **brim**, visor. **4** *the peak of his career* **height**, high point/spot, pinnacle, summit, top, climax, culmination, apex, zenith, crowning point, acme, apogee, prime, heyday.
▶ v. *Labour support has peaked* **reach its height**, climax, reach a climax, come to a head.
▶ adj. *peak loads* **maximum**, top, greatest, highest; ultimate, best, optimum.

peaky adj. **pale**, pasty, wan, drained, washed out, drawn, pallid, anaemic, ashen, grey, pinched, sickly, sallow; ill, unwell, poorly, indisposed, run down; Brit. off (colour); informal under the weather, rough, lousy, seedy; Brit. informal grotty, ropy.

peal n. **1** *a peal of bells* **chime**, carillon, ring, ringing, tintinnabulation. **2** *peals of laughter* **shriek**, shout, scream, howl, gale, fit, roar, hoot. **3** *a peal of thunder* **rumble**, roar, boom, crash, clap, crack.
▶ v. **1** *the bell pealed* **ring (out)**, chime (out), clang, sound, ding, jingle. **2** *the thunder pealed* **rumble**, roar, boom, crash, resound.

peasant n. **1** *peasants working the land* **agricultural worker**, small farmer, rustic, swain, villein, serf. **2** informal *you peasants!* See **boor**.

peccadillo n. **misdemeanour**, petty offence, indiscretion, lapse, misdeed.

peck v. **1** *the cockerel pecked my heel* **bite**, nip, strike, hit, tap, rap, jab. **2** *he pecked her on the cheek* **kiss**, give someone a peck. **3** informal *the old lady pecked at her food* **nibble**, pick

at, take very small bites from, toy with, play with.

peculiar adj. **1** *something peculiar began to happen* **strange**, unusual, odd, funny, curious, bizarre, weird, queer, unexpected, unfamiliar, abnormal, atypical, anomalous, out of the ordinary; exceptional, extraordinary, remarkable; puzzling, mystifying, mysterious, perplexing, baffling; suspicious, eerie, unnatural; informal fishy, creepy, spooky. **2** *peculiar behaviour* **bizarre**, eccentric, strange, odd, weird, queer, funny, unusual, abnormal, idiosyncratic, unconventional, outlandish, quirky; informal wacky, freaky, oddball, offbeat, off the wall; N. Amer. informal wacko. **3** informal *I feel a bit peculiar*. See **unwell**. **4** *mannerisms peculiar to the islanders* **characteristic of**, typical of, representative of, indicative of, suggestive of, exclusive to. **5** *their own peculiar contribution* **distinctive**, characteristic, distinct, individual, special, unique, personal.
– OPPOSITES ordinary.

peculiarity n. **1** *a legal peculiarity* **oddity**, anomaly, abnormality. **2** *a physical peculiarity* **idiosyncrasy**, mannerism, quirk, foible. **3** *one of the peculiarities of the city* **characteristic**, feature, (essential) quality, property, trait, attribute, hallmark, trademark. **4** *the peculiarity of this notion* **strangeness**, oddness, bizarreness, weirdness, queerness, unexpectedness, unfamiliarity, anomalousness, incongruity. **5** *there is a certain peculiarity about her appearance* **outlandishness**, bizarreness, unconventionality, idiosyncrasy, weirdness, oddness, eccentricity, unusualness, abnormality, queerness, strangeness, quirkiness; informal wackiness, freakiness.

pecuniary adj. **financial**, monetary, money, fiscal, economic.

pedagogic adj. **educational**, educative, pedagogical, teaching, instructional, instructive, didactic; academic, scholastic.

pedagogue formal n. **teacher**, schoolteacher, schoolmaster, schoolmistress, master, mistress, tutor; lecturer, academic, don, professor, instructor, educator, educationalist, educationist; Austral./NZ informal chalkie.

pedant n. **dogmatist**, purist, literalist, formalist, doctrinaire, perfectionist; quibbler, hair-splitter, casuist, sophist; informal nitpicker.

pedantic adj. **overscrupulous**, scrupulous, precise, exact, perfectionist, punctilious, meticulous, fussy, fastidious, finical, finicky; dogmatic, purist, literalist, literalistic, formalist; casuistic, casuistical, sophistic, sophistical; captious, hair-splitting, quibbling; informal nitpicking, pernickety; old use overnice.

pedantry n. **dogmatism**, purism, literalism, formalism; overscrupulousness, scrupulousness, perfectionism, fastidiousness, punctiliousness, meticulousness; captiousness, quibbling, hair-splitting, casuistry, sophistry; informal nitpicking.

peddle v. **1** *they are peddling water filters* **sell (from door to door)**, hawk, tout, vend; trade (in), deal in, traffic in. **2** *peddling unorthodox views* **advocate**, champion, preach, put forward, proclaim, propound, promote.

pedestal n. *a bust on a pedestal* **plinth**, base, support, mounting, stand, foundation, pillar, column, pier; Architecture socle.

□ **put someone on a pedestal** idealize, lionize, look up to, respect, hold in high regard, think highly of, admire, esteem, revere, worship.

pedestrian n. *accidents involving pedestrians* **walker**, person on foot.
– OPPOSITES driver.

▸ adj. *pedestrian lives* **dull**, boring, tedious, monotonous, uneventful, unremarkable, tiresome, wearisome, uninspired, unimaginative, unexciting, uninteresting; unvarying, unvaried, repetitive, routine, commonplace, workaday, ordinary, everyday, run-of-the-mill, mundane, humdrum; informal bog-standard, (plain) vanilla; Brit. informal common or garden.
– OPPOSITES exciting.

pedigree n. *a long pedigree* **ancestry**, descent, lineage, line (of descent), genealogy, family tree, extraction, derivation, origin(s), heritage, parentage, bloodline, background, roots.

▸ adj. *a pedigree cat* **pure-bred**, thoroughbred, pure-blooded.

pedlar n. **1** *pedlars of watches* **travelling salesman**, door-to-door salesman, huckster; street trader, hawker; Brit. informal fly-pitcher; old use chapman, packman. **2** *a drug pedlar* **trafficker**, dealer; informal pusher.

peek v. **1** *they peeked from behind the curtains* **(have a) peep**, have a peek, spy, take a sly/ stealthy look, sneak a look; informal take a gander, have a squint; Brit. informal have a dekko, have/take a butcher's, take a shufti. **2** *the deer's antlers peeked out from the trees* **appear (slowly/partly)**, show, come into view/sight, become visible, emerge, peep (out).

▸ n. *a peek at the map* **secret look**, sly look, stealthy look, sneaky look, peep, glance, glimpse, hurried/quick look; informal gander, squint; Brit. informal dekko, butcher's, shufti.

peel v. **1** *peel and core the fruit* **pare**, skin, take the skin/rind off; hull, shell, husk, shuck; technical decorticate. **2** *use a long knife to peel the veneer* **trim (off)**, peel off, pare, strip (off), shave (off), remove. **3** *the wallpaper was peeling* **flake (off)**, peel off, come off in layers/strips.

▸ n. *orange peel* **rind**, skin, covering, zest; hull, pod, integument, shuck.

□ **keep one's eyes peeled** keep a (sharp) lookout, look out, keep one's eyes open, keep watch, be watchful, be alert, be on the alert, be on the qui vive, be on guard; Brit. keep one's eyes skinned.

peel something off Brit. informal take off, strip off, remove.

peep[1] v. **1** *I peeped through the keyhole* **look quickly**, take a quick look, sneak a look, (have a) peek, glance; informal take a gander, have a squint; Brit. informal have a dekko, have/take a butcher's, take a shufti. **2** *the moon peeped through the clouds* **appear (slowly/partly)**, show, come into view/sight, become visible, emerge, peek, peer out.

▸ n. *I'll just take a peep at it* **quick look**, brief look, sneaky look, peek, glance; informal gander, squint; Brit. informal dekko, butcher's, shufti.

peep[2] n. **1** *I heard a quiet peep* **cheep**, chirp, chirrup, tweet, twitter, chirr, warble. **2** *there's been not a peep out of the children* **sound**, noise, cry, word. **3** *the painting was sold without a peep* **complaint**, grumble, mutter, murmur, grouse, objection, protest, protestation; informal moan, gripe, grouch.

▸ v. *the phone peeped* **cheep**, chirp, chirrup, tweet, twitter, chirr.

peephole n. **opening**, gap, cleft, spyhole, slit, crack, chink, keyhole, squint, judas (hole).

peer[1] v. *he peered at the manuscript* **look closely**, try to see, narrow one's eyes, screw up one's eyes, squint.

peer[2] n. **1** *hereditary peers* **aristocrat**, lord, lady, peer of the realm, peeress, noble, nobleman, noblewoman, titled man/woman, patrician. **2** *his academic peers* **equal**, coequal, fellow, confrère; contemporary; formal compeer.

peerage n. **aristocracy**, nobility, peers and peeresses, lords and ladies, patriciate; the House of Lords, the Lords.

peerless adj. **incomparable**, matchless, unrivalled, inimitable, beyond compare/comparison, unparalleled, unequalled, without equal, second to none, unsurpassed, unsurpassable, nonpareil; unique, consummate, perfect, rare, transcendent, surpassing; formal unexampled.

peeve v. informal **irritate**, annoy, vex, anger, exasperate, irk, gall, pique, nettle, put out, get on someone's nerves, try someone's patience, ruffle someone's feathers; Brit. rub up the wrong way; informal aggravate, rile, needle, get to, bug, hack off, get someone's goat, get/put someone's back up, get up someone's nose, give someone the hump; Brit. informal wind up, get on someone's wick; N. Amer. informal tee off, tick off.

peeved adj. informal **irritated**, annoyed, cross, angry, vexed, displeased, disgruntled, indignant, exasperated, galled, irked, put out, aggrieved, offended, affronted, piqued, nettled, in high dudgeon; informal aggravated, miffed, riled, hacked off, browned off; Brit. informal narked, cheesed off, brassed off, not best pleased; N. Amer. informal teed off, ticked off, sore.

peevish adj. **irritable**, fractious, fretful, cross, petulant, querulous, pettish, crabby,

p

crotchety, cantankerous, curmudgeonly, sullen, grumpy, bad-tempered, short-tempered, testy, touchy, tetchy, snappish, irascible, waspish, prickly, crusty, dyspeptic, splenetic, choleric; N. English mardy; Brit. informal ratty, like a bear with a sore head; N. Amer. informal cranky, ornery.
– OPPOSITES good-humoured.

peg n. **pin**, nail, dowel, skewer, spike, rivet, brad, screw, bolt, hook, spigot; Mountaineering piton; Golf tee.
▶ v. **1** *the flysheet is pegged to the ground* **fix**, pin, attach, fasten, secure, make fast. **2** *we decided to peg our prices* **hold down**, keep down, fix, set, hold, freeze.
□ **peg away** informal work hard, slog away, plod away, hammer away, grind away, slave away, exert oneself; persevere, persist, keep at it; informal beaver away, plug away, stick at it, soldier on; Brit. informal graft away.
take someone down a peg or two humble, humiliate, mortify, bring down, shame, embarrass, abash, put someone in their place, chasten, subdue, squash, deflate, make someone eat humble pie; informal show up, settle someone's hash, cut down to size; N. Amer. informal make someone eat crow.

pejorative adj. **disparaging**, derogatory, denigratory, deprecatory, defamatory, slanderous, libellous, abusive, insulting, slighting; informal bitchy.
– OPPOSITES complimentary.

pellet n. **1** *a pellet of mud* **little ball**, little piece. **2** *pellet wounds* **bullet**, shot, lead shot, buckshot. **3** *rabbit pellets* **excrement**, excreta, droppings, faeces, dung.

pell-mell adv. **1** *men streamed pell-mell from the building* **helter-skelter**, headlong, (at) full tilt, hotfoot, post-haste, hurriedly, hastily, recklessly, precipitately; old use hurry-scurry. **2** *the sacks' contents were thrown pell-mell to the ground* **untidily**, anyhow, in disarray, in a mess, in a muddle; informal all over the place, every which way, any old how; Brit. informal all over the shop; N. Amer. informal all over the map, all over the lot.

pellucid adj. **1** *the pellucid waters* **translucent**, transparent, clear, crystal clear, crystalline, glassy, limpid, unclouded. **2** *pellucid prose* **lucid**, limpid, clear, crystal clear, articulate; coherent, comprehensible, understandable, intelligible, straightforward, simple, well constructed; formal perspicuous.

pelt¹ v. **1** *they pelted him with snowballs* **bombard**, shower, attack, assail, pepper. **2** *rain was pelting down* **pour down**, teem down, stream down, tip down, rain cats and dogs, rain hard; Brit. informal bucket down, come down in stair rods. **3** informal *they pelted into the factory* **dash**, run, race, rush, sprint, bolt, dart, career, charge, shoot, hurtle, hare, fly, speed, zoom, streak; hasten, hurry; informal tear, belt, hotfoot it, scoot, leg it, go like a bat out of hell; Brit. informal bomb; N. Amer. informal hightail it.

pelt² n. *an animal's pelt* **skin**, hide, fleece, coat, fur; old use fell.

pen¹ n. *you'll need a pen and paper* fountain pen, ballpoint (pen), rollerball; fibre tip (pen), felt tip (pen), highlighter, marker pen; Brit. trademark biro.
▶ v. *he penned a number of articles* **write**, compose, draft, dash off; write down, jot down, set down, take down, scribble.

pen² n. *a sheep pen* **enclosure**, fold, sheepfold, pound, compound, stockade; sty, coop; N. Amer. corral.
▶ v. *the hostages had been penned up in a basement* **confine**, coop (up), cage, shut in, box up/in, lock up/in, trap, kettle, imprison, incarcerate, immure.

penal adj. **1** *a penal institution* **disciplinary**, punitive, corrective, correctional. **2** *penal rates of interest* **exorbitant**, extortionate, excessive, outrageous, preposterous, unreasonable, inflated, sky-high.

penalize v. **1** *if you break the rules you will be penalized* **punish**, discipline. **2** *people with certain medical conditions would be penalized* **handicap**, disadvantage, put at a disadvantage, cause to suffer.
– OPPOSITES reward.

penalty n. **1** *increased penalties for dumping oil at sea* **punishment**, sanction, punitive action, retribution; fine, forfeit, sentence; penance; formal mulct. **2** *the penalties of old age* **disadvantage**, difficulty, drawback, handicap, downside, minus; trial, tribulation, bane, affliction, burden, trouble.
– OPPOSITES reward.

penance n. **atonement**, expiation, self-punishment, self-mortification, self-abasement, amends; punishment, penalty.

penchant n. **liking**, fondness, preference, taste, relish, appetite, partiality, soft spot, love, passion, desire, fancy, whim, weakness, inclination, bent, bias, proclivity, predilection, predisposition.

pencil n. **1** *a sharpened pencil* **lead pencil**, propelling pencil. **2** *a pencil of light* **beam**, ray, shaft, finger, gleam.
▶ v. **1** *he pencilled his name inside the cover* **write**, write down, jot down, scribble, note, take down. **2** *pencil a line along the top of the moulding* **draw**, trace, sketch.

pendant n. **necklace**, locket, medallion.

pendent adj. **hanging**, suspended, dangling, pendulous, pensile, pendant, drooping, droopy, trailing.

pending adj. **1** *nine cases were still pending* **unresolved**, undecided, unsettled, awaiting decision/action, undetermined, open, hanging fire, (up) in the air, ongoing, outstanding, not done, unfinished, incomplete; informal on the back burner. **2** *with a general election pending* **imminent**, impending, about to happen, forthcoming, upcoming, on the way, coming, approaching, looming, gathering, near, nearing, close, close at hand, in the offing, to come.
▶ prep. *they were released on bail pending an appeal* **awaiting**, until, till, until there is/are.

pendulous adj. **drooping**, dangling, trailing, droopy, sagging, saggy, floppy; hanging, pendent, pensile.

penetrable adj. **1** *a penetrable subsoil* **permeable**, pervious, porous. **2** *books which are barely penetrable to anyone under 50* **understandable**, fathomable, comprehensible, intelligible.

penetrate v. **1** *the knife penetrated his lungs* **pierce**, puncture, make a hole in, perforate, stab, prick, gore, spike. **2** *they penetrated the enemy territory* **infiltrate**, slip into, sneak into, insinuate oneself into. **3** *fear penetrated her bones* **permeate**, pervade, fill, spread throughout, suffuse, seep through. **4** *he seemed to have penetrated the mysteries of nature* **understand**, comprehend, apprehend, fathom, grasp, perceive, discern, get to the bottom of, solve, resolve, make sense of, interpret, puzzle out, work out, unravel, decipher, make head or tail of; informal crack, get, figure out; Brit. informal suss out. **5** *his words finally penetrated* **register**, sink in, be understood, be comprehended, become clear, fall into place; informal click.

penetrating adj. **1** *a penetrating wind* **piercing**, cutting, biting, stinging, keen, sharp, harsh, raw, freezing, chill, wintry, cold. **2** *a penetrating voice* **shrill**, strident, piercing, carrying, loud, high, high-pitched, piping, ear-splitting, screechy, intrusive. **3** *a penetrating smell* **pungent**, pervasive, strong, powerful, sharp, acrid; heady, aromatic. **4** *her penetrating gaze* **observant**, searching, intent, alert, shrewd, perceptive, probing, piercing, sharp, keen. **5** *a penetrating analysis* **perceptive**, insightful, keen, sharp, sharp-witted, intelligent, clever, smart, incisive, piercing, razor-edged, trenchant, astute, shrewd, clear, acute, percipient, perspicacious, discerning, sensitive, thoughtful, deep, profound.
– OPPOSITES mild, soft.

penetration n. **1** *skin penetration by infective larvae* **perforation**, piercing, puncturing, puncture, stabbing, pricking. **2** *remarks of great penetration* **insight**, discernment, perception, perceptiveness, intelligence, sharp-wittedness, cleverness, incisiveness, keenness, sharpness, trenchancy, astuteness, shrewdness, acuteness, clarity, acuity, percipience, perspicacity, discrimination, sensitivity, thoughtfulness, profundity; formal perspicuity.

peninsula n. **cape**, promontory, point, head, headland, foreland, ness, horn, bill, bluff, mull.

penitence n. **repentance**, contrition, regret, remorse, ruefulness, sorrow, sorrowfulness, pangs of conscience, self-reproach, shame, guilt, compunction; old use rue.

penitent adj. **repentant**, contrite, remorseful, sorry, apologetic, regretful, conscience-stricken, rueful, ashamed, shamefaced, abject, in sackcloth and ashes.
– OPPOSITES unrepentant.

pen name n. **pseudonym**, nom de plume, assumed name, alias, professional name.

pennant n. **flag**, standard, ensign, colour(s), banner, banderole, guidon; Brit. pendant; Nautical burgee.

penniless adj. **destitute**, poverty-stricken, impoverished, poor, indigent, impecunious, in penury, moneyless, without a sou, necessitous, needy, on one's beam-ends; bankrupt, insolvent; Brit. on the breadline, without a penny (to one's name); informal (flat) broke, cleaned out, cash-strapped, on one's uppers, without a brass farthing, bust; Brit. informal stony broke, skint; N. Amer. informal stone broke; formal penurious.
– OPPOSITES wealthy.

penny n.
▢ **a pretty penny** informal a lot of money, millions, billions, a king's ransom; informal a (small) fortune, lots/pots/heaps of money, a mint, a killing, a bundle, a packet, a tidy sum, big money, telephone numbers, an arm and a leg; Brit. informal a bomb, loadsamoney; N. Amer. informal big bucks; Austral. informal big bickies, motser, motza.
two/ten a penny informal numerous, abundant, thick on the ground, plentiful; in large numbers, by the yard; very common, ubiquitous; N. Amer. informal a dime a dozen.

penny-pincher n. **miser**, Scrooge, niggard; informal skinflint, meanie, money-grubber, cheapskate; N. Amer. informal tightwad.
– OPPOSITES spendthrift.

penny-pinching adj. **mean**, miserly, niggardly, parsimonious, close-fisted, cheese-paring, grasping, Scrooge-like; informal stingy, mingy, tight, tight-fisted, money-grubbing; formal penurious; old use near.
– OPPOSITES generous.

pension n. **old-age pension**, retirement pension, regular payment, superannuation; allowance, benefit, support, welfare.

pensioner n. **retired person**, old-age pensioner, OAP, senior citizen; N. Amer. senior, retiree.

pensive adj. **thoughtful**, reflective, contemplative, musing, meditative, introspective, ruminative, absorbed, preoccupied, deep/lost in thought, in a brown study, brooding; formal cogitative.

pent-up adj. **repressed**, suppressed, stifled, smothered, restrained, confined, bottled up, held in/back, kept in check, curbed, bridled.

penurious adj. formal **1** *a penurious student* **poor**, as poor as a church mouse, poverty-stricken, destitute, necessitous, impecunious, impoverished, indigent, needy, in need/want, badly off, in reduced/straitened circumstances, hard up, on one's beam-ends, unable to make ends meet, penniless, without a sou; Brit. on the breadline, without a penny (to one's name); informal (flat) broke, strapped for cash, on one's uppers; Brit. informal stony broke, skint, without a brass farthing, in Queer Street; N. Amer. informal stone broke. **2** *a penurious old skinflint* **mean**, miserly, niggardly,

p

parsimonious, penny-pinching, close-fisted, cheese-paring, Scrooge-like; informal stingy, mingy, tight, tight-fisted, money-grubbing; old use near.
– OPPOSITES wealthy, generous.

penury n. **extreme poverty**, destitution, pennilessness, impecuniousness, impoverishment, indigence, pauperism, privation, beggary.

people plural n. **1** *crowds of people* **human beings**, persons, individuals, humans, mortals, (living) souls, personages, {men, women, and children}; informal folk, peeps. **2** *the British people* **citizens**, subjects, electors, voters, taxpayers, residents, inhabitants, (general) public, citizenry, nation, population, populace. **3** *a man of the people* **the common people**, the proletariat, the masses, the populace, the rank and file, the commonality, the commonalty, the third estate, the plebeians; derogatory the hoi polloi, the common herd, the great unwashed, the proles, the plebs. **4** *her people don't live far away* **family**, parents, relatives, relations, folk, kinsmen, kinswomen, kin, kith and kin, kinsfolk, flesh and blood, nearest and dearest; informal folks.
▸n. *the peoples of Africa* **race**, (ethnic) group, tribe, clan.
▸v. *the Indians who once peopled Newfoundland* **populate**, settle (in), colonize, inhabit, live in, occupy; formal reside in, be domiciled in, dwell in.

> **WORD LINKS**
> **anthropology** the study of peoples and human origins
> **ethnology** the study of the differences and relationships between different peoples
> **ethnic** relating a group of people with a common national or cultural tradition

pep informal n. *a performance full of pep* **dynamism**, life, energy, spirit, liveliness, animation, bounce, sparkle, effervescence, verve, spiritedness, ebullience, high spirits, enthusiasm, vitality, vivacity, fire, dash, panache, elan, zest, exuberance, vigour, gusto, brio; informal feistiness, get-up-and-go, oomph, pizzazz, vim.
□ **pep something up** enliven, animate, liven up, put some/new life into, invigorate, vitalize, revitalize, vivify, ginger up, energize, galvanize, stimulate, get something going, perk up; brighten up, cheer up; informal buck up.

pepper v. **1** *salt and pepper the potatoes* **add pepper to**, season, flavour. **2** *stars peppered the desert skies* **sprinkle**, fleck, dot, spot, stipple; cover, fill. **3** *another burst of bullets peppered the tank* **bombard**, pelt, shower, rain down on, attack, assail, batter, strafe, rake, blitz, hit.

peppery adj. **1** *a peppery sauce* **spicy**, spiced, peppered, hot, highly seasoned, piquant, pungent, sharp. **2** *a peppery old man* **irritable**, cantankerous, irascible, bad-tempered, ill-tempered, grumpy, grouchy, crotchety, short-tempered, tetchy, testy, crusty, crabby, curmudgeonly, peevish, cross, fractious, pettish, prickly, waspish; informal snappish, snappy, chippy; N. Amer. informal cranky, ornery.
– OPPOSITES mild, bland, affable.

perceive v. **1** *I immediately perceived the flaws in her story* **discern**, recognize, become aware of, see, distinguish, realize, grasp, understand, take in, make out, find, identify, hit on, comprehend, apprehend, appreciate, sense, divine; informal figure out; Brit. informal twig; formal become cognizant of. **2** *he perceived a flush creeping up her neck* **see**, discern, detect, catch sight of, spot, observe, notice. **3** *he was perceived as too negative* **regard**, look on, view, consider, think of, judge, deem, adjudge.

perceptible adj. **noticeable**, perceivable, detectable, discernible, visible, observable, recognizable, appreciable; obvious, apparent, evident, manifest, patent, clear, distinct, plain, conspicuous.

perception n. **1** *our perception of our own limitations* **recognition**, awareness, consciousness, appreciation, realization, knowledge, grasp, understanding, comprehension, apprehension; formal cognizance. **2** *popular perceptions of old age* **impression**, idea, conception, notion, thought, belief, judgement, estimation. **3** *he talks with great perception* **insight**, perceptiveness, percipience, perspicacity, understanding, sharpness, sharp-wittedness, intelligence, intuition, cleverness, incisiveness, trenchancy, astuteness, shrewdness, acuteness, acuity, discernment, sensitivity, penetration, thoughtfulness, profundity; formal perspicuity.

perceptive adj. **insightful**, discerning, sensitive, intuitive, observant; piercing, penetrating, percipient, perspicacious, penetrative, clear-sighted, far-sighted, intelligent, clever, canny, keen, sharp, sharp-witted, astute, shrewd, quick, smart, acute, discriminating; informal on the ball; N. Amer. informal heads-up.
– OPPOSITES obtuse.

perch n. *the budgerigar's perch* **pole**, rod, branch, roost, rest, resting place.
▸v. **1** *three swallows perched on the telegraph wire* **roost**, sit, rest; alight, settle, land, come to rest. **2** *she perched her glasses on her nose* **put**, place, set, rest, balance. **3** *the church is perched on a hill* **be located**, be situated, be positioned, be sited, stand.

perchance adv. literary **maybe**, perhaps, possibly, for all one knows, it could be, it's possible, conceivably; N. English happen; literary peradventure.

percipient adj. See **perceptive**.

percolate v. **1** *water percolated through the soil* **filter**, drain, drip, ooze, seep, trickle, dribble, leak, leach. **2** *these views began to percolate through society as a whole* **spread**, be disseminated, filter, pass; permeate, pervade. **3** *he put some coffee on to percolate* **brew**; informal perk.

perdition n. **damnation**, eternal punishment; hell, hellfire, doom.

peremptory adj. **1** *a peremptory reply* **brusque**, imperious, high-handed, brisk, abrupt, summary, commanding, dictatorial, autocratic, overbearing, dogmatic, arrogant, overweening, lordly, magisterial, authoritarian; emphatic, firm, insistent; informal bossy. **2** *a peremptory order of the court* **irreversible**, binding, absolute, final, conclusive, decisive, definitive, categorical, irrefutable, incontrovertible; Law unappealable.

perennial adj. **abiding**, enduring, lasting, everlasting, perpetual, eternal, continuing, unending, unceasing, never-ending, endless, undying, ceaseless, persisting, permanent, constant, continual, unfailing, unchanging, never-changing.

perfect adj. **1** *she strove to be the perfect wife* **ideal**, model, without fault, faultless, flawless, consummate, quintessential, exemplary, best, ultimate, copybook; unrivalled, unequalled, matchless, unparalleled, beyond compare, without equal, second to none, too good to be true, Utopian, incomparable, nonpareil, peerless, inimitable, unsurpassed, unsurpassable. **2** *an E-type Jaguar in perfect condition* **flawless**, mint, as good as new, pristine, impeccable, immaculate, superb, superlative, optimum, prime, optimal, peak, excellent, faultless, as sound as a bell, unspoiled, unblemished, undamaged, spotless, unmarred; informal tip-top, A1. **3** *a perfect copy* **exact**, precise, accurate, faithful, correct, unerring, right, true, strict; Brit. informal spot on; N. Amer. informal on the money. **4** *the perfect Christmas present for golfers everywhere* **ideal**, just right, right, appropriate, fitting, fit, suitable, apt, made to order, tailor-made; very; Brit. informal spot on, just the job. **5** *she felt a perfect idiot* **absolute**, complete, total, real, out-and-out, thorough, thoroughgoing, downright, utter, sheer, arrant, unmitigated, unqualified, veritable, in every respect, unalloyed; Brit. informal right; Austral./NZ informal fair.
▸v. *he's busy perfecting his bowling technique* **improve**, better, polish (up), hone, refine, put the finishing/final touches to, brush up, fine-tune.

perfection n. **1** *the perfection of his technique* **improvement**, betterment, refinement, refining, honing. **2** *for her, he was still perfection* **the ideal**, a paragon, the ne plus ultra, the beau idéal, a nonpareil, the crème de la crème, the last word, the ultimate; informal one in a million, the tops, the best/greatest thing since sliced bread, the bee's knees; old use a nonsuch.

perfectionist n. **purist**, stickler for perfection, idealist; pedant; old use precisian.

perfectly adv. **1** *a perfectly cooked meal* **superbly**, superlatively, excellently, flawlessly, faultlessly, to perfection, without fault, ideally, inimitably, incomparably, impeccably, immaculately, exquisitely, consummately; N. Amer. to a fare-thee-well; informal like a dream, to a T. **2** *I think we understand each other perfectly* **absolutely**, utterly, completely, altogether, entirely, wholly, totally, thoroughly, fully, in every respect. **3** *you know perfectly well that is not what I meant* **very**, quite, full; informal damn, damned; Brit. informal jolly, bloody; N. Amer. informal darned; N. English right.

perfidious adj. literary **treacherous**, duplicitous, deceitful, disloyal, faithless, unfaithful, traitorous, treasonous, false, false-hearted, double-dealing, two-faced, Janus-faced, untrustworthy.
– OPPOSITES faithful.

perfidy n. literary **treachery**, duplicity, deceit, deceitfulness, disloyalty, infidelity, faithlessness, unfaithfulness, betrayal, treason, double-dealing, untrustworthiness, breach of trust; literary perfidiousness.

perforate v. **pierce**, penetrate, enter, puncture, prick, bore through, riddle.

perforce adv. formal **necessarily**, of necessity, inevitably, unavoidably, by force of circumstances, needs must; informal like it or not; formal nolens volens.

perform v. **1** *I have my duties to perform* **carry out**, do, execute, discharge, bring about, bring off, accomplish, achieve, fulfil, complete, conduct, effect, dispatch, work, implement; informal pull off; formal effectuate; old use acquit oneself of. **2** *a car which performs well at low speeds* **function**, work, operate, run, go, respond, behave, act, acquit oneself/itself. **3** *the play has been performed in Britain* **stage**, put on, present, mount, enact, act, produce. **4** *the band performed live in Hyde Park* **appear**, play, be on stage.
– OPPOSITES neglect.

performance n. **1** *the evening performance* **show**, production, showing, presentation, staging; concert, recital; Brit. house; informal gig. **2** *their performance of Mozart's concerto in E flat* **rendition**, rendering, interpretation, playing, acting, representation. **3** *the continual performance of a single task* **carrying out**, execution, discharge, accomplishment, completion, fulfilment, dispatch, implementation; formal effectuation. **4** *the performance of the processor* **functioning**, working, operation, running, behaviour, capabilities, capability, capacity, power, potential. **5** *he made a great performance of telling her about it* **fuss**, production, palaver, scene; NZ bobsy-die; informal song and dance, to-do, hoo-ha, business, pantomime.

performer n. **entertainer**, actor, actress, thespian, artiste, artist, trouper, player, musician, singer, dancer, comic, comedian, comedienne.

perfume n. **1** *a bottle of perfume* **scent**, fragrance, eau de toilette, toilet water, eau de cologne, cologne, aftershave. **2** *the heady perfume of lilacs* **smell**, scent, fragrance, aroma, bouquet, redolence.

p

perfumed adj. **sweet-smelling**, scented, fragrant, fragranced, perfumy, aromatic.

perfunctory adj. **cursory**, desultory, quick, brief, hasty, hurried, rapid, fleeting, token, casual, superficial, careless, half-hearted, sketchy, mechanical, automatic, routine, offhand, inattentive.
– OPPOSITES careful, thorough.

perhaps adv. **maybe**, for all one knows, it could be, it may be, it's possible, possibly, conceivably; N. English happen; literary peradventure, perchance.

peril n. **danger**, jeopardy, risk, hazard, insecurity, uncertainty, menace, threat, perilousness; pitfall, problem.

perilous adj. **dangerous**, fraught with danger, hazardous, risky, unsafe, treacherous; precarious, vulnerable, uncertain, insecure, exposed, at risk, in jeopardy, in danger, touch-and-go; informal dicey.
– OPPOSITES safe.

perimeter n. **1** *the perimeter of a circle* **circumference**, outside, outer edge. **2** *the perimeter of the vast estate* **boundary**, border, limits, bounds, confines, edge, margin, fringe(s), periphery, borderline, verge; literary bourn, marge.

period n. **1** *a six-week period* **time**, spell, interval, stretch, term, span, phase, bout, run, duration, chapter, stage; while; Brit. informal patch. **2** *the post-war period* **era**, age, epoch, time, days, years; Geology aeon. **3** *a double maths period* **lesson**, class, session. **4** *women who suffer from painful periods* **menstruation**, menstrual flow; informal the curse, monthlies, time of the month; technical menses. **5** N. Amer. *a comma instead of a period* **full stop**, full point, point, stop.

periodic adj. **regular**, periodical, at fixed intervals, recurrent, recurring, repeated, cyclical, cyclic, seasonal; occasional, infrequent, intermittent, sporadic, spasmodic, odd.

periodical n. *he wrote for two periodicals* **journal**, publication, magazine, newspaper, paper, review, digest, gazette, newsletter, organ, quarterly; informal mag, book, glossy.
▶ adj. *the island has periodical earthquakes.* See **periodic**.

peripatetic adj. **nomadic**, itinerant, travelling, wandering, roving, roaming, migrant, migratory, unsettled.

peripheral adj. **1** *the city's peripheral housing estates* **outlying**, outer, on the edge/outskirts, surrounding. **2** *peripheral issues* **secondary**, subsidiary, incidental, tangential, marginal, minor, unimportant, lesser, inessential, non-essential, immaterial, ancillary.
– OPPOSITES central.

periphery n. **edge**, outer edge, margin, fringe, boundary, border, perimeter, rim, verge, borderline; outskirts, outer limits/reaches, bounds; literary bourn, marge.
– OPPOSITES centre.

periphrastic adj. **circumlocutory**, circuitous, roundabout, indirect, tautological, pleonastic, prolix, verbose, wordy, long-winded, rambling, wandering, tortuous, diffuse.

perish v. **1** *millions of soldiers perished* **die**, lose one's life, be killed, fall, expire, meet one's death, be lost, lay down one's life, breathe one's last, pass away, go the way of all flesh, give up the ghost, go to glory, meet one's maker, go to one's last resting place, cross the great divide; informal kick the bucket, turn up one's toes, shuffle off this mortal coil, buy it, croak, flatline; Brit. informal snuff it, pop one's clogs; N. Amer. informal bite the big one, buy the farm; old use decease, depart this life. **2** *must these hopes perish so soon?* **come to an end**, die (away), disappear, vanish, fade, dissolve, evaporate, melt away, wither. **3** *the wood had perished* **go bad**, go off, spoil, rot, go mouldy, moulder, putrefy, decay, decompose.

perjure v.
☐ **perjure oneself** lie under oath, lie, commit perjury, give false evidence/testimony; formal forswear oneself, be forsworn.

perjury n. **lying under oath**, making false statements, wilful falsehood.

perk[1] v.
☐ **perk up** *you seem to have perked up* **cheer up**, brighten up, liven up, take heart; informal buck up. **2** *the economy has been slow to perk up* **recover**, rally, improve, revive, take a turn for the better, look up, pick up, bounce back.
perk someone/something up *you could do with something to perk you up* cheer up, liven up, brighten up, raise someone's spirits, give someone a boost/lift, revitalize, invigorate, energize, enliven, ginger up, put new life/heart into, rejuvenate, refresh, vitalize; informal buck up, pep up.

perk[2] n. *a job with a lot of perks* **fringe benefit**, additional benefit, benefit, advantage, bonus, extra, plus; informal freebie; Brit. informal golden hello; formal perquisite.

perky adj. **cheerful**, lively, vivacious, animated, bubbly, effervescent, bouncy, spirited, high-spirited, in high spirits, cheery, merry, buoyant, ebullient, exuberant, jaunty, frisky, sprightly, spry, bright, sunny, jolly, full of the joys of spring, sparkly, pert; informal full of beans, bright-eyed and bushy-tailed, chirpy, chipper; N. Amer. informal peppy; dated gay.

permanence n. **stability**, durability, permanency, fixity, fixedness, changelessness, immutability, endurance, constancy, continuity, immortality, indestructibility, perpetuity, endlessness.

permanent adj. **1** *permanent brain damage* **lasting**, enduring, indefinite, continuing, perpetual, everlasting, eternal, abiding, constant, irreparable, irreversible, lifelong, indissoluble, indelible, standing, perennial, unending, endless, never-ending, immutable,

undying, imperishable, indestructible, ineradicable; literary sempiternal, perdurable. **2** *a permanent job* **long-term**, stable, secure, durable.
– OPPOSITES temporary.

permanently adv. **1** *the attack left her permanently disabled* **for all time**, forever, for good, for always, for ever and ever, (for) evermore, until hell freezes over, in perpetuity, indelibly, immutably, until the end of time; N. Amer. forevermore; informal for keeps, until the cows come home, until doomsday, until kingdom come; old use for aye. **2** *I was permanently hungry* **continually**, constantly, perpetually, always.

permeable adj. **porous**, pervious, penetrable, absorbent, absorptive.

permeate v. **1** *the delicious smell permeated the entire flat* **pervade**, spread through, fill, filter through, diffuse through, imbue, penetrate, pass through, percolate through, perfuse, charge, suffuse, steep, impregnate, inform. **2** *these resins are able to permeate the timber* **soak through**, penetrate, seep through, saturate, percolate through, leach through.

permissible adj. **permitted**, allowable, allowed, acceptable, legal, lawful, legitimate, admissible, licit, authorized, sanctioned, tolerated; informal legit, OK.
– OPPOSITES forbidden.

permission n. **authorization**, consent, leave, authority, sanction, licence, dispensation, assent, acquiescence, agreement, approval, seal of approval, approbation, endorsement, blessing, imprimatur, clearance, allowance, tolerance, sufferance, empowerment; informal the go-ahead, the thumbs up, the OK, the green light, say-so.

permissive adj. **liberal**, broad-minded, open-minded, free, free and easy, easy-going, live-and-let-live, latitudinarian, laissez-faire, libertarian, unprescriptive, tolerant, forbearing, indulgent, lenient; overindulgent, lax, soft.
– OPPOSITES intolerant, strict.

permit v. *I cannot permit you to leave* **allow**, let, authorize, give someone permission, sanction, grant, give someone the right, license, empower, enable, entitle, qualify; consent to, assent to, give one's blessing to, give the nod to, acquiesce in, agree to, tolerate, countenance, admit of; legalize, legitimatize, legitimate; informal give the go-ahead to, give the thumbs up to, OK, give the OK to, give the green light to, say the word; formal accede to; old use suffer.
– OPPOSITES ban, forbid.

▸ n. *I need to see your permit* **authorization**, licence, pass, ticket, warrant, document, certification; passport, visa.

permutation n. **variation**, alteration, modification, change, shift, transformation, transmutation, mutation; humorous transmogrification.

pernicious adj. **harmful**, damaging, destructive, injurious, hurtful, detrimental, deleterious, dangerous, adverse, inimical, unhealthy, unfavourable, bad, evil, baleful, wicked, malign, malevolent, malignant, noxious, poisonous, corrupting; literary maleficent.
– OPPOSITES beneficial.

pernickety adj. informal **fussy**, difficult to please, difficult, finicky, over-fastidious, fastidious, over-particular, particular, faddish, punctilious, hair-splitting, critical, overcritical; informal nitpicking, choosy, picky; Brit. informal faddy; N. Amer. informal persnickety.
– OPPOSITES easy-going.

peroration n. **1** *the peroration of his speech* **conclusion**, ending, close, closing remarks; summation, summing-up. **2** *an hour-long peroration* **speech**, lecture, talk, address, oration, sermon, disquisition, discourse, declamation, harangue, diatribe; informal spiel.

perpendicular adj. **1** *the perpendicular stones* **upright**, vertical, erect, plumb, straight (up and down), on end, standing, upended. **2** *lines perpendicular to each other* **at right angles**, at 90 degrees. **3** *the perpendicular hillside* **steep**, sheer, precipitous, abrupt, bluff, vertiginous.
– OPPOSITES horizontal.

perpetrate v. **commit**, carry out, perform, execute, do, effect, bring about, accomplish; be guilty of, be to blame for, be responsible for, inflict, wreak; informal pull off; formal effectuate.

perpetual adj. **1** *deep caves in perpetual darkness* **everlasting**, never-ending, eternal, permanent, unending, endless, without end, lasting, long-lasting, constant, abiding, enduring, perennial, timeless, ageless, deathless, undying, immortal; unfailing, unchanging, never-changing, changeless, unfading; literary sempiternal, perdurable. **2** *a perpetual state of fear* **constant**, permanent, uninterrupted, continuous, unremitting, unending, unceasing, persistent, unbroken. **3** *her mother's perpetual nagging* **interminable**, incessant, ceaseless, endless, without respite, relentless, unrelenting, persistent, continual, continuous, non-stop, never-ending, recurrent, repeated, unremitting, sustained, round-the-clock, unabating; informal eternal.
– OPPOSITES temporary, intermittent.

perpetuate v. **keep alive**, keep going, preserve, conserve, sustain, maintain, continue, extend, carry on, keep up, prolong; immortalize, commemorate, memorialize, eternalize.

perpetuity n.
□ **in perpetuity** forever, permanently, for always, for good, for good and all, perpetually, (for) evermore, for ever and ever, for all time, until the end of time, until hell freezes over, eternally, for eternity, everlastingly; N. Amer. forevermore; informal for keeps, until doomsday; old use for aye.

perplex v. **puzzle**, baffle, mystify, bemuse, bewilder, confound, confuse, nonplus, disconcert, dumbfound, throw, throw/catch off balance, exercise, worry; informal flummox, be all Greek to, stump, bamboozle, floor, beat, faze, fox; N. Amer. informal discombobulate; old use wilder, maze.

perplexing adj. **puzzling**, baffling, mystifying, mysterious, bewildering, confusing, disconcerting, worrying, unaccountable, difficult to understand, beyond one, paradoxical, peculiar, funny, strange, weird, odd.

perplexity n. **1** *he scratched his head in perplexity* **confusion**, bewilderment, puzzlement, bafflement, incomprehension, mystification, bemusement; informal bamboozlement; N. Amer. informal discombobulation. **2** *the perplexities of international relations* **complexity**, complication, intricacy, problem, difficulty, mystery, puzzle, enigma, paradox.

perquisite n. formal See **perk²**.

per se adv. **in itself**, of itself, by itself, as such, intrinsically; by its very nature, in essence, by definition, essentially.

persecute v. **1** *they were persecuted for their religious beliefs* **oppress**, abuse, victimize, ill-treat, mistreat, maltreat, tyrannize, torment, torture; martyr. **2** *she was persecuted by the press* **harass**, hound, plague, badger, harry, intimidate, pick on, pester, bother, bedevil, bully, victimize, terrorize; N. Amer. devil; informal hassle, give someone a hard time, get on someone's back; Austral. informal heavy.

persecution n. **1** *victims of religious persecution* **oppression**, victimization, maltreatment, ill-treatment, mistreatment, abuse, ill-usage, discrimination, tyranny; informal witch hunt. **2** *the persecution I endured at school* **harassment**, hounding, intimidation, bullying.

perseverance n. **persistence**, tenacity, determination, staying power, indefatigability, steadfastness, purposefulness; patience, endurance, application, diligence, dedication, commitment, doggedness, assiduity, tirelessness, stamina; intransigence, obstinacy; informal stickability; N. Amer. informal stick-to-it-iveness; formal pertinacity.

persevere v. **persist**, continue, carry on, go on, keep on, keep going, struggle on, hammer away, be persistent, be determined, see/follow something through, keep at it, press on/ahead, not take no for an answer, be tenacious, stand one's ground, stand fast/firm, hold on, go the distance, stay the course, plod on, plough on, stop at nothing, leave no stone unturned; informal soldier on, hang on, plug away, peg away, stick to one's guns, stick it out, hang in there.
– OPPOSITES give up.

persist v. **1** *Corbett persisted with his questioning.* See **persevere**. **2** *if dry weather persists, water the lawn thoroughly* **continue**,

hold, carry on, last, keep on, keep up, remain, linger, stay, endure.

persistence n. See **perseverance**.

persistent adj. **1** *a very persistent man* **tenacious**, persevering, determined, resolute, purposeful, dogged, single-minded, tireless, indefatigable, patient, unflagging, untiring, insistent, importunate, relentless, unrelenting; stubborn, intransigent, obstinate, obdurate; formal pertinacious. **2** *persistent rain* **constant**, continuous, continuing, continual, non-stop, never-ending, steady, uninterrupted, unbroken, interminable, incessant, unceasing, endless, unending, perpetual, unremitting, unrelenting, relentless, unrelieved, sustained. **3** *a persistent cough* **chronic**, permanent, nagging, frequent; repeated, habitual.
– OPPOSITES irresolute, intermittent.

person n. **human being**, individual, man/woman, human, being, (living) soul, mortal, creature; personage, figure, character, customer; informal type, sort, beggar, cookie; Brit. informal bod; informal dated body, dog, cove; old use wight.
□ **in person** physically, in the flesh, in propria persona, personally; oneself; informal as large as life.

persona n. **image**, face, public face, character, personality, identity, self; front, facade, guise, exterior, role, part.

personable adj. **pleasant**, agreeable, likeable, nice, amiable, affable, charming, congenial, genial, engaging, pleasing; attractive, presentable, good-looking, nice-looking, pretty, appealing; Scottish couthy; Scottish & N. English bonny, canny; dated taking.
– OPPOSITES disagreeable, unattractive.

personage n. **important person**, VIP, luminary, celebrity, personality, name, famous name, household name, public figure, star, leading light, dignitary, notable, notability, worthy, panjandrum; person; informal celeb, somebody, big shot, big noise; Brit. informal nob; N. Amer. informal big wheel, big kahuna.

personal adj. **1** *a highly personal style* **distinctive**, characteristic, unique, individual, one's own, particular, peculiar, idiosyncratic, individualized, personalized. **2** *a personal appearance* **in person**, in the flesh, actual, live, physical. **3** *his personal life* **private**, intimate, confidential, secret. **4** *a personal friend* **intimate**, close, dear, great, bosom. **5** *I have personal knowledge of the family* **direct**, empirical, first-hand, immediate, experiential. **6** *personal remarks* **derogatory**, disparaging, belittling, insulting, critical, rude, slighting, disrespectful, offensive, pejorative.
– OPPOSITES public, general.

personality n. **1** *her cheerful personality* **character**, nature, disposition, temperament, make-up, persona, psyche. **2** *she had loads of personality* **charisma**, magnetism, strength/force of personality, character, charm, presence. **3** *a famous personality* **celebrity**, VIP, star, superstar, name, famous name, household name, big name, somebody, leading light, luminary, notable, personage, notability; informal celeb.

personalize v. **1** *products which can be personalized to your requirements* **customize**, individualize. **2** *attempts to personalize God* **personify**, humanize, anthropomorphize.

personally adv. **1** *I'd like to thank him personally* **in person**, oneself. **2** *personally, I think it's a good idea* **for my part**, for myself, to my way of thinking, to my mind, in my estimation, as far as I am concerned, in my view/opinion, from my point of view, from where I stand, as I see it, if you ask me, for my money, in my book; privately.
□ **take something personally** take offence, take something amiss, be offended, be upset, be affronted, take umbrage, take exception, feel insulted, feel hurt.

personification n. **embodiment**, incarnation, epitome, quintessence, essence, type, symbol, soul, model, exemplification, exemplar, image, representation.

personify v. **epitomize**, embody, be the incarnation of, typify, exemplify, represent, symbolize, stand for, body forth.

personnel n. **staff**, employees, workforce, workers, labour force, manpower, human resources; informal liveware.

perspective n. **1** *her perspective on things had changed* **outlook**, view, viewpoint, point of view, standpoint, position, stand, stance, angle, slant, attitude, frame of mind, frame of reference, approach, way of looking, interpretation. **2** *a perspective of the whole valley* **view**, vista, panorama, prospect, bird's-eye view, outlook, aspect.

perspicacious adj. **discerning**, shrewd, perceptive, astute, penetrating, observant, percipient, sharp-witted, sharp, smart, alert, clear-sighted, far-sighted, acute, clever, canny, intelligent, insightful, wise, sage, sensitive, intuitive, understanding, aware, discriminating; informal on the ball; N. Amer. informal heads-up.
– OPPOSITES stupid.

perspicuous adj. formal See **clear** (sense 1 of the adjective).

perspiration n. **sweat**, moisture; a lather; informal a muck sweat; Medicine diaphoresis, hidrosis.

perspire v. **sweat**, be dripping/pouring with sweat, glow; informal be in a muck sweat.

persuadable adj. **malleable**, tractable, pliable, compliant, amenable, adaptable, accommodating, cooperative, flexible, acquiescent, yielding, biddable, complaisant, like putty in one's hands, suggestible.

persuade v. **1** *he tried to persuade her to come with him* **prevail on**, talk into, coax, convince, make, get, induce, win over, bring round, coerce, influence, sway, inveigle, entice, tempt, lure, cajole, wheedle; Law procure; informal sweet-talk, twist someone's

arm. **2** *shortage of money persuaded them to abandon the scheme* **cause**, lead, move, dispose, incline.
– OPPOSITES dissuade, deter.

persuasion n. **1** *Monica needed plenty of persuasion* **coaxing**, persuading, coercion, inducement, convincing, blandishment, encouragement, urging, inveiglement, cajolery, enticement, wheedling; informal sweet-talking, arm-twisting; formal suasion. **2** *various political and religious persuasions* **group**, grouping, sect, denomination, party, camp, side, faction, affiliation, school of thought, belief, creed, credo, faith, philosophy.

persuasive adj. **convincing**, cogent, compelling, potent, forceful, powerful, eloquent, impressive, influential, sound, valid, strong, effective, winning, telling, plausible, credible.
– OPPOSITES unconvincing.

pert adj. **1** *a pert little hat* **jaunty**, neat, trim, stylish, smart, perky, rakish; informal natty; N. Amer. informal saucy. **2** *a young girl with a pert manner* **impudent**, impertinent, cheeky, irreverent, forward, insolent, disrespectful, flippant, familiar, presumptuous, bold, as bold as brass, brazen; informal fresh, lippy, saucy; N. Amer. informal sassy; old use malapert.

pertain v. **1** *developments pertaining to the economy* **concern**, relate to, be related to, be connected with, be relevant to, apply to, be pertinent to, refer to, have a bearing on, appertain to, bear on, affect, involve, touch; old use regard. **2** *the stock and assets pertaining to the business* **belong to**, be a part of, be included in. **3** *the economic situation which pertained in Britain at that time* **exist**, be the order of the day, be the case, prevail; formal obtain.

pertinacious adj. formal **determined**, tenacious, persistent, persevering, purposeful, resolute, dogged, indefatigable, insistent, single-minded, unrelenting, relentless, tireless, unshakeable; stubborn, obstinate, inflexible, unbending.
– OPPOSITES irresolute, tentative.

pertinent adj. **relevant**, to the point, apposite, appropriate, suitable, fitting, fit, apt, applicable, material, germane, to the purpose, apropos; formal ad rem.
– OPPOSITES irrelevant.

perturb v. **worry**, upset, unsettle, disturb, concern, trouble, disquiet; disconcert, discomfit, unnerve, alarm, bother, distress, dismay, gnaw at, affect, agitate, fluster, ruffle, discountenance, exercise; informal rattle.
– OPPOSITES reassure.

perturbed adj. **upset**, worried, unsettled, disturbed, concerned, troubled, anxious, ill at ease, uneasy, disquieted, fretful; disconcerted, discomposed, distressed, unnerved, alarmed, bothered, dismayed, agitated, flustered, ruffled, shaken, discountenanced; informal twitchy, rattled, fazed; N. Amer. informal discombobulated.
– OPPOSITES calm.

p

peruse v. **read**, study, scrutinize, inspect, examine, wade through, look through; browse through, leaf through, scan, run one's eye over, glance through, flick through, skim through, thumb through, dip into; old use con.

pervade v. **permeate**, spread through, fill, suffuse, be diffused through, imbue, penetrate, filter through, percolate through, infuse, perfuse, flow through; charge, steep, saturate, impregnate, inform.

pervasive adj. **prevalent**, pervading, permeating, extensive, ubiquitous, omnipresent, universal, rife, widespread, general.

perverse adj. **1** *he is being deliberately perverse* **awkward**, contrary, difficult, unreasonable, uncooperative, unhelpful, obstructive, disobliging, recalcitrant, stubborn, obstinate, obdurate, mulish, pig-headed, bullheaded; informal cussed; Brit. informal bloody-minded, bolshie; N. Amer. informal balky; formal refractory; old use froward, contumacious. **2** *a verdict that is manifestly perverse* **illogical**, irrational, unreasonable, wrong, wrong-headed. **3** *an evil life dedicated to perverse pleasure* **perverted**, depraved, unnatural, abnormal, deviant, degenerate, immoral, warped, twisted, corrupt; wicked, base, evil; informal kinky, sick, pervy.
– OPPOSITES accommodating, reasonable.

perversion n. **1** *a twisted perversion of the truth* **distortion**, misrepresentation, falsification, travesty, misinterpretation, misconstruction, twisting, corruption, subversion, misuse, misapplication, debasement. **2** *sexual perversion* **deviance**, abnormality, depravity, degeneracy, debauchery, corruption, vice, wickedness, immorality.

perversity n. **1** *out of sheer perversity, he refused* **contrariness**, awkwardness, recalcitrance, stubbornness, obstinacy, obduracy, mulishness, pig-headedness; informal cussedness; Brit. informal bloody-mindedness; formal refractoriness. **2** *the perversity of the decision* **unreasonableness**, irrationality, illogicality, wrong-headedness.

pervert v. **1** *people who attempt to pervert the rules* **distort**, corrupt, subvert, twist, bend, abuse, misapply, misuse, misrepresent, misinterpret, falsify. **2** *men can be perverted by power* **corrupt**, lead astray, debase, warp, pollute, poison, deprave, debauch.
▸ n. *a sexual pervert* **deviant**, degenerate; informal perv, dirty old man, sicko.

perverted adj. **unnatural**, deviant, warped, corrupt, twisted, abnormal, unhealthy, depraved, perverse, aberrant, immoral, debauched, debased, degenerate, evil, wicked, vile, amoral, wrong, bad; informal sick, sicko, kinky, pervy.

pessimism n. **defeatism**, negativity, doom and gloom, gloominess, cynicism, fatalism; hopelessness, depression, despair, despondency, angst; informal looking on the black side.

pessimist n. **defeatist**, fatalist, prophet of doom, cynic, doomsayer, doomster, Cassandra; sceptic, doubter, doubting Thomas; misery, killjoy, Job's comforter; informal doom (and gloom) merchant, wet blanket; N. Amer. informal gloomy Gus.
– OPPOSITES optimist.

pessimistic adj. **gloomy**, negative, defeatist, downbeat, cynical, bleak, fatalistic, dark, black, despairing, despondent, depressed, hopeless; suspicious, distrustful, doubting.
– OPPOSITES optimistic.

pest n. **nuisance**, annoyance, irritation, irritant, thorn in one's flesh/side, vexation, trial, the bane of one's life, menace, trouble, problem, worry, bother; informal pain (in the neck), aggravation, headache; Scottish informal skelf; N. Amer. informal nudnik; Austral./NZ informal nark.

pester v. **badger**, hound, harass, plague, annoy, bother, trouble, keep after, persecute, torment, bedevil, harry, worry, beleaguer, chivvy, nag; informal hassle, bug, get on someone's back; N. English informal mither; N. Amer. informal devil.

pestilential adj. **1** *pestilential fever* **plague-like**, infectious, contagious, communicable, epidemic, virulent; informal catching; literary pestiferous. **2** informal *a pestilential man* **annoying**, irritating, infuriating, exasperating, maddening, tiresome, irksome, vexing, vexatious; informal aggravating, pesky, infernal.

pet[1] n. *the teacher's pet* **favourite**, darling, the apple of one's eye; Brit. informal blue-eyed boy/girl; N. Amer. informal fair-haired boy/girl.
▸ adj. **1** *a pet lamb* **tame**, domesticated, domestic; Brit. house-trained; N. Amer. housebroken. **2** *his pet theory* **favourite**, favoured, cherished, dear to one's heart; particular, special, personal.
▸ v. **1** *the cats came to be petted* **stroke**, caress, fondle, pat. **2** *she had always been petted by her parents* **pamper**, spoil, mollycoddle, coddle, cosset, baby, indulge, overindulge, wrap in cotton wool. **3** *couples were petting in their cars* **kiss and cuddle**, kiss, cuddle, embrace, caress; informal canoodle, neck, smooch; Brit. informal snog; N. Amer. informal make out, get it on; informal dated spoon.
□ **pet name** affectionate name, term of endearment, endearment, nickname, diminutive, hypocoristic.

pet[2] n. *Mum's in a pet* **bad mood**, mood, bad temper, temper, sulk, fit of pique, huff; Brit. informal paddy, strop.

peter v.
□ **peter out** fizzle out, fade (away), die away/out, dwindle, diminish, taper off, tail off, trail away/off, wane, ebb, melt away, evaporate, disappear, come to an end, subside.

petite adj. **small**, dainty, diminutive, slight, little, tiny, elfin, delicate, small-boned; Scottish wee; informal pint-sized.

petition n. **1** *over 1,000 people signed the petition* **appeal**, round robin. **2** *petitions to*

Allah **entreaty**, supplication, plea, prayer, appeal, request, invocation, suit; old use orison.
▶ v. *they petitioned the king to revoke the decision* **appeal to**, request, ask, call on, entreat, beg, implore, plead with, apply to, press, urge; formal adjure; literary beseech.

petrified adj. **1** *she looked petrified* **terrified**, terror-stricken, horrified, scared/frightened out of one's wits, scared/frightened to death. **2** *petrified remains of prehistoric animals* **ossified**, fossilized, calcified.

petrify v. **terrify**, horrify, frighten, scare, scare/frighten to death, scare/frighten the living daylights out of, scare/frighten the life out of, strike terror into, put the fear of God into; paralyse, transfix; informal scare the pants off; Irish informal scare the bejesus out of.

petrol n. **fuel**, unleaded, superunleaded, diesel; N. Amer. gasoline, gas; informal juice.

petticoat n. **slip**, underskirt, half-slip, underslip, undergarment; historical crinoline; old use kirtle.

petty adj. **1** *petty regulations* **trivial**, trifling, minor, small, unimportant, insignificant, inconsequential, inconsiderable, negligible, paltry, footling, pettifogging; informal piffling, piddling, fiddling. **2** *a petty form of revenge* **small-minded**, mean, ungenerous, shabby, spiteful.
– OPPOSITES important, magnanimous.

petulant adj. **peevish**, bad-tempered, querulous, pettish, fretful, cross, irritable, sulky, snappish, crotchety, touchy, tetchy, testy, fractious, grumpy, disgruntled, crabbed, crabby; informal grouchy; Brit. informal ratty; N. English informal mardy; N. Amer. informal cranky.
– OPPOSITES good-humoured.

phantasmagorical adj. **dreamlike**, psychedelic, kaleidoscopic, surreal, unreal, hallucinatory, fantastic, fantastical, chimerical.

phantom n. **1** *a phantom who haunts lonely roads* **ghost**, apparition, spirit, spectre, wraith; informal spook; literary phantasm, shade. **2** *the phantoms of an overactive imagination* **delusion**, figment of the imagination, hallucination, illusion, chimera, vision, mirage.

phase n. **1** *the final phase of the campaign* **stage**, period, chapter, episode, part, step, point, time, juncture. **2** *he's going through a difficult phase* **period**, stage, time, spell; Brit. informal patch. **3** *the phases of the moon* **aspect**, shape, form, appearance, state, condition.
□ **phase something in** introduce gradually, begin to use, ease in.
phase something out withdraw gradually, discontinue, stop using, run down, wind down.

phenomenal adj. **remarkable**, exceptional, extraordinary, amazing, astonishing, astounding, sensational, stunning, incredible, unbelievable; marvellous, magnificent, wonderful, outstanding, singular, out of the ordinary, unusual,

unprecedented; informal fantastic, terrific, tremendous, stupendous, awesome, out of this world; literary wondrous.
– OPPOSITES ordinary.

phenomenon n. **1** *a rare phenomenon* **occurrence**, event, happening, fact, situation, circumstance, experience, case, incident, episode. **2** *the band was a pop phenomenon* **marvel**, sensation, wonder, prodigy, miracle, rarity, nonpareil.

philander v. **womanize**, have affairs, flirt; informal play around, carry on, play the field, play away, sleep around; N. Amer. informal fool around.

philanderer n. **womanizer**, Casanova, Don Juan, Lothario, flirt, ladies' man, playboy, rake, roué; informal stud, skirt-chaser, ladykiller, wolf; informal dated gay dog.

philanthropic adj. **charitable**, generous, benevolent, humanitarian, public-spirited, altruistic, magnanimous, munificent, open-handed, bountiful, liberal, beneficent, caring, compassionate, unselfish, kind, kind-hearted, big-hearted; formal eleemosynary.
– OPPOSITES selfish, mean.

philanthropist n. **benefactor**, benefactress, patron, patroness, donor, contributor, sponsor, backer, helper, good Samaritan; do-gooder, Lady Bountiful; historical almsgiver.

philanthropy n. **benevolence**, generosity, humanitarianism, public-spiritedness, altruism, social conscience, charity, charitableness, brotherly love, fellow feeling, magnanimity, munificence, liberality, largesse, open-handedness, beneficence, unselfishness, humanity, kindness, kind-heartedness, compassion; historical almsgiving.

philistine adj. **uncultured**, lowbrow, anti-intellectual, uncultivated, uncivilized, uneducated, unenlightened, commercial, materialist, bourgeois; ignorant, crass, boorish, barbarian.

philosopher n. **thinker**, theorist, theorizer, theoretician, metaphysicist, metaphysician; scholar, intellectual, sage, wise man.

philosophical adj. **1** *a philosophical question* **theoretical**, metaphysical. **2** *a philosophical mood* **thoughtful**, reflective, pensive, meditative, contemplative, introspective, ruminative; formal cogitative. **3** *he was philosophical about losing the contract* **calm**, composed, cool, collected, {cool, calm, and collected}, self-possessed, serene, tranquil, stoical, impassive, dispassionate, phlegmatic, unperturbed, imperturbable, unruffled, patient, forbearing, long-suffering, resigned, rational, realistic.

philosophize v. **theorize**, speculate; pontificate, preach, sermonize, moralize.

philosophy n. **1** *the philosophy of Aristotle* **thinking**, thought, reasoning. **2** *her political philosophy* **beliefs**, credo, convictions, ideology, ideas, thinking, notions, theories, doctrine, tenets, principles, views, school of thought.

p

phlegm n. **1** mucus, catarrh. **2** *British phlegm and perseverance* **calmness**, coolness, composure, equanimity, tranquillity, placidity, placidness, impassivity, stolidity, imperturbability, impassiveness, dispassionateness; informal cool, unflappability.

phlegmatic adj. **calm**, cool, composed, {cool, calm, and collected}, controlled, serene, tranquil, placid, impassive, stolid, imperturbable, unruffled, dispassionate, philosophical; informal unflappable.
– OPPOSITES excitable.

phobia n. **abnormal fear**, irrational fear, obsessive fear, dread, horror, terror, hatred, loathing, detestation, aversion, antipathy, revulsion; complex, neurosis; informal thing, hang-up.

phone n. **1** *she spent hours on the phone* **telephone**, mobile (phone), car phone, cordless phone, speakerphone; extension; N. Amer. cell phone; Brit. informal blower; Brit. rhyming slang dog and bone. **2** *give me a phone sometime* **call**, telephone call, phone call; Brit. ring; informal buzz; Brit. informal tinkle, bell.
▸ v. *I'll phone you later* **telephone**, call, give someone a call; Brit. ring, ring up, give someone a ring; informal call up, give someone a buzz; Brit. informal give someone a bell/tinkle, get on the blower to; N. Amer. informal get someone on the horn.

phoney informal adj. *a phoney address* **bogus**, false, fake, fraudulent, spurious; counterfeit, forged, feigned; pseudo, imitation, sham, man-made, mock, ersatz, synthetic, artificial, faux; simulated, pretended, contrived, affected, insincere; informal pretend, put-on; Brit. informal cod.
– OPPOSITES authentic.
▸ n. **1** *he's nothing but a phoney* **impostor**, sham, fake, fraud, charlatan; informal con artist. **2** *the diamond's a phoney* **fake**, imitation, counterfeit, forgery.

photocopy n. **copy**, facsimile, duplicate, photostat; trademark Xerox, Ozalid.

photograph n. *a photograph of her father* **picture**, photo, snap, snapshot, shot, likeness, print, slide, transparency, still, enlargement; Brit. enprint; informal tranny, mugshot.
▸ v. *she was photographed leaving the castle* **take someone's picture/photo**, snap, shoot, film.

photographer n. **lensman**, paparazzo; cameraman; informal snapper; N. Amer. informal shutterbug.

photographic adj. **1** *a photographic record* **pictorial**, in photographs; cinematic, filmic. **2** *a photographic memory* **detailed**, graphic, exact, precise, accurate, vivid.

phrase n. *familiar words and phrases* **expression**, group of words, construction, locution, term, turn of phrase; idiom, idiomatic expression; saying, tag.
▸ v. *how could I phrase the question?* **express**, put into words, put, word, style, formulate, couch, frame, articulate, verbalize.

phraseology n. **wording**, choice of words, phrasing, way of speaking/writing, usage, idiom, diction, parlance, words, language, vocabulary, terminology; jargon; informal lingo, -speak, -ese.

physical adj. **1** *physical pleasure* **bodily**, corporeal, corporal, somatic; carnal, fleshly, non-spiritual. **2** *hard physical work* **manual**, labouring, blue-collar. **3** *the physical universe* **material**, concrete, tangible, palpable, solid, substantial, real, actual, visible.
– OPPOSITES mental, spiritual.

physician n. **doctor**, doctor of medicine, MD, medical practitioner, consultant; informal doc, medic; Brit. informal quack; informal dated sawbones.

physiognomy n. **face**, features, countenance, expression, look, mien; informal mug; Brit. informal phizog, phiz; Brit. rhyming slang boat race; N. Amer. informal puss; literary visage, lineaments.

physique n. **body**, build, figure, frame, anatomy, shape, form, proportions; muscles, musculature; informal vital statistics, bod.

pick v. **1** *I got a job picking apples* **harvest**, gather (in), collect, pluck; literary cull. **2** *pick the time that suits you best* **choose**, select, pick out, single out, take, opt for, plump for, elect, decide on, settle on, fix on, sift out, sort out; name, nominate. **3** *Beth picked at her food* **nibble**, toy with, play with, eat like a bird. **4** *people were singing and picking guitars* **strum**, twang, thrum, pluck. **5** *he tried to pick a fight* **provoke**, start, cause, incite, stir up, whip up, instigate, prompt, bring about.
▸ n. **1** *take your pick* **choice**, selection, option, decision; preference, favourite. **2** *the pick of the crop* **best**, finest, top, choice, choicest, prime, cream, flower, prize, pearl, gem, jewel, jewel in the crown, crème de la crème, elite.
□ **pick on** bully, victimize, tyrannize, torment, persecute, criticize, harass, hound, taunt, tease; informal get at, have it in for, have a down on, be down on, needle.
pick something out 1 *one painting was picked out for special mention* **choose**, select, pick, single out, opt for, plump for, decide on, elect, settle on, fix on, sift out, sort out; name, nominate. **2** *she picked out Jessica in the crowd* **see**, make out, distinguish, discern, spot, perceive, detect, notice, recognize, identify, catch sight of, glimpse; literary espy, behold, descry.
pick up improve, recover, be on the road to recovery, rally, make a comeback, bounce back, perk up, look up, take a turn for the better, turn the/a corner, be on the mend, make headway, make progress.
pick someone/something up lift, take up, raise, hoist, scoop up, gather up, snatch up.
pick someone up 1 *I'll pick you up after lunch* **fetch**, collect, call for. **2** *informal he was picked up by the police* **arrest**, apprehend, detain, take into custody, seize; informal nab, run in, bust; Brit. informal nick. **3** *informal he*

picked her up in a club **take up with**; informal get off with, pull, cop off with.

pick something up 1 *we picked it up at a flea market* **find**, discover, come across, stumble across, happen on, chance on; acquire, obtain, come by, get, procure; purchase, buy; informal get hold of, get/lay one's hands on, get one's mitts on, bag, land. **2** *he picked up the story in the 1950s* **resume**, take up, start again, recommence, continue, carry on with, go on with. **3** *she picked up a virus* **catch**, contract, get, go/come down with. **4** *he told us the bits of gossip he'd picked up* **hear**, hear tell, get wind of, be told, learn; glean, garner. **5** *we're picking up a distress signal* **receive**, detect, get, hear.

picket n. **1** *forty pickets were arrested* **striker**, demonstrator, protester, objector, picketer; flying picket. **2** *fences made of cedar pickets* **stake**, post, paling; upright, stanchion, pier, piling.
▶v. *over 200 people picketed the factory* **demonstrate at**, form a picket at, man the picket line at; blockade, shut off.

pickle n. **1** *a jar of pickle* **relish**, chutney, piccalilli. **2** *steep the vegetables in pickle* **marinade**, brine, vinegar. **3** informal *they got into an awful pickle* **plight**, predicament, mess, difficulty, trouble, dire/desperate straits, problem; informal tight corner, tight spot, jam, fix, scrape, bind, hole, hot water, fine kettle of fish; Brit. informal spot of bother.
▶v. *fish pickled in brine* **preserve**, souse, marinate, conserve; bottle, can, tin.

pick-me-up n. informal **1** *a drink that's a very good pick-me-up* **tonic**, restorative, energizer, stimulant, refresher, reviver; informal bracer; Medicine analeptic. **2** *his winning goal was a perfect pick-me-up* **boost**, boost to the spirits, fillip, stimulant, stimulus; informal shot in the arm.

pickpocket n. **thief**, petty thief, sneak thief; informal dipper; old use cutpurse.

pickup n. **improvement**, recovery, revival, upturn, upswing, rally, comeback, resurgence, renewal, turn for the better.
– OPPOSITES slump.

picnic n. **1** *a picnic on the beach* **outdoor meal**, alfresco meal; N. Amer. cookout. **2** informal *working for him was no picnic* **easy task/job**, child's play, five-finger exercise, gift, walkover; informal doddle, piece of cake, walk in the park, money for old rope, money for jam, cinch, breeze, kids' stuff, cakewalk, pushover; N. Amer. informal duck soup; Austral./NZ informal bludge.

pictorial adj. **illustrated**, in pictures, in picture form, in photographs, photographic, graphic.

picture n. **1** *pictures in an art gallery* **painting**, **drawing**, sketch, oil painting, watercolour, print, canvas, portrait, portrayal, illustration, artist's impression, artwork, depiction, likeness, representation, image, icon, miniature; fresco, mural, wall painting; informal oil. **2** *we were told not to take pictures* **photograph**, photo, snap, snapshot,

shot, print, slide, transparency, exposure, still, enlargement; Brit. enprint. **3** *a picture of the sort of person the child should be* **concept**, idea, impression, view, (mental) image, vision, visualization, notion. **4** *the picture of health* **personification**, embodiment, epitome, essence, quintessence, perfect example, soul, model. **5** *a picture starring Robert De Niro* **film**, movie, feature film, motion picture; informal flick; dated moving picture. **6** *we went to the pictures* **the cinema**, the movies, the silver screen, the big screen; informal the flicks.
▶v. **1** *he was pictured with his guests* **photograph**, snap, shoot, film. **2** *in the drawing they were pictured against a snowy background* **paint**, **draw**, sketch, depict, delineate, portray, show, illustrate. **3** *Anne still pictured Richard as he had been* **visualize**, see in one's mind's eye, conjure up a picture/image of, imagine, see, evoke.
□ **put someone in the picture** inform, fill in, explain the situation to, bring up to date, update, brief, keep posted; informal clue in, bring up to speed.

picturesque adj. **1** *a picturesque village* **attractive**, pretty, beautiful, lovely, scenic, charming, quaint, pleasing, delightful. **2** *a picturesque description* **vivid**, graphic, colourful, impressive, striking.
– OPPOSITES ugly, dull.

piddling adj. informal **trivial**, trifling, petty, footling, slight, small, insignificant, unimportant, inconsequential, inconsiderable, negligible; meagre, inadequate, insufficient, paltry, scant, scanty, derisory, pitiful, miserable, puny, niggardly, beggarly, mere; informal measly, pathetic, piffling, mingy, poxy; N. Amer. informal nickel-and-dime.

pie n. **pastry**, tart, tartlet, quiche, pasty, patty, turnover, strudel.

piebald adj. See **pied**.

piece n. **1** *a piece of cheese | a piece of wood* **bit**, slice, chunk, segment, section, lump, hunk, wedge, slab, block, cake, bar, cube, stick, length; offcut, sample, fragment, sliver, splinter, wafer, chip, crumb, scrap, remnant, shred, shard, snippet; mouthful, morsel; Brit. informal wodge. **2** *the pieces of a clock* **component**, part, bit, section, segment, constituent, element; unit, module. **3** *a piece of furniture* **item**, article, specimen. **4** *a piece of the profit* **share**, portion, slice, quota, part, bit, percentage, amount, quantity, ration, fraction, division; informal cut, rake-off; Brit. informal whack. **5** *pieces from his private collection* **work (of art)**, creation, production; composition, opus. **6** *the reporter who wrote the piece* **article**, item, story, report, essay, study, review, composition, column. **7** *the pieces on a chess board* **token**, counter, man, disc, chip, marker.
□ **in one piece 1** *the camera was still in one piece* **unbroken**, entire, whole, intact, undamaged, unharmed. **2** *I'll bring her back in one piece* **unhurt**, uninjured, unscathed,

p

safe, safe and sound.
in pieces broken, in bits, shattered,
smashed, in smithereens; informal bust.
go/fall to pieces have a breakdown, break
down, go out of one's mind, lose control,
lose one's head, fall apart; informal crack up,
lose it, come/fall apart at the seams, freak,
freak out.

pièce de résistance n. **masterpiece**,
magnum opus, chef-d'œuvre, masterwork,
tour de force, showpiece, prize, jewel in the
crown.

piecemeal adv. **a little at a time**, piece by
piece, bit by bit, gradually, slowly, in stages,
in steps, step by step, little by little, by
degrees, in/by fits and starts.

pied adj. **particoloured**, multicoloured,
variegated, black and white, brown and
white, piebald, skewbald, dappled, brindle,
spotted, mottled, speckled, flecked; N. Amer.
pinto.

pier n. **1** *a boat was tied to the pier* **jetty**, quay,
wharf, dock, landing, landing stage. **2** *the
piers of the bridge* **support**, cutwater, pile,
piling, abutment, buttress, stanchion, prop,
stay, upright, pillar, post, column.

pierce v. **1** *the metal pierced his flesh*
penetrate, puncture, perforate, prick, lance;
stab, spike, stick, impale, transfix, bore
through, drill through. **2** *his anguish pierced
her to the quick* **hurt**, wound, pain, sting,
sear, grieve, distress, upset, trouble, harrow,
afflict; affect, move.

piercing adj. **1** *a piercing shriek* **shrill**,
ear-splitting, high-pitched, penetrating,
strident, loud. **2** *the piercing wind* **bitter**,
biting, cutting, penetrating, sharp, keen,
stinging, raw; freezing, frigid, glacial, arctic,
chill. **3** *a piercing pain* **intense**, excruciating,
agonizing, sharp, stabbing, shooting,
stinging, severe, extreme, fierce, searing,
racking. **4** *his piercing gaze* **searching**,
probing, penetrating, penetrative, shrewd,
sharp, keen. **5** *his piercing intelligence*
perceptive, percipient, perspicacious,
penetrating, discerning, discriminating,
intelligent, quick-witted, sharp, sharp-
witted, shrewd, insightful, keen, acute,
astute, clever, smart, incisive, razor-edged,
trenchant.

piety n. **devoutness**, devotion, piousness,
religion, holiness, godliness, saintliness;
veneration, reverence, faith, religious duty,
spirituality, religious zeal, fervour; pietism,
religiosity.

piffle n. informal See **nonsense** (sense 1).

piffling adj. informal **inadequate**, insufficient,
tiny, small, minimal, trifling, paltry, pitiful,
negligible; miserly, miserable; informal measly,
stingy, lousy, pathetic, piddling, mingy, poxy.

pig n. **1** *a herd of pigs* **hog**, boar, sow, porker,
swine, piglet; children's word piggy. **2** *informal
he's eaten the lot, the pig* **glutton**, guzzler;
informal hog, greedy guts; Brit. informal gannet.
3 *informal he's been an absolute pig lately* informal
bastard, beast, louse, swine; Brit. informal
toerag; informal dated rotter, heel, stinker.

WORD LINKS
porcine relating to pigs
farrow (of a sow) give birth to piglets
swineherd a person who tends pigs
mast the fruit of forest trees, as food for pigs
pannage (in the past) the right of feeding pigs
in a wood

pigeonhole n. *journalistic pigeonholes*
category, categorization, class, classification,
group, grouping, designation, slot.
▶v. **1** *they were pigeonholed as an indie
guitar band* **categorize**, compartmentalize,
classify, characterize, label, brand, tag,
designate. **2** *the plan was pigeonholed last
year* **postpone**, put off, put back, defer,
shelve, hold over, put to one side, put on ice,
mothball, put in cold storage; N. Amer. table;
informal put on the back burner.

pig-headed adj. **obstinate**, stubborn (as
a mule), mulish, bullheaded, obdurate,
headstrong, self-willed, wilful, perverse,
contrary, recalcitrant, stiff-necked,
uncooperative, inflexible, uncompromising,
intractable, intransigent, unyielding;
Brit. informal bloody-minded, bolshie; formal
refractory.

pigment n. **colouring matter**, colouring,
colourant, colour, tint, dye, dyestuff.

pile¹ n. **1** *a pile of stones* **heap**, stack, mound,
pyramid, mass, quantity; collection,
accumulation, assemblage, store, stockpile,
hoard. **2** *informal I've a pile of work to do* **great
deal**, lot, large quantity/amount, quantities,
reams, mountain; abundance, cornucopia,
plethora; informal load, heap, mass, slew, ocean,
stack, ton; Brit. informal shedload; Austral./NZ
informal swag. **3** *informal he'd made his pile in the
fur trade* **fortune**, millions, billions; informal
small fortune, bomb, packet, bundle, wad; Brit.
informal loadsamoney. **4** *a huge Victorian pile*
mansion, stately home, manor, manor house,
country house; formal edifice.
▶v. **1** *he piled up the plates* **heap (up)**, stack
(up), put on top of each other. **2** *he piled his
plate with fried eggs* **load**, heap, fill (up),
lade, stack, charge, stock. **3** *his debts were
piling up* **increase**, grow, mount up, escalate,
soar, spiral, leap up, shoot up, rocket, climb,
accumulate, accrue, build up, multiply.
4 *we piled into the car* **crowd**, climb, pack,
squeeze, push, shove.
□ **pile it on** informal exaggerate, overstate
the case, make a mountain out of a molehill,
overdo it, overplay it, overdramatize,
catastrophize; informal lay it on thick, lay it on
with a trowel.

pile² n. *a wall supported by timber piles* **post**,
stake, pillar, column, support, foundation,
piling, abutment, pier, cutwater, buttress,
stanchion, upright.

pile³ n. *a carpet with a short pile* **nap**, fibres,
threads.

pile-up n. **crash**, multiple crash, collision,
multiple collision, smash, accident, road
accident; Brit. RTA (road traffic accident);
N. Amer. wreck; informal smash-up; Brit. informal
shunt.

pilfer v. **steal**, thieve, take, snatch, purloin, loot; informal swipe, rob, nab, rip off, lift, 'liberate', 'borrow', filch, snaffle; Brit. informal pinch, half-inch, nick, whip, knock off, nobble; N. Amer. informal heist.

pilgrim n. worshipper, devotee, believer; traveller, crusader, haji; literary wayfarer; historical palmer.

pilgrimage n. **religious journey**, religious expedition, hajj, crusade, mission.

pill n. **tablet**, capsule, caplet, pellet, lozenge, pastille; Veterinary Medicine bolus.

pillage v. **1** the abbey was pillaged **ransack**, rob, plunder, despoil, raid, loot; sack, devastate, lay waste, ravage, rape. **2** columns pillaged from an ancient town **steal**, pilfer, thieve, take, snatch, purloin, loot; informal swipe, rob, nab, rip off, lift, 'liberate', 'borrow', filch, snaffle; Brit. informal pinch, half-inch, nick, whip, knock off, nobble; N. Amer. informal heist.
▶ n. the rebels were intent on pillage **robbery**, robbing, raiding, plunder, looting, sacking, rape, marauding; literary rapine.

pillar n. **1** stone pillars **column**, post, support, upright, baluster, pier, pile, pilaster, stanchion, prop, newel; obelisk, monolith. **2** a pillar of the community **stalwart**, mainstay, bastion, rock; leading light, worthy, backbone, support, upholder, champion.

pillory n. offenders were put in the pillory **stocks**.
▶ v. **1** he was pilloried by the press **attack**, criticize, censure, condemn, denigrate, lambaste, savage, stigmatize, denounce; informal knock, slam, pan, bash, crucify, hammer; Brit. informal slate, rubbish, slag off; N. Amer. informal pummel; Austral./NZ informal bag, monster; formal excoriate. **2** they were pilloried at school **ridicule**, jeer at, sneer at, deride, mock, scorn, make fun of, poke fun at, laugh at, scoff at, tease, taunt, rag.

pillow n. his head rested on the pillow **cushion**, bolster, pad; headrest.
▶ v. she pillowed her head on folded arms **cushion**, cradle, rest, lay, support.

pilot n. **1** a fighter pilot **airman/airwoman**, flyer; captain, commander, co-pilot, wingman; informal skipper; N. Amer. informal jock; dated aviator, aeronaut. **2** a harbour pilot **navigator**, helmsman, steersman, coxswain. **3** a pilot for a TV series **trial episode**; sample, experiment.
▶ adj. a pilot project **experimental**, exploratory, trial, test, sample, speculative; preliminary.
▶ v. **1** he piloted the jet to safety **navigate**, guide, manoeuvre, steer, control, direct, captain, shepherd; fly, aviate; drive; sail; informal skipper. **2** the questionnaire has been piloted **test**, trial, try out; assess, investigate, examine, appraise, evaluate.

pimp n. **procurer**, procuress; brothel-keeper, madam; informal ponce; old use bawd.

pimple n. **spot**, pustule, bleb, boil, swelling, eruption, blackhead, carbuncle, blister; (**pimples**) acne; informal whitehead, zit; Scottish informal plook; technical comedo, papule.

pin n. **1** fasten the hem with a pin **tack**, safety pin, nail, staple, fastener. **2** a broken pin in the machine **bolt**, peg, rivet, dowel, screw. **3** they wore name pins **badge**, brooch.
▶ v. **1** she pinned the brooch to her dress **attach**, fasten, affix, fix, tack, clip; join, secure. **2** they pinned him to the ground **hold**, press, hold fast, hold down; restrain, pinion, immobilize. **3** they pinned the crime on him **blame for**, hold responsible for, attribute to, impute to, ascribe to; lay something at someone's door; informal stick on.
□ **pin someone/something down 1** our troops can pin down the enemy **confine**, **trap**, hem in, corner, close in, shut in, hedge in, pen in, restrain, entangle, enmesh, immobilize. **2** she tried to pin him down to a plan **constrain**, make someone commit themselves, pressure, pressurize, tie down, nail down. **3** it evoked a memory but he couldn't pin it down **define**, put one's finger on, put into words, express, name, specify, identify, pinpoint, place.

pinch v. **1** he pinched my arm **nip**, tweak, squeeze, grasp. **2** my new shoes pinch my toes **hurt**, pain; squeeze, crush, cramp; be uncomfortable. **3** I scraped and pinched to afford it **economize**, scrimp (and save), be sparing, be frugal, cut back, tighten one's belt, retrench, cut one's coat according to one's cloth; informal be stingy, be tight. **4** informal he was pinched for drink-driving **arrest**, apprehend, take into custody, detain, seize, catch, take in, haul in; informal collar, nab, pick up, run in, nick, bust, nail, do. **5** Brit. informal you pinched his biscuits **steal**, thieve, take, snatch, pilfer, purloin, loot; informal swipe, rob, nab, lift, 'liberate', 'borrow', filch; Brit. informal nick, half-inch, whip, knock off, nobble; N. Amer. informal heist.
▶ n. **1** he gave her arm a pinch **nip**, tweak, squeeze. **2** a pinch of salt **bit**, touch, dash, spot, trace, soupçon, speck, taste; informal smidgen, tad.
□ **at a pinch** if necessary, if need be, in an emergency, just possibly, with difficulty; N. Amer. in a pinch; Brit. informal at a push.
feel the pinch suffer hardship, be short of money, be poor, be impoverished.

pinched adj. their pinched faces **strained**, stressed, fraught, tense, taut; tired, worn, drained, sapped; wan, peaky, pale, grey, blanched; thin, drawn, haggard, gaunt.
– OPPOSITES healthy.

pine v. **1** I am pining away from love **languish**, decline, weaken, waste away, wilt, wither, fade, sicken, droop; brood, mope, moon. **2** he was pining for his son **yearn**, long, ache, sigh, hunger, languish; miss, mourn, lament, grieve over, shed tears for, bemoan, rue, eat one's heart out over; informal itch.

pinion v. **hold down**, pin down, restrain, hold fast, immobilize; tie, bind, truss (up), shackle, fetter, hobble, manacle, handcuff; informal cuff.

p

pink adj. **rose**, rosy, rosé, pale red, salmon, coral; flushed, blushing.
▶ n. informal *she's in the pink of condition* **prime**, perfection, best, finest, height; utmost, greatest, apex, zenith, acme, bloom.
□ **in the pink** informal in good health, very healthy, in rude health, very well, hale and hearty; blooming, flourishing, thriving, vigorous, strong, lusty, robust, in fine fettle, (as) fit as a fiddle, in excellent shape.

pinnacle n. **1** *pinnacles of rock* **peak**, needle, aiguille, hoodoo, crag, tor; summit, mountaintop, crest, apex, tip; Geology inselberg. **2** *the pinnacles of the clock tower* **turret**, minaret, spire, finial, shikara, mirador. **3** *the pinnacle of the sport* **highest level**, peak, height, high point, top, apex, zenith, apogee, acme.
– OPPOSITES nadir.

pinpoint n. *a pinpoint of light* **point**, spot, speck, dot, speckle.
▶ adj. *pinpoint accuracy* **precise**, strict, exact, meticulous, scrupulous, punctilious, accurate, careful.
▶ v. *pinpoint the cause of the trouble* **identify**, determine, distinguish, discover, find, locate, detect, track down, spot, diagnose, recognize, pin down, home in on, put one's finger on.

pioneer n. **1** *the pioneers of the Wild West* **settler**, colonist, colonizer, frontiersman/ frontierswoman, explorer, trailblazer. **2** *a pioneer of motoring* **developer**, innovator, trailblazer, groundbreaker, spearhead; founder, founding father, architect, creator; formal neoteric.
▶ v. *he pioneered the sale of insurance* **introduce**, develop, evolve, launch, instigate, initiate, spearhead, institute, establish, found, be the father/mother of, originate, set in motion, create; lay the groundwork, prepare the way, blaze a trail, break new ground.

pious adj. **1** *a pious family* **religious**, devout, God-fearing, churchgoing, spiritual, prayerful, holy, godly, saintly, dedicated, reverent, dutiful, righteous. **2** *a pious platitude* **sanctimonious**, hypocritical, insincere, self-righteous, holier-than-thou, pietistic, churchy; informal goody-goody; Brit. informal pi. **3** *a pious hope* **forlorn**, vain, doomed, hopeless, desperate; unlikely, unrealistic.
– OPPOSITES irreligious, sincere.

pip n. **seed**, stone, pit.

pipe n. **1** *a central-heating pipe* **tube**, conduit, hose, main, duct, line, channel, pipeline, drain; tubing, piping, siphon. **2** *he smokes a pipe* briar (pipe), meerschaum, chibouk; hookah, narghile, hubble-bubble, bong; Brit. churchwarden; Scottish & N. English cutty. **3** *she was playing a pipe* **whistle**, penny whistle, flute, recorder, fife; chanter. **4** *regimental pipes and drums* **bagpipes**, uillean pipes; pan pipes.
▶ v. **1** *the beer is piped into barrels* **siphon**, feed, channel, run, convey. **2** *programmes*

piped in from London **transmit**, feed, patch. **3** *he heard a tune being piped* **whistle**, tootle; literary flute. **4** *a curlew piped* **chirp**, cheep, chirrup, twitter, warble, trill, peep, sing, shrill.
□ **pipe down** informal be quiet, be silent, hush, stop talking, hold one's tongue; informal shut up, shut one's mouth, button it, button one's lip, belt up, put a sock in it; N. Amer. informal can it.

pipe dream n. **fantasy**, false hope, illusion, delusion, daydream, chimera; castle in the air, castle in Spain; informal pie in the sky.

pipeline n. *a gas pipeline* **pipe**, conduit, main, line, duct, tube.
□ **in the pipeline** on the way, coming, forthcoming, upcoming, imminent, about to happen, near, close, brewing, in the offing, in the wind.

pipsqueak n. informal **nobody**, nonentity, insignificant person, non-person, cipher, small fry; upstart, stripling; informal squirt, whippersnapper; N. Amer. informal picayune; old use dandiprat.

piquant adj. **1** *a piquant sauce* **spicy**, tangy, peppery, hot; tasty, flavoursome, flavourful, appetizing, savoury; pungent, sharp, tart, zesty, strong, salty. **2** *a piquant story* **intriguing**, stimulating, interesting, fascinating, colourful, exciting, lively; spicy, provocative, racy; informal juicy.
– OPPOSITES bland, dull.

pique n. *a fit of pique* **irritation**, annoyance, resentment, anger, displeasure, indignation, petulance, ill humour, vexation, exasperation, disgruntlement, discontent; offence, umbrage.
▶ v. **1** *his curiosity was piqued* **stimulate**, arouse, rouse, provoke, whet, awaken, excite, kindle, stir, galvanize. **2** *she was piqued by his neglect* **irritate**, annoy, bother, vex, displease, upset, offend, affront, anger, exasperate, infuriate, gall, irk, nettle; informal peeve, aggravate, miff, rile, bug, needle, get someone's back up, hack off, get someone's goat; Brit. informal nark, give someone the hump; N. Amer. informal tick off, tee off.

piracy n. **1** *piracy on the high seas* **robbery at sea**, freebooting; old use buccaneering. **2** *software piracy* **illegal copying**, plagiarism, copyright infringement, bootlegging.

pirate n. **1** *pirates boarded the ship* **freebooter**, marauder, raider; historical privateer; old use buccaneer, corsair. **2** *software pirates* **copyright infringer**, plagiarist, plagiarizer.
▶ v. *designers may pirate good ideas* **reproduce illegally**, copy illegally, plagiarize, poach, steal, appropriate, bootleg; informal crib, lift, rip off; Brit. informal nick, pinch.

pirouette n. *she did a little pirouette* **spin**, twirl, whirl, turn.
▶ v. *she pirouetted before the mirror* **spin round**, twirl, whirl, turn round, revolve, pivot.

pistol n. **revolver**, gun, handgun, side arm; automatic, six-shooter, thirty-eight, derringer; informal gat; N. Amer. informal piece, shooting iron; trademark Colt, Luger.

pit[1] n. **1** *a pit in the ground* **hole**, ditch, trench, trough, hollow, excavation, cavity, crater, pothole; shaft, mineshaft. **2** *pit closures* **coal mine**, colliery, quarry. **3** *the pits in her skin* **pockmark**, pock, hollow, indentation, depression, dent, dint, dimple.
▶ v. **1** *his skin had been pitted by acne* **mark**, pockmark, scar, blemish, disfigure.
2 *raindrops pitted the bare earth* **make holes in**, make hollows in, dent, indent, dint.
□ **pit someone/something against** set against, match against, put in opposition to, put in competition with; compete with, contend with, vie with, wrestle with.
the pits informal the worst, the lowest of the low; rock bottom, awful, abysmal, appalling, terrible, dreadful, deplorable; informal lousy, dire; Brit. informal chronic.

pit[2] n. *cherry pits* **stone**, pip, seed.

pitch[1] n. **1** *the pitch was unfit for cricket* **playing field**, field, ground, sports field; stadium, arena; Brit. informal park. **2** *her voice rose in pitch* **tone**, timbre, key, modulation, frequency. **3** *the pitch of the roof* **gradient**, slope, slant, angle, steepness, tilt, incline, inclination. **4** *her anger reached such a pitch that she screamed* **level**, intensity, point, degree, height, extent. **5** *a pitch of the ball* **throw**, fling, hurl, toss, lob; delivery; informal chuck, heave. **6** *his sales pitch* **patter**, talk; informal spiel, line. **7** *street traders reserved their pitches* **site**, place, spot, station; Scottish stance; Brit. informal patch.
▶ v. **1** *he pitched the note into the fire* **throw**, toss, fling, hurl, cast, lob, flip, propel, bowl; informal chuck, sling, heave, bung; N. Amer. informal peg; Austral. informal hoy; NZ informal bish; dated shy. **2** *he pitched overboard* **fall**, tumble, topple, plunge, plummet. **3** *they pitched their tents* **put up**, set up, erect, raise. **4** *the boat pitched* **lurch**, toss (about), plunge, roll, reel, sway, rock, keel, list, wallow, labour.
□ **make a pitch for** try to obtain, try to acquire, try to get, bid for, make a bid for.
pitch in help (out), assist, lend a hand, join in, participate, contribute, do one's bit, chip in, cooperate, collaborate; Brit. informal muck in.
pitch into attack, turn on, lash out at, set upon, assault, fly at, tear into, weigh into, belabour; informal lay into, let someone have it, take a pop at; N. Amer. informal light into.

pitch[2] n. *cement coated with pitch* **bitumen**, asphalt, tar.

pitch-black adj. **black**, dark, pitch-dark, inky, jet-black, coal-black, jet, ebony; starless, moonless; literary Stygian.

pitcher n. **jug**, ewer, jar; N. Amer. creamer; historical jorum.

piteous adj. **sad**, pitiful, pitiable, pathetic, heart-rending, heartbreaking, moving, touching; plaintive, poignant, forlorn; poor, wretched, miserable.

pitfall n. **hazard**, danger, risk, peril, difficulty, issue, problem, catch, snag, stumbling block, drawback.

pith n. **1** *the pith of the argument* **essence**, main point, fundamentals, heart, substance, nub, core, quintessence, crux, gist, meat, kernel, marrow, burden; informal nitty-gritty. **2** *he writes with pith and exactitude* **succinctness**, conciseness, concision, pithiness, brevity; cogency, weight, depth, force.

pithy adj. **succinct**, terse, concise, compact, short (and sweet), brief, condensed, to the point, epigrammatic, crisp, thumbnail; significant, meaningful, expressive, telling; formal compendious.
– OPPOSITES verbose.

pitiful adj. **1** *a child in a pitiful state* **distressing**, sad, piteous, pitiable, pathetic, heart-rending, heartbreaking, moving, touching, tear-jerking; plaintive, poignant, forlorn; poor, sorry, wretched, abject, miserable. **2** *a pitiful £50 a month* **paltry**, miserable, meagre, insufficient, trifling, negligible, pitiable, derisory; informal pathetic, measly, piddling, mingy; Brit. informal poxy. **3** *his performance was pitiful* **dreadful**, awful, terrible, appalling, abysmal, lamentable, hopeless, poor, bad, feeble, pitiable, woeful, inadequate, below par, deplorable, laughable; informal pathetic, useless, lousy, dire.

pitiless adj. **merciless**, unmerciful, unpitying, ruthless, cruel, heartless, remorseless, hard-hearted, cold-hearted, harsh, callous, severe, unsparing, unforgiving, unfeeling, uncaring, unsympathetic, uncharitable, brutal, inhuman, inhumane, barbaric, sadistic.
– OPPOSITES merciful.

pittance n. **a tiny amount**, next to nothing, very little; informal peanuts, chicken feed, slave wages; N. Amer. informal chump change.

pitted adj. **1** *his skin was pitted* **pockmarked**, pocked, scarred, marked, blemished. **2** *the pitted lane* **potholed**, rutted, rutty, holey, bumpy, rough, uneven.
– OPPOSITES smooth.

pity n. **1** *a voice full of pity* **compassion**, commiseration, condolence, sympathy, fellow feeling, understanding; sorrow, regret, sadness. **2** *it's a pity he never had children* **shame**, sad thing, bad luck, misfortune; informal crime, bummer, sin.
– OPPOSITES indifference, cruelty.
▶ v. *they pitied me* **feel sorry for**, feel for, sympathize with, empathize with, commiserate with, take pity on, be moved by, condole with, grieve for.
□ **take pity on** feel sorry for, relent, be compassionate towards, be sympathetic towards, have mercy on, help (out), put someone out of their misery.

pivot n. **1** *the machine turns on a pivot* **fulcrum**, axis, axle, swivel; pin, shaft, hub, spindle, hinge, kingpin, gudgeon. **2** *the pivot of government policy* **centre**, focus, hub,

heart, nucleus, crux, keystone, cornerstone, linchpin, kingpin.
▸ v. **1** *the panel pivots inwards* **rotate**, turn, swivel, revolve, spin. **2** *it all pivoted on his response* **depend**, hinge, turn, centre, hang, rely, rest; revolve around.

pivotal adj. **central**, crucial, vital, critical, focal, essential, key, decisive.

pixie n. **elf**, fairy, sprite, imp, brownie, puck, leprechaun; literary faerie, fay.

placard n. **notice**, poster, sign, bill, advertisement; banner; informal ad; Brit. informal advert.

placate v. **pacify**, calm, appease, mollify, soothe, win over, conciliate, propitiate, make peace with, humour; Austral./NZ square someone off.
– OPPOSITES provoke.

place n. **1** *an ideal place for dinner* **location**, site, spot, setting, position, situation, area, region, locale; venue; technical locus. **2** *foreign places* **country**, state, area, region, town, city; locality, district; literary clime. **3** *a place of her own* **home**, house, flat, apartment; accommodation, property, pied-à-terre; rooms, quarters; informal pad, digs; Brit. informal gaff; formal residence, abode, dwelling (place), domicile, habitation. **4** *if I were in your place, I'd agree* **situation**, position, circumstances; informal shoes. **5** *a place was reserved for her* **seat**, chair, space. **6** *I offered him a place in the company* **job**, position, post, appointment, situation, office; employment. **7** *I know my place* **status**, position, standing, rank, niche; dated estate, station. **8** *it was not her place to sort it out* **responsibility**, duty, job, task, role, function, concern, affair, charge; right, privilege, prerogative.
▸ v. **1** *books were placed on the table* **put (down)**, set (down), lay, deposit, position, plant, rest, stand, station, situate, leave; informal stick, dump, bung, park, plonk, pop; N. Amer. informal plunk. **2** *the trust you placed in me* **put**, lay, set, invest. **3** *a survey placed the company sixth* **rank**, order, grade, class, classify, categorize; put, set, assign. **4** *Joe couldn't quite place her* **identify**, recognize, remember, put a name to, pin down; locate, pinpoint. **5** *we were placed with foster-parents* **accommodate**, house; allocate, assign, appoint.
□ **in place 1** *the veil was held in place by pearls* **in position**, in situ. **2** *the plans are in place* **ready**, set up, all set, established, arranged, in order.
in place of instead of, rather than, as a substitute for, as a replacement for, in exchange for, in lieu of; in someone's stead.
out of place 1 *she never had a hair out of place* **out of position**, out of order, in disarray, disarranged, in a mess, messy, topsy-turvy, muddled. **2** *he said something out of place* **inappropriate**, unsuitable, unseemly, improper, untoward, out of keeping, unbecoming, wrong. **3** *she seemed out of place in a launderette* **incongruous**, like a fish out of water; uncomfortable, uneasy.

put someone in their place humiliate, take down a peg or two, deflate, crush, squash, humble; informal cut down to size, settle someone's hash; N. Amer. informal make someone eat crow.
take place happen, occur, come about, transpire, crop up, materialize, arise; N. Amer. informal go down; literary come to pass, befall, betide.
take the place of replace, stand in for, substitute for, act for, fill in for, cover for, relieve.

placement n. **1** *the placement of the chairs* **positioning**, placing, arrangement, position, deployment, location, disposition. **2** *teaching placements* **job**, post, assignment, posting, position, appointment, engagement.

placid adj. **1** *she's normally very placid* **even-tempered**, calm, tranquil, equable, equanimous, unexcitable, serene, mild, {cool, calm, and collected}, composed, self-possessed, poised, easy-going, level-headed, steady, unruffled, unperturbed, phlegmatic; informal unflappable. **2** *a placid village* **quiet**, calm, tranquil, still, peaceful, undisturbed, restful, sleepy.
– OPPOSITES excitable, bustling.

plagiarism n. **copying**, infringement of copyright, piracy, theft, stealing; informal cribbing.

plagiarize v. **copy**, infringe the copyright of, pirate, steal, poach, appropriate; informal rip off, crib, 'borrow'; Brit. informal pinch, nick.

plague n. **1** *they died of the plague* **bubonic plague**, pneumonic plague, the Black Death; disease, sickness, epidemic; dated contagion; old use pestilence. **2** *a plague of cat fleas* **infestation**, epidemic, invasion, swarm, multitude, host. **3** *theft is the plague of restaurants* **bane**, curse, scourge, affliction, blight.
▸ v. **1** *he was plagued by poor health* **afflict**, bedevil, torment, trouble, beset, dog, curse. **2** *he plagued her with questions* **pester**, harass, badger, bother, torment, persecute, bedevil, harry, hound, trouble, irritate, nag, annoy, vex, molest; informal hassle, bug, aggravate; N. English informal mither; N. Amer. informal devil.

plain adj. **1** *it was plain that something was wrong* **obvious**, (crystal) clear, evident, apparent, manifest, patent; discernible, perceptible, noticeable, recognizable, unmistakable, transparent; pronounced, marked, striking, conspicuous, self-evident, indisputable; as plain as a pikestaff, writ large; informal standing/sticking out like a sore thumb, standing/sticking out a mile. **2** *plain English* **intelligible**, comprehensible, understandable, clear, coherent, uncomplicated, lucid, unambiguous, simple, straightforward, user-friendly; formal perspicuous. **3** *plain speaking* **candid**, frank, outspoken, forthright, direct, honest, truthful, blunt, bald, explicit, unequivocal; informal upfront. **4** *a plain dress* **simple**, ordinary, unadorned, unembellished,

unornamented, unostentatious, unfussy, homely, basic, modest, unsophisticated, without frills; restrained, muted; everyday, workaday. **5** *a plain girl* **unattractive**, unprepossessing, ugly, ill-favoured, unlovely, ordinary; N. Amer. homely; informal not much to look at; Brit. informal no oil painting. **6** *it was plain bad luck* **sheer**, pure, downright, out-and-out, unmitigated.
– OPPOSITES obscure, fancy, attractive, pretentious.
▸ adv. *this is just plain stupid* **downright**, utterly, absolutely, completely, totally, really, thoroughly, positively, simply, unquestionably, undeniably; informal plumb.
▸ n. *the plains of North America* **grassland**, flatland, lowland, pasture, meadowland, prairie, savannah, steppe; tableland, tundra, pampas, veld.

plain-spoken adj. **candid**, frank, outspoken, forthright, direct, honest, truthful, open, blunt, straightforward, explicit, unequivocal, unambiguous, not afraid to call a spade a spade; informal upfront.
– OPPOSITES evasive.

plaintive adj. **mournful**, sad, wistful, doleful, pathetic, pitiful, piteous, melancholy, sorrowful, unhappy, wretched, woeful, forlorn, woebegone; literary dolorous.

plan n. **1** *a plan for raising money* **scheme**, idea, proposal, proposition, suggestion; project, programme, system, method, procedure, strategy, stratagem, formula, recipe; way, means, measure, tactic. **2** *her plan was to win a medal* **intention**, aim, idea, intent, objective, object, goal, target, ambition. **3** *plans for the clubhouse* **blueprint**, drawing, diagram, sketch, layout, artist's impression; illustration, representation; N. Amer. plat.
▸ v. **1** *plan your route in advance* **organize**, arrange, work out, design, outline, map out, prepare, schedule, formulate, frame, develop, devise, concoct; plot, scheme, hatch, brew; N. Amer. slate. **2** *he plans to buy a house* **intend**, aim, propose, mean, hope, want, wish, desire, envisage; formal purpose. **3** *I'm planning a new garden* **design**, draw up, sketch out, map out; N. Amer. plat.

plane[1] n. **1** *a horizontal plane* **flat surface**, level surface; the flat, horizontal. **2** *a higher plane of achievement* **level**, degree, standard, stratum; position, rung, echelon.
▸ adj. *a plane surface* **flat**, level, horizontal, even; smooth, regular, uniform; technical planar.
▸ v. **1** *seagulls planed overhead* **soar**, glide, float, drift, wheel. **2** *boats planed across the water* **skim**, glide.

plane[2] n. *the plane took off* **aircraft**, airliner, jet, jetliner; flying machine; Brit. aeroplane; N. Amer. airplane, ship.

planet n. **celestial body**, heavenly body, satellite, moon, earth, asteroid, planetoid; literary orb.

plangent adj. literary **melancholy**, mournful, plaintive; sonorous, resonant, loud.

plank n. **board**, floorboard, timber, stave.

planning n. **preparation(s)**, organization, arrangement, design; forethought, groundwork.

plant n. **1** *garden plants* flower, vegetable, herb, shrub, weed; (**plants**) vegetation, greenery, flora, herbage, verdure. **2** *a CIA plant* **spy**, informant, informer, (secret) agent, mole, infiltrator, operative; N. Amer. informal spook. **3** *the plant commenced production* **factory**, works, foundry, mill, workshop, yard; old use manufactory.
▸ v. **1** *plant the seeds this autumn* **sow**, scatter, seed; bed out, transplant. **2** *he planted his feet on the ground* **place**, put, set, position, situate, settle; informal plonk. **3** *she planted the idea in his mind* **instil**, implant, impress, imprint, put, place, introduce, fix, establish, lodge. **4** *letters were planted to embarrass them* **hide**, conceal, secrete.

> **WORD LINKS**
>
> **botany** the scientific study of plants
> **herbivore** an animal that feeds on plants
> **herbicide** a substance used to kill plants
> **photosynthesis** the process by which green plants use sunlight to form nutrients
> **chlorophyll** the green pigment in plants which enables photosynthesis

plaque n. **plate**, tablet, panel, sign, plaquette, cartouche; Brit. brass.

plaster n. **1** *the plaster covering the bricks* **plasterwork**, stucco, pargeting; trademark Artex. **2** *a statuette made of plaster* **plaster of Paris**, gypsum. **3** *waterproof plasters* **sticking plaster**, (adhesive) dressing, bandage; trademark Elastoplast, Band-Aid.
▸ v. **1** *bread plastered with butter* **cover thickly**, smother, spread, smear, cake, coat. **2** *his hair was plastered down with sweat* **flatten** (**down**), smooth down, slick down.

plastic adj. **1** *at high temperatures the rocks become plastic* **malleable**, mouldable, pliable, pliant, ductile, flexible, soft, workable, bendable; informal bendy. **2** *the plastic minds of children* **impressionable**, malleable, receptive, pliable, pliant, flexible; compliant, tractable, biddable, persuadable, susceptible, manipulable. **3** *a plastic smile* **artificial**, false, fake, superficial, pseudo, bogus, unnatural, insincere; informal phoney, pretend.
– OPPOSITES rigid, intractable, genuine.

plate n. **1** *a dinner plate* **dish**, platter, salver, paten; historical trencher; old use charger. **2** *a plate of spaghetti* **plateful**, helping, portion, serving. **3** *steel plates* **panel**, sheet, layer, pane, slab. **4** *a brass plate on the door* **plaque**, sign, tablet, plaquette, cartouche; Brit. brass. **5** *the book has colour plates* **picture**, print, illustration, photograph, photo.
▸ v. *the roof was plated with steel* **cover**, coat, overlay, laminate, veneer; electroplate, galvanize, gild.

plateau n. **1** *a windswept plateau* **upland**, tableland, plain, mesa, highland. **2** *prices*

p

reached a plateau quiescent period; let-up, respite, lull.

platform n. **1** *he made a speech from the platform* stage, dais, rostrum, podium, soapbox. **2** *the Democratic Party's platform* policy, programme, party line, manifesto, plan, principles, objectives, aims.

platitude n. cliché, truism, commonplace, banality, old chestnut, bromide.

platitudinous adj. **hackneyed**, overworked, overused, clichéd, banal, trite, commonplace, well worn, stale, tired, unoriginal; informal corny, old hat.
– OPPOSITES original.

platonic adj. **non-sexual**, non-physical, chaste; intellectual, friendly.
– OPPOSITES sexual.

platoon n. **unit**, patrol, troop, squad, squadron, team, company, corps, outfit, detachment, contingent.

platter n. **plate**, dish, salver, paten, tray; historical trencher; old use charger.

plaudits plural n. **praise**, acclaim, commendation, congratulations, accolades, compliments, cheers, applause, tributes, bouquets; a pat on the back; informal a (big) hand.
– OPPOSITES criticism.

plausible adj. **credible**, reasonable, believable, likely, feasible, tenable, possible, conceivable, imaginable; convincing, persuasive, cogent, sound, rational, logical, thinkable.
– OPPOSITES unlikely.

play v. **1** *the children played with toys* **amuse oneself**, entertain oneself, enjoy oneself, have fun; relax, occupy oneself, divert oneself; frolic, frisk, romp, caper; informal mess about/around, lark (about/around); dated sport. **2** *I used to play football* **take part in**, participate in, be involved in, compete in, do. **3** *Liverpool play Oxford on Sunday* **compete against**, take on, challenge, vie with. **4** *he was to play Macbeth* **act (the part of)**, take the role of, appear as, portray, depict, impersonate, represent, render, perform; formal personate. **5** *he learned to play the flute* **perform on**, make music on; blow, sound. **6** *the sunlight played on the water* **dance**, flit, ripple, touch; sparkle, glint.
▶ n. **1** *a balance between work and play* **amusement**, entertainment, relaxation, recreation, diversion, distraction, leisure; enjoyment, pleasure, fun, games, fun and games; horseplay, merrymaking, revelry; informal living it up; dated sport. **2** *a Shakespeare play* **drama**, comedy, tragedy; production, performance, show, sketch. **3** *she knew the play of the real world* **action**, activity, operation, working, function; interaction, interplay. **4** *there was a little play in the rope* **movement**, slack, give; room to manoeuvre, scope, latitude.
□ **play around** informal womanize, philander, have affairs, flirt; informal carry on, mess about/around, play the field, sleep around; Brit. informal play away; N. Amer. informal fool around.

play at pretend to be, pass oneself off as, masquerade as, profess to be, pose as, impersonate; fake, feign, simulate, affect; N. Amer. informal make like.

play ball informal cooperate, collaborate, play the game, show willing, help, lend a hand, assist, contribute; informal pitch in.

play something down make light of, make little of, gloss over, de-emphasize, downplay, understate; soft-pedal, tone down, diminish, trivialize, underrate, underestimate, undervalue; disparage, belittle, scoff at, sneer at, shrug off; informal pooh-pooh.

play for time stall, temporize, delay, hold back, hang fire, procrastinate, drag one's feet.

play it by ear improvise, extemporize, ad lib; make it up as one goes along, think on one's feet; informal busk it, wing it.

play on *they play on our fears* exploit, take advantage of, use, turn to (one's) account, profit by, capitalize on, trade on, milk, abuse.

play the fool clown about/around, fool about/around, mess about/around, lark about/around, monkey about/around, joke; informal horse about/around, act the goat; Brit. informal muck about/around.

play the game play fair, be fair, play by the rules, conform, be a good sport, toe the line.

play up Brit. informal **1** *the boys really did play up* **misbehave**, be bad, be naughty, get up to mischief, be disobedient, cause trouble. **2** *the boiler's playing up* **malfunction**, not work, be defective, be faulty; informal go on the blink, act up. **3** *his leg was playing up* **be painful**, hurt, ache, be sore, cause discomfort; informal kill someone, give someone gyp.

play something up emphasize, accentuate, call attention to, point up, underline, highlight, spotlight, foreground, feature, stress, accent.

play up to ingratiate oneself with, curry favour with, court, fawn over, make up to, keep someone sweet, toady to, crawl to, pander to, flatter; informal soft-soap, suck up to, butter up, lick someone's boots.

playboy n. **socialite**, pleasure-seeker, sybarite; ladies' man, womanizer, philanderer, rake, roué; informal ladykiller.

player n. **1** *a tournament for young players* **participant**, contestant, competitor, contender; sportsman/sportswoman, athlete. **2** *the players in the orchestra* **musician**, performer, instrumentalist, soloist, virtuoso. **3** *the players of the Royal Shakespeare Company* **actor**, actress, performer, thespian, entertainer, artist(e), trouper.

playful adj. **1** *a playful mood* **frisky**, jolly, lively, full of fun, sportive, high-spirited, exuberant, perky; mischievous, impish, rascally, tricksy; informal full of beans; literary frolicsome; dated gay; formal ludic. **2** *a playful remark* **light-hearted**, in jest, joking, jokey, teasing, humorous, jocular, good-natured, tongue-in-cheek, facetious, frivolous, flippant, arch; informal waggish.
– OPPOSITES serious.

p

playground n. **play area**, park, playing field, recreation ground; Brit. informal rec.

playmate n. **friend**, playfellow, companion; informal chum, pal; Brit. informal mate; N. Amer. informal buddy.

plaything n. **toy**, game.

playwright n. **dramatist**, dramaturge, scriptwriter, screenwriter, writer, scenarist; tragedian.

plea n. **1** *a plea for aid* **appeal**, entreaty, supplication, petition, request, call, suit, solicitation. **2** *her plea of a headache was unconvincing* **claim**, explanation, defence, justification; excuse, pretext.

plead v. **1** *he pleaded with her to stay* **beg**, implore, entreat, appeal to, supplicate, petition, request, ask, call on; literary beseech. **2** *she pleaded ignorance* **claim**, use as an excuse, assert, allege, argue, state.

pleasant adj. **1** *a pleasant evening* **enjoyable**, pleasurable, nice, agreeable, pleasing, satisfying, gratifying, good; entertaining, amusing, delightful, charming; fine, balmy; informal lovely, great. **2** *the staff are pleasant* **friendly**, amiable, amicable, nice, genial, cordial, likeable, amicable, good-humoured, good-natured, personable; hospitable, approachable, gracious, courteous, polite, obliging, helpful, considerate; charming, lovely, delightful, sweet, sympathetic; N. English & Scottish canny; Scottish couthy.
– OPPOSITES unpleasant, disagreeable.

pleasantry n. **1** *we exchanged pleasantries* **banter**, badinage; polite remark, casual remark; N. Amer. informal josh. **2** *he laughed at his own pleasantry* **joke**, witticism, quip, jest, gag, bon mot; informal wisecrack, crack.

please v. **1** *he'd do anything to please her* **make happy**, give pleasure to, make someone feel good; delight, charm, amuse, entertain; satisfy, gratify, humour, oblige, content, suit; informal tickle someone pink. **2** *do as you please* **like**, want, wish, desire, see fit, think fit, choose, will, prefer.
– OPPOSITES annoy.
▶ adv. *please sit down* **if you please**, if you wouldn't mind, if you would be so good; kindly, pray; old use prithee.

pleased adj. **happy**, glad, delighted, gratified, grateful, thankful, content, contented, satisfied; thrilled, elated, overjoyed, cock-a-hoop; informal over the moon, tickled pink, on cloud nine; Brit. informal chuffed; N. English informal made up; Austral. informal wrapped; humorous gruntled.
– OPPOSITES unhappy.

pleasing adj. **1** *a pleasing day* **nice**, agreeable, pleasant, pleasurable, satisfying, gratifying, good, enjoyable, entertaining, amusing, delightful; informal lovely, great. **2** *her pleasing manner* **friendly**, amiable, pleasant, agreeable, affable, nice, genial, likeable, good-humoured, charming, engaging, delightful; informal lovely.

pleasurable adj. **pleasant**, enjoyable, delightful, nice, pleasing, agreeable, gratifying; fun, entertaining, amusing, diverting; informal lovely, great.

pleasure n. **1** *she smiled with pleasure* **happiness**, delight, joy, gladness, glee, satisfaction, gratification, contentment, enjoyment, amusement. **2** *his greatest pleasures in life* **joy**, amusement, diversion, recreation, pastime; treat, thrill. **3** *don't mix business and pleasure* **enjoyment**, fun, entertainment; recreation, leisure, relaxation; informal jollies. **4** *a life of pleasure* **hedonism**, indulgence, self-indulgence, self-gratification, lotus-eating. **5** *what's your pleasure?* **wish**, desire, preference, will, inclination, choice.
□ **take pleasure in** enjoy, delight in, love, like, adore, appreciate, relish, savour, revel in, glory in; informal get a kick out of, get a thrill out of.
with pleasure gladly, willingly, happily, readily; by all means, of course; old use fain.

> **WORD LINKS**
> **sybarite, hedonist, voluptuary** a person who is very fond of pleasure

pleat n. *a curtain pleat* **fold**, crease, gather, tuck, crimp; pucker.
▶ v. *the dress is pleated at the front* **fold**, crease, gather, tuck, crimp; pucker.

plebeian n. *plebeians and gentry lived together* **proletarian**, commoner, working-class person, worker; peasant; informal pleb, prole.
– OPPOSITES aristocrat.
▶ adj. **1** *people of plebeian descent* **lower-class**, working-class, proletarian, common, peasant; mean, humble, lowly. **2** *plebeian tastes* **uncultured**, uncultivated, unrefined, lowbrow, philistine, uneducated; coarse, uncouth, common, vulgar; informal plebby; Brit. informal non-U.
– OPPOSITES noble, refined.

plebiscite n. **vote**, referendum, ballot, poll.

pledge n. **1** *his election pledge* **promise**, undertaking, vow, word (of honour), commitment, assurance, oath, guarantee. **2** *he gave it as a pledge to a creditor* **surety**, bond, security, collateral, guarantee, deposit. **3** *a pledge of my sincerity* **token**, symbol, sign, earnest, mark, testimony, proof, evidence.
▶ v. **1** *he pledged to root out corruption* **promise**, vow, swear, undertake, engage, commit oneself, declare, affirm, avow. **2** *they pledged £100 million* **promise (to give)**, donate, contribute, give, put up; Brit. covenant. **3** *his home is pledged as security against the loan* **mortgage**, put up as collateral, guarantee, pawn.

plenary adj. **1** *the council has plenary powers* **unconditional**, unlimited, unrestricted, unqualified, absolute, sweeping, comprehensive; plenipotentiary. **2** *a plenary session of the parliament* **full**, complete, entire.

plenipotentiary n. *a plenipotentiary in Paris* **diplomat**, dignitary, ambassador, minister, emissary, chargé d'affaires, envoy.

p

▸ adj. *plenipotentiary powers.* See **plenary** (sense 1).

plenitude n. formal **abundance**, lot, wealth, profusion, cornucopia, plethora, superabundance; informal load, slew, heap, ton; Brit. informal shedload.

plenteous adj. literary See **plentiful**.

plentiful adj. **abundant**, copious, ample, profuse, rich, lavish, generous, bountiful, large, great, bumper, superabundant, inexhaustible, prolific; informal a gogo, galore; literary plenteous.
– OPPOSITES scarce.

plenty n. *times of plenty* **prosperity**, affluence, wealth, opulence, comfort, luxury; plentifulness, abundance; literary plenteousness.
▸ pron. *there are plenty of books* **a lot of**, many, a great deal of, a plethora of, enough (and to spare), no lack of, sufficient, a wealth of; informal loads of, lots of, heaps of, stacks of, masses of, tons of, oodles of, scads of, a slew of.

plethora n. **excess**, abundance, superabundance, surplus, glut, superfluity, surfeit, profusion, too many, too much, enough and to spare; informal more —— than one can shake a stick at.
– OPPOSITES dearth.

pliable adj. **1** *leather is pliable* **flexible**, pliant, bendable, elastic, supple, malleable, workable, plastic, springy, ductile; informal bendy. **2** *pliable teenage minds* **malleable**, impressionable, flexible, adaptable, pliant, compliant, biddable, tractable, yielding, amenable, susceptible, suggestible, persuadable, manipulable, receptive.
– OPPOSITES rigid, obdurate.

pliant adj. See **pliable** (senses 1 & 2).

plight n. **predicament**, difficult situation, dire straits, trouble, difficulty, extremity, bind; informal dilemma, tight corner, tight spot, hole, pickle, jam, fix.

plod v. **1** *Mum plodded wearily upstairs* **trudge**, walk heavily, clump, stomp, tramp, lumber, slog; Brit. informal trog. **2** *I have to plod through the whole book* **wade**, plough, trawl, toil, labour; informal slog.

plot n. **1** *a plot to overthrow him* **conspiracy**, intrigue, secret plan; machinations. **2** *the plot of her novel* **storyline**, story, scenario, action, thread; formal diegesis. **3** *a three-acre plot of ground*, patch, area, tract, acreage; Brit. allotment; N. Amer. lot, plat; N. Amer. & Austral./NZ homesite.
▸ v. **1** *he plotted their downfall* **plan**, scheme, arrange, organize, hatch, concoct, devise, dream up; informal cook up. **2** *his brother was plotting against him* **conspire**, scheme, intrigue, collude, connive, machinate. **3** *the fifty-three sites were plotted* **mark**, chart, map, represent, graph.

plotter n. **conspirator**, schemer, intriguer, machinator; planner.

plough v. **1** *the fields were ploughed* **till**, furrow, harrow, cultivate, work, break up.

2 *the car ploughed into a lamp post* **crash**, smash, career, plunge, bulldoze, hurtle, cannon, run, drive; N. Amer. informal barrel. **3** *they ploughed through deep snow* **trudge**, plod, toil, wade; informal slog; Brit. informal trog.

ploy n. **ruse**, tactic, move, device, stratagem, scheme, trick, gambit, plan, manoeuvre, dodge, subterfuge, wile; Brit. informal wheeze.

pluck v. **1** *he plucked a thread from his lapel* **remove**, pick (off), pull (off/out), extract, take (off). **2** *she plucked at his T-shirt* **pull (at)**, tug (at), clutch (at), snatch (at), grab, catch (at), tweak, jerk; informal yank. **3** *she plucked the guitar strings* **strum**, pick, thrum, twang; play pizzicato. **4** *the turkeys are plucked by machine* **deplume**, remove the feathers from.
▸ n. *the task took a lot of pluck* **courage**, bravery, nerve, backbone, spine, daring, spirit, intrepidity, fearlessness, mettle, grit, determination, fortitude, resolve, stout-heartedness, dauntlessness, valour, heroism, audacity; informal guts, spunk, gumption; Brit. informal bottle; N. Amer. informal moxie.

plucky adj. **brave**, courageous, bold, daring, fearless, intrepid, spirited, game, valiant, valorous, stout-hearted, dauntless, resolute, determined, undaunted, unflinching, audacious, unafraid, doughty, mettlesome; informal gutsy, spunky.
– OPPOSITES timid.

plug n. **1** *she pulled out the plug* **stopper**, bung, cork, seal, spigot, spile; N. Amer. stopple. **2** *a plug of tobacco* **wad**, quid, twist, chew. **3** informal *a plug for his new book* **advertisement**, promotion, commercial, recommendation, mention, good word; informal hype, push, puff, ad, boost, ballyhoo; Brit. informal advert.
▸ v. **1** *plug the holes* **stop (up)**, seal (up/off), close (up/off), cork, stopper, bung, block (up/off), fill (up); N. Amer. stopple. **2** informal *she plugged her new film* **publicize**, promote, advertise, mention, bang the drum for, draw attention to; informal hype (up), push, puff. **3** informal *don't move or I'll plug you* **shoot**, gun down; informal blast, pump full of lead.
□ **plug away** informal toil, labour, slave away, soldier on, persevere, persist, keep on, plough on; informal slog away, beaver away, peg away.

plum adj. informal *a plum job* **excellent**, very good, wonderful, marvellous, choice, first-class; informal great, terrific, cushy.

plumb¹ v. *an attempt to plumb her psyche* **explore**, probe, delve into, search, examine, investigate, fathom, penetrate, understand.
▸ adv. **1** informal *it went plumb through the screen* **right**, exactly, precisely, directly, dead, straight; informal (slap) bang. **2** N. Amer. informal *he's plumb crazy* **utterly**, absolutely, completely, downright, totally, quite, thoroughly. **3** old use *the bell hangs plumb* **vertically**, perpendicularly, straight down.
▸ adj. *a plumb drop* **vertical**, perpendicular, straight.
□ **plumb the depths** experience the

extremes, reach the lowest point; reach rock bottom.

plumb² v. *he plumbed in the washing machine* **install**, put in, fit.

plume n. *ostrich plumes* **feather**, quill; Ornithology plumule, covert.
  ▢ **plume oneself** congratulate oneself, preen oneself, pat oneself on the back, pride oneself, boast about.

plummet v. **1** *the plane plummeted to the ground* **plunge**, nosedive, dive, drop, fall, descend, hurtle. **2** *share prices plummeted* **fall steeply**, plunge, tumble, drop rapidly, go down, slump; informal crash, nosedive.

plummy adj. Brit. informal *a plummy voice* **upper-class**, refined, aristocratic, grand; Brit. Home Counties; Scottish Kelvinside, Morningside; Brit. informal posh, Sloaney.

plump¹ adj. *a plump child* **chubby**, fat, stout, rotund, well padded, ample, round, chunky, portly, overweight, fleshy, paunchy, bulky, corpulent; informal tubby, roly-poly, pudgy, beefy, porky, blubbery; Brit. informal podgy, fubsy; N. Amer. informal zaftig, corn-fed.
– OPPOSITES thin.

plump² v. **1** *Jack plumped down on to a chair* **flop**, **collapse**, sink, fall, drop, slump; informal plonk oneself; N. Amer. informal plank oneself. **2** *she plumped her bag on the table* **put (down)**, set (down), place, deposit, dump, stick; informal plonk; Brit. informal bung; N. Amer. informal plunk. **3** *I plumped for a cream cake* **choose**, decide on, go for, opt for, pick, settle on, select, take, elect.

plunder v. **1** *they plundered the countryside* **pillage**, loot, rob, raid, ransack, despoil, strip, ravage, lay waste, devastate, sack, rape. **2** *money plundered from pension funds* **steal**, purloin, thieve, seize, pillage; embezzle.
  ▸n. **1** *the plunder of the villages* **looting**, pillaging, plundering, raiding, ransacking, devastation, sacking; literary rapine. **2** *the army took huge quantities of plunder* **booty**, loot, stolen goods, spoils, ill-gotten gains; informal swag.

plunge v. **1** *Joy plunged into the sea* **dive**, jump, throw oneself, launch oneself. **2** *the aircraft plunged to the ground* **plummet**, nosedive, drop, fall, pitch, tumble, descend. **3** *the car plunged down an alley* **charge**, hurtle, career, plough, cannon, tear; N. Amer. informal barrel. **4** *oil prices plunged* **fall sharply**, plummet, drop, go down, tumble, slump; informal crash, nosedive. **5** *he plunged the dagger into her back* **thrust**, jab, stab, sink, stick, ram, drive, push, shove, force. **6** *plunge the pears into water* **immerse**, submerge, dip, dunk. **7** *the room was plunged into darkness* **throw**, cast, pitch.
  ▸n. **1** *a plunge into the deep end* **dive**, jump, nosedive, fall, pitch, drop, plummet, descent. **2** *a plunge in profits* **fall**, drop, slump; informal nosedive, crash.
  ▢ **take the plunge** commit oneself, go for it, throw caution to the wind(s), risk it; informal jump in at the deep end, go for broke.

plurality n. *a plurality of theories* **wide variety**, diversity, range, lot, multitude, multiplicity, galaxy, wealth, profusion, abundance, plethora, host; informal load, stack, heap, mass.

plus prep. **1** *three plus three makes six* **and**, added to. **2** *he wrote four novels plus various poems* **as well as**, together with, along with, in addition to, and, not to mention, besides.
– OPPOSITES minus.
  ▸n. *one of the pluses of the job* **advantage**, good point, asset, pro, (fringe) benefit, bonus, extra, attraction; informal perk; formal perquisite.
– OPPOSITES disadvantage.

plush adj. informal **luxurious**, luxury, deluxe, sumptuous, palatial, lavish, opulent, magnificent, lush, rich, expensive, fancy, grand; Brit. upmarket; informal posh, ritzy, swanky, classy; Brit. informal swish; N. Amer. informal swank.
– OPPOSITES austere.

plutocrat n. **rich person**, magnate, millionaire, billionaire, multimillionaire, nouveau riche; informal fat cat, moneybags.

ply¹ v. **1** *the gondolier plied his oar* **use**, wield, work, manipulate, handle, operate, utilize, employ. **2** *he plied a profitable trade* **engage in**, carry on, pursue, conduct, practise; old use prosecute. **3** *ferries ply between all lake resorts* **go regularly**, travel, shuttle, go back and forth. **4** *she plied me with scones* **provide**, supply, lavish, shower, regale. **5** *he plied her with questions* **bombard**, assail, beset, pester, plague, harass, importune; informal hassle.

ply² n. *a three-ply tissue* **layer**, thickness, strand, sheet, leaf.

poach v. **1** *he's been poaching salmon* **hunt illegally**, catch illegally; steal. **2** *workers were poached by other firms* **steal**, appropriate, purloin, take; informal nab, swipe; Brit. informal nick, pinch.

pocket n. **1** *a bag with two pockets* **pouch**, compartment. **2** *the jewellery was beyond her pocket* **means**, budget, resources, finances, funds, money, wherewithal; N. Amer. pocketbook. **3** *pockets of disaffection* **(isolated) area**, patch, region, island, cluster, centre.
  ▸adj. *a pocket dictionary* **small**, little, miniature, mini, compact, fun-size, concise, abridged, potted, portable; N. Amer. vest-pocket.
  ▸v. *he pocketed $900,000 of their money* **steal**, take, appropriate, thieve, purloin, misappropriate, embezzle; informal filch, swipe, snaffle; Brit. informal pinch, nick, whip.

pockmark n. **scar**, pit, pock, mark, blemish.

pod n. **shell**, husk, hull, case; N. Amer. shuck; Botany pericarp, capsule.

podgy adj. Brit. informal **chubby**, plump, fat, stout, rotund, well padded, ample, round, chunky, portly, overweight, fleshy, paunchy, bulky, corpulent; informal tubby, roly-poly, pudgy, beefy, porky, blubbery; N. Amer. informal

p

zaftig, corn-fed.
– OPPOSITES thin.

podium n. **platform**, stage, dais, rostrum, stand, soapbox.

poem n. **verse**, rhyme, ode, sonnet, ballad, lyric, song, limerick, ditty.

poet n. versifier, rhymester, rhymer, sonneteer, lyricist, lyrist; laureate; literary bard; derogatory poetaster; historical troubadour, balladeer; old use rhymist.

poetic adj. **1** *poetic compositions* **poetical**, verse, metrical, lyrical, lyric, elegiac. **2** *poetic language* **expressive**, figurative, symbolic, flowery, artistic, elegant, fine, beautiful; sensitive, imaginative, creative.

poetry n. **poems**, verse, versification, metrical composition, rhymes, balladry; old use poesy.

pogrom n. **massacre**, slaughter, mass murder, annihilation, extermination, decimation, carnage, bloodbath, bloodletting, butchery, genocide, holocaust, ethnic cleansing.

poignancy n. **pathos**, pitifulness, piteousness, sadness, sorrow, mournfulness, wretchedness, misery, tragedy.

poignant adj. **touching**, moving, sad, affecting, pitiful, piteous, pathetic, sorrowful, mournful, wretched, miserable, distressing, heart-rending, tear-jerking, plaintive, tragic.

point[1] n. **1** *the point of a needle* **tip**, (sharp) end, extremity; prong, spike, tine, nib, barb. **2** *points of light* **pinpoint**, dot, spot, speck, fleck. **3** *a meeting point* **place**, position, location, site, spot, area. **4** *this point in her life* **time**, stage, juncture, period, phase. **5** *the tension had reached such a high point* **level**, degree, stage, pitch, extent. **6** *an important point* **detail**, item, fact, thing, argument, consideration, factor, element; subject, issue, topic, question, matter. **7** *get to the point* **heart of the matter**, most important part, essence, nub, keynote, core, pith, crux; meaning, significance, gist, substance, thrust, burden, relevance; informal brass tacks, nitty-gritty. **8** *what's the point of this?* **purpose**, aim, object, objective, goal, intention; use, sense, value, advantage. **9** *he had his good points* **attribute**, characteristic, feature, trait, quality, property, aspect, side.
▸v. **1** *she pointed the gun at him* **aim**, direct, level, train. **2** *the evidence pointed to his guilt* **indicate**, suggest, evidence, signal, signify, denote, bespeak, reveal, manifest.
□ **beside the point** irrelevant, immaterial, unimportant, neither here nor there, inconsequential, incidental, out of place, unconnected, peripheral, tangential, extraneous.
in point of fact in fact, as a matter of fact, actually, in actual fact, really, in reality, as it happens, in truth.
make a point of make an effort to, go out of one's way to, put emphasis on.
on the point of (just) about to, on the verge of, on the brink of, going to, all set to.

point of view opinion, view, belief, attitude, feeling, sentiment, thoughts; position, perspective, viewpoint, standpoint, outlook.
point something out identify, show, designate, draw attention to, indicate, specify, detail, mention.
point something up emphasize, highlight, draw attention to, accentuate, underline, spotlight, foreground, put emphasis on, stress, play up, accent, bring to the fore.
to the point relevant, pertinent, apposite, germane, applicable, apropos, appropriate, apt, fitting, suitable, material; formal ad rem.
up to a point partly, to some extent, to a certain degree, in part, somewhat, partially.

point[2] n. *the ship rounded the point* **promontory**, headland, foreland, cape, peninsula, bluff, ness, horn.

point-blank adv. **1** *he fired the pistol point-blank* **at close range**, close up, close to. **2** *she couldn't say it point-blank* **bluntly**, directly, straight, frankly, candidly, openly, explicitly, unequivocally, unambiguously, plainly, flatly, categorically, outright.
▸adj. *a point-blank refusal* **blunt**, direct, straight, straightforward, frank, candid, forthright, explicit, unequivocal, plain, clear, flat, decisive, unqualified, categorical, outright.

pointed adj. **1** *a pointed stick* **sharp**, tapering, tapered, conical, jagged, spiky, spiked, barbed; informal pointy. **2** *a pointed remark* **cutting**, trenchant, biting, incisive, acerbic, caustic, scathing, venomous, sarcastic; informal sarky; N. Amer. informal snarky.

pointer n. **1** *the pointer moved to 100 rpm* **indicator**, needle, arrow, hand. **2** *he used a pointer on the chart* **stick**, rod, cane; cursor. **3** *a pointer to the outcome of the election* **indication**, indicator, clue, hint, sign, signal, evidence, intimation, inkling, suggestion. **4** *I can give you a few pointers* **tip**, hint, suggestion, guideline, recommendation.

pointless adj. **senseless**, futile, hopeless, fruitless, useless, needless, in vain, unavailing, aimless, idle, worthless, valueless; absurd, insane, stupid, silly, foolish.
– OPPOSITES valuable.

poise n. **1** *poise and good deportment* **grace**, gracefulness, elegance, balance, control. **2** *in spite of the setback she retained her poise* **composure**, equanimity, self-possession, aplomb, presence of mind, self-assurance, self-control, nerve, calm, sangfroid, dignity; informal cool, unflappability.
▸v. **1** *she was poised on one foot* **balance**, hold (oneself) steady, be suspended, remain motionless, hang, hover. **2** *he was poised for action* **prepare oneself**, ready oneself, brace oneself, gear oneself up, stand by.

poison n. **1** *a deadly poison* **toxin**, toxicant, venom; old use bane. **2** *Marianne would spread her poison* **malice**, ill will, hate, malevolence, bitterness, spite, spitefulness, venom, acrimony, rancour; bad influence, cancer,

corruption, pollution.
▸ v. **1** *her mother poisoned her* **give poison to**; murder. **2** *a blackmailer poisoning baby foods* **contaminate**, put poison in, adulterate, spike, lace, doctor. **3** *the Amazon is being poisoned* **pollute**, contaminate, taint, blight, spoil; literary befoul. **4** *they poisoned his mind* **prejudice**, bias, jaundice, embitter, sour, envenom, warp, corrupt, subvert.

> **WORD LINKS**
> **toxicology** the branch of science concerned with poisons
> **antidote, antivenin** a substance taken to counteract a poison
> **antitoxin** an antibody that counteracts a toxin

poisonous adj. **1** *a poisonous snake* **venomous**, deadly. **2** *a poisonous chemical* **toxic**, noxious, deadly, fatal, lethal, mortal, death-dealing. **3** *a poisonous glance* **malicious**, malevolent, hostile, vicious, spiteful, bitter, venomous, vindictive, vitriolic, rancorous, malign, pernicious, mean, nasty; informal bitchy, catty.
– OPPOSITES harmless, non-toxic, benevolent.

poke v. **1** *she poked him in the ribs* **prod**, jab, dig, nudge, butt, shove, jolt, stab, stick. **2** *leave the cable poking out* **stick out**, jut out, protrude, project, extend.
▸ n. **1** *Carrie gave him a poke* **prod**, jab, dig, elbow, nudge. **2** *a poke in the arm* **jab**, dig, nudge, shove, stab.
□ **poke about/around** search, hunt, rummage (around), forage, grub, root about/around, scavenge, nose around, ferret (about/around); sift through, rifle through, scour, comb, probe; Brit. informal rootle (around).
poke fun at mock, make fun of, ridicule, laugh at, jeer at, sneer at, deride, scorn, scoff at, pillory, lampoon, tease, taunt, rag, chaff, jibe at; informal send up, take the mickey out of, kid, rib; Brit. informal wind up; N. Amer. informal goof on, rag on; Austral./NZ informal poke mullock at.
poke one's nose into pry into, interfere in, intrude on, butt into, meddle with; informal snoop into.

poky adj. **small**, little, tiny, cramped, confined, restricted, boxy; euphemistic compact, bijou.
– OPPOSITES spacious.

polar adj. **1** *polar weather* **Arctic, Antarctic**; cold, freezing, icy, glacial, chilly, gelid. **2** *two polar types of interview* **opposite**, opposed, dichotomous, extreme, contrary, contradictory, antithetical.

polarity n. **difference**, dichotomy, separation, opposition, contradiction, antithesis, antagonism.

pole¹ n. **post**, pillar, stanchion, paling, stake, stick, support, prop, batten, bar, rail, rod, beam; staff, stave, cane, baton.

pole² n. *points of view at opposite poles* **extremity**, extreme, limit, antipode.
□ **poles apart** completely different, directly opposed, antithetical, incompatible,

irreconcilable, worlds apart, at opposite extremes; Brit. like chalk and cheese.

polemic n. **1** *a polemic against injustice* **diatribe**, invective, rant, tirade, broadside, attack, harangue, condemnation, criticism, stricture, admonition, rebuke; abuse; informal blast; formal castigation; literary philippic. **2** *he is skilled in polemics* **argumentation**, argument, debate, contention, disputation, discussion, altercation; formal contestation.
▸ adj. *his famous polemic book.* See **polemical**.

polemical adj. **critical**, hostile, bitter, polemic, virulent, vitriolic, venomous, caustic, trenchant, cutting, acerbic, sardonic, sarcastic, scathing, sharp, incisive, devastating.

police n. the police force, police officers, policemen, policewomen, officers of the law, the forces of law and order; Brit. constabulary; informal the cops, the fuzz, (the long arm of) the law, the boys in blue; Brit. informal the (Old) Bill, coppers, bobbies, busies, the force; N. Amer. informal the heat; informal derogatory pigs, the filth.
▸ v. **1** *we must police the area* **guard**, watch over, protect, defend, patrol; control, regulate. **2** *the regulations will be policed by the ministry* **enforce**, regulate, oversee, supervise, monitor, observe, check.

police officer n. **policeman, policewoman**, officer (of the law); Brit. constable; N. Amer. patrolman, trooper, roundsman; informal cop; Brit. informal copper, bobby, rozzer, busy, (PC) plod; N. Amer. informal uniform; informal derogatory pig; old use peeler.

policy n. **plans**, strategy, stratagem, approach, code, system, guidelines, theory; line, position, stance, attitude.

polish v. **1** *I polished his shoes* **shine**, wax, buff, rub up/down; gloss, burnish; varnish, oil, glaze, lacquer, japan, shellac. **2** *polish up your essay* **perfect**, refine, improve, hone, enhance; brush up, revise, edit, correct, rewrite, go over, touch up; informal clean up.
▸ n. **1** *furniture polish* **wax**, glaze, varnish; lacquer, japan, shellac. **2** *a good surface polish* **shine**, gloss, lustre, sheen, sparkle, patina, finish. **3** *his polish made him stand out* **sophistication**, refinement, urbanity, suaveness, elegance, style, grace, finesse, cultivation, civility, gentility, breeding, courtesy, (good) manners; informal class; humorous couth.
□ **polish something off** informal **1** *he polished off an apple pie* **eat**, finish, consume, devour, guzzle, wolf down, down, bolt; drink up, drain, quaff, gulp (down); informal binge on, stuff oneself with, hoover up, get outside of, murder, put away, scoff, shovel down, pig out on, sink, swill, knock back; Brit. informal shift, gollop; N. Amer. informal scarf (down/up), snarf (down/up), chug. **2** *the enemy tried to polish him off* **destroy**, finish off, dispatch, do away with, eliminate, kill, liquidate; informal bump off, knock off, do in, take out, dispose of; N. Amer. informal rub out. **3** *I'll polish off the last few pages* **complete**, finish,

p

deal with, accomplish, discharge, do; end, conclude, close, finalize, round off, wind up; informal wrap up, sew up.

polished adj. **1** *a polished table* **shiny**, glossy, gleaming, lustrous, glassy; waxed, buffed, burnished; varnished, glazed, lacquered, japanned, shellacked. **2** *a polished performance* **expert**, accomplished, masterly, masterful, skilful, adept, adroit, dexterous; impeccable, flawless, perfect, consummate, exquisite, outstanding, excellent, superb, superlative, first-rate, fine; informal ace. **3** *polished manners* **refined**, cultivated, civilized, well bred, polite, courteous, genteel, decorous, respectable, urbane, suave, sophisticated.
– OPPOSITES dull, inexpert, gauche.

polite adj. **1** *a very polite girl* **well mannered**, civil, courteous, mannerly, respectful, deferential, well behaved, well bred, gentlemanly, ladylike, genteel, gracious, urbane; tactful, diplomatic. **2** *polite society* **civilized**, refined, cultured, sophisticated, genteel, courtly.
– OPPOSITES rude, uncivilized.

politic adj. **wise**, prudent, sensible, judicious, canny, sagacious, shrewd, astute; recommended, advantageous, beneficial, profitable, desirable, advisable; appropriate, suitable, fitting, apt.
– OPPOSITES unwise.

political adj. **1** *the political affairs of the nation* **governmental**, government, constitutional, ministerial, parliamentary, diplomatic, legislative, administrative, bureaucratic; public, civic, state. **2** *he's a political man* **politically active**, party (political); militant, factional, partisan.

politician n. **legislator**, elected official, Member of Parliament, MP, minister, statesman, stateswoman, public servant; senator, congressman, congresswoman, assemblyman, assemblywoman; informal politico, pol.

politics n. **1** *a career in politics* **government**, affairs of state, public affairs; diplomacy. **2** *he studies politics* **political science**, civics, statecraft. **3** *what are his politics?* **political views**, political leanings, party politics. **4** *office politics* **power struggle**, machinations, manoeuvring, opportunism, realpolitik.

poll n. **1** *a second-round poll* **vote**, ballot, show of hands, referendum, plebiscite; election. **2** *the poll was unduly low* **voting figures**, vote, returns, count, tally. **3** *a poll to investigate holiday choices* **survey**, opinion poll, straw poll, canvass, market research, census.
▶v. **1** *most of those polled supported him* **canvass**, survey, ask, question, interview, ballot. **2** *she polled 119 votes* **get**, gain, register, record, return.

pollute v. **1** *fish farms will pollute the lake* **contaminate**, adulterate, taint, poison, foul, dirty, soil, infect; literary befoul. **2** *propaganda polluted this nation* **corrupt**, poison, warp,

pervert, deprave, defile, blight, sully; literary besmirch.
– OPPOSITES purify.

pollution n. **1** *pollution in the rivers* **contamination**, adulteration, impurity; dirt, filth, infection. **2** *the pollution of young minds* **corruption**, defilement, poisoning, warping, depravation, sullying, violation.

pomp n. **ceremony**, ceremonial, solemnity, ritual, display, spectacle, pageantry; show, showiness, ostentation, splendour, grandeur, magnificence, majesty, stateliness, glory, opulence, brilliance, drama, resplendence, splendidness; informal razzmatazz.

pompous adj. **self-important**, imperious, overbearing, domineering, magisterial, pontifical, sententious, grandiose, affected, pretentious, puffed up, arrogant, vain, haughty, proud, conceited, egotistic, supercilious, condescending, patronizing; informal snooty, uppity, uppish.
– OPPOSITES modest.

pond n. **pool**, waterhole, lake, tarn, reservoir, swim; Brit. stew; Scottish lochan; N. Amer. pothole; Austral./NZ tank.

ponder v. **think about**, contemplate, consider, review, reflect on, mull over, meditate on, muse on, deliberate about, cogitate on, dwell on, brood on, ruminate on, chew over, puzzle over, turn over in one's mind.

ponderous adj. **1** *a ponderous dance* **clumsy**, heavy, awkward, lumbering, slow, cumbersome, ungainly, graceless, uncoordinated, blundering; informal clodhopping, clunky. **2** *his ponderous sentences* **laboured**, laborious, awkward, clumsy, forced, stilted, unnatural, artificial; stodgy, lifeless, plodding, pedestrian, boring, dull, tedious, monotonous; over-elaborate, convoluted, windy.
– OPPOSITES light, lively.

pontifical adj. **pompous**, cocksure, self-important, arrogant, superior; opinionated, dogmatic, doctrinaire, authoritarian, domineering; adamant, obstinate, stubborn, single-minded, inflexible.
– OPPOSITES humble.

pontificate v. **hold forth**, expound, declaim, preach, lay down the law, sound off, dogmatize, sermonize, moralize, lecture; informal preachify, mouth off.

pooh-pooh v. informal **dismiss**, reject, spurn, rebuff, wave aside, disregard, discount; play down, make light of, belittle, deride, mock, scorn, scoff at, sneer at; Austral./NZ informal wipe.

pool¹ n. **1** *pools of water* **puddle**, pond; literary plash. **2** *the hotel has a pool* **swimming pool**, baths, lido; Brit. swimming bath(s); N. Amer. natatorium.

pool² n. **1** *a pool of skilled labour* **supply**, reserve(s), reservoir, fund; store, stock, accumulation, cache. **2** *a pool of money for emergencies* **fund**, reserve, kitty, pot, bank, purse.
▶v. *they pooled their skills* **combine**, amalgamate, group, join, unite, merge; fuse,

conglomerate, integrate; share.

poor adj. **1** *a poor family* **poverty-stricken**, penniless, moneyless, impoverished, necessitous, impecunious, indigent, needy, destitute, pauperized, on one's beam-ends, unable to make ends meet, without a sou; insolvent, in debt; Brit. on the breadline, without a penny (to one's name); informal (flat) broke, hard up, cleaned out, strapped, on one's uppers, without two pennies to rub together; Brit. informal skint, in Queer Street; formal penurious. **2** *poor workmanship* **substandard**, below par, bad, deficient, defective, faulty, imperfect, inferior; appalling, abysmal, atrocious, awful, terrible, dreadful, unsatisfactory, second-rate, third-rate, shoddy, crude, lamentable, deplorable, inadequate, unacceptable; informal crummy, rubbishy, dire, dismal, bum, rotten, tenth-rate; Brit. informal ropy, duff, rubbish, pants. **3** *a poor crop* **meagre**, scanty, scant, paltry, disappointing, limited, reduced, modest, insufficient, inadequate, sparse, spare, deficient, insubstantial, skimpy, short, small, lean, slender; informal measly, stingy, pathetic, piddling; formal exiguous. **4** *poor soil* **unproductive**, barren, unyielding, unfruitful, uncultivable; arid, sterile. **5** *the waters are poor in nutrients* **deficient**, lacking, wanting; short of, low on. **6** *you poor thing!* **unfortunate**, unlucky, luckless, unhappy, hapless, ill-fated, ill-starred, pitiable, pitiful, wretched.
– OPPOSITES rich, superior, good, fertile, lucky.

poorly adv. *the text is poorly written* **badly**, deficiently, defectively, imperfectly, incompetently; appallingly, abysmally, atrociously, awfully, dreadfully; crudely, shoddily, inadequately.
▸ adj. *she felt poorly* **ill**, unwell, not (very) well, ailing, indisposed, out of sorts, under/below par, peaky; sick, queasy, nauseous; Brit. off colour; informal under the weather, funny, peculiar, lousy, rough; Brit. informal ropy, grotty; Scottish informal wabbit; Austral./NZ informal crook; Brit. informal dated queer; dated seedy.

pop v. **1** *champagne corks popped* **go bang**, go off; crack, snap, burst, explode. **2** *I'm just popping home* **go**; drop in, stop by, visit; informal tootle, whip; Brit. informal nip. **3** *pop a bag over the pot* **put**, place, slip, slide, stick, set, lay, install, position, arrange.
▸ n. **1** *the balloons burst with a pop* **bang**, crack, snap; explosion, report. **2** informal *a bottle of pop* **fizzy drink**, soft drink, carbonated drink; N. Amer. soda; Scottish informal scoosh.
□ **pop up** appear (suddenly), occur (suddenly), arrive, materialize, come along, happen, emerge, arise, crop up, turn up, present itself, come to light; informal show up.

pope n. **pontiff**, Bishop of Rome, Holy Father, Vicar of Christ, His Holiness.

WORD LINKS

papal, pontifical relating to a pope
papacy the position or period of office of a pope
bull an announcement by the pope
encyclical a letter sent by the pope to all Roman Catholic bishops
nuncio an official representative of the pope in a foreign country
legate a member of the clergy who represents the pope
Vatican the official residence of the pope in Rome
Curia the papal court at the Vatican

poppycock n. informal **nonsense**, rubbish, claptrap, balderdash, blather, moonshine, garbage; informal rot, tripe, hogwash, baloney, drivel, bilge, bosh, bunk, eyewash, piffle, phooey, twaddle; Brit. informal cobblers, codswallop, tosh; N. Amer. informal applesauce, bushwa; informal dated bunkum, tommyrot.

populace n. **population**, inhabitants, residents, natives; community, country, (general) public, people, nation; common people, man/woman in the street, masses, multitude, rank and file, commonality, commonalty, third estate, plebeians, proletariat; informal proles, plebs; Brit. informal Joe Public; formal denizens; derogatory the hoi polloi, common herd, rabble, riff-raff.

popular adj. **1** *the restaurant is very popular* **well liked**, favoured, sought-after, in demand, desired, wanted; commercial, marketable, fashionable, in vogue, all the rage, hot; informal in, cool, big; Brit. informal dated all the go. **2** *popular science* **non-specialist**, non-technical, amateur, lay person's, general, middle-of-the-road; accessible, simplified, plain, simple, easy, straightforward, understandable; mass-market, middlebrow, lowbrow, pop. **3** *popular opinion* **widespread**, general, common, current, prevalent, prevailing, standard, stock; ordinary, usual, accepted, established, acknowledged, conventional, orthodox. **4** *a popular movement for independence* **mass**, general, communal, collective, social, collaborative, group, civil, public.
– OPPOSITES unpopular, highbrow.

popularize v. **1** *tobacco was popularized by Sir Walter Raleigh* **make popular**, make fashionable; market, publicize; informal hype. **2** *he popularized the subject* **simplify**, make accessible; informal dumb down. **3** *the report popularized the unfounded notion* **give currency to**, spread, propagate, give credence to.

popularly adv. **1** *old age is popularly associated with illness* **widely**, generally, universally, commonly, usually, customarily, habitually, conventionally, traditionally, as a rule. **2** *the rock is popularly known as 'Arthur's Seat'* **informally**, unofficially.

populate v. **1** *the state is populated by 40,000 people* **inhabit**, occupy, people; live in, reside in. **2** *an attempt to populate the island* **settle**, colonize, people, occupy, move into, make one's home in.

population n. **inhabitants**, residents, people, citizens, citizenry; public, community, populace, society, natives, occupants; formal denizens.

populous adj. **densely populated**, heavily populated, congested, crowded, packed, jammed, crammed, teeming, swarming, seething, crawling; informal jam-packed.
– OPPOSITES deserted.

porch n. **vestibule**, foyer, entrance (hall), entry, portico, lobby; N. Amer. ramada, stoop; Architecture lanai, tambour, narthex.

pore[1] n. *pores in the skin* **opening**, orifice, aperture, hole, outlet, inlet, vent; Biology stoma, foramen.

pore[2] v. *they pored over the map* **study**, read intently, peruse, scrutinize, scan, examine, go over.

pornographic adj. **obscene**, indecent, crude, lewd, dirty, vulgar, smutty, filthy; erotic, titillating, arousing, suggestive, sexy, risqué; off colour, adult, X-rated, hard-core, soft-core; informal porn, porno, blue, skin.
– OPPOSITES wholesome.

pornography n. **erotica**, pornographic material, dirty books; smut, filth, vice; informal (hard/soft) porn, porno, girlie magazines, skin flicks.

porous adj. **permeable**, penetrable, pervious, cellular, holey; absorbent, absorptive, spongy.
– OPPOSITES impermeable.

port[1] n. **1** *the German port of Kiel* **seaport**, entrepôt. **2** *shells exploded down by the port* **harbour**, dock(s), haven, marina; anchorage, moorage, harbourage, roads.

port[2] n. *push the supply pipes into the ports* **aperture**, opening, outlet, inlet, socket, vent.

portable adj. **transportable**, movable, mobile, travel; lightweight, compact, handy, convenient.

portal n. **doorway**, gateway, entrance, exit, opening; door, gate; N. Amer. entryway; formal egress.

portend v. **presage**, augur, foreshadow, foretell, prophesy; be a sign, warn, be an omen, indicate, herald, signal, bode, promise, threaten, signify, spell, denote; literary betoken, foretoken, forebode.

portent n. **1** *a portent of things to come* **omen**, sign, signal, token, forewarning, warning, foreshadowing, prediction, forecast, prophecy, harbinger, augury, auspice, presage; writing on the wall, indication, hint; literary foretoken. **2** *the word carries terrifying portent* **significance**, importance, import, consequence, meaning, weight; formal moment.

portentous adj. **1** *portentous signs* **ominous**, warning, premonitory, prognosticatory; threatening, menacing, ill-omened, foreboding, inauspicious, unfavourable. **2** *portentous dialogue* **pompous**, bombastic, self-important, pontifical, solemn, sonorous, grandiloquent.

porter[1] n. *a porter helped with the bags* **carrier**, bearer; N. Amer. redcap, skycap.

porter[2] n. Brit. *the college porter* **doorman**, doorkeeper, commissionaire, gatekeeper.

portion n. **1** *the upper portion of the chimney* **part**, piece, bit, section, segment. **2** *her portion of the allowance* **share**, slice, quota, quantum, part, percentage, amount, quantity, ration, fraction, division, allocation, measure; informal cut, rake-off; Brit. informal whack. **3** *a portion of cake* **helping**, serving, amount, quantity; plateful, bowlful; slice, piece, chunk, wedge, slab, hunk; Brit. informal wodge.
▶v. *she portioned out the food* **share out**, allocate, allot, apportion; distribute, hand out, deal out, dole out, give out, dispense, mete out; informal divvy up.

portly adj. **stout**, plump, fat, overweight, heavy, corpulent, fleshy, paunchy, pot-bellied, well padded, rotund, stocky, bulky; informal tubby, roly-poly, beefy, porky, pudgy; Brit. informal podgy; N. Amer. informal corn-fed.
– OPPOSITES slim.

portrait n. **1** *a portrait of the King* **painting**, picture, drawing, sketch, likeness, image, study, miniature; informal oil; formal portraiture. **2** *a vivid portrait of Italy* **description**, portrayal, representation, depiction, impression, account; sketch, vignette, profile.

portray v. **1** *he portrays Windermere in sunny weather* **paint**, draw, sketch, picture, depict, represent, illustrate, render. **2** *the dons portrayed by Waugh* **describe**, depict, characterize, represent, delineate, evoke. **3** *he portrays her as a doormat* **represent**, depict, characterize, describe, present. **4** *the actor portrays a spy* **play**, act the part of, take the role of, represent, appear as; formal personate.

portrayal n. **1** *a portrayal of a parrot* **painting**, picture, portrait, drawing, sketch, artist's impression, representation, depiction, study. **2** *her portrayal of adolescence* **description**, representation, characterization, depiction, evocation. **3** *Brando's portrayal of Corleone* **performance as**, representation, interpretation, rendering; formal personation.

pose v. **1** *pollution poses a threat to health* **constitute**, present, create, cause, produce, be. **2** *the question posed earlier* **raise**, ask, put, set, submit, advance, propose, suggest, moot. **3** *she posed for the artist* **be a model**, model, sit. **4** *he posed her on the sofa* **position**, place, put, arrange, dispose, locate, situate. **5** *fashion victims were posing at the bar* **behave affectedly**, strike a pose, posture, attitudinize, put on airs; informal show off.
▶n. **1** *a sexy pose* **posture**, position, stance, attitude, bearing. **2** *her pose of aggrieved innocence* **pretence**, act, affectation, facade, show, front, display, masquerade, posture.

p

▢ **pose as** pretend to be, impersonate, pass oneself off as, masquerade as, profess to be, represent oneself as; formal personate.

poser¹ n. *this situation's a bit of a poser* **difficult question**, vexed question, awkward problem, tough one, puzzle, mystery, conundrum, puzzler, enigma, riddle; informal dilemma, facer, toughie, stumper.

poser² n. *he's such a poser* **exhibitionist**, poseur, poseuse, posturer, attention-seeker; informal show-off, pseud.

poseur n. See **poser²**.

posh adj. **1** informal *a posh hotel* **smart**, stylish, fancy, high-class, fashionable, chic, luxurious, luxury, deluxe, exclusive, opulent, lavish, grand, showy; Brit. upmarket; informal classy, swanky, snazzy, plush, ritzy, flash, la-di-da; Brit. informal swish; N. Amer. informal swank, tony. **2** Brit. informal *a posh accent* **upper-class**, aristocratic; Brit. upmarket, Home Counties; informal upper-crust, top-drawer; Brit. informal plummy, Sloaney, U.

posit v. **postulate**, put forward, advance, propound, submit, hypothesize, propose, assert.

position n. **1** *the aircraft's position* **location**, place, situation, spot, site, locality, setting, area; whereabouts, bearings, orientation; technical locus. **2** *a standing position* **posture**, stance, attitude, pose. **3** *our financial position* **situation**, state, condition, circumstances; predicament, plight, strait(s). **4** *the two parties jockeyed for position* **advantage**, the upper hand, the edge, the whip hand, primacy; Austral./NZ the box seat; N. Amer. informal the catbird seat. **5** *their position in society* **status**, place, level, rank, standing, stature, prestige, influence, reputation, importance, consequence, class; dated station. **6** *a secretarial position* **job**, post, situation, appointment, role, occupation, employment; office, capacity, duty, function; opening, vacancy, placement. **7** *the government's position on the matter* **viewpoint**, opinion, outlook, attitude, stand, standpoint, stance, perspective, approach, slant, thinking, policy, feelings.

▸ v. *he positioned a chair between them* **put**, place, locate, situate, set, site, stand, station; plant, stick, install; arrange, dispose; informal plonk, park.

positive adj. **1** *a positive response* **affirmative**, favourable, good, approving, enthusiastic, supportive, encouraging. **2** *do something positive* **constructive**, practical, useful, productive, helpful, worthwhile, beneficial, effective. **3** *she seems a lot more positive* **optimistic**, hopeful, confident, cheerful, sanguine, buoyant; informal upbeat. **4** *positive economic signs* **favourable**, good, promising, encouraging, heartening, propitious, auspicious. **5** *positive proof* **definite**, conclusive, certain, categorical, unequivocal, incontrovertible, indisputable, undeniable, unmistakable, irrefutable, reliable, concrete, tangible, clear-cut, explicit, firm, decisive, real, actual.

6 *I'm positive he's coming back* **certain**, sure, convinced, confident, satisfied, assured; as sure as eggs is eggs.

– OPPOSITES negative, pessimistic, doubtful, unsure.

positively adv. **1** *I could not positively identify the voice* **confidently**, definitely, emphatically, categorically, with certainty, conclusively, unquestionably, undoubtedly, indisputably, unmistakably, assuredly. **2** *he was positively livid* **absolutely**, really, downright, thoroughly, completely, utterly, totally, extremely, fairly; informal plain.

possess v. **1** *the only hat she possessed* **own**, have (to one's name), hold. **2** *he did not possess a sense of humour* **have**, be blessed with, be endowed with; enjoy, boast. **3** *a supernatural force possessed him* **take control of**, take over, control, dominate, influence; bewitch, enchant, enthral. **4** *she was possessed by a need to talk to him* **obsess**, haunt, preoccupy, consume; eat someone up, prey on one's mind.

▢ **possess oneself of** acquire, obtain, get (hold of), procure, get one's hands on; take, seize; informal get one's mitts on.

possessed adj. **mad**, demented, insane, crazed, berserk, out of one's mind; bewitched, enchanted, haunted, under a spell.

possession n. **1** *the estate came into their possession* **ownership**, control, hands, keeping, care, custody, charge, hold, title, guardianship. **2** *her possession of the premises* **occupancy**, occupation, tenure, holding, tenancy. **3** *she packed her possessions* **belongings**, things, property, (worldly) goods, (personal) effects, assets, chattels, movables, valuables; stuff, bits and pieces; luggage, baggage; informal gear, junk; Brit. informal clobber. **4** *colonial possessions* **colony**, dependency, territory, holding, protectorate.

▢ **take possession of** seize, appropriate, impound, expropriate, sequestrate, sequester, confiscate; take, get, acquire, obtain, procure, possess oneself of, get hold of, get one's hands on; capture, commandeer, requisition; Law distrain; Scottish Law poind; informal get one's mitts on.

possessive adj. **1** *he was very possessive* **proprietorial**, overprotective, controlling, dominating, jealous, clingy. **2** *kids are possessive of their own property* **covetous**, selfish, unwilling to share; grasping, greedy, acquisitive; N. Amer. informal grabby.

possibility n. **1** *there is a possibility that he might be alive* **chance**, likelihood, probability, hope; risk, hazard, danger, fear. **2** *they discussed the possibility of launching a new project* **feasibility**, practicability, chances, odds, achievability, probability. **3** *buying a smaller house is one possibility* **option**, alternative, choice, course of action, solution. **4** *the idea has distinct possibilities* **potential**, promise, prospects.

p

possible adj. **1** *it's not possible to check the figures* **feasible**, practicable, viable, within the bounds/realms of possibility, attainable, achievable, workable; informal on, doable. **2** *a possible reason for his disappearance* **conceivable**, plausible, imaginable, believable, likely, potential, probable, credible. **3** *a possible future leader* **potential**, prospective, likely, probable.
– OPPOSITES unlikely.

possibly adv. **1** *possibly he took the boy with him* **perhaps**, maybe, it is possible, for all one knows, very likely; literary peradventure, perchance, mayhap. **2** *you can't possibly refuse* **conceivably**, under any circumstances, by any means. **3** *could you possibly help me?* **please**, kindly, be so good as to.

post[1] n. *wooden posts* **pole**, stake, upright, shaft, prop, support, picket, strut, pillar, pale, paling, stanchion, puncheon.
▶ v. **1** *the notice posted on the wall* **affix**, attach, fasten, display, pin (up), put up, stick (up), tack (up). **2** *the group posted a net profit* **announce**, report, make known, publish.

post[2] n. Brit. **1** *the winners will be notified by post* **mail**, the postal service; airmail, surface mail, registered mail; informal snail mail. **2** *did we get any post?* **letters**, correspondence, mail.
▶ v. **1** Brit. *post the order form today* **send (off)**, mail, put in the post/mail, get off. **2** *post the transaction in the second column* **record**, write in, enter, register.
□ **keep someone posted** keep informed, keep up to date, keep in the picture, keep briefed, update, fill in; informal keep up to speed.

post[3] n. **1** *there were seventy candidates for the post* **job**, position, appointment, situation, place; vacancy, opening; Austral. informal grip. **2** *Back to your posts!* **(assigned) position**, station, observation post.
▶ v. **1** *he'd been posted to Berlin* **send**, assign to a post, dispatch. **2** *armed guards were posted beside the exit* **put on duty**, station, position, situate, locate.

poster n. **notice**, placard, bill, sign, advertisement, affiche, playbill; Brit. fly-poster.

posterior adj. **1** *the posterior part of the skull* **rear**, hind, back, hinder; technical dorsal, caudal. **2** formal *a date posterior to the Reform Bill* **later than**, subsequent to, following, after.
– OPPOSITES anterior, previous.
▶ n. humorous *her plump posterior.* See **bottom** (sense 6 of the noun).

posterity n. **future generations**, the future.

post-haste adv. **as quickly as possible**, without delay, (very) quickly, speedily, without further/more ado, with all speed, promptly, immediately, at once, straight away, right away; informal pronto, straight off.

postman, **postwoman** n. **postal worker**; N. Amer. mailman; Brit. informal postie.

post-mortem n. **1** *the hospital carried out a post-mortem* **autopsy**, PM, necropsy. **2** *a post-mortem of her failed relationship* **analysis**, evaluation, assessment, appraisal, examination, review.

postpone v. **put off/back**, delay, defer, reschedule, adjourn, shelve; N. Amer. put over, take a rain check on; informal put on ice, put on the back burner; rare remit, respite.
– OPPOSITES bring forward.

postponement n. **deferral**, deferment, delay, putting off/back, rescheduling, adjournment, shelving.

postscript n. **1** *a handwritten postscript* **afterthought**, PS, additional remark. **2** *he added postscripts of his own* **addendum**, supplement, appendix, codicil, afterword, addition.

postulate v. **put forward**, suggest, advance, posit, hypothesize, propose; assume, presuppose, presume.

posture n. **1** *a kneeling posture* **position**, pose, attitude, stance. **2** *good posture* **bearing**, carriage, stance, comportment; Brit. deportment. **3** *trade unions adopted a militant posture* **attitude**, stance, standpoint, point of view, opinion, position, frame of mind.
▶ v. *Keith postured, flexing his biceps* **pose**, strike an attitude, strut.

posy n. **bouquet**, bunch (of flowers), spray, nosegay, corsage; buttonhole, boutonnière.

pot n. **1** *pots and pans* **cooking utensil**, pan, saucepan, casserole, stewpot, stockpot, dixie. **2** *earthenware pots* **flowerpot**, planter, jardinière. **3** *Jim raked in half the pot* **bank**, kitty, pool, purse, jackpot.
□ **go to pot** informal deteriorate, decline, degenerate, go to (rack and) ruin, go downhill, go to seed, become run down; informal go to the dogs, go down the tubes; Austral./NZ informal go to the pack.

pot-bellied adj. **paunchy**, beer-bellied, portly, rotund; informal tubby, roly-poly.

pot belly n. **paunch**, (beer) belly; informal beer gut, pot, tummy.

potency n. **1** *the potency of his words* **forcefulness**, force, effectiveness, persuasiveness, cogency, influence, strength, authoritativeness, authority, power, powerfulness; literary puissance. **2** *the potency of the drugs* **strength**, powerfulness, power, effectiveness; formal efficacy; efficaciousness.

potent adj. **1** *a potent political force* **powerful**, strong, mighty, formidable, influential, dominant, forceful; puissant. **2** *a potent argument* **forceful**, convincing, cogent, compelling, persuasive, powerful, strong. **3** *a potent drug* **strong**, powerful, effective; formal efficacious.
– OPPOSITES weak.

potentate n. **ruler**, monarch, sovereign, king, queen, emperor, empress.

potential adj. *a potential source of conflict* **possible**, likely, prospective, future, probable; latent, inherent, undeveloped.

▶ n. *economic potential* **possibilities**, potentiality, prospects; promise, capability, capacity.

potion n. **concoction**, mixture, brew, elixir, philtre, drink, decoction; medicine, tonic; literary draught.

potpourri n. **mixture**, assortment, collection, selection, assemblage, medley, miscellany, mix, variety, mixed bag, patchwork; ragbag, hotchpotch, mishmash, jumble, farrago; N. Amer. hodgepodge.

potter v. *we pottered down to the library* **amble**, wander, meander, stroll, saunter, maunder; informal mosey, tootle, toddle; N. Amer. informal putter.

  □ **potter about/around** pass the time, fiddle about/around, footle about/around; informal mess about/around; Brit. informal muck about/around; N. Amer. informal putter about/ around, lollygag.

pottery n. **china**, crockery, ceramics.

potty adj. Brit. informal **1** *I'm going potty.* See **crazy** (sense 1). **2** *she's potty about you.* See **crazy** (sense 3).

pouch n. **1** *a leather pouch* **bag**, purse, sack, sac, pocket; Scottish sporran. **2** *a kangaroo's pouch* Zoology marsupium.

pounce v. *two men pounced on him* **jump**, spring, leap, dive, lunge; fall on, set on, attack suddenly; informal mug.

▶ n. *a sudden pounce* **leap**, spring, jump, dive, lunge, bound.

pound[1] v. **1** *the two men pounded him with their fists* **beat**, strike, hit, batter, thump, pummel, punch, rain blows on, belabour, hammer, thrash, set on, tear into; informal bash, clobber, wallop, beat the living daylights out of, whack, thwack, lay into, pitch into; Brit. informal slosh; N. Amer. informal light into, whale. **2** *waves pounded the seafront* **beat against**, crash against, batter, dash against, lash, buffet. **3** *gunships pounded the capital* **bombard**, bomb, shell, fire on; old use cannonade. **4** *pound the cloves with salt* **crush**, grind, pulverize, mill, mash, pulp; technical triturate; old use levigate. **5** *I heard him pounding along the gangway* **walk/run heavily**, stomp, lumber, clomp, clump, tramp, trudge. **6** *her heart was pounding* **throb**, thump, thud, hammer, pulse, race, go pit-a-pat; literary pant, thrill.

pound[2] n. **1** *a pound of apples* **pound weight**, lb. **2** *ten pounds* **pound sterling**, £; Brit. informal quid, smacker, nicker.

pound[3] n. *a dog pound* **enclosure**, compound, pen, yard.

pour v. **1** *blood was pouring from his nose* **stream**, flow, run, gush, course, jet, spurt, surge, spill. **2** *Amy poured wine into his glass* **tip**, let flow, splash, spill, decant; informal slosh, slop. **3** *it was pouring with rain* **rain heavily/hard**, teem down, pelt down, tip down, come down in torrents/sheets, rain cats and dogs; informal be chucking it down; Brit. informal bucket down, come down in stair rods; N. Amer. informal rain pitchforks. **4** *people poured off the train* **throng**, crowd, swarm,

stream, flood.

pout v. *Crystal pouted sullenly* **look petulant**, pull a face, look sulky.

▶ n. *a childish pout* **petulant expression**, sulky expression, moue.

poverty n. **1** *abject poverty* **penury**, destitution, pauperism, pauperdom, indigence, pennilessness, impoverishment, neediness, need, hardship, impecuniousness. **2** *the poverty of choice* **scarcity**, deficiency, dearth, shortage, paucity, insufficiency, absence, lack. **3** *the poverty of her imagination* **inferiority**, mediocrity, poorness, sterility.
– OPPOSITES wealth, abundance.

poverty-stricken adj. **extremely poor**, impoverished, destitute, penniless, on one's beam-ends, as poor as a church mouse, in penury, impecunious, indigent, needy, in need/want; Brit. on the breadline, without a penny (to one's name); informal on one's uppers, without two pennies/farthings to rub together; Brit. informal in Queer Street; formal penurious.

powder n. **dust**, fine particles; talcum powder, talc; historical pounce.

▶ v. **1** *the floor was powdered with broken glass* **sprinkle**, cover. **2** *the grains are powdered* **crush**, grind, pulverize, pound, mill; technical comminute; old use levigate.

powdered adj. **dried**, freeze-dried; technical lyophilized.

powdery adj. **fine**, dry, fine-grained, powder-like, dusty, chalky, floury, sandy, crumbly, friable.

power n. **1** *the power of speech* **ability**, capacity, capability, potential, faculty, competence. **2** *the unions wield enormous power* **control**, authority, influence, dominance, mastery, domination, dominion, sway, weight, leverage; informal clout, teeth; N. Amer. informal drag; literary puissance. **3** *police have the power to stop and search* **authority**, right, authorization, warrant, licence. **4** *a major European power* **state**, country, nation. **5** *he hit the ball with as much power as he could* **strength**, powerfulness, might, force, forcefulness, vigour, energy; brawn, muscle; informal punch; Brit. informal welly; literary thew. **6** *the power of his arguments* **forcefulness**, powerfulness, potency, strength, force, cogency, persuasiveness. **7** *the new engine has more power* **driving force**, horsepower, hp, acceleration; informal oomph, grunt. **8** *generating power from waste* **energy**, electrical power. **9** informal *the holiday did him a power of good* **a great deal of**, a lot of, much; informal lots of, loads of.
– OPPOSITES inability, weakness.

  □ **have someone in/under one's power** have control over, have influence over, have under one's thumb, have at one's mercy, have in one's clutches, have in the palm of one's hand; N. Amer. have in one's hip pocket; informal have over a barrel.

  the powers that be the authorities, the people in charge, the government.

p

WORD LINKS
megalomania an obsession with power
omnipotent having unlimited power

powerful adj. **1** *powerful shoulders* **strong**, muscular, muscly, sturdy, strapping, robust, brawny, burly, athletic, manly, well built, solid; informal beefy, hunky; dated stalwart; literary stark, thewy. **2** *a powerful drink* **intoxicating**, hard, strong, stiff; formal spirituous. **3** *a powerful blow* **violent**, forceful, hard, mighty. **4** *he felt a powerful desire to kiss her* **intense**, keen, fierce, passionate, ardent, burning, strong, irresistible, overpowering, overwhelming. **5** *a powerful nation* **influential**, strong, important, dominant, commanding, potent, forceful, formidable; literary puissant. **6** *a powerful critique* **cogent**, compelling, convincing, persuasive, forceful; dramatic, graphic, vivid, moving.
– OPPOSITES weak, gentle.

powerless adj. **impotent**, helpless, ineffectual, ineffective, useless, defenceless, vulnerable; literary impuissant.

practicable adj. **realistic**, feasible, possible, within the bounds/realms of possibility, viable, reasonable, sensible, workable, achievable; informal doable.

practical adj. **1** *practical experience* **empirical**, hands-on, actual, active, applied, heuristic, experiential. **2** *there are no practical alternatives* **feasible**, practicable, realistic, viable, workable, possible, reasonable, sensible; informal doable. **3** *practical clothes* **functional**, sensible, utilitarian, workaday. **4** *try to be more practical* **realistic**, sensible, down-to-earth, businesslike, commonsensical, hard-headed, no-nonsense; informal hard-nosed. **5** *a practical certainty* **virtual**, effective, near.
– OPPOSITES theoretical.

practicality n. **1** *the practicality of the proposal* **feasibility**, practicability, viability, workability. **2** *practicality of design* **functionalism**, functionality, serviceability, utility. **3** *his calm practicality* **(common) sense**, realism, pragmatism. **4** *the practicalities of army life* **practical details**; informal nitty gritty, nuts and bolts.

practical joke n. **trick**, joke, prank, jape, hoax; informal leg-pull.

practically adv. **1** *the cinema was practically empty* **almost**, (very) nearly, virtually, just about, all but, more or less, as good as, wellnigh, to all intents and purposes, verging on, bordering on; informal pretty nearly, pretty well. **2** *'You can't afford it,' he pointed out practically* **realistically**, sensibly, reasonably.

practice n. **1** *the practice of radiotherapy* **application**, exercise, use, operation, implementation, execution. **2** *common practice* **custom**, procedure, policy, convention, tradition; formal praxis. **3** *it takes lots of practice | the team's final practice* **training**, rehearsal, repetition, preparation;

practice session, dummy run, run-through; informal dry run. **4** *the practice of medicine* **profession**, career, business, work. **5** *a small legal practice* **business**, firm, office, company; informal outfit.
□ **in practice** in reality, realistically, practically.
out of practice rusty, unpractised.
put something into practice use, make use of, put to use, utilize, apply.

practise v. **1** *he practised the songs every day* **rehearse**, go over/through, run through, work on/at; polish, perfect. **2** *the performers were practising* **train**, rehearse, prepare, go through one's paces. **3** *we still practise these rituals today* **carry out**, perform, observe. **4** *she practises medicine* **work at**, pursue a career in.

practised adj. **expert**, experienced, seasoned, skilled, skilful, accomplished, proficient, talented, able, adept, consummate, master, masterly; informal crack, ace, mean; N. Amer. informal crackerjack.

pragmatic adj. **practical**, matter-of-fact, sensible, down-to-earth, commonsensical, businesslike, having both/one's feet on the ground, hard-headed, no-nonsense; informal hard-nosed.
– OPPOSITES impractical.

praise v. **1** *the police praised Pauline for her courage* **commend**, express admiration for, applaud, pay tribute to, speak highly of, eulogize, compliment, congratulate, sing the praises of, rave about, go into raptures about, wax lyrical about, make much of, pat on the back, take one's hat off to, lionize, admire, hail; N. Amer. informal ballyhoo; formal laud. **2** *we praise God* **worship**, glorify, honour, exalt, adore, pay tribute to, give thanks to, venerate, reverence; formal laud; old use magnify.
– OPPOSITES criticize.
▶ n. **1** *James was full of praise for the medical teams* **approval**, acclaim, admiration, approbation, acclamation, plaudits, congratulations, commendation; tribute, accolade, compliment, a pat on the back, eulogy, panegyric; N. Amer. informal kudos; formal laudation, encomium. **2** *give praise to God* **honour**, thanks, glory, worship, devotion, adoration, reverence.

praiseworthy adj. **commendable**, admirable, laudable, worthy (of admiration), meritorious, estimable, exemplary.

pram n. Brit. pushchair; N. Amer. baby carriage, stroller; Brit. trademark baby buggy; formal perambulator.

prance v. **cavort**, dance, jig, trip, caper, jump, leap, spring, bound, skip, hop, frisk, romp, frolic.

prank n. **(practical) joke**, trick, piece of mischief, escapade, stunt, caper, jape, game, hoax, antic; informal lark, leg-pull.

prattle v. *he prattled on for ages.* See **chat** (verb).
▶ n. *childish prattle.* See **chatter** (noun).

pray v. **1** *let us pray* **say one's prayers**, make one's devotions. **2** *she prayed God to forgive her* **invoke**, call on, implore, appeal to, entreat, beg, petition, supplicate; literary beseech.

prayer n. **1** *the priest's murmured prayers* **invocation**, intercession, devotion; old use orison. **2** *a quick prayer that she wouldn't bump into him* **appeal**, plea, entreaty, petition, supplication, invocation; rare obsecration.

preach v. **1** *he preached to a large congregation* **give a sermon**, sermonize, address, speak; evangelize. **2** *preaching the good news of Jesus* **proclaim**, teach, spread, propagate, expound. **3** *they preach toleration* **advocate**, recommend, advise, urge, teach, counsel. **4** *who are you to preach at me?* **moralize**, sermonize, pontificate, lecture, harangue; informal preachify.

> **WORD LINKS**
> **homiletics** the art of preaching or writing sermons

preacher n. **minister (of religion)**, parson, clergyman, clergywoman, member of the clergy, priest, man/woman of the cloth, man/woman of God, cleric, churchman, churchwoman, evangelist; informal reverend, padre, Holy Joe, sky pilot; N. Amer. informal preacher man; Austral. informal josser.

preaching n. **religious teaching**, message, sermons.

preachy adj. informal **moralistic**, moralizing, sanctimonious, self-righteous, holier-than-thou, sententious.

preamble n. **introduction**, preface, prologue; foreword, prelude, front matter; informal intro, prelims; formal exordium, proem, prolegomenon.

prearranged adj. **arranged beforehand**, agreed in advance, predetermined, pre-established, pre-planned.

precarious adj. **uncertain**, insecure, unpredictable, risky, parlous, hazardous, dangerous, unsafe; unsettled, unstable, unsteady, shaky; informal dicey, chancy, iffy; Brit. informal dodgy.
– OPPOSITES safe.

precaution n. **safeguard**, preventative/preventive measure, safety measure, insurance; informal backstop.

precautionary adj. **preventative**, preventive, safety.

precede v. **1** *adverts preceded the film* **go/come before**, lead (up) to, pave/prepare the way for, herald, introduce, usher in; old use forego. **2** *Catherine preceded him into the studio* **go ahead of**, go in front of, go before, go first, lead, show the way. **3** *he preceded the book with a poem* **preface**, introduce, begin, open.
– OPPOSITES follow.

precedence n. *quarrels over precedence* **priority**, rank, seniority, superiority, primacy, pre-eminence, eminence.
□ **take precedence over** take priority over, outweigh, prevail over, come before.

precedent n. **model**, exemplar, example, pattern, previous case, prior instance/example; paradigm, criterion, yardstick, standard.

preceding adj. **foregoing**, previous, prior, former, precedent, earlier, above, aforementioned, antecedent; formal anterior, prevenient.

precept n. **1** *the precepts of Orthodox Judaism* **principle**, rule, tenet, canon, doctrine, command, order, decree, dictate, dictum, injunction, commandment; Judaism mitzvah; formal prescript. **2** *precepts that her grandmother used to quote* **maxim**, saying, adage, axiom, aphorism, apophthegm.

precinct n. **1** *a pedestrian precinct* **area**, zone, sector. **2** *within the precincts of the City* **bounds**, boundaries, limits, confines. **3** *the cathedral precinct* **enclosure**, close, court.

precious adj. **1** *precious works of art* **valuable**, costly, expensive; invaluable, priceless, beyond price. **2** *her most precious possession* **valued**, cherished, treasured, prized, favourite, dear, dearest, beloved, darling, adored, loved, special. **3** *his precious manners* **affected**, over-refined, pretentious; informal la-di-da; Brit. informal poncey.

precipice n. **cliff (face)**, steep cliff, rock face, sheer drop, crag, bluff, escarpment, scarp; literary steep.

precipitate v. **1** *the incident precipitated a crisis* **bring about/on**, cause, lead to, give rise to, instigate, trigger, spark, touch off, provoke, hasten, accelerate, expedite. **2** *they were precipitated down the mountain* **hurl**, catapult, throw, plunge, launch, fling, propel.
▶ adj. **1** *their actions were precipitate* **hasty**, overhasty, rash, hurried, rushed; impetuous, impulsive, spur-of-the-moment, precipitous, incautious, imprudent, injudicious, ill-advised, reckless, harum-scarum; informal previous; literary temerarious. **2** *a precipitate decline.* See **precipitous** (sense 2).

precipitous adj. **1** *a precipitous drop* **steep**, sheer, perpendicular, abrupt, sharp, vertical. **2** *his fall from power was precipitous* **sudden**, rapid, swift, abrupt, headlong, speedy, quick, fast, precipitate. **3** *he was too precipitous.* See **precipitate** (sense 1 of the adjective).

precis n. *a precis of the report* **summary**, synopsis, résumé, abstract, outline, summarization, summation; abridgement, digest, overview, epitome; N. Amer. wrap-up; rare conspectus.
▶ v. *precising a passage* **summarize**, sum up, give a summary/precis of, give the main points of; abridge, condense, shorten, synopsize, abstract, outline, abbreviate; old use epitomize.

precise adj. **1** *precise measurements* **exact**, accurate, correct, specific, detailed, explicit, unambiguous, definite. **2** *at that precise moment the car stopped* **exact**, particular, very, specific. **3** *the attention to detail is very precise* **meticulous**, careful, exact, scrupulous, punctilious, conscientious,

p

particular, methodical, strict, rigorous.
– OPPOSITES inaccurate.

precisely adv. **1** *at 2 o'clock precisely* **exactly**, sharp, on the dot; promptly, prompt, dead (on), on the stroke of ——, on the dot of ——; informal bang (on); Brit. informal spot on; N. Amer. informal on the button/nose. **2** *precisely the kind of man I am looking for* **exactly**, absolutely, just, in all respects; informal to a T. **3** *fertilization can be timed precisely* **accurately**, exactly; clearly, distinctly, strictly. **4** *'So it's all done?' 'Precisely.'* **yes**, exactly, absolutely, (that's) right, quite so, indubitably, definitely; informal you bet, I'll say.

precision n. **exactness**, exactitude, accuracy, correctness, preciseness; care, carefulness, meticulousness, scrupulousness, punctiliousness, rigour, rigorousness.

preclude v. **prevent**, make it impossible for, rule out, stop, prohibit, debar, bar, hinder, impede, inhibit, exclude.

precocious adj. **advanced for one's age**, forward, mature, gifted, talented, clever, intelligent, quick; informal smart.
– OPPOSITES backward.

preconceived adj. **predetermined**, prejudged; prejudiced, biased.

preconception n. **preconceived idea/ notion**, presupposition, assumption, presumption, prejudgement; prejudice.

precondition n. **prerequisite**, (necessary/ essential) condition, requirement, necessity, essential, imperative, sine qua non; informal must.

precursor n. **1** *a three-stringed precursor of the guitar* **forerunner**, predecessor, forefather, father, antecedent, ancestor, forebear. **2** *a precursor of disasters to come* **harbinger**, herald, sign, indication, portent, omen.

precursory adj. **preliminary**, prior, previous, introductory, preparatory, prefatory; formal anterior, prevenient.

predatory adj. **1** *predatory birds* **predacious**, carnivorous, hunting, raptorial; of prey. **2** *a predatory gleam in his eyes* **exploitative**, wolfish, rapacious, vulturine, vulturous.

predecessor n. **1** *the Prime Minister's predecessor* **forerunner**, precursor, antecedent. **2** *our Victorian predecessors* **ancestor**, forefather, forebear, antecedent.
– OPPOSITES successor, descendant.

predestined adj. **preordained**, ordained, predetermined, destined, fated.

predetermined adj. **1** *a predetermined budget* **prearranged**, established in advance, preset, set, fixed, agreed. **2** *our predetermined fate* **predestined**, preordained.

predicament n. **difficult situation**, mess, difficulty, problem, issue, plight, quandary, muddle, mare's nest; informal hole, fix, jam, pickle, scrape, bind, tight spot/corner, dilemma.

predicate v. **base**, be dependent, found, establish, rest, ground, premise.

predict v. **forecast**, foretell, foresee, prophesy, anticipate, tell in advance, envision, envisage; literary previse; old use augur, presage.

predictable adj. **foreseeable**, (only) to be expected, anticipated, foreseen, unsurprising; informal inevitable.

prediction n. **forecast**, prophecy, prognosis, prognostication, augury; projection, conjecture, guess.

predilection n. **liking**, fondness, preference, partiality, taste, penchant, weakness, soft spot, fancy, inclination, leaning, bias, propensity, bent, proclivity, predisposition, appetite.
– OPPOSITES dislike.

predispose v. **1** *lack of exercise may predispose an individual to high blood pressure* **make susceptible**, make liable, make prone, make vulnerable, put at risk of. **2** *attitudes which predispose people to behave badly* **lead**, influence, sway, induce, prompt, dispose; bias, prejudice.

predisposed adj. **inclined**, prepared, ready, of a mind, disposed, minded, willing.

predisposition n. **1** *a predisposition to heart disease* **susceptibility**, proneness, tendency, liability, inclination, disposition, vulnerability. **2** *their political predispositions* **preference**, predilection, inclination, leaning.

predominance n. **1** *the predominance of women carers* **prevalence**, dominance, preponderance. **2** *American military predominance* **supremacy**, mastery, control, power, ascendancy, dominance, pre-eminence, superiority.

predominant adj. **1** *our predominant objectives* **main**, chief, principal, most important, primary, prime, central, leading, foremost, key, paramount; informal number-one. **2** *the predominant political forces* **controlling**, dominant, predominating, more/most powerful, pre-eminent, ascendant, superior, in the ascendancy.
– OPPOSITES subsidiary.

predominantly adv. **mainly**, mostly, for the most part, chiefly, principally, primarily, predominately, in the main, on the whole, largely, by and large, typically, generally, usually.

predominate v. **1** *small-scale producers predominate* **be in the majority**, preponderate, be predominant, prevail, be most prominent. **2** *private interest predominates over the public good* **prevail**, dominate, be dominant; override, outweigh.

pre-eminence n. **superiority**, supremacy, greatness, excellence, distinction, prominence, predominance, eminence, importance, prestige, stature, fame, renown, celebrity.

pre-eminent adj. **greatest**, leading, foremost, best, finest, chief, outstanding, excellent, distinguished, prominent,

p

eminent, important, top, famous, renowned, celebrated, illustrious, supreme; N. Amer. marquee.
– OPPOSITES undistinguished.

pre-eminently adv. **primarily**, principally, above all, chiefly, mostly, mainly, in particular.

pre-empt v. **1** *his action may have pre-empted war* **forestall**, prevent. **2** *many tables were already pre-empted by family parties* **commandeer**, occupy, seize, arrogate, appropriate, take over, secure, reserve.

preen v. **1** *the robin preened its feathers* **clean**, tidy, groom, smooth, arrange; old use plume. **2** *she preened before the mirror* **admire oneself**, primp oneself, prink oneself, groom oneself, spruce oneself up; informal titivate oneself, doll oneself up; Brit. informal tart oneself up; N. Amer. informal gussy oneself up.
□ **preen oneself** congratulate oneself, be pleased with oneself, be proud of oneself, pat oneself on the back, feel self-satisfied.

preface n. *the preface to the novel* **introduction**, foreword, preamble, prologue, prelude; front matter; informal prelims, intro; formal exordium, proem, prolegomenon.
▶ v. *the chapter is prefaced by a poem* **precede**, introduce, begin, open, start.

prefatory adj. **introductory**, preliminary, opening, initial, preparatory, initiatory, precursory.
– OPPOSITES closing.

prefect n. Brit. **monitor**; Brit. praepostor.

prefer v. **1** *I prefer white wine to red* **like better**, would rather (have), would sooner (have), favour, be more partial to; choose, select, pick, opt for, go for, plump for. **2** formal *do you want to prefer charges?* **bring**, press, file, lodge, lay. **3** old use *he was preferred to the post* **promote**, upgrade, raise, elevate.

preferable adj. **better**, best, more desirable, more suitable, advantageous, superior, preferred, recommended.

preferably adv. **ideally**, if possible, for preference, from choice.

preference n. **1** *her preference for boys' games* **liking**, partiality, predilection, proclivity, fondness, taste, inclination, leaning, bias, bent, penchant, predisposition. **2** *my preference is rock* **favourite**, (first) choice, selection; informal cup of tea, thing; N. Amer. informal druthers. **3** *preference will be given to applicants speaking Japanese* **priority**, favour, precedence, preferential treatment.
□ **in preference to** rather than, instead of, in place of, sooner than.

preferential adj. **special**, better, privileged, superior, favourable; partial, discriminatory, partisan, biased.

preferment n. **promotion**, advancement, elevation, being upgraded, a step up (the ladder); informal a kick upstairs.
– OPPOSITES demotion.

prefigure v. **foreshadow**, presage, be a harbinger of, herald; literary foretoken.

pregnant adj. **1** *she is heavily pregnant* **expecting a baby**, expectant, carrying a child; informal expecting, in the family way, preggers, with a bun in the oven; Brit. informal up the duff, in the (pudding) club, up the spout; N. Amer. informal knocked up, having swallowed a watermelon seed; Austral. informal with a joey in the pouch; informal dated in trouble; old use with child, in a delicate condition, in an interesting condition; technical gravid, parturient. **2** *a ceremony pregnant with religious significance* **filled**, charged, heavy; full of. **3** *a pregnant pause* **meaningful**, significant, suggestive, expressive, charged.

> **WORD LINKS**
> **gestation** the process of developing in the womb.
> See also **birth**.

prehistoric adj. **1** *prehistoric times* **primitive**, primeval, primordial, primal, ancient, early, antediluvian. **2** informal *the special effects look prehistoric* **out of date**, outdated, outmoded, old-fashioned, démodé, passé, antiquated, superannuated, archaic, behind the times, primitive, antediluvian; informal out of the ark; Brit. informal past its sell-by date; N. Amer. informal horse-and-buggy, clunky.
– OPPOSITES modern.

prejudice n. **1** *male prejudices about women* **preconceived idea**, preconception, prejudgement. **2** *they are motivated by prejudice* **bigotry**, bias, partisanship, partiality, intolerance, discrimination, unfairness, inequality. **3** *without prejudice to the interests of others* **detriment**, harm, damage, injury, hurt, loss.
▶ v. **1** *the article could prejudice the jury* **bias**, influence, sway, predispose, make biased, make partial, colour. **2** *this could prejudice his chances of victory* **damage**, be detrimental to, be prejudicial to, injure, harm, hurt, spoil, impair, undermine, hinder, compromise, drive a nail into the coffin of.

prejudiced adj. **biased**, bigoted, discriminatory, partisan, intolerant, narrow-minded, unfair, unjust, inequitable, coloured.
– OPPOSITES impartial.

prejudicial adj. **detrimental**, damaging, injurious, harmful, disadvantageous, hurtful, deleterious.
– OPPOSITES beneficial.

preliminary adj. *the discussions are still at a preliminary stage* **preparatory**, introductory, initial, opening, prefatory, precursory; early, exploratory.
– OPPOSITES final.
▶ n. **1** *he began without any preliminaries* **introduction**, preamble, opening/prefatory remarks, formalities. **2** *a preliminary to the resumption of war* **prelude**, preparation, preparatory measure, preliminary action.

p

□ **preliminary to** in preparation for, before, in advance of, prior to, preparatory to.

prelims plural n. informal **front matter**, preliminary material, introduction, foreword, preface, preamble; informal intro; formal exordium, proem, prolegomenon.

prelude n. **1** *a ceasefire was a prelude to peace negotiations* **preliminary**, overture, opening, preparation, introduction, start, commencement, beginning, lead-in, precursor. **2** *an orchestral prelude* **overture**, introductory movement, introduction, opening. **3** *the passage forms a prelude to Part III* **introduction**, preface, prologue, foreword, preamble; informal intro; formal exordium, proem, prolegomenon.

premature adj. **1** *his premature death* **untimely**, (too) early, unseasonable, before time. **2** *a premature baby* **preterm**; informal prem. **3** *such a step would be premature* **rash**, overhasty, hasty, precipitate, precipitous, impulsive, impetuous; informal previous.
– OPPOSITES overdue.

prematurely adv. **1** *Sam was born prematurely* **too soon**, too early, ahead of time; preterm. **2** *don't act prematurely* **rashly**, overhastily, hastily, precipitately, precipitously.

premeditated adj. **planned**, intentional, deliberate, pre-planned, calculated, cold-blooded, conscious, prearranged.
– OPPOSITES spontaneous.

premeditation n. **(advance) planning**, forethought, pre-planning, (criminal) intent; Law malice aforethought.

premier adj. *a premier chef* **leading**, foremost, chief, principal, head, top-ranking, top, prime, primary, first, highest, pre-eminent, senior, outstanding, master; N. Amer. ranking; informal top-notch.
▸ n. *the Italian premier* **head of government**, prime minister, PM, president, chancellor.

premiere n. **first performance**, first night, opening night.

premise n. *the premise that human life consists of a series of choices* **proposition**, assumption, hypothesis, thesis, presupposition, postulation, postulate, supposition, presumption, surmise, conjecture, speculation, assertion, belief.
▸ v. *they premised that the cosmos is indestructible* **postulate**, hypothesize, conjecture, posit, theorize, suppose, presuppose, surmise, assume.

premises plural n. **building(s)**, property, site, office.

premium n. **1** *monthly premiums of £30* **(regular) payment**, instalment. **2** *you must pay a premium for organic fruit* **surcharge**, additional payment, extra amount. **3** *a foreign service premium* **bonus**, extra; incentive, inducement; informal perk; formal perquisite.
□ **at a premium** scarce, in great demand, hard to come by, in short supply, thin on the ground.
put/place a premium on 1 *I place a high*

premium on our relationship **value greatly**, attach great/special importance to, set great store by, put a high value on. **2** *the high price of oil put a premium on the coal industry* **make valuable**, make invaluable, make important.

premonition n. **foreboding**, presentiment, intuition, (funny) feeling, hunch, suspicion, feeling in one's bones; misgiving, apprehension, fear; old use presage.

preoccupation n. **1** *she had an air of preoccupation* **pensiveness**, concentration, engrossment, absorption, self-absorption, musing, thinking, deep thought, brown study, brooding; abstraction, absent-mindedness, distraction, forgetfulness, inattentiveness, wool-gathering, daydreaming. **2** *their main preoccupation was feeding their family* **obsession**, concern; passion, enthusiasm, hobby horse.

preoccupied adj. **1** *officials preoccupied with their careers* **obsessed**, concerned, absorbed, engrossed, focused, intent, involved, wrapped up. **2** *she looked preoccupied* **lost/deep in thought**, in a brown study, pensive, absent-minded, distracted, abstracted.

preoccupy v. **engross**, concern, absorb, take up someone's attention, distract, obsess, occupy, prey on someone's mind.

preordain v. **predestine**, destine, foreordain, ordain, fate, predetermine, determine.

preparation n. **1** *the preparation of contingency plans* **devising**, putting together, drawing up, construction, composition, production, getting ready, development. **2** *preparations for the party* **arrangements**, planning, plans, preparatory measures. **3** *preparation for exams* **instruction**, teaching, coaching, training, tutoring, drilling, priming. **4** *a preparation to kill off mites* **mixture**, compound, concoction, solution, tincture, medicine, potion, cream, ointment, lotion.

preparatory adj. *preparatory work* **preliminary**, initial, introductory, prefatory, opening, preparative, precursory.
□ **preparatory to** in preparation for, before, prior to, preliminary to.

prepare v. **1** *I want you to prepare a report* **make/get ready**, put together, draw up, produce, arrange, assemble, construct, compose, formulate. **2** *the meal was easy to prepare* **cook**, make, get, put together, concoct; informal fix, rustle up; Brit. informal knock up. **3** *they are preparing for war* **get ready**, make preparations, arrange things, make provision. **4** *athletes preparing for the Olympics* **train**, get into shape, practise, get ready. **5** *I must prepare for my exams* **study**, revise; Brit. informal swot. **6** *this course prepares students for their exams* **instruct**, coach, train, tutor, drill, prime. **7** *prepare yourself for a shock* **brace**, make ready, tense, steel, steady.

prepared adj. **1** *he needs to be well prepared* **ready**, (all) set, equipped, primed; waiting, on hand, poised, in position. **2** *I'm not prepared to cut the price* **willing**, ready, disposed, predisposed, (favourably) inclined, of a mind, minded.

preponderance n. **1** *the preponderance of women among older people* **prevalence**, predominance, dominance. **2** *the preponderance of the evidence* **bulk**, majority, greater quantity, larger part, best/better part, most; almost all. **3** *the preponderance of the trade unions* **predominance**, dominance, ascendancy, supremacy, power.

preponderant adj. **dominant**, predominant, pre-eminent, in control, more/most powerful, superior, supreme, ascendant, in the ascendancy.

preponderate v. **be in the majority**, predominate, be predominant; be more/most important, prevail, dominate.

prepossessing adj. **attractive**, beautiful, pretty, handsome, good-looking, fetching, charming, delightful, enchanting, captivating; old use fair.
– OPPOSITES ugly.

preposterous adj. **absurd**, ridiculous, foolish, stupid, ludicrous, farcical, laughable, comical, risible, nonsensical, senseless, insane; outrageous, monstrous; informal crazy.
– OPPOSITES sensible.

prerequisite n. *a prerequisite for the course* **(necessary) condition**, precondition, essential, requirement, requisite, necessity, sine qua non; informal must.
▶ adj. *the prerequisite qualifications* **necessary**, required, called for, essential, requisite, obligatory, compulsory.
– OPPOSITES unnecessary.

prerogative n. **entitlement**, right, privilege, advantage, due, birthright.

presage v. *the owl's hooting presages death* **portend**, augur, foreshadow, foretell, prophesy, be an omen of, herald, be a sign of, be the harbinger of, warn of, be a presage of, signal, bode, promise, threaten; literary betoken, foretoken, forebode.
▶ n. *a sombre presage of his final illness* **omen**, sign, indication, portent, warning, forewarning, harbinger, augury, prophecy, foretoken.

prescience n. **far-sightedness**, foresight, foreknowledge; psychic powers, clairvoyance; prediction, prognostication, divination, prophecy, augury; insight, intuition, perception, percipience.

prescient adj. **prophetic**, predictive, visionary; psychic, clairvoyant; far-sighted, prognostic, divinatory; insightful, intuitive, perceptive, percipient.

prescribe v. **1** *the doctor prescribed antibiotics* **write a prescription for**. **2** *marriage is often prescribed as a universal remedy* **advise**, recommend, advocate, suggest, endorse, champion, promote. **3** *rules prescribing five acts for a play are purely arbitrary* **stipulate**, lay down, dictate, specify, determine, establish, fix.

prescription n. **1** *the doctor wrote a prescription* **instruction**, authorization; informal script; old use recipe. **2** *he fetched the prescription from the chemist* **medicine**, drug, medication. **3** *a painless prescription for improvement* **method**, measure; recommendation, suggestion, recipe, formula.

prescriptive adj. **dictatorial**, narrow, rigid, authoritarian, arbitrary, repressive, dogmatic.

presence n. **1** *the presence of a train was indicated electrically* **existence**, being there. **2** *I requested the presence of an adjudicator* **attendance**, appearance; company, companionship. **3** *a woman of great presence* **aura**, charisma, (strength/force of) personality; poise, self-assurance, self-confidence. **4** *she felt a presence in the castle* **ghost**, spirit, spectre, phantom, apparition, supernatural being; informal spook; literary shade.
– OPPOSITES absence.
□ **presence of mind** composure, equanimity, self-possession, level-headedness, self-assurance, calmness, sangfroid, imperturbability; alertness, quick-wittedness; informal cool, unflappability.

present[1] adj. **1** *a doctor must be present at the ringside* **in attendance**, here, there, near, nearby, (close/near) at hand, available. **2** *organic compounds are present in the waste* **in existence**, existing, existent. **3** *the present economic climate* **current**, present-day, existing; old use instant.
– OPPOSITES absent.
▶ n. *forget the past and think about the present* **now**, today, the present time/moment, the here and now.
– OPPOSITES past, future.
□ **at present** at the moment, just now, right now, at the present time, currently, at this moment in time.
for the present for the time being, for now, for the moment, for a while, temporarily, pro tem.
the present day modern times, nowadays.

present[2] v. **1** *Eddy presented a cheque to the winner* **hand over/out**, give (out), confer, bestow, award, grant, accord. **2** *the committee presented its report* **submit**, set forth, put forward, proffer, offer, tender, table. **3** *may I present my wife?* **introduce**, make known, acquaint someone with. **4** *I called to present my warmest compliments* **offer**, give, express. **5** *they presented their new product last month* **demonstrate**, show, put on show/display, exhibit, display, launch, unveil. **6** *presenting good quality opera* **stage**, put on, produce, perform. **7** *she presents a TV show* **host**, introduce, compère, be the presenter of; N. Amer. informal emcee. **8** *the authorities present him as a common criminal* **represent**, describe, portray, depict.
□ **present oneself 1** *he presented himself at ten* **be present**, make an appearance, appear, turn up, arrive. **2** *an opportunity that presented itself* **occur**, arise, happen, come about/up, appear, crop up, turn up.

p

present³ n. *a birthday present* **gift**, donation, offering, contribution; informal prezzie, freebie; formal benefaction.

presentable adj. **1** *I'm making the place look presentable* **tidy**, neat, straight, clean, spick and span, in good order, shipshape (and Bristol fashion). **2** *make yourself presentable* **smartly dressed**, tidily dressed, tidy, well groomed, trim, spruce; informal natty. **3** *presentable videos* **fairly good**, passable, all right, satisfactory, moderately good, not (too) bad, average, fair; informal OK.

presentation n. **1** *the presentation of his certificate* **awarding**, presenting, giving, handing over/out, bestowal, granting, award. **2** *the presentation of food* **appearance**, arrangement, packaging, disposition, display, layout. **3** *her presentation to the Queen* **introduction**, making known. **4** *the presentation of new proposals* **submission**, proffering, offering, tendering, advancing, proposal, suggestion, mooting, tabling. **5** *a sales presentation* **demonstration**, talk, lecture, address, speech, show, exhibition, display, introduction, launch, launching, unveiling. **6** *a presentation of his latest play* **staging**, production, performance, mounting, showing.

present-day adj. **current**, present, contemporary, latter-day, present-time, modern, twenty-first-century; up to date, up to the minute, fashionable, trendsetting, the latest, new, newest, newfangled; informal trendy, now.

presentiment n. **premonition**, foreboding, intuition, (funny) feeling, hunch, feeling in one's bones, sixth sense; old use presage.

presently adv. **1** *I shall see you presently* **soon**, shortly, directly, quite soon, in a short time, in a little while, at any moment/minute/second, in next to no time, before long; N. Amer. momentarily; informal pretty soon, any moment now, in a jiffy, before you can say Jack Robinson, in two shakes of a lamb's tail; Brit. informal in a mo; literary ere long. **2** *he is presently abroad* **at present**, currently, at the/this moment, at the present moment/time, now, nowadays, these days; Brit. informal at the minute.

preservation n. **1** *wood preservation* **conservation**, protection, care. **2** *the preservation of the status quo* **continuation**, conservation, maintenance, upholding, sustaining, perpetuation. **3** *the preservation of food* **conserving**, bottling, canning, freezing, drying; curing, smoking, pickling.

preserve v. **1** *oil helps preserve wood* **conserve**, protect, maintain, care for, look after. **2** *they wish to preserve the status quo* **continue (with)**, conserve, keep going, maintain, uphold, sustain, perpetuate. **3** *preserving him from harassment* **guard**, protect, keep, defend, safeguard, shelter, shield. **4** *spices enable us to preserve food* **conserve**, bottle, can, freeze, dry; cure, smoke, pickle.
▶ n. **1** *strawberry preserve* **jam**, jelly, marmalade, conserve. **2** *the preserve of an educated middle class* **domain**, area, field, sphere, orbit, realm, province, territory; informal turf, bailiwick. **3** *a game preserve* **sanctuary**, (game) reserve, reservation.

preside v. *the chairman presides at the meeting* **chair**, be chairman/chairwoman/chairperson, officiate (at), conduct, lead.
□ **preside over** be in charge of, be responsible for, be at the head/helm of, head, be head of, manage, administer, be in control of, control, direct, lead, govern, rule, command, supervise, oversee; informal head up, be boss of, be in the driving/driver's seat, be in the saddle.

president n. **1** *the president of the society* **head**, chief, director, leader, governor, principal, master; N. Amer. informal prexy. **2** *the president of the company* **chairman**, chairwoman; managing director, MD, chief executive (officer), CEO. **3** *the president of the United States* **head of state**, chief of state.

press v. **1** *press the paper down firmly* **push (down)**, press down, depress, hold down, force, thrust, squeeze, compress. **2** *his shirt was pressed* **smooth (out)**, iron. **3** *we pressed the grapes* **crush**, squeeze, squash, mash, pulp, pound, pulverize, macerate. **4** *she pressed the child to her bosom* **clasp**, hold close, hug, cuddle, squeeze, clutch, grasp, embrace. **5** *Winnie pressed his hand* **squeeze**, grip, clutch. **6** *the crowd pressed round* **cluster**, gather, converge, congregate, flock, swarm, throng, crowd. **7** *the government pressed its claim* **plead**, urge, advance insistently, present, submit, put forward. **8** *they pressed him to agree* **urge**, put pressure on, pressurize, force, push, coerce, dragoon, steamroller, browbeat; informal lean on, put the screws on, twist someone's arm, railroad, bulldoze. **9** *they pressed for a ban on the ivory trade* **call**, ask, clamour, push, campaign, demand.
▶ n. **1** *a private press* **publishing house**, printing company; printing press. **2** *the freedom of the press* **the media**, the newspapers, the papers, the news media, the fourth estate; journalists, reporters, newspapermen, newsmen, pressmen, presswomen; informal journos, newshounds; N. Amer. informal newsies; Brit. dated Fleet Street. **3** *the company had some bad press* **reports**, press coverage, press articles, press reviews.
□ **be pressed for** have too little, be short of, have insufficient, lack, be lacking (in), be deficient in, need, be/stand in need of; informal be strapped for.

press on proceed, keep going, continue, carry on, make progress, make headway, press ahead, forge on/ahead, push on, keep on, struggle on, persevere, keep at it, stay with it, plod on, plough on; informal soldier on, plug away, peg away, stick at it.

pressing adj. **1** *a pressing problem* **urgent**, critical, crucial, acute, desperate, serious, grave, life-and-death. **2** *a pressing engagement* **important**, high-priority, critical, crucial, compelling, inescapable.

pressure n. **1** *a confined gas exerts a constant pressure* **physical force**, load, stress, thrust; compression, weight. **2** *they put pressure on us to borrow money* **coercion**, force, compulsion, constraint, duress; pestering, harassment, nagging, badgering, intimidation, arm-twisting, pressurization, persuasion. **3** *she had a lot of pressure from work* **strain**, stress, tension, trouble, difficulty; informal hassle.
▸ v. *they pressured him into resigning.* See **pressurize**.

> **WORD LINKS**
> **barometer** an instrument for measuring atmospheric pressure
> **manometer, piezometer** an instrument for measuring the pressure of fluids

pressurize v. *he tried to pressurize Buffy into selling* **coerce**, pressure, put pressure on, press, push, persuade, force, bulldoze, hound, harass, nag, harry, badger, goad, pester, browbeat, bully, bludgeon, intimidate, dragoon, twist someone's arm; informal railroad, lean on; N. Amer. informal hustle.

prestige n. **status**, standing, stature, prestigiousness, reputation, repute, regard, fame, note, renown, honour, esteem, celebrity, importance, prominence, influence, eminence; kudos, cachet; informal clout.

prestigious adj. **1** *prestigious journals* **reputable**, distinguished, respected, esteemed, eminent, august, highly regarded, well thought of, acclaimed, authoritative, celebrated, illustrious, leading, renowned. **2** *a prestigious job* **impressive**, important, prominent, high-ranking, influential, powerful, glamorous; well paid, expensive; Brit. upmarket.
– OPPOSITES obscure, minor.

presumably adv. **I presume**, I expect, I assume, I take it, I suppose, I imagine, I dare say, I guess, in all probability, probably, in all likelihood, as likely as not, doubtless, undoubtedly, no doubt.

presume v. **1** *I presumed that it had once been an attic* **assume**, suppose, dare say, imagine, take it, expect, believe, think, surmise, guess, judge, conjecture, speculate, postulate, presuppose. **2** *let me presume to give you some advice* **venture**, dare, have the audacity/effrontery, be so bold as, take the liberty of.
▫ **presume on** take (unfair) advantage of, exploit, take liberties with; count on, bank on.

presumption n. **1** *this presumption may be easily rebutted* **assumption**, supposition, presupposition, belief, guess, judgement, surmise, conjecture, speculation, hypothesis, postulation, inference, deduction, conclusion. **2** *he apologized for his presumption* **brazenness**, audacity, boldness, audaciousness, temerity, arrogance, presumptuousness, forwardness; cockiness, insolence, impudence,

bumptiousness, impertinence, effrontery, cheek, cheekiness; rudeness, impoliteness, disrespect, familiarity; informal nerve, brass neck, chutzpah; N. Amer. informal sass, sassiness; old use assumption.

presumptive adj. **1** *a presumptive diagnosis* **conjectural**, speculative, tentative; theoretical, unproven, unconfirmed. **2** *the heir presumptive* **probable**, likely, prospective, assumed, supposed, expected.

presumptuous adj. **brazen**, overconfident, arrogant, bold, audacious, forward, familiar, impertinent, insolent, impudent, cocky; cheeky, rude, impolite, uncivil, bumptious; N. Amer. informal sassy; old use assumptive.

presuppose v. **1** *this presupposes the existence of a policy-making group* **require**, necessitate, imply, entail, mean, involve, assume. **2** *I had presupposed that theme parks make people happy* **presume**, assume, take it for granted, take it as read, suppose, surmise, think, accept, consider.

presupposition n. **presumption**, assumption, preconception, supposition, hypothesis, surmise, thesis, theory, premise, belief, postulation.

pretence n. **1** *cease this pretence* **make-believe**, acting, dissembling, shamming, faking, feigning, simulation, dissimulation, play-acting, posturing; deception, deceit, deceitfulness, fraud, fraudulence, duplicity, subterfuge, trickery, dishonesty, hypocrisy, falsity, lying, mendacity. **2** *he made a pretence of being unconcerned* **(false) show**, semblance, affectation, (false) appearance, outward appearance, impression, (false) front, guise, facade, display. **3** *she had dropped any pretence to faith* **claim**, profession. **4** *he was absolutely without pretence* **pretentiousness**, display, ostentation, affectation, showiness, posturing, humbug.
– OPPOSITES honesty.

pretend v. **1** *they just pretend to listen* **make as if**, profess, affect; dissimulate, dissemble, put it on, put on a false front, go through the motions, sham, fake it. **2** *I'll pretend to be the dragon* **put on an act**, make believe, play at, act, play-act, impersonate. **3** *it was useless to pretend innocence* **feign**, sham, fake, simulate, put on, counterfeit, affect. **4** *he cannot pretend to sophistication* **claim**, lay claim to, purport to have, profess to have.
▸ adj. informal *a pretend conversation* **imaginary**, imagined, pretended, make-believe, made-up, fantasy, fantasized, dreamed-up, unreal, invented, fictitious, mythical, feigned, fake, mock, sham, simulated, artificial, ersatz, false, pseudo; informal phoney.

pretended adj. **fake**, faked, affected, assumed, professed, spurious, mock, imitation, simulated, make-believe, pseudo, sham, false, bogus; informal pretend, phoney.

pretender n. **claimant**, aspirant.

pretension n. **1** *the author has no pretension to exhaustive coverage* **aspiration**, claim, assertion, pretence, profession. **2** *she spoke* *without pretension* **pretentiousness,** affectation, ostentation, ostentatiousness, artificiality, airs, posing, posturing, show, flashiness; pomposity, pompousness, grandiosity, grandiloquence, magniloquence.

pretentious adj. **affected,** ostentatious, showy; overambitious, pompous, artificial, inflated, overblown, high-sounding, flowery, grandiose, elaborate, extravagant, flamboyant, ornate, grandiloquent, magniloquent; N. Amer. sophomoric; informal flashy, highfalutin, la-di-da, pseudo; Brit. informal poncey.

preternatural adj. **extraordinary,** exceptional, unusual, uncommon, singular, unprecedented, remarkable, phenomenal, abnormal, inexplicable, unaccountable; strange, mysterious, fantastic.

pretext n. **(false) excuse,** ostensible reason, alleged reason; guise, ploy, pretence, ruse.

prettify v. **beautify,** make attractive, make pretty, titivate, adorn, ornament, decorate, smarten (up); informal doll up, do up, give something a facelift; Brit. informal tart up.

pretty adj. *a pretty child* **attractive,** lovely, good-looking, nice-looking, personable, fetching, prepossessing, appealing, charming, delightful, cute, as pretty as a picture; Scottish & N. English bonny; informal easy on the eye; literary beauteous; old use fair, comely.
– OPPOSITES plain, ugly.
▸ adv. *a pretty large sum* **quite,** rather, somewhat, fairly, reasonably, comparatively, relatively.
▸ v. *she's prettying herself* **beautify,** make attractive, make pretty, prettify, titivate, adorn, ornament, smarten; informal do oneself up; Brit. informal tart oneself up.

p

prevail v. **1** *common sense will prevail* **win (out/through),** triumph, be victorious, carry the day, come out on top, succeed, prove superior, conquer, overcome; rule, reign. **2** *the conditions that prevailed in the 1950s* **exist,** be in existence, be present, be the case, occur, be prevalent, be current, be the order of the day, be customary, be common, be widespread, be in force/effect; formal obtain.
□ **prevail on** persuade, induce, talk someone into, coax, convince, make, get, press someone into, argue someone into, urge, pressure someone into, pressurize someone into, coerce; informal sweet-talk, soft-soap.

prevailing adj. **current,** existing, prevalent, usual, common, general, widespread.

prevalence n. **commonness,** currency, widespread presence, generality, popularity, pervasiveness, universality, extensiveness; rampancy, rifeness.

prevalent adj. **widespread,** prevailing, frequent, usual, common, current, popular, general, universal; endemic, rampant, rife.
– OPPOSITES rare.

prevaricate v. **be evasive,** beat about the bush, hedge, fence, shilly-shally, dodge (the issue), sidestep (the issue), equivocate; temporize, stall (for time); Brit. hum and haw;

old use palter; rare tergiversate.

prevent v. **stop,** put a stop to, avert, nip in the bud, fend off, stave off, ward off; hinder, impede, hamper, obstruct, balk, foil, thwart, forestall, counteract, inhibit, curb, restrain, preclude, pre-empt, save, help; disallow, prohibit, forbid, proscribe, exclude, debar, bar; literary stay.
– OPPOSITES allow.

preventive adj. **1** *preventive maintenance* **pre-emptive,** deterrent, precautionary, protective. **2** *preventive medicine* **prophylactic,** disease-preventing.
▸ n. **1** *a preventive against crime* **precautionary measure,** deterrent, safeguard, security, protection, defence. **2** *disease preventives* **prophylactic (device),** prophylactic medicine, preventive drug.

previous adj. **1** *the previous five years* | *her previous boyfriend* **foregoing,** preceding, antecedent; old, earlier, prior, former, ex-, past, last, sometime, one-time, erstwhile, as was; formal quondam, anterior; old use whilom. **2** informal *I was a bit previous* **overhasty,** hasty, premature, precipitate, impetuous; informal ahead of oneself.
– OPPOSITES next.
□ **previous to** before, prior to, until, (leading) up to, earlier than, preceding; formal anterior to.

previously adv. **formerly,** earlier (on), before, hitherto, once, at one time, in the past, in days/times gone by, in bygone days, in times past, in former times; in advance, already, beforehand; formal heretofore.

prey n. **1** *the lions killed their prey* **quarry,** kill. **2** *she was easy prey* **victim,** target, dupe, gull; informal sucker, soft touch, pushover; N. Amer. informal patsy, sap, schlemiel; Austral./NZ informal dill.
– OPPOSITES predator.
□ **prey on 1** *hoverfly larvae prey on aphids* **hunt,** catch; eat, feed on, live on/off. **2** *they prey on the elderly* **exploit,** victimize, pick on, take advantage of; trick, swindle, cheat, hoodwink, fleece; informal con. **3** *the problem preyed on his mind* **oppress,** weigh (heavily) on, lie heavy on, gnaw at; trouble, beset, disturb, distress, haunt, nag, torment, plague, obsess.

price n. **1** *the purchase price* **cost,** asking price, charge, fee, fare, levy, amount, sum; outlay, expense, expenditure; valuation, quotation, estimate; humorous damage. **2** *spinsterhood was the price of her career* **consequence,** result, cost, penalty, sacrifice; downside, snag, drawback, disadvantage, minus. **3** *he had a price on his head* **reward,** bounty, premium.
▸ v. *a ticket is priced at £5.00* **fix/set the price of,** cost, value, rate; estimate.
□ **at a price** at a high price/cost, at considerable cost, for a great deal of money.
beyond price See **priceless** (sense 1).

priceless adj. **1** *priceless works of art* **of incalculable value/worth,** of immeasurable value/worth, invaluable, beyond price;

irreplaceable, incomparable, unparalleled.
2 informal *that's priceless!* See **hilarious**
(sense 1).
– OPPOSITES worthless, cheap.
pricey adj. informal See **expensive**.
prick v. **1** *prick the potatoes with a fork*
pierce, puncture, nick/put a hole in, stab,
perforate, nick, jab. **2** *his eyes began to prick*
sting, smart, burn, prickle. **3** *his conscience*
pricked him **trouble**, worry, distress,
perturb, disturb, cause someone anguish,
afflict, torment, plague, prey on, gnaw at.
4 *ambition pricked him on to greater effort*
goad, prod, incite, provoke, urge, spur,
stimulate, encourage, inspire, motivate,
push, propel, impel. **5** *the horse pricked up its*
ears **raise**, erect.
▸ n. **1** *a prick in the leg* **jab**, sting, pinprick,
stab. **2** *the prick of tears behind her eyelids*
sting, stinging, smart, smarting, burning.
3 *the prick of conscience* **pang**, twinge, stab.
□ **prick up one's ears** listen carefully, pay
attention, become attentive, begin to take
notice, attend; informal be all ears; literary hark.
prickle n. **1** *the cactus is covered with prickles*
thorn, needle, barb, spike, point, spine;
technical spicule. **2** *Willie felt a cold prickle of*
fear **tingle**, tingling (sensation), prickling
sensation, chill, thrill; Medicine paraesthesia.
▸ v. *its tiny spikes prickled his skin* **sting**, prick.
prickly adj. **1** *a prickly hedgehog* **spiky**,
spiked, thorny, barbed, spiny; briary,
brambly; rough, scratchy; technical spiculate,
spicular, aculeate, spinose. **2** *my skin*
feels prickly **tingly**, tingling, prickling.
3 *a prickly character.* See **irritable**. **4** *the*
prickly question of the refugees **problematic**,
awkward, ticklish, tricky, delicate, sensitive,
difficult, knotty, thorny, irksome, tough,
troublesome, bothersome, vexatious.
pride n. **1** *their triumphs were a source*
of pride **self-esteem**, dignity, honour,
self-respect, self-worth, self-regard, pride
in oneself. **2** *take pride in a good job well*
done **pleasure**, joy, delight, gratification,
fulfilment, satisfaction, sense of
achievement. **3** *he refused her offer out of*
pride **arrogance**, vanity, self-importance,
hubris, conceit, conceitedness, self-love,
self-adulation, self-admiration, narcissism,
egotism, superciliousness, haughtiness,
snobbery, snobbishness; informal big-
headedness; literary vainglory. **4** *the bull is*
the pride of the herd **best**, finest, top, cream,
pick, choice, prize, glory, the jewel in the
crown. **5** *the vegetable garden was the pride*
of the gardener **source of satisfaction**, pride
and joy, treasured possession, joy, delight.
– OPPOSITES shame, humility.
□ **pride oneself on** be proud of, be proud of
oneself for, take pride in, take satisfaction
in, congratulate oneself on, pat oneself on
the back for.
priest n. **clergyman**, **clergywoman**, minister
(of religion), cleric, clerk in holy orders,
ecclesiastic, vicar, rector, pastor, parson,
father, curé, churchman, churchwoman,
man/woman of the cloth, man/woman of

God; Scottish kirkman; N. Amer. dominie; informal
reverend, padre, Holy Joe, sky pilot; Austral.
informal josser; dated divine.

WORD LINKS
clerical, **hieratic**, **sacerdotal** relating to priests
ordain make someone a priest
defrock officially remove a priest from their job
  because of wrongdoing
seminary a training college for priests
cassock, **vestment** robes worn by Christian
  priests
soutane a robe worn by Roman Catholic priests

priestly adj. **clerical**, pastoral, priestlike,
ecclesiastical, sacerdotal, hieratic, rectorial;
old use vicarial.
prig n. **prude**, puritan, killjoy, Mrs Grundy;
informal goody-goody, Holy Joe; N. Amer. informal
bluenose.
priggish adj. **self-righteous**, holier-than-
thou, sanctimonious, moralistic, prudish,
puritanical, prim, strait-laced, stuffy, prissy,
narrow-minded; informal goody-goody, starchy.
– OPPOSITES broad-minded.
prim adj. **demure**, (prim and) proper, formal,
stuffy, strait-laced, prudish; prissy, mimsy,
priggish, puritanical; Brit. po-faced; informal
starchy.
primacy n. **greater importance**, priority,
precedence, pre-eminence, superiority,
supremacy, ascendancy, dominance,
dominion, leadership.
prima donna n. **1** **leading soprano**, leading
lady, diva, (opera) star, principal singer.
2 **temperamental person**, unpredictable
person.
primal adj. **1** *primal masculine instincts*
basic, fundamental, essential, elemental,
vital, central, intrinsic, inherent. **2** *the*
primal source of living things **original**,
initial, earliest, first, primitive, primeval.
primarily adv. **1** *the bishop was primarily*
a leader of the local community **first (and**
foremost), firstly, essentially, in essence,
fundamentally, principally, predominantly,
basically. **2** *such work is undertaken*
primarily for large institutions **mostly**, for
the most part, chiefly, mainly, in the main,
on the whole, largely, to a large extent,
especially, generally, usually, typically,
commonly, as a rule.
primary adj. **1** *our primary role* **main**, chief,
key, prime, central, principal, foremost, first,
most important, predominant, paramount;
informal number-one. **2** *the primary cause*
original, earliest, initial, first; essential,
fundamental, basic.
– OPPOSITES secondary.
prime¹ adj. **1** *his prime reason for leaving*
main, chief, key, primary, central, principal,
foremost, first, most important, paramount,
major; informal number-one. **2** *the prime cause*
of flooding **fundamental**, basic, essential,
primary, central. **3** *prime agricultural land*
top-quality, top, best, first-class, first-rate,
top-tier, grade A, superior, supreme, choice,
select, finest; excellent, superb, fine; informal

tip-top, A1, top-notch. **4** *a prime example* **archetypal**, prototypical, typical, classic, excellent, characteristic, quintessential.
– OPPOSITES secondary, inferior.
▸ n. *he is in his prime* **heyday**, best days/years, prime of one's life; youth, salad days; peak, pinnacle, high point/spot, zenith.

prime[2] v. **1** *he primed the gun* **prepare**, load, get ready. **2** *Lucy had primed him carefully* **brief**, fill in, prepare, put in the picture, inform, advise, instruct, coach, drill; informal clue in, give someone the low-down.

prime minister n. **premier**, first minister, head of (the) government; Brit. First Lord of the Treasury.

primeval adj. **1** *primeval forest* **ancient**, earliest, first, prehistoric, antediluvian, primordial; pristine, original, virgin. **2** *primeval fears* **instinctive**, primitive, basic, primal, primordial, intuitive, inborn, innate, inherent.

primitive adj. **1** *primitive times* **ancient**, earliest, first, prehistoric, antediluvian, primordial, primeval, primal. **2** *primitive peoples* **uncivilized**, barbarian, barbaric, barbarous, savage, ignorant, uncultivated. **3** *primitive tools* **crude**, simple, rough (and ready), basic, rudimentary, unrefined, unsophisticated, rude, makeshift. **4** *primitive art* **simple**, natural, unsophisticated, unaffected, undeveloped, unpretentious.
– OPPOSITES sophisticated, civilized.

primordial adj. **1** *the primordial oceans* **ancient**, earliest, first, prehistoric, antediluvian, primeval. **2** *their primordial desires* **instinctive**, primitive, basic, primal, primeval, intuitive, inborn, innate, inherent.

primp v. **groom**, tidy, arrange, brush, comb; smarten (up), spruce up; informal titivate, doll up; Brit. informal tart up; N. Amer. informal gussy up.

prince n. **ruler**, sovereign, monarch, king, princeling; Crown prince; emir, sheikh, sultan, maharaja, raja.

princely adj. **1** *princely buildings*. See **splendid** (sense 1). **2** *a princely sum*. See **handsome** (sense 3).

principal adj. *the principal cause of poor air quality* **main**, chief, primary, leading, foremost, first, most important, predominant, dominant, (most) prominent; key, crucial, vital, essential, basic, prime, central, focal; premier, paramount, major, overriding, cardinal, pre-eminent, uppermost, highest, top, topmost; informal number-one.
– OPPOSITES minor.
▸ n. **1** *the principal of the firm* **chief**, chief executive (officer), CEO, chairman, chairwoman, managing director, MD, president, director, manager, head; informal boss; Brit. informal gaffer, governor. **2** *the school's principal* **head (teacher)**, headmaster, headmistress; dean, rector, chancellor, vice chancellor, president, provost; N. Amer. informal prexy. **3** *a principal in a soap opera* **leading actor/actress**, leading player/performer, leading role, lead, star.

4 *repayment of the principal* **capital (sum)**, debt, loan.

principally adv. **mainly**, mostly, chiefly, for the most part, in the main, on the whole, largely, to a large extent, predominantly, basically, primarily.

principle n. **1** *elementary principles* **truth**, proposition, concept, idea, theory, assumption, fundamental, essential. **2** *the principle of laissez-faire* **doctrine**, belief, creed, credo, (golden) rule, criterion, tenet, code, ethic, dictum, canon, law. **3** *a woman of principle* | *sticking to one's principles* **morals**, morality, (code of) ethics, beliefs, ideals, standards; integrity, uprightness, righteousness, virtue, probity, (sense of) honour, decency, conscience, scruples.
□ **in principle 1** *there is no reason, in principle, why we couldn't work together* **in theory**, theoretically, on paper. **2** *he has accepted the idea in principle* **in general**, in essence, on the whole, in the main.

principled adj. **moral**, ethical, virtuous, righteous, upright, upstanding, high-minded, honourable, honest, incorruptible, anti-corruption.

prink v. **groom**, tidy, arrange, smarten (up), spruce up, preen, primp; informal titivate, doll up; Brit. informal tart up; N. Amer. informal gussy up.

print v. **1** *a thousand copies of the book were printed* **run off**; reprint. **2** *patterns were printed on the cloth* **imprint**, impress, stamp, mark. **3** *they printed 30,000 copies* **publish**, issue, release, circulate. **4** *the incident is printed on her memory* **register**, record, impress, imprint, engrave, etch, stamp, mark.
▸ n. **1** *small print* **type**, printing, letters, lettering, characters, type size, typeface, font. **2** *prints of his left hand* **impression**, fingerprint, footprint. **3** *sporting prints* **picture**, design, engraving, etching, lithograph, linocut, woodcut. **4** *prints and negatives* **photograph**, photo, snap, snapshot, picture, still; Brit. enprint. **5** *soft floral prints* **printed cloth/fabric**, patterned cloth/fabric, chintz.

prior adj. *by prior arrangement* **earlier**, previous, preceding, foregoing, antecedent, advance; formal anterior.
– OPPOSITES subsequent.
□ **prior to** before, until, till, up to, previous to, earlier than, preceding, leading up to; formal anterior to.

priority n. **1** *safety is our priority* **prime concern**, most important consideration, primary issue. **2** *giving priority to primary education* **precedence**, greater importance, preference, pre-eminence, predominance, primacy, first place. **3** *traffic on the roundabout has priority* **right of way**.

priory n. **religious house**, abbey, cloister; monastery, friary; convent, nunnery.

prise v. **1** *I prised the lid off* **lever**, jemmy; wrench, wrest, twist; N. Amer. pry, jimmy. **2** *he had to prise information from them* **wring**, wrest, worm out, winkle out, screw, squeeze, extract.

p

prison n. **jail**, lock-up, penal institution, detention centre; Brit. young offender institution; N. Amer. jailhouse, penitentiary, correctional facility; informal clink, cooler, slammer, stir, jug, brig; Brit. informal nick; N. Amer. informal can, pen, pokey, slam; Brit. informal dated chokey, quod; Brit. historical approved school, borstal, bridewell; Brit. Military glasshouse; (**be in prison**) informal be inside, be behind bars, do time; Brit. informal do bird, do porridge.

WORD LINKS

custodial relating to prison
penology the study of prison management
panopticon (in the past) a circular prison, allowing prisoners to be observed at all times
warden, warder a prison officer

---

prisoner n. **1** *a prisoner serving a life sentence* **convict**, detainee, inmate; informal jailbird, con; Brit. informal (old) lag; N. Amer. informal yardbird. **2** *the army took many prisoners* **prisoner of war**, POW, internee, captive.

prissy adj. **prudish**, priggish, prim, prim and proper, strait-laced, Victorian, old-maidish, schoolmistressy, schoolmarmish; Brit. po-faced; informal starchy.
– OPPOSITES broad-minded.

pristine adj. **immaculate**, perfect, in mint condition, as new, unspoilt, spotless, flawless, clean, fresh, new, virgin, pure, unused.
– OPPOSITES dirty, spoilt.

privacy n. **seclusion**, solitude, isolation; peace.

private adj. **1** *his private plane* **personal**, own, individual, special, exclusive, privately owned. **2** *private talks* **confidential**, secret, classified, unofficial, off the record, closet, in camera; backstage, privileged, one-on-one, tête-à-tête. **3** *private thoughts* **intimate**, personal, secret; innermost, undisclosed, unspoken, unvoiced. **4** *a very private man* **reserved**, introvert, introverted, self-contained, reticent, discreet, uncommunicative, unforthcoming, retiring, unsociable, withdrawn, solitary, reclusive, hermitic. **5** *they found a private place in which to talk* **secluded**, solitary, undisturbed, concealed, hidden, remote, isolated, out of the way, sequestered. **6** *we can be private here* **undisturbed**, uninterrupted; alone, by ourselves. **7** *the Queen attended in a private capacity* **unofficial**, personal. **8** *private industry* **independent**, non-state; privatized, denationalized; commercial, private-enterprise.
– OPPOSITES public, open, extrovert, busy, crowded, official, state, nationalized.
▶ n. *a private in the army* **private soldier**, common soldier; trooper; Brit. sapper, gunner, ranker; US GI; Brit. informal Tommy, squaddie.
□ **in private** in secret, secretly, privately, behind closed doors, in camera, à huis clos; in confidence, confidentially, between ourselves, entre nous, off the record; formal sub rosa.

private detective n. **private investigator**; Brit. enquiry agent; informal private eye, PI, sleuth, snoop; N. Amer. informal shamus, gumshoe; informal dated private dick.

privately adv. **1** *we must talk privately* **in secret**, secretly, in private, behind closed doors, in camera, à huis clos; in confidence, confidentially, between ourselves, entre nous, off the record; formal sub rosa. **2** *privately, I am glad* **secretly**, inwardly, deep down, personally, unofficially. **3** *he lived very privately* **out of the public eye**, out of public view, in seclusion, in solitude, alone.
– OPPOSITES publicly.

privation n. **deprivation**, hardship, destitution, impoverishment, want, need, neediness, austerity.
– OPPOSITES plenty, luxury.

privilege n. **1** *senior pupils have certain privileges* **advantage**, benefit; prerogative, entitlement, right; concession, freedom, liberty. **2** *it was a privilege to meet her* **honour**, pleasure. **3** *parliamentary privilege* **immunity**, exemption, dispensation.

privileged adj. **1** *a privileged background* **wealthy**, rich, affluent, prosperous; **lucky**, fortunate, elite, favoured; (socially) advantaged. **2** *privileged information* **confidential**, private, secret, restricted, classified, not for publication, off the record, inside; informal hush-hush. **3** *MPs are privileged* **immune (from prosecution)**, protected, exempt, excepted.
– OPPOSITES underprivileged, disadvantaged, public, liable.

privy adj. *he was not privy to the discussions* **in the know about**, acquainted with, in on, informed of, advised of, apprised of; informal genned up on, clued up on, wise to; formal cognizant of.
▶ n. *he went out to the privy.* See **toilet** (sense 1).

prize n. **1** *an art prize* **award**, reward, premium, purse; trophy, medal; honour, accolade, crown, laurels, palm. **2** *the prizes of war* **spoils**, booty, plunder, loot, pickings.
▶ adj. **1** *a prize bull* **champion**, award-winning, prize-winning, winning, top, best. **2** *a prize example* **outstanding**, excellent, superlative, superb, supreme, very good, prime, fine, magnificent, marvellous, wonderful; informal great, terrific, tremendous, fantastic. **3** *a prize idiot* **utter**, complete, total, absolute, real, perfect, positive, veritable; Brit. informal right, bloody; Austral./NZ informal fair.
– OPPOSITES second-rate.
▶ v. *many collectors prize his work* **value**, set great store by, rate highly, attach great importance to, esteem, hold in high regard, think highly of, treasure, cherish.

prized adj. **treasured**, precious, cherished, much loved, beloved, valued, esteemed, highly regarded.

prizewinner n. **champion**, winner, gold medallist, victor; informal champ, number one.

p

probability n. **1** *the probability of winning* **likelihood**, prospect, expectation, chance, chances, odds. **2** *relegation is a distinct probability* **probable event**, prospect, possibility, good/fair/reasonable bet.

probable adj. **likely**, most likely, odds-on, expected, anticipated, predictable, foreseeable, ten to one; informal on the cards, a good/fair/reasonable bet.
– OPPOSITES improbable, unlikely.

probably adv. **in all likelihood**, in all probability, as like(ly) as not, (very/most) likely, ten to one, the chances are, doubtless, no doubt; old use like enough.

probation n. **trial period**, test period, experimental period, trial.

probe n. *a probe into an air crash* **investigation**, enquiry, examination, inquest, exploration, study, analysis.
▸ v. **1** *hands probed his body* **examine**, feel, feel around, explore, prod, poke, check. **2** *police probed the tragedy* **investigate**, enquire into, look into, study, examine, scrutinize, go into, carry out an inquest into.

probity n. **integrity**, honesty, uprightness, decency, morality, rectitude, goodness, virtue, right-mindedness, trustworthiness, truthfulness, honour.
– OPPOSITES untrustworthiness.

problem n. **1** *they ran into a problem* **difficulty**, issue, trouble, worry, complication, difficult situation; snag, hitch, drawback, stumbling block, obstacle, hurdle, hiccup, setback, catch; predicament, plight; misfortune, mishap, misadventure; informal dilemma, headache, prob, facer.
2 *I don't want to be a problem* **nuisance**, bother, pest, irritant, thorn in one's side/flesh, vexation; informal drag, pain, pain in the neck. **3** *arithmetical problems* **puzzle**, question, poser, enigma, riddle, conundrum; informal teaser, brain-teaser.
▸ adj. *a problem child* **troublesome**, difficult, unmanageable, unruly, disobedient, uncontrollable, recalcitrant, delinquent.
– OPPOSITES well behaved, manageable.

problematic adj. **difficult**, hard, taxing, troublesome, tricky, awkward, controversial, ticklish, complicated, complex, knotty, thorny, prickly, vexed; informal sticky, like herding cats; Brit. informal dodgy.
– OPPOSITES easy, simple, straightforward.

procedure n. **course of action**, line of action, policy, series of steps, method, system, strategy, way, approach, formula, mechanism, methodology, MO (modus operandi), technique; routine, drill, practice.

proceed v. **1** *she was uncertain how to proceed* **begin**, make a start, get going, move, set something in motion; **take action**, act, go on, go ahead, make progress, make headway. **2** *he proceeded down the road* **go**, make one's way, advance, move, progress, carry on, press on, push on. **3** *we should proceed with the talks* **go ahead**, carry on, go on, continue, keep on, get on, get ahead; pursue, prosecute. **4** *there is not enough evidence to*

proceed against him **take someone to court**, start/take proceedings against, start an action against, sue. **5** *all power proceeds from God* **originate**, spring, stem, come, derive, arise, issue, flow, emanate.
– OPPOSITES stop.

proceedings plural n. **1** *the evening's proceedings* **events**, activities, happenings, goings-on, doings. **2** *the proceedings of the meeting* **report**, transactions, minutes, account, record(s); annals, archives. **3** *legal proceedings* **legal action**, court/judicial proceedings, litigation; lawsuit, case, prosecution.

proceeds plural n. **profits**, earnings, receipts, returns, takings, income, revenue; Sport gate (money/receipts); N. Amer. take.

process n. **1** *investigation is a long process* **procedure**, operation, action, activity, exercise, affair, business, job, task, undertaking. **2** *a new canning process* **method**, system, technique, means, practice, way, approach, methodology.
▸ v. *applications are processed rapidly* **deal with**, attend to, see to, sort out, handle, take care of, action.
▢ **in the process of** in the middle of, in the course of, in the midst of, in the throes of, busy with, occupied in/with, taken up with/by, involved in.

procession n. **1** *a procession through the town* **parade**, march, march past, cavalcade, motorcade, cortège; column, file, train. **2** *a procession of dance routines* **series**, succession, stream, string, sequence, run.

proclaim v. **1** *messengers proclaimed the good news* **declare**, announce, pronounce, state, make known, give out, advertise, publish, broadcast, promulgate, trumpet, blazon. **2** *the men proclaimed their innocence* **assert**, declare, profess, maintain, protest. **3** *he proclaimed himself president* **declare**, pronounce, announce. **4** *cheap paint soon proclaims its cheapness* **demonstrate**, indicate, show, reveal, manifest, betray, testify to, signify.

proclamation n. **declaration**, announcement, pronouncement, statement, notification, publication, broadcast, promulgation, blazoning; assertion, profession, protestation; **decree**, order, edict, ruling.

proclivity n. **inclination**, tendency, leaning, disposition, proneness, propensity, bent, bias, penchant, predisposition; predilection, partiality, liking, preference, taste, fondness, weakness.

procrastinate v. **delay**, put off doing something, postpone action, defer action, be dilatory, use delaying tactics, stall, temporize, drag one's feet/heels, take one's time, play for time, play a waiting game.

procreate v. **produce offspring**, reproduce, multiply, propagate, breed.

procure v. **1** *he managed to procure a coat* **obtain**, acquire, get, find, come by, secure, pick up; buy, purchase; informal get hold of, get

p

one's hands on. **2** *the police found that he was procuring* **pimp**; Brit. informal ponce.

prod v. **1** *Cassie prodded him in the chest* **poke**, jab, dig, elbow, butt, stab. **2** *they hoped to prod the government into action* **spur**, stimulate, stir, rouse, prompt, drive, galvanize; persuade, urge, chivvy; incite, goad, egg on, provoke.
▶ n. **1** *a prod in the ribs* **poke**, jab, dig, elbow, butt, thrust. **2** *they need a prod to get them to act* **stimulus**, push, prompt, reminder, spur; incitement, goad.

prodigal adj. **1** *prodigal habits die hard* **wasteful**, extravagant, spendthrift, profligate, improvident, imprudent. **2** *a composer who is prodigal with his talents* **generous**, lavish, liberal, unstinting, unsparing; literary bounteous. **3** *a dessert prodigal with whipped cream* **abounding in**, abundant in, rich in, covered in, awash with.
– OPPOSITES thrifty, mean, deficient.

prodigious adj. **enormous**, huge, colossal, immense, vast, great, massive, gigantic, mammoth, tremendous, inordinate, monumental; amazing, astonishing, astounding, staggering, stunning, remarkable, phenomenal, terrific, miraculous, impressive, striking, startling, sensational, spectacular, extraordinary, exceptional, breathtaking, incredible; informal humongous, stupendous, fantastic, fabulous, mega, awesome; Brit. informal ginormous; literary wondrous.
– OPPOSITES small, unexceptional.

prodigy n. **1** *a seven-year-old prodigy* **genius**, mastermind, virtuoso, wunderkind, wonder child; informal whizz-kid, whizz, wizard. **2** *Germany seemed a prodigy of industrial discipline* **model**, classic example, paragon, paradigm, epitome, exemplar, archetype.

produce v. **1** *the company produces furniture* **manufacture**, make, construct, build, fabricate, put together, assemble, turn out, create; mass-produce; informal churn out. **2** *the vineyards produce excellent wines* **yield**, grow, give, supply, provide, furnish, bear, bring forth. **3** *she produced ten puppies* **give birth to**, bear, deliver, bring forth, bring into the world. **4** *he produced five novels* **create**, originate, fashion, turn out; compose, write, pen; paint. **5** *she produced an ID card* **pull out**, extract, fish out; present, offer, proffer, show. **6** *no evidence was produced* **present**, offer, provide, furnish, advance, put forward, bring forward, come up with. **7** *that will produce a reaction* **give rise to**, bring about, cause, occasion, generate, engender, lead to, result in, effect, induce, set off; provoke, precipitate, breed, spark off, trigger; literary beget. **8** *James produced the play* **stage**, put on, mount, present.
▶ n. *fresh produce* **food**, foodstuff(s), products; harvest, crops, fruit, vegetables, greens; Brit. greengrocery.

producer n. **1** *a Japanese car producer* **manufacturer**, maker, builder, constructor, fabricator. **2** *coffee producers* **grower**,

farmer. **3** *the producer of the show* **impresario**, manager, administrator, promoter, regisseur.

product n. **1** *a household product* **artefact**, commodity, manufactured article; creation, invention; (**products**) goods, wares, merchandise, produce, solutions. **2** *his skill is a product of experience* **result**, consequence, outcome, effect, upshot, fruit, by-product, spin-off.

production n. **1** *the production of cars* **manufacture**, making, construction, building, fabrication, assembly, creation; mass production. **2** *the production of literary works* **creation**, origination, fashioning; composition, writing. **3** *literary productions* **work**, opus, creation; publication, composition, piece; work of art, painting, picture. **4** *agricultural production* **output**, yield; productivity. **5** *admission only on production of a ticket* **presentation**, proffering, showing. **6** *a theatre production* **performance**, staging, presentation, show, piece, play.

productive adj. **1** *a productive artist* **prolific**, inventive, creative; energetic. **2** *productive talks* **useful**, constructive, profitable, fruitful, gainful, valuable, effective, worthwhile, helpful. **3** *productive land* **fertile**, fruitful, rich, fecund.
– OPPOSITES sterile, barren.

productivity n. **1** *workers have boosted productivity* **efficiency**, work rate; output, yield, production. **2** *the productivity of the soil* **fruitfulness**, fertility, richness, fecundity.
– OPPOSITES sterility, barrenness.

profane adj. **1** *subjects both sacred and profane* **secular**, lay, non-religious, temporal; formal laic. **2** *a profane man* **irreverent**, irreligious, ungodly, godless, unbelieving, impious, disrespectful, sacrilegious. **3** *profane language* **obscene**, blasphemous, indecent, foul, vulgar, crude, filthy, dirty, smutty, coarse, rude, offensive, indecorous.
– OPPOSITES religious, sacred, reverent, decorous.
▶ v. *invaders profaned our temples* **desecrate**, violate, defile, treat sacrilegiously.

profanity n. **1** *he hissed a profanity | an outburst of profanity* **oath**, swear word, expletive, curse, obscenity, four-letter word, dirty word; blasphemy, swearing, foul language, bad language, cursing; informal cuss, cuss word; Brit. informal industrial language; formal imprecation; old use execration. **2** *some traditional festivals were tainted with profanity* **sacrilege**, blasphemy, irreligion, ungodliness, impiety, irreverence, disrespect.

profess v. **1** *he professed his love* **declare**, announce, proclaim, assert, state, affirm, avow, maintain, protest; formal aver. **2** *she professed to loathe publicity* **claim**, pretend, purport, affect; make out; informal let on. **3** *the Emperor professed Christianity* **affirm one's faith in**, affirm one's allegiance to, avow, confess.

p

professed adj. **1** *his professed ambition* **claimed**, supposed, ostensible, self-styled, apparent, pretended, purported. **2** *a professed Christian* **declared**, self-acknowledged, self-confessed, confessed, sworn, avowed, confirmed.

profession n. **1** *his chosen profession of teaching* **career**, occupation, calling, vocation, métier, line (of work), walk of life, job, business, trade, craft; informal racket. **2** *a profession of allegiance* **declaration**, affirmation, statement, announcement, proclamation, assertion, avowal, vow, claim, protestation; formal averment.

professional adj. **1** *people in professional occupations* **white-collar**, non-manual. **2** *a professional cricketer* **paid**, salaried. **3** *a thoroughly professional performance* **expert**, accomplished, skilful, masterly, masterful, fine, polished, skilled, proficient, competent, able, experienced, practised, trained, seasoned, businesslike, deft; informal ace, crack, top-notch. **4** *not a professional way to behave* **appropriate**, fitting, proper, honourable, ethical, correct, comme il faut.
– OPPOSITES manual, amateur, amateurish, inappropriate, unethical.
▸ n. **1** *affluent young professionals* **white-collar worker**, office worker. **2** *his first season as a professional* **professional player**, paid player, salaried player; informal pro. **3** *she was a real professional on stage* **expert**, virtuoso, old hand, master, maestro, past master; informal pro, ace, wizard, whizz, hotshot; Brit. informal dab hand; N. Amer. informal maven, crackerjack.
– OPPOSITES manual worker, amateur.

proffer v. **offer**, tender, submit, extend, volunteer, suggest, propose, put forward; hold out.
– OPPOSITES refuse, withdraw.

proficiency n. **skill**, expertise, experience, accomplishment, competence, mastery, prowess, professionalism, deftness, adroitness, dexterity, finesse, ability, facility; informal know-how.
– OPPOSITES incompetence.

proficient adj. **skilled**, skilful, expert, experienced, accomplished, competent, masterly, adept, adroit, deft, dexterous, able, professional, consummate, complete, master; informal crack, ace, mean.
– OPPOSITES incompetent.

profile n. **1** *his handsome profile* **side view**, outline, silhouette, contour, shape, form, figure, lines. **2** *she wrote a profile of the organization* **description**, account, study, portrait, portrayal, depiction, rundown, sketch, outline.
▸ v. *he was profiled in the Irish Times* **describe**, write about, give an account of, portray, depict, sketch, outline.
□ **keep a low profile** lie low, keep quiet, keep out of the public eye, avoid publicity, keep out of sight.

profit n. **1** *the firm made a profit* **(financial) gain**, return(s), yield, proceeds, earnings, winnings, surplus, excess; informal pay dirt, bottom line. **2** *there was little profit in going on* **advantage**, benefit, value, use, good, avail; informal mileage.
– OPPOSITES loss, disadvantage.
▸ v. **1** *the company will not profit from the disposal* **make money**, make a profit; informal rake it in, clean up, make a packet, make a killing, make a bundle; N. Amer. informal make big bucks, make a fast/quick buck. **2** *how will that profit us?* **benefit**, be beneficial to, be of benefit to, be advantageous to, be of advantage to, be of use to, be of value to, do someone good, help, be of service to, serve, assist, aid.
– OPPOSITES lose, disadvantage.
□ **profit by/from** benefit from, take advantage of, derive benefit from, capitalize on, make the most of, turn to one's advantage, put to good use, do well out of, exploit, gain from; informal cash in on.

profitable adj. **1** *a profitable company* **moneymaking**, profit-making, commercial, successful, money-spinning, solvent, in the black, gainful, remunerative, financially rewarding, paying, lucrative, bankable. **2** *profitable study* **beneficial**, useful, advantageous, valuable, productive, worthwhile; rewarding, fruitful, illuminating, informative, well spent.
– OPPOSITES loss-making, fruitless, useless.

profiteer v. *a shopkeeper was charged with profiteering* **overcharge**, racketeer; cheat someone, fleece someone; informal rip someone off, rob someone.
▸ n. *he was a war profiteer* **racketeer**, exploiter, black marketeer; informal bloodsucker.

profligate adj. **1** *profligate local authorities* **wasteful**, extravagant, spendthrift, improvident, prodigal. **2** *a profligate lifestyle* **dissolute**, degenerate, dissipated, debauched, corrupt, depraved; **promiscuous**, loose, wanton, licentious, libertine, decadent, abandoned, fast; **sybaritic**, voluptuary.
– OPPOSITES thrifty, frugal, moral, upright.
▸ n. *he was an out-and-out profligate* **libertine**, debauchee, degenerate, dissolute, roué, rake, loose-liver; sybarite, voluptuary; dated rip.

profound adj. **1** *profound relief* **heartfelt**, intense, keen, great, extreme, acute, severe, sincere, earnest, deep, deep-seated, overpowering, overwhelming, fervent, ardent. **2** *profound silence* **complete**, utter, total, absolute. **3** *a profound change* **far-reaching**, radical, extensive, sweeping, exhaustive, thoroughgoing. **4** *a profound analysis* **wise**, learned, clever, intelligent, scholarly, sage, erudite, discerning, penetrating, perceptive, astute, thoughtful, insightful, percipient, perspicacious; formal sapient. **5** *profound truths* **complex**, abstract, deep, weighty, difficult, abstruse, recondite, esoteric.
– OPPOSITES superficial, mild, slight, simple.

profuse adj. **1** *profuse apologies* **copious**, prolific, abundant, liberal, unstinting, fulsome, effusive, extravagant, lavish,

gushing; informal over the top, gushy.
2 *profuse blooms* **luxuriant**, plentiful,
copious, abundant, lush, rich, exuberant,
riotous, teeming, rank, rampant; informal
jungly.
– OPPOSITES meagre, sparse.

profusion n. **abundance**, mass, host,
cornucopia, riot, plethora, superabundance;
informal sea, wealth; formal plenitude.

progenitor n. **1** *the progenitor of an
illustrious family* **ancestor**, forefather,
forebear, parent, primogenitor; Law stirps;
old use begetter. **2** *the progenitor of modern
jazz* **originator**, creator, founder, architect,
inventor, pioneer.

progeny n. **offspring**, young, babies,
children, sons and daughters, family, brood;
descendants, heirs, scions; Law issue; old use
seed, fruit of one's loins.

prognosis n. **forecast**, prediction,
prognostication, prophecy, divination,
augury.

prognosticate v. **forecast**, predict,
prophesy, foretell, foresee, forewarn of.

prognostication n. **prediction**, forecast,
prophecy, prognosis, divination, augury.

programme n. **1** *our programme for the
day* **schedule**, agenda, calendar, timetable;
order of events, line-up. **2** *the government's
reform programme* **scheme**, plan of action,
initiative, series of measures, strategy,
solution. **3** *a television programme*
broadcast, production, show, presentation,
transmission, performance, telecast; informal
prog. **4** *a programme of study* **course**,
syllabus, curriculum. **5** *a theatre programme*
guide, list of performers; N. Amer. playbill.
▶ v. *they programmed the day well* **arrange**,
organize, schedule, plan, map out, timetable,
line up; N. Amer. slate.

progress n. **1** *boulders made progress
difficult* **forward movement**, advance,
going, progression, headway, passage.
2 *scientific progress* **development**, advance,
advancement, headway, step(s) forward;
improvement, betterment, growth.
– OPPOSITES relapse.
▶ v. **1** *they progressed slowly down the road* **go**,
make one's way, move, move forward, go
forward, proceed, advance, go on, continue,
make headway, work one's way. **2** *the school
has progressed rapidly* **develop**, make
progress, advance, make headway, move on,
get on, gain ground; improve, get better,
come on, come along, make strides; thrive,
prosper, blossom, flourish; informal be getting
there.
– OPPOSITES relapse.
□ **in progress** under way, going on,
ongoing, happening, occurring, taking place,
proceeding, continuing; unfinished, on the
stocks; N. Amer. in the works.

progression n. **1** *progression to the next
stage* **progress**, advancement, movement,
passage, march; development, evolution,
growth. **2** *a progression of peaks on the graph*
succession, series, sequence, string, stream,

chain, concatenation, train, row, cycle.

progressive adj. **1** *progressive deterioration*
continuing, continuous, increasing,
growing, developing, ongoing, accelerating,
escalating; gradual, step-by-step, cumulative.
2 *progressive views* **modern**, liberal,
advanced, forward-thinking, enlightened,
enterprising, innovative, pioneering,
dynamic, bold, avant-garde, reforming,
reformist, radical, disruptive; informal go-
ahead.
– OPPOSITES conservative, reactionary.
▶ n. *he is very much a progressive* **innovator**,
reformer, reformist, liberal, libertarian.

prohibit v. **1** *state law prohibits gambling*
forbid, ban, bar, interdict, proscribe, make
illegal, embargo, outlaw, disallow, veto; Law
enjoin. **2** *a cash shortage prohibited the visit*
prevent, stop, rule out, preclude, make
impossible.
– OPPOSITES allow.

prohibited adj. **forbidden**, verboten, taboo;
illegal, illicit, against the law; Islam haram;
informal not on, out, no go; formal non licet. See
also **prohibit**.
– OPPOSITES permitted.

prohibition n. **1** *the prohibition of
cannabis* **banning**, forbidding, prohibiting,
barring, debarment, vetoing, proscription,
interdiction, outlawing. **2** *a prohibition was
imposed* **ban**, bar, interdict, veto, embargo,
injunction, moratorium.

prohibitive adj. **1** *prohibitive costs*
excessively high, sky-high, overinflated;
out of the question, beyond one's means;
extortionate, unreasonable, exorbitant;
informal steep, criminal. **2** *prohibitive
regulations* **proscriptive**, prohibitory,
restrictive, repressive.

project n. **1** *an engineering project* **scheme**,
plan, programme, enterprise, undertaking,
venture; proposal, idea, concept. **2** *a history
project* **assignment**, piece of work, piece of
research, task.
▶ v. **1** *profits are projected to rise* **forecast**,
predict, expect, estimate, calculate, reckon.
2 *his projected book* **intend**, plan, propose,
devise, design, outline. **3** *balconies projected
over the lake* **stick out**, jut (out), protrude,
extend, stand out, bulge out, poke out,
thrust out, cantilever. **4** *seeds are projected
from the tree* **propel**, discharge, launch,
throw, cast, fling, hurl, shoot. **5** *the sun
projected his shadow on the wall* **cast**, throw,
send, shed, shine. **6** *she tried to project a
calm image* **convey**, put across, put over,
communicate, present, promote.

projectile n. **missile**.

projecting adj. **sticking out**, protuberant,
protruding, prominent, jutting, overhanging,
proud, bulging; informal sticky-out.
– OPPOSITES sunken, flush.

projection n. **1** *a sales projection* **forecast**,
prediction, prognosis, expectation,
estimate. **2** *tiny projections on the cliff face*
protuberance, protrusion, sticking-out bit,
prominence, eminence, outcrop, outgrowth,

p

jut, jag, snag; overhang, ledge, shelf; informal sticky-out bit.

proletarian adj. *a proletarian background* **working-class**, plebeian, cloth-cap, common.
– OPPOSITES aristocratic.
▶ n. *disaffected proletarians* **working-class person**, worker, plebeian, commoner, man/woman/person in the street; derogatory prole.
– OPPOSITES aristocrat.

proletariat n. **the workers**, working-class people, wage-earners, the labouring classes, the common people, the lower classes, the masses, the commonalty, the rank and file, the third estate, the plebeians; derogatory the hoi polloi, the plebs, the proles, the great unwashed, the mob, the rabble.
– OPPOSITES aristocracy.

proliferate v. **increase rapidly**, grow rapidly, multiply, rocket, mushroom, snowball, burgeon, run riot.
– OPPOSITES decrease, dwindle.

prolific adj. **1** *a prolific crop of tomatoes* **plentiful**, abundant, bountiful, profuse, copious, luxuriant, rich, lush; fruitful, fecund; literary plenteous, bounteous.
2 *a prolific composer* **productive**, creative, inventive, fertile.

prolix adj. **long-winded**, verbose, wordy, pleonastic, discursive, rambling, long-drawn-out, overlong, lengthy, protracted, interminable; informal windy; Brit. informal waffly.

prologue n. **introduction**, foreword, preface, preamble, prelude; informal intro; formal exordium, proem, prolegomenon.
– OPPOSITES epilogue.

prolong v. **lengthen**, extend, draw out, drag out, protract, spin out, stretch out, string out, elongate; carry on, continue, keep up, perpetuate.
– OPPOSITES shorten.

promenade n. **1** *the tree-lined promenade* **esplanade**, front, seafront, parade, walk, boulevard, avenue; N. Amer. boardwalk; Brit. informal prom. **2** *our nightly promenade* **walk**, stroll, turn, amble, airing; dated constitutional.
▶ v. *we promenaded in the park* **walk**, stroll, saunter, wander, amble, stretch one's legs, take a turn.

prominence n. **1** *his rise to prominence* **fame**, celebrity, eminence, pre-eminence, importance, distinction, greatness, note, notability, prestige, stature, standing, position, rank. **2** *the press gave prominence to the reports* **good coverage**, importance, precedence, weight, a high profile, top billing. **3** *a rocky prominence* **hillock**, hill, hummock, mound; outcrop, crag, spur, rise; ridge, arête; peak, pinnacle; promontory, cliff, headland.

prominent adj. **1** *a prominent surgeon* **important**, well known, leading, eminent, distinguished, notable, noteworthy, noted, illustrious, celebrated, famous, renowned, acclaimed, famed, influential; N. Amer. major-league. **2** *prominent cheekbones* **protuberant**, protruding, projecting, jutting

(out), standing out, sticking out, proud, bulging, bulbous. **3** *a prominent feature of the landscape* **conspicuous**, noticeable, easily seen, obvious, unmistakable, eye-catching, pronounced, salient, striking, dominant; obtrusive.
– OPPOSITES unimportant, unknown, inconspicuous.

promiscuity n. **licentiousness**, wantonness, immorality; informal sleeping around, sluttishness, whorishness; dated looseness.
– OPPOSITES chastity, virtue.

promiscuous adj. **1** *a promiscuous woman* **licentious**, sexually indiscriminate, wanton, immoral, of easy virtue, fast; informal easy, swinging, sluttish, whorish; N. Amer. informal roundheeled; Brit. informal slaggy; dated loose, fallen; old use light. **2** *promiscuous reading* **indiscriminate**, undiscriminating, unselective, random, haphazard, irresponsible, unthinking, unconsidered.
– OPPOSITES chaste, virtuous, selective.

promise n. **1** *you broke your promise* **word (of honour)**, assurance, pledge, vow, guarantee, oath, bond, undertaking, agreement, commitment, contract, covenant. **2** *he shows promise* **potential**, ability, aptitude, capability, capacity. **3** *a promise of fine weather* **indication**, hint, suggestion, sign.
▶ v. **1** *she promised to go* **give one's word**, swear, pledge, vow, undertake, guarantee, contract, engage, give an assurance, commit oneself, bind oneself, swear/take an oath, covenant; old use plight. **2** *the skies promised sunshine* **indicate**, lead one to expect, point to, denote, signify, be a sign of, be evidence of, give hope of, bespeak, presage, augur, herald, bode, portend; literary betoken, foretoken, forebode.

promising adj. **1** *a promising start* **good**, encouraging, favourable, hopeful, full of promise, auspicious, propitious, bright, rosy, heartening, reassuring. **2** *a promising actor* **with potential**, budding, up-and-coming, rising, coming, in the making.
– OPPOSITES unfavourable, hopeless.

promontory n. **headland**, point, cape, head, foreland, horn, bill, ness, naze, peninsula; Scottish mull.

promote v. **1** *she's been promoted at work* **upgrade**, give promotion to, elevate, advance, move up; old use prefer. **2** *an organization promoting justice* **encourage**, further, advance, assist, aid, help, contribute to, foster, nurture, develop, boost, stimulate, forward, work for. **3** *she is promoting her new film* **advertise**, publicize, give publicity to, beat/bang the drum for, market, merchandise; informal push, plug, hype, puff, boost; N. Amer. informal ballyhoo, flack.
– OPPOSITES demote, obstruct, play down.

promoter n. **advocate**, champion, supporter, backer, proponent, protagonist, campaigner; N. Amer. booster.

promotion n. **1** *her promotion at work* **upgrading**, preferment, elevation, advancement, step up (the ladder). **2** *the promotion of justice* **encouragement**, furtherance, furthering, advancement, assistance, aid, help, contribution to, fostering, boosting, stimulation; N. Amer. boosterism. **3** *the promotion of her new film* **advertising**, publicizing, marketing; publicity, campaign, propaganda; informal hard sell, plug, hype, puff; N. Amer. informal ballyhoo.

prompt v. **1** *curiosity prompted him to look* **induce**, make, move, motivate, lead, dispose, persuade, incline, encourage, stimulate, prod, impel, spur on, inspire. **2** *the statement prompted a hostile reaction* **give rise to**, bring about, cause, occasion, result in, lead to, elicit, produce, bring on, engender, induce, precipitate, trigger, spark off, provoke. **3** *the actors needed prompting* **remind**, cue, feed, help out; jog someone's memory.
– OPPOSITES deter.
▶ adj. *a prompt reply* **quick**, swift, rapid, speedy, fast, direct, immediate, instant, expeditious, early, punctual, in good time, on time, timely.
– OPPOSITES slow, late.
▶ adv. *at 3.30 prompt* **exactly**, precisely, sharp, on the dot, dead, punctually, on the nail; informal bang on; N. Amer. informal on the button, on the nose.
▶ n. *he stopped, and Julia supplied a prompt* **reminder**, cue, feed.

promptly adv. **1** *William arrived promptly at 7.30* **punctually**, on time; informal on the dot, bang on; Brit. informal spot on; N. Amer. informal on the button, on the nose. **2** *I expect the matter to be dealt with promptly* **without delay**, straight away, right away, at once, immediately, now, as soon as possible; quickly, swiftly, rapidly, speedily, fast, expeditiously; N. Amer. momentarily; informal pronto, ASAP, p.d.q. (pretty damn quick).
– OPPOSITES late, slowly.

promulgate v. **1** *they promulgated their own views* **make known**, make public, publicize, spread, communicate, propagate, disseminate, broadcast, promote, preach; literary bruit abroad. **2** *the law was promulgated in 1942* **put into effect**, enact, implement, enforce.

prone adj. **1** *malnourished people are prone to infection* **susceptible**, vulnerable, subject, open, liable, given, predisposed, likely, disposed, inclined, apt; at risk of. **2** *his prone body* **(lying) face down**, face downwards, on one's stomach/front; lying flat/down, horizontal, prostrate.
– OPPOSITES resistant, immune, upright.

prong n. **tine**, spike, point, tip, projection.

pronounce v. **1** *his name is difficult to pronounce* **say**, enunciate, articulate, utter, voice, sound, vocalize, get one's tongue round. **2** *the doctor pronounced that I had a virus* **announce**, proclaim, declare, affirm, assert; judge, rule, decree; rare asseverate.

pronounced adj. **noticeable**, marked, strong, conspicuous, striking, distinct,

prominent, unmistakable, obvious, recognizable, identifiable.
– OPPOSITES slight.

pronouncement n. **announcement**, proclamation, declaration, assertion; judgement, ruling, decree; formal ordinance; rare asseveration.

pronunciation n. **accent**, manner of speaking, speech, diction, delivery, elocution, intonation; articulation, enunciation, voicing, vocalization, sounding; rare orthoepy.

proof n. **1** *proof of ownership* **evidence**, verification, corroboration, authentication, confirmation, certification, documentation, validation, attestation, substantiation. **2** *the proofs of a book* **page proof**, galley proof, galley, pull, slip; revise.
▶ adj. *no system is proof against theft* **resistant**, immune, unaffected, invulnerable, impenetrable, impervious, repellent.

prop n. **1** *the roof is held up by props* **pole**, post, support, upright, brace, buttress, stay, strut, stanchion, shore, pier, pillar, pile, piling, bolster, truss, column. **2** *a prop for the economy* **mainstay**, pillar, anchor, backbone, support, foundation, cornerstone.
▶ v. **1** *he propped his bike against the wall* **lean**, rest, stand, balance, steady. **2** *this post is propping the wall up* **hold up**, shore up, bolster up, buttress, support, brace, underpin. **3** *they prop up loss-making industries* **subsidize**, underwrite, fund, finance.

propaganda n. **information**, promotion, advertising, publicity; agitprop, disinformation, counter-information, the big lie; informal info, hype, plugging.

propagandist n. **promoter**, champion, supporter, proponent, advocate, campaigner, crusader, publicist, evangelist, apostle; informal plugger.

propagate v. **1** *an easy plant to propagate* **breed**, grow, cultivate. **2** *these shrubs propagate easily* **reproduce**, multiply, proliferate, increase, spread, self-seed, self-sow. **3** *they propagated socialist ideas* **spread**, disseminate, communicate, make known, promulgate, circulate, broadcast, publicize, proclaim, preach, promote; literary bruit abroad.

propel v. **1** *a boat propelled by oars* **move**, power, push, drive. **2** *he propelled the ball into the air* **throw**, thrust, toss, fling, hurl, launch, pitch, project, send, shoot. **3** *confusion propelled her into action* **spur**, drive, prompt, precipitate, catapult, motivate, force, impel.

propeller n. **rotor**, screw, airscrew; informal prop.

propensity n. **tendency**, inclination, predisposition, proneness, proclivity, readiness, liability, disposition, leaning, weakness.

proper adj. **1** *he's not a proper scientist* **real**, genuine, actual, true, bona fide; informal kosher. **2** *the proper channels* **right**,

p

correct, accepted, orthodox, conventional, established, official, formal, regular, acceptable, appropriate; old use meet. **3** *they were terribly proper* **respectable**, decorous, seemly, decent, refined, ladylike, gentlemanly, genteel; formal, conventional, correct, comme il faut, done, orthodox, polite, punctilious. **4** Brit. informal *a proper mess* **complete**, absolute, real, perfect, total, thorough, utter, out-and-out, positive, unmitigated, consummate; Brit. informal right; Austral./NZ informal fair.
– OPPOSITES fake, inappropriate, wrong, unconventional.

property n. **1** *lost property* **possessions**, belongings, things, effects, stuff, chattels, movables; resources, assets, valuables, fortune, capital, riches, wealth; Law personalty, goods and chattels; informal gear. **2** *private property* **building(s)**, premises, house(s), land, estates; Law real property, realty; N. Amer. real estate. **3** *healing properties* **quality**, attribute, characteristic, feature, power, trait, mark, hallmark.

prophecy n. **1** *her prophecy is coming true* **prediction**, forecast, prognostication, prognosis, divination, augury. **2** *the gift of prophecy* **foretelling the future**, fortune telling, crystal-gazing, prediction, second sight, prognostication, divination, augury, soothsaying.

prophesy v. **predict**, foretell, forecast, foresee, forewarn of, prognosticate.

prophet, prophetess n. **seer**, soothsayer, fortune teller, clairvoyant, diviner; oracle, augur, sibyl.
□ **prophet of doom** pessimist, doom-monger, doomsayer, doomster, Cassandra, Jeremiah; informal doom (and gloom) merchant.

prophetic adj. **prescient**, predictive, far-seeing, prognostic, divinatory, sibylline, apocalyptic; rare vatic, mantic.

prophylactic adj. *prophylactic measures* **preventive**, preventative, precautionary, protective, inhibitory.
▶ n. *a prophylactic against malaria* **preventive measure**, precaution, safeguard, safety measure; preventive medicine.

prophylaxis n. **preventive treatment**, prevention, protection, precaution.

propitiate v. **appease**, placate, mollify, pacify, make peace with, conciliate, make amends to, soothe, calm.
– OPPOSITES provoke.

propitious adj. **favourable**, auspicious, promising, providential, advantageous, optimistic, bright, rosy, heaven-sent, hopeful; opportune, timely.
– OPPOSITES inauspicious, unfortunate.

proponent n. **advocate**, champion, supporter, backer, promoter, protagonist, campaigner; N. Amer. booster.

proportion n. **1** *a small proportion of the land* **part**, portion, amount, quantity, bit, piece, percentage, fraction, section, segment, share. **2** *the proportion of water to*

alcohol **ratio**, distribution, relative amount/number; relationship. **3** *the drawing is out of proportion* **balance**, symmetry, harmony, correspondence, correlation, agreement. **4** *men of huge proportions* **size**, dimensions, magnitude, measurements; mass, volume, bulk; expanse, extent, width, breadth.

proportional adj. **corresponding**, proportionate, comparable, in proportion, pro rata, commensurate, equivalent, consistent, relative, analogous.
– OPPOSITES disproportionate.

proposal n. **1** *the proposal was rejected* **scheme**, plan, idea, project, programme, manifesto, motion, proposition, suggestion, submission. **2** *the proposal of a new constitution* **putting forward**, proposing, suggesting, submitting.
– OPPOSITES withdrawal.

propose v. **1** *he proposed a solution* **put forward**, suggest, submit, advance, offer, present, move, come up with, lodge, table, nominate. **2** *do you propose to go?* **intend**, mean, plan, have in mind/view, resolve, aim, purpose, think of, aspire, want. **3** *you've proposed to her!* **ask someone to marry you**; informal pop the question; dated ask for someone's hand in marriage.
– OPPOSITES withdraw.

proposition n. **1** *the analysis derives from one proposition* **theory**, hypothesis, thesis, argument, premise, theorem, concept, idea, statement. **2** *a business proposition* **proposal**, scheme, plan, project, idea, programme, bid. **3** *doing it for real is a very different proposition* **task**, job, undertaking, venture, activity, affair, problem.
▶ v. *he never dared proposition her* **propose sex with**, make sexual advances to, make an indecent proposal to, make an improper suggestion to; informal give someone the come-on.

propound v. **put forward**, advance, offer, proffer, present, set forth, submit, tender, suggest, introduce, postulate, propose, pose, posit; advocate, promote, peddle, spread.

proprietor, proprietress n. **owner**, possessor, holder, master/mistress; landowner, landlord/landlady; innkeeper, hotel-keeper, hotelier, shopkeeper; Brit. publican.

propriety n. **1** *he behaves with the utmost propriety* **decorum**, respectability, decency, correctness, protocol, appropriateness, suitability, good manners, courtesy, politeness, rectitude, morality, civility, modesty, demureness; sobriety, refinement, discretion; humorous couth. **2** *he was careful to preserve the proprieties in public* **etiquette**, convention(s), social grace(s), niceties, protocol, standards, civilities, formalities, accepted behaviour, good form, the done thing, the thing to do, punctilio.
– OPPOSITES indecorum, impropriety.

propulsion n. **thrust**, motive force, impetus, impulse, drive, driving force, actuation, push, pressure, power.

prosaic adj. **ordinary**, everyday, commonplace, conventional, straightforward, routine, run-of-the-mill, workaday; **unimaginative**, uninspired, uninspiring, matter-of-fact, dull, dry, dreary, tedious, boring, humdrum, mundane, pedestrian, tame, plodding; bland, insipid, banal, trite, literal, factual, unpoetic, unemotional, unsentimental.
– OPPOSITES interesting, imaginative, inspired.

proscribe v. **1** *gambling was proscribed* **forbid**, prohibit, ban, bar, interdict, make illegal, embargo, outlaw, disallow, veto; Law enjoin. **2** *the book was proscribed by the Church* **condemn**, denounce, attack, criticize, censure, damn, reject.
– OPPOSITES allow, authorize, accept.

proscription n. **1** *the proscription of alcohol* **banning**, forbidding, prohibition, prohibiting, barring, debarment, vetoing, interdiction, outlawing. **2** *a proscription was imposed* **ban**, prohibition, bar, interdict, veto, embargo, moratorium. **3** *the proscription of his recordings* **condemnation**, denunciation, attacking, criticism, censuring, damning, rejection.
– OPPOSITES allowing, authorization, acceptance.

prosecute v. **1** *they prosecute offenders* **take to court**, institute legal proceedings against, take legal action against, sue, try, bring to trial, put on trial, put in the dock, indict, arraign; N. Amer. impeach; informal have the law on. **2** *they helped him prosecute the war* **pursue**, fight, wage, carry on, conduct, direct, engage in, proceed with, continue (with), keep on with.
– OPPOSITES defend, let off, give up.

proselyte n. **convert**, new believer, catechumen.

prospect n. **1** *there is little prospect of success* **likelihood**, hope, expectation, anticipation, (good/poor) chance, odds, probability, possibility, promise, lookout; fear, danger. **2** *her job prospects* **possibilities**, potential, promise, expectations, outlook. **3** *a daunting prospect* **vision**, thought, idea; task, undertaking. **4** *Jimmy is an exciting prospect* **candidate**, possibility; informal catch. **5** *there is a pleasant prospect from the lounge* **view**, vista, outlook, perspective, panorama, aspect, scene; picture, spectacle, sight.
▶ v. *they are prospecting for oil* **search**, look, explore, survey, scout, hunt, reconnoitre, examine, inspect.
◻ **in prospect** expected, likely, coming soon, on the way, to come, at hand, near, imminent, in the offing, in store, on the horizon, just around the corner, in the air, in the wind, brewing, looming; informal on the cards.

prospective adj. **potential**, possible, probable, likely, future, eventual, -to-be, soon-to-be, in the making; intending, aspiring, would-be; forthcoming, approaching, coming, imminent.

prospectus n. **brochure**, pamphlet, description, particulars, announcement, advertisement; syllabus, curriculum, catalogue, programme, list, scheme, schedule.

prosper v. **flourish**, thrive, do well, bloom, blossom, burgeon, progress, do all right for oneself, get ahead, get on (in the world), be successful; informal go places.
– OPPOSITES fail, flounder.

prosperity n. **success**, profitability, affluence, wealth, opulence, luxury, the good life, milk and honey, (good) fortune, ease, plenty, comfort, security, well-being.
– OPPOSITES hardship, failure.

prosperous adj. **thriving**, flourishing, successful, strong, vigorous, profitable, lucrative, expanding, booming, burgeoning; **affluent**, wealthy, rich, moneyed, well off, well-to-do, opulent, substantial, in clover; informal on a roll, on the up and up, in the money.
– OPPOSITES ailing, poor.

prostitute n. **whore**, sex worker, call girl; rent boy; informal tart, pro, moll, working girl, member of the oldest profession; Brit. informal tom, renter; N. Amer. informal hooker, hustler, chippy; black English ho; dated streetwalker, woman of the streets, lady/woman of the night, scarlet woman, cocotte; old use courtesan, strumpet, harlot, trollop, woman of ill repute, lady of pleasure, wench.
▶ v. *they prostituted their art* **betray**, sacrifice, sell, sell out, debase, degrade, demean, devalue, cheapen, lower, shame, misuse, pervert; abandon one's principles, be untrue to oneself.

prostitution n. **whoring**, the sex industry, streetwalking, Mrs Warren's profession, sex tourism; informal the oldest profession, the trade; rough trade; Brit. informal the game; N. Amer. informal hooking, hustling; dated whoredom; old use harlotry.

prostrate adj. **1** *the prostrate figure on the ground* **prone**, lying flat, lying down, stretched out, spreadeagled, sprawling, horizontal, recumbent; rare procumbent. **2** *his wife was prostrate with shock* **overwhelmed**, overcome, overpowered, brought to one's knees, stunned, dazed; speechless, helpless; informal knocked/hit for six. **3** *the fever left me prostrate* **worn out**, exhausted, fatigued, tired out, sapped, dog-tired, spent, drained, debilitated, enervated, laid low; informal all in, done in, dead, dead beat, dead on one's feet, ready to drop, fagged out, bushed, frazzled, worn to a frazzle; Brit. informal whacked, knackered; N. Amer. informal pooped.
– OPPOSITES upright, fresh.
▶ v. *she was prostrated by the tragedy* **overwhelm**, overcome, overpower, bring to one's knees, devastate, debilitate, weaken, enfeeble, enervate, lay low, wear out, exhaust, tire out, drain, sap, wash out, take it out of; informal knacker, frazzle, do in; N. Amer. informal poop.

□ **prostrate oneself** throw oneself down, lie down, stretch oneself out, throw oneself at someone's feet; dated measure one's length.

prostration n. **collapse**, weakness, debility, lassitude, exhaustion, fatigue, tiredness, enervation, emotional exhaustion.

protagonist n. **1** *the protagonist in the plot* **main/central character**, principal, hero/heroine, leading man/lady, title role, lead. **2** *a protagonist of deregulation* **champion**, advocate, upholder, supporter, backer, promoter, proponent, exponent, campaigner, fighter, crusader; apostle, apologist; N. Amer. booster.
– OPPOSITES opponent.

protean adj. **1** *the protean nature of mental disorders* **ever-changing**, variable, changeable, mutable, kaleidoscopic, inconstant, inconsistent, unstable, shifting, unsettled, fluctuating, fluid, wavering, vacillating, mercurial, volatile; technical labile. **2** *a remarkably protean composer* **versatile**, adaptable, flexible, all-round, multifaceted, multitalented, many-sided.
– OPPOSITES constant, consistent, limited.

protect v. **keep safe**, keep from harm, save, safeguard, preserve, defend, shield, cushion, insulate, hedge, shelter, screen, secure, fortify, guard, watch over, look after, take care of, keep; inoculate.
– OPPOSITES expose, neglect, attack, harm.

protection n. **1** *protection against frost* **defence**, security, shielding, preservation, conservation, safe keeping, safeguarding, safety, sanctuary, shelter, refuge, lee, immunity, insurance, indemnity. **2** *under the protection of the Church* **safe keeping**, care, charge, keeping, protectorship, guidance, aegis, auspices, umbrella, guardianship, support, patronage, championship, providence. **3** *good protection against noise* **barrier**, buffer, shield, screen, hedge, cushion, preventative, armour, refuge, bulwark.

protective adj. **1** *protective clothing* **preservative**, protecting, safeguarding, shielding, defensive, safety, precautionary, preventive, preventative. **2** *he felt protective towards the girl* **solicitous**, caring, warm, paternal/maternal, fatherly/motherly, gallant, chivalrous; overprotective, possessive, jealous.

protector n. **1** *a protector of the environment* **defender**, preserver, guardian, guard, champion, watchdog, ombudsman, knight in shining armour, guardian angel, patron, chaperone, escort, keeper, custodian, bodyguard, minder; informal hired gun. **2** *ear protectors* **guard**, shield, buffer, cushion, pad, screen.

protégé, protégée n. **pupil**, student, trainee, apprentice; disciple, follower; discovery, find, ward.

protest n. **1** *he resigned as a protest* **objection**, complaint, exception, disapproval, challenge, dissent, demurral, remonstration, fuss, outcry. **2** *women staged*

a protest **demonstration**, (protest) march, rally; sit-in, occupation; work-to-rule, industrial action, stoppage, strike, walkout, mutiny, picket, boycott; informal demo.
– OPPOSITES support, approval.

▶ v. **1** *residents protested at the plans* **express opposition**, object, dissent, take issue, make/take a stand, put up a fight, kick, take exception, complain, express disapproval, disagree, demur, remonstrate, make a fuss; cry out, speak out, rail, inveigh, fulminate; informal kick up a fuss/stink. **2** *people protested outside the cathedral* **demonstrate**, march, hold a rally, sit in, occupy somewhere; work to rule, take industrial action, stop work, down tools, strike, go on strike, walk out, mutiny, picket somewhere; boycott something. **3** *he protested his innocence* **insist on**, maintain, assert, affirm, announce, proclaim, declare, profess, contend, argue, claim, vow, swear (to), stress; formal aver, asseverate.
– OPPOSITES acquiesce, support, deny.

protestation n. **1** *his protestations of innocence* **declaration**, announcement, profession, assertion, insistence, claim, affirmation, assurance, oath, vow; rare aver, asseveration. **2** *we helped him despite his protestations* **objection**, protest, exception, complaint, disapproval, opposition, challenge, dissent, demurral, remonstration, fuss, outcry; informal stink.
– OPPOSITES denial, acquiescence, support.

protester n. **1** *the council lost protesters' letters* **objector**, opposer, opponent, complainant, complainer, dissenter, dissident, nonconformist. **2** *the protesters were moved on* **demonstrator**, protest marcher; striker, mutineer, picket.

protocol n. **1** *a stickler for protocol* **etiquette**, conventions, formalities, customs, rules of conduct, procedure, ritual, accepted behaviour, propriety, proprieties, decorum, good form, the done thing, the thing to do, punctilio. **2** *the two countries signed a protocol* **agreement**, treaty, entente, concordat, convention, deal, pact, contract, compact; formal concord.

prototype n. **1** *a prototype of the weapon* **original**, first example/model, master, mould, template, framework, mock-up, pattern, sample; design, guide, blueprint. **2** *the prototype of an ideal wife* **typical example**, paradigm, archetype, exemplar.

protract v. **prolong**, lengthen, extend, draw out, drag out, spin out, stretch out, string out, elongate; carry on, continue, keep up, perpetuate.
– OPPOSITES curtail, shorten.

protracted adj. **prolonged**, long-lasting, extended, long-drawn-out, spun out, dragged out, strung out, lengthy, long.
– OPPOSITES short.

protrude v. **stick out**, jut (out), project, extend, stand out, bulge out, poke out, thrust out, cantilever.

protruding adj. **sticking out**, protuberant, projecting, prominent, jutting, overhanging, proud, bulging; informal sticky-out.
– OPPOSITES sunken, flush.

protrusion n. **1** *the neck vertebrae have short vertical protrusions* **bump**, lump, knob, protuberance, projection, sticking-out bit, prominence, swelling, eminence, outcrop, outgrowth, jut, jag, snag; ledge, shelf, ridge; informal sticky-out bit. **2** *protrusion of the lips* **sticking out**, jutting, projection, obtrusion, prominence; swelling, bulging.

protuberance n. **1** *a protuberance can cause drag* **bump**, lump, knob, projection, protrusion, sticking-out bit, prominence, swelling, eminence, outcrop, outgrowth, jut, jag, snag; ledge, shelf, ridge; informal sticky-out bit. **2** *the protuberance of the incisors* **sticking out**, jutting, projection, obtrusion, prominence; swelling, bulging.

protuberant adj. **sticking out**, protruding, projecting, prominent, jutting, overhanging, proud, bulging; informal sticky-out.
– OPPOSITES sunken, flush.

proud adj. **1** *the proud parents beamed* **pleased**, glad, happy, delighted, joyful, overjoyed, thrilled, satisfied, gratified, content. **2** *a proud day* **pleasing**, gratifying, satisfying, cheering, heart-warming; happy, good, glorious, memorable, notable, red-letter. **3** *they were poor but proud* **self-respecting**, dignified, noble, worthy; independent. **4** *I'm not too proud to admit I'm wrong* **arrogant**, conceited, vain, self-important, full of oneself, puffed up, swollen-headed, jumped-up, smug, complacent, disdainful, condescending, scornful, supercilious, snobbish, imperious, pompous, overbearing, bumptious, haughty; informal big-headed, too big for one's boots, high and mighty, stuck-up, uppity, snooty, highfalutin; Brit. informal toffee-nosed; literary vainglorious; rare hubristic. **5** *the proud ships* **magnificent**, splendid, resplendent, grand, noble, stately, imposing, dignified, striking, impressive, majestic, glorious, awe-inspiring, awesome, monumental. **6** *the switch is proud of the wall* **projecting**, sticking out/up, jutting (out), protruding, prominent, raised, convex, elevated.
– OPPOSITES ashamed, shameful, humble, modest, unimpressive, concave, flush.

prove v. **1** *that proves I'm right* **show (to be true)**, demonstrate (the truth of), show beyond doubt, manifest, produce proof/evidence; witness to, give substance to, determine, substantiate, corroborate, verify, ratify, validate, authenticate, document, bear out, confirm; formal evince. **2** *the rumour proved to be correct* **turn out**, be found, happen.
– OPPOSITES disprove.
▢ **prove oneself** demonstrate one's abilities/qualities, show one's (true) mettle, show what one is made of.

provenance n. **origin**, source, place of origin; birthplace, fount, roots, pedigree,

derivation, root, etymology; N. Amer. provenience; formal radix.

proverb n. **saying**, adage, saw, maxim, axiom, motto, bon mot, aphorism, apophthegm, epigram, gnome, dictum, precept.

proverbial adj. **well known**, famous, famed, renowned, traditional, time-honoured, legendary; notorious, infamous.

provide v. **1** *the Foundation will provide funds* **supply**, give, issue, furnish, come up with, dispense, bestow, impart, produce, yield, bring forth, bear, deliver, donate, contribute, pledge, advance, spare, part with, allocate, distribute, allot, put up; informal fork out, lay out; N. Amer. informal ante up, pony up. **2** *he was provided with enough tools* **equip**, furnish, issue, supply, outfit; fit out, rig out, kit out, arm, provision; informal fix up. **3** *he had to provide for his family* **feed**, nurture, nourish; **support**, maintain, keep, sustain, provide sustenance for, fend for, finance, endow. **4** *the test may provide the answer* **make available**, present, offer, afford, give, add, bring, yield, impart. **5** *we have provided for further restructuring* **prepare**, allow, make provision, be prepared, arrange, get ready, plan, cater. **6** *the banks have to provide against bad debts* **take precautions**, take steps/measures, guard, forearm oneself; make provision for. **7** *the Act provides that factories must be kept clean* **stipulate**, lay down, require, order, ordain, demand, prescribe, state, specify.
– OPPOSITES refuse, withhold, deprive, neglect.

provided conj. **if**, on condition that, providing (that), provided that, presuming (that), assuming (that), on the assumption that, as long as, given (that), with the provision/proviso that, with/on the understanding that, contingent on.

providence n. **1** *a life mapped out by providence* **fate**, destiny, nemesis, kismet, God's will, divine intervention, predestination, predetermination, the stars; one's lot (in life); old use one's portion. **2** *he had a streak of providence* **prudence**, foresight, forethought, far-sightedness, judiciousness, shrewdness, circumspection, wisdom, sagacity, common sense; careful budgeting, thrift, economy.

provident adj. **prudent**, far-sighted, judicious, shrewd, circumspect, forearmed, wise, sagacious, sensible; thrifty, economical.
– OPPOSITES improvident.

providential adj. **opportune**, advantageous, favourable, auspicious, propitious, heaven-sent, welcome, golden, lucky, happy, fortunate, felicitous, timely, well timed, seasonable, convenient, expedient.
– OPPOSITES inopportune.

provider n. **supplier**, donor, giver, contributor, source.

providing conj. See **provided**.

province n. **1** *a province of the Ottoman Empire* **territory**, region, state, department, canton, area, district, sector, zone, division.

p

2 *people in the provinces* **non-metropolitan areas/counties**, Middle England/America, rural areas/districts, the countryside, the backwoods, the wilds; informal the sticks, the middle of nowhere; N. Amer. informal the boondocks. **3** *that's outside my province* **responsibility**, area of activity, area of interest, knowledge, department, sphere, world, realm, field, domain, territory, orbit, preserve, line of country; business, affair, concern; speciality, forte; jurisdiction, authority; informal pigeon, bailiwick, turf.

provincial adj. **1** *the provincial government* **regional**, state, territorial, district, local; sectoral, zonal, cantonal, county. **2** *provincial areas* **non-metropolitan**, small-town, non-urban, outlying, rural, country, rustic, backwoods, backwater; informal one-horse; N. Amer. informal hick, freshwater. **3** *they're so dull and provincial* **unsophisticated**, narrow-minded, parochial, small-town, suburban, insular, parish-pump, inward-looking, conservative; small-minded, blinkered, bigoted, prejudiced; N. Amer. informal jerkwater, corn-fed.
– OPPOSITES national, metropolitan, cosmopolitan, sophisticated, broad-minded.
▸ n. *they were dismissed as provincials* **(country) bumpkin**, country cousin, rustic, yokel, village idiot, peasant; Irish informal culchie; N. Amer. informal hayseed, hick, rube, hillbilly.
– OPPOSITES sophisticate.

provision n. **1** *the provision of weapons to guerrillas* **supplying**, supply, providing, giving, presentation, donation; equipping, furnishing. **2** *there has been limited provision for gifted children* **facilities**, services, amenities, resource(s), arrangements, solutions; means, funds, benefits, assistance, allowance(s). **3** *provisions for the trip* **supplies**, food and drink, stores, groceries, foodstuff(s), provender, rations; informal grub, eats, nosh; N. Amer. informal chuck; formal comestibles; literary viands; dated victuals. **4** *he made no provision for the future* **preparations**, plans, arrangements, prearrangement, precautions, contingency. **5** *the provisions of the Act* **term**, clause; requirement, specification, stipulation; proviso, condition, qualification, restriction, limitation.

provisional adj. **interim**, temporary, pro tem; transitional, changeover, stopgap, short-term, fill-in, acting, caretaker, TBC (to be confirmed), subject to confirmation; pencilled in, working, tentative, contingent.
– OPPOSITES permanent, definite.

provisionally adv. **temporarily**, short-term, pro tem, for the interim, for the present, for the time being, for now, for the nonce; subject to confirmation, in an acting capacity, conditionally, tentatively.

proviso n. **condition**, stipulation, provision, clause, rider, qualification, restriction, caveat.

provocation n. **1** *he remained calm despite severe provocation* **goading**, prodding, egging on, incitement, pressure; **annoyance**, irritation, nettling; harassment, plaguing, molestation; teasing, taunting, torment; affront, insults; informal hassle, aggravation. **2** *without provocation, Jones punched Mr Cartwright* **justification**, excuse, pretext, occasion, call, motivation, motive, cause, grounds, reason, need.

provocative adj. **1** *provocative remarks* **annoying**, irritating, exasperating, infuriating, maddening, vexing, galling; insulting, offensive, inflammatory, incendiary, controversial; informal aggravating, in-your-face. **2** *a provocative pose* **sexy**, sexually arousing, sexually exciting, alluring, seductive, suggestive, inviting, tantalizing, titillating; indecent, pornographic, indelicate, immodest, shameless; erotic, sensuous, slinky, coquettish, amorous, flirtatious; informal tarty, come-hither.
– OPPOSITES soothing, calming, modest, decorous.

provoke v. **1** *the plan has provoked outrage* **arouse**, produce, evoke, cause, give rise to, occasion, call forth, elicit, induce, excite, spark off, touch off, kindle, generate, engender, instigate, result in, lead to, bring on, precipitate, prompt, trigger; literary beget. **2** *he was provoked into replying* **goad**, spur, prick, sting, prod, egg on, incite, rouse, stir, move, stimulate, motivate, excite, inflame, work/fire up, impel. **3** *he wouldn't be provoked* **annoy**, anger, incense, enrage, irritate, infuriate, exasperate, madden, nettle, get/take a rise out of, ruffle, ruffle someone's feathers, make someone's hackles rise; harass, harry, plague, molest; tease, taunt, torment; Brit. rub up the wrong way; informal peeve, aggravate, hassle, miff, rile, needle, get, bug, hack off, make someone's blood boil, get under someone's skin, get in someone's hair, get/put someone's back up, get up someone's nose, get someone's goat, get across someone; Brit. informal wind up, nark; N. Amer. informal rankle, ride, gravel.
– OPPOSITES allay, deter, pacify, appease.

prow n. **bow(s)**, stem, front, nose, head, cutwater; Brit. humorous sharp end.

prowess n. **1** *his prowess as a winemaker* **skill**, expertise, mastery, facility, ability, capability, capacity, savoir faire, talent, genius, adeptness, aptitude, dexterity, deftness, competence, accomplishment, proficiency, finesse; informal know-how. **2** *the knights' prowess in battle* **courage**, bravery, gallantry, valour, heroism, intrepidity, nerve, pluck, pluckiness, boldness, daring, audacity, fearlessness; informal bottle, guts, spunk; N. Amer. informal moxie, sand.
– OPPOSITES inability, ineptitude, cowardice.

prowl v. **move stealthily**, slink, skulk, steal, nose, pussyfoot, sneak, stalk, creep; informal snoop.

proximity n. **closeness**, nearness, propinquity; accessibility, handiness; old use vicinity.

proxy n. **deputy**, representative, substitute, delegate, agent, surrogate, stand-in, attorney, go-between.

prude n. **puritan**, prig, killjoy, moralist, pietist; informal goody-goody; N. Amer. informal bluenose.

prudence n. **1** *you have gone beyond the bounds of prudence* **wisdom**, judgement, good judgement, common sense, sense, sagacity, shrewdness, advisability. **2** *financial prudence* **caution**, care, providence, far-sightedness, foresight, forethought, shrewdness, circumspection; thrift, economy.
– OPPOSITES folly, recklessness, extravagance.

prudent adj. **1** *it is prudent to obtain consent* **wise**, well judged, sensible, politic, judicious, sagacious, sage, shrewd, advisable, well advised. **2** *a prudent approach to borrowing* **cautious**, careful, provident, far-sighted, judicious, shrewd, circumspect; thrifty, economical.
– OPPOSITES unwise, reckless, extravagant.

prudish adj. **puritanical**, priggish, prim, prim and proper, moralistic, pietistic, sententious, censorious, strait-laced, Victorian, old-maidish, stuffy; informal goody-goody; rare starchy.
– OPPOSITES permissive.

prune v. **1** *I pruned the roses* **cut back**, trim, thin, pinch back, clip, shear, pollard, top, dock. **2** *prune lateral shoots of wisteria* **cut off**, lop (off), chop off, clip, snip (off), nip off, dock. **3** *staff numbers have been pruned* **reduce**, cut (back/down), pare (down), slim down, make reductions in, make cutbacks in, trim, decrease, diminish, downsize, axe, shrink; informal slash.
– OPPOSITES increase.

prurient adj. **salacious**, licentious, voyeuristic, lascivious, lecherous, lustful, lewd, libidinous, lubricious; formal concupiscent.

pry v. **enquire impertinently**, be inquisitive, be curious, poke about/around, ferret (about/around), spy, be a busybody; eavesdrop, listen in, intrude; informal stick/poke one's nose in/into, be nosy, nose, snoop; Austral./NZ informal stickybeak.
– OPPOSITES mind one's own business.

psalm n. **sacred song**, religious song, hymn, song of praise; chant, plainsong; (**psalms**) psalmody, psalter.

pseud n. **poser**, poseur, pretentious person, sham, fraud; informal show-off, phoney.

pseudo adj. **bogus**, sham, phoney, artificial, mock, ersatz, quasi-, fake, false, faux, spurious, deceptive, misleading, assumed, contrived, affected, insincere; informal pretend, put-on; Brit. informal cod.
– OPPOSITES genuine.

pseudonym n. **pen name**, nom de plume, assumed name, false name, alias, professional name, sobriquet, stage name, nom de guerre.

psych informal v.
▢ **psych someone out** intimidate, daunt, browbeat, bully, cow, tyrannize, scare, terrorize, frighten, dishearten, unnerve, subdue; informal bulldoze; N. Amer. informal buffalo.
psych oneself up nerve oneself, steel oneself, brace oneself, summon one's courage, prepare oneself, gear oneself up, urge oneself on, gird (up) one's loins.

psyche n. **soul**, spirit, (inner) self, ego, true being, inner man/woman, persona, subconscious, mind, intellect; technical anima, pneuma.
– OPPOSITES body.

psychiatrist n. **psychotherapist**, psychoanalyst; informal shrink, head doctor; Brit. humorous trick cyclist.

psychic adj. **1** *psychic powers* **supernatural**, paranormal, other-worldly, supernormal, preternatural, metaphysical, extrasensory, magic, magical, mystical, mystic, occult. **2** *I'm not psychic* **clairvoyant**, telepathic, having second sight, having a sixth sense. **3** *psychic development* **emotional**, spiritual, inner; cognitive, psychological, intellectual, mental, psychiatric, psychogenic.
– OPPOSITES normal, physical.
▸ n. *she is a psychic* **clairvoyant**, fortune teller, crystal-gazer; medium, spiritualist; telepathist, telepath, mind reader, palmist, palm-reader.

psychological adj. **1** *his psychological state* **mental**, emotional, intellectual, inner, cerebral, brain, rational, cognitive. **2** *her pain was psychological* **(all) in the mind**, psychosomatic, emotional, irrational, subjective, subconscious, unconscious.
– OPPOSITES physical.

psychology n. **1** *a degree in psychology* **study of the mind**, science of the mind. **2** *the psychology of the road user* **mindset**, mind, mental processes, thought processes, way of thinking, cast of mind, mentality, persona, psyche, (mental) attitude(s), make-up, character; informal what makes someone tick.

psychopath n. **madman, madwoman**, maniac, lunatic, psychotic, sociopath; informal loony, fruitcake, nutcase, nut, psycho, schizo, head case, headbanger, sicko; Brit. informal nutter; N. Amer. informal screwball, crazy, kook, meshuggener.

psychopathic adj. See **mad** (sense 1).

psychosomatic adj. **(all) in the mind**, psychological, irrational, stress-related, stress-induced, subjective, subconscious, unconscious.

psychotic adj. See **mad** (sense 1).

pub n. Brit. **bar**, inn, tavern, hostelry, wine bar, taproom, roadhouse; Brit. public house; Austral./NZ hotel; informal watering hole; Brit. informal local, boozer; dated alehouse; historical pot-house, beerhouse; N. Amer. historical saloon.

p

puberty n. **adolescence**, pubescence, sexual maturity, growing up; youth, young adulthood, teenage years, teens, the awkward age; formal juvenescence.

public adj. **1** *public affairs* **state**, national, federal, government; constitutional, civic, civil, official, social, municipal, community, communal, local; nationalized. **2** *by public demand* **popular**, general, common, communal, collective, shared, joint, universal, widespread. **3** *a public figure* **prominent**, well known, important, leading, eminent, distinguished, notable, noteworthy, noted, celebrated, household, famous, famed, influential; N. Amer. major-league. **4** *public places* **open (to the public)**, communal, accessible to all, available, free, unrestricted, community. **5** *the news became public* **known**, published, publicized, in circulation, exposed, overt, plain, obvious.
– OPPOSITES private, obscure, unknown, restricted, secret.
▸ n. **1** *the British public* **people**, citizens, subjects, general public, electors, electorate, voters, taxpayers, residents, inhabitants, citizenry, population, populace, community, society, country, nation, world; everyone. **2** *his adoring public* **audience**, spectators, concertgoers, theatregoers, followers, following, fans, devotees, aficionados, admirers; patrons, clientele, market, consumers, buyers, customers, readers.
▫ **in public** publicly, openly, in the open, in full view, for all to see, undisguisedly, blatantly, flagrantly, brazenly, overtly; formal coram populo.

> **WORD LINKS**
> **agoraphobia** fear of public places

p

publication n. **1** *the author of this publication* **book**, volume, title, work, tome, opus; newspaper, paper, magazine, periodical, newsletter, bulletin, journal, report; organ, booklet, brochure, catalogue; daily, weekly, monthly, quarterly, annual; informal rag, mag, zine. **2** *the publication of her new book* **issuing**, announcement, publishing, printing, notification, reporting, declaration, communication, proclamation, broadcasting, publicizing, advertising, distribution, spreading, dissemination, promulgation, issuance, appearance.

publicity n. **1** *the blaze of publicity* **public attention**, public interest, public notice, media attention/interest, exposure, glare, limelight. **2** *publicity should boost sales* **promotion**, advertising, propaganda; boost, push; informal hype, ballyhoo, puff, puffery, build-up, razzmatazz; plug.

publicize v. **1** *I never publicize the fact* **make known**, make public, publish, announce, report, post, communicate, broadcast, issue, put out, distribute, spread, promulgate, disseminate, circulate, air; disclose, reveal, divulge, leak. **2** *he just wants to publicize his book* **advertise**, promote, build up, talk up, push, beat the drum for, boost; informal hype,

plug, puff (up).
– OPPOSITES conceal, suppress.

public-spirited adj. **community-minded**, socially concerned, philanthropic, charitable; **altruistic**, humanitarian, generous, unselfish.

publish v. **1** *we publish novels* **issue**, bring out, produce, print. **2** *he ought to publish his views* **make known**, make public, publicize, announce, report, post, communicate, broadcast, issue, put out, distribute, spread, promulgate, disseminate, circulate, air; disclose, reveal, divulge, leak.

pucker v. *she puckered her forehead* **wrinkle**, crinkle, crease, furrow, crumple, rumple, ruck up, scrunch up, corrugate, ruffle, screw up, shrivel; cockle.
▸ n. *a pucker in the sewing* **wrinkle**, crinkle, crumple, corrugation, furrow, line, fold.

puckish adj. **mischievous**, naughty, impish, roguish, playful, arch, prankish; informal waggish.

pudding n. **dessert**, sweet, second course, last course; Brit. informal afters, pud.

puddle n. **pool**, spill, splash; literary plash.

puerile adj. **childish**, immature, infantile, juvenile, babyish; silly, inane, fatuous, jejune, asinine, foolish, petty.
– OPPOSITES mature, sensible.

puff n. **1** *a puff of wind* **gust**, blast, flurry, rush, draught, waft, breeze, breath. **2** *he took a puff at his cigar* **pull**; informal drag. **3** informal *they expected a puff in our review column* **favourable mention**, review, recommendation, good word, advertisement, promotion, commercial; informal ad; Brit. informal advert. **4** informal *a salesman's puff* **publicity**, advertising, promotion, marketing, propaganda, build-up; patter, line, pitch, sales talk; informal spiel.
▸ v. **1** *he walked fast, puffing a little* **breathe heavily**, pant, blow; gasp, fight for breath. **2** *she puffed at her cigarette* **smoke**, draw on, drag on, suck at/on. **3** informal *new ways to puff our products* **advertise**, promote, publicize, push, recommend, endorse, beat the drum for; informal hype (up), plug.
▫ **puff out/up** bulge, swell (out), stick out, distend, tumefy, balloon (up/out), expand, inflate, enlarge.
puff something out/up distend, expand, dilate, inflate, blow up, pump up, enlarge, bloat.

puffed adj. **out of breath**, breathless, short of breath; panting, puffing, gasping, wheezing, wheezy, winded; informal out of puff.

puffed-up adj. **self-important**, conceited, arrogant, bumptious, pompous, overbearing; affected, stiff, vain, proud; informal snooty, uppity, uppish.

puffy adj. **swollen**, puffed up, distended, enlarged, inflated, dilated, bloated, engorged, bulging, tumid, tumescent.

pugilist n. dated **boxer**, fighter, prizefighter; informal bruiser, pug.

pugnacious adj. **combative**, aggressive, antagonistic, belligerent, bellicose, warlike, quarrelsome, argumentative, contentious, disputatious, hostile, threatening, truculent; fiery, hot-tempered.
– OPPOSITES peaceable.

puke v. informal See **vomit** (senses 1 & 2 of the verb).

pukka adj. informal **1** *the pukka thing to do* **respectable**, decorous, proper, genteel, polite; conventional, right, correct, accepted, decent. **2** *pukka racing cars* **genuine**, authentic, proper, actual, real, true, bona fide, veritable, legitimate; informal kosher, the real McCoy. **3** *a pukka meal* **excellent**, very good, outstanding, exceptional, marvellous, wonderful, first-class; informal A1, ace, great, terrific, fantastic, fabulous, fab, awesome, wicked; Brit. informal brilliant, brill.
– OPPOSITES improper, imitation, bad.

pull v. **1** *he pulled the box towards him* **tug**, haul, drag, draw, tow, heave, lug, jerk, wrench; informal yank. **2** *he pulled the bad tooth out* **extract**, take out, remove. **3** *she pulled a muscle* **strain**, sprain, wrench, turn, rick, tear; damage. **4** *race day pulled big crowds* **attract**, draw, bring in, pull in, lure, seduce, entice, tempt, beckon, interest, fascinate.
– OPPOSITES push, repel.

▶ n. **1** *give the chain a pull* **tug**, jerk, heave; informal yank. **2** *she took a pull on her beer* **gulp**, draught, drink, swallow, mouthful, slug; informal swill, swig; N. Amer. informal chug. **3** *a pull on a cigarette* **puff**; informal drag. **4** *she felt the pull of the sea* **attraction**, draw, lure, allurement, enticement, magnetism, temptation, fascination, appeal. **5** *he has a lot of pull in finance* **influence**, sway, power, authority, say, prestige, standing, weight, leverage, muscle, teeth; informal clout.

□ **pull something apart** dismantle, disassemble, take/pull to pieces, take/pull to bits, take apart, strip down; demolish, destroy, break up.

pull back withdraw, retreat, fall back, back off; pull out, retire, disengage; flee, turn tail.

pull something down demolish, knock down, tear down, dismantle, raze (to the ground), level, flatten, bulldoze, destroy.

pull in stop, halt, come to a halt, pull over, pull up, draw up, brake, park.

pull someone/something in 1 *they pulled in big audiences.* See **pull** (sense 4 of the verb). **2** informal *the police pulled him in* arrest, apprehend, detain, take into custody, seize, capture, catch; informal collar, nab, nick, pinch, run in, bust, feel someone's collar.

pull someone's leg tease, fool, play a trick on, rag, pull the wool over someone's eyes; informal kid, rib, lead up the garden path, take for a ride; Brit. informal wind up, have on.

pull something off achieve, fulfil, succeed in, accomplish, bring off, carry off, perform, discharge, complete, clinch, fix, effect, engineer.

pull out withdraw, resign, leave, retire, step down, bow out, back out, give up; informal quit.

pull through get better, get well again, improve, recover, rally, come through, recuperate.

pull something to pieces 1 *don't pull my radio to pieces.* See **pull something apart**. **2** *they pulled the plan to pieces* criticize, attack, censure, condemn, find fault with, pillory, maul, savage; informal knock, slam, pan, bash, crucify, lay into, roast; Brit. informal slate, rubbish, slag off.

pull oneself together regain one's composure, recover, get a grip on oneself, get over it; informal snap out of it, get one's act together, buck up.

pull up See **pull in**.

pull someone up reprimand, rebuke, scold, chide, chastise, upbraid, berate, reprove, reproach, censure, take to task, admonish, lecture, read someone the Riot Act, haul over the coals; informal tell off, bawl out, dress down, give someone hell, give someone an earful; Brit. informal tick off, carpet, give someone a rollicking; N. Amer. informal chew out; Austral. informal monster; formal castigate.

pulp n. **1** *he kneaded it into a pulp* **mush**, mash, paste, purée, pomace, pap, slop, slush, mulch; informal gloop, goo; N. Amer. informal glop. **2** *the sweet pulp on cocoa seeds* **flesh**, marrow, meat.
▶ v. *pulp the gooseberries* **mash**, purée, cream, crush, press, liquidize, liquefy, sieve, squash, pound, macerate, grind, mince.
▶ adj. *pulp fiction* **trashy**, cheap, sensational, lurid, tasteless; informal tacky, rubbishy.

pulpit n. **stand**, lectern, platform, podium, stage, dais, rostrum.

pulsate v. **palpitate**, pulse, throb, pump, undulate, surge, heave, rise and fall; beat, thump, drum, thrum; flutter, quiver.

pulse n. **1** *the pulse in her neck* **heartbeat**, pulsation, pulsing, throbbing, pounding. **2** *the pulse of the train wheels* **rhythm**, beat, tempo, cadence, pounding, thudding, drumming. **3** *pulses of ultrasound* **burst**, blast, spurt, impulse, surge.
▶ v. *music pulsed through the building* **throb**, pulsate, vibrate, beat, pound, thud, thump, drum, thrum, reverberate, echo.

pulverize v. **1** *the seeds are pulverized into flour* **grind**, crush, pound, powder, mill, crunch, squash, press, pulp, mash, sieve, mince, macerate; technical comminute. **2** informal *he pulverized the opposition.* See **trounce**.

pummel v. **batter**, pound, belabour, drub, beat; punch, strike, hit, thump, thrash; informal clobber, wallop, bash, whack, beat the living daylights out of, give someone a (good) hiding, belt, biff, lay into, lam; Brit. informal slosh; N. Amer. informal bust, slug; Austral./NZ informal smite.

pump v. **1** *I pumped air out of the tube* **force**, drive, push; suck, draw, tap, siphon, withdraw, expel, extract, bleed, drain. **2** *she pumped up the tyre* **inflate**, aerate, blow up, fill up; swell, enlarge, distend, expand, dilate, puff up. **3** *blood was pumping from* *his leg* **spurt**, spout, squirt, jet, surge, spew, gush, stream, flow, pour, spill, well, cascade, run, course. **4** *informal I pumped them for information* **interrogate**, cross-examine, ask, question, quiz, probe, sound out, catechize, give someone the third degree; *informal* grill.

pun n. **play on words**, wordplay, double entendre, innuendo, witticism, quip, bon mot.

punch¹ v. *Jim punched him in the face* **hit**, strike, thump, jab, smash, welt, cuff, clip; batter, buffet, pound, pummel; *informal* sock, slug, biff, bop, wallop, clobber, bash, whack, thwack, clout, lam, whomp; *Brit. informal* stick one on, dot, slosh; *N. Amer. informal* boff, bust; *Austral./NZ informal* quilt; *literary* smite.

▶ n. **1** *a punch on the nose* **blow**, hit, knock, thump, box, jab, clip, welt; uppercut, hook; *informal* sock, slug, biff, bop, wallop, bash, whack, clout, belt; *N. Amer. informal* boff, bust; *dated* buffet. **2** *the album is full of punch* **vigour**, liveliness, vitality, drive, strength, zest, verve, enthusiasm; impact, bite, kick; *informal* oomph, zing.

punch² v. *he punched her ticket* **make a hole in**, perforate, puncture, pierce, prick, hole, spike, skewer; *literary* transpierce.

punch-up n. *Brit. informal* See **fight** (sense 1 of the noun).

punchy adj. *punchy dialogue* **forceful**, incisive, strong, powerful, vigorous, dynamic, effective, impressive, telling, compelling; dramatic, passionate, graphic, vivid, potent, authoritative, aggressive; *informal* in-your-face.
– OPPOSITES ineffectual.

punctilio n. **1** *a stickler for punctilio* **conformity**, conscientiousness, punctiliousness; etiquette, protocol, conventions, formalities, propriety, decorum, manners, politesse, good form, the done thing; *humorous* couth. **2** *the punctilios of court procedure* **nicety**, detail, fine point, subtlety, nuance, refinement.
– OPPOSITES informality.

punctilious adj. **meticulous**, conscientious, diligent, scrupulous, careful, painstaking, rigorous, perfectionist, methodical, particular, strict; fussy, fastidious, finicky, pedantic; *informal* nitpicking, pernickety; *N. Amer. informal* persnickety; *old use* nice.
– OPPOSITES careless.

punctual adj. **on time**, prompt, on schedule, in (good) time; *informal* on the dot.
– OPPOSITES late.

punctuate v. **1** *how to punctuate direct speech* **add punctuation to**, put punctuation marks in, dot, apostrophize. **2** *slides punctuated the talk* **break up**, interrupt, intersperse, pepper, sprinkle, scatter.

puncture n. **1** *the tyre developed a puncture* **hole**, perforation, rupture; cut, slit; leak. **2** *my car has a puncture* **flat tyre**; *informal* flat.
▶ v. **1** *he punctured her balloon* **make a hole in**, pierce, rupture, perforate, stab, cut, slit, prick, spike, stick, lance; deflate. **2** *she knows how to puncture his speeches* **put an end to**, cut short, deflate, reduce.

pundit n. **expert**, authority, specialist, doyen(ne), master, guru, sage, savant; *informal* buff, whizz.

pungent adj. **1** *a pungent marinade* **strong**, powerful, pervasive, penetrating; sharp, acid, sour, biting, bitter, tart, vinegary, tangy; highly flavoured, aromatic, spicy, piquant, peppery, hot. **2** *pungent remarks* **caustic**, biting, trenchant, cutting, acerbic, sardonic, sarcastic, scathing, acrimonious, barbed, sharp, tart, incisive, bitter, venomous, waspish.
– OPPOSITES bland, mild.

punish v. **1** *they punished their children* **discipline**, bring someone to book, teach someone a lesson; tan someone's hide; *informal* murder, wallop, come down on (like a ton of bricks), have someone's guts for garters; *Brit. informal* give someone what for; *dated* chastise. **2** *higher charges would punish the poor* **penalize**, unfairly disadvantage, handicap, hurt, wrong, ill-use, maltreat. **3** *the strikers punished the defence's mistakes* **exploit**, take advantage of, turn to account, profit from, capitalize on, cash in on; *informal* walk all over.

punishable adj. **illegal**, unlawful, illegitimate, criminal, felonious, actionable, indictable, penal; blameworthy, dishonest, fraudulent, unauthorized, outlawed, banned, forbidden, prohibited, interdicted, proscribed.

punishing adj. *a punishing schedule* **arduous**, demanding, taxing, onerous, burdensome, strenuous, rigorous, stressful, trying; hard, difficult, tough, exhausting, tiring, gruelling, crippling, relentless; *informal* killing.
– OPPOSITES easy.

punishment n. **1** *the punishment of the guilty* **penalizing**, punishing, disciplining; retribution; *dated* chastisement. **2** *the teacher imposed punishments* **penalty**, penance, sanction, sentence, one's just deserts; discipline, correction, vengeance, justice, judgement; *informal* comeuppance. **3** *both boxers took punishment* **a battering**, a thrashing, a beating, a drubbing; *informal* a hiding. **4** *ovens take continual punishment* **maltreatment**, mistreatment, abuse, ill-use, manhandling; damage, harm.

> **WORD LINKS**
> **punitive, penal** relating to punishment
> **penology** the study of the punishment of crime
> **condign** referring to punishment that is fitting and deserved
> **impunity** freedom from punishment
> **reprieve** the cancellation of a punishment

punitive adj. **1** *punitive measures* **penal**, disciplinary, corrective, correctional, retributive. **2** *punitive taxes* **harsh**, severe, stiff, stringent, burdensome, demanding, crushing, crippling; high, sky-high, inflated, exorbitant, extortionate, excessive, inordinate, unreasonable; *Brit.* swingeing.

punter n. **1** *informal each punter has a 1 in 39 chance* **gambler**, backer, staker, speculator, bettor; informal plunger, high roller. **2** Brit. informal *sales bring the punters in* **customer**, client, patron; buyer, purchaser, shopper, consumer; (**punters**) clientele, audience, trade, business; Brit. informal bums on seats.

puny adj. **1** *he grew up puny* **undersized**, undernourished, underfed, stunted, slight, small, little; weak, feeble, sickly, delicate, frail, fragile; informal weedy, pint-sized. **2** *puny efforts to save their homes* **pitiful**, pitiable, inadequate, insufficient, derisory, miserable, sorry, meagre, paltry, trifling, inconsequential; informal pathetic, measly, piddling; formal exiguous.
– OPPOSITES sturdy, substantial.

pupil n. **1** *former pupils of the school* **student**, scholar; schoolchild, schoolboy, schoolgirl. **2** *the guru's pupils* **disciple**, follower, student, protégé, apprentice, trainee, novice.

puppet n. **1** *a show with puppets* **marionette**; glove puppet, hand puppet, finger puppet. **2** *a puppet of the government* **pawn**, tool, instrument, cat's paw, poodle, creature, dupe; mouthpiece, minion, stooge.

purchase v. *we purchased the software* **buy**, pay for, acquire, obtain, pick up, snap up, take, procure; invest in; informal get hold of, score.
– OPPOSITES sell.
▸ n. **1** *he's happy with his purchase* **acquisition**, investment, order, bargain; shopping, goods; informal buy. **2** *he could get no purchase on the wall* **grip**, grasp, hold, foothold, toehold, anchorage, attachment, support; resistance, friction, leverage.
– OPPOSITES sale.

purchaser n. **buyer**, shopper, customer, consumer, patron; Law vendee.

pure adj. **1** *pure gold* **unadulterated**, uncontaminated, unmixed, undiluted, unalloyed, unblended; sterling, solid, refined, 100%; clarified, clear, filtered; flawless, perfect, genuine, real. **2** *the air is so pure* **clean**, clear, fresh, sparkling, unpolluted, uncontaminated, untainted; wholesome, natural, healthy; sanitary, uninfected, disinfected, germ-free, sterile, sterilized, aseptic. **3** *pure in body and mind* **virtuous**, moral, ethical, good, righteous, saintly, honourable, reputable, wholesome, clean, honest, upright, upstanding, exemplary, irreproachable; chaste, virginal, maidenly; decent, worthy, noble, blameless, guiltless, spotless, unsullied, uncorrupted, undefiled, anti-corruption; informal squeaky clean. **4** *pure maths* **theoretical**, abstract, conceptual, academic, hypothetical, speculative, conjectural. **5** *three hours of pure magic* **sheer**, utter, absolute, out-and-out, complete, total, perfect, unmitigated.
– OPPOSITES adulterated, polluted, immoral, practical.

pure-bred adj. **pedigree**, thoroughbred, full-bred, blooded, pedigreed, pure.
– OPPOSITES hybrid, mongrel.

purely adv. **entirely**, completely, absolutely, wholly, exclusively, solely, only, just, merely.

purgative n. **laxative**, evacuant; Medicine aperient; old use lenitive; dated purge.

purgatory n. **torment**, torture, misery, suffering, affliction, anguish, agony, woe, hell; an ordeal, a nightmare.
– OPPOSITES paradise.

purge v. **1** *he purged them of their doubt* **cleanse**, clear, purify, wash, shrive, absolve; rare lustrate. **2** *lawbreakers were purged from the army* **remove**, get rid of, expel, eject, exclude, dismiss, sack, oust, eradicate, clear out, weed out.
▸ n. *the purge of dissidents* **removal**, expulsion, ejection, exclusion, eviction, dismissal, sacking, ousting, eradication.

purify v. **1** *trees help to purify the air* **clean**, cleanse, refine, decontaminate; filter, clarify, clear, freshen, deodorize; sanitize, disinfect, sterilize. **2** *they purify themselves before the ceremony* **purge**, cleanse, unburden, deliver; redeem, shrive, exorcize, sanctify; rare lustrate.

purist n. **pedant**, perfectionist, formalist, literalist, stickler, traditionalist, doctrinaire, quibbler, dogmatist; informal nitpicker; old use precisian.

puritan n. **moralist**, pietist, prude, prig, killjoy; ascetic; informal goody-goody, Holy Joe; N. Amer. informal bluenose.

puritanical adj. **moralistic**, puritan, pietistic, strait-laced, stuffy, prudish, prim, priggish; narrow-minded, sententious, censorious; austere, severe, ascetic, abstemious; informal goody-goody, starchy.
– OPPOSITES permissive.

purity n. **1** *the purity of our tap water* **cleanness**, clearness, clarity, freshness; sterility. **2** *they sought purity in a foul world* **virtue**, morality, goodness, righteousness, saintliness, piety, honour, honesty, integrity, decency, ethicality, impeccability; innocence, chastity.

purloin v. **steal**, thieve, rob, take, snatch, pilfer, loot, appropriate; informal swipe, nab, rip off, lift, 'liberate', 'borrow', filch, snaffle; Brit. informal pinch, half-inch, nick, whip, knock off, nobble; N. Amer. informal heist.

purport v. *this work purports to be authoritative* **claim**, profess, pretend; appear, seem; be ostensibly, pose as, impersonate, masquerade as, pass for.
▸ n. **1** *the purport of his remarks* **gist**, substance, drift, implication, intention, meaning, significance, sense, essence, thrust, message. **2** *the purport of the attack* **intention**, purpose, object, objective, aim, goal, target, end, design, idea.

purpose n. **1** *the purpose of his visit* **motive**, motivation, grounds, cause, occasion, reason, point, basis, justification. **2** *their purpose was to subvert the economy* **intention**, aim, object, objective, goal, end, plan, scheme, target; ambition, aspiration. **3** *I cannot see any purpose in it* **advantage**, benefit, good, use, value, merit, worth, profit; informal mileage, percentage. **4** *the original purpose of the porch* **function**, role, use. **5** *they started*

p

the game with purpose **determination**, resolution, resolve, steadfastness, backbone, drive, push, enthusiasm, ambition, motivation, commitment, conviction, dedication; informal get-up-and-go.

▶v. formal *they purposed to reach the summit* **intend**, mean, aim, plan, design, have the intention; decide, resolve, determine, propose, aspire, set one's sights on.
□ **on purpose** deliberately, intentionally, purposely, by design, wilfully, knowingly, consciously, of one's own volition; expressly, specifically, especially, specially.

purposeful adj. **determined**, resolute, steadfast, single-minded; enthusiastic, motivated, driven, committed, dedicated, persistent, dogged, unfaltering, unshakeable.
– OPPOSITES aimless.

purse n. **1** *the money fell out of her purse* **wallet**, money bag; N. Amer. change purse, billfold. **2** N. Amer. *a woman's purse*. See **handbag**. **3** *the public purse* **fund(s)**, kitty, coffers, pool, bank, treasury, exchequer; money, finances, wealth, reserves, cash, capital, assets. **4** *the fight will net him a $75,000 purse* **prize**, reward, award; winnings, stake(s).
▶v. *he pursed his lips* **press together**, compress, tighten, pucker, pout.

pursuance n. formal **1** *he was arrested in pursuance of section 7 of this Act* **execution**, discharge, implementation, performance, accomplishment, fulfilment, dispatch, prosecution, enforcement. **2** *their pursuance of power* **search for**, pursuit of, quest for, hunt for.

pursue v. **1** *I pursued him down the garden* **follow**, run after, chase; hunt, stalk, track, trail, shadow, hound, course; informal tail. **2** *pursue the goal of political union* **strive for**, work towards, seek, search for, aim at/ for, aspire to. **3** *he had been pursuing her for weeks* **woo**, pay court to, chase, run after; informal make up to; dated court, make love to, romance, set one's cap at. **4** *she pursued a political career* **engage in**, be occupied in, practise, follow, prosecute, conduct, ply, take up, undertake, carry on. **5** *we will not pursue the matter* **investigate**, research, inquire into, look into, examine, scrutinize, analyse, delve into, probe.
– OPPOSITES avoid, shun.

pursuit n. **1** *the pursuit of profit* **striving towards**, quest after/for, search for; aim, goal, objective, dream. **2** *a worthwhile pursuit* **activity**, hobby, pastime, diversion, recreation, relaxation, divertissement, amusement; occupation, trade, vocation, business, work, job, employment.

purvey v. **sell**, supply, provide, furnish, cater, retail, deal in, trade, stock, offer; peddle, hawk, tout, traffic in; informal flog.

purveyor n. **seller**, vendor, retailer, supplier, stockist, trader, pedlar, hawker; trademark in US e-tailer; Brit. tout; Brit. informal flogger.

pus n. **suppuration**, matter; discharge, secretion.

WORD LINKS
purulent containing pus
maturate, suppurate form pus
---

push v. **1** *she tried to push him away* **shove**, thrust, propel; send, drive, force, prod, poke, nudge, elbow, shoulder; sweep, bundle, hustle, manhandle. **2** *she pushed her way into the flat* **force**, shove, thrust, squeeze, jostle, elbow, shoulder, bundle, hustle; work, inch. **3** *he pushed the panic button* **press**, depress, bear down on, hold down, squeeze; operate, activate. **4** *don't push her to join in* **urge**, press, pressure, pressurize, force, impel, coerce, nag; prevail on, browbeat into; informal lean on, twist someone's arm, bulldoze. **5** *they push their own products* **advertise**, publicize, promote, bang the drum for; sell, market, merchandise; informal plug, hype (up), puff, flog; N. Amer. informal ballyhoo.
– OPPOSITES pull.
▶n. **1** *I felt a push in the back* **shove**, thrust, nudge, ram, bump, jolt, butt, prod, poke. **2** *the enemy's eastward push* **advance**, drive, thrust, charge, attack, assault, onslaught, onrush, offensive, sortie, sally, incursion.
□ **at a push** Brit. informal if necessary, if need be, if needs must, if all else fails, in an emergency.

push someone around bully, domineer, ride roughshod over, trample on, bulldoze, browbeat, tyrannize, intimidate, threaten, victimize, pick on; informal lean on, boss about/around.

push for demand, call for, request, press for, campaign for, lobby for, speak up for; urge, promote, advocate, champion, espouse.

push off informal go away, depart, leave, get out; go, get moving, be off (with you), shoo; informal skedaddle, split, scram, run along, beat it, get lost, shove off, buzz off, clear off, on your bike; Brit. informal get stuffed, sling your hook, hop it, bog off, naff off; N. Amer. informal bug off, take a powder, take a hike; Austral./NZ informal rack off, nick off; literary begone.

push on press on, continue one's journey, carry on, advance, proceed, go on, progress, make headway, forge ahead.

pushover n. **1** *the teacher was a pushover* **weakling**, feeble opponent, man of straw; informal soft touch, easy touch, easy meat. **2** *this course is no pushover* **easy task**, walkover, five-finger exercise, gift; child's play; informal doddle, piece of cake, picnic, money for old rope, cinch, breeze, walk in the park; Brit. informal doss; N. Amer. informal duck soup, snap; Austral./NZ informal bludge; dated snip.

pushy adj. **assertive**, self-assertive, overbearing, domineering, aggressive, forceful, forward, bold, bumptious, officious; thrusting, ambitious, driven, overconfident, cocky; informal bossy; dated pushful.
– OPPOSITES submissive.

pusillanimous adj. **timid**, timorous, cowardly, fearful, faint-hearted, lily-livered,

spineless, craven, shrinking; informal chicken, gutless, wimpy, wimpish, sissy, yellow, yellow-bellied.
– OPPOSITES brave.

pussyfoot v. **1** *you can't pussyfoot around with this* **equivocate**, tergiversate, be evasive, be non-committal, sidestep the issue, prevaricate, quibble, hedge, beat about the bush; Brit. hum and haw; informal duck the question, sit on the fence, shilly-shally. **2** *I had to pussyfoot over the gravel* **creep**, tiptoe, pad, soft-shoe, steal, sneak, slink.

pustule n. **pimple**, spot, bleb, boil, swelling, eruption, carbuncle, blister, abscess; informal whitehead, zit; Scottish informal plook; technical comedo, papule.

put v. **1** *she put the parcel on a chair* **place**, set (down), lay (down), deposit, position, settle; leave, plant; informal stick, dump, bung, park, plonk, pop; N. Amer. informal plunk. **2** *he didn't want to be put in a category* **assign to**, consign to, allocate to, place in. **3** *don't put the blame on me* **lay**, pin, place, fix; attribute to, impute to, assign to, allocate to, ascribe to. **4** *the proposals put to the committee* **submit**, present, tender, offer, proffer, advance, suggest, propose. **5** *she put it bluntly* **express**, word, phrase, frame, formulate, render, convey, couch; state, say, utter. **6** *he put the cost at £8,000* **estimate**, calculate, reckon, gauge, assess, evaluate, value, judge, measure, compute, fix, set; informal guesstimate.
☐ **put something about** *the rumour had been put about* **spread**, circulate, make public, disseminate, broadcast, publicize, pass on, propagate, bandy about.
put something across/over communicate, convey, get across/over, explain, make clear, spell out, clarify; get through to someone.
put something aside 1 *we've got a bit put aside in the bank* **save**, put by, set aside, deposit, reserve, store, stockpile, hoard, stow, cache; informal salt away, squirrel away, stash away. **2** *they put aside their differences* **disregard**, set aside, ignore, forget, discount, bury.
put someone away informal *they put him away for life* **jail**, imprison, put in prison, put behind bars, lock up, incarcerate; informal cage; Brit. informal bang up, send down; N. Amer. informal jug.
put something away 1 *she never puts her things away* **replace**, put back, tidy away, tidy up, clear away. **2** informal *she can put away a lot of food.* See **eat** (sense 1).
put someone down 1 informal *he often puts me down* **criticize**, belittle, disparage, deprecate, denigrate, slight, humiliate, shame, crush, squash, deflate; informal show up, cut down to size. **2** *I put him down as shy* **consider to be**, judge to be, reckon to be, take to be; regard, have down, take for.
put something down 1 *he put his ideas down on paper* **write down**, note down, jot down, take down, set down; list, record, register, log. **2** *they put down the rebellion* **suppress**, check, crush, quash, squash, quell,

overthrow, stamp out, repress, subdue. **3** *the horse had to be put down* **destroy**, put to sleep, put out of its misery, put to death, kill. **4** *put it down to the heat* **attribute**, ascribe, chalk up, impute; blame on.
put something forward See **put** (sense 4).
put in for apply for, put in an application for, try for; request, seek, ask for.
put someone off deter, discourage, dissuade, daunt, unnerve, intimidate, scare off, repel, repulse; distract, disturb, divert, sidetrack; informal turn off.
put something off postpone, defer, delay, put back, adjourn, hold over, reschedule, shelve, table; informal put on ice, put on the back burner.
put it on pretend, play-act, make believe, fake it, go through the motions.
put something on 1 *she put on jeans* **dress in**, don, pull on, throw on, slip into, change into; informal doll oneself up in. **2** *I put the light on* **switch on**, turn on, activate. **3** *they put on an extra train* **provide**, lay on, supply, make available. **4** *the museum put on an exhibition* **organize**, stage, mount, present, produce. **5** *she put on an American accent* **feign**, fake, simulate, affect, assume. **6** *he put a fiver on Oxford United* **bet**, gamble, stake, wager; place, lay; risk, chance, hazard.
put someone out 1 *Maria was put out by the slur* **annoy**, anger, irritate, offend, affront, displease, irk, vex, pique, nettle, gall, upset; informal rile, miff, peeve; Brit. informal nark. **2** *I don't want to put you out* **inconvenience**, trouble, bother, impose on, disoblige; formal discommode.
put something out 1 *firemen put out the blaze* **extinguish**, quench, douse, smother; blow out, snuff out. **2** *he put out a press release* **issue**, publish, release, bring out, circulate, publicize, post.
put someone up 1 *we can put him up for a few days* **accommodate**, house, take in, lodge, quarter, billet; give someone a roof over their head. **2** *they put up a candidate* **nominate**, propose, put forward, recommend.
put something up 1 *the building was put up 100 years ago* **build**, construct, erect, raise. **2** *she put up a poster* **display**, pin up, stick up, hang up, post. **3** *we put up alternative schemes* **propose**, put forward, present, submit, suggest, tender. **4** *the chancellor put up taxes* **increase**, raise; informal jack up, hike, bump up. **5** *he put up most of the funding* **provide**, supply, furnish, give, contribute, donate, pledge, pay; informal fork out, cough up, shell out; N. Amer. informal ante up, pony up.
put upon informal take advantage of, impose on, exploit, use, misuse; informal walk all over.
put someone up to something informal persuade to, encourage to, urge to, egg on to, incite to, goad into.
put up with tolerate, take, stand (for), accept, stomach, swallow, endure, bear, support, take something lying down; informal abide, lump it; Brit. informal stick, be doing with; formal brook; old use suffer.

putative adj. **supposed**, assumed, presumed; accepted, recognized; commonly regarded, presumptive, alleged, reputed, reported, rumoured.

putrefy v. **decay**, rot, decompose, go bad, go off, spoil, fester, perish, deteriorate; moulder.

putrid adj. **decomposing**, decaying, rotting, rotten, bad, off, putrefied, putrescent, rancid, mouldy; foul, fetid, rank.

puzzle v. **1** *her decision puzzled me* **perplex**, confuse, bewilder, bemuse, baffle, mystify, confound, nonplus; informal flummox, faze, stump, beat; N. Amer. informal discombobulate. **2** *she puzzled over the problem* **think hard about**, mull over, muse over, ponder, contemplate, meditate on, consider, deliberate on, chew over, wonder about. **3** *she tried to puzzle out what he meant* **work out**, understand, comprehend, sort out, reason out, solve, make sense of, make head or tail of, unravel, decipher; informal figure out, suss out.
▸ n. *the poem has always been a puzzle* **enigma**, mystery, paradox, conundrum, poser, riddle, problem; informal stumper.

puzzled adj. **perplexed**, confused, bewildered, bemused, baffled, mystified, confounded, nonplussed, at a loss, at sea; informal flummoxed, stumped, fazed, clueless; N. Amer. informal discombobulated.

puzzling adj. **baffling**, perplexing, bewildering, confusing, complicated, unclear, mysterious, enigmatic, ambiguous, obscure, abstruse, unfathomable, incomprehensible, impenetrable, cryptic.
– OPPOSITES clear.

pyromaniac n. **arsonist**, incendiary; Brit. fire-raiser; informal firebug, pyro; N. Amer. informal torch.

p

Qq

quack n. **1** *a quack selling fake medicines* **swindler**, charlatan, mountebank, trickster, fraud, fraudster, impostor, hoaxer, sharper; informal con man, shark; Brit. informal twister; N. Amer. informal grifter; Austral. informal shicer. **2** Brit. informal *get the quack to examine you.* See **doctor** (noun).

quadrangle n. **courtyard**, quad, court, cloister, precinct; square, plaza, piazza.

quaff v. **drink**, swallow, gulp (down), guzzle, slurp, down, drain, empty; imbibe, partake of, consume, sup, sip; informal sink, kill, glug, swig, swill, slug, knock back, toss off; Brit. informal get outside (of), shift, murder, neck; N. Amer. informal chug, snarf (down).

quagmire n. **1** *the field became a quagmire* **swamp**, morass, bog, marsh, mire, slough; old use quag. **2** *a judicial quagmire* **muddle**, mix-up, mess, predicament, mare's nest, quandary, tangle, imbroglio; trouble, confusion, difficulty; informal sticky situation, pickle, stew, dilemma, fix, bind.

quail v. **cower**, cringe, flinch, shrink, recoil, shy (away), pull back; shiver, tremble, shake, quake, blench, blanch.

quaint adj. **1** *a quaint town* **picturesque**, charming, sweet, attractive, old-fashioned, old-world; Brit. twee; N. Amer. cunning; mock old use olde (worlde). **2** *quaint customs* **unusual**, different, out of the ordinary, curious, eccentric, quirky, bizarre, whimsical, unconventional; informal offbeat.
– OPPOSITES ugly, ordinary.

quake v. **1** *the ground quaked* **shake**, tremble, quiver, shudder, sway, rock, wobble, move, heave, convulse. **2** *we quaked when we saw the soldiers* **tremble**, shake, quiver, shiver; blench, blanch, flinch, shrink, recoil, cower, cringe.

qualification n. **1** *a teaching qualification* **certificate**, diploma, degree, licence, document, warrant; eligibility, acceptability, adequacy; proficiency, skill, ability, capability, aptitude. **2** *I can't accept it without qualification* **modification**, limitation, reservation, stipulation; alteration, amendment, revision, moderation, mitigation; condition, proviso, caveat.

qualified adj. **certified**, certificated, chartered, licensed, professional; trained, fit, competent, accomplished, proficient, skilled, experienced, expert.

qualify v. **1** *I qualify for free travel* **be eligible**, meet the requirements; be entitled to, be permitted. **2** *they qualify as refugees* **count**, be considered, be designated, be eligible. **3** *she qualified as a solicitor* **be certified**, be licensed; pass, graduate, make the grade, succeed, pass muster. **4** *the course qualified them to teach* **authorize**, empower, allow, permit, license; equip, prepare, train, educate, teach. **5** *they qualified their findings* **modify**, limit, restrict, make conditional; moderate, temper, modulate, mitigate.

quality n. **1** *a poor quality of signal* **standard**, grade, class, calibre, condition, character, nature, form, rank, value, level; sort, type, kind, variety. **2** *work of such quality* **excellence**, superiority, merit, worth, value, virtue, calibre, eminence, distinction, incomparability; talent, skill, virtuosity, craftsmanship. **3** *her good qualities* **feature**, trait, attribute, characteristic, point, aspect, facet, side, property.

qualm n. **misgiving**, doubt, reservation, second thought, worry, concern, anxiety; (**qualms**) hesitation, hesitance, hesitancy, demur, reluctance, disinclination, apprehension, trepidation, unease; scruples, remorse, compunction.

quandary n. **predicament**, plight, difficult situation, awkward situation; trouble, muddle, mess, confusion, difficulty, mare's nest; informal dilemma, sticky situation, pickle, hole, stew, fix, bind, jam.

quantity n. **1** *the quantity of food collected* **amount**, total, aggregate, sum, quota, mass, weight, volume, bulk; quantum, proportion, portion, part. **2** *a quantity of ammunition* **amount**, lot, great deal, good deal, an abundance, a wealth, a profusion, plenty; informal piles, oodles, tons, lots, loads, heaps, masses, stacks, bags; Brit. informal shedloads.

quarrel n. *they had a quarrel about money* **argument**, disagreement, squabble, fight, dispute, wrangle, clash, altercation, feud, contretemps, disputation, falling-out, war of words, shouting match; informal tiff, slanging match, run-in; Brit. informal barney, row, bust-up.
▸ v. *don't quarrel over it* **argue**, fight, disagree, fall out; differ, be at odds; bicker, squabble, cross swords, lock horns, be at each other's throats; informal argufy; Brit. informal row; Brit. informal, Football afters.
◻ **quarrel with** *you can't quarrel with the verdict* **fault**, criticize, object to, oppose, take

q

exception to; attack, take issue with, impugn, contradict, dispute, controvert; informal knock; formal gainsay.

quarrelsome adj. **argumentative**, disputatious, confrontational, captious, pugnacious, combative, antagonistic, bellicose, belligerent, cantankerous, choleric; Brit. informal stroppy; N. Amer. informal scrappy.
– OPPOSITES peaceable.

quarry n. **prey**, victim; object, goal, target; kill, game.

quarter n. **1** *the Latin quarter* **district**, area, region, part, side, neighbourhood, precinct, locality, sector, zone; ghetto, community, enclave. **2** *help from an unexpected quarter* **source**, direction, place, location; person. **3** *the servants' quarters* **accommodation**, lodgings, rooms, chambers; home; informal pad, digs; formal abode, residence, domicile. **4** *the riot squads gave no quarter* **mercy**, leniency, clemency, lenity, compassion, pity, charity, sympathy, tolerance.
▸v. **1** *they were quartered in a villa* **accommodate**, house, board, lodge, put up, take in, install, shelter; Military billet. **2** *I quartered the streets* **patrol**, range over, tour, reconnoitre, traverse, survey, scout; Brit. informal recce.

quash v. **1** *he may quash the sentence* **cancel**, reverse, rescind, repeal, revoke, retract, countermand, withdraw, overturn, overrule, veto, annul, nullify, invalidate, negate, void; Law vacate; formal abrogate. **2** *we want to quash these rumours* **put an end to**, put a stop to, stamp out, crush, put down, check, curb, nip in the bud, squash, quell, subdue, suppress, extinguish, stifle; informal squelch, put the kibosh on.
– OPPOSITES validate.

quasi- comb. form **1** *quasi-scientific* **supposedly**, seemingly, apparently, allegedly, ostensibly, on the face of it, on the surface, to all intents and purposes, outwardly, superficially, purportedly, nominally; pseudo-. **2** *a quasi-autonomous organization* **partly**, partially, part, to a certain extent, to some extent, half, relatively, comparatively, (up) to a point; almost, nearly, just about, all but.

quaver v. **tremble**, waver, quiver, shake, vibrate, oscillate, fluctuate, falter, warble.

quay n. **wharf**, pier, jetty, landing stage, berth; marina, dock, harbour.

queasy adj. **nauseous**, nauseated, bilious, sick; ill, unwell, poorly, green about the gills; Brit. off colour.

queen n. **1** *the Queen was crowned* **monarch**, sovereign, ruler, head of state; Her Majesty; king's consort, queen consort. **2** informal *the queen of soul music* **doyenne**, star, superstar, leading light, big name, queen bee, prima donna, idol, heroine, favourite, darling, goddess.

queer adj. **1** *it seemed queer to see him here* **odd**, strange, unusual, funny, peculiar, curious, bizarre, weird, uncanny, freakish,

eerie, unnatural; unconventional, unorthodox, unexpected, unfamiliar, abnormal, anomalous, atypical, untypical, out of the ordinary, incongruous, irregular; puzzling, perplexing, baffling, unaccountable; informal fishy, creepy, spooky, freaky; Brit. informal rum. **2** Brit. informal dated *the pills made her feel queer*. See **ill** (sense 1 of the adjective).
– OPPOSITES normal, well.
▸v. *he queered the whole deal* **spoil**, ruin, wreck, destroy, scotch, disrupt, undo, thwart, foil, blight, cripple, jeopardize, threaten, undermine, compromise; informal botch, blow, put the kibosh on; Brit. informal scupper.

quell v. **1** *troops quelled the unrest* **put an end to**, put a stop to, end, crush, put down, check, crack down on, curb, nip in the bud, squash, quash, subdue, suppress, overcome; informal squelch. **2** *he quelled his misgivings* **calm**, soothe, pacify, settle, quieten, quiet, silence, allay, assuage, mitigate, moderate; literary stay.

quench v. **1** *they quenched their thirst* **satisfy**, slake, sate, satiate, gratify, relieve, assuage, take the edge off, indulge; lessen, reduce, diminish, check, suppress, extinguish, overcome. **2** *the flames were quenched* **extinguish**, put out, snuff out, smother, douse.

querulous adj. **petulant**, peevish, pettish, complaining, fractious, fretful, irritable, testy, tetchy, cross, snappish, crabby, crotchety, cantankerous, miserable, moody, grumpy, bad-tempered, sullen, sulky, sour, churlish; informal snappy, grouchy, whingy; Brit. informal ratty, cranky; N. English informal mardy; N. Amer. informal soreheaded.

query n. **1** *we are happy to answer any queries* **question**, enquiry; Brit. informal quiz. **2** *there was a query as to who owned the hotel* **doubt**, uncertainty, question (mark), reservation; scepticism.
▸v. **1** *'Why do that?' queried Isobel* **ask**, enquire, question; Brit. informal quiz. **2** *folk may query his credentials* **question**, call into question, challenge, dispute, cast aspersions on, doubt, have suspicions about, have reservations about.

quest n. **1** *their quest for her killer* **search**, hunt; pursuance of. **2** *Sir Galahad's quest* **expedition**, journey, voyage, trek, travels, odyssey, adventure, exploration, search; crusade, mission, pilgrimage.
□ **in quest of** in search of, in pursuit of, seeking, looking for, on the lookout for, after.

question n. **1** *please answer my question* **enquiry**, query; interrogation; Brit. informal quiz. **2** *there is no question that he is ill* **doubt**, dispute, argument, debate, uncertainty, dubiousness, reservation; formal dubiety. **3** *the political questions of the day* **issue**, matter, business, problem, concern, topic, theme, case; debate, argument, dispute, controversy.
– OPPOSITES answer, certainty.
▸v. **1** *the magistrate questions the suspect*

interrogate, cross-examine, cross-question, quiz, catechize; interview, debrief, examine, give the third degree to; informal grill, pump. **2** *she questioned his motives* **query**, call into question, challenge, dispute, cast aspersions on, doubt, suspect, have suspicions about, have reservations about.

□ **beyond question 1** *her loyalty is beyond question* **undoubted**, beyond doubt, certain, indubitable, indisputable, incontrovertible, unquestionable, undeniable, clear, patent, manifest. **2** *the results demonstrated this beyond question* **indisputably**, irrefutably, incontestably, incontrovertibly, unquestionably, undeniably, undoubtedly, beyond doubt, without doubt, clearly, patently, obviously. **in question** at issue, under discussion, under consideration, on the agenda, to be decided.
out of the question impossible, impracticable, unfeasible, unworkable, inconceivable, unimaginable, unrealizable, unsuitable; informal not on.

> **WORD LINKS**
> **interrogative** relating to questions
> **catechism** questions and answers used for teaching the principles of Christianity
> **rhetorical** referring to a question asked for effect rather than to obtain an answer

questionable adj. **1** *jokes of questionable taste* **doubtful**, dubious, uncertain, debatable, controversial, contentious, arguable; unverified, unprovable, unresolved, unconvincing, implausible, improbable; borderline, marginal, moot; informal iffy; Brit. informal dodgy. **2** *questionable financial dealings* **suspicious**, suspect, dubious, irregular, odd, strange, murky, dark, unsavoury, disreputable; informal funny, fishy, shady, iffy; Brit. informal dodgy.
– OPPOSITES indisputable, honest.

questionnaire n. **question sheet**, survey form, opinion poll; test, exam, examination, quiz; Medicine questionary.

queue n. **1** *a queue of people* **line**, row, column, file, chain, string; procession, train, cavalcade; waiting list; N. Amer. wait list; Brit. informal crocodile. **2** *a traffic queue* **(traffic) jam**, tailback, gridlock; N. Amer. back-up; informal snarl-up.
▶ v. *we queued for ice creams* **line up**, form a queue, queue up, wait in line, form a line, fall in.

quibble n. *I have just one quibble* **criticism**, objection, complaint, protest, argument, exception, grumble, grouse, cavil; informal niggle, moan, gripe, beef, grouch.
▶ v. *no one quibbled with the title* **object to**, find fault with, complain about, cavil at; split hairs, chop logic; criticize, query, fault, pick holes in; informal nitpick; old use pettifog.

quick adj. **1** *a quick worker* **fast**, swift, rapid, speedy, high-speed, expeditious, brisk, smart; lightning, whirlwind, fast-track, breakneck, whistle-stop; informal nippy, zippy; literary fleet. **2** *she took a quick look* **hasty**,

hurried, cursory, perfunctory, desultory, superficial, summary; brief, short, fleeting, transient, transitory, short-lived, lightning, momentary. **3** *a quick end to the recession* **sudden**, instantaneous, immediate, instant, abrupt, precipitate. **4** *she isn't as quick as the others* **intelligent**, bright, clever, gifted, able, astute, quick-witted, sharp-witted, smart; observant, alert, sharp, perceptive; informal brainy, on the ball, quick on the uptake.
– OPPOSITES slow, long.

quicken v. **1** *she quickened her pace* **speed up**, accelerate, step up, hasten, hurry (up); informal gee up. **2** *the film quickened his interest in nature* **stimulate**, excite, arouse, rouse, stir up, activate, galvanize, whet, inspire, kindle; invigorate, revive, revitalize.

quickly adv. **1** *he walked quickly* **fast**, swiftly, briskly, rapidly, speedily, at the speed of light, at full tilt, at full pelt, as fast as one's legs can carry one, at a gallop, at the double, post-haste, hotfoot; informal double quick, p.d.q. (pretty damn quick), like (greased) lightning, hell for leather, like mad, like blazes, like the wind; Brit. informal like the clappers, like billy-o; N. Amer. informal lickety-split; literary apace. **2** *you'd better leave quickly* **immediately**, directly, at once, now, straight away, right away, instantly, forthwith, without delay, without further ado; soon, promptly, early; N. Amer. momentarily; informal like a shot, ASAP (as soon as possible), pronto, before you can say Jack Robinson, straight off. **3** *he quickly inspected it* **briefly**, fleetingly, briskly; hastily, hurriedly, cursorily, perfunctorily, superficially, desultorily.

quick-tempered adj. **irritable**, irascible, hot-tempered, short-tempered, snappish, fiery, touchy, volatile; cross, crabby, crotchety, cantankerous, grumpy, ill-tempered, bad-tempered, testy, tetchy, prickly, choleric; informal snappy, chippy, grouchy, cranky, on a short fuse; Brit. informal narky, ratty, eggy, like a bear with a sore head; N. Amer. informal soreheaded.
– OPPOSITES placid.

quick-witted adj. **intelligent**, bright, clever, gifted, able, astute, quick, smart, sharp-witted; observant, alert, sharp, perceptive; informal brainy, on the ball, quick on the uptake.
– OPPOSITES slow.

quid pro quo n. **exchange**, trade, trade-off, swap, switch, barter, substitute; reciprocation, return; amends, compensation, recompense, restitution, reparation.

quiescent adj. **inactive**, inert, idle, dormant, at rest, resting, inoperative, deactivated, quiet; still, motionless, immobile, passive.
– OPPOSITES active.

quiet adj. **1** *the whole pub went quiet* **silent**, still, hushed, noiseless, soundless; mute, dumb, speechless. **2** *a quiet voice* **soft**, low, muted, muffled, faint, indistinct, inaudible,

q

hushed, whispered, suppressed. **3** *a quiet village* **peaceful**, sleepy, tranquil, calm, still, restful, undisturbed, untroubled; unfrequented. **4** *can I have a quiet word?* **private**, confidential, secret, discreet, unofficial, off the record, between ourselves. **5** *quiet colours* **unobtrusive**, restrained, muted, understated, subdued, subtle, low-key; soft, pale, pastel. **6** *you can't keep it quiet for long* **secret**, confidential, classified, unrevealed, undisclosed, unknown, under wraps; informal hush-hush, mum; formal sub rosa. **7** *business is quiet* **slow**, stagnant, slack, sluggish, inactive, idle.
– OPPOSITES loud, busy, public.
▶ n. *the quiet of the countryside* **peacefulness**, peace, restfulness, calm, tranquillity, serenity; silence, quietness, stillness, still, quietude, hush, soundlessness.

quieten v. **1** *quieten the children down* **silence**, hush, shush, quiet; informal shut up. **2** *her companions quietened* **fall silent**, stop talking, break off, shush, hold one's tongue; informal shut up, clam up, shut it, pipe down, shut one's mouth, put a sock in it, button it. **3** *he tried to quieten manic patients* **pacify**, calm (down), soothe, subdue, tranquillize, relax, comfort, compose.

quietly adv. **1** *she quietly entered the room* **silently**, in silence, noiselessly, soundlessly, inaudibly; mutely, dumbly. **2** *he spoke quietly* **softly**, in a low voice, in a whisper, in a murmur, under one's breath, in an undertone, sotto voce, gently, faintly, weakly, feebly. **3** *some bonds were sold quietly* **discreetly**, privately, confidentially, secretly, unofficially, off the record. **4** *she is quietly confident* **calmly**, patiently, placidly, serenely.

quilt n. **duvet**, cover(s); Brit. eiderdown; N. Amer. comforter, puff; Austral. trademark Doona.

quintessence n. **1** *it's the quintessence of the modern home* **perfect example**, exemplar, prototype, stereotype, picture, epitome, embodiment, ideal; best, pick, prime, acme, crème de la crème. **2** *the quintessence of intelligence* **essence**, soul, spirit, nature, core, heart, crux, kernel, marrow, substance; informal nitty-gritty; Philosophy quiddity, esse.

quintessential adj. **typical**, prototypical, stereotypical, archetypal, classic, model, standard, stock, representative, conventional; ideal, consummate, exemplary, best, ultimate.

quip n. *the quip provoked a smile* **joke**, witty remark, witticism, jest, pun, sally, pleasantry, bon mot; informal one-liner, gag, crack, wisecrack, funny.
▶ v. *'Enjoy your trip?' he quipped* **joke**, jest, pun, sally; informal gag, wisecrack.

quirk n. **1** *they all know his quirks* **idiosyncrasy**, peculiarity, oddity, eccentricity, foible, whim, vagary, caprice, fancy, crotchet, habit, characteristic, trait, fad; informal hang-up. **2** *a quirk of fate* **chance**, fluke, freak, anomaly, twist.

quirky adj. **eccentric**, idiosyncratic, unconventional, unorthodox, unusual, off-centre, strange, bizarre, peculiar, odd, outlandish, zany; informal wacky, freaky, kinky, way-out, far out, kooky, offbeat.
– OPPOSITES conventional.

quisling n. **collaborator**, fraternizer, colluder, sympathizer; traitor, turncoat, back-stabber, double-crosser, defector, Judas, snake in the grass, fifth columnist.

quit v. **1** *he quit the office at 12.30* **leave**, vacate, exit, depart from, withdraw from; abandon, desert. **2** informal *he's decided to quit his job* **resign from**, leave, give up, hand in one's notice, stand down from, relinquish, vacate, walk out on, retire from; informal chuck, pack in. **3** informal *quit living in the past* **give up**, stop, cease, discontinue, drop, break off, abandon, abstain from, desist from, refrain from, avoid, forgo; informal pack (it) in, leave off.

quite adv. **1** *two quite different types* **completely**, entirely, totally, wholly, absolutely, utterly, thoroughly, altogether. **2** *red hair was quite common* **fairly**, rather, somewhat, slightly, relatively, comparatively, moderately, reasonably, to a certain extent; informal pretty, kind of, sort of.

quiver v. **1** *I quivered with terror* **tremble**, shake, shiver, quaver, quake, shudder. **2** *the bird quivers its wings* **flutter**, flap, beat, agitate, vibrate.
▶ n. *a quiver in her voice* **tremor**, tremble, shake, quaver, flutter, fluctuation, waver.

quixotic adj. **idealistic**, romantic, visionary, Utopian, extravagant, starry-eyed, unrealistic, unworldly; impracticable, unworkable, impossible.

quiz n. **1** *a music quiz* **competition**, test. **2** informal *jockey faces quiz over bribes* **interrogation**, questioning, interview, examination, the third degree; informal grilling.
▶ v. *a man was being quizzed by police* **question**, interrogate, cross-examine, cross-question, interview, sound out, give someone the third degree; informal grill, pump.

quizzical adj. **enquiring**, questioning, curious; puzzled, perplexed, baffled, mystified; amused, mocking, teasing.

quota n. **allocation**, share, allowance, limit, ration, portion, dispensation, slice (of the cake); percentage, commission; proportion, fraction, bit, amount, quantity; informal cut, rake-off; Brit. informal whack.

quotation n. **1** *a quotation from Dryden* **citation**, quote, excerpt, extract, passage, line, paragraph, verse, phrase; reference, allusion; N. Amer. cite. **2** *a quotation for the building work* **estimate**, quote, price, tender, bid, costing, charge, figure.

quote v. **1** *he quoted a sentence from the book* **recite**, repeat, reproduce, retell, echo, iterate; take, extract. **2** *she quoted one case in which a girl died* **cite**, mention, refer to, name, instance, specify, identify; relate, recount; allude to, point out, present, offer, advance.

q

▶ n. **1** *a Shakespeare quote.* See **quotation** (sense 1). **2** *ask the contractor for a quote.* See **quotation** (sense 2).

quotidian adj. **1** *the quotidian routine* **daily**, everyday, day-to-day, diurnal. **2** *her dreadfully quotidian car* **ordinary**, average, run-of-the-mill, everyday, standard, typical, middle-of-the-road, common, conventional, mainstream, unremarkable, unexceptional, workaday, commonplace, mundane, uninteresting; informal bog-standard, nothing to write home about, a dime a dozen; Brit. informal common or garden.
– OPPOSITES unusual.

Rr

rabbit n. buck, doe; Brit. coney; informal bunny.

> **WORD LINKS**
> **myxomatosis** an infectious and usually fatal
> disease of rabbits
> **scut** a rabbit's short tail
> **warren** a network of rabbit burrows

rabble n. **1** *a rabble of noisy youths* **mob**, crowd, throng, gang, swarm, horde, pack, mass, group. **2** *rule by the rabble* **the common people**, the masses, the populace, the multitude, the rank and file, the commonality, the commonalty, the plebeians, the proletariat, the peasantry, the hoi polloi, the lower classes, the riff-raff; informal the proles, the plebs.
– OPPOSITES nobility.

rabble-rouser n. **agitator**, troublemaker, instigator, firebrand, revolutionary, demagogue.

rabid adj. **1** *a rabid dog* rabies-infected, mad. **2** *a rabid anti-royalist* **extreme**, fanatical, overzealous, extremist, maniacal, passionate, fervent, diehard, uncompromising, illiberal; informal gung-ho.
– OPPOSITES moderate.

race[1] n. **1** *Dave won the race* **contest**, competition, event, fixture, heat, trial(s). **2** *the race for naval domination* **competition**, rivalry, contention; quest. **3** *the mill race* **channel**, waterway, conduit, sluice, spillway.
▶ v. **1** *he will race in the final* **compete**, contend; run. **2** *Claire raced after him* **hurry**, dash, rush, run, sprint, bolt, dart, gallop, career, charge, shoot, hurtle, hare, fly, speed, scurry; informal tear, belt, pelt, scoot, hotfoot it, leg it; Brit. informal bomb; N. Amer. informal hightail it. **3** *her heart was racing* **pound**, beat rapidly, throb, pulsate, thud, thump, hammer, palpitate, flutter, pitter-patter, quiver, pump.

race[2] n. **1** *pupils of many different races* **ethnic group**, racial type, (ethnic) origin. **2** *a bloodthirsty race* **people**, nation.

racial adj. **ethnic**, ethnological, race-related; cultural, national, tribal.

racism n. **racial discrimination**, racialism, racial prejudice, xenophobia, chauvinism, bigotry; anti-Semitism.

racist n. *he was exposed as a racist* **racial bigot**, racialist, xenophobe, chauvinist; anti-Semite.
▶ adj. *a racist society* **(racially) discriminatory**, racialist, prejudiced, bigoted; anti-Semitic.

rack n. *put the cake on a wire rack* **frame**, framework, stand, holder, trestle, support, shelf.
▶ v. *she was racked with guilt* **torment**, afflict, torture, agonize, harrow; plague, bedevil, persecute, trouble, worry.
□ **on the rack** under pressure, under stress, under a strain, in distress; in trouble, in difficulties, having problems.
rack one's brains think hard, concentrate, cudgel one's brains; informal scratch one's head.

racket n. **1** *the engine makes such a racket* **noise**, din, hubbub, clamour, uproar, tumult, commotion, rumpus, pandemonium, babel; informal hullabaloo; Brit. informal row. **2** informal *a gold-smuggling racket* **illegal scheme**, fraud, swindle; informal rip-off; N. Amer. informal shakedown.

raconteur n. **storyteller**, narrator, anecdotalist; Austral. informal magsman.

racy adj. **risqué**, suggestive, naughty, sexy, spicy, ribald; indecorous, indecent, immodest, off colour, dirty, rude, smutty, crude, salacious; N. Amer. gamy; informal raunchy, blue; Brit. informal saucy; euphemistic adult.
– OPPOSITES prim.

raddled adj. **haggard**, gaunt, drawn, tired, fatigued, drained, exhausted, worn out, washed out; unwell, unhealthy; informal the worse for wear.

radiance n. **1** *the radiance of the sun* **light**, brightness, brilliance, luminosity, beams, rays, illumination, blaze, glow, gleam, lustre, glare; luminescence, incandescence. **2** *her face flooded with radiance* **joy**, elation, jubilance, ecstasy, rapture, euphoria, delirium, happiness, delight, pleasure.

radiant adj. **1** *the radiant moon* **shining**, bright, illuminated, brilliant, gleaming, glowing, ablaze, luminous, luminescent, lustrous, incandescent, dazzling, shimmering; old use splendent. **2** *she looked radiant* **joyful**, elated, thrilled, overjoyed, jubilant, rapturous, ecstatic, euphoric, in seventh heaven, on cloud nine, delighted, very happy; informal on top of the world, over the moon; Austral. informal wrapped.
– OPPOSITES dark, gloomy.

radiate v. **1** *the stars radiate energy* **emit**, give off, give out, discharge, diffuse; shed, cast. **2** *light radiated from the hall* **shine**, beam, emanate. **3** *their faces radiate hope* **display**, show, exhibit; emanate, breathe, be a picture of. **4** *four spokes radiate from the hub* **fan out**, spread out, branch out/off, extend, issue.

radical adj. **1** *radical reform* **thoroughgoing**, thorough, complete, total, comprehensive, exhaustive, sweeping, far-reaching, wide-ranging, extensive, profound, major, stringent, rigorous. **2** *radical differences between the two theories* **fundamental**, basic, essential, quintessential; structural, deep-seated, intrinsic, organic, constitutive. **3** *a radical political movement* **revolutionary**, progressive, reformist, revisionist, progressivist; extreme, extremist, fanatical, militant, diehard.
– OPPOSITES superficial, minor, conservative.
▸ n. *the arrested man was a radical* **revolutionary**, progressive, reformer, revisionist; militant, zealot, extremist, fanatic, diehard; informal ultra.
– OPPOSITES conservative.

raffish adj. **rakish**, unconventional, bohemian; devil-may-care, casual, careless; louche, disreputable, dissolute, decadent.

raffle n. **lottery**, (prize) draw, sweepstake, sweep, tombola; N. Amer. lotto.

rag[1] n. **1** *an oily rag* **cloth**, scrap of cloth; N. Amer. informal schmatte. **2** *a man dressed in rags* **tatters**, torn clothing, old clothes; cast-offs, hand-me-downs.

rag[2] n. Brit. *the student rag* **fund-raising event**, charity event, charitable event.
▸ v. informal *he was ragged mercilessly.* See **tease**.

ragamuffin n. **urchin**, waif, guttersnipe; informal scarecrow; dated gamin(e).

ragbag n. **jumble**, hotchpotch, mishmash, mess, hash; assortment, mixture, miscellany, medley, mixed bag, melange, variety, diversity, potpourri; N. Amer. hodgepodge.

rage n. **1** *his rage is due to frustration* **fury**, anger, wrath, outrage, indignation, temper, spleen, resentment, pique, annoyance, vexation, displeasure; pet, tantrum, (bad) mood; air rage, road rage; informal grump, strop; literary ire, choler. **2** *the current rage for DIY* **craze**, passion, fashion, taste, trend, vogue, fad, enthusiasm, obsession, compulsion, fixation, fetish, mania, preoccupation; informal thing.
▸ v. **1** *she raged silently* **be angry**, be furious, be enraged, be incensed, seethe, be beside oneself, rave, storm, fume, spit; informal be livid, be wild, foam at the mouth, have a fit, be steamed up. **2** *he raged against the reforms* **protest about**, complain about, oppose, denounce; fulminate, storm, rail; informal kick up a stink about. **3** *a storm was raging* **blow**, howl, thunder, rampage.
□ **(all) the rage** popular, fashionable, in fashion, in vogue, the (latest) thing, in great demand, sought-after, le dernier cri; informal in, the in thing, cool, big, trendy, hot, hip.

ragged adj. **1** *ragged jeans* **tattered**, in tatters, torn, ripped, holey, in holes, moth-eaten, frayed, worn (out), falling to pieces, threadbare, scruffy, shabby; informal tatty. **2** *a ragged child* **shabby**, scruffy, down at heel,

unkempt. **3** *a ragged coastline* **jagged**, craggy, rugged, uneven, rough, irregular; serrated, sawtooth, indented; technical crenulate, crenulated.
– OPPOSITES smart.

raging adj. **1** *a raging mob* **angry**, furious, enraged, incensed, infuriated, irate, fuming, seething, ranting; informal livid, wild; literary wrathful. **2** *raging seas* **stormy**, violent, wild, turbulent, tempestuous. **3** *a raging headache* **excruciating**, agonizing, painful, throbbing, acute, bad. **4** *her raging thirst* **severe**, extreme, great, excessive.

raid n. **1** *the raid on Dieppe* **attack**, assault, descent, blitz, incursion, sortie; onslaught, storming, charge, offensive, invasion, blitzkrieg. **2** *a raid on a shop* **robbery**, burglary, hold-up, break-in, ram raid; looting, plunder; informal smash-and-grab, stick-up; Brit. informal blag; N. Amer. informal heist. **3** *a police raid on the flat* **swoop**, search; N. Amer. informal bust, takedown.
▸ v. **1** *they raided shipping in the harbour* **attack**, assault, set upon, descend on, swoop on, blitz, assail, storm, rush. **2** *armed men raided the store* **rob**, hold up, break into; plunder, steal from, pillage, loot, ransack, sack; informal stick up. **3** *homes were raided by police* **search**, swoop on; N. Amer. informal bust.

raider n. **robber**, burglar, thief, housebreaker, plunderer, pillager, looter, marauder; attacker, assailant, invader.

rail v. *he rails against injustice* **protest**, fulminate, inveigh, rage, speak out, make a stand; expostulate about, criticize, denounce, condemn; object to, oppose, complain about, challenge; informal kick up a fuss about.

railing n. **fence**, fencing, rail(s), paling, palisade, balustrade, banister, hurdle.

raillery n. **teasing**, mockery, chaff, ragging; banter, badinage; informal leg-pulling, ribbing, kidding; N. Amer. informal josh.

railroad v. informal **coerce**, force, compel, pressure, pressurize, badger, hustle, pester, hound, harass; browbeat, bludgeon, bulldoze, steamroller, dragoon, prevail on, strong-arm; Brit. informal bounce; N. Amer. informal fast-talk.

rain n. **1** *the rain had stopped* **rainfall**, precipitation, raindrops, wet weather; drizzle, mizzle, shower, rainstorm, cloudburst, torrent, downpour, deluge, storm. **2** *a rain of hot ash* **shower**, deluge, flood, torrent, avalanche, flurry; storm, hail.
▸ v. **1** *it rained heavily* **pour (down)**, pelt down, tip down, teem down, beat down, lash down, sheet down, rain cats and dogs; fall, drizzle, spit; informal be chucking it down; Brit. informal bucket down. **2** *bombs rained on the city* **fall**, hail, drop, shower.

WORD LINKS

pluvial relating to rainfall
nimbus a rain cloud
isohyet a line on a map connecting points having the same amount of rainfall

---

rainy adj. **wet**, showery, drizzly, damp, inclement.

r

raise v. **1** *he raised a hand in greeting* **lift (up)**, hold aloft, elevate, uplift, upraise, upthrust; hoist, haul up, hitch up; Brit. informal hoick up. **2** *he raised himself in the bed* **sit up**, stand up. **3** *they raised prices* **increase**, put up, push up, up, mark up, escalate, inflate; informal hike (up), jack up, bump up. **4** *he raised his voice* **amplify**, louden, magnify, intensify, boost, lift, increase, heighten, augment. **5** *the temple was raised in 900 BC* **build**, construct, erect, assemble, put up. **6** *how will you raise the money?* **get**, obtain, acquire; accumulate, amass, collect, fetch, net, make. **7** *the city raised troops to fight for them* **recruit**, enlist, sign up, conscript, call up, mobilize, rally, assemble; US draft. **8** *a tax raised on imports* **levy**, impose, exact, demand, charge. **9** *he raised several objections* **bring up**, air, ventilate; present, table, propose, submit, advance, suggest, moot, put forward. **10** *the disaster raised doubts about safety* **give rise to**, occasion, cause, produce, engender, elicit, create, result in, lead to, prompt, awaken, arouse, induce, kindle, incite, stir up, trigger, spark off, provoke, instigate, foment, whip up; literary beget. **11** *most parents raise their children well* **bring up**, rear, nurture, look after, care for, provide for, mother, parent, tend, cherish; educate, train. **12** *he raised cattle* **breed**, rear, nurture, keep, tend; grow, farm, cultivate, produce. **13** *he was raised to the peerage* **promote**, advance, upgrade, elevate, ennoble; informal kick upstairs; old use prefer.
– OPPOSITES lower, reduce, demolish.
▶n. *the workers wanted a raise* **pay rise**, pay increase, increment.

raised adj. **embossed**, relief, relievo, die-stamped.

rake¹ v. **1** *he raked the leaves into a pile* **scrape**, collect, gather. **2** *she raked the gravel* **smooth (out)**, level, even out, flatten, comb. **3** *the cat raked his arm with its claws* **scratch**, lacerate, scrape, rasp, graze, grate; Medicine excoriate. **4** *she raked a hand through her hair* **drag**, pull, scrape, tug, comb. **5** *I raked through my pockets* **rummage**, search, hunt, sift, rifle. **6** *machine-gun fire raked the streets* **sweep**, enfilade, pepper, strafe.
◻ **rake something in** informal earn, make, get, gain, obtain, acquire, accumulate, bring in, pull in, pocket, realize, fetch, return, yield, raise, net, gross.
rake something up remind people of, recollect, remember, call to mind; drag up, dredge up.

rake² n. *he was something of a rake* **playboy**, libertine, profligate; degenerate, roué, debauchee; lecher, seducer, womanizer, philanderer, adulterer, Don Juan, Lothario, Casanova; informal ladykiller, ladies' man, lech.

rake-off n. informal See **cut** (sense 3 of the noun).

rakish adj. **dashing**, debonair, stylish, jaunty, devil-may-care; raffish, disreputable, louche; informal sharp.

rally v. **1** *the troops rallied and held their ground* **regroup**, reassemble, re-form, reunite. **2** *he rallied an army* **muster**, marshal, mobilize, raise, call up, recruit, enlist, conscript; assemble, gather, round up; US draft; formal convoke. **3** *ministers rallied to denounce the rumours* **get together**, band together, assemble, join forces, unite, ally, collaborate, cooperate, pull together. **4** *share prices rallied* **recover**, improve, get better, pick up, revive, bounce back, perk up, look up, turn a corner.
– OPPOSITES disperse, disband, slump.
▶n. **1** *a rally in support of the strike* **(mass) meeting**, gathering, assembly, tweetup; demonstration, (protest) march; informal demo. **2** *a rally in oil prices* **recovery**, upturn, improvement, comeback, resurgence; Stock Exchange dead cat bounce.
– OPPOSITES slump.

ram v. **1** *he rammed his sword into its sheath* **force**, thrust, plunge, stab, push, sink, dig, stick, cram, jam, stuff, pack. **2** *a van rammed the police car* **hit**, strike, crash into, collide with, impact, run into, smash into, bump (into), butt.

ramble v. **1** *we rambled around the lanes* **walk**, hike, tramp, trek, backpack; wander, stroll, saunter, amble, roam, range, rove, traipse; Scottish & Irish stravaig; informal mosey, tootle; Brit. informal pootle; formal perambulate. **2** *she does ramble on* **chatter**, babble, prattle, prate, blather, gabble, jabber, twitter, rattle, maunder; informal jaw, gas, gab, yak, yabber; Brit. informal witter, chunter, natter, waffle, rabbit.
▶n. *a ramble in the hills* **walk**, hike, trek; wander, stroll, saunter, amble, roam, traipse, jaunt, promenade; informal mosey, tootle; Brit. informal pootle; formal perambulation.

rambler n. **walker**, hiker, backpacker, wanderer, rover; literary wayfarer.

rambling adj. **1** *a rambling speech* **long-winded**, verbose, wordy, prolix; digressive, maundering, roundabout, circuitous, circumlocutory; disconnected, disjointed, incoherent. **2** *rambling streets* **winding**, twisting, twisty, labyrinthine; sprawling. **3** *a rambling rose* **trailing**, creeping, climbing, vining.
– OPPOSITES concise.

ramification n. **consequence**, result, aftermath, outcome, effect, upshot; development, implication; product, by-product.

ramp n. **slope**, bank, incline, gradient, tilt; rise, ascent, acclivity; drop, descent, declivity.

rampage v. *mobs rampaged through the streets* **riot**, run riot, go on the rampage, run amok, go berserk; storm, charge, tear.
◻ **go on the rampage** riot, rampage, go berserk, get out of control, run amok; N. Amer. informal go postal.

rampant adj. **1** *rampant inflation* **uncontrolled**, unrestrained, unchecked, unbridled, widespread; out of control, out of hand, rife. **2** *rampant dislike* **vehement**, strong, violent, forceful, intense, passionate,

r

fanatical. **3** *rampant vegetation* **luxuriant**, exuberant, lush, rich, riotous, rank, profuse, vigorous; informal jungly. **4** Heraldry *a lion rampant* **upright**, erect, standing (up), rearing up.
– OPPOSITES controlled, mild.

rampart n. **defensive wall**, embankment, earthwork, parapet, breastwork, battlement, bulwark, outwork.

ramshackle adj. **tumbledown**, dilapidated, derelict, decrepit, neglected, run down, gone to rack and ruin, crumbling, decaying; rickety, shaky, unsound; informal shambly; N. Amer. informal shacky.
– OPPOSITES sound.

rancid adj. **sour**, stale, turned, rank, putrid, foul, rotten, bad, off; gamy, high, fetid, stinking, malodorous, foul-smelling; literary noisome.
– OPPOSITES fresh.

rancorous adj. **bitter**, spiteful, hateful, resentful, acrimonious, malicious, malevolent, hostile, venomous, vindictive, baleful, vitriolic, vengeful, pernicious, mean, nasty; informal bitchy, catty.
– OPPOSITES amicable.

rancour n. **bitterness**, spite, hate, hatred, resentment, malice, ill will, malevolence, animosity, antipathy, enmity, hostility, acrimony, venom, vitriol.

random adj. *random spot checks* **arbitrary**, unsystematic, unplanned, undirected, casual, indiscriminate, non-specific, haphazard, stray, erratic; chance, accidental.
– OPPOSITES systematic.
□ **at random** unsystematically, arbitrarily, randomly, unmethodically, haphazardly.

range n. **1** *his range of vision* **span**, scope, compass, sweep, extent, area, field, orbit, ambit, horizon, latitude; limits, bounds, confines, parameters. **2** *a range of mountains* **row**, chain, sierra, ridge, massif; line, string, series. **3** *a range of quality foods* **assortment**, variety, diversity, mixture, collection, array, selection, choice. **4** *she put the dish into the range* **stove**, cooker; trademark Aga. **5** *cows grazed on open range* **pasture**, pasturage, pastureland, grass, grassland, veld; Scottish shieling; literary greensward.
▶v. **1** *charges range from 1% to 5%* **vary**, fluctuate, differ; extend, stretch, reach, cover, go, run. **2** *on the stalls are ranged fresh foods* **arrange**, line up, order, position, dispose, set out, array. **3** *they ranged over the steppes* **roam**, rove, traverse, travel, journey, wander, drift, ramble, meander, stroll, traipse, walk, hike, trek.

rangy adj. **long-legged**, long-limbed, leggy, tall; slender, slim, lean, thin, gangling, gangly, lanky, spindly, skinny, spare.
– OPPOSITES squat.

rank[1] n. **1** *he was elevated to ministerial rank* **position**, level, grade, echelon; class, status, standing; dated station. **2** *a family of rank* **high standing**, blue blood, high birth, nobility, aristocracy; eminence, distinction, prestige; prominence, influence,

consequence, power. **3** *a rank of riflemen* **row**, line, file, column, string, train, procession.
▶v. **1** *the plant is ranked as endangered* **classify**, class, categorize, rate, grade, bracket, group, pigeonhole, designate; catalogue, file, list. **2** *he ranked below the others* **be graded**, have a status, be classed, be classified, be categorized; belong. **3** *tulips ranked like guardsmen* **line up**, align, order, arrange, dispose, set out, array, range.
□ **the rank and file 1** *the officers and the rank and file* **other ranks**, soldiers, NCOs, lower ranks; men, troops. **2** *a speech appealing to the rank and file* **the (common) people**, the proletariat, the masses, the populace, the commonality, the commonalty, the third estate, the plebeians; the hoi polloi, the rabble, the riff-raff, the great unwashed; informal the proles, the plebs.

rank[2] adj. **1** *rank vegetation* **abundant**, lush, luxuriant, dense, profuse, vigorous, overgrown; informal jungly. **2** *a rank smell* **offensive**, unpleasant, nasty, revolting, sickening, obnoxious, noxious; foul, fetid, smelly, stinking, reeking, high, off, rancid, putrid, malodorous; Brit. informal niffy, pongy, whiffy, humming; literary noisome. **3** *rank stupidity* **downright**, utter, outright, out-and-out, absolute, complete, sheer, arrant, thoroughgoing, unqualified, unmitigated, positive, perfect, patent, pure, total.
– OPPOSITES sparse, pleasant.

rankle v. **cause resentment**, annoy, upset, anger, irritate, offend, affront, displease, provoke, irk, vex, pique, nettle, gall; informal rile, miff, peeve, aggravate, hack off; Brit. informal nark; N. Amer. informal tick off.

ransack v. **plunder**, pillage, raid, rob, loot, sack, strip, despoil; ravage, devastate, turn upside down; scour, rifle, comb, search.

rant v. *she ranted on about the unfairness* **hold forth**, go on, fulminate, vociferate, sound off, spout, pontificate, bluster, declaim; shout, yell, bellow; informal mouth off.
▶n. *he went into a rant about them* **tirade**, diatribe, broadside, polemic; literary philippic.

rap[1] v. **1** *she rapped his fingers with a ruler* **hit**, strike; informal whack, thwack, bash, wallop; literary smite. **2** *I rapped on the door* **knock**, tap, bang, hammer, pound. **3** informal *banks were rapped for high charges.* See **reprimand** (verb).
▶n. **1** *a rap on the knuckles* **blow**, hit, knock, bang, crack; informal whack, thwack, bash, wallop. **2** *a rap at the door* **knock**, tap, rat-tat, bang, hammering, pounding.
□ **take the rap** informal be punished, take the blame, suffer (the consequences), pay (the price).

rap[2] n. *they didn't care a rap* **whit**, iota, jot, hoot, scrap, bit, fig; informal damn, monkey's.

rapacious adj. **grasping**, greedy, avaricious, acquisitive, covetous; mercenary, materialistic; insatiable, predatory; informal money-grubbing; N. Amer. informal grabby.
– OPPOSITES generous.

r

rape n. **1** *he was charged with rape* **sexual assault**, sexual abuse; old use ravishment, defilement. **2** *the rape of rainforest destruction*, violation, ravaging, pillaging, plundering, desecration, defilement, sacking, sack.

▸ v. **1** *he raped her at knifepoint* **sexually assault**, sexually abuse, violate, force oneself on; literary ravish; old use defile. **2** *they raped our country* **ravage**, violate, desecrate, defile, plunder, pillage, despoil; lay waste, ransack, sack.

rapid adj. **quick**, fast, swift, speedy, expeditious, express, brisk; lightning, meteoric, whirlwind; sudden, instantaneous, instant, immediate; hurried, hasty, precipitate; informal p.d.q. (pretty damn quick); literary fleet.
– OPPOSITES slow.

rapidly adv. **quickly**, fast, swiftly, speedily, at the speed of light, post-haste, hotfoot, at full tilt, briskly; hurriedly, hastily, in haste, in a rush, precipitately; informal like a shot, double quick, p.d.q. (pretty damn quick), in a flash, hell for leather, at the double, like a bat out of hell, like (greased) lightning, like mad, like the wind; Brit. informal like the clappers, at a rate of knots, like billy-o; N. Amer. informal lickety-split; literary apace.
– OPPOSITES slowly.

rapport n. **affinity**, close relationship, (mutual) understanding, bond, empathy, sympathy, accord.

rapt adj. **fascinated**, enthralled, spellbound, captivated, riveted, gripped, mesmerized, enchanted, entranced, bewitched; transported, enraptured, thrilled, ecstatic.
– OPPOSITES inattentive.

rapture n. *she gazed at him in rapture* **ecstasy**, bliss, exaltation, euphoria, elation, joy, enchantment, delight, happiness, pleasure.
□ **go into raptures** enthuse, rhapsodize, rave, gush, wax lyrical; praise something to the skies.

rapturous adj. **ecstatic**, joyful, elated, euphoric, enraptured, on cloud nine, in seventh heaven, transported, enchanted, blissful, happy; enthusiastic, delighted, thrilled, overjoyed, rapt; informal over the moon, on top of the world, blissed out; Austral. informal wrapped.

rara avis n. **rarity**, rare bird, wonder, marvel, nonpareil, nonsuch, one of a kind; curiosity, oddity, freak; Brit. informal one-off.

rare adj. **1** *rare moments of privacy* **infrequent**, scarce, sparse, few and far between, thin on the ground, like gold dust; occasional, limited, odd, isolated, unaccustomed, unwonted; Brit. out of the common. **2** *rare stamps* **unusual**, recherché, uncommon, unfamiliar, atypical, singular. **3** *a man of rare talent* **exceptional**, outstanding, unparalleled, peerless, matchless, unique, unrivalled, inimitable, beyond compare, without equal, second to none, unsurpassed; consummate, superior,

superlative, first-class; informal A1, top-notch.
– OPPOSITES common, commonplace.

rarefied adj. **esoteric**, exclusive, select; elevated, lofty.

rarely adv. **seldom**, infrequently, hardly (ever), scarcely, not often; once in a while, now and then, occasionally; informal once in a blue moon.
– OPPOSITES often.

raring adj. **eager**, keen, enthusiastic; impatient, longing, desperate; ready; informal dying, itching, gagging.

rarity n. **1** *the rarity of earthquakes in the UK* **infrequency**, rareness, unusualness, scarcity, scarceness. **2** *this book is a rarity* **collector's item**, rare thing, rare bird, rara avis; wonder, nonpareil, one of a kind; curiosity, oddity; Brit. informal one-off.

rascal n. **scallywag**, imp, monkey, mischief-maker, wretch; informal scamp, tyke, horror, monster; Brit. informal perisher; N. Amer. informal varmint; old use rapscallion.

rash[1] n. **1** *he broke out in a rash* **spots**, breakout, eruption; hives; Medicine erythema, exanthema, urticaria. **2** *a rash of articles in the press* **series**, succession, spate, wave, flood, deluge, torrent; outbreak, epidemic, flurry.

rash[2] adj. *a rash decision* **reckless**, impulsive, impetuous, hasty, foolhardy, incautious, precipitate; careless, heedless, thoughtless, imprudent, foolish; ill-advised, injudicious, ill-judged, misguided, hare-brained; literary temerarious.
– OPPOSITES prudent.

rasp v. **1** *enamel is rasped off the teeth* **scrape**, rub, abrade, grate, grind, sand, file, scratch, scour; Medicine excoriate. **2** *'Help!' he rasped* **croak**, squawk, caw, say hoarsely.

rasping adj. **harsh**, grating, jarring; raspy, scratchy, hoarse, rough, gravelly, croaky, gruff, husky, throaty, guttural.

rate n. **1** *a fixed rate of interest* **percentage**, ratio, proportion; scale, standard. **2** *an hourly rate of £30* **charge**, price, cost, tariff, fare, levy, toll; fee, remuneration, payment, wage, allowance. **3** *the rate of change* **speed**, pace, tempo, velocity, momentum.

▸ v. **1** *they rated their ability at driving* **assess**, evaluate, appraise, judge, weigh up, estimate, calculate, gauge, measure, adjudge; grade, rank, classify, categorize. **2** *the scheme was rated effective* **consider**, judge, reckon, think, hold, deem, find; regard as, look on as, count as. **3** *he rated only a brief mention* **merit**, deserve, warrant, be worthy of, be deserving of. **4** informal *Ben doesn't rate him* **think highly of**, think much of, set much store by; admire, esteem, value.
□ **at any rate** in any case, anyhow, anyway, in any event, nevertheless; whatever happens, come what may, regardless, notwithstanding.

rather adv. **1** *I'd rather you went sooner* **sooner**, by preference, preferably, by choice. **2** *it's rather complicated* **quite**, a bit, a little, fairly, slightly, somewhat, relatively, to some degree, comparatively; informal pretty, sort of, kind of. **3** *her true feelings—or rather, lack of feelings* **more precisely**, to be precise, to be exact, strictly speaking. **4** *she seemed sad rather than angry* **more**; as opposed to, instead of. **5** *it was not impulsive, but rather a considered decision* **on the contrary**, instead.

ratify v. **confirm**, approve, sanction, endorse, agree to, accept, uphold, authorize, formalize, validate, recognize; sign.
– OPPOSITES reject.

rating n. **grade**, grading, classification, ranking, rank, category, designation; assessment, evaluation, appraisal; mark, score.

ratio n. **proportion**, comparative number, correlation, relationship, correspondence; percentage, fraction, quotient.

ration n. **1** *a daily ration of chocolate* **allowance**, allocation, quota, quantum, share, portion, helping; amount, quantity, measure, proportion, percentage. **2** *the garrison ran out of rations* **supplies**, provisions, food, foodstuffs, eatables, edibles, provender; stores; informal grub, eats; N. Amer. informal chuck; formal comestibles; dated victuals.
▶ v. *fuel supplies were rationed* **control**, limit, restrict; conserve.

rational adj. **1** *a rational approach* **logical**, reasoned, sensible, reasonable, cogent, intelligent, judicious, shrewd, common-sense, commonsensical, sound, prudent; down-to-earth, practical, pragmatic. **2** *she was not rational at the time of signing* **sane**, compos mentis, in one's right mind, of sound mind; normal, balanced, lucid, coherent; informal all there. **3** *man is a rational being* **intelligent**, thinking, reasoning; cerebral, logical, analytical; formal ratiocinative.
– OPPOSITES illogical, insane.

rationale n. **reason(s)**, reasoning, thinking, logic, grounds, sense; principle, theory, argument, case; motive, motivation, explanation, justification, excuse; the whys and wherefores.

rationalize v. **1** *he tried to rationalize his behaviour* **justify**, explain (away), account for, defend, vindicate, excuse. **2** *an attempt to rationalize the industry* **streamline**, reorganize, modernize, update; trim, hone, simplify, downsize, prune.

rattle v. **1** *hailstones rattled against the window* **clatter**, patter; clink, clunk. **2** *he rattled some coins* **jingle**, jangle, clink, tinkle. **3** *the bus rattled along* **jolt**, bump, bounce, jounce, shake, judder. **4** *the government were rattled by the strike* **unnerve**, disconcert, disturb, fluster, shake, perturb, discompose, discomfit, ruffle, throw; informal faze.
▶ n. *the rattle of the bottles* **clatter**, clank, clink, clang; jingle, jangle.
◻ **rattle something off** reel off, recite, list, fire off, run through, enumerate.
rattle on/away prattle, babble, chatter, gabble, prate, go on, jabber, gibber, blether,

ramble; informal gab, yak, yap; Brit. informal witter, rabbit, chunter, waffle.

ratty adj. Brit. informal See **irritable**.

raucous adj. **1** *raucous laughter* **harsh**, strident, screeching, piercing, shrill, grating, discordant, dissonant; noisy, loud, cacophonous. **2** *a raucous hen night* **rowdy**, noisy, boisterous, roisterous, wild.
– OPPOSITES soft, quiet.

raunchy adj. informal See **sexy** (sense 2).

ravage v. **lay waste**, devastate, ruin, destroy, wreak havoc on, leave desolate; pillage, plunder, despoil, ransack, sack, loot; literary rape; old use spoil.

ravages plural n. **1** *the ravages of time* **damaging effects**, ill effects. **2** *the ravages of man* **(acts of) destruction**, damage, devastation, ruin, havoc, depredation(s).

rave v. **1** *he was raving about the fires of hell* **talk wildly**, babble, jabber, talk incoherently. **2** *I raved and swore at them* **rant (and rave)**, rage, lose one's temper, storm, fulminate, fume; shout, roar, thunder, bellow; informal fly off the handle, blow one's top, go up the wall, hit the roof; Brit. informal go spare; N. Amer. informal flip one's wig. **3** *he raved about her talent* **praise**, go into raptures about/over, wax lyrical about, sing the praises of, rhapsodize over, enthuse about/over, acclaim, eulogize, extol; N. Amer. informal ballyhoo; formal laud; old use panegyrize.
– OPPOSITES criticize.
▶ n. informal *the food won raves from the critics* **praise**, a rapturous reception, tribute, plaudits, acclaim.
– OPPOSITES criticism.
▶ adj. informal *rave reviews* **rapturous**, enthusiastic, glowing, ecstatic, excellent, highly favourable.

raven adj. *raven hair* **black**, jet-black, ebony; literary sable.

ravenous adj. **1** *I'm absolutely ravenous* **starving**, very hungry, famished; rare esurient. **2** *her ravenous appetite* **voracious**, insatiable; greedy, gluttonous; literary insatiate.

rave-up n. Brit. informal See **party** (sense 1 of the noun).

ravine n. **gorge**, canyon, gully, defile, couloir; chasm, abyss, gulf; S. English chine; N. English clough, gill, thrutch; N. Amer. gulch, coulee.

raving adj. **1** *she's raving mad.* See **mad** (sense 1). **2** *a raving beauty* **very great**, remarkable, extraordinary, singular, striking, outstanding, stunning.

ravings plural n. **gibberish**, rambling, babbling, wild/incoherent talk.

ravish v. **1** literary *he tried to ravish her* **rape**, sexually assault/abuse, violate, force oneself on, molest; old use dishonour, defile. **2** literary *you will be ravished by this wine* **enrapture**, enchant, delight, charm, entrance, enthral, captivate.

ravishing adj. **beautiful**, gorgeous, stunning, wonderful, lovely, striking, magnificent, dazzling, radiant, delightful, charming, enchanting; informal amazing,

sensational, fantastic, fabulous, terrific; Brit. informal smashing; N. Amer. informal bodacious.
– OPPOSITES hideous.

raw adj. **1** *raw carrot* **uncooked**, fresh.
2 *raw materials* **unprocessed**, untreated, unrefined, crude, natural. **3** *raw recruits* **inexperienced**, new, untrained, untried, untested; callow, immature, green, naive; informal wet behind the ears. **4** *his skin is raw* **sore**, red, painful, tender; abraded, chafed; Medicine excoriated. **5** *a raw morning* **bleak**, cold, chilly, freezing, icy, icy-cold, wintry, bitter; informal nippy; Brit. informal parky.
6 *raw emotions* **strong**, intense, passionate, fervent, powerful, violent; undisguised, unconcealed, unrestrained, uninhibited, naked. **7** *raw, contemporary images of Latin America* **realistic**, unembellished, unvarnished, brutal, harsh.
– OPPOSITES cooked, processed.
□ **in the raw** informal See **naked** (sense 1).

raw-boned adj. **thin**, lean, gaunt, bony, skinny, spare.
– OPPOSITES plump.

ray n. **1** *rays of light* **beam**, shaft, streak, stream. **2** *a ray of hope* **glimmer**, flicker, spark, hint, suggestion, sign.
▸ v. *her hair rayed out in the water* **spread out**, fan out.

raze v. **destroy**, demolish, raze to the ground, tear down, pull down, knock down, level, flatten, bulldoze, wipe out, lay waste.

re prep. **about**, concerning, regarding, with regard to, relating to, apropos (of), on the subject of, in respect of, with reference to, in connection with.

reach v. **1** *Travis reached out a hand* **stretch out**, hold out, extend, outstretch, thrust out, stick out. **2** *reach me that book* **pass**, hand, give. **3** *soon she reached Helen's house* **arrive at**, get to, come to; end up at. **4** *the temperature reached 94 degrees* **attain**, get to; rise to, climb to; fall to, sink to, drop to; informal hit. **5** *the leaders reached an agreement* **achieve**, work out, draw up, put together, negotiate, thrash out, hammer out. **6** *I have been trying to reach you all day* **get in touch with**, contact, get through to, get, speak to; informal get hold of. **7** *our concern is to reach more people* **influence**, sway, get (through) to, make an impression on, have an impact on.
▸ n. **1** *Bobby moved out of her reach* **grasp**, range. **2** *small goals within your reach* **capabilities**, capacity. **3** *beyond the reach of the law* **jurisdiction**, authority, influence; scope, range, compass, ambit.

react v. **1** *how would he react if she told him the truth?* **behave**, act, take it, conduct oneself; respond, reply, answer. **2** *he reacted against the new regulations* **rebel against**, oppose, rise up against.

reaction n. **1** *his reaction had bewildered her* **response**, answer, reply, rejoinder, retort, riposte; informal comeback. **2** *a reaction against modernism* **backlash**, counteraction. **3** *the forces of reaction* **conservatism**, the

right (wing), the extreme right.

reactionary adj. *a reactionary policy* **right-wing**, conservative, rightist, traditionalist, conventional, unprogressive.
– OPPOSITES progressive.
▸ n. *an extreme reactionary* **right-winger**, conservative, rightist, traditionalist, conventionalist.
– OPPOSITES radical.

read v. **1** *he was reading the newspaper* **peruse**, study, scrutinize, look through; pore over, be absorbed in; run one's eye over, cast an eye over, leaf through, scan, flick through, skim through, thumb through.
2 *he read a passage of the letter* **read out/aloud**, recite, declaim. **3** *I can't read my own writing* **decipher**, make out, make sense of, interpret, understand. **4** *his remark could be read as a criticism* **interpret**, take (to mean), construe, see, understand. **5** *the dial read 70 mph* **indicate**, register, record, display, show. **6** *he read modern history* **study**, take; N. Amer. & Austral./NZ major in.
▸ n. *have a read of this* **perusal**, study, scan; look (at), browse (through), leaf (through), flick (through), skim (through).
□ **read something into something** infer from, interpolate from, assume from, attribute to; read between the lines.
read up on study; informal bone up on; Brit. informal mug up on, swot; old use con.

> **WORD LINKS**
> **legible** clear enough to read
> **literacy** the ability to read and write
> **illiterate** unable to read and write
> **dyslexia** a disorder involving difficulty in learning to read

readable adj. **1** *the inscription is perfectly readable* **legible**, easy to read, decipherable, clear, intelligible, comprehensible. **2** *her novels are immensely readable* **enjoyable**, entertaining, interesting, absorbing, gripping, enthralling, engrossing, stimulating; informal unputdownable.
– OPPOSITES illegible.

readily adv. **1** *Durkin readily offered to drive him* **willingly**, without hesitation, unhesitatingly, ungrudgingly, gladly, happily, eagerly, promptly. **2** *the island is readily accessible* **easily**, with ease, without difficulty.
– OPPOSITES reluctantly.

readiness n. **1** *their readiness to accept change* **willingness**, enthusiasm, eagerness, keenness; promptness, quickness, alacrity.
2 *a state of readiness* **preparedness**, preparation. **3** *the readiness of his reply* **promptness**, quickness, rapidity, swiftness, speed, speediness.
□ **in readiness** (at the) ready, available, on hand, accessible, handy; prepared, primed, on standby, standing by, on full alert.

reading n. **1** *a cursory reading of the financial pages* **perusal**, study, scan, scanning; browse (through), look (through), glance (through), leaf (through), flick (through), skim (through). **2** *a man of wide reading*

r

(book) learning, scholarship, education, erudition. **3** *readings from the Bible* **passage**, lesson; section, piece; recital, recitation. **4** *my reading of the situation* **interpretation**, construal, understanding, explanation, analysis. **5** *a meter reading* **record**, figure, indication, measurement.

ready adj. **1** *are you ready?* **prepared**, (all) set, organized, primed; informal fit, psyched up, geared up. **2** *everything is ready* **completed**, finished, prepared, organized, done, arranged, fixed, in readiness. **3** *he's always ready to help* **willing**, prepared, game, pleased, inclined, disposed, predisposed; eager, keen, happy, glad. **4** *she looked ready to collapse* **about to**, on the point of, on the verge of, close to, liable to, likely to. **5** *a ready supply of food* **(easily) available**, accessible; handy, close/near at hand, to/on hand, convenient, within reach, at the ready, near, at one's fingertips. **6** *a ready answer* **prompt**, quick, swift, speedy, fast, immediate, unhesitating; clever, sharp, astute, shrewd, keen, perceptive, discerning; literary rathe.
▶ v. *he needed time to ready himself* **prepare**, get/make ready, organize; gear oneself up; informal psych oneself up.
◻ **at the ready** in position, poised, ready for use/action, waiting; N. Amer. on deck.
make ready prepare, make preparations, get everything ready, gear up for.

ready-made adj. **1** *ready-made clothing* **ready-to-wear**; Brit. off the peg; N. Amer. off the rack. **2** *ready-made meals* **pre-cooked**, oven-ready, convenience.
– OPPOSITES tailor-made.

real adj. **1** *is she a fictional character or a real person?* **actual**, non-fictional, factual; historical; material, physical, tangible, concrete, palpable. **2** *real gold* **genuine**, authentic, bona fide; informal pukka, kosher. **3** *my real name* **true**, actual. **4** *tears of real grief* **sincere**, genuine, true, unfeigned, heartfelt, unaffected. **5** *a real man* **proper**, true; informal regular; old use very. **6** *you're a real idiot* **complete**, utter, thorough, absolute, total, prize, perfect; Brit. informal right, proper; Austral./NZ informal fair.
– OPPOSITES imaginary, imitation.
▶ adv. N. Amer. informal *that's real good of you.* See **very** (adverb).

realism n. **1** *optimism tinged with realism* **pragmatism**, practicality, common sense, level-headedness. **2** *a degree of realism* **authenticity**, fidelity, verisimilitude, truthfulness, faithfulness; naturalism.

realistic adj. **1** *you've got to be realistic* **practical**, pragmatic, matter-of-fact, down-to-earth, sensible, commonsensical; rational, reasonable, level-headed, clear-sighted, businesslike; informal having both/one's feet on the ground, hard-nosed, no-nonsense. **2** *a realistic aim* **achievable**, attainable, feasible, practicable, viable, reasonable, sensible, workable; informal doable. **3** *a realistic portrayal of war* **true (to life)**, lifelike,

truthful, faithful, real-life, naturalistic, graphic.
– OPPOSITES idealistic, impracticable.

reality n. **1** *distinguishing fantasy from reality* **the real world**, real life, actuality; truth; physical existence. **2** *the harsh realities of life* **fact**, actuality, truth. **3** *the reality of the detail* **verisimilitude**, authenticity, realism, fidelity, faithfulness.
– OPPOSITES fantasy.
◻ **in reality** in (actual) fact, in point of fact, as a matter of fact, actually, really, in truth; in practice; old use in sooth.

realization n. **1** *a growing realization of the danger* **awareness**, understanding, comprehension, consciousness, appreciation, recognition, discernment; formal cognizance. **2** *the realization of our dreams* **fulfilment**, achievement, accomplishment, attainment; formal effectuation.

realize v. **1** *he suddenly realized what she meant* **register**, perceive, discern, be/become aware of (the fact that), be/become conscious of (the fact that), notice; understand, grasp, comprehend, see, recognize, work out, fathom (out), apprehend; informal latch on to, cotton on to, tumble to, savvy, figure out, get (the message); Brit. informal twig, suss; formal be/become cognizant of. **2** *they realized their dream* **fulfil**, achieve, accomplish, make a reality, make happen, bring to fruition, bring about/off, carry out/through; formal effectuate. **3** *the company realized significant profits* **make**, clear, gain, earn, return, produce. **4** *the goods realized £3000* **be sold for**, fetch, go for, make, net. **5** *he realized his assets* **cash in**, liquidate, capitalize.

really adv. **1** *he is really very wealthy* **in (actual) fact**, actually, in reality, in point of fact, as a matter of fact, in truth, to tell the truth; old use in sooth. **2** *he really likes her* **genuinely**, truly, honestly; undoubtedly, without a doubt, indubitably, certainly, assuredly, unquestionably; old use verily. **3** *they were really kind to me* **very**, extremely, thoroughly, decidedly, dreadfully, exceptionally, exceedingly, immensely, tremendously, uncommonly, remarkably, eminently, extraordinarily, most, downright; Scottish unco; N. Amer. quite; informal awfully, terribly, terrifically, fearfully, right, devilishly, ultra, too —— for words, seriously, majorly; Brit. informal jolly, ever so, dead, well, fair; N. Amer. informal real, mighty, awful, plumb, powerful, way; informal dated devilish, frightfully; old use exceeding.

realm n. **1** *peace in the realm* **kingdom**, country, land, dominion, nation. **2** *the realm of academia* **world**, domain, sphere, area, field, arena, province, territory.

reap v. **1** *the corn has been reaped* **harvest**, garner, gather in, bring in. **2** *reaping the benefits* **receive**, obtain, get, acquire, secure, realize.

rear[1] v. **1** *I was reared in Newcastle* **bring up**, care for, look after, nurture, parent; educate;

r

N. Amer. raise. **2** *he reared cattle* **breed**, raise, keep. **3** *laboratory-reared plants* **grow**, cultivate. **4** *Harry reared his head* **raise**, lift (up), hold up, uplift. **5** *Creagan Hill reared up before them* **rise (up)**, tower, soar, loom.

rear² n. **1** *the rear of the building* **back (part)**, hind part, back end; Nautical stern. **2** *the rear of the queue* **(tail) end**, rear end, back end, tail; N. Amer. tag end. **3** *he slapped her on the rear.* See **bottom** (sense 6 of the noun).
– OPPOSITES front.
▸ adj. *the rear bumper* **back**, end, rearmost; hind, hinder, hindmost; technical posterior.

rearrange v. **1** *the furniture has been rearranged* **reposition**, move round, change round, arrange differently. **2** *Tony had rearranged his schedule* **reorganize**, alter, adjust, change (round), reschedule; informal jigger.

reason n. **1** *the main reason for his decision* **cause**, ground(s), basis, rationale; motive, motivation, purpose, point, aim, intention, objective, goal; explanation, justification, argument, defence, vindication, excuse, pretext. **2** *postmodern voices railing against reason* **rationality**, logic, logical thought, reasoning, cognition; formal ratiocination. **3** *he was losing his reason* **sanity**, mind, mental faculties; senses, wits; informal marbles. **4** *he continues, against reason, to love her* **good sense**, good judgement, common sense, wisdom, sagacity, reasonableness.
▸ v. **1** *a young child is unable to reason* **think rationally**, think logically, use one's common sense, use one's head/brain; formal cogitate, ratiocinate. **2** *Scott reasoned that Annabel might be ill* **calculate**, come to the conclusion, conclude, reckon, think, judge, deduce, infer, surmise; informal figure. **3** *her husband tried to reason with her* **talk round**, bring round, win round, persuade, prevail on, convince, make someone see the light.
□ **reason something out** work out, think through, make sense of, get to the bottom of, puzzle out; informal figure out.
reason with someone talk round, bring round, persuade, prevail on, convince; make someone see the light.
with reason justifiably, justly, legitimately, rightly, reasonably.

> **WORD LINKS**
> **rational** based on reason or logic

reasonable adj. **1** *a reasonable man | a reasonable explanation* **sensible**, rational, logical, fair, fair-minded, just, equitable; intelligent, wise, level-headed, practical, realistic; sound, (well) reasoned, valid, commonsensical; tenable, plausible, credible, believable. **2** *you must take all reasonable precautions* **within reason**, practicable, sensible; appropriate, suitable. **3** *cars in reasonable condition* **fairly good**, acceptable, satisfactory, average, adequate, fair, all right, tolerable, passable; informal OK. **4** *reasonable prices* **inexpensive**, moderate, low, cheap, budget, bargain; competitive.

reasoned adj. **logical**, rational, well thought out, clear, lucid, coherent, cogent, well expressed, well presented, considered, sensible.

reasoning n. **thinking**, (train of) thought, thought process, logic, reason, analysis, interpretation, explanation, rationalization; reasons, rationale, arguments; formal ratiocination.

reassure v. **put/set someone's mind at rest**, put someone at ease, encourage, inspirit, hearten, buoy up, cheer up; comfort, soothe.
– OPPOSITES alarm.

rebate n. **(partial) refund**, repayment; discount, deduction, reduction, decrease.

rebel n. **1** *the rebels took control of the capital* **revolutionary**, insurgent, revolutionist, mutineer, insurrectionist, insurrectionary, guerrilla, terrorist, freedom fighter. **2** *the concept of the artist as a rebel* **nonconformist**, dissenter, dissident, iconoclast, maverick; informal bad boy.
▸ v. **1** *the citizens rebelled* **revolt**, mutiny, riot, rise up, take up arms, stage/mount a rebellion, be insubordinate. **2** *his stomach rebelled at the thought of food* **recoil**, show/feel repugnance. **3** *teenagers rebelling against their parents* **defy**, disobey, refuse to obey, kick against, challenge, oppose, resist.
– OPPOSITES obey.
▸ adj. **1** *rebel troops* **insurgent**, revolutionary, mutinous, rebellious, insurrectionary, insurrectionist. **2** *rebel MPs* **rebellious**, defiant, disobedient, insubordinate, subversive, resistant, recalcitrant; nonconformist, maverick, iconoclastic; old use contumacious.
– OPPOSITES compliant.

rebellion n. **1** *troops suppressed the rebellion* **uprising**, revolt, insurrection, mutiny, revolution, insurgence, insurgency; rioting, riot, disorder, unrest. **2** *an act of rebellion* **defiance**, disobedience, rebelliousness, insubordination, subversion, subversiveness, resistance.

rebellious adj. **1** *rebellious troops* **rebel**, insurgent, mutinous, mutinying, rebelling, rioting, riotous, insurrectionary, insurrectionist, revolutionary. **2** *a rebellious adolescent* **defiant**, disobedient, insubordinate, unruly, mutinous, wayward, obstreperous, recalcitrant, intractable; Brit. informal bolshie; formal refractory; old use contumacious.

rebirth n. **revival**, renaissance, resurrection, reawakening, renewal, regeneration; revitalization, rejuvenation; formal renascence.

rebound v. **1** *the ball rebounded off the wall* **bounce (back)**, spring back, ricochet, boomerang; N. Amer. carom. **2** *later sterling rebounded* **recover**, rally, pick up, make a recovery. **3** *Thomas's tactics rebounded on him* **backfire**, boomerang, have unwelcome repercussions; old use redound on.

rebuff v. *his offer was rebuffed* **reject**, turn down, spurn, refuse, decline, repudiate;

r

snub, slight, repulse, repel, dismiss, brush off, give someone the cold shoulder; informal give someone the brush-off; N. Amer. informal give someone the bum's rush.
– OPPOSITES accept.
▸ n. *the rebuff did little to dampen his ardour* **rejection**, snub, slight, repulse; refusal, spurning, cold-shouldering, discouragement; informal brush-off, kick in the teeth, slap in the face.

rebuild v. **reconstruct**, renovate, restore, remodel, remake, reassemble.
– OPPOSITES demolish.

rebuke v. *she never rebuked him in front of others* **reprimand**, reproach, scold, admonish, reprove, chastise, upbraid, berate, take to task, criticize, censure; informal tell off, give someone a telling-off, give someone a talking-to, give someone a dressing-down, give someone an earful; Brit. informal tick off; N. Amer. informal chew out, ream out; Austral. informal monster; formal castigate.
– OPPOSITES praise.
▸ n. *Damian was silenced by the rebuke* **reprimand**, reproach, reproof, scolding, admonishment, admonition, reproval, upbraiding; informal telling-off, dressing-down; Brit. informal ticking-off; formal castigation.
– OPPOSITES compliment.

rebut v. **refute**, deny, disprove; invalidate, negate, contradict, controvert, counter, discredit, give the lie to, explode; informal shoot full of holes; formal confute.
– OPPOSITES confirm.

rebuttal n. **refutation**, denial, countering, invalidation, negation, contradiction.

recalcitrant adj. **uncooperative**, intractable, insubordinate, defiant, rebellious, wilful, wayward, headstrong, self-willed, contrary, perverse, difficult, awkward; Brit. informal bloody-minded, bolshie, stroppy; formal refractory; old use contumacious, froward.
– OPPOSITES amenable.

recall v. **1** *he recalled his student days* **remember**, recollect, call to mind; think back on/to, look back on, reminisce about. **2** *their exploits recall the days of chivalry* **bring to mind**, call to mind, put one in mind of, call up, conjure up, evoke. **3** *the ambassador was recalled* **summon back**, order back, call back.
– OPPOSITES forget.
▸ n. **1** *the recall of the ambassador* **summoning back**, ordering back, calling back. **2** *their recall of dreams* **recollection**, remembrance, memory.

recant v. **1** *he was forced to recant his political beliefs* **renounce**, disavow, deny, repudiate, renege on; formal forswear, abjure. **2** *he refused to recant* **change one's mind**, be apostate; rare tergiversate. **3** *he recanted his testimony* **retract**, take back, withdraw.

recantation n. **renunciation**, renouncement, disavowal, denial, repudiation, retraction, withdrawal.

recapitulate v. **summarize**, sum up; restate, repeat, reiterate, go over, review; informal recap.

recede v. **1** *the flood waters receded* **retreat**, go back/down, move back/away, withdraw, ebb, subside, abate. **2** *the lights receded into the distance* **disappear**, fade (into the distance), be lost to view. **3** *fears of violence have receded* **diminish**, lessen, decrease, dwindle, fade, abate, subside, ebb, wane.
– OPPOSITES advance, grow.

receipt n. **1** *the receipt of a letter* **receiving**, getting, obtaining, gaining; arrival, delivery. **2** *make sure you get a receipt* **proof of purchase**, sales ticket, till receipt. **3** *receipts from house sales* **proceeds**, takings, money/payment received, income, revenue, earnings; profits, (financial) return(s); N. Amer. take.

receive v. **1** *Tony received an award | they received £650 in damages* **be given**, be presented with, be awarded, collect; get, obtain, gain, acquire; win, be paid, earn, gross, net. **2** *she received a letter* **be sent**, be in receipt of, accept (delivery of). **3** *Alec received the news on Monday* **be told**, be informed of, be notified of, hear, discover, find out (about), learn; informal get wind of. **4** *he received her suggestion with a complete lack of interest* **hear**, listen to; respond to, react to. **5** *she received a serious injury* **experience**, sustain, undergo, meet with; suffer, bear. **6** *they received their guests* **greet**, welcome, say hello to. **7** *she's not receiving visitors* **entertain**, be at home to.
– OPPOSITES give, send.

receiver n. **1** *the receiver of a gift* **recipient**, beneficiary, donee. **2** *a telephone receiver* **handset**.
– OPPOSITES donor.

recent adj. **1** *recent research* **new**, the latest, current, fresh, modern, contemporary, up to date, up to the minute. **2** *his recent visit* **not long ago**, just gone.
– OPPOSITES old.

recently adv. **not long ago**, a short time ago, in the past few days/weeks/months, a little while back; lately, latterly, just now.

receptacle n. **container**, holder, repository; box, tin, bin, can, canister, case, pot, bag.

reception n. **1** *the reception of the goods* **receipt**, receiving, getting. **2** *the reception of foreign diplomats* **greeting**, welcoming, entertaining. **3** *a chilly reception* **response**, reaction, treatment. **4** *a wedding reception* **party**, function, social occasion, soirée; N. Amer. levee; informal do, bash; Brit. informal rave-up, knees-up, beanfeast, bunfight, beano.

receptive adj. **open-minded**, responsive, amenable, well disposed, flexible, approachable, accessible; old use susceptive.
– OPPOSITES unresponsive.

recess n. **1** *two recesses fitted with bookshelves* **alcove**, bay, niche, nook, corner, hollow, oriel. **2** *the deepest recesses of Broadcasting House* **innermost parts**, heart, depths, bowels. **3** *the Christmas recess*

r

adjournment, break, interlude, interval, rest; holiday, vacation; informal breather.
▸ v. *let's recess for lunch* **adjourn**, stop, (take a) break; informal take five.

recession n. **economic decline**, downturn, depression, slump, slowdown.
– OPPOSITES boom.

recherché adj. **obscure**, rare, esoteric, abstruse, arcane, recondite, exotic, strange, unusual, unfamiliar, out of the ordinary.

recipe n. **1** *a tasty recipe* **cooking instructions**; old use receipt. **2** *a recipe for success* **means/ way of achieving**, prescription, formula, blueprint.

recipient n. **receiver**, beneficiary, legatee, donee.
– OPPOSITES donor.

reciprocal adj. **1** *reciprocal love* **given/ felt in return**, requited, reciprocated. **2** *reciprocal obligations and duties* **mutual**, common, shared, joint, corresponding, complementary.

reciprocate v. **1** *I was happy to reciprocate* **do the same (in return)**, return the favour. **2** *love that was not reciprocated* **requite**, return, give back.

recital n. **1** *a piano recital* **concert**, (musical) performance, solo (performance); informal gig. **2** *her recital of Adam's failures* **enumeration**, list, litany, catalogue, listing, detailing; account, report, description, recapitulation, recounting. **3** *a recital of the Lord's Prayer.* See **recitation** (sense 1).

recitation n. **1** *the recitation of his poem* **recital**, saying aloud, declamation, rendering, rendition, delivery, performance. **2** *a recitation of her life story* **account**, description, narration, narrative, story. **3** *songs and recitations* **reading**, passage; poem, verse, monologue.

recite v. **1** *he began to recite verses of the Koran* **repeat from memory**, say aloud, declaim, quote, deliver, render. **2** *John recited the facts they knew* **enumerate**, list, detail, reel off; recount, relate, describe, narrate, give an account of, recapitulate, repeat.

reckless adj. **rash**, careless, thoughtless, heedless, unheeding, hasty, overhasty, precipitate, precipitous, impetuous, impulsive, daredevil, devil-may-care; irresponsible, foolhardy, over-adventurous, audacious; ill-advised, injudicious, madcap, imprudent, unwise, ill-considered; literary temerarious.
– OPPOSITES careful.

reckon v. **1** *the cost was reckoned at £6,000* **calculate**, compute, work out, put a figure on, figure; count (up), add up, total; Brit. tot up. **2** *Anselm reckoned Hugh among his friends* **include**, count, consider to be, regard as, look on as. **3** informal *I reckon I can manage that* **believe**, think, be of the opinion/view, be convinced, dare say, imagine, guess, suppose, consider; informal figure. **4** *it was reckoned a failure* **regard as**, consider, judge, hold to be, think of as; deem, rate, gauge,

count. **5** *I reckon to get good value for money* **expect**, anticipate, hope to, be looking to; count on, rely on, depend on, bank on; N. Amer. informal figure on.
□ **to be reckoned with** important, of considerable importance, significant; influential, powerful, strong, potent, formidable, redoubtable.

reckon with 1 *it's her mother you'll have to reckon with* **deal with**, contend with, face (up to). **2** *they hadn't reckoned with her burning ambition* **take into account**, take into consideration, bargain for/on, anticipate, foresee, be prepared for, consider; formal take cognizance of.

reckon without overlook, fail to take account of, disregard.

reckoning n. **1** *by my reckoning, this comes to £2 million* **calculation**, estimation, estimate, computation, working out, summation, judgement, evaluation. **2** *the terrible reckoning that he deserved* **retribution**, fate, doom, nemesis, punishment.
□ **day of reckoning** Judgement Day, day of retribution, doomsday.

reclaim v. **1** *travelling expenses can be reclaimed* **get back**, claim back, recover, regain, retrieve, recoup. **2** *Henrietta had reclaimed him from a life of vice* **save**, rescue, redeem; reform.

recline v. **lie (down/back)**, lean back; be recumbent; relax, repose, loll, lounge, sprawl, stretch out; literary couch.

recluse n. **1** *a religious recluse* **hermit**, ascetic; historical anchorite, anchoress; old use eremite. **2** *a natural recluse* **loner**, solitary, lone wolf.

reclusive adj. **solitary**, secluded, isolated, hermit-like, hermitic, eremitic, eremitical, cloistered.
– OPPOSITES gregarious.

recognition n. **1** *there was no sign of recognition on his face* **identification**, recollection, remembrance. **2** *his recognition of his lack of experience* **acknowledgement**, acceptance, admission; realization, awareness, consciousness, knowledge, appreciation; formal cognizance. **3** *we have sought official recognition* **approval**, certification, accreditation, endorsement, validation. **4** *you deserve recognition for the tremendous job you are doing* **appreciation**, gratitude, thanks, congratulations, credit, commendation, acclaim, bouquets, acknowledgement.

recognizable adj. **identifiable**, noticeable, perceptible, discernible, detectable, distinguishable, observable, perceivable; distinct, unmistakable, clear; old use sensible.
– OPPOSITES imperceptible.

recognize v. **1** *Hannah recognized him at once* **identify**, place, know, put a name to; remember, recall, recollect; know by sight; Scottish & N. English ken. **2** *they recognized Alan's ability* **acknowledge**, accept, admit; realize, be aware of, be conscious of, perceive, discern, appreciate; formal be cognizant of.

3 *many therapists are recognized by the Society* **approve**, certify, accredit, endorse, sanction, validate. **4** *the Trust recognized their hard work* **pay tribute to**, show appreciation of, appreciate, be grateful for, acclaim, commend.

recoil v. **1** *she instinctively recoiled* **draw back**, jump back, pull back; flinch, shy away, shrink (back), blench. **2** *he recoiled from the thought* **feel revulsion at**, feel disgust at, be unable to stomach, shrink from, balk at. **3** *his rifle recoiled* **kick (back)**, jerk back, spring back. **4** *this will eventually recoil on him* **have an adverse effect on**, rebound on, affect badly, backfire, boomerang; old use redound on.
▸n. *the recoil of the gun* **kickback**, kick.

recollect v. **remember**, recall, call to mind, think of; think back to, look back on, reminisce about.
– OPPOSITES forget.

recollection n. **memory**, remembrance, impression, reminiscence.

recommend v. **1** *his former employer recommended him for the post* **advocate**, endorse, commend, suggest, put forward, propose, nominate, put up; speak favourably of, speak well of, put in a good word for, vouch for; informal plug. **2** *the committee recommended a cautious approach* **advise**, counsel, urge, exhort, enjoin, prescribe, argue for, back, support; suggest, advocate, propose. **3** *there was little to recommend her* **have in one's favour**, give an advantage to; informal have going for one.

recommendation n. **1** *the advisory group's recommendations* **advice**, counsel, guidance, direction, enjoinder; suggestion, proposal. **2** *a personal recommendation* **commendation**, endorsement, good word, favourable mention, testimonial; suggestion, tip; informal plug. **3** *a nonentity whose only recommendation is that he is obnoxious to no one* **advantage**, good point/feature, benefit, asset, boon, attraction, appeal.

recompense v. **1** *offenders should recompense their victims* **compensate**, indemnify, repay, reimburse, make reparation to, make restitution to, make amends to. **2** *she wanted to recompense him* **reward**, pay back; old use guerdon. **3** *nothing could recompense her loss* **make up for**, compensate for, make amends for, make restitution for, make reparation for, redress, make good.
▸n. *damages were paid in recompense* **compensation**, reparation, restitution, indemnification, indemnity; reimbursement, repayment, redress; old use guerdon.

reconcilable adj. **compatible**, consistent, congruous, congruent.

reconcile v. **1** *the news reconciled us* **reunite**, bring (back) together (again), restore friendly relations between, make peace between; pacify, appease, placate, mollify; formal conciliate. **2** *trying to reconcile his religious beliefs with his career* **make**

compatible, harmonize, square, make congruent, balance. **3** *the quarrel was reconciled* **settle**, resolve, sort out, mend, remedy, heal, rectify; informal patch up. **4** *they had to reconcile themselves to drastic losses* **(come to) accept**, resign oneself to, come to terms with, learn to live with, get used to.
– OPPOSITES estrange.

reconciliation n. **1** *the reconciliation of the disputants* **reuniting**, reunion, bringing together (again), conciliation, reconcilement; pacification, appeasement, placating, mollification. **2** *a reconciliation of their differences* **resolution**, settlement, settling, resolving, mending, remedying. **3** *there was little hope of reconciliation* **restoration of harmony**, agreement, compromise, understanding, peace; formal concord. **4** *the reconciliation of theory with practice* **harmonizing**, harmonization, squaring, balancing.

recondite adj. **obscure**, abstruse, arcane, esoteric, recherché, profound, difficult, complex, complicated, involved; incomprehensible, unfathomable, impenetrable, cryptic, opaque.

recondition v. **overhaul**, rebuild, renovate, restore, repair, reconstruct, remodel, refurbish; informal do up, revamp.

reconnaissance n. **(preliminary) survey**, exploration, observation, investigation, examination, inspection; patrol, search; reconnoitring; informal recce; N. Amer. informal recon.

reconnoitre v. **survey**, make a reconnaissance of, explore; investigate, examine, scrutinize, inspect, observe, take a look at; patrol; informal recce, make a recce of, check out; N. Amer. informal recon.

reconsider v. **rethink**, review, revise, re-examine, re-evaluate, reassess, reappraise; change, alter, modify; have second thoughts, change one's mind.

reconsideration n. **review**, rethink, re-examination, reassessment, re-evaluation, reappraisal.

reconstruct v. **1** *the building had to be reconstructed* **rebuild**, restore, renovate, recreate, remake, reassemble, remodel, refashion, revamp, recondition, refurbish. **2** *reconstructing the events of that day* **recreate**, build up a picture/impression of, piece together, re-enact.

record n. **1** *written records of the past* **account(s)**, document(s), documentation, data, file(s), dossier(s), evidence, report(s); annal(s), archive(s), chronicle(s); minutes, transactions, proceedings, transcript(s); certificate(s), instrument(s), deed(s); register, log, logbook; Law muniment(s). **2** *listening to records* album, vinyl; dated gramophone record, disc, LP, EP, single, forty-five, seventy-eight. **3** *his previous good record* **history**, track record, reputation. **4** *he's got a record* **criminal record**, police record; previous; Brit. informal form; N. Amer. informal rap sheet. **5** *a new British record*

r

best performance, highest achievement, personal best; best time, fastest time; world record. **6** *a lasting record of what they have achieved* **reminder**, memorial, souvenir, memento, remembrance, testament.

▸ adj. *record profits* **record-breaking**, best ever, unsurpassed, unparalleled, unequalled, second to none.

▸ v. **1** *the doctor recorded her blood pressure* **write down**, put in writing, take down, note, make a note of, jot down, put down on paper; document, put on record, enter, minute, register, log; list, catalogue. **2** *the thermometer recorded a high temperature* **indicate**, register, show, display. **3** *the team recorded their fourth away win* **achieve**, accomplish, chalk up, notch up; informal clock up. **4** *the recital was recorded live* **make a record/recording of**, tape, tape-record; video-record, videotape, video.

◻ **off the record 1** *his comments were off the record* **unofficial**, confidential, in (strict) confidence, not to be made public. **2** *they admitted, off the record, that they had made a mistake* **unofficially**, privately, in (strict) confidence, confidentially, between ourselves.

recorder n. **1** *he put a tape in the recorder* tape recorder, cassette recorder; video (recorder), VCR, videotape recorder. **2** *a recorder of rural life* **record keeper**, archivist, annalist, diarist, chronicler, historian.

recount v. **tell**, relate, narrate, give an account of, describe, report, outline, delineate, relay, convey, communicate, impart.

recoup v. **get back**, regain, recover, win back, retrieve, redeem, recuperate.

recourse n. *surgery may be the only recourse* **option**, possibility, alternative, resort, way out, hope, remedy, choice, expedient.
◻ **have recourse to** resort to, make use of, avail oneself of, turn to, call on, look to, fall back on.

recover v. **1** *he's recovering from a heart attack* **recuperate**, get better, convalesce, regain one's strength, get stronger, get back on one's feet; be on the mend, be on the road to recovery, pick up, rally, respond to treatment, improve, heal, pull through, bounce back. **2** *later, shares recovered* **rally**, improve, pick up, make a recovery, rebound, bounce back. **3** *the stolen material has been recovered* **retrieve**, regain (possession of), get back, recoup, reclaim, repossess, redeem, recuperate, find (again), track down. **4** *gold coins recovered from a wreck* **salvage**, save, rescue, retrieve.
– OPPOSITES deteriorate, lose.
◻ **recover oneself** pull oneself together, regain one's composure, regain one's self-control; informal get a grip (on oneself).

recovery n. **1** *her recovery may be slow* **recuperation**, convalescence. **2** *the economy was showing signs of recovery* **improvement**, rallying, picking up, upturn, upswing. **3** *the recovery of the stolen goods*

retrieval, regaining, repossession, getting back, reclamation, recouping, redemption, recuperation.
– OPPOSITES relapse, deterioration.

recreation n. **1** *she cycles for recreation* **pleasure**, leisure, relaxation, fun, enjoyment, entertainment, amusement; play, sport; informal R & R; N. Amer. informal rec; old use disport. **2** *his favourite recreations* **pastime**, hobby, leisure activity.
– OPPOSITES work.

recrimination n. **accusation(s)**, counter-accusation(s), countercharge(s), counter-attack(s), retaliation(s).

recruit v. **1** *more soldiers were recruited* **enlist**, call up, conscript; US draft, muster in; old use levy. **2** *the king recruited an army* **muster**, form, raise, mobilize. **3** *the company is recruiting staff* **hire**, employ, take on; enrol, sign up, engage.
– OPPOSITES disband, dismiss.

▸ n. **1** *new recruits were enlisted* **conscript**, new soldier; US draftee; Brit. informal sprog; N. Amer. informal yardbird. **2** *top-quality recruits* **trainee**, newcomer, initiate, beginner, novice; N. Amer. hire; informal rookie, newbie; N. Amer. informal tenderfoot, greenhorn.

rectify v. **correct**, (put) right, put to rights, sort out, deal with, amend, remedy, repair, fix, make good, resolve, settle; informal patch up.

rectitude n. **righteousness**, goodness, virtue, morality, honour, honourableness, integrity, principle, probity, honesty, trustworthiness, uprightness, decency, good character.

recumbent adj. **lying**, flat, horizontal, stretched out, sprawled (out), reclining, prone, prostrate, supine; lying down.
– OPPOSITES upright.

recuperate v. **1** *he went to France to recuperate* **get better**, recover, convalesce, get well, regain one's strength/health, get over something. **2** *he recuperated the money* **get back**, regain, recover, recoup, retrieve, reclaim, repossess, redeem.

recur v. **happen again**, reoccur, occur again, repeat (itself); come back (again), return, reappear, appear again; formal recrudesce.

recurrent adj. **repeated**, recurring, repetitive, periodic, cyclical, seasonal, perennial, regular, frequent; intermittent, sporadic, spasmodic.

recycle v. **reuse**, reprocess, reclaim, recover; salvage, save.

red adj. **1** *a red dress* scarlet, vermilion, ruby, cherry, cerise, cardinal, carmine, wine, blood-red; coral, cochineal, rose; brick-red, maroon, rusty, rufous; reddish; literary damask, vermeil, sanguine. **2** *he was red in the face* **flushed**, reddish, pink, pinkish, florid, rubicund; ruddy, rosy, glowing; burning, feverish; literary rubescent; old use sanguine. **3** *his eyes were red* **bloodshot**, swollen, sore. **4** *red hair* reddish, auburn, Titian, chestnut, carroty, ginger.

▸ n. informal derogatory *the war against the Reds*

Communist, socialist, left-winger, leftist, anti-capitalist; informal commie, lefty.

□ **in the red** overdrawn, in debt, in debit, in deficit, in arrears.

see red informal become very angry, become enraged, lose one's temper; informal go mad, go crazy, go wild, go bananas, hit the roof, go up the wall, fly off the handle, blow one's top, flip (one's lid), go ballistic; Brit. informal go spare, do one's nut; N. Amer. informal flip one's wig, blow one's lid/stack.

red-blooded adj. **manly**, masculine, virile, macho.

redden v. **go/turn red**, blush, flush, colour (up), burn.

redeem v. **1** *one feature redeems the book* **save**, compensate for the defects of, vindicate. **2** *he fully redeemed himself next time* **vindicate**, free from blame, absolve. **3** *you cannot redeem their sins* **atone for**, make amends for, make restitution for. **4** *redeeming sinners* **save**, deliver from sin, convert. **5** *Billy redeemed his drums from the pawnbrokers* **retrieve**, regain, recover, get back, reclaim, repossess; buy back. **6** *this voucher can be redeemed at any branch* **exchange**, cash in, convert, trade in. **7** *they could not redeem their debts* **pay off/back**, clear, discharge, honour. **8** *he made no effort to redeem his promise* **fulfil**, carry out, discharge, make good; keep (to), stick to, hold to, adhere to, abide by, honour.

redeeming adj. **compensating**, compensatory, extenuating, redemptive.

redemption n. **1** *God's redemption of his people* **salvation**, saving, deliverance. **2** *the redemption of their possessions* **retrieval**, recovery, reclamation, repossession, return. **3** *the redemption of credit vouchers* **exchange**, cashing in, conversion. **4** *the redemption of the mortgage* **paying off/back**, discharge, clearing, honouring. **5** *the redemption of his obligations* **fulfilment**, carrying out, discharge, performing, honouring, meeting.

red-handed adj. **in the act**, with one's fingers/hand in the till, in flagrante delicto; Brit. informal with one's trousers down; N. Amer. informal with one's pants down.

redolent adj. **evocative**, suggestive, reminiscent.

redoubtable adj. **formidable**, awe-inspiring, fearsome, daunting; impressive, commanding, indomitable, invincible, doughty, mighty.

redound v. formal **contribute to**, be conducive to, result in, lead to, have an effect; formal conduce to.

redress v. **1** *we redressed the problem* **rectify**, correct, right, put to rights, compensate for, amend, remedy, make good, resolve, settle. **2** *we aim to redress the balance* **even up**, regulate, equalize.

▶ n. *your best hope of redress* **compensation**, reparation, restitution, recompense, repayment, indemnity, indemnification, retribution, satisfaction; justice.

reduce v. **1** *the aim is to reduce pollution* **lessen**, make smaller, lower, bring down, decrease, diminish, minimize; shrink, narrow, contract, shorten; axe, cut (back/down), make cutbacks in, trim, slim (down), prune; rationalize, downsize; informal chop. **2** *he reduced her to tears* **bring to**, bring to the point of, drive to. **3** *he was reduced to the ranks* **demote**, downgrade, lower (in rank). **4** *bread has been reduced* **make cheaper**, lower the price of, cut (in price), mark down, discount, put on sale; informal slash, knock down.

– OPPOSITES increase, put up.

□ **in reduced circumstances** impoverished, in straitened circumstances, ruined, bankrupted; poor, indigent, impecunious, in penury, poverty-stricken, destitute; needy, badly off, hard up; informal flat (broke), without two pennies to rub together, strapped for cash; Brit. informal stony broke, skint, in Queer Street; N. Amer. informal stone broke; formal penurious.

reduction n. **1** *a reduction in pollution* **lessening**, lowering, decrease, diminution. **2** *a reduction in staff* **cut**, cutback, scaling down, rationalization, trimming, pruning, axing, chopping. **3** *a reduction in inflationary pressure* **easing**, lightening, moderation, alleviation. **4** *a reduction in status* **demotion**, downgrading, lowering. **5** *substantial reductions* **discount**, markdown, deduction, (price) cut, concession.

redundancy n. **1** *redundancy in language* **superfluity**, unnecessariness, excess. **2** *redundancies are in the offing* **sacking**, dismissal, lay-off, discharge; unemployment.

redundant adj. **1** *many churches are now redundant* **unnecessary**, not required, unneeded, uncalled for, surplus (to requirements), superfluous. **2** *2,000 workers were made redundant* **sacked**, dismissed, laid off, discharged; unemployed, jobless, out of work.

– OPPOSITES employed.

reef n. **shoal**, bar, sandbar, sandbank, spit; Scottish skerry.

reek v. *the whole place reeked* **stink**, smell (bad), stink to high heaven.

▶ n. *the reek of cattle dung* **stink**, bad smell, stench, malodour; Brit. informal niff, pong, whiff; literary miasma.

reel v. **1** *he reeled as the ship began to roll* **stagger**, lurch, sway, rock, stumble, totter, wobble, falter. **2** *we were reeling from the crisis* **be shaken**, be stunned, be in shock, be shocked, be taken aback, be staggered, be aghast, be upset. **3** *the room reeled* **go round (and round)**, whirl, spin, revolve, swirl, twirl, turn, swim.

□ **reel something off** recite, rattle off, list, run through, enumerate, detail, itemize.

refer v. **1** *he referred to errors in the article* **mention**, make reference to, allude to, touch on, reference, speak of/about, talk of/about, write about, comment on, deal with, point

r

out, call attention to. **2** *the matter has been referred to my insurers* **pass**, hand on/over, send on, transfer, remit, entrust, assign. **3** *these figures refer only to 2010* **apply to**, be relevant to, concern, relate to, be connected with, pertain to, appertain to, be pertinent to, have a bearing on, cover. **4** *the name refers to a Saxon village* **denote**, describe, indicate, mean, signify, designate. **5** *the constable referred to his notes* **consult**, turn to, look at, have recourse to.

referee n. **1** *the referee blew his whistle* **umpire**, judge, linesman, line judge; informal ref. **2** *include the names of two referees* **supporter**, character witness, advocate.
▸ v. **1** *he refereed the game* **umpire**, judge. **2** *they asked him to referee in the dispute* **arbitrate**, mediate; adjudicate.

reference n. **1** *his journal contains many references to railways* **mention of**, allusion to, comment on, remark about. **2** *references are given in the bibliography* **source**, citation, authority, credit; bibliographical data. **3** *reference to a higher court* **referral**, transfer, remission. **4** *a glowing reference* **testimonial**, character reference, recommendation; credentials; dated character.
□ **with reference to** apropos, with regard to, regarding, with respect to, on the subject of, re; in relation to, relating to, in connection with.

referendum n. **vote**, plebiscite, ballot, poll.

refine v. **1** *refining our cereal foods* **purify**, process, treat. **2** *helping students to refine their language skills* **improve**, perfect, polish (up), hone, fine-tune.

refined adj. **1** *refined sugar* **purified**, processed, treated. **2** *a refined lady* **cultivated**, cultured, polished, stylish, elegant, sophisticated, urbane; polite, gracious, well mannered, well bred, gentlemanly, ladylike, genteel. **3** *a person of refined taste* **discriminating**, discerning, fastidious, exquisite, impeccable, fine.
– OPPOSITES crude, coarse.

refinement n. **1** *the refinement of sugar* **purification**, refining, processing, treatment, treating. **2** *all writing needs endless refinement* **improvement**, polishing, honing, fine-tuning, touching up, finishing off, revision, editing. **3** *a woman of refinement* **style**, elegance, finesse, polish, sophistication, urbanity; politeness, grace, graciousness, good manners, good breeding, gentility; cultivation, taste, discrimination; humorous couth.

reflect v. **1** *the snow reflects light* **send back**, throw back, cast back. **2** *their expressions reflected their feelings* **indicate**, show, display, demonstrate, be evidence of, register, reveal, betray, disclose; express, communicate; formal evince. **3** *he reflected on his responsibilities* **think about**, give thought to, consider, give consideration to, review, mull over, contemplate, cogitate about/on, meditate on, muse on, brood on/over, turn over in one's mind; old use pore on;

rare cerebrate.
□ **reflect badly on** discredit, disgrace, shame, put in a bad light, damage, tarnish the reputation of, give a bad name to, bring into disrepute.

reflection n. **1** *the reflection of light* **sending back**, throwing back, casting back. **2** *her reflection in the mirror* **image**, likeness. **3** *your hands are a reflection of your well-being* **indication**, display, demonstration, manifestation; expression, evidence. **4** *a sad reflection on society* **slur**, aspersion, imputation, reproach, shame, criticism. **5** *after some reflection, he turned it down* **thought**, thinking, consideration, contemplation, deliberation, pondering, meditation, musing, rumination; formal cogitation; rare cerebration. **6** *write down your reflections* **opinion**, thought, view, belief, feeling, idea, impression, conclusion, assessment; comment, observation, remark.

reflex adj. **instinctive**, automatic, involuntary, reflexive, impulsive, intuitive, spontaneous, unconscious, unconditioned, untaught, unlearned.
– OPPOSITES conscious.

reform v. **1** *a plan to reform the system* **improve**, (make) better, ameliorate, refine; alter, make alterations to, change, adjust, make adjustments to, adapt, amend, revise, reshape, refashion, redesign, restyle, revamp, rebuild, reconstruct, remodel, reorganize. **2** *after his marriage he reformed* **mend one's ways**, change for the better, turn over a new leaf, improve.
▸ n. *the reform of the prison system* **improvement**, amelioration, refinement; alteration, change, adaptation, amendment, revision, reshaping, refashioning, redesigning, restyling, revamp, revamping, renovation, rebuilding, reconstruction, remodelling, reorganizing, reorganization.

refractory adj. formal **obstinate**, stubborn, mulish, pig-headed, obdurate, headstrong, self-willed, wayward, wilful, perverse, contrary, recalcitrant, obstreperous, disobedient; Brit. informal bloody-minded, bolshie, stroppy; N. Amer. informal balky; old use contumacious, froward.
– OPPOSITES obedient.

refrain v. **abstain**, desist, hold back, stop oneself, forbear, avoid, eschew, shun, renounce; informal swear off; formal forswear, abjure.

refresh v. **1** *the cool air will refresh me* **reinvigorate**, revitalize, revive, restore, fortify, enliven, perk up, stimulate, freshen, energize, exhilarate, reanimate, wake up, revivify, inspirit; blow away the cobwebs; informal buck up, pep up. **2** *let me refresh your memory* **jog**, stimulate, prompt, prod. **3** N. Amer. *I refreshed his glass* **refill**, top up, replenish, recharge.
– OPPOSITES weary.

refreshing adj. **1** *a refreshing drink* **invigorating**, revitalizing, reviving, restoring, bracing, fortifying, enlivening, inspiriting, stimulating, energizing, exhilarating. **2** *a refreshing change of direction* **welcome**, stimulating, fresh, imaginative, innovative.

refreshment n. **1** *refreshments were available in the interval* **food and drink**, sustenance, provender; snacks, titbits, eatables; informal nibbles, eats, grub, nosh; formal comestibles; literary viands; dated victuals; old use aliment. **2** *spiritual refreshment* **invigoration**, revival, stimulation, reanimation, revivification, rejuvenation, regeneration, renewal.

refrigerate v. **keep cold**, cool (down), chill.
– OPPOSITES heat.

refuge n. **1** *homeless people seeking refuge in subway stations* **shelter**, protection, safety, security, asylum, sanctuary. **2** *a refuge for mountain gorillas* **sanctuary**, shelter, place of safety, (safe) haven, sanctum; retreat, bolt-hole, hiding place, hideaway, hideout.

refugee n. **displaced person**, DP, fugitive, asylum seeker, exile, émigré, stateless person; Austral. informal reffo.

refund v. **1** *we will refund your money if you're not satisfied* **repay**, give back, return, pay back. **2** *they refunded the subscribers* **reimburse**, compensate, recompense, remunerate, indemnify.
▸ n. *a full refund* **repayment**, reimbursement, rebate.

refurbish v. **renovate**, recondition, rehabilitate, revamp, overhaul, restore, renew, redevelop, rebuild, reconstruct; redecorate, spruce up, upgrade, refit; N. Amer. bring up to code; informal do up; N. Amer. informal rehab.

refusal n. **1** *we had one refusal to our invitation* **non-acceptance**, no, dissent, demurral, negation, turndown; regrets. **2** *you can have first refusal* **option**, choice, opportunity to purchase. **3** *the refusal of planning permission* **withholding**, denial, turndown.

refuse[1] v. **1** *he refused their invitation* **decline**, turn down, say no to; reject, spurn, rebuff, dismiss; send one's regrets; informal pass up. **2** *the Council refused planning permission* **withhold**, not grant, deny.
– OPPOSITES accept, grant.

refuse[2] n. *piles of refuse* **rubbish**, waste, debris, litter, detritus, dross; dregs, leftovers; N. Amer. garbage, trash; Austral./NZ mullock; informal dreck, junk.

refute v. **1** *attempts to refute Einstein's theory* **disprove**, prove wrong/false, controvert, rebut, give the lie to, explode, debunk, discredit, invalidate; informal shoot full of holes; formal confute. **2** *she refuted the allegation* **deny**, reject, repudiate, rebut; contradict; formal gainsay.

regain v. **1** *government troops regained the capital* **recover**, get back, win back, recoup, retrieve, reclaim, repossess; take back, retake, recapture, reconquer. **2** *they regained dry land* **return to**, get back to, reach again, rejoin.

regal adj. **1** *a regal feast.* See **splendid** (sense 1). **2** *his regal forebears* **royal**, kingly, queenly, princely.

regale v. **1** *they were lavishly regaled* **entertain**, wine and dine, fete, feast, serve, feed. **2** *he regaled her with colourful stories* **entertain**, amuse, divert, delight, fascinate, captivate.

regard v. **1** *we regard these results as encouraging* **consider**, look on, view, see, think of, judge, deem, estimate, assess, reckon, adjudge, rate, gauge. **2** *he regarded her coldly* **look at**, contemplate, eye, gaze at, stare at; watch, observe, view, study, scrutinize; literary behold.
▸ n. **1** *he has no regard for human life* **consideration**, care, concern, thought, notice, heed, attention. **2** *doctors are held in high regard* **esteem**, respect, acclaim, admiration, approval, approbation, estimation. **3** *Jamie sends his regards* **best wishes**, good wishes, greetings, kind/kindest regards, felicitations, salutations, respects, compliments, best, love. **4** *his steady regard* **(fixed) look**, gaze, stare; observation, contemplation, study, scrutiny. **5** *in this regard I disagree with you* **respect**, aspect, point, item, particular, detail, specific; matter, issue, topic, question.
□ **with regard to** See **regarding**.

regarding prep. **concerning**, as regards, with/in regard to, with respect to, with reference to, relating to, respecting, re, about, apropos, on the subject of, in connection with, vis-à-vis.

regardless adv. *he decided to go, regardless* **anyway**, anyhow, in any case, nevertheless, nonetheless, despite everything, in spite of everything, even so, all the same, in any event, come what may; informal irregardless.
□ **regardless of** irrespective of, without regard to, without reference to, disregarding, without consideration of, discounting, ignoring, notwithstanding, no matter; informal irregardless of.

regenerate v. **revive**, revitalize, renew, restore, breathe new life into, revivify, rejuvenate, reanimate, resuscitate; informal give a shot in the arm to.

regime n. **1** *the former Communist regime* **government**, authorities, rule, authority, control, command, administration, leadership. **2** *a health regime* **system**, arrangement, scheme; order, pattern, method, procedure, routine, course, plan, programme.

regiment n. *the regiment was fighting in France* **unit**, outfit, force, corps, division, brigade, battalion, squadron, company, platoon.
▸ v. *their life is strictly regimented* **organize**, order, systematize, control, regulate, manage, discipline.

regimented adj. **strictly regulated**, organized, disciplined, controlled, ordered, systematic, orderly, rigid, inflexible.

region n. *the western region of the country* **district**, province, territory, division, area, section, sector, zone, belt, part, quarter; informal parts.

regional adj. **1** *regional variation* **geographical**, territorial; by region. **2** *a regional parliament* **local**, localized, provincial, district, parochial.
– OPPOSITES national.

register n. **1** *the register of electors* **list**, listing, roll, roster, index, directory, catalogue, inventory. **2** *the parish register* **record**, chronicle, log, logbook, ledger, archive; annals, files. **3** *the lower register of the piano* **range**, reaches; notes, octaves.
▶ v. **1** *I wish to register a complaint* **record**, put on record, enter, file, lodge, write down, put in writing, submit, report, note, minute, log. **2** *it is not too late to register* **enrol**, put one's name down, enlist, sign on/up, apply. **3** *the dial registered a speed of 100 mph* **indicate**, read, record, show, display. **4** *her face registered anger* **display**, show, express, exhibit, betray, evidence, reveal, manifest, demonstrate, bespeak; formal evince. **5** *the content of her statement did not register* **make an impression**, get through, sink in, penetrate, have an effect, strike home.

regress v. **revert**, retrogress, relapse, lapse, backslide, slip back; deteriorate, decline, go downhill, worsen, degenerate, get worse.
– OPPOSITES progress.

regret v. *they came to regret their decision* **be sorry about**, feel contrite about, feel remorse about/for, be remorseful about, rue, repent (of), feel repentant about, be regretful at/about.
▶ n. **1** *both players later expressed regret* **remorse**, sorrow, contrition, contriteness, repentance, penitence, guilt, compunction, ruefulness. **2** *please give your grandmother my regrets* **apology**, apologies; refusal. **3** *they left with genuine regret* **sadness**, sorrow, disappointment, unhappiness, grief.
– OPPOSITES satisfaction.

regretful adj. **sorry**, remorseful, contrite, repentant, rueful, penitent, conscience-stricken, apologetic, guilt-ridden, ashamed, shamefaced.
– OPPOSITES unrepentant.

regrettable adj. **undesirable**, unfortunate, unwelcome, sorry, woeful, disappointing; deplorable, lamentable, shameful, disgraceful.

regular adj. **1** *plant them at regular intervals* **uniform**, even, consistent, constant, unchanging, unvarying, fixed. **2** *a regular beat* **rhythmic**, steady, even, uniform, constant, unchanging, unvarying. **3** *the subject of regular protests* **frequent**, repeated, continual, recurrent, periodic, constant, perpetual, numerous. **4** *regular methods of business* **established**, conventional, orthodox, proper, official, approved, bona fide, standard, usual, traditional, tried and tested. **5** *a regular procedure* **methodical**, systematic,

structured, well ordered, well organized, orderly, efficient. **6** *his regular route to work* **usual**, normal, customary, habitual, routine, typical, accustomed, established. **7** informal dated *he's a regular charmer* **utter**, real, absolute, complete, thorough, total, out-and-out, perfect; N. Amer. full-bore; Brit. informal right, proper; Austral./NZ informal fair.
– OPPOSITES erratic, occasional.

regulate v. **1** *the flow of the river has been regulated* **control**, adjust, manage. **2** *a new act regulating businesses* **supervise**, police, monitor, check (up on), be responsible for; control, manage, direct, guide, govern.

regulation n. **1** *EU regulations* **rule**, ruling, order, directive, act, law, by-law, statute, edict, canon, pronouncement, dictate, dictum, decree, fiat, command, precept. **2** *the regulation of blood sugar* **adjustment**, control, management, balancing. **3** *the regulation of financial services* **supervision**, policing, superintendence, monitoring, inspection; control, management, responsibility for.
▶ adj. *regulation dress* **official**, prescribed, set, fixed, mandatory, compulsory, obligatory.
– OPPOSITES unofficial.

regurgitate v. **1** *a ruminant continually regurgitates food* **disgorge**, bring up; old use regorge. **2** *regurgitating facts* **repeat**, say again, restate, reiterate, recite, parrot; informal trot out.

rehabilitate v. **1** *efforts to rehabilitate patients* **restore to normality**, reintegrate, readapt; N. Amer. informal rehab. **2** *former dissidents were rehabilitated* **reinstate**, restore, bring back; pardon, absolve, exonerate, forgive; formal exculpate. **3** *rehabilitating vacant housing* **recondition**, restore, renovate, refurbish, revamp, overhaul, redevelop, rebuild, reconstruct; redecorate, spruce up; upgrade, refit, modernize; informal do up; N. Amer. informal rehab.

rehearsal n. **practice (session)**, trial, read-through, run-through; informal dry run.

rehearse v. **1** *I rehearsed the role* **practise**, read through, run through/over, go over, prepare. **2** *he rehearsed the Vienna Philharmonic* **train**, drill, prepare, coach, put someone through their paces. **3** *the document rehearsed all the arguments* **enumerate**, list, itemize, detail, spell out, catalogue, recite, rattle off; restate, repeat, reiterate, recapitulate, go over, run through; informal recap.

reign v. **1** *Robert II reigned for nineteen years* **be king/queen**, be monarch, be sovereign, sit on the throne, wear the crown, rule. **2** *chaos reigned* **prevail**, exist, be present, be the case, occur, be prevalent, be current, be rife, be rampant, be the order of the day, be in force, be in effect; formal obtain.
▶ n. **1** *during Henry's reign* **rule**, sovereignty, monarchy. **2** *his reign as manager* **time**, period, incumbency, managership, leadership.

reigning adj. **1** *the reigning monarch* **ruling**,
regnant; on the throne. **2** *the reigning
world champion* **incumbent**, current. **3** *the
reigning legal conventions* **prevailing**,
existing, current; usual, common,
recognized, established, accepted, popular,
widespread.

reimburse v. **1** *they will reimburse your
travel costs* **repay**, refund, return, pay
back. **2** *we'll reimburse you* **compensate**,
recompense, repay.

rein n. *there is no rein on his behaviour*
restraint, check, curb, constraint,
restriction, limitation, control, brake.
▸ v. *they reined back costs* **restrain**, check, curb,
constrain, hold back/in, keep under control,
regulate, restrict, control, curtail, limit.
◻ **free rein** freedom, a free hand, leeway,
latitude, flexibility, liberty, independence,
free play, licence, room to manoeuvre, carte
blanche.
keep a tight rein on exercise strict control
over, regulate, discipline, regiment, keep
in line.

reincarnation n. **rebirth**, transmigration of
the soul, metempsychosis.

reinforce v. **1** *troops reinforced the dam*
strengthen, fortify, bolster up, shore up,
buttress, prop up, underpin, brace, support.
2 *reinforcing links between colleges and
companies* **strengthen**, fortify, support;
cement, boost, promote, encourage, deepen,
enrich, enhance, intensify, improve. **3** *the
need to reinforce NATO troops* **augment**,
increase, add to, supplement, boost, top up.

reinforcement n. **1** *the reinforcement of
our defences* **strengthening**, fortification,
bolstering, shoring up, buttressing, bracing.
2 *reinforcement of the bomber force*
augmentation, increase, supplementing,
boosting, topping up. **3** *they returned later
with reinforcements* **additional troops**,
fresh troops, auxiliaries, reserves; support,
back-up, help.

reinstate v. **restore**, return to power, put
back, bring back, reinstitute, reinstall.

reiterate v. **repeat**, say again, restate,
recapitulate, go over (and over), rehearse.

reject v. **1** *the miners rejected the offer* **turn
down**, refuse, decline, say no to, spurn;
informal give the thumbs down to. **2** *Jamie
rejected her* **rebuff**, spurn, shun, snub,
repudiate, cast off/aside, discard, abandon,
desert, turn one's back on, have nothing
(more) to do with, wash one's hands of;
informal give someone the brush-off; Brit. informal
give someone the push, give someone the
elbow; literary forsake.
– OPPOSITES accept.
▸ n. **1** *I got it cheap— it's a reject* **second**,

discard. **2** *what a reject!* **failure**, loser,
incompetent.

rejection n. **1** *a rejection of the offer*
refusal, declining, turning down,
dismissal, spurning. **2** *Madeleine's rejection
of him* **repudiation**, rebuff, spurning,
abandonment, desertion; informal brush-off;
literary forsaking.

rejoice v. **1** *they rejoiced when she returned*
be joyful, be happy, be pleased, be glad, be
delighted, be elated, be ecstatic, be euphoric,
be overjoyed, be as pleased as Punch, be
cock-a-hoop, be jubilant, be in raptures,
be beside oneself with joy, be delirious, be
thrilled, be on cloud nine, be in seventh
heaven; celebrate, make merry; informal be
over the moon, be on top of the world; Austral.
informal be wrapped; literary joy; old use jubilate.
2 *he rejoiced in their success* **take delight**,
find/take pleasure, feel satisfaction, find joy,
enjoy, revel in, glory in, delight in, relish,
savour.
– OPPOSITES mourn.

rejoicing n. **happiness**, pleasure, joy,
gladness, delight, elation, jubilation,
exuberance, exultation, celebration, revelry,
merrymaking.

rejoin[1] v. *the path rejoins the main road
further on* **return to**, be reunited with, join
again, reach again, regain.

rejoin[2] v. *Eugene rejoined that you couldn't
expect much* **answer**, reply, respond, return,
retort, riposte, counter.

rejoinder n. **answer**, reply, response, retort,
riposte, counter; informal comeback.

rejuvenate v. **revive**, revitalize, regenerate,
breathe new life into, revivify, reanimate,
resuscitate, refresh, reawaken, put new life
into; informal give a shot in the arm to, pep up,
buck up.

relapse v. **1** *a few patients relapse* **become
ill again**, have/suffer a relapse, deteriorate,
degenerate, take a turn for the worse. **2** *she
relapsed into silence* **revert**, lapse; regress,
retrogress, slip back, slide back, degenerate.
– OPPOSITES improve.
▸ n. **1** *one patient suffered a relapse*
deterioration, turn for the worse. **2** *a
relapse into alcoholism* **decline**, lapse,
deterioration, degeneration, reversion,
regression, retrogression, fall, descent, slide.

relate v. **1** *he related many stories* **tell**,
recount, narrate, report, chronicle,
outline, delineate, retail, recite, repeat,
communicate, impart. **2** *mortality is related
to unemployment levels* **connect (with)**,
associate (with), link (with), correlate
(with), ally (with), couple (with). **3** *the
charges relate to offences committed
in August* **apply**, be relevant, concern,
pertain to, be pertinent to, have a bearing
on, appertain to, involve; old use regard.
4 *she cannot relate to her stepfather* **have
a rapport**, get on (well), feel sympathy,
feel for, identify with, empathize with,
understand; informal hit it off with.

related adj. **1** *related ideas* **connected**, interconnected, associated, linked, coupled, allied, affiliated, concomitant, corresponding, analogous, kindred, parallel, comparable, homologous, equivalent. **2** *are you two related?* **of the same family**, kin, akin, kindred, consanguineous; formal cognate.
– OPPOSITES unconnected.

relation n. **1** *the complex relation between church and state* **connection**, relationship, association, link, correlation, correspondence, parallel, alliance, bond, interrelation, interconnection. **2** *this had no relation to national security* **relevance**, applicability, reference, pertinence, bearing. **3** *are you a relation of his?* **relative**, member of the family, kinsman, kinswoman; (**relations**) family, (kith and) kin, kindred. **4** *improving relations with India* **dealings**, communication, relationship, connections, contact, interaction. **5** *sexual relations.* See **sex** (sense 1).

relationship n. **1** *the relationship between diet and diabetes* **connection**, relation, association, link, correlation, correspondence, parallel, alliance, bond, interrelation, interconnection. **2** *evidence of their relationship to a common ancestor* **family ties/connections**, blood relationship, kinship, affinity, consanguinity, common ancestry/lineage. **3** *the end of their relationship* **romance**, (love) affair, love, liaison, amour.

relative adj. **1** *the relative importance of each factor* **comparative**, respective, comparable, correlative, parallel, corresponding. **2** *the food required is relative to body weight* **proportionate**, proportional, in proportion, commensurate, corresponding. **3** *relative ease* **moderate**, reasonable, a fair degree of, considerable, comparative.
▶ n. *he's a relative of mine* **relation**, member of someone's/the family, kinsman, kinswoman; (**relatives**) family, (kith and) kin, kindred, kinsfolk.

relatively adv. **comparatively**, by comparison; quite, fairly, reasonably, rather, somewhat, to a certain degree/extent, tolerably, passably; informal pretty, kind of, sort of.

relax v. **1** *yoga is helpful in learning to relax* **unwind**, loosen up, ease up/off, slow down, de-stress, unbend, rest, put one's feet up, take it easy; informal chill (out), cool out; N. Amer. informal hang loose. **2** *a walk will relax you* **calm (down)**, unwind, loosen up, make less tense/uptight, soothe, pacify, compose. **3** *he relaxed his grip* **loosen**, loose, slacken, unclench, weaken, lessen. **4** *her muscles relaxed* **become less tense**, loosen, slacken, unknot. **5** *they relaxed the restrictions* **moderate**, modify, temper, ease (up on), loosen, lighten, dilute, weaken, reduce, decrease; informal let up on.
– OPPOSITES tense, tighten.

relaxation n. **1** *a state of relaxation* (**mental**) **repose**, calm, tranquillity, peacefulness, loosening up, unwinding. **2** *I just play for relaxation* **recreation**, enjoyment, amusement, entertainment, fun, pleasure, leisure; informal R & R. **3** *muscle relaxation* **loosening**, slackening, loosing. **4** *relaxation of censorship rules* **moderation**, easing, loosening, lightening; alleviation, mitigation, dilution, weakening, reduction; informal letting up.

relay n. *a live relay of the performance* **broadcast**, transmission, showing.
▶ v. *relaying messages through a third party* **pass on**, hand on, transfer, repeat, communicate, send, transmit, disseminate, spread, circulate.

release v. **1** *all prisoners were released* (**set**) **free**, let go/out, allow to leave, liberate, set at liberty. **2** *Burke released the animal* **untie**, undo, loose, let go, unleash, unfetter. **3** *this released staff for other duties* **make available**, free (up), put at someone's disposal, supply, furnish, provide. **4** *she released Stephen from his promise* **excuse**, exempt, discharge, deliver, absolve; informal let off. **5** *police released the news yesterday* **make public**, make known, issue, break, announce, declare, report, reveal, divulge, disclose, publish, broadcast, circulate, communicate, disseminate. **6** *the film has been released on DVD* **launch**, put on the market, put on sale, bring out, make available.
– OPPOSITES imprison, tie up.
▶ n. **1** *the release of political prisoners* **freeing**, liberation, deliverance; freedom, liberty. **2** *the release of the news* **issuing**, announcement, declaration, reporting, revealing, divulging, disclosure, publication, communication, dissemination. **3** *a press release* **announcement**, bulletin, newsflash, dispatch, proclamation. **4** *the group's last release* CD, album, single, record; video, film, DVD; book.

relegate v. **downgrade**, lower (in rank/status), put down, move down; demote, degrade.
– OPPOSITES upgrade.

relent v. **1** *the government finally relented* **change one's mind**, do a U-turn, back-pedal, back down, give way/in, capitulate; become merciful, become lenient, agree to something, allow something, concede something; Brit. do an about-turn; formal accede. **2** *the rain has relented* **ease (off/up)**, slacken, let up, abate, drop, die down, lessen, decrease, subside, weaken, tail off.

relentless adj. **1** *their relentless pursuit of quality* **persistent**, continuing, constant, continual, continuous, non-stop, never-ending, unabating, interminable, incessant, unceasing, endless, unending, unremitting, unrelenting, unrelieved; unfaltering, unflagging, untiring, unwavering, dogged, single-minded, tireless, indefatigable; formal pertinacious. **2** *a relentless taskmaster* **harsh**, grim, cruel, severe, strict, remorseless, merciless, pitiless, ruthless, unmerciful, heartless, hard-hearted, unforgiving; inflexible, unbending, uncompromising, obdurate, unyielding.

relevant adj. **pertinent**, applicable, apposite, material, apropos, to the point, germane; connected, related, linked.

reliable adj. **1** *reliable evidence* **dependable**, good, well founded, authentic, valid, genuine, sound, true. **2** *a reliable friend* **trustworthy**, dependable, good, true, faithful, devoted, steadfast, staunch, constant, loyal, trusty, dedicated, unfailing; truthful, honest. **3** *reliable brakes* **dependable**, safe, fail-safe. **4** *a reliable firm* **reputable**, dependable, trustworthy, honest, responsible, established, proven.
– OPPOSITES untrustworthy.

reliance n. **1** *reliance on the state* **dependence**, dependency. **2** *reliance on his own judgement* **trust**, confidence, faith, belief, conviction.

relic n. **1** *a Viking relic* **artefact**, historical object, ancient object, antiquity, antique. **2** *a saint's relics* **remains**, corpse, bones, reliquiae; Medicine cadaver.

relief n. **1** *it was such a relief to share my worries* **reassurance**, consolation, comfort, solace. **2** *the relief of pain* **alleviation**, alleviating, relieving, assuagement, assuaging, palliation, allaying, soothing, easing, lessening, reduction. **3** *relief from her burden* **freedom**, release, liberation, deliverance. **4** *a little light relief* **respite**, amusement, diversion, entertainment, jollity, jollification, recreation. **5** *bringing relief to the starving* **help**, aid, assistance, succour, sustenance; charity, gifts, donations. **6** *his relief arrived to take over* **replacement**, substitute, deputy, reserve, cover, stand-in, supply, locum (tenens), understudy.
– OPPOSITES intensification.
◻ **throw something into relief** highlight, spotlight, give prominence to, point up, show up, emphasize, bring out, stress, accent, underline, underscore, accentuate.

relieve v. **1** *this helps relieve pain* **alleviate**, mitigate, assuage, ease, dull, reduce, lessen, diminish. **2** *relieving the boredom* **counteract**, reduce, alleviate, mitigate; interrupt, vary, stop, dispel, prevent. **3** *the helpers relieved us* **replace**, take over from, stand in for, fill in for, substitute for, deputize for, cover for. **4** *this relieves the teacher of a heavy load* **(set) free**, release, exempt, excuse, absolve, let off, discharge.
– OPPOSITES aggravate.

relieved adj. **glad**, thankful, grateful, pleased, happy, easy/easier in one's mind, reassured.
– OPPOSITES worried.

religion n. **faith**, belief, worship, creed; sect, cult, church, denomination.

WORD LINKS
theology, divinity the study of religious belief
pilgrim a person travelling to a holy place for religious reasons
proselytize convert someone from one religion to another
fundamentalism the strict following of the basic doctrines of a religion
heresy belief or opinion which goes against traditional religious doctrine
apostate a person who abandons a system of religious belief
heathen, infidel a person who does not belong to a widely held religion
pagan a person who has religious beliefs other than those of established religions

religious adj. **1** *a religious person* **devout**, pious, reverent, godly, God-fearing, churchgoing, practising, faithful, devoted, committed. **2** *religious beliefs* **spiritual**, theological, scriptural, doctrinal, ecclesiastical, church, churchly, holy, divine, sacred. **3** *religious attention to detail* **scrupulous**, conscientious, meticulous, sedulous, punctilious, strict, rigorous, close.
– OPPOSITES atheistic, secular.

relinquish v. **1** *he relinquished control of the company* **renounce**, give up/away, hand over, let go of. **2** *he relinquished his post* **leave**, resign from, stand down from, bow out of, give up; informal quit, chuck. **3** *he relinquished his pipe-smoking* **discontinue**, stop, cease, give up, desist from; informal quit, leave off, kick; formal forswear. **4** *she relinquished her grip* **let go**, release, loose, loosen, relax.
– OPPOSITES retain, continue.

relish n. **1** *he dug into his food with relish* **enjoyment**, gusto, delight, pleasure, glee, rapture, satisfaction, contentment, appreciation, enthusiasm, appetite; humorous delectation. **2** *a hot relish* **condiment**, sauce, dressing, flavouring, seasoning, dip.
– OPPOSITES dislike.
▶ v. **1** *he was relishing his moment of glory* **enjoy**, delight in, love, adore, take pleasure in, rejoice in, appreciate, savour, revel in, luxuriate in, glory in. **2** *I don't relish the drive* **look forward to**, fancy, anticipate with pleasure.

reluctance n. **unwillingness**, disinclination; hesitation, wavering, vacillation; doubts, second thoughts, misgivings; old use disrelish.

reluctant adj. **1** *her parents were reluctant* **unwilling**, disinclined, unenthusiastic, resistant, resisting, opposed; hesitant. **2** *a reluctant smile* **shy**, bashful, coy, diffident, reserved, timid, timorous. **3** *he was reluctant to leave* **loath**, unwilling, disinclined, indisposed; not in favour of, against, opposed to.
– OPPOSITES willing, eager.

rely v. **1** *we can rely on his discretion* **depend**, count, bank, place reliance, reckon; be confident of, be sure of, believe in, have faith in, trust in; informal swear by; N. Amer. informal figure on. **2** *we rely on government funding* **be dependent**, depend, be unable to manage without.

remain v. **1** *the problem will remain* **continue to exist**, endure, last, abide, carry on, persist, stay (around), prevail, survive, live on. **2** *he remained in hospital* **stay (behind/put)**, wait (around), be left, hang on; informal hang

r

around/round; Brit. informal hang about; old
use bide. **3** *union leaders remain sceptical*
continue to be, stay, keep, persist in being,
carry on being.

remainder n. **residue**, balance, remaining
part/number, rest, others, those left,
remnant(s), surplus, extra, excess, overflow;
technical residuum.

remaining adj. **1** *the remaining workers*
residual, surviving, left (over); extra, surplus,
spare, superfluous, excess. **2** *his remaining*
jobs **unsettled**, outstanding, unfinished,
incomplete, to be done, unattended to. **3** *my*
only remaining memories **surviving**, lasting,
enduring, continuing, persisting, abiding,
(still) existing.

remains plural n. **1** *the remains of her drink*
remainder, residue, remaining part/number,
rest, remnant(s); technical residuum. **2** *Roman*
remains **antiquities**, relics, reliquiae. **3** *the*
saint's remains **corpse**, (dead) body, carcass;
bones, skeleton; Medicine cadaver.

remark v. **1** *'You're quiet,' he remarked*
comment, say, observe, mention, reflect,
state, declare, announce, pronounce, assert;
formal opine. **2** *many critics remarked on their*
rapport **comment**, mention, refer to, speak
of, pass comment on. **3** *he remarked the*
absence of policemen **note**, notice, observe,
take note of, perceive, discern.
▸ n. **1** *his remarks have been misinterpreted*
comment, statement, utterance,
observation, declaration, pronouncement.
2 *worthy of remark* **attention**, notice,
comment, mention, observation,
acknowledgement.

remarkable adj. **extraordinary**,
exceptional, amazing, astonishing,
astounding, marvellous, wonderful,
sensational, stunning, incredible,
unbelievable, phenomenal, outstanding,
momentous; out of the ordinary, unusual,
uncommon, surprising; informal fantastic,
terrific, tremendous, stupendous, awesome;
literary wondrous.
– OPPOSITES ordinary.

remediable adj. **curable**, treatable,
operable; solvable, reparable, rectifiable,
resolvable.
– OPPOSITES incurable.

remedy n. **1** *herbal remedies* **treatment**,
cure, medicine, medication, medicament,
drug; old use physic. **2** *a remedy for all kinds*
of problems **solution**, answer, cure, antidote,
curative, nostrum, panacea, cure-all; informal
magic bullet.
▸ v. **1** *remedying the situation* **put/set right**,
put/set to rights, right, rectify, solve,
sort out, straighten out, resolve, correct,
repair, mend, make good. **2** *anaemia can be*
remedied by iron tablets **cure**, treat, heal,
make better; relieve, ease, alleviate, palliate.

remember v. **1** *remembering happy times*
recall, call to mind, recollect, think of;
reminisce about, look back on; old use bethink
oneself of. **2** *can you remember all that?*
memorize, commit to memory, retain; learn

off by heart. **3** *you must remember she's*
only five **bear/keep in mind**, be mindful
of the fact; take into account, take into
consideration. **4** *remember to feed the cat* **be**
sure, be certain; mind that you, make sure
that you. **5** *remember me to Alice* **send one's**
best wishes to, send one's regards to, give
one's love to, send one's compliments to,
say hello to. **6** *the nation remembered those*
who gave their lives **commemorate**, pay
tribute to, honour, salute, pay homage to.
7 *she remembered them in her will* **bequeath**
something to, leave something to, bestow
something on.
– OPPOSITES forget.

remembrance n. **1** *an expression of*
remembrance **recollection**, reminiscence;
remembering, recalling, recollecting,
reminiscing. **2** *she smiled at the remembrance*
memory, recollection, reminiscence,
thought. **3** *we sold poppies in remembrance*
commemoration, memory, recognition.
4 *a remembrance of my father* **memento**,
reminder, keepsake, souvenir, memorial,
token.

remind v. **1** *I left a note to remind him*
jog someone's memory, help someone
remember, prompt. **2** *the song reminded me*
of my sister **make someone think of**, make
someone remember, put someone in mind
of, bring/call to mind, evoke.

reminder n. **prompt**, aide-memoire,
mnemonic.

reminisce v. **remember**, cast one's mind
back to, look back on, be nostalgic about,
recall, recollect, reflect on, call to mind.

reminiscences plural n. **memories**,
recollections, reflections, remembrances.

reminiscent adj. **similar to**, comparable
with, evocative of, suggestive of, redolent of.

remiss adj. **negligent**, neglectful,
irresponsible, careless, thoughtless,
heedless, lax, slack, sloppy, slipshod,
lackadaisical; N. Amer. derelict; formal
delinquent.
– OPPOSITES careful.

remission n. **1** *the remission of all fees*
cancellation, setting aside, suspension,
revocation; formal abrogation. **2** *the cancer*
is in remission **respite**, abeyance. **3** *the*
wind howled without remission **respite**,
lessening, abatement, easing, decrease,
reduction, diminution, dying down,
slackening, lull; informal let-up. **4** *the remission*
of sins **forgiveness**, pardoning, absolution,
exoneration; formal exculpation.

remit v. **1** *the fines were remitted* **cancel**,
set aside, suspend, revoke; formal abrogate.
2 *remitting duties to the authorities* **send**,
dispatch, forward, hand over; pay. **3** *the case*
was remitted to the Court of Appeal **pass**
(on), refer, send on, transfer. **4** *remitting*
their sins **pardon**, forgive; excuse.
▸ n. *that is outside his remit* **area of**
responsibility, sphere, orbit, scope, ambit,
province; brief, instructions, orders; informal
bailiwick.

remittance n. 1 *send the form with your remittance* **payment**, money, fee; cheque; formal monies. 2 *a monthly remittance* **allowance**, sum of money.

remnant n. 1 *the remnants of the picnic* **remains**, remainder, leftovers, residue, rest; technical residuum. 2 *remnants of cloth* **scrap**, piece, bit, fragment, shred, offcut, oddment.

remonstrate v. 1 *'I'm not a child!' he remonstrated* **protest**, complain, expostulate; argue with, take issue with. 2 *we remonstrated against this proposal* **object strongly to**, complain vociferously about, protest against, argue against, oppose strongly, make a fuss about, challenge; deplore, condemn, denounce, criticize; informal kick up a fuss/stink about.

remorse n. **contrition**, regret, repentance, penitence, guilt, compunction, ruefulness, contriteness; pangs of conscience.

remorseful adj. **sorry**, full of regret, regretful, contrite, repentant, penitent, guilt-ridden, conscience-stricken, guilty, chastened, self-reproachful.
– OPPOSITES unrepentant.

remorseless adj. 1 **heartless**, pitiless, merciless, ruthless, callous, cruel, hard-hearted, inhumane, unmerciful, unforgiving, unfeeling. 2 *remorseless cost-cutting* **relentless**, unrelenting, unremitting, unabating, inexorable, unstoppable.
– OPPOSITES compassionate.

remote adj. 1 *areas remote from hospitals* **faraway**, distant, far (off), far removed. 2 *a remote mountain village* **isolated**, out of the way, off the beaten track, secluded, lonely, in the back of beyond, godforsaken, inaccessible; N. Amer. in the backwoods, lonesome; Austral./NZ in the backblocks, in the booay; informal in the sticks, in the middle of nowhere; N. Amer. informal in the tall timbers; Austral./NZ informal beyond the black stump; old use unapproachable. 3 *events remote from modern times* **irrelevant to**, unrelated to, unconnected to, unconcerned with, not pertinent to, immaterial to, unassociated with; foreign to, alien to. 4 *a remote possibility* **unlikely**, improbable, implausible, doubtful, dubious; faint, slight, slim, small, slender. 5 *she seems very remote* **aloof**, distant, detached, withdrawn, reserved, uncommunicative, unforthcoming, unapproachable, unresponsive, unfriendly, unsociable, introspective, introverted; informal stand-offish.
– OPPOSITES close, central.

removal n. 1 *the removal of heavy artillery* **taking away**, moving, carrying away. 2 *his removal from office* **dismissal**, ejection, expulsion, ousting, displacement, deposition; N. Amer. ouster; informal sacking, firing. 3 *the removal of customs barriers* **withdrawal**, elimination, taking away. 4 *the removal of errors* **deletion**, elimination, erasing, effacing, obliteration. 5 *the removal of weeds* **uprooting**, eradication. 6 *the removal of old branches* **cutting off**, chopping off, hacking

off. 7 *her removal to France* **move**, transfer, relocation. 8 *the removal of a rival* **killing**, murder, elimination; informal liquidation.
– OPPOSITES installation.

remove v. 1 *remove the plug* **detach**, unfasten; pull out, take out, disconnect. 2 *she removed the lid* **take off**, undo, unfasten. 3 *he removed a note from his wallet* **take out**, extract, produce, bring out, get out, pull out, withdraw. 4 *police removed boxes of documents* **take away**, carry away, move, transport; confiscate; informal cart off. 5 *Sheila removed the mud* **clean off**, wash off, wipe off, rinse off, scrub off, sponge out. 6 *Henry removed his coat* **take off**, pull off, slip out of; Brit. informal peel off. 7 *he was removed from his post* **dismiss**, discharge, get rid of, dislodge, displace, expel, oust, depose; informal sack, fire, kick out, boot out; Brit. informal turf out. 8 *tax relief was removed* **withdraw**, abolish, eliminate, get rid of, do away with, stop, cut, axe. 9 *Gabriel removed two words* **delete**, erase, rub out, cross out, strike out, score out. 10 *weeds have to be removed* **uproot**, pull out, eradicate. 11 *removing branches* **cut off**, chop off, lop off, hack off. 12 dated *he removed to Edinburgh* **move (house)**, relocate, transfer; emigrate; Brit. informal up sticks; N. Amer. informal pull up stakes. 13 *the mobsters removed their enemies*. See **kill** (sense 1 of the verb).
– OPPOSITES attach, insert, replace.
▸ n. *it is impossible, at this remove, to reconstruct the accident* **distance**, space of time, interval.

removed adj. **distant**, remote, disconnected; unrelated, unconnected, alien, foreign.

remunerate v. **pay**, reward, reimburse, recompense.

remuneration n. **payment**, pay, salary, wages; earnings, fee(s), reward, recompense, reimbursement; formal emolument(s).

remunerative adj. **lucrative**, well paid, financially rewarding; profitable.

renaissance n. **revival**, renewal, resurrection, reawakening, re-emergence, rebirth, reappearance, resurgence, regeneration; formal renascence.

rend v. **tear/rip apart**, tear/rip in two, split, rupture, sever; literary tear/rip asunder, sunder; rare dissever; old use rive.

render v. 1 *her fury rendered her speechless* **make**, cause to be/become, leave. 2 *rendering assistance* **give**, provide, supply, furnish, contribute; offer, proffer. 3 *the invoices rendered by the accountants* **send in**, present, submit. 4 *the jury rendered their verdict* **deliver**, return, hand down, give, announce. 5 *paintings rendered in vivid colours* **paint**, draw, depict, portray, represent, execute; literary limn. 6 *she rendered all three verses* **perform**, sing. 7 *the characters are vividly rendered* **act**, perform, play, depict, interpret. 8 *the phrase was rendered into English* **translate**, put, express, rephrase, reword. 9 *he rendered up the stolen money* **give back**, return, restore, pay back, repay, hand over, give up, surrender. **10** *the fat can be rendered* **melt down**, clarify.

rendezvous n. *Edward was late for their rendezvous* **meeting**, appointment, assignation; informal date; literary tryst.
▸ v. *the bar where they had agreed to rendezvous* **meet**, come together, gather, assemble.

rendition n. **1** *our rendition of Beethoven's Fifth* **performance**, rendering, interpretation, presentation, execution, delivery. **2** *the artist's rendition of Adam and Eve* **depiction**, portrayal, representation, artist's impression. **3** *an interpreter's rendition of the message* **translation**, interpretation, version.

renegade n. **1** *he was denounced as a renegade* **traitor**, defector, deserter, turncoat, rebel, mutineer; rare tergiversator. **2** *old use a religious renegade* **apostate**, heretic, dissenter; old use recreant.
▸ adj. **1** *renegade troops* **treacherous**, traitorous, disloyal, treasonous, rebel, mutinous. **2** *a renegade monk* **apostate**, heretic, heretical, dissident; old use recreant.
– OPPOSITES loyal.

renege v. **default on**, fail to honour, go back on, break, back out of, withdraw from, retreat from, welsh on, backtrack on; break one's word/promise.
– OPPOSITES honour.

renew v. **1** *I renewed my search* **resume**, return to, take up again, come back to, begin again, start again, restart, recommence; continue (with), carry on (with). **2** *they renewed their vows* **reaffirm**, reassert, repeat, reiterate, restate. **3** *something to renew her interest in life* **revive**, regenerate, revitalize, reinvigorate, restore, resuscitate, breathe new life into; old use renovate. **4** *the hotel was completely renewed* **renovate**, restore, refurbish, modernize, overhaul, redevelop, rebuild, reconstruct, remodel; N. Amer. bring something up to code; informal do up; N. Amer. informal rehab. **5** *they renewed Jackie's contract* **extend**, prolong. **6** *I renewed my supply of toilet paper* **replenish**, restock, resupply, top up, replace.

renewal n. **1** *the renewal of our friendship* **resumption**, recommencement, re-establishment; continuation. **2** *spiritual renewal* **regeneration**, revival, reinvigoration, revitalization; old use renovation. **3** *the renewal of older urban areas* **renovation**, restoration, modernization, reconditioning, overhauling, redevelopment, rebuilding, reconstruction.

renounce v. **1** *Edward renounced his claim to the throne* **give up**, relinquish, abandon, abdicate, surrender, waive, forgo; Law disclaim; formal abnegate. **2** *Hungary renounced the agreement* **reject**, refuse to abide by, repudiate. **3** *she renounced her family* **repudiate**, deny, reject, abandon, wash one's hands of, turn one's back on, disown, spurn, shun; literary forsake. **4** *he renounced alcohol* **abstain from**, give up, desist from, refrain from, keep off, eschew;

informal quit, pack in, lay off; formal forswear.
– OPPOSITES assert, accept, embrace, turn to.

renovate v. **modernize**, restore, refurbish, revamp, recondition, rehabilitate, overhaul, redevelop; update, upgrade, refit; N. Amer. bring something up to code; informal do up; N. Amer. informal rehab.

renown n. **fame**, distinction, eminence, pre-eminence, prominence, repute, reputation, prestige, acclaim, celebrity, notability.

renowned adj. **famous**, celebrated, famed, eminent, distinguished, acclaimed, illustrious, pre-eminent, prominent, great, esteemed, of note, of repute, well known, well thought of.
– OPPOSITES unknown.

rent[1] v. **1** *she rented a car* **hire**, lease, charter. **2** *why don't you rent it out?* **let (out)**, lease (out), hire (out); sublet, sublease.

rent[2] n. **1** *the rent in his trousers* **rip**, tear, split, hole, slash, slit. **2** *a vast rent in the mountains* **gorge**, chasm, fault, rift, fissure, crevasse.

renunciation n. **1** *Henry's renunciation of his throne* **relinquishment**, giving up, abandonment, abdication, surrender, waiving, forgoing; Law disclaimer; rare abnegation. **2** *his renunciation of luxury* **abstention**, refraining, going without, giving up, eschewal; formal forswearing. **3** *their renunciation of terrorism* **repudiation**, rejection, abandonment.

reorganize v. **restructure**, change, alter, adjust, transform, shake up, rationalize, rearrange, reshape, overhaul.

repair[1] v. **1** *the car was repaired* **mend**, fix (up), put/set right, restore (to working order), overhaul, service; informal patch up. **2** *they repaired the costumes* **mend**, darn; informal patch up. **3** *repairing relations with other countries* **put/set right**, mend, fix, straighten out, improve; informal patch up. **4** *she sought to repair the wrong she had done* **rectify**, make good, (put) right, correct, make up for, make amends for, make reparation for.
▸ n. **1** *in need of repair* **restoration**, fixing (up), mending, renovation; old use reparation. **2** *an invisible repair* **mend**, darn. **3** *in good repair* **condition**, working order, state, shape, fettle; Brit. informal nick.
☐ **beyond repair** irreparable, irreversible, irretrievable, irremediable, irrecoverable, past hope.

repair[2] v. formal *we repaired to the sitting room* **go**, head for, adjourn, wend one's way; formal remove; literary betake oneself.

reparable adj. **rectifiable**, remediable, curable, restorable, recoverable, retrievable, salvageable.

reparation n. **amends**, restitution, redress, compensation, recompense, repayment, atonement.

repartee n. **banter**, badinage, bantering, raillery, witticism(s), ripostes, sallies, quips, joking, jesting, chaff, chaffing; formal persiflage.

repast n. formal **meal**, feast, banquet; informal spread, feed, bite (to eat); Brit. informal nosh-up; formal collation; literary refection.

repay v. **1** *repaying customers who have been cheated* **reimburse**, refund, pay back/off, recompense, compensate, indemnify. **2** *the grants have to be repaid* **pay back**, return, refund, reimburse. **3** *I'd like to repay her generosity* **reciprocate**, return, requite, recompense, reward. **4** *interesting books that would repay further study* **be well worth**, be worth one's while.

repayment n. **1** *the repayment of tax* **refund**, reimbursement, paying back. **2** *repayment for all they have done* **recompense**, reward, compensation.

repeal v. *the Act was repealed* **revoke**, rescind, cancel, reverse, annul, nullify, declare null and void, quash, abolish; Law vacate; formal abrogate; old use recall.
– OPPOSITES enact.
▸n. *the repeal of the law* **revocation**, rescinding, cancellation, reversal, annulment, nullification, quashing, abolition; formal abrogation; old use recall.

repeat v. **1** *she repeated her story* **say again**, restate, reiterate, go/run through again, recapitulate; informal recap. **2** *children can repeat large chunks of text* **recite**, quote, parrot, regurgitate; informal trot out. **3** *Steele was invited to repeat his work* **do again**, redo, replicate, duplicate. **4** *the episodes were repeated* **rebroadcast**, rerun, reshow, show again.
▸n. **1** *a repeat of the previous year's final* **repetition**, duplication, replication, duplicate. **2** *repeats of his TV show* **rerun**, rebroadcast, reshowing.
□ **repeat itself** reoccur, recur, occur again, happen again.

repeated adj. **recurrent**, frequent, persistent, continual, incessant, constant, regular, periodic, numerous, (very) many, a great many.
– OPPOSITES occasional.

repeatedly adv. **frequently**, often, again and again, over and over (again), time and (time) again, many times, many a time; persistently, recurrently, constantly, continually, regularly; N. Amer. oftentimes; informal 24-7; literary oft, oft-times.

repel v. **1** *the rebels were repelled* **fight off**, repulse, drive back/away, force back, beat back, push back; hold off, ward off, keep at bay; Brit. see off; old use rebut. **2** *the coating will repel water* **be impervious to**, be impermeable to, keep out, resist. **3** *the thought of kissing him repelled me* **revolt**, disgust, repulse, sicken, nauseate, turn someone's stomach, be repulsive, be distasteful, be repugnant; informal turn off; N. Amer. informal gross out.

repellent adj. **1** *a repellent stench* **revolting**, repulsive, disgusting, repugnant, sickening, nauseating, stomach-turning, nauseous, vile, nasty, foul, horrible, awful, dreadful, terrible, obnoxious, loathsome, offensive, objectionable; abhorrent, despicable, reprehensible, contemptible, odious, hateful, execrable; N. Amer. vomitous; informal ghastly, horrid, gross, rank, yucky, icky; literary noisome; old use disgustful. **2** *a repellent coating* **impermeable**, impervious; -proof, -resistant.
– OPPOSITES delightful.

repent v. **feel remorse**, regret, be sorry, rue, reproach oneself, be ashamed, feel contrite; be penitent, be remorseful, be repentant.

repentance n. **remorse**, contrition, contriteness, penitence, regret, ruefulness, shame, guilt; old use rue.

repentant adj. **penitent**, contrite, regretful, rueful, remorseful, apologetic, chastened, ashamed, shamefaced.
– OPPOSITES impenitent.

repercussion n. **consequence**, result, effect, outcome; reverberation, backlash, aftermath, fallout; US blowback.

repertoire n. **collection**, stock, range, repertory, reserve, store, repository, supply.

repetition n. **1** *the statistics bear repetition* **reiteration**, repeating, restatement, retelling. **2** *the repetition of words* **repeating**, echoing, parroting. **3** *a repetition of the scene in the kitchen* **recurrence**, reoccurrence, rerun, repeat. **4** *there is some repetition* **repetitiousness**, repetitiveness, redundancy, tautology.

repetitious adj. *repetitious work.* See **repetitive**.

repetitive adj. **monotonous**, tedious, boring, humdrum, mundane, dreary, tiresome; unvaried, unchanging, unvarying, recurrent, recurring, repeated, repetitious, routine, mechanical, automatic.

rephrase v. **reword**, put in other words, express differently, paraphrase.

repine v. literary **fret**, be/feel unhappy, mope, eat one's heart out, brood; lament, grieve, mourn, sorrow, pine.

replace v. **1** *Adam replaced the receiver* **put back**, return, restore. **2** *a new chairman came in to replace him* **take the place of**, succeed, take over from, supersede; stand in for, substitute for, deputize for, cover for, relieve; informal step into someone's shoes/boots. **3** *she replaced the spoon with a fork* **substitute**, exchange, change, swap.
– OPPOSITES remove.

replacement n. **1** *we have to find a replacement* **successor**; **substitute**, stand-in, locum, relief, cover. **2** *the wiring was in need of replacement* **renewal**, replacing.

replenish v. **1** *she replenished their glasses* **refill**, top up, fill up, recharge; N. Amer. freshen. **2** *their supplies were replenished* **stock up**, restock, restore, replace.
– OPPOSITES empty, exhaust.

replete adj. **1** *the guests were replete* **well fed**, sated, satiated, full (up); glutted, gorged; informal stuffed. **2** *a sumptuous environment replete with antiques* **filled**, full, well stocked, well supplied, crammed,

r

packed, jammed, teeming, overflowing, bursting; informal jam-packed, chock-a-block.

replica n. **1** *is it real or a replica?* **copy**, model, duplicate, reproduction, replication; dummy, imitation, facsimile, carbon copy. **2** *a replica of her mother* **perfect likeness**, double, lookalike, (living) image, twin, clone; informal spitting image, (dead) ringer.

replicate v. **copy**, reproduce, duplicate, recreate, repeat, perform again; clone.

reply v. **1** *Rachel didn't reply* **answer**, respond, come back, write back. **2** *he replied defensively* **respond**, answer, rejoin, retort, riposte, counter, come back.
▸n. *he waited for a reply* **answer**, response, rejoinder, retort, riposte; informal comeback.

report v. **1** *the government reported a fall in inflation* **announce**, describe, give an account of, detail, outline, communicate, divulge, disclose, reveal, make public, publish, broadcast, proclaim, publicize. **2** *the newspapers reported on the scandal* **investigate**, look into, inquire into; write about, cover, describe, give details of, commentate on. **3** *I reported him to the police* **inform on**, tattle on; informal shop, tell on, squeal on, rat on, peach on; Brit. informal grass on. **4** *Juliet reported for duty* **present oneself**, arrive, turn up, clock in, sign in; Brit. clock on; N. Amer. punch in; informal show up.
▸n. **1** *a full report on the meeting* **account**, review, record, description, statement; transactions, proceedings, transcripts, minutes. **2** *reports of drug dealing* **news**, information, word, intelligence; literary tidings. **3** *newspaper reports* **story**, account, article, piece, item, column, feature, bulletin, dispatch. **4** Brit. *a school report* **assessment**, evaluation, appraisal; N. Amer. report card. **5** *reports of his imminent resignation* **rumour**, whisper; informal buzz; old use bruit. **6** *the report of a gun* **bang**, blast, crack, shot, gunshot, explosion, boom.

reporter n. **journalist**, correspondent, newspaperman, newspaperwoman, newsman, newswoman, columnist; Brit. pressman; N. Amer. legman, wireman; Austral. roundsman; informal newshound, hack, stringer, journo; N. Amer. informal newsy.

repose n. **1** *a face in repose* **rest**, relaxation, inactivity; sleep, slumber. **2** *they found true repose* **peace (and quiet)**, peacefulness, quiet, quietness, calm, tranquillity. **3** *he lost his repose* **composure**, serenity, equanimity, poise, self-possession, aplomb.
▸v. *the diamond reposed on a bed of velvet* **lie**, rest, be placed, be situated.

repository n. **store**, storehouse, depository; reservoir, bank, cache, treasury, fund, mine.

reprehensible adj. **deplorable**, disgraceful, discreditable, despicable, blameworthy, culpable, wrong, bad, shameful, dishonourable, objectionable, opprobrious, repugnant, inexcusable, unforgivable, indefensible, unjustifiable; criminal, sinful, scandalous, iniquitous; formal exceptionable.
– OPPOSITES praiseworthy.

represent v. **1** *a character representing a single quality* **symbolize**, stand for, personify, epitomize, typify, embody, illustrate. **2** *the initials which represent her qualification* **stand for**, designate, denote; literary betoken. **3** *Hathor is represented as a woman with cow's horns* **depict**, portray, render, picture, delineate, show, illustrate; literary limn. **4** *he represented himself as the owner of the factory* **describe as**, present as, profess to be, claim to be, pass oneself off as, pose as, pretend to be. **5** *ageing represents a threat to one's independence* **constitute**, be, amount to, be regarded as. **6** *a panel representing a cross section of the public* **be a typical sample of**, be representative of, typify. **7** *his solicitor represented him in court* **appear for**, act for, speak on behalf of. **8** *the Queen was represented by Lord Lewin* **deputize for**, substitute for, stand in for.

representation n. **1** *Rossetti's representation of women* **portrayal**, depiction, delineation, presentation, rendition. **2** *representations of the human form* **likeness**, painting, drawing, picture, illustration, sketch, artist's impression, image, model, figure, figurine, statue, statuette. **3** formal *making representations to the council* **statement**, deposition, allegation, declaration, exposition, report, protestation.

representative adj. **1** *a representative sample* **typical**, prototypical, characteristic, illustrative, archetypal. **2** *a female figure representative of Britain* **symbolic**, emblematic. **3** *representative government* **elected**, elective, democratic, popular.
– OPPOSITES atypical, totalitarian.
▸n. **1** *a representative of the Royal Society* **spokesperson**, spokesman, spokeswoman, agent, official, mouthpiece. **2** *a sales representative* **(commercial) traveller**, (travelling) salesman, saleswoman, agent; informal rep; N. Amer. informal drummer. **3** *the Cambodian representative at the UN* **delegate**, commissioner, ambassador, attaché, envoy, emissary, chargé d'affaires, deputy. **4** *our representatives in parliament* **Member (of Parliament)**, MP; councillor; N. Amer. Member of Congress, senator. **5** *he acted as his father's representative* **deputy**, substitute, stand-in, proxy. **6** *fossil representatives of lampreys* **example**, specimen, exemplar, exemplification.

repress v. **1** *the rebellion was repressed* **suppress**, quell, quash, subdue, put down, crush, extinguish, stamp out, defeat, conquer, rout, overwhelm, contain. **2** *the peasants were repressed* **oppress**, subjugate, keep down, rule with a rod of iron, intimidate, tyrannize, crush. **3** *these emotions may well be repressed* **restrain**, hold back/in, keep back, suppress, keep in check, control, keep under control, curb, stifle, bottle up; informal button up, keep the lid on.

repressed adj. **1** *a repressed country* **oppressed**, subjugated, subdued,

tyrannized. **2** *repressed feelings* **restrained**, suppressed, held back/in, kept in check, stifled, pent up, bottled up. **3** *emotionally repressed* **inhibited**, frustrated, restrained; informal uptight, hung up.
– OPPOSITES democratic, uninhibited.

repression n. **1** *the repression of the protests* **suppression**, quashing, subduing, crushing, stamping out. **2** *political repression* **oppression**, subjugation, suppression, tyranny, despotism, authoritarianism. **3** *the repression of sexual urges* **restraint**, restraining, holding back, keeping back, suppression, control, stifling, bottling up.

repressive adj. **oppressive**, authoritarian, despotic, tyrannical, dictatorial, fascist, autocratic, undemocratic, anti-democratic, totalitarian.

reprieve v. **1** *she was reprieved* **grant a stay of execution to**, pardon, spare, grant an amnesty to, amnesty; informal let off (the hook); old use respite. **2** *the threatened pits could be reprieved* **save**, rescue.
▸n. *a last-minute reprieve* **stay of execution**, remission, pardon, amnesty; US Law continuance; informal let-off.

reprimand v. *he was publicly reprimanded* **rebuke**, admonish, chastise, chide, upbraid, reprove, reproach, scold, berate, take to task, lambaste, give someone a piece of one's mind, haul over the coals, lecture, criticize, censure; informal tell off, give someone a telling-off, give someone a talking-to, dress down, give someone a dressing-down, give someone an earful, give someone a roasting, rap over the knuckles, slap someone's wrist, bawl out, pitch into, lay into, lace into, blast; Brit. informal tick off, carpet, tear off a strip, give someone what for, give someone a wigging, give someone a rocket, give someone a rollicking; N. Amer. informal chew out, ream out; Austral. informal monster; formal castigate; dated give someone a rating; rare reprehend, objurgate.
– OPPOSITES praise.
▸n. *they received a severe reprimand* **rebuke**, reproof, admonishment, admonition, reproach, reproval, scolding, upbraiding, censure; informal telling-off, rap over the knuckles, slap on the wrist, flea in one's ear, dressing-down, earful, roasting, tongue-lashing; Brit. informal ticking-off, carpeting, wigging, rocket, rollicking; formal castigation; dated rating.
– OPPOSITES commendation.

reprisal n. **retaliation**, counter-attack, comeback; revenge, vengeance, retribution, requital; informal a taste of one's own medicine.

reproach v. *Albert reproached him for being late.* See **reprimand** (verb).
▸n. **1** *an expression of reproach.* See **reprimand** (noun). **2** *this party is a reproach to British politics* **disgrace**, discredit, source of shame, blemish, stain, blot; literary smirch.
□ **beyond/above reproach** perfect, blameless, above suspicion, without fault, faultless, flawless, irreproachable,

exemplary, impeccable, immaculate, unblemished, spotless, untarnished, stainless, unsullied, whiter than white; informal squeaky clean.

reproachful adj. **disapproving**, reproving, critical, censorious, disparaging, withering, accusatory, admonitory; formal castigatory.
– OPPOSITES approving.

reprobate n. *a hardened reprobate* **rogue**, rascal, scoundrel, miscreant, good-for-nothing, villain, wretch, rake, degenerate, libertine, debauchee; informal dated rotter, bounder; dated cad; old use blackguard, knave, rapscallion, scapegrace.
▸adj. *reprobate behaviour* **unprincipled**, bad, roguish, wicked, rakish, shameless, immoral, degenerate, dissipated, debauched, depraved; old use knavish.
▸v. old use *they reprobated his conduct* **criticize**, condemn, censure, denounce.

reproduce v. **1** *each artwork is reproduced in colour* **copy**, duplicate, replicate; photocopy, xerox, photostat, print. **2** *this work has not been reproduced in other laboratories* **repeat**, replicate, recreate, redo; simulate, imitate, emulate, mirror, mimic. **3** *some animals reproduce prolifically* **breed**, produce offspring, procreate, propagate, multiply.

reproduction n. **1** *colour reproduction* **copying**, duplication, duplicating; photocopying, xeroxing, photostatting, printing. **2** *a reproduction of the original* **print**, copy, reprint, duplicate, facsimile, carbon copy, photocopy; trademark Xerox. **3** *the process of reproduction* **breeding**, procreation, multiplying, propagation.

reproductive adj. **generative**, procreative, propagative; sexual, genital.

reproof n. **rebuke**, reprimand, reproach, admonishment, admonition; disapproval, censure, criticism, condemnation; informal telling-off, dressing down; Brit. informal ticking-off; dated rating.

reprove v. **reprimand**, rebuke, reproach, scold, admonish, chastise, chide, upbraid, berate, take to task, haul over the coals, criticize, censure; informal tell off, give someone a telling-off, give someone a talking-to, dress down, give someone a dressing-down, give someone an earful, give someone a roasting, rap over the knuckles, slap someone's wrist; Brit. informal tick off, carpet, tear off a strip, give someone a rocket, give someone a rollicking; formal castigate; dated give someone a rating; rare reprehend, objurgate.

reptile n.

WORD LINKS
herpetology the branch of zoology concerned with reptiles and amphibians

---

reptilian adj. **1** *reptilian species* **reptile**, reptile-like, saurian; cold-blooded. **2** *a reptilian smirk* **unpleasant**, distasteful, nasty, disagreeable, unattractive, off-putting, horrible, horrid; unctuous, ingratiating, oily, oleaginous; informal smarmy, slimy, creepy.

r

repudiate v. **1** *she repudiated communism* **reject**, renounce, abandon, give up, turn one's back on, disown, cast off, lay aside; formal forswear, abjure; literary forsake. **2** *Cranham repudiated the allegations* **deny**, refute, contradict, controvert, rebut, dispute, dismiss, brush aside; formal gainsay. **3** *Egypt repudiated the treaty* **cancel**, revoke, rescind, reverse, overrule, overturn, invalidate, nullify; disregard, flout, renege on; Law disaffirm; formal abrogate.
– OPPOSITES embrace, confirm.

repudiation n. **1** *the repudiation of one's religion* **rejection**, renunciation, abandonment, forswearing, giving up; rare abjuration. **2** *his repudiation of the allegations* **denial**, refutation, rebuttal, rejection. **3** *a repudiation of the contract* **cancellation**, revocation, reversal, invalidation, nullification; Law disaffirmation; formal abrogation.

repugnance n. **revulsion**, disgust, abhorrence, repulsion, loathing, hatred, detestation, aversion, distaste, antipathy, contempt; informal yuck factor; old use disrelish.

repugnant adj. **1** *the idea of cannibalism is repugnant* **abhorrent**, revolting, repulsive, repellent, disgusting, offensive, objectionable, vile, foul, nasty, loathsome, sickening, nauseating, hateful, detestable, horrible, execrable, abominable, monstrous, appalling, insufferable, intolerable, unacceptable, contemptible, unsavoury, unpalatable; informal ghastly, gross, horrid; literary noisome. **2** formal *the restriction is repugnant to the tenancy* **incompatible with**, in conflict with, contrary to, at variance with, inconsistent with.
– OPPOSITES pleasant.

repulse v. **1** *the rebels were repulsed* **repel**, drive back/away, fight back/off, put to flight, force back, beat off/back; ward off, hold off; Brit. see off; old use rebut. **2** *her advances were repulsed* **rebuff**, reject, spurn, snub, cold-shoulder; informal give someone the brush-off, freeze out; Brit. informal knock back; N. Amer. informal give someone the bum's rush. **3** *his bid for the company was repulsed* **reject**, turn down, refuse, decline. **4** *the brutality repulsed her* **revolt**, disgust, repel, sicken, nauseate, turn someone's stomach, be repugnant to; informal turn off; N. Amer. informal gross out.
▶ n. **1** *the repulse of the attack* **repelling**, driving back; warding off, holding off. **2** *he was mortified by this repulse* **rebuff**, rejection, snub, slight; informal brush-off, knock-back.

repulsion n. **disgust**, revulsion, abhorrence, repugnance, nausea, horror, aversion, abomination, distaste; informal yuck factor; old use disrelish.

repulsive adj. **revolting**, disgusting, abhorrent, repellent, repugnant, offensive, objectionable, vile, foul, nasty, loathsome, sickening, nauseating, hateful, detestable, execrable, abominable, horrible, monstrous, noxious, horrendous, awful, terrible, dreadful, frightful, obnoxious, unsavoury, unpleasant, disagreeable, distasteful; ugly, hideous, grotesque; informal ghastly, horrid, gross, rank; literary noisome; old use disgustful, loathly.
– OPPOSITES attractive.

reputable adj. **well thought of**, highly regarded, (well) respected, respectable, of (good) repute, prestigious, established; reliable, dependable, trustworthy; old use of good report.
– OPPOSITES untrustworthy.

reputation n. **(good) name**, character, repute, standing, stature, status, position, renown, esteem, prestige; N. Amer. informal rep, rap; old use honour, report.

repute n. **1** *a woman of ill repute* **reputation**, name, character; old use report. **2** *a firm of international repute* **fame**, renown, celebrity, distinction, high standing, stature, prestige.

reputed adj. **1** *they are reputed to be very rich* **thought**, said, reported, rumoured, believed, held, considered, regarded, deemed, alleged. **2** *a reputed naturalist* **well thought of**, (well) respected, highly regarded, of good repute.

reputedly adv. **supposedly**, by all accounts, so I'm told, so people say, allegedly.

request n. **1** *requests for assistance* **appeal**, entreaty, plea, petition, application, demand, call; formal adjuration; literary behest. **2** *Charlotte spoke, at Ursula's request* **bidding**, entreaty, demand, insistence. **3** *indicate your requests on the form* **requirement**, wish, desire; choice.
▶ v. **1** *the government requested military aid* **ask for**, appeal for, call for, seek, solicit, plead for, apply for, demand; formal adjure. **2** *I requested him to help* **call on**, beg, entreat, implore; literary beseech.

require v. **1** *the child required hospital treatment* **need**, be in need of. **2** *a situation requiring patience* **necessitate**, demand, call for, involve, entail. **3** *unquestioning obedience is required* **demand**, insist on, call for, ask for, expect. **4** *she was required to pay costs* **order**, instruct, command, enjoin, oblige, compel, force. **5** *do you require anything else?* **want**, wish to have, desire; lack, be short of.

required adj. **1** *required reading* **essential**, vital, indispensable, necessary, compulsory, obligatory, mandatory, prescribed. **2** *cut it to the required length* **desired**, preferred, chosen; correct, proper, right.
– OPPOSITES optional.

requirement n. **need**, wish, demand, want, necessity, essential, prerequisite, stipulation.

requisite adj. *he lacks the requisite skills* **necessary**, required, prerequisite, essential, indispensable, vital.
– OPPOSITES optional.
▶ n. **1** *toilet requisites* **requirement**, need, necessity, essential. **2** *a requisite for a successful career* **necessity**, essential (requirement), prerequisite, precondition,

sine qua non; informal must.

requisition n. **1** *requisitions for staff* **order**, request, call, application, claim, demand; Brit. indent. **2** *the requisition of cultural treasures* **appropriation**, commandeering, seizure, confiscation, expropriation.
▶ v. **1** *the house was requisitioned by the army* **commandeer**, appropriate, take over, take possession of, occupy, seize, confiscate, expropriate. **2** *she requisitioned statements* **request**, order, call for, demand.

requital n. **1** *in requital of your kindness* **repayment**, return, payment, recompense. **2** *personal requital* **revenge**, vengeance, retribution, redress.

requite v. **1** *requiting their hospitality* **return**, reciprocate, repay. **2** *Drake had requited the wrongs inflicted on them* **avenge**, exact revenge for, revenge, pay someone back for; take reprisals, settle the score, get even. **3** *she did not requite his love* **reciprocate**, return.

rescind v. **revoke**, repeal, cancel, reverse, overturn, overrule, annul, nullify, void, invalidate, quash, abolish; Law vacate; formal abrogate; old use recall.
– OPPOSITES enforce.

rescue v. **1** *an attempt to rescue the hostages* **save**, save the life of, come to the aid of; (set) free, release, liberate. **2** *Boyd rescued his papers* **retrieve**, recover, salvage, get back.
▶ n. *the rescue of 10 crewmen* **saving**, rescuing; release, freeing, liberation, deliverance, redemption.
□ **come to someone's rescue** help, assist, lend a (helping) hand to, bail out; informal save someone's bacon, save someone's neck, save someone's skin.

research n. **1** *medical research* **investigation**, experimentation, testing, analysis, fact-finding, examination, scrutiny, scrutinization. **2** *he continued his researches* **experiments**, experimentation, tests, inquiries, studies.
▶ v. **1** *the phenomenon has been widely researched* **investigate**, study, inquire into, look into, probe, explore, analyse, examine, scrutinize, review. **2** *I researched all the available material* **study**, read (up on), sift through; informal check out.

resemblance n. **similarity**, likeness, similitude, correspondence, congruity, congruence, coincidence, conformity, agreement, equivalence, comparability, parallelism, uniformity, sameness.

resemble v. **look like**, be similar to, be like, bear a resemblance to, remind one of, take after, favour, have the look of; approximate to, smack of, have (all) the hallmarks of, correspond to, echo, mirror, parallel.

resent v. **begrudge**, feel aggrieved at/about, feel bitter about, grudge, be annoyed at/about, be resentful of, dislike, take exception to, object to, take amiss, take offence at, take umbrage at, bear/harbour a grudge about.
– OPPOSITES welcome.

resentful adj. **aggrieved**, indignant, irritated, piqued, put out, in high dudgeon, dissatisfied, disgruntled, discontented, offended, bitter, jaundiced; envious, jealous; informal miffed, peeved; Brit. informal narked; N. Amer. informal sore.

resentment n. **bitterness**, indignation, irritation, pique, dissatisfaction, disgruntlement, discontentment, discontent, resentfulness, bad feelings, hard feelings, ill will, acrimony, rancour, animosity, jaundice; envy, jealousy.

reservation n. **1** *grave reservations* **doubt**, qualm, scruple; misgivings, scepticism, unease, hesitation, objection. **2** *group reservations* **(advance) booking**; dated engagement. **3** *the reservation of the room* **booking**, ordering, securing; dated engagement. **4** *Indian reservation* **reserve**, enclave, sanctuary, territory, homeland.
□ **without reservation** wholeheartedly, unreservedly, without qualification, fully, completely, totally, entirely, wholly, unconditionally.

reserve v. **1** *ask your newsagent to reserve you a copy* **put to one side**, put aside, set aside, keep (back), save, hold back, keep in reserve, earmark. **2** *he reserved a table* **book**, make a reservation for, order, arrange for, secure; formal bespeak; dated engage. **3** *the management reserves the right to alter the programme* **retain**, keep, hold. **4** *reserve your judgement until you know him better* **defer**, postpone, put off, delay, withhold.
▶ n. **1** *reserves of petrol* **stock**, supply, stockpile, pool, hoard, cache. **2** *the army are calling up reserves* **reinforcements**, extras, auxiliaries. **3** *a nature reserve* **national park**, sanctuary, preserve, conservation area. **4** *his natural reserve* **reticence**, detachment, distance, remoteness, coolness, aloofness, constraint, formality; shyness, diffidence, timidity, taciturnity, inhibition; informal stand-offishness. **5** *she trusted him without reserve* **reservation**, qualification, condition, limitation, hesitation, doubt.
▶ adj. *a reserve goalkeeper* **substitute**, stand-in, relief, replacement, fallback, spare, extra.
□ **in reserve** available, to/on hand, ready, in readiness, set aside, at one's disposal.

reserved adj. **1** *Sewell is rather reserved* **reticent**, quiet, private, uncommunicative, unforthcoming, undemonstrative, unsociable, formal, constrained, cool, aloof, detached, distant, remote, unapproachable, unfriendly, withdrawn, secretive, silent, taciturn; shy, retiring, diffident, timid, self-effacing, inhibited, introverted; informal stand-offish. **2** *that table is reserved* **booked**, taken, spoken for, prearranged; dated engaged; formal bespoken.
– OPPOSITES outgoing, free.

reservoir n. **1** *sailing on the reservoir* **lake**, pool, pond; water supply; Scottish loch. **2** *an ink reservoir* **receptacle**, container, holder, repository, tank. **3** *the reservoir of managerial talent* **stock**, store, stockpile, reserve(s), supply, bank, pool, fund.

r

reshuffle v. *the prime minister reshuffled his cabinet* **reorganize**, restructure, rearrange, change (around), shake up, shuffle.
▸n. *a management reshuffle* **reorganization**, restructuring, change, rearrangement; informal shake-up.

reside v. **1** *most students reside in flats* **live in**, occupy, inhabit, stay in, lodge in; formal dwell in, be domiciled in. **2** *the paintings reside in an air-conditioned vault* **be situated**, be found, be located, lie. **3** *executive power resides in the president* **be vested in**, be bestowed on, be conferred on, be in the hands of. **4** *the qualities that reside within each individual* **be inherent**, be present, exist.

residence n. **1** formal *her private residence* **home**, house, place of residence, address; quarters, lodgings; informal pad; formal dwelling (place), domicile, abode. **2** *his place of residence* **occupancy**, habitation, residency; formal abode.

resident n. **1** *the residents of New York City* **inhabitant**, local, citizen, native; householder, homeowner, occupier, tenant; formal denizen. **2** Brit. *the bar is open to residents only* **guest**, lodger.
▸adj. **1** *resident in the UK* **living**, residing, in residence; formal dwelling. **2** *a resident nanny* **live-in**, living in. **3** *the resident registrar in obstetrics* **permanent**, incumbent.

residential adj. **suburban**, commuter, dormitory.

residual adj. **1** *residual heat* **remaining**, leftover, unused, unconsumed. **2** *residual affection* **lingering**, enduring, abiding, surviving, vestigial.

residue n. **remainder**, remaining part, rest, remnant(s); surplus, extra, excess; remains, leftovers; technical residuum.

resign v. **1** *the senior manager resigned* **leave**, hand in one's notice, give notice, stand down, step down; informal quit. **2** *19 MPs resigned their seats* **give up**, leave, vacate, stand down from; informal quit, pack in; old use demit. **3** *he resigned his right to the title* **renounce**, relinquish, give up, abandon, surrender, forgo, cede; Law disclaim; literary forsake. **4** *we resigned ourselves to a long wait* **reconcile oneself to**, become resigned to, come to terms with.

resignation n. **1** *his resignation from his post* **departure**, leaving, standing down, stepping down; informal quitting. **2** *she handed in her resignation* **notice**, letter of resignation. **3** *he accepted his fate with resignation* **patience**, forbearance, stoicism, fortitude, fatalism, acceptance, acquiescence, compliance, passivity.

resigned adj. **patient**, long-suffering, uncomplaining, forbearing, stoical, philosophical, fatalistic, acquiescent, compliant, passive.

resilient adj. **1** *resilient materials* **flexible**, pliable, supple; durable, hard-wearing, stout, strong, sturdy, tough. **2** *young and resilient* **strong**, tough, hardy; quick to recover, buoyant, irrepressible.

resist v. **1** *built to resist cold winters* **withstand**, be proof against, combat, weather, endure, be resistant to, keep out. **2** *they resisted his attempts to change things* **oppose**, fight, refuse to accept, object to, defy, set one's face against, kick against; obstruct, impede, hinder, block, thwart, frustrate; informal be anti. **3** *I resisted the urge to retort* **refrain from**, abstain from, forbear from, desist from, not give in to, restrain oneself from, stop oneself from. **4** *she tried to resist him* **struggle with/against**, fight (against), stand up to, withstand, hold off; fend off, ward off.
– OPPOSITES welcome, submit.
□ **cannot resist** love, adore, relish, have a weakness for, be very keen on, like, delight in, enjoy, take great pleasure in; informal be mad about, get a kick/thrill out of.

resistance n. **1** *resistance to change* **opposition**, hostility, refusal to accept. **2** *a spirited resistance* **opposition**, fight, stand, struggle. **3** *the body's resistance to disease* **ability to fight off**, immunity from, defences against. **4** *the French resistance* **resistance movement**, freedom fighters, underground, partisans.

resistant adj. **1** *resistant to water* **impervious**, unsusceptible, immune, invulnerable, proof against, unaffected by. **2** *resistant to change* **opposed**, averse, hostile, inimical, against; informal anti.

resolute adj. **determined**, purposeful, resolved, adamant, single-minded, firm, unswerving, unwavering, steadfast, staunch, stalwart, unfaltering, unhesitating, persistent, indefatigable, tenacious, strong-willed, unshakeable; stubborn, dogged, obstinate, obdurate, inflexible, intransigent, implacable, unyielding, unrelenting; spirited, brave, bold, courageous, plucky, indomitable; N. Amer. rock-ribbed; informal gutsy, spunky; formal pertinacious.
– OPPOSITES half-hearted.

resolution n. **1** *her resolution not to smoke* **intention**, resolve, decision, intent, aim, plan; commitment, pledge, promise. **2** *the committee passed the resolution* **motion**, proposal, proposition; N. Amer. resolve. **3** *she handled the work with resolution* **determination**, purpose, purposefulness, resolve, resoluteness, single-mindedness, firmness (of purpose); steadfastness, staunchness, perseverance, persistence, indefatigability, tenacity, tenaciousness, staying power, dedication, commitment; stubbornness, doggedness, obstinacy, obduracy; boldness, spiritedness, braveness, bravery, courage, pluck, grit, courageousness; informal guts, spunk; formal pertinacity. **4** *a satisfactory resolution of the problem* **solution**, answer, end, ending, settlement, conclusion.

resolve v. **1** *this matter cannot be resolved overnight* **settle**, sort out, solve, find a solution to, fix, straighten out, deal with, put right, put to rights, rectify; informal hammer

out, thrash out, figure out. **2** *Charity resolved not to wait any longer* **determine**, decide, make up one's mind, take a decision. **3** *the committee resolved that the project should proceed* **vote**, pass a resolution, rule, decide formally, agree. **4** *the compounds were resolved into their active constituents* **break down/up**, separate, reduce, divide. **5** *the ability to resolve facts into their legal categories* **analyse**, dissect, break down. **6** *the orange light resolved itself into four roadwork lanterns* **turn**, change, be transformed.
▶ **n. 1** *their intimidation merely strengthened his resolve.* See **resolution** (sense 3).
2 N. Amer. *he made a resolve not to go there again* **decision**, resolution, commitment.

resolved adj. **determined**, hell-bent, intent, set.

resonant adj. **1** *a resonant voice* **deep**, low, sonorous, full, full-bodied, vibrant, rich, clear, ringing; loud, booming, thunderous. **2** *valleys resonant with the sound of church bells* **reverberating**, reverberant, resounding, echoing, filled. **3** *resonant words* **evocative**, suggestive, expressive, redolent.

resort n. **1** *a seaside resort* **holiday destination**, (tourist) centre; informal honeypot. **2** *settle the matter without resort to legal proceedings* **recourse to**, turning to, the use of, utilizing. **3** *strike action is our last resort* **expedient**, measure, step, recourse, alternative, option, choice, possibility, hope.
□ **in the last resort** ultimately, in the end, at the end of the day, in the long run, when all is said and done.
resort to have recourse to, fall back on, turn to, make use of, use, employ, avail oneself of; stoop to, descend to, sink to.

resound v. **1** *the explosion resounded round the silent street* **echo**, re-echo, reverberate, ring out, boom, thunder, rumble. **2** *resounding with the clang of hammers* **reverberate**, echo, re-echo, resonate, ring. **3** *nothing will resound like their earlier achievements* **be acclaimed**, be celebrated, be renowned, be famed, be glorified, be trumpeted.

resounding adj. **1** *a resounding voice* **reverberant**, reverberating, resonant, resonating, echoing, ringing, sonorous, deep, rich, clear; loud, booming. **2** *a resounding success* **enormous**, huge, very great, tremendous, terrific, colossal; emphatic, decisive, conclusive, outstanding, remarkable, phenomenal.

resource n. **1** *use your resources efficiently* **assets**, funds, wealth, money, capital; staff; supplies, materials, store(s), stock(s), reserve(s). **2** *your tutor is there as a resource* **facility**, amenity, aid, help, support, solution. **3** *tears were her only resource* **expedient**, resort, course, scheme, stratagem; trick, ruse, device. **4** *a person of resource* **initiative**, resourcefulness, enterprise, ingenuity, inventiveness; talent, ability, capability; informal gumption.

resourceful adj. **ingenious**, enterprising, inventive, creative; clever, talented, able, capable.

respect n. **1** *the respect due to a great artist* **esteem**, regard, high opinion, admiration, reverence, deference, honour. **2** *he spoke to her with respect* **due regard**, politeness, courtesy, civility, deference. **3** *paying one's respects* **(kind) regards**, compliments, greetings, best/good wishes, felicitations, salutations; old use remembrances. **4** *the report was accurate in every respect* **aspect**, regard, facet, feature, way, sense, particular, point, detail.
– OPPOSITES contempt.
▶ **v. 1** *he is highly respected for his industry* **esteem**, admire, think highly of, have a high opinion of, hold in high regard, hold in (high) esteem, look up to, revere, reverence, honour. **2** *they respected our privacy* **show consideration for**, have regard for, observe, be mindful of, be heedful of; formal take cognizance of. **3** *father respected her wishes* **abide by**, comply with, follow, adhere to, conform to, act in accordance with, defer to, obey, observe, keep (to).
– OPPOSITES despise, disobey.
□ **with respect to/in respect of** concerning, regarding, in/with regard to, with reference to, respecting, re, about, apropos, on the subject of, in connection with, vis-à-vis.

respectable adj. **1** *a respectable middle-class background* **reputable**, of good repute, upright, honest, honourable, trustworthy, decent, good, well bred, clean-living. **2** *a respectable salary* **fairly good**, decent, fair, reasonable, moderately good; substantial, considerable, sizeable.
– OPPOSITES disreputable, paltry.

respectful adj. **deferential**, reverent, reverential, dutiful; polite, well mannered, civil, courteous, gracious.
– OPPOSITES rude.

respective adj. **separate**, personal, own, particular, individual, specific, special, appropriate, different, various.

respite n. **1** *a brief respite* **rest**, break, breathing space, interval, intermission, interlude, recess, lull, pause, time out; relief, relaxation, repose; informal breather, let-up. **2** *respite from debts* **postponement**, deferment, delay, reprieve; US Law continuance.

resplendent adj. **splendid**, magnificent, brilliant, dazzling, glittering, gorgeous, impressive, imposing, spectacular, striking, stunning, majestic; informal splendiferous.

respond v. **1** *they do not respond to questions* **answer**, reply, make a response, make a rejoinder. **2** *'No,' she responded* **say**, answer, reply, rejoin, retort, riposte, counter. **3** *they were slow to respond* **react**, make a response, reciprocate, retaliate.

response n. **1** *his response to the question* **answer**, reply, rejoinder, retort, riposte; informal comeback. **2** *an angry response*

r

reaction, reply, retaliation; informal comeback.
– OPPOSITES question.

responsibility n. **1** *it was his responsibility to find witnesses* **duty**, task, function, job, role, business; Brit. informal pigeon. **2** *they denied responsibility for the bomb attack* **blame**, fault, guilt, culpability, liability. **3** *a sense of responsibility* **trustworthiness**, (common) sense, maturity, reliability, dependability. **4** *managerial responsibility* **authority**, control, power, leadership.

responsible adj. **1** *who is responsible for prisons?* **in charge of**, in control of, at the helm of, accountable for, liable for. **2** *I am responsible for the mistake* **accountable**, answerable, to blame, guilty, culpable, blameworthy, at fault, in the wrong. **3** *a responsible job* **important**, powerful, executive. **4** *he is responsible to the president* **answerable**, accountable. **5** *a responsible tenant* **trustworthy**, sensible, mature, reliable, dependable.

responsive adj. **quick to react**, reactive, receptive, open to suggestions, amenable, flexible, forthcoming.

rest[1] v. **1** *he needed to rest* **relax**, take a rest, ease up/off, let up, slow down, have/take a break, unbend, unwind, recharge one's batteries, be at leisure, take it easy, put one's feet up, lie down, go to bed, have/take a nap, catnap, doze, sleep; informal take five, have/take a breather, snatch forty winks, get some shut-eye; Brit. informal chill out; N. Amer. informal catch some Zs. **2** *his hands rested on the rail* **lie**, be laid, repose, be placed, be positioned, be supported by. **3** *she rested her basket on the ground* **support**, prop (up), lean, lay, set, stand, position, place, put. **4** *the film script rests on an improbable premise* **be based**, depend, be dependent, rely, hinge, turn on, be contingent, revolve around.
▸ n. **1** *get some rest* **repose**, relaxation, leisure, respite; time off, breathing space; sleep, nap, doze; informal shut-eye, snooze, lie-down, forty winks; Brit. informal kip. **2** *a short rest from work* **holiday**, vacation, break, breathing space, interval, interlude, intermission, time off/out; informal breather. **3** *she took the poker from its rest* **stand**, base, holder, support, rack, frame, shelf. **4** *we came to rest 100 metres lower* **a standstill**, a halt, a stop.

rest[2] n. *the rest of the board are appointees* **remainder**, residue, balance, remaining part/number/quantity, others, those left, remains, remnant(s), surplus, excess; technical residuum.
▸ v. *you may rest assured that he is there* **remain**, continue to be, stay, keep, carry on being.

restaurant n. bistro, brasserie, cafe, cafeteria; N. Amer. diner; informal eatery.

restful adj. **relaxed**, relaxing, quiet, calm, calming, tranquil, soothing, peaceful, placid, reposeful, leisurely, undisturbed, untroubled.
– OPPOSITES exciting.

restitution n. **1** *restitution of the land seized* **return**, restoration, handing back, surrender. **2** *restitution for the damage caused* **compensation**, recompense, reparation, damages, indemnification, indemnity, reimbursement, repayment, remuneration, redress; old use guerdon.

restive adj. **1** *Edward is getting restive.* See **restless** (sense 1). **2** *the militants are increasingly restive* **unruly**, disorderly, uncontrollable, unmanageable, wilful, recalcitrant, insubordinate; Brit. informal bolshie; formal refractory; old use contumacious.

restless adj. **1** *Maria was restless* **uneasy**, ill at ease, restive, fidgety, edgy, on edge, tense, nervy, worked up, nervous, agitated, anxious, on tenterhooks, keyed up; informal jumpy, jittery, twitchy, uptight, like a cat on a hot tin roof; Brit. informal like a cat on hot bricks. **2** *a restless night* **sleepless**, wakeful, fitful, broken, disturbed, troubled, unsettled.

restlessness n. **unease**, restiveness, edginess, tenseness, nervousness, agitation, anxiety, fretfulness, apprehension, disquiet; informal jitteriness.

restoration n. **1** *the restoration of democracy* **reinstatement**, reinstitution, re-establishment, reimposition, return. **2** *the restoration of derelict housing* **repair**, repairing, fixing, mending, refurbishment, reconditioning, rehabilitation, rebuilding, reconstruction, overhaul, redevelopment, renovation; informal facelift, refurb; N. Amer. informal rehab.

restore v. **1** *the aim to restore democracy* **reinstate**, bring back, reinstitute, reimpose, reinstall, re-establish. **2** *he restored it to its rightful owner* **return**, give back, hand back. **3** *the building has been restored* **repair**, fix, mend, refurbish, recondition, rehabilitate, rebuild, reconstruct, remodel, overhaul, redevelop, renovate; informal do up; N. Amer. informal rehab. **4** *a good sleep can restore you* **reinvigorate**, revitalize, revive, refresh, energize, fortify, revivify, stimulate, freshen.
– OPPOSITES abolish.

restrain v. **1** *Charles restrained his anger* **control**, keep under control, check, hold/keep in check, curb, suppress, repress, contain, dampen, subdue, smother, choke back, stifle, bottle up, rein back/in; informal keep the lid on. **2** *she could barely restrain herself from swearing* **prevent**, stop, keep, hold back. **3** *leg cuffs were used for restraining violent criminals* **tie up**, bind, tether, chain (up), fetter, shackle, manacle.

restrained adj. **1** *Julie was quite restrained* **self-controlled**, self-restrained, not given to excesses, sober, steady, unemotional, undemonstrative. **2** *restrained elegance* **muted**, soft, discreet, subtle, quiet, unobtrusive, unostentatious, understated, tasteful.

restraint n. **1** *a restraint on their impulsiveness* **constraint**, check, control, restriction, limitation, curtailment; rein, bridle, brake, damper, impediment, obstacle. **2** *the customary restraint of the police* **self-control**, self-restraint, self-discipline, control, moderation, prudence, judiciousness. **3** *the room has been decorated with restraint* **subtlety**, understatedness, taste, tastefulness, discrimination, discretion. **4** *a child restraint* **belt**, harness, strap.

restrict v. **1** *a busy working life restricted his leisure activities* **limit**, keep within bounds, regulate, control, moderate, cut down. **2** *the cuff supports the ankle without restricting movement* **hinder**, interfere with, impede, hamper, obstruct, block, check, curb. **3** *he restricted himself to a 15-minute speech* **confine**, limit.

restricted adj. **1** *restricted space* **cramped**, confined, constricted, small, narrow, tight; old use strait. **2** *a restricted calorie intake* **limited**, controlled, regulated, reduced. **3** *a restricted zone* **out of bounds**, off limits, private, exclusive. **4** *restricted information* **(top) secret**, classified; informal hush-hush.
– OPPOSITES unlimited.

restriction n. **1** *there is no restriction on the number of places* **limitation**, limit, constraint, control, check, curb; condition, proviso, qualification. **2** *the restriction of personal freedom* **reduction**, limitation, diminution, curtailment. **3** *restriction of movement* **hindrance**, impediment, slowing, reduction, limitation.

result n. **1** *stress is the result of overwork* **consequence**, outcome, upshot, sequel, effect, reaction, repercussion, ramification, conclusion, culmination. **2** *what is your result?* **answer**, solution; sum, total, product. **3** *exam results* **mark**, score, grade. **4** *the result of the trial* **verdict**, decision, outcome, conclusion, judgement, findings, ruling.
– OPPOSITES cause.
▶ v. **1** *differences between species could result from their habitat* **follow**, ensue, develop, stem, spring, arise, derive, evolve, proceed; occur, happen, take place, come about; be caused by, be brought about by, be produced by, originate in, be consequent on. **2** *the shooting resulted in five deaths* **end in**, culminate in, finish in, terminate in, lead to, prompt, precipitate, trigger; cause, bring about, occasion, effect, give rise to, produce, engender, generate; literary beget.

resume v. **1** *the government resumed negotiations* **restart**, recommence, begin again, start again, reopen; renew, return to, continue with, carry on with. **2** *the priest resumed his kneeling posture* **return to**, come back to, take up again, reoccupy.
– OPPOSITES suspend, abandon.

résumé n. **summary**, precis, synopsis, abstract, outline, summarization, summation, epitome; abridgement, digest, condensation, abbreviation, overview, review.

resumption n. **restart**, restarting, recommencement, reopening; continuation, carrying on, renewal, return to.

resurgence n. **renewal**, revival, recovery, comeback, reawakening, resurrection, reappearance, re-emergence, regeneration; resumption, recommencement, continuation; formal renascence.

resurrect v. **1** *Jesus was resurrected* **raise from the dead**, restore to life, revive. **2** *resurrecting his career* **revive**, restore, regenerate, revitalize, breathe new life into, reinvigorate, resuscitate, rejuvenate, stimulate, re-establish, relaunch, reinstitute.

resuscitate v. **1** *medics resuscitated him* **bring round**, revive, bring back to consciousness; give artificial respiration to, give the kiss of life to. **2** *measures to resuscitate the economy* **revive**, resurrect, restore, regenerate, revitalize, breathe new life into, reinvigorate, rejuvenate, stimulate.

retain v. **1** *the government retained a share in the industries* **keep (possession of)**, keep hold of, hold on to, hang on to. **2** *existing footpaths are to be retained* **maintain**, keep, preserve, conserve. **3** *some students retain facts easily* **remember**, memorize, keep in one's mind/memory. **4** *solicitors can retain a barrister* **employ**, contract, keep on the payroll.
– OPPOSITES give up, abolish.

retainer n. **1** *they're paid a retainer (retaining) fee*, periodic payment, advance, standing charge. **2** *a faithful retainer.* See **servant** (sense 1).

retaliate v. **fight back**, hit back, respond, react, reply, reciprocate, counter-attack, return like for like, get back at someone, give tit for tat, give someone a taste of their own medicine; have/get/take one's revenge, be revenged, avenge oneself, take reprisals, get even, pay someone back; informal get one's own back.

retaliation n. **revenge**, vengeance, reprisal, retribution, requital, recrimination, repayment; response, reaction, reply, counter-attack; old use a Roland for an Oliver.

retard v. **delay**, slow down/up, hold back/up, set back, postpone, put back, detain, decelerate; hinder, hamper, obstruct, inhibit, impede, check, restrain, restrict, trammel; literary stay.
– OPPOSITES accelerate.

retch v. **1** *the sour taste made her retch* **gag**, heave; informal keck. **2** *he retched all over the table.* See **vomit** (sense 1 of the verb).

reticence n. **reserve**, restraint, inhibition, diffidence, shyness; unresponsiveness, quietness, taciturnity, secretiveness.

reticent adj. **reserved**, withdrawn, introverted, inhibited, diffident, shy; uncommunicative, unforthcoming, unresponsive, tight-lipped, quiet, taciturn, silent, guarded, secretive.
– OPPOSITES expansive.

retinue n. **entourage**, escort, company, court, staff, personnel, household, train,

r

suite, following, bodyguard; aides, attendants, servants, retainers.

retire v. **1** *he has retired* **give up work**, stop working, stop work. **2** *we've retired him on full pension* **pension off**, force to retire. **3** *Gillian retired to her office* **withdraw**, go away, take oneself off, decamp, shut oneself away; formal repair; literary betake oneself. **4** *their forces retired* **retreat**, withdraw, pull back, fall back, disengage, back off, give ground. **5** *everyone retired early* **go to bed**, call it a day, go to sleep; informal turn in, hit the hay/sack.

retired adj. *a retired schoolteacher* **former**, ex-, past, in retirement; elderly.

retirement n. **1** *they are nearing retirement* **giving up work**, stopping work. **2** *he lived in retirement in Kent* **seclusion**, retreat, solitude, isolation; obscurity.

retiring adj. **1** *the retiring president* **departing**, outgoing. **2** *a retiring man* **shy**, diffident, self-effacing, unassuming, unassertive, reserved, reticent, quiet, timid, modest; private, secret, secretive, withdrawn, reclusive, unsociable.
– OPPOSITES incoming, outgoing.

retort v. *'No need to be rude!' she retorted* **answer**, reply, respond, say, return, counter, rejoin, riposte, retaliate, snap back.
▸n. *a sarcastic retort* **answer**, reply, response, return, counter, rejoinder, riposte, retaliation; informal comeback.

retract v. **1** *the sea otter can retract its claws* **pull in/back**, draw in. **2** *he retracted his allegation* **take back**, withdraw, recant, disavow, disclaim, repudiate, renounce, reverse, revoke, rescind, go back on, backtrack on, row back on; formal abjure.

retreat v. **1** *the army retreated* **withdraw**, retire, draw back, pull back/out, fall back, give way, give ground, beat a retreat. **2** *the tide was retreating* **go out**, ebb, recede, fall, go down. **3** *the government had to retreat* **change one's mind**, change one's plans; back down, climb down, do a U-turn, backtrack, back-pedal, row back, give in, concede defeat; Brit. do an about-turn.
– OPPOSITES advance.
▸n. **1** *the retreat of the army* **withdrawal**, pulling back. **2** *the President's retreat* **climbdown**, backdown, about-face, U-turn, rowback; Brit. about-turn. **3** *her rural retreat* **refuge**, haven, sanctuary; hideaway, hideout, hiding place; informal hidey-hole. **4** *a period of retreat from the world* **seclusion**, withdrawal, retirement, solitude, isolation, sanctuary.

retrench v. **1** *we have to retrench* **economize**, cut back, make cutbacks, make savings, make economies, reduce expenditure, be economical, be frugal, tighten one's belt. **2** *services have to be retrenched* **reduce**, cut (back/down), pare (down), slim down, make reductions in, make cutbacks in, trim, prune; informal slash.

retribution n. **punishment**, penalty, one's just deserts; revenge, reprisal, requital, retaliation, vengeance, an eye for an eye (and a tooth for a tooth), tit for tat; redress, reparation, restitution, recompense, repayment, indemnification, atonement, amends.

retrieve v. **1** *I retrieved our balls from their garden* **get back**, bring back, recover, regain (possession of), recoup, reclaim, repossess, redeem, recuperate. **2** *they were trying to retrieve the situation* **put/set right**, rectify, remedy, restore, sort out, straighten out, resolve.

retrograde adj. **1** *a retrograde step* **for the worse**, regressive, negative, downhill, unwelcome. **2** *retrograde motion* **backward(s)**, reverse, rearward.
– OPPOSITES positive, forward.

retrospect n.
□ **in retrospect** looking back, on reflection, in/with hindsight.

retrospective adj. **backdated**, retroactive, ex post facto.

return v. **1** *he returned to London* **go back**, come back, arrive back, come home. **2** *the symptoms returned* **recur**, reoccur, occur again, repeat (itself); reappear, appear again. **3** *he returned the money* **give back**, hand back; pay back, repay. **4** *Peter returned the book to the shelf* **restore**, put back, replace, reinstall. **5** *he returned the volley* **hit back**, throw back. **6** *she returned his kiss* **reciprocate**, requite, give in return, repay, give back. **7** *'Later,' returned Isabel* **answer**, reply, respond, counter, rejoin, retort. **8** *the jury returned a unanimous verdict* **deliver**, bring in, hand down. **9** *the club returned a profit* **yield**, earn, realize, net, gross, clear. **10** *the Labour candidate was returned* **elect**, vote in, choose, select.
– OPPOSITES depart, disappear, keep.
▸n. **1** *his return to Paris* **homecoming**. **2** *the return of hard times* **recurrence**, reoccurrence, repeat, repetition, reappearance, revival, resurrection, re-emergence, resurgence. **3** *I requested the return of my books* **giving back**, handing back, replacement, restoration, reinstatement, restitution. **4** *two returns to London* **return ticket/fare**; N. Amer. round trip ticket/fare. **5** *a quick return on investments* **yield**, profit, gain, revenue, interest, dividend. **6** *a census return* **statement**, report, submission, record, dossier; document, form.
– OPPOSITES departure, disappearance, single.
□ **in return for** in exchange for, as a reward for, as compensation for.

revamp v. **renovate**, redecorate, refurbish, recondition, rehabilitate, overhaul, make over; upgrade, refit, re-equip; remodel, refashion, redesign, restyle; informal do up, give something a facelift, vamp up; Brit. informal tart up; N. Amer. informal rehab.

reveal v. **1** *the police can't reveal his whereabouts* **divulge**, disclose, tell, let slip/drop, give away/out, blurt (out), release, leak; make known, make public, broadcast,

publicize, circulate, disseminate; informal let on; old use discover. **2** *he revealed his new car show*, display, exhibit, disclose, uncover; literary uncloak. **3** *the data reveals a good deal of information* **bring to light**, uncover, lay bare, unearth, unveil; formal evince; literary uncloak.
– OPPOSITES hide.

revel v. **1** *they revelled all night* **celebrate**, make merry, have a party, carouse, roister; informal party, live it up, whoop it up, make whoopee, rave, paint the town red. **2** *he revelled in the applause* **enjoy**, delight in, love, like, adore, be pleased by, take pleasure in, appreciate, relish, lap up, savour; informal get a kick out of.
▸ n. *late-night revels* **celebration**, festivity, jollification, merrymaking, carousal, carouse, spree; party, jamboree; informal rave, shindig, bash; Brit. informal rave-up, knees-up; N. Amer. informal wingding, blast; Austral. informal rage, ding, jollo.

revelation n. **1** *revelations about his personal life* **disclosure**, surprising fact, announcement, report; admission, confession. **2** *the revelation of a secret* **divulging**, divulgence, disclosure, disclosing, letting slip/drop, giving away/out, leaking, leak, betrayal, unveiling, making known, making public, broadcasting, publicizing, dissemination, reporting, report, declaring, declaration.

reveller n. **merrymaker**, partygoer, carouser, roisterer; old use wassailer.

revelry n. **celebration(s)**, parties, revels, festivity, festivities, jollification, merrymaking, carousing, carousal, roistering; informal partying.

revenge n. **1** *she is seeking revenge* **vengeance**, retribution, retaliation, reprisal, requital, recrimination, an eye for an eye (and a tooth for a tooth), redress, satisfaction. **2** *they were filled with revenge* **vengefulness**, vindictiveness, vitriol, spite, spitefulness, malice, maliciousness, malevolence, ill will, animosity, hate, hatred, rancour, bitterness; literary maleficence.
▸ v. **1** *he revenged his brother's murder* **avenge**, take/exact revenge for, exact retribution for, take reprisals for, get redress for, get satisfaction for. **2** *I'll be revenged on the whole pack of you* **take revenge on**, get one's revenge on, avenge oneself on, take vengeance on, get even with, settle a/the score with, pay back, take reprisals against; informal get one's own back on.

revenue n. **income**, takings, receipts, proceeds, earnings; profit(s).
– OPPOSITES expenditure.

reverberate v. **resound**, echo, re-echo, resonate, ring, boom, rumble.

reverberation n. **1** *natural reverberation* **resonance**, echo, echoing, re-echoing, resounding, ringing, booming, rumbling. **2** *political reverberations* **repercussions**, ramifications, consequences, shock waves; aftermath, fallout, backlash.

revere v. **respect**, admire, think highly of, have a high opinion of, esteem, hold in high esteem/regard, look up to.
– OPPOSITES despise.

reverence n. **esteem**, regard, respect, acclaim, admiration, appreciation, estimation, favour.
– OPPOSITES scorn.

reverent adj. **respectful**, reverential, admiring, devoted, devout, dutiful, awed, deferential.

reverie n. **daydream**, daydreaming, trance, musing; inattention, inattentiveness, wool-gathering, preoccupation, absorption, abstraction, lack of concentration.

reversal n. **1** *there was no reversal on this issue* **turnaround**, turnabout, about-face, volte-face, change of heart, U-turn, backtracking, rowback; Brit. about-turn; rare tergiversation. **2** *a reversal of roles* **swap**, exchange, change, swapping, interchange. **3** *the reversal of the decision* **alteration**, changing; countermanding, undoing, overturning, overthrow, disallowing, overriding, overruling, veto, vetoing, revocation, repeal, rescinding, annulment, nullification, voiding, invalidation; formal rescission, abrogation. **4** *they suffered a reversal* **setback**, reverse, upset, failure, misfortune, mishap, disaster, blow, disappointment, adversity, hardship, affliction, vicissitude, defeat; bad luck.

reverse v. **1** *the car reversed into a lamp post* **back**, drive back/backwards, move back/backwards. **2** *reverse the bottle in the ice bucket* **turn upside down**, turn over, upend, upturn, invert; old use overset. **3** *I reversed my jacket* **turn inside out**. **4** *reverse your roles* **swap (round)**, change (round), exchange, interchange, switch (round). **5** *the umpire reversed the decision* **alter**, change; overturn, overthrow, disallow, override, overrule, veto, revoke, repeal, rescind, annul, nullify, void, invalidate.
▸ adj. *in reverse order* **backward(s)**, reversed, inverted, transposed.
▸ n. **1** *the reverse is the case* **opposite**, contrary, converse, inverse, obverse, antithesis. **2** *successes and reverses*. See **reversal** (sense 4). **3** *the reverse of the page* **other side**, reverse side, back, underside, wrong side, verso.

revert v. **1** *life will soon revert to normal* **return**, go back, change back, default; fall back, regress, relapse. **2** *the property reverted to the landlord* **be returned**; historical escheat.

review n. **1** *the Council undertook a review* **analysis**, evaluation, assessment, appraisal, examination, investigation, inquiry, probe, inspection, study. **2** *the rent is due for review* **reconsideration**, reassessment, re-evaluation, reappraisal; change, alteration, modification, revision. **3** *book reviews* **criticism**, critique, assessment, evaluation, commentary; Brit. informal crit. **4** *a scientific review* **journal**, periodical, magazine, publication. **5** *their review of the economy*

r

survey, report, study, account, description, statement, overview. **6** *a military review* **inspection**, parade, tattoo, procession; Brit. march past.

▶ v. **1** *I reviewed the evidence* **survey**, study, research, consider, analyse, examine, scrutinize, explore, look into, probe, investigate, inspect, assess, appraise; informal size up. **2** *the referee reviewed his decision* **reconsider**, re-examine, reassess, re-evaluate, reappraise, rethink; change, alter, modify, revise. **3** *he reviewed the day* **remember**, recall, reflect on, think through, go over in one's mind, look back on. **4** *reviewing troops* **inspect**, view. **5** *she reviewed the play* **comment on**, evaluate, assess, appraise, judge, critique, criticize.

reviewer n. **critic**, **commentator**, judge, observer, pundit, analyst.

revile v. **criticize**, censure, condemn, attack, inveigh against, rail against, lambaste, denounce; slander, libel, malign, vilify, besmirch, abuse; informal knock, slam, pan, crucify, roast, bad-mouth; Brit. informal slate, rubbish, slag off; N. Amer. informal pummel; Austral./NZ informal bag, monster; formal excoriate, calumniate.
– OPPOSITES praise.

revise v. **1** *she revised her opinion* **reconsider**, review, re-examine, reassess, re-evaluate, reappraise, rethink; change, alter, modify. **2** *the editor revised the text* **amend**, emend, correct, alter, change, edit, rewrite, redraft, rephrase, rework. **3** Brit. *revise your lecture notes* **go over**, reread, memorize; cram; informal bone up on; Brit. informal swot up (on), mug up (on).

revision n. **1** *a revision of the Prayer Book* **emendation**, correction, alteration, adaptation, editing, rewriting, redrafting. **2** *a new revision* **version**, edition, rewrite. **3** *a major revision of the system* **reconsideration**, review, re-examination, reassessment, re-evaluation, reappraisal, rethink; change, alteration, modification. **4** Brit. *he was doing some revision* **rereading**, memorizing, cramming; Brit. informal swotting.

revitalize v. **reinvigorate**, re-energize, boost, regenerate, revive, revivify, rejuvenate, reanimate, resuscitate, refresh, stimulate, breathe new life into; informal give a shot in the arm to, pep up, buck up.

revival n. **1** *a revival in the economy* **improvement**, rallying, picking up, amelioration, turn for the better, upturn, upswing, resurgence. **2** *the revival of traditional crafts* **comeback**, re-establishment, reintroduction, restoration, reappearance, resurrection, regeneration, rejuvenation.
– OPPOSITES downturn, disappearance.

revive v. **1** *attempts to revive her failed* **resuscitate**, bring round, bring back to consciousness. **2** *the man soon revived* **regain consciousness**, come round, wake up. **3** *a cup of tea revived her* **reinvigorate**, revitalize, refresh, energize, reanimate,

resuscitate, revivify, rejuvenate, regenerate, enliven, stimulate. **4** *reviving old traditions* **reintroduce**, re-establish, reinstitute, restore, resurrect, bring back, regenerate, resuscitate.

revoke v. **cancel**, repeal, rescind, reverse, annul, nullify, void, invalidate, countermand, retract, withdraw, overrule, override; Law vacate; formal abrogate.

revolt v. **1** *the people revolted* **rebel**, rise (up), take to the streets, riot, mutiny. **2** *the smell revolted him* **disgust**, sicken, nauseate, make someone sick, make someone's gorge rise, turn someone's stomach, be repugnant to, be repulsive to, put off, be offensive to; informal turn off; N. Amer. informal gross out.

▶ n. *an armed revolt* **rebellion**, revolution, insurrection, mutiny, uprising, riot, rioting, insurgence, seizure of power, coup (d'état).

revolting adj. **disgusting**, sickening, nauseating, stomach-turning, stomach-churning, repulsive, repellent, repugnant, appalling, abominable, hideous, horrible, awful, dreadful, terrible, obnoxious, vile, nasty, foul, loathsome, offensive, objectionable, off-putting, distasteful, disagreeable; N. Amer. vomitous; informal ghastly, putrid, horrid, gross, gut-churning, yucky, rank, skanky, icky; formal rebarbative; literary noisome; old use disgustful, loathly.
– OPPOSITES attractive, pleasant.

revolution n. **1** *the French Revolution* **rebellion**, revolt, insurrection, mutiny, uprising, riot, rioting, insurgence, seizure of power, coup (d'état). **2** *a revolution in printing techniques* **dramatic change**, radical alteration, sea change, metamorphosis, transformation, innovation, reorganization, restructuring; informal shake-up; N. Amer. informal shakedown. **3** *one revolution of a wheel* **(single) turn**, rotation, circle, spin; circuit, lap. **4** *the revolution of the earth* **turning**, rotation, circling; orbit.

revolutionary adj. **1** *revolutionary troops* **rebellious**, rebel, insurgent, rioting, mutinous, renegade, insurrectionary, insurrectionist, seditious, subversive, extremist. **2** *revolutionary change* **thoroughgoing**, thorough, complete, total, absolute, radical, comprehensive, sweeping, far-reaching, extensive, profound. **3** *a revolutionary kind of wheelchair* **new**, novel, original, unusual, unconventional, unorthodox, off-centre, newfangled, innovative, innovatory, innovational, modern, state-of-the-art, futuristic, pioneering, groundbreaking, trailblazing, disruptive.

▶ n. *political revolutionaries* **rebel**, insurgent, revolutionist, mutineer, insurrectionist, agitator, subversive.

revolutionize v. **transform**, alter dramatically, shake up, turn upside down, restructure, reorganize, transmute, metamorphose; humorous transmogrify.

revolve v. **1** *a fan revolved slowly* **go round**, turn round, rotate, spin. **2** *the moon revolves* *around the earth* **circle**, travel, orbit. **3** *his life revolves around cars* **be concerned with**, be preoccupied with, focus on, centre around. **4** *her mind revolved the possibilities* **think about/over**, give thought to, consider, reflect on, mull over, muse on, cogitate about/on, chew over, weigh up; old use pore on.

revulsion n. **disgust**, repulsion, abhorrence, repugnance, nausea, horror, aversion, abomination, distaste; informal yuck factor; old use disrelish.
– OPPOSITES delight.

reward n. *a reward for its safe return* **recompense**, prize, award, honour, decoration, bonus, premium, bounty, present, gift, payment; informal pay-off, perk; formal perquisite.
▶v. *they were well rewarded* **recompense**, pay, remunerate, make something worth someone's while; give an award to.
– OPPOSITES punish.

rewarding adj. **satisfying**, gratifying, pleasing, fulfilling, enriching, edifying, beneficial, illuminating, worthwhile, productive, fruitful.

reword v. **rewrite**, rephrase, recast, put in other words, express differently, redraft, revise; paraphrase.

rewrite v. **revise**, recast, reword, rephrase, redraft.

rhetoric n. **1** *a form of rhetoric* **oratory**, eloquence, command of language, way with words. **2** *empty rhetoric* **bombast**, turgidity, grandiloquence, magniloquence, pomposity, extravagant language, purple prose; wordiness, verbosity, prolixity; informal hot air; rare fustian.

rhetorical adj. **1** *rhetorical devices* **stylistic**, oratorical, linguistic, verbal. **2** *rhetorical hyperbole* **extravagant**, grandiloquent, magniloquent, high-flown, orotund, bombastic, grandiose, pompous, pretentious, overblown, oratorical, turgid, flowery, florid; informal highfalutin; rare fustian.

rhyme n. **poem**, piece of poetry, verse; (**rhymes**) poetry, doggerel.

rhythm n. **1** *the rhythm of the music* **beat**, cadence, tempo, time, pulse, throb, swing. **2** *poetic features such as rhythm* **metre**, measure, stress, accent, cadence. **3** *the rhythm of daily life* **pattern**, flow, tempo.

rhythmic adj. **rhythmical**, with a steady pulse, measured, throbbing, beating, pulsating, regular, steady, even.

ribald adj. See **crude** (sense 3).

rich adj. **1** *rich people* **wealthy**, affluent, moneyed, well off, well-to-do, prosperous, opulent; N. Amer. silk-stocking; informal rolling in money, in the money, loaded, stinking rich, filthy rich, well heeled, made of money; informal dated oofy. **2** *rich furnishings* **sumptuous**, opulent, luxurious, luxury, deluxe, lavish, gorgeous, splendid, magnificent, costly, expensive, fancy; informal posh, classy, plush, ritzy, swanky, bling; Brit. informal swish; N. Amer. informal swank. **3** *a garden rich in flowers* **abounding**, well provided, well stocked, crammed, packed, teeming, bursting; informal jam-packed, chock-a-block, chock-full; Austral./NZ informal chocker. **4** *a rich supply of restaurants* **plentiful**, abundant, copious, ample, profuse, lavish, liberal, generous, bountiful; literary plenteous, bounteous. **5** *rich soil* **fertile**, productive, fecund, fruitful. **6** *a rich sauce* **creamy**, fatty, heavy, full-flavoured. **7** *a rich wine* **full-bodied**, heavy, fruity. **8** *rich colours* **strong**, deep, full, intense, vivid, brilliant. **9** *her rich voice* **sonorous**, full, resonant, deep, clear, mellow, mellifluous; rare mellifluent. **10** informal *that's rich!* **preposterous**, outrageous, absurd, ridiculous, ludicrous, laughable, risible; informal a bit much; Brit. informal a bit thick.
– OPPOSITES poor, light.

riches plural n. **1** *his new-found riches* **money**, wealth, funds, (hard) cash, (filthy) lucre, wherewithal, means, (liquid) assets, capital, resources, reserves; opulence, affluence, prosperity; informal dough, bread, loot, shekels, moolah, the necessary; Brit. informal dosh, brass, lolly, spondulicks, readies; N. Amer. informal bucks, mazuma, dinero; US informal greenbacks, simoleons, jack, rocks; Austral./NZ informal Oscar; Brit. dated l.s.d.; old use pelf. **2** *underwater riches* **resources**, treasure(s), bounty, jewels, gems.

richly adv. **1** *the richly furnished chamber* **sumptuously**, opulently, luxuriously, lavishly, gorgeously, splendidly, magnificently; informal poshly, plushly, ritzily, swankily, classily. **2** *the joy she richly deserves* **fully**, thoroughly, in full measure, well, completely, wholly, totally, entirely, absolutely, amply, utterly.
– OPPOSITES meanly.

rickety adj. **shaky**, unsteady, unsound, unsafe, tumbledown, broken-down, dilapidated, ramshackle; informal shambly; N. Amer. informal shacky.

rid v. *ridding the building of asbestos* **clear**, free, purge, empty, strip.
□ **get rid of 1** *we must get rid of some stuff* **dispose of**, throw away/out, clear out, discard, scrap, dump, bin, jettison; informal chuck (away), ditch, junk, get shut of; Brit. informal get shot of; N. Amer. informal trash. **2** *the cats got rid of the rats* **destroy**, eliminate, annihilate, obliterate, wipe out, kill.

riddle[1] n. *an answer to the riddle* **puzzle**, conundrum, brain-teaser, problem, question, poser, enigma, mystery; informal stumper.

riddle[2] v. **1** *his car was riddled by gunfire* **perforate**, hole, pierce, puncture, pepper. **2** *he was riddled with cancer* **permeate**, suffuse, fill, pervade, spread through, imbue, saturate, overrun, beset. **3** *the soil must be riddled* **sieve**, sift, strain, screen, filter; old use griddle.

ride v. **1** *she can ride a horse* **sit on**, mount, bestride; manage, handle, control. **2** *they rode home* **travel**, move, proceed, make one's way; trot, canter, gallop.

r

▶ n. *he took us for a ride* **trip**, journey, drive, run, excursion, outing, jaunt; lift; informal spin.

ridicule n. *he was subjected to ridicule* **mockery**, derision, laughter, scorn, scoffing, contempt, jeering, sneering, sneers, jibes, jibing, teasing, taunts, taunting, ragging, chaffing, sarcasm, satire; informal kidding, ribbing, joshing; N. Amer. informal goofing, razzing; Austral./NZ informal chiacking; dated sport.
– OPPOSITES respect.
▶ v. *his theory was ridiculed* **deride**, mock, laugh at, heap scorn on, jeer at, jibe at, sneer at, treat with contempt, scorn, make fun of, poke fun at, scoff at, satirize, lampoon, burlesque, caricature, parody, tease, taunt, rag, chaff; informal kid, rib, josh, take the mickey out of; N. Amer. informal goof on, rag on, razz, pull someone's chain; Austral./NZ informal chiack, poke mullock at, sling off at; dated make sport of, twit.

ridiculous adj. **stupid**, ludicrous, preposterous, laughable, farcical, risible, foolish, silly, senseless, absurd, inane, fatuous, childish, puerile, half-baked, hare-brained, ill-thought-out, crackpot, idiotic, nonsensical.
– OPPOSITES sensible.

rife adj. **1** *violence is rife* **widespread**, general, common, universal, extensive, ubiquitous, omnipresent, endemic, inescapable, insidious, prevalent. **2** *the village was rife with gossip* **overflowing**, bursting, alive, teeming, abounding.
– OPPOSITES unknown.

riff-raff n. **rabble**, scum, the lowest of the low, good-for-nothings, undesirables; informal peasants, Z-list.
– OPPOSITES elite.

rifle v. **1** *she rifled through her wardrobe* **rummage**, search, hunt, forage. **2** *a thief rifled her home* **burgle**, rob, steal from, loot, raid, plunder, ransack.

rift n. **1** *a deep rift in the ice* **crack**, fault, flaw, split, break, breach, fissure, fracture, cleft, crevice, cavity, opening. **2** *the rift between them* **breach**, division, split; quarrel, squabble, disagreement, falling-out, row, argument, dispute, conflict, feud, estrangement; informal spat, scrap; Brit. informal bust-up.

rig[1] v. **1** *the boats were rigged with a single sail* **equip**, kit out, fit out, supply, furnish, provide, arm. **2** *I rigged myself out in black* **dress**, clothe, attire, robe, garb, array, deck out, drape, accoutre, outfit, get up, trick out/up; informal doll up; old use apparel. **3** *he will rig up a shelter* **set up**, erect, assemble; throw together, cobble together, put together, whip up, improvise, contrive; Brit. informal knock up.
▶ n. **1** *a CB radio rig* **apparatus**, appliance, machine, device, instrument, contraption, system; tackle, gear, kit, outfit. **2** *the rig of the United States Air Force* **uniform**, costume, ensemble, outfit, livery, attire, clothes, clothing, garments, dress, garb, regimentals, regalia, trappings; Brit. strip;

informal get-up, gear, togs; Brit. informal kit; formal apparel; old use raiment, vestments.

rig[2] v. *they rigged the election* **manipulate**, engineer, distort, misrepresent, pervert, tamper with, doctor; falsify, fake, trump up; informal fix; Brit. informal fiddle.

right adj. **1** *it wouldn't be right to do that* **just**, fair, proper, good, upright, righteous, virtuous, moral, ethical, honourable, honest; lawful, legal. **2** *the right answer* **correct**, accurate, exact, precise; proper, valid, conventional, established, official, formal; Brit. informal spot on. **3** *the right person for the job* **suitable**, appropriate, fitting, correct, proper, desirable, preferable, ideal; old use meet. **4** *you've come at the right time* **opportune**, advantageous, favourable, propitious, good, lucky, happy, fortunate, providential, felicitous; timely, seasonable, convenient, expedient, suitable, appropriate. **5** *he's not right in the head* **sane**, lucid, rational, balanced, compos mentis; informal all there. **6** *he does not look right* **healthy**, well, (fighting) fit, normal, up to par; informal up to scratch, in the pink. **7** *my right hand* **dextral**, at three o'clock. **8** informal *it's a right mess* **absolute**, complete, total, real, thorough, perfect, utter, sheer, unmitigated, veritable.
– OPPOSITES wrong, insane, unhealthy.
▶ adv. **1** *she was right at the limit of her patience* **completely**, fully, totally, absolutely, utterly, quite. **2** *the pub's right in the middle of the village* **exactly**, precisely, directly, immediately, just, squarely, dead; informal (slap) bang, smack, plumb; N. Amer. informal smack dab. **3** *keep going right on* **straight**, directly, as the crow flies. **4** informal *I'll be right with you* **straight**, directly, forthwith, without further ado, promptly, quickly, ASAP, as soon as possible; N. Amer. in short order. **5** *I think I heard right* **correctly**, accurately, properly, precisely, aright, rightly, perfectly. **6** *make sure you're treated right* **well**, properly, justly, fairly, equitably, impartially, honourably, lawfully, legally. **7** *things will turn out right* **well**, for the best, favourably, happily, advantageously, profitably, providentially, luckily, conveniently.
– OPPOSITES wrong, badly.
▶ n. **1** *the difference between right and wrong* **goodness**, righteousness, virtue, integrity, rectitude, propriety, morality, truth, honesty, honour, justice, fairness, equity; lawfulness, legality. **2** *you have the right to say no* **entitlement**, prerogative, privilege, advantage, due, birthright, liberty, authority, power, licence, permission, dispensation, leave, sanction; Law, historical droit.
– OPPOSITES wrong.
▶ v. **1** *the way to right a capsized dinghy* **set upright**, turn back over. **2** *we must right the situation* **remedy**, put right, rectify, retrieve, fix, resolve, sort out, settle, square; straighten out, correct, repair, mend, redress, make good, ameliorate, better.
▫ **by rights** properly, correctly, technically, in fairness; legally, de jure.

r

right away at once, straight away, (right) now, this (very) minute, this instant, immediately, instantly, directly, forthwith, without further ado, promptly, quickly, without delay, ASAP, as soon as possible; N. Amer. in short order; informal straight off, p.d.q. (pretty damn quick), pronto; N. Amer. informal lickety-split.

within one's rights entitled, permitted, allowed, at liberty, empowered, authorized, qualified, licensed, justified.

> **WORD LINKS**
> **recto** the right-hand page in a book
> **starboard** the right-hand side of a ship or aircraft
> **dexter** (Heraldry) on the bearer's right-hand side of a coat of arms

righteous adj. **1** *righteous living* **good**, virtuous, upright, upstanding, decent; ethical, principled, moral, high-minded, law-abiding, anti-corruption, honest, honourable, blameless, irreproachable, noble; saintly, angelic, pure. **2** *righteous anger* **justifiable**, justified, legitimate, defensible, supportable, rightful; admissible, allowable, understandable, excusable, acceptable, reasonable.
– OPPOSITES sinful, unjustifiable.

rightful adj. **1** *the car's rightful owner* **legal**, lawful, real, true, proper, correct, recognized, genuine, authentic, acknowledged, approved, licensed, valid, bona fide, de jure; informal legit, kosher. **2** *their rightful place in society* **deserved**, merited, due, just, right, fair, proper, fitting, appropriate, suitable.

right-wing adj. **conservative**, rightist, ultra-conservative, blimpish, diehard; reactionary, traditionalist, conventional, unprogressive; fascist, fascistic.
– OPPOSITES left-wing.

rigid adj. **1** *a rigid container* **stiff**, hard, firm, inflexible, unbending, unyielding, inelastic. **2** *a rigid routine* **fixed**, set, firm, inflexible, unalterable, unchangeable, immutable, unvarying, invariable, hard and fast, cast-iron. **3** *a rigid approach to funding* **strict**, severe, stern, stringent, rigorous, inflexible, uncompromising, intransigent.
– OPPOSITES flexible, lenient.

rigmarole n. **1** *the rigmarole of dressing up* **fuss**, bother, trouble, folderol, ado, pother; NZ bobsy-die; informal palaver, song and dance, performance, to-do, pantomime, hassle; Brit. informal carry-on. **2** *that rigmarole about the house being haunted* **tale**, saga, yarn, shaggy-dog story; informal spiel.

rigorous adj. **1** *rigorous attention to detail* **meticulous**, conscientious, punctilious, careful, diligent, attentive, scrupulous, painstaking, exact, precise, accurate, thorough, particular, strict, demanding, exacting; informal pernickety. **2** *the rigorous enforcement of rules* **strict**, severe, stern, stringent, tough, harsh, rigid, relentless, unsparing, inflexible, draconian, intransigent, uncompromising, exacting. **3** *rigorous yachting conditions* **harsh**, severe,

bad, bleak, extreme, inclement; unpleasant, disagreeable, foul, nasty, filthy; stormy, wild, tempestuous.
– OPPOSITES slapdash, lax, mild.

rigour n. **1** *a mine operated under conditions of rigour* **strictness**, severity, stringency, toughness, harshness, rigidity, inflexibility, intransigence. **2** *intellectual rigour* **meticulousness**, thoroughness, carefulness, diligence, scrupulousness, exactness, exactitude, precision, accuracy, correctness, strictness. **3** *the rigours of the journey* **hardship**, harshness, severity, adversity; ordeal, misery, trial; discomfort, inconvenience, privation.

rile v. informal See **annoy**.

rim n. **1** *the rim of her cup* **brim**, edge, lip. **2** *the rim of the crater* **edge**, border, side, margin, brink, fringe, boundary, perimeter, limits, periphery; old use skirt.

rind n. **skin**, peel, zest, integument; Botany pericarp.

ring[1] n. **1** *a ring round the moon* **circle**, band, halo, disc. **2** *she wore a ring* **wedding ring**, band. **3** *a circus ring* **arena**, enclosure, field, ground; amphitheatre, stadium. **4** *a ring of onlookers* **circle**, group, knot, cluster, bunch, band, throng, crowd, flock, pack. **5** *a spy ring* **gang**, syndicate, cartel, mob, band, circle, organization, association, society, alliance, league, coterie, cabal.
▸v. *police ringed the building* **surround**, circle, encircle, encompass, girdle, enclose, hem in, confine, seal off.

> **WORD LINKS**
> **annular** ring-shaped

ring[2] v. **1** *church bells rang all day* **toll**, sound, peal, chime, clang, bong, ding, jingle, tinkle; literary knell. **2** *the room rang with laughter* **resound**, reverberate, resonate, echo. **3** *I'll ring you tomorrow* **telephone**, phone (up), call (up); reach, dial; informal give someone a buzz; Brit. informal give someone a bell, give someone a tinkle, get on the blower to; N. Amer. informal get someone on the horn.
▸n. **1** *the ring of a bell* **chime**, toll, peal, clang, clink, ding, jingle, tinkle, tintinnabulation, sound; literary knell. **2** *I'll give Chris a ring* **call**, telephone call, phone call; informal buzz; Brit. informal bell, tinkle.
□ **ring something in** herald, signal, announce, proclaim, usher in, introduce, mark, signify, indicate; literary betoken, knell.

rinse v. **wash (out)**, clean, cleanse, bathe; dip, drench, splash, swill, sluice, hose down.

riot n. **1** *a riot in the capital* **uproar**, commotion, upheaval, disturbance, furore, tumult, melee, scuffle, fracas, fray, brawl, free-for-all; violence, fighting, vandalism, mayhem, turmoil, lawlessness, anarchy; N. Amer. informal wilding; Law, dated affray. **2** *the garden was a riot of colour* **mass**, sea, splash, show, exhibition.
▸v. *the miners rioted* **(go on the) rampage**, run riot, fight in the streets, run wild, run amok, go berserk; informal raise hell.

r

□ **run riot 1** *the children ran riot* **(go on the) rampage**, riot, run amok, go berserk, go out of control; informal raise hell. **2** *the vegetation has run riot* **grow profusely**, spread uncontrolled, grow rapidly, spread like wildfire; burgeon, multiply, rocket.

riotous adj. **1** *the demonstration turned riotous* **unruly**, rowdy, disorderly, uncontrollable, unmanageable, undisciplined, uproarious, tumultuous; violent, wild, ugly, lawless, anarchic. **2** *a riotous party* **boisterous**, lively, loud, noisy, unrestrained, uninhibited, uproarious, unruly, rollicking; informal rumbustious; N. Amer. informal rambunctious.
– OPPOSITES peaceable.

rip v. **1** *he ripped the posters down* **tear**, wrench, wrest, pull, snatch, tug, prise, heave, drag, peel, pluck; informal yank. **2** *she ripped Leo's note into pieces* **tear**, claw, hack, slit, cut; literary rend.
▶ n. *a rip in my sleeve* **tear**, slit, split, rent, laceration, cut, gash, slash.

ripe adj. **1** *a ripe tomato* **mature**, ripened, full grown, ready to eat; luscious, juicy, succulent, tender, sweet. **2** *the dock is ripe for development* **ready**, fit, suitable, right. **3** *the ripe old age of ninety* **advanced**, hoary, venerable, old. **4** *the time is ripe for his return* **opportune**, advantageous, favourable, auspicious, propitious, promising, good, right, fortunate, benign, providential, felicitous, seasonable; convenient, suitable, appropriate, apt, fitting.
– OPPOSITES unsuitable, young.

ripen v. **become ripe**, mature, mellow.

rip-off n. informal **fraud**, swindle, confidence trick; informal con, scam, flimflam, gyp; Brit. informal swizz, daylight robbery; N. Amer. informal rip, shakedown, bunco; Austral. informal rort.

riposte n. *an indignant riposte* **retort**, counter, rejoinder, sally, return, answer, reply, response; informal comeback.
▶ v. *'Heaven help you,' riposted Sally* **retort**, counter, rejoin, return, retaliate, hurl back, answer, reply, respond, come back.

ripple n. *he blew ripples in his coffee* **wavelet**, wave, undulation, ripplet, ridge, ruffle.

rise v. **1** *the sun rose* **move up/upwards**, come up, make one's/its way up, arise, ascend, climb, mount, soar. **2** *the mountains rising above us* **loom**, tower, soar, rise up, rear (up). **3** *prices rose* **go up**, increase, soar, shoot up, surge, leap, jump, rocket, escalate, spiral. **4** *living standards have risen* **improve**, get better, advance, go up, soar, shoot up. **5** *his voice rose* **get higher**, get louder, increase, swell, intensify. **6** *he rose from his chair* **stand up**, get to one's feet, get up, jump up, leap up; formal arise. **7** *he rises at dawn* **get up**, get out of bed, rouse oneself, stir, bestir oneself, be up and about; informal rise and shine, shake a leg, surface; formal arise. **8** *the court rose at midday* **adjourn**, recess, be suspended, pause, take a break; informal knock off, take five. **9** *he rose through the ranks*

make progress, climb, advance, get on, work one's way, be promoted. **10** *he wouldn't rise to the bait* **react**, respond; take. **11** *Christ rose again* **come back to life**, be resurrected, revive. **12** *the dough started to rise* **swell**, expand, enlarge, puff up. **13** *the nation rose against its oppressors* **rebel**, revolt, mutiny, riot, take up arms. **14** *the Rhine rises in the Alps* **originate**, begin, start, emerge; issue from, spring from, flow from, emanate from. **15** *her spirits rose* **brighten**, lift, cheer up, improve, pick up; informal buck up. **16** *the ground rose gently* **slope upwards**, go uphill, incline, climb.
– OPPOSITES fall, descend, drop, sit, retire, resume, die, shelve.
▶ n. **1** *a price rise* **increase**, hike, leap, upsurge, upswing, climb, escalation. **2** *he got a rise of 11%* **raise**, pay increase, wage increase; hike, increment. **3** *a rise in standards* **improvement**, amelioration, upturn, leap. **4** *his rise to power* **progress**, climb, promotion, elevation, aggrandizement. **5** *we walked up the rise* **slope**, incline, acclivity, hillock, hill; formal eminence.

risible adj. **laughable**, ridiculous, absurd, comical, comic, amusing, funny, hilarious, humorous, droll, farcical, silly, ludicrous, hysterical; informal rib-tickling, priceless; informal dated killing.

risk n. **1** *there is a certain amount of risk* **chance**, uncertainty, unpredictability, precariousness, instability, insecurity, perilousness, riskiness. **2** *the risk of fire* **possibility**, chance, probability, likelihood, danger, peril, threat, menace, fear, prospect.
– OPPOSITES safety, impossibility.
▶ v. **1** *he risked his life to save them* **endanger**, imperil, jeopardize, hazard, gamble (with), chance; put on the line, put in jeopardy. **2** *you risk getting cold and wet* **run the risk of**, stand a chance of, be in danger of.
□ **at risk** in danger, in peril, in jeopardy, under threat.

risky adj. **dangerous**, hazardous, perilous, fraught with danger, unsafe, insecure, precarious, parlous, touch-and-go, treacherous; uncertain, unpredictable; informal chancy, dicey, hairy; N. Amer. informal gnarly.

risqué adj. **ribald**, rude, bawdy, racy, earthy, indecent, suggestive, improper, naughty, locker-room; vulgar, dirty, smutty, crude, coarse, obscene, lewd, X-rated; informal blue, raunchy; Brit. informal fruity, off colour, saucy; N. Amer. informal gamy.

rite n. **ceremony**, ritual, ceremonial; service, sacrament, liturgy, worship, office; act, practice, custom, tradition, convention, institution, procedure.

ritual n. *an elaborate civic ritual* **ceremony**, rite, ceremonial, observance; service, sacrament, liturgy, worship; act, practice, custom, tradition, convention, formality, procedure, protocol.
▶ adj. *a ritual burial* **ceremonial**, ritualistic, prescribed, set, formal; sacramental, liturgical; traditional, conventional.

ritzy adj. informal See **posh** (sense 1).

rival n. **1** *his rival for the nomination* **opponent**, challenger, competitor, contender; adversary, antagonist, enemy, nemesis; literary foe. **2** *the tool has no rival* **equal**, match, peer, equivalent, counterpart, like.
– OPPOSITES ally.
▶ v. *few countries can rival it for scenery* **match**, compare with, compete with, vie with, equal, measure up to, be in the same league as, be on a par with, touch, challenge; informal hold a candle to.
▶ adj. *rival candidates* **competing**, opposing, contending.

rivalry n. **competitiveness**, competition, contention, vying; opposition, conflict, feuding, antagonism, friction, enmity; informal keeping up with the Joneses.

riven adj. *a country riven by civil war* **torn apart**, split, rent, severed; literary cleft, torn asunder.

river n. **1 watercourse**, waterway, tributary, stream, rivulet, brook, inlet, rill, runnel, freshet; Scottish & N. English burn; N. English beck; S. English bourn; N. Amer. & Austral./NZ creek; Austral. billabong. **2** *a river of molten lava* **stream**, torrent, flood, deluge, cascade.

> **WORD LINKS**
>
> **fluvial** relating to or found in a river
> **riparian** relating to or found on the banks of a river
> **confluence** a place where two rivers join
> **delta** a triangular area where the mouth of a river has split into several channels
> **estuary** the mouth of a large river
> **oxbow** a loop formed by a horseshoe-shaped bend in a river
> **rapids, white water** a very fast-flowing stretch of a river
> **spate, freshet** a flood in a river
> **levee** an embankment built to prevent a river from overflowing
> **weir** a dam built to regulate the flow of a river
> **potamology** the study of rivers

riveted adj. **1** *she stood riveted to the spot* **fixed**, rooted, frozen, unable to move; motionless, unmoving, immobile, stock-still. **2** *he was riveted by the newsreels* **fascinated**, engrossed, gripped, captivated, enthralled, spellbound, mesmerized, transfixed. **3** *their eyes were riveted on the teacher* **fixed**, fastened, focused, concentrated, locked, glued.

riveting adj. **fascinating**, gripping, engrossing, interesting, intriguing, absorbing, captivating, enthralling, compelling, spellbinding, mesmerizing; informal unputdownable.
– OPPOSITES boring.

road n. **1** *the roads were crowded with traffic* **street**, thoroughfare, roadway, carriageway, avenue, broadway, bypass, ring road, trunk road, byroad; lane, crescent, drive, parade, row; corniche; Brit. dual carriageway, clearway, motorway; N. Amer. highway, freeway, parkway, throughway, expressway;

US turnpike, interstate. **2** *a step on the road to recovery* **way**, path, route, course. **3** *oil tankers waiting in the roads* **anchorage**, channel, haven, roadstead.
□ **on the road** on tour, touring, travelling.

roam v. **wander**, rove, ramble, drift, walk, traipse; range, travel, tramp, traverse, trek; Scottish & Irish stravaig; informal cruise, mosey; formal perambulate; old-use peregrinate.

roar n. **1** *the roars of the crowd* **shout**, bellow, yell, cry, howl; clamour; informal holler. **2** *the roar of the sea* **boom**, crash, rumble, roll, thundering. **3** *roars of laughter* **guffaw**, howl, hoot, shriek, gale, peal.
▶ v. **1** *'Get out!' roared Angus* **bellow**, yell, shout, bawl, howl; informal holler. **2** *thunder roared* **boom**, rumble, crash, roll, thunder. **3** *the movie left them roaring* **guffaw**, laugh, hoot; informal split one's sides, be rolling in the aisles, be doubled up, crack up, be in stitches, die laughing; Brit. informal crease up, fall about. **4** *a motorbike roared past* **speed**, zoom, whizz, flash; informal belt, tear, zip; Brit. informal bomb.

roaring adj. **1** *a roaring fire* **blazing**, burning, flaming. **2** informal *a roaring success* **enormous**, huge, massive, (very) great, tremendous; complete, out-and-out, thorough; informal rip-roaring, whopping, fantastic.

roast v. **1** *potatoes roasted in olive oil* **cook**, bake, grill; N. Amer. broil. **2** informal *they roasted him for wasting time.* See **criticize**.

roasting informal adj. *a roasting day* **hot**, sweltering, scorching, blistering, searing, torrid; informal boiling (hot), baking (hot).
▶ n. *the boss gave him a roasting.* See **lecture** (sense 2 of the noun).

rob v. **1** *the gang robbed the local bank* **burgle**, steal from, hold up, break into; raid, loot, plunder, pillage; N. Amer. burglarize; informal do, turn over, knock off, stick up. **2** *he robbed an old woman* **steal from**; informal mug, jump; N. Amer. informal clip. **3** *he was robbed of his savings* **cheat**, swindle, defraud; informal do out of, con out of, fleece; N. Amer. informal stiff. **4** informal *it cost £70—I was robbed* **overcharge**; informal rip off, sting, do, diddle; N. Amer. informal gouge. **5** *defeat robbed him of his title* **deprive**, strip, divest; deny.

robber n. **burglar**, thief, housebreaker, mugger, shoplifter; stealer, pilferer, raider, looter, plunderer, pillager; bandit, highwayman; informal crook, cracksman; Brit. informal tea leaf; N. Amer. informal yegg; literary brigand.

robbery n. **1** *they were arrested for the robbery* **burglary**, theft, thievery, stealing, breaking and entering, housebreaking, larceny, shoplifting; embezzlement, fraud; hold-up, break-in, raid; informal mugging, smash-and-grab, stick-up; Brit. informal blag; N. Amer. informal heist. **2** informal *Six quid? That's robbery* **a swindle**; informal a con, a rip-off; Brit. informal daylight robbery.

robe n. **1** *the women wore black robes* **cloak**, kaftan, djellaba, wrap, mantle, cape;

r

N. Amer. wrapper. **2** *coronation robes* **garb**,
regalia, costume, finery; garments, clothes;
formal apparel; old use raiment, habiliments,
vestments. **3** *priestly robes* **vestment**,
surplice, cassock, rochet, alb, dalmatic,
chasuble; canonicals. **4** *a towelling robe*
dressing gown, bathrobe, housecoat; N. Amer.
wrapper.
▶ v. *he robed for Mass* **dress**, clothe oneself;
formal enrobe.

robot n. **automaton**, android, golem; informal
bot, droid.

robust adj. **1** *a large, robust man* **strong**,
vigorous, sturdy, tough, powerful, solid,
muscular, sinewy, rugged, hardy, strapping,
brawny, burly, husky; healthy; (fighting)
fit, hale and hearty, lusty, in fine fettle;
informal beefy, hunky. **2** *these knives are
robust* **durable**, resilient, tough, hard-
wearing, long-lasting, sturdy, strong.
3 *her usual robust view of things* **down-
to-earth**, practical, realistic, pragmatic,
common-sense, commonsensical, matter-
of-fact, businesslike, sensible, unromantic,
unsentimental; informal no-nonsense. **4** *a
robust red wine* **strong**, full-bodied,
flavourful, flavoursome, rich.
– OPPOSITES frail, fragile, romantic, insipid.

rock[1] v. **1** *the ship rocked on the water* **move
to and fro**, move back and forth, sway, see-
saw; roll, pitch, plunge, toss, lurch, reel, list;
wobble, oscillate. **2** *the building began to rock*
shake, vibrate, quake, tremble. **3** *Wall Street
was rocked by the news* **stun**, shock, stagger,
astonish, startle, surprise, shake (up); take
aback, throw, unnerve, disconcert.

rock[2] n. **1** *a gully strewn with rocks* **boulder**,
stone, pebble; Austral. informal goolie. **2** *a castle
built on a rock* **crag**, cliff, outcrop. **3** *he was
the rock on which they relied* **foundation**,
cornerstone, support, prop, mainstay; tower
of strength, bulwark, anchor. **4** informal *she
wore a massive rock* **diamond (ring)**, jewel,
precious stone.
□ **on the rocks** informal **1** *her marriage is on
the rocks* **in difficulty**, in trouble, breaking
up, over; in tatters, in ruins, ruined. **2** *a
Scotch on the rocks* **with ice**, on ice.

> **WORD LINKS**
> **petrography, petrology, lithology** the
>   scientific study of rocks
> **moraine** a mass of rocks deposited by a glacier
> **stratum** a layer of rock

rocket n. **1** *guerrillas fired rockets at them*
missile, projectile. **2** *they lit some colourful
rockets* **firework**, Roman candle, banger.
3 Brit. informal *he got a rocket from the boss*. See
lecture (sense 2 of the noun).
▶ v. **1** *prices have rocketed* **shoot up**, soar,
increase, rise, escalate, spiral; informal go
through the roof. **2** *they rocketed into
the alley* **speed**, zoom, shoot, whizz, tear,
career; Brit. informal bomb; N. Amer. informal barrel,
hightail it.
– OPPOSITES plummet.

rocky[1] adj. *a rocky path* **stony**, pebbly,
shingly; rough, bumpy; craggy, mountainous.

rocky[2] adj. **1** *that table's rocky* **unsteady**,
shaky, unstable, wobbly, tottery, rickety,
flimsy. **2** *a rocky marriage* **difficult**,
problematic, precarious, unstable,
unreliable, undependable; informal iffy, up
and down.
– OPPOSITES steady, stable.

rococo adj. **ornate**, fancy, elaborate,
extravagant, baroque; fussy, busy,
ostentatious, showy; flowery, florid,
flamboyant, high-flown, magniloquent,
orotund, bombastic, overwrought,
overblown, inflated, turgid; informal
highfalutin.
– OPPOSITES plain.

rod n. **1** *an iron rod* **bar**, stick, pole, baton,
staff; shaft, strut, rail, spoke. **2** *the
ceremonial rod* **staff**, mace, sceptre.
3 *instruction was accompanied by the rod*
corporal punishment, the cane, the lash,
the birch; beating, flogging, caning, birching.

rogue n. **1** *a rogue without ethics* **scoundrel**,
villain, miscreant, reprobate, rascal, good-
for-nothing, ne'er-do-well, wretch; informal rat,
dog, louse, crook; informal dated rotter, bounder,
blighter; dated cad; old use blackguard, knave.
2 *your boy's a little rogue* **rascal**, imp, devil,
monkey; informal scamp, scallywag, monster,
horror, terror, tyke; Brit. informal perisher;
N. Amer. informal hellion.

roguish adj. **1** *a roguish character*
unprincipled, dishonest, deceitful,
unscrupulous, untrustworthy, shameless;
wicked, villainous; informal shady, scoundrelly,
rascally; old use knavish. **2** *a roguish grin*
mischievous, playful, teasing, cheeky,
naughty, wicked, impish, devilish, arch;
informal waggish.

roister v. **enjoy oneself**, celebrate, revel,
carouse, frolic, romp, have fun, make merry,
rollick; informal party, live it up, whoop it up,
have a ball, make whoopee.

role n. **1** *a small role in the film* **part**;
character. **2** *his role as President of the EC*
capacity, position, job, post, office, duty,
responsibility, mantle, place; function, part.

roll v. **1** *the bottle rolled down the table* **bowl**,
turn over and over, spin, rotate. **2** *waiters
rolled in the trolleys* **wheel**, push, trundle.
3 *we rolled past fields* **travel**, go, move, pass,
cruise, sweep. **4** *the months rolled by* **pass**,
go by, slip by, fly by, elapse, wear on, march
on. **5** *tears rolled down her cheeks* **flow**, run,
course, stream, pour, spill, trickle. **6** *the
mist rolled in* **billow**, undulate, tumble. **7** *he
rolled his handkerchief into a ball* **wind**, coil,
fold, curl; twist. **8** *roll out the pastry* **flatten**,
level; even out. **9** *they rolled about with
laughter* **stagger**, lurch, reel, totter, teeter,
wobble. **10** *the ship began to roll* **lurch**, toss,
rock, pitch, plunge, sway, reel, list, keel.
11 *thunder rolled* **rumble**, reverberate, echo,
resound, boom, roar, grumble.
▶ n. **1** *a roll of wrapping paper* **cylinder**, tube,
scroll; bolt. **2** *a roll of film* **reel**, spool. **3** *a
roll of notes* **wad**, bundle. **4** *a roll of the dice*
throw, toss, turn, spin. **5** *crusty rolls* **bread**

roll, bun, bagel; Brit. **bap**, muffin; N. English barm; N. Amer. **hoagie**; Military slang **wad**. **6** *the electoral roll* **list**, register, directory, record, file, index, catalogue, inventory; census. **7** *a roll of thunder* **rumble**, reverberation, echo, boom, clap, crack, roar, grumble.
◻ **roll in** informal **1** *money has been rolling in* **pour in**, flood in, flow in. **2** *he rolled in at nine o'clock* **arrive**, turn up, appear, show one's face; informal show up, roll up, blow in.
roll something out unroll, spread out, unfurl, unfold, open (out), unwind, uncoil.
roll something up fold (up), furl, wind up, coil (up), bundle up.

rollicking[1] n. Brit. informal *I got a rollicking for being late*. See **lecture** (sense 2 of the noun).

rollicking[2] adj. *a rollicking party* **lively**, boisterous, exuberant, spirited; riotous, noisy, wild, rowdy, roisterous; informal rumbustious; N. Amer. informal rambunctious.

roly-poly adj. informal **chubby**, plump, fat, stout, rotund, round, dumpy, chunky, portly, overweight, fleshy, paunchy, bulky, corpulent; informal tubby, pudgy, beefy, porky, blubbery; Brit. informal podgy; N. Amer. informal zaftig, corn-fed.
– OPPOSITES skinny.

romance n. **1** *their romance blossomed* **love**, passion, ardour, adoration, devotion; affection, fondness, attachment. **2** *he's had many romances* **love affair**, relationship, liaison, courtship, attachment; flirtation, dalliance. **3** *an author of historical romances* **love story**, novel; romantic fiction; informal tear-jerker. **4** *the romance of the Far East* **mystery**, glamour, excitement, exoticism, mystique; appeal, allure, charm.
▸ v. **1** dated *he was romancing Meg* **woo**, chase, pursue; go out with, pay court to; informal see, go steady with, date; dated court, make love to. **2** *I am romancing the past* **romanticize**, idealize, paint a rosy picture of.

romantic adj. **1** *he's so romantic* **loving**, amorous, passionate, tender, affectionate; informal lovey-dovey. **2** *romantic songs* **sentimental**, hearts-and-flowers, slushy, mushy, sloppy; mawkish, sickly, saccharine, syrupy; informal schmaltzy, gooey, treacly, cheesy, corny; Brit. informal soppy; N. Amer. informal cornball, sappy. **3** *a romantic setting* **idyllic**, picturesque, fairy-tale; beautiful, lovely, charming, pretty. **4** *romantic notions of rural communities* **idealistic**, idealized, unrealistic, fanciful, impractical; head-in-the-clouds, starry-eyed, optimistic, hopeful, visionary, utopian, fairy-tale.
– OPPOSITES unsentimental, realistic.
▸ n. *an incurable romantic* **idealist**, sentimentalist, romanticist; dreamer, visionary, utopian, Don Quixote, fantasist; N. Amer. fantast.
– OPPOSITES realist.

romp v. **1** *two fox cubs romped playfully* **play**, frolic, frisk, gambol, skip, prance, caper, cavort, rollick; dated sport. **2** *South Africa romped to a win* **sail**, coast, sweep; win hands down, run away with it; informal win by a mile, walk it.

room n. **1** *there isn't much room* **space**; headroom, legroom; area, expanse, extent; informal elbow room. **2** *there's room for improvement* **scope**, capacity, leeway, latitude, freedom; opportunity, chance; informal wiggle room. **3** *he had rooms in the Pepys building* **lodgings**, quarters; accommodation; a suite, an apartment; informal a pad, digs.
▸ v. *he roomed there in September* **lodge**, board, live, stay; be quartered, be housed; formal dwell, reside, sojourn.

roomy adj. **spacious**, capacious, sizeable, generous, big, large, extensive; voluminous, ample, loose-fitting, boyfriend; formal commodious.
– OPPOSITES cramped.

root n. **1** *a plant's roots* **rootstock**, tuber, rootlet; taproot; Botany rhizome, radicle. **2** *the root of the problem* **source**, origin, germ, beginnings, genesis; cause, reason, basis, foundation, bottom, seat; core, heart, nub, essence; formal radix. **3** *he rejected his roots* **origins**, beginnings, family, ancestors, predecessors, heritage; birthplace, homeland.
▸ v. **1** *has the shoot rooted?* **take root**, grow roots, establish, strike, take. **2** *root the cuttings* **plant**, bed out, sow. **3** *he rooted around in the cupboard* **rummage**, hunt, search, rifle, delve, forage, dig, nose, poke; Brit. informal rootle.
◻ **root and branch 1** *the firm should be eradicated, root and branch* **completely**, entirely, wholly, totally, thoroughly. **2** *a root-and-branch reform* **complete**, total, thorough, radical.
root for informal cheer (on), applaud, support, encourage.
root something out 1 *the hedge was rooted out* **uproot**, deracinate, pull up, grub out. **2** *a campaign to root out corruption* **eradicate**, eliminate, weed out, destroy, wipe out, stamp out, extirpate, abolish, end, put a stop to.
take root 1 *leave the plants to take root* **germinate**, sprout, establish, strike, take. **2** *Christianity took root in Persia* **become established**, take hold; develop, thrive, flourish.

┌─────────────────────────────────┐
│ **WORD LINKS**   │
│ **radical** relating to the root of a plant │
└─────────────────────────────────┘

rooted adj. **1** *views rooted in Indian culture* **embedded**, fixed, established, entrenched, ingrained. **2** *Neil was rooted to the spot* **frozen**, riveted, paralysed, glued, fixed; stock-still, motionless, unmoving.

rootless adj. **itinerant**, unsettled, drifting, roving, footloose; homeless, of no fixed abode.

rope n. **cord**, cable, line, hawser; string.
▸ v. *his feet were roped together* **tie**, bind, lash, truss; secure, moor, fasten, attach; hitch, tether, lasso.
◻ **rope someone in/into** persuade to/into, talk into, inveigle into; enlist, engage.

r

ropy adj. **1** *ropy strands of lava* **stringy**, thready, fibrous, filamentous; viscous, sticky, mucilaginous, thick. **2** Brit. informal *I feel a bit ropy.* See **ill** (sense 1 of the adjective). **3** Brit. informal *ropy defending from the home team.* See **substandard**.

roster n. **schedule**, list, listing, register, agenda, calendar, table; Brit. rota.

rostrum n. **dais**, platform, podium, stage; soapbox.

rosy adj. **1** *a rosy complexion* **pink**, pinkish, roseate, reddish; glowing, healthy, fresh, radiant, blooming; blushing, flushed; ruddy, high-coloured, florid. **2** *his future looks rosy* **promising**, optimistic, auspicious, hopeful, encouraging, favourable, bright, golden; informal upbeat.
– OPPOSITES pale, bleak.

rot v. **1** *the floorboards rotted* **decay**, decompose, become rotten; disintegrate, crumble, perish. **2** *the meat began to rot* **go bad**, go off, spoil; moulder, putrefy, fester. **3** *poor neighbourhoods have been left to rot* **deteriorate**, degenerate, decline, decay, go to rack and ruin, go to seed, go downhill; informal go to pot, go to the dogs.
– OPPOSITES improve.
▸n. **1** *the leaves turned black with rot* **decay**, decomposition, mould, mouldiness, mildew, blight, canker; putrefaction, putrescence. **2** *traditionalists said the rot had set in* **deterioration**, decline; corruption, cancer. **3** informal *stop talking rot.* See **nonsense** (sense 1).
– OPPOSITES sense.

rota n. Brit. See **roster**.

rotary adj. **rotating**, rotatory, rotational, revolving, turning, spinning, gyrating, gyratory.

rotate v. **1** *the wheels rotate continually* **revolve**, go round, turn (round), spin, gyrate, whirl, twirl, swivel, circle, pivot. **2** *many nurses rotate jobs* **alternate**, take turns, change, switch, interchange, exchange, swap; move around.

rotation n. **1** *the rotation of the wheels* **revolving**, turning, spinning, gyration, circling. **2** *a rotation of the Earth* **turn**, revolution, orbit, spin. **3** *each member is*

chair for six months in rotation **sequence**, succession; alternation, cycle.

rote n.
□ **by rote** mechanically, automatically, parrot-fashion, unthinkingly, mindlessly; from memory, by heart.

rotten adj. **1** *rotten meat* **decaying**, rotting, bad, off, decomposing, putrid, putrescent, perished, mouldy, mouldering, mildewy, rancid, festering, fetid; addled; maggoty, wormy, flyblown. **2** *rotten teeth* **decaying**, decayed, carious, black; disintegrating, crumbling. **3** *he's rotten to the core* **corrupt**, unprincipled, dishonest, dishonourable, unscrupulous, untrustworthy, immoral; villainous, bad, wicked, evil, iniquitous, venal; informal crooked, warped; Brit. informal bent. **4** informal *a rotten thing to do* **nasty**, unkind, unpleasant, obnoxious, vile, contemptible, despicable, shabby; spiteful, mean, malicious, hateful, hurtful; unfair, uncharitable, uncalled for; informal dirty, low-down; Brit. informal out of order. **5** informal *he was a rotten singer* **bad**, poor, dreadful, awful, terrible, frightful, atrocious, appalling, abysmal, hopeless, inadequate, inferior, substandard; informal crummy, pathetic, useless, lousy, dire; Brit. informal duff, rubbish, pants. **6** informal *I feel rotten about it* **guilty**, conscience-stricken, remorseful, ashamed, shamefaced, chastened, contrite, sorry, regretful, repentant, penitent. **7** informal *I felt rotten with that cold.* See **ill** (sense 1 of the adjective).
– OPPOSITES fresh, honourable, kind, good, well.

rotund adj. **1** *a small, rotund man* **plump**, chubby, fat, stout, portly, dumpy, round, chunky, overweight, heavy, paunchy, ample; flabby, fleshy, bulky, corpulent, obese; informal tubby, roly-poly, pudgy, beefy, porky, blubbery; Brit. informal podgy; N. Amer. informal zaftig, corn-fed. **2** *rotund cauldrons* **round**, bulbous, spherical, spheric; literary orbicular.
– OPPOSITES thin.

roué n. **libertine**, rake, debauchee, degenerate, profligate; lecher, seducer, womanizer, philanderer, adulterer, Don Juan, Lothario; informal ladykiller, lech, dirty old man.

rough adj. **1** *rough ground* **uneven**, irregular, bumpy, lumpy, knobbly, stony, rocky, rugged, rutted, pitted, rutty. **2** *the terrier's rough coat* **coarse**, bristly, scratchy, prickly; shaggy, hairy, bushy. **3** *rough skin* **dry**, leathery, weather-beaten; chapped, calloused, scaly, scabrous. **4** *his voice was rough* **gruff**, hoarse, harsh, rasping, raspy, husky, throaty, gravelly, guttural. **5** *rough red wine* **sharp**, sour, acidic, acid, vinegary, acidulous. **6** *he gets rough when he's drunk* **violent**, brutal, vicious; **aggressive**, belligerent, pugnacious, thuggish; boisterous, rowdy, disorderly, unruly, riotous. **7** *a machine that can take rough handling* **careless**, clumsy, inept, unskilful. **8** *rough manners* **boorish**, loutish, oafish, brutish, coarse, crude, uncouth, vulgar, unrefined, unladylike,

ungentlemanly, uncultured; unmannerly, impolite, discourteous, uncivil, ungracious, rude. **9** *rough seas* **turbulent**, stormy, tempestuous, violent, heavy, heaving, choppy. **10** informal *I've had a rough time* **difficult**, hard, tough, bad, unpleasant; demanding, arduous. **11** informal *you were a bit rough on her* **harsh**, hard, tough, stern, severe, unfair, unjust; insensitive, nasty, cruel, unkind, unsympathetic, brutal, heartless, merciless. **12** informal *I'm feeling rough.* See **ill** (sense 1 of the adjective). **13** *a rough draft* **preliminary**, hasty, quick, sketchy, cursory, basic, crude, rudimentary, raw, unpolished; incomplete, unfinished. **14** *a rough estimate* **approximate**, inexact, imprecise, coarse-grained, vague, estimated, hazy; N. Amer. informal **ballpark**. **15** *the accommodation is rather rough* **plain**, basic, simple, rough and ready, rude, crude, primitive, spartan.
– OPPOSITES smooth, sleek, soft, dulcet, sweet, gentle, careful, refined, calm, easy, kind, well, exact, luxurious.

▶n. **1** *the artist's initial roughs* **sketch**, draft, outline, mock-up. **2** Brit. *a bunch of roughs attacked him* **ruffian**, thug, lout, hooligan, hoodlum, rowdy; informal tough, roughneck, bruiser, gorilla, yahoo; Brit. informal yob, yobbo.

▶v. *rough the surface with sandpaper* **roughen**.
□ **rough something out** draft, sketch out, outline, block out, mock up; formal adumbrate.
rough someone up informal beat up, attack, assault, knock about/around, batter, manhandle; informal do over, beat the living daylights out of; Brit. informal duff up.

rough and ready adj. **basic**, simple, crude, unrefined, unsophisticated; makeshift, provisional, stopgap, improvised, extempory, ad hoc; hurried, sketchy.

rough and tumble n. **scuffle**, fight, brawl, melee, free-for-all, fracas, rumpus; horseplay; Law, dated affray; informal scrap, dust-up, punch-up, shindy; N. Amer. informal rough house.

roughly adv. **1** *he shoved her roughly away* **violently**, forcefully, forcibly, abruptly, unceremoniously. **2** *they treated him roughly* **harshly**, unkindly, unsympathetically; brutally, savagely, mercilessly, cruelly, heartlessly. **3** *roughly £2.4 million* **approximately**, (round) about, around, circa, in the region of, something like, of the order of, or so, or thereabouts, more or less, give or take; nearly, close to, approaching; Brit. getting on for.

roughneck n. informal See **ruffian**.

round adj. **1** *a round window* **circular**, disc-shaped, ring-shaped, hoop-shaped; spherical, spheroidal, globular, globe-shaped, orb-shaped; cylindrical; bulbous, rounded, rotund; technical annular, discoid, discoidal; literary orbicular. **2** *a short, round man* **plump**, chubby, fat, stout, rotund, portly, dumpy, chunky, overweight, pot-bellied, paunchy; flabby, corpulent, fleshy, bulky, obese; informal tubby, roly-poly, pudgy, beefy,

porky, blubbery; Brit. informal podgy; N. Amer. informal zaftig, corn-fed. **3** *his deep, round voice* **sonorous**, resonant, rich, full, mellow, mellifluous, orotund. **4** *a round dozen* **complete**, entire, whole, full. **5** *she berated him in round terms* **candid**, frank, direct, honest, truthful, straightforward, plain, blunt, forthright, bald, explicit, unequivocal.
– OPPOSITES thin, reedy.

▶n. **1** *mould the dough into rounds* **ball**, sphere, globe, orb, circle, disc, ring, hoop; technical annulus. **2** *a policeman on his rounds* **circuit**, beat, route, tour. **3** *the first round of the contest* **stage**, level; heat, game, bout, contest. **4** *an endless round of parties* **succession**, sequence, series, cycle. **5** *the gun fires thirty rounds a second* **bullet**, cartridge, shell, shot.

▶prep. & adv. **1** *the alleys round the station* **around**, about, encircling; near, in the vicinity of; orbiting. **2** *casinos dotted round France* **throughout**, all over, here and there in.

▶v. *the ship rounded the point* **go round**, travel round, skirt, circumnavigate, orbit.
□ **round about** approximately, about, around, circa, roughly, of the order of, something like, more or less, as near as dammit to, close to, near to, practically; or so, or thereabouts, give or take a few; not far off, nearly, almost, approaching; Brit. getting on for.
round the bend informal See **mad** (sense 1).
round the clock 1 *we're working round the clock* **day and night**, night and day, all the time, {morning, noon, and night}, continuously, non-stop, steadily, unremittingly; informal 24-7. **2** *round-the-clock supervision* **continuous**, constant, non-stop, continual, uninterrupted.
round something off 1 *the square edges were rounded off* **smooth off**, plane off, sand off, level off. **2** *the party rounded off a successful year* **complete**, finish off, crown, cap, top; conclude, close, end.
round on someone snap at, attack, turn on, weigh into, let fly at, lash out at, hit out at; informal bite someone's head off, jump down someone's throat, lay into, tear into; Brit. informal have a go at; N. Amer. informal light into.
round someone/something up gather together, herd together, muster, marshal, rally, assemble, collect, group; N. Amer. corral.

roundabout adj. **1** *a roundabout route* **circuitous**, indirect, meandering, serpentine, tortuous. **2** *I asked in a roundabout sort of way* **indirect**, oblique, circuitous, circumlocutory, periphrastic, digressive, long-winded; evasive.
– OPPOSITES direct.

▶n. Brit. **1** *I go straight on at the roundabout* N. Amer. rotary, traffic circle. **2** *a roundabout with wooden horses* **merry-go-round**, carousel; old use whirligig.

roundly adv. **1** *he was roundly condemned* **vehemently**, emphatically, fiercely, forcefully, severely; plainly, frankly, candidly. **2** *she was roundly defeated*

r

utterly, completely, thoroughly, decisively, conclusively, heavily, soundly.

round-up n. **1** *a cattle round-up* **assembly**, muster, rally; N. Amer. rodeo. **2** *the sports round-up* **summary**, synopsis, overview, review, outline, digest, precis; N. Amer. wrap-up; informal recap.

rouse v. **1** *he roused Ralph at dawn* **wake (up)**, awaken, arouse; Brit. informal knock up; formal waken. **2** *she roused and looked around* **wake up**, awake, awaken, come to, get up, rise, bestir oneself; formal arise. **3** *he roused the crowd* **stir up**, excite, galvanize, electrify, stimulate, inspire, inspirit, move, inflame, agitate, goad, provoke; incite, spur on; N. Amer. light a fire under. **4** *he's got a temper when he's roused* **provoke**, annoy, anger, infuriate, madden, incense, vex, irk; informal aggravate. **5** *her disappearance roused my suspicions* **arouse**, awaken, prompt, provoke, stimulate, pique, trigger, spark off, touch off, kindle, elicit.
– OPPOSITES calm, pacify, allay.

rousing adj. **stirring**, inspiring, exciting, stimulating, moving, electrifying, invigorating, energizing, exhilarating; enthusiastic, vigorous, spirited; inflammatory.

rout n. **1** *the army's ignominious rout* **retreat**, flight. **2** *Newcastle scored 13 tries in the rout* **crushing defeat**, trouncing, annihilation; debacle, fiasco; informal licking, hammering, thrashing, pasting, drubbing, massacre.
– OPPOSITES victory.
▶ v. **1** *his army was routed* **put to flight**, drive off, scatter; defeat, beat, conquer, vanquish, crush, overpower. **2** *he routed the defending champion* **beat hollow**, trounce, defeat, get the better of; informal lick, hammer, clobber, thrash, paste, demolish, annihilate, drub, cane, wipe the floor with, walk all over, make mincemeat of, massacre, slaughter; Brit. informal stuff; N. Amer. informal cream, shellac, skunk.

route n. *a different route to the shops* **way**, course, road, path, direction; passage, journey.
▶ v. *enquiries are routed to the relevant desk* **direct**, send, convey, dispatch, forward.

routine n. **1** *his morning routine* **procedure**, practice, pattern, drill, regime, regimen; programme, schedule, plan; formula, method, system; customs, habits; formal wont. **2** *a stand-up routine* **act**, performance, number, turn, piece; informal spiel, patter.
▶ adj. **1** *a routine health check* **standard**, regular, customary, normal, usual, ordinary, typical; everyday, common, commonplace, conventional, habitual; literary wonted. **2** *a routine action movie* **boring**, tedious, tiresome, wearisome, monotonous, humdrum, run-of-the-mill, prosaic, dreary, pedestrian; predictable, hackneyed, stock, unimaginative, unoriginal, banal, trite.
– OPPOSITES unusual.

rove v. **wander**, roam, ramble, drift, meander; range, travel; Scottish straivaig; old use

peregrinate.

rover n. **wanderer**, traveller, globetrotter, drifter, bird of passage, roamer, itinerant, transient; nomad, gypsy, Romany; tramp, vagrant, vagabond; N. Amer. hobo.

row[1] n. **1** *rows of children* **line**, column, file, queue; procession, chain, string, succession; informal crocodile. **2** *the middle row of seats* **tier**, line, rank, bank.
▫ **in a row** *three days in a row* consecutively, in succession; running, straight; informal on the trot.

row[2] Brit. informal n. **1** *have you two had a row?* **argument**, quarrel, squabble, fight, contretemps, falling-out, disagreement, dispute, clash, altercation, shouting match; informal tiff, set-to, run-in, slanging match, spat; Brit. informal barney, bust-up; Brit. informal, Football afters. **2** *the row the crowd was making* **din**, noise, racket, clamour, uproar, tumult, hubbub, commotion, brouhaha, rumpus, pandemonium, babel; informal hullabaloo. **3** *Mum gave me a row* **reprimand**, rebuke, reproof, admonition, reproach, remonstration, lecture, criticism; informal telling-off, slap on the wrist, dressing-down, roasting, tongue-lashing; Brit. informal ticking-off, carpeting, rollicking, rocket.
▶ v. *they rowed about money* **argue**, quarrel, squabble, bicker, fight, fall out, disagree, have words, dispute, wrangle, cross swords, lock horns, be at loggerheads; informal scrap, argufy.

rowdy adj. *rowdy youths* **unruly**, disorderly, obstreperous, riotous, undisciplined, uncontrollable, ungovernable, disruptive, out of control, rough, wild, lawless; boisterous, uproarious, noisy, loud, clamorous; informal rumbustious; N. Amer. informal rambunctious.
– OPPOSITES peaceful.
▶ n. *the pub filled up with rowdies* **ruffian**, troublemaker, lout, hooligan, thug, hoodlum; Brit. tearaway; informal tough, bruiser, yahoo; Brit. informal rough, yob, yobbo.

royal adj. **1** *the royal prerogative* **regal**, kingly, queenly, princely; sovereign, monarchical. **2** *a royal welcome* **excellent**, fine, magnificent, splendid, superb, wonderful, first-rate, first-class; informal fantastic, great, tremendous.

rub v. **1** *Polly rubbed her arm* **massage**, knead; stroke, pat. **2** *he rubbed sun lotion on her back* **apply**, smear, spread, work in. **3** *my shoes rub painfully* **chafe**, pinch; hurt, be painful.
▶ n. **1** *she gave his back a rub* **massage**, rub-down. **2** *I gave my shoes a rub* **polish**, wipe, clean. **3** *it's too complicated—that's the rub* **problem**, difficulty, trouble, drawback, hindrance, impediment; snag, hitch, catch.
▫ **rub along** Brit. informal manage, cope, get by, make do, muddle along/through; informal make out.
rub something down clean, sponge, wash; groom.
rub it in informal emphasize, stress, underline, highlight; go on, harp on; informal rub

r

someone's nose in it.
rub off on be transferred to, be passed on
to, be transmitted to, be communicated to;
affect, influence.
rub something out erase, delete, remove,
efface, obliterate, expunge.
rub shoulders with associate with, mingle
with, fraternize with, socialize with, mix
with, keep company with, consort with;
N. Amer. rub elbows with; informal hang around/
out with, hobnob with, knock about/around
with.
rub something up polish, buff up, burnish,
shine, wax; clean, wipe.
rub someone up the wrong way Brit. See
annoy.

rubbish n. **1** *throw away that rubbish*
refuse, waste, litter, debris, detritus,
scrap, dross; flotsam and jetsam, lumber;
sweepings, scraps, dregs; N. Amer. garbage,
trash; informal dreck, junk. **2** *she's talking
rubbish* **nonsense**, balderdash, gibberish,
claptrap, blarney, moonshine, garbage;
informal hogwash, baloney, tripe, drivel, bilge,
bunk, piffle, poppycock, phooey, twaddle,
gobbledegook; Brit. informal codswallop,
cobblers, tosh, cack; Scottish & N. English informal
havers; N. Amer. informal bushwa, applesauce.
▶ v. Brit. informal *they often rubbish trade unions*.
See **criticize**.
▶ adj. Brit. informal *a rubbish team*. See **hopeless**
(sense 3).
rubbishy adj. informal **worthless**, substandard,
trashy, inferior, second-rate, third-rate, poor-
quality, cheap, shoddy; bad, poor, dreadful,
awful, terrible, appalling; informal crummy,
lousy, dire, tacky; Brit. informal duff, chronic,
rubbish.
rubble n. **debris**, remains, ruins, wreckage.
ruction n. informal **disturbance**, noise, racket,
din, commotion, fuss, uproar, furore, hue
and cry, rumpus, fracas; (**ructions**) trouble,
hell to pay; informal to-do, hullabaloo, hoo-ha,
ballyhoo, stink, kerfuffle; Brit. informal row,
carry-on.
ruddy adj. **1** *a ruddy complexion* **rosy**, red,
pink, roseate, rubicund; healthy, glowing,
fresh; flushed, blushing; florid, high-
coloured; literary rubescent. **2** Brit. informal *you
ruddy idiot!* See **damned** (sense 2).
– OPPOSITES pale.
rude adj. **1** *a rude man* **ill-mannered**, bad-
mannered, impolite, discourteous, uncivil,
unmannerly, mannerless; impertinent,
insolent, impudent, disrespectful, cheeky;
churlish, curt, brusque, brash, offhand,
short, sharp; offensive, insulting, derogatory,
disparaging, abusive; tactless, undiplomatic,
uncomplimentary. **2** *rude jokes* **vulgar**,
coarse, smutty, dirty, filthy, crude, lewd,
obscene, off colour, offensive, indelicate,
tasteless; risqué, naughty, ribald, bawdy,
racy; informal blue; Brit. informal near the knuckle;
N. Amer. informal gamy; euphemistic adult. **3** *a rude
awakening* **abrupt**, sudden, sharp, startling;
unpleasant, nasty, harsh.
– OPPOSITES polite, clean, gentle.

rudimentary adj. **1** *rudimentary
carpentry skills* **basic**, elementary, primary,
fundamental, essential. **2** *the equipment
was rudimentary* **primitive**, crude, simple,
unsophisticated, rough (and ready),
makeshift. **3** *a rudimentary thumb* **vestigial**,
undeveloped, incomplete; Biology abortive,
primitive.
– OPPOSITES advanced, sophisticated,
developed.
rudiments plural n. **basics**, fundamentals,
essentials, first principles, foundation; informal
nuts and bolts, ABC.
rue v. **regret**, be sorry about, feel remorseful
about, repent of, reproach oneself for;
deplore, lament, bemoan, bewail.
rueful adj. **regretful**, apologetic, sorry,
remorseful, shamefaced, sheepish, hangdog,
contrite, repentant, penitent, conscience-
stricken, self-reproachful; sorrowful, sad.
ruffian n. **thug**, lout, hooligan, hoodlum,
vandal, delinquent, rowdy, scoundrel, villain,
rogue, bully boy, brute; informal tough, bruiser,
heavy, yahoo; Brit. informal rough, yob, yobbo;
N. Amer. informal goon.
ruffle v. **1** *he ruffled her hair* **disarrange**,
tousle, dishevel, rumple, riffle, disorder,
mess up, tangle; N. Amer. informal muss up. **2** *the
wind ruffled the water* **ripple**, riffle. **3** *don't
let him ruffle you* **annoy**, irritate, vex, nettle,
anger, exasperate; disconcert, unnerve,
fluster, agitate, harass, upset, disturb,
discomfit, put off, perturb, unsettle, bother,
worry, trouble; informal rattle, faze, throw, get
to, rile, needle, aggravate, bug, peeve; Brit.
informal wind up, nark.
– OPPOSITES smooth, soothe.
▶ n. *a shirt with ruffles* **frill**, flounce, ruff,
ruche, jabot, furbelow.
rug n. **1** *they sat on the rug* **mat**, carpet.
2 *he was wrapped in a tartan rug* **blanket**,
coverlet, throw, wrap; N. Amer. lap robe.
rugged adj. **1** *the rugged coast path* **rough**,
uneven, bumpy, rocky, stony, pitted, jagged,
craggy. **2** *a rugged vehicle* **robust**, durable,
sturdy, strong, tough, resilient. **3** *rugged
manly types* **well built**, burly, strong,
muscular, muscly, brawny, strapping, husky,
hulking; tough, hardy, robust, sturdy, lusty,
solid; informal hunky, beefy. **4** *his rugged
features* **strong**, craggy, rough-hewn; manly,
masculine; irregular, weathered.
– OPPOSITES smooth, flimsy, weedy, delicate.
ruin n. **1** *the buildings were saved from
ruin* **disintegration**, decay, disrepair,
dilapidation, ruination; destruction,
demolition, wreckage. **2** *the ruins of a church*
remains, remnants, fragments, relics;
rubble, debris, wreckage. **3** *electoral ruin for
Labour* **downfall**, collapse, defeat, undoing,
failure, breakdown, ruination; Waterloo.
4 *shopkeepers are facing ruin* **bankruptcy**,
insolvency, penury, poverty, destitution,
impoverishment, indigence; failure.
– OPPOSITES preservation, triumph, wealth.
▶ v. **1** *don't ruin my plans* **wreck**, destroy, spoil,
mar, blight, shatter, dash, torpedo, scotch,

r

mess up; sabotage; informal screw up, foul
up, put the kibosh on, do for, nix, queer;
Brit. informal scupper. **2** *the bank's collapse
ruined them all* **bankrupt**, make insolvent,
impoverish, pauperize, wipe out, break,
cripple; bring someone to their knees.
3 *a country ruined by civil war* **destroy**,
devastate, lay waste, ravage; raze, demolish,
wreck, wipe out, flatten.
– OPPOSITES save, rebuild.
▫ **in ruins 1** *the abbey is in ruins* **derelict**,
ruined, in disrepair, falling to pieces,
dilapidated, tumbledown, ramshackle,
decrepit, decaying, ruinous. **2** *his career is in
ruins* **destroyed**, ruined, in pieces, in ashes;
over, finished; informal in tatters, on the rocks,
done for.

ruined adj. **derelict**, in ruins, dilapidated,
ruinous, tumbledown, ramshackle, decrepit,
falling to pieces, crumbling, decaying,
disintegrating; informal shambly.

ruinous adj. **1** *a ruinous trade war*
disastrous, devastating, catastrophic,
calamitous, crippling, crushing, damaging,
destructive, harmful; costly. **2** *ruinous
interest rates* **extortionate**, exorbitant,
excessive, sky-high, outrageous, inflated;
Brit. over the odds; informal criminal, steep. **3** *a
ruinous chapel.* See **ruined**.

rule n. **1** *health and safety rules* **regulation**,
ruling, directive, order, act, law, statute,
edict, canon, mandate, command, dictate,
decree, fiat, injunction, commandment,
stipulation, requirement, guideline,
direction; formal ordinance. **2** *church
attendance on Sunday was the general rule*
procedure, practice, protocol, convention,
norm, routine, custom, habit; formal praxis,
wont. **3** *moderation is the golden rule*
precept, principle, standard, axiom, truth,
maxim. **4** *Punjab came under British rule*
control, jurisdiction, command, power,
dominion; government, administration,
sovereignty, leadership, supremacy,
authority; raj.
▸ v. **1** *El Salvador was ruled by Spain* **govern**,
preside over, control, lead, dominate, run,
head, administer, manage. **2** *Mary ruled for
six years* **be in power**, be in control, be in
command, be in charge, govern; reign, be
monarch, be sovereign. **3** *the judge ruled that
they be set free* **decree**, order, pronounce,
judge, adjudge, ordain; decide, find,
determine, resolve, settle. **4** *subversion ruled*
prevail, predominate, be the order of the
day, reign supreme; formal obtain.
▫ **as a rule** usually, generally, in general,
normally, ordinarily, customarily, for the
most part, on the whole, by and large, in the
main, mainly, mostly, commonly, typically.
rule something out exclude, eliminate,
disregard; preclude, prohibit, prevent,
disallow.

ruler n. **leader**, sovereign, monarch,
potentate, king, queen, emperor, empress,
prince, princess; crowned head, head of
state, president, premier, governor; overlord,
chief, chieftain, lord; dictator, autocrat.

– OPPOSITES subject.

ruling n. *the judge's ruling* **judgement**,
decision, adjudication, finding, verdict;
pronouncement, resolution, decree,
injunction.
▸ adj. **1** *the ruling monarch* **reigning**,
sovereign, regnant. **2** *Japan's ruling party*
governing, controlling, commanding,
supreme, leading, dominant, ascendant.
3 *football was their ruling passion* **main**,
chief, principal, major, prime, dominating,
foremost; predominant, central, focal; informal
number-one.

rumble v. **boom**, thunder, roll, roar, resound,
reverberate, echo, grumble.

rumbustious adj. informal See **boisterous**
(sense 1).

ruminate v. **1** *we ruminated on life* **think
about**, contemplate, consider, meditate
on, muse on, mull over, ponder on/over,
deliberate about/on, chew over, puzzle over;
formal cogitate about. **2** *cows ruminating*
chew the cud.

rummage v. **search**, hunt, root about/
around, ferret about/around, fish about/
around, poke around in, dig, delve, go
through, explore, sift through, rifle through;
Brit. informal rootle around.

rumour n. **gossip**, hearsay, talk, tittle-tattle,
speculation, word, on dit; (**rumours**)
reports, stories, whispers, canards; informal the
grapevine, the word on the street, the buzz;
N. Amer. informal scuttlebutt.

rump n. **1** *a smack on the rump* **rear (end)**,
seat; buttocks, cheeks; Brit. bottom; Scottish
bahookie; informal backside, behind, BTM, sit-
upon, derrière; Brit. informal bum, botty, jacksie;
N. Amer. informal butt, fanny, tush, tail, buns,
booty, heinie, bippy; humorous fundament,
posterior, stern; Anatomy nates. **2** *the rump of
the army* **remainder**, rest, remnant, remains.

rumple v. **1** *the sheet was rumpled* **crumple**,
crease, wrinkle, crinkle, ruck (up), scrunch
up; Brit. ruckle. **2** *Ian rumpled her hair* **ruffle**,
disarrange, tousle, dishevel, riffle; mess up;
N. Amer. informal muss up.
– OPPOSITES smooth.

rumpus n. **disturbance**, commotion, uproar,
furore, brouhaha, hue and cry, ruckus;
fracas, melee, tumult, noise, racket, din;
informal to-do, hullabaloo, kerfuffle, ballyhoo;
Brit. informal row, carry-on.

run v. **1** *she ran across the road* **sprint**, race,
dart, rush, dash, hasten, hurry, scurry,
scamper, hare, bolt, fly, gallop, career,
charge, shoot, hurtle, speed, zoom, go
like lightning, go hell for leather, go like
the wind; jog, trot; informal tear, pelt, scoot,
hotfoot it, leg it, belt, zip, whip; Brit. informal
bomb; N. Amer. informal hightail it, barrel. **2** *the
robbers turned and ran* **flee**, run away, run
off, run for it, take flight, make off, take off,
take to one's heels, make a break for it, bolt,
make one's getaway, escape; informal beat it,
clear off/out, vamoose, skedaddle, split, leg
it, scram; Brit. informal do a runner, scarper,
do a bunk; N. Amer. informal light out, take a

r

powder, skidoo; Austral. informal shoot through.
3 *he ran in the marathon* **compete**, take part,
participate. **4** *a shiver ran down my spine*
go, pass, slide, move, travel. **5** *he ran his eye
down the list* **cast**, pass, skim, flick. **6** *the road
runs the length of the valley* **extend**, stretch,
reach, continue. **7** *water ran from the eaves*
flow, pour, stream, gush, flood, cascade,
roll, course, spill, trickle, drip, dribble, leak.
8 *a bus runs to Sorrento* **travel**, shuttle, go.
9 *I'll run you home* **drive**, take, bring, ferry,
chauffeur, give someone a lift. **10** *he runs a
transport company* **be in charge of**, manage,
direct, control, head, govern, supervise,
superintend, oversee; operate, conduct,
own. **11** *it's expensive to run a car* **maintain**,
keep, own, possess, have; drive. **12** *they ran
some tests* **carry out**, do, perform, execute.
13 *he left the engine running* **operate**,
function, work, go; tick over, idle. **14** *the
lease runs for twenty years* **be valid**, last,
be in effect, be operative, continue, be
effective. **15** *the show ran for two years* **be
staged**, be performed, be on, be mounted, be
screened. **16** *he ran for president* **stand for**,
be a candidate for, be a contender for. **17** *the
paper ran the story* **publish**, print, feature,
carry, put out, release, issue. **18** *they run
drugs* **smuggle**, traffic in, deal in. **19** *they
were run out of town* **chase**, drive, hound.
▸ n. **1** *his morning run* **sprint**, jog, dash, gallop,
trot. **2** *she did the school run* **route**, journey;
circuit, round, beat. **3** *a run in the car* **drive**,
ride, turn; trip, excursion, outing, jaunt,
airing; informal spin, tootle; Scottish informal
hurl. **4** *an unbeaten run of victories* **series**,
succession, sequence, string, chain, streak,
spell, stretch, spate. **5** *a run on sterling*
demand for, rush on. **6** *they had the run of
her home* **free use of**, unrestricted access
to. **7** *the usual run of cafes* **type**, kind, sort,
variety, class. **8** *against the run of play,
he scored again* **trend**, tendency, course,
direction, movement, drift, tide. **9** *a chicken
run* **enclosure**, pen, coop. **10** *a ski run* **slope**,
track, piste; N. Amer. trail. **11** *a run in her
tights* **ladder**, rip, tear, snag, hole.
▫ **in the long run** eventually, in the end,
ultimately, when all is said and done, in the
fullness of time; Brit. informal at the end of the
day.
on the run on the loose, at large, loose;
running away, fleeing, fugitive; informal
AWOL; N. Amer. informal on the lam.
run across meet (by chance), come across,
run into, chance on, stumble on, happen on;
informal bump into.
run after informal pursue, chase; make
advances to, flirt with; informal make up to,
come on to, be all over, vamp; dated set one's
cap at.
run along informal go away, be off with you,
shoo; informal scram, buzz off, skedaddle,
scat, beat it, get lost, shove off, clear off; Brit.
informal hop it; literary begone.
run away 1 *her attacker ran away.* See **run**
(sense 2 of the verb). **2** *she ran away with the
championship* win easily, win hands down;

informal win by a mile, walk it, romp home.
run down decline, degenerate, go downhill,
go to seed, decay, go to rack and ruin; informal
go to pot, go to the dogs.
run someone down 1 *he was run down
by joyriders* **run over**, knock down/over;
hit, strike. **2** *she ran him down in front of
other people* **criticize**, denigrate, belittle,
disparage, deprecate, find fault with; informal
put down, knock, bad-mouth; Brit. informal
rubbish, slag off; formal derogate.
run something down 1 *she finally ran a
copy of the book down* **find**, discover, locate,
track down, trace, unearth. **2** *employers ran
down their workforces gradually* **reduce**, cut
back on, downsize, decrease, trim; phase out,
wind down/up.
run high *feelings were running high* be
strong, be fervent, be passionate, be intense.
run into 1 *a car ran into his van* **collide
with**, hit, strike, crash into, smash into,
plough into, ram, impact. **2** *I ran into
Hugo the other day* **meet (by chance)**, run
across, chance on, stumble on, happen on;
informal bump into. **3** *we ran into a problem*
experience, encounter, meet with, be faced
with, be confronted with. **4** *his debts run into
six figures* **reach**, extend to, be as much as.
run low *supplies were running low* dwindle,
diminish, become depleted, be used up, be in
short supply, be tight.
run off 1 *the youths ran off.* See **run** (sense 2
of the verb). **2** informal *he ran off with her
money.* See **steal** (sense 1 of the verb).
run something off 1 *would you run off
that list for me?* **copy**, photocopy, xerox,
duplicate, print, produce, do. **2** *run off some
of the excess water* **drain**, bleed, draw off,
pump out.
run on 1 *the call ran on for hours* **continue**,
go on, carry on, last, keep going, stretch.
2 *your mother does run on* **talk incessantly**,
talk a lot, go on, chatter on, ramble on;
informal yak, gab, yabber; Brit. informal rabbit on,
witter on, chunter on, talk the hind leg off a
donkey; N. Amer. informal run off at the mouth.
run out 1 *supplies ran out* **be used up**, dry
up, be exhausted, be finished, peter out.
2 *they ran out of cash* **be out of**; use up,
consume, eat up; informal be fresh out of, be
cleaned out of. **3** *her contract ran out* **expire**,
end, terminate, finish; lapse.
run over 1 *the bathwater ran over* **overflow**,
spill over, brim over; old use overbrim. **2** *the
project ran over budget* **exceed**, go over,
overshoot, overreach. **3** *he quickly ran over
the story* **recapitulate**, repeat, run through,
go over, reiterate, review; look over, read
through; informal recap on.
run someone over See **run someone
down** (sense 1).
run through 1 *they quickly ran through
their money* **squander**, spend, fritter away,
dissipate, waste, go through, consume, use up;
informal blow. **2** *the attitude that runs through
his writing* **pervade**, permeate, suffuse,
imbue, inform. **3** *he ran through his notes.*
See **run over** (sense 3). **4** *let's run through*

r

scene three **rehearse**, practise, go over, repeat; N. Amer. run down; informal recap on.

run to 1 *the bill ran to £22,000* **amount to**, add up to, total, come to, equal, reach, be as much as. **2** *we can't run to champagne* **afford**, stretch to, manage. **3** *he was running to fat* **tend to**, become, get, grow.

runaway n. *a teenage runaway* **fugitive**, escaper, escapee; refugee; truant; absconder, deserter.

▸ adj. **1** *a runaway horse* **out of control**, escaped, loose, on the loose. **2** *a runaway victory* **easy**, effortless; informal as easy as pie. **3** *runaway inflation* **rampant**, out of control, unchecked, unbridled.

rundown n. **summary**, synopsis, precis, run-through, summarization, summation, review, overview, briefing, sketch, outline; informal low-down, recap.

run down adj. **1** *a run-down area of London* **dilapidated**, tumbledown, ramshackle, derelict, ruinous, in ruins, crumbling; neglected, uncared-for, depressed, seedy, shabby, slummy, squalid; informal shambly; Brit. informal grotty. **2** *she was feeling rather run down* **unwell**, ill, poorly, unhealthy, peaky; tired, drained, exhausted, fatigued, worn out, below par, washed out; Brit. off colour; informal under the weather; Brit. informal off, ropy, knackered; Scottish informal wabbit; Austral./NZ informal crook; dated seedy.

run-in n. informal **disagreement**, argument, dispute, altercation, confrontation, contretemps, quarrel; brush, encounter, tangle, fight, clash; informal set-to, spat, scrap; Brit. informal row; Brit. informal, Football afters.

runner n. **1** *the runners were limbering up* **athlete**, sprinter, hurdler, racer, jogger. **2** *a strawberry runner* **shoot**, offshoot, sprout, tendril; Botany stolon. **3** *the bookmaker employed runners* **messenger**, courier, errand boy; informal gofer.
□ **do a runner** Brit. informal See **abscond**.

running n. **1** *his running was particularly fast* **sprinting**, sprint, racing, jogging, jog. **2** *the running of the school* **administration**, management, organization, coordination, orchestration, handling, direction, control, regulation, supervision. **3** *the smooth running of her department* **operation**, working, function, performance.

▸ adj. **1** *running water* **flowing**, gushing, rushing, moving. **2** *a running argument* **ongoing**, sustained, continuous, incessant, ceaseless, constant, perpetual; recurrent, recurring. **3** *she was late two days running* **in succession**, in a row, in sequence, consecutively; straight, together; informal on the trot.
□ **in the running** *he's in the running for a prize* likely to get, a candidate for, in line for, on the shortlist for, up for.

runny adj. **liquefied**, liquid, fluid, melted, molten; watery, thin.
– OPPOSITES solid.

run-of-the-mill adj. **ordinary**, average, middle-of-the-road, commonplace,

humdrum, mundane, standard, nondescript, characterless, conventional; unremarkable, unexceptional, uninteresting, dull, boring, routine, bland, lacklustre; N. Amer. garden-variety; informal bog-standard, nothing to write home about, nothing special, a dime a dozen; Brit. informal common or garden.
– OPPOSITES exceptional.

rupture n. **1** *pipeline ruptures* **break**, fracture, crack, burst, split, fissure. **2** *a rupture due to personal differences* **rift**, estrangement, falling-out, break-up, breach, split, separation, parting, division, schism; informal bust-up. **3** *an abdominal rupture* **hernia**.

▸ v. **1** *the reactor core might rupture* **break**, fracture, crack, breach, burst, split; informal bust. **2** *the problem ruptured their relationship* **sever**, break off, breach, disrupt; literary sunder.

rural adj. **country**, countryside, bucolic, rustic, pastoral; agricultural, agrarian; literary sylvan, georgic.
– OPPOSITES urban.

ruse n. **ploy**, stratagem, tactic, scheme, trick, gambit, cunning plan, dodge, subterfuge, machination, wile; Brit. informal wheeze.

rush v. **1** *she rushed home* **hurry**, dash, run, race, sprint, bolt, dart, gallop, career, charge, shoot, hurtle, hare, fly, speed, zoom, scurry, scuttle, scamper, hasten; informal tear, belt, pelt, scoot, zip, whip, hotfoot it, leg it; Brit. informal bomb; N. Amer. informal hightail it. **2** *water rushed along gutters* **flow**, pour, gush, surge, stream, cascade, run, course. **3** *the tax was rushed through parliament* **push**, hurry, hasten, speed, hustle, press, force. **4** *they rushed the cordon of troops* **attack**, charge, run at, assail, storm.

▸ n. **1** *Tim made a rush for the exit* **dash**, run, sprint, dart, bolt, charge, scramble, break. **2** *the lunchtime rush* **hustle and bustle**, commotion, hubbub, hurly-burly, stir. **3** *a last minute rush for flights* **demand**, clamour, call, request; run on. **4** *he was in no rush to leave* **hurry**, haste, urgency. **5** *a rush of adrenalin* **surge**, flow, flood, spurt, stream; dart, thrill, flash. **6** *a rush of cold air* **gust**, draught, flurry. **7** *I made a sudden rush at him* **charge**, onslaught, attack, assault, onrush.

▸ adj. *a rush job* **urgent**, high-priority, emergency; hurried, hasty, fast, quick, swift; N. Amer. informal hurry-up.

rushed adj. **1** *a rushed divorce* **hasty**, fast, speedy, quick, swift, rapid, hurried. **2** *he was too rushed to enjoy his stay* **pushed for time**, pressed for time, busy, in a hurry, run off one's feet.

rust v. **corrode**, oxidize, become rusty, tarnish.

WORD LINKS
ferruginous rust-coloured

---

rustic adj. **1** *a rustic setting* **rural**, country, countryside, countrified, pastoral, bucolic; agricultural, agrarian; literary sylvan, georgic.

2 *rustic wooden tables* **plain**, simple, homely, unsophisticated; rough, rude, crude. **3** *rustic peasants* **unsophisticated**, uncultured, unrefined, simple; artless, unassuming, guileless, naive, ingenuous; coarse, rough, uncouth, boorish; N. Amer. informal hillbilly, hick.
– OPPOSITES urban, ornate, sophisticated.
▶ n. *the rustics were carousing* **peasant**, countryman, countrywoman, bumpkin, yokel, country cousin; N. Amer. informal hillbilly, hayseed, hick; Austral./NZ informal bushy; old use swain, cottier.

rustle v. **1** *her dress rustled as she moved* **swish**, whoosh, whisper, sigh. **2** *he was rustling cattle* **steal**, thieve, take; abduct, kidnap.
▶ n. *the rustle of the leaves* **swish**, whisper, rustling; literary susurration, susurrus.
□ **rustle something up** informal prepare hastily, throw together, make; informal fix; Brit. informal knock up.

rusty adj. **1** *rusty wire* **rusted**, rust-covered, corroded, oxidized; tarnished, discoloured. **2** *his hair was a rusty colour* **reddish-brown**, chestnut, auburn, tawny, russet, coppery, copper, Titian, red. **3** *my French is a little rusty* **out of practice**, below par; unpractised, deficient, impaired, weak.

rut n. **1** *the car bumped across the ruts* **furrow**, groove, trough, ditch, hollow, pothole, crater. **2** *he was stuck in a rut* **boring routine**, humdrum existence, groove, dead end.

ruthless adj. **merciless**, pitiless, cruel, heartless, hard-hearted, cold-hearted, cold-blooded, harsh, callous, unmerciful, unforgiving, uncaring, unsympathetic, uncharitable; remorseless, unbending, inflexible, implacable; brutal, inhuman, inhumane, barbarous, barbaric, savage, sadistic, vicious.
– OPPOSITES merciful.

r

Ss

sabotage n. **vandalism**, wrecking, destruction, impairment, incapacitation, damage; subversion, obstruction, disruption, spoiling, undermining; Brit. a spanner in the works.
▶ v. **vandalize**, wreck, damage, destroy, cripple, impair, incapacitate; obstruct, disrupt, spoil, ruin, undermine, threaten, subvert.

sac n. **bag**, pouch; Medicine blister, cyst; Anatomy bladder, bursa, saccule, vesicle.

saccharine adj. **sentimental**, sickly, mawkish, mushy, slushy, cloying, sugary, sickening, nauseating; informal schmaltzy, weepy, gooey, drippy, cheesy, corny, toe-curling; Brit. informal soppy, twee; N. Amer. informal cornball, sappy.

sack[1] n. **1** a sack of flour **bag**, pouch, pocket, pack. **2** informal work hard or you'll get the sack **dismissal**, discharge, redundancy; informal the boot, the bullet, the axe, the heave-ho, the elbow, the push.
▶ v. informal she was sacked for stealing **dismiss**, discharge, lay off, make redundant, let go, throw out; Military cashier; informal fire, kick out, boot out, give someone the bullet, give someone the sack, give someone their marching orders, show someone the door, send packing; Brit. informal give someone their cards.
▫ **hit the sack** informal go to bed, retire, go to sleep; informal turn in, hit the hay, crash (out).

sack[2] v. raiders sacked the town **ravage**, lay waste, devastate, raid, ransack, strip, plunder, despoil, pillage, loot, rob.

sackcloth n. **hessian**, sacking, hopsack, burlap; N. Amer. gunny.
▫ **wearing sackcloth and ashes** penitent, contrite, regretful, sorrowful, rueful, remorseful, apologetic, ashamed, guilt-ridden, chastened, shamefaced, self-reproachful, guilty.

sacred adj. **1** the priest entered the sacred place **holy**, hallowed, blessed, consecrated, sanctified, venerated, revered; old use blest. **2** sacred music **religious**, spiritual, devotional, church, ecclesiastical. **3** the hill is sacred to the tribe **sacrosanct**, inviolable, inviolate, untouchable, protected, defended, secure.
– OPPOSITES secular, profane.

> **WORD LINKS**
> **blaspheme** speak disrespectfully about sacred things
> **desecrate, violate** treat something sacred with violent disrespect
> **sacrilege** the treating of something sacred with great disrespect
> **consecrate, sanctify** declare that something is sacred or holy
> **sanctum** a sacred or holy place
> **scriptures** the sacred writings of Christianity or another religion
> **hierophant** a person who interprets sacred mysteries

sacrifice n. **1** the sacrifice of animals **ritual slaughter**, offering, oblation, immolation. **2** the calf was a sacrifice **(votive) offering**, burnt offering, gift, oblation. **3** the sacrifice of sovereignty **surrender**, giving up, abandonment, renunciation, forfeiture, relinquishment, resignation, abdication.
▶ v. **1** two goats were sacrificed **offer up**, immolate, slaughter. **2** he sacrificed his principles **give up**, abandon, surrender, forgo, renounce, forfeit, relinquish, resign, abdicate; betray.

sacrificial adj. **votive**, oblatory, oblational; expiatory, propitiatory.

sacrilege n. **desecration**, profanity, profanation, blasphemy, impiety, irreligion, unholiness, irreverence, disrespect.
– OPPOSITES piety.

sacrilegious adj. **profane**, blasphemous, impious, sinful, irreverent, irreligious, unholy, disrespectful.

sacrosanct adj. **sacred**, hallowed, respected, inviolable, inviolate, unimpeachable, invulnerable, untouchable, inalienable; protected, defended, secure, safe.

sad adj. **1** we felt sad when we left **unhappy**, sorrowful, dejected, depressed, downcast, miserable, down, despondent, despairing, disconsolate, desolate, wretched, glum, gloomy, doleful, dismal, melancholy, mournful, woebegone, forlorn, crestfallen, heartbroken, inconsolable; informal blue, down in the mouth, down in the dumps. **2** they knew her sad story **tragic**, unhappy, unfortunate, awful, miserable, wretched, sorry, pitiful, pathetic, traumatic, heartbreaking, heart-rending, harrowing. **3** a sad state of affairs **unfortunate**, regrettable, sorry, deplorable, lamentable, pitiful, shameful, disgraceful.
– OPPOSITES happy, cheerful, fortunate.

sadden v. **depress**, dispirit, deject, dishearten, grieve, desolate, discourage, upset, get down, bring down, break someone's heart.

saddle v. *they were saddled with the children* **burden**, encumber, lumber, hamper; land, charge; impose something on, thrust something on, fob something off on to.

sadism n. **callousness**, barbarity, brutality, cruelty, cold-bloodedness, inhumanity, ruthlessness, heartlessness; perversion.

sadistic adj. **callous**, barbarous, vicious, brutal, cruel, fiendish, cold-blooded, inhuman, ruthless, heartless; perverted.

sadness n. **unhappiness**, sorrow, dejection, depression, misery, despondency, despair, desolation, wretchedness, gloom, gloominess, dolefulness, melancholy, mournfulness, woe, heartache, grief.

safe adj. **1** *the jewels are safe in the bank* **secure**, protected, shielded, sheltered, guarded, out of harm's way. **2** *the lost children are all safe* **unharmed**, unhurt, uninjured, unscathed, all right, well, in one piece, out of danger; informal OK. **3** *a safe place to hide* **secure**, sound, impregnable, unassailable, invulnerable. **4** *a safe driver* **cautious**, circumspect, prudent, attentive; unadventurous, conservative, unenterprising. **5** *the drug is safe* **harmless**, innocuous, benign, non-toxic, non-poisonous; wholesome.
– OPPOSITES insecure, dangerous, reckless, harmful.
▸n. *I keep the ring in a safe* **strongbox**, safety-deposit box, safe-deposit box, coffer, casket; strongroom, vault.

safeguard n. *a safeguard against crises* **protection**, defence, guard, screen, buffer, preventive, precaution, provision, security; surety, cover, insurance, indemnity.
▸v. *the contract will safeguard 1000 jobs* **protect**, preserve, conserve, save, secure, shield, guard, keep safe.
– OPPOSITES jeopardize.

safety n. **1** *the safety of the residents* **welfare**, well-being, protection, security. **2** *the safety of ferries* **security**, soundness, dependability, reliability. **3** *we reached the safety of the shore* **shelter**, sanctuary, refuge, haven.

sag v. **1** *he sagged back in his chair* **sink**, slump, loll, flop, crumple. **2** *the floors all sag* **dip**, droop; bulge, bag. **3** *production has sagged* **decline**, fall (off), drop, decrease, diminish, slump, plummet; informal nosedive.

saga n. **1** *Celtic tribal sagas* **epic**, tale, folk tale, chronicle, legend, romance, history, narrative, adventure, myth, fairy story. **2** *the saga of how they met* **long story**, rigmarole; informal spiel.

sagacious adj. **wise**, clever, intelligent, knowledgeable, sensible, sage; discerning, judicious, canny, perceptive, astute, shrewd, prudent, thoughtful, insightful, perspicacious; informal streetwise; formal sapient.
– OPPOSITES foolish.

sage n. *the Chinese sage Confucius* **wise man/woman**, learned person, philosopher, thinker, scholar, savant; authority, expert, guru.
▸adj. *some very sage comments.* See **sagacious**.

sail v. **1** *we sailed across the Atlantic* **voyage**, steam, navigate, cruise. **2** *you can learn to sail here* **yacht**, boat, go sailing; crew, helm. **3** *we sail tonight* **set sail**, put to sea, leave port, hoist sail, weigh anchor, shove off. **4** *he is sailing the ship* **steer**, pilot, navigate, con, helm, captain; informal skipper. **5** *clouds were sailing past* **glide**, drift, float, flow, sweep, skim, coast, flit. **6** *a pencil sailed past his ear* **whizz**, speed, streak, shoot, whip, buzz, zoom, flash; fly, wing, soar; informal zip.
□ **sail through** succeed easily at, pass easily, romp through, walk through.

sailor n. **seaman**, seafarer, mariner; boatman, yachtsman, yachtswoman; hand; informal (old) salt, sea dog, bluejacket; Brit. informal matelot; Brit. informal dated Jack tar.

saint n.

WORD LINKS
hagiography literature concerning the lives of saints
beatify declare a dead person to be in a state of bliss, the first step towards canonizing them
canonize officially declare a dead person to be a saint

saintly adj. **holy**, godly, pious, religious, devout, spiritual, prayerful; virtuous, righteous, good, moral, innocent, sinless, guiltless, irreproachable, spotless, uncorrupted, pure, angelic.
– OPPOSITES ungodly.

sake n. **1** *this is simplified for the sake of clarity* **purpose**, reason, aim, end, objective, object, goal, motive. **2** *she had to be brave for her daughter's sake* **benefit**, advantage, good, well-being, welfare, interest, profit.

salacious adj. *salacious writing* **pornographic**, obscene, indecent, crude, lewd, vulgar, dirty, filthy; erotic, titillating, arousing, suggestive, sexy, risqué, ribald, smutty, bawdy; X-rated; informal porn, porno, blue; euphemistic adult.

salary n. **pay**, wages, earnings, payment, remuneration, fee(s), stipend, income; formal emolument.

sale n. **1** *the sale of firearms* **selling**, vending; dealing, trading. **2** *they make a sale every minute* **deal**, transaction, bargain.
– OPPOSITES purchase.
□ **for sale** on the market, on sale, on offer, available, purchasable, obtainable.

salesperson n. **sales assistant**, salesman, saleswoman, shop assistant, seller, agent; shopkeeper, trader, merchant, dealer, pedlar, hawker; N. Amer. clerk; informal counter-jumper, rep; Brit. informal flogger.

salient adj. **important**, main, principal, major, chief, primary; notable, noteworthy, outstanding, conspicuous, striking, noticeable, obvious, remarkable, prominent, predominant, dominant; key, crucial, vital, essential, pivotal, prime, central, paramount.
– OPPOSITES minor.

saliva n. **spit**, spittle, dribble, drool, slaver, slobber, sputum.

sallow adj. **yellowish**, jaundiced, pallid, wan, pale, anaemic, bloodless, pasty; unhealthy, sickly, washed out, peaky; informal like death warmed up.

sally n. **1** *the garrison made a sally against us* **sortie**, charge, foray, thrust, drive, offensive, attack, assault, raid, incursion, invasion, onslaught; old use onset. **2** *a fruitless sally into Wales* **expedition**, excursion, trip, outing, jaunt, visit. **3** *he was delighted with his sally* **witticism**, smart remark, quip, barb, pleasantry; joke, pun, jest, bon mot; retort, riposte, counter, rejoinder; informal gag, wisecrack, comeback.

salon n. **1** *a hairdressing salon* **shop**, parlour, establishment, premises; boutique, store. **2** *the chateau's mirrored salon* **reception room**, drawing room, sitting room, living room, lounge; dated parlour.

salt n. *the potatoes need salt* **sodium chloride**.
▶ adj. *salt water* **salty**, saline, briny, brackish.
□ **salt something away** informal save, put aside, put by, set aside, reserve, keep, store, stockpile, hoard, stow away; informal squirrel away, stash away.

> **WORD LINKS**
> **saline** containing salt
> **desalinate** remove salt from seawater

salty adj. **1** *salty water* **salt**, salted, saline, briny, brackish. **2** *a salty sense of humour* **earthy**, colourful, spicy, racy, naughty, vulgar, rude; piquant, biting.

salubrious adj. **1** *I found the climate salubrious* **healthy**, health-giving, healthful, beneficial, wholesome; old use salutary. **2** *a salubrious area of London* **pleasant**, agreeable, nice, select, high-class; Brit. upmarket; informal posh, swanky, classy; Brit. informal swish; N. Amer. informal swank.
– OPPOSITES unhealthy, unpleasant.

salutary adj. *a salutary lesson on the fragility of nature* **beneficial**, advantageous, good, profitable, productive, helpful, useful, valuable, worthwhile; timely.
– OPPOSITES unwelcome.

salutation n. **greeting**, salute, address, welcome.

salute n. **1** *he gave the Brigadier a salute* **greeting**, salutation, gesture of respect, obeisance, acknowledgement, welcome, address. **2** *a salute to British courage* **tribute**, testimonial, homage, toast, honour, eulogy; celebration of, acknowledgement of.
▶ v. **1** *he saluted the ambassadors* **greet**, address, hail, welcome, acknowledge, toast; make obeisance to. **2** *we salute a great photographer* **pay tribute to**, pay homage to, honour, celebrate, acknowledge, take one's hat off to.

salvage v. **1** *an attempt to salvage the vessel* **rescue**, save, recover, retrieve, raise, reclaim. **2** *he salvaged a precious point for his club* **retain**, preserve, conserve; regain, recoup, redeem, snatch.
▶ n. *the salvage is taking place off the coast* **rescue**, recovery, reclamation.

salvation n. **1** *salvation by way of repentance* **redemption**, deliverance, reclamation. **2** *that conviction was her salvation* **lifeline**, preservation; means of escape.
– OPPOSITES damnation.

salve n. *lip salve* **ointment**, cream, balm, unguent, emollient; embrocation, liniment; old use unction.
▶ v. *she did it to salve her conscience* **soothe**, assuage, ease, allay, lighten, alleviate, comfort, mollify.

salver n. **platter**, plate, dish, paten, tray; old use charger.

same adj. **1** *we stayed at the same hotel* **identical**, selfsame, very same, one and the same. **2** *they had the same symptoms* **matching**, identical, alike, duplicate, carbon-copy, twin; indistinguishable, interchangeable, corresponding, equivalent, parallel, like, comparable, similar, congruent, concordant, consonant. **3** *it happened that same month* **selfsame**; aforesaid, aforementioned. **4** *they provide the same menu worldwide* **unchanging**, unvarying, unvaried, invariable, consistent, uniform, regular.
– OPPOSITES another, different, dissimilar, varying.
▶ n. *Louise said the same* **the same thing**, the aforementioned, the aforesaid, the above-mentioned.
□ **all the same 1** *I was frightened all the same* **in spite of everything**, despite that, nevertheless, nonetheless, even so, however, but, still, yet, though, be that as it may, just the same, at the same time, in any event, notwithstanding, regardless, anyway, anyhow; informal still and all. **2** *it's all the same to me* **immaterial**, of no importance, of no consequence, inconsequential, unimportant, of little account, irrelevant.

> **WORD LINKS**
> **contemporary, coeval** having the same age or date of origin
> **coterminous** having the same boundaries or extent
> **homogeneous** of the same kind, or consisting of parts all of the same kind
> **synonymous** having the same meaning
> **tautology** saying the same thing again in different words

sample n. **1** *a sample of the fabric* **specimen**, example, bit, snippet, swatch, exemplification, representative piece; prototype, test piece, dummy, pilot, trial, taste, taster, tester. **2** *a sample of 10,000 people nationwide* **cross section**, variety, sampling, test.
▶ v. *we sampled the culinary offerings* **try (out)**, taste, test, put to the test, experiment with; appraise, evaluate; informal check out.
▶ adj. **1** *the sample group is small* **representative**, illustrative, selected, specimen, test, trial, typical. **2** *a sample copy can be obtained* **specimen**, test, trial, pilot, dummy.

sanatorium n. **infirmary**, clinic, hospital, medical centre, hospice; sickbay, sickroom; N. Amer. sanitarium; informal san.

sanctify v. **1** *he came to sanctify the site* **consecrate**, bless, make holy, hallow, make sacred, dedicate to God. **2** *they sanctified themselves* **purify**, cleanse, free from sin, absolve, unburden, redeem; rare lustrate. **3** *we must not sanctify this outrage* **approve**, sanction, condone, vindicate, endorse, support, back, permit, allow, authorize, legitimize, legitimatize.

sanctimonious adj. **self-righteous**, holier-than-thou, pious, pietistic, churchy, moralizing, smug, superior, priggish, hypocritical, insincere; informal goody-goody, pi.

sanction n. **1** *trade sanctions* **penalty**, punishment, deterrent; (**sanctions**) punitive action, discipline, penalization, restriction; embargo, ban, prohibition, boycott. **2** *the scheme has the sanction of the court* **authorization**, consent, leave, permission, authority, warrant, licence, dispensation, assent, acquiescence, agreement, approval, approbation, endorsement, accreditation, ratification, validation, imprimatur, blessing; informal the go-ahead, the thumbs up, the OK, the green light.
– OPPOSITES reward, prohibition.
▸ v. **1** *the rally was sanctioned by the government* **authorize**, permit, allow, warrant, accredit, license, endorse, approve, accept, back, support; informal OK. **2** *the penalties available to sanction crime* **punish**, discipline someone for.
– OPPOSITES prohibit.

sanctity n. **1** *the sanctity of St Francis* **holiness**, godliness, blessedness, saintliness, spirituality, piety, piousness, devoutness, righteousness, goodness, virtue, purity; formal sanctitude. **2** *the sanctity of the family meal* **sacrosanctity**, inviolability; importance, paramountcy.

sanctuary n. **1** *the sanctuary at Delphi* **holy place**, temple; shrine, altar; sanctum, sacrarium, holy of holies, sanctum sanctorum. **2** *the island is our sanctuary* **refuge**, haven, harbour, port in a storm, oasis, shelter, retreat, bolt-hole, hideaway, fastness. **3** *he was given sanctuary in the embassy* **safety**, protection, shelter, immunity, asylum. **4** *a bird sanctuary* **reserve**, park, reservation, preserve.

sanctum n. **1** *the sanctum in the temple* **holy place**, shrine, sanctuary, holy of holies, sanctum sanctorum. **2** *a private sanctum for the bar's regulars* **refuge**, retreat, bolt-hole, hideout, hideaway, den.

sane adj. **1** *the accused is presumed to be sane* **of sound mind**, in one's right mind, compos mentis; lucid, rational, balanced, stable, normal; informal all there. **2** *it isn't sane to use nuclear weapons* **sensible**, practical, advisable, responsible, realistic, prudent, wise, reasonable, rational, level-headed, commonsensical, judicious, politic.
– OPPOSITES mad, foolish.

sangfroid n. **composure**, equanimity, self-possession, equilibrium, aplomb, poise, self-assurance, self-control, nerve, calm, presence of mind; informal cool, unflappability.

sanguine adj. **1** *he is sanguine about the advance of technology* **optimistic**, bullish, hopeful, buoyant, positive, confident, cheerful, cheery; informal upbeat. **2** old use *a sanguine complexion.* See **florid** (sense 1).
– OPPOSITES gloomy.

sanitary adj. **hygienic**, clean, antiseptic, aseptic, sterile, uninfected, disinfected, unpolluted, uncontaminated; salubrious, healthy, wholesome.

sanitize v. **1** *the best way to sanitize a bottle* **sterilize**, disinfect, clean, cleanse, purify, fumigate, decontaminate. **2** *the diaries have not been sanitized* **make presentable**, make acceptable, make palatable, clean up; expurgate, bowdlerize, censor, redact.

sanity n. **1** *she was losing her sanity* **mental health**, faculties, reason, rationality, saneness, stability, lucidity; sense, wits, mind. **2** *sanity has prevailed* **(common) sense**, wisdom, prudence, judiciousness, rationality, soundness, sensibleness.

sap n. **1** *sap from the roots of trees* **juice**, secretion, fluid, liquid. **2** *they're full of youthful sap* **vigour**, energy, drive, dynamism, life, spirit, liveliness, sparkle, verve, ebullience, enthusiasm, gusto, vitality, vivacity, fire, zest, zeal, exuberance; informal get-up-and-go, oomph, vim.
▸ v. *they sapped the will of the troops* **erode**, wear away/down, deplete, reduce, lessen, attenuate, undermine, exhaust, drain, bleed.

sarcasm n. **derision**, mockery, ridicule, scorn, sneering, scoffing; irony.

sarcastic adj. **sardonic**, ironic, ironical; derisive, snide, scornful, contemptuous, mocking, sneering, jeering; caustic, scathing, trenchant, cutting, sharp, acerbic; Brit. informal sarky; N. Amer. informal snarky.

sardonic adj. **mocking**, satirical, sarcastic, ironical, ironic; cynical, scornful, contemptuous, derisive, derisory, sneering, jeering; scathing, caustic, trenchant, cutting, sharp, acerbic; Brit. informal sarky.

sash n. **belt**, cummerbund, waistband, girdle, obi; literary cincture.

Satan n. See **devil** (sense 1).

satanic adj. **diabolical**, fiendish, devilish, demonic, demoniacal, ungodly, hellish, infernal, wicked, evil, sinful, iniquitous, nefarious, vile, foul, abominable, unspeakable, loathsome, monstrous, heinous, hideous, horrible, horrifying, shocking, appalling, dreadful, awful, terrible, ghastly, abhorrent, despicable, damnable.

sate v. See **satiate**.

satellite n. **1** *the European Space Agency's ERS-1 satellite* **space station**, space capsule, spacecraft; sputnik. **2** *the two small satellites of Mars* **moon**, secondary planet. **3** *Bulgaria was then a Russian satellite* **dependency**,

S

colony, protectorate, possession, holding; historical fief, vassal.
▶adj. *a satellite state* **dependent**, subordinate, subsidiary; puppet.

satiate v. **fill**, satisfy, sate; slake; quench; gorge, stuff, surfeit, glut, cloy, sicken, nauseate.

satiety n. **satiation**, satisfaction, repleteness, repletion, fullness; surfeit.

satiny adj. **smooth**, shiny, glossy, shining, gleaming, lustrous, sleek, silky.

satire n. **1** *a satire on American politics* **parody**, burlesque, caricature, lampoon, skit, pasquinade; informal spoof, take-off, send-up. **2** *he has become the subject of satire* **mockery**, ridicule, derision, scorn, caricature; irony, sarcasm.

satirical adj. **mocking**, ironic, ironical, satiric, sarcastic, sardonic; caustic, trenchant, mordant, biting, cutting, stinging, acerbic; critical, irreverent, disparaging, disrespectful.

satirize v. **mock**, ridicule, deride, make fun of, poke fun at, parody, lampoon, burlesque, caricature, take off; criticize; informal send up, take the mickey out of.

satisfaction n. **1** *he derived great satisfaction from his work* **contentment**, content, pleasure, gratification, fulfilment, enjoyment, happiness, pride; self-satisfaction, smugness, complacency. **2** *the satisfaction of consumer needs* **fulfilment**, gratification; appeasement, assuaging. **3** *investors turned to the courts for satisfaction* **compensation**, recompense, redress, reparation, restitution, repayment, payment, settlement, reimbursement, indemnification, indemnity.

satisfactory adj. **adequate**, all right, acceptable, good enough, sufficient, reasonable, quite good, competent, fair, decent, average, passable; fine, in order, up to scratch, up to the mark, up to standard, up to par; informal OK, so-so.
– OPPOSITES inadequate, poor.

satisfied adj. **1** *a satisfied smile* **pleased**, well pleased, content, contented, happy, proud, triumphant, smug, self-satisfied, pleased with oneself, complacent; Brit. informal like the cat that's got the cream. **2** *the pleasure of satisfied desire* **fulfilled**, gratified. **3** *I am satisfied that she is happy with the decision* **convinced**, certain, sure, positive, persuaded, easy in one's mind.
– OPPOSITES discontented, unhappy.

satisfy v. **1** *a last chance to satisfy his hunger for romance* **fulfil**, gratify, meet, fill; indulge, cater to, pander to; appease, assuage; quench, slake, satiate, sate, take the edge off. **2** *she satisfied herself that it had been an accident* **convince**, persuade, assure; reassure, put someone's mind at rest. **3** *products which satisfy the EU's criteria* **comply with**, meet, fulfil, answer, conform to; measure up to, come up to; suffice, be good enough, fit/fill the bill. **4** *there was insufficient collateral to satisfy the loan* **repay**, pay (off), settle, make

good, discharge, square, liquidate, clear.
– OPPOSITES frustrate.

satisfying adj. **fulfilling**, rewarding, gratifying, pleasing, enjoyable, pleasurable, to one's liking.

saturate v. **1** *heavy rain saturated the ground* **soak**, drench, waterlog, wet through; souse, steep, douse. **2** *the air was saturated with the stench of joss sticks* **permeate**, suffuse, imbue, pervade, charge, infuse, fill. **3** *the company has saturated the market* **flood**, glut, oversupply, overfill, overload.

saturated adj. **1** *his trousers were saturated* **soaked**, soaking (wet), wet through, sopping (wet), sodden, dripping, wringing wet, drenched; soaked to the skin, like a drowned rat. **2** *the saturated ground* **waterlogged**, soggy, squelchy, heavy, muddy, boggy.
– OPPOSITES dry.

saturnine adj. **1** *a saturnine temperament* **gloomy**, sombre, melancholy, moody, lugubrious, dour, glum, morose, unsmiling, humourless. **2** *his saturnine good looks* **swarthy**, dark, dark-skinned, dark-complexioned; mysterious, mercurial, moody.
– OPPOSITES cheerful.

sauce n. *a piquant sauce* **relish**, gravy, condiment; dip, dressing; jus, coulis.

saucepan n. **pan**, pot, casserole, skillet, stockpot, stewpot; billy, billycan.

saucy adj. informal **1** Brit. *saucy postcards* **suggestive**, titillating, risqué, rude, bawdy, racy, ribald, spicy; informal raunchy, smutty, nudge-nudge; Brit. informal fruity; N. Amer. informal gamy. **2** *you saucy little minx!* **cheeky**, impudent, impertinent, irreverent, forward, disrespectful, bold, as bold as brass, brazen; informal fresh, lippy, mouthy; N. Amer. informal sassy; old use malapert.
– OPPOSITES demure, polite.

saunter v. **stroll**, amble, wander, meander, drift, walk; stretch one's legs, take the air; informal mosey, tootle; Brit. informal pootle; formal promenade.

savage adj. **1** *savage dogs* **ferocious**, fierce; wild, untamed, undomesticated, feral. **2** *a savage assault* **vicious**, brutal, cruel, sadistic, ferocious, fierce, violent, bloody, murderous, homicidal, bloodthirsty; literary fell; old use sanguinary. **3** *a savage attack on European free-trade policy* **fierce**, blistering, scathing, searing, stinging, devastating, mordant, trenchant, caustic, cutting, biting, withering, virulent, vitriolic. **4** *a savage race* **primitive**, uncivilized, unenlightened, non-literate, in a state of nature. **5** *a savage landscape* **rugged**, rough, wild, inhospitable, uninhabitable. **6** *a savage blow for the town* **severe**, crushing, devastating, crippling, terrible, awful, dreadful, dire, catastrophic, calamitous, ruinous.
– OPPOSITES tame, mild, civilized.
▶n. **1** *she'd expected mud huts and savages* **barbarian**, wild man, wild woman, primitive. **2** *she described her son's assailants as savages* **brute**, beast, monster, barbarian,

sadist, animal.
▶v. **1** *he was savaged by a dog* **maul**, attack, tear to pieces, lacerate, claw, bite. **2** *critics savaged the film* **criticize severely**, attack, lambaste, condemn, denounce, pillory, revile; informal pan, tear to pieces, hammer, slam, do a hatchet job on, crucify; Brit. informal slate, rubbish; N. Amer. informal trash; Austral./NZ informal bag, monster; formal excoriate.

savant n. **intellectual**, scholar, sage, philosopher, thinker, wise/learned person; guru, master, pandit.
– OPPOSITES ignoramus.

save v. **1** *the captain was saved by his crew* **rescue**, come to someone's rescue, save someone's life; set free, free, liberate, deliver, extricate; bail out; informal save someone's bacon/neck/skin. **2** *the farmhouse has been saved from demolition* **preserve**, keep safe, keep, protect, safeguard; salvage, retrieve, reclaim, rescue. **3** *start saving old newspapers for wrapping china* **put aside**, set aside, put by, put to one side, save up, keep, retain, reserve, conserve, stockpile, store, hoard, save for a rainy day; informal salt away, squirrel away, stash away, hang on to. **4** *asking me first would have saved a lot of trouble* **prevent**, obviate, forestall, spare; stop; avoid, avert.
▶prep. & conj. formal *no one needed to know save herself* **except**, apart from, but, other than, besides, aside from, bar, barring, excluding, leaving out, saving; informal outside of.

saving n. **1** *a considerable saving in development costs* **reduction**, cut, decrease, economy. **2** *I'll have to use some of my savings* **nest egg**, money put by for a rainy day, life savings; capital, assets, funds, resources, reserves.

saving grace n. **redeeming feature**, good point, thing in its/one's favour, advantage, asset, selling point.

saviour n. **1** *the country's saviour* **rescuer**, liberator, deliverer, emancipator; champion, knight in shining armour, friend in need, good Samaritan. **2** *the Saviour is depicted with two archangels* **Christ**, Jesus (Christ), the Redeemer, the Messiah, Our Lord, the Lamb of God, the Son of God, the Son of Man, the Prince of Peace.

savoir faire n. **social skill**, social grace(s), urbanity, suavity, finesse, sophistication, poise, aplomb, adroitness, polish, style, smoothness, tact, tactfulness, diplomacy, soft skills, discretion, delicacy, sensitivity; informal savvy.
– OPPOSITES gaucheness.

savour v. **1** *she wanted to savour every moment* **relish**, enjoy (to the full), appreciate, delight in, revel in, smack one's lips over, luxuriate in, bask in. **2** *such a declaration savoured of immodesty* **suggest**, smack of, have the hallmarks of, seem like, have the air of, show signs of.
▶n. **1** *the subtle savour of wood smoke* **smell**, aroma, fragrance, scent, perfume, bouquet; **taste**, flavour, tang, smack. **2** *a savour of*

bitterness seasoned my feelings for him* **trace**, hint, suggestion, touch, smack. **3** *her usual diversions had lost their savour* **piquancy**, interest, attraction, flavour, spice, zest, excitement, enjoyment; informal zing.

savoury adj. **1** *sweet or savoury dishes* **salty**, spicy, piquant, tangy. **2** *a rich, savoury aroma* **appetizing**, mouth-watering, delicious, delectable, luscious; tasty, flavoursome, flavourful, palatable, toothsome; informal scrumptious, finger-licking, yummy, scrummy, moreish. **3** *one of the less savoury aspects of the affair* **acceptable**, pleasant, respectable, wholesome, honourable, proper, seemly.
– OPPOSITES sweet, unappetizing.
▶n. *cocktail savouries* **canapé**, hors d'oeuvre, appetizer, titbit.

savvy informal n. *his political savvy.* See **acumen**.
▶adj. *a savvy investor.* See **shrewd**.

saw n. **saying**, maxim, proverb, aphorism, axiom, adage, apophthegm, epigram, gnome.

say v. **1** *she felt her stomach flutter as he said her name* **speak**, utter, voice, pronounce, give voice to, vocalize. **2** *'I must go,' she said* **declare**, state, announce, remark, observe, mention, comment, note, add; reply, respond, answer, rejoin; informal come out with. **3** *Newall says he's innocent* **claim**, maintain, assert, hold, insist, contend; allege, profess; formal opine, aver; rare asseverate. **4** *I can't conjure up the words to say how I feel* **express**, put into words, phrase, articulate, communicate, make known, put/get across, convey, verbalize; reveal, divulge, impart, disclose; imply, suggest. **5** *they sang hymns and said a prayer* **recite**, repeat, utter, deliver, perform, declaim, orate. **6** *the dial of her watch said one twenty* **indicate**, show, read. **7** *I'd say it's about five miles* **estimate**, judge, guess, hazard a guess, predict, speculate, surmise, conjecture, venture; informal reckon. **8** *let's say you've just won a million pounds* **suppose**, assume, imagine, presume, hypothesize, postulate, posit.
▶n. **1** *everyone is entitled to their say* **chance to speak**, turn to speak, opinion, view, voice; informal twopence worth, twopenn'orth. **2** *don't I have any say in the matter?* **influence**, sway, weight, voice, input, share, part.
□ **that is to say** in other words, to put it another way; i.e., that is, to wit, viz, namely.

saying n. **proverb**, maxim, aphorism, axiom, adage, saw, tag, motto, apophthegm, epigram, dictum, gnome; expression, phrase, formula; slogan, catchphrase; platitude, cliché, commonplace, truism.

say-so n. informal **authorization**, (seal of) approval, agreement, consent, assent, permission, endorsement, sanction, ratification, approbation, acquiescence, blessing, leave; informal the OK, the go-ahead, the green light, the thumbs up.
– OPPOSITES refusal, denial.

S

scalding adj. **extremely hot**, burning, blistering, searing, red-hot; piping hot; informal boiling (hot), sizzling.

scale[1] n. **1** *the reptile's scales* **plate**; technical lamella, lamina, squama, scute, scutum. **2** *scales on the skin* **flake**; (**scales**) scurf, dandruff. **3** *scale in kettles* **limescale**, deposit, encrustation; Brit. fur.

scale[2] n. **1** *the Celsius scale of temperature* **calibrated system**, graduated system, system of measurement. **2** *opposite ends of the social scale* **hierarchy**, ladder, ranking, order, pecking order, spectrum; succession, sequence, series. **3** *the scale of the map* **ratio**, proportion, relative size. **4** *no one foresaw the scale of the disaster* **extent**, size, scope, magnitude, dimensions, range, breadth, compass, degree, reach.
▶v. *thieves scaled an 8ft high fence* **climb**, ascend, clamber up, shin (up), scramble up, mount; N. Amer. shinny (up).
□ **scale something down** reduce, cut down, cut back, cut, decrease, lessen, lower, trim, slim down, prune.
scale something up increase, expand, augment, build up, add to; step up, boost, escalate.

scaly adj. **1** *the dragon's scaly hide* technical squamous, squamulose, squamate, lamellose. **2** *scaly patches of dead skin* **dry**, flaky, flaking, scurfy, rough, scabrous, mangy, scabious; technical furfuraceous.

scam n. informal **fraud**, swindle, racket, trick, diddle; informal con (trick); Brit. informal ramp; N. Amer. informal hustle, grift, bunco.

scamp n. informal **rascal**, monkey, devil, imp, wretch, mischief-maker; informal scallywag, horror, monster, tyke; Brit. informal perisher; N. English informal scally; N. Amer. informal varmint; old use rapscallion, scapegrace.

scamper v. **scurry**, scuttle, dart, run, rush, race, dash, hurry, hasten; informal scoot; dated make haste.

scan v. **1** *Adam scanned the horizon* **scrutinize**, examine, study, inspect, survey, search, scour, sweep, rake; look at, stare at, gaze at, eye, watch; informal check out; N. Amer. informal scope. **2** *I scanned the papers* **glance through**, look through, have a look at, run/cast one's eye over, skim through, flick through, flip through, leaf through, thumb through.
▶n. **1** *a careful scan of the terrain* **inspection**, scrutiny, examination, survey. **2** *a quick scan through the report* **glance**, look, flick, browse. **3** *a brain scan* **examination**, screening.

scandal n. **1** *revelation of the sex scandal forced him to resign* **wrongdoing**, impropriety, misconduct, immoral behaviour, unethical behaviour; offence, transgression, crime, sin; skeleton in the closet; informal -gate. **2** *it's a scandal that the disease is not adequately treated* **disgrace**, outrage, injustice; (crying) shame. **3** *no scandal attached to her name* **malicious gossip**, malicious rumour(s), slander,

libel, calumny, defamation, aspersions, muckraking; informal dirt.

scandalize v. **shock**, appal, outrage, horrify, disgust; offend, affront, insult.
– OPPOSITES impress.

scandalous adj. **1** *a scandalous waste of taxpayers' money* **disgraceful**, shocking, outrageous, monstrous, criminal, wicked, shameful, appalling, deplorable, reprehensible, inexcusable, intolerable, insupportable, unforgivable, unpardonable. **2** *a series of scandalous liaisons* **discreditable**, disreputable, dishonourable, improper, unseemly, sordid. **3** *scandalous rumours* **scurrilous**, malicious, slanderous, libellous, defamatory.

scant adj. **little**, little or no, minimal, limited, negligible, meagre; insufficient, inadequate, deficient; formal exiguous.
– OPPOSITES abundant, ample.

scanty adj. **1** *their scanty wages* **meagre**, scant, minimal, limited, modest, restricted, sparse; tiny, small, paltry, negligible, insufficient, inadequate, deficient; scarce, in short supply, thin on the ground, few and far between; informal measly, piddling, mingy, pathetic; formal exiguous. **2** *her scanty nightdress* **skimpy**, revealing, short, brief; low, low-cut; indecent.
– OPPOSITES ample, plentiful.

scapegoat n. **whipping boy**, Aunt Sally; informal fall guy; N. Amer. informal patsy.

scar n. **1** *the scar on his left cheek* **cicatrix**, mark, blemish, disfigurement, discoloration; pockmark, pock, pit; lesion, stigma; birthmark, naevus. **2** *deep psychological scars* **trauma**, damage, injury.
▶v. **1** *he's likely to be scarred for life* **disfigure**, mark, blemish; pockmark, pit; Christianity stigmatize. **2** *a landscape which has been scarred by strip mining* **damage**, spoil, mar, deface, injure. **3** *she was profoundly scarred by the incident* **traumatize**, damage, injure; distress, disturb, upset.

scarce adj. **1** *food was scarce* **in short supply**, scant, scanty, meagre, sparse, hard to find, hard to come by, insufficient, deficient, inadequate; at a premium, like gold dust; paltry, negligible; informal not to be had for love nor money; formal exiguous. **2** *birds that prefer dense forest are becoming scarcer* **rare**, few and far between, thin on the ground; uncommon, unusual; Brit. out of the common.
– OPPOSITES plentiful.

scarcely adv. **1** *she could scarcely hear what he was saying* **hardly**, barely, only just; almost not. **2** *I scarcely ever see him* **rarely**, seldom, infrequently, not often, hardly ever, every once in a while; informal once in a blue moon. **3** *this could scarcely be accidental* **surely not**, not, hardly, certainly not, not at all, on no account, under no circumstances, by no means; N. Amer. noway.
– OPPOSITES often.

scarcity n. **shortage**, dearth, lack, undersupply, insufficiency, paucity, scantness, meagreness, sparseness, poverty;

deficiency, inadequacy; unavailability, absence; formal exiguity.

scare v. *stop it, you're scaring me* **frighten**, startle, alarm, terrify, petrify, unnerve, intimidate, terrorize, cow; strike terror into, put the fear of God into, chill someone to the bone/marrow, make someone's blood run cold; informal frighten/scare the living daylights out of, scare stiff, frighten/scare someone out of their wits, scare witless, frighten/scare to death, scare the pants off, make someone's hair stand on end, make someone jump out of their skin; Brit. informal put the wind up, make someone's hair curl; N. Amer. informal spook; Irish informal scare the bejesus out of; old use affright.
▶ n. *you gave me a scare—how did you get here?* **fright**, shock, start, turn, jump.

scared adj. **frightened**, afraid, fearful, nervous, panicky; terrified, petrified, horrified, panic-stricken, scared stiff, frightened/scared out of one's wits, scared witless, frightened/scared to death; Scottish feart; informal in a cold sweat, in a (blue) funk; Brit. informal funky, windy; N. Amer. informal spooked; dialect frit; old use afeared, affrighted.

scaremonger n. **alarmist**, prophet of doom, Cassandra, voice of doom, doom-monger; informal doom (and gloom) merchant.

scarf n. **muffler**, wrap, shawl, pashmina, snood; headscarf, headsquare, square; mantilla, stole, tippet; N. Amer. babushka.

scarper v. Brit. informal See **run** (sense 2 of the verb).

scary adj. informal **frightening**, alarming, terrifying, hair-raising, spine-chilling, blood-curdling, horrifying, nerve-racking, unnerving, eerie, sinister; informal creepy, spine-tingling, spooky, hairy.

scathing adj. **withering**, blistering, searing, devastating, fierce, ferocious, savage, severe, stinging, biting, cutting, mordant, trenchant, virulent, caustic, vitriolic, scornful, sharp, bitter, harsh, unsparing; formal mordacious.
– OPPOSITES mild.

scatter v. **1** *scatter the seeds as evenly as possible* **throw**, strew, toss, fling; sprinkle, spread, distribute, sow, broadcast, disseminate. **2** *the crowd scattered | onlookers were scattered in all directions* **disperse**, break up, disband, separate, go separate ways, dissolve; drive, send, put to flight, chase. **3** *the sky was scattered with stars* **fleck**, stud, dot, cover, sprinkle, stipple, spot, pepper; literary bestrew.
– OPPOSITES gather, assemble.

scatterbrained adj. **absent-minded**, forgetful, disorganized; dreamy, wool-gathering, with one's head in the clouds, feather-brained, giddy; informal scatty, with a mind/memory like a sieve, dizzy, dippy.

scavenge v. **search**, hunt, look, forage, rummage, root about/around, grub about/around.

scenario n. **1** *Walt wrote scenarios for a major Hollywood studio* **plot**, outline, storyline, framework; screenplay, script; formal diegesis. **2** *every possible scenario must be explored* **sequence of events**, course of events, chain of events, situation. **3** *this film has a more contemporary scenario* **setting**, background, context, scene, milieu.

scene n. **1** *the scene of the accident* **location**, site, place, position, point, spot; locale, whereabouts; technical locus. **2** *the scene is London, in the late 1890s* **background**, setting, context, milieu, backdrop, mise en scène. **3** *terrible scenes of violence* **incident**, event, episode, happening. **4** *an impressive mountain scene* **view**, vista, outlook, panorama, sight; landscape, scenery. **5** *she made an embarrassing scene* **fuss**, exhibition of oneself, performance, tantrum, commotion, disturbance, row, upset, furore, brouhaha; informal to-do; Brit. informal carry-on. **6** *the political scene* **arena**, stage, sphere, world, milieu, realm, domain; area of interest, field, province, preserve. **7** *a scene from a Laurel and Hardy film* **clip**, section, segment, part, sequence.
□ **behind the scenes** secretly, in secret, privately, in private, behind closed doors, surreptitiously; informal on the quiet, on the q.t.; formal sub rosa.

scenery n. **1** *the beautiful scenery of west Wales* **landscape**, countryside, country, terrain, topography, setting, surroundings, environment; view, vista, panorama. **2** *we all helped with the scenery and costumes* **stage set**, set, mise en scène, flats, backdrop, drop curtain; Brit. backcloth.

scenic adj. **picturesque**, pretty, pleasing, attractive, lovely, beautiful, charming, pretty as a picture, easy on the eye; impressive, striking, spectacular, breathtaking; panoramic.

scent n. **1** *the scent of freshly cut hay* **smell**, fragrance, aroma, perfume, redolence, savour, odour; bouquet, nose. **2** *a bottle of scent* **perfume**, fragrance, toilet water, eau de toilette, cologne; eau de cologne. **3** *the hounds picked up the scent of a hare* **spoor**, trail, track; Hunting foil, wind.
▶ v. **1** *a shark can scent blood from over half a kilometre away* **smell**, detect the smell of, get a whiff of. **2** *Rose looked at him, scenting a threat* **sense**, become aware of, detect, discern, recognize, get wind of.

scented adj. **perfumed**, fragranced, perfumy; sweet-smelling, fragrant, aromatic.

sceptic n. **1** *sceptics said the marriage wouldn't last* **cynic**, doubter; pessimist, prophet of doom. **2** *sceptics who have found faith* **agnostic**, atheist, unbeliever, non-believer, disbeliever, doubting Thomas; rare nullifidian.

sceptical adj. **dubious**, doubtful, taking something with a pinch of salt, doubting; cynical, distrustful, mistrustful, suspicious, disbelieving, unconvinced, incredulous, scoffing; pessimistic, defeatist.
– OPPOSITES certain, convinced.

scepticism n. **1** *his ideas were met with scepticism* **doubt**, doubtfulness, a pinch of

S

salt; disbelief, cynicism, distrust, mistrust, suspicion, incredulity; pessimism, defeatism; formal dubiety. **2** *he passed from scepticism to religious belief* **agnosticism**, doubt; atheism, unbelief, non-belief.

schedule n. **1** *we need to draw up a production schedule* **plan**, programme, timetable, scheme. **2** *I have a very busy schedule* **timetable**, agenda, diary, calendar; itinerary.
▸v. *another meeting has been scheduled for April 20* **arrange**, organize, plan, set up, programme, timetable, line up; N. Amer. slate.
□ **behind schedule** late, running late, overdue, behind time, behind, behindhand.

scheme n. **1** *adventurous fund-raising schemes* **plan**, project, plan of action, programme, strategy, stratagem, tactic, game plan, course/line of action; system, procedure, design, formula, recipe; Brit. informal wheeze; old use shift. **2** *police uncovered a scheme to steal the paintings* **plot**, intrigue, conspiracy; ruse, ploy, stratagem, manoeuvre, subterfuge; machinations; informal game, racket. **3** *the sonnet's rhyme scheme* **arrangement**, system, organization, configuration, pattern, format; technical schema.
▸v. *he schemed to bring about the collapse of the government* **plot**, hatch a plot, conspire, intrigue, connive, manoeuvre, plan.

scheming adj. **cunning**, crafty, calculating, devious, designing, conniving, wily, sly, tricky, artful, guileful, slippery, slick, manipulative, Machiavellian, unscrupulous, disingenuous; duplicitous, deceitful, Janus-faced, underhand, treacherous.
– OPPOSITES ingenuous, honest.

schism n. **division**, split, rift, breach, rupture, break, separation, severance; chasm, gulf; discord, disagreement, dissension.

schismatic adj. **separatist**, heterodox, dissident, dissentient, dissenting, heretical; breakaway, splinter.
– OPPOSITES orthodox.

schmaltzy adj. informal See **sentimental** (sense 2).

scholar n. **1** *a leading biblical scholar* **academic**, intellectual, learned person, man/woman of letters, mind, intellect, savant, polymath, highbrow, bluestocking; authority, expert; informal egghead; N. Amer. informal pointy-head; old use bookman. **2** old use *the school had 28 scholars* **pupil**, student, schoolchild, schoolboy, schoolgirl.

scholarly adj. **1** *an earnest, scholarly man* **learned**, erudite, academic, well read, widely read, intellectual, literary, lettered, educated, knowledgeable, highbrow; studious, bookish, donnish, bluestocking, cerebral; N. Amer. informal pointy-headed; old use clerkly. **2** *a scholarly career* **academic**, scholastic, pedagogic.
– OPPOSITES uneducated, illiterate.

scholarship n. **1** *a centre of medieval scholarship* **learning**, book learning, knowledge, erudition, education, letters,

culture, academic study, academic achievement. **2** *a scholarship of £200 per term* **grant**, award, endowment, payment; Brit. bursary, exhibition.

scholastic adj. **academic**, educational, school, scholarly.

school n. **1** *the village school* **educational institution**; academy, college; seminary; alma mater. **2** *the university's School of English* **department**, faculty, division. **3** *the Barbizon school* **group**, set, circle; followers, following, disciples, apostles, admirers, devotees, votaries; proponents, adherents. **4** *a school of linguistics* **way of thinking**, school of thought, persuasion, creed, credo, doctrine, belief, faith, opinion, point of view; approach, method, style.
▸v. **1** *he was schooled in Lyon* **educate**, teach, instruct. **2** *he schooled her in horsemanship* **train**, teach, tutor, coach, instruct, drill, discipline, direct, guide, prepare, groom; prime, verse.

> **WORD LINKS**
> **scholastic** relating to schools and education
> **alma mater** the school that a person attended
> **alumnus, alumna** a former student of a particular school

schooling n. **1** *his parents paid for his schooling* **education**, teaching, tuition, instruction, tutoring, tutelage, pedagogy; lessons; (book) learning. **2** *the schooling of horses* **training**, coaching, instruction, drill, drilling, discipline, disciplining.

schoolteacher n. **teacher**, schoolmaster, schoolmistress, tutor, educationist; Brit. master, mistress; N. Amer. informal schoolmarm; Austral./NZ informal chalkie, schoolie; formal pedagogue.

scientific adj. **1** *scientific research* **technological**, technical; research-based, knowledge-based, empirical. **2** *you need to approach it in a more scientific way* **systematic**, methodical, organized, well organized, ordered, orderly, meticulous, rigorous; exact, precise, accurate, mathematical; analytical, rational.

scientist n. **researcher**, technologist; Brit. informal boffin.

scintilla n. **particle**, iota, jot, whit, atom, speck, bit, trace, ounce, shred, crumb, fragment, grain, drop, spot, mite, modicum, hint, touch, suggestion, whisper, suspicion; informal smidgen, tad; old use scantling.

scintillate v. **sparkle**, shine, gleam, glitter, flash, shimmer, twinkle, glint, glisten, wink; literary glister, coruscate.

scintillating adj. **1** *a scintillating diamond necklace* **sparkling**, shining, bright, brilliant, gleaming, glittering, twinkling, coruscating, shimmering. **2** *a scintillating second-half performance* **brilliant**, dazzling, exciting, exhilarating, stimulating; sparkling, coruscating, lively, vivacious, vibrant, animated, ebullient, effervescent; witty, clever.
– OPPOSITES dull, boring.

scion n. **1** *a scion of the tree* **cutting**, graft, slip; shoot, offshoot, twig. **2** *the scion of an aristocratic family* **descendant**; heir, successor; child, offspring; Law issue.

scoff[1] v. *they scoffed at her article* **mock**, deride, ridicule, sneer at, jeer at, jibe at, taunt, make fun of, poke fun at, laugh at, scorn, laugh to scorn, dismiss, make light of, belittle; informal pooh-pooh.

scoff[2] v. informal *the bears scoffed our packed lunch* **eat**, devour, consume, guzzle, gobble, wolf down, bolt; informal put away, nosh, polish off, hoover up, demolish, shovel down, stuff one's face with, pig oneself on, pig out on, trough; Brit. informal gollop, shift; N. Amer. informal scarf (down/up), snarf (down/up).

scold v. *Mum took Anna away, scolding her for her bad behaviour* **rebuke**, reprimand, reproach, reprove, admonish, remonstrate with, chastise, chide, upbraid, berate, take to task, read someone the Riot Act, give someone a piece of one's mind, haul over the coals; informal tell off, dress down, give someone an earful, give someone a roasting, rap over the knuckles, let someone have it, bawl out, give someone hell; Brit. informal tick off, have a go at, carpet, tear someone off a strip, give someone what for, give someone some stick, give someone a rollicking/rocket/row; N. Amer. informal chew out, ream out; Austral. informal monster; formal castigate.
– OPPOSITES praise.
▸ n. old use *she is turning into a scold* **nag**, shrew, fishwife, harpy, termagant, harridan; complainer, moaner, grumbler; N. Amer. informal kvetch.

scolding n. **rebuke**, reprimand, reproach, reproof, admonishment, remonstration, lecture, upbraiding; informal telling-off, talking-to, rap over the knuckles, dressing-down, earful, roasting; Brit. informal ticking-off, carpeting, rocket, rollicking; formal castigation.

scoop n. **1** *a measuring scoop* **spoon**, ladle, dipper; bailer. **2** *a scoop of vanilla ice cream* **spoonful**, ladleful, portion, lump, ball; informal dollop. **3** informal *reporters competed for scoops* **exclusive (story)**, inside story, exposé, revelation.
▸ v. **1** *a hole was scooped out in the floor* **hollow out**, gouge out, dig, excavate, cut out. **2** *cut the tomatoes in half and scoop out the flesh* **remove**, take out, spoon out, scrape out. **3** *she scooped up armfuls of clothes* **pick up**, gather up, lift, take up; snatch up, grab.

scoot v. informal See **dash** (sense 1 of the verb).

scope n. **1** *the scope of the investigation* **extent**, range, breadth, width, reach, sweep, purview, span, horizon; area, sphere, field, realm, compass, orbit, ambit, terms/field of reference, jurisdiction, remit; confine, limit; gamut. **2** *The scope for change is limited by political realities* **opportunity**, freedom, latitude, leeway, capacity, liberty, room (to manoeuvre), elbow room; possibility, chance; informal wiggle room.

scorch v. **1** *the buildings were scorched by the fire* **burn**, sear, singe, char, blacken, discolour. **2** *grass scorched by the sun* **dry up**, desiccate, parch, wither, shrivel; burn, bake.

scorching adj. **1** *the scorching July sun* **extremely hot**, red-hot, blazing, flaming, fiery, burning, blistering, searing, sweltering, torrid; N. Amer. broiling; informal boiling (hot), baking (hot), sizzling. **2** *scorching criticism* **fierce**, savage, scathing, withering, blistering, searing, devastating, stringent, severe, harsh, stinging, biting, mordant, trenchant, caustic, virulent, vitriolic.
– OPPOSITES freezing, mild.

score n. **1** *the final score was 4–3* **result**, outcome; total, sum total, tally, count. **2** *an IQ score of 161* **rating**, grade, mark, percentage. **3** *I've got a score to settle with you* **grievance**, bone to pick, axe to grind, grudge, complaint; dispute, bone of contention. **4** informal *he knew the score before he got here* **the situation**, the position, the facts, the truth of the matter, the (true) state of affairs, the picture, how things stand, the lie of the land; Brit. the state of play; N. Amer. the lay of the land; informal the set-up, what's what. **5** *scores of complaints* **a great many**, a lot, a great/good deal, large quantities, plenty; informal lots, umpteen, a slew, loads, masses, stacks, scads, heaps, piles, bags, tons, oodles, dozens, hundreds, thousands, millions, billions; Brit. informal shedloads; N. Amer. informal a bunch, gazillions; Austral./NZ informal a swag.
▸ v. **1** *he's already scored 13 goals this season* **get**, gain, chalk up, achieve, make; record, rack up, notch up; informal bag, knock up. **2** *The piece was scored for flute, violin, and continuo* **orchestrate**, arrange, set, adapt; write, compose. **3** *score the wood in criss-cross patterns* **scratch**, cut, notch, incise, scrape, nick, snick, chip, gouge; mark; old use scotch.
□ **score points off** get the better of, gain the advantage over, outdo, worst, have the edge over; have the last laugh on, make a fool of, humiliate; informal get/be one up on, get one over on, best.
score something out/through cross out, strike out, put a line through, ink out, blue-pencil, scratch out; delete, obliterate, expunge.

scorn n. *he was unable to hide the scorn in his voice* **contempt**, derision, contemptuousness, disdain, derisiveness, mockery, sneering; old use contumely, despite.
– OPPOSITES admiration, respect.
▸ v. **1** *critics scorned the painting* **deride**, hold in contempt, treat with contempt, pour/heap scorn on, look down on, look down one's nose at, disdain, curl one's lip at, mock, scoff at, sneer at, jeer at, laugh at, laugh out of court; disparage, slight; dismiss, cock a snook at, thumb one's nose at; informal turn one's nose up at; old use contemn. **2** *'I am a woman scorned,' she thought* **spurn**, rebuff, reject, ignore, shun, snub. **3** *she would have scorned to stoop to such tactics* **refuse to**,

S

refrain from, not lower oneself to; be above, consider it beneath one.
– OPPOSITES admire, respect.

scornful adj. **contemptuous**, derisive, withering, mocking, scoffing, sneering, jeering, scathing, snide, disparaging, supercilious, disdainful, superior; old use contumelious.
– OPPOSITES admiring, respectful.

scotch v. **put an end to**, put a stop to, nip in the bud, put the lid on; ruin, wreck, destroy, smash, shatter, demolish, queer; frustrate, thwart; informal put paid to, put the kibosh on; Brit. informal scupper.

scot-free adv. **unpunished**, without punishment; unscathed, unhurt, unharmed, without a scratch.

scoundrel n. **rogue**, rascal, miscreant, good-for-nothing, reprobate; cheat, swindler, fraudster, trickster, charlatan; informal villain, bastard, beast, son of a bitch, SOB, rat, louse, swine, dog, skunk, heel, snake (in the grass), wretch, scumbag; Irish informal sleeveen, spalpeen; N. Amer. informal rat fink; informal dated rotter, hound, bounder, blighter; dated cad; old use blackguard, knave, varlet, whoreson.

scour[1] v. *she scoured the cooker and cleaned out the cupboards* **scrub**, rub, clean, wash, cleanse, wipe; polish, buff (up), shine, burnish; abrade.

scour[2] v. *Christine scoured the shops for a gift* **search**, comb, hunt through, rummage through, go through with a fine-tooth comb, root through, rake through, leave no stone unturned, look high and low in; ransack, turn upside-down; Austral./NZ informal fossick through.

scourge n. **affliction**, bane, curse, plague, menace, evil, misfortune, burden, cross to bear; blight, cancer, canker.
– OPPOSITES blessing, godsend.
▶ v. **afflict**, plague, torment, torture, curse, oppress, burden, bedevil, beset.

scout n. **1** *scouts reported that the enemy were massing ahead* **lookout**, outrider, advance guard, vanguard; spy. **2** *a lengthy scout round the area* **reconnaissance**, reconnoitre; exploration, search, expedition; informal recce; Brit. informal shufti; N. Amer. informal recon. **3** *a record company scout* **talent spotter**, talent scout; N. Amer. informal bird dog.
▶ v. **1** *I scouted around for some logs* **search**, look, hunt, ferret about/around, root about/around. **2** *a night patrol was sent to scout out the area* **reconnoitre**, explore, make a reconnaissance of, inspect, investigate, spy out, survey; examine, scan, study, observe; informal make a recce of, check out, case; Brit. informal take a shufti round; N. Amer. informal recon.

scowl v. **glower**, frown, glare, grimace, lour, look daggers at, give someone a black look; make a face, pull a face, pout; informal give someone a dirty look.
– OPPOSITES smile, grin.

scraggy adj. **scrawny**, thin, as thin as a rake, skinny, skin and bone, gaunt, bony, angular, gawky, raw-boned; dated spindle-shanked.
– OPPOSITES fat.

scramble v. **1** *we scrambled over the boulders* **clamber**, climb, crawl, claw one's way, scrabble, grope one's way, struggle; N. Amer. shinny. **2** *small children scrambled for the scattered coins* **jostle**, scuffle, tussle, struggle, strive, compete, contend, vie, jockey. **3** *scramble the letters and pick seven* **mix up**, jumble (up), disarrange, disorganize, disorder, muddle, confuse, disturb, mess up.
▶ n. **1** *a short scramble over the rocks* **clamber**, climb, trek. **2** *I lost Tommy in the scramble for a seat* **tussle**, jostle, scrimmage, scuffle, struggle, free-for-all, competition, contention, vying, jockeying; muddle, confusion, melee.

scrap[1] n. **1** *a scrap of paper* **fragment**, piece, bit, snippet, shred; offcut, oddment, remnant. **2** *there wasn't a scrap of evidence* **bit**, speck, iota, particle, ounce, whit, jot, atom, shred, scintilla, tittle, jot or tittle; informal smidgen, tad. **3** *he slept rough and lived on scraps* **leftovers**, leavings, crumbs, scrapings, remains, remnants, residue, odds and ends, bits and pieces. **4** *the whole thing was made from bits of scrap* **waste**, rubbish, refuse, litter, detritus; flotsam and jetsam; N. Amer. garbage, trash; informal junk.
▶ v. **1** *old cars which are due to be scrapped* **throw away**, throw out, dispose of, get rid of, toss out, throw on the scrapheap, discard, remove, dispense with, lose, bin; decommission, recycle, break up, demolish; informal chuck (away/out), ditch, dump, junk, get shut of; Brit. informal get shot of; N. Amer. informal trash. **2** *campaigners called for the plans to be scrapped* **abandon**, drop, abolish, withdraw, throw out, do away with, put an end to, cancel, axe, jettison; informal ditch, dump, junk.
– OPPOSITES keep, preserve.

scrap[2] informal n. *he and Joe had several scraps* **quarrel**, argument, row, fight, disagreement, difference of opinion, falling-out, dispute, squabble, contretemps, clash, altercation, brawl, tussle, conflict, shouting match; informal tiff, set-to, run-in, slanging match, shindy, spat, dust-up, ruction; Brit. informal barney, ding-dong, bust-up; Brit. informal, Football afters.
▶ v. *the older boys started scrapping with me* **quarrel**, argue, row, fight, squabble, brawl, bicker, spar, wrangle, lock horns, be at each other's throats.

scrape v. **1** *we scraped all the paint off the windows* **abrade**, grate, sand, sandpaper, scour, scratch, rub, file, rasp. **2** *their boots scraped along the floor* **grate**, creak, rasp, grind, scratch. **3** *she scraped her hair back behind her ears* **rake**, drag, pull, tug, draw. **4** *he scraped a hole in the ground* **scoop out**, hollow out, dig (out), excavate, gouge out. **5** *Ellen had scraped her shins on the wall* **graze**, scratch, abrade, scuff, rasp, skin, rub raw, cut, lacerate, bark, chafe; Medicine excoriate.

▶ n. **1** *the scrape of her key in the lock* **grating**, creaking, grinding, rasp, rasping, scratch, scratching. **2** *there was a long scrape on his shin* **graze**, scratch, abrasion, cut, laceration, wound. **3** informal *he's always getting into scrapes* **predicament**, plight, tight corner/spot, ticklish/tricky situation, problem, crisis, mess, muddle; informal jam, fix, stew, bind, hole, hot water, a pretty/fine kettle of fish; Brit. informal spot of bother.

□ **scrape by** manage, cope, survive, muddle through/along, make ends meet, get by/along, make do, keep the wolf from the door, keep one's head above water, eke out a living; informal make out.

scrappy adj. **disorganized**, untidy, disjointed, unsystematic, uneven, bitty, sketchy; piecemeal; fragmentary, incomplete, unfinished.

scratch v. **1** *the paintwork was scratched* **score**, abrade, scrape, scuff. **2** *thorns scratched her skin* **graze**, scrape, abrade, skin, rub raw, cut, lacerate, bark, chafe; wound; Medicine excoriate. **3** *many names had been scratched out* **cross out**, strike out, score out, delete, erase, remove, eliminate, expunge, obliterate. **4** *she was forced to scratch from the race* **withdraw**, pull out of, back out of, bow out of, stand down.

▶ n. **1** *he had two scratches on his cheek* **graze**, scrape, abrasion, cut, laceration, wound. **2** *a scratch on the paintwork* **score**, mark, line, scrape.

□ **up to scratch** good enough, up to the mark, up to standard, up to par, satisfactory, acceptable, adequate, passable, sufficient, all right; informal OK, up to snuff.

scrawl v. *he scrawled his name at the bottom of the page* **scribble**, write hurriedly, write untidily, dash off.

▶ n. *pages of handwritten scrawl* **scribble**, squiggle(s), hieroglyphics; rare cacography.

scrawny adj. **skinny**, thin, as thin as a rake, skin and bone, gaunt, bony, angular, gawky, scraggy, raw-boned; dated spindle-shanked.
– OPPOSITES fat.

scream v. *he screamed in pain* **shriek**, screech, yell, howl, shout, bellow, bawl, cry out, call out, yelp, squeal, wail, squawk; informal holler.

▶ n. **1** *a scream of pain* **shriek**, screech, yell, howl, shout, bellow, bawl, cry, yelp, squeal, wail, squawk; informal holler. **2** informal *the whole thing's a scream* **laugh**, hoot; informal gas, giggle, riot, bundle of fun/laughs. **3** informal *he's an absolute scream* **wit**, hoot, comedian, comic, entertainer, joker, clown, character; informal gas, giggle, riot; informal dated caution, case, card.

screech v. See **scream** (verb).

screen n. **1** *he dressed hurriedly behind the screen* **partition**, (room) divider; windbreak. **2** *a computer with a 15-inch screen* **display**, monitor, visual display unit, VDU. **3** *every window has a screen because of mosquitoes* **mesh**, net, netting. **4** *the hedge acts as a screen against the wind* **buffer**, protection,

shield, shelter, guard. **5** *the earth must be put through a screen* **sieve**, riddle, strainer, colander, filter.

▶ v. **1** *the end of the hall had been screened off* **partition off**, divide off, separate off, curtain off. **2** *the cottage was screened by the trees* **conceal**, hide, veil; shield, shelter, shade, protect, guard, safeguard. **3** *the prospective candidates will have to be screened* **vet**, check, check up on, investigate; informal check out. **4** *all donated blood is screened for the virus* **check**, test, examine, investigate. **5** *coal used to be screened by hand* **sieve**, riddle, sift, strain, filter, winnow. **6** *the programme is screened on Thursday evenings* **show**, broadcast, transmit, televise, put out, put on the air.

screw n. **1** *stainless steel screws* **bolt**, fastener; nail, pin, tack, spike, rivet, brad. **2** *the handle needs a couple of screws to tighten it* **turn**, twist, wrench. **3** *the ship's twin screws* **propeller**, rotor.

▶ v. **1** *he screwed the lid back on the jar* **tighten**, turn, twist, wind. **2** *the bracket was screwed in place* **fasten**, secure, fix, attach. **3** informal *she intended to screw money out of them* **extort**, force, extract, wrest, wring, squeeze; informal bleed.

□ **put the screws on** informal pressurize, put pressure on, pressure, coerce, browbeat, use strong-arm tactics on; hold a gun to someone's head; informal put the heat on, lean on.

screw something up 1 *Christina screwed up her face in disgust* **wrinkle (up)**, pucker, crumple, crease, furrow, contort, distort, twist, purse. **2** informal *they'll screw up the whole economy* **wreck**, ruin, destroy, wreak havoc on, damage, spoil, mar; dash, shatter, scotch, make a mess of, mess up; informal louse up, foul up, put the kibosh on, banjax, do for, nix, queer; Brit. informal scupper, cock up.

scribble v. *he scribbled a few lines on a piece of paper* **scrawl**, write hurriedly, write untidily, scratch, dash off, jot (down); doodle.

▶ n. *a page of scribble* **scrawl**, squiggle(s), jottings; doodle, doodlings; rare cacography.

scribe n. **1** historical *a medieval scribe* **clerk**, secretary, copyist, transcriber, amanuensis; historical penman, scrivener. **2** informal *a local cricket scribe* **writer**, author, penman; journalist, reporter; informal hack.

scrimmage n. **fight**, tussle, brawl, struggle, fracas, free-for-all, rough and tumble; Law, dated affray; informal scrap, dust-up, punch-up, set-to, shindy; Brit. informal scrum; Brit. informal, Football afters; N. Amer. informal rough house.

scrimp v. **economize**, skimp, scrimp and save, save; be thrifty, be frugal, tighten one's belt, cut back, husband one's resources, draw in one's horns, watch one's pennies; N. Amer. pinch the pennies.

script n. **1** *her neat, tidy script* **handwriting**, writing, hand, pen, penmanship, calligraphy. **2** *the script of the play* **text**, screenplay; libretto, score; lines, dialogue, words.

S

Scrooge n. **miser**, penny-pincher, pinchpenny, niggard; informal skinflint, meanie, money-grubber, cheapskate; N. Amer. informal tightwad.
– OPPOSITES spendthrift.

scrounge v. informal **beg**, borrow; informal cadge, sponge, bum, touch someone for; Brit. informal scab; N. Amer. informal mooch; Austral./NZ informal bludge.

scrounger n. informal **beggar**, borrower, parasite, cadger; informal sponger, freeloader, junketeer; N. Amer. informal mooch, moocher, schnorrer; Austral./NZ informal bludger.

scrub[1] v. **1** *he scrubbed the kitchen floor* **scour**, rub; clean, cleanse, wash, wipe.
2 informal *the plans were scrubbed* **abandon**, scrap, drop, cancel, call off, axe, jettison, discard, discontinue, abort; informal ditch, dump, junk.

scrub[2] n. *there the buildings ended and the scrub began* **brush**, brushwood, scrubland, undergrowth.

scruffy adj. **shabby**, worn, down at heel, ragged, tattered, mangy, dirty; untidy, unkempt, bedraggled, messy, dishevelled, ill-groomed; informal tatty, the worse for wear; N. Amer. informal raggedy.
– OPPOSITES smart, tidy.

scrumptious adj. informal **delicious**, delectable, mouth-watering, tasty, appetizing, rich, savoury, flavoursome, flavourful, toothsome; succulent, luscious; informal scrummy, yummy; Brit. informal moreish; N. Amer. informal finger-licking, nummy.
– OPPOSITES unpalatable.

scrunch v. **crumple**, crunch, crush, rumple, screw up, squash, squeeze, compress; informal squidge.

scruple v. *she would not scruple to ask them for money* **hesitate**, be reluctant, be loath, have qualms, have scruples, have misgivings, have reservations, think twice, balk, demur; recoil from, shrink from, shy away from, flinch from.

scruples plural n. *he had no scruples about eavesdropping* **qualms**, compunction, pangs/twinges of conscience, hesitation, reservations, second thoughts, doubt(s), misgivings, uneasiness, reluctance.

scrupulous adj. **1** *scrupulous attention to detail* **careful**, meticulous, painstaking, thorough, assiduous, sedulous, attentive, conscientious, punctilious, searching, close, minute, rigorous, particular, strict.
2 *a scrupulous man* **honest**, honourable, upright, upstanding, high-minded, right-minded, moral, ethical, good, virtuous, principled, incorruptible, anti-corruption.
– OPPOSITES careless, dishonest.

scrutinize v. **examine**, inspect, survey, study, look at, peruse; investigate, explore, probe, inquire into, go into, check.

scrutiny n. **examination**, inspection, survey, study, perusal; investigation, exploration, probe, inquiry; informal going-over.

scud v. **speed**, race, rush, sail, shoot, sweep, skim, whip, whizz, flash, fly, scurry, flit, scutter.

scuff v. **scrape**, scratch, rub, abrade; mark.

scuffle n. *there was a scuffle outside the pub* **fight**, struggle, tussle, brawl, fracas, free-for-all, rough and tumble, scrimmage; Law, dated affray; informal scrap, dust-up, punch-up, set-to, shindy; N. Amer. informal rough house; Brit. informal, Football afters.
▸v. *demonstrators scuffled with police* **fight**, struggle, tussle, exchange blows, come to blows, brawl, clash; informal scrap.

sculpt v. **carve**, model, chisel, sculpture, fashion, form, shape, cast, cut, hew.

sculpture n. *a bronze sculpture* **model**, carving, statue, statuette, figure, figurine, effigy, bust, head, likeness.
▸v. *the choir stalls were carefully sculptured.* See **sculpt**.

scum n. **1** *the water was covered with a thick green scum* **film**, layer, covering, froth; filth, dross, dirt. **2** informal *drug dealers are scum* **despicable people**, the lowest of the low, the dregs of society, vermin, riff-raff; informal the scum of the earth.

scupper Brit. v. **1** *the captain decided to scupper the ship* **sink**, scuttle, submerge, send to the bottom. **2** informal *he denied trying to scupper the agreement* **ruin**, wreck, destroy, sabotage, torpedo, spoil, mess up; informal screw up, foul up, put the kibosh on, banjax, do for; old use bring to naught.

scurrilous adj. **defamatory**, slanderous, libellous, scandalous, insulting, offensive, gross; abusive, vituperative, malicious; informal bitchy.

scurry v. *pedestrians scurried for cover* **hurry**, hasten, run, rush, dash; scamper, scuttle, scramble; Brit. scutter; informal scoot, beetle; dated make haste.
– OPPOSITES amble.
▸n. *there was a scurry to get out* **rush**, race, dash, run, hurry; scramble, bustle.

scuttle v. See **scurry** (verb).

sea n. **1** *the sea sparkled in the sun* **(the) ocean**, the waves; informal the drink; Brit. informal the briny; literary the deep, the main, the foam. **2** *the boat overturned in the heavy seas* **waves**, swell, breakers, rollers, combers; informal boomers. **3** *a sea of roofs and turrets* **expanse**, stretch, area, tract, sweep, blanket, sheet, carpet, mass; multitude, host, profusion, abundance, plethora.
– OPPOSITES land.
▸adj. *sea creatures* **marine**, ocean, oceanic; saltwater, seawater; ocean-going, seagoing, seafaring; maritime, naval, nautical; technical pelagic, thalassic.
□ **at sea** confused, perplexed, puzzled, baffled, mystified, bemused, bewildered, nonplussed, disconcerted, disoriented, dumbfounded, at a loss, at sixes and sevens; informal flummoxed, bamboozled, fazed; N. Amer. informal discombobulated; old use wildered, mazed.

seafaring adj. **maritime**, nautical, naval, seagoing, sea.

seal n. **1** *the seal round the bath* **sealant**, sealer, adhesive. **2** *the king put his seal on the letter* **emblem**, symbol, insignia, device, badge, crest, coat of arms, mark, monogram, stamp. **3** *the Minister gave his seal of approval to the project* **ratification**, approval, blessing, consent, agreement, permission, sanction, endorsement, clearance.
▶v. **1** *she quietly sealed the door behind her* **fasten**, secure, shut, close, lock, bolt. **2** *seal each bottle while it is hot* **stop up**, seal up, make airtight/watertight, cork, stopper, plug. **3** *police sealed off the High Street* **close off**, shut off, cordon off, fence off, isolate. **4** *he held out his hand to seal the bargain* **clinch**, secure, settle, conclude, complete, establish, set the seal on, confirm, guarantee; informal sew up.

seam n. **1** *the seam was coming undone* **join**, stitching; Surgery suture. **2** *a seam of coal* **layer**, stratum, vein, lode. **3** *the seams of his face* **wrinkle**, line, crow's foot, furrow, crease, corrugation, crinkle, pucker, groove, ridge.

seaman n. **sailor**, seafarer, mariner, boatman, hand; informal (old) salt, sea dog, bluejacket; Brit. informal **matelot**; informal dated tar, Jack Tar.
– OPPOSITES landlubber.

seamy adj. **sordid**, disreputable, seedy, sleazy, squalid, insalubrious, unwholesome, unsavoury, rough, unpleasant.
– OPPOSITES salubrious.

sear v. **1** *the heat of the blast seared his face* **scorch**, burn, singe, char. **2** *sear the meat before adding the other ingredients* **flash-fry**, seal, brown. **3** *his betrayal had seared her terribly* **hurt**, wound, pain, cut to the quick, sting; distress, grieve, upset, trouble, harrow, torment, torture.

search v. **1** *I searched for the key in my handbag* **hunt**, look, seek, forage, fish about/around, look high and low, cast about/around, ferret about/around, root about/around, rummage about/around; Brit. informal rootle about/around. **2** *he searched the house thoroughly* **look through**, hunt through, explore, scour, rifle through, go through, sift through, comb, go through with a fine-tooth comb; turn upside down, turn inside out, leave no stone unturned in; Austral./NZ informal fossick through. **3** *the guards searched him for weapons* **examine**, inspect, check, frisk.
▶n. *we continued our search for a hotel* **hunt**, look, quest; pursuit.
□ **in search of** searching for, hunting for, seeking, looking for, on the lookout for, in pursuit of.

searching adj. **penetrating**, piercing, probing, keen, shrewd, sharp, intent.

searing adj. **1** *the searing heat* **scorching**, blistering, sweltering, blazing (hot), burning, fiery, torrid; informal boiling (hot), baking (hot), sizzling, roasting. **2** *a searing pain* **intense**, excruciating, agonizing, sharp, stabbing, shooting, stinging, severe, extreme, racking. **3** *a searing attack* **fierce**, savage, blistering, scathing, stinging, devastating, mordant, trenchant, caustic, cutting, biting, withering.

seaside n. **coast**, shore, seashore, waterside; beach, sand, sands, littoral; literary strand.

season n. *the rainy season | the opera season* **period**, time, time of year, spell, term.
▶v. **1** *season the casserole to taste* **flavour**, add flavouring to, add salt/pepper to, spice. **2** *his albums include standard numbers seasoned with a few of his own tunes* **enliven**, leaven, spice (up), liven up; informal pep up.
□ **in season** available, obtainable, to be had, on offer, on the market; plentiful, abundant.

seasonable adj. **usual**, expected, predictable, normal for the time of year.

seasoned adj. **experienced**, practised, well versed, knowledgeable, established, habituated, veteran, hardened, battle-scarred.
– OPPOSITES inexperienced.

seasoning n. **flavouring**, salt and pepper, herbs, spices, condiments.

seat n. **1** *a wooden seat* **chair**, bench, stool, settle, stall; (**seats**) seating, room; Brit. informal pew. **2** *the seat of government* **headquarters**, base, centre, nerve centre, hub, heart; location, site, whereabouts, place. **3** *the family's country seat* **residence**, ancestral home, mansion, stately home; formal abode.
▶v. **1** *they seated themselves round the table* **position**, put, place; ensconce, install, settle; informal plonk, park. **2** *the hall seats 500* **have room for**, contain, take, sit, hold, accommodate.

seating n. **seats**, room, places, chairs, accommodation.

secede v. *the Kingdom of Belgium seceded from the Netherlands in 1830* **withdraw from**, break away from, break with, separate (oneself) from, leave, split with, split off from, disaffiliate from, resign from, pull out of; informal quit.
– OPPOSITES join.

secluded adj. **sheltered**, private, concealed, hidden, unfrequented, sequestered, tucked away.
– OPPOSITES public, busy.

seclusion n. **isolation**, solitude, retreat, privacy, retirement, withdrawal, purdah, concealment, hiding, secrecy.

second[1] adj. **1** *the second day of the trial* **next**, following, subsequent, succeeding. **2** *he keeps a second pair of glasses in his office* **additional**, extra, alternative, another, spare, back-up, relief, fallback; N. Amer. alternate. **3** *he dropped down to captain the second team* **secondary**, lower, subordinate,

S

subsidiary, lesser, inferior. **4** *the conflict could turn into a second Vietnam* **another**, new; repeat of, copy of, carbon copy of.
– OPPOSITES first.
▸ n. **1** *Eva had been working as his second* **assistant**, attendant, helper, aide, supporter, auxiliary, right-hand man/woman, girl/man Friday, second in command, number two, deputy, understudy, subordinate; informal sidekick. **2** informal *he enjoyed the pie and asked for seconds* **a second helping**, a further helping, more.
▸ v. *George Beale seconded the motion* **formally support**, give one's support to, vote for, back, approve, endorse.
□ **second to none** incomparable, matchless, unrivalled, inimitable, beyond compare/comparison, unparalleled, without parallel, unequalled, without equal, in a class of its own, peerless, unsurpassed, unsurpassable, nonpareil, unique; perfect, consummate, transcendent, surpassing, superlative, supreme; formal unexampled.

second² n. *I'll only be gone for a second* **moment**, bit, little while, short time, instant, split second; informal nanosecond, sec, jiffy; Brit. informal mo, tick, two ticks.
□ **in a second** very soon, in a minute, in a moment, in a trice, shortly, any minute (now), in the twinkling of an eye, in (less than) no time, in no time at all; N. Amer. momentarily; informal in a sec, in a nanosecond, in a jiffy, in two shakes (of a lamb's tail), before you can say Jack Robinson, in the blink of an eye; Brit. informal in a tick, in two ticks, in a mo; N. Amer. informal in a snap; literary ere long.

second³ v. *he was seconded to their Welsh office* **assign temporarily**, lend; transfer, move, shift, relocate, assign, reassign, send.

secondary adj. **1** *a secondary issue* **less important**, subordinate, lesser, minor, peripheral, incidental, ancillary, subsidiary, non-essential, inessential, of little account, unimportant. **2** *secondary infections* **accompanying**, attendant, concomitant, consequential, resulting, resultant.
– OPPOSITES primary, main.

second-class adj. **second-rate**, second-best, inferior, lesser, unimportant.

second-hand adj. **1** *second-hand clothes* **used**, old, worn, pre-owned, handed-down, hand-me-down, cast-off; Brit. informal reach-me-down. **2** *second-hand information* **indirect**, derivative; vicarious.
– OPPOSITES new, direct.
▸ adv. *I was discounting anything I heard second-hand* **indirectly**, at second hand, on the bush telegraph; informal on the grapevine.
– OPPOSITES directly.

second in command n. **deputy**, number two, subordinate, right-hand man/woman, wingman; understudy.

secondly adv. **furthermore**, also, moreover; second, in the second place, next; secondarily.

second-rate adj. **inferior**, substandard, low-quality, below par, bad, poor, deficient, defective, faulty, imperfect, shoddy, inadequate, insufficient, unacceptable; Brit. informal ropy, duff, rubbish.
– OPPOSITES first-rate, excellent.

secrecy n. **1** *the secrecy of the material* **confidentiality**, classified nature. **2** *a government which thrived on secrecy* **secretiveness**, covertness, furtiveness, surreptitiousness, stealth, stealthiness.

secret adj. **1** *a secret plan* **confidential**, top secret, classified, undisclosed, unknown, private, under wraps; informal hush-hush; formal sub rosa. **2** *a secret drawer in the table* **hidden**, concealed, disguised; invisible. **3** *a secret operation to infiltrate terrorist groups* **clandestine**, covert, undercover, underground, surreptitious, stealthy, furtive, cloak-and-dagger, hole-and-corner, closet; Military black; informal hush-hush. **4** *a secret message* | *a secret code* **cryptic**, encoded, coded; mysterious, abstruse, recondite, arcane, esoteric, cabbalistic. **5** *a secret place* **secluded**, private, concealed, hidden, unfrequented, out of the way, tucked away. **6** *a very secret person*. See **secretive**.
– OPPOSITES public, open.
▸ n. **1** *he just can't keep a secret* **confidential matter**, confidence, private affair; skeleton in the cupboard. **2** *the secrets of the universe* **mystery**, enigma, paradox, puzzle, conundrum, poser, riddle. **3** *the secret of their success* **recipe**, (magic) formula, blueprint, key, answer, solution.
□ **in secret** secretly, in private, privately, behind closed doors, behind the scenes, in camera, under cover, under the counter, discreetly, behind someone's back, furtively, stealthily, on the sly, on the quiet, conspiratorially, covertly, clandestinely, on the side; informal on the q.t.; formal sub rosa.

secret agent n. **spy**, double agent, counterspy, undercover agent, operative, plant, mole; N. Amer. informal spook.

secretary n. **assistant**, personal assistant, PA, administrator, amanuensis, girl/man Friday.

secrete¹ v. *a substance secreted by the prostate gland* **produce**, discharge, emit, excrete, release, send out.
– OPPOSITES absorb.

secrete² v. *we secreted ourselves in the bushes* **conceal**, hide, cover up, veil, shroud, screen, stow away; bury, cache; informal stash away.
– OPPOSITES reveal.

secretive adj. **uncommunicative**, secret, unforthcoming, playing one's cards close to one's chest, reticent, reserved, silent, non-communicative, quiet, tight-lipped, close-mouthed, taciturn.
– OPPOSITES open, communicative.

secretly adv. **1** *they met secretly for a year* **in secret**, in private, privately, behind closed doors, in camera, behind the scenes, under cover, under the counter, behind someone's back, furtively, stealthily, on the sly, on the quiet, conspiratorially, covertly, clandestinely, on the side; informal on the q.t.; formal sub rosa. **2** *he was secretly jealous of Bartholomew* **privately**, in one's heart (of hearts), deep down.

sect n. **(religious) cult**, religious group, denomination, persuasion, religious order; splinter group, faction.

sectarian adj. **factional**, separatist, partisan, parti pris; doctrinaire, dogmatic, extreme, fanatical, rigid, inflexible, bigoted, hidebound, narrow-minded.
– OPPOSITES tolerant, liberal.

section n. **1** *the separate sections of a train* **part**, piece, bit, segment, component, division, portion, element, unit, constituent. **2** *the last section of the questionnaire* **subdivision**, part, subsection, division, portion, bit, chapter, passage, clause. **3** *the reference section of the library* **department**, area, part, division. **4** *a residential section of the capital.* See **sector** (sense 2).

sector adj. **1** *every sector of the industry is affected* **part**, branch, arm, division, area, department, field, sphere. **2** *the north-eastern sector of the town* **district**, quarter, part, section, zone, region, area, belt.

secular adj. **non-religious**, lay, temporal, worldly, earthly, profane; formal laic.
– OPPOSITES holy, religious.

secure adj. **1** *check to make sure that all the bolts are secure* **fastened**, fixed, secured, done up; closed, shut, locked. **2** *an environment in which children can feel secure* **safe**, protected from harm/danger, out of danger, sheltered, safe and sound, out of harm's way, in a safe place, in safe hands, invulnerable; at ease, unworried, relaxed, happy, confident. **3** *a secure future* **certain**, assured, reliable, dependable, settled, fixed.
– OPPOSITES loose, vulnerable, uncertain.
▸v. **1** *pins secure the handle to the main body* **fix**, attach, fasten, affix, connect, couple. **2** *the doors had not been properly secured* **fasten**, close, shut, lock, bolt, chain, seal. **3** *he leapt out to secure the boat* **tie up**, moor, make fast; anchor. **4** *they sought to secure the country against attack* **protect**, make safe, fortify, strengthen. **5** *a written constitution would secure the rights of the individual* **assure**, ensure, guarantee, protect, confirm, establish. **6** *the division secured a major contract* **obtain**, acquire, gain, get, get possession of; informal get hold of, land.

security n. **1** *the security of the nation's citizens* **safety**, freedom from danger, protection, invulnerability. **2** *he could give her the security she needed* **peace of mind**, feeling of safety, stability, certainty, happiness, confidence. **3** *security at the court was tight* **safety measures**, safeguards, surveillance, defence, protection. **4** *additional security for your loan may be required* **guarantee**, collateral, surety, pledge, bond; old use gage.
– OPPOSITES vulnerability, danger.

sedate¹ v. *the patient had to be sedated* **tranquillize**, put under sedation, drug.

sedate² adj. **1** *a sedate pace* **slow**, steady, dignified, unhurried, relaxed, measured, leisurely, slow-moving, easy, easy-going, gentle. **2** *he had lived a very sedate and straightforward life* **calm**, placid, tranquil, quiet, uneventful; boring, dull.
– OPPOSITES exciting, fast.

sedative adj. *sedative drugs* **tranquillizing**, calming, calmative, relaxing, soporific; depressant; Medicine neuroleptic.
▸n. *the doctor gave him a sedative* **tranquillizer**, calmative, sleeping pill, narcotic, opiate; depressant; informal trank, sleeper, downer.

sedentary adj. **sitting**, seated, desk-bound; inactive.
– OPPOSITES active.

sediment n. **dregs**, lees, precipitate, deposit, grounds, settlings, residue, remains; silt, alluvium; technical residuum; old use grouts.

sedition n. **rabble-rousing**, subversion, troublemaking, provocation; rebellion, insurrection, mutiny, insurgence, civil disorder.

seditious adj. **rabble-rousing**, provocative, inflammatory, subversive, troublemaking; rebellious, insurrectionist, mutinous, insurgent.

seduce v. **1** *he took her to his hotel room and tried to seduce her* **persuade to have sex**; euphemistic have one's (wicked) way with, take advantage of; dated debauch. **2** *a firm which had seduced customers into buying worthless products* **attract**, allure, lure, tempt, entice, beguile, inveigle, manoeuvre.

seducer n. **womanizer**, philanderer, Romeo, Don Juan, Lothario, Casanova, playboy, ladies' man; informal ladykiller, wolf, skirt-chaser.

seductive adj. **sexy**, alluring, tempting, exciting, provocative, sultry, slinky; coquettish, flirtatious; informal vampish, come-hither, come-to-bed.

seductress n. **temptress**, siren, femme fatale, Mata Hari; flirt, coquette; informal vamp.

sedulous adj. **diligent**, careful, meticulous, thorough, assiduous, attentive, industrious, conscientious, ultra-careful, punctilious, scrupulous, painstaking, minute, rigorous, particular.

see¹ v. **1** *he saw her running across the road* **discern**, spot, notice, catch sight of, glimpse, catch/get a glimpse of, make out, pick out, spy, distinguish, detect, perceive, note; informal clap/lay/set eyes on, clock; literary behold, descry, espy. **2** *I saw a documentary about it last week* **watch**, look at, view; catch. **3** *would you like to see over the house?* **inspect**, view, look round, tour, survey, examine, scrutinize; informal give something a/ the once-over. **4** *I finally saw what she meant* **understand**, grasp, comprehend, follow, take in, realize, appreciate, recognize, work out, get the drift of, perceive, fathom (out);

S

informal get, latch on to, cotton on to, catch on to, tumble to, savvy, figure out, get a fix on; Brit. informal twig, suss (out). **5** *I must go and see what Victor is up to* **find out**, discover, learn, ascertain, determine, establish. **6** *see that no harm comes to him* **ensure**, make sure/certain, see to it, take care, mind. **7** *I see trouble ahead* **foresee**, predict, forecast, prophesy, anticipate, envisage, picture, visualize. **8** *about a year later, I saw him in town* **encounter**, meet, run into/across, come across, stumble on/across, happen on, chance on; informal bump into; old use run against. **9** *they see each other from time to time* **meet**, meet up with, get together with, socialize with. **10** *you'd better see a doctor* **consult**, confer with, talk to, speak to, have recourse to, call on, call in, turn to, ask. **11** *he's seeing someone else now* **go out with**, date, take out, be involved with; informal go steady with; Brit. informal dated walk out with; N. Amer. informal dated step out with; dated court. **12** *he saw her to her car* **escort**, accompany, show, walk, conduct, lead, take, usher, attend.

□ **see through** understand, get/have the measure of, read like a book; informal be wise to, have someone's number, know someone's (little) game.

see something through persevere with, persist with, continue (with), carry on with, keep at, follow through, stay with; informal stick at, stick it out, hang in there.

see to attend to, deal with, see about, take care of, look after, sort out, fix, organize, arrange.

see[2] n. *a bishop's see* **diocese**, bishopric.

seed n. **1** *sow the seeds in trays or pots* pip, stone, kernel; ovule. **2** *each war contains within it the seeds of a fresh war* **genesis**, source, origin, root, starting point, germ, beginnings, potential (for); cause, reason, motivation, motive, grounds. **3** old use *Abraham and his seed* **descendants**, heirs, successors, scions; offspring, children, sons and daughters, progeny, family; Law issue; derogatory spawn; old use fruit of someone's loins.

□ **go/run to seed** deteriorate, degenerate, decline, decay, fall into decay, go to rack and ruin, go downhill, moulder, rot; informal go to pot, go to the dogs.

> **WORD LINKS**
>
> **seminal** relating to the seed of a plant
> **germinate** (of a seed) begin to grow
> **cotyledon** the first leaf to grow from a germinating seed

seedy adj. **1** *the seedy world of prostitution* **sordid**, disreputable, seamy, sleazy, squalid, unwholesome, unsavoury. **2** *a seedy block of flats* **dilapidated**, tumbledown, ramshackle, falling to pieces, decrepit, gone to rack and ruin, run down, down at heel, shabby, dingy, slummy, insalubrious, squalid; informal crummy; Brit. informal grotty.

– OPPOSITES high-class.

seek v. **1** *they sought shelter from the winter snows* **search for**, try to find, look for, be on the lookout for, be after, hunt for, be in quest of. **2** *the company is seeking a judicial review of the decision* **try to obtain**, work towards, be intent on, aim at/for. **3** *he sought help from the police* **ask for**, request, solicit, call for, entreat, beg for, petition for, appeal for, apply for, put in for. **4** *we constantly seek to improve the service* **try**, attempt, endeavour, strive, work, do one's best; formal essay.

seem v. **appear (to be)**, have the appearance/ air of being, give the impression of being, look, look as though one is, look like, show signs of, look to be; come across as, strike someone as, sound.

seeming adj. **apparent**, ostensible, supposed, outward, surface, superficial; pretended, feigned.

– OPPOSITES actual, genuine.

seemingly adv. **apparently**, on the face of it, to all appearances, as far as one can see/tell, on the surface, to all intents and purposes, outwardly, superficially, supposedly.

seemly adj. **decorous**, proper, decent, becoming, fitting, suitable, appropriate, apt, apposite, meet, in good taste, genteel, polite, the done thing, right, correct, acceptable, comme il faut.

– OPPOSITES unseemly, unbecoming.

seep v. **ooze**, trickle, exude, drip, dribble, flow, issue, escape, leak, drain, bleed, filter, percolate, soak.

seer n. **soothsayer**, oracle, prophet(ess), augur, prognosticator, diviner, fortune teller, crystal-gazer, clairvoyant, psychic; Scottish spaewife; literary sibyl.

see-saw v. **fluctuate**, swing, go up and down, rise and fall, oscillate, alternate, yo-yo, vary.

seethe v. **1** *the brew seethed* **boil**, bubble, simmer, foam, froth, fizz, effervesce. **2** *the water seethed with fish* **teem**, swarm, boil, swirl, churn, surge. **3** *I seethed at the injustice of it all* **be angry**, be furious, be enraged, be incensed, be beside oneself, simmer, fume, smoulder; informal be hot under the collar.

see-through adj. **transparent**, translucent, clear, limpid, pellucid; thin, lightweight, flimsy, sheer, diaphanous, filmy, gossamer, chiffony, gauzy.

– OPPOSITES opaque.

segment n. **1** *orange segments* **piece**, bit, section, part, chunk, portion, division, slice; fragment, wedge, lump, tranche. **2** *all segments of society* **part**, section, sector, division, portion, constituent, element, unit, compartment; branch, wing.

▶ v. *they plan to segment their market share* **divide (up)**, subdivide, separate, split, cut up, carve up, slice up, break up; segregate, partition, section.

– OPPOSITES amalgamate.

segregate v. **separate**, set apart, keep apart, isolate, quarantine, closet; partition, divide,

S

detach, disconnect, sever, dissociate.
– OPPOSITES amalgamate.

seize v. **1** *she seized the microphone* **grab**, grasp, snatch, take hold of, get one's hands on; grip, clutch; Brit. informal nab. **2** *rebels seized the air base* **capture**, take, overrun, occupy, conquer, take over. **3** *the drugs were seized by customs* **confiscate**, impound, commandeer, requisition, appropriate, expropriate, take away; Law distrain; Scottish Law poind. **4** *terrorists seized his wife* **kidnap**, abduct, take captive, take prisoner, take hostage, hold to ransom; informal snatch.
– OPPOSITES relinquish, release.
□ **seize on** *they seized on the opportunity* take advantage of, exploit, grasp with both hands, leap at, jump at, pounce on.

seizure n. **1** *Napoleon's seizure of Spain* **capture**, takeover, annexation, invasion, occupation, colonization. **2** *the seizure of defaulters' property* **confiscation**, appropriation, expropriation, sequestration; Law distraint; Scottish Law poind. **3** *the seizure of UN staff by rebels* **kidnapping**, kidnap, abduction. **4** *the baby suffered a seizure* **convulsion**, fit, spasm, paroxysm; Medicine ictus; dated apoplexy.

seldom adv. **rarely**, infrequently, hardly (ever), scarcely (ever), almost never; now and then, occasionally, sporadically; informal once in a blue moon.
– OPPOSITES often.

select v. *select the correct tool for the job* **choose**, pick (out), single out, sort out, take; opt for, decide on, settle on, determine, nominate, appoint, elect.
▸ adj. **1** *a select group of SAS members* **choice**, hand-picked, prime, first-rate, first-class, superior, finest, best, top-class, supreme, A-list, superb, excellent; informal A1, top-notch. **2** *a select clientele* **exclusive**, elite, favoured, privileged; wealthy; informal posh.
– OPPOSITES inferior.

selection n. **1** *Jim made his selection of toys* **choice**, pick; option, preference. **2** *a wide selection of dishes* **range**, array, diversity, variety, assortment, mixture. **3** *a selection of his poems* **anthology**, assortment, collection, assemblage; miscellany, medley, potpourri.

selective adj. **discerning**, discriminating, discriminatory, critical, exacting, demanding, particular; fussy, fastidious, faddish; informal choosy, pernickety, picky; Brit. informal faddy.

self n. **ego**, I, oneself, persona, person, identity, character, personality, psyche, soul, spirit, mind, inner self.
– OPPOSITES other.

self-assembly n. *kits for self-assembly* **do-it-yourself**, DIY.
▸ adj. *self-assembly furniture* **flat-pack**, kit, self-build, do-it-yourself, DIY.

self-assurance n. **self-confidence**, confidence, assertiveness, self-reliance, self-possession, composure, presence of mind, aplomb.
– OPPOSITES diffidence.

self-assured adj. **self-confident**, confident, assertive, assured, authoritative, commanding, self-reliant, self-possessed, poised.

self-centred adj. **egocentric**, egotistic, egotistical, egomaniacal, self-absorbed, self-obsessed, self-seeking, self-interested, self-serving; narcissistic, vain; inconsiderate, thoughtless; informal looking after number one.

self-confidence n. **morale**, confidence, self-assurance, assurance, assertiveness, self-reliance, self-possession, composure.

self-conscious adj. **embarrassed**, uncomfortable, uneasy, nervous; unnatural, inhibited, gauche, awkward; modest, shy, diffident, bashful, retiring, shrinking.
– OPPOSITES confident.

self-contained adj. **1** *each train was a self-contained unit* **complete**, independent, separate, free-standing, enclosed. **2** *a very self-contained child* **independent**, self-sufficient, self-reliant; introverted, quiet, private, aloof, insular, reserved, reticent, secretive.

self-control n. **self-discipline**, restraint, self-possession, will power, composure, coolness; moderation, temperance, abstemiousness; informal cool.

self-denial n. **self-sacrifice**, selflessness, unselfishness; self-discipline, asceticism, self-deprivation, abstemiousness, abstinence, abstention; moderation, temperance.
– OPPOSITES self-indulgence.

self-discipline n. **self-control**; restraint, self-restraint; will power, purposefulness, strong-mindedness, resolve, moral fibre; doggedness, persistence, determination, grit.

self-employed adj. **freelance**, independent, casual; consultant, consulting; temporary, jobbing, visiting, outside, external; informal one's own boss.

self-esteem n. **self-respect**, pride, dignity, self-regard, faith in oneself; morale, self-confidence, confidence, self-assurance.

self-evident adj. **obvious**, clear, plain, evident, apparent, manifest, patent; distinct, transparent, overt, conspicuous, palpable, unmistakable, undeniable.
– OPPOSITES unclear.

self-explanatory adj. **easily understood**, comprehensible, intelligible, straightforward, unambiguous, accessible, crystal clear, user-friendly, simple, self-evident, obvious.
– OPPOSITES impenetrable.

self-governing n. **independent**, free, sovereign, autonomous; self-legislating, self-determining.
– OPPOSITES dependent.

self-important adj. **conceited**, arrogant, bumptious, full of oneself, puffed up, swollen-headed, pompous, overbearing, opinionated, cocky, presumptuous, sententious, vain, overweening, proud, egotistical; informal snooty, uppity, uppish.
– OPPOSITES humble.

S

self-indulgent adj. **hedonistic**, pleasure-seeking, sybaritic, indulgent, luxurious, lotus-eating, epicurean; intemperate, immoderate, overindulgent, excessive, extravagant, licentious, dissolute, decadent.
– OPPOSITES abstemious.

self-interest n. **self-seeking**, self-serving, self-obsession, self-absorption, self-regard, egocentrism, egotism, egomania, selfishness; informal looking after number one.
– OPPOSITES altruism.

self-interested adj. **self-seeking**, self-serving, self-obsessed, self-absorbed, wrapped up in oneself, egocentric, egotistic, egotistical, selfish.

selfish adj. **egocentric**, egotistic, egotistical, egomaniacal, self-centred, self-absorbed, self-obsessed, self-seeking, self-serving, wrapped up in oneself; inconsiderate, thoughtless, unthinking, uncaring, uncharitable; mean, miserly, grasping, greedy, mercenary, acquisitive, opportunistic; informal looking after number one.
– OPPOSITES altruistic.

selfless adj. **unselfish**, altruistic, self-sacrificing, self-denying; considerate, compassionate, kind, noble, generous, magnanimous, ungrudging, charitable, benevolent, open-handed.
– OPPOSITES inconsiderate.

self-possessed adj. **assured**, self-assured, calm, cool, composed, at ease, unperturbed, unruffled, confident, self-confident, poised, imperturbable; informal together, unfazed, unflappable.
– OPPOSITES unsure.

self-possession n. **composure**, assurance, self-assurance, self-control, imperturbability, impassivity, equanimity, nonchalance, confidence, self-confidence, poise, aplomb, presence of mind, nerve, sangfroid; informal cool.

self-reliant adj. **self-sufficient**, self-supporting, self-sustaining, able to stand on one's own two feet; independent, autarkic.

self-respect n. **self-esteem**, self-regard, amour propre, faith in oneself, pride, dignity, morale, self-confidence.

self-restraint n. **self-control**, restraint, self-discipline, self-possession, will power, moderation, temperance, abstemiousness, abstention.
– OPPOSITES self-indulgence.

self-righteous adj. **sanctimonious**, holier-than-thou, self-satisfied, smug, priggish, complacent, pious, moralizing, superior, hypocritical; informal goody-goody.
– OPPOSITES humble.

self-sacrifice n. **self-denial**, selflessness, unselfishness; self-discipline, asceticism, abnegation, self-deprivation, moderation, austerity, temperance, abstinence, abstention.

self-satisfied adj. **complacent**, self-congratulatory, smug, superior, puffed up, pleased with oneself; informal goody-goody,

I'm-all-right-Jack; Brit. informal like the cat that's got the cream.

self-seeking adj. **self-interested**, self-serving, selfish; egocentric, egotistic, egotistical, self-obsessed, self-absorbed; inconsiderate, thoughtless, unthinking; informal looking after number one.
– OPPOSITES altruistic.

self-styled adj. **would-be**, so-called, self-appointed, self-titled, professed, self-confessed, soi-disant.

self-sufficient adj. **self-supporting**, self-reliant, self-sustaining, able to stand on one's own two feet; independent, autarkic.

self-willed adj. **wilful**, contrary, perverse, uncooperative, wayward, headstrong, stubborn, obstinate, obdurate, pig-headed, mulish, intransigent, recalcitrant, intractable; Brit. informal bloody-minded; formal refractory.
– OPPOSITES biddable.

sell v. **1** *they are selling their house* **put up for sale**, offer for sale, put on sale, dispose of, vend, auction (off); trade, barter. **2** *he sells cakes* **trade in**, deal in, traffic in, stock, carry, offer for sale, peddle, hawk, retail, market. **3** *the book should sell well* **go**, be bought, be purchased; move, be in demand. **4** *it sells for £79.95* **cost**, be priced at, retail at, go for, be. **5** *he still has to sell the deal to Congress* **promote**; persuade someone to accept, talk someone into, bring someone round to, win someone over to, win approval for.
– OPPOSITES buy.
 □ **sell someone down the river** informal See **double-cross**.

sell out 1 *we've sold out of petrol* **have none left**, be out of stock, have run out; informal be fresh out, be cleaned out. **2** *the edition sold out quickly* **be bought up**, be depleted, be exhausted. **3** *they say the band has sold out* **abandon one's principles**, prostitute oneself, sell one's soul, betray one's ideals, be untrue to oneself; debase oneself, degrade oneself, demean oneself.

sell someone out betray, inform on; be disloyal to, be unfaithful to, double-cross, break faith with, stab in the back; informal tell on, sell down the river, blow the whistle on, squeal on, stitch up, peach on, do the dirty on; Brit. informal grass on, shop; N. Amer. informal finger.

sell someone short undervalue, underrate, underestimate, disparage, deprecate, belittle; formal derogate.

seller n. **vendor**, retailer, purveyor, supplier, stockist, trader, merchant, dealer; shopkeeper, salesperson, salesman, saleswoman, sales assistant, shop assistant, travelling salesperson, pedlar, hawker; auctioneer; trademark in US e-tailer; N. Amer. clerk; informal counter-jumper; Brit. informal flogger.

semblance n. **(outward) appearance**, air, show, facade, front, veneer, guise, pretence.

seminal adj. **influential**, formative, groundbreaking, pioneering, original, innovative; major, important.

seminar n. **1** *a seminar for education officials* **conference**, symposium, meeting, convention, forum, summit, discussion, consultation. **2** *teaching in the form of seminars* **study group**, workshop, tutorial, class, lesson.

seminary n. **theological college**, rabbinical college, Talmudical college; academy, training college, training institute, school.

send v. **1** *they sent a message to HQ* **dispatch**, post, mail, address, consign, direct, forward; transmit, convey, communicate; telephone, phone, broadcast, radio, fax, email; dated telegraph, wire, cable. **2** *we sent for a doctor* **call**, summon, contact; ask for, request, order. **3** *the pump sent out a jet of petrol* **propel**, project, eject, deliver, discharge, spout, fire, shoot, release; throw, let fly; informal chuck. **4** *the barrels send off nasty fumes* **emit**, give off, discharge, exude, send out, release, leak. **5** *it's enough to send one mad* **make**, drive, turn.
– OPPOSITES receive.
□ **send someone down 1** Brit. *she was sent down from Cambridge* **expel**, exclude; Brit. rusticate. **2** informal *he was sent down for life* **send to prison**, imprison, jail, incarcerate, lock up, confine, detain, intern; informal put away; Brit. informal bang up.
send someone off Sport order off, dismiss; show someone the red card; informal red-card, send for an early bath, sin-bin.
send someone/something up informal satirize, ridicule, make fun of, parody, lampoon, mock, caricature, imitate, ape; informal take off, spoof, take the mickey out of.

send-off n. **farewell**, goodbye, adieu, leave-taking, valediction; funeral; old use vale.
– OPPOSITES welcome.

send-up n. informal **satire**, burlesque, lampoon, pastiche, caricature, imitation, impression, impersonation; mockery, mimicry, travesty; informal spoof, take-off, mickey-take.

senile adj. **doddering**, doddery, decrepit, senescent, declining, infirm, feeble; aged, long in the tooth, in one's dotage; informal past it, gaga.

senior adj. **1** *senior school pupils* **older**, elder. **2** *a senior officer* **superior**, higher-ranking, high-ranking, more important; top, chief; N. Amer. ranking. **3** *Albert Stone Senior* **the Elder**; Brit. major; N. Amer. I, the First.
– OPPOSITES junior, subordinate.

senior citizen n. **retired person**, (old-age) pensioner, OAP; old person, elderly person, geriatric, dotard, Methuselah; N. Amer. senior, retiree, golden ager; informal old stager, old-timer, oldie, oldster, wrinkly, crumbly; Brit. informal buffer, josser.

seniority n. **rank**, superiority, standing, primacy, precedence, priority; age.

sensation n. **1** *a sensation of light* **feeling**, sense, awareness, consciousness, perception, impression. **2** *he caused a sensation by donating £1m* **commotion**, stir, uproar, furore, scandal, impact; interest, excitement; informal splash, to-do, hullabaloo. **3** *the new cars were a sensation* **triumph**, success, sell-out; talking point; informal smash (hit), hit, winner, crowd-puller, wow, knockout.

sensational adj. **1** *a sensational murder trial* **shocking**, scandalous, appalling; amazing, startling, astonishing, staggering; stirring, exciting, thrilling, electrifying; fascinating, interesting, noteworthy, significant, remarkable, momentous, historic, newsworthy. **2** *sensational stories* **overdramatized**, dramatic, melodramatic, exaggerated, sensationalist, sensationalistic; graphic, explicit, lurid; informal shock-horror, juicy. **3** informal *she looked sensational* **gorgeous**, stunning, wonderful, exquisite, lovely, radiant, delightful, charming, enchanting, captivating; striking, spectacular, remarkable, outstanding, arresting, eye-catching; marvellous, superb, excellent, fine, first-class; informal great, terrific, tremendous, super, fantastic, fabulous, fab, heavenly, divine, knockout, delectable, scrumptious, awesome, magic, wicked, out of this world; Brit. informal smashing, brilliant, brill.
– OPPOSITES dull, understated, unremarkable.

sense n. **1** *the sense of touch* **sensory faculty**, feeling, sensation, perception; sight, hearing, touch, taste, smell. **2** *a sense of guilt* **feeling**, awareness, sensation, consciousness, recognition. **3** *a sense of humour* **appreciation**, awareness, understanding, comprehension, discernment. **4** *she had the sense to press the panic button* **wisdom**, common sense, sagacity, discernment, perception; wit, intelligence, cleverness, shrewdness, judgement, reason, logic, brain(s); informal gumption, nous, horse sense, savvy; Brit. informal loaf, common; N. Amer. informal smarts. **5** *I can't see the sense in this* **purpose**, point, reason, object, motive; use, value, advantage, benefit. **6** *the different senses of 'well'* **meaning**, definition, import, signification, significance, purport, implication, nuance; drift, gist, thrust, tenor, message.
– OPPOSITES stupidity.
▶ v. *she sensed their hostility* **discern**, feel, observe, notice, recognize, pick up, be aware of, distinguish, make out, identify; comprehend, apprehend, see, appreciate, realize; suspect, have a funny feeling about, have a hunch, divine, intuit; informal catch on to; Brit. informal twig.

senseless adj. **1** *they found him senseless on the floor* **unconscious**, stunned, insensible, insensate, comatose, knocked out, out cold, out for the count; numb; informal KO'd, dead to the world; Brit. informal spark out. **2** *a senseless waste* **pointless**, futile, useless, needless, unavailing, in vain, purposeless, meaningless, unprofitable; absurd, foolish, insane, stupid, idiotic, ridiculous, ludicrous, mindless, illogical.
– OPPOSITES conscious, wise.

sensibility n. **1** *study leads to the growth of sensibility* **sensitivity**, finer

S

feelings, delicacy, taste, discrimination, discernment; understanding, insight, empathy, appreciation; feeling, intuition, responsiveness, receptiveness, perceptiveness, awareness. **2** *the wording might offend their sensibilities* (**finer**) **feelings**, emotions, sensitivities, moral sense.

sensible adj. **practical**, realistic, responsible, reasonable, commonsensical, rational, logical, sound, balanced, sober, no-nonsense, pragmatic, level-headed, thoughtful, down-to-earth, wise, prudent, judicious, sagacious, shrewd.
– OPPOSITES foolish.

sensitive adj. **1** *she's sensitive to changes in temperature* **responsive to**, reactive to, sentient of, sensitized to; aware of, conscious of, alive to; susceptible to, affected by, vulnerable to; attuned to. **2** *sensitive skin* **delicate**, fragile; tender, sore, raw. **3** *the matter needs sensitive handling* **tactful**, careful, thoughtful, diplomatic, delicate, subtle, kid-glove; sympathetic, compassionate, understanding, intuitive, responsive, insightful. **4** *he's sensitive about his bald patch* **touchy**, oversensitive, hypersensitive, easily offended, easily upset, easily hurt, thin-skinned, defensive; paranoid, neurotic; informal twitchy, uptight. **5** *a sensitive issue* **difficult**, delicate, tricky, awkward, problematic, ticklish; controversial, emotive; informal sticky.
– OPPOSITES impervious, resilient, clumsy, thick-skinned, uncontroversial.

sensitivity n. **1** *the sensitivity of the skin* **responsiveness**, sensitiveness, reactivity; susceptibility, vulnerability. **2** *the job calls for sensitivity* **consideration**, care, thoughtfulness, tact, diplomacy, delicacy, subtlety, finer feelings; understanding, empathy, soft skills, sensibility, feeling, intuition, responsiveness, receptiveness; perception, discernment, insight; savoir faire. **3** *her sensitivity on the subject of boyfriends* **touchiness**, oversensitivity, hypersensitivity, defensiveness. **4** *the sensitivity of the issue* **delicacy**, trickiness, awkwardness, ticklishness.

sensual adj. **1** *sensual pleasure* **physical**, carnal, bodily, fleshly, animal; hedonistic, epicurean, sybaritic, voluptuary. **2** *a beautiful, sensual woman* **sexually attractive**, sexy, voluptuous, sultry, seductive, passionate; sexually arousing, erotic, sexual.
– OPPOSITES spiritual, passionless.

sensualist n. **hedonist**, pleasure-seeker, sybarite, voluptuary; epicure, gastronome; bon vivant, bon viveur.

sensuality n. **sexiness**, sexual attractiveness, sultriness, seductiveness; sexuality, eroticism; physicality, carnality.

sensuous adj. **1** *big sensuous canvases* **aesthetically pleasing**, gratifying, rich, sumptuous, luxurious; sensory, sensorial. **2** *sensuous lips* **sexually attractive**, sexy,

seductive, voluptuous, luscious, lush.

sentence n. **prison term**, prison sentence; punishment; informal time, stretch, stint; Brit. informal porridge, bird.
▸ v. **pass judgement on**, punish, convict; condemn.

sententious adj. **moralistic**, moralizing, sanctimonious, self-righteous, pietistic, pious, priggish, judgemental; pompous, pontifical, self-important; informal preachifying, preachy; Brit. informal pi.

sentient adj. **(capable of) feeling**, living, live; conscious, aware, responsive, reactive.

sentiment n. **1** *the comments echo my own sentiments* **view**, feeling, attitude, thought, opinion, belief. **2** *there's no room for sentiment in sport* **sentimentality**, sentimentalism, mawkishness, emotionalism; emotion, sensibility, soft-heartedness, tender-heartedness; informal schmaltz, mush, slushiness, corniness, cheese; Brit. informal soppiness; N. Amer. informal sappiness.

sentimental adj. **1** *she kept the vase for sentimental reasons* **nostalgic**, tender, emotional, affectionate. **2** *the film is too sentimental* **mawkish**, overemotional, cloying, slushy, mushy, sickly, saccharine, sugary; romantic, hearts-and-flowers, touching; Brit. twee; informal weepy, tear-jerking, schmaltzy, lovey-dovey, gooey, drippy, cheesy, corny; Brit. informal soppy; N. Amer. informal cornball, sappy, hokey. **3** *she is sentimental about animals* **soft-hearted**, tender-hearted, soft; informal soppy.
– OPPOSITES practical, gritty.

sentry n. **guard**, sentinel, lookout, watch, watchman, patrol.

separable adj. **divisible**, distinct, independent, distinguishable; detachable, removable.

separate adj. **1** *his personal life was separate from his job* **unconnected**, unrelated, different, distinct, discrete; detached, divorced, disconnected, independent, autonomous. **2** *the infirmary was separate from the school* **set apart**, detached, disjoined; fenced off, cut off, segregated, isolated; free-standing, self-contained.
– OPPOSITES linked, attached.
▸ v. **1** *they separated two rioting mobs* **split (up)**, break up, part, pull apart, divide; literary sunder. **2** *the connectors can be separated* **disconnect**, detach, disengage, uncouple, unyoke, disunite, disjoin; split, divide, sever; disentangle. **3** *the wall that separated the two estates* **partition**, divide, come between, keep apart; bisect, intersect. **4** *the south aisle was separated off* **isolate**, partition off, section off; close off, shut off, cordon off, fence off, screen off. **5** *they separated at the airport* **part (company)**, go their separate ways, split up; say goodbye; disperse, disband, scatter. **6** *the road separated* **fork**, divide, branch, bifurcate, diverge. **7** *her parents separated* **split up**, break up, part, be estranged, divorce. **8** *separate fact*

from fiction **isolate**, set apart, segregate; distinguish, differentiate, dissociate; sort out, sift out, filter out, remove, weed out. **9** *those who separate themselves from society* **break away from**, break with, secede from, withdraw from, leave, quit, dissociate oneself from, resign from, drop out of, repudiate, reject.
– OPPOSITES unite, join, link, meet, merge, marry.

separately adv. **individually**, one by one, one at a time, singly, severally; apart, independently, alone, by oneself, on one's own.

separation n. **1** *the separation of the two companies* **disconnection**, detachment, severance, dissociation, disunion, disaffiliation, segregation, partition. **2** *her parents' separation* **break-up**, split, parting (of the ways), estrangement, rift, rupture, breach; divorce; Brit. informal bust-up. **3** *the separation between art and life* **distinction**, difference, differentiation, division, dividing line; gulf, gap, chasm.

septic adj. **infected**, festering, suppurating, pus-filled, putrid, putrefying, poisoned, diseased; Medicine purulent.

sepulchral adj. **gloomy**, lugubrious, sombre, melancholy, melancholic, sad, sorrowful, mournful, doleful, dismal; literary dolorous.
– OPPOSITES cheerful.

sepulchre n. **tomb**, vault, burial chamber, mausoleum, crypt, undercroft, catacomb; grave.

sequel n. **1** *the film inspired a sequel* **follow-up**, continuation. **2** *the sequel was an armed uprising* **consequence**, result, upshot, outcome, development, issue, postscript; effect, after-effect, aftermath; informal pay-off.

sequence n. **1** *the sequence of events* **succession**, order, course, series, chain, train, string, progression, chronology; pattern, flow; formal concatenation. **2** *a sequence from his film* **excerpt**, clip, extract, episode, section, scene.

sequester v. **1** *he sequestered himself from the world* **isolate oneself**, hide away, shut oneself away, seclude oneself, cut oneself off, segregate oneself; closet oneself, withdraw, retire. **2** *the government sequestered his property.* See **sequestrate**.

sequestrate v. **confiscate**, seize, take, sequester, appropriate, expropriate, impound, commandeer; Law distrain; Scottish Law poind.

seraphic adj. **blissful**, beatific, sublime, rapturous, ecstatic, joyful, rapt; serene, ethereal; cherubic, saintly, angelic.

serendipitous adj. **chance**, accidental, coincidental; lucky, fluky, fortuitous; unexpected, unforeseen.

serendipity n. **(happy) chance**, (happy) accident, fluke; luck, good luck, good fortune, fortuity, providence; happy coincidence.

serene adj. **1** *on the surface she seemed serene* **calm**, composed, tranquil, peaceful, untroubled, relaxed, at ease, unperturbed, unruffled, unworried; placid, equable; N. Amer. centered; informal together, unflappable. **2** *serene valleys* **peaceful**, tranquil, quiet, still, restful, relaxing, undisturbed.
– OPPOSITES agitated, turbulent.

series n. **1** *a series of lectures* **succession**, sequence, string, chain, run, round; spate, wave, rash; set, course, cycle; row, line; formal concatenation. **2** *a new drama series* **serial**, programme; soap opera; informal soap.

serious adj. **1** *a serious expression* **solemn**, earnest, grave, sombre, sober, unsmiling, poker-faced, stern, grim, dour, humourless, stony-faced; thoughtful, preoccupied, pensive. **2** *serious decisions* **important**, significant, consequential, momentous, weighty, far-reaching, major, grave; urgent, pressing, crucial, critical, vital, life-and-death, high-priority. **3** *give serious consideration to this* **careful**, detailed, in-depth, deep, profound, meaningful. **4** *a serious play* **intellectual**, highbrow, heavyweight, deep, profound, literary, learned, scholarly; informal heavy. **5** *serious injuries* **severe**, grave, bad, critical, acute, terrible, dire, dangerous, perilous, parlous; formal grievous. **6** *we're serious about equality* **in earnest**, earnest, sincere, wholehearted, genuine; committed, resolute, determined.
– OPPOSITES light-hearted, trivial, superficial, lowbrow, minor, half-hearted.

seriously adv. **1** *Faye nodded seriously* **solemnly**, earnestly, gravely, soberly, sombrely, sternly, grimly, dourly, humourlessly; pensively, thoughtfully. **2** *she was seriously injured* **severely**, gravely, badly, critically, acutely, dangerously; formal grievously. **3** *do you seriously expect me to come?* **really**, actually, honestly. **4** *seriously, I'm very pleased* **joking aside**, to be serious, honestly, truthfully, truly, I mean it; informal Scout's honour; Brit. informal straight up. **5** *informal he was seriously rich.* See **extremely**.

sermon n. **1** *he preached a sermon* **homily**, address, speech, talk, discourse, oration; lesson. **2** *the headmaster gave them a lengthy sermon* **lecture**, tirade, harangue, diatribe; speech, disquisition, monologue; reprimand, reproach, reproof, admonishment, admonition, reproval, remonstration, criticism; informal telling-off, talking-to, dressing-down, earful; Brit. informal ticking-off, row, rocket, rollicking; formal castigation.

serpentine adj. **1** *a serpentine path* **winding**, windy, zigzag, twisty, twisting and turning, meandering, sinuous, snaky, tortuous. **2** *serpentine election rules* **complicated**, complex, intricate, involved, tortuous, convoluted, elaborate, Byzantine, confusing, bewildering, baffling, impenetrable.
– OPPOSITES straight, simple.

serrated adj. **jagged**, sawtoothed, sawtooth, zigzag, notched, indented, toothed, denticulate, denticulated; Botany serrate; technical crenulated.
– OPPOSITES smooth.

serried adj. **close together**, packed together, close-set, dense, tight, compact.

servant n. **1** *servants were cleaning the hall* **attendant**, retainer; domestic (worker), (hired) help, cleaner; lackey, flunkey, minion; maid, housemaid, footman, page (boy), valet, butler, batman, manservant; housekeeper, steward; drudge, menial, slave, galley slave; Brit. informal Mrs Mop, daily (woman), skivvy, scout; Brit. dated charwoman, charlady, boots; old use abigail, scullion. **2** *a servant of the Labour Party* **helper**, supporter, follower.

serve v. **1** *they served their masters faithfully* **work for**, be in the service of, be employed by; obey. **2** *this job serves the community* **be of service to**, be of use to, help, assist, aid, make a contribution to, do one's bit for, do something for, benefit. **3** *she served on the committee for years* **be a member of**, work on, be on, sit on, have a place on. **4** *he served his apprenticeship in Scotland* **carry out**, perform, do, fulfil, complete, discharge; spend. **5** *serve the soup hot* **dish up/out**, give out, distribute; present, provide, supply; eat. **6** *she served another customer* **attend to**, deal with, see to; **assist**, help, look after. **7** *they served him with a writ* **present**, deliver, give, hand over. **8** *a saucer serving as an ashtray* **act as**, function as, do the work of, be a substitute for. **9** *official forms will serve in most cases* **suffice**, be adequate, be good enough, fit/fill the bill, do, answer, be useful, meet requirements, suit.

service n. **1** *your conditions of service* **work**, employment, employ, labour. **2** *he has done us a service* **favour**, kindness, good turn, helping hand; (**services**) **assistance**, help, aid, offices, ministrations. **3** *he took his car in for a service* **overhaul**, maintenance check, servicing. **4** *a marriage service* **ceremony**, ritual, rite, observance; liturgy, sacrament; formal ordinance. **5** *a range of local services* **amenity**, facility, resource, utility, solution. **6** *soldiers leaving the services* (**armed**) **forces**, armed services, military; army, navy, air force.

▶ v. *the appliances are serviced regularly* **overhaul**, check, go over, maintain; repair, mend, recondition.

□ **be of service** help, assist, benefit, be of assistance, be beneficial, serve, be useful, be of use, be valuable; do someone a good turn. **out of service** out of order, broken, broken-down, out of commission, unserviceable, faulty, defective, inoperative, in disrepair; down; informal conked out, bust, kaput, on the blink, acting up, shot; Brit. informal knackered.

serviceable adj. **1** *a serviceable heating system* **in working order**, working, functioning, functional, operational, operative; usable, workable, viable. **2** *serviceable lace-up shoes* **functional**, utilitarian, sensible, practical; **hard-wearing**, durable, tough, robust.
– OPPOSITES unusable, impractical.

servile adj. **obsequious**, sycophantic, deferential, subservient, fawning,

ingratiating, unctuous, grovelling, toadyish, slavish, humble, self-abasing; informal slimy, bootlicking, smarmy, sucky; N. Amer. informal apple-polishing.
– OPPOSITES assertive.

serving n. **portion**, helping, plateful, plate, bowlful; amount, quantity, ration.

servitude n. **slavery**, enslavement, bondage, subjugation, subjection, domination; historical serfdom.
– OPPOSITES liberty.

session n. **1** *a special session of the committee* **meeting**, sitting, assembly, conclave, plenary; hearing; conference, discussion, forum, symposium; Scottish sederunt, diet; N. Amer. & NZ caucus. **2** *training sessions* **period**, time, spell, stretch, bout. **3** *the next college session begins in August* **academic year**, school year; term, semester; N. Amer. trimester.

set¹ v. **1** *Beth set the bag on the table* **put (down)**, place, lay, deposit, position, settle, leave, stand, plant, posit; informal stick, dump, bung, park, plonk, pop; N. Amer. informal plunk. **2** *the cottage is set on a hill* **be situated**, be located, lie, stand, be sited, be perched. **3** *the fence is set in concrete* **fix**, embed, insert; mount. **4** *a ring set with precious stones* **adorn**, ornament, decorate, embellish; literary bejewel. **5** *I'll go and set the table* **lay**, prepare, arrange. **6** *we set them some easy tasks* **assign**, allocate, give, allot, prescribe. **7** *just set your mind to it* **apply**, address, direct, aim, turn, focus, concentrate. **8** *they set a date for the election* **decide on**, select, choose, arrange, schedule; fix (on), settle on, determine, designate, name, appoint, specify, stipulate. **9** *he set his horse towards her* **direct**, steer, orientate, point, aim, train. **10** *his jump set a national record* **establish**, create, institute. **11** *he set his watch* **adjust**, regulate, synchronize; calibrate; put right, correct; programme, activate, turn on. **12** *the adhesive will set in an hour* **solidify**, harden, stiffen, thicken, gel, gelatinize; cake, congeal, coagulate, clot; freeze, crystallize. **13** *the sun was setting* **go down**, sink, dip; vanish, disappear.
– OPPOSITES melt, rise.

□ **set about 1** *Mike set about raising £5000* **begin**, start, commence, go about, get to work on, get down to, embark on, tackle, address oneself to, undertake. **2** *the youths set about him* **attack**, assail, assault, hit, strike, beat, thrash, pummel, wallop, tear into, set upon, fall on; informal lay into, lace into, pitch into, let someone have it, do over, work over, rough up, knock about/around; Brit. informal duff up, have a go at; N. Amer. informal beat up on.
set someone apart distinguish, differentiate, mark out, single out, separate, demarcate.
set something apart isolate, separate, segregate, put to one side.
set something aside 1 *set aside some money each month* **save**, put by, put aside, put away, lay by, keep, reserve; store, stockpile, hoard,

stow away, cache, withhold; informal salt away, squirrel away, stash away. **2** *he set aside his cup* **put down**, cast aside, discard, abandon, dispense with. **3** *set aside your differences* **disregard**, put aside, ignore, forget, discount, shrug off, bury. **4** *the Appeal Court set aside the decision* **overrule**, overturn, reverse, revoke, countermand, nullify, annul, cancel, quash, dismiss, reject, repudiate; Law disaffirm; formal abrogate.

set someone/something back delay, hold up, hold back, slow down/up, retard, check, decelerate; hinder, impede, obstruct, hamper, inhibit, frustrate, thwart.

set something down 1 *he set down his thoughts* **write down**, put in writing, jot down, note down, make a note of; record, register, log. **2** *we set down a code of practice* **formulate**, draw up, establish, frame; lay down, determine, fix, stipulate, specify, prescribe, impose, ordain. **3** *I set it down to the fact that he was drunk* **attribute**, put down, ascribe, assign, chalk up; blame on, impute.

set someone free release, free, let go, turn loose, let out, liberate, deliver, emancipate.

set in *bad weather set in* begin, start, arrive, come, develop.

set off set out, start out, sally forth, leave, depart, embark, set sail; informal hit the road.

set something off 1 *the bomb was set off* **detonate**, explode, blow up, touch off, trigger; ignite. **2** *it set off a wave of protest* **give rise to**, cause, lead to, set in motion, occasion, bring about, initiate, precipitate, prompt, trigger (off), spark (off), touch off, provoke, incite. **3** *the blue dress set off her auburn hair* **enhance**, bring out, emphasize, show off, throw into relief; complement.

set on/upon attack, assail, assault, hit, strike, beat, thrash, pummel, wallop, set about, fall on; informal lay into, lace into, let someone have it, get stuck into, work over, rough up, knock about/around; Brit. informal duff up, have a go at; N. Amer. informal beat up on, light into.

set one's heart on want desperately, wish for, desire, long for, yearn for, hanker after, ache for, hunger for, thirst for, burn for; informal be itching for, be dying for.

set out 1 *he set out early.* See **set off**. **2** *you've done what you set out to achieve* aim, intend, mean, seek; hope, aspire, want.

set something out 1 *the gifts were set out on tables* **arrange**, lay out, put out, array, dispose, display, exhibit. **2** *they set out some guidelines* **present**, set forth, detail; state, declare, announce; submit, put forward, advance, propound.

set someone up 1 *his father set him up in business* **establish**, finance, fund, back, subsidize. **2** informal *she set him up for Newley's murder* **falsely incriminate**, frame, entrap; Brit. informal fit up.

set something up 1 *a monument to her memory was set up* **erect**, put up, construct, build, raise, elevate. **2** *she set up her own business* **establish**, start, begin, initiate,

institute, found, create. **3** *we set up a meeting* **arrange**, organize, fix (up), schedule, timetable, line up.

set² n. **1** *a set of colour postcards* **group**, collection, series; assortment, selection, compendium, batch, number; arrangement, array. **2** *the literary set* **clique**, coterie, circle, crowd, group, crew, band, company, ring, camp, fraternity, school, faction, league; informal gang, bunch. **3** *a chemistry set* **kit**, apparatus, equipment, outfit. **4** *a set of cutlery* **canteen**, box, case. **5** *a set of china* **service**. **6** *he's in the bottom set at school* **class**, form, group; stream, band. **7** *the set of his shoulders* **posture**, position, cast, attitude; bearing, carriage. **8** *a stage set* **scenery**, setting, backdrop, flats; mise en scène.

set³ adj. **1** *a set routine* **fixed**, established, predetermined, hard and fast, prearranged, prescribed, specified, defined; unvarying, unchanging, invariable, unvaried, rigid, inflexible, cast-iron, strict, settled, predictable; routine, standard, customary, regular, usual, habitual, accustomed; literary wonted. **2** *she had set ideas* **inflexible**, rigid, fixed, firm, deep-rooted, deep-seated, ingrained, entrenched. **3** *he had a set speech for such occasions* **stock**, standard, routine, rehearsed, well worn, formulaic, conventional. **4** *I was all set for the evening* **ready**, prepared, organized, equipped, primed; informal geared up, psyched up. **5** *he's set on marrying her* **determined to**, intent on, (hell) bent on, resolute about, insistent about. **6** *you were dead set against the idea* **opposed to**, averse to, hostile to, resistant to, antipathetic to, unsympathetic to; informal anti.
– OPPOSITES variable, flexible, original, unprepared, uncertain.

setback n. **problem**, difficulty, issue, hitch, complication, upset, disappointment, misfortune, mishap, reversal; blow, stumbling block, hindrance, impediment, obstruction; delay, hold-up; informal glitch, hiccup.
– OPPOSITES breakthrough.

settee n. **sofa**, couch, divan, chaise longue, chesterfield; Brit. put-you-up; N. Amer. davenport, day bed.

setting n. **1** *a rural setting* **surroundings**, position, situation, environment, background, backdrop, milieu, environs, habitat; spot, place, location, locale, site, scene; area, region, district. **2** *a garnet in a gold setting* **mount**, fixture, surround.

settle v. **1** *they settled the dispute* **resolve**, sort out, solve, clear up, end, fix, work out, iron out, straighten out, set right, rectify, remedy, reconcile; informal patch up. **2** *she settled their affairs* **put in order**, sort out, tidy up, arrange, organize, order, clear up. **3** *they settled on a date for the wedding* **decide on**, set, fix, agree on, name, establish, arrange, appoint, designate, assign; choose, select, pick. **4** *she went down to the lobby to settle her bill* **pay**, settle up, square, clear,

S

defray. **5** *they settled for a 4.2% pay rise* **accept**, agree to, assent to; formal accede to. **6** *he settled in London* **make one's home**, set up home, take up residence, put down roots, establish oneself; live, move to, emigrate to. **7** *immigrants settled much of Australia* **colonize**, occupy, inhabit, people, populate. **8** *Catherine settled down to her work* **apply oneself to**, get down to, set about, attack; concentrate on, focus on, devote oneself to. **9** *the class wouldn't settle down* **calm down**, quieten down, be quiet, be still; informal shut up. **10** *a brandy will settle your nerves* **calm**, quieten, quiet, soothe, pacify, quell; sedate, tranquillize. **11** *he settled into an armchair* **sit down**, seat oneself, install oneself, ensconce oneself, plant oneself; informal park oneself, plonk oneself. **12** *a butterfly settled on the flower* **land**, come to rest, alight, descend, perch; old use light. **13** *sediment settles at the bottom* **sink**, subside, fall, gravitate.
– OPPOSITES agitate, rise.

settlement n. **1** *a pay settlement* **agreement**, deal, arrangement, resolution, bargain, understanding, pact. **2** *the settlement of the dispute* **resolution**, settling, solution, reconciliation. **3** *a frontier settlement* **community**, colony, outpost, encampment, post; village, commune; historical plantation. **4** *the settlement of the area* **colonization**, settling, populating; historical plantation. **5** *the settlement of their debts* **payment**, discharge, defrayal, liquidation, clearance.

settler n. **colonist**, colonizer, frontiersman, frontierswoman, pioneer; immigrant, newcomer, incomer; N. Amer. historical homesteader.
– OPPOSITES native.

set-up n. **1** *a telecommunications set-up* **system**, structure, organization, arrangement, framework, layout, configuration. **2** informal *a set-up called Film International* **organization**, group, body, agency, association, operation; company, firm; informal outfit. **3** informal *the whole thing was a set-up* **trick**, trap; conspiracy; informal put-up job, frame-up.

seven cardinal number **septet**, septuplets.

WORD LINKS

septuple consisting of seven parts
heptagon a plane figure with seven sides
heptahedron a solid figure with seven faces
heptathlon a women's athletic event consisting of seven separate events
heptad a group or set of seven

---

sever v. **1** *the head was severed from the body* **cut off**, chop off, detach, disconnect, dissever, separate, part; amputate, dock; literary sunder. **2** *a knife had severed the artery* **cut (through)**, rupture, split, pierce. **3** *they severed diplomatic relations* **break off**, discontinue, suspend, end, terminate, cease, dissolve.
– OPPOSITES join, maintain.

several adj. **1** *several people* **some**, a number of, a few; various, assorted, sundry, diverse; literary divers. **2** *they sorted out their several responsibilities* **respective**, individual, own, particular, specific; separate, different, disparate, distinct; various.

severe adj. **1** *severe injuries* **acute**, very bad, serious, grave, critical, dreadful, terrible, awful; dangerous, parlous, life-threatening; formal grievous. **2** *severe storms* **fierce**, violent, strong, powerful, intense; tempestuous, turbulent. **3** *a severe winter* **harsh**, bitter, cold, bleak, freezing, icy, arctic, extreme. **4** *a severe headache* **excruciating**, agonizing, intense, dreadful, awful, terrible, unbearable, intolerable; informal splitting, pounding. **5** *a severe test of their stamina* **difficult**, demanding, tough, arduous, formidable, exacting, rigorous, punishing, onerous, gruelling. **6** *severe criticism* **harsh**, scathing, sharp, strong, fierce, savage, scorching, devastating, trenchant, caustic, biting, withering. **7** *severe tax penalties* **extortionate**, excessive, unreasonable, inordinate, outrageous, sky-high, harsh, stiff; punitive; Brit. swingeing. **8** *they received severe treatment* **harsh**, stern, hard, inflexible, uncompromising, unrelenting, merciless, pitiless, ruthless, draconian, oppressive, repressive, punitive; brutal, cruel, savage. **9** *his severe expression* **stern**, dour, grim, forbidding, disapproving, unsmiling, unfriendly, sombre, grave, serious, stony, steely; cold, frosty. **10** *a severe style of architecture* **plain**, simple, austere, unadorned, unembellished, unornamented, stark, spartan, ascetic; clinical, uncluttered.
– OPPOSITES minor, gentle, mild, easy, lenient, friendly, ornate.

severely adv. **1** *he was severely injured* **badly**, seriously, critically; fatally; formal grievously. **2** *she was severely criticized* **sharply**, roundly, soundly, fiercely, savagely. **3** *murderers should be treated more severely* **harshly**, strictly, sternly, rigorously, mercilessly, pitilessly, roughly, sharply; with a rod of iron; brutally, cruelly, savagely. **4** *she looked severely at Harriet* **sternly**, grimly, dourly, disapprovingly; coldly, frostily. **5** *she dressed severely in black* **plainly**, simply, austerely, starkly.

sew v. *she sewed the seams of the tunic* **stitch**, tack, baste, seam, hem; embroider.
▢ **sew something up 1** *the tear was sewn up* **darn**, mend, repair, patch. **2** informal *the company sewed up a deal with IBM* **secure**, clinch, pull off, bring off, settle, conclude, complete, finalize, tie up; informal swing.

sewing n. **stitching**, needlework, needlecraft, fancy-work.

sex n. **1** *they talked about sex* **sexual intercourse**, intercourse, lovemaking, making love, sex act, (sexual) relations; mating, copulation; informal nooky; Brit. informal rumpy pumpy, how's your father; formal fornication; technical coitus, coition; dated carnal knowledge. **2** *teach your children about sex* **the facts of life**, reproduction;

informal **the birds and the bees**. **3** *adults of both sexes* **gender**.

▢ **have sex** have sexual intercourse, make love, sleep with, go to bed; mate, copulate; seduce, rape; informal do it, go all the way, know in the biblical sense; Brit. informal bonk; N. Amer. informal get it on; euphemistic be intimate; literary ravish; formal fornicate.

sex appeal n. **sexiness**, seductiveness, sexual attractiveness, desirability, sensuality, sexuality; informal it, SA.

sexism n. **sexual discrimination**, chauvinism, prejudice, bias.

sexless adj. **asexual**, non-sexual, neuter; androgynous, epicene.

sexual adj. **1** *the sexual organs* **reproductive**, genital, sex, procreative. **2** *sexual activity* **carnal**, erotic; formal venereal; technical coital.

sexual intercourse n. See **sex** (sense 1).

sexuality n. **1** *she had a powerful sexuality* **sensuality**, sexiness, desirability, seductiveness, eroticism, physicality; sexual appetite, passion, desire, lust. **2** *I'm open about my sexuality* **sexual orientation**, sexual preference, leaning, persuasion; heterosexuality, homosexuality, lesbianism, bisexuality. **3** *sexuality within holy matrimony* **sexual activity**, sexual relations, sexual intercourse, sex, procreation.

sexy adj. **1** *she's so sexy* **sexually attractive**, seductive, desirable, alluring, sensual, sultry, slinky, provocative, tempting, tantalizing; nubile, voluptuous, luscious, lush; informal fanciable, beddable; Brit. informal fit; N. Amer. informal foxy, cute; Austral. informal spunky. **2** *sexy videos* **erotic**, sexually explicit, arousing, exciting, stimulating, hot, titillating, racy, naughty, risqué, adult, X-rated; rude, pornographic, crude, lewd; informal raunchy, steamy, porno, blue, skin. **3** *they weren't feeling sexy* **(sexually) aroused**, sexually excited, amorous, lustful, passionate; informal horny, hot, turned on, sexed up; Brit. informal randy. **4** informal *a sexy sales promotion* **exciting**, stimulating, interesting, appealing, intriguing.

shabby adj. **1** *a shabby little bar* **run down**, down at heel, scruffy, dilapidated, ramshackle, tumbledown; seedy, slummy, insalubrious, squalid, sordid; informal crummy, scuzzy, shambly; Brit. informal grotty; N. Amer. informal shacky. **2** *a shabby grey coat* **scruffy**, old, worn out, threadbare, ragged, frayed, tattered, battered, faded, moth-eaten, mangy; informal tatty, ratty, the worse for wear; N. Amer. informal raggedy. **3** *her shabby treatment of Ben* **contemptible**, despicable, dishonourable, discreditable, mean, low, dirty, hateful, shameful, sorry, ignoble, unfair, unworthy, unkind, shoddy, nasty; informal rotten, low-down; Brit. informal beastly.
– OPPOSITES smart, honourable.

shack n. **hut**, shanty, cabin, lean-to, shed; hovel; Scottish bothy, shieling.

▢ **shack up with** informal cohabit, live with; informal dated live in sin.

shackle v. **1** *he was shackled to the wall* **chain**, fetter, manacle; secure, tie (up), bind, tether, hobble; put in chains, clap in irons, handcuff. **2** *journalists were shackled by a new law* **restrain**, restrict, limit, constrain, handicap, hamstring, hamper, hinder, impede, obstruct, inhibit, check, curb.

shackles plural n. **1** *the men filed through their shackles* **chains**, fetters, irons, leg irons, manacles, handcuffs; bonds; informal cuffs, bracelets. **2** *the shackles of bureaucracy* **restrictions**, restraints, constraints, impediments, hindrances, obstacles, barriers, obstructions, checks, curbs; literary trammels.

shade n. **1** *they sat in the shade* **shadow(s)**, shadiness, shelter, cover; cool. **2** *shades of blue* **colour**, hue, tone, tint, tinge. **3** *shades of meaning* **nuance**, gradation, degree, difference, variation, variety; nicety, subtlety; undertone, overtone. **4** *her skirt was a shade too short* **a little**, a bit, a trace, a touch, a modicum, a tinge; slightly, rather, somewhat; informal a tad, a smidgen. **5** *the window shade* **blind**, curtain, screen, cover, covering; awning, canopy. **6** informal *he was wearing shades* **sunglasses**, dark glasses; Austral. informal sunnies.
– OPPOSITES light.

▸ v. **1** *vines shaded the garden* **cast a shadow over**, shadow, shade, shelter, cover, screen; darken. **2** *she shaded in the picture* **colour in**, pencil in, block in, fill in, darken; cross-hatch. **3** *the sky shaded from turquoise to blue* **change**, transmute, turn, go; merge, blend.

▢ **put someone/something in the shade** surpass, outshine, outclass, overshadow, eclipse, transcend, cap, top, outstrip, outdo, put to shame, beat, outperform, upstage; informal run rings around, be a cut above, leave standing.

shades of echoes of, a reminder of, memories of, suggestions of, hints of.

shadow n. **1** *he saw her shadow in the doorway* **silhouette**, outline, shape, contour, profile. **2** *he emerged from the shadows* **shade**, darkness, twilight; gloom, murkiness; old use umbrage. **3** *the shadow of war* **(black) cloud**, pall; gloom, blight; threat. **4** *she knew without any shadow of doubt* **trace**, scrap, shred, crumb, iota, scintilla, jot, whit, grain; informal smidgen, smidge, tad. **5** *a shadow of a smile* **trace**, hint, suggestion, suspicion, ghost, glimmer. **6** *he's a shadow of his former self* **inferior version**, poor imitation, apology, travesty; remnant. **7** *the dog became her shadow* **constant companion**, alter ego, second self; close friend, bosom friend, fidus Achates; informal Siamese twin.

▸ v. **1** *the market is shadowed by the church* **overshadow**, shade; darken, dim. **2** *he is shadowing a poacher* **follow**, trail, track, stalk, pursue, hunt; informal tail, keep tabs on.

shadowy adj. **1** *a shadowy corridor* **dark**, dim, gloomy, murky, crepuscular, shady, shaded; literary tenebrous. **2** *a shadowy figure* **indistinct**, hazy, indefinite, vague, nebulous, ill-defined, faint, blurred, blurry, unclear, indistinguishable, unrecognizable; ghostly,

S

spectral, wraithlike.
– OPPOSITES bright, clear.

shady adj. **1** *a shady garden* **shaded**, shadowy, dim, dark; sheltered, screened, shrouded; leafy; literary bosky, tenebrous. **2** informal *shady deals* **suspicious**, suspect, questionable, dubious, doubtful, disreputable, untrustworthy, dishonest, dishonourable, devious, underhand, unscrupulous, irregular, unethical; N. Amer. snide; informal fishy, murky; Brit. informal dodgy; Austral./NZ informal shonky.
– OPPOSITES bright, honest.

shaft n. **1** *the shaft of a golf club* **pole**, shank, stick, rod, staff; handle, hilt, stem. **2** *the shaft of a feather* **quill**; Ornithology rachis. **3** *shafts of sunlight* **ray**, beam, gleam, streak, finger. **4** *he directs his shafts against her* **cutting remark**, barb, jibe, taunt; informal dig. **5** *a ventilation shaft* **mineshaft**, tunnel, passage, pit, adit, downcast, upcast; borehole, bore; duct, well, flue, vent.

shaggy adj. **hairy**, bushy, thick, woolly; tangled, tousled, unkempt, dishevelled, untidy, matted; formal hirsute.
– OPPOSITES sleek.

shake v. **1** *the whole building shook* **vibrate**, tremble, quiver, quake, shiver, shudder, judder, jiggle, wobble, rock, sway; convulse. **2** *she shook the bottle* **jiggle**, joggle, agitate; informal waggle. **3** *he shook his stick at them* **brandish**, wave, flourish, swing, wield; informal waggle. **4** *the look in his eyes really shook her* **upset**, distress, disturb, unsettle, disconcert, discompose, disquiet, unnerve, trouble, throw off balance, agitate, fluster; shock, alarm, frighten, scare, worry; informal rattle. **5** *this will shake their confidence* **weaken**, undermine, damage, impair, harm; reduce, diminish, decrease.
– OPPOSITES soothe, strengthen.

▸n. **1** *he gave his coat a shake* **jiggle**, joggle; informal waggle. **2** *a shake of his fist* **flourish**, brandish, wave. **3** *it gives me the shakes* **tremors**, delirium tremens; informal DTs, jitters, willies, heebie-jeebies, yips; Austral. informal Joe Blakes.

□ **no great shakes** informal not very good, unexceptional, unmemorable, forgettable, uninspired, uninteresting, indifferent, unimpressive, lacklustre; informal nothing to write home about, nothing special, not up to much.

shake someone off get away from, escape, elude, dodge, lose, leave behind, get rid of, give someone the slip, throw off the scent; Brit. informal get shot of.

shake something off recover from, get over; get rid of, free oneself from; Brit. informal get shot of; N. Amer. informal shuck off.

shake someone/something up 1 *the accident shook him up.* See **shake** (sense 4 of the verb). **2** *plans to shake up the legal profession* **reorganize**, restructure, revolutionize, alter, change, transform, reform, overhaul.

shake-up n. informal **reorganization**, restructuring, reshuffle, change, overhaul,

makeover; upheaval; N. Amer. informal shakedown.

shaky adj. **1** *shaky legs* **trembling**, shaking, tremulous, quivering, quivery, unsteady, wobbly, weak; tottering, tottery, teetering, doddery; informal trembly. **2** *I feel a bit shaky* **faint**, dizzy, light-headed, giddy; weak, wobbly, quivery, groggy, muzzy; informal trembly, woozy. **3** *a shaky table* **unsteady**, unstable, wobbly, precarious, rocky, rickety, ramshackle; Brit. informal wonky. **4** *the evidence is shaky* **unreliable**, untrustworthy, questionable, dubious, doubtful, tenuous, suspect, flimsy, weak, unsound, unsupported, unsubstantiated, unfounded; informal iffy; Brit. informal dodgy.
– OPPOSITES steady, stable, sound.

shallow adj. **superficial**, facile, simplistic, oversimplified; flimsy, insubstantial, lightweight, empty, trivial, trifling; surface, skin-deep; frivolous, foolish, silly.
– OPPOSITES profound.

sham n. **1** *his tenderness had been a sham* **pretence**, fake, act, fiction, simulation, fraud, feint, lie, counterfeit; humbug. **2** *the doctor was a sham* **charlatan**, fake, fraud, impostor, pretender; quack, mountebank; informal phoney.
▸adj. *sham togetherness* **fake**, pretended, feigned, simulated, false, faux, artificial, bogus, insincere, contrived, affected, make-believe, fictitious; imitation, mock, counterfeit, fraudulent; informal pretend, put-on, phoney, pseudo; Brit. informal cod.
– OPPOSITES genuine.
▸v. **1** *she shams indifference* **feign**, fake, pretend, put on, simulate, affect. **2** *was he ill or just shamming?* **pretend**, fake, dissemble; malinger; informal put it on; Brit. informal swing the lead.

shaman n. **witch doctor**, medicine man/woman, healer, kahuna.

shamble v. **shuffle**, drag one's feet, lumber, totter, dodder; hobble, limp.

shambles plural n. **1** *we have to sort out this shambles* **chaos**, mess, muddle, confusion, disorder, havoc, mare's nest; Brit. informal dog's dinner/breakfast. **2** *the room was a shambles* **mess**, pigsty; informal disaster area; Brit. informal tip.

shambolic adj. Brit. informal See **chaotic**.

shame n. **1** *her face was scarlet with shame* **humiliation**, mortification, chagrin, ignominy, embarrassment, indignity, abashment, discomfort. **2** *I felt shame at telling a lie* **guilt**, remorse, contrition, compunction. **3** *he brought shame on the family* **disgrace**, dishonour, discredit, degradation, ignominy, disrepute, infamy, scandal, opprobrium, contempt; dated disesteem. **4** *it's a shame she never married* **pity**, misfortune, sad thing; bad luck; informal bummer, crime, sin.
– OPPOSITES pride, honour.
▸v. **1** *you shamed your family's name* **disgrace**, dishonour, discredit, degrade, debase; stigmatize, taint, sully, tarnish, besmirch,

blacken, drag through the mud. **2** *he was shamed in public* **humiliate**, mortify, chagrin, embarrass, abash, chasten, humble, take down a peg or two, cut down to size; informal show up; N. Amer. informal make someone eat crow.
– OPPOSITES honour.
□ **put someone/something to shame** outshine, outclass, eclipse, surpass, excel, outstrip, outdo, put in the shade, upstage; informal run rings around, leave standing; Brit. informal knock spots off.

shamefaced adj. **ashamed**, abashed, sheepish, guilty, conscience-stricken, guilt-ridden, contrite, sorry, remorseful, repentant, penitent, regretful, rueful, apologetic; embarrassed, mortified, red-faced, chagrined, humiliated; informal with one's tail between one's legs.
– OPPOSITES unrepentant.

shameful adj. **1** *shameful behaviour* **disgraceful**, deplorable, despicable, contemptible, dishonourable, discreditable, reprehensible, low, unworthy, ignoble, shabby; shocking, scandalous, outrageous, abominable, atrocious, appalling, vile, odious, heinous, egregious, loathsome, bad; inexcusable, unforgivable; informal low-down, hateful. **2** *a shameful secret* **embarrassing**, mortifying, humiliating, degrading, ignominious.
– OPPOSITES admirable.

shameless adj. **flagrant**, blatant, barefaced, overt, brazen, brash, audacious, outrageous, undisguised, unconcealed, transparent; immodest, indecorous; unabashed, unashamed, unblushing, unrepentant.
– OPPOSITES modest.

shanty n. **shack**, hut, cabin, lean-to, shed; hovel; Scottish bothy, shieling.

shape n. **1** *the shape of the dining table* **form**, appearance, configuration, formation, structure; figure, build, physique, body; contours, lines, outline, silhouette, profile. **2** *a spirit in the shape of a fox* **guise**, likeness, semblance, form, appearance, image. **3** *you're in pretty good shape* **condition**, health, trim, fettle, order; Brit. informal nick.
▶ v. **1** *the metal is shaped into tools* **form**, fashion, make, mould, model, cast; sculpt, sculpture, carve, cut, whittle. **2** *attitudes were shaped by his report* **determine**, form, fashion, mould, define, develop; influence, affect.
□ **shape up** *her work is shaping up nicely* **improve**, get better, progress, show promise; develop, take shape, come on, come along. **2** *a regime to help you shape up* **get fit**, get into shape, tone up; slim, lose weight.
take shape become clear, become definite, become tangible, crystallize, come together, fall into place.

shapeless adj. **1** *shapeless lumps* **formless**, amorphous, unformed, indefinite. **2** *a shapeless jumper* **baggy**, saggy, ill-fitting, sack-like, oversized, boyfriend, unshapely, formless.

shapely adj. **well proportioned**, clean-limbed, curvaceous, voluptuous, full-figured, Junoesque; attractive, sexy; informal curvy; old use comely.

shard n. **fragment**, sliver, splinter, shiver, chip, piece, bit, particle.

share n. *her share of the profits* **portion**, part, division, quota, quantum, allowance, ration, allocation, measure, due; percentage, commission, dividend; helping, serving; informal cut, slice, rake-off; Brit. informal whack, divvy.
▶ v. **1** *we share the bills* **split**, divide, go halves on; informal go fifty-fifty, go Dutch. **2** *they shared out the peanuts* **apportion**, divide up, allocate, portion out, ration out, parcel out, measure out; carve up; Brit. informal divvy up. **3** *we all share in the learning process* **participate in**, take part in, play a part in, be involved in, contribute to, have a hand in, partake in.

sharp adj. **1** *a sharp knife* **keen**, razor-edged; sharpened, honed. **2** *a sharp pain* **excruciating**, agonizing, intense, stabbing, shooting, severe, acute, keen, fierce, searing; exquisite. **3** *a sharp taste* **tangy**, piquant, strong; **acidic**, acid, sour, tart, pungent, acrid, bitter, acidulous. **4** *a sharp cry of pain* **loud**, piercing, shrill, high-pitched, penetrating, harsh, strident, ear-splitting, deafening. **5** *a sharp wind* **cold**, chilly, chill, brisk, keen, penetrating, biting, icy, bitter, freezing, raw; informal nippy; Brit. informal parky. **6** *sharp words* **harsh**, bitter, cutting, scathing, caustic, barbed, trenchant, acrimonious, acerbic, sarcastic, sardonic, spiteful, venomous, malicious, vitriolic, vicious, hurtful, nasty, cruel, abrasive; informal bitchy, catty. **7** *a sharp sense of loss* **intense**, acute, keen, strong, bitter, fierce, heartfelt, overwhelming. **8** *her nose is sharp* **pointed**, tapering, tapered; spiky; informal pointy. **9** *the lens brings it into sharp focus* **distinct**, clear, crisp; stark, obvious, marked, definite, pronounced. **10** *a sharp increase* **sudden**, abrupt, rapid; steep, precipitous. **11** *a sharp corner* **hairpin**, tight. **12** *a sharp drop* **steep**, sheer, abrupt, precipitous, vertical. **13** *sharp eyes* **keen**, perceptive, observant, acute, beady, hawklike. **14** *she was sharp and witty* **perceptive**, percipient, perspicacious, incisive, sensitive, keen, acute, quick-witted, clever, shrewd, canny, astute, intelligent, intuitive, bright, alert, smart, quick off the mark, insightful, knowing; informal on the ball, quick on the uptake, savvy; Brit. informal suss; Scottish & N. English informal pawky; N. Amer. informal heads-up. **15** informal *a sharp suit* **smart**, stylish, fashionable, chic, modish, elegant; informal trendy, cool, snazzy, classy, flash, snappy, natty, nifty; N. Amer. informal fly, spiffy.
– OPPOSITES blunt, mild, sweet, soft, kind, rounded, indistinct, gradual, slow, weak, stupid, naive, untidy.
▶ adv. **1** *nine o'clock sharp* **precisely**, exactly, on the dot; promptly, prompt, punctually, dead on; informal on the nose; N. Amer. informal on the button. **2** *the recession pulled people up sharp*

S

abruptly, suddenly, sharply, unexpectedly.
– OPPOSITES roughly.

sharpen v. 1 *sharpen the carving knife* **hone**, whet, strop, grind, file. 2 *the players are sharpening up their skills* **improve**, brush up, polish up, better, enhance; hone, fine-tune, perfect.

sharp-eyed adj. **observant**, perceptive, eagle-eyed, hawk-eyed, keen-eyed, gimlet-eyed; watchful, vigilant, alert, on the lookout; informal beady-eyed.

shatter v. 1 *the glasses shattered* **smash**, break, splinter, crack, fracture, fragment, disintegrate; informal bust. 2 *the announcement shattered their hopes* **destroy**, wreck, ruin, dash, crush, devastate, demolish, torpedo, scotch; informal put the kibosh on, banjax, do for, put paid to; Brit. informal scupper. 3 *we were shattered by the news* **devastate**, shock, stun, daze, traumatize, crush, distress; informal knock sideways; Brit. informal knock for six.

shattered adj. 1 *he was shattered by the reviews* **devastated**, shocked, shell-shocked, stunned, dazed, traumatized, crushed; heartbroken. 2 informal *I feel too shattered to move.* See **exhausted** (sense 1).
– OPPOSITES thrilled.

shave v. 1 *he shaved his beard* **cut off**, snip off; crop, trim, barber. 2 *shave off excess wood* **plane**, pare, whittle, scrape. 3 *shave Parmesan over the top* **grate**, shred. 4 *he shaved the MP's majority to 2,000* **reduce**, cut, lessen, decrease, pare down, shrink, slim down. 5 *his shot shaved the post* **graze**, brush, touch, glance off, kiss.

sheaf n. **bundle**, bunch, stack, pile, heap, mass; Brit. informal wodge.

sheath n. 1 *put the sword in its sheath* **scabbard**, case. 2 *the wire has a plastic sheath* **covering**, cover, case, casing, envelope, sleeve, wrapper, capsule. 3 *a contraceptive sheath.* See **condom**.

shed[1] n. *the rabbit lives in the shed* **hut**, lean-to, outhouse, outbuilding; shack; potting shed, woodshed; Brit. lock-up.

shed[2] v. 1 *the trees shed their leaves* **drop**, scatter, spill. 2 *the caterpillar shed its skin* **slough off**, cast off, moult; technical exuviate. 3 *we shed our jackets* **take off**, remove, shrug off, discard, doff, climb out of, slip out of, divest oneself of; Brit. informal peel off. 4 *much blood has been shed* **spill**, discharge. 5 *the firm is to shed ten workers* **make redundant**, dismiss, let go, discharge, get rid of, discard; informal sack, fire. 6 *they must shed their illusions* **discard**, get rid of, dispose of, do away with, drop, abandon, jettison, scrap, cast aside, dump, reject, repudiate; informal ditch, junk, get shut of; Brit. informal get shot of. 7 *the moon shed a watery light* **cast**, radiate, diffuse, disperse, give out.
– OPPOSITES don, hire, keep.
□ **shed tears** weep, cry, sob; lament, grieve, mourn; Scottish greet; informal blub, blubber, boohoo.

sheen n. **shine**, lustre, gloss, patina, shininess, burnish, polish, shimmer, brilliance, radiance.

sheep n. ram, ewe, lamb, wether, tup; Austral. informal jumbuck, woolly.

WORD LINKS

ovine relating to sheep
bellwether the leading sheep of a flock
shearling a sheep that has been shorn once
shepherd a person who looks after sheep
lanolin a fatty substance found on sheep's
  fleeces, used to make ointments
mutton the flesh of mature sheep used as food
scrapie a disease of sheep which affects the
  central nervous system

---

sheepish adj. **embarrassed**, uncomfortable, hangdog, self-conscious; shamefaced, ashamed, abashed, mortified, chastened, remorseful, contrite, apologetic, rueful, regretful, penitent, repentant.

sheer[1] adj. 1 *the sheer audacity of the plan* **utter**, complete, absolute, total, pure, downright, out-and-out, arrant, thorough, thoroughgoing, patent, veritable, unmitigated, plain; Austral./NZ informal fair. 2 *a sheer drop* **precipitous**, steep, vertical, perpendicular, abrupt, bluff, sharp. 3 *a sheer dress* **diaphanous**, gauzy, filmy, floaty, gossamer, thin, translucent, transparent, see-through, insubstantial.
– OPPOSITES gradual, thick.

sheer[2] v. 1 *the boat sheered off along the coast* **swerve**, veer, slew, skew, swing, change course. 2 *her mind sheered away from his image* **turn away**, flinch, recoil, shy away; avoid.

sheet n. 1 *she changed the sheets* **bedlinen**, linen, bedclothes. 2 *a sheet of ice* **layer**, stratum, covering, blanket, coating, coat, film, skin. 3 *a sheet of glass* **pane**, panel, piece, plate; slab. 4 *she put a fresh sheet in the typewriter* **piece of paper**, leaf, page, folio. 5 *a sheet of water* **expanse**, area, stretch, sweep.

shelf n. 1 *the plant on the shelf* **ledge**, sill, bracket, rack; mantelpiece; shelving. 2 *the waters above the shelf* **sandbank**, sandbar, bank, bar, reef, shoal.
□ **on the shelf** unmarried, single, unattached; lonely, unloved, neglected.

shell n. 1 *a crab shell* **carapace**, exterior; armour; Zoology exoskeleton. 2 *peanut shells* **pod**, husk, hull, casing, case, covering, integument; N. Amer. shuck. 3 *shells passing overhead* **projectile**, bomb, explosive; grenade; bullet, cartridge. 4 *the metal shell of the car* **framework**, frame, chassis, skeleton; hull, exterior.
▶ v. 1 *they were shelling peas* **hull**, pod, husk; N. Amer. shuck. 2 *rebel artillery shelled the city* **bombard**, fire on, shoot at, attack, bomb, blitz, strafe.

WORD LINKS

crustacean an animal with a hard outer shell
mollusc an animal with a soft body, often with
  an external shell

S

> **bivalve** a mollusc with a hinged shell, such as an oyster or mussel
> **conchology** the scientific study of shells
> **scrimshaw** decorative work consisting of shells with carved designs

shellfish n. **crustacean**, bivalve, mollusc.

shelter n. **1** *the trees provide shelter for animals* **protection**, cover, screening, shade; safety, security, refuge, sanctuary, asylum. **2** *a shelter for abandoned cats* **sanctuary**, refuge, home, haven, safe house; harbour, port in a storm.
– OPPOSITES exposure.
▸v. **1** *the hut sheltered him from the wind* **protect**, shield, screen, cover, shade, save, safeguard, preserve, defend, cushion, guard, insulate. **2** *the anchorage where the convoy sheltered* **take shelter**, take refuge, seek sanctuary, take cover; informal hole up.
– OPPOSITES expose.

sheltered adj. **1** *a sheltered stretch of water* **protected**, screened, shielded, covered; shady; cosy. **2** *she led a sheltered life* **secluded**, cloistered, isolated, protected, withdrawn, sequestered, reclusive; secure, privileged, safe, quiet.

shelve v. **postpone**, put off, delay, defer, put back, reschedule, hold over/off, put to one side, suspend, stay, keep in abeyance, mothball; abandon, drop, give up, stop, cancel, jettison, axe; N. Amer. put over, table; informal put on ice, put on the back burner, ditch, dump, junk.

shepherd n. *he worked as a shepherd* shepherdess, herdsman, herder, sheepman.
▸v. *we shepherded them away* **usher**, steer, herd, lead, take, escort, guide, conduct, marshal, walk; show, see, chaperone.

shield n. **1** *he used his shield to fend off blows* Heraldry escutcheon; historical buckler, target; old use targe. **2** *a shield against dirt* **protection**, guard, defence, cover, screen, security, shelter, safeguard, protector.
▸v. *he shielded his eyes* **protect**, cover, screen, shade; save, safeguard, preserve, defend, secure, guard; cushion, insulate.
– OPPOSITES expose.

shift v. **1** *he shifted some chairs* **move**, carry, transfer, transport, convey, lug, haul, fetch, switch, relocate, reposition, rearrange; informal cart. **2** *she shifted her position* **change**, alter, adjust, vary; modify, revise, reverse, retract, do a U-turn on, row back on. **3** *the cargo has shifted* **move**, slide, slip, be displaced. **4** *the wind shifted* **veer**, alter, change, turn, swing round. **5** Brit. *this brush really shifts the dirt* **get rid of**, remove, get off, budge, lift, expunge.
– OPPOSITES keep.
▸n. **1** *the southward shift of people* **movement**, move, transference, transport, transposition, relocation. **2** *a shift in public opinion* **change**, alteration, adjustment, amendment, variation, modification, revision, reversal, retraction, U-turn, rowback; Brit. about-turn. **3** *they worked three shifts* **stint**, stretch, spell of work. **4** *the night shift went home*

workers, crew, gang, team, squad, patrol. □ **shift for oneself** cope, manage, survive, make it, fend for oneself, take care of oneself, make do, get by/along, scrape by/ along, muddle through; stand on one's own two feet; informal make out.

shiftless adj. **lazy**, idle, indolent, slothful, lethargic, lackadaisical; spiritless, apathetic, feckless, good-for-nothing, worthless; unambitious, unenterprising.

shifty adj. informal **devious**, evasive, slippery, duplicitous, false, deceitful, underhand, untrustworthy, dishonest, shady, wily, crafty, tricky, sneaky, sly, treacherous, artful, scheming; N. Amer. snide; Brit. informal dodgy; Austral./NZ informal shonky.
– OPPOSITES honest.

shilly-shally v. **dither**, be indecisive, be irresolute, vacillate, waver, hesitate, blow hot and cold, falter, drag one's feet; Brit. haver, hum and haw; Scottish swither; informal dilly-dally.

shimmer v. *the lake shimmered* **glint**, glisten, twinkle, sparkle, flash, scintillate, gleam, glow, glimmer, glitter, wink; literary coruscate.
▸n. *the shimmer of lights from the traffic* **glint**, twinkle, sparkle, flash, gleam, glow, glimmer, lustre, glitter; literary coruscation.

shin v. **climb**, clamber, scramble, swarm, shoot, go; mount, ascend, scale; descend; N. Amer. shinny.

shine v. **1** *the sun shone* **emit light**, beam, radiate, gleam, glow, glint, glimmer, sparkle, twinkle, glitter, glisten, shimmer, flash, flare, glare, fluoresce, luminesce; literary glister, coruscate. **2** *she shone his shoes* **polish**, burnish, buff, wax, gloss, rub up. **3** *they shone at university* **excel**, be outstanding, be brilliant, be successful, stand out.
▸n. **1** *the shine of the moon on her face* **light**, brightness, gleam, glow, glint, glimmer, sparkle, twinkle, glitter, glisten, shimmer, beam, glare, radiance, illumination, luminescence, luminosity, incandescence. **2** *linseed oil restores the shine* **polish**, burnish, gleam, gloss, lustre, sheen, patina.

shining adj. **1** *a shining expanse of water* **gleaming**, bright, brilliant, illuminated, lustrous, glowing, glinting, sparkling, coruscating, twinkling, glittering, glistening, shimmering, dazzling, luminous, luminescent, incandescent; literary glistering, coruscating. **2** *a shining face* **glowing**, beaming, radiant, happy. **3** *shining chrome tubes* **shiny**, bright, polished, gleaming, glossy, glassy, sheeny, lustrous.

shiny adj. **glossy**, glassy, bright, polished, gleaming, satiny, sheeny, lustrous.
– OPPOSITES matt.

ship n. **boat**, vessel, craft.

> **WORD LINKS**
> **marine, maritime, nautical, naval** relating to ships or sailing
> **fleet, flotilla** a group of ships sailing together
> **port** the left-hand side of a ship, when one is facing forward
> **starboard** the right-hand side of a ship, when

S

one is facing forward

chandler a dealer in supplies and equipment for ships

stevedore a person employed to load and unload ships

dock, quay, wharf a place where ships may moor, load, and unload

bill of lading a full list of a ship's cargo

manifest a full list of a ship's contents, cargo, crew, and passengers

scupper, scuttle sink a ship deliberately

shipshape adj. **neat and tidy**, orderly, well ordered, in (good) order, well kept, spick and span, in apple-pie order, as neat as a new pin, immaculate, uncluttered, straight, trim, spruce; spotless, as fresh as paint; Brit. dated informal shipshape and Bristol fashion.
– OPPOSITES disorderly, untidy.

shirk v. **1** *she didn't shirk any task* **evade**, dodge, avoid, get out of, sidestep, shrink from, shun, slide out of, skip, miss; neglect; informal duck (out of), cop out of; Brit. informal skive off; N. Amer. informal cut; Austral./NZ informal duck-shove. **2** *no one shirked* **avoid one's duty**, be remiss, be negligent, play truant; Brit. informal skive (off), swing the lead, scrimshank, slack off; N. Amer. informal goof off, play hookey.

shirker n. **dodger**, truant, absentee, layabout, loafer, idler; informal slacker; Brit. informal skiver, scrimshanker; old use shirk.

shiver[1] v. *she was shivering with fear* **tremble**, quiver, shake, shudder, quaver, quake.
▸n. *she gave a shiver as the door opened* **tremble**, quiver, shake, shudder, quaver, quake, tremor, twitch.

shiver[2] n. *a shiver of glass* **splinter**, sliver, shard, fragment, chip, shaving, smithereen, particle, bit, piece.
▸v. *the window shivered into thousands of pieces* **shatter**, splinter, smash, fragment, crack, break.

shivery adj. **trembling**, trembly, quivery, shaky, shuddering, shuddery, quavery, quaking; cold, chilly.

shoal n. **sandbank**, bank, mudbank, bar, sandbar, tombolo, shelf, cay.

shock[1] n. **1** *the news came as a shock* **blow**, upset, disturbance; surprise, revelation, a bolt from the blue, thunderbolt, bombshell, rude awakening; informal eye-opener, whammy. **2** *you gave me a shock* **fright**, scare, jolt, start; informal turn. **3** *she was suffering from shock* **trauma**, traumatism, prostration; collapse, breakdown. **4** *the first shock of the earthquake* **vibration**, reverberation, shake, jolt, jar, jerk; impact, blow.
▸v. *the murder shocked the nation* **appal**, horrify, outrage, revolt, disgust, nauseate, sicken; traumatize, distress, upset, disturb, disquiet, unsettle; stun, rock, stagger, astound, astonish, amaze, startle, surprise, dumbfound, shake, take aback, throw, unnerve.

shock[2] n. *a shock of red hair* **mass**, mane, mop, thatch, head, crop, bush, frizz, tangle,

cascade, halo.

shocking adj. **appalling**, horrifying, horrific, dreadful, awful, frightful, terrible; scandalous, outrageous, disgraceful, vile, abominable, abhorrent, atrocious; odious, repugnant, disgusting, nauseating, sickening, loathsome; distressing, upsetting, disturbing, disquieting, unsettling; staggering, amazing, astonishing, startling, surprising.

shoddy adj. **1** *shoddy goods* **poor-quality**, inferior, second-rate, third-rate, cheap, cheapjack, trashy, jerry-built; informal tacky, rubbishy, junky; Brit. informal duff, rubbish. **2** *shoddy workmanship* **careless**, slapdash, sloppy, slipshod, scrappy, crude; negligent.
– OPPOSITES quality, careful.

shoemaker n. **cobbler**, bootmaker, clogger; Scottish & N. English souter.

shoot v. **1** *they shot him in the street* **gun down**, mow down, hit, wound, injure; pick off, bag, fell, kill; informal pot, blast, pump full of lead, plug. **2** *they shot at the enemy* **fire**, open fire, aim, snipe, let fly; bombard, shell. **3** *faster than a gun can shoot bullets* **discharge**, fire, launch, loose off, let fly, emit. **4** *a car shot past* **race**, speed, flash, dash, dart, rush, hurtle, streak, whizz, go like lightning, go hell for leather, zoom, charge; career, sweep, fly, wing; informal belt, scoot, scorch, tear, zip, whip, burn rubber; Brit. informal bomb, bucket, shift; N. Amer. informal clip, hightail it, barrel. **5** *the plant failed to shoot* **sprout**, bud, burgeon, germinate. **6** *the film was shot in Tunisia* **film**, photograph, take, snap, capture, record; televise, video.
▸n. *nip off the new shoots* **sprout**, bud, offshoot, scion, sucker, spear, runner, tendril, sprig.

shop n. **1** *a shop selling clothes* **store**, (retail) outlet, boutique, cash and carry, emporium, department store, supermarket, hypermarket, superstore, chain store, concession, market, mart, trading post; N. Amer. minimart. **2** *he works in the machine shop* **workshop**, workroom, plant, factory, works, industrial unit, mill, foundry, yard.
▸v. **1** *he was shopping for spices* **go shopping**; buy, purchase, get, stock up on; humorous indulge in retail therapy. **2** Brit. informal *he shopped his fellow robbers*. See **betray** (sense 1).

shopkeeper n. **shop-owner**, shop manager, vendor, retailer, dealer, seller, trader, wholesaler, salesperson, tradesman, distributor; N. Amer. storekeeper; Brit. informal flogger.

shopper n. **buyer**, purchaser, customer, consumer, client, patron; Law vendee.

shopping centre n. **shopping precinct**, (shopping) mall, (shopping) arcade, galleria, parade; marketplace, mart; N. Amer. plaza.

shore[1] n. *he swam out from the shore* **seashore**, beach, foreshore, sand(s), shoreline, waterside, front, coast, seaboard, littoral; literary strand.

shore[2] v. *we had to shore up the building* **prop up**, hold up, bolster, support, brace, buttress, strengthen, fortify, reinforce, underpin.

short adj. **1** *a short piece of string* **small**, little, tiny; informal teeny. **2** *short people* **small**, little, petite, tiny, diminutive, stubby, elfin, dwarfish, midget, pygmy, Lilliputian, minuscule, miniature; Scottish wee; informal pint-sized, teeny, knee-high to a grasshopper. **3** *a short report* **concise**, brief, succinct, compact, summary, economical, crisp, pithy, epigrammatic, laconic, thumbnail, abridged, abbreviated, condensed, synoptic, summarized, contracted, truncated; formal compendious. **4** *a short time* **brief**, momentary, temporary, short-lived, impermanent, cursory, fleeting, passing, fugitive, lightning, transitory, transient, ephemeral, quick. **5** *money is a bit short* **scarce**, in short supply, scant, meagre, sparse, insufficient, deficient, inadequate, lacking, wanting. **6** *he was rather short with her* **curt**, sharp, abrupt, blunt, brusque, terse, offhand, gruff, surly, testy, rude, uncivil; informal snappy.
– OPPOSITES long, tall, plentiful, courteous.
▸ adv. *she stopped short* **abruptly**, suddenly, sharply, all of a sudden, all at once, unexpectedly, without warning, out of the blue.
□ **in short** briefly, in a word, in a nutshell, in precis, in essence, to come to the point; in conclusion, in summary, to sum up.
short of 1 *we are short of nurses* **deficient in**, lacking, wanting, in need of, low on, short on, missing; informal strapped for, pushed for, minus. **2** *short of searching everyone, there is nothing we can do* **apart from**, other than, aside from, besides, except (for), excepting, without, excluding, not counting, save (for).

shortage n. **scarcity**, sparseness, sparsity, dearth, paucity, poverty, insufficiency, deficiency, inadequacy, famine, lack, want, deficit, shortfall, rarity.
– OPPOSITES abundance.

shortcoming n. **defect**, fault, flaw, imperfection, deficiency, limitation, failing, drawback, weakness, weak point, foible, frailty, vice.
– OPPOSITES strength.

shorten v. **make shorter**, abbreviate, abridge, condense, precis, synopsize, contract, compress, reduce, shrink, diminish, cut (down), dock, trim, crop, pare down, prune; curtail, truncate.
– OPPOSITES extend.

short-lived adj. **brief**, short, momentary, temporary, impermanent, cursory, fleeting, passing, fugitive, lightning, transitory, transient, ephemeral, quick.

shortly adv. **1** *she will be with you shortly* **soon**, presently, in a little while, at any moment, in a minute, in next to no time, before long, by and by; N. Amer. momentarily; informal anon, any time now, pretty soon, before one can say Jack Robinson, in a jiffy; Brit. informal in a mo, sharpish; dated directly.

2 *'I know,' he replied shortly* **curtly**, sharply, abruptly, bluntly, brusquely, tersely, gruffly, snappily, testily, rudely.

short-sighted adj. **1** *I'm a little short-sighted* **myopic**, nearsighted; informal as blind as a bat. **2** *short-sighted critics* **narrow-minded**, unimaginative, improvident, small-minded, insular, parochial, provincial.
– OPPOSITES long-sighted, imaginative.

short-staffed adj. **understaffed**, short-handed, undermanned, below strength.

short-tempered adj. **irritable**, irascible, hot-tempered, quick-tempered, snappish, fiery, touchy, volatile; cross, crabby, crotchety, cantankerous, grumpy, ill-tempered, bad-tempered, testy, tetchy, prickly, choleric; informal snappy, chippy, grouchy, cranky, on a short fuse; Brit. informal narky, ratty, eggy, like a bear with a sore head; N. Amer. informal soreheaded.
– OPPOSITES placid.

shot[1] n. **1** *a shot rang out* **report**, crack, bang, blast; (**shots**) gunfire. **2** *the cannon have run out of shot* **bullets**, cannonballs, pellets, ammunition. **3** *a winning shot* **stroke**, hit, strike; kick, throw, pitch, lob. **4** *Mike was an excellent shot* **marksman**, markswoman, shooter. **5** *a shot of us on holiday* **photograph**, photo, snap, snapshot, picture, print, slide, still; Brit. enprint. **6** informal *it's nice to get a shot at driving* **attempt**, try; turn, chance, opportunity; informal go, stab, crack, bash; formal essay. **7** *tetanus shots* **injection**, inoculation, immunization, vaccination, booster; informal jab.
□ **a shot in the arm** informal **boost**, fillip, tonic, stimulus, spur, impetus, encouragement.
a shot in the dark (wild) **guess**, surmise, supposition, conjecture, speculation.
like a shot informal **without hesitation**, unhesitatingly, eagerly, enthusiastically; immediately, at once, right away/now, straight away, instantly, instantaneously, without delay; informal in/like a flash, before one can say Jack Robinson.
not by a long shot by no (manner of) means, not at all, in no way, certainly not, absolutely not, definitely not; Brit. not by a long chalk.

shot[2] adj. *shot silk* **variegated**, mottled; multicoloured, varicoloured; iridescent, opalescent.

shoulder v. **1** *Britain shouldered the primary responsibility* **take on (oneself)**, undertake, accept, assume; bear, carry. **2** *another lad shouldered him aside* **push**, shove, thrust, jostle, force, bulldoze, bundle.
□ **give someone the cold shoulder** **snub**, shun, cold-shoulder, ignore, cut (dead), blank, rebuff, spurn, ostracize; informal give someone the brush-off, freeze out; Brit. informal send to Coventry.

shout v. *'Help,' he shouted* **yell**, cry (out), call (out), roar, howl, bellow, bawl, call at the top of one's voice, clamour, shriek, scream; raise

one's voice, vociferate; informal holler.
– OPPOSITES whisper.
▸ n. *a shout of pain* **yell**, cry, call, roar, howl, bellow, bawl, clamour, vociferation, shriek, scream; informal holler.

shove v. **1** *she shoved him back into the chair* **push**, thrust, propel, drive, force, ram, knock, elbow, shoulder; jostle, bundle, hustle, manhandle. **2** *she shoved past him* **push (one's way)**, force one's way, barge (one's way), elbow (one's way), shoulder one's way.
▸ n. *a hefty shove* **push**, thrust, bump, jolt.

shovel n. *a pick and shovel* **spade**; Austral./NZ banjo.
▸ v. *shovelling snow* **scoop (up)**, dig, excavate.

show v. **1** *the stitches do not show* **be visible**, be seen, be in view, be obvious. **2** *he wouldn't show the picture* **display**, exhibit, put on show/display, put on view, parade, uncover, reveal. **3** *Frank showed his frustration* **manifest**, exhibit, reveal, convey, communicate, make known; express, proclaim, make plain, make obvious, disclose, betray; formal evince. **4** *I'll show you how to make a daisy chain* **demonstrate**, explain, describe, illustrate; teach, instruct, give instructions. **5** *recent events show this to be true* **prove**, demonstrate, confirm, show beyond doubt; substantiate, corroborate, verify, establish, attest, certify, testify, bear out; formal evince. **6** *a young woman showed them to their seats* **escort**, accompany, take, conduct, lead, usher, guide, direct, steer, shepherd. **7** informal *they never showed* **appear**, arrive, come, get here/there, put in an appearance, materialize, turn up; informal show up.
– OPPOSITES conceal.
▸ n. **1** *a spectacular show of bluebells* **display**, array, exhibition, presentation, exposition, spectacle. **2** *the motor show* **exhibition**, exposition, fair, extravaganza, spectacle; N. Amer. exhibit. **3** *they took in a show* **(theatrical) performance**, musical, play. **4** *she's only doing it for show* **appearance**, display, impression, ostentation, image. **5** *Drew made a show of looking busy* **pretence**, outward appearance, (false) front, guise, semblance, pose, parade. **6** informal *I don't run the show* **undertaking**, affair, operation, proceedings, enterprise, business, venture.
□ **show off** informal behave affectedly, put on airs, put on an act, swagger around, swank, strut, strike an attitude, posture; draw attention to oneself; N. Amer. informal cop an attitude.
show something off display, show to advantage, exhibit, demonstrate, parade, draw attention to, flaunt.
show up 1 *cancers show up on X-rays* be visible, be obvious, be seen, be revealed. **2** informal *only two waitresses showed up*. See **show** (sense 7 of the verb).
show someone/something up 1 *the sun showed up the shabbiness of the room* expose, reveal, make visible, make obvious,

highlight. **2** informal *they showed him up in front of his friends*. See **humiliate**.

showdown n. **confrontation**, clash, face-off.

shower n. **1** *a shower of rain* **(light) fall**, drizzle, sprinkling, mizzle. **2** *a shower of arrows* **volley**, hail, salvo, bombardment, barrage, fusillade, cannonade. **3** *a shower of awards* **avalanche**, deluge, flood, spate, flurry; profusion, abundance, plethora.
▸ v. **1** *confetti showered down on us* **rain**, fall, hail. **2** *she showered them with gifts* **deluge**, flood, inundate, swamp, engulf; overwhelm, overload, snow under. **3** *showering honours on his cronies* **lavish**, heap, bestow freely.

showing n. **1** *another showing of the series* **presentation**, broadcast, airing, televising. **2** *the party's present showing* **performance**, (track) record, results, success, achievement.

showman n. **1** *a travelling showman* **impresario**, stage manager; ringmaster, host, compère, master of ceremonies, MC; presenter; N. Amer. informal emcee. **2** *he is a great showman* **entertainer**, performer, virtuoso; extrovert, self-publicist, show-off, attention-seeker.

show-off n. informal **exhibitionist**, extrovert, poser, poseur, peacock, swaggerer, self-publicist; informal pseud.

showy adj. **ostentatious**, conspicuous, pretentious, flamboyant, gaudy, garish, brash, vulgar, loud, extravagant, fancy, ornate, over-elaborate, kitsch; informal flash, flashy, bling, glitzy, ritzy, swanky; N. Amer. informal superfly.
– OPPOSITES restrained.

shred n. **1** *her dress was torn to shreds* **tatter**, scrap, strip, ribbon, rag, fragment, sliver, (tiny) bit/piece. **2** *not a shred of evidence* **scrap**, bit, speck, iota, particle, ounce, whit, jot, crumb, morsel, fragment, grain, drop, trace, scintilla, spot; informal smidgen.
▸ v. *shredding vegetables* **chop finely**, cut up, tear up, grate, mince, macerate, grind.

shrew n. **virago**, dragon, termagant, fishwife, witch, tartar, hag; informal battleaxe, old bag, old bat; old use scold.

shrewd adj. **astute**, sharp-witted, sharp, smart, acute, intelligent, clever, canny, perceptive, perspicacious, sagacious, wise; informal on the ball, savvy; N. Amer. informal heads-up; formal sapient.
– OPPOSITES stupid.

shrewdness n. **astuteness**, sharp-wittedness, acuteness, acumen, acuity, intelligence, cleverness, wit, canniness, common sense, discernment, insight, understanding, perception, perceptiveness, perspicacity, perspicaciousness, discrimination, sagacity, sageness; informal nous, horse sense, savvy; formal sapience.

shrewish adj. **bad-tempered**, quarrelsome, spiteful, sharp-tongued, scolding, nagging; venomous, rancorous.

shriek v. *she shrieked with laughter* **scream**, screech, squeal, squawk, roar, howl, shout, yelp; informal holler.

S

▸ n. *a shriek of laughter* **scream**, screech, squeal, squawk, roar, howl, shout, yelp; informal holler.

shrill adj. **high-pitched**, piercing, high, sharp, ear-piercing, ear-splitting, penetrating, screeching, shrieking, screechy.

shrine n. **1** *the shrine of St James* **holy place**, temple, church, chapel, tabernacle, sanctuary, sanctum. **2** *a shrine to the Beatles* **memorial**, monument.

shrink v. **1** *the number of competitors shrank* **get smaller**, become/grow smaller, contract, diminish, lessen, reduce, decrease, dwindle, decline, fall off, drop off. **2** *he shrank against the wall* **draw back**, recoil, back away, retreat, withdraw, cringe, cower, quail. **3** *he doesn't shrink from naming names* **recoil**, shy away, demur, flinch, have scruples, have misgivings, have qualms, be loath, be reluctant, be unwilling, be averse, fight shy of, be hesitant, be afraid, hesitate, balk at; old use disrelish something.
– OPPOSITES expand, increase.

shrivel v. **wither**, shrink; wilt; dry up, desiccate, dehydrate, parch, frazzle.

shroud n. **1** *the Turin Shroud* **winding sheet**; historical cerements. **2** *a shroud of mist | a shroud of secrecy* **covering**, cover, cloak, mantle, blanket, layer, cloud, veil.
▸ v. *a mist shrouded the jetties* **cover**, envelop, veil, cloak, blanket, screen, conceal, hide, mask, obscure; literary enshroud.

shrug v.
▫ **shrug something off** disregard, dismiss, take no notice of, ignore, pay no heed to, play down, make light of.

shudder v. *she shuddered at the thought* **shake**, shiver, tremble, quiver, vibrate, palpitate.
▸ n. *a shudder racked his body* **shake**, shiver, tremor, tremble, trembling, quiver, quivering, vibration, palpitation.

shuffle v. **1** *they shuffled along the passage* **shamble**, drag one's feet, totter, dodder. **2** *she shuffled her feet* **scrape**, drag, scuffle, scuff. **3** *he shuffled the cards* **mix (up)**, mingle, rearrange, jumble.

shun v. **avoid**, evade, eschew, steer clear of, shy away from, fight shy of, keep one's distance from, give a wide berth to, have nothing to do with; snub, give someone the cold shoulder, cold-shoulder, ignore, cut (dead), blank, look right through; reject, rebuff, spurn, ostracize; informal give someone the brush-off, freeze out, stiff-arm; Brit. informal send to Coventry; N. Amer. informal give someone the bum's rush.

shut v. *please shut the door* **close**, pull/push to, slam, fasten; put the lid on, bar, lock, secure.
– OPPOSITES open, unlock.
▫ **shut down** cease activity, close (down), cease operating, cease trading, be shut (down); informal fold, flatline.
shut someone/something in confine, enclose, impound, shut up, kettle, pen (in/ up), fence in, immure, lock up/in, cage,

imprison, intern, incarcerate; N. Amer. corral.
shut someone/something out 1 *he shut me out of the house* **lock out**, keep out, refuse entrance to. **2** *she shut out the memories* **block**, suppress. **3** *the bamboo shut out the light* **keep out**, block out, screen, veil.
shut up informal be quiet, keep quiet, hold one's tongue, keep one's lips sealed; stop talking, quieten (down); informal keep mum, button it, cut the cackle, shut it, shut your face/mouth/trap, belt up, put a sock in it, give it a rest; Brit. informal shut your gob; N. Amer. informal save it.
shut someone/something up 1 *I haven't shut the hens up yet.* See **shut someone/ something in**. **2** informal *that should shut them up* quieten (down), silence, hush, shush, quiet, gag, muzzle.

shuttle v. **ply**, run, commute, go/travel back and forth, go/travel to and fro; ferry.

shy[1] adj. *I was painfully shy* **bashful**, diffident, timid, sheepish, reserved, reticent, introverted, retiring, self-effacing, withdrawn, timorous, mousy, nervous, insecure, unconfident, inhibited, repressed, self-conscious, embarrassed.
– OPPOSITES confident.
▫ **shy away from** flinch, demur, recoil, hang back, have scruples, have misgivings, have qualms, be chary, be diffident, be bashful, fight shy, be coy; be loath, be reluctant, be unwilling, be disinclined, be hesitant, hesitate, balk at; informal boggle at; old use disrelish.

shy[2] v. dated *they began shying stones* **throw**, toss, fling, hurl, cast, lob, launch, pitch; informal chuck, heave, sling, bung.

shyness n. **bashfulness**, diffidence, sheepishness, reserve, reservedness, introversion, reticence, timidity, timidness, timorousness, mousiness, lack of confidence, inhibitedness, self-consciousness, embarrassment, coyness, demureness.

sibling n. brother, sister; Zoology sib.

sick adj. **1** *the children are sick* **ill**, unwell, poorly, ailing, indisposed, not oneself; Brit. off colour; informal laid up, under the weather; Austral./NZ informal crook. **2** *he was feeling sick* **nauseous**, nauseated, queasy, bilious, green about the gills; seasick, carsick, airsick, travel-sick; informal about to throw up. **3** informal *we're sick about the plans* **disappointed**, depressed, dejected, despondent, downcast, unhappy; angry, cross, annoyed, displeased, disgruntled; informal fed up; Brit. informal cheesed off. **4** *I'm sick of this music* **bored**, tired, weary; informal fed up. **5** informal *a sick joke* **macabre**, black, ghoulish, morbid, perverted, gruesome, sadistic, cruel.
– OPPOSITES well.
▫ **be sick** Brit. vomit, retch, heave, gag; informal throw up, chunder, chuck up, hurl, spew, keck; Brit. informal honk; N. Amer. informal spit up, barf, upchuck, toss one's cookies.

sicken v. **1** *the stench sickened him* **turn someone's stomach**, revolt, disgust; informal

S

make someone want to throw up; N. Amer. informal **gross out. 2** *she sickened and died* **become ill**, fall ill, be taken ill/sick, catch something. **3** *I'm sickening for something* **become ill with**, fall ill with, be taken ill with, show symptoms of, develop, come down with; Brit. go down with; N. Amer. informal take sick with.

sickening adj. **nauseating**, stomach-turning, stomach-churning, repulsive, revolting, disgusting, repellent, repugnant, appalling, obnoxious, nauseous, vile, nasty, foul, loathsome, offensive, objectionable, off-putting, distasteful, obscene, gruesome, grisly; N. Amer. **vomitous**; informal **gross**; formal **rebarbative**; old use **disgustful**.

sickly adj. **1** *a sickly child* **unhealthy**, in poor health, delicate, frail, weak. **2** *sickly faces* **pale**, wan, pasty, sallow, pallid, ashen, anaemic. **3** *a sickly green* **insipid**, pale, light, light-coloured, washed out, faded. **4** *sickly love songs* **sentimental**, mawkish, cloying, mushy, slushy, sugary, syrupy, saccharine; informal **schmaltzy**, weepy, lovey-dovey, corny; Brit. informal **soppy**; N. Amer. informal **cornball**, sappy, hokey, three-hankie.
– OPPOSITES healthy.

sickness n. **1** *she was absent through sickness* **illness**, disease, ailment, complaint, infection, malady, infirmity, indisposition; informal **bug**, virus; Brit. informal **lurgy**; Austral. informal **wog**. **2** *a wave of sickness* **nausea**, biliousness, queasiness. **3** *he suffered sickness and diarrhoea* **vomiting**, retching, gagging, travel-sickness, seasickness, carsickness, airsickness, motion sickness; informal **throwing up**, puking.

side n. **1** *the side of the road* **edge**, border, verge, boundary, margin, fringe(s), flank, bank, perimeter, extremity, periphery, (outer) limit, limits, bounds; literary **marge, bourn. 2** *the wrong side of the road* **half**, part; carriageway, lane. **3** *the east side of the city* **district**, quarter, area, region, part, neighbourhood, sector, section, zone, ward. **4** *one side of the paper* **surface**, face, plane. **5** *his side of the argument* **point of view**, viewpoint, perspective, opinion, way of thinking, standpoint, position, outlook, slant, angle. **6** *the losing side in the war* **faction**, camp, bloc, party, wing. **7** *the players in their side* **team**, squad, line-up. **8** Brit. informal *there's absolutely no side about her.* See **affectation** (sense 1).
– OPPOSITES centre, end.
▸adj. **1** *elaborate side pieces* **lateral**, wing, flanking. **2** *a side issue* **subordinate**, lesser, lower-level, secondary, minor, peripheral, incidental, ancillary, subsidiary, of little account, extraneous.
– OPPOSITES front, central.
▸v. *siding with the underdog.* See **take someone's side**.
▫ **side by side 1** *they cycled along side by side* **alongside (each other)**, beside each other, abreast, shoulder to shoulder, close together. **2** *most transactions proceed side by side* **at (one and) the same time**,

simultaneously, contemporaneously.
take someone's side support, take someone's part, side with, be on someone's side, stand by, back, give someone one's backing, be loyal to, defend, champion, ally (oneself) with, sympathize with, favour.

WORD LINKS

lateral relating to the side or sides

---

sideline n. *he founded the company as a sideline* **secondary occupation**, second job; hobby, leisure activity/pursuit, recreation.
▫ **on the sidelines** without taking part, without getting involved.

sidelong adj. *a sidelong glance* **indirect**, oblique, sideways, sideward; surreptitious, furtive, covert, sly.
– OPPOSITES overt.
▸adv. *he looked sidelong at her* **indirectly**, obliquely, sideways, out of the corner of one's eye; surreptitiously, furtively, covertly, slyly.

side-splitting adj. informal See **funny** (sense 1).

sidestep v. **avoid**, evade, dodge, circumvent, skirt round, bypass; informal **duck**.

sidetrack v. **distract**, divert, deflect, draw away.

sideways adv. **1** *I slid off sideways* **to the side**, laterally. **2** *the expansion slots are mounted sideways* **edgewise**, sidewards, side first, edgeways, end on. **3** *he looked sideways at her.* See **sidelong** (adverb).
▸adj. **1** *sideways force* **lateral**, sideward, on the side, side to side. **2** *a sideways look.* See **sidelong** (adjective).

sidle v. **creep**, sneak, slink, slip, slide, steal, edge, inch, move furtively.

siege n. **blockade**, encirclement; old use investment.

siesta n. **afternoon sleep**, nap, catnap, doze, rest; informal **snooze**, lie-down, forty winks; Brit. informal **kip**, zizz.

sieve n. *use a sieve to strain the mixture* **strainer**, sifter, filter, riddle, screen.
▸v. **1** *sieve the mixture into a bowl* **strain**, sift, screen, filter, riddle; old use **bolt. 2** *the coins were sieved from the ash* **separate out**, filter out, sift, sort out, divide, segregate, extract.

sift v. **1** *sift the flour into a large bowl* **sieve**, strain, screen, filter, riddle; old use **bolt. 2** *we sift out unsuitable applications* **separate out**, filter out, sort out, put to one side, weed out, get rid of, remove. **3** *investigators are sifting through the wreckage* **search through**, look through, examine, inspect, scrutinize, pore over, investigate, analyse, dissect, review.

sigh v. **1** *she sighed with relief* **breathe out**, exhale; groan, moan. **2** *the wind sighed in the trees* **rustle**, whisper, murmur, sough. **3** *he sighed for days gone by* **yearn**, long, pine, ache, grieve, cry for/over, weep for/over, rue, miss, mourn, lament, hanker for/after.

sight n. **1** *she has excellent sight* **eyesight**, vision, eyes, faculty of sight, visual perception. **2** *her first sight of it* **view**, glimpse, glance, look. **3** *within sight of the* enemy **range of vision**, field of vision, view. **4** dated *we are all equal in the sight of God* **perception**, judgement, belief, opinion, point of view, view, viewpoint, mind, perspective, standpoint. **5** *historic sights* **landmark**, place of interest, monument, spectacle, view, marvel, wonder. **6** informal *I must look a sight* **eyesore**, spectacle, mess; informal fright.

▶ v. *one of the helicopters sighted wreckage* **glimpse**, catch/get a glimpse of, catch sight of, see, spot, spy, notice, observe; literary espy, descry.

□ **catch sight of** glimpse, catch/get a glimpse of, see, spot, spy, make out, pick out, sight, have sight of; literary espy, descry.

set one's sights on aspire to, aim at/for, try for, strive for/towards, work towards.

> WORD LINKS
>
> **optic**, **optical**, **visual** relating to sight or vision
> **optometry** the occupation of measuring eyesight
> **myopia** short-sightedness
> **presbyopia** long-sightedness
> **nyctalopia** abnormal inability to see in very dim light

sightseer n. **1** *sightseers to the city* **tourist**, visitor, tripper, holidaymaker; Brit. informal grockle. **2** *gawping sightseers* **busybody**, gawker; informal rubberneck; Brit. informal gawper.

sign n. **1** *a sign of affection* **indication**, signal, symptom, pointer, suggestion, intimation, mark, manifestation, demonstration, token, evidence. **2** *a sign of things to come* **portent**, omen, warning, forewarning, augury, presage; promise, threat. **3** *at his sign the soldiers followed* **gesture**, signal, wave, gesticulation, cue, nod. **4** *signs saying 'keep out'* **notice**, signpost, signboard, warning sign, road sign, traffic sign. **5** *the dancers were daubed with signs* **symbol**, mark, cipher, letter, character, figure, hieroglyph, ideogram, rune, sigil, emblem, device, logo.

▶ v. **1** *he signed the letter* **write one's name on**, autograph, endorse, initial, countersign; formal subscribe. **2** *the government signed the agreement* **endorse**, validate, certify, authenticate, sanction, authorize; agree to, approve, ratify, adopt; informal give something the go-ahead, give something the green light, give something the thumbs up. **3** *he signed his name* **write**, inscribe, pen. **4** *we have signed a new player* **recruit**, hire, engage, employ, take on, appoint, sign on/up, enlist. **5** *she signed to Susan to leave* **gesture**, signal, give a sign to, motion; wave, beckon, nod.

□ **sign on/up** enlist, take a job, join (up), enrol, register, volunteer.

sign someone on/up See **sign** (sense 4 of the verb).

sign something over transfer, make over, hand over, bequeath, pass on, transmit, cede; Law devolve, convey.

signal¹ n. **1** *a signal to stop* **gesture**, sign, wave, gesticulation, cue, indication, warning, motion. **2** *a clear signal that the company is*

in trouble **indication**, sign, symptom, hint, pointer, intimation, clue, demonstration, evidence, proof. **3** *the encroaching dark is a signal for people to emerge* **cue**, prompt, impetus, stimulus; informal go-ahead.

▶ v. **1** *the driver signalled to her to cross* **gesture**, sign, give a sign to, direct, motion; wave, beckon, nod. **2** *they signalled displeasure by refusing to cooperate* **indicate**, show, express, communicate, proclaim, declare. **3** *his death signals the end of an era* **mark**, signify, mean, be a sign of, be evidence of, herald; literary betoken, foretoken.

signal² adj. *a signal failure* **notable**, noteworthy, remarkable, striking, glaring, significant, momentous, memorable, unforgettable, obvious, special, extraordinary, exceptional, conspicuous.

significance n. **1** *a matter of considerable significance* **importance**, import, consequence, seriousness, gravity, weight, magnitude, momentousness; formal moment. **2** *the significance of his remarks* **meaning**, sense, signification, import, thrust, drift, gist, implication, message, essence, substance, point.

significant adj. **1** *a significant increase* **notable**, noteworthy, worthy of attention, remarkable, important, of importance, of consequence; serious, crucial, weighty, momentous, uncommon, unusual, rare, extraordinary, exceptional, special; formal of moment. **2** *a significant look* **meaningful**, expressive, eloquent, suggestive, knowing, telling.

significantly adv. **1** *results are significantly better* **notably**, remarkably, outstandingly, importantly, crucially, materially, appreciably; markedly, considerably, obviously, conspicuously, strikingly, signally. **2** *he paused significantly* **meaningfully**, expressively, eloquently, revealingly, suggestively, knowingly.

signify v. **1** *this signified a fundamental change* **be evidence of**, be a sign of, mark, signal, mean, spell, be symptomatic of, herald, indicate; literary betoken. **2** *the egg signifies life* **mean**, denote, designate, represent, symbolize, stand for; literary betoken. **3** *signify your agreement by signing below* **express**, indicate, show, proclaim, declare. **4** *the locked door doesn't signify* **mean anything**, be of importance, be important, be significant, be of significance, be of account, count, matter, be relevant.

silence n. **1** *the silence of the night* **quietness**, quiet, quietude, still, stillness, hush, tranquillity, noiselessness, soundlessness, peacefulness, peace (and quiet). **2** *she was reduced to silence* **speechlessness**, wordlessness, dumbness, muteness, taciturnity. **3** *the politicians continue to keep their silence* **secretiveness**, secrecy, reticence, taciturnity, uncommunicativeness.
– OPPOSITES sound.

▶ v. **1** *he silenced her with a kiss* **quieten**, quiet, hush, shush; gag, muzzle, censor. **2** *silencing* outside noises **muffle**, deaden, soften, mute, smother, dampen, damp down, mask, suppress, reduce. **3** *this would silence their complaints* **stop**, put an end to, put a stop to.

silent adj. **1** *the night was silent* **completely quiet**, still, hushed, inaudible, noiseless, soundless. **2** *the right to remain silent* **speechless**, quiet, unspeaking, dumb, mute, taciturn, uncommunicative, tight-lipped; informal mum. **3** *silent thanks* **unspoken**, wordless, unsaid, unexpressed, unvoiced, tacit, implicit, understood.
– OPPOSITES audible, noisy.

silently adv. **1** *Nancy crept silently up the stairs* **quietly**, inaudibly, noiselessly, soundlessly, in silence. **2** *they drove on silently* **without a word**, saying nothing, in silence. **3** *I silently said goodbye* **without words**, wordlessly, in one's head, tacitly, implicitly.
– OPPOSITES audibly, out loud.

silhouette n. *the silhouette of the dome* **outline**, contour(s), profile, form, shape, figure, shadow.
▶ v. *the castle was silhouetted against the sky* **outline**, delineate, define; stand out.

silky adj. **smooth**, soft, sleek, fine, glossy, satiny, silken.

silly adj. **1** *don't be so silly* **foolish**, stupid, unintelligent, idiotic, brainless, mindless, witless, imbecilic, doltish; imprudent, thoughtless, rash, reckless, foolhardy, irresponsible; mad, feather-brained, scatterbrained; frivolous, giddy, inane, immature, childish, puerile, empty-headed; informal crazy, dotty, scatty, loopy, screwy, thick, thickheaded, birdbrained, pea-brained, dopey, dim, dim-witted, half-witted, dippy, blockheaded, boneheaded, lamebrained; Brit. informal daft, divvy; N. Amer. informal chowderheaded; dated tomfool. **2** *that was a silly thing to do* **unwise**, imprudent, thoughtless, foolish, stupid, idiotic, senseless, mindless; rash, reckless, foolhardy, irresponsible, injudicious, misguided, irrational; informal crazy; Brit. informal daft. **3** *he would brood about silly things* **trivial**, trifling, frivolous, footling, petty, small, insignificant, unimportant; informal piffling, piddling; N. Amer. informal small-bore. **4** *he drank himself silly* **senseless**, insensible, unconscious, stupid, into a stupor.
– OPPOSITES sensible.

silt n. *the flooding brought more silt* **sediment**, deposit, alluvium, mud.
▶ v. *the harbour had silted up* **become blocked**, become clogged, fill up (with silt).

silver n. **1** *freshly polished silver* **silverware**, (silver) plate; cutlery. **2** *a handful of silver* **coins**, coinage, specie; (small) change, loose change. **3** *she won three silvers* **silver medal**, second prize.
▶ adj. **1** *silver hair* **grey**, greyish, white. **2** *the silver water* **silvery**, shining, lustrous, gleaming; literary argent.

similar adj. **1** *you two are very similar* **alike**, (much) the same, indistinguishable, almost

identical, homogeneous; informal much of a muchness. **2** *northern India and similar areas* **comparable**, like, corresponding, homogeneous, equivalent, analogous. **3** *other parts were similar to Wales* **like**, much the same as, comparable to.
– OPPOSITES different, unlike.
□ **be similar to** resemble, look like, have the appearance of.

similarity n. **resemblance**, likeness, sameness, similitude, comparability, correspondence, parallel, equivalence, homogeneity, indistinguishability, uniformity; old use semblance.

similarly adv. **likewise**, in similar fashion, in like manner, comparably, correspondingly, uniformly, indistinguishably, analogously, homogeneously, equivalently, in the same way, the same, identically.

similitude n. See **similarity**.

simmer v. **1** *the soup was simmering on the stove* **boil gently**, cook gently, bubble. **2** *she was simmering with resentment* **be furious**, be enraged, be angry, be incensed, be infuriated, seethe, fume, smoulder; informal be steamed up, be hot under the collar.
□ **simmer down** become less angry, cool off/down, be placated, control oneself, become calmer, calm down, become quieter, quieten down.

simper v. **smile affectedly**, smile coquettishly, look coy.

simple adj. **1** *it's really pretty simple* **straightforward**, easy, uncomplicated, uninvolved, effortless, painless, undemanding, elementary, child's play; informal as easy as falling off a log, as easy as pie, as easy as ABC, a piece of cake, a cinch, no sweat, a doddle, a pushover, money for old rope, kids' stuff, a breeze, a walk in the park; Brit. informal easy-peasy, a doss; N. Amer. informal duck soup, a snap; Austral./NZ informal a bludge, a snack. **2** *simple language* **clear**, plain, straightforward, intelligible, comprehensible, uncomplicated, in words of one syllable, accessible; informal user-friendly. **3** *a simple white blouse* **plain**, unadorned, undecorated, unembellished, unornamented, basic, unsophisticated, no-frills; classic, understated, uncluttered, restrained. **4** *the simple truth* **candid**, frank, honest, sincere, plain, absolute, unqualified, bald, stark, unadorned, unvarnished, unembellished. **5** *simple country people* **unpretentious**, unsophisticated, ordinary, unaffected, unassuming, natural, honest-to-goodness; N. Amer. cracker-barrel. **6** *simple chemical substances* **non-compound**, non-complex, uncombined, unblended, unalloyed, pure, single. **7** *he's a bit simple* **of low intelligence**, simple-minded, unintelligent, backward.
– OPPOSITES difficult, complex, fancy, compound.

simpleton n. See **fool** (sense 1 of the noun).

simplicity n. **1** *the simplicity of the recipes* **straightforwardness**, ease, easiness, simpleness, effortlessness. **2** *the simplicity of the language* **clarity**, clearness, plainness, simpleness, intelligibility, comprehensibility, understandability, straightforwardness, accessibility. **3** *the building's simplicity* **plainness**, lack/absence of adornment, lack/absence of decoration, austerity, spareness, clean lines. **4** *the simplicity of their lifestyle* **unpretentiousness**, ordinariness, lack of sophistication, lack of affectation, naturalness.

simplify v. **make simple/simpler**, make easy/easier to understand, make plainer, clarify, make more comprehensible/intelligible; paraphrase, put in words of one syllable.
– OPPOSITES complicate.

simplistic adj. **facile**, superficial, oversimple, oversimplified; shallow, jejune, naive; N. Amer. informal dime-store.

simply adv. **1** *he spoke simply and forcefully* **straightforwardly**, directly, clearly, plainly, intelligibly, lucidly, unambiguously. **2** *she was dressed simply* **plainly**, without adornment, without decoration, without ornament/ornamentation, soberly, unfussily, classically. **3** *they lived simply* **unpretentiously**, modestly, quietly. **4** *they are welcomed simply because they have plenty of money* **merely**, just, purely, solely, only. **5** *Mrs Marks was simply livid* **utterly**, absolutely, completely, positively, really; informal plain. **6** *it's simply the best thing ever written* **without doubt**, unquestionably, undeniably, incontrovertibly, certainly, categorically.

simulate v. **1** *they simulated pleasure* **feign**, pretend, fake, sham, affect, put on, give the appearance of. **2** *simulating conditions in space* **imitate**, reproduce, replicate, duplicate, mimic.

simulated adj. **1** *simulated fear* **feigned**, fake, mock, affected, sham, insincere, false, bogus; informal pretend, put-on, phoney. **2** *simulated leather* **artificial**, imitation, fake, faux, mock, synthetic, man-made, ersatz.
– OPPOSITES real.

simultaneous adj. **concurrent**, contemporaneous, happening at the same time, concomitant, coinciding, coincident, synchronous, synchronized.

simultaneously adv. **at (one and) the same time**, at the same instant/moment, at once, concurrently, concomitantly; (all) together, in unison, in concert, in chorus.

sin n. **1** *a sin in the eyes of God* **immoral act**, wrong, wrongdoing, act of evil/wickedness, transgression, crime, offence, misdeed, misdemeanour; old use trespass. **2** *the human capacity for sin* **wickedness**, wrongdoing, wrong, evil, evildoing, sinfulness, immorality, iniquity, vice, crime. **3** informal *wasting money—it's a sin* **scandal**, crime, disgrace, outrage.
– OPPOSITES virtue.
▶ v. *I have sinned* **commit a sin**, commit an

offence, transgress, do wrong, commit a crime, break the law, misbehave, go astray; old use trespass.

sincere adj. **1** *our sincere gratitude* **heartfelt**, wholehearted, profound, deep; genuine, real, unfeigned, unaffected, true, honest, bona fide. **2** *a sincere person* **honest**, genuine, truthful, straightforward, direct, frank, candid; informal straight, upfront, on the level; N. Amer. informal on the up and up.
– OPPOSITES hypocritical, devious.

sincerely adv. **genuinely**, honestly, really, truly, truthfully, wholeheartedly, earnestly, fervently.

sincerity n. **honesty**, genuineness, truthfulness, integrity, probity, trustworthiness; straightforwardness, openness, candour, candidness.

sinecure n. **easy job**, soft option; informal cushy number, money for old rope, picnic, doddle, cinch; Austral. informal bludge.

sinewy adj. **muscular**, muscly, brawny, powerfully built, burly, strapping, sturdy, rugged, strong, powerful, athletic, muscle-bound; informal hunky, beefy; dated stalwart; literary thewy.
– OPPOSITES puny.

sinful adj. **1** *sinful conduct* **immoral**, wicked, (morally) wrong, wrongful, evil, bad, iniquitous, corrupt, criminal, nefarious, depraved, degenerate; rare peccable. **2** *a sinful waste of money* **reprehensible**, scandalous, disgraceful, deplorable, shameful, criminal.
– OPPOSITES virtuous.

sinfulness n. **immorality**, wickedness, sin, wrongdoing, evil, evildoing, iniquitousness, corruption, depravity, degeneracy, vice; formal turpitude; rare peccability.
– OPPOSITES virtue.

sing v. **1** *Miguelito began to sing* **croon**, carol, trill, troll, chant, intone, chorus. **2** *the birds were singing* **warble**, trill, chirp, chirrup, cheep, peep. **3** *he sang out a greeting* **call (out)**, cry (out), shout, yell; informal holler.

singe v. **scorch**, burn, sear, char.

singer n. **vocalist**, soloist, songster, songstress, cantor; informal songbird.

single adj. **1** *a single red rose* **one (only)**, sole, lone, solitary, by itself/oneself, unaccompanied, alone. **2** *she wrote down every single word* **individual**, separate, distinct, particular. **3** *is she single?* **unmarried**, unwed, unwedded, unattached,

free, a bachelor, a spinster; old use sole.
– OPPOSITES double, married.
◻ **single someone/something out** select, pick out, choose, decide on; target, earmark, mark out, separate out, set apart/aside.

single-handed adv. **by oneself**, alone, on one's own, solo, unaided, unassisted, without help.

single-minded adj. **determined**, committed, unswerving, unwavering, resolute, purposeful, devoted, dedicated, uncompromising, tireless, tenacious, persistent, indefatigable, dogged; formal pertinacious.
– OPPOSITES half-hearted.

singly adv. **one by one**, one at a time, one after the other, individually, separately, by oneself, on one's own.
– OPPOSITES together.

singular adj. **1** *the gallery's singular capacity to attract sponsors* **remarkable**, extraordinary, exceptional, outstanding, signal, notable, noteworthy; rare, unique, unparalleled, unprecedented, amazing, astonishing, phenomenal, astounding; informal fantastic, terrific. **2** *why was Betty behaving in so singular a fashion?* **strange**, unusual, odd, peculiar, funny, curious, extraordinary, bizarre, eccentric, weird, queer, unexpected, unfamiliar, abnormal, atypical, unconventional, out of the ordinary, off-centre, untypical, puzzling, mysterious, perplexing, baffling, unaccountable.

singularity n. **1** *the singularity of their concerns* **uniqueness**, distinctiveness. **2** *his singularities* **idiosyncrasy**, quirk, foible, peculiarity, oddity, eccentricity.

singularly adv. See **extremely**.

sinister adj. **1** *there was a sinister undertone in his words* **menacing**, threatening, ominous, forbidding, baleful, frightening, alarming, disturbing, disquieting, dark, black; formal minatory; literary direful. **2** *a sinister motive* **evil**, wicked, criminal, corrupt, nefarious, villainous, base, vile, malevolent, malicious; informal shady.
– OPPOSITES innocent.

S

sink v. **1** *the coffin sank below the waves* **become submerged**, be engulfed, go down, drop, fall, descend. **2** *the cruise liner sank yesterday* **founder**, go under, submerge. **3** *they sank their ships* **scuttle**, send to the bottom; Brit. scupper. **4** *the announcement sank hopes of a recovery* **destroy**, ruin, wreck, put an end to, demolish, smash, shatter, dash; informal put the kibosh on, put paid to; Brit. informal scupper; old use bring to naught. **5** *they agreed to sink their differences* **ignore**, overlook, disregard, forget, put aside, set aside, bury. **6** *I sank myself in student life* **immerse**, plunge, lose, bury. **7** *the plane sank towards the airstrip* **descend**, drop, go down/downwards. **8** *the sun was sinking* **set**, go down/downwards. **9** *Loretta sank into an armchair* **lower oneself**, flop, collapse, drop down, slump; informal plonk oneself. **10** *her voice sank to a whisper* **fall**, drop, become/

get quieter, become/get softer. **11** *she would never sink to your level* **stoop**, lower oneself, descend. **12** *he was sinking fast* **deteriorate**, decline, go downhill, fade, grow weak, flag, waste away; be at death's door, be on one's deathbed, be slipping away; informal be on one's last legs, be giving up the ghost. **13** *sink the pots into the ground* **embed**, insert, drive, plant. **14** *sinking a gold mine* **dig**, excavate, bore, drill. **15** informal *he sank five pints of lager* **drink**, quaff; informal down, knock back, polish off; N. Amer. informal chug, scarf down. **16** *they sank their life savings in the company* **invest**, venture, risk.
– OPPOSITES float, rise.
▸ n. *he washed himself at the sink* **basin**, washbasin, handbasin; dated lavabo.
◻ **sink in** register, be understood, be comprehended, be grasped, get through.

sinless adj. **innocent**, pure, virtuous, as pure as the driven snow, uncorrupted, faultless, blameless, guiltless, immaculate.
– OPPOSITES wicked.

sinner n. **wrongdoer**, evildoer, transgressor, miscreant, offender, criminal; old use trespasser.

sinuous adj. **1** *a sinuous river* **winding**, windy, serpentine, curving, twisting, meandering, snaking, zigzag, curling, coiling. **2** *sinuous grace* **lithe**, supple, agile, graceful, loose-limbed, limber, lissom.

sip v. *Amanda sipped her coffee* **drink (slowly)**; dated sup.
▸ n. *a sip of whisky* **mouthful**, swallow, drink, drop, dram, nip; informal swig; dated sup.

siren n. **1** *an air-raid siren* **alarm**, warning bell, danger signal; old use tocsin. **2** *the siren's allure* **seductress**, temptress, femme fatale; flirt, coquette; informal mantrap, vamp.

sissy informal n. *he's a real sissy.* See **drip** (sense 2 of the noun).
▸ adj. *don't be so sissy* **cowardly**, weak, feeble, spineless, effeminate, effete, unmanly; informal wet, weedy, wimpish, wimpy.

sister n. **1** *I have two sisters* **sibling**. **2** *our European sisters* **comrade**, partner, colleague. **3** *the sisters in the convent* **nun**, novice, abbess, prioress.

> **WORD LINKS**
> **sororal** relating to a sister
> **fratricide** the killing of one's sister or brother

sit v. **1** *you'd better sit down* **take a seat**, seat oneself, be seated, perch, ensconce oneself, plump oneself, flop; informal take the load/weight off one's feet, plonk oneself; Brit. informal take a pew. **2** *she sat the package on the table* **put (down)**, place, set (down), lay, deposit, rest, stand; informal stick, bung, dump, park, plonk. **3** *the chapel sat about 3,000 people* **hold**, seat, have seats for, have space/room for, accommodate. **4** *she sat for Picasso* **pose**, model. **5** *a hotel sitting on the bank of the River Dee* **be situated**, be located, be sited, stand. **6** *the committee sits on Saturday* **be in session**, meet, be convened. **7** *women jurists sit on the tribunal* **serve on**,

have a seat on, be a member of. **8** *his shyness doesn't sit easily with Hollywood tradition* **be harmonious**, go, fit in, harmonize. **9** *Mrs Hillman will sit for us* **babysit**, childmind.
– OPPOSITES stand.
□ **sit back** relax, unwind, lie back; informal let it all hang out, chill out, cool out, veg out; N. Amer. informal hang loose.
sit in for stand in for, fill in for, cover for, substitute for, deputize for; informal sub for.
sit in on attend, be present at, be an observer at, observe; N. Amer. audit.
sit tight informal **1** *just sit tight* **stay put**, wait there, remain in one's place. **2** *we're advising our clients to sit tight* **take no action**, wait, hold back, bide one's time; informal hold one's horses.
site n. *the site of the battle* **location**, place, position, situation, locality, whereabouts; technical locus.
▶ v. *bins sited at police stations* **place**, put, position, situate, locate.
sitting n. *all-night sittings* **session**, meeting, assembly; hearing.
▶ adj. *a sitting position* **sedentary**, seated.
– OPPOSITES standing.
sitting room n. **living room**, lounge, front room, drawing room, reception room, family room; dated parlour.
situate v. **locate**, site, position, place, station, build.
situation n. **1** *their financial situation* **circumstances**, (state of) affairs, state, condition. **2** *I'll fill you in on the situation* **the facts**, how things stand, the lie of the land, what's going on; Brit. the state of play; N. Amer. the lay of the land; informal the score. **3** *the hotel's pleasant situation* **location**, position, spot, site, setting, environment; technical locus. **4** *he was offered a situation in America* **job**, post, position, appointment; employment; old use employ.
six cardinal number **sextet**, sextuplets.

> **WORD LINKS**
> **sextuple** consisting of six parts
> **hexagon** a plane figure with six sides
> **hexahedron** a solid figure with six faces
> **hexad** a group or set of six
> **hexameter** a line of verse with six metrical feet

size n. *the room was of medium size* **dimensions**, measurements, proportions, magnitude, largeness, bigness, area, expanse; breadth, width, length, height, depth; immensity, hugeness, vastness.
▶ v. *the drills are sized in millimetres* **sort**, categorize, classify.
□ **size someone/something up** informal assess, appraise, form an estimate of, take the measure of, judge, take stock of, evaluate; Brit. informal suss out.
sizeable adj. **fairly large**, substantial, considerable, respectable, significant, largish, biggish, goodly.
– OPPOSITES small.
sizzle v. **crackle**, frizzle, sputter, spit.

sizzling adj. informal **1** *sizzling temperatures* **extremely hot**, unbearably hot, blazing, burning, scorching, sweltering; N. Amer. broiling; informal boiling (hot), baking (hot). **2** *a sizzling affair* **passionate**, torrid, ardent, lustful, erotic; informal steamy, hot.
– OPPOSITES freezing.
skedaddle v. informal See **run** (sense 2 of the verb).
skeletal adj. **1** *a skeletal man* **emaciated**, very thin, as thin as a rake, cadaverous, skin and bone, skinny, bony, gaunt; informal anorexic. **2** *a skeletal account* **lacking in detail**, incomplete, outline, fragmentary, sketchy; thumbnail.
– OPPOSITES fat, detailed.
skeleton n. **1** *the human skeleton* **bones**. **2** *she was no more than a skeleton* **skin and bone**; informal bag of bones. **3** *a concrete skeleton* **framework**, frame, shell. **4** *the skeleton of a report* **outline**, (rough) draft, abstract, (bare) bones.
▶ adj. *a skeleton staff* **minimum**, minimal, basic; essential.
sketch n. **1** *a sketch of the proposed design* **(preliminary) drawing**, outline; diagram, design, plan, artist's impression; informal rough. **2** *she gave a rough sketch of what had happened* **outline**, brief description, rundown, main points, thumbnail sketch, (bare) bones; summary, synopsis, summarization, precis, résumé; N. Amer. wrap-up. **3** *a biographical sketch* **description**, portrait, profile, portrayal, depiction. **4** *a hilarious sketch* **skit**, scene, piece, act, item, routine.
▶ v. **1** *he sketched the garden* **draw**, make a drawing of, draw a picture of, pencil, rough out, outline. **2** *the company sketched out its plans* **describe**, outline, give a brief idea of, rough out; summarize, precis.
sketchily adv. **perfunctorily**, cursorily, incompletely, patchily, vaguely, imprecisely; hastily, hurriedly.
sketchy adj. **incomplete**, patchy, fragmentary, cursory, perfunctory, scanty, vague, imprecise; hurried, hasty.
– OPPOSITES detailed.
skew-whiff adj. Brit. informal See **crooked** (sense 3).
skilful adj. **expert**, accomplished, skilled, masterly, master, virtuoso, consummate, proficient, talented, gifted, adept, adroit, deft, dexterous, able, good, competent, capable, brilliant, handy; informal mean, wicked, crack, ace, wizard; N. Amer. informal crackerjack.
skill n. **1** *his skill as a politician* **expertise**, skilfulness, expertness, adeptness, adroitness, deftness, dexterity, ability, prowess, mastery, competence, capability, aptitude, artistry, virtuosity, talent. **2** *bringing up a family gives you many skills* **accomplishment**, strength, gift.
– OPPOSITES incompetence.
skilled adj. **experienced**, trained, qualified, proficient, practised, accomplished, expert,

skilful, talented, gifted, adept, adroit, deft, dexterous, able, good, competent; informal crack; N. Amer. informal crackerjack.
– OPPOSITES inexperienced.

skim v. 1 *skim off the scum* **remove**, cream off, scoop off. 2 *the boat skimmed over the water* **glide**, move lightly, slide, sail, skate, float. 3 *he skimmed the pebble across the water* **throw**, toss, cast, pitch; bounce. 4 *she skimmed through the newspaper* **glance**, flick, flip, leaf, thumb, read quickly, scan, run one's eye over. 5 *Hannah skimmed over this part of the story* **mention briefly**, pass over quickly, skate over, gloss over.
– OPPOSITES elaborate on.

skimp v. 1 *don't skimp on the quantity* **stint on**, scrimp on, economize on, cut back on, be sparing, be frugal, be mean, be parsimonious, cut corners; informal be stingy, be mingy, be tight. 2 *the process cannot be skimped* **do hastily**, do carelessly.

skimpy adj. 1 *a skimpy black dress* **revealing**, short, low, low-cut; flimsy, thin, see-through, indecent. 2 *my information is rather skimpy* **meagre**, scanty, sketchy, limited, paltry, deficient, sparse.

skin n. 1 *these chemicals could damage the skin* **epidermis**, dermis, derma. 2 *Mary's fair skin* **complexion**, colouring, skin colour/tone, pigmentation. 3 *leopard skins* **hide**, pelt, fleece; old use fell. 4 *a banana skin* **peel**, rind, integument. 5 *milk with a skin on it* **film**, layer, membrane. 6 *the plane's skin was damaged* **casing**, exterior.
▶ v. 1 *skin the tomatoes* **peel**, pare, hull; technical decorticate. 2 *he skinned his knee* **graze**, scrape, abrade, bark, rub something raw, chafe; Medicine excoriate. 3 informal *Dad would skin me alive if I forgot it* **punish severely**; informal murder, come down on someone (like a ton of bricks); Brit. informal give someone what for.
□ **by the skin of one's teeth** (only) just, narrowly, by a hair's breadth, by a very small margin; informal by a whisker.
get under someone's skin informal 1 *the children really got under my skin.* See **irritate** (sense 1). 2 *she got under my skin* obsess, intrigue, captivate, charm; enthral, enchant, entrance.

> **WORD LINKS**
>
> **cutaneous** relating to the skin
> **subcutaneous, hypodermic** beneath the skin
> **dermatology** the branch of medicine concerned with skin disorders
> **dermatitis** inflammation of the skin
> **eczema, psoriasis** conditions that cause dry, itchy patches on the skin
> **pruritis** severe itching of the skin
> **melanoma** a form of skin cancer
> **slough** (of a snake) shed an old skin
> **ecdysis** the process of shedding an old skin

skin-deep adj. **superficial**, (on the) surface, external, outward, shallow.

skinflint n. informal See **miser**.

skinny adj. See **thin** (sense 3 of the adjective).

skip v. 1 *skipping down the path* **caper**, prance, trip, dance, bound, bounce, gambol, frisk, romp, cavort. 2 *we skipped the boring stuff* **omit**, leave out, miss out, dispense with, pass over, skim over, disregard; informal give something a miss. 3 *I skipped school* **play truant from**, miss; N. Amer. cut; informal sag off; Brit. informal skive off; N. Amer. informal play hookey from; Austral./NZ informal play the wag from. 4 *I skipped through the magazine* **have a quick look at**, flick through, flip through, leaf through. 5 informal *they skipped off again* **run off/away**, take off; informal beat it, clear off, cut and run; Brit. informal do a runner, do a bunk, scarper; N. Amer. informal light out, cut out; Austral. informal shoot through.

skirmish n. 1 *the unit was caught up in a skirmish* **fight**, battle, clash, conflict, encounter, engagement, fray, combat. 2 *there was a skirmish over the budget* **argument**, quarrel, squabble, contretemps, disagreement, difference of opinion, falling-out, dispute, clash, altercation; informal tiff, spat; Brit. informal row, barney, ding-dong; Brit. informal, Football afters.
▶ v. *they skirmished with enemy soldiers* **fight**, (do) battle with, engage with, close with, combat, clash with.

skirt v. 1 *he skirted the city* **go round**, walk round, circle. 2 *the fields that skirt the highway* **border**, edge, flank, line, lie alongside. 3 *he carefully skirted round the subject* **avoid**, evade, sidestep, dodge, pass over, gloss over; informal duck; Austral./NZ informal duck-shove.

skit n. **comedy sketch**, comedy act, parody, pastiche, burlesque, satire, pasquinade; informal spoof, take-off, send-up.

skittish adj. 1 *she grew increasingly skittish* **playful**, lively, high-spirited, sportive, frisky; literary frolicsome, wanton. 2 *his horse was skittish* **restive**, excitable, nervous, skittery, highly strung; informal jumpy.

skive v. Brit. informal **malinger**, play truant, truant, shirk, idle; N. Amer. cut; informal sag off; Brit. informal bunk off, swing the lead, scrimshank; N. Amer. informal gold-brick, play hookey, goof off; Austral./NZ informal play the wag.

skulduggery n. **trickery**, fraudulence, sharp practice, underhandedness, chicanery; informal shenanigans, funny business, monkey business; Brit. informal monkey tricks, jiggery-pokery; N. Amer. informal monkeyshines.

skulk v. **lurk**, loiter, hide; creep, sneak, slink, prowl, pussyfoot.

skull n.

> **WORD LINKS**
>
> **cranial** relating to the skull
> **phrenology** (in the past) the study of the shape of a person's skull as a supposed guide to character
> **trepan** (in the past) a saw used by surgeons to perforate the skull

S

sky n. **air**, atmosphere, airspace; literary the heavens, the firmament, the blue, the (wide) blue yonder, the welkin, the azure, the empyrean.

□ **to the skies** effusively, profusely, very highly, very enthusiastically, unreservedly, fervently, fulsomely, extravagantly.

> WORD LINKS
>
> **celestial** relating to the sky
> **nadir** the point in the sky directly opposite the zenith, below an observer
> **zenith** the highest point in the sky reached by the sun or moon

slab n. **piece**, block, hunk, chunk, lump; cake, tablet, brick.

slack adj. **1** *the rope went slack* **loose**, limp, hanging, flexible. **2** *slack skin* **flaccid**, flabby, loose, sagging, saggy. **3** *business is slack* **sluggish**, slow, quiet, slow-moving, flat, depressed, stagnant. **4** *slack accounting procedures* **lax**, negligent, remiss, careless, slapdash, sloppy, slipshod, lackadaisical, inefficient, casual; informal slap-happy.
– OPPOSITES tight, taut.
▶ n. **1** *the rope had some slack in it* **looseness**, play, give. **2** *foreign demand will help pick up the slack* **surplus**, excess, residue, spare capacity. **3** *a little slack in the daily routine* **lull**, pause, respite, break, hiatus, breathing space; informal let-up, breather.
▶ v. **1** *the horse slacked his pace* **reduce**, lessen, slacken, slow. **2** Brit. informal *no slacking!* **idle**, shirk, be lazy, be indolent, waste time, lounge about; Brit. informal skive; N. Amer. informal goof off.
□ **slack off 1** *the rain has slacked off* **decrease**, subside, let up, ease off, abate, diminish, die down, fall off. **2** *slack off a bit!* **relax**, take things easy, let up, ease up/off, loosen up, slow down; informal chill out; N. Amer. informal hang loose.
slack up *the horse slacked up* **slow (down)**, decelerate, reduce speed.

slacken v. **1** *he slackened his grip* **loosen**, release, relax, loose, lessen, weaken. **2** *he slackened his pace* **slow (down)**, become/ get/make slower, decelerate, slack (up). **3** *the rain is slackening* **decrease**, lessen, subside, ease up/off, let up, abate, slack off, diminish, die down, fall off.
– OPPOSITES tighten.

slacker n. informal See **layabout**.

slake v. **quench**, satisfy, sate, satiate, relieve, assuage.

slam v. **1** *he slammed the door behind him* **bang**, shut/close with a bang, shut/close noisily, shut/close with force. **2** *the car slammed into a lamp post* **crash into**, smash into, collide with, hit, strike, ram, plough into, run into, bump into; N. Amer. impact. **3** informal *he was slammed by the critics*. See **criticize**.

slander n. *he could decide to sue us for slander* **defamation (of character)**, character assassination, calumny, libel; scandalmongering, malicious gossip, disparagement, denigration, aspersions, vilification, traducement, obloquy; lie, slur, smear, false accusation; informal mud-slinging, bad-mouthing; old use contumely.
▶ v. *they were accused of slandering the minister* **defame (someone's character)**, blacken someone's name, tell lies about, speak ill/evil of, sully someone's reputation, libel, smear, cast aspersions on, spread scandal about, besmirch, tarnish, taint; malign, traduce, vilify, disparage, denigrate, run down; N. Amer. slur; formal derogate, calumniate.

slanderous adj. **defamatory**, denigratory, disparaging, libellous, pejorative, false, misrepresentative, scurrilous, scandalous, malicious, abusive, insulting; informal mud-slinging.
– OPPOSITES complimentary.

slang n. **informal language**, argot, colloquialisms, patois, cant; informal lingo, -speak.

slanging match n. informal See **quarrel** (noun).

slant v. **1** *the floor was slanting* **slope**, tilt, incline, be at an angle, tip, cant, lean, dip, pitch, shelve, list, bank. **2** *their findings were slanted in our favour* **bias**, distort, twist, skew, weight, give a bias to.
▶ n. **1** *the slant of the roof* **slope**, incline, tilt, gradient, pitch, angle, cant, camber, inclination. **2** *a feminist slant* **point of view**, viewpoint, standpoint, stance, angle, perspective, approach, view, attitude, position; bias, leaning.

slanting adj. **oblique**, sloping, at an angle, on an incline, inclined, tilting, tilted, slanted, aslant, diagonal, canted, cambered.

slap v. **1** *he slapped her hard* **hit**, strike, smack, clout, cuff, thump, punch, spank; informal whack, thwack, wallop, biff, bash; Brit. informal slosh; N. Amer. informal boff, slug, bust; Austral./NZ informal dong, quilt; old use smite. **2** *he slapped down a £10 note* **fling**, throw, toss, slam, bang; informal plonk. **3** *slap on a coat of paint* **daub**, plaster, spread. **4** informal *they slapped a huge tax on imports* **impose**, levy, put on.
▶ n. *a slap across the cheek* **smack**, blow, thump, cuff, clout, punch, spank; informal whack, thwack, wallop, clip, biff, bash.
▶ adv. informal *the bypass goes slap through the green belt* **straight**, right, directly, plumb; informal smack, (slap) bang; N. Amer. informal spang, smack dab.
□ **a slap in the face** rebuff, rejection, snub, insult, put-down, humiliation.
a slap on the back congratulations, commendation, approbation, approval, accolades, compliments, tributes, a pat on the back, praise, acclaim, acclamation; N. Amer. informal kudos; formal laudation.
a slap on the wrist reprimand, rebuke, reproof, scolding, admonishment; informal telling-off, rap over the knuckles, dressing-down; Brit. informal ticking-off, wigging; Austral./ NZ informal serve.
slap someone down informal See **berate**.

S

slapdash adj. **careless**, slipshod, sloppy, hurried, haphazard, unsystematic, untidy, messy, hit-or-miss, negligent, neglectful, lax; informal slap-happy; Brit. informal shambolic.
– OPPOSITES meticulous.

slap-happy adv. informal **1** *his slap-happy friend* **happy-go-lucky**, devil-may-care, carefree, easy-going, nonchalant, insouciant, blithe, airy, casual. **2** *slap-happy work.* See **slapdash**. **3** *she's a bit slap-happy after such a narrow escape* **dazed**, stupefied, punch-drunk.

slap-up adj. Brit. informal **lavish**, sumptuous, elaborate, expensive, fit for a king, princely, splendid.
– OPPOSITES meagre.

slash v. **1** *her tyres had been slashed* **cut (open)**, gash, slit, split open, lacerate, knife, make an incision in. **2** informal *the company slashed prices* **reduce**, cut, lower, bring down, mark down. **3** informal *they have slashed 10,000 jobs* **get rid of**, axe, cut, shed.
▸ n. **1** *a slash across his temple* **cut**, gash, laceration, slit, incision; wound. **2** *sentence breaks are indicated by slashes* **solidus**, oblique, forward slash, backslash.

slate v. Brit. informal See **criticize**.

slatternly adj. **slovenly**, untidy, messy, scruffy, unkempt, ill-groomed, dishevelled, frowzy; N. Amer. informal raggedy.

slaughter v. **1** *the animals were slaughtered* **kill**, butcher. **2** *innocent civilians are being slaughtered* **massacre**, murder, butcher, kill (off), annihilate, exterminate, liquidate, eliminate, destroy, decimate, wipe out, put to death; literary slay. **3** informal *their team were slaughtered.* See **defeat** (sense 1 of the verb).
▸ n. **1** *the slaughter of 20 demonstrators* **massacre**, murdering, (mass) murder, mass killing, mass execution, annihilation, extermination, liquidation, decimation, carnage, butchery, genocide; literary slaying. **2** *a scene of slaughter* **carnage**, bloodshed, bloodletting, bloodbath. **3** informal *their electoral slaughter.* See **defeat** (sense 1 of the noun).

slaughterhouse n. **abattoir**; Brit. butchery; old use shambles.

slave n. **1** *the work was done by slaves* historical serf, vassal, thrall; old use bondsman, bondswoman. **2** *Anna was his willing slave* **drudge**, servant, man/maid of all work, lackey, galley slave; informal gofer, bitch; Brit. informal skivvy, dogsbody, poodle.
– OPPOSITES freeman, master.
▸ v. *slaving away for a pittance* **toil**, labour, grind, sweat, work one's fingers to the bone, work like a Trojan/dog; informal work one's socks off, kill oneself, sweat blood, slog away; Brit. informal graft; Austral./NZ informal bullock; literary travail; old use drudge, moil.

WORD LINKS
servile relating to or like a slave
emancipate, manumit free someone from slavery

slaver v. **drool**, slobber, dribble, salivate; old use drivel.

slavery n. **1** *thousands were sold into slavery* **bondage**, enslavement, servitude; historical thrall, serfdom, vassalage. **2** *this work is sheer slavery* **drudgery**, toil, (hard) slog, hard labour, grind; literary travail; old use moil.
– OPPOSITES freedom.

slavish adj. **1** *slavish lackeys of the government* **servile**, subservient, fawning, obsequious, sycophantic, toadying, unctuous; informal bootlicking, forelock-tugging; N. Amer. informal apple-polishing. **2** *slavish copying* **unoriginal**, uninspired, unimaginative, uninventive, imitative.

slay v. literary **kill**, murder, put to death, butcher, cut down, cut to pieces, slaughter, massacre, shoot down, gun down, mow down, eliminate, annihilate, exterminate, liquidate; informal wipe out, bump off, do in/for.

slaying n. literary **murder**, killing, butchery, slaughter, massacre, extermination, liquidation.

sleazy adj. **1** *sleazy arms dealers* **corrupt**, immoral, unsavoury, disreputable; informal shady, sleazoid. **2** *a sleazy bar* **squalid**, seedy, seamy, sordid, insalubrious, mean, cheap, low-class, run down; informal scruffy, scuzzy, crummy, skanky; Brit. informal grotty.
– OPPOSITES reputable, upmarket.

sledge n. **toboggan**, bobsleigh, sleigh; N. Amer. sled.

sleek adj. **1** *his sleek dark hair* **smooth**, glossy, shiny, shining, lustrous, silken, silky. **2** *the car's sleek lines* **streamlined**, trim, elegant, graceful. **3** *sleek young men in city suits* **well groomed**, stylish, wealthy-looking.

sleep n. *go and have a sleep* **nap**, doze, siesta, catnap, beauty sleep; informal snooze, forty winks, a bit of shut-eye; Brit. informal kip, zizz; children's language bye-byes; literary slumber.
▸ v. *she slept for about an hour* **be asleep**, doze, take a siesta, take a nap, catnap, sleep like a log/top; informal snooze, snatch forty winks, get some shut-eye; Brit. informal (have a) kip, get one's head down, (get some) zizz; N. Amer. informal catch some Zs; humorous be in the land of Nod; literary slumber.
– OPPOSITES wake up.
□ **go to sleep** fall asleep, get to sleep; informal drop off, nod off, drift off, crash out, flake out; N. Amer. informal sack out, zone out.

WORD LINKS
sedative, soporific causing drowsiness or sleep
narcolepsy an extreme tendency to fall asleep

sleepiness n. **drowsiness**, tiredness, somnolence, languor, languidness, doziness; lethargy, sluggishness, lassitude, enervation.

sleepless adj. **wakeful**, restless, without sleep, insomniac; (wide) awake, unsleeping, tossing and turning; old use watchful.

sleeplessness n. **insomnia**, wakefulness.

sleepwalker n. **somnambulist**; rare noctambulist.

S

sleepy adj. **1** *she felt very sleepy* **drowsy**, tired, somnolent, languid, languorous, heavy-eyed, asleep on one's feet; lethargic, sluggish, enervated, torpid; informal dopey; literary slumberous. **2** *the sleepy heat of the afternoon* **soporific**, sleep-inducing, somnolent. **3** *a sleepy little village* **quiet**, peaceful, tranquil, placid, slow-moving; dull, boring.
– OPPOSITES awake, alert.

sleight of hand n. **1** *impressive sleight of hand* **dexterity**, adroitness, deftness, skill. **2** *financial sleight of hand* **deception**, deceit, dissimulation, chicanery, trickery, sharp practice.

slender adj. **1** *her tall slender figure* **slim**, lean, willowy, sylphlike, svelte, lissom, graceful; slight, slightly built, thin, skinny. **2** *slender evidence* **meagre**, limited, slight, scanty, scant, sparse, paltry, insubstantial, insufficient, deficient, negligible; formal exiguous. **3** *the chances seemed slender* **faint**, remote, flimsy, tenuous, fragile, slim; unlikely, improbable.
– OPPOSITES plump.

sleuth n. informal **(private) detective**, (private) investigator; informal private eye, snoop, sleuth-hound; N. Amer. informal shamus, gumshoe.

slice n. **1** *a slice of fruitcake* **piece**, portion, slab, rasher, sliver, wafer, shaving. **2** *a huge slice of public spending* **share**, part, portion, tranche, piece, proportion, allocation, percentage.
▶v. **1** *slice the cheese thinly* **cut (up)**, carve. **2** *one man had his ear sliced off* **cut off**, sever, chop off, shear off.

slick adj. **1** *a slick advertising campaign* **efficient**, smooth, smooth-running, polished, well organized, well run, streamlined. **2** *his slick use of words* **glib**, smooth, fluent, plausible. **3** *a slick salesman* **suave**, urbane, polished, assured, self-assured, smooth-talking, glib; informal smarmy. **4** *her slick brown hair* **shiny**, glossy, shining, sleek, smooth, oiled. **5** *the pavements were slick with rain* **slippery**, slithery, wet, greasy; informal slippy.
▶v. *his hair was slicked down* **smooth**, sleek, grease, oil, gel; informal smarm.

slide v. **1** *the glass slid across the table* **glide**, move smoothly, slip, slither, skim, skate; skid, slew. **2** *tears slid down her cheeks* **trickle**, run, flow, pour, stream. **3** *four men slid out of the shadows* **creep**, steal, slink, slip, tiptoe, sidle. **4** *the country is sliding into recession* **sink**, fall, drop, descend; decline, degenerate.
▶n. **1** *the current slide in house prices* **fall**, decline, drop, slump, downturn, downswing. **2** *a slide show* **transparency**, diapositive.
– OPPOSITES rise.
◻ **let something slide** neglect, pay little/no attention to, not attend to, be remiss about, let something go downhill.

slight adj. **1** *I'm afraid the chance of success is slight* **small**, modest, tiny, minute, inappreciable, negligible, insignificant, minimal, remote, slim, faint; informal minuscule; formal exiguous. **2** *the book is a slight work* **minor**, inconsequential, trivial, unimportant, lightweight, superficial, shallow. **3** *Elizabeth's slight figure* **slim**, slender, petite, diminutive, small, delicate, dainty.
– OPPOSITES considerable.
▶v. *he had been slighted* **insult**, snub, rebuff, repulse, spurn, treat disrespectfully, give someone the cold shoulder, cut (dead), scorn; informal give someone the brush-off, freeze out, stiff-arm.
– OPPOSITES respect.
▶n. *an unintended slight* **insult**, affront, snub, rebuff; informal put-down, dig.
– OPPOSITES compliment.

slighting adj. **insulting**, disparaging, derogatory, disrespectful, denigratory, pejorative, abusive, offensive, defamatory, slanderous, scurrilous; disdainful, scornful, contemptuous; old use contumelious.

slightly adv. **a little**, a bit, somewhat, rather, moderately, to a certain extent, faintly, vaguely, a shade.
– OPPOSITES very.

slim adj. **1** *she was tall and slim* **slender**, lean, thin, willowy, sylphlike, svelte, lissom, trim, slight, slightly built. **2** *a slim silver bracelet* **narrow**, slender, slimline. **3** *a slim chance of escape* **slight**, small, slender, faint, poor, remote, unlikely, improbable.
– OPPOSITES plump.
▶v. **1** *I'm trying to slim* **lose weight**, get thinner, get into shape; N. Amer. slenderize. **2** *the number of staff had been slimmed down* **reduce**, cut (down/back), scale down, decrease, diminish, pare down.

slime n. **ooze**, sludge, muck, mud; mire; informal goo, gunk, gook, gloop; Brit. informal gunge; N. Amer. informal guck, glop.

slimy adj. **1** *the floor was slimy* **slippery**, slithery, greasy, muddy, mucky, sludgy, wet, sticky; informal slippy, gooey, gloopy. **2** informal *her slimy press agent*. See **obsequious**.

sling n. **1** *she had her arm in a sling* **(support) bandage**, support, strap. **2** *armed only with a sling* **catapult**, slingshot; Austral./NZ shanghai.
▶v. **1** *a hammock was slung between two trees* **hang**, suspend, string, swing. **2** informal *she slung her jacket on the sofa*. See **throw** (sense 1 of the verb).

slink v. **creep**, sneak, steal, slip, slide, sidle, tiptoe, pussyfoot.

slinky adj. informal **1** *a slinky black dress* **tight-fitting**, close-fitting, figure-hugging, sexy. **2** *her slinky elegance* **sinuous**, willowy, graceful, sleek.

slip[1] v. **1** *she slipped on the ice* **slide**, skid, slither, glide; fall (over), lose one's balance, tumble. **2** *the envelope slipped through Luke's fingers* **fall**, drop, slide. **3** *we slipped out by a back door* **creep**, steal, sneak, slide, sidle, slope, slink, tiptoe. **4** *standards have slipped* **decline**, deteriorate, degenerate, worsen, get worse, go downhill, fall (off), drop; informal

S

go to the dogs, go to pot. **5** *the bank's shares slipped 1.5p* **drop**, go down, sink, slump, decrease, depreciate. **6** *the hours slipped by* **pass**, elapse, go by/past, roll by/past, fly by/past, tick by/past. **7** *she slipped the map into her pocket* **put**, tuck, shove; informal pop, stick, stuff. **8** *Sarah slipped into a black skirt* **put on**, pull on, don, dress/clothe oneself in; change into. **9** *she slipped out of her clothes* **take off**, remove, pull off, doff; Brit. informal peel off. **10** *he slipped the knot of his tie* **untie**, unfasten, undo.

▶n. **1** *a single slip could send them plummeting downwards* **false step**, misstep, slide, skid, fall, tumble. **2** *a careless slip* **mistake**, error, blunder, gaffe, slip of the tongue/pen; oversight, omission, lapse, inaccuracy; informal slip-up, boo-boo, howler, fail; Brit. informal boob, clanger, bloomer; N. Amer. informal goof, blooper, bloop. **3** *a silk slip* **underskirt**, petticoat, underslip.

□ **give someone the slip** informal escape from, get away from, evade, dodge, elude, lose, shake off, throw off (the scent), get clear of.

let something slip reveal, disclose, divulge, let out, give away, blurt out; give the game away; informal let on, blab, let the cat out of the bag, spill the beans; Brit. informal blow the gaff.

slip away 1 *they managed to slip away* escape, get away, break free; informal fly the coop; Brit. informal do a bunk, do a runner; N. Amer. informal take a powder. **2** *she slipped away in her sleep.* See **die** (sense 1).

slip up informal make a mistake, (make a) blunder, get something wrong, make an error, err; informal make a bloomer, make a boo-boo; Brit. informal boob, drop a clanger; N. Amer. informal goof up.

slip² n. **1** *a slip of paper* **piece of paper**, scrap of paper, sheet, note; chit; informal sticky. **2** *they took slips from rare plants* **cutting**, graft; scion, shoot, offshoot.

□ **a slip of a —** small, slender, slim, slight, slightly built, petite, little, tiny, diminutive; informal pint-sized.

slipper n. **1** *he pulled on his slippers* carpet slipper, bedroom slipper, house shoe; N. Amer. slipperette. **2** *satin slippers* pump, mule.

slippery adj. **1** *the roads are slippery* **slithery**, greasy, oily, icy, glassy, smooth, slimy, wet; informal slippy. **2** *a slippery customer* **evasive**, unreliable, unpredictable; devious, crafty, cunning, wily, tricky, artful, slick, sly, sneaky, scheming, untrustworthy, deceitful, duplicitous, dishonest, treacherous, two-faced, Janus-faced; N. Amer. snide; informal shady, shifty; Brit. informal dodgy; Austral./NZ informal shonky.

slipshod adj. **careless**, lackadaisical, slapdash, sloppy, disorganized, haphazard, hit-or-miss, untidy, messy, unsystematic, unmethodical, casual, negligent, neglectful, remiss, lax, slack; informal slap-happy.
– OPPOSITES meticulous.

slip-up n. informal **mistake**, slip, error, blunder, oversight, omission, gaffe, slip of the tongue/pen, inaccuracy; informal boo-boo, howler, fail; Brit. informal boob, clanger, bloomer; N. Amer. informal goof, blooper, bloop.

slit n. **1** *three diagonal slits* **cut**, incision, split, slash, gash, laceration. **2** *a slit in the curtains* **opening**, gap, chink, crack, aperture, slot.
▶v. *he threatened to slit her throat* **cut**, slash, split open, slice open, gash, lacerate, make an incision in.

slither v. **slide**, slip, glide, wriggle, crawl; skid.

sliver n. **splinter**, shard, shiver, chip, flake, shred, scrap, slither, shaving, paring, piece, fragment.

slob n. informal **layabout**, good-for-nothing, sluggard, slug, laggard; informal slacker, couch potato; old use sloven.

slobber v. **drool**, slaver, dribble, salivate; old use drivel.

slog v. **1** *they were all slogging away* **work hard**, toil, labour, work one's fingers to the bone, work like a Trojan/dog, exert oneself, grind, slave, grub, plough, plod, peg; informal beaver, plug, work one's socks off, sweat blood; Brit. informal graft; Austral./NZ informal bullock; literary travail; old use drudge, moil. **2** *they slogged around the streets* **trudge**, tramp, traipse, toil, plod, trek, footslog, drag oneself.
– OPPOSITES relax.
▶n. **1** *10 months' hard slog* **hard work**, toil, toiling, labour, effort, exertion, grind, drudgery; informal sweat; Brit. informal graft; Austral./NZ informal (hard) yakka; literary travail; old use moil. **2** *a steady uphill slog* **trudge**, tramp, traipse, plod, trek, footslog.
– OPPOSITES leisure.

slogan n. **catchphrase**, catchline, jingle; N. Amer. informal tag line.

slop v. *water slopped over the edge* **spill**, flow, overflow, run, slosh, splash.
□ **slop around/about** Brit. informal laze (around/about), lounge (around/about), loll (around/about), loaf (around/about), slouch (about/around); informal hang around; Brit. informal hang about, mooch about/around; N. Amer. informal bum around, lollygag.

slope n. **1** *the slope of the roof* **gradient**, incline, angle, slant, inclination, pitch, decline, ascent, declivity, acclivity, rise, fall, tilt, tip, downslope, upslope; N. Amer. grade, downgrade, upgrade. **2** *a grassy slope* **hill**, hillside, hillock, bank, escarpment, scarp; literary steep. **3** *the ski slopes* **piste**, run, nursery slope, dry slope; N. Amer. trail.
▶v. *the garden sloped down to a stream* **slant**, incline, tilt; drop away, fall away, decline, descend, shelve, lean; rise, ascend, climb.
□ **slope off** informal leave, go away, slip away, steal away, slink off, creep off, sneak off; informal push off, clear off.

sloping adj. **at a slant**, on the slant, at an angle, slanting, slanted, leaning, inclining, inclined, angled, cambered, canted, tilting, tilted, dipping, declivitous, acclivitous.
– OPPOSITES level.

sloppy adj. **1** *sloppy chicken curry* **runny**, watery, thin, liquid, semi-liquid, mushy; informal gloopy. **2** *their defending was sloppy* **careless**, slapdash, slipshod, lackadaisical, haphazard, lax, slack, slovenly; informal slap-happy; Brit. informal shambolic. **3** *sloppy T-shirts* **baggy**, loose-fitting, loose, generously cut; shapeless, sack-like, oversized. **4** *sloppy letters* **sentimental**, mawkish, cloying, slushy, saccharine, sugary, syrupy; romantic, hearts-and-flowers; informal schmaltzy, lovey-dovey; Brit. informal soppy; N. Amer. informal cornball, sappy, hokey, three-hankie.

slosh v. **1** *beer sloshed over the side of the glass* **spill**, slop, splash, flow, overflow. **2** *workers sloshed round in boots* **splash**, swash, squelch, wade; informal splosh. **3** *she sloshed more wine into her glass* **pour**, slop, splash. **4** Brit. informal *Gary sloshed him.* See **hit** (sense 1 of the verb).

slot n. **1** *he slid a coin into the slot* **aperture**, slit, crack, hole, opening. **2** *a mid-morning slot* **spot**, time, period, niche, space; informal window.
▶v. *he slotted a CD into the machine* **insert**, put, place, slide, slip.

sloth n. **laziness**, idleness, indolence, slothfulness, inactivity, inertia, sluggishness, shiftlessness, apathy, accidie, listlessness, lassitude, lethargy, languor, torpidity; literary hebetude.
– OPPOSITES industriousness.

slothful adj. **lazy**, idle, indolent, work-shy, inactive, sluggish, apathetic, lethargic, listless, languid, torpid; informal bone idle; old use otiose.

slouch v. **slump**, hunch; loll, droop.

slovenly adj. **1** *his slovenly appearance* **scruffy**, untidy, messy, unkempt, ill-groomed, slatternly, dishevelled, bedraggled, tousled, rumpled, frowzy; informal slobbish, slobby; N. Amer. informal raggedy, raunchy. **2** *his work is slovenly* **careless**, slapdash, sloppy, slipshod, haphazard, hit-or-miss, untidy, messy, negligent, lax, lackadaisical, slack; informal slap-happy.
– OPPOSITES tidy, careful.

slow adj. **1** *their slow walk home* **unhurried**, leisurely, steady, sedate, slow-moving, plodding, dawdling, sluggish, sluggardly. **2** *a slow process* **long-drawn-out**, time-consuming, lengthy, protracted, prolonged, gradual. **3** *he can be so slow* **obtuse**, stupid, unperceptive, insensitive, bovine, stolid, slow-witted, dull-witted, unintelligent, doltish, witless; informal dense, dim, dim-witted, thick, slow on the uptake, dumb, dopey, boneheaded; Brit. informal dozy; N. Amer. informal chowderheaded. **4** *they were slow to voice their opinions* **reluctant**, unwilling, disinclined, loath, hesitant, afraid, chary, shy. **5** *the slow season* **sluggish**, slack, quiet, inactive, flat, depressed, stagnant, dead. **6** *a slow narrative* **dull**, boring, uninteresting, unexciting, uneventful, tedious, tiresome, wearisome, monotonous, dreary, lacklustre.
– OPPOSITES fast.

▶v. **1** *the traffic forced him to slow down* **reduce speed**, go slower, decelerate, brake. **2** *you need to slow down* **take it easy**, relax, ease up/off, take a break, slack off, let up; informal chill out; N. Amer. informal hang loose. **3** *this would slow down economic growth* **hold back/up**, delay, retard, set back; restrict, check, curb, inhibit, impede, obstruct, hinder, hamper; old use stay.
– OPPOSITES accelerate.

slowly adv. **1** *Rose walked off slowly* **at a slow pace**, without hurrying, unhurriedly, steadily, at a leisurely pace, at a snail's pace; Music adagio, lento, largo. **2** *her health is improving slowly* **gradually**, bit by bit, little by little, slowly but surely, step by step.
– OPPOSITES quickly.

sludge n. **mud**, muck, mire, ooze, silt, alluvium; informal gunk, crud, gloop, gook, goo; Brit. informal gunge, grot; N. Amer. informal guck, glop.

sluggish adj. **1** *Alex felt tired and sluggish* **lethargic**, listless, lacking in energy, lifeless, inert, inactive, slow, torpid, languid, apathetic, weary, tired, fatigued, sleepy, drowsy, enervated; lazy, idle, indolent, slothful, sluggardly; Medicine asthenic; N. Amer. logy; informal dozy, dopey. **2** *the economy is sluggish* **inactive**, quiet, slow, slack, flat, depressed, stagnant.
– OPPOSITES vigorous.

sluice v. **1** *crews sluiced down the decks* **wash (down)**, rinse, clean, cleanse. **2** *the water sluiced out* **pour**, flow, run, gush, stream, course, flood, surge, spill.

slum n. **hovel**; (**slums**) ghetto, shanty town.

slumber literary v. *the child slumbered fitfully.* See **sleep** (verb).
▶n. *an uneasy slumber.* See **sleep** (noun).

slummy adj. **seedy**, insalubrious, squalid, sleazy, run down, down at heel, shabby, dilapidated; informal scruffy, skanky; Brit. informal grotty; N. Amer. informal shacky.
– OPPOSITES upmarket.

slump v. **1** *he slumped into a chair* **sit heavily**, flop, flump, collapse, sink, fall; informal plonk oneself. **2** *houses prices slumped* **fall steeply**, plummet, tumble, drop, go down; informal crash, nosedive. **3** *reading standards have slumped* **decline**, deteriorate, degenerate, worsen, slip, go downhill.
▶n. **1** *a slump in profits* **steep fall**, drop, tumble, downturn, downswing, slide, decline, decrease; informal nosedive. **2** *an economic slump* **recession**, economic decline, depression, slowdown, stagnation.
– OPPOSITES rise, boom.

slur v. *she was slurring her words* **mumble**, speak unclearly, garble.
▶n. *a gross slur* **insult**, slight, slander, slanderous statement, aspersion, smear, allegation.

slush n. **1** *he wiped the slush off his shoes* **melting snow**, wet snow, mush, sludge. **2** informal *the slush of romantic films* **sentimentality**, mawkishness, sentimentalism; informal schmaltz, mush,

S

slushiness, corniness; Brit. informal soppiness; N. Amer. informal sappiness, hokeyness.

slut n. **promiscuous woman**, prostitute, whore; informal tart, floozie, pro; Brit. informal scrubber, slag, slapper; N. Amer. informal tramp, hooker, hustler, roundheel; dated scarlet woman, loose woman, hussy, trollop; old use harlot, strumpet, wanton.

sly adj. **1** *she's rather sly* **cunning**, crafty, clever, wily, artful, guileful, tricky, scheming, devious, deceitful, duplicitous, dishonest, underhand, sneaky; old use subtle. **2** *a sly grin* **roguish**, mischievous, impish, playful, wicked, arch, knowing. **3** *she took a sly sip of water* **surreptitious**, furtive, stealthy, covert.
□ **on the sly** in secret, secretly, furtively, surreptitiously, covertly, clandestinely, on the quiet, behind someone's back.

smack¹ n. **1** *she gave him a smack* **slap**, clout, cuff, blow, spank, rap, swat, crack, thump, punch; informal whack, thwack, clip, biff, wallop, swipe, bop, belt, bash, sock. **2** *the parcel landed with a smack* **bang**, crash, crack, thud, thump. **3** *informal a smack on the lips* **kiss**, peck; informal smacker.
▸v. **1** *he tried to smack her* **slap**, hit, strike, spank, cuff, clout, thump, punch, swat; box someone's ears; informal whack, clip, wallop, biff, swipe, bop, belt, bash, sock; Scottish & N. English informal skelp; N. Amer. informal boff, slug, bust. **2** *the waiter smacked a plate down* **bang**, slam, crash, thump; sling, fling; informal plonk; N. Amer. informal plunk.
▸adv. *informal smack in the middle* **exactly**, precisely, straight, right, directly, squarely, dead, plumb, point-blank; informal slap bang; N. Amer. informal smack dab.

smack² n. **1** *the beer has a smack of hops* **taste**, flavour, savour. **2** *a smack of bitterness in his words* **trace**, tinge, touch, suggestion, hint, overtone, suspicion, whisper.
□ **smack of 1** *the tea smacked of tannin* **taste of**, have the flavour of. **2** *the plan smacked of self-promotion* **suggest**, hint at, have overtones of, give the impression of, have the stamp of, seem like; smell of, reek of.

small adj. **1** *a small flat* **little**, compact, bijou, tiny, miniature, mini; minute, microscopic, nanoscopic, minuscule; toy, baby; poky, cramped, boxy; Scottish wee; informal tiddly, teeny, teensy, itsy-bitsy, itty-bitty, pocket-sized, half-pint, dinky, ickle; Brit. informal titchy; N. Amer. informal little-bitty. **2** *a very small man* **short**, little, petite, diminutive, elfin, tiny; puny, undersized, stunted, dwarfish, midget, pygmy, Lilliputian; Scottish wee; informal teeny, pint-sized. **3** *a few small changes* **slight**, minor, unimportant, trifling, trivial, insignificant, inconsequential, negligible, nugatory, infinitesimal; informal minuscule, piffling, piddling. **4** *small helpings* **inadequate**, meagre, insufficient, ungenerous; informal measly, stingy, mingy, pathetic. **5** *they made him feel small* **foolish**, stupid, insignificant, unimportant; embarrassed, humiliated, uncomfortable, mortified, ashamed; crushed. **6** *a small*

farmer **small-scale**, small-time; modest, unpretentious, humble.
– OPPOSITES big, tall, major, ample, substantial.

small change n. **coins**, change, coppers, silver, cash, specie.

small-minded adj. **narrow-minded**, petty, mean-spirited, uncharitable; close-minded, short-sighted, myopic, blinkered, inward-looking, unimaginative, parochial, provincial, insular, small-town; intolerant, illiberal, conservative, hidebound, dyed-in-the-wool, set in one's ways, inflexible; prejudiced, bigoted; Brit. parish-pump, blimpish.
– OPPOSITES tolerant.

small-time adj. **minor**, small-scale; petty, unimportant, insignificant, inconsequential; N. Amer. minor-league; informal penny-ante, piddling; N. Amer. informal two-bit, bush-league, picayune.
– OPPOSITES major.

smarmy adj. *informal* **unctuous**, ingratiating, slick, oily, greasy, obsequious, sycophantic, fawning; informal slimy, sucky.

smart adj. **1** *you look very smart* **well dressed**, stylish, chic, fashionable, modish, elegant, neat, spruce, trim, dapper; N. Amer. trig; informal snazzy, natty, snappy, sharp, cool; N. Amer. informal sassy, spiffy, fly, kicky. **2** *a smart restaurant* **fashionable**, stylish, high-class, exclusive, chic, fancy; Brit. upmarket; N. Amer. high-toned; informal trendy, posh, ritzy, plush, classy, swanky, glitzy; Brit. informal swish; N. Amer. informal swank. **3** *informal he's the smart one* **clever**, bright, intelligent, sharp-witted, quick-witted, shrewd, astute, able, perceptive, percipient; informal brainy, savvy, quick on the uptake. **4** *a smart pace* **brisk**, quick, fast, rapid, swift, lively, spanking, energetic, vigorous; informal snappy, cracking. **5** *a smart blow on the snout* **sharp**, severe, forceful, violent.
– OPPOSITES untidy, downmarket, stupid, slow, gentle.
▸v. **1** *her eyes were smarting* **sting**, burn, tingle, prickle; hurt, ache. **2** *she smarted at the accusations* **feel annoyed**, feel upset, take offence, feel aggrieved, feel indignant, be put out, feel hurt.
□ **look smart** Brit. be quick, hurry up, speed up; informal make it snappy, get cracking, get moving, step on it, get a wiggle on; Brit. informal get one's skates on, stir one's stumps.

smarten v. **spruce up**, clean up, tidy up, neaten, tidy; groom, freshen, preen, primp, beautify; redecorate, refurbish, modernize; informal do up, titivate, doll up; Brit. informal tart up, posh up; N. Amer. informal gussy up.

smash v. **1** *he smashed a window* **break**, shatter, splinter, crack, shiver; informal bust. **2** *she's smashed the car* **crash**, wreck; Brit. write off; Brit. informal prang; N. Amer. informal total. **3** *they smashed into a wall* **crash into**, collide with, hit, strike, ram, smack into, slam into, plough into, run into, bump into; N. Amer. impact. **4** *Don smashed him over the*

S

head **hit**, strike, thump, punch, smack; informal whack, bash, biff, bop, clout, wallop, crown; Brit. informal slosh, dot; N. Amer. informal slug. **5** *he smashed their hopes of glory* **destroy**, wreck, ruin, shatter, dash, crush, devastate, demolish, overturn, scotch; informal put the kibosh on, do for, put paid to, queer; Brit. informal scupper.
▶ n. **1** *the smash of glass* **breaking**, shattering, crash. **2** *a motorway smash* **crash**, collision, accident, bump; Brit. RTA; N. Amer. wreck; informal pile-up, smash-up; Brit. informal prang, shunt. **3** informal *a box-office smash* **success**, sensation, sell-out, triumph; informal (smash) hit, winner, crowd-puller, knockout, wow, biggie.

smashing adj. Brit. informal See **marvellous** (sense 2).

smattering n. **bit**, little, modicum, touch, soupçon; nodding acquaintance; rudiments, basics; informal smidgen, smidge, tad.

smear v. **1** *the table was smeared with grease* **streak**, smudge, mark, soil, dirty; informal splotch, splodge; literary besmear. **2** *smear the meat with olive oil* **cover**, coat, grease; literary bedaub. **3** *she smeared sunblock on her skin* **spread**, rub, daub, slap, slather, smother, plaster, cream, slick; apply; literary besmear. **4** *they are trying to smear our reputation* **sully**, tarnish, blacken, drag through the mud, taint, damage, defame, discredit, malign, slander, libel; N. Amer. slur; informal do a hatchet job on; formal calumniate; literary besmirch.
▶ n. **1** *smears of blood* **streak**, smudge, daub, dab, spot, patch, blotch, mark; informal splotch, splodge. **2** *press smears about his closest aides* **false accusation**, lie, untruth, slur, slander, libel, defamation, calumny.

smell n. *the smell of the kitchen* **odour**, aroma, fragrance, scent, perfume, redolence; bouquet, nose; stench, stink, reek; Brit. informal pong, niff, whiff, hum; Scottish informal guff; N. Amer. informal funk; literary miasma.
▶ v. **1** *he smelled her perfume* **scent**, get a sniff of, detect. **2** *the dogs smelled each other* **sniff**, nose. **3** *the cellar smells* **stink**, reek, have a bad smell; Brit. informal pong, hum, niff, whiff. **4** *it smells like a hoax to me* **smack of**, have the hallmarks of, seem like, have the air of, suggest.

> **WORD LINKS**
> **olfactory** relating to the sense of smell
> **olfaction** the sense of smell
> **deodorant** a substance which prevents or conceals bodily odours

smelly adj. **foul-smelling**, stinking, reeking, fetid, malodorous, pungent, rank, noxious; off, gamy, high; musty, fusty; informal stinky; Brit. informal pongy, whiffy, humming; N. Amer. informal funky; literary miasmic, noisome.

smile v. *he smiled at her* **beam**, grin (from ear to ear), dimple, twinkle; smirk, simper; leer.
– OPPOSITES frown.
▶ n. *the smile on her face* **beam**, grin, twinkle; smirk, simper; leer.

smirk v. **smile smugly**, simper, snigger; leer.

smitten adj. **1** *he was smitten with cholera* **struck down**, laid low, suffering, affected, afflicted, plagued, stricken. **2** *Jane's smitten with you* **infatuated**, besotted, in love, obsessed, head over heels; enamoured of, attracted to, taken with; captivated, enchanted, under someone's spell; informal bowled over, swept off one's feet, crazy about, mad about, keen on, gone on, sweet on; Brit. informal potty about.

smog n. **fog**, haze; fumes, smoke, pollution; Brit. informal pea-souper.

smoke v. **1** *the fire was smoking* **smoulder**, emit smoke; old use reek. **2** *he smoked his cigarette* **puff on**, draw on, pull on; inhale; light; informal drag on. **3** *they smoke their salmon* **cure**, preserve, dry.
▶ n. *the smoke from the bonfire* **fumes**, exhaust, gas, vapour; smog.

smoky adj. **1** *the smoky atmosphere* **smoke-filled**, sooty, smoggy, hazy, foggy, murky, thick; Brit. informal fuggy. **2** *her smoky eyes* **grey**, sooty, dark, black.

smooth adj. **1** *the smooth flat rocks* **even**, level, flat, plane; unwrinkled, featureless; glassy, glossy, silky, polished. **2** *his face was smooth* **clean-shaven**, hairless. **3** *a smooth sauce* **creamy**, velvety, blended. **4** *a smooth sea* **calm**, still, tranquil, undisturbed, unruffled, even, flat, waveless, like a millpond. **5** *the smooth running of the equipment* **steady**, regular, uninterrupted, unbroken, fluid, fluent; straightforward, easy, effortless, trouble-free. **6** *a smooth wine* **mellow**, mild, agreeable, pleasant. **7** *the smooth tone of the clarinet* **dulcet**, soft, soothing, mellow, sweet, silvery, honeyed, mellifluous, melodious, lilting, lyrical, harmonious. **8** *a smooth, confident man* **suave**, urbane, sophisticated, polished, debonair; smooth-talking, glib, slick, ingratiating, unctuous; informal smarmy.
– OPPOSITES uneven, rough, hairy, lumpy, irregular, raucous, gauche.
▶ v. **1** *she smoothed the soil* **flatten**, level (out/off), even out/off; press, roll, steamroll, iron, plane. **2** *a plan to smooth the way for the agreement* **ease**, facilitate, clear the way for, pave the way for, expedite, assist, aid, help, oil the wheels of, lubricate.

smoothly adv. **1** *her hair was combed smoothly back* **evenly**, level, flat, flush. **2** *the door closed smoothly* **fluidly**, fluently, steadily, frictionlessly, easily; quietly. **3** *the plan had gone smoothly* **without a hitch**, like clockwork, without difficulty, easily, effortlessly, according to plan, swimmingly, satisfactorily, very well; informal like a dream.

smooth-talking adj. informal **persuasive**, glib, plausible, silver-tongued, slick, eloquent, fast-talking; ingratiating, flattering, unctuous, obsequious, sycophantic; informal smarmy.
– OPPOSITES blunt.

smother v. **1** *Othello smothered Desdemona with her pillow* **suffocate**, asphyxiate, stifle, choke. **2** *we smothered the flames*

extinguish, put out, snuff out, dampen, douse, stamp out, choke. **3** *we smothered ourselves with suncream* **smear**, daub, spread, cover; literary besmear, bedaub. **4** *their granny always smothers them* **overwhelm**, inundate, envelop, cocoon; Brit. wrap someone in cotton wool. **5** *she smothered a sigh* **stifle**, muffle, strangle, repress, suppress, hold back, fight back, bite back, swallow, contain, bottle up, conceal, hide; bite one's lip; informal keep a/the lid on.

smoulder v. **1** *the bonfire still smouldered* **smoke**, glow, burn; old use reek. **2** *she was smouldering with resentment* **seethe**, boil, fume, burn, simmer, be boiling over, be beside oneself; informal be livid.

smudge n. *a smudge of blood* **streak**, smear, mark, stain, blotch, stripe, blob, dab, patch, pop; informal splotch, splodge.
▶ v. **1** *her face was smudged with dust* **streak**, mark, dirty, soil, blotch, blacken, smear, blot, daub, stain; informal splotch, splodge; literary bedaub, besmirch. **2** *she smudged her make-up* **smear**, streak, mess up.

smug adj. **self-satisfied**, self-congratulatory, complacent, superior, pleased with oneself, self-approving; Brit. informal like the cat that got the cream, I'm-all-right-Jack.

smuggle v. **import/export illegally**, traffic in, run.

smuggler n. **contrabandist**, runner, courier; informal mule, moonshiner.

smutty adj. **vulgar**, rude, crude, dirty, filthy, salacious, coarse, obscene, lewd, pornographic, X-rated; risqué, racy, earthy, bawdy, suggestive, naughty, ribald, off colour; informal blue, raunchy; Brit. informal near the knuckle, saucy; N. Amer. informal gamy; euphemistic adult.

snack n. *she made herself a snack* **light meal**, sandwich, treat, refreshments, nibbles, titbit(s); informal bite (to eat); Brit. informal elevenses.
▶ v. *don't snack on sugary foods* **eat between meals**, nibble, munch; informal graze.

snaffle v. informal See **steal** (sense 1 of the verb).

snag n. **1** *the snag is that this might affect inflation* **complication**, difficulty, catch, hitch, obstacle, stumbling block, pitfall, problem, issue, impediment, hindrance, inconvenience, setback, hurdle, disadvantage, downside, drawback. **2** *smooth rails with no snags* **sharp projection**, jag; thorn, spur. **3** *a snag in her tights* **tear**, rip, hole, gash, slash; ladder, run.
▶ v. **1** *she snagged her tights* **tear**, rip, ladder. **2** *the zip snagged on the fabric* **catch**, get caught, hook.

snake n. *the snake shed its skin* literary serpent; Austral./NZ rhyming slang Joe Blake.
▶ v. *the road snakes inland* **twist**, wind, meander, zigzag, curve.
□ **snake in the grass** traitor, turncoat, betrayer, informer, back-stabber, double-crosser, quisling, Judas; fraudster, trickster, charlatan; informal two-timer, rat.

> **WORD LINKS**
>
> **colubrine, ophidian, serpentine** relating to or resembling a snake
> **gorgon** (in Greek mythology) each of three sisters who had snakes as hair
> **slough** (of a snake) shed an old skin

---

snap v. **1** *the ruler snapped* **break**, fracture, splinter, come apart, split, crack; informal bust. **2** *she snapped after years of violence* **flare up**, lose one's self-control, freak out, go to pieces, get worked up; informal crack up, lose one's cool, blow one's top, fly off the handle; Brit. informal throw a wobbly. **3** *a dog was snapping at his heels* **bite**; gnash its teeth. **4** *'Shut up!' Anna snapped* **say roughly**, say brusquely, say abruptly, say angrily, bark, snarl, growl; retort, rejoin, retaliate; round on someone; informal jump down someone's throat. **5** *photographers snapped the royals* **photograph**, picture, take, shoot, film, capture.
▶ n. **1** *she closed her purse with a snap* **click**, crack, pop. **2** *a cold snap* **period**, spell, time, interval, stretch; Brit. informal patch. **3** informal *holiday snaps* **photograph**, picture, photo, shot, snapshot, print, slide, frame, still; Brit. enprint.
□ **snap out of it** informal recover, get a grip, pull oneself together, get over it, get better, cheer up, perk up; informal buck up.
snap something up buy eagerly, accept eagerly, jump at, take advantage of, grab, seize (on), grasp with both hands, pounce on.

snappy adj. informal **1** *a snappy mood* **irritable**, irascible, short-tempered, quick-tempered, hot-tempered, snappish, fiery, touchy, volatile; cross, crabby, crotchety, cantankerous, grumpy, bad-tempered, testy, tetchy; informal chippy, grouchy, cranky, on a short fuse; Brit. informal narky, ratty, eggy, like a bear with a sore head; N. Amer. informal soreheaded. **2** *a snappy catchphrase* **concise**, succinct, memorable, catchy, neat, clever, crisp, pithy, witty, incisive, brief, short. **3** *a snappy dresser* **smart**, fashionable, stylish, chic, modish, elegant, neat, spruce, trim, dapper; informal snazzy, natty, sharp, nifty, cool; N. Amer. informal sassy, spiffy, fly.
– OPPOSITES peaceable, long-winded, slovenly.

snare n. **1** *the hare was caught in a snare* **trap**, gin, net, noose. **2** *avoid the snares of the new law* **pitfall**, trap, catch, danger, hazard, peril; web, mesh; literary toils.
▶ v. **1** *game birds were snared* **trap**, catch, net, bag, ensnare, entrap. **2** *he managed to snare an heiress* **ensnare**, catch, get hold of, bag, hook, land.

snarl¹ v. **1** *the wolves are snarling* **growl**, gnash one's teeth. **2** *'Shut it!' he snarled* **say roughly**, say brusquely, say nastily, bark, snap, growl; informal jump down someone's throat.

snarl² v. **1** *the rope got snarled up in a bush* **tangle**, entangle, entwine, enmesh, ravel, knot, foul. **2** *this case has snarled up the*

S

court process **complicate**, confuse, muddle, jumble; informal mess up.

snarl-up n. informal **1** *a snarl-up in Edinburgh traffic jam*, tailback, gridlock. **2** *a snarl-up in terminology* **muddle**, mess, tangle, jumble; misunderstanding, misinterpretation, misconception, confusion; mistake, mix-up, bungle; informal hash, foul-up, screw-up; N. Amer. informal snafu.

snatch v. **1** *she snatched the sandwich* **grab**, seize, take hold of, get one's hands on, take, pluck; grasp at, clutch at. **2** informal *someone snatched my bag.* See **steal** (sense 1 of the verb). **3** informal *she snatched the newborn from the hospital.* See **abduct**. **4** *he snatched victory* **seize**, pluck, wrest, achieve, secure, obtain; scrape.
▸ n. **1** *brief snatches of sleep* **period**, spell, time, fit, bout, interval, stretch. **2** *a snatch of conversation* **fragment**, snippet, bit, scrap, part, extract, excerpt, portion.

snazzy adj. informal See **stylish**.

sneak v. **1** *I sneaked out* **creep**, slink, steal, slip, slide, sidle, edge, move furtively, tiptoe, pussyfoot, pad, prowl. **2** *she sneaked a camera in* **bring/take surreptitiously**, bring/take secretly, bring/take illicitly, smuggle, spirit, slip. **3** *he sneaked a doughnut* **take furtively**, take surreptitiously; steal; informal snatch. **4** Brit. informal *the little squirt sneaked on me* **inform**, tell tales; report, give someone away, be disloyal, sell out, stab in the back; informal squeal, rat, blow the whistle, peach, snitch, stitch up; Brit. informal grass, split, shop; Scottish informal clype; N. Amer. informal finger; Austral./NZ informal dob.
▸ n. Brit. informal *Ethel was the class sneak* **informer**, traitor; informal snitch, squealer, rat, whistle-blower; Brit. informal grass; Scottish informal clype; N. Amer. informal fink; Austral./NZ informal dobber.
▸ adj. *a sneak preview* **furtive**, secret, stealthy, sly, surreptitious, clandestine, covert; private, quick.

sneaking adj. **1** *she had a sneaking admiration for him* **secret**, private, hidden, concealed, unvoiced, undisclosed, undeclared, unavowed. **2** *a sneaking feeling* **niggling**, nagging, lurking, insidious, lingering, gnawing, persistent.

sneaky adj. **sly**, crafty, cunning, wily, artful, scheming, devious, guileful, deceitful, duplicitous, underhand, unscrupulous; furtive, secretive, secret, stealthy, surreptitious, clandestine, covert; Military black; informal foxy, shifty, dirty.
– OPPOSITES honest.

sneer n. **1** *she had a sneer on her face* **smirk**, curl of the lip, disparaging smile, contemptuous smile, cruel smile. **2** *the sneers of others* **jibe**, barb, jeer, taunt, insult, slight, affront, slur; informal dig.
▸ v. **1** *he looked at me and sneered* **smirk**, curl one's lip, smile disparagingly, smile contemptuously, smile cruelly. **2** *it is easy to sneer at them* **scoff at**, scorn, disdain, mock, jeer at, hold in contempt, ridicule, deride,

insult, slight; N. Amer. slur.

snicker v. *they all snickered at her* **snigger**, titter, giggle, chortle, simper.
▸ n. *he could not suppress a snicker* **snigger**, titter, giggle, chortle, simper.

snide adj. **disparaging**, derogatory, deprecating, denigratory, insulting, contemptuous; mocking, taunting, sneering, scornful, derisive, sarcastic, spiteful, nasty, mean; Brit. informal sarky.

sniff v. **1** *she sniffed and blew her nose* **inhale**, breathe in; snuffle. **2** *Tom sniffed the fruit* **smell**, scent, get a whiff of.
▸ n. **1** *she gave a loud sniff* **snuffle**, inhalation. **2** *a sniff of fresh air* **smell**, scent, whiff; lungful. **3** informal *the first sniff of trouble* **indication**, hint, whiff, inkling, suggestion, whisper, trace, sign, suspicion.
□ **sniff at** scorn, disdain, hold in contempt, look down one's nose at, treat as inferior, look down on, sneer at, scoff at; informal turn one's nose up at.
sniff something out informal detect, find, discover, bring to light, track down, dig up, hunt out, ferret out, root out, uncover, unearth, run to earth/ground.

snigger v. *they snigger at him behind his back* **snicker**, titter, giggle, chortle, laugh; sneer, smirk.
▸ n. *the joke got hardly a snigger* **snicker**, titter, giggle, chortle, laugh; sneer, smirk.

snip v. **1** *an usher snipped our tickets* **cut**, clip, snick, slit, nick, notch. **2** *snip off the faded flowers* **cut off**, trim (off), clip, prune, chop off, lop (off), dock, crop, sever, detach, remove, take off.
▸ n. **1** *make snips along the edge* **cut**, slit, snick, nick, notch, incision. **2** *snips of wallpaper* **scrap**, snippet, cutting, shred, remnant, fragment, sliver, bit, piece. **3** Brit. informal *the book was a snip.* See **bargain** (sense 2 of the noun). **4** informal *the job was a snip.* See **cinch** (sense 1).

snippet n. **piece**, bit, scrap, fragment, particle, shred; excerpt, extract.

snivel v. **1** *he slumped in a chair, snivelling* **sniffle**, snuffle, whimper, whine, weep, cry; Scottish greet; informal blub, blubber, boohoo; Brit. informal grizzle. **2** *don't snivel about what you get* **complain**, mutter, grumble, grouse, groan, carp, bleat, whine; informal gripe, moan, grouch, beef, bellyache, whinge, sound off; Brit. informal create; N. Amer. informal kvetch.

snobbery n. **affectation**, pretension, pretentiousness, arrogance, haughtiness, airs and graces, elitism; disdain, condescension, superciliousness; informal snootiness, uppitiness; Brit. informal side.

snobbish adj. **elitist**, snobby, superior, supercilious; arrogant, haughty, disdainful, condescending; pretentious, affected; informal snooty, uppity, high and mighty, la-di-da, stuck-up, hoity-toity, snotty; Brit. informal toffee-nosed.

snoop informal v. **1** *don't snoop into our affairs* **pry**, inquire, be inquisitive, be curious, poke about/around, be a busybody, poke one's

S

nose into; interfere (in/with), meddle (in/with), intrude (on); informal be nosy; Austral./NZ informal stickybeak. **2** *they snooped around the building* **investigate**, explore, search, nose, have a good look; prowl around.
▸ n. **1** *he went for a snoop around* **search**, nose, look, prowl, ferret, poke, investigation. **2** *FBI snoops.* See **snooper**.

snooper n. **meddler**, busybody, eavesdropper; investigator, detective; informal nosy parker, Paul Pry, snoop, private eye, PI, sleuth; N. Amer. informal gumshoe; Austral./NZ informal stickybeak.

snooty adj. informal **arrogant**, proud, haughty, conceited, aloof, superior, self-important, disdainful, supercilious, snobbish, snobby, patronizing, condescending; informal uppity, high and mighty, la-di-da, stuck-up, hoity-toity; Brit. informal toffee-nosed.
– OPPOSITES modest.

snooze informal n. *a good place for a snooze* **nap**, doze, sleep, rest, siesta, catnap; informal forty winks; Brit. informal kip; literary slumber.
▸ v. *she gently snoozed* **nap**, doze, sleep, rest, take a siesta, catnap; informal snatch forty winks, get some shut-eye; Brit. informal kip, get one's head down; N. Amer. informal catch some Zs; literary slumber.

snout n. **muzzle**, nose, proboscis, trunk; Scottish & N. English neb.

snow n. **snowflakes**, flakes, snowfall, snowstorm, blizzard, sleet; snowdrift, avalanche.

> **WORD LINKS**
> niveous (literary) resembling snow

snub v. *they snubbed their hosts* **rebuff**, spurn, repulse, cold-shoulder, brush off, give the cold shoulder to, keep at arm's length; cut (dead), ignore; insult, slight, affront, humiliate; informal freeze out, knock back; N. Amer. informal stiff.
▸ n. *a very public snub* **rebuff**, repulse, slap in the face; humiliation, insult, slight, affront; informal brush-off, put-down.

snuff v. **extinguish**, put out, douse, smother, choke, blow out, quench, stub out.

snug adj. **1** *our tents were snug* **cosy**, comfortable, warm, homely, welcoming, restful, reassuring, intimate, sheltered, secure; informal comfy. **2** *a snug dress* **tight**, skintight, close-fitting, figure-hugging, slinky.
– OPPOSITES bleak, loose.

snuggle v. **nestle**, curl up, huddle (up), cuddle up, nuzzle, settle; N. Amer. snug down.

soak v. **1** *soak the beans in water* **immerse**, steep, submerge, submerse, dip, dunk, bathe, douse, marinate, souse. **2** *we got soaked outside* **drench**, wet through, saturate, waterlog, deluge, inundate, submerge, drown, swamp. **3** *the sweat soaked through his clothes* **permeate**, penetrate, percolate, seep into, spread through, infuse, impregnate. **4** *use towels to soak up the water* **absorb**, suck up, blot (up), mop (up), sponge up, sop up.

soaking adj. **drenched**, wet (through), soaked (through), sodden, soggy, waterlogged, saturated, sopping wet, dripping wet, wringing wet.
– OPPOSITES parched.

soar v. **1** *the bird soared into the air* **fly**, wing, ascend, climb, rise; take off, take flight. **2** *the gulls soared on the winds* **glide**, plane, float, drift, wheel, hover. **3** *the cost of living soared* **increase**, escalate, shoot up, rise, spiral; informal go through the roof, skyrocket.
– OPPOSITES plummet.

sob v. **weep**, cry, shed tears, snivel, whimper; howl, bawl; Scottish greet; informal blub, blubber, boohoo; Brit. informal grizzle.

sober adj. **1** *they were drunk more often than sober* **not drunk**, clear-headed; teetotal, abstinent, abstemious, dry; informal on the wagon. **2** *a sober view of life* **serious**, solemn, sensible, thoughtful, grave, sombre, staid, level-headed, businesslike, down-to-earth, commonsensical, pragmatic, conservative; unemotional, dispassionate, objective, matter-of-fact, no-nonsense, rational, logical, straightforward; Scottish douce. **3** *a sober suit* **sombre**, subdued, severe; conventional, traditional, quiet, drab, plain.
– OPPOSITES drunk, frivolous, sensational, flamboyant.
▸ v. **1** *I ought to sober up* **become sober**; informal dry out. **2** *his expression sobered her* **make serious**, subdue, calm down, quieten, steady; bring down to earth, make someone stop and think, give someone pause for thought.

sobriety n. **1** *she noted his sobriety* **abstinence**, teetotalism, non-indulgence, abstemiousness, temperance; clear-headedness. **2** *the mayor is a model of sobriety* **seriousness**, solemnity, gravity, dignity, level-headedness, common sense, pragmatism, practicality, self-control, self-restraint, conservatism.

so-called adj. **supposed**, ostensible, alleged, presumed; nominal, titular, self-styled, professed, would-be, self-appointed, soi-disant.

soccer n. **Association football**; Brit. football, the beautiful game.

sociable adj. **friendly**, affable, companionable, gregarious, convivial, clubbable, amicable, cordial, warm, genial; communicative, responsive, forthcoming, open, outgoing, extrovert, hail-fellow-well-met, approachable; informal chummy, clubby; Brit. informal matey.
– OPPOSITES unfriendly.

social adj. **1** *a major social problem* **communal**, community, collective, group, general, popular, civil, public, societal. **2** *a social club* **recreational**, leisure. **3** *a uniquely social animal* **gregarious**, interactional; organized.
– OPPOSITES individual.
▸ n. *the club has a social once a month* **party**, gathering, function, get-together; celebration, reunion, jamboree; informal bash, shindig, do; Brit. informal rave-up, knees-up,

S

beano, bunfight, jolly.

socialism n. **leftism**, Fabianism, labourism, welfarism; radicalism, progressivism, social democracy; communism, Marxism, Leninism, Maoism; historical Bolshevism.

socialist adj. *the socialist movement* **left-wing**, leftist, Labour, Labourite, labourist, anti-capitalist, Fabian, progressive, reform; radical, revolutionary, militant, red; communist, Marxist, Leninist, Maoist; informal derogatory lefty, Bolshie, commie.
– OPPOSITES conservative.
▸ n. *a well-known socialist* **left-winger**, leftist, Fabian, Labourite, labourist, anti-capitalist, progressive, progressivist, reformer; radical, revolutionary, militant, red; communist, Marxist, Leninist, Maoist; informal derogatory lefty, Bolshie, commie.
– OPPOSITES conservative.

socialize v. **interact**, converse, be sociable, mix, mingle, get together, meet, fraternize, consort; entertain, go out; informal hobnob.

society n. **1** *a danger to society* **the community**, the (general) public, the people, the population; civilization, humankind, mankind, humanity. **2** *an industrial society* **culture**, community, civilization, nation, population. **3** *Lady Angela will help you enter society* **high society**, polite society, the upper classes, the elite, the county set, the smart set, the beautiful people, the beau monde, the haut monde; informal the upper crust, the top drawer. **4** *a local history society* **association**, club, group, circle, fellowship, guild, lodge, fraternity, brotherhood, sisterhood, sorority, league, union, alliance. **5** *the society of others* **company**, companionship, fellowship, friendship, comradeship, camaraderie.

> **WORD LINKS**
> **sociology** the study of human society

sodden adj. **1** *his clothes were sodden* **soaking**, soaked (through), wet (through), saturated, drenched, sopping wet, wringing wet. **2** *sodden fields* **waterlogged**, soggy, saturated, boggy, swampy, miry, marshy; heavy, squelchy, soft.
– OPPOSITES arid.

sofa n. **settee**, couch, divan, chaise longue, chesterfield; Brit. put-you-up; N. Amer. davenport, day bed.

soft adj. **1** *soft fruit* **mushy**, squashy, pulpy, pappy, slushy, squelchy, squishy, doughy; informal gooey; Brit. informal squidgy. **2** *soft ground* **swampy**, marshy, boggy, miry, oozy; heavy, squelchy. **3** *a soft cushion* **squashy**, spongy, compressible, supple, springy, pliable, pliant, resilient, malleable. **4** *soft fabric* **velvety**, smooth, fleecy, downy, furry, silky, silken, satiny. **5** *a soft wind* **gentle**, light, mild, moderate. **6** *soft light* **dim**, low, faint, subdued, muted, mellow. **7** *soft colours* **pale**, pastel, muted, understated, restrained, subdued, subtle. **8** *soft voices* **quiet**, low, faint, muted, subdued, muffled, hushed, whispered, stifled, murmured,

gentle, dulcet; indistinct, inaudible. **9** *soft outlines* **blurred**, vague, hazy, misty, foggy, nebulous, fuzzy, blurry, indistinct, unclear. **10** *he seduced her with soft words* **kind**, gentle, sympathetic, soothing, tender, sensitive, affectionate, loving, warm, sweet, sentimental, mushy, slushy; informal schmaltzy. **11** *she's too soft with her pupils* **lenient**, easy-going, tolerant, forgiving, forbearing, indulgent, clement, permissive, liberal, lax. **12** informal *he's soft in the head* **foolish**, stupid, simple, brainless, mindless; mad, scatterbrained, feather-brained; slow, weak, feeble; informal dopey, dippy, dotty, scatty, loopy; Brit. informal daft; Scottish & N. English informal glaikit.
– OPPOSITES hard, firm, rough, strong, harsh, lurid, strident, sharp, strict, sensible.

soften v. **1** *he tried to soften the blow of new taxes* **alleviate**, ease, relieve, soothe, take the edge off, assuage, cushion, moderate, mitigate, palliate, diminish, blunt, deaden. **2** *the winds softened* **die down**, abate, subside, moderate, let up, calm, diminish, slacken, weaken.
□ **soften someone up** charm, win over, persuade, influence, weaken, disarm, sweeten; informal butter up, soft-soap.

soft-hearted adj. **kind**, kindly, tender-hearted, tender, gentle, sympathetic, compassionate, humane; generous, indulgent, lenient, merciful, benevolent.

softly-softly adj. **cautious**, circumspect, discreet, gentle, patient, tactful, diplomatic.

soggy adj. **mushy**, squashy, pulpy, slushy, squelchy, squishy; swampy, marshy, boggy, miry; soaking, soaked through, wet, saturated, drenched; Brit. informal squidgy.

soil¹ n. **1** *acid soil* **earth**, loam, dirt, clay, sod, turf; ground. **2** *British soil* **territory**, land, domain, dominion, region, country.

soil² v. **1** *he soiled his tie* **dirty**, stain, splash, spot, spatter, splatter, smear, smudge, sully, spoil, foul; informal muck up; literary begrime. **2** *our reputation is being soiled* **dishonour**, damage, sully, stain, blacken, tarnish, taint, blemish, defile, blot, smear, drag through the mud; literary besmirch.

sojourn formal n. *a sojourn in France* **stay**, visit, stop, stopover; holiday, vacation.
▸ v. *they sojourned in the monastery* **stay**, live, put up, stop (over), lodge, room, board; holiday, vacation.

solace n. *they found solace in each other* **comfort**, consolation, cheer, support, relief.
▸ v. *she was solaced with tea and sympathy* **comfort**, console, cheer, support, soothe, calm.

soldier n. **fighter**, trooper, serviceman, servicewoman; warrior; US GI; Brit. informal squaddie; old use man-at-arms.
□ **soldier on** informal **persevere**, persist, continue, carry on, go on, keep on, keep going, struggle on, hammer away, be persistent, be determined, see/follow something through, keep at it, press on/ahead, stand one's ground, go the distance,

S

stay the course, plod on; informal plug away, peg away, stick it out.

> **WORD LINKS**
>
> **military** relating to soldiers
> **cavalry** soldiers who fought on horseback
> **infantry** soldiers who fight on foot
> **mercenary** a professional soldier hired to serve in a foreign army

sole adj. **only**, one (and only), single, solitary, lone, unique, exclusive.

solecism n. **1** *a poem marred by solecisms* **(grammatical) mistake**, error, blunder; informal howler, blooper; Brit. informal boob. **2** *it would have been a solecism to answer* **faux pas**, gaffe, impropriety, social indiscretion, infelicity, slip, error, blunder, lapse; informal slip-up, boo-boo, fail; Brit. informal boob, clanger, bloomer; N. Amer. informal goof, blooper.

solely adv. **only**, simply, just, merely, uniquely, exclusively, entirely, wholly; alone.

solemn adj. **1** *a solemn occasion* **dignified**, ceremonious, ceremonial, stately, formal, courtly, majestic; imposing, awe-inspiring, splendid, magnificent, grand. **2** *he looked very solemn* **serious**, grave, sober, sombre, unsmiling, stern, grim, dour, humourless; pensive, meditative. **3** *a solemn promise* **sincere**, earnest, honest, genuine, firm, heartfelt, wholehearted, sworn.
– OPPOSITES frivolous, light-hearted, insincere.

solemnize v. **perform**, celebrate; officiate at, formalize.

solicit v. **1** *Phil tried to solicit his help* **ask for**, request, seek, apply for, put in for, call for, press for, beg, plead for; dated crave. **2** *they are solicited for their opinions* **ask**, beg, implore, plead with, entreat, appeal to, lobby, petition, importune, supplicate, call on, press; literary beseech. **3** *the girls gathered to solicit* **work as a prostitute**, make sexual advances, tout (for business); N. Amer. informal hustle.

solicitor n. Brit. **lawyer**, legal representative, legal practitioner, notary (public), advocate, attorney; Brit. articled clerk; Scottish law agent; informal brief.

solicitous adj. **concerned**, caring, considerate, attentive, mindful, thoughtful, interested; anxious, worried.

solid adj. **1** *the ice cream was solid* **hard**, rock-hard, rigid, firm, solidified, set, frozen, concrete. **2** *solid gold* **pure**, 24-carat, unalloyed, unadulterated, genuine. **3** *a solid line* **continuous**, uninterrupted, unbroken, non-stop, undivided. **4** *solid houses* **well built**, sound, substantial, strong, sturdy, durable. **5** *a solid argument* **well founded**, valid, sound, reasonable, logical, authoritative, convincing, cogent, plausible, credible, reliable. **6** *a solid friendship* **dependable**, reliable, firm, unshakeable, trustworthy, stable, steadfast, staunch, constant. **7** *solid citizens* **sensible**, dependable, trustworthy, decent, law-abiding, upright, upstanding, worthy. **8** *the company is very solid* **financially sound**, secure, creditworthy, profit-making, solvent, in credit, in the black; Finance ungeared, unlevered. **9** *solid support from their colleagues* **unanimous**, united, consistent, undivided.
– OPPOSITES liquid, alloyed, broken, flimsy, untenable, unreliable.

solidarity n. **unanimity**, unity, like-mindedness, agreement, accord, harmony, consensus, concurrence, cooperation, cohesion; formal concord.

solidify v. **harden**, set, freeze, thicken, stiffen, congeal, cake, dry, bake; ossify, fossilize, petrify.
– OPPOSITES liquefy.

soliloquy n. **monologue**, speech, address, lecture, oration, sermon, homily, aside.

solitary adj. **1** *a solitary life* **lonely**, companionless, unaccompanied, by oneself, on one's own, alone, friendless; antisocial, unsociable, withdrawn, reclusive, cloistered, hermitic; N. Amer. lonesome. **2** *solitary farmsteads* **isolated**, remote, lonely, out of the way, in the back of beyond, outlying, off the beaten track, godforsaken, obscure, inaccessible, cut-off; secluded, private, sequestered, desolate; N. Amer. in the backwoods; Austral./NZ in the backblocks; informal in the sticks, in the middle of nowhere; N. Amer. informal in the boondocks; Austral./NZ informal beyond the black stump; literary lone. **3** *a solitary piece of evidence* **single**, lone, sole, unique; only, one, individual; odd.
– OPPOSITES sociable, accessible.
▸ n. *he became a solitary* **recluse**, loner, hermit; historical anchorite; old use eremite.

solitude n. **1** *she savoured her solitude* **loneliness**, solitariness, isolation, seclusion, sequestration, withdrawal, privacy, peace. **2** *solitudes like the area around the loch* **wilderness**, rural area, wilds, backwoods; desert, emptiness, wasteland; Austral. the bush, the outback; N. Amer. & Austral./NZ backcountry; informal the sticks; N. Amer. informal the boondocks.

solo adj. *a solo flight* **unaccompanied**, single-handed, companionless, unescorted, unattended, unchaperoned, independent, solitary; alone, on one's own, by oneself.
– OPPOSITES accompanied.
▸ adv. *she sailed solo* **unaccompanied**, alone, on one's own, single-handed(ly), by oneself, unescorted, unattended, unchaperoned, unaided, independently.
– OPPOSITES accompanied.

solution n. **1** *an easy solution to the problem* **answer**, result, resolution, way out, panacea; key, formula, explanation, interpretation. **2** *a solution of ammonia in water* **mixture**, mix, blend, compound, suspension, tincture, infusion, emulsion.

solve v. **resolve**, answer, work out, find a solution to, find the key to, puzzle out, fathom, decipher, decode, clear up, straighten out, get to the bottom of, unravel, piece together, explain; informal figure out, crack; Brit. informal suss out.

solvent adj. **financially sound**, debt-free, in the black, in credit, creditworthy, solid, secure, profit-making; Finance ungeared, unlevered.

sombre adj. **1** *sombre clothes* **dark**, drab, dull, dingy; restrained, subdued, sober, funereal. **2** *a sombre expression* **solemn**, earnest, serious, grave, sober, unsmiling, stern, grim, dour, humourless; gloomy, depressed, sad, melancholy, dismal, doleful, mournful, lugubrious.
– OPPOSITES bright, cheerful.

somebody n. *she wanted to be a somebody* **important person**, VIP, public figure, notable, dignitary, worthy; someone, (big/household) name, celebrity, star, superstar; grandee, luminary; informal celeb, bigwig, big shot, big cheese, hotshot, megastar.
– OPPOSITES nonentity.

some day adv. **sometime**, one day, one of these (fine) days, at a future date, sooner or later, by and by, in due course, in the fullness of time, in the long run.

somehow adv. **by some means**, by any means, in some way, one way or another, no matter how, by fair means or foul, by hook or by crook, come what may.

sometime adv. **1** *I'll visit sometime* **some day**, one day, one of these (fine) days, at a future date, sooner or later, by and by, in due course, in the fullness of time, in the long run. **2** *it happened sometime on Sunday* **at some time**, at some point; during, in the course of.
– OPPOSITES never.
▸ adj. *the sometime editor of the paper* **former**, past, previous, prior, foregoing, late, erstwhile, one-time, as was, ex-; formal quondam.

sometimes adv. **occasionally**, from time to time, now and then, every so often, once in a while, on occasion, at times, off and on, at intervals, periodically, sporadically, spasmodically, intermittently.

somewhat adv. **1** *matters have improved somewhat* **a little**, a bit, to some extent, (up) to a point, in some measure, rather, quite; N. Amer. informal some; informal kind of, sort of. **2** *a somewhat thicker book* **slightly**, relatively, comparatively, moderately, fairly, rather, quite, marginally.
– OPPOSITES greatly.

somnolent adj. **1** *he felt somnolent after lunch* **sleepy**, drowsy, tired, languid, dozy, groggy, lethargic, sluggish, enervated, torpid; informal snoozy, dopey, yawny; literary slumberous. **2** *a somnolent village* **quiet**, restful, tranquil, calm, peaceful, relaxing, soothing, undisturbed, untroubled.

song n. **1** *a beautiful song* **air**, strain, ditty, melody, tune, number, track. **2** *the song of the birds* **call(s)**, chirping, cheeping, peeping, chirruping, warble(s), warbling, trilling, twitter; birdsong.

□ **song and dance** informal See **fuss** (sense 1 of the noun).

songster, songstress n. **singer**, vocalist, soloist, crooner, chorister, choirboy, choirgirl; alto, bass, baritone, contralto, tenor, soprano; balladeer; informal warbler, popster, soulster, folkie, songbird; historical minstrel, troubadour; old use melodist.

sonorous adj. **1** *a sonorous voice* **resonant**, rich, full, round, booming, deep, clear, mellow, orotund, fruity, strong, resounding, reverberant. **2** *sonorous words of condemnation* **impressive**, imposing, grandiloquent, magniloquent, high-flown, lofty, orotund, bombastic, grandiose, pompous, pretentious, overblown, turgid; oratorical, rhetorical; informal highfalutin.

soon adv. **1** *we'll be there soon* **shortly**, presently, in the near future, before long, in a little while, in a minute, in a moment, in an instant, in the twinkling of an eye, in no time, before you know it, any minute (now), any day (now), by and by; informal pronto, in a jiffy, before you can say Jack Robinson, anon; Brit. informal sharpish, in a tick, in two ticks; dated directly. **2** *how soon can you get here?* **early**, quickly, promptly, speedily, punctually.

sooner adv. **1** *he should have done it sooner* **earlier**, before, beforehand, in advance, ahead of time; already. **2** *I would sooner stay* **rather**, preferably, by preference, by choice, more willingly, more readily.

soothe v. **1** *Rachel tried to soothe him* **calm (down)**, pacify, comfort, hush, quiet, subdue, settle (down), lull, tranquillize; appease, conciliate, mollify; Brit. quieten (down). **2** *an analgesic to soothe the pain* **alleviate**, ease, relieve, take the edge off, assuage, allay, lessen, palliate, diminish, decrease, dull, blunt, deaden.
– OPPOSITES agitate, aggravate.

soothing adj. **1** *soothing music* **relaxing**, restful, calm, calming, tranquil, peaceful, reposeful, tranquillizing, soporific. **2** *soothing ointment* **palliative**, mild, calmative.

soothsayer n. **seer**, oracle, augur, prophet(ess), sage, prognosticator, diviner, fortune teller, crystal-gazer, clairvoyant, psychic; Scottish spaewife; literary sibyl.

sophisticated adj. **1** *sophisticated techniques* **advanced**, modern, state-of-the-art, the latest, new, up to the minute; innovatory, trailblazing, revolutionary, futuristic, avant-garde; complex, complicated, intricate. **2** *a sophisticated woman* **worldly**, worldly-wise, experienced, enlightened, cosmopolitan, knowledgeable, urbane, cultured, cultivated, civilized, polished, refined; elegant, stylish; informal cool.
– OPPOSITES crude, naive.

sophistication n. **worldliness**, experience; urbanity, culture, civilization, polish, refinement; elegance, style, poise, finesse, savoir faire; informal cool; humorous couth.

S

sophistry n. **1** *to claim this is pure sophistry* **specious reasoning**, fallacy, sophism, casuistry. **2** *he went along with her sophistry* **fallacious argument**, sophism, fallacy; Logic paralogism.

soporific adj. *soporific drugs* **sleep-inducing**, sedative, somnolent, calmative, tranquillizing, narcotic, opiate; drowsy, sleepy, somniferous; Medicine hypnotic.
– OPPOSITES invigorating.
▶ n. *she was given a soporific* **sleeping pill**, sedative, calmative, tranquillizer, narcotic, opiate; Medicine hypnotic.
– OPPOSITES stimulant.

soppy adj. Brit. informal **1** *the songs are really soppy.* See **sentimental** (sense 2). **2** *they were too soppy for our games.* See **feeble** (sense 3).

sorcerer, sorceress n. **wizard**, witch, magician, warlock, enchanter, enchantress, magus; shaman, witch doctor; old use mage.

sorcery n. **(black) magic**, the black arts, witchcraft, wizardry, enchantment, spells, incantation, witching, witchery, thaumaturgy; shamanism; Irish pishogue.

sordid adj. **1** *a sordid love affair* **sleazy**, seedy, seamy, unsavoury, tawdry, cheap, debased, degenerate, dishonourable, disreputable, discreditable, contemptible, ignominious, shameful, wretched, abhorrent. **2** *a sordid little street* **squalid**, slummy, dirty, filthy, mucky, grimy, shabby, messy, soiled, scummy, unclean; informal cruddy, grungy, crummy, scuzzy; Brit. informal grotty.
– OPPOSITES respectable, immaculate.

sore adj. **1** *a sore leg* **painful**, hurting, hurt, aching, throbbing, smarting, stinging, agonizing, excruciating; inflamed, sensitive, tender, raw, bruised, wounded, injured. **2** *we are in sore need of you* **dire**, urgent, pressing, desperate, parlous, critical, crucial, acute, grave, serious, drastic, extreme, life-and-death, great, terrible; formal exigent. **3** N. Amer. informal *they were sore at us* **upset**, angry, annoyed, cross, furious, vexed, displeased, disgruntled, dissatisfied, exasperated, irritated, galled, irked, put out, aggrieved, offended, affronted, piqued, nettled; informal aggravated, miffed, peeved, hacked off, riled; Brit. informal narked, cheesed off, brassed off, not best pleased; N. Amer. informal teed off, ticked off.
▶ n. *a sore on his leg* **inflammation**, swelling, lesion; wound, scrape, abrasion, cut, laceration, graze, contusion, bruise; ulcer, boil, abscess, carbuncle.

sorrow n. **1** *he felt sorrow at her death* **sadness**, unhappiness, misery, despondency, regret, depression, despair, desolation, dejection, wretchedness, gloom, dolefulness, melancholy, woe, heartache, grief; literary dolour. **2** *the sorrows of life* **trouble**, difficulty, problem, adversity, misery, woe, affliction, trial, tribulation, misfortune, setback, reverse, blow, failure, tragedy.
– OPPOSITES joy.
▶ v. *they sorrowed over her grave* **mourn**,
lament, grieve, be sad, be miserable, be despondent, despair, suffer, ache, agonize, anguish, pine, weep, wail.
– OPPOSITES rejoice.

sorrowful adj. **1** *sorrowful eyes* **sad**, unhappy, dejected, regretful, downcast, miserable, downhearted, despondent, despairing, disconsolate, desolate, glum, gloomy, doleful, dismal, melancholy, mournful, woeful, woebegone, forlorn, crestfallen, heartbroken; informal blue, down in the mouth, down in the dumps. **2** *sorrowful news* **tragic**, sad, unhappy, awful, miserable, sorry, pitiful; traumatic, upsetting, depressing, distressing, dispiriting, heartbreaking, harrowing; formal grievous.

sorry adj. **1** *I was sorry to hear about his accident* **sad**, unhappy, sorrowful, distressed, upset, downcast, downhearted, disheartened, despondent; heartbroken, inconsolable, grief-stricken. **2** *he felt sorry for her* **full of pity**, sympathetic, compassionate, moved, consoling, empathetic, concerned. **3** *I'm sorry if I was brusque* **regretful**, remorseful, contrite, repentant, rueful, penitent, apologetic, abject, guilty, self-reproachful, ashamed, sheepish, shamefaced. **4** *he looks a sorry sight* **pitiful**, pitiable, heart-rending, distressing; unfortunate, unhappy, wretched, unlucky, shameful, regrettable, awful.
– OPPOSITES glad, unsympathetic, unrepentant.

sort n. **1** *what sort of book is it?* **type**, kind, nature, manner, variety, class, category, style; calibre, quality, form, group, set, bracket, genre, species, family, order, generation, vintage, make, model, brand, stamp, ilk, kidney, cast, grain, mould; N. Amer. stripe. **2** informal *he's a good sort* **person**, individual, soul, creature, human being; character, customer; informal fellow, type, beggar, cookie; Brit. informal bod; informal dated body, dog, cove.
▶ v. **1** *they sorted things of similar size* **classify**, class, categorize, catalogue, grade, group; organize, arrange, order, marshal, assemble, systematize, systemize, pigeonhole. **2** *the problem was soon sorted* **resolve**, settle, solve, fix, work out, straighten out, deal with, put right, set right, rectify, iron out; answer, explain, fathom, unravel, clear up; informal sew up, hammer out, thrash out, patch up, figure out.
□ **out of sorts 1** *I'm feeling out of sorts* **unwell**, ill, poorly, sick, queasy, nauseous, peaky, run down, below par; Brit. off colour; informal under the weather, funny, rough, lousy, rotten, awful; Brit. informal off, ropy; Scottish informal wabbit, peely-wally; Austral./ NZ informal crook; dated seedy. **2** *I've been out of sorts and I'd like a chat* **unhappy**, sad, miserable, down, depressed, melancholy, gloomy, glum, dispirited, despondent, forlorn, woebegone, low, in the doldrums; informal blue, fed up, down in the dumps, down in the mouth.

sort of informal **1** *you look sort of familiar*

slightly, faintly, remotely, vaguely; somewhat, moderately, quite, rather, fairly, reasonably, relatively; informal pretty, kind of. **2** *he sort of pirouetted* **as it were**, kind of, somehow.
sort something out 1 *she sorted out the clothes.* See **sort** (sense 1 of the verb).
2 *they must sort out their problems.* See **sort** (sense 2 of the verb).

sortie n. **1** *a sortie against their besiegers* **foray**, sally, charge, offensive, attack, assault, onslaught, thrust, drive; old use onset. **2** *a bomber sortie* **raid**, flight, mission, operation.

so-so adj. informal **mediocre**, indifferent, average, middle-of-the-road, middling, moderate, ordinary, adequate, fair; uninspired, undistinguished, unexceptional, unremarkable, run-of-the-mill, lacklustre; informal bog-standard, no great shakes, not up to much; NZ informal half-pie.

soul n. **1** *seeing the soul through the eyes* **spirit**, psyche, (inner) self, inner being, life force, vital force; individuality, make-up, subconscious, anima; Philosophy pneuma; Hinduism atman. **2** *he is the soul of discretion* **embodiment**, personification, incarnation, epitome, quintessence, essence; model, exemplification, exemplar, image, manifestation. **3** *not a soul in sight* **person**, human being, individual, man, woman, mortal, creature. **4** *their music lacked soul* **inspiration**, feeling, emotion, passion, animation, intensity, fervour, ardour, enthusiasm, warmth, energy, vitality, spirit.

soulful adj. **emotional**, deep, profound, fervent, heartfelt, sincere, passionate; meaningful, significant, eloquent, expressive; moving, stirring; sad, mournful, doleful.

soulless adj. **1** *a soulless room* **characterless**, featureless, bland, dull, colourless, lacklustre, dreary, drab, uninspiring, undistinguished, anaemic, insipid. **2** *it was soulless work* **boring**, dull, tedious, dreary, humdrum, tiresome, wearisome, uninteresting, uninspiring, unexciting, soul-destroying, mind-numbing, dry; monotonous, repetitive.
– OPPOSITES exciting.

sound¹ n. **1** *the sound of the car* **noise**, note; din, racket, row, hubbub; resonance, reverberation. **2** *she did not make a sound* **utterance**, cry, word, noise, peep; informal cheep. **3** *the sound of the flute* **music**, tone, notes. **4** *I don't like the sound of that* **idea**, thought, concept, prospect, description. **5** *we're within sound of the sea* **earshot**, hearing (distance), range.
– OPPOSITES silence.
▶v. **1** *the buzzer sounded* **make a noise**, resonate, resound, reverberate, go off, blare; ring, chime, peal. **2** *drivers must sound their horns* **blow**, blast, toot, blare; operate, set off; ring. **3** *do you sound the 'h'?* **pronounce**, verbalize, voice, enunciate, articulate, vocalize, say. **4** *she sounded a warning* **utter**, voice, deliver, express, speak, announce,

pronounce. **5** *it sounds a crazy idea* **appear**, look (like), seem, strike someone as being, give every indication of being.

> **WORD LINKS**
>
> **acoustic, sonic** relating to sound or sound waves
> **decibel** a unit for measuring the intensity of sound
> **phonetics** the study of speech sounds
> **sonar** a system for detecting objects underwater, based on sound pulses

sound² adj. **1** *your heart is sound* **healthy**, in good condition, in good shape, fit, hale and hearty, in fine fettle; undamaged, unimpaired. **2** *a sound building* **well built**, solid, substantial, strong, sturdy, durable, stable, intact, unimpaired. **3** *sound advice* **well founded**, valid, reasonable, logical, weighty, authoritative, reliable. **4** *a sound judge of character* **reliable**, dependable, trustworthy, fair; good, sensible, wise, judicious, sagacious, shrewd, perceptive. **5** *financially sound* **solvent**, debt-free, in the black, in credit, creditworthy, secure. **6** *a sound sleep* **deep**, undisturbed, uninterrupted, untroubled, peaceful. **7** *a sound thrashing* **thorough**, proper, real, complete, unqualified, out-and-out, thoroughgoing, severe; informal right (royal).
– OPPOSITES unhealthy, unsafe, unreliable, insolvent, light.

sound³ v. *sound the depth of the river* **measure**, gauge, determine, test, investigate, survey, plumb, fathom, probe.
□ **sound someone/something out** investigate, test, check, examine, probe, research, look into; canvass, survey, poll, question, interview, sample; informal pump.

sound⁴ n. *an oil spill in Prince William Sound* **channel**, (sea) passage, strait(s), narrows, waterway; inlet, arm (of the sea), fjord, creek, bay; estuary, firth.

soup n. **broth**, potage, consommé, bouillon, chowder, bisque.

sour adj. **1** *sour wine* **acid**, acidic, acidy, acidulated, tart, bitter, sharp, vinegary, pungent; N. Amer. acerb; technical acerbic. **2** *sour milk* **bad**, off, turned, curdled, rancid, high, rank, foul, fetid. **3** *a sour old man* **embittered**, resentful, rancorous, jaundiced, bitter; nasty, spiteful, irritable, peevish, fractious, cross, crabby, crotchety, cantankerous, disagreeable, petulant, querulous, grumpy, bad-tempered, ill-humoured, sullen, surly, sulky, churlish; informal snappy, grouchy; Brit. informal ratty, stroppy, shirty; N. Amer. informal cranky, soreheaded.
– OPPOSITES sweet, fresh, amiable.
▶v. **1** *the war had soured him* **embitter**, disillusion, disenchant, poison, alienate; dissatisfy, frustrate. **2** *the dispute soured relations* **spoil**, mar, damage, harm, impair, wreck, upset, poison, blight, tarnish.
– OPPOSITES improve.

source n. **1** *the source of the river* **spring**, origin, (well) head, headspring, headwater(s); literary wellspring. **2** *the source*

S

of the rumour **origin**, birthplace, spring, fountainhead, fount, starting point; history, provenance, derivation, root, beginning, genesis, start, rise; author, originator, initiator, inventor; N. Amer. provenience. **3** *a historian uses primary and secondary sources* **reference**, authority, informant; document.

souse v. **drench**, douse, soak, steep, saturate, plunge, immerse, submerge, dip, sink, dunk.

soused adj. **1** *a soused herring* **pickled**, marinated, soaked, steeped. **2** informal *he was well and truly soused*. See **drunk** (adjective).

south adj. **southern**, southerly, meridional, austral.

souvenir n. **memento**, keepsake, reminder, remembrance, token, memorial; trophy, relic.

sovereign n. **ruler**, monarch, crowned head, head of state, potentate, suzerain, overlord, dynast, leader.
▸adj. **1** *sovereign control* **supreme**, absolute, unlimited, unrestricted, boundless, ultimate, total, unconditional, full; principal, chief, dominant, predominant, ruling; royal, regal, monarchical. **2** *a sovereign state* **independent**, autonomous, self-governing, self-determining; non-aligned, free. **3** dated *a sovereign remedy for all ills* **effective**, effectual, efficient, powerful, potent; useful, helpful, valuable, worthwhile; excellent, reliable, unfailing; informal sure-fire; formal efficacious.

sovereignty n. **1** *their sovereignty over the islands* **jurisdiction**, rule, supremacy, dominion, power, ascendancy, suzerainty, hegemony, domination, authority, control, influence. **2** *full sovereignty was achieved in 1955* **autonomy**, independence, self-government, self-rule, home rule, self-determination, freedom.

sow v. **1** *sow the seeds in rows* **plant**, scatter, spread, broadcast, disperse, strew, disseminate, distribute; drill, dibble, seed. **2** *the new policy has sown confusion* **cause**, bring about, occasion, create, lead to, produce, engender, generate, prompt, initiate, precipitate, trigger, provoke; culminate in, entail, necessitate; foster, foment; literary beget.

space n. **1** *there was not enough space* **room**, capacity, area, volume, expanse, extent, scope, latitude, margin, leeway, play, clearance. **2** *green spaces in London* **area**, expanse, stretch, sweep, tract. **3** *the space between the timbers* **gap**, interval, opening, aperture, cavity, cranny, fissure, crack, interstice, lacuna. **4** *write your name in the appropriate space* **blank**, gap, box. **5** *a space of seven years* **period**, span, time, duration, stretch, course, interval. **6** *the first woman in space* **outer space**, deep space; the universe, the galaxy, the solar system; infinity.
▸v. *the chairs were spaced widely* **position**, arrange, range, array, dispose, lay out, locate, situate, set, stand.

spaceman, **spacewoman** n. **astronaut**, cosmonaut, taikonaut, space traveller, space cadet; N. Amer. informal **jock**.

spacious adj. **roomy**, capacious, palatial, airy, sizeable, generous, large, big, vast, immense; extensive, expansive, sweeping, rolling, rambling, open; formal commodious.
– OPPOSITES cramped.

spadework n. **groundwork**, preliminary work, preliminaries, preparatory measures, preparations, planning, foundations; hard work, donkey work, labour, drudgery, toil; informal grind; Brit. informal graft.

span n. **1** *a six-foot wing span* **extent**, length, width, reach, stretch, spread, distance, range. **2** *the span of one working day* **period**, space, time, duration, course, interval.
▸v. **1** *an arch spanned the stream* **bridge**, cross, traverse, pass over. **2** *his career spanned twenty years* **last**, cover, extend, spread over, comprise.

spank v. **smack**, slap, hit, beat, cuff; informal wallop, belt, whack, give someone a hiding; Scottish & N. English skelp.

spar v. **quarrel**, argue, fight, disagree, differ, be at odds, be at variance, fall out, dispute, squabble, wrangle, bandy words, cross swords, lock horns, be at loggerheads; informal scrap, argufy, spat; Brit. informal row.

spare adj. **1** *a spare set of keys* **extra**, supplementary, additional, second, other, alternative; emergency, reserve, back-up, relief, fallback, substitute; fresh; N. Amer. alternate. **2** *they sold off the spare land* **surplus**, superfluous, excessive; redundant, unnecessary, inessential, unessential, unneeded, uncalled for, dispensable, disposable, expendable, unwanted; informal going begging. **3** *your spare time* **free**, leisure, own. **4** *a spare woman* **slender**, lean, willowy, svelte, lissom, rangy, clean-limbed, trim, slight; thin, skinny, gaunt, lanky, spindly; informal skin and bone.
▸v. **1** *he could not spare any money* **afford**, do without, manage without, dispense with, part with, give, provide. **2** *they were spared by their captors* **pardon**, let off, forgive, reprieve, release, free; leave uninjured, leave unhurt; be merciful to, show mercy to, have mercy on, be lenient to, have pity on.
▫ **go spare** Brit. informal See **get angry** at **angry**.
to spare left (over), remaining, unused, unneeded, not required, still available, surplus (to requirements), superfluous, extra; informal going begging.

sparing adj. **thrifty**, economical, frugal, canny, careful, prudent, cautious; mean, miserly, niggardly, parsimonious, close, close-fisted, penny-pinching, cheese-paring, ungenerous, grasping; informal stingy, tight-fisted, tight, mingy, money-grubbing; N. Amer. informal cheap.
– OPPOSITES lavish.

spark n. **1** *a spark of light* **flash**, glint, twinkle, flicker, flare, pinprick. **2** *not a spark of truth in the story* **particle**, iota, jot, whit, glimmer, atom, bit, trace, vestige, ounce, shred, crumb, grain, mite, hint, touch, suggestion, whisper, scintilla; informal smidgen, tad.

▶v. *the trial sparked a furious row* **cause**, give rise to, lead to, occasion, bring about, start, initiate, precipitate, prompt, trigger (off), provoke, stimulate, stir up.

sparkle v. **1** *her earrings sparkled* **glitter**, glint, glisten, twinkle, flash, blink, wink, shimmer, shine, gleam; literary coruscate, glister. **2** *she sparkled as the hostess* **be lively**, be vivacious, be animated, be ebullient, be exuberant, be bubbly, be effervescent, be witty, be full of life.

▶n. *the sparkle of the pool* **glitter**, glint, twinkle, flicker, shimmer, flash, shine, gleam; literary coruscation.

sparkling adj. **1** *sparkling wine* **effervescent**, fizzy, carbonated, aerated, gassy, bubbly, frothy; mousseux, spumante. **2** *a sparkling performance* **brilliant**, dazzling, scintillating, exciting, exhilarating, stimulating, invigorating; vivacious, lively, vibrant, animated.
– OPPOSITES still, dull.

sparse adj. **scant**, scanty, scattered, scarce, infrequent, few and far between; meagre, paltry, skimpy, limited, in short supply.
– OPPOSITES abundant.

spartan adj. **austere**, harsh, hard, frugal, stringent, rigorous, strict, stern, severe; ascetic, abstemious; bleak, joyless, grim, bare, stark, plain.
– OPPOSITES luxurious.

spasm n. **1** *a muscle spasm* **contraction**, convulsion, cramp; twitch, jerk, tic, shudder, shiver, tremor. **2** *a spasm of coughing* **fit**, paroxysm, attack, burst, bout, seizure, outburst, outbreak, access; informal splurt; formal boutade.

spasmodic adj. **intermittent**, fitful, irregular, sporadic, erratic, occasional, infrequent, scattered, patchy, isolated, periodic, periodical, on and off.

spate n. **series**, succession, run, cluster, string, rash, epidemic, outbreak, wave, flurry, rush, flood, deluge, torrent.

spatter v. **splash**, bespatter, splatter, spray, sprinkle, spritz, shower, speck, speckle, fleck, mottle, blotch, mark, cover; informal splotch; Brit. informal splodge.

spawn v. **give rise to**, bring about, occasion, generate, engender, originate; lead to, result in, effect, induce, initiate, start, set off, precipitate, trigger; breed, bear; literary beget.

speak v. **1** *she refused to speak about it* **talk**, say anything/something; utter, state, declare, tell, voice, express, pronounce, articulate, enunciate, vocalize, verbalize. **2** *we spoke the other day* **converse**, have a conversation, talk, communicate, chat, pass the time of day, have a word, gossip; informal have a confab, chew the fat; Brit. informal natter; N. Amer. informal shoot the breeze; formal confabulate. **3** *the Minister spoke for two hours* **give a speech**, talk, lecture, hold

forth, discourse, expound, expatiate, orate, sermonize, pontificate; informal spout, spiel, speechify, jaw, sound off. **4** *he was spoken of as a promising student* **mention**, talk about, discuss, refer to, remark on, allude to. **5** *his expression spoke disbelief* **indicate**, show, display, register, reveal, betray, exhibit, manifest, express, convey, impart, bespeak, communicate, evidence; suggest, denote, reflect; formal evince. **6** *you must speak to him about his rudeness* **reprimand**, rebuke, admonish, chastise, chide, upbraid, reprove, reproach, scold, remonstrate with, take to task, pull up; informal tell off, dress down, rap over the knuckles, come down on; Brit. informal tick off; formal castigate.

□ **speak for 1** *she speaks for the Liberal Democrats* **represent**, act for, appear for, express the views of, be spokesperson for. **2** *I spoke for the motion* **advocate**, champion, uphold, defend, support, promote, recommend, back, endorse, sponsor, espouse. **speak out** speak publicly, speak openly, speak frankly, speak one's mind, sound off, stand up and be counted. **speak up** speak loudly, speak clearly, raise one's voice; shout, yell, bellow; informal holler.

speaker n. **speech-maker**, lecturer, talker, speechifier, orator, declaimer, rhetorician; spokesperson, spokesman/woman, mouthpiece; reader, lector, commentator, broadcaster, narrator; informal tub-thumper, spieler; historical demagogue, rhetor.

spear n. **javelin**, lance, assegai, harpoon, bayonet; gaff, leister; historical pike.

spearhead n. *the spearhead of the struggle against Fascism* **leader(s)**, driving force; forefront, front runner(s), front line, vanguard, van, cutting edge.

▶v. *she spearheaded the campaign* **lead**, head, front; lead the way, be in the van, be in the vanguard.

special adj. **1** *a very special person* **exceptional**, unusual, singular, uncommon, notable, noteworthy, remarkable, outstanding, unique. **2** *our town's special character* **distinctive**, distinct, individual, particular, specific, peculiar. **3** *a special occasion* **momentous**, significant, memorable, signal, important, historic, festive, gala, red-letter. **4** *a special tool for cutting tiles* **specific**, particular, purpose-built, tailor-made, custom-built.
– OPPOSITES ordinary, general.

specialist n. **expert**, authority, pundit, professional; connoisseur; master, maestro, adept, virtuoso; informal pro, buff, ace, whizz, hotshot; Brit. informal dab hand; N. Amer. informal maven.
– OPPOSITES amateur.

speciality n. **1** *his speciality was watercolours* **forte**, strong point, strength, métier, strong suit, talent, skill, bent, gift; informal bag, thing, cup of tea. **2** *a speciality of the region* **delicacy**, specialty, fine food/product, traditional food/product.

S

species n. **type**, kind, sort; genus, family, order, breed, strain, variety, class, classification, category, set, bracket; style, manner, form, genre; generation, vintage.

specific adj. **1** *a specific purpose* **particular**, specified, fixed, set, determined, distinct, definite; single, individual, peculiar, discrete, express, precise. **2** *I gave specific instructions* **detailed**, explicit, express, clear-cut, unequivocal, precise, exact, meticulous, strict, definite.
– OPPOSITES general, vague.

specification n. **1** *clear specification of objectives* **statement**, identification, definition, description, setting out, framing, designation, detailing, enumeration; stipulation, prescription. **2** *a shelter built to their specifications* **instructions**, guidelines, parameters, stipulations, requirements, conditions, provisions, restrictions, order; description, details.

specify v. **state**, name, identify, define, describe, set out, frame, itemize, detail, list, spell out, enumerate, particularize, cite, instance; stipulate, prescribe.

specimen n. **sample**, example, instance, illustration, demonstration, exemplification; bit, snippet; model, prototype, pattern, dummy, pilot, trial, taster, tester.

specious adj. **misleading**, deceptive, false, fallacious, unsound, casuistic, sophistic; plausible but wrong.

speck n. **1** *a mere speck in the distance* **dot**, pinprick, spot, fleck, speckle. **2** *a speck of dust* **particle**, grain, atom, molecule; bit, trace.

speckled adj. **flecked**, speckly, specked, freckled, freckly, spotted, spotty, dotted, mottled, dappled.

spectacle n. **1** *a spectacle fit for a monarch* **display**, show, pageant, parade, performance, exhibition, extravaganza, spectacular. **2** *they were rather an odd spectacle* **sight**, vision, scene, prospect, vista, picture. **3** *don't make a spectacle of yourself* **exhibition**, laughing stock, fool, curiosity.

spectacles plural n. **glasses**, eyewear; N. Amer. eyeglasses; informal specs.

spectacular adj. **1** *a spectacular victory* **impressive**, magnificent, splendid, dazzling, sensational, dramatic, remarkable, outstanding, memorable, unforgettable. **2** *a spectacular view* **striking**, picturesque, eye-catching, breathtaking, arresting, glorious; informal out of this world.
– OPPOSITES unimpressive, dull.
▶ n. *a spectacular put on for the tourists.* See **spectacle** (sense 1).

spectator n. **watcher**, viewer, observer, onlooker, bystander, witness; commentator, reporter, monitor; literary beholder.
– OPPOSITES participant.

spectral adj. **ghostly**, phantom, wraithlike, shadowy, incorporeal, insubstantial, disembodied, unearthly, other-worldly; informal spooky.

spectre n. **1** *the spectres in the crypt* **ghost**, phantom, apparition, spirit, wraith, shadow, presence; informal spook; literary phantasm, shade. **2** *the looming spectre of war* **threat**, menace, shadow, cloud; prospect; danger, peril, fear, dread.

spectrum n. **range**, gamut, sweep, scope, span; compass, orbit, ambit.

speculate v. **1** *they speculated about my private life* **conjecture**, theorize, hypothesize, guess, surmise; think, wonder, muse. **2** *investors speculate on the stock market* **gamble**, take a risk, venture, wager; invest, play the market; Brit. informal have a flutter, punt.

speculative adj. **1** *any discussion is largely speculative* **conjectural**, suppositional, theoretical, hypothetical, putative, academic, notional, abstract; tentative, unproven, unfounded, groundless, unsubstantiated. **2** *a speculative investment* **risky**, hazardous, unsafe, uncertain, unpredictable; informal chancy, dicey, iffy; Brit. informal dodgy.

speech n. **1** *he doesn't have the power of speech* **speaking**, talking, verbal expression, verbal communication. **2** *her speech was slurred* **diction**, elocution, articulation, enunciation, pronunciation; utterance, words. **3** *an after-dinner speech* **talk**, address, lecture, discourse, oration, disquisition, peroration, deliverance, presentation; sermon, homily; monologue, soliloquy; informal spiel. **4** *Spanish popular speech* **language**, tongue, parlance, idiom, dialect, vernacular, patois; informal lingo, patter, -speak, -ese.

> **WORD LINKS**
> **oral, lingual, phonic** relating to speech or speech sounds
> **oracy** the ability to express oneself fluently and grammatically in speech
> **phonetics** the study of speech sounds
> **aphasia** inability to understand or produce speech as a result of brain damage
> **glossolalia** the phenomenon of apparently speaking in an unknown language during religious worship

speechless adj. **lost for words**, dumbstruck, bereft of speech, tongue-tied, inarticulate, mute, dumb, voiceless, silent; informal mum; old use mumchance.
– OPPOSITES verbose.

speed n. **1** *the speed of their progress* **rate**, pace, tempo, momentum. **2** *the speed with which they responded* **rapidity**, swiftness, speediness, quickness, dispatch, promptness, immediacy, briskness, sharpness; haste, hurry, precipitateness; acceleration, velocity; informal lick, clip; literary celerity.
▶ v. **1** *I sped home* **hurry**, rush, dash, run, race, sprint, bolt, dart, gallop, career, charge, shoot, hurtle, hare, fly, zoom, scurry, scuttle, scamper, hasten; informal tear, belt, pelt, scoot, zip, whip, hotfoot it, leg it; Brit. informal bomb; N. Amer. informal hightail it. **2** *he was caught speeding* **drive too fast**, exceed the speed limit. **3** *a holiday will speed his recovery*

hasten, expedite, speed up, accelerate, advance, further, promote, boost, stimulate, aid, assist, facilitate.
– OPPOSITES slow, hinder.
□ **speed up** hurry up, accelerate, go faster, get a move on, put a spurt on, pick up speed, gather speed; informal get cracking, get moving, step on it, shake a leg, get a wiggle on; Brit. informal get one's skates on.

> **WORD LINKS**
> **supersonic** faster than the speed of sound
> **Mach** used with a numeral to indicate the speed of sound, twice the speed of sound, etc.
> **tachometer** an instrument measuring the speed of an engine
> **tachograph** a tachometer used in commercial vehicles to record vehicle speed over a period of time

speedily adv. **rapidly**, swiftly, quickly, fast, post-haste, at the speed of light, at full tilt; promptly, immediately, briskly; hastily, hurriedly, precipitately; informal p.d.q. (pretty damn quick), double quick, hell for leather, at the double, like the wind, like (greased) lightning; Brit. informal like the clappers, like billy-o; N. Amer. informal lickety-split; literary apace.

speedy adj. **1** *a speedy reply* **rapid**, swift, quick, fast; prompt, immediate, expeditious, express, brisk, sharp; whirlwind, lightning, meteoric; hasty, hurried, precipitate, breakneck, rushed; informal p.d.q. (pretty damn quick), snappy, quickie. **2** *a speedy hatchback* **fast**, high-speed; informal nippy, zippy; literary fleet.
– OPPOSITES slow.

spell[1] v. *the drought spelled disaster for them* **signal**, signify, mean, amount to, add up to, constitute; portend, augur, herald, bode, promise; involve; literary betoken, foretoken, forebode.
□ **spell something out** explain, make clear, make plain, elucidate, clarify; specify, itemize, detail, enumerate, list, expound, particularize, catalogue.

> **WORD LINKS**
> **orthography** the conventional spelling system of a language

spell[2] n. **1** *the witch recited a spell* **incantation**, charm, conjuration, formula; (**spells**) magic, sorcery, witchcraft; N. Amer. hex. **2** *she surrendered to his spell* **influence**, (animal) magnetism, charisma, allure, lure, charm, attraction, enticement; magic, romance, mystique.
□ **cast a spell on** bewitch, enchant, entrance; curse, jinx, witch; N. Amer. hex.

spell[3] n. **1** *a spell of dry weather* **period**, time, interval, season, stretch, run, course, streak; Brit. informal patch. **2** *a spell of dizziness* **bout**, fit, attack.

spellbinding adj. *a spellbinding film* **fascinating**, enthralling, entrancing, bewitching, captivating, riveting, engrossing, gripping, absorbing, compelling, compulsive, mesmerizing, hypnotic; informal unputdownable.
– OPPOSITES boring.

spellbound adj. **enthralled**, fascinated, rapt, riveted, transfixed, gripped, captivated, bewitched, enchanted, mesmerized, hypnotized; informal hooked.

spend v. **1** *she spent £185 on shoes* **pay out**, dish out, expend, disburse; squander, waste, fritter away; lavish; informal fork out, lay out, shell out, cough up, blow, splash out, splurge; Brit. informal stump up, blue; N. Amer. informal pony up. **2** *the morning was spent gardening* **pass**, occupy, fill, take up, while away. **3** *I've spent hours on this essay* **put in**, devote; waste. **4** *the storm had spent its force* **use up**, consume, exhaust, deplete, drain.

spendthrift n. *he is such a spendthrift* **profligate**, prodigal, squanderer, waster; informal big spender.
– OPPOSITES miser.
▶ adj. *his spendthrift father* **profligate**, improvident, thriftless, wasteful, extravagant, prodigal.
– OPPOSITES frugal.

spent adj. **1** *a spent force* **used up**, consumed, exhausted, finished, depleted, drained; informal burnt out. **2** *that's enough—I'm spent* **exhausted**, tired (out), weary, worn out, dog-tired, on one's last legs, drained, fatigued, ready to drop; informal done in, all in, dead on one's feet, dead beat, bushed, wiped out, frazzled; Brit. informal knackered, whacked; N. Amer. informal pooped, tuckered out.

spew v. **1** *factories spewed out yellow smoke* **emit**, discharge, eject, expel, belch out, pour out, spout, gush, spurt, disgorge. **2** informal *he wanted to spew.* See **vomit** (sense 1 of the verb).

sphere n. **1** *a glass sphere* **globe**, ball, orb, spheroid, globule, round; bubble. **2** *our sphere of influence* **area**, field, compass, orbit; range, scope, extent. **3** *the sphere of foreign affairs* **domain**, realm, province, field, area, territory, arena, department.

spherical adj. **round**, globular, globose, globoid, globe-shaped, spheroidal, spheric; literary orbicular.

spice n. **1** *the spices in curry powder* **seasoning**, flavouring, condiment. **2** *the risk added spice to their affair* **excitement**, interest, colour, piquancy, zest; an edge; informal a kick; literary salt.
□ **spice something up** enliven, make more exciting, vitalize, perk up, put some life into, ginger up, galvanize, electrify, boost; informal pep up, jazz up, buck up.

spick and span adj. **neat**, tidy, orderly, well kept, shipshape (and Bristol fashion), in apple-pie order; immaculate, uncluttered, trim, spruce; spotless.
– OPPOSITES untidy.

spicy adj. **1** *a spicy casserole* **piquant**, tangy, peppery, hot, picante; spiced, seasoned; tasty, flavoursome, zesty, strong, pungent. **2** *spicy stories* **entertaining**, colourful, lively, spirited, exciting, piquant, zesty; risqué, racy, scandalous, ribald, titillating,

S

bawdy, naughty, salacious, dirty, smutty; informal raunchy, juicy; Brit. informal saucy, fruity; N. Amer. informal gamy.
– OPPOSITES bland, boring.

spider n.

> **WORD LINKS**
> **arachnid** a creature of a class including spiders and scorpions
> **arachnophobia** fear of spiders

spiel n. informal **speech**, patter, (sales) pitch, talk; monologue; rigmarole, story, saga.

spike n. **1** *a metal spike* **prong**, barb, point; skewer, stake, spit; tine, pin; spur; Mountaineering piton. **2** *the spikes of a cactus* **thorn**, spine, prickle, bristle; Zoology spicule.
▸v. **1** *she spiked an oyster* **impale**, spear, skewer; pierce, penetrate, perforate, stab, stick, transfix; literary transpierce. **2** *informal his drink was spiked with drugs* **adulterate**, contaminate, drug, lace; informal dope, doctor, cut.

spill v. **1** *Kevin spilled his drink* **knock over**, tip over, upset, overturn. **2** *the bath water spilled on to the floor* **overflow**, flow, pour, run, slop, slosh, splash; leak, escape; old use overbrim. **3** *students spilled out of the building* **stream**, pour, surge, swarm, flood, throng, crowd. **4** *the horse spilled his rider* **unseat**, throw, dislodge, unhorse. **5** informal *he's spilling out his troubles to her* **reveal**, disclose, divulge, blurt out, babble, betray, tell; informal blab.
▸n. **1** *an oil spill* **spillage**, leak, leakage, overflow, flood. **2** *he took a spill in the opening race* **fall**, tumble; informal header, cropper, nosedive.
□ **spill the beans** informal reveal all, tell all, give the game away, talk; informal let the cat out of the bag, blab, come clean.

spin v. **1** *the bike wheels are spinning* **revolve**, rotate, turn, go round, whirl, gyrate, circle. **2** *she spun round to face him* **whirl**, wheel, twirl, turn, swing, twist, swivel, pirouette, pivot. **3** *her head was spinning* **reel**, whirl, go round, swim. **4** *she spun me a yarn* **tell**, recount, relate, narrate; weave, concoct, invent, fabricate, make up.
▸n. **1** *a spin of the wheel* **rotation**, revolution, turn, whirl, twirl, gyration. **2** *a positive spin on the campaign* **slant**, angle, twist, bias. **3** *a spin in the car* **trip**, jaunt, outing, excursion, journey; drive, ride, run, turn, airing; informal tootle; Scottish informal hurl.
□ **spin something out** prolong, protract, draw out, drag out, string out, extend, carry on, continue; fill out, pad out; old use wire-draw.

spindle n. pivot, pin, rod, axle, capstan; axis.

spindly adj. **1** *he was pale and spindly* **lanky**, thin, skinny, lean, spare, gangling, gangly, scrawny, bony, rangy, angular; dated spindle-shanked. **2** *spindly chairs* **rickety**, flimsy, wobbly, shaky.
– OPPOSITES stocky.

spine n. **1** *he injured his spine* **backbone**, spinal column, vertebral column; back;

technical rachis. **2** *the spine of his philosophy* **core**, centre, cornerstone, foundation, basis. **3** *the spines of a hedgehog* **needle**, quill, bristle, barb, spike, prickle; thorn; technical spicule.

spine-chilling adj. **terrifying**, blood-curdling, petrifying, hair-raising, frightening, scaring, chilling, horrifying, fearsome; eerie, sinister, ghostly; Scottish eldritch; informal scary, creepy, spooky.
– OPPOSITES comforting, reassuring.

spineless adj. **weak**, weak-willed, weak-kneed, feeble, soft, ineffectual, irresolute, indecisive; **cowardly**, timid, timorous, fearful, faint-hearted, pusillanimous, craven, unmanly, namby-pamby, lily-livered, chicken-hearted; informal wimpish, wimpy, sissy, chicken, yellow, yellow-bellied, gutless; Brit. informal wet.
– OPPOSITES bold, brave, strong-willed.

spiny adj. **prickly**, spiky, thorny, bristly, bristled, spiked, barbed, scratchy, sharp; technical spinose, spinous.

spiral adj. *a spiral column of smoke* **coiled**, helical, corkscrew, curling, winding, twisting, whorled; technical voluted, helicoid, helicoidal.
▸n. *a spiral of smoke* **coil**, helix, corkscrew, curl, twist, gyre, whorl, scroll; technical volute, volution.
▸v. **1** *smoke spiralled up* **coil**, wind, swirl, twist, wreathe, snake, gyrate; literary gyre. **2** *prices spiralled* **soar**, shoot up, rocket, increase rapidly, rise rapidly, escalate, climb; informal skyrocket, go through the roof. **3** *the economy is spiralling downward* **deteriorate**, decline, go downhill, degenerate, worsen, get worse; informal take a nosedive, go to pot, go to the dogs, hit the skids, go down the tubes.
– OPPOSITES fall, improve.

spire n. steeple, flèche.

spirit n. **1** *harmony between body and spirit* **soul**, psyche, (inner) self, inner being, inner man/woman, mind, ego, id; Philosophy pneuma. **2** *a spirit haunts the island* **ghost**, phantom, spectre, apparition, wraith, presence; informal spook; literary shade. **3** *that's the spirit* **attitude**, frame of mind, way of thinking, point of view, outlook, thoughts, ideas. **4** *she was in good spirits when I left* **mood**, frame of mind, state of mind, emotional state, humour, temper. **5** *team spirit* **morale**, esprit de corps. **6** *the spirit of the age* **ethos**, prevailing tendency, motivating force, essence, quintessence; atmosphere, mood, feeling, climate; attitudes, beliefs, principles, standards, ethics. **7** *his spirit never failed him* **courage**, bravery, pluck, valour, strength of character, fortitude, backbone, mettle, stout-heartedness, determination, resolution, resolve, fight, grit; informal guts, spunk; Brit. informal bottle; N. Amer. informal sand, moxie. **8** *they played with great spirit* **enthusiasm**, eagerness, keenness, liveliness, vivacity, vivaciousness, animation, energy, verve, vigour, dynamism, zest, dash, elan, panache, sparkle, exuberance, gusto, brio,

S

pep, fervour, zeal, fire, passion; informal get-up-and-go. **9** *the spirit of the law* **real/true meaning**, true intention, essence, substance. **10** *he drinks spirits* **strong liquor/drink**; informal hard stuff, firewater, hooch.
– OPPOSITES body, flesh.

  □ **spirit someone/something away** whisk away/off, vanish with, make off with, run away with, abscond with, carry off, steal someone/something away, abduct, kidnap, snatch, seize.

spirited adj. **lively**, vivacious, vibrant, full of life, vital, animated, high-spirited, sparkling, sprightly, energetic, active, vigorous, dynamic, dashing, enthusiastic, passionate; determined, resolute, purposeful; informal feisty, spunky, have-a-go, gutsy; N. Amer. informal peppy.
– OPPOSITES timid, apathetic, lifeless.

spiritless adj. apathetic, passive, unenthusiastic, lifeless, listless, weak, feeble, spineless, languid, bloodless, insipid, characterless, submissive, meek, irresolute, indecisive; lacklustre, flat, colourless, passionless, uninspired, wooden, dry, anaemic, vapid, dull, boring, wishy-washy.
– OPPOSITES spirited, lively.

spiritual adj. **1** *your spiritual self* **non-material**, incorporeal, intangible; inner, mental, psychological; transcendent, ethereal, other-worldly, mystic, mystical, metaphysical; rare extramundane. **2** *spiritual writings* **religious**, sacred, divine, holy, non-secular, church, ecclesiastical, devotional.
– OPPOSITES physical, secular.

spit[1] v. **1** *Cranston coughed and spat* **expectorate**, hawk; Brit. informal gob. **2** *'Go to hell,' she spat* **snap**, say angrily, hiss. **3** *the fat began to spit* **sizzle**, hiss; crackle, sputter. **4** Brit. *it began to spit* **rain lightly**, drizzle, spot; N. English mizzle; N. Amer. sprinkle.
  ▶ n. **1** *spit dribbled from his mouth* **spittle**, saliva, sputum, slobber, dribble; Brit. informal gob. **2** informal *he is the spit of his father* **exact likeness**, image, very/living image, double, twin, lookalike, duplicate, copy, Doppelgänger; informal spitting image, ringer, dead ringer.

spit[2] n. *chicken cooked on a spit* **skewer**, brochette, rotisserie.

spite n. *he said it out of spite* **malice**, malevolence, ill will, vindictiveness, vengefulness, revenge, malignity, evil intentions, animus, enmity; informal bitchiness, cattiness; literary maleficence.
– OPPOSITES benevolence.
  ▶ v. *he did it to spite me* **upset**, hurt, make miserable, grieve, distress, wound, pain, torment, injure.
– OPPOSITES please.
  □ **in spite of** despite, notwithstanding, regardless of, for all; undeterred by, in defiance of, in the face of; even though, although.

spiteful adj. **malicious**, malevolent, evil-intentioned, vindictive, vengeful, malign, mean, nasty, hurtful, mischievous,

wounding, cruel, unkind; informal bitchy, catty; literary malefic, maleficent.
– OPPOSITES benevolent.

splash v. **1** *splash your face with cool water* **sprinkle**, spray, spritz, shower, splatter, slosh, slop, squirt; daub; wet. **2** *his boots were splashed with mud* **spatter**, bespatter, splatter, speck, speckle, blotch, smear, stain, mark; Scottish & Irish slabber; informal splotch, splodge; literary bedabble. **3** *waves splashed on the beach* **swash**, wash, break, lap; dash, beat, lash, batter, crash, buffet; literary plash. **4** *children splashed in the water* **paddle**, wade, slosh; wallow; informal splosh. **5** *the story was splashed across the front pages* **blazon**, display, spread, plaster, trumpet, publicize; informal splatter.
  ▶ n. **1** *a splash of fat on his shirt* **spot**, blob, dab, daub, smudge, smear, speck, fleck, patch, pop; mark, stain; informal splotch, splodge. **2** *a splash of lemonade* **drop**, dash, bit, spot, soupçon, dribble, driblet; Scottish informal scoosh. **3** *a splash of colour* **patch**, burst, streak.
  □ **make a splash** informal cause a sensation, cause a stir, attract attention, draw attention to oneself/itself, get noticed, make an impression, make an impact.
  splash out Brit. informal be extravagant, go on a spending spree, spare no expense, spend lavishly; informal lash out, splurge; Brit. informal push the boat out.

spleen n. **bad temper**, bad mood, ill temper, ill humour, anger, wrath, vexation, annoyance, irritation, displeasure, dissatisfaction, resentment, rancour; spite, ill feeling, malice, maliciousness, bitterness, animosity, antipathy, hostility, malevolence, venom, gall, malignance, malignity, acrimony, bile, hatred, hate; literary ire, choler.
– OPPOSITES good humour.

splendid adj. **1** *splendid costumes* **magnificent**, sumptuous, grand, impressive, imposing, superb, spectacular, resplendent, opulent, luxurious, deluxe, rich, fine, costly, expensive, lavish, ornate, gorgeous, glorious, dazzling, elegant, handsome, beautiful; stately, majestic, princely, noble, proud, palatial; informal plush, posh, swanky, ritzy, splendiferous; Brit. informal swish; N. Amer. informal swank; literary brave. **2** informal *we had a splendid holiday* **excellent**, wonderful, marvellous, superb, glorious, sublime, lovely, delightful, first-class, first-rate; informal super, great, amazing, fantastic, terrific, tremendous, phenomenal, sensational, heavenly, gorgeous, dreamy, grand, fabulous, fab, awesome, magic, ace, cool, mean, bad, wicked, mega, crucial, far out, A1, sound, out of this world; Brit. informal smashing, brilliant, brill; N. Amer. informal dandy, neat; Austral./NZ informal beaut, bonzer; black English def; informal dated divine, capital; Brit. informal dated champion, wizard, ripping, cracking, spiffing, top-hole; N. Amer. informal dated swell; old use goodly.
– OPPOSITES modest, awful.

S

splendour n. **magnificence**, sumptuousness, grandeur, impressiveness, resplendence, opulence, luxury, richness, fineness, lavishness, ornateness, glory, beauty, elegance; majesty, stateliness; informal ritziness, splendiferousness.
– OPPOSITES ordinariness, simplicity, modesty.

splenetic adj. **bad-tempered**, ill-tempered, angry, cross, peevish, petulant, pettish, irritable, irascible, choleric, dyspeptic, testy, tetchy, snappish, waspish, crotchety, crabby, querulous, resentful, rancorous, bilious; **spiteful**, malicious, ill-natured, hostile, acrimonious, sour, bitter, malevolent, malignant, malign; informal bitchy.
– OPPOSITES good-humoured.

splice v. *the ropes are spliced together* **interweave**, braid, plait, entwine, intertwine, interlace, knit, mesh; Nautical marry.
□ **get spliced** informal See **marry** (sense 1).

splinter n. *a splinter of wood* **sliver**, shiver, chip, shard; fragment, piece, bit, shred; Scottish skelf; (**splinters**) matchwood, flinders.
▸v. *the windscreen splintered* **shatter**, break into tiny pieces, smash, smash into smithereens, fracture, split, crack, disintegrate, crumble.

split v. **1** *the axe split the wood* **break**, chop, cut, hew, lop, cleave; snap, crack. **2** *the ice cracked and split* **break apart**, fracture, rupture, fissure, snap, come apart, splinter. **3** *her dress was split* **tear**, rip, slash, slit; literary rend. **4** *the issue could split the Party* **divide**, disunite, separate, sever; bisect, partition; literary tear asunder. **5** *they split the money between them* **share (out)**, divide (up), apportion, allocate, allot, distribute, dole out, parcel out, measure out; carve up, slice up; informal divvy up. **6** *the path split* **fork**, divide, bifurcate, diverge, branch. **7** *they split up last year* **break up**, separate, part, part company, become estranged; divorce, get divorced; Brit. informal bust up.
– OPPOSITES join, unite.
▸n. **1** *a split in the rock face* **crack**, fissure, cleft, crevice, break, fracture, breach. **2** *a split in the curtain* **rip**, tear, cut, rent, slash, slit. **3** *a split in the Party* **division**, rift, breach, schism, rupture, partition, separation, severance, scission, break-up. **4** *the acrimonious split with his wife* **break-up**, split-up, separation, parting, estrangement, rift; divorce; Brit. informal bust-up.
– OPPOSITES marriage.
□ **split hairs** quibble, cavil, carp, niggle, chop logic; informal nitpick; old use pettifog.

> WORD LINKS
> fissile easily split

split-up n. **break-up**, separation, split, parting, estrangement, rift; divorce; Brit. informal bust-up.

spoil v. **1** *too much sun spoils the complexion* **mar**, damage, impair, blemish, disfigure,

blight, flaw, deface, scar, injure, harm; ruin, destroy, wreck; be a blot on the landscape. **2** *rain spoiled my plans* **ruin**, wreck, destroy, upset, undo, mess up, make a mess of, dash, sabotage, scotch, torpedo; Brit. throw a spanner in the works of; informal foul up, louse up, muck up, screw up, put the kibosh on, banjax, do for; Brit. informal cock up, scupper; old use bring to naught. **3** *his sisters spoil him* **overindulge**, pamper, indulge, mollycoddle, cosset, coddle, baby, wait on hand and foot, kill with kindness; nanny; old use cocker. **4** *stockpiled food may spoil* **go bad**, go off, go rancid, turn, go sour, go mouldy, go rotten, rot, perish.
– OPPOSITES improve, enhance, further, help, neglect, be strict with, keep.
□ **spoiling for** eager for, looking for, keen to have, after, bent on, longing for; informal itching for.

spoils plural n. **1** *the spoils of war* **booty**, loot, stolen goods, plunder, ill-gotten gains, haul, pickings; informal swag, boodle. **2** *the spoils of office* **benefits**, advantages, perks, prize; formal perquisites.

spoilsport n. **killjoy**, dog in the manger, misery, damper; informal wet blanket, party pooper.

spoken adj. *spoken communication* **verbal**, oral, vocal, viva voce, uttered, said, stated; unwritten; by word of mouth.
– OPPOSITES non-verbal, written.
□ **spoken for 1** *the money is spoken for* **reserved**, set aside, claimed, owned, booked. **2** *Claudine is spoken for* **attached**, in a relationship; informal going steady; dated courting.

spokesman, **spokeswoman** n. **spokesperson**, representative, agent, mouthpiece, voice, official; informal spin doctor.

sponge v. **1** *I'll sponge your face* **wash**, clean, wipe, swab; mop, rinse, sluice, swill. **2** informal *he lived by sponging off others* **beg**, be a parasite; live off; informal scrounge, freeload, cadge, bum; N. Amer. informal mooch; Austral./NZ bludge.

sponger n. informal **parasite**, hanger-on, leech, scrounger, beggar; informal freeloader, junketeer, cadger, bum, bloodsucker; N. Amer. informal mooch, moocher, schnorrer; Austral./NZ informal bludger.

spongy adj. **soft**, squashy, cushioned, cushiony, compressible, yielding; springy, resilient, elastic; porous, absorbent, permeable; technical spongiform; Brit. informal squidgy.
– OPPOSITES hard, solid.

sponsor n. *the money came from sponsors* **backer**, patron, promoter, benefactor, benefactress, supporter, contributor, subscriber, friend, guarantor, underwriter; informal angel.
▸v. *a bank sponsored the event* **finance**, put up the money for, fund, subsidize, back, promote, support, contribute to, be a patron of, guarantee, underwrite; informal foot the

bill for, pick up the tab for; N. Amer. informal bankroll.

sponsorship n. **backing**, support, promotion, patronage, subsidy, funding, financing, aid, financial assistance.

spontaneous adj. **1** *a spontaneous display of affection* **unplanned**, unpremeditated, unrehearsed, impulsive, impetuous, unstudied, impromptu, spur-of-the-moment, extempore, extemporaneous; unforced, voluntary, unconstrained, unprompted, unbidden, unsolicited; informal off-the-cuff. **2** *a spontaneous reaction to danger* **reflex**, automatic, mechanical, natural, knee-jerk, involuntary, unthinking, unconscious, instinctive, instinctual; informal gut. **3** *a spontaneous kind of person* **natural**, uninhibited, relaxed, unselfconscious, unaffected, open, genuine, easy, free and easy; impulsive, impetuous.
– OPPOSITES planned, calculated, conscious, voluntary, inhibited.

spontaneously adv. **1** *they applauded spontaneously* **without being asked**, of one's own accord, voluntarily, on impulse, impulsively, on the spur of the moment, extempore, extemporaneously; informal off the cuff. **2** *he reacted spontaneously* **without thinking**, automatically, mechanically, unthinkingly, involuntarily, instinctively, naturally, by oneself/itself.

spooky adj. informal **eerie**, sinister, ghostly, uncanny, weird, unearthly, mysterious; **frightening**, spine-chilling, hair-raising; informal creepy, scary, spine-tingling.

sporadic adj. **occasional**, infrequent, irregular, periodic, scattered, patchy, isolated, odd; intermittent, spasmodic, fitful, desultory, erratic, unpredictable.
– OPPOSITES frequent, steady, continuous.

sport n. **1** *we did a lot of sport at school* **(competitive) game(s)**, physical recreation, physical activity, physical exercise. **2** dated *they were rogues out for a bit of sport* **fun**, pleasure, enjoyment, entertainment, diversion, amusement.
▶ v. *he sported a beard* **wear**, have on, dress in; **display**, exhibit, show off, flourish, parade, flaunt.

sporting adj. **sportsmanlike**, generous, gentlemanly, considerate; fair, just, honourable; Brit. informal decent.
– OPPOSITES dirty, unfair.

sporty adj. informal **1** *he's quite a sporty type* **athletic**, fit, active, energetic. **2** *a sporty outfit* **stylish**, smart, jaunty; **casual**, informal; informal trendy, cool, snazzy; N. Amer. informal sassy. **3** *a sporty car* **fast**, speedy; informal nippy, zippy.
– OPPOSITES unfit, lazy, formal, sloppy, slow.

spot n. **1** *a grease spot on the wall* **mark**, patch, pop, dot, fleck, smudge, smear, stain, blotch, blot, splash; informal splotch, splodge. **2** *a spot on his nose* **pimple**, pustule, blackhead, boil, swelling, eruption, wen, sty; **(spots)** acne; technical comedo, papule; informal zit, whitehead; Scottish informal plook.

3 *a secluded spot* **place**, location, site, position, point, situation, scene, setting, locale, locality, area, neighbourhood, region; venue; technical locus. **4** *social policy has a regular spot on the agenda* **position**, place, slot, space. **5** *a spot to eat or drink* **bit**, little, some, small amount, morsel, bite, mouthful; drop, splash; informal smidgen, tad. **6** informal *in a tight spot* **predicament**, mess, difficulty, trouble, plight, corner, quandary, dilemma; informal fix, jam, hole, sticky situation, pickle, scrape, hot water.
▶ v. **1** *she spotted him in his car* **notice**, see, observe, note, discern, detect, perceive, make out, recognize, identify, locate; catch sight of, glimpse; Brit. informal clock; literary behold, espy. **2** *her clothes were spotted with grease* **stain**, mark, fleck, speckle, smudge, streak, splash, spatter; informal splotch, splodge. **3** *it was spotting with rain* **lightly**, drizzle; Brit. spit; N. English mizzle; N. Amer. sprinkle.
□ **on the spot** immediately, at once, straight away, right away, without delay, without hesitation, that instant, directly, there and then, then and there, forthwith, instantly, summarily; N. Amer. in short order; old use straightway, instanter.

spot on Brit. informal accurate, correct, right, perfect, exact, unerring; Brit. informal bang on; N. Amer. informal on the money, on the nose.

spotless adj. **1** *the kitchen was spotless* **perfectly clean**, ultra-clean, pristine, immaculate, shining, shiny, gleaming, spick and span. **2** *a spotless reputation* **unblemished**, unsullied, untarnished, untainted, unstained, pure, whiter than white, innocent, impeccable, blameless, irreproachable, above reproach; informal squeaky clean.
– OPPOSITES dirty, tarnished, impure.

spotlight n. *she was constantly in the spotlight* **public eye**, glare of publicity, limelight; focus of public/media attention.
▶ v. *this article spotlights the problem* **focus attention on**, highlight, point up, draw/call attention to, give prominence to, throw into relief, turn the spotlight on, bring to the fore.

spotted adj. **1** *the spotted leaves* **mottled**, dappled, speckled, flecked, freckled, freckly, dotted, stippled, brindle(d); informal splotchy. **2** *a black-and-white spotted dress* **polka-dot**, spotty, dotted.
– OPPOSITES plain.

spotty adj. **1** *a spotty dog* **spotted**, mottled, speckled, speckly, flecked, specked, stippled; informal splodgy, splotchy. **2** *a spotty dress* **polka-dot**, spotted, dotted. **3** Brit. *his spotty face* **pimply**, pimpled, acned.

spouse n. **partner**, mate, consort; informal better half; Brit. informal other half. See also **husband** (noun), **wife**.

spout v. **1** *lava was spouting from the crater* **spurt**, gush, spew, erupt, shoot, squirt, spray; disgorge, discharge, emit, belch forth. **2** *he spouts on foreign affairs* **hold forth**, sound off, go on, talk at length, expatiate; informal

S

mouth off, speechify, spiel.
▸ n. *a can with a spout* **nozzle**, lip, rose.
□ **up the spout** Brit. informal **1** *my computer's up the spout.* See **broken** (sense 3). **2** *his daughter's up the spout.* See **pregnant** (sense 1).

sprawl v. **1** *he sprawled on a sofa* **stretch out**, lounge, loll, lie, recline, drape oneself, slump, flop, slouch. **2** *the town sprawled ahead of them* **spread**, stretch, extend, be strung out, be scattered, straggle, spill.

spray[1] n. **1** *a spray of water* **shower**, sprinkling, sprinkle, spritz, jet, mist, drizzle; spume, spindrift; foam, froth. **2** *a perfume spray* **atomizer**, vaporizer, aerosol, sprinkler; nebulizer.
▸ v. **1** *water was sprayed around* **sprinkle**, shower, spritz, spatter; scatter, disperse, diffuse; mist; douche; literary besprinkle.
2 *water sprayed into the air* **spout**, jet, gush, spurt, shoot, squirt.

spray[2] n. **1** *a spray of holly* **sprig**, twig.
2 *a spray of flowers* **bouquet**, bunch, posy, nosegay; corsage, buttonhole, boutonnière.

spread v. **1** *he spread the map out* **lay out**, open out, unfurl, unroll, roll out; straighten out, fan out; stretch out, extend; literary outspread. **2** *the landscape spread out below* **extend**, stretch, open out, be displayed, be exhibited, be on show; sprawl. **3** *papers were spread all over his desk* **scatter**, strew, disperse, distribute. **4** *he's been spreading rumours* **disseminate**, circulate, pass on, put about, communicate, diffuse, make public, make known, purvey, broadcast, publicize, propagate, promulgate; repeat; literary bruit about/abroad. **5** *she spread cold cream on her face* **smear**, daub, plaster, slather, lather, apply, put; smooth, rub. **6** *he spread the toast with butter* **cover**, coat, layer, daub, smother; butter.
– OPPOSITES fold up, suppress.
▸ n. **1** *the spread of learning* **expansion**, proliferation, extension, growth; dissemination, diffusion, transmission, propagation. **2** *a spread of six feet* **span**, width, extent, stretch, reach. **3** *the immense spread of the heavens* **expanse**, area, sweep, stretch. **4** *a wide spread of subjects* **range**, span, spectrum, sweep; variety. **5** informal *his mother laid on a huge spread* **large/elaborate meal**, feast, banquet; informal blowout, nosh; Brit. informal nosh-up, slap-up meal.

spree n. **1** *a shopping spree* **unrestrained bout**, orgy; informal binge, splurge; humorous retail therapy. **2** *a drinking spree* **drinking bout**, debauch; informal binge, bender, session, booze-up, blind; Scottish informal skite; N. Amer. informal jag, toot; literary bacchanal, bacchanalia; old use wassail.

sprig n. **small stem**, spray, twig.

sprightly adj. **spry**, lively, agile, nimble, energetic, active, full of energy, vigorous, spirited, animated, vivacious, frisky; informal full of vim and vigour; N. English informal wick.
– OPPOSITES doddery, lethargic.

spring v. **1** *the cat sprang off her lap* **leap**, jump, bound, vault, hop. **2** *the branch sprang back* **fly**, whip, flick, whisk, kick, bounce. **3** *all art springs from feelings* **originate**, derive, arise, stem, emanate, proceed, issue, evolve, come. **4** *fifty men sprang from nowhere* **appear suddenly**, appear unexpectedly, materialize, pop up, shoot up, sprout, develop quickly; proliferate, mushroom. **5** *he sprang the truth on me* **announce suddenly/unexpectedly**, reveal suddenly/unexpectedly, surprise someone with.
▸ n. **1** *with a sudden spring he leapt on to the table* **leap**, jump, bound, vault, hop; pounce. **2** *the mattress has lost its spring* **springiness**, bounciness, bounce, resilience, elasticity, flexibility, stretch, stretchiness, give. **3** *there was a spring in his step* **buoyancy**, bounce, energy, liveliness, jauntiness, sprightliness, confidence. **4** *a mineral spring* **well head**, source; spa, geyser; literary wellspring, fount. **5** *the springs of his own emotions* **origin**, source, fountainhead, root, roots, basis.

┌─────────────────────────────────────┐
│ **WORD LINKS** │
│ **vernal** relating to the season of spring │
└─────────────────────────────────────┘

springy adj. **elastic**, stretchy, stretchable, tensile; flexible, pliant, pliable, whippy; bouncy, resilient, spongy.
– OPPOSITES rigid, squashy.

sprinkle v. **1** *he sprinkled water over the towel* **splash**, trickle, spray, shower, spritz; spatter. **2** *sprinkle sesame seeds over the top* **scatter**, strew; drizzle. **3** *sprinkle the cake with icing sugar* **dredge**, dust. **4** *the sky was sprinkled with stars* **dot**, stipple, stud, fleck, speckle, spot, pepper; scatter, cover; literary besprinkle.

sprinkling n. **1** *a sprinkling of nutmeg* **scattering**, sprinkle, scatter, dusting; pinch, dash. **2** *mainly women, but a sprinkling of men* **few**, one or two, couple, handful, small number, trickle, scattering.

sprint v. **run**, race, dart, rush, dash, hasten, hurry, scurry, scamper, hare, bolt, fly, gallop, career, charge, shoot, hurtle, speed, zoom, go like lightning, go hell for leather, go like the wind; jog, trot; informal tear, pelt, scoot, hotfoot it, leg it, belt, zip, whip; Brit. informal bomb; N. Amer. informal hightail it, barrel.
– OPPOSITES walk.

sprite n. **fairy**, elf, pixie, imp, brownie, puck, peri, kelpie, leprechaun; nymph, nixie, sylph, naiad.

sprout v. **1** *the weeds begin to sprout* **germinate**, put/send out shoots, bud, burgeon. **2** *he had sprouted a beard* **grow**, develop, put/send out. **3** *parsley sprouted from the pot* **spring up**, shoot up, come up, grow, burgeon, develop, appear.

spruce adj. *the Captain looked very spruce* **neat**, well groomed, well turned out, well dressed, smart, trim, dapper, elegant, chic; informal natty, snazzy; N. Amer. informal spiffy, trig.
– OPPOSITES untidy.
▸ v. **1** *the cottage had been spruced up* **smarten**,

tidy, neaten, put in order, clean; informal do up; Brit. informal tart up, posh up; N. Amer. informal gussy up. **2** *Sarah had spruced herself up* **groom**, tidy, smarten, preen, primp, prink; N. Amer. trig; informal titivate, doll up; Brit. informal tart up.

spry adj. **sprightly**, lively, agile, nimble, energetic, active, full of energy, vigorous, spirited, animated, vivacious, frisky; informal full of vim and vigour; N. English informal wick.
– OPPOSITES doddery, lethargic.

spume n. **foam**, froth, surf, spindrift, bubbles.

spunk n. informal **courage**, bravery, valour, nerve, confidence, daring, audacity, pluck, spirit, grit, mettle, spine, backbone; informal guts, gumption; Brit. informal bottle; N. Amer. informal moxie.

spur n. **1** *competition can be a spur* **stimulus**, incentive, encouragement, inducement, fillip, impetus, prod, motivation, inspiration; informal kick up the backside, shot in the arm. **2** *a spur of bone* **projection**, spike, point; technical process.
– OPPOSITES disincentive, discouragement.
▸ v. *the thought spurred him into action* **stimulate**, encourage, prompt, propel, prod, induce, impel, motivate, move, galvanize, inspire, incentivize, urge, drive, egg on, stir; incite, goad, provoke, prick, sting; N. Amer. light a fire under.
– OPPOSITES discourage.
□ **on the spur of the moment** impulsively, on impulse, impetuously, without thinking, without premeditation, unpremeditatedly, impromptu, extempore, spontaneously; informal off the cuff.

spurious adj. **bogus**, fake, false, counterfeit, forged, fraudulent, sham, artificial, imitation, simulated, feigned, deceptive, misleading; informal phoney, pretend; Brit. informal cod.
– OPPOSITES genuine.

spurn v. **reject**, rebuff, scorn, turn down, treat with contempt, disdain, look down one's nose at, despise; snub, slight, jilt, dismiss, brush off, turn one's back on; give someone the cold shoulder, cold-shoulder; informal turn one's nose up at, give someone the brush-off, kick in the teeth; Brit. informal knock back; N. Amer. informal give someone the bum's rush.
– OPPOSITES welcome, accept.

spurt v. *water spurted from the tap* **squirt**, shoot, jet, erupt, gush, pour, stream, pump, surge, spew, course, well, spring, burst; disgorge, discharge, emit, belch forth, expel, eject; Brit. informal sloosh.
▸ n. **1** *a spurt of water* **squirt**, jet, spout, gush, stream, rush, surge, flood, cascade, torrent. **2** *a spurt of courage* **burst**, fit, bout, rush, spate, surge, attack, outburst, blaze. **3** *Daisy put on a spurt* **burst of speed**, turn of speed, sprint, rush, burst of energy.

spy n. *a foreign spy* **secret agent**, intelligence agent, double agent, counterspy, mole, plant, scout; informal snooper; N. Amer. informal spook; old

use intelligencer.
▸ v. **1** *he spied for the West* **be a spy**, gather intelligence; informal snoop. **2** *investigators spied on them* **observe furtively**, keep under surveillance/observation, watch, keep a watch on, keep an eye on. **3** *she spied a coffee shop* **notice**, observe, see, spot, sight, catch sight of, glimpse, make out, discern, detect; informal clap/lay/set eyes on; literary espy, behold, descry.

spying n. **espionage**, intelligence gathering, surveillance, infiltration, undercover work, cloak-and-dagger activities.

squabble n. *there was a squabble over which way they should go* **quarrel**, disagreement, row, argument, contretemps, falling-out, dispute, clash, altercation, shouting match, exchange, war of words; informal tiff, set-to, run-in, slanging match, shindig, shindy, stand-up, spat, scrap, dust-up; Brit. informal barney, ding-dong; Brit. informal, Football afters; N. Amer. informal rhubarb.
▸ v. *the boys were squabbling over a ball* **quarrel**, row, argue, bicker, fall out, disagree, have words, dispute, spar, cross swords, lock horns, be at loggerheads; informal scrap, argufy.

squad n. **1** *an assassination squad* **team**, crew, gang, band, cell, body, mob, outfit, force. **2** *a firing squad* **detachment**, detail, unit, platoon, battery, troop, patrol, squadron, cadre, commando.

squalid adj. **1** *a squalid prison* **dirty**, filthy, grubby, grimy, mucky, slummy, foul, vile, poor, sorry, wretched, miserable, mean, seedy, shabby, sordid, insalubrious; **neglected**, uncared-for, broken-down, run down, down at heel, depressed, dilapidated, ramshackle, tumbledown, gone to rack and ruin, crumbling, decaying; informal scruffy, crummy, shambly, ratty; Brit. informal grotty; N. Amer. informal shacky. **2** *a squalid deal with the opposition* **improper**, sordid, unseemly, unsavoury, sleazy, seedy, seamy, shoddy, cheap, base, low, corrupt, dishonest, dishonourable, disreputable, despicable, discreditable, disgraceful, contemptible, shameful; informal sleazoid.
– OPPOSITES clean, pleasant, smart, upmarket, proper, decent.

squall n. **gust**, storm, blast, flurry, shower, gale, blow, rush.

squally adj. **stormy**, gusty, gusting, blustery, blustering, windy, blowy; wild, tempestuous, rough.

squalor n. **dirt**, filth, grubbiness, grime, muck, foulness, vileness, poverty, wretchedness, meanness, seediness, shabbiness, sordidness, sleaziness, insalubrity; **neglect**, decay, dilapidation; informal scruffiness, crumminess, grunge, rattiness; Brit. informal grottiness.
– OPPOSITES cleanliness, pleasantness, smartness.

squander v. **waste**, misspend, misuse, throw away, fritter away, spend recklessly, spend unwisely, spend like water; informal blow, go

through, splurge, pour down the drain; Brit. informal **blue**.
– OPPOSITES save.

square n. **1** *a shop in the square* market square, marketplace, plaza, piazza. **2** informal *you're such a square!* (**old**) **fogey**, conservative, traditionalist, conventionalist, conformist, bourgeois, fossil; Brit. museum piece; informal stick-in-the-mud, fuddy-duddy, back number, stuffed shirt.
– OPPOSITES trendy.

▶ adj. **1** *a square table* **quadrilateral**, rectangular, oblong, right-angled, at right angles, perpendicular; straight, level, parallel, horizontal, upright, vertical, true, plane. **2** *the sides were square at half-time* **level**, even, drawn, equal, tied; neck and neck, level pegging, nip and tuck, side by side, evenly matched; informal even-steven(s). **3** *I'm going to be square with you* **fair**, honest, just, equitable, straight, true, upright, above board, ethical, decent, proper; informal on the level. **4** informal *don't be square!* **old-fashioned**, behind the times, out of date, conservative, traditionalist, conventional, conformist, bourgeois, strait-laced, fogeyish, stuffy; informal stick-in-the-mud, fuddy-duddy.
– OPPOSITES crooked, uneven, underhand, trendy.

▶ v. **1** *the theory does not square with the data* **agree**, tally, be in agreement, be consistent, match up, correspond, fit, coincide, accord, conform, be compatible. **2** *his goal squared the match 1–1* **level**, even, make equal. **3** *would you square up the bill?* **pay**, settle, discharge, clear, meet. **4** informal *they tried to square the press* **bribe**, buy off, buy, corrupt, suborn; informal grease someone's palm, give a backhander to. **5** *Tom squared things with his boss* **resolve**, sort out, settle, clear up, work out, iron out, smooth over, straighten out, deal with, put right, set right, put to rights, rectify, remedy; informal patch up.

squash v. **1** *the fruit got squashed* **crush**, squeeze, flatten, compress, press, smash, distort, pound, trample, stamp on; pulp, mash, cream, liquidize, beat, pulverize. **2** *she squashed her clothes inside the bag* **force**, ram, thrust, push, cram, jam, stuff, pack, compress, squeeze, wedge, press. **3** *the proposal was immediately squashed* **reject**, block, cancel, scotch, frustrate, thwart, suppress, put a stop to, nip in the bud, put the lid on; informal put paid to, put the kibosh on, stymie; Brit. informal dish, scupper.

squashy adj. **1** *a squashy pillow* **springy**, resilient, spongy, soft, pliant, pliable, yielding, elastic, cushiony, compressible. **2** *squashy pears* **mushy**, pulpy, pappy, slushy, squelchy, squishy, oozy, doughy, soft; Brit. informal squidgy.
– OPPOSITES firm, hard.

squat v. *I was squatting on the floor* **crouch (down)**, hunker (down), sit on one's haunches, sit on one's heels; N. Amer. informal scooch.

▶ adj. *he was muscular and squat* **stocky**, thickset, dumpy, stubby, stumpy, short,

small; Brit. informal fubsy.

squawk v. & n. *a pheasant squawked | the gull gave a squawk* **screech**, squeal, shriek, scream, croak, crow, caw, cluck, cackle, hoot, cry, call.

squeak n. & v. **1** *the vole's dying squeak | the rat squeaked* **peep**, cheep, pipe, piping, squeal, tweet, yelp, whimper. **2** *the squeak of the hinge | the hinges of the gate squeaked* **screech**, creak, scrape, grate, rasp, jar, groan.

squeal n. *the harsh squeal of a fox* **screech**, scream, shriek, squawk.

▶ v. **1** *a dog squealed* **screech**, scream, shriek, squawk. **2** *the bookies only squealed because we beat them* **complain**, protest, object, grouse, grumble, whine, wail, carp, squawk; informal kick up a fuss, kick up a stink, gripe, grouch, bellyache, moan, bitch, beef, whinge; N. English informal mither. **3** informal *he squealed on the rest of the gang to the police* **inform**, tell tales, sneak; report, give away, be disloyal, sell out, stab in the back; informal rat, peach, snitch, put the finger on, sell down the river, stitch up; Brit. informal grass, split, shop; N. Amer. informal rat out, finger, drop a/the dime on; Austral. informal dob, pimp on, pool.

squeamish adj. **1** *I'm too squeamish to gut fish* **easily nauseated**; (**be squeamish about**) be put off by, cannot stand the sight of. **2** *less squeamish nations will sell them arms* **scrupulous**, principled, fastidious, particular, punctilious, honourable, upright, upstanding, high-minded, righteous, right-minded, moral, ethical.

squeeze v. **1** *I squeezed the bottle* **compress**, press, crush, squash, pinch, nip, grasp, grip, clutch, flatten. **2** *squeeze the juice from both oranges* **extract**, press, force, express. **3** *Sally squeezed her feet into the sandals* **force**, thrust, cram, ram, jam, stuff, pack, wedge, press, squash. **4** *we all squeezed into Steve's van* **crowd**, crush, cram, pack, jam, squash, wedge oneself, shove, push, force one's way; N. Amer. informal scooch. **5** *he would squeeze more money out of Bill* **extort**, force, extract, wrest, wring, milk; informal bleed someone of something.

▶ n. **1** *he gave her hand a squeeze* **press**, pinch, nip; grasp, grip, clutch, hug, clasp; compression. **2** *it was a tight squeeze in the tiny hall* **crush**, jam, squash, press, huddle; congestion. **3** *a squeeze of lemon juice* **few drops**, dash, splash, dribble, trickle, spot, hint, touch.

squint v. *the sun made them squint* **screw up one's eyes**, narrow one's eyes, peer, blink.

▶ n. **1** informal *we must have another squint at his record card* **look**, glance, peep, peek, glimpse; view, examination, study, inspection, scan, sight; informal eyeful, dekko, butcher's, gander, look-see, once-over, shufti. **2** *he has a squint* **cross-eyes**, strabismus; Brit. informal boss-eye.

squire n. **1** *the squire of the village* **landowner**, landholder, landlord, lord of the manor, country gentleman. **2** historical *his squire carried a banner* **attendant**, courtier,

S

equerry, aide, steward, page boy.

squirm v. **1** *I tried to squirm away* **wriggle**, wiggle, writhe, twist, slide, slither, turn, shift, fidget, jiggle, twitch, thresh, flounder, flail, toss and turn. **2** *he squirmed as everyone laughed* **wince**, shudder, feel embarrassed, feel ashamed.

squirt v. **1** *a jet of ink squirted out of the tube* **spurt**, shoot, spray, spritz, fountain, jet, erupt; gush, rush, pump, surge, stream, spew, well, spring, burst, issue, emanate; emit, belch forth, expel, eject; Brit. informal sloosh. **2** *she squirted me with scent* **splash**, wet, spray, shower, spatter, splatter, sprinkle; Scottish & Irish slabber; literary besprinkle.
▶ n. **1** *a squirt of water* **spurt**, jet, spray, spritz, fountain, gush, stream, surge. **2** informal *he was just a little squirt* **impudent person**, insignificant person, gnat, insect; informal pipsqueak, whippersnapper; Brit. informal squit; Scottish informal nyaff; N. Amer. informal bozo, picayune, pisher.

stab v. **1** *he stabbed him in the stomach* **knife**, run through, skewer, spear, bayonet, gore, spike, stick, impale, transfix, pierce, prick, puncture; literary transpierce. **2** *she stabbed at the earth with a fork* **lunge**, thrust, jab, poke, prod, dig.
▶ n. **1** *a stab in the leg* **knife wound**, puncture, incision, prick, cut, perforation. **2** *they made stabs into the air* **lunge**, thrust, jab, poke, prod, dig, punch. **3** *a stab of pain* **twinge**, pang, throb, spasm, cramp, dart, blaze, prick, flash, thrill. **4** informal *he had a stab at writing* **attempt**, try, effort, endeavour; guess; informal go, shot, crack, bash, whack; formal essay.
▫ **stab someone in the back** betray, be disloyal to, be unfaithful to, desert, break one's promise to, double-cross, break faith with, sell out, play false, inform on/against; informal tell on, sell down the river, squeal on, stitch up, peach on, do the dirty on; Brit. informal grass on, shop; N. Amer. informal rat out, finger, drop a/the dime on; Austral. informal pimp on, pool, put someone's pot on.

stability n. **1** *the stability of play equipment* **firmness**, solidity, steadiness, strength, security, safety. **2** *his mental stability* **balance of mind**, mental health, sanity, normality, soundness, rationality, reason, sense. **3** *the stability of their relationship* **steadiness**, firmness, solidity, strength, durability, lasting nature, enduring nature, permanence, changelessness, invariability, immutability, indestructibility, reliability, dependability.

stable adj. **1** *a stable tent* **firm**, solid, steady, secure, fixed, fast, safe, moored, anchored, stuck down, immovable. **2** *a stable person* **well balanced**, of sound mind, compos mentis, sane, normal, right in the head, rational, steady, reasonable, sensible, sober, down-to-earth, matter-of-fact, having both one's feet on the ground; informal all there. **3** *a stable relationship* **secure**, solid, strong, steady, firm, sure, steadfast, unwavering, unvarying, unfaltering; established, abiding, durable, enduring, lasting, permanent,

reliable, dependable.
– OPPOSITES loose, wobbly, unbalanced, rocky, changeable.

stack n. **1** *a stack of boxes* **heap**, pile, mound, mountain, pyramid, tower. **2** *a stack of hay* **haystack**, rick, hayrick, stook, mow, shock; dated cock. **3** informal *a stack of money*. See **lot** (pronoun). **4** **chimney**, smokestack, funnel, exhaust pipe.
– OPPOSITES few, little.
▶ v. **1** *Leo was stacking plates* **heap (up)**, pile (up), make a heap/pile/stack of; assemble, put together, collect, hoard, store, stockpile. **2** *they stacked the shelves* **load**, fill (up), lade, pack, charge, stuff, cram; stock.
– OPPOSITES empty.

stadium n. **arena**, field, ground, pitch; bowl, amphitheatre, coliseum, ring, dome, manège; track, course, racetrack, racecourse, speedway, velodrome; in ancient Rome circus.

staff n. **1** *there is a reluctance to take on new staff* **employees**, workers, workforce, personnel, human resources, manpower, labour; informal liveware. **2** *he carried a wooden staff* **stick**, stave, pole, crook. **3** *a staff of office* **rod**, tipstaff, cane, mace, wand, sceptre, crozier, verge; Greek Mythology caduceus.
▶ v. *the centre is staffed by teachers* **man**, people, crew, work, operate, occupy.

stage n. **1** *this stage of the development* **phase**, period, juncture, step, point, time, moment, instant, level. **2** *the last stage of the race* **part**, section, portion, stretch, leg, lap, circuit. **3** *a theatre stage* **platform**, dais, stand, grandstand, staging, apron, rostrum, podium. **4** *she has written for the stage* **theatre**, drama, dramatics, dramatic art, thespianism; informal the boards. **5** *the political stage* **scene**, setting; context, frame, sphere, field, realm, arena, backdrop; affairs.
▶ v. **1** *they staged two plays* **put on**, put before the public, present, produce, mount, direct; perform, act, give. **2** *workers staged a protest* **organize**, arrange, coordinate, lay on, put together, get together, set up; orchestrate, choreograph, mastermind, engineer; take part in, participate in, join in.

stagger v. **1** *he staggered to the door* **lurch**, walk unsteadily, reel, sway, teeter, totter, stumble, wobble. **2** *I was absolutely staggered* **amaze**, astound, astonish, surprise, startle, stun, confound, dumbfound, stupefy, daze, nonplus, take aback, leave open-mouthed, leave aghast; informal flabbergast, bowl over; Brit. informal knock for six. **3** *meetings are staggered throughout the day* **spread (out)**, space (out), time at intervals, overlap.

stagnant adj. **1** *stagnant water* **still**, motionless, static, stationary, standing, dead, slack; **foul**, stale, putrid, smelly. **2** *a stagnant economy* **inactive**, sluggish, slow-moving, lethargic, static, flat, depressed, declining, moribund, dying, dead, dormant.
– OPPOSITES flowing, fresh, active, vibrant.

stagnate v. **1** *obstructions allow water to stagnate* **stop flowing**, become stagnant,

become trapped; stand; become foul, become stale; fester, putrefy. **2** *exports stagnated* **languish**, decline, deteriorate, fall, become stagnant, do nothing, stand still, be sluggish.
– OPPOSITES flow, rise, boom.

staid adj. **sedate**, respectable, quiet, serious, serious-minded, steady, conventional, traditional, unadventurous, unenterprising, set in one's ways, sober, proper, decorous, formal, stuffy, stiff; informal starchy, stick-in-the-mud.
– OPPOSITES frivolous, daring, informal.

stain v. **1** *her clothing was stained with blood* **discolour**, blemish, soil, mark, muddy, spot, spatter, splatter, smear, splash, smudge, blotch, blacken. **2** *the report stained his reputation* **damage**, injure, harm, sully, blacken, tarnish, taint, smear, bring discredit to, dishonour, drag through the mud; literary besmirch. **3** *the wood was stained* **colour**, tint, dye, tinge, pigment, colour-wash.
▶ n. **1** *a mud stain* **mark**, spot, spatter, splatter, blotch, smudge, smear. **2** *a stain on his character* **blemish**, injury, taint, blot, smear, discredit, dishonour; damage. **3** *dark wood stain* **tint**, colour, dye, tinge, pigment, colourant, colour wash.

stake[1] n. *a stake in the ground* **post**, pole, stick, spike, upright, support, prop, strut, pale, paling, picket, pile, piling, cane.
▶ v. **1** *the plants have to be staked* **prop up**, tie up, tether, support, hold up, brace, truss. **2** *he staked his claim* **assert**, declare, proclaim, state, make, lay, put in.
◻ **stake something out 1** *builders staked out the plot* **mark off/out**, demarcate, measure out, delimit, fence off, section off, close off, shut off, cordon off. **2** informal *the police staked out his flat* **observe**, watch, keep an eye on, keep under observation, keep watch on, monitor, keep under surveillance, surveil; informal keep tabs on, keep a tab on, case.

stake[2] n. **1** *playing dice for high stakes* **bet**, wager, ante. **2** *they are racing for record stakes* **prize money**, purse, pot, winnings. **3** *low down in the popularity stakes* **competition**, contest, battle, challenge, rivalry, race, running, struggle, scramble. **4** *a 40% stake in the business* **share**, interest, ownership, involvement.
▶ v. *he staked all his week's pay* **bet**, wager, lay, put on, gamble, chance, venture, risk, hazard.

stale adj. **1** *stale food* **old**, past its best, past its sell-by date; off, dry, hard, musty, rancid. **2** *stale air* **stuffy**, close, musty, fusty, stagnant, frowzy; Brit. frowsty, fuggy. **3** *stale beer* **flat**, turned, spoiled, off, insipid, tasteless. **4** *stale jokes* **hackneyed**, tired, worn out, overworked, threadbare, warmed-up, banal, trite, clichéd, platitudinous, unoriginal, unimaginative, uninspired, flat; out of date, outdated, outmoded, passé, archaic, obsolete; N. Amer. warmed-over; informal old hat, corny, out of the ark, played out.
– OPPOSITES fresh, original.

stalemate n. **deadlock**, impasse, stand-off; draw, tie, dead heat.

stalk[1] n. *the stalk of a plant* **stem**, shoot, trunk, stock, cane, bine, bent, haulm, straw, reed.

stalk[2] v. **1** *a stoat was stalking a rabbit* **creep up on**, trail, follow, shadow, track down, go after, be after, course, hunt; informal tail. **2** *she stalked out* **strut**, stride, march, flounce, storm, stomp, sweep.

stall n. **1** *a market stall* **stand**, table, counter, booth, kiosk. **2** *stalls for larger animals* **pen**, coop, sty, corral, enclosure, compartment. **3** Brit. *theatre* stalls N. Amer. orchestra, parterre.
▶ v. **1** *the Government has stalled the project* **obstruct**, impede, interfere with, hinder, hamper, block, interrupt, hold up, hold back, thwart, balk, sabotage, delay, stonewall, check, stop, halt, derail, put a brake on; informal stymie; N. Amer. informal bork. **2** *quit stalling* **use delaying tactics**, play for time, temporize, gain time, procrastinate, hedge, beat about the bush, drag one's feet, delay, filibuster, stonewall. **3** *stall him for a bit* **delay**, divert, distract; **hold off**, stave off, fend off, keep off, ward off, keep at bay.

stalwart adj. **staunch**, loyal, faithful, committed, devoted, dedicated, dependable, reliable, steady, constant, trusty, hard-working, steadfast, redoubtable, unwavering.
– OPPOSITES disloyal, unfaithful, unreliable.

stamina n. **endurance**, staying power, tirelessness, fortitude, strength, energy, toughness, determination, tenacity, perseverance, grit.

stammer v. *he began to stammer* **stutter**, stumble over one's words, hesitate, falter, pause, halt, splutter.
▶ n. *he had a stammer* **stutter**, speech impediment, speech defect.

stamp v. **1** *he stamped on my toe* **trample**, step, tread, tramp; **crush**, squash, flatten. **2** *John stamped off, muttering* **stomp**, stump, clomp, clump. **3** *the name is stamped on the cover* **imprint**, print, impress, punch, inscribe, emboss, brand, frank. **4** *his face was stamped on Martha's memory* **fix**, inscribe, etch, carve, imprint, impress. **5** *his style stamps him as a player to watch* **identify**, characterize, brand, distinguish, classify, mark out, set apart, single out.
▶ n. **1** *the stamp of authority* **mark**, hallmark, indication, sign, seal, sure sign, telltale sign, quality, smack, smell, savour, air. **2** *he was of a very different stamp* **type**, kind, sort, variety, class, category, classification, style, description, condition, calibre, status, quality, nature, ilk, kidney, cast, grain, mould; N. Amer. stripe.
◻ **stamp something out** put an end/stop to, end, stop, crush, put down, crack down on, curb, nip in the bud, scotch, squash, quash, quell, subdue, suppress, extinguish, stifle, abolish, get rid of, eliminate, eradicate, beat, overcome, defeat, destroy, wipe out.

stamp collecting n. **philately**.

stampede n. *the noise caused a stampede* **charge**, panic, rush, flight, rout.

▸ v. *the sheep stampeded* **bolt**, charge, flee, take flight; race, rush, career, sweep, run.

stance n. 1 *a natural golfer's stance* **posture**, position, pose, attitude. 2 *a liberal stance* **attitude**, stand, point of view, viewpoint, opinion, way of thinking, outlook, standpoint, position, angle, perspective, approach, line, policy.

stand v. 1 *Lionel stood in the doorway* **be on one's feet**, be upright, be erect, be vertical. 2 *the men stood up* **rise**, get/rise to one's feet, get up, straighten up, pick oneself up, find one's feet, be upstanding; formal arise. 3 *today a house stands on the site* **be**, be situated, be located, be positioned, be sited, have been built. 4 *he stood the book on the shelf* **put**, set, set up, erect, upend, place, position, locate, prop, lean, stick, install, arrange; informal park. 5 *my decision stands* **remain in force**, remain valid/effective/operative, remain in operation, hold, hold good, apply, be the case, exist; formal obtain. 6 *his heart could not stand the strain* **withstand**, endure, bear, put up with, take, cope with, handle, sustain, resist, stand up to. 7 informal *I won't stand cheek* **endure**, tolerate, bear, put up with, stomach, take, abide, support, countenance; Scottish thole; informal **swallow**; Brit. informal stick, wear; formal brook.

– OPPOSITES sit, lie, sit down, lie down.

▸ n. 1 *the party's stand on immigration* **attitude**, stance, point of view, viewpoint, opinion, way of thinking, outlook, standpoint, position, approach, thinking, policy, line. 2 *a stand against tyranny* **opposition**, resistance, objection, hostility, animosity. 3 *a large mirror on a stand* **base**, support, mounting, platform, rest, plinth, bottom; tripod, rack, trivet. 4 *a beer stand* **stall**, counter, booth, kiosk, tent. 5 *a taxi stand* **rank**, station, park, bay. 6 *the train drew to a stand* **stop**, halt, standstill, dead stop. 7 *a stand of trees* **copse**, spinney, thicket, grove.

□ **stand by** wait, be prepared, be in (a state of) readiness, be ready for action, be on full alert, wait in the wings.

stand by someone/something 1 *she stood by her husband* **remain/be loyal to**, stick with/by, remain/be true to, stand up for, support, back up, defend, stick up for. 2 *the government must stand by its pledges* **abide by**, keep (to), adhere to, hold to, stick to, observe, comply with.

stand for 1 *V stands for volts* **mean**, be an abbreviation of, represent, signify, denote, indicate, symbolize. 2 informal *I won't stand for any nonsense* **put up with**, endure, tolerate, stomach, accept, take, abide, stand, support, countenance; informal swallow; Brit. informal stick, wear; formal brook. 3 *we stand for animal welfare* **advocate**, champion, uphold, defend, stand up for, support, back, endorse, be in favour of, promote, recommend, urge.

stand in deputize, act, act as deputy, substitute, fill in, sit in, do duty, take over,

act as locum, be a proxy, cover, hold the fort, step into the breach; replace, relieve, take over from; informal sub, fill someone's shoes, step into someone's shoes; N. Amer. pinch-hit.

stand out 1 *his veins stood out* **project**, stick out, bulge (out), be proud, jut (out). 2 *she stood out in the crowd* **be noticeable**, be visible, be obvious, be conspicuous, stick out, be striking, be distinctive, be prominent, attract attention, catch the eye, leap out, show up; informal stick/stand out a mile, stick/stand out like a sore thumb.

stand up remain/be valid, be sound, be plausible, hold water, hold up, stand questioning, survive investigation, bear examination, be verifiable.

stand someone up fail to keep a date with, fail to meet, jilt.

stand up for someone/something support, defend, back, back up, stick up for, champion, promote, uphold, take someone's part, take the side of, side with.

stand up to someone/something 1 *she stood up to her parents* **defy**, confront, challenge, resist, take on, put up a fight against, argue with, take a stand against. 2 *the old house has stood up to the war* **withstand**, survive, come through (unscathed), outlast, outlive, weather, ride out, ward off.

standard n. 1 *the standard of Elizabeth's work* **quality**, level, grade, calibre, merit, excellence. 2 *a safety standard* **guideline**, norm, yardstick, benchmark, measure, criterion, guide, touchstone, model, pattern, example, exemplar. 3 *a standard to live by* **principle**, ideal; (**standards**) code of behaviour, code of honour, morals, scruples, ethics. 4 *the regiment's standard* **flag**, banner, pennant, ensign, colour(s), banderole, guidon; Brit. pendant; Nautical burgee.

▸ adj. 1 *the standard way of doing it* **normal**, usual, typical, stock, common, ordinary, customary, conventional, established, settled, set, fixed, traditional, prevailing; literary wonted. 2 *the standard work on the subject* **definitive**, established, classic, recognized, accepted, authoritative, most reliable, exhaustive.

– OPPOSITES unusual, special.

standardize v. **systematize**, make consistent, make uniform, make comparable, regulate, normalize, bring into line, equalize, homogenize, regiment.

stand-in n. *a stand-in for the minister* **substitute**, replacement, deputy, surrogate, proxy, understudy, locum, supply, fill-in, cover, relief, stopgap; informal temp; N. Amer. informal pinch-hitter.

▸ adj. *a stand-in goalkeeper* **substitute**, replacement, deputy, fill-in, stopgap, supply, surrogate, relief, acting, temporary, provisional, caretaker; N. Amer. informal pinch-hitting.

standing n. 1 *his standing in the community* **status**, rank, ranking, position; reputation, estimation, stature; dated station. 2 *a person*

S

of some standing **seniority**, rank, eminence, prominence, prestige, repute, stature, esteem, importance, account, consequence, influence, distinction; informal clout; dated mark. **3** *a squabble of long standing* **duration**, existence, continuance, endurance, life.
▶ adj. **1** *standing stones* **upright**, erect, vertical, plumb, upended, on end, perpendicular; on one's feet; Heraldry rampant. **2** *standing water* **stagnant**, still, motionless, static, stationary, dead, slack. **3** *a standing invitation* **permanent**, perpetual, everlasting, continuing, abiding, indefinite, open-ended; regular, repeated.
– OPPOSITES flat, lying down, seated, flowing, temporary, occasional.

stand-off n. **deadlock**, stalemate, impasse; draw, tie, dead heat; suspension of hostilities, lull.

stand-offish adj. informal **aloof**, distant, remote, detached, withdrawn, reserved, uncommunicative, unresponsive, unforthcoming, unapproachable, unfriendly, unsociable, introspective, introverted.
– OPPOSITES friendly, approachable, sociable.

standpoint n. **point of view**, viewpoint, vantage point, attitude, stance, view, opinion, position, way of thinking, outlook, perspective.

standstill n. **halt**, stop, dead stop, stand.

staple adj. **main**, principal, chief, major, primary, leading, foremost, first, most important, predominant, dominant, (most) prominent, basic, standard, prime, premier; informal number-one.

star n. **1** *the sky was full of stars* **celestial body**, heavenly body, sun; asteroid, planet. **2** *the stars of the film* **principal**, leading lady/man, lead, female/male lead, hero, heroine. **3** *a star of the world of chess* **celebrity**, superstar, big name, famous name, household name, someone, somebody, lion, leading light, VIP, personality, personage, luminary; informal celeb, big shot, big noise, megastar.
– OPPOSITES nobody.
▶ adj. **1** *a star pupil* **brilliant**, talented, gifted, able, exceptional, outstanding, bright, clever, masterly, consummate, precocious, prodigious. **2** *the star attraction* **top**, leading, best, greatest, foremost, major, pre-eminent, champion.
– OPPOSITES poor, minor.

> **WORD LINKS**
> **astral, stellar, sidereal** relating to stars
> **astronomy** the science of stars, planets, and the universe
> **astrology** the study of the supposed influence of stars and planets on human affairs
> **constellation** a group of stars forming a fixed pattern
> **galaxy** a system of millions or billions of stars
> **magnitude** the degree of a star's brightness
> **pentagram** a drawing of a five-pointed star, used as a magical symbol

starchy adj. informal See **staid**.

stare v. **gaze**, gape, goggle, glare, ogle, peer; informal gawk, rubberneck; Brit. informal gawp.

stark adj. **1** *a stark silhouette* **sharp**, sharply defined, well focused, crisp, distinct, obvious, evident, clear, clear-cut, graphic, striking. **2** *a stark landscape* **desolate**, bare, barren, arid, vacant, empty, forsaken, godforsaken, bleak, sombre, depressing, cheerless, joyless; literary drear. **3** *a stark room* **austere**, severe, bleak, plain, simple, bare, unadorned, unembellished, undecorated. **4** *stark terror* **sheer**, utter, complete, absolute, total, pure, downright, out-and-out, outright; rank, thorough, consummate, unqualified, unmitigated, unalloyed. **5** *the stark facts* **blunt**, bald, bare, simple, basic, plain, unvarnished, harsh, grim.
– OPPOSITES fuzzy, indistinct, pleasant, ornate, disguised.
▶ adv. *stark naked* **completely**, totally, utterly, absolutely, downright, dead, entirely, wholly, fully, quite, altogether, thoroughly, truly.

start v. **1** *the meeting starts at 7.45* **begin**, commence, get under way, go ahead, get going; informal kick off. **2** *this was how her illness had started* **come into being**, begin, commence, be born, come into existence, appear, arrive, come forth, emerge, erupt, burst out, arise, originate, develop. **3** *she started her own charity* **establish**, set up, found, create, bring into being, institute, initiate, inaugurate, introduce, open, launch, float, kick-start, get something off the ground, pioneer, organize, mastermind; informal kick something off. **4** *we had better start on the work* **make a start**, begin, commence, take the first step, make the first move, get going, go ahead, set things moving, start/get/set the ball rolling, take something forward, buckle to/down, turn to; informal get moving, get cracking, get stuck in, get down to it, get down to business, get one's finger out, get the show on the road, take the plunge, kick off, get off one's backside, fire away; Brit. informal get weaving. **5** *he started across the field* **set off**, set out, set forth, begin one's journey, get on the road, depart, leave, get under way, make a start, sally forth, embark, sail; informal hit the road. **6** *you can start the machine* **activate**, set in motion, switch on, start up, turn on, fire up; energize, actuate, set off, start off, set something going/moving. **7** *the machine started* **begin working**, start up, get going, spring into life. **8** *'Oh my!' she said, starting* **flinch**, jerk, jump, twitch, recoil, shy, shrink, blench, wince.
– OPPOSITES finish, stop, clear up, wind up, hang about, give up, arrive, stay, close down.
▶ n. **1** *the start of the event* **beginning**, commencement, inception. **2** *the start of her illness* **onset**, commencement, emergence, (first) appearance, arrival, eruption, dawn, birth. **3** *a quarter of an hour's start* **lead**, head start, advantage. **4** *a start in life* **advantageous beginning**, flying start, helping hand, lift, assistance, support, encouragement, boost, kick-start; informal

break, leg up. **5** *she awoke with a start* **jerk**, twitch, flinch, wince, spasm, convulsion, jump.
– OPPOSITES end, finish, handicap.

startle v. **surprise**, frighten, scare, alarm, give someone a shock/fright/jolt, make someone jump; **perturb**, unsettle, agitate, disturb, disconcert, disquiet; informal give someone a turn.

startling adj. **surprising**, astonishing, amazing, unexpected, unforeseen, staggering, shocking, stunning; extraordinary, remarkable, dramatic; disturbing, unsettling, perturbing, disconcerting, disquieting; frightening, alarming, scary.
– OPPOSITES predictable, ordinary.

starvation n. **extreme hunger**, lack of food, famine, undernourishment, malnourishment.

starving adj. **dying of hunger**, deprived of food, undernourished, malnourished, starved, half-starved; very hungry, ravenous, famished, empty, hollow; fasting.
– OPPOSITES well fed, full.

stash informal v. *he stashed his things away* **store**, stow, pack, load, cache, hide, conceal, secrete; hoard, save, stockpile; informal salt away, squirrel away.
▶ n. *a stash of money* **cache**, hoard, stock, stockpile, store, supply, accumulation, collection, reserve.

state[1] n. **1** *the state of the economy* **condition**, shape, situation, circumstances, position; predicament, plight. **2** informal *don't get into a state* **fluster**, frenzy, fever, fret, panic, state of agitation/anxiety; informal flap, tizzy, dither, stew, sweat; N. Amer. informal twit. **3** informal *your room is in a state* **mess**, chaos, disorder, disarray, confusion, muddle, heap, shambles; clutter, untidiness, disorganization. **4** *an autonomous state* **country**, nation, land, sovereign state, nation state, kingdom, realm, power, republic, confederation, federation. **5** *the country is divided into thirty-two states* **province**, federal state, region, territory, canton, department, county, district; Brit. shire. **6** *the power of the state* **government**, parliament, administration, regime, authorities.
▶ adj. *a state visit to China* **ceremonial**, official, formal, governmental, national, public.
– OPPOSITES unofficial, private, informal.

state[2] v. *I stated my views* **express**, voice, utter, put into words, declare, affirm, assert, announce, make known, put across/over, communicate, air, reveal, disclose, divulge, proclaim, present, expound; set out, set down; informal come out with.

stated adj. **specified**, fixed, settled, set, agreed, declared, designated, laid down.
– OPPOSITES undefined, irregular, tacit.

stately adj. **dignified**, majestic, ceremonious, courtly, imposing, impressive, solemn, awe-inspiring, regal, elegant, grand, glorious, splendid, magnificent, resplendent; slow-moving, measured, deliberate.

statement n. **declaration**, affirmation, assertion, announcement, utterance, communication, proclamation, presentation, expounding; account, testimony, evidence, report, bulletin, communiqué.

state-of-the-art adj. **modern**, ultra-modern, the latest, new, the newest, up to the minute; advanced, highly developed, innovatory, trailblazing, revolutionary; sophisticated.

static adj. **1** *static prices* **unchanged**, fixed, stable, steady, unchanging, changeless, unvarying, invariable, constant, consistent. **2** *a static display* **stationary**, motionless, immobile, unmoving, still, stock-still, at a standstill, at rest, not moving a muscle, like a statue, rooted to the spot, frozen, inactive, inert, lifeless, inanimate.
– OPPOSITES variable, mobile, active, dynamic.

station n. **1** *a railway station* **stopping place**, stop, halt, stage; terminus, terminal, depot. **2** *a research station* **establishment**, base, camp; post, depot; mission; site, facility, installation, yard. **3** *a police station* **office**, depot, base, headquarters; N. Amer. precinct, station house; informal cop shop; Brit. informal nick. **4** *a radio station* **channel**, broadcasting organization; wavelength. **5** Austral./NZ *a sheep station* **ranch**, range; farm. **6** *the lookout resumed his station* **post**, position, place. **7** dated *Karen was getting ideas above her station* **rank**, place, status, position in society, social class, stratum, level, grade; caste; old use condition, degree.
▶ v. *the regiment was stationed at Woolwich* **put on duty**, post, position, place; establish, install; deploy, base, garrison.

stationary adj. **1** *a stationary car* **static**, parked, stopped, motionless, immobile, unmoving, still, stock-still, at a standstill, at rest; not moving a muscle, like a statue, rooted to the spot, frozen, inactive, inert, lifeless, inanimate. **2** *a stationary population* **unchanging**, unvarying, invariable, constant, consistent, unchanged, changeless, fixed, stable, steady.
– OPPOSITES moving, shifting.

statue n. **sculpture**, figure, effigy, statuette, figurine, idol; carving, bronze, graven image, model; bust, head.

statuesque adj. **tall and dignified**, imposing, striking, stately, majestic, noble, magnificent, splendid, impressive, regal.

stature n. **1** *she was small in stature* **height**, tallness; size, build. **2** *an architect of international stature* **reputation**, repute, standing, status, position, prestige, distinction, eminence, pre-eminence, prominence, importance, influence, note, fame, celebrity, renown, acclaim.

status n. **1** *the status of women* **standing**, rank, ranking, position, social position, level, place, estimation; dated station. **2** *wealth and status* **prestige**, kudos, cachet, standing, stature, regard, fame, note, renown, honour, esteem, image, importance, prominence, consequence, distinction, influence, authority, eminence.

S

statute n. **law**, regulation, enactment, act, bill, decree, edict, rule, ruling, resolution, dictum, command, order, directive, pronouncement, proclamation, dictate, diktat, fiat, by-law; N. Amer. formal ordinance.

staunch[1] adj. *a staunch supporter* **stalwart**, loyal, faithful, committed, devoted, dedicated, dependable, reliable, steady, constant, trusty, hard-working, steadfast, redoubtable, unwavering.
– OPPOSITES disloyal, unfaithful, unreliable.

staunch[2] v. *she tried to staunch the flow of blood* **stem**, stop, halt, check, hold back, restrain, restrict, control, contain, curb; block, dam; slow, lessen, reduce, diminish, retard; N. Amer. stanch; old use stay.

stave v.
□ **stave something in** break in, smash in, put a hole in, push in, kick in, cave in.
stave something off avert, prevent, avoid, counter, preclude, forestall, nip in the bud; ward off, fend off, head off, keep off, keep at bay.

stay[1] v. **1** *he stayed where he was* **remain (behind)**, stay behind, stay put; wait, linger, stick, be left, hold on, hang on, lodge; informal hang around/round; Brit. informal hang about; old use bide, tarry. **2** *they won't stay hidden* **continue (to be)**, remain, keep, persist in being, carry on being, go on being. **3** *our aunt is staying with us* **visit**, spend time, put up, stop (off/over); holiday; lodge, room, board, have rooms, be housed, be accommodated, be quartered, be billeted; N. Amer. vacation; formal sojourn; old use bide. **4** *legal proceedings were stayed* **postpone**, put off, delay, defer, put back, hold over/off; adjourn, suspend, prorogue; N. Amer. put over, table, lay on the table, take a rain check on; US Law continue; informal put on ice, put on the back burner.
– OPPOSITES leave, resume.
▶ n. **1** *a stay at a hotel* **visit**, stop, stop-off, stopover, break, holiday; N. Amer. vacation; formal sojourn. **2** *a stay of judgement* **postponement**, putting off, delay, deferment, deferral, putting back; adjournment, suspension, prorogation; N. Amer. tabling; US Law continuance.

stay[2] n. *the stays holding up the mast* **strut**, **wire**, brace, tether, guy, prop, rod, support, truss; Nautical shroud.
▶ v. *her masts were well stayed* **brace**, tether, strut, wire, guy, prop, support, truss.

steadfast adj. **1** *a steadfast friend* **loyal**, faithful, committed, devoted, dedicated, dependable, reliable, steady, true, constant, staunch, trusty. **2** *a steadfast policy* **firm**, determined, resolute, relentless, implacable, single-minded; unchanging, unwavering, unhesitating, unfaltering, unswerving, unyielding, unflinching, uncompromising.
– OPPOSITES disloyal, irresolute.

steady adj. **1** *the ladder must be steady* **stable**, firm, fixed, secure, fast, safe, immovable, unshakeable, dependable; anchored, moored, jammed, rooted, braced. **2** *keep the camera steady* **motionless**, still, static, stationary, unmoving. **3** *a steady gaze* **fixed**, intent, unwavering, unfaltering. **4** *a steady young man* **sensible**, level-headed, rational, settled, mature, down-to-earth, full of common sense, reliable, dependable, sound, sober, serious-minded, responsible, serious. **5** *a steady income* **constant**, unchanging, regular, consistent, invariable; continuous, continual, unceasing, ceaseless, perpetual, unremitting, unwavering, unfaltering, unending, endless, round-the-clock, all-year-round. **6** *a steady boyfriend* **regular**, usual, established, settled, firm, devoted, faithful.
– OPPOSITES unstable, loose, shaky, darting, flighty, immature, fluctuating, sporadic, occasional.
▶ v. **1** *he steadied the rifle* **stabilize**, hold steady; brace, support; balance, poise; secure, fix, make fast. **2** *she needed to steady her nerves* **calm**, soothe, quieten, compose, settle; subdue, quell, control, get a grip on.

steal v. **1** *the raiders stole a laptop* **purloin**, thieve, take, take for oneself, help oneself to, loot, pilfer, run off with, carry off, shoplift; embezzle, misappropriate; have one's fingers/hand in the till; informal walk off with, rob, swipe, nab, rip off, lift, 'liberate', 'borrow', filch, snaffle, snitch; Brit. informal nick, pinch, half-inch, whip, knock off, nobble; N. Amer. informal heist; formal peculate. **2** *his work was stolen by his tutor* **plagiarize**, copy, pass off as one's own, pirate, poach, borrow; informal rip off, lift, pinch, nick, crib. **3** *he stole a kiss* **snatch**, sneak, get stealthily/surreptitiously. **4** *he stole out of the room* **creep**, sneak, slink, slip, slide, glide, tiptoe, sidle, slope, edge.
▶ n. informal *at £30 it's a steal*. See **bargain** (sense 2 of the noun).

> **WORD LINKS**
> **kleptomania** a recurrent urge to steal things
> **fence** a dealer in stolen goods
> **receiver** a person who knowingly buys or accepts stolen goods

stealing n. **theft**, thieving, thievery, robbery, larceny, burglary, shoplifting, pilfering, looting, misappropriation; embezzlement; formal peculation.

stealth n. **furtiveness**, secretiveness, secrecy, surreptitiousness, sneakiness, slyness.
– OPPOSITES openness.

stealthy adj. **furtive**, secretive, secret, surreptitious, sneaking, sly, clandestine, covert, conspiratorial; Military black.
– OPPOSITES open.

steam n. **1** *steam from the kettle* **water vapour**, condensation, mist, haze, fog, moisture. **2** *he ran out of steam* **energy**, vigour, vitality, stamina, enthusiasm; **momentum**, impetus, force, strength, thrust, impulse, push, drive; speed, pace.
▶ v. informal *he steamed into the shop*. See **run** (sense 1 of the verb).
□ **let off steam** informal give vent to one's feelings, speak one's mind, speak out, sound

off, lose one's inhibitions, let oneself go.
steam up mist (up/over), fog (up), become misty/misted.

steamy adj. **1** *the steamy jungle* **humid**, muggy, sticky, dripping, moist, damp, clammy, sultry, sweaty, steaming. **2** informal *a steamy love scene.* See **erotic**. **3** informal *they had a steamy affair* **passionate**, torrid, amorous, ardent, lustful; informal sizzling, hot, red-hot.

steel v.
▫ **steel oneself** brace oneself, nerve oneself, summon (up) one's courage, screw up one's courage, gear oneself up, prepare oneself, get in the right frame of mind; fortify oneself, harden oneself; informal psych oneself up; literary gird (up) one's loins.

steely adj. **1** *steely light* **blue-grey**, grey, steel-coloured, steel-grey, iron-grey. **2** *steely muscles* **hard**, firm, toned, rigid, stiff, tense, tensed, taut. **3** *steely eyes* **cruel**, unfeeling, merciless, ruthless, pitiless, heartless, hard-hearted, hard, stony, cold-blooded, cold-hearted, harsh, callous, severe, unrelenting, unpitying, unforgiving, uncaring, unsympathetic; literary adamantine. **4** *steely determination* **resolute**, firm, steadfast, dogged, single-minded; bitter, burning, ferocious, fanatical; ruthless, iron, grim, gritty; unquenchable, unflinching, unswerving, unfaltering, untiring, unwavering.
– OPPOSITES flabby, kind, half-hearted.

steep¹ adj. **1** *steep cliffs* **precipitous**, sheer, abrupt, sharp, perpendicular, vertical, bluff, vertiginous. **2** *a steep increase* **sharp**, sudden, precipitate, precipitous, rapid. **3** informal *steep prices* **expensive**, dear, costly, high, stiff; unreasonable, excessive, exorbitant, extortionate, outrageous, prohibitive; Brit. over the odds.
– OPPOSITES gentle, gradual, reasonable.

steep² v. **1** *the ham is then steeped in brine* **marinade**, marinate, soak, souse, macerate; pickle. **2** *winding sheets were steeped in mercury sulphate* **soak**, saturate, immerse, wet through, drench; technical ret. **3** *a city steeped in history* **imbue with**, fill with, permeate with, pervade with, suffuse with, infuse with, soak in.

steeple n. spire, tower; bell tower, belfry, campanile; minaret.

steer v. **1** *he steered the boat* **guide**, direct, manoeuvre, drive, pilot, navigate; Nautical con, helm. **2** *Luke steered her down the path* **guide**, conduct, direct, lead, take, usher, shepherd, marshal, herd.
▫ **steer clear of** keep away from, keep one's distance from, keep at arm's length, give a wide berth to, avoid, avoid dealing with, have nothing to do with, shun, eschew.

stem¹ n. *a plant stem* **stalk**, shoot, trunk, stock, cane, bine.
▫ **stem from** have its origins in, arise from, originate from, spring from, derive from, come from, emanate from, flow from, proceed from; be caused by, be brought on/

about by, be produced by.

stem² v. *he stemmed the flow of blood* **staunch**, stop, halt, check, hold back, restrict, control, contain, curb; block, dam; slow, lessen, reduce, diminish; N. Amer. stanch; old use stay.

stench n. **stink**, reek; Brit. informal niff, pong, whiff, hum; Scottish informal guff; N. Amer. informal funk; literary miasma.

stentorian adj. **loud**, thundering, thunderous, ear-splitting, deafening; powerful, strong, carrying; booming, resonant; strident.
– OPPOSITES quiet, soft.

step n. **1** *Frank took a step forward* **pace**, stride. **2** *she heard a step on the stairs* **footstep**, footfall, tread. **3** *she left the room with a springy step* **gait**, walk, tread. **4** *it is only a step to the river* **short distance**, stone's throw, spitting distance; informal {a hop, skip, and jump}. **5** *the top step* **stair**, tread; (**steps**) stairs, staircase, stairway. **6** *each step of the ladder* **rung**, tread. **7** *resigning is a very serious step* **course of action**, measure, move, act, action, initiative, manoeuvre, operation. **8** *a significant step towards a ceasefire* **advance**, development, move, movement; breakthrough. **9** *the first step on the managerial ladder* **stage**, level, grade, rank, degree; notch.
▸ v. **1** *she stepped forward* **walk**, move, tread, pace, stride. **2** *the bull had stepped on his hat* **tread**, stamp, trample; squash, crush, flatten.
▫ **in step** *he is in step with mainstream thinking* **in accord**, in harmony, in agreement, in tune, in line, in keeping, in conformity.

mind/watch one's step be careful, take care, step/tread carefully, exercise care/caution, mind how one goes, look out, watch out, be wary, be on one's guard, be on the qui vive.

out of step *the paper was often out of step with public opinion* **at odds**, at variance, in disagreement, out of tune, out of line, not in keeping, out of harmony.

step by step one step at a time, bit by bit, gradually, in stages, by degrees, slowly, steadily.

step down resign, stand down, give up one's post/job, bow out, abdicate; informal quit.

step in *nobody stepped in to save the bank* **intervene**, intercede, involve oneself, become/get involved, take a hand. **2** *I stepped in for a sick colleague* **stand in**, sit in, fill in, cover, substitute, take over; replace, take someone's place; informal sub.

step on it informal hurry up, get a move on, speed up, go faster, be quick; informal get cracking, get moving, get a wiggle on, step on the gas; Brit. informal get one's skates on; dated make haste.

step something up 1 *the army stepped up its offensive* **increase**, intensify, strengthen, augment, escalate; informal up, crank up. **2** *I stepped up my pace* **speed up**, increase, accelerate, quicken, hasten.

stereotype n. *the stereotype of the rancher* **standard/conventional image**, received idea, cliché, hackneyed idea, formula.
▶ v. *women are often stereotyped as scheming* **typecast**, pigeonhole, conventionalize, categorize, label, tag.

stereotyped adj. **stock**, conventional, stereotypical, standard, formulaic, predictable; hackneyed, clichéd, cliché-ridden, banal, trite, unoriginal; typecast; informal corny, old hat.
– OPPOSITES unconventional, original.

sterile adj. **1** *mules are sterile* **infertile**, unable to have children/young; technical infecund; old use barren. **2** *sterile desert* **unproductive**, infertile, unfruitful, uncultivable, barren. **3** *a sterile debate* **pointless**, unproductive, unfruitful, unrewarding, useless, unprofitable, profitless, futile, vain, idle; old use bootless. **4** *sterile academicism* **unimaginative**, uninspired, uninspiring, unoriginal, stale, lifeless, musty. **5** *sterile conditions* **aseptic**, sterilized, germ-free, antiseptic, disinfected; uncontaminated, unpolluted, pure, clean; sanitary, hygienic.
– OPPOSITES fertile, productive, creative, original, septic.

sterilize v. **1** *the scalpel was first sterilized* **disinfect**, fumigate, decontaminate, sanitize; pasteurize; clean, cleanse, purify; technical autoclave. **2** *stray pets are usually sterilized* **neuter**, castrate, spay, geld, cut, fix, desex; N. Amer. & Austral. alter; Brit. informal doctor.
– OPPOSITES contaminate.

sterling adj. Brit. **excellent**, first-rate, first-class, exceptional, outstanding, splendid, superlative, praiseworthy, laudable, commendable, admirable, valuable, worthy, deserving.
– OPPOSITES poor, unexceptional.

stern[1] adj. **1** *a stern expression* **serious**, unsmiling, frowning, severe, forbidding, grim, unfriendly, austere, dour, stony, flinty, steely, unrelenting, unforgiving, unbending, unsympathetic, disapproving; Brit. informal boot-faced. **2** *stern measures* **strict**, severe, stringent, harsh, drastic, hard, tough, extreme, rigid, ruthless, rigorous, exacting, demanding, uncompromising, unsparing, inflexible, authoritarian, draconian.
– OPPOSITES genial, friendly, lenient, lax.

stern[2] n. *the stern of the ship* **rear (end)**, back, after end, poop, transom, tail.
– OPPOSITES bow.

stew n. **1** *a beef stew* **casserole**, hotpot, ragout, goulash, carbonnade, daube, grillade; N. Amer. burgoo. **2** informal *she's in a right old stew* **panic**, fluster, fret, fuss, fever; informal flap, sweat, lather, tizzy, dither, twitter, state; N. Amer. informal twit; literary pother.
▶ v. **1** *stew the meat for an hour* **braise**, casserole, simmer, boil; jug; old use seethe. **2** informal *there's no point stewing over it*. See **worry** (sense 1 of the verb). **3** informal *the girls sat stewing in the heat* **swelter**, be very hot, perspire, sweat; informal roast, bake, be boiling.

steward n. **1** *an air steward* **flight attendant**, cabin attendant; stewardess, air hostess; N. Amer. informal stew. **2** *the race stewards* **official**, marshal, organizer. **3** *the steward of the estate* **(estate) manager**, agent, overseer, custodian, caretaker; Brit. land agent, bailiff; Scottish factor; historical reeve.

stick[1] n. **1** *a fire made of sticks* **piece of wood**, twig, small branch. **2** *he walks with a stick* **walking stick**, cane, staff, alpenstock, crook, crutch; trademark Zimmer frame. **3** *the plants need supporting on sticks* **cane**, pole, post, stake, upright. **4** *he beat me with a stick* **club**, cudgel, bludgeon, shillelagh; truncheon, baton; cane, birch, switch, rod; Brit. informal cosh. **5** Brit. informal *he'll get stick for this*. See **criticism** (sense 1).
– OPPOSITES praise, commendation.
□ **the sticks** informal the country, the countryside, rural areas, the provinces; the backwoods, the back of beyond, the wilds, the hinterland, a backwater; N. Amer. the backcountry, the backland; Austral./NZ the backblocks, the booay; S. African the backveld, the platteland; informal the middle of nowhere; N. Amer. informal the boondocks, the boonies; Austral./NZ informal Woop Woop, beyond the black stump.

stick[2] v. **1** *he stuck his fork into the sausage* **thrust**, push, insert, jab, poke, dig, plunge. **2** *the bristles stuck into his skin* **pierce**, penetrate, puncture, prick, stab. **3** *the cup stuck to its saucer* **adhere**, cling, be fixed, be glued. **4** *stick the stamp there* **affix**, attach, fasten, fix; paste, glue, gum, tape, Sellotape, pin, tack. **5** *the wheels stuck fast* **become trapped**, become jammed, jam, catch, become wedged, become lodged, become fixed, become embedded. **6** *that sticks in his mind* **remain**, stay, linger, dwell, persist, continue, last, endure. **7** *the charges won't stick* **be upheld**, hold, be believed; informal hold water. **8** informal *just stick that sandwich on my desk* **put (down)**, place, set (down), lay (down), deposit, position; leave, stow; informal dump, bung, park, plonk, pop; N. Amer. informal plunk. **9** Brit. informal *I can't stick it any longer* **tolerate**, put up with, take, stand, stomach, endure, bear; Scottish thole; informal abide.
□ **stick at** persevere with, persist with, keep at, work at, continue with, carry on with, hammer away at, stay with; go the distance, stay the course; informal soldier on with, hang in there.
stick by be loyal to, be faithful to, be true to, stand by, keep faith with, keep one's promise to.
stick it out put up with it, grin and bear it, keep at it, keep going, stay with it, see it through; persevere, persist, carry on, struggle on; informal hang in there, soldier on, tough it out.
stick out 1 *his front teeth stuck out* **protrude**, jut (out), project, stand out, extend, poke out; bulge, overhang. **2** *they stuck out in their strange clothes*

be noticeable, be visible, be obvious, be conspicuous, stand out, be obtrusive, be prominent, attract attention, catch the eye, leap out, show up; informal stick/stand out a mile, stick/stand out like a sore thumb.
stick to *he stuck to his promise* abide by, keep, adhere to, hold to, comply with, fulfil, make good, stand by.
stick up for support, take someone's side, side with, be on the side of, stand by, stand up for, take someone's part, defend, come to the defence of, champion, speak up for, fight for.

stick-in-the-mud n. informal **(old) fogey**, conservative, fossil, troglodyte; Brit. museum piece; informal fuddy-duddy, square, stuffed shirt.

sticky adj. **1** *sticky tape* **(self-)adhesive**, gummed; technical adherent. **2** *sticky clay* **glutinous**, viscous, viscid, ropy; gluey, tacky, gummy, treacly, syrupy; mucilaginous; Brit. claggy; informal gooey, gloopy, icky; Brit. informal gungy; N. Amer. informal gloppy. **3** *sticky weather* **humid**, muggy, close, sultry, steamy, sweaty. **4** *a sticky situation* **awkward**, difficult, tricky, ticklish, problematic, delicate, touch-and-go, embarrassing, sensitive, uncomfortable; informal hairy.
– OPPOSITES dry, fresh, cool, easy.

stiff adj. **1** *stiff cardboard* **rigid**, hard, firm, inelastic, inflexible. **2** *a stiff paste* **semi-solid**, viscous, viscid, thick, stiffened, firm. **3** *I'm stiff all over* **aching**, achy, painful; arthritic, rheumatic; informal creaky, rheumaticky, rusty. **4** *a rather stiff manner* **formal**, reserved, unfriendly, chilly, cold, frigid, icy, austere, wooden, forced, strained, stilted; informal starchy, uptight, stand-offish. **5** *a stiff fine* **harsh**, severe, heavy, crippling, punishing, stringent, drastic, draconian; Brit. swingeing. **6** *stiff resistance* **vigorous**, determined, full of determination, strong, spirited, resolute, tenacious, steely, four-square, unflagging, unyielding, dogged, stubborn, obdurate; N. Amer. rock-ribbed. **7** *a stiff climb* **difficult**, hard, arduous, tough, strenuous, laborious, uphill, exacting, tiring, demanding, formidable, challenging, punishing, gruelling; informal killing, hellish; Brit. informal knackering. **8** *a stiff breeze* **strong**, fresh, brisk. **9** *a stiff drink* **strong**, potent, alcoholic.
– OPPOSITES flexible, plastic, limp, runny, supple, limber, relaxed, informal, lenient, mild, half-hearted, easy, gentle, weak.

stiffen v. **1** *stir until the mixture stiffens* **become stiff**, thicken; set, become solid, solidify, harden, gel, congeal, coagulate, clot. **2** *she stiffened her muscles | without exercise, joints will stiffen* **make/become stiff**, tense (up), tighten, tauten. **3** *intimidation stiffened their resolve* **strengthen**, harden, toughen, fortify, reinforce, give a boost to.
– OPPOSITES soften, liquefy, relax, weaken.

stifle v. **1** *she stifled him with a bolster* **suffocate**, choke, asphyxiate, smother. **2** *Eleanor stifled a giggle* **suppress**, smother, restrain, fight back, choke back, gulp back,

check, swallow, curb, silence. **3** *cartels stifle competition* **constrain**, hinder, hamper, impede, hold back, curb, check, restrain, prevent, inhibit, suppress.
– OPPOSITES let out, encourage.

stifling adj. **airless**, suffocating, oppressive; very hot, sweltering; humid, close, muggy; informal boiling.
– OPPOSITES fresh, airy, cold.

stigma n. **shame**, disgrace, dishonour, ignominy, opprobrium, humiliation.
– OPPOSITES honour, credit.

stigmatize v. **condemn**, denounce; brand, label, mark out; disparage, vilify, pillory, pour scorn on, defame.

still adj. **1** *Polly lay still* **motionless**, unmoving, not moving a muscle, stock-still, immobile, like a statue, as if turned to stone, rooted to the spot, transfixed, static, stationary. **2** *a still night* **quiet**, silent, hushed, soundless, noiseless, undisturbed; calm, peaceful, serene, windless; literary stilly. **3** *the lake was still* **calm**, flat, even, smooth, placid, tranquil, pacific, waveless, glassy, like a millpond, unruffled.
– OPPOSITES moving, active, noisy, rough.
▸ n. *the still of the night* **quietness**, quiet, quietude, silence, stillness, hush, soundlessness; calm, tranquillity, peace, serenity.
– OPPOSITES noise, disturbance, hubbub.
▸ adv. **1** *he's still here* **up to this time**, up to the present time, until now, even now, yet. **2** *He's crazy. Still, he's harmless* **nevertheless**, nonetheless, all the same, just the same, anyway, anyhow, even so, yet, but, however, notwithstanding, despite that, in spite of that, for all that, be that as it may, in any event, at any rate; informal still and all.
▸ v. **1** *he stilled the crowd* **quieten**, quiet, silence, hush; calm, settle, pacify, soothe, lull, allay, subdue. **2** *the wind stilled* **abate**, die down, lessen, subside, ease up/off, let up, moderate, slacken, weaken.
– OPPOSITES stir up, get stronger, get up.

stilted adj. **strained**, forced, contrived, constrained, laboured, stiff, self-conscious, awkward, unnatural, wooden.
– OPPOSITES natural, effortless, spontaneous.

stimulant n. **1** *caffeine is a stimulant* **tonic**, restorative; antidepressant; informal pep pill, upper, pick-me-up, bracer; Medicine analeptic. **2** *a stimulant to discussion* **stimulus**, incentive, encouragement, impetus, inducement, fillip, boost, spur, prompt; informal shot in the arm.
– OPPOSITES sedative, downer, deterrent.

stimulate v. **encourage**, act as a stimulus to, prompt, prod, move, motivate, trigger, spark, spur on, galvanize, activate, kindle, fire, fire with enthusiasm, fuel, whet, nourish; inspire, incentivize, inspirit, rouse, excite, animate, electrify; N. Amer. light a fire under.
– OPPOSITES discourage.

stimulating adj. **1** *a stimulating effect on the circulation* **restorative**, tonic, invigorating, bracing, energizing, reviving, refreshing,

S

revitalizing, revivifying; Medicine analeptic.
2 *a stimulating lecture* **thought-provoking**,
interesting, fascinating, inspiring,
inspirational, lively, sparkling, exciting,
stirring, rousing, intriguing, giving one
food for thought, refreshing; provocative,
challenging.
– OPPOSITES sedative, uninspiring,
uninteresting, boring.

stimulus n. **spur**, stimulant, encouragement,
impetus, boost, prompt, prod, incentive,
inducement, inspiration, fillip; motivation,
impulse; informal shot in the arm.
– OPPOSITES deterrent, discouragement.

sting n. **1** *a bee sting* **prick**, wound, injury,
puncture. **2** *this cream will take the sting
away* **smart**, pricking; pain, soreness,
hurt, irritation. **3** *the sting of his betrayal*
heartache, heartbreak, agony, torture,
torment, hurt, pain, anguish. **4** *there was
a sting in her words* **sharpness**, severity,
bite, edge, pointedness, asperity; sarcasm,
acrimony, malice, spite, venom. **5** informal *the
victim of a sting* **swindle**, fraud, deception;
trickery, sharp practice; informal rip-off, con,
con trick, fiddle; N. Amer. informal bunco.
▶ v. **1** *she was stung by a scorpion* **prick**, wound;
poison. **2** *the smoke made her eyes sting*
smart, burn, hurt, be irritated, be sore.
3 *the criticism stung her* **upset**, wound,
cut to the quick, sear, grieve, hurt, pain,
torment, mortify. **4** *he was stung into action*
provoke, goad, incite, spur, prick, prod,
rouse, drive, galvanize. **5** informal *they stung a
bank for thousands* **swindle**, defraud, cheat,
fleece, gull; informal rip off, screw, shaft, bilk,
do, rook, diddle, take for a ride, skin; N. Amer.
informal chisel, gouge; Brit. informal dated rush.
– OPPOSITES deter.

stingy adj. informal **mean**, miserly, niggardly,
close-fisted, parsimonious, penny-pinching,
cheese-paring, Scrooge-like; informal tight-
fisted, tight, mingy, money-grubbing; N. Amer.
informal cheap; formal penurious; old use near,
niggard.
– OPPOSITES generous, liberal.

stink v. **1** *his clothes stank of sweat* **reek**,
smell (foul/bad/disgusting), stink/smell to
high heaven. **2** informal *the whole idea stinks*
be very unpleasant, be abhorrent, be
despicable, be contemptible, be disgusting,
be vile, be foul; N. Amer. informal suck. **3** informal
the whole affair stinks of a set-up **smack**,
reek, give the impression, have all the
hallmarks; strongly suggest.
▶ n. **1** *the stink of sweat* **stench**, reek, foul/bad
smell, malodour; Brit. informal pong, niff, hum;
Scottish informal guff; N. Amer. informal funk; literary
miasma. **2** informal *she kicked up a stink* **fuss**,
commotion, rumpus, ruckus, trouble, outcry,
uproar, brouhaha, furore; informal song and
dance, to-do, kerfuffle, hoo-ha; Brit. informal
row, carry-on.

stinking adj. **1** *stinking rubbish* **foul-
smelling**, smelly, reeking, fetid, malodorous,
rank, putrid, noxious; informal stinky, reeky;
Brit. informal niffing, niffy, pongy, whiffy,
humming; N. Amer. informal funky; literary

miasmic, noisome. **2** informal *a stinking cold*
dreadful, awful, terrible, frightful, ghastly,
nasty, foul, vile; Brit. informal rotten, shocking.
– OPPOSITES sweet-smelling, aromatic, mild,
slight.

stint v. *we saved by stinting on food* **skimp**,
scrimp, be economical, economize, be
sparing, hold back, be frugal; be mean,
be parsimonious; limit, restrict; informal be
stingy, be mingy, be tight.
▶ n. *a two-week stint in the office* **spell**, stretch,
turn, session, term, shift, tour of duty.

stipulate v. **specify**, set down, set out, lay
down; demand, require, insist on, make a
condition of, prescribe, impose; Law provide.

stipulation n. **condition**, precondition,
proviso, provision, prerequisite,
specification; demand, requirement; rider,
caveat, qualification.

stir v. **1** *stir the mixture well* **mix**, blend,
agitate; beat, whip, whisk, fold in; N. Amer.
muddle. **2** *Travis stirred in his sleep* **move
slightly**, change one's position, shift.
3 *a breeze stirred the leaves* **disturb**, rustle,
shake, move, flutter, agitate. **4** *he finally
stirred at ten o'clock* **get up**, get out of bed,
rouse oneself, rise; **wake (up)**, awaken;
informal rise and shine, surface, show signs
of life; formal arise; literary waken. **5** *I never
stirred from here* **move**, budge, make a move,
shift, go away; leave. **6** *symbolism can stir
the imagination* **arouse**, rouse, fire, kindle,
inspire, stimulate, excite, awaken, quicken;
literary waken. **7** *the war stirred him to action*
spur, drive, rouse, prompt, propel, prod,
motivate, encourage; urge, impel; provoke,
goad, prick, sting, incite; N. Amer. light a fire
under.
– OPPOSITES go to bed, retire, go to sleep,
stultify, stay, stay put.
▶ n. *the news caused a stir* **commotion**,
disturbance, fuss, excitement, turmoil,
sensation; informal to-do, hoo-ha, hullabaloo,
flap, splash.
□ **stir something up** whip up, work up,
foment, fan the flames of, trigger, spark off,
precipitate, excite, provoke, incite.

stirring adj. **exciting**, thrilling, rousing,
stimulating, moving, inspiring, inspirational,
passionate, impassioned, emotional, heady.
– OPPOSITES boring, pedestrian.

stitch v. *the seams are stitched by hand* **sew**,
baste, tack; seam, hem; darn.
□ **stitch someone up** Brit. informal falsely
incriminate, get someone into trouble;
informal frame, set up; Brit. informal fit someone
up, drop someone in it.

stock n. **1** *the shop carries little stock*
merchandise, goods, wares, items/articles
for sale, inventory. **2** *a stock of fuel* **store**,
supply, stockpile, reserve, hoard, cache,
bank, accumulation, quantity, collection.
3 *farm stock* **animals**, livestock, beasts;
flocks, herds. **4** *blue-chip stocks* **shares**,
securities, equities, bonds. **5** *his stock is low
with most voters* **popularity**, favour, regard,
estimation, standing, status, reputation,

name, prestige. **6** *his mother was of French stock* **descent**, ancestry, origin(s), parentage, pedigree, lineage, line (of descent), heritage, birth, extraction, family, blood, bloodline. **7** *chicken stock* **bouillon**, broth. **8** *the stock of a weapon* **handle**, butt, haft, grip, shaft, shank.

▸**adj. 1** *a stock size* **standard**, regular, normal, established, set; common, readily/widely available; staple. **2** *the stock response* **usual**, routine, predictable, set, standard, staple, customary, familiar, conventional, traditional, stereotyped, clichéd, hackneyed, unoriginal, formulaic.
– OPPOSITES non-standard, original, unusual.

▸**v. 1** *we do not stock GM food* **sell**, carry, keep (in stock), offer, have (for sale), retail, supply. **2** *the fridge was well stocked with milk* **supply**, provide, furnish, provision, equip, fill, load.
□ **in stock** for/on sale, (immediately) available, on the shelf.
stock up on/with amass supplies of, stockpile, hoard, cache, lay in, buy up/in, put away/by, put/set aside, collect, accumulate, save; informal squirrel away, salt away, stash away.
take stock of review, assess, weigh up, appraise, evaluate; informal size up.

stockings plural n. **nylons**, stay-ups; tights; hosiery, hose; N. Amer. pantyhose.

stockpile n. *a stockpile of weapons* **stock**, store, supply, accumulation, collection, reserve, hoard, cache; informal stash.
▸**v.** *food had been stockpiled* **store up**, amass, accumulate, stock up on, hoard, cache, collect, lay in, put away, put/set aside, put by, put away for a rainy day, stow away, save; informal salt away, stash away.

stock-still adj. **motionless**, completely still, unmoving, not moving a muscle, immobile, like a statue, as if turned to stone, rooted to the spot, transfixed, static, stationary.
– OPPOSITES moving, active.

stocky adj. **thickset**, sturdy, heavily built, chunky, burly, strapping, brawny, solid, heavy, hefty, beefy.
– OPPOSITES slender, skinny.

stodgy adj. **1** *a stodgy pudding* **solid**, substantial, filling, hearty, heavy, starchy, indigestible. **2** *stodgy writing* **boring**, dull, uninteresting, dreary, turgid, tedious, dry, heavy going, unimaginative, uninspired, unexciting, unoriginal, monotonous, humdrum, prosaic, staid; informal deadly, square.
– OPPOSITES light, interesting, lively.

stoical adj. **long-suffering**, uncomplaining, patient, forbearing, accepting, tolerant, resigned, phlegmatic, philosophical.
– OPPOSITES complaining, intolerant.

stoicism n. **patience**, forbearance, resignation, fortitude, endurance, acceptance, tolerance, phlegm; Brit. Dunkirk spirit.
– OPPOSITES intolerance.

stoke v. **add fuel to**, mend, keep burning, tend.

stolid adj. **impassive**, phlegmatic, unemotional, cool, calm, placid, unexcitable; dependable; unimaginative, dull.
– OPPOSITES emotional, lively, imaginative.

stomach n. **1** *a pain in the stomach* **abdomen**, belly, gut, middle; informal tummy, tum, breadbasket, insides. **2** *his fat stomach* **paunch**, pot belly, beer belly, girth; informal beer gut, pot, tummy, spare tyre, middle-aged spread; N. Amer. informal bay window; dated humorous corporation. **3** *he had no stomach for it* **appetite**, taste, hunger, thirst; inclination, desire, relish, fancy.
▸**v. 1** *I can't stomach butter* **digest**, keep down, manage to eat/consume, tolerate, take. **2** *they couldn't stomach the sight* **tolerate**, put up with, take, stand, endure, bear; Scottish thole; informal hack, abide; Brit. informal stick.

> **WORD LINKS**
> **gastric** relating to the stomach
> **gastritis** inflammation of the stomach lining
> **gastroenterology** the branch of medicine that deals with the stomach and intestines

stomach ache n. **indigestion**, dyspepsia; colic, gripe; informal bellyache, tummy ache, gut ache, collywobbles.

stone n. **1** *someone threw a stone at me* **rock**, pebble, boulder. **2** *a commemorative stone* **tablet**, monument, monolith, obelisk; gravestone, headstone, tombstone. **3** *paving stones* **slab**, flagstone, flag, sett. **4** *a precious stone* **gem**, gemstone, jewel, semi-precious stone, brilliant; informal rock, sparkler. **5** *a peach stone* **kernel**, seed, pip, pit.

> **WORD LINKS**
> **lapidary** relating to the cutting or polishing of stones and gems
> **lithic** relating to or like stone
> **mason** a person who builds with stone or shapes stone for building
> **petrify** change organic matter into stone

stony adj. **1** *a stony path* **rocky**, pebbly, gravelly, shingly; rough, hard. **2** *a stony stare* **unfriendly**, hostile, cold, chilly, frosty, icy; hard, flinty, steely, stern, severe; fixed, expressionless, blank, poker-faced, deadpan; unfeeling, uncaring, unsympathetic, indifferent, cold-hearted, callous, heartless, hard-hearted, stony-hearted, merciless, pitiless.
– OPPOSITES smooth, friendly, sympathetic.

stooge n. **1** *a government stooge* **underling**, minion, lackey, subordinate; henchman; **puppet**, pawn, cat's paw; informal sidekick; Brit. informal dogsbody, poodle. **2** *a comedian's stooge* **butt**, foil, straight man.

stoop v. **1** *she stooped to pick up the pen* **bend (over/down)**, lean, lean over/down, crouch (down). **2** *he stooped his head* **lower**, bend, incline, bow, duck. **3** *he stoops when he walks* **hunch one's shoulders**, walk with a stoop, be round-shouldered. **4** *Davis would stoop to crime* **lower oneself**, sink, descend, resort; go as far as, sink as low as.

S

▸n. *a man with a stoop* **hunch**, round shoulders; curvature of the spine; Medicine kyphosis.

stop v. **1** *we can't stop the decline* **put an end to**, bring to an end, end, halt; finish, terminate, wind up, discontinue, cut short, interrupt, nip in the bud; deactivate, shut down. **2** *he stopped running* **cease**, discontinue, desist from, break off; give up, abandon, abstain from, cut out; informal quit, leave off, knock off, pack in, lay off, give over; Brit. informal jack in. **3** *the car stopped* **pull up**, draw up, come to a standstill, come to a halt, come to rest, pull in, pull over; park. **4** *the music stopped* **come to an end**/, cease, end, finish, draw to a close, be over, conclude, terminate; pause, break off; peter out, fade away. **5** *divers stopped the flow of oil* **stem**, staunch, hold back, check, curb, block, dam; N. Amer. stanch; old use stay. **6** *the police stopped her leaving* **prevent**, hinder, obstruct, impede, block, bar, preclude; dissuade from. **7** *the council stopped the Kilmarnock scheme* **thwart**, balk, foil, frustrate, stand in the way of; scotch, derail; informal put paid to, put the kibosh on, do for, stymie; Brit. informal scupper. **8** *the firm stops your tax* **withhold**, keep back, hold back, deduct, take away, refuse to pay. **9** *just stop the bottle with your thumb* **block (up)**, plug, close (up), fill (up); seal, caulk, bung up; technical occlude.
– OPPOSITES start, begin, continue, allow, encourage, expedite, pay, open.
▸n. **1** *all business came to a stop* **halt**, end, finish, close, standstill; cessation, conclusion, stoppage, discontinuation. **2** *a brief stop in the town* **break**, stopover, stop-off, stay, visit; formal sojourn. **3** *the next stop is Oxford Circus* **stopping place**, halt, station, stage. **4** *a full stop* **(full) point**; N. Amer. period.
– OPPOSITES start, beginning, continuation.
▫ **put a stop to** See **stop** (senses 1 & 7 of the verb).

stop off/over break one's journey, take a break, pause; stay, remain, put up, lodge, rest; formal sojourn.

stopgap n. *that old plane was merely a stopgap* **temporary solution**, expedient, makeshift; substitute, stand-in.
▸adj. *a stopgap measure* **temporary**, provisional, interim, pro tem, short-term, working, makeshift, emergency; caretaker, acting, fill-in, stand-in.
– OPPOSITES permanent.

stopover n. **break**, stop, stop-off, visit, stay; formal sojourn.

stoppage n. **1** *the stoppage of production* **discontinuation**, stopping, halting, cessation, termination, end, finish; interruption, suspension, breaking off. **2** *a stoppage of the blood supply* **obstruction**, blocking, blockage, block; Medicine occlusion, stasis. **3** *a stoppage over pay* **strike**, walkout; industrial action. **4** Brit. *she was paid £3.40 an hour before stoppages* **deduction**, subtraction.
– OPPOSITES start, continuation.

stopper n. **bung**, plug, cork, spigot, spile; seal; N. Amer. stopple.

store n. **1** *a store of food* **stock**, supply, stockpile, hoard, cache, reserve, bank, pool. **2** *a grain store* **storeroom**, storehouse, repository, depository, stockroom, depot, warehouse, magazine; informal lock-up. **3** *ship's stores* **supplies**, provisions, stocks, necessities; food, rations, provender; materials, equipment, hardware; Military materiel, accoutrements; Nautical chandlery. **4** *a DIY store* **shop**, (retail) outlet, boutique, department store, chain store, emporium; supermarket, hypermarket, superstore, megastore.
▸v. *rabbits don't store food* **keep**, keep in reserve, stockpile, lay in, put/set aside, put away/by, put away for a rainy day, save, collect, accumulate, hoard, cache; informal squirrel away, salt away, stash away.
– OPPOSITES use, discard.
▫ **set (great) store by** value, attach great importance to, put a high value on, put a premium on; think highly of, hold in (high) regard, have a high opinion of; informal rate.

storehouse n. **warehouse**, depository, repository, store, storeroom, depot.

storey n. **floor**, level, deck.

storm n. **1** *battered by a storm* **tempest**, squall; gale, hurricane, tornado, cyclone, typhoon, superstorm; thunderstorm, rainstorm, monsoon, hailstorm, snowstorm, blizzard; N. Amer. williwaw, windstorm. **2** *a storm of bullets* **volley**, salvo, fusillade, barrage, cannonade; shower, spray, hail, rain. **3** *there was a storm over his remarks* **uproar**, outcry, fuss, furore, brouhaha, rumpus, trouble, hue and cry, controversy; informal to-do, hoo-ha, hullabaloo, ballyhoo, ructions, stink; Brit. informal row. **4** *a storm of protest* **outburst**, outbreak, explosion, eruption, outpouring, surge, blaze, flare-up, wave.
▸v. **1** *she stormed out* **stride angrily**, stomp, march, stalk, flounce, stamp, fling. **2** *his mother stormed at him* **rant**, rave, shout, bellow, roar, thunder, rage. **3** *police stormed the building* **attack**, charge, rush, assail, descend on, swoop on.

stormy adj. **1** *stormy weather* **blustery**, squally, windy, gusty, blowy; rainy, thundery; wild, tempestuous, turbulent, violent, rough, foul. **2** *a stormy debate* **angry**, heated, fiery, fierce, furious, passionate, 'lively'.
– OPPOSITES calm, fine, peaceful.

story n. **1** *an adventure story* **tale**, narrative, account, anecdote; informal yarn, spiel. **2** *the novel has a good story* **plot**, storyline, scenario; formal diegesis. **3** *the story appeared in the papers* **news item**, news report, article, feature, piece. **4** *there have been a lot of stories going round* **rumour**, piece of gossip, whisper; speculation; Austral./NZ informal furphy. **5** *Harper changed his story* **testimony**, statement, report, account, version. **6** *Ellie never told stories.* See **falsehood** (sense 1).

S

storyteller n. **narrator**, teller of tales, raconteur, raconteuse, fabulist, anecdotalist; Austral. informal magsman.

stout adj. **1** *a short stout man* **fat**, plump, portly, rotund, dumpy, chunky, corpulent; stocky, burly, bulky, hefty, solidly built, thickset; informal tubby, pudgy; Brit. informal podgy, fubsy; N. Amer. informal zaftig, corn-fed; old use pursy. **2** *stout leather shoes* **strong**, sturdy, solid, substantial, robust, tough, durable, hard-wearing. **3** *stout resistance* **determined**, vigorous, forceful, spirited; staunch, steadfast, stalwart, firm, resolute, unyielding, dogged; brave, bold, courageous, valiant, valorous, gallant, fearless, doughty, intrepid; informal gutsy, spunky.
– OPPOSITES thin, flimsy, feeble.

stout-hearted adj. **brave**, determined, courageous, bold, plucky, spirited, valiant, valorous, gallant, fearless, doughty, intrepid, stalwart; informal gutsy, spunky.

stove n. **oven**, range, cooker.

stow v. *Barney stowed her luggage in the boot* **pack**, load, store, place, put (away), deposit, stash.
– OPPOSITES unload.
□ **stow away** hide, conceal oneself, travel secretly.

straddle v. **1** *she straddled the motorbike* **sit/stand astride**, bestride, mount, get on. **2** *a mountain range straddling the border* **lie on both sides of**, extend across, span. **3** N. Amer. *he straddled the issue of taxes* **be equivocal about**, be undecided about, equivocate about, vacillate about, waver about; informal sit on the fence.

strafe v. **bomb**, shell, bombard, fire on, machine-gun, rake with gunfire, enfilade; old use fusillade.

straggle v. **trail**, lag, dawdle, walk slowly; fall behind, bring up the rear.

straggly adj. **untidy**, messy, unkempt, straggling, dishevelled.

straight adj. **1** *a long, straight road* **unswerving**, undeviating, linear, as straight as an arrow, uncurving, unbending. **2** *that picture isn't straight* **level**, even, in line, aligned, square; vertical, upright, perpendicular; horizontal. **3** *we must get the place straight* **in order**, (neat and) tidy, neat, shipshape (and Bristol fashion), orderly, spick and span, organized, arranged, sorted out, straightened out. **4** *a straight answer* **honest**, direct, frank, candid, truthful, sincere, forthright, straightforward, plain-spoken, blunt, straight from the shoulder, unequivocal, unambiguous; informal upfront. **5** *straight thinking* **logical**, rational, clear, lucid, sound, coherent. **6** *three straight wins* **successive**, in succession, consecutive, in a row, running; informal on the trot. **7** *straight brandy* **undiluted**, neat, pure; N. Amer. informal straight up. **8** informal *she's very straight* **respectable**, conventional, conservative, traditional, old-fashioned, strait-laced; informal stuffy, square, fuddy-duddy.
– OPPOSITES winding, crooked, untidy, evasive.

▶ adv. **1** *he looked me straight in the eyes* **right**, directly, squarely, full; informal smack, (slap) bang; N. Amer. informal spang, smack dab. **2** *she drove straight home* **directly**, right, by a direct route. **3** *I'll call you straight back* **right away**, straight away, immediately, directly, at once; old use straightway. **4** *I told her straight* **frankly**, directly, candidly, honestly, forthrightly, plainly, point-blank, bluntly, flatly, straight from the shoulder, without beating about the bush, without mincing one's words, unequivocally, unambiguously, in plain English, to someone's face; Brit. informal straight up. **5** *he can't think straight* **logically**, rationally, clearly, lucidly, coherently, cogently.
□ **go straight** reform, mend one's ways, turn over a new leaf, get back on the straight and narrow.

straight away at once, right away, (right) now, this/that (very) minute, this/that instant, immediately, instantly, directly, forthwith, without further/more ado, promptly, quickly, without delay, then and there, here and now, ASAP, as soon as possible, as quickly as possible; N. Amer. in short order; informal straight off, in double quick time, p.d.q., pretty damn quick, pronto, before you can say Jack Robinson; N. Amer. informal lickety-split; old use straightway.

straight from the shoulder See **straight** (sense 4 of the adverb).

straighten v. **1** *Rory straightened his tie* **make straight**, adjust, arrange, rearrange, (make) tidy, spruce up. **2** *we must straighten things out with Viola* **put/set right**, sort out, clear up, settle, resolve, put in order, regularize, rectify, remedy; informal patch up. **3** *he straightened up* **stand up (straight)**, stand upright.

straightforward adj. **1** *the process was remarkably straightforward* **uncomplicated**, simple, easy, effortless, painless, undemanding, plain sailing, child's play; informal as easy as falling off a log, as easy as pie, a piece of cake, a cinch, a snip, a doddle, a breeze, a cakewalk, a walk in the park; Brit. informal easy-peasy, a doss; N. Amer. informal duck soup, a snap; Austral./NZ informal a bludge, a snack. **2** *a straightforward man* **honest**, frank, candid, open, truthful, sincere, on the level; forthright, plain-speaking, direct, unambiguous; informal upfront; N. Amer. informal on the up and up.
– OPPOSITES complicated.

strain¹ v. **1** *take care that you don't strain yourself* **overtax**, overwork, overextend, overreach, drive too far, overdo it; exhaust, wear out; informal knacker, knock oneself out. **2** *you have strained a muscle* **injure**, damage, pull, wrench, twist, sprain. **3** *we strained to haul the guns up the slope* **struggle**, labour, toil, make every effort, try very hard, break one's back, push/drive oneself to the limit; informal pull out all the stops, go all out, bust a gut; Austral. informal go for the doctor. **4** *the flood of refugees is straining the relief services* **make excessive demands on**, overtax, be

too much for, test, tax, put a strain on. **5** *the bear strained at the chain* **pull**, tug, heave, haul, jerk; informal yank. **6** *strain the mixture* **sieve**, sift, filter, screen, riddle; rare filtrate.
▸n. **1** *the rope snapped under the strain* **tension**, tightness, tautness. **2** *muscle strain* **injury**, sprain, wrench, twist. **3** *the strain of her job* **pressure**, demands, burdens; stress; informal hassle. **4** *Melissa was showing signs of strain* **stress**, (nervous) tension; exhaustion, fatigue, pressure of work, overwork. **5** *the strains of Brahms's lullaby* **sound**, music; melody, tune.

strain² n. **1** *a different strain of flu* **variety**, kind, type, sort; breed, genus. **2** *Hawthorne was of Puritan strain* **descent**, ancestry, origin(s), parentage, lineage, extraction, family, roots. **3** *there was a strain of insanity in the family* **tendency**, susceptibility, propensity, proneness; trait, disposition. **4** *a strain of solemnity* **element**, strand, vein, note, trace, touch, suggestion, hint.

strained adj. **1** *relations between them were strained* **awkward**, tense, uneasy, uncomfortable, edgy, difficult, troubled. **2** *Jean's strained face* **drawn**, careworn, worn, pinched, tired, exhausted, drained, haggard. **3** *a strained smile* **forced**, constrained, unnatural; artificial, insincere, false, affected, put-on.
– OPPOSITES friendly, relaxed, natural.

strainer n. **sieve**, colander, filter, sifter, riddle, screen; old use griddle.

strait n. **1** *a strait about six miles wide* **channel**, sound, inlet, stretch of water. **2** *the company is in desperate straits* **a bad/difficult situation**, difficulty, trouble, crisis, a mess, a predicament, a plight; informal hot/deep water, a jam, a hole, a bind, a fix, a scrape.

straitened adj. **impoverished**, poverty-stricken, poor, destitute, penniless, on one's beam-ends, as poor as a church mouse, in penury, impecunious, unable to make ends meet, in reduced circumstances; Brit. on the breadline; informal (flat) broke, strapped for cash, on one's uppers; Brit. informal stony broke, skint, in Queer Street; N. Amer. informal stone broke; formal penurious.

strait-laced adj. **prim (and proper)**, prudish, puritanical, prissy, mimsy, niminy-piminy; conservative, old-fashioned, stuffy, staid, narrow-minded; informal starchy, square, fuddy-duddy.
– OPPOSITES broad-minded.

strand¹ n. **1** *strands of wool* **thread**, filament, fibre; length, ply. **2** *the various strands of the ecological movement* **element**, component, factor, ingredient, aspect, feature, strain, trope.

strand² n. literary *a walk along the strand* **seashore**, shore, beach, sands, foreshore, shoreline, seaside, waterfront, front, waterside.

stranded adj. **1** *a stranded ship* **beached**, grounded, run aground, high and dry; shipwrecked, wrecked, marooned. **2** *she was* *stranded in a strange city* **helpless**, without resources, in difficulties; in the lurch, abandoned, deserted.

strange adj. **1** *strange things have been happening* **unusual**, odd, curious, peculiar, funny, bizarre, weird, uncanny, queer, unexpected, unfamiliar, atypical, anomalous, out of the ordinary, extraordinary, puzzling, mystifying, mysterious, perplexing, baffling, unaccountable, inexplicable, singular, freakish; suspicious, questionable; eerie, unnatural; informal fishy, creepy, spooky. **2** *strange clothes* **weird**, eccentric, odd, peculiar, funny, bizarre, unusual, unconventional, outlandish, freakish, quirky, zany; informal wacky, way out, freaky, kooky, offbeat, off the wall; N. Amer. informal screwy, wacko. **3** *visiting a strange house* **unfamiliar**, unknown, new. **4** *Jean was feeling strange* **ill**, unwell, poorly, peaky; Brit. off colour; informal under the weather, funny, peculiar, lousy; Brit. informal off, ropy, grotty; Austral./NZ informal crook; dated queer. **5** *she felt strange with him* **ill at ease**, uneasy, uncomfortable, awkward, self-conscious.
– OPPOSITES ordinary, familiar, well, at ease.

strangeness n. **oddity**, eccentricity, peculiarity, curiousness, bizarreness, weirdness, queerness, unusualness, abnormality, unaccountability, inexplicability, incongruousness, outlandishness, singularity.

stranger n. **newcomer**, new arrival, visitor, outsider; Austral. informal blow-in.
▫ **a stranger to** unaccustomed to, unfamiliar with, unused to, new to, fresh to, inexperienced in; old use strange to.

strangle v. **1** *the victim was strangled with a scarf* **throttle**, choke, garrotte; informal strangulate. **2** *she strangled a sob* **suppress**, smother, stifle, repress, restrain, fight back, choke back. **3** *bureaucracy is strangling commercial activity* **hamper**, hinder, impede, restrict, inhibit, curb, check, constrain, squash, crush, suppress, repress.

strap n. *thick leather straps* **thong**, tie, band, belt.
▸v. **1** *a bag was strapped to the bicycle* **fasten**, secure, tie, bind, make fast, lash, truss. **2** *his knee was strapped up* **bandage**, bind. **3** *his father strapped him*. See **lash** (sense 1 of the verb).

strapping adj. **big**, strong, well built, brawny, burly, broad-shouldered, muscular, rugged; informal hunky, beefy; dated stalwart.
– OPPOSITES weedy.

stratagem n. **plan**, scheme, tactic, manoeuvre, ploy, device, trick, ruse, plot, machination, dodge; subterfuge, artifice; Brit. informal wheeze; Austral. informal lurk; old use shift.

strategic adj. **planned**, calculated, tactical, politic, judicious, prudent, shrewd.

strategy n. **1** *the government's economic strategy* **master plan**, grand design, game plan, plan (of action), policy, programme; tactics. **2** *military strategy* **the art of war**, (military) tactics.

S

stratum n. **1** *a stratum of flint* **layer**, vein, seam, lode, bed. **2** *this stratum of society* **level**, class, echelon, rank, grade, group, set; caste; dated station, estate.

stray v. **1** *the gazelle had strayed from the herd* **wander off**, go astray, get separated, get lost. **2** *we strayed from our original topic* **digress**, deviate, wander, get sidetracked, go off at a tangent; get off the subject. **3** *the young men were likely to stray* **be unfaithful**, have affairs, philander; informal play around, play the field. **4** *he strayed from the path of righteousness* **sin**, transgress, err, go astray; old use trespass.
▸adj. **1** *a stray dog* **homeless**, lost, strayed, gone astray, abandoned. **2** *a stray bullet* **random**, chance, freak, unexpected, isolated, lone, single.
▸n. *wardens who deal with strays* **homeless animal**, stray dog/cat, waif.

streak n. **1** *a streak of orange light* **band**, line, strip, stripe, vein, slash, ray. **2** *green streaks on her legs* **mark**, smear, smudge, stain, blotch; informal splotch. **3** *a streak of self-destructiveness* **element**, vein, touch, strain; trait, characteristic. **4** *a winning streak* **period**, spell, stretch, run; Brit. informal patch.
▸v. **1** *the sky was streaked with red* **stripe**, band, fleck; old use freak. **2** *overalls streaked with paint* **mark**, daub, smear; informal splotch. **3** *Miranda streaked across the road.* See **run** (sense 1 of the verb).

streaky adj. **striped**, stripy, streaked, banded, veined, brindled.

stream n. **1** *a mountain stream* **brook**, rivulet, rill, runnel, streamlet, freshet; tributary; Scottish & N. English burn; N. English beck; S. English bourn; N. Amer. & Austral./NZ creek; Austral. billabong. **2** *a stream of boiling water* **jet**, flow, rush, gush, surge, torrent, flood, cascade, outpouring, outflow; technical efflux. **3** *a steady stream of visitors* **succession**, series, string.
▸v. **1** *tears were streaming down her face* **flow**, pour, course, run, gush, surge, flood, cascade, spill. **2** *children streamed out of the classrooms* **pour**, surge, flood, swarm, pile, crowd. **3** *a flag streamed from the mast* **flutter**, float, flap, fly, blow, waft, wave.

streamer n. **pennant**, pennon, flag, banderole, banner.

streamlined adj. **1** *streamlined cars* **aerodynamic**, smooth, sleek, elegant. **2** *a streamlined organization* **efficient**, smooth-running, well run, slick; time-saving, labour-saving.

street n. *Amsterdam's narrow cobbled streets* **road**, thoroughfare, avenue, drive, boulevard, parade; side street/road, lane; N. Amer. highway.
□ **the man/woman in the street** an ordinary person, Mr/Mrs Average; Brit. informal Joe Bloggs, Joe Public, the man on the Clapham omnibus; N. Amer. informal John Doe, Joe Sixpack.
on the streets homeless, sleeping rough, down and out.

strength n. **1** *enormous physical strength* **power**, brawn, muscle, muscularity, burliness, sturdiness, robustness, toughness, hardiness; vigour, force, might; informal beef; literary thew. **2** *Oliver began to regain his strength* **health**, fitness, vigour, stamina. **3** *her great inner strength* **fortitude**, resilience, spirit, backbone, strength of character; courage, bravery, pluck, pluckiness, courageousness, grit; Brit. Dunkirk spirit; informal guts, spunk. **4** *the strength of the retaining wall* **robustness**, sturdiness, firmness, toughness, soundness, solidity, durability. **5** *Europe's military strength* **power**, influence, dominance, ascendancy, supremacy; informal clout; literary puissance. **6** *the strength of feeling against the president* **intensity**, vehemence, force, forcefulness, depth, ardour, fervour. **7** *the strength of their argument* **cogency**, forcefulness, force, weight, power, potency, persuasiveness, soundness, validity. **8** *what are your strengths?* **strong point**, advantage, asset, forte, aptitude, talent, skill; speciality. **9** *the strength of the army* **size**, extent, magnitude.
– OPPOSITES weakness.
□ **on the strength of** because of, by virtue of, on the basis of.

strengthen v. **1** *calcium strengthens growing bones* **make strong/stronger**, build up, give strength to. **2** *engineers strengthened the walls* **reinforce**, make stronger, buttress, shore up, underpin. **3** *strengthened glass* **toughen**, temper, anneal. **4** *the wind had strengthened* **become strong/stronger**, gain strength, intensify, pick up. **5** *his insistence strengthened her determination* **fortify**, bolster, make stronger, boost, reinforce, harden, stiffen, toughen, fuel. **6** *they strengthened their efforts* **step up**, increase, escalate; informal up, crank up, beef up. **7** *the argument is strengthened by this evidence* **reinforce**, lend more weight to; support, back up, confirm, bear out, corroborate.
– OPPOSITES weaken.

strenuous adj. **1** *a strenuous climb* **arduous**, difficult, hard, tough, taxing, demanding, exacting, exhausting, tiring, gruelling, back-breaking; informal killing; Brit. informal knackering; old use toilsome. **2** *strenuous efforts* **vigorous**, energetic, zealous, forceful, strong, spirited, intense, determined, resolute, tenacious, tireless, indefatigable, dogged; formal pertinacious.
– OPPOSITES easy, half-hearted.

stress n. **1** *he's under a lot of stress* **strain**, pressure, (nervous) tension, worry, anxiety, trouble, difficulty; informal hassle. **2** *laying greater stress on education* **emphasis**, importance, weight. **3** *the stress falls on the first syllable* **emphasis**, accent, accentuation; beat; Prosody ictus. **4** *the stress is uniform across the bar* **pressure**, tension, strain.
▸v. **1** *they stressed the need for reform* **emphasize**, draw attention to, underline, underscore, point up, place emphasis on, lay stress on, highlight, accentuate, press

home. **2** *the last syllable is stressed* **place the emphasis on**, emphasize, place the accent on. **3** *all the staff were stressed* **overstretch**, overtax, push to the limit, pressurize, pressure, make tense, worry, harass; informal hassle.
– OPPOSITES play down.

stressful adj. **demanding**, trying, taxing, difficult, hard, tough; fraught, traumatic, pressured, tense, frustrating.
– OPPOSITES relaxing.

stretch v. **1** *this material stretches* **be elastic**, be stretchy, be tensile. **2** *he stretched the elastic* **pull (out)**, draw out, extend, lengthen, elongate, expand. **3** *stretch your weekend into a vacation* **prolong**, lengthen, make longer, extend, spin out. **4** *my budget won't stretch to a new car* **be sufficient for**, be enough for, cover; afford, have the money for. **5** *the court case stretched their finances* **put a strain on**, overtax, overextend, drain, sap. **6** *stretching the truth* **bend**, strain, distort, exaggerate, embellish. **7** *she stretched out her hand to him* **reach out**, hold out, extend, outstretch, proffer; literary outreach. **8** *he stretched his arms* **extend**, straighten (out). **9** *she stretched out on the sofa* **lie down**, recline, lean back, be recumbent, sprawl, lounge, loll. **10** *the desert stretches for miles* **extend**, spread, continue.
– OPPOSITES shorten.
▸n. **1** *magnificent stretches of forest* **expanse**, area, tract, belt, sweep, extent. **2** *a four-hour stretch* **period**, time, spell, run, stint, session, shift. **3** informal *a ten-year stretch* **(prison) sentence**; N. Amer. informal rap.
▸adj. *stretch fabrics* **stretchy**, stretchable, elastic.

strew v. **scatter**, spread, disperse, litter, toss; literary bestrew.

stricken adj. **troubled**, (deeply) affected, afflicted, struck, hit.

strict adj. **1** *a strict interpretation of the law* **precise**, exact, literal, faithful, accurate, careful, meticulous, rigorous. **2** *strict controls on spending* **stringent**, rigorous, severe, harsh, hard, rigid, tough. **3** *strict parents* **stern**, severe, harsh, uncompromising, authoritarian, firm, austere. **4** *this will be treated in strict confidence* **absolute**, utter, complete, total. **5** *a strict Roman Catholic* **orthodox**, devout, conscientious.
– OPPOSITES loose, liberal.

strictness n. **1** *the strictness of the laws* **severity**, harshness, rigidity, rigidness, stringency, rigorousness, sternness.
2 *the provision has been interpreted with strictness* **precision**, preciseness, accuracy, exactness, faithfulness; meticulousness, scrupulousness.
– OPPOSITES imprecision.

stricture n. **1** *the constant strictures of the nuns* **criticism**, censure, condemnation, reproof, reproach, admonishment. **2** *the strictures on Victorian women* **constraint**, restriction, limitation, restraint, straitjacket, curb, impediment, barrier, obstacle. **3** *an intestinal stricture* **narrowing**, constriction.
– OPPOSITES praise, freedom.

stride v. *she came striding down the path* **march**, pace, step.
▸n. *long swinging strides* **(long/large) step**, pace.
□ **take something in one's stride** deal with easily, cope with easily, not bat an eyelid.

strident adj. **harsh**, raucous, rough, grating, rasping, jarring, loud, shrill, screeching, piercing, ear-piercing.
– OPPOSITES soft.

strife n. **conflict**, friction, discord, disagreement, dissension, dispute, argument, quarrelling, wrangling, bickering, controversy; ill/bad feeling, falling-out, bad blood, hostility, animosity.
– OPPOSITES peace.

strike v. **1** *the teacher struck Mary* **hit**, slap, smack, beat, thrash, spank, thump, punch, cuff; cane, lash, whip, club; Austral./NZ informal quilt; informal clout, wallop, belt, whack, thwack, bash, clobber, bop, biff; literary smite. **2** *he struck the gong* **bang**, beat, hit; informal bash, wallop. **3** *the car struck a tree* **crash into**, collide with, hit, run into, bump into, smash into; N. Amer. impact. **4** *Jennifer struck the ball* **hit**, drive, propel; informal clout, wallop, swipe; Brit. informal welly. **5** *he struck a match* **light**. **6** *she was asleep when the killer struck* **attack**, set upon someone, fall on someone, assault someone. **7** *the disease is striking 3,000 people a year* **affect**, afflict, attack, hit. **8** *striking a balance* **achieve**, reach, arrive at, find, attain, establish. **9** *we have struck a bargain* **agree (on)**, come to an agreement on, settle on; informal clinch. **10** *he struck a heroic pose* **assume**, adopt, take on/up, affect; N. Amer. informal cop. **11** *they have struck oil* **discover**, find, come upon. **12** *a thought struck her* **occur to**, come to (mind), dawn on one, hit, spring to mind, enter one's head. **13** *you strike me as intelligent* **seem to**, appear to, give the impression of. **14** *train drivers are striking* **take industrial action**, go on strike, down tools, walk out. **15** *they struck the big tent* **take down**, pull down. **16** *Lord Bridport struck his flag* **lower**, take down, bring down. **17** *we should strike south* **go**, make one's way, head.
▸n. **1** *a 48-hour strike* **industrial action**, walkout. **2** *a military strike* **(air) attack**, assault, bombing. **3** *a gold strike* **find**, discovery.
□ **strike something out** delete, cross out, erase, rub out.
strike something up 1 *the band struck up another tune* **begin to play**, start playing. **2** *we struck up a friendship* **begin**, start, commence, embark on, establish.

striking adj. **1** *Lizzie bears a striking resemblance to her sister* **noticeable**, obvious, conspicuous, evident, marked, notable, unmistakable, strong; remarkable, extraordinary, incredible, amazing,

astounding, astonishing, staggering.
2 *Kenya's striking landscape* **impressive**,
imposing, grand, splendid, magnificent,
spectacular, breathtaking, superb,
marvellous, wonderful, stunning,
staggering, sensational, dramatic. **3** *striking
good looks* **stunning**, attractive, good-
looking, beautiful, glamorous, gorgeous,
prepossessing, ravishing, handsome, pretty;
informal knockout; old use fair, comely.
– OPPOSITES unremarkable.

string n. **1** *a ball of string* **twine**, cord,
yarn, thread, strand. **2** *a string of brewers*
chain, group, firm, company. **3** *a string
of convictions* **series**, succession, chain,
sequence, run, streak. **4** *a string of wagons*
queue, procession, line, file, column,
convoy, train, cavalcade. **5** *a string of pearls*
strand, rope, necklace. **6** *a guaranteed loan
with no strings* **conditions**, qualifications,
provisions, provisos, caveats, stipulations,
riders, prerequisites, limitations, limits,
constraints, restrictions; informal catches.
▸ v. **1** *lights were strung across the promenade*
hang, suspend, sling, stretch, run; thread,
loop, festoon. **2** *beads strung on a silver chain*
thread, loop, link.
▫ **string along** go along, come too,
accompany, join (up with).
string someone along informal mislead,
deceive, take advantage of, dupe, hoax, fool,
make a fool of, play with, toy with, dally
with, trifle with; informal lead up the garden
path, take for a ride.
string something out 1 *stringing out a
story* **spin out**, drag out, lengthen. **2** *airfields
strung out along the Gulf* **spread out**, space
out, distribute, scatter.
string someone up informal hang, lynch,
gibbet.

stringent adj. **strict**, firm, rigid, rigorous,
severe, harsh, tough, tight, exacting,
demanding, inflexible, hard and fast.

stringy adj. **1** *stringy hair* **straggly**, lank,
thin. **2** *a stringy brunette* **lanky**, gangling,
gangly, rangy, wiry, bony, skinny, scrawny,
thin, spare, gaunt. **3** *stringy meat* **fibrous**,
gristly, sinewy, chewy, tough, leathery.

strip[1] v. **1** *he stripped and got into bed*
undress, strip off, take one's clothes off,
unclothe, disrobe, strip naked. **2** *stripping
off paint* **peel**, remove, take off, scrape, rub,
clean. **3** *they stripped him of his doctorate*
take away from, dispossess, deprive,
confiscate, divest, relieve. **4** *they stripped
down my engine* **dismantle**, disassemble,
take to bits/pieces, take apart. **5** *the house
had been stripped* **empty**, clear, clean out,
plunder, rob, burgle, loot, pillage, ransack,
despoil, sack; old use spoil.
– OPPOSITES dress.
▸ n. *the team's new strip* **outfit**, clothes,
clothing, garments, dress, garb; Brit. kit;
informal gear, get-up; Brit. informal rig-out.

strip[2] n. *a strip of paper* **(narrow) piece**, bit,
band, belt, ribbon, slip, shred.

stripe n. **line**, band, strip, belt, bar, streak,
vein, flash, blaze; technical stria, striation.

striped adj. See **stripy**.

stripling n. **youth**, adolescent, youngster,
boy, schoolboy, lad, teenager, juvenile,
minor, young man; Scottish laddie; informal kid,
young 'un, nipper, whippersnapper, shaver.

stripy adj. **striped**, barred, lined, banded;
streaky, variegated; technical striated.

strive v. **1** *I shall strive to be virtuous* **try
(hard)**, attempt, endeavour, aim, venture,
make an effort, exert oneself, do one's best,
do all one can, do one's utmost, labour, work;
informal go all out, give it one's best shot, pull
out all the stops; formal essay. **2** *scholars must
strive against bias* **struggle**, fight, battle,
combat; campaign, crusade.

stroke n. **1** *five strokes of the axe* **blow**, hit,
thump, punch, slap, smack, cuff, knock;
informal wallop, clout, whack, thwack, bash,
biff, swipe; old use smite. **2** *cricket strokes*
shot, hit, strike. **3** *light upward strokes*
movement, action, motion. **4** *a stroke of
genius* **feat**, accomplishment, achievement,
master stroke. **5** *broad brush strokes* **mark**,
line. **6** *the budget was full of bold strokes*
detail, touch, point. **7** *he suffered a stroke*
thrombosis, seizure; Medicine ictus.
▸ v. *she stroked the cat* **caress**, fondle, pat, pet,
touch, rub, massage, soothe.

stroll v. *they strolled along the river*
saunter, amble, wander, meander, ramble,
promenade, walk, go for a walk, stretch one's
legs; informal mosey; formal perambulate.
▸ n. *a stroll in the park* **saunter**, amble, wander,
walk, turn, promenade; informal mosey; dated
constitutional; formal perambulation.

strong adj. **1** *a strong lad* **powerful**,
muscular, brawny, powerfully built,
strapping, sturdy, burly, meaty, robust,
athletic, tough, rugged, lusty, strong as
an ox/horse; informal beefy, hunky, husky;
dated stalwart. **2** *she isn't very strong* **well**,
healthy, in good health, (fighting) fit,
robust, vigorous, blooming, thriving, hale
and hearty, in fine fettle; informal in the pink.
3 *a strong character* **forceful**, determined,
spirited, self-assertive, tough, tenacious,
formidable, redoubtable, strong-minded;
informal gutsy, feisty. **4** *a strong fortress*
secure, well built, indestructible, well
fortified, well protected, impregnable, solid.
5 *strong cotton bags* **durable**, hard-wearing,
heavy-duty, tough, sturdy, well made, long-
lasting. **6** *the current is very strong* **forceful**,
powerful, vigorous, fierce, intense. **7** *a strong
interest in literature* **keen**, eager, passionate,
fervent. **8** *strong feelings* **intense**, forceful,
passionate, ardent, fervent, fervid, deep-
seated; literary perfervid. **9** *a strong supporter*
keen, eager, enthusiastic, dedicated,
staunch, loyal, steadfast. **10** *strong
arguments* **compelling**, cogent, forceful,
powerful, potent, weighty, convincing,
sound, valid, well founded, persuasive,
influential. **11** *a need for strong action* **firm**,
forceful, drastic, extreme. **12** *she bore a
very strong resemblance to Vera* **marked**,
noticeable, pronounced, distinct, definite,
unmistakable, notable. **13** *a strong voice*

loud, powerful, forceful, resonant, sonorous, rich, deep, booming. **14** *strong language* **bad,** foul, obscene, profane. **15** *a strong blue colour* **intense,** deep, rich, bright, brilliant, vivid. **16** *strong lights* **bright,** brilliant, dazzling, glaring. **17** *strong black coffee* **concentrated,** undiluted. **18** *strong cheese* **highly flavoured,** flavourful, flavoursome; piquant, tangy, spicy. **19** *strong drink* **alcoholic,** intoxicating, hard, stiff; formal spirituous.
– OPPOSITES weak, gentle, mild.

strong-arm adj. **aggressive,** forceful, bullying, coercive, threatening, intimidatory; informal bully-boy.

strongbox n. **safe,** safe-deposit box, cash/money box.

stronghold n. **1** *the enemy stronghold* **fortress,** fort, castle, citadel, garrison. **2** *a Tory stronghold* **bastion,** centre, hotbed.

strong-minded adj. **determined,** firm, resolute, purposeful, strong-willed, uncompromising, unbending, forceful, persistent, tenacious, dogged; informal gutsy, spunky.

strong point n. **strength,** strong suit, forte, speciality.
– OPPOSITES weakness.

strong-willed adj. **determined,** resolute, stubborn, obstinate, wilful, headstrong, strong-minded, self-willed, unbending, unyielding, intransigent, intractable, obdurate, recalcitrant; formal refractory.

stroppy adj. Brit. informal See **bad-tempered**.

structure n. **1** *a vast Gothic structure* **building,** construction, erection, pile; formal edifice. **2** *the structure of local government* **construction,** form, formation, shape, composition, anatomy, make-up, constitution; organization, system, arrangement, design, framework, configuration, pattern.
▸ v. *the programme is structured around periods of residential study* **arrange,** organize, design, shape, construct, build, put together.

struggle v. **1** *they struggled to do better* **strive,** try hard, endeavour, make every effort, do one's best/utmost, bend over backwards, put oneself out; informal go all out, give it one's best shot; formal essay. **2** *James struggled with the raiders* **fight,** grapple, wrestle, scuffle, brawl, spar; informal scrap. **3** *the teams struggled to be first* **compete,** contend, vie, fight, battle, jockey. **4** *she struggled over the dunes* **scramble,** flounder, stumble, fight/battle one's way, labour.
▸ n. **1** *the struggle for justice* **endeavour,** striving, effort, exertion, labour; campaign, battle, crusade, drive, push. **2** *they were arrested without a struggle* **fight,** scuffle, brawl, tussle, wrestling bout, skirmish, fracas, melee; breach of the peace; informal scrap, dust-up, punch-up; Brit. informal bust-up, ding-dong; Law, dated affray. **3** *many perished in the struggle* **conflict,** fight, battle, confrontation, clash, skirmish; hostilities, fighting, war, warfare, campaign. **4** *a struggle within the leadership* **contest,** competition, fight, clash; rivalry, friction, feuding, conflict. **5** *life has been a struggle for me* **effort,** trial, trouble, stress, strain, battle; informal grind, hassle.

strumpet n. old use See **prostitute** (noun).

strut v. **swagger,** swank, parade, stride, sweep; N. Amer. informal sashay.

stub n. **1** *a cigarette stub* **butt,** (tail) end; informal dog-end. **2** *a ticket stub* **counterfoil,** ticket slip, tab. **3** *a stub of pencil* **stump,** remnant, (tail) end.

stubble n. **1** *a field of stubble* **stalks,** straw. **2** *grey stubble* **bristles,** whiskers, facial hair; informal five o'clock shadow.

stubbly adj. **bristly,** unshaven, whiskered; prickly, rough, coarse, scratchy.

stubborn adj. **1** *you're too stubborn to admit it* **obstinate,** stubborn as a mule, headstrong, wilful, strong-willed, pig-headed, obdurate, difficult, contrary, perverse, recalcitrant, inflexible, iron-willed, uncompromising, unbending; informal stiff-necked; Brit. informal bolshie, bloody-minded; N. Amer. informal balky; formal pertinacious, refractory; old use contumacious, froward. **2** *stubborn stains* **indelible,** permanent, persistent, tenacious, resistant.
– OPPOSITES compliant.

stubby adj. **dumpy,** stocky, chunky, chubby, squat; short, stumpy, dwarfish.
– OPPOSITES slender, tall.

stuck adj. **1** *a message was stuck to his screen* **fixed,** fastened, attached, glued, pinned. **2** *the gate was stuck* **immovable,** stuck fast, jammed. **3** *if you get stuck, leave a blank* **baffled,** beaten, at a loss, at one's wits' end; informal stumped, bogged down, flummoxed, fazed, bamboozled.
□ **get stuck into** informal get down to, make a start on, commence, embark on, get to work at, tackle, throw oneself into.

stuck on informal infatuated with, besotted with, smitten with, (head over heels) in love with, obsessed with; informal struck on, crazy about, mad about, wild about, carrying a torch for.

stuck with lumbered with, left with, made responsible for.

stuck-up adj. informal See **conceited**.

studded adj. **dotted,** scattered, sprinkled, covered, spangled; literary bespangled, bejewelled.

student n. **1** *a university student* **undergraduate,** postgraduate, scholar; freshman, freshwoman, finalist; N. Amer. sophomore; Brit. informal fresher. **2** *a former student* **pupil,** schoolchild, schoolboy, schoolgirl, scholar. **3** *a nursing student* **trainee,** apprentice, probationer, recruit, novice; informal rookie.

studied adj. **deliberate,** careful, considered, conscious, calculated, intentional; affected, forced, strained, artificial.

studio n. **workshop,** workroom, atelier.

studious adj. **1** *a studious nature* **scholarly,** academic, bookish, intellectual, erudite, learned, donnish. **2** *studious attention* **diligent**, careful, attentive, assiduous, painstaking, thorough, meticulous. **3** *his studious absence from public view* **deliberate**, wilful, conscious, intentional.

study n. **1** *two years of study* **learning**, education, schooling, academic work, scholarship, tuition, research; informal swotting, cramming. **2** *a study of global warming* **investigation**, enquiry, research, examination, analysis, review, survey. **3** *Father was in his study* **office**, workroom, studio. **4** *a critical study* **essay**, article, work, review, paper, dissertation, disquisition.
▶ v. **1** *Anne studied hard* **work**, revise; informal swot, cram, mug up; old use con. **2** *he studied electronics* **learn**, read, be taught. **3** *Thomas was studying child development* **investigate**, inquire into, research, look into, examine, analyse, explore, review, appraise. **4** *she studied her friend thoughtfully* **scrutinize**, examine, inspect, consider, regard, look at, eye, observe, watch, survey; informal check out; N. Amer. informal eyeball.
□ **in a brown study** lost in thought, in a reverie, musing, ruminating, cogitating, dreaming, daydreaming; informal miles away.

stuff n. **1** *suede is tough stuff* **material**, fabric, cloth, textile; matter, substance. **2** *first-aid stuff* **items**, articles, objects, goods; informal things, bits and pieces, odds and ends. **3** *all my stuff is in the suitcase* **belongings**, (personal) possessions, effects, goods (and chattels), paraphernalia; informal gear, things, kit; Brit. informal clobber, gubbins. **4** *he knows his stuff* **facts**, information, data, subject; informal onions.
▶ v. **1** *stuffing pillows* **fill**, pack, pad, upholster. **2** *Robyn stuffed her clothes into a bag* **shove**, thrust, push, ram, cram, squeeze, force, jam, pack, pile, stick. **3** informal *they stuffed themselves with chocolate* **fill**, gorge, overindulge; gobble, devour, wolf; informal pig (out), make a pig of oneself. **4** *my nose was stuffed up* **block**, bung, congest, obstruct. **5** Brit. informal *Scotland stuffed Chile.* See **trounce**.
□ **stuff and nonsense** Brit. informal See **nonsense** (sense 1).

stuffing n. **1** *the stuffing is coming out of the armchair* **padding**, wadding, filling, upholstery, packing, filler. **2** *sage and onion stuffing* **filling**, forcemeat, salpicon; N. Amer. dressing.
□ **knock the stuffing out of** informal devastate, shatter, crush, shock; informal knock sideways; Brit. informal knock for six.

stuffy adj. **1** *a stuffy atmosphere* **airless**, close, musty, stale; Brit. frowsty; Brit. informal fuggy. **2** *a stuffy young man* **staid**, sedate, sober, prim, priggish, strait-laced, conformist, conservative, old-fashioned; informal square, straight, starchy, fuddy-duddy. **3** *a stuffy nose* **blocked**, stuffed up, bunged up.
– OPPOSITES airy, clear.

stultify v. **1** *the free market was stultified by the welfare state* **hamper**, impede, thwart,

frustrate, foil, suppress, smother. **2** *he stultifies her with too much gentleness* **bore**, make bored, dull, numb, benumb, stupefy.

stumble v. **1** *he stumbled and fell heavily* **trip (over/up)**, lose one's balance, lose/miss one's footing, slip. **2** *he stumbled back home* **stagger**, totter, teeter, dodder, blunder, hobble, move clumsily. **3** *he stumbled through his speech* **stammer**, stutter, hesitate, falter, speak haltingly; informal fluff one's lines.
□ **stumble across/on** come across/upon, chance on, happen on, light on; discover, find, unearth, uncover; informal dig up.

stumbling block n. **obstacle**, hurdle, barrier, bar, hindrance, impediment, handicap, disadvantage; snag, fly in the ointment, hitch, catch, drawback, difficulty, problem, weakness, issue, defect, pitfall; informal hiccup.

stump v. **1** informal *they were stumped by the question* **baffle**, perplex, puzzle, confuse, confound, nonplus, defeat, put at a loss; informal flummox, fox, throw, floor; N. Amer. informal discombobulate. **2** *she stumped along the landing* **stomp**, stamp, clomp, clump, lumber, thump, thud.
□ **stump something up** Brit. informal pay (up), dish out, contribute; informal fork out, shell out, lay out, cough up, chip in; N. Amer. informal ante up, pony up.

stumpy adj. **short**, stubby, squat, stocky, chunky.
– OPPOSITES long, thin.

stun v. **1** *a glancing blow stunned Gary* **daze**, stupefy, knock unconscious, knock out, lay out. **2** *she was stunned by the news* **astound**, amaze, astonish, dumbfound, stupefy, stagger, shock, take aback; informal flabbergast, knock sideways, bowl over; Brit. informal knock for six.

stunner n. informal See **beauty** (sense 2).

stunning adj. **1** *a stunning win* **remarkable**, extraordinary, staggering, incredible, outstanding, amazing, astonishing, marvellous, phenomenal, splendid; informal fabulous, fantastic, tremendous. **2** *she was looking stunning.* See **beautiful**.
– OPPOSITES ordinary.

stunt[1] v. *a disease that stunts growth* **inhibit**, impede, hamper, hinder, restrict, retard, slow, curb, check.
– OPPOSITES encourage.

stunt[2] n. *acrobatic stunts* **feat**, exploit, trick.

stunted adj. **small**, undersize(d), diminutive.

stupefaction n. **1** *alcoholic stupefaction* **oblivion**, obliviousness, unconsciousness, insensibility, stupor, daze. **2** *Don shook his head in stupefaction* **bewilderment**, confusion, perplexity, wonder, amazement, astonishment.

stupefy v. **1** *the blow had stupefied her* **stun**, daze, knock unconscious, knock out, lay out. **2** *they were stupefied* **drug**, sedate, tranquillize, intoxicate, inebriate; informal dope. **3** *the amount stupefied us* **shock**, stun, astound, dumbfound, overwhelm, stagger,

S

amaze, astonish, take aback, take someone's breath away; informal flabbergast, knock sideways, bowl over, floor; Brit. informal knock for six.

stupendous adj. **1** *stupendous achievements* **amazing**, astounding, astonishing, extraordinary, remarkable, phenomenal, staggering, breathtaking; informal fantastic, mind-boggling, awesome; literary wondrous. **2** *a building of stupendous size* **colossal**, immense, vast, gigantic, massive, mammoth, huge, enormous.
– OPPOSITES ordinary.

stupid adj. **1** *they're rather stupid* **unintelligent**, ignorant, dense, foolish, dull-witted, slow, simple-minded, vacuous, vapid, idiotic, imbecilic, imbecile, obtuse, doltish; informal thick (as two short planks), dim, dumb, dopey, dozy, moronic, cretinous, pea-brained, half-witted, soft in the head, scatterbrained, boneheaded, thickheaded, wooden-headed, muttonheaded; Brit. informal barmy, daft, not the full shilling. **2** *a stupid mistake* **foolish**, silly, unintelligent, idiotic, nonsensical, senseless, unthinking, ill-advised, ill-considered, unwise, injudicious; inane, absurd, ludicrous, ridiculous, laughable, risible, fatuous, asinine, mad, insane, lunatic; informal crazy, dopey, cracked, half-baked, cockeyed, hare-brained, nutty, dotty, batty, gormless, cuckoo, loony, loopy, off one's head, off one's trolley; Brit. informal potty. **3** *he drank himself stupid* **into a stupor**, into a daze, into oblivion; stupefied, dazed, unconscious.
– OPPOSITES intelligent, sensible.

stupidity n. **1** *he cursed their stupidity* **lack of intelligence**, foolishness, denseness, brainlessness, ignorance, dull-wittedness, slow-wittedness, doltishness, slowness; informal thickness, dimness, dopiness, doziness. **2** *she blushed at her stupidity* **foolishness**, folly, silliness, idiocy, brainlessness, senselessness, injudiciousness, ineptitude, inaneness, inanity, absurdity, ludicrousness, ridiculousness, fatuousness, madness, insanity, lunacy; informal craziness; Brit. informal daftness.

stupor n. **daze**, state of unconsciousness, torpor, insensibility, oblivion.

sturdy adj. **1** *a sturdy lad* **strapping**, well built, muscular, athletic, strong, hefty, brawny, powerful, solid, burly, rugged, robust, tough, hardy, lusty; informal husky, beefy, meaty; dated stalwart; literary thewy, stark. **2** *sturdy boots* **robust**, strong, strongly made, well built, solid, stout, tough, resilient, durable, long-lasting, hard-wearing. **3** *sturdy resistance* **vigorous**, strong, stalwart, firm, determined, resolute, staunch, steadfast.
– OPPOSITES weak.

stutter v. *he stuttered over a word* **stammer**, stumble, falter.
▶n. *a bad stutter* **stammer**, speech impediment, speech defect.

style n. **1** *differing styles of management* **manner**, way, technique, method, methodology, approach, system, mode, form, modus operandi; informal MO. **2** *a non-directive style of counselling* **type**, kind, variety, sort, genre, school, brand, pattern, model. **3** *wearing clothes with style* **flair**, stylishness, elegance, grace, gracefulness, poise, polish, suaveness, sophistication, urbanity, chic, dash, panache, elan; informal class, pizzazz. **4** *Laura travelled in style* **comfort**, luxury, elegance, opulence, lavishness. **5** *modern styles* **fashion**, trend, vogue, mode.
▶v. **1** *sportswear styled by Karl* **design**, fashion, tailor. **2** *men who were styled 'knight'* **call**, name, title, entitle, dub, designate, term, label, tag, nickname; formal denominate.

stylish adj. **fashionable**, modish, voguish, modern, up to date; smart, sophisticated, elegant, chic, dapper, dashing; informal trendy, natty, classy, nifty, ritzy, snazzy; N. Amer. informal fly, kicky, tony, spiffy.
– OPPOSITES unfashionable.

stymie v. informal See **hamper²**.

suave adj. **charming**, sophisticated, debonair, urbane, polished, refined, poised, self-possessed, dignified, civilized, gentlemanly, gallant; smooth, polite, well mannered, civil, courteous, affable, tactful, diplomatic.
– OPPOSITES unsophisticated.

suavity n. **charm**, sophistication, polish, urbanity, suaveness, refinement, poise; politeness, courtesy, courteousness, civility, tact; humorous couth.

subconscious adj. *subconscious desires* **unconscious**, latent, suppressed, repressed, subliminal, dormant, underlying, innermost; informal bottled up.
▶n. *the creative powers of the subconscious* **(unconscious) mind**, imagination, inner self, psyche.

subdue v. **1** *he subdued all his enemies* **conquer**, defeat, vanquish, overcome, overwhelm, crush, quash, beat, trounce, subjugate, suppress, bring someone to their knees; informal lick, thrash, hammer. **2** *she could not subdue her longing* **curb**, restrain, hold back, constrain, contain, repress, suppress, stifle, smother, keep in check, rein in, control, master, quell; informal keep a/the lid on.

subdued adj. **1** *Lewis's subdued air* **sombre**, low-spirited, downcast, sad, dejected, depressed, gloomy, despondent, dispirited, disheartened, forlorn, woebegone; withdrawn, preoccupied; informal down in the mouth, down in the dumps, in the doldrums. **2** *subdued voices* **hushed**, muted, quiet, low, soft, faint, muffled, indistinct. **3** *subdued light* **dim**, muted, softened, soft, lowered, subtle.
– OPPOSITES cheerful, bright.

subject n. **1** *the subject of this chapter* **theme**, subject matter, topic, issue, question, concern, point; substance, essence, gist. **2** *popular university subjects* **branch of**

S

study, discipline, field. **3** *six subjects did the trials* **participant**, volunteer; informal guinea pig. **4** *British subjects* **citizen**, national; taxpayer, voter. **5** *a loyal subject* **liege**, liegeman, vassal, henchman, follower.
▶ v. *they were subjected to violence* **put through**, treat with, expose to.
□ **subject to 1** *it is subject to budgetary approval* **conditional on**, contingent on, dependent on. **2** *horses are subject to coughs* **susceptible to**, liable to, prone to, vulnerable to, predisposed to, at risk of; old use susceptive of. **3** *we are all subject to the law* **bound by**, constrained by, accountable to.

subjection n. **subjugation**, domination, oppression, mastery, repression, suppression.

subjective adj. **personal**, individual, emotional, instinctive, intuitive.
– OPPOSITES objective.

subjugate v. **conquer**, vanquish, defeat, crush, quash, bring someone to their knees, enslave, subdue, suppress.
– OPPOSITES liberate.

sublimate v. **channel**, control, divert, transfer, redirect, convert.

sublime adj. **1** *sublime music* **exalted**, elevated, noble, lofty, awe-inspiring, majestic, magnificent, glorious, superb, wonderful, marvellous, splendid; informal fantastic, fabulous, terrific, heavenly, divine, out of this world. **2** *the sublime confidence of youth* **supreme**, total, complete, utter, consummate.

subliminal adj. **subconscious**; hidden, concealed.
– OPPOSITES explicit.

submerge v. **1** *the U-boat submerged* **go under water**, dive, sink. **2** *submerge the bowl in water* **immerse**, plunge, sink. **3** *the farmland was submerged* **flood**, inundate, deluge, swamp. **4** *she was submerged in work* **overwhelm**, inundate, deluge, swamp, bury, engulf, snow under.
– OPPOSITES surface.

submission n. **1** *submission to authority* **yielding**, capitulation, acceptance, consent, compliance. **2** *Tim raised his hands in submission* **surrender**, capitulation, resignation, defeat. **3** *he wanted her total submission* **compliance**, submissiveness, acquiescence, passivity, obedience, docility, deference, subservience, servility, subjection. **4** *a report for submission to the Board* **presentation**, presenting, proffering, tendering, proposal, proposing. **5** *his original submission* **proposal**, suggestion, proposition, recommendation. **6** *the judge rejected his submission* **argument**, assertion, contention, statement, claim, allegation.
– OPPOSITES defiance, resistance.

submissive adj. **compliant**, yielding, acquiescent, unassertive, passive, obedient, biddable, dutiful, docile, pliant; informal under someone's thumb.

submit v. **1** *she submitted under duress* **give in/way**, yield, back down, cave in, capitulate; surrender, knuckle under. **2** *he refused to submit to their authority* **be governed by**, abide by, be regulated by, comply with, accept, adhere to, be subject to, agree to, consent to, conform to. **3** *we submitted an unopposed bid* **put forward**, present, offer, proffer, tender, propose, suggest; put in, send in, register. **4** *they submitted that the judgement was inappropriate* **contend**, assert, argue, state, claim, posit, postulate.
– OPPOSITES resist, withdraw.

subordinate adj. **1** *subordinate staff* **lower-ranking**, junior, lower, supporting. **2** *a subordinate rule* **secondary**, lesser, minor, subsidiary, subservient, ancillary, auxiliary, peripheral, marginal; supplementary, accessory.
– OPPOSITES senior.
▶ n. *the manager and his subordinates* **junior**, assistant, second (in command), number two, right-hand man/woman, deputy, aide, underling, minion; informal sidekick.
– OPPOSITES superior.

subordination n. **inferiority**, subjection, subservience, submission, servitude.

subscribe v. **1** *we subscribe to 'Punch'* **pay a subscription**, take, buy regularly. **2** *millions subscribe to the NSPCC* **donate**, make a donation, give (money), contribute towards. **3** *I can't subscribe to that theory* **agree with**, accept, believe in, endorse, back, support, champion; formal accede to. **4** formal *he subscribed the document* **sign**, countersign, initial, autograph, witness.

subscriber n. **(regular) reader**, member, patron, supporter, backer, contributor.

subscription n. **1** *the club's subscription* **membership fee**, dues, annual payment, charge. **2** *we put your subscription to good use* **donation**, contribution, gift, grant; formal benefaction. **3** *their subscription to capitalism* **agreement**, belief, endorsement, backing, support. **4** formal *the subscription was witnessed* **signature**, initials; addition, appendage.

subsequent adj. *the subsequent months* **following**, ensuing, succeeding, later, future, coming, to come, next.
– OPPOSITES previous.

subsequently adv. **later (on)**, at a later date, afterwards, in due course, following this/that, eventually; informal after a bit; formal thereafter.

subservient adj. **1** *subservient women* **submissive**, deferential, compliant, obedient, dutiful, biddable, docile, passive, unassertive, subdued, downtrodden; informal under someone's thumb. **2** *individual rights are subservient to the interests of the state* **subordinate**, secondary, subsidiary, peripheral, ancillary, auxiliary, less important.
– OPPOSITES independent.

subside v. **1** *wait until the storm subsides* **abate**, let up, quieten down, calm,

S

slacken (off), ease (up), relent, die down, recede, lessen, soften, diminish, decline, dwindle, weaken, fade, wane, ebb; old use remit. **2** *the flood has subsided* **recede**, ebb, fall, go down, get lower, abate. **3** *the volcano is gradually subsiding* **sink**, settle, cave in, collapse, crumple, give way. **4** *Sarah subsided into a chair* **slump**, flop, sink, collapse; informal flump, plonk oneself.
– OPPOSITES intensify, rise.

subsidiary adj. *a subsidiary company* **subordinate**, secondary, ancillary, auxiliary, subservient, supplementary, peripheral.
– OPPOSITES principal.
▸ n. *two major subsidiaries* **subordinate company**, branch, division, subdivision, derivative, offshoot.

subsidize v. **give money to**, pay a subsidy to, contribute to, invest in, sponsor, support, fund, finance, underwrite; informal shell out for, fork out for, cough up for; N. Amer. informal bankroll.

subsidy n. **grant**, allowance, endowment, contribution, donation, bursary, handout; backing, support, sponsorship, finance, funding; formal benefaction.

subsist v. **1** *he subsists on his pension* **survive**, live, stay alive, exist, eke out an existence; support oneself, manage, get along/by, make (both) ends meet. **2** *the tenant's rights of occupation subsist* **continue**, last, persist, endure, prevail, carry on, remain.

subsistence n. **1** *they depend on fish for subsistence* **survival**, existence, living, life, sustenance, nourishment. **2** *the money needed for his subsistence* **maintenance**, keep, upkeep, livelihood, board (and lodging), nourishment, food.

substance n. **1** *an organic substance* **material**, matter, stuff. **2** *ghostly figures with no substance* **solidity**, body, corporeality; density, mass, weight, shape, structure. **3** *none of the objections has any substance* **meaningfulness**, significance, importance, import, validity, foundation; formal moment. **4** *the substance of the tale is very thin* **content**, subject matter, theme, message, essence. **5** *Rangers are a team of substance* **character**, backbone, mettle. **6** *independent men of substance* **wealth**, fortune, riches, affluence, prosperity, money, means.

substandard adj. **inferior**, second-rate, low-quality, poor, below par, imperfect, faulty, defective, shoddy, shabby, unsound, unsatisfactory; informal tenth-rate, crummy, lousy; Brit. informal duff, ropy, rubbish, chronic.

substantial adj. **1** *substantial beings* **real**, true, actual; physical, solid, material, concrete, corporeal. **2** *substantial progress had been made* **considerable**, real, significant, important, notable, major, valuable, useful. **3** *substantial damages* **sizeable**, considerable, significant, large, ample, appreciable, goodly. **4** *substantial Victorian villas* **sturdy**, solid, stout, strong, well built, durable, long-lasting, hard-

wearing. **5** *substantial country gentlemen* **hefty**, stout, sturdy, large, solid, bulky, burly, well built, portly. **6** *substantial City companies* **successful**, profitable, prosperous, wealthy, affluent, moneyed, well-to-do, rich; informal loaded, stinking rich. **7** *substantial agreement* **fundamental**, essential, basic.

substantially adv. **1** *the cost has fallen substantially* **considerably**, significantly, to a great/large extent, greatly, markedly, appreciably. **2** *the draft was substantially accepted* **largely**, for the most part, by and large, on the whole, in the main, mainly, in essence, basically, fundamentally, to all intents and purposes.
– OPPOSITES slightly.

substantiate v. **prove**, show to be true, give substance to, support, uphold, bear out, justify, vindicate, validate, corroborate, verify, authenticate, confirm, endorse, give credence to.
– OPPOSITES disprove.

substitute n. *substitutes for permanent employees* **replacement**, deputy, relief, proxy, reserve, surrogate, cover, stand-in, locum (tenens), understudy; informal sub.
▸ adj. *a substitute teacher* **acting**, replacement, deputy, relief, reserve, surrogate, stand-in, temporary, caretaker, interim, provisional.
– OPPOSITES permanent.
▸ v. **1** *curd cheese can be substituted for yogurt* **exchange**, replace with, use instead of, use as an alternative to, use in place of, swap. **2** *the Senate was empowered to substitute for the President* **deputize**, act as deputy, act as a substitute, stand in, cover; replace, relieve, take over from; informal sub, fill someone's boots/shoes.

substitution n. **exchange**, change; replacement, replacing, swapping, switching.

subterfuge n. **1** *the use of subterfuge by journalists* **trickery**, intrigue, deviousness, deceit, deception, dishonesty, cheating, duplicity, guile, cunning, craftiness, chicanery, pretence, fraud, fraudulence. **2** *a disreputable subterfuge* **trick**, hoax, ruse, wile, ploy, stratagem, artifice, dodge, bluff, pretence, deception, fraud, blind, smokescreen; informal con, scam.

subtle adj. **1** *subtle colours* **understated**, muted, subdued; delicate, faint, pale, soft, indistinct. **2** *subtle distinctions* **fine**, fine-drawn, nice, overnice, hair-splitting. **3** *a subtle mind* **astute**, keen, quick, fine, acute, sharp, shrewd, perceptive, discerning, discriminating, penetrating, sagacious, wise, clever, intelligent. **4** *a subtle plan* **ingenious**, clever, cunning, crafty, wily, artful, devious.

subtlety n. **1** *the subtlety of the flavour* **delicacy**, delicateness, subtleness; understatedness, mutedness, softness. **2** *classification is fraught with subtlety* **fineness**, subtleness, niceness, nicety, nuance. **3** *the subtlety of the human mind* **astuteness**, keenness, acuteness, sharpness, canniness, shrewdness, perceptiveness, discernment, discrimination, percipience, perspicacity, wisdom, cleverness, intelligence. **4** *the subtlety of their tactics* **ingenuity**, cleverness, skilfulness, adroitness, cunning, guile, craftiness, wiliness, artfulness, deviousness.

subtract v. **take away/off**, deduct, debit, dock; informal knock off, minus.
– OPPOSITES add.

suburb n. **residential area**, dormitory area, commuter belt; suburbia.

suburban adj. **1** *a suburban area* **residential**, commuter, dormitory. **2** *her drab suburban existence* **dull**, boring, uninteresting, conventional, ordinary, commonplace, unremarkable, unexceptional; provincial, unsophisticated, parochial, bourgeois, middle-class.

subversive adj. *subversive activities* **disruptive**, troublemaking, inflammatory, insurrectionary; seditious, revolutionary, rebellious, rebel, renegade, dissident.
▸ n. *a dangerous subversive* **troublemaker**, dissident, agitator, revolutionary, renegade, rebel.

subvert v. **1** *a plot to subvert the state* **destabilize**, unsettle, overthrow, overturn; bring down, topple, depose, oust; disrupt, wreak havoc on, sabotage, ruin, undermine, weaken, damage. **2** *attempts to subvert Soviet youth* **corrupt**, pervert, deprave, contaminate, poison, embitter.

subway n. **1** *he walked through the subway* **underpass**, (pedestrian) tunnel. **2** *Tokyo's subway* **underground (railway)**, metro; Brit. informal tube.

succeed v. **1** *Darwin succeeded where others had failed* **triumph**, achieve success, be successful, do well, flourish, thrive; informal make it, make the grade, make a name for oneself. **2** *the plan succeeded* **be successful**, turn out well, work (out), be effective; informal come off, pay off. **3** *Rosebery succeeded Gladstone as Prime Minister* **replace**, take the place of, take over from, follow, supersede; informal step into someone's shoes. **4** *he succeeded to the throne* **inherit**, assume, acquire, attain; formal accede to. **5** *embarrassment was succeeded by fear* **follow**, come after, follow after.
– OPPOSITES fail, precede.

succeeding adj. **subsequent**, successive, following, ensuing, later, future, coming.

success n. **1** *the success of the scheme* **favourable outcome**, successfulness, successful result, triumph. **2** *the trappings of success* **prosperity**, prosperousness, affluence, wealth, riches, opulence. **3** *a West End success* **triumph**, best-seller, box-office success, sell-out; informal (smash) hit, winner. **4** *an overnight success* **star**, superstar, celebrity, big name, household name; informal celeb, megastar.
– OPPOSITES failure.

successful adj. **1** *a successful campaign* **victorious**, triumphant; fortunate, lucky. **2** *a successful designer* **prosperous**,

affluent, wealthy, rich; doing well, famous, eminent, top; informal on the up and up. **3** *successful companies* **flourishing**, thriving, booming, buoyant, doing well, profitable, moneymaking, lucrative; informal on the up and up.

succession n. **1** *a succession of exciting events* **sequence**, series, progression, chain, cycle, round, string, train, line, run, flow, stream. **2** *his succession to the throne* **accession**, elevation, assumption.
□ **in succession** one after the other, in a row, consecutively, successively, in sequence; running; informal on the trot.

successive adj. **consecutive**, in a row, straight, sequential, in succession, running; informal on the trot.

successor n. **heir (apparent)**, inheritor, next-in-line.
– OPPOSITES predecessor.

succinct adj. **concise**, short (and sweet), brief, compact, condensed, crisp, laconic, terse, to the point, pithy, epigrammatic, synoptic, gnomic; formal compendious.
– OPPOSITES verbose.

succour n. *providing succour in times of need* **aid**, help, a helping hand, assistance; comfort, ease, relief, support.
▸ v. *the prisoners were succoured* **help**, aid, bring aid to, give/render assistance to, assist, lend a (helping) hand to; minister to, care for, comfort, bring relief to, support, take care of, look after, attend to.

succulent adj. **juicy**, moist, luscious, soft, tender; choice, mouth-watering, appetizing, flavoursome, tasty, delicious; informal scrumptious, scrummy.
– OPPOSITES dry.

succumb v. **1** *she succumbed to temptation* **yield**, give in/way, submit, surrender, capitulate, cave in. **2** *he succumbed to the disease* **die from/of**; catch, develop, contract, fall ill with; informal come/go down with.
– OPPOSITES resist.

suck v. **1** *they sucked orange juice through straws* **sip**, sup, siphon, slurp, draw, drink. **2** *Fran sucked in a deep breath* **draw**, pull, breathe, gasp; inhale, inspire. **3** *they got sucked into petty crime* **implicate in**, involve in, draw into; informal mix up in. **4** N. Amer. informal *the weather sucks* **be very bad**, be awful, be terrible, be dreadful, be horrible; informal stink.
□ **suck up** informal *they suck up to him, hanging on to his every word* **grovel**, creep, toady, be obsequious, be sycophantic, kowtow, bow and scrape, truckle; fawn on; informal lick someone's boots, be all over.

suckle v. **breastfeed**, feed, nurse.

sudden adj. **unexpected**, unforeseen, unanticipated, unlooked-for; immediate, instantaneous, instant, precipitous, precipitate, abrupt, rapid, swift, quick.

suddenly adv. **immediately**, instantaneously, instantly, straight away, all of a sudden, all at once, promptly, abruptly, swiftly; unexpectedly, without warning,

S

without notice, out of the blue; informal straight off, in a flash, like a shot.
– OPPOSITES gradually.

suds plural n. **lather**, foam, froth, bubbles, soap.

sue v. **1** *he sued for negligence* **take legal action**, take to court, proceed against; informal have the law on. **2** *suing for peace* **appeal**, petition, ask, solicit, request, seek.

suffer v. **1** *I hate to see him suffer* **hurt**, ache, be in pain, feel pain; be in distress, be upset, be miserable. **2** *he suffers from asthma* **be afflicted by**, be affected by, be troubled with, have. **3** *England suffered a humiliating defeat* **undergo**, experience, be subjected to, receive, endure, face. **4** *the school's reputation has suffered* **be impaired**, be damaged, deteriorate, decline. **5** old use *he was obliged to suffer her intimate proximity* **tolerate**, put up with, bear, stand, abide, endure; formal brook. **6** old use *my conscience would not suffer me to accept* **allow**, permit, let, give leave to, sanction.

suffering n. **hardship**, distress, misery, wretchedness, adversity, tribulation; pain, agony, anguish, trauma, torment, torture, hurt, affliction, sadness, unhappiness, sorrow, grief, woe, angst, heartache, heartbreak, stress; literary dolour.

suffice v. **be enough**, be sufficient, be adequate, do, serve, meet requirements, fit/fill the bill, satisfy demands, answer/meet one's needs, answer/serve the purpose; informal hit the spot.

sufficient adj. & determiner **enough**, adequate, plenty of, ample.
– OPPOSITES inadequate.

suffocate v. **1** *she suffocated her victim* **smother**, asphyxiate, stifle; choke, strangle. **2** *she was suffocating in the heat* **be breathless**, struggle for air; be too hot, swelter; informal roast, bake, boil.

suffrage n. **franchise**, right to vote, the vote, enfranchisement, ballot.

suffuse v. **permeate**, spread over, spread throughout, cover, bathe, pervade, wash, saturate, imbue.

sugary adj. **1** *sugary snacks* **sweet**, sugared, sickly. **2** *sugary romance* **sentimental**, mawkish, cloying, slushy, mushy, sloppy, sickly (sweet), saccharine, syrupy; informal soppy, schmaltzy, cutesy, corny.
– OPPOSITES sour.

suggest v. **1** *Ruth suggested a holiday* **propose**, put forward, recommend, advocate; advise, urge, encourage, counsel. **2** *evidence suggests that teenagers are responsive to price increases* **indicate**, lead to the belief, argue, demonstrate, show; formal evince. **3** *sources suggest that the Prime Minister will change his cabinet* **hint**, insinuate, imply, intimate, indicate. **4** *the seduction scenes suggest his guilt and her loneliness* **convey**, express, impart, imply, intimate, smack of, evoke, conjure up; formal evince.

suggestion n. **1** *some suggestions for tackling this problem* **proposal**, proposition,

motion, submission, recommendation; advice, counsel, hint, tip, clue, idea. **2** *the suggestion of a smirk* **hint**, trace, touch, suspicion, dash, soupçon; ghost, semblance, shadow, glimmer, impression, whisper. **3** *there is no suggestion that he was party to a conspiracy* **insinuation**, hint, implication, intimation, innuendo, imputation.

suggestive adj. **1** *suggestive remarks* **indecent**, indelicate, improper, unseemly, sexual, sexy, smutty, dirty, ribald, bawdy, racy, risqué, lewd, vulgar, coarse, salacious. **2** *an odour suggestive of a brewery* **redolent**, evocative, reminiscent; characteristic, indicative, typical.

suicide n. **self-destruction**, taking one's own life, self-murder; informal topping oneself.

suit n. **1** *a pinstriped suit* **outfit**, set of clothes, ensemble. **2** informal *suits in faraway boardrooms* **businessman**, **businesswoman**, executive, bureaucrat, administrator, manager. **3** *a medical malpractice suit* **legal action**, lawsuit, (court) case, action, (legal/judicial) proceedings, litigation. **4** *they spurned his suit* **entreaty**, request, plea, appeal, petition, supplication, application. **5** *his suit came to nothing* **courtship**, wooing, attentions.
▸ v. **1** *blue really suits you* **look good on**, become, flatter, look attractive on, do something for. **2** *savings schemes to suit all pockets* **be convenient for**, be acceptable to, be suitable for, meet the requirements of; fit/fill the bill. **3** *recipes ideally suited to students* **tailor**, fashion, adjust, adapt, modify, fit, gear, design.

suitable adj. **1** *suitable employment opportunities* **acceptable**, satisfactory, fitting; informal right up someone's street. **2** *a drama suitable for all ages* **appropriate**, fitting, fit, acceptable, right. **3** *music suitable for a lively dinner party* **appropriate**, suited, befitting, in keeping with; informal cut out for. **4** *they treated him with suitable respect* **proper**, seemly, decent, appropriate, fitting, befitting, correct, due. **5** *suitable candidates* **well qualified**, well suited, appropriate, fitting.
– OPPOSITES inappropriate.

suitcase n. **travelling bag**, travel bag, case, valise, overnight case, portmanteau, vanity case; (**suitcases**) luggage, baggage.

suite n. **1** *a penthouse suite* **apartment**, flat, (set of) rooms. **2** *the Queen and her suite* **retinue**, entourage, train, escort, royal household, court; attendants, retainers, servants.

suitor n. **admirer**, wooer, boyfriend, sweetheart, lover; literary swain; dated beau.

sulk v. *Dad was sulking* **mope**, brood, be sullen, have a long face, be in a bad mood, be in a huff, be grumpy, be moody; informal be down in the dumps.
▸ n. *he sank into a deep sulk* **(bad) mood**, fit of pique, pet, huff, (bad) temper, the sulks, the blues; informal grump.

sulky adj. *sulky faces* **sullen**, surly, moping, pouting, moody, sour, piqued, petulant, disgruntled, ill-humoured, in a bad mood, out of humour, put out; bad-tempered, grumpy, huffy, glum, gloomy, morose; informal grouchy, fed up.
– OPPOSITES cheerful.

sullen adj. **surly**, sulky, pouting, sour, morose, resentful, glum, moody, gloomy, grumpy, bad-tempered, ill-tempered; unresponsive, uncommunicative, uncivil, unfriendly.
– OPPOSITES cheerful.

sully v. **taint**, defile, soil, tarnish, stain, blemish, pollute, spoil, mar; literary besmirch, befoul.

sultry adj. **1** *a sultry day* **humid**, close, airless, stifling, oppressive, muggy, sticky, sweltering, tropical, heavy; hot; informal boiling, roasting. **2** *a sultry film star* **passionate**, attractive, sensual, sexy, voluptuous, erotic, seductive.
– OPPOSITES refreshing.

sum n. **1** *a large sum of money* **amount**, quantity, volume. **2** *just a small sum of money* **amount**, price, charge, fee, cost. **3** *the sum of two numbers* **(sum) total**, grand total, tally, aggregate, summation. **4** *the sum of his wisdom* **entirety**, totality, total, whole, aggregate, summation, beginning and end. **5** *we did sums at school* **(arithmetical) problem**, calculation; (**sums**) arithmetic, mathematics, computation; Brit. informal maths; N. Amer. informal math.
– OPPOSITES difference.
▫ **sum up** summarize the evidence, review the evidence, give a summing-up.
sum someone/something up 1 *one reviewer summed it up as 'compelling'* **evaluate**, assess, appraise, rate, weigh up, gauge, judge, deem, adjudge, estimate, form an opinion of. **2** *he summed up his reasons* **summarize**, make/give a summary of, precis, outline, give an outline of, recapitulate, review; informal recap.

summarily adv. **immediately**, instantly, right away, straight away, at once, on the spot, promptly; speedily, swiftly, rapidly, without delay; arbitrarily, without formality, peremptorily, without due process.

summarize v. **sum up**, abridge, condense, encapsulate, outline, give an outline of, put in a nutshell, recapitulate, give/make a summary of, give a synopsis of, precis, give a résumé of, give the gist of; informal recap; old use epitomize.

summary n. *a summary of the findings* **synopsis**, precis, résumé, abstract, digest, encapsulation, abbreviated version; outline, sketch, rundown, review, summing-up, overview, recapitulation, epitome, conspectus; informal recap.
▸ adj. **1** *a summary financial statement* **abridged**, abbreviated, shortened, condensed, concise, succinct, short, brief, pithy; formal compendious. **2** *summary execution* **immediate**, instant,

instantaneous, on-the-spot; speedy, swift, rapid, without delay, sudden; arbitrary, without formality, peremptory.

summer n.

WORD LINKS
aestival relating to or appearing in summer

summer house n. **gazebo**, pavilion, belvedere; literary bower.

summit n. **1** *the summit of Mont Blanc* **top**, peak, mountaintop, crest, crown, apex, tip, cap; brow, crag, tor; hilltop. **2** *the summits of world literature* **acme**, peak, height, pinnacle, zenith, climax, high point/spot, highlight, crowning glory, best, finest, nonpareil. **3** *the next superpower summit* **meeting**, negotiation, conference, talk(s), discussion.
– OPPOSITES base, nadir.

summon v. **1** *he was summoned to the Embassy* **send for**, call for, request the presence of; ask, invite. **2** *they were summoned as witnesses* **serve with a summons**, summons, subpoena, cite. **3** *the chair summoned a meeting* **convene**, assemble, order, call, announce; formal convoke. **4** *he summoned the courage to move closer* **muster**, gather, collect, rally, screw up. **5** *summoning up their memories of home* **call to mind**, call up/forth, conjure up, evoke, recall, revive, arouse, kindle, awaken, spark (off). **6** *they summoned spirits of the dead* **conjure up**, call up, invoke.

summons n. **1** *the court issued a summons* **writ**, subpoena, warrant, court order; Law citation. **2** *a summons to go to the boss's office* **order**, directive, command, instruction, demand, decree, injunction, edict, call, request.
▸ v. *he was summonsed to appear in court* **serve with a summons**, subpoena, summon, cite.

sumptuous adj. **lavish**, luxurious, opulent, magnificent, resplendent, gorgeous, splendid, grand, lavishly appointed, palatial, rich; informal plush, ritzy; Brit. informal swish.
– OPPOSITES plain.

sun n. **sunshine**, sunlight, daylight, light, warmth; beams, rays.

WORD LINKS
solar relating to the sun
solstice each of the two times in the year when the sun reaches its highest or lowest point in the sky at noon
heliocentric referring to an astronomical system having the sun at its centre
aphelion the point in a planet's orbit at which it is furthest from the sun
perihelion the point in a planet's orbit at which it is closest to the sun
parhelion a bright spot in the sky on either side of the sun
zenith the highest point in the sky reached by the sun

sunbathe v. **sun oneself**, bask, get a tan, tan oneself; informal catch some rays.

sunburnt adj. **1** *his sunburnt shoulders* **burnt**, sunburned, red, scarlet. **2** *a handsome sunburnt face* **tanned**, suntanned, brown, bronzed, bronze.
– OPPOSITES pale.

Sunday n. **the Sabbath**, the Lord's Day.

> **WORD LINKS**
> **dominical** relating to Sunday

sundry adj. **various**, varied, miscellaneous, assorted, mixed, diverse, diversified; several, numerous, many, manifold, multifarious, multitudinous; literary divers.

sunken adj. **1** *sunken eyes* **hollowed**, hollow, depressed, deep-set, concave, indented. **2** *a sunken garden* **below ground level**, at a lower level, lowered.

sunless adj. **1** *a cold sunless day* **dark**, overcast, cloudy, grey, gloomy, dismal, murky, dull. **2** *the sunless side of the house* **shady**, shadowy, dark, gloomy.

sunlight n. **daylight**, sun, sunshine, sun's rays, (natural) light.

sunny adj. **1** *a sunny day* **bright**, sunshiny, sunlit, clear, fine, cloudless, without a cloud in the sky. **2** *a sunny disposition* **cheerful**, cheery, happy, light-hearted, bright, merry, joyful, bubbly, jolly, jovial, animated, buoyant, ebullient, upbeat, vivacious; literary blithe. **3** *look on the sunny side* **optimistic**, rosy, bright, hopeful, auspicious, favourable.
– OPPOSITES dull, miserable.

sunrise n. **(crack of) dawn**, daybreak, break of day, first light, (early) morning, cockcrow; N. Amer. sunup; literary aurora, dayspring.

sunset n. **nightfall**, close of day, twilight, dusk, evening; N. Amer. sundown; literary eventide, gloaming.

sunshine n. **1** *relaxing in the sunshine* **sunlight**, sun, sun's rays, daylight, (natural) light. **2** *his smile was all sunshine* **happiness**, cheerfulness, cheer, gladness, laughter, gaiety, merriment, joy, joyfulness, joviality, jollity; literary blitheness. **3** Brit. informal *hello, sunshine* **my friend**; informal pal, chum; Brit. informal mate, matey, squire, mush; N. Amer. informal bud, buddy, buster.

super adj. informal **excellent**, superb, superlative, first-class, outstanding, marvellous, magnificent, wonderful, splendid, glorious; informal great, fantastic, fabulous, terrific, ace, divine, A1, wicked, cool; Brit. informal smashing, brilliant, brill.
– OPPOSITES rotten.

superannuated adj. **1** *a superannuated civil servant* **pensioned (off)**, retired; elderly, old. **2** *superannuated computing equipment* **old**, old-fashioned, antiquated, out of date, outmoded, broken-down, obsolete, disused, defunct; informal clapped out.

superb adj. **1** *he scored a superb goal* **excellent**, superlative, first-rate, first-class, outstanding, top-tier, remarkable, marvellous, magnificent, wonderful, splendid, admirable, noteworthy, impressive, fine, exquisite, exceptional, glorious; informal great, fantastic, fabulous, terrific, super, awesome, ace, cool, A1; Brit. informal brilliant, brill, smashing. **2** *a superb diamond necklace* **magnificent**, majestic, splendid, grand, impressive, imposing, awe-inspiring, breathtaking; gorgeous.
– OPPOSITES poor, inferior.

supercilious adj. **arrogant**, haughty, conceited, disdainful, overbearing, pompous, condescending, superior, patronizing, imperious, proud, snobbish, snobby, smug, scornful, sneering; informal hoity-toity, high and mighty, uppity, snooty, stuck-up, snotty, jumped up, too big for one's boots.

superficial adj. **1** *superficial burns* **surface**, exterior, external, outer, outside, slight. **2** *a superficial friendship* **shallow**, surface, skin-deep, artificial; empty, hollow, meaningless. **3** *a superficial investigation* **cursory**, perfunctory, casual, sketchy, desultory, token, slapdash, offhand, rushed, hasty, hurried. **4** *a superficial resemblance* **apparent**, seeming, outward, ostensible, cosmetic, slight. **5** *a superficial biography* **trivial**, lightweight. **6** *a superficial person* **facile**, shallow, flippant, empty-headed, trivial, frivolous, silly, inane.
– OPPOSITES deep, thorough.

superficially adv. **apparently**, seemingly, ostensibly, outwardly, on the surface, on the face of it, to all intents and purposes, at first glance, to the casual eye.

superfluity n. **surplus**, excess, overabundance, glut, surfeit, profusion, plethora.
– OPPOSITES shortage.

superfluous adj. **1** *superfluous material* **surplus (to requirements)**, redundant, unneeded, excess, extra, (to) spare, remaining, unused, left over, in excess, waste. **2** *words seemed superfluous* **unnecessary**, unneeded, redundant, uncalled for, unwarranted.
– OPPOSITES necessary.

superhuman adj. **1** *a superhuman effort* **extraordinary**, phenomenal, prodigious, stupendous, exceptional, immense, heroic. **2** *superhuman power* **divine**, holy, heavenly. **3** *superhuman beings* **supernatural**, preternatural, paranormal, other-worldly, unearthly; rare extramundane.
– OPPOSITES mundane.

superintend v. **supervise**, oversee, be in charge of, be in control of, preside over, direct, administer, manage, run, be responsible for.

superintendent n. **1** *the superintendent of the museum* **manager**, director, administrator, supervisor, overseer, controller, chief, head, governor; informal boss. **2** N. Amer. *the building's superintendent* **caretaker**, janitor, warden, porter.

superior adj. **1** *a superior officer* **higher-ranking**, higher-level, senior, higher, higher-up. **2** *the superior candidate* **better**, more expert, more skilful; worthier, fitter, preferred. **3** *superior workmanship* **finer**, better, higher-grade, of higher quality,

S

greater; accomplished, expert. **4** *superior chocolate* **good-quality**, high-quality, first-class, first-rate, top-quality; choice, select, exclusive, prime, prize, fine, excellent, best, choicest, finest. **5** *a superior hotel* **high-class**, upper-class, select, exclusive; Brit. upmarket; informal classy, posh. **6** *Jake regarded her with superior amusement* **condescending**, supercilious, patronizing, haughty, disdainful, pompous, snobbish; informal high and mighty, hoity-toity, snooty, stuck-up.
– OPPOSITES junior, inferior.
▶ n. *my immediate superior* **manager**, chief, supervisor, senior, controller, foreman; informal boss.
– OPPOSITES subordinate.

superiority n. **supremacy**, advantage, lead, dominance, primacy, ascendancy, eminence.

superlative adj. **excellent**, magnificent, wonderful, marvellous, supreme, consummate, outstanding, remarkable, fine, choice, first-rate, first-class, top-tier, premier, prime, unsurpassed, unequalled, unparalleled, unrivalled, pre-eminent; informal crack, ace, wicked; Brit. informal brilliant.
– OPPOSITES mediocre.

supernatural adj. **1** *supernatural powers* **paranormal**, psychic, magic, magical, occult, mystic, mystical, superhuman, supernormal; rare extramundane. **2** *a supernatural being* **ghostly**, phantom, spectral, other-worldly, unearthly, unnatural.

supersede v. **replace**, take the place of, take over from, succeed; supplant, displace, oust, overthrow, remove, unseat; informal fill someone's shoes/boots.

superstition n. **1** *the old superstitions held by sailors* **myth**, belief, old wives' tale; legend, story. **2** *medicine was riddled with superstition* **unfounded belief**, credulity, fallacy, delusion, illusion; magic, sorcery.

superstitious adj. **1** *superstitious beliefs* **mythical**, irrational, illusory, groundless, unfounded; traditional. **2** *he's incredibly superstitious* **credulous**, naive, gullible.
– OPPOSITES factual, sceptical.

supervise v. **1** *he had to supervise the loading* **superintend**, oversee, be in charge of, preside over, direct, manage, run, look after, be responsible for, govern, organize, handle. **2** *you may need to supervise the patient* **watch**, oversee, keep an eye on, observe, monitor, mind.

supervision n. **1** *the supervision of the banking system* **administration**, management, control, charge; superintendence, regulation, government, governance. **2** *keep your children under supervision* **observation**, guidance, custody, charge, safe keeping, care, guardianship; control.

supervisor n. **manager**, director, overseer, controller, superintendent, governor, chief, head; steward, foreman; Brit. ganger, gangmaster; informal boss; Brit. informal gaffer.

supine adj. **1** *she lay supine on the sand* **flat on one's back**, face upwards, flat, horizontal, recumbent, stretched out. **2** *a supine media* **weak**, spineless, yielding, effete; docile, acquiescent, pliant, submissive, passive, inert, spiritless.
– OPPOSITES prostrate, strong.

supper n. **dinner**, evening meal, main meal; snack, bite to eat; Brit. tea; formal repast; literary refection.

supplant v. **1** *motorways supplanted the network of A-roads* **replace**, supersede, displace, take over from, substitute for, override. **2** *the man he supplanted as Prime Minister* **oust**, usurp, overthrow, remove, topple, unseat, depose, dethrone; succeed, come after; informal fill someone's shoes/boots.

supple adj. **1** *her supple body* **lithe**, limber, lissom(e), willowy, flexible, loose-limbed, agile, acrobatic, nimble, double-jointed. **2** *supple leather* **pliant**, pliable, flexible, soft, bendable, workable, malleable, stretchy, elastic, springy, yielding, rubbery.
– OPPOSITES stiff, rigid.

supplement n. **1** *the handout is a supplement to the official manual* **addition**, supplementation, supplementary, extra, add-on, accessory, adjunct, appendage. **2** *a single room supplement* **surcharge**, addition, increase. **3** *a supplement to the essay* **appendix**, addendum, end matter, tailpiece, codicil, postscript, addition, coda. **4** *a special supplement with today's paper* **pull-out**, insert, extra section.
▶ v. *they supplemented their incomes by spinning* **augment**, increase, add to, boost, swell, amplify, enlarge, top up.

supplementary adj. **1** *supplementary income* **additional**, supplemental, extra, more, further; add-on, subsidiary, auxiliary, ancillary. **2** *a supplementary index* **appended**, attached, added, extra, accompanying.

suppliant n. *they were not mere suppliants* **petitioner**, supplicant, pleader, beggar, applicant.
▶ adj. *those around her were suppliant* **pleading**, begging, imploring, entreating, supplicating; on bended knee.

supplicate v. **entreat**, beg, plead with, implore, petition, appeal to, call on, urge, enjoin, importune, sue, ask, request; literary beseech.

supply v. **1** *they supplied money to rebels* **give**, contribute, provide, furnish, donate, bestow, grant, endow, impart; dispense, disburse, allocate, assign; informal fork out, shell out. **2** *the lake supplies the city with water* **provide**, furnish, endow, serve, confer; equip, arm. **3** *windmills supply their power needs* **satisfy**, meet, fulfil, cater for.
▶ n. **1** *a limited supply of food* **stock**, store, reserve, reservoir, stockpile, hoard, cache; storehouse, repository; fund, mine, bank. **2** *the supply of alcoholic liquor* **provision**, dissemination, distribution, serving. **3** *go to a supermarket for supplies* **provisions**, stores, stocks, rations, food, foodstuffs, eatables, produce, necessities; informal eats;

S

formal comestibles.
▶ adj. *a supply teacher* **substitute**, stand-in, fill-in, locum, temporary, stopgap.

support v. **1** *a roof supported by pillars* **hold up**, bear, carry, prop up, keep up, brace, shore up, underpin, buttress, reinforce. **2** *he struggled to support his family* **provide for**, maintain, sustain, keep, take care of, look after. **3** *she supported him to the end* **comfort**, encourage, sustain, buoy up, hearten, fortify, console, solace, reassure; informal buck up. **4** *evidence to support the argument* **substantiate**, back up, bear out, corroborate, confirm, attest to, verify, prove, validate, authenticate, endorse, ratify. **5** *the money supports charitable projects* **help**, aid, assist; contribute to, back, subsidize, fund, finance; N. Amer. informal bankroll. **6** *an independent candidate supported by locals* **back**, champion, help, assist, aid, abet, favour, encourage; vote for, stand behind, defend; sponsor, second, promote, endorse, sanction; informal throw one's weight behind. **7** *they support human rights* **advocate**, promote, champion, back, espouse, be in favour of, recommend, defend, subscribe to. **8** *I could not support the grief* **endure**, bear, tolerate, stand, put up with, abide, stomach, sustain; formal brook; old use suffer.
– OPPOSITES neglect, contradict, oppose.
▶ n. **1** *bridge supports* **pillar**, post, prop, upright, crutch, plinth, brace, buttress; base, substructure, foundation, underpinning. **2** *he pays support for his wife* **maintenance**, keep, sustenance, subsistence. **3** *I was lucky to have their support* **encouragement**, friendship, strength, consolation, solace, succour, relief. **4** *he was a great support* **comfort**, help, assistance, tower of strength, prop, mainstay. **5** *support for community services* **contributions**, backing, donations, money, subsidy, funding, funds, finance, capital. **6** *they voiced their support for him* **backing**, help, assistance, aid, endorsement, approval; votes, patronage. **7** *a surge in support for decentralization* **advocacy**, backing, promotion, championship, espousal, defence, recommendation.

supporter n. **1** *supporters of gun control* **advocate**, backer, adherent, promoter, champion, defender, upholder, crusader, proponent, campaigner, apologist. **2** *Labour supporters* **backer**, helper, adherent, follower, ally, voter, disciple; member. **3** *the charity relies on its supporters* **contributor**, donor, benefactor, sponsor, backer, patron, subscriber, well-wisher. **4** *the team's supporters* **fan**, follower, enthusiast, devotee, admirer; informal buff, addict.

supportive adj. **1** *a supportive teacher* **encouraging**, caring, sympathetic, reassuring, understanding, concerned, helpful, kind, kindly. **2** *we are supportive of the proposal* **in favour of**, favourable to, pro, on the side of, sympathetic to, well disposed to, receptive to.

suppose v. **1** *I suppose he's used to this* **assume**, presume, expect, dare say, take it (as read); believe, think, fancy, suspect, sense, trust; guess, surmise, reckon, conjecture, deduce, infer, gather; formal opine. **2** *suppose you had a spacecraft* **assume**, imagine, (let's) say; hypothesize, theorize, speculate. **3** *the theory supposes rational players* **require**, presuppose, imply, assume; call for, need.

supposed adj. **1** *the supposed phenomena* **apparent**, ostensible, seeming, alleged, putative, reputed, rumoured, claimed, purported; professed, declared, assumed, presumed. **2** *I'm supposed to meet him at 8.30* **meant**, intended, expected; required, obliged.

supposition n. **belief**, surmise, idea, notion, suspicion, conjecture, speculation, inference, theory, hypothesis, postulation, guess, feeling, hunch, assumption, presumption.

suppress v. **1** *they could suppress the rebellion* **subdue**, repress, crush, quell, quash, squash, stamp out; defeat, conquer, overpower, put down, crack down on; end, stop, terminate, halt. **2** *she suppressed her irritation* **conceal**, restrain, stifle, smother, bottle up, hold back, control, check, curb, contain, bridle, inhibit, keep a rein on, put a lid on. **3** *the report was suppressed* **censor**, redact, keep secret, conceal, hide, hush up, gag, withhold, cover up, stifle; ban, proscribe, outlaw; sweep under the carpet.
– OPPOSITES incite, reveal.

suppurate v. **fester**, form pus, discharge, run, weep, become septic; Medicine maturate.

supremacy n. **ascendancy**, predominance, primacy, dominion, hegemony, authority, mastery, control, power, rule, sovereignty, influence; dominance, superiority, advantage, the upper hand, the whip hand, the edge; distinction, greatness.

supreme adj. **1** *the supreme commander* **highest ranking**, chief, head, top, foremost, principal, superior, premier, first, prime; greatest, dominant, predominant, pre-eminent. **2** *a supreme achievement* **extraordinary**, remarkable, incredible, phenomenal, rare, exceptional, outstanding, great, incomparable, unparalleled, peerless. **3** *the supreme sacrifice* **ultimate**, final, last; utmost, extreme, greatest, highest.
– OPPOSITES subordinate, insignificant.

sure adj. **1** *I am sure they didn't mind* **certain**, positive, convinced, confident, definite, assured, satisfied, persuaded; unhesitating, unwavering, unshakeable. **2** *someone was sure to be blamed* **bound**, likely, destined, fated. **3** *a sure winner with the children* **guaranteed**, unfailing, infallible, unerring, assured, certain, inevitable, as sure as eggs is eggs; informal sure-fire. **4** *he entered in the sure knowledge that he would win* **unquestionable**, indisputable, irrefutable, incontrovertible, undeniable, indubitable, undoubted, absolute, categorical, true, certain; obvious, evident, plain, clear, conclusive, definite. **5** *a sure sign that he's worried* **reliable**, dependable, trustworthy,

S

unfailing, infallible, certain, unambiguous, true, foolproof, established, effective; informal sure-fire; formal efficacious. **6** *the sure hand of the soloist* **firm**, steady, stable, secure, confident, steadfast, unfaltering, unwavering.
– OPPOSITES uncertain, unlikely.

▶ exclam. *'Can I come too?' 'Sure.'* **yes**, all right, of course, indeed, certainly, absolutely, agreed; informal OK, yeah, yep, uh-huh, you bet, I'll say, sure thing.
□ **make sure** check, confirm, make certain, ensure, assure; verify, corroborate, substantiate.

surely adv. **1** *surely you remembered?* **it must be the case that**, assuredly, without question. **2** *I will surely die* **certainly**, for sure, definitely, undoubtedly, without doubt, doubtless, indubitably, unquestionably, without fail, inevitably. **3** *slowly but surely manipulating the public* **firmly**, steadily, confidently, assuredly, unhesitatingly, unfalteringly, unswervingly, determinedly, doggedly.

surety n. **1** *she's a surety for his obligations* **guarantor**, sponsor. **2** *bail of £10,000 with a further £10,000 surety* **pledge**, collateral, guaranty, guarantee, bond, assurance, insurance, deposit; security, indemnity, indemnification; earnest.

surface n. **1** *the surface of the door* **outside**, exterior; top, side; finish, veneer. **2** *the surface of police culture* **outward appearance**, facade. **3** *a floured surface* **worktop**, top, work surface, counter, table.
– OPPOSITES inside, interior.

▶ adj. *surface appearances* **superficial**, external, exterior, outward, ostensible, apparent, cosmetic, skin deep.
– OPPOSITES underlying.

▶ v. **1** *a submarine surfaced* **come to the surface**, come up, rise. **2** *the idea first surfaced in the sixties* **emerge**, arise, appear, come to light, crop up, materialize, spring up. **3** informal *she eventually surfaces for breakfast* **get up**, get out of bed, rise, wake, awaken, appear.
– OPPOSITES dive.
□ **on the surface** at first glance, to the casual eye, outwardly, to all appearances, apparently, ostensibly, superficially, externally.

surfeit n. *a surfeit of apples* **excess**, surplus, abundance, oversupply, superabundance, superfluity, glut, avalanche, deluge; overdose; too much; informal bellyful.
– OPPOSITES lack.

▶ v. *we'll all be surfeited with food* **satiate**, gorge, overfeed, overfill, glut, cram, stuff, overindulge, fill.

surge n. **1** *a surge of water* **gush**, rush, outpouring, stream, flow. **2** *a surge in oil production* **increase**, rise, growth, upswing, upsurge, escalation, leap. **3** *a sudden surge of anger* **rush**, storm, torrent, blaze, outburst, eruption. **4** *the surge of sea* **swell**, heaving, rolling, roll, swirling; tide.

▶ v. **1** *the water surged into people's homes* **gush**, rush, stream, flow, burst, pour, cascade, spill, overflow, sweep, roll. **2** *the Dow Jones index surged 47.63 points* **increase**, rise, grow, escalate, leap. **3** *the sea surged* **swell**, heave, rise, roll.

surly adj. **sullen**, sulky, moody, sour, unfriendly, unpleasant, scowling, unsmiling; bad-tempered, grumpy, crotchety, prickly, cantankerous, irascible, testy, short-tempered; abrupt, brusque, curt, gruff, churlish, ill-humoured, crabby, uncivil; informal grouchy.
– OPPOSITES pleasant.

surmise v. **guess**, conjecture, suspect, deduce, infer, conclude, theorize, speculate, divine; assume, presume, suppose, understand, gather, feel, sense, think, believe, imagine, fancy, reckon; formal opine.

surmount v. **1** *his reputation surmounts language barriers* **overcome**, conquer, prevail over, triumph over, beat, vanquish; clear, cross, pass over; resist, endure. **2** *they surmounted the ridge* **climb over**, top, ascend, scale, mount. **3** *the dome is surmounted by a statue* **cap**, top, crown, finish.
– OPPOSITES descend.

surname n. **family name**, last name; patronymic.

surpass v. **excel**, exceed, transcend; outdo, outshine, outstrip, outclass, overshadow, eclipse; improve on, top, trump, cap, beat, better, outperform.

surplus n. *a surplus of grain* **excess**, surfeit, superabundance, superfluity, oversupply, glut, profusion, plethora; remainder, residue, remains, leftovers.
– OPPOSITES dearth.

▶ adj. *surplus adhesive* **excess**, leftover, unused, remaining, extra, additional, spare; superfluous, redundant, unwanted, unneeded, dispensable, expendable.
– OPPOSITES insufficient.

surprise n. **1** *Kate looked at me in surprise* **astonishment**, amazement, wonder, incredulity, bewilderment, stupefaction, disbelief. **2** *the test came as a big surprise* **shock**, bolt from the blue, bombshell, revelation, rude awakening; informal turn-up for the books, eye-opener, shocker.

▶ v. **1** *I was so surprised that I dropped it* **astonish**, amaze, startle, astound, stun, stagger, shock; leave open-mouthed, take someone's breath away, dumbfound, daze, take aback, shake up; informal bowl over, floor, flabbergast; Brit. informal knock for six. **2** *she surprised a burglar* **take by surprise**, catch unawares, catch off guard, catch red-handed, catch in the act, catch out; Brit. informal catch on the hop.

surprised adj. **astonished**, amazed, astounded, startled, stunned, staggered, nonplussed, shocked, shell-shocked, taken aback, stupefied, dumbfounded, dumbstruck, speechless, thunderstruck, confounded, shaken up; informal bowled over, flabbergasted, floored, flummoxed; Brit. informal gobsmacked.

S

surprising adj. **unexpected**, unforeseen, unpredictable; astonishing, amazing, startling, astounding, staggering, incredible, extraordinary, breathtaking, remarkable; informal mind-blowing.

surrender v. **1** *the army surrendered* **capitulate**, give in, give (oneself) up, give way, yield, concede (defeat), submit, climb down, back down, cave in, relent, crumble; lay down one's arms, raise the white flag, throw in the towel/sponge. **2** *they surrendered power to the government* **give up**, relinquish, renounce, forgo, forswear; cede, abdicate, waive, forfeit, sacrifice; hand over, turn over, yield, resign, transfer, grant. **3** *surrender all hope of changing things* **abandon**, give up, cast aside.
– OPPOSITES resist, seize.
▸ n. **1** *the surrender of the hijackers* **capitulation**, submission, yielding, succumbing, acquiescence; fall, defeat. **2** *a surrender of power to the shop floor* **relinquishment**, renunciation, cession, abdication, resignation, transfer.

surreptitious adj. **secret**, secretive, stealthy, clandestine, sneaky, sly, furtive; concealed, hidden, undercover, covert, veiled, cloak-and-dagger; Military black.
– OPPOSITES blatant.

surrogate n. **substitute**, proxy, replacement; deputy, representative, stand-in, standby, stopgap, relief, understudy.

surround v. *we were surrounded by cops* **encircle**, enclose, encompass, ring; fence in, hem in, confine, bound, circumscribe, cut off; besiege, trap.
▸ n. *a fireplace with a wood surround* **border**, edging, edge, perimeter, boundary, margin, skirting, fringe.

surrounding adj. **neighbouring**, nearby, near, neighbourhood, local; adjoining, adjacent, bordering, abutting; encircling, encompassing.

surroundings plural n. **environment**, setting, milieu, background, backdrop; conditions, circumstances, situation, context; vicinity, locality, habitat.

surveillance n. **observation**, scrutiny, watch, view, inspection, supervision; spying, espionage, infiltration, reconnaissance; informal bugging, wiretapping, recon.

survey v. **1** *he surveyed his work* **look at**, look over, observe, view, contemplate, regard, gaze at, stare at, eye; scrutinize, examine, inspect, scan, study, consider, review, take stock of; informal size up; literary behold. **2** *they surveyed 4000 drug users* **interview**, question, canvass, poll, cross-examine, investigate, research, study, probe, sample. **3** *he was asked to survey the house* **appraise**, assess, prospect; make a survey of, value.
▸ n. **1** *a survey of the current literature* **study**, review, consideration, overview; scrutiny, examination, inspection, appraisal. **2** *a survey of sexual behaviour* **poll**, review, investigation, inquiry, study, probe, questionnaire, census, research. **3** *a thorough*

survey of the property **appraisal**, assessment, valuation, estimate, estimation.

survive v. **1** *he survived by escaping through a hole* **remain alive**, live, sustain oneself, pull through, get through, hold on/out, make it, keep body and soul together. **2** *the theatre must survive* **continue**, remain, persist, endure, live on, persevere, abide, go on, carry on, be extant, exist. **3** *he was survived by his sons* **outlive**, outlast; live longer than.

susceptible adj. **1** *susceptible children* **impressionable**, credulous, gullible, innocent, ingenuous, naive, easily led; defenceless, vulnerable; persuadable, tractable; sensitive, responsive, thin-skinned. **2** *people susceptible to blackmail* **open to**, receptive to, vulnerable to; an easy target for. **3** *he is susceptible to ulcers* **liable to**, prone to, subject to, inclined to, predisposed to, disposed to, given to, at risk of; old use susceptive of. **4** *the database will be susceptible of exploitation* **open to**, capable of, admitting of, receptive of, responsive to.
– OPPOSITES sceptical, immune, resistant.

suspect v. **1** *I suspected she'd made a mistake* **have a suspicion**, have a feeling, feel, (be inclined to) think, fancy, reckon, guess, surmise, conjecture, conclude, have a hunch; suppose, presume, deduce, infer, sense, imagine; fear. **2** *he had no reason to suspect my honesty* **doubt**, distrust, mistrust, have misgivings about, be sceptical about, have qualms about, be suspicious of, be wary of, harbour reservations about; informal smell a rat.
▸ n. *a murder suspect* **suspected person**, accused, defendant.
▸ adj. *a suspect package* **suspicious**, dubious, doubtful, untrustworthy; odd, queer; informal fishy, funny, shady; Brit. informal dodgy.

suspend v. **1** *the court case was suspended* **adjourn**, interrupt, break off, postpone, delay, defer, shelve, put off, intermit, prorogue, hold over, hold in abeyance; cut short, discontinue, dissolve, disband, terminate; N. Amer. table; informal put on ice, put on the back burner, mothball; N. Amer. informal take a rain check on. **2** *he was suspended from his duties* **exclude**, debar, remove, eliminate, expel, eject. **3** *lights were suspended from the ceiling* **hang**, sling, string; swing, dangle.

suspense n. *I can't bear the suspense* **tension**, uncertainty, doubt, anticipation, expectation, expectancy, excitement, anxiety, apprehension, strain.
□ **in suspense** eagerly, agog, with bated breath, on tenterhooks; on edge, anxious, edgy, keyed up, uneasy; informal uptight, jumpy, jittery.

suspension n. **1** *the suspension of army operations* **adjournment**, interruption, postponement, delay, deferral, deferment, stay, prorogation; armistice; cessation, end, halt, stoppage, dissolution, disbandment, termination. **2** *his suspension from school* **exclusion**, debarment, removal, elimination, expulsion, ejection; Brit. rustication.

suspicion n. **1** *she had a suspicion that he didn't like her* **intuition**, feeling, impression, inkling, hunch, fancy, notion, supposition, belief, idea, theory; presentiment, premonition; informal gut feeling, sixth sense. **2** *I confronted him with my suspicions* **misgiving**, doubt, qualm, reservation, hesitation, question; scepticism, uncertainty, distrust, mistrust. **3** *wine with a suspicion of soda* **trace**, touch, suggestion, hint, soupçon, tinge, shade, whiff, bit, drop, dash, taste, jot, mite.

suspicious adj. **1** *she gave Jonathan a suspicious look* **doubtful**, unsure, dubious, wary, chary, sceptical, distrustful, mistrustful, disbelieving, cynical. **2** *a highly suspicious character* **disreputable**, unsavoury, dubious, suspect, dishonest-looking, funny-looking, slippery; informal shifty, shady; Brit. informal dodgy. **3** *she disappeared in suspicious circumstances* **questionable**, odd, strange, dubious, irregular, queer, funny, doubtful, mysterious, murky; informal fishy; Brit. informal dodgy.
– OPPOSITES trusting, honest, innocent.

sustain v. **1** *the balcony might not sustain the weight* **bear**, support, carry, stand, keep up, prop up, shore up, underpin. **2** *her memories sustained her* **comfort**, help, assist, encourage, succour, support, give strength to, buoy up, carry, cheer up, hearten; informal buck up. **3** *they were unable to sustain a coalition* **continue**, carry on, keep up, keep alive, maintain, preserve, conserve, perpetuate, retain. **4** *she had bread and cheese to sustain her* **nourish**, feed, nurture; maintain, preserve, keep alive, keep going, provide for. **5** *she sustained slight injuries* **undergo**, experience, suffer, endure. **6** *the allegation was not sustained* **uphold**, validate, ratify, vindicate, confirm, endorse; verify, corroborate, substantiate, bear out, prove, authenticate, back up, evidence, justify.

sustained adj. **continuous**, ongoing, steady, continual, constant, prolonged, persistent, non-stop, perpetual, unabating, relentless, unrelieved, unbroken, never-ending, incessant, unceasing, ceaseless, round the clock.
– OPPOSITES sporadic.

sustenance n. **1** *the creature needs sustenance* **nourishment**, food, nutriment, nutrition, provisions, provender, rations; informal grub, chow, scoff; formal comestibles; literary viands; dated victuals. **2** *the sustenance of his family* **support**, maintenance, keep, living, livelihood, subsistence, income.

swagger v. **1** *we swaggered into the arena* **strut**, parade, stride; walk confidently; informal sashay. **2** *he likes to swagger about his kindness* **boast**, brag, bluster, crow, gloat; strut, posture, blow one's own trumpet, lord it; informal show off, swank.
▸n. **1** *a slight swagger in his stride* **strut**; confidence, arrogance, ostentation. **2** *he was full of swagger* **bluster**, braggadocio,

bumptiousness, vainglory; informal swank.

swallow v. **1** *she couldn't swallow anything* **eat**, gulp down, consume, devour, put away; ingest, assimilate; drink, guzzle, quaff, imbibe, sup, slug; informal polish off, scoff, swig, swill, down; Brit. informal neck; N. Amer. informal chug. **2** *I can't swallow any more of your insults* **tolerate**, endure, stand, put up with, bear, abide, countenance, stomach, take, accept; informal hack; Brit. informal stick; formal brook. **3** *he swallowed my story* **believe**, credit, accept, trust; informal fall for, buy, go for, {swallow hook, line, and sinker}. **4** *she swallowed her pride* **restrain**, repress, suppress, hold back, fight back; overcome, check, control, curb, rein in; silence, muffle, stifle, smother, hide, bottle up; informal keep a/the lid on.
□ **swallow someone/something up 1** *the darkness swallowed them up* **engulf**, swamp, devour, overwhelm, overcome. **2** *the colleges were swallowed up by universities* **take over**, engulf, absorb, assimilate, incorporate.

swamp n. *his horse got stuck in a swamp* **marsh**, bog, quagmire, mire, morass, fen; quicksand; N. Amer. bayou; old use quag.
▸v. **1** *the rain was swamping the dry roads* **flood**, inundate, deluge, immerse; soak, drench, saturate. **2** *he was swamped by media attention* **overwhelm**, inundate, flood, deluge, engulf, snow under, overload, overpower, weigh down, besiege, beset.

swampy adj. **marshy**, boggy, fenny, miry; soft, soggy, muddy, spongy, heavy, squelchy, waterlogged, sodden, wet; old use quaggy.

swap v. **1** *I swapped some toys for a set of dice* **exchange**, trade, barter, interchange, bargain; switch, change, replace. **2** *we swapped jokes* **bandy**, exchange, trade, reciprocate.
▸n. *a job swap* **exchange**, interchange, trade, switch, trade-off, substitution.

swarm n. **1** *a swarm of bees* **hive**, flock, collection. **2** *a swarm of gendarmes* **crowd**, multitude, horde, host, mob, gang, throng, mass, army, troop, herd, pack; literary myriad.
▸v. *reporters were swarming all over the place* **flock**, crowd, throng, surge, stream.
□ **be swarming with** be crowded with, be thronged with, be overrun with, be full of, abound in, be teeming with, bristle with, be alive with, be crawling with, be infested with, overflow with, be prolific in, be abundant in; informal be thick with.

swarthy adj. **dark-skinned**, olive-skinned, dusky, tanned, saturnine, black; old use swart.
– OPPOSITES pale.

swashbuckling adj. **daring**, heroic, daredevil, dashing, adventurous, bold, valiant, valorous, fearless, lionhearted, dauntless, devil-may-care; gallant, chivalrous, romantic.
– OPPOSITES timid.

swathe v. **wrap**, envelop, bind, swaddle, bandage, cover, shroud, drape, wind, enfold, sheathe.

S

sway v. **1** *the curtains swayed in the breeze* **swing**, shake, oscillate, undulate, move to and fro, move back and forth. **2** *she swayed on her feet* **stagger**, wobble, rock, lurch, reel, roll, list, stumble, pitch. **3** *we are swayed by the media* **influence**, affect, bias, persuade, talk round, win over; manipulate, bend, mould. **4** *you must not be swayed by emotion* **rule**, govern, dominate, control, guide.
▶ n. **1** *the sway of her hips* **swing**, roll, shake, oscillation, undulation. **2** *a province under the sway of the Franks* **jurisdiction**, rule, government, sovereignty, dominion, control, command, power, authority, ascendancy, domination, mastery.
□ **hold sway** hold power, wield power, exercise power, rule, be in control, predominate; have the upper hand, have the edge, have the whip hand; informal run the show, be in the driving seat, be in the saddle.

swear v. **1** *they swore to marry each other* **promise**, vow, pledge, give one's word, take an oath, undertake, guarantee; Law depose; formal aver. **2** *she swore she would never go back* **insist**, avow, pronounce, declare, proclaim, assert, profess, maintain, contend, emphasize, stress; formal aver. **3** *Kate spilled wine and swore* **curse**, blaspheme, utter profanities, utter oaths, use bad language, take the Lord's name in vain; informal cuss, eff and blind; old use execrate.
□ **swear by** informal express confidence in, have faith in, trust, believe in; set store by, value; informal rate.
swear off informal renounce, forswear, forgo, abstain from, go without, shun, avoid, eschew, steer clear of; give up, dispense with, stop, discontinue, drop; informal kick, quit; Brit. informal jack in.

swearing n. **bad language**, strong language, cursing, blaspheming, blasphemy; profanities, obscenities, curses, oaths, expletives, swear words; informal cussing, effing and blinding, four-letter words; Brit. informal industrial language; formal imprecation.

sweat n. **1** *he was drenched with sweat* **perspiration**, moisture, dampness, wetness; Medicine diaphoresis, hidrosis. **2** informal *the sweat of the working classes* **labour**, hard work, toil(s), effort(s), exertion(s), industry, drudgery, slog; informal graft, grind, elbow grease.
▶ v. **1** *she was sweating heavily* **perspire**, swelter, glow; be damp, be wet; secrete. **2** *I've sweated over this for six months* **work (hard)**, work like a Trojan, labour, toil, slog, slave, work one's fingers to the bone; informal graft, plug away; old use drudge.

> **WORD LINKS**
> **sudorific** relating to or causing sweating
> **diaphoresis** excessive sweating as caused by a disease or drug

sweaty adj. **perspiring**, sweating, clammy, sticky, glowing; moist, damp.
sweep v. **1** *she swept the floor* **brush**, clean, scrub, wipe, mop, dust, scour; informal do.

2 *I swept the crumbs off* **remove**, brush, clean, clear, whisk. **3** *he was swept out to sea* **carry**, pull, drag, tow. **4** *riots swept the country* **engulf**, overwhelm, flood. **5** *he swept down the stairs* **glide**, sail, breeze, drift, flit, flounce; stride, stroll, swagger. **6** *a limousine swept past* **glide**, sail, rush, race, streak, speed, fly, zoom, whizz, hurtle; informal tear, whip. **7** *police swept the conference room* **search**, probe, check, explore, go through, scour, comb.
▶ n. **1** *a great sweep of his hand* **gesture**, stroke, wave, movement. **2** *a security sweep* **search**, hunt, exploration, probe. **3** *a long sweep of golden sand* **expanse**, tract, stretch, extent, plain. **4** *the broad sweep of our interests* **range**, span, scope, compass, reach, spread, ambit, remit, gamut, spectrum, extent.
□ **sweep something aside** disregard, ignore, take no notice of, dismiss, shrug off, forget about, brush aside.
sweep something under the carpet hide, conceal, suppress, hush up, keep quiet about, censor, redact, gag, withhold, cover up, stifle.

sweeping adj. **1** *sweeping changes* **extensive**, wide-ranging, global, broad, comprehensive, all-inclusive, all-embracing, far-reaching, across the board; thorough, radical; informal wall-to-wall. **2** *a sweeping victory* **overwhelming**, decisive, thorough, complete, total, absolute, out-and-out, unqualified. **3** *sweeping statements* **wholesale**, blanket, generalized, all-inclusive, unqualified, indiscriminate, universal, oversimplified, imprecise. **4** *sweeping banks of heather* **broad**, extensive, expansive, vast, spacious, boundless, panoramic.
– OPPOSITES limited, narrow, focused, small.

sweet adj. **1** *sweet biscuits* **sugary**, sweetened, saccharine; sugared, honeyed, candied, glacé; sickly, cloying. **2** *the sweet scent of roses* **fragrant**, aromatic, perfumed; literary ambrosial. **3** *her sweet voice* **dulcet**, melodious, lyrical, mellifluous, musical, tuneful, soft, harmonious, silvery, honeyed, mellow, rich, golden. **4** *life was still sweet* **pleasant**, pleasing, agreeable, delightful, nice, satisfying, gratifying, good, acceptable, fine; informal lovely, great. **5** *the sweet March air* **pure**, wholesome, fresh, clean, clear. **6** *she has a sweet nature* **likeable**, appealing, engaging, amiable, pleasant, agreeable, genial, friendly, nice, kind, thoughtful, considerate; charming, enchanting, captivating, delightful, lovely. **7** *she looks quite sweet* **cute**, lovable, adorable, endearing, charming, attractive, dear. **8** *my sweet Lydia* **dear**, dearest, darling, beloved, loved, cherished, precious, treasured.
– OPPOSITES sour, savoury, harsh, disagreeable.
▶ n. **1** *sweets for the children* **confectionery**, bonbon, chocolate, toffee; N. Amer. candy; informal sweetie; old use sweetmeat. **2** *a delicious sweet for the guests* **dessert**, pudding, second course, last course; Brit. informal afters, pud. **3** *happy birthday,*

my sweet! **dear**, darling, dearest, love, sweetheart, beloved, honey, pet, treasure, angel.

◻ **sweet on** informal fond of, taken with, attracted to, in love with, enamoured of, captivated by, infatuated with, keen on, devoted to, smitten with; informal gone on, mad about.

sweeten v. **1** *sweeten the milk with honey* **make sweet**, add sugar to, sugar, sugar-coat. **2** *he chewed gum to sweeten his breath* **freshen**, refresh, purify, deodorize, perfume. **3** *try to sweeten the bad news* **soften**, ease, alleviate, mitigate, temper, cushion; embellish, embroider. **4** informal *a bigger dividend to sweeten shareholders* **mollify**, placate, soothe, soften up, pacify, appease, win over.

sweetheart n. **1** *you look lovely, sweetheart* **darling**, dear, dearest, love, beloved, sweet; informal honey, sweetie, sugar, baby, babe, poppet. **2** *my high-school sweetheart* **lover**, love, girlfriend, boyfriend, beloved, significant other, lady-love, loved one, suitor, admirer; informal steady, flame; literary swain; dated beau; old use paramour.

swell v. **1** *her lip swelled up* **expand**, bulge, distend, inflate, dilate, bloat, puff up, balloon, fatten, fill out, tumefy; rare intumesce. **2** *the population swelled* **grow**, enlarge, increase, expand, rise, escalate, multiply, proliferate, snowball, mushroom. **3** *she swelled with pride* **be filled**, be bursting, brim, overflow. **4** *the graduate scheme swelled entry numbers* **increase**, enlarge, augment, boost, top up, step up, multiply. **5** *the music swelled to fill the house* **grow loud**, grow louder, amplify, intensify, heighten.
– OPPOSITES shrink, decrease, quieten.
▸ n. **1** *a brief swell in the volume* **increase**, rise, escalation, surge, boost. **2** *a heavy swell on the sea* **surge**, wave, undulation, roll.
– OPPOSITES decrease, dip.
▸ adj. N. Amer. informal dated *a swell idea* **excellent**, marvellous, wonderful, splendid, magnificent, superb; informal super, great, fantastic.
– OPPOSITES bad.

swelling n. **bump**, lump, bulge, protuberance, enlargement, distension, prominence, protrusion, node, nodule, tumescence; boil, blister, bunion, carbuncle.

sweltering adj. **hot**, stifling, humid, sultry, sticky, muggy, close, stuffy; tropical, torrid, searing, blistering; informal boiling (hot), baking, roasting, sizzling.
– OPPOSITES freezing.

swerve v. *a car swerved into her path* **veer**, deviate, skew, diverge, sheer, weave, zigzag, change direction; Sailing tack.
▸ n. *the bowler regulated his swerve* **curve**, curl, deviation, twist; N. Amer. English.

swift adj. **1** *a swift decision* **prompt**, rapid, sudden, immediate, instant, instantaneous; abrupt, hasty, hurried, precipitate, headlong.
2 *swift runners* **fast**, rapid, quick, speedy,

high-speed, brisk, lively; express, breakneck; fleet-footed; informal nippy, supersonic.
– OPPOSITES slow, leisurely.

swill v. **1** informal *she was swilling pints* **drink**, quaff, swallow, down, gulp, drain, imbibe, sup, slurp, consume, slug; informal swig, knock back, toss off, put away; Brit. informal neck; N. Amer. informal chug. **2** *he swilled out a glass* **wash**, rinse, sluice, clean, flush.
▸ n. **1** informal *he took a swill of coffee* **gulp**, swallow, drink, draught, mouthful, slug; informal swig. **2** *swill for the pigs* **pigswill**, mash, slops, scraps, refuse, scourings, leftovers; old use hogwash.

swim v. **1** *they swam in the pool* **bathe**, take a dip, splash around; float, tread water. **2** *his food was swimming in gravy* **be saturated in**, be drenched in, be soaked in, be steeped in, be immersed in, be covered in, be full of.

swimmingly adv. **well**, smoothly, easily, effortlessly, like clockwork, without a hitch, as planned, to plan; informal like a dream, like magic.

swimming pool n. **pool**, baths, lido, piscina; Brit. swimming bath(s); N. Amer. natatorium.

swimsuit n. **bathing suit**, bathing dress, (swimming) trunks, bikini; swimwear; Brit. bathing costume, swimming costume; informal cossie; Austral./NZ informal bathers.

swindle v. *I was swindled out of money* **defraud**, cheat, trick, dupe, deceive, fool, hoax, hoodwink, bamboozle; informal fleece, do, con, sting, diddle, swizzle, rip off, take for a ride, pull a fast one on, put one over on, take to the cleaners, gull; N. Amer. informal stiff, euchre; literary cozen; old use sharp.
▸ n. *an insurance swindle* **fraud**, trick, deception, deceit, cheat, sham, artifice, ruse, dodge, racket, wile; sharp practice; informal con, fiddle, diddle, rip-off, flimflam, swizzle, swizz; N. Amer. informal bunco.

swindler n. **fraudster**, fraud, (confidence) trickster, cheat, rogue, mountebank, charlatan, impostor, hoaxer; informal con man, con artist, shark, sharp, hustler, phoney, crook.

swing v. **1** *the sign swung in the wind* **sway**, oscillate, move back and forth, move to and fro, wave, wag, rock, flutter, flap. **2** *Helen swung the bottle* **brandish**, wave, flourish, wield, shake, wag, twirl. **3** *this road swings off to the north* **curve**, bend, veer, turn, bear, wind, twist, deviate, slew, skew, drift, head. **4** *the balance swung from one party to the other* **change**, fluctuate, shift, alter, oscillate, waver, alternate, see-saw, yo-yo, vary. **5** informal *their persistence finally swung it for him* **accomplish**, achieve, obtain, acquire, get, secure, net, win, attain, bag, hook; informal wangle, land, fix (up).
▸ n. **1** *a swing of the pendulum* **oscillation**, sway, wave. **2** *the swing to the Conservatives* **change**, move; turnaround, turnabout, reversal, about-turn, about-face, volte-face, change of heart, U-turn, sea change. **3** *a swing towards plain food* **trend**,

S

tendency, drift, movement. **4** *a mood swing* **fluctuation**, change, shift, variation, oscillation.

swingeing adj. Brit. **severe**, extreme, serious, substantial, drastic, harsh, punishing, excessive, heavy.
– OPPOSITES minor.

swipe informal v. **1** *he swiped at her head* **swing**, lash out; strike, hit, slap, cuff; informal belt, wallop, sock, biff, clout. **2** *they're always swiping sweets* **steal**, thieve, take, pilfer, purloin, snatch, shoplift; informal filch, lift, snaffle, rob, nab; Brit. informal nick, pinch, whip; N. Amer. informal glom.
▶n. *she took a swipe at his face* **swing**, stroke, strike, hit, slap, cuff, clip; informal belt, wallop.

swirl v. **whirl**, eddy, billow, spiral, circulate, revolve, spin, twist; flow, stream, surge, seethe.

switch n. **1** *the switch on top of the telephone* **button**, lever, control, dial. **2** *a switch from direct to indirect taxation* **change**, move, shift, transition, transformation; reversal, turnaround, U-turn, rowback, changeover, transfer, conversion; substitution, exchange. **3** *a switch of willow* **branch**, twig, stick, rod.
▶v. **1** *he switched sides* **change**, shift; reverse; Brit. informal chop and change. **2** *he managed to switch envelopes* **exchange**, swap, interchange, trade, substitute, replace, rotate.
□ **switch something on** turn on, put on, activate, start, set going, set in motion, operate, initiate, actuate, initialize, energize. **switch something off** turn off, shut off, stop, cut, halt, deactivate.

swivel v. **turn**, rotate, revolve, pivot, swing; spin, twirl, whirl, wheel, gyrate, pirouette.

swollen adj. **distended**, expanded, enlarged, bulging, inflated, dilated, bloated, puffed up, puffy, tumescent; inflamed.

swoop v. **1** *pigeons swooped down after the grain* **dive**, descend, sweep, pounce, plunge, pitch, nosedive; rush, dart, speed, zoom. **2** *police swooped on the flat* **raid**, search; pounce on, attack, assault, assail, charge; N. Amer. informal bust.
▶n. *an early morning swoop by police* **raid**; attack, assault; N. Amer. informal bust, takedown.

sword n. *a ceremonial sword* **blade**, foil, épée, cutlass, rapier, sabre, scimitar; literary brand.
□ **cross swords** quarrel, disagree, dispute, wrangle, bicker, be at odds, be at loggerheads, lock horns; fight, contend; informal scrap.
put to the sword kill, execute, put to death, murder, butcher, slaughter, massacre, cut down; literary slay.

sybarite n. **hedonist**, sensualist, voluptuary, libertine, pleasure-seeker, epicure, bon vivant, bon viveur.
– OPPOSITES puritan.

sybaritic adj. **luxurious**, extravagant, lavish, self-indulgent, pleasure-seeking, sensual, voluptuous, hedonistic, epicurean, lotus-eating, libertine, debauched, decadent.
– OPPOSITES ascetic.

sycophant n. **toady**, creep, crawler, fawner, flatterer, truckler, groveller, doormat, lickspittle, kowtower, Uriah Heep; informal bootlicker, yes-man.

sycophantic adj. **obsequious**, servile, subservient, deferential, grovelling, toadying, fawning, flattering, ingratiating, cringing, unctuous, slavish; informal smarmy, bootlicking.

syllabus n. **curriculum**, course (of study), programme of study, course outline; timetable, schedule.

symbol n. **1** *the lotus is the symbol of purity* **emblem**, token, sign, representation, figure, image; metaphor, allegory. **2** *the chemical symbol for helium* **sign**, character, mark, letter, ideogram. **3** *the Red Cross symbol* **logo**, emblem, badge, stamp, trademark, crest, insignia, coat of arms, seal, device, monogram, hallmark, flag, motif.

symbolic adj. **1** *the Colosseum is symbolic of the Roman Empire* **emblematic**, representative, typical, characteristic, symptomatic. **2** *symbolic language* **figurative**, representative, illustrative, emblematic, metaphorical, allegorical, parabolic, allusive, suggestive; meaningful, significant.
– OPPOSITES literal.

symbolize v. **represent**, stand for, be a sign of, exemplify; denote, signify, mean, indicate, convey, express, imply, suggest, allude to; embody, epitomize, encapsulate, personify, typify; literary betoken.

symmetrical adj. **regular**, uniform, consistent; evenly shaped, aligned, equal; mirror-image; balanced, proportional, even.

symmetry n. **regularity**, evenness, uniformity, consistency, conformity, correspondence, equality; balance, proportions; formal concord.

sympathetic adj. **1** *a sympathetic listener* **compassionate**, caring, concerned, solicitous, empathetic, understanding, sensitive; commiserative, pitying, consoling, comforting, supportive, encouraging; considerate, kind, tender-hearted. **2** *the most sympathetic character in the book* **likeable**, pleasant, agreeable, congenial, friendly, genial. **3** *I was sympathetic to his cause* **in favour of**, in sympathy with, pro, on the side of, supportive of, encouraging of; well disposed to, favourably disposed to, receptive to.
– OPPOSITES unfeeling, opposed.

sympathize v. **1** *he sympathized with his wife* **pity**, feel sorry for, show compassion for, commiserate, offer condolences to, feel for, show concern, show interest; console, comfort, solace, soothe, support, encourage; empathize with, identify with, understand, relate to. **2** *they sympathize with the critique* **agree with**, support, be in favour of, go along with, favour, approve of, back, side with.

sympathizer n. **supporter**, backer, well-wisher, advocate, ally, partisan; collaborator, fraternizer, conspirator, quisling.

sympathy n. **1** *he shows sympathy for the poor* **compassion**, caring, concern, solicitude, empathy; commiseration, pity, condolence, comfort, solace, support, encouragement; consideration, kindness. **2** *sympathy with a fellow journalist* **rapport**, fellow feeling, affinity, empathy, harmony, accord, compatibility; fellowship, camaraderie. **3** *their sympathy with the Republicans* **agreement**, favour, approval, approbation, support, encouragement, partiality; association, alignment, affiliation.
– OPPOSITES indifference, hostility.

symptom n. **1** *the symptoms of the disease* **manifestation**, indication, indicator, sign, mark, feature, trait; Medicine prodrome. **2** *a symptom of the country's present turmoil* **expression**, sign, indication, mark, token, manifestation; portent, warning, clue, hint; testimony, evidence, proof.

symptomatic adj. **indicative**, characteristic, suggestive, typical, representative, symbolic.

synopsis n. **summary**, summarization, precis, abstract, outline, digest, rundown, round-up, abridgement.

synthesis n. **combination**, union, amalgam, blend, mixture, compound, fusion, composite, alloy; unification, amalgamation, marrying.

synthetic adj. **artificial**, fake, imitation, mock, false, faux, simulated, ersatz, substitute; pseudo, so-called; man-made, manufactured, fabricated; informal phoney, pretend.
– OPPOSITES natural.

syrupy adj. **1** *syrupy medicine* **oversweet**, sweet, sugary, treacly, honeyed, saccharine; thick, sticky, gluey, viscid, glutinous; informal gooey. **2** *syrupy romantic drivel* **sentimental**, mawkish, cloying, mushy, slushy, sloppy, sickly, saccharine, trite; informal soppy, schmaltzy, lovey-dovey, cheesy, corny.

system n. **1** *a system of canals* **structure**, organization, arrangement, complex, network; informal set-up. **2** *a system for regulating sales* **method**, methodology, technique, process, procedure, approach, practice; means, way, mode, framework, modus operandi; scheme, plan, policy, programme, regimen, formula, routine. **3** *there was no system in his work* **order**, method, orderliness, systematization, planning, logic, routine. **4** *youngsters have no faith in the system* **the establishment**, the administration, the authorities, the powers that be; bureaucracy, officialdom; the status quo.

systematic adj. **structured**, methodical, organized, orderly, planned, systematized, regular, routine, standardized, standard; logical, coherent, consistent; efficient, businesslike, practical.
– OPPOSITES disorganized.

Tt

tab n. **1** *his name is on the tab of his jacket* **tag**, label, flap. **2** informal *the company will pick up the tab* **bill**, invoice, account, charge, expense, cost; N. Amer. check.

table n. **1** *put the plates on the table* bench, buffet, stand, counter, work surface, worktop; desk, bar. **2** *he provides an excellent table* **meal**, food, fare, menu, nourishment; eatables, provisions; informal spread, grub, chow, eats, nosh; literary viands; dated victuals. **3** *the report has numerous tables* **chart**, diagram, figure, graph, plan; list, tabulation, index.
▶v. *she tabled a question in parliament* **submit**, put forward, propose, suggest, move, lodge, file, introduce, air, moot.

tableau n. **1** *mythic tableaux* **picture**, painting, representation, illustration, image. **2** *the first act consists of a series of tableaux* **pageant**, tableau vivant, parade, diorama, scene. **3** *a domestic tableau around the fireplace* **scene**, arrangement, grouping, group; picture, spectacle, image, vignette.

tablet n. **1** *a carved tablet* **slab**, stone, panel, plaque, plate, sign. **2** *a headache tablet* **pill**, capsule, lozenge, caplet, pastille, drop, pilule; informal tab. **3** *a tablet of soap* **bar**, cake, slab, brick, block, chunk, piece.

taboo n. *the taboo against healing on the sabbath* **prohibition**, proscription, veto, interdiction, interdict, ban, restriction.
▶adj. *taboo language* **forbidden**, prohibited, banned, proscribed, interdicted, non licet, outlawed, illegal, illicit, unlawful, restricted, off limits; unmentionable, unspeakable, unutterable, ineffable; rude, impolite; Islam haram; NZ tapu; informal no go.
– OPPOSITES acceptable.

tabulate v. **chart**, arrange, order, organize, systematize, systemize, catalogue, list, index, classify, class, codify; compile, group, log, grade, rate.

tacit adj. **implicit**, understood, implied, inferred, hinted, suggested; unspoken, unstated, unsaid, unexpressed, unvoiced; taken for granted, taken as read.
– OPPOSITES explicit.

taciturn adj. **reticent**, uncommunicative, unforthcoming, quiet, secretive, tight-lipped, close-mouthed; silent, mute, dumb, inarticulate; reserved, withdrawn.
– OPPOSITES talkative.

tack n. **1** *tacks held the carpet down* **pin**, drawing pin, nail, staple, rivet, stud.
2 *the brig bowled past on the opposite tack* **heading**, bearing, course, track, path, line. **3** *the defender changed his tack* **approach**, way, method; policy; procedure, technique, tactic, plan, strategy, stratagem; path, line, angle, direction, course.
▶v. **1** *a photo tacked to the wall* **pin**, nail, staple, fix, fasten, attach, secure, affix. **2** *the dress was roughly tacked together* **stitch**, baste, sew, bind. **3** *the yachts tacked back and forth* **change course**, change direction, swerve, zigzag, veer; Nautical go/come about, beat. **4** *poems tacked on at the end of the book* **add**, append, join, tag.

tackle n. **1** *fishing tackle* **gear**, equipment, apparatus, kit, hardware; implements, instruments, accoutrements, paraphernalia, trappings, appurtenances; informal things, stuff, clobber, bits and pieces; old use equipage. **2** *lifting tackle* **pulleys**, gear, hoist, crane, winch, davit, windlass, sheave. **3** *a tackle by the scrum half* **challenge**, interception, block, attack.
▶v. **1** *we must tackle environmental problems* **get to grips with**, address, get to work on, set one's hand to, approach, take on, take forward, attend to, see to; deal with, take care of, handle, manage; informal get stuck into, have a crack at, have a go at. **2** *I tackled Nina about it* **confront**, speak to, interview, question, cross-examine; accost, waylay; remonstrate with. **3** *he tackled a masked intruder* **confront**, face up to, take on, contend with, challenge; seize, grab, grapple with, intercept, block, stop; bring down, floor, fell, rugby-tackle; informal have a go at. **4** *the winger got tackled* **challenge**, rugby-tackle, intercept, block, stop, attack.

tacky[1] adj. *the paint was still tacky* **sticky**, wet, gluey, gummy, adhesive, viscous, viscid, treacly; informal gooey.

tacky[2] adj. informal *a tacky game show* **tawdry**, tasteless, kitsch, vulgar, crude, garish, gaudy, showy, trashy, cheap, common, second-rate; informal cheesy; Brit. informal naff.
– OPPOSITES tasteful.

tact n. **diplomacy**, tactfulness, sensitivity, understanding, thoughtfulness, consideration, delicacy, discretion, prudence, judiciousness, subtlety, savoir faire; informal savvy.

tactful adj. **diplomatic**, discreet, considerate, sensitive, understanding, thoughtful, delicate, judicious, politic, perceptive, subtle; courteous, polite, decorous, respectful; informal savvy.

tactic n. **1** *a tax-saving tactic* **scheme**, stratagem, strategy, plan, manoeuvre; method, expedient, gambit, move, approach, tack; device, trick, ploy, dodge, ruse, machination, contrivance; informal wangle; old use shift. **2** *our fleet's superior tactics* **battle plans**, game plan, policy, campaign, manoeuvres, logistics; generalship, organization, planning, direction, orchestration.

tactical adj. **calculated**, planned, strategic; prudent, politic, diplomatic, judicious, shrewd, cunning, artful.

tactless adj. **insensitive**, inconsiderate, thoughtless, indelicate, undiplomatic, impolitic, indiscreet, unsubtle, clumsy, heavy-handed, graceless, awkward, inept, gauche; blunt, frank, outspoken, abrupt, gruff, rough, crude, coarse; imprudent, injudicious, unwise; rude, impolite, uncouth, discourteous, crass, tasteless, disrespectful, boorish.

tag n. **1** *a price tag* **label**, ticket, badge, mark, marker, tab, sticker, docket, stub, counterfoil, flag. **2** *his jacket was hung up by its tag* **tab**, loop, label. **3** *he gained a 'bad boy' tag* **designation**, label, description, characterization, identity; nickname, name, epithet, title, sobriquet; informal handle, moniker; formal denomination, appellation. **4** *tags from Shakespeare* **quotation**, quote, phrase, platitude, cliché, excerpt; saying, proverb, maxim, adage, aphorism, motto, epigram; slogan, catchphrase.
▶ v. **1** *bottles tagged with coloured stickers* **label**, mark, ticket, identify, flag, indicate. **2** *he is tagged as a 'thinking' actor* **label**, class, categorize, characterize, designate, describe, identify, classify; mark, stamp, brand, pigeonhole, stereotype, typecast, compartmentalize, typify; name, call, title, entitle, dub, term, style. **3** *a poem tagged on as an afterthought* **add**, tack, join; attach, append. **4** *he was tagging along behind her* **follow**, trail; come after, go after, shadow, dog; accompany, attend, escort; informal tail.

tail n. **1** *the animal's tail* brush, scut; tailpiece, tail feathers; hindquarters. **2** *the tail of the queue* **rear**, end, back, extremity; bottom; Brit. informal fag end. **3** *the tail of the hunting season* **close**, end, conclusion, tail end. **4** informal *put a tail on that man* **detective**, investigator, shadow; informal sleuth, private eye, tec; N. Amer. informal gumshoe.
– OPPOSITES head, front, start.
▶ v. informal *the paparazzi tailed them* **follow**, shadow, stalk, trail, track, hunt, hound, dog, pursue, chase.
□ **tail off/away** fade, wane, ebb, dwindle, decrease, lessen, diminish, decline, subside, abate, drop off, peter out, taper off; let up, ease off, die away, die down, come to an end.
turn tail run away, flee, bolt, make off, take to one's heels, cut and run, beat a (hasty) retreat; informal scram, scarper, skedaddle, vamoose.

WORD LINKS
caudal relating to an animal's tail
dock cut an animal's tail short

tailback n. **traffic jam**, queue, line; congestion.

tailor n. **outfitter**, dressmaker, couturier, (fashion) designer; clothier, costumier, seamstress; dated modiste.
▶ v. *services can be tailored to customer requirements* **customize**, adapt, adjust, modify, change, convert, alter, attune, mould, gear, fit, cut, shape, tune.

taint n. *the taint of corruption* **trace**, touch, suggestion, hint, tinge; stain, blot, blemish, stigma, black mark, blot on one's escutcheon; discredit, dishonour, disgrace, shame.
▶ v. **1** *the wilderness is tainted by pollution* **contaminate**, pollute, adulterate, infect, blight, spoil, soil, ruin, destroy; literary befoul. **2** *fraudulent firms taint our firm's reputation* **tarnish**, sully, blacken, stain, blot, blemish, stigmatize, mar, corrupt, defile, soil, muddy, damage, harm, hurt; drag through the mud; literary besmirch.
– OPPOSITES clean, improve.

take v. **1** *she took his hand* **lay hold of**, get hold of; grasp, grip, clasp, clutch, grab. **2** *he took an envelope from his pocket* **remove**, pull, draw, withdraw, extract, fish. **3** *a passage taken from my book* **extract**, quote, cite, excerpt, derive, abstract, copy, cull. **4** *she took a little wine* **drink**, imbibe; consume, swallow, eat, ingest. **5** *many prisoners were taken* **capture**, seize, catch, arrest, apprehend, take into custody; carry off, abduct. **6** *someone's taken my car* **steal**, remove, appropriate, make off with, pilfer, purloin; informal filch, swipe, snaffle; Brit. informal pinch, nick. **7** *take four from the total* **subtract**, deduct, remove; discount; informal knock off, minus. **8** *all the seats had been taken* **occupy**, use, utilize, fill, hold; reserve, engage; informal bag. **9** *I have taken a room nearby* **rent**, lease, hire, charter; reserve, book, engage. **10** *I took the job* **accept**, undertake. **11** *I'd take this over the other option* **pick**, choose, select; prefer, favour, opt for, plump for, vote for. **12** *take, for instance, the English word 'one'* **consider**, contemplate, ponder, think about, weigh up, mull over, examine, study, meditate over, ruminate about. **13** *he takes 'The Observer'* **subscribe to**, buy, read. **14** *she took his temperature* **ascertain**, determine, establish, measure, find out, discover; calculate, compute, evaluate, rate, assess, appraise, gauge. **15** *he took notes* **write**, note (down), jot (down), scribble, scrawl, record, register, document, minute. **16** *I took it back to London* **bring**, carry, bear, transport, convey, move, transfer, shift, ferry; informal cart, tote. **17** *the priest took her home* **escort**, accompany, help, assist, show, lead, guide, see, usher, convey. **18** *he took the train* **travel on/by**, journey on, go via; use. **19** *the town takes its name from the lake* **derive**, get, obtain, come by, acquire, pick up. **20** *she took the prize*

for best speaker **receive**, obtain, gain, get, acquire, collect, accept, be awarded; secure, come by, win, earn, pick up, carry off; informal land, bag, net, scoop. **21** *I took the chance to postpone it* **act on**, take advantage of, capitalize on, use, exploit, make the most of, leap at, jump at, pounce on, seize, grasp, grab, accept. **22** *he took great pleasure in painting* **derive**, draw, acquire, obtain, get, gain, extract, procure; experience, undergo, feel. **23** *Liz took the news badly* **receive**, respond to, react to, meet, greet; deal with, cope with. **24** *do you take me for a fool?* **regard as**, consider to be, view as, see as, believe to be, reckon to be, imagine to be, deem to be. **25** *I take it that you are hungry* **assume**, presume, suppose, imagine, expect, reckon, gather, dare say, trust, surmise, deduce, guess, conjecture, fancy, suspect. **26** *I take your point* **understand**, grasp, get, comprehend, apprehend, see, follow; accept, appreciate, acknowledge, sympathize with, agree with. **27** *Shirley was rather taken with him* **captivate**, enchant, charm, delight, attract, beguile, enthral, entrance, infatuate, dazzle; amuse, divert, entertain; informal tickle someone's fancy. **28** *I can't take much more* **endure**, bear, tolerate, stand, put up with, abide, stomach, accept, allow, countenance, support, shoulder; formal brook; old use suffer. **29** *applicants must take a test* **carry out**, do, complete, conduct, perform, execute, discharge, accomplish, fulfil. **30** *I took English and French* **study**, learn, have lessons in; take up, pursue; Brit. read; informal do. **31** *the journey took six hours* **last**, continue for, go on for, carry on for; require, call for, need, necessitate, entail, involve. **32** *it would take an expert to know that* **require**, need, necessitate, demand, call for, entail, involve. **33** *I take size three shoes* **wear**, use; require, need. **34** *the dye did not take* **be effective**, take effect, hold, root, be productive, be effectual, be useful; work, operate, succeed, function; formal be efficacious.
– OPPOSITES give, free, add, refuse, miss.
▸ n. **1** *the whalers' commercial take* **catch**, haul, bag, yield, net. **2** *the state's tax take* **revenue**, income, gain, profit; takings, proceeds, returns, receipts, winnings, pickings, earnings, spoils; purse. **3** *a clapperboard for the start of each take* **scene**, sequence, (film) clip. **4** *a wry take on gender issues* **view of**, reading of, version of, interpretation of, understanding of, account of, analysis of, approach to.
□ **take after** resemble, look like; remind one of, make one think of, recall, conjure up, suggest, evoke; informal favour, be a chip off the old block, be the spitting image of.
take something apart 1 *we took the machine apart* dismantle, pull to pieces, pull apart, disassemble, break up; tear down, demolish, destroy, wreck. **2** informal *the scene was taken apart by the director.* See **criticize**.
take someone back 1 *the dream took me back to Vienna* evoke, remind one of, conjure up, summon up; echo, suggest. **2** *I will never*

take that girl back **be reconciled to**, forgive, pardon, excuse, exonerate, absolve; let bygones be bygones, bury the hatchet.
take something back 1 *I take back every word* **retract**, withdraw, renounce, disclaim, unsay, disavow, recant, repudiate; formal abjure. **2** *I must take the keys back* **return**, bring back, give back, restore.
take something down write down, note down, jot down, set down, record, commit to paper, register, draft, document, minute, pen.
take someone in 1 *she took in paying guests* **accommodate**, board, house, feed, put up, admit, receive; harbour. **2** *you were taken in by a hoax* **deceive**, delude, hoodwink, mislead, trick, dupe, fool, cheat, defraud, swindle, outwit, gull, hoax, bamboozle; informal con, put one over on.
take something in 1 *she could hardly take in the news* **comprehend**, understand, grasp, follow, absorb; informal get. **2** *this route takes in some great scenery* **include**, encompass, embrace, contain, comprise, cover, incorporate, comprehend, hold.
take someone in hand control, be in charge of, dominate, master; reform, improve, correct, change, rehabilitate.
take something in hand deal with, apply oneself to, get to grips with, set one's hand to, grapple with, take on, attend to, see to, sort out, take care of, handle, manage; informal get stuck into.
take it out of someone exhaust, drain, enervate, tire, fatigue, wear out, weary, debilitate; informal knacker, poop.
take off 1 *the horse took off at great speed* **run away/off**, flee, abscond, take flight, decamp, leave, go, depart, make off, bolt, take to one's heels, escape; informal split, clear off, skedaddle, vamoose. **2** *the plane took off* **become airborne**, take to the air, take wing; lift off, blast off. **3** *the idea really took off* **succeed**, do well, become popular, catch on, prosper, flourish, thrive, boom.
take someone off mimic, impersonate, imitate, ape, parody, mock, caricature, satirize, burlesque, lampoon, ridicule; informal spoof, send up.
take someone on 1 *there was no challenger to take him on* **compete against**, oppose, challenge, confront, face, fight, vie with, contend with, stand up to. **2** *we took on extra staff* **engage**, hire, employ, enrol, enlist, sign up; informal take on board.
take something on 1 *he took on more responsibility* **undertake**, accept, assume, shoulder, acquire, carry, bear. **2** *the study took on political meaning* **acquire**, assume, come to have.
take one's time go slowly, dally, dawdle, delay, linger, drag one's feet, waste time, kill time; informal dilly-dally; old use tarry.
take something over assume control of, take charge of, take command of.
take to 1 *he took to carrying his money in his sock* **make a habit of**, resort to, turn to, have recourse to; start, commence. **2** *Ruth took to*

him instantly **like**, get on with, be friendly towards; informal take a shine to. **3** *the dog has really taken to racing* **become good at**, develop an ability for; like, enjoy.

take something up 1 *he took up abstract painting* **engage in**, practise; begin, start, commence. **2** *the meetings took up all her time* **consume**, fill, absorb, use, occupy; waste, squander. **3** *her cousin took up the story* **resume**, recommence, restart, carry on, pick up, return to. **4** *he took up their offer of a job* **accept**, say yes to, agree to, adopt; formal accede to. **5** *take the skirt up an inch* **shorten**, turn up; raise, lift.

take up with become friends with, go around with, fall in with, string along with, get involved with, start seeing; informal knock around with, hang out with.

take-off n. **1** *the plane crashed on take-off* **departure**, lift-off, launch, blast-off; ascent, flight. **2** informal *a take-off of a talent show* **parody**, pastiche, mockery, caricature, travesty, satire, lampoon, mimicry, imitation, impersonation, impression; informal send-up, spoof.
– OPPOSITES landing, touchdown.

takeover n. **buyout**, merger, amalgamation; purchase, acquisition.

takings plural n. **proceeds**, returns, receipts, earnings, winnings, pickings, spoils; profit, gain, income, revenue; gate, purse.

tale n. **1** *a tale of witches* **story**, narrative, anecdote, report, account, history; legend, fable, myth, parable, allegory, saga; informal yarn. **2** *she told tales to her mother* **lie**, fib, falsehood, story, untruth, fabrication, fiction; informal tall story, fairy story/tale, cock and bull story.

talent n. **flair**, aptitude, facility, gift, knack, technique, touch, bent, ability, expertise, capacity, faculty; strength, forte, genius, brilliance; dexterity, skill, artistry.

talented adj. **gifted**, skilful, skilled, accomplished, brilliant, expert, consummate, masterly, adroit, dexterous, able, competent, capable, apt, deft, adept, proficient; informal crack, ace.
– OPPOSITES inept.

talisman n. **(lucky) charm**, fetish, amulet, mascot, totem, juju.

talk v. **1** *I was talking to a friend* **speak**, chat, chatter, gossip, prattle, babble, rattle on, blather; informal yak, gab, jaw, chew the fat; Brit. informal natter, rabbit, witter, chunter; N. Amer. informal rap; Austral./NZ informal mag. **2** *you're talking rubbish* **utter**, speak, say, voice, express, articulate, pronounce, verbalize, vocalize. **3** *they were able to talk in peace* **converse**, communicate, speak, confer, consult; negotiate, parley; informal have a confab, chew the fat/rag, rap; formal confabulate. **4** *he talked of suicide* **mention**, refer to, speak about, discuss. **5** *I was able to talk English* **speak (in)**, talk in, communicate in, converse in, express oneself in; use. **6** *nothing would make her talk* **confess**, speak out/up, reveal all, tell tales, give the game away, open one's mouth; informal come clean, blab, squeal, let the cat out of the bag, spill the beans, grass, sing, rat. **7** *the others will talk* **gossip**, pass comment, make remarks; criticize.

▶ n. **1** *he was bored with all this talk* **chatter**, gossip, prattle, jabbering, babbling, gabbling; informal yakking, gabbing; Brit. informal nattering, rabbit. **2** *she needed a talk with Vi* **conversation**, chat, discussion, tête-à-tête, heart-to-heart, dialogue, parley, powwow, consultation, conference, meeting; informal confab, jaw, chit-chat, gossip; Austral. informal convo; formal colloquy, confabulation. **3** *peace talks* **negotiations**, discussions; conference, summit, meeting, consultation, dialogue, symposium, seminar, conclave, parley; mediation, arbitration; informal powwow. **4** *she gave a talk on her travels* **lecture**, speech, address, discourse, oration, presentation, report, sermon; informal spiel. **5** *there was talk of a takeover* **gossip**, rumour, hearsay, tittle-tattle; news, report. **6** *baby talk* **speech**, language, slang, idiom, idiolect; words; informal lingo.

□ **talk back** answer back, be impertinent, be cheeky, be rude; contradict, argue with, disagree with.

talk big informal See **boast** (sense 1 of the verb).

talk something down denigrate, deprecate, disparage, belittle, diminish, criticize; informal knock, put down.

talk down to condescend to, patronize, look down one's nose at, put down.

talk someone into something persuade into, argue into, cajole into, coax into, bring round to, inveigle into, wheedle into, prevail on someone to; informal sweet-talk into, hustle, fast-talk.

talkative adj. **chatty**, loquacious, garrulous, voluble, conversational, communicative; gossipy, babbling, blathering; long-winded, wordy, verbose; informal gabby, mouthy.
– OPPOSITES taciturn.

talker n. **conversationalist**, speaker, communicator, raconteur, orator; chatterbox, gossip.

talking-to n. informal See **reprimand** (noun).

tall adj. **1** *a tall man* **big**, large, huge, towering, colossal, gigantic, giant, monstrous; leggy; informal long. **2** *tall buildings* **high**, big, lofty, towering, elevated, sky-high; multistorey. **3** *she's five feet tall* **in height**, high, from head to toe; from top to bottom. **4** *a tall tale* **unlikely**, improbable, exaggerated, far-fetched, implausible, dubious, unbelievable, incredible, absurd, untrue; informal cock-and-bull. **5** *a tall order* **demanding**, exacting, difficult; unreasonable, impossible.
– OPPOSITES short, low, wide, credible, easy.

tally n. **1** *he keeps a tally of the score* **running total**, count, record, reckoning, register, account, roll; census, poll. **2** *his tally of 1,816 wickets* **total**, score, count, sum.

▶ v. **1** *these statistics tally with government*

figures **correspond**, agree, accord, concur, coincide, match, fit, be consistent, conform, equate, harmonize, be in tune, dovetail, correlate, parallel; informal square; N. Amer. informal jibe. **2** *votes were tallied with abacuses* **count**, calculate, add up, total, compute; figure out, work out, reckon, measure, quantify; Brit. tot up; formal enumerate.
– OPPOSITES disagree.

tame adj. **1** *a tame elephant* **domesticated**, domestic, docile, tamed, broken, trained; gentle, mild; pet; Brit. house-trained; N. Amer. housebroken. **2** informal *he has a tame lawyer* **amenable**, biddable, cooperative, willing, obedient, tractable, acquiescent, docile, submissive, compliant, meek. **3** *it was a pretty tame affair* **unexciting**, uninteresting, uninspiring, dull, bland, flat, insipid, spiritless, pedestrian, colourless, run-of-the-mill, mediocre, ordinary, humdrum, boring; harmless, safe, inoffensive.
– OPPOSITES wild, uncooperative, exciting.
▶ v. **1** *wild rabbits can be tamed* **domesticate**, break, train, master, subdue. **2** *she learned to tame her emotions* **subdue**, curb, control, calm, master, moderate, overcome, discipline, suppress, repress, mellow, temper, soften, bridle, get a grip on; informal lick.

tamper v. **1** *she saw them tampering with her car* **interfere**, monkey around, meddle, tinker, fiddle, fool around, play around; doctor, alter, change, adjust, damage, deface, vandalize; informal mess about/around; Brit. informal muck about/around. **2** *the defendant tampered with the jury* **influence**, get at, rig, manipulate, bribe, corrupt, bias; informal fix; Brit. informal nobble.

tan adj. *a tan waistcoat* **yellowish-brown**, light brown, pale brown, tawny.
▶ v. **1** *use a sunscreen to help you tan* **become suntanned**, get a suntan, (go) brown, bronze. **2** informal *I'll tan his hide.* See **thrash** (sense 1).

tang n. **flavour**, taste, savour; sharpness, zest, bite, edge, smack, piquancy, spice; smell, odour, aroma, fragrance, perfume, redolence; informal kick, pep.

tangible adj. **1** *we offer a tangible product rather than a service* **actual**, palpable, material, physical, real, substantial, corporeal, solid, concrete. **2** *organizations want to see some tangible benefit from the scheme* **visible**, noticeable, actual, definite, clear, clear-cut, distinct, manifest, evident, unmistakable, perceptible, discernible.
– OPPOSITES abstract.

tangle v. **1** *the wool got tangled up* **entangle**, snarl, catch, entwine, twist, ravel, knot, enmesh, coil, mat, jumble, muddle. **2** *he tangled with his old rival* **come into conflict**, dispute, argue, quarrel, fight, wrangle, squabble, contend, cross swords, lock horns.
▶ n. **1** *a tangle of branches* **snarl**, mass, knot, mesh, mishmash. **2** *the defence got into an awful tangle* **muddle**, jumble, mix-up, confusion, shambles.

tangled adj. **1** *tangled hair* **knotted**, knotty, ravelled, entangled, snarled (up), twisted, matted, tangly, messy; tousled, unkempt, ratty; informal mussed up. **2** *a tangled bureaucratic mess* **confused**, jumbled, mixed up, messy, chaotic, complicated, involved, complex, intricate, knotty, tortuous.
– OPPOSITES simple.

tangy adj. **zesty**, sharp, acid, acidic, tart, sour, bitter, piquant, spicy, tasty, flavoursome, pungent.
– OPPOSITES bland.

tank n. **1** *a hot water tank* **container**, receptacle, vat, cistern, repository, reservoir, basin. **2** *a tank full of fish* **aquarium**, bowl. **3** *the army's use of tanks* **armoured vehicle**, armoured car, combat vehicle; Panzer.

tantalize v. **tease**, torment, torture, bait; tempt, entice, lure, allure, beguile; excite, fascinate, titillate, intrigue.

tantamount adj. *this is tantamount to mutiny* **equivalent to**, equal to, as good as, more or less, much the same as, comparable to, on a par with, commensurate with.

tantrum n. **fit of temper**, fit of rage, fit, outburst, pet, paroxysm, frenzy, (bad) mood, huff, scene; informal paddy, wax, wobbly; Brit. informal dated bate; N. Amer. informal hissy fit.

tap¹ n. **1** *she turned the tap on* **valve**, stopcock, cock, spout; N. Amer. faucet, spigot, spile. **2** *a phone tap in the embassy* **listening device**, wiretap, wire, bug, bugging device, microphone, receiver.
▶ v. **1** *several barrels were tapped* **drain**, bleed, milk; broach, open. **2** *butlers were tapping ale* **pour (out)**, draw off, siphon off, pump out, decant. **3** *their telephones were tapped* **bug**, wiretap, hack (into), monitor, overhear, eavesdrop on, spy on. **4** *the resources were to be tapped for our benefit* **draw on**, exploit, milk, mine, use, utilize, turn to account.
□ **on tap** *beers on tap* **on draught**, cask-conditioned, real-ale, from barrels. **2** informal *trained staff are on tap* **on hand**, at hand, available, ready, handy, accessible, standing by.

tap² v. **1** *she tapped on the door* **knock**, rap, strike, beat, drum. **2** *Dad tapped me on the knee* **pat**, hit, strike, slap, jab, poke, dig.
▶ n. **1** *a sharp tap at the door* **knock**, rap, rat-tat. **2** *a tap on the shoulder* **pat**, blow, slap, jab, poke, dig.

tape n. **1** *a package tied with tape* **binding**, ribbon, string, braid. **2** *secure the bandage with tape* **adhesive tape**, sticky tape, masking tape; trademark Sellotape. **3** *they listened to tapes* **(audio) cassette**, (tape) recording, audio tape, reel, spool; video.
▶ v. **1** *a card was taped to the box* **bind**, stick, fix, fasten, secure, attach; tie, strap. **2** *they taped off the area* **cordon**, seal, close, shut, mark, fence; isolate, segregate. **3** *police taped his confession* **record**, tape-record; video.

taper v. **1** *the leaves taper at the tip* **narrow**, thin (out), come to a point, attenuate. **2** *the meetings soon tapered off* **decrease**, lessen, dwindle, diminish, reduce, decline, die

down, peter out, wane, ebb, slacken (off),
fall off, let up, thin out.
– OPPOSITES thicken, increase.
▸ n. *a lighted taper* **candle**, spill, sconce; historical
rushlight.

tardy adj. **late**, unpunctual, behind schedule,
running late; behind, overdue, belated,
delayed; slow, dilatory.
– OPPOSITES punctual.

target n. **1** *targets at a range of 200 yards*
mark, bullseye, goal. **2** *eagles can spot their
targets from half a mile* **prey**, quarry, game,
kill. **3** *their profit target* **objective**, goal,
aim, end; plan, intention, intent, design,
aspiration, ambition, ideal, desire, wish.
4 *she was the target for a wave of abuse*
victim, butt, recipient, focus, object, subject.
▸ v. **1** *he was targeted by a gunman* **pick out**,
single out, earmark, fix on; attack, aim at,
fire at. **2** *the product is targeted at a specific
market* **aim**, direct, level, intend, focus.
□ **on target 1** *the striker was bang on target*
accurate, precise, unerring, sure, on the
mark; Brit. informal spot on. **2** *the project was
on target* **on schedule**, on track, on course,
on time.

tariff n. **tax**, duty, toll, excise, levy, charge,
rate, fee; price list.

tarnish v. **1** *gold does not tarnish easily*
discolour, rust, oxidize, corrode, stain, dull,
blacken. **2** *it tarnished his reputation* **sully**,
blacken, stain, blemish, blot, taint, soil,
ruin, disgrace, mar, damage, harm, hurt,
undermine, dishonour, stigmatize; literary
besmirch.
– OPPOSITES polish, enhance.
▸ n. **1** *the tarnish on the candlesticks*
discoloration, oxidation, rust; film. **2** *the
tarnish on his reputation* **smear**, stain,
blemish, blot, taint, stigma.

tarry v. old use **linger**, loiter, procrastinate,
delay, wait, dawdle; informal hang around/
round.
– OPPOSITES hurry.

tart[1] n. *a jam tart* **pastry**, flan, tartlet, quiche,
pie.

tart[2] informal n. *a tart on a street corner.* See
prostitute (noun).
▸ v. **1** *she tarted herself up* **dress up**, make
up, smarten up, preen oneself, beautify
oneself, groom oneself; informal doll oneself
up, titivate oneself. **2** *we must tart this
place up a bit* **decorate**, renovate, refurbish,
redecorate; smarten up; informal do up, fix up.

tart[3] adj. **1** *a tart apple* **sour**, sharp, acid,
acidic, zesty, tangy, piquant; lemony, acetic.
2 *a tart reply* **acerbic**, sharp, biting, cutting,
astringent, caustic, trenchant, incisive,
barbed, scathing, sarcastic, acrimonious,
nasty, rude, vicious, spiteful, venomous.
– OPPOSITES sweet, kind.

task n. *a daunting task* **job**, duty, chore,
charge, assignment, detail, mission,
engagement, occupation, undertaking,
exercise, business, responsibility, burden,
endeavour, enterprise, venture.
□ **take someone to task** rebuke,

reprimand, reprove, reproach, remonstrate
with, upbraid, scold, berate, lecture, censure,
criticize, admonish, chide, chasten, arraign;
informal tell off, bawl out, give someone a
dressing-down; Brit. informal tick off, carpet;
formal castigate.

taste n. **1** *a distinctive sharp taste* **flavour**,
savour, relish, tang, smack. **2** *a taste of
brandy* **mouthful**, drop, bit, sip, nip,
swallow, touch, soupçon, dash, modicum.
3 *it's too sweet for my taste* **palate**, taste
buds, appetite, stomach. **4** *a taste for
adventure* **liking**, love, fondness, fancy,
desire, preference, penchant, predilection,
inclination, partiality; hankering, appetite,
hunger, thirst, relish. **5** *my first taste of
prison* **experience**, impression; exposure
to, contact with, involvement with. **6** *the
house was furnished with taste* **judgement**,
discrimination, discernment, tastefulness,
refinement, finesse, elegance, grace, style.
7 *the photo was rejected on grounds of taste*
decorum, propriety, etiquette, politeness,
delicacy, nicety, sensitivity, discretion,
tastefulness.
– OPPOSITES dislike.
▸ v. **1** *Adam tasted the wine* **sample**, test,
try, savour; sip, sup. **2** *he could taste blood*
perceive, discern, make out, distinguish. **3** *a
beer that tasted of cashews* **have a flavour**,
savour, smack, be reminiscent; suggest. **4** *it'll
be good to taste real coffee again* **consume**,
drink, partake of; eat, devour. **5** *he tasted
defeat* **experience**, encounter, come face to
face with, come up against, undergo; know.

> **WORD LINKS**
>
> **gustatory, gustative** relating to the sense of
> taste
> **palatable** pleasant to taste
> **supertaster** a person who is very sensitive to
> particular tastes

tasteful adj. **1** *the decor is simple and tasteful*
aesthetically pleasing, in good taste,
refined, cultured, elegant, stylish, smart,
chic, attractive, exquisite. **2** *this video is
erotic but tasteful* **decorous**, proper, seemly,
respectable, appropriate, modest.
– OPPOSITES tasteless, improper.

tasteless adj. **1** *the vegetables are tasteless*
flavourless, bland, insipid, unappetizing,
savourless, watery, weak. **2** *tasteless leather
panelling* **vulgar**, crude, tawdry, garish,
gaudy, loud, trashy, showy, ostentatious,
cheap, inelegant; informal flash, flashy,
tacky, kitsch; Brit. informal naff. **3** *a tasteless
remark* **crude**, vulgar, indelicate, uncouth,
crass, tactless, undiplomatic, indiscreet,
inappropriate, offensive.
– OPPOSITES tasty, tasteful, seemly.

tasty adj. **delicious**, palatable, luscious,
mouth-watering, delectable, ambrosial,
toothsome, dainty, flavoursome, flavourful;
appetizing, tempting; informal yummy,
scrummy, scrumptious, finger-licking,
moreish; dated flavorous.
– OPPOSITES bland.

t

tatters plural n. *the satin had frayed to tatters* **rags**, scraps, shreds, bits, pieces, ribbons.
□ **in tatters 1** *his clothes were in tatters* **ragged**, tattered, torn, ripped, frayed, in pieces, worn out, moth-eaten, falling to pieces, threadbare. **2** *her marriage is in tatters* **in ruins**, on the rocks, destroyed, finished, devastated.

tattle v. **1** *we were tattling about him* **gossip**, tittle-tattle, chatter, chat, prattle, babble, jabber, gabble, rattle on, jaw, yak, gab; Brit. informal natter, chinwag, chit-chat. **2** *I would tattle on her if I had evidence* **inform**; report, talk, tell all, spill the beans; informal squeal, sing, let the cat out of the bag.
▸ n. *tabloid tattle* **gossip**, rumour, tittle-tattle, hearsay, scandal.

taunt n. *the taunts of his classmates* **jeer**, jibe, sneer, insult, barb, catcall; (**taunts**) teasing, provocation, goading, derision, mockery; informal dig, put-down.
▸ v. *she taunted him about his job* **jeer at**, sneer at, scoff at, poke fun at, make fun of, get at, insult, tease, chaff, torment, goad, ridicule, deride, mock, heckle; N. Amer. ride; informal rib, needle, rag, guy.

taut adj. **1** *the rope was pulled taut* **tight**, stretched, rigid. **2** *his muscles remained taut* **flexed**, tense, hard, solid, firm, rigid, stiff. **3** *a taut expression* **fraught**, strained, stressed, tense; informal uptight. **4** *a taut tale of gang life* **concise**, controlled, crisp, pithy, sharp, succinct, compact, terse. **5** *he ran a taut ship* **orderly**, tight, trim, neat, disciplined, tidy, spruce, smart, shipshape (and Bristol fashion).
– OPPOSITES slack, relaxed.

tavern n. **bar**, inn, hostelry, taphouse; Brit. pub, public house; informal watering hole; Brit. informal local, boozer; dated alehouse; N. Amer. historical saloon.

tawdry adj. **gaudy**, flashy, showy, garish, loud; tasteless, vulgar, trashy, junky, cheap (and nasty), cheapjack, shoddy, shabby, gimcrack; informal rubbishy, tacky, kitsch.
– OPPOSITES tasteful.

tax n. **1** *higher taxes will dampen consumer spending* **duty**, excise, customs, dues; levy, tariff, toll, impost, tithe, charge, fee; VAT, community charge, income tax. **2** *a heavy tax on one's attention* **burden**, load, weight, demand, strain, pressure, stress, drain, imposition.
– OPPOSITES rebate.
▸ v. **1** *they tax foreign companies more harshly* **charge (duty on)**, tithe; formal mulct. **2** *his whining taxed her patience* **strain**, stretch, overburden, overload, encumber, push too far; overwhelm, try, wear out, exhaust, sap, drain, weary, weaken.

WORD LINKS
fiscal relating to government revenue raised through taxes
progressive referring to taxes that increase in rate as the amount taxed increases
regressive referring to taxes that take a proportionally greater amount from people on lower incomes

taxing adj. **demanding**, exacting, challenging, burdensome, arduous, onerous, difficult, hard, tough, laborious, back-breaking, strenuous, rigorous, punishing; tiring, exhausting, enervating, wearing, stressful; informal murderous.
– OPPOSITES easy.

teach v. **1** *she teaches small children* **educate**, instruct, school, tutor, coach, train; enlighten, illuminate, verse, indoctrinate; drill, discipline; formal edify. **2** *I taught English* **give lessons in**, lecture in, be a teacher of. **3** *teach your teenager how to negotiate* **train**, show, guide, instruct, demonstrate; instil, inculcate.

WORD LINKS
didactic, **pedagogic** intended to teach, or relating to teaching
pedagogy the profession or theory of teaching
academia the world of teaching and research conducted at universities
autodidact a self-taught person

teacher n. **educator**, tutor, instructor, master, mistress, schoolmarm, governess, educationist, preceptor; coach, trainer; lecturer, professor, don; guide, mentor, guru, counsellor; informal teach; Brit. informal beak; Austral./NZ informal chalkie, schoolie; formal pedagogue; historical schoolman.

team n. **1** *the sales team* **group**, squad, company, party, crew, troupe, band, side, line-up; informal bunch, gang, posse. **2** *a team of horses* **pair**, span, yoke, duo, set, tandem.
▸ v. **1** *the horses are teamed in pairs* **harness**, yoke, hitch, couple. **2** *team a T-shirt with matching shorts* **match**, coordinate, complement, pair up. **3** *team up with another artist for an exhibition* **join (forces)**, collaborate, get together, work together; unite, combine, cooperate, link, ally, associate, club together.

tear[1] v. **1** *I tore up the letter* **rip up**, rip in two, pull to pieces, shred. **2** *his flesh was torn* **lacerate**, cut (open), gash, slash, scratch, hack, pierce, stab; injure, wound. **3** *the traumas tore her family apart* **divide**, split, sever, break up, disunite, rupture; literary rend, sunder, cleave. **4** *Gina tore the book from his hands* **snatch**, grab, seize, rip, wrench, wrest, pull, pluck; informal yank. **5** informal *Jack tore down the street* **sprint**, race, run, dart, rush, dash, hasten, hurry, hare, bolt, fly, career, charge, shoot, hurtle, speed, whizz, zoom, go like lightning, go like the wind; informal pelt, scoot, hotfoot it, leg it, belt, zip, whip; Brit. informal go like the clappers, bomb, bucket; N. Amer. informal hightail it.
– OPPOSITES unite, stroll.
▸ n. *a tear in her dress* **rip**, hole, split, slash, slit; ladder, snag.
□ **tear something down** demolish, knock down, raze (to the ground), flatten, level, bulldoze; dismantle, disassemble.

tear[2] n. *tears in her eyes* **teardrop**.

◻ **in tears** crying, weeping, sobbing, wailing, howling, bawling, whimpering; tearful, upset; informal weepy, teary, blubbing, blubbering.

> **WORD LINKS**
> **lachrymal, lacrimal** connected with tears

tearaway n. **hooligan**, hoodlum, ruffian, lout, rowdy, roughneck; Austral. larrikin; informal yahoo; Brit. informal yob, yobbo; Scottish informal ned; Austral./NZ informal roughie.

tearful adj. **1** *Georgina was tearful* **close to tears**, emotional, upset, distressed, sad, unhappy; in tears, crying, weeping, sobbing, snivelling; informal weepy, teary; formal lachrymose. **2** *a tearful farewell* **emotional**, upsetting, distressing, sad, heartbreaking, sorrowful; poignant, moving, touching, tear-jerking; literary dolorous.
– OPPOSITES cheerful.

tease v. **make fun of**, poke fun at, chaff, laugh at, guy, make a monkey (out) of; taunt, bait, goad, pick on; deride, mock, ridicule; informal take the mickey out of, rag, send up, rib, josh, have on, pull someone's leg; Brit. informal wind up; N. Amer. informal pull someone's chain, razz; Austral./NZ informal poke mullock at; dated twit.

technical adj. **1** *an important technical achievement* **practical**, scientific, technological, high-tech. **2** *this might seem very technical* **specialist**, specialized, scientific; complex, complicated, esoteric. **3** *a technical fault* **mechanical**.

technique n. **1** *different techniques for solving the problem* **method**, approach, procedure, system, modus operandi, MO, way; means, strategy, tack, tactic, line; routine, practice. **2** *I was impressed with his technique* **skill**, ability, proficiency, expertise, mastery, talent, genius, artistry, craftsmanship; aptitude, adroitness, deftness, dexterity, facility, competence; performance, delivery; informal know-how.

tedious adj. **boring**, dull, monotonous, repetitive, unrelieved, unvaried, uneventful; characterless, colourless, lifeless, insipid, uninteresting, unexciting, uninspiring, flat, bland, dry, stale, tired, lacklustre, stodgy, dreary, humdrum, mundane; mind-numbing, soul-destroying, wearisome, tiring, tiresome, irksome, trying, frustrating; informal deadly, not up to much; Brit. informal samey; N. Amer. informal dullsville.
– OPPOSITES exciting.

tedium n. **monotony**, boredom, ennui, uniformity, routine, dreariness, dryness, banality, vapidity, insipidity.
– OPPOSITES variety.

teem[1] v. *the pond was teeming with fish* **be full of**, be filled with, be alive with, be brimming with, abound in, be swarming with; be packed with, be crawling with, be overrun by, bristle with, seethe with, be thick with; informal be jam-packed with, be chock-a-block with, be chock-full with.

teem[2] v. *the rain was teeming down* **pour**, pelt, tip, beat, lash, sheet; come down in torrents, rain cats and dogs; informal be chucking it down; Brit. informal bucket down.

teenage adj. **adolescent**, teenaged, youthful, young, juvenile; informal teen.

teenager n. **adolescent**, youth, young person, minor, juvenile; informal teen, teenybopper.

teeny adj. informal See **tiny**.

teeter v. **1** *Daisy teetered towards them* **totter**, wobble, toddle, sway, stagger, stumble, reel, lurch, pitch. **2** *the situation teetered between tragedy and farce* **see-saw**, veer, fluctuate, oscillate, swing, alternate, waver.

teetotal adj. **abstinent**, abstemious; sober, dry; informal on the wagon.
– OPPOSITES alcoholic.

telegram n. **telemessage**, telex; informal wire; dated radiogram; historical cable, cablegram.

telepathic adj. **psychic**, clairvoyant.

telepathy n. **mind reading**, thought transference; extrasensory perception, ESP; clairvoyance, sixth sense; psychometry.

telephone n. *Sophie picked up the telephone* **phone**, handset, receiver; Brit. mobile, mobile phone; N. Amer. cell, cell phone; informal blower; N. Amer. informal horn.
▸ v. *he telephoned me last night* **phone**, call, dial; get, reach; Brit. ring (up); informal call up, give someone a buzz, get on the blower to; Brit. informal give someone a bell, give someone a tinkle; N. Amer. informal get someone on the horn.

telescope n. **spyglass**; informal scope.
▸ v. **1** *the front of the car was telescoped* **concertina**, compact, compress, crush, squash. **2** *his experience can be telescoped into a paragraph* **condense**, shorten, reduce, abbreviate, abridge, summarize, precis, abstract, shrink, consolidate; truncate, curtail.

televise v. **broadcast**, screen, air, telecast; transmit, relay.

television n. **TV**; informal the small screen; Brit. informal telly, the box; N. Amer. informal the tube.

tell v. **1** *why didn't you tell me before?* **inform**, notify, apprise, let know, make aware, acquaint with, advise, put in the picture, brief, fill in; alert, warn; informal clue in/up. **2** *she told the story slowly* **relate**, recount, narrate, unfold, report, recite, describe, sketch, weave, spin; utter, voice, state, declare, communicate, impart, divulge. **3** *she told him to leave* **instruct**, order, command, direct, charge, enjoin, call on, require; literary bid. **4** *I tell you, I did nothing wrong* **assure**, promise, give one's word, swear, guarantee. **5** *the figures tell a different story* **reveal**, show, indicate, be evidence of, disclose, convey, signify. **6** *promise you won't tell?* **give the game away**, talk, tell tales, tattle; informal spill the beans, let the cat out of the bag, blab; Brit. informal blow the gaff. **7** *she was bound to tell on him* **inform on**, tell tales on, give away, denounce, sell out; informal split on,

blow the whistle on, rat on, peach on, squeal on; Brit. informal grass on, sneak on, shop; N. Amer. informal finger; Austral./NZ informal dob on. **8** *it was hard to tell what he said* **ascertain**, determine, work out, make out, deduce, discern, perceive, see, identify, recognize, understand, comprehend; informal figure out; Brit. informal suss out. **9** *he couldn't tell one from the other* **distinguish**, differentiate, discriminate. **10** *the strain began to tell on him* **take its toll**, leave its mark; affect.
□ **tell someone off** informal See **reprimand** (verb).

teller n. **1** *a bank teller* **cashier**, clerk. **2** *a teller of tales* **narrator**, raconteur; storyteller, anecdotalist.

telling adj. **revealing**, significant, weighty, important, meaningful, influential, striking, potent, powerful, compelling.
– OPPOSITES insignificant.

telling-off n. informal See **reprimand** (noun).

telltale adj. *the telltale blush on her face* **revealing**, revelatory, suggestive, meaningful, significant, meaning; informal giveaway.
▸ n. *'Sue did it,' said a telltale* **informer**, whistle-blower; N. Amer. tattletale; informal snitch, squealer; Brit. informal sneak; Scottish informal clype; dated talebearer.

temerity n. **audacity**, nerve, effrontery, impudence, impertinence, cheek, gall, presumption; daring; informal face, front, (brass) neck, chutzpah.

temper n. **1** *he walked out in a temper* **(fit of) rage**, fury, fit of pique, tantrum, (bad) mood, pet, sulk, huff; informal grump, snit; Brit. informal strop, paddy; Brit. informal dated bate, wax; N. Amer. informal hissy fit. **2** *a display of temper* **anger**, fury, rage, annoyance, vexation, irritation, irritability, ill humour, spleen, pique, petulance, testiness, tetchiness, crabbiness; Brit. informal stroppiness; literary ire, choler. **3** *she struggled to keep her temper* **composure**, equanimity, self-control, self-possession, sangfroid, calm, good humour; informal cool.
▸ v. **1** *the steel is tempered by heat* **harden**, strengthen, toughen, fortify, anneal. **2** *his idealism is tempered with realism* **moderate**, modify, modulate, mitigate, alleviate, reduce, weaken, lighten, soften.
□ **lose one's temper** get angry, fly into a rage, erupt, lose control, go berserk, breathe fire, flare up, boil over; informal go mad, go crazy, go bananas, have a fit, see red, fly off the handle, blow one's top, do one's nut, hit the roof, go off the deep end, go ape, flip, lose one's rag, freak out; Brit. informal go spare, go crackers, throw a wobbly.

temperament n. **disposition**, nature, character, personality, make-up, constitution, mind, spirit; stamp, mettle, mould; mood, frame of mind, attitude, outlook, humour.

temperamental adj. **1** *a temperamental chef* **volatile**, excitable, emotional, mercurial, capricious, erratic, unpredictable,

changeable, inconsistent; hot-headed, fiery, quick-tempered, irritable, irascible, impatient; touchy, moody, sensitive, oversensitive, highly strung, neurotic, melodramatic. **2** *a temperamental dislike of conflict* **inherent**, innate, natural, inborn, constitutional, deep-rooted, ingrained, congenital.
– OPPOSITES placid.

temperance n. **teetotalism**, abstinence, abstention, sobriety, self-restraint; prohibition.
– OPPOSITES alcoholism.

temperate adj. **1** *temperate climates* **mild**, clement, benign, gentle, balmy. **2** *he was temperate in his consumption* **self-restrained**, restrained, moderate, self-controlled, disciplined; abstemious, self-denying, austere, ascetic; teetotal, abstinent.
– OPPOSITES extreme.

tempest n. **storm**, gale, hurricane, superstorm; tornado, whirlwind, cyclone, typhoon.

tempestuous adj. **1** *the day was tempestuous* **stormy**, blustery, squally, wild, turbulent, windy, gusty, blowy, rainy; foul, nasty, inclement. **2** *the tempestuous political environment* **turbulent**, stormy, tumultuous, wild, lively, heated, explosive, feverish, frenetic, frenzied. **3** *a tempestuous woman* **emotional**, passionate, impassioned, fiery, intense; temperamental, volatile, excitable, mercurial, capricious, unpredictable, quick-tempered.
– OPPOSITES calm, peaceful, placid.

temple n. **house of God**, shrine, sanctuary; church, cathedral, mosque, synagogue, shul, gurdwara, mandir, pagoda; old use fane.

tempo n. **1** *the tempo of the music* **cadence**, speed, rhythm, beat, time, pulse; measure, metre. **2** *the tempo of life in Western society* **pace**, rate, speed, velocity.

temporal adj. **secular**, non-spiritual, worldly, profane, material, mundane, earthly, terrestrial; non-religious, lay.
– OPPOSITES spiritual.

temporarily adv. **1** *the girl was temporarily placed with a foster family* **for the time being**, for the moment, for now, for the present, in the interim, for the nonce, in/for the meantime, in the meanwhile; provisionally, pro tem; informal for the minute. **2** *he was temporarily blinded by the light* **briefly**, for a short time, momentarily, fleetingly.
– OPPOSITES permanently.

temporary adj. **1** *temporary accommodation | the temporary captain* **short-term**, interim; provisional, pro tem, makeshift, stopgap; acting, fill-in, stand-in, caretaker. **2** *a temporary loss of self-control* **brief**, short-lived, momentary, fleeting, passing.
– OPPOSITES permanent, lasting.

temporize v. **equivocate**, procrastinate, play for time, play a waiting game, stall, use delaying tactics, delay, hang back, prevaricate; Brit. hum and haw; rare tergiversate.

tempt v. **1** *the manager tried to tempt him to stay* **entice**, persuade, convince, inveigle, induce, cajole, coax, woo; informal sweet-talk. **2** *more customers are being tempted by credit* **allure**, attract, appeal to, whet the appetite of; lure, seduce, beguile, tantalize, draw.
– OPPOSITES discourage, deter.

temptation n. **1** *Mary resisted the temptation to answer back* **desire**, urge, itch, impulse, inclination. **2** *the temptations of London* **lure**, allurement, enticement, seduction, attraction, draw, pull; siren song. **3** *the temptation of travel to exotic locations* **allure**, appeal, attraction, fascination.

tempting adj. **1** *the tempting shops of the Via Nazionale* **enticing**, alluring, attractive, appealing, inviting, captivating, seductive, beguiling, fascinating, tantalizing; irresistible. **2** *a plate of tempting cakes* **appetizing**, mouth-watering, delicious, toothsome; informal scrumptious, scrummy, yummy.
– OPPOSITES off-putting, uninviting.

temptress n. **seductress**, siren, femme fatale, Mata Hari; informal vamp.

ten cardinal number **decade**.

> **WORD LINKS**
>
> **decimal** relating to a system of numbers based on ten
> **decagon** a plane figure with ten sides
> **decahedron** a solid figure with ten faces
> **decathlon** an athletic event consisting of ten different activities
> **decennial** lasting for or recurring every ten years
> **Decalogue** the Ten Commandments

tenable adj. **defensible**, justifiable, supportable, sustainable, arguable, able to hold water, reasonable, rational, sound, viable, plausible, credible, believable, conceivable.
– OPPOSITES indefensible.

tenacious adj. **1** *his tenacious grip* **firm**, tight, fast, clinging; strong, forceful, powerful, unshakeable, immovable, iron. **2** *a tenacious man* **persevering**, persistent, determined, dogged, strong-willed, tireless, indefatigable, resolute, patient, purposeful, unflagging, staunch, steadfast, untiring, unwavering, unswerving, unshakeable, unyielding, insistent; stubborn, intransigent, obstinate, obdurate, stiff-necked; N. Amer. rock-ribbed; formal pertinacious.
– OPPOSITES weak, irresolute.

tenacity n. **persistence**, determination, perseverance, doggedness, strength of purpose, bulldog spirit, tirelessness, indefatigability, resolution, resoluteness, resolve, firmness, patience, purposefulness, staunchness, steadfastness, staying power, application; stubbornness, intransigence, obstinacy, obduracy; formal pertinacity.

tenancy n. **occupancy**, occupation, period of occupancy/occupation, residence, habitation, holding, possession; tenure, lease, rental, leasehold.

tenant n. **occupant**, resident, inhabitant; leaseholder, lessee, renter; Brit. occupier, sitting tenant.
– OPPOSITES owner, freeholder.

tend[1] v. **1** *I tend to get very involved in my work* **be inclined**, be apt, be disposed, be prone, be liable, have a tendency, have a propensity. **2** *younger voters tended towards the tabloid press* **incline**, lean, gravitate, move; prefer, favour; N. Amer. trend.

tend[2] v. *she tended her cattle* **look after**, take care of, care for, minister to, attend to, see to, wait on; watch over, keep an eye on, mind, protect, watch, guard; nurse, nurture, cherish.
– OPPOSITES neglect.

tendency n. **1** *his tendency to take the law into his own hands* **propensity**, proclivity, proneness, aptness, likelihood, inclination, disposition, predisposition, bent, leaning, penchant, predilection, susceptibility, liability; readiness; habit. **2** *this tendency towards cohabitation* **trend**, movement, drift, swing, gravitation, direction, course; orientation, bias.

tender[1] adj. **1** *a gentle, tender man* **caring**, kind, kindly, kind-hearted, soft-hearted, tender-hearted, compassionate, sympathetic, warm, warm-hearted, fatherly, motherly, maternal, gentle, mild, benevolent, generous, giving, humane. **2** *a tender kiss* **affectionate**, fond, loving, emotional, warm, gentle, soft; amorous, adoring; informal lovey-dovey. **3** *tender love songs* **romantic**, sentimental, emotional, emotive, touching, moving, poignant; Brit. informal soppy. **4** *simmer until the meat is tender* **easily chewed**, soft; succulent, juicy; tenderized. **5** *tender plants* **delicate**, easily damaged, fragile. **6** *her ankle was swollen and tender* **sore**, painful, sensitive, inflamed, raw, red, chafed, bruised; hurting, aching, throbbing, smarting. **7** *the tender age of fifteen* **young**, youthful; impressionable, inexperienced, immature, unsophisticated, unseasoned, juvenile, callow, green, raw; informal wet behind the ears. **8** *the issue of conscription was a particularly tender one* **difficult**, delicate, tricky, awkward, problematic, troublesome, ticklish; controversial, emotive; informal sticky.
– OPPOSITES hard-hearted, callous, tough.

tender[2] v. **1** *she tendered her resignation* **offer**, proffer, present, put forward, propose, suggest, advance, submit, extend, give, render; hand in. **2** *firms of interior decorators tendered for the work* **put in a bid**, bid, quote, give an estimate.
▸ n. *six contractors were invited to submit tenders* **bid**, offer, quotation, quote, estimate, price; proposal, submission.

tender-hearted adj. See **tender**[1] (sense 1).

tenderness n. **1** *I felt an enormous tenderness for her* **affection**, fondness, love, devotion, loving kindness, emotion, sentiment. **2** *with unexpected tenderness, he told her what had happened* **kindness**, kindliness, kind-heartedness, tender-

t

heartedness, compassion, care, concern, sympathy, warmth, fatherliness, motherliness, gentleness, benevolence, generosity. **3** *abdominal tenderness* **soreness**, pain, inflammation, bruising; ache, aching, smarting, throbbing.

tenet n. **principle**, belief, doctrine, precept, creed, credo, article of faith, dogma, canon; theory, thesis, conviction, idea, view, opinion, position, hypothesis, postulation; (**tenets**) ideology, code of belief, teaching(s).

tenor n. **1** *the general tenor of his speech* **sense**, meaning, theme, drift, thread, import, purport, intent, intention, burden, thrust, significance, message; gist, essence, substance, spirit. **2** *the even tenor of life in the village* **course**, direction, movement, drift, current, trend.

tense adj. **1** *the tense muscles of his neck* **taut**, tight, rigid, stretched, strained, stiff. **2** *Loretta was feeling tense and irritable* **anxious**, nervous, on edge, edgy, strained, stressed, under pressure, agitated, ill at ease, uneasy, nervy, restless, worked up, keyed up, overwrought, on tenterhooks, with one's stomach in knots, worried, apprehensive, panicky; informal a bundle of nerves, jittery, jumpy, twitchy, uptight, stressed out; N. Amer. informal spooky, squirrelly. **3** *a tense moment* **nerve-racking**, stressful, anxious, worrying, fraught, charged, strained, nail-biting, difficult, uneasy, uncomfortable; exciting, cliffhanging, knife-edge.
– OPPOSITES slack, calm.
▶v. *Hebden tensed his muscles* **tighten**, tauten, tense up, flex, contract, brace, stiffen; screw up, knot, strain, stretch; N. Amer. squinch up.
– OPPOSITES relax.

tension n. **1** *the tension of the rope* **tightness**, tautness, rigidity; pull, traction. **2** *the tension was unbearable* **strain**, stress, anxiety, pressure; worry, apprehensiveness, apprehension, agitation, nerves, nervousness, jumpiness, edginess, restlessness; suspense, uncertainty, anticipation, excitement; informal butterflies (in one's stomach), collywobbles. **3** *months of tension between the military and the government* **strained relations**, strain; ill feeling, friction, antagonism, antipathy, hostility, enmity.

tentative adj. **1** *tentative arrangements | a tentative conclusion* **provisional**, unconfirmed, pencilled in, preliminary, to be confirmed, TBC, subject to confirmation; speculative, conjectural, untried, unproven, exploratory, experimental, trial, test, pilot. **2** *he took a few tentative steps* **hesitant**, uncertain, cautious, timid, hesitating, faltering, shaky, unsteady, halting; wavering, unsure.
– OPPOSITES definite, confident.

tenterhooks plural n.
□ **on tenterhooks** in suspense, waiting with bated breath; anxious, nervous, nervy, apprehensive, worried, worried sick,

on edge, edgy, tense, strained, stressed, agitated, restless, worked up, keyed up, with one's stomach in knots, with one's heart in one's mouth, like a cat on a hot tin roof; informal with butterflies in one's stomach, jittery, jumpy, twitchy, in a state, uptight; N. Amer. informal spooky, squirrelly.

tenuous adj. **1** *a tenuous connection* **slight**, insubstantial, flimsy, weak, doubtful, dubious, questionable, suspect; vague, nebulous, hazy. **2** *a tenuous thread* **fine**, thin, slender, delicate, gossamer, fragile.
– OPPOSITES convincing, strong.

tenure n. **1** *residents should have security of tenure* **tenancy**, occupancy, holding, occupation, residence; possession, title, ownership. **2** *his tenure as Secretary of State for Industry* **incumbency**, term (of office), period (of/in office), time (in office).

tepid adj. **1** *tepid water* **lukewarm**, warmish, slightly warm; at room temperature. **2** *a tepid response* **unenthusiastic**, apathetic, half-hearted, indifferent, cool, lukewarm, uninterested; informal unenthused.
– OPPOSITES hot, cold, enthusiastic.

term n. **1** *scientific and technical terms* **word**, expression, phrase, turn of phrase, idiom, locution; name, title, designation, label; formal appellation, denomination. **2** *a protest in the strongest terms* **language**, mode of expression, manner of speaking, phraseology, terminology; words, phrases, expressions. **3** *the terms of the contract* **conditions**, stipulations, specifications, provisions, provisos; restrictions, qualifications; particulars, details, points. **4** *a policy offering more favourable terms* **rates**, prices, charges, costs, fees; tariff. **5** *the President is elected for a four-year term* **period**, period of time, length of time, spell, stint, duration; stretch, run; period of office, incumbency. **6** old use *the whole term of your natural life* **duration**, length, span. **7** *the summer term* **session**; N. Amer. semester, trimester, quarter.
▶v. *he has been termed the father of modern theology* **call**, name, entitle, title, style, designate, describe as, dub, label, tag; nickname; formal denominate.
□ **come to terms 1** *the two sides came to terms* **reach an agreement/understanding**, make a deal, reach a compromise, meet each other halfway. **2** *she eventually came to terms with her situation* **accept**, come to accept, reconcile oneself to, learn to live with, become resigned to, make the best of; face up to.

terminal adj. **1** *a terminal illness* **incurable**, untreatable, inoperable; fatal, mortal, deadly. **2** *terminal patients* **dying**, near death; incurable. **3** *a terminal bonus may be payable when a policy matures* **final**, last, concluding, closing, end. **4** informal *you're making a terminal ass of yourself* **complete**, utter, absolute, total, real, thorough, out-and-out, downright, perfect; Brit. informal right, proper; Austral./NZ informal fair.

▶ **n. 1** *a railway terminal* **station**, last stop, end of the line; depot; Brit. terminus. **2** *a computer terminal* **workstation**, VDU, visual display unit.

terminate v. **1** *treatment was terminated* **bring to an end**, end, bring to a close/conclusion, close, conclude, finish, stop, put an end to, wind up, discontinue, cease, cut short, abort, axe; informal pull the plug on. **2** *the train will terminate in Stratford* **end its journey**, finish up, stop. **3** *the pregnancy was terminated* **abort**, end.
– OPPOSITES begin, start, continue.

termination n. **1** *the termination of a contract* **ending**, end, closing, close, conclusion, finish, stopping, winding up, discontinuance, discontinuation; cancellation, dissolution; informal wind-up. **2** *she had a termination* **abortion**; rare feticide.
– OPPOSITES start, beginning.

terminology n. **phraseology**, terms, expressions, words, language, parlance, vocabulary, nomenclature; usage, idiom; jargon, cant, argot; informal lingo, -speak, -ese.

terminus n. Brit. *the bus terminus* **station**, last stop, end of the line, terminal; depot, garage.

terrain n. **land**, ground, territory; topography, landscape, countryside, country.

terrestrial adj. **earthly**, worldly, mundane, earthbound; literary sublunary.

terrible adj. **1** *a terrible crime* | *terrible injuries* **dreadful**, awful, appalling, horrific, horrifying, horrible, horrendous, atrocious, abominable, abhorrent, frightful, shocking, hideous, ghastly, grim, dire, unspeakable, gruesome, monstrous, sickening, heinous, vile; serious, grave, acute; formal grievous. **2** *a terrible smell* **nasty**, disgusting, awful, dreadful, ghastly, horrid, horrible, vile, foul, abominable, frightful, loathsome, revolting, repulsive, odious, nauseating, repellent, horrendous, hideous, appalling, offensive, objectionable, obnoxious; informal gruesome, putrid, diabolical, yucky, sick-making, God-awful, gross, rank; Brit. informal beastly; old use disgustful. **3** *he was in terrible pain* **severe**, extreme, intense, excruciating, agonizing, unbearable, intolerable, unendurable. **4** *that's a terrible thing to say* **unkind**, nasty, unpleasant, foul, obnoxious, vile, contemptible, despicable, wretched, shabby; spiteful, mean, malicious, poisonous, mean-spirited, cruel, hateful, hurtful; unfair, uncharitable, uncalled for, below the belt, unwarranted; Brit. informal beastly. **5** *the film was terrible* **very bad**, dreadful, awful, frightful, appalling, abysmal, atrocious, hopeless, poor; informal pathetic, pitiful, useless, lousy, dire; Brit. informal duff, chronic, poxy, rubbish, pants. **6** informal *you're a terrible flirt* **incorrigible**, outrageous; real, awful, dreadful, frightful, shocking; informal impossible, fearful; Brit. informal right, proper. **7** *I feel terrible—I've been in bed all day* **ill**, poorly, sick, queasy, nauseous, nauseated, green about the gills; faint, dizzy; informal rough, lousy, awful, dreadful; Brit. informal grotty, ropy. **8** *he still feels terrible about what he did to John* **guilty**, conscience-stricken, remorseful, guilt-ridden, ashamed, chastened, contrite, sorry.
– OPPOSITES minor, slight, pleasant, wonderful.

terribly adv. **1** informal *she's terribly upset* **very**, extremely, really, terrifically, tremendously, immensely, thoroughly, dreadfully, exceptionally, remarkably, extraordinarily, exceedingly; N. English right; informal awfully, devilishly, seriously, majorly; Brit. informal jolly, ever so, dead, well; N. Amer. informal real, mighty, awful; informal dated frightfully; old use exceeding. **2** *he played terribly* **very badly**, atrociously, awfully, dreadfully, appallingly, abysmally, execrably; informal pitifully, diabolically. **3** informal *I shall miss you terribly* **very much**, greatly, a great deal, a lot; informal loads.

terrific adj. **1** *a terrific bang* **tremendous**, huge, massive, gigantic, colossal, mighty, great, prodigious, formidable, sizeable, considerable; intense, extreme, extraordinary; informal mega, whopping great, humongous; Brit. informal whacking great, ginormous. **2** informal *a terrific game of top-quality football* **marvellous**, wonderful, sensational, outstanding, superb, excellent, first-rate, first-class, dazzling, out of this world, breathtaking; informal great, fantastic, fabulous, fab, mega, super, ace, magic, cracking, cool, wicked, awesome; Brit. informal brilliant, brill, smashing; Austral./NZ informal bonzer; Brit. informal dated spiffing. **3** old use *terrific scenes of slaughter and destruction* **dreadful**, terrible, appalling, awful, horrific, horrible, horrendous, horrifying, hideous, grim, ghastly, gruesome, frightful, fearful.

terrified adj. **petrified**, frightened, scared, scared/frightened to death, scared stiff, scared/frightened out of one's wits, scared witless, horrified, with one's heart in one's mouth, shaking in one's shoes.

terrify v. **petrify**, horrify, frighten, scare, scare/frighten to death, scare/frighten the living daylights out of, scare/frighten the life out of, scare/frighten someone out of their wits, scare witless, strike terror into, put the fear of God into; paralyse, transfix; informal scare the pants off; Irish informal scare the bejesus out of.

territory n. **1** *British overseas territories* **area of land**, area, region, enclave; country, state, land, dependency, colony, dominion, protectorate, fief, possession, holding. **2** *mountainous territory* **terrain**, land, ground, countryside. **3** *the territory of biblical scholarship* **domain**, area of concern/interest/knowledge, province, department, field, preserve, sphere, arena, realm, world. **4** *Sheffield was his territory* **sphere of operations**, area, section; informal turf; Brit. informal patch, manor.

t

terror n. **1** *she screamed in terror* **fear**, dread, horror, fear and trembling, fright, alarm, panic, shock. **2** *the terrors of her own mind* **demon**, fiend, devil, monster; horror, nightmare. **3** informal *he turned out to be a right little terror* **rascal**, devil, imp, monkey, scallywag, mischief-maker; informal scamp, horror; Brit. informal perisher; N. English informal scally; N. Amer. informal varmint.

terrorist n. **bomber**, arsonist; gunman, assassin; hijacker; revolutionary, radical, guerrilla, urban guerrilla, anarchist, freedom fighter.

terrorize v. **persecute**, victimize, torment, tyrannize, intimidate, menace, threaten, bully, browbeat; scare, frighten, terrify, petrify; Brit. informal put the frighteners on.

terse adj. **brief**, short, to the point, concise, succinct, crisp, pithy, incisive, short and sweet, laconic, elliptical; **brusque**, abrupt, curt, clipped, blunt, ungracious.
– OPPOSITES long-winded, polite.

test n. **1** *a series of scientific tests* **trial**, experiment, pilot study, try-out; check, examination, assessment, evaluation, appraisal, investigation, inspection, analysis, scrutiny, study, probe, exploration; screening; technical assay. **2** *candidates may be required to take a test* **exam**, examination; N. Amer. quiz. **3** *the test of a good sparkling wine* **criterion**, proof, indication, yardstick, touchstone, standard, measure, litmus test, acid test.
▶v. **1** *a small-scale prototype was tested* **try out**, trial, put to the test, put through its paces, experiment with, pilot; check, examine, assess, evaluate, appraise, investigate, analyse, scrutinize, study, probe, explore; sample; screen; technical assay. **2** *such behaviour would test any marriage* **put a strain on**, strain, tax, try; make demands on, stretch, challenge.

testament n. *an achievement which is a testament to his professionalism and dedication* **testimony**, witness, evidence, proof, attestation; demonstration, indication, exemplification; monument, tribute.

testify v. **1** *you may be required to testify in court* **give evidence**, bear witness, be a witness, give one's testimony, attest; Law make a deposition. **2** *he testified that he had been threatened by a fellow officer* **attest**, swear, state on oath, state, declare, assert, affirm; allege, submit, claim; Law depose. **3** *the exhibits testify to the talents of the local sculptors* **be evidence/proof of**, attest to, confirm, prove, corroborate, substantiate, bear out; show, demonstrate, bear witness to, indicate, reveal, bespeak.

testimonial n. **reference**, character reference, letter of recommendation, commendation.

testimony n. **1** *Smith was in court to hear her testimony* **evidence**, sworn statement, attestation, affidavit; statement, declaration, assertion, affirmation; allegation, submission, claim; Law deposition. **2** *the work is a testimony to his professional commitment* **testament**, proof, evidence, attestation, witness; confirmation, corroboration; demonstration, indication.

testing adj. **difficult**, challenging, tough, hard, demanding, taxing, stressful.
– OPPOSITES easy.

testy adj. See **tetchy**.

tetchy adj. **irritable**, cantankerous, irascible, bad-tempered, grumpy, grouchy, crotchety, crabby, testy, crusty, curmudgeonly, ill-tempered, ill-humoured, peevish, cross, fractious, pettish, crabbed, prickly, waspish; informal snappish, snappy, chippy; Brit. informal shirty, stroppy, narky, ratty; N. Amer. informal cranky, ornery.
– OPPOSITES good-humoured.

tête-à-tête n. **conversation**, chat, talk, heart-to-heart, one-on-one, one-to-one; informal confab; Brit. informal natter, chinwag; Austral. informal convo; formal confabulation.

tether v. *the horse had been tethered to a post* **tie (up)**, hitch, rope, chain; fasten, secure.
– OPPOSITES unleash.
▶n. *a dog on a tether* **rope**, chain, cord, lead, leash; restraint; halter.
◻ **at the end of one's tether** at one's wits' end, desperate, not knowing which way to turn, unable to cope; N. Amer. at the end of one's rope.

text n. **1** *a text which explores pain and grief* **book**, textbook, work, publication. **2** *the pictures are clear and relate well to the text* **words**, wording; content, body, main body. **3** *a text from the First Book of Samuel* **passage**, extract, quotation, verse, line; reading. **4** *he took as his text the fact that Australia is a paradise* **theme**, subject, topic, motif; thesis, argument.

textile n. **fabric**, cloth, material.

texture n. **feel**, touch; appearance, finish, surface, grain; quality, consistency; weave, nap.

thank v. **express (one's) gratitude to**, express one's thanks to, offer/extend thanks to, say thank you to, show one's appreciation to.

thankful adj. **grateful**, filled with gratitude, relieved, pleased, glad.

thankless adj. **1** *a thankless task* **unenviable**, difficult, unpleasant, unrewarding; unappreciated, unrecognized, unacknowledged. **2** *her thankless children* **ungrateful**, unappreciative, unthankful.
– OPPOSITES rewarding, grateful.

thanks plural n. *they expressed their thanks and wished her well* **gratitude**, appreciation; acknowledgement, recognition, credit.
▶exclam. *thanks for being so helpful* **thank you**, many thanks, thanks very much, thanks a lot, thank you kindly, much obliged, much appreciated, bless you; informal cheers, thanks a million; Brit. informal ta.
◻ **thanks to** as a result of, owing to, due to, because of, through, as a consequence of, on

t

account of, by virtue of, by dint of; formal by reason of.

thaw v. **melt**, unfreeze, soften, liquefy, dissolve; defrost; N. Amer. unthaw.
– OPPOSITES freeze.

theatre n. **1** *the local theatre* **playhouse**, auditorium, amphitheatre. **2** *what made you want to go into the theatre?* **acting**, performing, the stage; drama, the dramatic arts, dramaturgy, the thespian art; show business; informal the boards, showbiz. **3** *the lecture theatre* **hall**, room, auditorium. **4** *the theatre of war* **scene**, arena, field/sphere of action.

theatrical adj. **1** *a theatrical career* **stage**, dramatic, thespian, dramaturgical; show-business; informal showbiz; formal histrionic. **2** *Henry looked over his shoulder with theatrical caution* **exaggerated**, ostentatious, actressy, stagy, showy, melodramatic, overacted, overdone, histrionic, actorly, affected, mannered; informal hammy, ham, camp.

theft n. **robbery**, stealing, thieving, larceny, thievery, shoplifting, burglary, misappropriation, embezzlement; raid, hold-up; informal smash-and-grab; N. Amer. informal heist, stick-up; formal peculation.

> **WORD LINKS**
> **kleptomania** compulsive theft

theme n. **1** *the theme of her speech* **subject**, topic, subject matter, matter, thesis, argument, text, burden, thrust; thread, motif, trope, keynote. **2** *the first violin takes up the theme* **melody**, tune, air; motif, leitmotif.

then adv. **1** *I was living in Cairo then* **at that time**, in those days; at that point (in time), at that moment, on that occasion. **2** *she won the first and then the second game* **next**, after that, afterwards, subsequently. **3** *and then there's another problem* **in addition**, also, besides, as well, additionally, on top of that, over and above that, moreover, furthermore, what's more, to boot; too. **4** *well, if that's what he wants, then he should leave* **in that case**, that being so, it follows that.

theological adj. **religious**, scriptural, ecclesiastical, doctrinal; divine, holy.

theoretical adj. **hypothetical**, conjectural, academic, suppositional, speculative, notional, postulatory, assumed, presumed, untested, unproven, unsubstantiated; conceptual, abstract.
– OPPOSITES actual, real.

theorize v. **speculate**, conjecture, hypothesize, postulate, propose, posit, suppose.

theory n. **1** *I reckon that confirms my theory* **hypothesis**, thesis, conjecture, supposition, speculation, postulation, postulate, proposition, premise, surmise, assumption, presupposition; opinion, view, belief, contention. **2** *modern economic theory* **principles**, ideas, concepts; philosophy,

ideology, system of ideas, science.
□ **in theory** in principle, on paper, in the abstract, all things being equal, in an ideal world; hypothetically.

therapeutic adj. **healing**, curative, remedial, medicinal, restorative, health-giving, tonic, reparative, corrective, beneficial, good, salutary; calming, relaxing, soothing; old use sanative.
– OPPOSITES harmful.

therapist n. **psychologist**, psychotherapist, analyst, psychoanalyst, psychiatrist; informal shrink; Brit. humorous trick cyclist.

therapy n. **1** *a wide range of complementary therapies* **treatment**, remedy, cure. **2** *he's currently in therapy* **psychotherapy**, psychoanalysis, analysis.

thereabouts adv. **1** *the land thereabouts* **near there**, around there. **2** *they sold it for five million or thereabouts* **approximately**, or so, give or take a bit, plus or minus a bit, in round numbers, not far off; Brit. getting on for; N. Amer. informal in the ballpark of.

thereafter adv. **after that**, following that, afterwards, subsequently, then, next.

therefore adv. **consequently**, so, as a result, hence, thus, accordingly, for that reason, ergo, that being the case, on that account; formal whence; old use wherefore.

thesis n. **1** *the central thesis of his lecture* **theory**, contention, argument, line of argument, proposal, proposition, premise, assumption, hypothesis, postulation, surmise, supposition. **2** *a doctoral thesis* **dissertation**, essay, paper, treatise, disquisition, composition, monograph, study; N. Amer. theme.

thick adj. **1** *the walls are five feet thick* **in extent/diameter**, across, wide, broad, deep. **2** *his short, thick legs* **stocky**, sturdy, chunky, hefty, thickset, beefy, meaty, big, solid; fat, stout, plump. **3** *a thick Aran sweater* **chunky**, bulky, heavy, cable-knit; woollen, woolly. **4** *the station was thick with people* **crowded**, full, filled, packed, teeming, seething, swarming, crawling, crammed, thronged, bursting at the seams, solid, overflowing, choked, jammed, congested; informal jam-packed, chock-a-block, stuffed; Austral./NZ informal chocker. **5** *the thick summer vegetation* **plentiful**, abundant, profuse, luxuriant, bushy, rich, riotous, exuberant, rank, rampant; dense, close-packed, impenetrable, impassable; serried; informal jungly. **6** *a thick paste* **semi-solid**, firm, stiff, stiffened, heavy; clotted, coagulated, viscid, viscous, gelatinous; concentrated. **7** *thick fog* **dense**, heavy, opaque, impenetrable, soupy, murky. **8** informal *he's a bit thick.* See **stupid** (sense 1). **9** *Guy's voice was thick with desire* **husky**, hoarse, throaty, guttural, gravelly, rough. **10** *a thick Scottish accent* **obvious**, pronounced, marked, broad, strong, rich, decided, distinct. **11** *she's very thick with him* **friendly**, intimate, familiar, on the best of terms, hand in glove; close to, devoted to, inseparable from; informal pally, chummy,

t

matey, buddy-buddy, as thick as thieves, well in.
– OPPOSITES thin, slender, sparse.

▸ n. *in the thick of the crisis* **midst**, centre, hub, middle, core, heart.

□ **a bit thick** Brit. informal unreasonable, unfair, unjust, unjustified, uncalled for, unwarranted, unnecessary, excessive; informal below the belt, a bit much; Brit. informal out of order.

thicken v. **become thick/thicker**, stiffen, condense; solidify, set, gel, congeal, clot, coagulate, cake, inspissate.

thicket n. **copse**, coppice, grove, brake, covert, clump; wood; Brit. spinney; old use hurst.

thickhead n. informal See **fool** (sense 1 of the noun).

thickness n. **1** *the gateway is several feet in thickness* **width**, breadth, depth, diameter. **2** *several thicknesses of limestone* **layer**, stratum, stratification, seam, vein; sheet, lamina.

thickset adj. **stocky**, sturdy, heavily built, well built, chunky, burly, strapping, brawny, solid, heavy, hefty, beefy, meaty; Physiology pyknic.
– OPPOSITES slight.

thick-skinned adj. **insensitive**, unfeeling, tough, impervious, hardened, case-hardened; informal hard-boiled.
– OPPOSITES sensitive.

thief n. **robber**, burglar, housebreaker, cat burglar, shoplifter, pickpocket, sneak thief, mugger; embezzler, swindler; criminal, villain; kleptomaniac; bandit, pirate, highwayman; informal crook, cracksman; Brit. rhyming slang tea leaf; literary brigand.

thieve v. **steal**, take, purloin, help oneself to, snatch, pilfer; embezzle, misappropriate; have one's fingers/hand in the till; informal rob, swipe, nab, rip off, lift, 'liberate', 'borrow', filch, snaffle; Brit. informal nick, pinch, half-inch, whip, knock off, nobble; N. Amer. informal heist; formal peculate.

thievery n. See **thieving**.

thieving n. **theft**, stealing, thievery, robbery, larceny, pilfering; burglary, shoplifting, embezzlement; formal peculation.

thin adj. **1** *a thin white line* **narrow**, fine, attenuated. **2** *a thin cotton nightdress* **lightweight**, light, fine, delicate, floaty, flimsy, diaphanous, gossamer, insubstantial; sheer, gauzy, filmy, chiffony, transparent, see-through. **3** *a tall, thin woman* **slim**, lean, slender, rangy, willowy, svelte, sylphlike, spare, slight; **skinny**, underweight, scrawny, scraggy, bony, angular, raw-boned, hollow-cheeked, gaunt, as thin as a rake/reed, stick-like, skin and bone, emaciated, skeletal, wasted, pinched, undernourished, underfed; lanky, spindly, gangly, gangling, weedy; informal anorexic, like a bag of bones; dated spindle-shanked; old use starveling. **4** *his thin grey hair* **sparse**, scanty, wispy, thinning. **5** *a bowl of thin soup* **watery**, weak, dilute,

diluted; runny, sloppy. **6** *her thin voice* **weak**, faint, feeble, small, soft; reedy, high-pitched. **7** *the plot is very thin* **insubstantial**, flimsy, slight, feeble, lame, poor, weak, tenuous, inadequate, insufficient, unconvincing, unbelievable, implausible.
– OPPOSITES thick, broad, fat, abundant.

▸ v. **1** *some paint must be thinned down before use* **dilute**, water down, weaken. **2** *the crowds were beginning to thin out* **disperse**, dissipate, scatter; become less dense/numerous, decrease, diminish, dwindle.

thing n. **1** *the room was full of strange things* **object**, article, item, artefact, commodity; device, gadget, instrument, utensil, tool, implement; entity, body; informal doodah, whatsit, whatchamacallit, thingummy, thingy, thingamabob, thingamajig; Brit. informal gubbins; N. Amer. informal doodad, dingus. **2** *I'll come back tomorrow to collect my things* **belongings**, possessions, stuff, property, worldly goods, (personal) effects, paraphernalia, bits and pieces, bits and bobs; luggage, baggage, bags; Law goods and chattels; informal gear, junk; Brit. informal clobber. **3** *his gardening things* **equipment**, apparatus, gear, kit, tackle, stuff; implements, tools, utensils; accoutrements. **4** *I've got several things to do today* **activity**, act, action, deed, undertaking, exploit, feat; task, job, chore. **5** *I've got other things on my mind just now* **thought**, notion, idea; concern, matter, worry, preoccupation. **6** *I keep remembering things he said* **remark**, statement, comment, utterance, observation, declaration, pronouncement. **7** *quite a few odd things happened* **incident**, episode, event, happening, occurrence, phenomenon. **8** *how are things with you?* **matters**, affairs, circumstances, conditions, relations; state of affairs, situation, life. **9** *one of the things I like about you is your optimism* **characteristic**, quality, attribute, property, trait, feature, point, aspect, facet. **10** *there's another thing you should know* **fact**, piece of information, point, detail, particular, factor. **11** *the thing is, I'm not sure if it's what I want* **fact of the matter**, fact, point, issue, problem. **12** *you lucky thing!* **person**, soul, creature, wretch; informal devil, beggar, bastard. **13** *Dora developed a thing about noise* **phobia**, fear, dislike, aversion; obsession, fixation; complex, neurosis; informal hang-up, bee in one's bonnet. **14** *she had a thing about men who wore glasses* **penchant**, preference, taste, inclination, partiality, predilection, soft spot, weakness, fancy, fondness, liking, love; fetish, obsession, fixation. **15** *books aren't really my thing* **what one likes**, what interests one; informal one's cup of tea, one's bag, what turns one on. **16** *it's the latest thing* **fashionable**, in fashion, popular, all the rage; informal trendy, cool, big, hip, happening.

think v. **1** *I think he's gone home* **believe**, be of the opinion, be of the view, be under the impression; expect, imagine, anticipate; surmise, suppose, conjecture, guess, fancy;

t

conclude, determine, reason; informal reckon, figure; formal opine; old use ween. **2** *his family was thought to be enormously rich* **deem**, judge, hold, reckon, consider, presume, estimate; regard as, view as. **3** *Jack thought for a moment* **ponder**, reflect, deliberate, consider, meditate, contemplate, muse, ruminate, be lost in thought, be in a brown study, brood; concentrate, rack one's brains; informal put on one's thinking cap, sleep on it; formal cogitate. **4** *she thought of all the visits she had made to her father* **recall**, remember, recollect, call to mind, think back to. **5** *she forced herself to think of how he must be feeling* **imagine**, picture, visualize, envisage; dream about, fantasize about.
□ **think better of** have second thoughts about, think twice about, think again about, change one's mind about; reconsider, decide against; informal get cold feet about.
think something over consider, contemplate, deliberate about, weigh up, consider the pros and cons of, mull over, ponder, reflect on, muse on, ruminate on.
think something up devise, dream up, come up with, invent, create, concoct, make up; hit on.

thinker n. **theorist**, ideologist, philosopher, scholar, savant, sage, intellectual, intellect, mind; informal brain.

thinking adj. *he seemed a thinking man* **intelligent**, sensible, reasonable, rational; logical, analytical; thoughtful, reflective, meditative, contemplative, pensive, philosophical.
– OPPOSITES stupid, irrational.
▶ n. *the thinking behind the campaign* **reasoning**, idea(s), theory, thoughts, line of thought, philosophy, beliefs; opinion(s), view(s), position, judgement, assessment, evaluation.

thin-skinned adj. **sensitive**, oversensitive, hypersensitive, easily upset/offended/hurt, touchy, defensive.
– OPPOSITES insensitive.

third-rate adj. **substandard**, bad, inferior, poor, poor-quality, low-grade, inadequate, unsatisfactory, unacceptable, appalling, abysmal, atrocious, awful, terrible, dreadful, execrable, frightful, miserable, wretched, pitiful; jerry-built, shoddy, tinny, trashy; N. Amer. cheapjack; informal lousy, diabolical, rotten, dire, bum, crummy, rubbishy; Brit. informal ropy, duff, pants.
– OPPOSITES excellent.

thirst n. **1** *I need a drink—I'm dying of thirst* **thirstiness**, dryness; dehydration; Medicine polydipsia; old use drought. **2** *his thirst for knowledge* **craving**, desire, longing, yearning, hunger, hankering, keenness, eagerness, lust, appetite; informal yen, itch; old use appetency.
▶ v. *she thirsted for power* **crave**, want, covet, desire, hunger for, lust after, hanker after, have one's heart set on; wish, long.

thirsty adj. **1** *the boys were hot and thirsty longing for a drink*, dry, dehydrated;

informal parched, gasping; Brit. informal spitting feathers; Austral./NZ informal spitting chips. **2** *the thirsty soil* **dry**, arid, dried up/out, as dry as a bone, parched, baked, desiccated. **3** *she was thirsty for power* **eager**, hungry, greedy, thirsting, craving, longing, yearning, lusting, burning, desirous, hankering; informal itching, dying.

thorn n. **prickle**, spike, barb, spine.

thorny adj. **1** *dense thorny undergrowth* **prickly**, spiky, barbed, spiny, sharp; technical spinose, spinous. **2** *the thorny subject of confidentiality* **problematic**, tricky, ticklish, delicate, controversial, awkward, difficult, knotty, tough, taxing, trying, troublesome; complicated, complex, involved, intricate; vexed; informal sticky.

thorough adj. **1** *a thorough investigation* **rigorous**, in-depth, exhaustive, thoroughgoing, minute, detailed, close, meticulous, methodical, careful, complete, comprehensive, full, extensive, widespread, sweeping, all-embracing, all-inclusive. **2** *he is slow but thorough* **meticulous**, scrupulous, assiduous, conscientious, painstaking, punctilious, methodical, careful, diligent, industrious, hard-working. **3** *the child is being a thorough nuisance* **utter**, downright, thoroughgoing, absolute, complete, total, out-and-out, arrant, real, perfect, proper, sheer, unqualified, unmitigated; Brit. informal right; Austral./NZ informal fair.
– OPPOSITES superficial, cursory, careless.

thoroughbred adj. **pure-bred**, pedigree, pure, pure-blooded.

thoroughfare n. **1** *the park is being used as a thoroughfare* **through route**, access route; Brit. informal rat run. **2** *the teeming thoroughfares of central London* **street**, road, roadway, avenue, boulevard, main road, high road, A road, B road; N. Amer. highway, freeway, throughway.

thoroughly adv. **1** *we will investigate all complaints thoroughly* **rigorously**, in depth, exhaustively, from top to bottom, minutely, closely, in detail, meticulously, scrupulously, assiduously, conscientiously, painstakingly, methodically, carefully, comprehensively, fully. **2** *she is thoroughly spoilt* **utterly**, downright, absolutely, completely, totally, entirely, really, perfectly, positively, in every respect, through and through; informal plain, clean.

though conj. *though she smiled bravely, she looked pale and tired* **although**, even though/if, in spite of the fact that, despite the fact that, notwithstanding (the fact) that, for all that.
▶ adv. *You can't always do that. You can try, though* **nevertheless**, nonetheless, even so, however, be that as it may, for all that, despite that, having said that; informal still and all.

thought n. **1** *what are your thoughts on the matter?* **idea**, notion, opinion, view, impression, feeling, theory; judgement, assessment, conclusion. **2** *he gave up any* *thought of taking a degree* **hope**, aspiration, ambition, dream; intention, idea, plan, design, aim. **3** *it only took a moment's thought* **thinking**, contemplation, musing, pondering, consideration, reflection, introspection, deliberation, rumination, meditation, brooding, reverie, brown study, concentration; formal cogitation. **4** *have you no thought for others?* **compassion**, sympathy, care, concern, regard, solicitude, empathy; consideration, understanding, sensitivity, thoughtfulness, charity.

thoughtful adj. **1** *a thoughtful expression* **pensive**, reflective, contemplative, musing, meditative, introspective, philosophical, ruminative, absorbed, engrossed, rapt, preoccupied, deep/lost in thought, in a brown study, brooding; formal cogitative. **2** *how very thoughtful of you!* **considerate**, caring, attentive, understanding, sympathetic, solicitous, concerned, helpful, friendly, obliging, accommodating, neighbourly, unselfish, kind, compassionate, charitable.
– OPPOSITES vacant, inconsiderate.

thoughtless adj. **1** *I'm so sorry—how thoughtless of me* **inconsiderate**, uncaring, insensitive, uncharitable, unkind, tactless, undiplomatic, indiscreet, careless. **2** *a few minutes of thoughtless pleasure* **unthinking**, heedless, careless, unmindful, absent-minded, injudicious, ill-advised, ill-considered, imprudent, unwise, foolish, silly, stupid, reckless, rash, precipitate, negligent, neglectful, remiss.
– OPPOSITES considerate, careful.

thousand cardinal number informal K, grand, thou.

> **WORD LINKS**
> **millennium, millenary** a period of a thousand years

thrall n. **power**, clutches, hands, control, grip, yoke, enslavement, subjection, subjugation, tyranny.

thrash v. **1** *she thrashed him across the head and shoulders* **hit**, beat, strike, batter, thump, hammer, pound, rain blows on; assault, attack; cudgel, club, birch; informal wallop, belt, bash, whack, thwack, clout, clobber, slug, tan, biff, bop, sock, beat the living daylights out of, give someone a good hiding. **2** informal *Newcastle were thrashed 8–1.* See **trounce**. **3** *he was thrashing around in pain* **flail**, writhe, thresh, jerk, toss, twist, twitch.
□ **thrash something out 1** *it's better if we can thrash out our difficulties first* **resolve**, settle, sort out, straighten out, iron out, clear up; talk through, discuss, debate, air, ventilate. **2** *they tried to thrash out an agreement* **work out**, negotiate, agree on, bring about, hammer out, produce, effect.

thread n. **1** *a needle and thread* **cotton**, yarn, filament, fibre. **2** literary *the Thames was a thread of silver below them* **streak**, strand, stripe, line, strip, seam, vein. **3** *she lost the thread of the conversation* **train of thought**, drift, direction, theme, motif, tenor; storyline, plot.
▶ v. **1** *he threaded the rope through a pulley* **pass**, string, work, ease, push, poke. **2** *she threaded her way through the tables* **weave one's way**, inch one's way, wind one's way, squeeze one's way, make one's way.

threadbare adj. **worn**, well worn, old, thin, worn out, holey, moth-eaten, mangy, ragged, frayed, tattered, battered; decrepit, shabby, scruffy, unkempt; having seen better days, falling apart at the seams, falling to pieces; informal tatty, ratty, the worse for wear; N. Amer. informal raggedy.

threat n. **1** *Maggie ignored his threats* **threatening remark**, warning, ultimatum. **2** *a possible threat to aircraft* **danger**, peril, hazard, menace, risk. **3** *the company faces the threat of liquidation proceedings* **possibility**, chance, probability, likelihood, risk; sword of Damocles.

threaten v. **1** *how dare you threaten me!* **menace**, intimidate, browbeat, bully, terrorize; make/issue threats to. **2** *these events could threaten the stability of Europe* **endanger**, be a danger/threat to, jeopardize, imperil, put at risk, put in jeopardy, drive a nail into the coffin of. **3** *the grey skies threatened snow* **herald**, bode, warn of, presage, augur, portend, foreshadow, be a harbinger of, indicate, point to, be a sign of, signal, spell; literary foretoken. **4** *as rain threatened, the party moved indoors* **seem likely**, seem imminent, be on the horizon, be brewing, be gathering, be looming, be on the way, be impending; hang over someone.

threatening adj. **1** *a threatening letter* **menacing**, intimidating, bullying, frightening, hostile; formal minatory. **2** *banks of threatening clouds* **ominous**, sinister, menacing, dark, black, thunderous.

three cardinal number **trio**, threesome; triplets.

> **WORD LINKS**
> **treble, triple, ternary** consisting of three parts
> **hat-trick** three successes of the same kind
> **tercentenary** a three-hundredth anniversary
> **triad** a group of three people or things
> **triangle** a three-sided figure
> **triathlon** an athletic contest consisting of three different events
> **triennial** lasting for or recurring every three years
> **trilogy** a group of three related novels, plays, or films
> **trimester** a period of three months
> **trinity** a group of three people or things
> **triptych** a painting on three hinged panels
> **triumvirate** a group of three powerful people
> **troika** a group of three political leaders or managers

threesome n. **trio**, triumvirate, triad, trinity, troika; triplets.

threnody n. **lament**, dirge, requiem, elegy, monody; Irish keen; Irish & Scottish coronach.

threshold n. **1** *the threshold of the church* **doorstep**, doorway, entrance, entry, door, gate, gateway, portal. **2** *the threshold of a new era* **start**, beginning, commencement, brink, verge, dawn, inception, day one, opening, debut; informal kick-off. **3** *the human threshold of pain* **lower limit**, minimum; Psychology limen.

> **WORD LINKS**
> **liminal** at or on a threshold
> **subliminal** (of a mental process) below the threshold of sensation or consciousness
> **first-footer** the first person to cross someone's threshold in the New Year

thrift n. **frugality**, economy, economizing, thriftiness, providence, prudence, good management/husbandry, saving, scrimping and saving, abstemiousness, parsimony, penny-pinching.
– OPPOSITES extravagance.

thriftless adj. **extravagant**, profligate, spendthrift, wasteful, improvident, imprudent, free-spending, prodigal, lavish; immoderate, excessive, reckless, irresponsible.

thrifty adj. **frugal**, economical, sparing, careful with money, provident, prudent, abstemious, parsimonious, penny-pinching; N. Amer. forehanded.
– OPPOSITES extravagant.

thrill n. **1** *the thrill of jumping out of an aeroplane* **excitement**, stimulation, pleasure, tingle, fun, enjoyment, amusement, delight, joy; informal buzz, kick; N. Amer. informal charge. **2** *a thrill of excitement ran through her* **wave**, rush, surge, flash, blaze, stab, dart, throb, tremor, quiver, flutter, shudder.
▸ v. **1** *his words thrilled her* **excite**, stimulate, arouse, rouse, inspire, delight, exhilarate, intoxicate, stir, electrify, galvanize, move, fire (with enthusiasm), fire someone's imagination; informal give someone a buzz, give someone a kick; N. Amer. informal give someone a charge. **2** *he thrilled at the sound of her voice* **be/feel excited**, tingle; informal get a buzz out of, get a kick out of; N. Amer. informal get a charge out of. **3** *shivers of anticipation thrilled through her* **rush**, race, surge, course, flood, flow, wash, sweep, flash, blaze.
– OPPOSITES bore.

thrilling adj. **exciting**, stirring, action-packed, rip-roaring, gripping, riveting, fascinating, dramatic, hair-raising; rousing, stimulating, moving, inspiring, inspirational, electrifying, heady, soul-stirring.
– OPPOSITES boring.

thrive v. **flourish**, prosper, burgeon, bloom, blossom, do well, advance, make strides, succeed, boom.
– OPPOSITES decline, wither.

thriving adj. **flourishing**, prosperous, prospering, growing, developing, burgeoning, blooming, healthy, successful, booming, profitable, expanding; informal going strong.
– OPPOSITES decline.

throat n. **gullet**, oesophagus; windpipe, trachea; maw; informal dated the red lane; old use throttle, gorge.

> **WORD LINKS**
> **jugular** relating to the throat or neck
> **guttural** (of a speech sound) produced in the throat
> **croup, quinsy** inflammation of the throat
> **diphtheria** a serious infectious disease causing inflammation of the throat

throaty adj. **gravelly**, husky, rough, guttural, deep, thick, gruff, growly, growling, hoarse, croaky, croaking; rasping, raspy.
– OPPOSITES high-pitched.

throb v. *her arms and legs throbbed with tiredness* **pulsate**, beat, pulse, palpitate, pound, thud, thump, drum, thrum, vibrate, pitter-patter, go pit-a-pat, quiver.
▸ n. *the throb of the ship's engines* **pulsation**, beat, beating, pulse, palpitation, pounding, thudding, thumping, drumming, thrumming, pit-a-pat, pitter-patter.

throes plural n. *the throes of childbirth* **agony**, pain, pangs, suffering, torture; literary travail.
□ **in the throes of** in the middle of, in the process of, in the midst of, busy with, occupied with, taken up with/by, involved in; struggling with, wrestling with, grappling with.

thrombosis n. **blood clot**, embolism, embolus, thrombus, infarction.

throne n. *the tsar risked losing his throne* **sovereign power**, sovereignty, rule, dominion.

throng n. *throngs of people blocked her way* **crowd**, horde, mass, multitude, host, army, herd, flock, drove, swarm, sea, troupe, pack, press, crush; collection, company, gathering, assembly, assemblage, congregation; informal gaggle, bunch, gang; old use rout.
▸ v. **1** *the pavements were thronged with tourists* **fill**, crowd, pack, cram, jam. **2** *people thronged to see the play* **flock**, stream, swarm, troop. **3** *visitors thronged round him* **crowd**, cluster, mill, swarm, congregate, gather.

throttle v. **1** *he tried to throttle her* **choke**, strangle, strangulate, garrotte. **2** *attempts to throttle the criminal supply of drugs* **suppress**, inhibit, stifle, control, restrain, check, contain, put a/the lid on; stop, put an end to, end, stamp out.

through prep. **1** *we drove through the tunnel* **into and out of**, to the other/far side of, from one side to the other of. **2** *he got the job through an advertisement* **by means of**, by way of, by dint of, via, using, thanks to, by virtue of, as a result of, as a consequence of, on account of, owing to, because of. **3** *he worked through the night* **throughout**, all through, for the duration of, until/to the end of.
▸ adv. **1** *as soon as we opened the gate they came streaming through* **from one side to the other**, from one end to another, in and out the other side. **2** *I woke up, but Anthony slept through* **the whole time**, all the time, from start to finish, without a break, without an interruption, non-stop, continuously, throughout.

t

▸adj. *a through train* **direct**, non-stop.
□ **through and through** in every respect, to the core; thoroughly, utterly, absolutely, completely, totally, wholly, fully, entirely, unconditionally, unreservedly, altogether, out-and-out.

throughout prep. **1** *it had repercussions throughout Europe* **all over**, in every part of, everywhere in, all through, right through, all round. **2** *Rose had generally been very fit throughout her life* **all through**, all, for the duration of, for the whole of, until the end of.

throw v. **1** *she threw the ball back* **hurl**, toss, fling, pitch, cast, lob, launch, catapult, project, propel, bowl; informal chuck, heave, sling, bung; N. Amer. informal peg; Austral. informal hoy; NZ informal bish; dated shy. **2** *he threw the door open* **push**, thrust, fling, bang, force. **3** *a chandelier threw its light over the walls* **cast**, send, give off, emit, radiate, project. **4** *he threw another punch* **deliver**, give, land. **5** *she threw a withering glance at him* **direct**, cast, send, dart, shoot. **6** *the horse threw his rider* **unseat**, dislodge. **7** *his question threw me* **disconcert**, unnerve, fluster, ruffle, agitate, discomfit, put off, throw off balance, discountenance, unsettle, confuse; informal rattle, faze; N. Amer. informal discombobulate. **8** *the pots were thrown on a wheel* **shape**, form, mould, fashion. **9** *he threw a farewell party for them* **give**, host, hold, have, provide, put on, lay on, arrange, organize.
▸n. **1** *we were allowed two throws each* **lob**, pitch; go; bowl, ball. **2** informal *drinks are only £1 a throw* **each**, apiece, per item.
□ **throw something away 1** *she hated throwing old clothes away* **discard**, throw out, dispose of, get rid of, do away with, toss out, scrap, throw on the scrapheap, clear out, dump, jettison; informal chuck (away/out), ditch, bin, junk, get shut of; Brit. informal get shot of. **2** *Cambridge threw away a 15–0 lead* **squander**, waste, fritter away, fail to exploit, lose, let slip; informal blow, throw something down the drain.
throw someone off shake off, get away from, escape, elude, give someone the slip, throw off the scent, dodge, lose.
throw someone out expel, eject, evict, drive out, force out, oust, remove; get rid of, depose, topple, unseat, overthrow, bring down, overturn, dislodge, displace, supplant, show someone the door; banish, deport, exile; informal boot out, kick out, give someone the boot; Brit. informal turf out.
throw something out 1 *throw out food that's past its sell-by date.* See **throw something out** (sense 1). **2** *his case was thrown out by the magistrate* **reject**, dismiss, turn down, refuse, disallow, veto; informal give the thumbs down to. **3** *a thermal light bulb throws out a lot of heat* **radiate**, emit, give off, send out, diffuse.
throw someone over abandon, leave, desert, discard, turn one's back on, cast aside/off; jilt, break up with, finish with, leave in the lurch, leave high and dry; informal

dump, ditch, chuck, drop, walk out on, run out on, leave flat, give someone the push/elbow, give someone the big E; literary forsake.
throw up informal See **vomit** (sense 1 of the verb).
throw something up give up, abandon, relinquish, resign (from); leave; informal quit, chuck, pack in; Brit. informal jack in.

throwaway adj. **1** *throwaway packaging* **disposable**, non-returnable; biodegradable, photodegradable. **2** *throwaway remarks* **casual**, passing, careless, unthinking, unstudied, unconsidered, offhand.

thrust v. **1** *she thrust her hands into her pockets* **shove**, push, force, plunge, stick, drive, propel, ram, poke. **2** *fame had been thrust on him* **force**, foist, impose, inflict. **3** *he thrust his way past her* **push**, shove, force, elbow, shoulder, barge.
▸n. **1** *a hard thrust* **shove**, push, lunge, poke. **2** *a thrust by the Third Army* **advance**, push, drive, attack, assault, onslaught, offensive, charge, sortie, foray, raid, sally, invasion, incursion. **3** *only one engine is producing thrust* **force**, propulsive force, propulsion, power, impetus, momentum. **4** *the thrust of the speech* **gist**, substance, drift, burden, meaning, significance, signification, sense, theme, message, import, tenor.

thrusting adj. **ambitious**, pushy, forceful, aggressive, assertive, self-assertive, full of oneself, determined, driven, power-hungry.
– OPPOSITES meek.

thud n. & v. **thump**, clunk, clonk, crash, smack, bang; stomp, stamp, clump, clomp; informal wham.

thug n. **ruffian**, lout, hooligan, bully boy, vandal, hoodlum, gangster, villain, criminal; informal tough, bruiser, heavy, hired gun; Brit. informal rough, bovver boy; N. Amer. informal hood, goon.

thumb n. technical pollex, opposable digit.
▸v. **1** *he thumbed through his notebook* **leaf**, flick, flip, riffle, skim, browse, look. **2** *his dictionaries were thumbed and ink-stained* **soil**, mark, make dog-eared. **3** *he was thumbing his way across France* **hitch-hike**; informal hitch, hitch/thumb a lift.
□ **all thumbs** Brit. informal clumsy, awkward, maladroit, inept, unskilful, heavy-handed, inexpert; informal butterfingered, cack-handed, ham-fisted, having two left feet; Brit. informal all fingers and thumbs; N. Amer. informal klutzy.
thumbs down informal rejection, refusal, veto, no, negation, rebuff; informal knock-back.
thumbs up informal approval, seal of approval, endorsement; permission, authorization, consent, yes, leave, authority, sanction, ratification, licence, dispensation, nod, assent, blessing, rubber stamp, clearance; informal go-ahead, OK, green light, say-so.

thumbnail adj. **concise**, short, brief, succinct, to the point, compact, crisp, short and sweet, quick, rapid; potted.

thump v. **1** *the two men kicked and thumped him* **hit**, strike, smack, cuff, punch; beat, thrash, batter, belabour, pound, pummel, box

someone's ears; informal whack, wallop, bash, biff, bop, lam, clout, clobber, sock, swipe, crown, beat the living daylights out of, give someone a (good) hiding, belt, tan, lay into, let someone have it; Brit. informal stick one on, slosh; N. Amer. informal slug, boff; literary smite. **2** *her heart thumped with fright* **throb**, pound, thud, hammer, pulsate, pulse, pump, palpitate, race, beat heavily.
▸**n. 1** *a well-aimed thump on the jaw* **blow**, punch, box, cuff, smack; thrashing; hiding; informal whack, thwack, wallop, bash, belt, biff, clout, swipe; Brit. informal slosh; N. Amer. informal boff, slug. **2** *she put the box down with a thump* **thud**, clunk, clonk, crash, smack, bang.

thumping adj. **1** *the thumping beat of her heart* **thudding**, pounding, throbbing, pulsating, banging, hammering, drumming. **2** *informal a thumping 64 per cent majority* | *a thumping victory* **enormous**, huge, massive, vast, tremendous, substantial, prodigious, gigantic, giant, terrific, fantastic, colossal, immense, mammoth, monumental, stupendous; emphatic, decisive, conclusive, striking, impressive, outstanding, notable, memorable, remarkable, extraordinary, resounding, phenomenal; informal whopping, thundering; Brit. informal whacking.
▸**adv.** *informal a thumping good read.* See **very** (adverb).

thunder n. **1** *thunder and lightning* **thunderclap**, roll/rumble of thunder, crack/crash of thunder; literary thunderbolt. **2** *the ceaseless thunder of the traffic* **rumble**, rumbling, boom, booming, roar, roaring, pounding, thud, thudding, crash, crashing, reverberation.
▸**v. 1** *below me the surf thrashed and thundered* **rumble**, boom, roar, pound, thud, thump, bang; resound, reverberate, beat. **2** *he thundered against the evils of the age* **rail**, fulminate, inveigh, rage; condemn, denounce. **3** *'Answer me!' he thundered* **roar**, bellow, bark, yell, shout, bawl; informal holler.

thundering adj. *a thundering noise.* See **thunderous**.
▸**adv.** *a thundering good read.* See **very** (adverb).

thunderous adj. **very loud**, deafening, ear-splitting, tumultuous, booming, roaring, resounding, reverberating, reverberant, ringing, noisy.

thunderstruck adj. **astonished**, amazed, astounded, staggered, surprised, startled, stunned, shocked, shell-shocked, aghast, taken aback, dumbfounded, dumbstruck, stupefied, dazed, speechless; informal flabbergasted; Brit. informal gobsmacked, knocked for six.

thus adv. **1** *the studio handled production, thus cutting its costs* **consequently**, as a consequence, in consequence, so, that being so, therefore, thereby, ergo, accordingly, hence, as a result, for that reason, because of that, on that account. **2** *legislation forbids such data being held thus* **like that**, in that way, so, like so.

thwack v. *informal* **hit**, strike, slap, smack, cuff, punch, thump; beat, thrash, batter, belabour, pound, pummel, box someone's ears; whip, flog, cane; informal whack, wallop, bash, biff, bop, lam, clout, clobber, sock, swipe, crown, beat the living daylights out of, give someone a (good) hiding, belt, tan, lay into, let someone have it, deck, floor; Brit. informal stick one on, slosh; N. Amer. informal slug, boff; literary smite.

thwart v. **foil**, frustrate, balk, stand in the way of, forestall, derail, dash; stop, check, block, prevent, defeat, impede, obstruct, snooker, hinder, hamper; spike someone's guns; informal put paid to, put the kibosh on, do for, stymie; Brit. informal scupper, queer someone's pitch.
– OPPOSITES facilitate.

tic n. **twitch**, spasm, jerk, tremor.

tick n. **1** *put a tick against the item of your choice* **mark**, stroke; N. Amer. check, check mark. **2** *the tick of his watch* **ticking**, tick-tock, click, clicking, tap, tapping. **3** *Brit. informal I won't be a tick* **moment**, second, minute, bit, little while, instant; informal sec, jiffy; Brit. informal mo, two ticks.
▸**v. 1** *tick the appropriate box* **put a tick in/against**, mark, check off, indicate; N. Amer. check. **2** *I could hear the clock ticking* **tick-tock**, click; tap.
□ **in a tick** *Brit. informal* **(very) soon**, in a second, in a minute, in a moment, in a trice, in a flash, shortly, any second, any minute, in no time (at all); N. Amer. momentarily; informal in a sec, in a jiffy, in two shakes (of a lamb's tail), before you can say Jack Robinson; Brit. informal in two ticks, in a mo; N. Amer. informal in a snap; dated directly.
□ **tick someone off** *Brit. informal* See **reprimand** (verb).

ticket n. **1** *can I see your ticket?* **pass**, authorization, permit; token, coupon, voucher. **2** *a price ticket* **label**, tag, sticker, tab, marker, docket.

tickle v. **1** *he tried to tickle her under the chin* **stroke**, pet, chuck. **2** *he found something that tickled his imagination* **stimulate**, interest, appeal to, arouse, excite. **3** *the idea tickled Lewis* **amuse**, entertain, divert, please, delight; informal tickle someone pink.

ticklish adj. **difficult**, problematic, tricky, delicate, sensitive, awkward, prickly, thorny, tough; vexed; informal sticky.

tide n. **1** *ships come up the river with the tide* **tidal flow**, ebb and flow, tidewater, ebb, current. **2** *the tide of history* **course**, movement, direction, trend, current, drift, run, turn, tendency, tenor.
□ **tide someone over** **sustain**, keep someone going, keep someone's head above water, see someone through; keep the wolf from the door; help out, assist, aid.

tidings plural n. *literary* **news**, information, intelligence, word, reports, notification, communication, the latest; informal info, the low down.

tidy adj. **1** *a tidy room* **neat**, neat and tidy, as neat as a new pin, orderly, well ordered, in (good) order, well kept, shipshape (and Bristol fashion), in apple-pie order, immaculate, spick and span, uncluttered, straight, trim, spruce. **2** *he's a very tidy person* **neat**, trim, spruce, dapper, well groomed, well turned out; organized, well organized, methodical, meticulous; fastidious; informal natty. **3** informal *a tidy sum* **large**, sizeable, considerable, substantial, generous, significant, appreciable, handsome, respectable, decent, goodly; informal not to be sneezed at.
– OPPOSITES messy.
▶v. **1** *I'd better tidy up the living room* **put in order**, clear up, sort out, straighten (up), clean up, spruce up. **2** *she tidied herself up in the bathroom* **groom oneself**, spruce oneself up, freshen oneself up, smarten oneself up; informal titivate oneself.

tie v. **1** *they tied Max to a chair* **bind**, tie up, tether, hitch, strap, truss, fetter, rope, chain, make fast, moor, lash, attach, fasten, fix, secure, join, connect, link, couple. **2** *he bent to tie his shoelaces* **do up**, lace, knot. **3** *women can feel tied by childcare responsibilities* **restrict**, restrain, limit, tie down, constrain, trammel, confine, cramp, hamper, handicap, hamstring, encumber, shackle, inhibit; cramp someone's style. **4** *a pay deal tied to a productivity agreement* **link**, connect, couple, relate, join, marry; make conditional on, bind up with. **5** *they tied for second place* **draw**, be equal, be even, be neck and neck.
▶n. **1** *he tightened the ties of his robe* **lace**, string, cord, fastening, fastener. **2** *a collar and tie* **necktie**, bow tie, string tie; Brit. bootlace tie. **3** *family ties* **bond**, connection, link, relationship, attachment, affiliation, allegiance, friendship; kinship, interdependence. **4** *pets can be a tremendous tie* **restriction**, constraint, curb, limitation, restraint, hindrance, encumbrance, handicap; obligation, commitment. **5** *there was a tie for first place* **draw**, dead heat, deadlock. **6** Brit. *Turkey's World Cup tie against Holland* **match**, game, contest, fixture, event; Brit. clash.
□ **tie someone down** *she was afraid of being tied down.* See **tie** (sense 3 of the verb).
tie in be consistent, tally, agree, be in agreement, accord, concur, fit in, harmonize, be in tune, dovetail, correspond, match; informal square; N. Amer. informal jibe.
tie someone/something up 1 *robbers tied her up and ransacked her home* **bind**, bind hand and foot, fasten together, truss (up), fetter, chain up. **2** *he is tied up in meetings all morning* **occupy**, engage, keep busy. **3** *they were anxious to tie up the contract* **finalize**, conclude, complete, finish off, seal, set the seal on, settle, secure, clinch; informal wrap up.
tie-in n. **connection**, link, association, correlation, tie-up, interrelation, relationship, relation, interconnection; parallel, similarity.

tier n. **1** *tiers of empty seats* **row**, rank, bank, line; layer, level. **2** *the most senior tier of management* **grade**, level, echelon, rung on the ladder.

tiff n. informal **quarrel**, squabble, argument, disagreement, fight, falling-out, difference of opinion, dispute, wrangle, altercation, contretemps, disputation, shouting match; informal slanging match, run-in, spat, set-to; Brit. informal barney, row, bust-up.

tight adj. **1** *a tight grip* **firm**, fast, secure, fixed, clenched. **2** *the rope was pulled tight* **taut**, rigid, stiff, tense, stretched, strained. **3** *tight jeans* **tight-fitting**, close-fitting, narrow, figure-hugging, skintight; informal sprayed on. **4** *a tight mass of fibres* **compact**, compacted, compressed, dense, solid. **5** *a tight space* **small**, tiny, narrow, limited, restricted, confined, cramped, constricted, uncomfortable. **6** *the joint will be perfectly tight against petrol leaks* **impervious**, impenetrable, sealed, sound, hermetic; watertight, airtight. **7** *tight limits on the use of pesticides* **strict**, rigorous, stringent, tough, rigid, firm, uncompromising. **8** *he's in a tight spot* **difficult**, tricky, delicate, awkward, problematic, worrying, precarious; informal sticky; Brit. informal dodgy. **9** *a tight piece of writing* **succinct**, concise, pithy, incisive, crisp, condensed, well structured, to the point. **10** *a tight race* **close**, even, evenly matched, well matched; hard-fought, neck and neck, nip and tuck. **11** *money is a bit tight just now* **limited**, restricted, in short supply, scarce, depleted, diminished, low, inadequate, insufficient. **12** informal *he's tight with his money* **mean**, miserly, parsimonious, niggardly, close-fisted, penny-pinching, cheese-paring, Scrooge-like, close; informal stingy, tight-fisted; N. Amer. informal cheap; formal penurious; old use near. **13** informal *he came home tight from the pub.* See **drunk** (adjective).
– OPPOSITES slack, loose, generous.

tighten v. **1** *I tightened up the screws* **make tighter**, make fast, screw up. **2** *he tightened his grip* **strengthen**, make stronger, harden. **3** *she tightened the rope* **tauten**, make/draw taut, make/draw tight, stretch, strain, stiffen, tense. **4** *he tightened his lips* **narrow**, constrict, contract, compress, screw up, pucker, purse; N. Amer. informal squinch. **5** *security in the area has been tightened up* **increase**, make stricter, toughen up, heighten, scale up.
– OPPOSITES loosen, slacken, relax.

tight-fisted adj. informal **mean**, miserly, parsimonious, niggardly, close-fisted, penny-pinching, cheese-paring, Scrooge-like, close; informal stingy, tight; N. Amer. informal cheap; formal penurious; old use near.
– OPPOSITES generous.

tight-lipped adj. **reticent**, uncommunicative, unforthcoming, playing one's cards close to one's chest, close-mouthed, silent, taciturn; informal mum.
– OPPOSITES forthcoming.

t

till[1] prep. & conj. *he stayed till 7* | *I'll stay here till you get back.* See **until**.

till[2] n. *she counted the money in the till* **cash register**, cash box, cash drawer, strongbox; checkout, cash desk.

till[3] v. *he went back to tilling the land* **cultivate**, work, farm, plough, dig, turn over, prepare.

tilt v. **1** *the ground seemed to tilt* **slope**, tip, lean, list, bank, slant, incline, pitch, cant, careen, angle. **2** historical *he tilts at his prey* **charge**, rush, run; lunge, thrust, jab. **3** historical *knights tilting at a tournament* **joust**, tourney, enter the lists; contend, spar, fight.
▶n. **1** *a tilt of some 45°* **slope**, list, camber, gradient, bank, slant, incline, pitch, cant, bevel, angle. **2** historical *knights would take part in a tilt* **joust**, tournament, tourney, lists, combat, contest, fight, duel. **3** *another tilt at the Champions League* **attempt**, bid; informal go, crack, shot.
□ **(at) full tilt 1** *they charged full tilt down the side of the hill* **(at) full speed**, (at) full pelt, as fast as one's legs can carry one, at a gallop, helter-skelter, headlong, pell-mell, at breakneck speed; informal hell for leather, at the double, a mile a minute, like the wind, like a bat out of hell, like a scalded cat, like (greased) lightning; Brit. informal like the clappers, at a rate of knots, like billy-o; N. Amer. informal lickety-split; literary apace. **2** *the marketing blitz has raged at full tilt for some time now* **with great force**, with full force, full blast, with all the stops out, all out, with a vengeance; informal like crazy, like mad.

timber n. **1** *houses built of timber* **wood**; N. Amer. lumber. **2** *the timbers of wrecked ships* **beam**, spar, plank, batten, lath, board, joist, rafter.

timbre n. **tone**, tonality, sound, voice, colour, resonance.

time n. **1** *what time is it?* **hour**; dated o'clock. **2** *late at night was the best time to leave* **moment**, point (in time), occasion, hour, minute, second, instant, juncture, stage. **3** *he worked there for a time* **while**, spell, stretch, stint, span, season, interval, period (of time), length of time, duration, run, space, phase, stage, term; Brit. informal patch. **4** *the time of the dinosaurs* **era**, age, epoch, period, years, days; generation, date. **5** *I've known a lot of women in my time* **lifetime**, life, life span, days, time on earth, existence, threescore years and ten. **6** *he had been a professional actor in his time* **heyday**, day, best days/years, prime. **7** *times are hard at the moment* **conditions**, circumstances, life, state of affairs, experiences. **8** *tunes in waltz time* **rhythm**, tempo, beat; metre, measure, cadence, pattern.
▶v. *the meeting was timed for three o'clock* **schedule**, set, set up, arrange, organize, fix, fix up, book, line up, slot in, prearrange, timetable, plan; N. Amer. slate.
□ **ahead of time** early, in good time, with time to spare, in advance.

ahead of one's/its time revolutionary, avant-garde, futuristic, innovatory, innovative, trailblazing, pioneering, groundbreaking, advanced, disruptive.
all the time constantly, the entire time, around the clock, day and night, night and day, {morning, noon, and night}, {day in, day out}, at all times, always, without a break, ceaselessly, endlessly, incessantly, perpetually, permanently, interminably, continuously, continually, eternally, unremittingly, remorselessly, relentlessly; N. Amer. without surcease; informal 24-7.
at the same time *they arrived at the same time* simultaneously, at the same instant/moment, together, all together, as a group, at once, at one and the same time; in unison, in concert, in chorus, as one.
at times occasionally, sometimes, from time to time, now and then, every so often, once in a while, on occasion, off and on, at intervals, periodically, sporadically.
behind time late, behind, behind schedule, behindhand, running late, overdue.
behind the times old-fashioned, out of date, outmoded, outdated, dated, old, passé; informal square, not with it, out of the ark; N. Amer. informal horse-and-buggy, clunky.
for the time being for now, for the moment, for the present, in the interim, for the nonce, in/for the meantime, in the meanwhile, for a short time, briefly; temporarily, provisionally, pro tem; informal for the minute.
from time to time occasionally, sometimes, now and then, every so often, once in a while, on occasion, off and on, at intervals, periodically, sporadically.
in no time (very) soon, in a second, in a minute, in a moment, in a trice, in a flash, shortly, any second, any minute (now); N. Amer. momentarily; informal in a sec, in a nanosecond, in a jiffy, in two shakes (of a lamb's tail), before you can say Jack Robinson; Brit. informal in a tick, in two ticks, in a mo; N. Amer. informal in a snap; dated directly.
in time 1 *I came back in time for the party* **early enough**, in good time, punctually, on time, not too late, with time to spare, on schedule. **2** *in time, she forgot about it* **eventually**, in the end, in due course, by and by, finally; one day, some day, sometime, sooner or later.
many a time frequently, regularly, often, very often, all the time, habitually, customarily, routinely; again and again, time and again, over and over again, repeatedly, recurrently, continually; N. Amer. oftentimes; literary oft, oft-times.
on time punctually, in good time, to/on schedule, when expected; informal on the dot, bang on time.
time after time repeatedly, frequently, often, again and again, over and over (again), time and (time) again, many times, many a time; persistently, recurrently, constantly, continually; N. Amer. oftentimes; literary oft, oft-times.

t

time-honoured adj. **traditional**, established, long-established, long-standing, long-lived, age-old, enduring, lasting, tried and tested.

timeless adj. **lasting**, enduring, classic, ageless, permanent, perennial, abiding, unfailing, unchanging, unvarying, never-changing, changeless, unfading, unending, undying, deathless, immortal, eternal, everlasting, immutable.
– OPPOSITES ephemeral.

timely adj. **opportune**, well timed, at the right time, convenient, appropriate, expedient, seasonable, felicitous.
– OPPOSITES ill-timed.

timetable n. *a bus timetable | I have a very full timetable* **schedule**, programme, agenda, calendar; list, itinerary.
▸ v. *German lessons were timetabled on Wednesday* **schedule**, set, arrange, organize, fix, time, line up; N. Amer. slate.

time-worn adj. **1** *the carpet was old and time-worn* **worn out**, worn, well worn, old, tattered, battered, dog-eared, shabby, having seen better days; informal tatty. **2** *time-worn faces* **old**, aged, weathered, lined, wrinkled, hoary. **3** *a time-worn aphorism* **hackneyed**, trite, banal, platitudinous, clichéd, stock, conventional, unoriginal, overused, overworked, tired, stale; informal old hat.
– OPPOSITES new, fresh.

timid adj. **easily frightened**, fearful, afraid, faint-hearted, timorous, nervous, scared, frightened, cowardly, pusillanimous, lily-livered, spineless; shy, diffident, self-effacing; informal wimpish, wimpy, chicken, gutless.
– OPPOSITES bold.

timorous adj. See **timid**.

tincture n. **1** *tincture of iodine* **solution**, suspension, infusion, elixir. **2** *a tincture of bitterness* **trace**, note, tinge, touch, suggestion, hint, bit, element, suspicion, soupçon.

tinge v. **1** *a mass of white blossom tinged with pink* **tint**, colour, stain, shade, wash. **2** *his optimism is tinged with realism* **influence**, affect, touch, flavour, colour, modify.
▸ n. **1** *the light had a blue tinge to it* **tint**, colour, shade, tone, hue. **2** *a tinge of cynicism* **trace**, note, touch, suggestion, hint, bit, scintilla, savour, flavour, element, streak, vein, suspicion, soupçon, tincture.

tingle v. *her flesh still tingled from the shock* **prickle**, sting; tremble, quiver, shiver.

▸ n. *she felt a tingle of anticipation* **prickling**, tingling, pricking, sting, stinging; tremor, thrill, quiver, shiver; goose pimples; N. Amer. goosebumps.

tinker v. *a workman was tinkering with the engine* **fiddle with**, adjust, try to mend, play about with; tamper with, interfere with, mess about with, meddle with; informal rearrange the deckchairs on the Titanic; Brit. informal muck about with.

tinkle v. **1** *the bell tinkled* **ring**, jingle, jangle, chime, peal, ding, ping. **2** *cool water tinkled in the stone fountain* **splash**, purl, babble, burble; literary plash.
▸ n. **1** *the tinkle of the doorbell* **ring**, chime, peal, ding, ping, jingle, jangle, tintinnabulation. **2** *the faint tinkle of water* **splash**, purl, babble, burble; literary plash.

tinny adj. **1** *tinny music* **jangly**, jangling, jingling, jingly. **2** *a tinny little car* **cheap**, cheapjack, poor-quality, inferior, low-grade, gimcrack, shoddy, jerry-built; informal tacky, tatty, rubbishy.

tinsel n. *the tinsel of Hollywood* **ostentation**, showiness, show, glitter, flamboyance, gaudiness; attractiveness, glamour; informal flashiness, glitz, glitziness, razzle-dazzle, razzmatazz.
▸ adj. *tinsel stardom* **ostentatious**, showy, glittering, flamboyant, gaudy; informal flash, flashy, over the top, OTT, glitzy, ritzy; N. Amer. informal superfly.

tint n. **1** *the sky was taking on an apricot tint* **shade**, colour, tone, hue, tinge, cast, tincture, flush, blush. **2** *a hair tint* **dye**, colourant, colouring, wash; highlights, lowlights.

tiny adj. **minute**, minuscule, microscopic, nanoscopic, very small, little, mini, diminutive, miniature, scaled down, baby, toy, dwarf, pygmy, Lilliputian; Scottish wee; informal teeny, teeny-weeny, teensy, teensy-weensy, itsy-bitsy, eensy, eensy-weensy, tiddly, pint-sized; Brit. informal titchy; N. Amer. informal little-bitty.
– OPPOSITES huge.

tip¹ n. **1** *the tip of the spear* **point**, end, extremity, head, sharp end, spike, prong, tine, nib. **2** *the tips of the mountains* **peak**, point, top, summit, apex, crown, crest, pinnacle. **3** *the sticks have tips fitted to protect them* **cap**, cover, ferrule.
▸ v. *mountains tipped with snow* **cap**, top, crown.

tip² v. **1** *the boat tipped over* **overturn**, turn over, topple (over), fall (over); keel over, capsize, turn turtle; Nautical pitchpole. **2** *a whale could tip over a small boat* **upset**, overturn, topple over, turn over, knock over, push over, upend, capsize; informal roll; old use overset. **3** *the car tipped to one side* **lean**, tilt, list, slope, bank, slant, incline, pitch, cant, heel, careen. **4** *she tipped the water into the trough* **pour**, empty, drain, unload, dump, discharge; decant.
▸ n. Brit. *rubbish must be taken to the tip* **dump**, rubbish dump; Canadian nuisance grounds.

tip³ n. **1** *a generous tip* **gratuity**, baksheesh; present, gift, reward; Brit. informal dropsy. **2** *useful tips* **piece of advice**, suggestion, word of advice, pointer, recommendation; clue, hint; informal wrinkle, tip-off.

tip-off n. informal **piece of information**, warning, lead, forewarning; hint, clue; advice, information, notification.

tipple v. *boys discovered tippling were punished* **drink alcohol**, drink; informal booze, wet one's whistle, hit the bottle; Brit. informal bevvy; N. Amer. informal bend one's elbow; old use tope.
▸ n. informal *their favourite tipple was claret* **alcoholic drink**, drink, liquor; informal booze, poison.

tippler n. **drinker**, imbiber; alcoholic, drunk, drunkard, dipsomaniac, inebriate, sot; informal boozer, alky, lush, barfly, sponge, dipso, wino, soak; Austral./NZ informal hophead; old use toper.
– OPPOSITES teetotaller.

tipsy adj. **merry**, mellow, slightly drunk; Brit. informal tiddly, squiffy.
– OPPOSITES sober.

tirade n. **diatribe**, harangue, rant, onslaught, attack, polemic, denunciation, broadside, fulmination, condemnation, censure, criticism, tongue-lashing; informal blast; literary philippic.

tire v. **1** *the ascent grew steeper and he began to tire* **get tired**, weaken, grow weak, flag, droop. **2** *the journey had tired him* **fatigue**, tire out, exhaust, wear out, drain, weary, wash out, overtire, enervate; informal knock out, take it out of, do in, fag out, wear to a frazzle; Brit. informal knacker. **3** *they tired of his difficult behaviour* **weary**, get tired, get sick, get bored; informal get fed up, have had something up to here.

tired adj. **1** *you're just tired from travelling* **exhausted**, worn out, weary, fatigued, dog-tired, bone-tired, ready to drop, drained, enervated, jaded; informal done in, all in, dead beat, shattered, bushed, knocked out, wiped out, bushwhacked; Brit. informal knackered, whacked (out), jiggered; N. Amer. informal pooped, tuckered out; Austral./NZ informal stonkered. **2** *are you tired of having him here?* **bored with/by**, weary of, sick (and tired) of; informal fed up with, up to here with. **3** *tired jokes* **hackneyed**, overused, overworked, worn out, stale, clichéd, hoary, stock, stereotyped, predictable, unimaginative, unoriginal, uninspired, dull, boring, routine; informal old hat, corny, played out.
– OPPOSITES energetic, lively, fresh.

tiredness n. **fatigue**, weariness, exhaustion, enervation, inertia; sleepiness, drowsiness, somnolence.
– OPPOSITES energy.

tireless adj. **vigorous**, energetic, industrious, determined, enthusiastic, keen, zealous, spirited, dynamic, dogged, tenacious, persevering, stout, untiring, unwearying, indefatigable, unflagging.

– OPPOSITES lazy.

tiresome adj. **boring**, dull, tedious, wearisome, wearing, uninteresting, uneventful, humdrum; annoying, irritating, trying, irksome, vexatious, troublesome; informal aggravating, pesky.
– OPPOSITES interesting, pleasant.

tiring adj. **exhausting**, wearying, taxing, fatiguing, wearing, enervating, draining; hard, heavy, arduous, strenuous, onerous, uphill, demanding, gruelling; informal killing, murderous; Brit. informal knackering.

tissue n. **1** *living tissue* **matter**, material, substance; flesh. **2** *a box of tissues* **paper handkerchief**, paper towel; trademark Kleenex. **3** *a tissue of lies* **web**, network, nexus, complex, mass, set, series, chain.

> **WORD LINKS**
>
> **histology** the branch of biology concerned with tissue structure
> **atrophy** the wasting away of body tissue
> **dystrophy** a disorder in which body tissue wastes away
> **gangrene, necrosis** the death and decay of body tissue
> **sclerosis** abnormal hardening of body tissue

titanic adj. **huge**, great, enormous, gigantic, massive, colossal, monumental, mammoth, immense, cosmic, tremendous, terrific, mighty, stupendous, prodigious, gargantuan, Herculean; informal humongous, whopping, thumping, mega; Brit. informal whacking, ginormous.

titbit n. **1** *tasty titbits* **delicacy**, tasty morsel, dainty, bonne bouche, treat; snack, nibble, savoury, appetizer; informal goody; N. Amer. tidbit. **2** *a fascinating titbit* **piece of gossip**, bit of scandal, piece of information.

tit for tat n. **retaliation**, reprisal, counter-attack, counterstroke, comeback; revenge, vengeance, retribution, an eye for an eye, a tooth for a tooth, as good as one gets, payback; informal a taste of someone's own medicine.

titillate v. **arouse**, excite, tantalize, stimulate, stir, thrill, interest, attract, fascinate; informal turn on.
– OPPOSITES bore.

titillating adj. **arousing**, exciting, stimulating, sexy, thrilling, provocative, tantalizing, interesting, fascinating; suggestive, salacious, lurid; Brit. informal saucy.
– OPPOSITES boring.

titivate v. informal *she titivated herself in front of the hall mirror* **groom**, smarten (up), spruce up, freshen up, preen, primp, prink; tidy, arrange; informal doll up, tart up; N. Amer. informal gussy up.

title n. **1** *the title of the book* **name**. **2** *the cartoon title* **caption**, legend, inscription, label, heading, subheading; credit. **3** *the company publishes 400 titles a year* **publication**, work, book, newspaper, paper, magazine, periodical. **4** *the title of Duke of Marlborough* **designation**, name, form of address; epithet, style; rank, office, position;

t

informal moniker, handle; **formal** appellation, denomination. **5** *an Olympic title* **championship**, crown, first place; laurels, bays, palm. **6** *the vendor is obliged to prove his title to the land* **ownership**, proprietorship, possession, holding, freehold, entitlement, right, claim.

▸v. *a policy paper titled 'Law and Order'* **call**, entitle, name, dub, designate, style, term; **formal** denominate.

titter v. & n. **giggle**, snigger, snicker, tee-hee, chuckle, laugh; **informal** chortle.

tittle n. See **iota**.

tittle-tattle n. *she would never listen to tittle-tattle* **gossip**, rumour(s), idle talk, hearsay, whispers, titbits; scandal; **informal** dirt, buzz; **Brit. informal** goss; **N. Amer. informal** scuttlebutt.

▸v. *he was tittle-tattling all over the village* **gossip**, spread rumours, spread gossip, tattle, talk, whisper, tell tales.

titular adj. **1** *the titular head of a university* **nominal**, in title/name only, ceremonial; token, puppet. **2** *the work's titular song* **eponymous**, identifying.

toad n.

> **WORD LINKS**
> **batrachian, anuran** relating to toads

toady n. *a conniving little toady* **sycophant**, fawner, flatterer, creep, crawler, lickspittle; **informal** bootlicker, yes-man; **old use** toad-eater.

▸v. *she imagined him toadying to his rich clients* **grovel to**, ingratiate oneself with, be obsequious to, kowtow to, pander to, crawl to, truckle to, bow and scrape to, dance attendance on, curry favour with, make up to, fawn on/over; **informal** suck up to, lick someone's boots, butter up.

toast n. **1** *he raised his glass in a toast* **tribute**, salute, salutation; **old use** pledge. **2** *he was the toast of the West End* **darling**, favourite, pet, heroine, hero; talk; **Brit. informal** blue-eyed boy/ girl; **N. Amer. informal** fair-haired boy/girl.

▸v. **1** *she toasted her hands in front of the fire* **warm (up)**, heat, heat (up). **2** *we toasted the couple with champagne* **drink (to) the health of**, drink to, salute, honour, pay tribute to; **old use** pledge.

today adv. **1** *the work must be finished today* **this (very) day**, this morning, this afternoon, this evening. **2** *the complex tasks demanded of computers today* **nowadays**, these days, at the present time, in these times, in this day and age, now, currently, at the moment, at present, at this moment in time; in the present climate; **N. Amer.** presently.

toddle v. **1** *the child toddled towards him* **totter**, teeter, wobble, falter, waddle, stumble. **2** **informal** *I toddled down to the quay* **amble**, potter, wander, meander, stroll, saunter; **informal** mosey, tootle; **N. Amer. informal** putter.

to-do n. **informal** **commotion**, fuss, ado, excitement, agitation, bother, stir, palaver,

confusion, disturbance, brouhaha, uproar, furore, storm in a teacup, much ado about nothing; **informal** hoo-ha, ballyhoo, kerfuffle, song and dance, performance, pantomime; **Brit. informal** carry-on; **N. Amer. informal** fuss and feathers.

together adv. **1** *friends who work together* **with each other**, in conjunction, jointly, in cooperation, in collaboration, in partnership, in combination, in league, side by side, hand in hand, shoulder to shoulder, cheek by jowl; in collusion, hand in glove; **informal** in cahoots. **2** *they both spoke together* **simultaneously**, at the same time, at one and the same time, at once, all together, as a group, in unison, in concert, in chorus, as one, with one accord. **3** *I was not able to get up for days together* **in succession**, in a row, at a time, successively, consecutively, running, straight, on end, one after the other, continuously, without a break, without interruption; **informal** on the trot.

– OPPOSITES separately.

▸adj. **informal** *a very together young woman*. See **level-headed**.

toil v. **1** *she toiled all night* **work hard**, labour, exert oneself, slave (away), grind away, strive, work one's fingers to the bone, work like a Trojan/slave, keep one's nose to the grindstone; **informal** slog away, plug away, peg away, beaver away, work one's socks off, sweat blood; **Brit. informal** graft; **literary** travail; **old use** moil. **2** *she began to toil up the cliff path* **struggle**, trudge, tramp, traipse, slog, plod, trek, footslog, drag oneself; **Brit. informal** yomp; **N. Amer. informal** schlep.

– OPPOSITES rest, relax.

▸n. *a life of toil* **hard work**, labour, exertion, slaving, drudgery, effort, industry, {blood, sweat, and tears}; **informal** slog, elbow grease; **Brit. informal** graft; **literary** travail; **old use** moil.

toilet n. **1** *he had to go to the toilet* **lavatory**, WC, water closet, (public) convenience, cloakroom, powder room, urinal, privy, latrine, jakes; **N. Amer.** washroom, bathroom, rest room, men's/ladies' room, commode, comfort station; **Nautical** head; **informal** little girls'/boys' room, smallest room; **Brit. informal** loo, bog, the Ladies, the Gents, khazi, lav; **N. Amer. informal** can, john; **Austral./NZ informal** dunny; **old use** closet, garderobe. **2** *she had always taken a long time over her toilet* **washing**, bathing, showering; grooming, dressing, make-up; **formal or humorous** ablutions; **dated** toilette.

token n. **1** *a token of our appreciation* **symbol**, sign, emblem, badge, representation, indication, mark, manifestation, expression, pledge, demonstration, recognition; evidence, proof. **2** *he kept the menu as a token of their golden wedding* **memento**, souvenir, keepsake, reminder, remembrance, memorial. **3** *a book token* **voucher**, coupon. **4** *a telephone token* **counter**, disc, jetton, chip, piece, man.

▸adj. **1** *a one-day token strike* **symbolic**, emblematic, indicative; peppercorn. **2** *the practice now meets only token resistance* **perfunctory**, slight, nominal, minimal, minor, mild, superficial, inconsequential.

tolerable adj. **1** *a tolerable noise level*
bearable, endurable, supportable,
acceptable. **2** *he had a tolerable voice*
fairly good, passable, adequate, all right,
acceptable, satisfactory, not (too) bad,
average, fair; mediocre, middling, ordinary,
indifferent, unremarkable, unexceptional;
informal OK, so-so, nothing to write home
about, no great shakes.
– OPPOSITES unacceptable.

tolerance n. **1** *an attitude of tolerance
towards other people* **acceptance**, toleration;
open-mindedness, broad-mindedness,
forbearance, liberality, liberalism; patience,
charity, indulgence, understanding. **2** *the
plant's tolerance of pollution* **endurance**,
resilience, resistance, immunity. **3** *a
1% maximum tolerance in measurement*
deviation, variation, play; inaccuracy,
imprecision.

tolerant adj. **open-minded**, forbearing,
broad-minded, liberal, unprejudiced,
unbiased; patient, long-suffering,
understanding, charitable, lenient,
indulgent, permissive, free and easy, easy-
going, lax.
– OPPOSITES intolerant.

tolerate v. **1** *a regime unwilling to tolerate
serious dissent* **allow**, permit, condone,
accept, swallow, countenance; formal brook;
old use suffer. **2** *he couldn't tolerate her moods
any longer* **endure**, put up with, bear, take,
stand, support, stomach; informal hack, abide;
Brit. informal stick, wear, be doing with.

toleration n. **acceptance**, tolerance,
endurance; forbearance, liberality, open-
mindedness, broad-mindedness, liberalism;
patience, charity, indulgence, understanding.

toll[1] n. **1** *a motorway toll* **charge**, fee,
payment, levy, tariff, tax. **2** *the toll of dead
and injured* **number**, count, tally, total, sum
total, grand total, sum; record, list, listing.
3 *the toll on the environment has been high*
adverse effect(s), detriment, harm, damage,
injury, hurt; cost, price, loss, disadvantage,
suffering, penalty.

toll[2] v. *I heard the bell toll* **ring (out)**,
chime, strike, peal; sound, clang, resound,
reverberate; literary knell.

tomb n. **burial chamber**, sepulchre,
mausoleum, vault, crypt, undercroft,
catacomb; last/final resting place, grave,
barrow, burial mound; dolmen, cromlech;
historical charnel house.

> **WORD LINKS**
> **sepulchral** relating to a tomb
> **epitaph** an inscription on a tomb

tombstone n. **gravestone**, headstone,
stone; memorial, monument.

tome n. **volume**, book, work, opus,
publication, title.

tomfoolery n. **silliness**, fooling around,
clowning, capers, antics, pranks, tricks,
buffoonery, skylarking, nonsense, horseplay,
mischief, foolishness, foolery; informal larks,
shenanigans.

tone n. **1** *the tone of the tuba* **timbre**, sound,
sound quality, voice, voice quality, colour,
tone colour, tonality. **2** *his friendly tone*
intonation, tone of voice, modulation,
accentuation. **3** *the somewhat impatient tone
of his letter* **mood**, air, feel, flavour, note,
attitude, character, temper; tenor, vein, drift,
gist. **4** *a dialling tone* **note**, signal, beep,
bleep. **5** *tones of primrose, lavender, and rose*
shade, colour, hue, tint, tinge.
▸ v. *the caramel shirt toned well with her cream
skirt* **harmonize**, go, blend, coordinate,
team; match, suit, complement.
▫ **tone something down 1** *the colour needs
to be toned down a bit* **soften**, lighten, mute,
subdue. **2** *the papers refused to tone down
their criticism* **moderate**, modify, modulate,
mitigate, temper, dampen, soften, subdue.

tongue n. **1** *a foreign tongue* **language**,
dialect, patois, vernacular, mother tongue,
native tongue; informal lingo. **2** *her sharp
tongue* **way of speaking**, speech, parlance.

> **WORD LINKS**
> **lingual** relating to the tongue

tongue-tied adj. **lost for words**, speechless,
unable to get a word out, struck dumb,
dumbstruck; mute, dumb, silent; informal
mum.
– OPPOSITES loquacious.

tonic n. **1** *ginseng can be used as a natural
tonic* **stimulant**, restorative, refresher;
informal pick-me-up, bracer; Medicine analeptic.
2 *we found the change of scene a tonic*
stimulant, boost, fillip; informal shot in the
arm, pick-me-up.

too adv. **1** *invasion would be too risky*
excessively, overly, over, unduly,
immoderately, inordinately, unreasonably,
extremely, very; informal too-too. **2** *he was
unhappy, too, you know* **also**, as well, in
addition, additionally, into the bargain,
besides, furthermore, moreover, on top of
that, to boot.

tool n. **1** *garden tools* **implement**,
utensil, instrument, device, apparatus,
gadget, appliance, machine, contrivance,
contraption; informal gizmo. **2** *the beautiful
Estella is Miss Havisham's tool* **puppet**, pawn,
creature, cat's paw; minion, lackey; informal
stooge.
▸ v. *red leather, tooled in gold* **ornament**,
embellish, decorate, work, cut, chase.

tooth n. **fang**, tusk; molar, incisor, canine;
Zoology denticle; informal gnasher; Brit. informal
pearly white.

> **WORD LINKS**
> **dental** relating to teeth
> **dentition** the arrangement of the teeth in a
> particular species
> **occlusion** the position of the teeth when the
> jaws are closed
> **odontology** the scientific study of teeth
> **orthodontics** the treatment of irregularities in
> the teeth

t

> **caries** tooth decay
> **plaque** a sticky deposit on teeth
> **tartar, scale** a hard deposit formed on teeth

toothsome adj. **tasty**, delicious, luscious, mouth-watering, delectable, succulent; tempting, appetizing, inviting; informal scrumptious, yummy, scrummy, finger-licking; Brit. informal moreish.

top n. **1** *the top of the cliff* **summit**, peak, mountaintop, pinnacle, crest, crown, brow, head, tip, apex, vertex. **2** *the top of the table* **upper part**, upper surface, upper layer. **3** *the carrots' green tops* **leaves**, shoots, stem, stalk. **4** *the top of the coffee jar* **lid**, cap, cover, stopper, cork. **5** *a short-sleeved top* **sweater**, jumper, jersey, sweat shirt; T-shirt, shirt; blouse. **6** *by 1981 he was at the top of his profession* **high point**, height, peak, pinnacle, zenith, acme, culmination, climax, crowning point; prime.
– OPPOSITES bottom, base.
▶adj. **1** *the top floor* **highest**, topmost, uppermost, upmost. **2** *the world's top scientists* **foremost**, leading, principal, pre-eminent, greatest, best, finest, elite; informal top-notch. **3** *the organization's top management* **chief**, principal, main, leading, highest, highest-ranking, ruling, commanding, most powerful, most important. **4** *a top Paris hotel* **prime**, excellent, superb, superior, choice, select, top-quality, top-tier, top-grade, first-rate, first-class, grade A, best, finest, premier, superlative, second to none; informal A1, top-notch. **5** *they are travelling at top speed* **maximum**, maximal, greatest, utmost.
– OPPOSITES bottom, lowest, minimum.
▶v. **1** *sales are expected to top £1.3 billion* **exceed**, surpass, go beyond, better, best, beat, outstrip, outdo, outshine, eclipse, go one better than. **2** *their debut CD is currently topping the charts* **lead**, head, be at the top of. **3** *they topped the rise of a mist-shrouded valley* **reach the top of**, crest, climb, scale, ascend, mount. **4** *chocolate mousse topped with cream* **cover**, cap, coat, smother; finish, garnish.
☐ **over the top** informal excessive, immoderate, inordinate, extreme, exaggerated, extravagant, overblown, too much, unreasonable, disproportionate, undue, unwarranted, uncalled for, unnecessary, going too far; informal a bit much, OTT.

top something up fill, refill, refresh, freshen, replenish, recharge, resupply; supplement, add to, augment.

topic n. **subject**, subject matter, theme, issue, matter, point, talking point, question, concern, argument, thesis, text, keynote.

topical adj. **current**, up to date, up to the minute, contemporary, recent, relevant; newsworthy, in the news.
– OPPOSITES out of date.

topmost adj. **1** *the tree's topmost branches* **highest**, top, uppermost, upmost. **2** *the topmost authority on the subject* **foremost**,

leading, principal, premier, prime, top, greatest, best, supreme, pre-eminent, outstanding, most important, main, chief; N. Amer. ranking; informal number-one.

top-notch adj. informal **first-class**, first-rate, top-quality, top-tier, five-star; superior, prime, premier, premium, grade A, superlative, best, finest, select, exclusive, excellent, superb, outstanding, splendid; informal tip-top, A1.

topple v. **1** *she toppled over* **fall**, tumble, overbalance, overturn, tip, keel; lose one's balance. **2** *protesters toppled a huge statue* **knock over**, upset, push over, tip over, upend. **3** *a plot to topple the government* **overthrow**, oust, unseat, overturn, bring down, defeat, get rid of, dislodge, eject.

topsy-turvy adj. **1** *a topsy-turvy flag* **upside down**, the wrong way/side up, inverted. **2** *everything in the flat was topsy-turvy* **in disarray**, in a mess, in a muddle, in disorder, disordered, in chaos, chaotic, disorganized, awry, upside down, at sixes and sevens; informal every which way, higgledy-piggledy.
– OPPOSITES neat.

torch n. **1** *an electric torch* **lamp**, light, flashlight. **2** historical *a flaming torch* **firebrand**, brand; historical cresset, flambeau.
▶v. informal *one of the shops had been torched* **burn**, set fire to, set on fire, set light to, set alight, incinerate, put/set a match to.

torment n. **1** *months of mental and emotional torment* **agony**, suffering, torture, pain, anguish, misery, distress, affliction, trauma, wretchedness; hell, purgatory. **2** *it was a torment to see him like that* **ordeal**, affliction, scourge, curse, plague, bane, thorn in someone's side/flesh, cross to bear; sorrow, tribulation, trouble.
▶v. **1** *she was tormented by shame* **torture**, afflict, rack, harrow, plague, haunt, distress, agonize. **2** *she began to torment the two younger boys* **tease**, taunt, bait, harass, provoke, goad, plague, bother, trouble, persecute; informal needle.

torn adj. **1** *a torn shirt* **ripped**, rent, cut, slit; ragged, tattered, in tatters, in ribbons. **2** *she was torn between the two options* **wavering**, vacillating, irresolute, dithering, uncertain, unsure, undecided, in two minds.

tornado n. **whirlwind**, windstorm, cyclone, typhoon, storm, superstorm, hurricane; N. Amer. informal twister.

torpid adj. **lethargic**, sluggish, inert, inactive, slow, lifeless; languid, listless, lazy, idle, indolent, slothful, supine, passive, apathetic, somnolent, sleepy, weary, tired.
– OPPOSITES energetic.

torpor n. **lethargy**, sluggishness, inertia, inactivity, lifelessness, listlessness, languor, lassitude, laziness, idleness, indolence, sloth, accidie, passivity, somnolence, weariness, sleepiness.

torrent n. **1** *a torrent of water* **flood**, deluge, inundation, spate, cascade, rush, stream, current, flow, overflow, tide. **2** *a torrent of abuse* **outburst**, outpouring, stream, flood,

t

volley, barrage, tide, spate.
– OPPOSITES trickle.

torrential adj. **copious**, heavy, teeming, severe, relentless, violent.

torrid adj. **1** *a torrid summer* **hot**, dry, scorching, searing, blazing, blistering, sweltering, burning; informal boiling (hot), baking (hot), sizzling. **2** *a torrid affair* **passionate**, ardent, lustful, amorous; informal steamy, sizzling, hot.
– OPPOSITES cold.

tortuous adj. **1** *a tortuous route* **twisting**, twisty, twisting and turning, winding, windy, zigzag, sinuous, snaky, meandering, serpentine. **2** *a tortuous argument* **convoluted**, complicated, complex, labyrinthine, involved, confusing, difficult to follow, lengthy, overlong.
– OPPOSITES straight, straightforward.

torture n. **1** *the torture of political prisoners* **abuse**, ill-treatment, maltreatment, persecution. **2** *the torture of losing a loved one* **torment**, agony, suffering, pain, anguish, misery, distress, heartbreak, affliction, trauma, wretchedness; hell, purgatory.
▸ v. **1** *the security forces routinely tortured suspects* **inflict pain on**, ill-treat, abuse, mistreat, maltreat, persecute; informal work over, give someone the works. **2** *he was tortured by grief* **torment**, rack, afflict, harrow, plague, agonize, crucify.

toss v. **1** *he tossed his tools into the boot* **throw**, hurl, fling, sling, cast, pitch, lob, propel, project, launch; informal heave, chuck, bung; dated shy. **2** *he tossed a coin and it landed heads up* **flip**, flick, spin. **3** *the ship tossed about on the waves* **pitch**, lurch, rock, roll, plunge, reel, list, keel, sway, wallow, make heavy weather. **4** *toss the salad ingredients together* **shake**, stir, turn, mix, combine.

tot[1] n. **1** *the tot looks just like her mum* **infant**, baby, toddler, tiny tot, child, little one, mite; Scottish bairn, wean. **2** *a tot of rum* **dram**, drink, nip, drop, slug; informal shot, finger, snifter.

tot[2] v. **1** *he totted up some figures* **add**, total, count, calculate, compute, reckon, tally. **2** *we've totted up 89 victories* **accumulate**, build up, amass, accrue.

total adj. **1** *the total cost* **entire**, complete, whole, full, comprehensive, combined, aggregate, gross, overall. **2** *a total disaster* **complete**, utter, absolute, thorough, perfect, downright, out-and-out, outright, thoroughgoing, all-out, sheer, arrant, positive, prize, rank, unmitigated, unqualified; Brit. informal right, proper.
– OPPOSITES partial.
▸ n. *a total of £160,000* **sum**, sum total, grand total, aggregate; whole, entirety, totality.
▸ v. **1** *the prize money totalled £33,050* **add up to**, amount to, come to, run to, make, work out as. **2** *he totalled up his score* **add (up)**, count, reckon, tot up, compute, work out.

totalitarian adj. **autocratic**, undemocratic, one-party, dictatorial, tyrannical, despotic, undemocratic, anti-democratic, fascist, oppressive, repressive, illiberal; authoritarian, autarchic, absolute, absolutist.
– OPPOSITES democratic.

totality n. **entirety**, whole, total, aggregate, sum, sum total; all, everything.

totally adv. **completely**, entirely, wholly, thoroughly, fully, utterly, absolutely, perfectly, unreservedly, unconditionally, quite, altogether, downright; in every way, in every respect, one hundred per cent, every inch, to the hilt; informal dead, deadly.
– OPPOSITES partly.

totter v. **1** *he tottered off down the road* **teeter**, walk unsteadily, stagger, wobble, stumble, shuffle, shamble, toddle; reel, sway, roll, lurch. **2** *the foundations began to heave and totter* **shake**, sway, tremble, quiver, teeter, shudder, judder, rock, quake.

touch v. **1** *his shoes were touching the end of the bed* **be in contact with**, come into contact with, meet, join, connect with, converge with, be contiguous with, be against. **2** *he touched her cheek* **press lightly**, tap, pat; feel, stroke, fondle, caress, pet; brush, graze. **3** *sales touched twenty grand last year* **reach**, attain, come to, make; rise to, soar to; sink to, plummet to; informal hit. **4** *nobody can touch him when he's on form* **compare with**, be on a par with, equal, match, be a match for, be in the same class/league as, parallel, rival, come/get close to, measure up to; better, beat; informal hold a candle to. **5** *you're not supposed to touch the computer* **handle**, hold, pick up, move; meddle with, play about with, fiddle with, interfere with, tamper with, disturb, lay a finger on; use, employ, make use of. **6** *state companies which have been touched by privatization* **affect**, have an effect/impact on, make a difference to. **7** *Lisa felt touched by her kindness* **affect**, move, tug at someone's heartstrings; leave an impression on, have an effect on.
▸ n. **1** *her touch on his shoulder* **tap**, pat; stroke, caress; brush, graze. **2** *his political touch* **skill**, skilfulness, expertise, dexterity, deftness, adroitness, adeptness, ability, talent, flair, facility, proficiency, knack, technique, approach, style. **3** *there was a touch of bitterness in her voice* | *add a touch of vinegar* **trace**, bit, suggestion, suspicion, hint, scintilla, tinge, overtone, undertone; dash, taste, spot, drop, dab, pinch, speck, soupçon. **4** *the gas lights are a nice touch* **detail**, feature, point; addition, accessory. **5** *have you been in touch with him?* **contact**, communication, correspondence; connection, association.
□ **touch down** land, alight, come down, put down, arrive.

touch something off 1 *he touched off two of the bombs* **detonate**, set off, trigger, explode. **2** *the plan touched off a major political storm* **cause**, spark off, trigger (off), start, set in motion, ignite, stir up, provoke, give rise to, lead to, generate.

touch on 1 *many television programmes*

have touched on the subject **refer to**, mention, comment on, remark on, bring up, raise, broach, allude to; cover, deal with. **2** *a self-confident manner touching on the arrogant* **come close to**, verge on, border on, approach.

touch someone up Brit. informal fondle, molest, feel up; informal grope, paw, maul, goose; N. Amer. informal cop a feel.

touch something up 1 *these paints are handy for touching up small areas* **repaint**, retouch, patch up, fix up; renovate, refurbish, revamp; informal do up. **2** *touch up your CV and improve your interview skills* **improve**, enhance, make better, refine; informal tweak.

> **WORD LINKS**
>
> **tactile** relating to the sense of touch
> **tangible, palpable** able to be touched
> **palpate** examine a part of the body by touch

touch-and-go adj. **uncertain**, precarious, risky, hazardous, dangerous, critical, suspenseful, cliffhanging, hanging by a thread.
– OPPOSITES certain.

touched adj. **1** *he was visibly touched by their plight* **affected**, moved. **2** informal *her mother was a bit touched*. See **mad** (sense 1).

touching adj. **moving**, affecting, heart-warming, emotional, emotive, tender, sentimental; poignant, sad, tear-jerking.

touchstone n. **criterion**, standard, yardstick, benchmark, barometer, litmus test; measure, point of reference, norm, gauge, test, guide, exemplar, model, pattern.

touchy adj. **1** *she can be so touchy* **sensitive**, oversensitive, hypersensitive, easily offended, thin-skinned, highly strung, tense; irritable, tetchy, testy, crotchety, peevish, querulous, bad-tempered, petulant, pettish; informal snappy, ratty; N. Amer. informal cranky. **2** *a touchy subject* **delicate**, sensitive, tricky, ticklish, embarrassing, awkward, difficult; contentious, controversial.
– OPPOSITES affable.

tough adj. **1** *tough leather gloves* **durable**, strong, resilient, sturdy, rugged, solid, stout, hard-wearing, long-lasting, heavy-duty, well built, made to last. **2** *the steak was tough* **chewy**, leathery, gristly, stringy, fibrous. **3** *he'll survive—he's pretty tough* **robust**, resilient, strong, hardy, rugged, fit; informal hard, (as) tough as old boots; dated stalwart. **4** *tough sentencing for persistent offenders* **strict**, stern, severe, stringent, rigorous, hard, firm, hard-hitting, uncompromising; unsentimental, unsympathetic. **5** *the training was pretty tough* **arduous**, onerous, strenuous, gruelling, exacting, difficult, demanding, hard, heavy, taxing, tiring, exhausting, punishing, laborious, stressful, Herculean; old use toilsome. **6** *these are tough questions for American policy-makers* **difficult**, hard, knotty, thorny, tricky.
– OPPOSITES soft, weak, easy.

▶ n. informal *a gang of toughs* **ruffian**, thug,

hoodlum, hooligan, bully boy; Brit. rough; informal roughneck, heavy, bruiser, gorilla, yahoo; Brit. informal yob, yobbo.

toughen v. **1** *the process toughens the wood fibres* **strengthen**, fortify, reinforce, harden, temper, anneal. **2** *measures to toughen up prison discipline* **make stricter**, make more severe, stiffen, tighten up; informal beef up.

tour n. **1** *a three-day walking tour* **trip**, excursion, journey, expedition, jaunt, outing, trek, safari; old use peregrination. **2** *a tour of the factory* **visit**, inspection, guided tour, walkabout. **3** *his tour of duty in Ulster* **stint**, stretch, period, spell, turn, assignment.
▶ v. **1** *this hotel is well placed for touring Somerset* **travel round**, explore, holiday in; informal do. **2** *the prince toured a local factory* **visit**, go round, walk round, inspect.

tourist n. **holidaymaker**, traveller, sightseer, visitor, backpacker, globetrotter, day tripper, tripper; N. Amer. vacationer, vacationist, out-of-towner; Brit. informal grockle.
– OPPOSITES local.

tournament n. **1** *a golf tournament* **competition**, contest, championship, meeting, meet, event, match, fixture; Brit. clash. **2** historical *a knight preparing for a tournament* **joust**, tourney, tilt; the lists.

tousled adj. **untidy**, dishevelled, wind-blown, messy, disordered, disarranged, messed up, rumpled, uncombed, ungroomed, tangled, wild, unkempt; informal mussed up.
– OPPOSITES neat, tidy.

tout v. **1** *street merchants were touting their wares* **peddle**, sell, hawk, offer for sale; informal flog. **2** *minicab drivers were touting for business* **solicit**, seek, drum up; ask, petition, appeal, canvass. **3** *he's being touted as the next Scotland manager* **recommend**, speak of, talk of; predict; Brit. tip.

tow v. *the car was towed back to the garage* **pull**, haul, drag, draw, tug, lug.
□ **in tow** *he arrived with his new girlfriend in tow* **in attendance**, by one's side, in one's charge; accompanying, following.

towards prep. **1** *they were driving towards her flat* **in the direction of**, to; on the way to, on the road to, en route for. **2** *towards evening dark clouds gathered* **just before**, shortly before, near, nearing, around, approaching, close to, coming to, getting on for. **3** *her attitude towards politics* **with regard to**, as regards, regarding, in/with regard to, respecting, in relation to, concerning, about, apropos. **4** *a grant towards the cost of new buses* **as a contribution to**, for, to help with.

tower n. *a church tower* **steeple**, spire; minaret; turret; bell tower, belfry, campanile.
▶ v. **1** *snow-capped peaks towered over the valley* **soar**, rise, rear; overshadow, overhang, hang over, dominate. **2** *he towered over most other theologians of his generation* **dominate**, overshadow, outshine, outclass, eclipse, be head and shoulders above, put someone/something in the shade.

towering adj. **1** *a towering skyscraper* **high**, tall, lofty, soaring, sky-high, sky-scraping, multistorey; giant, gigantic, enormous, huge, massive; informal ginormous. **2** *a towering intellect* **outstanding**, pre-eminent, leading, foremost, finest, top, surpassing, supreme, great, incomparable, unrivalled, unsurpassed, peerless. **3** *a towering rage* **extreme**, fierce, terrible, intense, overpowering, mighty, violent, vehement, passionate.

town n. **urban area**, conurbation, municipality; city, metropolis, megalopolis; Brit. borough; Scottish burgh; N. Amer. informal burg.
– OPPOSITES country.

> **WORD LINKS**
> civic, municipal, urban relating to a town

toxic adj. **poisonous**, virulent, noxious, dangerous, harmful, injurious, pernicious.
– OPPOSITES harmless.

toy n. **1** *a cuddly toy* **plaything**, game. **2** *an executive toy* **gadget**, device; trinket, knick-knack; informal gizmo.
▸ adj. **1** *a toy gun* **model**, imitation, replica; miniature. **2** *a toy poodle* **miniature**, small, tiny, fun-size, diminutive, dwarf, midget, pygmy.
□ **toy with 1** *I was toying with the idea of writing a book* **think about**, consider, flirt with, entertain the possibility of; informal kick around. **2** *Adam toyed with his glasses* **fiddle with**, play with, fidget with, twiddle; finger. **3** *she toyed with her food* **nibble**, pick at, peck at, eat listlessly, eat like a bird.

trace v. **1** *police hope to trace the owner of the jewellery* **track down**, find, discover, detect, unearth, turn up, hunt down, ferret out, run to ground. **2** *she traced a pattern in the sand with her toe* **draw**, outline, mark. **3** *the analysis traces out the consequences of such beliefs* **outline**, map out, sketch out, delineate, depict, show, indicate.
▸ n. **1** *no trace had been found of the missing plane* **vestige**, sign, mark, indication, evidence, clue; remains, remnant, relic; survival. **2** *a trace of bitterness crept into her voice* **bit**, touch, hint, suggestion, suspicion, shadow, whiff; drop, dash, tinge, speck, shred, jot, iota; informal smidgen, tad. **3** *the ground was hard and they left no traces* **trail**, tracks, marks, prints, footprints; spoor.

track n. **1** *a gravel track* **path**, pathway, footpath, lane, trail, route, way, course. **2** *the final lap of the track* **course**, racecourse, racetrack; velodrome; Brit. circuit. **3** *he found the tracks of a grey fox* **traces**, marks, prints, footprints, trail, spoor. **4** *Orkney lies on the track of the Atlantic winds* **course**, path, line, route, way, trajectory. **5** *commuters had to walk along the tracks* **rail**, line, railway line. **6** *the album's title track* **song**, recording, number, piece.
▸ v. *he tracked a bear for 40 km* **follow**, trail, trace, pursue, shadow, stalk, keep an eye on, keep in sight; informal tail.

□ **keep track of** monitor, follow, keep up with, keep an eye on; keep in touch with, keep up to date with; informal keep tabs on.
track someone/something down discover, find, detect, hunt down/out, unearth, uncover, turn up, dig up, ferret out, bring to light, run to earth, run to ground.

tract[1] n. *large tracts of land* **area**, region, belt, expanse, sweep, stretch, extent, swathe, zone.

tract[2] n. *a political tract* **treatise**, essay, article, paper, work, monograph, disquisition, dissertation, thesis, homily; pamphlet, booklet, leaflet.

tractable adj. **malleable**, manageable, amenable, pliable, governable, yielding, complaisant, compliant, persuadable, accommodating, docile, biddable, obedient, submissive, meek.
– OPPOSITES recalcitrant.

traction n. **grip**, purchase, friction, adhesion.

trade n. **1** *the illicit trade in stolen cattle* **commerce**, buying and selling, dealing, traffic, trafficking, business, marketing, merchandising; dealings, transactions. **2** *the glazier's trade* **craft**, occupation, job, career, profession, business, line (of work), métier, vocation, calling, walk of life, field; work, employment.
▸ v. **1** *he made his fortune trading in beaver pelts* **deal**, buy and sell, traffic, market, merchandise, peddle; informal hawk, flog. **2** *the business is trading at a loss* **operate**, run, do business. **3** *I traded the old machine for a newer model* **swap**, exchange, switch; barter.
□ **trade on** exploit, take advantage of, capitalize on, profit from, use, make use of; milk; informal cash in on.

> **WORD LINKS**
> mercantile relating to trade

trademark n. **1** *the company's trademark* **logo**, emblem, sign, mark, stamp, symbol, device, badge, crest, monogram, colophon; trade name, brand name, proprietary name. **2** *it had all the trademarks of a Mafia hit* **characteristic**, hallmark, telltale sign, sign, trait, quality, attribute, feature, peculiarity, idiosyncrasy.

trader n. **dealer**, merchant, buyer, seller, buyer and seller, marketeer, merchandiser, broker, agent; distributor, vendor, purveyor, supplier, trafficker; shopkeeper, retailer, wholesaler; trademark in US e-tailer; Brit. informal flogger.

tradesman, tradeswoman n.
1 *tradesmen standing nonchalantly outside their stores* **shopkeeper**, retailer, vendor, wholesaler; N. Amer. storekeeper. **2** *a qualified tradesman* **craftsman**, craftswoman, workman, artisan.

tradition n. **1** *during a maiden speech, by tradition, everyone keeps absolutely silent* **historical convention**, unwritten law; oral history, lore, folklore. **2** *an age-old tradition* **custom**, practice, convention, ritual, observance, way, usage, habit, institution; formal praxis.

traditional adj. **1** *traditional Christmas fare* **long-established**, customary, time-honoured, established, classic, accustomed, standard, regular, normal, conventional, usual, orthodox, habitual, set, fixed, routine, ritual; old, age-old; literary wonted. **2** *traditional beliefs* **handed-down**, folk, unwritten, oral.

traditionalist n. *she married an old-guard traditionalist* **conservative**, right-winger, rightist, reactionary, conformist; informal square, stick-in-the-mud, fuddy-duddy.
– OPPOSITES radical.
▶ adj. *a traditionalist splinter group* **conservative**, traditional, established, accepted, orthodox, conventional, conformist, reactionary.
– OPPOSITES radical.

traduce v. **defame**, slander, speak ill of, misrepresent, malign, vilify, denigrate, disparage, slur, impugn, smear, besmirch, run down, blacken the name of, cast aspersions on; informal bad-mouth; formal calumniate.

traffic n. **1** *the bridge is not open to traffic* **vehicles**, cars, lorries, trucks. **2** *they might be stuck in traffic* **traffic jams**, congestion, gridlock, tailbacks, hold-ups, queues; informal snarl-ups. **3** *the increased use of railways for goods traffic* **transport**, transportation, freight, conveyancing, shipping. **4** *the illegal traffic in stolen art* **trade**, trading, trafficking, dealing, commerce, business, buying and selling; smuggling, bootlegging, black market; dealings, transactions.
▶ v. *he confessed to trafficking in gold and ivory* **trade**, deal, do business, buy and sell; smuggle, bootleg; informal run.

tragedy n. **disaster**, calamity, catastrophe, cataclysm, misfortune, reverse, vicissitude, trial, tribulation, affliction, adversity.

tragic adj. **1** *a tragic accident* **disastrous**, calamitous, catastrophic, cataclysmic, devastating, terrible, dreadful, awful, appalling, horrendous; fatal, deadly, mortal, lethal. **2** *a tragic tale* **sad**, unhappy, pathetic, moving, distressing, painful, harrowing, heart-rending, piteous, wretched, sorry; melancholy, doleful, mournful. **3** *a tragic waste of talent* **dreadful**, terrible, awful, deplorable, lamentable, regrettable; formal grievous.
– OPPOSITES fortunate, happy.

trail n. **1** *he left a trail of clues | a trail of devastation* **series**, string, chain, succession, sequence; aftermath. **2** *wolves on the trail of their prey* **track**, spoor, path, scent; traces, marks, signs, prints, footprints. **3** *the plane's vapour trail* **wake**, tail, stream. **4** *a trail of ants* **line**, column, train, file, procession, string, chain, convoy; queue. **5** *country parks with nature trails* **path**, pathway, way, footpath, track, course, route.
▶ v. **1** *her robe trailed along the ground* **drag**, sweep, be drawn; dangle, hang (down), droop. **2** *the roses grew wild, their stems trailing over the banks* **hang**, droop, fall, spill, cascade. **3** *Sharpe suspected that they were trailing him* **follow**, pursue, track, shadow, stalk, hunt (down); run to earth, run to ground; informal tail. **4** *the defending champions were trailing 10–5 at half time* **lose**, be down, be behind, lag behind. **5** *I hate trailing round the shops* **trudge**, plod, drag oneself, traipse, trek; N. Amer. informal schlep. **6** *her voice trailed off* **fade**, tail off/away, grow faint, die away, dwindle, subside, peter out, fizzle out.

train v. **1** *an engineer trained in remote-sensing techniques* **instruct**, teach, coach, tutor, school, educate, prime, drill, ground; inculcate, indoctrinate. **2** *she's training to be a hairdresser* **study**, learn, prepare, take instruction. **3** *with the Olympics in mind, athletes are training hard* **exercise**, do exercises, work out, get into shape, practise. **4** *she trained the gun on his chest* **aim**, point, direct, level, focus; take aim, zero in on.
▶ n. **1** *the train for London* **railway train**; baby talk choo-choo. **2** *a minister and his train of attendants* **retinue**, entourage, cortège, following, staff, household, court, suite, attendants, retainers, followers, bodyguards. **3** *a train of elephants* **procession**, line, file, column, convoy, cavalcade, caravan, queue, string, succession. **4** *a bizarre train of events* **chain**, string, series, sequence, succession, set, course, cycle, concatenation.

trainer n. **coach**, instructor, teacher, tutor; handler.

training n. **1** *in-house training for staff* **instruction**, teaching, coaching, tuition, tutoring, schooling, education, pedagogy; indoctrination, inculcation. **2** *four months' hard training before the match* **exercise**, exercises, working out; practice, preparation.

traipse v. **trudge**, trek, tramp, trail, plod, drag oneself, slog; Brit. informal trog; N. Amer. informal schlep.

trait n. **characteristic**, attribute, feature, (essential) quality, property; habit, custom, mannerism, idiosyncrasy, peculiarity, quirk, oddity, foible.

traitor n. **betrayer**, back-stabber, double-crosser, double-dealer, renegade, Judas, quisling, fifth columnist; turncoat, defector, deserter; collaborator, informer, double agent; informal snake in the grass, two-timer.

traitorous adj. **treacherous**, disloyal, treasonous, back-stabbing; double-crossing, double-dealing, faithless, unfaithful, two-faced, Janus-faced, false-hearted, duplicitous, deceitful, false; informal two-timing; literary perfidious.
– OPPOSITES loyal.

trajectory n. **course**, path, route, track, line, orbit.

trammel literary n. *the trammels of tradition* **restraint**, constraint, curb, check, impediment, obstacle, barrier, handicap, bar, hindrance, encumbrance, disadvantage, drawback, snag, stumbling block; straitjacket, shackles, fetters, bonds.
▶ v. *those less trammelled by convention than*

himself **restrict**, restrain, constrain, hamper, confine, hinder, handicap, obstruct, impede, hold back, hamstring, shackle, fetter.

tramp v. 1 *men were tramping through the shrubbery* **trudge**, plod, stamp, trample, lumber, clump, clomp, stump, stomp; informal traipse, galumph. 2 *he spent ten days tramping through the jungle* **trek**, slog, footslog, trudge, drag oneself, walk, hike, march; informal traipse; Brit. informal yomp; N. Amer. informal schlep.
▸ n. 1 *a dirty old tramp* **vagrant**, vagabond, homeless person, down-and-out; traveller, drifter, beachcomber; beggar, mendicant; N. Amer. hobo; Austral./NZ bagman; informal bag lady; N. Amer. informal bum. 2 *the regular tramp of the sentry's boots* **footstep**, step, footfall, tread, stamp, stomp. 3 *a tramp round Norwich* **trek**, slog, trudge, hike, march, walk; Brit. informal yomp; N. Amer. informal schlep.

trample v. 1 *someone had trampled on the tulips* **tread**, tramp, stamp, stomp, walk over; squash, crush, flatten. 2 *we do nothing but trample over their feelings* **treat with contempt**, ride roughshod over, disregard, set at naught, show no consideration for, abuse; encroach on, infringe.

trance n. **daze**, stupor, hypnotic state, half-conscious state, dream; Scottish dwam.

tranquil adj. 1 *a wonderfully tranquil village* **peaceful**, calm, restful, quiet, still, relaxing, undisturbed. 2 *Martha smiled, perfectly tranquil* **calm**, serene, relaxed, unruffled, unperturbed, unflustered, untroubled, composed, {cool, calm, and collected}; equable, even-tempered, placid, phlegmatic; informal unflappable.
– OPPOSITES busy, excitable.

tranquillity n. 1 *the tranquillity of the Norfolk countryside* **peace**, peacefulness, restfulness, repose, calm, calmness, quiet, quietness, stillness. 2 *the incident jolted her out of her tranquillity* **composure**, calmness, serenity; equanimity, equability, placidity; informal cool, unflappability.

tranquillize v. **sedate**, put under sedation, narcotize, drug.

tranquillizer n. **sedative**, barbiturate, calmative, sleeping pill, narcotic, opiate; informal trank, downer.
– OPPOSITES stimulant.

transact v. **conduct**, carry out, negotiate, do, perform, execute, take care of; settle, conclude, finish, clinch, accomplish.

transaction n. 1 *property transactions* **deal**, business deal, undertaking, arrangement, bargain, negotiation, agreement, settlement; proceedings. 2 *the transactions of the Historical Society* **proceedings**, report, record(s), minutes, account; archives. 3 *the transaction of government business* **conduct**, carrying out, negotiation, performance, execution.

transcend v. 1 *an issue that transcended party politics* **go beyond**, rise above, cut across. 2 *his military exploits far transcended those of his predecessors* **surpass**, exceed,

beat, top, cap, outdo, outclass, outstrip, leave behind, outshine, eclipse, overshadow, throw into the shade, upstage.

transcendence n. **excellence**, supremacy, incomparability, matchlessness, magnificence.

transcendent adj. 1 *the search for a transcendent level of knowledge* **mystical**, mystic, transcendental, spiritual; metaphysical. 2 *a transcendent genius* **incomparable**, matchless, peerless, unrivalled, inimitable, beyond compare/comparison, unparalleled, unequalled, without equal, second to none, unsurpassed, unsurpassable, nonpareil; exceptional, consummate, unique, perfect, rare, surpassing, magnificent; formal unexampled.

transcendental adj. See **transcendent** (sense 1).

transcribe v. 1 *each interview was taped and transcribed* **write out**, copy out, put in writing, put on paper. 2 *a person who can take and transcribe shorthand* **transliterate**, interpret, translate.

transcript n. **written version**, printed version, text, transliteration, record, reproduction.

transfer v. 1 *the hostages were transferred to a safe house* **move**, convey, take, bring, shift, remove, carry, transport; transplant, relocate, resettle. 2 *the property was transferred to his wife* **hand over**, pass on, make over, turn over, sign over, consign, devolve, assign, delegate.
▸ n. *he died shortly after his transfer to hospital* **move**, conveyance, transferral, transference, relocation, removal, transplantation.

transfigure v. **transform**, transmute, change, alter, metamorphose; humorous transmogrify.

transfix v. 1 *he was transfixed by the images on the screen* **mesmerize**, hypnotize, spellbind, bewitch, captivate, entrance, enthral, fascinate, enrapture, grip, rivet; root to the spot, paralyse. 2 *a field mouse is transfixed by the owl's curved talons* **impale**, stab, spear, pierce, spike, skewer, gore, stick, run through; literary transpierce.

transform v. **change**, alter, convert, metamorphose, transfigure, transmute; revolutionize, overhaul; remodel, reshape, remould, redo, reconstruct, rebuild, reorganize, rearrange, rework, renew, revamp, remake; humorous transmogrify.

transformation n. **change**, alteration, conversion, metamorphosis, transfiguration, transmutation, sea change; revolution, overhaul; remodelling, reshaping, remoulding, redoing, reconstruction, rebuilding, reorganization, rearrangement, reworking, renewal, revamp, remaking; humorous transmogrification.

transgress v. 1 *if they transgress the punishment is harsh* **misbehave**, behave badly, break the law, err, fall from grace, stray from the straight and narrow, sin, do wrong, go astray; old use trespass. **2** *she had transgressed an unwritten social law* **infringe**, breach, contravene, disobey, defy, violate, break, flout.

transgression n. **1** *a punishment for past transgressions* **offence**, crime, sin, wrong, wrongdoing, misdemeanour, misdeed, lawbreaking; error, lapse, fault; old use trespass. **2** *Adam's transgression of God's law* **infringement**, breach, contravention, violation, defiance, disobedience, non-observance.

transgressor n. **wrongdoer**, offender, miscreant, lawbreaker, criminal, villain, felon, malefactor, guilty party, culprit; sinner, evildoer; old use trespasser.

transient adj. **transitory**, temporary, short-lived, short-term, ephemeral, impermanent, brief, short, momentary, fleeting, passing, fugitive, here today and gone tomorrow; literary evanescent.
– OPPOSITES permanent.

transit n. *the transit of goods between states* **transport**, transportation, movement, conveyance, shipment, haulage, freightage, carriage, transfer.
□ **in transit** en route, on the journey, on the way, along/on the road, during transport.

transition n. **change**, passage, move, transformation, conversion, metamorphosis, alteration, changeover, shift, switch, jump, leap, progression, progress, development, evolution.

transitional adj. **1** *a transitional period* **intermediate**, interim, changeover; changing, fluid, unsettled. **2** *the transitional government* **interim**, temporary, provisional, pro tem, acting, caretaker.

transitory adj. **transient**, temporary, brief, short, short-lived, short-term, impermanent, ephemeral, momentary, fleeting, passing, fugitive, here today and gone tomorrow; literary evanescent.
– OPPOSITES permanent.

translate v. **1** *the German original had been translated into English* **render**, put, express, convert, change; transcribe, transliterate. **2** *be prepared to translate the jargon into normal English* **render**, paraphrase, reword, rephrase, convert, decipher, decode, gloss, explain. **3** *interesting ideas cannot always be translated into effective movies* **change**, convert, transform, alter, adapt, turn, transmute; humorous transmogrify. **4** *in 1228 the bishop was translated from Salisbury to Durham* **relocate**, transfer, move, remove, shift, transplant.

translation n. **1** *the translation of the Bible into English* **rendition**, rendering, conversion; transcription, transliteration. **2** *the translation of these policies into practice* **conversion**, change, transformation, alteration, adaptation, transmutation; humorous transmogrification.

translucent adj. **semi-transparent**, pellucid, limpid, clear; diaphanous, gossamer, sheer.

– OPPOSITES opaque.

transmission n. **1** *the transmission of knowledge and culture* **transference**, transferral, communication, conveyance; dissemination, spreading, circulation. **2** *the transmission of the film* **broadcasting**, relaying, airing, televising. **3** *a live transmission* **broadcast**, programme, show, videocast, podcast.

transmit v. **1** *the use of computers to transmit information* **transfer**, pass on, hand on, communicate, convey, impart, channel, carry, relay, dispatch; disseminate, spread, circulate. **2** *the programme will be transmitted on Sunday* **broadcast**, relay, send out, air, televise, videocast, podcast.

transmute v. **change**, alter, adapt, transform, convert, metamorphose, translate; humorous transmogrify.

transparency n. **1** *the transparency of the glass* **translucency**, limpidity, glassiness, clearness, clarity. **2** *colour transparencies* **slide**, diapositive.

transparent adj. **1** *transparent blue water* **clear**, crystal clear, see-through, translucent, pellucid, limpid, glassy. **2** *fine transparent fabrics* **see-through**, sheer, filmy, gauzy, diaphanous. **3** *the symbolism of this myth is transparent* **obvious**, unambiguous, unequivocal, clear, crystal clear, plain, (as) plain as the nose on your face, apparent, unmistakable, manifest, conspicuous, patent, palpable, indisputable, evident, self-evident, undisguised, unconcealed.
– OPPOSITES opaque, obscure.

transpire v. **1** *it transpired that her family had moved away* **become known**, emerge, come to light, be revealed, turn out, come out, be discovered, prove to be the case. **2** *I'm going to find out exactly what transpired* **happen**, occur, take place, arise, come about, turn up, chance, befall; literary come to pass.

transplant v. **1** *it was proposed to transplant the club to the vacant site* **transfer**, move, remove, shift, relocate, take. **2** *the seedlings should be transplanted in larger pots* **replant**, repot, relocate. **3** *kidneys must be transplanted within 48 hours of removal* **transfer**, implant.

transport v. **1** *the concrete blocks were transported by lorry* **convey**, carry, take, transfer, move, shift, send, deliver, bear, ship, ferry; informal cart. **2** *he was convicted of theft and transported* **banish**, exile, deport, expatriate, extradite. **3** *she was completely transported by the excitement* **thrill**, delight, carry away, enrapture, entrance, enchant, enthral, electrify, captivate, bewitch, fascinate, spellbind, charm; informal send; literary ravish.
▶ n. **1** *alternative forms of transport* **conveyance**, transportation; vehicle. **2** *the transport of crude oil* **transportation**, conveyance, carriage, freight, freightage, shipment, shipping, haulage; transit. **3** *transports of delight* **rapture**, ecstasy, elation, exaltation, exhilaration, euphoria,

bliss, seventh heaven, heaven, paradise, high; passion, strong feeling/emotion; informal cloud nine.

transpose v. **1** *the blue and black plates were transposed* **interchange**, exchange, switch, swap (round), reverse, invert. **2** *the themes are transposed from the sphere of love to that of work* **transfer**, shift, relocate, transplant, move, displace.

transverse adj. **crosswise**, crossways, cross, horizontal, diagonal, oblique.

trap n. **1** *an animal caught in a trap* **snare**, net, mesh, gin, springe; N. Amer. deadfall. **2** *the question was set as a trap* **trick**, ploy, ruse, deception, subterfuge; booby trap; informal set-up. **3** informal *shut your trap!* See **mouth** (sense 1 of the noun).
▸ v. **1** *police trapped the two men, who admitted blackmail* **snare**, entrap, ensnare, lay a trap for; capture, catch, corner, ambush; old use ambuscade. **2** *a rat trapped in a barn* **confine**, cut off, corner, shut in, pen in, hem in; imprison, hold captive. **3** *I hoped to trap him into an admission* **trick**, dupe, deceive, lure, inveigle, beguile, fool, hoodwink; catch out, trip up.

trappings plural n. **accessories**, accoutrements, appurtenances, trimmings, frills, accompaniments, extras, ornamentation, adornment, decoration; regalia, panoply, paraphernalia, apparatus, finery, equipment, gear, effects, things.

trash n. **1** N. Amer. *the subway entrance was blocked with trash* **rubbish**, refuse, waste, litter, junk, detritus; N. Amer. garbage. **2** informal *if they read at all, they read trash* **rubbish**, nonsense, trivia, pulp (fiction), pap; N. Amer. garbage; informal drivel, dreck. **3** informal *they're just trash* **scum**, vermin, the dregs of society, the scum of the earth, the lowest of the low; informal dirt.
▸ v. N. Amer. informal **1** *the apartment had been totally trashed* **wreck**, ruin, destroy, wreak havoc on, devastate; vandalize; informal total. **2** *his play was trashed by the critics.* See **lambaste**.

trauma n. **1** *the trauma of divorce* **shock**, upheaval, distress, stress, strain, pain, anguish, suffering, upset, agony, misery, sorrow, grief, heartache, heartbreak, torture; ordeal, trial, tribulation, trouble, worry, anxiety; nightmare. **2** *the trauma to the liver* **injury**, damage, wound; cut, laceration, lesion, abrasion, contusion.

traumatic adj. **disturbing**, shocking, distressing, upsetting, heartbreaking, painful, agonizing, hurtful, stressful, damaging, injurious, harmful, awful, terrible, devastating, harrowing.

travail literary n. **1** *years of bitter travail* **ordeals**, trials, tribulations, trials and tribulations, trouble, hardship, privation, stress; drudgery, toil, slog, effort, exertion, labour, work, endeavour, sweat, struggle. **2** *a woman in travail* **labour**, childbirth; contractions, labour pains; old use childbed.

travel v. **1** *he spent much of his time travelling abroad* **journey**, tour, take a trip, voyage, go sightseeing, globetrot, backpack; informal gallivant; old use peregrinate. **2** *we travelled the length and breadth of the island* **journey through**, cross, traverse, cover; roam, rove, range, trek. **3** *light travels faster than sound* **move**, be transmitted.
▸ n. *he amassed great wealth during his travels* **journeys**, expeditions, trips, tours, excursions, voyages, treks, safaris, explorations, wanderings, odysseys, pilgrimages, jaunts; travelling, touring, sightseeing, backpacking, globetrotting; informal gallivanting; old use peregrinations.

traveller n. **1** *thousands of travellers were left stranded* **tourist**, tripper, holidaymaker, sightseer, visitor, globetrotter, backpacker; pilgrim; passenger, commuter, fare; N. Amer. vacationer, vacationist. **2** *a travellers' site* **gypsy**, Romany, tzigane; nomad, migrant, wanderer, itinerant, drifter; tramp, vagrant; dialect didicoi; Brit. derogatory tinker.

travelling adj. **1** *the travelling population* **nomadic**, itinerant, peripatetic, wandering, roaming, roving, wayfaring, migrant, vagrant, of no fixed address/abode; gypsy, Romany. **2** *a little travelling clock* **portable**, easily carried, easy to carry, lightweight, compact.

traverse v. **1** *he traversed the forest* **travel over/across**, cross, journey over/across, pass over; cover; ply; wander, roam, range. **2** *a ditch traversed by a wooden bridge* **cross**, bridge, span; extend across, lie across, stretch across.

travesty n. *a travesty of justice* **misrepresentation**, distortion, perversion, corruption, poor imitation, poor substitute, mockery, parody, caricature; farce, charade, pantomime, sham; informal apology for, excuse for.

treacherous adj. **1** *her treacherous brother betrayed her* **traitorous**, disloyal, faithless, unfaithful, duplicitous, false-hearted, deceitful, false, back-stabbing, double-crossing, double-dealing, two-faced, untrustworthy, unreliable; apostate, renegade; informal two-timing; literary perfidious. **2** *treacherous driving conditions* **dangerous**, hazardous, perilous, unsafe, precarious, risky, deceptive, unreliable; informal dicey, hairy.
– OPPOSITES loyal, faithful, reliable.

treachery n. **betrayal**, disloyalty, faithlessness, unfaithfulness, infidelity, breach of trust, duplicity, deceit, deception, stab in the back, back-stabbing, double-dealing, untrustworthiness; treason; informal two-timing; literary perfidy.

tread v. **1** *he trod purposefully down the hall* **walk**, step, stride, pace, go; march, tramp, plod, stomp, trudge. **2** *the snow had been trodden down by the horses* **crush**, flatten, press down, squash; trample on, tramp on, stamp on, stomp on.
▸ n. *we heard his heavy tread on the stairs* **step**, footstep, footfall, tramp.

t

treason n. **treachery**, lese-majesty; disloyalty, betrayal, faithlessness; sedition, subversion, mutiny, rebellion; high treason; literary perfidy.
– OPPOSITES allegiance, loyalty.

treasonable adj. **traitorous**, treacherous, disloyal; seditious, subversive, mutinous, rebellious; literary perfidious.
– OPPOSITES loyal.

treasure n. **1** *a casket of treasure* **riches**, valuables, jewels, gems, gold, silver, precious metals, money, cash; wealth, fortune; Brit. treasure trove. **2** *art treasures* **valuable object**, valuable, work of art, objet of virtu, masterpiece. **3** informal *she's a real treasure* **paragon**, gem, angel, nonpareil; find, prize; informal star, one of a kind, one in a million, the tops.
▶ v. *I treasure the photographs I took of Jack* **cherish**, hold dear, prize, set great store by, value greatly; adore, dote on, love dearly, be devoted to, worship.

treasury n. **1** *the national treasury* **exchequer**, purse; bank, coffers; revenues, finances, funds, moneys. **2** *the area is a treasury of early fossils* **rich source**, repository, storehouse, treasure house; fund, mine, bank. **3** *a treasury of stories* **anthology**, collection, miscellany, compilation, compendium.

treat v. **1** *Charlotte treated him very badly* **behave towards**, act towards, use; deal with, handle. **2** *police are treating the fires as arson* **regard**, consider, view, look on; put down as. **3** *the book treats its subject with insight and responsibility* **deal with**, tackle, handle, discuss, explore, investigate; consider, study, analyse. **4** *she was treated at Addenbrooke's Hospital* **care for**, nurse, tend, attend to; medicate. **5** *the plants may prove useful in treating cancer* **cure**, heal, remedy. **6** *he treated her to a slap-up lunch* **buy**, take out for, stand, give; pay for; entertain, wine and dine; informal foot the bill for. **7** *delegates were treated to authentic Indonesian dance performances* **regale with**, entertain with/by, fete with, amuse with, divert with. **8** formal *propagandists claimed that he was treating with the enemy* **negotiate**, discuss terms, have talks, consult, parley, talk, confer.
▶ n. **1** *a birthday treat* **celebration**, entertainment, amusement; surprise; party, excursion, outing. **2** *I bought you some chocolate as a treat* **present**, gift; titbit, delicacy, luxury, indulgence, extravagance; informal goody. **3** *it was a real treat to see them* **pleasure**, delight, thrill, joy.

treatise n. **disquisition**, essay, paper, work, exposition, discourse, dissertation, thesis, monograph, study, critique; tract, pamphlet.

treatment n. **1** *the company's treatment of its workers* **behaviour towards**, conduct towards; handling of, dealings with. **2** *she's responding well to treatment* **medical care**, therapy, nursing; medication, drugs, medicaments; cure, remedy. **3** *her*

treatment of the topic **discussion**, handling, investigation, exploration, consideration, study, analysis, critique.

treaty n. **agreement**, settlement, pact, deal, entente, concordat, accord, protocol, compact, convention, contract, covenant, bargain, pledge; formal concord.

tree n. sapling, conifer, evergreen.

> **WORD LINKS**
>
> **arboreal** living in trees, or relating to trees
> **arboretum** a botanical garden devoted to trees
> **dendrology** the scientific study of trees
> **silviculture**, **arboriculture** the cultivation of trees

trek n. *a three-day trek across the desert* **journey**, trip, expedition, safari, odyssey; hike, march, slog, footslog, tramp, walk; long haul; Brit. informal yomp, trog.
▶ v. *we trekked through the jungle* **hike**, tramp, march, slog, footslog, trudge, traipse, walk; travel, journey; Brit. informal yomp, trog.

trellis n. **lattice**, framework, espalier; network, mesh, tracery, grille, grid, grating; latticework, trelliswork; technical reticulation.

tremble v. **1** *Joe's hands were trembling* **shake**, shake like a leaf, quiver, twitch; quaver, waver. **2** *the entire building trembled* **shake**, shudder, judder, wobble, rock, vibrate, move, sway, totter, teeter. **3** *she trembled at the thought of what he had in store for her* **be afraid**, be frightened, be apprehensive, worry, shake in one's shoes; quail, shrink, blench; informal be in a blue funk, be all of a tremble.
▶ n. *the slight tremble in her hands* **tremor**, shake, shakiness, trembling, quiver, twitch.
– OPPOSITES steadiness.

tremendous adj. **1** *tremendous sums of money* **huge**, enormous, immense, colossal, massive, prodigious, stupendous, monumental, mammoth, vast, gigantic, giant, mighty, epic, titanic, cosmic, towering, king-size(d), gargantuan, Herculean; substantial, considerable; informal whopping, thumping, astronomical, humongous; Brit. informal whacking, ginormous. **2** *a tremendous explosion* **very loud**, deafening, ear-splitting, booming, thundering, thunderous, resounding. **3** informal *I've seen him play and he's tremendous* **excellent**, splendid, wonderful, marvellous, magnificent, superb, glorious, sublime, lovely, delightful, too good to be true; informal super, great, amazing, fantastic, terrific, sensational, heavenly, divine, gorgeous, grand, fabulous, fab, awesome, to die for, magic, ace, wicked, mind-blowing, far out, out of this world; Brit. informal smashing, brilliant, brill; N. Amer. informal boss; Austral./NZ informal beaut, bonzer; Brit. informal dated champion, wizard, corking, ripping, spiffing, top-hole; N. Amer. informal dated swell.
– OPPOSITES tiny, small, poor.

tremor n. **1** *the sudden tremor of her hands* **trembling**, shaking, shakiness, tremble, shake, quivering, quiver, twitching, twitch, tic; quavering, quaver. **2** *a tremor of fear ran through her* **frisson**, shiver, spasm, thrill, tingle, stab, dart, shaft; wave, surge, rush, ripple. **3** *the epicentre of the tremor* **earthquake**, earth tremor, shock; informal quake; N. Amer. informal tremblor.

tremulous adj. **1** *a tremulous voice* **shaky**, trembling, shaking, unsteady, quavering, wavering, quivering, quivery, quaking, weak; informal trembly, all of a tremble. **2** *a tremulous smile* **timid**, diffident, shy, hesitant, uncertain, nervous, timorous, fearful, frightened, scared, anxious, apprehensive; informal trepidatious.
– OPPOSITES steady, confident.

trench n. **ditch**, channel, trough, excavation, furrow, rut, conduit, cut, drain, waterway, watercourse; earthwork, entrenchment, moat; Archaeology fosse.

trenchant adj. **incisive**, penetrating, sharp, keen, acute, shrewd, razor-sharp, rapier-like, piercing; vigorous, forceful, strong, telling, emphatic, forthright; mordant, cutting, biting, pungent.
– OPPOSITES vague.

trend n. **1** *an upward trend in unemployment* **tendency**, movement, drift, swing, shift, course, current, direction, inclination, leaning; bias, bent. **2** *the latest trend in dance music* **fashion**, vogue, style, mode, craze, mania, rage; informal fad, thing.
▸ v. *interest rates are trending up* **move**, go, head, drift, gravitate, swing, shift, turn, incline, tend, lean, veer.

trendy adj. informal **fashionable**, in fashion, in vogue, popular, (bang) up to date, up to the minute, modern, all the rage, modish, à la mode, trendsetting; stylish, chic, designer; informal cool, funky, in, the in thing, hot, big, hip, happening, sharp, groovy, snazzy, with it; N. Amer. informal tony, kicky.
– OPPOSITES unfashionable.

trepidation n. **fear**, apprehension, dread, fearfulness, agitation, anxiety, worry, nervousness, tension, misgivings, unease, uneasiness, foreboding, disquiet, dismay, consternation, alarm, panic; informal butterflies, jitteriness, the jitters, a cold sweat, a blue funk, the heebie-jeebies, the willies, the shakes, the jim-jams, collywobbles, cold feet; Brit. informal the (screaming) abdabs/habdabs.
– OPPOSITES equanimity, composure.

trespass v. **1** *there is no excuse for trespassing on railway property* **intrude on**, encroach on, enter without permission, invade. **2** *I must not trespass on your good nature* **take advantage of**, impose on, play on, exploit, abuse; encroach on, infringe. **3** old use *he would be the last among us to trespass* **sin**, transgress, offend, do wrong, err, go astray, fall from grace, stray from the straight and narrow.
▸ n. **1** *his alleged trespass on council land* **unlawful entry**, intrusion, encroachment, invasion. **2** old use *he asked forgiveness for his trespasses* **sin**, wrong, wrongdoing,

transgression, crime, offence, misdeed, misdemeanour, error, lapse, fall from grace.

trespasser n. **1** *a high stone wall discouraged would-be trespassers* **intruder**, interloper, unwelcome visitor, encroacher. **2** old use *trespassers asking for forgiveness* **sinner**, transgressor, wrongdoer, evildoer, malefactor, offender, criminal.

tresses plural n. **hair**, head of hair, mane, mop of hair, shock of hair; locks, curls, ringlets.

trial n. **1** *the trial is expected to last several weeks* **court case**, case, lawsuit, suit, hearing, inquiry, tribunal, litigation, (legal/judicial) proceedings, legal action; court martial; appeal, retrial. **2** *the drug is undergoing clinical trials* **test**, try-out, experiment, pilot study; examination, check, assessment, evaluation, appraisal; trial/test period, trial/test run, dummy run; informal dry run. **3** *she could be a bit of a trial at times* **nuisance**, pest, bother, irritant, problem, inconvenience, plague, thorn in one's flesh, the bane of one's life, one's cross to bear; bore; informal pain, pain in the neck/backside, headache, drag, nightmare; Scottish informal skelf; N. Amer. informal pain in the butt, nudnik, burr under someone's saddle. **4** *a long account of her trials and tribulations* **trouble**, anxiety, worry, burden, affliction, ordeal, tribulation, adversity, hardship, tragedy, trauma, reverse, setback, difficulty, problem, misfortune, bad luck, mishap, misadventure; informal hassle; literary travails.
▸ adj. *a three-month trial period* **test**, experimental, pilot, exploratory, probationary, provisional.
▸ v. *the electronic cash card has been trialled by several banks* **test**, try out, put to the test, put through its paces; pilot.

tribe n. **1** *the nomadic tribes of the Sahara* **ethnic group**, people; family, dynasty, house; clan, sept. **2** *a tribe of children trailed after her* **group**, crowd, gang, company, body, band, host, bevy, party, pack, army, herd, flock, drove, horde; informal bunch, crew, gaggle, posse.

tribulation n. **1** *the tribulations of her personal life* **trouble**, difficulty, problem, worry, anxiety, burden, cross to bear, ordeal, trial, adversity, hardship, tragedy, trauma, affliction; reverse, setback, blow; informal hassle. **2** *his time of tribulation was just beginning* **suffering**, distress, trouble, misery, wretchedness, unhappiness, sadness, heartache, woe, grief, pain, anguish, agony; literary travail.

tribunal n. **1** *a rent tribunal* **arbitration board/panel**, board, panel, committee. **2** *an international war-crimes tribunal* **court**, court of justice, court of law, law court; court of inquiry; N. Amer. forum.

tributary n. **branch**, headwater, feeder, side stream, influent; N. Amer. & Austral./NZ creek.

tribute n. **1** *tributes flooded in from friends and colleagues* **accolade**, praise, commendation, salute, testimonial, homage, eulogy, paean, panegyric; congratulations,

compliments, plaudits, bouquet; gift, present, offering; formal laudation, encomium. **2** *it is a tribute to his determination that he ever played again* **testimony**, indication, manifestation, evidence, proof, attestation. **3** *the Vikings demanded tributes in silver* **payment**, contribution, dues, levy, tax, duty, impost.
– OPPOSITES criticism, condemnation.
□ **pay tribute to** praise, sing the praises of, speak highly of, commend, acclaim, take one's hat off to, applaud, salute, honour, show appreciation of, recognize, acknowledge, pay homage to, extol; formal laud.

trice n.
□ **in a trice** very soon, in a moment/second/instant, shortly, any minute (now), in a short time, in (less than) no time, in the twinkling of an eye, in a flash, before you know it, before long; informal anon, in a jiffy, in a nanosecond, in two shakes (of a lamb's tail), before you can say Jack Robinson; Brit. informal in a tick, in a mo, in two ticks; N. Amer. informal in a snap; dated directly.

trick n. **1** *he's capable of any mean trick* **stratagem**, ploy, ruse, scheme, device, manoeuvre, contrivance, machination, artifice, wile, dodge; deceit, deception, trickery, subterfuge, chicanery, sharp practice; swindle, hoax, fraud, confidence trick; informal con (trick), set-up, game, scam, sting, flimflam; Brit. informal wheeze; N. Amer. informal bunco; old use shift. **2** *I think he's playing a trick on us* **practical joke**, joke, prank, jape; informal leg-pull, spoof, put-on; Brit. informal cod. **3** *conjuring tricks* **feat**, stunt; (**tricks**) **sleight of hand**, legerdemain, prestidigitation; magic. **4** *it was probably a trick of the light* **illusion**, optical illusion, figment of the imagination; mirage. **5** *the tricks of the trade* **knack**, art, skill, technique; secret. **6** *he sat biting his fingernails, a trick of his when he was excited* **mannerism**, habit, quirk, idiosyncrasy, peculiarity, foible, way; characteristic, trait.
▶v. *many people have been tricked by villains with false identity cards* **deceive**, delude, hoodwink, mislead, take in, dupe, fool, double-cross, cheat, defraud, swindle, catch out, gull, hoax, bamboozle; informal con, diddle, rook, put one over on, pull a fast one on, pull the wool over someone's eyes, take for a ride, lead up the garden path, shaft, do, flimflam; N. Amer. informal sucker, snooker, gold-brick; Austral. informal pull a swifty on; literary cozen.
□ **trick someone/something out** dress (up), attire, array, rig out, garb, get up; adorn, decorate, deck (out), bedeck, embellish, ornament, festoon; literary bedizen, caparison; old use apparel.

trickery n. **deception**, deceit, dishonesty, cheating, duplicity, double-dealing, legerdemain, sleight of hand, guile, craftiness, deviousness, subterfuge, skulduggery, chicanery, fraud, fraudulence,

swindling, sharp practice; informal monkey business, funny business, jiggery-pokery.
– OPPOSITES honesty.

trickle v. *blood was trickling from two cuts in his lip* **drip**, dribble, ooze, leak, seep, spill.
– OPPOSITES pour, gush.
▶n. *trickles of water* **dribble**, drip, thin stream, rivulet.

trickster n. **swindler**, cheat, fraud, fraudster; charlatan, mountebank, quack, impostor, sham, hoaxer; rogue, villain, scoundrel; informal con man, sharp, flimflammer; Brit. informal twister; N. Amer. informal grifter, bunco artist; Austral. informal illywhacker, magsman; dated confidence man.

tricky adj. **1** *a tricky situation* **difficult**, awkward, problematic, delicate, ticklish, sensitive, embarrassing, touchy; risky, uncertain, precarious, touch-and-go; thorny, knotty; informal sticky, dicey; N. Amer. informal gnarly. **2** *a tricky and unscrupulous politician* **cunning**, crafty, wily, guileful, artful, devious, sly, scheming, calculating, designing, sharp, shrewd, astute, canny, duplicitous, dishonest, deceitful; informal foxy.
– OPPOSITES straightforward, honest.

tried and trusted adj. **reliable**, dependable, trustworthy, trusted, certain, sure; proven, proved, tested, tried and tested, put to the test, established, fail-safe; reputable.

trifle n. **1** *we needn't bother the headmaster over such trifles* **unimportant thing**, trivial thing, triviality, thing of no importance/consequence, bagatelle, inessential, nothing; technicality; (**trifles**) trivia, minutiae. **2** *he bought it for a trifle* **next to nothing**, very small amount; pittance; informal peanuts; N. Amer. informal chump change. **3** *he went to buy a few trifles for Christmas* **bauble**, trinket, knick-knack, gimcrack, gewgaw, toy.
□ **a trifle** a little, a bit, somewhat, a touch, a spot, a mite, a whit; informal a tad.

trifle with play with, amuse oneself with, toy with, dally with, flirt with, play fast and loose with; informal mess about with; dated sport with.

trifling adj. **trivial**, unimportant, insignificant, inconsequential, petty, minor, of little/no account, of little/no consequence, footling, pettifogging, incidental, silly, idle, superficial, small, tiny, inconsiderable, nominal, negligible, nugatory; informal piffling, piddling, fiddling; formal exiguous.
– OPPOSITES important.

trigger v. **1** *the incident triggered an acrimonious debate* **precipitate**, prompt, trigger off, set off, spark (off), touch off, provoke, stir up; cause, give rise to, lead to, set in motion, occasion, bring about, generate, engender, begin, start, initiate; literary enkindle. **2** *burglars triggered the alarm* **activate**, set off, set going, trip.

trill v. **warble**, sing, chirp, chirrup, tweet, twitter, cheep, peep.

trim v. **1** *his hair had been washed and trimmed* **cut**, barber, crop, bob, shorten,

clip, snip, shear; neaten, shape, tidy up. **2** *trim off the lower leaves using a sharp knife* **cut off**, remove, take off, chop off, lop off; prune, pollard. **3** *production costs need to be trimmed* **reduce**, decrease, cut down, cut back on, scale down, prune, slim down, pare down, dock. **4** *the story was severely trimmed for the film version* **shorten**, abridge, condense, abbreviate, telescope, truncate. **5** *a pair of black leather gloves trimmed with fake fur* **decorate**, adorn, ornament, embellish; edge, pipe, border, hem, fringe.
▸ **n. 1** *white curtains with a blue trim* **decoration**, trimming, ornamentation, adornment, embellishment; border, edging, piping, rickrack, hem, fringe, frill; old use purfle. **2** *an unruly mop in desperate need of a trim* **haircut**, cut, barbering, clip, snip; pruning; tidy-up.
▸ **adj. 1** *a cropped, fitted jacket looks trim with a long-line skirt* **smart**, stylish, chic, spruce, dapper, elegant, crisp; N. Amer. trig; informal natty, sharp; N. Amer. informal spiffy. **2** *a trim little villa* **neat**, tidy, neat and tidy, as neat as a new pin, orderly, in (good) order, uncluttered, well kept, well maintained, shipshape (and Bristol fashion), in apple-pie order, immaculate, spick and span. **3** *her trim figure* **slim**, slender, lean, clean-limbed, sleek, willowy, lissom, sylphlike, svelte; streamlined.
– OPPOSITES untidy, messy.
▢ **in trim** fit, fighting fit, as fit as a fiddle, in good health, in fine fettle; slim, in shape.

trimming n. **1** *a black party dress with lace trimming* **decoration**, trim, ornamentation, adornment, passementerie, embroidery; border, edging, piping, rickrack, fringes, fringing, frills; old use purfles. **2** *roast turkey with all the trimmings* **accompaniments**, extras, frills, accessories, accoutrements, trappings, paraphernalia; garnishing, garnish. **3** *hedge trimmings* **cuttings**, clippings, parings, shavings.

trinket n. **knick-knack**, bauble, ornament, bibelot, curio, trifle, toy, novelty, gimcrack, gewgaw; N. Amer. kickshaw; N. Amer. informal tchotchke; old use whim-wham, bijou, gaud.

trio n. **threesome**, three, triumvirate, triad, troika, trinity; trilogy, triptych; triplets.

trip v. **1** *he tripped on the loose stones* **stumble**, lose one's footing, catch one's foot, slip, lose one's balance, fall (down), tumble, topple, take a spill. **2** *taxpayers often trip up by not declaring taxable income* **make a mistake**, miscalculate, make a blunder, blunder, go wrong, make an error, err; informal slip up, screw up, make a boo-boo; Brit. informal boob; N. Amer. informal goof up. **3** *the question was intended to trip him up* **catch out**, trick, outwit, outsmart; throw off balance, disconcert, unsettle, discountenance, discomfit; informal throw, wrong-foot; Brit. informal catch on the hop. **4** *they tripped up the terrace steps* **skip**, run, dance, prance, bound, spring, scamper. **5** *Hoffman tripped the alarm* **set off**, activate, trigger; turn on, switch on, throw.

▸ **n. 1** *a trip to Paris* **excursion**, outing, jaunt; holiday, visit, tour, journey, expedition, voyage, transfer; drive, run, day out, day trip; informal junket, spin. **2** *trips and falls cause nearly half such accidents* **stumble**, slip, misstep, false step; fall, tumble, spill.

tripe n. informal See **nonsense** (sense 1).

triple adj. **1** *a triple alliance* **three-way**, tripartite; threefold. **2** *they paid him triple the going rate* **three times**, treble.

tripper n. Brit. informal **tourist**, holidaymaker, sightseer, day tripper, visitor, traveller; N. Amer. vacationer, vacationist, out-of-towner; Brit. informal grockle.

trite adj. **banal**, hackneyed, clichéd, platitudinous, vapid, commonplace, stock, conventional, stereotyped, overused, overdone, overworked, stale, worn out, time-worn, tired, hoary, hack, unimaginative, unoriginal, uninteresting, dull; informal old hat, corny, played out; N. Amer. informal cornball.
– OPPOSITES original, imaginative.

triumph n. **1** *Napoleon's many triumphs* **victory**, win, conquest, success; achievement. **2** *his eyes shone with triumph* **jubilation**, exultation, elation, delight, joy, happiness, glee, pride, satisfaction. **3** *a triumph of Victorian engineering* **tour de force**, masterpiece, crowning example, coup, wonder, sensation, master stroke.
– OPPOSITES defeat, disappointment.
▸ **v. 1** *he triumphed in the British Grand Prix* **win**, succeed, come first, be victorious, carry the day, carry all before one, prevail, take the honours, come out on top. **2** *they had no chance of triumphing over the Nationalists* **defeat**, beat, conquer, trounce, vanquish, worst, overcome, overpower, overwhelm, get the better of; bring someone to their knees, prevail against, subdue, subjugate; informal lick, best. **3** *'You can't touch me,' she triumphed* **crow**, gloat; rejoice, exult.
– OPPOSITES lose.

triumphant adj. **1** *the triumphant British team* **victorious**, successful, winning, conquering; undefeated, unbeaten. **2** *a triumphant expression* **jubilant**, exultant, elated, rejoicing, joyful, joyous, delighted, gleeful, proud, cock-a-hoop; gloating.
– OPPOSITES unsuccessful, despondent.

trivia plural n. **(petty) details**, minutiae, niceties, technicalities, trivialities, trifles, non-essentials.

trivial adj. **1** *trivial problems* **unimportant**, insignificant, inconsequential, minor, of no account, of no consequence, of no importance; incidental, inessential, non-essential, petty, trifling, pettifogging, footling, small, slight, little, inconsiderable, negligible, paltry, nugatory; informal piddling, piffling, fiddling, penny-ante. **2** *I used to be quite a trivial person* **frivolous**, superficial, shallow, unthinking, empty-headed, feather-brained, lightweight, foolish, silly.
– OPPOSITES important, significant, serious.

triviality n. **1** *the triviality of the subject matter* **unimportance**, insignificance, inconsequence, inconsequentiality, pettiness. **2** *he need not concern himself with such trivialities* **minor detail**, petty detail, thing of no importance/consequence, trifle, non-essential, nothing; technicality; (**trivialities**) trivia, minutiae.

trivialize v. **minimize**, play down, underestimate, underplay, make light of, treat lightly, dismiss; informal pooh-pooh.

troop n. **1** *a troop of tourists* **group**, party, band, gang, bevy, body, company, troupe, crowd, throng, horde, pack, drove, flock, swarm, multitude, host, army; informal bunch, gaggle, crew, posse. **2** *British troops were stationed here* **soldiers**, armed forces, servicemen, servicewomen; the services, the army, the military, soldiery.
▸v. **1** *we trooped out of the hall* **walk**, march, file; flock, crowd, throng, stream, swarm, surge, spill. **2** *Caroline trooped wearily home* **trudge**, plod, traipse, trail, drag oneself, tramp; N. Amer. informal schlep.

trophy n. **1** *a swimming trophy* **cup**, medal; prize, award. **2** *a cabinet full of trophies from his travels* **souvenir**, memento, keepsake; spoils, booty.

tropical adj. *tropical weather* **very hot**, sweltering, humid, sultry, steamy, sticky, oppressive, stifling, suffocating, heavy; informal boiling.
– OPPOSITES cold, arctic.

trot v. *Doyle trotted across the patio* **run**, jog, jogtrot, dogtrot; scuttle, scurry, bustle, scamper.
□ **on the trot** Brit. informal in succession, one after the other, in a row, consecutively, successively; running, straight.
trot something out informal recite, repeat, regurgitate, churn out; come out with, produce.

troubadour n. historical **minstrel**, singer, balladeer, poet; historical jongleur, trouvère.

trouble n. **1** *you've caused enough trouble already* **problems**, difficulty, issues, bother, inconvenience, worry, anxiety, distress, stress, agitation, harassment, unpleasantness; informal hassle. **2** *she poured out all her troubles* **problem**, misfortune, difficulty, issue, trial, tribulation, trauma, burden, pain, woe, grief, heartache, misery, affliction, suffering. **3** *he's gone to a lot of trouble to help you* **bother**, inconvenience, fuss, effort, exertion, work, labour; pains, care, attention, trouble. **4** *I wouldn't want to be a trouble to her* **nuisance**, bother, inconvenience, irritation, irritant, problem, trial, pest, thorn in someone's flesh/side; informal headache, pain, pain in the neck/backside, drag; N. Amer. informal pain in the butt, burr under someone's saddle, nudnik. **5** *you're too gullible, that's your trouble* **shortcoming**, weakness, weak point, failing, fault, imperfection, defect, blemish; problem, difficulty. **6** *he had a history of heart trouble* **disease**, illness, sickness, ailments, complaints, problems; disorder, disability. **7** *the crash was due to engine trouble* **malfunction**, dysfunction, failure, breakdown. **8** *a match marred by serious crowd trouble* **disturbance**, disorder, unrest, fighting, ructions, fracas, breach of the peace; Law, dated affray.
▸v. **1** *this matter had been troubling her for some time* **worry**, bother, concern, disturb, upset, agitate, distress, perturb, annoy, irritate, vex, irk, nag, niggle, prey on someone's mind, weigh down, burden; informal bug. **2** *he was troubled by bouts of ill health* **afflict**, burden; suffer from, be cursed with; informal be a martyr to. **3** *there is nothing you need trouble about* **worry**, upset oneself, fret, be anxious, be concerned, concern oneself. **4** *don't trouble to see me out* **bother**, take the trouble, go to the trouble, exert oneself, go out of one's way. **5** *I'm sorry to trouble you* **inconvenience**, bother, impose on, disturb, put out, disoblige; informal hassle; formal discommode.
□ **in trouble** in difficulty, in difficulties, in a mess, in a bad way, in a predicament; informal in a tight corner/spot, in a fix, in a hole, in hot water, in a pickle, in the soup, up against it; Brit. informal up a gum tree.

troubled adj. **1** *Joanna looked troubled* **anxious**, worried, concerned, perturbed, disturbed, bothered, ill at ease, uneasy, unsettled, agitated; distressed, upset, dismayed. **2** *we live in troubled times* **difficult**, problematic, full of problems, unsettled, hard, tough, stressful, dark.

troublemaker n. **mischief-maker**, agitator, rabble-rouser, firebrand, agent provocateur, ringleader, incendiary; demagogue; scandalmonger, gossipmonger, meddler; informal stirrer.

troublesome adj. **1** *a troublesome problem* **annoying**, irritating, exasperating, maddening, infuriating, irksome, vexatious, vexing, bothersome, tiresome, worrying, worrisome, disturbing, upsetting, niggling, nagging; difficult, awkward, problematic, taxing; informal aggravating; N. Amer. informal pesky. **2** *a troublesome child* **difficult**, awkward, trying, demanding, uncooperative, rebellious, unmanageable, unruly, obstreperous, disruptive, badly behaved, attention-seeking, disobedient, naughty, recalcitrant; formal refractory.
– OPPOSITES simple, cooperative.

trough n. **1** *a large feeding trough* **manger**, feedbox, feeder, fodder rack, crib. **2** *a thirty-yard trough* **channel**, conduit, trench, ditch, gully, drain, culvert, cut, flume, gutter.

trounce v. **defeat utterly**, beat hollow, rout, crush, overwhelm; informal hammer, clobber, thrash, drub, pulverize, massacre, crucify, demolish, destroy, annihilate, wipe the floor with, make mincemeat of, murder; Brit. informal stuff; N. Amer. informal shellac, cream, skunk.

troupe n. **group**, company, band, ensemble, set; cast.

trousers plural n. **slacks**, chinos, jeans; N. Amer. pants; Brit. informal trews, strides, kecks, breeches; Austral. informal daks.

t

truant n. **absentee**; Brit. informal skiver; Austral./ NZ informal wag.
▶ v. *pupils who truant.* See **play truant**.
☐ **play truant** stay away from school, truant; informal sag off; Brit. informal skive (off), bunk off; Irish informal mitch (off); N. Amer. informal play hookey, goof off; Austral./NZ informal play the wag.

truce n. **ceasefire**, armistice, suspension of hostilities, peace; respite, lull; informal let-up.

truck[1] n. *a heavily laden truck* **lorry**, wagon, heavy goods vehicle, juggernaut; van, pickup (truck); Brit. HGV; dated pantechnicon.

truck[2] n. *we are to have no truck with him* **dealings**, association, contact, communication, connection, relations; business, trade.

truckle v. *an ambitious woman who truckled to no man* **kowtow**, submit, defer, yield, bow and scrape, be obsequious, pander, toady, prostrate oneself, grovel; fawn on, dance attendance on, curry favour with, ingratiate oneself with; informal suck up, crawl, lick someone's boots; Austral./NZ informal smoodge.

truculent adj. **defiant**, aggressive, antagonistic, belligerent, pugnacious, confrontational, ready for a fight, obstreperous, argumentative, quarrelsome, uncooperative; bad-tempered, short-tempered, cross, snappish; informal feisty, spoiling for a fight; Brit. informal stroppy, bolshie.
– OPPOSITES cooperative, amiable.

trudge v. **plod**, tramp, drag oneself, walk heavily/slowly, plough, slog, footslog, toil, trek; informal traipse, galumph; Brit. informal trog.

true adj. **1** *you'll see that what I say is true* **correct**, accurate, right, verifiable, in accordance with the facts, what actually/ really happened, the case, so; faithful, literal, factual, unvarnished. **2** *people are still willing to pay for true craftsmanship* **genuine**, authentic, real, actual, bona fide, proper; informal honest-to-goodness, kosher, pukka, legit, the real McCoy; Austral./ NZ informal dinkum. **3** *the true owner of the goods* **rightful**, legitimate, legal, lawful, authorized, bona fide, de jure. **4** *the necessity for true repentance* **sincere**, genuine, real, unfeigned, heartfelt, from the heart. **5** *a true friend* **loyal**, faithful, constant, devoted, staunch, steadfast, unswerving, unwavering; trustworthy, trusty, reliable, dependable. **6** *a true reflection of life in the 50s* **accurate**, true to life, faithful, telling it like it is, fact-based, realistic, close, lifelike.
– OPPOSITES untrue, false, disloyal, inaccurate.

true-blue adj. **staunch**, loyal, faithful, stalwart, committed, card-carrying, confirmed, dyed-in-the-wool, devoted, dedicated, firm, steadfast, unswerving, unwavering, unfaltering; informal deep-dyed.

truism n. **platitude**, commonplace, cliché, stock phrase, banality, old chestnut, old saw, bromide.

truly adv. **1** *tell me truly what you want* **truthfully**, honestly, frankly, candidly, openly, to someone's face, laying one's cards on the table; informal pulling no punches. **2** *I'm truly grateful to them* **sincerely**, genuinely, really, indeed, from the bottom of one's heart, heartily, profoundly; very, extremely, dreadfully, immensely, tremendously, incredibly, most; informal awfully, terribly, terrifically, fearfully; Brit. informal jolly, ever so; informal dated frightfully. **3** *a truly dreadful song* **really**, absolutely, simply, utterly, totally, perfectly, thoroughly, positively, completely. **4** *this is truly a miracle* **without (a) doubt**, unquestionably, undoubtedly, certainly, surely, definitely, beyond doubt/ question, indubitably, undeniably, beyond the shadow of a doubt; in truth, really, in reality, actually, in fact; old use forsooth, in sooth, verily. **5** *the streaming system does not truly reflect children's ability* **accurately**, correctly, exactly, precisely, faithfully.

trump v. *by wearing the simplest of dresses, she had trumped them all* **outshine**, outclass, upstage, put in the shade, eclipse, surpass, outdo, outperform; beat, better, top, cap; informal be a cut above, be head and shoulders above, leave standing; Brit. informal knock spots off; old use outrival.
☐ **trump something up** invent, make up, fabricate, concoct, contrive, manufacture, devise, hatch; fake, falsify; informal cook up.

trumped up adj. **bogus**, spurious, specious, false, fabricated, invented, manufactured, contrived, made-up, fake, factitious; informal phoney.
– OPPOSITES genuine.

trumpet v. **1** *'Come on!' he trumpeted* **shout**, bellow, roar, yell, cry out, call out; informal holler. **2** *companies trumpeted their enthusiasm for the multimedia revolution* **proclaim**, announce, declare, noise abroad, shout from the rooftops.
☐ **blow one's own trumpet** boast, brag, sing one's own praises, show off, swank, congratulate oneself; N. Amer. informal blow/toot one's own horn; Austral./NZ informal skite.

truncate v. **shorten**, cut, cut short, curtail, bring to an untimely end; abbreviate, condense, reduce.
– OPPOSITES lengthen, extend.

truncheon n. Brit. **club**, baton, cudgel, bludgeon; stick, staff; Brit. life preserver; N. Amer. billy, blackjack, nightstick; Brit. informal cosh.

trunk n. **1** *the trunk of a tree* **main stem**, bole, stock. **2** *his powerful trunk* **torso**, body. **3** *an elephant's trunk* **proboscis**, nose, snout. **4** *an enormous tin trunk* **chest**, box, crate, coffer; case, portmanteau. **5** N. Amer. *the trunk of his car* **luggage compartment**; Brit. boot.

truss n. **1** *the bridge is supported by three steel trusses* **support**, buttress, joist, brace, prop, strut, stay, stanchion, pier. **2** *a hernia truss* **surgical appliance**, support, pad.
▶ v. *they trussed us up with ropes and chains* **tie up**, bind, chain up; pinion, fetter, tether, secure.

t

trust n. **1** *good relationships are built on trust* **confidence**, belief, faith, certainty, assurance, conviction, credence; reliance. **2** *a position of trust* **responsibility**, duty, obligation. **3** *the money is to be held in trust for his son* **safe keeping**, keeping, protection, charge, care, custody; trusteeship, guardianship.

▸ v. **1** *I should never have trusted her* **put one's trust in**, have faith in, have (every) confidence in, believe in, pin one's hopes/faith on. **2** *he can be trusted to carry out an impartial investigation* **rely on**, depend on, bank on, count on, be sure of. **3** *I trust we shall meet again* **hope**, expect, take it, assume, presume. **4** *they don't like to trust their money to anyone outside the family* **entrust**, consign, commit, give, hand over, turn over, assign; formal commend.
– OPPOSITES distrust, mistrust, doubt.

> WORD LINKS
> **fiduciary** (Law) involving trust

trustee n. **administrator**, agent; custodian, keeper, steward, depositary; executor, executrix; Law fiduciary, feoffee.

trustful adj. See **trusting**.

trusting adj. **trustful**, unsuspecting, unquestioning, unguarded, unwary; naive, innocent, childlike, ingenuous, wide-eyed, credulous, gullible, easily taken in.
– OPPOSITES distrustful, suspicious.

trustworthy adj. **reliable**, dependable, honest, honourable, upright, principled, true, truthful, as good as one's word, ethical, virtuous, incorruptible, unimpeachable, above suspicion; responsible, sensible, level-headed; loyal, faithful, staunch, steadfast, trusty; safe, sound, reputable; informal on the level; N. Amer. informal straight-up.
– OPPOSITES unreliable.

trusty adj. **reliable**, dependable, trustworthy, never-failing, unfailing, trusted; loyal, faithful, true, staunch, steadfast, constant, unswerving, unwavering.
– OPPOSITES unreliable.

truth n. **1** *he doubted the truth of her statement* **veracity**, truthfulness, verity, sincerity, candour, honesty; accuracy, correctness, validity, factuality, authenticity. **2** *it's the truth, I swear it* **what really happened**, the case, so; gospel (truth), the honest truth. **3** *truth is stranger than fiction* **fact(s)**, reality, real life, actuality. **4** *scientific truths* **fact**, verity, certainty, certitude; law, principle.
– OPPOSITES lies, fiction, falsehood.
□ **in truth** in (actual) fact, in point of fact, in reality, really, actually, to tell the truth, if truth be told.

truthful adj. **1** *a truthful answer* **honest**, sincere, trustworthy, genuine; candid, frank, open, forthright, straight; informal upfront, on the level; N. Amer. informal on the up and up. **2** *a truthful account* **true**, accurate, correct, factual, faithful, reliable; unvarnished, unembellished; formal veracious, veridical.
– OPPOSITES deceitful, untrue.

try v. **1** *try to help him* **attempt**, endeavour, make an effort, exert oneself, strive, do one's best, do one's utmost, move heaven and earth; undertake, aim, take it on oneself; informal have a go, give it one's best shot, bend over backwards, bust a gut, do one's damnedest, pull out all the stops, go all out, knock oneself out; formal essay; old use assay. **2** *try it and see what you think* **test**, put to the test, sample, taste, inspect, investigate, examine, appraise, evaluate, assess; informal check out, give something a whirl. **3** *Mary tried everyone's patience* **tax**, strain, test, stretch, sap, drain, exhaust, wear out. **4** *the case is to be tried by a jury* **adjudicate**, consider, hear, adjudge, examine.

▸ n. *I'll have one last try* **attempt**, effort, endeavour; informal go, shot, crack, stab, bash, whack; formal essay.
□ **try something out** test, trial, experiment with, pilot; put through its paces; assess, evaluate.

trying adj. **1** *a trying day* **stressful**, taxing, demanding, difficult, tough, hard, pressured, frustrating, fraught; arduous, gruelling, tiring, exhausting; informal hellish. **2** *Steve was very trying* **annoying**, irritating, exasperating, maddening, infuriating; tiresome, irksome, troublesome, bothersome; informal aggravating.
– OPPOSITES easy, accommodating.

tub n. **1** *a wooden tub* **container**, butt, barrel, cask, drum, keg. **2** *a tub of yogurt* **pot**, carton. **3** *a soak in the tub* **bath**, bathtub; hot tub.

tubby adj. informal **chubby**, plump, stout, dumpy, chunky, portly, rotund, round, fat, overweight, fleshy, paunchy, pot-bellied, corpulent; informal pudgy, beefy, porky, roly-poly, blubbery; Brit. informal podgy; N. Amer. informal corn-fed.
– OPPOSITES skinny.

tuck v. **1** *he tucked his shirt into his trousers* **push**, insert, slip; thrust, stuff, stick, cram; informal pop. **2** *the dress was tucked all over* **pleat**, gather, fold, ruffle. **3** *he tucked the knife behind his seat* **hide**, conceal, secrete; store, stow; informal stash.

▸ n. **1** *a dress with tucks* **pleat**, gather, fold, ruffle. **2** Brit. informal *they pinched his tuck* **food**; informal eats, grub, nosh, chow; Brit. informal scoff; N. Amer. informal chuck; literary viands; dated victuals.
□ **tuck someone in/up** make comfortable, settle down, cover up; put to bed.
tuck in/into informal eat heartily, devour, consume, gobble up, wolf down; informal get stuck into, dispose of, polish off, hoover up, get outside of, put away, scoff (down), trough; Brit. informal shift; N. Amer. informal scarf (down/up), snarf (down/up).

tuft n. **clump**, bunch, knot, cluster, tussock, tuffet; lock, wisp; crest, topknot; tassel.

tug v. **1** *Ben tugged his sleeve* **pull**, pluck, tweak, twitch, jerk, wrench; catch hold of; informal yank. **2** *she tugged him towards the door* **drag**, pull, lug, draw, haul, heave, tow, trail.

▸ n. *one good tug would loosen it* **pull**, jerk, wrench, heave; informal yank.

tuition n. **instruction**, teaching, coaching, tutoring, tutelage, lessons, education, schooling, pedagogy; training, drill, preparation, guidance.

tumble v. **1** *he tumbled over* **fall (over/down)**, topple over, lose one's balance, keel over, take a spill, go headlong, go head over heels, trip (up), stumble; informal come a cropper. **2** *they all tumbled from the room* **hurry**, rush, scramble, scurry, bound, pile, bundle. **3** *a brook tumbled over the rocks* **cascade**, fall, flow, pour, spill, stream. **4** *oil prices tumbled* **plummet**, plunge, fall, dive, nosedive, drop, slump, slide, decrease, decline; informal crash. **5** informal *I tumbled to what was happening.* See **realize** (sense 1).
– OPPOSITES rise.

▸ n. **1** *I took a tumble in the nettles* **fall**, trip, spill; informal nosedive, header, cropper. **2** *a tumble in share prices* **drop**, fall, plunge, dive, nosedive, slump, decline, collapse; informal crash.
– OPPOSITES rise.

tumbledown adj. **dilapidated**, ramshackle, decrepit, neglected, run down, gone to rack and ruin, falling to pieces, decaying, derelict, crumbling; rickety, shaky; N. Amer. informal shacky.

tumbler n. **(drinking) glass**, beaker, highball glass.

tumid adj. **1** *her tumid belly* **swollen**, distended, tumescent, engorged, enlarged, bloated, bulging, protuberant, bulbous. **2** *tumid oratory* **bombastic**, pompous, turgid, overblown, inflated, high-flown, pretentious, grandiose, florid, flowery, magniloquent, grandiloquent, orotund; informal highfalutin, purple, windy.
– OPPOSITES shrunken, simple.

tummy n. informal **stomach**, abdomen, belly, gut, middle; informal tum, insides; Austral. informal bingy.

tumour n. **cancerous growth**, malignant growth, cancer, malignancy; lump, growth, swelling; Medicine carcinoma, sarcoma.

tumult n. **1** *she added her voice to the tumult* **clamour**, din, noise, racket, uproar, commotion, ruckus, rumpus, hubbub, pandemonium, babel, bedlam, brouhaha, furore, fracas, melee, frenzy; Scottish & N. English stramash; informal hullabaloo; Brit. informal row. **2** *years of political tumult* **turmoil**, confusion, disorder, disarray, unrest, chaos, turbulence, mayhem, havoc, upheaval, ferment, agitation, trouble.
– OPPOSITES tranquillity.

tumultuous adj. **1** *tumultuous applause* **loud**, deafening, thunderous, uproarious, noisy, clamorous, vociferous. **2** *a tumultuous crowd* **disorderly**, unruly, rowdy, turbulent, boisterous, excited, agitated, restless, wild, riotous, frenzied; informal rumbustious.
– OPPOSITES soft, orderly.

tune n. *she hummed a cheerful tune* **melody**, air, strain, theme; song, jingle, ditty.

▸ v. **1** *they tuned their guitars* **adjust**, fine-tune. **2** *a body clock tuned to the tides* **attune**, adapt, adjust, fine-tune; regulate, modulate.
□ **in tune** in accord, in keeping, in accordance, in agreement, in harmony, in step, in line, in sympathy.

tuneful adj. **melodious**, melodic, musical, mellifluous, dulcet, euphonious, harmonious, lyrical, lilting, sweet.
– OPPOSITES discordant.

tuneless adj. **discordant**, unmelodious, dissonant, harsh, cacophonous.
– OPPOSITES melodious.

tunnel n. *a tunnel under the hills* **underground passage**, underpass, subway; shaft; burrow, hole; historical mine, sap.
▸ v. *he tunnelled under the fence* **dig**, burrow, mine, bore, drill.

turbid adj. **murky**, opaque, cloudy, muddy, thick; N. Amer. roily.
– OPPOSITES clear.

turbulent adj. **1** *the country's turbulent past* **tempestuous**, stormy, unstable, unsettled, tumultuous, chaotic; violent, anarchic, lawless. **2** *turbulent seas* **rough**, stormy, tempestuous, storm-tossed, heavy, violent, wild, seething, choppy, agitated, boisterous.
– OPPOSITES peaceful, calm.

turf n. **1** *they walked across the turf* **grass**, lawn, sod; literary sward, greensward. **2** *devotees of the turf* **horse racing**; racecourses, racetracks. **3** informal *he was keen to protect his turf* **territory**, domain, province, preserve, sphere of influence; stamping ground; informal bailiwick; Brit. informal patch, manor.
▸ v. *the lawns have been turfed* **grass (over)**.
□ **turf someone/something out** informal See **eject** (sense 3).

turgid adj. **1** *his turgid prose* **bombastic**, pompous, overblown, inflated, tumid, high-flown, affected, pretentious, grandiose, florid, ornate, magniloquent, grandiloquent, orotund; informal highfalutin, purple, windy. **2** *the tissues become turgid* **swollen**, distended, tumescent, engorged, bloated.
– OPPOSITES simple.

turmoil n. *political turmoil* **confusion**, upheaval, turbulence, tumult, disorder, disturbance, agitation, ferment, unrest, trouble, disruption, chaos, mayhem; uncertainty; N. Amer. informal tohubohu.
– OPPOSITES peace.
□ **in turmoil** confused, in a whirl, at sixes and sevens; reeling, disorientated; informal all over the place.

turn v. **1** *the wheels were still turning* **go round**, revolve, rotate, spin, roll, circle, wheel, whirl, gyrate, swivel, pivot. **2** *I turned and headed back* **change direction**, change course, make a U-turn, turn about/round, wheel round. **3** *the car turned the corner* **go round**, round, negotiate, take. **4** *the path turned to right and left* **bend**, curve, wind, twist, meander, snake, zigzag. **5** *he turned his pistol on Liam* **aim at**, point at, level at, direct at, train on. **6** *he turned his* *ankle* **sprain**, twist, wrench; hurt. **7** *their honeymoon turned into a nightmare* **become**, develop into, turn out to be; be transformed into, metamorphose into. **8** *Emma turned red* **become**, go, grow, get. **9** *he turned the house into flats* **convert**, change, transform, make; adapt, modify, rebuild, reconstruct. **10** *I've just turned forty* **reach**, get to, become; informal **hit**. **11** *the milk had turned* **(go) sour**, go off, curdle, become rancid, go bad, spoil. **12** *he turned to politics* **take up**, become involved in, go in for, enter, undertake. **13** *we can now turn to another topic* **move on to**, go on to, consider, attend to, address; take up. **14** *she turned a somersault* **perform**, execute, do, carry out. **15** *an object turned on a lathe* **fashion**, make, shape, form.

▶ n. **1** *a turn of the wheel* **rotation**, revolution, spin, whirl, gyration, swivel. **2** *a turn to the left* **change of direction**, veer, divergence. **3** *we're approaching the turn* **bend**, corner, dog-leg; turning, junction, crossroads; N. Amer. turnout; Brit. hairpin bend. **4** *you'll get your turn in a minute* **opportunity**, chance, say; stint, time; try; informal go, shot, stab, crack. **5** *a comic turn* **act**, routine, performance, number, piece. **6** *a turn around the garden* **stroll**, walk, saunter, amble, wander, airing, promenade; outing, excursion, jaunt; informal mosey, tootle, spin; Brit. informal pootle. **7** *you gave me quite a turn!* **shock**, start, surprise, jolt; fright, scare. **8** *she did me some good turns* **service**, deed, act; favour, kindness; disservice, wrong.

□ **in turn** one after the other, one by one, one at a time, in succession, successively, sequentially.

take a turn for the better improve, pick up, look up, perk up, rally, turn the corner; recover, revive.

take a turn for the worse deteriorate, worsen, decline, go downhill.

turn back retrace one's steps, go back, return; retreat.

turn someone/something down 1 *his novel was turned down* **reject**, spurn, rebuff, refuse, decline; Brit. informal knock back. **2** *Pete turned the sound down* **reduce**, lower, decrease, lessen; muffle, mute.

turn someone in betray, inform on, denounce, sell out, stab someone in the back; informal split on, blow the whistle on, rat on, peach on, squeal on; Brit. informal grass on, shop; N. Amer. informal finger; Austral./NZ informal dob on.

turn someone off informal put off, leave cold, repel, disgust, revolt, offend; disenchant, alienate; bore; N. Amer. informal gross out.

turn something off switch off, shut off, put off, extinguish, deactivate; informal kill, cut.

turn on *the decision turned on the law* depend on, rest on, hinge on, be contingent on, be decided by.

turn someone on informal See **arouse** (sense 3).

turn something on switch on, put on, start up, activate, trip.

turn on someone attack, set on, fall on, let fly at, lash out at, hit out at, round on; informal lay into, tear into, let someone have it, bite someone's head off, jump down someone's throat; Brit. informal have a go at; N. Amer. informal light into.

turn out 1 *a huge crowd turned out* **come**, be present, attend, appear, turn up, arrive; assemble, gather; informal show up. **2** *it turned out that she had been abroad* **transpire**, emerge, come to light, become apparent. **3** *things didn't turn out as I'd intended* **happen**, occur, come about; develop, work out, come out, end up; informal pan out; formal eventuate.

turn something out 1 *turn out the light.* See **turn something off**. **2** *they turn out a million engines a year* **produce**, make, manufacture, fabricate, put out, churn out. **3** *she turned out the cupboards* **clear out**, clean out, empty (out).

turn over overturn, upturn, capsize, keel over, turn turtle, be upended.

turn something over 1 *I turned over a few pages* **flip over**, flick through, leaf through. **2** *she turned the proposal over in her mind* **think about/over**, consider, weigh up, ponder, contemplate, reflect on, chew over, mull over, muse on, ruminate on.

turn of phrase expression, idiom, phrase, term, word.

turn someone's stomach nauseate, sicken, make someone's gorge rise.

turn to someone/something seek help from, have recourse to, approach, apply to, appeal to; take to, resort to.

turn up 1 *the missing documents turned up* **be found**, be discovered, be located, reappear. **2** *the police turned up* **arrive**, appear, present oneself; informal show (up), rock up, show one's face. **3** *something better will turn up* **present itself**, occur, happen, crop up.

turn something up 1 *she turned up the volume* **increase**, raise, amplify, intensify. **2** *they turned up lots of information* **discover**, uncover, unearth, find, dig up, ferret out, root out, expose.

turncoat n. **traitor**, renegade, defector, deserter, betrayer, Judas; fifth columnist, quisling; informal rat.

turning n. **turn-off**, turn, side road, exit; N. Amer. turnout.

turning point n. **watershed**, critical moment, decisive moment, moment of truth, crossroads, crisis.

turnout n. **1** *the lecture attracted a good turnout* **attendance**, audience, house; crowd, gathering, throng, assembly, assemblage, congregation. **2** *his turnout was very elegant* **outfit**, clothes, clothing, dress, garb, attire, ensemble; informal get-up, gear, togs; Brit. informal clobber, kit; formal apparel.

turnover n. **1** *an annual turnover of £2.25 million* **(gross) revenue**, income, yield; sales. **2** *a high turnover of staff* rate of replacement, change, movement.

turpitude n. formal See **depravity**.

tussle n. *his glasses were smashed in the tussle* **scuffle**, fight, struggle, skirmish, brawl, scrum, rough and tumble, free-for-all, fracas, fray, rumpus, melee; Irish, N. Amer., & Austral. donnybrook; informal scrap, dust-up, punch-up, spat, ruck; Brit. informal ding-dong, bust-up; Brit. informal, Football afters; Scottish informal rammy; Law, dated affray.
▶v. *demonstrators tussled with police* **scuffle**, fight, struggle, brawl, grapple, wrestle, clash; informal scrap; N. Amer. informal rough-house.

tutor n. *a history tutor* **teacher**, instructor, educator, educationist, lecturer, trainer, mentor; informal teach; formal pedagogue.
▶v. *he was tutored at home* **teach**, instruct, educate, school, coach, train, drill.

tutorial n. **lesson**, class, seminar.

twaddle n. informal See **nonsense** (sense 1).

tweak v. 1 *he tweaked the boy's ear* **pull**, jerk, tug, twist, twitch, pinch, squeeze. 2 informal *the programme can be tweaked to suit your needs* **adjust**, modify, alter, change, adapt; refine.
▶n. 1 *he gave her a tweak* **pull**, jerk, tug, twist, pinch, twitch, squeeze. 2 informal *a few minor tweaks were required* **adjustment**, modification, alteration, change; refinement.

twee adj. Brit. 1 *twee little shops* **quaint**, sweet, dainty, pretty; informal cute, cutesy. 2 *the lyrics are too twee in places* **sentimental**, over-sentimental, mawkish, sickly; Brit. informal soppy.

twelve cardinal number **dozen**.

> WORD LINKS
>
> **duodecimal** relating to a counting system with twelve as a base
> **dodecagon** a plane figure with twelve straight sides
> **dodecahedron** a solid figure with twelve faces
> **gross** twelve dozen
> **zodiac** an area of the sky divided by astrologers into twelve equal parts

twenty cardinal number **score**.

> WORD LINKS
>
> **icosahedron** a solid figure with twenty faces
> **vigesimal** relating to the number twenty

twiddle v. *she twiddled the dials* **turn**, twist, swivel, twirl; adjust, move, jiggle; fiddle with, play with.
□ **twiddle one's thumbs** be idle, kick one's heels, kill time, waste time; informal hang around/round; Brit. informal hang about.

twig¹ n. *leafy twigs* **stick**, sprig, withy, shoot, stem, branchlet.

twig² v. Brit. informal *she finally twigged what I was on about* **realize**, understand, grasp, comprehend, take in, fathom, see, recognize; informal latch on to, cotton on to, tumble to, get, get wise to, figure out; Brit. informal suss.

twilight n. 1 *we arrived at twilight* **dusk**, sunset, sundown, nightfall, evening, close of day; literary eventide, the gloaming. 2 *it was scarcely visible in the twilight* **half-light**, semi-darkness, gloom. 3 *the twilight of his career* **decline**, waning, ebb; autumn, final years.
– OPPOSITES dawn.
▶adj. *he inhabited a sinister twilight world of treason and murder* **shadowy**, dark, shady, dim, gloomy, obscure.

> WORD LINKS
>
> **crepuscular** resembling or relating to twilight

twin n. *a sitting room that was the twin of her own* **duplicate**, double, carbon-copy, exact likeness, mirror image, replica, lookalike, clone; counterpart, match, pair; informal spitting image, dead ringer.
▶adj. 1 *the twin towers of the stadium* **matching**, identical, matched, paired. 2 *the twin aims of conservation and recreation* **twofold**, double, dual; related, linked, connected; corresponding, parallel, complementary, equivalent.
▶v. *the company twinned its brewing with distilling* **combine**, join, link, couple, pair.

twine n. *a ball of twine* **string**, cord, thread, yarn.
▶v. 1 *she twined her arms around him* **wind**, entwine, wrap, wreathe. 2 *convolvulus twined around the tree* **entwine itself**, coil, loop, twist, spiral, curl. 3 *a bloom was twined in her hair* **weave**, interlace, intertwine, braid, twist.

twinge n. 1 *twinges in her stomach* **pain**, spasm, ache, throb; cramp, stitch. 2 *a twinge of guilt* **pang**, prick, dart; qualm, scruple, misgiving.

twinkle v. 1 *the lights of the city twinkled* **glitter**, sparkle, shine, glimmer, shimmer, glint, gleam, glisten, flicker, flash, wink; literary coruscate, glister. 2 *his feet twinkled over the ground* **dart**, dance, skip, flit, glide.
▶n. *the twinkle of the lights* **glitter**, sparkle, glimmer, shimmer, glint, gleam, flicker, flash, wink; literary coruscation.

twinkling adj. **sparkling**, glistening, glittering, glimmering, glinting, gleaming, flickering, winking, shining, scintillating; literary coruscating.

twirl v. 1 *she twirled her parasol* **spin**, whirl, turn, gyrate, pivot, swivel, twist, revolve, rotate. 2 *she twirled her hair round her fingers* **wind**, twist, coil, curl, wrap.
▶n. *she did a quick twirl* **pirouette**, spin, whirl, turn, twist, rotation, revolution, gyration.

twist v. 1 *the impact twisted the chassis* **crumple**, crush, buckle, mangle, warp, deform, distort. 2 *her face twisted with rage* **contort**, screw up. 3 *Ma anxiously twisted a handkerchief* **wring**, squeeze. 4 *he twisted round in his seat* **turn (round)**, swivel (round), spin (round), pivot, rotate, revolve. 5 *she twisted out of his grasp* **wriggle**, squirm, worm, wiggle. 6 *I twisted my ankle* **sprain**, wrench, turn, rick, crick. 7 *you are twisting my words* **distort**, misrepresent, change, alter, pervert, falsify, warp, skew, misinterpret, misconstrue, misstate, misquote; garble. 8 *he twisted the radio knob* **twiddle**, adjust, turn, rotate, swivel. 9 *she*

t

twisted her hair round her finger **wind**, twirl, coil, curl, wrap. **10** *the wires were twisted together* **intertwine**, twine, interlace, weave, plait, braid, coil, wind. **11** *the road twisted and turned* **wind**, bend, curve, turn, meander, weave, zigzag, swerve, snake.
▶n. **1** *the twist of a dial* **turn**, twirl, spin. **2** *a personality twist* **quirk**, idiosyncrasy, foible, eccentricity, peculiarity, oddity, kink; aberration, fault, flaw, imperfection, defect, failing, weakness. **3** Brit. *a twist of tobacco* **wad**, quid, plug, chew; Brit. screw. **4** *long twists of black hair* **ringlet**, curl, corkscrew, coil; lock, hank. **5** *the twists of the road* **bend**, curve, turn, zigzag, kink, dog-leg; Brit. hairpin bend. **6** *the twists of the plot* **convolution**, complication, complexity, intricacy; surprise, revelation. **7** *a new twist on an old theme* **interpretation**, slant, outlook, angle, approach, treatment; variation.
□ **twist someone's arm** informal pressurize, coerce, force; persuade; informal lean on, bulldoze, railroad, put the screws on.

twisted adj. **1** *twisted metal* **crumpled**, bent, crushed, buckled, warped, misshapen, distorted, deformed. **2** *a twisted smile* **crooked**, lopsided; contorted, wry. **3** *his twisted mind* **perverted**, warped, deviant, depraved, corrupt, abnormal, unhealthy, aberrant, distorted, corrupted, debauched, debased; informal sick, kinky, pervy.

twisty adj. **winding**, windy, twisting, bendy, zigzag, meandering, curving, sinuous, snaky.
– OPPOSITES straight.

twit n. Brit. informal See **fool** (sense 1 of the noun).

twitch v. **1** *he twitched and then lay still* **jerk**, convulse, quiver, tremble, shiver, shudder. **2** *he twitched the note out of my hand* **snatch**, tweak, pluck, pull, tug; informal yank.
▶n. **1** *a twitch of her lips* **spasm**, convulsion, quiver, tremor, shiver, shudder; tic. **2** *he gave a twitch at his moustache* **pull**, tug, tweak; informal yank. **3** *he felt a twitch of annoyance* **pang**, twinge, dart, stab, prick.

twitter v. **1** *sparrows twittered under the eaves* **chirp**, chirrup, cheep, tweet, peep, chatter, trill, warble, sing. **2** *stop twittering about Francis* **prattle**, babble, chatter, gabble, jabber, go on, yap, blether, blither, ramble; informal yak, yabber; Brit. informal witter, rabbit, chunter, waffle.
▶n. **1** *a bird's twitter* **chirp**, chirrup, cheep, tweet, peep, trill, warble, song. **2** *her non-stop twitter* **prattle**, chatter, babble, talk, gabble, blether; informal wittering, nattering, chuntering; Brit. informal yackety-yak; Brit. informal wittering, nattering, chuntering. **3** informal *she got into a real twitter*. See **stew** (sense 2 of the noun).

two cardinal number **pair**, duo, duet, double; old use twain.

WORD LINKS

binary, **dual** composed of or involving two parts or things
biannual taking place twice a year
biennial taking place every two years
bicentenary, **bicentennial** the two-hundredth
---

anniversary of an event
biped an animal that walks on two feet
bisect divide into two parts
dichotomy a division or contrast between two things
diptych a painting on two hinged panels
duple referring to musical rhythm based on two main beats to the bar
dyad a thing consisting of two elements or parts

two-faced adj. **deceitful**, insincere, double-dealing, hypocritical, back-stabbing, false, untrustworthy, duplicitous, deceiving, dissembling, dishonest; disloyal, treacherous, faithless; lying, untruthful, mendacious; literary perfidious.
– OPPOSITES sincere.

twosome n. **couple**, pair, duo.

tycoon n. **magnate**, mogul, businessman, captain of industry, industrialist, financier, entrepreneur; millionaire, multimillionaire; informal big shot, bigwig, honcho; Brit. informal supremo; N. Amer. informal big wheel, kahuna; derogatory fat cat.

type n. **1** *a curate of the old-fashioned type* **kind**, sort, variety, class, category, set, genre, species, order, breed, race; style, nature, manner, rank; generation, vintage; stamp, ilk, kidney, cast, grain, mould; N. Amer. stripe. **2** informal *sporty types* **person**, individual, character, sort; Brit. informal bod. **3** *his sayings are the type of modern wisdom* **epitome**, quintessence, essence, archetype, paradigm, model, embodiment. **4** *italic type* **print**, typeface, face, characters, lettering, letters; font; Brit. fount.

typhoon n. **cyclone**, tropical storm, storm, tornado, hurricane, whirlwind.

typical adj. **1** *a typical example of art deco* **representative**, classic, quintessential, archetypal, model, prototypical, stereotypical. **2** *a fairly typical day* **normal**, average, ordinary, standard, regular, routine, run-of-the-mill, conventional, unremarkable, unexceptional; informal bog-standard. **3** *it's typical of him to forget* **characteristic**, in keeping, usual, normal, par for the course, predictable, true to form; customary, habitual.
– OPPOSITES unusual, exceptional, uncharacteristic.

typify v. **1** *he typified the civil servant* **epitomize**, exemplify, characterize, be representative of; personify, embody. **2** *the sun typified the Greeks* **symbolize**, represent, stand for, be emblematic of.

tyrannical adj. **dictatorial**, despotic, autocratic, oppressive, repressive, totalitarian, undemocratic, anti-democratic, illiberal; authoritarian, high-handed, imperious, harsh, strict, iron-handed, severe, cruel, brutal, ruthless.
– OPPOSITES liberal.

tyrannize v. **dominate**, dictate to, browbeat, intimidate, bully, lord it over; persecute, victimize, torment; oppress, rule with a rod of iron, repress, crush, subjugate; informal push around.

t

tyranny n. **despotism**, absolute power,
autocracy, dictatorship, totalitarianism,
fascism; oppression, repression, subjugation,
enslavement; authoritarianism, bullying,
severity, cruelty, brutality, ruthlessness.

tyrant n. **dictator**, despot, autocrat,
authoritarian, oppressor; slave-driver,
martinet, bully.

tyro n. **novice**, beginner, learner, neophyte,
newcomer, initiate, fledgling; apprentice,
trainee, probationer; N. Amer. tenderfoot;
informal rookie, newie, newbie; N. Amer. informal
greenhorn.
– OPPOSITES veteran.

Uu

ubiquitous adj. **omnipresent**, ever-present, everywhere, all over the place, all-pervasive; universal, worldwide, global; rife, prevalent, far-reaching, inescapable.
– OPPOSITES rare.

ugly adj. **1** *an ugly face* **unattractive**, ill-favoured, hideous, plain, unlovely, unprepossessing, unsightly, horrible, frightful, awful, ghastly, unpleasant, vile, revolting, repellent, repugnant; grotesque, monstrous, reptilian, misshapen, deformed, disfigured; N. Amer. homely; informal not much to look at; Brit. informal no oil painting. **2** *things got pretty ugly* **unpleasant**, nasty, disagreeable, alarming, tense, charged, serious, grave; dangerous, perilous, threatening, menacing, hostile, ominous, sinister. **3** *an ugly rumour* **horrible**, despicable, reprehensible, nasty, appalling, objectionable, offensive, obnoxious, vile, dishonourable, rotten, vicious, spiteful.
– OPPOSITES beautiful, pleasant.

ulcer n. sore, ulceration, abscess, boil, carbuncle, blister, gumboil, wen; Medicine aphtha, chancre, furuncle.

ulterior adj. **underlying**, undisclosed, undivulged, concealed, hidden, covert, secret, personal, private, selfish.
– OPPOSITES overt.

ultimate adj. **1** *the ultimate collapse of the Empire* **eventual**, final, concluding, terminal, end; resulting, ensuing, consequent, subsequent. **2** *ultimate truths about civilization* **fundamental**, basic, primary, elementary, elemental, absolute, central, key, crucial, essential, pivotal. **3** *the ultimate gift for cat lovers* **best**, ideal, greatest, supreme, paramount, superlative, highest, utmost, optimum, quintessential.
▸ n. *the ultimate in luxury living* **utmost**, optimum, last word, height, epitome, peak, pinnacle, acme, zenith, nonpareil, dernier cri, ne plus ultra; informal the bee's knees, the cat's pyjamas/whiskers.

ultimately adv. **1** *the cost will ultimately fall on us* **eventually**, in the end, in the long run, at length, finally, sooner or later, in time, in the fullness of time, when all is said and done, one day, some day, sometime; informal when push comes to shove; Brit. informal at the end of the day. **2** *two ultimately contradictory reasons* **fundamentally**, basically, primarily, essentially, at heart, deep down.

ultra- comb. form *an ultra-conservative view* **extremely**, exceedingly, excessively, immensely, especially, exceptionally; N. English right; informal mega, mucho, majorly, oh-so; Brit. informal dead, ever so, well; N. Amer. informal real; informal dated devilish; old use exceeding.
▸ n. *ultras in the animal rights movement* **extremist**, radical, fanatic, zealot, diehard, militant.

umbrage n.
□ **take umbrage** take offence, take exception, be aggrieved, be affronted, be annoyed, be angry, be indignant, be put out, be insulted, be resentful, be disgruntled; informal be miffed, have one's nose put out of joint; Brit. informal get the hump.

umbrella n. **1** *they huddled under the umbrella* parasol, sunshade; Brit. informal brolly; Brit. informal dated gamp. **2** *the groups worked under the umbrella of the Liberal Party* **aegis**, auspices, patronage, protection, guardianship, support, backing, agency, guidance, care, charge, responsibility, cover.

umpire n. *the umpire reversed his decision* **referee**, linesman, line judge, judge, adjudicator, arbitrator, moderator; informal ref; N. Amer. informal ump.
▸ v. *he umpired a boat race* **referee**, adjudicate, arbitrate, judge, moderate, oversee; Cricket stand; informal ref.

umpteen adj. informal See **countless**.

unabashed adj. **unashamed**, shameless, unembarrassed, brazen, audacious, barefaced, blatant, flagrant, bold, unrepentant, undaunted, unconcerned, fearless.
– OPPOSITES sheepish.

unable adj. **powerless**, impotent, at a loss, inadequate, incompetent, unfit, unqualified, incapable.

unabridged adj. **complete**, entire, whole, intact, uncut, unshortened, unexpurgated.

unacceptable adj. **intolerable**, insufferable, unsatisfactory, inadmissible, inappropriate, unsuitable, undesirable, unreasonable, insupportable; offensive, obnoxious, disagreeable, disgraceful, deplorable, beyond the pale, bad; informal not on, a bit much, too much, out of order; Brit. informal a bit thick, a bit off, not cricket; formal exceptionable.
– OPPOSITES satisfactory.

unaccompanied adj. **alone**, on one's own, by oneself, solo, lone, solitary, single-handed; unescorted, unattended, unchaperoned; informal by one's lonesome; Brit. informal on one's tod, on one's Jack Jones; Austral./NZ informal on one's Pat Malone.

unaccomplished adj. **1** *unaccomplished works* **uncompleted**, incomplete, unfinished, undone, half-done, unfulfilled, neglected. **2** *an unaccomplished poet* **inexpert**, unskilful, unskilled, amateur, amateurish, unqualified, untrained; incompetent, maladroit.
– OPPOSITES complete, skilful.

unaccountable adj. **1** *for some unaccountable reason* **inexplicable**, insoluble, incomprehensible, unfathomable, impenetrable, puzzling, perplexing, baffling, bewildering, mystifying, mysterious, inscrutable, peculiar, strange, queer, odd, obscure; informal weird, freaky; Brit. informal rum. **2** *the Council is unaccountable to anyone* **unanswerable**, not liable; free, exempt, immune; unsupervised.

unaccustomed adj. **1** *she was unaccustomed to being bossed about* **unused**, new, fresh; unfamiliar with, inexperienced in, unacquainted with. **2** *he showed unaccustomed emotion* **unusual**, unfamiliar, uncommon, unwonted, exceptional, extraordinary, rare, surprising, abnormal, atypical.
– OPPOSITES habitual.

unacquainted adj. **unfamiliar**, unaccustomed, unused; inexperienced, ignorant, uninformed, unenlightened; informal in the dark; literary nescient.
– OPPOSITES familiar.

unadorned adj. **unembellished**, unornamented, undecorated, unfussy, no-nonsense, no-frills; plain, basic, restrained; bare, bald, austere, stark, spartan, clinical.
– OPPOSITES ornate.

unadventurous adj. **cautious**, careful, circumspect, wary, hesitant, timid; conservative, conventional, unenterprising, unexciting, unimaginative; boring, strait-laced, stuffy, narrow-minded; informal square, straight, stick-in-the-mud.
– OPPOSITES enterprising.

unaffected adj. **1** *they are unaffected by the cabinet reshuffle* **unchanged**, unaltered, uninfluenced; untouched, unmoved, unresponsive to; proof against, impervious to, immune to. **2** *his manner was unaffected* **unassuming**, unpretentious, down-to-earth, natural, easy, uninhibited, open, artless, guileless, ingenuous, unsophisticated. **3** *she was welcomed with unaffected warmth* **genuine**, real, sincere, honest, earnest, wholehearted, heartfelt, true, bona fide, frank, open; informal upfront.
– OPPOSITES influenced, pretentious, false, feigned.

unafraid adj. **undaunted**, unabashed, fearless, brave, courageous, plucky, intrepid, stout-hearted, bold, daring, confident, audacious, mettlesome, unshrinking; informal gutsy, spunky.
– OPPOSITES timid.

unanimous adj. **1** *doctors were unanimous about the effects* **united**, in agreement, in accord, of one mind, in harmony, concordant, undivided. **2** *a unanimous vote* **uniform**, consistent, united, concerted, congruent.
– OPPOSITES divided.

unanswerable adj. **1** *an unanswerable case* **irrefutable**, indisputable, undeniable, incontestable, incontrovertible; conclusive, absolute, positive. **2** *unanswerable questions* **insoluble**, unsolvable, insolvable, inexplicable, unexplainable.
– OPPOSITES weak, obvious.

unanswered adj. **unresolved**, undecided, unsettled, undetermined; pending, open to question, up in the air, doubtful, disputed.

unappetizing adj. **unpalatable**, uninviting, unappealing, unpleasant, off-putting, disagreeable, distasteful, unsavoury, insipid, tasteless, flavourless, dull; inedible, uneatable, revolting; informal yucky, gross.
– OPPOSITES tempting.

unapproachable adj. *her boss appeared unapproachable* **aloof**, distant, remote, detached, reserved, withdrawn, uncommunicative, guarded, undemonstrative, unresponsive, unforthcoming, unfriendly, unsympathetic, unsociable; cool, cold, frosty, stiff, formal; informal stand-offish.
– OPPOSITES accessible, friendly.

unarmed adj. **defenceless**, weaponless; unprotected, undefended, unguarded, unshielded, vulnerable, exposed, assailable, pregnable.

unassailable adj. **1** *an unassailable fortress* **impregnable**, invulnerable, impenetrable, inviolable, invincible, unconquerable; secure, safe, strong, indestructible. **2** *his logic was unassailable* **indisputable**, undeniable, unquestionable, incontestable, incontrovertible, irrefutable, indubitable, watertight, sound, good, sure, manifest, patent, obvious.
– OPPOSITES defenceless.

unassertive adj. **passive**, retiring, unforthcoming, submissive, unassuming, self-effacing, modest, humble, meek, unconfident, diffident, shy, timid, insecure; informal mousy.
– OPPOSITES bold.

unassuming adj. **modest**, self-effacing, humble, meek, reserved, diffident; unobtrusive, unostentatious, unpretentious, unaffected, natural, artless, ingenuous.

unattached adj. **1** *they were both unattached* **single**, unmarried, unwed, partnerless, uncommitted, available, footloose and fancy free, on one's own; on the shelf, unloved. **2** *we are unattached to any organization* **unaffiliated**, unallied; autonomous, independent, non-aligned, self-governing, neutral, separate, unconnected, detached.
– OPPOSITES married.

unattainable adj. **unreachable**, unachievable, unobtainable, impossible,

unwinnable; unrealistic, implausible.
– OPPOSITES attainable.

unattended adj. **1** *his cries went unattended*
ignored, disregarded, neglected, passed
over. **2** *an unattended vehicle* **unguarded**,
unwatched, alone, solitary; abandoned.
3 *she had to walk there unattended*
unaccompanied, unescorted, partnerless,
unchaperoned, alone, on one's own, by
oneself, solo; Brit. informal on one's tod.

unattractive adj. **ugly**, plain, ill-favoured,
unappealing, unsightly, unlovely,
unprepossessing, displeasing; hideous,
monstrous, grotesque; N. Amer. homely; informal
not much to look at, as ugly as sin; Brit. informal
no oil painting.
– OPPOSITES beautiful.

unauthorized adj. **unofficial**, unsanctioned,
unaccredited, unlicensed, unwarranted,
unapproved; disallowed, prohibited, banned,
barred, forbidden, outlawed, illegal, against
the law, illegitimate, illicit, proscribed.
– OPPOSITES official.

unavailing adj. **ineffective**, ineffectual,
inefficacious, vain, futile, useless,
unsuccessful, fruitless, profitless,
unprofitable, to no avail, abortive; old use
bootless.
– OPPOSITES effective.

unavoidable adj. **inescapable**, inevitable,
inexorable, assured, certain, predestined,
predetermined, ineluctable, unpreventable;
necessary, compulsory, required, obligatory,
mandatory.

unaware adj. **ignorant**, unknowing,
unconscious, heedless, unmindful, oblivious,
unsuspecting, uninformed, unenlightened,
unwitting, innocent; inattentive,
unobservant, unperceptive, blind, deaf;
informal in the dark; literary nescient.
– OPPOSITES conscious.

unawares adv. **1** *brigands caught them
unawares* **by surprise**, unexpectedly,
without warning, suddenly, abruptly,
unprepared, off-guard; informal with one's
trousers down, napping; Brit. informal on
the hop. **2** *the roach approached the pike
unawares* **unknowingly**, unwittingly,
unconsciously; unintentionally,
inadvertently, accidentally, by mistake.
– OPPOSITES prepared, knowingly.

unbalanced adj. **1** *he is unbalanced and
dangerous* **unstable**, mentally ill, deranged,
demented, disturbed, unhinged, insane,
mad, out of one's mind, non compos
mentis; informal crazy, loopy, loony, nuts,
nutty, cracked, screwy, batty, dotty, cuckoo,
bonkers, mental, off one's head, round the
bend/twist; Brit. informal barmy, potty, crackers,
barking, off one's rocker; N. Amer. informal
nutso, squirrelly; dated touched. **2** *a most
unbalanced article* **biased**, prejudiced, one-
sided, partisan, inequitable, unjust, unfair,
parti pris.
– OPPOSITES sane, unbiased.

unbearable adj. **intolerable**, insufferable,
insupportable, unendurable, unacceptable,

unmanageable, more than flesh and blood
can stand, overpowering; informal too much.
– OPPOSITES tolerable.

unbeatable adj. **invincible**, unstoppable,
unassailable, indomitable, unconquerable,
unsurpassable, matchless, peerless; supreme.

unbeaten adj. **undefeated**, unconquered,
unsurpassed, unequalled, unrivalled;
triumphant, victorious, supreme, matchless,
second to none.

unbecoming adj. **1** *an unbecoming sundress*
unflattering, unattractive, unsightly,
plain, ugly, hideous; unsuitable. **2** *conduct
unbecoming to the Senate* **inappropriate**,
unfitting, unbefitting, unsuitable, unsuited,
inapt, out of keeping, untoward, incorrect,
unacceptable; unworthy, improper,
unseemly, undignified.
– OPPOSITES flattering, appropriate.

unbelief n. **atheism**, non-belief, agnosticism,
apostasy, irreligion, godlessness, nihilism;
scepticism, cynicism, disbelief, doubt.
– OPPOSITES faith.

unbelievable adj. **incredible**, beyond
belief, inconceivable, unthinkable,
unimaginable; unconvincing, far-fetched,
implausible, improbable; informal hard to
swallow.
– OPPOSITES credible.

unbend v. **1** *I couldn't unbend my knees*
straighten (out), extend, flex, uncurl.
2 *if you'd only unbend a little* **relax**, unwind,
de-stress, loosen up, let oneself go; informal
let one's hair down, let it all hang out, hang
loose.

unbending adj. **1** *an unbending man* **aloof**,
formal, stiff, reserved, remote, forbidding,
cool, unfeeling, unemotional, unfriendly,
austere; informal uptight, stand-offish.
2 *unbending attitudes* **uncompromising**,
inflexible, unyielding, hard-line, tough,
strict, firm, resolute, determined,
unrelenting, relentless, inexorable,
intransigent, immovable.

unbiased adj. **impartial**, unprejudiced,
neutral, non-partisan, disinterested,
detached, dispassionate, objective, open-
minded, equitable, even-handed, fair.
– OPPOSITES prejudiced.

unbidden adj. **1** *an unbidden guest*
uninvited, unasked, unsolicited; unwanted,
unwelcome. **2** *unbidden excitement*
spontaneous, unprompted, voluntary,
unforced, unplanned, unpremeditated;
informal off-the-cuff.

unbind v. **untie**, unchain, unfetter,
unshackle, unfasten, untether, undo, loosen;
release, free, liberate.

unblemished adj. **impeccable**, flawless,
faultless, perfect, pure, whiter than
white, clean, spotless, unsullied, unspoilt,
undefiled, untouched, untarnished,
unpolluted; incorrupt, guiltless, sinless,
innocent, blameless; informal squeaky clean.
– OPPOSITES flawed.

unborn adj. **1** *your unborn child* **embryonic**,
fetal, in utero; expected. **2** *the unborn*

generations **future**, coming, forthcoming, subsequent.

unbounded adj. **unlimited**, boundless, limitless, illimitable; unrestrained, unrestricted, unconstrained, uncontrolled, unchecked, unbridled; untold, immeasurable, endless, unending, interminable, everlasting, infinite, cosmic, inexhaustible.
– OPPOSITES limited.

unbreakable adj. **shatterproof**, indestructible, imperishable, durable, long-lasting; toughened, sturdy, stout, resistant, hard-wearing, heavy-duty.
– OPPOSITES fragile.

unbridled adj. **unrestrained**, unconstrained, uncontrolled, uninhibited, unrestricted, unchecked, uncurbed, rampant, runaway, irrepressible, unstoppable, intemperate, immoderate.
– OPPOSITES restrained.

unbroken adj. **1** *the last unbroken window* **undamaged**, unimpaired, unharmed, unscathed, untouched, sound, intact, whole, perfect. **2** *an unbroken horse* **untamed**, undomesticated, wild, feral. **3** *an unbroken chain of victories* **uninterrupted**, continuous, endless, constant, unremitting, ongoing. **4** *his record is still unbroken* **unbeaten**, undefeated, unsurpassed, unrivalled, unmatched, supreme.

unburden v. *she had a sudden wish to unburden herself* **open one's heart**, confess, tell all; informal **come clean**; old use **unbosom** oneself.

uncalled for adj. **gratuitous**, unnecessary, needless, inessential; undeserved, unmerited, unwarranted, unjustified, unreasonable, unfair, inappropriate, pointless; unasked, unsolicited, unrequested, unprompted, unprovoked, unwelcome.

uncanny adj. **1** *the silence was uncanny* **eerie**, unnatural, unearthly, other-worldly, ghostly, strange, abnormal, weird, bizarre, freakish; Scottish **eldritch**; informal **creepy**, spooky, freaky. **2** *an uncanny resemblance* **striking**, remarkable, extraordinary, exceptional, incredible, noteworthy, notable, arresting.

unceasing adj. **incessant**, ceaseless, constant, continual, unabating, interminable, endless, unending, never-ending, everlasting, eternal, perpetual, continuous, non-stop, uninterrupted, unbroken, unremitting, persistent, relentless, unrelenting, unrelieved, sustained.

unceremonious adj. **1** *an unceremonious dismissal* **abrupt**, sudden, hasty, hurried, summary, perfunctory, undignified; rude, impolite, discourteous, offhand. **2** *an unceremonious man* **informal**, casual, relaxed, easy-going, familiar, natural, open; informal **laid-back**.
– OPPOSITES formal.

uncertain adj. **1** *the effects are uncertain* **unknown**, debatable, open to question, in doubt, undetermined, unsure, in the balance, up in the air; unpredictable, unforeseeable, incalculable; risky, chancy; informal **iffy**. **2** *uncertain weather* **changeable**, variable, changeful, irregular, unpredictable, unreliable, unsettled, erratic, fluctuating. **3** *Ed was uncertain about the decision* **unsure**, doubtful, dubious, undecided, irresolute, hesitant, blowing hot and cold, vacillating, vague, unclear, ambivalent, in two minds. **4** *an uncertain smile* **hesitant**, tentative, faltering, unsure, unconfident.
– OPPOSITES predictable, sure, confident.

unchangeable adj. **unalterable**, immutable, invariable, changeless, fixed, hard and fast, cast-iron, set in stone, established, permanent, enduring, abiding, lasting, indestructible, ineradicable, irreversible.
– OPPOSITES variable.

unchanging adj. **consistent**, constant, regular, unvarying, predictable, stable, steady, fixed, permanent, perpetual, eternal; sustained, lasting, persistent.

uncharitable adj. **mean**, mean-spirited, unkind, selfish, self-centred, inconsiderate, thoughtless, insensitive, unfriendly, unsympathetic, uncaring, ungenerous, ungracious, unfair.

uncharted adj. **unexplored**, undiscovered, unmapped, untravelled, unfamiliar, unplumbed, unknown.

uncivil adj. **impolite**, rude, discourteous, disrespectful, unmannerly, bad-mannered, impertinent, impudent, ungracious; brusque, sharp, curt, offhand, gruff, churlish; informal **off**, fresh.
– OPPOSITES polite.

uncivilized adj. **uncouth**, coarse, rough, boorish, vulgar, philistine, uneducated, uncultured, uncultivated, benighted, unsophisticated, unpolished; ill-bred, ill-mannered, thuggish, loutish; barbarian, primitive, savage, brutish; old use **rude**.

unclean adj. **1** *unclean premises* **dirty**, filthy, grubby, grimy, mucky, foul, impure, tainted, soiled, unwashed; polluted, contaminated, infected, insanitary, unhygienic, unhealthy, germy, disease-ridden; informal **yucky**, cruddy; Brit. informal **grotty**, gungy. **2** *sex was considered unclean* **sinful**, immoral, bad, wicked, evil, corrupt, impure, unwholesome, sordid, disgusting, debased, degenerate, depraved. **3** *an unclean meat* **impure**; forbidden, taboo.
– OPPOSITES pure, halal, kosher.

unclear adj. **uncertain**, unsure, unsettled, up in the air, debatable, open to question, in doubt, doubtful; ambiguous, equivocal, indefinite, vague, mysterious, obscure, hazy, foggy, nebulous; informal **iffy**.
– OPPOSITES evident.

unclothed adj. **naked**, bare, nude, stripped, undressed, in a state of nature; informal **in one's birthday suit**, in the buff, in the raw, in the altogether, in the nuddy; Brit. informal **starkers**; Scottish informal **in the scud**; N. Amer. informal **buck naked**.
– OPPOSITES dressed.

u

uncomfortable adj. **1** *an uncomfortable chair* **painful**, disagreeable, intolerable, unbearable, confining, cramped. **2** *I felt uncomfortable in her presence* **uneasy**, awkward, nervous, tense, strained, edgy, restless, embarrassed, troubled, worried, anxious, unquiet, fraught; informal rattled, twitchy; N. Amer. informal discombobulated, antsy.
– OPPOSITES relaxed.

uncommitted adj. **1** *uncommitted voters* **floating**, undecided, non-partisan, unaffiliated, neutral, impartial, independent, undeclared, uncertain; informal sitting on the fence. **2** *the uncommitted male* **unmarried**, unattached, unwed, partnerless; footloose and fancy free, available, single, lone.
– OPPOSITES aligned, attached.

uncommon adj. **1** *an uncommon plant* **unusual**, abnormal, rare, atypical, unconventional, unfamiliar, strange, odd, curious, extraordinary, outlandish, novel, singular, peculiar, queer, bizarre; alien; informal weird, oddball, offbeat. **2** *abductions are uncommon* **rare**, scarce, few and far between, exceptional, abnormal, isolated, infrequent, irregular; Brit. out of the common. **3** *an uncommon capacity for hard work* **remarkable**, extraordinary, exceptional, singular, particular, marked, outstanding, noteworthy, significant, especial, special, signal, superior, unique, unparalleled, prodigious; informal mind-boggling.

uncommonly adv. **unusually**, remarkably, extraordinarily, exceptionally, singularly, particularly, especially, decidedly, notably, eminently, extremely, very; N. English right; informal awfully, terribly, seriously; Brit. informal jolly, dead.

uncommunicative adj. **taciturn**, quiet, unforthcoming, reserved, reticent, laconic, tongue-tied, mute, silent, tight-lipped; guarded, secretive, close, private; distant, remote, aloof, withdrawn, unsociable; informal mum, stand-offish.
– OPPOSITES talkative.

uncomplicated adj. **simple**, straightforward, clear, accessible, undemanding, unchallenging, unsophisticated, trouble-free, painless, effortless, easy, elementary, idiot-proof, plain sailing; informal a piece of cake, child's play, a cinch, a doddle, a breeze, a walk in the park; Brit. informal easy-peasy.
– OPPOSITES complex.

uncompromising adj. **inflexible**, unbending, unyielding, unshakeable, resolute, rigid, hard-line, immovable, intractable, firm, determined, iron-willed, obstinate, stubborn, adamant, obdurate, intransigent, headstrong, pig-headed; Brit. informal bloody-minded.
– OPPOSITES flexible.

unconcerned adj. **1** *he is unconcerned about their responses* **indifferent**, unmoved, apathetic, uninterested, incurious, dispassionate, heedless, unmindful; cool, lukewarm, unenthusiastic. **2** *she tried to look unconcerned* **untroubled**, unworried, unruffled, insouciant, nonchalant, blasé, carefree, casual, relaxed, at ease, {cool, calm, and collected}; informal laid-back.
– OPPOSITES interested, anxious.

unconditional adj. **unquestioning**, unqualified, unreserved, unlimited, unrestricted, wholehearted; complete, total, entire, full, absolute, out-and-out, unequivocal.

unconnected adj. **1** *the earth wire was unconnected* **detached**, disconnected, loose. **2** *unconnected tasks* **unrelated**, dissociated, separate, independent, distinct, different, disparate, discrete. **3** *unconnected chains of thought* **disjointed**, incoherent, disconnected, rambling, wandering, diffuse, disorderly, haphazard, disorganized, garbled, mixed, muddled, aimless.
– OPPOSITES attached, related, coherent.

unconscionable adj. **1** *the unconscionable use of test animals* **unethical**, amoral, immoral, unprincipled, indefensible, wrong; unscrupulous, unfair, underhand, dishonourable. **2** *we had to wait an unconscionable time* **excessive**, unreasonable, unwarranted, uncalled for, unfair, inordinate, immoderate, undue, inexcusable, unnecessary, needless; informal over the top, OTT.
– OPPOSITES ethical, acceptable.

unconscious adj. **1** *she made sure he was unconscious* **insensible**, senseless, insentient, insensate, comatose, inert, knocked out, stunned; motionless, immobile, prostrate; informal out cold, out for the count, dead to the world; Brit. informal spark out. **2** *she was unconscious of the pain* **heedless**, unmindful, disregarding, oblivious to, insensible to, impervious to, unaffected by, unconcerned by, indifferent to; unaware, unknowing. **3** *an unconscious desire* **subconscious**, latent, suppressed, subliminal, sleeping, inherent, instinctive, involuntary, uncontrolled, spontaneous; unintentional, unthinking, unwitting, inadvertent; informal gut.
– OPPOSITES aware, voluntary.
▶ n. *fantasies raging in the unconscious* **subconscious**, psyche, ego, id, inner self.

uncontrollable adj. **1** *the crowds were uncontrollable* **unmanageable**, out of control, ungovernable, wild, unruly, disorderly, recalcitrant, turbulent, disobedient, delinquent, defiant, undisciplined; formal refractory. **2** *an uncontrollable rage* **ungovernable**, irrepressible, unstoppable, unquenchable; wild, violent, frenzied, furious, mad, hysterical, passionate.
– OPPOSITES compliant.

unconventional adj. **unusual**, irregular, unorthodox, unfamiliar, uncommon, unwonted, out of the ordinary, atypical, singular, alternative, different; new, novel, innovative, groundbreaking, pioneering, original, unprecedented; eccentric,

idiosyncratic, quirky, odd, strange, bizarre, weird, outlandish, off-centre, curious; abnormal, anomalous, aberrant, extraordinary; nonconformist, bohemian, avant-garde; informal way out, far out, offbeat, wacky, madcap, zany; Brit. informal rum; N. Amer. informal kooky, wacko.
– OPPOSITES orthodox.

unconvincing adj. **improbable**, unlikely, implausible, incredible, unbelievable, questionable, dubious, doubtful; strained, laboured, far-fetched, unrealistic, fanciful, fantastic; feeble, weak, transparent, poor, lame, ineffectual, half-baked; informal hard to swallow.
– OPPOSITES persuasive.

uncooperative adj. **unhelpful**, awkward, disobliging, recalcitrant, perverse, contrary, stubborn, wilful, stiff-necked, unyielding, unbending, inflexible, immovable, obstructive, difficult, obstreperous, disobedient; Brit. informal bloody-minded.
– OPPOSITES obliging.

uncoordinated adj. **clumsy**, awkward, blundering, bumbling, lumbering, flat-footed, heavy-handed, graceless, gawky, ungainly, ungraceful; inept, unhandy, unskilful, inexpert, maladroit, bungling; informal butterfingered, cack-handed, ham-fisted; Brit. informal all (fingers and) thumbs; N. Amer. informal klutzy.
– OPPOSITES dexterous.

uncouth adj. **uncivilized**, uncultured, uncultivated, unrefined, unpolished, unsophisticated, common, low, rough, coarse, crude, loutish, boorish, oafish; churlish, uncivil, rude, impolite, discourteous, disrespectful, unmannerly, bad-mannered, ill-bred, indecorous, vulgar, crass, indelicate; Brit. informal yobbish.
– OPPOSITES refined.

uncover v. **1** *she uncovered the sandwiches* **expose**, reveal, lay bare; unwrap, unveil; strip, denude. **2** *they uncovered a money-laundering plot* **detect**, discover, come across, stumble on, chance on, find, turn up, unearth, dig up; expose, bring to light, unmask, unveil, reveal, lay bare, make known, make public, betray, give away; informal blow the whistle on.

unctuous adj. **sycophantic**, ingratiating, obsequious, fawning, servile, grovelling, subservient, cringing, humble, hypocritical, insincere, gushing, effusive; glib, smooth, slick, slippery, oily, greasy; informal smarmy, slimy, sucky, soapy.

undaunted adj. **unafraid**, undismayed, unflinching, unshrinking, unabashed, fearless, dauntless, intrepid, bold, valiant, brave, courageous, plucky, mettlesome, gritty, indomitable, confident, audacious, daring; informal gutsy, spunky.
– OPPOSITES fearful.

undecided adj. **unresolved**, uncertain, unsure, unclear, unsettled, indefinite, undetermined, unknown, in the balance, up in the air, debatable, arguable, moot, open

to question, doubtful, dubious, borderline, ambiguous, vague; indecisive, irresolute, hesitant, tentative, wavering, vacillating, uncommitted, ambivalent, in two minds; informal iffy.
– OPPOSITES certain.

undefined adj. **1** *some matters are still undefined* **unspecified**, unexplained, unspecific, indeterminate, unsettled; unclear, woolly, imprecise, inexact, indefinite, vague. **2** *undefined shapes* **indistinct**, indefinite, formless, indistinguishable, vague, hazy, misty, shadowy, nebulous, blurred, blurry.
– OPPOSITES definite, distinct.

undemonstrative adj. **unemotional**, unaffectionate, impassive, dispassionate, restrained, reserved, unresponsive, uncommunicative, unforthcoming, stiff, guarded, aloof, distant, detached, remote, withdrawn; cool, cold, frosty, frigid; informal stand-offish.

undeniable adj. **indisputable**, indubitable, unquestionable, beyond doubt, beyond question, undebatable, incontrovertible, incontestable, irrefutable, unassailable; certain, sure, definite, positive, conclusive, plain, obvious, unmistakable, self-evident, patent, emphatic, categorical, unequivocal.
– OPPOSITES questionable.

under prep. **1** *they hid under a bush* **beneath**, below, underneath. **2** *the rent is under £250* **less than**, lower than, below. **3** *branch managers are under the retail director* **subordinate to**, junior to, inferior to, subservient to, answerable to, responsible to, subject to, controlled by. **4** *forty homes are under construction* **undergoing**, in the process of. **5** *the town was under water* **flooded by**, immersed in, submerged by, sunk in, engulfed by, inundated by. **6** *our finances are under pressure* **subject to**, liable to, at the mercy of.
– OPPOSITES above, over.

▸ adv. *coughing and spluttering she went under* **down**, lower, below, underneath, beneath; underwater.

underclothes plural n. **underwear**, undergarments, underclothing, underthings, lingerie; informal undies, frillies; Brit. informal smalls; old use underlinen.

undercover adj. **covert**, secret, clandestine, underground, surreptitious, furtive, cloak-and-dagger, hole-and-corner, hugger-mugger, stealthy, hidden, concealed; informal hush-hush, sneaky; Military black.
– OPPOSITES overt.

undercurrent n. **1** *dangerous undercurrents in the cove* **undertow**, underflow, underswell, underset. **2** *the undercurrent of despair in his words* **undertone**, overtone, suggestion, connotation, intimation, hint, nuance, trace, suspicion, whisper, tinge; feeling, atmosphere, aura, echo; informal vibes.

undercut v. **1** *the firm undercut their rivals* **charge less than**, undersell, underbid. **2** *his authority was being undercut* **undermine**,

u

weaken, impair, sap, threaten, subvert, sabotage, ruin, destabilize, wreck.

underdog n. **weaker party**, victim, loser, scapegoat; informal little guy, fall guy, stooge.

underestimate v. **underrate**, undervalue, do an injustice to, be wrong about, sell short, play down, understate; minimize, de-emphasize, underemphasize, diminish, downgrade, gloss over, trivialize; miscalculate, misjudge, misconstrue, misread.

– OPPOSITES exaggerate.

undergo v. **go through**, experience, undertake, face, submit to, be subjected to, come in for, receive, sustain, endure, brave, bear, tolerate, stand, withstand, weather; Brit. informal wear.

underground adj. **1** *an underground car park* **subterranean**, buried, sunken, basement. **2** *underground organizations* **clandestine**, secret, surreptitious, covert, undercover, closet, hole-and-corner, cloak-and-dagger, hugger-mugger, back-alley, hidden, sneaky, furtive; resistance, subversive; Military black; informal hush-hush. **3** *the underground art scene* **alternative**, radical, revolutionary, unconventional, unorthodox, avant-garde, experimental, innovative.

▸n. **1** *he took the underground* **underground railway**, metro; N. Amer. subway; Brit. informal tube. **2** *information from the French underground* **resistance (movement)**; partisans, guerrillas, freedom fighters; historical Maquis.

undergrowth n. **shrubbery**, vegetation, greenery, ground cover, underwood, brushwood, brush, scrub, covert, thicket, copse; bushes, plants, brambles, herbage; N. Amer. underbrush.

underhand adj. **deceitful**, dishonest, dishonourable, disreputable, unethical, unprincipled, immoral, unscrupulous, fraudulent, dubious, unfair; treacherous, duplicitous, double-dealing; devious, artful, crafty, conniving, scheming, sly, wily; clandestine, sneaky, furtive, covert, cloak-and-dagger; N. Amer. snide; informal crooked, shady, bent, low-down; Brit. informal dodgy; Austral./NZ informal shonky.

– OPPOSITES honest.

underline v. **1** *she underlined a phrase* **underscore**, mark, pick out, emphasize, highlight. **2** *the programme underlines the benefits of exercise* **emphasize**, stress, highlight, accentuate, accent, focus on, spotlight, point up, play up; informal rub in.

underling n. **subordinate**, inferior, junior, minion, lackey, flunkey, menial, retainer, vassal, subject, hireling, servant, henchman, factotum, gofer; informal bitch; Brit. informal skivvy, dogsbody.

– OPPOSITES boss.

underlying adj. **1** *the underlying aims of the research* **fundamental**, basic, primary, prime, central, principal, chief, key, elementary, intrinsic, essential.

2 *an underlying feeling of irritation* **latent**, repressed, suppressed, unrevealed, undisclosed, unexpressed, concealed, hidden, masked.

undermine v. **1** *their integrity is being undermined* **subvert**, sabotage, threaten, weaken, compromise, diminish, reduce, impair, mar, spoil, ruin, damage, hurt, injure, cripple, sap, shake. **2** *we undermined the building* **tunnel under**, dig under, burrow under, sap. **3** *the damp had so undermined the wall that it collapsed* **erode**, wear away, eat away at.

– OPPOSITES strengthen, support.

underprivileged adj. **needy**, deprived, disadvantaged, poor, destitute, in straitened circumstances, on one's uppers, on one's beam-ends, impoverished, poverty-stricken, indigent; Brit. on the breadline; formal penurious.

– OPPOSITES wealthy.

underrate v. **undervalue**, underestimate, do an injustice to, sell short, play down, understate, minimize, diminish, downgrade, trivialize.

– OPPOSITES exaggerate.

undersized adj. **underdeveloped**, stunted, small, short, little, tiny, petite, slight, compact, miniature, mini, diminutive, dwarfish, pygmy; Scottish wee; informal pint-sized, pocket-sized, knee-high to a grasshopper, baby, teeny-weeny, itsy-bitsy.

– OPPOSITES overgrown.

understand v. **1** *he couldn't understand anything we said* **comprehend**, grasp, take in, see, apprehend, follow, make sense of, fathom; unravel, decipher, interpret; informal work out, figure out, make head or tail of, get one's head around, take on board, get the drift of, catch on to, get; Brit. informal twig, suss (out). **2** *she understood how hard he'd worked* **appreciate**, recognize, realize, acknowledge, know, be aware of, be conscious of; informal be wise to; formal be cognizant of. **3** *I understand that you wish to go* **believe**, gather, take it, hear (tell), notice, see, learn; conclude, infer, assume, surmise, fancy.

understandable adj. **1** *make it understandable to the layman* **comprehensible**, intelligible, coherent, clear, explicit, unambiguous, transparent, plain, straightforward, digestible, user-friendly. **2** *an understandable desire to be happy* **unsurprising**, expected, predictable, inevitable; reasonable, acceptable, logical, rational, normal, natural; justifiable, justified, defensible, excusable, pardonable, forgivable.

understanding n. **1** *test your understanding of the language* **comprehension**, apprehension, grasp, mastery, appreciation, assimilation, absorption; knowledge, awareness, insight, skill, expertise, proficiency; informal know-how; formal cognizance. **2** *a young man of brilliant understanding* **intellect**, intelligence, brainpower, brains, judgement, reasoning,

mentality; insight, intuition, shrewdness, acumen, sagacity, wisdom, wit; informal nous, savvy, know-how. **3** *it was my understanding that this was free* **belief**, perception, view, conviction, feeling, opinion, intuition, impression, assumption, supposition. **4** *he treated me with understanding* **compassion**, sympathy, pity, feeling, concern, consideration, kindness, sensitivity, decency, humanity, charity, goodwill, mercy, tolerance. **5** *we had a tacit understanding* **agreement**, arrangement, deal, bargain, settlement, pledge, pact, compact, contract, covenant, bond.
– OPPOSITES ignorance, indifference.
▶ adj. *an understanding friend* **compassionate**, sympathetic, sensitive, considerate, tender, kind, thoughtful, tolerant, patient, forbearing, lenient, merciful, forgiving, humane; approachable, supportive, perceptive.

understate v. **play down**, downplay, underrate, underplay, de-emphasize, trivialize, minimize, diminish, downgrade, brush aside, gloss over; informal soft-pedal, sell short.
– OPPOSITES exaggerate.

understudy n. **stand-in**, substitute, replacement, reserve, fill-in, locum, proxy, back-up, relief, standby, stopgap, second, ancillary; informal sub; N. Amer. informal pinch-hitter.

undertake v. **tackle**, take on, assume, shoulder, handle, manage, deal with, take forward, be responsible for; engage in, take part in, go about, set about, get down to, get to grips with, embark on; attempt, try, endeavour; informal have a go at; formal essay.

undertaker n. **funeral director**; N. Amer. mortician.

undertaking n. **1** *a risky undertaking* **enterprise**, venture, project, campaign, scheme, plan, operation, endeavour, effort, task, activity, pursuit, exploit, business, affair, procedure; mission, quest. **2** *sign this undertaking to comply with the rules* **pledge**, agreement, promise, oath, covenant, vow, commitment, guarantee, assurance, contract.

undertone n. **1** *he said something in an undertone* **low voice**, murmur, whisper, mutter. **2** *the story's dark undertones* **undercurrent**, overtone, suggestion, nuance, vein, atmosphere, aura, tenor, flavour; vibrations.

undervalue v. **underrate**, underestimate, play down, understate, underemphasize, diminish, minimize, downgrade, reduce, brush aside, gloss over, trivialize, hold cheap; informal sell short.

underwater adj. **submerged**, immersed, sunken, subaqueous; undersea, submarine.

underwear n. **underclothes**, underclothing, undergarments, underthings, lingerie; informal undies, frillies; Brit. informal smalls; old use underlinen.

underworld n. **1** *Osiris, god of the underworld* **the netherworld**, the nether

regions, hell, the abyss; eternal damnation; Gehenna, Tophet, Sheol, Hades; Brit. the other place; literary the pit. **2** *the violent underworld of Southwark* **criminal world**, gangland; criminals, gangsters; informal mobsters.
– OPPOSITES heaven.

> **WORD LINKS**
>
> **chthonic** relating to or inhabiting the underworld
> **Cerberus** (in Greek mythology) the dog guarding the entrance to the underworld
> **Charon** (in Greek mythology) the man who ferried the souls of the dead to the underworld
> **Styx** (in Greek mythology) a river in the underworld

underwrite v. **sponsor**, support, back, insure, indemnify, subsidize, pay for, finance, fund; informal foot the bill for; N. Amer. informal bankroll.

undesirable adj. **1** *undesirable side effects* **unpleasant**, disagreeable, nasty, unwelcome, unwanted, unfortunate, infelicitous. **2** *some very undesirable people* **unpleasant**, disagreeable, obnoxious, nasty, awful, terrible, dreadful, frightful, repulsive, repellent, abhorrent, loathsome, hateful, detestable, deplorable, horrible, appalling, insufferable, intolerable, despicable, contemptible, odious, vile, unsavoury; informal ghastly, horrid; Brit. informal beastly.
– OPPOSITES pleasant, agreeable.

undignified adj. **unseemly**, demeaning, unbecoming, unworthy, unbefitting, degrading, shameful, dishonourable, ignominious, discreditable, ignoble, untoward, unsuitable; scandalous, disgraceful, indecent, low, base; informal infra dig.

undisciplined adj. **unruly**, disorderly, disobedient, badly behaved, recalcitrant, wilful, wayward, delinquent, naughty, rebellious, insubordinate, disruptive, attention-seeking, errant, out of control, uncontrollable, wild; disorganized, unsystematic, unmethodical, lax, slapdash, slipshod, sloppy; Brit. informal stroppy, bolshie; formal refractory.

undisguised adj. **obvious**, evident, patent, manifest, transparent, overt, unconcealed, unhidden, unmistakable, undeniable, plain, clear, clear-cut, explicit, naked, visible; blatant, flagrant, glaring, bold; informal standing/sticking out a mile.

undisputed adj. **undoubted**, indubitable, uncontested, incontestable, unchallenged, incontrovertible, unequivocal, undeniable, irrefutable, unmistakable, sure, certain, definite, accepted, acknowledged, recognized.
– OPPOSITES doubtful.

undistinguished adj. **unexceptional**, indifferent, run-of-the-mill, middle-of-the-road, ordinary, average, commonplace, mediocre, humdrum, lacklustre, forgettable, uninspired, uneventful, unremarkable, inconsequential, featureless, nondescript, middling, moderate; N. Amer. garden-variety; informal nothing special, no great shakes,

u

nothing to write home about, OK, so-so, bog-standard; Brit. informal common or garden; N. Amer. informal bush-league.
– OPPOSITES extraordinary.

undivided adj. **complete**, full, total, whole, entire, absolute, unqualified, unreserved, unmitigated, unbroken, consistent, thorough, exclusive, dedicated; focused, engrossed, absorbed, attentive, committed.

undo v. **1** *he undid another button* **unfasten**, unbutton, unhook, untie, unlace; unlock, unbolt; loosen, disentangle, extricate, release, detach, free, open; disconnect, disengage, separate. **2** *they will undo a decision by the law lords* **revoke**, overrule, overturn, repeal, rescind, reverse, countermand, cancel, annul, nullify, invalidate, void, negate; Law vacate; formal abrogate. **3** *she undid much of the good work done* **ruin**, undermine, subvert, overturn, scotch, sabotage, spoil, impair, mar, destroy, wreck, eradicate, obliterate; cancel out, neutralize, thwart, foil, frustrate, hamper, hinder, obstruct; informal blow, put the kibosh on, foul up, muck up; Brit. informal scupper; N. Amer. informal rain on someone's parade.
– OPPOSITES fasten, ratify, enhance.

undoing n. **1** *she plotted the king's undoing* **downfall**, defeat, conquest, deposition, overthrow, ruin, ruination, elimination, end, collapse, failure, debasement; Waterloo. **2** *their complacency was their undoing* **fatal flaw**, Achilles' heel, weakness, weak point, failing, misfortune, affliction, curse.

undone adj. **1** *some work was left undone* **unfinished**, incomplete, half-done, unaccomplished, unfulfilled, unconcluded; omitted, neglected, disregarded, ignored; remaining, outstanding, deferred, pending, on ice; informal on the back burner. **2** formal *she had lost and was utterly undone* **done for**, finished, ruined, destroyed, doomed, lost, defeated, beaten; informal washed up.
– OPPOSITES finished, successful.

undoubted adj. **undisputed**, unchallenged, unquestioned, indubitable, incontrovertible, irrefutable, incontestable, sure, certain, unmistakable; definite, accepted, acknowledged, recognized.

undoubtedly adv. **doubtless**, indubitably, doubtlessly, no doubt, without (a) doubt; unquestionably, indisputably, undeniably, incontrovertibly, clearly, obviously, patently, certainly, definitely, surely, of course, indeed.

undress v. *he undressed and got into bed* **strip (off)**, disrobe, take off one's clothes; Brit. informal peel off.
□ **in a state of undress** naked, (in the) nude, bare, stripped, unclothed, undressed, in a state of nature; informal in one's birthday suit, in the raw, in the buff, in the nuddy; Brit. informal starkers.

undue adj. **excessive**, immoderate, intemperate, inordinate, disproportionate; uncalled for, unneeded, unnecessary, non-essential, needless, unwarranted,

unjustified, unreasonable; inappropriate, unmerited, unsuitable, improper.
– OPPOSITES appropriate.

undulate v. **rise and fall**, surge, swell, heave, ripple, flow; wind, wobble, oscillate.

undying adj. **abiding**, lasting, enduring, permanent, constant, infinite; unceasing, perpetual, ceaseless, incessant, unending, never-ending; immortal, eternal, deathless.

unearth v. **1** *workmen unearthed an artillery shell* **dig up**, excavate, exhume, disinter, root out, unbury. **2** *I unearthed an interesting fact* **discover**, uncover, find, come across, hit on, bring to light, expose, turn up, hunt out, nose out.

unearthly adj. **1** *an unearthly chill in the air* **other-worldly**, supernatural, preternatural, alien; ghostly, spectral, phantom, mysterious, spine-chilling, hair-raising; uncanny, eerie, strange, weird, unnatural, bizarre; Scottish eldritch; informal spooky, creepy, scary. **2** informal *they rose at some unearthly hour* **unreasonable**, preposterous, abnormal, extraordinary, absurd, ridiculous, unheard of; informal ungodly, unholy.
– OPPOSITES normal, reasonable.

uneasy adj. **1** *the doctor made him feel uneasy* **worried**, anxious, troubled, disturbed, agitated, nervous, tense, nervy, overwrought, edgy, apprehensive, restless, discomfited, perturbed, fearful, uncomfortable, unsettled; informal jittery. **2** *he had an uneasy feeling* **worrying**, disturbing, troubling, alarming, dismaying, disquieting, unsettling, disconcerting, upsetting. **3** *the victory ensured an uneasy peace* **tense**, awkward, strained, fraught; precarious, unstable, insecure.
– OPPOSITES calm, stable.

uneconomic, **uneconomical** adj. **unprofitable**, uncommercial, non-viable, loss-making, worthless; wasteful, inefficient, improvident.

uneducated adj. **untaught**, unschooled, untutored, untrained, unread, unscholarly, illiterate, unlettered, ignorant, ill-informed, uninformed; uncouth, unsophisticated, uncultured, unaccomplished, unenlightened, philistine, benighted, backward.
– OPPOSITES learned.

unemotional adj. **reserved**, undemonstrative, sober, restrained, passionless, emotionless, unsentimental, unexcitable, impassive, phlegmatic, stoical, equable; cold, cool, unfeeling.

unemployed adj. **jobless**, out of work, between jobs, unwaged, unoccupied, redundant, laid off; on benefit; Brit. signing on; N. Amer. on welfare; Brit. informal on the dole, 'resting'.

unending adj. **endless**, never-ending, interminable, perpetual, eternal, ceaseless, incessant, unceasing, non-stop, uninterrupted, continuous, continual, constant, persistent, unbroken, unabating, unremitting, relentless.

unendurable adj. **intolerable**, unbearable, insufferable, insupportable, more than flesh and blood can stand.

unenthusiastic adj. **indifferent**, apathetic, half-hearted, lukewarm, casual, cool, lacklustre, offhand, unmoved; cursory, perfunctory.
– OPPOSITES keen.

unenviable adj. **disagreeable**, nasty, unpleasant, undesirable, horrible, thankless; unwanted, unwished-for.

unequal adj. **1** *they are unequal in length* **different**, dissimilar, unlike, unalike, disparate, unmatched, uneven, irregular, varying, variable. **2** *the unequal distribution of wealth* **unfair**, unjust, disproportionate, inequitable, biased. **3** *an unequal contest* **one-sided**, uneven, unfair, ill-matched, unbalanced, lopsided. **4** *she felt unequal to the task* **inadequate for**, incapable of, unqualified for, unsuited to, incompetent at, not up to; informal not cut out for.
– OPPOSITES identical, fair.

unequalled adj. **unbeaten**, matchless, unmatched, unrivalled, unsurpassed, unparalleled, peerless, incomparable, inimitable, second to none, unique.

unequivocal adj. **unambiguous**, unmistakable, indisputable, incontrovertible, indubitable, undeniable; clear, clear-cut, plain, explicit, specific, categorical, straightforward, blunt, candid, emphatic, manifest.
– OPPOSITES ambiguous.

unerring adj. **unfailing**, infallible, perfect, flawless, faultless, impeccable, unimpeachable; sure, true, assured, deadly; informal sure-fire.

unethical adj. **immoral**, amoral, unprincipled, unscrupulous, dishonourable, dishonest, wrong, deceitful, unconscionable, fraudulent, underhand, wicked, evil, corrupt; unprofessional, improper.

uneven adj. **1** *uneven ground* **bumpy**, rough, lumpy, stony, rocky, potholed, rutted, pitted, jagged. **2** *uneven teeth* **irregular**, unequal, unbalanced, lopsided, askew, crooked, asymmetrical, unsymmetrical. **3** *uneven quality* **inconsistent**, variable, varying, fluctuating, irregular, erratic, patchy. **4** *an uneven contest* **one-sided**, unequal, unfair, unjust, inequitable, ill-matched, unbalanced.
– OPPOSITES flat, regular, equal.

uneventful adj. **unexciting**, uninteresting, monotonous, boring, dull, tedious, humdrum, routine, unvaried, ordinary, run-of-the-mill, pedestrian, mundane, predictable.
– OPPOSITES exciting.

unexceptional adj. **ordinary**, average, typical, everyday, mediocre, run-of-the-mill, middle-of-the-road, indifferent; informal OK, so-so, nothing special, no great shakes, fair-to-middling.

unexpected adj. **unforeseen**, unanticipated, unpredicted, unlooked-for, without warning; sudden, abrupt, surprising, out of the blue.

unfailing adj. *his unfailing good humour* **constant**, reliable, dependable, steadfast, steady; endless, undying, unfading, inexhaustible, boundless, ceaseless.

unfair adj. **1** *the trial was unfair* **unjust**, inequitable, prejudiced, biased, discriminatory; one-sided, unequal, uneven, unbalanced, partisan. **2** *his comments were unfair* **undeserved**, unmerited, uncalled for, unreasonable, unjustified; Brit. informal out of order. **3** *unfair play* **unsporting**, unsportsmanlike, dirty, below the belt, underhand, dishonourable. **4** *you're being very unfair* **inconsiderate**, thoughtless, insensitive, selfish, mean, unkind, unreasonable.
– OPPOSITES just, justified.

unfaithful adj. **1** *her husband had been unfaithful* **adulterous**, faithless, fickle, untrue, inconstant; informal cheating, two-timing. **2** *an unfaithful friend* **disloyal**, treacherous, traitorous, untrustworthy, unreliable, undependable, false, two-faced, Janus-faced, double-crossing, deceitful; literary perfidious.
– OPPOSITES loyal.

unfaltering adj. **steady**, resolute, resolved, firm, steadfast, fixed, decided, unswerving, unwavering, tireless, indefatigable, persistent, unyielding, relentless, unremitting, unrelenting.
– OPPOSITES unsteady.

unfamiliar adj. **1** *an unfamiliar part of the city* **unknown**, new, strange, foreign, alien. **2** *the unfamiliar sounds* **unusual**, uncommon, unconventional, novel, different, exotic, unorthodox, odd, peculiar, curious, uncharacteristic, anomalous, out of the ordinary. **3** *investors unfamiliar with the stock market* **unacquainted**, unused, unaccustomed, inexperienced, uninformed, unenlightened, ignorant, new to, a stranger to.

unfashionable adj. **out of fashion**, outdated, old-fashioned, outmoded, out of style, dated, unstylish, passé, démodé; informal out, square, out of the ark.

unfasten v. **undo**, open, disconnect, remove, untie, unbutton, unzip, loose, loosen, free, unlock, unbolt.

unfathomable adj. **1** *his dark and unfathomable eyes* **inscrutable**, incomprehensible, enigmatic, indecipherable, obscure, esoteric, mysterious, mystifying, deep, profound. **2** *unfathomable water* **deep**, immeasurable, unfathomed, unplumbed, bottomless.
– OPPOSITES penetrable.

unfavourable adj. **1** *unfavourable comment* **adverse**, critical, hostile, inimical, unfriendly, unsympathetic, negative; discouraging, disapproving, uncomplimentary, unflattering. **2** *the unfavourable economic climate* **disadvantageous**, adverse, inauspicious, unpropitious, gloomy; unsuitable, inappropriate, inopportune.
– OPPOSITES positive.

u

unfeeling adj. *he is not an unfeeling man* **uncaring**, unsympathetic, unemotional, uncharitable; heartless, hard-hearted, hard, harsh, austere, cold, cold-hearted.
– OPPOSITES compassionate.

unfeigned adj. **sincere**, genuine, real, true, honest, unaffected, unforced, heartfelt, wholehearted.
– OPPOSITES insincere.

unfettered adj. **unrestrained**, unrestricted, unconstrained, free, unbridled, unchecked, uncontrolled.
– OPPOSITES restricted.

unfinished adj. **1** *an unfinished essay* **incomplete**, uncompleted; partial, undone, half-done; imperfect, unpolished, unrefined, sketchy, fragmentary, rough. **2** *the door can be supplied unfinished* **unpainted**, unvarnished, untreated.
– OPPOSITES complete.

unfit adj. **1** *the film is unfit for children | unfit for duty* **unsuitable**, unsuited, inappropriate, unequipped, inadequate, not designed; incapable of, unable to do something, not up to, not equal to; informal not cut out for, not up to scratch. **2** *I am unfit* **unhealthy**, out of condition/shape, in poor condition.

unflagging adj. **tireless**, persistent, dogged, tenacious, determined, resolute, staunch, single-minded, unrelenting, unfaltering, unfailing.
– OPPOSITES inconstant.

unflappable adj. informal **imperturbable**, unexcitable, cool, calm, {cool, calm, and collected}, self-controlled, cool-headed, level-headed; informal laid-back.
– OPPOSITES excitable.

unflattering adj. **1** *an unflattering review* **unfavourable**, uncomplimentary, harsh, unsympathetic, critical, hostile, scathing. **2** *an unflattering dress* **unattractive**, unbecoming, unsightly, ugly, plain, ill-fitting.
– OPPOSITES complimentary, becoming.

unflinching adj. **resolute**, determined, single-minded, dogged, resolved, firm, committed, steady, unwavering, unflagging, unswerving, unfaltering, untiring, undaunted, fearless.

unfold v. **1** *May unfolded the map* **open out**, spread out, flatten, straighten out, unroll. **2** *I watched the events unfold* **develop**, evolve, happen, take place, occur, transpire, progress. **3** *she unfolded her tale to Joanna* **narrate**, relate, recount, tell, reveal, disclose, divulge, communicate, report, recite.

unforeseen adj. **unpredicted**, unexpected, unanticipated, unimagined, unplanned, unlooked-for, not bargained for.
– OPPOSITES expected.

unforgettable adj. **memorable**, not/never to be forgotten, haunting, catchy; striking, impressive, outstanding, extraordinary, exceptional.
– OPPOSITES unexceptional.

unforgivable adj. **inexcusable**, unpardonable, unjustifiable, indefensible, inexpiable, irremissible.
– OPPOSITES venial.

unfortunate adj. **1** *unfortunate people* **unlucky**, hapless, out of luck, luckless, wretched, miserable, forlorn, poor, pitiful; informal down on one's luck. **2** *an unfortunate start to our holiday* **adverse**, disadvantageous, unfavourable, unlucky, unwelcome, unpromising, inauspicious, unpropitious; formal grievous. **3** *an unfortunate remark* **regrettable**, inappropriate, unsuitable, infelicitous, tactless, injudicious.
– OPPOSITES lucky, auspicious.

unfortunately adv. **unluckily**, sadly, regrettably, unhappily, alas, sad to say; informal worse luck.

unfounded adj. **groundless**, baseless, unsubstantiated, unproven, unsupported, uncorroborated, unconfirmed, unverified, unattested, without basis, without foundation, speculative, conjectural.
– OPPOSITES proven.

unfriendly adj. **1** *an unfriendly look* **hostile**, disagreeable, antagonistic, aggressive; ill-natured, unpleasant, surly, sour, uncongenial; inhospitable, unneighbourly, unwelcoming, unkind, unsympathetic; unsociable, antisocial; aloof, cold, cool, frosty, distant, unapproachable; informal stand-offish, starchy. **2** *unfriendly terrain* **unfavourable**, disadvantageous, unpropitious, inauspicious, hostile.
– OPPOSITES amiable, favourable.

ungainly adj. **awkward**, clumsy, ungraceful, graceless, inelegant, gawky, maladroit, gauche, uncoordinated; old use lubberly.
– OPPOSITES graceful.

ungodly adj. **1** *ungodly behaviour* **unholy**, godless, irreligious, impious, blasphemous, sacrilegious; immoral, corrupt, depraved, sinful, wicked, evil, iniquitous. **2** informal *he called at an ungodly hour* **unreasonable**, unsocial, antisocial; informal unearthly.

ungovernable adj. **uncontrollable**, unmanageable, anarchic, intractable; unruly, disorderly, rebellious, riotous, wild, mutinous, undisciplined.

ungracious adj. **rude**, impolite, uncivil, discourteous, ill-mannered, bad-mannered, uncouth, disrespectful, insolent, impertinent, offhand.
– OPPOSITES polite.

ungrateful adj. **unappreciative**, unthankful, ungracious.
– OPPOSITES thankful.

unguarded adj. **1** *an unguarded frontier* **undefended**, unprotected, unfortified; vulnerable, insecure, open to attack. **2** *an unguarded remark* **careless**, ill-considered, incautious, thoughtless, rash, foolhardy, foolish, indiscreet, imprudent, injudicious, ill-judged, insensitive; literary temerarious. **3** *an unguarded moment* **unwary**,

u

unhappiness n. **sadness**, sorrow, dejection, depression, misery, cheerlessness, downheartedness, despondency, despair, desolation, wretchedness, glumness, gloom, gloominess, dolefulness; melancholy, low spirits, mournfulness, woe, heartache, distress, chagrin, grief, pain; informal the blues.

unhappy adj. **1** *an unhappy childhood* **sad**, miserable, sorrowful, dejected, despondent, disconsolate, morose, broken-hearted, heartbroken, down, downcast, dispirited, downhearted, depressed, melancholy, mournful, gloomy, glum, despairing, doleful, forlorn, woebegone, woeful, long-faced, joyless, cheerless; informal down in the mouth/dumps, fed up, blue. **2** *in the unhappy event of litigation* **unfortunate**, unlucky, luckless; ill-starred, ill-fated, doomed; informal jinxed; literary star-crossed. **3** *I was unhappy with the service I received* **dissatisfied**, displeased, discontented, disappointed, disgruntled; Brit. informal not best pleased. **4** *'disorganized capitalism' seems an unhappy term* **inappropriate**, unsuitable, inapt, unfortunate; regrettable, ill-chosen.
– OPPOSITES cheerful.

unharmed adj. **1** *they released the hostage unharmed* **uninjured**, unhurt, unscathed, safe (and sound), alive and well, in one piece, without a scratch. **2** *the tomb was unharmed* **undamaged**, unbroken, unmarred, unspoiled, unsullied, unmarked; sound, intact, perfect, unblemished, pristine.
– OPPOSITES injured, damaged.

unhealthy adj. **1** *an unhealthy lifestyle* **harmful**, detrimental, destructive, injurious, damaging, deleterious; malign, noxious, poisonous, insalubrious, baleful. **2** *an unhealthy pallor* **ill-looking**, ill, unwell, in poor health, ailing, sick, sickly, poorly, indisposed, weak, frail, delicate, infirm, washed out, run down, peaky. **3** *an unhealthy obsession with drugs* **unwholesome**, morbid, macabre, twisted, abnormal, warped, depraved, unnatural; informal sick.

unheard of adj. **1** *such behaviour was unheard of* **unprecedented**, exceptional, extraordinary, out of the ordinary, unthought of, undreamed of, unbelievable, inconceivable, unimaginable, unthinkable; formal unexampled. **2** *a game unheard of in the UK* **unknown**, unfamiliar, new.
– OPPOSITES common, well known.

unheeded adj. **disregarded**, ignored, neglected, overlooked, unnoted, unrecognized.

unhinged adj. **deranged**, demented, unbalanced, out of one's mind, crazed, mad, insane, disturbed; informal crazy, mental, bonkers, batty, loopy, bananas, touched.
– OPPOSITES sane.

unholy adj. **1** *a grin of unholy amusement* **ungodly**, godless, irreligious, impious, blasphemous, sacrilegious, profane, irreverent; wicked, evil, immoral, corrupt, depraved, sinful. **2** informal *an unholy row* **shocking**, dreadful, outrageous, appalling, terrible, horrendous, frightful. **3** *an unholy alliance* **unnatural**, unusual, improbable, made in Hell.

unhoped for adj. **unexpected**, unanticipated, unforeseen, unlooked-for, undreamed of, out of the blue.
– OPPOSITES expected.

unhurried adj. **leisurely**, easy, easy-going, relaxed, slow, deliberate, measured, calm.
– OPPOSITES hasty.

unhygienic adj. **insanitary**, unsanitary, dirty, filthy, contaminated, unhealthy, unwholesome, insalubrious, polluted, foul.
– OPPOSITES sanitary.

unidentified adj. **unknown**, unnamed, anonymous, incognito, nameless, unfamiliar, strange.
– OPPOSITES known.

unification n. **union**, merger, fusion, fusing, amalgamation, coalition, combination, confederation, federation, synthesis, joining.

uniform adj. **1** *a uniform temperature* **constant**, consistent, steady, invariable, unvarying, unchanging, stable, static, regular, fixed, even, equal. **2** *pieces of uniform size* **identical**, matching, similar, equal; same, like, homogeneous, consistent.
– OPPOSITES variable.
▶ n. *a soldier in uniform* **costume**, livery, regalia, suit, ensemble, outfit; regimentals, colours; informal get-up, rig, gear; old use habit.

uniformity n. **1** *uniformity in tax law* **constancy**, consistency, conformity, invariability, stability, regularity, evenness, homogeneity, homogeneousness, equality. **2** *a dull uniformity* **monotony**, tedium, tediousness, dullness, dreariness, flatness, sameness.
– OPPOSITES variation, variety.

unify v. **unite**, bring together, join (together), merge, fuse, amalgamate, coalesce, combine, blend, mix, bind, consolidate.
– OPPOSITES separate.

unimaginable adj. **unthinkable**, inconceivable, incredible, unbelievable, unheard of, unthought of, unimagined, untold, undreamed of, beyond one's wildest dreams.

unimaginative adj. **uninspired**, uninventive, unoriginal, uncreative, commonplace, pedestrian, mundane, ordinary, routine, humdrum, workaday, run-of-the-mill, hackneyed, trite.

unimagined adj. **unthought of**, unpredicted, unforeseen, unanticipated, unplanned, accidental, unlooked for, unsought, unexpected, not bargained for/on.
– OPPOSITES expected, predictable.

unimpeachable adj. **trustworthy**, reliable, dependable, above suspicion, irreproachable.
– OPPOSITES unreliable.

unimpeded adj. **unrestricted**, unhindered, unblocked, unhampered, free, clear.

u

unimportant adj. **insignificant**, inconsequential, trivial, minor, trifling, of little/no importance, of little/no consequence, of no account, irrelevant, peripheral, extraneous, petty, paltry; informal piddling; formal of no moment.

uninhabited adj. **1** *much of this land was uninhabited* **unpopulated**, unpeopled, unsettled. **2** *an uninhabited hut* **vacant**, empty, unoccupied, untenanted, to let.

uninhibited adj. **1** *uninhibited dancing* **unrestrained**, unrepressed, abandoned, wild, reckless; unrestricted, uncontrolled, unchecked, intemperate, wanton. **2** *I'm pretty uninhibited* **unreserved**, unrepressed, liberated, unselfconscious, free and easy, relaxed, informal, open, outgoing, extrovert, outspoken, frank, forthright; informal upfront.
– OPPOSITES repressed.

uninspired adj. **unimaginative**, uninventive, pedestrian, mundane, unoriginal, commonplace, ordinary, routine, humdrum, run-of-the-mill, hackneyed, trite; spiritless, passionless.

uninspiring adj. **boring**, dull, dreary, unexciting; dry, colourless, bland, lacklustre, tedious, humdrum, run-of-the-mill.

unintelligent adj. **stupid**, ignorant, dense, brainless, mindless, foolish, dull-witted, slow, simple-minded, vacuous, vapid, idiotic, obtuse; informal thick, dim, dumb, dopey, half-witted, dozy.

unintelligible adj. **1** *unintelligible sounds* **incomprehensible**, indiscernible, mumbled, indistinct, unclear, slurred, inarticulate, incoherent, garbled. **2** *unintelligible graffiti* **illegible**, indecipherable, unreadable.

unintentional adj. **unintended**, accidental, inadvertent, involuntary, unwitting, unthinking, unpremeditated, unconscious.
– OPPOSITES deliberate.

uninterested adj. **indifferent**, unconcerned, uninvolved, apathetic, lukewarm, unenthusiastic.

uninteresting adj. **unexciting**, boring, dull, tiresome, wearisome, tedious, dreary, lifeless, humdrum, colourless, bland, insipid, banal, dry, pedestrian; informal samey.
– OPPOSITES exciting.

uninterrupted adj. **unbroken**, continuous, continual, undisturbed, untroubled.
– OPPOSITES intermittent.

uninvited adj. **1** *an uninvited guest* **unasked**, unexpected; unwelcome, unwanted. **2** *uninvited suggestions* **unsolicited**, unrequested, unsought.

uninviting adj. **unappealing**, unattractive, unappetizing, off-putting; bleak, cheerless, dreary, dismal, depressing, grim, inhospitable.
– OPPOSITES tempting.

union n. **1** *the union of art and nature* **unification**, uniting, joining, merging, merger, fusion, fusing, amalgamating, amalgamation, coalition, combination, synthesis, blend, blending, mingling. **2** *the crowd moved in union* **unity**, accord, unison, harmony, agreement, concurrence; formal concord. **3** *his daughter's union* **marriage**, wedding, alliance; coupling, intercourse, copulation. **4** *representation by a union* **association**, trade union, league, guild, confederation, federation.
– OPPOSITES separation, parting.

unique adj. **1** *each site is unique* **distinctive**, individual, special, idiosyncratic; single, sole, lone, unrepeated, unrepeatable, solitary, exclusive, rare, uncommon, unusual; informal one-off. **2** *a unique insight into history* **remarkable**, special, singular, noteworthy, notable, extraordinary; unequalled, unparalleled, unmatched, unsurpassed, incomparable; formal unexampled. **3** *species unique to the island* **peculiar**, specific.

unison n.
□ **in unison 1** *they lifted their arms in unison* **simultaneously**, at (one and) the same time, (all) at once, (all) together. **2** *we are in complete unison* **in agreement**, in accord, in harmony, as one; formal in concord.

unit n. **1** *the family is the fundamental unit of society* **component**, element, constituent, subdivision. **2** *a unit of currency* **quantity**, measure, denomination. **3** *a guerrilla unit* **detachment**, contingent, division, company, squadron, corps, regiment, brigade, platoon, battalion; cell, faction.

unite v. **1** *uniting the nation* **unify**, join, link, connect, combine, amalgamate, fuse, weld, bond, bring together, knit together. **2** *environmentalists and activists united* **join together**, join forces, combine, band together, ally, cooperate, collaborate, work together, pull together, team up. **3** *he sought to unite comfort with elegance* **merge**, mix, blend, mingle, combine; literary commingle.
– OPPOSITES divide.

united adj. **1** *a united Germany* **unified**, integrated, amalgamated, joined, merged; federal, confederate. **2** *a united response* **common**, shared, joint, combined, communal, cooperative, collective, collaborative; concerted. **3** *they were united in their views* **in agreement**, agreed, in unison, of the same opinion, like-minded, as one, in accord, in harmony, in unity.

unity n. **1** *European unity* **union**, unification, integration, amalgamation; coalition, federation, confederation. **2** *unity between opposing factions* **harmony**, accord, cooperation, collaboration, agreement, consensus, solidarity; formal concord. **3** *the organic unity of the universe* **oneness**, singleness, wholeness, uniformity, homogeneity.
– OPPOSITES division, discord.

universal adj. **general**, ubiquitous, comprehensive, common, omnipresent, all-inclusive; global, worldwide, international, widespread.

universally adv. **invariably**, always, without exception, in all cases; everywhere, worldwide, globally, internationally; widely, commonly, generally.

u

universe n. **1** *the physical universe* **cosmos**, macrocosm, totality; infinity, all existence. **2** *the universe of computer hardware* **province**, world, sphere, preserve, domain.

> **WORD LINKS**
>
> **cosmic** relating to the universe
> **cosmology** the science of the origin and development of the universe
> **astronomy** the study of stars, planets, and the universe
> **Big Bang** the explosion of dense matter said to have marked the origin of the universe

university n. **college**, academy, institute; alma mater; N. Amer. **school**; historical polytechnic.

> **WORD LINKS**
>
> **matriculation** university enrolment
> **freshman** a first-year university student
> **undergraduate** a student who has not taken their first degree
> **graduate** a person who has been awarded a degree
> **postgraduate** a student studying for a second degree
> **don, professor** a university teacher
> **campus** a university's grounds and buildings
> **tenure** a permanent teaching post at a university

unjust adj. **1** *the attack was unjust* **biased**, prejudiced, unfair, inequitable, discriminatory, partisan, partial, one-sided. **2** *an unjust law* **wrongful**, unfair, undeserved, unmerited, unwarranted, uncalled for, unreasonable, unjustifiable, indefensible.
– OPPOSITES fair.

unjustifiable adj. **1** *an unjustifiable extravagance* **indefensible**, inexcusable, unforgivable, unpardonable, uncalled for, without justification, unwarrantable; excessive, immoderate. **2** *an unjustifiable slur on his character* **groundless**, unfounded, baseless, unsubstantiated, unconfirmed, uncorroborated.
– OPPOSITES reasonable.

unkempt adj. **untidy**, messy, scruffy, disordered, dishevelled, disarranged, rumpled, wind-blown, ungroomed, bedraggled, in a mess, messed up; tousled, uncombed; N. Amer. informal mussed up.
– OPPOSITES tidy.

unkind adj. **1** *everyone was being unkind to him* **uncharitable**, unpleasant, disagreeable, nasty, mean, mean-spirited, cruel, vicious, spiteful, malicious, callous, unsympathetic, unfeeling, uncaring, hurtful, ill-natured, hard-hearted, cold-hearted; unfriendly, uncivil, inconsiderate, insensitive, hostile; informal bitchy, catty; Brit. informal beastly. **2** *unkind weather* **inclement**, intemperate, rough, severe, filthy.

unkindness n. **nastiness**, unpleasantness, disagreeableness, cruelty, malice, meanness, mean-spiritedness, viciousness, callousness, hard-heartedness, cold-heartedness; unfriendliness, inconsiderateness, hostility; informal bitchiness, cattiness.

unknown adj. **1** *the outcome was unknown* **undisclosed**, unrevealed, secret; undetermined, undecided, unresolved, unsettled, unsure, unascertained. **2** *unknown country* **unexplored**, uncharted, unmapped, untravelled, undiscovered. **3** *persons unknown* **unidentified**, unnamed, nameless, anonymous. **4** *Uranus was unknown to the ancients* **unfamiliar**, unheard of, new, novel, strange. **5** *unknown artists* **obscure**, unheard of, unsung, minor, insignificant, unimportant, undistinguished.
– OPPOSITES familiar.

unlawful adj. **illegal**, illicit, illegitimate, against the law; criminal, felonious; prohibited, banned, outlawed, proscribed, forbidden.
– OPPOSITES legal.

unleash v. **let loose**, release, (set) free, unloose, untie, untether, unchain.

unlettered adj. **illiterate**, uneducated, poorly educated, unschooled, unlearned, ignorant.
– OPPOSITES educated.

unlike prep. **1** *England is totally unlike Jamaica* **different from**, unalike, dissimilar to. **2** *unlike Linda, Chrissy was a bit of a radical* **in contrast to**, as opposed to.
– OPPOSITES similar to.
▸ adj. *a meeting of unlike minds* **dissimilar**, unalike, disparate, contrasting, antithetical, different, diverse, heterogeneous, divergent, at variance, varying, at odds; informal like chalk and cheese.

unlikely adj. **1** *it is unlikely they will ever recover* **improbable**, doubtful, dubious. **2** *an unlikely story* **implausible**, improbable, questionable, unconvincing, far-fetched, unrealistic, incredible, unbelievable, inconceivable, unimaginable; informal tall, cock-and-bull.
– OPPOSITES probable, believable.

unlimited adj. **1** *unlimited supplies of water* **inexhaustible**, limitless, illimitable, boundless, immeasurable, incalculable, untold, infinite, endless, never-ending, cosmic. **2** *unlimited travel* **unrestricted**, unconstrained, unrestrained, unchecked, unbridled, uncurbed. **3** *unlimited power* **total**, unqualified, unconditional, unrestricted, absolute, supreme.
– OPPOSITES finite, restricted.

unload v. **1** *we unloaded the van* **unpack**, empty; old use unlade. **2** *they unloaded the cases from the lorry* **remove**, offload, discharge. **3** *the state unloaded its 25 per cent stake* **sell**, discard, jettison, offload, get rid of, dispose of; palm something off on someone, foist something on someone, fob something off on someone; informal dump, junk, get shot/shut of.

unlock v. **unbolt**, unlatch, unbar, unfasten, open.

unlooked-for adj. **unexpected**, unforeseen, unanticipated, unsought, unpredicted, undreamed of, fortuitous, chance, serendipitous.

u

unloved adj. **uncared-for**, unwanted, friendless, unvalued; rejected, unwelcome, shunned, spurned, neglected, abandoned.

unlucky adj. **1** *he was unlucky not to score* **unfortunate**, luckless, out of luck, hapless, ill-fated, ill-starred, unhappy; informal down on one's luck; literary star-crossed. **2** *an unlucky number* **unfavourable**, inauspicious, unpropitious, ominous, cursed, ill-fated, ill-omened, disadvantageous, unfortunate.
– OPPOSITES fortunate, favourable.

unmanageable adj. **1** *the huge house was unmanageable* **troublesome**, awkward, inconvenient; cumbersome, bulky, unwieldy. **2** *his behaviour was becoming unmanageable* **uncontrollable**, ungovernable, unruly, disorderly, out of hand, difficult, disruptive, undisciplined, wayward; informal stroppy; old use contumacious.

unmanly adj. **effeminate**, effete, unmasculine; weak, soft, timid, timorous, limp-wristed; informal sissy, wimpish, wimpy.
– OPPOSITES virile.

unmannerly adj. **rude**, impolite, uncivil, discourteous, bad-mannered, ill-mannered, disrespectful, impertinent, impudent, insolent; uncouth, boorish, oafish, loutish, ill-bred, coarse.
– OPPOSITES polite.

unmarried adj. **unwed(ded)**, single; spinster, bachelor; unattached, available, eligible, free.

unmatched adj. **1** *a talent for publicity unmatched by any other politician* **unequalled**, unrivalled, unparalleled, unsurpassed. **2** *unmatched clarity and balance* **peerless**, matchless, without equal, without parallel, incomparable, inimitable, superlative, second to none, in a class of its own.

unmentionable adj. **taboo**, censored, forbidden, banned, proscribed, prohibited, not to be spoken of, ineffable, unspeakable, unutterable, unprintable, off limits; informal no go.

unmerciful adj. **ruthless**, cruel, harsh, merciless, pitiless, cold-blooded, hard-hearted, callous, brutal, severe, unforgiving, inhumane, inhuman, heartless, unsympathetic, unfeeling.

unmistakable adj. **distinctive**, distinct, telltale, indisputable, indubitable, undoubted; plain, clear, definite, obvious, evident, self-evident, manifest, patent, unambiguous, unequivocal, pronounced, as plain as the nose on your face.

unmitigated adj. **absolute**, unqualified, categorical, complete, total, downright, outright, utter, out-and-out, undiluted, unequivocal, veritable, perfect, consummate, pure, sheer.

unmoved adj. **1** *he was totally unmoved by her outburst* **unaffected**, untouched, unimpressed, undismayed, unworried; aloof, cool, cold, dry-eyed; unconcerned, uncaring, indifferent, impassive, unemotional, stoical, phlegmatic, equable; impervious (to), oblivious (to), heedless (of), deaf to. **2** *he remained unmoved on the crucial issues* **steadfast**, firm, unwavering, unswerving, resolute, decided, resolved, inflexible, unbending, implacable, adamant.

unnatural adj. **1** *wanting to help other people is not unnatural* **abnormal**, unusual, uncommon, extraordinary, strange, freak, odd, peculiar, unorthodox, exceptional, irregular, untypical. **2** *a flash of unnatural colour* **artificial**, man-made, synthetic, manufactured. **3** *unnatural vice* **perverted**, warped, twisted, deviant, depraved, degenerate; informal kinky, pervy, sick. **4** *her voice sounded unnatural* **affected**, artificial, stilted, forced, laboured, strained, false, fake, insincere; informal put on, phoney. **5** *they condemned her as an unnatural woman* **uncaring**, unfeeling, heartless, cold-blooded, hard-hearted, callous, cruel, inhumane.
– OPPOSITES normal, genuine.

unnecessary adj. **unneeded**, inessential, not required, uncalled for, useless, unwarranted, unwanted, undesired, dispensable, unimportant, optional, extraneous, expendable, disposable, redundant, pointless, purposeless.
– OPPOSITES essential.

unnerve v. **demoralize**, discourage, dishearten, dispirit, daunt, alarm, frighten, dismay, disconcert, discompose, perturb, upset, discomfit, take aback, unsettle, disquiet, fluster, agitate, shake, ruffle, throw off balance; informal rattle, faze, shake up; Brit. informal put the wind up; N. Amer. informal discombobulate.
– OPPOSITES hearten.

unobtrusive adj. **1** *she was unobtrusive and shy* **self-effacing**, retiring, unassuming, quiet; shy, bashful, timid, timorous, reserved, withdrawn, introvert(ed), unforthcoming, unassertive. **2** *unobtrusive service* **inconspicuous**, unnoticeable, low-key, discreet, circumspect, understated, unostentatious.
– OPPOSITES extrovert, conspicuous.

unoccupied adj. **1** *an unoccupied house* **vacant**, empty, uninhabited; free, available, to let. **2** *an unoccupied territory* **uninhabited**, unpopulated, unpeopled, unsettled. **3** *many young people were unoccupied* **at leisure**, idle, free, with time on one's hands, at a loose end.
– OPPOSITES inhabited, populated, busy.

unofficial adj. **1** *unofficial figures* **unauthenticated**, unconfirmed, uncorroborated, unsubstantiated, off the record. **2** *an unofficial committee* **informal**, casual; unauthorized, unsanctioned, unaccredited.
– OPPOSITES confirmed, formal.

unorthodox adj. **1** *unorthodox views on management* **unconventional**, unusual, radical, nonconformist, avant-garde, eccentric, off-centre; informal off the wall,

way out, offbeat. **2** *unorthodox religious views* **heterodox**, heretical, nonconformist, dissenting.
– OPPOSITES conventional.

unpaid adj. **1** *unpaid bills* **unsettled**, outstanding, due, overdue, owing, owed, payable, undischarged; N. Amer. delinquent, past due. **2** *unpaid charity work* **voluntary**, volunteer, honorary, unremunerative, unsalaried, pro bono (publico).

unpalatable adj. **1** *unpalatable food* **unappetizing**, unappealing, unsavoury, inedible, uneatable; disgusting, revolting, nauseating, tasteless, flavourless. **2** *the unpalatable truth* **disagreeable**, unpleasant, regrettable, unwelcome, lamentable, dreadful, hateful.
– OPPOSITES tasty.

unparalleled adj. **exceptional**, unique, singular, rare, unequalled, unprecedented, without parallel, without equal; matchless, peerless, unrivalled, unsurpassed, incomparable, second to none; formal unexampled.

unperturbed adj. **untroubled**, undisturbed, unworried, unconcerned, unmoved, unflustered, unruffled, undismayed; calm, composed, cool, collected, unemotional, self-possessed, self-assured, level-headed, unfazed, laid-back.

unpleasant adj. **1** *a very unpleasant situation* **disagreeable**, irksome, troublesome, annoying, irritating, vexatious, displeasing, distressing, nasty, horrible, terrible, awful, dreadful, hateful, miserable, invidious, objectionable, offensive, obnoxious, repugnant, repulsive, repellent, revolting, disgusting, distasteful, nauseating, unsavoury. **2** *an unpleasant man* **nasty**, disagreeable, unfriendly, rude, spiteful, mean, mean-spirited; insufferable, unbearable, obnoxious, annoying, irritating. **3** *an unpleasant taste* **unappetizing**, unpalatable, unsavoury, unappealing, bitter, sour, rancid; disgusting, revolting, nauseating, sickening.
– OPPOSITES agreeable, likeable.

unpolished adj. **1** *unpolished wood* **unvarnished**, unfinished, untreated, natural. **2** *his unpolished ways* **unsophisticated**, unrefined, uncultured, uncultivated, coarse, vulgar, crude, rough (and ready), awkward, clumsy, gauche. **3** *an unpolished performance* **slipshod**, rough, crude, uneven.
– OPPOSITES varnished, sophisticated.

unpopular adj. **disliked**, friendless, unliked, unloved; unwelcome, avoided, ignored, rejected, shunned, spurned, cold-shouldered.

unprecedented adj. **unparalleled**, unequalled, unmatched, unrivalled, without parallel, without equal, out of the ordinary, unusual, exceptional, singular, remarkable, unique; unheard of, unknown, new, groundbreaking, revolutionary, pioneering; formal unexampled.

unpredictable adj. **1** *unpredictable results* **unforeseeable**, uncertain, unsure, doubtful, dubious, in the balance, up in the air, arbitrary. **2** *unpredictable behaviour* **erratic**, moody, volatile, unstable, capricious, temperamental, mercurial, changeable, variable.

unprejudiced adj. **1** *unprejudiced observation* **objective**, impartial, unbiased, neutral, non-partisan, detached, disinterested. **2** *unprejudiced attitudes* **unbiased**, non-discriminatory, tolerant, liberal, broad-minded, unbigoted.
– OPPOSITES partisan, intolerant.

unpremeditated adj. **unplanned**, unprepared, spontaneous, impromptu, spur-of-the-moment, unrehearsed; informal off-the-cuff.
– OPPOSITES planned.

unprepared adj. **1** *we were unprepared for the new VAT regime* **unready**, off (one's) guard, surprised, taken aback; informal caught napping, caught on the hop. **2** *they are unprepared to support the reforms* **unwilling**, disinclined, loath, reluctant, resistant, opposed.
– OPPOSITES ready, willing.

unpretentious adj. **1** *he was thoroughly unpretentious* **unaffected**, modest, unassuming, without airs, natural, straightforward, open, honest, sincere, frank. **2** *an unpretentious hotel* **simple**, plain, modest, humble, unostentatious, homely, unsophisticated.

unprincipled adj. **immoral**, unethical, unscrupulous, dishonourable, dishonest, deceitful, devious, corrupt, crooked, wicked, evil, villainous, shameless, base, low.
– OPPOSITES ethical.

unproductive adj. **1** *unproductive soil* **sterile**, barren, infertile, unfruitful, poor. **2** *unproductive meetings* **fruitless**, futile, vain, idle, useless, worthless, valueless, pointless, ineffective, ineffectual, unprofitable, unrewarding.
– OPPOSITES fruitful.

unprofessional adj. **1** *unprofessional conduct* **improper**, unethical, unprincipled, unscrupulous, dishonourable, disreputable, unseemly, unbecoming, indecorous; informal shady, crooked. **2** *he accused the detectives of being unprofessional* **amateurish**, amateur, unskilled, unskilful, inexpert, unqualified, inexperienced, incompetent, second-rate, inefficient.

unpromising adj. **inauspicious**, unfavourable, unpropitious, discouraging, disheartening, gloomy, bleak, black, portentous, ominous, ill-omened.
– OPPOSITES auspicious.

unqualified adj. **1** *an unqualified accountant* **uncertified**, unlicensed, untrained, inexperienced. **2** *those unqualified to look after children* **unsuitable**, unfit, ineligible, incompetent, unable, incapable. **3** *unqualified support* **unconditional**, unreserved, unlimited, without reservations,

u

categorical, unequivocal, unambiguous, wholehearted; complete, absolute, downright, undivided, total, utter.

unquestionable adj. **indubitable**, undoubted, beyond question, beyond doubt, indisputable, undeniable, irrefutable, incontestable, incontrovertible, unequivocal; certain, sure, definite, self-evident, evident, manifest, obvious, apparent, patent.

unravel v. **1** *he unravelled the strands* **untangle**, disentangle, separate out, unwind, untwist. **2** *detectives are trying to unravel the mystery* **solve**, resolve, clear up, puzzle out, get to the bottom of, explain, clarify, make head or tail of; *informal* figure out, suss (out). **3** *society is starting to unravel* **fall apart**, fail, collapse, go wrong.
– OPPOSITES entangle.

unreadable adj. **1** *unreadable writing* **illegible**, hard to read, indecipherable, unintelligible, scrawled, crabbed. **2** *heavy, unreadable novels* **dull**, tedious, boring, uninteresting, dry, wearisome, difficult, heavy. **3** *Nathan's expression was unreadable* **inscrutable**, enigmatic, impenetrable, cryptic, mysterious, deadpan, poker-faced.
– OPPOSITES legible, accessible.

unreal adj. **imaginary**, fictitious, pretend, make-believe, made-up, dreamed-up, mock, false, illusory, mythical, fanciful; hypothetical, theoretical; *informal* phoney.

unrealistic adj. **1** *it is unrealistic to expect changes overnight* **impractical**, impracticable, unfeasible, non-viable; unreasonable, irrational, illogical, senseless, silly, foolish, fanciful, idealistic, romantic, starry-eyed. **2** *unrealistic images* **unlifelike**, non-realistic, unnatural, non-representational, abstract.
– OPPOSITES pragmatic, lifelike.

unreasonable adj. **1** *an unreasonable woman* **uncooperative**, unhelpful, disobliging, unaccommodating, awkward, contrary, difficult; obstinate, obdurate, wilful, headstrong, pig-headed, intractable, intransigent, inflexible; irrational, illogical, prejudiced, intolerant. **2** *unreasonable demands* **unacceptable**, preposterous, outrageous; excessive, immoderate, disproportionate, undue, inordinate, intolerable, unjustified, unwarranted, uncalled for.

unrecognizable adj. **unidentifiable**, unknowable; disguised.

unrefined adj. **1** *unrefined clay* **unprocessed**, untreated, crude, raw, natural, unprepared, unfinished. **2** *unrefined men* **uncultured**, uncultivated, uncivilized, uneducated, unsophisticated; boorish, oafish, loutish, coarse, vulgar, rude, uncouth.
– OPPOSITES processed, cultured.

unrelated adj. **1** *unrelated incidents* **separate**, unconnected, independent, unassociated, distinct, discrete, disparate. **2** *a reason unrelated to my work* **irrelevant**, immaterial, inapplicable, unconcerned, beside the point, not pertinent, not germane.

unrelenting adj. **1** *the unrelenting heat* **continual**, constant, continuous, relentless, unremitting, unabating, unrelieved, incessant, unceasing, endless, unending, persistent. **2** *an unrelenting opponent* **implacable**, inflexible, uncompromising, unyielding, unbending, relentless, determined, dogged, tireless, unflagging, unshakeable, unswerving, unwavering.
– OPPOSITES intermittent.

unreliable adj. **1** *unreliable volunteers* **undependable**, untrustworthy, irresponsible, fickle, capricious, erratic, unpredictable, inconstant, faithless. **2** *an unreliable indicator* **questionable**, open to doubt, doubtful, dubious, suspect, unsound, tenuous, fallible; risky, chancy, inaccurate; *informal* iffy, dicey.

unremitting adj. **relentless**, unrelenting, continual, constant, continuous, unabating, unrelieved, sustained, unceasing, ceaseless, endless, unending, persistent, perpetual, interminable.

unrepentant adj. **impenitent**, unrepenting, remorseless, unashamed, unapologetic, unabashed.

unreserved adj. **1** *unreserved support* **unconditional**, unqualified, without reservations, unlimited, categorical, unequivocal, unambiguous; absolute, complete, thorough, wholehearted, total, utter, undivided. **2** *an unreserved young man* **uninhibited**, extrovert, outgoing, unrestrained, open, unconstrained, unselfconscious, outspoken, frank, candid. **3** *unreserved seats* **unbooked**, unallocated, unoccupied, free, empty, vacant.
– OPPOSITES qualified, reticent, booked.

unresolved adj. **undecided**, unsettled, undetermined, uncertain, open, pending, open to debate/question, doubtful, in doubt, up in the air.
– OPPOSITES decided.

unrest n. **disruption**, disturbance, trouble, turmoil, disorder, chaos, anarchy; discord, dissension, dissent, strife, protest, rebellion, uprising, rioting.
– OPPOSITES peace.

unrestrained adj. **uncontrolled**, unconstrained, unrestricted, unchecked, unbridled, unlimited, unfettered, uninhibited, unbounded, undisciplined.

unrestricted adj. **unlimited**, open, free, clear, unhindered, unimpeded, unhampered, unchecked, unrestrained, unconstrained, unblocked, unbounded, unconfined, unqualified.
– OPPOSITES limited.

unripe adj. **immature**, unready, green, sour.

unrivalled adj. **unequalled**, without equal, unparalleled, without parallel, unmatched, unsurpassed, incomparable, beyond compare, inimitable, second to none.

unruffled adj. **1** *an unruffled voice* **calm**, composed, self-controlled, self-possessed, untroubled, unperturbed, at ease, relaxed, serene, cool, {cool, calm, and collected}, cool-headed, unemotional, equanimous, equable, stoical; informal unfazed. **2** *an unruffled sea* **tranquil**, calm, smooth, still, flat, motionless, placid, waveless, pacific, like a millpond.

unruly adj. **disorderly**, rowdy, wild, unmanageable, uncontrollable, disobedient, disruptive, attention-seeking, undisciplined, wayward, wilful, headstrong, irrepressible, obstreperous, difficult, intractable, out of hand, recalcitrant; boisterous, lively; formal refractory; old use contumacious.
– OPPOSITES disciplined.

unsafe adj. **1** *the building was unsafe* **dangerous**, risky, perilous, hazardous, life-threatening, high-risk, treacherous, insecure, unsound; harmful, injurious, toxic. **2** *the verdict was unsafe* **unreliable**, insecure, unsound, questionable, open to question/doubt, doubtful, dubious, suspect, fallible; informal iffy.
– OPPOSITES harmless, secure.

unsaid adj. **unspoken**, unuttered, unstated, unexpressed, unvoiced, untalked-of, suppressed; tacit, implicit, understood, not spelled out, taken as read, inferred, implied.

unsanitary adj. **unhygienic**, insanitary, dirty, filthy, unclean, contaminated, unhealthy, germ-ridden, disease-ridden, infested, insalubrious, polluted.
– OPPOSITES hygienic.

unsatisfactory adj. **disappointing**, dissatisfying, undesirable, disagreeable, displeasing; inadequate, unacceptable, poor, bad, substandard, weak, mediocre, not good enough, not up to par, defective, deficient, imperfect, inferior; informal leaving a lot to be desired, no great shakes, not much cop.

unsavoury adj. **1** *unsavoury portions of food* **unpalatable**, unappetizing, distasteful, disagreeable, unappealing, unattractive; inedible, uneatable, disgusting, revolting, nauseating, sickening, foul, nasty, vile; tasteless, bland, flavourless; informal yucky. **2** *an unsavoury character* **disreputable**, unpleasant, disagreeable, nasty, mean, rough; immoral, degenerate, dishonourable, dishonest, unprincipled, unscrupulous, low, villainous; informal shady, crooked.
– OPPOSITES tasty, appetizing.

unscathed adj. **unharmed**, unhurt, uninjured, undamaged, in one piece, intact, safe (and sound), unmarked, untouched, unscratched.
– OPPOSITES harmed, injured.

unscrupulous adj. **unprincipled**, unethical, immoral, conscienceless, shameless, reprobate, exploitative, corrupt, dishonest, dishonourable, deceitful, devious, underhand, unsavoury, disreputable, evil, wicked, villainous; informal crooked, shady; dated dastardly.

unseat v. **1** *the horse unseated his rider* **dislodge**, throw, dismount, upset, unhorse. **2** *an attempt to unseat the party leader* **depose**, oust, remove from office, topple, overthrow, bring down, dislodge, supplant, usurp, overturn, eject.

unseemly adj. **indecorous**, improper, unbecoming, unfitting, unbefitting, unworthy, undignified, indiscreet, indelicate, ungentlemanly, unladylike.
– OPPOSITES decorous.

unseen adj. **hidden**, concealed, obscured, camouflaged, out of sight, imperceptible, undetectable, unnoticeable, unnoticed, unobserved.

unselfish adj. **altruistic**, disinterested, selfless, self-denying, self-sacrificing; generous, philanthropic, public-spirited, charitable, benevolent, caring, kind, considerate, noble.

unsettle v. **discompose**, unnerve, upset, disturb, disquiet, perturb, discomfit, disconcert, alarm, dismay, trouble, bother, agitate, fluster, ruffle, shake (up), throw, unbalance, destabilize; informal rattle, faze.

unsettled adj. **1** *an unsettled life* **aimless**, directionless, purposeless, without purpose; rootless, nomadic. **2** *an unsettled child* **restless**, restive, fidgety, anxious, worried, troubled, fretful; agitated, ruffled, uneasy, disconcerted, discomposed, unnerved, ill at ease, edgy, on edge, tense, nervous, apprehensive, disturbed, perturbed; informal rattled. **3** *unsettled weather* **changeable**, changing, variable, varying, inconstant, inconsistent, ever-changing, erratic, unstable, undependable, unreliable, uncertain, unpredictable, protean. **4** *the question remains unsettled* **undecided**, to be decided, unresolved, undetermined, uncertain, open to debate, doubtful, in doubt, up in the air. **5** *the debt remains unsettled* **unpaid**, payable, outstanding, owing, owed, to be paid, due, undischarged; N. Amer. delinquent, past due. **6** *unsettled areas* **uninhabited**, unpopulated, unpeopled, desolate, lonely.

unshakeable adj. **steadfast**, resolute, staunch, firm, decided, determined, unswerving, unwavering; unyielding, inflexible, dogged, obstinate, persistent, indefatigable, tireless, unflagging, unremitting, unrelenting, relentless.

unsightly adj. **ugly**, unattractive, unprepossessing, unlovely, disagreeable, displeasing, hideous, horrible, repulsive, revolting, offensive, grotesque, monstrous, ghastly.
– OPPOSITES attractive.

unskilful adj. **inexpert**, incompetent, inept, unskilled, amateurish, unprofessional, inexperienced, untrained, unpractised; informal ham-fisted, ham-handed, cack-handed.

unskilled adj. **untrained**, unqualified; manual, blue-collar, labouring, menial; inexpert, inexperienced, unpractised, amateurish, unprofessional.

unsociable adj. **unfriendly**, uncongenial, unneighbourly, unapproachable, introverted, reticent, reserved, withdrawn, aloof, distant, remote, detached, unsocial, antisocial, taciturn, silent, quiet; informal stand-offish.
– OPPOSITES friendly.

u

unsolicited adj. **uninvited**, unsought, unasked for, unrequested.

unsophisticated adj. **1** *she seemed terribly unsophisticated* **unworldly**, naive, simple, innocent, ignorant, green, immature, callow, inexperienced, childlike, artless, guileless, ingenuous, natural, unaffected, unassuming, unpretentious. **2** *unsophisticated software* **simple**, crude, basic, rudimentary, primitive, rough and ready; straightforward, uncomplicated, uninvolved.

unsound adj. **1** *structurally unsound* **rickety**, flimsy, wobbly, unstable, crumbling, damaged, rotten, ramshackle, insubstantial, unsafe, dangerous. **2** *this submission appears unsound* **untenable**, flawed, defective, faulty, ill-founded, flimsy, unreliable, questionable, dubious, tenuous, suspect, fallacious, fallible; informal iffy. **3** *of unsound mind* **disordered**, deranged, disturbed, demented, unstable, unbalanced, unhinged, insane; informal touched.
– OPPOSITES strong.

unsparing adj. **1** *he is unsparing in his criticism* **merciless**, pitiless, ruthless, relentless, remorseless, unmerciful, unforgiving, implacable, uncompromising; stern, strict, severe, harsh, tough, rigorous. **2** *unsparing approval* **ungrudging**, unstinting, willingly given, free, free-handed, ready; lavish, liberal, generous, magnanimous, open-handed.

unspeakable adj. **1** *unspeakable delights* **indescribable**, beyond description, inexpressible, unutterable, indefinable, unimaginable, inconceivable, marvellous, wonderful. **2** *an unspeakable crime* **dreadful**, awful, appalling, horrific, horrifying, horrendous, abominable, frightful, fearful, shocking, ghastly, gruesome, monstrous, heinous, egregious, deplorable, despicable, execrable, vile.

unspecified adj. **unnamed**, unstated, unidentified, undesignated, undefined, unfixed, undecided, undetermined, uncertain; nameless, unknown, indefinite, indeterminate, vague.

unspectacular adj. **unremarkable**, unexceptional, undistinguished, unmemorable; ordinary, average, commonplace, mediocre, run-of-the-mill, indifferent.
– OPPOSITES remarkable.

unspoilt adj. **unimpaired**, as good as new/before, perfect, pristine, immaculate, unblemished, unharmed, undamaged, untouched, unmarked, untainted.

unspoken adj. **unstated**, unexpressed, unuttered, unsaid, unvoiced, unarticulated, undeclared, not spelled out; tacit, implicit, implied, understood, taken as read.
– OPPOSITES explicit.

unstable adj. **1** *icebergs are notoriously unstable* **unsteady**, rocky, wobbly, rickety, shaky, unsafe, insecure, precarious. **2** *unstable coffee prices* **changeable**, volatile, variable, fluctuating, irregular, unpredictable, erratic. **3** *he was mentally unstable* **unbalanced**, of unsound mind, mentally ill, deranged, demented, disturbed, unhinged.
– OPPOSITES steady, firm.

unsteady adj. **1** *she was unsteady on her feet* **unstable**, rocky, wobbly, rickety, shaky, tottery, doddery, insecure. **2** *an unsteady flow* **irregular**, uneven, varying, variable, erratic, spasmodic, changeable, changing, fluctuating, inconstant, intermittent, fitful.
– OPPOSITES stable, regular.

unstinted, unstinting adj. *unstinted praise* **lavish**, liberal, generous, open-handed, ungrudging, unsparing, willingly given, ready, profuse, abundant, ample.

unstudied adj. **natural**, easy, unaffected, unforced, uncontrived, unstilted, unpretentious, without airs, artless.

unsubstantiated adj. **unconfirmed**, unsupported, uncorroborated, unverified, unattested, unproven; unfounded, groundless, baseless, without foundation.

unsuccessful adj. **1** *an unsuccessful attempt* **failed**, without success, abortive, ineffective, fruitless, profitless, unproductive; vain, futile, useless, pointless, worthless. **2** *an unsuccessful business* **unprofitable**, loss-making. **3** *an unsuccessful candidate* **failed**, losing, beaten; unlucky, out of luck.

unsuitable adj. **1** *an unsuitable product* **inappropriate**, unsuited, ill-suited, inapt, inapposite, unacceptable, unfitting, unbefitting, incompatible, out of place/keeping. **2** *an unsuitable moment* **inopportune**, infelicitous; formal malapropos.
– OPPOSITES appropriate, opportune.

unsullied adj. **spotless**, untarnished, unblemished, unspoilt, untainted, impeccable, undamaged, unimpaired, stainless, immaculate.
– OPPOSITES tarnished.

unsung adj. **unacknowledged**, uncelebrated, unacclaimed, unapplauded, unhailed; neglected, unrecognized, overlooked, forgotten.
– OPPOSITES celebrated.

unsure adj. **1** *she felt very unsure* **unconfident**, unassertive, insecure, hesitant, diffident, anxious, apprehensive. **2** *Sally was unsure what to do* **undecided**, irresolute, dithering, equivocating, in two minds, in a quandary. **3** *some teachers are unsure about the proposed strike* **dubious**, doubtful, sceptical, uncertain, unconvinced. **4** *the date is unsure* **not fixed**, undecided, uncertain.
– OPPOSITES confident, certain.

unsurpassed adj. **unmatched**, unrivalled, unparalleled, unequalled, matchless, peerless, without equal, inimitable, incomparable, unsurpassable; formal unexampled.

unsurprising adj. **predictable**, foreseeable, (only) to be expected, foreseen, anticipated, par for the course; informal inevitable, on the cards.

unsuspecting adj. **unsuspicious**, unwary, unaware, unconscious, ignorant, unwitting; trusting, gullible, credulous, ingenuous, naive.
– OPPOSITES wary.

unswerving adj. **unwavering**, unfaltering, steadfast, unshakeable, staunch, firm, resolute, stalwart, dedicated, committed, constant, single-minded, dogged, indefatigable, unyielding, unbending, indomitable.

unsympathetic adj. **1** *unsympathetic staff* **uncaring**, unconcerned, unfeeling, insensitive, unkind, pitiless, heartless, hard-hearted. **2** *the government was unsympathetic to these views* **opposed**, against, (dead) set against, antagonistic, ill-disposed; informal anti. **3** *an unsympathetic character* **unlikeable**, disagreeable, unpleasant, objectionable, unsavoury; uncongenial, unfriendly, unneighbourly, unapproachable.
– OPPOSITES caring.

unsystematic adj. **unmethodical**, uncoordinated, disorganized, unplanned, indiscriminate; random, inconsistent, irregular, erratic, casual, haphazard, chaotic.

untamed adj. **wild**, feral, undomesticated, unbroken.

untangle v. **1** *I untangled the fishing tackle* **disentangle**, unravel, unsnarl, straighten out, untwist, untwine, unknot. **2** *untangling a mystery* **solve**, resolve, puzzle out, fathom, clear up, clarify, get to the bottom of; informal figure out; Brit. informal suss out.

untarnished adj. **unsullied**, unblemished, untainted, impeccable, undamaged, unspoilt, unimpaired, spotless, stainless.

untenable adj. **indefensible**, insupportable, unsustainable, unjustified, unjustifiable, flimsy, weak, shaky.

unthinkable adj. **unimaginable**, inconceivable, unbelievable, incredible, beyond belief, implausible.

unthinking adj. **1** *an unthinking woman* **thoughtless**, inconsiderate, insensitive; tactless, undiplomatic, indiscreet. **2** *an unthinking remark* **absent-minded**, heedless, thoughtless, careless, injudicious, imprudent, unwise, foolish, reckless, rash, precipitate; involuntary, inadvertent, unintentional, spontaneous, impulsive, unpremeditated.
– OPPOSITES thoughtful, intentional.

untidy adj. **1** *untidy hair* **scruffy**, tousled, dishevelled, unkempt, messy, disordered, disarranged, messed up, rumpled, bedraggled, uncombed, ungroomed, straggly, ruffled, tangled, matted, wind-blown; informal mussed up; N. Amer. informal raggedy. **2** *the room was untidy* **disordered**, messy, in a mess, disorderly, disorganized, in disorder, cluttered, in a muddle, muddled, in chaos, chaotic, haywire, topsy-turvy, in disarray, at sixes and sevens; informal higgledy-piggledy.
– OPPOSITES neat, orderly.

untie v. **undo**, unknot, unbind, unfasten, unlace, untether, unhitch, unmoor; loose, (set) free, release, let go.

until prep. & conj. **1** *I was working until midnight* **(up) till**, up to, up until; N. Amer. through. **2** *this did not happen until 1998* **before**, prior to, previous to, up until, (up) till, earlier than.

untimely adj. **1** *an untimely interruption* **ill-timed**, badly timed, mistimed; inopportune, inappropriate; inconvenient, unwelcome, infelicitous; formal malapropos. **2** *his untimely death* **premature**, (too) early, too soon, before time.
– OPPOSITES opportune.

untiring adj. **vigorous**, energetic, determined, resolute, enthusiastic, keen, zealous, spirited, dogged, tenacious, persistent, persevering, staunch; tireless, unflagging, unfailing, unfaltering, unwavering, indefatigable, unrelenting, unswerving; formal pertinacious.

untold adj. **1** *untold damage* **boundless**, measureless, limitless, unlimited, infinite, immeasurable, incalculable. **2** *untold billions* **countless**, innumerable, endless, limitless, numberless, an infinite number of, without number, uncountable; numerous, many, multiple; literary multitudinous, myriad. **3** *the untold story* **unreported**, unrecounted, unrevealed, undisclosed, undivulged, unpublished.
– OPPOSITES limited.

untouched adj. **1** *the food was untouched* **uneaten**, unconsumed, undrunk. **2** *one of the few untouched areas* **unspoilt**, unmarked, unblemished, unsullied, undefiled, undamaged, unharmed; pristine, natural, immaculate, in perfect condition, unaffected, unchanged, unaltered.

untoward adj. **unexpected**, unanticipated, unforeseen, unpredictable, unpredicted, surprising, unusual; unwelcome, unfavourable, adverse, unfortunate, infelicitous; formal malapropos.

untrained adj. **unskilled**, untaught, unschooled, untutored, unpractised, inexperienced; unqualified, unlicensed, amateur, non-professional.

untried adj. **untested**, unestablished, new, experimental, unattempted, trial, test, pilot, unproven.
– OPPOSITES established.

untroubled adj. **unworried**, unperturbed, unconcerned, unruffled, undismayed, unbothered, unagitated, unflustered; insouciant, nonchalant, blasé, carefree, serene, relaxed, at ease, happy-go-lucky; informal laid-back.

untrue adj. **1** *these suggestions are totally untrue* **false**, untruthful, fabricated, made up, invented, concocted, trumped up; erroneous, wrong, incorrect, inaccurate, fallacious, unsound, unfounded, misguided. **2** *he was untrue to his friends* **unfaithful**, disloyal, faithless, false, treacherous, traitorous, deceitful, deceiving, duplicitous,

u

double-dealing, two-faced, Janus-faced, insincere, unreliable, undependable, inconstant; informal two-timing; literary perfidious.
– OPPOSITES correct, faithful.

untrustworthy adj. **dishonest**, deceitful, double-dealing, treacherous, traitorous, two-faced, duplicitous, dishonourable, unprincipled, unscrupulous, corrupt; unreliable, undependable.
– OPPOSITES reliable.

untruth n. **1** *a patent untruth* **lie**, falsehood, fib, fabrication, invention, falsification, cock and bull story, half-truth, exaggeration; story, myth, piece of fiction; informal tall story, fairy tale, whopper; Brit. informal porky (pie). **2** *the total untruth of the story* **falsity**, falsehood, falseness, untruthfulness, fallaciousness, fictitiousness; fabrication, dishonesty, deceit, deceitfulness.

untruthful adj. **1** *the answers may be untruthful* **false**, untrue, fabricated, made up, invented, trumped up; erroneous, wrong, incorrect, inaccurate, fallacious, fictitious. **2** *an untruthful person* **lying**, mendacious, dishonest, deceitful, duplicitous, false, double-dealing, two-faced, Janus-faced; informal crooked, bent; literary perfidious.
– OPPOSITES honest.

untutored adj. **uneducated**, untaught, unschooled, ignorant, unsophisticated, uncultured, unenlightened.
– OPPOSITES educated.

untwine v. See **untwist**.

untwist v. **untwine**, disentangle, unravel, unsnarl, unwind, unroll, uncoil, unfurl, open (out), straighten (out).

unused adj. **1** *the notebook is unused | unused food* **unutilized**, unemployed, unexploited, not in service; left over, remaining, uneaten, unconsumed, unneeded, not required, to spare, surplus. **2** *he was unused to such directness* **unaccustomed**, new, a stranger, unfamiliar, unacquainted; old use strange.
– OPPOSITES accustomed.

unusual adj. **1** *an unusual sight* **uncommon**, abnormal, atypical, unexpected, surprising, unfamiliar, different; strange, odd, curious, out of the ordinary, extraordinary, unorthodox, unconventional, outlandish, off-centre, singular, peculiar, bizarre; rare, scarce, few and far between, thin on the ground, exceptional, isolated, occasional, infrequent; informal weird, offbeat, way out, freaky. **2** *a man of unusual talent* **remarkable**, extraordinary, exceptional, singular, particular, outstanding, notable, noteworthy, distinctive, striking, significant, special, unique, unparalleled, prodigious.
– OPPOSITES common.

unutterable adj. **1** *an existence of unutterable boredom* **indescribable**, beyond description, inexpressible, unspeakable, undefinable, inconceivable; extreme, great, overwhelming; dreadful, awful, appalling, terrible. **2** *unutterable joy* **marvellous**, wonderful, superb, splendid, unimaginable,

profound, deep.

unvarnished adj. **1** *unvarnished wood* **bare**, unpainted, unpolished, unfinished, untreated. **2** *the unvarnished truth* **straightforward**, plain, simple, stark; truthful, realistic, candid, honest, frank, forthright, direct, blunt, straight from the shoulder.

unveil v. **reveal**, present, disclose, divulge, make known, make public, communicate, publish, broadcast; display, show, exhibit, put on display; release, bring out.

unwanted adj. **1** *an unwanted development* **unwelcome**, undesirable, undesired, unpopular, unfortunate, unlucky, unfavourable, untoward; unpleasant, disagreeable, displeasing, distasteful, objectionable; regrettable, deplorable, lamentable; unacceptable, intolerable, awful, terrible, wretched, appalling. **2** *tins of unwanted pet food* **unused**, left over, surplus, superfluous; uneaten, unconsumed, untouched. **3** *an unwanted guest* **uninvited**, unbidden, unasked, unrequested, unsolicited. **4** *many ageing people feel unwanted* **friendless**, unloved, uncared-for, forsaken, rejected, shunned; superfluous, useless, unnecessary.
– OPPOSITES welcome.

unwarranted adj. **1** *the criticism is unwarranted* **unjustified**, unjustifiable, indefensible, inexcusable, unforgivable, unpardonable, uncalled for, unnecessary, unreasonable, unjust, groundless, excessive, immoderate, disproportionate. **2** *an unwarranted invasion of privacy* **unauthorized**, unsanctioned, unapproved, uncertified, unlicensed; illegal, unlawful, illicit, illegitimate, criminal, actionable.
– OPPOSITES justified.

unwary adj. **incautious**, careless, thoughtless, heedless, inattentive, unwatchful, off one's guard.

unwavering adj. **steady**, fixed, resolute, resolved, firm, steadfast, unswerving, unfaltering, untiring, tireless, indefatigable, unyielding, relentless, unremitting, unrelenting, sustained.
– OPPOSITES unsteady.

unwelcome adj. **1** *I was made to feel unwelcome* **unwanted**, uninvited. **2** *even a small increase is unwelcome* **undesirable**, undesired, unpopular, unfortunate, unlucky; disappointing, upsetting, distressing, disagreeable, displeasing; regrettable, deplorable, lamentable.

unwell adj. **ill**, sick, poorly, indisposed, ailing, not (very) well, not oneself, under/below par, peaky, queasy, nauseous; Brit. off colour; informal under the weather, not up to snuff, funny, peculiar, lousy, rough; Brit. informal grotty; Austral./NZ informal crook; dated queer.

unwholesome adj. **1** *unwholesome air* **unhealthy**, noxious, poisonous; insalubrious, unhygienic, insanitary; harmful, injurious, detrimental,

destructive, damaging, deleterious, baleful. **2** *unwholesome web pages* **improper**, immoral, indecent, corrupting, depraving, salacious.
– OPPOSITES healthy, seemly.

unwieldy adj. **cumbersome**, unmanageable, unmanoeuvrable; awkward, clumsy, massive, heavy, hefty, bulky, weighty.
– OPPOSITES manageable.

unwilling adj. **1** *unwilling conscripts* **reluctant**, unenthusiastic, hesitant, resistant, grudging, involuntary, forced. **2** *he was unwilling to take on that responsibility* **disinclined**, reluctant, averse, loath; (**be unwilling to do something**) not have the heart to, balk at, demur at, shy away from, flinch from, shrink from, have qualms about, have misgivings about, have reservations about.
– OPPOSITES keen.

unwillingness adj. **disinclination**, reluctance, hesitation, diffidence, wavering, vacillation, resistance, objection, opposition, doubts, second thoughts, scruples, qualms, misgivings; old use disrelish.

unwind v. **1** *Ella unwound the scarf from her neck* **unroll**, uncoil, unravel, untwine, untwist, disentangle, open (out), straighten (out). **2** *unwinding after work* **relax**, loosen up, ease up/off, slow down, de-stress, unbend, rest, put one's feet up, take it easy; informal chill out, wind down, let it all hang out, cool out; N. Amer. informal hang loose.

unwise adj. **injudicious**, ill-advised, imprudent, foolish, silly, inadvisable, impolitic, misguided, foolhardy, irresponsible, rash, hasty, overhasty, reckless.
– OPPOSITES sensible.

unwitting adj. **1** *an unwitting accomplice* **unknowing**, unconscious, unsuspecting, oblivious, unaware, innocent. **2** *an unwitting mistake* **unintentional**, unintended, inadvertent, involuntary, unconscious, accidental.
– OPPOSITES conscious.

unwonted adj. **unusual**, uncommon, unaccustomed, unfamiliar, unprecedented, exceptional, extraordinary, remarkable, singular, surprising.
– OPPOSITES usual.

unworldly adj. **1** *a gauche, unworldly girl* **naive**, simple, inexperienced, innocent, green, raw, callow, immature, unsophisticated, gullible, ingenuous, artless, guileless, childlike, trusting, credulous. **2** *unworldly beauty* **unearthly**, other-worldly, ethereal, ghostly, preternatural, supernatural, paranormal, mystical; rare extramundane. **3** *an unworldly religious order* **non-materialistic**, spiritualistic, religious.

unworthy adj. **1** *he was unworthy of trust* **undeserving**, ineligible, unqualified, unfit. **2** *unworthy behaviour* **unbecoming**, unsuitable, inappropriate, unbefitting, unfitting, unseemly, improper; discreditable,

shameful, dishonourable, despicable, ignoble, contemptible, reprehensible.
– OPPOSITES deserving, becoming.

unwritten adj. **tacit**, implicit, unvoiced, taken for granted, accepted, recognized, understood; traditional, customary, conventional; oral, verbal, spoken, vocal, word-of-mouth.

unyielding adj. **1** *unyielding spikes of cane* **stiff**, inflexible, unbending, inelastic, firm, hard, solid, tough, tight, compact, compressed, dense. **2** *an unyielding policy* **resolute**, inflexible, uncompromising, unbending, unshakeable, unwavering, immovable, intractable, intransigent, rigid, stiff, firm, determined, dogged, obstinate, stubborn, adamant, obdurate, tenacious, relentless, implacable, single-minded; formal pertinacious.

up-and-coming adj. **promising**, budding, rising, on the up and up, with potential; talented, gifted, able.

upbeat adj. informal **optimistic**, cheerful, cheery, positive, confident, hopeful, sanguine, bullish, buoyant.
– OPPOSITES pessimistic, negative.

upbraid v. **reprimand**, rebuke, admonish, chastise, chide, reprove, reproach, scold, berate, take to task, lambaste, give someone a piece of one's mind, haul over the coals, lecture; informal tell off, give someone a talking-to, dress down, give someone an earful, rap over the knuckles, bawl out, lay into; Brit. informal tick off, carpet, tear off a strip, give someone what for, give someone a rocket/rollicking; N. Amer. informal chew out, ream out; Austral. informal monster; formal castigate; rare reprehend.

upbringing n. **childhood**, early life, formative years, teaching, instruction, care, bringing-up, rearing.

update v. **1** *security measures are continually updated* **modernize**, upgrade, bring up to date, improve, overhaul; N. Amer. bring up to code. **2** *I'll update him on today's developments* **brief**, bring up to date, inform, fill in, tell, notify, apprise, keep posted; informal clue in, put in the picture, bring/keep up to speed.

upgrade v. **1** *there are plans to upgrade the rail system* **improve**, modernize, update, bring up to date, make better, ameliorate, reform; rehabilitate, recondition, refurbish, renovate; N. Amer. bring up to code. **2** *he was upgraded to a seat in the cabinet* **promote**, give promotion to, elevate, move up, raise; old use prefer.
– OPPOSITES downgrade, demote.

upheaval n. **disruption**, disturbance, trouble, turbulence, disorder, confusion, turmoil, pandemonium, chaos, mayhem, cataclysm; revolution, change.

uphill adj. **1** *an uphill path* **upward**, rising, ascending, climbing. **2** *an uphill job* **arduous**, difficult, hard, tough, taxing, demanding, exacting, stiff, formidable, exhausting, tiring, wearisome, laborious,

u

gruelling, back-breaking, punishing, burdensome, onerous, Herculean; informal no picnic, killing; old use toilsome.
– OPPOSITES downhill, easy.

uphold v. **1** *the court upheld his claim for damages* **confirm**, endorse, sustain, approve, support, back (up), stand by, champion, defend. **2** *they've a tradition to uphold* **maintain**, sustain, continue, preserve, protect, keep, hold to, keep alive, keep going.
– OPPOSITES overturn, oppose.

upkeep n. **1** *the upkeep of the road* **maintenance**, repair(s), service, servicing, care, preservation, conservation; running. **2** *the child's upkeep* (**financial**) **support**, maintenance, keep, subsistence, care.

uplift v. *she needs something to uplift her spirits* **boost**, raise, buoy up, lift, cheer up, perk up, enliven, brighten up, lighten, stimulate, inspire, ginger up, revive, restore; informal buck up.

uplifted adj. **raised**, upraised, elevated, upthrust; held high, erect, proud.

uplifting adj. **inspiring**, stirring, inspirational, rousing, moving, touching, affecting, cheering, heartening, encouraging, life-affirming.

upper adj. **1** *the upper floor* **higher**, superior; top. **2** *the upper echelons of the party* **senior**, superior, higher-level, higher-ranking, top.
– OPPOSITES lower.
□ **the upper hand** an advantage, the edge, the whip hand, a lead, a head start, ascendancy, superiority, supremacy, sway, control, power, mastery, dominance, command.

upper-class adj. **aristocratic**, noble, of noble birth, patrician, titled, blue-blooded, high-born, well born, elite, landowning, landed, born with a silver spoon in one's mouth; Brit. county, upmarket; informal upper-crust, top-drawer, {huntin', shootin', and fishin'}, classy; Brit. informal posh; old use gentle, of gentle birth.

uppermost adj. **1** *the uppermost branches* **highest**, top, topmost. **2** *their own problems remained uppermost in their minds* **predominant**, of greatest importance, to the fore, foremost, dominant, principal, chief, main, paramount, major.

uppish adj. informal **arrogant**, bumptious, full of oneself, puffed up, conceited, swollen-headed, pompous, self-assertive, overbearing, throwing one's weight about, cocky, cocksure, haughty, self-important, superior, presumptuous, overweening; informal snooty, uppity, high and mighty, too big for one's boots.

upright adj. **1** *an upright position* **vertical**, perpendicular, plumb, straight (up), straight up and down, bolt upright, erect, on end; on one's feet; Heraldry rampant. **2** *an upright member of the community* **honest**, honourable, upstanding, respectable, high-minded, law-abiding, right-minded, worthy, moral, ethical, righteous, decent, good, virtuous, principled, high-principled,

of principle, noble, incorruptible, anti-corruption.
– OPPOSITES horizontal, dishonourable.

uprising n. **rebellion**, revolt, insurrection, mutiny, revolution, insurgence, rioting, riot; civil disobedience, unrest, anarchy; coup, coup d'état, putsch.

uproar n. **1** *the uproar in the kitchen continued for some time* **turmoil**, disorder, confusion, chaos, commotion, disturbance, rumpus, tumult, turbulence, mayhem, pandemonium, bedlam, noise, din, clamour, hubbub, racket; shouting, yelling, babel; informal hullabaloo; Brit. informal row. **2** *there was an uproar when he was dismissed* **outcry**, furore; fuss, commotion, hue and cry, rumpus, ruckus, brouhaha; informal hullabaloo, stink, ructions; Brit. informal row.
– OPPOSITES calm.

uproarious adj. *an uproarious party* **riotous**, rowdy, noisy, loud, wild, unrestrained, unruly, rip-roaring, rollicking, boisterous; informal rumbustious; N. Amer. informal rambunctious.
– OPPOSITES quiet.

uproot v. **1** *don't pick or uproot wild flowers* **pull up**, root out, deracinate, grub out/up. **2** *a revolution is necessary to uproot the social order* **eradicate**, get rid of, eliminate, root out, destroy, put an end to, do away with, wipe out, stamp out.
– OPPOSITES plant.

upset v. **1** *the accusation upset her* **distress**, trouble, perturb, dismay, disturb, discompose, unsettle, disconcert, disquiet, worry, bother, agitate, fluster, throw, ruffle, unnerve, shake; hurt, sadden, grieve. **2** *he upset a tureen of soup* **knock over**, overturn, upend, tip over, topple (over); spill; old use overset. **3** *the dam will upset the ecological balance* **disrupt**, interfere with, disturb, throw out, turn topsy-turvy, throw into confusion, mess up.
▶ n. **1** *a legal dispute will cause worry and upset* **distress**, trouble, perturbation, dismay, disquiet, worry, bother, agitation; hurt, grief. **2** *a stomach upset* **disorder**, complaint, ailment, illness, sickness, malady; informal bug; Brit. informal lurgy.
▶ adj. **1** *I was upset by the news* **distressed**, troubled, perturbed, dismayed, disturbed, unsettled, disconcerted, worried, bothered, anxious, agitated, flustered, ruffled, unnerved, shaken; hurt, saddened, grieved; informal cut up, choked; Brit. informal gutted. **2** *an upset stomach* **disturbed**, unsettled, queasy, bad, poorly; informal gippy.
– OPPOSITES unperturbed, calm.

upshot n. **result**, end result, consequence, outcome, conclusion; effect, repercussion, reverberations, ramification; dated issue.
– OPPOSITES cause.

upside down adj. **1** *an upside-down canoe* **upturned**, upended, wrong side up, overturned, inverted; capsized. **2** *they left the flat upside down* **in disarray**, in disorder, jumbled up, in a muddle, untidy, disorganized, chaotic, all over the place, in chaos, in confusion, topsy-turvy, at sixes and sevens; informal higgledy-piggledy.

upstanding adj. **1** *an upstanding member of the community* **honest**, honourable, upright, respectable, high-minded, law-abiding, right-minded, worthy, moral, ethical, righteous, decent, good, virtuous, principled, high-principled, of principle, noble, incorruptible, anti-corruption. **2** *the upstanding feathered plumes* **upright**, erect, vertical; standing, on one's feet; Heraldry rampant.
– OPPOSITES dishonourable.

upstart n. **parvenu(e)**, arriviste, nouveau riche, vulgarian; status-seeker, social climber.

up to date adj. **1** *up-to-date equipment* **modern**, contemporary, the latest, state-of-the-art, new, present-day, up to the minute; advanced; informal bang up to date, mod. **2** *the newsletter will keep you up to date* **informed**, up to speed, in the picture, in touch, au fait, au courant, conversant, familiar, knowledgeable, acquainted, aware; informal plugged-in.
– OPPOSITES out of date, old-fashioned.

upturn n. **improvement**, upswing, turn for the better; recovery, revival, rally, resurgence, increase, rise, jump, leap, upsurge, boost, escalation.
– OPPOSITES fall, slump.

upward adj. *an upward trend* **rising**, on the rise, ascending, climbing, mounting; uphill.
– OPPOSITES downward.
▸ adv. *the smoke drifts upward.* See **upwards**.

upwards adv. *he inched his way upwards* **up**, upward, uphill; to the top.
– OPPOSITES downward.
□ **upward(s) of** more than, above, over, in excess of, exceeding, beyond.

urban adj. **town**, city, municipal, metropolitan, built-up, inner-city, suburban.
– OPPOSITES rural.

urbane adj. **suave**, sophisticated, debonair, worldly, cultivated, cultured, civilized; smooth, polished, refined, self-possessed; courteous, polite, civil, well mannered, mannerly, charming, gentlemanly, gallant.
– OPPOSITES uncouth, unsophisticated.

urchin n. **ragamuffin**, waif, stray; imp, rascal; derogatory guttersnipe; dated gamin; old use mudlark, scapegrace, street Arab.

urge v. **1** *she urged him to try again* **encourage**, exhort, enjoin, press, entreat, implore, call on, appeal to, beg, plead with; egg on, spur, push, pressure, pressurize; formal adjure; literary beseech. **2** *she urged her horse down the lane* **spur (on)**, force, drive, impel. **3** *I urge caution in interpreting these results* **advise**, counsel, advocate, recommend.
▸ n. *his urge to travel* **desire**, wish, need, compulsion, longing, yearning, hankering, craving, appetite, hunger, thirst; fancy, impulse; informal yen, itch.

urgent adj. **1** *the urgent need for more funding* **acute**, pressing, dire, desperate, critical, serious, grave, intense, crying, burning, compelling, extreme, high-priority, top-priority; life-and-death. **2** *an urgent whisper* **insistent**, persistent, importunate, earnest, pleading, begging.

urinate v. **pass water**, relieve oneself; informal spend a penny, have/take a leak, pee, piddle, widdle; Brit. informal wee, have a Jimmy (Riddle), have a slash; N. Amer. informal take a whizz; formal micturate.

usable adj. **ready/fit for use**, able to be used, at someone's disposal; working, in working order, functioning, functional, serviceable, operational, up and running.

usage n. **1** *energy usage* **use**, consumption, utilization. **2** *the usage of equipment* **use**, utilization, operation, manipulation, running, handling. **3** *the intricacies of English usage* **phraseology**, parlance, idiom, way of speaking/writing, mode of expression; idiolect. **4** *the usages of polite society* **custom**, practice, habit, tradition, convention, rule, observance; way, procedure, form; formal praxis, wont; (**usages**) mores.

use v. **1** *she used her key to open the front door* **utilize**, make use of, avail oneself of, employ, work, operate, wield, ply, apply, manoeuvre, manipulate, put to use, put into service. **2** *the court will use its discretion in making an order* **exercise**, employ, bring into play, practise, apply. **3** *use your troops well and they will not let you down* **manage**, handle, treat, deal with, behave/act towards. **4** *I couldn't help feeling that she was using me* **take advantage of**, exploit, manipulate, take liberties with, impose on, abuse; capitalize on, profit from, trade on, milk; informal cash in on, walk all over. **5** *we have used all the available funds* **consume**, get/go through, exhaust, deplete, expend, spend; waste, fritter away, squander, dissipate.
▸ n. **1** *the use of such weapons* **utilization**, usage, application, employment, operation, manipulation. **2** *his use of other people for his own ends* **exploitation**, manipulation; abuse. **3** *what is the use of that?* **advantage**, benefit, service, utility, usefulness, help, good, gain, avail, profit, value, worth, point, object, purpose, sense, reason. **4** *composers have not found much use for the device* **need**, necessity, call, demand, requirement.

used adj. *a used car* **second-hand**, pre-owned, nearly new, old; worn, hand-me-down, handed-down, cast-off; Brit. informal reach-me-down.
– OPPOSITES new.
□ **used to** accustomed to, no stranger to, familiar with, at home with, in the habit of, experienced in, versed in, conversant with, acquainted with.

useful adj. **1** *a useful multi-purpose tool* **functional**, practical, handy, convenient, utilitarian, serviceable, of use, of service; informal nifty. **2** *a useful experience* **beneficial**, advantageous, helpful, worthwhile, profitable, rewarding, productive, constructive, valuable, fruitful. **3** informal *they had some very useful players* **competent**,

u

capable, able, skilful, skilled, talented, proficient, accomplished, good, handy.
– OPPOSITES useless, disadvantageous, incompetent.

useless adj. **1** *it was useless to try | a piece of useless knowledge* **futile**, to no avail, in vain, vain, pointless, to no purpose, unavailing, hopeless, ineffectual, ineffective, to no effect, fruitless, unprofitable, profitless, unproductive; broken, kaput; old use bootless. **2** informal *he was useless at his job* **incompetent**, inept, ineffective, incapable, inadequate, hopeless, bad; informal pathetic, a dead loss.
– OPPOSITES useful, beneficial, competent.

usher v. *she ushered him to a window seat* **escort**, accompany, take, show, see, lead, conduct, guide, steer, shepherd.
▸ n. *ushers showed them to their seats* **guide**, attendant, escort.
◻ **usher something in** herald, mark the start of, signal, ring in, show in, set the scene for, pave the way for; start, begin, introduce, open the door to, get going, set in motion, get under way, kick off, launch.

usual adj. **habitual**, customary, accustomed, normal, routine, regular, standard, typical, established, set, settled, stock, conventional, traditional, expected, predictable, familiar; average, general, ordinary, everyday; literary wonted.
– OPPOSITES exceptional.

usually adv. **normally**, generally, habitually, customarily, routinely, typically, ordinarily, commonly, conventionally, traditionally; as a rule, in general, more often than not, in the main, mainly, mostly, for the most part.

usurp v. **1** *Richard usurped the throne* **seize**, take over, take possession of, take, commandeer, assume. **2** *the Hanoverian dynasty had usurped the Stuarts* **oust**, overthrow, remove, topple, unseat, depose, dethrone; supplant, replace.

utensil n. **implement**, tool, instrument, device, apparatus, gadget, appliance, contrivance, contraption, aid; informal gizmo.

utilitarian adj. **practical**, functional, serviceable, useful, sensible, efficient, utility, workaday; plain, unadorned.
– OPPOSITES decorative.

utility n. **usefulness**, use, benefit, value, advantage, help, helpfulness, profitability, practicality, effectiveness, avail, service; formal efficacy.

utilize v. **use**, make use of, put to use, employ, avail oneself of, bring/press into service, bring into play, deploy, draw on, exploit.

utmost adj. **1** *a matter of the utmost importance* **greatest**, highest, maximum, most, uttermost; extreme, supreme, paramount. **2** *the utmost tip of Shetland* **furthest**, farthest, furthermost, farthermost, extreme, very, uttermost, outermost, endmost.
▸ n. *a plot that stretches credulity to the utmost* **uttermost**, maximum, limit.

Utopia n. **paradise**, heaven, heaven on earth, Eden, Garden of Eden, Shangri-La, Elysium; idyll, nirvana, ideal place; literary Arcadia.

Utopian adj. **idealistic**, visionary, romantic, starry-eyed, fanciful, unrealistic; ideal, perfect, paradisal, heavenly, idyllic, blissful, Elysian; literary Arcadian.

utter[1] adj. *that's utter nonsense* **complete**, total, absolute, thorough, perfect, downright, out-and-out, outright, thoroughgoing, all-out, sheer, arrant, positive, prize, rank, pure, real, veritable, consummate, categorical, unmitigated, unqualified, unadulterated, unalloyed.

utter[2] v. **1** *he uttered an exasperated snort* **emit**, let out, give, produce. **2** *he hardly uttered a word* **say**, speak, voice, express, articulate, pronounce, enunciate, verbalize, vocalize.

utterance n. **remark**, comment, word, statement, observation, declaration, pronouncement.

utterly adv. **completely**, totally, absolutely, entirely, wholly, fully, thoroughly, quite, altogether, one hundred per cent, downright, outright, in all respects, unconditionally, perfectly, really, to the hilt, to the core; informal dead.

uttermost adj. & n. See **utmost**.

U-turn n. *a complete U-turn in economic policy* **volte-face**, turnaround, about-face, reversal, rowback, shift, change of heart, change of mind, backtracking, change of plan; Brit. about-turn.

u

Vv

vacancy n. **1** *there are vacancies for computer technicians* **opening**, position, situation vacant, post, job, opportunity, place. **2** *Cathy stared into vacancy, seeing nothing* **empty space**, emptiness, nothingness, void. **3** *a vacancy of mind* **empty-headedness**, lack of intelligence, brainlessness, vacuousness, vacuity, stupidity.

vacant adj. **1** *a vacant house* **empty**, unoccupied, available, not in use, free, unfilled; uninhabited, untenanted. **2** *a vacant look* **blank**, expressionless, unresponsive, emotionless, impassive, uninterested, vacuous, empty, glazed, glassy; unintelligent, dull-witted, dense, brainless, empty-headed.
– OPPOSITES full, occupied, expressive.

vacate v. **1** *he was forced to vacate the premises* **leave**, move out of, evacuate, quit, depart from; abandon, desert. **2** *he will be vacating his post next year* **resign from**, leave, stand down from, give up, bow out of, relinquish, retire from; informal quit.
– OPPOSITES occupy, take up.

vacation n. **1** *his summer vacations in France* **holiday**, trip, tour, break, mini-break; leave, time off, recess, furlough; informal hol, vac, staycation; formal sojourn. **2** *the squatters' vacation of the occupied land* **departure**, evacuation, abandonment, desertion.

vacillate v. **dither**, be indecisive, be undecided, waver, hesitate, be in two minds, blow hot and cold, keep changing one's mind; Brit. haver, hum and haw; informal dilly-dally, shilly-shally.

vacillating adj. **irresolute**, indecisive, dithering, undecided, hesitant, wavering, ambivalent, divided, uncertain, in two minds, blowing hot and cold; informal dilly-dallying, shilly-shallying.
– OPPOSITES resolute.

vacuous adj. **silly**, inane, unintelligent, foolish, stupid, fatuous, idiotic, brainless, witless, vapid, vacant, empty-headed; informal dumb, gormless, moronic, brain-dead.
– OPPOSITES intelligent.

vacuum n. **1** *people longing to fill the spiritual vacuum in their lives* **emptiness**, void, nothingness, vacancy. **2** *the political vacuum left by the Emperor's death* **gap**, space, lacuna, void. **3** informal *I use the vacuum for cleaning the rug* **vacuum cleaner**; Brit. informal vac; trademark Hoover.

vagabond n. See **vagrant** (noun).

vagary n. **change**, fluctuation, variation, quirk, peculiarity, oddity, eccentricity, unpredictability, caprice, foible, whim, whimsy, fancy.

vagrant n. *a temporary home for vagrants* **tramp**, drifter, down-and-out, derelict, beggar, itinerant, wanderer, nomad, traveller, vagabond, transient, homeless person, beachcomber; informal knight of the road; N. Amer. hobo; Austral. bagman; informal bag lady; N. Amer. informal bum; literary wayfarer.
▸ adj. *vagrant beggars* **homeless**, drifting, transient, roving, roaming, itinerant, wandering, nomadic, travelling, vagabond, rootless, of no fixed address/abode.

vague adj. **1** *a vague shape* **indistinct**, indefinite, indeterminate, unclear, ill-defined; hazy, fuzzy, misty, blurred, blurry, faint, shadowy, dim, obscure, nebulous, amorphous. **2** *a vague description* **imprecise**, rough, approximate, inexact, non-specific, generalized, ambiguous, equivocal, hazy, woolly. **3** *they had only vague plans* **hazy**, uncertain, undecided, unsure, unclear, unsettled, indefinite, indeterminate, unconfirmed, up in the air, speculative. **4** *she was so vague in everyday life* **absent-minded**, forgetful, dreamy, abstracted, with one's head in the clouds; informal scatty, not with it.
– OPPOSITES clear, precise, certain.

vaguely adv. **1** *she looks vaguely familiar* **slightly**, a little, a bit, somewhat, rather, in a way; faintly, obscurely; informal sort of, kind of. **2** *he fired his rifle vaguely in our direction* **roughly**, more or less, approximately. **3** *he smiled vaguely* **absent-mindedly**, abstractedly, vacantly.
– OPPOSITES very, exactly.

vain adj. **1** *he was vain about his looks* **conceited**, narcissistic, self-loving, self-admiring, self-regarding, egotistic, egotistical; proud, arrogant, boastful, cocky, immodest, swaggering; informal big-headed; literary vainglorious. **2** *a vain attempt* **futile**, useless, pointless, to no purpose, in vain; ineffective, ineffectual, inefficacious, impotent, unavailing, to no avail, fruitless, profitless, unproductive, unsuccessful, failed, abortive, for nothing; thwarted, frustrated, foiled; old use bootless.
– OPPOSITES modest, successful.
□ **in vain 1** *they tried in vain to save him* **unsuccessfully**, without success, to no avail, to no purpose, fruitlessly. **2** *his efforts were in vain.* See **vain** (sense 2).

V

valediction n. **farewell**, goodbye, adieu, leave-taking.

valedictory adj. **farewell**, goodbye, leaving, parting; last, final.

valet n. **manservant**, man, personal attendant, gentleman's gentleman, Jeeves; Military, dated batman.

valetudinarian n. *an elderly valetudinarian* **hypochondriac**; invalid.
▸adj. *he was earnest, fussy, and valetudinarian* **hypochondriac**, obsessed with one's health, neurotic; sickly, ailing, poorly, in poor health, weak, infirm, valetudinary.

valiant adj. **brave**, courageous, plucky, valorous, intrepid, heroic, gallant, lionhearted, bold, fearless, daring, audacious; unflinching, unshrinking, unafraid, dauntless, undaunted, doughty, indomitable, mettlesome, stout-hearted, spirited; informal game, gutsy, spunky.
– OPPOSITES cowardly.

valid adj. **1** *a valid criticism* **well founded**, sound, reasonable, rational, logical, justifiable, defensible, viable, bona fide; cogent, effective, powerful, convincing, credible, forceful, strong, weighty. **2** *a valid contract* **legally binding**, lawful, legal, official, signed and sealed, contractual; in force, in effect, effective.

validate v. **1** *clinical trials now exist to validate this claim* **prove**, substantiate, corroborate, verify, support, back up, bear out, confirm, justify, vindicate, authenticate. **2** *250 course proposals were validated* **ratify**, endorse, approve, agree to, accept, authorize, legalize, legitimize, warrant, license, certify, recognize.
– OPPOSITES disprove.

valley n. **dale**, vale; hollow, gully, gorge, ravine, canyon, rift; Brit. combe, dene; N. English clough; Scottish glen, strath; literary dell, dingle.

valour n. **bravery**, courage, pluck, intrepidity, nerve, daring, fearlessness, audacity, boldness, dauntlessness, stout-heartedness, heroism, backbone, spirit; informal guts, spunk; Brit. informal bottle; N. Amer. informal moxie.
– OPPOSITES cowardice.

valuable adj. **1** *a valuable watch* **precious**, costly, high-priced, high-cost, expensive, dear; worth its weight in gold, worth a king's ransom, priceless. **2** *a valuable contribution* **useful**, helpful, beneficial, invaluable, productive, constructive, effective, advantageous, worthwhile, worthy, important.
– OPPOSITES cheap, worthless, useless.

valuables plural n. **precious items**, costly items, prized possessions, personal effects, treasures.

value n. **1** *houses exceeding £250,000 in value* **price**, cost, worth; market price, monetary value, face value. **2** *the value of adequate preparation cannot be overstated* **worth**, usefulness, advantage, benefit, gain, profit, good, help, helpfulness, avail; importance, significance. **3** *society's values are passed on to us as children* **principles**, ethics, moral code, morals, standards, code of behaviour.
▸v. **1** *his estate was valued at £45,000* **evaluate**, assess, estimate, appraise, price, put/set a price on. **2** *she valued his opinion* **think highly of**, have a high opinion of, hold in high regard, rate highly, esteem, set (great) store by, appreciate, respect; prize, cherish, treasure.

valued adj. **cherished**, treasured, dear, prized; esteemed, respected, highly regarded.

valueless adj. **worthless**, of no value, useless, to no purpose, (of) no use, profitless, futile, pointless, vain, in vain, to no avail, to no effect, fruitless, unproductive, idle, ineffective, unavailing; old use bootless.

vamp¹ v. informal *the design had been vamped up* **improve**, revamp, redesign, remodel, restyle, rework, make over; renovate, refurbish, redecorate, recondition, rehabilitate, overhaul, repair; informal do up, give something a facelift; N. Amer. informal rehab.

vamp² n. informal *a raven-haired vamp* **seductress**, temptress, siren, femme fatale, Mata Hari; flirt, coquette, tease.

van n. *he was in the van of the movement.* See **vanguard**.

vanguard n. **forefront**, van, advance guard, spearhead, front, front line, fore, lead, cutting edge; leaders, founders, founding fathers, pioneers, trailblazers, trendsetters, innovators, groundbreakers.
– OPPOSITES rear.

vanish v. **1** *he vanished into the darkness* **disappear**, be lost to sight/view, become invisible, vanish into thin air, recede from view. **2** *all hope of freedom vanished* **fade (away)**, evaporate, melt away, come to an end, end, cease to exist, pass away, die out, be no more.
– OPPOSITES appear, materialize.

vanity n. **1** *she had none of the vanity often associated with beautiful women* **conceit**, narcissism, self-love, self-admiration, self-regard, egotism; pride, arrogance, boastfulness, cockiness, swagger; informal big-headedness; literary vainglory. **2** *the vanity of all desires of the will* **futility**, uselessness, pointlessness, worthlessness, fruitlessness.
– OPPOSITES modesty.

vanquish v. **conquer**, defeat, beat, trounce, rout, triumph over, be victorious over, get the better of, worst; overcome, overwhelm, overpower, overthrow, quash, subdue, subjugate, quell, crush, bring someone to their knees; informal lick, hammer, clobber, thrash, demolish, wipe the floor with, make mincemeat of, massacre, slaughter, annihilate; Brit. informal stuff; N. Amer. informal cream, shellac.

vapid adj. **insipid**, uninspired, colourless, uninteresting, feeble, flat, dull, boring, tedious, tired, unexciting, uninspiring, unimaginative, lifeless, tame, vacuous, bland, trite.

V

– OPPOSITES lively, colourful.

vapour n. **haze**, mist, steam, condensation; fumes, exhalation, fog, smog, smoke.

variable adj. **changeable**, changing, varying, shifting, fluctuating, changeful, irregular, inconstant, inconsistent, fluid, unsteady, unstable, unsettled, fitful, mutable, protean, wavering, vacillating, capricious, fickle, volatile, unpredictable, unreliable; informal up and down.
– OPPOSITES constant.

variance n. **difference**, variation, discrepancy, dissimilarity, disagreement, conflict, divergence, deviation, contrast, contradiction, imbalance, incongruity.
□ **at variance 1** *his recollections were at variance with documentary evidence* **inconsistent**, at odds, not in keeping, out of keeping, out of line, out of step, in conflict, in disagreement, different, differing, divergent, discrepant, dissimilar, contrary, incompatible, contradictory, irreconcilable, incongruous. **2** *they were at variance with their previous allies* **in disagreement**, at odds, at cross purposes, at loggerheads, in conflict, in dispute, at outs, quarrelling.

variant n. *there are a number of variants of the same idea* **variation**, form, alternative, adaptation, alteration, modification, permutation.
▸ adj. *a variant spelling* **alternative**, other, different, divergent, derived, modified.

variation n. **1** *regional variations in farming practice* **difference**, dissimilarity; disparity, contrast, discrepancy, imbalance; technical differential; formal dissimilitude. **2** *opening times are subject to variation* **change**, alteration, modification; diversification. **3** *there was very little variation from an understood pattern* **deviation**, variance, divergence, departure, fluctuation. **4** *hurling is an Irish variation of hockey* **variant**, form, alternative form; development, adaptation, alteration, diversification, modification.

varied adj. **diverse**, assorted, miscellaneous, mixed, sundry, wide-ranging, heterogeneous, multifarious; disparate, motley.

variegated adj. **multicoloured**, particoloured, multicolour, many-coloured, many-hued, polychromatic, colourful, prismatic, rainbow-like, kaleidoscopic; mottled, striated, marbled, streaked, speckled, flecked, dappled; informal splotchy, splodgy.
– OPPOSITES plain, monochrome.

variety n. **1** *the lack of variety in the curriculum* **diversity**, variation, diversification, multifariousness, heterogeneity, many-sidedness; change, difference. **2** *a wide variety of flowers and shrubs* **assortment**, miscellany, range, array, collection, selection, mixture, medley, multiplicity; mixed bag, motley collection, potpourri. **3** *fifty varieties of pasta* **sort**, kind, type, class, category, style, form; make, model, brand; strain, breed, genus.
– OPPOSITES uniformity.

various adj. **diverse**, different, differing, varied, varying, a variety of, assorted, mixed, sundry, miscellaneous, heterogeneous, disparate, motley; literary divers.

varnish n. & v. **lacquer**, shellac, japan, enamel, glaze; polish.

vary v. **1** *estimates of the development cost vary* **differ**, be different, be dissimilar. **2** *rates of interest vary over time* **fluctuate**, rise and fall, go up and down, change, alter, shift, swing. **3** *the diaphragm is used for varying the aperture of the lens* **modify**, change, alter, adjust, regulate, control, set; diversify. **4** *the routine never varied* **change**, alter, deviate, differ, fluctuate.

vassal n. historical **villein**, liegeman, man, vavasour, serf, helot.

vast adj. **huge**, extensive, expansive, broad, wide, boundless, immeasurable, limitless, infinite; enormous, immense, great, massive, colossal, tremendous, mighty, prodigious, gigantic, gargantuan, mammoth, monumental; giant, towering, mountainous, titanic, Brobdingnagian; informal jumbo, mega, monster, whopping, humongous, astronomical; Brit. informal ginormous.
– OPPOSITES tiny.

vat n. **tub**, tank, cistern, barrel, butt, cask, tun, drum, basin; vessel, receptacle, container, holder, reservoir.

vault[1] n. **1** *the highest Gothic vault in Europe* **arched roof**, dome, arch. **2** *the vault under the church* **cellar**, basement, underground chamber; crypt, undercroft, catacomb, burial chamber. **3** *valuables stored in the vault* **strongroom**, safe deposit, safety deposit.

vault[2] v. *he vaulted over the gate* **jump over**, leap over, spring over, bound over; hurdle, clear.

vaunt v. **boast about**, brag about, make much of, crow about, parade, flaunt; acclaim, praise, extol, celebrate; informal show off about; formal laud.

veer v. **turn**, swerve, swing, sheer, career, weave, wheel; change direction/course, go off course, deviate.

vegetate v. **do nothing**, idle, languish, laze, lounge, loll; moulder, stagnate; informal veg out, slob out; Brit. informal slummock; N. Amer. informal bum around, lollygag.

vegetation n. **plants**, flora; greenery, foliage, herbage, verdure.

> **WORD LINKS**
> **herbicide** a substance used to kill vegetation

vehemence n. **passion**, force, forcefulness, ardour, fervour, violence, urgency, strength, vigour, intensity, keenness, enthusiasm, zeal.

vehement adj. **passionate**, forceful, ardent, impassioned, heated, spirited, urgent, fervent, violent, fierce, strong, forcible, powerful, emphatic, vigorous, intense, earnest, keen, enthusiastic, zealous.
– OPPOSITES mild, apathetic.

vehicle n. **1** *a stolen vehicle* **means of transport**, conveyance; car, automobile, motorcycle, motorbike, van, bus, coach, lorry, truck; N. Amer. informal auto. **2** *a vehicle for the communication of original ideas* **channel**, medium, means (of expression), agency, agent, instrument, mechanism, organ, apparatus.

> **WORD LINKS**
>
> **automotive** relating to vehicles
> **tare** the weight of a vehicle without its fuel or load
> **weighbridge** a machine for weighing vehicles
> **tachograph** a device recording a commercial road vehicle's speed over a period of time

veil n. *a thin veil of high cloud made the sun hazy* **covering**, cover, screen, curtain, mantle, cloak, mask, blanket, shroud, canopy, cloud, pall.
▸ v. *the peak was veiled in mist* **envelop**, surround, swathe, enfold, cover, conceal, hide, screen, shield, cloak, blanket, shroud, obscure; literary enshroud, mantle.

veiled adj. *veiled threats* **disguised**, camouflaged, masked, covert, hidden, concealed, suppressed, underlying, implicit, implied, indirect.
– OPPOSITES overt.

vein n. **1** *a vein in his neck pulsed* **blood vessel**. **2** *the mineral veins in the rock* **layer**, lode, seam, stratum, stratification, deposit. **3** *white marble with grey veins* **streak**, marking, mark, line, stripe, strip, band, thread, strand; technical stria, striation. **4** *he closes the article in a humorous vein* **mood**, humour, frame of mind, temper, disposition, attitude, tenor, tone, key, spirit, character, feel, flavour, quality, atmosphere; manner, way, style.

> **WORD LINKS**
>
> **vascular**, **venous** relating to veins
> **phlebotomy** surgical incision of a vein

velocity n. **speed**, pace, rate, tempo, momentum, impetus; swiftness, rapidity; literary fleetness, celerity.

venal adj. **corrupt**, corruptible, bribable, open to bribery; dishonest, dishonourable, untrustworthy, unscrupulous, unprincipled; mercenary, greedy; informal bent.
– OPPOSITES honourable, honest.

vendetta n. **feud**, blood feud, quarrel, argument, falling-out, dispute, fight, war; bad blood, enmity, rivalry, conflict, strife.

vendor n. **seller**, retailer, purveyor, dealer, trader, tradesman, shopkeeper, merchant, supplier, stockist; huckster, pedlar, hawker; trademark in US e-tailer; N. Amer. storekeeper; Brit. informal flogger.

veneer n. **1** *American cherry wood with a maple veneer* **surface**, lamination, layer, overlay, facing, covering, finish, exterior. **2** *a veneer of sophistication* **facade**, front, false front, show, outward display, appearance, impression, semblance, guise, disguise, mask, masquerade, pretence, camouflage, cover.

venerable adj. **respected**, venerated, revered, reverenced, honoured, esteemed, hallowed, august, distinguished, eminent, great.

venerate v. **revere**, reverence, worship, hallow, hold sacred, exalt, adore, honour, respect, esteem; old use magnify.

veneration n. **reverence**, worship, adoration, exaltation, devotion, honour, respect, esteem, high regard.

vengeance n. **revenge**, retribution, retaliation, requital, reprisal, satisfaction, an eye for an eye (and a tooth for a tooth).
▫ **with a vengeance** vigorously, strenuously, energetically, with a will, with might and main, with all the stops out, for all one is worth, all out, flat out, at full tilt; informal hammer and tongs, like crazy, like mad; Brit. informal like billy-o.

vengeful adj. **vindictive**, revengeful, out for revenge, unforgiving, grudge-bearing.
– OPPOSITES forgiving.

venial adj. **forgivable**, pardonable, excusable, allowable, permissible; slight, minor, unimportant, insignificant, trivial, trifling.
– OPPOSITES unforgivable, mortal.

venom n. **1** *snake venom* **poison**, toxin; old use bane. **2** *his voice was full of venom* **rancour**, malevolence, vitriol, spite, vindictiveness, malice, maliciousness, ill will, animosity, animus, bitterness, antagonism, hostility, bile, hate, hatred; informal bitchiness, cattiness.

venomous adj. **1** *a venomous snake | the spider's venomous bite* **poisonous**, toxic; dangerous, deadly, lethal, fatal, mortal. **2** *venomous remarks* **vicious**, spiteful, rancorous, malevolent, vitriolic, vindictive, malicious, poisonous, virulent, bitter, acrimonious, antagonistic, hostile, cruel; informal bitchy, catty; literary malefic, maleficent.
– OPPOSITES harmless, benevolent.

vent n. *an air vent* **outlet**, **inlet**, opening, aperture, hole, gap, orifice, space; duct, flue, shaft, well, passage, airway.
▸ v. *the crowd vented their fury on the pitch* **let out**, give vent to, give free rein to, release, pour out, express, give expression to, air, voice, give voice to, ventilate.

ventilate v. **1** *the greenhouse must be properly ventilated* **air**, aerate, oxygenate, air-condition; freshen, cool. **2** *the workers ventilated their discontent* **express**, give expression to, air, communicate, voice, give voice to, verbalize, discuss, debate, talk over.

venture n. *a business venture* **enterprise**, undertaking, project, scheme, operation, endeavour, speculation, plunge, gamble, experiment.
▸ v. **1** *we ventured across the moor* **set out**, go, travel, journey. **2** *may I venture an opinion?* **put forward**, advance, proffer, offer, air, suggest, submit, propose, moot, ventilate. **3** *I ventured to ask her to come and dine with me* **dare**, make so bold as, presume; take the liberty of; informal stick one's neck out, go out on a limb.

veracious adj. formal See **truthful**.

verbal adj. **oral**, spoken, stated, said, verbalized; unwritten.

verbatim adv. **word for word**, letter for letter, line for line, to the letter, literally, exactly, precisely, closely, faithfully; formal literatim.

verbiage n. **verbosity**, padding, wordiness, prolixity, long-windedness; Brit. informal waffle.

verbose adj. **wordy**, loquacious, garrulous, talkative, voluble; long-winded, lengthy, prolix, tautological, pleonastic, periphrastic, circumlocutory, circuitous, discursive, digressive, rambling; informal mouthy, gabby; Brit. informal waffly, gobby.
– OPPOSITES succinct, laconic.

verbosity n. **wordiness**, loquacity, garrulity, talkativeness, volubility; long-windedness, lengthiness, verbiage, prolixity, tautology, circumlocution, discursiveness; Brit. informal waffle.

verdant adj. **green**, leafy, grassy; lush, rich; literary verdured, verdurous.

verdict n. **judgement**, adjudication, decision, finding, ruling, resolution, pronouncement, conclusion, opinion; Law determination.

verge n. 1 *the verge of the lake* **edge**, border, margin, side, brink, rim, lip; fringe, boundary, perimeter; literary bourn, marge, skirt. 2 *Spain was on the verge of an economic crisis* **brink**, threshold, edge, point.
▶ v. *a degree of caution that verged on the obsessive* **approach**, border on, be close/near to, be tantamount to; tend towards, approximate to, resemble.

verification n. **confirmation**, substantiation, proof, corroboration, support, attestation, validation, authentication, endorsement.

verify v. **substantiate**, confirm, prove, corroborate, back up, bear out, justify, support, uphold, attest to, testify to, validate, authenticate, endorse, certify.
– OPPOSITES refute.

vernacular n. 1 *he wrote in the vernacular to reach a wider audience* **everyday language**, colloquial language, conversational language, common parlance; dialect, regional language, regionalisms, patois; informal lingo, local lingo. 2 *informal the vernacular of today's youth* **language**, parlance; idiom, slang, jargon; informal lingo, -speak, -ese.

versatile adj. **adaptable**, flexible, all-round, multifaceted, multitalented, resourceful; adjustable, multi-purpose, all-purpose, handy.

verse n. 1 *Elizabethan verse* **poetry**, versification; poems, lyrics, balladry; literary poesy. 2 *a verse he'd composed to mark my anniversary* **poem**, lyric, ballad, sonnet, ode; limerick, rhyme, ditty. 3 *a poem with sixty verses* **stanza**, canto, couplet; strophe.
– OPPOSITES prose.

version n. 1 *his version of events* **account**, report, statement, description, record, story,

rendering, interpretation, explanation, understanding, reading, impression, side. 2 *the English version will be published next year* **edition**, translation, impression. 3 *they have replaced coal-burning fires with gas versions* **form**, sort, kind, type, variety, variant.

vertex n. **apex**, peak, tip, top.

vertical adj. **upright**, erect, perpendicular, plumb, straight up and down, on end, standing, upstanding, bolt upright, upended.
– OPPOSITES horizontal.

vertigo n. **dizziness**, giddiness, light-headedness, loss of balance; Veterinary Medicine sturdy.

verve n. **enthusiasm**, vigour, energy, pep, dynamism, go, elan, vitality, vivacity, buoyancy, liveliness, animation, zest, sparkle, spirit, ebullience, life, brio, gusto, eagerness, keenness, passion, zeal, relish, feeling, ardour, fire; informal zing, zip, vim, pizzazz, oomph.

very adv. *that's very kind of you* **extremely**, exceedingly, exceptionally, extraordinarily, tremendously, immensely, hugely, intensely, acutely, abundantly, singularly, uncommonly, unusually, decidedly, particularly, supremely, highly, remarkably, really, truly, mightily; informal terrifically, awfully, fearfully, terribly, devilishly, majorly, seriously, mega, ultra, damn, damned; Brit. informal ever so, well, hellish, dead, jolly; N. Amer. informal real, mighty, awful, darned; informal dated devilish, frightfully; old use exceeding.
– OPPOSITES slightly.
▶ adj. 1 *those were his very words* **exact**, actual, precise. 2 *the very thought of food made her feel ill* **mere**, simple, pure; sheer.

vessel n. 1 *a fishing vessel* **boat**, ship, craft, watercraft; literary barque. 2 *pour the mixture into a heatproof vessel* **container**, receptacle; basin, bowl, pan, pot; urn, cask, barrel, drum, butt, vat.

vest v. *executive power is vested in the President* **confer on**, entrust to, invest in, bestow on, grant to, give to; endow, lodge, lay, place.

vestibule n. **entrance hall**, hall, hallway, entrance, porch, portico, foyer, lobby, anteroom, antechamber, waiting room.

vestige n. 1 *the last vestiges of colonialism* **remnant**, fragment, relic, echo, indication, sign, trace, mark, legacy, reminder; remains. 2 *she showed no vestige of emotion* **bit**, touch, hint, suggestion, suspicion, shadow, scrap, tinge, speck, shred, jot, iota, whit, scintilla, glimmer; informal smidgen, tad.

vestigial adj. 1 *vestigial limbs* **rudimentary**, undeveloped; non-functional; Biology primitive. 2 *he felt a vestigial flicker of anger from last night* **remaining**, surviving, residual, leftover, lingering.

vestments plural n. **robes**, clothes, garments, attire, costume, garb, uniform, trappings, finery, regalia.

V

vet v. *press releases are vetted by an executive council* **check**, examine, scrutinize, investigate, inspect, look over, screen, assess, evaluate, appraise; informal check out.
▸ n. *I took the cat to the vet* **veterinary surgeon**, animal doctor, horse doctor; N. Amer. veterinarian; dated veterinary.

veteran n. *a veteran of 16 political campaigns* **old hand**, past master, doyen; informal old-timer, old stager, old warhorse.
– OPPOSITES novice.
▸ adj. *a veteran diplomat* **long-serving**, seasoned, old, hardened; adept, expert, well trained, practised, experienced; informal battle-scarred.

veto n. *parliament's right of veto* **rejection**, dismissal; prohibition, proscription, embargo, ban, interdict.
– OPPOSITES approval.
▸ v. *the president vetoed the bill* **reject**, turn down, throw out, dismiss; prohibit, forbid, interdict, proscribe, disallow, embargo, ban; informal kill, put the kibosh on, give the thumbs down to.
– OPPOSITES approve.

vex v. **annoy**, irritate, anger, infuriate, exasperate, irk, gall, pique, put out, antagonize, get on someone's nerves, ruffle someone's feathers, make someone's hackles rise; Brit. rub up the wrong way; informal aggravate, peeve, miff, rile, nettle, needle, get (to), bug, hack off, get up someone's nose, get someone's goat, get someone's back up, give someone the hump, get someone's dander up; Brit. informal wind up, nark, get on someone's wick; N. Amer. informal tee off, tick off, burn up, rankle; informal dated give someone the pip.

vexation n. **annoyance**, irritation, exasperation, indignation, anger, crossness, displeasure, pique, disgruntlement; informal aggravation.

vexatious adj. **annoying**, irritating, infuriating, exasperating, maddening, trying, tiresome, troublesome, bothersome, irksome, vexing, galling; informal aggravating, pesky.

vexed adj. **1** *a vexed expression* **annoyed**, irritated, cross, angry, infuriated, exasperated, irked, piqued, displeased, put out, disgruntled; informal aggravated, peeved, nettled, miffed, miffy, riled, hacked off, hot under the collar; Brit. informal narked, shirty, not best pleased; N. Amer. informal teed off, ticked off, sore, bent out of shape; old use wroth. **2** *the vexed issue of immigration* **disputed**, in dispute, contested, in contention, contentious, debated, at issue, controversial, moot; problematic, difficult, knotty, thorny.

viable adj. **feasible**, workable, practicable, practical, usable, possible, realistic, achievable, attainable, realizable; informal doable.
– OPPOSITES impracticable.

vibrant adj. **1** *a vibrant and passionate woman* **spirited**, lively, full of life, energetic,

vigorous, vital, full of vim and vigour, animated, sparkling, effervescent, vivacious, dynamic, stimulating, exciting, passionate, fiery; informal peppy, feisty. **2** *she was vibrant with excitement* **quivering**, trembling, shaking, shivering, shuddering, quavering, quaking. **3** *vibrant colours* **vivid**, bright, striking, brilliant, strong, rich. **4** *his vibrant voice* **resonant**, sonorous, reverberant, resounding, ringing, echoing; strong, rich, full.
– OPPOSITES lifeless, pale.

vibrate v. **1** *the floor beneath them vibrated* **quiver**, shake, tremble, shiver, shudder, judder, throb, pulsate; rock, oscillate, swing, sway, move to and fro. **2** *a low rumbling sound began to vibrate through the car* **reverberate**, resonate, resound, ring, echo.

vibration n. **tremor**, shaking, quivering, quaking, judder, juddering, shuddering, throb, throbbing, pulsation.

vicar n. **minister**, rector, priest, parson, clergyman, clergywoman, cleric, churchman, churchwoman, ecclesiastic, pastor, father, man/woman of the cloth, man/woman of God, curate, chaplain, preacher; Scottish kirkman; N. Amer. dominie; informal reverend, padre, Holy Joe, sky pilot; Austral. informal josser; dated divine.

vicarious adj. **indirect**, second-hand, secondary, derivative, derived, surrogate, substitute; empathetic, empathic.

vice n. **1** *youngsters may be driven to vice* **immorality**, wrongdoing, wickedness, badness, evil, iniquity, villainy, corruption, misconduct; sin, sinfulness, ungodliness; depravity, degeneracy, dissolution, dissipation, debauchery, decadence, lechery; crime, transgression; formal turpitude; old use trespass. **2** *smoking is my only vice* **shortcoming**, failing, flaw, fault, defect, weakness, deficiency, limitation, imperfection, blemish, foible, frailty.
– OPPOSITES virtue.

vice versa adv. **conversely**, inversely, contrariwise; reciprocally.

vicinity n. **1** *she lives in the vicinity* **neighbourhood**, surrounding area, locality, locale, (local) area, district, region, quarter, zone; environs, surroundings, precincts; N. Amer. vicinage; informal neck of the woods. **2** old use *the forest's vicinity to the dockyards.* See **proximity**.
▫ **in the vicinity of** around, about, nearly, circa, approaching, roughly, something like, more or less; in the region of, in the neighbourhood of, near to, close to; Brit. getting on for.

vicious adj. **1** *a vicious killer* **brutal**, ferocious, savage, violent, dangerous, ruthless, remorseless, merciless, heartless, callous, cruel, harsh, cold-blooded, inhuman, fierce, barbarous, barbaric, brutish, bloodthirsty, fiendish, sadistic, monstrous, murderous, homicidal. **2** *a vicious hate campaign* **malicious**, malevolent, malignant, malign, spiteful, vindictive, venomous,

poisonous, rancorous, mean, cruel, bitter, acrimonious, hostile, nasty; defamatory, slanderous; informal catty.
– OPPOSITES gentle, kindly.

vicissitude n. **change**, alteration, transition, shift, reversal, downturn; inconstancy, instability, uncertainty, unpredictability, chanciness, fickleness, variability, changeability, fluctuation, vacillation; ups and downs.

victim n. **1** *a victim of crime* **sufferer**, injured party, casualty; fatality, loss; loser. **2** *the victim of a confidence trick* **dupe**, stooge, gull, fool; target, prey, quarry, object, subject, focus, recipient; informal sucker, fall guy, chump, muggins, charlie; N. Amer. informal patsy, pigeon, sap. **3** *a sacrificial victim* **sacrifice**, (burnt) offering, scapegoat.
□ **fall victim to** fall ill with, be stricken with, catch, develop, contract, pick up; succumb to; informal go down with.

victimize v. **persecute**, pick on, push around, bully, abuse, discriminate against, ill-treat, mistreat, maltreat, terrorize; exploit, prey on, take advantage of, dupe, cheat, double-cross; informal get at, have it in for, give someone a hard time, hassle, lean on.

victor v. **winner**, champion, conqueror, vanquisher, hero; prizewinner, medallist; informal champ, top dog.
– OPPOSITES loser.

victorious adj. **triumphant**, conquering, vanquishing, winning, champion, successful, top, first.

victory n. **success**, triumph, conquest, win, favourable result, landslide, {game, set, and match}, coup; mastery, superiority, supremacy; informal walkover, thrashing, trouncing.
– OPPOSITES defeat.

victuals plural n. dated See **food** (sense 1).

vie v. **compete**, contend, contest, struggle, fight, battle, cross swords, lock horns, jockey; war, feud.

view n. **1** *the view from her flat* **outlook**, prospect, panorama, vista, scene, aspect, perspective, spectacle, sight; scenery, landscape. **2** *we agree with this view* **opinion**, point of view, viewpoint, belief, judgement, thinking, notion, idea, conviction, persuasion, attitude, feeling, sentiment, concept, hypothesis, theory; stance, standpoint, approach. **3** *the church came into view* **sight**, perspective, vision, visibility.
▶ v. **1** *they viewed the landscape* **look at**, eye, observe, gaze at, stare at, ogle, contemplate, regard, scan, survey, inspect, scrutinize; informal check out, get a load of, gawp at; Brit. informal clock; N. Amer. informal eyeball; literary espy, behold. **2** *the law was viewed as a last resort* **consider**, regard, look on, see, perceive, judge, deem, reckon.
□ **in view of** considering, bearing in mind, taking into account, on account of, in the light of, owing to, because of, as a result of.
on view on display, on exhibition, on show.

viewer n. **watcher**, spectator, onlooker, observer; (**viewers**) audience, crowd; literary beholder.

viewpoint n. See **view** (sense 2 of the noun).

vigilant adj. **watchful**, observant, attentive, alert, eagle-eyed, hawk-eyed, on the lookout, on one's toes, on the qui vive; wide awake, on one's guard, cautious, wary, circumspect, heedful, mindful; informal beady-eyed.
– OPPOSITES inattentive.

vigorous adj. **1** *the child was vigorous* **robust**, healthy, hale and hearty, strong, sturdy, fit; hardy, tough, athletic; bouncing, thriving, flourishing, blooming; energetic, lively, active, perky, spirited, vibrant, vital, zestful; informal peppy, bouncy, in the pink. **2** *a vigorous defence of policy* **strenuous**, powerful, forceful, spirited, mettlesome, determined, aggressive, eager, zealous, ardent, fervent, vehement, passionate; tough, blunt, hard-hitting; informal punchy.
– OPPOSITES weak, feeble.

vigorously adv. **strenuously**, strongly, powerfully, forcefully, energetically, heartily, with might and main, for dear life, for all one is worth, all out, fiercely, hard; informal like mad, like crazy; Brit. informal like billy-o.

vigour n. **robustness**, health, hardiness, strength, sturdiness, toughness; bloom, radiance, energy, life, vitality, verve, spirit; zeal, passion, determination, dynamism, zest, pep, drive; informal oomph, get-up-and-go; Brit. informal welly.
– OPPOSITES lethargy.

vile adj. **foul**, nasty, unpleasant, bad, disagreeable, horrid, horrible, dreadful, abominable, atrocious, offensive, obnoxious, odious, unsavoury, repulsive, disgusting, distasteful, loathsome, hateful, nauseating, sickening; disgraceful, appalling, shocking, sorry, shabby, shameful, dishonourable, execrable, heinous, abhorrent, deplorable, monstrous, wicked, evil, iniquitous, depraved, debased; contemptible, despicable, reprehensible; informal gross, rank, God-awful, low-down, lousy; Brit. informal beastly; old use scurvy.
– OPPOSITES pleasant.

vilify v. **disparage**, denigrate, defame, run down, revile, abuse, speak ill of, criticize, condemn; malign, slander, libel; N. Amer. slur; informal pull apart, lay into, slam, bad-mouth; Brit. informal rubbish, slate; Austral./NZ informal bag, monster; formal derogate, calumniate.
– OPPOSITES commend.

villain n. **criminal**, lawbreaker, offender, felon, convict, malefactor, miscreant, wrongdoer; gangster, gunman, thief, robber; rogue, scoundrel, reprobate, ruffian, hoodlum; Law malfeasant; informal crook, con, crim, baddy; dated cad, knave; old use blackguard.

villainous adj. **wicked**, evil, iniquitous, sinful, nefarious, vile, foul, monstrous, outrageous, atrocious, abominable,

reprehensible, hateful, odious, contemptible, horrible, heinous, egregious, diabolical, fiendish, vicious, murderous; criminal, illicit, unlawful, illegal, lawless; immoral, corrupt, degenerate, sordid, depraved, dishonourable, dishonest, unscrupulous, unprincipled; informal crooked, bent, low-down, dirty, shady; dated dastardly.
– OPPOSITES virtuous.

villainy n. wickedness, badness, evil, iniquity, wrongdoing, dishonesty, unscrupulousness, roguery, delinquency; crime, vice, criminality, lawlessness, lawbreaking, corruption; Law malfeasance; informal crookedness; formal turpitude; old use knavery.

vindicate v. 1 *he was vindicated by the jury* **acquit**, clear, absolve, exonerate; discharge, liberate, free, redeem; informal let off (the hook); formal exculpate. 2 *I had fully vindicated my request* **justify**, warrant, substantiate, ratify, authenticate, verify, confirm, corroborate, prove, defend, support, back, evidence, endorse.

vindictive adj. **vengeful**, revengeful, unforgiving, resentful, acrimonious, bitter; spiteful, mean, rancorous, venomous, malicious, malevolent, nasty, cruel, unkind; informal catty.
– OPPOSITES forgiving.

vintage n. 1 *1986 was a classic vintage* **year**. 2 *he lost a vintage through frost* **(grape) harvest**, crop, yield. 3 *furniture of Louis XV vintage* **period**, era, epoch, time, origin; genre, style, kind, sort, type.
▶ adj. 1 *vintage French wine* **high-quality**, quality, choice, select, superior, best. 2 *vintage motor vehicles* **classic**, ageless, timeless; old, antique, heritage, historic. 3 *his reaction was vintage Francis* **characteristic**, typical, pure.

violate v. 1 *this violates fundamental human rights* **contravene**, breach, infringe, break, transgress, overstep, disobey, defy, flout; disregard, ignore. 2 *the tomb was violated* **desecrate**, profane, defile, degrade, debase; damage, vandalize, deface, destroy. 3 *he drugged and then violated her* **rape**, assault, force oneself on, abuse, molest, interfere with; dated deflower, defile, dishonour, ruin; literary ravish.
– OPPOSITES respect.

violation n. 1 *a violation of human rights* **contravention**, breach, infringement, infraction, transgression, defiance; neglect. 2 *a violation of their private lives* **invasion**, breach, infraction; trespass, intrusion, encroachment. 3 *she was threatened with violation* **rape**, (sexual) assault, (sexual) abuse, molestation, interference; dated defloration, defilement, dishonour; old use ravishment.

violence n. 1 *police violence* **brutality**, brute force, ferocity, savagery, cruelty, sadism, barbarity, brutishness. 2 *the violence of the blow* **forcefulness**, force, power, strength, might, savagery, ferocity, brutality. 3 *the violence of his passion* **intensity**, severity, strength, force, vehemence, power, potency, fervency, ardency, ferocity, fury.

violent adj. 1 *a violent alcoholic* **brutal**, vicious, savage, rough, aggressive, threatening, fierce, wild, ferocious; barbarous, barbaric, thuggish, cut-throat, homicidal, murderous, cruel. 2 *a violent blow* **powerful**, forceful, hard, sharp, smart, strong, vigorous, mighty, hefty; savage, ferocious, brutal, vicious. 3 *violent jealousy* **intense**, extreme, strong, powerful, vehement, intemperate, unbridled, uncontrollable, ungovernable, inordinate, consuming, passionate.
– OPPOSITES gentle, weak, mild.

VIP n. celebrity, famous person, very important person, personality, big name, star, superstar; dignitary, luminary, worthy, grandee, lion, notable, notability, personage; informal heavyweight, celeb, bigwig, big shot, big cheese, nob, honcho, top dog, megastar; N. Amer. informal big wheel, (big) kahuna, high muckamuck.

virago n. harridan, shrew, dragon, termagant, vixen; fishwife, witch, hellcat, she-devil, tartar, martinet, spitfire, ogress; informal battleaxe; old use scold.

virgin n. *she remained a virgin* **chaste woman**, celibate; formal virgo intacta; literary maiden, maid, vestal.
▶ adj. 1 *virgin forest* **untouched**, unspoilt, untainted, immaculate, pristine, flawless; spotless, unsullied, unpolluted, undefiled, perfect; unchanged, intact; unexplored, uncharted, unmapped. 2 *virgin girls* **chaste**, virginal, celibate, abstinent; unmarried, unwed, maiden, maidenly; pure, uncorrupted, incorrupt, undefiled, unsullied, innocent; literary vestal.

virginal adj. See **virgin** (sense 2 of the adjective).

virginity n. chastity, maidenhood, honour, purity, innocence; celibacy, abstinence; informal cherry; old use virtue.

virile adj. manly, masculine, male; strong, tough, vigorous, robust, muscular, muscly, brawny, rugged, sturdy, husky; red-blooded, fertile; informal macho, laddish, butch, beefy, hunky.
– OPPOSITES effeminate.

virtual adj. effective, in effect, near (enough), essential, practical, to all intents and purposes; indirect, implied, implicit, unacknowledged, tacit.

virtually adv. almost, practically, nearly, close to, verging on, just about, as good as, essentially, to all intents and purposes, effectively, in effect, all but, more or less, as near as dammit; roughly, approximately; informal pretty much, pretty well.

virtue n. 1 *the simple virtue of peasant life* **goodness**, virtuousness, righteousness, morality, integrity, dignity, rectitude, honour, decency, respectability, nobility, worthiness, purity; principles, ethics. 2 *promptness was not one of his virtues* **good**

point, good quality, strong point, asset, forte, attribute, strength, talent. **3** *I can see no virtue in this* **merit**, advantage, benefit, usefulness, strength, efficacy.
– OPPOSITES vice, failing, disadvantage.
□ **by virtue of** because of, on account of, by dint of, by means of, by way of, via, through, as a result of, as a consequence of, on the strength of, owing to, thanks to, due to, by reason of.

virtuosity n. **skill**, skilfulness, mastery, expertise, prowess, proficiency, ability, aptitude; excellence, brilliance, talent, genius, artistry, flair, panache, finesse, wizardry; informal know-how.

virtuoso n. *the pianist is clearly a virtuoso* **genius**, expert, (past) master, maestro, artist, prodigy, marvel, adept, professional, doyen, veteran; star, champion; informal hotshot, wizard, pro, ace; Brit. informal dab hand.
– OPPOSITES duffer.
▸ adj. *a virtuoso violinist* **skilful**, expert, accomplished, masterly, master, consummate, proficient, talented, gifted, adept, able, good, competent, capable; impressive, outstanding, exceptional, magnificent, supreme, first-rate, brilliant, excellent; informal superb, mean, ace.
– OPPOSITES incompetent.

virtuous adj. **righteous**, good, moral, ethical, upright, upstanding, high-minded, principled, anti-corruption, exemplary; law-abiding, irreproachable, blameless, guiltless, unimpeachable, honest, honourable, reputable, decent, respectable, noble, worthy, meritorious; pure, whiter than white, saintly, angelic; informal squeaky clean.

virulent adj. **1** *virulent herbicides* **poisonous**, toxic, venomous, noxious, deadly, lethal, fatal, mortal, dangerous, harmful, injurious, pernicious, damaging, destructive; literary deathly, nocuous. **2** *a virulent epidemic* **infectious**, infective, contagious, communicable, transmittable, transmissible, spreading, pestilential; informal catching. **3** *a virulent attack on morals* **vitriolic**, malicious, malevolent, hostile, spiteful, venomous, vicious, vindictive, bitter, rancorous, acrimonious, scathing, caustic, withering, nasty, savage, harsh.
– OPPOSITES harmless, amicable.

viscous adj. **sticky**, gummy, gluey, adhesive, tacky, adherent, treacly, syrupy; glutinous, gelatinous, thick, viscid, mucous, mucoid, mucilaginous; informal gooey, gloopy; N. Amer. informal gloppy.

visible adj. **perceptible**, perceivable, seeable, observable, noticeable, detectable, discernible; in sight, in/on view, on display; evident, apparent, manifest, transparent, plain, clear, conspicuous, obvious, patent, unmistakable, unconcealed, undisguised, prominent, salient, striking, glaring.

vision n. **1** *her vision was blurred by tears* **eyesight**, sight, observation, (visual) perception; eyes; view, perspective. **2** *nightmarish visions of the dead*

apparition, spectre, phantom, ghost, wraith, manifestation; hallucination, illusion, mirage; informal spook; literary phantasm, shade. **3** *visions of a better future* **dream**, daydream, reverie; plan, hope; fantasy, pipe dream, delusion. **4** *his speech lacked vision* **imagination**, creativity, inventiveness, innovation, inspiration, intuition, perception, insight, foresight, prescience. **5** *Melissa was a vision in lilac* **beautiful sight**, feast for the eyes, pleasure to behold, delight, dream, beauty, picture, joy, marvel, sensation; informal sight for sore eyes, stunner, knockout, looker, peach; Brit. informal smasher.

> **WORD LINKS**
> **visual, optical** relating to vision

visionary adj. *a visionary leader* **inspired**, imaginative, creative, inventive, ingenious, enterprising, innovative; insightful, perceptive, intuitive, prescient, discerning, shrewd, wise, clever, resourceful; idealistic, romantic, quixotic, dreamy; informal starry-eyed.
▸ n. **1** *a visionary pictured him in hell* **seer**, mystic, oracle, prophet(ess), soothsayer, augur, diviner, clairvoyant, crystal-gazer; Scottish spaewife; literary sibyl. **2** *a visionary can't run a business effectively* **dreamer**, daydreamer, idealist, romantic, fantasist, utopian.

visit v. **1** *I visited my dear uncle* **call on**, pay a visit to, go to see, look in on; stay with, holiday with; stop by, drop by; N. Amer. visit with, go see; informal pop in on, drop in on, look up. **2** *Alex was visiting America* **stay in**, stop over in, spend time in, holiday in, vacation in; tour, explore, see; informal do. **3** *they were visited with many epidemics* **afflict**, attack, trouble, torment; old use smite.
▸ n. **1** *she paid a visit to her mum* **(social) call**. **2** *a visit to the museum* **trip to**, tour of, look round; stopover, stay; holiday, break, vacation; formal sojourn.

visitation n. **1** *the bishop's pastoral visitations* **(official) visit**, tour of inspection, survey, examination. **2** *a visitation from God* **apparition**, vision, appearance, manifestation, materialization. **3** *Jehovah punished them by visitations* **affliction**, scourge, bane, curse, plague, blight, disaster, tragedy, catastrophe; punishment, retribution, vengeance.

visitor n. **1** *I am expecting a visitor* **guest**, caller; company; old use visitant. **2** *the monument attracts foreign visitors* **tourist**, traveller, holidaymaker, day tripper, tripper, vacationer, vacationist, sightseer; pilgrim; foreigner, outsider, stranger, alien; Brit. informal emmet, grockle.

vista n. **view**, prospect, panorama, aspect, perspective, spectacle, sight; scenery, landscape.

visual adj. **1** *visual defects* **optical**, optic, ocular, eye; vision, sight. **2** *a visual indication that the alarm works* **visible**, perceptible, perceivable, discernible.

V

visualize v. **envisage**, envision, conjure up, picture, call to mind, see, imagine, evoke, dream up, fantasize about, conceptualize, contemplate.

vital adj. **1** *it is vital that action is taken* **essential**, of the essence, critical, crucial, indispensable, all-important, imperative, mandatory, urgent, pressing, burning, compelling, high-priority; informal earth-shattering, world-shaking. **2** *the vital organs* **major**, main, chief; essential, necessary. **3** *he is young and vital* **lively**, energetic, active, sprightly, spry, spirited, vivacious, exuberant, bouncy, enthusiastic, vibrant, zestful, sparkling, dynamic, vigorous, lusty, hale and hearty; informal peppy, spunky, full of beans, bright-eyed and bushy-tailed.
– OPPOSITES unimportant, minor, listless.

vitality n. **liveliness**, life, energy, spirit, vivacity, exuberance, buoyancy, bounce, verve, vim, pep, brio, zest, sparkle, dynamism, passion, fire, vigour, drive; informal get-up-and-go.

vitriolic adj. **acrimonious**, rancorous, bitter, caustic, mordant, acerbic, trenchant, virulent, spiteful, savage, venomous, poisonous, malicious, splenetic; nasty, mean, cruel, unkind, harsh, vindictive, scathing, barbed, wounding, sharp, cutting, withering, sarcastic; informal bitchy, catty.

vituperate v. old use See **revile**.

vituperation n. **invective**, revilement, condemnation, opprobrium, scolding, criticism, disapprobation, fault-finding; blame, abuse, insults, vilification, denunciation, obloquy, denigration, disparagement, slander, libel, defamation, slurs, aspersions; vitriol, venom; informal flak; Brit. informal stick; formal castigation.
– OPPOSITES praise.

vivacious adj. **lively**, spirited, bubbly, ebullient, buoyant, sparkling, light-hearted, jaunty, merry, happy, jolly, cheery, cheerful, perky, sunny, breezy, enthusiastic, irrepressible, vibrant, vital, zestful, energetic, dynamic; informal peppy, bouncy, upbeat, chirpy; dated gay.
– OPPOSITES dull.

vivid adj. **1** *a vivid blue sea* **bright**, colourful, brilliant, radiant, vibrant, strong, bold, deep, intense, rich, warm. **2** *a vivid account of urban poverty* **graphic**, evocative, realistic, lifelike, faithful, authentic, clear, detailed, lucid, striking, arresting, impressive, colourful, rich, dramatic, lively, stimulating, interesting, fascinating, scintillating; memorable, powerful, stirring, moving, haunting.
– OPPOSITES dull, vague.

viz. adv. **namely**, that is to say, in other words, to wit, specifically; such as, as, like, for instance, for example; formal videlicet.

vocabulary n. **1** *she has an extensive vocabulary* **lexicon**, lexis. **2** *we listed the terms in a vocabulary* **wordbook**, dictionary, wordfinder, glossary, lexicon, thesaurus.

vocal adj. **1** *vocal sounds* **vocalized**, voiced, uttered, articulated, oral; spoken, said. **2** *a vocal critic of the government* **vociferous**, outspoken, forthright, plain-spoken, blunt, frank, candid, open; vehement, vigorous, emphatic, insistent, forceful, zealous, clamorous.

vocation n. **calling**, life's work, mission, purpose, function; profession, occupation, career, job, employment, trade, craft, business, line (of work), métier.

vociferous adj. See **vocal** (sense 2).

vogue n. *the skirt is enjoying a new vogue* **fashion**, trend, fad, fancy, craze, rage, enthusiasm, passion, obsession, mania; fashionableness, popularity, currency, favour; informal trendiness.
□ **in vogue** fashionable, voguish, stylish, modish, up to date, up to the minute, modern, current; prevalent, popular, in favour, in demand, sought-after, all the rage; chic, smart, le dernier cri; informal trendy, hip, cool, big, happening, now, in, with it; N. Amer. informal tony, kicky.

voice n. **1** *she lost her voice* **power of speech**. **2** *he gave voice to his anger* **expression**, utterance, verbalization, vocalization. **3** *the voice of the people* **opinion**, view, feeling, wish, desire, vote, input. **4** *a powerful voice for conservation* **mouthpiece**, representative, spokesperson, intermediary; forum, vehicle, instrument, channel, organ, agent.
▶ v. *they voiced their opposition* **express**, vocalize, communicate, declare, state, assert, reveal, proclaim, announce, table, air, ventilate, vent; utter, say, speak, articulate; informal come out with.

> **WORD LINKS**
>
> **vocal** relating to the human voice
> **register** a particular part of the range of a voice
> **falsetto** a high-pitched voice above the normal range
> **inflection, intonation, lilt, modulation** variation in the tone or pitch of the voice
> **ventriloquist** an entertainer who seems to make their voice come from a dummy

void n. *the void of space* **vacuum**, emptiness, nothingness, blankness, vacuity; (empty) space, gap, cavity, chasm, abyss, gulf, pit.
▶ v. **1** *the contract was voided* **invalidate**, annul, nullify; negate, quash, cancel, countermand, repeal, revoke, rescind, retract, withdraw, reverse, undo, abolish; Law vacate; formal abrogate. **2** *they voided their bladders* **evacuate**, empty, drain, clear, purge. **3** *bacteria are voided in the urine* **eject**, expel, emit, discharge, pass, excrete, exude, eliminate.
– OPPOSITES validate, fill.
▶ adj. **1** *vast void spaces* **empty**, vacant, blank, bare, clear, free, unfilled, unoccupied, uninhabited. **2** *a country void of man or beast* **devoid of**, empty of, vacant of, bereft of, free from; lacking, wanting, without. **3** *the election was void* **invalid**, null, ineffective, non-viable, useless, worthless, nugatory.

V

– OPPOSITES full, occupied, valid.

volatile adj. **1** *a volatile personality* **unpredictable**, changeable, variable, inconstant, inconsistent, erratic, irregular, unstable, turbulent, blowing hot and cold, varying, shifting, fluctuating, fluid, mutable; mercurial, capricious, whimsical, fickle, flighty, impulsive, temperamental, highly strung, excitable, emotional, fiery, moody, tempestuous. **2** *the atmosphere is too volatile for an election* **tense**, strained, fraught, uneasy, uncomfortable, charged, explosive, inflammatory, turbulent, nail-biting; Brit. informal dodgy. **3** *a volatile organic compound* **evaporative**, vaporous; explosive, inflammable; unstable, labile.
– OPPOSITES stable, calm.

volition n.
□ **of one's own volition** of one's own free will, of one's own accord, by choice, by preference; voluntarily, willingly, readily, freely, intentionally, consciously, deliberately, on purpose, purposely; gladly, with pleasure.

volley n. **barrage**, cannonade, battery, bombardment, salvo, fusillade; storm, hail, shower, deluge, torrent; historical broadside.

voluble adj. **talkative**, loquacious, garrulous, verbose, wordy, chatty, gossipy, effusive, gushing, forthcoming, conversational, communicative, expansive; articulate, fluent; informal mouthy, gabby, gassy, windy; Brit. informal able to talk the hind legs off a donkey, gobby.
– OPPOSITES taciturn.

volume n. **1** *a volume from the library* **book**, publication, tome, hardback, paperback, title; manual, almanac, compendium. **2** *a glass syringe of known volume* **capacity**, cubic measure, size, magnitude, mass, bulk, extent; dimensions, proportions, measurements. **3** *a huge volume of water* **quantity**, amount, proportion, measure, mass, bulk. **4** *she turned the volume down* **loudness**, sound, amplification.

voluminous adj. **capacious**, roomy, spacious, ample, full, big, large, generous; billowing, baggy, loose-fitting, boyfriend; formal commodious.

voluntarily adv. **of one's own free will**, of one's own accord, of one's own volition, by choice, by preference; willingly, readily, freely, intentionally, deliberately, on purpose, purposely, spontaneously; gladly, with pleasure.

voluntary adj. **1** *attendance is voluntary* **optional**, discretionary, elective, non-compulsory, volitional; Law permissive. **2** *voluntary work* **unpaid**, unsalaried, for free, without charge, for nothing; honorary, volunteer; Law pro bono (publico).
– OPPOSITES compulsory, paid.

volunteer v. **1** *I volunteered my services* **offer**, tender, proffer, put forward, put up, venture. **2** *he volunteered as a driver* **offer one's services**, present oneself, make oneself available.

▸ n. *each volunteer was tested three times* **subject**, participant, case, client, patient; informal guinea pig.

voluptuous adj. **1** *a voluptuous model* **curvaceous**, shapely, ample, buxom, full-figured, Junoesque, Rubenesque; seductive, alluring, sultry, sensuous, sexy; informal curvy, busty. **2** *she was voluptuous by nature* **hedonistic**, sybaritic, epicurean, pleasure-loving, self-indulgent; decadent, intemperate, immoderate, dissolute, sensual, licentious.
– OPPOSITES scrawny, ascetic.

vomit v. **1** *he needed to vomit* **be sick**, spew, fetch up; heave, retch, reach, gag; N. Amer. get sick; informal throw up, puke, chunder, chuck up, hurl; Brit. informal honk; Scottish informal boke; N. Amer. informal barf, upchuck. **2** *I vomited my breakfast* **regurgitate**, bring up, spew up, cough up; informal chuck up, throw up, puke; Brit. informal sick up; N. Amer. informal spit up. **3** *the printer is vomiting paper* **eject**, issue, emit, expel, discharge, disgorge, throw out, spew out, belch.

▸ n. *a coat stained with vomit* **sick**; informal chunder, puke, spew; N. Amer. informal barf; Medicine vomitus.

voracious adj. **insatiable**, unquenchable, unappeasable, prodigious, uncontrollable, compulsive, gluttonous, greedy, rapacious; enthusiastic, eager, keen, avid, desirous, hungry, ravenous; informal piggish.

vortex n. **whirlwind**, whirlpool, gyre, maelstrom, eddy, swirl.

vote n. **1** *a rigged vote* **ballot**, poll, election, referendum, plebiscite; show of hands. **2** *in 1918 women got the vote* **suffrage**, voting rights, franchise; voice, say.

▸ v. **1** *only half of them voted* **go to the polls**, cast one's vote. **2** *I vote we have one more game* **suggest**, propose, recommend, advocate, move, table, submit.
□ **vote someone in** elect, return, select, choose, pick, adopt, appoint, designate, opt for, plump for, decide on.

> **WORD LINKS**
>
> **psephology** the study of elections and voting
> **electorate** all the people entitled to vote
> **enfranchise** give someone the right to vote
> **abstain** formally choose not to vote
> **teller** a person appointed to count votes

vouch v.
□ **vouch for** attest to, confirm, affirm, verify, swear to, testify to, bear out, back up, support, stick up for, corroborate, substantiate, prove, uphold, give credence to, endorse, certify, warrant, validate.

voucher n. **coupon**, token, ticket, licence, permit, carnet, pass; chit, slip, stub, docket; Brit. informal chitty; N. Amer. informal ducat, comp.

vouchsafe v. **1** *the grace which God had vouchsafed him* **grant**, give, accord; confer on, bestow on, favour with. **2** *you never vouchsafed that information before* **disclose**, reveal, divulge, impart, give away, make known, broadcast, air; informal blab, spill;

V

Brit. informal cough. **3** *if he would only vouchsafe to talk with them* **deign**, condescend, stoop, lower oneself, humble oneself, demean oneself.
– OPPOSITES withhold, conceal.

vow n. *a vow of silence* **oath**, pledge, promise, bond, covenant, commitment, avowal, profession, affirmation, attestation, assurance, guarantee; word (of honour); formal troth.
▸ v. *I vowed to do better* **swear**, pledge, promise, avow, undertake, engage, make a commitment, give one's word, guarantee; old use plight.

> **WORD LINKS**
> **votive** offered in fulfilment of a vow
> **votary** a person who has taken vows to dedicate their life to God

voyage n. *the voyage lasted 120 days* **journey**, trip, expedition, excursion, tour; hike, trek; pilgrimage, quest, crusade, odyssey; cruise, passage, flight, drive.
▸ v. *he voyaged through Peru* **travel**, journey, tour, globetrot; sail, steam, cruise, fly, drive; informal gallivant; old use peregrinate.

vulgar adj. **1** *a vulgar joke* **rude**, indecent, indelicate, offensive, distasteful, coarse, crude, ribald, risqué, naughty, suggestive, racy, earthy, off colour, bawdy, obscene, lewd, salacious, smutty, dirty, filthy, pornographic, X-rated; informal sleazy, raunchy, blue, locker-room; Brit. informal saucy, close to the bone; N. Amer. informal gamy; euphemistic adult. **2** *the decor was lavish but vulgar* **tasteless**, crass, tawdry, ostentatious, flamboyant, overdone, showy, gaudy, garish, brassy, kitsch, tinselly, loud; informal flash, flashy, tacky, over the top. **3** *it was vulgar for a woman to whistle* **impolite**, ill-mannered, unmannerly, indecorous, unseemly, ill-bred, boorish, uncouth, crude, rough; unsophisticated, unrefined, common.
– OPPOSITES tasteful, decorous.

vulnerable adj. **1** *a vulnerable city* **in danger**, in peril, in jeopardy, at risk, endangered, unsafe, unprotected, unguarded; open to attack, assailable, exposed, wide open; undefended, unfortified, unarmed, defenceless, helpless, pregnable. **2** *he is vulnerable to criticism* **exposed to**, open to, liable to, prone to, prey to, susceptible to, subject to, an easy target for; old use susceptive of.
– OPPOSITES resilient.

v

Ww

wacky adj. informal See **eccentric** (adjective).

wad n. **1** *a wad of cotton wool* **lump**, clump, mass, plug, pad, hunk, wedge, ball, cake, nugget; bit, piece; Brit. informal wodge. **2** *a wad of dollar bills* **bundle**, roll, pile, stack, sheaf; N. Amer. bankroll. **3** *a wad of tobacco* **quid**, twist, plug, chew.
▶v. *the teddy bear was wadded with cotton stuff*, pad, fill, pack; wrap, cover, cushion.

wadding n. **stuffing**, filling, filler, packing, padding, cushioning, quilting.

waddle v. **toddle**, dodder, totter, wobble, shuffle; duckwalk.

wade v. **1** *they waded in the icy water* **paddle**, wallow, dabble, squelch; informal splosh. **2** *I had to wade through some hefty documents* **plough**, plod, trawl, labour, toil; study, browse; informal slog.

waffle Brit. informal v. *they waffled on about the baby* **prattle**, chatter, babble, ramble, jabber, gibber, gabble, prate, drivel; informal blather; Brit. informal rabbit, witter, natter.
▶n. *my panic reduced the interview to waffle* **prattle**, drivel, nonsense, twaddle, gibberish, mumbo jumbo; informal hot air, poppycock, bunk, hogwash, gobbledegook.

waft v. **1** *smoke wafted through the air* **drift**, float, glide, whirl, travel. **2** *a breeze wafted the smell towards us* **convey**, carry, transport, bear; blow, puff.

wag¹ v. **1** *the dog's tail wagged frantically* **swing**, swish, switch, sway, shake, quiver, twitch, whip; informal waggle. **2** *he wagged his stick at them* **shake**, wave, wiggle, flourish, brandish.
▶n. **1** *a feeble wag of her tail* **swing**, shake, swish, switch, quiver, twitch, whip; informal waggle. **2** *a wag of the finger* **shake**, flourish, wiggle, wobble, wave; informal waggle.

wag² n. informal *he's a bit of a wag.* See **joker**.

wage n. **1** *the farmworkers' wages* **pay**, payment, remuneration, salary, stipend, fee, honorarium; income, revenue; profit, gain, reward; earnings; formal emolument. **2** *the wages of sin is death* **reward**, recompense, retribution; returns, deserts.
▶v. *they waged war on the guerrillas* **engage in**, carry on, conduct, execute, pursue, prosecute, proceed with.

wager n. *a wager of £100* **bet**, gamble, speculation; stake, pledge, ante; Brit. informal flutter.
▶v. *I'll wager a pound on the home team* **bet**, gamble, lay odds, put money on; stake,

pledge, risk, venture, hazard, chance; informal punt.

waggle v. & n. informal See **wag**¹.

waif n. **ragamuffin**, urchin; foundling, orphan, stray; derogatory guttersnipe; dated gamin.

wail n. *a wail of anguish* **howl**, bawl, yowl, cry, moan, groan; shriek, scream, yelp.
▶v. *the children began to wail* **howl**, weep, cry, sob, moan, groan, keen, lament, yowl, snivel, whimper, whine, bawl, shriek, scream, yelp, caterwaul; Scottish greet; informal blubber, blub.

wait v. **1** *we'll wait in the airport* **stay (put)**, remain, rest, stop, halt, pause; linger, loiter, dally; informal stick around; old use tarry. **2** *she had to wait until her bags arrived* **stand by**, hold back, bide one's time, hang fire, mark time, kill time, waste time, kick one's heels, twiddle one's thumbs; informal hold on, hang around, sit tight, hold one's horses. **3** *they were waiting for the kettle to boil* **await**; anticipate, expect, be ready. **4** *that job will have to wait* **be postponed**, be delayed, be put off, be deferred; informal be put on the back burner, be put on ice.
▶n. *a long wait* **delay**, hold-up, interval, interlude, intermission, pause, break, stay, cessation, suspension, stoppage, halt, interruption, lull, respite, recess, moratorium, hiatus, gap, rest.
□ **wait on someone** serve, attend to, cater for/to; minister to, take care of, look after, see to.

waiter, **waitress** n. **server**, stewardess, steward, attendant, garçon; hostess, host; butler, servant, page; N. Amer. waitperson.

waive v. **1** *he waived his right to a hearing* **relinquish**, renounce, give up, abandon, surrender, yield, reject, dispense with, abdicate, sacrifice, refuse, turn down, spurn. **2** *the manager waived the rules* **disregard**, ignore, overlook, set aside, forgo, drop.

wake¹ v. **1** *at 4.30 am Mark woke up* **awake**, waken (up), awaken, rouse oneself, stir, come to, come round, bestir oneself. **2** *she woke her husband* **rouse**, waken; Brit. informal knock up. **3** *the shock woke him up a bit* **activate**, stimulate, galvanize, enliven, stir up, spur on, ginger up, buoy up, invigorate, perk up, revitalize; informal pep up. **4** *they woke up to what we were saying* **realize**, become aware of, become conscious of, become mindful of. **5** *the name woke an old memory* **evoke**, conjure up, rouse,

stir, revive, awaken, rekindle, rejuvenate, stimulate.
– OPPOSITES sleep.
▸n. *a mourner at a wake* **vigil**, watch; funeral.
wake² n. *the cruiser's wake* **backwash**, wash, slipstream, turbulence; trail, path.
▫ **in the wake of** in the aftermath of, after, subsequent to, following, as a result of, as a consequence of, on account of, because of, owing to.
wakeful adj. **1** *he had been wakeful all night* **awake**, restless, restive, tossing and turning; old use watchful. **2** *I was suddenly wakeful* **alert**, watchful, vigilant, on the lookout, on one's guard, attentive, heedful, wary.
– OPPOSITES asleep, inattentive.
waken v. See **wake¹** (senses 1 & 2 of the verb).
walk v. **1** *they walked along the road* **stroll**, saunter, amble, trudge, plod, hike, tramp, trek, march, stride, troop, patrol, step out, wander, ramble, tread, prowl, footslog, promenade, roam, traipse; stretch one's legs; informal mosey, pootle, hoof it; Brit. informal yomp; formal perambulate. **2** *he walked her home* **accompany**, escort, guide, show, see, usher, take, chaperone, steer, shepherd.
▸n. **1** *country walks* **stroll**, saunter, amble, promenade; ramble, hike, tramp, march; turn, airing; dated constitutional. **2** *her elegant walk* **gait**, step, stride, tread. **3** *the riverside walk* **pathway**, path, footpath, track, walkway, promenade, footway, pavement, trail, towpath.
▫ **walk all over someone** informal *be firm or they'll walk all over you* take advantage of, impose on, exploit, use, abuse, misuse, manipulate, take liberties with; informal take for a ride, run rings around.
walk of life class, status, rank, caste, sphere, arena; profession, career, vocation, job, occupation, employment, business, trade, craft; province, field; dated station.
walk out 1 *he walked out in a temper* **leave**, depart, get up and go, storm off/out, flounce out, absent oneself; informal take off. **2** *teachers walked out in protest* **(go on) strike**, stop work; protest, mutiny, revolt; Brit. informal down tools.
walk out on someone desert, abandon, leave, betray, throw over, jilt, run out on, rat on; informal chuck, dump, ditch.
walker n. **hiker**, rambler, traveller, roamer, rover, stroller; pedestrian; literary wayfarer.
walkout n. **strike**, stoppage, industrial action; revolt, rebellion.
walkover n. **easy victory**, rout, landslide, {game, set, and match}; informal piece of cake, doddle, pushover, cinch, breeze, picnic, whitewash; N. Amer. informal duck soup; dated snip.
wall n. **1** *brick walls* **barrier**, partition, enclosure, screen, panel, separator. **2** *an ancient city wall* **fortification**, rampart, barricade, bulwark, stockade. **3** *break down the walls that stop world trade* **obstacle**, barrier, fence; impediment, hindrance, block, check.

▸v. **1** *tenements walled in the courtyard* **enclose**, bound, encircle, confine, hem, close in, shut in, fence in. **2** *the doorway had been walled up* **block**, seal, close, brick up.

WORD LINKS

buttress a projecting support built against a wall
cornice a moulding round the wall of a room, just below the ceiling
dado rail a waist-high moulding round the wall of a room
skirting a wooden board running along the base of an interior wall
wainscot, wainscoting wooden panelling on the lower part of the walls of a room
mural a picture painted directly on a wall
fresco a painting done on wet plaster on a wall or ceiling

---

wallet n. **purse**; N. Amer. billfold, pocketbook; Brit. dated notecase.
wallop v. informal See **thump** (sense 1 of the verb).
wallow v. **1** *buffalo wallowed in the lake* **loll about/around**, lie about/around, splash about/around; slosh, wade, paddle; informal splosh. **2** *a ship wallowing in stormy seas* **roll**, lurch, toss, plunge, reel, rock, flounder, keel, list; labour. **3** *she seems to wallow in self-pity* **luxuriate**, bask, take pleasure, take satisfaction, indulge (oneself), delight, revel, glory; enjoy, like, love, relish, savour; informal get a kick out of.
wan adj. **1** *she looked so wan and frail* **pale**, pallid, ashen, white, grey; anaemic, colourless, bloodless, waxen, chalky, pasty, peaky, sickly, washed out, drained, drawn, ghostly. **2** *the wan light of the moon* **dim**, faint, weak, feeble, pale, watery.
– OPPOSITES flushed, bright.
wand n. **baton**, stick, staff, bar, dowel, rod; twig, cane, birch, switch; historical caduceus.
wander v. **1** *I wandered around the estate* **stroll**, amble, saunter, walk, dawdle, potter, ramble, meander; roam, rove, range, drift, prowl; Scottish & Irish stravaig; informal traipse, mosey, tootle; Brit. informal mooch. **2** *we are wandering from the point* **stray**, depart, diverge, veer, swerve, deviate, digress, drift, get sidetracked. **3** *the child wandered off* **get lost**, lose one's way, go astray. **4** *the road wanders along the shore* **meander**, wind, twist, curve, zigzag, bend, snake.
▸n. *let's go for a wander* **stroll**, amble, saunter, walk, potter, ramble, prowl, promenade; turn, breather, airing; informal traipse, mosey, tootle; Brit. informal mooch; dated constitutional.
wanderer n. **traveller**, rambler, hiker, migrant, globetrotter, roamer, rover; itinerant, rolling stone, bird of passage, nomad; tramp, drifter, vagabond, vagrant; Brit. informal dosser; N. Amer. informal hobo, bum; literary wayfarer.
wane v. **1** *the moon is waning* **decrease**, diminish, dwindle. **2** *their support was waning* **decline**, diminish, decrease, dwindle, shrink, tail off, ebb, fade (away), lessen, peter out, fall off, recede, slump, flag, weaken, give way, wither, evaporate, die out;

literary evanesce.

– OPPOSITES wax, grow.

□ **on the wane** declining, decreasing, diminishing, dwindling, shrinking, contracting, tapering off, subsiding, ebbing, fading away, dissolving, petering out, winding down, falling off, on the way out, receding, flagging, melting away, crumbling, withering, disintegrating, evaporating, dying out.

wangle v. informal See **contrive**.

want v. **1** *do you want more coffee?* **desire**, wish for, hope for, fancy, care for, like; long for, yearn for, crave, hanker after, hunger for, thirst for, cry out for, covet; need; informal have a yen for, be dying for. **2** informal *his toaster wants repairing* **need**, require, demand, cry out for. **3** informal *you want to be more careful* **should**, ought, need, must.

▸ n. **1** *the want of vigilance* **lack**, absence, non-existence, unavailability; dearth, deficiency, inadequacy, insufficiency, paucity, shortage, scarcity, deficit. **2** *a time of want* **need**, neediness, austerity, privation, deprivation, poverty, impoverishment, penury, destitution; famine, drought. **3** *all her wants would be taken care of* **wish**, desire, demand, longing, yearning, fancy, craving, hankering; need, requirement; informal yen.

wanting adj. **1** *the defences were found wanting* **deficient**, inadequate, lacking, insufficient, imperfect, unacceptable, flawed, faulty, defective, unsound, substandard, inferior, second-rate, poor, shoddy; Brit. informal not much cop. **2** *the kneecap is wanting in amphibians* **absent**, missing, lacking, non-existent. **3** *millions were left wanting for food* **without**, lacking, deprived of, devoid of, bereft of, in need of; deficient in, short on; informal minus.

– OPPOSITES sufficient, present.

wanton adj. **1** *wanton destruction* **deliberate**, wilful, malicious, spiteful, wicked, cruel; gratuitous, unprovoked, motiveless, arbitrary, groundless, unjustifiable, needless, unnecessary, uncalled for, senseless, pointless, purposeless, meaningless, empty. **2** *a wanton seductress* **promiscuous**, immoral, immodest, indecent, shameless, unchaste, fast, impure, abandoned, lustful, lecherous, lascivious, libidinous, licentious, dissolute, debauched, degenerate, corrupt, whorish, disreputable; dated loose.

– OPPOSITES justifiable, chaste.

war n. **1** *the Napoleonic wars* **conflict**, warfare, combat, fighting, (military) action, bloodshed, struggle; battle, skirmish, fight, clash, engagement, encounter; offensive, attack, campaign; hostilities; jihad, crusade. **2** *the war against drugs* **campaign**, crusade, battle, fight, struggle, movement, drive.

– OPPOSITES peace.

▸ v. *rival emperors warred against each other* **fight**, battle, combat, wage war, take up arms; feud, quarrel, struggle, contend, wrangle, cross swords; attack, engage, take on, skirmish with.

WORD LINKS

martial relating to war

belligerent engaged in a war

combatant a person or nation fighting during a war

friendly fire weapon fire from one's own side that kills or injures one's own forces

collateral damage unintentional casualties or destruction in civilian areas during a war

armistice, ceasefire, truce an agreement to stop fighting for a time

reparations compensation for war damage paid by a defeated state

---

warble v. *larks warbled in the sky* **trill**, sing, chirp, chirrup, cheep, twitter, tweet, chatter, peep.

▸ n. *a warble pierced the air* **trill**, song, chirp, chirrup, chirr, cheep, twitter, tweet, chatter, peep, call.

ward n. **1** *the surgical ward* **room**, department, unit, area. **2** *the most marginal ward in Westminster* **district**, constituency, division, quarter, zone, parish. **3** *the boy is my ward* **dependant**, charge, protégé.

□ **ward someone off** fend off, repel, repulse, beat back, chase away; informal send packing.

ward something off 1 *she warded off the blow* **parry**, avert, deflect, block; evade, avoid, dodge. **2** *garlic is worn to ward off evil spirits* **rebuff**, avert, keep at bay, fend off, stave off, resist, prevent, obstruct, foil, frustrate, thwart, check, stop.

warden n. **1** *the flats have a resident warden* **superintendent**, caretaker, janitor, porter, custodian, watchman, concierge, doorman. **2** *a game warden* **ranger**, custodian, keeper, guardian, protector. **3** *he was handcuffed to a warden* **prison officer**, guard, jailer, warder, wardress, keeper, sentry; informal screw. **4** Brit. *the college warden* **principal**, head, governor, master, mistress, rector, provost, president, director, chancellor; N. Amer. informal prexy.

warder, wardress n. See **warden** (sense 3).

wardrobe n. **1** *she opened the wardrobe* **cupboard**, cabinet, locker; N. Amer. closet. **2** *her wardrobe has an outfit for every mood* **collection of clothes**; garments, attire, outfits; trousseau.

warehouse n. **storeroom**, storehouse, store, depot, depository, stockroom; magazine; granary; informal lock-up.

wares plural n. **merchandise**, goods, products, produce, stock, commodities, solutions; lines, range.

warfare n. **fighting**, war, combat, conflict, (military) action, hostilities; bloodshed, battles, skirmishes.

warlike adj. **aggressive**, belligerent, warring, bellicose, pugnacious, combative, bloodthirsty, jingoistic, sabre-rattling; hostile, threatening, quarrelsome; militaristic, militant; informal gung-ho.

warlock n. **sorcerer**, wizard, magus, (black) magician, enchanter; old use mage.

w

warm adj. **1** *a warm kitchen* **hot**, cosy, snug; informal toasty. **2** *a warm day in spring* **balmy**, summery, sultry, hot, mild, temperate; sunny, fine. **3** *warm water* **heated**, tepid, lukewarm. **4** *a warm sweater* **thick**, chunky, thermal, winter, woolly. **5** *a warm welcome* **friendly**, cordial, amiable, genial, kind, pleasant, fond; welcoming, hospitable, benevolent, benign, charitable; sincere, genuine, wholehearted, heartfelt, enthusiastic, eager, hearty. **6** informal *they haven't found it, but they're warm* **close**, near; informal hot.
– OPPOSITES cold, chilly, light, hostile.
▶ v. *warm the soup in that pan* **heat (up)**, reheat, cook; thaw (out), melt; N. Amer. warm over; informal zap; Brit. informal hot up.
– OPPOSITES chill.
□ **warm to/towards** *everyone warmed to him* like, take to, get on (well) with; informal hit it off with.
warm up limber up, loosen up, stretch, work out, exercise; prepare, rehearse.
warm someone up *the compère warmed up the crowd* enliven, liven, stimulate, animate, rouse, stir, excite; informal get going.

warm-blooded adj. **1** *mammals are warm-blooded* Zoology **homeothermic**, homeothermal. **2** *a warm-blooded woman* **passionate**, ardent, red-blooded, emotional, intense, impetuous, lively, spirited, fiery, tempestuous.
– OPPOSITES cold-blooded, reserved.

warmed-up adj. **1** *a warmed-up pasty* **reheated**; N. Amer. warmed-over. **2** *warmed-up ideas* **unoriginal**, derivative, imitative, uninspired; copied, plagiarized, rehashed; hackneyed, stale, tired, banal; informal old hat.
– OPPOSITES original.

warm-hearted adj. **kind**, warm, big-hearted, tender-hearted, tender, loving, caring, feeling, unselfish, selfless, benevolent, humane, good-natured; friendly, sympathetic, understanding, compassionate, charitable, generous.

warmonger n. **militarist**, hawk, jingoist, sabre-rattler, aggressor, belligerent.

warmth n. **1** *the warmth of the fire* **heat**, warmness, hotness; cosiness. **2** *the warmth of their welcome* **friendliness**, amiability, geniality, cordiality, kindness, tenderness, fondness; benevolence, charity; enthusiasm, eagerness, ardour, fervour, effusiveness.

warn v. **1** *David warned her that it was too late* **notify**, alert, apprise, inform, tell, make someone aware, forewarn, remind; informal tip off, put wise. **2** *police are warning galleries to be alert* **advise**, exhort, urge, counsel, caution.

warning n. **1** *the earthquake came without warning* **(advance) notice**, forewarning, alert; hint, signal, sign, alarm bells; informal a tip-off. **2** *a health warning* **caution**, notification, information; exhortation, injunction; advice. **3** *a warning of things to come* **omen**, premonition, foreboding, prophecy, prediction, forecast, token,

portent, signal, sign; literary foretoken. **4** *his sentence is a warning to other drunk drivers* **example**, deterrent, lesson, caution, exemplar, message, moral. **5** *a written warning* **admonition**, caution, remonstrance, reprimand, censure; informal dressing-down, talking-to, telling-off.

warp v. **1** *timber which is too dry will warp* **buckle**, twist, bend, distort, deform, misshape, malform, curve, bow, contort. **2** *he warped the mind of her child* **corrupt**, twist, pervert, deprave.
– OPPOSITES straighten.

warrant n. **1** *a warrant for his arrest* **authorization**, order, licence, permit, document; writ, summons, subpoena; mandate, decree, fiat, edict. **2** *a travel warrant* **voucher**, chit, slip, ticket, coupon, pass. **3** *there's no warrant for this assumption* **justification**, grounds, cause, rationale, basis, authority, licence, sanction, vindication.
▶ v. **1** *the charges warranted a severe sentence* **justify**, vindicate, call for, sanction, validate; permit, authorize; deserve, excuse, account for, legitimate; support, license, approve of; merit, qualify for, rate, be worthy of, be deserving of. **2** *we warrant that the texts do not infringe copyright* **guarantee**, affirm, swear, promise, vow, pledge, undertake, state, assert, declare, profess, attest; vouch, testify, bear witness; formal aver.

warranty n. **guarantee**, assurance, promise, commitment, undertaking, agreement.

warring adj. **opposing**, conflicting, at war, fighting, battling, quarrelling; competing, hostile, rival.

warrior n. **fighter**, soldier, serviceman, combatant.

wary adj. **1** *he was trained to be wary* **cautious**, careful, circumspect, on one's guard, chary, alert, on the lookout, on one's toes, on the qui vive; attentive, heedful, watchful, vigilant, observant; informal wide awake. **2** *we are wary of strangers* **suspicious**, chary, leery, careful, distrustful, mistrustful, sceptical, doubtful, dubious.
– OPPOSITES inattentive, trustful.

wash v. **1** *he washed in the bath* **clean oneself**, have a wash; bathe, bath, shower, soak, freshen up; formal perform one's ablutions; dated make one's toilet. **2** *she washed her hands* **clean**, cleanse, sponge, scrub, wipe, scour; shampoo, lather; sluice, swill, douse, swab, disinfect. **3** *she washed off the blood* **remove**, expunge, eradicate; sponge off, scrub off, wipe off, rinse off. **4** *the women were washing clothes* **launder**, clean, rinse; literary lave. **5** *waves washed against the hull* **splash**, lap, splosh, dash, break, beat, surge, ripple, roll. **6** *the wreckage was washed up downriver* **sweep**, carry, convey, transport; deposit. **7** *guilt washed over her* **affect**, rush through, surge through, course through, flood over, flow over. **8** *the stonework was washed with pastel paint* **paint**, colour, tint, shade, dye, stain;

coat, cover. **9** informal *this story just won't wash* **be accepted**, be acceptable, be plausible, be convincing, hold up, hold water, stand up, bear scrutiny.
– OPPOSITES dirty, soil.

▸ n. **1** *she needs a wash* **clean**, shower, dip, bath, soak; formal ablutions. **2** *that shirt should go in the wash* **laundry**, washing. **3** *antiseptic skin wash* **lotion**, salve, preparation, rinse, liquid; liniment, embrocation. **4** *the wash of a motor boat* **backwash**, wake, trail, path. **5** *the wash of the waves on the beach* **surge**, flow, swell, sweep, rise and fall, roll, splash. **6** *water thinned out the crayon into a wash* **paint**, stain, film.
□ **wash one's hands of** disown, renounce, reject, forswear, disavow, give up on, turn one's back on, cast aside, abandon; formal abjure.

washed out adj. **1** *a washed-out denim jacket* **faded**, bleached, decolorized, stonewashed; pale, light, drab, muted. **2** *he looked washed out after his exams* **exhausted**, tired, worn out, weary, fatigued, spent, drained, enervated, run down; informal all in, done in, dog-tired, bushed, beat, zonked; Brit. informal knackered; N. Amer. informal pooped, tuckered out.
– OPPOSITES bold, energetic.

washout n. informal See **failure** (sense 2).

waspish adj. **irritable**, touchy, testy, cross, snappish, cantankerous, splenetic, short-tempered, bad-tempered, moody, crotchety, crabby, ratty; informal grouchy.

waste v. **1** *he doesn't like to waste money* **squander**, misspend, misuse, fritter away, throw away, lavish, dissipate, throw around; informal blow, splurge. **2** *kids are wasting away in the streets* **grow weak**, grow thin, shrink, decline, wilt, fade, flag, deteriorate, degenerate, languish. **3** *the disease wasted his legs* **emaciate**, atrophy, wither, debilitate, shrivel, shrink, weaken, enfeeble. **4** N. Amer. informal *I saw them waste the guy.* See **murder** (sense 1 of the verb).
– OPPOSITES conserve, thrive.

▸ adj. **1** *waste material* **unwanted**, excess, superfluous, left over, spare, useless, worthless; unusable, unprofitable. **2** *waste ground* **uncultivated**, barren, desert, arid, bare; desolate, void, uninhabited, unpopulated; wild.

▸ n. **1** *a waste of money* **misuse**, misapplication, misemployment, abuse; extravagance, wastefulness, lavishness. **2** *household waste* **rubbish**, refuse, litter, debris, dross, junk, detritus, scrap; dregs, scraps; sewage, effluent; N. Amer. garbage, trash. **3** *the frozen wastes of the South Pole* **desert**, wasteland, wilderness, emptiness, wilds.
□ **lay waste** See **lay**¹.

wasted adj. **1** *a wasted effort* **squandered**, misspent, misdirected, misused, dissipated; pointless, useless, needless, unnecessary. **2** *a wasted opportunity* **missed**, lost, forfeited, neglected, squandered, bungled; informal down the drain. **3** *I'm wasted in this job* **underemployed**, underused, too good

for; neglected, forgotten, disregarded. **4** *his wasted legs* **emaciated**, atrophied, withered, shrivelled, weak, frail, shrunken, skeletal, rickety, scrawny, wizened. **5** informal *everybody at the party was wasted.* See **drunk** (adjective).

wasteful adj. **prodigal**, profligate, uneconomical, extravagant, lavish, excessive, imprudent, improvident; thriftless, spendthrift; needless, useless.
– OPPOSITES frugal.

wasteland n. **wilderness**, desert; wilds, wastes, badlands.

waster n. informal **idler**, loafer, good-for-nothing, ne'er-do-well, slob, lounger, shirker, sluggard, slug, laggard; informal loser, skiver, slacker, lazybones; N. Amer. informal bum; literary wastrel.

wastrel n. literary See **waster**.

watch v. **1** *she watched him as he spoke* **observe**, view, look at, eye, gaze at, stare at, gape at, peer at; contemplate, survey, keep an eye on; inspect, scrutinize, scan, examine, study, ogle, regard, mark; informal check out, get a load of, recce; N. Amer. informal eyeball; literary behold. **2** *he was being watched by the police* **spy on**, keep in sight, track, monitor, survey, follow, keep under surveillance; informal keep tabs on, stake out. **3** *will you watch the kids?* **look after**, mind, keep an eye on, take care of, supervise, tend, attend to; guard, safeguard, protect. **4** *we stayed to watch the boat* **guard**, protect, shield, defend, safeguard; cover, patrol, police. **5** *watch what you say* **be careful**, mind, be aware of, pay attention to, consider, pay heed to.
– OPPOSITES ignore, neglect.

▸ n. **1** *Bill looked at his watch* **timepiece**, chronometer; wristwatch, pocket watch, stopwatch. **2** *we kept watch on the yacht* **guard**, vigil, lookout, an eye; observation, surveillance, vigilance.
□ **watch out** be careful, be watchful, be on your guard, beware, be wary, be cautious, mind out, look out, pay attention, take heed, take care, keep an eye open/out, keep one's eyes peeled, be vigilant.

watchdog n. **1** *they use watchdogs to ward off trespassers* **guard dog**. **2** *a consumer watchdog* **ombudsman**, monitor, scrutineer, inspector, supervisor; custodian, guardian, protector.

watcher n. **onlooker**, spectator, observer, viewer, fly on the wall; witness, bystander; spy; informal rubberneck; literary beholder.

watchful adj. **observant**, alert, vigilant, attentive, awake, aware, heedful, sharp-eyed, eagle-eyed; on the lookout, on the qui vive, wary, cautious, careful, chary.

watchman n. **security guard**, custodian, warden; sentry, guard, patrolman, lookout, sentinel, scout, watch.

watchword n. **guiding principle**, motto, slogan, maxim, mantra, catchword, catchphrase, byword; informal buzzword.

w

water n. **1** *a glass of water* technical H$_2$O; dated Adam's ale. **2** *a house down by the water* sea, ocean; lake, river.
▶ v. **1** *water the plants* **sprinkle**, moisten, dampen, wet, spray, splash; soak, douse, souse, drench, saturate; hose (down). **2** *my mouth watered* **moisten**, become wet, leak; salivate.
□ **hold water** be tenable, ring true, bear scrutiny, make sense, stand up, hold up, be convincing, be plausible, be sound.
water something down 1 *staff had watered down the drinks* **dilute**, water, thin (out), weaken; adulterate, doctor, mix; informal cut. **2** *the proposals were watered down* **moderate**, temper, mitigate, tone down, soften, tame; understate, play down, soft-pedal.

> **WORD LINKS**
>
> **aquatic**, **aqueous** relating to water
> **aqueduct** a structure for carrying water across a valley
> **reservoir** a large lake used as a water supply
> **dowse**, **divine** search for undergound water with a divining rod
> **irrigate** supply water to land or crops
> **hydropathy**, **hydrotherapy** the treatment of illness through the use of water
> **hydrophilic** tending to mix with or dissolve in water
> **hydrophobic** tending to repel or fail to mix with water
> **hydrophobia** extreme fear of water, as a symptom of rabies
> **dehydration** the loss or removal of water

waterfall n. **cascade**, cataract, falls, rapids; N. English force.
waterproof adj. *a waterproof jacket* **watertight**, water-repellent, water-resistant, damp-proof; impermeable, impervious; rubberized, waxed.
▶ n. Brit. *she put on a waterproof* **raincoat**, anorak, oilskin, cagoule; Brit. mackintosh; Brit. informal mac.
watertight adj. **1** *a watertight plastic container* **impermeable**, impervious, (hermetically) sealed; waterproof, water-repellent, water-resistant, damp-proof. **2** *a watertight alibi* **indisputable**, unquestionable, incontrovertible, irrefutable, unassailable, impregnable; foolproof, sound, flawless, airtight, conclusive.
– OPPOSITES leaky, flawed.
watery adj. **1** *a watery discharge* **liquid**, fluid, aqueous; technical hydrous. **2** *a watery meadow* **wet**, damp, moist, sodden, soggy, squelchy, soft; saturated, waterlogged; boggy, marshy, swampy, miry, muddy. **3** *watery porridge* **thin**, runny, weak, sloppy, dilute, diluted; tasteless, flavourless, insipid, bland. **4** *the light was watery and grey* **pale**, wan, faint, weak, feeble; informal wishy-washy. **5** *watery eyes* **tearful**, moist, rheumy; informal teary, weepy; formal lachrymose.
– OPPOSITES dry, thick, bright.

wave v. **1** *he waved his flag furiously* **move up and down**, move to and fro, wag, shake, swish, sweep, swing, brandish, flourish, wield; flick, flutter; informal waggle. **2** *the grass waved in the breeze* **ripple**, flutter, undulate, stir, flap, sway, shake, quiver, move. **3** *the waiter waved them closer* **gesture**, gesticulate, signal, beckon, motion.
▶ n. **1** *she gave him a friendly wave* **gesture**, gesticulation; signal, sign, motion. **2** *he surfs the big waves* **breaker**, roller, comber, boomer, ripple, white horse; (**waves**) swell, surf, froth; Austral. bombora; old use billow. **3** *a wave of immigrants* **flow**, rush, surge, flood, stream, tide, deluge, spate. **4** *a wave of self-pity* **surge**, rush, stab, dart, upsurge; thrill, frisson; feeling. **5** *his hair grew in thick waves* **curl**, kink, corkscrew, twist, ringlet, coil. **6** *electromagnetic waves* vibration, oscillation, ripple.
□ **make waves** informal cause trouble, be disruptive, be troublesome; make an impression, get noticed.
wave something aside dismiss, reject, brush aside, shrug off, disregard, ignore, discount, play down; informal pooh-pooh.
wave someone/something down flag down, hail, stop, summon, call, accost.
waver v. **1** *the candlelight wavered in the draught* **flicker**, quiver, twinkle, glimmer, wink, blink. **2** *his voice wavered* **falter**, wobble, tremble, quaver. **3** *he wavered between the choices* **be undecided**, be irresolute, hesitate, dither, equivocate, vacillate, fluctuate; think twice, change one's mind, blow hot and cold; Brit. haver, hum and haw; informal shilly-shally, sit on the fence.
wavy adj. **curly**, curvy, curved, undulating, squiggly, rippled, crinkly, kinked, zigzag.
wax v. **1** *the moon is waxing* **get bigger**, increase, enlarge. **2** literary *price sensitivity is waxing* **increase**, grow, develop, rise, expand, escalate, intensify, spread, mushroom, snowball.
– OPPOSITES wane.
□ **wax lyrical** be enthusiastic, enthuse, rave, gush, get carried away.
waxen adj. **pallid**, pale, pasty, wan, ashen, colourless, anaemic, bloodless, washed out, white, grey, whitish, waxy, drained, sickly.
– OPPOSITES ruddy.
waxy adj. See **waxen**.
way n. **1** *a way of reducing the damage* **method**, process, procedure, technique, system; plan, strategy, scheme; means, mechanism, approach. **2** *she kissed him in her brisk way* **manner**, style, fashion, mode; modus operandi, MO. **3** *I've changed my ways* **practice**, habit, custom, policy, procedure, convention, routine, modus vivendi; trait, attribute, peculiarity, idiosyncrasy; conduct, behaviour, manner, style, nature, personality, temperament, disposition, character; formal wont. **4** *which way leads home?* **route**, course, direction; road, street, track, path. **5** *I'll go out the back way* **door**, gate, exit, entrance, entry; route. **6** *a short way downstream* **distance**, length, stretch,

w

journey; space, interval, span. **7** *April is a long way away* **time**, stretch, term, span, duration. **8** *a car coming the other way* **direction**, bearing, course, orientation, line, tack. **9** informal *what do they call it down your way?* **area**, region, district, neighbourhood, locality, locale; informal neck of the woods, parts; Brit. informal **manor**; N. Amer. informal **hood**, nabe. **10** *in some ways, he may be better off* **respect**, regard, aspect, facet, sense; detail, point, particular. **11** *the country is in a bad way* **state**, condition, situation, circumstances, position; predicament, plight; informal shape.
□ **by the way** incidentally, by the by, in passing, en passant.
give way 1 *the government gave way and passed the bill* **yield**, back down, surrender, concede defeat, give in, submit, succumb; acquiesce, agree, assent; informal throw in the towel/sponge, cave in. **2** *the door gave way* **collapse**, give, cave in, fall in, come apart, crumple. **3** *grief gave way to guilt* **be replaced by**, be succeeded by, be followed by, be supplanted by.
on the way coming, imminent, forthcoming, approaching, impending, close, near, on us; proceeding, en route, in transit.
wayfarer n. literary See **wanderer**.
waylay v. **1** *we were waylaid and robbed* **ambush**, hold up, attack, assail, rob; informal mug, stick up. **2** *several people waylaid her to chat* **accost**, detain, intercept, take aside, pounce on, importune; informal buttonhole.
way-out adj. informal **unconventional**, avant-garde, outlandish, eccentric, off-centre, quirky, unusual, bizarre, strange, peculiar, odd, uncommon; informal far out, offbeat, oddball, off the wall; Brit. informal **rum**.
– OPPOSITES ordinary.
wayward adj. **wilful**, headstrong, stubborn, obstinate, obdurate, perverse, contrary, disobedient, insubordinate, undisciplined; rebellious, defiant, uncooperative, recalcitrant, unruly, wild, unmanageable, erratic, difficult, impossible; formal refractory.
– OPPOSITES docile.

weak adj. **1** *they are too weak to move* **frail**, feeble, delicate, fragile; infirm, sick, sickly, debilitated, incapacitated, ailing, indisposed, decrepit; tired, fatigued, exhausted; informal weedy. **2** *bats have weak eyes* **inadequate**, poor, feeble; defective, faulty, deficient, imperfect, substandard. **3** *a weak excuse* **unconvincing**, untenable, tenuous, implausible, unsatisfactory, poor, inadequate, feeble, flimsy, lame, hollow; informal pathetic. **4** *I was too weak to be a rebel* **spineless**, craven, cowardly, pusillanimous, timid; irresolute, indecisive, ineffectual, inept, effete, meek, tame, ineffective, impotent, soft, faint-hearted; informal yellow, weak-kneed, gutless, chicken. **5** *a weak light* **dim**, pale, wan, faint, feeble, muted. **6** *a weak voice* **indistinct**, muffled, muted, hushed, faint, low. **7** *weak coffee* **watery**, diluted, dilute, watered down, thin, tasteless, flavourless, bland, insipid, wishy-washy. **8** *a weak smile* **unenthusiastic**, feeble, half-hearted, lame.
– OPPOSITES strong, powerful, convincing, resolute, bright, loud.
weaken v. **1** *the virus weakened him terribly* **enfeeble**, debilitate, incapacitate, sap, enervate, tire, exhaust, wear out; wither, cripple, disable. **2** *she tried to weaken the shock for him* **reduce**, decrease, diminish, lessen, moderate, temper, dilute, blunt, mitigate, soften. **3** *our morale weakened* **decrease**, dwindle, diminish, wane, ebb, subside, peter out, fizzle out, tail off, decline, falter. **4** *the move weakened her authority* **impair**, undermine, compromise; invalidate, negate, discredit.
weakling n. **milksop**, namby-pamby, coward, pushover; informal wimp, weed, sissy, drip, softie, doormat, chicken, yellow-belly, scaredy-cat; N. Amer. informal **wuss**, pussy.
weakness n. **1** *with old age came weakness* **frailty**, feebleness, enfeeblement, fragility, delicacy; infirmity, sickness, sickliness, debility, incapacity, indisposition, decrepitude; informal weediness. **2** *he has worked on his weaknesses* **fault**, flaw, defect, deficiency, weak point, failing, shortcoming, imperfection, Achilles' heel. **3** *a weakness for champagne* **fondness**, liking, partiality, preference, love, penchant, soft spot, predilection, inclination, taste, eye; enthusiasm, appetite. **4** *the President was accused of weakness* **timidity**, cravenness, cowardliness, pusillanimity; indecision, irresolution, ineffectuality, ineptitude, meekness, powerlessness, ineffectiveness, impotence. **5** *the weakness of this argument* **untenability**, implausibility, poverty, inadequacy, transparency; flimsiness, hollowness. **6** *the weakness of the sound* **indistinctness**, mutedness, faintness, feebleness, lowness; dimness, paleness.
weak-willed adj. **spineless**, weak, irresolute, indecisive; impressionable, persuadable, persuasible, submissive, unassertive, compliant, pusillanimous; informal wimpish, chicken.
weal n. **welt**, wound, lesion, swelling; scar, cicatrix, mark, blemish.
wealth n. **1** *a gentleman of wealth* **affluence**, prosperity, riches, means, substance, fortune; money, cash, lucre, capital, treasure, finance; assets, possessions, resources, funds; property, stock, reserves, securities, holdings; informal wherewithal, dough, bread. **2** *a wealth of information* **abundance**, profusion, plethora, mine, store, treasury, bounty, cornucopia; informal lot, load, heap, mass, mountain, stack, ton; Brit. informal shedload; formal plenitude.
– OPPOSITES poverty, dearth.

W

> **WORD LINKS**
>
> **Mammon** wealth seen as an evil or corrupting influence
> **El Dorado** a legendary place of great wealth
> **plutocrat** a person who is powerful because of their wealth

parvenu a person who has recently become wealthy.
See also **money**.

wealthy adj. **rich**, affluent, moneyed, well off, well-to-do, prosperous, comfortable, propertied; of substance; informal well heeled, rolling in it, in the money, made of money, filthy rich, stinking rich, loaded, flush, quids in.
– OPPOSITES poor.

wear v. **1** *he wore a suit* **dress in**, be clothed in, have on, sport; put on, don. **2** *Barbara wore a smile* **bear**, have (on one's face), show, display, exhibit; give, put on, assume. **3** *the bricks have been worn down* **erode**, abrade, rub away, grind away, wash away, crumble (away), wear down; corrode, eat away (at), dissolve. **4** *the tyres are wearing well* **last**, endure, hold up, bear up, prove durable. **5** *Brit. informal I've asked him twice, but he won't wear it* **allow**, permit, authorize, sanction, condone, indulge, agree to, approve of; put up with, take, stand, support; accept, stomach, swallow, tolerate, countenance; informal hack, abide; Brit. informal stick; formal brook; old use suffer.
▶ n. **1** *you won't get much wear out of that* **use**, wearing, service, utility, value; informal mileage. **2** *evening wear* **clothes**, clothing, garments, dress, attire, garb, wardrobe; informal get-up, gear, togs; Brit. informal kit, clobber; formal apparel; literary array. **3** *the varnish which will withstand wear* **damage**, friction, erosion, attrition, abrasion.
□ **wear something down** *he wore down her resistance* gradually overcome, slowly reduce, erode, wear away, exhaust, undermine.
wear off *the novelty soon wore off* fade, diminish, lessen, dwindle, decrease, wane, ebb, peter out, fizzle out, pall, disappear, vanish, run out.
wear on *the afternoon wore on* pass, elapse, proceed, advance, progress, go by, roll by, march on, slip by/away, fly by/past.
wear out deteriorate, become worn, wear thin, fray, become threadbare, wear through.
wear something out use up, consume, go through.
wear someone out fatigue, tire out, weary, exhaust, drain, sap, overtax, enervate, debilitate, jade, prostrate; informal whack, poop, shatter, frazzle, do in; Brit. informal knacker.

wearing adj. **tiring**, exhausting, wearying, wearisome, fatiguing, enervating, draining, sapping; demanding, exacting, taxing, arduous, gruelling, punishing, difficult, hard, tough, laborious, strenuous, rigorous.

wearisome adj. See **wearing**.

weary adj. **1** *he was weary after cycling* **tired**, worn out, exhausted, fatigued, sapped, dog-tired, spent, drained, prostrate, enervated; informal all in, done in, dead beat, ready to drop, bushed, worn to a frazzle, shattered; Brit. informal knackered, whacked; N. Amer. informal pooped, tuckered out. **2** *she was weary of*

the arguments **tired of**, bored by, sick of; informal fed up with. **3** *a weary journey* **tiring**, exhausting, wearying, fatiguing, enervating, draining, sapping, wearing, trying, demanding, taxing, arduous, gruelling, difficult, hard, tough.
– OPPOSITES fresh, keen, refreshing.
▶ v. **1** *she was wearied by her illness* **tire**, fatigue, wear out, overtire, exhaust, drain, sap, enervate, debilitate, enfeeble, prostrate; informal whack, bush, shatter, frazzle, poop, do in; Brit. informal knacker. **2** *don't risk wearying the reader* **bore**, tire; irk, irritate, exasperate. **3** *he wearied of the struggle* **tire of**, become bored by, sicken of; have had enough of; informal become fed up with.
– OPPOSITES refresh, interest.

wearying adj. See **wearing**.

weather n. *what's the weather like?* **meteorological conditions**, climate, atmospheric pressure, temperature; elements; forecast, outlook.
▶ v. *we weathered the recession* **survive**, come through, ride out, pull through; withstand, endure, rise above, surmount, overcome, resist; informal stick out.

weathered adj. **weather-beaten**, worn; tanned, bronzed; lined, creased, wrinkled, gnarled.

weave¹ v. **1** *flowers were woven into their hair* **entwine**, lace, twist, knit, intertwine, braid, plait. **2** *he weaves colourful plots* **invent**, make up, fabricate, construct, create, contrive, spin; tell, recount, relate.

weave² v. *he had to weave his way through the crowds* **thread**, wind, wend; dodge, zigzag.

web n. **1** *a spider's web* **mesh**, net, lattice, latticework, lacework, webbing; gauze, gossamer. **2** *a web of friendships* **network**, nexus, complex, set, chain.

wed v. **1** *they are old enough to wed* **marry**, get married, become husband and wife; informal tie the knot, walk down the aisle, get spliced, get hitched. **2** *he will wed his girlfriend* **marry**, take as one's wife/ husband, lead to the altar; informal make an honest woman of; old use espouse. **3** *she wedded the two forms of spirituality* **unite**, unify, join, combine, amalgamate, fuse, integrate, bond, merge.
– OPPOSITES divorce, separate.

wedded adj. **1** *wedded bliss* **married**, matrimonial, marital, conjugal, nuptial; Law spousal; literary connubial. **2** *he is wedded to his work* **dedicated to**, devoted to, attached to, fixated on, single-minded about.

wedding n. **marriage (service/rites)**, nuptials, union; old use espousal.

WORD LINKS
nuptial relating to a wedding

wedge n. **1** *the door was secured by a wedge* **tapered block**, chock, stop. **2** *a wedge of cheese* **triangle**, segment, slice, section; chunk, lump, slab, hunk, block, piece.
▶ v. *she wedged her case between two bags* **squeeze**, cram, jam, ram, force, push, shove;

W

informal **stuff, bung.**

wedlock n. **marriage,** (holy) matrimony, married state, union.

wee adj. Scottish **little,** small, tiny, minute, miniature, mini, compact, undersized, diminutive, dwarf, midget, infinitesimal, microscopic, nanoscopic, minuscule; informal teeny, teeny-weeny, itsy-bitsy, half-pint, dinky; Brit. informal titchy, diddy; N. Amer. informal little-bitty.
– OPPOSITES big.

weed v.
□ **weed something/someone out** isolate, separate out, sort out, sift out, winnow out, filter out, set apart, segregate; eliminate, get rid of, remove; informal lose.

weedy adj. informal **puny,** feeble, weak, frail, undersized, slight, skinny; informal pint-sized.

weekly adj. *weekly instalments* **once a week;** lasting a week; formal hebdomadal.
▶ adv. *the directors meet weekly* **once a week,** every week, each week, on a weekly basis; by the week, per week, a week.

weep v. *even the toughest soldiers wept* **cry,** shed tears, sob, snivel, whimper, whine, wail, bawl, keen; Scottish greet; informal boohoo, blub, blubber; Brit. informal grizzle.
▶ n. *you sit and have a weep* **cry,** sob, snivel, whimper, bawl; informal blub, blubber; Brit. informal grizzle.

weepy adj. informal **tearful,** close to tears, upset, distressed, sad, unhappy; in tears, crying, weeping, snivelling; informal teary; formal lachrymose.

weigh v. **1** *she weighs the vegetables* **measure the weight of,** put on the scales. **2** *he weighed 118 kg* **have a weight of,** tip the scales at. **3** *the situation weighed heavily on him.* See **weigh someone down** (sense 2). **4** *he has to weigh up the possibilities* **consider,** contemplate, think about, mull over, chew over, reflect on, ruminate about, muse on; assess, appraise, analyse, investigate, inquire into, look into, examine, review, explore, take stock of. **5** *they need to weigh benefit against risk* **balance,** evaluate, compare, juxtapose, contrast.
□ **weigh someone down 1** *my fishing gear weighed me down* **burden,** saddle, overload, overburden, encumber, hamper, handicap. **2** *the silence weighed me down* **oppress,** depress, lie heavy on, burden, cast down, hang over, gnaw at, prey on (one's mind); trouble, worry, bother, disturb, upset, haunt, nag, torment, afflict, plague.

weight n. **1** *the weight of the book* **heaviness,** mass, load, burden, pressure, force; poundage, tonnage. **2** *his recommendation will carry great weight* **influence,** force, leverage, sway, pull, importance, significance, consequence, value, substance, power, authority; informal clout. **3** *a weight off her mind* **burden,** load, millstone, albatross, encumbrance; trouble, worry, strain. **4** *the weight of the evidence is against him* **preponderance,** majority, bulk, body, lion's share, predominance; most, almost all.

weighty adj. **1** *a weighty tome* **heavy,** thick, bulky, hefty, cumbersome, ponderous. **2** *a weighty subject* **important,** significant, momentous, consequential, far-reaching, key, major, vital, critical, crucial; serious, grave, solemn. **3** *a weighty responsibility* **burdensome,** onerous, heavy, oppressive, taxing, troublesome. **4** *weighty arguments* **compelling,** cogent, strong, forceful, powerful, potent, effective, sound, valid, telling; impressive, persuasive, convincing, influential, authoritative.
– OPPOSITES light, trivial, weak.

weird adj. **1** *weird apparitions* **uncanny,** eerie, unnatural, supernatural, unearthly, other-worldly, ghostly, mysterious, strange, abnormal, unusual; Scottish eldritch; informal creepy, spooky, freaky. **2** informal *a weird sense of humour* **bizarre,** quirky, outlandish, eccentric, unconventional, unorthodox, idiosyncratic, surreal, crazy, peculiar, odd, strange, queer, freakish, zany, madcap, outré; informal wacky, freaky, way-out, offbeat, off the wall; Brit. informal rum; N. Amer. informal wacko.
– OPPOSITES normal, conventional.

weirdo n. informal See **eccentric** (noun).

welcome n. *a welcome from the vicar* **greeting,** salutation; reception, hospitality; the red carpet.
▶ v. **1** *welcome your guests in their own language* **greet,** salute, receive, meet, usher in. **2** *we welcomed their decision* **be pleased by,** be glad about, approve of, appreciate, embrace; informal give the thumbs up to.
▶ adj. *welcome news* **pleasing,** agreeable, encouraging, gratifying, heartening, promising, favourable, pleasant; gladly received, wanted, appreciated, popular, desirable.

weld v. **fuse,** bond, stick, join, attach, seal, splice, melt, solder.

welfare n. **1** *the welfare of children* **well-being,** health, comfort, security, safety, protection, prosperity, success, fortune; interest, good. **2** *we cannot claim welfare* **social security,** (state) benefit, public assistance; pension, credit, support; sick pay, unemployment benefit; Brit. informal the dole.

well[1] adv. **1** *please behave well* **satisfactorily,** nicely, correctly, properly, fittingly, suitably, appropriately. **2** *they get on well together* **harmoniously,** agreeably, pleasantly, nicely, happily, amicably, amiably, peaceably; informal famously. **3** *he plays the piano well* **skilfully,** ably, competently, proficiently, adeptly, deftly, expertly, admirably, excellently. **4** *treat your employees well* **decently,** fairly, kindly, generously, honestly. **5** *mix the ingredients well* **thoroughly,** completely, effectively, rigorously, carefully. **6** *I know her quite well* **intimately,** thoroughly, deeply, profoundly, personally. **7** *they studied the car market well* **carefully,** closely, attentively, rigorously, in depth, exhaustively, in detail,

W

meticulously, scrupulously, conscientiously, methodically, completely, comprehensively, fully, extensively. **8** *they speak well of him* **admiringly**, highly, approvingly, favourably, appreciatively, warmly, enthusiastically, glowingly. **9** *she makes enough money to live well* **comfortably**, in (the lap of) luxury, prosperously. **10** *you may well be right* **quite possibly**, conceivably, probably; undoubtedly, certainly, unquestionably. **11** *he is well over forty* **considerably**, very much, a great deal, substantially, easily, comfortably, significantly. **12** *she could well afford it* **easily**, comfortably, readily, effortlessly.
– OPPOSITES badly.
▸adj. **1** *she was completely well again* **healthy**, fine, fit, robust, strong, vigorous, blooming, thriving, hale and hearty, in good shape, in good condition, in good trim, in fine fettle; informal in the pink. **2** *all is not well* **satisfactory**, all right, fine, in order, as it should be, acceptable; informal OK, hunky-dory; N. Amer. & Austral./NZ informal jake; Brit. informal dated tickety-boo. **3** *it would be well to tell us in advance* **advisable**, sensible, prudent, politic, commonsensical, wise, judicious, expedient, recommended, advantageous, beneficial, profitable, desirable; a good idea.
– OPPOSITES unwell, unsatisfactory, inadvisable.
▫ **as well** too, also, in addition, additionally, into the bargain, besides, furthermore, moreover, to boot.
as well as together with, along with, besides, plus, and, with, on top of, not to mention, to say nothing of, let alone.

well² n. **1** *she drew water from the well* **borehole**, bore, spring, waterhole. **2** *he's a bottomless well of forgiveness* **source**, supply, fount, reservoir, mine, fund, treasury.
▸v. *tears welled up in her eyes* **flow**, spill, stream, run, rush, gush, roll, cascade, flood, spout; seep, trickle; burst, issue.

well advised adj. **wise**, prudent, sensible.

well balanced adj. See **balanced**

well behaved adj. **orderly**, obedient, disciplined, peaceable, docile, controlled, restrained, cooperative, compliant; mannerly, polite, civil, courteous, respectful, proper, decorous, refined, polished.
– OPPOSITES naughty.

well-being n. See **welfare** (sense 1).

well bred adj. **well brought up**, polite, civil, mannerly, courteous, respectful; ladylike, gentlemanly, genteel, cultivated, urbane, proper, refined, polished, well behaved.

well built adj. **sturdy**, strapping, brawny, burly, hefty, muscular, muscly, strong, rugged, lusty, Herculean; informal hunky, beefy, husky, hulking.
– OPPOSITES puny.

well dressed adj. **smart**, fashionable, stylish, chic, modish, elegant, neat, spruce, trim, dapper; N. Amer. trig; informal snazzy,

natty, snappy, sharp; N. Amer. informal spiffy, fly.
– OPPOSITES scruffy.

well founded adj. **justifiable**, justified, warranted, legitimate, defensible, valid, admissible, allowable, understandable, excusable, acceptable, reasonable, sensible, sound.
– OPPOSITES groundless.

well heeled adj. informal See **wealthy**.

well known adj. **1** *well-known principles* **familiar**, widely known, popular, common, everyday, established. **2** *a well-known family of architects* **famous**, famed, prominent, notable, renowned, distinguished, eminent, illustrious, celebrated, acclaimed, important.
– OPPOSITES obscure.

well mannered adj. **polite**, courteous, civil, mannerly, genteel, decorous, respectful, refined, polished, civilized, urbane, well bred.

well-nigh adv. **almost**, nearly, just about, more or less, practically, virtually, all but, as good as, nearing, approaching, nigh on; roughly, approximately; informal pretty much.

well off adj. **1** *her family's very well off.* See **well-to-do**. **2** *the prisoners were relatively well off* **fortunate**, lucky, comfortable; informal sitting pretty. **3** *the island is not well off for harbours* **well supplied with**, well stocked with, well furnished with, well equipped with.

well read adj. **knowledgeable**, well informed, well versed, erudite, scholarly, literate, educated, cultured, bookish, studious; dated lettered.
– OPPOSITES ignorant.

well spoken adj. **articulate**, nicely spoken; refined, polite; Brit. informal posh.

well-to-do adj. **wealthy**, rich, affluent, moneyed, well off, prosperous, comfortable, propertied; informal rolling in it, in the money, loaded, well heeled, flush, made of money, quids in, worth a packet, on easy street.

welter n. **confusion**, jumble, tangle, mess, hotchpotch, mishmash, mass.

wend v. **meander**, make one's way, wander, amble, stroll, saunter, drift, roam, swan, traipse, walk; journey, travel; informal mosey, tootle.

west adj. **western**, westerly, occidental.

wet adj. **1** *wet clothes* **damp**, moist, soaked, drenched, saturated, sopping, dripping, soggy; waterlogged, squelchy. **2** *it was cold and wet* **rainy**, raining, pouring, teeming, showery, drizzly, drizzling; damp. **3** *the paint is still wet* **sticky**, tacky; fresh. **4** *a wet mortar mix* **aqueous**, watery, sloppy. **5** Brit. informal *the cadets were a bit wet* **feeble**, silly, weak, foolish, inept, ineffectual, effete, soft, namby-pamby, timid, spiritless, cowardly, spineless; informal sissy, pathetic, drippy, wimpish, weedy, chicken; Brit. informal soppy.
– OPPOSITES dry, fine, brave.
▸v. *wet the clothes before ironing them* **dampen**, damp, moisten; sprinkle, spray, splash; soak, saturate, flood, douse, souse, drench.

w

– OPPOSITES dry.

▶ **n. 1** *the wet of his tears* **wetness**, damp, moisture, moistness, sogginess; wateriness. **2** *the race was held in the wet* **rain**, drizzle, precipitation; spray, dew, damp. **3** Brit. informal *come on, don't be such a wet* **namby-pamby**, weakling, milksop, Milquetoast, baby, coward; informal wimp, weed, drip, sissy, softie, chicken, scaredy-cat; Brit. informal big girl's blouse; N. Amer. informal pantywaist, pussy.

whack informal v. *she whacked him on the head.* See **strike** (sense 1 of the verb).

▶ **n. 1** *he got a whack with a stick.* See **blow²** (sense 1). **2** Brit. *everyone will get their whack.* See **share** (noun).

wharf n. **quay**, pier, dock, berth, landing, jetty; harbour, dockyard, marina.

wheedle v. **coax**, cajole, inveigle, induce, entice, charm, tempt, beguile, flatter, persuade, influence, win someone over, bring someone round, convince, prevail on, get round; informal sweet-talk, soft-soap.

wheel n. *a wagon wheel* disc, hoop, ring, circle.

▶ **v. 1** *she wheeled the trolley away* **push**, trundle, roll. **2** *the flock of doves wheeled round* **turn**, go round, circle, orbit.

wheeze v. *the illness left her wheezing* **breathe noisily**, gasp, whistle, hiss, rasp, croak, pant, cough.

▶ **n. 1** *she still had a slight wheeze* **rasp**, croak, whistle, hiss, pant, cough. **2** Brit. informal *I've thought of a brilliant wheeze.* See **ruse**.

whereabouts n. **location**, position, site, place, situation, spot, point, vicinity; home, address, locale, neighbourhood; bearings, orientation.

wherewithal n. **money**, cash, capital, finance(s), funds; resources, means, ability, capability; informal dough, bread, loot, the necessary, boodle, dibs, ducats; Brit. informal dosh, brass, lolly, readies; N. Amer. informal bucks; US informal greenbacks.

whet v. **1** *he whetted his knife on a stone* **sharpen**, hone, strop, grind, file. **2** *something to whet your appetite* **stimulate**, excite, arouse, rouse, kindle, trigger, spark, quicken, stir, inspire, animate, fuel, fire, activate, tempt, galvanize.

– OPPOSITES blunt.

whiff n. **1** *I caught a whiff of perfume* **faint smell**, trace, sniff, scent, odour, aroma. **2** Brit. informal *there's a terrible whiff in here* **stench**, stink, smell, reek; Brit. informal pong, niff, hum; Scottish informal guff; N. Amer. informal funk. **3** *the faintest whiff of irony* **trace**, hint, suggestion, impression, suspicion, soupçon, nuance, intimation, tinge, vein, shred, whisper, air, element, overtone. **4** *whiffs of smoke from the boiler* **puff**, gust, flurry, breath, draught, waft.

while n. *we chatted for a while* **time**, spell, stretch, stint, span, interval, period; duration, phase; Brit. informal patch.

▶ **v.** *tennis helped to while away the time* **pass**, spend, occupy, use up, kill.

whim n. **1** *she bought it on a whim* **impulse**, urge, notion, fancy, foible, caprice, conceit, vagary, crotchet, inclination. **2** *human whim* **capriciousness**, whimsy, caprice, volatility, fickleness, idiosyncrasy.

whimper v. *he was whimpering in pain* **whine**, cry, sob, moan, snivel, wail, groan; Brit. informal grizzle.

▶ **n.** *she gave a whimper of protest* **whine**, cry, sob, moan, bleat, wail, groan.

whimsical adj. **1** *a whimsical sense of humour* **fanciful**, playful, mischievous, waggish, quaint, curious, droll; eccentric, quirky, idiosyncratic, unconventional, outlandish, queer; informal offbeat, freaky. **2** *the whimsical arbitrariness of autocracy* **volatile**, capricious, fickle, changeable, unpredictable, variable, erratic, mercurial, mutable, inconstant, inconsistent, unstable, protean.

whine n. **1** *the dog gave a whine* **whimper**, cry, mewl, howl, yowl. **2** *the whine of the motor* **hum**, drone. **3** *a whine about the quality of service* **complaint**, grouse, grumble, murmur; informal gripe, moan, grouch, whinge, bellyache, beef.

▶ **v. 1** *a child was whining* **wail**, whimper, cry, mewl, moan, howl, yowl. **2** *the lift began to whine* **hum**, drone. **3** *he's always whining about something* **complain**, grouse, grouch, grumble, moan, carp, mutter, murmur; informal gripe, bellyache, whinge.

whinge informal v. *I whinged about the weather.* See **whine** (sense 3 of the verb).

▶ **n.** *his tale is one long whinge.* See **whine** (sense 3 of the noun).

whip n. *he would use a whip on his dogs* **lash**, scourge, strap, belt; historical cat-o'-nine-tails.

▶ **v. 1** *he whipped the boy* **flog**, scourge, flagellate, lash, strap, belt, thrash, beat, tan someone's hide. **2** *whip the cream* **whisk**, beat. **3** *he whipped his listeners into a frenzy* **rouse**, stir up, excite, galvanize, electrify, stimulate, inspire, fire up, get someone going, inflame, agitate, goad, provoke. **4** informal *he whipped round the corner.* See **dash** (sense 1 of the verb). **5** informal *then he whipped out a revolver* **pull**, whisk, snatch, pluck, jerk; informal yank; Scottish informal wheech. **6** Brit. informal *he whipped the necklace.* See **steal** (sense 1 of the verb).

whippersnapper n. informal **upstart**, stripling; informal pipsqueak, squirt; Brit. informal squit; N. Amer. informal snip.

whirl v. **1** *leaves whirled in eddies of wind* **rotate**, circle, wheel, turn, revolve, orbit, spin, twirl; Scottish informal birl. **2** *they whirled past* **hurry**, race, dash, rush, run, sprint, bolt, dart, gallop, career, charge, shoot, hurtle, hare, fly, speed, scurry; informal tear, belt, pelt, scoot; Brit. informal bomb; N. Amer. informal hightail it. **3** *his mind was whirling* **spin**, reel, swim.

▶ **n. 1** *a whirl of dust* **swirl**, flurry, eddy. **2** *the mad social whirl* **hurly-burly**, activity, bustle, rush, flurry, fuss, turmoil, merry-go-round; informal to-do. **3** *Laura's mind was in a whirl* **spin**, daze, stupor, muddle, jumble;

w

confusion; informal **dither**. **4** informal *go on, give it a whirl* **try**, test; informal go, shot, bash, stab.

whirlpool n. **1** *a river full of whirlpools* **eddy**, vortex, maelstrom; N. Amer. informal suckhole. **2** *the health club has a whirlpool* spa bath, hot tub; trademark jacuzzi.

whirlwind n. **1** *the building was hit by a whirlwind* **tornado**, hurricane, typhoon, cyclone, vortex; Austral. willy-willy; N. Amer. informal twister. **2** *a whirlwind of activity* **maelstrom**, welter, bedlam, mayhem, babel, swirl, tumult, hurly-burly, commotion, confusion; informal madhouse; N. Amer. three-ring circus.
▶ adj. *a whirlwind romance* **rapid**, lightning, headlong, impulsive, breakneck, meteoric, sudden, swift, fast, quick, speedy; informal quickie.

whisk v. **1** *the cable car will whisk you to the top* **speed**, hurry, rush, sweep, hurtle, shoot; Scottish informal wheech. **2** *she whisked the cloth away* **pull**, snatch, pluck, tug, jerk; informal whip, yank; Scottish informal wheech. **3** *he whisked out of sight* **dash**, rush, race, bolt, dart, gallop, career, charge, shoot, hurtle, hare, fly, speed, zoom, scurry, scuttle, scamper; informal tear, belt, pelt, scoot, zip, whip. **4** *horses whisk their tails* **flick**, twitch, wave. **5** *whisk the egg yolks* **whip**, beat, mix.
▶ n. **1** *the horse gave a whisk of its tail* **flick**, twitch, wave, sweep. **2** *blend the eggs with a whisk* **beater**, mixer, blender.

whisky n. the water of life; Irish & Scottish usquebaugh.

whisper v. **1** *Alison whispered in his ear* **murmur**, mutter, mumble, speak softly, breathe. **2** literary *the wind whispered in the grass* **rustle**, murmur, sigh, moan, whoosh, whir, swish, blow, breathe.
– OPPOSITES roar.
▶ n. **1** *she spoke in a whisper* **murmur**, mutter, mumble, low voice, undertone. **2** literary *the wind died to a whisper* **rustle**, murmur, sigh, whoosh, swish. **3** *I heard a whisper that he's left town* **rumour**, story, report, speculation, insinuation, suggestion, hint; informal buzz. **4** *not a whisper of interest.* See **whit**.

whit n. **scrap**, bit, speck, iota, jot, atom, crumb, shred, grain, mite, touch, trace, shadow, suggestion, whisper, suspicion, scintilla; informal smidgen, smidge.

white adj. **1** *a clean white bandage* **colourless**, unpigmented, bleached, natural; snowy, milky, chalky, ivory. **2** *her face was white with fear* **pale**, pallid, wan, ashen, bloodless, waxen, chalky, pasty, peaky, washed out, drained, drawn, ghostly, deathly. **3** *white hair* **snowy**, grey, silver, silvery, hoary, grizzled. **4** *a whiter than white government* **virtuous**, moral, ethical, good, righteous, honourable, reputable, wholesome, honest, upright, upstanding, irreproachable, decent, worthy, noble, blameless, spotless, impeccable, unsullied, unblemished, uncorrupted, untainted; informal squeaky clean.
– OPPOSITES black, flushed, immoral.

white-collar adj. **clerical**, professional, executive, salaried, office.

whiten v. **make white**, make pale, bleach, blanch, lighten, fade; Brit. Military blanco; old use white.

whitewash n. **1** *the report was a whitewash* **cover-up**, camouflage, deception, facade, veneer, pretext. **2** *a four-match whitewash* **walkover**, rout, landslide; informal pushover, cinch, breeze.
– OPPOSITES exposé.
▶ v. *don't whitewash what happened* **cover up**, sweep under the carpet, hush up, suppress, draw a veil over, conceal, veil, obscure, keep secret; gloss over, downplay, soft-pedal.
– OPPOSITES expose.

whittle v. **1** *he sat whittling a piece of wood* **pare**, shave, trim, carve, shape, model. **2** *his powers were whittled away* **erode**, wear away, eat away, reduce, diminish, undermine, weaken, subvert, compromise, impair, impede, hinder, cripple, disable, enfeeble, sap. **3** *the ten teams have been whittled down to six* **reduce**, cut down, cut back, prune, trim, slim down, pare down, shrink, decrease, diminish.

whole adj. **1** *the whole report* **entire**, complete, full, unabridged, uncut. **2** *a whole marble mantelpiece* **intact**, in one piece, unbroken; undamaged, flawless, faultless, unmarked, perfect.
– OPPOSITES incomplete.
▶ n. **1** *a single whole* **entity**, unit, body, discrete item, ensemble. **2** *the whole of the year* **all**, every part, the lot, the sum (total).
□ **on the whole** overall, all in all, all things considered, for the most part, in the main, in general, generally (speaking), as a (general) rule, by and large; normally, usually, more often than not, almost always, most of the time, typically, ordinarily.

wholehearted adj. **committed**, positive, emphatic, devoted, dedicated, enthusiastic, unshakeable, unswerving; unqualified, unreserved, without reservations, unconditional, unequivocal, unmitigated; complete, full, total, absolute.
– OPPOSITES half-hearted.

wholesale adv. *the images were removed wholesale* **extensively**, on a large scale, comprehensively; indiscriminately, without exception.
– OPPOSITES selectively.
▶ adj. *wholesale destruction* **extensive**, widespread, large-scale, wide-ranging, comprehensive, total, mass; indiscriminate.
– OPPOSITES partial.

wholesome adj. **1** *wholesome food* **healthy**, health-giving, healthful, good (for one), nutritious, nourishing; natural, uncontaminated, organic. **2** *wholesome fun* **moral**, ethical, good, clean, virtuous, pure, innocent, chaste; uplifting, edifying, proper, correct, decent; informal squeaky clean.

wholly adv. **1** *the measures were wholly inadequate* **completely**, totally, absolutely, entirely, fully, thoroughly, utterly, quite, perfectly, downright, in every respect, in all respects; informal one hundred per cent. **2** *they rely wholly on you* **exclusively**, only, solely, purely, alone.

whoop n. *whoops of delight* **shout**, cry, call, yell, roar, scream, shriek, screech, cheer; informal holler.

▸ v. *he whooped for joy* **shout**, cry, call, yell, roar, scream, shriek, screech, cheer; informal holler.

whopper n. informal **1** *what a whopper!* **monster**, brute, giant, colossus, mammoth, monstrosity; informal jumbo. **2** *Joseph's story is a whopper.* See **lie¹** (noun).

whopping adj. informal See **huge**.

whorehouse n. See **brothel**.

whorl n. **loop**, coil, hoop, ring, curl, twirl, twist, spiral, helix.

wicked adj. **1** *wicked deeds* **evil**, sinful, immoral, wrong, morally wrong, wrongful, bad, iniquitous, corrupt, black-hearted, base, mean, vile; villainous, nefarious, erring, foul, monstrous, shocking, outrageous, atrocious, abominable, reprehensible, hateful, detestable, despicable, odious, contemptible, horrible, heinous, egregious, execrable, fiendish, vicious, murderous, barbarous; criminal, illicit, unlawful, illegal, lawless, felonious, dishonest, unscrupulous; Law malfeasant; informal crooked; Brit. informal beastly; dated dastardly; rare peccable. **2** *the wind was wicked* **disagreeable**, unpleasant, foul, bad, nasty, irksome, troublesome, annoying, irritating, displeasing, hateful, detestable. **3** *a wicked sense of humour* **mischievous**, playful, naughty, impish, roguish, arch, puckish, cheeky. **4** informal *she makes wicked cakes.* See **excellent**.
– OPPOSITES virtuous.

wickedness n. **evildoing**, evil, sin, sinfulness, iniquity, vileness, baseness, badness, wrongdoing, dishonesty, unscrupulousness, roguery, villainy, viciousness, degeneracy, depravity, immorality, vice, corruption, corruptness, devilry, fiendishness; Law malfeasance; informal crookedness; formal turpitude.

wide adj. **1** *a wide river* **broad**, extensive, spacious, vast, spread out. **2** *their mouths were wide with shock* **fully open**, agape, wide open. **3** *a wide range of opinion* **comprehensive**, ample, broad, extensive, large, large-scale, wide-ranging, exhaustive, general, all-inclusive. **4** *his shot was wide* **off target**, off the mark, wide of the mark/target, inaccurate.
– OPPOSITES narrow.

▸ adv. **1** *he opened his eyes wide* **fully**, to the fullest/furthest extent, as far/much as possible. **2** *he shot wide* **off target**, wide of the mark/target, inaccurately.

wide awake adj. **fully awake**, conscious, sleepless, insomniac; old use watchful.
– OPPOSITES asleep.

wide-eyed adj. **1** *the whole class was wide-eyed* **staring in amazement**, goggle-eyed, open-mouthed, dumbstruck, amazed,

surprised, astonished, astounded, stunned, staggered; informal flabbergasted; Brit. informal gobsmacked. **2** *wide-eyed visitors* **innocent**, naive, impressionable, ingenuous, childlike, unsophisticated, credulous, trusting, unquestioning, gullible.

widen v. **1** *a proposal to widen the motorway* **broaden**, make/become wider, open up/out, expand, extend, enlarge. **2** *the Party must widen its support* **increase**, augment, boost, swell, enlarge.

wide open adj. **1** *his eyes were wide open* **fully open**, open wide, agape. **2** *the championship is wide open* **unpredictable**, uncertain, unsure, in the balance, up in the air; informal anyone's guess. **3** *they were wide open to attacks* **vulnerable**, exposed, unprotected, defenceless, undefended, at risk, in danger.

widespread adj. **general**, extensive, universal, common, global, worldwide, international, omnipresent, ubiquitous, across the board, predominant, prevalent, rife, broad, rampant, pervasive.
– OPPOSITES limited.

width n. **1** *the width of the river* **wideness**, breadth, broadness, thickness, span, diameter, girth. **2** *the width of experience required* **range**, breadth, compass, scope, span, scale, extent, extensiveness, comprehensiveness.
– OPPOSITES length, narrowness.

wield v. **1** *he was wielding a sword* **brandish**, flourish, wave, swing; use, employ, handle. **2** *he has wielded power since 1972* **exercise**, exert, hold, maintain, command, control.

wife n. **spouse**, partner, mate, consort, woman, helpmate, helpmeet, bride; informal old lady, wifey, better half, missus; Brit. informal other half, her indoors, trouble and strife.

> **WORD LINKS**
> **uxorial** relating to a wife
> **uxorious** very fond of one's wife
> **uxoricide** the killing of one's wife

wiggle v. **jiggle**, wriggle, twitch, shimmy, joggle, wag, wobble, shake, twist, squirm, writhe; informal waggle.

wild adj. **1** *wild animals* **untamed**, undomesticated, feral; fierce, ferocious, savage. **2** *wild flowers* **uncultivated**, native, indigenous. **3** *wild tribes* **primitive**, uncivilized, uncultured; savage, barbarous, barbaric. **4** *wild hill country* **uninhabited**, unpopulated, uncultivated; rugged, rough, inhospitable, desolate, barren. **5** *a wild night* **stormy**, squally, tempestuous, turbulent, boisterous. **6** *her wild black hair* **dishevelled**, tousled, tangled, windswept, untidy, unkempt; N. Amer. mussed up. **7** *wild behaviour* **uncontrolled**, unrestrained, out of control, undisciplined, unruly, rowdy, disorderly, riotous, attention-seeking. **8** *wild with excitement* **very excited**, delirious, in a frenzy; tumultuous, passionate, vehement, unrestrained. **9** informal *I was wild with jealousy* **distraught**, frantic, beside

W

oneself, in a frenzy, hysterical, deranged, berserk; informal mad, crazy. **10** informal *Hank went wild when he found out*. See **furious** (sense 1). **11** informal *his family weren't wild about me* **very keen**, very enthusiastic, enamoured, infatuated, smitten; informal crazy, mad, nutty, nuts. **12** *Bill's wild schemes* **madcap**, ridiculous, ludicrous, foolish, stupid, foolhardy, idiotic, absurd, silly, ill-considered, senseless, nonsensical, impractical, impracticable, unworkable; informal crazy, crackpot, cockeyed. **13** *a wild guess* **random**, arbitrary, haphazard, uninformed.
– OPPOSITES tame, cultivated, calm, disciplined.

wilderness n. **1** *the Siberian wilderness* **wilds**, wastes, inhospitable region; desert. **2** *a litter-strewn wilderness* **wasteland**.

wildlife n. **(wild) animals**, fauna.

wilds plural n. **remote areas**, wilderness; backwoods; N. Amer. backcountry, backland; Austral./NZ outback, bush, backblocks, booay; N. Amer. informal boondocks, tall timbers.

wiles plural n. **tricks**, ruses, ploys, schemes, dodges, manoeuvres, subterfuges, artifices; guile, artfulness, cunning, craftiness.

wilful adj. **1** *an act of wilful destruction* **deliberate**, intentional, done on purpose, premeditated, planned, conscious. **2** *a wilful child* **headstrong**, strong-willed, obstinate, stubborn, pig-headed, recalcitrant, uncooperative, obstreperous, ungovernable, unmanageable; Brit. informal bloody-minded, bolshie; N. Amer. informal balky; formal refractory; old use froward, contumacious.
– OPPOSITES accidental, amenable.

will[1] v. *accidents will happen* **have a tendency to**, are bound to, do.

will[2] n. **1** *the will to succeed* **determination**, will power, strength of character, resolution, resolve, resoluteness, single-mindedness, purposefulness, drive, commitment, dedication, doggedness, tenacity, tenaciousness, staying power. **2** *they stayed against their will* **desire**, wish, preference, inclination, intention, intent. **3** *God's will* **wish**, desire, decision, choice; decree, command. **4** *his father's will* **(last will and) testament**.
▸ v. **1** *do what you will* **want**, wish, please, see/think fit, think best, like, choose, prefer. **2** *God willed it* **decree**, order, ordain, command. **3** *she willed the money to her husband* **bequeath**, leave, hand down, pass on, settle on; Law devise.

> **WORD LINKS**
> **intestate** not having made a will before dying
> **testator** a person who has made a will
> **executor** a person appointed to carry out the terms of a will
> **probate** the official process of proving that a will is valid
> **codicil** a supplement to a will
> **bequest, legacy** something left in a will

willing adj. **1** *I'm willing to give it a try* **ready**, prepared, game, disposed, inclined,

of a mind, minded; happy, glad, pleased, agreeable, amenable. **2** *willing help* **readily given**, willingly given, ungrudging.
– OPPOSITES reluctant.

willingly adv. **voluntarily**, of one's own free will, of one's own accord; readily, without reluctance, ungrudgingly, cheerfully, happily, gladly, with pleasure.

willingness n. **readiness**, inclination, will, wish, desire.

willowy adj. **tall**, **slim**, slender, svelte, lissom, sylphlike, long-limbed, graceful, lithe; informal slinky.

will power n. See **will**[2] (sense 1 of the noun).

willy-nilly adv. **1** *cars were parked willy-nilly* **haphazardly**, at random, randomly. **2** *we are, willy-nilly, in a new situation* **whether one likes it or not**, of necessity; informal like it or lump it; formal perforce, nolens volens.

wilt v. **1** *the roses had begun to wilt* **droop**, sag, become limp, flop; wither, shrivel (up). **2** *wilting in the heat* **languish**, flag, droop, become listless. **3** *Shelley's happy mood wilted* **fade**, ebb, wane, evaporate, melt away.
– OPPOSITES flourish.

wily adj. **shrewd**, clever, sharp, sharp-witted, astute, canny, smart; crafty, cunning, artful, sly, scheming, calculating, devious; informal tricky, foxy; old use subtle.
– OPPOSITES naive.

wimp n. informal **coward**, namby-pamby, milksop, weakling; informal drip, sissy, weed, pansy, scaredy-cat, chicken; Brit. informal wet, mummy's boy, big girl's blouse; N. Amer. informal cupcake, pantywaist, wuss, pussy; Austral./NZ informal sook; old use poltroon.

win v. **1** *Steve won the race* **be the victor in**, be the winner of, come first in, take first prize in, triumph in, be successful in. **2** *she was determined to win* **come first**, be the winner, be victorious, carry/win the day, come out on top, succeed, triumph, prevail. **3** *he won a cash prize* **secure**, gain, collect, pick up, walk away/off with, carry off; informal land, net, bag, scoop. **4** *Ilona won his heart* **captivate**, steal.
– OPPOSITES lose.
▸ n. *a 3–0 win* **victory**, triumph, conquest.
– OPPOSITES defeat.
☐ **win someone round/over** persuade, talk round, convince, sway, prevail on.

wince v. *he winced at the pain* **grimace**, pull a face, flinch, blench, start.
▸ n. *a wince of pain* **grimace**, flinch, start.

winch n. *the winch was used to haul furniture into the building* **crane**, derrick, hoist, davit, windlass, tackle, block and tackle, lifting gear, hoisting gear, system of pulleys, sheave; Nautical sheerlegs.
▸ v. *the crew were winched to safety* **haul**, pull, drag, hoist, crane, lift, tug, heave, trail, draw, tow, manhandle.

wind[1] n. **1** *the trees were swaying in the wind* **breeze**, current of air; gale, hurricane; informal blow; literary zephyr. **2** *Jez got his wind back* **breath**; informal puff. **3** **flatulence**, gas; formal flatus.

W

□ **get wind of** informal hear about/of, learn of, find out about, be told about, be informed of; informal hear something on the grapevine.
in the wind on the way, coming, about to happen, in the offing, in the air, on the horizon, approaching, looming, brewing, afoot; informal on the cards.

> **WORD LINKS**
> **anemometer** an instrument for measuring wind speed
> **Beaufort scale** a scale for wind speed

wind² v. **1** *the road winds up the mountain* **twist (and turn)**, bend, curve, loop, zigzag, weave, snake. **2** *he wound a towel around his waist* **wrap**, furl, entwine, lace. **3** *Anne wound the wool into a ball* **coil**, roll, twist, twine.
□ **wind down 1** informal *he needed to wind down* **relax**, unwind, calm down, cool down/off, ease up/off, take it easy, rest, put one's feet up; informal chill (out), cool out; N. Amer. informal hang loose. **2** *the campaign was winding down* **draw to a close**, come to an end, tail off, slack(en) off, slow down.
wind something down bring to a close/end, wind up, close down.
wind up informal end up, finish up, find oneself, land up; informal fetch up.
wind someone up 1 Brit. informal *Katie was just winding me up* **tease**, make fun of, chaff; informal take the mickey out of, send up, rib, josh, kid, have on, pull someone's leg; N. Amer. informal pull someone's chain; Austral./NZ informal poke mullock at. **2** *David was winding him up on purpose* **annoy**, anger, irritate, exasperate, get on someone's nerves, provoke, goad; Brit. rub up the wrong way; informal aggravate, rile, niggle, bug, put someone's back up, get up someone's nose, hack off; Brit. informal nark; N. Amer. informal ride.
wind something up 1 *Richard wound up the meeting* **conclude**, bring to an end/close, end, terminate; informal wrap up. **2** *the company has been wound up* **close (down)**, dissolve, put into liquidation.

winded adj. **out of breath**, breathless, gasping for breath, panting, puffing, puffed out; informal out of puff.

windfall n. **bonanza**, jackpot, pennies from heaven.

winding n. *the windings of the stream* **twist**, turn, turning, bend, loop, curve, zigzag, meander.
▸ adj. *the winding country roads* **twisting and turning**, meandering, windy, twisty, bending, curving, zigzag, zigzagging, serpentine, sinuous, snaking.
– OPPOSITES straight.

windpipe n. **trachea**, pharynx; throat.

windswept adj. **1** *the windswept moors* **exposed**, bleak, bare, desolate. **2** *his windswept hair* **dishevelled**, tousled, wind-blown, unkempt, untidy; N. Amer. mussed up.

windy adj. **1** *a windy day* **breezy**, blowy, fresh, blustery, gusty; wild, stormy, squally, tempestuous, boisterous. **2** *a windy hillside*

windswept, exposed, open to the elements, bare, bleak. **3** informal *windy speeches*. See **long-winded**. **4** Brit. informal *she still felt a bit windy*. See **anxious** (sense 1).
– OPPOSITES still, sheltered.

wine n. informal plonk, vino, the grape; literary vintage.

> **WORD LINKS**
> **vinous** relating to wine
> **oenology** the study of wines
> **oenophile** a connoisseur of wines
> **viticulture** the cultivation of grape vines
> **vintner** a wine merchant
> **sommelier** a wine waiter

wing n. **1** *a bird's wings* literary pinion. **2** *the east wing of the house* **part**, section, side; annexe, extension; N. Amer. ell. **3** *the radical wing of the party* **faction**, camp, caucus, arm, branch, group, section, set, coterie, cabal.
▸ v. **1** *a seagull winged its way over the sea* **fly**, glide, soar. **2** *the bomb winged past* **hurtle**, speed, shoot, whizz, zoom, streak, fly. **3** *she was shot at and winged* **wound**, graze, hit.
□ **wing it** informal improvise, play it by ear, extemporize, ad lib; informal busk it.

wink v. **1** *he winked an eye at her* **blink**, flutter, bat. **2** *the diamond winked in the moonlight* **sparkle**, twinkle, flash, glitter, gleam, shine, scintillate.
▸ n. *a wink of light* **glimmer**, gleam, glint, flash, flicker, twinkle, sparkle.
□ **wink at** turn a blind eye to, close one's eyes to, ignore, overlook, disregard; connive at, condone, tolerate.

winkle v.
□ **winkle something out** worm out, prise out, dig out, extract, draw out, obtain, get.

winner n. **victor**, champion, conqueror, vanquisher, hero; medallist; Brit. victor ludorum; informal champ, top dog.
– OPPOSITES loser.

winning adj. **1** *the winning team will receive £5,000* **victorious**, successful, triumphant, vanquishing, conquering; first, top. **2** *a winning smile* **engaging**, charming, appealing, endearing, sweet, cute, winsome, attractive, pretty, prepossessing, fetching, lovely, adorable, delightful, disarming, captivating; dated taking.

winnings plural n. **prize money**, gains, prize, booty, spoils; proceeds, profits, takings, purse.

winnow v. **separate (out)**, divide, sort out, sift out, filter out; isolate, find, identify; remove, get rid of.

winsome adj. See **winning** (sense 2).

wintry adj. **1** *wintry weather* **bleak**, cold, chilly, chill, frosty, freezing, icy, snowy, arctic, glacial, bitter, raw; informal nippy; Brit. informal parky. **2** *a wintry smile* **unfriendly**, unwelcoming, cool, cold, frosty, frigid.
– OPPOSITES summery, warm.

wipe v. **1** *Beth wiped the table* **rub**, mop, sponge, swab; clean, dry, polish. **2** *he wiped the marks off the window* **rub off**, clean off, clear up, remove, get rid of, take off, erase,

w

efface. **3** *she wiped the memory from her mind* **obliterate**, expunge, erase, blot out, blank out.

▶ n. *he gave the table a wipe* **rub**, mop, sponge, swab; clean, polish.

□ **wipe someone/something out** destroy, annihilate, eradicate, eliminate; slaughter, massacre, kill, exterminate; demolish, raze to the ground; informal take out, zap; N. Amer. informal waste; literary slay.

wire n. **cable**, lead, flex.

wiry adj. **1** *a wiry man* **sinewy**, tough, athletic, strong; lean, spare, thin, stringy, skinny. **2** *wiry hair* **coarse**, rough, strong; curly, wavy.
– OPPOSITES flabby, smooth.

wisdom n. **1** *we questioned the wisdom of the decision* **sagacity**, intelligence, sense, common sense, shrewdness, astuteness, smartness, judiciousness, judgement, prudence, circumspection; logic, rationale, rationality, soundness, advisability. **2** *the wisdom of the East* **knowledge**, learning, erudition, scholarship, philosophy; lore.
– OPPOSITES folly.

wise adj. *a wise old man* **sage**, sagacious, intelligent, clever, learned, knowledgeable, enlightened; astute, smart, shrewd, sharp-witted, canny, knowing; sensible, prudent, discerning, judicious, perceptive, insightful, perspicacious; rational, logical, sound, sane; Brit. informal fly; formal sapient.
– OPPOSITES foolish.

□ **wise to** informal aware of, familiar with, acquainted with; formal cognizant of.

wisecrack n. informal **joke**, witticism, quip, jest, sally; pun, bon mot; informal crack, gag, funny, one-liner.

wish v. **1** *I wished for power* **desire**, want, hope for, covet, dream of, long for, yearn for, crave, hunger for, lust after; aspire to, set one's heart on, seek, fancy, hanker after; informal have a yen for, itch for; old use be desirous of. **2** *they can do as they wish* **want**, desire, feel inclined, feel like, care; choose, please, think fit. **3** *I wish you to send them a message* **want**, desire, require. **4** *I wished him farewell* **bid**.

▶ n. **1** *his wish to own a Mercedes* **desire**, longing, yearning, inclination, urge, whim, craving, hunger; hope, aspiration, aim, ambition, dream; informal hankering, yen, itch. **2** *her parents' wishes* **request**, requirement, bidding, instruction, direction, demand, order, command; want, desire; will; literary behest.

wishy-washy adj. **1** *he's so wishy-washy* **feeble**, ineffectual, weak, vapid, effete, spineless, limp, namby-pamby, spiritless, indecisive; informal wet, pathetic. **2** *wishy-washy soup* **watery**, weak, thin; tasteless, flavourless, insipid. **3** *a wishy-washy colour* **pale**, insipid, pallid, muted.
– OPPOSITES strong, tasty, vibrant.

wisp n. **strand**, tendril, lock; scrap, shred, thread.

wispy adj. **thin**, fine, feathery, flyaway.

wistful adj. *a long, wistful sigh* **nostalgic**, yearning, longing; plaintive, regretful, rueful, melancholy, mournful; pensive, reflective, contemplative.

wit n. **1** *he needed all his wits to escape* **intelligence**, shrewdness, astuteness, cleverness, canniness, (common) sense, wisdom, sagacity, judgement, acumen, insight; brains, mind; informal nous, gumption, savvy, horse sense; Brit. informal common; N. Amer. informal smarts. **2** *my sparkling wit* **wittiness**, humour, funniness, drollery; repartee, badinage, banter, wordplay; jokes, witticisms, quips, puns. **3** *she's such a wit* **comedian**, humorist, comic, joker, jokester; informal wag; informal dated card, caution.

witch n. **1** *the witch cast a spell* **sorceress**, enchantress, hex; Wiccan; old use pythoness. **2** informal *she's a right old witch* **hag**, crone, harpy, harridan, she-devil; informal battleaxe.

witchcraft n. **sorcery**, (black) magic, witching, witchery, wizardry, thaumaturgy, spells, incantations; Wicca; Irish pishogue.

witch doctor n. **medicine man**, medicine woman, shaman, healer.

with prep. **accompanied by**, escorted by; alongside, in addition to, as well as.

withdraw v. **1** *she withdrew her hand from his* **remove**, extract, pull out, take out; take back, take away. **2** *the ban on advertising was withdrawn* **abolish**, cancel, lift, set aside, end, stop, remove, reverse, revoke, rescind, repeal, annul, void. **3** *she withdrew the allegation* **retract**, take back, go back on, recant, disavow, disclaim, repudiate, renounce; back down, climb down, backtrack, row back, back-pedal, do a U-turn, eat one's words. **4** *the troops withdrew from the city* **leave**, pull out of, evacuate, quit, retreat from. **5** *his partner withdrew from the project* **pull out of**, back out of, bow out of; get cold feet. **6** *they withdrew to their rooms* **retire**, retreat, adjourn, decamp; leave, depart, absent oneself; formal repair; dated remove; literary betake oneself.
– OPPOSITES insert, introduce, deposit, enter.

withdrawal n. **1** *the withdrawal of subsidies* **removal**, abolition, cancellation, discontinuation, termination, elimination. **2** *the withdrawal of the troops* **departure**, pull-out, exit, exodus, evacuation, retreat.

withdrawn adj. **introverted**, quiet, unsociable, inhibited, uncommunicative, unforthcoming, reticent, reserved, retiring, private, reclusive; shy, timid; aloof; informal stand-offish.
– OPPOSITES outgoing.

wither v. **1** *the flowers withered in the sun* **shrivel (up)**, dry up; wilt, droop, go limp, fade, perish. **2** *the muscles in his leg withered* **waste (away)**, shrivel (up), shrink, atrophy. **3** *her confidence withered* **diminish**, dwindle, shrink, lessen, fade, ebb, wane; evaporate, disappear.
– OPPOSITES thrive, grow.

withering adj. **scornful**, contemptuous, scathing, stinging, devastating; humiliating,

mortifying.
– OPPOSITES admiring.

withhold v. **1** *he withheld important information* **hold back**, keep back, refuse to give; retain, hold on to; hide, conceal, keep secret; informal sit on. **2** *she could not withhold her tears* **suppress**, repress, hold back, fight back, choke back, control, check, restrain, contain.

within prep. **1** *within the prison walls* **inside**, in, enclosed by, surrounded by; within the bounds of, within the confines of. **2** *within a few hours* **in less than**, in under, after only.
– OPPOSITES outside.

without prep. **1** *thousands were without food* **lacking**, short of, deprived of, in need of, wanting, needing, requiring. **2** *I don't want to go without you* **unaccompanied by**, unescorted by; in the absence of.
– OPPOSITES with.

withstand v. **resist**, weather, survive, endure, cope with, stand, tolerate, bear, defy, brave, hold out against, bear up against; stand up to, face, confront.

witless adj. **foolish**, stupid, unintelligent, idiotic, brainless, mindless; fatuous, inane, half-baked, empty-headed, slow-witted; informal thick, birdbrained, pea-brained, dopey, dim, dim-witted, half-witted, dippy, lamebrained, wooden-headed; Brit. informal daft; Scottish & N. English informal glaikit.

witness n. **1** *witnesses claimed that he started the fight* **observer**, onlooker, eyewitness, spectator, viewer, watcher; bystander, passer-by. **2** *a whisky bottle was the only witness of his mood* **evidence**, indication, proof, testimony.
▸ v. **1** *who witnessed the incident?* **see**, observe, watch, view, notice, spot; be present at, attend; literary behold. **2** *the will is correctly witnessed* **countersign**, sign, endorse, validate; N. Amer. notarize. **3** *his writings witness an inner toughness* **attest to**, testify to, bear witness to, confirm, evidence, prove, verify, corroborate, substantiate; show, demonstrate, indicate, reveal, bespeak.

witter v. Brit. informal See **gabble** (verb).

witticism n. **joke**, quip, jest, pun, play on words, bon mot; informal one-liner, gag, funny, crack, wisecrack.

witty adj. **humorous**, amusing, droll, funny, comic, comical, chucklesome; jocular, facetious, waggish; sparkling, scintillating, entertaining; clever, quick-witted.

wizard n. **1** *the wizard cast a spell over them* **sorcerer**, warlock, magus, (black) magician, enchanter; old use mage. **2** *a financial wizard* **genius**, expert, master, virtuoso, maestro, marvel, wunderkind; informal hotshot, demon, whizz-kid, buff, pro, ace; Brit. informal dab hand; N. Amer. informal maven.

wizardry n. **sorcery**, witchcraft, witchery, witching, (black) magic, enchantment; spells, charms; Irish pishogue.

wizened adj. **wrinkled**, lined, creased, shrivelled (up), withered, weather-beaten, shrunken, gnarled.

wobble v. **1** *the table wobbled* **rock**, teeter, jiggle, sway, see-saw, shake. **2** *he wobbled across to the door* **teeter**, totter, stagger, lurch. **3** *her voice wobbled* **tremble**, shake, quiver, quaver, waver. **4** *for a few days the minister wobbled* **hesitate**, vacillate, waver, dither, shilly-shally, blow hot and cold; Scottish swither.
▸ n. **1** *she stood up with a wobble* **totter**, teeter, sway. **2** *the operatic wobble in her voice* **tremor**, quiver, quaver, trembling, vibrato.

wobbly adj. **1** *a wobbly table* **unsteady**, unstable, shaky, rocky, rickety; unsafe, precarious; uneven, unbalanced; informal wonky. **2** *her legs were a bit wobbly* **shaky**, quivery, weak, unsteady; informal trembly, like jelly. **3** *I feel so wobbly* **faint**, dizzy, light-headed, giddy, weak (at the knees), groggy, muzzy; informal woozy.
– OPPOSITES stable.

woe n. **1** *a long tale of woe* **misery**, sorrow, distress, wretchedness, sadness, unhappiness, heartache, heartbreak, despondency, despair, depression, gloom, melancholy; adversity, misfortune, disaster, suffering, hardship; literary dolour. **2** *financial woes* **trouble**, difficulty, problem, trial, tribulation, misfortune, setback, reverse.
– OPPOSITES joy.

woebegone adj. **sad**, unhappy, miserable, dejected, disconsolate, forlorn, crestfallen, downcast, glum, gloomy, doleful, downhearted, despondent, melancholy, sorrowful, mournful, woeful, depressed, wretched, desolate; informal down in the mouth, down in the dumps, blue.
– OPPOSITES cheerful.

woeful adj. **1** *her face was woeful.* See **woebegone**. **2** *a woeful tale* **tragic**, sad, miserable, cheerless, gloomy, sorry, pitiful, pathetic, traumatic, depressing, heartbreaking, heart-rending, tear-jerking. **3** *the team's woeful performance* **dreadful**, awful, terrible, atrocious, appalling, abysmal, disgraceful, deplorable, shameful, hopeless, lamentable; substandard, poor, inadequate, inferior, unsatisfactory; informal rotten, crummy, pathetic, pitiful, lousy, dire; Brit. informal duff, chronic, rubbish.
– OPPOSITES cheerful, excellent.

wolf v. **devour**, gobble (up), guzzle, gulp down, bolt; informal put away, demolish, shovel down, scoff (down), get outside of, hoover up, trough; Brit. informal gollop; N. Amer. informal scarf (down/up), snarf (down/up).

> **WORD LINKS**
> **lupine** relating to wolves
> **werewolf, lycanthrope** (in folklore) a person who periodically changes into a wolf

wolfish adj. informal **lascivious**, lecherous, lustful; predatory, rapacious.

woman n. **1** *a woman got out of the car* **lady**, girl, female; matron; Scottish & N. English lass, lassie; Irish colleen; informal chick, girlie, filly, biddy; Brit. informal bird; Scottish & N. English informal wifie; N. Amer. informal sister, dame, broad, gal,

w

jane; Austral./NZ informal sheila; humorous the female of the species; literary maid, maiden, damsel; old use wench, gentlewoman. **2** *he found himself a new woman* **girlfriend**, sweetheart, partner, significant other, inamorata, lover, mistress; fiancée; wife, spouse; informal bird, fancy woman, missus, better half; Brit. informal other half, Dutch, trouble and strife; Irish informal mot; N. Amer. informal squeeze; dated lady friend, lady-love; old use leman.

> **WORD LINKS**
> **female, feminine** relating to women
> **distaff side** the female side of a family
> **gynaecology** the branch of medicine concerning women
> **matriarchy** a society in which women hold the power
> **matrilineal** based on relationship with the mother or female line of descent
> **misogyny** hatred of women
> **yin** (in Chinese philosophy) the passive female principle of the universe

womanhood n. **1** *she was on the brink of womanhood* **adulthood**, maturity; literary muliebrity. **2** *she's an ideal of womanhood* **womanliness**, femininity. **3** *the stereotype of French womanhood* **women**, womenfolk; womankind, womenkind, woman; the female sex.

womanish adj. **effeminate**, girlish, girlie, unmanly, unmasculine.
– OPPOSITES manly.

womanizer n. **philanderer**, Casanova, Don Juan, Romeo, Lothario, ladies' man, playboy, seducer, rake, roué, libertine, lecher; informal skirt-chaser, ladykiller, lech.

womankind n. **women**, woman, the female sex, womenkind, womanhood, womenfolk.

womanly adj. **1** *womanly virtues* **feminine**, female; old use feminal. **2** *her womanly figure* **voluptuous**, curvaceous, shapely, ample, Junoesque, Rubenesque, buxom, full-figured; informal curvy, busty.
– OPPOSITES masculine, boyish.

wonder n. **1** *she was speechless with wonder* **awe**, admiration, wonderment, fascination; surprise, astonishment, amazement. **2** *the wonders of nature* **marvel**, miracle, phenomenon, sensation, spectacle, beauty; curiosity.
▶v. **1** *I wondered what was on her mind* **ponder**, think about, meditate on, reflect on, muse on, speculate about, conjecture; be curious about. **2** *people wondered at such bravery* **marvel**, be amazed, be astonished, stand in awe, be dumbfounded, gape, goggle; informal be flabbergasted.

wonderful adj. **marvellous**, magnificent, superb, glorious, sublime, lovely, delightful; informal super, great, fantastic, terrific, tremendous, sensational, incredible, fabulous, fab, awesome, magic, ace, wicked, far out; Brit. informal smashing, brilliant, brill; N. Amer. informal peachy, dandy, neat; Austral./NZ informal beaut, bonzer; Brit. informal dated champion, wizard, spiffing, topping; N. Amer.

informal dated swell.
– OPPOSITES awful.

wonky adj. Brit. informal **1** *a wonky picture.* See **crooked** (sense 3). **2** *wonky stools.* See **wobbly** (sense 1).

wont adj. literary *he was wont to arise at 5.30* **accustomed**, used, given, inclined.
▶n. formal *Paul drove fast, as was his wont* **custom**, habit, way, practice, convention, rule.

wonted adj. literary **customary**, habitual, usual, accustomed, familiar, normal, conventional, routine, common.

woo v. **1** *Richard wooed Joan* **pay court to**, pursue, chase (after); dated court, romance, seek the hand of, set one's cap at, make love to. **2** *the party wooed voters with promises* **seek**, pursue, curry favour with, try to win, try to attract, try to cultivate. **3** *an attempt to woo him out of retirement* **entice**, tempt, coax, persuade, wheedle; informal sweet-talk.

wood n. **1** *polished wood* **timber**, planks, planking; logs; N. Amer. lumber. **2** *a walk through the woods* **forest**, woodland, trees; copse, coppice, grove; Brit. spinney; old use greenwood.

> **WORD LINKS**
> **ligneous** consisting of wood
> **carpenter, joiner, cabinetmaker** a person who makes wooden objects or structures
> **lathe** a machine for shaping wood

wooded adj. **forested**, afforested, tree-covered, woody; literary sylvan, bosky.

wooden adj. **1** *a wooden door* **wood**, timber, woody; ligneous. **2** *wooden acting* **stilted**, stiff, unnatural, awkward, leaden; dry, flat, stodgy, lifeless, passionless, spiritless, soulless. **3** *her face was wooden* **expressionless**, impassive, poker-faced, emotionless, blank, vacant, unresponsive.

woodland n. **woods**, wood, forest, trees; old use greenwood.

woodwork n. **carpentry**, joinery.

wool n. **1** *sheep's wool* **fleece**, hair, coat; floccus. **2** *a sweater made of cream wool* **yarn**.
□ **pull the wool over someone's eyes** informal **deceive**, fool, trick, hoodwink, dupe, delude; informal lead up the garden path, put one over on, bamboozle, con.

wool-gathering n. **daydreaming**, dreaming, reverie, musing, abstraction, preoccupation; absent-mindedness, forgetfulness.

woolly adj. **1** *a woolly hat* **woollen**, wool, fleecy. **2** *a sheep's woolly coat* **fleecy**, shaggy, hairy, fluffy, flocculent. **3** *woolly generalizations* **vague**, ill-defined, hazy, unclear, fuzzy, blurry, foggy, nebulous, imprecise, inexact, indefinite; confused, muddled.
▶n. informal **sweater**, pullover, jersey, cardigan; Brit. jumper; Brit. informal cardy.

woozy adj. informal See **groggy**.

word n. **1** *the Italian word for 'ham'* **term**, name, expression, designation, locution,

vocable; formal appellation. **2** *his words were meant kindly* **remark**, comment, observation, statement, utterance, pronouncement. **3** *I've got three weeks to learn the words* **script**, lyrics, libretto. **4** *I give you my word* **promise**, word of honour, assurance, guarantee, undertaking; pledge, vow, oath, bond; formal troth. **5** *I want a word with you* **talk**, conversation, chat, tête-à-tête, heart-to-heart, one-to-one; discussion, consultation; informal confab, powwow; formal confabulation. **6** *there's no word from the hospital* **news**, information, communication, intelligence; message, report, communiqué, dispatch, bulletin; informal info, gen, dope; literary tidings. **7** *word has it he's turned over a new leaf* **rumour**, hearsay, talk, gossip; informal the grapevine, the word on the street. **8** *I'm waiting for the word from HQ* **instruction**, order, command; signal, prompt, cue, tip-off; informal go-ahead, thumbs up, green light. **9** *his word was law* **command**, order, decree, edict; bidding, will. **10** *our word now must be success* **motto**, watchword, slogan, catchword, buzz word.
▸ v. *the question was carefully worded* **phrase**, express, put, couch, frame, formulate, style; say, utter.
□ **have words** quarrel, argue, disagree, squabble, bicker, fight, wrangle, dispute, fall out, clash; Brit. informal row.
in a word briefly, to be brief, in short, in a nutshell, to come to the point, to cut a long story short, not to put too fine a point on it; to sum up, to summarize, in summary.
word for word 1 *they took down the speeches word for word* **verbatim**, letter for letter, to the letter; exactly, faithfully. **2** *a word-for-word translation* **verbatim**, literal, exact, direct, accurate, faithful; unadulterated, unabridged.

> **WORD LINKS**
>
> **verbal**, **lexical** relating to words
> **semantic** relating to the meaning of words
> **syntax** the arrangement of words to make a well-formed sentence
> **etymology** an account of the origins of a word

wording n. **phrasing**, phraseology, words, language, expression, terminology.
wordplay n. **punning**, puns, play on words; wit, witticisms, repartee.
wordy adj. **long-winded**, verbose, prolix, lengthy, protracted, long-drawn-out, rambling, circumlocutory, periphrastic, pleonastic; loquacious, garrulous, voluble; informal windy; Brit. informal waffly.
– OPPOSITES succinct.

work n. **1** *a day's work in the fields* **labour**, toil, slog, drudgery, exertion, effort, industry, service; informal grind, sweat, elbow grease; Brit. informal graft, fag; Austral./NZ informal yakka; literary travail. **2** *I'm looking for work* **employment**, a job, a post, a position, a situation; occupation, profession, career, vocation, calling. **3** *haven't you got any work?* **tasks**, jobs, duties, assignments, projects; chores. **4** *works of literature* **composition**,

piece, creation; opus, oeuvre. **5** *this is the work of a radical faction* **handiwork**, doing, act, deed. **6** *a lifetime spent doing good works* **deeds**, acts, actions. **7** *the complete works of Shakespeare* **writings**, oeuvre, canon, output. **8** *a car works* **factory**, plant, mill, foundry, yard, workshop, shop. **9** *the works of a clock* **mechanism**, machinery, workings, parts, movement, action; informal insides. **10** informal *for only $60 you can get the works* **everything**, the full treatment; informal the lot, the whole shebang, the full nine yards; Brit. informal the full monty.
– OPPOSITES leisure.
▸ v. **1** *staff worked late into the night* **toil**, labour, exert oneself, slave (away); keep at it, keep one's nose to the grindstone; informal slog (away), beaver away, plug away, put one's back into it, knock oneself out, sweat blood; Brit. informal graft, fag; literary travail. **2** *he worked in education for years* **be employed**, have a job, earn one's living, do business. **3** *farmers worked the land* **cultivate**, farm, till, plough. **4** *his car was working perfectly* **function**, go, run, operate; informal behave. **5** *how do I work this machine?* **operate**, use, handle, control, manipulate, run. **6** *their ploy worked* **succeed**, work out, turn out well, go as planned, get results, be effective; informal come off, pay off, do the trick. **7** *blusher can work miracles* **bring about**, accomplish, achieve, produce, perform, create, engender, contrive, effect. **8** informal *the chairman was prepared to work it for Phil* **arrange**, manipulate, contrive; pull strings; N. Amer. pull wires; informal fix, swing, wangle. **9** *he worked the crowd into a frenzy* **stir (up)**, excite, drive, move, rouse, fire, galvanize; whip up, agitate. **10** *work the mixture into a paste* **knead**, squeeze, form; mix, stir, blend. **11** *he worked the blade into the padlock* **manoeuvre**, manipulate, guide, edge. **12** *her mouth worked furiously* **twitch**, quiver, convulse. **13** *he worked his way through the crowd* **manoeuvre**, make, thread, wind, weave, wend.
– OPPOSITES rest, fail.
□ **work on someone** persuade, manipulate, influence; coax, cajole, wheedle, soften up; informal twist someone's arm, lean on.
work out 1 *the bill works out at £50* **amount to**, add up to, come to, total; Brit. tot up to. **2** *my idea worked out*. See **work** (sense 6 of the verb). **3** *things didn't work out the way she planned* **end up**, turn out, go, come out, develop; happen, occur; informal pan out. **4** *he works out at the local gym* **exercise**, train.
work something out 1 *work out what you can afford* **calculate**, compute, reckon up, determine. **2** *I'm trying to work out what she meant* **understand**, comprehend, puzzle out, sort out, make sense of, get to the bottom of, make head or tail of, unravel, decipher, decode; informal figure out; Brit. informal suss out. **3** *they worked out a plan* **devise**, formulate, draw up, put together, develop, construct, arrange, organize, contrive, concoct; hammer out, negotiate.

w

work something up stimulate, rouse, raise, arouse, awaken, excite.

workable adj. **practicable**, feasible, viable, possible, achievable; realistic, reasonable, sensible, practical; informal doable.
– OPPOSITES impracticable.

workaday adj. **ordinary**, average, run-of-the-mill, middle-of-the-road, conventional, unremarkable, unexceptional, undistinguished, commonplace, mundane, humdrum, pedestrian; routine, everyday, day-to-day; N. Amer. garden-variety; informal bog-standard, nothing to write home about, ten a penny, a dime a dozen; Brit. informal common or garden.
– OPPOSITES exceptional.

worker n. **1** *a strike by 500 workers* **employee**, member of staff; workman, labourer, hand, operative, operator; proletarian; artisan, craftsman, craftswoman; wage-earner, breadwinner. **2** informal *I got a reputation for being a worker* **hard worker**, toiler, workhorse, galley slave; informal busy bee, eager beaver, workaholic; N. Amer. informal wheel horse.

workforce n. **employees**, staff, workers, personnel, labour force, manpower; human resources; informal liveware.

working adj. **1** *working mothers* **employed**, in (gainful) employment, in work, waged. **2** *a working waterwheel* **functioning**, operating, running, active, operational, functional, serviceable; informal up and running. **3** *a working knowledge of contract law* **sufficient**, adequate, viable; useful, effective.
– OPPOSITES unemployed, faulty.
▶ n. **1** *the working of a carburettor* **functioning**, operation, running, action, performance. **2** *the workings of a watch* **mechanism**, machinery, parts, movement, action, works; informal insides.

workman n. **(manual) worker**, labourer, hand, operative, operator; employee; journeyman, artisan.

workmanlike adj. *the team put up a solid, workmanlike performance* **efficient**, competent, professional, proficient, skilful, adept, masterly.

workmanship n. **craftsmanship**, artistry, craft, art, artisanship, handiwork; skill, expertise, technique.

workout n. **exercise session**, keep-fit session, training session, drill; warm-up; exercises, aerobics; informal dated daily dozen.

workshop n. **1** *a car repair workshop* **factory**, works, plant; garage. **2** *the craftsmen had a chilly workshop* **workroom**, studio, atelier. **3** *a workshop on combating stress* **study group**, discussion group, seminar, class.

world n. **1** *he travelled the world* **earth**, globe, planet. **2** *life on other worlds* **planet**, satellite, moon, star, heavenly body, orb. **3** *the academic world* **sphere**, society, circle, arena, milieu, province, domain, orbit, preserve, realm, field, discipline,

W

area. **4** *she would show the world that she was strong* **everyone**, everybody, people, mankind, humankind, humanity, the (general) public, the population, the populace, all and sundry, every mother's son, {every Tom, Dick, and Harry}, every man jack. **5** *a world of difference* **huge amount**, good deal, great deal, abundance, wealth, profusion, mountain; plenty; informal heap, lot, load, ton, masses; Brit. informal shedload. **6** *she renounced the world* **society**, secular interests, temporal concerns, earthly concerns.

> **WORD LINKS**
> **global**, **mondial** relating to the whole world

worldly adj. **1** *his youth was wasted on worldly pursuits* **earthly**, terrestrial, temporal, mundane; mortal, human, material, materialistic, physical, carnal, fleshly, bodily, corporeal, sensual. **2** *a worldly man* **sophisticated**, experienced, worldly-wise, knowledgeable, knowing, enlightened, shrewd, mature, seasoned, cosmopolitan, urbane, cultivated, cultured.
– OPPOSITES spiritual, naive.

worldly-wise adj. See **worldly** (sense 2).

worldwide adj. **global**, international, intercontinental, universal; ubiquitous, extensive, widespread, far-reaching, wide-ranging, all-embracing.
– OPPOSITES local.

worm n.

> **WORD LINKS**
> **vermiform** resembling a worm
> **vermicide** a substance used to kill worms

worn adj. **1** *his hat was worn* **shabby**, worn out, threadbare, tattered, in tatters, holey, falling to pieces, ragged, frayed, moth-eaten, scruffy, having seen better days; informal tatty, ratty, the worse for wear; N. Amer. informal raggedy. **2** *her face looked worn.* See **worn out** (sense 2).
– OPPOSITES smart, fresh.

worn out adj. **1** *a worn-out shirt.* See **worn** (sense 1). **2** *by evening they looked worn out* **exhausted**, fatigued, tired (out), weary, drained, worn, drawn, wan, sapped, spent; careworn, haggard, hollow-eyed, pinched, pale, peaky; informal all in, done in, dog-tired, dead beat, fit to drop, shattered; Brit. informal knackered; N. Amer. informal pooped, tuckered out. **3** *worn-out ideas* **obsolete**, antiquated, old, stale, hackneyed, trite, overused, overworked, clichéd, unoriginal, commonplace, pedestrian, prosaic, stock, conventional; informal played out, old hat.
– OPPOSITES smart, fresh.

worried adj. **anxious**, perturbed, troubled, bothered, concerned, upset, distressed, distraught, disquieted, uneasy, fretful, agitated, nervous, edgy, on edge, tense, overwrought, worked up, keyed up, stressed; apprehensive, fearful, afraid, frightened, scared; informal uptight, a bundle of nerves, on tenterhooks, jittery, jumpy, twitchy, in a

stew, all of a dither, in a flap, in a sweat, het up, rattled; Brit. informal windy, having kittens; N. Amer. informal antsy, squirrelly.
– OPPOSITES carefree.

worrisome adj. See **worrying**.

worry v. **1** *she worries about his health* **fret**, be concerned, be anxious, agonize, brood, panic, lose sleep, get worked up; informal get stressed, get in a flap, get in a state, stew, torment oneself. **2** *is something worrying you?* **trouble**, bother, make anxious, disturb, distress, upset, concern, disquiet, fret, agitate, unsettle, perturb, scare, fluster, stress, tax, torment, plague, bedevil; prey on one's mind, weigh down, gnaw at; informal rattle, bug, get to. **3** *a dog worried his sheep* **attack**, savage, maul, mutilate, mangle, go for; molest, torment, persecute.
▸ n. **1** *I'm beside myself with worry* **anxiety**, perturbation, distress, concern, uneasiness, unease, disquiet, fretfulness, restlessness, nervousness, nerves, agitation, edginess, tension, stress; apprehension, fear, dread, trepidation, misgiving, angst; informal butterflies (in the stomach), the willies, the heebie-jeebies. **2** *the rats are a worry* **problem**, cause for concern; nuisance, pest, plague, trial, trouble, vexation, bane, bugbear; informal pain (in the neck), headache, hassle, stress.

worrying adj. **alarming**, worrisome, daunting, perturbing, niggling, bothersome, troublesome, unsettling, nerve-racking; distressing, disquieting, upsetting, traumatic, problematic; informal scary, hairy.

worsen v. **1** *insomnia can worsen a patient's distress* **aggravate**, exacerbate, compound, add to, intensify, increase, magnify, heighten, inflame, augment; informal add fuel to the fire. **2** *the recession worsened* **deteriorate**, degenerate, decline, go downhill; informal go to pot, go to the dogs, hit the skids, nosedive.
– OPPOSITES improve.

worship n. **1** *the worship of saints* **reverence**, veneration, adoration, glorification, glory, exaltation; devotion, praise, thanksgiving, homage, honour; dulia, latria; formal laudation; old use magnification. **2** *morning worship* **service**, religious rite, prayer, praise, devotion, religious observance; matins, vespers, evensong. **3** *he contemplated her with worship* **admiration**, adulation, idolization, lionization, hero-worship.
▸ v. *they worship pagan gods* **revere**, reverence, venerate, pay homage to, honour, adore, praise, pray to, glorify, exalt, extol; hold dear, cherish, treasure, esteem, adulate, idolize, deify, hero-worship, lionize; informal put on a pedestal; formal laud; old use magnify.

worst v. **defeat**, beat, prevail over, triumph over, trounce, rout, vanquish, conquer, master, overcome, overwhelm, overpower, crush; outdo, outclass, outstrip, surpass; informal thrash, lick, best, clobber, drub, slaughter, murder, wipe out, crucify, demolish, wipe the floor with, take to the cleaners, walk all over, make mincemeat of;

Brit. informal stuff; N. Amer. informal shellac.

worth n. **1** *evidence of the rug's worth* **value**, price, cost; valuation, quotation, estimate. **2** *the intrinsic worth of education* **benefit**, advantage, use, value, virtue, utility, service, profit, help, aid; desirability, appeal; significance, sense; informal mileage, percentage; old use behoof. **3** *a sense of personal worth* **worthiness**, merit, value, excellence, calibre, quality, stature, eminence, consequence, importance, significance, distinction.

worthless adj. **1** *the item was worthless* **valueless**; poor quality, inferior, second-rate, low-grade, cheap, shoddy, tawdry; informal crummy, rubbishy, ten a penny; Brit. informal twopenny-halfpenny; N. Amer. informal nickel-and-dime. **2** *your conclusions are worthless* **useless**, no use, ineffective, ineffectual, fruitless, unproductive, unavailing, pointless, nugatory, valueless, inadequate, deficient, meaningless, senseless, insubstantial, empty, hollow, trifling, petty, inconsequential, lame, paltry, pathetic; informal a dead loss. **3** *his worthless son* **good-for-nothing**, ne'er-do-well, useless, despicable, contemptible, low, ignominious, corrupt, villainous, degenerate, shiftless, feckless; informal no-good, lousy.
– OPPOSITES valuable, useful.

worthwhile adj. **valuable**, useful, of use, of service, beneficial, rewarding, advantageous, positive, helpful, profitable, gainful, fruitful, productive, constructive, effective, effectual, meaningful, worthy.

worthy adj. *a worthy citizen* **virtuous**, righteous, good, moral, ethical, upright, upstanding, high-minded, principled, exemplary; law-abiding, irreproachable, blameless, guiltless, unimpeachable, honest, honourable, reputable, decent, respectable, noble, meritorious, admirable; pure, whiter than white, saintly, angelic; informal squeaky clean.
– OPPOSITES disreputable.
▸ n. *local worthies* **dignitary**, personage, grandee, VIP, notable, notability, pillar of society, luminary, leading light, big name; informal heavyweight, bigwig, top dog, big shot, big cheese; N. Amer. informal big wheel, big kahuna.
– OPPOSITES nobody.
□ **be worthy of** deserve, merit, warrant, rate, justify, earn, be entitled to, qualify for.

would-be adj. **aspiring**, budding, promising, prospective, potential, hopeful, keen, eager, ambitious; informal wannabe.

wound n. **1** *a chest wound* **injury**, lesion, cut, gash, laceration, tear, slash; graze, scratch, abrasion; bruise, contusion; Medicine trauma. **2** *the wounds inflicted by the media* **insult**, blow, slight, offence, affront; hurt, damage, injury, pain, distress, grief, anguish, torment.
▸ v. **1** *he was critically wounded* **injure**, hurt, harm; maim, mutilate, disable, incapacitate, cripple; lacerate, cut, graze, gash, stab, slash. **2** *her words had wounded him* **hurt**, scar, damage, injure; insult, slight,

W

offend, affront, distress, disturb, upset, trouble; grieve, sadden, pain, sting, shock, traumatize, torment.

wraith n. **ghost**, spectre, spirit, phantom, apparition, manifestation; informal spook; literary shade, phantasm.

wrangle n. *a wrangle over money* **argument**, dispute, disagreement, quarrel, falling-out, fight, squabble, altercation, war of words, shouting match, tiff; informal set-to, run-in, slanging match; Brit. informal barney, row, bust-up; Brit. informal, Football afters.
▸v. *we wrangled over the details* **argue**, quarrel, bicker, squabble, fall out, have words, disagree, be at odds, fight, battle, feud, clash; informal scrap; Brit. informal row.

wrap v. **1** *she wrapped herself in a towel* **swathe**, bundle, swaddle, muffle, cloak, enfold, envelop, encase, cover, fold, wind. **2** *I wrapped the vase carefully* **parcel (up)**, package, pack (up), bundle (up); gift-wrap.
▸n. *he put a wrap round then* **shawl**, stole, cloak, cape, mantle, scarf, pashmina, poncho, serape; historical pelisse.
□ **wrap something up** informal conclude, finish, end, wind up, round off, terminate, stop, cease, finalize, complete, tie up; informal sew up.

wrapper n. **1** *a sweet wrapper* **wrapping**, packaging, paper, cover, covering; jacket, sheath. **2** N. Amer. *she wore a cotton wrapper* **housecoat**, bathrobe, dressing gown, robe, kimono, peignoir.

wrath n. **anger**, rage, fury, outrage, spleen, vexation, (high) dudgeon, crossness, displeasure, annoyance, irritation; literary ire, choler.
– OPPOSITES happiness.

wreak v. **inflict**, bestow, mete out, administer, deliver, impose, exact, create, cause, result in, effect, engender, bring about, perpetrate, unleash, vent; formal effectuate.

wreath n. **garland**, circlet, chaplet, crown, festoon, lei; ring, loop, circle.

wreathe v. **1** *a pulpit wreathed in holly* **festoon**, garland, drape, cover, bedeck, deck, decorate, ornament, adorn. **2** *blue smoke wreathed upwards* **spiral**, coil, loop, wind, curl, twist, snake, curve.

wreck n. **1** *salvage teams landed on the wreck* **shipwreck**, wreckage, sunken ship, derelict; shell, hull. **2** *the wreck of a stolen car* **wreckage**, debris, remainder, ruins, remains.
▸v. **1** *he had wrecked her car* **demolish**, crash, smash up, damage, destroy; vandalize, deface, desecrate, write off; N. Amer. informal trash, total. **2** *his ship was wrecked* **shipwreck**, sink, capsize, run aground. **3** *the crisis wrecked his plans* **ruin**, spoil, disrupt, undo, put a stop to, frustrate, blight, crush, quash, dash, destroy, scotch, shatter, devastate, sabotage; informal mess up, screw up, foul up, put paid to, stymie, put the kibosh on, nix; Brit. informal scupper, dish.

wreckage n. See **wreck** (noun).

wrench n. **1** *she felt a wrench on her shoulders* **tug**, pull, jerk, jolt, heave; informal yank. **2** *hold the piston with a wrench* **spanner**, monkey wrench. **3** *a wrench in his arm* **sprain**, twist, strain, rick, crick. **4** *leaving was an immense wrench* **painful parting**, traumatic event; pang, trauma.
▸v. **1** *he wrenched the gun from her hand* **tug**, pull, jerk, wrest, heave, twist, pluck, grab, seize, snatch, force, prise; N. Amer. pry; informal yank. **2** *she wrenched her ankle* **sprain**, twist, turn, strain, rick, crick, pull; injure, hurt.

wrest v. **wrench**, snatch, seize, grab, prise, pluck, tug, pull, jerk, dislodge; N. Amer. pry; informal yank.

wrestle v. **grapple**, fight, struggle, contend, vie, battle, wrangle; scuffle, tussle, brawl; informal scrap.

wretch n. **1** *the wretches killed themselves* **poor creature**, poor soul, poor thing, poor unfortunate; informal poor devil, poor beggar. **2** *I wouldn't trust the old wretch* **scoundrel**, villain, ruffian, rogue, rascal, reprobate, criminal, miscreant, good-for-nothing; informal heel, creep, louse, rat, swine, dog, lowlife, scumbag; informal dated rotter, bounder, blighter; old use blackguard.

wretched adj. **1** *I felt so wretched without you* **miserable**, unhappy, sad, heartbroken, grief-stricken, sorrowful, distressed, desolate, devastated, despairing, disconsolate, downcast, dejected, crestfallen, cheerless, depressed, melancholy, morose, gloomy, mournful, doleful, dismal, forlorn, woebegone; informal blue; literary dolorous. **2** *I feel wretched* **ill**, unwell, poorly, sick, below par; Brit. off colour; informal under the weather, out of sorts. **3** *their living conditions are wretched* **harsh**, hard, grim, stark, difficult; poor, impoverished; pitiful, pathetic, miserable, cheerless, sordid, shabby, seedy, dilapidated; informal scummy; Brit. informal grotty. **4** *the wretched dwellers of the slums* **unfortunate**, unlucky, luckless, ill-starred, blighted, hapless, poor, pitiable, downtrodden, oppressed; literary star-crossed. **5** *he's a wretched coward* **despicable**, contemptible, reprehensible, base, vile, loathsome, hateful, detestable, odious, ignoble, shameful, shabby, worthless; informal dirty, rotten, low-down, lousy. **6** *wretched weather* **terrible**, awful, dire, atrocious, dreadful, bad, poor, lamentable, deplorable; informal God-awful; Brit. informal beastly. **7** *I don't want the wretched money* informal damn, damned, blasted, blessed, flaming, confounded, rotten; Brit. informal flipping, blinking, blooming, bloody.
– OPPOSITES cheerful, well, comfortable, fortunate, excellent.

wriggle v. **1** *she tried to hug him but he wriggled* **squirm**, writhe, wiggle, jiggle, jerk, thresh, flounder, flail, twitch, twist and turn; snake, worm, slither. **2** *he wriggled out of his responsibilities* **avoid**, shirk, dodge, evade, elude, sidestep; escape from; informal duck.
▸n. *the baby gave a wriggle* **squirm**, jiggle, wiggle, twitch, twist.

wring v. **1** *wring out the clothes* **twist**, squeeze, screw, scrunch, knead, press, mangle. **2** *concessions were wrung from the government* **extract**, elicit, force, exact, wrest, wrench, squeeze, milk; informal bleed. **3** *his expression wrung her heart* **rend**, tear at, harrow, pierce, stab, wound, rack; distress, pain, hurt.

wrinkle n. **1** *fine wrinkles around her mouth* **crease**, fold, pucker, line, crinkle, furrow, ridge, groove; informal crow's feet. **2** informal *learn the wrinkles from someone more experienced* **guideline**, hint, tip, pointer, clue, suggestion; (**wrinkles**) advice, guidance.
▸ v. *his coat tails wrinkled up* **crease**, pucker, gather, line, crinkle, crimp, crumple, rumple, ruck up, scrunch up.

writ n. **summons**, subpoena, warrant, arraignment, indictment, citation, court order.

write v. **1** *he wrote her name in the book* **put in writing**, write down, put down, jot down, note (down), take down, record, register, log, list; inscribe, sign, scribble, scrawl, pencil. **2** *I wrote a poem* **compose**, draft, think up, formulate, compile, pen, dash off, produce. **3** *he had her address and promised to write* **correspond**, write a letter, communicate, get in touch, keep in contact; informal drop someone a line.
□ **write someone/something off 1** *they have had to write off loans* **forget about**, disregard, give up on, cancel, annul, wipe out. **2** *he wrote off his new car* **wreck**, smash up, crash, destroy, demolish, ruin; N. Amer. informal total. **3** *who would write off a player of his stature?* **disregard**, dismiss, ignore.

writer n. **author**, wordsmith, man/woman of letters, penman; novelist, essayist, biographer; journalist, columnist, correspondent; scriptwriter, playwright, dramatist, dramaturge, tragedian; poet; informal scribbler, scribe, pen-pusher, hack.

writhe v. **squirm**, wriggle, thrash, flail, toss, toss and turn, twist, twist and turn, struggle.

writing n. **1** *I can't read his writing* **handwriting**, hand, script, print; penmanship, calligraphy, chirography; informal scribble, scrawl. **2** *the writings of Gertrude Stein* **works**, compositions, books, publications, oeuvre; papers, articles, essays.

WORD LINKS

graphology the study of handwriting
palaeography the study of ancient writing systems
holograph, **autograph** a manuscript in an author's own handwriting
transcribe put something into written form

---

wrong adj. **1** *the wrong answer* **incorrect**, mistaken, in error, erroneous, inaccurate, inexact, imprecise, fallacious, wide of the mark, off target, unsound, faulty; informal off beam, out. **2** *he knew he had said the wrong thing* **inappropriate**, unsuitable, inapt, inapposite, undesirable; ill-advised,

ill-considered, ill-judged, impolitic, injudicious, infelicitous, unfitting, out of keeping, improper; informal out of order. **3** *I've done nothing wrong* **illegal**, against the law, unlawful, illicit, criminal, dishonest, dishonourable, corrupt; unethical, immoral, bad, wicked, sinful, iniquitous, nefarious, blameworthy, reprehensible; informal crooked. **4** *there's something wrong with the engine* **amiss**, awry, out of order, not right, faulty, defective.
– OPPOSITES right, correct, appropriate, legal.
▸ adv. *she guessed wrong* **incorrectly**, wrongly, inaccurately, erroneously, mistakenly.
▸ n. **1** *the difference between right and wrong* **immorality**, sin, sinfulness, wickedness, evil; unlawfulness, crime, corruption, villainy, dishonesty, injustice, wrongdoing, misconduct, transgression. **2** *an attempt to compensate for past wrongs* **misdeed**, offence, injury, crime, transgression, peccadillo, sin; injustice, outrage, atrocity; Law tort; old use trespass.
– OPPOSITES right.
▸ v. **1** *she was determined to forget the man who had wronged her* **ill-use**, mistreat, do an injustice to, do wrong to, ill-treat, abuse, harm, hurt, injure; informal do the dirty on. **2** *perhaps I am wronging him* **malign**, misrepresent, do a disservice to, impugn, defame, slander, libel.
□ **get someone/something wrong** misunderstand, misinterpret, misconstrue, mistake, misread, take amiss; get the wrong idea/impression; informal get the wrong end of the stick, be barking up the wrong tree.
go wrong 1 *I've gone wrong somewhere* **make a mistake**, make an error, miscalculate; informal slip up, screw up, make a boo-boo; Brit. informal boob. **2** *their plans went wrong* **go awry**, go amiss, fail, be unsuccessful, fall through, come to nothing; backfire, misfire, rebound; informal come to grief, come a cropper, go up in smoke; Brit. informal go adrift. **3** *the radio's gone wrong* **break down**, malfunction, fail, stop working, crash, give out; informal be on the blink, conk out, go kaput; Brit. informal play up, pack up.
in the wrong to blame, blameworthy, at fault, reprehensible, responsible, culpable, answerable, guilty; old use peccant.

wrongdoer n. **offender**, lawbreaker, criminal, felon, delinquent, villain, culprit, evildoer, sinner, transgressor, malefactor, miscreant, rogue, scoundrel; informal crook, wrong 'un; Law malfeasant; old use trespasser.

wrongdoing n. **crime**, lawbreaking, lawlessness, criminality, misconduct, misbehaviour, malpractice, corruption, immorality, sin, sinfulness, wickedness, evil, vice, iniquity, villainy; offence, felony, wrong, misdeed, misdemeanour, fault, peccadillo, transgression; Law malfeasance, tort; formal malversation; old use trespass.

wrongful adj. **unjustified**, unjust, unwarranted, unfair, undue, undeserved,

w

unreasonable, groundless, indefensible, inappropriate, improper, unlawful, illegal, illegitimate.
– OPPOSITES rightful.

wrought up adj. **agitated**, tense, stressed, overwrought, nervous, on edge, edgy, keyed up, worked up, anxious, nervy, flustered, fretful, upset; informal in a state, in a stew, het up, wound up, uptight, jumpy, in a tizz/tizzy; Brit. informal **strung up**; N. Amer. informal spooky, squirrelly.
– OPPOSITES calm.

wry adj. **1** *his wry humour* **ironic**, sardonic, satirical, mocking, sarcastic; dry, droll, witty, humorous. **2** *a wry expression* **unimpressed**, displeased, annoyed, irritated, irked, vexed, piqued, disgruntled, dissatisfied; informal peeved. **3** *a wry neck* **twisted**, crooked, contorted, distorted, deformed, misshapen; Scottish thrawn.

xenophobic adj. **jingoistic**, chauvinistic, flag-waving, excessively nationalistic, isolationist, insular; prejudiced, bigoted, intolerant.

Xerox n. trademark **photocopy**, photostat, copy, duplicate, reproduction.

X-ray n. **radiograph**, roentgenogram, radiogram.

WORD LINKS

radiography the making of images using X-rays

radiology the science dealing with X-rays

radiotherapy the treatment of disease using X-rays

tomography displaying a cross section through the body using X-rays

barium meal substance swallowed so that the digestive system can be X-rayed

Yy

yahoo n. informal **boor**, lout, oaf, thug, barbarian, Neanderthal, brute, bully boy; informal clod, roughneck, bruiser; Brit. informal yobbo, yob, oik.

yank v. informal **jerk**, pull, tug, wrench; snatch, seize.

yap v. **1** *the dogs yapped about his heels* **bark**, woof, yelp. **2** informal *what are they yapping on about?* See **babble** (sense 1 of the verb).

yardstick n. **standard**, measure, gauge, scale, guide, guideline, indicator, test, touchstone, barometer, criterion, benchmark, point of reference, model, pattern.

yarn n. **1** *you need to use a fine yarn* **thread**, cotton, wool, fibre, filament; ply. **2** informal *a far-fetched yarn* **story**, tale, anecdote, saga, narrative; informal tall tale/story, cock and bull story, shaggy-dog story, spiel.

yawning adj. **gaping**, wide open, wide, cavernous, deep; huge, great, big.

year n. **twelve-month period**, calendar year; literary sun, summer, winter; old use twelvemonth.

> **WORD LINKS**
>
> **annual** happening once a year or lasting a year
> **biannual** happening twice a year
> **biennial** taking place every other year
> **annuity** a fixed sum of money paid each year
> **decade** a period of ten years
> **century** a period of a hundred years
> **millennium** a period of a thousand years

yearly adj. *a yearly payment* **annual**, once a year, every year, each year.
▸ adv. *the guide is published yearly* **annually**, once a year, per annum, every year, each year.

yearn v. **long**, pine, crave, desire, want, wish, hanker, covet, lust, pant, hunger, thirst, ache, eat one's heart out, have one's heart set on; informal have a yen, itch.

yearning n. **longing**, craving, desire, want, wish, hankering, urge, hunger, thirst, appetite, lust, ache; informal yen, itch.

yell v. *he yelled in agony* **cry out**, call out, call at the top of one's voice, shout, howl, yowl, wail, scream, shriek, screech, yelp, squeal; roar, bawl; informal holler.
▸ n. *a yell of rage* **cry**, shout, howl, yowl, scream, shriek, screech, yelp, squeal; roar; informal holler.

yellow adj. **1** *yellow hair* | *a yellow shirt* **flaxen**, golden, gold, blonde, fair; lemon, daffodil-yellow, mustard. **2** informal *he'll have to prove he's not yellow.* See **cowardly**.

yelp n. & v. **squeal**, shriek, howl, yowl, yell, cry, shout, yawp; informal holler.

yen n. informal **hankering**, yearning, longing, craving, urge, desire, want, wish, hunger, thirst, lust, appetite, ache; fancy, inclination; informal itch.

yes adv. **all right**, very well, of course, by all means, sure, certainly, absolutely, indeed, affirmative, in the affirmative, agreed, roger; Scottish, N. English, & old use aye; Nautical aye aye; informal yeah, yep, yup, uh-huh, okay, OK, okey-dokey, okey-doke; Brit. informal righto, righty-ho; N. Amer. informal surely; old use or formal yea.
– OPPOSITES no.

yes-man n. informal **sycophant**, toady, creep, fawner, flatterer, lickspittle, doormat; informal bootlicker; Brit. informal poodle; N. Amer. informal suck-up.

yet adv. **1** *he hasn't made up his mind yet* **so far**, thus far, as yet, up till/to now, until now. **2** *don't celebrate just yet* **now**, right now, at this time; already, so soon. **3** *he was doing nothing, yet he appeared purposeful* **nevertheless**, nonetheless, even so, but, however, still, notwithstanding, despite that, in spite of that, for all that, all the same, just the same, at the same time, be that as it may; old use natheless. **4** *he supplied yet more unsolicited advice* **even**, still, further, in addition, additionally, besides, into the bargain, to boot.

yield v. **1** *too many projects yield poor returns* **produce**, bear, give, supply, provide, afford, return, bring in, earn, realize, generate, deliver, pay out. **2** *the nobility had yielded power to the new capitalist class* **relinquish**, surrender, cede, remit, part with, hand over; make over, bequeath, leave. **3** *the Duke was forced to yield* **surrender**, capitulate, submit, relent, admit defeat, back down, climb down, give in, give up the struggle, lay down one's arms, raise/show the white flag, throw in the towel/sponge. **4** *he yielded to her demands* **give in to**, give way to, submit to, bow down to, comply with, agree to, consent to, go along with; grant, permit, allow; informal cave in to; formal accede to. **5** *the floorboards yielded underfoot* **bend**, give, give way.
– OPPOSITES withhold, resist, defy.
▸ n. *risky investments usually have higher yields* **profit**, gain, return, dividend, earnings.

yob, yobbo n. Brit. informal See **hooligan**.

yoke n. **1** *the horses were loosened from the yoke* **harness**, collar, coupling. **2** *countries struggling under the yoke of imperialism* **tyranny**, oppression, domination, hegemony, enslavement, servitude, subjugation, subjection, bondage, thrall; bonds, chains, fetters, shackles. **3** *the yoke of marriage* **bond**, tie, connection, link.

▸v. **1** *a pair of oxen were yoked together* **harness**, hitch, couple, tether, fasten, attach, join. **2** *their aim of yoking biology and mechanics* **unite**, join, link, connect; tie, bind, bond.

yokel n. **bumpkin**, peasant, provincial, rustic, country cousin, countryman/woman; Irish informal culchie; N. Amer. informal hayseed, hillbilly, hick; Austral. informal bushy.

young adj. **1** *young people* **youthful**, juvenile, underage; junior, adolescent, teenage; in the springtime of life, in one's salad days. **2** *she's very young for her age* **immature**, childish, inexperienced, unsophisticated, naive, unworldly; informal wet behind the ears. **3** *the young microbrewery industry* **fledgling**, developing, budding, in its infancy, emerging.
– OPPOSITES old, elderly, mature.

▸n. **1** *a robin feeding its young* **offspring**, progeny, family, babies. **2** *the young don't care nowadays* **young people**, children, youngsters, youth, the younger generation, juveniles, minors; informal kids, young 'uns.

youngster n. **child**, teenager, adolescent, youth, juvenile, minor, junior; boy, girl; Scottish & N. English lass, lassie; informal lad, kid, whippersnapper, young 'un, teen.

youth n. **1** *he had been a keen sportsman in his youth* **early years**, young days, teens, teenage years, adolescence, boyhood, girlhood, childhood; minority; formal juvenescence. **2** *she had kept her youth and beauty* **youthfulness**, freshness, bloom, vigour, energy. **3** *local youths* **young man**, boy, juvenile, teenager, adolescent, junior, minor; informal lad, kid. **4** *the youth of the nation* **young people**, young, younger generation, next generation; informal kids.
– OPPOSITES adulthood, old age.

youthful adj. **young-looking**, spry, sprightly, vigorous, active; young, boyish, girlish; fresh-faced, in the springtime of life, in one's salad days.
– OPPOSITES old, elderly.

y

Zz

zany adj. **eccentric**, peculiar, odd, unconventional, off-centre, strange, bizarre, weird; mad, crazy, comic, madcap, funny, quirky, idiosyncratic; informal wacky, screwy, nutty, oddball, off the wall; Brit. informal daft; N. Amer. informal kooky, wacko.
– OPPOSITES conventional, sensible.

zap v. informal **1** *they were zapped by anti-radar missiles.* See **destroy** (sense 5). **2** *racing cars zapped past.* See **speed** (sense 1 of the verb).

zeal n. **passion**, ardour, love, fervour, fire, avidity, devotion, enthusiasm, eagerness, keenness, appetite, relish, gusto, vigour, energy, intensity; fanaticism.
– OPPOSITES apathy.

zealot n. **fanatic**, enthusiast, extremist, radical, Young Turk, diehard, activist, militant; bigot, dogmatist, sectarian, partisan; informal fiend, maniac, ultra, nut.

zealous adj. **fervent**, ardent, fervid, fanatical, passionate, impassioned, devout, devoted, committed, dedicated, enthusiastic, eager, keen, avid, vigorous, energetic, intense, fierce; literary perfervid.
– OPPOSITES apathetic.

zenith n. **highest point**, high point, crowning point, height, top, acme, peak, pinnacle, apex, apogee, crown, crest, summit, climax, culmination, prime, meridian.
– OPPOSITES nadir.

zero n. **1** *the sum's wrong—you've left off a zero* **nought**, nothing, nil, o; Computing null character; dated cipher; old use naught. **2** *I rated my chances as zero* **nothing (at all)**, nil, none; N. English nowt; informal zilch, nix, sweet Fanny Adams, sweet FA, not a dicky bird; Brit. informal damn all, not a sausage; N. Amer. informal zip, nada, diddly-squat; old use naught, nought.
□ **zero in on** focus on, focus attention on, centre on, concentrate on, home in on, fix on, pinpoint, highlight, spotlight; informal zoom in on.

zero hour n. **the appointed time**, the critical moment, the moment of truth, the point/moment of decision, the Rubicon, the crux; informal the crunch.

zest n. **1** *she had a great zest for life* **enthusiasm**, gusto, relish, appetite, eagerness, keenness, avidity, zeal, fervour, ardour, passion; verve, vigour, liveliness, sparkle, fire, animation, vitality, dynamism, energy, brio, pep, spirit, exuberance, high spirits; informal zing, zip, oomph, vim, pizzazz, get-up-and-go. **2** *he wanted to add some zest to his life* **piquancy**, tang, flavour, savour, taste, spice, spiciness, relish, bite; excitement, interest, an edge; informal kick, punch, zing, oomph. **3** *the zest of an orange* **rind**, peel, skin.
– OPPOSITES apathy, indifference, blandness.

zigzag adj. **twisting**, twisty, full of twists and turns, serpentine, meandering, snaking, snaky, winding, crooked.
– OPPOSITES straight.

zing n. informal See **zest** (sense 1).

zip informal n. *he's full of zip.* See **energy**.
▶ v. *I zipped back along the M20.* See **speed** (sense 1 of the verb).

zone n. **area**, sector, section, belt, stretch, region, territory, district, quarter, precinct, locality, neighbourhood, province.

zoom v. informal See **speed** (sense 1 of the verb).